W9-CHK-208

ZONDERVAN
ILLUSTRATED
BIBLE DICTIONARY

ZONDERVAN ILLUSTRATED BIBLE DICTIONARY

J. D. DOUGLAS AND MERRILL C. TENNEY
REVISED BY MOISÉS SILVA

ZONDERVAN®

ZONDERVAN.com/
AUTHORTRACKER
follow your favorite authors

ZONDERVAN

Zondervan Illustrated Bible Dictionary
Copyright © 1987, 2011 by Zondervan

This title is also available as a Zondervan ebook.
Visit www.zondervan.com/ebooks.

Requests for information should be addressed to:

Zondervan, *Grand Rapids, Michigan 49530*

Library of Congress Cataloging-in-Publication Data

Zondervan illustrated Bible dictionary / [edited by] J. D. Douglas and Merrill C. Tenney; revised by Moisés Silva.
    p.   cm.
   Includes bibliographical references.
   ISBN 978-0-310-22983-4 (hardcover, printed)
   1. Bible—Dictionaries. I. Douglas, J. D. (James Dixon) II. Tenney, Merrill C. (Merrill Chapin), 1904-1985.
III. Silva, Moisés. IV. Zondervan encyclopedia of the Bible.
BS440.Z66 2011
220.3—dc22   2010034210

All Scripture quotations, unless otherwise indicated, are taken from the Holy Bible, *New International Version*®, *NIV*®. Copyright © 1973, 1978, 1984 by Biblica, Inc.™ Used by permission of Zondervan. All rights reserved.

Maps by International Mapping. Copyright © 2009 by Zondervan. All rights reserved.

Any Internet addresses (websites, blogs, etc.) and telephone numbers printed in this book are offered as a resource. They are not intended in any way to be or imply an endorsement by Zondervan, nor does Zondervan vouch for the content of these sites and numbers for the life of this book.

All rights reserved. No part of this publication may be reproduced, stored in a retrieval system, or transmitted in any form or by any means—electronic, mechanical, photocopy, recording, or any other—except for brief quotations in printed reviews, without the prior permission of the publisher.

Interior design: Mark Sheeres

Printed in the United States of America

14 15 16 17 18 19 20 /DCI/ 23 22 21 20 19 18 17 16 15 14 13 12 11 10 9 8 7 6 5

INTRODUCTION

When the *Zondervan Pictorial Bible Dictionary* appeared in 1963, under the general editorship of the well-known New Testament scholar Merrill C. Tenney, it quickly established itself as a standard one-volume reference work for the study of Scripture. Almost twenty-five years later, a completely revised edition, which came to be known as the *New International Bible Dictionary*, was published under the capable direction of J. D. Douglas. The present revision preserves a fundamental continuity with the two previous editions, yet in many important respects it represents a new work.

The most obvious difference is of course its general appearance. Printed in full color throughout, the *Zondervan Illustrated Bible Dictionary* (*ZIBD*) includes more than 470 striking photographs and more than 17 freshly produced maps. The new artistic design and use of fonts greatly enhance the attractiveness and clarity of the work.

More substantial, however, are the changes in content. Almost 1,800 new entries have been added, bringing the total to over 7,200 (including many useful cross-references that make it easier for the user to find desired information). Articles dealing with the books of the Bible now include a sidebar with concise information concerning authorship, historical setting, purpose, and contents. Every article has been revised and updated, and although in some cases the changes required were minor, most entries involved thorough revision or even total rewriting. In this process, the editor had the advantage of being able to make use of the revised edition of the *Zondervan Encyclopedia of the Bible* (*ZEB*). Particularly in the case of shorter articles, material from *ZEB* was often transferred (with only minor revisions) to the corresponding *ZIBD* entries. Thus the one-volume work, while retaining many distinctive features not found in *ZEB*, may be regarded to some extent as an abbreviated version of its multivolume cousin.

What this means for the reader is the benefit of using *ZIBD* with greater confidence. One-volume Bible dictionaries often report information or make claims that—because of space limitations or for other reasons—are not properly documented. If an item seems unusual (e.g., a statement is made that contradicts an alternate work of reference), readers may find it quite difficult to verify the information. Users of *ZIBD*, in contrast, knowing that most of the material is treated more fully in *ZEB* (which usually includes argumentation, some technical data, and extensive bibliographies), can readily consult the larger work for further details.

Although much of the material in *ZIBD* can still be traced back to one or both of the previous editions, the changes have been so extensive that attributing articles to individual authors would in most cases prove misleading. Rather than make arbitrary decisions in specific cases, all the entries now appear unsigned. The revising editor and all readers, however, will continue to be indebted to the original writers, whose names appear listed in both of the earlier editions.

All biblical quotations, unless otherwise noted, come from the NIV/TNIV. Because using this dual reference is cumbersome and usually unnecessary, the abbreviation NIV should be assumed to include TNIV; when the latter has a different rendering relevant to the discussion, the difference is noted. Other translations, especially the NRSV, are often noted to indicate alternate interpretations. Quotations of the Apocrypha are taken from the NRSV. Because of the historical significance and continued use of the KJV, attention is given to its distinct name forms, to selected problems related to it (such as words and phrases not easily understood today), and to some of its influential renderings.

For the benefit of readers who are not proficient in the biblical languages, the Goodrick-Kohlenberger numbers are included with individual Hebrew, Aramaic, and Greek words. The transliteration of such words follows the academic style adopted in *The SBL Handbook of Style* (1999), chapter 5. To aid the user in finding relevant material, thousands of cross-references are included; these are indicated with small caps. Within the body of the articles, cross-references are normally marked only on first mention.

Alphabetization

The entries in this dictionary are alphabetized according to the so-called letter-by-letter system: a parenthesis or a comma interrupts the alphabetizing, but all other punctuation marks and word spaces are ignored (cf. *The Chicago Manual of Style*, 15th ed. [2003], sect. 18.56–59). Note the order in the following example:

> Beth Anoth
> Bethany
> Beth Ashbea

Some dictionaries and encyclopedias follow the word-by-word method, according to which any punctuation mark or word space also interrupts the alphabetizing. In the example above, they would place "Beth Ashbea" and many other "Beth-" compounds before "Bethany." Usually these differences do not create obstacles, but in certain cases—when a large number of items or a long article separates similar entries—the user may on first try be unable to find a particular entry where expected. Note the potential confusion in the following example:

> sea
> sea, brazen
> Sea, Great
> sea, molten
> sea cow
> sea gull
> seah
> seal
> sea monster
> sea of glass

Because the article on "seal" extends several paragraphs—so that the entry "sea monster" could pass unnoticed—the reader may infer that "sea gull" is the last "sea" entry. In short, users should not assume that an article is missing if they do not find it on first try.

The only exception to strict alphabetical order is in the case of dual articles that treat the same topic focusing respectively on the OT and the NT. For example, "chronology (OT)" comes before "chronology (NT)."

Proper Names

The representation of Middle Eastern names in English is fraught with difficulties, resulting in a bewildering diversity of spellings (except in the case of widely used names whose English orthography has become conventional). Some writers adopt a precise transliteration, using numerous diacritical markings that distinguish between fairly subtle sound differences; others prefer a greatly simplified system that ignores even important distinctions. The present work seeks a middle ground. For example, in the representation of Arabic names (used for most archaeological sites and modern villages in the Holy Land), vowel length is ignored, but differences in the consonants have been carefully preserved (e.g., h / $ḥ$ / $ḫ$).

With regard to biblical names specifically, the spelling follows the NIV, but alternate forms are also included (primarily from the TNIV, KJV, and NRSV). The articles begin with initial parenthetical information that gives the original form in transliterated Hebrew, Aramaic, or Greek, followed by the meaning of the name, if known. Most of these meanings cannot be confirmed definitively, however, and even when there is a reasonable degree of certainty, one cannot be sure what may have motivated the parents to choose a particular name (a characteristic of the child? an event at the time of birth? a parental hope? the desire to honor an ancestor or an important figure by using that person's name? an ascription of praise to God not specifically related to the child? merely the perception that the name had a pleasant sound?).

Pronunciation guides have been provided for all biblical names as well as for selected names found outside the Bible. With relatively few exceptions, the information is taken from W. O. Walker Jr. et al., *The HarperCollins Bible Pronunciation Guide* (1989), which uses a simple system for indicating English sounds, as shown below. There exists of course a standard pronunciation for a large number of well-known biblical names. Numerous other names, however, are not in common use and thus there is no "accepted" or conventional pronunciation for them. The approach used by Walker and his associate editors gives preference to what would likely be considered a natural English pronunciation (i.e., consistent with how similarly spelled words in English are usually pronounced). Biblical scholars, however, frequently favor a pronunciation that comes closer to that of the original languages, particularly in the case of Hebrew names. Thus for the name Hazor, Walker gives the pronunciation hay′zor, but many biblical students prefer hah-tsor′. In short, then, the pronunciation guides included in this dictionary are not presented as authoritative prescriptions; many of them should be regarded only as reasonable suggestions.

Moisés Silva

PRONUNCIATION KEY

a	cat	ihr	**ear**	ou	h**ow**
ah	f**a**ther	j	**j**oke	p	**p**at
ahr	l**ar**d	k	**k**ing	r	**r**un
air	c**are**	kh	**ch** as in German *Buch*	s	**s**o
aw	j**aw**			sh	**s**ure
ay	p**ay**	ks	ve**x**	t	**t**oe
b	**b**ug	kw	**qu**ill	th	**th**in
ch	**ch**ew	l	**l**ove	*th*	**th**en
d	**d**o	m	**m**at	ts	**ts**etse
e, eh	p**e**t	n	**n**ot	tw	**tw**in
ee	s**ee**m	ng	si**ng**	uh	**a**go
er	**er**ror	o	h**o**t	uhr	h**er**
f	**f**un	oh	g**o**	v	**v**ow
g	**g**ood	oi	b**oy**	w	**w**eather
h	**h**ot	oo	f**oo**t	y	**y**oung
hw	**wh**ether	*oo*	b**oo**t	z	**z**one
i	**i**t	oor	p**oor**	zh	vi**s**ion
i	sk**y**	or	f**or**		

Stress accents are printed after stressed syllables:
   ′ primary stress
   ‵ secondary stress

PREFACE TO THE SECOND EDITION (ABBREVIATED)

For more than two decades the *Zondervan Pictorial Bible Dictionary* has been a best-seller. During that period, however, more background information has become available. Archaeological excavations have been carried out on biblical sites. New books have been written to enhance our understanding of the Bible. A further dimension was added with the publication of the New International Version of the Bible.

These developments are reflected in this revision. The revision has been so thorough, in fact, that the dictionary merits a new name: *New International Dictionary of the Bible*. There is, for example, a completely new entry on archaeology, and, where necessary, notes have been added to the individual entries dealing with particular sites.

Every reviser is in debt to the original editors and writers and lives with a nagging feeling of presumptuousness in setting out to amend or supersede the work of bygone saints. Why did they say this or that? Did they know something we don't know? This haunting and not-unlikely possibility is a healthy inhibiting factor for brandishers of blue pencils.

This is especially relevant when confronting a presentation that is put a little more forcefully than one would expect in a dictionary of the Bible. In the following pages a reasonable amount of idiosyncrasy has been perpetuated in certain entries; with a certain affectionate indulgence we recognize that that was the way in which some of our elders drew attention to the importance of their topics.

Dictionaries are particularly vulnerable because a writer has to say in a few words what others expand into whole books. Contributors to dictionaries of the Bible are further at risk because some of their subjects lend themselves to controversy. In treating them, mention may be made either of opinions not within the Evangelical tradition or of widely divergent interpretations within that tradition. We hope that this policy will have no adverse effect on anyone's blood pressure. It was, indeed, an eminent physician, Sir Wilfred Grenfell, who reminded us that two men can think differently without either being wicked.

The consulting editors are not to be held accountable for the finished revision. None of them has seen all of it. All of them responded to the initial invitation to comment on what needed to be done. Moreover, all were contributors as well as consultants, and the work has greatly benefited. But someone had to see the work last, so for the final choice of material the revising editor alone is responsible.

In addition to article writers, a number of people worked very hard and lightened the editorial task. Doug Buckwalter and David Lazell shared their expertise in the peculiarly demanding job of adapting some of the omnibus articles to NIV usage. Myra Wilson cheerfully did a mass of accurate typing and checking; Ruj Vanavisut meticulously performed a daunting load of secretarial and kindred chores; Louan and Walter Elwell selflessly provided a second home and library facilities for a traveling editor. For the publisher, Stan Gundry was a model of restraint in letting the editor get on with the project unhindered but was ready to respond promptly to editorial requests.

J. D. DOUGLAS

PREFACE TO THE FIRST EDITION (ABBREVIATED)

Robert A. Millikan, American physicist and Nobel prizewinner, once said that a knowledge of the Bible is an indispensable qualification of a well-educated man. No other single book in the history of literature has been so widely distributed or read, or has exercised so powerful an influence upon civilization. It is the fountainhead of Western culture, and is the sole source of spiritual life and revelation for all Christians. For the development of Christian experience and for the propagation of faith, a study of the Scriptures is absolutely necessary. The history, laws, prophecies, sermons and letters which they contain provide God's estimate of man and His disclosure of Himself through the historic process of revelation culminating in the person of His Son, Jesus Christ.

Understanding the Bible is often difficult for the average reader because of the unfamiliar names of persons, places, and objects to which it alludes. The historical and cultural backgrounds are alien to those of the modern day and presuppose knowledge that is not easily attainable. The function of a Bible dictionary is to render accessible a body of information that will enable one to comprehend the meaning of the text he is reading, and to obtain ready and complete data concerning any related subject.

Within recent years, the need for a new, up-to-date reference work has become increasingly urgent. Fresh discoveries in archaeology, better understanding of the history and geography of the Middle East, and the fruit of multiplied research have provided new insights and interpretations. The advance of the graphic arts has improved greatly the effectiveness of photography, so that the artifacts and inscriptions of the past can be reproduced vividly for public exhibition. Realizing the opportunity for a fresh venture in this field, the Zondervan Publishing House, inspired by the interest and foresight of Mr. Peter deVisser, Director of Publications, has undertaken the task of creating a totally new dictionary, enlisting the cooperation of sixty-five competent scholars in every field from archaeology to zoology. The content includes more than 5,000 entries, among which may be found a number of important monographs on biblical and theological topics. In addition, the dictionary contains an extensive series of articles on Christian doctrines.

This *Pictorial Bible Dictionary* is a completely new, fully illustrated one-volume work. It is designed to provide quick access to explanatory data, both by the verbal exposition of biographical, chronological, geographical, and historical aspects of the Bible, and by the illustrations related to them. The pictures have been selected for their relevance to the subject matter, for their historical value, and also with an eye to human interest.

The scope of a one-volume dictionary is necessarily limited. The articles are not intended to be exhaustive, nor are they planned primarily for professional scholars. They are gauged for the use of pastors, Sunday-school teachers, Bible-class leaders, and students who desire concise and accurate information on questions raised by ordinary reading. For intensive research, a more detailed and critical work is recommended.

Although the articles are written from a conservative viewpoint, each writer has been free to express his own opinions and is responsible for the material that appears over his signature. There may be minor disagreements between statements by different persons; in such instances there is room for debate, and the contributors have liberty to differ. Uncertainty still exists in some fields, since sufficient data are not available for final conclusions.

Special acknowledgments are due to Dr. Steven Barabas, Associate Editor, who collaborated in preparing articles for publication, and who contributed many himself; to Dr. E. M. Blaiklock, Professor Wick Broomall, Dr. Howard Z. Cleveland, the Rev. Charles Cook, Dr. Carl De Vries, the Rev. Arthur B. Fowler, the Rev. J. P. Freeman, Dr. Guy B. Funderburk, the Rev. Clyde E. Harrington, Dr. D. Edmond Hiebert, the Rev. John G. Johansson, the Rev. Brewster Porcella,

Professor Arthur M. Ross, Dr. Emmet Russell, and Dr. Walter Wessel, who, in addition to the initialed articles published under their names, contributed many of the unsigned articles; to Miss Verda Bloomhuff and the Rev. Briggs P. Dingman, who assisted in correction of copy and proof; and to Mrs. Carol Currie and Mrs. Alice Holmes for invaluable secretarial service. The General Editor wishes to express his gratitude to all those scholars named in the list of contributors who have lent their time and counsel to the production of this book.

MERRILL C. TENNEY

ABBREVIATIONS

General Abbreviations

Akk.	Akkadian
ANE	Ancient Near East(ern)
ANET	*Ancient Near East Texts Relating to the Old Testament*, ed. J. B. Pritchard, 3rd ed. (1969)
aor.	aorist
Apoc.	Apocrypha
approx.	approximate(ly)
Arab.	Arabic
Aram.	Aramaic
Assyr.	Assyrian
ASV	American Standard Version
b.	born
c.	*circa*, about, approximately
cent.	century
cf.	*confer*, compare
ch(s).	chapter(s)
cm.	centimeters
contra	in contrast to
d.	died, date of death
DSS	Dead Sea Scrolls
E	east
ed(s).	editor(s), edited, edition
e.g.	*exempli gratia*, for example
Egyp.	Egyptian
Eng.	English
ERV	English Revised Version
esp.	especially
ESV	English Standard Version
et al.	*et alii*, and others
f.	and following (*pl.* ff.)
fem.	feminine
fig.	figure, figurative(ly)
fl.	*floruit*, flourished
ft.	feet
Ger.	German
Gk.	Greek
GNB	Good News Bible
Heb.	Hebrew
Hitt.	Hittite
ibid.	*ibidem*, in the same place
i.e.	*id est*, that is
illus.	illustration
impf.	imperfect
impv.	imperative

in.	inches
JB	Jerusalem Bible
Jos.	Josephus
JPS	Jewish Publication Society, *The Holy Scriptures according to the Masoretic Text: A New Translation ... (1945)*
KJV	King James Version
km.	kilometers
l.	liters
Lat.	Latin
lit.	literal; literally
LXX	Septuagint
m.	meters
masc.	masculine
mg.	margin
mi.	miles
MS(S)	manuscript(s)
MT	Masoretic Text
N	north
n.	note (*pl.* nn.)
NAB	New American Bible
NASB	New American Standard Bible
NCV	New Century Version
NE	northeast
NEB	New English Bible
neut.	neuter
NIV	New International Version (1984 ed.)
NJB	New Jerusalem Bible
NJPS	*Tanakh: The Holy Scriptures. The New JPS translation according to the Traditional Hebrew Text*
NKJV	New King James Version
NLT	New Living Translation
no.	number
NT	New Testament
NW	northwest
orig.	original(ly)
OT	Old Testament
p., pp.	page, pages
pass.	passive
pf.	perfect
pl.	plural
prob.	probably
ptc.	participle
REB	Revised English Bible
rev.	revised
Rom.	Roman
RSV	Revised Standard Version

RV	Revised Version
S	south
SE	southeast
sect.	section
sing.	singular
Sumer.	Sumerian
s.v.	*sub verbo*, under the word
SW	southwest
Syr.	Syriac
TEV	Today's English Version
TNIV	Today's New International Version
TR	Textus Receptus
trans.	translated by; translation
Ugar.	Ugaritic
v., vv.	verse, verses
vol(s).	volume(s)
vs.	versus
Vulg.	Vulgate
W	west

II. Books of the Bible

Old Testament

Gen.	Genesis
Exod.	Exodus
Lev.	Leviticus
Num.	Numbers
Deut.	Deuteronomy
Josh.	Joshua
Jdg.	Judges
Ruth	Ruth
1 Sam.	1 Samuel
2 Sam.	2 Samuel
1 Ki.	1 Kings
2 Ki.	2 Kings
1 Chr.	1 Chronicles
2 Chr.	2 Chronicles
Ezra	Ezra
Neh.	Nehemiah
Esth.	Esther
Job	Job
Ps.	Psalm(s)
Prov.	Proverbs
Eccl.	Ecclesiastes
Cant.	Canticles (Song of Songs)
Isa.	Isaiah
Jer.	Jeremiah
Lam.	Lamentations

Ezek.	Ezekiel
Dan.	Daniel
Hos.	Hosea
Joel	Joel
Amos	Amos
Obad.	Obadiah
Jon.	Jonah
Mic.	Micah
Nah.	Nahum
Hab.	Habakkuk
Zeph.	Zephaniah
Hag.	Haggai
Zech.	Zechariah
Mal.	Malachi

New Testament

Matt.	Matthew
Mk.	Mark
Lk.	Luke
Jn.	John
Acts	Acts
Rom.	Romans
1 Cor.	1 Corinthians
2 Cor.	2 Corinthians
Gal.	Galatians
Eph.	Ephesians
Phil.	Philippians
Col.	Colossians
1 Thess.	1 Thessalonians
2 Thess.	2 Thessalonians
1 Tim.	1 Timothy
2 Tim.	2 Timothy
Tit.	Titus
Phlm.	Philemon
Heb.	Hebrews
Jas.	James
1 Pet.	1 Peter
2 Pet.	2 Peter
1 Jn.	1 John
2 Jn.	2 John
3 Jn.	3 John
Jude	Jude
Rev.	Revelation

Apocrypha

1 Esd.	1 Esdras
2 Esd.	2 Esdras (= *4 Ezra*)
Tob.	Tobit
Jdt.	Judith
Add. Esth.	Additions to Esther
Wisd.	Wisdom of Solomon
Sir.	Ecclesiasticus (Wisdom of Jesus the Son of Sirach)
Bar.	Baruch
Ep. Jer.	Epistle of Jeremy
Pr. Azar.	Prayer of Azariah
Sg.	ThreeSong of the Three Children (or Young Men)
Sus.	Susanna
Bel	Bel and the Dragon
Pr. Man.	Prayer of Manasseh
1 Macc.	1 Maccabees
2 Macc.	2 Maccabees

III. Pseudepigrapha

As. Moses	*Assumption of Moses*
2 Bar.	*2 Baruch*
3 Bar.	*3 Baruch*
1 En.	*1 Enoch*
2 En.	*2 Enoch*
4 Ezra	*4 Ezra (= 2 Esdras)*
Jub.	*Book of Jubilees*
Let. Aris.	*Letter of Aristeas*
Life Adam	*Life of Adam and Eve*
3 Macc.	*3 Maccabees*
4 Macc.	*4 Maccabees*
Mart. Isa.	*Martyrdom of Isaiah*
Pss. Sol.	*Psalms of Solomon*
Sib. Or.	*Sibylline Oracles*
T. Benj.	*Testament of Benjamin* (etc.)
T. 12 Patr.	*Testaments of the Twelve Patriarchs*
Zad. Frag.	*Zadokite Fragments*

Other Christian, Jewish, and Greco-Roman texts are referred to by their standard abbreviations. See, e.g., *The SBL Handbook of Style* (1999), chapter 8, appendix F, and appendix H.

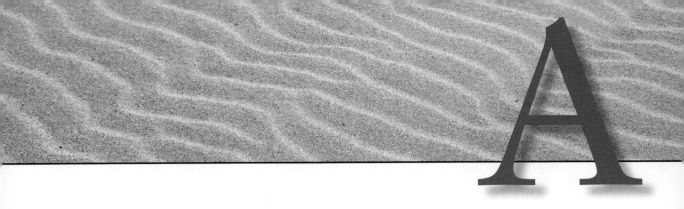

A

A. The symbol used to designate Codex Alexandrinus. See Septuagint; text and versions (NT).

Aaron. air´uhn (Heb. *ʾahărôn H195*, derivation uncertain, possibly an Egyp. name; Gk. *Aarōn G2*). The oldest son of Amram and Jochebed, of the tribe of Levi, and brother of Moses and Miriam (Exod. 6:20; Num. 26:59). He was born during the captivity in Egypt, before Pharaoh's edict that all male infants should be destroyed, and was three years older than Moses (Exod. 7:7). His name first appears in God's commission to Moses. When Moses protested that he did not have sufficient ability in public speaking to undertake the mission to Pharaoh, God declared that Aaron should be spokesman for his brother (4:10-16). So Aaron met Moses at "the mountain of God" (4:27) after forty years' separation, and took him back to the family home in Goshen. Aaron introduced him to the elders of the people and persuaded them to accept him as their leader. Together Moses and Aaron went to Pharaoh's court, where they carried on the negotiations that finally brought an end to the oppression of the Israelites and precipitated the exodus from Egypt.

According to Islamic tradition, the tomb of Aaron lies atop Jebel Harun (Mt. Hor) located a few miles S of Petra. (View to the N.W.)

© Dr. James C. Martin

During Moses' forty years in the wilderness Aaron had married ELISHEBA, daughter of AMMINADAB and sister of NAHSHON, a prince of the tribe of JUDAH (Exod. 6:23; 1 Chr. 2:10). They had four sons: NADAB, ABIHU, ELEAZAR, and ITHAMAR (Exod. 6:23).

After the Israelites left Egypt, Aaron assisted his brother during the wandering in the wilderness. On the way to SINAI, in the battle with AMALEK, Aaron and HUR held up Moses' hands (Exod. 17:9-13), in which was the staff of God. Israel consequently won the battle. With the establishment of the TABERNACLE, Aaron became high priest in charge of the national WORSHIP and the head of the hereditary priesthood (see PRIEST).

In character Aaron was weak and occasionally jealous. He and Miriam criticized Moses for having married a Cushite woman (Num. 12:1-2; see CUSH #3). This complaint may have been an intentionally insulting reference to ZIPPORAH. (See Hab. 3:7 for a linking of MIDIAN and Cush; Zipporah is always elsewhere described as a Midianite.) Behind this personal slight lies a more serious threat to Moses' position. Aaron was high priest and thus the supreme religious leader of Israel; Miriam was a prophetess (Exod. 15:20). The great issue was not whether Moses had married a particular person but whether he could any longer be considered the sole, authoritative mouthpiece of God. As Aaron and Miriam said, "Hasn't he [the LORD] also spoken through us?" (Num. 12:2). It is in the light of this basic challenge to Moses' God-given status that we must understand and appreciate the prompt and dramatic response of the Lord (12:4-15).

We may further note that Aaron's own authority as priest did not go unchallenged. It becomes clear that when KORAH and his company (Num. 16) challenged Moses' leadership, Aaron's priesthood too was called into question. By the miraculous sign of the flowering and fruit-bearing staff, the Lord identified Aaron as his chosen priest (17:1-9) and accorded him a perpetual priesthood by ordering his staff to be deposited in the sanctuary (17:10).

When Moses went up Mount Sinai to receive the tablets of the law from God, Aaron acceded to the people's demand for a visible god that they could worship. Taking their personal jewelry, he melted it in a furnace and made a golden calf similar to the familiar bull-god of Egypt. The people hailed this image as the god who had brought them out of Egypt. Aaron did not remonstrate with them but built an altar and proclaimed a feast to the Lord on the next day, which the people celebrated with revelry and debauchery (Exod. 32:1-6). When Moses returned from the mountain and rebuked Aaron for aiding this abuse, Aaron gave this naive answer: "They gave me the gold, and I threw it into the fire, and out came this calf!" (32:24). It may be that Aaron meant to restrain the people by a compromise, but he was wholly unsuccessful. See also CALF WORSHIP.

In the biblical narrative much is made of the consecration of Aaron and his sons as priests. The "dignity and honor" (Exod. 28:2) of their office was expressed in garments of great beauty and significance: the breastpiece, ephod, robe, tunic, turban, and sash. The ceremony of appointment is described in Exod. 29 and enacted in Lev. 8. It involved presenting a sin offering and a burnt offering on behalf of the priests-to-be (Exod. 29:10-14, 15-18), for though they were priests, they were first of all sinners needing the grace of God in atonement (Heb. 5:2-3). See SACRIFICE AND OFFERINGS.

The consecration included three special ceremonies: (1) their ears, hands, and feet were touched with the blood of a ram (Exod. 29:19-20), signifying respectively the hallowing of the mind and of the acts and directions of life—what they would hear, what they would do, where they would go; (2) they were anointed with oil mingled with the sacrificial blood (29:21), symbolizing the grace of God in atonement (blood) and endowment (oil); (3) their hands were filled with some of the fat of the slain beasts along with various sorts of bread, and the whole was lifted up in offering to the Lord (29:22-23). Just as we say that a busy person "has his hands full," so they consecrated to the Lord the whole business of living—life's special duties, seen in the fat of the sacrifices, and life's ordinary cares and needs, seen in the bread. After eight days (Lev. 9:1) Aaron and his sons entered their public ministry, presenting the sin offering, burnt offering, and fellowship offering on behalf of the people. This first act of ministry received divine ratification in the appearing of the glory of the Lord and the fire of God that fell on the offering (9:23-24).

At the end of the wilderness wandering, Aaron was warned of his impending death. He and Moses went up Mount HOR, where Aaron was stripped of his priestly robes, which passed in succession to his son Eleazar. Aaron died at the age of 123 and was buried on the mountain (Num. 20:22-29; 33:38; Deut. 10:6; 32:50). The people mourned for him thirty days.

The Psalms speak of the priestly line as the "house of Aaron" (Ps. 115:10, 12; 118:3; 135:19), and Aaron is mentioned in Hebrews as a type of Christ, who was "called by God, just as Aaron was" (Heb. 5:4-5), though the eternal priesthood of Christ is stated explicitly to be derived from MELCHIZEDEK and not from Aaron (7:11).

Aaronites. air'uh-nīts. This term is used by the KJV in two passages where the Hebrew simply has AARON, but where the reference is clearly to his descendants (1 Chr. 12:27; 27:17; in the former passage the NIV translates, "the family of Aaron").

Aaron's staff (rod). When KORAH and his confederates challenged the leadership of MOSES and AARON (Num. 16-17, possibly the most important event during the thirty-seven years of wandering described in chs. 15-19), Moses demanded that the staffs of each of the princes of the tribes be given him; and he placed their staffs with Aaron's "before the LORD in the Tent of the Testimony" (17:7). The next day Aaron's staff was found to have budded, vindicating the divine authority of Aaron as high priest (17:8). It was then placed before the ARK OF THE COVENANT in the Holy of Holies to be preserved as a witness against all who might rebel against his authority (17:8-10). (It is possible that the staff was subsequently placed inside the ark, as Heb. 9:4 suggests.)

The staff referred to is very likely the same shepherd's staff Moses was carrying at the time of his call (Exod. 4:2). When turned into a serpent, it became a sign to Moses and Aaron, to Israel, and to Pharaoh of the divine mission and authority of Moses (v. 17). It is twice called "the staff of God" (4:20; 17:9). In the battle with AMALEK the staff

was in Moses' hand; and Aaron and Hur supported his arms when he was weary (17:9-13). Moses was commanded to take the staff, and he and Aaron were told to "speak to that rock" (Num. 20:8). Instead of following these instructions implicitly, Moses (evidently with Aaron's support) spoke arrogantly to the people, and Moses lifted up his hand with his staff and smote the rock twice (v. 11), acts of presumption for which he and Aaron were severely punished.

All of the expressions used are natural in view of the significance of the staff. It was called "the staff of God," for it was the symbol of God's authority; it was Moses' staff, because it belonged to him and was carried by him; it was also Aaron's staff, because Aaron at times spoke and acted for Moses.

Ab. ab. The fifth month (July-August) in the Babylonian CALENDAR used by postexilic Israel. This name is not found in the Bible.

Abaddon. uh-bad'uhn (Gk. *Abaddōn G3*). This Hebrew name, with its Greek equivalent Apollyon, is used once in the NT with reference to the evil angel who reigns over the infernal regions of the ABYSS (Rev. 9:11). The Hebrew noun *ʾăbaddôn H11*, meaning "[place of] destruction, ruin," but variously translated, occurs only in a few poetic passages (Job 26:6; 28:22; 31:12; Ps. 88:11; Prov. 15:11; 27:20).

Abagtha. uh-bag'thuh (Heb. *ʾăbagtāʾ H5*, possibly an Iranian name). One of the seven EUNUCHS sent by the Persian king XERXES (Ahasuerus) to bring Queen VASHTI to a royal feast (Esth. 1:10).

Abana. ab'uh-nuh (Heb. *ʾăbānâ H76*, "stony"). Also Abanah. The name of a river that flows through DAMASCUS, mentioned in the Bible only once, when NAAMAN asked, "Are not Abana and Pharpar, the rivers of Damascus, better than any of the waters of Israel?" (2 Ki. 5:12; an alternate reading in the Heb. MSS is AMANA). The Greeks called it the Chrysorrhoas ("golden stream"); it is the same as the modern Barada River. Beginning 23 mi. (37 km.) NW of Damascus in the Antilebanon Mountains, this river makes Damascus, though bordering on a desert, a very lovely and fertile area.

A

It divides into nine or ten branches and spreads out like an open fan into the plain E of Damascus.

Abarim. ab´uh-rim (Heb. ʿăbārîm *H6305*, "the regions beyond"). The region E of the JORDAN (TRANSJORDAN), and specifically a mountain range in NW MOAB that includes Mount NEBO. The Israelites encamped here just before crossing the Jordan, and from one of its peaks MOSES saw the Promised Land (Num. 27:12; 33:47-48; Deut. 32:49; Jer. 22:20).

Abba. ah´buh, ab´uh (Gk. *abba G5*). An ARAMAIC term meaning "father," transliterated into Greek in the NT and thence into English. It occurs in three NT prayers (Mk. 14:36; Rom. 8:15; Gal. 4:6) together with the Greek word for "father" (*abba ho patēr*). It is probable that Jesus used this word also in many of the instances where the Greek Gospels record that he addressed or referred to God as FATHER. Because Jewish children used *Abba* when speaking to or about their fathers, some have argued that the term should be translated "Daddy." However, *Abba* was the standard expression used also by adults, even when referring very respectfully to a rabbi. See also SON OF GOD.

Abda. ab´duh (Heb. ʿabdāʾ *H6272*, "servant, worshiper"; possibly short form of OBADIAH, "servant of Yahweh"). **(1)** Father of ADONIRAM, who was a high official of SOLOMON in charge of forced labor (1 Ki. 4:6).
(2) Son of Shammua and a postexilic chief LEVITE in Jerusalem (Neh. 11:17; called Obadiah son of Shemaiah in 1 Chr. 9:16).

Abdeel. ab´dee-uhl (Heb. ʿabdĕʾēl *H6274*, "servant of God" [cf. ABDA]). Father of an official named SHELEMIAH; the latter, with two other officials, was instructed by King JEHOIAKIM to arrest BARUCH the scribe and JEREMIAH the prophet (Jer. 36:26).

Abdi. ab´di (Heb. ʿabdî *H6279*, possibly short form of OBADIAH, "servant of Yahweh"). **(1)** A LEVITE of the family of MERARI whose grandson ETHAN was made a songmaster by DAVID (1 Chr. 6:44 [Heb. v. 29]).
(2) Father of KISH, a Levite of the family of MERARI; Kish took part in the cleansing and con-

secration of the temple under King HEZEKIAH (2 Chr. 29:12).
(3) One of the descendants of Elam who agreed to put away their foreign wives (Ezra 10:26).

Abdiel. ab´dee-uhl (Heb. ʿabdîʾēl *H6280*, "servant of God" [cf. ABDEEL]). Son of Guni and father of Ahi; the latter was head of a clan in the tribe of GAD that lived in GILEAD and BASHAN (1 Chr. 5:15).

Abdon (person). ab´duhn (Heb. ʿabdôn *H6277*, "servant" or "servile"). **(1)** Son of Hillel and the eleventh mentioned judge of Israel in the book of JUDGES. Abdon "judged" Israel eight years, probably from PIRATHON in the hill country of EPHRAIM. The reference to his "forty sons and thirty grandsons, who rode on seventy donkeys" probably signifies the wealth and prominence of his family. Abdon was buried in Pirathon (Jdg. 12:13-15). Nothing is said about his rule. JOSEPHUS suggests that his reign was a peaceful one, and therefore "he had no occasion to perform glorious actions" (*Ant.* 5.7.15 §273).
(2) Oldest son of Jeiel (KJV, "Jehiel") and Maacah of GIBEON, included in the two lists of SAUL's genealogy (1 Chr. 8:30; 9:36). See also ABIEL.
(3) Son of Micah, sent by King JOSIAH with other officials to inquire of HULDAH the prophetess, after the book of the law of the Lord was read before him (2 Chr. 34:20; called Acbor son of Micaiah in 2 Ki. 22:12, 14; Jer. 26:22).
(4) Son of Shashak (1 Chr. 8:23, cf. v. 25), a Benjamite living in Jerusalem, probably in NEHEMIAH's time (see vv. 1, 28).

Abdon (place). ab´duhn (Heb. ʿabdôn *H6278*, possibly "service"). One of the four Levitical towns in the territory of ASHER (Josh. 21:30; 1 Chr. 6:74), probably located at modern Khirbet ʿAbdah about 15 mi. (24 km.) S of TYRE; perhaps to be identified with the EBRON of Josh. 19:28 (where some Heb. MSS read "Abdon" instead of "Ebron").

Abednego. uh-bed´ni-goh (Heb. ʿăbēd nĕgô *H6284* [Aram. *H10524*], possibly "servant of [the god] NEBO"). The Babylonian name that ASHPENAZ, chief officer of NEBUCHADNEZZAR king of BABYLON, gave to AZARIAH, one of the three

Israelite youths who were companions of DANIEL (Dan. 1:7). The other two were SHADRACH and MESHACH. Daniel and his three friends belonged to the Hebrew royal family and are described as "young men without any physical defect, handsome, showing aptitude for every kind of learning, well informed, quick to understand, and qualified to serve in the king's palace" (1:3-4). They were to be educated for three years in the "language and literature of the Babylonians." They determined, however, not to defile themselves with the "royal food and wine"; instead, they ate vegetables and drank water for ten days (vv. 8-14). At the end of this trial period, it was obvious that "they looked healthier and better nourished than any of the young men who ate the royal food" (v. 15). Later, the three youths were appointed provincial administrators (2:49). They also proved to be of stalwart faith and piety, and withstood all pressures to worship the pagan image set up by NEBUCHADNEZZAR. In consequence of this, all three were cast into a fiery furnace, but they were miraculously delivered (3:1-30; see DANIEL, BOOK OF). The NT alludes to them when it mentions the heroes of faith who "quenched the fury of the flames" (Heb. 11:34).

Abel (person). ay´buhl (Heb. *hebel H2040*, "breath, vanity," or "son, heir"; Gk. *Abel G6*, also *Habel*). ADAM and EVE's second son, who was murdered by his brother CAIN (Gen. 4). "Abel kept flocks, and Cain worked the soil" (4:2). The problem that caused disaffection between the brothers arose when Cain brought a vegetable offering to the Lord, and Abel brought a lamb from the flock. "The Lord looked with favor on Abel and his offering, but on Cain and his offering he did not look with favor" (4:4-5). What this precisely means the Bible does not make clear. Perhaps the Lord had previously made his will known that he must be approached with blood-sacrifice (cf. 3:21); or possibly with this incident between Cain and Abel the Lord revealed that he required such an offering. Two things tend to suggest

an earlier revelation of this requirement: first, the Genesis account has "Abel and his offering," "Cain and his offering," in each case putting the person first and suggesting that the one came in a correct spirit whereas the other did not. Second, the epistle to the Hebrews suggests the same view: "By faith Abel offered God a better sacrifice than Cain did" (Heb. 11:4; cf. 12:24). How could he have acted in faith if there had not been a prior word from the Lord for him to believe and obey? Cain, by contrast, came in a defiant spirit, as is revealed in his hurt refusal of the Lord's reminder that the right way was open to him and in his resentful murder of his brother. Thus Abel became the first exemplar of the way of righteousness through faith (Matt. 23:35; Lk. 11:51; 1 Jn. 3:12).

Abel (place). ay´buhl (Heb. *ʾābēl H64*, "meadow"). A name found in various compounds, apparently used to describe the nature of a site or its surroundings. In 2 Sam. 20:18 Abel is the shortened form of ABEL BETH MAACAH. In 1 Sam. 6:18 the KJV reads, "the great *stone of* Abel," but the Hebrew text probably means, "the great meadow"; the NIV translates "the large rock," following a few Hebrew MSS and the SEPTUAGINT (similarly other English versions).

Abel Acacia Grove. See SHITTIM.

Abel Beth Maacah. ay´buhl-beth-may´uh-kuh (Heb. *ʾābēl bêt maʿăkâ H68* [with spelling variations], "meadow of the house of oppression"). Sometimes

Excavated area of Abel Beth Maacah (view to the NE).

© Dr. James C. Martin

A

A

translated "Abel of Beth-maacah," and also known as Abel Maim (2 Chr. 16:4). A town in the extreme N of Palestine, modern Abil el-Qamḥ, about 12 mi. (19 km.) N of Lake Huleh and a few miles W of the city of DAN, in the tribal territory of NAPHTALI (2 Sam. 20:15; 1 Ki. 15:20). Abel Beth Maacah is mentioned in some early Egyptian sources. SHEBA son of Bicri fled to it when his revolt against DAVID failed. The town was saved from assault by JOAB when, with its proverbial shrewdness, it followed the advice of "a wise woman" that the people sacrifice Sheba (2 Sam. 20:14-22). About eighty years later it was seized by BEN-HADAD (1 Ki. 15:20) and in 734 B.C. by TIGLATH-PILESER, who carried off its inhabitants to ASSYRIA (2 Ki. 15:29).

Abel Keramim. ay´buhl-ker´uh-mim (Heb. *ʾābēl kĕrāmîm H70*, "meadow of vineyards"). Also Abel-cheramim. A place in AMMON, E of the JORDAN. JEPHTHAH is said to have "devastated twenty towns from Aroer to the vicinity of Minnith, as far as Abel Keramim" (Jdg. 11:33; KJV, "the plain of the vineyards"). Its location is uncertain, but it was probably S of the JABBOK River, near modern Amman.

Abel Maim. ay´buhl-may´im (Heb. *ʾābēl mayim H72*, "meadow of water"). Also Abel-maim. An alternate name for ABEL BETH MAACAH; it occurs only in 2 Chr. 16:4.

Abel Meholah. ay´buhl-mi-hoh´luh (Heb. *ʾābēl mĕḥôlâ H71*, "meadow of dancing"). The hometown of ELISHA the prophet (1 Ki. 19:16). This is where ELIJAH, returning from HOREB on his way to DAMASCUS, found Elisha and his servants plowing with twelve yoke of oxen. Previously, Abel Meholah had figured in GIDEON's smashing victory over the Midianite camp in the JEZREEL Valley (Jdg. 7:22). The identification of this town is debated, but during SOLOMON's reign it was included in the same district as BETH SHAN (1 Ki. 4:12), so many scholars locate it S of Beth Shan and W of the Jordan. Abel Meholah was probably the hometown of "Adriel the Meholathite," a man to whom SAUL gave his eldest daughter, MERAB (1 Sam. 18:19; 2 Sam. 21:8; NIV, "Adriel of Meholah"). See ADRIEL.

Abel Mizraim. ay´buhl-miz´ray-im (Heb. *ʾābēl miṣrayim H73*, "meadow of Egypt," apparently a wordplay on *ʾēbel H65*, "mourning"). A place near the JORDAN River at which the funeral cortège of JACOB stopped to mourn for seven days before proceeding to MACHPELAH to bury the patriarch (Gen. 50:10-11). The site was known as the "threshing floor of Atad," but it was renamed the "mourning of Egypt" because Pharaoh's officials, as well as Egyptian chariots and horsemen, took part in the funeral rites (vv. 8-9). The site is often thought to have been E of the river, but the Hebrew phrase rendered "beyond the Jordan" by most versions can mean more generally "the region of the Jordan."

Abel Shittim. ay´buhl-shit´im (Heb. *ʾābēl haššiṭṭîm H69*, "meadow of the acacias"). A locality in the plains of MOAB where the Israelites camped before entering the Promised Land (Num. 33:49). See SHITTIM.

Abez. ay´bez. See EBEZ.

Abi, Abia(h). ay´bi, uh-bi´uh. See ABIJAH.

Abi-Albon. ay´bi-al´buhn (Heb. *ʾăbî-ʿalbôn H50*, meaning uncertain). Identified as an Arbathite (meaning prob. that he was from BETH ARABAH), Abi-Albon was a member of DAVID's thirty mighty warriors (2 Sam. 23:31). Many think this form of the name is corrupt, for he is called ABIEL in the parallel (1 Chr. 11:32).

Abiasaph. uh-bi´uh-saf (Heb. *ʾăbîʾāsāp H25*, "[my] father has gathered"; spelled *ʾebyāsāp H47* in 1 Chr.). Also Ebiasaph. Son (or descendant) of KORAH and descendant of LEVI (Exod. 6:24; 1 Chr. 9:19). The order of succession in Exod. 6:16-24 and 1 Chr. 6:37-38 is Kohath, Izhar, Korah, A/Ebiasaph; but in 1 Chr. 6:22-23 it is given as Kohath, Amminadab, Korah, Assir, Elkanah, Ebiasaph. He is apparently called ASAPH in 1 Chr. 26:1 (cf. LXX).

Abiathar. uh-bi´uh-thahr (Heb. *ʾebyātār H59*, "father of abundance"). Son of the high priest AHIMELECH. The latter, along with eighty-four other priests, was killed at Nob on Saul's instructions, after Doeg had told the king that Ahimelech had helped David by inquiring of the Lord for him and by giving him Goliath's sword (1 Sam. 22). Abiathar somehow escaped the slaughter and joined David, bringing the oracular ephod with him (22:20-23). Subsequently, Abiathar and Zadok seem to have functioned as joint high priests, an arrangement that continued through David's reign (cf. 2 Sam. 15:24, 27, 29). Abiathar did not, however, give the same loyalty to Solomon, but associated himself with the cause of Adonijah, the eldest surviving son of David (1 Ki. 1:7, 19, 25). It would appear that, even after the failure of Adonijah's attempt to succeed David, Abiathar was in some way still linked with him, for when Adonijah was executed on suspicion of plotting a coup, Abiathar was banished from Jerusalem (2:22-27). This act terminated the joint priesthood of Zadok and Abiathar (as still referred to in 1 Ki. 4:4), and also fulfilled the prediction, made 150 years earlier, of the end of the priestly rule of the house of Eli (1 Sam. 2:31-35).

Abib. ay´bib, ah-veev´ (Heb. *ʾābîb H26,* "ripened head of grain"). TNIV Aviv. The first month in the Jewish religious calendar (corresponding to March-April), during which the Passover took place (Exod. 13:4; 23:15; 34:18; Deut. 16:1). Abib is the older and presumably Canaanite name for the month of Nisan.

Abib, Tel. See Tel Abib.

Abida. uh-bi´duh (Heb. *ʾăbîdāʿ H30,* "father of knowledge" or "my father knows/has acknowledged [me]"). Also Abidah (some eds. of KJV at Gen. 25:4). The fourth of the five sons of Midian, who was a son of Abraham by his concubine Keturah (Gen. 25:4; 1 Chr. 1:33). Abraham gave gifts to the sons of his concubines and sent them to the E while he was still living so that Isaac's inheritance would not be compromised.

Abidan. uh-bi´duhn (Heb. *ʾăbîdān H29,* "[my] father has judged"). Son of Gideoni; he was a leader who represented the tribe of Benjamin as a census taker in the wilderness of Sinai (Num. 1:11; 2:22;

10:24). As one of the twelve tribal princes, he made an offering for his tribe at the dedication of the tabernacle in the wilderness. Benjamin's offering was on the ninth day (7:60, 65).

Abiel. ay´bee-uhl (Heb. *ʾăbîʾēl H24,* "my father is God"). **(1)** A man of Benjamin who is mentioned as the father of Kish and the grandfather of King Saul and Abner (1 Sam. 9:1; 14:51). It is conjectured that Jeiel in 1 Chr. 8:29 and 9:35, the father of Ner, is the same as Abiel. In that case, Abiel (Jeiel) was the grandfather of Kish and the great-grandfather of Saul. Other solutions have been proposed.

(2) One of David's thirty mighty warriors (1 Chr. 11:32), also called Abi-Albon (2 Sam. 23:31). He was probably a native of Beth Arabah in the N of Judah (Josh. 15:6) and was therefore known as Abiel the Arbathite.

Abiezer. ay´bi-ee´zuhr (Heb. *ʾăbîʿezer H48,* "[my] father is help"; gentilic *ʾăbîʿezrî H49,* "Abiezrite"). **(1)** A descendant of Manasseh, the son of Joseph. Abiezer, who settled on the W side of the Jordan (Josh. 17:2), is probably the same as Iezer (a contraction of Abiezer), regarded as the son of Gilead (Num. 26:30). If 1 Chr. 7:18 refers to the same individual, he was apparently Gilead's nephew, in which case he may have been considered a son for genealogical purposes. The district of Manasseh inhabited by the Abiezrites (Jdg. 6:34) was the native region from which Gideon came (6:11). The site of the appearance of the angel of the Lord to Gideon was Ophrah of the Abiezrites (6:24), the town from which Gideon drew his first support of men to fight the Midianites (6:34). See Ophrah (place).

(2) One of David's military elite, the Thirty; a native of Anathoth in Benjamin (2 Sam. 23:27; 1 Chr. 11:28). He was one of David's month-by-month army commanders, having his turn in the ninth month (1 Chr. 27:12).

Abiezrite. ay´bi-ez´rit. See Abiezer.

Abigail, Abigal. ab´uh-gayl, ab´uh-gal (Heb. *ʾăbigayil H28,* "[my] father rejoices" or "source of joy"; also *ʾăbigal* [1 Sam. 25:32; 2 Sam. 3:3 *Ketib;*

17:25]). **(1)** The wife of Nabal, a rich man of Maon in Judah. When Nabal refused to give provisions to David and his men in payment for the protection they had given him, Abigail, a wise and beautiful woman, herself brought provisions to David, persuading him not to take vengeance on her husband. About ten days later Nabal died, and subsequently Abigail became David's wife (1 Sam. 25:2-42). Abigail bore to David his second son, Kileab (2 Sam. 3:3, called Daniel in 1 Chr. 3:1).

(2) Sister of King David and of Zeruiah (2 Sam. 17:25; 1 Chr. 2:16-17). David's father, however, was Jesse (cf. 1 Chr. 2:13), whereas Abigail is identified as the daughter of Nahash. It has been suggested that "daughter of Nahash" might be a textual corruption, or that Nahash was another name for Jesse, or that Jesse married the widow of Nahash; if the latter, Abigail was David's half-sister. Whether or not any of these surmises is true, Abigail and David had the same mother. Abigal became the wife of Ithra (Jether) and the mother of Amasa, who for a while was commander of David's army.

Abihail. ab´uh-hayl (Heb. *ăbîḥayil H38*, "my father is strength" or "strong father"; the form *ăbîḥayil H35* [1 Chr. 2:29; 2 Chr. 11:18] may be a variant spelling or a different name). **(1)** Father of Zuriel; the latter was head of the Levitical house of Merari (Num. 3:35).

(2) Wife of Abishur son of Shammai (1 Chr. 2:29).

(3) Son of Huri; he was a man of the tribe of Gad who lived in Gilead (1 Chr. 5:14).

(4) Daughter of David's brother Eliab. She probably married her cousin Jerimoth (David's son) and was the mother of Mahalath, one of the wives of Rehoboam (2 Chr. 11:18). Ambiguity in the Hebrew text leaves open the possibility that Abihail was another wife of Rehoboam (cf. KJV, but the singular in the Heb. of the next two verses suggests that he had only one wife).

(5) Father of Queen Esther and uncle of Mordecai (Esth. 2:15; 9:29).

Abihu. uh-bi´hyoo (Heb. *ăbîhûʾ H33*, "he is [my] father"). The second of the four sons of Aaron and Elisheba (Exod. 6:23; Num. 3:2; 26:60;

1 Chr. 6:3; 24:1). Aaron, his sons Nadab and Abihu, and seventy elders went part of the way up Mount Sinai with Moses at the command of the Lord, and they "saw the God of Israel" (Exod. 24:1, 9-10). Abihu, along with his father and three brothers, was later consecrated as priest (Exod. 28:1; Num. 3:2-3; 1 Chr. 24:1). Abihu and his older brother Nadab were slain by God when "they offered unauthorized fire before the Lord, contrary to his command" (Lev. 10:1-2). Neither Nadab nor Abihu had any sons (Num. 3:4; 1 Chr. 24:2).

Abihud. uh-bi´huhd (Heb. *ăbîhûd H34*, "[my] father is majesty"). Son of Bela and grandson of Benjamin (1 Chr. 8:3; however, some scholars believe that the text should read "the father of Ehud" rather than "Abihud").

Abijah, Abijam. uh-bi´juh, uh-bi´juhm (Heb. *ăbiyyâ H31*, "[my] father is Yahweh"; also *ăbiyyāhû H32* [2 Chr. 13:20-21] and *ăbiyyam H41* [1 Ki. 14:31—15:1, not in NIV]). KJV also Abia, Abiah. **(1)** Seventh son of Beker and grandson of Benjamin (1 Chr. 7:8).

(2) Second son of Samuel. Along with his older brother Joel, he was appointed by his father to be a judge in Beersheba (1 Sam. 8:2). However, the brothers took bribes, perverted justice, and incurred the wrath of the people to such an extent that the Israelites came to Samuel and demanded a king (1 Sam. 8:3-6).

(3) According to 1 Chr. 2:24, a woman named Abijah was the wife of Hezron (grandson of Judah by Perez) and the mother of Ashhur, father (or founder) of Tekoa. The MT is difficult, and some of the ancient versions read differently. The RSV rendering, "Caleb went in to Ephrathah, the wife of Hezron his father, and she bore him Ashhur," involves an emendation of Abijah (*ăbiyyâ*) to "his father" (*ăbîhû*).

(4) A descendant of Aaron who became the head of the eighth priestly division (1 Chr. 24:10). Twenty-four divisions were appointed by lot for the service of the temple in the time of David. Zechariah, the father of John the Baptist, belonged to the division of Abijah (Lk. 1:5; KJV, "Abia").

(5) Son of JEROBOAM I of Israel (1 Ki. 14:1-18). He died from illness when still a child, in fulfillment of a prediction by the prophet AHIJAH, to whom the queen had gone in disguise to inquire regarding the outcome of the child's illness. The death was a judgment for the apostasy of Jeroboam.

(6) Son of REHOBOAM and the second king of Judah after the division of the kingdom (1 Ki. 14:31—15:8 [where the Heb. text calls him "Abijam"]; 2 Chr. 12:16—14:1). Abijah made war on Jeroboam in an effort to recover the ten tribes of Israel. In a speech before an important battle in which his army was greatly outnumbered, he appealed to Jeroboam not to oppose the God of Israel, for God had given the kingdom to David and his sons forever. Abijah gained a decisive victory. Prosperity tempted him to multiply wives and to follow the evil ways of his father. He reigned three years.

(7) Mother of HEZEKIAH, king of Judah (2 Chr. 29:1); she was also known as "Abi" (2 Ki. 18:2; see NIV mg.).

(8) One of the priests in the days of NEHEMIAH who sealed the covenant of reform in which the people promised to serve the Lord (Neh. 10:7). Some believe that this is a clan name, connected with the individual listed in 12:4 (see next item).

(9) A priest who returned from Babylon with ZERUBBABEL (Neh. 12:4). In the chronology of the priests given in Neh. 12:10-21, Zicri is listed as next descendant to rule the house of Abijah (12:17).

Abilene. ab´uh-lee´nee (Gk. *Abilēnē G9*). A region in SYRIA near the Antilebanon mountains (see LEBANON). The area was named after its principal city, Abila (modern Suq Wadi Barada), which lay some 18 mi. (29 km.) NW of DAMASCUS (thus not to be confused with Abila in the DECAPOLIS).

LUKE identifies Abilene as the tetrarchy of LYSANIAS when JOHN THE BAPTIST began his ministry (Lk. 3:1). In A.D. 37 this area, with other territories, was given to AGRIPPA I. After his death in 44, Abilene was administered by procurators until 53, when it was conferred on AGRIPPA II. Toward the end of the century, it was made a part of the Roman province of Syria.

Abijah and his brother Joel, sons of Samuel, may have exercised their functions as judges here at the gate complex of Beersheba, identified by the U-shaped chambers (view to the E).

© Dr. James C. Martin

Abimael. uh-bim´ay-uhl (Heb. *ʾăbîmāʾēl H42*, possibly "[my] father is truly God"). Son of JOKTAN and descendant of SHEM (Gen. 10:28; 1 Chr. 1:22).

Abimelech. uh-bim´uh-lek (Heb. *ʾăbîmelek H43*, "my father is king" or "father of a king"). TNIV Abimelek. **(1)** A PHILISTINE king of GERAR, near GAZA. It was at his court that ABRAHAM, out of fear, said that SARAH was his sister. Struck by her beauty, Abimelech took her to marry her but when he was warned by God in a dream, he immediately returned her to Abraham (Gen. 20:1-18). Later, when their servants contended over a well, the two men made a covenant (21:22-34). Some believe that the name Abimelech was a title (comparable to PHARAOH). See also #2 and #4 below.

(2) A second king of Gerar, probably the son of the first-mentioned Abimelech. At his court ISAAC tried to pass off his wife REBEKAH as his sister (Gen. 26:1-11). Abimelech rebuked Isaac when the falsehood was detected. Later their servants quarreled, and they made a covenant between them, as Abraham and the first Abimelech had done.

(3) The son of GIDEON by a concubine (Jdg. 8:31; 9:1-57). After Gideon's death, Abimelech, aspiring to be king, murdered seventy sons of his father. Only one son, JOTHAM, escaped. Abimelech was then made king of SHECHEM. After he had reigned only three years, rebellion broke out against him; in the course of the rebellion he attacked and destroyed his own city of Shechem. Later he was killed while besieging the nearby town of THEBEZ.

(4) A Philistine king mentioned in the title of Ps. 34. He is very likely the same as ACHISH king of Gath (1 Sam. 21:10—22:1), with whom DAVID sought refuge when he fled from SAUL. As mentioned above, it is possible that Abimelech was a royal Philistine title, not a personal name.

(5) Son of ABIATHAR; he was a PRIEST in the days of David (1 Chr. 18:16 KJV, but see NIV mg.). Elsewhere he is called AHIMELECH (24:6), and most scholars believe that the form Abimelech is a scribal error.

Abinadab. uh-bin′uh-dab (Heb. ʾăbînādāb H44, prob. "[my] father is generous"). (1) The second son of JESSE (1 Sam. 16:8; 1 Chr. 2:13). When GOLIATH challenged the Israelites in the Valley of ELAH and was killed by DAVID (1 Sam. 17), Abinadab and two of his brothers were in SAUL's army (v. 13).

(2) One of the sons of Saul who died with his father and his two brothers on Mount GILBOA in battle with the PHILISTINES (1 Sam. 31:2; 1 Chr. 8:33; 9:39; 10:2).

(3) A man of KIRIATH JEARIM at whose place on a hill the ARK OF THE COVENANT remained after it was returned from the Philistines in the days of SAMUEL (1 Sam. 7:1). His son ELEAZAR was chosen by the city fathers to have charge of the ark. Much later his other sons (or descendants) UZZAH and AHIO were among those who assisted David in his first attempt to bring the ark to Jerusalem (2 Sam. 6:3-4; 1 Chr. 13:7).

(4) The father of one of SOLOMON's sons-in-law (1 Ki. 4:11 KJV). However, the Hebrew ben-ʾăbînādāb ("son of Abinadab") should probably be translated as the personal name BEN-ABINADAB (as in NIV).

Abinoam. uh-bin′oh-uhm (Heb. ʾăbînōʿam H45, prob. "father of pleasantness"). The father of BARAK, mentioned in the narrative of Barak's victory over the Canaanites under JABIN and SISERA and in the song of DEBORAH (Jdg. 4:6, 12; 5:1, 12).

Abiram. uh-bi′ruhm (Heb. ʾăbîrām H53, "[my] father is exalted"). (1) One of three men of the tribe of REUBEN who, with KORAH the Levite, led 250 leaders of the Israelites in rebellion against MOSES, declaring that Moses and AARON had exalted themselves "above the assembly of the Lord" (Num. 16:1-3). Abiram and his household, along with Korah's and DATHAN's, were swallowed up alive into the earth as a punishment of God (16:25-33).

(2) Son of HIEL of BETHEL. When Hiel rebuilt JERICHO during the reign of AHAB, "He laid its foundations at the cost of his firstborn son Abiram, and he set up its gates at the cost of his youngest son Segub, in accordance with the word of the LORD spoken by Joshua son of Nun" (1 Ki. 16:34; cf. Josh. 6:26). See SEGUB.

Abishag. ab′uh-shag (Heb. ʾăbîšag H54, possibly "[my] father is a wanderer"). A Shunammite woman who nursed DAVID in his old age (1 Ki. 1:3, 15). After David died, ADONIJAH, SOLOMON's elder half-brother, asked permission to marry her (2:13-18). Solomon evidently interpreted this request as a claim to the throne (cf. 1:5-7), for the household women of a former king were sometimes used for such purposes (cf. ABSALOM's behavior in 2 Sam. 16:20-22). Thus Solomon had Adonijah executed (1 Ki. 2:22-25).

Abishai. uh-bi′shi (Heb. ʾăbîšay H57, meaning uncertain; also ʾabšay H93 in 1 Chronicles). Son of DAVID's sister ZERUIAH, and brother of JOAB and ASAHEL. He was impetuous and courageous, cruel and hard to his foes, but always intensely loyal to David. Abishai counseled David to kill the sleeping SAUL (1 Sam. 26:6-9). He aided Joab in the murder of ABNER, an act of revenge for the slaying of their brother Asahel (2 Sam. 3:30). He was loyal

A

to David when ABSALOM and SHEBA revolted, and he wanted to kill SHIMEI for cursing David (16:5-14). He defeated a large army of Edomites (1 Chr. 18:12-13). Late in David's life Abishag rescued the king in the fight with Ishbi-Benob, the PHILISTINE giant (2 Sam. 21:17), and he was considered chief of the three top Israelite warriors (23:18-19, although the meaning of the Heb. text is disputed).

Abishalom. See ABSALOM.

Abishua. uh-bish´*oo*-uh (Heb. ʾăbîšûaʿ *H55*, "[my] father is salvation"). **(1)** Son of PHINEHAS and great-grandson of AARON (1 Chr. 6:4, 50). An ancestor of EZRA the scribe, Abishua is included in the genealogy of LEVI among the descendants of Aaron serving the altar (Ezra 7:5).

(**2**) Son of BELA and grandson of BENJAMIN (1 Chr. 8:4).

Abishur. uh-bi´shuhr (Heb. ʾăbîšûr *H56*, "[my] father is a wall [of protection]"). Son of Shammai and descendant of JUDAH through PEREZ and JERAHMEEL; his wife's name was Abihail (1 Chr. 2:28-29).

Abital. uh-bi´tuhl (Heb. ʾăbîṭāl *H40*, "[my] father is dew," or possibly "source of protection"). A wife of DAVID and mother of Shephatiah, the fifth son born to DAVID in HEBRON (2 Sam. 3:4; 1 Chr. 3:3).

Abitub. uh-bi´tuhb (Heb. ʾăbîṭûb *H39*, "[my] father is good"). Son of Shaharaim by his first wife, Hushim; he is included among the descendants of BENJAMIN, but the precise genealogical connection is not stated (1 Chr. 8:11; cf. v. 8).

Abiud. uh-bi´uhd (Gk. *Abioud G10*). A son of ZERUBBABEL listed in Matthew's GENEALOGY OF JESUS CHRIST (Matt. 1:13); this name does not occur in the OT.

Abner. ab´nuhr (Heb. ʾabnēr *H79*, also ʾăbînēr *H46*, "[my] father is Ner [*or* a lamp]"). Son of NER and cousin (or uncle) of King SAUL. During Saul's reign, Abner was the commander-in-chief of the Israelite army (1 Sam. 14:50). It was Abner who brought DAVID to Saul following the slaying of GOLIATH (17:55-58). He accompanied Saul in his

pursuit of David (26:5) and was rebuked by David for his failure to keep better watch over his master (26:13-16).

At Saul's death, Abner had ISH-BOSHETH, Saul's son, made king over Israel (2 Sam. 2:8). Abner and his men met David's servants in combat by the pool of GIBEON and were overwhelmingly defeated. During the retreat from this battle, Abner was pursued by ASAHEL, JOAB's brother, and in self-defense killed him (2:12-32).

Soon after this, Abner and Ish-Bosheth had a quarrel over Saul's concubine, Rizpah. Ish-Bosheth probably saw Abner's behavior with Rizpah as tantamount to a claim to the throne. This resulted in Abner's entering into negotiations with David to go to his side, and he promised to bring all Israel with him. David graciously received him; Abner had not been gone long when Joab heard of the affair, and, believing or pretending to believe that Abner had come as a spy, Joab invited him to a friendly conversation and murdered him "to avenge the blood of his brother Asahel" (2 Sam. 3:6-27). This seems to have been a genuine grief to David, who composed a lament for the occasion (3:33-34).

abomination. This English term, applied to that which causes disgust or hatred, occurs frequently in the KJV but only a few times in the NIV and other modern versions (e.g., Prov. 26:25; Isa. 66:3; Dan. 9:27; 11:31; 12:11; cf. "abominable," Isa. 66:17; Jer. 32:34). The idea is most often expressed in the NIV by the verb *detest* and the adjective *detestable*. Two main Hebrew words are involved: (1) *šiqqûṣ H9199* is used of idols (e.g., 2 Ki. 23:24; Jer. 7:30), of the gods represented by idols (e.g., 2 Ki. 23:13), of forbidden practices (e.g., 23:24), and generally of anything contrary to the worship and religion of the Lord (e.g., 2 Chr. 15:8; Isa. 66:3; Jer. 4:1). The related noun *šeqeṣ H9211* is used of idols in animal form (Ezek. 8:10), of forbidden foods (Lev. 11:10, 13, 42), and generally of anything bringing ceremonial defilement (7:21). (2) The more common term *tôʿēbâ H9359* is applied to wider areas of life. It is used of things related to idols (Deut. 7:25; 27:15) and of the false gods themselves (32:16); but it is used also, for example, of forbidden sexual practices (e.g., Lev. 18:22, 26-27), of prophecy leading to the worship of other gods (Deut. 13:13-14), of offering blemished animals in sacrifice (17:1), and of heathen divination (18:9, 12). Basic to the use of these words, then, is the active abhorrence the Lord feels toward that which challenges his position as the sole God of his people, or contradicts his will, whether in the way he is to be worshiped or in the way his people are to live.

abomination of desolation. The interpretation of the references of Daniel to some notable and frightful "abomination that causes desolation" (Dan. 9:27; 11:31; 12:11) has caused much difficulty and difference among interpreters. Many continue to hold that Dan. 11:31 was fulfilled in 165 B.C., when the Seleucid king ANTIOCHUS Epiphanes set up an altar in the Jerusalem TEMPLE and sacrificed a pig on it. But that event could not have exhausted the meaning of the passage, for Matt. 24:15 and Mk. 13:14 make it clear that the Lord Jesus understood the "abomination" as still to come. Some understand the Lord to refer to some horrifying act of sacrilege during the period of the Jewish revolt and the sack of JERUSALEM by the Romans in A.D. 70. It cannot, however, be the entry of the Romans into the Most Holy Place, for the setting up of the abomination is offered by the Lord as a sign to his true followers that they must leave the city without delay to avoid being caught up in its overthrow. Once the city fell to the Romans, the time of flight would be past. It is more likely, therefore, that the reference is to Jewish zealot rebels who actually set up their military headquarters in the Holy Place. Other interpreters, however, understand the Lord to be speaking not of the fall of Jerusalem but of the end-time itself, immediately prior to his own coming; and they link the setting up of the abomination with the appearance and activity of the man of sin (2 Thess. 2:3-4, 8-9).

Abraham, Abram. ay′bruh-ham, ay′bruhm (Heb. ʾabrāhām H90, etymology uncertain, but interpreted as "father of a multitude" [Gen. 17:5, perhaps a play on words]; his original name, used from Gen. 11:26 to 17:5, was ʾabrām H92, possibly short form of ʾăbîrām H53, "[my] father is exalted" [see ABIRAM]). Son of TERAH, founder of the Hebrew nation, and father of the people of

God, he traced his ancestry back to NOAH through SHEM (11:10-27) and came into the Bible story out of an idolatrous background (Josh. 24:2). After the death of his brother HARAN (Gen. 11:28), Abram moved in obedience to a divine vision (Acts 7:2-4) from UR of the Chaldees in MESOPOTAMIA to the city of Haran in N SYRIA. He was accompanied by his father Terah, his wife and half-sister Sarai (SARAH), and his nephew LOT (Gen. 11:31-32).

Abraham's renown in the Bible as a man of faith and the father of the people of faith is a direct consequence of the way the Bible tells his story. Like all history writing, the Bible is selective in the facts it records, choosing those that are most significant to bring out the meaning of the events. The Genesis account of Abraham's life records the development of his FAITH—from the imperfect faith of Gen. 12-13, through the growing faith of chs. 14-17, and on to the mature faith of chs. 18-25.

At age seventy-five (Gen. 12:4) Abram was commanded to leave all and go out into the unknown, sustained only by the promises of God (12:1-3). In faith he obeyed, but with an imperfect obedience. Contrary to the command to leave his "father's household," he took his nephew Lot with him, laying the foundation for considerable future trouble (chs. 13; 19). When Abram arrived in Canaan (12:6), God confirmed the promise that this was the land Abram's descendants would possess (12:7), but the imperfection of Abram's faith again appeared. Although assured by God that he was in the right place, Abram deserted Canaan for Egypt in a time of famine and, still uncertain whether the Lord could preserve him in trouble, tried to pass off Sarai as his sister, hoping to purchase his own safety at her expense (12:10-20). Yet Abram's imperfection of faith did not shake the promises of God, who first acted to protect the chosen family in Egypt (12:17-20) and then, when Abram tried to solve family problems (13:7) by dividing up the Promised Land, reaffirmed (13:14-17) that none but Abram and his descendants could inherit the promises.

The fascinating glimpse into the international tensions of the ancient world given in Gen. 14 allows us to see Abram's growing faith. Clearly he is now more aware of himself as the man separated to God from the world. He first opposed the kings

(14:13-16) and then refused the world's wealth (14:21-24). These are plainly the acts of a man confident in the protection and provision of God. The Lord was not slow to respond in both regards (15:1). But the richness of the divine response provoked Abram to question the point of it all, for he had no son to inherit what the Lord would give more sure. First, he made Abram and Sarai into new people (17:3-5, 15-16). This is the significance of the gift of new names: they are themselves made new, with new capacities. Second, the Lord restated and amplified his spoken promises so as to leave no doubt of his seriousness in making them (17:6-8). Third, he sealed his promises with the

The Egyptian tomb paintings at Beni Hasan, dating approximately to the period of Abraham, depict Semitic travelers to Egypt.

© Dr. James C. Martin. Egyptian Ministry of Antiquity. Photographed by permission.

him. This leads to that high moment of faith when Abram, fully aware that every human aspect of the situation was against him (Rom. 4:18-21), rested wholly and absolutely on God's word of promise; this is the faith that justifies (Gen. 15:4-6). But though Abram had leaped onto a pinnacle of faith, he was still only learning to walk in the way of faith.

The Lord confirmed his promises of children and land in a great COVENANT sign (Gen. 15:7-21), but Abram and Sarai, tired of waiting (ch. 16), turned from the way of faith to a human expedient that was permitted—even expected—by the laws of the day: a childless couple might "have children" through the medium of a secondary wife. Poor, mistreated HAGAR fell into this role. Yet the Lord was not diverted from his chosen course: in gentle grace he picked up the pieces of Hagar's broken life (16:7-16) and reaffirmed his covenant with Abram (ch. 17). In three ways the Lord made his promises

sign of CIRCUMCISION (17:9-14) so that forever after Abraham and his family would be able to look at their own bodies and say, "The Lord has indeed kept his promises to me!"

Out of this experience of becoming the new man, Abraham, and having the promises confirmed and sealed, Abraham's faith grew to maturity. Genesis 17:17—22:19 is the tale of two sons. Abraham deeply loved his sons ISHMAEL and ISAAC (17:18; 21:11-12), yet he was called to give them both up—in faith that the Lord would keep his promises concerning them (21:11-13; 22:1-18). The Lord did not spring these great decisions on Abraham, but prepared him for them by his experience over Lot and SODOM (chs. 18-19). In this connection Abraham would learn two lessons: First, that it is not a vain thing to leave matters in the hand of God—he prayed, and the Lord answered prayer (18:22-33); second, that the Lord really meant the "family" aspect of his promises—even Lot was preserved because the Lord "remembered Abraham" (19:29). To be linked with the covenant man was to come under the sovereign hand of the covenant God. And if Lot, how much more Ishmael, and how very much more the son of promise himself, Isaac! Thus Abraham came to the maturity of faith that enabled him to say (22:5), "We will go ... we will worship ... we will come back"—knowing that the worship in question involved raising the knife over Isaac.

Quietly the underlining of the maturity of Abraham's faith proceeds: Sarah was laid to rest within the Promised Land by her husband, who was planning to be buried there himself, awaiting the fulfillment of the promise of possession. Sternly Abraham's servant was forbidden to move Isaac away from the place of promise (Gen. 24:6-8).

Three main streams of NT thought focus on Abraham as the exemplar of faith. Paul stresses faith as simple trust in the promises of God (Rom. 4:18-22); Hebrews takes note especially of the patience of faith (Heb. 11:8-16; cf. 6:11-13); and James brings out the essential obedience that proves faith to be genuine (Jas. 2:21-23).

Abraham's bosom (side). A figure of speech used by Jesus in the parable of Lazarus and the rich man to designate the blessedness with which the beggar was honored upon his death (Lk. 16:22-23). The figure derives either from the Roman custom of reclining on the left side at meals—Lazarus being in the place of honor at ABRAHAM's right, leaning on his breast—or from its appropriateness as expressing closest fellowship (cf. Jn. 1:18; 13:23). Since Abraham was the founder of the Hebrew nation, such closeness was the highest honor and bliss.

Abram. See ABRAHAM.

abrech, abrek. ay′brek (Heb. ʾabrēk *H91*). A word shouted to warn of the approach of JOSEPH, presumably so proper respect could be shown to him (Gen. 41:43 KJV mg., JB, et al.). The term may be Egyptian, but its derivation and meaning are debated. Proposed translations include "Make way!" (e.g., NIV, NEB), "Bow the knee!" (e.g., KJV,

NRSV, as if from Heb. *bārak H1384,* "to kneel"), and others.

Abronah. uh-broh′nuh (Heb. ʿabrōnâ *H6307,* perhaps "crossing, ford"). KJV Ebronah. A camp of the Israelites during their wilderness journey, one stop before EZION GEBER at the Gulf of AQABAH on the border of EDOM (Num. 33:34-35; not mentioned in Deut. 10:6-7). Possible identifications include ʿAin ed-Defiyeh (Heb. ʿEin Avrona, about 9 mi./14 km. N of Ezion Geber) and ELATH (on the northern shore of the gulf).

Absalom, Abishalom. ab′suh-luhm, uh-bish′uh-luhm (Heb. ʾabšālôm *H94* and ʾăbîšālôm *H58* [only 1 Ki. 15:2, 10], "[my] father is peace"). Third son of DAVID, born in HEBRON; his mother was MAACAH, daughter of TALMAI king of GESHUR, a small district NE of Lake Galilee (2 Sam. 3:3; 1 Chr. 3:2). The circumstances that brought Absalom into prominence are as follows. AMNON, David's eldest son and Absalom's half-brother, raped Absalom's sister TAMAR (2 Sam. 13:1-19). David, though greatly angered, never punished Amnon (13:21). Absalom nursed his hatred for two years, then treacherously plotted Amnon's assassination (13:22-29). Absalom fled to his grandfather Talmai and remained with him three years (13:37-38), while David "longed to go to Absalom, for he was consoled concerning Amnon's death" (13:39). At the end of that time JOAB by stratagem induced David to recall Absalom, but David would not see him for two years more (14:1-24). Then Absalom by a trick of his own moved Joab to intercede with the king and was restored to favor (14:28, 33).

"In all Israel there was not a man so highly praised for his handsome appearance as Absalom," and for the abundance of his hair (2 Sam. 14:25-27). He had three sons and a daughter, whom he named Tamar after his sister. Absalom now began to act like a candidate for the kingship (15:1-6), parading a great retinue and subtly indicating how he would improve the administration of justice in the interests of the people.

"At the end of four years" (2 Sam. 15:7 NIV, following some versional evidence; KJV "forty," following MT), Absalom pretended to have a proper motive for visiting Hebron, the capital of

Judah when David began his reign and Absalom's birthplace (3:2-3). There Absalom proclaimed himself king and attracted the disaffected to his standard (15:7-14). David realized at once that this was a serious threat to his throne. He plainly could have chosen to remain in the safety of the all-but-impregnable fortress city of JERUSALEM, but this would have been both strategically a mistake and practically a needless involvement of an innocent population in the harsh realities of a prolonged siege. David did not explain his decision to depart hastily from the city, but what we know of him from the Bible suggests these two motives: first, out in the open country he was in his natural element both as a man and as a soldier; second, he could rally troops to his cause and, as a commander actually in the field—not confined in the city—he could direct operations. But it was a sad and hurried flight, marked by partings from friends and the defection of valued counselors such as AHITHOPHEL. David sent back to the capital the intensely loyal priests, ZADOK and ABIATHAR, that with their sons as messengers they might keep David informed of events. HUSHAI the Arkite also was asked to return and feign loyalty to Absalom, and so help David by "frustrating Ahithophel's advice" (15:20-37).

Ahithophel advised Absalom to attack David at once, before he could gather a large following (2 Sam. 17:1-4). Hushai advised delay until all the military power of the realm could be gathered under the command of Absalom himself, to make sure they had a force large enough to defeat the warlike David and his loyal soldiers (17:5-14). Absalom actually followed a compromise plan. The armies met in the woods of Ephraim, where Absalom's forces were disastrously defeated (18:1-8; see EPHRAIM, FOREST OF). Absalom was caught by his head in the branches of an oak, and the mule he was riding went on and left him dangling helpless there. Joab and his men killed him, though David, in the hearing of the whole army, had forbidden anyone to harm him. Absalom was buried in a pit and covered with a heap of stones in the wood where he fell (18:9-17).

David's great and prolonged grief over the death of his son nearly cost him the loyalty of his subjects (2 Sam. 18:33—19:8). Absalom's rebellion was the most serious threat to David's throne, but its significance for the future lay in the weakness already existing in the kingdom in David's day. Plainly David's administration was faulty. The ease with which Absalom detached the northern tribes from allegiance to David not only exposed the fact that as a Judahite David was guilty of neglecting the Israelite section of his kingdom, but also, more seriously, showed how fragile were the bonds between Judah and Israel. SOLOMON's more rigorous administrative methods staved off the inevitable division that needed only the ineptitude of his son and successor REHOBOAM to make it a reality (1 Ki. 12:1-19). In these ways, as much as in its more explicit predictions, the OT prepared the way for Christ. It records the golden days of David; yet the flaws in his character and kingdom give rise to the people's yearning for great David's greater Son.

abstinence. This English noun occurs once in the KJV in the context of PAUL's shipwreck, when the people went without food for a long period (Acts 27:21). The verb *abstain* occurs a few times in most English versions (usually as the rendering of Gk. *apechō* **G600**) and means "to refrain from an action." The decree of the Council of Jerusalem (15:20, 29) commanded abstinence from "food sacrificed to idols, from blood, from the meat of strangled animals and from sexual immorality," practices abhorrent to Jewish Christians. PAUL (1 Thess. 4:3) connects abstaining from sexual immorality with SANCTIFICATION. In 1 Thess. 5:22 he exhorts Christians to abstinence "from all appearance of evil" (KJV; NIV, "Avoid every kind of evil"). In 1 Tim. 4:3 he refers to false teachers who commanded believers "to abstain from certain foods, which God created to be received with thanksgiving by those who believe and who know the truth." PETER exhorts, "Dear friends, I urge you, as aliens and strangers in the world, to abstain from sinful desires, which war against your soul" (1 Pet. 2:11).

Abstinence from eating blood antedates the Mosaic law (see Gen. 9:4) but was rigorously reinforced when the Lord spoke through MOSES. The sacred function of BLOOD within the sacrificial system (Lev. 17:11) made it something set apart from any common use. Israel abstained voluntarily

A

from eating the sinew on the thigh for the reason given in Gen. 32:32. The book of Leviticus defined what animals the children of Israel might not eat, to "distinguish between the unclean and the clean" (Lev. 11:47), and to keep Israel separate from other nations. The priests were forbidden to drink "wine or other fermented drink" while they were ministering (10:8-9). The NAZIRITES were to abstain from the fruit of the vine absolutely. The Recabites (see RECAB) took a similar vow in deference to their ancestor JONADAB (Jer. 35). God's people are to abstain from participation in idol feasts (Exod. 34:15; Ps. 106:28; Rom. 14:21; 1 Cor. 8:4-13).

Many Christians believe that the injunctions regarding drunkenness and sobriety (1 Cor. 5:11; 6:9-10; Eph. 5:18; 1 Tim. 3:3, 8; Tit. 2:2-4) point to the wisdom of total abstinence from alcoholic beverages (cf. Col. 3:17). Abstinence is not a virtue in itself, but it can be a means to make virtue possible. See also FASTING.

abyss. The Greek term *abyssos G12* (originally an adjective, "bottomless, unfathomable," then a noun, "deep place") is rendered by the KJV with "the deep" (Lk. 8:31; Rom. 10:7) and "bottomless pit" (Rev. 9:1-2, 11; 11:7; 17:8; 20:1, 3). The NIV treats it as a proper name, "Abyss" (except in Romans). In classical Greek the term was applied to the primeval deep of ancient cosmogonies, an ocean surrounding and under the earth. In the LXX it can refer to the primal waters (Gen. 1:2), but also to the world of the dead (e.g., Ps. 71:20). In later JUDAISM it means also the interior depths of the earth and the prison of evil spirits. The NT writers use it with reference to the world of the dead (Rom. 10:7) or the nether world, the prison of disobedient spirits (Lk. 8:31; Rev. 9:1-2, 11; 11:7; 17:8; 20:1-3). The use of "abyss" in Rom. 10:7 is parallel with the use of "the lower, earthly regions" in Eph. 4:9 (see Ps. 106:28); both contrast the highest heaven and the lowest depth. In Lk. 8:31 the demons had a great dread of the primal abyss; even so, they may have caused themselves to go there when the pigs were drowned in the sea. In Revelation the horror of infinite deeps is intensified. See also ABADDON.

acacia. See PLANTS.

Acbor. ak′bor (Heb. *ʿakbôr H6570*, "mouse"). TNIV Akbor. (1) Father of BAAL-HANAN, an Edomite king (Gen. 36:38-39; 1 Chr. 1:49).

(2) Son of Micaiah and father of ELNATHAN; King JOSIAH commanded him to go with some others to consult HULDAH the prophetess concerning the newly discovered book of the law (2 Ki. 22:12, 14; Jer. 26:22; called Abdon son of Micah in 2 Chr. 34:20).

Accad. See AKKAD.

accent. This term is used once by the NIV and other versions to render Greek *lalia G3282*, "talking, speech" (Matt. 26:73). The Greek word likely refers to the dialectical peculiarity of one like PETER, who spoke Jewish ARAMAIC in a way characteristic of GALILEE. "Accent" may be too restricted a rendering, for *lalia* probably included the peculiar use of words and idioms as well as mere accent or intonation.

acceptance. The act of receiving something or someone with approval; the state of being thus received. In the Bible the most vital need of the person is to be acceptable to God. SIN separates; acceptance is a condition of restoration to God. It is clear that God determines who is acceptable to him, and he it is who provides the means of RECONCILIATION of the estranged. God instituted reconciling SACRIFICES, but sacrifices in themselves are of no use if the worshipers are profane in their manner of life (Isa. 1:11-16). The NT gives the final word on the solution: God provided access to himself through Jesus Christ by his cross (Eph. 2:18; 3:12). Acceptance is, in more personal terms, the equivalent of the idea of JUSTIFICATION, which comes through accepting God's gift by FAITH (Rom. 5:1-2). We are accepted by accepting God's gift. Since this is so, believers can offer themselves acceptably to God (12:1); and their spiritual sacrifices, such as acts of praise and well-doing, are acceptable through Christ (Phil 4:18; Heb. 13:15-16; 1 Pet. 2:5). Because God has received believers, moreover, they are to forgive and accept each other in the fellowship of LOVE (Eph. 4:32; 5:2).

access. A word used to translate Greek *prosagōgē G4643*, which appears three times in the NT (Rom.

5:2; Eph. 2:18; in Eph. 3:12 NIV uses the term "approach"). Commentators are not agreed as to whether the word should be taken in the transitive sense, meaning "introduction," or in the intransitive sense, meaning "access, personal approach." In the NT it is always used of the work of Christ. He introduces a person into the royal presence of God. The redemptive blessings that belong to the believer are made possible through Christ, by FAITH.

Accho. See Acco.

Acco. ak′oh (Heb. *ʿakkô H6573*; Gk. *Ptolemais G4767*). KJV Accho; TNIV Akko. A Canaanite-Phoenician coastal city, known as Ptolemais in NT times; identified as modern Acre, some 8 mi. (13 km.) N of Mount CARMEL and 30 mi. (50 km.) S of TYRE. The river Belus flows into the Mediterranean Sea close to the town. Acco was in the portion assigned to the tribe of ASHER, but the Hebrews did not drive out the original inhabitants (Jdg. 1:31). In the Hellenistic period it received the name Ptolemais from the Ptolemies of Egypt (see PTOLEMY). PAUL stayed there a day with Christian brethren on his way from Tyre to CAESAREA (Acts 21:7). The Crusaders occupied the town and named it St. Jean d'Acre. In modern times it was part of the Turkish empire, except for a time when it was occupied by Egypt, being restored to the Turks with British help. Today it is in the nation of Israel, opposite the larger city of Haifa.

accommodation. A term used in theology to indicate God's act of revealing himself in ways that are compatible with human understanding (see REVELATION). When God spoke, he used the thought forms of the day and not the scientific terminology of a later age. HEAVEN is described in terms of human values: gold, silver, jewels. HELL is described in terms of fire and brimstone. God himself is spoken of as having a face, eyes, ears, mouth, hands, feet, and so on (see ANTHROPOMORPHISM). In no way does this accommodation affect the truth or the religious value of the passage. That which is declared is real, but intelligible to human beings only through their language and in their thought forms (see also ALLEGORY; INTERPRETATION). In a somewhat different sense, one may say that God accommodated himself supremely in the INCARNATION of Jesus Christ.

Aerial view of the Crusader city of Acco (looking NE).

© Dr. James C. Martin

accord. See UNITY.

accursed. See ANATHEMA; CURSE; DEVOTED THING.

Accuser. See SATAN.

Aceldama. See AKELDAMA.

Achaea. See ACHAIA.

Achaia. uh-kay′uh (Gk. *Achaia G938*). Also Achaea. The name of a region, later a Roman PROVINCE, in S GREECE that included the Peloponnesus; CORINTH was its capital. The areas N of Achaia were districts of MACEDONIA, and the phrase "Macedonia and Achaia" generally means all Greece (Acts 19:21; Rom. 15:26; 1 Thess. 1:7-8). In Acts 20:2 "Greece" refers specifically to Achaia. In Acts 18:12, GALLIO is accurately called PROCONSUL of Achaia, for CLAUDIUS had just made this region a senatorial province (the governors of imperial provinces were called PREFECTS and later

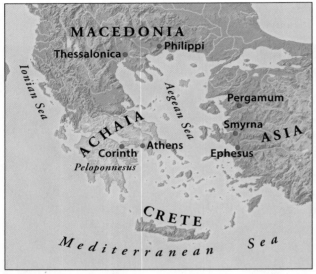

Achaia.

PROCURATORS). Achaia is mentioned in five other NT passages (Acts 18:27; 1 Cor. 16:15; 2 Cor. 1:1; 9:2; 11:10; in Rom. 16:5, KJV has Achaia, but the earliest textual evidence supports ASIA).

Achaicus. uh-kay´uh-kuhs (Gk. *Achaikos G939*, "belonging to Achaia"). A respected Christian of CORINTH. He is mentioned only in 1 Cor. 16:17 as the third member of a three-man delegation coming to PAUL in EPHESUS with a letter from the Corinthian church (7:1; some MSS also insert the three names of the delegation in 16:15). Their arrival refreshed Paul, and when they returned to Corinth, they may have taken with them 1 Corinthians (cf. the subscription after 16:24 in most MSS).

Achan. ay´kan (Heb. *ʿākān H6575*, derivation unknown; in 1 Chr. 2:7 the name appears as *ʿākār*

H6580, "Achar," which means "troubler"; LXX has *Achar* throughout). Son of Carmi and descendant of JUDAH through ZERAH (one of the twins born to Judah by his own daughter-in-law, TAMAR). Achan was stoned to death for violating the ban (see DEVOTED THING) during the conquest of JERICHO (Josh. 7:1-26). Achan stole 200 shekels of silver, a Babylonian garment, and a wedge of gold weighing 50 shekels, and hid them in the earthen floor of his tent (7:21). JOSHUA had devoted the metals to God (6:17-19). All else was to be destroyed. Because of this one man's disobedience, Israel was defeated at AI. God revealed the reason to Joshua. By a process of elimination Achan was found out. He confessed, and he and his family and possessions were brought down to the Valley of ACHOR.

In spite of some difficulty in understanding the Hebrew text in Josh. 7:25-26, there is little ground for holding that Joshua's command (6:17) was not carried out in the execution of both Achan and his entourage. In the Scriptures the Lord often allows us to see the full significance of our sinful ways. Achan's experience illustrates the biblical revelation that we never sin alone: there is always a family involvement (cf. Exod. 20:5-6) and also a wider pollution touching the whole people of God and bringing them under judgment. Joshua expressed this thought in his epitaph: "Why have you brought this trouble on us?" (Josh. 7:25), allowing the name Achan to slip over into the similar-sounding verb *ʿākar H6579*, "to trouble, bring disaster." This in turn became the name of the place itself, Achor, "disaster"; and in 2 Chr. 2:7, Achan himself is referred to as Achar, meaning "troubler, man of disaster."

Achar. See ACHAN.

Achaz. See AHAZ.

Achbor. See ACBOR.

Achim. See AKIM.

Achish. ay´kish (Heb. *ʾākîš H429*, possibly from Hurrian *akk sha(rur)*, "the king gives"). A PHILISTINE king of GATH to whom DAVID fled for protection (1 Sam. 21:10-15). Initially, David was fearful and pretended insanity; when Achish repulsed him, he fled. At a later point David again sought refuge with Achish, this time behaving so as to win his confidence (27:1-12). David consented to join Achish against Israel, but when the Philistine lords objected, the king sent him away (29:1-11). He may be the same Achish to whom Shimei's servant fled many years later (1 Ki. 2:39-40). In the title to Ps. 34 Achish is called ABIMELECH, which may have been a dynastic name of Philistine kings (cf. Gen. 20:2, 22; 26:1, 26).

Achmetha. See ECBATANA.

Achor. ay´kohr (Heb. ʿākôr *H6574*, "trouble"). The valley in which ACHAN, apparently with his family, was stoned to death because he had taken forbidden booty (Josh. 7:24-26). The place is often identified with modern el-Buqeʿah, SW of JERICHO. This area certainly suits the symbolic reference in Hos. 2:15, where the transformation of Achor into "a door of hope" typifies the changed expectations of the people of God in the messianic day (cf. Isa. 65:10).

Achsah, Achsa. See ACSAH.

Achshaph. See ACSHAPH.

Achzib. See ACZIB.

acre. This English term, referring to a unit of area, is used twice (1 Sam. 14:14; Isa. 5:10) to render the Hebrew word *ṣemed H7538*, which literally means "yoke." In both passages the area involved is the average amount a yoke of oxen could plow in a day. What precise measurements are involved is not known, and the translation "acre" is merely conventional. (For the proper name Acre, see ACCO.)

Acropolis. uh-krop´uh-lis (Gk. *Akropolis*, from *akros*, "top, extremity," and *polis*, "city"). The higher city, citadel, or castle of a Greek municipality; especially the citadel of ATHENS, where the treasury was. The crowning glory of Athens is the Parthenon, usually regarded as the finest exemplar of Greek architecture. During PAUL's stay in Athens (Acts 17:15—18:1), "he was greatly distressed to see that the city was full of idols" (17:16). The images of gods and of heroes worshiped as gods filled Athens and were inescapably conspicuous on the Acropolis. As Paul stood on Mars' Hill, before the court of the AREOPAGUS, he could see the temples on the Acropolis directly to the E, and the AGORA (marketplace) below it. Many other towns mentioned in the NT—e.g., CORINTH, PHILIPPI, SAMARIA—had an acropolis, which served as the town's civic and religious center, while the agora constituted the central shopping plaza.

acrostic. This term (Gk. *akrostichis*, from *akros*, "top, extremity," and *stichos*, "line" of verse) refers to a poem in which the first letters of consecutive lines or stanzas follow the alphabet or form words. The NT contains no acrostics. The OT, however, contains fourteen acrostic poems, in which the twenty-two letters of the Hebrew alphabet appear in order at the beginning of a line or stanza. This literary form may have been intended as an aid to memory, but more likely it was a poetic way of saying that a total coverage of the subject was being offered—as we would say, "from A to Z." Acrostics occur in Ps. 111 and 112, where each letter begins a line; in Ps. 25; 34; and 145, where each letter begins a half-verse (cf. Nah. 1:2–10); in Ps. 9; 10; 37; Prov. 31:10-31; and Lam. 1; 2; and 4, where each letter begins a whole verse; and in Lam. 3, where each letter begins three verses. Palm 119 is the most elaborate demonstration of the acrostic method where, in each section of eight verses, the same opening letter is used, and the twenty-two sections of the psalm move through the Hebrew alphabet, letter after letter. It is the genius of Hebrew poetry to allow the demands of the sense to take precedence over the demands of form, and this accounts for "broken acrostics" (there is a letter missing in Ps. 25 and in Ps. 34) or acrostics in which letters are taken out of order (as in Lam. 2:16-17).

Acsah. ak´suh (Heb. ʿaksâ *H6578*, possibly meaning "anklet"). Also Achsah; TNIV Aksah. A daughter of CALEB who was given in marriage to OTHNIEL, son of Caleb's younger brother KENAZ (Josh. 15:16-19; Jdg. 1:12-15; 1 Chr. 2:49). The

A

arrangement was made in fulfillment of a promise Caleb had made to give his daughter "to the man who attacks and captures Kiriath Sepher." The bride persuaded her husband to ask her father for a field. It was given him, but Acsah was not satisfied. Out riding one day, she met Caleb and asked him for springs to water the field. Caleb gave her both the upper and lower springs.

Acshaph. ak´shaf (Heb. *ʾakšāp H439*, "sorcery, enchanted [place]"). Also Achshaph; TNIV Akshaph. An old (Bronze Age) Canaanite town on the border of the territory given to ASHER at SHILOH (Josh. 19:25) after JOSHUA led the Israelites into northern Palestine against a coalition of kings under JABIN, king of HAZOR. The king of Acshaph, with many other kings, was defeated by Joshua in a battle by the waters of MEROM (11:1-12; 12:20). Acshaph is tentatively identified either with Tell Keisan, c. 6 mi. (10 km.) SE of Acco, or with Khirbet el-Harbaj, c. 12 mi. (19 km.) S of Acco.

Acts of the Apostles. The book that gives the history of early Christianity from the ASCENSION OF CHRIST to the end of two years of Paul's imprisonment in Rome.

I. Title of the Book. An early MS has the title "Acts" (Gk. *Praxeis*, "doings, transactions, achievements"). Other early titles are "Acts of Apostles," "The Acts of the Apostles," "Acts of the Holy Apostles." The book, however, narrates actions and speeches chiefly of PETER and PAUL. There is some information about JUDAS ISCARIOT (Acts 1:16-20), the man chosen to succeed him (1:21-26), JOHN THE APOSTLE (3:1—4:31; 8:14-17), and John's brother, JAMES (12:12). The Twelve, except the betrayer, are listed in 1:13. Acts is not a history of all the apostles; rather, it is a selection from the deeds and words of some who illustrate the progress of first-century Christianity in those phases that interested the author as he was moved by the Holy Spirit. The title "Acts of the Holy Spirit" has often been suggested, and the contents of the book bear out the appropriateness of such a title.

II. Author. Not until A.D. 160-200 do we have positive statements as to the authorship of Acts. From that time onward, all who mention the subject agree that the two books dedicated to THEOPHILUS (Luke and Acts) were written by "Luke, the beloved physician." Only in modern times have there been attempts to ascribe both books to TITUS or some other author. See LUKE; LUKE, GOSPEL OF.

By writing "we" instead of "they" in recounting events when he was present, the author indicates that he was a companion of Paul. Luke evidently joined Paul, SILAS, and TIMOTHY at TROAS during the second missionary journey and accompanied them to PHILIPPI but did not go on with them when they left there (Acts 16:10-17). The author next indicates that he was in Philippi toward the end of the third missionary journey, when Paul was about to sail for Palestine with the contributions of the Gentile churches for the poor at Jerusalem (20:6 et al.). We do not know

© Dr. James C. Martin

Aerial view of Herod's palace in Caesarea (looking SE). The Roman Governor, Felix, ordered Paul kept under guard here, where he remained for two years. Porcius Festus then succeeded Felix and took charge over Paul's trial (Acts 23-25).

whether Luke spent all the interval at Philippi. From this point Luke accompanied Paul to Jerusalem (Acts 20:6—21:18). Nor do we know how Luke spent the two years during which Paul was imprisoned at CAESAREA, but Luke enters the narrative again in 27:1 ("when it was decided that we would sail for Italy"); he continued with Paul, giving us a vivid account of the voyage to Rome.

Acts breaks off abruptly at the end of Paul's two years of ministry in Rome, when he was enjoying the relative freedom of "his own rented house," where he "welcomed all who came to see him. Boldly and without hindrance he preached the kingdom of God and taught about the Lord Jesus Christ" (28:30-31). If a later writer had incorporated these "we" sections, he would have named their author to enhance their authority. But the style of the "we" passages cannot be distinguished from the style of the rest of Acts nor from that of Luke's gospel. The author of Luke and Acts is the author of the "we" sections of Acts and a companion of Paul.

The question remains: Which of the companions of Paul is the author of Acts? He cannot be one of those referred to by name in the "we" sections as distinct from the author. He is not likely to have been one of those named in Paul's letters written at times other than those included in the "we" sections. Of those named in Paul's letters written when the "we" author might have been with Paul, early Christian writers chose "our dear friend Luke, the doctor" (Col. 4:14). Luke is not otherwise prominent in the NT. Why should he have been chosen, unless he was the author? The medical language in Acts is not sufficient to prove that the author was a physician, but it is sufficient to confirm other evidence to that effect. Luke was with Paul shortly before the apostle's expected death (2 Tim. 4:11).

Luke cannot be certainly identified with either of two Christians named LUCIUS (Acts 13:1; Rom. 16:21). There is wide and ancient support for connecting Luke with ANTIOCH in Syria. It is not probable that he was from Philippi. The tradition that he was a painter cannot be traced earlier than the tenth century. From 2 Cor. 8:18 it is possible to infer that Titus was Luke's brother and that Luke was "the brother who is praised by all the churches for his service to the gospel." Titus and Luke are named together in 2 Tim. 4:10-11. The conjecture that Luke was the "man of Macedonia" of Paul's vision (Acts 16:9) is attractive and inherently possible but not certain.

III. Place. The place where Acts was written is not named, though the sudden ending of the

Overview of ACTS

Author: Anonymous, but traditionally attributed to LUKE the physician.

Historical setting: Covers the period from the ASCENSION OF CHRIST (A.D. 30 or 33) to PAUL'S imprisonment in ROME (c. 61-63). The book was probably written in Rome soon after the last events narrated, but some date it to the 70s or even later.

Purpose: To provide a historical-theological account of the early CHURCH, focusing on the rapid expansion of Christianity as a result of the powerful outpouring of the HOLY SPIRIT.

Contents: Promise and fulfillment of the Spirit's power (Acts 1-2). Spread of the GOSPEL in JERUSALEM, JUDEA, SAMARIA, and ANTIOCH, with emphasis on the ministry of PETER (chs. 3-12). Spread of the gospel in ASIA MINOR and Europe as far as Rome, with emphasis on the ministry of PAUL (chs. 13-28).

A

book, while Paul is residing at Rome awaiting trial, makes Rome an appropriate choice. The question of place is tied in with that of Luke's purpose in writing and with the occasion for the publication of the book.

IV. Date. Allusions to Acts in the APOSTOLIC FATHERS are too indefinite to compel the setting of a date much before the end of the first century. If Acts is dependent on JOSEPHUS for information, it cannot be earlier than 93. But such dependence is not proved and is highly unlikely. Acts must have been finished after the latest date mentioned in the book (Acts 28:30). The abrupt close indicates that it was written at that time, c. 61 or 62. Luke's Gospel has an appropriate ending; Acts does not. We are not told how the trial of Paul came out. There is no hint of Paul's release or of his death. The attitude toward Roman officials is friendly, and that would not have been the case after the persecution under Nero in 64. The Jewish War of 66-70 and the destruction of Jerusalem are not referred to. Chapters 1-15 accurately picture conditions in Jerusalem before its destruction. It would be attractive to think that Luke's two books were written to inform and influence well-disposed Roman officials in their handling of Paul's case.

V. The Speeches in Acts. Do the speeches report what was actually said? We do not expect stenographic reporting, but Luke is a careful writer, as a comparison of his Gospel with Mark and Matthew shows. The style of the speeches in Acts is not Luke's, but that which is appropriate to each speaker, whether Peter, Stephen, Paul, or even the minor characters such as Gamaliel (Acts 5:34-39), the Ephesian town clerk (19:35-40), and Tertullus (24:2-8). Similarities between the speeches of Peter and Paul are explained by the fact that Paul explicitly preached the same gospel as Peter did. Speeches by the same person are varied in type, each suited to the occasion.

VI. Contents

Introduction. (1) Summary of ground covered by the "former treatise," especially the resurrection ministry of Jesus, Acts 1:1-11. (2) The period of waiting; a ten-day prayer meeting in the upper room, 1:12-14. (3) The choice of a successor to the betrayer as one of the Twelve, 1:15-26.

A. The Day of Pentecost, the birthday of the church. (1) The occasion and the event, 2:1-13. (2) Peter's sermon, 2:14-36. (3) The result: the beginning of the church, 2:37-47.

B. Pictures of the first church in Jerusalem. (1) A lame man healed, 3:1-11. (2) Peter's sermon to the crowd on this occasion, 3:12-26. (3) Attempted suppression of the new church met by prayer-power, 4:1-30. (4) A contrast in givers, 4:31—5:11: Barnabas, the generous giver, 4:31-37, and Ananias and Sapphira, the grudging givers, 5:1-11. (5) Growth of the healing ministry of the church, 5:12-16. (6) Another attempt at suppression of the church met by obedience to God, 5:17-42. (7) An administrative problem solved leads to further advance, 6:1-8. (8) The attempt of the Council (Sanhedrin) to suppress the new leader, Stephen, 6:9-15. (9) Stephen's defense, 7:1-53. (10) Stephen's martyrdom, 7:54-60.

C. The gospel spread to all Judea and Samaria, 8:1-25. (1) The stimulus to expansion: Saul as persecutor, 8:1-4. (2) Problems in Samaria, 8:5-25.

D. Three "continental" conversions. (1) From Africa: the eunuch from Ethiopia, 8:26-40. (2) From Asia: Saul of Tarsus, 9:1-31. (Interlude: Peter in W Palestine, 9:32-43.) (3) From Europe: Cornelius of Italy, 10:1-48.

E. The Judean church accepts the mission to the Gentiles, 11:1-30. (1) Peter convinces the Jewish Christians, 11:1-18. (2) The extent of the early mission to the Gentiles, 11:19-21. (3) Barnabas and Saul minister in Antioch of Syria, 11:22-26. "The disciples were called Christians first at Antioch," 11:26. (4) Response of the church in Antioch to need in Judea, 11:27-30. (5) A further attempt to suppress the Christian movement frustrated by the miraculous escape of Peter from prison, 12:1-19. (Note: The death of Herod, 12:20-23.)

F. Paul's first missionary journey. (1) The church at Antioch commissions Barnabas and Saul as missionaries to the Gentiles, 12:24—13:3. (2) The mission to Cyprus, 13:4-12. (3) The mission at Antioch in Pisidia, 13:13-50. (4) The mission to Iconium, 13:51—14:5. (5) The mission to Lystra, 14:6-20. (6) The mission to Derbe, 14:20-21. (7) Return through the cities visited and formally established churches, 14:21-25. (8) Furlough in Antioch, 14:26-28.

A

G. The Council at Jerusalem: Terms of admission of Gentile believers settled, 15:1-29.

H. Paul's second missionary journey. (1) Completion of furlough in Antioch and reporting the council's proceedings, 15:30-35. (2) Paul and Barnabas part, Barnabas to Cyprus, Paul to Cilicia, 15:36-41. (3) The journey to Troas, 16:1-8. (4) Invitation to Europe accepted, 16:9-11. (5) The mission to Philippi, 16:12-40. (6) The mission to Thessalonica, 17:1-9. (7) The mission to Berea, 17:10-14. (8) The mission to Athens, 17:15-34. (9) The mission to Corinth, 18:1-18. (10) Beginning of the mission to Ephesus and the journey to Jerusalem and Antioch, 18:18-23.

I. Paul's third missionary journey. (1) Confirming the disciples in Galatia and Phrygia, 18:23. (2) Apollos at Ephesus, 18:24-28. (3) The mission to Ephesus, 19:1—20:1. (4) Journeyings through Greece and Macedonia to Troas, 20:1-6. (5) The mission to Troas, 20:6-12. (6) The journey to Jerusalem, 20:13—21:16.

J. Paul's arrest and voyage to Rome. (1) Paul in Jerusalem, 21:17—23:30. (2) Paul in Caesarea, 23:31—26:32. (3) The voyage to Rome, 27:1—28:15. (4) Paul in Rome, 28:16-31.

Aczib. ak'zib (Heb. *ʾakzîb H424*, "lying, deceptive, disappointing"). Also Achzib; TNIV Akzib. (1) A boundary city of the tribe of ASHER on the Mediterranean coast (Josh. 19:29) from which the Asherites were not able to drive out the Canaanites (Jdg. 1:31). In NT times Aczib was called Ecdippa, now identified with modern ez-Zib, 11 mi. (18 km.) N of Acco.

(2) A city in the SHEPHELAH of JUDAH, listed between KEILAH and MARESHAH (Josh. 15:44). This Aczib is probably to be identified with KEZIB, where SHELAH son of Judah was born (Gen. 38:5), and with COZEBA, whose inhabitants are called "sons of Shelah son of Judah" (1 Chr. 4:21-22). Micah makes a play on the meaning of the name when he says: "Aczib will prove deceptive [*ʾakzîb lĕʾakzāb*] to the kings of Israel" (Mic. 1:14). It is tentatively identified with modern Tell el-Beida, 20 mi. (32 km.) SW of JERUSALEM (but see LIBNAH).

Adad. See HADAD.

Adadah. ad'uh-duh (Heb. *ʿadʿādâ H6368*, derivation uncertain). A city of the tribe of JUDAH on its SE border near EDOM (Josh. 15:22). Many scholars emend the text to *ʿarʿārâ* and identify the place as AROER (= Khirbet ʿArʿarah), some 12 mi. (19 km.) SE of BEERSHEBA.

Adah. ay'duh (Heb. *ʿādāh H6336*, "ornament, adornment"). (1) A wife of LAMECH and the mother of JABAL and JUBAL (Gen. 4:19-21).

(2) The first-mentioned wife of ESAU and daughter of ELON the HITTITE (Gen. 36:2). Adah was the mother of Eliphaz (vv. 4, 10), whose sons in turn are called the sons of Adah (vv. 12, 16). The marriage of Esau and Adah introduced Canaanite blood and influence into ISAAC's family. See also BASEMATH.

Adaiah. uh-day'yuh (Heb. *ʿădāyâ H6347* and *ʿădāyāhû H6348* [only 2 Chr. 23:1], "Yahweh has adorned" or "pleasing to Yahweh"; see IDDO). (1) A man of Bozkath; he was the father of Jedidah and thus grandfather of King JOSIAH (2 Ki. 22:1).

(2) A Levite of the family of GERSHON, ancestor of ASAPH, the temple singer (1 Chr. 6:41; apparently the same as IDDO in v. 21).

(3) The seventh of nine sons of Shimei listed among the Benjamite heads of family living in Jerusalem (1 Chr. 8:21, 28). Shimei (Shema in v. 13) was the fifth son of Elpaal.

(4) Son of Jehoram; a priest and head of family who returned to Jerusalem after the EXILE (1 Chr. 9:12; a fuller genealogy is given in Neh. 11:12).

(5) Father of MAASEIAH; the latter was one of the commanders who helped JEHOIADA destroy ATHALIAH and enthrone Joash (JEHOASH) in Judah (2 Chr. 23:1).

(6) A descendant of Bani. He is listed among those who married foreign women during the exile but put them away during the reformation under EZRA (Ezra 10:29; 1 Esd. 9:30 [KJV, "Jedeus"]). Some believe this is the same individual as #7 below. See also BANI #6.

(7) A descendant of Binnui (Ezra 10:39). See #6 above.

(8) An ancestor of Maaseiah; the latter was a Judahite in Jerusalem in NEHEMIAH's time whose lineage descended through PEREZ (Neh. 11:5).

A

Adalia. uh-day′lee-uh (Heb. *ʾădalyāʾ H130*, meaning unknown). The fifth of the ten sons of Haman who were put to death by the Jews (Esth. 9:8).

Adam (person). ad′uhm (Heb. *ʾādām H134*, "man, human being, humankind"; Gk. *Adam G77*). In Hebrew this term is both a personal name and a general noun, "mankind." The latter meaning is found over 500 times in the OT. Both usages are found in Gen. 1-3, where Adam as a personal name occurs at 2:20 (for further references see 3:17, 21; 4:25; 5:2-5; 1 Chr. 1:1). As the first and representative man, Adam was made in the image of God, provided with a garden and a wife, and given work to do (Gen. 1-2). His rejection of God's authority led to the breaking of communion with God (see fall), his expulsion from the garden, and a life of toil (ch. 3). From the physical descendants of Adam and Eve the human race emerged.

Adam is mentioned nine times in the NT (Lk. 3:38; Rom. 5:14 [twice]; 1 Cor. 15:22, 45 [twice]; 1 Tim. 2:13-14; Jude 14). In all these he is assumed to be the first human being to live on the earth. Paul developed a theology of the identity and role of Jesus through a comparison with the identity and role of Adam (Rom. 5:12-19; 1 Cor. 15:20-22, 45-49). In these comparisons Paul made use of the double meaning of the Hebrew word for Adam. He also developed a theology of the relationship between man and woman from the details of the Genesis account of Adam and Eve (1 Tim. 2:11-15). Jesus referred to the union of Adam and Eve in marriage as a union of one flesh (Matt. 19:4-6 and Mk. 10:6-9, where Gen. 1:27 and 2:24 are cited).

Adam (place). ad′uhm (Heb. *ʾādām*, "man, human being"). A city in the Jordan Valley where the second largest river of Transjordan, the Jabbok, empties into the Jordan River. Here, according to Josh. 3:15-16, the Jordan was dammed, probably by the collapse of the banks (40 ft./12 m. high) along this narrow stretch of the river, allowing Israel to pass over dryshod opposite Jericho (c. 16 mi./26 km. S of Adam). The site is identified with modern Tell ed-Damiyeh.

Adamah. ad′uh-muh (Heb. *ʾădāmāh H142*, "ground"). One of the nineteen fortified and fenced cities of Naphtali listed in Josh. 19:36. Not to be confused with Adami Nekeb (v. 33) or with Adam (3:16), its location has been disputed, but its position in the list would place it N of the Sea of Galilee. It is often identified with modern Qarn Ḥaṭṭin, some 5 mi. (8 km.) W of Tiberias.

adamant. This English noun, referring to an extremely hard stone (such as diamond), is used twice in the KJV to render *šāmîr H9032* (Ezek. 3:9; Zech. 7:12; it also occurs in Jer. 17:1, where KJV has "diamond"). The precise meaning of the Hebrew word is uncertain, and modern versions often render it with "flint." See also minerals.

Adami Nekeb. ad′uh-mi-nee′keb (Heb. *ʾădāmî hanneqeb H146*, "ground of the pass" or "red pass"). A site on the border of Naphtali (Josh. 19:33). The KJV, following the Septuagint, divides the name into two, Adami and Nekeb. It is probably to be located at Khirbet Damiyeh (or Khirbet et-Tell, just above it), a Bronze Age site 5 mi. (8 km.) SW of Tiberias on the W side of the Sea of Galilee, controlling a pass on a caravan route from the area E of Galilee to the plain of Acco.

Adar. ay′dahr (Heb. *ʾădār H160*; Aram. *ʾădār H10009*). **(1)** The twelfth month (late February to early March) in the Babylonian calendar used by postexilic Israel (Ezra 6:15; Esth. 3:7, 13; 8:12; 9:1, 15-21).

(2) KJV alternate form of Addar (Josh. 15:3).

Adbeel. ad′bee-uhl (Heb. *ʾadbĕʾēl H118*, possibly "languishing for God" or "grief of God"). Third son of Ishmael and grandson of Abraham by Hagar the Egyptian (Gen. 25:13; 1 Chr. 1:29). The descendants of Adbeel should perhaps be identified with the Idibaʾileans, a bedouin Aramean tribe mentioned in the Assyrian records of Tiglath-Pileser.

Addan. See Addon.

Addar (person). ad′ahr (Heb. *ʾaddār H161*, prob. "glorious"). Son of Bela and grandson of Benjamin (1 Chr. 8:3), also called Ard (Num. 26:40; in Gen. 46:21, Ard is included among the "sons" [prob. meaning "descendants"] of Benjamin).

A

Addar (place). ad´ahr (Heb. *addār H162*, "glorious" or "threshing floor"). A fortified city on the S border of JUDAH near KADESH BARNEA (Josh. 15:3; KJV, "Adar"). Addar may be the same as HAZAR ADDAR (Num. 34:4), and a possible location is modern ʿAin Qedeis, about 5 mi. (8 km.) SE of Kadesh Barnea.

adder. See ANIMALS.

Addi. ad´i (Gk. *Addi G79*). Son of Cosam, included in Luke's GENEALOGY OF JESUS CHRIST (Lk. 3:28).

Additions to Esther and Daniel. See APOCRYPHA.

Addon. ad´uhn (Heb. *addôn H124* [Neh. 7:61] and *addān H150* [Ezra 2:59], meaning unknown). One of five Babylonian places from which certain Jewish exiles returned who were unable to prove their Israelite ancestry (Ezra 2:59 [KJV and other versions, "Addan"]; Neh. 7:61). If Addon here is a place name, its location is unknown. However, the parallel in the APOCRYPHA reads, "The following are those who came up from Tel-melah and Tel-harsha, under the leadership of Cherub, Addan, and Immer" (1 Esd. 5:36 NRSV, following a generally accepted conjectural emendation), and some scholars argue that this reading is original.

Ader. See EDER.

Adiel. ay´dee-uhl (Heb. *ʿădîʾēl H6346*, "ornament of God"). **(1)** A clan leader from the tribe of SIMEON (1 Chr. 4:36). He is listed among those who increased their lands by defeating the people of Gedor during the reign of HEZEKIAH (cf. vv. 38-43).
(2) Son of Jahzerah; his son Maasai was among the priests who returned to Jerusalem after the Babylonian EXILE (1 Chr. 9:12; cf. Azarel in the parallel list in Neh. 11:13).
(3) The father of Azmaveth, who was in charge of the royal treasures of David (1 Chr. 27:25).

Adin. ay´din (Heb. *ʿādîn H6350*, "luxuriant"). A man whose descendants returned from the Babylonian EXILE. They were among the family heads who sealed the covenant with NEHEMIAH (Ezra 2:15; 8:6; Neh. 7:20; 10:16).

Adina. ad´uh-nuh (Heb. *ʿădînāʾ H6351*, "adorned"). Son of Shiza and descendant of REUBEN; a tribal chief who was one of DAVID's mighty warriors (1 Chr. 11:42).

Adino. ad´uh-noh. The KJV has the name "Adino the Eznite" in 2 Sam. 23:8 as a transliteration of the words *ʿădînô hāʿeṣnî*. On the basis of the parallel passage (1 Chr. 11:11), modern translations usually emend the words to read *ʿôrēr ʾet-ḥănîtô* (NIV, "he raised his spear").

Adithaim. ad´uh-thay´im (Heb. *ʿădîtayim H6353*, meaning uncertain). A city in the SHEPHELAH of Judah (Josh. 15:36). The site is unknown, although some identify it with modern el-Ḥaditheh (see HADID).

adjuration. See CURSE.

Adlai. ad´li (Heb. *ʿadlay H6354*, perhaps "Yahweh is just"). Father of Shaphat; the latter was herdsman of the royal flocks in the time of DAVID (1 Chr. 27:29).

Admah. ad´muh (Heb. *admâ H144*, "ground"). One of the CITIES OF THE PLAIN. Along with SODOM, GOMORRAH, and ZEBOIIM, Admah is mentioned as marking CANAAN's southern border (Gen. 10:19) and as having been destroyed (Deut. 29:23; Hos. 11:8). With its king SHINAB, Admah is also mentioned as one of the five cities that were attacked by the four eastern kings (Gen. 14:2). Its location is unknown.

Admatha. ad-may´thuh (Heb. *admātāʾ H148*, Pers. name possibly meaning "unconquered"). One of "the seven nobles of Persia and Media who had special access to the king and were highest in the kingdom" (Esth. 1:14). Queen VASHTI was banished by Ahasuerus (XERXES) on their advice.

Admin. ad´min (Gk. *Admin G98* [not in NIV]). Son of Amminadab, included in Luke's GENEALOGY OF JESUS CHRIST, according to some MSS (Lk. 3:33 NRSV; the NIV follows a different reading).

administration. See DISPENSATION.

A

Adna. ad'nuh (Heb. *'adnā'* H6363, "delight"). **(1)** The head of a priestly house who returned from EXILE with ZERUBBABEL (Neh. 12:15).

(2) One of the descendants of PAHATH-MOAB who agreed to put away their foreign wives (Ezra 10:30).

Adnah. ad'nuh (Heb. *'adnaḥ* H6367 [1 Chr. 12:20] and *'adnâ* H6365 [2 Chr. 17:14], both meaning "delight"). **(1)** A soldier from the tribe of MANASSEH who defected SAUL's army and joined DAVID in ZIKLAG (1 Chr. 12:20).

(2) A military commander of JEHOSHAPHAT's army (2 Chr. 17:14).

Adonai. ad'oh-ni' (Heb. *'ădōnāy* H151 [a pl. form with 1st person sg. pronoun], from *'ādôn* H123, a common term for "lord, master"). Also Adonay. A divine name usually translated "the Lord." When in combination with the Tetragrammaton (YHWH), the NIV renders the phrase "Sovereign LORD." See JEHOVAH.

Adoni-Bezek. uh-doh'ni-bee'zek (Heb. *'ădōni bezeq* H152, "lord of Bezek"). The title of the king of a town named BEZEK in N Palestine. He was pursued and captured by the tribes of JUDAH and SIMEON; he then suffered the same kind of incapacitation to which he subjected seventy other kings, namely, the amputation of their thumbs and great toes (Jdg. 1:3-7). Judah was probably threatened or attacked by Canaanite forces in the N under Adoni-Bezek, and therefore they turned to meet him before they could begin clearing out their own tribal territory.

Adonijah. ad'uh-ni'juh (Heb. *'ădōniyyâ* H153 and *'ădōniyyāhû* H154, "my Lord is Yahweh"). **(1)** The fourth son of DAVID, born at HEBRON; his mother was HAGGITH (2 Sam. 3:2-4; 1 Chr. 3:2). The story of his attempt and failure to seize the crown is told in 1 Ki. 1:5—2:25.

AMMON and ABSALOM, David's first and third sons, had died; the second, KILEAB, is not mentioned after his birth and may have died also. Adonijah, as the eldest living son, aspired to the throne. He was a spoiled, handsome lad (1:6), and now he "got chariots and horses ready, with fifty men to run ahead of him" (1:5). He won over JOAB and the priest ABIATHAR, but failed to gain ZADOK the priest, NATHAN the prophet, and David's guard (1:7-8).

Adonijah held a great feast at EN ROGEL, to which he invited "all his brothers, the king's sons, and all the men of Judah who were royal officials, but he did not invite Nathan the prophet or Benaiah or the special guard or his brother Solomon" (1 Ki. 1:9-10). Nathan spoke to BATHSHEBA, SOLOMON's mother, and together they warned David of what Adonijah was doing. David, roused to action, had Solomon proclaimed king at GIHON (1:11-40). Adonijah and his guests heard the shout and the sound of the trumpet (1:41). Immediately Jonathan, the son of Abiathar, brought a full account of what had happened (1:42-48). The guests fled, and Adonijah sought refuge at the altar (1:49-50). Solomon pardoned him, and he returned home (1:51-53). But after the death of David, Adonijah emboldened himself to ask Bathsheba to persuade King Solomon to give him ABISHAG, David's nurse in his last illness, for a wife (2:13-18). This revived Solomon's suspicions, for in ancient times claiming a former monarch's concubines was tantamount to

Reconstruction of the tabernacle with the altar out front. Upon hearing of Solomon's rise to the throne, Adonijah went to the tabernacle, which had been set up in Jerusalem, and held on to the horns of the altar until the king made an oath not to put him to death (1 Ki. 1:51).

© Dr. James C. Martin

claiming his throne. Solomon had Adonijah killed (2:19-25).

(2) One of the Levites sent by JEHOSHAPHAT to teach the people in the cities of Judah the law of God (2 Chr. 17:8).

(3) One of the leaders of the people who sealed the covenant in Ezra's time (Neh. 10:16). Some believe he is to be identified with ADONIKAM.

Adonikam. ad´uh-ni´kuhm (Heb. ʾădōniqām H156, "my lord has risen"). The name of one of the families that returned from EXILE (Ezra 2:13; Neh. 7:18). The descendants of Adonikam are given as 666 in Ezra and 667 in Nehemiah (also in 1 Esd. 5:14). Adonikam is also mentioned in Ezra 8:13 (= 1 Esd. 8:39) and possibly in Neh. 10:16 (if he is the same as ADONIJAH).

Adoniram. ad´uh-ni´ruhm (Heb. ʾădōnirām H157, "[my] Lord is exalted"; alternately, ʾădōrām H164 [not in NIV; 2 Sam. 20:24; 1 Ki. 12:18] and hădôrām H2067 [not in NIV; 2 Chr. 10:18], possibly meaning "[the deity] Adad/HADAD is exalted"). Son of Abda; an official in charge of forced labor under SOLOMON (1 Ki. 4:6; 5:14). He is also identified with an official at the end of DAVID's reign, and the opening of REHOBOAM's, who functioned in the same office and who evidently was known by a contracted form of the name, Adoram (2 Sam. 20:24; 1 Ki. 12:18) or Hadoram (2 Chr. 10:18). Rehoboam sent him on a mission of some kind to the now rebel tribes of Israel (1 Ki. 12:18), who stoned him to death.

Adonis. uh-doh´nis (Gk. *Adōnis*, from Heb. ʾādōn H123, "lord"). The Syrian deity of vegetation, which wilts under the hot summer sun. He was called Dumuzi or TAMMUZ in MESOPOTAMIA (cf. Ezek. 8:14). In SYRIA and PHOENICIA he was known as ʾadōnī, from which comes his Greek name, Adonis. He was venerated throughout the ANE, Egypt, and Greece. There is a possible reference to the worship of this god in Isa. 17:10, where the "finest plants" may refer to Adonis gardens, as the herbs planted in his honor were called (cf. NEB).

Adoni-Zedek. uh-doh´ni-zee´dek (Heb. ʾădoni-ṣedeq H155, "my lord is righteousness"). AMORITE king of JERUSALEM when the Israelites invaded Canaan under JOSHUA (Josh. 10:1, 3). Having heard how JOSHUA had destroyed AI and JERICHO and how GIBEON had made peace with Israel, Adoni-Zedek invited four other Amorite kings to join him in attacking Gibeon. Joshua came to the aid of the Gibeonites, and God defeated the kings, both in battle and with great hailstones. This was the day when Joshua called on the sun and moon to stand still until the people had avenged themselves on their enemies. The kings hid in a cave, which Joshua sealed with great stones. When he had completed the victory, Joshua ordered the kings brought out. He killed them and hanged them on trees until sunset, when they were cut down and buried in the cave where they had hidden. An earlier king of Jerusalem (Salem) bore a name of similar form and almost identical meaning: MELCHIZEDEK, "king of righteousness" (Gen. 14:18-20). Some have thought this detail indicates the continuation of the same dynasty, but even if the dynasty changed, there was some reason why the pre-Davidic kings of Jerusalem thought it important to preserve the name or title.

adoption. The practice of adoption is exemplified in the OT. For example, PHARAOH's daughter adopted MOSES (Exod. 2:10) as her son; HADAD the Edomite married the sister of the Egyptian queen, and their son GENUBATH was brought up "with Pharaoh's own children," whether formally adopted or not (1 Ki. 11:20); ESTHER was adopted by MORDECAI (Esth. 2:7, 15). These cases were outside Palestine, in Egypt or Persia. Whether adoption was practiced in the Hebrews' own land is not clear. Abram (ABRAHAM) thought of ELIEZER of Damascus as his heir, but God told him otherwise (Gen. 15:2-4). Sarai (SARAH) gave her maid HAGAR to Abram that she might obtain children by her (16:1-3). RACHEL (30:1-5) and LEAH (30:9-12) gave JACOB their maids for a like purpose, a kind of adoption by the mother but not by the father. Jacob adopted his grandsons MANASSEH and EPHRAIM to be as REUBEN and SIMEON (48:5). The case of JAIR (1 Chr. 2:21-22) is one of inheritance rather than adoption. Some have inferred (from Matt. 1:16; Lk. 3:23) that MARY, MOTHER OF JESUS or JOSEPH her husband, or both,

A

A

were adopted, but there is no clear evidence. LEVI-RATE MARRIAGE (Deut. 25:5-6) involved a sort of posthumous adoption of a brother's later-born son.

But none of the OT instances has a direct bearing on the NT usage of the Greek term *huiothesia G5625*. PAUL is the only writer to use it, and with him it is a metaphor derived from Hellenistic usage and Roman law. The legal situation of a son in early Roman times was little better than that of a SLAVE, though in practice its rigor would vary with the disposition of the father. A son was the property of his father, who was entitled to the son's earnings. The father could transfer ownership of him by adoption or by a true sale and could, under certain circumstances, even put him to death. An adopted son was considered like a son born in the family. He could no longer inherit from his natural father. He was no longer liable for old debts (a loophole eventually closed). So far as his former family was concerned, he was dead. Modifications of the rigor of sonship were at intervals introduced into Roman law, and a more liberal Hellenistic view was doubtless in the mind of Paul.

In Gal. 4:1-3 Paul states accurately the Roman law of sonship. Then we read that God sent his Son to be born into the human condition under law, and that God's purpose in so doing was "to redeem those under law, that we might receive the full rights of sons" (vv. 4-5). We were not merely children who needed to grow up; we had become slaves of sin and as such needed to be redeemed, bought out of our bondage, that we might enter the new family Christ brought into being by his death and resurrection. Adoption expresses both the redemption and the new relation of trust and love, for "because you are sons, God sent the Spirit of his Son into our hearts, the Spirit who calls out, '*Abba*, Father'" (v. 6). The adoption brought us from slavery to sonship and heirship (v. 7).

The same thought appears in Rom. 8:15. The first part of the chapter demonstrates that the adoption is more than a matter of position or status; when God adopted us, he put his Spirit within us, and we became subject to his control. This involves chastisement (Heb. 12:5-11) as well as inheritance (Rom. 8:16-18).

In Rom. 8:23 "our adoption" is spoken of as future, in the sense that its full effects are to be consummated at the time of "the redemption of our bodies." This "redemption" is not the "buying out" mentioned above, but the release, the loosing from all restraints that the limitation of a mortal body imposes. We are part of a suffering creation (8:22). The spiritual body, the resurrection body, pictured in the vivid terms of 1 Cor. 15:35-57, is the object of Paul's longing (2 Cor. 5:1-8; Phil. 3:21). The present effects of God's adoption of us as sons are marvelous, yet they are only a small indication (2 Cor. 1:22; 5:5; Eph. 1:13-14) of what the adoption will mean when we come into our inheritance in heaven.

In Rom. 9:4 Paul begins his enumeration of the privileges of the Israelites with "the adoption." God says, "Israel is my firstborn son" (Exod. 4:22); "When Israel was a child, I loved him, and out of Egypt I called my son" (Hos. 11:1). MOSES expressed the relationship in this way, "You are the children of the LORD your God" (Deut. 14:1). Israel's sonship, however, was not the natural relationship by creation, but a peculiar one by a COVENANT of promise, a spiritual relationship by FAITH, under the sovereign grace of God, as Paul goes on to explain in Rom. 9-11. Thus a clear distinction is drawn between the "offspring" of God by creation (Acts 17:28) and the children of God by adoption into the obedience of faith.

With utmost compression of language Paul expresses, in Eph. 1:4-5, God's action that resulted in his adoption of us and enumerates its effects in vv. 6-12. This action began with God's ELECTION ("For he chose us in him before the creation of the world. ... In love he predestined us"), having Jesus Christ as the agent and he himself as the adopting parent. God's sovereign act is stressed by the concluding phrase of v. 5: "in accordance with his pleasure and will." Adoption, however, is not a mere matter of position, as is made plain in the statement of the purpose of election: "he chose us ... to be holy and blameless in his sight" (1:4).

Adoption is a serious matter under any system of law. As a figure of speech expressing spiritual truth it emphasizes the sovereign and gracious character of the act of God in our salvation, our solemn obligation as adopted sons of our adopting Parent, the newness of the family relationship established, a climate of intimate trust and love,

A

and the immensity of an inheritance that eternity alone can reveal to us.

Adoraim. ad´uh-ray´im (Heb. ʾădôrayim *H126*, perhaps "[pair of] hills"). One of the fifteen cities fortified by REHOBOAM (2 Chr. 11:9). It is identified with the modern village of Dura in JUDAH, 5 mi. (8 km.) SW of HEBRON. In 1 Maccabees (see APOCRYPHA) and in JOSEPHUS the name appears as Adora.

Adoram. See ADONIRAM.

adoration. See WORSHIP.

adorn. The Greek word *kosmeō G3175* ("to arrange, put in order, decorate, embellish") is used in Scripture in both a literal and a figurative sense. The figurative use can be traced back to the OT (cf. Isa. 61:10). Paul says that slaves are to live in such a way that they will "make attractive" the doctrine of God (Tit. 2:10). The book of Revelation compares the beauty of the new Jerusalem to a bride "beautifully dressed" (Rev. 21:2). Both Paul and Peter urge women not to be overly concerned about personal adornment, but to dress modestly and sensibly, and to be concerned about the beauty of good deeds (1 Tim. 2:9; 1 Pet. 3:5). The words of the apostles harmonize with the general teaching of Scripture that emphasis should be placed upon spiritual beauty rather than upon physical adornment.

Adrammelech. uh-dram´uh-lek (Heb. ʾadrammelek *H165* and *H166*, possibly "the lordship of the king," but more likely represents an original *Adad-Milki,* "[the god] HADAD is king"). TNIV Adrammelek. **(1)** A god of the natives of SEPHARVAIM (possibly Sabraim in E central SYRIA) whom the Assyrians transplanted to SAMARIA after 722 B.C. (2 Ki. 17:31).

(2) A son of SENNACHERIB who, with his brother SHAREZER, murdered their father in the temple of NISROCH (2 Ki. 19:37; Isa. 37-38). Recent discoveries indicate that Sennacherib's murder was the result of a conspiracy led by his son Arad-Ninlil, who should have been named successor but was bypassed in favor of ESARHADDON, his younger brother. The name Adrammelech

This votive gift to Adad or Hadad, regarded as god of the weather, dates about 1300 B.C. (The wavy lines on the top and sides are thought to be thunderbolts.) The god Adrammelech may have been viewed as a manifestation of Adad.

© Dr. James C. Martin. The British Museum. Photographed by permission.

may be a (deliberate?) corruption of Arad-Ninlil (the Assyrian script allows other spellings, such as Arda-Mulissu).

Adramyttium. ad´ruh-mit´ee-uhm (Gk. *Adramytteion*). Ancient port city of MYSIA in ASIA MINOR. PAUL sailed in a ship of Adramyttium along the coast from CAESAREA in Palestine to MYRA in LYCIA, where an Alexandrian ship bound for Italy took him on board (Acts 27:2, where the name appears in the adjectival form *Adramyttēnos G101,* "of Adramyttium").

Adria, Adriatic Sea. ay´dree-uh, ay´dree-a´tik (Gk. *Adrias G102*). The entire body of water lying between ITALY on the W and the Balkan Peninsula (including GREECE) on the E; it extends into the central Mediterranean to include the waters between CRETE and MALTA, where Paul's ship encountered the storm on the voyage to Rome

A

(Acts 27:27; KJV, "Adria"; NRSV, "sea of Adria"; NIV, "Adriatic Sea"). Originally the name referred to that part of the gulf between Italy and the Dalmatian coast near the mouth of the Po River, named for the town of Adria (Atria).

Adriel. ay'dree-uhl (Heb. *ʿadrîʾēl H6377*, "God is my help"; prob. an Aram. name, equivalent to Heb. AZRIEL). A son of BARZILLAI who lived in ABEL MEHOLAH in the Jordan Valley. SAUL gave his daughter MERAB to Adriel, although he had promised to give her to DAVID (1 Sam. 18:19). Adriel and Merab had five sons, all of whom perished in David's dreadful and sinful acquiescence in the demand of the Gibeonites for scapegoats (2 Sam. 21:8, where most Heb. MSS read "Michal" for "Merab," apparently a scribal error).

Adullam. uh-duhl'uhm (Heb. *ʿădullām H6355*, "retreat, refuge"). A very ancient city in the SHEPHELAH or lowland, between the hill country of Judah and the sea, 13 mi. (21 km.) SW of BETHLEHEM (Gen. 38:1, 12, 20; Josh. 15:35). Adullam was the seat of one of the thirty-one petty kings conquered by JOSHUA (Josh. 12:15). It was later fortified by REHOBOAM (2 Chr. 11:7). Because of its beauty it was called "the glory of Israel" (Mic. 1:15). Adullam was reoccupied on the return from the Babylonian EXILE (Neh. 11:30).

David hid with his family and about 400 men in one of the many limestone caves near Adullam (1 Sam. 22:1-2) at a time when SAUL sought his life. While David was here, three of his "mighty men" risked their lives to fulfill his expressed desire for water from the well of Bethlehem, but David refused to drink it, rightly recognizing that the extreme devotion that put life itself at risk was due to the Lord alone. For this reason he "poured it out before the LORD" (2 Sam. 23:13-17; 1 Chr. 11:15-19).

adultery. Voluntary sexual intercourse between a married person and someone other than his or her spouse. In the OT, the Hebrew verb *nāʾap H5537* is applied usually to such an act between a man, married or unmarried, and the wife of another. One of the Ten Commandments forbids it (Exod. 20:14; Deut. 5:18; see COMMANDMENTS, TEN). The punishment for both man and woman was death, probably by stoning (Deut. 22:22-24; Jn. 8:3-7).

From the earliest times, even outside the people of God, adultery was regarded as a serious sin (Gen. 26:10; 39:9). Along with other sexual offenses (e.g., Gen. 34:7; Deut. 22:21; Jdg. 19:23; 2 Sam. 13:12) it is an "outrageous thing" (Jer. 29:23; Heb. *nĕbālâ H5576*, referring to behavior that lacks moral principle or any recognition of proper obligation). MARRIAGE is a COVENANT relationship (e.g., Mal. 2:14), and for this reason it not only imposes obligations on the partners, but also on the community within which they have entered into their solemn, mutual vows. Thus the OT finds adultery a ready figure for APOSTASY from the Lord and attachment to false gods (e.g., Isa. 57:3; Jer. 3:8-9; 13:27; Ezek. 23:27, 43; Hos. 2:4).

While FORNICATION is frequently and severely condemned in the OT, special solemnity attaches to the reproof of adultery, both in the relations of individual men and women and, figuratively, in the relations of the covenant people Israel, conceived of as a wife with God, their spiritual husband. Isaiah, Jeremiah, and Ezekiel use the figure (see references above). Hosea, from his personal experience with an adulterous wife, develops an allegory of God's love for his unfaithful people. Adultery in the marriage relation is reprehensible; how much more infidelity in the behavior of human beings toward a God who loves them with a love that can well be expressed as that of a husband for his wife! Thus the figurative use enhances the literal sense, emphasizing the divine institution and nature of marriage.

The NT uses the corresponding Greek verb *moicheuō G3658* (and derivatives). Jesus quotes the seventh commandment (Matt. 5:27-30; 19:18; Mk. 10:19; Lk. 18:20), broadening its application to include the lustful look that betrays an adulterous heart. He teaches that such evils as adultery come from the heart (Matt. 15:19; Mk. 7:21). Dealing with DIVORCE, Jesus declares remarriage of a divorced man or woman to be adultery (Matt. 5:31-32; 19:3-9; Mk. 10:2-12; Lk. 16:18), with one exception (Matt. 5:32; 19:9), the interpretation of which is debated. The PHARISEE in a parable rejoices that he is not an adulterer (Lk. 18:11). Jesus uses the term figuratively of a people

A

unfaithful to God (Matt. 12:39; 16:4; Mk. 8:38). In Jn. 8:2-11, the account of a woman taken in adultery reveals Jesus' insistence on the equal guilt of the man. Without belittling the seriousness of adultery, Jesus exercises the sovereign pardoning power of the GRACE of God, coupled with a solemn injunction against future offenses. Jesus' attitude toward adultery springs from his conception of marriage as God intended it and as it must be in the new Christian society.

Paul names adultery as one of the tests of obedience to the law (Rom. 2:22), quotes the commandment (13:9), uses adultery as an analogy of our relation to God (7:3), says that adulterers "will not inherit the kingdom of God" (1 Cor. 6:9), and lists adultery among works of the flesh (Gal. 5:19). The sanctity of marriage is the point stressed in Heb. 13:4. In Jas. 2:1 the writer uses adultery and murder as examples of the equal obligation of all the commandments of God. In 4:4 adultery is a figure of speech for unfaithfulness to God. Spiritual adultery is condemned in Rev. 2:20-23.

The NT treatment of adultery, following the implications of the OT concept, supports marriage as a lifelong monogamous union. Adultery is a special and aggravated case of fornication. In the teaching of Jesus and the apostles in the NT, all sexual impurity is sin against God, against self, and against others. Spiritual adultery (unfaithfulness to God) violates the union between Christ and his own.

Adummim. uh-duhm´im (Heb. *ădummîm H147*, perhaps meaning "red [rocks]"). A pass about 6 mi. (10 km.) SW of JERICHO that was possibly used as a trade route at an early date. It leads from the JORDAN Valley in the vicinity of JERICHO to the hill country, including JERUSALEM. It was a part of Judah's northern boundary (Josh. 15:7) and was used as a point of reference in establishing the location of GELILOTH on BENJAMIN's southern border (18:17). Adummim is convincingly held to be the scene of Jesus' parable of the Good Samaritan (Lk. 10:30-35).

advent. This English term, which refers to the arrival of someone or something important, is used especially of the coming of CHRIST at the INCAR-

NATION. In Christian liturgy it refers to the period that begins the fourth Sunday before Christmas. The term is also used with reference to the second coming (see ESCHATOLOGY).

adversary. See SATAN.

advocate. One that pleads the cause of another. The term is commonly used to render Greek *paraklētos G4156*, found in 1 Jn. 2:1: "My little children, I am writing these things to you so that you may not sin. But if any one does sin, we have an advocate with the Father, Jesus Christ the righteous" (NRSV; the NIV renders, "we have one who speaks to the Father in our defense"). John means that Christ is the legal advocate and intercessor with the Father when one falls into sin. The next verse shows that the basis of the intercession is Christ's propitiatory death for sin. This term occurs four other times in the NT (Jn. 14:16, 26; 15:26; 16:7), but in these passages it is a title given to the HOLY SPIRIT. In all four occurrences the KJV translates it "Comforter," but recent English versions prefer renderings such as "Counselor" (NIV), "Helper" (NASB), "Advocate" (NRSV).

Aeneas. i-nee´uhs (Gk. *Aineas G138*, "praise"). A resident at LYDDA, bedridden with paralysis for eight years, whom PETER miraculously healed (Acts 9:33-35). His healing caused many to accept Christianity.

Aenon. ee´nuhn (Gk. *Ainōn G143*, possibly from Heb. *ʿayin H6524*, "spring"). A place near SALIM where JOHN THE BAPTIST was baptizing during the time Jesus was ministering in Judea (Jn. 3:22-23). The site of Aenon is debated. Some identify Salim with modern Tell Sheikh es-Selim, about 8 mi. (13 km.) S of BETH SHAN in the JORDAN Valley, but it would seem unnecessary to mention "much water" (3:23) if Aenon had been close to the Jordan River. Thus other scholars prefer the modern village of Salim a few miles E of Nablus SHECHEM, in which case Aenon can easily be identified with modern ʿAinun, which is near the springs of Wadi Fariʿa. Evidently, John must have moved from "Bethany on the other side of the Jordan" (1:28) to an area W of the Jordan.

A

aeon. This term, meaning "a long period of time," does not occur in most English translations of the Bible. However, the corresponding Greek word (*aiōn G172*, "age") is found frequently in the NT and also in the Septuagint (esp. to render Heb. *ʿôlām H6409*). A common translation in the NT is "world," in which case its duration in time is involved. Good examples of the meaning of the word as a period of time are Heb. 9:26, where "the end of the ages" is the period ushered in by the first coming of Christ, and Matt. 24:3 and 28:20, where "the end of the age" is its culmination at his second coming. We live in the in-between period (1 Cor. 10:11). "This present age [time]" and "the age [world] to come" are distinguished (e.g., Matt. 12:32; Mk. 10:30). "This [the present] world [age]" (e.g., Rom. 12:2; 2 Tim. 4:10; Tit. 2:12) implies the existence of another world. In Eph. 1:21 "the present age" precedes "the one to come." Hebrews 6:5 speaks of "the powers of the coming age," which believers already experience. See WORLD. The Gnostic concept of aeons as beings emanating from and standing between God and the world is foreign to the NT.

affliction. See PERSECUTION; SORROW.

Africa. Although this name does not occur in the Bible, there are numerous references either to the continent in general or more specifically to Roman Proconsular Africa (that is, modern Tunisia, to which were added Numidia and Mauretania). The OT often refers to EGYPT and a few times to ETHIOPIA (e.g., Isa. 45:14; Jer. 13:23). In the NT, Egypt, its Greek city of ALEXANDRIA (Acts 18:24), Ethiopia (8:27), and the port of CYRENE in modern Libya (Mk. 15:21) are mentioned primarily because of the Jewish settlements there. Jesus himself went into Egypt (Matt. 2:13-14), and Jews from Africa were present on the Day of Pentecost (Acts 2:10).

Agabus. ag´uh-buhs (Gk. *Hagabos G13*, meaning uncertain). One of the prophets from JERUSALEM who came to ANTIOCH of Syria and prophesied that there would be "a severe famine … over the entire Roman world." The prediction, which came to pass during the reign of Claudius, led Christians at Antioch "to provide help for … Judea …

by Barnabas and Saul" (Acts 11:27-30). Years later, a "prophet named Agabus" (almost surely the same man) came down from Jerusalem to CAESAREA and by a dramatic action warned PAUL that he would be put in bonds if he persisted in going to Jerusalem (21:10-11).

Agag. ay´gag (Heb. *ʾăgag H97*, possibly "angry, warlike"). An important king of AMALEK (Num. 24:7). BALAAM prophesied that a king of Jacob (Israel) would surpass Agag. Israel's oldest enemy following the exodus was Amalek (Exod. 17:8-15), and Balaam foresaw Israel's future glory in terms of the defeat of the Amalekites under a king whom he identified as Agag. Some believe this prediction was fulfilled when SAUL met Agag in battle and defeated him (1 Sam. 15:1-33, though he only partly obeyed the command to wreak the Lord's vengeance). It is possible, however, that Agag was a dynastic title.

Agagite. See HAMAN.

agape. Transliteration of the Greek term *agapē G27*, the more frequent of two NT words for LOVE. It is used in Jude 12 (KJV "feasts of charity"; NIV, "love feasts") of common meals that cultivated brotherly love among Christians. They may be referred to elsewhere (Acts 20:11; 1 Cor. 11:21-22, 33-34; 2 Pet. 2:13). In Acts 2:46, "broke bread" refers to the LORD's SUPPER (cf. v. 42), but "ate together" requires a full meal. PAUL rebukes Christians for the abuses that had crept into the love feasts and had marred the Lord's Supper (1 Cor. 11:20-34). Apparently the Lord's Supper properly followed, but was distinct from, the love feast.

Agar. See HAGAR.

agate. See MINERALS.

age. See AEON.

age, old. According to the Ten Commandments, attaining old age is the reward of filial obedience (Exod. 20:12). The Mosaic legislation spelled out the respect that should be shown to the aged (Lev. 19:32). Younger men waited till their elders had spoken (Job 32:4). God promised ABRAHAM "a good old age" (Gen. 15:15). When PHARAOH received him, JACOB lamented that he had not lived as long as his ancestors (47:7-9). There are many Hebrew words relating to old age in the OT, showing the honor in which the aged were usually held; yet the gray hairs that were so much respected also had their sorrows (44:29-31). Official positions went to older men or ELDERS (e.g., Exod. 3:16; Matt. 21:23; Acts 14:23). Aged men and women are given sound advice in Tit. 2:2-5. There is a fine picture of old age in Eccl. 12:1-7. Jesus Christ is portrayed with the white hair of old age in Rev. 1:14.

Agee. ay'gee (Heb. *ʾāgēʾ* H96, derivation uncertain). A HARARITE and the father of SHAMMAH; the latter was one of DAVID's mighty warriors (2 Sam. 23:11).

Aggadah. See HAGGADAH.

agony. This English word is derived from Greek *agōnia G75* (itself from *agōn G74*, "contest, struggle, race"), which is found in the NT only in Lk. 22:44, used to describe the Lord's "anguish" in the Garden of GETHSEMANE (the cognate verb *agōnizomai G76* was often used to describe the exhausting struggles and sufferings of athletes and gladiators). It is equivalent to "sorrowful and troubled" in Matt. 26:37 and "deeply distressed and troubled" in Mk. 14:33. Luke alone records that Christ's agony was such that "his sweat was like drops of blood falling to the ground," though Matthew and Mark speak of the change in his countenance and manner and record his words as he spoke of his overwhelming sorrow "even unto death" (cf. Heb. 5:7-8).

Jesus' struggle was in part with the powers of darkness, which were then returning with double force, having retreated after SATAN's defeat at the temptation "until an opportune time" (Lk. 4:13). Chiefly, however, Jesus' agony was caused by the prospect of the darkness on CALVARY, when he was to experience a horror never known before, the hiding of the Father's face, the climax of his vicarious suffering for our sins. The one who knew no sin was to be made sin for mankind (2 Cor. 5:21). The hour was before him when he would cry out in wretchedness of soul, "My God, my God, why have you forsaken me?" The prospect of this dreadful cup caused the struggle in the garden. In this supreme spiritual conflict, the Captain of our salvation emerged triumphant, as is evident in the language of his final victory of faith over the sinless infirmity of his flesh: "Shall I not drink the cup the Father has given me?" (Jn. 18:11).

agora. ag'uh-ruh. Transliteration of a Greek term (*agora G59*) that refers to a marketplace, usually the center of public life, where people met for the exchange of merchandise, information, and ideas. The agorae of GALILEE and JUDEA were the scenes for many of the healing miracles of Christ (Mk. 6:56). Here the village idlers, as well as those seeking work, would gather (Matt. 20:3). Here the vain and the proud could parade in order to gain public recognition (Matt. 23:7; Mk. 12:38; Lk. 11:43; 20:46). Here also the children would gather for play (Matt. 11:16-17; Lk. 7:32). In Gentile cities, the agorae served also as forums and tribunals. The agora of PHILIPPI was the scene of the trial of PAUL and SILAS (Acts 16:19-21) following the deliverance of a "slave girl who had a spirit by which she predicted the future" (v. 16). In ATHENS Paul's daily disputations in the agora led directly to his famed message before the AREOPAGUS, the court that met on Mars' Hill, N of the ACROPOLIS (17:17-34).

agrapha. ag'ruh-fuh. Transliteration of the neuter plural form of Greek *agraphos*, meaning "unrecorded." The term does not appear in the NT, but in the ancient church was applied to those sayings of the apostolic church that were not incorporated in the canonical NT. Modern scholars use the term with reference to units of tradition concerning Christ, mostly sayings ascribed to him, transmitted to us outside of the canonical Gospels. The entire collection of agrapha, gathered from all sources, is not large; and when what is obviously apocryphal or spurious is eliminated, the small remainder is of limited value.

Several sources of agrapha may be noted. The best authenticated are those found in the NT outside of the Gospels: four in Acts (Acts 1:4-5; 1:7-8; 11:16; 20:35); two in Paul's letters (1 Cor. 11:24-25; 1 Thess. 4:15); and one in James (Jas. 1:12).

A

A second source of agrapha is found in ancient MSS of the NT. Most often, sayings preserved in such documents are of the nature of textual variations: parallel forms or expansions or combinations of sayings found in the canonical Gospels. A few, however, cannot be fitted into this category; the following, for example, is found after Lk. 6:5 in an important fifth-century MS called Codex Bezae: "On the same day, seeing someone working on the Sabbath, he [Jesus] said to him, 'Man, if indeed you know what you are doing, you are blessed; but if you do not know, you are cursed and a transgressor of the Law.'"

Another source of agrapha is patristic literature. Papias, bishop of Hierapolis (c. A.D. 80-155), was the first of the church fathers to make a collection of the sayings of Jesus not recorded in the Gospels, but very little of his work survives. Agrapha are found in the works of Justin Martyr, Clement of Alexandria, Origen, and a few others. Origen, for example, wrote, "I have read somewhere that the Saviour said … 'He that is near me is near the fire; he that is far from me is far from the kingdom.'"

Still another source of agrapha consists of papyri that have been discovered in Egypt during the past century, especially some found by Oxford scholars B. P. Grenfell and A. S. Hunt at Oxyrhynchus. In some of these documents one agraphon follows another without context, introduced by the simple formula, "Jesus says," as in the following: "Jesus says: Wheresoever there are two, they are not with God, and where there is one alone, I say, I am with him. Lift up the stone, and there shalt thou find me; cleave the wood, and I am there."

Agrapha are found also in the apocryphal gospels, like the *Gospel According to the Hebrews* and the *Gospel According to the Egyptians*, but few, if any, of these can be regarded as genuine. The recently discovered (1945 or 1946) Gnostic Coptic *Gospel of Thomas*, found near Nag Hammadi in Upper Egypt, which is dated around A.D. 150, consists of more than one hundred short sayings of Jesus, the majority of which begin with the words, "Jesus said," or they give a reply by Jesus when asked by his disciples to instruct them on a doubtful point. See also Thomas, Gospel of. Many sayings ascribed to Jesus are found in Islamic sources, but these traditions are for the most part of no value.

Although the number of agrapha collected by scholars seems imposing, only a very few have anything like a strong claim to acceptance on the grounds of early and reliable source and internal character. Some scholars reject the agrapha completely; others think that they are the remains of a considerable body of extracanonical sayings that circulated in early Christian circles, and that a few of them, at least, may be genuine.

agriculture. The cultivation of plants and care of livestock for crops and products. In the form of horticulture, this activity is as old as Adam (Gen. 2:5, 8-15). Caring for the Garden of Eden became labor after the curse (3:17-19). Nomad and farmer began to be differentiated with Abel and Cain (4:2-4). As animal husbandry took its place along with tillage as part of the agricultural economy, the farmer gained in social status. Yet as late as shortly before the Babylonian exile, nomads still felt a sense of superiority over the settled agricultural people (cf. the Recabites, Jer. 35:1-11).

Noah is described as "a man of the soil" who planted a vineyard (Gen. 9:20). Abraham and his descendants were nomad herdsmen in Canaan, though Isaac and Jacob at times also tilled the soil (26:12; 37:7). Recurrent famines and the sojourn in Egypt taught the Israelites to depend more on agriculture, so that the report of the spies regarding the lush growth in Canaan interested them (Num. 13:23; Deut. 8:8). Agriculture became the basis of the Mosaic commonwealth, since the land of Palestine was suited to an agricultural rather than a pastoral economy. The soil is fertile wherever water

Women from the village of Bet Sahour on the outskirts of Bethlehem harvesting wheat by hand.

© Direct Design

can be applied abundantly. The HAURAN district is productive. The soil of GAZA is dark and rich, though porous, and retains rain; olive trees abound there.

The Israelites cleared away most of the wood that they found in Canaan (Josh. 17:18). Wood became scarce; dung and hay heated their ovens (Ezek. 4:12-15; Matt. 6:30). Their WATER supply came from RAIN, from brooks that ran from the hills, and from the JORDAN. Irrigation was made possible by ducts from cisterns hewn out of rock. As population increased, the more difficult cultivation of the hills was resorted to and yielded abundance. Terraces were cut, one above another, and faced with low stone walls. Rain falls chiefly in autumn and winter, November and December, rarely after March, almost never as late as May. The "early" rain falls from about the September equinox to sowing time in November or December, the "latter" rain comes in January and February (Joel 2:23; Jas. 5:7). Drought two or three months before HARVEST meant FAMINE (Amos 4:7-8).

Wheat, barley, and rye (millet rarely) were the staple cereals. "Corn" in the KJV, according to British usage, refers to any grain, not specifically to maize (NIV renders "grain"). The barley harvest was earlier than the wheat harvest: "The flax and barley were destroyed, since the barley had headed and the flax was in bloom. The wheat and spelt, however, were not destroyed, because they ripen later" (Exod. 9:31-32). Accordingly, at the Passover the barley was ready for the sickle, and the wave sheaf was offered. At the Pentecost feast fifty days later, the wheat was ripe for cutting, and the first-fruit loaves were offered. The vine, olive, and fig abounded, and traces remain everywhere of wine and olive presses. Cummin, peas, beans, lentils, lettuce, endive, leek, garlic, onion, cucumber, and cabbage were also cultivated.

The Passover in the month of Nisan (March-April) occurred in the green stage of produce; the Feast of Weeks in Sivan (May-June), to the ripening stage; and the Feast of Tabernacles in Tishri (September-October), to the harvest. See FEASTS. The six months from Tishri to Nisan were occupied with cultivation; the six months from Nisan to Tishri, with gathering fruits. Rain from the equinox in Tishri to Nisan was pretty continuous but was heavier at the beginning (the early rain) and the end (the latter rain). Rain in harvest was almost unknown (Prov. 26:1).

Viticulture (the cultivation of grapes) is pictured in Isa. 5:1-7 and Matt. 21:33-41. Some farming procedures are described in Isa. 28:24-28. The plow was light and drawn by yokes of oxen (1 Ki. 19:19). Oxen were urged on with a spearlike goad, which could double as a deadly weapon (Jdg. 3:31). Fallow ground was broken and cleared early in the year (Jer. 4:3; Hos. 10:1). Seed was scattered broadcast, as in the parable of the sower (Matt. 13:1-8), and plowed in afterward, the stubble of the preceding crop becoming mulch by decay. In irrigated fields, the seed was trodden in by cattle (Isa. 32:20). The contrast between the exclusive dependence on irrigation in Egypt and the larger dependence on rain in Palestine is drawn in Deut. 11:10-12. To sow among thorns was deemed bad husbandry (Job 5:5; Prov. 24:30-32). Hoeing and weeding were seldom needed in their fine tilth. Seventy days sufficed between barley sowing and the offering of the wave sheaf of ripe grain at Passover.

Harvest customs in the time of the Judges are described in Ruth 2 and 3. The sowing of varied seed in a field was forbidden (Deut. 22:9). Oxen, unmuzzled (25:4) and five abreast, trod out the grain on a threshing floor of hard beaten earth, to separate the grain from chaff and straw. Flails were used for small quantities and lighter grains (Isa. 28:27). A threshing sledge (41:15) was also used, probably like the Egyptian sledge still in use (a stage with three rollers ridged with iron, which cut the straw for fodder, while crushing out the grain). The shovel and fan winnowed the grain afterward with the help of the evening breeze (Ruth 3:2; Isa. 30:24); lastly it was shaken in a sieve (Amos 9:9; Lk. 22:31). The fruit of newly planted trees was not to be eaten for the first three years. In the fourth it was offered as firstfruits. In the fifth year it might be eaten freely (Lev. 19:23-25). We have glimpses of the relations of farm laborers, steward (manager or overseer), and owner in the book of Ruth, in Matt. 20:1-16, and in Lk. 17:7-9.

Agriculture was beset with pests: locust, cankerworm, caterpillar, and palmerworm (Joel 2:25 KJV); God calls them "my great army," as

A

destructive as an invasion by human enemies. Haggai speaks of blight, mildew, and hail (Hag. 2:17). Modern development of agriculture in Palestine under the British mandate and since the establishment of the State of Israel, and parallel but lesser development in the country of Jordan, are restoring the coastal plain, the plains of Esdraelon and Dothan, the Shephelah, the Negev, and the Hauran to their ancient prosperity. See also FARMING; OCCUPATIONS AND PROFESSIONS.

Agrippa I. uh-grip´uh (Gk. *Agrippas G68*). King Herod Agrippa I, referred to simply as Herod in Acts 12, was the son of Aristobulus and Bernice and grandson of HEROD the Great. Through friendship with the emperors CALIGULA and CLAUDIUS he gained the rulership first of ITUREA and TRACONITIS, then of GALILEE and PEREA, and ultimately of JUDEA and SAMARIA. He ruled over this reunited domain of Herod the Great from A.D. 40 until his death in 44 at the age of fifty-four. While owing his position to the favor of Rome, he recognized the importance of exercising great tact in his contacts with the Jews. Thus it was that his natural humanity gave way to expediency in the severe conflict between Judaism and the growing Christian movement. He killed JAMES (brother of JOHN THE APOSTLE), an act that "pleased the Jews," and imprisoned PETER with the intention of bringing him before the people for execution after the Passover (Acts 12:2-4). Agrippa's sudden death shortly thereafter, noted in Acts 12:20-23, is fully recorded by JOSEPHUS (*Ant.* 19.8.2 §§343-52). On the second day of a festival held in CAESAREA in honor of Claudius, Agrippa put on a silver garment of "wonderful" texture and entered the amphitheater early in the morning. When the sun's rays shone on his garment, the brilliant glare caused his flatterers to cry out that he was a god. Josephus adds that "the king did neither rebuke them nor reject their impious flattery." Almost immediately a severe pain arose in his abdomen; five days later he died in great agony.

Agrippa II. uh-grip´uh (Gk. *Agrippas G68*). King Herod Agrippa II, referred to simply as Agrippa in Acts 25-26, was the son of AGRIPPA I. Only seventeen at the death of his father, he was thought too young to succeed to the throne. Six years later (A.D. 50), he was placed over the kingdom of Chalcis, which included the right to appoint the high priest of the temple in Jerusalem. In 53 he was transferred to the tetrarchies formerly held by Philip (ITUREA and TRACONITIS) and Lysanias (ABILENE) and given the title of king. After the death of CLAUDIUS in 54, NERO added to Agrippa's realm several cities of GALILEE and PEREA. When FESTUS became procurator of Judea, Agrippa went to CAESAREA to pay his respects. He was accompanied by his sister BERNICE, with whom he was rumored to have an incestuous relationship (the reliability of this rumor is doubtful). It was at this time that PAUL appeared before him, as recorded in Acts 25:23—26:32. In the final revolt of the Jews against Rome, Agrippa sided with the Romans in the destruction of his nation in the same cynical spirit with which he met the impassioned appeal of the apostle. Following the fall of Jerusalem in 70, he retired with Bernice to Rome, where he died in 100.

ague. A term used in the KJV (Lev. 26:16) with reference to fever. See DISEASE (under *malaria*).

Agur. ay´guhr (Heb. *ʾāgûr H101*, possibly "hireling" or "gatherer"). Son of Jakeh; an otherwise unknown writer of maxims who may have been from a place named MASSA (Prov. 30:1; cf. NIV mg., RSV, NJPS). Agur's proverbs were written to two unknown men, ITHIEL and UCAL, although the meaning of the text is debated. Most early rabbis and church fathers thought that SOLOMON was designated by the name Agur, but it is difficult to see why he should be referred to by a pseudonym. It has also been conjectured that Agur was the brother of LEMUEL (Prov. 31:1).

Ahab. ay´hab (Heb. *ʾaḥʾāb H281*, "father's brother" [possibly suggesting that the son is just like the father]). (1) Son of OMRI and seventh king of the northern kingdom of ISRAEL. He reigned twenty-two years, 874-853 B.C. Politically, Ahab was one of the strongest kings of Israel. In his days Israel was at peace with Judah (see JUDAH, KINGDOM OF) and maintained her dominion over MOAB, which paid a considerable tribute (2 Ki. 3:4). He went into battle on three different occasions in later years against BEN-HADAD, king of SYRIA. While he had great success in the first two campaigns, he was defeated and mortally wounded in the third. Not mentioned in the Bible is Ahab's participation in the Battle of Qarqar in 854/53. The "Monolith Inscription" of the Assyrian king SHALMANESER III contains a description of this battle that the Assyrians fought against a Syrian coalition of twelve kings. Of these, "Hadadezer," king of Damascus, is named first; Irhuleni of Hamath follows; and in third place is "Ahab, the Israelite." The inscription states that Ahab commanded 2,000 chariots and 10,000 men. The number of his chariots was far greater than the number credited to any other king.

Successful as he might have been politically, however, Ahab owes his prominence in the OT to the religious APOSTASY that occurred in Israel during his reign. Of him it is said, he "did more evil in the eyes of the LORD than any of those before him" (1 Ki. 16:30). His marriage to JEZEBEL, daughter of the king of the Sidonians, was politically advantageous but religiously disastrous. Jezebel introduced the idolatrous worship of BAAL into Israel as well as the licentious orgies of the goddess ASHTORETH. She also instituted a severe persecution against the followers of the Lord and killed all the prophets of the Lord with the sword, except the one hundred who had been hidden by OBADIAH (18:4; cf. 19:14). At this critical period in the history of Israel, God raised up ELIJAH, whose faithful ministry culminated in the conflict with the prophets of Baal on Mount Carmel (ch. 18).

Ahab's religious corruption was equaled by his love of material wealth and display. He was well known, for example, for his elaborately ornamented ivory palace (1 Ki. 22:39). Not content with what he had, however, he coveted the vineyard of NABOTH, which adjoined his palace at JEZREEL. Naboth refused to sell the land and Ahab was utterly dejected. Seeing his state, Jezebel asked him to remember who was king in Israel, and proceeded unscrupulously to charge Naboth with blasphemy, doing so in the name of the king, who weakly maintained silence. False witnesses testified against Naboth, he was stoned to death, and Ahab took possession of the vineyard. This crime sealed the doom not only of Ahab, but also of his family. The judgment of the Lord was that all of his pos-

terity would be cut off (21:21), even as had been the case with the two previous dynasties, those of JEROBOAM and BAASHA. The ringing condemnatory sentence of Elijah (21:19) was fulfilled to the letter on Ahab's son Joram (JEHORAM, 2 Ki. 9:24-26) and in part on Ahab himself (1 Ki. 22:38). Execution of the sentence was, however, delayed

© Dr. James C. Martin. The British Museum. Photographed by permission.

The Black Obelisk of Shalmaneser III (859-824 B.C.), whose conquests resulted in forced tribute by a number of the northern tribes of Israel. Here (side C), five Israelite emissaries bring tribute to the Assyrian empire.

by Ahab's repentance (21:27-29). Ahab also sinned by failing to discern the Lord's will and sparing the defeated Ben-Hadad of Syria (20:20-43). The prediction of his own death (20:42) was fulfilled when he was killed in battle at RAMOTH GILEAD (22:34).

Ahab's character is succinctly summarized by the historian: "There was never a man like Ahab, who sold himself to do evil in the eyes of the LORD, urged on by Jezebel his wife" (1 Ki. 21:25).

(2) Ahab son of Kolaiah, a false (i.e., self-appointed) prophet who, along with a certain ZEDEKIAH, was guilty of immorality and claimed to speak in Yahweh's name among the exiles of Babylon; he is known only from Jer. 29:21-23.

Aharah. uh-hair′uh (Heb. ʾaḥraḥ H341, derivation unknown). Third son of BENJAMIN (1 Chr. 8:1). The name is probably a scribal corruption of AHIRAM (Num. 26:38).

Aharhel. uh-hahr′hel (Heb. ʾaḥarḥēl H342, derivation uncertain). Son of Harum and descendant of JUDAH; a clan leader (1 Chr. 4:8).

A

Ahasai. See AHZAI.

Ahasbai. uh-haz'bi (Heb. *ʾăḥasbay H335*, derivation uncertain). Father of ELIPHELET, who was one of DAVID's mighty warriors (2 Sam. 23:34). Described as "the Maacathite" (lit., "son of the Maacathite"), Ahasbai may have been from a Judean family named MAACAH (1 Chr. 2:48; 4:19), or from the city of ABEL BETH MAACAH (2 Sam. 20:14), or from the Aramean city of Maacah (2 Sam. 10:6-8). Because the parallel passage reads differently (1 Chr. 11:35b-36a), some scholars suspect scribal corruption.

Ahasuerus. uh-hash'yoo-er'uhs (Heb. *ʾăḥašwērôš H347*, from Pers. *ḫšayāršā*, possibly "mighty man"). See XERXES.

Ahava. uh-hay'vuh (Heb. *ʾahăwāʾ H178*, meaning unknown). The name of a canal and its surrounding area in BABYLON, mentioned only in Ezra 8:15, 21, and 31 (the parallel passage in the APOCRYPHA has the name "Theras," 1 Esd. 8:41, 61). No such location has ever been found, and there is little evidence to support the supposition of the older commentators that it was a city. Ahava was the gathering place for the Israelites returning to Jerusalem with EZRA.

Ahaz. ay'haz (Heb. *ʾāḥāz H298*, short form of JEHOAHAZ, "Yahweh has taken hold [for protection]"). KJV NT Achaz. **(1)** Reigning over the southern kingdom of Judah, c. 735-715 B.C., Ahaz was a king of great significance both historically and theologically (see JUDAH, KINGDOM OF). Historically, during his reign and as a result of his policies, the people of God became vassals of ASSYRIA and never again did the throne of DAVID exist in its fully sovereign right. Ahaz began that prolonged period of foreign domination that continued beyond the time of the coming of Christ. The dominant political power changed—Assyria, Babylon, Persia, Greece, Rome—but the vassalage did not. In addition, Ahaz is significant theologically, for his policies involved a denial of the way of faith. The essential cause of the demeaning of the throne of David and its enslavement was unbelief. The message of the reign of Ahaz remains as ISA-

IAH summarized it: "If you do not stand firm in your faith, you will not stand at all" (Isa. 7:9).

Ahaz is often represented as a weak, ineffective king. This is not the case. He gave his country firm and resolute leadership—but in the wrong direction. In 745 B.C. TIGLATH-PILESER gained the throne of Assyria, the contemporary "superpower"; at once the Assyrians threw off the lethargy of the previous years and began to pursue imperialist policies. The states W of Assyria, particularly ARAM (SYRIA) and ISRAEL (the northern kingdom of the people of God), felt their security threatened and determined on a defensive, military alliance. Desiring a united Palestinian front, these northern powers determined to coerce Judah into their anti-Assyrian bloc.

From the time of JOTHAM, Ahaz's father, Judah had been under this pressure (2 Ki. 15:37), but it was not until Ahaz's day that events reached a climax. A large-scale invasion brought the northern powers the successes reported in 2 Chr. 28:5-8, though for reasons no longer clear they failed to capitalize on these achievements by taking JERUSALEM (Isa. 7:1). A further incursion was planned. This time the armies of EDOM and of the PHILISTINES (2 Chr. 28:17-18) also took the field, with the clearly defined objective of bringing the monarchy of David to an end and replacing the Davidic king, perhaps with an Aramean puppet (Isa. 7:6). This threat to the dynasty of David made the events of the reign of Ahaz crucially significant. In the face of the threat we may well ask, What made the people of God secure? How did they keep hold of their God-given possessions and privileges?

Isaiah answered these questions with one word: "Faith." Those who trust the Lord's promises will find that he keeps his promises. Isaiah revealed the Lord's mind: the dreaded threat from the N would come to nothing (Isa. 7:7), whereas trusting in the apparent security of her military alliance with Syria would bring Ephraim (Israel) to a total end (7:8). Only the way of faith would keep Judah secure (7:9). When Isaiah made this appeal to Ahaz, that resolute monarch was already committed to the beginning of a militarist solution. Isaiah reveals him reviewing Jerusalem's most vulnerable point: its overground water supply that could easily be cut off by a besieging enemy (7:3). King Ahaz could not be moved to the position of simple faith. To the offer of a sign from the Lord of even cosmic proportions (7:10-11) he gave the sort of answer that is often the resort of the outwardly religious man (7:12), and the die was cast.

Ahaz refused the way of faith and embraced instead the way of works—the military-political solution. He showed all his astute hard-headedness in the course he followed. In fear of Assyria, Syria and Israel were threatening him. What better way to deal with them than to appeal over their heads to Assyria, secure an alliance with the super-power, and leave it to Assyrian armed might to disperse the Syro-Ephraimite armies? This is exactly what Ahaz did (2 Ki. 16:7-8; 2 Chr. 28:16). But he learned the risk of taking a tiger by the tail: once Assyria had disposed of the N Palestine kingdoms it was the turn of Judah, and Ahaz became the first vassal king in David's line.

The Bible makes it clear that Ahaz had prepared the way for his own spiritual downfall by religious apostasy long before the decisive moment arrived (2 Ki. 16:14; 2 Chr. 28:1-4). It comes as no surprise that his decisions to abandon the way of faith opened the door to further and greater religious decline (2 Ki. 16:10-18; 2 Chr. 28:22-23).

(2) Son of Micah and great-grandson of King SAUL (1 Chr. 8:35-36; 9:41-42). Nothing else is known about him.

Ahaz, dial of. See DIAL.

Ahaziah. ay´huh-zi´uh (Heb. ʾăḥazyâ *H301*, also ʾăḥazyāhû *H302*, "Yahweh has taken hold [for protection]" or "whom Yahweh sustains"; cf. JEHO-AHAZ, AHZAI). **(1)** Son of AHAB and JEZEBEL; eighth king of ISRAEL, reigning only briefly, 853-852 B.C. Ahaziah was a worshiper of JEROBOAM's calves and of his mother's idols, BAAL and ASH-TORETH. The most notable event of his reign was the revolt of MOAB, which had been giving a yearly tribute of 100,000 lambs and 100,000 rams (2 Ki. 1:1; 3:4-5). Ahaziah was prevented from trying to put down the revolt by a fall through a lattice in his palace at SAMARIA. Injured severely, he sent messengers to inquire of BAAL-ZEBUB, god of EKRON, whether he would recover. ELIJAH the prophet was sent by God to intercept the messengers and

proclaimed to them that Ahaziah would die. The king in anger tried to capture the prophet, but two groups of fifty men were consumed by fire from heaven in making the attempt. A third contingent was sent to seize the prophet but instead implored Elijah to deliver them from the fate of their predecessors (2 Ki. 1:13-14). Elijah then went down to Samaria and gave the message directly to the king, who died shortly afterward. He was succeeded by his brother Joram/Jehoram (1:17; cf. 8:16). See JEHORAM #2.

(2) Son of Jehoram of Judah (see JEHORAM #1) and ATHALIAH; thus grandson of JEHOSHAPHAT and of AHAB, and nephew of Ahaziah of Israel. He was the sixth king of Judah in the divided monarchy (see JUDAH, KINGDOM OF) and reigned only one year (2 Chr. 22:2), c. 842 B.C. In 2 Chr. 21:17 and 25:23, his name appears also as Jehoahaz (a simple transposition of the component parts of the compound name; in 22:6 the KJV, following most Heb. MSS, has Azariah). According to 2 Ki. 8:26, Ahaziah was twenty-two years old when he began to reign, and his father, Jehoram, only lived to age forty (21:20). However, 2 Chr. 22:2 states that he was forty-two years old when he ascended the throne. Some have thought that this last reference is a scribal error, but it may indicate a coregency. Ahaziah walked in all the idolatries of the house of Ahab, "for his mother encouraged him in doing wrong" (22:3). He sinned also in allying himself with Joram/Jehoram of Israel against Hazael of Syria, going into battle at RAMOTH GILEAD (22:5). Joram was wounded and Ahaziah went to see him at JEZREEL. Here judgment came on him through the hand of JEHU, who fell on Joram and all the house of Ahab. When Ahaziah saw the slaughter, he fled, but "they wounded him in his chariot ... he escaped to Megiddo and died there" (2 Ki. 9:27). The account given in Chronicles presents different though not irreconcilable details of his death (2 Chr. 22:6-9). Ahaziah was buried with his fathers in Jerusalem (2 Ki. 9:28). Jehu allowed this honorable burial because Ahaziah was the grandson of Jehoshaphat, who sought the Lord with all his heart (2 Chr. 22:9). Following the death of Ahaziah, his mother Athaliah seized the throne. She killed all the royal sons of the house of Judah except Joash (JEHOASH), Ahaziah's son, who was hidden by

JEHOSHEBA, sister of Ahaziah and wife of JEHOIADA the high priest (22:10-12).

Ahban. ah´ban (Heb. *ʾaḥbān H283*, derivation uncertain). Son of Abishur and descendant of JUDAH through PEREZ and JERAHMEEL (1 Chr. 2:29).

Aher. ay´huhr (Heb. *ʾaḥēr H338*, "another" [possibly indicating a substitute for a sibling who has died]). A Benjamite identified as the father or ancestor of the Hushites (1 Chr. 7:12; see HUSHIM #2). The text is emended by some scholars, but if it is sound, the name may be a contracted form of AHIRAM (Num. 26:38).

Ahi. ay´hi (Heb. *ʾāḥi H306*, "my brother"; perhaps a contraction of AHIJAH). (1) Son of Abdiel and descendant of GAD; head of a family (1 Chr. 5:15).

(2) Son of SHOMER (KJV, "Shamer"; NRSV, "Shemer") and descendant of ASHER (1 Chr. 7:34); some read the text not as a name but as *ʾāḥîw*, meaning "his brother" (cf. RSV and NIV mg.).

The form *Ahi* is also used in the composition of many Hebrew names with various possible meanings, such as "brother of" and "my brother is" (where "brother" can be a reference to God).

Ahiah. uh-hi´uh (Heb. *ʾāḥiyyâ H308*, short form of AHIJAH, "[my] brother is Yahweh"). One of the leaders of the people who sealed the covenant of reform with NEHEMIAH (Neh. 10:26). Here the KJV has "Ahijah," but in several passages where other versions have "Ahijah," the KJV reads "Ahiah" (1 Sam. 14:3, 18; 1 Ki. 4:3; 1 Chr. 8:7). No English version seems to be completely consistent in the spelling of this name.

Ahiam. uh-hi´uhm (Heb. *ʾāḥiʾām H307*, possibly short form of *ʾāḥiʾāmî* "my brother is indeed [Yahweh]"; see ABIJAH #5). Son of Sharar the HARARITE; he was one of DAVID's mighty warriors (2 Sam. 23:33; called "son of Sacar" in 1 Chr. 11:35).

Ahian. uh-hi´uhn (Heb. *ʾaḥyān H319*, possibly "little brother"). Son of Shemida and descendant of MANASSEH (1 Chr. 7:19).

Ahiezer. ay´hi-ee´zuhr (Heb. *ʾāḥîʿezer H323*, "my brother is help"). (1) Son of Ammishaddai; in the time of MOSES he represented the tribe of DAN on a number of important occasions (Num. 1:12; 2:25; 7:66, 71; 10:25).

(2) Son of Shemaah of GIBEAH; he and his brother Joash were warriors from the tribe of BENJAMIN who left SAUL and joined DAVID at ZIKLAG (1 Chr. 12:3; cf. v. 1).

Ahihud. uh-hi´huhd (Heb. *ʾāḥîhûd H310*, "[my] brother is majesty"). (1) Son of Sheloni and a leader of the tribe of ASHER; he was appointed by MOSES to help divide the land W of the Jordan after the Israelites settled there (Num. 34:27).

(2) The head of a Benjamite family (1 Chr. 8:7). The Hebrew text is difficult; he may have been the son of Ehud (KJV) or of Gera (NIV) or of Heglam (NRSV).

Ahijah. uh-hi´juh (Heb. *ʾāḥiyyâ H308*, also *ʾāḥiyyāhû H309*, "[my] brother is Yahweh"; see AHIAH). (1) Son of AHITUB and a priest in the days of SAUL. He was a descendant of ELI through PHINEHAS's line (1 Sam. 14:3, 18; KJV, "Ahiah"). He is also called AHIMELECH (possibly a short form of Ahijah, 22:9, 11, 20). He was the father of ABIATHAR and served as priest at NOB. Ahijah consulted the oracles of God for Saul on the field at MICMASH (14:18-19). He is the same one who offered the showbread to DAVID when he was hungry and fleeing from Saul (21:1-10).

(2) A Pelonite who was one of David's Thirty, the military élite of the nation (1 Chr. 11:36). However, the parallel list at this point reads, "Eliam the son of Ahithophel the Gilonite" (2 Sam. 23:34; this reading is to be preferred).

(3) A Levite in the time of David who was in charge of the treasuries of the temple (1 Chr. 26:20 KJV, NRSV). The NIV, following the SEPTUAGINT and most commentators, reads *ʾāḥêhem* ("their brothers") and translates, "Their fellow Levites."

(4) Son of Shisha; he and his brother Elihoreph were secretaries for SOLOMON (1 Ki. 4:3; KJV, "Ahiah").

(5) A prophet from SHILOH who predicted to JEROBOAM that he would reign over ten of the twelve tribes, and that his dynasty would be

A

an enduring one if he did what was right in the eyes of the Lord (1 Ki. 11:29-39; 12:15). However, Jeroboam ignored the condition attached to the prediction, and it fell to Ahijah to foretell not only the death of Jeroboam's son but also the end of Jeroboam's line (14:1-18). The fulfillment of these words continued to roll in during subsequent days (1 Ki. 15:29; 2 Chr. 10:15). "The prophecy of Ahijah the Shilonite" was one of the sources used in the history of Solomon (2 Chr. 9:29).

(6) Father of King BAASHA of Israel; the latter conspired against NADAB, the son of Jeroboam, and then ruled in his place (1 Ki. 15:27, 33; 21:22; 2 Ki. 9:9). He was from the tribe of ISSACHAR.

(7) Son of JERAHMEEL and descendant of JUDAH (1 Chr. 2:25).

(8) Son of EHUD and descendant of BENJAMIN (1 Chr. 8:7; KJV, "Ahiah"). The text is difficult, and some argue that the names Naaman, Ahijah, and Gera are a dittography (from vv. 4-5). Further, both Ahijah (v. 7) and Ahoah (v. 4), as well as Ehi (Gen. 46:21), may be scribal variations for an original reading of AHIRAM (Num. 26:38-40).

(9) One of the leaders of the people who sealed the covenant of reform with NEHEMIAH (Neh. 10:26 KJV; other English versions spell it AHIAH).

Ahikam. uh-hi´kuhm (Heb. ʾăḥîqām H324, "my brother has arisen" [possibly a reference to God as rising for battle]). Son of SHAPHAN; royal secretary during the reign of King JOSIAH and a prominent man in the following decades (2 Ki. 22:12, 14; 25:22; 2 Chr. 34:20; Jer. 26:24; 39:14; 40:5—41:18; 43:6). Josiah made him a member of the deputation to consult with the prophetess HULDAH concerning the Book of the Law. In the reign of JEHOIAKIM, Ahikam protected JEREMIAH from death. Ahikam was the father of GEDALIAH, whom NEBUCHADNEZZAR made governor of the land after the destruction of Jerusalem.

Ahilud. uh-hi´luhd (Heb. ʾăḥîlûd H314, perhaps "my brother is born"). The father of a certain Jehoshaphat who served as "recorder" during the reigns of DAVID and SOLOMON (2 Sam. 8:16; 20:24; 1 Ki. 4:3; 1 Chr. 18:15). This Ahilud is probably also the one identified as the father of BAANA, one of Solomon's district governors (1 Ki. 4:12).

Ahimaaz. uh-him´ay-az (Heb. ʾăḥimaʿaṣ H318, perhaps "my brother is wrath"). (1) The father of SAUL's wife, AHINOAM (1 Sam. 14:50).

(2) Son of ZADOK the high priest (1 Chr. 6:8). During ABSALOM's rebellion he and JONATHAN, son of ABIATHAR, served as messengers between DAVID and HUSHAI, David's counselor and spy. They brought to David Hushai's news that AHITHOPHEL had urged Absalom to make an immediate attack and Hushai's warning that David should cross the Jordan at once (2 Sam. 15:24-27; 17:15-22). David's estimate of Ahimaaz appears in his remark at his approach after the battle: "He's a good man. … He comes with good news" (18:27). Ahimaaz announced the victory but evaded the question concerning Absalom's fate, wishing to spare the feelings of the king. While Ahimaaz was still in David's presence, another messenger identified as "a Cushite" (see CUSH #3) arrived and unfeelingly broke the news concerning Absalom's death. Comparing 1 Ki. 4:2 with 1 Chr. 6:8-10, some infer that Ahimaaz died before he attained the priesthood and before the death of his father Zadok, who was succeeded by Ahimaaz's son, Azariah.

(3) One of SOLOMON's twelve commissary officers (1 Ki. 4:15). He married BASEMATH, the daughter of Solomon. In contrast to the other officers in the list, the name of this man's father is missing. Some therefore conjecture that it is the man's own name that has dropped out of the text and that only the name of his father, Ahimaaz, has remained. If so, this Ahimaaz is probably the same as #2, above.

Ahiman. uh-hi´muhn (Heb. ʾăḥîman H317, perhaps "my brother is fortune"). (1) One of the three sons or descendants of ANAK living in HEBRON when the twelve spies reconnoitered the land in the time of Moses (Num. 13:22; Josh. 15:14; Jdg. 1:10). They were so tall and strong that ten of the spies were terrified of them and persuaded the Israelites not to enter the land that God had promised them. Ahiman was probably the name of an individual and of a clan or group of clans. The three clans were driven out from Hebron by CALEB (Josh. 15:14) and later defeated again by the tribe of JUDAH (Jdg. 1:10).

(2) A Levite in the postexilic period. He was one of the chief gatekeepers of Jerusalem (1 Chr.

A

9:17). Since he is not included in the parallel list (Neh. 11:19, "Akkub, Talmon and their associates [*lit.*, brothers]"), some emend the text to read *ʾăḥêhem*, "their brothers."

Ahimelech. uh-him′uh-lek (Heb. *ʾăḥimelek H316*, "my brother is [the god] Melek" or "my brother is king"). TNIV Ahimelek. **(1)** Son of AHITUB and father of ABIATHAR, DAVID's high priest (1 Sam. 21:1-2, 8; 22:9-23; 23:6; 30:7). This priest of NOB gave assistance to David by offering him the showbread (21:6), and when SAUL learned of this aid, it cost Ahimelech his life (22:11-19). AHIJAH (14:3, 18) may be (a) a short form of the name Ahimelech, (b) another name for Ahimelech, or (c) Ahimelech's father in a fuller genealogy. One of the eight fugitive psalms refers to the evil use of the tongue by DOEG, the Edomite, against Ahimelech (Ps. 52, title).

(2) Son of Abiathar (2 Sam. 8:17; cf. 1 Chr. 18:16), that is, a grandson of #1 above. Most scholars regard this as an inadvertent transposition for "Abiathar the son of Ahimelech." While such a textual corruption is possible, the detailed account of 1 Chr. 24:3, 6, 31 would seem to rule against it.

(3) A HITTITE who followed David while he was a fugitive in the wilderness hiding from Saul (1 Sam. 26:6).

Ahimoth. uh-hi′moth (Heb. *ʾăḥimôt H315*, possibly "my brother is death"). Son of ELKANAH, included in a list of Levites descended from KOHATH (1 Chr. 6:25). He was an ancestor of SAMUEL.

Ahinadab. uh-hin′uh-dab (Heb. *ʾăḥinādāb H320*, "my brother is noble"). Son of Iddo (1 Ki. 4:14) and one of SOLOMON's "twelve district governors over all Israel, who supplied provisions for the king and the royal household" (v. 7). His district was S GILEAD, and his headquarters, MAHANAIM.

Ahinoam. uh-hin′oh-uhm (Heb. *ʾăḥinōʿam H321*, "my brother is delight"). **(1)** Daughter of Ahimaaz and wife of SAUL (1 Sam. 14:50), thus the first queen of Israel.

(2) A woman from JEZREEL whom DAVID married after Saul took MICHAL from him and gave her to another husband. Ahinoam was probably his first wife, even though his marriage to ABIGAIL is mentioned first (1 Sam. 25:39-44). Three other times they are mentioned together, and Ahinoam is always mentioned first (27:3; 30:5; 2 Sam. 2:2). She was the mother of David's first son, AMNON, and Abigail was mother of his second (2 Sam. 3:2; 1 Chr. 3:1).

Ahio. uh-hi′oh (Heb. *ʾaḥyô H311*, perhaps "little brother" or short form of AHIHAH, "[my] brother is Yahweh"). **(1)** Son of ABINADAB and brother of UZZA (2 Sam. 6:3-4; 1 Chr. 13:7). He went before the cart that carried the ARK OF THE COVENANT from the house of Abinadab to JERUSALEM.

(2) Son of BERIAH and descendant of BENJAMIN, listed among the heads of families living in postexilic Jerusalem (1 Chr. 8:14; cf. v. 28). The NRSV and other versions, however, include him among the sons of ELPAAL.

(3) Son of Jeiel and brother of KISH (1 Chr. 8:29-31; 9:35-37), possibly the uncle of King SAUL (cf. 8:33; 9:39).

Ahira. uh-hi′ruh (Heb. *ʾăḥiraʿ H327*, possibly "my brother is a friend"). Son of Enan and a leader of the tribe of NAPHTALI in the time of MOSES, whom he assisted in the census (Num. 1:15). He commanded his tribe when on the march (10:27) and made the tribal offering (2:29; 7:78-83).

Ahiram. uh-hi′ruhm (Heb. *ʾăḥirām H325*, "my brother is exalted"). Third son of BENJAMIN and grandson of JACOB (Num. 26:38). In 1 Chr. 8:1, where the sons of Benjamin are explicitly numbered, the third name, AHARAH, may be a corrupt form of AHIRAM (cf. also the forms AHOAH in v. 4, AHIJAH in v. 7, and AHER in 7:12). In the Benjamite genealogy found in Gen. 46:21, EHI may be an abbreviated form of Ahiram. In this genealogy ten sons of Benjamin are mentioned, but some of them are referred to as more remote descendants in other lists.

Ahisamach. uh-his′uh-mak (Heb. *ʾăḥisāmāk H322*, "my brother has supported"). TNIV Ahisamak. Father of OHOLIAB; the latter assisted BEZALEL in building the TABERNACLE and its furniture (Exod. 31:6; 35:34; 38:23).

Ahishahar. uh-hish´uh-hahr (Heb. *ʾăhîšāhar H328*, "brother of the dawn"). Son of Bilhan and descendant of BENJAMIN (1 Chr. 7:10); he was a head of family in the clan of JEDIAEL (v. 11).

Ahishar. uh-hi´shahr (Heb. *ʾăhîšār H329*, meaning uncertain). A man who was in charge of SOLOMON's household (1 Ki. 4:6).

Ahithophel. uh-hith´uh-fel (Heb. *ʾăhîtōpel H330*, perhaps "brother of foolishness"; the name may have been *ʾăhîpelet*, "my brother is deliverance" [cf. ELIPHELET, 2 Sam. 23:34] or *ʾăhîbaʿal*, "my brother is Baal" [cf. ISH-BOSHET], purposely distorted). DAVID's counselor who joined the conspiracy of ABSALOM. His oracular wisdom was proverbial (2 Sam. 16:23), and it seems clear that he was a mainspring of the rebellion (15:12). Some suggest, in looking for motivation for his treachery, that he was the grandfather of BATHSHEBA, for she was the daughter of Eliam (11:3), and an Eliam, the son of Ahithophel the Gilonite, is listed as one of David's valiant men (23:34). Thus it is suggested that Ahithophel had a certain bitterness toward David for corrupting his granddaughter and murdering her husband. Others note, however, that the time element seems insufficiently long for Ahithophel to have a married granddaughter at the time of David's great sin, and that it seems easier to believe that there was more than one man in Israel named Eliam. Furthermore, it seems unlikely that a man such as Ahithophel would conspire against the interests of his granddaughter and her son. His main motivation appears to have been ambition for personal power. His proposal to Absalom that he pursue David immediately with 12,000 men, smiting the king while he was still weary and underprotected, indicates his wisdom and boldness. David's prayer turned his counsel into foolishness (15:31), for Absalom deferred to HUSHAI's advice that they take time to muster all Israel against such a mighty man of war as David. Ahithophel, seeing his counsel rejected, realized that the cause of Absalom was lost; he went to his home and hanged himself (17:1-23).

Ahitub. uh-hi´tuhb (Heb. *ʾăhîtûb H313*, "my brother is goodness"). **(1)** Son of PHINEHAS and father of the priest AHIJAH (also called AHIMELECH, 1 Sam. 14:3; 22:9, 11-12, 20).

(2) Son of AMARIAH and father of ZADOK, the high priest during the time of DAVID (2 Sam. 8:17; 1 Chr. 6:7-8; 6:52-53; 18:16; Ezra 7:2). Some argue (on the basis of 1 Chr. 9:11 and Neh. 11:11) that this Ahitub was really the grandfather of Zadok; however, see #3 below.

(3) Son of Amariah II and father of Zadok II (1 Chr. 6:11; 9:11; Neh. 11:11). Some scholars believe that this Ahitub is the same as #2 and that there is confusion in the lists.

Ahlab. ah´lab (Heb. *ʾahlāb H331*, possibly "forest" or "fruitful"). A town within the boundaries of ASHER, probably located at Khirbet el-Maḥalib, near the coast, c. 4 mi. (6 km.) NE of TYRE. The tribe of Asher was unable to drive out the Canaanite inhabitants of the town (Jdg. 1:31). Possibly the same as HELBAH and MAHALAB.

Ahlai. ah´li (Heb. *ʾahlāy H333*, possibly "the brother is my God" or derived from the interjection *ʾahălay H332*, "O would that!"). **(1)** Son or daughter of SHESHAN and descendant of JUDAH through JERAHMEEL (1 Chr. 2:31). The name is introduced in the Hebrew with the words, "the sons of Sheshan," but we are later told that "Sheshan had no sons—only daughters" (v. 34). Ahlai may have been the daughter that Sheshan gave in marriage to his Egyptian servant JARHA (v. 35). The phrase "the sons of Sheshan" may indicate that Ahlai was regarded as the one through whom Sheshan's line was preserved and as the progenitor of an important Jerahmeelite clan. See also #2 below.

(2) Father of ZABAD; the latter was one of DAVID's mighty warriors (1 Chr. 11:41). Some argue (on the basis of 2:35-36) that this Ahlai was a woman, an ancestress of Zabad, identical with #1 above.

Ahoah. uh-hoh´uh (Heb. *ʾăhôah H291*, derivation uncertain). Son of BELA and grandson of BENJAMIN (1 Chr. 8:4). It is possible that the name is a scribal error for AHIJAH (cf. v. 7).

Ahohi. uh-hoh´hi (Heb. *ʾăhôhî H292*, apparently a gentilic of *ʾăhôah H291*). The NRSV renders

2 Sam. 23:9 literally as "Dodo son of Ahohi," whereas KJV and NIV, on the basis of the parallel passage (1 Chr. 11:12), have "Dodo [Dodai] the Ahohite." See AHOHITE.

Ahohite. uh-hoh′hit (Heb. *ʾăḥôḥî H292*, apparently a gentilic of *ʾăḥôaḥ H291*). Probably a patronymic used by the descendants of AHOAH. The term is used only in connection with military heroes in DAVID's time: DODAI (2 Sam. 23:9; 1 Chr. 11:12; 27:14) and ZALMON (2 Sam. 23:28; called ILAI in 1 Chr. 11:29).

Aholah; Aholiab; Aholibah; Aholibamah. KJV forms of OHOLAH; OHOLIAB; OHOLIBAH; OHOLIBAMAH.

Ahumai. uh-hyoo′mi (Heb. *ʾăḥûmay H293*, "it is indeed a brother"). Son of JAHATH and descendant of JUDAH through SHOBAL (1 Chr. 4:2). He and his brother LAHAD are referred to as "the clans of the Zorathites" (see ZORAH).

Ahuzam. See AHUZZAM.

Ahuzzam. uh-huh′zuhm (Heb. *ʾăḥuzzām H303*, possibly "possessor"). KJV Ahuzam. Son of ASHHUR and descendant of JUDAH (1 Chr. 4:6).

Ahuzzath. uh-huh′zath (Heb. *ʾăḥuzzat H304*, possibly "possession"). A personal adviser (Heb. *mērēʿa*, lit., "friend") of ABIMELECH, PHILISTINE king of GERAR, who with PHICOL, commander of the army, went with Abimelech to make a covenant with ISAAC at BEERSHEBA (Gen. 26:26-31).

Ahzai. ah′zi (Heb. *ʾaḥzay H300*, short form AHAZIAH, "Yahweh has taken hold [for protection]"). KJV Ahasai. Son of Meshillemoth, descendant of IMMER, and grandfather (or ancestor) of AMASHSAI; the latter is mentioned among the priestly leaders who resettled Jerusalem in EZRA's time (Neh. 11:13). Ahzai is probably the same as JAHZERAH (1 Chr. 9:12).

Ai. *i*, ay′*i* (Heb. *ʿay H6504* [always written with the definite article, *hāʿay*], "the heap" or "the ruin"; also *ʿayyat H6569* [Isa. 10:28] and possibly *ʿayyâ H6509* [1 Chr. 7:28; Neh. 11:31]). **(1)** A city of central Palestine, E of BETHEL. ABRAHAM pitched his tent between Ai and Bethel when he arrived in Canaan (Gen. 12:8). Ai figures most prominently in the account of the conquest of the land; it was the second Canaanite city taken by the forces under JOSHUA (Josh. 7-8). Having conquered JERICHO, the Israelites felt that a portion of the armies would be sufficient to conquer the much smaller Ai. The Israelite contingent was routed, however. It was then disclosed that ACHAN had sinned in taking articles from the consecrated spoil of Jericho. After Achan had confessed his sin and he and his family had been stoned to death, the Israelites made a second attack, which resulted in the total destruction of the city and the annihilation of all its 12,000 inhabitants. The city, the site of which belonged to the tribe of BENJAMIN following the partition of the land, had not been rebuilt when the book of Joshua was written (Josh. 8:28). It was, however, rebuilt in later days, for men of Ai returned from Babylon with ZERUBBABEL (Ezra 2:28; Neh. 7:32).

The work of Joseph Callaway (1964-72) at Khirbet et-Tell, generally identified with bibli-

Early Bronze Age excavations at the site of Khirbet et-Tell, generally identified with the biblical city of Ai. (View to the SW.)

© Dr. James C. Martin

cal Ai, has shown that no city stood here from the Early Bronze Age destruction in about 2300 B.C. till a pre-Israelite settlement was built in the Early Iron Age (c. 1200 B.C.). Thus it appears that no town existed here in the time of the conquest under Joshua during the Late Bronze Age (c. 1550 to 1200 B.C.). Alternate identifications of Ai have been suggested, such as the nearby sites of Khirbet el-Maqatir and Khirbet Nisya, but few scholars accept these proposals. The discrepancy between the biblical account and the archaeological data remains an unsolved problem.

(2) A town in AMMON mentioned only once (Jer. 49:3); its location is unknown.

Aiah. ay′yuh (Heb. ʾayyāh H371, "falcon"). (1) Son of Zibeon, a HORITE; ancestor of a clan in EDOM (Gen. 36:24 [KJV, "Ajah"]; 1 Chr. 1:40).

(2) Father of Rizpah, a concubine of SAUL; ISH-BOSHETH falsely accused ABNER of having an affair with her (2 Sam. 3:7). Years later her sons were handed over to the Gibeonites by DAVID for hanging (21:8-11).

Aiath. ay′yath. Alternate form of AI (Isa. 10:28).

Aija. ay′juh. Alternate form of AI (Neh. 11:31).

Aijalon. ay′juh-lon (Heb. ʾayyālôn H389, "[place of the] deer"). KJV also Ajalon. (1) A city within the tribal territory of DAN (Josh. 19:42), assigned to the Levite sons of KOHATH (1 Chr. 6:69). It is mentioned most notably in the memorable words of Joshua, "O sun, stand still over Gibeon, / O moon, over the Valley of Aijalon" (Josh. 10:12). SAUL and JONATHAN won a great victory against the PHILISTINES in the vicinity of Aijalon (1 Sam. 14:31). At one stage, the town was inhabited by Ephraimites (1 Chr. 6:69) and at another by Benjamites (8:13). Under the divided kingdom, Aijalon fell to Judah and REHOBOAM fortified it (2 Chr. 11:10). In the reign of AHAZ, the Philistines raided the cities of the SHEPHELAH ("lowlands") and occupied Aijalon (28:18). It is identified with the modern Yalo, about 13 mi. (21 km.) NW of Jerusalem, N of the Jaffa road.

(2) A town within the tribal territory of ZEBULUN, mentioned only once (Jdg 12:12); its location

is unknown. The judge ELON is said to have been buried there.

Aijeleth Shahar. ay′juh-leth-shay′hahr. KJV transliteration of Hebrew ʾayyelet haššaḥar in the title of Ps. 22; NIV understands it as a tune name, "The Doe of the Morning." Others take the first word in the phrase as related to ʾĕyālût H394 in v. 19, meaning "strength" or "help." If this is correct, the words actually entitle the psalm "Help at Daybreak" suitably, as vv. 22-31 show.

Ain. ayn (Heb. ʿayin H6526, "spring"). (1) A town in the NE corner of Canaan named, no doubt, for the presence of a spring there (Num. 34:11). Some MSS of the VULGATE have *fontem Daphnim* ("the spring of Daphne"), and the identification of Ain with modern Khirbet Dufna (less than 2 mi./3 km. W of DAN) has support in some rabbinic texts. Some scholars identify Ain with modern Khirbet ʿAyyun, about 3 mi. (5 km.) E of the S tip of the Sea of Galilee. See also RIBLAH.

(2) A Levitical city in the NEGEV appearing in the Judah/Simeon list (Josh. 21:16, although some emend the text to read "Ashan" on the basis of some MSS of the SEPTUAGINT as well as the parallel list in 1 Chr. 6:59). The name also appears in Josh. 15:32; 19:7; 1 Chr. 4:32 (unless it is combined with the next name and read as EN RIMMON). The site is unknown.

The word *Ain* (*En*) is also used in the composition of various place names, such as EN GEDI and ENDOR.

air. In the OT and the Gospels this word is usually found in expressions speaking of the birds or fowl of the air (Job 41:16 is the only exception) and representing words normally translated "heaven." Elsewhere in the NT it stands for the atmosphere. An ineffective Christian is pictured as a boxer "beating the air" (1 Cor. 9:26). "Speaking into the air" describes unintelligible utterance (14:9). Satan is called "the prince of the power of the air" (Eph. 2:2), that is, the ruler of the demonic beings that fill the air. The rapture of the church will culminate in her meeting the Lord and Savior, Jesus Christ, "in the air" (1 Thess. 4:17).

Ajah. See AIAH.

A

Ajalon. See Aijalon.

Akan. ay´kan. (*ʿăqān H6826*, derivation uncertain). Son of Ezer and grandson of Seir the Horite; he probably became the progenitor of a clan in Edom (Gen. 36:27; in 1 Chr. 1:42 most Heb. MSS have Jaakan [KJV, "Jakan"]).

Akbor. See Acbor.

Akeldama. uh-kel´duh-muh (Gk. *Hakeldamach G192*, from Aram. *hăqēl dĕmāʾ*, "field of blood"). KJV Aceldama; other versions, Hakeldama. The field purchased with the money Judas Iscariot received for betraying Christ (Acts 1:18-19). Matthew, with a fuller account of the purchase, says the priests bought it "as a burial place for foreigners" (Matt. 27:3-10). Acts 1:18-19 is a parenthesis, an explanation by Luke, not part of Peter's speech. These verses say that "with the reward he got for his wickedness, Judas bought a field." The priests apparently bought it in Judas's name, the money having been his. The field was called "the place of blood" in Aramaic. Some think the Aramaic word means "field of sleep," or "cemetery," but the meaning "field of blood"

is preferable, and it is appropriate because of the manner of Judas's death, the gruesome details being given in Acts 1:18.

Akhenaten. akh´uh-nah´tuhn (Egyp. "Blessed Spirit of Aten" or "Beneficial to Aten"). Also Akhenaton. The name chosen by Amenhotep IV (1370-1353 B.C.), ruler in the 18th dynasty of Egypt, when he changed the religion of his country, demanding that all his subjects worship only the sun god under the name Aten (Aton). Politically his reign was disastrous. Internal disorders prevailed, and Egypt's Asian possessions began to slip away. His external troubles are illustrated by clay tablets found at Tell el-Amarna, the site of Akhet-Aten, the capital he established. Hundreds of letters from vassal governors in Syria and Palestine tell of invasions and intrigue and make appeals for help. Many of these tablets refer to invaders called the Habiru. Some feel that this name designates the Hebrew people; others say that it speaks of a non-Semitic people. Akhenaten is credited by many as being the first monotheist and, indeed, the inspiration for the monotheism of Moses. However, Akhenaten clearly worshiped the sun itself and not the Creator of the sun.

© Dr. James C. Martin

The Greek Monastery of St. Onuphrius lies on the southern edge of Jerusalem's Hinnom Valley and marks the traditional site of Akeldama. (View to the SW.)

Akim. ay′kim (Gk. *Achim G943*). Also Achim. An ancestor of Jesus and descendant of ZERUBBABEL (mentioned only in Matt. 1:14). Some scholars consider this name a shortened form of JEHOIAKIM or of AHIMAAZ. See also GENEALOGY OF JESUS CHRIST.

Akkad. ak′ad (ʾakkad *H422*, meaning uncertain). One of the cities or districts of NIMROD's kingdom, with BABEL, ERECH, and CALNEH (Gen. 10:10). Babel and Erech are located on or near the lower EUPHRATES, Erech being not far from what was then the head of the Persian Gulf. Calneh, formerly identified with Nippur between Babel and Erech, is thought by many to be, not the name of a city, but a word meaning "all of them" (cf. NRSV) referring to Babel, the capital, and to Akkad and Erech, the chief cities of the northern and southern districts of Babylonia respectively. The location of Akkad is uncertain, though it is thought to be identified with Agade, the chief city of a district of the same name in northern Babylonia, which Sargon I, the Semitic conqueror of the Sumerian Akkadians, made his capital in c. 2350 B.C. The kingdom called Nimrod's had evidently fallen into disorder, and Sargon united the warring city-states under his firm rule. With the help of invaders, first from the NE and then from the NW, Akkadian civilization flourished sporadically and precariously until Semitic AMORITES from the W founded a dynasty at BABYLON about 1894. The most illustrious ruler of this dynasty was HAMMURABI (1792-1750). Sumerian or Akkadian civilization now finally came to an end. As Nimrod cannot be certainly identified with any person otherwise known, so Akkad remains a shadowy city or region.

Akkadian. uh-kay′dee-uhn. The Eastern Semitic language spoken by Assyrians and Babylonians, the oldest written form of which stems from documents composed during the reign of Sargon of AKKAD. The discovery and decipherment of thousands of Akkadian CLAY TABLETS inscribed in the cuneiform (wedge-shaped) script have been of inestimable value for the better understanding of the Semitic languages (including Hebrew and Aramaic), as well as the history, culture, and religions of the ANE.

Akko. See ACCO.

Akkub. ak′uhb (Heb. ʿaqqûb *H6822*, perhaps "protector" or "protected"). (1) Son of Elioenai and descendant of King JEHOIACHIN, from the line of DAVID (1 Chr. 3:24).

(2) Name of a family of Levitical gatekeepers in the temple after the EXILE (1 Chr. 9:17; Ezra 2:42; Neh. 7:45; 11:19; 12:25).

(3) Name of a family of NETHINIM or temple servants (Ezra 2:45).

(4) A Levite who assisted EZRA in expounding the law (Neh. 8:7-8).

Akrabbim. uh-krab′im (Heb. ʿaqrābbîm, from ʿaqrāb *H6832*, "scorpion"). The "ascent of Akrabbim" (NIV, "Scorpion Pass") was a mountain pass on the S side of the DEAD SEA (Num. 34:4; Josh. 15:3 [KJV, "Maaleh-acrabbim"]; Jdg. 1:36). It is usually identified with the modern Naqb eṣ-Ṣafa, some 20 mi. (32 km.) SW of the southern tip of the DEAD SEA, but some suggest Umm el-ʿAqarab, on the W side of the Dead Sea. This may be the area where Judas MACCABEE defeated the Edomites (1 Macc. 5:3).

Aksah. See ACSAH.

Akshaph. See ACSHAPH.

Akzib. See ACZIB.

alabaster. See MINERALS.

Alameth. See ALEMETH.

Alammelech. See ALLAMMELECH.

alamoth. al′uh-moth (Heb. ʿălāmôt *H6628*, meaning unknown). Probably the name of a musical tune (1 Chr. 15:20; Ps. 46, title). Because the word is possibly related to the Hebrew word for "maiden," some have thought it may indicate a women's choir, or musical instruments set in a high pitch, or instruments played by virgins.

Alcimus. al′si-muhs (Gk. *Alkimos*). High priest in Jerusalem from 163 to 161 B.C.; an opponent of

Judas Maccabee and his followers (1 Macc. 7:4-50; 9:1-57; 2 Macc. 14:1-27; Jos. *Ant.* 12.10).

alcoholism. See DRUNKENNESS.

Alemeth (person). al'uh-meth (Heb. *ʿālemet H6631*, possibly "concealment"). (**1**) Son of BEKER and grandson of BENJAMIN (1 Chr. 7:8; KJV, "Alameth").

(**2**) Son of JEHOADDAH and descendant of SAUL through JONATHAN (1 Chr. 8:36; in 9:42, the father's name is given as JADAH [most Heb. MSS, "Jarah"]).

Alemeth (place). al'uh-meth (Heb. *ʿālemet H6630*, possibly "concealment"). A Levitical city in the tribal territory of BENJAMIN (1 Chr. 6:60), also called Almon (Josh. 21:18). Identified with Khirbet ʿAlmit, 4 mi. (6 km.) NE of JERUSALEM.

aleph. ah'lef (from Heb. *ʾelep H546*, "cattle"). The first letter of the Hebrew alphabet (א, transliterated as ʾ), with a numerical value of one. It is named for the shape of the letter, which in its older form resembled the head of an ox. This letter indicates a glottal stop, which functions as a consonant, but it was later used by the Greeks to represent the vowel *alpha*, "A." The letter is also used as the symbol for Codex Sinaiticus, a very important fourth-century Greek biblical MS.

Alexander.   al'ig-zan'duhr (Gk. *Alexandros*, "defender of men"). A name common from Hellenistic times. (**1**) ALEXANDER THE GREAT. See separate article.

(**2**) Alexander Balas, pretended son of the Seleucid King ANTIOCHUS IV. He overthrew DEMETRIUS I in 150 B.C. and was in turn supplanted by the latter's son, Demetrius II, in 145 B.C. These civil wars hastened the decline of Seleucid powers, and provided Jonathan, the brother and successor of Judas MACCABEE, with the opportu-

nity of securing the high priesthood in Jerusalem (1 Macc. 10:1—11:19).

(**3**) Alexander Jannaeus, ruler of the Jews from 103-76 B.C. See MACCABEE.

(**4**) Son of SIMON of Cyrene (Mk. 15:21). Alexander and his brother RUFUS are mentioned here presumably because they were known to Mark's intended readers (in Rome?).

(**5**) A member of the high-priestly family, mentioned at the inquiry into PETER's preaching (Acts 4:6); otherwise unknown.

(**6**) The Jewish spokesman at the time of the riot in EPHESUS (Acts 19:33).

(**7**) An apostate from the Christian faith who, along with HYMENEUS, was "handed over to Satan to be taught not to blaspheme" (1 Tim. 1:20).

(**8**) A coppersmith who did PAUL great harm and opposed his message (2 Tim. 4:14).

Alexander the Great. Son of Philip, king of Macedon, and Olympias, an Epirote princess; born 356 B.C. Although not named in the Bible, he appears to be described prophetically in Daniel as the "goat" from the W with a notable horn between his eyes. He came against the ram with two horns, who was standing before the river, defeated the ram, and became very great until the great horn was broken and four notable ones came up from it (Dan. 8:5-8; see DANIEL, BOOK OF). The prophecy identifies the ram as the kings of MEDIA

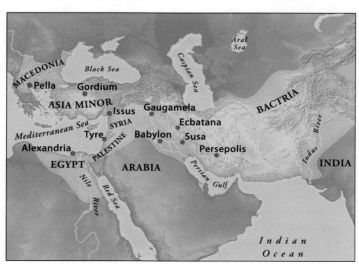

The empire of Alexander the Great.

and PERSIA, the goat as the king of GREECE, the great horn being the first king. When he fell, four kings arose in his place (8:18-22).

The historical fulfillment is striking: Alexander led the Greek armies across the Hellespont into Asia Minor in 334 B.C. and defeated the Persian forces at the river Granicus. Moving with amazing rapidity ("without touching the ground," Dan. 8:5), he again met and defeated the Persians at Issus. Turning S, he moved down the Syrian coast, advancing to EGYPT, which fell to him without a blow. Turning again to the E, he met the armies of DARIUS for the last time, defeating them in the battle of Arbela, E of the TIGRIS River. Rapidly he occupied BABYLON, then SUSA and Persepolis, the capitals of Persia.

The next years were spent in consolidating the new empire. Alexander took Persians into his army, encouraged his soldiers to marry Asians, and began to hellenize Asia through the establishment of Greek cities in the eastern empire. He marched his armies eastward as far as India, where they won a great battle at the Hydaspes River. The army, however, refused to advance farther, and Alexander was forced to return to Persepolis. While still making plans for further conquests, he contracted a fever. Weakened by the strenuous campaign and his increasing dissipation, he was unable to throw off the fever and died in Babylon in 323 B.C. at the age of thirty-three. His empire was then divided among four of his generals. While Alexander was outstanding as a conqueror, his notable contributions to civilization came via his hellenizing efforts. The fact that GREEK became the language of literature and

Statue of Alexander the Great (reigned 336-323 B.C.).

© Dr. James C. Martin. The Istanbul Archaeological Museum. Photographed by permission.

commerce throughout the "inhabited world," for example, was of inestimable importance to the spread of the gospel.

Alexandra. al´ig-zan´druh (Gk. *Alexandra*). Wife of Aristobulus, king of the Jews (104-103 B.C.). Upon his death, she made her brother-in-law, Alexander Jannaeus, king and married him. After he died, Alexandra ruled wisely from 76-67 during a period of peace and prosperity. John Hyrcanus II and Aristobulus II were her sons. See MACCABEE.

Alexandria. al´ig-zan´dree-uh. Founded by Alexander the Great in 332 B.C., this city became the capital of EGYPT during the Hellenistic and Roman periods (to be distinguished from other cities in the ANE that he also named Alexandria). Its harbors, formed by the island Pharos and the headland Lochias, were suitable for both commerce and war. It was the chief grain port for Rome. Its merchant ships, the largest and finest of the day, usually sailed directly to Puteoli, but at times because of the severity of the weather sailed under the coast of Asia Minor, as did the vessel that carried PAUL (Acts 27:6). Alexandria was also an important cultural center, boasting an excellent university. Patterned after the great school at ATHENS, it soon outstripped its model. It was especially noted for the study of mathematics, astronomy, medicine, and poetry. Literature and art also flourished. The library of Alexandria became the largest and best known in the world.

The population of Alexandria had three prominent elements: Jews, Greeks, and Egyptians. The Jews enjoyed equal privileges with the Greeks, so that they became established there. While continuing to regard JERUSALEM as "the holy city,"

A

they looked on Alexandria as the metropolis of the Jews throughout the world. Here the translation of the Hebrew PENTATEUCH into Greek, known as the SEPTUAGINT, was made in the third century before Christ. It became the popular Bible of the Jews of the DISPERSION, generally used by the writers of the NT. At Alexandria the OT rev-

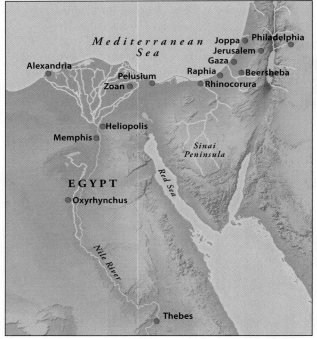

Alexandria.

elation was brought into contact with Greek philosophy. The consequent synthesis became of great importance in later religious thought. The influence of Alexandrian philosophy on the thought of the writers of the NT is debatable, but its impact on subsequent theological and biblical studies in the Christian church was great.

According to tradition, Mark the evangelist carried the gospel to Alexandria and established the first church there (see MARK, JOHN). From this city Christianity reached out into all Egypt and the surrounding countries. A theological school flourished here as early as the second century. Among its great teachers were Clement and Origen, pioneers in biblical scholarship and Christian philosophy.

Alexandrinus, Codex. See SEPTUAGINT; TEXT AND VERSIONS (NT).

algum. See PLANTS.

Aliah. See ALVAH.

Alian. See ALVAN.

alien. See STRANGER.

Allammelech. uh-lam′uh-lek (Heb. ʾallammelek H526, "terebinth of the king"). KJV Alammelech. A town in the tribe of ASHER (Josh. 19:26). It was probably located in the southern part of the tribe's territory, but the precise site has not been identified.

allegory. This term (derived from the Greek verb *allēgoreō*, which originally meant "to speak in a way other than what is meant") can be used simply of an extended metaphor or a narrative that makes use of symbols. To speak allegorically is thus to set forth one thing in the image of another, the principal subject being inferred from the figure rather than by direct statement. In this sense, allegory is a literary device used extensively in Scripture, for example in Isa. 5:1-7 and in the SONG OF SOLOMON (but it should be distinguished from PARABLE). The term often refers, however, to the expression of hidden, mysterious truths by the use of words that also have a literal meaning. Even if the writer did not intend a hidden meaning, the allegorical method is a way of interpreting a poet, a story teller, or a Scripture passage in such a way that the interpreter sees a mysterious meaning the writer may not have intended.

Allegorizing (to be distinguished from the drawing out of spiritual truths from factual presentations) has had broad application in Bible teaching. Alexandrian Jews such as PHILO JUDAEUS were inclined to spiritualize Scripture, sometimes minimizing or even denying the literal meaning. The church fathers followed, reaching a sophisticated approach in the school of Origen and leading to much emphasis on mystical and moral meanings. In the "allegory" in Gal. 4:21-31 Isaac, the child of promise, corresponds to (or typifies) the Christian who is justified in Christ and is free to love and serve his Father; while Ishmael, the child of contrivance, typifies the legalist who is under the law and is bound to serve it and to seek justification in obedience to it. Thus in spite of Paul's use of the verb *allēgoreō* in v. 24, the apostle does not downplay the historical meaning, and many believe that the term *typology* more accurately describes the passage.

alleluia. See HALLELUJAH.

alliance. See COVENANT.

Allon. al´on (Heb. *ʾallôn H474*, "oak"). **(1)** Son of Jedaiah and descendant of SIMEON (1 Chr. 4:37); included in the genealogy of Ziza, a clan leader.

(2) KJV rendering in Josh. 19:33, where modern translations, correctly, have "the oak" (NRSV) or "the large tree" (NIV).

Allon Bacuth. al´uhn-bak´uhth (Heb. *ʾallôn bākût H475*, "oak of weeping"). TNIV Allon Bakuth. The burial site of DEBORAH, REBEKAH's nurse, somewhere in the vicinity of BETHEL (Gen. 35:8). Some modern scholars allege that the text confuses this person with the later Deborah, who is described as holding court under a palm tree "between Ramah and Bethel" (Jdg. 4:5).

allotment. This English term is used primarily in reference to the allocation of PALESTINE to the tribes of Israel (Josh. 15-17). Such practice stems, not from the land's originally communal ownership, as is sometimes alleged, but from its divine ownership (Josh. 22:19); the human residents were "aliens" and "tenants" before God (Lev. 25:23). Even as God chose Israel for his INHERITANCE (Exod. 19:5; Deut. 4:20), so he in turn became the "portion" of his people (Ps. 16:5; 73:26). Specifically, he promised to the seed of ABRAHAM the land of Canaan (Gen. 13:15; 17:8; cf. Josh. 21:43) and then provided for its distribution to their tribes and families (Num. 26:53; 33:54). Precise amounts depended upon the size of each group (26:54); but assignments were to be made by lot (26:55-56; cf. Josh. 16:1; 17:1), indicative of God's ultimate control (Prov. 16:33; Isa. 34:17). See LOTS.

Almighty. This English term is often used to render Hebrew *šadday H8724*, which occurs in the OT forty-eight times (thirty-one of these in the book of Job), either alone or in combination with *ʾēl H446*, "God." See EL SHADDAI. In the NT the Greek term *pantokratōr G4120* occurs ten times (nine of these in Revelation).

Almodad. al´moh´dad (Heb. *ʾalmôdād H525*, possibly "God is loved"). Eldest son of JOKTAN and descendant of SHEM (Gen. 10:26; 1 Chr. 1:20). He was presumably the eponymous ancestor of a S Arabian tribe, and some believe the name is preserved in el-Mudad, famous in Arabian history as the reputed father of ISHMAEL's wife and as chief of Jurham, supposedly a Joktanite tribe.

Almon. al´muhn (Heb. *ʿalmôn H6626*, possibly "signpost"). See ALEMETH (PLACE).

Almon Diblathaim. al´muhn-dib´luh-thay´im (Heb. *ʿalmôn diblātayim H6627*, possibly "signpost of the [double] fig cakes"). A stopping place in the wilderness journeys of the Israelites (Num. 33:46-47) in MOAB. It is usually identified with BETH DIBLATHAIM (Jer. 48:22).

almond tree. See PLANTS.

alms. Benevolent giving for the relief of the POOR. This term is not found in the NIV, though the practice is of Mosaic legislation and NT injunction. The English word is derived from Greek *eleēmosynē G1797*, which means "pity," but is also used in the sense of "charity, donation" (e.g., Matt. 6:2-3; Acts 9:36; 10:2; 24:17). In the OT the law prescribed gleanings from the harvest, the vineyards, and the grain in the corners of the field for the poor (Lev. 19:9-10), stipulating further gleanings from the orchards and olive groves (Deut. 24:10-22). It also protected the rights of the poor and unfortunate concerning wages, working conditions, and pledges, preventing the poor from being deprived of necessary garments or other needs. Almsgiving is set forth in Deut. 15:11: "There will always be poor people in the land. Therefore I command you to be openhanded toward your brothers and toward the poor and needy in your land."

The righteousness of almsgiving could become somewhat legalistic and professional. The lame man at the Gate Beautiful exemplified professional

A

begging in that daily he "asked … for money" (Acts 3:2-3 NIV; KJV, "to ask alms"). Perversion in receiving alms is seen in a beggar's cry (if it suggests the idea, "bless yourself by giving to me") and in benefactors who "announce it with trumpets," probably to be taken figuratively, and who want "to be seen" by people (Matt. 6:1-2). In Judaism almsgiving was of two kinds: "alms of the dish" (food and money received daily for distribution) and "alms of the chest" (coins received on the Sabbath for widows, orphans, strangers, and the poor).

The practice of the NT church was foreshadowed in Jesus' admonitions: "give to the poor" (Lk. 11:41; cf. 1 Cor. 16:2) and "sell your possessions and give to the poor" (Lk. 12:33; cf. 2 Cor. 8:3). Alms in the NT church were seen in the churches of Macedonia, who in "their extreme poverty … beyond their ability … [shared] in this service to the saints" (2 Cor. 8:1-4). True purpose and spirit were shown: "At the present time your plenty will supply what they need, so that in turn their plenty will supply what you need" (8:14). The full measure of ministry, blessings, and ability to give by God's grace is delineated in 2 Cor. 8 and 9, to be done liberally, prayerfully, and cheerfully. See also Jas. 2:15-16 and 1 Jn. 3:17. A primary function of deacons was to distribute alms (Acts 6).

almug. See PLANTS.

aloe. See PLANTS.

Aloth. ay′loth (Heb. ʿālôt H6599, meaning unknown). One of the Solomonic districts (1 Ki. 4:16); the Hebrew text can be read as either the phrase "in Aloth" (KJV, NIV) or the name "Bealoth" (NRSV, NJPS). See BEALOTH #2.

alpha and omega. al′fuh, oh-meg′uh. The first and last letters of the Greek alphabet, *alpha* being roughly equivalent to our letter *a*, and *omega* (literally, *great o*) to our *o*. The phrase "I am the Alpha and the Omega" occurs at least three times in the NT (Rev. 1:8; 21:6; 22:13), and always with the repeated definite article. It is probable that the occurrences in Revelation were intended as allusions to Isa. 44:6 and 48:12, "I am the first, and I am the last," asserting the eternal and transcen-

dent greatness of Yahweh. Perhaps also they were intended as allusions to Rom. 11:36 and Eph. 1:10, not in the actual words but in the theological concepts involved. Such language points to the preexistence and eternity of CHRIST and thus constitutes a strong assertion of his divine nature.

alphabet. See WRITING.

Alphaeus. al-fee′uhs (Gk. *Halphaios G271*, from Heb. *ḥalpî*). **(1)** The father of Levi (Mk. 2:14), who is identified with the apostle MATTHEW (Matt. 9:9; 10:3). Nothing more is known about him.

(2) Father of JAMES the apostle (Matt. 10:3; Mk. 3:18; Lk. 6:15; Acts 1:13; called "James the younger" in Mk. 15:40); Alphaeus's name is included to distinguish this James from the son of Zebedee who was also brother of John. Some have thought that this Alphaeus is the same as #1, in which case Levi/Matthew and James were brothers. Others have speculated that he is the same person as CLOPAS (Jn. 19:25), on the assumption that MARY the wife of Clopas, who was present at the crucifixion of Jesus with some other women, is the same as Mary the mother of James, who was also present at that time (Matt. 27:56; Mk. 15:40).

altar. A structure used for WORSHIP, especially for offering SACRIFICES. The first altar we read about (Gen. 8:20) was erected by Noah after leaving the ark. Subsequent altars were built by Abraham (12:7-8; 13:4, 18; 22:9), Isaac (26:25), Jacob (35:1-7), Moses (Exod. 17:15), and Joshua (Josh. 8:30-31). Some of these must have been very simple in structure, as the context of Gen. 22:9 seems to indicate. Most of the altars were built for sacrificial purposes, but some seem to have been largely memorial in character (Exod. 17:15-16; Josh. 22:26-27). Sometimes God stated just how the altar was to be built and of what materials (e.g., Exod. 20:24-26).

With the erection of the TABERNACLE, altars were constructed by the Hebrews for two chief purposes: the offering of sacrifices and the burning of INCENSE. Moses was told to build the altar of burnt offering out of acacia wood, overlaid with BRONZE (Exod. 27:1-2). The shape was a square of five cubits (c. 7.5 ft./2.3 m.), three cubits high (c. 4.5 ft./1.4 m.). At each corner of the altar there was

A

The Canaanite round altar at Megiddo was used between 2700 and 2200 B.C. (View to the S.)

to be a projection or "horn." This feature is found outside Israel, as in the tenth-century B.C. altar discovered at MEGIDDO. The purpose of the horns is not stated, although apparently it was thought to provide refuge from justice (1 Ki. 1:50-53; but see 2:28-34). A bronze grating was placed in the center of the altar that projected through the opening on two sides. Four rings were fastened to it in which two poles of the same material as the altar were to be placed to carry the altar. Steps leading up to the altar were forbidden (Exod. 20:26). For seven days ATONEMENT was to be made for the altar—apparently to sanctify it for the uses to which it was to be devoted (29:37); it was to be cleansed on the Day of Atonement after the presentation of sin offerings for the high priest and the nation (Lev. 16:19-20). See ATONEMENT, DAY OF.

Certain bronze utensils were made in connection with the altar. There were pans to hold the ashes, shovels for removing the ashes, basins to receive the blood and to convey it to the varied places for sprinkling, three-pronged flesh hooks with which to remove the flesh, and censers for carrying coals from the altar (Exod. 27:3). Once the fire on this altar was kindled, it was required that it burn continually (Lev. 6:13).

The altar of burnt offering was also included in Solomon's TEMPLE, the second temple, and in the temple built by HEROD. Its form was altered to fit into the varying sizes of these structures. Solomon made his altar of bronze, extending its length and width to twenty cubits (30 ft./9 m.) and its height to ten cubits (15 ft./4.5 m., 2 Chr. 4:1). After its construction it had a very interesting history.

Because idols had polluted it, King ASA rededicated it (15:8). Later on URIAH the priest removed it from its regular place, in order it seems to make room for another altar that he had patterned after the one King AHAZ had seen in DAMASCUS (2 Ki. 16:11-14). The terrible pollution of spiritual things in the reign of Ahaz led HEZEKIAH to cleanse the altar (2 Chr. 29:12-18). Finally it was repaired and restored to its place by MANASSEH (33:16).

In ZERUBBABEL's temple the altar was built first (Ezra 3:2), supposedly on the exact spot where it previously stood (Jos. *Ant.* 11.4.1). After it had been desecrated by ANTIOCHUS Epiphanes, it was rebuilt by Judas MACCABEE with unhewn stones (1 Macc. 4:47).

Moses was also commanded by God to make "an altar … for burning incense" (Exod. 30:1), sometimes called "the gold altar" (39:38; Num. 4:11). It was to be a cubit square and two cubits high (1.5 x 1.5 x 3 ft. [45 x 45 x 90 cm.], Exod. 30:2) with horns at each corner. It was made of acacia wood overlaid with pure gold. Around the top of this structure a crown of gold was placed, beneath which were fixed two golden rings, one on each side. Staves of the same construction as the altar were placed through these rings to carry it (30:1-5).

This altar was to be located before the veil that separated the Holy Place from the Most Holy Place, midway between the walls (Exod. 30:6; 40:5). Because of its special location, it was referred to as "the altar before the LORD" (Lev. 16:12). Elsewhere in the Bible it is referred to as "the altar that belonged to the inner sanctuary" (1 Ki. 6:22; cf. Heb. 9:3-4) and "the golden altar before the throne" (Rev. 8:3). Incense was burned on this altar twice each day (Exod. 30:7-8), and the blood of the atonement was sprinkled on it (30:10). The burning of incense on this altar symbolized the offering up of the believers' prayers (Rev. 8:3). It was while ZECHARIAH was officiating at this altar that the angel appeared to him (Lk. 1:10).

There are no altars recognized in the NT church. While Heb. 13:10 is sometimes used to prove the contrary, the context makes clear that Jesus Christ is the true altar of each believer. PAUL mentions in Acts 17:23 the inscription on an altar, "TO AN UNKNOWN GOD," which he saw in ATHENS. See UNKNOWN GOD.

© Dr. James C. Martin

A

There is good reason to believe that the need for altars was revealed very early as basic in approaching God. The altar played a leading role in all OT worship of the true God, as well as a prominent part in most pagan religions. A careful study of the use of this article of furniture in Israel's worship furnishes us with many spiritual lessons today. It was the place of sacrifice where God was propitiated and where man was pardoned and sanctified. It looked to the great sacrifice that the Son of God was about to make on the cross. The altar of sacrifice, the first thing visible as one approached the tabernacle, spoke loudly to sinners that without the shedding of blood there would be no access to God and no forgiveness of sin (Heb. 9:9, 22).

Al-taschith. al-tas'kith. A word found in KJV in the titles of Ps. 57-59 and 75 as a transliteration of the Hebrew phrase ʾal-tašḥēt, meaning "Do not destroy" (some versions transliterate "Altashheth"). This phrase may form the beginning of an old tune, normally sung at the harvesting of grapes, as described in Isa. 65:8. But David's word about Saul, "Don't destroy him" (1 Sam. 26:9), and the words of Moses' prayer (Deut. 9:26) both imply a spirit of trust in the Lord suited to the content of these psalms. The purpose of the title may, therefore, be to indicate the type of praise that follows. See also Aijeleth Shahar.

Alush. ay'luhsh (Heb. ʾālûš H478, meaning unknown). A stopping place of the Israelites in their journey through the wilderness (Num. 33:13-14). Alush was apparently located between Dophkah and Rephidim, but the site has not been identified.

Alvah. al'vuh (Heb. ʿalwāh H6595, meaning unknown). Descendant of Esau, listed among the clan chiefs of Edom (Gen. 36:40; 1 Chr. 1:51; in the latter passage, the KJV and other versions have "Aliah," following the *Ketib* or variant reading). The name was probably applied to a territory as well. Some identify Alvah with Alvan.

Alvan. al'vuhn (Heb. ʿalwān H6597, perhaps "tall" or "ascending"). Son of Shobal and grandson of Seir the Horite (Gen. 36:23; 1 Chr. 1:40; in the latter passage, the KJV and other versions have "Alian," following most Heb. MSS). Some identify Alvan with Alvah.

Amad. ay'mad (Heb. ʿamʿād H6675, derivation unknown). A town in the tribal territory of Asher (Josh. 19:26). The site is unknown.

Amal. ay'muhl (Heb. ʿāmāl H6663, possibly "laborer"). Son of Helem, listed among the brave warriors who were heads of families of the tribe of Asher (1 Chr. 7:35; cf. v. 40).

Amalek. am'uh-lek (Heb. ʿămālēq H6667, derivation uncertain). Son of Eliphaz (by his concubine Timna), grandson of Esau, and a tribal chief of Edom (Gen. 36:12, 15-16; 1 Chr. 1:36). The name is frequently applied to his descendants. See Amalekites.

The Amalekites roamed throughout this region in SE Israel referred to in the Bible as the Desert of Zin.

© Dr. James C. Martin

Amalekite. uh-mal'uh-kit (Heb. ʿămālēqî H6668, "of Amalek"). A descendant of Amalek (but see below). The Amalekites were an ancient and nomadic marauding people dwelling mainly in the Negev from early in the second millennium to c. 700 B.C.

The first mention of them is among those conquered by Kedorlaomer in the days of Abraham

(Gen. 14:7). Moses felt their fury in the unprovoked attack on the Israelites at Rephidim, for which God decreed continual war and ultimate obliteration (Exod. 17:8-16). Joshua and the other spies encountered them in Canaan, and they and the Canaanites repulsed the Israelites at Hormah (Num. 14:45). During the period of the judges they sided with Ammon and Moab against the Israelites in the days of Ehud (Jdg. 3:13) and with Midian and other eastern peoples against Gideon (6:3, 33). Another judge, Abdon, was buried "in the hill country of the Amalekites" (12:15).

During the monarchy, Saul was commissioned to destroy them utterly but failed to do so and spared their leader, Agag (1 Sam. 15:8-9). An Amalekite later killed Saul (2 Sam. 1:1-10). David invaded the land of the Amalekites and other ancient inhabitants from Shur to Egypt (1 Sam. 27:8) and struck them severely in recovering his wives and property stolen during the raid on Ziklag (30:18). They are numbered among nations subdued by him (2 Sam. 8:12; 1 Chr. 18:11). The Simeonites during the time of Hezekiah finally exterminated them (1 Chr. 4:43).

Distribution of the Amalekites was primarily in the Negev, SW of the Dead Sea, but also in the Sinai Peninsula from Rephidim (Exod. 17:8) to the border of Egypt (1 Sam. 27:8); northward at Jezreel (Jdg. 6:33), Pirathon (12:15), and at or near Jericho (3:13); and eastward to Mount Seir (1 Chr. 4:42). See also Num. 13:29.

The origin of the Amalekites is debated. If Amalek, the grandson of Esau (Gen. 36:12), is the nation's father, the note in Gen. 14:7 must be seen as proleptic (i.e., the term is used to identify the land that later became the home of the Amalekite descendants of Esau). Accordingly, their description as "first among the nations" in Num. 24:20 can be first in time, first in preeminence, or most likely first to molest liberated Israel (at Rephidim). Arab traditions, late and conflicting, have the Amalekites stem from Ham.

In character the Amalekites were warlike, usually confederate with the Canaanites (Num. 14:45) or Moabites (Jdg. 3:13), but sometimes alone, as at Rephidim (Exod. 17:8) and Ziklag (1 Sam. 10:1). They "cut off all who were lagging behind; they had no fear of God" (Deut. 25:18), and they destroyed crops (Jdg. 6:4).

At Rephidim the Lord said, "I will completely blot out the memory of Amalek from under heaven" (Exod. 17:14), and Balaam prophesied, "Amalek ... will come to ruin at last" (Num. 24:20). Saul failed to destroy the Amalekites, but David reduced them to inactivity, and the Simeonites at Mount Seir "killed the remaining Amalekites who had escaped" (1 Chr. 4:43). Archaeology has produced no evidence of them thus far.

Amam. ay'mahm (Heb. *ʾāmām H585*, derivation uncertain). An unidentified city in the Negev that the tribe of Judah received in the allotment of the land (Josh. 15:26).

Amana. uh-may'nuh (Heb. *ʾāmānāh H592*, perhaps "constant"). Also Amanah. A mountain in the Antilebanon range (Cant. 4:8), near the course of the river Abana (2 Ki. 5:12, where the river too is called "Amana" in a variant reading).

amanuensis. uh-man'yoo-en'sis. This Latin term, meaning "secretary," is used specifically of someone who takes dictation or copies a MS. Amanuenses were frequently used by writers in antiquity. Peter speaks of being assisted by Silas in writing a letter (1 Pet. 5:12). When Paul refers to writing a greeting with his own hand (1 Cor. 16:21; 2 Thess. 3:17; cf. also Phlm. 19 and esp. Gal. 6:10-18), he implies that the rest of the letter was written by a secretary. One of them, Tertius, identifies himself in Rom. 16:22. The use of amanuenses may serve to account for stylistic differences between letters that have the same author, but there is debate about how much freedom these secretaries were given in the composition of documents.

Amariah. am'uh-ri'uh (Heb. *ʾămaryâ H618* and *ʾămaryāhhû H619*, "Yahweh has said"). **(1)** Son of Meraioth and descendant of Aaron in the line of Eleazar; grandfather (or ancestor) of Zadok the priest (1 Chr. 6:7, 52).

(2) Son of Hebron and descendant of Levi in the line of Kohath; contemporary of David (1 Chr. 23:19; 24:23).

(3) Son of Azariah and descendant of Aaron in the line of Eleazar; ancestor of Ezra (1 Chr. 6:11; Ezra 7:3).

A

(4) A chief priest in the reign of Jehoshaphat (2 Chr. 19:11); some identify him with #3 above.

(5) A Levite who faithfully assisted Kore in distributing the contributions made to the temple during the reign of Hezekiah (2 Chr. 31:15).

(6) One of the descendants of Binnui who agreed to put away their foreign wives (Ezra 10:42 [cf. v. 38 NIV and NRSV]).

(7) A priest who returned to Jerusalem and sealed the covenant under Nehemiah (Neh. 10:3). Some believe he is the same as the Amariah who returned from Babylon with Zerubbabel (12:2; cf. v. 13).

(8) Son of Shephatiah, descendant of Judah, and ancestor of Athaiah (Neh. 11:4).

(9) Ancestor of the prophet Zephaniah and son of Hezekiah, possibly the king (Zeph. 1:1).

Amarna, Tell-el. tel´el-uh-mahr´nuh. Name given to a mound of ruins in Egypt, halfway between Thebes (present Luxor) and Memphis (near Cairo); it was the site of a major city built by one of the Egyptian pharaohs, Amenhotep (Amenophis) IV, better known as Akhenaten (c. 1370-1353 B.C.). The city's ancient name was

© Dr. James C. Martin. The Cairo Museum. Photographed by permission.

This small cuneiform tablet from Tell el-Amarna describes diplomatic correspondence between the Egyptian court and the rulers of neighboring states.

Akhet-Aten (Egyptian ʾḫt-ʾtn, "the horizon of Aten," referring to the deified sun disk). In A.D. 1887, a peasant woman, seeking the dust from ancient buildings with which to fertilize her garden, dug in the ruins of Tell el-Amarna. She found some clay tablets, which she pulverized and took to her home. Finally an American missionary stationed at Luxor, Chauncey Murch, heard of this find and notified some cuneiform scholars. After the site producing these tablets had been identified, it was excavated by Sir Flinders Petrie.

The excavation yielded 320 clay tablets of varying sizes with Akkadian cuneiform writing on both sides. There are now 82 in the British Museum, 160 in Berlin, 60 at Giza Museum, and the rest in private hands. They contain the private correspondence between the ruling Egyptian pharaohs at the time and the political leaders in Palestine. It is believed they reflect the prevailing conditions that existed during the time Joshua carried on his campaigns in Palestine. These tablets have cast considerable light on the cultural and historical background to the biblical world. These tablets have also provided valuable linguistic information (e.g., regarding the Egyptian vowel system). In addition, the excavations uncovered much about Egyptian art, architecture, and theology that was previously unknown.

Amasa. uh-may´suh (Heb. *ʿămāśāʾ* H6690, possibly short form of Amasiah, "Yahweh has carried [*i.e.*, protected]"). **(1)** Son of Jether (Ithra) and captain of the Israelite army appointed by Absalom when the latter attempted to overthrow David's rule in Israel (2 Sam. 17:25; 1 Chr. 2:16-17). Abigail, sister of Zeruiah and David, was his mother, making him nephew to David and cousin to Absalom. Following the defeat of the rebels under Amasa and the death of Absalom by Joab in the forest of Ephraim (2 Sam. 18:6-17), David made Amasa captain of the army in place of Joab (19:13). When Sheba and the men of Israel rebelled, David set three days for Amasa to assemble the men of Judah (20:4). Amasa delayed beyond the set time, so David sent Abishai, brother of Joab, and a body of armed men after Sheba. Amasa joined forces with Abishai at "the great rock in Gibeon," where Joab, in feigned greeting, "took Amasa by the beard with his right hand to kiss him" and ran him through with his sword (20:8-10).

(2) Son of Hadlai; he was one of the princes of EPHRAIM who supported ODED the prophet in warning the Israelites not to take captives from Judah (2 Chr. 28:9-15).

Amasai. uh-may′si (Heb. *ʿămāśay H6691*, possibly short form of AMASIAH, "Yahweh has carried [*i.e.*, protected]"). **(1)** Son of ELKANAH and descendant of LEVI in the line of KOHATH (1 Chr. 6:25 [Heb. v. 10]). Somehow he also is linked with the genealogy of the musician HEMAN and thus is listed as the father of Mahath (v. 35 [Heb. v. 20]).

(2) One of the priests appointed by DAVID to blow the trumpets before the ARK OF THE COVENANT when it was brought to Jerusalem (1 Chr. 15:24).

(3) Father of Mahath, a Levite who served in the time of HEZEKIAH's revival (2 Chr. 29:12). Since the Amasai in #1 above also had a son named Mahath, it might appear that they are the same person, but 1 Chr. 6:25 and 35 refer to someone who served much earlier, during the time of SOLOMON.

(4) The "chief of the Thirty," upon whom the Spirit came when he met DAVID at ZIKLAG (1 Chr. 12:18). Some identify him with AMASA, captain of Absalom's army (2 Sam. 17:25), and others with ABISHAI, the brother of JOAB (1 Chr. 11:20; cf. 2 Sam. 23:18; 1 Chr. 2:16; 18:12). The problem would remain, however, in that none of the three (Amasai, Amasa, or Abishai) appears in the lists of the Thirty given in 2 Sam. 23 and 1 Chr. 11.

Amashai. uh-mash′i. KJV form of AMASHSAI.

Amashsai. uh-mash′si (Heb. *ʿămašsay H6692*, possibly a scribal error for *ʿămāśay H6691*, "Amasai"). KJV Amashai. Son of Azarel and descendant of IMMER; a postexilic priest (Neh. 11:13). Some identify him with MAASAI in the parallel list (1 Chr. 9:12).

Amasiah. am′uh-si′uh (Heb. *ʿămasyâ H6674*, "Yahweh has carried [for protection]"). Son of Zicri; a Judahite commander under JEHOSHAPHAT "who volunteered himself for the service of the LORD" (2 Chr. 17:16).

Amaw. ay′maw (Heb. *ʿammô*). Also Amau. According to some scholars, this term refers to the land near the EUPHRATES River from which BALAK, king of MOAB, summoned BALAAM to curse Israel (Num. 22:5 NRSV). If this translation is correct, Amaw (or Amaʾe) may be identified with a region in the valley of the river Sajur in N Syria. A few Hebrew MSS, supported by several ancient versions, read AMMON, preferred by some scholars because of this country's closer proximity to Moab. It is better, however, to read the Hebrew text not as a proper noun, but as the word for "his people" (cf. KJV), thus NIV, "his native land." See also PETHOR.

Amaziah. am uh-zi′uh (Heb. *ʾămaṣyâ H604* and *ʾămaṣyāhû H605*, "strength of Yahweh" or "Yahweh is powerful"). **(1)** Son of Joash (JEHOASH) and his successor as king of Judah. His mother was a certain Jehoaddin of Jerusalem (2 Ki. 14:2; 2 Chr. 25:1). The length of his reign is given as twenty-nine years in 2 Ki. 14:2, but such a long reign is difficult to reconcile with other data, unless the figure includes a period of coregency with his son Azariah (UZZIAH); thus some scholars date his reign c. 800-783 B.C., others 796-767. Amaziah ascended the throne in the midst of trying circumstances, when his father was murdered by some of his courtiers (2 Ki. 14:5-6; 2 Chr. 25:3-4). He was quite successful against the Edomites in the S along the Jordan Valley but was foolish to challenge the more powerful Jehoash, king of Israel, as a result of which he lost his kingdom (2 Ki. 14:7-14; 2 Chr. 25:17-24). He then fell the victim of a court intrigue and was pursued to LACHISH, where he was murdered. His body was brought back in a funeral cortège, and he was buried in the royal tombs outside the Mount of Zion.

(2) Father of Joshah, a clan leader in the tribe of SIMEON (1 Chr. 4:34; cf. v. 38).

(3) Son of Hilkiah and descendant of LEVI in the line of MERARI (1 Chr. 6:45); he is listed among those who "ministered with music before the tabernacle, the Tent of Meeting, until Solomon built the temple of the LORD in Jerusalem" (v. 32).

(4) A minor figure named Amaziah is mentioned as a priest at the shrine of BETHEL during the reign of the second JEROBOAM. He attempted

A

to deter Amos from prophesying there and reported the prophet's denunciations to the king (Amos 7:10-17).

ambassador. An official representative of a ruler or government. Ambassadors and envoys are mentioned throughout most of the biblical period (e.g., Num. 20:14; Jdg. 11:12; 2 Chr. 32:31; Isa. 30:4). Disrespect shown to them was regarded as a serious insult to their sovereign and his people, and sometimes led to war (2 Sam. 10). In the NT the term is used only in a figurative sense. Paul called himself "an ambassador in chains" (Eph. 6:20); he also said, "We are therefore Christ's ambassadors, as though God were making his appeal through us" (2 Cor. 5:20). See MESSENGER.

amber. A yellow translucent fossil tree resin. Deeply colored translucent to transparent varieties are prized as gem material and have been used, since prehistoric times, for ornaments. The term *amber* is used by some English versions to translate a Hebrew word of uncertain meaning (Ezek. 1:4, 27; 8:2; NIV, "metal").

amen. A Hebrew term (*ʾāmēn H589*; cf. Gk. *amēn G297*) used to express assent. In both Greek and English (and many other languages), this term is a transliteration of a Hebrew adverb meaning "truly, verily," itself derived from a verb meaning "to be reliable, have stability." In the OT it appears with doxologies (1 Chr. 16:36; Neh. 8:6; Ps. 41:13) as an assent by the congregation to laws (Num. 5:22; Deut. 27:15-26), with oaths (Neh. 5:13), with appointments (1 Ki. 1:36), and as a call to divine witness (Jer. 28:6). In the NT it is used in various contexts. For example, it can introduce a solemn saying of Jesus, always in the sense of "I tell you the truth" (KJV, "Verily I say," Jn. 3:5; cf. Ps. 41:13). It is also used following a doxology (Rom. 11:36), following a benediction (15:33), as a concluding particle at the end of most NT books, as an assent to forebodings (Rev. 1:7; 22:20), in reverence to God (Rom. 1:25; 9:5; Rev. 1:18), and as a title of God (Rev. 3:14; cf. Isa. 65:15). The word may indicate the agreement or consent of the congregation to utterances of leaders (1 Cor. 14:16); it is also equated with certainty of the promises of God (2 Cor. 1:20).

American Standard Version. See BIBLE VERSIONS, ENGLISH.

amethyst. See MINERALS.

Ami. ay′mi (Heb. *ʾāmî H577*, "trustworthy"). See AMON #3.

amillennialism. See KINGDOM OF GOD.

Aminadab. See AMMINADAB.

Amittai. uh-mit′i (Heb. *ʾămittay H624*, "faithful"). Father of the prophet JONAH, from GATH HEPHER in the tribal territory of ZEBULUN (2 Ki. 14:25; Jon. 1:1).

Ammah. am′uh (Heb. *ʾammāh H565*, prob. "[water] canal"; cf. METHEG AMMAH). A hill near GIAH in BENJAMIN, somewhere E of GIBEON, where JOAB and ABISHAI halted in their pursuit of ABNER and his forces (2 Sam. 2:24). The site has not been identified.

Amman. ah-mahn′. The capital city of the modern country of Jordan. See RABBAH.

Ammi. am′i (Heb. *ʿammî* [from *ʿam H6639*], "my people"). The new name to be applied to Israel in the time of restoration (Hos. 2:1; NIV, "My people"), in contrast to rejected Israel, called LO-AMMI, "Not my people," the name given to HOSEA's third child by GOMER (1:9; cf. Rom. 9:25-26).

Ammiel. am′ee-uhl (Heb. *ʿammîʾēl H6653*, "my kinsman is God"). (1) Son of Gemalli, of the tribe of DAN; one of the twelve spies sent by MOSES into Canaan (Num. 13:12).

(2) Father of MAKIR, in whose house MEPHIBOSHETH was hidden from DAVID (2 Sam. 9:4-5). Makir later befriended David (17:27).

(3) Father of BATHSHEBA, a wife of David and the mother of SOLOMON (1 Chr. 3:5 NIV; the NRSV, following most MSS, has "Bath-shua, daughter of Ammiel"). Elsewhere he is called ELIAM (2 Sam. 11:3; note that the two names have the same meaning, but with the components *ʿam* and *ʾēl* reversed).

(4) Sixth son of Obed-Edom, whose family took care of the South Gate of the temple and the storehouse in the time of David (1 Chr. 26:5, 15).

Ammihud. uh-mi′huhd (Heb. ʿammîhûd *H6654*, "my kinsman is glorious" or "my people have majesty"). **(1)** Father of Elishama; the latter was head of the tribe of Ephraim during the sojourn in the wilderness (Num. 1:10; 2:18; 7:48, 53; 10:22). Ammihud is listed in the genealogy of Joshua (1 Chr. 7:26).

(2) Father of Shemuel; the latter was one of the leaders of the tribe of Simeon appointed by Moses to help divide the land of Canaan (Num. 34:20).

(3) Father of Pedahel; the latter was one of the leaders of the tribe of Naphtali appointed by Moses to help divide the land of Canaan (Num. 34:28).

(4) Father of Talmai, king of Geshur, to whom Absalom fled after the murder of his brother Amnon (2 Sam. 13:37, where "Ammihur" is a variant [*Ketib*]).

(5) Son of Omri and father of Uthai; listed among leaders from the tribe of Judah who were the first to resettle after the exile (1 Chr. 9:4).

Amminadab. uh-min′uh-dab (Heb. ʿammînādāb *H6657*, "my kinsman is noble" or "my people are generous"; Gk. *Aminadab G300*). **(1)** Father of Nahshon; the latter was the head of a family in the tribe of Judah (Num. 1:7; 2:3; 7:12, 17; 10:14). Amminadab was also the father of Elisheba, the wife of Aaron (Exod. 6:23). He descended from Perez, Judah's son (Gen. 38:29; 46:12), was an ancestor of David (Ruth 4:19-20), and is included in the genealogy of Jesus Christ (Matt. 1:4; Lk. 3:33).

(2) The name Amminadab is listed in the MT of 1 Chr. 6:22 (= v. 7 in MT and LXX), possibly by textual corruption, as a son of Kohath (who was a son of Levi) and as the father of Korah. However, according to vv. 37-38 (and in Exod. 6:18, 21; cf. Num. 3:19), Kohath's son who fathered Korah was Izhar (the reading of some MSS of the LXX in 1 Chr. 6:22).

(3) The head of the Levitical family of Uzziel; he helped to bring the ark of the covenant to Jerusalem in David's time (1 Chr. 15:10-12).

(4) According to the Septuagint, Amminadab was the name of Esther's father, but the MT reading, Abihail, is probably correct (Esth. 2:15; 9:29).

Amminadib. uh-min′uh-dib (Heb. ʿammî-nādîb [from ʿam *H6639* + nādîb *H5618*], "my people are noble" or "my kinsman is generous willing"). A name found only in an obscure passage, "my soul made me *like* the chariots of Amminadib" (Cant. 6:12 KJV). However, the NIV interprets the term as two common nouns and renders, "my desire set me among the royal chariots of my people" (similarly NRSV, "my fancy set me in a chariot beside my prince").

Ammishaddai. am-i-shad′i (Heb. ʿammîšadday *H6659*, "Shaddai is my kinsman"). The father of Ahiezer; the latter was a leader of the tribe of Dan in the wilderness journey (Num. 1:12; 2:25; 7:66, 71; 10:25).

Ammizabad. uh-miz′uh-bad (Heb. ʿammîzābād *H6655*, "my kinsman has bestowed"). Son of Benaiah; the latter was one of David's bodyguards and captain of the elite Thirty, while Ammizabad was in charge of the division led by his father (1 Chr. 27:6).

Ammon. am′uhn (Heb. ʿammôn *H6648*, derivation uncertain). An ancient nation in Transjordan; its inhabitants were descendants of Ben-Ammi, one of the sons of Lot born to him by his youngest daughter in the neighborhood of Zoar (Gen. 19:38). See Ammonite.

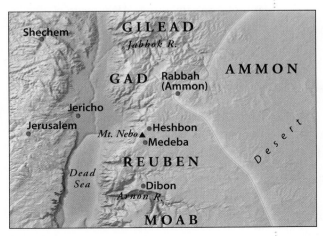

Ammon.

A

© Dr. James C. Martin. Amman Archaeological Museum. Photographed by permission.

This statue of the Ammonite king Yerah ʿAzar, discovered at the Amman Citadel, dates to the end of the 8th cent. B.C.

Ammonite. amʹuh-nit (Heb. *ʿammônî H6649*). A descendant of BEN-AMMI (Gen. 19:38). The Ammonites constituted a nation E of the JORDAN River, S of GILEAD, and N of MOAB. They were closely related to the Moabites by ancestry and often appear in Scripture in united effort with them. Because they were also related to Israel (through LOT, nephew of ABRAHAM), the Israelites were told by the Lord not to enter into battle with them as they journeyed toward the land of Canaan (Deut. 2:19). Lot fled from the destruction of the cities of SODOM and GOMORRAH and dwelt in the mountains to the E of the Dead Sea. The land God gave the Ammonites stretched to the N as far as the JABBOK River and to the S to the hills of EDOM. Many years later the Ammonites made

war with Israel in order to extend their borders farther W. Although this land never really belonged to the Ammonites, they claimed it and gave this as a reason for their aggression (Jdg. 11:13).

Unable to expand westward and not desiring the desert tract of land on the E, the Ammonites were confined to a small area. Although they were a nomadic people, they did have a few cities, their capital RABBAH (Rabbath-Ammon) being the most famous.

The people were fierce in nature and rebellious and, apart from the period when NAHASH was a friendly ally of DAVID's (2 Sam. 10:2), hostile to Israel. They threatened to gouge out the right eyes of all in JABESH GILEAD (1 Sam. 11:2). They were given to brutal murder (Jer. 40:14; 41:5-7; Amos 1:14). Though related to Israel, they refused to help them when asked, and they joined with Moab in securing BALAAM to curse them (Deut. 23:3-4). Later in Israel's history they united with SANBALLAT to oppose the work of NEHEMIAH in restoring the walls of JERUSALEM (Neh. 2:10-19). In religion the Ammonites were a degraded, idolatrous people. Their chief idol was MOLECH, to whom they were guilty of offering human sacrifices (1 Ki. 11:7).

Because of their sins and especially because they constantly opposed Israel, EZEKIEL predicted their complete destruction (Ezek. 25:1-7). Their last stand seems to have been against Judas MACCABEE (1 Macc. 5:6).

Amnon. amʹnon (Heb. *ʾamnôn H596*, "faithful"). (1) Firstborn son of DAVID by AHINOAM (2 Sam. 3:2; 1 Chr. 3:1). He dishonored his half-sister TAMAR and was subsequently slain (2 Sam. 13). See discussion under ABSALOM.

(2) Son of Shimon and descendant of JUDAH (1 Chr. 4:20).

Amok. ayʹmok (Heb. *ʿamôq H6651*, "deep" or "wise"). A leader among the priests who returned from EXILE with ZERUBBABEL and JESHUA; Amok's son or descendant Eber was head of his family in the time of JOIAKIM (Neh. 12:7, 20; cf. v. 12).

Amon. amʹuhn (Heb. *ʾāmôn H571* [*ʾāmōn* in 1 Ki. 22:26], "faithful" [Egyp. deity *ʾāmôn H572*]; Gk. *Amōn G321*). (1) Son of MANASSEH and fifteenth king of Judah. The brief biblical accounts of Amon (2 Ki. 21:18-26 and 2 Chr. 33:20-25) describe him as an evil king who after only two years of reign (c. 642-640 B.C.) was slain by officials of his household. His son, however, was the illustrious King JOSIAH. Amon is included in Matthew's GENEALOGY OF JESUS CHRIST (Matt. 1:10, where the NRSV reads "Amos," the form found in the earliest Gk. MSS and other important witnesses; because this form is also a variant reading in the SEPTUAGINT, Matthew may have used it deliberately).

(2) Governor of the city of SAMARIA who was ordered by AHAB king of Israel to put MICAIAH the prophet in prison (1 Ki. 22:26; 2 Chr. 18:25).

(3) One of SOLOMON's servants whose descendants returned from EXILE under ZERUBBABEL (Neh. 7:59); called Ami in the parallel passage (Ezra 2:57).

(4) The name of an Egyptian deity who resided at No (meaning "the city," i.e., THEBES, Jer. 46:25; KJV here reads "the multitude of No"). Often spelled Amun or Amen. In Nah. 3:8, "Thebes" is a translation of *nōʾ ʾāmôn H5531* (lit., "the city of Amon"; KJV, "populous No"). Since Amon, the king of Judah, bore this name—which is one of relatively few Hebrew names with no Semitic divine element incorporated into it—some scholars have connected him with this Egyptian deity. This supposition is strengthened in the light of the unorthodoxy of Amon's father, Manasseh. The Thebian god Amon, a fertility deity, was often pictured having elements of sacred animals (the ram and the goose). When Thebes became the capital of EGYPT, Amon was connected with RE, the sun god. Amon-Reᶜ thus came to be worshiped as the supreme god.

Amorite. am´uh-rit (Heb. *ʾĕmōrî H616*, prob. "westerner"). Although this word in the Hebrew occurs always in the singular, it is used collectively of that tribe of people who, according to Gen. 10:16, descended from CANAAN. They were prominent in pre-Israelite days, for it is believed that at one time their kingdom occupied the larger part of MESOPOTAMIA and SYRIA, with their capital at HARAN. The MARI tablets throw a flood of light on them, and some have thought that AMRAPHEL of SHINAR (Gen. 14:1) was one of their

kings. When people from the N drove them from this region, they settled Babylonia and brought the entire area under their control, giving to Babylonia one of the richest periods in her history. After several hundred years they were defeated by the HITTITES, and they settled throughout a large portion of Canaan. They may even have ruled in Egypt for a time.

We do know that during their supremacy in Canaan they marched on the kingdom of MOAB and under the leadership of SIHON king of HESHBON subdued a large portion of this land, in which they settled (Num. 21:13, 26-31). JOSHUA speaks of their land as E of the JORDAN (Josh. 24:8), but elsewhere it is described as being on the W shore of the DEAD SEA (Gen. 14:7), on the plain of MAMRE (14:13), and around Mount HERMON (Deut. 3:8). They were apparently a very wicked people, for God told ABRAHAM that his descendants would mete out divine vengeance on them when their iniquity was full (Gen. 15:16). Under MOSES' leadership this judgment was dealt to Sihon and to OG of BASHAN, the kings of the Amorites E of the Jordan. Their territory was subdued and given to the tribe of REUBEN, who held it for 500 years until it fell to Moab. This land was very rich, attractive to both farmers and herdsmen. Joshua met these people in battle in the united campaign of the five Amorite kings of JERUSALEM, HEBRON, MARMUTH, LACHISH, and EGLON (Josh. 10:1-43). These battles (11:1-14), fought by Joshua under divine leadership, ended forever Amorite hostilities against Israel (1 Sam. 7:14; 1 Ki. 9:20-21).

Amos. ay´muhs (Heb. *ʿāmôs H6650*, "burdenbearer" or "supported [by Yahweh]" [cf. AMASAH]; Gk. *Amōs G322*). (1) An 8th-cent. B.C. literary prophet. See AMOS, BOOK OF.

(2) According to some MSS of Matt. 1:10, the son of King MANASSEH. See AMON #1.

(3) Son of Nahum, included in Luke's GENEALOGY OF JESUS CHRIST (Lk. 3:25).

Amos, Book of. The third book among the twelve Minor Prophets. The prophet Amos was one of the colorful personalities in an era that saw the rise of several towering prophetic figures. His ministry occurred in the reign of JEROBOAM II (c. 786-746

A

Overview of AMOS

Author: Amos, a shepherd from Tekoa (near Bethlehem) who was called to serve as prophet, possibly for only a limited period of time.

Historical setting: Amos received his revelation about the year 760 B.C., during the latter part of the prosperous reign of Jeroboam II of Israel. His ministry was directed primarily to the northern kingdom, making special reference to the region of Samaria and the city of Bethel.

Purpose: To condemn the idolatry prevalent in Israel and to challenge the social injustice of its wealthy inhabitants.

Contents: The book begins with a general indictment of various nations (Amos 1-2), followed by an extensive condemnation of the northern kingdom of Israel (chs. 3-6) and by predictions of its destruction (chs. 7-9), although the prophecy ends with a promise of restoration (9:11-15).

B.C.), son of King Jehoash of the Jehu dynasty of Israel. Due to the removal of Ben-Hadad III of Syria as a military threat, the northern kingdom had been able to consolidate its hold on Damascus and extend its borders northward to the pass of Hamath. To the S and E, its territorial acquisitions equaled those of the early kingdom period under David and Solomon. Although Assyria was becoming an increasingly serious political threat, its military might under Tiglath-Pileser III was still a distant prospect when Jeroboam II began to rule Israel.

Jeroboam's forty-year reign was one of great prosperity for the northern kingdom, approaching in character the "golden age" of David and Solomon. With the threat of war removed, a cultural, social, and economic revival took place. The expansion of trade and commerce resulted in a steady drift from country to city, and the small towns in the northern kingdom gradually became overcrowded. But prosperity was accompanied by an almost unprecedented degree of social corruption (Amos 2:6-8; 5:11-12), caused principally by the demoralizing influence of Canaanite Baal worship, which had been fostered at the local shrines from the time when the northern kingdom had assumed a separate existence.

Archaeological discoveries in Palestine have furnished a dramatic picture of the extent to which this depraved, immoral religion exerted its corrupting influences over the Israelites. Characteristic of the ritual observances were drunkenness, violence, gross sensuality, and idolatrous worship. The effect was seen in the corruption of justice, in wanton and luxurious living, and in the decay of social unity in Hebrew society. The rich manifested no sense of responsibility toward the poor, and instead of relieving their economic distress seemed bent on devising new means of depriving them of their property.

To this perilous situation Amos brought a message of stern denunciation. Although he was not an inhabitant of the northern kingdom, he was painfully aware of its moral, social, and religious shortcomings. Amos lived in the small mountain village of Tekoa, which lay to the S of Jerusalem on the borders of the extensive upland pastures of Judah. By trade he was a herdsman of sheep and goats (Amos 7:14) and was also engaged in dressing the sycamore-fig tree, whose fruit needs to be incised about four days before the harvest to hasten the ripening process. His background was of a strictly agricultural nature, and his work afforded him ample time for meditating on God's laws and their meaning for wayward Israel.

On receiving his call, Amos protested vigorously against the luxurious and careless lifestyle characteristic of SAMARIA, castigated the elaborate offerings made at the shrines of BEERSHEBA and GILGAL, and stated flatly that ritual could never form an acceptable substitute for righteousness. He asserted the moral jurisdiction of God over all nations (Amos 1:3, 6, 9, 11, 13; 2:1, 4, 6) and warned the Israelites that unless they repented of their idolatry and, following a renewed spiritual relationship with God, commenced to redress social inequalities, they would fall victim to the invader from the E. So great was the impact of this vigorous personality that Amos was accused of sedition by AMAZIAH, the idolatrous high priest of BETHEL (7:10-13). In reply, Amos pointed out that he had no connection with any prophetic order, nor was he linked in any way politically with the house of David. Instead he was called by God to prophesy the captivity of an unrepentant Israel.

The style of his book, though simple, is picturesque, marked by striking illustrations taken from his rural surroundings. His work as a herdsman was clearly not incompatible either with a knowledge of history (Amos 9:7) or with an ability to assess the significance of contemporary political and religious trends. The integrity of his book has suffered little at the hands of modern critical scholars.

Contents

Amos 1-2. The indictment of foreign nations, including Judah and Israel.

3:1—5:17. The condemnation of wicked Samaria.

5:18—6:14. False security exposed; judgment foretold.

7:1—9:10. Five visions illustrate divine forbearance and justice; Amos's reception at Bethel (7:10-17).

9:11-15. Epilogue promising restoration and prosperity.

Amoz. ay´muhz (Heb. ʾāmôṣ *H576*, prob. short form of AMAZIAH, "strength of Yahweh"). The father of the prophet ISAIAH (2 Ki. 19:2; Isa. 1:1).

Amphipolis. am-fip´uh-lis (Gk. *Amphipolis G315*, "city on both sides"). A city of MACEDONIA, situated on a bend of the River Strymon. It was founded by the Athenians in the fifth century B.C. and under the Romans it became the capital of one of the four districts into which Macedonia was divided. It was a military post on the Via Egnatia, 33 mi. (53 km.) SW of PHILIPPI. PAUL passed through it on the way from Philippi to THESSALONICA (Acts 17:1).

Excavated area of Amphipolis. (View to the S.)

© Dr. James C. Martin

Amplias. am′plee-uhs. See Ampliatus.

Ampliatus. am′pli-ay′tuhs (Gk. *Ampliatos G309*; the shortened form *Amplias* is a textual variant, thus KJV, "Amplias"). A Christian living in Rome to whom Paul sends greetings and to whom he refers as one "whom I love in the Lord" (Rom. 16:8). His name was common in ancient Rome, especially among slaves and freedmen.

Amram. am′ram (Heb. *ʿamrām H6688*, "exalted people" or "the kinsman [referring to a deity] is eminent"; gentilic *ʿamrāmî H6689*, "Amramite"). (1) A Levite, son or descendant of Kohath; he was the husband (and nephew) of Jochebed and the father of Moses, Aaron, and Miriam (Exod. 6:18, 20; Num. 3:19; 26:59; 1 Chr. 6:3). The Amramites, descended from him, had special duties in the wilderness tabernacle and in the temple (Num. 3:27; 1 Chr. 26:23). (2) One of the descendants of Bani who agreed to put away their wives during Ezra's reforms (Ezra 10:34). (3) KJV form of Hamran (1 Chr. 1:41; see Hemdan).

Amraphel. am′ruh-fel (Heb. *ʾamrāpel H620*, meaning disputed). A member of a league of four kings (Amraphel of Shinar, Arioch of Ellasar, Kedorlaomer of Elam, and Tidal of Goiim) that fought an opposing league of Palestinian kings (of Sodom, Gomorrah, Admah, Zeboiim, and Bela) and defeated them (Gen. 14). The head of the eastern league was Kedorlaomer, king of Elam. Although identifications of several of these kings have been suggested (e.g., Amraphel = Hammurabi of Babylon, Tidal = Tudhalia I of Hatti), few scholars have accepted them.

amulet. The prophet Isaiah speaks of the women of his day as wearing "charms" (Isa. 3:20; NRSV, "amulets"). The Hebrew word there (*laḥaš H4318*) means "whispering" and is used in Eccl. 10:11 and Jer. 8:17 specifically of snake-charming (cf. the related verb in Ps. 58:4-5). Isaiah sees the existence of those "instructed in whispering" (NIV, "clever enchanter," i.e., holding whispered communication with the dead, with spirits, or making whis-

pered communication purporting to come from "the other side") as evidence that society is about to collapse (Isa. 3:3). The same word (in 3:20) also refers to objects, personal ornaments, into which some magic charm has been whispered, supposed therefore to afford protection or some other "lucky" benefit to the wearer. Archaeology has revealed such practices all over the ancient world.

Amzi. am′zi (Heb. *ʾamṣî H603*, "my strength" or short form of Amaziah, "strength of Yahweh"). (1) Son of Bani, descendant of Levi in the line of Merari, and ancestor of Ethan, who was a musician in the temple (1 Chr. 6:46 [Heb. v. 31]; cf. v. 44 [Heb. v. 29]). (2) Son of Zechariah and ancestor of Adaiah; the latter was a priest who returned to Jerusalem after the exile (Neh. 11:12).

Anab. ay′nab (Heb. *ʿănāb H6693*, "[place of the] grape"). A city in the hill country of Judah, near Debir, from which Joshua drove out the Anakites (Josh. 11:21; 15:50). The modern site is Khirbet ʿUnnab eṣ-Ṣaghir, some 12 mi. (19 km.) SW of Hebron.

Anah. ay′nuh (Heb. *ʿănâ H6704*, derivation uncertain). The name of one or more individuals mentioned in Gen. 36:2, 14, 18, 20, 24-25, 29 (cf. also 1 Chr. 1:38-41). The first two references in the MT describe Anah as the *daughter* of Zibeon the Hivite, but the NRSV says *son*, following several ancient versions. (The NIV translates, "Oholibamah daughter of Anah and *granddaughter* of Zibeon the Hivite." This rendering, which assumes that in this clause the second occurrence of *bat*, "daughter," also refers to Oholibamah, leaves open the question whether Anah was her father or her mother.) If this Anah was indeed a man, he is probably the same as the Horite in Gen. 36:24, identified as a son of Zibeon who discovered some "hot springs" (KJV, "mules"; the Hebrew word is of uncertain meaning) in the desert.

Anaharath. uh-nay′huh-rath (Heb. *ʾănāḥărat H637*, meaning unknown). A city in the tribal territory of Issachar (Josh. 19:19). It is no. 52 in Thutmose III's list, and should probably be identified with Tell el-Mukharkhash (Tel Rekhesh), about 8 mi. (13 km.) SW of the southern tip of the Sea of Galilee, close to Shunem.

Anaiah. uh-nay′yuh (Heb. *‘ănāyâ H6717*, "Yahweh has answered"). One of the men who stood beside Ezra when he read the law to the people (Neh. 8:4). He is probably the same individual listed among the leaders of the people who sealed the covenant with Nehemiah (10:22).

Anak. ay′nak (Heb. *‘ănāq H6737*, possibly "long-necked"). Descendant of Arba (Josh. 15:13) and ancestor of the Anakites (Num. 13:33 et al.).

Anakim. an′uh-kim. See Anakites.

Anakites. an′uh-kits (Heb. *anāqîm*, apparently gentilic pl. of *‘ănāq H6737*). Also Anakim. Descendants of Anak. The Anakites were a tribe inhabiting Palestine in pre-Israelite times. The spies compared them to the Nephilim or giants of Gen. 6:4; also they were reckoned among the Rephaites (Deut. 2:11). Three chiefs of the Anakites were in Hebron (Num. 13:22) from the time of the spies until Caleb took it (Josh. 15:13-14). Remnants of them remained in the Philistine cities of Gaza, Gath, and Ashdod (11:21-22).

Anamim. an′uh-mim. See Anamites.

Anamites. an′uh-mits (Heb. *‘ănāmîm H6723*, meaning unknown). A tribe or nation related to the Egyptians (Mizraim) and mentioned in the ethnographic lists of Gen. 10:13 and 1 Chr. 1:11. Various suggestions have been made regarding their location (such as Cyrene, the desert of Libya, and an area W of Alexandria), but the identification of the Anamites remains uncertain.

Anammelech. uh-nam′uh-lek (Heb. *‘ănammelek H6724*, perhaps "Anath is queen [*lit.*, king]"). TNIV Anammelek. A deity of the natives of Sepharvaim (Sabraim in E central Syria) whom the Assyrians transplanted to Samaria after 722 B.C. (2 Ki. 17:31). Some scholars hold that the name should be spelled "Anu-melech" (Anu was the great sky-god of the Sumerians). Others suggest

that the name alludes to the Canaanite goddess Anath. See also Adrammelech.

Anan. ay′nuhn (Heb. *‘ānān H6728*, possibly "cloud" or short form of Ananiah, "Yahweh has heard me"). One of the leaders of the people who sealed the covenant with Nehemiah (Neh. 10:26).

Anani. uh-nay′ni (Heb. *‘ănānî H6730*, short form of Ananiah, "Yahweh has heard me"). Son of Elioenai and descendant of King Jehoiachin (1 Chr. 3:24).

Ananiah (person). an′uh-ni′uh (Heb. *‘ănānyāh H6731*, prob. "Yahweh has heard/answered [me]"). Father of Maaseiah and grandfather of Azariah; the latter was an Israelite who helped rebuild the walls of Jerusalem under Nehemiah (Neh. 3:23).

Ananiah (place). an′uh-ni′uh (Heb. *‘ănānyāh H6732*, prob. "Yahweh has heard/answered"). A town in the tribal territory of Benjamin occupied by Jews after their return from exile (Neh. 11:32); it is probably modern el-‘Azariyeh (= NT Bethany).

Ananias. an′uh-ni′uhs (Gk. *Ananias G393*, from Heb. *ḥănanyâ H2863*, "Yahweh is gracious"). **(1)** Husband of Sapphira (Acts 5:1-11). He and his wife pretended to give to the church all they received from a sale of property but kept back part. When Peter denounced his deceit, Ananias fell down dead. The generosity of others (4:32-37) accentuates the meanness of Ananias. Yet lying to the Holy Spirit, rather than greed, was the sin for which he was punished. That his was the first gross act of disobedience within the church justifies the severity of the punishment. Peter prophesied rather than decreed his death, which was a penalty God inflicted.

(2) A disciple at Damascus who, obeying a vision, was the means of healing the sight of Saul of Tarsus (Paul) and of introducing him to the Christians of Damascus (Acts 9:10-19). In Acts 22:12-16 Paul recalls Ananias's part in his conversion and speaks of him as "a devout observer of the law and highly respected by all the Jews living" in Damascus.

A

(3) A high priest before whom Paul was tried in Jerusalem (Acts 23:1-5). Paul, whether because of poor eyesight or momentary forgetfulness or Ananias's unpriestly behavior, reviled him, was rebuked, and promptly apologized. Ananias came down to CAESAREA in person to accuse Paul before the Roman governor FELIX (24:1). According to JOSEPHUS, Ananias was sent to Rome in the year A.D. 52 to answer charges of cruelty, but he was acquitted by CLAUDIUS through the efforts of AGRIPPA II the Younger (*Ant.* 20.6.2-3) and retained office until the year 58. He was a typical SADDUCEE, haughty, wealthy, and unscrupulous (*Ant.* 20.9.2). Because of his collaborations with the Romans, he was hated by the nationalistic Jews. When the war broke out in 66, he was hunted down and murdered (Jos. *War* 2.17.9). He has been called one of the most unworthy men to hold the office of "high priest."

Anath. ay´nath, ah´nath (Heb. *ănāt H6742*, meaning unknown). (1) Father of SHAMGAR; the latter was one of the judges in Israel (Jdg. 3:31; 5:6). It has been suggested that the phrase "son of Anath" is really a military title; others emend the phrase and regard it as a reference to the city of BETH ANATH (1:33).

(2) Anath (or Anat) was also the name of a warrior-goddess worshiped by various nations in the ANE. She is especially prominent in the texts found at UGARIT, where she is referred to as the sister (perhaps not in a literal sense) and consort of BAAL. This goddess is not explicitly mentioned in the OT, although perhaps she is alluded to in the names of various cities (e.g., ANATHOTH, BETH ANATH, BETH ANOTH).

anathema. uh-nath´uh-muh. This English term, borrowed directly from Greek (*anathema G353* or *anathēma G356*, "that which is devoted, dedicated, banned, cursed"), occurs once in the KJV (1 Cor. 16:22), but not at all in most modern versions. The SEPTUAGINT uses the Greek term frequently, though not exclusively, to translate *ḥērem H3051*, a noun that occurs almost thirty times in the OT. This word refers primarily to that which is devoted to God, becomes his, and is therefore irrevocably withdrawn from common use. A person so devoted

is doomed to death—a death implying moral worthlessness (Lev. 27:28-29; Rom. 3:9; 1 Cor. 12:3; 16:22; Gal. 1:9). See also DEVOTED THING.

anathema maranatha. See MARANATHA.

Anathoth (person). an´uh-thoth (Heb. *ănātôt H6744*, prob. from ANATH). (1) One of the leaders of the people who sealed the covenant along with NEHEMIAH after the return from the Babylonian captivity (Neh. 10:19).

(2) Son of BEKER and grandson of BENJAMIN (1 Chr. 7:8).

Anathoth (place). an´uh-thoth (Heb. *ănātôt H6743*; gentilic *annĕtôtî H6745*, "Anathothite," KJV "Anet(h)othite"). One of the forty-eight cities allotted to the Levites from the territory of the tribe of BENJAMIN (Josh. 21:18). The name may derive from ANATH, a Canaanite goddess, thus suggesting that the city was devoted to the worship of that deity before the Hebrew occupation. Anathoth was the native place of ABIATHAR the priest (1 Ki. 2:26) and JEREMIAH the prophet (Jer. 1:1). Two of DAVID's distinguished soldiers, Abiezer (2 Sam. 23:27) and Jehu (1 Chr. 12:3), were Anathothites. SOLOMON banished Abiathar to Anathoth for his part in the unsuccessful attempt of ADONIJAH to lay claim to the throne (1 Ki. 2:26). In a prophetic oracle depicting the advance of the Assyrian invaders, ISAIAH speaks of Anathoth as one of the places standing in the path of the invading armies (Isa. 10:30). After the EXILE, 128 men of Anathoth returned in the contingent that came with ZERUBBABEL (Ezra 2:23). The city was settled in the time of NEHEMIAH (Neh. 11:32), and its name apparently lives on in the modern Anata. Ancient Anathoth, however, is usually identified with the nearby site of Ras el-Kharrubeh, 2.5 mi. (4 km.) NE of JERUSALEM, where excavations have revealed settlements from early Israelite times.

Anatolia. a´-nuh-toh´lee-uh (from *anatolē G424*, "rising [of the sun]," referring to the east). A term equivalent to ASIA MINOR. The Anatolian languages include several that belong to the Indo-European family (e.g., HITTITE) and some that do not (e.g., HURRIAN).

anchor. In ancient times every ship carried several anchors. In successive periods they were made of stone, iron, lead, and perhaps other metals. Each had two flukes and was held by a cable or a chain. The word is used in Acts in connection with PAUL's journey to Rome (Acts 27:13, 17, 29, 30, 40 and Heb. 6:19). The author of Hebrews uses it as a powerful figure for Christian confidence: "We have this hope as an anchor for the soul, firm and secure" (6:19). See ASSURANCE; HOPE.

Ancient of Days. This elegant Semitic expression, which refers simply to someone old, occurs only in Dan. 7:9, 13, and 22. It was probably chosen to contrast God and his kingdom with the temporary limited duration of the four successive kingdoms, under the figures of four wild beasts, which appear earlier in the chapter. The eternal Yahweh of all the universe appropriately defeats them and establishes his own eternal kingdom under the matchless "son of man" and his "saints" who appear in the same scene (vv. 13-14, 22). See DANIEL, BOOK OF; SON OF MAN.

Andrew. an′droo (Gk. *Andreas G436*, "manly"). The brother of Simon PETER and one of the first disciples of Jesus. Although a native Palestinian Jew, Andrew bore a Greek name. He was the son of Jonah (Matt. 16:17) or John (Jn. 1:42; 21:15-17; see JOHN #4), whose home was in BETHSAIDA in GALILEE (Jn. 1:44; 12:21). Andrew was a fisherman, like his brother, with whom he lived at CAPERNAUM (Mk. 1:29). He was a disciple of JOHN THE BAPTIST, who directed him to Jesus as the Lamb of God. Convinced that Jesus was the MESSIAH, he quickly brought his brother Peter to Jesus (Jn. 1:25-42). Subsequently Jesus called the two brothers to abandon their fishing and take up permanent fellowship with him (Matt. 4:18-19); later Jesus appointed Andrew an apostle (Matt. 10:2; Mk. 3:18; Lk. 6:14; Acts 1:13). In the lists of the apostles his name always appears next to that of PHILIP, who was also from Bethsaida. He is associated with the feeding of the 5,000, where he expressed doubt that the multitude could be fed with the lad's five loaves and two fishes (Jn. 6:6-9), and also with the request of the Greeks to see Jesus (12:22). Andrew was one of the four who asked Jesus about the destruction of the TEMPLE and the time of the second coming. After Acts 1:13 he is never mentioned again. According to tradition he preached in Scythia and suffered martyrdom in Achaia, crucified on an X-shaped cross, now called a St. Andrew's cross.

Andronicus. an-dron′uh-kuhs (Gk. *Andronikos G438*, "conqueror of men"). A Christian at Rome to whom PAUL sent greetings (Rom. 16:7). The apostle calls him and JUNIAS "my relatives," though the Greek term (*syngenēs G5150*) may indicate simply fellow-Jews (cf. 9:3). The apostle says that they became Christians before he did and that they shared imprisonment with him (where or when is not known). They are further described as "outstanding among the apostles," meaning either that they were held in high esteem by the apostles or that they were themselves distinguished "apostles" (in a wider sense, i.e., early authorized preachers of the gospel).

Anem. ay′nuhm (Heb. *ʿānēm H6722*, meaning uncertain). One of the Levitical cities of ISSACHAR assigned to the descendants of GERSHON (1 Chr. 6:73). The parallel list reads EN GANNIM (Josh. 21:29). If they are not the same site, Anem may be identified either with ʿOlam, some 8 mi. (13 km.) SE of Mount TABOR or with the nearby location Khirbet ʿAnim.

Aner (person). ay′nuhr (Heb. *ʿānēr H6738*, meaning unknown). One of three AMORITE brothers, including MAMRE and ESHCOL, allies of ABRAHAM in his pursuit after the four kings who had taken LOT captive (Gen. 14:13, 24). Since Mamre is an old name for HEBRON (Gen. 23:19), and Eshcol is the name of a valley near Hebron (Num. 13:23), it is likely that Aner was also the name of a locality.

Aner (place). ay′nuhr (Heb. *ʿānēr H6739*, meaning unknown). One of the Levitical cities of MANASSEH assigned to the descendants of KOHATH (1 Chr. 6:70). The parallel list reads TAANACH (Josh. 21:25). If they are not the same site, the location of Aner remains unknown.

Anet(h)othite. an′uh-t(h)oh-thit. See ANATHOTH (PLACE).

A

angel. A supernatural, heavenly being. The English term is derived from Greek *angelos* **G34** and corresponds to Hebrew *maPāk* **H4855**, both meaning "messenger." Angels are created beings (Ps. 148:2-5; Col. 1:16). Scripture does not tell us the time of their creation, but it was certainly before the creation of man (Job 38:7). They are described as "spirits" (Heb. 1:14). Although without a bodily organism, they have often revealed themselves in bodily form. Jesus said that they do not marry and do not die (Lk. 20:34-36). They therefore constitute a company, not a race developed from one original pair.

According to Scripture, angels are not mere personifications of abstract good and evil but rather personal beings. Although possessed of superhuman intelligence, they are not omniscient (Matt. 24:36; 1 Pet. 1:12); and although stronger than human beings, they are not omnipotent (Ps. 103:20; 2 Thess. 1:7; 2 Pet. 2:11). They are not glorified human beings but are distinct from men and women (1 Cor. 6:3; Heb. 1:14). There is a vast multitude of them. John says that he "heard the voice of many angels, numbering thousands upon thousands, and ten thousand times ten thousand" (Rev. 5:11). They are of various ranks and endowments (Col. 1:16), but only one—MICHAEL—is expressly called an archangel in Scripture (Jude 9). The great hosts of angels, both good and bad, are highly organized (Rom. 8:38; Eph. 1:21; 3:10; Col. 1:16; 2:15).

Angels were created holy (Gen. 1:31; Jude 6), but after a period (of probation?) some fell from their state of innocence (2 Pet. 2:4; Jude 6). Scripture is silent regarding the time and cause of their sin, but it is clear that it occurred before the FALL of ADAM and EVE (for SATAN deceived Eve in the Garden of Eden) and that it was due to a deliberate, self-determined rebellion against God. As a result these angels lost their original holiness, became corrupt, and were confirmed in evil. Some were "sent … to hell," where they are held in chains until the Day of Judgment (2 Pet. 2:4); others were left free, and they oppose the work of God.

The work of the angels is varied. Good angels stand in the presence of God and worship him (Matt. 18:10; Heb. 1:6; Rev. 5:11). They assist, protect, and deliver God's people (Gen. 19:11; Ps. 91:11; Dan. 3:28; 6:22; Acts 5:19). The author of

Modern replica of a carved Assyrian relief depicting a guardian angel.

© Dr. James C. Martin. Musée du Louvre; Autorisation de photographer et de filmer—LOUVRE. Paris, France. Photographed by permission.

Hebrews says, "Are not all angels ministering spirits sent to serve those who will inherit salvation?" (Heb. 1:14). They sometimes guide God's children, as when one told PHILIP to go into the desert near GAZA (Acts 8:26); and they bring encouragement, as when one spoke to PAUL in CORINTH (27:23-24). Sometimes they interpret God's will to people (Dan. 7:16; 10:5, 11; Zech. 1:9, 13-14, 19). They execute God's will toward individuals and nations (Gen. 19:12, 13; 2 Sam. 24:16; Ezek. 9:2, 5, 7; Acts 12:23). The affairs of nations are guided by them (Dan. 10:12-13, 20). God uses them to punish his enemies (2 Ki. 19:35; Acts 12:23).

Angels had a large place in the life and ministry of Christ. At his birth they made their appearance to Mary, Joseph, and the shepherds. After the wilderness temptation of Christ they ministered to him (Matt. 4:11); an angel strengthened him in the garden (Lk. 22:43); an angel rolled away the stone from the tomb (Matt. 28:2-7); and angels were with him at the ascension (Acts 1:10-11).

As for the evil angels, it is clear that their principal purpose is to oppose God and to try to defeat his will and frustrate his plans. Evil angels endeavor to separate believers from God (Rom. 8:38). They oppose good angels in their work (Dan. 10:12-13). They hinder our temporal and eternal welfare by a limited control over natural phenomena (Job 1:12-13, 19; 2:7), by inflicting disease (Lk. 13:11, 16; Acts 10:38; 2 Cor. 12:7), by tempting us to sin (Matt. 4:3; Jn. 13:27; 1 Pet. 5:8), and by spreading false doctrine (1 Ki. 22:21-23; 2 Thess. 2:2; 1 Tim. 4:1). They cannot, however, exercise over people any moral power independent of the human will, and whatever power they have is limited by the permissive will of God. The word *Satan* means "adversary," and Scripture shows him to be the adversary of both God and human beings. All of his many other names show his extremely wicked character.

Scripture shows that good angels will continue in the service of God in the future age, whereas evil angels will have their part in the eternal fire (Matt. 25:41).

angel of the Lord. This phrase (or its equivalent, "the angel of God") occurs frequently in the OT, and in almost every case the angel or messenger is regarded as deity and yet is distinguished from God (Gen. 16:7-14; 22:11-18; 31:11, 13; Exod. 3:2-5; Num. 22:22-35; Jdg. 6:11-23; 13:2-25; 1 Ki. 19:5-7; 1 Chr. 21:15-17). These references show that the angel is the Lord himself adopting a visible form (and therefore a human appearance) for the sake of speaking with people (e.g., Jdg. 13:6, 10, 21). Many students of the Bible regard these appearances as Christophanies, manifestations of the preincarnate Christ. While himself holy as God is holy (e.g., Exod. 3:2-5), the angel expresses the Holy One's condescension to walk among sinners (32:34; 33:3). He is also the executant of divine WRATH (e.g., 2 Sam. 24:16; 2 Ki. 19:35). In all these ways, as we can see from the NT perspective, the angel of the Lord is part of the OT preparation for the Lord Jesus Christ.

anger. The English rendering of at least ten biblical words, of which the most common is Hebrew

ʾap *H678* (lit., "nose," thought of as the seat of anger, from its use in hard breathing). The OT condemns anger because it encourages folly and evil (Ps. 37:8; Prov. 14:29) and because vengeance belongs to God (Deut. 32:35). Elsewhere it calls for restraint from those confronted by anger (Prov. 16:14; Eccl. 10:4). In the NT anger is among those emotions that provoke God's WRATH (Eph. 5:6) and is regarded as alien to godliness (1 Tim. 2:8; Jas. 1:19-20). There is righteous anger, however, as when Jesus condemned the misuse of the temple (Jn. 2:12-17), the corruption of others (Mk. 9:42), and lack of compassion (3:5).

Aniam. uh-niʹuhm (Heb. ʾănîʿām *H642*, "lament of the people" or "I am kinsman"). Son of Shemida and descendant of MANASSEH (1 Chr. 7:19). Some scholars emend Manasseh's genealogy here on the basis of Num 26:30-32.

Anim. ayʹnim (Heb. ʿānîm *H6719*, possibly "springs"). A city in the hill country of JUDAH (Josh. 15:50). It is identified with modern Khirbet Ghuwein et-Taḥta, 11 mi. (18 km.) S of HEBRON.

animals. This article deals with all kinds of animal life appearing in the Bible, with the exception of birds, which are the subject of a separate entry.

adder. See *snake*, below.

ant. The two references to ants in Proverbs cite the excellent example given to a sluggard and no doubt other people (Prov. 6:6; 30:25). Study of the ant's behavior will provide wisdom, declares the author, drawing special attention to the ant's wise use of its "little strength" to "store up [its] food" and prepare for the future. The type of ant mentioned here is the harvester ant, found in regions of relative food shortage and therefore dependent on a diet of seeds. There are thousands of species worldwide belonging to this insect family, *Formicidae*. Most species maintain underground colonies that, like those of bees, work on a division-of-labor principle. Some attend to the cultivation of fungi, others milk the aphids for their secreted honeydew, others guard the colony. Most ants are wingless sterile workers, but the short-lived male has wings.

antelope. A hoofed ruminant of the *Bovidae* family, the antelope is most often found in Africa.

A

It is included among the permitted edible animals in Deut. 14:5 (KJV wrongly, "wild ox"). Hunting of antelope, using net, is indicated in Isa. 51:20. In Deut. 14:5 KJV also uses the word "pygarg" (which means "white-rumped") to translate a Hebrew word of uncertain meaning, but thought to refer either to a type of antelope known as the addax, a native of desert areas of northern Africa and the Sudan, or to the ibex. See *deer; gazelle; ibex.*

ape. The modern use of this word has more specific reference to a species excluding the monkey. The biblical record did not anticipate our contemporary classification when it recorded that King SOLOMON's fleet journeyed every three years and returned with "gold, silver and ivory, and apes and baboons" (1 Ki. 10:22; 2 Chr. 9:21). It is likely that the rhesus monkey of India is meant by the word "ape."

asp. See *snake.*

ass. See *donkey.*

baboon. The NIV translation of a Hebrew word that the KJV and other versions render as "peacock" (1 Ki. 10:22; 2 Chr. 9:21; peacocks were for generations an adornment of royal courts.) A large, short-tailed monkey, the baboon is found mainly in Africa, but the Arabian baboon was once considered sacred to the Egyptians. With its dog-like appearance, the baboon lives in the wild in large social groups.

badger. The species *Meles meles* is found throughout Europe and northern Asia, while the American badger, *Taxidea taxus*, is a smaller species. This mainly underground dweller is not found in Bible lands. An uncertain word for the coverings used in the TABERNACLE (Exod. 25:5 et al.) is rendered "badgers' skins" by the KJV, but modern versions have such translations as "fine leather" (NRSV) and "goatskins" (RSV). Partly on the basis of a cognate Arabic term, many scholars believe that the reference is to a marine species, either the porpoise/dolphin (NASB, NEB, NJPS) or the dugong/sea cow (NIV; but TNIV, "durable leather"). In addition, the NRSV uses "rock badger" for another term that probably refers to the hyrax or coney (Lev. 11:5; cf. Ps. 104:18), which is similar in appearance to a rabbit, but for the absence of a tail and comparatively short legs and ears. The four-toed foot of the coney has earned it the description, "little cousin of the elephant." Vegetarian, with molars similar to those of the rhinoceros, the coney has a jaw action reminiscent of an animal "chewing the cud," though its digestive system does not allow for rumination. Although it is timid, the coney is a very active creature. It is found throughout the Middle East and much of Africa.

bald locust. See *grasshopper.*

bat. The Bible classifies bats as unclean (Lev. 11:19; Deut. 14:18), while Isaiah's vision of the last days refers to people throwing their various idols made of precious metals to "rodents and bats" (Isa. 2:20). Although since biblical times rumor and legend have given the bat an unfavorable reputation, this only true flying mammal is wonderfully equipped with a natural radar system for locating its prey, usually insects. An estimated two thousand different types of bats are found throughout the world, most of them nocturnal in habit. Some tropical species are fruit-eating, but those found in Bible lands are usually insect-eating. Gregarious creatures—living in great numbers in remote caves, for example—bats are classified with birds in Scrip-

© Dr. James C. Martin

The donkey was a common mode of transportation and an important agricultural asset in antiquity.

ture, as in the Leviticus and Deuteronomy references above.

bear. With a mainly vegetable diet, the bear could have been far more frequently encountered in an afforested Palestine than is sometimes supposed. The bear killed by DAVID (1 Sam. 17:34-37) was the Syrian brown bear, *Ursus syriacus*, the species referred to elsewhere in the OT. Reference is made to the ferocity of a female bear robbed of her cubs (2 Sam. 17:8), and a readiness to attack humans is indicated in 2 Ki. 2:23-25, when two bears mauled some forty-two youths who had been jeering at ELISHA's bald head. A bald man was not a common sight, and the attitude of the youths seems to have been more threatening than mere banter. The NRSV refers to the attacking animals as "she-bears," surmising perhaps that they had been provoked to defend their cubs, apparently or really threatened by the youths. The sole reference to cubs is made in 2 Sam. 17:8. In terms of a symbol for other powers, the bear featured prominently in visions given to Isaiah, Daniel, and John.

beast. This generic description is derived from some thirteen Hebrew and five Greek words, providing the following criteria: (1) A mammal, not including humans and clearly different from birds and fishes and sometimes from reptiles also (cf. Gen. 1:30). (2) A wild, undomesticated animal, as in Lev. 26:22 and Isa. 13:21; 34:14 ("desert creatures"); Mk. 1:13 refers to the Lord's time in the desert with "wild animals." (3) Any of the "inferior" animals, in relation to the Mosaic law's definition of ceremonially clean or unclean animals or beasts. (4) An APOCALYPTIC symbol of brute force, opposed to God's rule and thereby to man's best interests: in Dan. 7:3 four great beasts symbolize four successive world empires (Babylon, Medo-Persia, Greece, and Rome), while in Rev. 13:1-10 a beast coming out of the sea is identified as a world ruler with great, if temporary, authority; many take the beast that comes out of the earth (Rev. 13:11-18) to be ANTICHRIST. (5) The celestial beings that worship God (Rev. 4:6-9 et al.) are referred to as "beasts" by the KJV, but the Greek term is more appropriately rendered "living creatures."

bee, hornet. The term *hornet* applies to several species of large social wasps belonging to the family *Vespidae*. Usually colored yellow and black, the hor-

net is a medium-sized insect deriving its diet from flies; its paper nest may be above or below ground level and, though basically beneficial to humans, the hornet possesses a severe sting and an evident determination to deliver it when stimulated to do so. Bees—the agents of pollination—have four wings. They may be social or solitary in behavior. Colonies function on what may be described as a division-of-labor system, with as many as fifty thousand members. Expansion is not unlimited, however, and swarms represent waves of emigration from the old hive (which remains in use) to a new home to be created elsewhere. HONEY is made from the nectar collected by bees in their pollination activity, developed in the honey sac of the workers, and stored in the wax cells of the honeycomb. Although there is little evidence that the ancient Hebrews cultivated bees for the manufacture of honey, the link was obvious enough. Bees would be plentiful in any land flowing with milk and honey, as indeed they always have been in Palestine. The abundance of flora in the land insured a large bee community. Biblical references speak of God's use of the hornet in driving away the enemies of Israel (Exod. 23:28; Deut. 7:20; Josh. 24:12). On occasion, enemies of Israel were compared to a swarm of bees (e.g., Deut. 1:44; Ps. 118:12). Isaiah prophesies about the day when "the LORD will whistle ... for bees from the land of Assyria" (Isa. 7:18). SAMSON is said to have found a swarm of bees and honey in a lion's carcass, a discovery that shaped one of the most famous riddles in history (Jdg. 14:8-19).

beetle. See *grasshopper*.

behemoth. The graphic description of the behemoth in Job 40:15-24 is often thought to refer to the hippopotamus. Sometimes described as "the river horse of Africa," the hippopotamus is certainly a herbivorous heavyweight, sometimes reaching four tons (three and one-half metric tons). Despite its ungainly, even lethargic appearance, it is versatile in terms of its environment. It can swim or float, sink to the bottom of the river bed, and run along on the bottom. The species *Hippopotamus amphibius* is found in Central Africa; the pygmy hippopotamus, *Choeropsis liberiensis*, is found in Liberia. Like the elephant, the hippopotamus is a source of ivory through the large tusks in its lower jaw. There was extensive trading in ivory in biblical times, with at least a dozen biblical references to its use. King SOLOMON overlaid his IVORY throne with gold (1 Ki. 10:18); King AHAB made great use of ivory in his palace. See also *elephant*.

boar. See *pig*.

bull. See *cattle*.

butterfly. See *moth*.

calf. See *cattle*.

camel, dromedary. The importance of the camel to life in Bible lands is confirmed by the many references (over sixty) to it in Scripture. As the original root word is almost identical in Hebrew and Arabic, one may conclude that the camel was well known to the patriarchs, long before the horse came into widespread use. Despite its reportedly grumbling disposition, the camel is well named the "ship of the desert," with its marvelous adaptation to terrain and climate. It can travel long distances without the need to take in water and can withstand high temperatures while being surefooted in undulating terrain. Of further value to the desert-dweller is the camel's long life, perhaps forty or fifty years.

Two basic forms are found: the single-humped dromedary and the slower-moving Bactrian camel with its two humps. The dromedary has longer legs and can move considerably faster. With a load that may be up to 400 pounds (182 kg.), the Bactrian camel may cover little more than 30 mi. (50 km.) in a single day; a dromedary, lightly burdened, can cover up to 150 mi. (240 km.). The two forms are thus complementary: the dromedary for personal travel or the fast conveying of important messages, the Bactrian camel for commerce and trade. Earlier translations, especially KJV, referred to dromedaries in 1 Ki. 4:28 and Esth. 8:10, but these are now translated as (swift) horses.

Camels feature prominently in OT narrative and are included among ABRAHAM's acquisitions while in EGYPT (Gen. 12:16). When Abraham's servant went out to find a wife for ISAAC in NW MESOPOTAMIA (Gen. 24), the journey was accomplished with ten camels—the encounter with REBEKAH commencing as the camels were watered. Inventory of JACOB's wealth includes camels (Gen. 30:43), as does that of JOB (Job 1:3; 42:12). The camel was ceremonially unclean (Lev. 11:4), though its milk was utilized (Gen. 32:15). Probably the most familiar biblical reference to the camel is that of Matt. 19:24, in which our Lord compares the difficulty of rich people securing entry into the kingdom of God with that of a camel making its way through the eye of a NEEDLE. Even in our technologically advanced age, the camel remains an important aspect of economy in Bible lands. Its flesh and milk are valued by some inhabitants, together with the use of its hair.

cankerworm. See *grasshopper*.

caterpillar. See *moth*.

cattle. Cattle are mentioned in the first chapter of the Bible ("livestock" in NIV), symbolic of their importance to the well-being of the human race. Eleven Hebrew and two Greek words are translated to indicate cattle, the species descended from wild members of the family *Bovidae*, true ruminants with four-chambered stomachs for leisurely and thorough mastication.

Canaan was portrayed as a place of great prosperity, a place flowing with milk and honey—an abundance of cattle and good grazing ground. The patriarchs were accounted wealthy largely on the basis of their ownership of cattle, as in the case of Abraham (Gen. 13:2). Included in Jacob's gift for his brother Esau were "forty cows and

© Dr. James C. Martin

Camels grazing in the Negev during winter.

ten bulls" (32:15) taken from his own substantial herds. Joseph's destiny was shaped by Pharaoh's dream of seven cows, sleek and fat, succeeded by seven cows, ugly and gaunt (41:1-7), symbolic of years of plenteous harvests followed by bad ones. Joseph's life as prime minister and his relationship to his formerly estranged brothers includes reference to their cattle (45:10; 46:34). Loss of cattle represented a catastrophe, yet the Egyptians did not heed Moses' warning (Exod. 9:1-7) of the destruction of their cattle as part of God's judgment. Later, Moses' defeat of the Midianites brought considerable "plunder" including 72,000 cattle (Num. 31:33).

Calves (young bulls or cows) were valued for food as well as sacrifice. A choice, tender calf was chosen by Abraham in entertaining his three mysterious visitors (Gen. 18:7). Visions given to Isaiah, Ezekiel, and John included the calf, and Jesus concluded the story of the prodigal's homecoming with a great feast—at which a calf was prepared as appropriate to the celebration. Calves used for sacrifice were usually one-year-old males, specified by Moses in Lev. 9:3, 8. Corruption of the sacrificial aspect resulted in occasional lapses into calf worship, similar to that followed by the Egyptians. Moses' anger at witnessing such behavior was so great that he broke the tablets of the law that were in his hands (Exod. 32:19).

Bulls were important in the lives of the people and for the nation, playing a part in the sin offerings for the congregation and in consecration of the Levites and the work of the priests. At times of national and religious revival in the OT, substantial numbers of bulls, as well as rams and lambs, were offered in sacrifice. King Solomon's temple included a molten sea of brass supported by twelve bulls cast in bronze (1 Ki. 7:25). David also made the bull a figure of threat in distress when, hunted by Saul, he wrote, "Many bulls surround me; / strong bulls of Bashan encircle me" (Ps. 22:12).

A heifer is a young cow. It was often used in sacrifice, or at the direct request of the Lord. Abraham killed a heifer on direct instruction (Gen. 15:9), and Samuel was instructed by the Lord to take a heifer for sacrifice. Religious ceremonial law involving the use of a heifer is restricted to Deut. 21:1-9. Ashes of the red heifer were used to

Mummy of a young bull from Thebes (c. A.D. 30).

remove ceremonial uncleanness, as in purification of the leper or of one who had touched a dead person (Num. 19:9). From the bright perspective of the Christian era, Paul encouraged converts from the Jewish tradition by referring to the fact that Christ's finished work superseded the old forms of sacrifice (Heb. 9:13).

During the creation, God made the livestock according to their kinds (Gen. 1:25). In Exod. 9 the word is used in referring to the disaster that would befall Egypt if Pharaoh refused to permit the Israelites to leave in peace: the plague would fall "on your livestock in the field—on your horses and donkeys and camels and on your cattle and sheep and goats." In Num. 32 the word "livestock" is synonymous with "very large herds and flocks" (32:1).

Oxen, in addition to their use for food and in religious ceremonies, were important working members of the agricultural community. Six covered carts and twelve oxen were presented to the Lord's work at the dedication of the tabernacle (Num. 7:3), to "be used in the work at the Tent of Meeting" (7:5). Property rights pertaining to oxen, as well as those relevant to other animals, were defined by the Lord (Exod. 22:1) in recognition of their importance to the well-being of the people. Jesus referred to the care owed to animals (including oxen) in his response to those who attacked

A

him for healing on the Sabbath (Lk. 13:15). There were, even for the strict Sabbatarians, "animal rights" that were to be observed, whatever the day of the week.

Elisha was plowing with twelve yoke of oxen when Elijah encountered him (1 Ki. 19:19), just as Amos was following the plow when he heard the call of God. Although the ox is not especially regarded today as a religious symbol, it should be noted that Ezekiel's vision of the four celestial living creatures referred to one having the face of an ox (Ezek. 1:10).

The "unicorn" (KJV at Num. 23:22; Deut. 33:17), distinct from the mythological figure of that name, was probably the extinct auroch (NIV and other versions, "wild ox"). When seen in profile, it gave the appearance of having one horn rather than two. A very powerful animal, standing some 6 ft. (2 m.) high, the auroch was once a familiar sight in Bible lands.

chameleon. See *lizard.*

chamois. See *sheep.*

cobra. See *snake.*

cockatrice. See *snake.*

colt. See *horse.*

coney. See *badger.*

coral. Red coral, *Corallium nobile,* is native to the central and western Mediterranean and was greatly prized in ancient times. Its substance consists of the calcareous skeleton of a branching colony of polyps that remains long after the jellylike body of the polyp has perished and disappeared. Used in the making of jewelry, coral is mentioned in Job 28:18 in a celebrated passage on the value of wisdom. Ezekiel's lament concerning Tyre (Ezek. 27:16) includes reference to trade in coral, which might be expected of a coastal city.

cow. See *cattle.*

creeping thing. This expression is used by the KJV and other versions to render a Hebrew term referring to small animals and reptiles (the NRSV translates this term "crawling things" in Hab. 1:14). The Genesis account lists only three general groups of land animals: livestock, wild animals, and creeping things (Gen. 1:24; NIV, "creatures that move along the ground"). The term may include most of the invertebrates. The KJV uses the English expression also in the NT to render a Greek

word that is better translated "reptile" (Acts 10:12; 11:6; Rom. 1:23).

cricket. See *grasshopper.*

crocodile. See *Leviathan; lizard.*

deer. The family of ruminant mammals, *Cervidae,* includes deer, elks, reindeer, moose, found worldwide except in Australia. The deer is included in the list of animals that may be eaten (Deut. 14:5) and also in Solomon's list of daily provisions (1 Ki. 4:23). As with other Bible animals, the special qualities of the deer are praised as models for human beings. David's song of praise compares his feet to those of the deer (2 Sam. 22:34). David begins Ps. 42 with a comparison of his soul's thirst for God with that of a deer panting for streams of water. The writer of Lamentations likens the plight of princes to that of deer without pasture (Lam. 1:6). Isaiah's description of the job of the redeemed anticipates the leaping of the lame like a deer (Isa. 35:6).

The doe, the female of the species (traditionally of the fallow deer), "bears beautiful fawns" (Gen. 49:21). Proverbs 5:19 compares the wife of one's youth with "a loving doe, a graceful deer." The Lord inquires of Job, "Do you watch when the doe bears her fawn?" (Job 39:1). The "hart" of KJV was either the red deer of Europe and Asia (*Cervus elephus*) or the Syrian deer (*Cervus barbatus*). The former is similar to the American elk, but smaller. Harts are stags or male deer, the word "stag" appearing only in the Song of Songs (Cant. 2:9, 17; 8:14), and then in a lyrical sense. A single hart may weigh as much as 300 lbs. (136 kg.). Every year the six-branched antlers are shed, to be replaced by new ones in due course. See also *antelope; gazelle; ibex.*

desert creature. A term used in Isaiah's prophecies against Babylon (Isa. 13:21), Tyre (23:13), and Edom (34:14). Jeremiah's prophecy against Babylon also refers to desert creatures (Jer. 50:39). No particular species is intended, and the description seemingly applies to a variety of wild creatures, great or small (though primarily the latter), that would be found in places remote from human habitation.

devourer. See *grasshopper.*

doe. See *deer.*

dog. Domesticated member of the *Canidae* family to which the wolf and jackal also belong.

The Bible's forty references to dogs are not complimentary to these UNCLEAN animals. Proverbs 26:11 reflects a contemporary opinion that dogs return to their own vomit. Their readiness to bark at people or animals is alluded to in Exod. 11:7, though here God declares that among the Israelites not a dog will bark at any man or animal. In NT times dogs—often strays—were regarded as nuisances. One licked the sores of the beggar named Lazarus (Lk. 16:21). Job's reference to his sheep dogs (Job 30:1) suggests that good training could make even these despised animals useful, since he was hardly a man to take chances with his stock. Especially evocative is the Canaanite woman's plea for help, met when she reminded the Lord that "even the dogs" were permitted to eat the crumbs from the master's table (Matt. 15:26-27). The KJV and a few other versions use "greyhound" for a rare Hebrew word that possibly means "rooster" (Prov. 30:31).

donkey. This small mammal, genus *Equus*, with some similarity in appearance to a horse (though usually smaller), has served mankind for thousands of years. It is probably descended from the Abyssinian or Somali wild ass. Among its special characteristics are endurance and sure-footedness, though occasional stupidity is not unknown. Found wild in semidesert regions, the species includes the African and Asian varieties.

Abraham's journey of testing, with his son Isaac, was made with a donkey (Gen. 22:3, 5). Balaam's donkey was given the temporary power of speech in order to rebuke the foolish prophet (Num. 22:21-33). In a rhetorical question Job (Job 6:5) asks if a wild donkey would bray if preoccupied with good pasture. Donkeys were a fundamental part of the economy, and a person's wealth was measured by the number he owned. Sometimes donkeys were acquired in battle as plunder, as when the Israelites captured some 61,000 from the Midianites (Num. 31:34). But Israelites were commanded neither to covet a donkey nor to attempt to plow with a donkey and an ox together (Deut. 5:21; 22:10).

Donkeys undertook heavy work on the farm but were used for personal transportation too. White donkeys were highly prized by their owners, who would in any case be careful of their choice of an animal for a long journey. Jesus' triumphal entry into Jerusalem, celebrated on Palm Sunday in the church calendar, fulfilled the prophecy of Zech. 9:9 as he came "riding on a donkey, on a colt, the foal of a donkey" (Matt. 21:2-7). The donkey did not then have the lowly status it has today but was an appropriate choice for a procession of importance.

The mule is the offspring of a male donkey and a horse mare, and is itself sterile. The Israelites were forbidden to breed mules under a general prohibition on mating different animals (Lev. 19:19), but mules were secured in the course of trading and were used for carrying goods and merchandise, as well as for personal transportation. King David reputedly introduced the use of the mule for riding. That mules might be urged to move quickly if required is indicated in 2 Sam. 13:29, where the king's sons mounted their mules and fled. Absalom was deserted by his mule when his head became caught in the branches of a thick oak (18:9), the mule plodding on while his master remained suspended in midair. Mules ridden by kings, officials, and army officers were chosen with care, but at the best of times the mule might prove unpredictable. In comparatively recent times itinerant preachers used mules as transportation to local engagements.

dragon. This English term is used in some Bible versions to render Hebrew *tannin H9490* (NIV, "monster") in passages that speak of cosmic combat (Job 7:12; Ps 74:13; Isa. 27:1; 57:9; Ezek. 29:3; 32:2; the Heb. word can also mean "snake," Exod. 7:9 et al.). See also *Leviathan*. In the book of Revelation it stands for Greek *drakōn G1532* and designates SATAN (Rev. 12:3-17; 13:1-11; 16:13; 20:2). In a few passages, the KJV uses "dragons" to translate the similar-sounding term *tanim* (pl. of *tan H9478*), which however means "jackals" (Job 30:29; Isa. 13:22; et al.). See *jackal*.

dromedary. See *camel*.

elephant. The elephant had many practical uses in ancient times, even in battle, as the books of 1 and 2 Maccabees confirm (1 Macc. 1:17 et al.). Some have thought that the elephant, with its instinctive grandeur, may better fit Job's description of *behemoth* (e.g., "his tail sways like a cedar" [Job 40:17] could possibly refer to the elephant's trunk).

ewe. See *sheep*.

fallow deer. See *deer*.

fawn. See *deer*.

A

fish. In Gen. 1, Adam is instructed to rule over the fish of the sea, as well as the rest of creation. Many references to fish and the means of catching them are found in the Scriptures. Later, the outline of a fish became symbolic in the early church. Specific species are not mentioned, though the striped mullet *(Mugil cephalus)* was well known in Bible times, found in the Mediterranean area, and the barbel—represented by various species— was almost certainly known too, being found from British waters eastward to the East Indies.

There is no doubt about the importance of fish in everyday diet. One of the judgments that befell Egypt was the destruction of the nation's fish stock, and during their sojourn in the desert the Israelites grieved for the good fish they had eaten in Egypt (Num. 11:5). The great fish that swallowed JONAH (Jon. 1:17) is not identified by species, though in popular parlance it is thought of as a "whale." Our Lord's miraculous feeding of the 5,000 involved use of five loaves and two fishes (Matt. 14:17). Significantly, the final chapter of John's gospel records Christ's resurrection appearance to the disciples as coinciding with a miraculous draught of fish, caught after the previously daunted fishermen let down their nets at his command (Jn. 21).

flea. Common throughout Bible lands, as elsewhere in the world, the flea is mentioned in 1 Sam. 24:14; 26:20. The flea is any of the *Aphaniptera* order of small, wingless insects possessing a flattened body and legs highly developed for leaping. An estimated 500 species of fleas present a threat as well as an irritant to mankind, as their bite can transmit disease, more particularly bubonic plague. Endemic typhus is also transmitted by fleas. David's rhetorical question in 1 Sam. 24:14 refers to the folly of pursuing a flea, while 1 Sam. 26:20 compares the task of looking for a flea with that of hunting a partridge in the mountains. With its natural agility and tiny size, the flea is difficult to catch. Some reportedly can jump 13 in. (33 cm.) horizontally and almost 8 in. (21 cm.) vertically.

fly. This widely occurring species includes not only the house fly, but the tsetse fly and the malaria-carrying mosquito. Flies may carry disease by germs on their body or by bloodsucking. True flies have a single pair of functional membranous wings, plus a pair of halteres, that is, small clublike appendages that by rapid movement in flight are the fly's gyro, or balance mechanism.

Ruination of Egypt by flies (Exod. 8:24) was one of God's judgments described (8:20-32) as the plague of flies, following the plague of gnats described in earlier verses. The flies were possibly mosquitoes. In addition to threats to health, flies could also ruin crops. Failure of the olive crop (Deut. 28:40) was due to the olive fly, a pest that deposits its eggs beneath the skin of the ripening olive. The maggot emerging from the egg destroys the fruit. See *worm*. Such loss is anticipated by Mic. 6:15 in speaking to an unrepentant Israel, while Habakkuk also refers to the failure of the olive crop (Hab. 3:17), apparently through similar assault. The threat to Egypt prophesied by Jeremiah (Jer. 46:20) is described as "destruction" in KJV, but NIV renders the word as "gadfly"—a biting, pestering nuisance. Socrates was described as "the gadfly of Athens," suggesting that the ancients were well aware of the gadfly's persistent attacks.

The gnat, a sharp-biting member of the mosquito family, was used in one of the judgments on Egypt (Exod. 8:16-18), though the reference may be to some kind of sandfly with an especially painful sting. An alternative rendering of the Hebrew is "lice" (so KJV; see also Ps. 105:31). Jesus rebuked the teachers of the law for straining at a gnat but swallowing a camel (Matt. 23:24). Man's insignificant status is emphasized in Job 25:6 as that of a maggot. In ancient times the fate of corpses, as of unguarded or unfresh food, was obvious enough. Isaiah's prophecy against the king of Babylon (Isa. 14:11) refers to the presence of maggots in his grave. The narrative of the manna and quail in the wilderness (Exod. 16:20, 24) demonstrates that food could not be stored, except by the grace of God, as when it remained fresh over the Sabbath.

foal. See *horse*.

fox. The relatively few references in Scripture are to the common fox of Palestine, *Vulpes vulgaris*, a wild carnivore of the dog family, living usually on a diet of small animals and fruit, though its European relations may sometimes be found looking into trash cans during daylight hours as well as at night. This natural predator usually lives in burrows, the American red fox being a related species. Damage to vineyards by "the little foxes" (Cant.

© Dr. James C. Martin

With retractable pads and claws, Blanford's fox is well adapted for climbing on rocks.

2:15) may have been a reference to jackals rather than to foxes. Similarly the 300 foxes caught by Samson in order to pair them for raids on Philistine corn fields, with lit torches tied to their tails (Jdg. 15:4-5), may have been jackals, which would have been more readily caught. Tobiah the Ammonite poured scorn on the rebuilding of the wall of Jerusalem by suggesting that even the tread of a fox would break the stones (Neh. 4:3). The craftiness of the fox was emphasized by our Lord's description of HEROD Antipas (Lk. 13:32). See also *jackal*.

frog. Exodus 8 speaks of the plague of frogs, summoned by Aaron from their natural habitat of streams, canals, and ponds. References in Ps. 78:45 and 105:30 recall the plague, and as the frog had some cultic significance to the Egyptians the significance of the plague would not have been overlooked. A tailless amphibian of the order *Anura*, the frog was represented by two species in Egypt, toads by three. Revelation 16:13 tells of evil spirits with the appearance of frogs, possibly with the plague narrative in mind.

gadfly. See *fly*.

gazelle. Comprising about twelve species, gazelles are medium-sized antelopes inhabiting dry grasslands and desert (Deut. 12:15 et al.; the KJV renderings "roe" and "roebuck" are not correct). The Greek name (*dorkas G1520*, cf. Acts 9:36 and see DORCAS) is still found in the scientific name of *Gazella dorcas*, one of the two species found in W Palestine today. The other, much more common, is the Palestine gazelle (*G. arabica*); this is one of the smallest, standing just over 2 ft. (0.6 m.) at the shoulders. Gazelles are usually of pale brown or sandy color, often with

a dark line along the side demarcating the almost white underparts. This provides good camouflage, but their main defense is speed, and the figurative passages outside SONG OF SOLOMON refer to this distinctive (e.g., 2 Sam. 2:18). In Song of Solomon the word is used as a symbol of grace and beauty (Cant. 2:9 et al.). The delicacy of the meat is indicated in Deut. 12:15, 22, coupled with that of the deer. Solomon's list of provisions included gazelles (1 Ki. 4:23). See also *antelope; deer; ibex*.

gecko. See *lizard*.

gnat. See *fly*.

grasshopper, locust, cricket, palmerworm. Grasshoppers and locusts are included in the insect family *Locustidae*, itself part of the order *Orthoptera*, which includes crickets, katydids, cockroaches, mantids, and walking sticks as well. Grasshoppers are the most frequently mentioned insects in the Bible, and man is sometimes compared to them in terms of his insignificance before great enemies (Num. 13:3) or in the sight of God (Isa. 40:22). In Eccl. 12:5 the grasshopper's painful progress as he "drags himself along" is contained in a passage pointing to human mortality.

Locusts had significance beyond the natural order, often having been sent as a judgment from God (Exod. 10:4). Such visitations could be devastating, and even in our technological age, locust swarms can quickly denude an area of its vegetation. Most species of locust are nonmigratory, but some migrate in great swarms, traveling over great distances if necessary and proving themselves omnivorous consumers of all kinds of vegetation. Where natural food is lacking, they can become cannibalistic and carnivorous. The awesome sight and power of locusts depicted in Rev. 9:3, 7 is beyond anything yet known to human experience. The author of the book knew well the tradition of locusts as a form of judgment from God. Joel's description of utter devastation through a visitation by locusts (Joel 1:4) precedes a passage (2:1-11) in which locusts are described in terms of a great army (the various Heb. terms used in 1:4 and 2:25 are of uncertain meaning, but may refer to various phases of the migratory locust).

Locusts, however, were not without benefit to the human race and represented a useful diet for the poor—that is, in normal times. Edible locusts

A

are listed in Lev. 11:21-22, while the TALMUD provides a description of edible locusts in order that readers could identify them. John the Baptist ate locusts and wild honey (Mk. 1:6), a diet that was not considered unusual by his contemporaries. One of the edible locusts is identified as "katydid" by NIV (Lev. 11:22; KJV and other versions, "bald locust"); this is an insect of the long-horned grasshopper family found in the tropics and in the eastern USA. The same passage refers to the "cricket" (KJV, "beetle"), referring to an insect of the *Gryllidae* family related to the grasshopper and locust, but with long antennae and an apparent liking for human company.

   great lizard. See *lizard.*
   greyhound. See *dog.*
   hare. See *rabbit.*
   hart. See *deer.*
   heifer. See *cattle.*
   hind. See *deer.*
   hippopotamus. See *behemoth.*
   hopper. See *grasshopper.*
   hornet. See *bee.*

horse. Most references concern the use of the horse in warfare, though some religious significance is attached to this animal, as in the visions of Rev. 9:17-19; 6:1-8. Domesticated on the plains of Asia more than 4,000 years ago, the horse—a herbivorous hoofed mammal, *Equus caballus*—was used in the military campaigns of ALEXANDER THE GREAT and was probably introduced into the American continent by conquerors from Europe. Scripture refers to the beneficial use of the horse among its more than 150 references. Joseph exchanged food for horses and for other animals during the great famine in Egypt (Gen. 47:17). A very large company of chariots and horses accompanied the body of Jacob to his last resting place (50:9).

Although horses, with other livestock, perished under the judgment of God (Exod. 9:3), Pharaoh secured further war horses and chariots in order to pursue the departing Israelites (14:23), though the Lord swept them into the sea (14:27-28). David's victories included the acquisition of large numbers of chariots, charioteers, and horses (2 Sam. 8:4; 10:18). Solomon's accumulation of chariots and horses (1 Ki. 10:26) involved importation of horses from Egypt and Kue at considerable expense that, in

view of his drift away from his former moral convictions, would have affronted the prophets (Isa. 31).

Isaiah refers to the agricultural use of the horse, that is, for plowing (Isa. 28:24-29). The use of horsemen to convey messages (2 Ki. 9:18) and for royal processions (Esth. 6:8-11) was familiar to the ancients. Ending of the idolatrous use of horses and chariots dedicated to the sun is reported in 2 Ki. 23:11 as Josiah renewed the covenant with God. The sun religion, like the horses, was probably imported from Egypt.

As the stallion is a horse used for breeding purposes, its use in the OT is aligned to the sinful behavior of the people. Jeremiah likens his careless contemporaries to well-fed, lusty stallions considering their neighbors' wives (Jer. 5:8; cf. 50:11). Stallions were large and strong and were used as symbols of enemy power, as in the Lord's declaration that the whole land trembled at the neighing of the enemy's stallions (8:16). The steed is a spirited horse especially chosen for battle, probably for its speed and daring. Deborah's song recites the galloping of the mighty steeds (Jdg. 5:22). We learn that the Israelites used steeds for battle against Egypt (Jer. 46:4) and against the Philistines (47:3).

horse leech. See *leech.*

hyena. This carnivorous animal allied to the dog was common in Palestine. Isaiah's prophecy against Babylon speaks of hyenas howling in the strongholds of the fallen city (Isa. 13:22)—a fate reserved for the citadels of Edom (34:14). Jeremiah speaks in similar vein against Babylon (Jer. 50:39). The hyena, like the *jackal*, was associated with desolation and with dwelling among ruins.

ibex. This term may be generally applied to any of several species of mountain goats or wild goats, with their horns curving backward. Included in the list of permitted edible animals (Deut. 14:5; KJV, "pygarg"), the variety known to the people was that of the Nubian ibex, occurring in Palestine as well as in Egypt and Arabia.

jackal. The usual Hebrew term for "jackal" is *tan H9478* (always pl. and used in figurative contexts), but *šûʿāl H8785*, which most often refers to the *fox*, can be used with the same meaning (Lam. 5:18; Ezek. 13:4), as can perhaps other terms (cf. Isa. 13:21 NIV; NRSV, "howling creatures"). Jackals are related to foxes and even more closely to domestic dogs. The Palestine species is the oriental jackal (*Canis aureus*), with head and body 24-30 in. in length, and a tail of up to 12 in.; its color is a dirty yellow mixed with reds and blacks. Jackals usually go about in packs of up to a dozen, feeding mostly at night, and it is interesting that in all cases the Hebrew word is plural. The jackal is basically a scavenger, living rather as a *hyena* in game country, where it can clean up after the larger carnivores have killed. In contrast, the fox is more solitary, feeding on a wide range of vegetable matter and small animals, and taking less refuse than the jackal. Several times it is prophesied that lands (e.g., Babylon, Jer. 51:37; Edom, Mal. 1:3) shall become the haunt of jackals, which are almost a symbol of desolation (more than half of the passages have this theme). To the casual observer foxes and jackals look very similar, and it is possible that they were often given the same name.

katydid. See *grasshopper*.

kine. Archaic KJV plural term for "cow." See *cattle*.

leech. This term occurs only once in the Bible (Prov. 30:15; KJV, "horseleach"), though the meaning of the Hebrew word is uncertain. The leech is of the class of annelids (*Hirudinea*) living in water or swampy territory. A sucker at either end of its segmented body fixes onto the body of an animal or human, sucking blood. A natural anticoagulant (hirudin) keeps the blood liquid. At one time the use of leeches was thought to have beneficial properties, and a type of leech, *Hirudo medicinalis*, was well known to physicians of past generations.

leopard. The reference to "mountain haunts of the leopards" (Cant. 4:8) reminds us that these awesome animals were well known in Palestine, as well as in the mountainous regions of Lebanon, at the time of Solomon's reign. A mammal of the cat family (*Panthera pardus*) with a black-spotted yellowish coat, the leopard is today found only in Africa and Asia. Its ferocity and intelligence were apparent to dwellers in Bible lands, though, as with the rest of the wayward creation, transformation was promised in the messianic age (Isa. 11:6). Jeremiah regarded the leopard as an instrument of God's judgment on the wicked (Jer. 5:6), and in a later passage raised

Close-up photo of a leopard.

© Direct Design

the rhetorical question whether a leopard could change his spots (13:23). Several references to the leopard appear in the Bible, including the figurative usage in Dan. 7:6 and Rev. 13:2.

Leviathan. That the Leviathan was strong and probably very large is confirmed by the question put in Job 41:1. The NIV footnote suggests a hippopotamus or elephant, neither of which would be pulled in with a fishhook. Job's cursing (3:8) refers to those who are ready to rouse Leviathan. Crushing the heads of Leviathan (Ps. 74:14) immediately follows reference to the destruction of monsters of the sea. This may echo the song of praise to God following the safe journey of the Israelites through the Red Sea. Crocodiles or other threatening creatures would have been rendered harmless to the Israelites, as the pursuing Egyptians were. Not all allusions to Leviathan concern threatening species, however; Ps. 104:26 refers to its frolicking in the sea. Probably this is the sperm whale, which has been seen in the Mediterranean and which surfaces suddenly before submerging, giving the impression of play activity.

lice. See *fly*.

lion. A large carnivore of the cat family (*Panthera leo*) today found in Africa S of the Sahara and in NW India. In biblical times the lion was far more widespread and was found even in Greece as well as in Asia Minor, Iran, Iraq, and Syria. A social animal, the lion is a member of a group known as a pride and will live in isolation only when old or wounded—conditions in which it is most dangerous to humans. In usual circumstances the lion will not attack them, though "man-eaters"

A

have been known, becoming part of local legends and hunters' tales.

Daniel's testing in the lions' den (Dan. 6) demonstrates an oriental ruler's use of lions as a means of execution, but it is more importantly an example of protection by the Almighty. Although a wayward prophet was killed by a lion (1 Ki. 13:24-28), this event is told in terms of God's judgment rather than any initiative by a roving lion. A young lion attacked Samson but was speedily dealt with (Jdg. 14:5-6), and David also killed a lion (1 Sam. 17:34-37), both triumphs being ascribed to God's protection.

The power, speed, and ferocity of the lion were compared to those of Israel's foes; and throughout Scripture the lion is used as a symbol of might. Jacob compared his son Judah to a lion (Gen. 49:9), and the Lord Jesus Christ is often called the Lion of the Tribe of Judah (or the Lion of Judah). Daniel described Babylon as a winged lion—a religious symbol used in the ancient pagan world—while Peter warned his contemporaries that the devil prowls around like a roaring lion (1 Pet. 5:8).

lioness. Ezekiel's lament on the princes of Israel refers to the lioness as their mother (Ezek. 19:2), whose cubs might be scattered (Job 4:11). Joel's prophecy (Joel 1:6) speaks of the fangs of the lioness as a characteristic of an invading nation.

livestock. See *cattle.*

lizard. A reptile of the suborder *Lacertila*, with four legs usually, but some species—like the slowworm—have none. With scaly skin and long body and tail, the lizard may be small or comparatively large. The species includes the iguana, monitor, and gecko. Leviticus 11:29-30 classifies as unclean any kind of great lizard, the gecko, monitor lizard (NRSV, "land crocodile"), wall lizard, skink (NRSV, "sand lizard"), and chameleon. The most common lizard in Palestine was the *Agama stellio*, part of a family of dragon lizards. These reptiles are active during the daylight hours, possess crests and dewlaps, and somewhat resemble the iguanids.

The chameleon is any member of the *Chamaeleontidae* family of reptiles, resembling lizards, but having the interesting characteristic of controlling its color to match its environment. This reptile catches insects by its tongue. Its eyes are able to operate independently of each other. The gecko is a harmless lizard, a member of the *Gekkonidae* family, found in tropical or subtropical regions. Some geckos are able to move readily on a vertical wall or other smooth surface, using a natural adhesive pad on their feet. Their diet consists of insects. An interesting feature is the gecko's ability to grow a new tail when its old one is broken off by a predator or overinquisitive human being.

The great lizard, another unclean animal, is possibly the Arabian thorny-tailed, color-changing lizard (*Uromastix spinipes*) common in Egypt and also found in Syria and Arabia. The monitor lizard is a member of the *Varanidae* family of large carnivorous lizards and is found in Africa, Asia, and Australia, its largest species being the Komodo dragon. It is recognized additionally by its elongated snout, long neck, and forked tongue. The Nile monitor, *Varanus niloticus*, is the largest four-footed reptile in Africa, with the exception of the crocodile, and may attain a length of 6 ft. (almost 2 m.).

A reptile called the sand lizard, *Lacerta agilis*, is found in sandy regions in central and western Europe. The NIV identifies the Hebrew word with the skink, some 600 species of which represent the largest family of lizards. Snakelike and found most often in desert regions, their features include a scaly tongue and elongated body, with limbs either of small size or absent altogether. The skink mentioned in Lev. 11:30 was the common skink *(Scincus scincus)* of Africa. The wall lizard is included in the list of unclean reptiles, but its precise species is uncertain. Small lizards or reptiles living close to human habitation would be commonly found on walls.

locust. See *grasshopper.*

maggot. See *fly.*

mole. See *rodent.*

monitor lizard. See *lizard.*

monster. See *dragon.*

moth, butterfly. Both belong to the order *Lepidoptera*, the moth being distinguished from the butterfly by its nocturnal activity, its threadlike antenna, and wings that wrap around its body (most butterflies fold their wings vertically). Butterflies have two pairs of wings, and most have eye-catching color displays, using their proboscis to suck nectar. America has more than 9,000 species of moths and butterflies. Throughout the world some species have either disappeared or seem to be on the verge of extinction. To counter this problem, at least in part, new work in butterfly farming is occurring.

The moth of Scripture is usually the clothes moth of the large family, *Tineidae*. Human frailty is like that of the moth (Job 4:19), a sentiment echoed in Job 13:28, where a person's own wasting away is likened to that of a garment eaten by moths (or moth larvae). Psalm 39:11 and Isa. 50:9; 51:8 offer similar reflections. Man's habitation is akin to that of a moth's cocoon (Job 27:18). Insignificant and fragile though it is (Hos. 5:12), the clothes moth is no less able to destroy those transient possessions that people set their hearts on (Matt. 6:19). It lays its eggs at night on wool, fur, feathers, or other materials; when the larvae hatch about ten days later, they immediately start eating the host material.

Silkworms, larvae of the Chinese silkworm moth (*Bombyx mori*), produce the natural fiber of silk garments known to the ancients and worn by the most wealthy. Silk is included among the cargoes of merchants that in the apocalyptic vision of Rev. 18:12 no one buys any more. Raw silk is derived from the cocoon of larvae that pupate in thick oval, white or yellow silken cocoons. As larvae are easily reared on a commercial basis—if one has the appropriate skills and resources—silk has been a source of wealth to many traders over the centuries. Even in our age of modern fibers, silk remains a symbol of luxury and status.

A lepidopterous larva was probably the "worm" that chewed the vine under which Jonah sat (Jon. 4:7), since such larvae have voracious appetites. Most references to "worm" in Scripture refer to the larvae of flies, generally known as "maggots" (see *fly*). The rendering "caterpillar" (larva of a butterfly or moth) is used by the NRSV and other versions in some passages (e.g., 1 Ki. 8:37; Isa. 33:4), but the meaning of the Hebrew is uncertain.

mouse. See *rat*.

mule. See *donkey*.

onager. See *wild ass*.

ox. See *cattle*.

palmerworm. See *grasshopper*.

peacock. See *baboon*.

pig. The Mosaic law includes the pig (KJV, "swine") among the unclean animal (Lev. 11:7; Deut. 14:8), but it seems to have been present in considerable numbers in areas of Palestine inhabited primarily by non-Jews. Destruction of a large herd occurred when evil spirits entered them following Jesus' healing of a demon-possessed man (Mk. 5:1-17; Lk. 8:27-39). The parable of the prodigal son demonstrated the desperate plight of the young man in becoming a pig-feeder (Lk. 15:15), employment degrading to any self-respecting Israelite. Jesus advised against throwing pearls before pigs (Matt. 7:6), as they are likely to be trampled underfoot by the undiscerning creatures. Solomon compared a beautiful woman devoid of discretion with a gold ring in a pig's snout (Prov. 11:22). Peter speaks of a washed sow returning to wallow in the mud (2 Pet. 2:22).

The domestic pig, member of the *Suidae* family of hoofed animals, was probably developed from the wild boar of the Orient, with widespread domestication for food and other uses. The sole reference to "boar" is in Ps. 80:13, where the ravaging actions of wild boars are indicated. With its enlarged canine tusk, the wild boar could cause damage to property or crops and inflict wounds on the unsuspecting.

pygarg. See *ibex*.

rabbit. The rabbit was classified as unclean (Lev. 11:6; Deut. 14:7) because it did not have a split hoof. The KJV and other versions have the word "hare," because some think rabbits did not exist in Palestine at the time of the Pentateuch's composition. At least two species of hare were thought to be present, both members of the order *Lagomorpha*, though the hare was originally classified as a rodent. Rabbits live in burrows and are born hairless and blind, whereas hares do not use burrows and are born with a coat of hair and with effective vision. The hare also has longer ears and hind legs. Like the rabbit, it is found extensively in Europe.

ram. See *sheep*.

rat. Like mice, rats followed human exploitation and habitation of previously inhabited areas. Rats are mentioned in the list of unclean animals (Lev. 11:29) and in the narrative of the plague on the Philistines (1 Sam. 6). Isaiah prophesied against those who had followed heathen practices of eating pig's flesh and rats (Isa. 66:17). In these passages the KJV and other versions have "mouse"

A

(or "mice"), one of the many long-tailed rodents of the *Muridae* family.

red heifer. See *cattle.*

reptile. See *snake.*

rock badger. See *badger.*

rodent. This term is used by the NIV in Isa. 2:20 to translate a Hebrew text of uncertain meaning. Here the KJV and other versions read "moles" (the KJV uses "mole" also at Lev. 11:30 for a word that prob. refers to the chameleon).

roe. See *gazelle.*

sand lizard, sand reptile. See *lizard.*

scorpion. Found in the vast, thirsty land of the wilderness journey, the scorpion (Deut. 8:15) is notorious for its venomous sting delivered from its long, segmented tail. The name applies to any of the order *Scorpionidae* of arachnids of tropical or hot regions. Large pincers at the front of the body, as well as the curving, sting-laden tail, give the scorpion a distinctive and formidable appearance. Rehoboam unwisely threatened to scourge the people with scorpions (1 Ki. 12:11, 14). Followers of Jesus were given authority to tread on scorpions (Lk. 10:19), an authority related to the work of the kingdom of God. In Lk. 11:12 Jesus mentions the scorpion in a rhetorical question.

sea cow. The NIV rendering of a Hebrew term of uncertain meaning (Exod. 25:5 et al.). See discussion under *badger.*

serpent. See *snake.*

sheep. This animal is the one most often mentioned in Scripture, perhaps because of its importance in the economy of the age. The most familiar picture of Jesus Christ is probably that of the Good Shepherd; and the most easily recalled parable may be that of the lost sheep.

A ruminant mammal of the *Ovidae* family, sheep come in many breeds today, some with special advantages for their wool, others for meat. For centuries sheep have been largely domesticated. In Bible lands sheep were kept for their milk more than for their meat. Religious ceremonies included the sacrifice of sheep, and rams' horns were used to summon the congregation. Job's wealth consisted of flocks and herds, including 7,000 sheep (Job 1:3), which were all destroyed by a divinely permitted catastrophe (1:16). The life of shepherds and their flocks is reported in several places (Gen. 29;

Exod. 22:1, 4; Num. 31:36). Sheep were watered at midday, and the well became an important meeting place. Need for water and at least reasonable pasture shaped the shepherd's way of life. His care for his sheep is reflected in Ps. 23. The Bible often refers to bad or good shepherds in terms of their care not merely of sheep but also of their fellow human beings in the eyes of God. Women also served as shepherds, as in the case of seven daughters of the priest of Midian (Exod. 2:16).

Several Hebrew words are translated "ewe," that is, a female sheep. Seven ewe lambs were presented by Abraham to Abimelech (Gen. 21:28-29) to seal the treaty made at Beersheba. Jacob's gift to Esau included two hundred ewes and twenty rams (32:14). Use of a female lamb without defect was permitted as a sin offering (Lev. 4:32). Nathan's parable (2 Sam. 12:3) referred to a man whose "one ewe lamb" was taken from him by a rich and greedy man.

The list of unclean foods in Deut. 14:5 includes "mountain sheep" (KJV incorrectly, "chamois"), a ruminant mammal halfway between a goat and an antelope, found usually in mountainous regions of Europe and SW Asia. The ram, the horned male sheep, was used in breeding. Although most biblical references are to the ram's role in priestly ceremony or sacrifice (Gen. 15:9; Exod. 29; Num. 7), the skipping action of the ram is poetically portrayed by the psalmist (Ps. 114).

skink. See *lizard.*

slug, snail. The slug is herbivorous and often creates considerable damage to plant life. Like the snail, the slug is a gastropod mollusc, moving on a muscular foot with a natural form of lubrication that appears as a trail of slime. The snail has a spiral protective shell and exists in varying species in salt water, fresh water, and on land. The most common species is that of the garden snail (*Helix aspera*), to be distinguished from the edible variety (*Helix pomatia*). The action of the slug or snail is described in Ps. 58:8 (in Lev. 11:30 the KJV also has "snail" for what is prob. a kind of lizard).

snake. Member of the suborder *Ophidia* of limbless, elongated reptiles, with scaly skin, a forked tongue, and a mouth that opens sufficiently wide to swallow prey (e.g., rodents or eggs). Poisonous snakes carry venom in their salivary glands, delivered through the fangs and acting either on the central nervous system to paralyze or on cells to cause hemorrhages. The snake has special significance in the OT. One of the signs of authority given to Moses was that of his staff turning into a snake when thrown to the ground (Exod. 3:3-4). Venomous snakes invaded the Israelite camp when the people complained about God and Moses. Those affected were healed when they looked at an emblem of a snake cast in bronze by Moses (Num. 21). The symbol of the snake on the staff is today an emblem of healing used by the medical profession.

The proper translation of various Hebrew terms for poisonous snakes is not certain. Jeremiah speaks of "vipers that cannot be charmed" as one of God's judgments (Jer. 8:17)—an allusion perhaps to the so-called charming of snakes that are actually not "charmed" but controlled more subtly by their masters. Job 20:16 refers to the destruction of the wicked by the fangs of the adder, just as Isa. 59:5 anticipates the infliction of vipers on the wicked. In modern language the viper and adder are the same species, but the scriptural reference is probably to the northern viper, *Vipera berus*, found also in Africa. Ps. 91:13 assures the godly that they will tread on the cobra and the serpent without any harm, through divine protection. The cobra was doubtless the Egyptian cobra, used throughout Egypt as a religious symbol and attaining a length of more than 8 ft. (2.5 m.). It is found along the coast of N and E Africa, with a subspecies occurring in the Arabian peninsula. Where "cockatrice" is used by the KJV and other translations (Isa. 11:8; 14:29; 59:5; Jer. 8:17), the word was probably associated with a poisonous reptile generally, rather than with specific species.

In the millennial age the cobra and the viper will be the harmless companions of children (Isa. 11:8)—further confirmation of the reconciliation of human beings with the natural order following the creation's renewal. Isaiah, then, does not anticipate a banishing of such reptiles but their transformation. His prophecy against the Philistines (14:29) involves a viper. The use of the word "asp" in some translations denotes a poisonous reptile, that is, the Egyptian cobra.

Solomon's wisdom led him to teach about reptiles, as well as mammals, birds, and fish (1 Ki. 4:33). Peter's remarkable vision included reptiles to be eaten, confirming that nothing God had made could now be called unclean (Acts 10:12; 11:6), symbolizing the now-clean Gentiles in the new covenant.

No single species is identified in the word *serpent*, but the meaning is that of a crafty and very dangerous creature, albeit a persuasive one. It was a symbol of evil (Gen. 3), but God was able to pierce it (Job 26:13). Paul referred to the cunning of the serpent (2 Cor. 11:3).

spider. A member of the order *Araneida* of arachnids, many species of which are armed with poison glands for killing prey. The black widow spider and the Australian funnel-web spider are especially dangerous to humans, unlike most species. The spider's abdomen has two or more pairs of spinnerets that produce the silk thread for webs and cocoons. One who forgets God has hope as fragile as a spider's web (Job 8:14) and finds his own fabrications useless (Isa. 59:5). Proverbs 30:28 refers to the presence of spiders in kings' palaces, though NIV here has the word "lizard" rather than "spider."

sponge. Known scientifically as *Porifera*, the sponge is a class of the sessile aquatic animal family. A sponge filled with wine vinegar was offered to Jesus on the cross (Matt. 27:48; Mk. 15:36). John notes that a stalk of the hyssop plant was used to lift the sponge to the Lord's lips (Jn. 19:29). Such use of a sponge to provide liquid refreshment was common in biblical times. The sponge would absorb the wine or water in a vessel, then was usually squeezed into the upturned mouth of the user.

stag. See *deer*.

stallion, steed. See *horse*.

steer. See *cattle*.

swine. See *pig*.

tortoise. KJV rendering of a word that refers to some kind of *lizard* (Lev. 11:29).

unicorn. See *cattle*.

viper. See *snake*.

weasel. Classed as unclean (Lev. 11:29), the weasel is a small, carnivorous mammal, genus *Mustela*, resembling a small ermine. Its diet consists of small rodents and its distribution is apparently worldwide.

whale. The KJV translates as "whale" those words rendered by NIV as "great creatures" (Gen. 1:21),

A

"monster of the deep" (Job 7:12), and "monster in the seas" (Ezek. 32:2). The KJV and other versions also use "whale" with reference to the fish that swallowed Jonah (Matt. 12:40; but "great fish" in Jon. 1:17). The whale, a large marine fishlike mammal (order *Cetacea*), is one of nature's most amazing wonders. One group includes the toothed whales, another the whalebone whales in which teeth are not present, using instead thin, parallel whalebone plates to extract plankton from sea water. Toothed whales include porpoises, dolphins, and sperm whales. Whalebone whales include the blue whale, largest of all mammals.

wild ass. This English term (NIV, "wild donkey") is the usual translation of Hebrew *pere*' *H7230* (Gen. 16:12 et al.), but the name preferred for the biblical or Asian wild ass is *onager* (*Equus onager*). It is rightly classed as "half-ass," belonging to a species distinct from the true wild ass of N Africa (*E. asinus*, from which the donkey is derived). The onager once had a wide distribution, divided into several geographical types, extending from the borders of Europe and Palestine in the W through to India and Mongolia. Job describes its habitat precisely: "the steppe for its home, the salt land for its dwelling place" (Job 39:6).

wolf. A carnivorous, intelligent mammal, genus *Canis*, the wolf usually hunts in packs and will readily attack more powerful animals. The N American timber or grey wolf is a subspecies of the European *Canis lupus*. The behavior of this animal has fascinated many writers. Mentioned thirteen times in Scripture, the wolf would have been a familiar threat to shepherds, especially in Palestine with its forest terrain. False prophets were described as "ferocious wolves" in sheep's clothing (Matt. 7:15), while Gen. 49:27 declares the tribe of Benjamin to be like the ravenous wolf. Isaiah's anticipation of the millennium includes the wolf living with the lamb (Isa. 11:6; 65:25).

worm. In every mention of the worm in Scripture, the reference is to the maggot rather than to the earthworm, which is apparently nowhere mentioned in the Bible. Maggots are hatched from eggs laid by flies such as the flesh fly (of the family *Sarcophagidae*) or the blow fly (of the family *Calliphoridae*). See *fly*. The blow fly is well known even to our hygienic times, being the large and noisy fly

with blue or green iridescent body. Such flies lay their eggs in the bodies of dead animals, in effect accelerating the decaying process, as the maggots feed on the corpse during their larval period. In that sense they serve a beneficial purpose in the natural process. The presence of worms on the human body, alive (Job 7:5) or dead (Job 17:14; 21:26; Isa. 14:11; 66:24), was a further reminder of the transient nature of life. The condition of hell, warned Jesus, was one in which the worm does not die (Mk. 9:48). See also *moth*.

Herod AGRIPPA I's death (Acts 12:23) is described as caused by his being eaten by worms. This demise was probably accomplished by the screw worm, as the adult female fly lays eggs not only on decaying animal matter, but in wounds and sores and even in the nostrils and ears of people and cattle. In severe attacks, in the ancient world especially, infection of the nasal passages by larvae could produce collapse of the septum and palate. Herod's affliction is not, however, regarded as accidental, but as a judgment arising from his pride and his aspiration to divine status.

anise. See PLANTS.

anklet. An ornament for the ankles, consisting of metal or glass spangles, worn by women. Sometimes anklets were linked together by ankle chains (Isa. 3:20). See also DRESS.

Anna. an'uh (Gk. *Anna* or *Hanna G483*, the equivalent of Heb. *ḥannâ H2839*, "grace"). Daughter of Phanuel of the tribe of ASHER. Widowed after seven years of marriage, she became a prophetess. At the age of eighty-four, when the infant Jesus was brought into the temple to be dedicated, she recognized and proclaimed him as the MESSIAH (Lk. 2:36-38).

Annas. an'uhs (Gk. *Hannas G484*, shortened form of *Hananos* = *ḥănanyâ H2863*, "Yahweh is gracious"). A high PRIEST of the Jews from A.D. 6 to 15, and who as long as he lived was the virtual head of the priestly party in Jerusalem. In his thirty-seventh year, he was appointed to this office by QUIRINIUS, governor of SYRIA. He was deposed c. A.D. 15 by Valerius Gratus, governor of JUDEA. His five sons became high priests, and he was father-in-law of CAIAPHAS (Jn. 18:13). Annas and Caiaphas are described as the high priests when JOHN THE BAPTIST began his public ministry (Lk. 3:2), perhaps because as family head Annas was the most influential priest and still bore the title. Therefore when Jesus was arrested, he was led first to Annas (Jn. 18:13), and only later was sent bound to Caiaphas (18:24). Similarly, Annas is called the high priest in Acts 4:6 when Peter and John were arrested, although Caiaphas was probably the actual high priest.

annunciation. This term, though not found in Scripture, is used in theology with reference to the supernatural announcement made by the angel GABRIEL to Mary that she would conceive and give birth (Lk. 1:26-38). (The term is sometimes applied also to two other announcements: the one of Jesus' birth made to Joseph, and the one of JOHN THE BAPTIST's birth made to ZECHARIAH. Moreover, the name Annunciation is used of the festival held on March 25, nine months before Christmas Day, to celebrate the visit of Gabriel to the Virgin Mary.)

Mary, a virgin, was betrothed but not yet married to JOSEPH (see MARY, MOTHER OF JESUS). They lived in NAZARETH, a town of GALILEE. In his message Gabriel assured the frightened Mary that she was highly favored and that the Lord was with her. The young lady was overcome with surprise and fear, not only by the presence of the angel, but also by his message. Gabriel, however, assured her that she had no need to fear. God had chosen her to be the mother of a unique boy: "He will be great and will be called the Son of the Most High" (Lk. 1:32). Her son would be God's Son, and, like David, he would reign over the people of God; yet, unlike David's kingdom, his would be an everlasting kingdom. When Mary asked how this could occur since she was not yet married, Gabriel explained that she would conceive through the direct agency of the HOLY SPIRIT. Like her relative ELIZABETH (who had conceived in her old age and was carrying John the Baptist), she would know the power of God in her life. Overwhelmed by this amazing message, Mary submitted to the will of the Lord, and the angel left her.

anoint. To apply OIL to a person or thing, a practice common in the ANE. Anointing was of three kinds: ordinary, sacred, and medical. Ordinary anointing with scented oils was a common operation (Ruth 3:3; Ps. 104:15; Prov. 27:9). It was discontinued during a time of mourning (2 Sam. 14:2; Dan. 10:3; Matt. 6:17). Guests were anointed as a mark of respect (Ps. 23:5; Lk. 7:46). The dead were prepared for burial by anointing (Mk. 14:8; 16:1). The leather of shields was rubbed with oil to keep it from cracking (Isa. 21:5), but this could be called also a sacred anointing—a consecration to the war in the name of whatever god was invoked to bless the battle.

The purpose of sacred anointing was to dedicate the thing or person to God. JACOB anointed the stone he had used for a pillow at BETHEL (Gen. 28:18). The TABERNACLE and its furniture were anointed (Exod. 30:22-29). Prophets (1 Ki. 19:16; 1 Chr. 16:22), priests (Exod. 28:41; 29:7; Lev. 8:12, 30), and kings (Saul—1 Sam. 9:16; 10:1; David—1 Sam. 16:1, 12-13; 2 Sam. 2:7; Solomon—1 Ki. 1:34; Jehu—1 Ki. 19:16) were anointed, the oil symbolizing the HOLY SPIRIT. They were thus set apart and empowered for a particular work in the service of God. "The Lord's anointed" was the common term for a theocratic king (1 Sam. 12:3; Lam. 4:20).

The terms MESSIAH and CHRIST mean "the anointed one" (respectively from the Heb. and Gk. verbs meaning "to anoint," *māšaḥ H5417* and *chriō G5987*). In the OT, Messiah is twice used of the coming Redeemer (Ps. 2:2; Dan. 9:25-26). Jesus was anointed with the Holy Spirit at his baptism (Jn. 1:32-33), marking him as the Messiah of the OT (Lk. 4:18, 21; Acts 9:22; 17:2-3; 18:5, 28). His disciples, through union with him, are anointed with the Holy Spirit too (2 Cor. 1:21; 1 Jn. 2:20).

Medical anointing, not necessarily with oil, was customary for the sick and wounded (Isa. 1:6; Lk. 10:34). Mark 6:13 and Jas. 5:14 speak of the use of anointing oil by disciples of Jesus.

ant. See ANIMALS.

antediluvians. People who lived before the FLOOD ("deluge"). They apparently were familiar with AGRICULTURE (ADAM kept the garden

A

of EDEN, Gen. 2:15; Adam and ABEL tilled the ground, 3:17-19; 4:2), botany (thorns and thistles, 3:18; cypress wood, 6:14; fig tree, 3:7; pitch, 6:14), metallurgy (bronze and iron tools, 4:22), architecture (CAIN built a city, 4:17), and music (harp and flute, 4:21). The hints of government seem to be patriarchal and possibly city states. With regard to religion, SACRIFICES appear to have been established (4:4; 8:20), and NOAH was familiar with "clean" animals (7:2; 8:20). Of the lineage of SETH and ENOSH it is said, "At that time men began to call on the name of the LORD" (4:26). A contrast with the descendants of Cain, who presumably did not call upon God, seems to be implied.

antelope. See ANIMALS.

Anthothijah. an´thoh-thi´juh (Heb. ʿantōtiyyâ *H6746*, possibly "belonging to Anathoth"). KJV Antothijah. Son of Shashak and descendant of BENJAMIN (1 Chr. 8:24); he is included among the clan chiefs who lived in Jerusalem (v. 28).

anthropology. (1) The study of human beings in relation to history, geography, culture, and so forth. (2) The biblical and theological doctrine regarding the origin, nature, and destiny of human beings. See HUMAN NATURE.

anthropomorphism. A figure of speech whereby the deity is referred to in terms of human bodily parts or human passions. To speak of God's hands, eyes, anger, or even love is to speak anthropomorphically. Some anthropomorphisms picture God in bodily form and others refer to God as possessing various aspects of human personality. In a sense, it can be argued that only those of the first type are true anthropomorphisms. They speak as if God possessed bodily form, which of course he does not. The second type of anthropomorphism may be called factual description and not a figure of speech at all (though the term *anthropopathism* is sometimes used specifically with reference to the ascription of human feeling to God). It is the Christian teaching that the living and true God is actually possessed of these personal characteristics, which human beings recognize in themselves as attributes of personality.

antichrist. This word derives directly from the Greek compound *antichristos G532*, meaning literally "against Christ" or "instead of Christ"; thus it may refer either to an enemy of CHRIST or to one who usurps Christ's name and rights. The word is found in only four verses (1 Jn. 2:18, 22; 4:3; 2 Jn. 7), but the idea conveyed by it appears throughout Scripture. It is evident from the way John and Paul refer to the antichrists or the Antichrist that they took for granted a tradition well known at the time (2 Thess. 2:6, "you know"; 1 Jn. 4:3, "you have heard").

The OT gives evidence of a belief in a hostile person or power who in the end time will bring an attack against God's people—an attack that will be crushed by the Lord or his MESSIAH. Psalm 2 gives a picture of the rebellion of the world kingdoms "against the LORD and against his Anointed One." The same sort of contest is described in Ezek. 38-39 and in Zech. 12-14. In the book of Daniel there are vivid descriptions of the Antichrist that find their echo in the writings of the apostles (cf. 2 Thess. 2:4 with Dan. 11:36-37; and cf. Rev. 13:1-8 with Dan. 7:8, 20-21; 8:24; 11:28, 30).

In his eschatological discourse Christ warns against the "false Christs" and the "false prophets" who would lead astray, if possible, even the elect (Matt. 24:24; Mk. 13:22). In Matt. 24:15 he refers to "the abomination that causes desolation" spoken of by Daniel.

In 2 Thess. 2:1-12 PAUL gives us a very full description of the working of Antichrist, under the name of "the man of lawlessness," in which he draws on the language and imagery of the OT. The Thessalonian Christians seem to have been under the erroneous impression that the "day of the Lord" was at hand, and Paul told them that before that day could come two things would have to take place: an apostasy and the revelation of the man of lawlessness, the son of perdition. The "secret power of lawlessness" (2:7) is already at work, he said, but is held in check by some restraining person or power. With the removal of this restraining force, the man of lawlessness is revealed. He will oppose and exalt himself above God and will actually sit in the temple of God and claim to be God. With satanic power he will perform signs and deceitful wonders, bringing great deception to people who reject God's truth. In spite of his extraordinary power, however, "the Lord Jesus will overthrow [him] with the breath of his mouth" (2:8).

In 1 Jn. 2:18 JOHN THE APOSTLE shows that the coming of the Antichrist was an event generally expected by the church. It is apparent, however, that he is more concerned about directing the attention of Christians to anti-Christian forces already at work ("even now many antichrists have come"). He says that teachers of erroneous views of the person of Christ (evidently referring to GNOSTICISM) are antichrists (1 Jn. 2:22; 4:3; 2 Jn. 7).

In the book of Revelation, the beast of Rev. 17:8 recalls the horned beast of Dan. 7-8. He claims and is accorded divine homage and makes war on God's people. For a period of three and one-half years he rules over the earth and is finally destroyed by the Lord in a great battle. With his defeat the contest of good and evil comes to its final decision.

Antilebanon. Also Anti-Lebanon. See LEBANON.

antimony. A hard, brittle, and lustrous metallic element (symbol Sb). The term is used twice for Hebrew *pûk H7037* in the NRSV and some other versions (1 Chr. 29:2; Isa. 54:11). In both of these instances, the NIV translates "turquoise" (see MINERALS); some believe that the meaning is "hard cement." The Hebrew word occurs also in two other contexts, where it seems to refer to (black) eye paint (2 Ki. 9:30; Jer. 4:30).

antinomianism.   an'ti-noh'mee-uh-niz-uhm. This term (from Gk. *anti G505*, "against," and *nomos G3795*, "law") refers to a theology that interprets biblical teaching, particularly that of PAUL, to mean that Christians are so wholly in GRACE that they have no obligation to keep the LAW. Because salvation does not come through works but through grace, it is held, moral effort can be discounted. Paul found that this kind of heresy had crept into the church (1 Cor. 5-6). Others had chosen to misrepresent his own teaching on grace (Rom. 3:8), and he pointed out the absurdity of the charge (6:1, 15). From the first century to our own day, some individuals or groups have sought to combine the spiritual life with moral license, but Scripture leaves no doubt that the new life in Christ means death to the old evil desires (Gal. 5:24).

Antioch. an'tee-ok (Gk. *Antiocheia G522*). (1) Antioch of SYRIA was built in 301 B.C. by Seleucus I (Nicator) and became the capital of the SELEUCID empire, which had been the Asiatic part of the vast empire of ALEXANDER THE GREAT. It was the greatest of sixteen Antiochs he founded in honor of his father ANTIOCHUS. The city was a great commercial center. Caravan roads converged on it from the E, and its situation on the ORONTES River, 15 navigable mi. (24 km.) from the Mediterranean, made it readily available to ships as well. Antioch was set in a broad and fertile valley, shielded by majestic snow-covered mountains, and was called "Antioch the Beautiful and the Golden." In 65 B.C. the Romans took the city and made it the capital of the Roman province of Syria. Seleucid kings and early Roman emperors extended and adorned the city until it became the third largest in the empire (after ROME and ALEXANDRIA), with a population in the first century A.D. of about 500,000. A cosmopolitan city from its foundation, its inhabitants included many Jews, who were given privileges similar to those of the Greeks. Its citizens were a vigorous and aggressive race, famous for their commercial aptitude, their licentiousness, and their biting wit.

Antioch has an important place in the early history of Christianity. One of the original deacons of the apostolic church was NICOLAS, a proselyte

Antioch in Pisidia and Syria.

A

© Dr. James C. Martin

Byzantine church ruins in Pisidian Antioch; beneath them lie the remnants of an ancient synagogue.

of Antioch (Acts 6:5). The first Gentile church, the mother of all the others, was founded there. Many fugitive Christians, scattered at the death of STEPHEN, went to Antioch and inaugurated a new era by preaching not only to the Hellenist Jews but to "Greeks also" (11:20). The Jerusalem church sent BARNABAS to assist in the work; after laboring there for a while Barnabas summoned PAUL from TARSUS to assist him. After they had worked there for a year, they were sent with relief to the famine-stricken saints in Jerusalem. The disciples were called Christians first in Antioch (11:19-26), a designation probably coming from the populace, who were well known for their invention of nicknames. The church at Antioch sent Paul and Barnabas out on their missionary work (13:1-3), and they reported to this church on their return from the first journey (14:26-27; cf. also 18:22 after the second journey). The Antiochene Christians submitted the question of the CIRCUMCISION of Gentile converts to a council at Jerusalem (Acts 15), winning for the church at large a great victory over Judean narrowness.

After NT times, Antioch gave rise to a school of thought distinguished by literal interpretation of the Scriptures; its best-known representative was John Chrysostom (c. A.D. 345-407). During the third and fourth centuries, ten church councils were held there. The city was taken and destroyed in 538 by the Persians, rebuilt by the Roman emperor Justinian shortly afterward, and in 635 was taken by the Muslims, by whom it has since, except for a brief period, been retained. Today the city is called Antakya, with a population of about 150,000.

In 1916 an announcement was made that Arabs in or near Antioch had found what has come to be known as "The Chalice of Antioch." It is a plain silver cup surrounded by an outer shell decorated with vines and with the figures of Christ and the apostles; it is set on a solid silver base. The cup was vigorously claimed to be the Holy Grail, used by Jesus at the Last Supper, the figures on the shell interpreted as first-century portraits. But the authenticity of the chalice has been called into question. Serious scholars have virtually proved that at most the cup is a piece of early Christian silver from the fourth or fifth century and had nothing to do with the Last Supper in Jerusalem.

(2) Antioch of PISIDIA, a town in southern ASIA MINOR, was also founded by Seleucus I and named in honor of his father Antiochus. It was in fact situated in PHRYGIA, but not far from Pisidia, and was therefore called Antioch of Pisidia and Pisidian Antioch to distinguish it from another city of the same name in Phrygia. In 25 B.C. it became a part of the Roman province of GALATIA. Soon after, it was made the capital of southern Galatia,

and a Roman colony. The Romans made it a strong garrison center to hold down the surrounding wild tribes. Paul and Barnabas preached in the synagogue there on their first missionary journey; but the Jews, jealous of the many Gentile converts that were made, drove the missionaries from the city to ICONIUM and followed them even to LYSTRA (Acts 13:14—14:19). On Paul's return journey he revisited Antioch to establish the disciples and probably returned on his second (16:6) and third journeys as well (18:23).

Antiochus. an-ti'uh-kuhs (Gk. *Antiochos*, "opposer, withstander"). A favorite name of the Seleucid kings of SYRIA from 280 B.C. onward. The most significant rulers who bore that name were the following:

(1) Antiochus III (the Great), sixth ruler of the dynasty (223-187 B.C.). By his victory over the Egyptians in 198 Syria gained control of Palestine. He was decisively defeated by the Romans in 190 and thereby lost control over ASIA MINOR. He was murdered by a mob while plundering a temple.

(2) Antiochus IV (Epiphanes), son of Antiochus III and eighth ruler of the dynasty (175-163 B.C.). In his attempt to hellenize the Jews he had a pig sacrificed on the altar in Jerusalem, forbade circumcision, and destroyed all the OT books he could find. These outrages involved him in the Maccabean war in which the Syrian armies were repeatedly defeated by the brilliant Judas MACCABEE (1 Macc. 1:10-64; 3:1-11; et al.).

(3) Antiochus V (Eupator), son of Antiochus IV. He reigned as a minor for two years and then was assassinated.

Antipas. an'tee-puhs (Gk. *Antipas G525*, possibly short form of *Antipatros*). (1) The name of several men in the Herodian family, especially a son of Herod the Great who was made tetrarch of GALILEE and PEREA. See HEROD.

(2) In the letter to the church in PERGAMUM, a Christian named Antipas is described as "my faithful witness, who was put to death in your city" (Rev. 2:13). Nothing more is known about him, although later legends arose concerning his martyrdom.

Antipater. See HEROD.

Antipatris. an-tip'uh-tris (Gk. *Antipatris G526*). The NT city that occupied the site of the OT PHILISTINE town of APHEK, in the Plain of SHARON (1 Sam. 4:1; 29:1). The new city was built by HEROD the Great in 9 B.C. He named it Antipatris in honor of his father Antipater, who had been procurator of JUDEA under Julius CAESAR. The modern name of the ruins is Ras el-ʿAin. There is only one mention of Antipatris in Scripture, when PAUL was taken following his arrest in Jerusalem from that city to CAESAREA (Acts 23:31). It marked the NW limit of JUDEA.

Antonia, Tower of. A great fortress rebuilt by HEROD the Great for the defense of the TEMPLE area and located at its NW corner. He named it in honor of Mark Antony, his patron. A Roman legion was stationed in the castle to guard against excesses on the part of the people. The Tower of Antonia may have been the site of the PRAETORIUM, where Jesus was tried by PILATE. When PAUL was seized in the temple by the Jews, he was carried to this castle ("the barracks"), from the stairs of which he addressed the people (Acts 21:34-40).

The Romans used the Antonia fortress, consisting of four towers, to keep watch over Jewish activities taking place on the temple courts. (Modern reconstruction; view to the SE.)

© Dr. James C. Martin. Holy Land Hotel, Jerusalem. Photographed by permission.

Antothijah. an'toh-thi'juh. See ANTHOTHIJAH.

Antothite. an'tuh-thit. See ANATHOTH (PLACE).

Anub. ay'nuhb (Heb. *ʿānûb H6707*, meaning uncertain). Son of Koz and descendant of JUDAH (1 Chr. 4:8). There may be a connection between Anub and the town of ANAB.

anvil. The Hebrew term *paʿam H7193*, which has various uses, is found with the meaning "anvil" only in Isa. 41:7, where reference is made to the custom of workmen encouraging one another with their work. The metal anvil was driven into a block of wood or into the ground to keep it stable. It was used by various artificers: blacksmiths, silversmiths, tinsmiths, and shoemakers.

anxiety. See FEAR.

ape. See ANIMALS.

Apelles. uh-pel'eez (Gk. *Apellēs G593*). A Christian in ROME to whom PAUL sent greetings, referring to him as one who was "approved in Christ" (Rom. 16:10). The reason for the approval is not given, but it is clear that Apelles had been tested and found faithful. The name was a common one among Jews at Rome.

Apharsachite, Apharsathchite, Apharsite. uh-fahr'suh-kit, uh-fahr'-suth-kit, uh-fahr'sit (Aram. *ʾăparseˈkāy H10061*, *ʾăparsatkāy H10062*, *ʾăpārsāy H10060*). These terms in the KJV are transliterations of Aramaic words in Ezra 4:9; 5:6; 6:6. They refer to people listed among the signers of a letter in which complaint is made to the Persian rulers against the Jewish rebuilding of the temple. The first two terms are probably variant forms of Old Persian loanwords meaning "investigator" or, more generally, "official." The third term possibly has the same meaning, but some believe that it should be translated "Persian" (cf. NIV).

Aphek. ay'fek (Heb. *ʾăpēq H707* [*ʾăpîq* in Jdg. 1:31], perhaps "stream-bed" or "fortress"). A place name that appears in widely scattered areas of Palestine. (1) A city of the tribal inheritance of ASHER taken from the Canaanites (Josh. 19:30; Jdg. 1:31 [KJV and other versions, "Aphik"]). The tribe was not able to drive out its inhabitants so they dwelt among them. The city was strategically located on the coastal highway connecting PHOENICIA and EGYPT. It is usually identified with Tell Kurdaneh, near the sources of the River Naʿaman on the Plain of Acco, 3 mi. (5 km.) inland from the Bay of Haifa.

(2) A site located on the N boundary of the Canaanite territory adjoining "the region of the Amorites" (Josh. 13:4). This Aphek is probably to be identified with modern Afqa (ancient Aphaca) in LEBANON, SE of Jebeil (biblical GEBAL).

(3) One of an important chain of cities on the Plain of SHARON ("level country" or "forested region"). It is to be identified with Tell Ras el-ʿAin at the source of the Yarkon, just NE of JOPPA. Its king was slain by JOSHUA and the Israelites during the conquest of Canaan (Josh. 12:18). The town is elsewhere associated with the PHILISTINES (1 Sam. 4:1; 29:1). In NT times, HEROD the Great built ANTIPATRIS on this site.

(4) A city in the N TRANSJORDAN district of BASHAN. It was near here that BEN-HADAD I and II, the Aramean rulers, were defeated by the Israelites (1 Ki. 20:26-34; 2 Ki. 13:14-25). Some have identified this city with two distinct sites near the E shore of the Sea of Galilee: Fiq (Upper Aphek) and ʿEn-Gev (Lower Aphek).

Aphekah. uh-fee'kuh (Heb. *ʾăpēqâ H708*, perhaps "stream-bed" or "fortress"). One of the cities listed as part of a district of JUDAH (Josh. 15:53). It should probably be identified with Khirbet el-Ḥadab, some 4 mi. (6 km.) SW of HEBRON.

Aphiah. uh-fi'uh (Heb. *ʾăpîaḥ H688*, perhaps "large forehead" or "sooty"). A Benjamite who was one of SAUL's ancestors (1 Sam. 9:1).

Aphik. See APHEK.

Aphrah. See BETH OPHRAH.

Aphses. See HAPPIZZEZ.

Apiru. See HABIRU.

Apis. ay´pis (Gk. *Apis*). A fertility god (see FERTIL-ITY CULTS) in the form of a living bull, worshiped by the ancient Egyptians in MEMPHIS (where he was associated with Ptah, a creator god, and with OSIRIS, god of the dead). Some have suggested that the Apis bull inspired the CALF WORSHIP of the Israelites (at Mount Sinai, Exod. 32:4-35, and under JEROBOAM, 1 Ki. 12:28-29). According to some scholars, this god is mentioned at Jer. 46:15 (LXX 26:15), "Why has Apis fled?" (thus NRSV). Such a rendering is based on the SEPTUAGINT, which evidently interpreted the Hebrew verb *nishap* ("was swept away"; NIV, "laid low") as two words, *nās hap* ("fled Apis").

Apocalypse. uh-pok´uh-lips´. Alternate name for the book of Revelation. See APOCALYPTIC LITERA-TURE; REVELATION, BOOK OF.

apocalyptic literature. A type of Jewish (and subsequently Christian) religious writing that developed during the intertestamental period and had it roots in OT prophecy. The word *apocalyptic* derives from Greek *apokalypsis G637* ("uncover-ing, disclosure, revelation") and is applied to these writings because they contain alleged revelation of the secret purposes of God, the end of the world, and the establishment of God's kingdom on earth. The same Greek word is translated "revelation" in Rev. 1:1.

After the days of the postexilic PROPHETS, God no longer spoke to Israel through the living voice of inspired prophecy. The prophetic forecasts of the coming of God's kingdom and the salvation of Israel had not been fulfilled. Instead of God's kingdom, a succession of evil kingdoms ruled over Israel: Medo-Persia, Greece, and finally Rome. Evil reigned supreme. The hope of God's kingdom grew dim. God no longer offered words of comfort and salvation to his people.

The apocalypses were written to meet this reli-gious need. Following the pattern of canonical Daniel (see DANIEL, BOOK OF), various unknown authors wrote alleged revelations of God's purposes that explained present evils, comforted Israel in her sufferings and afflictions, and gave fresh assurances that God's kingdom would shortly appear. See ESCHATOLOGY. Many modern critics place Daniel

in these times, but there are valid reasons for an earlier date.

The outstanding apocalypses in the first two centuries B.C. are *1 Enoch* (or *Ethiopic Enoch*), a composite book that is notable for its description of the heavenly SON OF MAN; *Jubilees*, an alleged rev-elation to MOSES of the history of the world from creation to the end; and the *Assumption of Moses*. A work known as either *2 Esdras* or *4 Ezra* (see APOCRYPHA) was written after the fall of Jerusa-lem in A.D. 70 and reflects that tragedy; the same is true of the *Apocalypse of Baruch*. The apocalypse entitled *2 Enoch* or *Slavonic Enoch* is of uncertain date. Other apocalyptic writings have been discov-ered among the DEAD SEA SCROLLS.

Some additional documents are usually included in the discussion of apocalyptic literature although they are not, properly speaking, apocalypses. The *Testaments of the Twelve Patriarchs* (from the 2nd cent. B.C., but with substantial Christian additions) imitate OT predictive prophecy and contain impor-tant eschatological materials. The seventeenth and eighteenth *Psalms of Solomon*, first century B.C., portray the hope of the coming of the Lord's Anointed to establish God's kingdom. The *Sibylline Oracles*, which follow the pattern of Greek oracular literature, also contain eschatological passages.

Certain characteristics mark these apocalypses. (1) *Revelation*. They describe alleged revelations of God's purposes given through the media of dreams, visions, or journeys to heaven by which the seer learns the secrets of God's world and the future. (2) *Imitation*. These writings seldom embody any genuine subjective visionary experi-ences. Their "revelations" have become a literary form imitating the visions of the true prophets in a thinly veiled literary fiction. (3) *Pseudonym-ity*. These books, although actually written close to NT times, are usually attributed to some OT saint who lived long ago. Pseudonymity was used as a means of validating the message of these authors to their own generation. Since God was no lon-ger speaking through the spirit of prophecy, no one could speak in his own name or directly in the name of the Lord. Instead, the apocalyptists placed their "revelations" in the mouths of OT saints. (4) *Symbolism*. These works employ an elaborate sym-bolism, similar to that appearing in Daniel, as a

A

means of conveying their predictions of the future. (5) *Pseudo-predictive*. The authors take their stand in the distant past and rewrite history under the guise of prophecy down to their own day when the end of the world and the kingdom of God were expected shortly to come.

There are distinct similarities but even more important differences between canonical and noncanonical apocalypses. The visions of Daniel provide the archetype that the later apocalypses imitate, and the Revelation of John records visions given to the apostle in similar symbolic forms. Both Daniel and the Revelation contain revelations conveyed through symbolism; but they differ from noncanonical apocalypses in that they are genuine experiences rather than imitative literary works, are not pseudonymous, and do not rewrite history under the guise of prophecy.

The importance of these apocalyptic writings is that they reveal first-century Jewish ideas about God, evil, and history, and they disclose Jewish hopes for the future and the coming of God's kingdom. They show us what such terms as the "kingdom of God," "Messiah," and the "Son of Man" meant to first-century Jews to whom our Lord addressed his gospel of the kingdom.

Apocrypha. Interspersed among the canonical books of the OT in the Latin Vulgate Bible, and thus also in Roman Catholic versions, are certain additional books and parts of books that were first part of the SEPTUAGINT. It is to these that Protestant usage generally assigns the term *Apocrypha*, indicating that they are not to be regarded as authoritative or canonical (the Gk. adjective *apokryphos* **G649**, "hidden," was used originally as a literary term with regard to books considered unsuitable for public reading because of their esoteric content). When these books are included in Protestant versions, they are usually grouped together as fifteen separate books between the OT and the NT. (See also APOCRYPHAL NEW TESTAMENT.)

At the Council of Trent (A.D. 1546) the Roman Catholic Church received as canonical the additional materials in the Vulgate (except for 1 and 2 Esdras and the Prayer of Manasseh) and designated them *deuterocanonical*, that is, officially accepted as part of the canon on a second or later occasion. That decision was made in contradiction of the best tradition of even the Roman Church itself. It was a reaction to the Reformers, who recognized as divinely inspired and as their infallible rule of faith and practice only those books that were in the canon of the Jews, the group of books that Protestants believe were sanctioned by the Lord Jesus Christ. See CANONICITY. The books that are part of the Apocrypha are the following.

1 Esdras (called 3 Esdras in post-Trentian editions of the Vulgate, where the canonical Ezra and Nehemiah are called 1 and 2 Esdras respectively). Except for the story of the wisdom contest (1 Esd. 3:1—5:6), the contents are a version of the history narrated in 2 Chr. 35:1—36:23, the book of Ezra, and Neh. 7:73—8:12, embracing the period from JOSIAH's Passover to EZRA's reformation. Nothing is known of the author except that he produced it some time before JOSEPHUS, who in his *Antiquities* strangely prefers it to the canonical record.

2 Esdras (called 4 Esdras in the Vulgate; usually referred to as *4 Ezra*). Some call it Apocalyptic Esdras because the central kernel (chs. 3-14) presents seven revelations allegedly given to Ezra in exile, several in visionary form and of largely eschatological import. To this original composed by an unknown Jew, probably near the end of the first century A.D., and later translated into Greek, Christian authors subsequently added some material (chs. 1-2, 15-16). The Jewish original offers its apocalyptic prospects as an answer to the theodicy problem (God's goodness in relation to the evil in the world), acutely posed for Judaism by the fall of Jerusalem in A.D. 70. The Christian addition assigns the casting off of Israel in favor of the Gentiles to Israel's APOSTASY.

Tobit. This romantic tale with religious didactic purpose was composed at least as early as the second century B.C. It is named after its hero, who is pictured as an eighth-century-B.C. Naphtalite carried into exile to NINEVEH. His story becomes entwined with that of his kinswoman Sarah, exiled in Ecbatana. The tragedies of both are remedied through the adventures of Tobit's son Tobias, whom Sarah marries, and all under the angel Raphael's supervision. Prayer, fasting, and almsgiving are stressed but unfortunately in a context of autosoterism (salvation by one's own efforts).

Judith. Like Tobit, this is Jewish historical fiction with a religious moral. It includes elements from two centuries (7th to 5th B.C.) of Israelite fortunes, not always in their proper historical order or setting. Using Jael-like tactics (Jdg. 4:14-22), Judith, a beautiful Jewish woman, saves the besieged town of Bethulia by slaying Holofernes, the enemy commander. Possibly the grotesque anachronisms are intentional; Luther interpreted it as an allegory of Israel's triumphing, under God, over her enemies. The book evidences appreciation of Israel's peculiar theocratic privileges but magnifies a ceremonial piety that would exceed the requirements of Moses. Some think it was composed to inspire zeal during the Maccabean revolt in the second century B.C.

Additions to Esther. The canonical Hebrew text of Esther has 163 verses; the Greek version has 270. The additional material is divided into seven sections and is distributed at the appropriate points throughout the narrative in this way: (1) before Esth. 1:1; (2) after 3:13; (3) and (4) after 7:17; (5) after 8:12; (6) after 10:3. Inasmuch as genuine Esther contains explicit references neither to God nor traditional Jewish religious practices other than fasting (see ESTHER, BOOK OF), it is significant that prayers of MORDECAI and ESTHER and also frequent mention of God are included in the additions. The Greek additions contradict details of canonical Esther and contain other obviously fictional elements. They appeared as an appendix to Esther in the Vulgate and this fusion of disconnected fragments constitutes a "book" in the Apocrypha.

Wisdom of Solomon. The LXX uses this title; the Vulgate, *Liber Sapientiae*. The author, who identifies himself with the figure of SOLOMON, apparently was an Alexandrian Jew writing in Greek in the first century B.C. or A.D. (some, however, judge the book to be of composite authorship). The influence of Greek philosophy is evidenced by the dependence on *logos* speculations in the treatment of personified Wisdom and by the acceptance of various pagan teachings: the creation of the world out of preexistent matter; the preexistence of souls; the impedimentary character of the body; perhaps too, the doctrine of emanation. In tracing Wisdom's government of history from Adam to Moses, numerous fanciful and false embellishments of the biblical record are included.

Ecclesiasticus. This second representative of the wisdom style of literature in the Apocrypha is also called, after its author, The Wisdom of Jesus ben Sira(ch). Written in Hebrew, 180 B.C. or earlier, it was translated into Greek for the Alexandrian Jews by the author's grandson c. 130. Ben Sira, apparently a professional scribe and teacher, patterned his work after the style of Proverbs. In it he expounds the nature of wisdom, applying its counsel to all areas of social and religious life. Though often reflecting sentiments of the canonical books, Ben Sira also echoes the ethical motivations of pagan wisdom literature. Moreover, he contradicts the biblical teaching that salvation is through faith alone by writing that almsgiving makes atonement for sin (Sir. 3:30).

Baruch. This pseudepigraphic book was evidently written by several authors at different times. The first part, Bar. 1:1—3:8, dated by some as early as the third century B.C., was probably written in Hebrew, as was possibly also the remainder, which is of later origin. Composed in a prophetic prose, this section purports to have been produced by JEREMIAH's secretary in Babylonian exile and sent to Jerusalem. It is a confession of national sin (in imitation of Daniel's), petitioning for God's mercy. Actually Baruch went to Egypt with Jeremiah, and there is no evidence that he was ever in Babylonia. Beginning at 3:9, the book is poetry. In 3:9—4:4 Israel is recalled to wisdom. In 4:5—5:9 Jerusalem laments her exiled children, but assurances of restoration are offered.

Epistle of Jeremiah (Jeremy). In some Greek and Syriac MSS this "epistle" is found after Lamentations; in others and in the Vulgate it is attached to Baruch and therefore appears as a sixth chapter of Baruch in most English editions. A superscription describes it as an epistle sent by Jeremiah to certain captives about to be led into Babylon (cf. Jer. 29). The true author is unknown and the original language uncertain. A baffling reference to "seven generations" of exile (contrast Jer. 29:10) has figured in speculation as to its date, which was no later than the second century B.C. It ridicules the foolishness of idol worship as represented by the worship of the god BEL and so served as a

A

warning to the Jews and as an accusation against Gentiles.

The Prayer of Azariah and the Song of the Three Children. This is one of the three sections (the other two being Susanna and Bel and the Dragon) added to the canonical Daniel. Between Dan. 3:23 and 3:24 the Greek and Latin versions insert: (1) a prayer of national confession with supplication for deliverance, which Daniel's friend Azariah (cf. Dan. 1:7) offers while he and his two companions are in the fiery furnace; (2) a psalm of praise (dependent on Ps. 148 and 136), uttered by the three; and (3) a narrative framework containing details not warranted by the genuine Daniel. This section is itself perhaps of composite authorship and was probably written in Hebrew.

Susanna. In the Vulgate, Susanna follows canonical Daniel as ch. 13; in Greek MSS it is prefixed to ch. 1. Two crucial word plays at the climax of the tale suggest it was composed in Greek but there is no consensus. Its origin and date are unknown; ALEXANDRIA about 100 B.C. is one theory. The story relates how two Israelite elders in Babylon, their lustful advances having been resisted by Susanna, falsely accuse her of adultery. But young Daniel effects Susanna's deliverance and the elders' doom by ensnaring them in contradictory testimony.

Bel and the Dragon. These fables ridiculing heathenism appear as ch. 13 of Daniel in the Greek and as ch. 14 in the Vulgate. They date from the first or second century B.C.; their original language is uncertain. Daniel plays detective to expose to CYRUS the fraud of the priests who clandestinely consumed the food-offerings of Bel (i.e., MARDUK). After destroying Bel, Daniel concocts a recipe that explodes a sacred dragon. Consigned to a den of lions, Daniel is miraculously fed and delivered.

The Prayer of Manasseh. According to 2 Chr. 33:11-13, when the wicked King MANASSEH had been carried into exile, he repented and God restored him to Jerusalem. Verses 18-19 refer to sources that contained Manasseh's prayer of repentance. The origin of the apocryphal book that purports to be that prayer is unknown; possibly it was produced in Palestine a century or two before Christ. It contains confession of sin and petition for forgiveness. The view is expressed that certain sinless men need no repentance. In Greek MSS the prayer appears in the Odes attached to the Psalter. In the Vulgate it came to be placed after 2 Chronicles.

1 Maccabees. Beginning with the accession of ANTIOCHUS Epiphanes (176 B.C.), the history of the Jewish struggle for religious-political liberation is traced to the death of Simon (136 B.C.). This apocryphal book is our most valuable historical source for that period. It narrates the exploits of the priest Mattathias and of his sons—Judas, Jonathan, and Simon—who successively led the Hasidim to remarkable victories. Judas was given the surname MACCABEE, afterward applied to his brothers and four books (1-4 Maccabees). The author wrote in Hebrew and was a contemporary of John Hyrcanus, son and successor of Simon. According to one theory, the last three chapters were added and the whole reedited after the destruction of the temple.

2 Maccabees. Independent of 1 Maccabees, this history partly overlaps it, extending from the last year of Seleucus IV (176 B.C.) to the defeat of Nicanor by Judas (161). The author states that he has epitomized the (now lost) five-volume history of Jason of Cyrene (1 Macc. 2:23). Both Jason and the Epitomist wrote in Greek. Suggested dates for 2 Maccabees vary from c. 120 B.C. to the early first century A.D. Two introductory letters (1:1—2:18) were perhaps lacking in the first edition. While there are various errors in 1 Maccabees, legendary exaggeration is characteristic of the moralizing in 2 Maccabees. It also includes doctrinal errors such as the propriety of prayers for the dead. (The books of 3 and 4 Maccabees are quite different in character; though included in the LXX, they are not accepted as part of the Apocrypha. See also PSEUDEPIGRAPHA.)

Apocryphal New Testament. The collective title given to a number of documents, ranging in date from the early Christian centuries to the Middle Ages and even into modern times, all similar in form to the NT books (gospels, epistles, acts, apocalypses) but never finally received into the canon. The *Apocalypse of Peter* and the *Acts of Paul* did enjoy a measure of temporary or local CANONICITY, but no others attained even to this level of recognition. It should be noted that whereas the books of the

OT APOCRYPHA are recognized in certain branches of the church, with the NT Apocrypha this is not the case. Aside from the two books above, none of these works has ever been accorded recognition or authority in any branch of the Christian tradition. It is important to emphasize this point, since it is sometimes suggested that the canonical NT is the result of an arbitrary selection by the church from a large mass of documents that had an equal claim to recognition. Comparison of the apocryphal NT with the canonical books is in itself sufficient to reveal the inferiority of the former.

Broadly speaking, the NT Apocrypha may be divided into two groups: books intended to propagate a particular kind of teaching, usually heretical; and those intended to make good the deficiencies, as they appeared to a later age, in the canonical reports of the activity of Jesus and his apostles. The significance of this literature does not lie in its content, often merely legendary and fictitious, but in the insights it provides into the popular Christianity of the early centuries, which was often on an entirely different level from the theological speculation and theorizing of the early Fathers. Authentic early historical tradition is scarcely to be expected, and is likely to be found only in the earliest documents, if at all. These writings provide a useful standard of comparison with the canonical books and show the difference between documents still controlled by authentic recollection of events and those in which inventive imagination has been given free rein.

Apocryphal gospels. These may be grouped under three categories. (1) Early texts that unfortunately are for the most part fragmentary. For example, a *Gospel of the Egyptians* is quoted by Clement of Alexandria, who did not entirely disapprove of it; but since only his quotations are available, it is difficult to assess its character. It may have been the gospel of Gentile Christians in Egypt, while the *Gospel of the Hebrews* was that of the Jewish Christians; it appears to have been rather more Gnostic in character, and certainly was used by some Gnostic sects. A fragment of the *Gospel of Peter*, previously known only from references in Eusebius, was found in 1886; it is of interest for its original and unorthodox account of the passion and resurrection of Jesus.

(2) The Gnostic gospels and related documents. A common feature of these is their presentation of revelations given to the disciples by the risen Christ in the period between the resurrection and the ascension, a period extended by the Gnostics from 40 to 550 days (or 18 months). The scene is usually a mountain, often the Mount of Olives; one or more of the disciples meet with Jesus, ply him with questions, and receive his answers. Occasionally there is some kind of visionary experience. Some of these works (such as the *Apocryphon of John*) are associated with the names of particular disciples; others, like the *Sophia Jesu Christi* or the *Pistis Sophia*, have more general titles. An important group is formed by the three "gospels" found at NAG HAMMADI, the *Gospel of Truth* (a meditation on the theme of the gospel message), the *Gospel of Thomas* (a collection of sayings), and the *Gospel of Philip* (sayings and meditations loosely strung together). More recently, a *Gospel of Judas* has come to light that presents a positive picture of Judas Iscariot.

(3) Infancy gospels and other later texts. These owe their origin to the desire to make up for the apparent deficiencies of the canonical Gospels and fill in the gaps in the story. In them Jesus is depicted as possessing miraculous powers while still a child, and in the *Infancy Gospel of Thomas* (to be distinguished from the Coptic *Gospel of Thomas*) he sometimes makes use of them in a way quite incompatible with the character presented in the canonical tradition. The *Protevangelium of James* is much less crude, and indeed its use of legendary material is comparatively restrained; it was written mainly for the glorification of MARY MOTHER OF JESUS and carries the story back beyond the birth of Jesus to the miraculous birth of Mary herself and her upbringing in the temple.

Apocryphal epistles. These are comparatively few and some are not really epistles. For example, the Latin work *Epistle to the Laodiceans* is a patchwork of Pauline phrases, although it is found in some MSS of the Bible. The *Letters of Paul and Seneca*, known already to Jerome, are clearly intended to enlist the prestige and authority of the Roman philosopher in support of the Christian faith. A letter from Corinth to Paul and his reply (sometimes referred to as *3 Corinthians*) are

A

now known to have formed part of the *Acts of Paul*, although they also circulated independently.

Apocryphal acts. These are more extensive and more significant, especially the five major works from the 2nd and 3rd centuries attributed to Andrew, John, Paul, Peter, and Thomas. In general it may be said that these were intended to supplement, rather than to replace, the canonical Acts by providing fuller information about the deeds of the apostles and in particular about their martyrdoms. These works testify to the high regard in which the apostles were held, as guarantors of the authentic gospel message and pioneers of the Christian mission; but at the same time their use of legendary motifs and their delight in miracle for its own sake, as a means of glorifying the apostles, place them in the category of romance rather than of history. The important point, however, is their popularity and their influence on later writings. They were themselves the basis of, and often a quarry for, numerous later works. In time, similar *Acts* were composed for other apostles also: Philip, Matthew, Bartholomew, Simon and Judas, Thaddaeus, Barnabas.

Apocryphal apocalypses. The early church shared to a large extent in the temper and thought world of Jewish APOCALYPTIC and took over and adapted several of its documents, but there is of course a shift of emphasis, with interest now centering in the return of Christ. The *Ascension of Isaiah*, for example, derives its title from a vision describing the prophet's ascent through the seven heavens; the work may date from the second century A.D. Also from this century, since it was known to Clement of Alexandria, is the *Apocalypse of Peter*, which is significant both for the way in which it incorporates ideas of heaven and hell from non-Christian sources and also for its influence on later writing, down through the *Apocalypse of Paul* and other works to the *Divina comedia* of Dante. It should be added that not all the works that include "Apocalypse" or "Revelation" in their titles are necessarily apocalyptic in the full sense; and, conversely, revelations of an apocalyptic character sometimes occur in writings that do not bear the title.

Apollonia. ap´uh-loh´nee-uh (Gk. *Apollōnia G662*). There were several towns of this name. The Apollonia of the NT was in MACEDONIA, on the VIA EGNATIA, c. 27 mi. (43 km.) WSW of AMPHIPOLIS. PAUL and SILAS passed through the town on their way between THESSALONICA and PHILIPPI (Acts 17:1).

Apollos. uh-pol´uhs (Gk. *Apollōs G663*, prob. an abbreviated form of *Apollōnios*). A gifted, scholarly, zealous preacher in the early Christian church (Acts 18:24-28; 19:1; 1 Cor. 1:12; 3:4-6, 22; 4:6; 16:12; Tit. 3:13). A native of ALEXANDRIA, he is initially described as mighty in the Scriptures and eloquent, but knowing only the baptism of John. He came to EPHESUS after PAUL had visited that city on his second missionary journey. There he met AQUILA and PRISCILLA, who had been left there to minister pending the apostle's return. They heard Apollos speak boldly in the synagogue and, observing that he was deficient in his knowledge of the gospel, they "explained to him the way of God more adequately" (Acts 18:26). It is not easy to determine from the brief account in Acts the precise character of his religious knowledge. Before long he went to ACHAIA with letters of recommendation from the Ephesian brothers. When he arrived in CORINTH, "he was a great help to those who by grace had believed. For he vigorously refuted the Jews in public debate, proving from the Scriptures that Jesus was the Christ" (18:27-28).

Apollos's gifts and methods of presenting the gospel were undoubtedly different from those of Paul, and he put the impress of his own mode of thinking on many who heard him. Before long a party arose in the Corinthian church with the watchword, "I follow Apollos" (1 Cor. 3:4). There does not, however, appear to have been any feeling of rivalry between Paul and Apollos. Paul urged Apollos to revisit Corinth (16:12), and he also asked TITUS to help Apollos, apparently then or when he was on his way to Crete (Tit. 3:13). Luther suggested the theory, since accepted by a few scholars, that Apollos wrote the letter to the Hebrews.

Apollyon. See ABADDON.

apostasy. The abandonment of one's religion. The word is seldom found in English translations of the Bible, but it is a description of Israel's rebellion against God (Josh. 22:22; 2 Chr. 29:19; Jer. 2:19).

In Greek, where it has the implication of deserting a post, it refers generally to the abandonment of Christianity for unbelief (1 Tim. 4:1; 2 Tim. 2:18), though many believe that this refers to those who had never truly believed (1 Jn. 1:19; cf. Jn. 15:6). The writer of the letter to the Hebrews declares apostasy to be irrevocable (Heb. 6:4-6; 10:26), and Paul applies it eschatologically to the coming of a time of great rebellion against God (2 Thess. 2:3).

apostle. This term derives from Greek *apostolos G693*, which means literally "one sent out" but usually referred to naval expeditions and sometimes to messengers or ambassadors. In the NT it is a title applied in various ways. First of all, it once describes CHRIST himself ("Jesus, the apostle and high priest," Heb. 3:1), pointing to Jesus' role on earth as the ambassador of the Father. Second, the twelve disciples whom Jesus chose to be with him and whom he commissioned and sent out to preach are also called "apostles" (Matt. 10:2; Mk. 3:14; 6:30; Lk. 6:13; 9:10; 11:49; 17:5; 22:14; 24:10). These men (without Judas but with Matthias, Acts 1:26) were primary witnesses of the resurrection of Jesus, and their task was to proclaim the gospel of God, establish churches, and teach sound doctrine (Acts 4:33; 5:12; 5:29; 8:1, 14-18). They did this as they lived in spiritual union with the exalted Jesus through the HOLY SPIRIT promised by Jesus in Jn. 14-16.

Since PAUL met the resurrected and glorified Jesus and was given a commission by him to be the messenger to the Gentiles and the planter of churches in Gentile cities, he called himself an apostle (Rom. 1:1; Gal. 1:1), he defended his right to be known as an apostle (2 Cor. 11-12; Gal. 1), and he was described as an apostle by Luke (Acts 14:14). He believed that suffering was an inescapable part of his apostolic role (1 Cor. 4:9-13; 2 Cor. 4:7-12; 11:23-29), and he held that the church of God was built on Christ as the chief cornerstone and on the apostles as primary foundational stones (Eph. 2:20).

Further, and this information prevents neat and tidy definitions of an apostle, there are others who are called "apostles" in the NT. Included here are fellow-workers of Paul such as BARNABAS (Acts 14:4, 14), SILAS (1 Thess. 2:6), and probably ANDRONICUS and JUNIAS (Rom. 16:7); it is also possible that Paul refers to JAMES, brother of the Lord Jesus, as an apostle in Gal. 1:19, but the meaning of this statement is debated. In any case, these individuals were not of the Twelve (Rev. 21:14) and not on the same footing as Paul, who was uniquely *the* apostle to the Gentiles.

apostolic age. The period in the history of the Christian church when the apostles were alive, beginning with the Day of Pentecost and ending with the death of the apostle John near the end of the first century. See ACTS OF THE APOSTLES.

Apostolic Council. See COUNCIL.

Apostolic Fathers. A collection of early Christian writings (also referred to as Post-Apostolic or Sub-Apostolic) produced by authors thought to have been associated with the apostles. These documents are significant in that they help to close a gap between the NT and later writers. In addition, the Apostolic Fathers provide information about the Christian church in the period immediately after the apostles. The subjects to which one or another refer include the officers of the church, its form of worship, its sacramental observances, its treatment by the civil government, its system of discipline, its ethical teaching, and its ultimate source of authority. The information needs, of course, to be subjected to the usual critical tests before its value can be ascertained.

Usually included in the collection are the following writings. (1) The so-called epistles of Clement: *1 Clement*, written in Rome c. A.D. 95; *2 Clement*,

Codex Sinaiticus, a 4th-cent. MS of the NT that includes two books from the Apostolic Fathers.

© Dr. James C. Martin. St. Catherine's Monastery. Photographed by permission.

A

which is really a sermon by a different author, perhaps originating in Rome c. 140. (2) The epistles of Ignatius, written c. 115 to six churches and one individual: *Ephesians, Magnesians, Trallians, Romans, Philadelphians, Smyrnaeans, Polycarp.* (3) Two documents concerned with Polycarp: his letter to the *Philippians,* c. 115, and the *Martyrdom of Polycarp,* c. 160. (4) The *Didache,* probably from Syria c. 90. (5) The so-called *Epistle of Barnabas,* probably from Egypt, c. 130. (6) The *Shepherd of Hermas,* from Rome, c. 150. (7) The quotations from Papias of Hierapolis, c. 125. (8) The *Epistle to Diognetus.*

apothecary. See OCCUPATIONS AND PROFESSIONS.

Appaim. ap´ay-im (Heb. *ʾappayim H691,* possibly "little-nosed" or "big-nosed" or "angry"). Son of Nadab and descendant of JUDAH (1 Chr. 2:30-31).

apparel. See DRESS.

appeal. No provision was made in the OT for the reconsideration from a lower to a higher court of a case already tried. Exodus 18:26 shows, however, that MOSES provided for lower and higher courts: "The difficult cases they brought to Moses, but the simple ones they decided themselves." In Deut. 17:8-13 provision was made for a lower court, under certain conditions, to seek instructions as to procedure from a higher court; but the decision itself belonged to the lower court.

In NT times the Roman government allowed each synagogue to exercise discipline over Jews, but only the Romans had the power of life and death. A Roman citizen could, however, claim exemption from trial by the Jews and appeal to be tried by a Roman court. PAUL did this when he said, "I appeal to Caesar!" (Acts 25:11). In such cases the litigant either pronounced the Latin word *appellō,* as Paul probably did, or submitted the appeal in writing. In either case the presiding magistrate was under obligation to transmit the file, together with a personal report, to the competent higher magistrate.

Apphia. af´ee-uh (Gk. *Apphia G722,* prob. a native Phrygian name). A lady included in the salutation of Paul's letter to PHILEMON, designated "our [*lit.,* the] sister," probably in the Christian

sense, indicating that she was a member of some prominence in the church (Phlm 2; KJV, following the TR, reads "our beloved Apphia"). Some have argued that she was Philemon's wife; others have suggested that she was his (biological) sister.

Appian Way. ap´ee-uhn. The *Via Appia* was the first of the paved roads that were the supreme engineering achievement of ROME. It was named after Appius Claudius Caecus, the censor, one of the first clear-cut personalities of Roman history. Begun in 312 B.C., the Appian Way ran from Rome to Capua, with a later extension to Brundisium. Parts of the road are still in use. PAUL must have traveled by it from PUTEOLI to Rome (Acts 28:13-16).

Appius, Forum of. ap´ee-uhs, for´uhm. A *forum* was the public square or marketplace of an ancient Roman city (cf. the Gk. AGORA), and the Forum of Appius was a traveler's stop on the APPIAN WAY, about 40 mi. (64 km.) S of ROME, where PAUL was met by Roman Christians on his way to the capital under guard (Acts 28:15).

apple. See PLANTS.

apple of the eye. An English idiom denoting the pupil of the eye, which is precious and, therefore, most carefully guarded. The phrase is used to translate a comparable Hebrew idiom occurring in passages that speak of God's care of his people (Deut. 32:10; Ps. 17:8; Zech. 2:8) and of the preciousness of the divine law (Prov. 7:2). The KJV uses the phrase also in Lam. 2:18, which refers to the literal eye.

apricot. See PLANTS.

apron. See DRESS.

Aqabah, Gulf of. ah´kuh-bah. Also Aqaba. The NE arm of the RED SEA bounded on the W by the SINAI Peninsula and on the E by the Land of MIDIAN (Arabian Desert). SOLOMON's seaport city of EZION GEBER (see also ELATH) situated on this gulf is said to be on the Red Sea (1 Ki. 9:26). During the wilderness wanderings, the Israelites were ordered to go from KADESH BARNEA into the wilderness by the way to the Red Sea, which most naturally refers to the Gulf of Aqabah (Num. 14:25; Deut. 1:40; 2:1). Similarly, after a second stay at Kadesh Barnea, Israel went by way of the Red Sea to go around EDOM, which lay E of the ARABAH (Num. 21:4; Jdg. 11:16).

aqueduct. A channel, covered or open, cut in the rock; a waterway built of stone and sometimes faced with smooth cement; a waterway carried on stone arches across depressions. Aqueducts are used to convey WATER from reservoirs, pools, cisterns, or springs to the places where it is to be used. Aqueducts may have existed even in pre-Israelite times, and continued to be developed until the excellent work of the NABATEAN period (100 B.C. to A.D. 100). The Roman period shows many fine examples. HEZEKIAH excavated the SILOAM tunnel (conduit) to bring water into Jerusalem by a way that could not be stopped up in time of siege (2 Ki. 20:20; 2 Chr. 32:30), and this served the purpose of an aqueduct.

Aquila. ak´wi-luh, uh-kwi´luh (Gk. *Akylas*, "eagle"). A Jewish Christian whom PAUL found at CORINTH on his arrival from ATHENS (Acts 18:2, 18, 26; Rom. 16:3-4; 1 Cor. 16:19; 2 Tim. 4:19). A characteristic feature of Aquila and his wife PRISCILLA is that their names are always mentioned together. All that they accomplished was the result of their unity of spiritual nature and purpose in Christ. Having been among the Jews expelled from ROME, they opened a tentmaking business in Corinth. Because Paul followed the same trade, he was attracted to them. Being in full sympathy with the apostle, they hospitably received him into their home, where he remained for a year and a half. Their willingness to "risk their lives" for him earned the gratitude of all the churches. APOLLOS and many others were helped by their spiritual insight. Aquila and Priscilla had a "church that [met] at their house." Priscilla is usually named first, possibly because she became a Christian first, or because she was more active in Christian endeavors, or perhaps for some other unknown reason.

Ar. ahr (Heb. ʿār *H6840*, possibly "city"). A city in MOAB, E of the DEAD SEA, apparently near the

ARNON River (Num. 21:14-15, 28; Deut. 2:9, 18, 29; Isa. 15:1). The suggestion that Ar was the capital of the Moabites is worth noting. Its location is uncertain, and some think the name could refer to a larger region within Moab.

Ara. air´uh (Heb. ʾărā ʾ *H736*, possibly "lion"). Son of JETHER (1 Chr. 7:38), listed among the "heads of families, choice men, brave warriors and outstanding leaders" of the tribe of ASHER (v. 40).

Arab (people group). a´ruhb, air´uhb. See ARABIA.

Arab (place). a´ruhb, air´uhb (Heb. ʾărāb *H742*, possibly "ambush"). A city in the hill country of the tribe of JUDAH (Josh. 15:52); the site is uncertain, but it is usually identified with modern Khirbet er-Rabiyeh, 8 mi. (13 km.) SW of HEBRON.

Arabah. air´uh-buh (Heb. ʿărābāh *H6858*, "wilderness"). When this Hebrew word is used with the definite article, as it most frequently is, it refers to the great rift valley running S from the Sea of Galilee, including the JORDAN Valley and the DEAD SEA, and extending all the way to the Gulf of AQABAH. As such, it forms a major geographical area of the land of the Bible and certainly the most important feature of the relief of the land. In the KJV, the word is rendered as the proper name "Arabah" only in Josh. 18:18, elsewhere as "desert," "plain," "wilderness." Modern translations more consistently take it as a proper name. Without the Hebrew definite article, the term can be used to refer to desert steppe land in general (e.g., Job 24:5; 39:6; Isa. 33:9; Jer. 17:6). In the plural it could be applied to certain desert sections within the Arabah as a whole (e.g., Num. 26:3; Josh. 5:10; 2 Sam. 15:28; et al.). The modern terms used are *Ghor* ("depression") for the Jordan Valley portion of the Arabah and ʿArabah or *Wadi el-ʿArabah* for that portion S of the Dead Sea.

The Dead Sea is sometimes also referred to as the "Sea of the Arabah" (Deut. 4:49; Josh. 3:16; 12:3; 2 Ki. 14:25). The name "Wadi Arabah" (Amos 6:14 NRSV; "valley of the Arabah" in NIV) may refer to the ZERED River, but some scholars locate it NE of the Dead Sea.

A

Arabia. uh-ray′bee-uh (Heb. *ărāb H6851*, "desert"; Gk. *Arabia G728*). A large peninsula of SW Asia consisting of (1) Arabia Petraea, including PETRA and the peninsula of SINAI; (2) Arabia Deserta, that is, the Syrian desert, between the JORDAN Valley and the EUPHRATES River; (3) Arabia Felix, the southern section. The peninsula is bounded N by the Fertile Crescent, E by the Persian Gulf, SE and S by the Indian Ocean, SW and W by the Red Sea. Arabia is an arid steppe, a rocky tableland with enough rainfall in the interior and S to support considerable population, yet with resources so meager they encourage emigration. With water barriers on three sides, expansion was toward the more fertile lands northward, in successive waves of Canaanites, Israelites, Amorites, Babylonians, Assyrians, Arameans ("Syrians"), Idumeans, and Nabateans, all Semitic peoples. They collided with Indo-Europeans pressing down from Asia Minor and Iran. Israel's proximity to Arabia—with a border ill-defined and difficult to defend, and with a "have-not" population ready to plunder—was a major factor influencing the history of the Hebrew people.

The first mention of Arabia in the Bible by name is in the reign of SOLOMON, when its kings brought gold and spices, either as tribute or in trade (1 Ki. 10:15; 2 Chr. 9:14). Arabians brought tribute to JEHOSHAPHAT (2 Chr. 17:11). They joined the PHILISTINES against JEHORAM, defeating him disastrously (21:16—22:1). At desolate Babylon not even the Arabian nomad would pitch his tent (Isa. 13:20). Isaiah 21:13-17 laid a burden on Arabia. Moral depravity is indicated in Jer. 3:2. The kings of Arabia were involved in judgment on the nations after the Babylonian captivity (Jer. 25:24). Arabia sold cattle to TYRE (Ezek. 27:21). Arabians gave NEHEMIAH trouble when he was rebuilding the walls of Jerusalem (Neh. 2:19; 4:7; 6:1). Arabians were among those present at PENTECOST (Acts 2:11). PAUL went into Arabia, meaning probably the NABATEAN environments of Damascus, soon after his conversion (Gal. 1:17; the belief that he went to Mount Sinai is based on the experiences of Moses and Elijah there and on his mention of "Mount Sinai in Arabia," 4:25).

Arad (person). a′rad, air′ad (Heb. *ărād H6865*, possibly "wild ass" or "fugitive"). Son of Beriah and descendant of BENJAMIN (1 Chr. 8:15).

Arad (place). a′rad, air′ad (Heb. *ărād H6866*, meaning uncertain). A settlement in the NE

Aerial view of ancient Arad (looking N). The Early Bronze (2600 B.C.) lower city is encompassed by a massive wall. The Israelite fortress is situated on the upper area of the tell.

© Dr. James C. Martin

A

NEGEV, modern Tell ʿArad, some 17 mi. (27 km.) S of HEBRON. Arad occupied an excellent strategic position in the middle of a wide, gently rolling plain. The city was a center of civilization as early as the fourth millennium B.C. and again in Abrahamite times (some argue, however, that this Canaanite Arad should be identified with Tell el-Milḥ, c. 8 mi./13 km. SW of Tell ʿArad). Near the NW corner of the fortress at Tell ʿArad stood a sanctuary whose design was similar, but not identical, to that of the nearly contemporary Solomonic TEMPLE. The city is mentioned only four times in the OT (Num. 21:1; 33:40; Josh. 12:14; Jdg. 1:16; in the first two passages the KJV takes it incorrectly as the name of a king). According to Num. 21:1-3, the "king" (or chieftain) of Arad joined battle with the Israelites, the latter being victorious and calling the place Hormah ("destruction"). Numerous fragmentary OSTRACA in Hebrew and Aramaic, dating from the tenth to the fourth century, have been discovered at the site; they provide significant paleographical data and make intriguing, but uncertain, historical allusions.

Arah (person). air´uh (Heb. ʾārah *H783*, possibly "he wonders" or "ox"). **(1)** Son of Ulla and descendant of ASHER, included among the "heads of families, choice men, brave warriors and outstanding leaders" (1 Chr. 7:39-40).

(2) Head of a family that returned from the EXILE with ZERUBBABEL (Ezra 2:5; Neh. 7:10; the numbers of those who returned vary in these passages). He is possibly the same person identified as the father of Shecaniah (Neh. 6:18).

Arah (place). air´uh (Heb. ʿārāh *H6869*, perhaps "bulrush"). Possibly a Sidonian city (Josh. 13:4). The MT reading, *mĕʿārâ* (MEARAH, KJV, NRSV), should perhaps be vocalized so as to read *mēʿārâ*, "from Arah" (so NIV; cf. LXX, "before Gaza," apparently reading the Heb. as *mēʿazzâ*). No city by the name of either Arah or Mearah is known.

Aram. air´uhm (Heb. ʾărām *H806*, "high, exalted"). **(1)** One of the five sons of SHEM and the father of Uz, Hul, Gether, and Mash in the Table of Nations (Gen. 10:22-23, cf. 1 Chr. 1:17); regarded as the ancestor of the ARAMEANS. His name is also used

for a country or region N of Israel and extending eastward to MESOPOTAMIA (called "Syria" in the KJV and other versions). The major Aramean city was DAMASCUS. For further description see SYRIA; see also ARAM NAHARAIM, MAACAH, PADDAN ARAM, and ZOBAH.

(2) Son of Kemuel and grandson of NAHOR, ABRAHAM's brother (Gen. 22:20-21).

(3) Son of Shemer and descendant of ASHER (1 Chr. 7:34).

(4) Son of Hezron, included in the GENEALOGY OF JESUS CHRIST (Matt. 1:3-4 KJV, NRSV; Lk. 3:33 KJV [NRSV, "Arni," following a variant reading]). Here the name represents the Greek *Aram*, which however refers to RAM (cf. NIV in both passages).

Aramaic. air´uh-may´ik. A NW Semitic language, closely related to HEBREW. Already in Gen. 31:47 Aramaic is mentioned as the language used by LABAN in contrast to JACOB's use of Hebrew. By the eighth century B.C. Aramaic had become the language of Assyrian diplomacy, and sufficiently different from Hebrew that the people of Jerusalem did not understand the former (2 Ki. 18:26; Isa. 36:11). Some Aramaic place names and personal names occur in the OT, such as TABRIMMON (1 Ki. 15:18) and HAZAEL (2 Ki. 8:8). Aramaic texts in the OT include one verse in Jeremiah (Jer. 10:11, an answer by the Jews to their Aramaic-speaking conquerors who would seduce them to worship idols) and more substantial sections in Ezra and Daniel (Ezra 4:8—6:18; 7:12-26; Dan. 2:4—7:28), reflecting the adoption of this language by the Jews during the Babylonian EXILE and the Persian period. The Jews also adopted the so-called "square" script of Aramaic to write not only Aramaic but also Hebrew, which previously had been written in a Phoenician-type script known as paleo-Hebrew (see WRITING).

In NT times, GREEK was widely used in Palestine and Hebrew was still spoken to some extent, especially in JUDEA. It is generally recognized, however, that Aramaic was predominant, particularly in GALILEE. Almost certainly it was Jesus' mother tongue, and the NT preserves a number of Aramaic words and phrases spoken by him: ABBA (Mk. 14:36; cf. Rom. 8:15; Gal. 4:6), EPHPHATHA (Mk. 7:34), ELOI, ELOI, LAMA SABACHTHANI

A

(Matt. 27:46; Mk. 15:34), TALITHA KOUM (Mk. 5:41). Aramaic was probably also the language of the early Jewish Christian church, as reflected in the word MARANATHA (1 Cor. 16:22).

Numerous dialects of the language can be distinguished. Examples of Old Aramaic, in various forms, survive in inscriptions dated as early as the tenth century B.C. The language characteristic of the Persian period and used by Ezra and Daniel is known as Official or Imperial Aramaic, subsequent to which a distinction is made between western and eastern dialects. The most important western dialect was Jewish Palestinian Aramaic (prob. Jesus' language), used in the DEAD SEA SCROLLS and in Palestinian rabbinic literature; the NABATEANS and other groups also used a western form of Aramaic. Among the eastern dialects, the most significant were Jewish Babylonian Aramaic (the language of the official TALMUD), Syriac, and Mandaic. Some forms of the language are still spoken today. On the Aramaic Targums, see TEXT AND VERSIONS (OT).

Aramean. air′uh-mee′uhn (Heb. *ʾărammî H812*). Also Aramaean. A descendant of ARAM. More generally, the Arameans were a desert people who had already settled parts of SYRIA and W MESOPOTAMIA prior to the time of ABRAHAM. Centuries later, some of the groups that lived NE of Israel established kingdoms and formed loose confederacies that frequently interacted with the Israelites, usually as enemies. The most important Aramean city was DAMASCUS. Prominent Aramean kings included several by the name (or title) of BEN-HADAD, as well as HADADEZER and REZON, who were rulers in ZOBAH.

Aramitess. air′uh-mi-tes (Heb. *ʾărammîâ*, fem. of *ʾărammî H812*). Term used by KJV with reference to the concubine mother of MAKIR, the father of GILEAD (1 Chr. 7:14; NIV, "Aramean"). See ARAMEAN.

Aram Maacah. air′uhm-may′uh-kuh (Heb. *ʾăram*

maʿăkâ H807). Alternate name of MAACAH (1 Chr. 19:6).

Aram Naharaim. air′uhm-nay-huh-ray′im (Heb. *ʾăram nahărayim H808*, "Aram of the [two] rivers"). This name, usually rendered MESOPOTAMIA by the KJV (following the LXX), refers to the same general area as PADDAN ARAM, roughly between the rivers EUPHRATES and HABOR. Aram Naharaim is identified as the place to which ABRAHAM's servant went in search of a wife for ISAAC (Gen. 24:10) and as the home of BALAAM son of Beor (Deut. 23:4). After the death of JOSHUA, Israel was delivered into the hands of CUSHAN-RISHATHAIM king of Aram Naharaim for eight years (Jdg. 3:8-10), and the AMMONITES later hired horsemen and chariots from Aram Naharaim against DAVID (1 Chr. 19:6; cf. title of Ps. 60).

Aram Zobah. air′uhm-zoh′buh (Heb. *ʾăram ṣôbâ H809*). Alternate name of ZOBAH (Ps. 60, title; cf. 2 Sam. 10:6-8; 1 Chr. 19:6).

Aran. air′an (Heb. *ʾărān H814*, possibly "wild goat"). Son of Dishan (Gen. 36:28; 1 Chr. 1:42), who was a son of SEIR and a HORITE chief (Gen. 36:20-21). Some scholars believe that Aran is a variant of OREN.

Ararat. air′uh-rat (Heb. *ʾărāraṭ H827*, meaning unknown). A country in Armenia, a mountainous tableland from which flow the TIGRIS, EUPHRATES,

Mount Ararat.

© Dr. James C. Martin

Aras (Araxes), and Choruk rivers. Near its center lies Lake Van, which, like the Dead Sea, has no outlet. Its general elevation is about 6,000 ft. (1,830 m.), above which rise mountains to as high as 17,000 ft. (5,180 m.), the height of the extinct volcano that in modern times is called Mount Ararat and on which the ark is supposed to have rested, though the plural in Gen. 8:4 is indefinite: "On the mountains of Ararat." There the sons of SENNACHERIB fled after murdering their father (2 Ki. 19:37; Isa. 37:38). Jeremiah 51:27 associates the kingdoms of Ararat, Minni, and Ashkenaz with the kings of the Medes as prophesied conquerors of Babylonia. The region is now part of Turkey. The Babylonian name was Urartu.

Ararite. See HARARITE.

Araunah (Ornan). uh-raw′nuh, or′nuhn (Heb. *ʾărawnâ H779* in 2 Sam., *ʾornān H821* in 1-2 Chr., possibly the Hurrian term for "lord"). The JEBUSITE who owned the threshing floor on Mount MORIAH that DAVID purchased in order to erect an altar. Because of David's sin in numbering the people, the land was stricken with a plague. When the plague was stayed, David presented a costly offering to the Lord (2 Sam. 24:15-25; called Ornan in 1 Chr. 21:15-28 [KJV and most versions]). The difference between 2 Sam. 24:24 (50 shekels) and 1 Chr. 21:25 (600 shekels) may indicate that Samuel speaks of an immediate transaction covering what David purchased then and there (perhaps only the oxen?), while 1 Chronicles records the (subsequent?) purchase of the whole site. In 2 Sam. 24:16 the Hebrew text has "the Araunah" and in v. 23, "Araunah the king." Was Araunah, then, the last Jebusite king of JERUSALEM, permitted to live on in his city after David captured it? This is no more than an interesting conjecture.

Arba. ahr′buh (only in the name *qiryat ʾarbaʿ H7957*, "city of Arba [= four]"). The ancestor of the ANAKITES and the greatest hero of that race. In the book of Joshua he is described as "the greatest man among the Anakites" (Josh. 14:15) and "the forefather of Anak" (15:13; 21:11). He was the founder of the city named for him, on the site of which HEBRON was built (21:11). At the time of the conquest JOSHUA gave CALEB the city of Hebron as his inheritance because of his confidence that God would enable him to drive out the Anakites (14:6-15). See KIRIATH ARBA.

Arbathite. ahr′buh-thīt (Heb. *ʿarbātî H6863*). A native of the ARABAH or, more likely, of BETH ARABAH. It is the designation given to ABI-ALBON, one of David's "Thirty" (2 Sam. 23:31, named Abiel in 1 Chr. 11:32).

Arbite. ahr′bīt (Heb. *ʾarbî H750*, apparently gentilic of *ʾărāb H742*). This term was probably applied to the inhabitants of ARAB in S Judah (Josh. 15:52). The epithet is used to describe PAARAI, one of David's "Thirty" (2 Sam. 23:35). The parallel list reads "Naarai son of Ezbai" (1 Chr. 11:37). See EZBAI.

arbitrate. See MEDIATOR.

arch. This term is used by the KJV incorrectly in Ezek. 40:16-36, which refers rather to the porches of the temple gates.

archaeology. The study of antiquity through material remains (fossils, artifacts). In modern times it has graduated from a treasure hunt into a highly scientific discipline. W. F. Albright once wrote that next to nuclear science, archaeology has become the fastest-growing discipline in the country. Excavation is only one aspect of the total effort of an archaeological enterprise. Geographical regional surveys, geological analyses, evaluation of artifacts, translation of inscriptions, reconstruction of architecture, examination of human remains, identification of art forms, construction of ceramic pottery typology for chronological purposes, and many other highly complex scientific endeavors constitute a major part of the expedition's work. The end result of it all is to enrich our understanding of unknown aspects of ancient civilizations.

I. **Biblical Archaeology.** G. E. Wright has insisted that biblical archaeology is an armchair variety of general archaeology, but William Dever has correctly emphasized that archaeology is biblical only where and when the scientific methodology of general archaeology uncovers something

A

relative to the Bible. There is no special science or technique available to the biblical scholar. One who digs a biblical site is a biblical archaeologist in the same way that one who digs a classical site is a classical archaeologist. The methods are the same. There are no special methods or aims for biblical archaeology.

Special emphasis should be given to the fact that all reputable archaeology strives for the same total reconstruction of the past and presupposes the same standards of objectivity. As Roland de Vaux pointed out, archaeology cannot prove the Bible. Spiritual truth is of such a nature that it cannot be proven or disproven by the material discoveries of archaeology. The truths of the Bible do not need proving; they are self-evident. But as the Israeli scholar Gaalyah Cornfeld commented in a recent book, "The net effect of archaeology has been to support the general trustworthiness and substantial historicity of the biblical tradition where data are available."

The study of the Bible and the pursuit of archaeology belong together. When Middle-Eastern archaeology began about a century ago, the majority of the excavators were biblical scholars. They recognized the fact that the greatest contribution archaeology could make to biblical studies would be to illuminate our understandings of the cultural settings in which the various books of the Bible were written and which they reflect. That information will, at times, significantly affect our interpretation of relevant sections of the text.

II. The history of Palestinian archaeology. Although some exploration was done as early as medieval times, no real interest was kindled in Middle-Eastern antiquities until after 1600, when cuneiform documents from Persepolis reached Europe. Napoleon took a team of scholars with him in 1798 to study the antiquities of Egypt once he had conquered it. One of his officers discovered the Rosetta Stone, whose identical inscription in three languages unlocked the mystery of Egyptian hieroglyphs and opened the history of Egypt. Palestine was explored in the mid-1800s by Edward Robinson, Charles Warren, C. R. Conder, H. H. Kitchener, and others. A British officer named Henry Rawlinson found a trilingual inscription at Behistun, Persia, that unlocked the mysteries of

cuneiform, and this "Rosetta Stone of Persia" further heightened interest in the lands of the Bible.

Although exploration of Palestine had been remarkably well done by the end of the nineteenth century, excavation was quite rare and virtually worthless. Systematic excavation got underway only after 1870 when Heinrich Schliemann discovered in Troy on the W coast of Turkey that the mounds dotting the horizon all over Bible lands were actually the remains of ancient cities successively destroyed and rebuilt, one on top of another. Lack of understanding about these mounds had reflected itself in Bible translations prior to that time. In Josh. 11:13 the KJV says: "But as for the cities that stood still in their strength, Israel burned none of them save Hazor only." The word "strength" renders Hebrew *tēl H9424* (in Arabic spelled *tell*), a word whose meaning was unknown at that time. Schliemann's work showed that the word rather meant "mound," and modern versions translate the phrase correctly: "the cities that stood on their mounds" (NRSV).

Nevertheless, his work was still of little influence in Palestinian excavation. He realized that these mounds consisted of strata, layers of civilization superimposed one on the other like layers of cake, but he did not know how to date them other than the obvious fact that the oldest ones were at the bottom. It remained for Sir Flinders Petrie to provide the means of dating these strata that has remained our most important method until the present time. In Egypt he became familiar with ceramic pottery that could be dated by tomb inscriptions. In his work in Israel in 1890 he discovered that the same forms of pottery could be found in various strata of his excavation at Tell el-Ḥesi (in SW Palestine, c. 16 mi./26 km. E of GAZA). He observed that the pottery styles changed from layer to layer and that he could date the strata by the changing forms, in much the same way that automobiles can be dated by their changing styles. His work was supplemented by that of W. F. Albright at Tell Beit Mirsim in 1926-32, and an extensive ceramic typology was published that has become a standard basis of comparison for Palestinian archaeologists. This has proven to be the single most important method of dating ancient sites, because the pottery is virtually indestructible and was so easily made that people never bothered to take it when they moved.

III. The future of Palestinian archaeology. Albright trained a generation of archaeologists, both American and Israeli, and work today continues at a feverish pace both by his students and those whom they have trained. These in turn are training a new generation. The "new archaeology," which became prominent in the 1970s, sought to go beyond the concern these scholars had with structures and chronology by attempting to reconstruct the total picture of the society that lived in a given period of history. Such an approach to excavation requires a vast array of expertise, and expeditions are regularly staffed now with such specialists as paleoethnobotanists, geologists, architects, ceramicists, numismatists, stratigraphers, historians, linguists, photographers, geographers, and the like. The days of treasure hunting are over; excavations have become scientific expeditions.

Archaeology is a rapidly developing science. Its potential for significant contribution to the interpretation of the Bible is well established and the future is bright for the discipline. There is much that remains to be done. Paul Lapp estimated in 1963 that of a total of 5,000 sites in Palestine there had been scientific excavations at about 150, including only 26 major excavations. Of the more than 5,000 mounds located in Iraq, ancient Babylonia, and Assyria, fewer than 30 major excavations are documented in Beek's *Atlas of Mesopotamia* (1962), less than 1 percent of the total sites. Yigael Yadin estimated that at the rate of his normal excavation progress at HAZOR in Galilee it would take 8,000 years to thoroughly excavate the site. Hazor covers about 200 acres in its upper and lower sections. How long would it take to thoroughly excavate the 8,000 acres of CAESAREA Maritima?

IV. Recent contributions of archaeology to the study of the Bible.

A. Old Testament. Until recently it was commonly believed that ABRAHAM lived in the Middle Bronze Period (c. 2000-1500 B.C.), but an electrifying new discovery in Syria in 1974 at Tell Mardikh (EBLA) caused Noel Freedman to place him in the Early Bronze period, at a time when Ebla was at its height of power and influence. A royal library was found here consisting of perhaps 20,000 clay

This ostracon from Arad is a letter that reads in part: "To Eliashib. And now, issue from the wine 3 baths. And Hananyahu has commanded you to Beer-Sheba with 2 donkeys' load and you shall wrap up the dough with them. And count the wheat and the bread … "

© Dr. James C. Martin. The Israel Museum. Photographed by permission.

tablets, 80 percent of which were written in Sumerian and the rest in an unknown Semitic language akin to Hebrew that is now called Eblaite. Located halfway between modern Aleppo and Hama, at the top of the Fertile Crescent, the city was in the heart of Abraham's ancestral home territory of HARAN and flourished in c. 2200 B.C. Names similar to those in the Bible (e.g., Eve, Noah) appear in the texts.

The impact of archaeology can also be illustrated by reference to the controversial question of the date of the EXODUS. A thirteenth-century B.C. date has been indicated by destruction levels that date to that century in excavations of Hazor, Jericho, Ai, Lachish, and other sites mentioned in the book of Joshua. John Bimson argued in a publication in 1978 that neither the archaeological nor the biblical evidence militates against an early date. His selectivity in handling archaeological data, however, has limited the influence of his book among archaeologists. A growing trend sees the exodus not as an event but as a series of events beginning with some sort of violent intrusion followed by a more socioeconomic upheaval of people within the land. Both Yigael Yadin and Yohanan Aharoni held such a view. The early date has also been argued, among others, by Eugene Merrill, who points out that the thirteenth-century evidence of destruction is irrelevant because the Bible does not really say Joshua destroyed these cities, only that he conquered them and reused them. He considers Hazor an exception to this policy (Josh. 11:13). Therefore he does not expect to find destruction levels associated with Joshua's conquest. But it should be pointed out that Jericho was burned (6:24)! The more daring views of Norman Gottwald and Robert Boling, that the conquest was not a military invasion at all, are so at variance with the straightforward reading of the biblical text that they will not likely secure a large following. To call it merely an economically based sociological upheaval is inadequate.

The period of the monarchy has been significantly touched by the excavations at Hazor, Megiddo, Jerusalem, and Gezer. These cities, which were renovated by Solomon (1 Ki. 9:15), have been found to have unique water systems, and all but Jerusalem have unique city gates. Jerusalem has not been thoroughly excavated, however, because it continues to be a living city. The water systems consist of hidden underground springs outside the city walls. Water is brought through a secret tunnel into the city to a pool that is reached by a stairway. The gates have four protruding sections facing each other from two separate structures, producing three compartments within, and are unique in ancient Palestine. Excavations on Mount Ophel by Yigal Shiloh in the early 1980s have produced a part of the city wall just S of the temple mount that may belong to Solomon, extending below and not into sixth-century-B.C. buildings as Kathleen Kenyon had previously thought when she first excavated the wall and dated it to the time of Nehemiah.

Asher Kaufmann has found convincing evidence of foundational cuttings for the temples of Solomon and Zerubbabel/Herod on the NW corner of the temple platform. The cuttings coincide with the 16.7-inch (42.8-cm.) cubit used in the construction of the first temple and the 17-inch (43.7-cm.) cubit used in the second temple. These line up the Most Holy Place with the modern Golden Gate, solving a previously inexplicable problem of the misalignment of this gate in relation to the cur-

rent Dome of the Rock, which has been assumed to sit over the temple site. In 1983 James Fleming published his discovery of another gate beneath this one belonging either to the second or tenth centuries B.C., possibly built by Solomon.

A stunning discovery was made in 1980 during the excavation of a sixth-century-B.C. burial cave in Jerusalem. It was a silver amulet, 3.82 in. (9.8 cm.) long, containing the ancient Hebrew name of God (Yahweh) inscribed on it. Although the name is found more than 6,800 times in the OT, this is the first time that the name has been found in excavations in Jerusalem.

In 1977 the tomb of Philip II of Macedon was found in Vergina, Greece, containing the bones, armor, and gold diadem of this king. His son ALEXANDER THE GREAT made Greek the universal language of the empire, the language in which the books of the NT were originally written. The lid of his golden casket was decorated with the golden sunburst, symbol of the Macedonian kings.

Equally important but not so recent are a number of finds that significantly contribute to our understanding of the OT. A number of discoveries have greatly weakened the Wellhausian theory of the evolutionary development of the Israelite religion. This theory advocated that Moses could not have written the PENTATEUCH because neither language nor the concept of law had yet developed to the advanced stage represented in the law of Moses. In refutation of this, James Pritchard has published in *ANET* four law codes found in Mesopotamia that are older than those of Moses and are almost identical in the casuistic ("if … then") portions. The Ur-Nammu Law Code was produced by the founder of the third dynasty of Ur and builder of the best preserved ziggurat in Mesopotamia. He ruled from 2112 to 2095 B.C. Twenty-nine laws are extant. The Eshunna Code found in a suburb of Baghdad (also called the Code of Bilalama) was published by Bilalama, who reigned about 1950 B.C. Sixty laws are extant. The Lipit Ishtar Code was produced by this fifth ruler of the dynasty of Isin who ruled from 1864 to 1854. Thirty-eight laws are extant. The Hammurabi Code dates from his reign, 1728 to 1686, and there are 282 laws inscribed on a stela preserved in the Louvre in Paris. All of these are casuistic in nature, like the

Book of the Covenant in Exod. 21-24. No apodictic laws ("You shall not ...") have yet been found in the Middle East corresponding to Exod. 20.

An account of the FLOOD, called the Gilgamesh Epic, was found in 1853 in the midst of a long and beautiful Babylonian poem, excavated as a part of ASHURBANIPAL's library in NINEVEH. It contains remarkable parallels to the biblical account, such as a warning of the coming flood, the building of an ark, the flood coming, the ark resting on a mountain, and birds being sent out to find land. The hero of the story corresponding to the biblical Noah is Utnapishtim who, like Noah, offers a sacrifice after the flood. Pritchard dates the original composition of the work to c. 2000 B.C. The story is found in many ancient languages including Assyrian, Hittite, Hurrian, and Sumerian.

The period of the patriarchs has been illuminated by the discovery in 1925 of approximately one thousand clay tablets at Nuzi in Mesopotamia, written in Akkadian cuneiform and dating to the fifteenth century B.C. Even though they were written about three centuries after the patriarchal period, they are generally acknowledged to reflect much older material, throwing light on customs that existed in the very region inhabited by the family of Abraham. There are parallels to numerous customs mentioned in Genesis, such as the importance of the patriarchal blessing that Isaac gave Jacob, the giving of a handmaid to one's husband as Sarah gave Hagar to Abraham, the transfer of a birthright as Isaac did from Esau to Jacob, the proof of ownership of property by the possession of one's family idols (explaining why Rachel stole her father's teraphim). These indicate that the appropriate setting for the stories told in Genesis is the second millennium B.C. and not the first, as some radical critics claimed.

For the period of the exodus and conquest much of the older evidence has been reevaluated by later digs and better dating techniques, though, as discussed above, there is still no substantial agreement about either the nature or date of these events. Garstang's dates for Jericho and Hazor have been shown to be wrong by Kenyon and Yadin respectively, while work in the past seventy years at other sites mentioned in Joshua—such as Gibeon, Ai, Azekah, and Lachish—have yielded dates for destruction levels later than most readings of the biblical data will easily warrant. Kenyon dated the fall of Jericho earlier than the usual late date (13th cent. B.C.) but much later than the early date (15th cent.). Both archaeological methodology and the handling of biblical chronology are still imperfect, and the results yielded are less than certain.

Our understanding of the religion of the Canaanites at the time of the conquest has been greatly increased by the discovery of ancient Ugarit (RAS SHAMRA) in 1928 and its subsequent excavation. A library was found there by Claude Schaeffer dating to the period of the city's greatest literary and cultural achievements (1600-1200 B.C.), and written in what we now call Ugaritic. It testifies to the depraved nature of Canaanite religion at this time, including the boiling of a goat kid in its mother's milk, a practice warned against in Exod. 23:19 and 34:26 and which probably lies at the heart of the kosher laws. In addition to considerable information about the Canaanite idol BAAL, against whom strong invectives are made in the Bible, there appears also the astonishing fact that the chief deity of the Canaanites was named EL, the same name used by the Jews for their God. Help is being found in this library for correcting our misimpressions of some words in our Hebrew Bibles.

Considerably more information was gained about the various cities of Palestine about the time of the exodus and conquest by the discovery of the AMARNA Letters dating to the reign of Amenhotep IV (Akhenaten) and his father in the late fourteenth century B.C. These clay tablets, written in the Babylonian language, were found in Tell el-Amarna, Egypt, in 1887. They refer to a marauding class of people called Habiru, who may possibly be the Hebrews, though this is not certain.

In the fifth year of the Pharaoh Merneptah (c. 1223-1211 B.C.) he commemorated his military achievements over the eastern Mediterranean by setting up a black granite stela with an extensive inscription containing among other references these words: "Canaan is plundered with every evil; Ashkelon is taken; Gezer is captured ... Israel lies desolate." This is the earliest reference to Israel in antiquity.

Important references to people mentioned in the Bible have been found in the centuries following the monarchy. The divided kingdom after SOLO-MON (9th to 6th centuries B.C.) was affected by Syrians, Moabites, Assyrians, and Babylonians, all of whom left witness of their relation to biblical events in official monuments. The ninth-century MOABITE STONE, erected by Mesha, king of Moab, was found at Diban in Jordan in 1868. It contains references to OMRI, king of Israel (2 Ki. 3). The Zakir Stele, also ninth century, found in 1907 S of Aleppo, commemorates a victory of Zakir, king of HAMATH, over BEN-HADAD. The Assyrian sources have been shown to be basically reliable, as have those of the Neo-Babylonian period. Historical texts from these two empires have been found in Nineveh, Nimrud, Ashur, and Babylon. The Kurkh Stele, erected in the mid-ninth century, contains the name of AHAB the Israelite (1 Ki. 16:29). The Black Obelisk of SHALMANESER III not only contains the name of "Jehu, son of Omri," a king of Israel (2 Ki. 10:28-29) in the late ninth century, but also has a depiction of him bowing before Shalmaneser. Jehu is bearded and wears a sleeveless mantle over a long fringed and girded tunic. This is the only contemporary depiction of any Israelite king.

In the eighth century B.C. the Annals of TIGLATH-PILESER III mention that King MENAHEM paid tribute, the amount being clearly stated in 2 Ki. 15:19-20. This document also refers to a certain Azriau of Yaudi, probably Azariah (UZZIAH) of Judah (2 Chr. 26:6-15). The Nimrud Tablet of the same century claims that Tiglath-Pileser set HOSHEA over Israel after PEKAH was deposed (2 Ki. 15:29-31). A slab inscription from the SE palace at Nimrud states that Jehoahaz (long form of AHAZ) of Judah paid tribute to Tiglath-Pileser (16:8). There is frequent mention in this century of Israel, called "the House of Omri," in the various inscriptions of SARGON II (722-205).

SENNACHERIB, his successor (705-681), left a fascinating reference to a Jewish king in the Taylor Prism, which says that "Hezekiah the Jew [*lit.* Judean]" resisted the Assyrian monarch and "he himself I shut up like a caged bird within Jerusalem" (cf. 2 Ki. 18:13-14). Interestingly the prism makes no mention of the actual conquest of Jerusalem. The reason is that he never conquered it. He lost 185,000 troops by the hand of God during the siege, and he went back to Nineveh (19:35-36).

The Bull Inscription, however, boasts that Sennacherib "laid waste the district of Judah [Iaudi] and made the overbearing and proud Hezekiah, its king, bow submissively at my feet." A slab inscription found at Nineveh claims, "I overthrew the wide district of Judah. I imposed my [yoke-] ropes upon Hezekiah, its king." The Annals of Assyria, which detail the exploits of ESARHADDON (681-669), successor of Sennacherib, mention the subservience of "Manasseh, king of Judah" (2 Ki. 21). Esarhaddon is mentioned in 2 Ki. 19:37; Isa. 37:38; Ezra 4:2.

One of the most important documents of the period is the Babylonian Chronicle, containing a running and probably contemporary record of the exploits of the Babylonians in Syria, Palestine, and other countries. It states that "the Babylonian king [Nebuchadnezzar] … on the second day of the month of Adar [March 16, 597 B.C.] took the city and captured the king [Jehoichin]" (2 Ki. 24:12-13). This gives a firm date for OT and Babylonian chronology. CYRUS the Persian, who conquered the Babylonians in October of 539, left a clay cylinder inscribed in cuneiform that tells of his decree allowing conquered peoples to rebuild their cities and religious shrines. This is consistent with the biblical record of the return of the Jews from Persia to Palestine in the books of Ezra and Nehemiah.

B. New Testament. HEROD the Great was king of the Jews when Jesus was born. He was the greatest builder in Jewish history, having completed projects in twenty different sites in Palestine and thirteen outside the land. Extensive remains of his program have been found in recent excavations that supplement what we already know about him. At CASEAREA Maritima portions of his wall around the city have been found since 1972, including the northern gate. His harbor and about a hundred vaulted warehouses stretching along the harbor have been discovered in underwater excavation. The high-level aqueduct and the small theater in which he dedicated his newly built city have long been identified. An inscription bearing the name of Pontius PILATE was found in the theater.

Herod's desert palace at Herodium, S of BETHLEHEM, has been shown to have seven levels in the large donut-shaped mound. The lower palace has an esplanade and large square pool found by Ehud

Netzer. The esplanade leads to a building complex that Netzer thinks may contain the tomb of Herod. A unique circular pavilion with concentric walls stood in the middle of a pool, its unique design appearing in Palestine only in Herod's building projects, for example, in the middle level pavilion

© Dr. James C. Martin

Volunteers excavate the area of the Essene Gate in Jerusalem.

at Masada's northern palace and in the frigidarium (unheated bathing pool) of the Roman bath in his palace at JERICHO. A portion of a similar structure has been found in the area just N of the Damascus Gate in Jerusalem which Netzer thinks may be the family tomb of Herod. This structural oddity may have influenced the design of the similar edifice in Hadrian's villa outside Rome. Yadin's excavation of Masada, on the W side of the Dead Sea, revealed a massive complex of buildings constructed by Herod, consisting of casemate walls, a northern palace in three tiers, a large bathhouse, a swimming pool, many huge cisterns, warehouses, and a dining hall later converted into a synagogue.

In the 1970s Herod's winter palace at Jericho was found by Ehud Netzer and Eric Meyers and was extensively excavated, revealing a large reception hall with an adjoining apse leading to a large Roman bath. Included in the complex was the older Hasmonean winter palace containing many pools, including the large one in which Herod had Aristobulus drowned. It also contained several of the oldest mikvehs (Jewish pools for ritual bathing) yet found in Palestine (2nd cent. B.C.).

Evidence of his work in Jerusalem is seen in the tower still standing in the Jaffa Gate, which Titus left to show the greatness of the city he had conquered. A considerable portion of the Herodian courses of stone undergirding his expansion of the temple mount have been exposed, including some monoliths that weigh 400 tons (364 metric tons). The arches holding up the southern end of the temple mount are Herodian, not Solomonic.

Excavations at CAPERNAUM have revealed that the synagogue there is not earlier than the fourth century A.D. but that it was built over a first-century synagogue whose basalt stone floors and walls have been found directly beneath the floor of the fourth-century prayer hall. This no doubt was the synagogue that Jesus attended while in Capernaum with Simon Peter. The house of PETER may have been located immediately S of the synagogue, built of the same basalt stone found in the earlier synagogue. A large room in the center of the house has evidently been venerated since the mid-first century when the pottery found in the room ceased to be domestic. The walls were plastered about this time, the only excavated house in Capernaum so done. On the wall 130 graffiti in several languages mention Jesus as Lord and Christ, among other things. The room was designated by an arch and then covered in the fourth century by a square Byzantine church building, over which a fifth-century octagonal church was built with a mosaic floor that remained there until the recent excavations.

In Jerusalem the pool of BETHESDA (Jn. 5:2) has been excavated just inside the eastern Lion Gate, and farther to the S the pool of SILOAM (9:7) is easily identified by HEZEKIAH's tunnel connecting it with the GIHON Spring. Thirty steps leading up to the temple mount through the southern gates of Hulda, 200 ft. (60 m.) in width, have been found along with adjacent houses from the time of Christ.

A

Underground walkways and aqueducts have been excavated in this area dating to the same period. A portion of an aqueduct built by Pontius Pilate has recently been found in Bethlehem; this aqueduct brought water to Jerusalem from S of Hebron. The stone pavement on which Jesus stood before Pilate (Jn. 19:13) is almost certainly to be identified with the courtyard of the Fortress of ANTONIA, beneath the Sisters of Zion Convent. Excavations of Kathleen Kenyon have shown that the modern Church of the Holy Sepulchre, the probable site of the crucifixion and burial of Jesus, was outside the first-century city wall. Ancient burials for everyone but kings and high officials were outside the walls.

In 1947 the DEAD SEA SCROLLS were found on the NW shore of the Dead Sea in a number of caves, deposited there by a sect of Jews generally identified as ESSENES. Their walled community nearby was excavated from 1953 to 1956, revealing several large cisterns used for baptisms and for storage of water brought in by aqueduct from the cliffs to the west. It is possible that JOHN THE BAPTIST was acquainted with this sect in his earlier life. They not only baptized, but, like John, used Isa. 40:3 to justify their being in the wilderness. He preached in this area and baptized Jesus not far away. Ten of eleven caves found produced tens of thousands of fragments of ancient books including some of every book of the OT. A full copy of Isaiah was found dating to the second century B.C., the oldest copy of a book of the Hebrew Bible. The Essenes' documents were produced between 200 B.C. and A.D. 50. The community, consisting of perhaps 200 members, was destroyed by the Romans about A.D. 68.

In recent decades many papyri containing books of the NT dating into the third and even the second century A.D. have been found, such as the Bodmer II papyrus of the complete Gospel of John, the Chester Beatty papyri of Paul's letters, and the John Rylands fragment of Jn. 18 (which dates to the early 2nd cent., making it the oldest surviving piece of any book of the NT). A third-century Greek inscription of Rom. 13:3 was found in 1972 in excavations at Caesarea Maritima. It is part of a mosaic floor belonging to a building that was constructed in the third century and destroyed in the seventh.

In 1945 a complete library was discovered at NAG HAMMADI, Egypt, that contains many apocryphal NT books along with other books related to the religion of second-century Gnostic sects. Originally produced in Greek, they were translated into Coptic in the fourth century. These documents are extremely valuable for studying the milieu of early Christianity. Gnostic-type groups constituted a challenge to mainline Christianity in these early centuries, replacing the biblical emphasis on faith with that of a special kind of knowledge (*gnosis*; see GNOSTICISM). They seem to have prompted the finalizing of the limits of the NT canon.

An important discovery bearing on the chronology of the NT was reported privately by Jerry Vardaman, who has found coins with an accession date of A.D. 56 for FESTUS, before whom Paul appeared (Acts 25:1; unfortunately, Vardaman has not published his material). Very important is the older discovery of the GALLIO inscription in Delphi, Greece, which places this proconsul in Greece in the spring of 51, and thus PAUL's arrival there about eighteen months earlier (18:11).

An inscription dating probably to the middle of the first century A.D. was found in the pavement NE of the large theater in Corinth, reading ERASTUS. PRO. AED/S.P.STRAVIT. It means that Erastus, in return for his aedileship (an aedile was a Roman official in charge of public works), laid the pavement at his own expense. Unabbreviated it would read "Erastus pro aedilitate sua pecunia stravit." This must refer to the same Erastus whom Paul mentions as "treasurer of the city" of Corinth, for whom Rom. 16:23 was undoubtedly written! Also found in excavations at Corinth is the *bema* (referred to in a Latin inscription in Corinth as *rostra*), the tribunal or platform where Paul would have stood before Gallio (Acts 18:12-17).

Excavations in EPHESUS have revealed the 22,000-seat theater where an irate crowd assembled to express opposition to Paul's attack on ARTEMIS, the patron goddess of the city (Acts 19:29). Her temple was one of the seven wonders of the ancient world. Two magnificent statues of Artemis were found, illuminating references to her in Acts 19:24-25.

Luke's accuracy as a witness to the historical circumstances of early Christian missionary activity is indicated by the discovery of an inscription, now in the British Museum, that stood in an arch at the W end of the Egnatian Way in THESSALONICA. It begins "In the days of the politarchs ... ," using a word for Roman officials that critics said Luke had mistakenly used in Acts 17:6, since it has not been found anywhere else in Greek literature. A number of inscriptions have now been found that contain the word.

archangel. See ANGEL.

Archelaus. ahr´kuh-lay´uhs (Gk. *Archelaos G793*). Son of Herod the Great; he succeeded his father as ruler of IDUMEA, SAMARIA, and JUDEA in 4 B.C., but was deposed by the Roman government in A.D. 6. Archelaus is mentioned once in the NT (Matt. 2:22). See HEROD.

archers. Bowmen, hunters, or warriors with bow and arrows. ISHMAEL is the first man so named in the Bible (Gen. 21:20). JOSEPH is represented as victor in a battle of archery (49:23-24). Archery played a part in a crisis in the relations of DAVID and JONATHAN (1 Sam. 20:17-42). PHILISTINE archers mortally wounded SAUL (1 Sam. 31:3; 1 Chr. 10:3). It is said of the sons of Ulam, descendants of BENJAMIN, that they "were brave warriors who could handle the bow" (1 Chr. 8:40). JOSIAH was killed by archers (2 Chr. 35:23), and JOB compared his troubles to being surrounded by archers (Job 16:13). Archers are mentioned elsewhere (e.g., Isa. 21:17; 22:3; Jer. 50:29). Light-armed, mobile, effective at a distance, archers were valuable in any ARMY, and their skill was no less useful in hunting.

Archevite. ahr´kuh-vit (Aram. *ʾarkěwāy H10074*, gentilic derived from a place name; cf. Heb. *ʾerek H804*). This term in the KJV transliterates a name referring to people from the Babylonian city of ERECH (Uruk). Along with the Persians, Babylonians, Elamites, and others, they were transplanted by ASHURBANIPAL (Osnappar) to the cities of SAMARIA and other parts of the province (Ezra 4:9-10).

Archi. ahr´ki. See ARKITE.

Archippus. ahr-kip´uhs (Gk. *Archippos G800*, "master of the horse"). A Christian at COLOSSE, conspicuous as a champion of the gospel, a close friend (or perhaps the son or brother) of PHILEMON, an office-bearer in the church (Col. 4:17; Phlm. 2). Because of the spiritual laxity at Colosse (like LAODICEA, Rev. 3:14-19), it is not surprising to find that PAUL exhorts this fellow soldier to maintain his zeal and fidelity.

Archite. See ARKITE.

architecture. The art or science of building. As a form of art, architecture is the effort to make a building aesthetically pleasing as well as useful. It must be classified as an abstract art, for it is the least representational of all the arts. For example, an artist who wished to portray the Madonna and Child could hardly use architecture as his medium; some architects, especially in modern times, have indeed attempted to use symbolism in order to make it representational, but even this is greatly limited. Architecture could further be described as the most social of the arts, since a building is usually designed for more than one person, whether it is a church, a railroad station, or a home. The sole exception probably would be the monument or tomb that is intended simply to contain the remains of a single individual.

The materials of architecture in antiquity were wood, clay, brick (formed of clay, whether sunbaked or kiln-fired), and stone. In general, local availability determined the material used. It is well known that wooden beams were exported from LEBANON (the famed "cedars of Lebanon") to practically all parts of the ANE; likewise the beautiful and distinctive rose granite was exported from the quarries at Aswan in Upper Egypt to many lands to be used for columns and statues, but these are notable exceptions.

One of the earliest materials for building is known as "wattle and daub," formed by driving stakes into the ground and interlacing reeds or flexible twigs to form the framework, and then covering both sides with clay. When the clay had dried in the sun it was quite permanent and required only a periodic coat of plaster to preserve it. Wattle-and-daub walls have been found dating

A

back to the earliest period of building, namely the late Neolithic period. Buildings of this material can be included under the subject of architecture only in the broadest sense of the word, however, for they give little indication of any aesthetic quality.

Clay bricks seem to have been invented by the Obeid people in PERSIA before they descended to the Mesopotamian plain early in the fourth millennium B.C. The temple of Abu Shahrein (known in ancient times as Eridu) in S Mesopotamia and that at Tepe Gawra in N Mesopotamia (both from

The Giza pyramids and sphinx are representatives of early Egyptian art and architecture.

the early part of the fourth millennium) can clearly be described as architectural buildings, incorporating several features that became characteristic of Mesopotamian architecture. We mention here only the use of the buttress, designed not so much to strengthen the construction as to break up the monotonous expanse of a clay-brick wall.

In Egypt early builders experimented not only with clay and brick but also with wood, and then they made a remarkable transition to stone masonry. The genius traditionally connected with this new building technique was Imhotep, the designer and builder of the Step Pyramid at Saqqara in the time of Zoser (or Djoser) of the 3rd dynasty (c. 2780 B.C.). From an examination of the remains at Saqqara there seems to be little doubt that the builders were seeking to imitate wood through the medium of stone. We find simulated hinges, boards carved in stone doors that obviously could

not function, and other features that would be useful in wood but only ornamental in stone.

In the same building compound at Saqqara are found such remarkable features as the proto-Doric column (which seems to have been formed in stone after the pattern of papyrus bundles), the cornice, corner posts, and other architectural elements. The columns, it should be added, are not freestanding but are an integral part of the stone building; yet they cannot properly be identified as pilasters, since they have all of the other features of the column. Fluting is not only concave in the customary Doric manner but also convex, and the capitals appear to be papyrus and palm leaves, which compare to the acanthus leaves of the Corinthian columns of Greek architecture of a much later period. If the columns were freestanding, the fluting would number from fourteen to twenty around the circumference of the column, which compares to twenty flutes in the classical Doric order.

One of the early problems to be faced in building was the construction of the roof, and the solutions led to two main forms of architecture: *trabeated* and *arcuated*. The trabeated form is designed and constructed using horizontal beams supported by vertical posts, commonly called "post and lintel." The arcuated form makes use of various modifications of the arch. In the trabeated form the length of span between vertical supports is limited by the strength of the material used for the lintel. If, for example, the lintels were constructed of stone, as in ancient Egypt, it was only by using stone of great thickness that a span of any reasonable length could be obtained; as a result the space between columns in Egyptian temples is not much greater than the diameter of the columns. Wooden beams, on the other hand, permitted more useful space between the uprights. With the modern invention of structural steel and reinforced concrete, the span reaches probably its greatest limit.

An attempt to solve this problem resulted in the development of the arch. The first step was probably the corbelled vault, which is formed by stepping out successive courses of brick or stone beyond the supporting wall or column to meet similar corbelling from the adjacent vertical support. Corbelled vaults can be found at Ur in Mesopotamia as early as the Early Dynastic Period (c. 3000-2340

A

B.C.) and in Egypt as early as the tombs of the 3rd dynasty (c. 2780-2680) at Reqaqnah and Beit Khallaf. To judge from predynastic drawings from Egypt, the true arch may have developed from the practice of bending reeds, which had been erected vertically to form side walls, so they would join overhead to form a roof. The arch, which is but a refinement of corbelling to effect a curved line rather than a steplike appearance, is found also in some of the buildings of Ur. However, the arch does not seem to have been used successfully in large buildings until the Roman period and is generally attributed to the Etruscans. A modification of the corbelled vault, in which the stones form the sides of a triangle coming to an apex overhead, is found in Mycenaean tombs at Mycenae and Ugarit, dating from the fifteenth or fourteenth century B.C.

Unusual styles of architecture include the pyramid-shaped building. The ZIGGURAT in Mesopotamia is generally believed to be the representative of a mountain; it was built of clay brick with exterior staircases or a sloping ramp and probably a shrine at the top. One of the best preserved has recently been excavated at Choga Zambil, 23 mi. (37 km.) SE of Susa in Iran. The pyramids in Egypt were built as tombs and were constructed of stone, having an inner room or rooms. The Egyptians developed great precision in squaring and orienting their pyramids.

The Levant (the lands on the eastern shore of the Mediterranean) exhibited very poor architecture in the early second millennium B.C., and what little there is of quality can be traced to external origins. Original architecture does, however, seem to have developed in N Syria, the most characteristic being the *bit ḫilani*, a temple or palace compound that incorporates a portico and a throne room with their long axis parallel to the façade, behind which are small rooms, probably bedrooms and a storeroom. This pattern was developed in the second millennium but became characteristic of the early first millennium B.C. One feature of N Syrian architecture that should be mentioned is the use of a zoomorphic (animal form) base to support a column and often a human figure for the column itself.

Among the Israelites architecture does not seem to have been developed as an art or a skill; rather,

Phoenician craftsmen were brought in to build Solomon's PALACE and TEMPLE. Phoenician elements appear to be present also in the buildings of subsequent Israelite periods; it is difficult to classify these, however, for the Phoenicians made use of many techniques and styles, some of which can be traced to Cyprus and Egypt. Their use of metal work in architecture (e.g., the columns in front of Solomon's temple) was possibly derived from Asia Minor. See PHOENICIA.

The HITTITES made use of stone foundations, often using large stones, at first rough but later dressed; characteristically the first course was set with the long dimension vertical. The upper portions of their buildings were frequently built of sun-dried brick strengthened by wooden beams, a type of architecture that can be found in the same areas of Asia Minor to the present time.

Late Assyrian architecture is perhaps best understood through the excavations of the palace of SARGON II at Khorsabad (720-704 B.C.). Regularity and a notable use of symmetry in the buildings are characteristic. Much of the work was still of clay brick, with the use of glazed bricks (a technique that had been imported by the Mitanni from Crete) to protect the exterior or exposed surfaces, as well as to lend a decorative element.

Persian architecture seems to have developed the use of the cyclopean foundation, which may have come from the Urartians in the region of Lake Van. This use of huge stones, sometimes with drafting around the edges, is comparable to the well-known Herodian use of large stones; particularly true of Taht-i-Sulayman N of Pasargadae in Iran, the foundation stones there could easily be mistaken for those at Ramat el-Khalil near HEBRON, a town built by HEROD several centuries later. The Persians apparently brought in the Ionic column from the Greek world and developed and used it widely. The base of Persian columns is characteristically Ionic with fluting; the double volute or spiral at the capital is likewise Ionic, but the columns are more slender and graceful. Some idea of the gracefulness of Persian columns may be gained from the fact that the ratio of the height to the diameter, which in Egyptian columns is rarely more than six to one and which attained a maximum of ten to one in the Corinthian order,

A

is twelve to one in the Hall of XERXES at Persepolis. Likewise the distance between the columns, which in Egypt is rarely much more than one diameter and in Greek architecture from one to slightly less than three diameters, in Persian buildings is between three and one-half and seven diameters. This gave the halls a sense of spaciousness not found in other large buildings of antiquity. One feature of the capital of the Persian column is unique, namely the use of a stylized bull with a head at either end, the heads serving to support the longitudinal beams, while the hollow of the back supported the transverse beams.

The supreme achievement in architecture is admittedly the Periclean architecture of GREECE (460-400 B.C.). This is the Doric order characterized by simplicity and symmetry. There are certain optical refinements, among which may be mentioned the use of *entasis* (a slight convexity in columns to avoid the impression of hollowness that straight lines would give), similarly a slight convexity of long horizontal lines (to avoid the appearance of sagging), deviation from perpendicular at the corners of the building and from exact intervals of spacing between the columns (to avoid the appearance that the end columns are leaning outward and that the central columns are too close together). We can clearly see the developments of the Doric order if we consult first of all the Temple of Apollo at CORINTH (about the 6th cent.), then the great temple of Poseidon at Paestum in Italy (early 5th cent.). The Ionic order achieved its classical form during this same period, having originated along the Asiatic coast of the Aegean Sea. The Corinthian order developed toward the end of the fifth and the beginning of the fourth century and reached its zenith in the Greco-Roman period a few centuries later.

Roman architecture owed much to the Greeks but adopted some elements from the Etruscans; among the latter is principally the arch. In general we may say that Roman is not as subtle, but at the same time it is more utilitarian. The Greeks had developed the skill of masonry to a high degree of perfection and fit marble blocks together with remarkable accuracy without mortar or cement. The Romans, on the other hand, developed the use of pozzolana, a volcanic earth that was mixed with lime to make a hydraulic cement. Using this as mortar, they were able to bond courses of stone without exact precision in masonry, increase the span in arches, and build two-story structures. Roman architecture, even more than Greek, included memorial arches and columns, amphitheaters, theaters, forums (or marketplaces), and many other forms familiar to us from the numerous remains of the Roman world to be found all over the Middle East.

Arcturus. ahrk-toor´uhs. One of the brightest stars in the sky, found in the constellation Boötes. It is the KJV rendering of two Hebrew terms (in Job 9:9; 38:2) that are now usually understood as a reference to the constellation of the Great Bear (Ursa Major or Big Dipper). See ASTRONOMY.

Ard. ahrd (Heb. *ʾard H764*, possibly "hunchbacked"; gentilic *ʾardi H766*, "Ardite"). Listed among the "sons" of BENJAMIN in Gen. 46:21, but identified more specifically as a son of BELA and therefore as Benjamin's grandson in Num. 26:40, which also describes him as head of the Ardite clan; called ADDAR in 1 Chr. 8:3.

Ardon. ahr´don (Heb. *ʾardôn H765*, possibly "hunchbacked"). Son of CALEB (apparently by AZUBAH) and descendant of JUDAH (1 Chr. 2:18).

Areli. uh-ree´li (Heb. *ʾarʾēli H739* [possibly variant of *ʾărîʾēl H791*; see ARIEL], gentilic *ʾarʾēli H740*, "Arelite"). Son of GAD and ancestral head of the Arelite clan (Gen. 46:16; Num. 26:17).

Areopagite. See DIONYSIUS.

Areopagus. air´ee-op´uh-guhs (Gk. *Areios pagos G740*, "hill of Ares," also known as "Mars' Hill"; Ares was the Gk. god of war, corresponding to Mars in the Roman pantheon). A large, irregular outcropping of limestone about 380 ft. (115 m.) high. It lies NW of the ACROPOLIS, to which it is connected by a low, narrow saddle, and overlooks the AGORA, the marketplace of classical and Hellenistic ATHENS. Areopagus is also the name of the council that met on Mars' Hill, a court dating back to legendary times, and in NT days still

A

Looking from the Acropolis in Athens, we see the Areopagus (the limestone outcrop also known as Mars' Hill) with the agora or market place below it. (View to the N.)

charged with questions of morals and the rights of teachers who lectured in public. Its importance was enhanced under the Romans. PAUL was brought to the Areopagus to be examined regarding his teaching (Acts 17:19-22). Before these "solid citizens," the bulwark of civic and religious conservatism, Paul met the mocking taunts of the EPICUREANS and the STOICS, adherents of two of that day's most popular philosophies. His address is today more widely read than any of the writings of the philosophers and is almost the only means by which we remember the Council of Areopagus. Paul's mission in Athens produced numerically scant results, and the founding of no church is recorded; but DIONYSIUS the Areopagite, one of the members of this honorable court, and a woman named DAMARIS were among those who "became followers of Paul and believed" (17:34).

Aretas. air´uh-tuhs (Gk. *Haretas G745*, from Nabatean *Hariṭat*). A NABATEAN king whose deputy sought to apprehend PAUL at Damascus (2 Cor. 11:32; cf. Acts 9:24). The name (or title?) was borne by several rulers. The king mentioned in the NT was Aretas IV, whose daughter was married to HEROD Antipas for a time.

Argob. ahr´gob (Heb. *ʾargōb H758* and *H759*, prob. "mound"). **(1)** A region in BASHAN (Deut. 3:4, 13-14; 1 Ki. 4:13) in the kingdom of OG containing "sixty cities," but possibly distinguished from the "settlements of Jair" (see HAVVOTH JAIR), which belonged to GILEAD (cf. Num. 32:41; Jdg. 10:4; 1 Ki. 4:13). The precise location of Argob is uncertain, but it probably covered the southern part of Bashan.

(2) An uncertain text (2 Ki. 15:25) leaves the question open whether the names Argob and Arieh refer to men or places. If they are men, it cannot be determined whether they were fellow-conspirators with PEKAH or victims slain with PEKAHIAH. If they are places, Argob would be the region discussed above (#1), and Arieh may be a reference to Havvoth Jair.

Aridai. air´uh-di (Heb. *ʾăriday H767*, a Persian name of uncertain meaning). One of the ten sons of HAMAN who were put to death by the Jews (Esth. 9:9).

Aridatha. air´uh-day´thuh (Heb. *ʾăridātāʾ H792*, a Persian name of uncertain meaning). One of the ten sons of HAMAN who were put to death by the Jews (Esth. 9:8).

A

Arieh. air´ee-uh (Heb. *ʾaryēh H794*, "lion"). Possibly a man who was assassinated along with PEKAHIAH and Argob (2 Ki. 15:25). For other interpretations of the text, see ARGOB #2.

Ariel (person). air´ee-uhl (Heb. *ʾărîʾēl H791*, possibly "lion of God"; see also ARELI). (1) One of the leaders sent by EZRA to IDDO and to the temple servants (NETHINIM) in CASIPHIA, with an order to bring attendants for the house of God (Ezra 8:16-17).

(2) In 2 Sam. 23:20 the NRSV, following the SEPTUAGINT, states that Benaiah son of Jehoiada "struck the two sons of Ariel of Moab." However, the Hebrew term here (*ʾărîʾēl H738*) is possibly not a proper name, and the NIV translates, "two of Moab's best men [KJV, lionlike]."

Ariel (place). air´ee-uhl (Heb. *ʾărîʾēl H790*, possibly "altar hearth of God" or "lion of God"). A symbolical designation for JERUSALEM (Isa. 29:1-2, 7), possibly suggested by metonymy as the place where the altar of God with its worship was located. Those who identify this name with "God's hearth" suppose that the word comes from a root *ʾrh* "to burn." Various commentators, following the Aramaic TARGUM, favor this view and point to Ezek. 43:15-16, where the term refers to an altar of four cubits with four horns on its corners. Others argue that the word means "God's lion" (cf. 2 Sam. 23:20; Isa. 33:7). Less likely is the meaning "the light of God."

Arimathea. air´uh-muh-thee´uh (Gk. *Harimathaia G751*). Also Arimathaea. The native town of JOSEPH, a member of the SANHEDRIN who, after the crucifixion, obtained the body of Jesus and placed it in his own unused tomb (Matt. 27:57-60; Mk. 15:43; Lk. 23:50-53; Jn. 19:38). Arimathea is mentioned in the NT only in connection with this story. The exact site is uncertain, but it is thought to be identical with the modern Rentis, 20 mi. (32 km.) NW of Jerusalem, in the hills of the SHEPHELAH area. It may be the same as the OT RAMATHAIM, where the prophet SAMUEL lived (1 Sam. 1:1).

Arioch. air´ee-ok (Heb. *ʾaryôk H796*, meaning unknown; in Daniel, Aram. *ʾaryôk H10070*). (1) King of ELLASAR and an ally of KEDORLAOMER

king of ELAM, who with three other kings led a punitive expedition against the kings of the CITIES OF THE PLAIN (Gen. 14:1, 9). Attempts to identify Arioch (e.g., with Eri-Aku king of Larsa) have not been successful.

(2) Captain of the king's guard at BABYLON under NEBUCHADNEZZAR (Dan. 2:14-25). He was commanded to execute the "wise men" who had failed to interpret the royal dream.

Arisai. air´uh-si (Heb. *ʾărîsay H798*, Persian name of uncertain meaning). One of the ten sons of HAMAN who were put to death by the Jews (Esth. 9:9).

Aristarchus. air´is-tahr´kuhs (Gk. *Aristarchos G752*, "best ruler"). A Macedonian Christian from THESSALONICA, one of PAUL's travel companions. In EPHESUS, he and GAIUS were seized by the mob and rushed into the theater (Acts 19:29). Subsequently, Aristarchus was one of the delegates from the Thessalonian church accompanying Paul to Jerusalem with the collection (20:4); he was present also when the apostle left CAESAREA headed for ROME. Paul himself refers to Aristarchus as a "fellow prisoner" and "fellow laborer" (Col. 4:10; Phlm. 24).

Aristobulus. air´is-tob´yuh-luhs (Gk. *Aristoboulos G755*, "best adviser"). A Christian in ROME to whose household PAUL sent greetings (Rom. 16:10). There is a tradition that he was one of the seventy disciples and that he preached in Britain.

Arkite. ahr´kit (*ʿarqî H6909* and *ʾarkî H805*). This name serves as the rendering of two different Hebrew words. (1) The first term refers to an inhabitant of the Phoenician town of Arka/Irqata (modern Tell ʿArqa, about 12 mi./19 km. NE of Tripoli, Lebanon, and about 4 mi./6 km. from the Mediterranean Sea). Arkites are mentioned in the genealogy of NOAH as descendants of CANAAN (Gen. 10:17; 1 Chr. 1:15).

(2) The other term (spelled "Archite" by KJV and other versions) refers to a clan mentioned in connection with the allotment of the descendants of JOSEPH; these Arkites inhabited ATAROTH, between BETHEL and Lower BETH HORON (Josh. 16:2; KJV, "Archi"). Its most famous member was

Hushai, the adviser of David and later of Absalom (2 Sam. 15:32; 16:16; 17:5, 14; 1 Chr. 27:33).

ark of bulrushes. Term used by the KJV to describe the small papyrus basket made for the infant Moses, in which he was floated on the Nile in order to escape detection by the Egyptians (Exod. 2:3). Only this basket and the ark of Noah are called by the name *tēbâ H9310*, which is possibly an Egyptian loanword for "box" or "coffin" (the usual word in Heb. for "box" or for the ark of the covenant being *ʾărôn H778*). No description is given of the shape or construction of the basket, except that it was daubed with waterproofing substances (NIV, "tar and pitch"). It was made with some sort of cover over the top (cf. v. 6); this feature could account for the name "ark" even if the general shape was that of the papyrus boats of the Nile.

ark of Noah. A vessel that God ordered Noah to build for the purpose of preserving through the time of the flood a remnant of the human race, together with two each of all animals (Gen. 6:14-16). God told Noah what to bring into it (6:18-21), and Noah obeyed (6:22—7:10). The ark floated during the flood (7:11—8:3), then came to rest "on the mountains of Ararat" (8:4). After Noah abandoned the ark (8:18-19), what happened to it is unknown, despite many traditions and expeditions. We do not even know on which peak of the mountains in the land of Ararat the ark grounded. The ark of Noah is referred to in Matt. 24:38 and Lk. 17:27 in a warning of coming judgment; in Heb. 11:7 its construction is an example of faith; and in 1 Pet. 3:20 "the days of Noah while the ark was being built" are held up as an example of the long-suffering of God, followed by disaster for the disobedient and salvation for the few who entered the ark.

ark of the covenant. Also called *ark of the testimony*. A wooden chest containing the tablets of the law, resting in the tabernacle and later in the temple. God directed Moses (Exod. 25:10-22; Deut. 10:2-5) to make the ark of acacia (shittim) wood, of precise dimensions, and to overlay it with pure gold within and without, with a crown of gold about it. Rings of gold at the corners, as well as gold-covered staves to put through the rings, were

made to carry the ark. Moses placed inside the ark the stone tablets on which the commandments were written. An atonement cover of gold, with two winged cherubim of gold, covered the top of the ark. Moses made the ark after the golden calf was destroyed (Deut. 10:1, "at that time") and set it up in the tabernacle (Exod. 40:20).

The ark went before Israel in the wilderness journeys "to find them a place to rest" (Num. 10:33). The ark was instrumental in the crossing of Jordan on dry land under Joshua (Josh. 3) and in the capture of Jericho (4:7-11). Joshua prayed

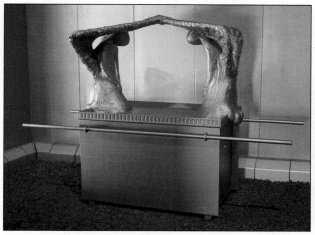

Reconstruction of the ark of the covenant.

© Dr. James C. Martin

before the ark after the defeat at Ai (7:6) and after the subsequent victory at Mount Ebal with the ark present (8:33). In the days of Eli the ark was in the tabernacle at Shiloh (1 Sam. 3:3). Eli's sons took it into battle against the Philistines, who captured it; because of this tragedy it was said, "The glory has departed from Israel" (4:3-22). The Philistines held the ark until a plague convinced them that it was too dangerous to keep, and they ceremoniously sent it back to Beth Shemesh (5:1—6:16). The men of this place also suffered a plague for looking into the ark, and it was removed to Kiriath Jearim (6:19-21). Here it was treated with due respect, kept in the house of Abinadab under the care of his son Eleazar (7:1-2).

David brought the ark to Jerusalem, after some misadventures (2 Sam. 6; 1 Chr. 13 and 15). When Uriah said to David, "The ark and Israel and Judah are staying in tents" (2 Sam. 11:11), he may have meant that the ark had been taken by the army into the field or merely that the ark was in a tent (the tabernacle) just as the armies of Israel and Judah were in tents. At the time of ABSALOM's rebellion, ZADOK and the LEVITES carried the ark out of Jerusalem, but David had them take it back (15:24-29). The priests brought the ark into SOLOMON's temple (1 Ki. 8:3-9). There was nothing in it at this time "except the two stone tablets that Moses had placed in it at Horeb" (8:9).

Before the ark was made, Moses directed that a pot of MANNA be kept before the Lord (Exod. 16:32-34) and Heb. 9:4 says that the "ark contained the gold jar of manna, Aaron's staff that had budded, and the stone tablets of the covenant," though it need not be understood to imply that these were the contents of the ark throughout its history. JEREMIAH, writing after the destruction of Jerusalem by NEBUCHADNEZZAR, prophesied that in time to come the ark would no longer be of significance for worship (Jer. 3:16). Psalm 132:8 speaks of the ark poetically as representing the strength of the Lord. Hebrews 9 uses the tabernacle and all its furnishings, including the ark, as an analogy in explaining salvation by the high priesthood of Christ. After the destruction of the first temple, there is no evidence as to what happened to the ark, but only highly speculative tradition and conjecture. SYNAGOGUES, from our earliest knowledge of them to the present, have had arks in the side wall toward Jerusalem; the scrolls of the Law are stored in them behind a curtain.

The ark was set in the very heart of the tabernacle, the Most Holy Place (Exod. 26:34), symbolizing its central significance in Israel. When the high priest, once each year (Lev. 16:15; Heb. 9:7), penetrated to the innermost shrine, he came into the very presence of the God of Israel (Exod. 30:6; Lev. 16:1-2). That presence, however, was not visibly expressed in any image form (Deut. 4:12), but by the presence of the law of the Lord, that is, the stone tablets and the atonement cover ("mercy seat") that was over them. In other words, the ark by its contents declared the divine holiness by which all stand condemned and by its form (specifically the atonement cover) declared the divine redeeming mercy through the shed blood.

ark of the testimony. See ARK OF THE COVENANT.

arm. In the Bible, the upper human limb is often used as a figure for personal, active power. Thus the Lord lays "bare his holy arm" (Isa. 52:10), rather as we might say of someone about to undertake some task, "he rolled up his sleeves." The Lord's arm (53:1) is figurative of his personal intervention. In particular, the figure of the "arm" looks back to what the Lord did at the EXODUS (Exod. 6:6; Deut. 4:34; 5:15; Isa. 51:9-11).

Armageddon. ahr´muh-ged´uhn (Gk. *Harmagedōn* G762, usually derived from Heb. *har* H2215 and *mĕgiddô* H4459, "mountain[s] of Megiddo"). Also Har-magedon. A name found only in Rev. 16:16 for the final battleground between the forces of good and the forces of evil. The Valley of JEZREEL (Plain of Esdraelon) at the foot of Mount MEGIDDO was the scene of many decisive incidents in the history of Israel: the victory over SISERA sung by DEBORAH and BARAK (Jdg. 5:19-20); GIDEON's defeat of MIDIAN (6:33); SAUL's death at the hands of the PHILISTINES (1 Sam. 31; cf. 2 Sam. 4:4); JOSIAH's death in battle with Pharaoh NECO (2 Ki. 23:29-30); AHAZIAH's death when he fled there (9:27). The town of Megiddo guarded the pass that formed the easiest caravan route between the Plain of SHARON and the Valley of Jezreel, and the low mountains around were silent witnesses of perhaps more bloody encounters than any other spot on earth, continuing down to recent times. Hence the appropriateness of this place for the vast conflict pictured in Rev. 16.

Armenia. ahr-mee´nee-uh. An upland region in western Asia (SE of the Black Sea and SW of the Caspian Sea), earlier occupied by the kingdom of Urartu (see ARARAT). "Armenia" is used by the KJV to render Hebrew *ʾărāraṭ* H827 (only 2 Ki. 19:37 = Isa. 37:38), referring to the place where the two sons of SENNACHERIB, king of Assyria, escaped after murdering their father.

armlet. An ornamental band circling the upper arm, as a bracelet would do on the lower arm or wrist. The English term is used by some versions to render Hebrew *ʾeṣʿādâ H731* (Num. 31:50; 2 Sam. 1:10; for the latter passage, NIV renders "band"). The NRSV uses the term also in Isa 3:20 for Hebrew *ṣĕʿādāh H7578* (NIV, "ankle chains"). See also BRACELET.

Armoni. ahr-moh′ni (Heb. *ʾarmōnî H813*, "palatial" [i.e., born in a palace] or "my citadel"). One of the two sons of SAUL by his concubine RIZPAH (2 Sam. 21:8). DAVID delivered the brothers (and five grandsons of Saul) to the Gibeonites (see GIBEON) to satisfy their vengeance (vv. 1-9).

armor. See ARMS AND ARMOR.

armor-bearer. A personal servant who carried additional weapons for the commanders of Israel's armies. Armor-bearers are mentioned some eighteen times in the OT with reference to such commanders as ABIMELECH (Jdg. 9:54), JONATHAN (1 Sam. 14:7-17), King SAUL (1 Sam. 16:21; 31:4-6), and JOAB (2 Sam. 18:15; 23:37; 1 Chr. 11:39). Another of their duties was to slay those wounded in the onslaught of their masters. While the chieftains threw the heavy javelins and shot the arrows, the armor-bearers used clubs and thick swords to dispatch the enemy wounded.

armory. A place where military equipment is stored. The development of BRONZE and IRON weapons, and the introduction of the HORSE and CHARIOT in WAR, necessitated a specialized division of labor for both armorers and their arsenals. One important location was the "Palace of the Forest of Lebanon" (1 Ki. 7:2-12; 10:16-17). Certain arms were stored in the temple compound (2 Ki. 11:10), and in the later days of the commonwealth, arsenals were located around Jerusalem (2 Ki. 20:13; Neh. 3:19). See ARMS AND ARMOR.

arms and armor. These are mentioned often in the Bible, both literally and as illustrative of spiritual conflicts. Here only hand weapons and body armor are considered, not chariots or machines used in siege.

I. **Offensive weapons**. The *sword* is the first offensive weapon mentioned in the Bible: "A flaming sword flashing back and forth to guard the way to the tree of life" (Gen. 3:24). The common Hebrew term is *ḥereb H2995*. A sword for punishment is ascribed to God (Exod. 5:3; 22:24). Figurative and literal are united in the phrase, "a sword for the Lord and for Gideon" (Jdg. 7:20); GIDEON's men were executing the judgment of God. In NT Greek the more common word is *machaira G3479*, referring to a short sword, dagger, or saber (Matt. 26:27-53; Rom. 8:35; 13:4); figuratively, PAUL speaks of "the sword of the Spirit" (Eph. 6:17). Another Greek term, *rhomphaia G4855*, originally referring to a large, broad sword, occurs with symbolic meaning once in Lk. 2:35 and six times in the book of Revelation (e.g., Rev. 1:16).

A *rod*, a stick loaded at one end, could be used as a weapon (Ps. 2:9). The *sling* was a band of leather, wide in the middle to receive a stone. With the ends held together, it was swung around the head, then one end was released so that the stone could fly to its mark (1 Sam. 17:40, 49; Jdg. 20:16; 2 Ki. 3:25). The *bow* is first mentioned as used in hunting (Gen. 27:3), and the practice of archery is described in 1 Sam. 20:20-22, 35-40. In the NT the bow is mentioned only once (Rev. 6:2). The *spear* (*lance, javelin*) was a sharp-pointed instrument to be thrust or thrown (Josh. 8:18; Jdg. 5:8; 1 Sam. 17:7; 18:11; Ps. 68:30). Spearmen are mentioned in Acts 23:23, and a Roman lance pierced the body of Jesus on the cross (Jn. 19:34). Flame-tipped darts were used also (Eph. 6:16).

II. **Defensive armor**. *Shields* were either small and round (Gen. 15:1; Jdg. 5:8; Heb. *māgēn H4482*) or large (1 Sam. 17:7, 41; Heb. *ṣinnāh H7558*), and were sometimes used for display (2 Chr. 9:16). The NT Greek term is *thyreos G2599* referring to a long, oblong shield (Eph. 6:16). *Helmets* (1 Sam. 17:5; Isa. 59:17), sometimes of bronze (1 Sam. 17:38), protected the head (Eph. 6:17; 1 Thess. 5:8). The *coat of mail* or *scale armor* is mentioned in 1 Sam. 17:5 and elsewhere; the Hebrew term can refer to a *breastplate* (Isa. 59:17). The NT has several figurative or symbolic references to the breastplate (Eph. 6:14; 1 Thess. 5:8; Rev. 9:9, 17). *Greaves*, for protection of the legs, are mentioned only in 1 Sam. 17:6. The description of a heavily armed soldier in Eph. 6:11-18 is evidently drawn from Paul's intimate contact, as a prisoner, with Roman guards. The phrase "whole armor" renders Greek *panoplia*

A

G4110, a technical term for such armament. Note also the detailed description of the armor of GOLIATH (1 Sam. 17:4-7).

army. A large body of personnel armed and organized for warfare. The Hebrew term *gĕdûd H1522* generally refers to a band of light troops going out on forays (1 Sam. 30:8; 2 Sam. 22:30), though in the time of King AMAZIAH it was used of his great army of 300,000 chosen men of Judah and Benjamin with, at first, 100,000 mercenaries from the northern kingdom (2 Chr. 25:9; cf. vv. 5-6). These were drafted and put under colonels and captains. The very common Hebrew word *ḥayil H2657*, meaning "power" and often implying valor, is translated "army" in numerous contexts (Exod. 14:4 et al.). Another frequent term, *ṣābā᾽ H7372*, often translated "host" (as in the KJV phrase "the LORD of hosts"), may be used to highlight the vast number of the soldiers. When used of God's army, the "soldiers" may be people (Exod. 7:4), angels (Ps. 103:21), or even locusts (Joel 2). The corresponding Greek word *stratia G5131* in the NT is used of angels (Lk. 2:13) and of stars and planets (Acts 7:42).

The armies of Israel, when directed and led by God, were uniformly successful (Josh. 1:3; 5:14), but when men like SAUL (1 Sam. 15) and Amaziah (2 Chr. 25:14) refused to listen to God, defeat and death followed. For some reason, God did not want Israel to use or to depend on cavalry (Deut. 17:16; 20:1; Isa. 31:1). In the days of the judges, God raised up from time to time men of special ability to save Israel when the people had suffered for their apostasies and had been brought to repentance. These judges saved Israel from foreign oppressors and they varied greatly in character, from the godly DEBORAH (Jdg. 4-5) to the rather erratic champion SAMSON (ch. 14-16). Israel's armies down to Solomon's time were composed mostly of footmen, armed with swords, spears, bows and arrows, and slings, and protected by small shields. They were led by a judge, general, or king.

Numbers 1 contains a military census of Israel at SINAI just after the EXODUS, and Num. 26 records a second census taken forty years later in the plains of MOAB. According to the plain sense of the English versions, the number of military men was immense: over 603,000 at the exodus and nearly as many at

the Jordan. These figures imply a total population of something like three million men, women, and children, accompanied by herds and flocks. It is hard to picture them drinking at a common spring, even a large one. The Hebrew word for "thousand" (*᾽elep H547*) can also refer to a tribal subdivision or "clan," and such a meaning would make the numbers more comprehensible (e.g., Num. 1:21 could read "forty-six families, five hundred men" instead of "46,500"). This approach also would explain the remarkable numerical phenomenon that in all the twenty-four numbers recorded, in the hundreds' digits we have not a single "zero," "one," "eight," or "nine." The trouble with this theory, however, lies in the totals: if *᾽elep* here means "family," the total in Num. 1:46 would become "598 families, 5,500 men" instead of "603,500 men."

Israel, on the condition of obedience (Deut. 28:1-7), could have become the paramount power of the earth; but when the nation had gone into hopeless APOSTASY, God began to raise up great universal world powers to overturn Israel (Dan. 2; Ezek. 21:27), preparing for the coming of our Lord. The Babylonians with their hordes were overthrown by the Persians, originally a hardy race whose armies were mostly cavalry; but when the Persian king XERXES (Esth. 1) attempted to invade Europe, he was defeated. The book of Esther tells of his great "feast" of six months, which was really a military council preparing for his invasion of GREECE in 480 B.C. The eastern army was defeated by the Greeks with their phalanxes of heavily armed infantry, arranged closely in ranks and files. The Greek armies, in turn, were conquered by ROME. The Romans had a genius for government and for military organization, and the various NT references mention their "commanders" (Acts 21:31), whom we would call colonels, and their "centurions" (10:1), implying their organization into legions and armies. Jesus hints at a possible angelic army divided into legions like the Roman army (Matt. 26:53). The smallest group mentioned in reference to the Roman army is the "quaternion" (Acts 12:4 KJV), comprising only four soldiers.

Arnan. ahr´nuhn (Heb. *᾽arnān H820*, possibly "ibex" or "quick"). A descendant of DAVID through

Hananiah, son of ZERUBBABEL (1 Chr. 3:21). According to the NRSV (which follows LXX), Arnan was the son of Rephaiah and the father of Obadiah, but the precise relationship is left ambiguous by the NIV (following the MT, which says lit., "the sons of Rephaiah, the sons of Arnan, the sons of Obadiah").

Arni. ahr′ni (Gk. *Arni G767* [not in NIV]). Son of Hezron, included in Luke's GENEALOGY OF JESUS CHRIST (Lk. 3:33 NRSV). However, the Lukan genealogy is textually uncertain at this point. The NIV, following many MSS, reads "Ram" (KJV, "Aram"; see Matt. 1:3; Ruth 4:19; 1 Chr. 2:9-10). See ARAM #4.

Arnon. ahr′nuhn (Heb. *ʾarnôn H818*, possibly "rushing [stream]"). The swift "roaring stream" and the valley of the same name that descend to the E side of the DEAD SEA a little N of its center. The river begins in the hills of N ARABIA, flows NW a while, and then turns westward to descend precipitously into the Dead Sea, emptying at about the lowest point on the earth's surface. It is now a "wadi," implying that it is dry most of the year. It is first mentioned as the boundary between MOAB and the AMORITES in the time of MOSES (Num. 21:13); Israel encamped on its N side so as not to invade Moab. In Jdg. 11:18-26 JEPHTHAH tells the AMMONITES how Israel had held the land N of the

Looking NE into the valley of the Arnon River (Wadi el-Mujib).

© Dr. James C. Martin

Arnon for 300 years previous to this time (c. 1560-1260 B.C.). For all those years, and for a long time after, the Arnon was the S boundary of the tribe of REUBEN. In the days of King JEHU (9th cent. B.C.), HAZAEL king of Aram overpowered Israel E of the Jordan as far as Arnon (2 Ki. 10:32-33). Today the Arnon (Wadi el-Mujib) flows through the kingdom of Jordan.

Arod. air′od. See ARODI.

Arodi. air′uh-di (Heb. *ʾărôdî H771*; gentilic *ʾărôdî H772*, "Arodite"). Son of GAD and eponymous ancestor of the Arodite clan (Gen. 46:16; Num. 26:17; in the latter passage, the KJV and other versions, following the MT, have "Arod," but "Arodi" is supported by several ancient versions).

Aroer. uh-roh′uhr (Heb. *ʿărōʿēr H6876*, prob. "juniper"; gentilic *ʿărōʿērî H6901*, "Aroerite"). **(1)** An ancient city E of the JORDAN on the N bank of the river ARNON about 14 mi. (23 km.) from the DEAD SEA and known as ʿAroʿir in modern times. Initially it indicated the southern limit of the AMORITE kingdom of SIHON and was taken by Israel under MOSES (Deut. 2:36; 3:12; 4:48; Josh. 12:2). Aroer was evidently repaired by the descendants of GAD (Num. 32:34) before being assigned to REUBEN (Josh. 13:7, 16; Jdg. 11:26; cf. 1 Chr. 5:8). It was one of twenty towns that JEPHTHAH took from the AMMONITES (Jdg. 11:33). JOAB's census for DAVID began at Aroer (2 Sam. 24:5). In the days of JEHU, HAZAEL, the powerful Aramean king, took the city from Israel (2 Ki. 10:33). Also about this time, MESHA, king of MOAB, "built Aroer and ... made the highway in the Arnon (valley)" (MOABITE STONE, line 26; see *ANET*, 320). Aroer evidently remained Moabite until the time of Jeremiah, who prophesied against it (Jer. 48:18-20).

(2) A city near RABBAH (Josh. 13:25; Jdg. 11:33). The site has not been positively identified; some think it is the same as #1 above.

(3) A city in the NEGEV some 20 mi. (32 km.) SE of BEERSHEBA and known today as Khirbet ʿArʿarah. David shared his Amalekite spoils with the people of Aroer (1 Sam. 30:28). Two sons of "Hotham the Aroerite" were among David's

A

mighty warriors (1 Chr. 11:44); however, some argue that the allusion here is to a site in TRANS-JORDAN (thus #1 or #2 above).

Arpachshad. ahr-pak´shad. See ARPHAXAD.

Arpad. ahr´pad (Heb. *'arpād H822*, meaning uncertain). KJV also Arphad (Isa. 36:19; 37:13). The name of a province and its chief city located in the northern region of SYRIA near the city of HAMATH, with which it is invariably associated in the Bible. The modern Tell er-Refad, 25 mi. (40 km.) N of Aleppo, most probably marks the site today. The city was overrun by the Assyrians in 740 B.C. under TIGLATH-PILESER III and in 720 B.C. by SARGON II. The inability of Arpad and Hamath to withstand such attacks led to the Assyrian claim that Israel too would not be able to stand (2 Ki. 18:34; 19:13; Isa. 10:9; 36:19; 37:13).

Arphad. ahr´fad. See ARPAD.

Arphaxad. ahr-fak´sad (Heb. *'arpakšad H823*, derivation uncertain; Gk. *Arphaxad G790*). Also Arpachshad. Son of SHEM and grandfather of EBER (Gen. 10:22-24; 11:10-13; 1 Chr. 1:17-18, 24; Lk. 3:36). The birth of Arphaxad is the first recorded birth after the FLOOD. Many suggestions have been made concerning the nation of which he was the progenitor. One reasonable proposal is that his name should be linked to the CHALDEANS.

arrogance. See PRIDE.

arrow. See ARMS AND ARMOR.

arsenal. See ARMS AND ARMOR.

art. The application of human skills to produce a pleasing effect. The word is also used in a broader sense with reference to the good and the useful, but the narrower meaning, referring to the beautiful, is more common. The six major arts are music, dance, architecture, sculpture, painting, and literature.

It is difficult to date the beginning of art. If some human being found pleasure in the shape of a stone axe or flint sickle, this might be described as the beginning of art. By any definition, the line drawings in the cave of La Madelaine from the Old Stone Age seem to be art. Architecture might be traced to the first building of a house, although some effort at an aesthetic quality should be added to the utilitarian value in order for the building to qualify as "art." Artistic attempts can be found in the early temples in MESOPOTAMIA from the fourth millennium B.C. and in EGYPT only slightly later. Sculpture is found in Mesopotamia and Egypt as early as the beginning of the third millennium. Literature must be placed before the time of writing, for the folk stories and legends had already taken on forms that gave pleasure to the hearers in the preliterary period—again toward the end of the fourth millennium. To judge from wall paintings in Egypt, music and dance must go back to about the same time. Hence it seems reasonable to date the beginning of art in historical cultures to some time in the fourth millennium. The origin of the arts may be intended in Gen. 4:21-22, where JUBAL and TUBAL-CAIN are mentioned.

The arts can be classified as spatial (architecture, sculpture, painting) and temporal (music, literature), with the dance extending over both categories. Spatial art can be seen as a whole before the parts become meaningful; temporal art on the other hand must be seen or heard in the parts before the whole is comprehended. The temporal forms therefore require a greater use of the memory on the part of the observer, and a certain amount of repetition and interpretation on the part of the artist. Music and in many cases literature might be called aural arts, whereas the others are visual arts.

© Dr. James C. Martin. The British Museum. Photographed by permission.

Various geometric and floral designs are exhibited on this artistic ossuary from Jerusalem that may be as early as the 1st cent. B.C.

In each of the arts, categories of matter, form, and content can be distinguished. Matter involves all the material available to the artist to select, arrange, and use for the purpose intended; form involves all the ways in which the artist can organize the material; content involves what is actually expressed when the work of art is finished. The artist's innate ability is discernible in the selection of matter and form; it would be ludicrous if an artist were to attempt to present a sunset at sea by sculpturing in marble, or a thunderstorm by a piccolo solo.

It becomes increasingly apparent, as we think on the subject of art, that something of the IMAGE OF GOD as Creator is to be found in humans as artists. Artists create. In fact, some authors claim that there is no art in nature and no art without the creativity of the artist.

Each art has certain limitations imposed on it. Music and dance can convey certain emotional messages, but in spite of the saying that "music is the universal language," it is seriously limited in the intellectual message it can convey. Sculpture and painting can convey messages from the visible world but are more limited in conveying ideas or emotions. Literature is by far the most communicative of all the arts and can be used to convey conceptual, emotional, and other ideas. In keeping with this fact is the presentation of God's revelation through the medium of literature.

In Israel, probably because of the commandment against representational art (Exod. 20:4), there were no great contributions to the arts of painting or sculpturing. The major architectural work in Israel—the TEMPLE—is a notable exception, yet even that was constructed with some help from Phoenician craftsmen. References to dance in the OT are extremely limited and afford no information on the form or content. The development of music in Israel, on the other hand, is noteworthy; and to judge from the titles we may assume that many of the psalms, if not all, were sung to music and accompanied by musical instruments. Literature, however, was the most thoroughly developed art in Israel and reached a level not surpassed in all antiquity. See also DANCING; MUSIC AND MUSICAL INSTRUMENTS.

Artaxerxes. ahr´tuh-zuhrk´seez (Heb. *ʾartaḥšastāʾ* H831; Aram. *ʾartaḥšastēʾ* H10078; from Pers. *Artakhshathra*, "Arta's Kingdom"). There were three Persian kings with the name (or title?) of Artaxerxes, but external evidence indicates which of the three was NEHEMIAH's patron. The Elephantine papyri show that in 408 B.C. SANBALLAT was an old man whose work as governor of SAMARIA was to all intents and purposes in the hands of his two sons. This means that the Artaxerxes in whose reign Nehemiah lived must have been Artaxerxes I Longimanus (464-424), since obviously Sanballat was then in the prime of life. EZRA came to Jerusalem in 458, that is, the seventh year of Artaxerxes I (Ezra 7:7), and Nehemiah in 445, the twentieth year of the same reign (Neh. 2:1; 5:14; 13:6). Prior to these events, the Persian king had for a time halted the rebuilding of JERUSALEM (Ezra 4:7-23; 6:14).

Artemas. ahr´tuh-muhs (Gk. *Artemas G782*, contracted form of *Artemidōros*, "gift of Artemis"). One of two men whom PAUL contemplated sending as a replacement for TITUS on CRETE (Tit. 3:12). He must have been a coworker of considerable ability and experience. Tradition makes him bishop of LYSTRA.

Artemis. ahr´tuh-mis (Gk. *Artemis G783*, meaning uncertain). Identified with the goddess Diana by the Romans, Artemis was worshiped throughout the Greek world. Her sphere was the uncultivated earth, the forests, and the hills. Homer gave her the title, "lady of wild things," the virgin huntress, armed with bow and arrows. "Artemis of the Ephesians" is mentioned only in Acts 19:24-35 ("Diana" in KJV). Her silver "shrines" (19:24) were little "temples" containing an image of Artemis as imagined by the Asiatics, a combination of the Greek virgin goddess with the many-breasted and lewd Semitic moon goddess ASHTORETH. For the Ephesians, Artemis was the great Asiatic nursing mother of gods, men, animals, and plants, and was the patroness of the sexual instinct. Her images, instead of being artistically beautiful like those of the Greeks, were ugly, more like the lascivious images of India and Tyre and Sidon. Her special worship was centered in the great temple at EPHESUS, probably because of the discovery of a very interesting aerolite that supposedly fell from heaven (19:35). The feasts of Artemis, "who is worshiped throughout the province of Asia and the world" (19:27), were commercialized, and among the silversmiths there was a large industry in making shrines and idols for the worship of this goddess. The preaching of PAUL interfered with this commerce and aroused violent opposition. It seems that Paul and his companions had preached the gospel from the positive side instead of directly attacking the idolatry, for the city clerk testified that they "neither robbed temples nor blasphemed our goddess" (19:37).

artificer, artisan. See OCCUPATIONS AND PROFESSIONS.

Arubboth. uh-ruhb′oth (Heb. *ʾărubbôt H749*, from a word referring to a lattice or window). KJV Aruboth. A town in one of the twelve administrative districts from which provisions for SOLOMON's household were obtained by BEN-HESED, an official of Solomon's court (1 Ki. 4:10, mentioned with "Socoh, and all the land of Hepher"). The site is now identified by various scholars with Khirbet el-Ḥammam, 17 mi. (27 km.) NW of SHECHEM and thus within the hill country of MANASSEH. The name may be preserved in the nearby town of ʾArrabeh.

Aruboth. See ARUBBOTH.

Arumah. uh-roo′mah (Heb. *ʾărûmâ H777*, "lofty"). The town in which ABIMELECH, the son of Jerub-Baal (GIDEON), lived after he had been driven from SHECHEM (Jdg. 9:41; NRSV also reads "Arumah" as a conjecture in v. 31). The site is identified with modern Khirbet el-ʿOrmah, 5 mi. (8 km.) SE of Shechem.

Arvad. ahr′vad (Heb. *ʾarwād H770*, derivation uncertain; gentilic *ʾarwādî H773*, "Arvadite"). The most northerly town in PHOENICIA, situated on a rocky island called now Ruad (opposite the coastal town of Tartus, Syria). The island lies a short distance off the Syrian coast directly opposite CYPRUS. In Greek and later sources it is called Arados/Aradus. In ancient times it was heavily built over to spite its diminutive size of less than a mile in circumference. There are remains of the sea walls with immense stones 12 ft. (3.6 m.) long and 10 ft. (3 m.) high, indented with deep grooves, perhaps for tying up boats. Arvad ruled over much of the neighboring coast for centuries. Although few surface remains are extant, various scenes of the town appear on Assyrian reliefs. Arvad is mentioned only twice in the OT as a place that supplied sailors and soldiers for TYRE (Ezek. 27:8, 11). Its inhabitants, the Arvadites, are also mentioned in the Table of Nations as descendants of CANAAN (Gen. 10:18; 1 Chr. 1:16).

Arza. ahr′zuh (Heb. *ʾarṣāʾ H825*, perhaps "pleasing" or "woodworm"). The steward of ELAH, king of Israel, at the palace in TIRZAH, where ZIMRI murdered the king during a drinking debauch (1 Ki. 16:9-10).

Asa. ay′suh (Heb. *ʾāsāʾ H654*, perhaps "healer" or "gatherer"). **(1)** Third king of Judah, reigning from 911/10 to 870/69 B.C. (1 Ki. 15:9-24; 2 Chr. 14-16). He was the first of the five kings of Judah (Asa, Jehoshaphat, Joash, Hezekiah, Josiah) who were outstanding for godliness, and he deserves special credit considering his idolatrous ancestors. He was the son of ABIJAH and grandson of REHOBOAM. Asa's grandmother was MAACAH (2 Chr. 15:10; lit., "mother"), a daughter of ABSALOM and a confirmed idolatress who greatly influenced Judah toward idolatry. Asa began his reign by deposing his wicked and powerful grandmother and by destroying a fearful, impure image that she had set up. He then drove out the male shrine prostitutes and destroyed idols that his fathers had worshiped (15:12), commanding the nation of Judah to seek the Lord God of their fathers (14:4).

In the early peaceful days of his reign, he gathered into the temple the dedicated things that he and his father had dedicated to the Lord (1 Ki. 15:15). Then about 897 B.C. ZERAH the Ethiopian came against him with an immense force. The Lord helped Judah defeat them at MARESHAH in the west-central part of Judah, because Asa trusted the Lord (2 Chr. 14:9-15). In 2 Chr. 15:1-13 we see how the Lord approved and encouraged Asa in his faith and in his work of reformation. Later, c. 895/94, BAASHA of the northern kingdom made

A

war against Judah. The people this time did not put their whole trust in the Lord, but Asa bribed BEN-HADAD of Aram (SYRIA) to break his league with Baasha so as to draw off the forces of Israel. This Ben-Hadad did, but the Lord, through his prophet Hanani, rebuked Asa for trusting in politics rather than in God (1 Ki. 15:16-22; 2 Chr. 16:1-10). In the thirty-ninth year of his reign Asa was taken with a severe disease of the feet, and because he trusted his physicians rather than the Lord, he died two years later (2 Chr. 16:11-14).

(2) Son of Elkanah and father of Berekiah, listed among the Levites who resettled in their towns after the EXILE (1 Chr. 9:16).

Asahel. as′uh-hel (Heb. *ʿăśāhʾēl H6915*, "God has made"; cf. ASAIAH). **(1)** Son of ZERUIAH (DAVID's sister) and brother of JOAB and ABISHAI (1 Chr. 2:16). As one of David's thirty mighty men (2 Sam. 23:24), he was made commander of a division of 24,000 soldiers in David's army (1 Chr. 27:7). Asahel was noted for bravery and fleetness (2 Sam. 2:18; 23:24). In the Battle of GIBEON he pursued ABNER, the commander of ISH-BOSHETH's troops, to kill him. Abner was aware that the hour had arrived for David to lead the nation, and that contention among the military leaders could only be a detriment to the best interests of the nation; thus he slew Asahel, after warning him, in vain, to forbear (2 Sam. 2:18-23).

(2) A Levite sent by King JEHOSHAPHAT to instruct the people throughout the realm in the law of MOSES (2 Chr. 17:8).

(3) A Levite overseer of the temple who supervised the offerings during the reign of HEZEKIAH (2 Chr. 31:13).

(4) The father of a certain Jonathan who opposed EZRA the scribe when the latter told those who had returned from the EXILE to divorce their non-Jewish wives (Ezra 10:15).

Asahiah. as′uh-hi′uh. KJV alternate form of ASAIAH (2 Ki. 22:12, 14).

Asaiah. uh-zay′yuh (Heb. *ʿăśāyâ H6919*, "Yahweh has made"; cf. ASAHEL). **(1)** Son of Haggiah and a descendant of MERARI. He is listed among the Levites whom DAVID put in charge of the MUSIC in

the tabernacle. He also had a part in bringing the ARK OF THE COVENANT from the house of OBED-EDOM to Jerusalem (1 Chr. 6:30; 15:6, 11).

(2) A clan leader of the tribe of SIMEON (1 Chr. 4:36). He assisted in dispossessing the inhabitants of GEDOR during the reign of HEZEKIAH (vv. 38-40).

(3) An official under King JOSIAH; he was part of the deputation sent by the king to consult HULDAH the prophetess regarding the book of the law found by HILKIAH (2 Ki. 22:12, 14 [KJV, "Asahiah"]; 2 Chr. 34:20).

(4) The firstborn of the SHILONITES; he and his family were among the first to resettle in Judah after the Babylonian captivity (1 Chr. 9:5 NIV and most versions; the TNIV reads "Shelanites" on the basis of Num. 26:20).

Asaph. ay′saf (Heb. *ʾāsāp H666*, "gatherer" or "[God] has added"). **(1)** A LEVITE descended from GERSHON, appointed over the service of praise in the time of DAVID and SOLOMON (1 Chr. 16:5; 2 Chr. 5:12). He led the singing and sounded cymbals before the ark and apparently set up a school of music (Neh. 7:44). Twelve psalms are credited to Asaph (Ps. 50; 73-83). This accreditation does not necessarily imply authorship (see PSALMS) and may mean no more than that these psalms constituted an Asaphic collection, begun by the great man and then prolonged over the years by the Asaph singers. The psalms themselves cover a long span of time, for psalms like 74 are best understood in an exilic context. The psalms of Asaph have certain points in common: God as Judge (50:3-4; 75:8; 76:8-9), a call to true spirituality reminiscent of the prophets (50:7, 14-15, 22-23; 81:8-10), the use of history to teach spiritual lessons (78), the Lord as Shepherd (74:1; 77:20; 79:13; 80:1). These psalms have a deep and contemplative nature.

(2) The father of Joah, who was the recorder under King HEZEKIAH (2 Ki. 18:18; Isa. 36:3, 22).

(3) An officer under ARTAXERXES Longimanus of Persia (465-445 B.C.) who was designated as the keeper of the king's forest in Palestine (Neh. 2:8).

(4) The name Asaph in 1 Chr. 26:1 is probably an abbreviation or a scribal error for Ebiasaph (cf. LXX and 9:19; see ABIASAPH).

(5) The earliest Greek MSS read "Asaph" in the Matthean GENEALOGY OF JESUS CHRIST (Matt.

A

1:7-8), but the reference is certainly to ASA (a secondary reading found in most witnesses). It is not clear why Matthew would have spelled the name as he did.

Asareel. uh-sair´ee-uhl. See ASAREL.

Asarel. as´uh-rel (Heb. *ʾăśarʾēl H832*, possibly "God has bound [with a vow]" or "God has filled with joy"). KJV Asareel. Son of Jehallelel and descendant of JUDAH (1 Chr. 4:16).

Asarelah. as´uh-ree´luh (Heb. *ʾăśarʾēlâ H833*, possibly "God has bound [with a vow]" or "God has filled with joy"). One of the sons of ASAPH who assisted their father in the prophetic ministry of MUSIC (1 Chr. 25:2; RSV, "Asharelah"). The pattern into which the sons of Asaph fall in 1 Chr. 25:9-14 indicates that Jesarelah, who was the head of the seventh company of temple musicians appointed by lot under David (v. 14), should be identified with Asarelah.

ascension of Christ. The EXALTATION of the eternal Son, in his assumed and glorified humanity, from earth to heaven in order to sit at the right hand of the Father as coregent. The witness of the NT to the ascension of CHRIST is of three kinds. First, there is the descriptive material in Mk. 16:19; Lk. 24:51; Acts 1:9-11. Second, there is the prophetic or anticipatory reference found in Jn. 6:62; 20:17. Third, there is the reference that assumes that Christ is ascended and exalted and therefore proclaims his present exalted position or future coming in glory (Eph. 4:8-11; Heb. 4:14; 6:19-20; Rev. 12:1-6). Much of the latter teaching is molded in the light of Ps. 110:1, 4. Ascension presupposes bodily RESURRECTION, for it was in his body that Jesus went up to heaven. The term *exaltation* covers both resurrection and ascension, while *session* means his sitting at the Father's right hand. The position of the exalted Jesus has often been portrayed in biblical imagery as that of King (= Lord) of the universe and church, Priest of the people of God, and Prophet to the people of God and the world. The HOLY SPIRIT is sent by the Father in the name of the Lord Jesus so that he comes bearing the virtues and characteristics of Christ and so is the Paraclete (Jn. 16:5-14). As Jesus ascended into heaven, so he will return from heaven to judge the world (Acts 1:11).

Ascension of Isaiah. See PSEUDEPIGRAPHA.

ascent. This English term is used a number of times in the Bible, especially in the description "song of ascent" (see ASCENTS, SONG OF). It also occurs in the KJV and other versions with reference to mountain passes (Num. 34:4; Josh. 15:7; et al.). The Hebrew word is used in other contexts as well, such as 2 Ki. 20:9-10, where HEZEKIAH is told that his sundial would go back ten "degrees" (KJV; the NIV has "steps"); see DIAL.

ascents, song of. A description that occurs in the titles of Ps. 120-34 (KJV, "Song of degrees"). There is uncertainty about its origin. Some Jewish authorities attributed it to the use made of fifteen steps leading to the court of women in the TEMPLE. The Levitical musicians performed with these steps as the stage. Some scholars attribute the title to the way in which the thought advances from step to step, as seen in Ps. 121:4-5 and 124:1-4, but not all the songs have this characteristic. The most logical

© Dr. James C. Martin

Tower of the Church of the Ascension on the Mount of Olives. (View to the N.)

explanation is that the title was given to the series of hymns because they were used by pilgrims *going up* to the three annual pilgrimage FEASTS of Jerusalem.

These lovely pilgrim songs should be studied in groups of three. In each group, the first psalm finds the pilgrim far away (e.g., Ps. 120, he feels himself an alien in Kedar; Ps. 129, still among enemies); the second in each triad concentrates on the Lord's power to preserve, whatever the vicissitudes of the way; and the third is a psalm of arrival and security in ZION. In this way the whole "pilgrim hymnbook" is vibrant with the theme of going up and going home to the Holy City.

asceticism. Although this word is not used in the Bible, the concept is found frequently. In the positive sense of self-discipline, asceticism normally occurs in the OT in connection with particular circumstances such as repentance (1 Sam. 7:6) or religious regulations (Lev. 10:9; Num. 6:1-8). In the NT, however, self-discipline affects the whole lifestyle, calling for renunciation of everything that hinders discipleship (Matt. 19:21-22; Mk. 10:29-30). Self-control is listed as a fruit of the Spirit (Gal. 5:23). It is demanded of the contestant (1 Cor. 9:25), of church elders (Tit. 1:8), and of Christians generally (2 Pet. 1:6), who must not let the "good things" of this world rob them of the best things. The term *asceticism*, however, more frequently has a negative connotation, referring to severe self-denial and austerity, and the Bible condemns regulations that involve a "harsh treatment of the body" (Col. 3:20-23; cf. 1 Tim. 4:3). Both within and outside the Christian church, asceticism has often been fueled by a nonbiblical, dualistic philosophy that views the body in negative terms, for example, as a prison from which the soul needs to be released.

Asenath. as´uh-nath (Heb. *ʾāsĕnat H664*, "she belongs to [the goddess] Neit"). Also Aseneth. Daughter of POTIPHERA, priest of ON. The PHARAOH gave her to JOSEPH as a wife, and she became the mother of EPHRAIM and MANASSEH (Gen. 41:45, 50; 46:20). Asenath is a subject of interest in Jewish tradition, especially in the apocryphal work *Joseph and Asenath*, according to which she renounced her heathen religion and became a worshiper of Yahweh when she married Joseph.

Aser. See ASHER.

Ashan. ay´shuhn (Heb. *ʿāšān H6941*, prob. "smoke," perhaps suggesting a desolate place). A town in the SHEPHELAH originally assigned to the tribe of JUDAH (Josh. 15:42; possibly the same as BOR ASHAN, 1 Sam. 30:30). Later it was either transferred to SIMEON or considered a border town (Josh. 19:7); it was also designated a Levitical city of refuge (1 Chr. 6:59). The location of Ashan is uncertain, but some identify it with modern Khirbet ʿAsan, 1.5 mi. (2 km.) NW of BEERSHEBA.

Asharelah. ash´uh-ree´luh. See ASARELAH.

Ashbea. See BETH ASHBEA.

Ashbel. ash´bel (Heb. *ʾašbēl H839*, derivation disputed; gentilic *ʾašbēli H840*, "Ashbelite"). Second son of BENJAMIN (1 Chr. 8:1; listed as third in Gen. 46:21) and the progenitor of the Ashbelite clan (Num. 26:38).

Ashchenaz. ash´kuh-naz. See ASHKENAZ.

Ashdod. ash´dod (Heb. *ʾašdôd H846*, perhaps "fortress"; gentilic *ʾašdôdi H847*, "Ashdodite"; Gk. *Azōtos G111*). One of the five chief cities of the PHILISTINES; the other four were GAZA, ASHKELON, GATH, and EKRON (Josh. 13:3; KJV, "Ashdothite"). Three of them were on or near the coast, and Ashdod was the northernmost of them, about 10 mi. (16 km.) N of Ashkelon. These cities were assigned to the tribe of JUDAH, but Judah failed to drive out the inhabitants "because they had iron chariots" (Jdg. 1:19). Ashdod was a center of DAGON worship, and when the Philistines thought to honor the ARK OF THE COVENANT by placing it in their temple (1 Sam. 5:1-7), God cast down and destroyed their idol. The Philistines found by careful testing that their plagues (ch. 5-6) were from God, so they sent back the ark with a guilt offering. UZZIAH, king of Judah early in the eighth century B.C., conquered the city (2 Chr. 26:6). Amos predicted Ashdod's destruction (Amos 1:8). About the year 711, SARGON II of ASSYRIA took it (Isa. 20:1). In Jeremiah's prophecy (Jer. 25:15-29) Ashdod was to drink with the nations "this cup filled with the wine" of God's

A

wrath. Zephaniah prophesied the destruction of the Philistines (Zeph. 2:4), and Zechariah said that "foreigners will occupy Ashdod" (Zech. 9:6). In NEHEMIAH's time (c. 444) the men of Ashdod combined with others to hinder the Jews (Neh. 4:7-9). Failing in this, they tried intermarrying with them (13:23-24) to produce a mongrel race, but Nehemiah foiled them. In the SEPTUAGINT and in the NT Ashdod is called by its Hellenistic name, "Azotus." PHILIP the evangelist found himself there after the Holy Spirit had taken him away from the ETHIOPIAN EUNUCH (Acts 8:40).

Ashdodite, Ashdothite. ash′duh-dit, -thit. See ASHDOD.

Ashdoth Pisgah. See PISGAH.

Asher. ash′uhr (Heb. ʾāšēr *H888*, "happy, fortunate"; gentilic ʾāšērî *H896*, "Asherite"; Gk. *Asēr G818*). KJV NT Aser. **(1)** Son of JACOB by ZILPAH, the handmaid whom LABAN gave to LEAH his daughter; his name reflects Leah's happiness at his birth. Asher was born at PADAN-ARAM (in the plain of MESOPOTAMIA) during Jacob's service with Laban (Gen. 30:13). We know little of his personal history except the names of his five children (46:17).

(2) The tribe that descended from Asher (Num. 1:13 et al.). Jacob had predicted, "Asher's food will be rich; / he will provide delicacies fit for a king" (Gen. 49:20), and MOSES said of this tribe, "Most blessed of sons is Asher; / let him be favored by his brothers, / and let him bathe his feet in oil" (Deut. 33:24). The Asherites were given the territory along the Mediterranean in the NW corner of Palestine (Josh. 19:24-31), but they failed to drive out the inhabitants of SIDON, ACCO, and other Canaanite towns (Jdg. 1:31-32). The tribe does not figure prominently in Israelite history, and it is not even referred to in the list of DAVID's tribal officers (1 Chr. 27:16-22). The prophetess ANNA was from the tribe of Asher (Lk. 2:36).

(3) According to some scholars, Asher in Josh. 17:7 may be a reference to a town rather than to the tribe. If so, the site is unknown.

Asherah. uh-shihr′uh (Heb. ʾāšērâ *H895*, derivation uncertain). A Canaanite deity, goddess of the sea and the consort of EL; the same Hebrew term can also refer to the sacred wooden poles associated with her cult (usually masc. pl. form ʾăšērîm, but sometimes fem. pl. ʾăšērôt). The KJV translates this word with "grove," following the SEPTUAGINT. These poles were associated with incense stands (Isa. 17:8), altars (Jer. 17:2), high places (2 Chr. 17:6), and other images (2 Chr. 34:4). It is twice called an "abominable image" (NRSV, 1 Ki. 15:13; 2 Chr. 15:16; NIV, "repulsive Asherah pole"). Prior to the discovery of Ugarit (RAS SHAMRA), the deity Asherah was sometimes confused with ASHTORETH (Astarte). In the Ugaritic texts, however, Asherah (Athirat) is described as the progenitress of several gods, including BAAL, who was also associated with her (cf. Jdg. 3:7; 6:26-30; 1 Ki. 18:19; 2 Ki. 23:4). Asherah is not mentioned in connection with the PATRIARCHS, but the Israelites were commanded to cut down or burn the Asherim of the Canaanites; they also were forbidden to plant any tree as an Asherah beside the altar of the Lord (Exod. 34:13; Deut. 12:3; 16:21). Unfortunately, the Israelite invaders appropriated for their own religious worship the "high places" of the Canaanites and also adopted Asherah (1 Ki. 14:23; 2 Ki. 17:10, 16; Isa. 17:8; 27:9; Jer. 17:2; Mic. 5:13-14). GIDEON was told to destroy his father's Asherah pole (Jdg. 6:25-26). The deity is not associated with the kings of the monarchy, but later, after the kingdom split, she is mentioned in connection with both the northern and southern kingdoms. King MANASSEH even introduced Asherah into the temple at Jerusalem (2 Ki. 21:3, 7); subsequently, JOSIAH brought the image out of the temple and burned it (23:4).

Asherim. uh-shihr′im. See ASHERAH.

Asherite. ash′uh-rit. See ASHER.

Asheroth. uh-shihr′oth. See ASHERAH.

ashes. The expression "dust and ashes" (e.g., Gen. 18:27) is a play on words (Heb. ʿāpār *H6760* and ʾēper *H709*) and alludes to the origin of the human body from the ordinary chemical elements. It contrasts the lowliness of mortals with the dignity of God. Ashes were sprinkled over a person, or a person sat among ashes, as a sign of MOURNING

(2 Sam. 13:19; Job 2:8). The word is often united with SACKCLOTH to express mourning (Jer. 6:26). The lovely expression "beauty [*pě'ēr H6996*] for ashes" (Isa. 61:3 KJV) is also a play on words. Another word for ashes (*dešen H2016*) is used for the remains of the burnt offering (e.g., Lev. 6:10-11). See SACRIFICE AND OFFERINGS.

Ashhur. ash'uhr (Heb. *'ašḥûr H858*, possibly "black"). KJV Ashur. Son of HEZRON, descendant of JUDAH, and "father of Tekoa," which probably means that he was the founder or leader of the village of TEKOA (1 Chr. 2:24; 4:5; the name Ashhur is not to be confused with ASSHUR.)

Ashima. uh-shi'muh (Heb. *'ăšîmā' H860*, possibly Aram., "the name"). A deity worshiped by the inhabitants of HAMATH who had settled in SAMARIA (2 Ki. 17:30). Some have thought that the name is a corruption of ASHERAH, the Canaanite mother goddess. Others associate Ashima with Eshmun, the chief god of SIDON. It is also possible that the name could designate any of the Semitic goddesses thought to be consorts of BAAL. (In Amos 8:14, the NRSV reads, "Those who swear by Ashimah of Samaria," which involves a slight emendation of the Hebrew.)

Ashkelon. ash'kuh-lon (Heb. *'ašqělôn H884*, meaning uncertain; gentilic *'ašqělônî H885*, "Ashkelonite" [Josh. 13:3; KJV, "Eshkalonite"]). One of the five chief cities of the PHILISTINES, situated on the Mediterranean sea coast about midway between ASHDOD and GAZA (the other two cities in the Philistine pentapolis were ASHDOD and GATH). Ashkelon was taken by the tribe of JUDAH shortly after the death of JOSHUA (Jdg. 1:18), but was retaken by the Philistines and remained in their hands through much of the OT period. In the eighth century B.C. Amos denounced the city for its complicity with PHOENICIA and EDOM in their warfare on Israel (Amos 1:6-8). Zephaniah, writing in the dark days before the captivity of Judah (Zeph. 2:4, 7) and looking far into the future, saw the restoration of Judah with the Jews occupying the desolate ruins of Ashkelon. Zechariah, writing about 518, prophesied that Ashkelon would see the destruction of TYRE and then that Ashkelon itself

Figurine of a kneeling worshiper discovered at Ashkelon.

© Dr. James C. Martin. The Rockefeller Museum, Jerusalem. Photographed by permission.

would be destroyed (Zech. 9:5). Apparently it was rebuilt, for HEROD the Great was born there and Roman ruins have been found. During the Crusades, it came to life again, and Richard Coeur de Lion held court there. Later the town reverted to the Saracens. Archaeological remains are sparse: a ruined and overgrown Byzantine church, a quadrangle with some preserved columns and foundation walls of an odeum (tiered council chamber) attributed to Herod the Great by the excavators, some statues belonging to the façade of the odeum, and a third-century A.D. painted tomb. The oldest evidence of occupation here is from the area near the beach and dates to c. 2000 B.C.

Ashkenaz. ash'kuh-naz (Heb. *'aškěnaz H867*). KJV also Ashchenaz. Son of GOMER and grandson

A

of JAPHETH (Gen. 10:3; 1 Chr. 1:6). He was the eponymous ancestor of a people mentioned by Jeremiah in association with ARARAT and MINNI (Jer. 51:27). Probably Ashkenaz is to be identified with the SCYTHIANS, a people who had settled near Lake Urmia in the region of Ararat (Urartu) in the time of Jeremiah. The name Ashkenaz is used also with reference to Germany in medieval Hebrew, and thus today the term *Ashkenazi* refers to Yiddish-speaking Jews from central and northern Europe (in contrast to *Sephardi* [see SEPHARAD], which designates someone who descends from the Jews who lived in Spain).

Ashnah. ash′nuh (Heb. *ʾašnâ H877*, derivation uncertain). **(1)** A town in the SHEPHELAH of JUDAH, listed between ZORAH and ZANOAH (Josh. 15:33); it should perhaps be identified with modern ʿAslin, near the edge of the maritime plain of Judah.

(2) Another town of Judah, also in the Shephelah, but apparently farther S, between IPHTAH and NEZIB (Josh. 15:43); this Ashnah may be the same as modern Idna, some 8 mi. (13 km.) WNW of HEBRON.

Ashpenaz. ash′puh-naz (Heb. *ʾašpĕnaz H881*, perhaps Old Pers., "[keeper of the] inn"). The name (or title) of the chief official in NEBUCHADNEZZAR's court, responsible for bringing to Babylon certain Hebrew youths for training (Dan. 1:3; NRSV, "palace master"; lit., "chief of his eunuchs" [see EUNUCH]).

Ashriel. ash′ree-uhl. See ASRIEL.

Ashtaroth. ash′tuh-roth (Heb. *ʿaštārōt H6958*, from the name of the Canaanite goddess, Ashtoreth; gentilic *ʿaštĕrātî H6960*, "Ashterathite"). **(1)** A city in northern TRANSJORDAN, near ancient EDREI and N of the village of JAIR; home of OG, king of BASHAN (Deut. 1:4 [KJV, "Astaroth"]; Josh. 9:10; 12:4; 13:12). After the Israelite conquest, Ashtaroth was allotted to the half-tribe of MANASSEH and settled by the descendants of MAKIR (13:31). It was then given to the Levite clans descended from GERSHON (1 Chr. 6:71; cf. also Josh. 21:27, where BE ESHTARAH may be a scribal mistake for Ashtaroth). One of DAVID's mighty men was Uzzia the Ashterathite. Most scholars identify Ashtaroth

with ASHTEROTH KARNAIM, modern Tell ʿAshtarah, some 20 mi. (32 km.) E of the Sea of Galilee.

(2) The KJV and other versions use the form Ashtaroth to transliterate the plural of ASHTORETH, the Canaanite goddess (Jdg. 2:13 et al.). The NRSV has "Astartes," while the NIV renders it "Ashtoreths."

Ashterathite. ash′tuh-ruh-thit. See ASHTAROTH.

Ashteroth Karnaim. ash′tuh-roth-kahr-nay′im (Heb. *ʿaštĕrōt qarnayim H6959*). A city inhabited by the REPHAITES, located on the KING'S HIGHWAY and sacked by four kings under the leadership of KEDORLAOMER in ABRAHAM's time (Gen. 14:5). Some have taken the name as meaning "Ashtoreth of the two horns," finding support for this interpretation in art work from GEZER and BETH SHAN that depicts a female goddess with two horns. It seems much more probable, however, that the name refers to the city of ASHTAROTH and was so designated because of its proximity to the city of KARNAIM (modern Sheikh Saʿd, c. 23 mi./37 km. E of the Sea of Galilee; see Amos 6:3).

Ashtoreth. ash′tuh-reth (Heb. *ʿaštōret H6956*). The OT Hebrew name of the Canaanite goddess otherwise known as Astarte (from Gk. sources), and corresponding to the Mesopotamian deity Ishtar. The plural form *ʿaštārōt*, referring to the idols representing her, is transliterated as Ashtaroth in the KJV and other versions (Jdg. 2:13 et al.). Her male consort was apparently BAAL, and the two were worshiped with lewd fertility rites. In Jdg. 2:11-23 we are told that the Israelites forsook their God and served "Baal and the Ashtoreths." The prophet SAMUEL brought about a great revival, but before Israel could be saved from the PHILISTINES, they had to give up Ashtoreth and turn to the Lord (1 Sam. 7:3-4). Israel kept fairly close to the Lord through the times of Samuel, SAUL, and DAVID, as well as the early days of SOLOMON, until that "wise" man lost his wisdom by marrying various heathen women for political reasons. They succeeded in turning his heart from the Lord to worship of the Ashtoreth and other idols (1 Ki. 11:4-8). These idols remained more than three and a half centuries till JOSIAH defiled and demolished them (2 Ki. 23:13-14).

A

Ashur. See ASHHUR and ASSHUR.

Ashurbanipal. ash´uhr-ban´uh-puhl (Assyr. *Aššur-bān-apli*, "Ashur has created an heir"). King of ASSYRIA, 669 to c. 626 B.C. He was grandson of the famous SENNACHERIB and son of ESAR-HADDON. Ashurbanipal, or, as he was known to the Greeks, Sardanapalus, was contemporary with several kings of Judah: MANASSEH, JOTHAM, and JOSIAH. Modern scholars have reason to be grateful to Ashurbanipal because he was a lover of learning and collected a great library of cuneiform tablets in NINEVEH (over 22,000 in number) that have

© Dr. James C. Martin. The British Museum. Photographed by permission.

This cuneiform text is known as the Autobiography of Ashurbanipal; it recounts his early life and education prior to being crowned king.

given to us most of what we know of Babylonian and Assyrian literature. It is generally thought that Hebrew *ʾosnappar H10055* (Ezra 4:10; KJV, "Asnapper"; NRSV, "Osnappar") corresponds to Ashurbanipal.

Ashuri. ash´uh-ri (Heb. *ʾăšûrî H856*). Also Ashurite. The name of a region or of a people group in N Israel over whom ISH-BOSHETH, son of SAUL, ruled in his brief reign of two years (2 Sam. 2:9). If the term refers to a place, its location is unknown. It is unlikely that the name refers to the Assyrians (who had not yet occupied any part of Canaan) or to the Arabian ASSHURITES (Gen. 25:3; these inhabited regions outside of Israel). The TARGUM interprets the name as a reference to the tribe of

ASHER, and some scholars agree by emending the text to read "Asherites."

Ashurite. ash´uh-rit. See ASHURI; ASSHURITES.

Ashvath. ash´vath (Heb. *ʿašwāt H6937*, perhaps "blind" or "unintelligent"). Son of Japhlet and descendant of ASHER (1 Chr. 7:33).

Asia. ay´zhuh (Gk. *Asia G823*, derivation uncertain). The ancient Greeks used this term in a general way to refer to the lands E of them, that is, the blunt peninsula later known as ASIA MINOR, as well as the countries beyond it. In the NT, however, this name refers invariably to a Roman province that comprised nearly one-third of the W end of Asia Minor. Asia was the richest and best endowed part of the great peninsula. It contained the whole western coastline and the adjacent islands. Its great cities were ancient seats and centers of Hellenic and Hellenistic civilization, with its science, philosophy, and literature. Its capital was EPHESUS, where PAUL labored; in this city too JOHN THE APOSTLE administered the group of Christian communities to which he wrote his letters. Most of the cities of Asia have disappeared, but SMYRNA (Rev. 2:8-11) remains a great city even now (called Izmir, in modern Turkey). PHILADELPHIA remained till the Middle Ages.

Asia Minor. The Greek phrase *hē mikra Asia* (the Little Asia) was first used after NT times to denote the westernmost part of the Asian continent, that is, the peninsular mass between the Aegean Sea and the EUPHRATES River, and roughly equivalent to modern Turkey. It is also known as Anatolia (from Gk. *anatolē G424*, "rising [of the sun]," i.e., "east") and as the Levant (though the latter term usually includes the other countries bordering on the eastern Mediterranean Sea). In the second millennium B.C., the heartland of Asia Minor was the center of the great HITTITE empire, but the area was also home to various other people groups. During the first millennium B.C., it was frequently the scene of wars and political changes. By NT times, it had been organized into provinces under the Roman empire. See separate articles for the regions within Asia Minor mentioned or alluded to in the Bible: ASIA (which in the NT refers only to the westernmost Roman province), BITHYNIA, CAPPADOCIA, CARIA, CILICIA, GALATIA, LYCIA, LYDIA (PLACE), MYSIA, PAMPHYLIA, PISIDIA, PHRYGIA.

Asiarch. ay′zhee-ahrk (Gk. *Asiarchēs G825*). This word is used in some Bible versions as a straight transliteration of the Greek term in Acts 19:31 (NRSV, "officials of the province of Asia"; cf. also NIV). Similar officials are found in other provincial contexts. Little is known about this office, although it appears possible that the title was permanent, and that once a citizen had held the office, he continued to bear the honorary title. It is likely that a number of Asiarchs were in EPHESUS at the time of PAUL's clash with the guild of the silversmiths. Perhaps they functioned collectively, with the year's incumbent performing the duties of the office.

Asiel. as′ee-uhl (Heb. *ʿăśîʾēl H6918*, prob. "God has made"). A Simeonite whose great-grandson, Jehu, is listed as a clan leader in the days of King HEZEKIAH (1 Chr. 4:35; cf. vv. 38-43).

Asnah. as′nuh (Heb. *ʾasnâ H663*, perhaps "thornbush"). The head of a family of temple servants (NETHINIM) who returned from the EXILE with ZERUBBABEL (Ezra 2:50).

Asnapper. See ASHURBANIPAL.

asp. See ANIMALS.

Aspatha. as-pay′thuh (Heb. *ʾaspātāʾ H672*, a Pers. name of uncertain meaning). One of the ten sons of HAMAN who were put to death by the Jews (Esth. 9:7).

Asriel. as′ree-uhl (Heb. *ʾaśrîʾēl H835*, meaning uncertain; gentilic *ʾaśrîʾēlî H834*, "Asrielite"). Son of GILEAD, great-grandson of MANASSEH, and eponymous ancestor of the Asrielite clan (Num. 26:31; Josh. 17:2). In 1 Chr. 7:14 (KJV, "Ashriel") he is described as the son (NIV, "descendant") of Manasseh through an Aramean concubine.

ass. See ANIMALS.

assembly. See CONGREGATION.

Asshur. ash′uhr (Heb. *ʾaššûr H855*, meaning uncertain). KJV and TNIV Ashur; KJV also Assur. One of the three sons of SHEM (Gen. 10:22; 1 Chr. 1:17; not to be confused with an Israelite named ASHHUR). His name was borne also by the patron deity, people, territory (cf. Gen. 2:14), and capital city of ASSYRIA (out of almost 140 occurrences of the name in the OT, all but half a dozen or so are usually rendered "Assyria" or "Assyrians"). Asshur son of Shem was considered to be the founder of the Assyrian nation, whose king list refers to the earliest founders as tent-dwellers in the southern and western deserts (cf. Gen. 10:11). The name of the national god (often spelled Ashur) is not found in the Bible, although some see allusions to it (e.g., Num. 24:22-24; Ps. 83:8). It occurs as an element in many personal names (e.g., ASHURBANIPAL, ESARHADDON) and may well account for the name given to the capital city. The ruins of the city of Asshur (modern Qalaʿat Sherqat) lie c. 56 mi. (90 km.) S of Mosul (NINEVEH) on the W bank of the TIGRIS River, bordering the great desert.

Asshurim. ash′uh-rim. See ASSHURITES.

Asshurites. ash′uh-rits (Heb. *ʾaššûrim H857*). Also Ashurites, Asshurim. An Arabian tribe descended (along with the LETUSHITES and LEUMMITES) from ABRAHAM and KETURAH through DEDAN (Gen. 25:3). They are not related to ASSHUR and the Assyrians.

Assir. as′uhr (Heb. *ʾassîr H661*, possibly "captive"). **(1)** Son of KORAH and descendant of LEVI (Exod. 6:24; 1 Chr. 6:22).

(2) A son of Ebiasaph (see ABIASAPH) and grandson of #1 above (1 Chr. 6:23, 37). Some scholars believe these genealogical lists are textually corrupt and that there was only one Assir.

(3) According to the KJV, a son of Jeconiah (i.e., JEHOIACHIN, 1 Chr. 3:17), king of Judah. Most scholars, however, regard the Hebrew word here not as a proper name, but as an adjective (cf. NIV, "Jehoiachin the captive").

Assos. as′os (Gk. *Assos G840*). Also Assus. Modern Behramkoy, seaport of MYSIA in ASIA MINOR on the N coast of the gulf of Adramyttium, 7 mi. (11 km.)

from the island of Lesbos to the S near Methymna, and 20 mi. (32 km.) S of Troas (Acts 20:13-14). The ship with Luke and others sailed from Troas around Cape Lectum, while Paul walked the shorter way (20 mi./32 km.) overland to Assos, where he reached the ship in time for her arrival that evening at Mity-lene, a port on the SE coast of Lesbos.

Assur. as'uhr. See Asshur.

assurance. The Christians' confidence that God is their Father and Christ their Savior and Lord. Thus they know that what the gospel declares about Jesus is true and that in Jesus they have a new relationship with God. The term *assurance* can also refer to the external evidence supporting that confidence.

Faith as belief in, trust of, and commitment to God through Jesus Christ carries with it a certain assurance. This is because true faith includes the acceptance of God's own testimony concerning himself and his relation to a sinner (Acts 17:31; 1 Cor. 2:10-13; 1 Thess. 2:13). Thus the believer approaches the Father in prayer and worship with humble conviction and "full assurance" (Gk. *plērophoria G4443*, Heb. 10:22; cf. 6:11; Col. 2:2). In fact the Christian is "fully persuaded" that God is what he says he is and does what he claims to do (Rom. 4:21; cf. 8:38; 2 Tim. 1:12).

There is also the internal witness of the Holy Spirit bringing the knowledge that the believer is truly a child of God (Rom. 8:15-16) as well as the external testimony of a changed life (1 Jn. 2:3-5, 29; 3:9-14, 18-19; 4:7). Because of the presence of the indwelling Spirit, assurance in the new cov-enant is of a much deeper order than in the old covenant. However, assurance was a reality for believers within the Mosaic covenant (Isa. 32:17).

Assyria. uh-sihr'ee-uh. Originally a land between the upper Tigris and Zab rivers, with its capital first at Asshur, later at Nineveh. Assyria was taken over in the third millennium B.C. by Sem-ites from Arabia. First mentioned in the Bible in Gen. 2:14, Assyria and the Assyrians are frequently named, sometimes as Asshur (KJV, Assur). By 1900 B.C. Assyrian traders had a colony in Hit-tite territory, at Kanish in Asia Minor. In the

The Assyrian Empire.

A

thirteenth century Assyrian military expeditions crossed the Euphrates, and by 1100 they reached the Mediterranean. But Assyria was not strong enough to maintain their advance. By 1000 the Aramean kingdom of ZOBAH reached the EUPHRATES, but DAVID conquered Zobah and stopped its invasion of Assyria, an irony of history enabling Assyria to become strong. The tenth century B.C. was one of powerful and systematic advance. Assyria rounded out its borders N and E, con-quered Babylonia (see BABY-LON), and advanced westward through Aramean territory to the Mediterranean. Under SHALMANESER III the Assyr-ians turned toward Palestine. In 853 they were defeated at Qarqar but claimed a victory over BEN-HADAD of DAMAS-cus and a coalition including AHAB, king of Israel. They failed to follow up their effort.

After the religious revival under ELIJAH and ELISHA, the coalition of Israel with SYRIA broke up. When JEHU gained the throne (2 Ki. 9-10), Shalmaneser III seized the opportunity to claim trib-ute from Jehu and to weaken Damascus. Internal difficul-ties kept Assyria from further Palestinian inroads for nearly a century, until shortly after the middle of the eighth cen-tury B.C., when TIGLATH-PILESER III invaded the W, divided the territory into subject provinces, and exchanged populations on a large scale to make rebellion more difficult. In 733-732 he conquered GALILEE, the Plain of SHARON, and GILEAD, making both Israel and Judah pay tribute (15:29; 16:9). Isaiah prophesied that this attempt to sub-jugate Judah would eventually fail. Shalmaneser V besieged Samaria for three years. He died during the siege, and his successor SARGON II took the city in 721 and carried its more prosperous citizens into exile, replacing them with colonists from other provinces of his empire (17:6-41).

Assyrian human-headed winged bull and protective spirit (c. 710 B.C.). These enormous figures guarded one of the gates into the citadel of Khorsabad; the weight of one of them has been estimated at sixteen tons.

For nearly a century thereafter, Assyria was troubled from all sides—from Babylon, Elam, the Medes, Phrygia, and Egypt. Yet SENNACHERIB nearly captured JERUSALEM in 701-700 B.C. (2 Ki. 18:13—19:37; Isa. 36-37), the danger ending only when "the angel of the LORD went out and put to death a hundred and eighty-five thousand men in the Assyrian camp," an event followed by the assassi-nation of Sennacherib by his own sons. MANASSEH, king of Judah, paid tribute to Assyria, except during a short rebellion for which he was car-ried to Babylon but released after he sought the Lord (2 Chr. 33:11-13). The last quarter of the seventh century saw the fall and decline of the Assyr-ian empire and its subjugation by the Chaldean conquerors of Babylonia with the Medes. Nineveh was taken in 612. For a short time Babylonia replaced Assyria as the great power. The prophets Elijah, Elisha, and Isaiah are largely concerned with Assyria; several other prophets—Jeremiah, Ezekiel, Hosea, Micah, Nahum, Zepha-niah, and Zechariah—refer to it. Jonah was actually sent to prophesy to Nineveh, and the revival he unwillingly promoted saved the city from destruction for a long period of time.

Assyrian kings during the centuries in which Assyria had its closest contact with Israel and Judah, with approximate dates for their reigns (all B.C.) from the list found at Khor-sabad in Mesopotamia, are as follows:

Shalmaneser III	859-824
Shamshi-Adad V	823-811
Adad-Nirari III	810-783
Shalmaneser IV	782-772
Ashur-dan III	771-754
Ashur-Nirari V	753-746
Tiglath-Pileser III	745-727
Shalmaneser V	726-722
Sargon III (II)	722-705

© Dr. James C. Martin. The British Museum. Photographed by permission.

Sennacherib	705-681
Esarhaddon	681-669
Ashurbanipal	669-627
Ashur-eti-ilani	627-623
Sin-shum-lishir	623-623
Sin-shar-ishkun	623-612
Ashur-uballit	611-608

Assyrian art, architecture, and technology were successively influenced by Sumerians, Akkadians, and Babylonians and early attained high levels, exciting the admiration and imitation of AHAZ, king of Judah (2 Ki. 16:10-13). Literature was largely utilitarian—legal, historical, commercial, scientific, pseudoscientific, and religious—but it exists in abundance, notably the library of ASHUR-BANIPAL, consisting of thousands of clay tablets. The Assyrians early added to their worship of the primitive national god Asshur the Babylonian deities with their cultic apparatus. Wherever they influenced Israel and Judah, the effort was demoralizing, as the historical books of the Bible and the prophets bear abundant witness.

Astaroth. as'tuh-roth. See ASHTAROTH.

Astarte. as-tahr'tee. NRSV form of ASHTORETH.

astrologer. This term is used in the NIV and other English translations of Daniel to render the Hebrew word *kaśdîm H4169* (Dan. 2:2 et al.; Aram. *kaśdāy H10373* in 2:10 et al.), which could also be translated "Chaldean" (cf. NRSV and see CHALDEA). In the same passages, the KJV uses "astrologer" as a translation of *ʾaśśāp H879* (Aram. *ʾāśap H10081*), which means "enchanter." In addition, both the KJV and the NIV use "astrologers" to represent a difficult Hebrew phrase in Isa. 47:13 (lit., "dividers of heaven"). The MAGI from the east mentioned in Matt. 2:1 (*magos G3407*) were high-ranking Persian priests expert in ASTROLOGY and other occult arts.

astrology. The observation of the sun, moon, planets, and stars for the purpose of determining the character of individuals and the course of events. In warning his people against Canaanite superstition (Deut. 18:10-13), Moses made no reference to astrology or any sort of fortune-telling by means of the stars, for it was essentially a Babylo-nian or Mesopotamian profession, though it later came into Palestine. Although the term ASTROLO-GER appears several times in the English Bible (e.g., Dan. 2:2; 5:7 NIV), the only unequivocal references to the practice and its practitioners are found in Isa. 47:13 ("those stargazers who make predictions month by month") and in Jer. 10:2 (where people are urged not to be "terrified by signs in the sky"). It was a characteristic of Babylonian wisdom, as well as Egyptian, to ponder the movement of the stars, taking note of variations and conjunctions, so as to predict events on earth. See also ASTRONOMY.

astronomy. The study of celestial bodies and phenomena. While the word *astronomy* is not found in the Bible, there are many passages that refer to some aspects of the subject. God is recognized as the maker of the stars (Gen. 1:16) as well as the one who knows their number and names (Ps. 147:4). In the beautiful poem of Ps. 19 the psalmist asserts that the heavenly bodies (referring to the stars) show forth the glory of their Creator. A reference is made also to the sun as one of the heavenly bodies.

There are hundreds of biblical references to stars, sun, moon, and planets. When God wished to tell ABRAHAM how numerous his descendants would be, he took him out and showed him the stars. Then God said, "Look up at the heavens and count the stars—if indeed you can count them" (Gen. 15:5). The Bible refers in a most striking manner to the height of the stars—that is, to their distance from the earth: "Is not God in the heights of heaven? And see how lofty are the highest stars!" (Job 22:12). Another reference to the great height of the stars is found in Isa. 14:13, "I will ascend to heaven; I will raise my throne above the stars of God." The implication here is that it must be a very great distance to the stars, but it was not until recent times that scientists became aware of the astonishing distances involved.

It appears that the biblical writers were aware that the stars differ greatly from each other. PAUL, writing to the church at CORINTH, says, "The sun has one kind of splendor, the moon another and the stars another; and star differs from star in splendor" (1 Cor. 15:41). This has been verified by the astronomers. Not only do stars have different colors, but they also differ widely in size, in density, in tem-

A

perature, and in total amount of light emitted. The sun, around which the earth revolves, is an average star. While it is over one million times as large as the earth, there are some stars that are one million times as large as the sun. On the other hand, there are other stars smaller than the planet Mercury.

One of the many sins of the children of Israel was that of worshiping idols. They wanted to worship also the sun, the moon, and the stars. In Deut. 4:19 they were warned not to indulge in such worship. In spite of such warnings, sun worship prevailed many times. ASA and JOSIAH, kings of Judah, found it necessary to take away the sun images that had been kept at the entrance to the temple. See IDOLATRY; SUN.

While there is little evidence in the Bible that the Hebrew people had indulged very much in the study of astronomy, it is clear that they recognized a sublime order in the movements of the heavenly bodies. They observed carefully the daily rising of the sun, its majestic movement across the sky, and its final setting in the west. This is vividly portrayed in the story of the battle with the AMORITES as recorded in Josh. 10, when the sun stood still in the middle of the sky. Many theories have been proposed in an attempt to give a scientific explanation to this "long day of Joshua." None is completely satisfactory, and they will not be discussed here. It is sufficient to add that this is one of many miracles recorded in the Bible to show us that God is the ruler and sustainer of the universe.

More remarkable than the long day of Joshua when the sun apparently stood still, is the story of the return of the shadow on the sundial of AHAZ. In this case the Lord gave King HEZEKIAH a sign saying, "I will make the shadow cast by the sun go back the ten steps it has gone down on the stairway of Ahaz" (Isa. 38:8). This is, indeed, a remarkable miracle. If taken literally, it means not only that the earth stopped rotating on its axis, but that it reversed its direction of rotation for a short time. Again the scientists have no answer to explain such an event.

There are a number of allusions in the Bible to eclipses of the sun and of the moon. In Isa. 13:10 it is stated, "The rising sun will be darkened," while in Joel 2:31 we have the statement, "The sun will be turned to darkness and the moon to blood." These two descriptions accord quite well with observa-

Babylonian text (164-163 BC) recording an observation of Halley's comet to about 22-28 September, 164 BC.

Dr. James C. Martin. The British Museum. Photographed by permission.

tions of eclipses of the sun and of the moon. As the shadow of the moon sweeps across the face of the sun it appears that the sun is turned to darkness. When the earth comes directly between the sun and the moon, there is an eclipse of the moon. When the eclipse is complete, it is still possible to see the surface of the moon, due to the fact that the atmosphere of the earth bends the light rays from their straight line path. Thus sunlight is bent somewhat as it passes the earth; it is then reflected by the moon and returned to the earth. Just as the sun appears to be red when it is setting, due to the passage of the light through more atmosphere, so the eclipsed moon appears strange in color. The Bible uses the apt expression "turned ... to blood" to describe this astronomical phenomenon.

Calculated eclipses of the sun that occurred in Palestine during OT times are as follows: July 31, 1063; August 15, 831; June 15, 763; May 18, 603; May 28, 585. Very likely the prophets Amos and Joel witnessed the eclipse of August 15, 831. Such an eclipse is vividly described by Amos: "I will make the sun go down at noon and darken the earth in broad daylight" (Amos 8:9).

The subject of ASTROLOGY has been connected with astronomy since early times. The reference in

Jdg. 5:20 no doubt refers to the influence of the stars in the lives of people. The writer states, "From the heavens the stars fought, from their courses they fought against Sisera." However, the Hebrew people seemed to have had little to do with the subject. In the book of Daniel there are repeated statements made concerning the astrologers. It is to be noted that Daniel and his three friends, though closely associated with astrologers, are always mentioned as keeping themselves separated and undefiled. Again and again when the magicians and the astrologers were unable to perform a task, it was Daniel who was able to do important things for the king. Thus it is apparent that the Bible condemns the pseudoscience of astrology.

Probably the most fascinating part of biblical astronomy concerns the star of Bethlehem. This story is told in the second chapter of Matthew. When the wise men from the E came to Jerusalem they asked, "Where is the one who has been born king of the Jews? We saw his star in the east and have come to worship him" (Matt. 2:2). Even King Herod was greatly disturbed over the news, and he inquired of them diligently at what time the star appeared. This star seemed to be their ever-present guide, for it is stated that "the star they had seen in the east went ahead of them until it stopped over the place where the child was" (2:9).

The question is: What kind of a star can continually guide travelers to a definite point on the earth? Many answers have been proposed. One is that this was an unusual conjunction of bright planets (the coming together on the same meridian at the same time of two or more celestial objects). Another theory is that this star was a nova (an explosion that makes a star look suddenly much brighter), although it is unclear how such a bright star could serve as a guide to the wise men. Still another theory is that this was the planet Venus at its greatest brilliance, but these Magi knew the movements of the planets, and therefore the bright appearance of Venus would hardly have served as a guide to lead them to the Christ child.

Evidently here is another of the many biblical miracles that modern science is unable to explain. This miraculous appearance, which is called a star, aroused the curiosity of the wise men to such an extent that they followed it for many miles until finally it pointed out the exact place where they wished to go.

There is much evidence in the Bible that some of the constellations were known to the writers. The Lord asked Job, "Can you bind the beautiful Pleiades? / Can you loose the cords of Orion?" (Job 38:31; cf. also v. 32; 9:9; Isa. 13:10; Amos 5:8). One constellation that has a special significance to some Christians is Cygnus (the flying swan), also known as the Northern Cross. Its six stars form a huge Roman cross in the summer sky, about the size of the Big Dipper. This constellation sinks westward in the sky until at Christmas time it stands upright just above the horizon in the NW. Some see rich symbolism in the fact that the star Deneb at the top of the cross, where the head of Christ was, is a supergiant, while the one at the bottom, Albireo, where his feet were, is a beautiful telescopic double-star.

In the last chapter of the last book of the Bible, the Lord Jesus is called "the bright Morning Star" (Rev. 22:16). Evidently the writer, the apostle John, had frequently waited for the morning light and had watched for the bright morning star, which is usually a planet. Its beauty had greatly inspired him, so he used this striking figure for the Lord Jesus Christ. Many Christians watch for his coming as people of old have watched for the morning and have seen the bright stars of the morning!

Asuppim. uh-suhp′im (pl. of ʾāsōp *H667*). KJV transliteration of a Hebrew word that is more correctly interpreted as a common noun (1 Chr. 26:15, 17); the phrase of which it is a part is rendered "storehouse" by the NIV and other versions (the Heb. word occurs also in Neh. 12:25, where KJV renders it with "thresholds").

Aswan. as-wahn′. See Syene.

asylum. See Cities of Refuge.

Asyncritus. uh-sin′kri-tuhs (Gk. *Asynkritos G850*, "incomparable"). A Christian in Rome, named with four other men, to whom Paul sent greetings (Rom. 16:14). Mentioned first, he may have been the leader of this group of believers.

A

Atad. ay′tad (Heb. *ʾăṭād H354*, "thornbush"). A threshing floor where the funeral cortège of JACOB stopped on its way northward to HEBRON (Gen. 50:10-11). Here the Egyptians mourned seven days for Joseph's father, and therefore the place was given the name ABEL MIZRAIM, "mourning [*or* meadow] of the Egyptians." A geographical problem is seen in the statement that Atad was "beyond the Jordan" (NRSV), since the direct route from Egypt to HEBRON would be W of the river. It is possible that the cortège followed an old trade route through the Sinai peninsula or that the phrase should be translated "near the Jordan" (NIV). The site has not been identified.

Atarah. at′uh-ruh (Heb. *ʿăṭārāh H6499*, "crown"). The second wife of JERAHMEEL and the mother of Onam, mentioned in the genealogy of JUDAH (1 Chr. 2:26).

Ataroth. at′uh-roth′ (Heb. *ʿăṭārôt H6500*, "crowns," or perhaps "[cattle] pens"). **(1)** One of the towns built by the descendants of GAD in the TRANSJORDAN (Num. 32:3, 34) along with DIBON and AROER. It is mentioned by King MESHA on his MOABITE STONE (lines 10-14) as being the city where "the men of Gad had always dwelt." The site is usually identified with Khirbet ʿAṭṭarus, 9 mi. (15 km.) NW of Dibon.

(2) A border town of the tribe of EPHRAIM, part of the territory of the ARKITES (Josh. 16:2, 7). It was apparently located between BETHEL and Lower BETH HORON, but the precise site has not been identified. Some believe that the town mentioned in v. 2 is the same as ATAROTH ADDAR in v. 5, but that the Ataroth of v. 7 was a different town on the NE boundary of Ephraim (perhaps modern Tell Sheikh edh-Dhiab or Tell el-Mazar, but see JOKMEAM).

(3) The KJV reads "Ataroth, the house of Joab" in 1 Chr. 2:54, but this phrase is better rendered as one proper name, ATROTH BETH JOAB (cf. NIV; some have suggested translating it, "the crowns [i.e., chiefs] of the house of Joab").

Ataroth Addar. at′uh-roth-ad′uhr (Heb. *ʿaṭrôt ʾaddār H6501*, "crowns of Addar" or "[cattle] pens at the threshing floor"). A town included in the bound-ary lists for the tribes of EPHRAIM and MANASSEH (Josh. 16:5; 18:13; the S boundary of the Joseph tribes coincides with the N boundary of BENJAMIN). The precise location is uncertain, though one suggestion is Khirbet Raddana, about 9 mi. (15 km.) NNW of Jerusalem. Some believe that this town should be identified with ATAROTH #2.

Ater. ay′tuhr (Heb. *ʾāṭēr H359*, perhaps "binder" or "crippled"). **(1)** The ancestor of a family that returned from the Babylonian captivity with ZERUBBABEL (Ezra 2:16; Neh. 7:21). The unusual Hebrew expression (lit., "the sons of Ater [belonging] to Hezekiah") can be rendered "of Ater, namely of Hezekiah" (cf. NRSV), which might indicate that Hezekiah was an older family name; the NIV translates, "of Ater (through Hezekiah)." Ater was among those who sealed the covenant of NEHEMIAH (Neh. 10:17; in this passage, Ater and Hezekiah are listed as though they were two distinct individuals).

(2) Ancestor of a family of temple gatekeepers who returned from exile with Zerubbabel (Ezra 2:42; Neh. 7:45).

Athach. ay′thak (Heb. *ʿāṯāk H6973*, derivation uncertain). TNIV Athak. A city in the S foothills of the tribal territory of JUDAH to which DAVID sent booty taken from the AMALEKITES (1 Sam. 30:30). The site is unknown, unless the name is a variant (or scribal corruption) of ETHER, as some scholars believe.

Athaiah. uh-thay′yuh (Heb. *ʿăṯāyâ H6970*, perhaps "Yahweh has shown himself superior"). Son of Uzziah and descendant of PEREZ; he was one of the Judahites who after the return from the Babylonian captivity lived in Jerusalem (Neh. 11:4).

Athak. See ATHACH.

Athaliah. ath′uh-li′uh (Heb. *ʿăṯalyâ H6975* and *ʿăṯalyāhû H6976*, possibly "Yahweh is exalted"). One woman and two men in the OT bore this name. **(1)** The wife of JEHORAM, king of Judah, and daughter of AHAB, king of Israel (2 Ki. 8:18). She is called OMRI's "daughter" (2 Ki. 8:26; 2 Chr. 22:2), which probably should be understood to mean "granddaughter." The union between Athaliah and Jehoram was a marriage of political convenience with disastrous spiritual results. Athaliah inherited the unscrupulous nature of her mother JEZEBEL. Her influence over her husband and her son AHAZIAH was for evil. She was responsible for introducing into Judah the worship of the Phoenician BAAL. After the death of Ahaziah, Athaliah became the only woman to reign over Judah in OT times. She put to death all Ahaziah's sons except Joash (JEHOASH), who was hidden by JEHOSHEBA, sister of Ahaziah and wife of JEHOIADA the priest. Then, in the seventh year of her reign, Jehoiada conspired to put Joash on the throne. Coming into the temple to see what the excitement meant, Athaliah found that the coronation had already taken place. She was allowed to leave the temple, that it might not be defiled with her blood, but was killed as she went out the door (2 Ki. 11:1-20; 2 Chr. 22:10—23:21).

(2) Son of Jeroham and descendant of BENJAMIN; he is listed among the heads of families who lived in Jerusalem (1 Chr. 8:26).

(3) Descendant of Elam and father of Jeshaiah; the latter is listed among those who returned with EZRA from the Babylonian captivity (Ezra 8:7).

Atharim. ath´uh-rim (Heb. *ʾătārim H926*, derivation uncertain). According to Num. 21:1, the Israelites, during their wilderness wanderings, were attacked by the Canaanite king of ARAD "along the road to Atharim." Following some ancient versions, the KJV incorrectly translates, "the way of the spies." Atharim may have been a town in the NEGEV, but the site is unknown. The road in question must have been a significant route, and it probably went from KADESH BARNEA N through AROER and ARAD and on to HEBRON.

Athens. ath´inz (Gk. *Athēnai G121*). Chief city of the ancient city-state of Attica and capital of modern GREECE. The city was named after its patron goddess Athene. Centered around a rocky hill called the ACROPOLIS, the city is 4.5 mi. (7 km.) from the sea. Two walls, 250 ft. (76 m.) apart, connected the city with its harbor (Peiraeus). According to tradition, the city was founded by Cecrops, who came from Egypt about 1556 B.C. The city was ruled by kings until about 1068, when archons (magistrates) began to rule. Two of the most famous archons were Draco, who in c. 620 issued laws "written in blood," and Solon, who in 594 gave the state a constitution. The Athenians defeated the Persians at Marathon in 490 and again in 480 at Salamis. They then built a small empire, with a powerful fleet for its support.

The period of Athens' greatest glory was during the rule of Pericles (459-431), who erected many beautiful public buildings in the city and under whose administration literature and art flourished. The Peloponnesian War (431-404) ended with the submission of Athens to Sparta. Later wars sapped the strength of Athens. Philip of Macedon crushed the city in 338. In 146 the Romans made it a part of the province of ACHAIA. The city was the seat of Greek art, science, and philosophy, and was the most important university center in the ancient world, even under Roman sway. Although politically conquered, it conquered its conquerors with its learning and culture.

PAUL visited the city on his second missionary journey and spoke to an interested but somewhat disdainful audience (Acts 17). He reminded them of their altar inscribed with the words "TO AN UNKNOWN GOD," which he had seen in the city,

Athenian forum and Stoa of Attalus. (View to the N.)

© Dr. James C. Martin

and declared that he could tell them about this God. He made some converts in the city, but there is no record of his establishing a church there or of his returning on any later occasion. From Athens he went to CORINTH, where he remained for a year and a half, establishing a strong church.

Athlai. ath′li (Heb. ʿatlāy *H6974*, prob. short form of ATHALIAH, "Yahweh is exalted"). One of the descendants of Bebai who agreed to put away their foreign wives in the time of EZRA (Ezra 10:28).

athlete. See GAMES.

atonement. In early English, this term (from *at one*, i.e., in agreement) meant "reconciliation," the bringing together into harmony of those who have been separated, enemies. Such a term brings a basic biblical concept into focus, but at the same time it leaves unanswered the really crucial questions: What has caused the separation? What has brought about peace? How has it been accomplished?

In the OT, atonement is mainly expressed by the verb *kāpar H4105*, whose root meaning is apparently "to cover over." In secular use, for example, NOAH "covered over" the woodwork of the ark with pitch (Gen. 6:14). The noun related to this verb, *kōper H4111*, is mainly used of the ransom price that "covers" an offense—not by sweeping it out of sight but by making an equivalent payment so that the offense has been actually and exactly paid for (e.g., Exod. 30:12; Num. 35:31; Ps. 49:7; Isa. 43:3). Perhaps arising from this use of the noun, certain forms of the verb (the Heb. piel and pual stems) came to be set aside to express only the idea of removing offense by equivalent payment and so bringing the offender and the offended together. The means of atonement—the actual price paid as equivalent to the sin committed—was the sacrificial BLOOD, the life laid down in death.

The ritual of the Day of Atonement should be studied, and in particular the part played by the two goats (Lev. 16:15-17, 20-22). The Lord wanted his people to know the significance of what had happened in secret when the high priest sprinkled the blood on the "mercy seat" or "atonement cover" (Heb. *kappōret H4114*). Therefore he commanded the ceremony of the live goat so that they might

actually see their sins being laid on another and see their sins being borne away never to return again. See also ATONEMENT, DAY OF; LAYING ON OF HANDS.

In Christian theology, atonement is the central doctrine of faith and can properly include all that Jesus accomplished for us on the cross. It was a vicarious (substitutionary) atonement. On the Day of Atonement, the goat that was substituted was not as valuable as a person; but God in his matchless grace provided a Substitute who was *infinitely* better than the sinner, absolutely sinless and holy, and dearer to the Father than all creation. "The wages of sin is death" (Rom. 6:23) and "God made him who had no sin to be sin for us, so that in him we might become the righteousness of God" (2 Cor. 5:21).

There are two opposite facts that the ingenuity of the theologians could not have reconciled without God's solution: First, that God is holy and he hates sin, and that by his holy law sin is a capital crime; and second, that "God is love" (1 Jn. 4:8). So the problem was, "How can God be just and at the same time justify the sinner?" (cf. Rom. 3:26). John 3:16 tells us that God so loved that he gave—but our blessed Lord was not just a means to an end, he was not a martyr to a cause. In the eternal counsels of the Trinity, he offered himself to bear our sins (Rev. 13:8). He voluntarily set aside the divine trappings of omnipotence, omniscience, and glory (Phil. 2:5-8), that he might be truly human, becoming the babe of Bethlehem. For some thirty-three years he perfectly fulfilled the law on our behalf (Matt. 5:18) and then paid the penalty for our sins in his death for us on the cross. Our Lord's work of atonement looks in three directions: toward sin and Satan (1 Pet. 1:18-19), toward us (Rom. 5:6-11), and toward the Holy Father (1 Jn. 2:2).

Atonement, Day of. Theologically and spiritually, the Day of Atonement is the center of LEVITICUS, "the book of holiness." The sixteenth chapter gives the law for the Day of Atonement. The divinely inspired commentary on this chapter is found in Heb. 9:1—10:25. Israel had two beginnings for its years, six months apart. In the first month (approx. March-April) on the fourteenth day, they ate the Passover as a memorial of the events leading to the EXODUS from Egypt; half a year later, in the seventh month (approx. September-October) on the tenth day (Lev. 16:29), they afflicted their souls and the priest made atonement for them. The Jews now celebrate their New Year's Day (Rosh Hashanah) on the first day of the seventh month, and the Day of Atonement (Yom Kippur) on the tenth day.

The purpose of the Day of Atonement seems to have been at least fourfold: first, to show God's hatred of sin, that the "wages of sin is death" (Rom. 6:23) and that "without the shedding of blood there is no forgiveness" (Heb. 9:22); second, to show the contagious nature of sin, for even the Most Holy Place had to be cleansed "because of the uncleanness and rebellion of the Israelites, whatever their sins have been" (Lev. 16:16); third, to point forward by three types to the death of "the Lamb of God," our blessed Savior; and fourth, by its repetition year after year to signify that the way into the very presence of God had not been made manifest before the death of Christ (Heb. 9:7-9). When our Lord offered himself on Calvary, the veil of the temple was torn (Mk. 15:38), and God signified that from that moment on we were under a new covenant—a covenant of grace, not of law. "For the law was given through Moses; grace and truth came through Jesus Christ" (Jn. 1:17). The OT ceremonies were but symbols and types and shadows: the NT records the realities. In OT times God was teaching his people by "kindergarten" methods—godliness brought health, long life, and prosperity; sin brought quick, visible, corporeal punishment. Today, under grace, we look back to Calvary, when the great Day of Atonement took place once for all.

atonement cover. See TABERNACLE.

Atroth. See ATROTH SHOPHAN.

Atroth Beth Joab. at´roth-beth-joh´ab (Heb. *ʿaṭrôt bêt yôʾāb H6502*, "crowns [*or* cattle pens] of the house of Joab"). Apparently a village near BETHLEHEM listed among the descendants of Salma in the genealogy of JUDAH (1 Chr. 2:54; KJV reads, "Ataroth, the house of Joab"). However, the words could be translated, "the chief ones of Joab's clan," and be taken as a description of the Netophathites or of the towns of Bethlehem and NETOPHAH. See also ATAROTH.

Atroth Shophan. at´roth-shoh´fan (Heb. *ʿaṭrôt šōpān H6503*, "crowns [*or* cattle pens] of Shophan"). A city of the Gadites built in the territory conquered from SIHON (Num. 32:35). The KJV reads, "Atroth, Shophan," as though two places are meant (cf. Vulg. MSS, *Etroth et Sophan*). Some scholars identify the site with Rujm ʿAttarus, which is less than 2 mi. (3 km.) NE of ATAROTH of GAD.

Attai. at´i (Heb. *ʿattay H6968*, perhaps "timely, ready"). **(1)** Son of Jarha (an Egyptian slave) and descendant of JUDAH through JERAHMEEL (1 Chr. 2:35-36).

(2) A warrior, sixth in rank among the brave and skillful Gadite officers who served DAVID at ZIKLAG (1 Chr. 12:9).

(3) A son of REHOBOAM by his favorite wife MAACAH; grandson of SOLOMON (2 Chr. 11:20).

Attalia. at´uh-li´uh (Gk. *Attaleia G877*). A seaport in PAMPHYLIA in the S of ASIA MINOR. Returning to ANTIOCH OF SYRIA from their missionary journey, PAUL and BARNABAS embarked at Atta-

The seaport of Attalia.

© Dr. James C. Martin

lia (Acts 14:25-26), where they had presumably landed earlier, on their way from PAPHOS to PERGA (13:13). The city was founded by Attalus II of PERGAMUM between 165 and 138 B.C., and subsequently passed under Roman domination. Attalia later became a Roman colony, and today, with the name Andaliya (Antalya, Adalia), it is one of the principal seaports of Turkey.

Attica, Attic Greek. See ATHENS; GREECE; GREEK LANGUAGE.

attire. See DRESS.

Augustan Cohort. This term is used by some Bible versions to render the Greek *speira Sebastē*, which corresponds to Latin *cohors Augusta* and occurs in Acts 27:1 with reference to troops commanded by "a centurion named Julius" (KJV, "Augustus' band"; NIV, "Imperial Regiment"). A COHORT was normally a tenth part of a LEGION and was itself divided into six centuries, each under a CENTURION. The cohorts, therefore, comprised 600 men; in the auxiliary troops the cohorts were the basic unit of division and each numbered 500 or 1,000 men. They were commanded by prefects or tribunes, and so it is uncertain why in the present instance the cohort was led by a centurion. See also ITALIAN REGIMENT.

Augustus Caesar. aw-guhs´tuhs see´zuhr (Gk. *Augoustos Kaisar G880 + G2790*). Augustus was the honorific title conferred in 27 B.C. on Octavian (Gaius Octavius, 63 B.C. to A.D. 14), the adoptive heir of Julius CAESAR, who, by the hindsight of history, is called the first of the Roman "emperors." Early in his life Octavian became influential through his great-uncle Julius Caesar. He was studying quietly in Illyria when he heard of Caesar's murder in 44. Hastening to Italy, he learned that Caesar had adopted him and made him his heir. Thus in his early manhood, by skillful manipulation of his friends, he conquered his rival Antony at Actium. The beginning of the Roman empire may be reckoned from that date—September 2, 31 B.C. By his adoption he had become "Caesar," and then the Roman senate added the title "Augustus." Although he preserved

Marble bust of Augustus Caesar. Discovered at Pergamum (modern Bergama).

the forms of a republic, he gradually assumed all the power into his hands. He reigned till his death on A.D. 14. Augustus Caesar is mentioned just once in the NT as the emperor under whose reign Jesus was born (Lk. 2:1).

author. This English word, only in the sense of "one who begins or originates," is sometimes used to render Greek *archēgos G795* ("founder, prince, originator") in several NT passages with reference to CHRIST. The writer of Hebrews calls Jesus the author of our salvation and of our faith (Heb. 2:10 [KJV, "captain"]; 12:2 [in both passages, NRSV has "pioneer"]). It is significant that Peter refers to Jesus as "the author of life" in a context dealing with his death and resurrection (Acts 3:15, truly a fulfillment of Isa. 53:10-12). The Greek term appears frequently in the SEPTUAGINT with the sense "leader, prince," a meaning found at least

© Dr. James C. Martin. The Istanbul Archaeological Museum. Photographed by permission.

once in the NT, again with reference to Jesus (Acts 5:31). Some scholars argue that all the passages in which the word occurs speak of Jesus not so much as *originator*, but rather as the eschatological trail blazer who *leads* his people to salvation, faith, and life.

authority. The legal and/or moral right to exercise power, or power that is rightly possessed. In the Bible God is presented as the ultimate, personal authority and the source of all authority. All exercise of authority in the created order, by angels or human beings, is therefore subordinate and derivative. The important statements of Daniel (Dan. 4:34-35; cf. 2:21; 7:13-14) and Paul (Rom. 13:1) point to the sovereign, final, and incontestable authority of God, Creator, Judge, and Redeemer over and in his creation. Thus, the Lord exercises power as the One with authority.

In the life of the people of Israel, the Lord exercised his authority through the authority he gave to king, priest, and prophet. It was the duty of the king to reign in righteousness and justice, of the priest rightly to order the worship and service of God, and of the prophet to declare the word of the sovereign Lord, whether the people would or would not hear. When the word of the Lord came to be written down as Scripture, it was seen as authoritative because of its source (see Ps. 119).

Since Jesus was uniquely sent by God, he has authority; and since he was anointed by the Holy Spirit in order to perform the ministry of MESSIAH, he has power. Authority (Gk. *exousia G2026*) and power (*dynamis G1539*) are related concepts (see Lk. 4:36, "with authority and power he gives orders to evil spirits"). Jesus is a man under authority and with authority (Matt. 8:9; 7:29; Mk. 1:27); he empowers his disciples to cast out demons (Matt. 10:1; Mk. 3:15); he does what only God can do—he forgives sins (Matt. 9:6); he has control over nature (Mk. 4:41); he exercises power over death (Jn. 10:18); and as the resurrected Lord he has all authority in earth and heaven (Matt. 28:18). As those who believed that Jesus had been exalted to the right hand of the Father, the apostles developed the theme of the authority of Jesus, presenting him as coregent of the Father and possessing authority over the whole cosmos (Eph. 1:20-23;

Phil. 2:1-11; Col. 2:9-10). He is the "Lord of lords and King of kings" (Rev. 17:14).

The NT also recognizes other forms of authority as delegated by God and Christ. There is the authority of the state (Rom. 13:1-7), of the apostles as unique pillars of the church and recipients of divine revelation (Lk. 6:13; Eph. 2:20), and of the husband as head of the family (1 Cor. 11:3). In each case the exercise of power is to be within the will of God, and the one exercising authority must be mindful that God is Judge. The possession of authority and power by SATAN (Lk. 22:53; Col. 1:13) has been abused and will be punished.

Authorized Version. See BIBLE VERSIONS, ENGLISH.

Ava. See AVVA.

avarice. See GREED.

Aven. ay′ven (Heb. *ʾāwen H225*, "emptiness, wickedness"). This name appears by itself only once in the NIV, "the Valley of Aven," probably the plain between the LEBANON and Antilebanon ranges (Amos 1:5). Elsewhere it occurs as part of another name, BETH AVEN. In the KJV and NRSV the name also occurs in Hos. 10:8 in what appears to be a derogatory reference to Beth Aven; however, some scholars prefer to take the word here as a common noun (cf. NIV, "The high places of wickedness"). Finally, the KJV uses the name in Ezek. 30:17 (following the MT), but it is better to interpret the Hebrew as a reference to ON, that is, HELIOPOLIS (thus NIV).

avenger. The Hebrew word *gōʾēl* (participle of the verb *gāʾal H1457*, "to loose, set free, vindicate, deliver as kinsman") has a two-sided application of its basic meaning. At heart it is a very gracious word: it refers to the "next of kin" who possesses the right to take on himself whatever need may have overwhelmed his kinsman or kinswoman. We see this at its human best in the book of RUTH (Ruth 3:12-13; 4:2-10) and at its highest when the Lord himself is called our *gōʾēl* (Isa. 43:14). But there is a darker side. Suppose someone has committed the ultimate crime against us and we lie dead through murder. What then? The *gōʾēl* comes to take our part and to exact the vengeance that the law demands (Num. 35:11-34). This is how the word that means "redeemer" also means "avenger." OT law was rightly dominated by the concept of equality: an exact equivalence between crime and punishment. It expressed this in characteristically vigorous terms—for example, "eye for eye" (Exod. 21:23-24; Lev. 24:20; Deut. 19:21). We should note that these passages all refer to punishments imposed by courts of law and are not rules for private conduct. In the case of murder, where life must be taken for life, the next of kin took up the dreadful duty, carefully circumscribed in his actions by the clear OT distinction between capital murder and accidental manslaughter and by the limitation of vengeance to the murderer only (Deut. 24:16).

Avim, Avites. See Avvim; Avvites.

Avith. ay′vith (Heb. *ʿăwît H6400*, possibly "ruin"). The royal city of a king of Edom named Hadad son of Bedad (Gen. 36:35; 1 Chr. 1:46). Site unknown.

Aviv. ah-veev′. See Abib.

Avva. av′uh (Heb. *ʿawwāʾ H6379*, possibly "ruin"). KJV Ava. A city conquered in the eighth century B.C. by Shalmaneser V of Assyria; its inhabitants were then resettled in Samaria (2 Ki. 17:24; cf. v. 31). It is probably identical with Ivvah, but the site has not been identified.

Avvim. av′im (Heb. *ʿawwîm H6399*, possibly "ruins"). KJV Avim. (1) A town near Bethel allotted to the tribe of Benjamin (Josh. 18:23). Because the form can be interpreted as a gentilic, however, many scholars believe that it refers to a people group, perhaps the inhabitants of Ai or Aiath.

(2) Alternate form of Avvites in NRSV and other versions.

Avvites. av′its (Heb. *ʿawwîm H6398*; see also Avvim). Also Avims, Avites, Avvim, Avvites. (1) The inhabitants of some villages in the S coastal region who were conquered by the people of Caphtor (Deut. 2:23); they are later mentioned as continuing to live among the Philistines or just S of them (Josh. 13:3).

(2) The inhabitants of Avva (2 Ki. 17:31).

awe. See fear.

Awel-Marduk. See Evil-Merodach.

awl. A sharp, piercing tool (Exod. 21:6; Deut. 15:17).

awning. This English term is used once with reference to a ship's covered deck, probably to protect the passengers from the sun (Ezek. 27:7). The awning was made of "blue and purple" woven material.

ax, axhead. Various Hebrew words are translated "ax" ("axe") in the English versions. The one term specifically meaning "ax" in the modern sense is *garzen H179*, a bronze or iron implement for hewing wood, skiving stone, or using as a weapon (Deut. 19:5; 20:19; 1 Ki. 6:7 [NIV, "chisel"]; Isa. 10:15). The word *qardōm H7935* (Jdg. 9:48; 1 Sam. 13:20, 21; Ps. 74:5; Jer. 46:22) is perhaps better translated "adze" (i.e., with a curved blade at right angles with the handle). The word "axhead" in 2 Ki. 6:5 translates Hebrew *barzel H1366*, "iron" (cf. also Deut. 19:5, "the head"). In the NT, the common Greek term *axinē G544* is found twice (Matt. 3:10 = Lk. 3:9).

axle. See wheel.

ayin. i′yin (Heb. *ʿayin H6524*, "eye, fountain"; cf. such place names as Ain and En Gedi). The sixteenth letter of the Hebrew alphabet (ע, transliterated as ʿ), with a numerical value of seventy. It is named for the shape of the letter, which in its older form resembled an eye. Its sound probably involved a contraction of the pharynx (as in Arabic).

Ayyah. ah′yuh (Heb. *ʿayyâ H6509*, "heap, ruin"). The possessions of the tribe of Ephraim are described as including "Shechem and its villages all the way to Ayyah and its villages" (1 Chr. 7:28). Here the KJV has Gaza, which reflects the reading of many ancient MSS; if correct, it would refer

A

to an otherwise unknown site in the hill country (certainly not the PHILISTINE Gaza). Those who prefer the reading Ayyah often identify it with AI (cf. esp. Neh. 11:31, where English versions use the form "Aija") or with modern Turmus ʿAjja (near SHILOH).

Azal. ayʹzuhl (Heb. ʾāṣal, prob. "noble"). An unknown place not far from JERUSALEM (Zech. 14:5; NIV, AZEL). Some scholars emend the text (e.g., RSV, "the side of it").

Azaliah. azʹuh-liʹuh (Heb. ʾăṣalyāhû H729, "Yahweh has reserved" or "Yahweh has been noble"). The father of SHAPHAN the secretary, who brought to JOSIAH's attention the book of the law that HILKIAH the high priest had found in the temple (2 Ki. 22:3; 2 Chr. 34:8).

Azaniah. azʹuh-niʹuh (Heb. ʾăzanyâ H271, "Yahweh has heard"). The father of Jeshua, who was one of the Levites that affixed their seals to the covenant of NEHEMIAH (Neh. 10:9).

Azarael, Azareel. azʹuh-rayʹuhl, azʹuh-reeʹuhl. See AZAREL.

Azarel. azʹuh-rel (Heb. ʿăzarʾēl H6475, "God has helped"; cf. AZRIEL and AZARIAH). KJV Azareel (Azarael in Neh. 12:36). **(1)** One of several Korahite warriors who joined DAVID at ZIKLAG (1 Chr. 12:6; cf. vv. 1-2). These soldiers may have been Levites from the family of KORAH, but some argue that the reference is to a different Korah or even to a locality in the tribe of BENJAMIN.

(2) Son of HEMAN, the king's seer (1 Chr. 25:18, called UZZIEL in v. 4 [note that King Azariah is usually called UZZIAH]). The fourteen sons of Heman, along with the sons of ASAPH and JEDUTHUN, were set apart for the ministry of music.

(3) Son of Jehoram; he was an officer over the tribe of DAN during David's reign (1 Chr. 27:22).

(4) A descendant of BINNUI, listed among those who had married foreign wives (Ezra 10:41). Instead of "the descendants of Binnui" (10:38, following LXX), the KJV follows the MT and reads "Bani, and Binnui."

(5) Son of Ahzai and descendant of IMMER; Azarel's son, AMASHSAI, was one of the priests who came to live in Jerusalem after the exile (Neh. 11:13).

(6) One of the musicians who took part in the procession when the wall of Jerusalem was dedicated (Neh. 12:36); perhaps identical with #5 above.

Azariah. azʹuh-riʹuh (Heb. ʿăzaryāhû H6482 and ʿăzaryâ H6481, "Yahweh has helped"; cf. AZAREL, AZRIEL). The name Azariah is one of the most common in the OT, being attributed to approximately thirty persons, although in some cases it is difficult to distinguish between them.

(1) King of Judah, more frequently known as UZZIAH (2 Ki. 14:21; 15:1, 6-8, 17, 23, 27; 1 Chr. 3:12; cf. AZAREL #3, who is also called UZZIEL).

(2) Son (grandson?) of ZADOK, listed among the chief officials under SOLOMON and called "the priest," possibly indicating that he was the high priest at that time (1 Ki. 4:2); maybe the same as #6 or #7 below.

(3) Son of NATHAN and an official in the court of SOLOMON (1 Ki. 4:5); possibly Solomon's nephew (cf. 2 Sam. 5:14).

(4) Son of Ethan and descendant of JUDAH (1 Chr. 2:8).

(5) Son of Jehu and descendant of Judah (1 Chr. 2:38-39).

(6) Son of AHIMAAZ and grandson of Zadok (1 Chr. 6:9; for this and the following items, note that 6:1-81 corresponds to MT and LXX 5:27—6:66). It is thought by some that the statement, "it was he who served as priest in the temple Solomon built in Jerusalem" (v. 10b), applies to him. If so, he may be the same as #2 above.

(7) Son of Johanan and grandson of #6 above (1 Chr. 6:10). If the comment that he served as priest in Solomon's temple applies to him, this Azariah may be the same as either #2 above or #14 below. Some think, moreover, that he should be identified with #19.

(8) Son of Hilkiah and descendant of Zadok, included in several genealogies (1 Chr. 6:13-14; 9:11; Ezra 7:1; Neh. 11:11).

(9) Son of Zephaniah, listed in the genealogy of KOHATH (1 Chr. 6:36).

A

(10) Son of Oded and a prophet during the reign of Asa; he inspired the king to destroy the idols and to renew the temple worship (2 Chr. 15:1-15).

(11) Son of Jehoshaphat (2 Chr. 21:2, where NIV and NJPS distinguish between Azariah and Azariahu); when Jehoram, also son of Jehoshaphat, became king, he killed all his brothers, including Azariah (v. 4).

(12) Son of Jeroham and a commander in the Judean army that deposed Athaliah and enthroned Joash/Jehoash (2 Chr. 23:1).

(13) Son of Obed and a colleague of #12 above (2 Chr. 23:1).

(14) The chief priest who protested King Uzziah's intrusion into the priest's office (2 Chr. 26:17, 20); possibly the same as #18 below.

(15) Son of Jehohanan (Johanan), a leader in Ephraim who protested against the capture of Judeans by the Israelite army, supplied them with food and clothing, and released them (2 Chr. 28:12).

(16) Father of Joel, who was a Kohathite that served during Hezekiah's reign (2 Chr. 29:12); possibly the same as #18 below.

(17) Son of Jehallelel; he was a Merarite who served during Hezekiah's reign (2 Chr. 29:12).

(18) The high priest under Hezekiah (2 Chr. 31:10, 13); possibly the same as #14 or #16 above.

(19) Son (or descendant) of Meraioth and an ancestor of Ezra (Ezra 7:3).

(20) Son of Maaseiah; he was a priest who assisted Nehemiah in building the wall (Neh. 3:23).

(21) A companion of Zerubbabel in the return from the exile (Neh. 7:7).

(22) A man who stood to the right of Ezra as he read the law (1 Esd. 9:43, not mentioned in the parallel passage, Neh. 8:4).

(23) A Levite who assisted Ezra in instructing the people in the law (Neh. 8:7).

(24) A priest who signed Nehemiah's covenant (Neh. 10:2); apparently the same as Ezra (12:1).

(25) A participant in the dedication of the rebuilt wall of Jerusalem (Neh. 12:32).

(26) Son of Hoshaiah and a leader in the group who opposed Jeremiah's counsel (Jer. 43:2; cf. 42:1 NRSV, following LXX [MT, Jezaniah]).

(27) One of Daniel's three companions, renamed Abednego, whom Nebuchadnezzar condemned to the fiery furnace (Dan. 1:6, 7, 11, 19; 2:17; 3:12-30).

Azariahu. az´uh-ri´uh-hyoo (Heb. *ʿazaryāhû H6482*, "Yahweh has helped"). KJV and other versions, Azariah. Son of Jehoshaphat (2 Chr. 21:2). See Azariah #11.

Azaz. ay´zaz (Heb. *ʿāzāz H6452*, prob. short form of Azaziah, "Yahweh is strong"). Son of Shema and descendant of Reuben; his son Bela and other Reubenites settled in a large area of Transjordan (1 Chr. 5:8).

Azazel. See scapegoat.

Azaziah. az´uh-zi´uh (Heb. *ʿazazyāhû H6453* "Yahweh is strong"). **(1)** One of the Levites assigned to play the harp when the ark of the covenant was brought to Jerusalem (1 Chr. 15:21).

(2) Father of Hoshea; the latter was an officer over the tribe of Ephraim during the reign of David (1 Chr. 27:20).

(3) One of the temple supervisors under Conaniah, who was in charge of the contributions during the reign of Hezekiah (2 Chr. 31:13).

Azbuk. az´buhk (Heb. *ʿazbûq H6443*, derivation unknown). The father of a certain man named Nehemiah; the latter ruled part of Beth Zur and helped the better-known Nehemiah rebuild the wall of Jerusalem (Neh. 3:16).

Azekah. uh-zee´kuh (Heb. *ʿăzēqâ H6467*, possibly "hoed [ground]"). A town in NW Judah, mentioned as a place to which Joshua pursued the kings at the battle of Gibeon (Josh. 10:10-11). The town is mentioned in a few other passages (e.g., Josh. 15:35; 1 Sam. 17:1; 2 Chr. 11:9). Azekah was one of the last towns to fall to Nebuchadnezzar before he attacked Jerusalem c. 588 B.C. (Jer. 34:7). In Lachish letter # 4, Hoshaiah, who commanded a garrison N of Lachish, informed his superior Yoash at Lachish that he could no longer see the signals (fire or smoke) from Azekah N of his post. This indicated that Azekah had already fallen. After the exile the city was reoccupied (Neh. 11:30). Azekah is identified with Tell

Zakariyeh, a triangular mound that rises about 350 ft. (105 m.) above the Valley of ELAH, some 15 mi. (24 km.) NW of HEBRON.

Azel. ay′zuhl (Heb. *ʾāṣēl H727*, "noble"). (1) Son of Eleasah and descendant of King SAUL through JONATHAN (1 Chr. 8:37-38; 9:43-44).

(2) NIV form of AZAL.

Azem. See EZEM.

Azgad. az′gad (Heb. *ʿazgād H6444*, possibly "Gad is strong"). Ancestor of a family that returned from the EXILE. They returned in two contingents, one with ZERUBBABEL (Ezra 2:12; Neh. 7:17) and the other with EZRA (Ezra 8:12). Azgad (or a descendant representing the clan) was among those who signed NEHEMIAH's covenant (Neh. 10:15).

Aziel. ay′zee-uhl (Heb. *ʿăzîʾēl H6456*, prob. "God is [my] strength"). One of the Levites who played the lyre when the ARK OF THE COVENANT was brought to Jerusalem (1 Chr. 15:20; called JAAZIEL in v. 18; some also identify him with the first JEIEL listed in 16:5).

Aziza. uh-zi′zuh (Heb. *ʿăzîzāʾ H6461*, "strong one," or short form of AZAZIAH, "Yahweh is strong"; see AZAZIAH). One of the descendants of Zattu who agreed to put away their foreign wives in the time of EZRA (Ezra 10:27).

Azmaveth (person). az′muh-veth (Heb. *ʿazmāwet H6462*, possibly "Mot [Death] is fierce"). (1) A member of DAVID's military elite known as the Thirty; he was apparently from BAHURIM (2 Sam. 23:31, "the Barhumite"; 1 Chr. 11:33, "the Baharumite").

(2) The father of two warriors named JEZIEL and PELET, from the tribe of BENJAMIN. Both men were ambidextrous stone slingers and archers. They joined David at ZIKLAG while David was fleeing from SAUL (1 Chr. 12:3). He may be the same man as #1 above.

(3) Son of Jehoaddah (or Jarah/Jadah) and descendant of King SAUL through JONATHAN (1 Chr. 8:36; 9:42).

(4) Son of Adiel and supervisor of the royal treasuries in Jerusalem during David' reign (1 Chr. 27:25).

Azmaveth (place). az′muh-veth (Heb. *ʿazmāwet H6463*, possibly "Mot [Death] is fierce"). A town in the Judean hills listed between ANATHOTH and KIRIATH JEARIM in postexilic census lists (Ezra 2:24; called "Beth Azmaveth" in Neh. 7:28). This village supplied some of the singers for the dedication of the temple (Neh 12:29). It has been identified with modern Ḥizmeh, c. 5 mi. (8 km.) NNE of Jerusalem.

Azmon. az′mon (Heb. *ʿaṣmôn H6801*, "strong" or "[place of] bones"). A site on the S border of the tribe of JUDAH (Num. 34:4; Josh. 15:4). Its location is uncertain, but it was probably not far from KADESH BARNEA.

Aznoth Tabor. az′noth-tay′buhr (Heb. *ʾaznôt tābôr H268*, possibly "peaks of Tabor"). A place in the SW border of the tribe of NAPHTALI, evidently in the area of Mount TABOR (Josh. 19:34); some scholars identify it with Khirbet el-Jebeil, about 3 mi. (5 km.) N of the mountain.

Azor. ay′zor (Gk. *Azōr G110*). Son of Eliakim, included in Matthew's GENEALOGY OF JESUS CHRIST (Matt. 1:13-14).

Azotus. See ASHDOD.

Azriel. az′ree-uhl (Heb. *ʿazrîʾēl H6480*, "God is my help"; cf. AZAREL, AZARIAH). (1) A chief of the half-tribe of MANASSEH, E of the Jordan; he and six other men are described as "brave warriors, famous men, and heads of their families" (1 Chr. 5:24).

(2) Father of JERIMOTH; the latter was an officer over the tribe of NAPHTALI in the reign of King DAVID (1 Chr. 27:19).

(3) Father of Seraiah; the latter was one of the officers sent by King JEHOIAKIM to arrest JEREMIAH and BARUCH (Jer. 36:26).

Azrikam. az′ri-kuhm (Heb. *ʿazrîqām H6483*, "my help has arisen"). (1) Son of Neariah and descendant of DAVID through ZERUBBABEL (1 Chr. 3:23); scholars differ regarding the precise way to reconstruct this genealogy.

(2) Son of Azel and descendant of SAUL through JONATHAN (1 Chr. 8:38; 9:44). Perhaps the same as #4 below.

(3) Son of Hashabiah and descendant of Levi through Merari (1 Chr. 9:14; Neh. 11:15).

(4) A high-ranking official during the reign of Ahaz. Described as "the officer in charge of the palace," Azrikam was slain in battle by Zicri, a warrior from Ephraim (2 Chr. 28:7).

Azubah. uh-zoo´buh (Heb. *ʿăzûbāh H6448*, "forsaken"). **(1)** Daughter of Shilhi, wife of king Asa, and mother of King Jehoshaphat (1 Ki. 22:42; 2 Chr. 20:31).

(2) Wife of Caleb son of Hezron; she was apparently the mother of Jesher, Shobab, and Ardon (1 Chr. 2:18-19 NIV). The Hebrew text is very difficult, and some believe that she was Caleb's daughter. It is also possible that Jerioth was not a second wife but another name for Azubah.

Azur. See Azzur.

Azzah. See Gaza.

Azzan. az´uhn (Heb. *ʿazzān H6464*, "strong" or "[God] has shown strength"). Father of Paltiel; the latter was a leader from the tribe of Issachar, chosen to help distribute the territory W of the Jordan among the various tribes who settled there (Num. 34:26).

Azzur. az´uhr (Heb. *ʿazzur H6473*, possibly "helper"). **(1)** Father of Hananiah; the latter was a false prophet from Gibeon in the days of King Zedekiah (Jer. 28:1; KJV, "Azur"). **(2)** An Israelite leader who sealed the covenant with Nehemiah after the return from Babylon (Neh. 10:17). **(3)** Father of Jaazaniah; the latter was one of a group of Israelite leaders against whom Ezekiel was told to prophesy (Ezek. 11:1; KJV, "Azur").

B. The symbol used to designate Codex Vaticanus. See Septuagint; text and versions (NT).

Baal (deity). bay´uhl, bah-ahl´ (Heb. *ba῾al H1251*, "owner, lord"). This Hebrew word appears in the OT with a variety of meanings. Originally it was not a proper noun, but later it came to be so used. Sometimes it is used in the primary sense of "master" or "owner" (as in Exod. 21:28, 34; Jdg. 19:22; Isa. 16:8). Since the Hebrew husband was regarded as the literal owner of his wife, *ba῾al* was the common term for "husband" (as in Exod. 21:3; 2 Sam. 11:26; Hos. 2:16). Most often, however, the word refers to a Semitic deity. Baal became the proper name for the most significant god in the Canaanite pantheon or company of gods. He was the presiding deity in many localities. Its plural form, Baalim, may be used of the different manifestations or attributes of the one Baal or may indicate that in popular thought local Baals came to have independent existence. The Baals were the gods of the land, owning and controlling it; and the increase of crops, fruits, and cattle was under their control. The farmer was completely dependent on them. Some Baals were greater than others. Some were in control of cities, as Melkart of Tyre. The name Baal occurs as early as the Hyksos period (c. 1700 B.C.). The Amarna letters and the Ras Shamra texts (c. 1400) make Baal a prominent Semitic deity, and in the latter texts the name is not only applied to local gods but is also used as the name of a distinct god Baal.

Baal was worshiped on high places in Moab in the time of Balaam and Balak (Num. 22:41). In the period of the judges there were altars to Baal in Palestine (Jdg. 2:13; 6:28-32); and in the time of Ahab and his wife Jezebel, the daughter of the heathen king of the Sidonians, the worship of the Lord in the northern kingdom was almost supplanted by that of Baal. The struggle between Baalism and the worship of the true God came to a head on Mount Carmel when the prophet Elijah met the priests of Baal and had 450 of them killed (1 Ki. 16:32; 18:17-40). The cult quickly revived, however, and prospered until crushed by Jehu (2 Ki. 10:18-28). Jezebel's daughter Athaliah, wife of King Jehoram of Judah, gave the worship of Baal a new impulse (2 Chr. 17:3; 21:6; 22:2). When she was overthrown, the temple of Baal at Jerusalem was destroyed and the chief priest killed before the altar (2 Ki. 11:18). Before long, however, there was another revival of the worship of Baal (2 Chr. 28:2; 2 Ki. 21:3). Josiah again destroyed the temple of Baal at Jerusalem and caused the public worship of the god to cease for a time (2 Ki. 23:4-5). The prophets of Israel, especially Jeremiah, often denounced Baal worship (Jer. 19:4-5).

Incense and sacrifice—even human sacrifice—were offered to Baal (Jer. 7:9; 19:5), but the worship of Baal was chiefly marked by fertility rites. The main function of Baal was thought to be to make the land, animals, and people fertile. To prompt the god to perform these functions, worshipers themselves performed human sexual acts of fertility, and the Baal shrines were staffed with male and female attendants for this purpose. The same function of prompting Baal to do what is sought from him is seen in 1 Ki. 18:26, 28. The priests desired fire from heaven and tried to represent this by making blood pour down their bodies, hoping that Baal might see and perform a similar action himself.

Since the term *ba῾al* means simply "lord, master," in early years the title Baal seems to have been

B

© Dr. James C. Martin. The Israel Museum, Jerusalem. Photographed by permission.

Bronze statuette of a storm-god, probably Baal, with bull and serpent; discovered at Hazor (1500-1000 B.C.).

used for the God of Israel, Yahweh. When the Lord's people came into Canaan, they naturally thought of him as the "possessor" and "lord" of the land—as indeed he was. Even DAVID applied the name to Yahweh (2 Sam. 5:20). But later it was seen that this opened the door to thinking of the God of Israel as though he were only a Canaanite Baal, and the practice was dropped. We see this change in the alteration of certain names, such as JERUB-BAAL to Jerubesheth (Jdg. 6:32; 2 Sam. 11:21; see also ISH-BOSHETH and MEPHIBOSHETH).

Baal (person). bay'uhl, bah-ahl' (Heb. *ba'al H1252*, "owner, lord"). (1) Son of Reaiah and descendant of REUBEN through Joel; Baal's son Beerah was a clan leader deported by TIGLATH-PILESER (1 Chr. 5:5-6). (2) Son of Jeiel and descendant of BENJAMIN (1 Chr. 8:30; 9:36).

Baal (place). See BAALATH #2.

Baalah. bay'uh-luh (Heb. *ba'ălāh H1267*, "lady, mistress"). (1) An alternate name for KIRIATH JEARIM, first mentioned in connection with the border designating the territory of JUDAH (Josh. 15:9-10; 1 Chr. 13:6). Baalah may have been an ancient Canaanite name reflecting the worship of a goddess (see BAAL).

(2) One of the "southernmost towns of the tribe of Judah in the Negev toward the boundary of Edom" (Josh. 15:29; cf. v. 21). The site is unknown, though it has been variously identified with BAAL-ATH BEER, BALAH, BEALOTH, and BILHAH.

(3) Mount Baalah was a ridge on the N border of Judah, NW of EKRON (Josh. 15:11); it is often identified with a hill known today as Mughar (cf. BAALATH #1).

Baalath. bay'uh-lath (Heb. *ba'ălāt H1272*, "lady, mistress"). (1) One of the towns included in the territory allotted to the tribe of DAN (Josh. 19:44); the site is usually identified with modern el-Mughar (cf. BAALAH #3). It is probably the same city that was later rebuilt by SOLOMON (1 Ki. 9:18; 2 Chr. 8:6; but some believe that these verses refer to Baalah #3).

(2) The NIV, following a SEPTUAGINT variant, reads "Baalath" in 1 Chr. 4:33 (NRSV and other versions, "Baal," following the MT). The name is evidently an alternative form of the Simeonite border town of BAALATH BEER.

Baalath Beer. bay'uh-lath-bee'uhr (Heb. *ba'ălat bĕ'ēr H1273*, "mistress of the well"). A border town, possibly the shrine of a goddess, in the southern part of the territory allotted to the tribe of SIMEON; it may be the same as "Ramah in the Negev" (Josh. 19:8; but see RAMAH #4). It is elsewhere called Baal (1 Chr. 4:33, where NIV has "Baalath," following a LXX variant). Its location is uncertain; see BAALATH #2.

Baalbek. bay'uhl-bek (from Baal of Beqa', "Lord of the Valley"). A city in LEBANON about 40 mi. (64 km.) NW of DAMASCUS and the same distance ENE of Beirut, celebrated for its magnificence in the first centuries of the Christian era and famous since then for its ruins. The Greeks named it Heliopolis, "city of the sun" (to be distinguished from HELIOPOLIS in Egypt). Baalbek is not mentioned in the Bible, but it became a place of importance after it was made a Roman colony. Chief of the ruins is the great Temple of the Sun, 290 ft. (90 m.) x 160 ft. (50 m.), built of incredibly huge stones from nearby quarries. The city was completely destroyed by earthquake in A.D. 1759.

The Prussian government undertook its excavation in 1902.

Baal-Berith. bay'uhl-bi-rith' (Heb. *ba'al běrit H1253*, "lord of the covenant"). A god worshiped by Israel after the death of GIDEON (Jdg. 8:33). ABIMELECH, Gideon's son, took seventy pieces of silver from the house of this god to hire followers in his time of rebellion (9:4). It is possible that Baal-Berith and EL-BERITH (9:46) are alternate ways of referring to the same god, but some scholars believe that two different sanctuaries with two distinct deities were found in SHECHEM. The idol was undoubtedly worshiped by the Shechemites during, and particularly after, Gideon's time.

Baale of Judah. bay'uh-lee. The KJV rendering of a place name in 2 Sam. 6:2 (NRSV, "Baale-judah"). The NIV correctly interprets it to mean "Baalah of Judah," that is, KIRIATH JEARIM, the place from which DAVID left to bring up the ARK OF THE COVENANT to Jerusalem (6:2). See BAALAH #1.

Baal Gad. bay'uhl-gad' (Heb. *ba'al gād H1254*, "lord of fortune"). A Canaanite town, located "in the Valley of Lebanon below Mount Hermon"; it marked the northern extremity of JOSHUA's conquests (Josh. 11:17; 12:7; 13:5; cf. the last reference with Jdg. 3:3, which suggests a connection between this town and Mount BAAL HERMON). The exact location is unknown, but it should be near the Damascus road on the NW slope of Mount HERMON.

Baal Hamon. bay'uhl-hay'muhn (Heb. *ba'al hāmôn H1255*, "lord [*or* possessor] of abundance"). A place mentioned in the Song of Songs as a fertile region where SOLOMON had a vineyard (Cant. 8:11). The context would indicate that its fruit was exceptionally fine. The location of Baal Hamon is not known, and some have thought that the language is only a poetic expression, not a reference to a real vineyard.

Baal-Hanan. bay'uhl-hay'nuhn (Heb. *ba'al hānān H1257*, "Baal [*or* the master] has been gracious"). **(1)** Son of Acbor and one of "the kings who reigned in Edom before any Israelite king reigned";

he was Shaul's successor (Gen. 36:38-39 [cf. v. 31]; 1 Chr. 1:49-50).

(2) A man from GEDER who was in charge of DAVID's "olive and sycamore-fig trees in the western foothills" (1 Chr. 27:28).

Baal Hazor. bay'uhl-hay'zor (Heb. *ba'al hāṣôr H1258*, "lord of the court"). A location near the border of EPHRAIM where ABSALOM's sheepshearers had gathered (2 Sam. 13:23). It was here that Absalom planned a feast for his brothers, also inviting his father DAVID, who did not accept. In this remote place marked by rugged limestone slopes, Absalom avenged the rape of his sister TAMAR by having AMNON killed. It was possibly a mountain home, being more than 3,000 ft. (915 m.) above sea level. The site is identified with Jebel el-'Aṣur, some 5 mi. (8 km.) N of BETHEL.

Baal Hermon. bay'uhl-huhr'muhn (Heb. *ba'al hermôn H1259*, "lord of Hermon [consecrated place]"). A mountain that marked the S border of the land occupied by the HIVITES, whom God had left to test Israel (Jdg. 3:3). It also marked the N border of the half-tribe of MANASSEH (1 Chr. 5:23). This last reference associates Baal Hermon closely with SENIR and Mount HERMON; it may be one of the peaks comprising the mountain. See also BAAL GAD.

Baali. bay'uh-l*i*. KJV transliteration of Hebrew *ba'lî* ("my BAAL," that is, "my master"), a name used by some in HOSEA's day to describe God (Hos. 2:16). Because of this name's pagan associations, God preferred and demanded that he be called *'îšî* ("my husband"), which emphasized the COVENANT relationship he had established between his people and himself.

Baalim. bay'-uh-lim. KJV transliteration of Hebrew *habbě'ālîm*, which is the plural form of BAAL with the definite article (Jdg. 2:11 et al.).

Baalis. bay'uh-lis (Heb. *ba'ālis H1271*, possibly "the lord is salvation"). King of AMMON in the early sixth century B.C. (Jer. 40:14). He sent ISHMAEL son of Nethaniah to kill GEDALIAH, the governor of Israel appointed by NEBUCHADNEZZAR, king of Babylon. The murder occurred soon after

Jerusalem was captured (41:1-2). Baalis is probably to be identified with Baʿal-yišʿa ("the lord is salvation"), whose name is found in a seal discovered in 1984 at Tell el-ʿUmeiri, near Amman.

Baal Meon. bay´uhl-mee´on (Heb. *baʿal mĕʿôn H1260*, "lord of the dwelling [*or* of refuge]"). A city built by the tribe of REUBEN across the JORDAN (Num. 32:38; 1 Chr. 5:8). It is described as one of the glorious cities on the frontier of MOAB (Ezek. 25:9). Baal Meon is also called BETH BAAL MEON (Josh. 13:17), BETH MEON (Jer. 48:23), and probably BEON (Num. 32:3). MESHA, king of Moab, claimed to have built Baal Meon, making a reservoir for it (MOABITE STONE, line 9; Beth Baal Meon is also mentioned on line 30; see *ANET*, 320-21). Possession must have passed alternately between Moab and Israel several times in its history. The city is identified with modern Maʿin, about 10 mi. (16 km.) E of the DEAD SEA and 3 mi. (5 km.) SW of MEDEBA.

Baal Peor, Baal of Peor. bay´uhl-pee´or (Heb. *baʿal pĕʿôr H1261*, "lord of Peor"). The "Baal of Peor" was a local deity (see BAAL) worshiped by the Israelites while encamped at SHITTIM in MOAB (Num. 25:3-5). The heinous nature of the sin, which involved licentious practice with Moabite women (Num. 25:1-2), was not soon forgotten, as is clear from subsequent references (Ps. 106:28; Hos. 9:10). The same Hebrew name is used as a place name equivalent to Mount PEOR (Deut. 4:3; Hos. 9:10). In some passages, it is ambiguous whether the single name Peor refers to the deity or to the place (cf. Num. 25:18; 31:16; Josh. 22:17). See also BETH PEOR.

Baal Perazim. bay´uhl-pi-ray´zim (Heb. *baʿal-pĕrāṣîm H1262*, "lord of breaches [i.e., breach-maker]"). A name given to the place where DAVID smote the PHILISTINES after he was made the king of Israel (2 Sam. 5:20; 1 Chr. 14:11). The place was so named because the Lord "broke out" (Heb. *pāraz H7287*) against David's enemies there. It is thought to be the same place that Isaiah calls "Mount Perazim" (Isa. 28:21). Baal Perazim is perhaps to be identified with modern ez-Zuhur, 4 mi. (6 km.) SW of JERUSALEM.

Baal Shalishah. bay´uhl-shal´uh-shuh (Heb. *baʿal šālišâ H1264*, "lord of Shalishah [third part?]"). The home of the unnamed man who brought to ELISHA twenty loaves of barley bread and some heads of new grain by which 100 people were fed (2 Ki. 4:42). The location of the site is uncertain, partly depending on what is meant by GILGAL (v. 38).

Baal Tamar. bay´uhl-tay´mahr (Heb. *baʿal tāmār H1265*, "lord of the palm tree"). The place where the Israelites awaited the pursuing Benjamites when the nation went to war to punish the tribe of BENJAMIN for the violent rape and death of a Levite's concubine (Jdg. 20:33). Its precise location is not known, but it was near GIBEAH of Benjamin (some 3 mi./5 km. N of JERUSALEM) on the way to BETHEL (another 8 mi./13 km. farther N).

Baal-zebub. bay´uhl-zee´buhb (Heb. *baʿal zĕbûb H1256*, "lord of the flies"). The name under which BAAL was worshiped by the PHILISTINES of EKRON (2 Ki. 1:2, 3, 6, 16). ELIJAH rebuked AHAZIAH for consulting this god to find out whether he would recover from his illness. The name is peculiar and various explanations have been proposed (e.g., that he protected his worshipers from flies); others have argued that it was originally Baal-Zebul (perhaps from Heb. *zĕbul H2292*, "lofty dwelling") and that it was deliberately distorted by Hebrew scribes as a way of mocking pagan worship. The name appears as "Beelzebul" in NT MSS (Matt. 10:25 et al.), but probably for a different reason; see BEELZEBUB.

Baal Zephon. bay´uhl-zee´fon (Heb. *baʿal ṣĕpōn H1263*, "lord of the north"). A place near which the Israelites encamped just before they crossed the RED SEA (Exod. 14:2, 9; Num. 33:7). The site is unknown, though some scholars believe that Baal Zephon was an earlier name for the city of TAHPANHES.

Baana. bay´uh-nuh (Heb. *baʿānāʾ H1275*, perhaps "son of oppression"). **(1)** Son of AHILUD; he was one of twelve district governors of SOLOMON commissioned to supply provisions for the royal household (1 Ki. 4:12). He may have been a brother of Jehoshaphat the recorder (v. 3).

(2) Son of HUSHAI; he was another of Solomon's district governors (1 Ki. 4:16; KJV, "Baanah").

(3) Father (ancestor?) of a certain Zadok who helped to repair the walls of Jerusalem under the supervision of Nehemiah (Neh. 3:4); possibly the same as Baanah #3.

Baanah. bay'uh-nuh (Heb. *ba'ănâ H1276*, perhaps "son of oppression"). **(1)** Son of Rimmon; he and his brother Recab were captains in the army of Ish-Bosheth, king of Israel during the time when David was king of Judah in Hebron. Baanah and his brother plotted to unify the kingdom under David. They journeyed to Ish-Bosheth's house and, arriving when the king was taking his noontime nap, eluded the doorkeeper and murdered the king in his bed. They took his severed head to David in Hebron expecting commendation and probably advancement from the king. David, however, angrily accused them of murdering an innocent man in his sleep. He ordered them killed, their hands and feet severed, and their bodies publicly hung by the pool in Hebron (2 Sam. 4:2-12). **(2)** A man of Netophah and father of Heled (Heleb); the latter was one of David's renowned Thirty (2 Sam. 23:29; 1 Chr. 11:30). **(3)** A leader who returned with Zerubbabel to Judah after the exile (Ezra 2:2; Neh. 7:7). He is probably to be identified with the Baanah who affixed his seal to the covenant of Nehemiah (10:27), and the same as Baana #3.

Baara. bay'uh-ruh (Heb. *ba'ărā' H1281*, possibly "passionate"). One of the three wives of Shaharaim, a Benjamite who lived in Moab (1 Chr. 8:8). It is possible that Shaharaim divorced Baara and Hushim because they did not bear him any children.

Baaseiah. bay'uh-see'yuh (Heb. *ba'ăśêâ H1283*, derivation uncertain). An ancestor of Asaph, the Levite musician (1 Chr. 6:40 [MT v. 25]).

Baasha. bay'uh-shuh (Heb. *ba'šā' H1284*, meaning uncertain). Son of Ahijah, of the tribe of Issachar. Baasha became the third king of Israel by assassinating Nadab, when that king, the son of Jeroboam, was directing the siege of Gibbethon in the land of the Philistines. Baasha exterminated the house of Jeroboam and made Tirzah his capital. He ascended the throne in the third year of Asa, king of Judah (1 Ki. 15-16), and carried on a long war with him. About the sixteenth year of Asa, Baasha began to fortify Ramah, 5 mi. (8 km.) N of Jerusalem, in order to blockade the northern frontier of Judah. He was prevented from completing this work by Ben-Hadad, king of Damascus, whom Asa had hired (1 Ki. 15:16-21; 2 Chr. 16:1-6). Asa then tore down Baasha's defenses, and for his own protection built up the bulwarks of Geba (between Ramah and Jerusalem). Baasha continued the calf worship begun by Jeroboam, and Jehu the prophet threatened him and his house with a worse fate than Jeroboam's. After a reign of twenty-four years he died a natural death and was succeeded by his son Elah, who, along with every member of the house of Baasha, was killed by Zimri.

babbler. In the NT, the Greek term *spermologos G5066* (lit., "picker up of seeds," but applied to those who scavenge for information) occurs only in an offhand remark attributed to the Epicurean and Stoic philosophers who listened to Paul's address on the Areopagus and accused him of being a charlatan (Acts 17:18). The translation "babbler" is also used by the NRSV to render a Hebrew phrase that means literally "one who opens his lips" (Prov. 20:19); moreover, the KJV uses it incorrectly to render another phrase ("master of the tongue") that really means "charmer," apparently with reference to a pagan shaman (Eccl. 10:11). The NIV uses the verb "babble" to render Greek *battalogeō G1006*, with reference to the meaningless prayer of pagans (Matt. 6:7).

Babel, Tower of. bay'buhl (Heb. *bābel H951*, from Akk. *bāb-ilī*, "gate of God"). An expression not found in the Bible, but used popularly for the structure built in the plain of Shinar, as the story is told in Gen. 11:1-9. The men of Shinar intended to build a tower that reached "to the heavens," but the Lord frustrated them by confusing their tongues. The author of Genesis assumes that before this the whole human species was a single tribe moving from place to place and speaking one language. The event took place not very long after the flood.

The remains of large towers called ziggurats can be found at the sites of many ancient cities in

B

Mesopotamia. These sacred temple-towers were built in steplike stages of brick and asphalt, usually with a shrine at the top. The Tower of Babel was, however, not a temple-tower but simply a tower, apparently the first one ever attempted. The ziggurats may have been imitations of this tower. It is not known for certain whether the ruins of the Tower of Babel are still extant. There are rival claimants for the honor.

baboon. See ANIMALS.

baby. This English term is sometimes used literally in the Bible to denote an infant or very young child (e.g., Exod. 2:6; Ps 8:2; Lk. 1:41; 2:12). Its figurative use in the NT may reflect the imagery of spiritual REGENERATION (new birth): young Christians, as well as believers who are undeveloped or stunted in their spiritual growth, are referred to as "babes in Christ" (1 Cor. 3:1 KJV; NIV, "infants") and as "newborn babies" (1 Pet. 2:2). Just as human babies can assimilate only milk, not solid food, so spiritual infants can grasp only fundamental or basic doctrines (cf. also Heb. 5:12-14).

Babylon. bab′uh-luhn (Heb. *bābel* H951, from Akk. *bāb-ilī, bāb-ilāni*, "the gate of god[s]"; Gk. *Babylōn G956*). Capital of the land of Babylonia, from which the land takes its name. Though not the oldest city in that region, it soon became the most important from the standpoint of both size and influence. Babylon was situated in central MESOPOTAMIA on the river EUPHRATES, some 50 mi. (80 km.) S of modern Baghdad, capital of Iraq. A huge plantation of palm trees added to the beauty of the ancient city, and a permanent water supply assured fertility for the surrounding areas. It was within easy reach of the Persian Gulf and, being situated on an important caravan-trade route, was in contact with all the most important cultural centers of the ANE.

The date of its foundation is still disputed. The connection between AKKAD, CALNEH, ERECH, and Babylon (Gen. 10:10) indicates a period at least as early as 3000 B.C. Babylon may have been founded originally by the Sumerians, and an early tablet recorded that Sargon of Akkad (c. 2400) destroyed Babylon and took some of its sacred earth to his own capital city, Akkad. Whatever the date of its foundation, the earliest archaeological levels of the mound that once was stately Babylon come from the first dynasty period, that is, the nineteenth to sixteenth centuries B.C.

The history of Babylon is complicated by the fact that it was governed by rulers from several lands who were successively engaged in struggles for its capture and retention. It was the scene of many a decisive battle, its magnificent buildings plundered in various periods and its walls and temples leveled from time to time. Yet this apparently indestructible city rose from its ruins on each occasion more splendid than before, until during the reign of NEBUCHADNEZZAR II (c. 605-562 B.C.) it was probably the largest and most elaborate city in the ancient world. All that now remains of its former glory is a series of mounds some 5 mi. (8 km.) in extent, lying mostly on the left bank of the Euphrates.

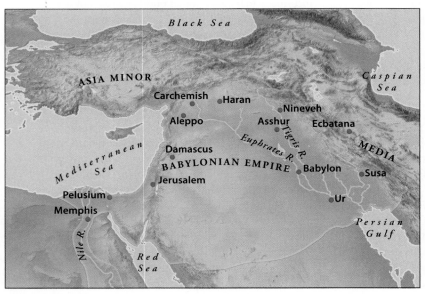

The Babylonian Empire.

The political history of Babylon was bound up with that of Babylonia and ASSYRIA, though from the beginning of the eighteenth century B.C. (about the period of TERAH's migration from UR, Gen. 11:31) until the time of the Assyrian regime (ninth to sixth centuries), Babylon was the dominant influence in Mesopotamia. Under HAMMURABI (c. 1704-1662), the last great king of the first dynasty, the Babylonian empire stretched from the Persian Gulf to the middle Euphrates and upper TIGRIS regions. Archaeological discoveries have brought to light many of the achievements of this remarkable scholar-statesman, the most interesting of which is his celebrated legal code. His attempts to unify and organize social life led him to collect and expand existing minor law codes. The resulting legislation was of a most comprehensive nature, and Hammurabi ordered it to be incised on a basalt column and placed in the temple of Shamash, god of justice, for all to see. This column is in every sense a monument of ancient jurisprudence. It was carried away as a trophy by invading Elamites (see ELAM) in a surprise raid during the twelfth century and was unearthed only in A.D. 1901 at SUSA by J. de Morgan.

The first dynasty of Babylon fell about 1596 B.C. when the HITTITE king Mursilis I advanced from Anatolia (ASIA MINOR) with an army and sacked the city. For about 300 years Babylon was at the mercy of the Kassites who lived to the N, the Elamites, and other warlike nomadic people. An early Assyrian monarch named Tukulti-Ninurta I (c. 1250) occupied Babylon and took the sacred statue of MARDUK, patron deity of the city, to ASSHUR. From the end of the tenth century Babylon became a vassal of Assyria, controlled by the kings of NINEVEH. Occasionally the vassal ruler revolted and attempted to form a new dynasty in Babylon, but by the time of TIGLATH-PILESER III of Assyria (c. 745-727) Babylon was completely under Assyrian control. This redoubtable monarch (known as Pul in 2 Ki. 15:19 and 1 Chr. 5:26) attacked the northern kingdom of Israel, carried away captives from Gilead, Galilee, and Naphtali (2 Ki. 15:29), demanded booty, and reduced Israel to a series of provinces.

One of the more vigorous vassal rulers of Babylon who revolted against Assyria was Mardukapal-

Reconstruction of the Ishtar Gate at Babylon.

© Dr. James C. Martin

iddin (c. 722-711 B.C.), the MERODACH-BALADAN of 2 Ki. 20:12-13 and Isa. 39:1. He endeavored to organize a coalition against his overlord SARGON II (c. 722-705) and sought the kingdom of Judah as an ally. ISAIAH dissuaded HEZEKIAH from such a course on the ground that it would be futile. A small stone tablet has been unearthed in Babylonia depicting Merodach-Baladan as a stout man with the long curled hair and beard typical of Babylonian men. He held a scepter in his left hand, and on his head he wore a conical helmet quite unlike the usual Assyrian crown. Merodach-Baladan's schemes were ended by Sargon, who subdued him with difficulty and occupied the throne of Babylon.

Sargon was succeeded by his son SENNACHERIB (c. 705-681 B.C.), who employed vassal princes to keep Babylon in subjugation. When this device failed, he attacked the city and sacked it in 689, removing the statues of its gods to Assyria. It was left to his son ESARHADDON (c. 681-669) to repair the damage and restore the city, perhaps at the instigation of his mother, who was apparently of Aramean descent. When Esarhaddon died, his kingdom was divided between his two sons. One of them, ASHURBANIPAL (c. 669-626), the last great Assyrian ruler, reigned in Nineveh while his brother Shamash-Shumukin occupied the throne of Babylon. They quarreled bitterly, and in 651

B

Ashurbanipal attacked and burned Babylon. His brother was killed, and a vassal was appointed to succeed him. Toward the end of Ashurbanipal's life this man became increasingly rebellious, and from 631-612 the influence of Babylon increased to the point where NABOPOLASSAR founded an independent dynasty in 626, known as the neo-Babylonian, or Chaldean, regime.

Under Nabopolassar (c. 626-605 B.C.) and his son Nebuchadnezzar II (c. 605-562), ancient Babylon attained the height of its splendor. While both men were notable military strategists they were also individuals of cultural interests, and they set about rebuilding the old Babylonian empire so as to make it the most splendid and notable of all time. Military expeditions brought numbers of captive peoples to Babylonia, and these were employed as artisans and craftsmen on the vast reconstruction projects. As a result of the energy and imagination of Nabopolassar and his son, the influence of Babylon far outstripped that of Nineveh, and in 616 the Babylonians began a military campaign against the middle Euphrates region that ended in the destruction of the Assyrian empire.

Nabopolassar first marched to the Balikh River and sacked a number of towns but returned to Babylon the same year. In 615 B.C. he set out to attack Asshur, and after a year's siege the city capitulated. A revolt in the central Euphrates region delayed a further attack on Assyria, but in 612 a combined force of Babylonians and Medes marched against Nineveh, captured it, and burned it to the ground. The remnant of the Assyrian forces fled to HARAN (PLACE) in NW Mesopotamia, and despite their attempts to ally with Egypt they were decisively defeated in 610, ending the power of the Assyrian regime.

A battle at CARCHEMISH in 605 B.C. against the Egyptians gave the Babylonian forces a decided military advantage, and Nabopolassar determined to occupy S Palestine, probably intending to use it as an advance base for a subsequent attack on Egypt. Nebuchadnezzar directed the operation on the death of Nabopolassar in 605, and in 597 the first attack on Judah took place. This was followed by others in 586 and 581, when several thousand inhabitants of Judah were sent to Babylon as captives. This group joined other previously enslaved peoples, supplementing the already large labor force employed on the gigantic tasks of reconstruction and expansion current in the empire.

Once Nebuchadnezzar felt reasonably secure, he devoted an increasing amount of attention to the expansion of cultural interests in imperial territory, and more particularly in Babylon. His objective was to make this capital the most notable city in the world, and to this end he constructed new canals and navigable waterways, erected magnificent buildings, and laid out extensive parks. A number of travelers who visited Babylon at this time have left their impressions of the city. The description furnished by Herodotus in particular clearly indicates his amazement at the city's great size and splendor.

According to this notable historian of antiquity, the city occupied an area of about 200 sq. mi. (518 sq. km.) and was built on both sides of the Euphrates. It was protected by a double defensive brick wall reinforced with towers. Outside the city wall, about 60 ft. (18 m.) distant, was an additional defensive wall of burnt bricks set in bitumen. The outer portion of the twin walls extended over 17 mi. (27 km.) and was constructed under Nebuchadnezzar, while his predecessors were responsible for other parts of the fortification. Excavations at the mound have shown that the earliest attempt at constructing a defensive system goes back to the nineteenth century B.C.

According to cuneiform sources, access to the city was gained by eight gates, four of which have been excavated. Probably the most impressive of these is the Ishtar gate, located at the northern end of the mound. To reach it one passed down part of the great stone-paved processional street that was about 3,000 ft. (937.5 m.) in length. It was decorated on either side with figures of lions passant in enameled brick. Assyrian art was at its height at this period, and the craftmanship and execution of these animals indicate an advanced degree of artistic skill. The Ishtar gate was also decorated with animals, consisting of about a dozen rows of bulls and mythological dragons placed alternately. The decor was executed predominantly in blue and brown enamel and was done in the time of Nebuchadnezzar.

When the city was at the height of its influence, there were more than fifty temples in Babylon.

© Dr. James C. Martin. The British Museum. Photographed by permission.

Babylonian weight of 166 grams. The inscription (in Old Persian, Elamite, and Babylonian) gives the names and titles of Darius I (521-486 B.C.).

When some of these were excavated, they were found to be in a reasonably good state of preservation. The temple of Ninmah, goddess of the underworld, was built by Ashurbanipal near the Ishtar gate. The ground plan indicated that when the city was approached from the N, a vestibule led into a larger courtyard, the S end of which was decorated with pillars. Beyond these was an antechapel, while to the S of this area was the shrine of the deity; this shrine contained among other structures an elevated platform designed to support a statue of the goddess. In addition there were living quarters for the priests and stairways that gave access to other parts of the building. A great number of terra-cotta figurines were uncovered at the site but proved to be of little importance.

The southern citadel that was adjacent to the processional street comprised a huge complex of buildings whose main sections were the work of Nabopolassar and Nebuchadnezzar. Several blocks of buildings and courtyards finally led to the royal palace, many of whose rooms were ornately decorated with blue enameled bricks incorporating motifs similar to those used in Greece at a later time. The living quarters provided for the royal family, the court officers, and the retinue of servants, and displayed the grandeur and pomp characteristic of an eastern court.

In this complex was situated one of the seven wonders of the world, the celebrated "hanging gardens" of Babylon. They actually consisted of terraces supported on huge masonry arches, on which carefully tended gardens had been laid out at different levels. Most probably they were designed and executed under Nebuchadnezzar, who had married a Median princess and perhaps intended the raised gardens to be a comforting reminder of her mountainous homeland. They included many species of Babylonian and Persian plants in addition to the palm trees that were a characteristic feature of Babylonia at that time. Water was raised to these elevated terraces by a number of mechanical hoists. The interesting feature of these raised gardens was that they were visible above the tops of the buildings, providing a welcome contrast of greenery against an otherwise unrelieved expanse of white roofs or blue sky.

In an enclosed area SW of the Ishtar gate was the huge ZIGGURAT of Babylon, which was closely linked with the temple of Marduk lying immediately to the south. A ziggurat was a staged or terraced tower crowned with a small shrine dedicated to a particular deity. The structure was generally erected on a mound or artificial brick platform, presumably to serve as a protection against floodwaters. Sometimes the term *ziggurat* is used to include the platform as well as the tower itself. This great staged tower of Babylon may have been the original Tower of BABEL (Gen. 11:1-9), modified by subsequent reconstruction and additions, although efforts to prove so have been unsuccessful. From archaeological and other sources it appears that it was a seven-story building of sun-dried mud brick faced with kiln-dried brick. An eighth story probably consisted of a small shrine dedicated to Marduk, and in the time of Nebuchadnezzar it was faced with blue enameled bricks. Access to the various levels was gained by means of stairways or ramps. The ground plan of the ziggurat was approximately 300 ft. (90 m.) square, and the structure as it stood in the sixth century B.C. exceeded 300 ft. (90 m.) in height.

The associated temple of Marduk consisted of an annex leading to the principal building. In the latter were a number of chapels devoted to deities other than Marduk, but his shrine was by far the most ornate, richly decorated with gold, alabaster, cedar-wood paneling, lapis lazuli, obsidian, and other semiprecious stones. Much of this work was done in the sixth century B.C.

B

B

Nebuchadnezzar died in 562 B.C., and during the next five years three kings, one of whom was EVIL-MERODACH (2 Ki. 25:27), occupied the throne until NABONIDUS came to power in 556. Nabonidus was a mystic who had antiquarian interests, and after a short rule he made his son Bēl-šar-uṣur (Belshazzar) regent while he retired to Teima (see TEMA) in ARABIA. After nine years he returned to Babylon only to witness the overthrow of the city by CYRUS in 539. This conqueror did not pillage Babylon, but acted respectfully toward the shrines and deities of the land. Enslaved populations were liberated, including the captive Hebrews, and Cyrus, "king of Babylon," set about building up his vast Persian empire. See PERSIA.

DARIUS I (c. 521-485 B.C.) continued the political tendencies begun by Cyrus, but in later years the center of influence of the Achaemenid regime moved from Babylon to Persepolis and Ecbatana. When the Persian empire fell to ALEXANDER THE GREAT in 330, Babylon was destroyed. Alexander intended to reconstruct the great ziggurat, and ordered the rubble removed from the site, but at his death in 323 the task was left unfinished. Although remaining an inhabited site, Babylon declined still further in importance under the PARTHIANS (c. 125 B.C.).

Babylon is mentioned several times in the NT. One controversial passage is at the end of 1 Peter: "She who is in Babylon, chosen together with you, sends you her greetings" (1 Pet. 5:13). This statement appears to be a greeting from a "sister church" (so NRSV), but what city is in view? Although some have thought that Mesopotamian Babylon is in view, there is no evidence that PETER ever visited this city; moreover, it would seem an extraordinary coincidence for Mark and Silvanus, Paul's companions, to have been in Mesopotamia also. Most scholars take this verse as a reference to ROME, indicating the place in which the letter was written. See PETER, FIRST LETTER OF.

In the book of Revelation, "Babylon" is described as a great city that was to fall dramatically, as had Mesopotamian Babylon (Rev. 14:8; 16:19; 18:2, 10, 21). It was the "mother of prostitutes," the very antithesis of the new Jerusalem, and as such the fount of all earth's abominations (17:5). Some have interpreted this apocalyptic city as an extension of that Mesopotamian metropolis (just as they would posit the heavenly Jerusalem to be described in terms of an extended Palestinian Jerusalem), but the name of Babylon is clearly stated to be a "mystery" that is to be allegorically interpreted (17:5, 7). Most commentators see Rome as fulfilling all the characteristics of the Babylon of Revelation. Faced by that city's opposition to the kingdom of God, it would be natural for Jews and Christians alike to see in the new world power of Rome a "Babylon" such as had oppressed Judah. Since God had overthrown the Mesopotamian city and delivered his people, in the same way the downfall of the Roman empire could be envisaged.

Babylonian captivity. See EXILE.

Baca, Valley of. bay′kuh (Heb. *bākā* H1133, "balsam tree" or "weeping"). TNIV Baka. This name occurs only in Ps. 84:6, which says of those who trust in God and are blessed: "As they pass through the Valley of Baca, / they make it a place of springs." The name possibly refers to a plant that exuded gum or that dripped tear-like drops of moisture. In any case, the psalmist appears to use this name, not in reference to an actual geographical location, but as a symbol of the pilgrim's affliction.

Bacchides. bak′uh-deez (Gk. *Bakchidēs*). A SELEUCID official who figures prominently in the book of 1 Maccabees. As general, Bacchides was required to conduct a number of campaigns against Judas MACCABEE and his followers. The first one took place when the Seleucid king Demetrius sent Bacchides to Judea to establish ALCIMUS as high priest; the general succeeded in this task, but in the process alienated many (1 Macc. 7:5-20). In a second campaign Bacchides attacked with a large force that killed Judas and dispersed the Jewish army (9:1-18). The Jews elected Jonathan, Judas's brother, as their leader, and two years later Demetrius sent Bacchides against Jonathan. The siege proved unsuccessful and Bacchides withdrew permanently from Judea, providing a basis for a truce (9:57-63).

Bachrites. See BEKER.

backsliding. This English term occurs especially in the book of Jeremiah (Jer. 2:19; 3:22; 5:6; 14:7). In these and similar instances, the relevant Hebrew terms were used when Israel turned away from the true and living God to worship the heathen nature gods and idols, usually referred to with the name BAAL. See APOSTASY. The term "backsliding" does not appear in the NT, but the idea is implied (Mk. 4:16, 17; Lk. 9:62; Gal. 3:1-5; 1 Tim. 5:15; 2 Tim. 4:10; Rev. 2:4; 3:17). The NT concept carries with it the idea that those who once made profession of the Christian faith have turned aside or have reverted to a life of sin and spiritual indifference.

badger. See ANIMALS.

bag. This term is used in English versions of the Bible to translate various Hebrew and Greek nouns. The most common Hebrew word is *kîs H3967*, used especially of a "weight bag" (e.g., Deut. 25:13; Isa. 46:6). A frequent Greek noun in the NT is *pēra G4385*, which probably refers to a knapsack (e.g., Matt. 10:10; it is distinguished from *ballantion G964*, "purse," in Lk. 22:35). See also PURSE.

bagpipe. See MUSIC AND MUSICAL INSTRUMENTS.

Baharum. buh-hair´uhm. See BAHURIM.

Baharumite, Barhumite. buh-hair´uh-mit, bahr-hyoo´mit (Heb. *bahărûmî H1049, barhumî H1372*). Apparently, two alternate ways of designating someone from BAHURIM (1 Chr. 11:33; 2 Sam. 23:31).

Bahurim. buh-hyoor´im (Heb. *bahûrîm H1038*, possibly "[village of] young men"). NRSV also Baharum (in 1 Chr. 11:33). A village in the territory of BENJAMIN, often identified with modern Ras et-Temim, just NNE of the Mount of OLIVES, on the N side of the Roman road to JERICHO from JERUSALEM. Bahurim is mentioned in several historical passages (2 Sam. 3:16; 16:5; 17:18-20). Bahurim happened to be the home of SHIMEI, who ran along the ridge throwing stones at DAVID and cursing the king (19:16; 1 Ki. 2:8). This town also had some loyal supporters of David,

for an unnamed woman concealed David's spying messengers in a well at Bahurim (2 Sam. 17:18-20). Further, one of David's elite military heroes, AZMAVETH, was apparently a native of this town (2 Sam. 23:31, "the Barhumite"; 1 Chr. 11:33, "the Baharumite").

Bajith. bay´jith (Heb. *bayit H1074*, "house"). Also Bayith. According to the KJV and other versions, this is the name of an otherwise unknown city, mentioned alongside DIBON (Isa. 15:2). The Hebrew text is difficult, and many scholars take the word as a common noun (cf. NIV and NRSV).

Bakbakkar. bak-bak´uhr (Heb. *baqbaqqar H1320*, meaning uncertain). One of the Levites who ministered in the temple after the return from the EXILE (1 Chr. 9:15; possibly identical to BAKBUKIAH).

Bakbuk. bak´buhk (Heb. *baqbûq H1317*, possibly short form of BAKBUKIAH). The head of a family of temple servants (NETHINIM) who returned from the EXILE with ZERUBBABEL (Ezra 2:51; Neh. 7:53).

Bakbukiah. bak´buh-ki´uh (Heb. *baqbuqyâ H1319*, perhaps "Yahweh has emptied, poured out"). A Levite who served after the EXILE; he is described as an associate of MATTANIAH, the director of worship (Neh. 11:17; 12:9). In another reference (12:25), Bakbukiah and Mattaniah are grouped with the gatekeepers, so it is not certain whether the same persons are meant. See also BAKBAKKAR,

baker. See OCCUPATIONS AND PROFESSIONS.

Balaam. bay´luhm (Heb. *bilʿām H1189*, possibly "devourer, glutton"; Gk. *Balaam G962*). Son of Beor from the city of PETHOR on the EUPHRATES, a diviner with a remarkable history (Num. 22:22—24:25; 31:8, 16; Deut. 23:4; Josh. 13:22; 24:9; Neh. 13:2; Mic. 6:5; 2 Pet. 2:15; Jude 11; Rev. 2:14). Balaam figures when the Israelites pitched their tents in the plains of MOAB after their victory over SIHON and OG. BALAK, the king of the Moabites, sent an embassy of elders of Moab and MIDIAN to Balaam, offering to reward him if he would curse the Israelites. After looking to God about the matter, he replied that God had forbidden him

B

to comply with the request. Balak then sent some messengers of a higher rank with more alluring promises. This time God permitted Balaam to go, cautioning him, however, to deliver only the message God gave him. On his way to Balak, Balaam had this command strongly impressed on his mind by the strange behavior of his donkey and his encounter with the angel of the Lord.

Balak took Balaam to BAMOTH BAAL, from which a part of the camp of the Israelites could be seen. To Balak's disappointment, Balaam pronounced a blessing on the Israelites instead of a curse. Surprised and incensed at the words of the diviner, Balak thought that a fuller view of the camp of Israel might change his disposition. He took him to the top of Mount PISGAH, but the only result was further blessing instead of cursing. Balaam compared the children of Israel to a lion who will not lie down until he has eaten his prey. In desperation Balak now suggested that the issue be tried from a third locality. They went to the top of PEOR, and there the Spirit of God came on Balaam and caused him to declare not only that God would bless Israel, but that he who blessed her would be blessed and he who cursed her would be cursed. In his bitter disappointment, Balak angrily reproached Balaam and ordered him to go home without the promised reward. Before he left, Balaam reminded the king that at the very beginning he had said that no amount of money could make him give anything other than the commandment of the Lord. He then uttered a last prophecy—the most remarkable so far—in which he foretold the coming of a star from Jacob and a scepter out of Israel that would defeat Israel's enemies, including Moab.

Nothing else is said of Balaam until Num. 31. There the seer, who had failed to turn away the Lord from his people, tried before long to turn the people from the Lord. He knew that if he succeeded in this, the consequences to Israel would be just as Balak had desired, God's curse on Israel. By his advice the Israelites were seduced into idolatry and all the vile abominations connected with it. In the judgment that followed, no fewer than 24,000 Israelites perished, until it was evident that the nation abhorred idolatry as a great crime against God. By God's command Israel brought vengeance on her seducers, the Midianites; and in the universal slaughter Balaam also perished.

In the NT Balaam is several times held up as an example of the pernicious influence of hypocritical teachers who attempt to lead God's people astray (2 Pet. 2:15; Jude 11; Rev. 2:14). No Bible character is more severely excoriated. The experience of Balaam brings into focus some basic elements in the biblical understanding of God's rule in the world. First, we see how the Lord overrules man's sinful will and desire to bring his own purposes to pass. Balaam already knew God's will (Num. 22:12-13). The fact that he responded to the second deputation (22:15) with a reference to abundant reward (22:18) and a renewed approach to the Lord indicates not a sincere desire to do God's will but a determination if at all possible to do his own. It is in this light that we should understand what is expressed as a divine directive (22:20): Balaam hears from the Lord only what he wants to hear. But when he went to Balak, all he could do was what the Lord determined he should do. It is the Lord who reigns. Second, we ought to note that against all odds the Lord's promises prevail: Balak may wish to reverse them, and Balaam, if only he could, might try to overturn them, but the promises stand. It is to highlight this truth that Balaam is brought before us in a manner that challenges the promise to Abraham (Num. 22:6; cf. Gen. 12:3). But in any event it is not the word that Balaam speaks but the people's attitude to the descendants of Abraham that is decisive: Balak is unable to hurt them; Balaam and the Midianites perish. Third, we learn that the Lord guards his people from overwhelming threats of which they are not even aware. Balaam certainly possessed a mysterious power (Num. 22:6) and, without their knowledge, it was to be directed against Israel from the hills overlooking their camp. But the Lord turned the curse into a blessing and they knew nothing about it until long after (31:8). This is the truth expressed in 1 Cor. 10:13.

Balac. See BALAK.

Baladan. bal′uh-duhn (Heb. *balʾădān H1156*, Akk. *Apla-iddin*, "[God] gave a son"). The father of MERODACH-BALADAN king of BABYLON (2 Ki.

20:12; Isa. 39:1). His name is not attested outside the Bible.

Balah. bay′luh (Heb. *bālāh H1163*, possibly "old"). A town within the territory of JUDAH that was allotted to the tribe of SIMEON (Josh. 19:3; cf. v. 1). See BAALAH #2.

Balak. bay′lak (Heb. *bālāq H1192*, "devastator"; Gk. *Balak G963*). Son of Zippor and king of MOAB when Israel emerged from the wilderness to enter Canaan. Having seen what the Hebrews had done to the AMORITES, he attempted to prevent Israel's advance by hiring BALAAM to curse them (Num. 22–24). He built altars at three different sites for the purpose, but each attempt failed. He remains throughout Hebrew history as an example of the folly of attempting to thwart Yahweh's will (Josh. 24:9; Jdg. 11:25; Mic. 6:5; cf. Rev. 2:14 [KJV, "Balac"]).

balance. The English word is from the Latin *bilanx* and means "having two scales." The balances of the Hebrews consisted of a horizontal bar, either suspended from a cord that was held in the hand or pivoted on a perpendicular rod. Scales were suspended from the ends of the bar, one for the object to be weighed, the other for the weight. At first the weights were of stone. Weighing with such balances could be accurately done, but the system was liable to fraud, so that in the OT there is much denunciation of "dishonest scales" (Mic. 6:11).

Bronze pair of scales from the Roman period.

bald locust. See ANIMALS.

baldness. Natural baldness is seldom mentioned in the Bible. It was believed to result from hard work (Ezek. 29:18) or disease (Isa. 3:17, 24). Baldness produced by shaving the head, however, is frequently referred to. It was done as a mark of mourning for the dead (Lev. 21:5; Isa. 15:2; 22:12; Mic. 1:16). Shaving the head as a sacrifice to the deity was the custom of the heathens in the land, and the Israelites were strictly forbidden to practice it (Lev. 21:5; Deut. 14:1). The custom among neighboring nations of shaving all but a small patch in the center of the head was also forbidden (Lev. 19:27; 21:5). When a NAZIRITE completed his vow, the shaven hair was offered as a sacrifice to the Lord (Num. 6:18; cf. Acts 18:18; 21:24).

balm. An aromatic resin perhaps obtained in GILEAD (Gen. 37:25; Jer. 8:22; 46:11) and exported from Palestine. It was used as an ointment for healing wounds (Jer. 51:8). It came from a small tree not now found in Gilead, and perhaps it never grew there. See also PLANTS.

balsam. See PLANTS.

Bamah. bay′muh (Heb. *bāmāh H1196*, "high place"). This name occurs only in Ezek. 20:29, where the prophet is instructed to ask the Israelites, with scorn and an apparent word play, "What [*mâ*] is the high place [*habbāmâ*] to which you go [*habbā'îm*]?" Then follows the comment, "And its name is called Bamah to this day" (lit. trans.). The location of this HIGH PLACE is not known, although some scholars speculate that it may be a reference to a prominent center of worship such as the one at GIBEON (cf. 1 Ki. 3:4).

Bamoth, Bamoth Baal. bay′moth, bay′moth-bay′uhl (Heb. *bāmôt H1199*, *bāmôt ba'al H1200*, "high places of Baal"). A place in TRANSJORDAN, N of the ARNON River, where the Israelites stopped (Num. 21:19–20). Bamoth is probably the shortened form of Bamoth Baal (22:41). This Moabite town probably was named for the special cultic installation found at this spot, where King BALAK brought the prophet BALAAM to curse Israel.

© Dr. James C. Martin. The British Museum. Photographed by permission.

Subsequently, the tribe of REUBEN was assigned this city as part of its inheritance (Josh. 13:17). The precise location is not known, but most fix it on the W edge of the Transjordanian plateau, S of Mount Nebo (see NEBO, MOUNT).

ban. See DEVOTED THING.

band. This English term has various meanings and translates several Hebrew nouns and verbs. For example, the noun *ḥāšûq H3122* is used with reference to the silver rings (KJV, "fillets") put on the posts of the TABERNACLE (Exod. 27:10 et al.). The very different meaning "a group of people" is often expressed in Hebrew with the term *gĕdûd H1522*, which usually refers to a raiding party (Gen. 49:19 et al.). In the NT, the KJV uses English "band" to render the military Greek noun *speira G5061* (e.g., Jn. 18:3; NIV, "detachment"). Other Hebrew and Greek terms may be rendered with "band" or its synonyms in various English translations.

Bani. bay´ni (Heb. *bānî H1220*, possibly a short form of BENAIAH). This name, which was popular in the postexilic period, is easily confused with others that have a similar form (e.g., Binnui), and it may have also been used as a clan name; the items included here may therefore not correspond precisely with the number of individuals referred to in the Bible.

(1) "Bani the Gadite" was one of DAVID's Thirty, the military elite of its time (2 Sam. 23:36 NRSV and other versions). The NIV, however, has "the son of Hagri" on the basis of the parallel passage (1 Chr. 11:38). See HAGRI.

(2) Son of Shemer, descendant of LEVI through MERARI, and ancestor of ETHAN; the latter ministered with music in the TABERNACLE during the time of David (1 Chr. 6:46).

(3) Descendant of JUDAH through PEREZ and ancestor of Uttai; the latter was among the first to resettle in Jerusalem after the EXILE (1 Chr. 9:4).

(4) The ancestor of a large group that returned from the EXILE with ZERUBBABEL (Ezra 2:10; called Binnui in Neh. 7:15).

(5) Ancestor of Shelomith; the latter accompanied EZRA as a representative from Babylon (Ezra 8:10, on the basis of LXX and of 1 Esd. 8:36; KJV, following the MT, omits the name).

(6) In the list of exiles who had married foreign women, the (clan?) name Bani occurs three times according to the MT (Ezra 10:29, 34, 38). The first two occurrences may refer to the same family head. The third occurrence probably reflects a scribal mistake, so that the name Bani should be emended to "descendants of" (Heb. *bĕnê*; so NIV and NRSV, following LXX).

(7) A Levite whose son Rehum helped to repair the wall of Jerusalem (Neh. 3:17).

(8) A LEVITE who along with others assisted Ezra in expounding the law of God (Neh. 8:7). He is probably the same person mentioned twice among those who led the people in confession and worship (9:4a, 5; the Bani mentioned in 4b, if not a textual corruption, is a different individual).

(9) One of the Levitical representatives who signed the covenant of NEHEMIAH (Neh. 10:13).

(10) One of the leaders of the people who signed the covenant of Nehemiah (Neh. 10:14).

(11) Father of Uzzi; the latter, who was "chief officer of the Levites in Jerusalem" after the return from the exile, is also described as "one of Asaph's descendants, who were the singers responsible for the service of the house of God" (Neh. 11:22).

banking. An early form of banking business was first established in Israel only after the EXILE. Previously, people generally buried their treasures and valuables (Josh. 7:21; cf. Matt. 13:44; Lk. 19:20). Functions associated with banking, however, are recorded throughout the Bible. Money could be received on deposit, loaned out, and exchanged for smaller denominations or for foreign money. Israelites were not permitted to charge each other INTEREST (Exod. 22:25) but could lend with interest to Gentiles (Deut. 23:20).

banner. A standard or ensign, generally on a high pole or carried on a staff, to represent a cause or to indicate a rallying point for battle. Banners were used in ancient times for military, national, and ecclesiastical purposes very much as they are today. In connection with Israel's wilderness journey we read, "The Israelites are to camp around the Tent of Meeting some distance from it, each man under his standard with the banners of his family" (Num. 2:2). The word occurs frequently in the figurative sense of a rallying point for God's people (Isa. 5:26; 11:10; Jer. 4:21).

banquet. The Hebrews, like other peoples of the ANE, were very fond of social feasting. At the three great religious feasts, which all males were expected to attend, the family had its feast. Sacrifices were accompanied by a feast (Exod. 34:15; Jdg. 16:23-25). There were feasts for birthdays (Gen. 40:20; Job 1:4; Matt. 14:6), marriages (Gen. 29:22; Matt. 22:2), funerals (2 Sam. 3:35; Jer. 16:7), laying of foundations (Prov. 9:1-5), vintage (Jdg. 9:27), sheep-shearing (1 Sam. 25:2, 36), and on other occasions. A banquet always included wine drinking; it was not simply a feast in our sense. At a large banquet a second invitation was often sent on the day of the feast, or a servant brought the guests to the feast (Matt. 22:2-14; Lk. 14:17-24). The host provided robes for the guests; these were worn in his honor and were a token of his regard. Guests were welcomed by the host with a kiss (Lk. 7:45), and their feet were washed because of the dusty roads (Gen. 18:4; Jdg. 19:21; Lk. 7:44). The head was anointed (Ps. 23:5; Lk. 7:46), and sometimes the beard, the feet, and the clothes were also anointed. The head was decorated with garlands (Isa. 28:1). The guests were seated according to their respective rank (1 Sam. 9:22; Lk. 14:8), the hands were washed (2 Ki. 3:11), and prayers for blessing on the food were said (1 Sam. 9:13; Matt. 15:35; Lk. 22:17). The PHARISEES made hand washing and the blessing of food burdensome rituals. The feast was put under the superintendence of a "governor of the feast," usually one of the guests, whose task it was to taste the food and the drinks and to settle about the toasts and amusements. The most honored guests received either larger portions or more choice ones than the rest (Gen. 43:34; 1 Sam. 9:23-24). Portions were sometimes sent to friends not attending the feast (2 Sam. 11:8; Neh. 8:10). Often the meal was enlivened with music, singing, and dancing (2 Sam. 19:35; Lk. 15:25), or with riddles (Jdg. 14:12). A great banquet sometimes lasted seven days, but excess in eating and drinking was condemned by the sacred writers (Eccl. 10:16-17; Isa. 5:11-12).

baptism. The significance of the Greek verb *baptizō G966* often has been obscured by a lack of exegetical clarity and by forced interpretation. Its true meaning can be found only in its usage and its theological significance. Its antecedent meaning involves the Judaic usage in OT times and the practice of JOHN THE BAPTIST. Its incipient meaning lies in CHRIST's own baptism and his interpretation of it. Its formal meaning is to be found in its apostolic interpretation, particularly by PAUL.

The idea of ceremonial washing, or cleansing, appears repeatedly in the Mosaic laws of purification (e.g., Exod. 29:4, 17; 30:17-21; 40:12, 30; Lev. 1:9, 13; 6:27; 9:14; 11:25; 14:8-9, 47; 15:5-27; 16:4-28; 17:15-16; 22:6; Num. 8:7; 19:7-21; 31:23-24; Deut. 21:6; 23:11). It is clear that later JUDAISM incorporated this connotation of cleansing and purification into its idea of the new covenant relation and used baptism as a rite of initiation, as reflected in the practices of the Qumran sect (see DEAD SEA SCROLLS).

While later Judaism certainly attached a deeply pietistic significance to the cleansing act, John the Baptist, who followed in this tradition, infused into the ritual act of initiation and purification an ethical quality that baptism had not had before. His was a moral community of penitent souls seeking personal righteousness, and he associated with the act of baptism the imperative necessity for a thorough change in the condition of the soul, manifested in a remission of sins through REPENTANCE. His fervent exhortation to repent and flee from the wrath to come (Matt. 3:7-8) was not a mere invitation to a religious ceremony, but was, rather, an indication of the change brought on by the act of baptism itself. The meaning of the act was deepened. Baptism was transformed from a rite to which one submitted oneself to a positive moral act initiated by the individual as a decisive commitment to personal piety.

John's baptism was, nevertheless, only transitory—his baptism of repentance was but preparatory to a baptism of identification. The meaning and efficacy of baptism can be understood only in the light of the redemptive death and resurrection of Christ. Christ referred to his death in the words, "I have a baptism to undergo" (Lk. 12:50), and in the question, "Can you drink the cup I drink or be baptized with the baptism I am baptized with?" (Matt. 20:22; Mk. 10:38). Here the

B

noun *baptisma* **G967**, which indicates the state or condition, is used instead of *baptismos* **G968**, which applies to Jewish rites and refers only to the act itself. The term *baptisma*, used only in the NT and in Christian writings, never refers to the act alone but always incorporates into its meaning the entire scope of the redemptive significance of the incarnate person of Christ.

John's baptism of Jesus, therefore, connects the act of water baptism with the meaning of the salvation events through Jesus's own person and work. To the act of water baptism Jesus added the promise of the baptism with the HOLY SPIRIT, the means by which his redemptive work is applied to human beings (Matt. 3:11; Mk. 1:8; Lk. 3:16; Acts 1:4-5; 11:16). Using the initiatory and purificatory meaning found in water baptism, Christ made spiritual baptism (by the Holy Spirit) synonymous with the actual application of the virtues of his death and resurrection to sinners.

Ritual purification pool used by the Qumran community.

The apostolic writers, particularly Paul, related Spirit baptism to the whole of the redemptive act. The act of water baptism symbolizes cleansing, but Spirit baptism gives the believer entry into the righteousness of Christ through an identification with Christ himself. Through Spirit baptism the redeemed sinner is incorporated into the spiritual BODY OF CHRIST, not merely as an act of initiation but as a state or condition of personal righteousness. It is, therefore, the only access to identification with the redeeming Christ.

Baptism may, therefore, be regarded from two perspectives. *Subjectively*, the baptism by the Holy Spirit brings the believer into positive relationship to God; *symbolically*, water baptism is the objective manifestation of the believer's acquiescence in that relationship. Its subjective significance is represented in the NT by many analogies. It is regarded as the means of *participation in the death and resurrection* of Jesus. In Rom. 6:3-5, Paul relates the actual spiritual condition of his readers to such a participation in Jesus' death and resurrection through Spirit baptism. "Do you not know that all of us who have been baptized into Christ Jesus were baptized into his death? We were buried therefore with him *by baptism* into death, so that as Christ was raised from the dead by the glory of the Father, we too might walk in newness of life." This identification has reference not merely to the death of Christ, in which the believer has also died to sin, but to the resurrection of Christ, in which the believer has found "newness of life." Spirit baptism is, therefore, an *entry into the new life in Christ*—a passage from the old creation into the new creation. This involves not merely forgiveness of sins but also an impartation of the life and righteousness of Christ to the believer (2 Pet. 1:4). The believer is "in Christ," and Christ is in the believer. Moreover, the identification effected through Spirit baptism *cleanses the believer through the blood of Christ* (Tit. 3:5-6). Thus, Spirit baptism is the incorporation of the believer into Christ's righteousness and an infusion of that righteousness into the believer.

Its symbolic significance is depicted in its objective form. While much debate has focused on the varying interpretations of the forms of baptism, each form (immersion, sprinkling, or pouring) is clearly associated with the concept of cleansing

© Dr. James C. Martin

and identification, which are the two integral parts of Spirit baptism. Many believe that immersion depicts more clearly the symbolic aspect of baptism since its three steps—*im*mersion (going into the water), *sub*mersion (going under the water), and *e*mersion (coming out of the water)—more closely parallel the concept of entering into the death of Christ, experiencing the forgiveness of sins, and rising to walk in the newness of Christ's resurrected life. Others argue that Rom. 6 is not the only passage that speaks of baptism; elsewhere Paul uses the symbolism of drinking (1 Cor. 12:13) and of being clothed (Gal. 3:27).

The genius of Christian baptism, however, is to be found not merely in its symbolic significance but in its actual effect in the life of the believer. Spirit baptism is always vitally related to FAITH. Only through responsive faith to the regenerative work of Christ does the soul participate in Spirit baptism and, simultaneously, in vital union with God. Subsequently, the symbolic form of baptism (water baptism) should also be related to, and on the basis of, personal faith, as a public commitment to the person of Christ.

While much recent emphasis among evangelicals has been on the "symbol only" concept of baptism, and while the NT pointedly abstains from ascribing a sacramental value to the act itself, a renewed emphasis on Spirit baptism will restore to its proper place a much neglected aspect of this doctrine. No statement of the doctrine can be a truly biblical one if it fails to emphasize that beyond the symbolic and commemorative act performed by a person there is also the Holy Spirit's inward operation. Spirit baptism brings the regenerated person into a redemptive relationship through his participation in and identification with the death, burial, and resurrection of Christ and the subsequent infusion of the merits of that death and resurrection into the life of the believer, by which he may live as one dead to sin but alive to God (Rom. 6:11).

baptism for the dead. In the midst of his discussion of the RESURRECTION, the apostle PAUL argues: "Now if there is no resurrection, what will those do who are baptized for the dead? If the dead are not raised at all, why are people baptized for them?" (1 Cor. 15:29). Opinion concerning the

meaning of this verse has been divided since early times, and there can be few passages of Scripture concerning which the views of modern commentators are so bewilderingly diverse. Only a selection of the more important views can be given: (1) Vicarious baptism to benefit those who died unbaptized. (2) Baptism for the sake of the dead, that is, in order to secure reunion with Christian relatives after death. (3) Baptism on account of the dead, that is, because of the witness in life of Christians martyred for the faith, such faith leading to the conversion and subsequent baptism of others. (4) Baptism to take the place of the dead, that is, to make up their number and so, perhaps, to hasten the second coming by assisting the completion of one of its preconditions. (5) Baptism over the dead, that is, over their graves, to express solidarity with them if they are Christian believers; if they are not, to involve them in salvation by this ritual. (6) Ceremonial ablution because of defilement through contact with a dead body. (7) Prayer for the dead described figuratively as baptism for them, comparable to the way "sacrifice" is sometimes spiritualized as prayer in the NT. (8) Death for the dead: the death of Christians regarded as redemptive and as securing salvation for the dead, and described as baptism because this symbolizes death. (9) Baptism to wash away mortal sins. (10) Baptism to confess the resurrection of the dead, because it symbolizes death and resurrection. (11) Baptism to secure benefit after death, because the thought of death has hastened the act of baptism. (12) Baptism "on account of the apostles," whose suffering makes them "truly dead."

The issue is anything but simple to decide. A number of the above interpretations are very forced, especially in their understanding of the Greek. Number 10 is popular because it presents no theological problems, but is grammatically suspect. Number 2 has been strongly advocated by some scholars. Number 1 still seems much the most natural. The postapostolic heretical sect of the Marcionites certainly practiced vicarious baptism, although possibly in misinterpretation of this passage. It does not seem likely that Paul was expressing approval of the practice; rather, he was only seeking to show the inconsistency of those who follow the practice while doubting or denying the resurrection.

baptism of the Holy Spirit. This phrase is sometimes used today in the sense of a "second blessing," an in-filling of the HOLY SPIRIT subsequent to, and quite distinct from, conversion, and usually regarded as a deeper spiritual experience, ushered in by spiritual phenomena, such as glossolalia (see TONGUES, GIFT OF). Without discussing the rightness or wrongness of the view in question, it would seem to be more proper to describe such an experience or state by using a different biblical phrase, "filled with the Holy Spirit" (Acts 2:4 et al.). In biblical usage "baptism of the Holy Spirit" is more general and somewhat different, as will be seen from the examination of the texts.

The origins of the phrase probably go back to JOHN THE BAPTIST, who contrasted his own preparatory rite of water baptism, a mere token of REPENTANCE, with the Spirit-baptism that will be given by the "more powerful" one who is to succeed him (Lk. 3:16 and parallels). Since the baptism of Christ is the pattern of all Christian baptism, it is not surprising that Lk. 3:21-22 shows the "baptism of the Spirit" being fulfilled (doubtless in a very special sense) in the case of CHRIST himself, after his water baptism at the hands of John. In addition, Christ is recorded having said to NICODEMUS, "no one can enter the kingdom of God unless he is born of water and the Spirit" (Jn. 3:5).

Later references to this concept are surprisingly few. It is clear from Acts 1:5 that the promise of "baptism of the Spirit" was to be fulfilled for the first disciples at PENTECOST. In the account of that day, however, and on subsequent occasions in the NT, the phrase used is "filled with the Holy Spirit" (Acts 2:4; 9:17). This event was apparently something that could happen repeatedly to the same group (cf. 2:5; 4:8, 31). One clear instance of the original metaphor is in 1 Cor. 12:13, "we were all baptized by one Spirit." Here Paul, by the wording, must be appealing to the universal spiritual experience of all true Christians, not to something unusual belonging to a minority. "Filling with the Spirit," by contrast, appears to be something that can take place repeatedly.

Bar-. bahr (Aram. *bar* H10120, "son, descendant"). This form occurs in English Bibles only as a prefix in patronymics. For example, Acts 13:6 refers to a Jewish sorcerer in PAPHOS who was named BAR-JESUS, that is, "the son of Jesus [= Joshua]." The same pattern is found in several other names, such as BARABBAS, BARNABAS, and BARTHOLOMEW.

Barabbas. buh-rab´uhs (Gk. *Barabbas G972*, from Aram. *bar ʾabbāʾ*, "son of Abba [= the father]"). A criminal chosen by the Jerusalem mob, at the instigation of the chief priests, in preference to Christ, to be released by PILATE on the feast of the Passover. Matthew calls him a notorious prisoner, and the other evangelists say he was arrested with others for robbery, sedition, and murder (Matt. 27:16; Mk. 15:15; Lk. 23:18; Jn. 18:40). The custom here mentioned of releasing a prisoner on the Passover is otherwise unknown. The reading "Jesus Barabbas" for his full name in Matt. 27:16-17 was found by Origen in many MSS and is attested in other witnesses; it is possibly due to a scribe's error in transcription.

Barachel. See BARAKEL.

Barachias. See BEREKIAH.

Barak. bair´ak (Heb. *bārāq H1399*, "lightning"; Gk. *Barak G973*). Son of Abinoam, from KADESH in the tribal territory of NAPHTALI. Barak became a significant part of Israel's history during the period of the judges when he was summoned by DEBORAH, the prophetess, to lead volunteers from ZEBULUN and Naphtali against the forces of JABIN, king of the Canaanites, who was located at HAZOR (Jdg. 4:1-24). For twenty years Israel had been oppressed by the Canaanites. The farm lands were plundered; traffic almost ceased; and the fighting men of Israel were disarmed, so that not a shield nor a spear was to be seen among them. Barak raised an army of 100,000 men, mostly from a few faithful tribes. They encamped on Mount TABOR, where wooded slopes would protect them against the chariots of the Canaanites. The army of Israel routed Jabin's 800 iron chariots and heavily armed host in the plain of JEZREEL (ESDRAELON). A heavy rainfall caused the alluvial plain to become a morass in which the Canaanite army found it impossible to move. Sisera abandoned his chariot and ran away on foot. Barak

B

pursued him and found him dead; he had been killed by Jael in her tent. A peace of forty years followed. In Heb. 11:32 Barak's name appears among those who achieved great things through faith. The period of the judges is probably to be dated from 1200 B.C., with Deborah and Barak c. 1125.

Barakel. bair´uh-kuhl (Heb. *barak'ēl H1387*, "God blesses"). Father of ELIHU, who was the last of the friends to reason with JOB (Job 32:2, 6). Barakel is also described as "the Buzite" (BUZ was a country in the eastern part of ARABIA).

barbarian. In English this term has a negative connotation, indicating that a person or culture is "uncivilized," lacking in refinement. The Greek word *barbaros G975*, however, simply meant "foreign," that is, "non-Greek." PAUL uses it in this sense in Rom. 1:14, where the combination of "Greeks" and "barbarians" means the whole human race. Similarly, in 1 Cor. 14:11 Paul uses the word to describe one who spoke in an unintelligible foreign tongue (NIV, "foreigner"); and in Acts 28:2, 4 it is applied to the inhabitants of the island of MALTA (NIV, "islanders"; NRSV, "natives"). In Col. 3:11 the word refers to those who did not belong to the cultivated Greek race, and its occurrence in this type of context leads easily to a pejorative use.

barber. See OCCUPATIONS AND PROFESSIONS.

Bar Cochba. See BAR KOKHBA.

Barhumite. bahr-hyoo´mit. See BAHARUMITE.

Bariah. buh-ri´uh (Heb. *bāriaḥ H1377*, possibly "fugitive"). Son of Shemaiah and descendant of DAVID through SOLOMON (1 Chr. 3:22).

Bar-Jesus. bahr-jee´zuhs (Gk. *Bariēsous G979*, from Aram. *bar yēšûaʿ*, "son of JOSHUA"). A "Jewish sorcerer and false prophet" at PAPHOS on CYPRUS who became temporarily blind when PAUL denounced him (Acts 13:6-11). He opposed the preaching of the gospel for fear of losing his influential position with the governor. Paul's empow-

ered denunciation, exposing his character and deeds (vv. 10-11), defeated the opposition. Luke's added words, "But Elymas the sorcerer (for that is what his name means) … " (v. 8), are obscure; possibly the simple meaning is that Bar-Jesus was his Jewish patronymic while ELYMAS was his personal Greek name.

Barjona. bahr-joh´nuh (Gk. *Bariōna G980*, from Aram. *bar yônâ*, "son of Jonah"). A family name identifying Simon PETER by his father, JONAH (Matt. 16:17 KJV; modern versions translate "son of Jonah"). In Jn. 1:42 and 21:15-17 Peter is called the "son of John."

Bar Kokhba. bahr-kohk´buh (Aram. *bar kôkbāʾ*, "son of the star"). Also Bar Cochba. Sobriquet given to Simon ben Kosiba, leader of the Jews in their disastrous second war with Rome, A.D. 132-135. This revolt was apparently precipitated by Emperor Hadrian's move to found a non-Jewish city, Aelia Capitolina, on the site of JERUSALEM. Bar Kokhba proclaimed an independent Jewish state and issued coinage struck from defaced Roman currency; it took the Romans three years to stamp resistance down. The rebel headquarters were in the wadis and cliffs where the Judean wilderness breaks into the DEAD SEA. In this area is found an inaccessible cave-complex where the rebels hid and were finally starved to death or committed suicide. The cave was lined in one part by baskets of bones. A basket was found containing a bundle of PAPYRUS documents, women's sandals, and farm and household implements. Among the letters cached in a remote rear corner of the cave were some apparently from Bar Kokhba himself. His name may have been given him as a messianic allusion to Num 24:17, but later rabbis were critical of him and apparently came up with a different sobriquet, Bar Koziba, meaning "son of a lie."

Barkos. bahr´kos (Heb. *barqôs H1401*, "son of Kos"). The ancestor of some temple servants (NETHINIM) who returned from the EXILE with ZERUBBABEL (Ezra 2:53; Neh. 7:55).

barley. See PLANTS.

B

barn. In ancient Palestine, grain was usually stored in dry CISTERNS in the ground, but sometimes in buildings. God promised to send a blessing on the barns of the Israelites if they obeyed him (Deut. 28:8; cf. Prov. 3:10). The Greek term *apothēkē G630* occurs several times in the Gospels, once metaphorically in JOHN THE BAPTIST's eschatological warning (Matt. 3:12; Lk. 3:17), elsewhere in the teachings of Jesus (Matt. 6:26; 13:30; Lk. 12:18, 24).

Barnabas. bahr′nuh-buhs (Gk. *Barnabas G982*, possibly from Aram. *bar něbûʾâ*, "son of prophecy"; Luke gives the meaning "son of encouragement" [Acts 4:36] not as a scientific etymology but as an indication of character). A noted member of the early Jerusalem church and an active missionary to the Gentiles. His original name was JOSEPH, while the surname Barnabas marked his ability to comfort and encourage (or perhaps his skills in exhortation). Barnabas was a LEVITE from CYPRUS who in the early days of the church sold a field and gave the proceeds to the support of the poorer members of the church in Jerusalem (4:37). Later, when the church hesitated to receive Saul (PAUL) into their fellowship, Barnabas removed their fears by speaking in the apostle's behalf (9:27). He is also described as "a good man and full of the Holy Spirit and faith," traits that early brought him into leadership (11:24).

After the start of the work at ANTIOCH in Syria, the church in Jerusalem sent Barnabas there to give the work direction. After laboring in that city for some time, he went to TARSUS and brought back Paul as his associate (Acts 11:22-26). At the end of a year the two men were sent to carry alms from the infant church to the believers at Jerusalem, who were suffering from famine (11:27-30). Returning from Jerusalem, they were ordained as missionaries and, accompanied by John Mark, proceeded on a mission to the Gentiles (13:2-5; see MARK, JOHN). Barnabas and Paul together are referred to as APOSTLES (14:14). Together the two men labored at Cyprus, Antioch in Pisidia, Iconium, Lystra, and Derbe. Initially, the leadership is ascribed to Barnabas, but Paul seems to have taken the lead after the events in Cyprus ("Paul and his companions," 13:13). At LYSTRA, after a cripple was healed, the inhabitants worshiped Barnabas as ZEUS, and Paul,

the chief speaker, as HERMES (14:8-28). After their return to Antioch, the church sent them to the council at Jerusalem (15:2). They were commissioned to carry the decrees of the council to the churches in SYRIA and ASIA MINOR (15:22-35).

The beginning of a difference between the two men is suggested by Paul in Gal. 2:13, where he says that Barnabas went along with PETER in the latter's inconsistent course. This was followed by a more serious break when, after Paul had suggested a second missionary journey, he refused to take along Barnabas's cousin Mark on the ground that he had left them on their first journey. The two men separated, Barnabas going with Mark to Cyprus, and Paul to Asia Minor (Acts 15:36-41). The mutual affection of the two evangelists did not cease, however. Paul's allusions to Barnabas in his letters shows that he continued to hold his former associate in high esteem (1 Cor. 9:6; Gal. 2:1, 9, 13; Col. 4:10).

After the apostolic period, Barnabas was still regarded highly. Some early church leaders attributed to him the authorship of the letter to the HEBREWS. A work that came to be known as the *Epistle of Barnabas* (included among the APOSTOLIC FATHERS) was produced in the first decades of the second century, but this document is anonymous and much of its content is inconsistent with NT teaching.

barrenness. To be a wife without motherhood has always been regarded in the E not merely as a matter of regret, but also of reproach and humiliation. Notice SARAH's sad laughter of despair (Gen. 18:12), HANNAH's silent pleading (1 Sam. 1:10-17), and RACHEL's passionate alternative of children or death (Gen. 30:1; cf. also REBEKAH, 25:21). It is significant that the mothers of the Hebrew race were by nature sterile (Gen. 11:30; 25:21; 29:31), and therefore God's special intervention showed his favor to Israel (cf. also ELIZABETH, Lk. 1:7, 36). Barrenness was removed by the mercy of God, often through prayer (Gen. 25:21; 1 Sam. 1:12; cf. Ps. 113:9; Lk. 23:29). ISAIAH compared the nation of Israel with a barren woman who will sing because of the promise of children (Isa. 54:1), and PAUL appealed to that promise to illustrate the principle of freedom from the law (Gal. 4:27).

Barsabas. See BARSABBAS.

Barsabbas. bahr´suh-buhs (Gk. *Barsabbas G984*, possibly from Aram. *bar sāʾbāʾ*, "son of the elder"). KJV Barsabas. A patronymic of two early Jewish Christians, possibly brothers. (1) JOSEPH, surnamed JUSTUS, who must have had a close acquaintance with Jesus, since he was one of the two men nominated to succeed JUDAS ISCARIOT in the apostolic band (Acts 1:23).

(2) JUDAS, a Christian prophet who, along with SILAS, was sent to ANTIOCH of Syria with the decision of the Jerusalem conference (Acts 15:22, 32).

Bartholomew. bahr-thol´uh-myoo (Gk. *Bartholomaios G978*, from Aram. *bar talmay*, "son of Talmai"). One of the twelve apostles. His name immediately follows that of PHILIP in the lists of Jesus' disciples in the Synoptic Gospels (Matt. 10:3; Mk. 3:18; Lk. 6:14; in Acts 1:13 the name of THOMAS comes between them). John never mentions Bartholomew, while the Synoptic Gospels and Acts never mention NATHANAEL, who according to Jn. 1:45-46 was led to Christ by Philip. Thus it is reasonable to infer that Bartholomew was Nathanael's surname, although we have no conclusive proof for this view. Bartholomew figures in some early Christian traditions, but these are not reliable.

Bartimaeus. bahr´tuh-mee´uhs (Gk. *Bartimaios G985*, possibly from Aram. *bar ṭimay*, "son of Timai"). Son of Timaeus. A blind man healed by Jesus as he went out from JERICHO on his way to JERUSALEM shortly before Passion Week (Mk. 10:46-52). A similar account is given by Luke (Lk. 18:35-43), except that he reports the miracle as occurring before Jesus reached Jericho, and the blind man's name is not given. Matthew, for his part, tells of Jesus healing two blind men on the way out of Jericho (Matt. 20:29-34). On the surface the stories seem irreconcilable, but various explanations have been proposed. For example, some have speculated that a blind man made his request as Jesus approached Jericho, but Jesus did not heed him, perhaps to test his faith; later, when Jesus left Jericho, the blind man was accompanied by another and both were healed. Neither this solution nor other suggestions have proved to be fully persuasive.

Baruch. bair´uhk (Heb. *bārûk H1358*, "blessed"). (1) Son of Neriah and devoted friend of JEREMIAH (Jer. 32:12 et al.). His brother was Seraiah, King ZEDEKIAH's staff officer (51:59). Baruch served as Jeremiah's secretary (36:4). A man of unusual qualities, he might have risen to a high position if he had not thrown in his lot with the prophet (45:5). Jeremiah dictated his prophecies to Baruch, who read them to the people (36:5-8). King JEHOIAKIM, on hearing the opening sentences of the prophecy, became greatly angered and burned the scroll. He ordered the arrest of Baruch and Jeremiah, but they escaped. Baruch rewrote the prophet's oracles with additions (36:27-32). In the reign of Zedekiah, during the final siege of Jerusalem, Jeremiah bought his ancestral estate in ANATHOTH. Since he was at that time a prisoner, he placed the deed in Baruch's hands and testified that Israel would again possess the land (ch. 32). JOSEPHUS (*Ant.* 10.9.1) says that Baruch continued to live with Jeremiah at MIZPAH after the fall of Jerusalem. After the murder of GEDALIAH, the leaders

Beneath this modern asphalt road lies the ancient Jericho road on which Jesus probably met blind Bartimaeus. (View to the E.)

© Dr. James C. Martin

B

accused him of unduly influencing Jeremiah when the latter urged the people to remain in Judah (Jer. 43:3), a fact that shows how great Baruch's influence was thought to be over his master. He was taken to Egypt with Jeremiah (43:6). After that, all reliable records about him cease. Jerome preserves a tradition that he died in Egypt soon after his arrival. Other traditions say that he was taken by NEBUCHADNEZZAR to BABYLON after this king conquered Egypt and that he died there twelve years later. The high regard in which Baruch was held is shown by the large number of spurious writings that were attributed to him (see APOCRYPHA; PSEUDEPIGRAPHA).

(2) Son of Zabbai; he aided NEHEMIAH in rebuilding the Jerusalem walls by repairing the section from the ANGLE to the house of the high priest, ELIASHIB (Neh. 3:20).

(3) A leader who affixed his seal to Nehemiah's covenant (Neh. 10:6).

(4) Son of Colhozeh and a descendant of JUDAH through PEREZ (Neh. 11:5).

Baruch, Book of. See APOCRYPHA.

Barzillai. bahr-zil′i (Heb. *barzillay H1367*, "made of iron"). **(1)** An aged and wealthy Gileadite of ROGELIM who, with others, brought provisions to DAVID and his army at MAHANAIM while they were fleeing from ABSALOM (2 Sam. 17:27). After David defeated Absalom and was returning to Jerusalem, Barzillai escorted him over the Jordan but, because of his age, declined the king's invitation to come and live at the capital. In his place he sent his son, KIMHAM (19:31-39). When SOLOMON was about to become king, David urged him to show kindness to Barzillai's sons in recognition of their father's loyalty (1 Ki. 2:7).

(2) A Meholathite whose son, ADRIEL, married SAUL's daughter, MERAB (2 Sam. 21:8; KJV, "Michal," following MT); Adriel's five sons were given over to the GIBEONITES to avenge Saul's blood guilt (v. 9).

(3) Father or ancestor of a family of priests who returned from the EXILE with ZERUBBABEL (Ezra 2:61-63; Neh. 7:63-64). The family members could not trace their genealogy to prove they belonged to the priesthood. Barzillai had taken his name from

his wife's family when he married a descendant of Barzillai the Gileadite (see #1 above); it has been suggested that by adopting a nonpriestly family name he compromised the priestly status of his own family.

Basemath. bas′uh-math (Heb. *bāśĕmat H1412*, "fragrant"; cf. IBSAM, MIBSAM). KJV Bashemath (in 1 Ki. 4:15, Basmath). **(1)** A wife of ESAU and daughter of ELON the HITTITE (Gen. 26:34). Esau's marriage to a Canaanite brought great bitterness to ISAAC and REBEKAH. Another of Esau's wives, ADAH, is also identified as a daughter of Elon the Hittite (36:2). Some believe that Adah was Basemath's sister. Others argue that 26:34 is corrupt and should read Adah rather than Basemath. See also #2 below.

(2) A wife of Esau, identified as the daughter of ISHMAEL and the sister of NEBAIOTH (Gen. 36:3). She is apparently the same as MAHALATH, who is described in identical terms earlier (28:6-9).

(3) Daughter of SOLOMON and wife of AHIMAAZ; the latter was an officer in charge of providing food for the king's household one month of the year (1 Ki. 4:15). The only other daughter of Solomon mentioned in the Bible is TAPHATH, who was also married to a district governor (v. 11).

Bashan. bay′shuhn (Heb. *bāšān H1421* [always with the definite article], "smooth plain"). The fertile tract of country on the E side of the upper JORDAN, adjacent to the Sea of Galilee (see GALILEE, SEA OF). Although it is impossible to determine its exact boundaries, Bashan appears to have been bounded by Mount HERMON on the N, SALECAH on the E, GILEAD on the S, GESHUR and MAACAH on the W. The YARMUK River coursed through the southern area. Bashan included the regions of ARGOB (Deut. 3:4) and GOLAN (4:43, also a city), and the cities of EDREI (3:1), KARNAIM (1:4), ASHTAROTH (Josh. 9:10), and Salecah (Deut. 3:10). In the Greek period its cities included Hippos, Dion, Gamala, and Seleucia. JOSEPHUS identifies Bashan with Gaulanitis and Batanea (cf. *Ant.* 4.5.3 with 1 Ki. 4:13; and *Ant.* 9.8.1 with 2 Ki. 10:33). In the days of ABRAHAM it was occupied by a people called the REPHAITES (Gen. 14:5). OG, the last king of the race, was defeated and killed by the Israelites at Edrei in the time of Moses (Num. 21:33-35; Deut. 3:1-7). The entire district was assigned to the half-tribe of Manasseh (Deut. 3:13). Solomon taxed the land (1 Ki. 4:13). It was lost to Israel in the wars with the Arameans (1 Ki. 22; 2 Ki. 8:28; 10:32, 35). Tiglath-Pileser incorporated Bashan into the Assyrian empire (2 Ki. 15:29). It was included in the kingdom of Herod the Great and then belonged to Philip, Herod's son. It was celebrated for its cattle (Ps. 22:12), its breed of sheep (Deut. 32:14), and its oak trees (Isa. 2:13; Ezek. 27:6).

Bashan-havoth-jair. See Havvoth Jair.

Bashemath. See Basemath.

basin. This English term is used in the NIV normally as a translation of Hebrew *kiyyôr H3963*, traditionally rendered "laver." Other English versions also use "basin" to translate *mizrāq H4670* (NIV, "sprinkling bowl"); this was a vessel for pouring or scattering a considerable amount of liquid in one motion, and one can picture a broad shallow basin from which the blood of the sacrifice cascades upon the sides or top of the altar (Exod. 29:16, 20; Lev. 1:5-6, 7:2; Num. 4:14; 1 Ki. 7:40; Jer. 52:18-19; Zech. 9:15). The same type of vessel was used for wine consumption (Amos 6:6) and for meal oil offerings by rulers (Num. 7:13-14). In the NT the only reference to a basin is the occasion when Jesus washed the disciples' feet (Jn. 13:5; Gk. *niptēr G3781*).

basket. Several kinds of baskets are mentioned in the OT, but we cannot tell from their names their differences in size, shape, and use. They were made of various materials—leaves, reeds, rushes, twigs, or ropes. Some were small enough to be carried in the hands; others had to be carried on the shoulder or head or on a pole between two persons. They were used for a variety of purposes: for carrying fruit (Deut. 26:2); bread, cake, and meat (Gen. 40:17; Exod. 29:2-3); clay to make bricks, and earth for embankments (Ps. 81:6). In the NT two kinds of baskets are referred to. The *kophinos G3186* (Matt. 14:20; Mk. 6:43; Jn. 6:13) was a relatively small basket that could be carried on the

back to hold provisions. Twelve of these baskets were used to gather the food that remained after the feeding of the 5,000. The *spyris G5083* must have been considerably larger, since it was used to let Paul down from the wall at Damascus (Acts 9:25). Seven of these were needed to gather the food that was left after the feeding of the 4,000 (Matt. 16:9-10).

Basmath. See Basemath.

bastard. KJV rendering of Hebrew *mamzēr H4927* (Deut. 23:2 [NIV, "one born of a forbidden marriage"]; Zech. 9:6 [NIV, "foreigners"]) and Greek *nothos G3785* (Heb. 12:8 [NIV, "illegitimate children"], used figuratively of those who reject God's authority and discipline).

bat. See Animals.

bath. See Weights and Measures.

bathing. The act of bathing in the ordinary, nonreligious sense, whether for physical cleanliness or refreshment, is not often mentioned in the Scriptures. The average Hebrew had neither the water nor the inclination for bathing. In most cases "bathe" means partial washing. Public baths of the Greek type were unknown among the Hebrews until Greek culture invaded Palestine under Antiochus Epiphanes (c. 168 B.C.). The dusty roads of Palestine made frequent washing of the feet necessary, and this was always done when staying at a house (Gen. 18:4; 19:2; Jn. 13:10). In the Bible bathing stands chiefly for ritual acts—purification from ceremonial defilement because of contact with the dead, defiled persons or things, or things under the ban. Priests washed their hands and feet before entering the sanctuary or making an offering on the altar (Exod. 30:19-21). The high priest bathed on the Day of Atonement before each act of expiation (Lev. 16:4, 24). In the time of Christ, the Jews washed their hands before eating (Mk. 7:3-4). According to Josephus, the Essenes practiced daily bathing for ceremonial reasons.

Bath Rabbim. bath-rab'im (Heb. *bat-rabbim H1442*, "daughter of a multitude"). A gate in the

B

Transjordanian city of HESHBON; the beautiful eyes of a woman are compared to the pools near this gate (Cant. 7:4).

Bathsheba. bath-shee′buh (Heb. *bat-šebaʿ H1444*, prob. "daughter of abundance"; in 1 Chr. 3:5 she is called *bat-šûaʿ*, [see BATH-SHUA], which can be interpreted as "daughter is salvation" but more probably is a textual or orthographic variant of Bathsheba). Daughter of ELIAM (Ammiel in 3:5) and wife of URIAH the HITTITE, a soldier in DAVID's army. During Uriah's absence in the wars David used his royal authority to commit adultery with her (2 Sam. 11). Bathsheba became pregnant and Uriah was then treacherously killed by David's order. After a period of mourning, David married her, but the Lord was displeased and their child died soon after birth (11:27—12:23). Subsequently, David and Bathsheba had four sons, including SOLOMON (2 Sam. 5:14; 1 Chr. 3:5). With the help of the prophet NATHAN she defeated the plot of ADONIJAH to usurp the kingdom and succeeded in having David choose Solomon as his successor (1 Ki. 1:11-35). She was a woman of resourcefulness and energy and retained her influence over David until his death. Her sons Nathan and Solomon were both ancestors of Jesus Christ through different genealogical lines (Matt. 1:6; Lk. 3:31).

Bathshua. bath-shoo′uh (Heb. *bat-šûaʿ*, perhaps "daughter is salvation"). Also Bath-shua. **(1)** According to some scholars, she was the Canaanite wife of JUDAH who bore him three sons, ER, ONAN, and SHELAH (1 Chr. 2:3; cf. NRSV, NJPS). Others, however, prefer to translate the phrase as "the daughter of Shua" (cf. KJV, NIV; see also Gen. 38:2, 12), in which case we do not know her given name. See SHUA #1.

(2) Alternate form of BATHSHEBA (1 Chr. 3:5 KJV and other versions).

battering ram. See WAR.

battle. In ancient times a trumpet signal by the commander opened each battle (Jdg. 7:18) and, when necessary, called the soldiers away from the fight (2 Sam. 2:28; 18:16). When the army drew

near the battle, a priest or the commander encouraged the soldiers by reminding them of God's presence and help. The fainthearted were exempted (Deut. 20:8). Military science was relatively simple. A force was usually divided into two attacking divisions, the one in the rear serving as a reserve or as a means of escape for the leader in case of defeat. Spearmen probably formed the first line, bowmen or archers the second, and slingers the third. Horses and chariots were not used by Israel until quite late. Most of the fighting was done by footmen. Sometimes the battle was preceded by duels between individuals, and these on occasion determined the outcome of the battle (1 Sam. 17:3-10; 2 Sam. 2:14-16). Night attacks and ambushes were often resorted to (Jdg. 7:16; Josh. 8:2). See also ARMS AND ARMOR; WAR.

battlement. See PARAPET.

Bavai. bay′vi (Heb. *bawway H1002* [not in NIV]). Son (or descendant) of Henadad; he was the ruler of one of the half-districts of KEILAH and helped repair the wall of Jerusalem under NEHEMIAH (Neh. 3:18 KJV; RSV, "Bavvai"). The MT reading, however, is probably a scribal error for BINNUI (cf. v. 24).

bay. **(1)** With the meaning "inward extension of the sea," this English term is used with reference to the N and S ends of the DEAD SEA (Josh. 15:2, 5; 18:19). In the NT it is used once with reference to an inlet on the island of MALTA where PAUL's ship foundered (Acts 27:39; KJV, "creek"); the site is identified as the traditional Bay of St. Paul, c. 8 mi. (13 km.) NW of the town of Valetta.

(2) With the meaning "reddish-brown," the term *bay* is used by the KJV to describe the fourth group of horses in Zechariah's vision (Zech. 6:3, 7). The Hebrew term here actually means "strong" (cf. NIV), but the context leads many scholars to interpret the word as referring to a color.

bay tree. See PLANTS.

bazaar. This term is used by some English Bibles in 1 Ki. 20:34, which states that a defeated BEN-HADAD allowed King AHAB to set up "market areas" (NIV) in the streets of DAMASCUS.

Bazlith. baz'lith. See Bazluth.

Bazluth, Bazlith. baz'luhth (Heb. *baṣlût H1296* and *baṣlît H1297* [not in NIV], possibly "onion"). Also Bazlith (in Neh. 7:54). Ancestor of a family of temple servants (Nethinim) who returned from the exile with Zerubbabel (Ezra 2:52; Neh. 7:54).

bdellium. A substance mentioned in Gen. 2:12 and Num. 11:7, variously taken to be a gum or resin (cf. NIV), a precious stone, or a pearl. It was the same color as manna and was found like gold and the onyx stone or the beryl in the land of Havilah. The Greeks gave the name bdellium to a gum obtained from a tree growing in Arabia, Babylonia, India, and Media.

Bealiah. bee´uh-li´uh (Heb. *bĕ'alyâ H1270*, "Yahweh is Lord"). One of a score of ambidextrous warriors, kinsmen of Saul from the tribe of Benjamin, who joined David at Ziklag in opposition to Saul (1 Chr. 12:5; cf. vv. 1-2).

Bealoth. bee´uh-loth (Heb. *bĕ'ālôt H1268*, "ladies" [from *ba'al H1251*, "lord"]). **(1)** A city in the extreme S of the tribe of Judah (Josh. 15:24). Its precise location is unknown, but it is sometimes identified with Baalah and with Baalath Beer.

(2) A city in the N of Israel, associated with the tribe of Asher and included in the list of Solomon's administrative districts (1 Ki. 4:16 NRSV). Many scholars understand the Hebrew to mean "in Aloth" (cf. NIV). In either case, however, the location is unknown.

beam. Used in the OT to refer to beams used in constructing the upper floors and roofs of buildings (1 Ki. 7:3) and to the beam of a weaver's loom (Jdg. 16:14). Jesus uses the term in a figurative sense in Matt. 7:3 and Lk. 6:41 (NIV "plank" in both cases) in contrast to a mote, in order to show how inconsistent it is to criticize minor faults in others when ours are so much greater.

bean. See plants.

bear. See animals.

beard. With Asiatics a badge of manly dignity, in contrast to the Egyptians, who usually shaved the head and the face. As a sign of mourning, it was the custom to pluck it out or cut it off. The Israelites were forbidden to shave off the corners of their beards, probably because that act was regarded as a sign of paganism (Lev. 19:27). To force a man to cut off his beard was to inflict on him a shameful disgrace (2 Sam. 10:4-5).

beast. See animals.

beaten gold, beaten silver. The phrase "beaten gold" is used by some English versions in descriptions of ornamental and military hardware, referring to gold inlay and overlay (1 Ki. 10:16-17; 2 Chr. 9:15-16; NIV, "hammered gold"). Some believe, however, that the word rendered "beaten" or "hammered" indicates "to be alloyed, mixed." In the case of the phrase "beaten silver," which occurs only once (Jer. 10:9; NIV, "hammered silver"), the verb is a different one and certainly means "to stamp, hammer." Ancient cultures were well aware of the unusual malleability of silver. An important use of thin leaves of silver was the incrustation of idols (cf. Isa. 30:22; Hab. 2:19). Some parts of the tabernacle court were overlaid with silver (Exod. 38:17). See minerals.

beaten oil. The KJV and other versions use this rendering for a Hebrew phrase that probably refers to oil obtained from the first pressing of the olives, that is, the best quality, before the addition of water needed to extract the lower grades (Exod. 29:40 et al.; NIV, "oil from pressed olives").

beating. See scourge.

Beatitudes. bee-at´uh-tyoods (from the Lat. *beatus*, "blessed, happy," used in the Vulg. to render Heb. *'ašrê H897* and Gk. *makarios G3421*). This term, referring to a state of bliss, is not found in the English Bible, but declarations of blessedness occur frequently in the OT (e.g., Ps. 32:1-2; 41:1; 65:4), and the Gospels contain isolated beatitudes by Christ (Matt. 11:6; 13:16; 16:17; 24:46 [with the Lukan parallels]; Jn. 13:17; 20:29). Most frequently, however, "the Beatitudes" is the title given

B

to Jesus' initial declarations in the SERMON ON THE MOUNT (Matt. 5:3-11; cf. Lk. 6:20-22).

The Beatitudes do not describe separate types of Christian character. Rather, they set forth qualities and experiences that are combined in the ideal character. In Matthew there are nine beatitudes and no woes; Luke has four beatitudes and four corresponding woes. In Matthew all the sayings except the last are in the third person; in Luke they are in the second. In Matthew all the blessings except the last are attached to spiritual qualities; in Luke they relate to outward conditions of poverty and suffering. Luke omits the third, fifth, sixth, and seventh beatitudes of Matthew. Some scholars profess to find a gradation in the order in which the Beatitudes are recorded. Much has been written on the grouping of the Beatitudes, but no grouping is generally accepted.

Beautiful Gate. A gate of the TEMPLE built by HEROD the Great and renowned for its splendor. This name occurs only in the NT, which mentions it as the place where PETER and JOHN THE APOSTLE healed a lame man (Acts 3:2, 10). Some uncertainty exists concerning the identification of the gate, but the evidence seems to favor the Nicanor Gate, which according to rabbinic literature was made of bronze that "shone like gold."

Bebai. bee´bi (Heb. *bēbay H950*, possibly "child"). (1) The ancestor of an Israelite family that returned from the EXILE with Ezra (Ezra 2:11; 8:11; 10:28; Neh. 7:16).

(2) A leader of the people who affixed his seal to the covenant of NEHEMIAH (Neh. 10:15).

Becher. See BEKER.

Bechorath. See BECORATH.

Becorath. bi-kor´ath (Heb. *bĕkôrat H1138*, "firstborn"). KJV Bechorath; TNIV Bekorath. Son of Aphiah, descendant of BENJAMIN, and ancestor of King SAUL (1 Sam. 9:1). Because the form of the name is feminine, some believe Becorath was the daughter of Aphiah.

bed. In the East, in ancient times as now, the very poor slept on the ground, their outer garments serving as both mattress and blanket. The law, therefore, did not allow such a garment to be kept in pledge after sunset, or the man would be without covering (Deut. 24:13). In more advanced conditions a rug or a mat was used as a bed. At first it was laid on the floor, usually near a wall; later it was put on an elevation, either a raised part of the floor or a bedstead, which gave rise to the expression "go

© Dr. James C. Martin

The so-called Mount of Beatitudes (looking N). On top of the hill, the Church of Beatitudes overlooks an area known as Heptapegon.

up on a bed" (cf. Ps. 132:3 Heb.). Beds on raised platforms along the walls of a room were covered with cushions and used as sofas during the day. The mats from such beds were rolled up and put away in a closet or another room for the day. The bedroom where Joash (JEHOASH) was hidden was not a chamber for sleeping but a storeroom in which bedding was kept (2 Ki. 11:2). Still later, in some cases, a mattress took the place of the mat, and a pillow was also used, along with a blanket of some kind. Bedsteads must have been used occasionally, for the giant OG had one made of iron, a marvel in those days (Deut. 3:11). The very wealthy had more elaborate and ornamented bedsteads. Amos speaks of "beds inlaid with ivory" (Amos 6:4), and in Esth. 1:6 we read of "couches of gold and silver." Such bedsteads were sometimes further furnished with posts and a canopy (Cant. 3:10), and they had rich coverings (Prov. 7:16).

Bedad. bee′dad (Heb. *bĕdad H971*, "alone"). Father of King HADAD of EDOM (Gen. 36:35; 1 Chr. 1:46).

Bedan. bee′dan (Heb. *bĕdān H979*, derivation uncertain). (1) Son of Ulam and descendant of MANASSEH through MAKIR (1 Chr. 7:17).

(2) A judge in Israel, according to the KJV and Hebrew text of 1 Sam. 12:11, where Bedan is listed along with three prominent judges (JERUB-BAAL, JEPHTHAH, and SAMSON). Since such a leader is nowhere else mentioned, most modern versions of the Bible emend the text to BARAK, following some early versional evidence. A few scholars, however, interpret Bedan here as a shortened form of ABDON (Jdg. 12:13); other suggestions have been proposed.

Bedeiah. bi-dee′yah (Heb. *bēdyâ H973*, possibly "branch of Yahweh"). One of the descendants of Bani who agreed to put way their foreign wives (Ezra 10:35).

bedouin. (from Arab. *badāwī* [pl. *badāwīn*], "dessert dweller"). Often capitalized. An Arab belonging to a nomadic tribe. In ANE studies, the term is applied specifically to nonsedentary societies that specialized in camel breeding. Some of these societies acquired considerable power and may

accurately be described as "bedouin states," though they usually lasted for only a few generations. One group that evolved into a more permanent statehood was that of the NABATEANS. See NOMAD.

bee. See ANIMALS.

Beeliada. bee-uh-li′uh-duh (Heb. *bĕʿelyādāʿ H1269*, "the lord [Baal] knows"). A son of DAVID, born at Jerusalem (1 Chr. 14:7). The name was apparently changed to ELIADA ("God knows," 2 Sam. 5:16; 1 Chr. 3:8) when the term BAAL became distasteful because of its associations with idolatry.

Beelzebub, Beelzebul. bee-el′zi-buhb, -buhl (Gk. *Beelzeboul G1015*, derivation uncertain). The traditional spelling *Beelzebub*, which comes from the VULGATE (also attested in the Syriac tradition), links this name with BAAL-ZEBUB, "lord of the flies." Most Greek MSS of the NT, however, spell it *Beelzebul* (a few have *Beezebul*). In the Gospel of Matthew, the term is used first by Jesus (Matt. 10:25), but evidently because the name had been applied to him by the Jewish leaders. In another context, Jesus is accused of casting out DEMONS by the power of Beelzebub (12:24; cf. Mk. 3:22). Here Beelzebub is further defined as the prince of demons, indicating that Jesus himself is regarded as a demon. Jesus answers his accusers by showing the inconsistency of what they say (Matt. 12:25-27; Lk. 11:18-19). It is uncertain whether the term referred to *the* prince of demons and thus became synonymous with SATAN (as would appear from Matt. 12:26-27), or whether it was applied to a lesser prince in the demonic hierarchy.

Beer. bee′uhr (Heb. *bĕʾēr H932*, "well, cistern"). (1) A stopping place for the wandering Israelites probably N of the River ARNON in MOAB (Num. 21:16). Yahweh provided water there for the people. The BEER ELIM of Isa. 15:8 may be the same place, but the site has not been identified.

(2) The place to which JOTHAM fled after declaring the parable in which he denounced his brother ABIMELECH's violent seizure of power (Jdg. 9:21). Some have thought that this site should be identified with modern el-Bireh, c. 7 mi. (11 km.) NW of BETH SHAN.

B

beer (drink). See WINE.

Beera. bee´uh-ruh (Heb. *bĕ’ērā’ H938*, "well, cistern"). Son of Zophah and descendant of ASHER (1 Chr. 7:37). He is listed among the "heads of families, choice men, brave warriors and outstanding leaders" (v. 40).

Beerah. bee´uh-ruh (Heb. *bĕ’ērâ H939*, "well, cistern"). Son of Baal; he was a leader of the tribe of REUBEN who was taken into exile by TIGLATH-PILESER, king of Assyria (1 Chr. 5:6).

Beer Elim. bee´uhr-ee´lim (Heb. *bĕ’ēr ’ēlîm H935*, "well of Elim [mighty trees]"). A city of MOAB (Isa. 15:8); perhaps the same as BEER (Num. 21:16).

Beeri. bee´uhr-i (Heb. *bĕ’ērî H941*, apparently a gentilic of BEER). **(1)** Father of JUDITH, one of ESAU's wives; he is identified as a HITTITE (Gen. 26:34).
   (2) Father of the prophet HOSEA (Hos. 1:1).

Beer Lahai Roi. bee´uhr-luh-hi´roi (Heb. *bĕ’ēr laḥay rō’î H936*, possibly "the well of the Living One who sees me"). A spring in the desert, by the road to SHUR, between KADESH and BERED (Gen. 16:14, cf. v. 7), where the angel of the Lord appeared to the fleeing Egyptian slave girl HAGAR. Later this NEGEV site was visited by ISAAC (24:62; 25:11). Some have thought that Beer Lahai Roi may be identified with modern ‘Ain el-Muweileh, about 50 mi. (80 km.) SW of BEERSHEBA.

Beeroth. bee´uh-roth (Heb. *bĕ’ērôt H940*, "wells, cisterns"; gentilic *bĕ’ērôtî H943*, "Beerothite"). One of four Canaanite towns whose inhabitants succeeded in deceiving Israel by making a covenant with them (Josh. 9:17). When the deceit was discovered, they were made slaves by the Israelites (9:22-23). They were apparently HIVITES (9:7), and their village was located in the territory assigned to the tribe of BENJAMIN (18:25; 2 Sam. 4:2). The murderers of ISH-BOSHETH (2 Sam. 4:2) and JOAB's armor-bearer (23:37) came from Beeroth; and Beerothites returned from Babylon after the EXILE (Ezra 2:25). The location of the town is disputed; one possibility is modern el-Bireh, about 8 mi. (13 km.) N of JERUSALEM.

Beeroth-bene-jaakan. bee´uh-roth-ben´i-jay´-uh-kuhn (Heb. *bĕ’ērôt bĕnê-ya‘āqān*, "the wells of the sons of Jaakan"). One of the stations during the wilderness wanderings of the Israelites, on the way to MOSERAH (where AARON died) and near the border of EDOM (Deut. 10:6 NRSV). The KJV renders it "Beeroth of the children of Jaakan," while the NIV has "the wells of the Jaakanites," and the TNIV, "the wells of Bene Jaakan." The name could apparently be shortened to BENE JAAKAN (Num. 33:31). The site must have been near Mount HOR, but the precise location is unknown; some have suggested modern Birein. See also JAAKAN.

Beerothite. bee´uh-ruh-thit. See BEEROTH.

Beersheba. bee´uhr-shee´buh (Heb. *bĕ’ēr šeba‘ H937*, "the well of seven" or "the well of swearing"). The most southerly town of the Hebrews, hence the nation's practical boundary line; "the river of Egypt" (Wadi el-‘Arish, Gen. 15:18) was only about 60 mi. (100 km.) to the south. In the days of the conquest of Canaan, it was allotted to the tribe of SIMEON (Josh. 19:2). The familiar expression "from Dan to Beersheba" is used to designate the

Beersheba.

The ancient site of Beersheba during the period of the kings of Israel. (View to the NW.)

© Dr. James C. Martin

northern and southern extremities of the nation of Israel (2 Sam. 3:10; 17:11; 24:2).

HAGAR wandered in the wilderness of Beersheba when she fled from her mistress SARAH (Gen. 21:14). ABRAHAM made a covenant with the PHILISTINE princes here (21:32), and he made this his residence after the "offering up" of ISAAC (22:19). Here God appeared to JACOB and promised his continued presence when Jacob was on his way down into Egypt to be reunited with his son JOSEPH (46:1). ELIJAH the prophet sought refuge in Beersheba from the terror of the wicked JEZEBEL, wife of King AHAB of Israel (1 Ki. 19:3). The prophet AMOS rebuked the idolatrous tendencies he saw infiltrating the religious life of Beersheba from BETHEL and from DAN (Amos 8:14). The town is identified with modern Tell es-Sabaᶜ.

Be Eshtarah. bee-esh′tuh-ruh (Heb. *běᶜeštěrâ H1285*, possibly "house of ASHTORETH"). Also Beeshterah. One of the cities given to the LEVITE clans descended from GERSHON within the territory of the half-tribe of MANASSEH on the E side of the Jordan (Josh. 21:27). However, this form may be a scribal mistake or an alternate name for ASHTAROTH (see the parallel passage, 1 Chr. 6:71).

beetle. See ANIMALS.

beggar. See OCCUPATIONS AND PROFESSIONS; POOR.

beggarly elements. See ELEMENTS.

beginning. See ALPHA AND OMEGA; CREATION; TIME.

begotten. The Hebrew and Greek verbs for "beget" (*yālad H3528*; *gennaō G1164*) are frequent in both the literal sense (Deut. 23:8) and the metaphorical (Job 38:28, referring to the deposit of dew). Modern versions often use phrases such as "become father" to render these verbs. The Hebrew word is used in Ps. 2:7 (quoted in Acts 13:33; Heb. 1:5; 5:5) of God's relationship to the messianic king. In the NT, the literal sense is still common (e.g., Matt. 1:1-16), but the metaphorical use is greatly extended, especially when used to describe the relation of the believers to God (Jn. 1:13; 1 Pet. 1:3; et al.), so that Christians are regarded as "children" of God (e.g., Jn. 1:12). See also ONLY BEGOTTEN.

behavior. See OBEDIENCE; SANCTIFICATION.

beheading. The OT records several instances of a man's head being cut off after his death (1 Sam.

B

17:51; 2 Sam. 4:7, 12; 20:22). The term is used with reference to HEROD Antipas's execution of JOHN THE BAPTIST (Matt. 14:10; Mk. 6:16, 27; Lk. 9:9) and in the description of "the souls of those who had been beheaded because of their testimony for Jesus and because of the word of God" (Rev. 20:4).

behemoth. See ANIMALS.

beka. See WEIGHTS AND MEASURES.

Beker. bee´kuhr (Heb. *beker H1146,* "young camel"; gentilic *bakrî H1151,* "Bekerite"). Also Becher. **(1)** Son of BENJAMIN and grandson of JACOB (Gen. 46:21; 1 Chr. 7:6). This name and also Gera and Rosh are missing in the parallel list (Num. 26:38-40), possibly because they died childless. See also #2 below.

(2) Son of EPHRAIM and founder of a family called Bekerites (KJV, "Bachrites," Num. 26:35). Since he is called BERED in the parallel passage (1 Chr. 7:20), some scholars argue that the name Beker here is a scribal error and that it belongs a few verses later in the Benjamite genealogy (Num. 26:38-40). If so, this Beker would be the same as #1 above.

Bekorath. See BECORATH.

Bel. bel (Heb. *bēl H1155,* "lord" [cognate of *ba῾al H1251;* see BAAL]). The Sumerian equivalent of Bel was *En,* a title of Enlil, the god of wind and storm and one of the original triad of Sumerian deities (see SUMER). With the rise to supremacy of BABYLON, its chief god MARDUK took over the attributes of Enlil, and so was given Bel as an honorific title, which gradually superseded Marduk in ordinary use (Isa. 46:1; Jer. 50:2; 51:44).

Bela (person). bee´luh (Heb. *bela῾ H1185,* perhaps "devourer" or "eloquent"; gentilic *bal῾i H1188,* "Belaite"). **(1)** Son of BEOR and an early king of EDOM; his capital city was Dinhabah, otherwise unknown (Gen. 36:32-33; 1 Chr. 1:4-44). Cf. also BELA (PLACE).

(2) Son of BENJAMIN (prob. his firstborn), grandson of JACOB, and eponymous ancestor of the Belaite clan (Gen. 46:21 [KJV, "Belah"]; Num.

26:38-40; 1 Chr. 7:6-7; 8:1-3). The lists of Benjamin's sons display some striking differences; Bela's name is the only one that occurs in all four passages.

(3) Son of Azaz and descendant of REUBEN through JOEL (1 Chr. 5:8).

Bela (place). bee´luh (Heb. *bela῾ H1186,* possibly from a root meaning "devour"). Alternate name for ZOAR, one of the five cities that joined forces against KEDORLAOMER (Gen. 14:2, 8).

Bel and the Dragon. See APOCRYPHA.

Belial. bee´lee-uhl (Heb. *bĕliyya῾al H1175,* "worthlessness, wickedness"; Gk. *Beliar G1016*). A KJV epithet of scorn and disdain that appears often throughout the OT, especially in the phrase "sons of Belial" (Deut. 13:13 et al. [NIV, "wicked men"]). The Hebrew word is probably not a name but a term that combines two common Hebrew words meaning "without" and "to profit," thus "worthlessness"; and "son of" is an idiom indicating a person's characteristic or membership in a group. It is therefore equivalent to our "good-for-nothing." NABAL receives such a description from the lips of ABIGAIL, his wife (1 Sam. 25:25 KJV). The apostle PAUL employs the term once (2 Cor. 6:15; the only place where the term appears in the NIV) where Belial (Beliar) stands as opposed to Christ, thus approaching the diabolical status of ANTICHRIST.

belief, believer. See FAITH.

bell. See MUSIC, MUSICAL INSTRUMENTS.

bellows. An ancient device for fanning the flames of the fires of the smelting furnace (Jer. 6:29). The Egyptian type of bellows was operated by the feet, as one alternately trod on two inflated skins. This created a forced draft by means of reed tubes tipped with iron; the air thus jettisoned into the glowing fire caused the flames to burn more brilliantly and hotly. As each skin was exhausted of its supply of air, the workman would raise it by a cord attached for that purpose and inflate the skin again. This process was then repeated as many times as was necessary.

B

belly. This English term renders several Hebrew words that occur with a variety of meanings. The abdominal region of human beings was described as *beṭen H1061* (Jdg. 3:21, 22; Ps. 17:14; Prov. 13:25; et al.), a word that also was used of the womb (e.g., Ps. 22:9; 139:13) or the abdomen (distended in a woman undergoing the "jealousy ordeal," Num. 5:21-27) or figuratively of the locale of the emotions (e.g., Isa. 16:11; Jer. 4:19; Hab. 3:16). In NT Greek the word *koilia G3120* was used of the stomach or intestines (Matt. 12:40; 15:17) or, following the SEPTUAGINT, of the womb (Lk. 1:41-44; Jn. 3:4; Gal. 1:15). Metaphorically, it could be used of the HEART (Jn. 7:38). See also BODY.

Beloved Disciple. The "disciple whom Jesus loved" is referred to only in the Gospel of John, but never identified by name. He is mentioned in the following passages: Jn. 13:23; 19:26-27; 20:2; 21:7, 20, 24. In addition, 18:15 and 19:35 are also usually taken to refer to the Beloved Disciple. This figure is represented as the one "who testifies to these things and who wrote them down" (21:24; cf. vv. 20-23), suggesting that he is the (primary) author of this gospel. See JOHN, GOSPEL OF.

Who was the Beloved Disciple? Several views are held: (1) He was not a particular disciple of Jesus, a man of flesh and blood like Peter, but an ideal figure representing any true disciple of Christ. (2) He was LAZARUS, of whom it is said three times in the Gospel of John that Jesus loved him (Jn. 11:3, 5, 36). (3) He was an otherwise unknown Jerusalem disciple of Jesus connected with the high priest. (4) Some modern writers speculate that the Beloved Disciple was an otherwise unidentified Christian leader who may or may not have been a true disciple of Jesus, but who became the head of the so-called Johannine Community. (5) He was JOHN THE APOSTLE.

Both internal and external support is given for the last view. He must have been one of three apostles who are described in the Gospels as having been particularly close to Jesus—PETER, JAMES, and John. He cannot have been Peter, with whom he is contrasted (Jn. 21:20-21), or James, who was martyred early in the apostolic period, long before the Gospel of John was written (Acts 12:2). In the Lukan writings, moreover, Peter and John appear together (Lk. 22:8; Acts 3:1; 8:14), as Peter and the Beloved Disciple do in the fourth gospel. Most important, if the Beloved Disciple is not John, then John is not mentioned at all in this gospel, which would be very strange indeed. It seems most likely that John is identifying himself indirectly through this figure.

Belshazzar. bel-shaz′uhr (Heb. *bēlʾšaṣṣar H1157* and Aram. *bēlšaʾṣṣar H10109*, probably from Babylonian *Bēl-šar-uṣur*, "[the god] BEL has protected the king"). King of BABYLON, known for the writing on the wall that appeared during a great banquet and that predicted his fall (Dan. 5; 7:1; 8:1). Belshazzar was the son of, and coregent with, NABONIDUS (556-539 B.C.), the Chaldean ruler at the time of the capture of Babylon by the Persians. For many years Belshazzar was regarded as a fictitious literary creation of a postexilic author; now, however, it is well authenticated through archaeological studies that Belshazzar was a historic personage. In Dan. 5 he is referred to as the son of NEBUCHADNEZZAR (vv. 2, 11, 13, 18, 22), a description that conforms with general Semitic usage where one's descendant is often referred to as his "son."

Nebuchadnezzar died in 562 B.C., after a forty-two-year reign, and was followed in quick succession by Amel-Marduk (562-560, referred to as EVIL-MERODACH in Jer. 52:31 and 2 Ki. 25:27). He was replaced by Nergal Shar-usar (Nergal-Sharezer) who reigned from 560 to 556. He was succeeded by Labashi-Marduk, his weak son, who reigned but a few months and was then overthrown by revolution. One of the conspirators, Nabonidus (Nabonaid), then ascended the throne. Though a revolutionary, he was still a man of culture and religious zeal for the gods of Babylon. He is sometimes called "the world's first archaeologist." Nabonidus is thus the last true king of BABYLON and the father of Belshazzar. Nabonidus made Belshazzar coregent when he retired to Arabia, presumably to consolidate the weakening empire. The Nabonidus chronicle was written after the capture of Babylon in 539 B.C. CYRUS of Persia declares how he was able to take the city without a struggle. He describes his leniency toward the population, regarding himself as an "Enlightened Despot" and

B

executioner of the will of the gods. His estimation of the character of Belshazzar is exceedingly low, not at all out of harmony with that represented by the biblical account.

Regarding the latter account, Belshazzar's miserable doom came about at the end of, and largely as a consequence of, a drunken orgy held October 29, 539 B.C. (Dan. 5). Suddenly the fingers of a man's hand appeared, writing in fiery letters a message that Belshazzar could not decipher but which he still recognized as ominous. After the failure of his advisers to decipher the "cryptogram," he followed the suggestion of the queen mother and summoned the venerable Hebrew prophet DANIEL. After verbally castigating Belshazzar, Daniel interpreted the message ("You have been weighed on the scales and found wanting"). The judgment was swift and inevitable. Babylon fell to the Medo-Persians, Belshazzar was killed, and DARIUS in the name of Cyrus took the throne.

belt. See DRESS.

Belteshazzar. bel'ti-shaz'uhr (Heb. *bēltĕšaʾṣṣar H1171* [Aram. *H10108*], possibly from Babylonian *[Bēl-]balāṭsu-uṣur*, "[may BEL] protect his life"). The Babylonian name given to DANIEL (Dan. 1:7; 10:1; used mostly in the ARAMAIC section of the book, as follows: 2:26; 4:8-9, 18-19; 5:12). Not to be confused with the name BELSHAZZAR.

bema. See JUDGMENT SEAT.

Ben (person). ben (Heb. *bēn H1202* [not in NIV] "son"). According to the MT, a LEVITE musician (1 Chr. 15:18; cf. KJV). Most modern versions, following the SEPTUAGINT (cf. also the MT, v. 20), omit this name.

Ben (prefix and idiom). ben (Heb. *bēn H1201*, "son of"; also in the pl. construct, *bĕnê*; in Aram. *bar H10120*; cf. *bat H1426*, "daughter"). A Hebrew term prefixed to many names or otherwise used to indicate a wide variety of states and relationships. among the most important are these: (1) Actual sonship— by far the most frequent usage—including the more general relationship of children, both male and female, to parents (Gen. 3:16). (2) The relationship of descendants, however far removed (e.g., "the children of Israel"). (3) Membership in a profession or group, such as "son of a prophet" probably meaning "belonging to a prophetic guild" (Amos 7:14), or "daughter of a foreign god" meaning "an idolatrous woman" (Mal. 2:11). (4) Nonliving objects, such as "sons of flame" meaning "sparks" (Job 5:7), or "daughter of the eye" as equivalent to the English "apple of the eye" (Ps. 17:8). (5) An outstanding feature or characteristic of a person, animal, or thing, as in "sons of wickedness" meaning "wicked men" (2 Sam. 3:34), or "son of scourgings" meaning "deserving to be beaten" (Deut. 25:2), or "son of fat" meaning "fertile" (Isa. 5:1).

Ben-Abinadab. ben'uh-bin'uh-dab (Heb. *ben-ʾăbînādāb H1203*, "son of ABINADAB"). A son-in-law of SOLOMON and one of the twelve district governors who supplied provisions for the king and his household; he was in charge of the territory around the port city of DOR (1 Ki. 4:11; KJV, "The son of Abinadab").

Benaiah. bi-nay'yuh (Heb. *bĕnāyāhû H1226*, prob. "Yahweh has built"). A popular name, particularly among the LEVITES. (1) Son of Jehoiada and commander over the KERETHITES and Pelethites, a special unit from DAVID's earlier days (2 Sam. 8:18; 20:23). He is described as "a valiant fighter," a native of KABZEEL, who through a number of daring exploits distinguished himself as one of David's mighty warriors and was put in charge of the king's bodyguard (2 Sam. 23:20-23; 1 Chr. 11:22-25; 27:5-6). Because he did not take part in the attempted usurpation of ADONIJAH (1 Ki. 1:8), he was among those chosen to make arrangements for the proclamation of SOLOMON as king (1:32-40). Under the new king, Benaiah replaced JOAB as head of the army (2:35; 4:4) and executed Adonijah (2:25), Joab (2:29), and SHIMEI (2:46).

(2) An Ephraimite warrior from the town of PIRATHON and one of David's Thirty (2 Sam. 23:30; 1 Chr. 11:31). He became army commander for the eleventh month and had 24,000 men in his division (1 Chr. 27:14).

(3) A clan leader in the tribe of SIMEON (1 Chr. 4:36). He is listed among those whose families increased greatly during the days of King HEZE-

KIAH and who dispossessed the Hamites (see HAM) and MEUNITES near GEDOR (vv. 38-41).

(4) A Levite appointed to the second order of singers and assigned to play the lyre with others "according to *alamoth*" (1 Chr. 15:18, 20; 16:5).

(5) One of the priests assigned to blow the trumpets regularly before the ARK OF THE COVENANT (1 Chr. 15:24; 16:6).

(6) Father of Jehoiada; the latter succeeded AHITHOPHEL as royal counselor (1 Chr. 27:34).

(7) Grandfather of Jahaziel and descendant of ASAPH (2 Chr. 20:14); possibly the same as #4 above.

(8) A supervisor under CONANIAH and SHIMEI, who were ordered by King Hezekiah to prepare storerooms in the temple (2 Chr. 31:13).

(9) Father of Pelatiah; the latter was one of the evil leaders of the people in EZEKIEL's time (Ezek. 11:1, 13).

(10-13) Four different Israelites listed among those who had taken foreign wives in the days of EZRA (Ezra 10:25, 30, 35, 43).

Ben-Ammi. ben-am´i (Heb. *ben-ʿammî H1214*, possibly "son of my people"). Son of the younger daughter of LOT (Gen. 19:38) whom she conceived through her own father following the destruction of SODOM. He was the progenitor of the AMMONITES. See also MOAB.

Ben-Deker. ben-dee´kuhr (Heb. *ben-deqer H1206*, "son of Deker [piercing]"). One of the twelve district governors who supplied provisions for SOLOMON and the royal household; he was in charge of the second administrative district in the northern part of the SHEPHELAH, roughly the area of southern DAN (1 Ki. 4:9; KJV, "The son of Dekar").

Bene Berak. bin´ee-bihr´ak (Heb. *bēnê-bĕraq H1222*, "sons of Barak [lightning]"). One of the towns originally allotted to the tribe of DAN (Josh. 19:45), but the Danites were unable to occupy the territory (v. 47). It is identified with the modern el-Kheiriyeh, 4.5 mi. (7 km.) E of JOPPA.

benediction. A prayer in which divine blessings are invoked or in which there is recognition that such blessings are present. See BLESS.

Benedictus. ben´uh-dik´toohs (Latin term used to translate Greek *eulogētos G2329*, "blessed, praised"). The name given to ZECHARIAH's thanksgiving hymn at the birth of JOHN THE BAPTIST (Lk. 1:68-79), because the first line in the Latin Vulgate reads, *Benedictus Dominus Deus Israel*, "Blessed be the Lord God of Israel."

benefactor. This term represents Greek *euergetēs G2309*, "well-doer," which could function as a title sometimes assumed by kings (e.g., PTOLEMY III, 247-242 B.C.) and sometimes conferred by them upon outstanding citizens as a reward for some unusual service. The concept was of cultural importance and provides the background for various words in the NT that describe people who qualify for special recognition. The specific Greek term, however, occurs only once in the NT: when a dispute arose among the apostles as to which of them was to be regarded as the greatest, Jesus rebuked them, saying that those in authority over the Gentiles were called benefactors, but that the apostles should humbly serve others (Lk. 22:25).

Bene Jaakan. ben´ee-jay´uh-kuhn (Heb. *bēnê yaʿăqān H1223*, "sons of Jaakan"). One of the stations during the wilderness wanderings of the Israelites, near the border of EDOM (Num. 33:31-32; cf. Deut. 10:6). See also BEEROTH-BENE-JAAKAN; JAAKAN.

Ben-Geber. ben-gee´buhr (Heb. *ben-geber H1205*, "son of Geber [strength]"). One of the twelve district governors who supplied provisions for SOLOMON and the royal household; he was in charge of the sixth district in central TRANSJORDAN, with RAMOTH GILEAD as its capital (1 Ki. 4:13; KJV, "The son of Geber"). This territory, initially part of MANASSEH, was later what remained of DAVID's Aramean conquests.

Ben-Hadad. ben-hay´dad (Heb. *ben-hădad H1207*, "son of HADAD [thunderer]"). The name or title of three (according to some scholars, two) Aramean kings. See SYRIA.

(1) Ben-Hadad I, son of TABRIMMON and grandson of HEZION, ruled in DAMASCUS and was a contemporary with ASA, king of Judah from 910

B

to 869 B.C. (1 Ki. 15:18-20). At the request of Asa, Ben-Hadad severed his alliance with BAASHA of Israel and aligned himself with the southern kingdom. Though his assistance was of temporary value, the price that Asa was obliged to pay for such aid was tremendous, as Ben-Hadad not only gained control of the treasures of Asa's kingdom but was able through his alliance to extend his territory into the Hebrew kingdoms themselves.

(2) Ben-Hadad II (1 Ki. 20:1-34; 2 Ki. 6:24; 8:7-9) was in all probability the son of Ben-Hadad I (although some scholars argue that that they are one and the same person; others have proposed that Ben-Hadad II and III are the same). Ben-Hadad II should likely be identified with Adad-ʾidri (Hadadezer) of Damascus, who is mentioned in Assyrian records. He was contemporary with AHAB of Israel (873-853 B.C.), against whom he waged war, laying siege to the newly constructed capital, SAMARIA. Because of the ungracious terms of surrender demanded by Ben-Hadad, Ahab refused to capitulate. With divine aid, Ahab was able to rout the Syrian army utterly at the battle of APHEK. Ahab spared the life of Ben-Hadad, thus never fully realizing the victory that otherwise would have been his.

(3) Ben-Hadad III (796-770 B.C.) was son of the usurper HAZAEL, hence not in direct line (2 Ki. 13:3). His name was adopted from the illustrious kings before him. He was a contemporary of AMAZIAH of Judah and JEHOAHAZ of Israel. He reduced the fighting personnel of Israel till it was "like the dust at threshing time" (13:7). JEHOASH son of Jehoahaz was able to defeat Ben-Hadad on three different occasions and to recover the cities of Israel (13:25; cf. Amos 1:4-5; Jer. 49:27).

Ben-Hail. ben-hay′uhl (Heb. *ben-ḥayil H1211*, "son of strength"). One of the princes sent by King JEHOSHAPHAT to teach the law of the Lord in the cities of Judah (2 Chr. 17:7).

Ben-Hanan. ben-hay′nuhn (Heb. *ben-ḥānān H1212*, "son of grace"). Son of Shimon and descendant of JUDAH (1 Chr. 4:20).

Ben-Hesed. ben-hee′sed (Heb. *ben-ḥesed H1213*, "son of mercy"). One of the twelve district gover-

nors who supplied provisions for SOLOMON and the royal household; he was in charge of the third district, NW of SHECHEM in the western territory of MANASSEH (1 Ki. 4:10; KJV, "The son of Hesed").

Ben-Hinnom. See HINNOM, VALLEY OF.

Ben-Hur. ben-huhr′ (Heb. *ben-ḥûr H1210*, "son of Hur"). One of the twelve district governors who supplied provisions for SOLOMON and the royal household; he was in charge of the first district, the hill country of EPHRAIM (1 Ki. 4:8; KJV, "The son of Hur").

Beninu. bi-ni′nyoo (Heb. *běnînû H1231*, possibly "our son"). One of the Levites who affixed their seals to the covenant with NEHEMIAH (Neh. 10:13).

Benjamin. ben′juh-muhn (Heb. *binyāmin H1228*, "son of the right hand"; gentilic *ben-yĕmîni H1229*, "Benjamite" or "Benjaminite"). Youngest son of the patriarch JACOB (Gen. 35:16-18). His mother RACHEL did not survive the difficulties of childbirth, and just before she died she named the baby Ben-Oni ("son of my sorrow"), but Jacob gave him the name Benjamin ("son of my right hand"). Of all the children of Jacob, he alone was born in Palestine, between EPHRATHAH and BETHEL. Together with his brother JOSEPH, he appears as a special object of parental love and devotion, no doubt, in part at least, because of the sad circumstances surrounding his birth. He seems to have played no part in the sale of Joseph into Egypt. The intercession on the part of JUDAH in behalf of Benjamin (44:18-34) is one of the most moving speeches in all of literature. No doubt the brothers had been softened in their attitude as they had observed the continued suffering of their father over the fate of Joseph, whom he believed irrevocably lost. At the time of Jacob's descent into Egypt, Benjamin is reported to have had ten sons (46:21; puzzling differences appear in the other lists, Num. 26:38-40; 1 Chr. 7:6; 8:1-2). Jacob's blessing suggests that Benjamin was to have a fruitful life (Gen. 49:27). See also BENJAMIN, TRIBE OF.

(2) Son of Bilhan and great-grandson of Benjamin son of Jacob (1 Chr. 7:10).

(3) One of the descendants of Harim who agreed to put away their foreign wives in the time of EZRA (Ezra 10:32).

(4) An Israelite who helped repair the wall of Jerusalem (Neh. 3:23); probably the same Benjamin as the leader who took part in the dedication of the wall (12:34). He may be the same as #3 above.

Benjamin, tribe of. Named for Jacob's youngest son. On the basis of the first census taken after the EXODUS, the tribe numbered 35,400; at the second census, it numbered 45,600 (Num. 1:37; 26:41). Later, in the division of territory by JOSHUA among the twelve tribes, Benjamin was assigned the portion between JUDAH on the S and EPHRAIM on the N (Josh. 18:11-28). Benjamin thus occupied a strategic position commercially and militarily. Benjamin loyally participated in DEBORAH's rebellion against SISERA (Jdg. 5:14). The civil war with Benjamin constitutes a sad and strange story (Jdg. 19-20).

King SAUL, son of Kish, came from this tribe (1 Sam. 9:1-2). After the death of Saul there was tension and actual fighting between the forces of DAVID and the men of Benjamin. ISH-BOSHETH, Saul's weak son, was set up as David's rival (2 Sam. 2:8). SHIMEI of Bahurim, who cursed David, was a Benjamite (16:5, 11). At the time of the schism after the death of SOLOMON, however, the Benjamites threw in their lot with the tribe of Judah and followed the Davidic house, as represented by REHOBOAM, against JEROBOAM in the north. Saul of Tarsus (PAUL) was a member of the tribe of Benjamin (Phil. 3:5).

Benjamin Gate. One of the city gates of preexilic JERUSALEM (Jer. 37:13; 38:7). Its name may suggest that it led to the tribal territory of BENJAMIN, but its location is uncertain. Proposed identifications include the MUSTER GATE at the N end of the city's E wall (Neh. 3:31), the SHEEP GATE at the E end of the N wall (3:32), and the Upper Benjamin Gate into the TEMPLE (Jer. 20:2; cf. 2 Ki. 15:35; Ezek. 9:2).

Benjaminite, Benjamite. ben´juh-muh-n*i*t, ben´juh-m*i*t. Alternate gentilic forms of BENJAMIN.

Beno. bee´noh (Heb. *bĕnô H1217*, "his son"). Son of Jaaziah and descendant of LEVI through MERARI (1 Chr. 24:26-27). The text is difficult, and some scholars emend it; others believe it is not a proper name and should rather be translated "his son" (cf. NRSV mg.).

Ben-Oni. ben-oh´n*i* (Heb. *ben-ʾônî H1204*, "son of my sorrow"). The name RACHEL gave to her son at birth; later JACOB changed it to BENJAMIN (Gen. 35:18).

Aerial view of the tribal region of Benjamin, including Jerusalem, looking NE toward Jericho.

Ben Sira(ch). ben-si′ruh(k). See APOCRYPHA.

Ben-zoheth. ben-zoh′heth (Heb. *ben-zôḥēt H1209*, "son of Zoheth"). Son (or descendant) of Ishi, included in the genealogy of JUDAH (1 Chr. 4:20).

Beon. bee′on (Heb. *bĕʿōn H1274*). A town in TRANSJORDAN within the tribal territory of REUBEN (Num. 32:1), probably to be identified with BAAL MEON.

Beor. bee′or (Heb. *bĕʿôr H1242*, possibly "burning"; Gk. *Beōr G1027*). (1) Father of BELA; the latter was an Edomite king before Israel became a monarchy (Gen. 36:32; 1 Chr. 1:43).

(2) Father of the seer BALAAM, who was summoned by BALAK to curse Israel (Num. 22:5; 24:3, 15; 31:8; Deut. 23:4; Josh. 13:22; 24:9; Mic. 6:5; 2 Pet. 2:15 [variant BOSOR]).

Bera. bihr′uh (*beraʿ H1396*, derivation uncertain). The king of SODOM who, with four allies, rebelled against KEDORLAOMER (Gen. 14:2; cf. vv. 8, 10–11, 17, 22).

Beracah. ber′uh-kuh (Heb. *bĕrākāh H1389*, "blessing"). KJV Berachah; TNIV Berakah. (1) One of the ambidextrous Benjamite warriors, kinsmen of SAUL, who joined DAVID at ZIKLAG (1 Chr. 12:3; cf. v. 2).

(2) An area in the Judean wilderness near TEKOA where King JEHOSHAPHAT and the men of Judah celebrated their victory against a Transjordanian coalition (2 Chr. 20:26). The precise identification is uncertain, but most scholars locate it between BETHLEHEM and HEBRON.

Berachah. See BERACAH.

Berachiah. See BEREKIAH.

Beraiah. bi-ray′yuh (Heb. *bĕrāʾyâ H1349*, "Yahweh has created"). Son of Shimei and descendant of BENJAMIN (1 Chr. 8:21).

Berakah. See BERACAH.

Berakiah. See BEREKIAH.

Berea. bi-ree′uh (Gk. *Beroia G1023*). Also Beroea. A city in SW MACEDONIA (Acts 17:10-15; 20:4). Lying at the foot of Mount Bermius, situated on a tributary of the Haliacmon, its origins appear lost in the mists of time, but it was counted in the third of the four divisions of the empire of ALEXANDER THE GREAT. By NT times Berea had become a desirable city, one of the most populous centers of Macedonia. The apostle PAUL and his party visited Berea on the second missionary journey. Here they found some open-minded people who were willing to study the teachings of Paul in the light of the Scripture. This happy situation was disrupted, however, when Jews from THESSALONICA arrived, turning the Bereans against the message and forcing Paul to flee to ATHENS. Silas and Timothy remained there briefly instructing the true believers. A Christian from Berea, SOPATER, accompanied Paul back to Jerusalem at the end of the apostle's third journey.

Berechiah. See BEREKIAH.

Bered (person). bihr′ed (Heb. *bered H1355*, possibly "coolness"). Apparently son of SHUTHELAH and grandson of EPHRAIM (1 Chr. 7:20), but the text is difficult, especially when compared with the alternate Ephraimite genealogy (Num. 26:35). Some believe the name should be emended to BEKER, that is, Ephraim's son.

Bered (place). bihr′ed (Heb. *bered H1354*, possibly "cool [well]"). A settlement or region in the NEGEV near KADESH (Gen. 16:14). HAGAR stopped in this area with her son ISHMAEL when they were met by the angel of the Lord at the well called BEER LAHAI ROI. Its location is unknown, though some identify it with a mountain SE of Kadesh.

Berekiah. ber′uh-ki′uh (Heb. *berekyâ H1392* and *berekyāhû H1393*, "Yahweh has blessed"; Gk. *Barachias G974*). Also Berachiah and Berechiah (OT), Barachiah and Barachias (NT). (1) Son of ZERUBBABEL and descendant of DAVID through SOLOMON (1 Chr. 3:20), possibly born in Palestine (see HASHUBAH).

(2) Father of ASAPH the musician (1 Chr. 6:39; 15:17).

(3) Son of a certain Asa; he was a LEVITE who returned to Judah from Babylon and settled among the Netophathites (1 Chr. 9:16; see NETOPHAH).

(4) A doorkeeper for the ARK OF THE COVENANT at the time of David's restructuring of the Levitical service (1 Chr. 15:23). Possibly the same as #2 above.

(5) Son of Meshillemoth; he was one of the leaders in Ephraim who opposed the bringing of captives from their countrymen in Judah into Samaria in the days of AHAZ (2 Chr. 28:12).

(6) Son of Meshezabel and father of MESHULLAM; the latter was one of the priests that helped to repair the wall of Jerusalem under NEHEMIAH, and whose daughter married TOBIAH's son, Jehohanan (Neh. 3:4, 30; 6:18).

(7) Son of IDDO and father of the prophet ZECHARIAH (Zech. 1:1, 7; Matt. 23:35).

Beri. bihr´i (Heb. *bērî H1373*, perhaps a gentilic of BEER). Son of Zophah and descendant of ASHER (1 Chr. 7:36). The name is not mentioned in the parallel genealogies (Gen. 46:17-18; Num. 26:44-47). Beri has no connection with the BERIITE clan (Num. 26:44) or with the BERITES (2 Sam. 20:14).

Beriah. bi-ri´uh (Heb. *bērî˓â H1380*, possibly "prominent"). **(1)** Son of ASHER and father of Heber and Malkiel; ancestral head of the BERIITE clan (Gen. 46:17; Num. 26:44; 1 Chr. 7:30-31).

(2) Son of EPHRAIM, who gave him the name Beriah "because there had been misfortune in his family" (1 Chr. 7:23; apparently a play on Heb. *rā˓âh H8288*, "evil"). Other sons of Ephraim had been put to death by the people of GATH (vv. 21-22).

(3) Son of ELPAAL and descendant of BENJAMIN; he and his brother SHEMA, heads of families in AIJALON, put to flight the inhabitants of Gath (1 Chr. 8:13, 16).

(4) Son of SHIMEI and descendant of LEVI through GERSHON; both he and his brother Jeush had few sons, "so they were counted as one family with one assignment" among the Levites (1 Chr. 23:10-11).

Beriites. bi-ri´its (Heb. *bērî˓î H1381*, gentilic of *bērî˓â H1380*). An Asherite clan (Num. 26:44). See BERIAH #1.

Berites. bihr´its (Heb. *bērîm H1379*, derivation uncertain). Apparently an Israelite clan that joined SHEBA in his rebellion against DAVID (2 Sam. 20:14). Many scholars, however, believe the name is a scribal error and read "Bichrites" (cf. NRSV). See BICRI.

Berith. See EL-BERITH; see also COVENANT.

Bernice. buhr-nees´ (Gk. *Bernikē G1022*, "bringer of victory"). Three times in the book of Acts reference is made to Bernice (Acts 25:13, 23; 26:30), Herod AGRIPPA I's eldest daughter (12:1), who was born in A.D. 28. According to JOSEPHUS (*Ant.* 19.5.1; 20.7.1-3), she was first married to a certain Marcus, and after his death she became the wife of Herod of Chalcis, her own uncle. When the latter died (A.D. 48), Bernice returned home to share the household of her brother AGRIPPA II, leading to rumors about an incestuous union, for which there is no real evidence (to meet the scandal, Bernice married another petty monarch, Polemon II of Olba in CILICIA, but the union did not last long). Bernice was present in CAESAREA when Agrippa II listened to PAUL's noble defense. Later, she shared with her brother the self-sacrificing endeavor to prevent the outbreak of the great rebellion of A.D. 66, confronting the mad procurator Gessius Florus at peril of her life. During the Jewish war she cultivated the goodwill of VESPASIAN, and the latter's son, TITUS, subsequently took her as his mistress for a time.

Berodach-Baladan. See MERODACH-BALADAN.

Beroea. See BEREA.

Berothah. bi-roh´thuh (Heb. *bērôtâ H1363*, perhaps "well"; cf. BEEROTH). In Ezekiel's vision, Berothah is one of the places marking the N boundary of Israel, near the border between DAMASCUS and HAMATH (Ezek. 47:16). This city was once thought to be the site of modern Beirut (which lies on the coast), but the more likely identification is with Bereitan, about 30 mi. (50 km.) NW of Damascus. It is probably the same as BEROTHAI.

Berothai. bi-roh´thi (Heb. *bērōtay H1408*, possibly "my well"). A city belonging to the Aramean king HADADEZER and from which DAVID took a

B

great quantity of bronze (2 Sam. 8:8). The parallel passage reads Cun (1 Chr. 18:8), but that is probably a different place. Most scholars identify Berothai with BEROTHAH.

Berothite. bihr′uh-thit. KJV form of Beerothite; see BEEROTH.

beryl. See MINERALS.

Besai. bee′si (Heb. *bēsay H1234*, derivation uncertain). Head of a family of temple servants (NETHINIM) who returned from the EXILE with ZERUBBABEL (Ezra 2:49; Neh. 7:52).

Besodeiah. bes′uh-dee′yah (Heb. *bĕsôdyâ H1233*, "in the council of Yahweh"). Father of Meshullam; the latter helped to repair the OLD GATE (Jeshanah) in the wall of Jerusalem under NEHEMIAH (Neh. 3:6).

besom. This English term, which refers to a broom made with twigs, is used by the KJV in one passage (Isa. 14:23; NIV, "broom"), where the prophet is portraying a figurative sweeper with which God will sweep away Babylon.

Besor. bee′sor (Heb. *bĕsôr H1410*, derivation uncertain). A wadi or ravine DAVID crossed in pursuit of the AMALEKITES, who had just raided ZIKLAG (1 Sam. 30:9-10, 21). Here David left 200 of his men who were too exhausted to pursue the Amalekites further. It is identified with Wadi Ghazzeh, one of the largest rivers in the NEGEV. It flows NW from the highlands to the coast, below GAZA.

Betah. bee′tuh (Heb. *beṭaḥ H1056* [not in NIV], "security"). A city belonging to the Aramean king HADADEZER and from which DAVID took a great quantity of bronze (2 Sam. 8:8 KJV and other versions). On the basis of some Greek MSS and the parallel passage (1 Chr. 18:8), the NIV emends the text to TEBAH.

Beten. bee′tuhn (Heb. *beṭen H1062*, "womb"). A town in the territory of the tribe of ASHER (Josh. 19:25). Some scholars identify the city with Khirbet Ibtin, about 11 mi. (18 km.) SSE of Acco.

beth (letter). beth (from *bayit H1074*, "house"). The second letter of the Hebrew alphabet (ב), with a numerical value of two. It is named for the shape of the letter, which in its older form resembled the outline of a house. Its sound corresponds to that of English *b* (following a vowel, it later became spirantized, with a sound similar to that of English *v*).

Beth- (name element). beth. This form (construct of the noun *bayit H1074*) is used as the initial element of numerous place names. Although its literal meaning is "house," usually the sense is more general, "place." For example, the name BETH EMEK probably means simply "valley-place."

Bethabara. beth-ab′uh-ruh (Gk. *Bēthabara*). According to the KJV (following the TR), the place across the JORDAN where JOHN THE BAPTIST ministered (Jn. 1:28). However, the majority of MSS, including the earliest witnesses, read BETHANY.

Beth Anath. beth-ay′nath (Heb. *bêt-ʿănāt H1117*, "house of [the goddess] ANATH"). A fortified city in the territory assigned to the tribe of NAPHTALI (Josh. 19:38). The Naphtalites failed to dislodge its inhabitants, but they enslaved the Canaanites living in this pagan town (Jdg. 1:33). The location of Beth Anath is uncertain, but some scholars place it about 15 mi. (24 km.) SE of TYRE.

Beth Anoth. beth-ay′noth (Heb. *bêt-ʿănôt H1116*, possibly "house of [the goddess] Anath [pl. form]"). A town in the hill country of the tribe of JUDAH (Josh. 15:59). It was probably an archaic Canaanite altar and shrine (see ANATH). It is identified with modern Khirbet Beit ʿAnun, some 3 mi. (5 km.) NE of HEBRON.

Bethany. beth′uh-nee (Gk. *Bēthania G1029*, possibly from *bêt ʿāniyyâ*, "house of the poor," or *bêt ʿănānyāh*, "house of Ananiah"). **(1)** A village less than 2 mi. (3 km.) SE of JERUSALEM, on the E side of the Mount of Olives and on the road to JERICHO (Mk. 11:1; Lk. 19:29; Jn. 11:18). MARY, MARTHA, and LAZARUS lived in Bethany, and it was there that Lazarus was raised from the dead. It seems generally to have served as Jesus' abode when in JUDEA (Matt. 21:17; Mk. 11:11). Bethany

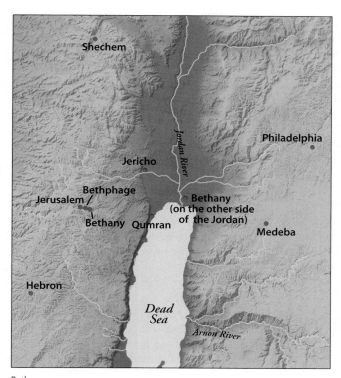

Bethany.

The village of Bethany in 1905. (View to the SE.)

© Dr. James C. Martin

B

(Lk. 24:50-51). Bethany still exists as a settled town today and is known as el-ʿAziriyeh, "the place of Lazarus." The traditional tomb of Lazarus is marked. Cf. also ANANIAH (PLACE).

(2) A place E of the JORDAN where JOHN THE BAPTIST ministered and where his confrontation with the delegation of priests and Levites from Jerusalem took place (Jn. 1:28, where the KJV has BETHABARA). Considerable debate surrounds the identification of this site, though a strong possibility is the traditional location at the Wadi el-Kharar, some 6 mi. (10 km.) E of Jericho. Some scholars believe that this Bethany should be identified with #1 above.

Beth Arabah. beth-air′uh-buh (Heb. *bêt hāʿărābâ H1098*, "house of the ARABAH [desert]") A town belonging to the tribe of JUDAH on its N boundary with the tribe of BENJAMIN (Josh. 15:6, 61; 18:18 [the last reference involves an emendation based on the LXX]). However, Beth Arabah is also included among the possessions of Benjamin (18:22); it is possible that the town changed hands at some time by an incident not recorded in the text. Beth Arabah is usually identified with the modern Arab village of ʿAin el-Gharabeh, located in the wilderness about 4 mi. (6 km.) SE of JERICHO, on the N bank of the Wadi Qelt.

Beth-aram. beth-air′uhm. KJV form of BETH HARAM.

Beth Arbel. beth-ahr′buhl (Heb. *bêt ʾarbēʾl H1079*, "house of Arbel"). An Israelite town devastated by a certain SHALMAN (Hos. 10:14). There is no other mention of either this town or the king. Beth Arbel is usually identified with the modern Irbid, which is situated on a crossroads in northern TRANSJORDAN, c. 20 mi. (32 km.) SE of the S tip of the Sea of GALILEE.

also was the home of Simon the leper, in whose house our Lord was anointed with the alabaster jar of ointment at the hands of a woman (Mk. 14:3-9; Lk. 7:36-50; cf. Jn. 12:1-8). According to Luke, the ASCENSION OF CHRIST took place near Bethany

Beth Ashbea. beth-ash′bee-uh (Heb. *bêt ʾašbēaʿ H1080*, "house of Ashbea"). A town of unknown location; it was home to some clans of linen workers that descended from JUDAH through SHELAH (1 Chr. 4:21). The KJV interprets the Hebrew as referring not to a town but to a family (i.e., the linen workers "of the house of Ashbea").

Beth Aven. beth-ay′vuhn (Heb. *bêt ʾāwen H1077*, "house of trouble [*or* idolatry]"). A town belonging to the tribe of BENJAMIN on its N boundary; it was near AI, to the E of BETHEL and just to the W of MICMASH (Josh. 7:2; 18:12; 1 Sam. 13:5; 14:23). The precise location is disputed, but a likely site is Tell Maryam, some 7 mi. (11 km.) NE of JERUSALEM. The prophet HOSEA, however, appears to use the name in a derogatory way as a reference to Bethel (Hos. 4:15; 5:8; 10:5; cf. also the wordplay in the Heb. of Amos 5:5). See also AVEN.

Beth Azmaveth. See AZMAVETH (PLACE).

Beth Baal Meon. beth-bay′uhl-mee′on (Heb. *bêt baʿal mĕʿôn H1081*, "house of the lord of the dwelling"). A town within the tribal territory of REUBEN in TRANSJORDAN (Josh. 13:17), probably to be identified with BAAL MEON. Both names occur in the MOABITE STONE.

Beth Barah. beth-bair′uh (Heb. *bêt bārâ H1083*, "house of Barah"). A place near the JORDAN River; GIDEON instructed the men of EPHRAIM to seize that area so as to head off the fleeing army of MIDIAN (Jdg. 7:24). Because the Hebrew construction is unusual, some scholars emend the text so that it reads, "up to the fords of the Jordan." Others have attempted to link the place with BETHABARA, but the site remains unidentified.

Beth Bieri. beth-bihr′ee-*i*. KJV form of BETH BIRI.

Beth Biri. beth-bihr′*i* (Heb. *bêt birʾi H1082*, "house of Biri"). KJV Beth-birei. An unidentified town inhabited by descendants of SIMEON (1 Chr. 4:31); apparently a postexilic name for BETH LEBAOTH (Josh. 19:6).

Beth Car. beth-kahr′ (Heb. *bêt kār H1105*, "house of pasture"). TNIV Beth Kar. A town of unknown

location, but apparently to the W of MIZPAH, in the territory of the tribe of BENJAMIN; the Israelites pursued the PHILISTINES all the way to an area near this town (1 Sam. 7:11).

Beth Dagon. beth-day′gon (Heb. *bêt-dāgôn H1087*, "house of [the god] Dagon"). **(1)** A site in the SHEPHELAH or lowlands of JUDAH (Josh. 15:41). The exact location of the site is unknown. A town by that name is mentioned in extrabiblical sources, but the biblical Beth Dagon is probably a different site.

(2) A border city in the territory of the tribe of ASHER and E of Mount CARMEL (Josh. 19:27). The location is unknown, although some identify it with modern Tell Regeb, about 5 mi. (8 km.) SE of Haifa.

Beth Diblathaim. beth′dib-luh-thay′im (Heb. *bêt diblātayim H1086*, "house of [double] fig cakes"). One of the cities of MOAB against which JEREMIAH announced judgment (Jer. 48:22). The town is mentioned in the MOABITE STONE, which suggests it was situated between MEDEBA and BETH BAAL MEON. It is probably the same location as ALMON DIBLATHAIM (Num. 33:46-47). Some scholars identify the town with modern Khirbet Deleilat esh-Sherqiyeh, about 21 mi. (34 km.) SE of Amman, Jordan.

Beth Eden. beth-ee′duhn (Heb. *bêt ʿeden H1114*, prob. "house of delight"). An Aramean principality (see SYRIA) against which AMOS prophesied (Amos 1:5; KJV, "house of Eden"). Known as Bit-Adini in Assyrian sources, it was situated in the watershed of the EUPHRATES and thrived after the collapse of the great powers in the ninth-eighth century B.C. SENNACHERIB boasted that his Assyrian forefathers had destroyed "the people [children] of Eden," probably a reference to the same place (2 Ki. 19:12 = Isa. 37:12; perhaps also Ezek. 27:23).

Beth Eked. beth-ee′kid (Heb. *bêt-ʿēqed H1118*, possibly "binding-house"). A place on the way from JEZREEL to SAMARIA where JEHU executed some relatives of King AHAZIAH (2 Ki. 10:12, 14). *Targum Jonathan* interprets the words not as a proper name but as a description, "meeting house [of the shepherds]" (so also KJV, "shearing house"). It probably does refer to a town, however, and some scholars have identified it with modern Beit Qad, a few miles SSE of JEZREEL, but this location is disputed.

Bethel (deity). beth´uhl (Heb. *bêt-ʾēl H1078*, "house of God"). A W Semitic deity attested with various names in extrabiblical literature. A probable biblical reference is Jer. 48:13, where Bethel stands in parallelism with CHEMOSH. However, no notice is ever given to the presence of this god in the northern tribes, so it is possible that, as is likely in Amos 5:5, the name Bethel is given, by metonymy, with reference to the golden calf found in the city. In Zech. 7:2, the KJV renders the name as "the house of God," but a reference to the Jerusalem temple is very unlikely. The Hebrew text may reflect the personal name Bethel-sharezer (see SHAREZER); some modern versions (e.g., NAB, NEB, NJPS) have adopted this interpretation, but others (e.g., NIV, NRSV) understand the text as a reference to the town (or inhabitants) of Bethel.

Bethel (place). beth´uhl (Heb. *bêt-ʾēl H1078*, "house of God"). **(1)** A town originally known as LUZ, 12 mi. (19 km.) N of JERUSALEM (Gen. 28:19), and a short distance W of AI. ABRAHAM stopped near this spot on his way to the NEGEV and offered a sacrifice (12:8; 13:3). JACOB called Luz "Bethel" (28:10-22), since God met him here and confirmed the Abrahamic covenant to him. Jacob revisited this town when he returned from PADDAN ARAM in response to the command of God (35:1). He built an altar and worshiped, calling the place EL BETHEL ("the God of Bethel," 35:7). Here Jacob buried DEBORAH, the nurse of REBEKAH (35:8). It was a logical stopping place, for it lay on a well-known route running from the Plain of ESDRAELON to BEERSHEBA.

Bethel seems to have been a Canaanite city originally, and after the conquest by JOSHUA it was given to the tribe of BENJAMIN (Josh. 18:21-22). JOSEPH's descendants, under the guidance of the Lord, went up against Bethel and took it (Jdg. 1:22-26). It remained on the southern border of EPHRAIM. During the period of the judges, because of the wickedness of the tribe of Ephraim,

the Israelites marched against them. They stopped at Bethel to ascertain God's will (20:18). The ARK OF THE COVENANT was kept there at this time (20:26-28). SAMUEL went to this city from time to time to conduct business and to worship (1 Sam. 7:16; 10:3).

At a later period, after the kingdom was divided, JEROBOAM, in order to nullify the influence of JERUSALEM as the center of religious activity for the people, chose Bethel as one of the two centers in which he set up golden calves (1 Ki. 12:26-30). Here he sacrificed to the calves and placed priests to minister in the high places (12:32). See CALF WORSHIP. Because of these and other sins, Amos cried out against this city (Amos 3:14; 4:4-6). Hosea too pronounced judgment on Bethel, even calling it BETH AVEN, "the house of trouble" (Hos. 4:15). An Israelite priest returned here to teach the people resettled in the area by ASSYRIA (2 Ki. 17:27-28). They combined worship of their heathen gods with worship of the Lord (17:33). It was not until JOSIAH became king that this idolatry was removed from Bethel and the true worship of the Lord established (23:15-23). When the Jews returned from the Babylonian captivity, Ezra and Nehemiah both record that some returned to Bethel (Ezra 2:28; Neh. 7:32) and, as one might suppose, they are listed as Benjamites (Neh. 11:31). Bethel is also mentioned in the APOCRYPHA as being fortified by BACCHIDES (1 Macc. 9:50).

Most scholars identify Bethel with the modern village of Beitin, which was excavated by Albright and Kelso intermittently from 1934 to 1961. City walls from the Middle Bronze Age (2200 to 1550 B.C.), the time of the patriarchs, were found. In the Late Bronze Age (1550-1200) there were well-built houses here with much imported pottery. In the thirteenth century a destruction layer of ashes and burned bricks testifies to its demise, which some attribute to Joshua.

(2) Another city in S Judah (1 Sam. 30:27) is also called Bethel. See BETHUEL.

Beth Emek. beth-ee´mik (Heb. *bêt hāʿēmeq H1097*, "house of the valley"). A town on the northern border of the tribe of ASHER (Josh. 19:27). It is usually identified with modern Tell Mimas, about 5 mi. (8 km.) NE of Acco.

Bether. bee-thuhr′ (Heb. *beter H1441*, possibly "cutting, piece"). The KJV and other versions take the Hebrew word as a proper name in Cant. 2:7 and render the text, "the mountains of Bether." Although there is some evidence for the existence of a town by that name, it is doubtful that Song of Solomon is referring to it, so many scholars take the word as a reference to a plant-name or to a fragrance (cf. 8:14, "spice-laden mountains"). According to a different interpretation, the phrase can be translated "the rugged hills" (NIV; similarly NRSV, "the cleft mountains").

Bethesda. buh-thez′duh (Gk. *Bēthesda G1031*, possibly from Aram. *bêt ḥisdā᾿*, "house of mercy").

This view of the wall that divides the northern and southern pools of Bethesda reveals bedrock (lower right of photo) that was part of the original pool dating as early as the 3rd cent. B.C. (View to the NW.)

A spring-fed pool at JERUSALEM, near the SHEEP GATE and surrounded by five porches (Jn. 5:2; the variant reading BETH-ZATHA is accepted by the NRSV; another variant is BETHSAIDA). Sick people waited to step down into these waters, which were thought to have healing properties. Here Jesus healed a man who had been sick for thirty-eight years (5:1-16; note that v. 4 is omitted by most other modern versions because some early MSS and versions omit it). In A.D. 1888, while the church of St. Anne in NE Jerusalem was being repaired, twin reservoirs were discovered, one 55 ft. (17 m.) long and the other 65 ft. (20 m.). The former one was spanned by five arches with five corresponding porches. The Crusaders regarded this as the site mentioned by John and built a church over it, with a crypt imitating the five porches and an opening in the floor to get down to the water.

Beth Ezel. beth-ee′zuhl (Heb. *bēt hā᾿ēṣel H1089*, possibly "house of proximity," i.e., "nearby place"). A town against which MICAH prophesied (Mic. 1:11). The imprecation is against the enemies of Judah and refers to various sites mostly in the SHEPHELAH. The location of Beth Ezel is uncertain.

Beth Gader. beth-gay′duhr (Heb. *bêt-gādēr H1084*, "house of stone wall"). A place name appearing as part of JUDAH's genealogical list (1 Chr. 2:51, "Hareph the father [*i.e.*, founder, ruler] of Beth Gader"). Some scholars identify it with GEDER. The town was probably in the vicinity of the other towns listed, such as BETHLEHEM, but its precise location is unknown.

Beth Gamul. beth-gay′muhl (Heb. *bêt gāmûl H1085*, "house of recompense"). One of the cities of the tableland of MOAB against which JEREMIAH prophesied (Jer. 48:23). Some have identified it with Khirbet el-Jemeil, c. 5 mi. (8 km.) E of AROER.

Beth Gilgal. beth-gil′gal (Heb. *bêt haggilgāl H1090*, "house of Gilgal [circle]"). One of the villages around JERUSALEM from which singers came to celebrate the dedication of the wall rebuilt after

© Dr. James C. Martin

the EXILE (Neh. 12:29; KJV, "the house of Gilgal"). It is often identified with the better-known town of GILGAL, which lies c. 4 mi. (6 km.) SE of JERICHO, but some scholars argue that Beth Gilgal was probably closer to Jerusalem.

Beth-haccerem, Beth-haccherem. beth-hak´uh-rem. See BETH HAKKEREM.

Beth Haggan. beth-hag´uhn (Heb. *bêt haggān H1091*, "house of the garden"). A town S of the Valley of JEZREEL toward which AHAZIAH fled when pursued by JEHU (2 Ki. 9:27; KJV, "the garden house"). It is identified with modern Jenin, 11 mi. (18 km.) SE of MEGIDDO.

Beth Hakkerem. beth-hak´uh-rem (Heb. *bêt-hakkerem H1094*, "house of the vineyard"). Also Beth-haccerem, Beth-haccherem. The chief city of a district in JUDAH; its ruler, MALKIJAH, repaired the DUNG GATE as the wall was rebuilt after the EXILE (Neh. 3:14). It was a suitable location for a signaling station (Jer. 6:1). Some scholars have identified the city with ʿAin Karim, c. 6 mi. (10 km.) W of JERUSALEM, but a more likely site is Ramat Raḥel, a high hill less than 3 mi. (5 km.) SSW of Jerusalem.

Beth Haram. beth-hair´uhm (Heb. *bêt hārām H1099*, "house of high place"). KJV Beth-aram. A town allotted to the tribe of GAD (Josh. 13:27); it is doubtless the same as Beth Haran (Num. 32:36). Taken from the Amorites, it held a high point E of the JORDAN River in the Jordan valley and was fortified by the tribe of Gad to protect their families and cattle while they shared with the other tribes in the conquest W of Jordan. The site is identified with the modern Tell Iktanu, 8 mi. (13 km.) NE of the mouth of the Jordan.

Beth Haran. beth-hair´uhn. Alternate form of BETH HARAM.

Beth Hoglah. beth-hog´luh (Heb. *bêt-ḥaglâ H1102*, "house of Hoglah [partridge]"). One of fourteen cities assigned to the tribe of BENJAMIN (Josh. 18:21). It was located in the ARABAH on the

S boundary of the tribe (18:19), which is also the N boundary of JUDAH (15:6). Beth Hoglah should possibly be identified with modern Deir Ḥajlah, 3.5 mi. (5.5 km.) SE of JERICHO.

Beth Horon. beth-hor´uhn (Heb. *bêt-ḥōrôn H1103*, "house of a caves"). The name of twin towns belonging to the tribe of EPHRAIM and assigned to the Kohathites (Josh. 16:3, 5; 21:22; 1 Chr. 7:24; 2 Chr. 8:5). Beit ʿUr el-Foka ("the upper") is c. 800 ft. (245 m.) higher than Beit ʿUr et-Taḥta ("the lower"). Built by a woman named SHEERAH (1 Chr. 7:24), Beth Horon lay on the boundary line between BENJAMIN and Ephraim (Josh. 16:3, 5), on the road from GIBEON to AZEKAH (10:10-11).

For centuries a strategic route into the heart of JUDEA went up from JOPPA (modern Jaffa) on the coast through the Valley of AIJALON (modern Yalo), ascending through the two Beth Horons to Gibeon (4 mi./6 km. distant) on its way to Jerusalem. It was in this valley that Joshua commanded the sun and moon to stand still while he fought the AMORITE kings in his defense of the Gibeonites. He chased these five kings over the pass to Beth Horon (Josh. 10:10-13). Along this route the PHILISTINES fled after they had been defeated at MICMASH (1 Sam. 14:31), and it was there that Judas MACCABEE overthrew the army of Seron, a SELEUCID commander (1 Macc. 3:13-24). The importance of the Beth Horon pass as a key route into Palestine explains the fortification of its towns by SOLOMON (2 Chr. 8:5). It is no longer important, but great foundation stones can be seen there yet today.

Beth Jeshimoth. beth-jesh´uh-moth (Heb. *bêt hayšîmôt H1093*, "house of deserts"). A city in the plains of MOAB; it had been ruled by SIHON king of the AMORITES and was allotted to the tribe of REUBEN (Num. 33:49 [KJV, "Beth-jesimoth"]; Josh. 12:3; 13:20). It is described as one of the glorious cities on the frontier of Moab (Ezek. 25:9). Beth Jeshimoth is identified with Tell el-ʿAzeimeh, about 4 mi. (6 km.) from the NE end of the DEAD SEA.

Beth-jesimoth. See BETH JESHIMOTH.

Beth Kar. See BETH CAR.

Beth-leaphrah. beth´li-af´-ruh. See BETH OPHRAH.

Beth Lebaoth. beth´li-bay´oth (Heb. *bêt lĕbāʾôt H1106*, "house of lionesses"). One of the cities "taken from the share of Judah" and assigned to the tribe of SIMEON (Josh. 19:6; cf. v. 9). It is probably the same as LEBAOTH (15:32; cf. v. 21); and in the Chronicler's parallel list, it is apparently referred to as BETH BIRI, possibly its postexilic name (1 Chr. 4:31). Its precise location in the NEGEV is unknown.

Bethlehem. beth´li-hem (Heb. *bêt leḥem H1107*, "house of bread"; gentilic *bêt-hallaḥmî H1095*, "Bethlehemite"). **(1)** A town 5 mi. (8 km.) SW of JERUSALEM, 2,550 ft. (780 m.) above sea level, in the hill country of JUDEA on the main highway to HEBRON and EGYPT. In JACOB's time it was called EPHRATH ("fruitful") and was the burial place of RACHEL (Gen. 35:16, 19; 48:7). Little is known of the origin of the town, though in 1 Chr. 2:51 SALMA the son of CALEB is described as the "father [*i.e.*, founder or first Israelite leader] of Bethlehem." Bethlehem may have been the home of IBZAN, the tenth judge (Jdg. 12:8-10, but see #2 below); it certainly was the home of ELIMELECH, father-in-law of RUTH (Ruth 1:1-2), and of Ruth's husband BOAZ (2:1, 4). Here their great-grandson

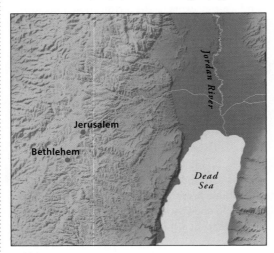

Bethlehem.

DAVID kept his father's sheep and was anointed king by SAMUEL (1 Sam. 16:13, 15). Hence it was known as "the city of David" (Lk. 2:4, 11). It was once occupied by a PHILISTINE garrison (2 Sam. 23:14-16), later fortified by REHOBOAM (2 Chr. 11:6).

In JEREMIAH's time (Jer. 41:17) the caravan inn of KIMHAM (see 2 Sam. 19:37-40) near Bethlehem was the usual starting place for Egypt. The inn mentioned in Lk. 2 must have been a similar one and some have speculated that it was the same. Here the MESSIAH was born (Matt. 2:1; Lk. 2:1-7), for whom this town that was "small among the clans of Judah" (Mic. 5:2) achieved its great fame. Its male children under two years of age were murdered in HEROD's attempt to kill the King of the Jews (Matt. 2:16).

Justin Martyr, a Christian writer in the second century, said that our Lord's birth took place in a cave close to the village. Over this traditional manger site the emperor Constantine (A.D. 330) and Helena his mother built the Church of the Nativity. Rebuilt more sumptuously by Justinian in the sixth century, it still has part of the original structure and is a popular attraction for tourists today. The grotto of the nativity is beneath a crypt, c. 39 ft. (12 m.) long, 11 ft. (3.5 m.) wide, and 9 ft. (3 m.) high, hewn out of the rock and lined with marble. A rich altar is over the supposed site of the Savior's birth. Modern Bethlehem is a village of fewer than 10,000 inhabitants. The slopes abound in figs, vines, almonds, and olives. The shepherds' fields are still seen to the NE.

(2) A town within the tribal territory of ZEBULUN (Josh. 19:15). Some believe that this Bethlehem, and not the one in Judah, was the home and burial place of IBZAN the judge (Jdg. 12:8, 10). The town, modern Beit Laḥm, is about 7 mi. (11 km.) NW of NAZARETH, and some remains have been found indicating its importance in earlier times.

Bethlehem, Star of. See ASTRONOMY.

Beth Maac(h)ah. See ABEL BETH MAACAH.

Beth Marcaboth. beth-mahr´kuh-both (Heb. *bêt-hammarkābôt H1096* and *bêt markābôt H1112*, "house of [the] chariots"). TNIV Beth Markaboth.

One of the cities "taken from the share of Judah" and apportioned to the tribe of SIMEON (Josh. 19:5, cf. v. 9; 1 Chr. 4:31). It is probably the same town as MADMANNAH, which appears in its place in the corresponding list (Josh. 15:31).

Beth Meon. beth-mee'on (Heb. *bêt mĕʿôn H1110*, "house of habitation"). A town in the Moabite plateau against which JEREMIAH prophesied judgment (Jer. 48:23). It is probably to be identified with BAAL MEON.

Beth Millo. beth-mil'oh (Heb. *bêt millôʾ H1109*, "house of Millo [filling]"). **(1)** A place associated with SHECHEM (Jdg. 9:6, 20; KJV, "the house of Millo") and usually identified with "the tower of Shechem" (9:46-49). Some think it may refer to an area of earth fill and thus to the foundation of the upper city, which would have been inhabited by priests and soldiers.

(2) A place near JERUSALEM, "on the road down to Silla," where King Joash (JEHOASH) was assassinated by his officials (2 Ki. 12:20; KJV and other versions, "the house of Millo"). It may have been a prominent building in an area of Jerusalem known as the MILLO.

Beth Nimrah. beth-nim'ruh (Heb. *bêt nimrâ H1113*, perhaps "house of a leopard"). A town allotted to the tribe of GAD (Num. 32:36; Josh. 13:27), also called simply Nimrah (Num. 32:3). Taken from the AMORITES, it was fortified by the Gadites to protect their families and cattle while they shared with the other tribes in the conquest W of Jordan. The ancient city is identified as Tell el-Bleibil, some 10 mi. (16 km.) NE of JERICHO.

Beth Ophrah. beth-of'ruh (Heb. *bêt lĕʿaprâ H1108*, "house of dust"). A town in the SHEPHELAH mentioned in Micah's lament (Mic. 1:10; KJV, "the house of Aphrah"; NRSV and other versions, "Beth-leaphrah"). Since the expression is clearly a play on words ("in the dusty place roll in the dust"), some think it may be an allusion to another city, such as OPHRAH or BETHEL.

Beth-palet. See BETH PELET.

Beth Pazzez. beth-paz'iz (Heb. *bêt paṣṣēṣ H1122*, "house of dispersion"). A city included in the territory of the tribe of ISSACHAR (Josh. 19:21). It was located to the E of Mount TABOR, but the site has not been identified.

Beth Pelet. beth-pee'lit (Heb. *bêt peleṭ H1120*, "house of escape"). One of the "southernmost towns of the tribe of Judah in the Negev toward the boundary of Edom" (Josh. 15:27 [KJV, "Beth-palet"]; cf. v. 21). It was rebuilt and inhabited by the people of JUDAH after their return from EXILE in Babylon (Neh. 11:26 [KJV, "Beth-phelet"]). HELEZ the Paltite, one of DAVID's famous Thirty, was likely from this city (2 Sam. 23:26). It is perhaps to be identified with Tell es-Saqati, about 6 mi. (10 km.) NNE of BEERSHEBA.

Beth Peor. beth-pee'or (Heb. *bêt pĕʿor H1121*, "house of Peor"). A city in MOAB that was assigned to the tribe of REUBEN (Josh. 13:20). Before entering the land of Canaan, the Israelites encamped in the valley near Beth Peor, where MOSES committed laws to them; in this same valley God buried him (Deut. 3:29; 4:46; 34:6). The name of the city may have been originally Beth Baal Peor and was likely the place where BAAL PEOR was worshiped as patron deity (Num. 25:3, 5, 18; see also PEOR). Possible identifications are Khirbet esh-Sheikh-Jayil and Khirbet ʿAyun Musa, both of them a short distance N of Mount NEBO.

Bethphage. beth'fuh-jee (Gk. *Bēthphagē G1036*, from Aram. *bêt paggēʾ*, "house of unripe figs"). A village on the Mount of OLIVES and near BETHANY. As Jesus approached this town on his way to JERUSALEM, he sent two of his disciples to procure a colt in preparation for the TRIUMPHAL ENTRY (Matt. 21:1; Mk. 11:1; Lk. 19:29). The site is generally identified with the present Kafr et-Tur, just W of Bethany.

Beth-phelet. See BETH PELET.

Beth Rapha. beth-ray'fuh (Heb. *bêt rāpāʾ H1125*, "house of Rapha [healing]"). Son of Eshton and descendant of JUDAH; he is described as one of "the men of Recah" (1 Chr. 4:12).

B

Beth Rehob. beth-ree´hob (Heb. *bêt-rĕḥôb H1124*, "house of Rehob [street]"). An Aramean town or principality near the city of LAISH (DAN) in the extreme N of Palestine (Jdg. 18:28). It is probably the same as the REHOB that marked the northern limit of the spies' inspection of Canaan (Num. 13:21). When the AMMONITES prepared to fight against King DAVID, they hired 20,000 Aramean mercenaries from this area and from the nearby kingdom of ZOBAH (2 Sam. 10:6; see SYRIA). The area was probably located between Dan and Zobah, but the precise location has not been identified

Bethsaida. beth-say´uh-duh (Gk. *Bēthsaida G1034*, from Heb. *bêt ṣaydâ*, "house of hunting [fishing]"). A town on the N shore of the Sea of GALILEE. The Gospel of John clearly states that PHILIP the disciple was from Bethsaida, the city of ANDREW and PETER (Jn. 1:44; 12:21). Apparently Jesus visited the town at this early point in his ministry (cf. 1:43). Bethsaida was the scene of the feeding of the 5,000 (Lk. 9:10-17). Both Matthew and Mark wrote of the scene of this feeding as a "solitary place" without naming it (Matt. 14:13; Mk. 6:31-32). Confusion arises from Mark's account, which first reports the event and then adds, "Immediately Jesus made his disciples get into the boat and go on ahead of him to Bethsaida" (6:45). Furthermore, John introduces his account of the same event by saying that "Jesus crossed to the far shore [presumably the E side] of the Sea of Galilee" (Jn. 6:1). Elsewhere John speaks of "Bethsaida in Galilee" (12:21). Tradition places the feeding of the 5,000 at ʿAin et-Tabghah, 1.5 mi. (2 km.) W of CAPERNAUM, but there are serious problems with this identification despite the presence of the Chapel of the Multiplication of the Loaves and Fishes at that site. It is generally agreed from the texts that Bethsaida is somewhere near the N end of the Sea of Galilee, but probably on the E side of the JORDAN's mouth.

After Jesus' trip toward TYRE and SIDON, he returned to the area of GALILEE, where he healed a deaf mute, fed the 4,000, argued with the PHARISEES, and then came again to Bethsaida (Mk. 8:22). He healed the blind man brought to him and from there went N to CAESAREA PHILIPPI with his disciples. Apparently Jesus' ministry was less than successful in Bethsaida in spite of the feeding of the 5,000; both that town and KORAZIN were cursed (Matt. 11:21-22; Lk. 10:13). The only other reference to Bethsaida in the Bible is as a textual variant (Jn. 5:2, where the original reading is prob. BETHESDA).

Some scholars argue that the Gospels refer to two different towns named Bethsaida, one E and

© Dr. James C. Martin

Excavation of a site thought by some to be ancient Bethsaida. The view is to the SE, and the Sea of Galilee is visible on the top right.

the other W of the Jordan. It is true that the name, being a fitting description of a fishing village, could refer to several towns on this productive lake, but it is not necessary to adopt such a solution. Bethsaida is often identified with modern el-ʿAraj, which is right on the lake and just E of the Jordan's mouth. It has a harbor and thus meets most of the specifications, but some argue that it does not fit the evidence from Josephus. About a mile N of el-ʿAraj, and connected by what was a fine road, is another site bearing the simple name of et-Tell ("the mound"). This location is near the Jordan and has evidence of being a larger city complete with wall, aqueduct, and fine buildings. This identification would solve most of the questions presented in the Gospels as well as those in ancient secular sources.

Beth Shan. beth-shan′ (Heb. *bêt-šĕʾān H1126* [*byt šn* in Samuel], "house of quietness"). Also Bethshean. A town allotted to the tribe of Manasseh, but within the territory of Issachar; the Manassites were not able to drive the Canaanites out of this town (Josh. 17:11-12; Jdg. 1:27). It lay 14 mi. (23 km.) S of the Sea of Galilee, overlooking the Plain of Esdraelon. After Saul died on Mount Gilboa, the Philistines fastened his body to the wall of Beth Shan and put his armor in the temple of the Ashtoreths as trophies of their victory (1 Sam. 31:8-12). Later the men of Jabesh Gilead stole the bones of Saul and his sons from the street of Beth Shan, but David recovered them and gave them a proper burial (2 Sam. 21:12-14).

Today the site of the city is a mound, called Tell el-Ḥusn ("Mound of the Fortress"), located near the Arab village of Beisan. Excavations have yielded rich finds, dating the history of the city from 3500 B.C. to the Christian era. A stratification of eighteen levels of debris and ruined houses can be seen as evidence of repeated destructions and eras of rebuilding. Because of its commanding location, it was fortified with double walls and was a strong Egyptian outpost from the fifteenth to the twelfth centuries. Temples and monument inscriptions by three pharaohs were discovered and date back to this time. The excavators have shown that Beth Shan was destroyed between 1050 and 1000, the approximate time of King David, who may have been responsible for its destruction. Four Canaanite temples were unearthed at the site, one of which has been identified with the "temple of the Ashtoreths" (1 Sam. 31:10), and another with the temple

The uplifted hill of Beth Shan inhabited during the OT period towers over the Greco-Roman and Byzantine ruins of Scythopolis. (View to the NNE.)

© Dr. James C. Martin

of DAGON where the Philistines fastened Saul's head (1 Chr. 10:10). In SOLOMON's reign Beth Shan was included in one of his commissary districts (1 Ki. 4:12). A Roman theater, erected about A.D. 200, still stands, and the remains of a synagogue from the fourth century have been found.

Beth Shemesh. beth-sheh′mish (Heb. *bêt šemeš H1127*, "house of the sun"). A place name, apparently applied to several towns where a shrine to the sun-god was consecrated in pre-Israelite times. **(1)** In Upper GALILEE. A Canaanite town in the tribal inheritance of NAPHTALI (Josh. 19:38); it maintained its independence during the period of the judges (Jdg. 1:33), probably until the reign of DAVID (cf. 2 Sam. 24:6-7). The biblical association of BETH ANATH with Naphtali's Beth Shemesh (Jdg. 1:33) points to a location in central upper Galilee, possibly Khirbet Tell er-Ruweisi, about 17 mi. (27 km.) NE of Acco.

(2) In Lower Galilee. Another town by this name appears near the border of the tribal territory of ISSACHAR (Josh. 19:22). Of the various suggestions for its identification, the most likely is Khirbet Sheikh esh-Shamsawi, which would place Beth Shemesh on the northern side of Issachar's district near the border with Naphtali, about 3 mi. (5 km.) SW of the S tip of the Sea of Galilee.

(3) In JUDAH. The most prominent Beth Shemesh in biblical history was the one on the northern boundary of Judah's tribal inheritance (Josh. 15:10). It was also known as IR SHEMESH (Josh. 19:41) and Mount HERES (Jdg. 1:35). The city served as a landmark on the N boundary of Judah (Josh. 15:10), but under the name Ir Shemesh its territory was apparently assigned to DAN, who were unable to occupy it. The town itself was given to the descendants of AARON (Josh. 21:16; 1 Chr. 6:59). When the ARK OF THE COVENANT was returned to Israel by the PHILISTINES, it was brought via the SOREK Valley to Beth Shemesh (1 Sam. 6). SOLOMON's second administrative district included Beth Shemesh (1 Ki. 4:9). The town figures in other biblical narratives (2 Ki. 14:8-14; 2 Chr. 25:17-24; 28:18). Beth Shemesh is identified with a large mound known as Tell er-Rumeileh, some 16 mi. (26 km.) W of JERUSALEM. Excavations have revealed six levels of occupation, the third of which dates to the time of SAUL and DAVID (1200-1000 B.C.). Implements of the late Canaanite and early Israelite period have been discovered here, such as pottery, weapons, and jewelry. Quantities of Philistine pottery indicate their domination of the Israelite population and also suggest a later Philistine occupancy (2 Chr. 28:18). Copper smelters and houses with underground cisterns were also found.

(4) In EGYPT. The Hebrew phrase *bêt šemeš* occurs also in Jer. 43:13 (cf. KJV), but the NIV renders it "the temple of the sun"; the reference may be to ON, that is, HELIOPOLIS (cf. NRSV).

Beth-shemite. beth-shem′it (Heb. *bêt-šimšî H1128*). Term used in the KJV and other versions with reference to a certain Joshua, in whose field the ARK OF THE COVENANT was set (1 Sam. 6:14, 18; NIV, "Joshua of Beth Shemesh"). See BETH SHEMESH #3.

Beth Shittah. beth-shit′uh (Heb. *bêt haššiṭṭâ H1101*, "house of Shittah [acacia]"). The place near the border of ABEL MEHOLAH to which the routed army of MIDIAN fled before GIDEON (Jdg. 7:22). The site was probably located SE of BETH SHAN, perhaps on the E side of the JORDAN.

Beth Tappuah. beth-tap′yoo-uh (Heb. *bêt-tappûaḥ H1130*, "house of [the clan of] Tappuah" or "place of the apple trees"). A town in the hill country of JUDAH; its district included HEBRON and seven other cities (Josh. 15:53). The site is identified with the modern village of Taffuḥ, 3.5 mi. (5.5 km.) NNW of Hebron. It stands on the edge of a high ridge that overlooks fertile terraces below.

Beth Togarmah. beth′toh-gahr′muh (Heb. *bêt tôgarmâ H1129*, "house of Togarmah"). A place in "the far north" that exchanged horses and mules for the merchandise of TYRE and that had military connections with GOG (Ezek. 27:14; 38:6). It was probably located in what is modern Armenia. See also TOGARMAH.

Bethuel (person). bi-thyoo′uhl (Heb. *bĕtûʾēl H1432*, possibly "man of God"). Son of NAHOR (ABRAHAM's brother) and father of REBEKAH and LABAN (Gen. 22:22-23; 24:15; et al.). He is referred to as "the Aramean from Paddan Aram" (25:20; cf. also 28:5). See PADDAN ARAM.

Bethuel (place). bi-thy*oo*'uhl (Heb. *bĕtû'ēl H1433*, derivation uncertain, but cf. previous item; also *bĕtûl H1434* [Josh. 19:4]). A town occupied by the clan of SHIMEI, descendant of SIMEON (1 Chr. 4:30). In a parallel list that describes the inheritance of Simeon within the territory of JUDAH, it is spelled Bethul (Josh. 19:4). It appears to be the same as KESIL (Josh. 15:30), and perhaps it occurs once in the alternate (or textually corrupt?) form "Bethel" (1 Sam. 30:27). Its precise location is unknown, although one proposal is Khirbet el-Qarjetein, a ruin some 12 mi. (19 km.) S of HEBRON.

Bethul. beth'uhl. See BETHUEL (PLACE).

Beth-zatha. beth-zay'thuh (Gk. *Bēthzatha*, possibly from Aram. *byt zyt'*, "house of the olive"). According to some Greek MSS, Beth-zatha was the name of the pool in JERUSALEM where Jesus healed a lame man (Jn. 5:2; this textual variant is accepted by the NRSV and other versions). The pool may have been given the name Beth-zatha (either initially or subsequent to NT times) because of its connection or proximity to a suburb of Jerusalem that had a similar name. However, the NIV takes BETHESDA as the original reading in John.

Beth Zur. beth-zuhr' (Heb. *bêt-ṣûr H1123*, "house [*or* place] of rocks"). A town in the hill country of JUDAH (Josh. 15:58), apparently founded by MAON, a descendant of CALEB (1 Chr. 2:45). Beth Zur was one of fifteen cities REHOBOAM fortified for the defense of the southern kingdom (11:7). After the EXILE, the town is described as a half-district ruled by a certain Nehemiah son of Azbuk (Neh. 3:16). Beth Zur was an important military stronghold where Judas MACCABEE defeated the Greek army under Lysias (1 Macc. 4:28-34). Beth Zur is identified with Khirbet eṭ-Ṭubeiqah, which is about 4.5 mi. (7 km.) N of HEBRON.

Betonim. bet'uh-nim (Heb. *bĕṭōnîm H1064*, "pistachio nuts"). A town in the AMORITE territory of JAZER allotted to the tribe of GAD (Josh. 13:26). It is usually identified with modern Khirbet Batneh, about 16 mi. (28 km.) NE of JERICHO, across the JORDAN.

betrothal. See MARRIAGE.

Beulah. by*oo*'luh (Heb. *bĕ'ûlâ H1241*, "married"). This name, as a transliteration of the Hebrew, occurs once in some English translations of the Bible, such as KJV and NIV (Isa. 62:4; NRSV, "Married"). In this passage God promises Israel that she will no longer be called Azubah (Deserted) but Hephzibah (My Delight is in Her); and her land will no longer be called Shemamah (Desolate) but Beulah (Married). The marriage relationship is often used in the Bible to portray God's relationship with his people (Isa. 54:5; Ezek. 16; 23; Hos. 1-3; et al.).

bewitch. A term used in most English versions to render the Greek verb *baskainō G1001* (Gal. 3:1), which meant, among other things, "to cast a spell." PAUL's use of such a strong metaphor indicates the seriousness of the error espoused by the GALATIANS. The English word is also used twice by the KJV to render *existēmi G2014* in the context of Simon's sorceries (Acts 8:9, 11); however, this Greek verb is better translated "to amaze."

Bezai. bee'zi (Heb. *bēṣay H1291*, prob. short form of *bĕṣal'ēl H1295*, "in the shadow of God"; see BEZALEL). (1) Ancestor of an Israelite clan that returned from the EXILE (Ezra 2:17; Neh. 7:23).

(2) One of the leaders who affixed their seals to the covenant of NEHEMIAH (Neh. 10:18). He was probably the head of the clan mentioned in #1 above.

Bezaleel. See BEZALEL.

Bezalel. bez'uh-lel (Heb. *bĕṣal'ēl H1295*, "in the shadow of God"). KJV Bezaleel. (1) Son of Uri and a descendant of JUDAH through PEREZ (1 Chr. 2:20). Bezalel was the chief artisan and foundryman of the TABERNACLE. He was appointed to this task by Yahweh, who filled him with the Spirit to perform the work. His special gift included the detailed

B

technical skills for metallurgy, casting, engraving, jewelry making, and wood carving (Exod. 31:2-5; 35:30-33; 36:1-2; 37:1; 38:22; 2 Chr. 1:5).

(2) One of the descendants of PAHATH-MOAB who agreed to put away their foreign wives (Ezra 10:30).

Bezek. bee´zik (Heb. *bezeq H1028*, possibly "scattering"). A town where the tribes of JUDAH and SIMEON conquered the Canaanites under ADONI-BEZEK (Jdg. 1:4). Some scholars locate the town in S Palestine, in the territory allotted to Judah, but it is probably the same Bezek where King SAUL mustered his troops to fight the AMMONITES at JABESH GILEAD (1 Sam. 11:8). It is thus to be located in the mountains of GILBOA and identified with modern Khirbet Ibziq, 13 mi. (21 km.) NE of SHECHEM.

Bezer (person). bee´zuhr (Heb. *beṣer H1310*, possibly "gold ore"). Son of Zophah and descendant of ASHER (1 Chr. 7:37).

Bezer (place). bee´zuhr (Heb. *beṣer H1311*, possibly "gold ore" or "fortress"). A Levitical city in the region of the tribe of REUBEN assigned to the descendants of MERARI (Josh. 21:36; 1 Chr. 6:78). It was also one of the three CITIES OF REFUGE appointed by MOSES on the E side of the Jordan (Deut. 4:43; Josh. 20:8). According to the MOABITE STONE, Bezer was one of the towns King MESHA fortified c. 830 B.C., possibly the same as BOZRAH of MOAB (Jer. 48:24, as opposed to Bozrah of EDOM). It is often identified with modern Umm el-ʿAmad, 8 mi. (13 km.) NE of MEDEBA.

Bible. The collection of books recognized and used by the Christian church as the inspired record of God's revelation of himself and of his will to mankind.

I. Names. The English word *Bible* is derived from the Greek word *biblion G1046*, a diminutive form of *byblos* (also *biblos G1047*), which refers to the bark of the PAPYRUS plant, used widely for writing material. Thus the term meant first "a strip of papyrus," then "document, scroll, book." The plural *biblia* ("books") was naturally used of the collection of holy writings, but it was sometimes mistaken for the feminine singular, which has an identical form, hence "books" became "the book" (Bible). In the NT, the OT is usually referred to as "the Scriptures" (Matt. 21:42; 22:29; Lk. 24:32; Jn. 5:39; Acts 18:24), "Scripture" (Acts 8:32; Gal. 3:22), and "holy Scriptures" (Rom. 1:2; 2 Tim. 3:15). The plural term *biblia* serves as a reminder that the Bible is a collection of books, while its use in the singular suggests that behind these many books there lies a wonderful unity.

The names "Old Testament" and "New Testament" have been used since the close of the second century A.D. to distinguish the Jewish and Christian Scriptures. The OT is composed of books produced by writers under God's COVENANT with Israel; the NT contains writings of the apostles (members of God's new covenant people). The term *Novum Testamentum* occurs first in Tertullian (A.D. 190-220); the Latin word *testamentum* is used to render Greek *diathēkē G1347*, which in classical usage meant "a will, testament" but in the SEPTUAGINT and in the NT was used to translate the Hebrew word *běrît*, "covenant."

II. Languages. Most of the OT was written in the HEBREW LANGUAGE, spoken by the Israelites in Canaan before the Babylonian captivity. After the return from exile, Hebrew gave way to ARAMAIC, a related dialect generally spoken throughout SW Asia. A few parts of the OT are in Aramaic (Ezra 4:8—6:18; 7:12-26; Jer. 10:11; Dan. 2:4—7:28). The ancient Hebrew text consisted only of consonants, since the Hebrew alphabet had no written vowels. Vowel signs were invented by the Jewish Masoretic scholars in the sixth century A.D. and later.

Except for a few words and sentences, the NT was composed in GREEK, the language of ordinary conversation in the Hellenistic world. The difference between NT Greek and classical Greek used to be a cause of bewilderment to scholars, but the discovery, since the 1890s, of many thousands of papyrus documents in the sands of Egypt has shown that the language of the NT is the Koine ("common"), that is, the form of Greek generally spoken in the Mediterranean world in the first century. The papyri have thrown a great deal of light on the meaning of many NT words.

III. Compass and Divisions. The Protestant Bible in general use today contains sixty-six books, thirty-nine in the OT and twenty-seven in the NT. The thirty-nine OT books are the same as those recognized by the Palestinian Jews in NT times. The Greek-speaking Jews of this period, on the other hand, made use of a larger number of books, and the Greek OT (LXX), which passed from them to the early Christian church, contained, in addition to the thirty-nine books of the Hebrew canon, a number of others, of which seven—Tobit, Judith, Wisdom, Ecclesiasticus, Baruch, 1 and 2 Maccabees, plus the two so-called additions to Esther and Daniel—are regarded as canonical by the Roman Catholic church, which therefore has an OT canon of forty-six books. See APOCRYPHA. Jews today consider canonical only the thirty-nine books accepted by Protestants.

The books in the Hebrew Bible are arranged in three groups: the Law, the Prophets, and the Writings. The Law comprises the PENTATEUCH. The Prophets consist of eight books: the Former Prophets (Joshua, Judges, Samuel, and Kings) and the Latter Prophets (Isaiah, Jeremiah, Ezekiel, and the book of the Minor Prophets). The Writings are the remaining books: Psalms, Proverbs, Job, Song of Songs, Ruth, Lamentations, Ecclesiastes, Esther, Daniel, Ezra-Nehemiah, and Chronicles. The total is traditionally reckoned as twenty-four, but these correspond to the Protestant thirty-nine, since in the latter reckoning the Minor Prophets are counted as twelve books, and Samuel, Kings, Chronicles, and Ezra-Nehemiah as two each. In ancient times there were also other enumerations, notably one by JOSEPHUS, who held twenty-two books as canonical (after the number of letters in the Hebrew alphabet), but his twenty-two are the same as the twenty-four in the traditional reckoning.

In the LXX both the number of books and the arrangement of them differ from the Hebrew Bible. The books of the Apocrypha are all late in date and are in Greek, though some of them had a Hebrew origin. The more scholarly of the church fathers (Melito, Origen, Athanasius, Jerome) did not regard the Apocrypha as canonical, although they permitted their use for edification.

The Protestant OT follow in general the grouping found in the LXX. It has, first, the five books of the Pentateuch; then the eleven historical books, beginning with Joshua and ending with Esther; after that what are often called the poetical books (Job, Psalms, Proverbs, Ecclesiastes, and the Song of Songs); and finally the Prophets, first the so-called Major Prophets (including Daniel) and then the Minor Prophets.

All branches of the Christian church are agreed on the NT canon. The grouping of the books

A portion of the great Isaiah scroll from Qumran (1QIsaᵃ).

© Dr. James C. Martin. Collection of the Israel Museum, Jerusalem and courtesy of the Israel Antiquities Authority, exhibited at the Shrine of the Book the Israel Museum, Jerusalem.

is a natural one: first the four Gospels; then the remaining historical book of the NT, the Acts of the Apostles; after that the letters to the churches, first the letters of Paul and then the General Epistles; and finally the Revelation.

IV. Text. Although the Bible was written over a period of approximately 1,400 years, from the time of MOSES to the end of the first century A.D., its text has come to us in a remarkable state of preservation. It is of course not identical with the text that left the hands of the original writers. Scribal errors have crept in. Until the invention of printing in the middle of the fifteenth century, all copies of the Scriptures were made by hand. There is evidence that the ancient Jewish scribes copied the books of the OT with extreme care. The recently discovered DEAD SEA SCROLLS, some going as far back as the second and third centuries B.C., contain either whole books or fragments of all but one (Esther) of the OT books; and they bear witness to a text remarkably like the Hebrew text left by the Masoretes (from A.D. 500 on). The Greek translation of the OT, the Septuagint, was begun about 250 B.C. and completed one or two centuries later. Although it differs in places from the Hebrew text current today, it is also a valuable witness to the accuracy of the OT text. See TEXT AND VERSIONS (OT).

In the NT the evidence for the reliability of the text is almost embarrassingly large and includes more than 5,700 Greek MSS (many fragmentary), numerous versions, and many thousands of scriptural quotations in the writings of the church fathers. The superabundance of textual evidence for the NT, some of which dates to the second century, may be appreciated when it is realized that very few MSS of most ancient Greek and Latin classical authors have survived, and those that have survived are almost all late in date. Among the oldest MSS of the Greek NT that have come down to us are the John Rylands fragment of the Gospel of John (c. 125); Papyrus Bodmer II, a MS of the Gospel of John dating c. 200; the Chester Beatty Papyri, consisting of three codices containing the Gospels and Acts, most of Paul's Letters, and the Revelation, dating from c. 200; and codices Vaticanus and Sinaiticus, both produced c. 350. See TEXT AND VERSIONS (NT).

V. Chapters and Verses. The books of the Bible originally had no chapter or verse divisions. For convenience of reference, Jewish scribes were the first to divide the OT into sections; similarly, some early NT MSS have sectional markings. The chapter divisions we use today were made by Stephen Langton, archbishop of Canterbury, who died in 1228. The division of the NT into its present verses is found for the first time in an edition of the Greek NT published in 1551 by a printer in Paris, Robert Estienne (Stephanus), who in 1555 also brought out the first edition of the entire Bible (Vulgate) to appear with our present chapters and verses. The first English Bible to be so divided was the Geneva edition of 1560.

VI. Translations. The Old and New Testaments appeared very early in translations. Most of the OT was translated into Greek (the LXX) between 250 and 150 B.C., and other translations in Greek, Jewish Aramaic, and Syriac appeared some time later. The NT began to be translated into Latin and Syriac c. 150 and into Coptic shortly after. In subsequent centuries versions appeared in the Armenian, Gothic, Ethiopic, Georgian, Arabic, Persian, and Slavonic languages. The Bible, in whole or in part, is now available in more than 2,300 different languages and dialects. Many languages have been reduced to writing in order that the Bible might be translated into them in written form, and this work still goes on in many lands.

VII. Message. Although the Bible consists of many different books written over a long period of time by a great variety of writers, most of whom did not know one another, it has an organic unity that can be explained only by assuming, as the book itself claims, that its writers were inspired by the Holy Spirit to give God's message to men and women. The theme of this message is the same in both Testaments, the redemption of sinners. The OT tells about the origin of sin and the preparation God made for the solution of this problem through his own Son, the Messiah. The NT describes the fulfillment of God's redemptive plan; the four Gospels telling about the Messiah's coming; the Acts of the Apostles describing the origin and growth of the church, God's redeemed people; the Epistles giving the meaning and implication of the incarnation; and the Revelation showing how some day all of history will be consummated in Christ. The two Testaments form two volumes of one work. The first is incomplete without the second; and the second cannot be understood without the first. Together they are God's revelation to people of the provision he has made for their salvation. See also OLD TESTAMENT; NEW TESTAMENT.

Bible, interpretation of the. See INTERPRETATION.

Bible versions, ancient. See TEXT AND VERSIONS (OT); TEXT AND VERSIONS (NT).

Bible versions, English. In the earliest days of English Christianity the only known Bible was the Latin Vulgate, made by Jerome between A.D. 383 and 405. This version could be read by the clergy and by monks, the only ones who were familiar with the language. In the medieval period, however, there were some attempts at producing English translations of portions of the Bible.

Early efforts. In 670 Caedmon, a monk at Whitby, produced in Old English a metrical version of some of the more interesting narratives of the OT. The first straightforward translation of any part of the Bible into the language of the people was the Psalter, made in about 700 by Aldhelm, the first bishop of Sherborne in Dorset. Some parts of the NT were translated into English by Bede, the learned monk of Jarrow, author of the famous *Ecclesiastical History of the English Nation*. According to a letter of his disciple Cuthbert, Bede was still engaged in translating the Gospel of John into English on his deathbed. It is not certain whether he completed it, but, unfortunately, his translation has not survived.

King Alfred (871-901) produced during his reign English versions of parts of the Old and New Testaments, including a part of the Psalter. Some Latin Gospels that survive from this period have written between the lines a word-for-word translation of the text into English, without regard to the idiom and usage of the vernacular.

From the same period come what are known as the Wessex Gospels, the first independent Old English version of the Gospels. Toward the end of the tenth century Aelfric, archbishop of Canterbury, translated parts of the first seven books of the OT, as well as parts of other OT books.

For nearly three centuries after the Norman Conquest in 1066 the uncertain conditions of the language prevented any real literary progress, but some MSS of translations of parts of the Bible into Anglo-Norman French survive. About the beginning of the thirteenth century an Augustinian monk named Orm (Ormin) produced a poetical version of the Gospels and the Acts of the Apostles called the *Ormulum*. From the first half of the fourteenth century there survive two prose translations of the Psalter, done in two different dialects; and from the end of the fourteenth century, a version of the principal NT letters, apparently made, however, not for the use of the common people but for monks and nuns. There was no thought as yet of providing ordinary layfolk with the Bible in their own tongue. It was Wycliffe who first entertained this revolutionary idea.

John Wycliffe. Born in Yorkshire about the year 1320, Wycliffe stands out as one of the most illustrious figures of the fourteenth century. This was a period of transition, neither the Middle Ages nor the Reformation—a kind of middle ground between the two. The old order was struggling with the new. Throughout the whole of this century the

The Gutenberg Bible (1455) opened to a page in Daniel.

© Dr. James C. Martin. Sola Scriptura. The Van Kampen Collection on display at the Holy Land Experience in Orlando, Florida. Photographed by permission.

B

prestige of the Roman Catholic church was very low. The "Babylonian Captivity" of the popes at Avignon (1309-1378) was followed by the "Great Schism," when for forty years there were two rival popes, one at Rome and the other at Avignon. In the struggle between the papacy and the English parliament over the papal tribute, Wycliffe sided with the parliament. The outstanding Oxford theologian of his day and an ardent ecclesiastical reformer, he is called the "Morning-star of the Reformation." He was convinced that the surest way of defeating Rome was to put the Bible into the hands of the common people, and he therefore decided to make such a translation available. Under his auspices, the NT came out in 1380 and the OT two years later.

It is uncertain exactly how much of the translation was done by Wycliffe himself. A number of scholars worked with him on the project, and one of them, Nicholas Hereford, did the greater part of the OT. The translation was made from the Latin, not from the original languages. Since printing was not known, copies were made by hand and were naturally very expensive (about 170 are in existence at present). It was not printed until 1850, when the Oxford Press published it. The original MS in the handwriting of at least five different men is preserved in the Bodleian Library at Oxford.

To help him in his efforts for reform, Wycliffe organized a kind of religious order of poor preachers, called Lollards, whom he sent throughout England to preach his doctrines and to read the Bible to all who wished to hear. Foxe reports that the people were so eager to read it that they would give a whole load of hay for the use of the NT for one day. There was opposition to Wycliffe on the part of the church, but contrary to his own expectations, he was permitted to retire to his rectory of Lutterworth, where he quietly died in 1384. Twelve years later, however, his bones were disinterred and burned, and the ashes scattered over the river that flows through Lutterworth. His translation has indelibly stamped itself on our present-day Bible. Some of the familiar expressions that are first found in his version are "strait gate," "make whole," "compass land and sea," "son of perdition," "enter thou into the joy of thy Lord."

From Wycliffe to Tyndale. Four years after Wycliffe's death his secretary, John Purvey, issued a careful revision of his translation, introduced with an interesting prologue and accompanied by notes. The church, however, did not approve of the new Bible. In 1408 a decree, known as the "Constitutions of Oxford," was issued forbidding anyone to translate or read any part of the Bible in the vernacular without the approval of his bishop or of a provincial council. Six years later a law was enacted that all persons who should read the Scriptures in their own language should "forfeit land, catel, life, and goods from their heyres for ever." Nicholas Hereford and John Purvey were imprisoned. The public demand for the Bible continued, however, in spite of the severe penalties attached to its circulation.

The fifteenth century was one of the great epochs of human history. In that century there lived such men as Columbus, Galileo, Frances Bacon, Kepler, and Marco Polo. Another great man of the time was the inventor of printing, Gutenberg, who in 1454 brought out in Germany the first dated printed work, a Latin Psalter, and two years later the famous Gutenberg Bible in the Latin Vulgate. After the capture of Constantinople in 1453, Christian scholars were compelled to leave the capital of the Eastern empire, where for a thousand years Greek learning had flourished. They brought with them to Western Europe many Greek MSS, which led to a revival of interest in biblical studies and made it possible for Erasmus to issue in 1516 the first printed edition of the Greek NT. At the beginning of the sixteenth century Greek was for the first time introduced as a subject of study in the universities of Oxford and Cambridge. By 1500 most of the countries of Europe had the Scriptures in the vernacular. England, however, had only scattered copies of the Wycliffe MS version, the language of which had by then become obsolete. The Constitutions of Oxford were still in force. England was ready for a new translation of the Bible, from the original languages.

William Tyndale. This great figure in the history of the English Bible was born about the year 1494 and spent ten years studying at Oxford and Cambridge. Soon after leaving Cambridge, while working as a chaplain and tutor, he said in a controversy with a clergyman, "If God spare my life, ere many years I will cause a boy that driveth a plough to know more of the Scripture than thou dost." This became the fixed resolve of his life. In his projected translation he tried to get the support of the bishop of London, but without success. A wealthy London cloth merchant finally came to his support, but after six months, in 1524, Tyndale left for the Continent because, he said, he "understood at the last not only that there was no room in my lord of London's palace to translate the NT, but also that there was no place to do it in all England, as experience doth now openly declare." He was never able to return to England. He seems to have visited Luther at Wittenberg, and then went to Cologne, where he found a printer for his NT. A priest discovered his plan, and Tyndale was obliged to flee. In Worms he found another printer, and there, in 1525, 3,000 copies of the first printed English NT were published. By 1530 six editions, numbering about 15,000 copies, were published. They were all smuggled into England—hidden in bales of cotton, sacks of flour, and bundles of flax.

As soon as Tyndale's NT reached England, there was a great demand for it: by the laity that they might read it, and by the ecclesiastical authorities that they might destroy it! A decree was issued for its destruction. Bishops bought up whole editions to consign to the flames. As a result, only a few imperfect copies survive. Tyndale's English NT began a new epoch in the history of the English Bible. It was not a translation from the Latin, as Wycliffe's had been, but from the original Greek, the text published by Erasmus. With each successive edition, Tyndale made corrections and improvements. So well did Tyndale do his work that the KJV reproduces about 90 percent of Tyndale in the NT. After the completion of the NT, Tyndale started to bring out a translation of the OT from the Hebrew text, but he lived only to complete the Pentateuch, Jonah, and probably the historical books from Joshua to 2 Chronicles. After ten years on the Continent, mostly in hiding, he was betrayed in Antwerp by an English Roman Catholic and was condemned to death for being a heretic. He was strangled and his body burned at the stake. His last words were a prayer, "Lord, open the King of England's eyes." But Tyndale

had won his battle. Although his NT was burned in large quantities by the church, it contributed greatly toward creating an appetite for the Bible in English. The government, moreover, began to see the wisdom and necessity of providing the Bible in English for common use. The break with the papacy in 1534 helped greatly in this development.

Miles Coverdale. While Tyndale was imprisoned in Belgium, an English Bible suddenly appeared in England in 1535. It had come from the Continent. The title page stated that it had been translated out of the German and Latin into English. This Bible was a rendering by Miles Coverdale, although in the NT and in those parts of the OT done by Tyndale, it was no more than a slight revision of the latter's work. It was the first complete printed Bible in the English language. It was not translated from the Hebrew and Greek, for in the dedication (to Henry VIII) Coverdale says that he used the work of five different translators. His version of the Psalms still appears in the Book of Common Prayer, used daily in the ritual of the Church of England. Two new editions of Coverdale's Bible appeared in 1537, the title page containing the significant words, "Set forth with the King's most gracious license." So within a year of Tyndale's death, the entire Bible was translated, printed, and distributed, apparently with royal approval.

Thomas Matthew. In 1537 another Bible appeared in England, this one by Thomas Matthew (a pen name for John Rogers, a former associate of Tyndale's), who was burned at the stake by Queen Mary in 1555. The whole of the NT and about half of the OT are Tyndale's, while the remainder is Coverdale's. It bore on its title page the words, "Set forth with the king's most gracious license." This Bible has the distinction of being the first edition of the whole English Bible actually to be printed in England. So now two versions of the English Bible circulated in England with the king's permission, Coverdale's and Matthew's, both of them heavily dependent on Tyndale.

The Great Bible. The next version to appear was a revision of the Matthew Bible, done by Coverdale. The printing was begun in Paris, but the Inquisition stepped in and the work was completed in England. It appeared in 1539 and was

B

called the Great Bible because of its large size and sumptuousness. In his revision Coverdale made considerable use of the Hebrew and Greek texts then available. Subsequent editions were called Cranmer's Bible because of a preface he wrote for it in which he commended the widespread reading of the Scriptures and declared that they were the sufficient rule of faith and life. At the foot of the title page were the words, "This is the Bible appointed to the use of the churches." This makes explicit an order that was issued in 1538, while this Bible was being printed, that a copy of it was to be placed in every church in the land. The people cordially welcomed the Great Bible, but its size and cost limited it largely to use in churches.

The later years of Henry VIII were marked by a serious reaction against the Reform movement. In 1543 Parliament passed an act to ban the use of Tyndale's NT, made it a crime for an unlicensed person to read or expound the Bible publicly to others, and restricted even the private reading of the Bible to the upper classes. Three years later Parliament prohibited the use of everything but the Great Bible. In London large quantities of Tyndale's NT and Coverdale's Bible were burned at St. Paul's Cross.

In the brief reign of Edward VI, who succeeded his father Henry VIII in 1547, no new translation work was done. However, great encouragement was given to the reading of the Bible and to the printing of existing versions, and injunctions were reissued that a copy of the Great Bible be placed in every parish church.

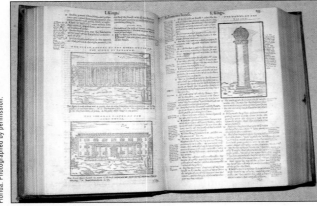

© Dr. James C. Martin. Sola Scriptura. The Van Kampen Collection on display at the Holy Land Experience in Orlando, Florida. Photographed by permission.

The Geneva Bible (1560).

The Geneva Bible. With the accession of Mary in 1553, hundreds of Protestants lost their lives, among them some men closely associated with Bible translation, like John Rogers and Thomas Cranmer. Coverdale escaped martyrdom by fleeing to the Continent. Some of the English Reformers escaped to Geneva, where the leading figure was John Calvin. One of their number, William Wittingham, who had married Calvin's sister, produced in 1557 a revision of the English NT. He and his associates then undertook the revision of the whole Bible. Appearing in 1560, the work is known as the Geneva Bible, but it also received the nickname "the Breeches Bible" from its rendering of Gen. 3:7, "They sewed fig tree leaves together, and made themselves breeches." The Geneva Bible enjoyed a long popularity, going through 160 editions, 60 of them during the reign of Queen Elizabeth alone, and continued to be printed even after the publication of the KJV in 1611.

The Bishops' Bible. Queen Elizabeth, who succeeded Mary Tudor as queen, restored the arrangements of Edward VI. The Great Bible was again placed in every church, and people were encouraged to read the Scriptures. The excellence of the Geneva Bible made obvious the deficiencies of the Great Bible, but some of the Geneva Bible's renderings and the marginal notes, which reflected the influence of John Calvin, made it unacceptable to many of the clergy. Archbishop Parker, aided by eight bishops and some other scholars, therefore made a revision of the Great Bible, which was completed and published in 1568 and came to be known as the Bishops' Bible. It gained considerable circulation, but the Geneva Bible was far more popular and was used more widely.

Rheims-Douai Version. This Roman Catholic work was produced by Gregory Martin, who with a number of other English Romanists left England at the beginning of Elizabeth's reign and settled in NE France, where in 1568 they founded a college. The NT, published in 1582, was done while the college was at Rheims, and hence is known as the Rheims NT; but the OT was not published until 1609-10, after the college had moved to Douai, and hence it is called the Douai OT. The whole work is often referred to as the Douay-Rheims Bible or simply as the Douay Bible. The preface warned readers against the then-existing "profane" translations and blames Protestants for casting what was holy to dogs. Like Wycliffe's version, this one was made not from the original languages but from Latin, and is therefore only a secondary translation. The main objection to it is its too close adherence to the words of the original Latin and the too great Latinizing of the English. It included the APOCRYPHA and contained a large number of notes, most of them to interpret the sacred text in conformity with Roman Catholic teaching and to reply to the arguments of the Reformers. The Douay Bible in use today is not the same as the one made by Gregory Martin, but is a thorough revision made of it between 1749 and 1763 by Bishop Richard Challoner. It was first authorized for use by American Roman Catholics in 1810.

King James (or Authorized) Version. When Elizabeth died in 1603, the crown passed to James I, who had been king of Scotland for thirty-six years as James VI. Several months after he ascended the throne of England he called a conference of bishops and Puritan clergy to harmonize the differences that existed in the church. At this conference John Reynolds, President of Corpus Christi College, Oxford, a leader of the Puritan party in the Church of England, suggested that a new translation of the Bible be made to replace the Bishops' Bible, which many people found unacceptable. The proposal pleased the king, who violently disliked the Geneva Bible; a resolution was passed to produce a new translation from the original Hebrew and Greek, without any marginal notes, for the use of all the churches in England.

Without delay King James nominated fifty-four of the best Hebrew and Greek scholars of the day. Only forty-seven actually took part in the work, which did not begin until 1607. They were divided into six groups: three for the OT, two for the NT, and one for the Apocrypha. Two of the groups met at Oxford, two at Cambridge, and two at Westminster. Elaborate rules were laid down for their guidance. When a group had completed its task, its work was submitted to twelve men, two from each panel. Final differences of opinion were settled at a general meeting of each company. In cases of special difficulty, learned men outside the board of revisers were consulted. Marginal notes were used only to explain Hebrew and Greek words and to draw attention to parallel passages. Italics were used for words not found in the original but necessary to complete the sense.

The revisers, who received no financial remuneration for their work, completed their task in two years; nine more months were devoted to a revision of their work by a special committee consisting of two members from each group. In 1611 the new version was published. Although the title page described it as "newly translated out of the original tongues" and as "appointed to be read in churches," neither statement is entirely in accord with the facts. The work was actually a revision of the Bishops' Bible on the basis of the Hebrew and Greek; and it was never officially sanctioned by king, Parliament, or the church. It did not win immediate universal acceptance, taking almost fifty years to displace the Geneva Bible in popular favor. In the course of time slight alterations were made, especially in spelling, to conform to changing usage, but these were all done piecemeal by private enterprise. Its excellence is shown by the fact that for almost three centuries it was virtually the only version used in the English-speaking Protestant world, for both public and private reading.

Revisions of the King James Version. During the second half of the nineteenth century a substantial revision of the KJV was seen as necessary for a number of reasons: (1) in the course of time some words had become obsolete, (2) a number of Greek MSS were discovered that were older than those available to the KJV translators, and (3) scholars' knowledge of the biblical languages and ancient culture had improved considerably. The English Revised Version (RV) had its origin in 1870 when, at the Convocation of Canterbury of the Church of England, a committee was appointed to invite outstanding Hebrew and Greek scholars, irrespective of religious denomination, to join in revising the KJV. Eventually a committee of fifty-four was formed, divided into two groups of twenty-seven each—one for the OT, the other for the NT. American scholars were also invited to cooperate, and they formed two groups corresponding to the British groups. It was agreed that American suggestions not accepted by the

B

British revisers be recorded in an appendix to the published volume and that the American revisers give their moral support to the new Bible and not issue an edition of their own until at least fourteen years later.

The revisers were guided by a number of rules, the most important being that they were to make as few alterations as possible in the text of the KJV, while basing their translation of the NT on a different Greek text. Altogether the Greek text underlying the revised NT differed in almost 5,800 readings from the Textus Receptus (the edition used by the KJV translators), but the vast majority of these differences do not affect the translation— and those that do require no change in established Christian doctrines. The English text of the NT contains about 36,000 changes, most of which however involve expressing the same meaning in a more understandable style. The new Bible differed from its predecessors also in printing poetical passages in the OT as poetry and in grouping verses into paragraphs according to sense units.

The NT was published in 1881, the OT in 1885. The work occupied the NT translators for about 40 days each year for ten years, while the OT group was occupied for 792 days over a period of fourteen years. The revisers gave their time and labor without charge. When they completed their work, they disbanded. Although the new version was widely accepted (three million copies being sold within the first year), it did not meet with immediate approval, nor did it ever surpass the KJV for supremacy among Bible translations; the English of the RV was not sufficiently readable to replace the time-honored KJV. Though not part of the original project, the Apocrypha was published in 1895.

The American scholars who cooperated with the English revisers on the RV were not entirely satisfied with it. The suggested changes printed in the appendix represented only a part of the changes they wanted made; and the English revisers retained a large number of words and phrases whose meanings and spellings were regarded as antiquated. These revisers also retained words that were English but not American in meaning. For these and other reasons the American scholars did not disband when the RV was published, but their own work, known as the American Standard Version, was not published until 1901. The ASV was regarded by many as being on the whole superior to the RV, and it was used widely, especially for study purposes, during much of the twentieth century.

The Revised Standard Version (RSV) was a revision of the ASV, the NT appearing in 1946 and the OT in 1952. Sponsored by the International Council of Religious Education, it was the work of thirty-two American scholars who worked in two sections, one dealing with the OT, the other with the NT. It was designed for use in public and private worship. In this version the language is modernized; direct speech is regularly indicated by the use of quotation marks; and the policy is followed (as already done to some extent in the KJV) of using a variety of synonyms to translate the Greek words where it is thought to be advisable. The RSV became very popular, especially in mainline Protestant denominations, and Catholic editions appeared in 1965 (NT) and 1966 (complete Bible), while a new edition in 1973 was accepted as a "common Bible" for Catholic, Protestant, and Orthodox Christians alike.

Many conservative Christians, however, objected to some of the features of the RV (e.g., "young woman" rather than "virgin" in Isa. 7:14). These concerns led to the production of the New American Standard Bible (NASB). This translation was prepared by fifty-eight originally anonymous (but now acknowledged) scholars under the auspices of the Lockman Foundation of La Habra, California. The NT appeared in 1963 and the whole Bible in 1971. Based on the ASV, the NASB is the most consistently literal of major English versions produced over the last half century. Examples include its use of italicization of English words that do not have Greek or Hebrew parallels and the identification of historical present tense verbs in the NT with an asterisk. An updated edition was released in 1995 that removed some archaic language, increased readability, and removed the archaic "thees" and "thous" with reference to deity.

The New King James Version (NKJV), a direct revision of the KJV, was sponsored by Thomas Nelson Publishers of Nashville, Tennessee. More than 130 evangelical scholars produced this work over a seven-year period. The NT appeared in

1979 and the whole Bible followed in 1982. The primary distinction of the NKJV is its textual basis, utilizing the Textus Receptus, the edition of the Greek NT behind the KJV (almost all other modern translations use the critical text derived from older Greek MSS). While updating archaic words, the NKJV consciously seeks to retain the literalness, cadence, style, and idiom of the KJV.

After the initial publication of the RSV in 1952, its translation committee continued to meet every few years to consider future changes and to make minor corrections to the text. In 1974 the National Council of Churches, which held the copyright to the RSV, authorized a new revision. The complete Bible of the New Revised Standard Version (NRSV) was published in 1990. Like its predecessors, the NRSV is a "formal-equivalence" version, but not slavishly so, being more sensitive to Greek and Hebrew idiom than other literal versions. It is widely used in academic and scholarly circles. The NRSV was also the first English version to introduce consistent gender-inclusive language for masculine generic terms in Hebrew and Greek.

The English Standard Version, published in 2001, is a light revision of the RSV (less than 5% changed) that seeks to move the latter in a more conservative and evangelical direction. In addition to "correcting" RSV readings viewed by some as liberal the ESV removes "thees" and "thous," updates other archaic language, and at times moves the text in a slightly more literal direction. The ESV also adopts a moderate (though sometimes inconsistent) use of gender-inclusive language.

Other Modern Versions. The discovery at the end of the nineteenth century of many thousands of Greek papyri in the sands of Egypt, all written in the everyday Greek language of the people, had a revolutionary influence on the study of NT Greek. The language of the NT had hitherto presented a vexing problem because it was so different from classical Greek. Now it was shown to be the colloquial language of Greek-speaking people in the first century. Many felt, therefore, that the NT should be translated into today's everyday speech, not in stilted and antiquated English. These developments created a keen interest in bringing out fresh translations of the NT in the spoken Eng-

lish of today. As a result, numerous modern-speech versions have been produced, both by individuals and by groups of scholars.

The first of these to appear was *The Twentieth Century New Testament: A Translation into Modern English Made from the Original Greek* (Westcott and Hort's Text); published in 1902, it was the work of about twenty translators whose names were not given. In 1903 R. F. Weymouth brought out *The New Testament in Modern Speech;* it was thoroughly revised in 1924 by J. A. Robertson. James Moffatt, the well-known Scottish NT scholar, brought out *The Bible: A New Translation* in 1913-14. The American counterpart of Moffatt was *The Complete Bible: An American Translation* (1927, rev. 1935); the NT first appeared in 1923 and was the work of E. J. Goodspeed, while four scholars, headed by J. M. Powis Smith, did the OT. *The New Testament: A Translation in the Language of the People*, by C. B. Williams, came out in 1937. *The New Testament in Modern English* (1958), by J. B. Phillips, is one of the most readable of the modern-speech translations. *The Amplified New Testament* (1958), which gives variant shades of meaning, was followed in 1961 by *The Amplified Old Testament*; it was the work of Frances E. Siewert and unnamed assistants. *The Holy Bible: The Berkeley Version in Modern English* (1959) was the work of Gerrit Verkuyl in the NT and of twenty American scholars in the OT. Kenneth Wuest's *The New Testament— An Expanded Translation* appeared complete in 1961. Also in 1961 *The Simplified New Testament* appeared, a new translation by Olaf M. Norlie.

During this period a number of new Roman Catholic versions were brought out also. *The New Testament of our Lord and Saviour Jesus Christ* (1941) was a revision of the Rheims-Challoner NT sponsored by the Episcopal Committee of the Confraternity of Christian Doctrine; therefore it was called the Confraternity Version. It was followed by the translation of the OT in four successive volumes (1948-69), which represented, not a revision of Douai-Challoner, but a new version from Hebrew. It seemed unreasonable to have a secondary version of the NT alongside a primary version of the OT; but when it was decided to make a new translation of the NT from Greek it was also decided to undertake a thorough revision of the whole Confraternity Version. This revision appeared in 1970 under the new title, the *New American Bible*. The *Westminster Version of the Sacred Scriptures* appeared under the editorship of Cuthbert Lattey—the NT in 1935, followed by parts of the OT. It was discontinued after Lattey's death in 1954. R. A. Knox's translation from the Latin Vulgate (NT, 1941; OT, 1949; rev. 1955) is a literary masterpiece and retains the charm of a period piece. The *Jerusalem Bible* (1966), a scholarly and widely appreciated translation, follows the pattern of the French *Bible de Jerusalem* (1956), produced by the Dominican faculty of the Biblical and Archaeological School in Jerusalem; a revision, the *New Jerusalem Bible*, appeared in 1985.

The standard English version for Jewish readers during most of the twentieth century was entitled *The Holy Scriptures According to the Masoretic Text*, published in 1917 under the auspices of the Jewish Publication Society (thus known as JPS). The style was very similar to that of the KJV. A revision, entitled *Tanakh*, was published in stages (Torah, 1962; Prophets, 1978, Writings, 1982) and released as a whole in 1985. This work is a highly respected version that utilizes the best of Jewish scholarship and a contemporary and idiomatic style.

The New English Bible (NEB) was a completely new translation, not a revision of previously existing versions. The first suggestion for this project came in 1946 from the General Assembly of the Church of Scotland, but it was the joint effort of all the major religious denominations (with the main Bible Societies) in the British Isles, apart from the Roman Catholic church. C. H. Dodd was the general director of the whole translation. The translators were assisted by a panel of advisers on literary and stylistic questions. The NT came out in 1961; the complete Bible (including the Apocrypha), in 1970. As with most earlier translations, this also was greeted with a mixture of praise and criticism. Criticisms of substance were brought under consideration, leading to the Revised English Bible (REB), which appeared in 1989.

The year 1971 saw the completion of *The Living Bible*, a paraphrase into simple English, the work of one man, Kenneth N. Taylor. It attained widespread popularity, especially among young people, but its free approach also received criticism. In response, the *New Living Translation* came out in 1996 (rev. 2004), a committee project involving some ninety evangelical scholars from various denominations. Although based on Taylor's work, it is not a paraphrase but a genuine translation that uses "functional equivalence." This term, previously known as "dynamic equivalence," has as its purpose producing the same effect on readers today as the Hebrew and Greek texts produced on the original readers or hearers. The first consistent attempt at a functional-equivalence translation, however, was the *Good News Bible*, completed in 1976 (the NT had been published ten years earlier under the title *Today's English Version* or *Good News for Modern Man*). It has proven to be a very popular version.

The Holman Christian Standard Version, which appeared in 2004, was produced by the Sunday School Board of the Southern Baptist Convention. Intended to serve as an alternative to the NIV (see below), the HCSB is more literal than the NIV but less so than other formal-equivalence versions. It is described as striving for "optimal equivalence" or "precision with clarity." Though following the critical Greek text, the HCSB is unique among modern versions in supplying many alternate readings from the Textus Receptus and the Majority text in its footnotes.

The most widely accepted modern English translation is the *New International Version*, the work of a team of over one hundred evangelical scholars drawn from most of the English-speaking countries. The NT appeared in 1973 and the entire Bible in 1978, with a minor revision released in 1984. It was advertised as being written in "the language of the common man," but its idiom is rather more elevated than that of the GNB. The NIV achieved huge success and by the mid-1980s began outselling even the KJV. Twenty-five years after its release over 110 million copies were in print. The NIV's success is largely due to its balance between formal correspondence and functional equivalence. It is readable yet closer to the cadence of the KJV tradition than other meaning-based versions.

Today's New International Version (TNIV) updated the NIV in light of advances in biblical scholarship, striving also for greater accuracy and clarity. About 7 percent of the NIV was altered, with approximately one third of these changes related to gender. The NT was released in 2001 and the whole Bible in 2005.

A new revision of the NIV, intended to replace both the 1984 NIV and the TNIV, is scheduled for publication in 2011.

Bichri. See BICHRI.

Bicri. bik′ri (Heb. *bikri H1152*, "firstborn" or "youthful"). Also Bichri; TNIV Bikri. Father of SHEBA, the Benjamite who rebelled against DAVID (2 Sam. 20:1-22). Because the name has a gentilic form, some scholars believe that Bicri refers to a clan rather than a person, possibly referring to the descendants of Benjamin's son BEKER. See also BERITES.

Bidkar. bid′kahr (Heb. *bidqar H982*, derivation uncertain). A military officer who sided with JEHU in his revolt and who assisted him at the slaying of King Joram (2 Ki. 9:25; see JEHORAM).

bier. This term is used in English Bibles in the accounts of the funerals of ABNER and King ASA (2 Sam. 3:31; 2 Chr. 16:14) and of the widow's son at NAIN (Lk. 7:14 KJV and other versions; NIV, "coffin"). The bier was an open bed or litter set in a bedroom where the body was placed for public viewing, while around the room hired mourners kept up lamentation. The body was carried to the grave on the same open stretcher, just as in poorer Muslim funerals the corpse is carried on boards.

Bigtha, Bigthan, Bigthana. big′thuh, big′thuhn, big′thuh-nuh (Heb. *bigtā' H960*, *bigtan H961*, *bigtānā' H962*, possibly from Pers. *bagadâ* or *bagadâna*, "gift of God"). The name of one or two EUNUCHS or officers in the court of XERXES (Ahasuerus). The three names occur respectively in Esth. 1:10; 2:1; 6:2. In the last two references, Bigthan and Bigthana are certainly one and the same (the NIV uses "Bigthana" in both passages); in them he and Teresh are described as "two of the king's officers [*lit.*, eunuchs] who guarded the doorway" and who had conspired to assassinate the king (they were subsequently hanged, 2:23). In

the first reference, Bigtha, who may be the same person, is listed as one of the seven eunuch chamberlains instructed by the king to bring Queen VASHTI to the royal feast.

Bigvai. big′vi (Heb. *bigway H958*, possibly from Pers. *baga*, "God"). An Israelite mentioned among leading individuals who returned from BABYLON with ZERUBBABEL (Ezra 2:2; Neh. 7:7). Presumably the same Bigvai (but possibly an ancestor) is then listed as the head of a family that numbered more than 2,000 (Ezra 2:14; Neh. 7:19). Some members of the family came later with EZRA (Ezra 8:14). The name Bigvai also occurs in the list of leaders who signed the covenant with NEHEMIAH (Neh. 10:16); this may be the same person or a representative of the clan. It is possible that two or even three different individuals are intended in these passages

Bikri. See BICRI.

Bildad. bil′dad (Heb. *bildad H1161*, possibly "[the god] Bel has loved"; cf. ELDAD). One of the three friends of JOB who came to comfort him but who really added to his grief (Job 2:11; 8:1; 18:1; 25:1; 42:9). He is called a "Shuhite," which may mean that he was descended from a son of ABRAHAM and KETURAH named SHUAH (Gen. 25:2); thus Bildad was possibly a member of an Aramean tribe of nomads who lived SE of Palestine (25:6; see ARAM). Three chapters (Job 8; 18; 25) are filled with Bildad's speeches, in which he shows himself blustering and relatively kind as he emphasizes the justice of God.

Bileam. bil′ee-uhm (Heb. *bil'ām H1190*, meaning uncertain; cf. BALAAM). One of the Levitical cities given to the descendants of KOHATH in the territory of the tribe of MANASSEH (1 Chr. 6:70; many scholars emend GATH RIMMON to Bileam in the parallel passage, Josh. 21:25). It is probably the same as IBLEAM, identified with modern Khirbet Bel'ameh, 12 mi. (19 km.) SE of MEGIDDO.

Bilgah. bil′guh (Heb. *bilgâ H1159*, "gleam, cheerfulness"). (1) The head of the fifteenth division of priests in the time of DAVID (1 Chr. 24:14).

(2) A leader among the priests who returned from the EXILE with ZERUBBABEL and who served in the days of JESHUA (Neh. 12:5; cf. v. 7). It is possible that he gave his name to the priestly family headed by Shammua (v. 18). In addition, Bilgah is probably to be identified with BILGAI, who affixed his seal to the covenant of NEHEMIAH (10:8).

Bilgai. bil′g*i* (Heb. *bilgay H1160*, "gleam, cheerfulness"). One of the priests who sealed the covenant of NEHEMIAH (Neh. 10:8); probably the same as BILGAH #2.

Bilhah (person). bil′huh (Heb. *bilhāh H1167*, possibly "carefree"). A slave girl given by LABAN to his daughter RACHEL (Gen. 29:29). Because Rachel was barren, she became jealous of her sister LEAH, and in order to build her own family she gave Bilhah to JACOB as a concubine. Bilhah bore Jacob two sons, whom Rachel named DAN and NAPHTALI, thus claiming them as her own (30:1-8; 35:25; 46:25). Bilhah later engaged in incest with REUBEN (35:22).

Bilhah (place). bil′huh (Heb. *bilhāh H1168*, possibly "carefree"). One of the towns inhabited by the clan of SHIMEI, descendant of SIMEON (1 Chr. 4:29). Its location is unknown, but it is often identified with BAALAH (Josh. 15:29) and BALAH (19:3).

Bilhan. bil′han (Heb. *bilhān H1169*, possibly "foolish"). **(1)** Son of EZER and grandson of SEIR the HORITE; he probably became the progenitor of a clan in EDOM (Gen. 36:27; 1 Chr. 1:42).

(2) Son of JEDIAEL and grandson (or more distant descendant) of BENJAMIN; he was also the father of seven men who became warriors and heads of families (1 Chr. 7:10-11).

bill. This English term is used by the KJV and other versions in the expression "bill of divorce(ment)" (Deut. 24:1-3; Isa. 50:1; Jer. 3:8; cf. also Mk. 10:4 KJV). The NIV uses the term "certificate." DIVORCE consisted of placing such a document in the hands of the rejected wife. The term "bill" is also used by most versions in the parable of the unjust steward (Lk. 16:6-7). The document referred to was of varied detail, given by the recipient of goods or property in acknowledgment of debt and obliga-

tion; it was a receipt. The rascally steward of Jesus' parable handed the documents back to the debtors and secured, in their own handwriting, a note of diminished obligation.

Bilshan. bil′shan (Heb. *billĕšān H1193*, perhaps "inquirer"). An Israelite mentioned among leading individuals who returned from Babylon with ZERUBBABEL (Ezra 2:2; Neh. 7:7).

Bimhal. bim′hal (Heb. *bimhāl H1197*, perhaps "son of circumcision"). Son of Japhlet and descendant of ASHER (1 Chr. 7:33). He is listed among the tribal "heads of families, choice men, brave warriors and outstanding leaders" (v. 40).

binding and loosing. The carrying of a key or keys was a symbol of the delegated power of opening and closing. In Matt. 16:19 our Lord gave the "power of the keys" to PETER, and Peter's use of the keys is narrated in what may be called the "three stages of Pentecost." On the Day of PENTECOST (Acts 2:14-40) Peter preached the first Christian sermon and opened "the kingdom of heaven" to what became a Hebrew-Christian church; then, with JOHN THE APOSTLE, he went to SAMARIA (8:14-17) and opened the same "kingdom" to the Samaritans; still later in the house of CORNELIUS (10:44-48) he opened it to the Gentiles. Thus, the church became universal. The medieval teaching about Peter standing at the gate of heaven to receive or reject souls of men has no basis in biblical teaching.

Binea. bin′ee-uh (Heb. *binʿāʾ H1232*, derivation uncertain). Son of Moza and a descendant of King SAUL through JONATHAN (1 Chr. 8:37; 9:43).

Binnui. bin′yoo-i (Heb. *binnûy H1218*, possibly short form BENAIAH, "Yahweh has built"). See also BANI. **(1)** Father of NOADIAH; the latter was a LEVITE appointed to the job of supervising the weighing of the gold and silver vessels that EZRA had brought from BABYLON (Ezra 8:33).

(2) Son (or descendant) of HENADAD; he repaired a section of the wall of Jerusalem and was among those who sealed the covenant of NEHEMIAH (Neh. 3:24; 10:9). Binnui was probably also the ruler of one of the half-districts of Keilah (3:18 NIV, NRSV; the MT has Bavvai [cf. KJV], likely a scribal error).

(3) The ancestor or head of a family that returned from the EXILE with ZERUBBABEL (Neh. 7:15; called Bani in Ezra 2:10).

(4) The ancestor of some Israelites who had married foreign wives (Ezra 10:38; he may be the same as the man called Bani in v. 34).

(5) One of the Levites who returned from the exile with Zerubbabel (Neh. 12:8; some scholars believe he may be the same as the man called Bani in 9:4-5).

(6) One of the descendants of PAHATH-MOAB who had married foreign wives (Ezra 10:30). Some identify this man with #4 above.

birds. PALESTINE is the home of some 375 kinds of birds, of which perhaps 25 are peculiar to that region. The Bible mentions about 50, using Hebrew or Greek names that can sometimes be identified with particular species of the present. Birds are mentioned in more than two-thirds of the biblical books. In English versions of the Bible there are often differences in the translations of the names of birds. Sometimes the identification of some creature as a bird has been questioned (see, e.g., *peacock* and *night creature* below). Where there are differences of translation, comparisons are often made with terms as they occur in different versions, but some of the more speculative translations that occur in only one version have been omitted. While the main aim is to put birds in their biblical context, some brief general details of birds are also given.

bird of prey. The Latin word *rapto* ("to seize and carry off") is the root for the general description of birds of prey as raptors, a group that includes some of the largest and strongest birds, all with hook-tipped beaks and sharp, curving claws (talons). ABRAHAM drove away birds of prey from his sacrifice (Gen. 15:11); this is the Bible's first reference to these troublesome creatures. JOB reflected that no bird of prey knew the hidden path of a mine of precious metals (Job 28:7). ISAIAH's prophecy against CUSH (Isa. 18:6) shows knowledge of the habits of birds of prey—which must also obey the call of God (46:11).

bittern. A wading bird of the heron family, equipped with a long pointed bill used for spearing fish, frogs, and other prey. Its speckled plumage aids camouflage in the bittern's marshland environment, where it easily blends with reeds and other plant life. With its somewhat mournful call, the bittern was considered a melancholy creature and therefore likely to live in places far from human habitation, in the wasteland that followed the downfall of EDOM (Isa. 34:11 KJV) or the decay of BABYLON (14:23 KJV). NINEVEH would suffer a similar fate, its terrain becoming a home for the bittern (Zeph. 2:14 KJV). The RSV gives the

Griffin vulture soaring above Israel.

alternative renderings "porcupine" and "hedgehog." The NIV translates this word "owl" (Isa. 14:23) or specifies a variety of owl (Isa. 34:11; Zeph. 2:14); such translations are more likely, given the desolation that might be expected to follow the prophesied catastrophes.

buzzard. A general description of any of a large number of heavily built hawks, mainly genus *Buteo*. With its short, broad wings and ability to soar, the buzzard is quite easily recognized. The European variety, *Buteo buteo*, is found from Scandinavia to the Mediterranean. The American use of "buzzard" is more widely applied to many types of hawk and vulture. Their main prey consists of small animals and insects, though the buzzard may occasionally attack small birds. It is included by the NRSV in

© Dr. James C. Martin

the lists of unclean birds, where the NIV uses "red kite" (Lev. 11:14; Deut. 14:13).

carrion bird. EZEKIEL declared that the enemies of Israel would be given "as food to all kinds of carrion birds" (Ezek. 39:4), the reference being to a variety of flesh-eating birds. In addition, the NRSV uses "carrion vulture" to render a Hebrew term that the NIV understands as a reference to the osprey (Lev. 11:18; Deut. 14:17).

chicken. Descended from the wild red jungle fowl of SE Asia, the domestic chicken or fowl is seen in many varieties throughout the world. It is mainly bred for food, the eggs of the female being a useful source of protein. Our Lord observed the hen's care of its chicks as a striking example of the concern he felt for JERUSALEM (Matt. 23:37; Lk. 13:34). Immature males, cockerels, are usually bred for food purposes, mature males for breeding.

cock. See *rooster*.

cormorant. A diving seabird of the Phalacrocoracidae family, equipped with a long neck and body that can reach a length of 3 ft. (1 m.). Although fast and powerful in flight—which is low over water—the cormorant has a rather laborious takeoff. With its diet of fish caught in short dives, the bird's hooked bill is ideal. Under water the cormorant swims with its feet only, while striking at its prey. Breeding harmoniously in colonies, the cormorant has been tamed in the Orient and trained to catch fish for its human owners. Because of its flesh-eating habits, the cormorant is included in the list of prohibited birds (Lev. 11:17; Deut. 14:17). The KJV uses "cormorant" also to render a Hebrew word of uncertain meaning in Isa. 34:11 and Zeph. 2:14.

crane. Any member of the Gruidae family of long-necked, long-legged wading birds, found throughout the world except for South America. The crane somewhat resembles the heron, but is larger and has a heavier bill, a partly naked head, and more compact plumage. When flying, it stretches its long neck forward, its stilt-like legs trailing behind. The crane's croak, or honk, may be heard over distances of several miles and is unmistakable. According to the KJV, HEZEKIAH's lament over his sickness was compared by Isaiah to the chatter of a crane, as if the king spoke loudly of his affliction, then fell away into muttering (Isa.

38:14); the NIV and other versions, however, use "swift" in this passage (cf. also Jer. 8:7 KJV).

cuckoo. This term (in the form "cuckow") is used by the KJV in the lists of unclean birds (Lev. 11:16; Deut. 14:15), but the Hebrew word is generally thought to refer to the *sea gull*.

desert owl. See *owl*.

dove, pigeon. The dove is a medium-sized bird of the family Columbidae, to which the pigeon also belongs, the latter being a somewhat larger bird. Domestic pigeons are descended from the rock dove, *Columba livia*, and a strong resemblance may be noted to the wild variety. A white domestic pigeon is usually called "the dove of peace," reproduction drawings showing a twig in its beak, commemorating the dispatch of the dove from the ark by NOAH (Gen. 8:8–12). Although not outstanding in its appearance, having a short neck and legs, nor in its cooing cry, the dove inspired the psalmist to write that he would indeed possess the wings of the dove (Ps. 55:6). In God's good time, the believer will share such glory as may be compared to the wings of the dove being sheathed with silver, its feathers with shining gold (68:13).

Some biblical references to the dove probably refer to the turtle dove (see *turtle dove*) as in Cant. 2:12, where the cooing of doves was associated with the season of singing. Hezekiah in contrast mourned about his illness, like a mourning dove (Isa. 38:14; cf. 59:11). Ezekiel prophesied that those people who escaped the sword in the city would moan like doves of the valley (Ezek. 7:16). Yet help was promised to those who flew like doves to their nests (Isa. 60:8); that is, those who returned to their true home, which is God. The security of the dove in the clefts of the rocks is noted in Cant. 2:14. It was not, however, reckoned to be a very intelligent bird, and EPHRAIM was compared to one because of the nation's lack of good sense (Hos. 7:11). Yet the NT spoke of the HOLY SPIRIT descending like a dove onto the head of Jesus Christ at his baptism (Matt. 3:18). This divinely given "dove" was indeed of power and grace, in contrast to the doves sold as merchandise in the temple, for ceremonial purification. The OT record clearly shows that doves were allowed for sacrifice because of their abundance: the temple authorities had made it hard for people to make their sacrifice by "cornering the market" in sacrificial doves. Jesus Christ charged his followers to be as shrewd as snakes and as innocent as doves (10:16), reflecting a prevailing public opinion of the bird.

eagle. For many centuries the eagle has been adopted as a symbol of power and majesty, appropriately, it might be said, in view of its powers and regal appearance. Carnivorous, equipped with long talons and remarkably keen eyesight, the eagle is a member of the Accipitridae family and is monogamous—mating for life—and using the same nest every year. Nests are built in inaccessible places, far from human and animal marauders. For the most part, the eagle's diet consists of live prey, not carrion, and stories of the swift appearance of an eagle, carrying away a small animal (a baby lamb, for example), are commonly heard among shepherds. Although the eagle is superbly equipped for flying because of its exceptionally broad wings, it is somewhat ponderous when pursuing prey. Thus it uses a sudden descent and the element of surprise, these characteristics being duly noted by the bird-watchers of Bible times. An eagle somewhat resembles a vulture, but it has a fully feathered head and, as already noted, prefers live prey. Among the many types found today is the crowned eagle, which may be some 3 ft. (1 m.) long and represents Africa's largest eagle; the snake-hunting harrier eagles of Europe, Asia, and Africa; and the lightly built hawk eagles found in the Mediterranean area and S Asia. Eagles were included among the unclean foods listed in Lev. 11.

Although in normal circumstances the town-dweller in Bible times might see an eagle only rarely, such an appearance was not to be forgotten. Indeed, the people of Israel were reminded that they had been borne from Egyptian captivity, as it were, on the wings of eagles (Exod. 19:4; Deut. 32:11). In similar praise, the psalmist declares that his youth was renewed like that of the eagle (Ps. 103:5). Isaiah promises similar power to those who hope in the Lord (Isa. 40:31) Two eagle's wings were provided to transport the woman mentioned in Rev. 12 to the place prepared for her in the desert. The power of the eagle was noted earlier; for example, the sudden descent of the eagle on its prey was appropriately compared to an attack

of a nation that would be "like an eagle swooping down" on a careless Israel (Deut. 28:49). Jeremiah prophesied in a similar vein, referring to an enemy equipped with horses swifter than eagles (Jer. 4:13). Yet the Lord would prevail even against those enemies who built their nest as high as that of the eagle (49:16, echoed in Obad. 4, in reference to Edom).

The face of the eagle was part of EZEKIEL's great vision of living creatures (Ezek. 1:10). Later, Ezekiel used two eagles and a vine in his allegory (ch. 17); appropriately, both eagles were "great" and had "powerful wings." DANIEL's dream of four beasts included a lion with the wings of an eagle (Dan. 7:4)—a reference to the mighty kingdom of NEBUCHADNEZZAR. Yet, among the warlike similes—necessary to warn a careless Israel—there is graciousness indeed, as that shown to SAUL and JONATHAN, who were in life swifter than eagles (2 Sam. 1:23). Job felt the passage of his days on earth as swift-passing as an eagle swooping on its prey (Job 9:26). In a no-less-reflective mood, the author of Proverbs believed that riches would fly away like an eagle (Prov. 23:5).

falcon. Found worldwide, this member of the Falconidae family is equipped with long, pointed wings, a powerful hooked beak, and a long tail. Species of falcon include the peregrine, kestrel, merlin, and South American caracara. Some nine classes of falcon were known in Bible times. The NIV and other versions use "falcon" to render Hebrew ʾayyāh *H370* (Job 28:7), a word elsewhere translated "black kite" (Lev. 11:14 et al.). The NIV uses it also to render dayyâ *H1901* (Deut. 14:13; Isa. 34:15), apparently a general term referring to various unclean birds of prey.

fowl. The KJV often uses this term with reference to birds in general (Gen. 1:20-22 et al.), but in modern speech it usually means "domestic fowl" or "poultry." We read that "choice fowl" was included in Solomon's inventory of daily provisions (1 Ki. 4:23), while the 150 Jews and officials who shared Nehemiah's table enjoyed meat of poultry as well as of oxen and choice sheep (Neh. 5:18). That people in Bible times set traps for wild fowl is clearly indicated in Ps. 91:3 and 124:7, where deliverance from one's enemy is compared to the escape of a bird from a fowler's snare.

B

B

gier eagle. See *osprey.*

glede. See *kite.*

great owl. See *owl.*

gull. An aquatic bird of the family Laridae, characterized by long wings and webbed feet. The NIV uses this term in the lists of unclean birds (Lev. 11:16; Deut. 14:15; NRSV, "sea gull"; KJV, "cuckow"). Ten true gulls and eight other members of the family are recorded in Palestine; five are only rare stragglers, but the others migrate. The winter visitors are the commonest, including lesser black-backed and black-headed gulls; their flocks may run into hundreds and they may be seen on the Mediterranean and Red Sea coasts, on the Lake of Galilee, and around the great complexes of fishponds. Only the herring gull nests in Palestine, along with the black, common, and little terns. Most gulls are scavengers and would certainly rank as unclean.

hawk. A general name applied to several small to medium-sized diurnal birds of prey, having short, rounded wings, hooked beaks, and claws. Kites, buzzards, harriers, falcons, and caracaras are included in the generic description, together with other members of the genus *Accipiter*. All hawks were unclean and were not to be eaten (Lev. 11:16; Deut. 14:15). The impressive flying abilities of the hawk were compared to those of the eagle as the Lord answered Job out of the storm (Job 39:26-27). Found worldwide, hawks usually nest in trees, though some, such as the marsh hawk, prefer a ground-level nest site in a suitable grassy environment. Others nest in cliffs.

hen. See *chicken.*

heron. Listed among the unclean birds (Lev. 11:19; Deut. 14:18), the heron is a long-necked, long-legged wading bird of the Ardeidae family, breeding in colonies with others in suitably high trees. Found throughout the world, herons are most concentrated in tropical regions, usually in marshy terrain. During biblical times large numbers of them populated the swamps surrounding Lake Huleh, and they were common also on the Jordan and the Kishon and on the coastal regions of Palestine. The heron's diet consists of fish, frogs, and other reptiles, caught while wading unobtrusively in shallow water. With its sharp-pointed, long and straight bill, the heron is ideally equipped to catch its prey.

hoopoe. A solitary and somewhat timid bird, possessing a slender, down-curved bill and a long black-tipped erect crest, the hoopoe is found from southern Europe and Africa to SE Asia. It secures its diet of insects by thrusting its bill into the ground and foraging. This, together with its habit of fouling its own nest, may show why it was considered unclean (Lev. 11:19; Deut. 14:18 [KJV, "lapwing"]).

horned owl. See *owl.*

ibis. A wading bird similar to the stork. The term is used once by the RSV (Lev. 11:17), but the Hebrew word is more properly translated "(great) owl," as the RSV itself does elsewhere (Deut. 14:16; Isa. 34:11). See *owl.*

kite. A member of the *hawk* family, equipped with a short beak and long, pointed wings, the kite is found worldwide in warm regions. Its diet consists mostly of carrion and small birds, though some kites live on insects. Lightly built, the kite flies by a slow flapping of its wings and by effective gliding action. Its scavenging characteristics may account for its inclusion in the list of prohibited birds (Lev. 11:14; Deut. 14:13 [KJV, "glede"]). American kites include the swallow-tailed kite, a black-and-white bird some 2 ft. (60 cm.) in length,

Limestone figurine of a falcon; from Egypt, c. 600 B.C.

© Dr. James C. Martin. The British Museum. Photographed by permission.

and the white-tailed kite, one of the few American birds of prey increasing in population.

lapwing. See *hoopoe.*

lilith. See *night creature.*

little owl. See *owl.*

night creature. The Hebrew word *lilit H4327* occurs only once in a passage describing the terrible desolation that will befall EDOM (Isa. 34:14). Because most (or perhaps all) of the other creatures mentioned in the context are real animals or birds thought to inhabit waste solitudes, this word has been rendered variously as "screech owl" (KJV), "night hag" (RSV), "night-jar" (NEB), "night creatures" (NIV). The NRSV and some other versions use the transliteration "Lilith," referring to a female Mesopotamian deity. More likely, the reference could be to any of those nocturnal birds thought to bring omens, or to which superstition might be attached.

nighthawk. A small-beaked, insect-eating bird with impressive flying abilities. The name is used by the KJV and other versions in the lists of prohibited birds (Lev. 11:16; Deut. 14:15 KJV), but it is probable that some kind of *owl* is in view (cf. NIV, "screech owl").

osprey. A large bird of the *hawk* family, the osprey is found in Europe, Asia, and North America. It has dark plumage with white underparts. Feeding on fish, the osprey is well-endowed with roughened pads on its feet in order to grasp its slippery prey. "Osprey" is the rendering of the NRSV and other versions for Hebrew *ʿozniyyâ H6465* (Lev. 11:13 and Deut. 14:12, where the NIV has "black vulture"), while the NIV uses it to render *rāḥām H8164* (Lev. 11:18 and Deut. 14:17, where the NRSV has "carrion vulture").

ossifrage. See *vulture.*

ostrich. The largest of all birds, up to 8 ft. (2.5 m.) tall, this nonflying, fast-running bird of Africa and Arabia is mainly vegetarian, able to do without water for considerable periods. Its long legs have two toes on each foot, and its long, featherless neck accounts for about half the total body weight. It is well adapted for its life in hot, dusty areas. In the wild, the ostrich lives in flocks and enjoys the company of other grazing animals. Job's essay on the ostrich (Job 39:13-18) confirms a keen observation of the bird. The NRSV and other versions

have "ostrich" in several passages where a more likely rendering is "owl" (Lev. 11:16 et al.).

owl. Any member of the order Strigformes, nocturnal birds of prey found throughout the world, in three families: typical owls (Strigidae), barn and grey owls (Tytonidae), and bay owls (Phodilidae). Equipped with a short, hooked beak set in a broad head, the owl has disc-shaped, forward-looking eyes, fringed with stiff feathers. Hearing and vision are acutely developed, fitting the owl for its nocturnal hunting pursuits. Prey consists of small birds and rodents. Hebrew names for the owl reflect the bird's own cry and nature. Thus Job confessed that he had become a companion of owls (Job 30:29; NRSV and other versions, "ostriches"), and the psalmist felt that he had become like an owl among the ruins (Ps. 102:6). Isaiah declared that the great owl, desert owl, and screech owl would nest in the ruins of Edom (Isa. 34:11), though the NIV footnote points out that precise identification is uncertain. Isaiah also referred to the owls nesting among the ruins of Edom (34:15). Several kinds of owls are listed among the unclean birds (Lev. 11:16-18; Deut. 14:15-17). One of them, the "little owl," is the most common owl in Palestine; it is noteworthy in its seeking of isolation, though its hoarse cry announces its presence to travelers.

partridge. A member of the order of birds to which chickens belong. Because of their swift and sneaky running, they are excellent game birds. When Saul was hunting him, David compared himself to a partridge (1 Sam. 26:20). It was supposed that partridges robbed eggs from other birds and hatched them, a symbol of getting riches unfairly (Jer. 17:11).

peacock. A male game bird, *Paro cristatus*, from India and SE Asia, best known for its handsome and long tail feathers, brought into a fan-shaped display during courtship. With their brightly colored bodies, peacocks were shown off in any self-respecting court in the ancient world and were a common feature of English country houses until fairly recent times. According to the KJV and other versions, large numbers of peacocks were imported for Solomon's palace (1 Ki. 10:22; 2 Chr. 9:21), but here the NIV prefers the alternate rendering "baboons" (see ANIMALS). (The KJV also has "peacock" in Job 39:13a, but the reference there is to the

B

ostrich, a word that the KJV incorrectly uses at the end of the verse.)

pelican. A gregarious web-footed water bird, equipped with a very large bill, beneath which is suspended a pouch for storing fish. The white pelican of Africa and Asia is the best-known species, though pelicans may be found in many parts of the world. With a wingspan of up to 10 ft. (3 m.) and a length up to 6 ft. (almost 2 m.), the pelican is one of the world's largest birds. Its pursuit and capture of fish is helped by the webs between all four toes. The KJV and some modern versions use "pelican" to render Hebrew *qāʾat H7684* in the lists of unclean birds (Lev. 11:18; Deut. 14:17; cf. also Ps. 102:6). However, the contexts in which the Hebrew term occurs (Ps. 102:6; Isa. 34:11; Zeph. 2:14) make this meaning unlikely, and many scholars believe that the word refers to a type of owl.

pigeon. See *dove, pigeon.*

quail. A small migratory game bird, in some 130 species. The quail lives at ground level, in pasture, scrub-land, arable crops, etc. Ready to fly short distances at a comparatively rapid speed, the quail has some similarity to the partridge but is somewhat smaller, reaching a length of only about 7 in. (18 cm.). Like the partridge, the quail is a dust-bather and shares a similar diet of fruit, leaves, and insects. In Bible times the quail was seen in large flocks, traveling most often over short distances. Its abundance as food for the Israelites in the wilderness came as large numbers of the Coturnix quail fell exhausted to the ground following the birds' long flight from Africa, where they had spent the winter (Exod. 16:13; Ps. 105:40). The abundance is graphically described in Num. 11:31. The flesh of the quail is delicious, as are its eggs. North American quail include the California or valley quail, as well as the desert quail—both being important game birds possessing forward curling head plume and somewhat stronger bills than are found in species of Europe, Asia, and Africa.

raven. This large bird—the male of which can reach a length of 2 ft. (60 cm.)—is a member of the crow family. It is found especially in the northern hemisphere in cliffs and mountainous terrain. In urban areas it is seen as a scavenger and will eat all kinds of animal flesh including carrion. Its head and shoulders are larger than those of a crow, and

its soaring action is similar to that of a buzzard. The raven is listed among the unclean birds (Lev. 11:15; Deut. 14:14). Ravens were themselves fed by the Lord (Job 38:41). Such birds would nest in the ruins of Edom, together with other birds of desolation (Isa. 34:11). Jesus referred to the ravens in his encouragement of the disciples and their immense significance to his heavenly Father (Lk. 12:24).

Noah is said to have sent a raven from the ark to ascertain if a landfall might be made (Gen. 8:7), apparently forgetting that, as the raven was a bird of prey, it was unlikely to return, given the abundance of carrion exposed by the receding waters. Nor did the raven have the homing instinct of the dove that subsequently carried out Noah's errand. The record of Noah's dispatch of the raven and its apparent disloyalty, together with the bird's deep hoarse croak, accounts for some old beliefs. Proverbs 30:17 declares that any who mocked their fathers might expect to have their eye pecked out by the ravens of the valley. Yet ravens were used by God to feed ELIJAH (1 Ki. 17:4), though some scholars have suggested here an alternative rendering to have Elijah fed by "human ravens" (itinerant peddlers). Another suggestion is that Elijah was fed by citizens of the nearby town of Orbo. However, ravens are ever generous in feeding their young, leaving some nests crowded with meat that could be eaten by a human being (after cooking or other preparation).

ravenous bird. See *bird of prey.*

rooster. In biblical times its early morning crowing was associated with the start of a new day (Matt. 13:35). The sound had a lamentable meaning for PETER, who denied his Lord before the cock crowed, according to Jesus' prophecy (26:74; Mk. 14:30; Lk. 22:34, 61; Jn. 13:38; 18:27).

screech owl. See *owl.*

sea gull. See *gull.*

sparrow. A small, short-beaked, seed-eating bird—noisy, active, and prolific. The house sparrow, member of genus *Passer*, possesses brown/gray streaked plumage and was originally native to northern Europe and Asia. It has been introduced into Australasia and North America, where it is sometimes called the "English sparrow." In fact, it is classed by ornithologists as a finch, not as a sparrow. True sparrows, with other finches, buntings, and grosbeaks, are members of the family Fringillidae, a large group with many subdivisions. In Bible times protection to the sparrow was provided within the temple precincts (Ps. 84:3). Sparrows were very cheap to buy, yet even this seemingly unimportant bird was of great concern to the Lord, without whose knowledge no sparrow fell to the ground, but who accounted people far more highly (Matt. 10:29, 31; Lk. 12:6, 7).

stork. A large migratory bird of the Ciconiidae family, nesting in trees. Equipped with long legs, neck, and bill, the stork usually lives on a diet of small animals caught at ground level. Some species, including the maribou stork of Africa and the adjutant stork of India, feed on carrion. Nesting characteristics of the stork "in the pine trees" were noted by the psalmist (Ps. 104:17), and Jeremiah confirmed that the stork knew its appointed seasons (Jer. 8:7). Here, as elsewhere in the passage, Jeremiah contrasted the alertness of the bird to natural law with the carelessness of God's people. Zechariah's vision included women equipped with the powerful wings of a stork (Zech. 5:9). The stork was included in the list of prohibited birds (Lev. 11:19; Deut. 14:18).

swallow. An insect-eating bird of the Hirundinidae family, small and with a long forked tail and long wings. Among the most agile of birds, it captures its insect prey while in flight. Its skill in executing maneuvers is noted in Prov. 26:2, while the piercing chatterlike call of the swallow was compared to the chattering of Hezekiah during his illness (Isa. 38:14; NIV, "swift"). Five species are still found in Bible lands. Two of these are known also in the United States—the bank swallow and the barn swallow, the latter recognized by its deeply forked tail feathers.

swan. This term is used by the KJV to translate a Hebrew word of uncertain meaning rendered "water hen" in the NRSV and "white owl" in the NIV (Lev. 11:18; Deut. 14:16).

swift. Any member of the Apodidae family of migratory birds, resembling swallows and having long wings reminiscent of the shape of a scythe. That the swift knew the time of its seasons (i.e., for migration) was confirmed by Jeremiah (Jer. 8:7). The record of Hezekiah's illness also refers to the swift (Isa. 38:14). Some versions prefer the rendering "swallow."

thrush. A term applied to many species of small, plain-colored, singing birds of the family Turdidae. It is used by the NIV to render a Hebrew word that occurs only twice (Isa. 38:14; Jer. 8:7).

turtledove. Found in S Europe and in Africa, the turtledove—a wild pigeon of migratory habit (*Streptopelia turtur*)—is similar to the "mourning dove," which sings early in spring. Canticles 2:12 probably refers to such a bird. These were the birds that, abundant in number, were readily acquired for ceremonial sacrifice (Gen. 15:9). Purification after childbirth involved sacrifice of this bird or a young pigeon (Lev. 12:6-8). It was used in ceremonial cleansing (Num. 6:10). Translations vary in Jer. 8:7.

vulture. A large carrion-eating bird equipped with a hooked beak and strong claws. Some twenty species in the order Falconiformes have featherless heads and necks, as well as large crops. The Andean condor is probably the best known of vultures found in the American continent, though vultures exist in central Europe, Asia, and parts of Africa. Also found in America is the black vulture, sometimes called "black buzzard" or "carrion crow," and the king vulture. One of the largest and heaviest birds in the world, the cinereous (gray colored) vulture (*Aegypius monachus*) has a wingspread of some 9 ft. (3 m.), is about 3 ft. (1 m.) long, and weighs over 27 lbs. (12 kg.). It is found in southern Europe, northern and eastern Africa, and the Middle East to Afghanistan and India. Another impressive member of the species is the Nubian or lappet-faced vulture found in Africa.

Little seems to discourage these large birds in their search for food, and the people of Bible times were accustomed to seeing vultures—and not merely on the battlefield or where carrion was plentiful. Sometimes they would descend to make a raid in some town. Some five species were known in those times. The bearded vulture was easily identified by its full-feathered head and black moustache feathers. The Egyptian vulture was a smaller bird with white feathers on its head, black flight feathers, and a weak, slender beak. Sometimes called Pharaoh's chicken, the Egyptian vulture grew to a length of about 2 ft. (60 cm.). Three further types found in the area were all black and virtually bald. The Mosaic law prohibited eating the vulture (Lev. 11:13; Deut. 14:12 [KJV, "ossifrage"]). Jesus reminded his hearers that vultures eagerly gather around a carcass (Matt. 24:28; Lk. 17:37). Translations vary in Isa. 34:15.

Birsha. bihr'shuh (Heb. *biršaᶜ H1407*, possibly "in [*or* son of] wickedness"). King of GOMORRAH who, with his allies, rebelled against KEDORLAOMER and was defeated (Gen. 14:2).

birth. The bringing forth of a separate life into the world. Childbirth is often accompanied by rending pain, but Gen. 3:16 seems to indicate that such travail was a direct result of the entrance of SIN. Apparently the ancient Hebrew women went through labor more easily than the Egyptians did (Exod. 1:19). The day of one's birth can be regarded, in a sense, as the most important day of his or her life, and so the celebration of birthdays goes back to very ancient times (Gen. 40:20). The Hebrew ceremonies connected with childbirth are given in Lev. 12. The permission to the poor to offer "a pair of turtledoves or two young pigeons" in place of a lamb (Lk. 2:24) gives touching testimony to the comparative poverty of Mary, the mother of Jesus. Our Lord, in Jn. 3:3-6, makes a clear distinction between the first and second births of a regenerate person; and when this distinction is applied, it seems almost to make two different species of the human race: the once-born and the regenerate (see REGENERATION). The former are depraved, and unless they repent they are destined for judgment (Heb. 9:27; 10:31); the latter are being made partakers in the divine nature (2 Pet. 1:4) and are destined for glory.

birth, new. See REGENERATION.

birth, virgin. See VIRGIN BIRTH.

birthright. From time immemorial the FIRSTBORN son has been given privileges above those of his younger brothers. This is illustrated today by the order of succession to the throne (in Britain, for instance). Among the Israelites God had a special claim on the firstborn, at least from the time of the EXODUS, when he destroyed the first-born of Egypt and claimed those of Israel by right of redemption (Exod. 13:2, 12-16). The birthright included a double portion of the inheritance (Deut. 21:15-17) and the privilege of priesthood (Exod. 13:1-2; 24:5); but in Israel God later set apart the tribe of LEVI instead of the firstborn for that service. (Note Num. 3:38-51, where the Levites are about the same in number as the firstborn of Israel.) ESAU lost his birthright by selling it to JACOB for some stew, and no regret could undo the loss he had brought on himself. (See Gen. 25:27-34; Heb. 12:16; and compare the destinies of Israel and of Edom; see also Obad. 17-18.) REUBEN lost his birthright through sin, and his brothers SIMEON and Levi lost theirs through violence; and so the blessing came to JUDAH (Gen. 49:3-10).

birthstool. This English term is used in some versions of the Bible to render Hebrew *ʾobnayim H78*, lit., "double stones," in one passage (Exod. 1:16; NIV, "delivery stool"). It apparently refers to a type of bench on which women sat while giving birth. The Hebrew word implies that it consisted of a pair of stones. Each stone would support a thigh, and the gap would allow the midwife to effect the delivery. According to a number of scholars, however, the word refers to the genitalia, which the Hebrew midwives were told to look at to determine the sex of the baby (if it was a boy, they were to kill him).

Birzaith. bihr-zay'ith (Heb. *birzāyit H1365*, "well of olive oil"). KJV Birzavith. Son of Malkiel and great-grandson of ASHER (1 Chr. 7:31). Some scholars, however, believe that the expression "father of Birzaith" means "founder [*or* leader] of Birzaith," in which case the name refers to a town, presumably modern Bir Zeit, about 13 mi. (21 km.) N of JERUSALEM. If so, Malkiel was its "father," that is, its founder or ruler. It is also possible that Birzaith was indeed a person, but that a town was named from him or populated by his offspring.

Birzavith. bihr-zay'vith. See BIRZAITH.

Bishlam. bish'luhm (Heb. *bišlām H1420*, perhaps "son of peace"). One of three Persian officials who wrote a letter of complaint against the Jews to King

ARTAXERXES (Ezra 4:7). The syntax in this passage is a little unusual, and the SEPTUAGINT renders the word not as a name but as the phrase "in peace," suggesting to some scholars that the term should be understood in the sense, "with the consent of."

bishop. The KJV and other versions use this term to render Greek *episkopos G2176*, which simply means "overseer." In the NT it evidently refers to the principal officer of the local church, the other being the DEACON (1 Tim. 3:1-7). The title ELDER (or "presbyter") generally applied to the same officer, "elder" alluding to his age and dignity, and "bishop" to his work of superintendence. As the churches multiplied, the bishop of a larger church would often be given special honor, and so gradually there grew up a hierarchy, all the way from presiding elders to bishops (over groups of churches), then archbishops.

Bishops' Bible. See BIBLE VERSIONS, ENGLISH.

bit and bridle. This expression is used in English versions to translate two words in Ps. 32:9. Both terms seem to include the whole controlling harness of the animal's head and thus may be translated "bridle." In the NT the term *chalinos G5903* undoubtedly means "bit" in Jas. 3:3 (cf. 1:26) but "bridle, reins" in Rev. 14:20.

Bithiah. bi-thi′uh (Heb. *bityâ H1437*, "daughter of Yahweh"). A daughter of PHARAOH who married MERED, a descendant of JUDAH through CALEB (1 Chr. 4:18; NRSV, v. 17). It is not certain whether "Pharaoh" here was an Egyptian king. Some understand "Pharaoh's daughter" to mean simply "Egyptian lady"; it has also been suggested that "Pharaoh" in this verse could be a Hebrew proper name.

Bithron. bith′ron (Heb. *bitrôn H1443*, "ravine" or "forenoon"). The KJV, as well as the NIV and other versions, treats "Bithron" as a place name, referring to a valley leading E from the JORDAN to MAHANAIM (2 Sam. 2:29). Some scholars, however, prefer to translate the term as a common noun, either "ravine" or "morning" (cf. NRSV, "the whole forenoon," opposite "all that night").

Bithynia. bi-thin′ee-uh (Gk. *Bithynia G1049*). A region in NW ASIA MINOR fronting on the Black Sea, the Bosphorus, and the Sea of Marmara. PAUL and his companions desired to enter Bithynia with the gospel (Acts 16:6-10), but the HOLY SPIRIT was leading toward Europe, and so they could not enter. However, there were Christians there in the first century (1 Pet. 1:1). At the beginning of the second century the Roman governor Pliny the Younger complained to Emperor Trajan concerning the Christians and asked how to deal with them. Bithynia was settled very early, and its known history goes back past the sixth century B.C. when Croesus made it a part of his kingdom. A king of Bithynia in the third century B.C. invited the Gauls into Asia, so originating GALATIA.

bitter, bitterness. These English terms usually render the Hebrew verb *mārar H5352* and its derivatives; in the NT, Greek *pikrainō G4393* and derivatives. Israel was commanded at the Feast of Passover to eat bitter herbs with the roast lamb and UNLEAVENED bread (Exod. 12:8). The observance was meant to symbolize the bitterness and agony of their Egyptian servitude (modern rabbis have allowed the eating of horseradish as the fulfillment of this commandment). A technical use is found in the ceremony of the BITTER WATER, which was a ritual test (or ordeal?) for a woman's faithfulness in the case of a jealous husband (Num. 5:18-27).

In speaking of the moral corruption of the nations in Canaan, MOSES refers to them figuratively as bitter clusters of grapes (Deut. 32:32). The sacred writer records the mental attitude and stern disposition of dethroned DAVID and his followers as "bitter of soul" (lit. trans. of 2 Sam. 17:8; NIV, "fierce"). Jeremiah describes Judah's wickedness as bitter, so much so that it overwhelms the heart (Jer. 4:18). Amos, in his denunciations of Israel's sins, predicts the loss of their feasts and music with the replacement by sackcloth and mourning, all of it constituting a bitter day (Amos 8:10). God foretells that his people will be punished by the Babylonians, a "bitter and hasty nation" (Hab. 1:6 KJV; NIV, "ruthless and impetuous people"). The reference is to their inconsiderate and cruel treatment of subject peoples, whom they considered much as the fisherman does his catch.

B

At SAMARIA the apostle PETER was constrained to rebuke SIMON Magus sternly when he attempted to buy the gift of the HOLY SPIRIT. He accused Simon of being "in the gall of bitterness" (Acts 8:23 NRSV; NIV, "full of bitterness"), an expression intended to awaken the offender to the depth of his depravity and ungodliness. Throughout the epistle to the Hebrews, professing Jewish believers are warned against the "bitter root" (Heb. 12:15), which may refer to any sin which could develop into APOSTASY (cf. also Rom. 3:14; Eph. 4:31; Jas. 3:14). The "waters that had become bitter" (Rev. 8:11) may describe figuratively any disasters yet to befall sinful humanity.

bitter herbs. See BITTER, BITTERNESS; PLANTS (under *herbs*).

bittern. See BIRDS.

bitter water. A drink consisting of holy water, dust from the TABERNACLE floor, and the ink of a written curse and designed to be used as an "ordeal" to establish the guilt or innocence of a suspected adulteress (Num. 5:11-31). The priest would set the woman "before the LORD," unbind her hair, and place in her hands the cereal offering. He would then declare a lengthy and frightening oath to which the woman would reply, "Amen, Amen." The woman was made to drink the mixture of dust and ink, and the cereal was offered up to Yahweh. If she had been unfaithful, the bitter water would cause great pain and distortion of the lower body, and she would be considered accursed by her people. If, on the other hand, the woman was innocent, she would be free to bear children. This ritual seems to have been peculiar to Israel among ANE peoples.

bitumen. A mineral pitch widely scattered over the earth, and one of the best waterproofing substances known. This English word is used by the NRSV to render the Hebrew noun *ḥēmār H2819*, which occurs three times in the OT (Gen. 11:3; 14:10; Exod. 2:3). The NIV translates this noun with English "tar" (KJV, "slime"). A similar term, "pitch," is used in most versions to translate other terms (Gen. 6:14; Exod. 2:3; Isa. 34:9). There were great deposits of bitumen or tar near the DEAD SEA and at different places in MESOPOTAMIA. The principal modern source is a great lake of pitch on the island of Trinidad.

Biziothiah. biz´ee-oh-thi´uh (Heb. *bizyôtyâ H1026*, perhaps "booty of Yahweh"). KJV Bizjoth-jah. According to the MT, a town in the NEGEV district of JUDAH (Josh. 15:28). Instead of "Beersheba, Biziothiah," however, many scholars prefer to read "Beersheba and its villages" (cf. LXX and Neh. 11:27).

Bizjothjah. biz-joth´juh . See BIZIOTHIAH.

Biztha, Bizthah. biz´thuh (Heb. *bizzĕtaʾ H1030*, possibly "eunuch" or "bound"). One of the seven EUNUCH chamberlains instructed by XERXES (Ahasuerus), king of Persia, to bring Queen VASHTI to the royal feast (Esth. 1:10).

black. This English term translates various Hebrew words. One of them is applied to horses (Zech. 6:2, 6, here signifying death and famine), to the suitor's locks (Cant. 5:11), and to the sunburnt look of SOLOMON's beloved (1:5; NIV "dark"). A cognate verb describes the state of JOB's skin as it peeled off under the ravages of the boils (Job 30:30). Another verb is used to describe storm-black clouds (1 Ki. 18:45; Jer. 4:28); metaphorically it refers to mourning (Jer. 8:21; Joel 2:6; Nah. 2:10) and is used of Job's unfaithful friends (6:16). In the NT, "black" can describe the color of hair (Matt. 5:36), horses (Rev. 6:5), the obscuring of the sun (v. 12), and ink (2 Cor. 3:3). See also DARKNESS.

blacksmith. See OCCUPATIONS AND PROFESSIONS.

blasphemy. The act of insulting or showing contempt for someone. To reproach or to bring a railing accusation against any one is bad enough (Jude 9), but to speak lightly or carelessly of God is an especially grievous sin. The third commandment, "You shall not misuse the name of the LORD your God" (Exod. 20:7), was observed so meticulously by the Jews that they would not speak the sacred name *YHWH* at all, and so no one knows today for certain how it was pronounced (see JEHOVAH).

Before his conversion, Paul blasphemed (1 Tim. 1:13) and tried to force Christians to blaspheme (Acts 26:11). God prescribed that in Israel the punishment for blasphemy would be death by stoning (Lev. 24:10-16). Naboth was falsely charged with blasphemy and was stoned to death (1 Ki. 21:10-13), as was Stephen (Acts 6:11). Stoning was also in the minds of those who charged Jesus with blasphemy (Matt. 9:3; 26:65; Lk. 5:31; Jn. 10:33); what Jesus said about himself would have been blasphemy were it not true. See also Unpardonable Sin.

Blastus. blas′tuhs (Gk. *Blastos* G1058, "bud, sprout"). The chamberlain of Herod Agrippa I, who apparently was easily bribed; the men of Tyre and Sidon used him in approaching the king (Acts 12:20). As the officer in charge of Herod's private quarters, he was in a position to influence the king favorably.

bless, blessing. The Bible states that God blesses nature (Gen. 1:22), mankind (1:28), the Sabbath (2:3), individuals (24:1), and whole nations (Ps. 33:12). The idea is clearly that of a divine announcement of favor; the assurance that God is conferring his grace. On the other hand, when godly men and women "bless" God, they adore him, worship him, and praise him (103:1-2). The same word is used for what worshipers offer to God and for what they seek from him. When we "bless" God, we bring his glories before our mind and respond in worship and adoration; when we ask him to "bless" us, we invite him to call our needs to mind and respond in meeting them.

Godly people by words and actions can bestow blessings on their fellows (Matt. 5:44; 1 Pet. 3:9). In Bible times, men under inspiration bestowed prophetic blessings on their progeny; for example, Noah blessed Japheth and Shem (Gen. 9:26-27), Isaac blessed Jacob and Esau (27:27-29, 39-40), Jacob blessed the tribes of Israel (ch 49), and Moses also blessed them (Deut. 33). We can bless things when we set them apart for sacred use (e.g., 1 Cor. 10:16 KJV).

blessing, cup of. This expression is found only in 1 Cor. 10:16 (NIV, "cup of thanksgiving"), and is best understood in light of the ancient Jewish custom of concluding meals with a prayer of thanksgiving over a cup of wine. This ritual act acknowledged God as the Giver of all good gifts,

According to Deut. 28-31, the Israelites were instructed to remember God's covenant by proclaiming God's blessings from Mt. Gerizim (left ridge) and potential curses from Mt. Ebal (right ridge). (View to the W.)

© Dr. James C. Martin

B

and consecrated the meal to the one who ate. Noteworthy is the fact that the third cup of the Jewish Passover feast was also called the "cup of blessing." Borrowing this expression from Judaism, Paul applied it to the cup of the LORD'S SUPPER. He meant by it, therefore, not the cup that imparts blessing, but the cup over which the Christian gives thanks to God for the death of Christ.

blindness. See DISEASES.

blood. The word occurs over 400 times in the Bible and is especially frequent in LEVITICUS. The circulation of the blood was not known until long after Scripture was written, and for the most part Bible references are directed toward the practical observation that loss of blood leads to loss of vitality and that a draining away of the blood leads to death. Genesis 9:5 says (literally), "Your blood, belonging to your lives, I will seek ... from the hand of man ... I will seek the life of man." In this verse "seek blood" is parallel with "seek life," and both refer to exacting the death penalty. When blood is shed, life is terminated, and the Lord seeks requital for the shedding of blood by demanding the life of the murderer (cf. Gen. 37:26; Ps. 30:9; 58:10). The statement "Your blood be on your own head" (e.g., 2 Sam. 1:16) witnesses to the same understanding of things: a person guilty of murder must pay with his life. Our concern here is not the question of the death penalty, but the way in which the Bible uses "blood" as a metaphor for "death." When blood is spoken of as the life of the flesh (Gen. 9:4; cf. Lev. 17:11), the meaning is the practical one that flesh and blood in their proper union constitute a living creature, beast or human, but that when they are separated death takes place. The bearing of this truth on the use of blood in sacrificial ritual is most important. For further discussion see SACRIFICE.

blood, avenger of. See AVENGER.

Blood, Field of. See AKELDAMA.

blood, issue (flow) of. See DISEASES (sect. VI).

bloodguilt. This term (KJV, "bloodguiltiness" in Ps. 51:14) is sometimes used as a rendering of the Hebrew word for BLOOD, *dām H1947*, in its plural (intensive) form, *dāmîm*. It occurs only twice in the NIV (Ps. 51:14; Joel 3:21), but more frequently in the NRSV (e.g., Exod. 22:2; Deut. 19:10; 1 Sam. 25:26). In these instances guilt incurred by bloodshed is denoted. The Hebrew term can also be used where other crimes are in view (e.g., Ezek. 18:13).

bloody sweat. See DISEASES (sect. VI).

blue. A color extracted from the mollusk *Helix ianthina*. The exact color on the fringe of every Hebrew garment cannot be defined (e.g., Num. 15:38); it may have been a shade of blue or violet. There is also no indication of how the dye was made, but no doubt the Israelites during the bondage in Egypt had learned to make the blue extract. See also PURPLE.

Boanerges. boh´uh-nuhr´jeez (Gk. *Boanērges G1065*, possibly from Heb. *bĕnĕ regeš H1201 + H8094*, "sons of commotion"). A surname interpreted as meaning "Sons of Thunder" and given by Jesus to JAMES and JOHN THE APOSTLE, the sons of ZEBEDEE, at the time they were chosen apostles (Mk. 3:17). The derivation of the name is debated, and Mark translates it without stating why the term was appropriate. Some have thought it referred to their fiery eloquence; others have taken it as referring to their fiery dispositions.

boar. See ANIMALS.

boast. This English term is used to translate various Hebrew words, especially the verb *hālal H2146* (Ps. 10:3; 34:2; et al.). In the NT, it is primarily a rendering of the Greek verb *kauchaomai G3016* and its derivatives; this word group is used mainly by PAUL, especially in 2 Cor. 10-12 (e.g., 10:13-17). The idea of boasting may convey both a good (e.g., Ps. 44:8; 2 Cor. 7:14) and a bad sense (e.g., Ps. 10:3; Rom. 2:17; 2 Tim. 3:2). The fundamental biblical principle is expressed by God's declaration, "let him who boasts boast about this: / that he understands and knows me, / that I am the LORD" (Jer. 9:24; quoted in 1 Cor. 1:31).

boat. See SHIPS.

Boaz met Ruth in the vicinity of the fields and threshing floors located on the E side of Bethlehem. (View to the N.)

© Dr. James C. Martin

Boaz. boh´az (Heb. *bōʿaz H1244*, possibly "quick [of mind]" or "in him is strength"; Gk. *Boes G1067* [Matt. 1:5] and *Boos G1078* [Lk. 3:32]). A well-to-do Bethlehemite in the days of the judges who became an ancestor of Jesus by marrying RUTH the Moabitess, widow of one of the sons of ELIM-ELECH (Ruth 2-4). This was in accordance with the levirate law of Deut. 25:5-10; Boaz could marry Ruth only after the nearer kinsman had refused the privilege—or the duty (Ruth 3:12; 4:1-8). The other refused because, if he had married Ruth and had had a son, a portion of his property would have gone to the credit of Elimelech's posterity, instead of his own by a former marriage. It is impossible to date Boaz exactly, because the genealogy of Ruth 4:18-22 (cf. Matt. 1:5-6; Lk. 3:32) is almost certainly a partial list, giving ten names to cover 800 years. The list in Matt. 1 is demonstrably schematic, as it omits names of four kings, and this one in Ruth is almost as surely partial also. They are both accurate but, like most genealogies, partial. SALMON (or Salmah), given here as the father of Boaz, lived at the time of the conquest, for he married RAHAB; but the general setting of the story is that of a later period of settled life.

Boaz and Jakin. See JAKIN AND BOAZ.

Bocheru. See BOKERU.

Bochim. See BOKIM.

body. The OT uses various names for parts and organs of the body to signify the physical, temporal, spatial, and tactual aspect of a human being. In the English versions some ten Hebrew words are loosely (and often incorrectly) translated "body." The Greek word *sōma G5393* has a wide range of meaning in the NT. It can refer to a corpse (Matt. 27:52), one's physical body (Mk. 5:29), and the human self expressed in and through a body (Heb. 10:10; 1 Pet. 2:24). As a Jewish thinker, PAUL saw the body not merely as an outer shell to house the soul/spirit, but as the expression of the whole person (Rom. 12:1). So he warned against the misuse of the body (1 Cor. 6:13-20), especially since it is the temple of the HOLY SPIRIT in the case of the believer (6:15, 19). However, the body is affected by sin and so may be called the "body of sin" (Rom. 6:6) and "body of death" (7:24). Even so, Paul's use of "body" must be distinguished from his use of FLESH. The latter almost always points to the principle of SIN endemic in human nature.

As there is a physical body for this life, so there is a spiritual and imperishable body for the life of the age to come after the RESURRECTION (1 Cor. 15:38-49). The present body, which is affected by sin, will be replaced by a body whose nature is spirit and which is pure and glorious—like

B

Christ's resurrection body. In the LORD's SUPPER the bread symbolizes the body of Jesus offered as a sacrifice for sin (Mk. 14:22; 1 Cor. 11:24). The CHURCH can also be understood as a body. See BODY OF CHRIST.

body of Christ. The NT applies the term *body* to Christ in three ways. (1) As the natural, human body of Jesus that the eternal Son made his own in the womb of Mary, and in which he offered himself as a sacrifice for the sin of the world (Heb. 10:10). This body was transformed from a physical into a spiritual body in resurrection and then taken to heaven in ascension. Yet it remains a human body, and thus he who sits at the right hand of the Father as coregent is still the God-Man. (2) As the people of God or the CHURCH (local and universal) united to Christ in grace by faith and through baptism. Believers are "one body in Christ" (Rom. 12:5) in each locality and, as a universal community, are the "body of Christ" (Eph. 4:12) ruled and sustained by Christ, the Head (5:23). (3) As the bread used at the Last Supper by Jesus and then as the bread used in Holy Communion by believers. "This is my body," said Jesus (Matt. 26:26). Just as Jesus' body was broken on the cross, and just as by eating the Passover meal the Israelites had been associated with delivery from Egypt and bondage, so believers participate in the saving work of Christ on the cross by taking this bread (and wine).

Bohan, Stone of. boh´han (Heb. *bōhan H992*, possibly "thumb"). The description of the N boundary of the tribe of JUDAH contains a reference to "the Stone of Bohan son of Reuben" (Josh. 15:6); the same language is then used to describe the S boundary of the tribe of BENJAMIN (18:17). The stone was apparently near JERICHO, and it is possible that at one time descendants of the tribe of REUBEN temporarily inhabited the NE corner of the territory of Judah before the final boundary settlements were made by JOSHUA.

boil. See DISEASES.

Bokeru. boh´kuh-roo (Heb. *bōkĕrû H1150*, possibly "youthful"). Also Bocheru. Son of Azel and

descendant of SAUL through JONATHAN (1 Chr. 8:38; 9:44). Some scholars (following the Greek and Syriac versions) take the word as a common noun with suffix, "his firstborn," applying the description to Azel's first son, Azrikam.

Bokim. boh´kim (Heb. *bōkim H1141*, "weepers"). Also Bochim. Name given to a place near GILGAL where the nation of Israel wept after being admonished by the angel of the Lord (Jdg. 2:1, 5). The SEPTUAGINT inserts a reference to BETHEL after Bokim, and the latter may be connected with ALLON BACUTH, meaning "oak of weeping," which is said to be "below Bethel" (Gen. 35:8).

boldness. Common translation of the Greek noun *parrēsia G4244*, which also means "frankness, sense of freedom, confidence." Luke uses it often to describe the bold witnessing of the early Christians (Acts 2:29; 4:29-31; et al.; cf. also the cognate verb *parrēsiazomai G4245*, "speak boldly, preach fearlessly," 9:27 et al.). PAUL uses it too in some key passages that focus either on the boldness required in his ministry (2 Cor. 3:12; Eph 6:19-20; et al.) or on the confidence believers have to approach God (Eph. 3:12; 1 Tim. 3:13; cf. also Heb. 3:16 et al.; 1 Jn. 2:28 et al.). For Christians, courage of every sort is possible in the measure that they know themselves to be in the almighty hands and under the beneficent protection of their heavenly Father. See also SHAME.

bolled. An archaic term used by the KJV once, referring to the flower bud or the seed pod of flax (Exod. 9:31; NIV, "in bloom"). The English term meant "having bolls" or "bearing pods," hence "in seed," though the corresponding Hebrew word may refer equally to the flower.

bondage. See SLAVE, SLAVERY.

bone. In the living body, bones form the strong framework, and the connotation is one of strength. "Bone of my bones and flesh of my flesh" (Gen. 2:23) was spoken in a literal sense of EVE; but almost the same words (29:14), spoken by LABAN to JACOB, are figurative and show only kinship. Strong chastening is thought of as a bone-breaking experience (Ps. 51:8), and the terrible writhing on the cross of Calvary literally threw bones out of joint (22:14). Dry bones form a picture of hopeless death (Ezek. 37:1-12). The Passover lamb, without a broken bone (Exod. 12:46), was a type of the Lamb of God (Jn. 19:36).

book. Generally a literary production having some unity of purpose. Books may be classified by their forms or subjects, but more particularly by the nature and quality of the written material within. In ancient ASSYRIA and Babylonia (see BABYLON) much of the WRITING that was thought to be of value was done in wedge-shaped characters on soft clay that was then baked, and the "libraries" were, in form, almost like piles of brick.

In ancient EGYPT, the people early learned to press and glue thin sheets of the PAPYRUS plant

© Dr. James C. Martin. The British Museum. Photographed by permission.

In ancient Mesopotamia, books were produced in the form of inscribed tablets like this one (19th cent. B.C.), commemorating the building of Ur by Warad-Sin, king of Larsa.

into sheets of "paper"; the writing was in narrow columns on sheets of regular size that were then glued together and wound around two sticks, thus forming a scroll or roll. Still later, people learned to bind the sheets together into a "codex," very similar to our modern books. *Book* in the Bible always refers to a scroll (see esp. Jer. 36). In PERGAMUM, in the second century B.C., due to the scarcity of paper, workers learned to dress the skin of calves and of kids as a writing material. This new substance was named *parchment* in honor of its place of origin and almost displaced papyrus in many regions.

In ancient books made of papyrus or parchment, the writing was generally done on one side of each sheet, but occasionally, owing to afterthoughts, material was written also on the back side (see Rev. 5:1). When a book was sealed, the contents were made secret, and when unsealed they were open (cf. Dan. 12:4, 9; Rev. 5:1-4 on the one hand and Rev. 5:5; 22:10 on the other). Only the Son of God was found worthy to open the seals of the book of the future that had been locked in the hands of "him that sat on the throne."

Judaism, Christianity, and Islam are all religions of a book, and their main books have greatly changed the history of the human race. The BIBLE is *the* book, God's Word, and it differs from all other books in that it alone is inspired (God-breathed). The Bible originally had sixty-three books, as the division of Samuel, Kings, and Chronicles into "First" and "Second" was not originally intended. The larger books were generally written on separate rolls (see Lk. 4:17) but sometimes the *Megilloth* (Ruth, Esther, Lamentations, Song of Songs, and Ecclesiastes) were bound together, as were also "The Twelve" (i.e., the Minor Prophets). Many books that have been lost are mentioned in the Bible (e.g., "the book of Jashar," Josh. 10:13; "the book of the annals of Solomon," 1 Ki. 11:41).

book of life. See LIFE, BOOK OF.

Book of the Covenant, Book of the Law. See COVENANT, BOOK OF THE.

booth. A simple, temporary shelter generally constructed of tree branches with the leaves left on.

It was used by the guardian of a vineyard or vegetable garden when the fruit was fit to be stolen. Sometimes this word describes a larger enclosure (Gen. 33:17) such as Jacob built for his cattle (cf. Isa. 1:8 NRSV).

Booths, Feast of. See FEASTS (sect. VI).

booty. Goods taken from a defeated enemy. In the law as given through Moses, very different arrangements were made for varying circumstances. In the case of some cities whose people were extremely wicked, everything was to be destroyed (see DEVOTED THING). Persons could sometimes be enslaved (Deut. 20:14), but in other cases they had to be utterly destroyed (20:16-18). The purpose here was to prevent the pagans from teaching their abominations to God's people Israel (cf. 1 Sam. 15, where Saul's hypocritical half-obedience brought ruin on himself and his house). The very practical question as to the division of the booty was solved partly by custom, as when Abram (Abraham) freely devoted a tenth of the spoil to the Lord by giving it to Melchizedek (Gen. 14:20), and partly by legislation, as when David ordered that booty be shared equally by those who because of weariness could not continue in battle (1 Sam. 30:21-25).

Booz. boh′oz. See Boaz.

Bor Ashan. bor-ay′shuhn (Heb. *bôr-ʿāšān H1016*, "smoking pit"). A city in the SW of Judah, mentioned among the places where David and his men roamed prior to his becoming king (1 Sam. 30:30; for the first consonant, many Heb. MSS have a *k* instead of a *b*, thus KJV "Chor-ashan"). It may be the same as Ashan, a city of uncertain location in the Shephelah (Josh. 19:7; 1 Chr. 4:32).

borrow. The KJV uses this verb three times in the context of the people of Israel "borrowing" extensively from the Egyptians (Exod. 3:22; 11:2; 12:35; the Heb. verb means literally "to ask"). The fact is that the Egyptians, thoroughly cowed by the rigors of the ten plagues, were willing to give generously in order to get rid of their troublesome "guests"; and God, in his providence, allowed Israel to despoil the Egyptians (12:36) in order to provide gold and silver for the TABERNACLE that was to be constructed. "Surely your wrath against men brings you praise" (Ps. 76:10).

The law of Moses gives careful direction concerning the responsibility of those who borrow or who hold property in trust or who are criminally careless in regard to the property of another (Exod. 22:1-15). Among the blessings promised Israel on condition of obedience is that they would be lenders, not borrowers (Deut. 15:6; 28:12). Also, Jesus instructed his followers to not turn away those who wanted to borrow from them (Matt. 5:42). Generally the borrower is the servant of the lender (Prov. 22:7), but God's judgment can erase differences (Isa. 24:2). See also DEBT; INTEREST.

Boscath. See Bozkath.

bosom. Although in English this word refers to the part of the body between the arms, in Scripture it is generally used in an affectionate sense; for example, "the only Son, who is in the bosom of the Father" (Jn. 1:18 RSV), carrying the lambs in his bosom (Isa. 40:11 KJV), or Lazarus resting in Abraham's bosom (Lk. 16:22-23 KJV). It can be almost synonymous with "heart" as the center of one's life (cf. Ps. 35:13; Eccl. 7:9 KJV). Quite commonly, of course, it refers to conjugal love, as in Mic. 7:5 (KJV; NIV, "embrace"). In Prov. 17:23 we read of the bosom as a place of hiding money (KJV; NIV, "accepts a bribe in secret").

Bosor. boh′sor (Gk. *Bosor G1082* [not in NIV]). An alternate name for Beor, the father of Balaam (2 Pet. 2:15 KJV, NRSV; but NIV reads Beor, following Codex Vaticanus and a few other witnesses). Some scholars have thought that the form *Bosor* in this passage is simply an ancient blunder that spread through virtually the whole MS tradition. Many others believe that it is the original form in this passage and that it was corrected to Beor by a few scribes to harmonize the text with the Septuagint spelling.

botch. See DISEASES.

bottle. A term used frequently by the KJV where modern versions have such renderings as "jar" and "wineskin" (or simply "skin"). The Hebrew noun *nō'd H5532* in particular refers to the hide of an animal sewn and sealed to be used as a WINE or WATER container (e.g., Josh. 9:4). In the NT, the Greek term *askos G929* appears several times (e.g., Matt. 9:17). See also PITCHER; POTTERY.

bottomless pit. See ABYSS.

boundary stones. God not only set careful bounds to the land of his people (Josh. 13-21), but also provided a curse for those who removed their neighbors' landmarks (Deut. 27:17; cf. 19:14). Figuratively, the expression implies a decent regard for ancient institutions (Prov. 22:28; 23:10).

bow. See ARMS AND ARMOR; RAINBOW.

bowels. In the KJV this English word occurs thirty-six times and in three principal senses: (1) literally (2 Chr. 21:15-19; Acts 1:18); (2) as the generative parts of the body, whether male or female (Gen. 15:4; Ps. 71:6); and (3) as the seat of the emotions (e.g. Lam. 1:20 [NIV, "heart"]; Phil. 1:8 [NIV, "affection"]).

bowl. Various Hebrew words are rendered "bowl" in the OT. One of these may refer to a large, flat earthenware dish for holding a liquid, such as milk (Jdg. 5:25). Another one is used of large costly bowls, like the silver bowls presented by the princes of the congregation (Num. 7:13-14). Still another

one is used in reference to the receptacle for oil in the candlestick of Zechariah's vision (Zech. 4:3), and to the bowl-shaped capitals of the temple pillars Jakin and Boaz (1 Ki. 7:41-42; 2 Chr. 4:12-13). In the NT, two Greek terms are used. One occurs in Jesus' statement at the Last Supper, "The one who has dipped his hand into the bowl with me will betray me" (Matt. 26:23). The other one is found frequently in the book of Revelation (Rev. 5:8; 15:7; et al. [KJV, "vial"]). See also CUP; POTTERY; VESSEL.

box tree. See PLANTS.

Bozez. boh´ziz (Heb. *bôṣēṣ H1010*, perhaps "gleaming [place]"). The northern of two cliffs (the southern was called SENEH) situated on either side of the pass of MICMASH (1 Sam. 14:4). It was apparently this crag, or near it, that JONATHAN and his armor-bearer climbed when attacking the PHILISTINE outpost. The exact spot has not been identified, although doubtless both cliffs lay near the sharp bend of the pass. The area is some 7 mi. (11 km.) NNE of JERUSALEM.

Bozkath. boz´kath (Heb. *boṣqat H1304*, "swollen" or "elevation"). One of the towns in the SHEPHELAH within the territory of the tribe of JUDAH (Josh. 15:39); it was the home of King JOSIAH's mother, Jedidah (2 Ki. 22:1; KJV, "Boscath"). Its precise location is unknown, but it must have been near LACHISH.

Bozrah. boz´ruh (Heb. *boṣrāh H1313*, possibly "enclosure [for sheep]"). (1) An ancient city in the mountains of EDOM, strongly fortified and virtually impregnable. It is probably to be identified with modern Buṣeirah, situated at the head of the Wadi Hamayideh on a rocky isolated bluff surrounded on three sides by steep valleys, approximately 30 mi. (50 km.) N of PETRA (SELA) and 25 mi. (40 km.) SE of the S tip of the DEAD SEA. It was the strongest

© Dr. James C. Martin. The Cairo Museum. Photographed by permission.

A collection of votive bowls dedicated to the Canaanite temple in Hazor (15th-13th cent. B.C.).

B

fortress of the northern half of Edom and as such controlled access to the king's highway, and hence to the ARABAH and the Red Sea port of ELATH. Bozrah is mentioned in Gen. 36:33 and 1 Chr. 1:44 as being the city of JOBAB, one of the early kings of Edom. It is particularly used by the prophets, along with TEMAN, to describe Edom in oracles of judgment, since both places were so impregnable (Isa. 34:6; 63:1; Jer. 49:13, 22; Amos 1:12). In Mic. 2:12 it is better translated "sheepfold," as in the modern versions.

(2) One of the cities of MOAB against which Jeremiah prophesied (Jer. 48:24). It is usually identified with BEZER.

bracelet. Properly a circlet for the wrist, but the word translates in the KJV five different Hebrew nouns. In 2 Sam. 1:10 the word probably means "armlet" as a mark of royalty (NIV, "band on his arm"); in Exod. 35:22 it could be "brooches" or "clasps"; in Gen. 38:18, 25 it represents the cord about the neck from which the signet ring was suspended; in Gen. 24:22, 30, 47, it is properly "bracelet," from the root meaning "something bound on"; in Ezek. 16:11; 23:42; and in Isa. 3:19, in the interesting inventory of twenty-one items of feminine adornment, it could be rendered "twisted chains." Bracelets and other showy adornments (anklets, nose-rings, armlets, etc.) were much admired in ancient days. See also DRESS.

braid. The braiding of the HAIR refers to a custom practiced by women of means during the Roman period. It involved the elaborate entwining of the hair, and it often included the use of thin threads of gold, pearls, or precious stones of various colors. Two of the NT church leaders speak against this practice because of its identification with the world system of that day (1 Tim. 2:9; 1 Pet. 3:3). The NIV uses the term "braid" with reference to SAMSON's hair (Jdg. 16:13, 19).

bramble. See PLANTS.

branch. A word representing eighteen different Hebrew and four Greek words in the Bible, most notably as a title applied to the MESSIAH as the offspring of DAVID (Jer. 23:5; 33:15; Zech. 3:8; 6:12).

brasen. See BRONZE SEA; BRONZE SNAKE.

brass. See MINERALS.

bray. This verb refers to the distinctive call of the donkey, horse, and mule. Its two exclusive biblical references occur in JOB. In his distress Job declares there was good reason for his rash words: "Does a wild donkey bray when it has grass, / or an ox bellow when it has fodder?" (Job 6:5). Later, he compares the "base and nameless brood" who mocked him to wild desert asses braying in the bushes (30:8-9). (The KJV uses the word in its other meaning of "grind" in Prov. 27:22.)

brazen sea, brazen serpent. See BRONZE SEA; BRONZE SNAKE.

bread. The "staff of life," generally baked from dough made of wheat flour that has been leavened (raised by means of fermenting yeast) and made into loaves of various shapes and sizes. At the time of the Passover (Exod. 12) the Israelites ate unleavened bread because of their haste, and ever afterward they memorialized this event in an annual feast (12:15-20). The poorer people usually used barley instead of wheat to make the bread for this feast, and in times of distress and of famine most of the people used barley. See PLANTS. In Jdg. 7:13, the Midianite's dream of a barley loaf, which was interpreted as "the sword of Gideon," perhaps hinted at the poverty of Israel under Midianite oppression; and in Jn. 6:9 the boy's store of five barley loaves suggests that he came from a family or a region that could not afford the more delicious and nutritious wheat bread. Ezekiel 4:9-17 gives a vivid picture of baking in famine times.

In the more primitive parts of Syria today there are several sorts of wheat bread. In some villages a barrel-shaped hole in the ground is used as an oven; the women adroitly knead the bread into large thin sheets that they lay on cushions and slap against the hot wall of the oven. Though dried dung mixed with straw is used as fuel to preheat the oven, the taste is not impaired. In other villages of Syria, a convex sheet of iron is placed over an open fire and the bread is similarly baked; but in the larger towns and cities there are bakeries to which the people bring their loaves for baking. The long stone oven is heated for hours, then the raised loaves, about 8 to 10 in. (21 to 26 cm.) in diameter and one-fourth inch (about 1 cm.) thick, are placed inside by means of a long wooden paddle. The heat quickly bakes the surface, and gas forming inside splits the loaves, which are then turned and soon removed (Hos. 7:8).

The word *bread*, depicting the most universal solid food, is often used figuratively for FOOD in general: "By the sweat of your brow you shall eat bread" (Gen. 3:19 NRSV); "Give us today our daily bread" (Matt. 6:11). The word is used by the Lord in a mystical but very true and precious sense in his discourse on "the bread of life" in Jn. 6:43-59. As important as bread (i.e., solid food) is to our bodies, so necessary is the Lord to spiritual life. And so, in the "breaking of bread" at our "communion" services, some partake in a very real way of Christ, while others, not recognizing the body of the Lord, eat and drink judgment on themselves (1 Cor. 11:29). In the tabernacle and in the temple, the "bread of the Presence" indicated the presence of the Lord, the "bread of life" among his people.

bread of the Presence. See TABERNACLE.

breastpiece. An elaborately decorated square of linen worn on the breast as part of the robes of Israel's high PRIEST (Exod. 28:15-30; 39:8-21; Lev. 8:8; KJV, "breastplate"). A piece of material of gold, blue, purple, scarlet, and fine linen was folded double into a square of 9 x 9 in. It was fastened from the top to the shoulder of the EPHOD by gold cords, and by a blue lace from the lower corners to gold rings on the ephod. On the front were four rows, each of three precious stones, and each stone inscribed with the name of one of the twelve tribes. Three times it is referred to as the "breastpiece of judgment" (Exod. 28:15, 29-30; NIV, "breastpiece for making decisions"). This term apparently refers to the oracular function of the URIM AND THUMMIM, commonly thought to have been objects held in the fold.

breastplate. See ARMS AND ARMOR; BREASTPIECE.

breath. The most important ingredient of physical LIFE. A person can live for thirty days without food, but only a few minutes without breathing. Because human beings owe their breath to God (Gen. 2:7; Job 27:3), the concept has strong theological associations. God will restore his people, who are like dry bones, when he breathes his Spirit, and thus life, into them (Ezek. 37:1-14; the Heb. word for "spirit," *rûaḥ H5972*, also means "breath, wind," and the same is true of the corresponding Gk. word, *pneuma G4460*). After his resurrection, Jesus breathed on his disciples, signifying their reception of the HOLY SPIRIT (Jn. 20:22). Moreover, the Scriptures are described as being "breathed out" by God (*theopneustos G2535*, 2 Tim. 3:16; see INSPIRATION).

breeches. See DRESS.

brethren of the Lord. See BROTHERS OF THE LORD.

bribery. Anything given to induce a person to do something illegal or wrong, or against his or her wishes. The taking of bribes is mentioned often in the OT. Bribery was used to condemn the innocent (Ps. 15:5; Isa. 5:23; Ezek. 22:12), to acquit the guilty (Isa. 5:23), to slay the innocent (Deut. 27:25). The law of Moses prohibited it (Exod. 23:8; Deut. 16:19), and those who take a bribe are described as cursed (Deut. 27:25). The prophets denounced it (Isa. 1:23; Amos 5:12; Mic. 3:11; 7:3). Rulers (Exod. 18:21; Isa. 1:23; Ezek. 22:12; Mic. 3:11; 7:3) and judges (2 Chr. 19:7) were especially given to it. The God of Israel is not partial and does not take a bribe (Deut. 10:17). The person who is approved by God does not take bribes (Ps. 15:5; Prov. 15:27; Isa. 33:15).

brick. Building material made of clay dried in the sun. The word for "brick" in Hebrew (*lĕbēnâ H4246*) is derived from the verb "to be white" (cf. LEBANON, so named for its snow-clad mountaintops). The very name would lead us to expect the oriental bricks to be whitish in color, rather than red like our more common bricks. The earliest mention of brick in the Bible (Gen. 11:3) shows that the molding of clay into bricks and its

B

thorough burning were known when the Tower of BABEL was built, possibly not more than a century after Noah's flood.

Owing to the prevalence of stone in EGYPT and its comparative rarity in lower MESOPOTAMIA, the use of brick for building was much more common in CHALDEA than in Egypt, though the record of the bondage of Israel (Exod. 1:11-14; 5:7-19) shows that at least some cities in Egypt were built of brick rather than of stone. In fact, the ruins of PITHOM have been found with three grades of brick *in situ:* bricks with binding material of straw at the bottom; above them, bricks made with stubble; and at the top, bricks of pure clay with no binding material at all. The ancient bricks were generally square instead of oblong and were much larger than ours, about 13 x 13 x 3.5 in. (33 x 33 x 9 cm.). Before being baked they were often stamped with the name of the monarch. Much of the ancient brickwork was of bricks merely baked in the sun, especially in Egypt, but at BABYLON the bricks were thoroughly burned.

Brickmaking is mentioned in DAVID's time (2 Sam. 12:31), and centuries later NAHUM, taunting the Ninevites, tells them: "Work the clay, tread the mortar, repair the brickwork!" (Nah. 3:14). In Isa. 9:9-10 the "pride and arrogance of heart" of the Israelites is rebuked because they intended to replace the overthrown bricks with stone, even as many a modern city has been rebuilt after a catastrophe. The sin was not in their desire for improvement, but in their impious and profane pride.

bride, bride-chamber, bridegroom. See WEDDING.

bride of Christ. See CHURCH.

bridle. See BIT AND BRIDLE.

brier. See PLANTS.

brimstone. Modern translations prefer the more common term "sulfur," referring to a nonmetallic element with a yellow color and usually found as well-formed crystals. It is soft and burns with a blue flame forming a noxious gas. The biblical use of the term is generally connected with judgment, as when the Lord rained "brimstone and fire" on SODOM and GOMORRAH (Gen. 19:24 KJV; NIV, "burning sulfur") or as when the dust of EDOM was to be turned into brimstone (Isa. 34:9 KJV). In the book of Revelation, burning sulfur is mentioned repeatedly in connection with divine punishment (Rev. 14:10 et al.).

Broad Wall. A portion of the walls of JERUSALEM in times of NEHEMIAH (Neh. 3:8; 12:38). It was apparently in the NW section of the city, between the Tower of the OVENS and the EPHRAIM GATE. In the course of exacavations during the 1970s, an impressive eighth-century B.C. wall (about 210 ft./64 m. long and 23 ft./7m. thick) was discovered in what is now the Jewish Quarter. It is very likely the wall that was built first by HEZEKIAH (2 Chr. 32:5).

broidered. See EMBROIDERY.

bronze. See MINERALS.

bronze sea. Name given to a very large laver (c. 15 ft. or 4.5 m.) that SOLOMON placed in front of the TEMPLE for washing the sacrifices and the bodies of the priests (2 Ki. 25:13; 1 Chr. 18:8; Jer. 52:17; KJV, "brasen sea"). It is also known as the "molten sea" (1 Ki. 7:23; 2 Chr. 4:2; NIV, "Sea of cast metal"). The tank was mounted on a base consisting

Mud bricks on stone foundation courses at the Beersheba excavation.

© Dr. James C. Martin

of twelve oxen, also cast from bronze, three facing toward each of the four cardinal points of the compass. The metal was cast a handbreadth in thickness, and the lip was curved over like the flower of a lily.

bronze snake. According to Num. 21:4-9, the people of Israel, as they were preparing to travel around the land of EDOM, complained against God and MOSES because they had no bread or water. In judgment God sent venomous snakes against them. When the people confessed their sin, Moses made a snake made of bronze and set it on a pole so that "anyone who is bitten can look at it and live." With the passage of time, however, Israel lost sight of the symbolical and typical function of the statue. By the later eighth century B.C., the Israelites were burning INCENSE to it, as if it were in itself a deity, and during HEZEKIAH's religious reform it was broken into pieces (2 Ki. 18:4; KJV, "brasen serpent").

brook. The usual Hebrew word for "brook" is *naḥal H5707* (to be distinguished from the similar-sounding term for "river," *nāhār H5643*). It is often rendered "valley," and this English term seems best in view of the places so named, such as the Valley of ESHCOL (Num. 13:23) and the Valley of SOREK (Jdg. 16:4). The Arabic word *wadi* is more accurate, since some "brooks" are nothing more than dry washes except during flood season. This feature is illustrated well in 2 Ki. 3:16-17. The Spanish *arroyo* describes the same phenomenon in the SW United States. The fact that the valley between JERUSALEM and the MOUNT OF OLIVES is called the Brook KIDRON is ample evidence that it may refer to a gully in which water rarely or never runs. Even though water is only occasionally present in some brooks, the dry bed is often the best place to dig for water or to plant. In some passages, the NIV renders the Hebrew term with "gorge," "ravine," etc. See also RIVER; VALLEY.

broom (tree). See PLANTS.

brother. This term is applied to various relationships. (1) A male person related to another person or other persons by having the same parents (Gen. 27:6) or only the same father or mother (28:2; Jdg.

8:19). (2) A member of the same tribe (2 Sam. 19:12); (3) A citizen of the same country (Exod. 2:11; Acts 3:22). (4) An ally (Amos 1:9). (5) A kindred nation (Num. 20:14). (6) Someone spiritually akin (Matt. 12:50; 23:8), used especially among Christians (Acts 9:17; 1 Cor. 6:6). (7) Someone of equal rank or office (1 Ki. 9:13; Ezra 3:2 KJV).

brothers of the Lord. The term is used in the NT in identifying four men: JAMES, JOSEPH, SIMON, and JUDE (Matt. 13:55; Mk. 6:3). It is also used collectively of a group of men whose names are not given (Jn. 7:3; Acts 1:14; 1 Cor. 9:5). The precise relationship of these men to Jesus has been much debated, with three different answers offered: (1) They were younger children of Mary and Joseph; this is suggested by the reference to Mary's "first" child (Lk. 2:7) but is rejected by those who insist that Mary remained a virgin throughout her life. (2) They were Joseph's children from a previous marriage; this view is possible, but it has no support in the NT. (3) They were cousins of Jesus, sons of his aunt Mary wife of CLEOPAS (Jn. 19:25), described as "the mother of James the Younger and of Joses" (Mk. 15:40); but if this James is the apostle listed in Mk. 3:18, Mary's husband was Alphaeus, not Cleopas, and this could be explained only if Alphaeus and Cleopas were alternative names for the same man, or if Mary had been married twice. Most Protestant scholars argue that the first option above is the most natural.

Bubastis. byoo-bas'tis (Gk. *Boubastis*; LXX *Boubastos*). A major city in EGYPT (Ezek. 30:17 NIV). See PI BESETH.

bucket. A pail made of leather used for drawing water from a WELL or CISTERN. It had two crosspieces at the top to keep it open. Such buckets are still in use in Palestine. The term is used figuratively in the OT (Num. 24:7; Isa. 40:15).

buckler. See ARMS AND ARMOR.

build, building. See ARCHITECTURE.

Bukki. buhk'i (Heb. *buqqî H1321*, short form of BUKKIAH). **(1)** Son of Jogli; as a leader from the tribe of DAN, he was one of the men entrusted with the division of the land of Canaan among the Israelites (Num. 34:22).

(2) Son of Abishua, descendant of LEVI through KOHATH, and ancestor of EZRA (1 Chr. 6:5, 51; Ezra 7:4).

Bukkiah. buh-ki´uh (Heb. *buqqiyyāhû H1322*, possibly "proved of Yahweh"). One of the fourteen sons of HEMAN, a Levite; he received the sixth lot that determined his duties in the temple (1 Chr. 25:4, 13). Along with the sons of ASAPH and JEDUTHUN, the sons of Heman were involved in "the ministry of prophesying, accompanied by harps, lyres and cymbals" (v. 1).

Bul. bool (Heb. *bûl H1004*, possibly "autumn rain" or "harvest"). The name of the eighth month of the year (corresponding to late October and early November), according to the preexilic Canaanite system of names. It occurs only once, in dating the completion of Solomon's TEMPLE (1 Ki. 6:38). See CALENDAR.

bull. See ANIMALS.

bullock. See ANIMALS.

bulrush. See ARK OF BULRUSHES; PLANTS.

Bunah. byoo´nuh (Heb. *bûnâ H1007*, possibly "intelligence"). Son of JERAHMEEL and descendant of JUDAH through PEREZ and HEZRON (1 Chr. 2:25).

Bunni. buhn´i (Heb. *bunnî H1221*, possibly short form of BENAIAH). (1) A LEVITE who was present at EZRA's public reading of the law (Neh. 9:4).

(2) An ancestor of a certain Shemaiah; the latter was one of the Levites who chose to live in Jerusalem at the time of NEHEMIAH (Neh. 11:15).

(3) A leader of the people who sealed the covenant with Nehemiah (Neh. 10:15).

burden. That which is laid on an animal or person in order to be carried. The word translates a variety of Hebrew and Greek terms. When literally used, it is easily understood and needs no special comment. Figuratively, it can refer to responsibility (Num. 11:11; Matt. 11:30) or to sorrow (Ps. 55:22 KJV; NIV, "cares"). The KJV uses "burden" also in passages where the Hebrew word (prob. a homonym) has the different meaning of "divine pronouncement, oracle" (Isa. 13:1 et al.).

burial. The act of placing a dead body in a tomb, in the earth, or in the sea, generally with appropriate ceremonies, as opposed to exposure to the beasts or abandonment or burning. Various peoples, notably the Egyptians, who believed that their dead would live and practice ordinary human occupations in "the land of the dead," often went to great lengths to preserve the bodies of their departed loved ones. They sometimes placed with the mummy tools or instruments or weapons, and occasionally killed and buried a wife or a servant to accompany the one whom they had buried.

Partly because of God's declaration to fallen Adam, "For dust you are and to dust you will return" (Gen. 3:19), the people of Israel almost always buried their dead; and because the land of Canaan had so many caves, these places were very frequently used as places of burial. Probably the prevailing motive for our respect for the dead, and even for the place of burial, is the sense of decency and our feeling of love for the person, often without regarding the fact that the real person has gone and that only his former "residence" remains.

The story of the treatment of the bodies of SAUL and of his sons sheds light on the subject. The PHILISTINES beheaded the bodies, exhibiting the heads throughout their land and fastening Saul's body to the city wall of BETH SHAN (1 Sam. 31:8-13). The men of Israel rescued the bodies, burned them, reverently buried the bones under a tree, and mourned seven days.

It is remarkable that although God had given to ABRAHAM the deed of the land of Canaan (Gen. 15:18-21), the only land that the patriarchs possessed before JOSHUA's time was the burial places for the original family: a cave at HEBRON and a field at SHECHEM (cf. Gen. 23; 49:29-32; Josh. 24:32-33). In Canaan, in ancient times and in the more primitive parts of the land even today, there was (and is) no embalming in most cases but immediate burial to avoid unpleasant odors (Acts 5:5-10) and ceremonial uncleanness (Num. 19:11-

22). In the time of Christ, the bodies were wrapped in clean linen (Matt. 27:57-60), and spices and ointments were prepared (Lk. 23:56).

The strange story of the dead Moabite reviving when he touched the bones of ELISHA (2 Ki.

© Dr. James C. Martin

This tomb, with its visible headrests, borders the SW corner of the Hinnom Valley in Jerusalem and dates to the time of Jeremiah.

13:20-21) shows not only the speedy decomposition of a body but also the informality of burials in times of war or necessity. The still stranger story of the disobedient prophet (1 Ki. 13) shows how a heathen altar could be defiled by burning bones on it (13:1-3) and shows also the desire of a prophet to be buried near another whom he honored (13:30-31). In several cases of sinful rulers, ordinary burial was denied to their bodies: the dogs ate JEZEBEL (2 Ki. 9:10); JEHORAM of Judah, who died with incurable diseases, was not buried with the kings (2 Chr. 21:18-20); UZZIAH was buried in a field, not in the tombs of the kings (26:23); and JEHOIAKIM was given the burial of a donkey (Jer. 22:18-19).

burning. The burning of the SACRIFICE (Lev. 1-7) was a symbolic way of conveying the offering, and thus the commitment of the sacrificer, to God: as the sacrifice was consumed and the smoke and odor arose to heaven, it symbolized the entrance into the divine presence. Burning as a means of judgment has been literally carried out in history, and it will again at the consummation of all things (Lev. 10:1-2; Josh. 6:24; 8:28; 1 Cor. 3:13). God himself in holiness and eternal might is represented by

the BURNING BUSH (Exod. 3:1-3), by the burning coals of Ezekiel's vision (Ezek. 1:13), and by the continually burning lamp of the sanctuary: "God is a consuming fire" (Heb. 12:29). Burning can also indicate zeal and passion, both in positive and in negative contexts (Lk. 24:32; Jn. 5:35; Rom. 1:27; 1 Cor. 7:9).

burning bush. A thorny bush that MOSES saw burning and from which he heard the Lord speak (Exod. 3:2-3; Deut. 33:16; Mk. 12:26). Many attempts have been made to identify the plant, but without success. The incident is important because it is the first direct statement in the Bible linking HOLINESS with the very life of God and making fire the symbol of that holiness. The flame that needs no fuel to maintain it ("the bush ... did not burn up") represents the eternal, self-sufficient life of God. Where this God is, holiness is, and sinners can draw near only by meeting the conditions God imposes ("take off your sandals"). This is the seed from which the whole Mosaic system grows. The unapproachable fire is seen in all its majesty on Mount SINAI (Exod. 19:18), and this in turn is reflected in the undying fire on the altar (Lev. 6:9). The same God who made the simple provision for Moses to draw nigh (Exod. 3:5; cf. Josh. 5:13) provided the sacrifices.

burnt Offering. See SACRIFICE AND OFFERINGS.

bush. See PLANTS.

bushel. See WEIGHTS AND MEASURES.

butler. See OCCUPATIONS AND PROFESSIONS.

butter. This English term is used by the KJV to render a Hebrew word that refers to curdled milk, comparable to yogurt. Modern versions usually render the Hebrew term with "curds" (e.g., Deut. 32:14; 2 Sam. 17:29; Isa. 7:15, 22) or "cream" (Job 20:17 and 29:6 NIV), though the word "butter" is sometimes retained (e.g., Prov. 30:33 NIV). After the milk has been churned and the "butter" (in our sense of the word) produced, the butter is boiled and the curds separated from the almost pure oil; this is poured into a goatskin and kept until slightly rancid (to Western taste) and then is used with food, but more generally for frying eggs or vegetables. See FOOD.

Buz. buhz (Heb. *bûz H998*, perhaps "contempt"; gentilic *bûzî H1000*, "Buzite"). **(1)** Son of NAHOR (ABRAHAM's brother) by MILCAH (Gen. 22:21).

(2) A descendant of GAD and ancestor of Abihail (1 Chr. 5:14).

(3) A tribe or city-state in ARABIA, listed with DEDAN and TEMA as objects of God's judgment (Jer. 25:23). It was apparently the home of ELIHU, whose father is called Barakel the Buzite (Job 32:2, 6). It is debated whether the Buzites were descendants of #1 above. Buz is usually connected with the E Arabian town of Bazu, mentioned in Assyrian texts.

Buzi. by*oo'zi* (Heb. *bûzî H1001*, perhaps "contempt" or "of Buz"). The father of EZEKIEL (Ezek. 1:3). It is unclear whether this name should be related to the Arabian tribe of BUZ.

buzzard. See BIRDS.

Byblos. See GEBAL.

byways. This English term is used by some versions to render a Hebrew phrase meaning "winding paths" (Jdg. 5:6). Cf. also the term "bypaths" to render a different Hebrew phrase that describes the way an erring people follow, in contrast to an open way or highway (Jer. 18:15).

cab. See WEIGHTS AND MEASURES.

Cabbon. kab'uhn (Heb. *kabbôn H3887*, derivation uncertain). TNIV Kabbon. A city in the SHEPHELAH, near LACHISH (Josh. 15:40). Some scholars have associated Cabbon with MACBENAH (Caleb's descendant according to 1 Chr. 2:49, but usually taken as a reference to a town) on the assumption that the two names are from the same Hebrew root.

Cabul. kay'buhl (Heb. *kābûl H3886*, meaning uncertain). TNIV Kabul. **(1)** A town on the E boundary of the tribe of ASHER (Josh. 19:27). It is usually identified with modern Kabul, nestled among the hills c. 9 mi. (15 km.) ESE of Acco (Acre), but another proposal is nearby Khirbet Ras ez-Zetun (Rosh Zayith).

(2) The "Land of Cabul" (1 Ki. 9:13) was a district in N GALILEE comprising twenty towns (presumably including the town of Cabul; see #1 above) that SOLOMON ceded to HIRAM for his help in building the TEMPLE at Jerusalem. When Hiram saw the cities he was so dissatisfied that he called them "Land of Cabul," apparently because this name can be interpreted to mean "like nothing," that is, worthless. The reason for Hiram's reaction is unclear, but it seems from 2 Chr. 8:2 that Hiram returned these cities and that Solomon rebuilt them.

Caesar. see'zuhr (Gk. *Kaisar G2790*). Cognomen of the Julian family, whose most eminent member was Caius Julius Caesar, the great soldier, statesman, orator, and author (102-44 B.C.). The name was then taken as a title by each of the Roman emperors; thus, for example, the first emperor was known as AUGUSTUS CAESAR. The title is mentioned by our Lord (Lk. 20:22-25) both literally as referring to TIBERIUS and figuratively as meaning any earthly ruler. The name Caesar came to be used as a symbol of the state in general and is often used in this sense in the NT (Matt. 22:17, 21; Mk. 12:14, 16-17; Lk. 20:22, 25).

Caesarea. ses'uh-ree'uh (Gk. *Kaisareia G2791*). Also known as Caesarea Maritima ("by the sea") to distinguish it from CAESAREA PHILIPPI. The city was built between 25 and 13 B.C. by HEROD the Great at a vast cost and named in honor of his

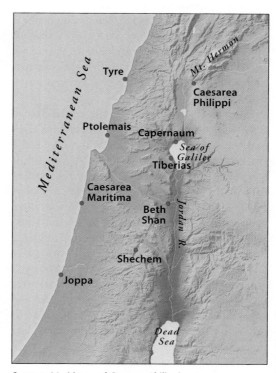

Caesarea Maritima and Caesarea Philippi.

235

C

© Dr. James C. Martin

The stadium at Caesarea Maritima. (View to the N.)

patron AUGUSTUS CAESAR. It lay on the coast of the Mediterranean about 25 mi. (40 km.) NW of the town of SAMARIA. Herod intended it as the port of his capital, and great stone blocks were used to top the reefs that helped to form the harbor. It is a rewarding but demanding site for archaeological investigation. Underwater explorations during the 1970s and 1980s demonstrated that the construction of the harbor under Herod was an engineering marvel.

Being the military headquarters for the Roman forces and the residence of the procurators, Caesarea was the home of CORNELIUS, in whose house PETER first preached to the Gentiles (Acts 10). It was the place of residence of PHILIP the evangelist with his four unmarried prophesying daughters (8:40; 21:8-9), who entertained PAUL and LUKE and their party on their return from the third missionary journey. Later it was the enforced residence of Paul while he was a prisoner for two years, and where he preached before King AGRIPPA II (23:31—26:32). The Jewish war that JOSEPHUS described with such power and pathos, and that culminated in the destruction of Jerusalem, had its origin in a riot in Caesarea. Here Vespasian was proclaimed emperor of Rome in the year A.D. 69, while he was engaged in the Jewish war. Caesarea became the birthplace of the church historian

Eusebius (c. 260) and the seat of his bishopric. It is still called Kaysariyeh.

Caesarea Philippi. ses´us-ree´uh-fil´i-pi´ (Gk. *Kaisareia tēs Philippou*). A town at the extreme N boundary of Palestine, about 30 mi. (50 km.) inland from TYRE and 50 mi. (80 km.) SW of DAMASCUS. It lies in the beautiful hill country on the southern slopes of Mount HERMON and was probably near the scene of Jesus' TRANSFIGURATION (cf. Matt. 16:13—17:8; Mk. 8:27—9:8). The town was very ancient, and some have speculated that it may be the BAAL GAD of Josh. 12:7; 13:5. Caesarea Philippi was a center of worship of the heathen god Pan, and thus the city came to be known as Paneas, whence the modern Arabic name Banias. AUGUSTUS CAESAR presented it, with the surrounding country, to HEROD the Great, who built a temple there in honor of the emperor. Herod's son, PHILIP the tetrarch, enlarged the town and named it Caesarea Philippi to distinguish it from the other Caesarea. It lies at the easternmost of the four sources of the JORDAN, and nearby these streams unite to form the main river. It was at a secluded spot near here that the Lord began to prepare his disciples for his approaching sufferings and death and resurrection, and that PETER made his famous confession (Matt. 16:13-17).

Caesar's household. A term referring to the imperial staff, composed of both slaves and freedmen; it was more commonly applied to the imperial civil service, usually at ROME, but also throughout the empire, particularly in the imperial provinces. When PAUL says to the PHILIPPIANS, "All the saints send you greetings, especially those who belong to Caesar's household" (Phil. 4:22), it is natural to infer that the apostle was writing from Rome. Some scholars, however, have argued that the epistle may have been written while he was imprisoned elsewhere (EPHESUS and CAESAREA have been suggested).

cage. This English term is used in Bible versions to render two rare Hebrew words that refer to an enclosure for confining birds (Jer. 5:27) or animals (Ezek. 19:9; Heb. *sûgar H6050*). The KJV uses the word also in the NT, where BABYLON is described as "a cage of every unclean and hateful bird" (Rev. 18:2; the NIV and other versions have "haunt").

Caiaphas. kay'uh-fuhs (Gk. *Kaiaphas G2780*). The official high priest during the ministry and trial of Jesus (Matt. 26:3, 57; Lk. 3:2; Jn. 11:49; 18:13-14, 24, 28; Acts 4:6). During the intertestamental period, the high priesthood evolved into a political office, the priests still coming from the descendants of AARON but being generally appointed for worldly considerations. When Pompey gained control of JUDEA in 63 B.C., the Romans took over the authority of appointing not only the civil rulers (e.g., HEROD) but the high priests also, with the result that the office declined spiritually. ANNAS, father-in-law of Caiaphas (Jn. 18:13), had been high priest by appointment of the Roman governor from A.D. 7 to 14 (see Lk. 3:2), and though three of his sons succeeded for a short period, Caiaphas held the office from 18 to 36, with Annas still a sort of "high priest emeritus."

After Jesus had raised LAZARUS from the dead (Jn. 11), many of the Jews believed in him (11:45-46), but some through jealousy reported the matter to the PHARISEES. With the chief priests they gathered a council, fearing, or pretending to fear, that if Jesus were let alone many would accept him and the Romans would destroy what was left of Jewish autonomy. Caiaphas declared that it would be better for Jesus to die than for the whole nation to be destroyed (11:41-53). When our Lord was betrayed into the hands of his enemies, the Roman soldiers and the Jewish officers took him first to the house of Annas, where by night he was given the pretense of a trial (18:12-23). Then Annas sent him bound to Caiaphas before whom the "trial" continued (18:24-27). Afterward he was delivered to PILATE because the Jews could not legally execute him. As a SADDUCEE opposed to the teaching of the RESURRECTION, Caiaphas took a leading part in the persecution of the early church. In Acts 4:6 he is named second among the Sadducean leaders who assembled to try Peter and John. That Annas rather than Caiaphas is here called "the high priest" is problematic, but seems to be further evidence of the continued power of the former high priest. Caiaphas is also probably the high priest mentioned in Acts as the bitter persecutor of the Christians (Acts 5:17-21, 27; 7:1; 9:1).

Cain. kayn (Heb. *qayin H7803*, possibly "metal worker," but by popular etymology, "acquired" [Gen. 4:1]; Gk. *Kain G2782*). (1) The first son of ADAM and EVE, and a farmer by occupation. As an offering to God, he brought some of the fruits of the ground, while his brother brought an animal sacrifice (Gen. 4). Angry when his offering was not received (Heb. 11:4 shows that he lacked a right disposition toward God), he murdered his brother. He added to his guilt before God by denying the act and giving no evidence of repentance. He fled to the land of NOD and there built a city, becoming the ancestor of a line that included JABAL, forefather of tent-dwelling cattle-keepers; JUBAL, forefather of musicians; TUBAL-CAIN, forefather of smiths; and LAMECH, a man of violence. Cain is described in the NT as being "of the evil one" (1 Jn. 3:12; cf. Jude 11).

(2) Alternate form of KAIN.

Cainan. kay'nuhn (Gk. *Kainam G2783*). (1) Son of ARPHAXAD and grandson of SHEM, included in Luke's GENEALOGY OF JESUS CHRIST (Lk. 3:36; this name is not found in the MT, but see the LXX at Gen. 10:24 and 11:12).

(2) Alternate form of KENAN.

cake. See RAISIN CAKE.

C

Calah. kay′luh (Heb. *kelaḥ H3996*, possibly "strength"). One of the capital cities of Assyria. Now called Nimrud and located in the NE angle of the confluence of the Tigris and Upper Zab rivers, it is c. 25 mi. (40 km.) S of Nineveh on the E bank of the Tigris. According to Gen. 10:8-12, Calah was built by Nimrod (the KJV and other versions understand the Heb. text to mean that it was built by Asshur). The city was apparently rebuilt by Shalmaneser I (1274-1245 B.C.) and then later abandoned until it was restored by Ashurnasirpal (883-859). Calah fell to the Medes and Babylonians in 612 B.C. Excavations at this site have revealed immense statuary in the form of winged bulls and lions. Also discovered at Calah was the famous Black Obelisk of Shalmaneser III that portrays, among other captives, Jehu of Israel.

calamus. See PLANTS.

Calcol. kal′kol (Heb. *kalkōl H4004*, possibly "sustaining"). TNIV Kalkol. Son or descendant of Mahol and one of the sages whom Solomon surpassed in wisdom (1 Ki. 4:31; KJV, "Chalcol"). Many believe, however, that "the sons of Mahol" refers to a guild of musicians. Calcol is elsewhere listed as a son or descendant of Zerah, Judah's son by Tamar (1 Chr. 2:6; cf. v. 4). See also Darda; Ethan.

caldron. A large earthenware or metal vessel in which meat is to be boiled; the word is sometimes translated "pot" in modern versions (Jer. 52:18, 19; Ezek. 11:3, 7, 11).

Caleb. kay′luhb (Heb. *kālēb H3979*, "dog"). (1) The son of Jephunneh the Kenizzite; he was a leader of the tribe of Judah whom Moses sent with eleven others to spy out the Promised Land (Num. 13:6). Most of the spies brought back a pessimistic report. Their names are almost forgotten; but two heroes of faith, Caleb and Joshua, who encouraged the people to go up and take the land, are still remembered. Because Israel in cowardice adopted the majority report, God imposed on them forty years of "wandering" in the wilderness until that generation died out. Caleb was forty years old when the spies were sent (Josh. 14:7). At the age of eighty-five, when the land of Canaan was being distributed, he asked for, and received, Hebron and the hill country. There lived the fearful Anakites who had terrorized ten of the spies. Later he became father-in-law of Othniel, the first of the "judges," by giving him Acsah his daughter (Jdg. 1:12-15, 20).

(2) Son of Hezron and descendant of Judah through Perez (1 Chr. 2:9 [KJV and other versions, "Chelubai" or "Kelubai"]; 18-19, 42).

Caleb Ephrathah. kay′luhb-ef′ruh-thuh (Heb. *kālēb ʾeprātâ H3980*). Possibly a village, otherwise unknown, where Hezron is said to have died (1 Chr. 2:24). Many scholars, however, emend the Hebrew on the basis of the Septuagint and read, "After the death of Hezron, Caleb went in to Ephrathah, the wife of Hezron his father" (thus RSV). See Ephrath.

calendar. A system of measuring time by reference to recurring phenomena or to computed intervals. Calendars are devised as a trustworthy means for recording history and determining dates in advance for social, civic, and religious anniversaries, and for economic planning. Comparatively little is known of the calendar of the early Israelites from the patriarchs to the exile, but a critical study of the biblical records and archaeological discoveries is rewarding. During the Bible period, time was reckoned primarily on astronomical observations. The early Chaldean and Egyptian astrologers became quite learned in the movements of astronomical bodies. Their discoveries, as well as those of other ANE neighbors, made their impact on the Jewish calendar. From earliest times the sun and moon were determinants of periods: days, months, and years.

I. Day. In the biblical record of time, days begin with the account of creation (Gen. 1:5, 8, et al.). While the Babylonian day began at sunrise, the Bible reckoned the twenty-four-hour span from sunset to sunset (Deut. 23:11), probably taking its clue from the repeated phrase in the creation narrative. Nehemiah 4:21 suggests that the end of one day and the beginning of the next was actually marked by the appearance of the stars. Days of the week were not named but were designated by ordinal numbers. The term SABBATH was not so much the name of the seventh day as it was a sacred designation.

Days were also subdivided in a manner set forth in the creation account. And God said, "Let there be lights in the expanse of the sky to separate the day from the night ... the greater light to govern the day" (Gen. 1:14-16; see also Num. 9:16; Ruth 3:13). In the OT the day, as distinguished from the night, was not divided into exact periods but by broad terms such as evening, morning, midday, and (literally) "between the evenings" (e.g., Exod. 12:6). The division of the day into hours is ancient in Babylonia, and Isa. 39:8 (cf. 2 Ki. 20:9-10) shows that timing devices were known among the Hebrews as well. Babylonians divided the day by sunwatches into twelve equal parts, which were subdivided by the sexagenary system into minutes and seconds.

The Egyptians divided the day plus the night into twenty-four hours, for which they had at least two calibrated measuring devices. One was a shadow clock, comprised of a horizontal piece of wood with markings to which was attached at one end a short T-like piece, set toward the E in the morning and toward the W in the afternoon. A specimen dating about 1400 B.C. is now in the Berlin Museum. Another Egyptian timepiece was the water-clock, clepsydra, the oldest-known specimen of which dates from the reign of Amenhotep III. It is of alabaster, shaped like a flower-pot, with calibrated marks inside and a small aperture near the bottom through which the water gradually flowed out.

Early Hebrews divided the night into three watches: "the morning watch" (Exod. 14:24); "the middle watch" (Jdg. 7:19); and "at the beginning of the watches" (Lam. 2:19 NRSV). The Romans divided the night into four watches, from which

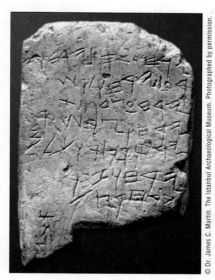

One of the earliest Hebrew texts (10th cent. B.C.), this limestone inscription discovered at Gezer lists the agricultural phases of the year.

© Dr. James C. Martin. The Istanbul Archaeological Museum. Photographed by permission.

Jesus drew an analogy in his eschatological warning of unpredictable time: ".... in the evening, or at midnight, or when the rooster crows, or at dawn" (Mk. 13:35). In the NT Jn. 11:9 records the rhetorical question of Jesus, "Are there not twelve hours of daylight?" (as distinguished from night). This kind of daily reckoning is also seen in the crucifixion account that mentions the third, sixth, and ninth hours (Mk. 15:25, 33, 34), referring approximately to 9 a.m., noon, and 3 p.m.

II. Week. The seven-day week appears to be of Semitic origin, but reckoned from various reference points. The Babylonians and Assyrians bound their weeks to the lunar cycle, corresponding with the four phases of the moon, and beginning anew with each new moon. The biblical week had its origin in the seven-day creation account and ran consecutively in a free-week system irrespective of lunar or solar cycles. This approach reflects the high esteem held for the Sabbath. The Egyptian week had ten days. In contrast to other time units (measured by the sun, moon, and stars), the week alone was not controlled by celestial bodies, but originated by divine command for man's economic, physical, and spiritual welfare.

Though God placed special emphasis on the seventh day at the time of creation (Gen. 2:2-3), the records are silent as to its observance during the long interlude between then and Moses' day. If the people of the pre-flood era or of the patriarchal period observed a "sabbath," there are no biblical records of it. However, since sabbath observance was kept alive in tradition until recorded in Genesis, it is a reasonable conjecture that it was preserved in practice also. Anyway, it was either revived or given special emphasis by Moses. The first recorded instance of the observance of "a day of rest, a holy Sabbath to the LORD" (Exod. 16:23) was when the Israelites were gathering manna in

C

the wilderness. Subsequently, the Sabbath became the most holy, as well as the most frequent, of all the sacred days observed by the Jews.

When Moses transmitted to Israel the fourth commandment in the Decalogue, "Remember the Sabbath day by keeping it holy" (Exod. 20:8), it was designated as a perpetual memorial sign of the COVENANT between God and his chosen people. "You must observe my Sabbaths. This will be a sign between me and you for the generations to come, so you may know that I am the LORD, who makes you holy" (31:12-13). It became a distinctive day with successive injunctions to observe it, describing the manner of doing so and the penalties for its desecration (23:12; 35:2-3). Emphasis on keeping the Sabbath is seen in the DEAD SEA SCROLLS and in the bitter accusations hurled at Jesus on this point (Mk. 2:24). Jesus confirmed the divine authenticity of this special day by going "into the synagogue, as was his custom" on the Sabbath day to teach, preach, and heal (Lk. 4:16), and by affirming, "The Sabbath was made for man" (Mk. 2:27a); but the additional comment, "not man for the Sabbath" (2:27b) reflects his displeasure with the misuse of the day by some of his contemporaries.

III. Month. This English term is derived from the word *moon*, and a similar connection is found in other languages, including Hebrew. Because of the moon's regular cycles, ancient peoples measured time by it and often worshiped it. The Egyptian moon-god Thoth was the god of measure. Even in Israel the moon and other heavenly bodies were worshiped at times (2 Ki. 23:5; Jer. 8:2). The early Israelites designated their months by names that they borrowed from the Canaanites or Phoenicians. These names had seasonal connotations as implied in the four that have survived in the early biblical records. ABIB (Exod. 13:4; Deut. 16:1), corresponding to Nisan in the later calendar, means "[month of the] ripening head of grain." ZIV (1 Ki. 6:1), corresponding to Iyyar, means "[month of] blossoms." ETHANIM (8:2), corresponding to Tishri, means "[month of] perennial streams." BUL (6:38), corresponding to Marchesvan, may mean "autumn rain" (being the first month in the rainy season) or "harvest."

The Gezer Calendar, dated in the tenth century B.C., gives an interesting glimpse into the agricultural life in Palestine at that early date. This archaeological find is a limestone plaque bearing a Hebrew inscription enumerating farm operations for eight months, mentioning sowing, flax harvest, barley harvest, and vine pruning. The prophet HAGGAI, about 520 B.C., at the time of the rebuilding of the temple, uses the numeral designation of months without names (Hag. 1:1; 2:1, 10), but his contemporary ZECHARIAH relates the numeral month to the Babylonian names, which came into popular use after the EXILE: "the eleventh month, the month of Shebat" (Zech. 1:7; see also 7:1). These postexilic names of months were not used for civil and historical purposes. The first month in the Jewish religious calendar, still used today, is Nisan (late March to early April), followed by Iyyar, Sivan, Tammuz, Ab, Elul, Tishri, Marchesvan (Cheshvan), Kislev, Tebeth, Shebat, and Adar. These, like the early Canaanite names, probably had their origin close to nature, but the derivation of some of them is uncertain. When religious responsibility was vested in the SANHEDRIN, three of their number, including the chief, were entrusted as watchmen to report the first appearance of the new moon. A declaration of the beginning of a new month was then quickly dispatched over the country by fire signals, and later by messengers.

IV. Year. The Hebrew calendar contained two concurrent years: the sacred year, beginning in the spring with the month Nisan, and the civil year, beginning in the fall with Tishri. The sacred year was instituted by Moses following the EXODUS and consists of twelve or thirteen lunar months of twenty-nine and a half days each. The civil year claims a more remote antiquity, reckoning from the creation, which according to tradition took place in autumn. It came into popular use in the third century of the Christian era. That this order of the year was kept by the ancient Hebrews is supported by the Mosaic command, "Celebrate the Feast of Ingathering at the end of the year, when you gather in your crops from the field" (Exod. 23:16). According to JOSEPHUS (*Ant.* 1.3.3), Moses ordered that the year of holy days and religious festivals begin with Nisan, the month in which the exodus transpired, but that he retained the old order of year for buying and selling and secular affairs. This observation has been confirmed by critical study and subsequent Jewish custom of keeping both a sacred and a civil year.

The Babylonians and Egyptians devised the intercalary month in order to reconcile the lunar and solar years. The Jewish leap years in their Metonic cycle of nineteen years were fixed, adding an intercalary month to the third, sixth, ninth, eleventh, fourteenth, seventeenth, and nineteenth years. If on the sixteenth of the month Nisan the sun had not reached the vernal equinox, the month was declared to be the second Adar and the following one Nisan. (In 46 B.C., a great advance was made by Julius CAESAR, whose calendar year contained 365 1/4 days; it had a discrepancy of eleven minutes in excess of the solar year, and so was superseded by the Gregorian Calendar in A.D. 1582, which has the very small error of gaining one day in 325 years.)

FEASTS and fasts were intricately woven into the lunar-solar sacred year. Three great historic feasts were instituted by Moses: Unleavened Bread, Harvest, and Ingathering (Exod. 23:14-16), corresponding roughly to Passover, Pentecost, and Thanksgiving. There were also numerous minor feasts. Beginning in the month Nisan or Abib (Neh. 2:1; Exod. 23:15), the sacred holidays of feasts and fasts came in the following order: On the fourteenth of Nisan, the Passover (Exod. 12:18-19; 13:3-10) was observed in preparation for the following week's festival and in eating the paschal supper (see Matt. 26:17-29). The fifteenth to twenty-first was the Feast of Unleavened Bread (Lev. 23:6), which included, on the fifteenth, a Sabbath, a day of holy convocation; on the sixteenth, Omer, or presenting the first sheaves of harvest; and on the twenty-first, another holy convocation. (The Christian Easter, fulfilling the Passover, is reckoned on solar-lunar cycles, coming on the first full moon on or after the vernal equinox, about March 21.).

On the tenth day of the second month, Iyyar (known formerly as Ziv), the Jews fasted in commemoration of the death of ELIJAH; the fourteenth was the Second or Little Passover for those who could not keep the regular one (cf. Num. 9:10-11); and on the sixteenth was a fast for the death of SAMUEL. Pentecost (also known as Feast of Weeks, or of Harvest, or of Firstfruits), when loaves as

firstfruits of the gathered harvest were presented (Exod. 23:16; 34:22; Lev. 23:17, 20; Num. 28:26; Deut. 16:9-10), was celebrated on the sixth or seventh of Sivan (Esth. 8:9; cf. Acts 2:1). This was the first of the two great agricultural feasts, coming at the end of seven weeks after the beginning of barley harvest, or fifty days after the Passover.

Next in annual order was the New Year (Rosh Hashanah), one of the most important feasts and possibly the oldest, observed on the first day of the civil year, in the month Tishri (formerly Ethanim or seventh month, 1 Ki. 8:2). It was called the Feast of Trumpets, a precursor of one emblem of modern New Year's celebrations. It was a day of holy convocation, of reading the law (Neh. 8:1-8), of blowing trumpets, of burnt offerings, of cereal offerings, and of profound solemnity, introducing "Ten Days of Repentance" (cf. Num. 29:1-16; Ezra 3:4-6). This protracted feast culminated in the Day of Atonement (Yom Kippur), the tenth of Tishri, the most holy day for the Jews. This is strictly a fast day and the only one commanded by law (Lev. 16:26-34; 23:27-32; called "the fast" in Acts 27:9). The Jewish calendar does not allow Rosh Hashanah or Yom Kippur to fall on the day before or the day after the Sabbath; the same is true for the seventh day of Tabernacles. From the fifteenth to the twenty-first of Tishri the Jews held the Feast of Ingatherings (or Tabernacles or Booths—recalling the wilderness wandering), when the firstfruits of wine and oil were offered (Exod. 23:16; Lev. 23:34-42; Deut. 16:13). It was a day of soulsearching and expiation of sins and of deep gratitude to God. It was the third of the three great feasts commanded by Moses, and the second of the two great agricultural feasts, corresponding to our modern Thanksgiving.

Winter holy days were few, though one of significance is mentioned in Jn. 10:22-23: "Then came the Feast of Dedication at Jerusalem. It was winter, and Jesus was in the temple area." Dedication of the temple was instituted by Judas MACCABEE in 164 B.C. This feast was held on the twenty-fifth of Kislev (Zech. 7:1). Besides the one divinely ordained fast, the Day of Atonement, there were minor fasts, some temporary (Ezra 9:5; Neh. 1:4) and some annual. One fast in memory of the destruction of Jerusalem by NEBUCHADNEZZAR

(2 Ki. 25:1-7), instituted after the exile, was observed on the ninth of Ab. Another, the fast of ESTHER, was observed on the thirteenth of Adar and was followed the next two days by the Feast of Purim.

V. Cycles. From God's hallowing of the seventh day there arose a special sacredness in relation to the number seven. Religious convocations and festivals were highly regarded on the seventh day (Sabbath), seventh week (Pentecost), seventh month (Trumpets), seventh year (sabbatical year), and seven times seven years (Jubilee). The sabbatical year was one of solemn rest for landlords, slaves, beasts of burden, and land, and of freedom for Hebrew slaves. Only what grew of itself on the farm and vineyard was to be gathered and consumed (Exod. 23:10-11; Lev. 25:3-7). The sabbatical and Jubilee years were synchronized with the civil or agricultural year, beginning in autumn. The Jubilee, every fiftieth year, following "seven weeks of years," was a hallowed year whose observance included family reunions, canceled mortgages, and the return of lands to their original owners (Lev. 25:8-17).

calf. See ANIMALS.

calf worship. A part of the religious worship of almost all ancient Semitic peoples. At least as early as the EXODUS, living bulls were worshiped in Egypt. The Babylonians looked on the bull as the symbol of their greatest gods. The bull was a sacred animal in PHOENICIA and SYRIA. Among the Semitic Canaanites the bull was the symbol of BAAL. It appears that the bull was in some way connected with the reproductive processes of plants and animals and with the sun. It symbolized strength, vigor, and endurance.

While MOSES was on the mountain receiving God's law, AARON made a golden image of a male calf in order that the people might worship the Lord under this form (Exod. 32:4). It is unlikely that the golden calf was a representation of an Egyptian deity; the feast held in connection with this worship was characterized as a "festival to the LORD" (32:5). Centuries later, after the division of the kingdom, JEROBOAM set up two golden calves in Israel, one at BETHEL and one at DAN (1 Ki.

12:28-29), because he feared that his people might desert him if they continued to worship in JERUSALEM. He was not trying to make heathenism the state religion, for the bull images were erroneously supposed to represent the God of Israel. In time, these images, at first recognized as symbols, came to be regarded as common idols (1 Ki. 12:30; Hos. 13:2).

Caligula. kuh-lig'yuh-luh. Gaius Julius Caesar Germanicus, nicknamed Caligula ("Little Boots") by the soldiers of the Rhine, was born in A.D. 12. After his father's death in 19 and his mother's arrest in 29, he lived with his uncle, the aging TIBERIUS. On the death of Tiberius in 37, Gaius was acclaimed emperor. In the first year of his principate Gaius was seriously ill, and on his recovery manifested those symptoms of sadistic madness and irresponsible folly for which he is chiefly remembered. Gaius's assassination in 41 ended a period of odious cruelty and dangerous tyranny, one effect of which would have been to anticipate the Jewish rebellion by thirty years. Gaius had given the order to set up his statue in the JERUSALEM Holy of Holies. It was only the brave temporizing of the legate of SYRIA, and Gaius's death, which averted disaster. PHILO JUDAEUS, the Alexandrian Jewish scholar, headed an embassy to Gaius in 39 or 40, and his vivid account (*Legatio ad Gaium*) sheds lurid light on the horrors of the young madman's brief principate.

call. This English term is very common in the Bible, representing over twenty Hebrew and Greek words, but principally with four different meanings: (1) To speak out in the way of prayer—"Call to me and I will answer you" (Jer. 33:3). (2) To summon or appoint—"I am calling all the tribes of the kingdoms of the north" (Jer. 1:15 NRSV). (3) To name a person or thing—"God called the light 'day'" (Gen. 1:5). (4) To invite people to accept salvation through Christ.

The last usage indicates a call by God through the HOLY SPIRIT; it is heavenly (Heb. 3:1) and holy (2 Tim. 1:9). This call comes to people in all situations and occupations (1 Cor. 1:26; 7:20). Often a distinction is made between the universal call ("many are called, but few are chosen," Matt. 22:14

NRSV) and the effectual call ("those he called, he also justified," Rom. 8:30). Christians are therefore described as "called" in the special sense that they have responded to the divine invitation (Rom. 1:6-7; 1 Cor. 1:2, 24; et al.).

Calneh, Calno. kal'neh, kal'noh (Heb. *kalnēh H4011*; *kalnô H4012*). TNIV Kalneh, Kalno. **(1)** One of the cities founded by NIMROD in SHINAR and cited in association with BABEL, ERECH, and AKKAD (Gen. 10:10). The location of the city, however, is unknown. As a result, some suggest a change in the Hebrew vowels, yielding the translation "all of them" (cf. NRSV).

(2) A city named "Calneh" appears in association with HAMATH and GATH (Amos 6:2). Elsewhere "Calno" is associated with CARCHEMISH (Isa. 10:9). Calneh and Calno are doubtless to be regarded as identical, but the contexts would seem to warrant a location to the N rather than in the area of Babel, Erech, and Akkad (see #1 above). Further support for a location in the N is claimed by those who believe that Calneh is the same as CANNEH (Ezek. 27:23). Many scholars identify Calneh with Kullania, a town mentioned in Assyrian documents in frequent association with Arpad. It is quite probably the modern Kullan Köy, located about 8 mi. (13 km.) NE of ALEPPO in SYRIA.

Calvary. See GOLGOTHA.

calves of our lips. The clause "so we will render the calves of our lips" is the KJV's rendering of a difficult Hebrew clause (Hos. 14:2 [Heb. v. 3]). The meaning is probably, "and instead of bulls, we will offer as sacrifice our lips in praise" (NIV, "that we may offer the fruit of our lips"; cf. Heb. 13:15).

camel. See ANIMALS.

camel's hair. A phrase mentioned only in Matt. 3:4 and Mk. 1:6, where we are told that JOHN THE BAPTIST wore a garment of that material. It is probable, however, that this was not a garment made of the relatively expensive woven camel's hair, but of dressed camel's skin. Such garments are still used in the Near East. Some think that Elijah's mantle was made of camel's hair (2 Ki. 1:8; cf. Zech. 13:4).

Camon. See KAMON.

camp, encampment. A group of tents intended for traveling or for temporary residence as in case of war—contrasted with villages, towns, or cities that are composed of houses and other more or less permanent buildings. The Hebrew word *maḥăneh H4722* occurs over two hundred times and is properly rendered "camp," but it is often translated "host" and occasionally "army," indicating the military purpose of the encampment. In Gen. 32:1-2, when the angels of God met JACOB, the patriarch exclaimed, "This is the camp of God!" and he named the place MAHANAIM, or "Two Camps," referring to God's host and his own.

In the wilderness the Israelites were given precise instructions as to the order and arrangements of their camp, both at rest and in traveling (Num. 2). The TABERNACLE in the center indicated the centrality of God in their life and worship. It was surrounded rather closely by the three families of the priests and Levites, and then farther back were the twelve tribes. In Deut. 23:9-14 the sanitary and ceremonial observances, which were used to keep the camp clean and wholesome, are given. Three tribes were grouped on each side of the tabernacle under the banners of the leading tribes: Judah eastward, with Issachar and Zebulun; Reuben southward, with Simeon and Gad; Ephraim westward, with Manasseh and Benjamin; and Dan northward, with Asher and Naphtali. When they marched, the Levites, carrying the tabernacle, occupied the center of the line. The high command was located there.

camphire. See PLANTS (under *henna*).

Cana. kay'nuh (Gk. *Kana G2830*, prob. "reed"). Cana of GALILEE is mentioned four times in the Gospel of John and nowhere else in Scripture. It was in the highlands of Galilee, as one had to go *down* from there to CAPERNAUM; but opinions differ as to its exact location. It may have been at Kefr Kenna, about 5 mi. (8 km.) NE of NAZARETH, or at Khirbet Qana, a little farther N. Here Jesus

The exposed bedrock (lower right of photo) reveals the partially excavated site of Khirbet Qana (prob. Cana of Galilee), situated on the lower slopes of the Bet Netofa ridge. (View to the NW.)

performed his first miracle, graciously relieving the embarrassment caused by the shortage of wine at a marriage feast (Jn. 2:1-11). It was here too that he announced to the nobleman from Capernaum the healing of his apparently dying son (4:46). NATHANAEL came from Cana (21:2).

Canaan, Canaanites. kay′nuhn, kay′nuh-n*i*ts (Heb. *kĕna‘an H4046*, gentilic *kĕna‘ănî H4050*; Gk. *Chanaan G5913* [KJV NT, "Chanaan"], gentilic *Chananaios G5914*). Fourth son of HAM, father of SIDON, and ancestor of many Canaanite people groups, such as the HITTITES, the JEBUSITES, and the AMORITES (Gen. 9:18; 10:6, 15-18). For reasons that are unclear, he received the curse from NOAH as a result of Ham's offense (9:22-27). In the Bible, the name is used almost always to designate the land W of JORDAN occupied by the Israelites at the time of the conquest, though in a wider sense it included part of SYRIA. The etymology of the name is unknown, but early Egyptian inscriptions use it for the coastland between EGYPT and ASIA MINOR. In the AMARNA letters of c. 1400 B.C. the name is applied to the Phoenician coast.

According to Jdg. 1:9-10, Canaanites lived throughout the land. According to some passages (Gen. 12:6; 24:3, 37; Josh. 3:10), the Canaanites included the whole pre-Israelite population, even E of the Jordan. The language of Canaan (Isa. 19:18) refers to the group of W Semitic languages of which Hebrew, Phoenician, and Moabite were dialects. The Canaanites were of Semitic stock and were part of a large migration of Semites from NE ARABIA in the third millennium B.C. They came under Egyptian control c. 1500. The Israelites were never able to exterminate the Canaanites completely, and many were undoubtedly absorbed by their Israelite conquerors. Their continued presence with their heathen practices created serious religious problems for the Hebrew nation.

The Canaanite social structure was akin to that which prevailed all over the ANE; that is, it was comprised of city states in which the king had wide powers to appoint and conscript his subjects for military service, to control lands and lease them for services rendered, to impose taxation of various kinds, and to compel his subjects to undertake public works (corvée). There were several strata in society, such as freemen, semifreemen (clients), and slaves. The slaves comprised war captives, foreign slaves, and native Canaanites who became slaves because of debt or unemployment, or because parents sold them or exposed them as children. Slaves might belong to the state, to the temple, to private landowners, or to craftsmen.

The economy was based on AGRICULTURE. All land was owned by the state, the temples, and private landowners, although tenant farmers possessed small areas. Since society was basically feudal, much of the land was held as a grant from the king. Members of the royal family, state officials, and others owed the king specified services and taxation in return for their lands. There was a severe difference in living standards between the upper class patricians and the wide range of lower-class people such as half-free serfs, slaves, etc. Some evidence of class distinction comes from excavations that reveal some fine houses and many inferior houses. The population was distributed in the larger towns and their numerous associated villages or suburbs (many references in Josh. 13-19).

The excavations at Ugarit (RAS SHAMRA) have revealed an unsuspected world of Canaanite literature. The texts, which date from the early fourteenth century B.C., are written on clay tablets in the special thirty-letter cuneiform alphabet. Among the more important epics are three: the Baal Epic, which recounts the deeds and fortunes of Baal or Hadad; the legend of Aqhat, the only son of the good King Danʾel; the story of King Keret, who was bereft of his family and took another wife by conquest, thus incurring the wrath of the gods. There are fragments of other stories as well as a wide variety of letters, treaties, etc. Important insights into Canaanite religious beliefs, and into numerous aspects of national and family life shine through these epics.

The OT gives hints of a Canaanite pantheon that is now known to have been extensive. The senior deity was EL, to whom matters were referred by other gods. For practical purposes, however, BAAL (Lord) was more significant. He is known in the OT in his various local manifestations as the fertility god par excellence and is to be equated with HADAD the storm god. Both he and DAGON had a temple in Ugarit. Among the goddesses were ANATH, ASHERAH, and ASHTORETH, deities of sex and war. At Ugarit there was a high priest and no less than twelve families of priests. In ancient times the king exercised some priestly

functions, which he retained in part in later times. Canaanite temples have been excavated in Syria and Palestine. Among the most famous of these is the Late Bronze Temple of LACHISH, the temples at MEGIDDO and JERICHO from c. 3000 B.C., three at Megiddo from c. 1900, two at BETH SHAN from the Late Bronze Age, and several important temples at HAZOR from the Late Bronze Age also.

Canaanite, Simon the. See CANANAEAN.

canals. This English term is used in Bible versions to translate the plural form of Hebrew *yeʾōr H3284* (Exod. 7:19; 8:5). The singular normally refers to the NILE, so the relevant passages indicate irrigation canals branching off from this river. Other Hebrew words for "river" are also rendered "canal" in the NIV (Ezra 8:15; Dan. 8:2-3, 6; et al.).

Cananaean. kayʹnuh-neeʹuhn (Gk. *Kananaios G2831*). Surname given to SIMON, one of Jesus' disciples (NRSV and other versions at Matt. 10:4; Mk. 3:18; NIV, "Simon the Zealot"). This epithet served to distinguish him from Simon PETER. The KJV, following many Greek MSS, reads the incorrect form "Canaanite," which properly means an inhabitant of CANAAN. The term "Cananaean" is rather a Greek transliteration of the Aramaic *qanʾān*, meaning "zealot, enthusiast." Accordingly, the Lukan lists have "the Zealot" (Lk. 6:15 and Acts 1:13; these passages are the basis for the NIV rendering in Matt. 10:4 and Mk. 3:18). Thus the identification of this Simon is essentially the same in all four accounts. The surname presumably was given to him because he had been a member of the ZEALOTS, a religio-political party in first-century Palestine.

cancer. See DISEASES.

Candace. kanʹduh-see (Gk. *Kandakē G2833*). TNIV Kandake. The title of the queen of ETHIOPIA, whose treasurer was baptized between JERUSALEM and GAZA by PHILIP the evangelist (Acts 8:26-27; see also ETHIOPIAN EUNUCH). By Ethiopia is meant the kingdom of Nubia in the N Sudan, whose capital was Meroē. Classical writers refer to several queens of Meroē in the first century B.C.

and the first century A.D. who had the title Candace (in the form Kadake). The Candace of Acts 8:27 was probably Amantitere, who ruled about A.D. 25-41. She and her husband built or added to several Nubian temples, and her pyramid and tomb have been discovered in Meroē.

candle. See LAMP.

candlestick. See LAMPSTAND.

cane. See PLANTS.

canker. See DISEASES.

cankerworm. See ANIMALS.

Canneh. kan'uh (Heb. *kannēh H4034*). TNIV Kanneh. A city in N MESOPOTAMIA, mentioned alongside HARAN and Eden (BETH EDEN) as places with which TYRE traded garments and fabric (Ezek. 27:23-24). Some scholars have identified Canneh with CALNEH (Amos 6:2). Others believe it is the same place as Kannuʾ, a city attested in Assyrian texts and apparently located on an important trade route on the E side of the TIGRIS, near ASSHUR. In either case, Canneh must have been a significant commercial center.

canonicity. The Greek word *kanōn G2834* means "measuring rule," hence more generally "rule" or "standard." In theology its chief application is to those books received as authoritative and making up our BIBLE. The Protestant canon includes thirty-nine books in the OT, twenty-seven in the NT. The Roman Catholic and Orthodox Canons add seven books and some additional pieces in the OT (See APOCRYPHA). The Jews accept as authoritative the same books of the OT as do Protestants.

It is commonly said that the Protestant test of canonicity is INSPIRATION. That is, Protestants accept into their canon those books they believe to be immediately inspired by God and therefore true, infallible, and inerrant, the very Word of God. To be sure, it is possible for an utterance or a writing to have been inspired by God but not divinely intended to be part of the canon (e.g., it is likely that the book of Isaiah does not include

every inspired message spoken by the prophet; and presumably, Paul's so-called "former letter" to the Corinthians [cf. 1 Cor. 5:9] was inspired even though it was not included in the NT). More important, some would argue that any "test" of canonicity necessarily elevates that test as a more ultimate criterion of authority than the Bible itself. The point that needs stressing, however, is that when the creeds of the Reformation age listed the books that were accepted as inspired, these were included not because of the decision of a church or council, but because the books themselves were recognized as true and inspired, having God for their author. The history of the acceptance of these books and the study of the principles on which this acceptance occurred is an important phase of Bible introduction.

I. The OT canon. The Jewish TALMUD names the books of the Hebrew canon in approximately the order found in our Hebrew Bibles today. By combining some of the books (e.g., 1 and 2 Samuel are regarded as one book, and so are the twelve Minor Prophets), the rabbis arrive at the number of twenty-four books. These were divided into five books of Torah or Law (Genesis to Deuteronomy), eight books of Prophets (the Former Prophets being Joshua, Judges, Samuel, and Kings; the Latter Prophets consisting of Isaiah, Jeremiah, Ezekiel, and the Twelve) and eleven books of Writings (Psalms, Proverbs, Job, Song of Songs, Ruth, Lamentations, Ecclesiastes, Esther, Daniel, Ezra-Nehemiah, Chronicles). The position of Chronicles at the end of the canon is reflected in Lk. 11:51, where ZECHARIAH (cf. 2 Chr. 24:20-22) is reckoned as the last martyr of pre-Christian times, as ABEL was the first. In earlier days they combined Ruth with Judges, and Lamentations with Jeremiah, thus making twenty-two books equivalent to the twenty-two letters in the Hebrew alphabet.

Origen, the Christian scholar of the third century, lists twenty-two OT books, but in the order of the SEPTUAGINT, not that of the Hebrew Bible (which is the order attested in the Talmud). Earlier, about 170, Melito of Sardis tells us that he went to Palestine to ascertain accurately the number of OT books. He lists the five books of the Law first, then the others follow in an order based on the Septuagint and rather similar to that of our English Bible. Before Melito, we have the vital witness of the Jewish historian JOSEPHUS. About A.D. 90 he wrote his work *Against Apion*. In it he says that the Jews receive twenty-two books: five of the Law of Moses, thirteen of prophecy, and four of hymns to God and precepts for life. These books, he says, the pious Jew would rather die than alter or deny. He says these books were written by Moses and the succeeding prophets from that time to the days of Artaxerxes (around 400 B.C.) and that other later books, not written by prophets, were not so highly regarded.

Some in the past have argued that the rabbis held a council at Jamnia around A.D. 90 to make formal decisions about the canon and that it was at this time that the Hebrew canon was officially closed. While it is true that for a number of decades after A.D. 70 Jewish sages gathered in Jamnia from time to time to debate a variety of problems, and that these meetings often led to decisions (whether by formal vote or by consensus), the use of such terms as *council* or *synod* is misleading. These gatherings should not be compared with the Christian ecumenical councils that reached decisions binding on the church as a whole. Moreover, there is no evidence that questions about the canon were a major concern when the rabbis met.

Earlier evidence on the OT canon gives us no listing but considerable valuable information. PHILO JUDAEUS, the Alexandrian philosopher of the first century A.D., evidently accepted the twenty-two Hebrew books, for he quotes from many of them and from them only, as authoritative. The NT evidence is in accord with this, for most of the OT books are quoted authoritatively. The NT gives no positive evidence on the order of the books, but it reveals in general a twofold division of the OT such as is found in Melito, rather than the threefold division. A dozen times the OT is referred to as the "Law and the Prophets" or "Moses and the Prophets." As is evident from NT usage, this twofold category included all twenty-two books. Only once does it adopt a threefold classification, "Moses, the Prophets and the Psalms" (Lk. 24:44; but cf. 24:27).

Pre-Christian evidence has been greatly augmented by the discovery in A.D. 1947 of the DEAD SEA SCROLLS of the Qumran community. Previously, only the apocryphal books and other Jewish writings were available. These sources occasionally quoted books of the OT, but not with great frequency. Of special importance was the prologue to Ecclesiasticus, dated in 132 B.C. Three times it refers to the "law, and the prophets, and the other books of our fathers." One time it refers to these as already translated into Greek—the LXX. Because of the antiquity of this witness, the threefold canon has been held to be original. The twofold canon as referred to in the NT was not then explained. The DSS, however, give four places where the OT is referred to in two categories, the Law and the Prophets, as is usual in the NT. That this twofold canon included all our present books seems apparent from the fact that the Qumran community quoted from most of the OT books, including those later classified in the third division of "Writings"; for example, even the book of Proverbs was treated as authoritative (cf. CD XI, 20). The DSS includes MSS of all the biblical books except Esther. Thus the twofold canon may be as early as, or possibly earlier than, the threefold.

From the above outline of evidence it is easily seen that the canonicity of the books of Tobit, Judith, Wisdom, Ecclesiasticus, Baruch, 1 and 2 Maccabees, and certain additions to Esther and Daniel, has no ancient authority and was not recognized by Christ, the apostles, or the Jewish people. The distinction between those books and the canonical OT writings was generally preserved by the Greek fathers; it was generally overlooked by the Latin fathers. Among the latter the outstanding exception was Jerome; his acquaintance with the Hebrew Bible enabled him to distinguish those books that belonged to the "Hebrew verity" from those of lesser authority. It was he who first called the latter the "apocryphal" books, meaning by that books that might be read in church "for example of life and instruction of manners," but not for the establishment of doctrine. Jerome's distinction was reaffirmed at the Reformation in the Anglican Articles of Religion (1562) and has been generally recognized by Lutherans. Those churches, however, that followed the Reformed tradition of Geneva tended to give no authoritative status at all to the Apocrypha. The Council of

Trent, by reaction to the Reformers, affirmed the full canonicity of most of the apocryphal books, which are referred to by the term *deuterocanonical* (i.e., recognized at a "second" or later time).

The fact is that those who spoke the word of God to Israel were called prophets. There is no record of any group of non-prophets who were inspired. Most of the OT books were clearly written by prophets. Also regarded as prophets were authors of some others, like Joshua and Proverbs, Song of Songs, most of the Psalms—at least they received revelations from God (Num. 12:6). For several books, information on authorship is lacking. Jewish tradition classifies the books of Joshua, Judges, Samuel, and Kings as "the Former Prophets." One has as much right to hold that Ruth, Job, Esther, or Chronicles were written by prophets as to say that Judges was. Apparently these books are included under the designation "Prophets" in the Qumran scrolls and in the NT. If books of prophetic origin were to be received by Israel, this is a practical test that would check on the authority of written teaching as well as oral (cf. Deut. 13:1-5; 18:15-22). On this basis it can be explained how it was that the writings of prophets were accorded prompt acceptance by the faithful (cf. Josh. 1:7, 8; Jer. 36:8-16; 26:18; Dan. 9:2). Hebrews 1:1 sums up the whole matter, "God spoke ... through the prophets."

II. The NT canon. Since the end of the fourth century there has been no question among most of the Christian churches as to which books belong in the NT. Nearly all branches of Christendom have accepted the current twenty-seven books as authoritative and canonical. They are so accepted because they are held to be true and immediately inspired by God. Earlier, there was a general agreement as to the books that the church at large accepted as canonical, but the evidence is not complete in detail for every book. Several books were accepted in some quarters but not in others. Contrary to statements sometimes made, no other books beside these twenty-seven were ever given significant or general acceptance.

One must not, however, confuse the acceptance of the books with the establishment of the canon. In a sense, the canon was established at once as soon as there were inspired books, for the NT books claim authority and recognize the authority of one another. But while canonicity presupposes this recognition of authority, it implies also the collection of authoritative books in such a way that it may be known by ordinary believers which books are authoritative and which are not. Some churches had some of the books early but it took time for all of the books to be distributed and for the evidence of their genuineness to be given to all and accepted by all. Fortunately for us, the early Christians were not gullible; they had learned to try the spirits. This testing of the spirits became especially necessary in the second half of the second century because of the rise of the Montanists, with their claim to the renewed gift of prophecy; it was necessary to submit prophetic utterances to the judgment of Holy Scripture, and this made it of practical importance to know what was Holy Scripture and what was not. Furthermore, the Gnostic heresy rather soon began to multiply spurious writings and this made people cautious. It took time to convince everybody of every book. The history of the collection of the books traces this process.

A. The Period of 170-200. In brief survey we may take three early periods for analysis. Irenaeus of Lyons (c. 180) has not left us a specific list of NT books, but it is evident from his extant writings that, in addition to the self-evident canonicity of the four Gospels, he regarded as canonical Acts, Paul's letters (including the Pastorals), 1 Peter, 1 John, and Revelation. More or less contemporary with Irenaeus is a Latin document known as the Muratorian Canon, which provides a list of books acknowledged to be of apostolic authority. Although some recent scholars have argued that the original Greek work from which the Muratorian Canon was translated may have been produced in Syria or Palestine as late as the fourth century, it is widely believed that this document is the earliest existing list of its kind, composed originally c. A.D. 180-190 in or near Rome. It includes the four Gospels and Acts, thirteen of Paul's letters (with a warning against some forgeries), two letters of John (probably in addition to 1 John, which is separately quoted), Jude, and Revelation. It mentions an apocalypse of Peter, "although some among us will not have this latter read in the churches." (This second-century apocalypse was popular because of its lurid description of the torments of the damned.) The Shepherd of Hermas is rejected from the canon because it is not apostolic and is too late to be included among the prophetic books. The omission of 1 Peter is surprising, especially if (as seems probable) the Muratorian list reflects the usage of the Roman church toward the end of the second century. The omission of Hebrews, on the other hand, is to be expected, because, while it was known in the Roman church from the first century on, it was not accepted there as canonical because it was known not to be the work of Paul.

B. The Period of 140-170. At the beginning of this period the most important figure is Marcion, who published an edition of Holy Scripture (an expurgated Greek NT) at Rome about 144. He rejected the OT as forming no part of Christian Scripture; his canon was a closed canon, comprising an edited text of the Gospel of Luke and ten letters of Paul (excluding the Pastorals). The use of Marcion's canon challenged orthodox churchmen to state more precisely what they believed constituted the canon of Christian Scripture. From this period we now have new evidence in the *Gospel of Truth* discovered recently in Egypt. This book, written by the Gnostic Valentinus, was referred to by Irenaeus and dates from about 150. It weaves into its pantheistic composition all our NT books except 1 and 2 Timothy, Titus, James, 2 Peter, 2 and 3 John, and Jude. Hebrews and Revelation are definitely included. One scholar has concluded that c. 140-150 a collection of writings known at Rome and accepted as authoritative was "virtually identical with our NT." Justin Martyr, who spent his later years in Rome and whose literary activity spans three decades (135-165), mentions "the memoirs of the apostles"—which, he says, "are called gospels"—and says that they were read in church along with the compositions of the prophets. His disciple Tatian showed

his appreciation of the distinctive authority of the four Gospels by arranging their contents into a continuous narrative known as the *Diatessaron*.

C. The Period of 95-118. Omitting many details, we may turn to the three great witnesses of the earliest age. Clement of Rome, Ignatius, and Polycarp all wrote between 95 and about 118. They show by quotation or clear allusion that they knew and used all our NT books except Luke, Colossians, Philemon, 2 Peter, 2 and 3 John, Jude, and Revelation. Moreover, these authors held the apostles in such high repute that their writings would obviously be treasured and accepted. Clement rather clearly ascribes inspiration to Paul.

D. Later Problems. Although our books were accepted at an early date, the history of their use is discontinuous. The Gospels were never challenged after the collection and publication of the fourfold Gospel until a later group of heretics questioned all of John's writings, claiming that they were spurious. Note that here, as usual, denial of apostolicity involved denial of authority. The book of Hebrews was continuously and from early days received and accepted as Pauline in Egypt. In Rome it was used by Clement, Justin, and Valentinus, although they did not accept it as the work of Paul. The witness of Irenaeus and Tertullian (c. 200) is hardly clear. Finally the views of Egypt and Palestine prevailed and Hebrews was fully accepted. The Roman church was persuaded

Greek minuscule MS (9th cent.) showing the beginning of the Gospel of Luke, with a painted image of the evangelist.

© Dr. James C. Martin. Sola Scriptura. The Van Kampen Collection on display at the Holy Land Experience in Orlando, Florida. Photographed by permission.

to include it in the canon in the fourth century under pressure from Athanasius; they agreed to do so not because he convinced them of its Pauline authorship but because they did not wish to be out of step with the rest of Christendom. Second Peter had least external authority, but it was certainly in circulation among the churches by the end of the second century.

E. The NT witness. We must not forget the vital witness of the NT itself. Paul claims the authority of an apostle (1 Cor. 9:1; 2 Cor. 12:11-12) and declares his letters are to be accepted (1 Cor. 14:37; 2 Thess. 3:14). John in Revelation does the same (Rev. 1:3; 22:18-19). Peter insists that Paul's writings are Scripture (2 Pet. 3:15; cf. 3:2). Jude quotes Peter as apostolic (Jude 18). It seems probable that 1 Tim. 5:18 quotes Lk. 10:7 as Scripture. The fact is that, as the early church knew, Christ had promised his apostles a special work of the Spirit, inspiring them as teachers of his revelation (Jn. 14:25; 16:13). It is true that a few, a very few, of the books were actually written by those not themselves apostles. But it is clear that the apostles used helpers in their writing (Rom. 16:22; 1 Pet. 5:12). The early church fathers called such men as Mark, Luke, and the author of Hebrews helpers or disciples of the apostles, and accepted their work as that of the apostles with whom they labored. At least the books were all written and apparently were all accepted within the period of the apostles.

Other indications combine to teach us that these twenty-seven books are rightly in our canon. The Holy Spirit has witnessed through the generations to the saving truth contained in them. These books have brought untold blessing where they have been received and obeyed. The church with one voice finds them to be the very word of God.

canopy. This English term is used a few times in modern versions of the OT to render various Hebrew words, such as *sukkâ H6109* (2 Sam 22:12 = Ps. 18:11; this Heb. noun is elsewhere usually translated "booth") and *ḥuppāh H2903* (Isa. 4:5). The NRSV uses it also to render *ʿāb H6264* (1 Ki. 7:6, NIV "overhanging roof"; Ezek. 41:25-26, NIV "overhang").

Canticles. See SONG OF SOLOMON.

caper, caperberry. See PLANTS.

Capernaum. kuh-puhr´nay-uhm (Gk. *Kapharnaoum G3019*; from Heb. *kĕpar naḥûm*, "village of Nahum"). A town on the NW shore of the Sea of Galilee where Jesus made his headquarters during his ministry in GALILEE (Matt. 4:13; Mk. 2:1). In Scripture it is mentioned only in the Gospels, and perhaps did not arise until after the EXILE. That it was a town of considerable size in the days of Christ is shown by a number of facts: a tax collector had his office there (Mk. 2:14); a high officer of King HEROD Antipas had his residence in Capernaum and built a synagogue for the people there (Matt. 8:5-13; Lk. 7:1-10). Jesus performed many striking miracles in the town, among them the healing of the centurion's palsied servant (Matt. 8:5-13), the paralytic who was lowered through a roof by four friends (Mk. 2:1-13), and a nobleman's son (Jn. 4:46-54). It was there that Jesus called Matthew to the apostleship as he was sitting at the

© Dr. James C. Martin

View of Capernaum looking W to the Sea of Galilee. The modern Catholic church (octangle) is built over Byzantine remains from the 4th-5th cent. The partial reconstruction of the white limestone synagogue sits on top of the basalt synagogue foundation dating to the 1st cent.

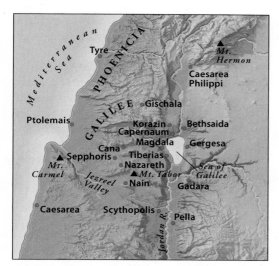

Capernaum.

tax-collector's booth (Matt. 9:9-13). Capernaum was also the setting for the discourse on the Bread of Life, which followed the feeding of the 5,000 (Jn. 6), and many other addresses (cf. Mk. 9:33-50). In spite of Jesus' remarkable works and teachings, the people did not repent, and Jesus predicted the complete ruin of the place (Matt. 11:23-24; Lk. 10:15). His prophecy was so completely fulfilled that the town has disappeared and its very site is a matter of debate. There are two main claimants for the honor of being the site: Tell Ḥum, which is about 2.5 mi. (4 km.) W of the mouth of the JORDAN, and Khan Minyeh, which is 2.5 mi. (4 km.) further SW of Tell Ḥum. Several strands of evidence favor Tell Ḥum, and archaeological excavations have given additional support to this identification.

caph. See KAPH.

Caphtor, Caphtorim, Caphtorite. kaf′tor, kaf′tuh-rim, kaf′tuh-rit (Heb. *kaptôr H4116*, meaning uncertain; gentilic *kaptôrî H4118*). KJV also Caphthorim (1 Chr. 1:12) and Caphtorims (Deut. 2:23). Explicit references to Caphtor are few. The PHILISTINES and the Caphtorites (or Caphtorim) are both said to have come from Caphtor (Deut. 2:23; Amos 9:7) and are probably to be identified or related. In the Table of Nations (Gen. 10:14; 1 Chr. 1:12), the Philistines are described as having come from the CASLUHITES,

but it is often assumed that the phrase in question has been misplaced and that the text should read, "Casluhim, and Caphtorim, from which the Philistines came" (NRSV). In these two passages the Caphtorites are identified as the descendants of MIZRAIM (i.e., EGYPT). The closest the OT comes to giving the location of Caphtor is in Jer. 47:4, where the Philistines are described as "the remnant from the coasts [*or* isle] of Caphtor," but even this comment is ambiguous. Most scholars believe that biblical Caphtor is used in the same sense as Akkadian *Kaptara* and Egyptian *Keftiu*, referring to Crete. Other proposals include the W part of CILICIA and the island of CYPRUS.

capital. The ornamental top of a PILLAR. This English term is used primarily in the description of the TEMPLE (1 Ki. 7:16-20 et al.), but some versions use it with reference to the posts of the TABERNACLE (e.g., NRSV at Exod. 36:38 et al.). For the sense "major city," see CITY.

capital punishment. See PUNISHMENT.

Cappadocia. kap′uh-doh′shee-uh (Gk. *Kappadokia G2838*). A large inland region of ASIA MINOR that apparently was given this name by the Persians. Later the region was divided into two territories of which the more northerly was subsequently named PONTUS and the southerly Cappadocia, the name it retained in NT times. It was bounded on the N by Pontus, on the E by SYRIA and ARMENIA, on the S by CILICIA, and on the W by LYCAONIA. The Romans built roads through the "Cilician gates" in the Taurus range so that Cappadocia could readily be entered from the south. Jews from Cappadocia (Acts 2:9) were among the hearers of the first Christian sermon along with men from other Anatolian provinces; and PETER directed his first letter (1 Pet. 1:1) in part to "God's elect … scattered throughout" various provinces in the north. It is almost certain that many of these Cappadocian Jews were converted on the Day of Pentecost, and so had the honor of being among the very earliest Christians.

captain. A military leader, although in the Bible the word is not to be understood in the modern sense designating a particular rank in order of command. Over a dozen Hebrew words (with such literal meanings as "head," "chief," "ruler," etc.) are rendered "captain" in the KJV, though modern versions use a greater variety of renderings. Especially frequent is the word *śar H8569*, referring to the military commander of an army or of a division (e.g., Gen. 21:22; Num. 31:48; Jdg. 5:14), to the keeper of a prison (Gen. 40:3), etc. In the NT it is used by modern versions to render Greek *stratēgos G5130* with reference to a temple officer who arrested the apostles (e.g., Acts 4:1; 5:24, cf. v. 26). According to rabbinic literature, this officer was in charge of twenty-four watches, or guard posts, located at important spots about the temple courtyard. See also ARMY. With regard to the application of the term "captain" to Christ in the KJV (Heb. 2:10), see AUTHOR.

captivity. See DISPERSION; EXILE.

caravan. A group of travelers united together for a common purpose or for mutual protection and generally equipped for a long journey, especially in desert country or through foreign and presumably hostile territory. JACOB'S "company" (Gen. 32-33) is a good example of a caravan organized to carry a clan to a new home; and the host of the AMALEKITES whom DAVID destroyed (1 Sam. 30:1-20) was also a caravan, but organized for raiding purposes. In the trackless desert where oases were few and far between and where savage beasts and more savage men were found, it was essential to go in caravans for protection. The word does not occur in the KJV, but "company" and "troop" could often have been "caravan."

caraway. See PLANTS.

carbuncle. A red precious stone. This term is used by the KJV and other versions in several passages where a better rendering would be "beryl" or "emerald" (Exod. 28:17 et al.). See MINERALS.

Carcas. kahr'kuhs (Heb. *karkas H4139*, possibly from Old Iranian *kahrkāsa*, "vulture"). Also Carkas, Karkas. One of seven EUNUCHS who served King XERXES of PERSIA (Esth. 1:10). They were

ordered by the king to bring Queen VASHTI before the princes of the empire, during a long banquet, to show off her beauty.

carcass. KJV *carcase*. The dead body of a person or beast. The word is used to render various words in Scripture with root ideas of something fallen, faded, exhausted; or it may simply denote "body," such as the lion's carcass in Jdg. 14:8-9. The law of Moses, probably partly for sanitary reasons, required that carcasses of "unclean" beasts be considered abominable. See Lev. 11:8-40.

Carchemish. kahr'kuh-mish (Heb. *karkĕmîš H4138*; Akk. and Hitt. *Kargamish*). Also Charchemish. An ancient city of the HITTITES located on the W bank of the EUPHRATES; the modern site is Jerablus, c. 60 mi. (100 km.) NE of Aleppo. Carchemish was important commercially and militarily. For many years it paid tribute to the kings of ASSYRIA. When SARGON captured it in 717 B.C., the Hittite empire fell with it (Isa. 10:9). It was the scene of a great victory by NEBUCHADNEZZAR over Pharaoh NECO in 605 (Jer. 46:2; 2 Chr. 35:20). Its site is called Jerabis or Jerablus.

Careah. See KAREAH.

Carite. kair'it (Heb. *kārî H4133*). The Carites were a military group, apparently mercenaries, mentioned along with commanders and guards who were assigned to protect young King Joash/JEHOASH (2 Ki. 11:4, 19; KJV, "captains"). Their identity is uncertain. Some scholars argue that they were mercenaries from CARIA; others identify the Carites with the KERETHITES (cf. the *Qere* reading in 2 Sam. 20:23).

Carkas. See CARCAS.

Carmel. kahr'muhl (Heb. *karmel H4150* and *H4151*, "orchard, plantation"; gentilic *karmĕlî H4153*, "Carmelite"). (1) A city of the MAON district within the tribal territory of JUDAH (Josh. 15:55); it is identified with modern Khirbet el-Kirmil, located 7.5 mi. (12 km.) SE of HEBRON. It lies on the edge of the Judean desert, in a pastoral region of broad hills and wide valleys. Some emphasis is placed upon

The Mt. Carmel ridge (looking SW). The Egyptian pharaoh Pepi I referred to it as the "antelope's nose."

this location in the accounts of King SAUL (1 Sam. 15:12) and of DAVID, especially in the latter's dealings with NABAL and his wife ABIGAIL, whom the young warrior eventually married after Nabal's death (1 Sam. 25:2-40; 27:3; 30:5; 2 Sam. 2:2; 3:3). One of David's warriors, HEZRO, was a Carmelite (2 Sam. 23:35; 1 Chr. 11:37).

(2) The mountainous promontory jutting into the Mediterranean Sea just S of the modern city of Haifa and straight W of the Sea of Galilee. On the map of PALESTINE it forms the principal deviation from a comparatively straight coastline and forms the southern wall of the magnificent bay (or gulf) of Acre (Acco), the best natural harbor S of Beirut. When the word occurs with the definite article, it generally refers to Mount Carmel and is often used to illustrate a beautiful and fruitful place (Isa. 35:2; but see 33:9, which pictures God's judgment). South of Carmel lies the fruitful plain of SHARON and NE of it flows the river KISHON through the Plain of ESDRAELON. At Carmel, ELIJAH stood against 450 heathen prophets and defeated them (1 Ki. 18). ELISHA also visited Carmel (2 Ki. 2:25; 4:25).

Carmi. kahr′mi (Heb. *karmî H4145*, "vineyard"; gentilic *karmî H4146*, "Carmite"). TNIV Karmi. **(1)** Fourth son of REUBEN (Gen. 46:9; Exod. 6:14; 1 Chr. 5:3). From him sprang the Carmites (Num. 26:6).

(2) Son of ZIMRI (or ZABDI), descendant of JUDAH, and father of ACHAN (Josh. 7:1, 18; 1 Chr. 2:7; in 4:1 he is described as a son of Judah in the sense of a descendant). Achan defiled all Israel by stealing from God what was devoted in JERICHO.

carnal. Traditional rendering of the Greek adjectives *sarkikos G4920* and *sarkinos G4921*. It means "fleshly," that is, in the manner of the FLESH (*sarx G4922*) or belonging to the realm of the flesh, and thus opposite of that which is spiritual. The word is used frequently in the KJV and has two main references. (1) *Physical:* that which is earthly, material, secular, in contrast to SPIRIT; something necessary to the physical (Rom. 15:27; 1 Cor. 9:11); subject to human sensibility (2 Cor. 3:3); weak (10:4); temporary (Heb. 7:16); also those appetites, desires, and urges that may be expressed in harmony with divine law and be satisfied without violation of God's law. (2) *Ethical (moral):* pertaining to or characterized by the flesh, hence weak and sinful (2 Cor. 1:12; Rom. 7:14); a disposition that is definitely antispiritual in its manifestation; the dynamic principle of sinfulness that alienate human beings from God (Rom. 8:5-8); also spiritual immaturity, not being delivered from that which is inherently evil (1 Cor. 3:3-4). Because in modern English the word *carnal* usually has a specific sexual meaning, the NIV uses various alternate renderings, such as "material," "human," "unspiritual," "worldly," and "sinful." (The distinction between the two Greek adjectives is not substantial and does not affect the translation.)

carnelian. See MINERALS.

carob. See PLANTS.

carpenter. See OCCUPATIONS AND PROFESSIONS.

carpet. This English term is used by some Bible versions in a passage referring to wares that traders sold to TYRE (Ezek. 27:24; NIV, "rugs"). Since the item was "bound with cords and made secure" (NRSV), some believe that chests covered with rich brocade are meant (so KJV; cf. Esth. 3:9; 4:7). In addition, the NRSV has "rich carpets" with reference to something on which people sit, apparently as they travel (Jdg. 5:10), but the NIV's "saddle blankets" is preferable. One should keep in mind that tent dwellers used only straw mats or a piece of leather on the floor. Assyrian and Persian palaces and wealthy villas in Hellenistic and Roman times had mosaic patterns in paved floors (cf. Esth. 1:6).

Carpus. kahr´puhs (Gk. *Karpos*, *G2842*). Carpus was a resident of TROAS, probably a Christian, with whom PAUL had left his cloak and perhaps also some important books (2 Tim. 4:13). Carpus is not mentioned elsewhere in Scripture, but according to Hippolytus (died c. A.D. 236) he later became the bishop of Berytus or Beroea in Thrace.

carriage. This term, in its older sense of "goods, baggage," is used several times by the KJV (e.g., 1 Sam. 17:22). The NIV uses the term to render two different Hebrew words referring to Solomon's litter (Cant. 3:7, 9). See also CART; CHARIOT.

carrion vulture. See BIRDS.

Carshena. kahr-shee´nuh (Heb. *karšĕnā᾿ H4161*, possibly from Old Iranian *Karša*, "furrows"). TNIV Karshena. One of the seven nobles of PERSIA and MEDIA in the time of XERXES "who had special access to the king and were highest in the kingdom" (Esth. 1:14).

cart. Carts and wagons are very ancient. In Gen. 45:19-21 PHARAOH provided carts for the wives and children of JACOB for their journey into Egypt. In the days of ELI, the PHILISTINES took the ARK OF THE COVENANT and, finding it a most unwelcome guest, put it on a cart and let it go back to Israel (1 Sam. 6). Later, when DAVID desired to bring the same ark to his city, he used a cart, and there was a disastrous event connected with that arrangement (see 2 Sam. 6:1-11).

carving. See IDOLATRY; OCCUPATIONS AND PROFESSIONS (under *craftsman* and *engraver*).

casement. See LATTICE.

Casiphia. kuh-sif´ee-uh (Heb. *kāsipyā᾿ H4085*, possibly "silversmiths"). TNIV Kasiphia. An unidentified town from which EZRA summoned Levites to return from Babylon and serve the newly restored Jewish community in Jerusalem (Ezra 8:17). The name has been a rich source of Jewish traditions, and other passages of the OT were related to it by the rabbis. Its location is unknown.

Casluhim. See CASLUHITES.

Casluhites. kas´luh-hits (Heb. *kasluḥîm H4078*, meaning unknown). Also Casluhim; TNIV Kasluhites. The name of an unidentified tribe sprung from MIZRAIM (EGYPT) and identified as the progenitor of the PHILISTINES (Gen. 10:14; 1 Chr. 1:12). Many scholars emend the text so as to link the Philistines with the CAPHTORITES rather than with the Casluhites (cf. NRSV).

cassia. See PLANTS.

castanets. See MUSIC AND MUSICAL INSTRUMENTS.

castaway. A word used once by the KJV to render Greek *adokimos G99*, "disapproved" (1 Cor. 9:27; NIV, "disqualified for the prize"). The Greek word elsewhere is translated in several ways (e.g., "depraved, rejected, unfit") by the English versions (Rom. 1:28; 2 Cor. 13:5-7; 2 Tim. 3:8; Tit. 1:16; Heb. 6:8).

castle. A large fortified building or set of buildings, as that of a prince or nobleman. The English word is used fifteen times by the KJV to translate various Hebrew and Greek terms that are better rendered "camp" (e.g., Gen. 25:16), "settlement" (e.g., 1 Chr. 6:54), "fortress" (e.g., 1 Chr. 11:5), "citadel" (e.g., Prov. 18:19), "barracks" (e.g., Acts 21:34, with reference to the Tower of Antonia), etc. See also Gabbatha; tower.

Castor and Pollux. kas´tuhr, pol´uhks. In Greek mythology they were "sons of Zeus" (Gk. *Dioskouroi G1483*, Acts 28:11) by Leda, one of his numerous mistresses. Castor was a horseman and Pollux an adept boxer. They were later put in the sky in the constellation known as Gemini ("the Twins") and were considered as tutelary deities favorable to sailors, a fact that explains why the ship in which Paul sailed was named in their honor. St. Elmo's fire used to be credited to Castor and Pollux.

caterpillar. See animals (under *moth*).

Catholic Epistles. Also *General Epistles*. A term applied to the letters of James, Peter, John, and Jude. It goes back to the early church fathers, but why the word *catholic* (meaning "universal" or "general") was chosen is uncertain. The most commonly accepted explanation is that these epistles were addressed, not to individual churches or persons, but to a number of churches, thus to the church at large. The seeming exceptions, 2 and 3 John, were probably included as properly belonging with 1 John and of value to the general reader.

cattle. See animals.

Cauda. kaw´duh (Gk. *Kauda G3007*; apparently the name could also be spelled *Klauda*, which is the reading of many MSS). KJV Clauda. A small island lying about 25 mi. (40 km.) to the S of Crete (Acts 27:16) and now called Gavdos. Here Paul and his companions were almost wrecked on their journey toward Rome.

cave. A hollowed-out place in the earth, whether formed by nature or by humans. In a mountainous land such as Palestine, where there is much limestone, caves are likely to be quite numerous. Caves were often used for regular human habitation, for hiding from the law or from enemies in warfare, for securing precious treasure (such as the Dead Sea Scrolls), for storehouses and cisterns, for stables and cattle, and for burial (Gen. 19:30; 1 Ki. 19:9).

cedar. See plants.

Cedron. See Kidron.

ceiling. This English word is used in 1 Ki. 6:15 (KJV "cieling") to translate a Hebrew term that normally means "walls" (as in v. 16 KJV, though here too the NIV has "ceiling"). Some scholars argue that in this passage the term should be emended to a very similar Hebrew word that means "beams" (cf. 2 Chr. 3:7). The NIV, on the basis of some ancient versions, uses "ceiling" also in 1 Ki. 7:7 where the Hebrew text repeats the word "floor."

celestial. See heaven.

celibacy. The state of being unmarried, particularly when this state is deliberately chosen. The Bible lays down no definitive rules about it. John the Baptist, for example, was unmarried, but Peter was married. Jesus himself did not marry, but he contributed notably to the wedding celebrations at Cana (Jn. 2:1-11). He realized that some "have renounced marriage because of the kingdom of heaven" (Matt. 19:12), and once he warned against wrong priorities if to become married would be a hindrance to discipleship (Lk. 14:20). Paul recognized the dangers of earthly ties and stressed basic principles: God has an assignment for every life, and whatever our situation, married or single, the main thing is to be able to exercise our God-given gifts to the full (1 Cor. 7:7-9, 17, 32-38). See marriage.

cellar. This English term is used twice by the KJV with reference to storage supplies of wine and oil (1 Chr. 27:27 [NIV, "vats"], 28 [NIV, "supplies"]). Excavations at Gibeon have revealed bedrock cellars that undoubtedly provided the best available refrigeration for wine. The word is also used by the NRSV to render Greek *kryptē G3219*, "hidden place," which occurs only once (Lk. 11:33).

Cenchrea. sen′kree-uh (Gk. *Kenchreai G3020*). Also Cenchreae. The eastern harbor of CORINTH, about 7 mi. (11 km.) from the city. A village, it existed solely for the transportation of goods to and from Corinth. Rather than sail around the

Remnants of the ancient roadway leading to the Cenchrea harbor. (View to the NE.)

dangerous southern tip of the Peloponnesus, ships were dragged across the isthmus from Cenchrea to Lechaeum, the western harbor of Corinth, on sleds. The cargo of larger ships was unloaded and moved the same way to a ship on the other side. PAUL in Rom. 16:1 commends to the Roman church a deaconess called PHOEBE of the church at Cenchrea, a church that the apostle may have founded on his second missionary journey. Paul stopped here to have his head shaved in fulfillment of a vow (Acts 18:18).

censer. A shallow vessel used to remove ashes (hot or cold) from an altar, or to gather burnt parts of wicks from the lampstand, or to burn INCENSE on hot coals placed on the pan (cf. Num. 16:6-7). The same Hebrew word can also mean "tray" (for the lampstand, e.g., Exod. 25:38) and "firepan" (e.g., 27:3). One of the angels in the book of Revelation hurled a golden censer to bring judgment on the earth (Rev. 8:3-5).

census. A numbering and registration of a people. The OT tells of three different occasions when a formal census was taken. The first was at Mount SINAI, soon after the Israelites left Egypt (Num. 1). The second was at SHITTIM near the end of the forty years' wilderness wandering. The third was made by DAVID (2 Sam. 24:1-9; 1 Chr. 21:1-5). The exiles who returned from Babylonia with ZERUBBABEL were also numbered (Ezra 2). Shortly before the birth of Christ, Emperor AUGUSTUS ordered a census throughout the Roman world (Lk. 2:1). See QUIRINIUS.

centurion. (*kentyriōn G3035* [from Lat. *centurio*], only in Mark; elsewhere *hekatontarchēs G1672*, "ruler of one hundred"). A commander of one hundred soldiers in the Roman army. The word is mentioned first in connection with the centurion of CAPERNAUM whose beloved servant was deathly sick (Matt. 8:5-13; Lk. 7:2-10). This officer had built a synagogue for the Jews, who therefore appreciated him and begged Jesus to heal the servant. The centurion showed real reverence for Jesus in saying, "I do not deserve to have you come under my roof," and Jesus responded, "I have not found anyone in Israel with such great faith." CORNELIUS (Acts 10), another centurion, was "devout and God-fearing." PETER was sent to him to open up salvation to the Gentiles as he had at JERUSALEM for the Jews (Acts 2) and at SAMARIA for its people (8:14-17). Another centurion, JULIUS, of the Imperial Regiment (27:1-43), had the duty of taking PAUL to ROME. He saved Paul's life when the soldiers wished to kill all the prisoners, and Paul by his presence and counsel saved the centurion and all the ship's company. Other unnamed centurions are mentioned elsewhere (Matt. 27:54; Mk. 15:39, 44-45; Acts 22:25-26; 23:1-18 et al.).

Cephas. see′fuhs (Gk. *Kēphas G3064*, from Aram. *kêpāʾ*, "rock, stone"). See PETER.

cereal. See PLANTS.

ceremonial law. A term applied to those commandments that involve rites or otherwise focus on external form. See LAW; PURIFICATION; SACRIFICE AND OFFERINGS; WORSHIP.

certainty. See ASSURANCE.

certificate of divorce. See DIVORCE.

chaff. The refuse of the grain that has been threshed and winnowed. This is partly dust and dirt, but the real chaff is the hard and inedible coat of the grain. By threshing, most of this is separated; then on a windy day the grain is tossed into the air and the chaff and the shorter pieces of straw are blown away. In Isa. 5:24 and 33:11, the word properly means "dry hay" fit for burning. The more common Hebrew word is generally used as a figure for worthless or godless people (e.g., Ps. 1:4, "Not so the wicked! They are like chaff that the wind blows away"). It is used also for godless nations (Isa. 17:13). The evanescence of the wicked is likened in Hos. 13:3 to the morning mist, the early dew, "chaff swirling from a threshing floor," and "smoke escaping through a window." In the preaching of John the Baptist (Matt. 3:12; Lk. 3:17) our Lord is to save the righteous ("gathering his wheat into his barn") and destroy the wicked ("burning up the chaff with unquenchable fire").

chain. The English word represents many Hebrew words meaning "chain, necklace, band, bracelet, clasp, hook, ring, rope." Chains were used for a variety of purposes.

(1) As marks of distinction. When JOSEPH was put in charge of the land of Egypt, the PHARAOH gave him a ring, dressed him in fine clothes, and "put a gold chain around his neck" (Gen. 41:42); and after DANIEL interpreted the writing on the wall, he too was given a gold chain (Dan. 5:29).

(2) As ornaments. Chains were used to adorn the TABERNACLE (Exod. 28:14, 22; 39:15, 17-18). The Midianites adorned their camels' necks with chains (Jdg. 8:21, 26). Wreaths of chainwork ornamented the tops of the pillars (1 Ki. 7:17; 2 Chr. 3:16) and other places in Solomon's TEMPLE (1 Ki.

6:21; 2 Chr. 3:5). As jewelry, chains are referred to in several passages (Prov. 1:9 et al.).

(3) As fetters. The OT describes those who are conquered as being in chains (Isa. 45:14; Nah. 3:10; et al.). According to Mk. 5:3-4 (= Lk. 8:29), chains were used to bind a demoniac. PETER in prison was bound with two chains, but he was miraculously released (Acts 12:6-7). When PAUL was in ROME, he lived with a chain (28:20) that probably bound his right hand to a soldier's left. In the book of Revelation, an angel binds SATAN with a chain (Rev. 20:1).

chalcedony. See MINERALS.

Chalcol. See CALCOL.

Chaldea, Chaldean. kal-dee´uh, -uhn (Heb. *kaśdîm H4169* [both place name and gentilic]; Aram. gentilic *kaśdāy H10373*; Gk. gentilic *Chaldaios G5900*). Also Chaldaea(n), Chaldee. Chaldea was the name of a district in S Babylonia, later applied to a dynasty that controlled all Babylonia (cf. the NIV rendering in Jer. 50:10; 51:24, 35; Ezek. 11:24; 16:29). See BABYLON; UR (CITY).

chamber. This English word is used frequently in the KJV and other versions as the rendering of various Hebrew words (e.g., Isa. 26:20; Ezek 40:17). For many of these occurrences, the NIV prefers "room" (however, see Ezra 8:29; Job 37:9; Ps. 45:13; Cant. 1:4; et al.). The KJV uses the term also in the NT, but only a few times (e.g., Matt. 24:26; Acts 9:37). See also CHAMBERS OF THE SOUTH.

chambering. This English term is used once by the KJV in the now obsolete sense of "lewdness" (Rom. 13:13).

chamberlain. See OCCUPATIONS AND PROFESSIONS.

chambers of the south. This expression is used in a context that mentions several star formations (Job 9:9 KJV and other versions). JOB is probably applying the term to one or more constellations visible in the southern part of the sky (cf. NIV). Others refer it to the vacant stretches of this region and identify it with the place from which the whirlwind is said to come (thus NJPS, "chambers of the south wind"; cf. 37:9).

chameleon. See ANIMALS (under *lizard*).

chamois. See ANIMALS (under *sheep*).

champaign. This English term, which refers to a broad expanse of plain, flat, open country, is used by the KJV once with reference to the ARABAH (Deut. 11:30; cf. also KJV Ezek. 37:2 mg.).

champion. This English word is used to render a Hebrew phrase that means literally, "the man of the middle"; it is used with reference to GOLIATH, who fought DAVID between the two armies that watched (1 Sam. 17:4, 23). It was common for individual champions from either side to decide conflicts, because the bloodshed of a full-scale war could thus be avoided. The word occurs occasionally to render other Hebrew terms (e.g., the NRSV in 1 Sam. 17:51; the NIV in Ps. 19:5 and Isa. 5:22; the NJPS in Jdg. 3:9 et al. [often as a verb, e.g., Isa. 3:13]). The phrase "David's champions" is often used today with reference to "the Thirty," the list of warriors who served as King David's military elite (2 Sam. 23:8-39 = 1 Chr. 11:40-47; cf. 2 Sam. 21:15-22).

Chanaan. kay′nuhn. See CANAAN.

chance. See PROVIDENCE.

chancellor. This term is used by the KJV to render the Aramaic phrase *bě'ēl-ṭě'ēm* (*H10116* + *H10302*), which was the title of the Persian official REHUM (Ezra 4:8-9, 17; NIV, "commanding officer"; NRSV, "royal deputy");

changers of money. The function of money changers was to convert the currency of a worshiper at the Jerusalem TEMPLE into a type of money acceptable for purposes of a sacrificial offering. It could not have been because of anything inherently reproachful in their activity that they aroused Christ's ire in the temple (Matt. 21:12; Mk. 11:15; Jn. 2:14-15). Undoubtedly they served the convenience of the public, especially where birds, animals, or cake-offerings had to be purchased by city dwellers not possessing livestock of their own. In these transactions it must have been necessary to make small change available if the buyer was not to be cheated, and of course the banker who provided this service was entitled to some sort of a fee, in order to make a living. There seem to be only two possible grounds on which they incurred our Lord's indignation: either their charges for money changing were excessive and tended to gouge the poor and pious, or else they had their tables set up so close to the section of the temple set apart for worship and sacrifice as to interfere with these sacred functions. On either count, or on both counts, Christ could have leveled the charge of turning the house of God into "a den of robbers." Money changers evidently sat at tables or benches, stacked high with various types of coins used in the Mediterranean world at the time. It is quite conceivable that the loud and passionate haggling that undoubtedly accompanied this activity, augmented by the bleating of sheep and goats, was completely disturbing to genuine devotion. At any rate, Jesus found it necessary to clear them all out, and thus relegate them to a suitable distance from the place of sacrifice and prayer.

chapiter. KJV term for CAPITAL.

character. See VIRTUE. For the meaning "letter," see WRITING.

Charashim. See GE HARASHIM.

Charchemish. See CARCHEMISH.

charcoal. See COAL.

charger. An obsolete term for a large flat dish (KJV Num. 7:13 et al.; Matt. 14:8 et al.).

chariot. A two-wheeled vehicle drawn by two horses. In EGYPT, JOSEPH rode in PHARAOH's second chariot (Gen. 41:43). Chariots were used in JACOB's funeral procession (50:9). Pharaoh pursued the children of Israel into the RED SEA with chariots (Exod. 14:7—15:19). The Canaanites used chariots against Israel (1 Sam. 13:5). DAVID hamstrung the chariot horses of his enemies (2 Sam. 8:4). ADONIJAH prepared chariots when he plotted to assume the throne (1 Ki. 1:5). SOLOMON built establishments to house many chariots (9:19). He imported chariots from Egypt at six hundred shekels each (10:28-29). Both divided kingdoms

This chariot was given to the Egyptian courtier Yuya by his son-in-law, Pharaoh Amenhotep III (14th cent. B.C.); made of wood and covered in most parts with leather.

used chariots in war (16:9; 22:34; 2 Ki. 23:30). The ETHIOPIAN EUNUCH was riding a chariot when PHILIP met him (Acts 8:27-29).

Some parts of a chariot are referred to in 1 Ki. 7:33. There was a pole to which the two horses were yoked, an axle, wheels with six or eight spokes, and a body fastened to the axle and pole. Often only two men rode in a chariot, a driver and a warrior (22:34); but sometimes the HITTITE practice of adding a shield-bearer was followed. The Assyrian chariot was heavier than the Egyptian or Hebrew and carried three or four men. Nahum 2:3-4 is a vivid picture of such chariots. ELIJAH was honored by being escorted up to heaven by a chariot of fire (2 Ki. 2:11), and his manner of going became a proverb (2:12; 13:14). God is represented as having thousands of chariots, showing his power (Ps. 68:17). Trust in chariots is vain compared with trust in God (20:7). Habakkuk speaks of God riding on his victorious chariots (Hab. 3:8). The chariots of the sun (2 Ki. 23:11) were used in sun worship (23:5). Chariots were used for riding (Cant. 1:9; 6:12), especially by royalty.

charismata. See GIFTS, SPIRITUAL.

charity. This term, which in present-day English means "almsgiving, benevolence," is used in the KJV with its older meaning, LOVE (1 Cor. 13:1 et al.; only in the Epistles and Revelation).

charms. See AMULET.

Charran. See HARAN.

chaste, chastity. See CLEAN.

chastisement. This English term, which in modern English means "punishment" or "severe censure," is used by the KJV and other versions to translate Hebrew and Greek words that mean more broadly "discipline, admonition, correction, chastening" (cf. Deut. 11:2; Job 5:17; et al.). The concept of instruction in wisdom is prominent in the book of Proverbs (e.g., Prov. 3:11-12, cited in Heb. 12:5-11). In Isa. 53:5 the term is used to speak of the substitution of the sinless Servant of the Lord for his guilty people. The Greek word *paideia G4082* in classical literature is strictly a positive term ("the rearing of a child [*pais G4090*], education, learning, culture"), but in the SEPTUAGINT, as a rendering of the corresponding Hebrew word, it begins to take on as well the negative sense of "punishment." PAUL counsels: "Fathers, do not exasperate your children; instead, bring them up in the training [*paideia*] and instruction of the Lord" (Eph. 6:4). He states that the commendable conduct of the Lord's servant is to correct or instruct (verb *paideuō G4084*) his opponents with gentleness (2 Tim. 2:25). And in his climactic admonition to TIMOTHY, he wrote, "All Scripture is God-breathed and is useful for teaching, rebuking, correcting and training [*paideia*] in righteousness" (2 Tim. 3:16). Civine training with discipline is the process by which God brings people to put their trust in him, and nurtures those whom he has received until they reach maturity.

Chebar. See KEBAR.

checker work. The expression "nets of checker work" is used by some English versions to render an unusual Hebrew phrase that means literally, "lattices—a work of lattice" (only in 1 Ki. 7:17; NIV simply, "network"). It refers to the seven-stranded link chains, four in warp and three in weft (to hold the four in line) draped over each of the pommels of the double capitals of the pillars named Jakin and Boaz in Solomon's TEMPLE.

Chedorlaomer. See KEDORLAOMER.

cheek. The lateral part of the mouth on each side of the face. The corresponding Hebrew term can refer to the jowls or jawbone of an animal (Deut. 18:3; Jdg. 15:15-17), but it is usually rendered "cheek" when the reference is to a person (e.g., Cant. 1:10; Lam. 1:2). To smite the cheek is an act of reproach (Job 16:10; Lam. 3:30; et al.). Christ's command to turn the other cheek (Matt. 5:39 = Lk. 6:29) forcefully states what he meant the Christian's attitude toward reproach should be. In line with this instruction, both PAUL and PETER, using different language, give expression to the special joy and blessing they experienced in thus enduring reproach for Christ's sake (2 Cor. 12:10; 1 Pet. 4:14).

cheese. This word occurs three times in the OT, each time as the rendering of a different Hebrew term (1 Sam. 17:18; 2 Sam. 17:29; Job 10:10). The reference in Job's speech ("Did you not pour me out like milk / and curdle me like cheese …") is the clearest reference to cheese as the modern world knows it. Milk of cows, goats, and sheep was stored in skins. In a warm climate, without refrigeration, it soon curdled.

Chelal. See KELAL.

Chelluh. See KELUHI.

Chelub. See KELUB.

Chelubai. See CALEB.

Cheluhi. kel'uh-hi. See KELUHI.

Chemarims. kem'uh-rims. This name occurs only once in the KJV as the transliteration of a Hebrew word that means "idol-priests" (Zeph. 1:4; the word is translated properly by the KJV in 2 Ki. 23:5 and Hos. 10:5).

Chemosh. kee'mosh (Heb. *kĕmôš H4019*, meaning uncertain). The god of MOAB, so named in an ancient Israelite song (Num. 21:29; alluded to in Jer. 48:7, 13, 46). JEPHTHAH refers to Chemosh as god of the AMMONITES (Jdg. 11:24), presumably because the nation of Ammon also worshiped this deity in addition to MOLECH. SOLOMON introduced the worship of Chemosh into Jerusalem to please a foreign wife, though by doing so he displeased God (1 Ki. 11:7, 33). JOSIAH defiled this high place of Chemosh (2 Ki. 23:13), putting an end to its use as a place of worship. MESHA, king of Moab, suffered a great disaster in his rebellion against Israel, in consequence of which he offered his son, the heir to the throne of Moab, as a burnt offering (3:4-27). His inscription on the MOABITE STONE shows that this sacrifice was made to Chemosh and describes the help that Mesha believed Chemosh had given his people in war and the chastisement that Chemosh meted out to them when they were unfaithful. The terms used are so similar in style to the terms used by the Israelites of the true God that they serve only to accentuate the contrast between the two.

Chenaanah. See KENAANAH.

Chenani. See KENANI.

Chenaniah. See KENANIAH.

Chephar-ammoni,   Chephar-haammonai. kee'fuhr-am'uh-ni, kee'fuhr-hay-am'uh-ni. See KEPHAR AMMONI.

Chephirah. See KEPHIRAH.

Cheran. See KERAN.

Cherethim, Cherethite. See KERETHITE.

Cherith. See KERITH.

cherub, cherubim. cher´uhb, cher´uh-bim (Heb. *kĕrûb* H4131 [usually in pl., *kĕrubîm*], meaning uncertain; Gk. *cheroub* G5938 [in the NT, only in the form *cheroubin*, Heb. 9:5]). For traditional reasons, most Bible versions use *cherubim* as the plural form (KJV has *cherubims*, a superfluous English pl. form), though *cherubs* would be more appropriate. The term refers to a winged angelic creature and is applied mainly to the images made for the TABERNACLE and the TEMPLE. The cherubim and a flaming sword were placed at the E of EDEN to guard the way to the TREE OF LIFE after ADAM and EVE were expelled from the garden (Gen. 3:24). The curtains of the TABERNACLE were embroidered with cherubim (Exod. 26:1). God directed MOSES to place two cherubim of beaten gold on the mercy seat above the ARK OF THE COVENANT in the Most Holy Place of the tabernacle; there God would commune with Moses (25:18-22; 37:7-9). God's glory rested between the cherubim in both the tabernacle and the TEMPLE (Num. 7:89; 1 Sam. 4:4; 2 Sam. 6:2; 2 Ki. 19:15; Ps. 80:1; 99:1; Isa. 37:16; Heb. 9:5). The cherubim in the temple were huge figures newly made for the purpose (1 Ki. 6:23-28; 2 Chr.

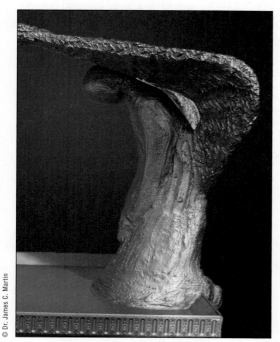

Artist's rendition of one of the cherubim that were placed on opposite ends of the mercy seat.

© Dr. James C. Martin

3:10-13; 5:7-8). Carved cherubim also adorned the walls of the temple (1 Ki. 6:29). David sings of God riding on a cherub (2 Sam. 22:11; Ps. 18:10).

That the cherubim were more than clouds or statues is plain from the description Ezekiel gives (Ezek. 9:3; 10:1-22), which shows that they are the "living creatures" of the first chapter. The four faces of each of the cherubim (1:10) stand for the four "excellencies" of the created order: the lion, the greatest of the wild beasts; the eagle, the greatest of the birds; the ox, the greatest of the domestic beasts; and man, the crown of creation. Ezekiel sees, over the heads of the cherubim, the throne of the God who is thus absolutely sovereign over his whole creation, in all its variety of life and being and in all its complexity of movement. The same explanation of the cherub-form suits their function both in Eden (CREATION in its ideal purity consents to the Creator's edict of exclusion from the garden) and on the mercy seat (all the created excellencies marvel and adore the Triune God for the shed blood of ATONEMENT). At the same time, Ezekiel's vision explains the OT allusion to the Lord as seated (or enthroned) on/between the cherubim (e.g., Ps. 99:1); it is a metaphor of his total sovereignty. Likewise when the Lord is said to ride on the cherubim (e.g., Ps. 18:10; Ezek. 10 passim), the thought is that all creation is subject to his sovereign rule and "intervention," and all its powers are at his disposal.

The book of Revelation mentions four "living creatures" (Rev. 4:6-9; 5:6-14; 6:1-11; 14:3; 15:7; 19:4 [not "beasts," as the KJV says]). They are described in terms that identify them with Ezekiel's living creatures or cherubim (Ezek. 1; 10). The first living creature was like a lion, the second like a calf, the third had a face as a man, the fourth was like a flying eagle (Rev. 4:7). They are the bearers of the judgments that follow the breaking of the first four seals.

The cherubim are the living chariot or carriers of God when appearing to human beings. They are heavenly creatures, servants of God in theophany and judgment, appearing in winged human-animal form with the faces of lion, ox, man, and eagle. Their representations in the tabernacle and temple as statues and in embroidery and carving are not a breach of the second commandment (Exod. 20:4). They are significant in prophecy (Ezekiel) and in the Apocalypse (Revelation). Their service is rendered immediately to God. They never come closer to man than when one took fire in his hand and gave it into the hands of "the man in linen" (Ezek. 10:7). Yet because the mercy seat, on which the blood of atonement was sprinkled, lay "between the cherubim," nothing can more nearly touch our salvation. In the OT sanctuary, where everything was done and taught by visible, tangible types and symbols, physical representations of the living heavenly cherubim were important.

Cherub (place). See Kerub.

Chesalon. See Kesalon.

Chesed. See Kesed.

Chesil. See Kesil.

Chest. A box (of any size) for keeping valuables. English versions use this term in a few passages (e.g., 2 Ki. 12:9-10; 2 Chr. 24:8-11) to render a Hebrew word that occurs elsewhere frequently with reference to the ark of the covenant. Another Hebrew term occurs only in one passage (1 Sam. 6:8, 11, 15). In addition, the KJV uses "chest" in a difficult verse (Ezek. 27:24; see carpet).

chestnut tree. See plants.

Chesulloth. See Kesulloth.

cheth. See heth.

Chezib. See Kezib.

chicken. See birds.

Chidon. See Kidon.

chief. See occupations and professions (under *ruler*).

chief priest. See priest.

child, children. Among the people of the OT and NT, as in most other cultures, children, especially male, were greatly desired (Gen. 15:2; 30:1; 1 Sam. 1:11, 20; Ps. 127:3; 128:3; Lk. 1:7, 28). Among the Hebrews all the firstborn belonged to God (cf. Num. 3:40-51). Children were sometimes dedicated to God for special service (Jdg. 13:2-7; 1 Sam. 1:11; Lk. 1:13-17, 76-79). Male descendants of Abraham were circumcised on the eighth day (Gen. 17:12; 21:4; Lk. 1:59; 2:21), when the name was given. Weaning often was delayed and then celebrated with a feast (Gen. 21:8). Education was primarily in the home and was the duty of parents (Exod. 12:26-27; Deut. 6:7; Josh. 4:21-24; Prov. 22:6; Eph. 6:4; Col. 3:21; 2 Tim. 3:15). Discipline was to be firm, with corporal punishment (Prov. 22:15; 23:13; 29:15). Much was expected of children (Prov. 20:11). Obedience and respect to parents was commanded (Exod. 21:17; Eph. 6:1-3; Col. 3:20; 1 Tim. 3:4, 12; Tit. 1:6).

Favoritism was sometimes shown (Gen. 25:28; 37:3). Affection for children is strikingly portrayed in many instances, as in David's love for his child who died (2 Sam. 12:15-23), and in the raising of children to life by Elijah (1 Ki. 17:17-24), by Elisha (2 Ki. 4:18-37), and by Jesus (Matt. 9:23-26; Mk. 5:35-43; Lk. 8:49-56). Jesus' love and concern for children is seen in Matt. 18:1-14; 19:13-15; Mk. 9:35-37; 10:13-16; Lk. 9:46-48; 18:15-17. Jesus recognized children's play (Matt. 11:16). There are many reports of attractive childhood, for example, Moses (Exod. 2:1-10), Samuel (1 Sam. 1:20—3:19), Jesus (Lk. 2:7-40), Timothy (2 Tim. 1:5; 3:14-15).

"Children" is an affectionate address, as in 1 John, of an old man to adults, who are nevertheless expected to act their age (1 Cor. 13:11; 14:20). The attention given to the childhood of the Messiah in prophecy (Isa. 7:14; 9:6) prepares us for the infancy narratives in Matt. 2 and Lk. 2. The Savior came as a helpless babe and apparently had a normal childhood. A return to childlike receptiveness and trust is required of those who would enter the kingdom of heaven (Matt. 18:1-14; 19:13-15; Mk. 9:35-37; 10:13-61; Lk. 9:46-48; 18:15-17).

childbearing. The word occurs in 1 Tim. 2:15 in a passage relating to the proper sphere and conduct of women. The statement, "Women will be saved through childbearing," cannot refer to salvation from sin, which is by grace through faith, but to safekeeping through the pain that became incidental to childbirth through the FALL (Gen. 3:16). Hebrew mothers had the assistance of midwives (Exod. 1:15-21). Newborn babies had the navel cut, were washed with water, salted, and wrapped in swaddling clothes (Ezek. 16:4; Lk. 2:7, 12). PURIFICATION rites were prescribed after childbirth (Lev. 12; Lk. 2:22-24).

children of God. See SONS OF GOD.

Chileab. See KILEAB.

Chilion. See KILION.

Chilmad. See KILMAD.

Chimham. See KIMHAM.

Chinnereth. See KINNERETH.

Chios. See KIOS.

chisel. See AX; PLANE.

Chisleu, Chislev. See KISLEV.

Chislon. See KISLON.

Chisloth-tabor. See KISLOTH TABOR.

Chithlish, Chitlish. See KITLISH.

Chittim. See KITTIM.

Chiun. See KAIWAN.

Chloe. kloh′ee (Gk. *Chloē G5951*, "verdure, green grass" [an epithet of the goddess Demeter]). A woman whose people reported to PAUL on conditions at CORINTH (1 Cor. 1:11). Chloe may have lived in Corinth or, more likely, in EPHESUS (where Paul was when he wrote 1 Corinthians).

choice, chosen. See ELECTION AND PREDESTINATION.

choinix. See WEIGHTS AND MEASURES.

choir. See MUSIC AND MUSICAL INSTRUMENTS.

Chor-ashan. See BOR ASHAN.

Chorazin. koh-ray′zin. See KORAZIN.

Christ, Jesus. kr*i*st, jee′zuhs (Gk. *Christos G5986*, "anointed" [see MESSIAH]; Gk. *Iēsous G2653*, from Heb. *yēšûʿa H3800*, short form of *yĕhôšuaʿ H3397*, "Yahweh is salvation" [see JOSHUA]).

I. **Comprehensive Life and Work**. Although the life of Christ, as ordinarily understood, embraces only the years our Lord spent on this earth as described in the four Gospels, his full career spans the ages and invites reflection on its several aspects. Fundamental to the various "I am" sayings of Jesus is his assertion of absolute existence (Jn. 8:58). Therefore it is reasonable to think of him as belonging to eternity. Scripture, in fact, affirms his preexistence and does so in terms of fellowship with the Father (1:1), glory (17:5), and designation in advance as the Savior of the world (1 Pet. 1:20). His more immediate relation to the realm of people and things belongs to his activity in CREATION. All things came into being through him (Jn. 1:3; 1 Cor. 8:6; Heb. 1:2), and in him they continue to have their cohesive principle (Col. 1:17).

Evidence is not lacking for his presence also in the OT. The manifestations of God in this period are apparently connected with the preincarnate Christ. When Isaiah glimpsed the glory of God, he was seeing Christ (Jn. 12:41). Moses and the prophets spoke of him (Lk. 24:27, 44; Jn. 5:46), with special reference to his sufferings and the glories that would follow (1 Pet. 1:11). Some of the more important passages of a predictive nature are Gen. 3:15; Deut. 18:15, 18; Ps. 2; 16; 22; 110; Isa. 7:14; 9:6, 7, 11; 42:1-4; 52:13—53:12; 61:1, 2; Jer. 23:5-6; Mic. 5:2. In addition there are covenantal statements that do not speak of the MESSIAH directly and personally, but that involve him in crucial ways (Gen. 12:3; 2 Sam. 7:12-16). As though in anticipation of the INCARNATION, the Son of God showed himself at times to the faithful in visible form as the ANGEL of the Lord (Gen. 18:1-19:1; Jdg. 13). Before his advent Christ had thoroughly identified himself with his people, so that when he came, he came to his own (Jn. 1:11).

By the incarnation, the Christ of God took on himself human nature in order to reveal God to people in a way they could grasp (Jn. 1:14, 18), to become their Savior by ransoming them from their sins (Mk. 10:45), and to deal sympathetically with their needs (Heb. 2:17-18). Today, in glory, he is still the God-man. The incarnation persists. The present ministry of Christ is being carried on in heaven, where he represents the saints before the throne of God (Heb. 7:25; 1 Jn. 2:1). By the successful completion of his work on earth he is exalted to be the head of the CHURCH (Eph. 1:22; 4:15) and by the HOLY SPIRIT directs the life and service of his saints on earth (Matt. 28:20).

One purpose of the incarnation was not achieved during the earthly ministry of our Lord but is reserved for his second coming. His kingly rule will then be introduced following his work as judge (Matt. 25:31-34). This future coming is one of the major truths set forth in the Epistles (Phil. 3:20-21; 2 Thess. 1:7-10) and is the leading theme of the Revelation. After the millennial kingdom, Christ will enter with his people the blessedness of the eternal state, which will be unmarred by the inroads of sin or death. See ESCHATOLOGY.

II. Earthly Ministry. The long-heralded Christ came in the fullness of time (Gal. 4:4). God providentially supplied the proper background for his appearing and mission. The world had become to a great extent homogeneous through the spread of the Greek language and culture and through the organizing genius of ROME. The means were thus provided for the spread of the GOSPEL once it had been forged out in the career of the Son of God. His advent occurred at a point in human history when the LAW of Moses had done its work of demonstrating the sinfulness of human beings and the impossibility of achieving righteousness by human effort.

Entirely in keeping with this divine control of the circumstances surrounding the incarnation is the careful selection of the Virgin Mary as the mother of Jesus. The birth of the Savior was natural, but his conception was supernatural by the power of the Holy Spirit (Matt. 1:18; Lk. 1:35). See VIRGIN BIRTH. Even the Roman emperor,

AUGUSTUS, was drawn into the circle of the instruments chosen by God when he ordered a universal enrollment for taxation, not realizing that by doing so he would make possible the birth of Jesus in the place appointed by prophetic announcement (Mic. 5:2; Lk. 2:1-7). The shepherds, by their readiness to seek out the babe in the manger and by their joy at seeing him, became prototypes of the humble souls in Judaism who in coming days would recognize in Jesus their Savior. An intimation of Gentile desire to participate in the Christ may be seen in the coming of the MAGI from the East. In darker perspective appears the figure of HEROD, emblematic of the hatred and opposition that would meet Jesus of Nazareth and work for his death. In the SCRIBES, conversant with the Scriptures but apathetic about seeking the One who fulfilled them, we see the shape of things to come—the leaders of a nation refusing to receive him when he came to his own.

In more theological terms the Christ-event is an incarnation. God was manifest in flesh. The One who was in the form of God took the form of a servant and was made in human likeness (Phil. 2:6-7). Therefore, when the Scriptures assert from time to time that God sent his Son into the world, this affirmation is not to be treated as though Christ is merely a messenger of God, like the ancient prophets. Rather, he is the eternal Son of God now clothing himself with human nature to accomplish the salvation of people. Though the expression "God-man" is not found in the sacred records, it faithfully expresses the truth regarding the person of Jesus Christ. God did not appropriate a man who already existed and make of him an instrument for the working out of the divine purposes. He took what is common to us all, our human nature, yet free from any taint of sin, and combined it with deity to become an actual person with his own individuality. This is the mystery of the incarnation. The gulf between the Creator and the creature is bridged, first by the person of Christ and then by his mediatorial work.

The boyhood of Jesus should be approached from the standpoint of the truth revealed about the incarnation. Deity did not eclipse humanity so as to render the process of learning unnecessary. Christ grew in body and advanced both in knowl-

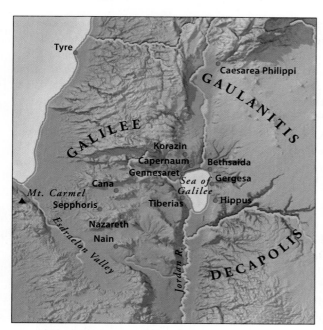

Jesus' ministry in Galilee.

break Christ's dependence on the Father, so that he would desert the standpoint of man and rely on special consideration as the Son of God. But Christ refused to be moved from his determined place of chosen identification with the human race. "Man does not live on bread alone" was his first line of defense. He maintained it in the two following episodes, quoting the obligation of Israel in relation to God as his own reason for refusing to be moved from a place of trustful dependence on the Almighty (Matt. 4:7, 10).

Only when equipped by the baptism and seasoned by the ordeal of temptation was Jesus ready for his life and work. No word of teaching and no work of power is attributed to him prior to these events, but immediately afterward he began moving in the power of the Spirit to undertake the work the Father had given him to do (Lk. 4:14).

The public ministry of Jesus was brief. Its length has to be estimated from the materials recorded in the Gospels. John gives more information on this point than the other evangelists. Judging from the number of PASSOVERS mentioned there (Jn. 2:23; 6:4; 13:1; perhaps also 5:1), the period was at least somewhat in excess of two years and possibly more than three.

John supplements the Synoptic Gospels also in the description of the place of ministry. The synoptists put chief stress on GALILEE and give notice of a visit to the regions of TYRE and SIDON (Matt. 15:21-28), CAESAREA PHILIPPI (16:13), the Gentile cities of the DECAPOLIS (Mk. 7:31; cf. also Mk. 5:1-20), SAMARIA (Lk. 9:51-56; 17:11), and the region E of the JORDAN River known as PEREA (Mk. 10:1). John, on the other hand, reports several visits to Jerusalem; in fact, most of his record is taken up with accounts of Jesus' ministry in JUDEA. The synoptists hint at such a ministry (e.g., Matt. 23:37; Lk. 10:38-42) but give little information.

During his Galilean mission, Jesus made the city of CAPERNAUM his headquarters. From this center he went out, usually in the company of his disciples, to challenge the people in city and town and village with his message. Several such tours are indicated

edge and in the wisdom that enabled him to make proper use of what he knew. He did not command his parents but rather obeyed them, fulfilling the law in this matter as in all others. The scriptural accounts have none of the fanciful extravagances of the apocryphal gospels, which present the boy Jesus as a worker of wonders during his early years (see APOCRYPHAL NEW TESTAMENT). They emphasize his progress in the understanding of the OT and affirm his consciousness of a special relation to his Father in heaven (Lk. 2:49).

At his BAPTISM Jesus received divine confirmation of the mission now opening out before him and also the anointing of the Holy Spirit for the fulfillment of it. The days of preparation were definitely at an end, so that retirement was put aside and contact begun with his people Israel. By the baptism he was fulfilling all righteousness (Matt. 3:15) in the sense that he was identifying himself with those he came to redeem.

Closely related to the baptism is the TEMPTATION, for it also includes this representative character. The first ADAM failed when put to the test; the last Adam succeeded, though weakened by hunger and harried by the desolation of the wilderness. In essence, the temptation was the effort of SATAN to

in the sacred text (Mk. 1:38; 6:6; Lk. 8:1). A part of his ministry consisted in healings and exorcisms, for many had diseases of various sorts and many were afflicted with demon possession. These miracles were not only tokens of divine compassion but also signs that in the person of Jesus of Nazareth the Promised One had come (cf. Matt. 11:2-6; Lk. 4:16-19). They were revelations of the mercy and power of God at work in God's Anointed. Jesus found fault with the cities of Galilee for rejecting him despite the occurrence of so many mighty works in their midst (Matt. 11:20-24).

The message proclaimed by Jesus during these journeys was epitomized in the phrase, the KINGDOM OF GOD. Fundamentally, this means the rule of God in human life and history. The phrase may have a more concrete significance at times, for Jesus spoke now and again about entering into the kingdom. In certain passages he spoke of the kingdom as future (Matt. 25:34), but in others as present (Lk. 11:20). This last reference is of special importance, for it connects the kingdom with the activity of Jesus in casting out DEMONS. To the degree that Jesus invades the kingdom of Satan in this fashion, the kingdom of God has already come. But in the more spiritual and positive aspects of kingdom teaching, where the individual life is concerned, the emphasis does not fall on invasion of personality or compulsive surrender to the power of God. The laws of discipleship are demanding indeed, but for their application they await the consent of the individual. No disciple is to be forced but is rather to be persuaded by the power of love and grace.

If we inquire more definitely into the relation of Jesus himself to the kingdom, we are obliged to conclude that he not only introduced the kingdom but also was its perfect embodiment. The appropriate response to the preaching of the kingdom is committal to the will of God (Matt. 6:10), and it is crystal clear that doing the will of God was the mainspring of Jesus' ministry (Matt. 12:50; Mk. 14:36; Jn. 4:34). It is evident, of course, that Jesus will also inaugurate the final phase of the kingdom when he comes again in power and glory. Entrance into the present aspect of the kingdom is obtained through FAITH in the Son of God and his successful mission.

Much of our Lord's teaching was conveyed through PARABLES. These were usually comparisons taken from various phases of nature or human life ("The kingdom of God is like ... "). This method of teaching preserved the interest of the hearers until the spiritual application could be made. If the truth so taught was somewhat veiled by this method, this served to seal the spiritual blindness of the unre-

© Dr. James C. Martin

View from Mt. Tabor looking NW over the Nazareth Ridge and the modern city of Nazareth. Despite Jesus' extended stay in Nazareth during his early years, the Gospels say very little about this time in his earthly life.

pentant and at the same time created a wholesome curiosity on the part of those who were disposed to believe, so that they could be led on to firm faith by more direct teaching.

The ministry of the Savior was predominantly to the multitudes during its earlier phase, as he sought out the people where they were, whether in the synagogue or on the city street or by the lakeside. "He went around doing good" is the way PETER described it (Acts 10:38). But much of Jesus' last year of ministry was given over to instruction of the twelve disciples whom he had chosen (for the two phases, see Matt. 4:17 and 16:21). This shift of emphasis was not due primarily to the lack of response on the part of the multitudes, although his following faded at times (Jn. 6:15, 66), but principally to his desire to instruct his disciples concerning himself and his mission. These men, nearly all Galileans and many of them fishermen, had been able to learn much through hearing Jesus address the crowds and through watching him heal the sick and relieve the distressed, and especially through being sent out by him to minister in his name (Lk. 9:1-6). However, they needed more direct teaching to prepare them for the part they would play in the life of the church after the ASCENSION.

What they saw and heard during those early days confirmed their understanding of the person of Jesus as the Messiah and the Son of God (Matt. 16:16), but they were quite unprepared to receive his teaching on the suffering and death that his earthly life would involve (16:21-23). Although this prospect was absolutely necessary for Jesus (16:21), for Peter it was something that the Lord should dismiss from consideration (16:22). If the most prominent one of the apostolic circle felt this way, no doubt the others were of the same mind. Their thoughts were so taken up with the prospect of a kingdom of external power and glory that they were perplexed and disturbed to find that their Master anticipated quite a different experience. His prediction of a RESURRECTION from the dead fell on deaf ears, for the blow of the announcement about his forthcoming death had been too heavy. Even the lessons of the TRANSFIGURATION scene, where death was the theme under discussion and the glory beyond was presented to their sight, did not completely effect the orientation of the disciples to the

teaching of Jesus. He had to repeat it more than once (Mk. 10:33-45). Their sorrow in the Garden of GETHSEMANE shows that they had reluctantly adjusted to it but could not look beyond it to resurrection nor could they realize how much that death itself could mean to their spiritual welfare. After the resurrection they were much more open to the Lord's instruction, so when he appeared to them, he revealed from the OT the divine purpose prewritten there concerning himself (Lk. 24:26-27, 44).

Christ's investment of time and patience with these men was well rewarded, for when the Spirit took up the work of instruction begun by him and gave them his own power for witness, they became effective instruments for declaring the Word of God and for the leadership of the Christian church. The record of the book of Acts vindicates the wisdom of Christ and his understanding of the future.

In contrast to the Twelve in their attitude to Jesus are the SCRIBES and PHARISEES. The former were experts in the law and the traditions that had grown up around it, and the latter were men dedicated to a meticulous devotion to this heritage of JUDAISM. These groups usually worked together, and they collided with Jesus on many occasions over many issues. They were shocked that he would declare sins forgiven and claim a special relation to God as Son that others did not have. They resented his rejection of the traditions that they kept so carefully, and stood aghast at his willingness to "break" the SABBATH (in their way of thinking) by doing deeds of mercy on that day. It was tragic that men who held to the Scriptures as God's Word should fail to see in Jesus Christ the One of whom that Word spoke. They refused to put their trust in him despite all his MIRACLES and the matchless perfection of his personal life. Because tradition meant more to them than truth, they stumbled in their apprehension of the Christ of God. In the end they plotted with their opponents the SADDUCEES in order to do away with Jesus.

Even as Christ was engaged in teaching his disciples from the days of the transfiguration on, he was ever moving toward Jerusalem to fulfill his course at the cross (Lk. 9:51). In those latter days some stirring events were unfolded—the triumphal entry into Jerusalem, the cleansing of the temple, the institution of the Lord's Supper, the soul conflict in the Garden of Gethsemane, the arrest and trial, the crucifixion, the resurrection, the appearances, the ascension into heaven. In all of them Jesus remained the central figure. In all of them he received testimony to himself or gave it. Nothing was unimportant. All contributed to the working out of the plan of God. The CROSS was the human decision respecting Christ, but it had already been his own decision and that of the Father. It underscored the sins of some even as it removed the sins of others. In the cross man's day erupted in violence and blasphemy. In the resurrection God's day began to dawn. It was his answer to the world and to the powers of darkness. In it Christ was justified and his claims illuminated.

III. Names, Titles, and Offices. Considerable help in understanding the person and work of Christ may be gleaned from a consideration of the terms used to designate him, especially as these are used by himself and his close associates. The name *Jesus* alludes to his role as Savior (it is the Gk. form of JOSHUA, "Yahweh is salvation"; cf. Matt. 1:21); it is used mostly in the narratives of the Gospels, and only rarely does it appear in direct address. For the most part this name is joined with "Christ" or "Lord" when used in the NT Epistles, but occasionally it stands alone, especially in Hebrews—doubtless for the purpose of emphasizing his humanity as a continuing element of his being (Heb. 2:9 et al.). Thus, it is legitimate for us today to use the simple name in unadorned fashion, but to do so exclusively could indicate a lack of appreciation of the rounded presentation that Scripture gives of him.

Christ, meaning "anointed one," is the Greek equivalent of the Hebrew word *Messiah*. Its function as a title is emphasized by the fact that often it occurs with the definite article, which gives it the force of "the promised Christ," the one who fulfills the concept of Messiah as set forth in the OT Scriptures. Our Lord uses it of himself in Lk. 24:46: "He told them, 'This is what is written: The Christ will suffer and rise from the dead on the third day.'" By extension of meaning, the same form is used by Paul with reference to the CHURCH as a body (1 Cor. 12:12), thus emphasizing the intimate bond between Christ and his people (see BODY OF CHRIST). Of special interest is the development that led to the use of "Christ" as a personal name.

It must have taken place early in the life of the church, for we find it reflected, for example, in the opening verse of Mark's Gospel—"The beginning of the gospel of Jesus Christ, the Son of God." Possibly our Lord himself is responsible for this usage (Jn. 17:3). In Acts and the Epistles it is not always clear whether "Christ" is being used as a name or as a title, but there are definitely some occurrences of this term alone as a name (e.g., 1 Cor. 15:3).

A circumstance that may strike the reader of the Gospels as odd is the prohibition against making Jesus known as the Christ or Messiah during the days of his ministry. He imposed this restriction on the disciples (Matt. 16:20) and somewhat similarly choked off any possible testimony from demons (Lk. 4:41). If this title should be used freely of him among the Jews, it would excite the populace to expect in him a political Messiah who would gain for them their national freedom and many accompanying benefits. Since this was not the purpose of Jesus, he did what he could to suppress the use of the term *Messiah* with regard to himself, though he welcomed it in the circle of the apostles (Matt. 16:16).

Only once does the name IMMANUEL occur, and then in connection with the conception of Jesus (Matt. 1:23). It is a Hebrew word meaning "God with us," and is especially appropriate when describing the incarnational aspect of Jesus' birth. For some reason the name did not gain currency in the church, perhaps because it was crowded out by Jesus and Christ.

Among the ancients it was common to distinguish a person not only by name but also by place of residence. Consequently Jesus was often called the NAZARENE because of his years spent in the village of NAZARETH (Lk. 24:19). When used of Jesus' followers by the Jews (Acts 24:5), the term took on an element of reproach that it did not possess in any recognizable way during his life on earth.

When Jesus referred to himself, he most often used the title SON OF MAN. It was more than a means of identification, however, for it linked him to a conception of majesty that had gathered around the term since its use in Dan. 7:13. Although it is possible that occasionally the title stresses Jesus' humanity, in the main it serves to point to his transcendence as a heavenly figure. Certainly the widespread notion that Son of Man expresses the humanity of Jesus, as Son of God expresses his deity, is quite misleading (cf. Lk. 22:69-70). By using this title publicly rather than Messiah, Jesus was able to avoid suggesting that his mission was political in nature, and instead could put into the title by his own use of it the content that he wanted to give to it. The church apparently recognized the Lord's right to exclusive use of the term and did not use it, out of deference to him (the one exception is STEPHEN's comment in Acts 7:56).

One of the most familiar designations for Jesus is SON OF GOD. Only in John's Gospel does he use it of himself (Jn. 5:25; 10:36; 11:4). But elsewhere he uses its equivalent, the Son (Matt. 11:27), which is especially appropriate when used opposite the Father, and which in such a passage clearly sets off the uniqueness of this particular Son. In the Synoptic Gospels considerable care is needed in order to impute to the term Son of God the exact nuance of meaning proper to its every occurrence. Geerhardus Vos discerned four meanings: the nativistic, which stresses the divine origination of the person of Jesus as a human figure; the ethico-religious, which points to the filial relation that Christ had with the Father within the context of his human life, similar to that which any child of God has; the messianic, which has to do with his appointment as the one anointed and sent by God, in fulfillment of OT prophecy; the trinitarian or ontological, in which the unique relation of Christ to the Father as the only Son is expressed. This latter, of course, represents the highest level of sonship.

Rather frequently in the course of his ministry Jesus was addressed as *Son of David* (Matt. 21:9; Lk. 18:38), which is a distinctly messianic title pointing to him as the One who fulfilled the Davidic covenant, the One who was expected to establish the kingdom and bring Israel to freedom, peace, and glory (cf. Matt. 1:1; Lk. 1:32-33).

A few passages proclaim outright that Jesus is *God* (Jn. 1:1 [in a preincarnate setting]; 1:18 [according to the strongest MS evidence]; 20:28; Rom. 9:5 [according to the most natural construction of the verse]; Tit. 2:13; Heb. 1:8). That the passages are relatively few in number is probably due to the fact that Jesus Christ, as known to human beings, was in a position of subordination to the heavenly Father, his deity veiled by his humanity, so that it was much more natural to assign to him the predicates of deity than to refer to him directly as God. The monotheistic background of the early Hebrew Christians doubtlessly exercised a restraining influence also. Some moderns who do not doubt Jesus' essential deity have also confessed to a feeling of restraint in referring to Jesus as God.

No term is more expressive of the faith of early believers in Jesus than LORD (Acts 2:36; 10:36; Rom. 10:9; 1 Cor. 8:6; 12:3; Phil. 2:11). It denotes the SOVEREIGNTY of Christ and his headship over the individual believer, the church as a body, and all things. For those who were strangers it was merely a title of respect and is translated "sir" (Jn. 4:11); but for those who were deeply attached to the Savior it had the highest import, calling alike for homage and obedience (Jn. 20:28; Acts 22:10). Used sparingly during the period of the earthly ministry prior to the resurrection, it takes on an increased use and heightened significance as a result of that momentous event.

Some titles pertain to the mission of Christ more than to his person. One of these is *Word* (Jn. 1:1, 14; 1 Jn. 1:1). See LOGOS. As such Christ is essentially the revealer of God, the One who opens to the understanding of people the nature and purposes

Model of the 1st-cent. Jerusalem temple, looking S over the Court of Women toward the two-story colonnades of the Royal Stoa where the money changers did business.

© Dr. James C. Martin

of the Almighty and discloses the higher wisdom that stands in contrast to the wisdom of those who are merely human beings. In keeping with such a title is the designation *Teacher*, by which our Lord was customarily addressed in the days of his flesh. This attests to the impact of his instruction and the authority that lay behind it. Despite the fact that Jesus lacked rabbinic training, he could not be denied the recognition of the wisdom that shone through his spoken word.

The classic designation of Christ as *Servant* is given by Paul in Phil. 2:7, but it was widely recognized in the early church that our Lord fulfilled the servant-of-God role (see Matt. 12:17-21). That it dominated the thinking of Christ himself may be safely affirmed in the light of such a passage as Mk. 10:45. See SERVANT OF THE LORD.

Central to the mission of Christ was his work as SAVIOR. We have already seen that the name Jesus has this meaning, the name suggesting the reason for his coming into the world. Several passages herald Christ under the aspect of his saviorhood (e.g., Lk. 2:11; Jn. 4:42). The idea in the word is not merely deliverance from sin and all the other woes that afflict the human race, but the provision of a state of wholeness and blessedness in which a person realizes the purpose of God for him or her. In reports of the healings of Jesus, the verb form calls attention to the state of soundness that resulted from the healing touch of the Savior.

Jesus' saving mission is declared also in the expression, LAMB OF GOD (Jn. 1:29, 36; cf. Rev. 5:6). Peter likewise uses the word "lamb" in reference to Jesus, with special reference to his qualification of sinlessness (1 Pet. 1:19).

The designation of Jesus as *High Priest* is confined to the letter to the Hebrews, where it occurs some ten times, his work being described as taking place in the heavenly sanctuary, in the presence of God, where the fruits of his death for sinners on the earth are conserved in his work of intercession (Heb. 9:11-12).

More general is the characterization of the Lord as the MEDIATOR between God and men (1 Tim. 2:5). This term takes account of the barrier that sin erected between the Creator and the creature, that Christ alone was qualified to remove. For the concept in the OT, see Job 9:33.

Paul uses the title *Last Adam* (1 Cor. 15:45) in contrast to the first Adam, suggesting the undoing of the consequences of sin brought on by Adam's transgression (cf. Rom. 5:12-21) and the new creation life that is to be the possession of all believers in resurrection glory even as it is already their portion in Christ in a spiritual sense.

This list of names and titles of Christ is not exhaustive. The resources of language are taxed in the sacred record to set forth the full excellence and worth of the Son of God. When his work is considered in its broad sweep, the most satisfying analysis divides it into the offices that he fulfills—those of PROPHET, PRIEST, and KING. The prophetic ministry relates especially to the testimony given in the days of his flesh as he heralded the kingdom of God, warned of coming judgment, and encouraged the people of God. He is still the faithful and true witness as he speaks to the church through the Spirit. As priest our Lord made the one sacrifice of himself that brought to an end animal sacrifices and put away sin forever (Heb. 9:26). Faithful and merciful, he ministers before God on behalf of this people who are compassed by sin and infirmity (2:17; 4:15-16). The term *king* relates especially to the future activity of our Lord as he comes again to supplant the kingdom of the world with his own gracious and sovereign rule (Rev. 11:15). He will be no ordinary ruler, but King of kings, without a peer.

IV. Character. "What manner of man is this?" Such was the amazed observation of the disciples of Jesus as they watched him in action and felt the strength and mystery of his personality as they associated with him. Certain ingredients of character deserve special mention, but it cannot be said that he was noted for some things above others, for this would involve disproportion and would reflect on the perfection of his being. He had integrity. After all, this is the kernel of character. The gospel appeal to put our faith in Christ would be impossible if he were not trustworthy. No taint of duplicity marred his dealings with others, for there was no mixture of motives within his heart. He could not deceive, for he was Truth incarnate. The claims of Jesus in areas where we have no means of testing them can be cordially received, because in areas where his affirmations can be judged they stand the test.

Christ had courage. When Aristotle advanced his famous doctrine of the mean, he illustrated it by courage, which lies midway between cowardice and recklessness. Judged by this standard the character of Jesus appears in a most favorable light, for in him one can detect no wild instability even in the most intense activity, nor any supineness in his passivity. Christ had physical courage. Without it he could never have cleared the temple single-handedly. He had the courage of conviction. Peter was probably his boldest disciple, yet he denied his Lord under pressure, whereas Jesus confessed his own person and mission before the SANHEDRIN even though it meant his death. The stamina of human beings is often attributable, at least in part, to the help and sympathy of their fellows, but Jesus stood alone as he faced his final ordeal.

Our Lord showed great compassion as he dealt with people. This is the word used in the Gospels. In the NT Epistles it is called LOVE. The sight of multitudes forlorn and forsaken by those who should have been their spiritual shepherds stirred Christ to the depths of his being. Out of his compassion he ministered to their physical needs for food and health and went on to tell them the secrets of the life of true godliness. Compassion was more than an emotion with Jesus. It was a call to action, to selfless ministry on behalf of the needy. He gave himself to one with the same intensity that he showed in dealing with the many. Virtue went out of him and he did not regret the loss, for it is the nature of love to give. To love the loveless and love them to the end and to the uttermost—this is the love that Paul says "surpasses knowledge" (Eph. 3:19). It is a love that proved itself through death—he "loved me and gave himself for me" (Gal. 2:20)—and yet remains deathless.

Jesus clothed himself with HUMILITY. He could talk about this as his own possession without affectation (Matt. 11:29). Christ wrought a revolution in ethics by dignifying humility in a world that despised it as weakness. Though the universe was his creation, though he was equal with the Father, and though every knee would one day bow before him, yet he was not lifted up with pride because of these things. The mind of Christ is that which takes every reason for exaltation and transforms it into a reason for selfless service. In essence his humility was his refusal to please himself. He came not to be ministered to but to minister.

Our Lord's character is crowned with perfection or sinlessness. This perfection was not simply the absence of sin, but the infusion of a heavenly HOLINESS into all that he said and did. It may be objected that when Jesus gave way to anger and spoke out in bitter denunciation of the Pharisees (Matt. 23), he revealed at least a trace of imperfection. But a character without the power of righteous indignation would be faulty. If Jesus had failed to expose these men, he would not have done his full duty as the exponent of truth. He is the image of the Father, and God is angry with the wicked every day.

V. Influence. A life so brief, so confined in its geographical orbit, so little noticed by the world in his own time, has yet become the most potent force for good in all of human history. This truth is seen in the Scriptures of the NT. In every single book that makes up this collection, Jesus Christ is the inevitable point of reference. Even so brief and personal a writing as Philemon owes its inspiration to the Son of God who came to make men free. The Gospels picture him in the flesh; the NT letters present him in the Spirit. The Acts of the Apostles depicts the victories of his grace in the extension of his church; the Revelation sets forth the triumph of his glory through his personal presence once more in history.

His influence on the saints is so radical and comprehensive that nothing can describe it better than the assertion that Christ is their life. They were not truly living until they came to know him by faith. Until he comes into the heart, self rules supreme. When he comes, he creates a new point of reference and a new set of values. To be Christ-centered is simply normal Christian experience.

What Christ can do in transforming a life may be seen to good advantage in the case of Saul of Tarsus. Apart from Christ the world might never have heard of him. Because in Christ he died to self and lived in the energy of the risen Christ to glorify God, his is a household name wherever Christians are found.

It is inevitable that sinners should feel the touch of Christ and never be the same afterward. Regarding the self-righteous leaders of his own time Jesus could say, "If I had not come and spoken to them, they would not be guilty of sin. Now, however, they have no excuse for their sin" (Jn. 15:22). Christ is the conscience of the world. Because he is the light of the world, when people stand in that light but then turn from it, they walk in deeper darkness and are without hope.

In a more general sense, Christ has mightily affected society in its organized state. He has taught the world the dignity of human life, the worth of the soul, the preciousness of personality. Because of this the status of women has steadily been improved under Christian influence, slavery has been abolished, and children, instead of being exposed as infants and neglected in formative years, are recognized as a primary responsibility for the lavishing of love and care. Even when human life becomes weak or deformed or diseased, it is not regarded as forfeiting a right to a place in society, but as being entitled to assistance. The fact that governments and scientific groups are now engaged in social service on a large scale ought not to disguise the fact that the impulse for these works of mercy has been the Christian church acting in the name and spirit of Christ.

The arts also owe their sublimest achievements to the desire to honor the Son of God. Beethoven called Handel the greatest composer of all time, a man who could not complete his oratorio *The Messiah* without being moved repeatedly to tears as he thought about the incarnation. Every cathedral spire that pierces the sky throughout Christendom bears its silent testimony to the loving outreach toward God that is induced through the knowledge of Christ the Lord. Moralists and philosophers, even when they lack faith in him for the saving of the soul, nevertheless are often found acknowledging wistfully that they wish they had a personal inheritance in him as they commend him to others as the one great hope for mankind.

Christian. (*Christianos G5985*, really a Latin formation, *Christianus*). The Latin termination *-ianus* is common and descriptive: in historical writings of classical times it is used to define a group in terms of its allegiance. The disciples of CHRIST were formally called Christians first in ANTIOCH of Syria (Acts 11:26). AGRIPPA II recognized that to believe

what PAUL preached would make him a Christian (26:28). PETER accepted the name as in itself a basis for persecution (1 Pet. 4:16). Thus gradually a name imposed by GENTILES was adopted by the disciples of Jesus. Some Jews had referred to them as "the Nazarene sect" (Acts 24:5); and Paul, when he was a persecutor, referred to them as those "who belonged to the Way" (9:2). The apostles wrote of themselves as servants (slaves) of Christ (Rom. 1:1; Jas. 1:1; 2 Pet. 1:1; Jude 1; Rev. 1:1). The NT calls the followers of Christ "brothers" (Acts 14:2); "disciples" (6:1-2); "saints" (Acts 9:13; Rom. 1:7; 1 Cor. 1:2); "believers" (1 Tim. 4:12); "the church of God" (Acts 20:28); "all who call on your name" (Acts 9:14; Rom. 10:12-13). To the first Christians, their own name mattered not at all; their concern was with the one Name of Jesus Christ (Acts 3:16; 4:10, 12; 5:28). Inevitably, the name that they invoked was given to them: Christians—those who belong to Christ.

Chronicles, Books of. In the Hebrew Bible, these two volumes bear the title *sēper dibrê hayyāmîm*, "book of the things of the days," that is, "record of the events of the times" or simply "annals." This Hebrew expression occurs some thirty-two times in the books of Kings (e.g., 1 Ki. 14:29; 2 Ki. 1:18) and several times elsewhere (1 Chr. 27:24; Neh. 12:23; Esth. 6:1; 10:2), referring probably to official court records. The title used in the SEPTUAGINT, *Paraleipomenōn*, meaning "things left over," reflects the view that 1-2 Chronicles contain events omitted in the accounts of Samuel and Kings, especially concerning the kingdom of Judah. The church father Jerome (c. A.D. 400) first entitled them "Chronicles." Originally they formed a single composition but were divided into 1 and 2 Chronicles in the LXX, about 150 B.C. In the Hebrew they stand as the last book of the OT canon. Christ (Lk. 11:51) thus spoke of all the martyrs from Abel in the first book (Gen. 4) to Zechariah in the last (2 Chr. 24).

Chronicles contains no statements about its own authorship or date. The last event it records is the decree of CYRUS in 538 B.C. that permitted the exiles to return from their Babylonian captivity (2 Chr. 36:22); and its genealogies extend to approximately 500 B.C., as far, that is, as Pelatiah and Jeshaiah (1 Chr. 3:21), two grandsons of ZERUBBABEL, the prince who led in the return

This cuneiform tablet (BM 21946, late 5th cent. or 4th cent. B.C.) records Babylonian history for the years 605-595 B.C. and includes Nebuchadnezzar's capture of Jerusalem in 598.

from exile. The language, however, and the contents of Chronicles closely parallel that of the book of EZRA, which continues the history of the Jews from the decree of Cyrus down to 457 B.C. Both documents are marked by lists and genealogies, by an interest in priestly ritual, and by devotion to the law of Moses. Moreover, the closing verses of Chronicles (2 Chr. 36:22-23) are repeated as the opening verses of Ezra (Ezra 1:1-3). Thus many believe that Ezra may have been the author of both volumes. If so, his complete work would then have been finished some time around 450 B.C.

Ezra's position as a "scribe" (Ezra 7:6) may also explain the care that Chronicles shows in acknowledging its written source materials. These include such records as those of Samuel (1 Chr. 29:29), Isaiah (2 Chr. 32:32), and a number of other prophets (9:29; 12:15; 20:34; 33:19), and above all else, "the book of the kings of Judah and Israel" (e.g., 16:11; 25:26). This latter work cannot be equated with our present-day 1-2 Kings, for verses such as 1 Chr. 9:1 and 2 Chr. 27:7 refer to "the book of the kings" for further details on matters about which 1-2 Kings is silent. The author's source must have

been a larger court record, now lost, from which the authors of both Kings and Chronicles subsequently drew much of their information.

The occasion for the writing of Chronicles appears to be Ezra's crusade to bring postexilic Judah back into conformity with the law of Moses (Ezra 7:10). From 458 B.C., Ezra sought to restore the temple worship (7:19-23, 27; 8:33-34), to eliminate the mixed marriages of Jews with their pagan neighbors (ch. 9-10), and to strengthen Jerusalem by rebuilding its walls (4:8-16). Chronicles, accordingly, consists of these four parts: genealogies, to enable the Jews to establish their lines of family descent (1 Chr. 1-9); the kingdom of David, as a pattern for the ideal theocratic state (10-29); the glory of Solomon, with an emphasis on the temple and its worship (2 Chr. 1-9); and the history of the southern kingdom, stressing in particular the religious reforms and military victories of Judah's more pious rulers (10-36).

As compared with the parallel histories in Samuel and Kings, the priestly annals of Chronicles put a greater emphasis on the structure of the temple (1 Chr. 22) and on Israel's ark, the Levites, and the singers (1 Chr. 13; 15-16). They omit, however, certain individualistic, moral acts of the kings (2 Sam. 9; 1 Ki. 3:16-28), as well as detailed biographies of the prophets (1 Ki. 17—22:28; 2 Ki. 1—8:15), features that account for the incorporation of Chronicles into the third (nonprophetic) section of the Hebrew canon, as distinguished from the location of the more homiletic books of Samuel and Kings in the second (prophetic) division. Finally, the chronicler foregoes discussion of David's disputed inauguration and later shame (2 Sam. 1-4; 11-21), of Solomon's failures (1 Ki. 11), and of the whole inglorious history of Saul (1 Sam. 8-30, except his death, v. 31), and of the northern kingdom of Israel. The disillusioned, impoverished Jews of 450 B.C. knew enough of sin and defeat; they needed an encouraging reminder of their former, God-given victories (e.g., 2 Chr. 13-14; 20; 25).

Because of these emphases, many modern critics have rejected Chronicles as being Levitical propaganda, a fiction of "what ought to have happened," with extensive (and conflicting) revisions as late as 250 B.C. The book's high numeric totals (such as the one million invading Ethiopians, 2 Chr. 14:9)

© Dr. James C. Martin. The British Museum. Photographed by permission.

C

Overview of 1-2 CHRONICLES

Author: Unknown, though Jewish tradition attributed it (as well as Ezra and Nehemiah) to EZRA.

Historical setting: Chronicles treats approximately the same period covered by the books of 2 Samuel and 1-2 Kings, but from the perspective of someone living after the Babylonian EXILE, probably in the fifth century B.C. (some date Chronicles as late as 250 B.C.).

Purpose: To provide a historical-theological account of the Hebrew nation from the reign of DAVID to the fall of JERUSALEM, focusing almost exclusively on the southern kingdom of JUDAH, and reminding the people of the glories of the Davidic dynasty, the importance of the TEMPLE for Jewish WORSHIP, and the divine principle of BLESSING and RETRIBUTION.

Contents: After a genealogical background establishing the continuity of postexilic ISRAEL with the people of God (1 Chr. 1-9), the writer provides a narrative of the united Hebrew kingdom under David and SOLOMON, with emphasis on both the preparations for and the actual building of the temple (1 Chr. 10 to 2 Chr. 9); the last section traces the history of Judah after the division of the kingdom (2 Chr. 10-36).

have been questioned despite the elucidations presented by several conservative scholars. Although Chronicles does stress the bright side of Hebrew history, it does not deny the defects (cf. 1 Chr. 29:22 on the successful *second* anointing of Solomon, and 2 Chr. 17:3 on the more exemplary *first* ways of David). The prophetic judgments of Kings and the priestly hopes of Chronicles are both true, and both are necessary. The morality of the former is invaluable, but the redemption of the latter constitutes the more distinctive feature of Christian faith.

While primarily historical in nature, the books of 1 and 2 Chronicles reflect a distinct theology. This theology is set forth in the selection and arrangement of historical events as well as in the chronicler's comments on these events. One of the important theological themes of the books of Chronicles is the necessity of obedience for divine blessing. The chronicler observes that Saul's death was due to unfaithfulness (1 Chr. 10:13-14), as was the exile of the southern kingdom (1 Chr. 9:1; see also 2 Chr. 6:24). On the other hand, obedi-

ence will bring blessing to the nation (1 Chr. 28:8; 2 Chr. 7:14-18). Even the lengthy genealogy that forms the preface to 1 Chronicles contains affirmations of this fact (4:10; 5:1, 25). The narration of selected events from the life of David focuses on the steps of obedience that led to his successful administration of the kingdom. Instances of David's disobedience are minimized. Thus the obedience of David was presented as an ideal for the postexilic community.

Another theological aspect of Chronicles is its emphasis on the Davidic theology. David's role in the establishment of Israelite worship receives prominence (1 Chr. 22:2-5; 23:1-32; 25:1—26:32). But most important to the Davidic theology is the restatement of the terms of the Abrahamic covenant to David (1 Chr. 17:1-27; cf. 2 Chr. 6:1-11). The Davidic covenant established the divine authority of the Davidic dynasty and guaranteed its perpetuity (1 Chr. 21:7).

The theology of worship in Chronicles acknowledges only one site where Israel may worship. The legitimacy of the postexilic temple and its personnel is established by virtue of its continuity with the temple built by Solomon under the sponsorship of David (1 Chr. 17:24; 2 Chr. 6:7-9).

chronology (OT). This topic presents complex and difficult problems. Because of insufficient data, many of these problems are at present insoluble. Even where the evidence is abundant, the exact meaning is often not immediately apparent, leaving room for considerable difference of opinion and giving rise to many variant chronological reconstructions. Only the most careful study of all the data, both biblical and extrabiblical, can hope to provide a reliable chronology.

I. From the creation to the flood. In this period the only biblical information consists of the ages of the patriarchs in Gen. 7:11 and the genealogical tables of Gen. 5. Calculations of the years from Adam to the flood vary in the ancient texts: 1,656 (Heb. Masoretic Text = MT), 1,307 (Samaritan Pentateuch = SP), and 2,242 (Gk. Septuagint = LXX). The numbers of the MT are in agreement with the SP except in the cases of Jared, Methuselah, and Lamech, where the numbers of the MT are higher by 100, 120, and 129 years respectively. For the eight patriarchs from Adam to Methuselah, the numbers of the LXX are a century higher in each instance than those of the SP, while for Lamech the number is 135 years higher.

Extrabiblical sources for this period are almost completely lacking. The early Sumerian king list names eight kings with a total of 241,200 years from the time when "the kingship was lowered from heaven" to the time when "the Flood swept" over the land and once more "the kingship was lowered from heaven" (Thorkild Jacobsen, *The Sumerian King List* [1939], 71, 77). Such a statement, however, makes no practical contribution to the solution of this phase of OT chronology. Nor is modern science in a position to supply a detailed and final solution.

II. From the flood to Abraham. For this period we are again dependent on the genealogical data in the Greek and Hebrew texts and the SP. Reckoning the age of Terah at the birth of Abraham as 70 (Gen. 11:26), the years from the flood to Abraham would be 292 according to the MT, 942 according to the SP, and 1,172 according to the LXX. But if the age of Terah at Abraham's birth is reckoned as 130 years (on the basis of Gen. 11:32; 12:4; Acts 7:4), the above totals would be raised by 60 years. On this basis, the Hebrew text would give 352 years from the flood to Abraham, and the Greek would be 1,232. In this area the testimony of the MT stands alone against the LXX and the Samaritan Pentateuch, where the numbers are 100 years higher than those of the MT for Arphaxad, Salah, Eber, Peleg, Reu, and Serug; while for Nahor, the grandfather of Abraham, the SP and the LXX are respectively 50 and 150 years higher than the MT.

Serious chronological difficulties are thus encountered in the period immediately beyond Abraham. This patriarch was 86 years old at the birth of Ishmael (Gen. 16:16) and 100 at the birth of Isaac (21:5). But how old was Terah at the birth of Abraham—70, 130, or some number not revealed? And how old was Nahor at the birth of Terah—29, 79, or 179? If Terah was 130 years old at the birth of Abraham, as seems to be indicated by the biblical evidence, it must be admitted that the numbers of the LXX for this period (135, 130, 130, 134, 130, 132, 130, 179, 130), are much more consistent with each other than the numbers of the Hebrew (35, 30, 34, 30, 32, 30, 29, 130). But notice that in the case of nine patriarchs in the LXX, five of them were 130 years old when their sons were born, while in the Hebrew three out of eight were 30, one was 130, while the others were all in their thirties with the exception of Nahor, who was 29—one year from 30. And if Terah was 130 years old when Abraham was born, why was it regarded as so very unusual for Abraham to have a son at the age of 100 (Gen. 17:17; 18:11; 21:2, 5)?

An endeavor to assess the relative values of the three sources involved accomplishes little, for the indications are that none is complete. Certainly the LXX had great weight in NT times, for in Luke's table of the ancestors of Christ, there is listed a second Cainan—son of Arphaxad (Lk. 3:36), in harmony with the LXX of Gen. 11:12-13—a Cainan not found in the MT. If the LXX is here to be followed rather than the MT, another 130 years should be added to the years of the flood and creation, for that is the age of Cainan in the LXX at the time of the birth of Salah.

Aerial view of red granite mountains in S Sinai.

© Dr. James C. Martin

The omission of the names of known individuals is frequent in biblical genealogical records. Thus, Matthew's table of the ancestors of Christ omits the names of three Judean kings—Ahaziah, Joash, and Amaziah—with the statement that "Jehoram [was] the father of Uzziah" (Matt. 1:8), whereas Uzziah was actually the great-great-grandson of Jehoram. A comparison of Ezra 7:1-5 with 1 Chr. 6:4-15 shows a block of six names missing in Ezra's tabulation.

Extrabiblical materials prior to Abraham are of little assistance in the establishment of an absolute chronology, for no exact synchronisms exist between biblical and secular chronology of this period. Because of the difficulties involved, it must be admitted that the construction of a definitive chronology from Adam to Abraham is not now possible on the basis of the available data.

III. From Abraham to Moses. From Abraham to Joseph the detailed patriarchal narratives provide more data than are available for the preceding periods, and we have the certainty that there are no missing links. There are also a number of correlations with later and better-known periods. Since Abraham was 75 years old at the time of his entrance into Canaan (Gen. 12:4), and since he was 100 at the birth of Isaac (21:5), there were 25 years from the entry into Canaan to Isaac. Isaac was 60

at the birth of Jacob (25:26), and Jacob was 130 at his entrance into Egypt (47:9, 28), making 215 years from the beginning of the sojourn in Canaan to the beginning of the sojourn in Egypt. The total length of the sojourn was 430 years (Exod. 12:40). Did this involve only the sojourn in Egypt or did it include also the sojourn in Canaan? If Israel was in Egypt 430 years, there were 645 years from the entrance into Canaan to Moses' departure from Egypt. However, if the 430 years includes the time spent by the patriarchs in Canaan, the length of the Egyptian sojourn would have been only 215 years.

According to 1 Ki. 6:1, the temple was founded in the 480th year after the exodus. Some have argued that this figure is not intended as a precise number (40 x 12 perhaps indicating an ideal number of generations). If taken literally, however, it provides an important chronological marker. Solomon began to build the temple in the fourth year of his reign. On the basis of a 40-year reign (1 Ki. 11:42) and in accord with the established chronology of the kings, the year must have been 966 B.C. This information yields 1445 as the date of the exodus and 1525 as the year of Moses' birth (Exod. 7:7). If the 430-year sojourn involved only the period in Egypt, Abraham entered Canaan in 2090. If it included the years in Canaan, the date was 1875.

The answer depends on the meaning of the prophecy of Gen. 15:13-16 and the reconstruction of the details from Abraham to Moses. From Abraham to Joseph the details are known, but from Joseph to Moses there is only genealogical evidence.

Due to omissions, repetitions, and other variations in the genealogical lists, the endeavor to establish dates by the evidence of such lists must be regarded as highly precarious. Compare, for instance, the line of descent of Samuel and his sons from Levi and Kohath as recorded in 1 Chr. 6:22-28 and in 6:33-38, and see 1 Sam. 8:2 for the names of these sons. Compare also the various lists of the sons of Benjamin and their descendants as found in Gen. 46:21; Num. 26:38-40; 1 Chr. 7:6-12; 8:1-40. The variations in existence here and in many other lists indicate the dangers involved in dogmatic reconstructions based only on genealogical evidence.

The ancestry of Moses from Jacob through Levi, Kohath, and Amram is repeatedly given (Num. 3:17-19; 26:57-59; 1 Chr. 6:1-3; 23:6, 12-13), including the ages of these men at the time of death (Exod. 6:16, 18, 20); but their ages at the time of their sons' births are not recorded. Jochebed, the wife of Amram and mother of Moses, is said to have been the sister of Kohath, who was the son of Levi and the grandfather of Moses (6:16, 18, 20), and to have been born to Levi in Egypt (Num. 26:59). This might appear to be conclusive evidence of a comparatively brief period in Egypt and to make a sojourn there of 430 years impossible. But there are difficulties. While four to five generations from Jacob to Moses may be indicated in the above line of descent, eleven generations may be counted from Jacob to Joshua (1 Chr. 7:20-27). And that some considerable period was involved is clear from the fact that Joseph before his death saw the children of the third generation of both his sons (Gen. 50:23), and that at the time of the exodus, Amram and his brothers were already regarded as founders of clans (Num. 3:27).

Levi was the elder brother of Joseph and must have been born not more than ten years before Joseph (Gen. 29:30-34; 30:22-43; 31:41). Since Joseph was 30 when he stood before Pharaoh (41:46), and since seven years of plenty and two years of famine had passed at the time Jacob entered Egypt (41:47, 53; 45:6), Joseph would have been 39 when Jacob was 130 (47:9, 28) and would thus have been born when Jacob was 91. That, however, would have made Jacob an old man of about 80 at the time of his marriage and the birth of his firstborn—possible but hardly probable. In view of the frequency of the numbers of 30 or 130 in age lists of biblical patriarchs, and in view of the significance of the number 30 in connection with the Sed Festival in Egypt (which honored a ruler on the thirtieth anniversary of his appointment as heir to the crown), the question might well be raised as to whether 130 as the age of Jacob is used in an absolute sense. If not, the chronological reckonings based on it are only approximate and not absolute.

We should also notice that if the sojourn in Egypt was 215 years and if there were only four generations from Jacob to Moses, then Levi must have been about 100 at the birth of Jochebed, and Jochebed 84 at the birth of Moses. Since the birth of Isaac to Sarah when she was 90 and to Abraham when he was 100 was regarded as in the nature of a miracle (Gen. 17:17; 18:11-14; Rom. 4:19), these ages are hardly probable.

On the basis of the OT data it is impossible to give a categorical answer as to exactly what was involved in the 430-year sojourn, nor is it possible to give an absolute date for Abraham's entry into Canaan. Paul regarded the 430 years as beginning at the time when the promises were made to Abraham (Gen. 12:1-4) and terminating with the giving of the law at Sinai (Gal. 3:16-17). On this basis the date of the entry into Canaan and the beginning of the sojourn was 1875 B.C.

An exodus date of 1445 calls for 1405 as the beginning of the conquest (Num. 33:38; Deut. 1:3; Josh. 5:6). If so, the exodus took place during the reigns of the famous rulers of Egypt's 18th dynasty (c. 1570-1325). Such a setting fits well with some of the evidence, but not all. Many scholars have argued for a date in the thirteenth century. See the discussion under EXODUS.

IV. From the conquest to the kingdom. The establishment of absolute dates from Moses through Joshua and the judges to the setting up of the monarchy is again not possible with the available data. Assuming the date 1405 B.C. for the beginning of the conquest, we infer 1399 as the year when Caleb received his inheritance, since he was

40 when he was sent as a spy from Kadesh Barnea (Josh. 14:7) in the second year after the departure from Egypt (Num. 10:11-12; Deut. 2:14), and he was 85 when he received his inheritance 45 years later (Josh. 14:10). The date of Joshua's death cannot be given, for we do not know how old he was when he was sent as a spy, although he was 110 when he died (24:29).

Many attempts have been made to set dates for the judges, but, with the data now available, absolute certainty regarding the chronology for this period is impossible. Here are the data:

Oppression under Cushan-Rishathaim	(Jdg. 3:8)	8
Deliverance under Othniel; peace	(Jdg. 3:11)	40
Oppression under Eglon of Moab	(Jdg. 3:14)	18
Deliverance by Ehud; peace	(Jdg. 3:30)	80
Oppression under Jabin of Hazor	(Jdg. 4:3)	20
Deliverance under Deborah; peace	(Jdg. 5:31)	40
Oppression under Midian	(Jdg. 6:1)	7
Deliverance under Gideon; peace	(Jdg. 8:28)	40
Reign of Abimelech	(Jdg. 9:22)	3
Judgeship of Tola	(Jdg. 10:2)	23
Judgeship of Jair	(Jdg. 10:3)	22
Oppression of Gilead by Ammon	(Jdg. 10:8)	18
Judgeship of Jephthah	(Jdg. 12:7)	6
Judgeship of Ibzan	(Jdg. 12:9)	7
Judgeship of Elon	(Jdg. 12:11)	10
Judgeship of Abdon	(Jdg. 12:14)	8
Oppression under the Philistines	(Jdg. 13:1)	40
Judgeship of Samson	(Jdg. 15:20; 16:31)	20
Judgeship of Eli	(1 Sam. 4:18)	40
Judgeship of Samuel	(1 Sam. 7:2)	20

The sum of the above numbers is 470 years. However, it seems clear that we can subtract the 20 years of Samson's judgeship, because that period is included in the 40 years of oppression under the Philistines (he "led Israel for twenty years in the days of the Philistines," Jdg. 15:20). This results in the grand total of 450 years for the period of the judges, the same number given by the apostle Paul when he spoke of this period in his speech in the synagogue at Antioch in Pisidia (Acts 13:20). On the other hand, some speculate that the judges were local rulers, exercising control over limited areas while others held office in other parts of the land (cf. Jephthah, who ruled over Gilead, Jdg.

10:18; 11:5-11; 12:4). They argue that the judgeships and oppressions at times overlapped (as with Samson); two oppressions might have been simultaneous in different parts of the land, as with the Ammonites in the NE and the Philistines in the SW (10:6-7). Furthermore, they say, the numerous 40s or multiples and submultiples of 40 (40, 80, 20, 40, 40, 10, 40, 20, 40) and Jephthah's 300 years after the conquest (11:26) are to be understood as merely approximate.

V. The united monarchy. Because of a number of uncertainties the absolute date for the establishment of the united monarchy cannot be given. The OT does not give the length of the reign of Saul, but Paul in a sermon at Antioch referred to it as forty years (Acts 13:21). If Saul reigned a full forty years, David was not born until ten years after Saul began his reign, for he was thirty when he took the throne (2 Sam. 5:4). The battle with the Philistines at Micmash, with Jonathan in command of a large part of the army, presumably took place early in Saul's reign, perhaps even in his second year (1 Sam. 13:1-2). In such a case Jonathan would have been well advanced in years when David was a mere youth, which is out of harmony with the picture in the biblical record. Other difficulties are also involved, all making it clear that Saul either did not reign a full forty years or that he must have been very young when he took the throne.

The reign of David, on the other hand, may be regarded as a full forty years, for he reigned seven years in Hebron and thirty-three in Jerusalem (2 Sam. 5:4-5; 1 Ki. 2:11; 1 Chr. 3:4), and one event is dated in the fortieth year (1 Chr. 26:31).

Solomon began his reign before the death of David (1 Ki. 1:32-48), but how long is not recorded. Presumably it was only a short time, but the indefiniteness of this period must be taken into consideration in any endeavor to establish an absolute chronology. And the forty years of his reign (11:42) might have been intended as a round number. Without certainty that the recorded numbers from the exodus to Solomon are absolute, we cannot provide a definitive chronology for the periods involved.

VI. The divided monarchy. For the period of the divided monarchy an entirely different situation is found. Here there is an abundance of data that may be checked against each other; and the numbers evidently are no longer round. Four biblical yardsticks are here provided—the lengths of reign of the rulers of Judah and those of Israel, and the synchronisms of Judah with Israel and of Israel with Judah. Furthermore, a number of synchronisms with the fixed years of contemporary Assyria make possible a check with an exact chronological yardstick and make possible the establishment of absolute years for the period of the kings.

Various methods were used in the ANE for reckoning the official years of kings. During the divided monarchy, Judah used a system whereby the year when a ruler took the throne was his "accession year." Israel, on the other hand, followed those nations where a king termed his initial year his "first year." According to this latter method, the year when a king began to reign was always counted twice—as the last year of his predecessor and his own first official year. Thus, reigns reckoned according to this method were always one year longer in official length than those reckoned according to the former method, and for every reign there was always a gain of one year over absolute time. The following tables will make these two methods of reckoning clear and will show how for every reign the totals of Israel for this period increase by one year over those of Judah:

		Old king	New king			
Accession-year reckoning (Judah)		last year	accession year	1st year	2nd year	3rd year
Non-accession-year reckoning (Israel)		last year	1st year	2nd year	3rd year	4th year

JUDAH, official years:	22	23	46	47	58	61	78	79
Rehoboam 17 Abijam 3 Asa 2nd	3rd	26th	27th	38th	41 Jehoshaphat 17th	18th		
Jeroboam	22 Nadab 2 Baasha 24 Elah 2 Zimri	Omri 12 Ahab 4th			22 Ahaziah 2	Jehoram		
ISRAEL, official years:	22	24	48	50	62	66	84	86
Excess years for Israel	0	1	2	3	4	5	6	7

The following table shows how the totals of both nations from the division to the death of Ahaziah in Israel in the eighteenth year of Jehoshaphat in Judah (omitting the seven-day reign of Zimri) are identical and perfectly correct when properly understood:

ISRAEL			JUDAH	
King	Official years	Actual years	King	Years
Jeroboam	22	21	Rehoboam	17
Nadab	2	1	Abijam	3
Baasha	24	23	Asa	41
Elah	2	1	Jehoshaphat	18
Omri	12	11		
Ahab	22	21		
Ahaziah	2	1		
Total	86	79		79

Based on biblical numbers that possess internal harmony and are in accord with the years of contemporary Assyria and Babylon, the following conditions make possible the construction of a chronological pattern of the kings: (1) regnal years that begin the month of Tishri in Judah and the month of Nisan in Israel; (2) accession-year reckoning for Judah except for Jehoram, Ahaziah, Athaliah, and Joash, who followed the nonaccession-year system then employed in Israel; (3) nonaccession-year reckoning in Israel for the early period, but accession-year reckoning from Jehoash to the end; (4) synchronisms of each nation in accord with its own current system of reckoning; (5) a number of coregencies or of overlapping reigns when rival rulers exercised control; (6) a double chronological pattern for both Israel and Judah involving the closing years of Israel's history.

The years of the kings based on the above principles are as follows:

ISRAEL			JUDAH		
Ruler	Overlapping Reign	Reign	Ruler	Overlapping Reign	Reign
Jeroboam I		931/30–910/9	Rehoboam		931/30–913
Nadab		910/9–909/8	Abijam		913–911
Baasha		909/8–886/85	Asa		911/10–870
Elah		886/85–885/84	Jehoshaphat	873/72–870/69	870/69–848
Zimri		885/84	Jehoram	853–848	848–841
Tibni		885/84–880	Ahaziah		841
Omri		885/84–880	Athaliah		841–835
Ahab		874/73–853	Joash		835–796
Ahaziah		853–852	Amaziah		796–767
Joram		852–841	Azariah (Uzziah)	972/91–767	767–740
Jehu		841–814/13			
Jehoahaz		814/13–798	Jotham	750–740/39	740/39–732
Jehoash		798–782/81			
Jeroboam II	793/92–782/81	782/81–753	Ahaz	735–732/31	732/31–716
Zachariah		753–752			
Shallum		752	Hezekiah		716/15–687
Menahem		752–742/41	Manasseh	697/96–687/86	687/86–643
Pekahiah		742/41–740/39	Amon		643/42–641
Pekah		752–740/39	Josiah		641/40–609
Hoshea		732/31–723/22	Jehoahaz		609
			Jehoiakim		609–598
			Jehoiachin		598–597
			Zedekiah		597–586

VII. The exile and return. The book of 2 Kings closes with the notice of the release of Jehoiachin from captivity on the twenty-seventh day of the twelfth month, in the thirty-seventh year of his captivity and the accession year of Evil-Merodach (2 Ki. 25:27). That was April 2, 561 B.C.

Babylon fell to the Persians on October 12, 539 B.C., and Cyrus in the first year of his reign issued a decree permitting the Jews to return and rebuild the temple (2 Chr. 36:22; Ezra 1:1). On the basis of Nisan regnal years, this would have been 538. However, Neh. 1:1 and 2:1 give evidence that the author of Nehemiah reckoned the years of the Persian kings not from Nisan as was the Persian custom, but from Tishri, in accord with the Jewish custom. The Aramaic papyri from Elephantine in Egypt give evidence that the same custom was followed by the Jewish colony there in the fifth century B.C. Since it is probable that Chronicles-Ezra-Nehemiah were originally one and came from the same author, the indications are that the first year of Cyrus referred to in Ezra 1:1 was reckoned on a Tishri basis, and that it was, therefore, in 537 that Cyrus issued his decree.

Haggai began his ministry on the first day of the sixth month in the second year of Darius (Hag. 1:1), August 29, 520; and Zechariah commenced his work in the eighth month of the same year (Zech. 1:1), in October or November of 520. The temple was completed on the third of Adar, the sixth year of Darius (Ezra 6:15), March 12, 515.

The return of Ezra from Babylon was begun the first day of the first month, in the seventh year of Artaxerxes (Ezra 7:7, 9). Artaxerxes came to the throne in December of 465, and this would bring the first of Nisan of his seventh year on April 8, 458, according to Persian reckoning, but on March 27, 457, according to Judean years. The evidence that this was the custom then employed has already been given above.

Word was brought to Nehemiah of the sad state of affairs at Jerusalem in the month Kislev of the twentieth year of Artaxerxes (Neh. 1:1), and in Nisan of that same twentieth year Nehemiah stood before the king and received permission to return to Jerusalem to rebuild the city (2:1-8). That was April, 444 B.C. With Nehemiah's return to Babylon in the thirty-second year of Artaxerxes (13:6), 433/32, the chronology of the OT proper comes to a close.

chronology (NT). The task of determining precise dates for the NT books and the historical events mentioned in them is beset with serious difficulty. The necessary evidence is often lacking, and the computations must be based on ancient documents that did not record historical events under exact calendar dates as modern historical records do. Neither sacred nor secular historians of that time were accustomed to record history under absolute dates; they felt that all demands were satisfied when some specific event was related to a well-known period, as the reign of a noted ruler or the time of some famous contemporary. Luke's method of dating the beginning of the ministry of John the Baptist (Lk. 3:1-2) is typical of the historian's method of that day. Further, the use of different local chronologies and different ways of computing years often leave the results tentative. NT chronology naturally falls into two parts: the life of Christ and the apostolic age.

I. Life of Christ. The erection of a chronology of the life of Christ turns around three points: his birth, baptism, and crucifixion. Luke's statement of the age of Jesus at his baptism (Lk. 3:23) links the first two, while the problem of the length of the ministry links the second and third.

The Christian era, now used almost exclusively in the Western world for civil chronology, was introduced at Rome by Abbot Dionysius Exiguus in the sixth century. It is now generally agreed that the beginning of the era should have been fixed at least four years later. According to the Gospels, Jesus was born some time before the death of Herod the Great. Josephus, the Jewish historian who was born A.D. 37, affirms that Herod died shortly after an eclipse of the moon (*Ant.* 17.6.4), which is astronomically fixed at March 12-13, 4 B.C. His death occurred shortly before Passover, which that year fell on April 4. His death in 4 B.C. is also confirmed from the known commencement of the rule of his three sons in that year. The age of Jesus at Herod's death is not certain. The "two years" for the age of the children killed at Bethlehem (Matt. 2:16) offers no sure indication, since Herod would allow a liberal margin for safety; also,

The altar and star located within the Church of the Nativity (Bethlehem) marking the traditional spot of Jesus' birth.

of taking the census among the Jews, may have delayed the actual census in Palestine for several years, bringing it down to the year 5 B.C.

Luke gives the age of Jesus at his baptism as "about thirty years" (Lk. 3:23). Although the statement of age is not specific, it may indicate that he was only a few months under or over thirty. Born in the latter part of 5 B.C., his baptism then occurred near the close of A.D. 26 or the beginning of 27. The forty-day period of the temptation plus the events recorded in Jn. 1:19—2:12 seem to require that the baptism occurred at least three months before the first Passover of his public ministry (2:13-22). Since Herod began the reconstruction of the temple in 20 B.C., the "forty and six years" mentioned by the Jews during this Passover, using the inclusive Jewish count, again brings us to A.D. 27 for this first Passover.

Apparently John began his ministry some six months before the baptism of Jesus, Scripture dating that beginning as "in the fifteenth year of the reign of Tiberius Caesar" (Lk. 3:1). Augustus died in August of A.D. 14, but fifteen years added to that would be two years too late for our previous dates. Since Tiberius had been reigning jointly with Augustus in the provinces for two years before his death, it seems only natural that Luke would follow the provincial point of view and count the fifteen years from the time of Tiberius' actual assumption of authority in the provinces. Thus counted, the date is in harmony with our other dates. The ministry of John, begun about six months before the baptism of Jesus, commenced about the middle of A.D. 26. (Others, however, argue that since there is no evidence that Tiberius's reign was ever reckoned as beginning prior to the year 14, John's ministry must have begun no earlier than 28.)

The time of the crucifixion will be determined by the length of the ministry of Jesus. Mark's Gospel seems to require at least two years: the plucking of the ears of grain (April-June) marks a first spring, the feeding of the 5,000 when the grass was fresh green (March-April) was a second, and the Passover of the crucifixion becomes the third. John's Gospel explicitly mentions three Passovers (Jn. 2:23; 6:4; 11:55). If the feast of Jn. 5:1 is also a Passover, as seems probable—a view having the

part of a year might be counted as a year. It does show that Jesus was born at least some months before Herod's death. Christ's presentation in the temple after he was forty days old (Lev. 12:1-8; Lk. 2:22-24) may indicate that the wise men came at least six weeks after his birth. The time spent in Egypt is uncertain, but it may have been several months. Thus, the birth of Jesus should likely be placed in the latter part of the year 5 B.C.

Luke's statement that Jesus was born in connection with the "first census" when "Quirinius was governor of Syria" (Lk. 2:1-2) was once fiercely assailed as erroneous, since Quirinius was known to be governor in connection with the census of A.D. 6. But it is now known that he was also connected with the Syrian government at some previous time (see QUIRINIUS). Papyrus evidence shows that Augustus inaugurated a periodic census every fourteen years, from 8 B.C. onward. Herod's war with the king of Arabia and his troubles with Augustus, as well as the problem of the method

traditional backing of Irenaeus—then the length of the ministry of Jesus was a full three years and a little over. This places the crucifixion at the Passover of A.D. 30. (An alternate reckoning dates the crucifixion in the year 33.)

II. Apostolic Age. Due to the uncertainties connected with the limited data for an apostolic chronology, authorities have arrived at varied dates. The book of Acts, with its many notes of time, mostly indefinite, offers but few points for the establishment of even relatively fixed dates. Even Paul's apparently precise chronological notes in Gal. 1:18 and 2:1 leave us in doubt as to whether "after three years" and "fourteen years later" are to be regarded as consecutive or as both counting from his conversion.

The death of Herod Agrippa I (Acts 12:23) and the proconsulship of Gallio (18:12) are important for the chronology of the period. The death of Herod Agrippa I, one of the fixed dates of the NT, is known to have taken place in A.D. 44. It establishes the year of Peter's arrest and miraculous escape from prison. The proconsulship of Gallio is also strongly relied on for an apostolic chronology. A fragmentary inscription found at Delphi associates his proconsulship with the twenty-sixth acclamation of Claudius as Imperator. This would place his proconsulship between May of 51 and 52, or between May of 52 and 53. The latter date is more probable since Gallio would assume office in May and not in midsummer as some advocates of the earlier date assumed. Since apparently Paul had already been at Corinth a year and a half when Gallio arrived, his ministry at Corinth began in the latter part of 50. Efforts to determine the time of the accession of Festus as governor, under whom Paul was sent to Rome, have not resulted in agreement. From the inconclusive data, advocates have argued for a date as early as 55 and as late as 60 or 61. The balance of the arguments seem to point to 60 or perhaps 59. If the latter, the suggested dates should be adjusted accordingly.

III. Chronological table. The dates for many NT events must remain tentative, but as indicated by Luke (Lk. 3:1-2), they have a definite correlation with secular history (as shown in the accompanying diagram). The following chronological table is regarded as approximately correct.

Birth of Jesus	5 B.C.
Baptism of Jesus	late A.D. 26 or early 27
First Passover of ministry	27
Crucifixion of Jesus	30
Conversion of Saul	34 or 35
Death of Herod Agrippa I	44
Letter of James	before 50
First missionary journey	48-49
Jerusalem conference	49 or 50
Second missionary journey	begun spring 50
Paul at Corinth	50-52
1 and 2 Thessalonians from Corinth	51
Galatians from Corinth (?)	early 52
Arrival of Gallio as proconsul	May 52
Third missionary journey	begun 54
Paul at Ephesus	54-57
1 Corinthians from Ephesus	spring 57
2 Corinthians from Macedonia	fall 57
Romans from Corinth	winter 57-58
Paul's arrest at Jerusalem	Pentecost 58
Imprisonment at Caesarea	58-60
On island of Malta	winter 60-61
Arrival at Rome	spring 61
Roman imprisonment	61-63
Colossians, Philemon, Ephesians	summer 62
Philippians	spring 63
Paul's release and further work	63-65
1 Timothy and Titus	63
Hebrews	64
Synoptic Gospels and Acts	before 67
1 and 2 Peter from Rome	64-65
Peter's death at Rome	65
Paul's second Roman imprisonment	66
2 Timothy	66
Death at Rome	late 66 or early 67
Jude	67-68
Writings of John	before 100
Death of John	98-100

C

chrysolite. See MINERALS.

chrysoprase. See MINERALS.

Chub. See CUB.

Chun. See CUN.

church. The English word *church* (cf. also Scottish *kirk*) is derived from the Greek adjective *kyriakos* G3258, signifying "the Lord's" or "belonging to the Lord." In the NT, however, *church* translates a different Greek term, *ekklēsia* G1711 (from a verb meaning "to call out"). This noun was originally employed in secular Greek society to denote an assembly or congregation of free citizens summoned or "called out" by a herald in connection with public affairs (cf. Acts 19:39). In the SEPTUAGINT the "congregation" of Israel is referred to as the *ekklēsia*, especially when gathered before the Lord for religious purposes (Deut. 31:30; Acts 7:38). In this latter sense the word is adopted to describe the new gathering or congregation of the disciples of Jesus Christ.

In the Gospels the term is found only in Matt. 16:18 and 18:17. This paucity is perhaps explained by the fact that both these verses seem to envisage a situation that would follow Christ's earthly ministry. Yet the verses show that Christ has this reconstitution in view, that the church thus reconstituted will rest on the apostolic confession, and that it will take up the ministry of reconciliation.

When we turn to Acts, the situation changes. The saving work has been fulfilled, and the NT church can thus have its birthday at PENTECOST. The term is now used regularly to describe local groups of believers. Thus, we read of the church at Jerusalem (Acts 5:11), Antioch (13:1), and Caesarea (18:22). At the same time the word is used for all believers (as is possibly the case in 9:31). From the outset the church has both a local and a general significance, denoting both the individual assembly and the worldwide community.

This twofold usage is also seen in PAUL. He addresses his letters to specific churches, such as those in Corinth (1 Cor. 1:2) or Thessalonica (1 Thess. 1:1). Indeed, he seems sometimes to localize further by referring to specific groups within the local community as churches, as though sending greetings to congregations within the one city (e.g., Rom. 16:5). Yet Paul also develops more fully the concept of a church that consists of all believers in all local churches, as in 1 Cor. 10:32 and 1 Tim. 3:15, and with an even grander sweep in Col. 1:18 and especially Ephesians. The other NT books give us mostly examples of the local usage (e.g., 3 Jn. 9; Rev. 1:4; 2:1).

There is no tension between the local and the universal sense. Each church or congregation is the church in its own setting, each a manifestation or concretion of the whole church. This means that there is room for great flexibility in organization and structure according to particular and varying needs. At the worldwide level, it is unlikely that there can ever be more than the loosest practical interconnection. Varying degrees of integration are possible at national, provincial, or municipal levels. But the basic unity is always the local church, not in isolation but as a concretion of the universal fellowship with a strong sense of belonging to it.

This leads us to the further consideration that the church is not primarily a human structure like a political, social, or economic organism. It is basically the church of Jesus Christ ("my church," Matt. 16:18) or of the living God (1 Tim. 3:15). The various biblical descriptions all emphasize this. It is metaphorically a building of which Jesus Christ is the chief cornerstone or foundation, "a holy temple in the Lord ... a dwelling in which God lives by his Spirit" (Eph. 2:20-22). It is the fellowship of saints or people of God (1 Pet. 2:9). It is the bride of Jesus Christ, saved and sanctified by him for union with himself (Eph. 5:25-26). Indeed, the church is the BODY OF CHRIST (Rom. 12:5; 1 Cor. 12:12-13; Eph. 4:4, 12, 16-17), and as such it is the fullness of Christ, who himself fills all in all (Eph. 1:23).

While there is an element of imagery in some of the terms used to refer to the church (Christ's temple, bride, or body), its true reality is found in the company of those who believe in Christ and are thus dead, buried, and raised in him, their Savior and substitute. Yet, this reality is not the visible one of earthly organization. The various local churches in this sinful age do not fully conform to their new and true reality any more than individual believers conform to what they are now in Christ. In its real life the church is known only in faith. It is thus hidden or, in the old phrase, "invisible." The visible life that it must also have, and that should be conformed to its true reality, may fall far short of it. Indeed, in visible organization even the membership cannot be fully identical with that of the true church (cf. Simon Magus). Yet the church invisible is not just ideal or mystical, but the real fact of the church is its being in Christ. In every manifestation, there should thus be the aim, not of conformity to the world, but of transformation by renewal into the likeness of him in whom it has its true life (cf. Rom. 12:2).

In this connection appears the relevance of the traditional "marks" or "notes" of the church. (1) The church is *one* (Eph. 4:4), for Jesus Christ has only one temple, bride, and body, and all divisions are overcome in death and resurrection with him and by endowment of his Spirit. In all its legitimate multiformity, the visible church should thus seek a unity corresponding to this reality. (2) The church is *holy*, for it is set apart and sanctified by himself (Gal. 1:4; Eph. 5:26). Even in its pilgrimage in the world, it is thus to attest its consecration by the manner of its life and the nature of its service (cf. 1 Pet. 1:15). (3) The church is *catholic* or universal, that is, constituted from among all people of all races, places, and ages (Eph. 2:14; Col. 1:6; 3:11; Rev. 5:9). For all its diversity of membership and form, it is thus to maintain its universality of outreach, yet also its identity and relevance in every age and place. (4) The church is *apostolic*, for it rests on the foundation of the apostles and prophets (Eph. 2:20), the apostles being raised up as the first authoritative witnesses (Acts 1:8) whose testimony is basic and by whose teaching it is called, instructed, and directed. In all its activity it is thus "devoted ... to the apostles' teaching and to the fellowship" (Acts 2:42), not finding apostolicity in mere externals but in conformity to apostolic teaching and practice as divinely perpetuated in Holy Scripture.

This brings us to the means of the church's life and its continuing function. It draws its life from Jesus Christ by the Holy Spirit; but it does so through the Word, from which it gets life (Jas. 1:18) and by which it is nourished and sanctified (Eph. 5:26; 1 Pet. 2:2). Receiving life by the Word, it also receives its function, namely, to pass on the Word that others may also be quickened and cleansed. It is to preach the gospel (Mk. 16:15), to take up the ministry of reconciliation (2 Cor. 5:19), to dispense the mysteries of God (1 Cor. 4:1).

The ministry of the church arises in this connection. The apostles were first commissioned, and they ordained others, yet no rigid form of ministry arose in the NT. Rather, we are given patterns (notably of speech, action, and rule), historically focused in the elders (also called bishops or overseers) and the deacons. There seems to be no biblical prescription, however, for the discharge of ministry in a fixed order, nor for the sharp isolation of an official ministry from the so-called laity or "mere" people of God. The Bible's concern is that there should be real ministry, that is, service, not in self-assertion and pride but in humility, obedience, and self-offering that conforms to the example of him who was among us as one who serves (see Matt. 23:11-12; Phil. 2:5-6; 1 Pet. 5:1-2).

Finally, the church's work is not exclusively for the salvation of people; it is primarily to the praise of God's glory (Eph. 1:6; 2:7). Hence neither the church nor its function ceases with the completion of its earthly task. There is ground, therefore, for the old distinction between the church triumphant and the church militant. All the church is triumphant in its true reality. But the warring and wayfaring church is still engaged in conflict between the old reality and the new. Its destiny, however, is to be brought into full conformity to the Lord (1 Jn. 3:2). Toward this it moves hesitantly yet expectantly, confident in its future glory when it will be wholly the church triumphant as graphically depicted in Rev. 7:9-17, enjoying its full reality as the bride and body of the Lord.

Chushan-rishathaim. See CUSHAN-RISHATHAIM.

Chuza. See CUZA.

ciel. This English word (now spelled "ceil") is used by the KJV to render several Hebrew verbs meaning "to cover, to panel" (2 Chr. 3:5; Jer. 22:14; Hag. 1:4; Ezek. 41:16).

Cilicia. suh-lish'ee-uh (Gk. *Kilikia G3070*). A country in SE ASIA MINOR, bounded on the N and

W by the Taurus range, and on the S by the Mediterranean. It had two parts, the western one called Rugged Cilicia; the eastern one, Plain Cilicia, the chief city of which was Tarsus, the birthplace of Paul (Acts 21:39; 22:3; 23:34). The early inhabitants must have been Hittites. Later, Syrians and

This mountainous region of Cilicia connects Tarsus to the region of Cappadocia. (View to the N.)

Phoenicians settled there. It came under Persian sway. After Alexander the Great, Seleucid rulers governed it from Antioch of Syria. It became a Roman province in 100 B.C. One of its governors was Cicero, the famous orator (51-50). Cilicia is accessible by land only by way of its two famous mountain passes, the Cilician Gates and the Syrian Gates. Jews from Cilicia disputed with Stephen (Acts 6:9). The gospel reached it early (15:23), probably through Paul (9:30; Gal. 1:21). On his second missionary journey the apostle confirmed the churches that had been established there (Acts 15:41), and on his way to Rome as a prisoner he sailed over the sea of Cilicia (27:5).

cinnamon. See PLANTS.

Cinneroth. See Kinnereth.

circle of the earth. The prophet Isaiah says that God "sits enthroned above the circle of the earth" (Isa. 40:22). The Hebrew word for "circle" here occurs in two other passages (Job 22:14, referring

to the "vault" or "dome" of heaven, and Prov. 8:27, which says that God traced the "horizon" of the ocean). The text neither assumes nor excludes the notion of a spherical earth. All the usage of the term indicates is that the horizon where the sea meets the sky was known by observation to be curved, that it was upon this arc that Yahweh set the limits of the seas, and that his power and sovereignty are shown by the fact that he is enthroned above it.

circumcision. The surgical removal of the foreskin or prepuce, a covering of skin on the head of the male sexual organ. This custom has prevailed among many peoples in different parts of the world, and in ancient times it was practiced among many western Semites—Hebrews, Arabians, Moabites, Ammonites, Edomites, and also Egyptians, but not among the Babylonians, Assyrians, Canaanites, and Philistines. Various theories are held regarding the origin and original significance of circumcision, but there can be no doubt that it was at first a religious act.

Among the Hebrews the rite was instituted by God as the sign of the COVENANT between him and ABRAHAM, shortly after the latter's sojourn in Egypt. God ordained that it be performed on Abraham, on his posterity and slaves, and on foreigners joining themselves to the Hebrew nation (Gen. 17:12). Every male child was to be circumcised on the eighth day. Originally the father performed the rite, but in exceptional cases a woman could do it (Exod. 4:25). In later times a Hebrew surgeon was called in. The child was given his name at the ceremony. Today in Jewish families the rite is performed either in the parent's home or in the synagogue. In former times flint or glass knives were preferred, but now steel is usually used.

According to the terms of the covenant symbolized by circumcision, the Lord undertook to be the God of Abraham and his descendants, and they were to belong to him, worshiping and obeying only him. The rite effected admission to the fellowship of the covenant people and secured for the individual, as a member of the nation, his share in the promises God made to the nation as a whole. Circumcision reminded the Israelites of God's promises to them and of the duties they had assumed. The prophets often reminded them that the outward rite, to have any significance, must be accompanied by a "circumcision of the heart" (Lev. 26:41; Deut. 30:6; Ezek. 44:7). Jeremiah said that his countrymen were no better than the pagans, for they were "uncircumcised in heart" (Jer. 9:25-26). Paul used a word meaning "mutilation" (KJV, "concision") for this outward circumcision not accompanied by a spiritual change (Phil. 3:2). In the early history of the Christian church, Judaizing Christians argued for the necessity of circumcising GENTILES who came into the church over against Paul, who insisted that the signs of the old covenant could not be forced on the children of the new covenant. Paul's view was affirmed by the Council of Jerusalem (Acts 15).

Cis. See KISH.

Cisjordan. The area W of the JORDAN river (see TRANSJORDAN).

cistern. An artificial tank or reservoir dug in the earth or rock for the collection and storage of rain WATER, or, sometimes, of spring water brought from a distance by a conduit. A cistern is distinguished from a pool by always being covered. Cisterns were very numerous in Palestine. The long, dry, rainless summers, lasting from May to September, and the small annual precipitation, together with a lack of natural springs, made the people largely dependent on RAIN water. Cisterns were fed from surface and roof drainage by gutters and pipes. The hilly character of the land allowed little rain to penetrate the soil. Most of it flowed down the steep hillsides through the many ravines and watercourses, and it was easily brought by conduits to pools and cisterns. Cisterns in Palestine varied in size and character. Some were cut wholly in the rock, often in the form of a bottle-shaped tank, with a long stairway leading to the surface of the ground. They were often of great depth, some more than 100 ft. (30 m.) deep. Very large ones were supported by rock pillars. The TEMPLE area in Jerusalem had at least thirty-seven great cisterns,

one of them holding between two and three million gallons (8-11 million liters). Public rock-cut cisterns were made within the city walls so that the inhabitants could hold out in time of siege.

Where the substratum of the soil was earth and not rock, cisterns of masonry were built. Some of these were large and had vaulted roofs supported by pillars. Besides the large public cisterns, there were many smaller private ones. Ancient sites are honeycombed with them. All cisterns had one or more openings for drawing water to the surface. They needed periodic cleaning because of the impurities washed in from the outside. Empty cisterns were sometimes used as prisons. Joseph was cast into one (Gen. 37:22), and Jeremiah was let down into one with a muddy bottom (Jer. 38:6). Zechariah 9:11 alludes to the custom of confining prisoners in an empty cistern.

citadel. Fortifications within Hebrew towns. The term should probably be applied only to the final defense unit of a city. This might include the palace (1 Ki. 16:18) or sometimes the temple (Neh. 2:8). See also CASTLE.

cities, Levitical. See LEVITICAL CITIES.

cities of refuge. Six cities, three on each side of the JORDAN, set apart by MOSES and JOSHUA as places of asylum for those who had committed manslaughter. Those E of the Jordan were BEZER in Reuben, RAMOTH GILEAD in Gad, and GOLAN in Manasseh (Deut. 4:41-43); those W of the Jordan were HEBRON in Judah, SHECHEM in Ephraim, and KEDESH in Naphtali (Josh. 20:7-8). To shelter the person guilty of manslaughter from the AVENGER of blood, provision was made that the principal roads leading to these cities should always be kept open. No part of Palestine was more than 30 mi. (50 km.) away from a city of refuge—a distance that could be covered in one day. Cities of refuge were provided to protect a person until his case could be properly adjudged. The right of asylum was only for those who had taken life unintentionally. Willful murderers were put to death at once.

The regulations concerning these cities of refuge are found in Num. 35; Deut. 19:1-13; and Josh. 20. If one guilty of unintentional killing reached a city of refuge before the avenger of blood could kill him, he was given asylum until a fair trial could be held. The trial took place where the accused had lived. If proved innocent of willful murder, he was brought back to the city of refuge. There he had to stay until the death of the high priest. After that he was free to return to his own home. But if during that period he passed beyond the limits of the city of refuge, the avenger of blood could kill him without blame.

cities of the plain. This phrase occurs twice in the OT (Gen. 13:12; 19:29) and refers to certain cities near the DEAD SEA, including SODOM, GOMORRAH, ADMAH, ZEBOIIM, and ZOAR. In the first reference we read that LOT, after ABRAHAM had given him the choice of where he wanted to live, decided to dwell in the cities of the plain and pitched his tent near Sodom. According to Gen. 14:2, each of the cities had its own king; this chapter recounts how Abraham delivered Lot when the cities were attacked and Lot taken captive. The story of the destruction of the cities because of their wickedness is given in ch. 19. It is thought that God may have accomplished this by causing an eruption of gases and petroleum to ignite. Only Lot and his two daughters were spared. The exact site of the cities is unknown; but though there are weighty arguments for believing that they were at the N end of the Dead Sea, scholars favor the S end, especially since asphalt in large quantities has been found only here. It is believed that the sea covers the site. Sodom and Gomorrah are often used as a warning example of sin and divine punishment (Deut. 29:23; Isa. 1:9; 3:9; Jer. 50:40; Ezek. 16:46; Matt. 10:15; Rom. 9:29).

citizenship. In the Gospels the use of the Greek word for "citizen" means nothing more than the inhabitant of a country (Lk. 15:15; 19:14). Among the ancient Jews emphasis was placed on Israel as a religious organization, not on relationship to city and state. The good citizen was the good Israelite, one who followed not just civil law but religious law as well. Non-Israelites had the same protection of the law as native Israelites, but they were required not to perform acts that violated the religious commitments of the people. The advantage of a Jew over a Gentile was thus strictly spiritual. He was a member of the theocracy.

Among the Romans, citizenship brought the right to be considered equal to natives of the city of Rome. Emperors sometimes granted it to whole provinces and cities, and also to single individuals for services rendered to the state or to the imperial family, or even for a certain sum of money. Roman citizens were exempted from shameful punishments, such as scourging and crucifixion, and they had the right of appeal to the emperor with certain limitations.

PAUL says he had become a Roman citizen by birth (see Acts 16:37-39; 22:25-29). Either his father or some other ancestor had acquired the right and had transmitted it to his son. He was proud of his Roman citizenship and, when occasion demanded, availed himself of his rights. When writing to the Philippians, who were members of a Roman colony and therefore Roman citizens, Paul emphasized that Christians are citizens of a heavenly commonwealth and ought to live accordingly (Phil. 1:27; 3:20).

citron. See PLANTS.

city. In ancient times cities owed their origin not to organized manufacture but to agriculture. When people left the pastoral life and settled down to the cultivation of the soil, they often found their cattle and crops endangered by wandering tribes of the desert; and it was to protect themselves from such enemies that they created first the village and then the city. Cities were built in areas where AGRICULTURE could be carried on, usually on the side of a mountain or the top of a hill, and where a sufficient supply of water was assured. The names of cities often indicate the feature that was determinative in the selection of the site. For example, the prefixes *Beer*, meaning "well," and *En*, meaning "spring," in such names as Beersheba and En Gedi, show that it was a local well or spring that determined the building of the city. Names like Ramah, Mizpah, and Gibeah (all from roots indicating height), which were very common in Palestine, indicate that a site on an elevation was preferred for a city. A ruling family sometimes gave its name to a city (with the word *Beth*, meaning "house of").

Ancient farmers did not have their own farms. At the end of a day's work they retired for the night

The city of Jerusalem played a crucial role throughout the history of Israel. (View to the N.)

to the village or city. Smaller villages sought the protection of nearby cities. That is the meaning of the expression, "and its surrounding settlements," added to the name of a city (Num. 21:25; 32:42). In return for the protection offered against nomadic attacks, the cities received payment in service and produce. Sometimes a city was protected by a feudal lord around or near whose fortress the city was built. Often it depended entirely on the strength of its walls and the bravery of its men.

The chief feature distinguishing a city from a village was that it had a WALL (Lev. 25:29-30). Walls 20-30 ft. (6-9 m.) thick were not unusual. Sometimes a city was also surrounded by a moat (Dan. 9:25; KJV "wall"; NIV "trench"), and even by a second smaller wall acting as a rampart (2 Sam. 20:15). The wall had one or more gates that were closed during the night (Josh. 2:5, 7), and in later times on the Sabbath (Neh. 13:19). The gates were strengthened with iron or bronze bars and bolts (Deut. 3:5; Jdg. 16:3) and had rooms overhead (2 Sam. 18:24). From the top of the wall or from a tower by the gate, a watchman was on the lookout for approaching danger (Jer. 6:17). The gates were approached by narrow roads easy to defend. From a distance, usually all that could be seen of a city was its walls, except possibly its inner fortress or citadel.

Within the walls, the important features of a city were the stronghold or fortress, the high place, the broad place by the gate, and the streets. The stronghold was an inner fort protected by a garrison to which the inhabitants could run when the outer walls were taken by an enemy. The people of SHECHEM tried unsuccessfully to hold out against ABIMELECH in such a stronghold (Jdg. 9:49), and the king was afterward killed by a woman who dropped a stone from the tower within the city of Thebez (9:50, 53). When DAVID captured the fortress of ZION, the whole city came into his possession (2 Sam. 5:7). Sometimes TOWERS abutted the inside of the city wall.

The HIGH PLACES were an important part of every Canaanite city. There sacrifices were offered and feasts held. Originally they were on an elevation, but the term became the general one for any local sanctuary even when it was on level ground.

The broad place was an open area—not a square, but only a widening of the street, just inside the city gate, serving as a place for social intercourse in general. It was the center of communal life. Here the people of the city administered justice, held deliberative assemblies, exchanged news, and transacted business. Strangers in the city passed the night there if they had no friends in the city. It had a defensive value in time of war, as it

© Dr. James C. Martin

permitted the concentration of forces in front of the city GATE.

The streets in ancient cities were not laid out on any fixed plan. They were narrow, winding, unpaved alleys. The streets of JERUSALEM were not paved until the time of Herod AGRIPPA II. Cities built on steep hillsides had streets on the roofs of houses. Streets were rarely cleaned and were unlighted. Certain streets were allocated to particular trades and guilds—for bakers, cheese-makers, goldsmiths, etc.

Little is known about how city government was administered. In Deut. 16:18 and 19:12 mention is made of elders and judges. SAMARIA had a governor (1 Ki. 22:26). Jerusalem must have had several high officials (2 Ki. 23:8).

city authorities, city officials. Although the NT can use general expressions referring to city officials (Acts 13:50; 25:23), the specific term *politarchēs* **G4485** is used in only one passage (Acts 17:6, 8; KJV, "rulers of the city"). Here it refers to the civic MAGISTRATES of THESSALONICA before whom JASON and some of the Christians were dragged by the mob following on the preaching of the gospel by PAUL and SILAS. The term does not occur in classical Greek literature and its use in this passage was once dismissed as a mistake, but it has since been found in many inscriptions dating as far back as the second century B.C. In most cases the word is used for magistrates in Macedonian cities, and five times it refers to Thessalonica itself.

city clerk. See OCCUPATIONS AND PROFESSIONS.

City of David. Although this expression is applied to BETHLEHEM in Luke's nativity story (Lk. 2:4, 11; NIV, "town of David"), the phrase refers primarily to ZION, that is, the JEBUSITE fortress that DAVID captured and made his royal residence (2 Sam. 5:7, 9, and frequently).

City of Destruction. According to Isa. 19:18, five Egyptian cities will swear allegiance to Yahweh in the end times, and one of them will bear the name City of Destruction. The Hebrew word for "Destruction" is *ḥeres* **H2239**, but the Great Isaiah Scroll from Qumran (see DEAD SEA SCROLLS), along with a few Masoretic MSS, has *ḥeres* **H3064**,

"Sun." This reading is also reflected in several ancient versions and has been adopted by some modern translations (e.g., NRSV). It is possible that a pun is implied—what was then "City of the Sun" was to be called "City of Destruction." Of Egyptian towns, one in particular was known as "City of the Sun," namely, HELIOPOLIS: the "destruction" could reflect the judgments expressed and the overthrow of Egyptian paganism.

city of Moab. A phrase used once by the KJV and other versions (Num. 22:36; NIV, "Moabite town"; NRSV, "Ir-moab"). It refers to the location near the river ARNON where BALAAM visited BALAK; it is often identified with the Moabite city of AR (cf. Num. 21:15, 28; Isa. 15:1).

City of Palms. Also "city of palm trees." An epithet for JERICHO (Deut. 34:3; Jdg. 1:16; 3:13; 2 Chr. 28:15).

City of Salt. One of six cities allotted to JUDAH in the desert (Josh. 15:62). Four of these—MIDDIN, SECACAH, NIBSHAN, and the City of Salt—are often identified with four Iron II settlements in el-Buqeʿah, a valley SW of JERICHO (see ACHOR), and many have thought that the City of Salt in particular is the same as Khirbet Qumran (see DEAD SEA SCROLLS). This identification is uncertain, however, and other proposals have been made.

City of the Sun. See CITY OF DESTRUCTION.

city of waters. This phrase is used by the KJV and other versions as the literal rendering of a Hebrew idiom that probably refers to a district in the Ammonite city of RABBAH where the water supply was found (2 Sam. 12:27).

clan. This English term is used frequently by the NIV and other versions to render Hebrew *mišpāḥâ* **H5476**, a unit of kinship larger than a FAMILY but smaller than a TRIBE (e.g., Gen. 10:5; 24:38; Num. 1:2; Josh. 7:14; et al.; less often it renders *ʾelep* **H548**, Jdg. 6:15 et al.). Unfortunately, the technical term *clan* in modern anthropology refers, as a rule, to an extended family within which marriage is not allowed (*exogamous*). The Hebrew word, in contrast, designates a large group made up of many families among whom marriage was not only permitted (*endogamous*) but might even be required in certain situations.

Clauda. See CAUDA.

Claudia. klaw′dee-uh (Gk. *Klaudia G3086*, apparently from Lat. *claudus*, "lame"). A Christian woman who, along with others (EUBULUS, LINUS, and PUDENS), was a friend of the apostle PAUL during his second Roman imprisonment and who sent greetings to TIMOTHY (2 Tim. 4:21). One ancient tradition identifies her as the mother (or possibly the wife) of Linus; others have speculated that she was married to Pudens.

Claudius. klaw′dee-uhs (Gk. *Klaudios G3087*, apparently from Lat. *claudus*, "lame"). The fourth Roman emperor (A.D. 41-54). His full name was Tiberius Claudius Drusus Nero Germanicus. A young man of physical disabilities, he lived a secluded life under Emperor TIBERIUS, who was his uncle. Under the next emperor, Caligula, he held several important posts. When Caligula was killed,

© Dr. James C. Martin. The Istanbul Archaeological Museum. Photographed by permission.

Marble bust (1st cent.) of the emperor Claudius.

Claudius was named emperor by the praetorian guard in return for a considerable largess. Despite his handicaps he ruled well during the early years of his reign. Claudius was favorable towards the Jews during this period: two edicts, one relating to ALEXANDRIA and the other to the empire, granted them religious toleration, exemption from military service, and partial self-government. Herod AGRIPPA I, grandson of HEROD the Great, had assisted him much in his advancement to the throne, and in consequence was given the whole of Palestine.

The latter part of Claudius's reign, however, was marked by intrigue and suspicion. The government was in the hands of his freedmen and the women around him. His niece Agrippina became his fourth wife, and she prompted him to set aside his own son Brittanicus in favor of NERO, her son by a former marriage. In A.D. 54 the emperor decided that Brittanicus should succeed him, but before he could make public his wish, Agrippina fed him poisoned mushrooms.

Claudius is mentioned twice in the NT. In Acts 11:28 a prophecy was made by AGABUS that there would be a "severe famine ... over the entire Roman world"; Luke adds, "This happened during the reign of Claudius." In 18:2 we are told that PAUL, while at Corinth, met AQUILA and his wife PRISCILLA, Jews who had come there "because Claudius had ordered all the Jews to leave Rome." This event is usually identified with an incident reported by Suetonius: "Because the Jews at Rome caused continuous disturbances at the instigation of Chrestus, he [Claudius] expelled them from the city" (*Claudius* 25; the name "Chrestus" is prob. a misunderstanding for "Christus").

Claudius Lysias. klaw′dee-uhs lis′ee-uhs (Gk. *Klaudios Lysias G3087 + G3385*). Commander of the Roman garrison in Jerusalem at the time of PAUL's arrest (Acts 21:31-39; 22:23-30; 23:10-35; the name occurs only in 23:26; 24:22). He was a military tribune in command of a cohort that was stationed at the fortress of ANTONIA near the temple area and connected to it by a staircase. His cognomen, Lysias, suggests that he was of Greek origin. When he learned who Paul was, he allowed him to address the Jewish mob from the steps of the castle. However, Paul's mention of his mission to the Gentiles renewed the uprising (21:27—22:24). Lysias was prepared to examine Paul by torture until he learned that he was a Roman citizen and therefore exempt from such treatment. The apostle was then turned over to the SANHEDRIN for examination. Dissension prevented Paul's conviction, but a group plotted to kill him. When informed of the plot by Paul's nephew, Lysias sent the apostle by night to FELIX, the governor at CAESAREA (23:23-33). The situation must have been serious, for Paul was guarded by 200 foot soldiers, 70 horsemen, and 200 spearmen. A letter from Lysias to FELIX concerning the essential facts in the matter is recorded in 23:26-30.

clay. A word that translates a number of different Hebrew words and one Greek word and is often used in the Bible in a literal or a metaphorical sense—in the latter sense meaning "dust" or "flesh" (as made from earth). Clay was widely used in OT times for the making of brick, mortar, and pottery, and, in some countries, for the making of tablets on which inscriptions were impressed (see CLAY TAB-LETS). Mud bricks were not always made of true clay, but of mud mixed with straw. True clay was variable in composition, giving variety to quality and color, and thus was suited for different uses. As a building material, clay has been used from very ancient times. BABYLON was made wholly of brick, either baked or dried in the sun. NINEVEH, the capital of ASSYRIA, was made mostly of brick. The villages of EGYPT were constructed of sun-dried clay.

clay tablets. In ancient times WRITING was done on papyrus, parchment, potsherds, and clay tablets. The latter were made of clean-washed, smooth clay. While still wet, the clay had wedge-shaped letters (a script now called *cuneiform*, from Latin *cuneus*, "wedge") imprinted on it with a stylus, and then was kiln fired or sun dried. Tablets were made of various shapes—cone-shaped, drum-shaped, and flat. They were often placed in a clay envelope. Vast quantities of these have been excavated in the Near East, though many remain unread. The oldest ones go back to c. 3000 B.C. They are practically imperishable; fire only hardens them more. Personal and business letters, legal documents, books, and communications between rulers are represented. The tablets reveal many details of everyday life in the ANE and shed light on obscure customs mentioned in the OT. Some provide versions of the creation and the flood. They have greatly increased our understanding of the biblical setting, at times confirming the scriptural record.

clean. The division found in the OT between clean and unclean is fundamental to Hebrew/Israelite religion. The Lord is to be served and worshiped only by a clean, pure, and chaste people. They were to be physically clean (Exod. 19:10-14; 30:18-21), ritually and ceremonially clean (Lev. 14-15), and morally clean in heart. DAVID prayed, "Cleanse me with hyssop, and I will be clean; / wash me, and I will be whiter than snow" (Ps. 51:7). While the NT supplies examples of Jewish ritual cleansing (e.g., Mk. 1:44; Acts 21:26), it makes clear that Christian believers have been freed from the ceremonial regulations of the Mosaic LAW (e.g., Eph. 2:14-15). Its emphasis is therefore on the clean heart and pure life. Jesus condemned the obsession with external purity with no related emphasis on internal purity/wholeness (Mk. 7:1-23). Further, by his atoning work Jesus cleanses believers from all sin (Eph. 5:25-26; 1 Jn. 1:7). As High Priest, Jesus cleanses the heart as well as the body (Heb. 10:2, 21-22). So believers are to be pure in heart (Matt. 5:8; 1 Tim. 1:5) and chaste in life (1 Tim. 4:2; 5:2). It is their duty to purify themselves (1 Pet. 2:22; 1 Jn. 3:3). See also PURIFICATION; SANCTIFICATION; UNCLEAN.

Cleanthes. klee-an'theez (Gk. *Kleanthēs*). Son of Phanius of Assos and head of the STOIC school in ATHENS from 263 to 232 B.C. His *Hymn to Zeus*, a surviving poem, contains the words quoted by PAUL in his address before the AREOPAGUS Court (Acts 17:28). He made Stoicism more religious in its orientation by teaching that the universe was a living being, that God was its soul, and that the sun was its heart.

Clement. klem'uhnt (Gk. *Klēmēs G3098*, from Lat. *clemens*, "gentle"). One of PAUL's fellow workers at PHILIPPI, of whom the apostle says that their "names are in the book of life" (Phil. 4:3). He was apparently one of those who labored in the establishment of the church there. Paul seems to accord

Clemens a place of special esteem since he alone is named in the group. Some early traditions identify him with Clement of Rome, who was bishop of that city at the end of the century and who wrote an important letter to the Corinthian church (see APOSTOLIC FATHERS), but most scholars think this is unlikely. The name Clement was very common.

Cleopas. klee´oh-puhs (Gk. *Kleopas G3093*, a short form of *Kleopatros*, possibly "renowned father"). One of the two disciples whom Jesus joined on the road to EMMAUS during the afternoon of the day of his resurrection (Lk. 24:13-32). The other disciple is not named. Tradition gives the name Simon to Cleopas's companion and includes both among the seventy(-two) whom Jesus sent out on a mission (Lk. 10:1-24; other suggestions regarding the identity of this disciple include Cleopas's wife or son, as well as NATHANAEL, NICODEMUS, et al.). Some of the church fathers identified Cleopas with the CLOPAS mentioned in Jn. 19:25. Because of the sound similarity, Cleopas (a genuine Greek name) may have functioned as the equivalent of Clopas (the Greek form of a Semitic name), but there is no evidence that these two persons were the same.

Cleophas. See CLOPAS.

clerk. See OCCUPATIONS AND PROFESSIONS.

cloak. See DRESS.

Clopas. kloh´puhs (Gk. *Klōpas G3116*, prob. an Aram. name). KJV Cleophas. The husband (or possibly the son or father—the Greek text is ambiguous) of a certain MARY, one of the women who stood at the foot of the cross when Jesus was crucified (Jn. 19:25). This Mary is distinguished from Mary Magdalene and from Jesus' mother. Matthew and Mark both mention a "Mary the mother of James and Joseph [Joses]" among the women who were at the cross (Matt. 27:56; Mk. 15:40). Mark identifies this JAMES as "James the younger" as if to distinguish him from James the son of Zebedee. It is interesting that in all four lists of the twelve disciples given in the Gospels and Acts, there is a James son of ALPHAEUS (Matt. 10:3; Mk. 3:18; Lk. 6:15; Acts 1:13). If the James mentioned in Matt. 27 and Mk.

15 is the son of Alphaeus, then Clopas is the same as Alphaeus. Some of the later church fathers identified Clopas with CLEOPAS, one of the disciples to whom Jesus appeared on the road to EMMAUS after his resurrection (Lk. 24:18), but Cleopas is clearly a Greek name while Clopas is Semitic.

closet. This English term is used by the KJV to render Hebrew *ḥuppāh H2903* (with reference to a bridal "chamber" or "canopy," Joel 2:16; cf. Ps. 19:5; Isa. 4:5) and Greek *tameion G5421*, "private room, inner chamber" (Matt. 6:6; Lk. 12:3).

cloth, clothes, clothing. See DRESS.

cloud. Biblical references to clouds seldom have anything do with actual weather conditions, because in PALESTINE the weather is not very varied. There were two recognized seasons: a rainy one from October to April, and one of sunshine from May to September. The Hebrews were not much given to making comments on the weather. In Scripture there are, however, many references to clouds in a metaphoric and figurative sense. They symbolize transitoriness. God says Judah's goodness is like a morning cloud (Hos. 6:4 KJV; "mist" in NIV), and Job compares his prosperity to the passing clouds (Job 30:15). Sometimes they are used as a type of refreshment, for they bring shade from the oppressive sun and give promise of rain. Clouds without water, therefore, symbolize a person who promises much but does not perform (Prov. 16:15; 25:14; Jude 12). The darkness of clouds is the symbol of mystery, especially that of creation (Job 3:5; 38:9; Ps. 97:2). Their distance from the earth is made to typify the unattainable (Job 20:6; Ps. 147:8; Isa. 14:14). One of the most frequent and suggestive uses of the figure is in connection with the presence of God. Clouds both veil and reveal the divine presence. God rides on the clouds (Isa. 19:1; Nah. 1:3); he is present in the cloud (Exod. 19:9; 24:16; 34:5). See also CLOUD, PILLAR OF. A cloud appeared at our Lord's TRANSFIGURATION (Matt. 17:5) and at his ASCENSION (Acts 1:9), and it has a place in his prediction that he would return (Matt. 24:30; 26:64).

cloud, pillar of. A symbol of the presence and guidance of God in the forty-year wilderness journey of the Israelites from Egypt to Canaan (Exod. 13:21-22). At night it became fire. When God wanted Israel to rest in any place, the cloud rested on the tabernacle above the mercy seat (29:42-43) or at the door of the tabernacle (33:9-10; Num. 12:5), or it covered the tabernacle (Exod. 40:34-38).

clout. See DRESS.

club. A specially made club for battle purposes seems to have been used as early as 3500 B.C. in the ANE. The head was a well-shaped stone or ball of metal with a hole through which the handle was thrust. When an adequate helmet was invented, the mace became obsolete as a crushing weapon, and the axe was developed to pierce the armor of the enemy. The club then became stylized as a symbol of authority. In the OT this is called a "rod of iron" (Ps. 2:9; Isa. 10:5; cf. Isa. 10:15). The shepherd's weapon was a wooden club (1 Sam. 17:40, 43; Ps. 23:4).

Cnidus. ni´duhs (Gk. *Knidos G3118*). A Greek colony on the SW tip of ASIA MINOR, in the region of CARIA, past which PAUL sailed on his journey to ROME (Acts 27:7). It was situated at the end of a long, narrow peninsula projecting between the islands of Cos and RHODES, and had two excellent harbors. It had the rank of a free city. Jews lived there as early as the second century B.C. Only ruins are left of a once-flourishing city, especially noted for its temple of Venus (Aphrodite), which housed a famous statue of this deity by Praxiteles.

coal. Often found in the English Bible, the word never refers to true mineral coal, which has not been found in Palestine proper, where the geological formation as a whole is recent. Coal of a poor quality has been found at SIDON, and for a time some was mined in Lebanon. The half dozen Hebrew and Greek words rendered "coal" refer either to charcoal or to live embers of any kind. Charcoal was used by the Hebrews to provide warmth in winter (Isa. 47:14; Jn. 18:18), for cooking (Isa. 44:19; Jn. 21:9), and for blacksmith work (Isa. 44:12; 54:16). It was made by covering a carefully stacked pile of wood with leaves and earth, and then setting fire to it. After several days of burning and smoldering,

the wood was converted into charcoal and the pile was opened.

In Ps. 120:4 there is mention of "coals of the broom tree." In 1 Ki. 19:6 and Isa. 6:6 the Hebrew word denotes a hot stone. Frequently the word is used metaphorically, as in Prov. 26:21 (NIV, "charcoal"). In Prov. 25:22 and Rom. 12:20, where we are told to give to an enemy good in return for evil, thus heaping coals of fire on his head, the coals of fire probably are not meant to suggest the pain of punishment to the guilty but the softening of his heart as he thinks with burning shame of his unworthy hatred. Love will melt and purify. In Lam. 4:8 the literal meaning of the Hebrew word translated "coal" by KJV (NIV, "soot") is "blackness."

coat. See DRESS.

coat of mail. See ARMS AND ARMOR.

cobra. See ANIMALS.

cock. See BIRDS.

cockatrice. See ANIMALS.

cock crowing. Literal rendering of a Greek term used once in the NT to designate the name of the third watch of the night, from midnight to about 3:00 a.m. (Mk. 13:35 NRSV; the KJV has "cockcrowing"; the NIV, "when the rooster crows"). In the time of Christ the night was divided by the Romans into four watches: late, midnight, cockcrow, and

This inscription found in the Jerusalem temple mount reads, "To the place of the trumpeting." At cockcrow in NT times, two priests blew the shofars from the SW corner of the temple platform.

© Dr. James C. Martin. The Israel Museum, Jerusalem. Photographed by permission.

early (see HOUR). In a literal sense, each of the evangelists refers to the crowing of the rooster in connection with PETER's denial of Jesus (Matt. 26:34, 74; Mk. 14:30; Lk. 22:34; Jn. 13:38).

cockle. See PLANTS.

code, written. This expression is used by the NIV to render two Greek words: *gramma G1207*, meaning "letter, document" (Rom. 2:26-27; 7:6), and *cheirographon G5934*, meaning "handwritten document, record of debts" (Col. 2:14). In both cases it refers to the Mosaic LAW viewed negatively. The first term focuses on the law as an outward requirement, contrasting with what is spiritual. The second speaks of its condemnatory function.

codex. A bound manuscript (pl. *codices*), contrasted with a SCROLL (which consists of sheets joined together in long rolls). The modern book descends from the codex form, which was already in existence, but rarely used, during the NT period. As early as the second century of our era, Christians were favoring the codex for the transcription of NT books and other religious literature. Although the original reason for this choice is debated, the codex provided some significant advantages over the scroll. A relatively long biblical book, such as the Gospel of Luke, would fill one large scroll, whereas the whole NT (and even the whole Greek Bible) could be bound together within the covers of one portable codex. Moreover, finding a specific text was far easier by turning pages than by unrolling a scroll that was 20-30 ft. (6-10 m.) long. By the fourth century, the codex had become the medium of choice also for the transcription of non-Christian literature. See also TEXT AND VERSIONS (NT).

coffin. This word is used by the KJV and other versions only in Gen. 50:26, where it renders a Hebrew word meaning "chest" or "box," though in this instance it may mean "mummy case." In EGYPT, where JOSEPH died, the dead were put in such a case after being embalmed. The term *coffin* is also used by the NIV in Lk. 7:14 with reference to the widow's son at NAIN, but the Israelites were usually carried to the grave on a BIER, a simple flat board with two or three staves.

cohort. Nominally the tenth part of a Roman LEGION, or 600 soldiers, but the actual number varied between 500 and 1,000. Although this English term often has the general sense of "a group of people," it is used by the NRSV and other versions in its precise military meaning to render Greek *speira G5061* (Matt. 27:27; Mk. 15:16; Jn. 18:3, 12; Acts 10:1; 21:31; 27:1). In the NT narratives, the cohorts function as garrison troops and as local military police. The NIV uses more general renderings, such as "detachment of soldiers" and "regiment." See also AUGUSTAN COHORT; ITALIAN REGIMENT.

coin. See MONEY.

Col-Hozeh. kol-hoh′zuh (Heb. *kol-ḥōzeh H3997*, possibly "everyone is a seer"). TNIV Kol-Hozeh. Father of a certain SHALLUN who ruled the district of MIZPAH and repaired the FOUNTAIN GATE (Neh. 3:15). He should probably be distinguished from another Col-Hozeh, identified as the father of a certain Baruch and as the son of Hazaiah, and included in a list of descendants of JUDAH who lived in Jerusalem (11:5).

collar. See DRESS.

collection. See CONTRIBUTION.

college. This English term is used twice by the KJV to render Hebrew *mišneh H5467*, "double, second," when it refers to a district in Jerusalem (2 Ki. 22:14; 2 Chr. 34:22). See SECOND DISTRICT.

colony. In the only occurrence of the word in the NT, Acts 16:12, the city of PHILIPPI is identified as a colony, that is, a settlement of Roman citizens, authorized by the government, in conquered territory. The settlers were usually retired Roman soldiers who settled in places where they could keep enemies of the empire in check. They were the aristocracy of the provincial towns where they lived. Such colonies had the rights of Italian cities: municipal self-government and exemption from poll and land taxes.

color. No word occurs in the Hebrew OT for the abstract idea of color; the Greeks had such a word (*chrōma*), but it is not used in the NT. It is possible that the first commandment inhibited many types of artistic efforts among the Israelites, including the extensive employment of color. On the other hand, the colors of the TABERNACLE hangings were prescribed by God, and likewise also the vestments of the high priest. But it was probably after contact developed with the Phoenicians that colors became more emphasized in Israelite culture. Individual colors are not numerous in the Bible, though the primary colors of red, yellow, and blue are found, as are purple, scarlet, and crimson, but the precision of quality or definition is unknown.

Colors appear principally as dyes, the most lavish use being seen in the tabernacle and on a reduced scale in Solomon's TEMPLE. These were extracted principally from plants or mollusks, and the resulting product was rather impure and often unstable. The most expensive was the PURPLE of the *murex*, which required 250,000 mollusks per ounce! In early times colors probably had little allegorical meaning. PHILO JUDAEUS (*Life of Moses* 2.17) makes white a symbol of the earth, and purple a symbol of the sea. The book of Revelation often mentions white, clearly as a symbol of purity and righteousness (e.g., Rev. 3:4-5; 19:8, 11, 14), while red represents the carnage of war (6:4), and black signifies the sorrow and death resulting therefrom (6:5, 12; cf. Zech. 6:2, 6).

Colossae. See COLOSSE.

Colosse. kuh-los′ee (*Kolossai G3145*). Also Colossae. An ancient city of PHRYGIA, situated on the S bank of the Lycus River. It was about 11 mi. (18 km.) from LAODICEA and 13 mi. (21 km.) from HIERAPOLIS. Colosse stood on the most important trade route from EPHESUS to the EUPHRATES River and was a place of great importance from early times. XERXES visited it in 481 B.C., and Cyrus the Younger in 401. The city was particularly renowned for a peculiar wool, probably purple in color (*colossinus*). The church at Colosse was probably established on PAUL's third missionary journey, during his three years in Ephesus, not by Paul himself (Col. 2:1), but by EPAPHRAS (1:7, 12-13). ARCHIPPUS also exercised a fruitful ministry there (4:17; Phlm. 2). PHILEMON was an active member of this church, and so also was ONESIMUS (Col. 4:9). During Paul's first Roman imprisonment, Epaphras brought to the apostle a report of the religious views and practices in Colosse that called forth his letter, in which he rebuked the church for its errors. Colosse lost its importance by the change of the road system. Laodicea became the greater city. During the seventh and eighth centuries A.D. its openness exposed it to the terrible raids of the Saracens, and the people moved to Chonae (now called Chonas), a fortress on the slope of Mount Cadmus, about 3 mi. (5 km.) farther south. In the twelfth century the Turks destroyed the city. Archaeologists have unearthed ruins of an ancient church.

Colossians, Epistle to the. A letter of PAUL to the church in COLOSSE. It was written by the apostle when he was a prisoner (Col. 4:3, 10, 18), about the year A.D. 62, probably during his first imprisonment in ROME (Acts 28:30-31), though CAESAREA (23:35; 24:27) and EPHESUS have also been suggested. The genuineness of Colossians has been disputed on the grounds that its style and content

Paul's letter to the Colossians was sent to Colosse, a city situated in the valley of the Lycus River. (View to the SE.)

© Dr. James C. Martin

Overview of COLOSSIANS

Author: The apostle PAUL.

Historical setting: Probably written from ROME during the apostle's first imprisonment in that city (c. A.D. 61-63), but some scholars prefer an earlier date and alternate places (EPHESUS or CAESAREA). The letter may have been written in response to news about heretical influences in the church at COLOSSE.

Purpose: To oppose false teachings concerning ceremonial and ascetic practices by exalting CHRIST as the one who holds supremacy over all and in whom true wisdom is to be found.

Contents: The preeminence of Christ over against human teachings (Col. 1-2), and the implications of this truth for Christian conduct (chs. 3-4).

C

contain non-Pauline features, but most scholars have not found this view persuasive.

The church at Colosse was very likely founded during Paul's three-year stay in Ephesus on his third missionary journey. It appears from Col. 2:1 that Paul himself had never preached in Colosse. EPAPHRAS, a native of Colosse (4:12), was probably converted under Paul's ministry at Ephesus and was then sent by the apostle to preach in his native city (1:7). Evidently he also evangelized the nearby cities of LAODICEA and HIERAPOLIS (4:13). When Paul wrote this letter, the minister of the church at Colosse was ARCHIPPUS (4:17), who may have been PHILEMON's son (Phlm. 2). Epaphras had recently come to Paul with a disturbing report of the condition of the church, and this led the apostle to write to the believers there. The bearer of the letter was TYCHICUS (Col. 4:7, 8), to whom Paul also entrusted his letter to the EPHESIANS (Eph. 6:21), probably written at the same time. With him went ONESIMUS (Col. 4:9), a runaway slave converted by Paul, bearing the letter to Philemon, a resident of Colosse, who was also one of Paul's converts, perhaps becoming a believer at Ephesus.

In the few years since Paul had been in the province of ASIA an insidious error had crept into the church at Colosse. Who the false teachers were we do not know; but it is clear that the trouble was different from that faced by Paul at GALATIA, where

JUDAIZERS had tried to undermine his work. The teaching attacked by Paul is described in Col. 2:8, 16-23. It was, at least in part, Judaistic, as is seen in his reference to circumcision (2:11; 3:11), ordinances (2:14), meats and drinks, feast days, new moons, and Sabbaths (2:16). There was also in it a strong ascetic element. Special self-denying rules were given that had as their purpose the mortification of the body (2:16, 20-23). Some sort of worship of ANGELS was apparently practiced—a custom that continued for several centuries (in the fourth century the Council of Laodicea condemned it in one of its canons, and in the fifth century Theodoret said that the archangel Michael was worshiped in the area). This heresy claimed to be a philosophy and made much of wisdom and knowledge (2:8). Plainly, the Colossians were beguiled by this religious syncretism and even took pride in it (2:8). The exact origin of the false teaching is unknown. Some find it in Essenism, others in incipient GNOSTICISM or in contemporary Judaism with a syncretistic addition of local Phrygian ideas.

Paul met these errors, not by controversy or personal authority, but by presenting the counter truth that Jesus Christ is the image of the invisible God (Col. 1:15), in whom are hid all the treasures of wisdom and knowledge, and in whom the fullness of the divine perfections find their perfect embodiment (1:19). He is the creator of all, and all power is from him. On the cross he revealed the impotence of all the powers that had tried to thwart his purposes (2:15). Freedom from the corruption of human nature is found in the newness of life that the death and resurrection of Christ provide. The letter to the Colossians may be divided into four parts: (1) The salutation and thanksgiving (1:1-8); (2) the doctrinal section (1:9—2:5); (3) practical exhortations (2:6—4:6); (4) concluding salutations (4:7-18). Toward the end of the document (4:16), Paul asks that the Colossian church exchange letters with the church at Laodicea, to which he has also written. It is possible that this letter to the Laodiceans is what we know as the letter to the Ephesians, sent as a circular letter to various churches in the Roman province of Asia.

colt. See ANIMALS.

column. See PILLAR.

comfort. See CONSOLATION.

Comforter. See ADVOCATE; HOLY SPIRIT.

commandment. This word is used in the English Bible to translate a variety of Hebrew and Greek terms. The idea of authority conveyed by these terms comes from the fact that God as sovereign Lord has a right to be obeyed. The instruction of Jesus is full of ethical teachings that have the force of divine commandments. What he says is as authoritative as what was said by God in OT times. That is true even when he does not use the word "commandment" or its equivalents, as he often does. But what is said of God and Jesus Christ is also true of the apostles. Paul, for example, does not hesitate to say, "What I am writing to you is the Lord's command" (1 Cor. 14:37). The Bible makes it very clear, however, that God is not satisfied with mere external compliance but expects willing and joyful obedience, coming from the heart. See also COMMANDMENTS, TEN; LAW.

commandment, new. That command given in the NT which emphasizes the substance and spiritual power of LOVE involved in the moral law (the TEN COMMANDMENTS). The kernel of this thought is imbedded in various passages in the Gospels (Matt. 19:16-22; 22:37-40; et al.), but the actual NT references where the term "new commandment" is found are Jn. 13:34-35; 1 Jn. 2:7-8; 2 Jn. 5. It had been stated in the OT that God's people should love their neighbors. Jesus puts new emphasis on this concept found in the law. "You who are My disciples," he says in effect, "must really show love *to one another, as I* have shown love *to you*. This will be a new thing for the world to see, that you, My disciples, have love for one another." In 1 Jn. 2:5-10 the commandment is called "old" in that the readers knew from the OT and from John's presentation of Jesus' teaching that they should love one another (cf. Jn. 15:12), but it was new in that there was renewed and continual emphasis to be placed on the Christian loving his brother through the power of God's own love.

Commandments, Ten. The OT is distinctly a religion of LAW, with creed, cult, and conduct prescribed minutely by God. The OT praises the revelational instruction of the Torah (God's law as set forth in the first five books of the OT; cf. Ps. 119:97), which has come to the elect nation as a gift of grace, invested with divine authority and sanction. The Torah is revered because it embodies the will and wisdom of the Creator. Expressing God's own nature, it demands of the creature only what the Creator's HOLINESS requires for fellowship with himself. The climax of Torah is the Decalogue, the Code of the Ten Words, received by MOSES on Mount SINAI. The Decalogue is specifically the gift of grace of God the Redeemer (Exod. 20:2), given to his people not to bring them

Replica of the ark of the covenant, which held the Ten Commandments, Aaron's staff that budded, and manna.

© Dr. James C. Martin

into bondage but because they have been brought out of bondage. That it is unique among the several codes found in the OT can scarcely be disputed. Originally spoken by God in a context calculated to produce unforgettable awe (19:9-25), it was afterward inscribed by his finger on two tablets of stone (31:18); in fact, it was inscribed by him a second time after Moses in anger shattered the first two tablets (Deut. 10:1-4). It was placed in the ARK OF THE COVENANT (Exod. 25:21) and thus enshrined at the very center of Israel's worship. Hence the Code of the Ten Words is indeed *sui generis*, a statement that gives the distillation of religion and morality: these principles, so simply phrased, are remarkably comprehensive and universally valid. Mount Sinai, therefore, was the scene of an epochal event in human history.

Before examining this code in any detail we must answer several questions concerning it. First, how do we explain the two somewhat dissimilar versions of it that the Pentateuch contains, one in Exod. 20:1-17, the other in Deut. 5:6-21? In the Exodus version the fourth commandment grounds the keeping of the SABBATH in God's own Sabbath-rest after his six days of CREATION; in the Deuteronomy version, however, Sabbath-keeping is grounded in the Egyptian deliverance. Moreover, the two versions do not agree with respect to the tenth commandment, which forbids covetousness; different verbs are used and the order of clauses varies. But surely these differences are trivial when we remember that the Deuteronomic version is part of an address Moses delivered. In an oral recital one scarcely expects notarial precision. Also, Moses, because of the Spirit's guidance, was free to introduce new elements and slight changes.

Second, how are the Ten Words to be numbered? W. S. Bruce helpfully clears away the complexities of this question by pointing out that the commandments were not numbered by Moses, and thus down the ages different schemes of arrangement have been found. According to one tradition, the commandments not to have other gods and not to make images are viewed as one, whereas the commandment against covetousness is analyzed as consisting of two. In the one most commonly known among English-speaking communities, "the preface is not made a commandment or part of one: but the first commandment simply forbids the worship of false deities, and the second prohibits the use of idols; while all the prohibitions of covetousness are included under the last command" (*The Ethics of the Old Testament* [1909], 101-2).

Third, how are the Ten Words to be divided between the two tables (tablets)? The Roman Catholic church puts three commandments on the first table, seven on the second. The Reformed church adheres to a four and six classification. Josephus, however, gives the traditional five and five arrangement, the first table dealing, as he says, with piety, the second with probity. Taking Josephus as his guide, C. E. Luthardt in his *History of Christian Ethics* gives what seems to be the most satisfactory division:

FIRST TABLE
1. No other gods.
2. No image of God.
3. No dishonoring of God's name.
4. No desecration of God's day.
5. No dishonoring of God's representatives (parents).

SECOND TABLE
1. No taking away of a neighbor's life.
2. No taking away of his wife, his dearest good.
3. No taking away of his goods.
4. No taking away of his good name.
5. No coveting of his good or his goods.

Fourth, is there any significance to the fact that the Ten Words are inscribed on two tables rather than one? Traditionally the reference to "two tables" has been understood to refer to the fact that the Decalogue falls, as we have seen, into the two sections of our duty to God and our duty to man. It has been assumed that each of these sections was given a tablet to itself. This explanation is unlikely because it would seem to put asunder what God has joined, making it appear as if the commandments Godward and the commandments manward are essentially separable. Some prefer to follow the line opened up by more recent knowledge of ancient COVENANT forms in which the stipulations of the covenant—the laws imposed by the covenant-lord—were written in duplicate. The covenant-lord retained one copy and deposited the other in the sanctuary of the god of the people on whom he was imposing his covenant. In the case of the Decalogue, Yahweh is both Covenant-Lord and also God of Israel. He, therefore, takes both copies into his care: the whole care, continuance, and maintenance of the covenant relationship rests with him.

Fifth, is this code merely negative or does it have a positive aspect also? Admittedly, the only commandment couched in positive terms is the fifth law, which enjoins respect for one's parents. But the seeming negativism of the Ten Words is only superficial. Whenever an evil is forbidden, the opposite good is implicitly demanded. Here we have far more than a forbidding: we have a requiring as well. When Jesus interprets and epitomizes this code, he reduces it to the positive virtue of love. Paul does exactly the same thing in Rom. 13:8-10. This law cannot be fulfilled only by concern and care; it calls for loving obedience to God and loving service to man.

Sixth, are the Ten Commandments to be viewed as "a yoke of slavery" (Gal. 5:1) or as a wise provision that God graciously made for his people? Undeniably in the course of the centuries there was a tendency for the Torah to be perverted into a grievous legalism; undeniably, too, the law as a whole had a pedagogic function, revealing as it did—and still does—our need of Jesus Christ (Rom. 7:7; Gal. 3:24). Yet the primary purpose of the Ten Words was to enable the Israelites, as the Lord's redeemed and peculiar treasure, to enter into a life of joyful fellowship with their Redeemer. This code issued from God's sovereign and saving relationship with his elect nation. It was imposed at his initiative and as the result of his covenantal activity. Passages like Exod. 20:2 and Deut. 4:32-40 show that Israel's Savior was Israel's Legislator. This law, then, was designed to bring the Lord's saving deed to its fulfillment by creating a holy community, a community reflecting his own nature, a community in which he could dwell and by which he could be magnified (Lev. 11:44; 20:8). Hence, used lawfully (1 Tim. 1:8), this code, which guided life rather than gave it, was a source of blessing (Ps. 19:8-9; 119:54).

With these six questions answered, let us now analyze briefly each of the Ten Words. The first commandment (Exod. 20:3) enjoins a confession of God's singularity, his absolute and exclusive deity. It predicates faith in him as the one and only God. Though not expressly teaching MONOTHEISM, it inferentially denounces polytheism as treason and unbelief. It demonstrates that God is not a class term but a proper name.

The second commandment (Exod. 20:4-6) enjoins the adoration of God's spirituality. Forbidding his worship by any false means, it rebukes the gross IDOLATRY that surrounded Israel. It shows that because of his very Being (Jn. 4:24) no visible or material representation of true Deity is possible. Thus it prevents wrong concepts of God from taking root in the human mind (Rom. 1:21-23).

The third commandment (Exod. 20:7) enjoins the reverence of the Lord's NAME. Since in the OT name and person are equivalent, with the name practically a reification of the person, this law prohibits blasphemy and profanity. It also interdicts immorality, any conduct that causes God's honor to suffer defilement by the sinner who bears his name (Rom. 2:24-25). With respect to the sacredness and significance of God's name, Mal. 3:16-17 is instructive.

The fourth commandment (Exod. 20:8-11) enjoins the observance of the Lord's day. For both humanitarian (Amos 8:5-6) and religious (Isa. 58:13-14) reasons, one day of rest in every seven is a blessed necessity. A Sabbath—whether on Saturday as commemorating a finished creation or on Sunday as commemorating a finished redemption—serves one's physical and spiritual welfare simultaneously (Mk. 2:27).

The fifth commandment (Exod. 20:12) enjoins the honor of God's surrogates, parents to whom he grants a kind of cocreatorship in the begetting of children and to whom he grants a kind of corulership in the governing of children. Let any nation abandon respect for the mystery, dignity, and authority of parenthood, and before long the moral fiber and social fabric of that nation are bound to disintegrate. That is why the OT statutes on this score are so severe (Exod. 21:15; Deut. 27:16; Prov. 20:20).

The sixth commandment (Exod. 20:13) is a prohibition of MURDER. Life is, patently, a person's one utterly indispensable possession; but, more than that, human beings bear the IMAGE OF GOD, and murder wantonly destroys God's image. Hence capital punishment is the penalty affixed to breaking this law (Gen. 9:5-6).

The seventh commandment (Exod. 20:24) is a prohibition of ADULTERY, a stringent prohibition that safeguards the sanctity of MARRIAGE and throws a bulwark around the home.

The eighth commandment (Exod. 20:15) is a prohibition of theft in any and all forms. Property is essentially an extension of one's personality, and thus this law indicates that the rights and achievements of one's neighbor must not be ignored.

The ninth commandment (Exod. 20:16) is a prohibition of falsehood in its many varieties, whether perjury, slander, or defamation (see LIE, LYING). TRUTH is the cement of community, the sine qua non of enduring interpersonal relationships on every level. Thus the OT, like the NT, stresses the need for a sanctified tongue (Ps. 5:9; 15:1-4; Prov. 18:21; Jer. 9:1-5).

The tenth commandment (Exod. 20:17) is a prohibition of COVETOUSNESS, and as such reveals that the Ten Words are not simply a civil code, but form a moral and spiritual code that strikes beneath the surface of the overt act (which is the exclusive province of civil law), tracing evil conduct to evil desire, probing the hidden motives of people (which is the province of morality and religion, God's province). This tenth commandment, therefore, highlights the pivotal importance of wrong appetites and intentions; it agrees with Paul that covetousness is idolatry (Col. 3:5), since inordinate craving means that a person's ego has become his or her god.

Except as the NT deepens and extends its principles, the Decalogue represents the high-water level of morality.

commerce. See TRADE AND TRAVEL.

common. This English term is used in Bible versions with various meanings ("shared, ordinary, public"). In the NT, the phrase "in common" is used to describe the early Christian practice of sharing possessions (Acts 2:44; 4:32; see COMMUNITY OF GOODS). The word "common" can also describe the faith and salvation shared by God's people

(Tit. 1:4; Jude 3). Of special interest is its use to render a Hebrew word meaning "profane, ritually neutral" (contrasted with "holy"; see Lev. 10:10; 1 Sam. 21:4-5; Ezek. 22:26; 42:20; 44:23; 48:14-15). The corresponding Greek adjective can also refer to that which is ritually UNCLEAN (Mk. 7:2, 5; Acts 10:14-15, 28; 11:8-9; Rom. 14:14; Heb. 10:29; Rev. 21:27). See CLEAN; HOLINESS.

communion. See FELLOWSHIP; LORD'S SUPPER.

community of goods. An expression not found in the NT but referring to Christian LOVE as expressed in the free sharing of material goods, as recorded in Acts 2:44 and 4:34—5:11. These two passages make clear that the social structure of the church at Jerusalem was not a communal program in the modern sense of the word, for the emphasis is placed first upon the sharing of *spiritual* blessings in Christ (2:42-43; 4:31-33). In addition, the Christians were willing to share their material goods, so that none of the saints at Jerusalem was impoverished (4:34). That the disciples were not forced to sell their property nor give it to the church is shown by the example of ANANIAS and SAPPHIRA, who were condemned not for failing to give their property (5:4), but for pretending to contribute more than they actually had given (5:1-3). Even this modified voluntary community of goods seems to have been practiced only in the Jerusalem church and for a limited time. Later this Christian community received gifts from non-Judean churches (Acts 11:27-30; 2 Cor. 8:1-5), one such church being instructed to lay aside offerings for the Lord's work each week (1 Cor. 16:1-2), with no suggestion of any community of goods. See CONTRIBUTION.

compassion. See MERCY; PITY.

Conaniah. kon´uh-ni´uh (Heb. *kānanyāhû H4042*, possibly "Yahweh sustains"). TNIV Konaniah. **(1)** A Levite who, with the help of his brother Shimei, was in charge of administering the collections under King HEZEKIAH (2 Chr. 31:12-13; KJV, "Cononiah").

(2) A leader of the Levites during the reign of King JOSIAH; along with his brothers Shemaiah and Nethanel, Conaniah provided five thousand offerings (lambs) and five head of cattle for the renewed celebration of the Passover (2 Chr. 35:9). He is thought by some to be a descendant of #1 above.

concision. See CIRCUMCISION.

concubine. In the Bible this word designates not a paramour, but rather a woman lawfully united in MARRIAGE to a man in a relation inferior to that of the regular wife. No moral stigma was attached to being a concubine; it was a natural part of a polygamous social system. Concubinage is assumed and provided for in the law of Moses, which tried to prevent its excesses and abuses (Exod. 21:7-11; Deut. 21:10-14). Concubines were commonly taken from among Hebrew or foreign slave girls, or Gentile captives taken in war, although free Hebrew women might also become concubines. They enjoyed no other right but lawful cohabitation. They had no authority in the family or in household affairs. Their husbands could send them away with a small present, and their children could, by means of small presents, be excluded from the heritage (Gen. 25:6). The children were regarded as legitimate, although the children of the first wife were preferred in the distribution of the inheritance. In patriarchal times, at least, the immediate cause of concubinage was the BARRENNESS of the lawful wife; sometimes the wife herself might suggest that her husband have children by her maidservant (Gen. 16; 30). Prominent OT figures who had concubines were Nahor (22:24), Abraham (25:6), Jacob (35:22), Eliphaz (36:12), Gideon (Jdg. 8:31), Saul (2 Sam. 3:7), David (5:13; 15:16; 16:21), Solomon (1 Ki. 11:3), Caleb (1 Chr. 2:46), Manasseh (7:14), Rehoboam (2 Chr. 11:21), Abijah (13:21), and Belshazzar (Dan. 5:2).

concupiscence. This English term (from Lat. *concupiscere*, "to desire intensely") is used in the KJV to render Greek *epithymia G2123*, "desire," in three passages where the context is negative (Rom. 7:8; Col. 3:5; 1 Thess. 4:5). In the Christian ethical tradition concupiscence, which often connotes inordinate sexual desire, is generally considered to be a sinful disposition either because it is abnormally intense or (more often) because it is wrongly directed. See LUST.

condemn, condemnation. These terms (and in the KJV sometimes "damnation") are used to render various Hebrew and Greek words that involve the thought of declaring JUDGMENT against someone or treating a person as guilty. Sometimes the sentence or penalty for the guilt or supposed guilt is expressed. Condemnation may be that of one person by another without any legal procedure—a person is simply reckoned guilty and perhaps made to suffer as guilty. Christ's injunction, however, is against all such judging: "Do not condemn, and you will not be condemned" (Lk. 6:37; cf. Rom. 2:1). In a different sense, it may be said that the integrity and God-fearing quality of one person's life condemns another: NOAH by his faith and action "condemned the world" (Heb. 11:7; cf. Matt. 12:41-42). Closely associated with this is the way that Scripture often says that people are condemned by their own words and actions (Job 9:20; 15:6; Tit. 3:11). John goes further in speaking of a person's own heart as being self-condemning (1 Jn. 3:20).

Scripture speaks also of the condemnation of a human magistrate, which may be perfectly just (Lk. 23:40), or—as in the case of Jesus' trial—completely unjust (Mk. 14:64). Earthly magistrates are considered God's ministers (Rom. 13:1-5), responsible to him for "acquitting the innocent and condemning the guilty" (Deut. 25:1). Ultimately all judgment is God's. He has judged and condemned men and women for their sin in the past (2 Pet. 2:6); all sin comes under his righteous condemnation (Rom. 5:16, 18); and in the end this will be perfectly manifest (Ps. 34:21; Matt. 12:37; Jude 4). It is made clear, however, that God's purpose in sending Jesus Christ was not "to condemn the world, but to save the world through him" (Jn. 3:17). Christ made this salvation possible by bearing the sin of men and women, because thus he "condemned sin" (Rom. 8:3); that is, he showed the guilt of sin and bore its consequences, so that "there is now no condemnation for those who are in Christ Jesus" (8:1).

conduit. See AQUEDUCT.

coney. See ANIMALS.

confectioner. See OCCUPATIONS AND PROFESSIONS.

confession. To confess is openly to acknowledge the truth in anything, as in the existence and authority of God or the sins of which one has been guilty. Occasionally it also means to concede or allow (Jn. 1:20; Acts 24:14; Heb. 11:13), or to praise God by thankfully acknowledging him (Rom. 14:11; Heb. 13:15). In the Bible, confession of SIN before God is recognized as a condition of FORGIVENESS. Christ taught the necessity of confessing offenses committed against other people (Matt. 5:24; Lk. 17:4).

confidence. See ASSURANCE; FAITH; HOPE.

confirm. This English term is used to render several verbs in the Bible that occur in a variety of contexts, such as strengthening persons, ratifying covenants, fulfilling promises, and verifying claims (e.g., Deut. 8:18; Esth. 9:29; Heb. 2:3).

congregation. A word used in Scripture most often to refer to the Hebrew people in a collective capacity, especially when viewed as an assembly summoned for a definite purpose (1 Ki. 8:65) or meeting on a festive occasion (Deut. 23:1). Sometimes it refers to an assembly of the whole people; sometimes, to any part of the people who might be present on a given occasion. Occasionally it conveys the idea of "horde." Every circumcised Hebrew was a member of the congregation and took part in its proceedings probably from the time he bore arms. He had, however, no political rights as an individual, but only as a member of a house, a family, or a tribe, which was usually represented by its head, known as an elder or a prince. The elders, summoned by the supreme governor or the high priest, represented the whole congregation, served as a national parliament, and had legislative and judicial powers. They sat as a court to deal with capital offenses (Num. 15:32-33), declared war, made peace, and concluded treaties (Josh. 9:15). The people were strictly bound by their acts, whether they approved of them or not (9:18). Occasionally the whole body of people was assembled for some solemn religious occasion (Exod. 12:47; Num. 25:6; Joel 2:15) or to receive some new commandments (Exod. 19:7-8; Lev. 8:4). After the conquest of Canaan the congregation was assembled only to consider very important matters.

The two primary Hebrew terms for "congregation" are ʿēdāh H6337 and qāhal H7735; the former is translated by the SEPTUAGINT with *synagōgē* G5252, and the latter with either *synagōgē* (esp. Exodus, Numbers, Leviticus) or *ekklēsia* G1711. In the NT, the Greek term *ekklēsia* can be used of Israel (Acts 7:38) and of secular assemblies among the Gentiles (19:32, 39, 41), but it is in the process of becoming a technical term for a definite group of people who meet for religious purposes (Acts 5:11; 8:3; 1 Cor. 14:23). It can describe the CHURCH universal to which all Christians belong (Matt. 16:18; Acts 9:31; 1 Cor. 12:28), or a body of Christians in a particular place (Acts 8:1; Rom. 16:1). The term *synagōgē* also could still be used to describe a Jewish-Christian assembly place (Jas. 2:2), although its main reference in the NT is to the place of Jewish assembly (Lk. 4:16; Acts 13:5). The references to "synagogue of Satan" (Rev. 2:9; 3:9) may indicate the increasing antagonism between the Christian

The "Western Wall" of the temple mount in Jerusalem is a popular assembly place for prayer. Ten Jewish men gathered for worship constitutes a synagogue.

© Dr. James C. Martin

church and the Jewish SYNAGOGUE. At the end of the first century these two Greek terms, which had hitherto been interchangeable and not in any sense confined to religious assemblies, had become fixed to denote rival religions.

congregation, mount of the. A phrase used by the KJV only once (Isa. 14:13; NIV and NRSV, "mount of assembly"). This phrase is widely thought to be an allusion to the mythological "assembly of the gods" mentioned especially in Ugaritic texts. A similar conception is thought to be found in the next phrase, "the utmost heights of the sacred mountain" (NIV; the TNIV says, "the utmost heights of Mount Zaphon"; see ZAPHON #2). The OT sometimes uses the language of ANE myth (which would have been familiar to the Israelites) for various purposes, such as polemics and conceptual analogies. There is no reason to think, however, that the present passage had its origins in a pagan Canaanite setting. The term does seem to be some kind of literary allusion and cannot be identified with any known place name.

Coniah. koh-ni′uh (Heb. *konyāhû H4037*, shortened form of *yĕkānyāhû H3527*, "Yahweh supports"). See JECONIAH and JEHOIACHIN.

Cononiah. kon′uh-ni′uh. See CONANIAH.

conquest of Canaan. See ISRAEL (sect. II); JOSHUA, BOOK OF.

conscience. The OT has no separate word for "conscience," but it is able to express the idea by other means. It is clear from Gen. 3:8 that the first result of the FALL was a guilty conscience, compelling ADAM and EVE to hide from God. Likewise, we read that DAVID's "heart smote him" (1 Sam. 24:5 KJV); the NIV correctly interprets this comment by rendering, "David was conscience-stricken." In everyday Greek the word *syneidēsis G5287* referred to the pain or guilt felt by persons who believed they had done wrong. The author of Hebrews states that as a result of accepting the gospel, people receive a purified, or perfected, conscience (Heb. 9:14; 10:22), through forgiveness and the gift of the Holy Spirit.

PAUL, who used the word more than other NT writers, developed the concept in several ways. (1) He described the universal existence of conscience as the internal moral witness found in all human beings (Rom. 2:14-16). (2) He believed that Christians should have clear and good consciences (2 Cor. 1:12; 1 Tim. 1:5, 19; 3:9), because their lives are lived for the glory of God and in the light of Christian teaching. (3) He knew of and gave advice about the weak or partially formed conscience of certain Christians ("conscience" occurs nine times in 1 Cor. 8:1-13 and 10:23—11:1); in certain cases mature Christians are to restrict their liberty of action in order not to offend the undeveloped conscience of their weaker brothers and sisters. (4) He was aware of the existence of evil consciences, corrupted by false teaching (1 Tim. 4:5; Tit. 1:15). A person who rejects the gospel and resolutely opposes God has an evil conscience. (5) Finally, it may be said that while Paul's use of the word *conscience* is that of the internal witness of the mind/heart judging past actions in the light of Christian teaching, he also appears to suggest that the conscience will guide present and future actions (e.g., Rom. 13:3; 1 Cor. 10:25).

consecration. An act by which a person or thing is dedicated to the service and worship of God. Frequently involved in the idea is the confirmation by religious ceremonies or rites; the word may also indicate an act by which a thing, event, or person becomes memorable or significant. The concept is especially prominent in the OT and in those portions of the NT that are most intimately related by content or symbolism to the Levitical system.

Among several Hebrew terms that convey the idea of consecration, the most common is the verb *qādaš H7727* and its cognates (e.g., Exod. 13:12; Lev. 8:10-12; 1 Ki. 8:64; Isa. 66:17; et al.). These terms are used to indicate separation from common or profane use, and DEDICATION to a sacral purpose or use. The application of "consecration" to objects includes, among other instances, the TABERNACLE and TEMPLE as well as their furnishings (Exod. 40:9-11; 2 Chr. 7:7). The booty taken at the conquest of JERICHO was so set apart (Josh. 6:19; see ANATHEMA). When applied to individuals, the terms suggest not only the motif of setting apart for a sacred service but also the acceptance by the subject of such a dedication. Thus AARON and his sons accept as the garb of their office the garments that symbolize it (Exod. 29:29, 33, 35).

In the NT, the primary Greek verb meaning "consecrate" is *hagiazō G39*, usually rendered "sanctify, set apart, make holy" (e.g., Jn. 10:36; 17:17, 19; 1 Cor. 7:14; 1 Tim. 4:5). As applied to the Lord, the usages signify the endowment with fullness of grace and truth, and his self-dedication to his redemptive work; as applied to the disciples, it suggests setting apart and personal SANCTIFICATION; as applied to food, it indicates rendering licit by prayer; and as applied to unbelieving marital partners, it suggests that Christian sanctity is, in some degree, passed over from the believing one as a concomitant of the intimacy of the relationship. See also HOLINESS.

consolation. ELIPHAZ says to JOB, "Are God's consolations not enough for you?" (Job 15:11), meaning, Do they seem beneath your notice? Job says to his friends that the consolation he asks from them is that they listen to him (21:2). JEREMIAH foretells that many in the land of Israel shall die, but no one will give the "cup of consolation" to a bereaved person who mourns for his parents (Jer. 16:7; NIV, "a drink to console"). When it is said of SIMEON that he looked for the "consolation [*paraklēsis G4155*] of Israel" (Lk. 2:25), the term is used by metonymy for the messianic salvation that will bring comfort to the people of Israel (cf. Isa. 40:1). PAUL describes God as "the Father of compassion and the God of all comfort" (2 Cor. 1:3; NRSV, "of all consolation"; see also vv. 4-7 and 7:6-7).

constellations. See ASTRONOMY.

contentment. The state of being content or satisfied. It is a virtue enjoined by the Scriptures upon believers (Lk. 3:14; Heb. 13:5), is intimately associated with godliness (1 Tim. 6:6), and is a marked feature of Pauline spirituality (Phil. 4:11; 1 Tim. 6:8). Having nothing to do with social insensitivity, complacency, or inertia, Christian contentment is centrally an acceptance of God's ministrations as these affect one's station and task in life, and also one's resources. It is thus a settled disposition to regard God's gifts as sufficient, and his assignments as appropriate. Contentment is opposed to petulance, self-rejection, despair, and panic on the one hand, and vaulting ambition on the other. It excludes envy (Jas. 3:16), avarice (Heb. 13:5; 1 Tim. 6:8), and repinings (1 Cor. 10:10). It is a glad, trustful, repose in God and a humble participation in his purposes and dealings.

contest. See GAMES.

contribution. This English term is used by the NIV and other versions of the OT primarily as a rendering of Hebrew *tĕrûmâ H9556*, "tribute, offering" (e.g., Exod. 29:28; 2 Chr. 31:10-14). In the NT it renders *koinōnia G3126* (which more frequently means "sharing"; see FELLOWSHIP) in one important passage, Rom. 15:26, where it designates the offering that the Gentile churches were giving "for the poor among the saints in Jerusalem" (cf. also 2 Cor. 9:13 RSV). PAUL refers to the same offering with the term *logeia G3356*, "collection," in 1 Cor. 16:1-2. During his third missionary journey, he devoted much attention and effort to raising this collection among the Gentile churches for the believers in JUDEA. (Part of the reason, in the view of many scholars, was the need to relieve the tensions that had arisen between Gentile and Jewish Christians over the issue of circumcision; cf. Gal. 2:10.) At least twice he wrote to the Corinthians about the matter (1 Cor. 16:1-4; 2 Cor. 9:1-5). Toward the end of his third journey (when he was about to leave Corinth), Paul hoped to go to Rome, but he felt constrained first to accompany the contribution to Jerusalem (Rom. 15:22-29). The apostle clearly viewed this offering not only as a generous act, but also as an important demonstration of the unity between the Jewish and Gentile branches of the church.

contrite. This English term is found a few times in the OT as the rendering of Hebrew terms that mean literally "crushed" or "stricken." God does not despise the "broken and contrite heart" (Ps. 51:17; 34:18). The contrite of spirit and heart are lowly and humble, trembling at the word of the "high and lofty One" (Isa. 57:15; 66:2).

conversation. This English term (from Latin *conversārī*, "to associate with"), is used by the KJV in its archaic sense of "conduct," to render several different words, especially Greek *anastrophē G419*, meaning "way of life." This word is found thirteen times in the NT, and almost half of the occurrences are in 1 Peter (Gal. 1:13; Heb. 13:7; 1 Pet. 1:15, 18; et al.). The modern meaning of *conversation* ("a spoken exchange") can be conveyed by other Hebrew and Greek words.

conversion. The verb *to convert* is used a number of times in the KJV primarily as the rendering of Hebrew *šûb H8740* and Greek *epistrephō G2188* (e.g., Ps. 51:13; Matt. 13:15), both of which mean "to turn, return." See REPENTANCE. The noun *convert* is used in modern versions to render Greek *prosēlytos G4670* (lit., "one who has arrived"; e.g., Matt. 23:15; Acts 6:5). See PROSELYTE.

conviction. The first stage of REPENTANCE, experienced when in some way the evil nature of SIN has been brought home to the penitent, who now recognizes that he or she is guilty of it. Although the word *conviction* is never used in the KJV and seldom in other versions, the Bible gives many illustrations of the experience. In the OT one of the most notable is found in Ps. 51, where DAVID, realizing he has sinned against God, is overwhelmed with sorrow for his transgression and cries out to God for forgiveness and cleansing. In the NT the central passage bearing on this theme is Jn. 16:7-11, where Jesus says that when the HOLY SPIRIT comes, "he will convict the world of guilt in regard to sin and righteousness and judgment." Here the verb *convict* means "convince" (so RSV) or "prove guilty" (cf. NRSV). The thought is that the Holy Spirit addresses the heart of the guilty and shows how inadequate ordinary standards of righteousness are. The purpose of conviction is to lead to godly repentance.

convocation, holy. The KJV rendering of a Hebrew phrase that the NIV translates as "sacred assembly." It is first mentioned in Exod. 12:16 with reference to the first and seventh days of the Passover feast; on those days no work was to be done, and only the preparation of food was allowed. In addition, Lev. 23 lists other holy convocations that took place during the seventh month. Offerings of various kinds were to be made on these days (cf. Num. 28:8, 25-26). The FEASTS were undoubtedly meant to be a foretaste of the great day of rest for all of God's people; they point to a day of hope when God's children will sit down with him in his kingdom.

cooking. See FOOD.

Coos. See Cos.

copper. See MINERALS.

coppersmith. See OCCUPATIONS AND PROFESSIONS.

cor. See WEIGHTS AND MEASURES.

coral. See ANIMALS; MINERALS.

corban. kor′ban. This term occurs only once in the NT (Mk. 7:11, where it is defined as a "gift [dedicated to God]"; cf. Matt. 15:5). In this passage Jesus condemns the "tradition of the elders" when it evades the plain intent of the TORAH. Under the pious pretext of dedicating his property to the Lord (and retaining a life estate in it himself), a man could sidestep his obligation to support his aged parents, alleging that he had no undedicated property from which he could support them. Literally, the Hebrew term *qorbān H7933* means "gift, offering," and can refer to a blood sacrifice or a vegetable offering (Lev. 1:2; 22:27; 23:14; Num. 7:25; Ezek. 20:28; 40:43). The term was later applied to the dedication of property (whether real or personal) intended for the Lord's use and thus forbidden to human beings.

cord. Throughout the ANE, ropes and cords were made of goats' or camels' hair spun into threads and then plaited or twisted into the larger and stronger form. Sometimes they were made of strips of skin from goats and cows twisted together. Ropes for temporary fastenings were sometimes made from vines twisted together and also from the bark of the branches of the mulberry tree. Frequently the word is used in a figurative sense in the Bible. Thus Job speaks of being "held fast by cords of affliction" (Job 36:8), and Solomon says of the wicked man that "the cords of his sin hold him fast" (Prov. 5:22). Other illustrations of this figurative use are Ps. 129:4; 140:5; Eccl. 4:12; Isa. 5:18; 54:2. The word is found also in the NIV with reference to the "lace of blue" (KJV) used to bind the high priest's breastplate to the EPHOD (Exod. 28:28, 37; 39:21, 31). Jesus made a whip out of cords to clear the temple of moneychangers (Jn. 2:15). Lifeboats were lashed to sailing ships by means of cords, or ropes (Acts 27:32).

Core. See KORAH.

coriander. See PLANTS.

Corinth. kor´inth (Gk. *Korinthos G3172*). A city of GREECE on the narrow isthmus between the Peloponnesus and the mainland. Under the Romans, ATHENS was still the educational center of Greece, but Corinth became the capital of the Roman province they called ACHAIA and was the most important city in the country. Land traffic between the N and S of Achaia had to pass the city, and much of the commerce between ROME and the E was brought to its harbors.

Corinth occupied a strategic geographical position. It was situated at the southern extremity of the isthmus, at the northern foot of the lofty (c. 2,000 ft./610 m.) and impregnable Acrocorinthus, which commanded a wonderful view over the Saronic Gulf on the E and the Corinthian Gulf on the W, as well as over central Greece and the Peloponnesus. From the Acrocorinthus it is possible on a clear day to see the Acropolis of Athens 40 mi. (65 km.) away. Corinth had three harbors: Lechaeum to the W, and CENCHREA and Schoenus to the E. Lechaeum was connected with Corinth by a double row of walls. Because of its highly favored commercial position, in ancient times the city was known as "two-sea'd Corinth."

Ancient sailors dreaded making the voyage round the southern capes of the Peloponnesus, and thus many of the smaller ships and their cargoes were hauled across the narrow isthmus on a track. Sometimes the cargo of large ships was removed

Corinth.

at the harbor, carried across the isthmus, and then loaded onto another ship on the other side. Several attempts were made in ancient times to cut a ship canal across the isthmus, notably one by NERO about A.D. 66, but none was successful. Finally a canal was opened in 1893 and is now in use.

Corinth had an ancient and very interesting history. Phoenician settlers were early attracted to it. They introduced many profitable manufactures and established the impure worship of the Phoenician deities. Later, Greeks from Attica became supreme. They probably changed the name of the city to Corinth, and glorified the games held there in honor of Poseidon, the god of the sea. About 1074 B.C. the Dorians conquered the city. After the invention of triremes (ships with three tiers of oars on each side) about 585, a series of important colonies was founded, and Corinth became a strong maritime force. The city was lukewarm in the Persian Wars and opposed Athens in the Peloponnesian War. Except for a brief period the Macedonians held the city from 335 to 197. The Romans declared Greece and Corinth free in 196; but in 146, because of a rebellion against Rome, the city was totally destroyed by the Roman consul Mummius, and its famous art treasures were taken as spoil to Rome. Julius Caesar rebuilt it as a Roman colony and made it the capital of Achaia in 46, and after that it rapidly came into prominence again. The Goths raided it in the third and fourth centuries A.D.; the Normans sacked it in 1147; the Venetians and Turks held it in the Middle Ages; from 1715 until 1822 it remained with the Turks. A severe earthquake in 1858 caused the

C

abandonment of the city and the building of a new town a few miles from the ancient site.

In Roman times Corinth was a city of wealth, luxury, and immorality. It had no rivals as a city of vice. "To live like a Corinthian" meant to live a life of profligacy and debauchery. It was customary in a stage play for a Corinthian to come on the scene drunk. The inhabitants were naturally devoted to the worship of Poseidon, since they drew so much of their wealth from the sea, but their greatest devotion was given to Aphrodite, the goddess of love. Her temple on the Acrocorinthus had more than a thousand *hierodouloi*—priestesses of vice not found in other shrines of Greece, and she attracted worshipers from all over the ancient world. Besides drawing vast revenues from the sea, Corinth had many important industries, its pottery and brass especially being famous all over the world. The Isthmian games, held every two years, made Corinth a great center of Hellenic life.

At the height of its power, Corinth probably had a free population of 200,000 plus a half million slaves. Its residents consisted of the descendants of

of Jews and also some Gentiles brought under the influence of Judaism because of its monotheism and lofty morality.

PAUL visited Corinth for the first time on his second missionary journey (Acts 18). He had just come from Athens, where he had not been well received, and he began his work in Corinth with a sense of weakness, fear, and trembling (1 Cor. 2:3). A special revelation from the Lord in a night vision altered his plans to return to THESSALONICA (Acts 18:9-10; 1 Thess. 2:17-18), and he was told to speak freely and boldly in the city. At his first arrival, he became acquainted with AQUILA and PRISCILLA, fellow Christians and, like himself, tentmakers. During his stay of a year and a half he resided in their home. He labored with his own hands, so that his motives as a preacher would be above suspicion. Soon after his arrival, SILAS and TIMOTHY rejoined him, Timothy bringing news from the church at Thessalonica (1 Thess. 3:6).

Every Sabbath Paul preached in the synagogue, but before long he met with strong opposition from the Jews, so that he turned from them and for the rest of his stay in Corinth gave his attention to the Gentiles (Acts 18:6). He was then offered the use of the house of TITUS JUSTUS, a God-fearing Gentile who lived next door to the synagogue. Many turned to Christ and were baptized as a result of Paul's preaching, among them CRISPUS, the ruler of the synagogue, and all his house. None of the baptisms in Corinth were performed by Paul himself, except those of Crispus, GAIUS (Paul's host on his later visit, Rom. 16:23), and the household of STEPHANAS, who were Paul's first converts (1 Cor. 16:15).

© Dr. James C. Martin

The ancient site of Corinth (bottom right of photo), strategically located near the gulf. (View to the NNW.)

the Roman colonists who were established there in 46 B.C., many Romans who came for business, a large Greek population, and many strangers of different nationalities attracted to the city for various reasons. In the last group was a considerable body

During Paul's stay in Corinth, GALLIO, the elder brother of the Roman philosopher Seneca, came to govern Achaia as proconsul. This was about the year A.D. 51, as an inscription found at Delphi in 1908 shows. The Jews brought an accusation

Overview of 1 CORINTHIANS

Author: The apostle PAUL.

Historical setting: Written from EPHESUS during Paul's third missionary journey (c. A.D. 56), in response to (a) reports from members of CHLOE's household (1 Cor. 1:11) and (b) a letter written by the Corinthian Christians themselves (7:1).

Purpose: To give instruction and directions concerning many problems faced by the church in CORINTH, including internal divisions, immorality, partaking of idol food, disorders in worship, and false teaching concerning the resurrection.

Contents: After an introductory paragraph (1 Cor. 1:1-9), the apostle first addresses the problems reported by Chloe's household—quarrels within the Corinthian church (1:10—4:21) and moral and ethical issues (5:1—6:20); he then responds to the questions raised by the Corinthians' letter—about marriage and divorce (ch. 7), food offered to idols (chs. 8-10), worship (ch. 11), spiritual gifts (chs. 12-14), the resurrection (ch. 15), and the collection and other matters (ch. 16).

C

before Gallio against Paul, charging that he was preaching a religion contrary to Roman law. Gallio, however, refused to admit the case to trial and dismissed them. It is evident that he looked on Christianity as being only an obscure variety of Judaism and that to him the quarrel between the Jews and Paul had its origin in nothing more than differing interpretations of the Jewish law. Following Gallio's decision, the Greek bystanders vented their hostility against the Jews by seizing and beating SOSTHENES, the ruler of the synagogue, and Gallio paid no attention to them (Acts 18:12-17). Gallio's action was highly important, for it amounted to an authoritative decision by a highly placed Roman official that Paul's preaching could not be interpreted as an offense against Roman law; and from this experience Paul gained a new idea of the protection the Roman law afforded him as a preacher of the gospel. After an extended period, Paul left Corinth to go to JERUSALEM and ANTIOCH, on his way stopping off briefly at EPHESUS.

Luke in the book of Acts tells little of the subsequent history of the church at Corinth. APOLLOS, a convert of Aquila and Priscilla at Ephesus, was sent from Ephesus to Corinth with a letter of recommendation, and he exercised an influential ministry there (Acts 18:27-28; 1 Cor. 1:12). There is evidence that during Paul's stay in Ephesus on his third missionary journey he paid a brief visit to Corinth (2 Cor. 12:14; 13:1), though some hold that he did this later from MACEDONIA. While at Ephesus he wrote a letter to Corinth that has not been preserved (1 Cor. 5:9). A reply to this, asking advice on important problems facing the church, and an oral report brought to him that all was not well in the church, led to his writing 1 Corinthians. This was probably brought by TITUS, who was sent to Corinth by Paul about this time (2 Cor. 7:13). Timothy was also sent there on some mission (1 Cor. 4:17). After the silversmiths' riot at Ephesus, Paul went to TROAS, hoping to meet Titus there with news from Corinth, but he was disappointed and went on to Macedonia, where he did meet him. From Titus's largely favorable report, Paul wrote 2 Corinthians, and probably sent Titus to deliver it. After some time in Macedonia, Paul went to Greece for three months (Acts 20:2-3), chiefly, no doubt, to Corinth. On Paul's third missionary journey he had busied himself getting offerings of money for the poor Christians in Jerusalem from

Overview of 2 CORINTHIANS

Author: The apostle PAUL.

Historical setting: Written from MACEDONIA during Paul's third missionary journey (c. A.D. 56) in response to a report brought by TITUS (2 Cor. 2:13; 7:6, 13).

Purpose: To commend the Corinthians for their positive response to Titus's mission; to help them understand the nature of Paul's ministry; to encourage them to participate in the collection for other Christians in need; and to admonish a rebellious group in the church.

Contents: After an introductory paragraph (2 Cor. 1:1-11), Paul gives an account of his recent activities (1:12—2:13), leading to an explanation of his apostolic ministry (2:14—6:10) and to various appeals (6:11—7:16); he then urges them to fulfill their intention of contributing to the collection being raised for the poor in Jerusalem (chs. 8-9); finally, he vindicates his apostolic authority by rebuking some false teachers who are still causing problems in the Corinthian church (chs. 10-13).

the various churches he had founded. The Corinthian church responded generously (2 Cor. 9:2-5). During this visit to Corinth, Paul wrote his letter to the ROMANS (Rom. 16:23). Whether he ever returned to the city is unknown.

About A.D. 97, Clement of Rome wrote a letter to the church at Corinth, now included among the APOSTOLIC FATHERS. It shows that in his time the Christians there were still vexed by divisions.

Corinthians, Letters to the. The letter we call First Corinthians was written by PAUL in EPHESUS on his third missionary journey (Acts 19:1; 1 Cor. 16:8, 19), probably in A.D. 56 or 57. He had previously written a letter to the Corinthians that has not come down to us; in it he had warned against associating with immoral persons (1 Cor. 5:9). In reply Paul received a letter (alluded to in 5:10; 7:1; 8:1) in which they declared it was impossible to follow his advice without going out of the world altogether, and submitted to him a number of problems on which they asked his opinion. This letter from Corinth was probably brought by three of their number—STEPHANAS, FORTUNATUS, and ACHAICUS (16:17)—who came to visit

Paul at Ephesus and undoubtedly told him about the condition of the church. Meanwhile, Paul had heard of factions in the church from the servants of CHLOE (1:11), probably from Corinth, and this news caused him much pain and anxiety. It was these various circumstances that led to the writing of 1 Corinthians.

The following subjects are discussed in the letter, after the introductory salutation (1 Cor. 1:1-9):

(1) In the first four chapters the apostle takes up the reported factionalism in the church and points out the danger and scandal of party spirit. He reminds them that Christ alone is their Master, their Christian teachers being only servants of Christ and fellow workers with God.

(2) In ch. 5 the apostle deals with a case of incestuous marriage and prescribes that the offender be put out of the church so that his soul may be saved.

(3) In ch. 6 Paul addresses their practice of bringing disputes between themselves before heathen judges for litigation. He shows that this is morally wrong and out of harmony with the spirit of love by which they as Christians should be animated. Paul also pleads with Christians to keep their bodies pure for God's glory.

(4) Various phases of the subject of marriage are considered in ch. 7. While commending a celibate life, Paul holds marriage to be wise and honorable.

(5) The eating of meat offered to idols was a problem of conscience to many Christians, and chs. 8-10 are devoted to it. Paul points out that while there is nothing inherently wrong in a Christian's eating such food, the law of love requires that it be avoided if it will offend another who regards the eating of it as sin. He illustrates this principle of self-control in his own life: lest his motives in preaching the gospel be misunderstood, he refuses to exercise his undoubted right of looking for material aid from the church. He warns against a spirit of self-confidence and urges them to be careful not to seem to countenance idolatry.

(6) Paul next takes up certain abuses in public worship: the matter of appropriate head apparel for women in their assemblies (1 Cor. 11:2-16) and the proper observance of the Lord's Supper (11:17-34), since there had been serious abuses in its administration.

(7) There then follows a long discussion of the use and abuse of spiritual gifts, especially speaking in tongues (ch. 12-14). The apostle, while commending the careful exercise of all the gifts, bids them cultivate above all God's greatest gift, love (ch. 13).

(8) In ch. 15 Paul turns to a consideration of one of the most important of their troubles—the doubt that some had concerning the resurrection of the dead. He meets the objections raised against the doctrine by showing that it is necessitated by the resurrection of Christ and that their salvation is inseparably connected with it.

(9) The letter concludes with directions about the collections being made for the saints in Jerusalem, the mother church; with comments about Paul's plans; and with personal messages to various friends.

Second Corinthians was written by Paul on his third missionary journey somewhere in Macedonia, where he had just met TITUS, who had brought him a report concerning the church at Corinth. The letter reveals that Judaizing teachers—perhaps recent arrivals from Jerusalem—had sought to discredit the apostle and had succeeded in turning the church as a whole against him. Paul was denounced as no minister of Christ at all. This revolt caused

Paul to make a brief visit to Corinth in order to restore his authority (2 Cor. 12:14; 13:1-2), but the visit did not have its expected effect. The report Titus brought Paul was, on the whole, most encouraging. The majority had repented of their treatment of Paul and had cast out of the church the man who had led the attack on him. Paul's authority was acknowledged once more. Titus seems to have helped greatly in bringing about this happy change. It was the report of Titus that chiefly occasioned the writing of this letter.

Paul's mention of a severe letter that had caused him great sorrow of heart to write (2 Cor. 2:3-4, 9; 7:8-12) has been the subject of considerable debate. Some scholars think he refers to 1 Corinthians; others hold that this letter, like the one referred to in 1 Cor. 5:9, is wholly lost; while still others believe that it is preserved in 2 Cor. 10-13, which, they say, was written by Paul at Ephesus some time after the writing of 1 Corinthians.

This second letter is the least methodical and the most personal of Paul's writings. It is very autobiographical and falls naturally into three main divisions:

(1) In chs. 1-7 Paul, after giving thanks to God for his goodness to him in trial (1:1-11), shares some thoughts on the crisis through which the church has just passed.

(2) In ch. 8-9 he admonishes the Corinthians to complete the collection for the poor in Jerusalem.

(3) Chapters 10-13 are a defense of Paul's ministry against the attacks of his enemies and a vindication of his apostleship.

The Greek temple of Apollo with the Acrocorinth in the background.

© Dr. James C. Martin

cormorant. See BIRDS.

corn. See PLANTS.

Cornelius. kor-neel'yuhs (Gk. *Kornēlios G3173*). A name of ancient and honorable standing among the Romans. Before the NT age, it was borne by such distinguished families as the Scipios and Sulla. Acts 10:1 speaks of a Cornelius who was a centurion of the ITALIAN REGIMENT. While stationed at CAESAREA, in obedience to instructions received in a vision, he sent for Simon PETER, who was staying at JOPPA; Cornelius wanted to learn how he and his household should be saved (11:14).

Cornelius is described as "devout and God-fearing" (Acts 10:2). His religious status prior to Peter's visit is ambiguous, but it is likely that Cornelius was a pious Roman, who, disillusioned by polytheism and disappointed by philosophy, had gravitated spiritually toward Judaism and was now what the rabbis called a "proselyte of the Gate." Any doubts that Peter was acting improperly by sharing the message with this first Gentile convert are dispelled by the twofold consideration of Peter's preparatory vision (10:9-16) and the subsequent outpouring of the Holy Spirit on Cornelius's household (10:44-47). On these grounds, Peter defended his conduct before his critics at Jerusalem (11:1-18).

Corner Gate. A gate that protected the NW approach to JERUSALEM. During the reign of AMAZIAH king of Judah, a long stretch of the wall leading to it was destroyed by Jehoash (JOASH) king of Israel (2 Ki. 14:13; 2 Chr. 25:23), so the gate was later rebuilt and fortified by UZZIAH (2 Chr. 26:9). After the destruction of the city, the Corner Gate figures in two prophecies (Jer. 31:38; Zech. 14:10). It is not mentioned in NEHEMIAH's description of Jerusalem, and its precise location is uncertain.

cornerstone. A stone that serves a foundational function as part of a corner or angle in a wall. Among the Canaanites, before the conquest of the land by JOSHUA, the laying of the foundation stone was accompanied by the dreadful rite of human sacrifice. Numerous skeletons have been unearthed, especially those of tiny babies in earthen jars. In the Bible the term *cornerstone* is commonly used figuratively. In particular, it occurs in several messianic contexts (Ps. 118:22 [NIV, "capstone"]; Isa. 28:16; Zech. 10:4). Jesus validated his ministry by citing the Psalms passage (Matt. 21:42 and parallels). Paul explained God's saving purposes by combining Isa. 28:16 and 8:14 (Rom. 9:33; cf. Eph. 2:20). Peter's description of Christians as "living stones" brings together the passages from both the book of Psalms and Isaiah (1 Pet. 2:4-8).

cornet. See MUSIC AND MUSICAL INSTRUMENTS.

correction. See CHASTISEMENT.

corruption. The KJV uses this term (NIV, "decay") mainly in passages that refer to the decaying of the physical body (e.g., Ps. 16:10; Acts 2:27; more broadly of creation, Rom. 8:21). See DEATH; SHEOL. The word and its cognates can be used also of moral DEPRAVITY (e.g., Hos. 9:9; 2 Pet. 1:4). See SIN.

Corruption, Hill (Mount) of. According to 1 Ki. 11:7, SOLOMON built a HIGH PLACE for several Canaanite gods on a hill to the E of JERUSALEM. Many years later, during a time of spiritual revival, King JOSIAH "desecrated the high places that were east of Jerusalem on the south of the Hill of

The forested area on the right side of the elevation marks the "Hill of Corruption," where Solomon built high places to foreign idols. (View to the NE.)

Corruption—the ones Solomon king of Israel had built for Ashtoreth the vile goddess of the Sidonians, for Chemosh the vile god of Moab, and for Molech the detestable god of the people of Ammon" (the same Hebrew phrase occurs in Jer. 51:25 with the sense "destroying mountain," referring to BABYLON). The site is usually identified with the southern height of the ridge known as the Mount of OLIVES. In modern times this hill is sometimes referred to by the Latin names *Mons Offensionis* (Mount of Offense, from the Vulgate of 2 Ki. 23:13) and *Mons Scandali* (Mount of Scandal).

Cos. kos (Gk. *Kōs G3271*). KJV Coos. An island of the Sporades group off the SW coast of ASIA MINOR. It is mountainous in terrain, especially in the southern sector, and it was the birthplace of Hippocrates, the father of medicine, and of Ptolemy Philadelphus. The name of its capital is also Cos. A large Jewish settlement was located there. It is mentioned in connection with PAUL's third missionary journey (Acts 21:1).

Cosam. koh´suhm (Gk. *Kōsam G3272*, prob. from Heb. *qāsam*, "diviner"). Son of Elmadam and descendant of DAVID through NATHAN; included in Luke's GENEALOGY OF JESUS CHRIST (Lk. 3:28).

cosmetics. See EYES, PAINTING OF; OINTMENTS AND PERFUMES.

cosmogony, cosmology. The term *cosmogony* refers to any view regarding the origin of the visible universe. A similar meaning is conveyed by the word *cosmology*, which can also be used more specifically of the modern astrophysical study of the origins, evolution, and structure of the universe. See also ASTRONOMY; CREATION; HEAVEN; WORLD.

cotton. Possible rendering of Hebrew word in Esth. 1:6 (so NRSV; the KJV mistranslates with "green"); others believe the word refers to LINEN (cf. NIV). Some Egyptian child mummies were wrapped in cotton bandages. The Hebrews would have learned about cotton growing while they were in captivity in Persia under King XERXES. It is uncertain whether cotton was grown in Palestine in biblical times.

couch. A piece of furniture for reclining. The couch became so ornate that Amos rebuked the rich for the costly display of their couches (Amos 6:4). Sometimes, however, the couch was no more than a rolled-up mat that could be easily transported (Matt. 9:6). See also BED.

coulter. See PLOWSHARE.

council. This English term can be used to render several Hebrew words, especially *sôd H6051*, which refers to an intimate circle of friends or confidants. In the OT God was frequently described as being in council with the host of heaven (Job 15:8; Ps. 89:7; Jer. 23:18; cf. Amos 3:7; see CONGREGATION, MOUNT OF). Likewise the ruler or king had his council of advisers and nobles; they were distinguished as those who were permitted in the royal presence to see his face (cf. NRSV at 2 Ki. 25:19; Jer. 52:25). In the NT, the Greek term *synedrion G5284* can refer to lesser courts among the Jews (Matt. 10:17; Mk. 13:9; each town in Palestine had such a council). The most frequent use of this term, however, is in reference to the high court of the Jews, the SANHEDRIN, which many of the rabbis wanted to believe went back to MOSES.

The expressions "Council of Jerusalem" and "Apostolic Council" are applied to a meeting of delegates of the church in ANTIOCH with the apostles and elders in JERUSALEM (Acts 15, though the text does not contain the word *council*; many believe that the same meeting is referred to by Paul in Gal. 2:1-10). The primary concern of this gathering was whether GENTILE converts should be required to submit to the Mosaic LAW, especially the rite of CIRCUMCISION. See discussion under PAUL.

counselor. See ADVOCATE; HOLY SPIRIT; OCCUPATIONS AND PROFESSIONS.

countenance. See FACE.

courage. See BOLDNESS.

course. This English word, which has a variety of meanings, can be used to translate several words or expressions. For example, a Hebrew noun meaning "highway" can refer figuratively to the paths of the heavenly bodies (Jdg. 5:20). The Greek noun *trochos G5580*, "wheel, race-course," is used in Jas. 3:6 with reference either to the course of a person's life (NIV) or to the cycle of nature (NRSV). The KJV uses "courses" of the groups into which PRIESTS were divided (e.g., 1 Chr. 23:6; Lk. 1:5).

court. During the biblical period, court proceedings were held normally in the forum or market square that faced the principal GATE of the city. The first definite reference to such a forum is found in Gen. 19:1, which speaks of LOT "sitting in the gateway" of SODOM when he noticed the two angelic visitors whom he invited to his home. Later allusions to the city gate as the place for public tribunals are found in the book of Deuteronomy (Deut. 16:18; 21:19; 25:7). On JETHRO's advice MOSES instituted a system of jurisprudence for the Israelites. He appointed judges over tens, fifties, hundreds, and thousands; Moses himself had the final decision in "difficult cases" (Exod. 18:25-26).

Judicial functions were taken over by the king after the Hebrew monarchy was instituted: DAVID maintained an "appellate court" for his entire kingdom (2 Sam. 15:2), and SOLOMON as well (1 Ki. 3:9; 7:7). By the time of JEHOSHAPHAT (2 Chr. 19:5-8) it became necessary to enlarge even the central tribunal at Jerusalem into a larger complex consisting of priests, Levites, and heads of clans. Perhaps it was from this measure that the later SANHEDRIN, or Council of Seventy, developed (although there is no specific mention of it until Hellenistic times), which functioned under the presidency of the high priest.

By NT times there had intervened several centuries of Greek influence and example, and it became more usual to hold court hearings inside a building constructed as a courthouse. In Greek cities like PHILIPPI, criminal cases could be tried in the open (Acts 19:38; cf. also 18:12-17). Another distinctive feature of NT times was the activity of the lawyer. Like the SCRIBES (to which order they themselves may have belonged), lawyers were careful students of the TORAH, but also of the "traditions of the elders," and could be relied upon to assist the judges with any interpretation or precedent that had previously arisen in Jewish history. Under the Roman government, the Jews of Palestine were permitted to adjudicate their own civil cases, and even their criminal cases if they did not involve the death penalty. But the Sanhedrin itself was not legally competent to execute capital punishment on Jesus (Jn. 18:31-32), and the later episode when STEPHEN was stoned (Acts 7:57-58) may have taken place in the reign of Herod AGRIPPA I, when there was no direct Roman authority present.

covenant. This English term translates the Hebrew noun *bĕrît H1382*, the etymology of which is uncertain. In the OT, the word identifies three different types of legal relationships. (1) A two-sided covenant between human parties who both voluntarily accept the terms of the agreement (for friendship, 1 Sam. 18:3-4; marriage, Mal. 2:14; or political alliance, Josh. 9:15; Obad. 7). God, however, does not enter into such a covenant of equality with human beings. (2) A one-sided disposition imposed by a superior party (Ezek. 17:13-14). God the Lord thus "commands" a covenant his servants are to obey (Josh. 23:16). In the original "covenant of works," as it is sometimes called, God placed ADAM on probation, bestowing life, should he prove faithful (Gen. 2:17). Humanity failed; but Christ, the last Adam (1 Cor. 15:45), did fulfill all righteousness (Matt. 3:15; Gal. 4:4), thereby earning restoration for all who are his. (3) God's self-imposed obligation for the reconciliation of sinners to himself (Deut. 7:6-8; Ps. 89:3-4). As he stated to ABRAHAM, "I will establish my covenant ... between me and you and your descendants after you for the generations to come (Gen. 17:7).

The SEPTUAGINT avoided the usual Greek term for covenant, *synthēkē*, probably because this word, which can also be rendered "contract," assumes

Platform for the throne and judgment room at the gate complex of Dan (8th-7th cent. B.C.).

© Dr. James C. Martin

C

that the parties are equals. Instead, it used *diathēkē G1347*, the primary meaning of which is "a disposition of property by a will." NT revelation makes clear the wonderful appropriateness of this term for describing the instrument of God's redemptive love (see Heb. 9:16-18). Although most scholars believe that *diathēkē* in the NT simply means "covenant," the sense of "will" or "testament" points to a specific form of covenant, the bequest; and it well describes God's OT *bĕrit*, because apart from the death of Christ the OT saints "should not be made perfect" (11:40 KJV).

The covenant then constitutes the heart of all God's special REVELATION; when put into writing, the "Book of the Covenant" becomes the objective source for religious hope (Exod. 24:7). Scripture consists of the "Old Testament" and the "New Testament." While there can be but one testament, corresponding to the one death of Christ ("my blood of *the* testament," according to the better MSS of Matt. 26:28), revelation yet organizes itself under the older testament, with its anticipatory symbols of Christ's coming (Jer. 31-32; 2 Cor. 3:14), and the newer testament, commemorative of his accomplished redemption (Jer. 31:31; 2 Cor. 3:6).

The following aspects compose the testamentary arrangements: the testator, God the Son, "the mediator" (Heb. 9:15); the heirs, "those who are called" (9:15); the objective method of effectuation, a gracious bequest (9:16); the subjective conditions by which the heir qualifies for the gift, namely, commitment (9:28: it is "to those who are waiting for him"); and the inheritance of reconciliation, eternal salvation (9:15, 28). Certain specific features then characterize this covenant. Its objective effectuation is always marked by a monergism ("one worker")—God exercising pure grace (cf. Gen. 15:18; Exod. 19:4), unassisted by human works (Eph. 2:8-9). Other features are the death of the testator (Exod. 24:8; Heb. 9:18-22); the promise, "I will be their God, and they will be my people" (Gen. 17:7 to Rev. 21:3); the eternity of the inheritance (Lev. 2:13; Num. 18:19; Ps. 105:8-10); and a confirmatory sign, such as the rainbow to Noah (Gen. 9:12-13), the exodus to Moses (Exod. 20:2), or Christ's resurrection to us (Rom. 1:4). Subjective appropriation of the covenant is likewise marked by unchangeable features of human response: faith (Gen. 15:6; Deut. 6:5; Heb. 11:6) and obedience—both moral (Gen. 17:1; Matt. 7:24; Eph. 2:10) and ceremonial (Gen. 17:10-14; Acts 22:16; 1 Cor. 11:24), for genuine faith must be demonstrated by works (Jas. 2:14-26).

Yet God's revelations of his covenant also exhibit historical progression (note plural "covenants," Rom. 9:4). Under the older testament appear: (1) the Edenic (Gen. 3:15), God's earliest promise of redemption, though at the cost of the bruising of the heel of the seed of woman; (2) the Noachian (9:9), for the preservation of the seed; (3) the Abrahamic (15:18), granting blessing through Abram's family; (4) the Sinaitic (Exod. 19:5-6), designating Israel as God's chosen people; (5) the Levitical (Num. 25:12-13), making reconciliation through priestly atonement; (6) the Davidic (2 Sam. 23:5), with messianic salvation promised through David's dynasty. Each of these covenants anticipated the same redemptive death; yet differences appear, particularly in their ceremonial response. A "dispensation" may thus be defined as a covenantal period during which faith in Christ is manifested by a distinct form of ceremonial obedience. Even our own, newer testament thus exhibits two stages: (7) the present new covenant in Christ, which is internal, "in their heart," reconciling (as always, "I will be their God"); direct, "they will all know me;" and with finished atonement, "for I will forgive their wickedness" (Jer. 31:33-34; Heb. 8:6-13). But its ceremony, the Lord's Supper, possesses a dispensational limit, exhibiting "the Lord's death *until he comes*" (1 Cor. 11:26). Thus Ezekiel speaks of (8) the future covenant of peace, when our internal salvation will reach out to embrace external nature (Ezek. 34:25), when direct spiritual communion will become "face to face" (20:35; 37:27), and when divine forgiveness will achieve the goal of peace among all nations (34:28).

covenant, ark of the. See ARK OF THE COVENANT.

Covenant, Book of the. An expression that occurs in Exod. 24:7 (also in 2 Ki. 23:2, 21; 2 Chr. 34:30 as a general reference to the law of Moses) and is used to designate Exod. 20-23. These chapters contain, in addition to the TEN COMMANDMENTS, a series of laws most of which begin with the word "if" in the English text. They are laws that express particular case types of domestic, economic, and criminal legislation common not only to the Hebrews but to many peoples of the ANE. See LAW.

covenant of salt. See SALT, COVENANT OF.

covering the head. Modern archaeological discovery has provided information about ancient head coverings from reliefs or wall paintings. Evidently early Palestinian men were bareheaded. Later a variety of head-coverings came into use. The simplest was the headband (1 Ki. 20:38, 41), but ornamental headdresses were worn in various contexts (e.g., Isa. 3:18, 20; 61:3). High priests had a special "turban" (Exod. 28:4; 29:9; 39:28; Lev. 8:13). Writing to the CORINTHIANS, PAUL says that "long hair is given to [women] as a covering" (1 Cor. 11:15; cf. vv. 4-7). When the apostle insists that men should pray with heads uncovered, but women should have their heads covered in public worship, he seems to refer to the use of an external material, such as a shawl, but some scholars argue that having the head covered means wearing the hair long. Unfortunately, it is difficult to reconstruct what first-century worship practice may have been.

covetousness. The act or quality of desiring inordinately and with ENVY that which belongs to another. It is a SIN mentioned frequently in both OT and NT, considered a root of other serious and mortal iniquities. The Hebrew verb that appears in the tenth commandment (Exod. 20:17) is *ḥāmad H2773*, meaning "to desire intensely." Clearly it refers to a desire that is given more than human and common importance and that becomes a substitute for the devotion and love due to God. Because of its intensity, this desire tends to overshadow the moral demands of the law and to allow the end, the possession of the coveted object, to justify any means for its achievement. The corresponding Greek verb, *epithymeō G2121* ("to desire, long for"), occurs in many NT passages, some of which speak of a positive longing (e.g., Lk. 22:15). Another common term is the noun *pleonexia G4432*, meaning literally "greediness, insatiable desire" (Lk. 12:15).

cow. See ANIMALS.

Coz. See KOZ.

Cozbi. koz´bi (Heb. *kozbî H3944*, perhaps "deceitful"). TNIV Kozbi. The daughter of Zur, one of the chiefs of MIDIAN (Num. 25:15, 18; cf. 31:8; Josh. 13:21). An Israelite named ZIMRI, who was one of the family heads in the tribe of SIMEON (Num. 25:14), apparently committed open immorality with Cozbi (v. 6, though the meaning of this text is debated). PHINEHAS the priest was outraged and executed them on the spot, an act that stopped the plague (vv. 7-8). It has been suggested that Cozbi may have played a significant role in leading the Israelites into the immoral worship of BAAL (vv. 1-3).

Cozeba. koh-zee´buh (Heb. *kōzēbāʾ H3943*, "liar"). KJV Chozeba; TNIV Kozeba. A small village located in the SHEPHELAH; it was home to some descendants of SHELAH son of JUDAH (1 Chr. 4:22). Most scholars think that Cozeba is the same as ACZIB and KEZIB, usually identified with modern Tell el-Beida (3 mi./5 km. W of ADULLAM).

cracknels. This English term is used by the KJV once to render a Hebrew word that probably refers to small hard cakes (1 Ki. 14:3).

craft, craftsman. See OCCUPATIONS AND PROFESSIONS.

Craftsmen, Valley of the. See GE HARASHIM.

crane. See BIRDS.

crawling thing. See ANIMALS (under *creeping thing*).

creation. The doctrine of creation is clearly presented in certain key passages (Gen. 1-2; Isa. 40-51; Heb. 11:3). The Bible teaches that the universe, including all matter, had a beginning and came into existence through the will of the eternal God. In Gen. 1:1 the words "the heavens and the earth" summarize all the materials of the universe. Thus even if one accepts the interpretation that this verse is a mere introduction to v. 2 ("When God began to create heaven and earth ... "), it would

© NASA GPN-2000-001138

In the beginning God created the heavens and the earth (Gen. 1:1).

six days of labor followed by one day of rest (Exod. 20:11). No end to the rest of the seventh day is mentioned. As far as the Bible tells us, God's rest from creating still continues.

There is much discussion about the question of evolution in relation to the creation, but the word *evolution* is used in many different ways. If taken in its most comprehensive biological and philosophical sense—the theory that everything now existing has come into its present condition as a result of strictly natural development—such an explanation of origins is sharply contradicted by the divine facts revealed in Gen. 1-2. These chapters indicate a number of specific divine commands bringing new factors into existence. God's activity is indicated throughout the entire creation narrative. It is explicitly stated several times that plants and animals are to reproduce "after their kind." The account nowhere indicates how large a "kind" is, and there is no ground for equating it with any particular modern definition of "species." Yet the narrative seems to indicate that a number (perhaps a large number) of "kinds" of plants and of animals did not come into existence by reproducing or evolving from one into the other. Nothing in the Bible, however, denies the possibility of change and development within the limits of a particular "kind."

Moreover, the creation of ADAM is sharply distinguished from other aspects of creation, and Gen. 2:7 does not seem to allow for the possibility that he existed as an animate being prior to becoming a man, created after the IMAGE OF GOD. Similarly, the creation of EVE is described as a distinct act of God.

It is sometimes said that the Bible begins with two contradictory accounts of creation, but that is to misconstrue the narrative. An atlas may begin with two different but overlapping maps: one of the world and one of the United States. The first would include a great deal of territory not included in the second; while the second would include a great deal of detail not mentioned in the first. Such is exactly the relation between the two creation accounts. Genesis 1 describes the creation of the universe as a whole, while 2:4-25 covers one special segment of that creation. One may say that 2:4 "steps back" into ch. 1 to begin the study of "what happened

not follow that v. 2 speaks of preexisting matter. In an attempt to reconcile the Genesis account with science (esp. the evidence for the existence of dinosaurs and other forms of life in remote times), some have held to a so-called "gap theory," according to which v. 2 should be rendered, "And the earth *became* formless and empty," implying that God's perfect creation came into chaos through a great catastrophe. The Hebrew syntax, however, does not naturally lend itself to such a translation.

The length of the creative days of Gen. 1 is not stated in the Bible. The Hebrew word *yôm H3427*, like "day" in English, may mean a period of light between two periods of darkness, a period of light together with the preceding period of darkness, or a long period of time. All three usages occur often in the Bible, and in this very context (2:4) *yôm* is used with reference to the whole week of creation. (The argument that when the Heb. word is accompanied by a number it always refers to a 24-hour period is in effect an ad hoc explanation; the use of a number with a word does not normally affect a word's meaning.) There is no indisputable indication as to which of the three is meant. The Bible gives no specific statement as to how long ago matter was created, how long ago the first day of creation began, or when the sixth day ended. On the seventh day (2:2-3) God ceased from his labors. God refers to this as an example for Israel to have

next," how out of God's creative work there came the beginnings of human life and history on earth. This explains the alleged differences and supposed contradictions between the chapters, for ch. 2 alludes to the creative work as a whole only insofar as it is necessary to do so in recording the beginnings of human history. It is reasonable, therefore, that it gives a more detailed account of the creation of Adam and Even but says nothing about that of matter, light, heavenly bodies, or plants.

Again, it is sometimes said that Gen. 1 begins with a watery chaos and Gen. 2:4 with a dry earth. But there is no contradiction, because the two have different starting points in the creative acts of God. Chapter 2 does not describe the creation of vegetation, as some assert; it simply mentions the planting of a garden. It is hardly reasonable to insist that God created man and then put him aside while the garden was planted and given time to mature. The verbs in 2:8-9 must be understood (as is perfectly proper to do) as pluperfects, and the same is true of 2:19 where the previous creation of animals is alluded to. Genesis 2 does not contradict ch. 1 in any way; instead, it opens up our understanding of the wonder of the creation of human beings and introduces us to the beginnings of human history on earth.

creation, new. See REGENERATION.

creature. Something created, although the term is usually applied to living beings, especially humans (see also LIVING CREATURE). PAUL explicitly contrasts "the creature" (NIV, "created things") with the Creator (Rom. 1:25). The well-known phrase in the KJV, "new creature" (2 Cor. 5:17; NIV, "new creation"), is a reference to REGENERATION.

credit, creditor. See BORROW; DEBT.

creed. An authoritative statement of the principal affirmations of the Christian faith. It is generally brief and concise, free of definition, proof, or explanation. It is at once personal, social, and historical in its impact. Insofar as possible, a creed attempts to witness to the universal CHURCH rather than to set forth those points of doctrine that would describe variance within that church. Thus creeds

give testimony to those universal beliefs that bind the whole church, not only in the day in which they were written but throughout history. Several passages in the Bible may be regarded as creedal in character (e.g., Deut. 6:4-5; Matt. 16:16; 1 Cor. 15:1-5; 1 Tim. 3:16), but the earliest formal Christian confession, the Apostles' Creed, probably originated about the middle of the second century. The most substantial and important confessions of the ancient church, such as the Nicene Creed, were produced in the fourth and fifth centuries.

creeping thing. See ANIMALS.

Crescens. kres´uhnz (Gk. *Krēskēs*, from Lat. *Crescens*, "growing"). A companion of PAUL in his last imprisonment (2 Tim. 4:10). He is said to have left the apostle and gone to GALATIA.

crescents. This term is used by some versions to render Hebrew *śahărōnîm H8448* (Jdg. 8:21, 26 [NIV, "ornaments"]; Isa. 3:18 [NIV, "crescent necklaces"]). The word refers to ornaments made of gold, silver, or bronze, and shaped in the form of the new moon. They were worn as necklaces or sewn on garments.

Cretan. kree´tuhn. See CRETE.

Crete. kreet (Gk. *Krētē G3207*; gentilic *Krēs G3205*, "Cretan"). A large island in the eastern Mediterranean, SE of the Greek mainland (see GREECE). Crete is about 160 mi. (260 km.) long, and its width varies from 7 to 35 mi. (11-55 km.). It is dominated by four mountain ranges, but in the eastern half there are fertile plains and upland basins that furnish summer pasturage. For this reason only the eastern half was settled in prehistoric times. Crete forms a natural bridge between Europe and Asia Minor, but despite this enviable geographical position, it has never attained a prominent place in history, partly because of internal dissensions and, in more modern times, because of its acceptance of Turkish rule and the Islamic faith until 1913, when it was formally incorporated into Greece, where the Orthodox Church predominates.

In mythology, Mount Ida is the legendary birthplace of ZEUS, the head of the Greek Pantheon.

King Minos, a half-historical and half-mythological character, alleged son of Zeus, was an early ruler of Crete. Both Thucydides and Aristotle accepted the existence of King Minos and claimed that he established maritime supremacy for Crete by putting down piracy. Aristotle compares the institutions of Crete to those of Sparta. Crete is said to have been colonized by the Dorians from the Peloponnesus. The most important of the ancient cities of Crete are Knossos (excavated by Arthur Evans), Gortyna, and Cydonia. Around 140 B.C. the Jews established a large enough colony on this island to be able to appeal successfully to the protection of ROME.

In the OT the KERETHITES (1 Sam. 30:14; Ezek. 25:16), related to the PHILISTINES, are usually held to be Cretans. In the NT a number of Cretans are represented as being present on the Day of PENTECOST (Acts 2:11). PAUL sailed on a grain ship along the southern coast of Crete on the way to ROME (27:12-13). The ship anchored at FAIR HAVENS just E of Cape Matala, then sailed to the harbor of PHOENIX, but the narrative does not specifically indicate that Paul actually landed on the island. It is not known who founded the churches on Crete. Paul implied that he did so when he stated that he left TITUS on the island to correct the churches and appoint elders in every town (Tit. 1:5). The Cretans were proverbially depraved. Paul quoted the poet Epimenides c. 600 B.C., "Cretans are always liars, evil beasts, lazy gluttons" (1:12), an opinion shared by many of the ancients.

crib. See MANGER.

cricket. See ANIMALS.

crimes and punishments. See PUNISHMENT.

crimson. A vivid or deep red color, similar to SCARLET. The latter term usually refers to a brighter red, but it is uncertain whether this distinction applies to the relevant Hebrew words (cf. the use of both in Isa. 1:18). All the standard English versions use "crimson" as the rendering of Hebrew *karmîl H4147*, which occurs only three times (2 Chr. 2:7, 14; 3:14). It is found more frequently in the NRSV, which uses it also to render *šānî H9106* (e.g., Exod.

28:5-6 and often), but this term is rendered "scarlet" in the KJV and NIV. The dye for red colors is extracted from the body of female cochineal insects.

crisping pin. An instrument for curling the hair. It is the KJV rendering of Hebrew *ḥārîṭ H3038* ("bag, handbag, purse") in Isa. 3:22. The Hebrew word occurs also in 2 Ki. 5:23, where the KJV correctly translates with "bag."

Crispus. kris′puhs (Gk. *Krispos G3214*, from Lat. *Crispus*, "curled, curly"). A superintendent of the SYNAGOGUE in CORINTH and an early convert there with his family (Acts 18:8); he was one of the few Corinthians baptized by PAUL (1 Cor. 1:14). Most Corinthian Jews opposed the gospel, and synagogue preaching became impossible (Acts 18:4-8, 12); the conversion of a prominent synagogue official must have been striking. (This name occurs, mistakenly, for CRESCENS in some ancient versions of 2 Tim. 4:10.) See also SOSTHENES.

crocodile. See ANIMALS.

crocus. See PLANTS.

crookbackt. KJV rendering of a Hebrew word meaning "hunchbacked" (Lev. 21:20).

crop. This English noun, when referring to a bird's enlarged gullet (craw), which was to be removed in sacrificial rites, occurs only once (Lev. 1:16). Otherwise, the word (usually in the pl. *crops*) occurs frequently in Bible versions with reference to the yield of cultivated plants and agricultural produce. See AGRICULTURE; HARVEST; PLANTS.

cross. This term in the Bible can refer not only literally to the wooden instrument of torture and death, but also (by metonymy) to the act of crucifixion, death on the cross; in addition, the cross can be a symbolic representation of REDEMPTION. The cross existed in four different forms: (1) the *crux immissa*, the type usually presented in art in which the upright beam extends above the cross beam, traditionally held to be the cross on which the Redeemer suffered and died. (2) The *crux commissa*, or "Saint Anthony's Cross" in the form of

C

Artistic reconstruction of a T-shaped cross used in crucifixion. In certain cases the arms may have been attached to the cross beam by ropes.

© Dr. James C. Martin. Illustration by Timothy Ladwig.

hanged was accursed, and as a Roman to whom one crucified was an object of scorn (Gal. 3:13), came to glory in the cross would be one of the absurdities of history were it not for the fact that the apostle held the Crucified as the Christ of God (2:20).

Crucifixion was one of the most cruel and barbarous forms of death known to man. It was practiced, especially in times of war, by the Phoenicians, Carthaginians, Egyptians, and later by the Romans. So dreaded was it that even in the pre-Christian era, the cares and troubles of life were often compared to a cross. The gory details of the crucifixion of Christ are passed over by the Evangelists, who say simply, "They crucified him" (Matt. 27:35; Mk. 15:24). Following his trial before the Jewish and Roman authorities, Christ was led forth for crucifixion. Before the actual ordeal itself, he was scourged. The prisoner was bent over and tied to a post, while the Roman soldier applied blow after blow on his bared back with a lash intertwined with pieces of bone or steel. This in itself was frequently sufficient to cause death.

The agony of the crucified victim was brought about by a number of factors. First, the painful but nonfatal character of the wounds inflicted. Although there were two distinctive methods of affixing a living victim to a cross, tying or nailing, it is well established that Christ underwent the horror of the latter, or possibly both. The second factor causing great suffering was the abnormal position of the body. The slightest movement brought on additional torture. The third factor was the traumatic fever induced by hanging for such a long period of time.

What was the physical reason for Christ's death? Recent medical studies have sought an answer to the question. When a person is suspended by his two hands, the blood sinks rapidly into the lower extremities of the body. Within six to twelve minutes the blood pressure has dropped to half, while the rate of the pulse has doubled. The heart is deprived of blood, and fainting follows. This leads to an orthorastic collapse through insufficient circulation. Death during crucifixion is due to heart failure. Victims of crucifixion did not generally succumb for two or three days. Death was hastened by the *crucifragium* or the breaking of the legs. "But when they came to Jesus and found

the letter "T." (3) The Greek cross in which the cross beams are of equal length. (4) The *crux decussata*, or "Saint Andrew's Cross," in the shape of the letter "X." Antedating these forms, the Assyrians impaled the body with a crude pointed stick.

Because of the sacrificial death of the Savior on the cross, the cross rapidly became interwoven into the theological construction of religious thinking, especially PAUL's. In 1 Cor. 1:17 the "preaching" of the cross is set forth as the "divine folly" in sharp contrast to earthly WISDOM. In Eph. 2:16 it is presented as the medium of RECONCILIATION. According to Col. 1:20, PEACE has been effected through the cross; and in 2:14 we read that the penalties of the law have been removed from the believer by the cross. How Paul as a pious Hebrew to whom one

that he was already dead, they did not break his legs" (Jn. 19:33). To such a death, the one who was coequal with God descended (Phil. 2:5).

crow. See BIRDS (under *raven*).

crown. This English word is used, with more than one meaning, to render several Hebrew and Greek terms. (1) It may simply indicate something of a particular form or shape (e.g., Exod. 25:11 KJV, referring to a part of the ornamentation of the ARK OF THE COVENANT). (2) It may be a symbol of kingship. In Ps. 21:3 Yahweh is spoken of as placing a crown of fine gold upon the head of DAVID, the theocratic king. According to 2 Sam. 12:30, the crown of the Ammonite king of RABBAH, weighing a talent of gold and set with a precious stone, was taken from his head and placed on the head of David, king of Israel, as a symbol of sovereignty over the country and people of AMMON. (3) In Ps. 8:5 human beings, as the representatives of God in ruling all the created existences of the world, are spoken of as crowned with glory and honor. (4) In the NT, the word is used twice to mean a symbol of

evil ruling powers, demonic or antichristian (Rev. 12:3; 13:1), and once of Jesus Christ (19:12). (5) In addition, Roman soldiers are said to have "twisted together a crown of thorns" (Matt. 27:29; Mk. 15:17; Jn. 19:2). What material or kind of tree or bush was used is unknown. The crown of thorns evidently served a double function as intended by the soldiers: to mock and humiliate Jesus with a travesty of royal honor, and to increase the physical torture that was inflicted upon him.

(6) Finally, the crown can be a symbol of victory. The background of this concept is the Greek athletic GAMES or contests, in which the victor was crowned with a garland or wreath of foliage. This crown had no intrinsic value; its worth consisted solely in the honor of victory that it symbolized and recognized. (Similar to a ribbon or medal given to the winner in an athletic contest today). This idea was lifted by the NT into the terminology of religion, and the crown became the symbol of victory over the forces and powers of evil (cf. Rev. 2:10; 3:11; 6:2). In 2 Tim. 4:8 the "crown of life" and "crown of righteousness" are not to be thought of as separate or distinct glories to be received by the Christian at the Lord's coming; rather, both signify absolute and total victory, the "crown of life" emphasizing the idea of victory over death, and the "crown of righteousness" stressing the idea of victory over sin.

crucible. A refining pot for silver and gold and other metals, made to resist great heat (Prov. 17:3; 27:21).

crucifixion. See CROSS.

cruse. This English term, meaning "a small earthenware jar (for holding water, oil, etc.)," is used by the KJV to render several Hebrew words, especially *ṣappaḥat H7608*, which seems to refer to the two-handled traveler's flask or canteen (1 Sam. 26:11-12, 16; 1 Ki. 19:6). It was ill-suited to contain olive oil, but perhaps necessary in the case of the poverty-stricken widow (1 Ki. 17:12; 14, 16). See also POTTERY.

cry. This English word is often used as a rendering of various terms (e.g., Gen. 27:34; Matt. 25:6). The

© Dr. James C. Martin. The Israel Museum, Jerusalem. Photographed by permission.

Dating to c. 3200 B.C., this copper crown used in religious ceremonies was discovered above the W shore of the Dead Sea in the area of En Gedi.

C

"cry" may or may not be uttered; it may express the anguish of the soul under dire and prolonged stress or burden and the lifting of perpetual petition in search of fulfillment, deliverance, or the answer to the riddles of life (cf. Heb. 5:7). At times the idea of prayer was uppermost, as in the cry of Jesus from the CROSS (Matt. 27:46). The two terms "pray" and "cry" can be used interchangeably (Ps. 39:12).

crystal. See MINERALS.

Cub. kuhb. Also Kub. Transliteration of Hebrew *kûb H3915* (not in NIV), a place mentioned only once (Ezek. 30:5 ASV; the KJV has "Chub" and identifies "Put" as "Libya"). On the basis of the SEPTUAGINT, most scholars emend the Hebrew text to read *lûb H4275*, that is, LIBYA. Cf. Nah. 3:9, where Libyans are referred to along with CUSH and PUT, as here.

cubit. See WEIGHTS AND MEASURES.

cuckoo, cuckow. See BIRDS.

cucumber. See PLANTS.

cummin. See PLANTS.

Cun. kuhn (Heb. *kûn H3923*). TNIV Kun. An Aramean town located in the northern part of ZOBAH (1 Chr. 18:8). Even though the parallel passage reads BEROTHAI (2 Sam. 8:8), this does not mean that they are necessarily the same place; DAVID took bronze booty from a number of the towns in this area. Some scholars identify Cun with modern Ras Baʿalbek, about 55 mi. (90 km.) NE of Beirut.

cuneiform. See WRITING.

cup. A drinking vessel made of POTTERY or metal. Cups were of various forms and designs; the cups of the Hebrews often carried designs borrowed from Phoenicia and Egypt. All of SOLOMON's drinking vessels were of gold (1 Ki. 10:21). The cups mentioned in the NT were doubtless of Roman style.

The cup is used as a symbol of prosperity or of the Lord's blessing, but also of his malediction on the wicked (Ps. 11:6; 16:5; 23:5). In other contexts the cup can represent drunkenness and other illicit pleasures (Prov. 23:31; Rev. 17:4; 18:6). "Cup of salvation" (Ps. 116:13), "cup of thanksgiving" (1 Cor. 10:16), and "cup of the Lord" (10:21) are also used. In the latter two passages, PAUL is referring to the communion cup, over which the blessing is said prior to the feast that commemorates the Lord's death and burial. The cup from ancient times signified FELLOWSHIP. Thus when the believer takes the cup of the Lord, he enters into fellowship with him. The "cup of demons" (10:21), mentioned in opposition to the cup of the Lord, can best be understood in this context. The apostle is saying in a figurative way that we cannot have fellowship with Christ and with the forces of darkness at the same time. At heathen feasts the cup was sacred to the name of the god in whose name the feast was being held. Thus, in the Christian communion service, the cup is sacred to the name of the Redeemer who instituted its practice (Matt. 26:27; Mk. 14:23-24; Lk. 22:20). The "cup of his wrath" (Isa. 51:17, 22), the "cup that sends all the surrounding peoples reeling" (Zech. 12:2), and the "cup of ruin and desolation" (Ezek. 23:33) are among other biblical occurrences of the term.

cupbearer. See OCCUPATIONS AND PROFESSIONS.

curds. See BUTTER.

curse. The expression (as by prayer) of a wish that evil fall on someone; the opposite of *blessing* (see BLESS). On the divine level, to curse is to impose JUDGMENT. In ANE thought the curse carried with it its own power of execution. A curse was imposed on the serpent (Gen. 3:14). NOAH cursed CANAAN (9:25). The curse of BALAAM, the pseudoprophet, turned to a blessing (Num. 24:10). After the Israelites reached the Promised Land, half of the tribes stood on Mount GERIZIM and half on Mount EBAL to utter blessings and curses respectively (Deut. 27:12-13; Josh. 8:33-34). The cursing of one's parents is sternly prohibited by Mosaic regulations. Christ commanded those who would be his disciples to bless and not to curse (Lk. 6:28). PAUL represents the curse of the LAW as borne by Christ on the CROSS for the believer (Gal. 3:13). See also BLASPHEMY.

curtain. Curtains were much more familiar in the ANE household than elsewhere. The nomad's tent was sewn together of narrow lengths of cloth woven from goats' and camels' hair mixed with sheep's wool. The majority of biblical references to curtains are in Exodus in connection with the TABERNACLE; in fact, one of the Hebrew words for "curtain" (*yĕrî'â H3749*) became virtually synonymous with the sacred tent (2 Sam. 7:2; cf. KJV). The weaving of the curtains was the work of the women (Exod. 35:25-26). In the tabernacle the curtains hung on 60 acacia pillars set in brass sockets 5 cubits apart. Curtains for the N and S sides were each 5 cubits high by 100 cubits long of fine white linen; that for the W side was 5 by 50 cubits. On the E side (the entrance) hung two short curtains, each 5 by 15 cubits, on three pillars.

Special importance attaches to another Hebrew word, *pārōket H7267*, a technical term applied only to the inner curtain (KJV, "veil") that divided the Holy Place from the Most Holy Place in the tabernacle. A symbol of God's unapproachability, this curtain was made of blue, purple, scarlet, and fine twisted linen embroidered with figures of CHERUBIM (Exod. 26:31-37; 36:35). It was hung with golden hooks upon four pillars of acacia wood overlaid with gold which were set in sockets or bases of silver. It is likely that the curtain was quite thick to correspond with its great size. Only the high priest was permitted to enter behind the veil, and that only one day each year—the Day of Atonement (Lev. 16; Num. 18:7; Heb. 9:7). Mention is made only once of this curtain in Solomon's TEMPLE (2 Chr. 3:14). During the crucifixion of Jesus (Lk. 23:45), or at the moment of his death (Matt. 27:51; Mk. 15:38), and at the time the priests were busy with the evening sacrifice, the veil of the temple was torn in two, from top to bottom, exposing the Holy of Holies and symbolizing that Jesus, as the High Priest who could enter the Most Holy Place (Heb. 6:19-20; 9:11-12), had opened the way for all believers to enter into the presence of God through his flesh, symbolized by the veil (10:19-20).

Cush. koosh (Heb. *kûš H3932* and *H3933*; gentilic *kûšî H3934*, "Cushite"). Also Kush. **(1)** Oldest son of HAM and grandson of NOAH (Gen. 10:6-8;

1 Chr. 1:8-10). From him descended several tribes, including the southernmost people group known to the Hebrews. See #3 below.

(2) A Benjamite mentioned in the title of Ps. 7. In this psalm DAVID prays for deliverance from his enemies, and Cush (identified by some with SAUL) may have been among them. It is also possible, however, that Cush was not an enemy; perhaps he is the same as the Cushite messenger mentioned in 2 Sam. 18:21-32.

(3) A land lying to the S of EGYPT, in the upper NILE region (Nubia), and corresponding roughly to ETHIOPIA. It would appear that Cush originally referred to a piece of territory lying between the second and the third cataracts of the Nile, but later it came to designate a broader area. At times the reference to Cush is merely one that implies a country lying as far off as possible (cf. Ezek. 29:10). A few problems are encountered in connection with the use of the term *kûš*. The first of these is that "the entire land of Cush" is said to be encircled by the GIHON River (Gen. 2:13). This reference demands a location near MESOPOTAMIA and lies therefore almost as far N as Cush lies S. There is also the problem of the wife of MOSES, the "Cushite woman" (Num. 12:1). She either came from the area adjacent to the SINAI peninsula (the ZIPPORAH of Exod. 2:21) or possibly after Zipporah's death may have been an Ethiopian who, in a manner not known to us, came into that same peninsula. Another problem has to do with ZERAH the Cushite, who appeared in the land of Judah in

© Dr. James C. Martin. The British Museum. Photographed by permission.

Cushites (Nubians) being taken prisoner by Assyrian soldiers after capturing a fortress in Egypt. Panel from a palace in Nineveh (c. 640 B.C.).

the days of King Asa with a huge army (2 Chr. 14:9, 12-13). History has yet to find an answer to the question how in a time when Ethiopia had no power in Egypt, Zerah should have been able to muster so large a force. (Other Cushites are mentioned in 2 Sam. 18:21-23 and Jer. 38:7-13.)

Cushan. koosh´an (Heb. *kûšān H3936*, derivation uncertain). Speaking of Yahweh's coming in judgment, the prophet says, "I saw the tents of Cushan in distress, / the dwellings of Midian in anguish" (Hab. 3:7). The SEPTUAGINT understood the passage to refer to ETHIOPIA (see CUSH), but this area is much farther S than the context suggests. Because of the parallelism in the verse, most scholars assume that Cushan was near (or even the same as) MIDIAN, in the desert E of the SINAI peninsula. Others see a connection with CUSHAN-RISHATHAIM ("king of Aram Naharaim," Jdg. 3:8) and place Cushan in N SYRIA.

Cushan-rishathaim. koosh´an-rish´uh-thay´im (Heb. *kûšan rišʿātayim H3937*, possibly a deliberate disfigurement of an uncertain name). A king of Aram Naharaim (MESOPOTAMIA) who ruled over Israel for eight years during the period of the judges (Jdg. 3:8, 10). When the Israelites cried to God, he raised a deliverer, OTHNIEL, who prevailed over Cushan-Rishathaim. The identity of this king and his kingdom are uncertain. Perhaps there is a connection between him and a district in N SYRIA (part of Aram Naharaim) known as Kûshân-rōm. It is also possible that Cushan-Rishathaim was a HITTITE ruler of that area or a member of an Assyrian or Babylonian dynasty.

Cushi. koosh´i (Heb. *kûšî H3935*; this form can also be used as the gentilic "Cushite," for which see CUSH). **(1)** The great-grandfather of JEHUDI, who was a prince in the court of JEHOIAKIM (Jer. 36:14).

(2) The father of the prophet ZEPHANIAH (Zeph. 1:1).

(3) KJV form of Cushite (2 Sam. 18:21-32).

Cushite. koosh´it. See CUSH.

custodian. This term is used by the RSV to render Greek *paidagōgos G4080* (lit., "boy's guide"), a word

used by PAUL to describe one of the functions of the LAW (Gal 3:24-25). The word was wrongly translated "schoolmaster" by the KJV, while the NRSV uses a negative term, "disciplinarian" (the NIV uses descriptive phrases, "put in charge of," "under the supervision of"). The *paidagōgos* was a trusted, often well-educated slave who was given constant supervision of a boy between the ages of six and sixteen. He was responsible for the disciplined training and the moral development of his charge, going to and from school with him and assisting with his home studies. Paul's point in using this image, however, has been debated: is he calling attention to the oppressive character of the law or to its positive function in leading sinners to Christ? The apostle seems to indicate that the purpose of the law in the economy of God was to prepare a people, and thereby perfect his plan, for the coming of Christ. It was necessary to place upon them severe restrictions in order to develop their racial and cultural identity, and to lay them under the moral discipline of the law. In addition, they needed to be instructed in the "promises" that pointed to Christ. The intent of the law went no farther than this.

custom, receipt of. The post from which MATTHEW (Levi) was called to follow Christ (Matt. 9:9; NIV, "tax collector's booth"). In postexilic days the TRIBUTE was usually in terms of a road toll. The Romans imposed tribute or TAXES on Jews as on all their subjects for the maintenance of their provincial government. Tax collectors or publicans were despised because of their notorious dishonesty and willingness to work for a foreign power.

Cuth. kooth. See CUTHAH.

Cuthah. kooth´uh (Heb. *kûtâ H3940* or *kût H3939*, from Akk. *Kūtū*). Also Cuth; TNIV Kuthah. One of the most important cities of ancient Babylonia—perhaps even the capital of an early Sumerian empire (2 Ki. 17:24, 30). Today the site is marked by Tel-Ibrahim (c. 20 mi./32 km. NE of BABYLON). Here contract tablets were found that give the name as *Gudua* or *Kūtū*. To the W lies a smaller mound crowned with a sanctuary in memory of *Ibrahim* (ABRAHAM). Cuthah had a temple (*E-shid-lam*) dedicated to NERGAL, king of the underworld. The city was probably important commercially because it had two rivers (or canals). SENNACHERIB boasts that he destroyed Cuthah in one of his campaigns; NEBUCHADNEZZAR later rebuilt its beautiful temple. Cuthah is one of the cities from which SARGON II deported colonists to repopulate N Israel after SAMARIA had capitulated (721 B.C.). Apparently these aliens were predominant, for the inhabitants of Samaria were long after called Cutheans.

Cuza. koo´zuh (Gk. *Chouzas*, from Aram. *kûzā*, "jug"). Also Chuza. The husband of JOANNA, one of the women from GALILEE who followed Jesus and helped support him and his disciples (Lk. 8:3; she also went to the tomb of Jesus to anoint his body with spices on the morning of his resurrection, 24:10). Cuza is said to have been a steward of HEROD Antipas. Some have speculated that Cuza had died before the time when Joanna followed Jesus.

cymbal. See MUSIC AND MUSICAL INSTRUMENTS.

cypress. See PLANTS.

Cyprus. si´pruhs (Gk. *Kypros G3251*). An island in the eastern part of the Mediterranean directly off the coast of Syria and Cilicia, about 150 mi. (240 km.) long and about 40 mi. (65 km.) across. The island, which is rich in copper deposits, has roots deep in the past. The aboriginal inhabitants of Cyprus seem to have been of Minoan stock. After the breakup of the Minoan civilization, the dark ages settled down on the island. The curtain rose again when settlers from the Greek mainland reached it. Cyprus has known various conquerors. SARGON in 709 B.C. made himself ruler of Cyprus, and it paid tribute to Assyria until the days of ESARHADDON. The demise of the Assyrian empire appears to have brought the island relative freedom, until it was annexed to Egypt in 540. With the rise of Cambyses

Cyprus.

(526), Cyprus passed under Persian rule until the time of ALEXANDER THE GREAT, to whom it surrendered voluntarily and helped with the siege of TYRE. During the late intertestamental period it fell into the hands of the Romans (cf. 1 Macc. 10:13), who accorded the island provincial status in 58 B.C.

In the pre-Christian era, a large colony of Jews settled there and later no doubt formed the nucleus of the Christian church ministered to by PAUL and his companions, who passed through the island from SALAMIS to PAPHOS (Acts 13:4-12). At Paphos, Sergius PAULUS, the imperial deputy of the island, came to believe in Christ. BARNABAS, who

Aerial view of the western section of the island of Cyprus (view to the N). The harbor of Paphos is located at the bottom right of the picture.

© Dr. James C. Martin

C

accompanied Paul on this first missionary journey, was a native of the island (Acts 4:36); with John Mark (see MARK, JOHN) he later returned to evangelize Cyprus after they had left Paul's company (15:36-39).

Cyrene. si-ree´nee (Gk. *Kyrēnē* G3255, from the name of the nature goddess, Kyrana). A Libyan city in N Africa, W of EGYPT, separated from it by a part of the Libyan Desert. It was situated some 2,000 ft. (610 m.) above and 10 mi. (16 km.) away from the Mediterranean. The coastline afforded a natural shelter from the heat of the Sahara. It was protected by steps of descending ranges about 80 mi. (130 km.) to the south. The fertility and climate of the city were delightful and productive.

Cyrene, originally a Greek colony, was founded by Battus in 603 B.C. This veritable "oasis in the desert" attracted travelers and commerce from early times. Among its distinguished citizens was Carneacles, the founder of the new academy at ATHENS. Aristippus, the Epicurean philosopher and friend of Socrates, also came from this city. PTOLEMY Euergetes I incorporated Cyrene as a part of Egypt in 231. It later passed into the hands of the Romans, being willed to them by the last Ptolemy.

Cyrene is not mentioned in the OT but becomes important in the NT. A native of Cyrene, SIMON by name, was impressed by the Roman soldiers into carrying the cross of Jesus (Lk. 23:26); thus did Simon immortalize his city. There were also representatives of Cyrene present in JERUSALEM on the day of PENTECOST (Acts 2:10). Its Jewish population warranted a synagogue (6:9). A certain Lucius of Cyrene was one of the leaders of the church in Syrian ANTIOCH (13:1). Archaeology has shown that it was the Greek plan to make Cyrene the "Athens of Africa." The most interesting remains are a great system of tombs cut out of solid rock into the cliff. Architecture and paintings adorn these tombs.

Cyrenius. See QUIRINIUS.

Cyrus. si´ruhs (Heb. *kôreš* H3931). Although this name was borne by more than one Persian ruler (see PERSIA), the most important by far was Cyrus II the Great (559-530 B.C.), son of Cambyses and founder of the Achaemenid empire, which continued for two centuries to the time of ALEXANDER THE GREAT. Seven years after the death of NEBUCHADNEZZAR, Nabonidus ascended the throne of BABYLON, in 555 B.C. He was destined to be the last ruling sovereign of the neo-Babylonian empire, for in the highlands of Iran another kingdom was forging out its own program of conquest. When the Medes and their king, Astyages, were defeated by Cyrus, the realm of Persia began to assume threatening proportions.

Cyrus himself announced his genealogy: "I am Cyrus, king of the hosts, the great king, king of Babylon, king of Sumer and Akkad ... son of Cambyses, the king, king of Anshan; the grandson of Cyrus ... the great-grandson of Teispes ... king of Anshan ... " In this same inscription Cyrus proceeds to relate how the city of Babylon opened its gates to him without resistance, confirming the biblical account recorded in Dan. 5 when DARIUS, acting as vice-regent for Cyrus, took the city of Babylon in the name of Cyrus the Great. The neo-Babylonian empire was in no condition to resist the advance of Cyrus, and fell easily into the hands of the Persians. The OT sets the framework of reference against the backdrop of BELSHAZZAR's impious feast (Dan. 5:1-30). Cyrus entered Babylon on October 29, 539 B.C., and presented himself in the role of the liberator of the people. He allowed the images of the gods to be transported back to their original cities and instituted a kindly policy of repatriation for captive peoples. His policies of moderation naturally extended to the Hebrews, whom he encouraged to return to Judea to rebuild their temple (2 Chr. 36:22-23; Ezra 1:1-6). Isaiah refers to Cyrus as "his [i.e., the Lord's] anointed" (Isa. 45:1).

D. The symbol used to designate two different NT MSS, Codex Bezae (for the Gospels and Acts) and Codex Claromontanus (Pauline Epistles). It is also an abbreviation used (along with E, J, and P) to designate one of the supposed sources of the PENTATEUCH, according to the Documentary Hypothesis. It refers primarily to the author or editor of the book of DEUTERONOMY, but also to the material or outlook peculiar to it.

Dabareh. See DABERATH.

Dabbasheth. See DABBESHETH.

Dabbesheth. dab´uh-sheth (Heb. *dabbešet H1833*, "hump"). KJV Dabbasheth. A town on the S border of the tribe of ZEBULUN between SARID and JOKNEAM (Josh. 19:11), perhaps a little E of the Brook KISHON. Dabbesheth should possibly be identified with Tell esh-Shammam, some 6 mi. (10 km.) NW of MEGIDDO.

Daberath. dab´uh-rath (Heb. *dāběrat H1829*, "pasture"). A town at the NW foot of Mount TABOR, in the territory of the tribe of ISSACHAR, allotted to the Levites descended from GERSHON (Josh. 21:28 [KJV, "Dabareh"]; 1 Chr. 6:72 [Heb. 6:57]); it was apparently on the border with ZEBULUN (Josh. 19:12). The site is identified with the village of Daburiyeh, 5 mi. (8 km.) E of NAZARETH. Some think Daberath is the same place as RABBITH (Josh. 19:20).

dagger. See ARMS AND ARMOR.

Dagon. day´gon (Heb. *dāgôn H1837*, derivation disputed). Chief god of the PHILISTINES, but possibly worshiped by the Canaanites before the Philistine invasion of Canaan, as suggested by place-names such as BETH DAGON in Judah (Josh. 15:41) and in Asher (19:27). Some have thought that Dagon was a sea god (the Heb. word *dāg H1834* means "fish") or an agricultural deity (from *dāgān H1841*, "grain") or, perhaps more likely, a storm god (as some Mesopotamian and Ugaritic texts suggest). The OT mentions Dagon in three contexts. (1) When the Philistines captured SAMSON, they "assembled to offer a great sacrifice to Dagon their god" (Jdg. 16:23). (2) Some years later the Philistines captured the ARK OF THE COVENANT, brought it into their temple, and set it beside an image of Dagon; but the statue fell twice on its face and broke, and moreover the Lord afflicted the people with tumors (1 Sam. 5:1-7). (3) Upon the death of SAUL and his sons on Mount GILBOA, the Philistines "hung up his head in the temple of Dagon" in BETH SHAN (1 Chr. 10:10; cf. 1 Sam. 31:10).

Dalaiah. See DELAIAH.

daleth. dah´leth (from *delet H1946*, "door"). The fourth letter of the Hebrew alphabet (ד), with a numerical value of four. This consonant was pronounced like *d* in English, although in later times it became spirantized (cf. the *th* sound in English *this*) when it was preceded by a vowel sound. Because its shape is very similar to that of the RESH (ר), these two consonants were often confused by the scribes.

Dalmanutha. dal-muh-n*oo*´thuh (Gk. *Dalmanoutha G1236*). A village near the W shore of the Sea of Galilee (only in Mk. 8:10). See GALILEE, SEA OF. Following the feeding of the 4,000, Jesus and his disciples came to this region, an area that must have been near (or the same as) MAGADAN, the name that occurs in the parallel passage (Matt. 15:39). The ruins on the W shore of the lake, 3 mi. (5 km.) NW of TIBERIAS near modern Majdel (Magdala), may be the location. The name Dalmanutha is not attested elsewhere.

Dalmatia. dal-may′shee-uh (Gk. *Dalmatia G1237*). A district in the southern part of ILLYRICUM to which TITUS went during PAUL's final imprisonment (2 Tim. 4:10). Dalmatia was a somewhat vaguely defined area of coast and mountain hinterland that lay E of the Adriatic Sea confronting Italy. It was a vital area in the prosecution of Rome's project of a Rhine-Danube frontier. Paul's brief and unexplained reference to Illyricum in writing to Rome (Rom. 15:19) may mean that the apostle himself had founded Christian churches in the southern and more hellenized parts of the region. He possibly visited the area from MACEDONIA after his Ephesian ministry (Acts 20:1).

Dalphon. dal′fon (Heb. *dalpôn H1943*, possibly from Akk. *dullupu*, "sleepless"). The second of the ten sons of HAMAN who were put to death by the Jews (Esth. 9:7).

Damaris. dam′uh-ris (Gk. *Damaris G1240*, possibly "wife" or "heifer"). One of Paul's converts at Mars' Hill in ATHENS (Acts 17:34; see AREOPAGUS). Beyond this we know nothing of her. Since LUKE singled her out as one of several converts, and since she was named with DIONYSIUS, one of the judges of the Athenian court, some have thought that she may have been a woman of high social rank; others, however, speculate that she was an educated courtesan and thus a woman of low moral character.

Damascene. dam′uh-seen. A resident of DAMASCUS.

Damascus. duh-mas′kuhs (Heb. *dammeśeq H1966* [with variant spellings]; Gk. *Damaskos G1242*, gentilic *Damaskēnos G1241*, "Damascene"). This name can be applied to (1) the well-known city NE of Mount HERMON, (2) the general geographic region in S SYRIA where the city was located, and (3) at times, the state of which the city was the

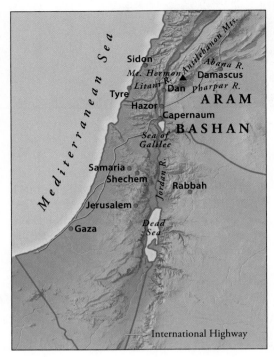

Damascus.

capital. Today Damascus is the capital of the modern state of Syria.

For more than 4,000 years, Damascus has been the capital of one government after another, a prize for which nation after nation went to war, a city whose boast for centuries has been, "The world began at Damascus, and the world will end there." It is a modern focal point between the Christian and the Muslim worlds, center of tourist interest and of international unrest. Damascus is watered by the Barada River and the Wady Awaj (the ABANA and PHARPAR of the OT, 2 Ki. 5:12). A 2,000-ft. (625 m.) elevation gives it a delightful climate. Its gardens and olive groves still flourish after millennia of cultivation. Caravan routes from the E, W, and S once crossed in the city, carrying treasures of silks, perfumes, carpets, and foods. It was a rich city whose merchandise was far-famed (Ezek. 27:16).

Damascus and Syria played an important part in biblical history. By the time of ABRAHAM, Damascus was well enough known to be a landmark (Gen. 14:15). En route from Ur, Abraham found in Syria a steward, ELIEZER, who was his heir presumptive until ISAAC came (15:2-3). From the days when Abraham liberated LOT (14:13-16), there were repeated periods of peace and war among his descendants, many of them involving Damascus. Abraham secured a wife for Isaac from Syria, hence Israel is of Syrian ancestry (Gen. 24; Deut. 26:5). JACOB labored long in Syria for RACHEL (Gen. 29).

According to JOSEPHUS, Hadad was the first king. DAVID subjugated and ruled the city for a time (2 Sam. 8:5-6; 1 Chr. 18:3-6). REZON, a deserter, killed King HADADEZER, whom David had defeated, and made himself king. He hated Israel and harassed SOLOMON all his life (1 Ki. 11:23-25). Solomon had made extensive purchases from Syria (10:29). ASA, king of Judah, bribed BEN-HADAD, grandson of Rezon of Syria, to aid him against Israel, paying him with temple treasures (15:16-21). ELIJAH, acting on instructions from God, anointed HAZAEL to be king of Syria and JEHU to rule Israel, to the end that Judah might be punished (19:15-17). In the meantime, Ben-Hadad attacked King Ahab of Israel with a great force, but during a drunken orgy was overwhelmed. Ahab foolishly allowed him to return to his throne (20:1-34). Later, becoming ill, Ben-Hadad sent Hazael to consult Elisha, who made a prophecy that led Hazael to assassinate Ben-Hadad and usurp the throne for which Elijah had anointed him (19:15; 2 Ki. 8:7-15). Hazael overcame AHAZIAH and Joram (2 Ki. 8:28; see JEHORAM), and ravaged the northern tribes (10:32-33; 13:3).

A strong kingdom was developed under Ahab, with merchants in Damascus (1 Ki. 20:34). Syrians defeated Joash (JEHOASH) after he failed in a test before ELISHA (2 Ki. 13:14-22). Ben-Hadad II succeeded Hazael, and Israel recovered her lost possessions (13:24-25). Under JEROBOAM II, Damascus was retaken by Israel (14:28). AHAZ, in order to save his kingdom from Syria, made an alliance with TIGLATH-PILESER (Pul), who destroyed Damascus and ended Syria's power for many decades (16:7-9). The city remained of little importance until 333 B.C., when an army of ALEXANDER THE GREAT captured it. Then followed two centuries of rise and fall. In 63 B.C. Syria became a province of the Roman Empire.

During NT days, Damascus was an important center, ruled by ARABIA under ARETAS (2 Cor. 11:32). A strong Christian community had developed by PAUL's day. It was while en route there to arrest the believers that he was converted (Acts 9:1-18). He escaped his Jewish enemies of the city by being let down from a wall in a basket (9:25; 2 Cor. 11:33). After a checkered history under Rome, Damascus was captured by Muslims in A.D. 635 and made the seat of the Muslim world. It remained the center of the Muslim faith until 1918, when it was put under French mandate after World War I. In 1946 Syria became a free state.

damnation. See CONDEMN, CONDEMNATION.

Dan. dan (Heb. *dan H1968* and *H1969*, "judge"; gentilic *dānî H1974*, "Danites"). The name of a man, of the tribe descended from him, and of a city within the tribe's territory.

(1) Son of JACOB through BILHAH. Jacob's wife RACHEL, unable to bear children (and thus jealous of her sister LEAH, who had already given birth to four sons), gave to Jacob her maid Bilhah as a wife. When the latter bore a son, Rachel said,

The tribal territory of Dan and, farther north, the city of Dan.

D

Aerial view of the ancient city of Dan (looking SSW).

"God has vindicated [*or* judged, *din H1906*] me," and so named him Dan (Gen. 30:6). Nothing more is said about Dan except that he had a son named HUSHIM (46:23; apparently the same as SHUHAM in Num. 26:42).

(2) A tribe descended from #1 above. By the time of the EXODUS Dan's offspring had increased to 62,700 men (Num. 1:39). The tribe acted as rear guard during the wilderness wanderings (10:25). After the conquest of Canaan, the Danites were given a fertile area lying between Judah and the Mediterranean Sea. This region, however, was occupied by the PHILISTINES, whose lands extended along the coast from EGYPT to the W of SHECHEM (Josh. 13:3). Failure to conquer Philistia made the Danites move northward, where by strategy they conquered Leshem (Laish of Jdg. 18:29) and renamed it Dan (Josh. 19:47; Jdg. 18:1-29; see #3 below). The heritage of Dan, though small, was productive and, with the acquisition of extra lands, provided for growth. OHOLIAB and SAMSON were Danites (Exod. 31:6; Jdg. 13:2, 24). The Assyrians eventually overran Israel and took many Danites into captivity (1 Chr. 5:26). Little is known of the tribe subsequent to that time.

(3) A city of the northern extremity of ancient Israel, situated on the S base of Mount HERMON close to one of the tributaries of the JORDAN River, the Nahr Leddan. It was commonly used as a sym-bol of the extent of Israelite territory in the phrase, "from Dan to Beersheba" (Jdg. 20:1, et al.). The mound where the ancient city stood is known in Arabic as Tell el-Qadi (in Hebrew as Tel Dan) and rises about 75 ft. (23 m.) above the grass land roundabout. In ancient Canaanite times it was known as LAISH (Jdg. 18:7; variant LESHEM, Josh. 19:47). It is known that the site was occupied as early as the Bronze Age and probably was inhabited by 3500 B.C. The town was on the trade route to the Syrian coast. After the revolt of JEROBOAM, Dan along with BETHEL became the locations of the two shrines that he set up with golden calves, probably as symbols of BAAL worship (1 Ki. 12:29; see CALF WORSHIP). So ingrained did this cult at the shrines become that even the massacre of Baal worshipers by JEHU did not stamp it out (2 Ki. 10:28-31). Subsequently it was one of the towns taken by the Aramean king BEN-HADAD, in fulfillment of the warning in 10:32: "the LORD began to trim off parts of Israel" (NRSV). Dan was recaptured by Israel under Jeroboam II (14:25), but was again taken by the Assyrian TIGLATH-PILESER III (745-727 B.C.).

dancing. Several Hebrew words describe the joyous, rhythmic movements of the dance, which evidently played a significant part in Israelite life. Dancing has formed a part of religious rites and has been associated with war and hunting, with marriage, birth, and other occasions since human records began to be written. It grew out of three basic motives: the desire to imitate movements of beasts, birds, even the sun and moon; the desire to express emotions by gestures; and gregarious impulses.

Throughout past ages, dancing has been linked with WORSHIP. In sacramental dance worshipers sought to express through bodily movements praise or penitence, worship or prayer. Out of the primitive dances the esthetic dance of civilized ancient nations slowly developed. In these the primary concern of the dancers was to reveal grace, speed, and rhythm, often to appeal to the carnal nature of both participants and spectators. VASHTI refused to expose herself to this end (Esth. 1:12). Priests of all pagan religions cultivated dancing but at times found it the source of dissipation and harm. For ages it has been accompanied by clapping of the hands. Percussion and other noise-making instruments seem to be native to dance (Jdg. 11:34; Ps. 68:25).

The Hebrew people developed their own type of dancing, associated in the main with worship. Basically, it was more like modern religious shouting by individuals, or processions of exuberant groups. Three things characterized it. First, the sexes apparently did not intermingle in it, except where pagan influences had crept in (cf. Exod. 32:19). Second, dancing was usually done by women, with one leading, as in the case of MIRIAM, when a form of antiphonal singing was used (15:20-21; cf. also Jdg. 21:20-23; 1 Sam. 18:6; Ps. 68:25). Third, dancing usually took place out of doors. Men might dance solo, as in the case of DAVID before the ARK OF THE COVENANT (2 Sam. 6:14-16), and in groups, as when Israel celebrated the victory over the AMALEKITES (1 Sam. 30:16). The time for dancing was recognized by the writer of Ecclesiastes (Eccl. 3:4). Job complained against the rich because of their ability to dance (Job 21:11). Jeremiah bemoaned the tragedy that made singing and dancing out of place (Lam. 5:15). The redemption of Israel was to be celebrated by dancing, both virgins and men and boys having part (Jer. 31:13). The Romans introduced the Greek dance to Palestine. Primitive Christian churches allowed dance, but it soon caused degeneracy and was banned, as is indicated by many of the early Christian writers.

Daniel. dan´yuhl (Heb. *dāniyyē'l H1975*, "God is my judge"; Gk. *Daniēl G1248*). **(1)** The second son of DAVID born to him in HEBRON (1 Chr. 3:1). See KILEAB (2 Sam. 3:3).

(2) A descendant of AARON through ITHAMAR and priest of the postexilic period; he was among those who affixed their seals to NEHEMIAH's covenant (Ezra 8:2; Neh. 10:6).

(3) An important and wise individual whom the prophet EZEKIEL mentions alongside NOAH and JOB (Ezek. 14:14, 20; 28:3). The consonantal Hebrew text (*Ketib*) in these passages spells the name *dn'l*, possibly pronounced "Danel." The fact that this figure is associated with ancient patriarchs has led many scholars to link him with a Phoenician king named Dan'ilu who is described in Ugaritic literature (see RAS SHAMRA) as someone revered for his wisdom and upright character. Other scholars prefer to identify him with the biblical Daniel who was a contemporary of Ezekiel (see #4 below).

(4) An exile who is traditionally regarded as the author of the book of Daniel (see DANIEL, BOOK OF). Born into an unidentified family of Judean nobility at the time of JOSIAH's reformation (621 B.C.), Daniel was among the select, youthful hostages of the first Hebrew deportation, taken to BABYLON by NEBUCHADNEZZAR in 605, the third year of King JEHOIAKIM (Dan. 1:1, 3). The reliability of this date and indeed of the whole account has been questioned by some critics. However, the method of dating used in the book of Daniel simply follows the customary Babylonian practice of numbering the years of a king's reign *after* his accession year (contrast Jer. 46:2, which speaks of this date as Jehoiakim's fourth year). The publication, moreover, of certain Nebuchadnezzar tablets demonstrates that after the Babylonian defeat of Egypt at CARCHEMISH in 605, this king did "conquer the whole area of Hatti" (Syria and Palestine) and "took away the heavy tribute of Hatti to Babylon" just as claimed in Dan. 1:2 (cf. 2 Chr. 36:6-7).

Daniel was assigned the Babylonian name BELTESHAZZAR (Dan. 1:7), which probably means, "[may Bel] protect his life!"—thereby invoking a pagan deity (4:8)—and for three years he and his companions were trained in all the wisdom of the Babylonians (1:4-5). These young men, however,

D

remained true to their ancestral faith, courteously refusing "the royal food and wine" (1:8, tainted with idolatry and contrary to the Levitical purity laws). God rewarded them with unsurpassed learning (1:20), which qualified them as official "wise men" (2:13). On Daniel, moreover, he bestowed the gift of visions and of interpreting dreams (1:17).

Near the close of this second year (602 B.C.), Nebuchadnezzar required his fellow Babylonians, who as the ruling strata in society had assumed the position of priestly diviners (Dan. 2:2), to identify and interpret an undisclosed dream that had troubled him the preceding evening (2:5, 8). The hoax of spiritism and astrology was duly exposed, and when judgment was pronounced on the enchanters, Daniel and his companions were included under the death sentence. But the "God in heaven who reveals mysteries" (2:28; cf. 2:11) answered Daniel's prayer for illumination (2:18-19). Daniel revealed both the dream, depicting a fourfold image, and its import of four world empires (Babylon, Persia, Greece, and Rome) that would introduce God's messianic kingdom (2:44). In appreciation, Nebuchadnezzar made Daniel ruler of the province of Babylon and chief over the wise men (2:48).

In the latter years of Nebuchadnezzar's reign (604-562 B.C.), Daniel's courage was demonstrated when he interpreted the king's dream of the fallen tree (Dan. 4:13-27). He tactfully informed his despotic master that for seven "times" pride would reduce him to beast-like madness, and reiterated that "the Most High is sovereign over the kingdoms of men" (4:24-25; cf. its historical fulfillment twelve months later, 4:28-33).

In 552 B.C., after the retirement of King Nabonidus to Arabian Teima and the accession of his son BELSHAZZAR, Daniel was granted his vision of the four great beasts (Dan. 7) that parallels Nebuchadnezzar's earlier dream of the composite image. Then in 550, at the time of CYRUS's amalgamation of the Median and Persian states and of the growing eclipse of Babylon, Daniel received the prophecy of the ram and the goat concerning Persia and Greece (8:20-21) down to ANTIOCHUS IV (8:25). On October 12, 539, Cyrus's general, Gobryas, after having routed the Babylonian armies, occupied the city of Babylon. During the profane revelries of Belshazzar's court that immediately preceded the end, Daniel was summoned to interpret God's handwriting on the wall, and the prophet fearlessly condemned the desperate prince (5:22-23). He predicted Medo-Persian victory (5:28), and that very night the citadel fell and Belshazzar was slain.

When Darius the Mede (presumably Gobryas or another official of similar name) was made king of Babylon by Cyrus (Dan. 5:31; 9:1), he at once sought out Daniel as one of his three "administrators" (6:2) because of his excellency, and was considering him for the post of chief administrator (6:3). Daniel's jealous colleagues, failing to uncover a valid charge of corruption (6:4), proceeded to contrive his downfall through a royal edict prohibiting for thirty days all prayers or petitions, except to Darius himself. Daniel was promptly apprehended in prayer to God; and Darius had no recourse but to cast him into a den of lions, as had been prescribed. God, however, intervened on behalf of his faithful servant (cf. 6:16) and shut the lions' mouths, though they subsequently devoured his accusers when they were condemned to a similar fate. It was in this same first year of Darius, as the seventy years of Babylonian exile drew to a close, that the angel GABRIEL answered Daniel's prayers and confessions with a revelation of the seventy "sevens" (9:24-27). "So Daniel prospered during the reign of Darius" (6:28; cf. 1:21).

The last-known event in the life of Daniel took place in the third year of Cyrus (536 B.C.), when he was granted an overpowering vision of the archangel MICHAEL contending with the demonic powers of pagan society (Dan. 10:10—11:1); of the course of world history, through the persecutions of Antiochus IV (11:2-39); and of the eschatological ANTICHRIST, the resurrections, and God's final judgment (11:40—12:4). The vision concluded with the assurance that though Daniel would go to his grave prior to these events he would yet receive his appointed reward in the consummation (12:13). Thus in his mid-eighties, after completing his inspired autobiography and apocalyptic oracles, he finished his honored course. The book of Daniel presents a timeless demonstration of separation from impurity, of courage against compromise, of efficaciousness in prayer, and of dedication to him whose "kingdom endures from generation to generation" (4:34).

Daniel, Additions to. See APOCRYPHA.

Daniel, Book of. Although it stands as the last of the Major Prophets in the English Bible, this book appears in the Hebrew OT (which consists of the Law, the Prophets, and the Writings) as one of the Writings. For though Christ spoke of Daniel's *function* as prophetic (Matt. 24:15), his *position* was that of a governmental official and inspired writer rather than ministering prophet (see Acts 2:29-30). See DANIEL #4.

The first half of the book (Dan. 1-6) consists of six narratives on the life of Daniel and his friends: their education (605-602 B.C.), Daniel's revelation of NEBUCHADNEZZAR's dream-image, the trial by fiery furnace, Daniel's prediction of Nebuchadnezzar's madness, his interpretation of the handwriting on the wall (539, the fall of Babylon), and his ordeal in the lions' den. The second half (chs. 7-12) consists of four apocalyptic visions predicting the course of world history.

The vision recorded in Dan. 7 envisions the rise of four beasts: a lion, bear, leopard, and monster with iron teeth explained as representing successive kings (kingdoms, 7:23). The description parallels that of Nebuchadnezzar's image, with its head, breast, trunk, and iron legs. The first empire must therefore be contemporary BABYLON (2:38). The fourth kingdom is regarded by most conservative scholars as ROME. Between them lie PERSIA and GREECE. The vision further describes the disintegration of Rome into a tenfold balance of power (2:42; 7:24; cf. Rev. 17:12, 16), the eventual rise of ANTICHRIST for an indefinite period of "times" (Dan. 7:8, 25), and his destruction when "one like a son of man" comes with the clouds of heaven (7:13). This figure is understood by most scholars as the MESSIAH because Christ applied this imagery to himself (Matt. 24:30). However, some understand it to symbolize the saints of the Most High (7:18, 22) epitomized in Jesus Christ, the "last Adam" (Mk. 14:62; 1 Cor. 15:45). Some scholars understand the KINGDOM OF GOD, represented by the rock (Dan. 2:34-35; cf. vv. 44-45), to be the CHURCH. Others see it as the eschatological kingdom (the millennium; see ESCHATOLOGY).

The section from Dan. 2:4b to 7:28 is composed in ARAMAIC, the international language of the day. But with ch. 8, Daniel resumes his use of HEBREW, probably because of the more Jewish orientation of the three remaining visions. The ram and the goat depict the coming victory of Greece (331 B.C.)

Overview of DANIEL

Author: Daniel, a member of the Hebrew nobility who was taken into EXILE and rose to prominence in the Babylonian administration. The narrative of the first six chapters refers to Daniel in the third person without explicit claim of authorship, but the visions in the second part of the book are related in the first person (e.g., "I, Daniel," Dan. 8:1).

Historical setting: The sixth century B.C. in BABYLON and SUSA, though many scholars reject this traditional view and date the book to the Maccabean period (second century B.C.).

Purpose: To encourage the believing community by stressing God's sovereignty over the oppressive nations of the world and his power to deliver those who trust him.

Contents: Six narratives on the life of Daniel and his friends (Dan. 1-6), followed by four apocalyptic visions predicting God's victory over evil (chs. 7-12).

Excavated mud-brick remains of Belshazzar's palace, where this king saw the writing on the wall.

over the amalgamated empire of Media and Persia (8:20-21) and the subsequent persecution of Judah by ANTIOCHUS IV (168-165; 8:9-14, 23-26).

The prophecy of the seventy "sevens" in Dan. 9:20-27 was given in response to Daniel's prayer concerning the end of JERUSALEM's desolations (9:16). The prophecy indicated that the suffering would cease at the end of seventy "sevens." Many scholars understand the designation "seven" to refer to a period of seven years. Sixty-nine "sevens" extend from the decree to rebuild Jerusalem (458 B.C.; cf. Ezra 7:18, 25) to Messiah. Those who do not hold to the future significance of the seventieth "seven" propose that the "cutting off" (9:26) of the Messiah is Christ's crucifixion in the midst of the seventieth "seven." Other scholars terminate the sixty-ninth "seven" with Christ's death and place the seventieth "seven" in the last days. It is in the seventieth "seven" that Antichrist will destroy Jerusalem according to this view. If the pointing of the Masoretic tradition is observed, the first seven "sevens" are separated from the sixty-two, and the seventieth "seven" witnesses either the devastations under Antiochus Epiphanes or the eschatological Antichrist.

The remaining chapters, after elaborating on the succession of Persian and Greek rulers through Antiochus (Dan. 10:1—11:39), move on to "the time of the end," foretelling Antichrist's tribulation (11:40—12:1), the resurrections of the saved and the lost (12:2; cf. Rev. 20:4-6, 12), and the final judgment (Dan. 12:2).

The authorship of the Book of Daniel is nowhere expressly defined but is indicated by the autobiographical, first-person composition from Dan. 7:2 onward. Unity of style and content (as admitted by several critical scholars), plus God's commitment of "the book" to Daniel (12:4), imply the latter's authorship, shortly after his last vision, 536 B.C. (10:1). Modern criticism, however, overwhelmingly denies the authenticity of Daniel as a product of the sixth century B.C. Indeed, as early as A.D. 275 the neo-Platonic philosopher Porphyry categorically repudiated the possibility of Daniel's miraculous predictions. Antisupernaturalism must bring the "prophecy" down to a time after the events described (especially after Antiochus's sacrilege of 168 B.C.); or, if the latest possible date has been reached, it must then reinterpret the predictions to apply to other events already accomplished. Consequently, since Daniel was extensively quoted (and misunderstood) as early as 140 B.C. (cf. *Sibylline Oracles* 3.381-400), rationalists have no alternative but to apply the supposed coming of the Messiah and the fulfillment of the seventy weeks to Maccabean times, rather than Christ's, even though this requires that the author has miscalculated the years involved.

The arguments for a late (Maccabean) date for the book of Daniel may be classed as historical, linguistic, and theological. A number of specific censures have been advanced against Daniel's historical authenticity. These may, however, be dismissed, either as arguments from silence or as answered by recent archaeology. More generally, it is asserted that Daniel conceived of a fictitious Median empire, existing as a separate kingdom between Babylon and Persia (thus allowing Daniel's fourth empire to be identified with Greece rather than Rome, as required by some critical presuppositions). But the very passage adduced (Dan. 5:31—6:1) speaks of unified Medo-Persia (6:8, 12; cf. 7:5; cf. 8:3, 29), while the third beast is described as four-headed, evidently the fourfold Greek empire (7:6; 8:8, 22). Again the fact that the apocryphal book of Ecclesiasticus, written about 180 B.C. (see APOCRYPHA), omits Daniel from its survey of Scripture, proves little other than the prejudice of its writer; for he likewise disregards the book of EZRA, whose high theology parallels that of Daniel. Fragments of Daniel, moreover, have been discovered among the DEAD SEA SCROLLS of Qumran, datable to the very second century B.C. in which the book's fraudulent composition is commonly said to have taken place.

Daniel has been questioned on linguistic grounds as well because it contains several terms of Persian or Greek origin. However, the Greek words are limited to the names of musical instruments, such as "harp" (Dan. 3:5). These words may have been imported to Babylon at an earlier time. Among the apocryphal literature from Qumran, there has been recovered a *Prayer of Nabonidus* that closely parallels Daniel's record of Nebuchadnezzar's madness (Dan. 4). Far, however, from proving Daniel to be a corruption of this third-century work, the Qumranic legend, though garbled, serves to suggest the essential historicity of Daniel's account. As to the so-called "late" Aramaic and Hebrew languages of Daniel, several specialists have concluded that there is nothing in the material that precludes a sixth-century B.C. authorship by Daniel.

Lastly, the theology of the book, with its APOCALYPTIC eschatology, biblicism, and developed angelology, are said to prohibit exilic origin. Yet Isaiah had composed an apocalypse, describing the RESURRECTION in terms similar to Daniel's, as early as 711 B.C. (Isa. 26:19; even those who deny the authenticity of this passage date it to the exilic period). When Daniel in 538 B.C. devoted himself to the inspired "Scriptures" (Dan. 9:2), the OT canon was complete, except for three minor prophets, the last two books of Psalms, and Chronicles-Esther (see CANONICITY). And Daniel's ANGELS, both in name and in function, stand naturally in the Hebraic religious development. His book was destined to inspire Jewish exiles with confidence in the Most High (4:34-37), and those of God's people today who will approach this book in faith believing will discover in it victorious supernaturalism that overcomes the world.

Danite. See DAN.

Dan Jaan. dan-jay´uhn (Heb. *dān yaʿan H1970*, meaning uncertain). A locality somewhere between GILEAD and SIDON (2 Sam. 24:6). According to the NIV, David's census takers "went to Gilead and the region of Tahtim Hodshi, and on to Dan Jaan and around toward Sidon." The NRSV emends the MT on the basis of the SEPTUAGINT and translates, "they came to Dan, and from Dan they went around to Sidon." Other emendations have been proposed.

Dannah. dan´uh (Heb. *dannâ H1972*, possibly "stronghold"). A town of the hill country of Judah, near SOCOH and DEBIR (Josh. 15:49). The exact location is unknown, but it must have been some 8-12 mi. (13-19 km.) SW of HEBRON.

Dara. dair´uh. See DARDA.

Darda. dahr´duh (Heb. *dardaʿ H1997*, derivation uncertain). One of the sons of MAHOL who were regarded as wise men (1 Ki. 4:31). The same group of names (plus Zimri) apparently occurs in 1 Chr. 2:6, although most Hebrew MSS here have "Dara" instead of "Darda." This latter text, however, purports to list the children of ZERAH son of JUDAH. The discrepancy is often explained by arguing that Zerah was a remote ancestor. Others believe that the phrase "sons of Mahol" in the Kings passage should be understood as "sons of dance" and thus as the designation of a musical guild serving in the temple. See also ETHAN.

daric. dair'ik. A Persian gold coin of great value (1 Chr. 29:7; Ezra 8:27; KJV, "dram"). See MONEY.

Darius. duh-ri'uhs (Heb. *doryāweš H2003* [Aram. *H10184*]). **(1)** A ruler described as "Darius the Mede" is mentioned only in the Bible (Dan. 5:31; 9:1). His identity is debated. He may have been the same as Gubaru, an officer in CYRUS's army who became governor of the Persian province of N BABYLON, but the evidence is rather more suited to the view that "Darius the Mede" was an alternative title for Cyrus the Persian himself.

(2) Darius I Hytaspes, also known as Darius the Great, was the fourth ruler of the Persian empire (521-486 B.C.) after Cyrus, Cambyses, and Gaumata. The background to his accession was as follows. Cambyses, the son of Cyrus, had continued the conquests started by his father. He did not, however, recognize the claims of the Jews (Jos. *Ant.* 11.1.2). In one of his campaigns he was defeated by the Egyptians, and on his way home he committed suicide. Taking advantage of the king's defeat, a pretender named Smerdis was made king by zealots of the Magian religious sect, and he ruled one year until killed by Darius and other princes, Darius having had himself made king. He was

© Dr. James C. Martin. The British Museum. Photographed by permission.

Clay tablet inscribed in Old Persian (Susa, 5th cent. B.C.) and recounting the achievements of Darius the Great (521-486).

of the same family line as Cyrus but not a direct descendant. Cyrus, according to tradition, had selected Darius to succeed him. Between the reign of Cyrus and that of Darius, the Jews had been mistreated, and work on rebuilding JERUSALEM had stopped (Ezra 4:1-6). An appeal was made to Darius who searched and discovered the original decree of Cyrus favoring the Jews. Under his lenient reign, they restored the walls of the city and rebuilt the temple (6:1-15). Darius was beset by rebellious subjects and spent much time in putting them down. He reorganized the government and extended its boundaries. He conducted many magnificent building enterprises and encouraged men of letters, especially the historians who extolled his prowess. The Greeks never yielded to him, however, and after some futile campaigns, his forces were overwhelmed in the battle at Marathon, 490 B.C. Darius planned another campaign against the Greeks, but rebellion in Egypt interfered, and death in 486 ended his career. He was succeeded by XERXES, a grandson of Cyrus the Great.

(3) Darius II Ochus, son of ARTAXERXES I by a Babylonian concubine, became the seventh ruler of the Persian empire (423-404 B.C.). The empire disintegrated at an accelerated pace under his administration, with revolts in Sardis, Media, Cyprus, Cadusia, and Egypt. In the latter case, the Jewish colony at ELEPHANTINE lost their temple (on an island in the Nile of Upper Egypt) and wrote desperate letters to Jerusalem and Samaria for help, all in vain. It was probably during the reign of Darius II that NEHEMIAH went to Jerusalem the second time and found that many abuses had arisen (Neh. 13:6-11; cf. 12:22), although some have argued that the ruler in view here is Darius III Codomannus (335-331 B.C.), the last king of the Persian empire, defeated by ALEXANDER THE GREAT.

darkness. This word first appears in Scripture as a description of the chaotic condition of the world before God created LIGHT (Gen. 1:2-3). The subsequent division between light and darkness resulted in "day" and "night." Darkness has a certain reality, being more than the absence of light (Isa. 45:7). Beyond its literal sense, the word is used metaphorically in association with various concepts: (1) mystery (Exod. 20:21; 2 Sam. 22:10; 1 Ki. 8:12;

Ps. 97:2; Isa. 8:22; Matt. 10:27); (2) ignorance, especially about God (Job 37:19; Prov. 2:13; Eccl. 2:14; Jn. 12:35; 1 Thess. 5:1-8); (3) the seat of evil (Prov. 4:19; Matt. 6:23; Lk. 11:34; 22:53; Jn. 8:12; Rom. 13:12; 1 Cor. 4:5; Eph. 5:11); (4) supernatural events (Gen. 15:12; Exod. 10:21; Matt. 27:45; Rev. 8:12; 16:10); (5) the Lord's return (Isa. 60:2; Joel 2:2; Amos 5:8; Matt. 24:29); (6) eternal punishment (Matt. 22:13; 2 Pet. 2:4, 17; Jude 6-7; cf. Job 2:1-5; 20:20); (7) spiritual blindness (Isa. 9:2; Jn. 1:5; Eph. 5:8; 1 Jn. 1:5; 2:8); (8) sorrow and distress (Isa. 8:22; 13:10; Ps. 23:4). Darkness, however, never holds sway where the Redeemer has come to shed his light (Col. 1:13).

Darkon. dahr´kon (Heb. *darqôn H2010*, meaning disputed). Ancestor of a group of "Solomon's servants" who returned from BABYLON with ZERUBBABEL and his associates (Ezra 2:56; Neh. 7:58).

dart. See ARMS AND ARMOR.

dates. See PLANTS (under *palm*).

Dathan. day´thuhn (Heb. *dātān H2018*, possibly "strong, warlike"). Son of Eliab and descendant of REUBEN. With his brother ABIRAM and another Reubenite, he joined the Levite KORAH in leading a rebellion of 250 chosen men against the leadership of MOSES and AARON (Num. 16:1, 12, 24-25, 27; 26:9). Moses specifically summoned Dathan and Abiram, but they refused to come. The next morning the glory of the Lord appeared to them all, the ground split apart, "and the earth opened its mouth and swallowed" the rebels and their families (16:31-32). Later Moses reminded Israel of this discipline of the Lord (Deut. 11:6; cf. also Ps. 106:17; Sir. 45:18; 4 Macc. 2:17).

daughter. In addition to the sense of "[direct] female offspring," the Hebrew term *bat H1426* can be used irrespective of age for a proximate circle of female relatives. See FAMILY. The word can also be applied to classes of females (e.g., "daughters [NIV, women] of Zion," Isa. 3:16 et al.), but this use is considerably less common than the construction "son/sons of," which can indicate a wide variety of relationships. See BEN (PREFIX AND IDIOM).

The word is compounded in some names: BATH RABBIM (daughter of a multitude), BATHSHEBA (daughter of an oath), BATH-SHUA (daughter of abundance?). There are also many figurative uses, such as "village" (Num. 21:25 et al.), "[beloved] offspring" in general (Isa. 22.4; Jer. 9:1), "city inhabitants" (Zech 9:9), and so forth.

David. day´vid (Heb. *dāwid H1858*, possibly related to *dôd H1856*, "beloved"). Son of JESSE of BETHLEHEM and second king of Israel (1 Sam. 16—1 Ki. 2:11; 1 Chr. 11-29). David ranks with MOSES as one of the most commanding figures in the OT. Born about 1040 B.C., he was the youngest son of Jesse of Bethlehem (1 Sam. 16:10-11), and developed in strength, courage, and attractiveness while caring for his father's sheep (16:12; 17:34-36). When God rejected SAUL, the prophet SAMUEL sought out David and secretly anointed him as Israel's next king; and God's Spirit came upon David from that time on (16:13). Saul, meanwhile, summoned David to periodic appearances at court to soothe his own troubled mind by skillful harp-playing (16:18; 17:15). While still in his teens, David gained national renown and the friendship of Saul's son JONATHAN (18:1-3; cf. 20:12-16; 23:16-17) through his faith-inspired victory over the taunting PHILISTINE champion GOLIATH (17:45-47). Saul's growing jealousy and four insidious attempts on David's life served only to increase the latter's popularity (cf. 18:13-16, 27). At length, urged on by David's rivals (cf. Ps. 59:12), Saul openly sought his destruction; and though frustrated by Samuel and the priests at NOB, he did succeed in driving David into exile (1 Sam. 19:11; 21:10).

David fled to the Philistine city of GATH, but his motives became suspect. Only by a stratagem and by the grace of God (1 Sam. 21:12; Ps. 56:3; 34:6-8) did he reach the wilderness cave of ADULLAM in Judah (Ps. 142:6). Here David was joined by a variety of people who were unhappy with conditions under Saul (1 Sam. 22:2), and also by the priest ABIATHAR, who had escaped Saul's retaliatory attack upon Nob (cf. Ps. 52:1). On three separate occasions Saul attempted to seize David: when fellow-Judeans from ZIPH betrayed his presence, after his deliverance of KEILAH (1 Sam. 23; Ps. 54:3); at the cave of EN GEDI by the Dead Sea where Saul was caught in his own trap (1 Sam. 24; Ps. 7:4; 57:6); and on David's return to Ziphite territory, when he again spared his pursuer's life (1 Sam. 26). Near the end of 1012 B.C., however (27:7), David in despair sought asylum in Gath, feigning vassalage (27:8—28:25).

Hearing of the death of Saul at Mount GIL-BOA in 1010 B.C. and the Philistine domination of Israel from BETH SHAN, David composed his moving lament of "The Bow" (2 Sam. 1:19-27). Shortly thereafter, David's forces advanced inland to HEBRON, where he was declared king over JUDAH. His appeal, however, to the northern and eastern tribes elicited no response (2:7); and for five years most of Israel lay under Philistine control.

In 1005 B.C. ABNER enthroned Saul's son ISH-BOSHETH, but in the conflict that followed David's arms gained ascendancy. Abner himself eventually transferred his support to David, only to be treacherously murdered by the vengeful commander JOAB (2 Sam. 3). Only after the death of Ish-Bosheth (ch. 4) did all Israel acclaim David king in 1003 (2 Sam. 5:1-5; 1 Chr. 11:10; 12:38).

Realizing that their "vassal" had gotten out of hand, the Philistines undertook an all-out attack on reunited Israel. David, however, after an initial retreat to Adullam (2 Sam. 5:17; 23:13-17), expelled the enemy in two divinely directed campaigns (5:18-25). He next established a new capital by capturing the JEBUSITE stronghold of JERUSALEM. This strategic site on the Benjamite border served not only as an incomparable fortress, but also as a neutral location between the rival tribes of N and S. David then constructed MILLO, a fortification that "filled up" Jerusalem's breached northern wall. Joab, for his bravery, was appointed commander (1 Chr. 11:6). Twelve corps of militia were organized under him, each with 24,000 men, on periods of one-month duty annually (ch. 27). David's military organization also included the professional KERETHITES and PELETHITES (Cretans and Philistines) and certain elite groups: "the six hundred" mighty men (2 Sam. 15:18; cf. 1 Sam. 27:2), "the thirty" heroes, and "the three" most distinguished (2 Sam. 23; 1 Chr. 11).

David also elevated Jerusalem into his religious capital by installing the ARK OF THE COVENANT in a tent on ZION (2 Sam. 6; cf. Ps. 24). He honored

© Dr. James C. Martin. The Israel Museum, Jerusalem. Photographed by permission.

The "House of David Inscription" discovered in 1994 at Tel Dan (basalt stela, 9th cent. B.C.). This unique monument, written in Aramaic, is part of a victory stela erected by an Aramean king (presumably Hazael) in which he, according to the usual interpretation of the text, claims to have killed Joram son of Ahab, king of Israel, and Ahaziah son of Jehoram, of the "House of David" (apparently the earliest extrabiblical occurrence of this expression).

it, both with a dedicatory psalm (1 Chr. 16, from Ps. 96; 105; 106) and with a permanent ministry of Levitical singers under ASAPH (1 Chr. 16:5, 37, 42; 25:1-31). Eventually David organized 38,000 Levites under hereditary leaders, appointing them as doorkeepers, treasurers, or even district judges (chs. 23-26). The Aaronic priests he divided into twenty-four rotating courses, which were continued into NT times (1 Chr. 24:10; Lk. 1:5).

From approximately 1002 to 995 B.C. David expanded his kingdom on all sides: W against the Philistines, taking Gath, one of its five ruling cities (2 Sam. 8:1); E against MOAB, (8:2); N against SYRIA, in two campaigns to the EUPHRATES River (10:13, 18; cf. 8:3); and S against stubborn EDOM (1 Ki. 11:15; Ps. 60:10). An alliance with HIRAM of TYRE enabled David to construct a palace in Jerusalem (2 Sam. 5:11). David's political organization shows analogies with Egypt's, his "cabinet" (8:15-18) including such officers as the recorder (public relations official), the scribe (secretary of state), and other later additions (20:23-26). Over all, however, whether tribal princes (1 Chr. 27:16-24) or royal officials (27:25-31), David reigned supreme.

Rest from war followed (2 Sam. 7:1; 22:1-51; Ps. 18), and David proposed a permanent TEMPLE for the Lord in Jerusalem. But while the prophet NATHAN denied David the privilege of building God's house (because of excessive bloodshed, 1 Chr. 22:8; 28:3), he revealed that God would build David's "house," raising up his son to construct the temple (2 Sam. 7:13a) and establishing his dynasty (7:13b). This "Davidic covenant" (Ps. 89:3; 132:12) mediates salvation for all (Isa. 55:3; Rev. 22:16), climaxing God's promises begun in Gen. 3:15 and accomplished in the new testament of Jesus Christ. God's Spirit then inspired David to compose messianic psalms, depicting the deity of the Lord's anointed Son (Ps. 2), his eternal priesthood (Ps. 110), his atoning death (Ps. 22), and his resurrection, ascension, and coming kingdom (Ps. 2; 16; 68). Some of David's greatest achievements lie in this literary sphere. Of the 150 canonical psalms, 73 possess titles asserting Davidic authorship. These references, moreover, appear in the oldest MSS and warrant full acceptance. David also composed some of the titleless psalms (cf. Ps. 2; 95; cf. Acts 4:25; Heb. 4:7) and stimulated Asaph and his associates to the inscripturation of others. One of the world's best-loved compositions is David's heart-affirmation, "The Lord is my shepherd" (Ps. 23).

Yet soon after this, David lapsed into a series of failures. He killed seven innocent descendants of Saul (but not MEPHIBOSHETH, 2 Sam. 21:7) to enforce a promise rashly made to pagan Gibeonites (contrast Num. 35:33). He committed adultery with BATHSHEBA and murdered her husband to conceal his crime (2 Sam. 10-11). When exposed by Nathan, he humbly confessed his sin (Ps. 32; 51); but the testimony of God's people had suffered compromise, and Nathan condemned the king to corresponding punishments (2 Sam. 12:10-14). David also became guilty of ineffective control over his sons. Thus in about 990 B.C. AMNON, following his father's shameful example, raped his sister TAMAR (13:1-14); and two years later ABSALOM avenged Tamar by murdering Amnon (13:23-29). Until about 983 (13:38; 14:28) David shunned Absalom's presence; and four years later (15:7 [KJV, "forty"]) Absalom revolted, driving his father from Jerusalem (cf. Ps. 3; 63) and specifically fulfilling

Nathan's curses (2 Sam. 16:20-22). Through fatal delay, Absalom was defeated and killed by Joab, though only the latter's stern rebuke could shake David from irresponsible grief over the death of his son (18:33-19:8). Even after David's restoration to Jerusalem, intertribal jealousies led SHEBA of Benjamin to prolong the disorder (ch. 20).

David's last years (975-970 B.C.) were occupied with Philistine wars (2 Sam. 21:15-22) and with a military census, motivated by David's pride in his armed forces (24:3, 9; Ps. 30:6). Plague resulted. But when the destroying angel halted at ARAUNAH's threshing floor on Mount MORIAH, just N of Jerusalem (2 Chr. 3:1), this area became marked as David's place of sacrifice and the very house of God (1 Chr. 22:1; Ps. 30 title). David subsequently undertook massive preparations for the temple (1 Chr. 22); he received in writing from God's Spirit the plans for its construction (28:12, 19); and he solemnly charged Solomon and the princes with their execution (chs. 22; 28; 29). As David became increasingly incapacitated by age, his oldest surviving son, ADONIJAH, attempted to usurp the throne from Solomon, the divinely designated heir. Nathan, however, aroused David to proclaim Solomon's coronation (1 Ki. 1). Thus in 970, after a final charge to his son (2:2-9), David died. His last words were a prophecy of the future Davidic MESSIAH and of his own salvation, springing from this COVENANT (2 Sam. 23:5).

David, City of. See CITY OF DAVID; JERUSALEM; ZION.

dawn. This English term, as a noun or a verb, can be used to render several words and expressions, especially Hebrew *šaḥar H8840* (e.g., Job 38:12; KJV, "dayspring"). Some believe this word refers to the AMORITE god Shahar. The light of dawn can be a symbol for truthfulness and discernment (Isa. 8:19-20). The Greek term *anatolē G424* ("rising"), rendered "dawn" by the NRSV in Lk. 1:78, is a figurative reference to the coming of MESSIAH.

day. A word often misinterpreted because of its various uses in the Bible. It often denotes the period of time from sunrise to sunset (Gen. 1:5; Ps. 74:16). At an early date it was divided into three parts—morning, noon, and evening (Ps. 55:17; Dan. 6:10). Probably due to Medo-Persian influence after the EXILE, it was divided into twelve hours (Jn. 11:9). Early morning was the first hour; the sixth hour was noon. Time could not be determined by clocks, so the length of an hour depended on the time of the year. The word also refers to time in general (Jdg. 18:30; Job 18:20; Obad. 12). It is also used figuratively, referring to the day of judgment (Isa. 2:12; Joel 1:15; Amos 5:18; Rom. 13:12), the length of life (Gen. 5:4), and the time of opportunity (Jn. 9:4).

Day of Atonement. See ATONEMENT, DAY OF.

Day of Christ. A phrase used by PAUL to indicate Jesus' eschatological intervention in human history (Phil. 1:6, 10). Sometimes it is called "the day of the [*or* our] Lord Jesus [Christ]" (1 Cor. 1:8; 2 Cor. 1:14) or simply "that day" (Matt. 7:22) or "the Day" (1 Cor. 3:13). See ESCHATOLOGY; DAY OF THE LORD.

day of the Lord. An eschatological term referring to the consummation of the KINGDOM OF GOD, the triumph over his foes, and the deliverance of his people. It begins at the second coming of Christ and will include the final judgment. It will remove class distinction (Isa. 2:12-21), abolish sins (2 Pet. 3:11-13), and will be accompanied by social calamities and physical cataclysms (Matt. 24; Lk. 21:7-33). It will include the millennial judgment (Rev. 4:1—19:6) and culminate in the new heaven and the new earth (Isa. 65:17; 66:22; Rev. 21:1; cf. also 1 Cor. 1:8; 5:5; 2 Cor. 1:14; Phil. 1:6, 10; 2:16; 1 Thess. 5:2; 2 Thess. 2:2). See ESCHATOLOGY.

day's journey, day's walk. The distance that a person can normally travel in one day. It would necessarily vary with the terrain and the method of travel—whether on foot, with an animal, with a caravan; also whether the journey was made in leisure or in haste. The Greek historian Herodotus in one place says that he reckons a day's journey at 25 mi. (40 km.), but in another at 18 mi. (29 km.; see *Histories* 4.101; 5.53). The Bible makes mention of a day's journey (Num. 11:31; 1 Ki. 19:4; Jon. 3:4; Lk. 2:44); of a three days' journey (Gen. 30:36;

Exod. 3:18; 5:3; 8:27; Num. 10:33; Jon 3:3); and of a seven days' journey (Gen. 31:23; 2 Ki. 3:9). It is said that LABAN and his relatives pursued JACOB from HARAN to GILEAD, a distance of 350 mi. (560 km.), in seven days, or an average of 50 mi. (80 km.) a day (Gen. 31:23), but they would have been riding camels.

daysman. This archaic term, referring to someone appointed to serve as arbiter (on a *day* fixed for trial), is used by the KJV in one passage where JOB expresses the longing for someone to mediate the conflict between God and himself (Job 9:33; NRSV, "umpire"; NIV, "someone to arbitrate"; cf. the use of the same Heb. term in Isa. 29:21 et al.). That longing of the human heart was fulfilled in the INCARNATION. See also MEDIATOR.

dayspring. See DAWN.

day star. See MORNING STAR.

deacon, deaconess. The Greek noun *diakonos* G1356 was a common term for "servant, assistant, messenger." It and its cognates are used with reference to table waiters (Lk. 22:26-27; Jn. 2:5, 9), royal servants (Matt. 22:13), service or ministry in general (Mk. 10:43-45 [Jesus]; Acts 1:17, 25 [apostles]; Rom. 11:13 [Paul]), and local Christian leaders, possibly an official title (Phil. 1:1; 1 Tim. 3:8, 12-13). In Rom. 13:4 the word is applied to secular rulers.

The diaconate as a CHURCH office is inferred from Acts 6:1-2, which says that some of the widows were not receiving the daily *diakonia* G1355 (NIV, "the daily distribution of food") and that the apostles believed it was not proper to set aside the preaching of the word of God in order to serve tables (verb *diakoneō* G1354). Thus seven men were chosen to meet the latter responsibility, though it should be noted that they are not specifically called "deacons" and that at least two of them, STEPHEN and PHILIP, also functioned as evangelists. At some point in the development of the church, however, deacons came to be recognized as church officers. Qualifications given in 1 Tim. 3 show that they were not considered ordinary lay members of the church. Paul's mention of deacons in connection with BISHOPS or "overseers" (Phil. 1:1) supports the view. The same Greek word is used of Phoebe in Rom. 16:1, but its meaning here is disputed: should it be understood in a general sense and rendered "servant" (KJV, NIV), or officially in the sense of "deacon" (TNIV, NRSV), or more specifically of a separate office, "deaconess" (RSV)? See discussion under PHOEBE.

dead. See DEATH; HADES; SHEOL; RESURRECTION.

Dead Sea. An intensely saline lake occupying the S end of the JORDAN Valley, called in Scripture the Salt Sea (Gen. 14:3; Num. 34:3, 12; Deut. 3:17; Josh. 3:16; 15:2, 5; 18:19), the Sea of the Arabah (Deut. 3:17; 4:49; Josh. 3:16; 2 Ki. 14:25), and "the eastern sea" (Ezek. 47:18; Joel 2:20). It has the earth's lowest surface, 1,290 ft. (393 m.) below sea level. Occupying a geologic fault that extends from SYRIA through the RED SEA into AFRICA, it is 47 mi. (75 km.) long and covers approximately 300 sq. mi. (780 sq. km.). Cliffs rise 1,500-2,500 ft. (460-760 m.) on either shore. North of the Lisan or "Tongue" peninsula, the water's depth attains 1,300 ft. (400 m.), though southward it averages less than 10 ft. (3 m.). The lake is slowly expanding, as the muddy Jordan extends its northern delta. Salt concentration reaches 25 percent, four times that of ocean water. Magnesium bromide prevents organic life; the climate is arid, and the heat extreme.

Though man's historical access to the Dead Sea has been slight, five streams S of the Lisan recommended this area to LOT as a "well-watered ... garden" (Gen. 13:10). Yet the text later explains that the plain, known as the Valley of SIDDIM, was the same as the Salt Sea (14:3), a fact suggested by the known growth of the lake (once crossable at the Lisan), by his mention of "tar pits" (14:10) now active on the Sea's floor (cf. JOSEPHUS's name for it, "Lake Asphaltites," *Ant.* 1.9.1), and by contemporaneous ruins discovered on the Lisan. God's destruction of SODOM may thus reflect the area's combustibleness (Gen. 19:24, 28); and Jebel Usdum, "mountain of Sodom," still identifies an extensive rock-salt formation opposite ZOAR (cf. Gen. 19:26; Lk. 17:32).

The Dead Sea constituted Israel's eastern border (Num. 34:12; Ezek. 47:18), although some of the tribes occupied parts of TRANSJORDAN. At EN GEDI, which terminates the principal descent from Judah, a spring provided refuge for DAVID (1 Sam. 24:1). The Valley of Salt, S of the Dead Sea, witnessed the victories of David and of AMAZIAH over EDOM (2 Ki. 14:7; 1 Chr. 18:12) and countermarches in the days of JEHOSHAPHAT (2 Ki. 3:8-9; 2 Chr. 20:1-2). On the E shore above the ARNON

Looking E across the Dead Sea towards the mountains of Moab (modern Kingdom of Jordan).

© Dr. James C. Martin

River, the springs of Callirrhoe served HEROD the Great during his final illness; and at MACHAERUS his son Herod Antipas imprisoned JOHN THE BAPTIST (Mk. 1:14; 6:17). On the W shore, above En Gedi, lies Khirbet Qumran, site of the community that preserved the DEAD SEA SCROLLS; and opposite Lisan rises Masada, Palestine's finest natural fortress, the refuge of Herod against Parthians in 42 B.C., and the last stand of Jerusalem's zealots in A.D. 70 (Jos. *War* 7.10.1). In modern times the Dead Sea has produced potash; but Ezekiel predicts a healing of its waters, granting abundant life in God's kingdom age (Ezek. 47:8-10).

Dead Sea Scrolls. The popular name given to a collection of manuscripts belonging originally to an ancient religious community living at a place now known as Khirbet Qumran, a short distance from the NW corner of the DEAD SEA (a copious spring of fresh water called ʿAin Feshkha is nearby). In the larger sense the designation Dead Sea Scrolls refers to all of the MSS found in numerous unrelated sites in the Judean desert in the area immediately surrounding the Dead Sea. The DSS were first discovered, probably in A.D. 1947, by a bedouin. They were seen by several scholars in the latter part of 1947, some of whom have admitted that they passed them up as forgeries. One of the scholars who recognized the antiquity of the scrolls was Eleazar L. Sukenik of the Hebrew University of Jerusalem, who was subsequently successful in purchasing some of them. Other scrolls were taken to the American School of Oriental Research in Jerusalem, where the acting director, John C. Trever, was convinced of their value and arranged to photograph the portions that were brought to him. One of his photographs was sent to William F. Albright, who promptly declared that this was "the most important discovery ever made in OT MSS."

The scrolls that were purchased by the Hebrew University included the *Hebrew University Isaiah Scroll* (1QIsaᵇ), also known as the Second Isaiah Scroll, a fragmentary MS; the *War of the Sons of Light against the Sons of Darkness* (1QM); and the *Thanksgiving Hymns*, or *Hodayot* (1QH). The scrolls purchased by the Syrian archbishop and published by the American Schools of Orien-

© Dr. James C. Martin. Collection of the Israel Museum, Jerusalem and courtesy of the Israel Antiquities Authority, exhibited at the Shrine of the Book the Israel Museum, Jerusalem.

Qumran Cave 1, where the first of the Dead Sea Scrolls were discovered.

tal Research included the *St. Mark's Isaiah Scroll* (1QIsaᵃ), better known as the First or Great Isaiah Scroll, which is complete; the *Habakkuk Commentary* (1QpHab) which contains the text of Hab. 1-2 with a running commentary; and the *Manual of Discipline* (1QS), which contains the rules for the members of the Qumran community. The DSS have subsequently come into the possession of the State of Israel; they have been published in numerous editions and translated into many languages, and are readily available for anyone who wishes to study them either in translation or in facsimile.

Following the discovery of these important scrolls, which are now all but unanimously accepted as having come from the last century B.C. and the first century A.D., the region from which they came was systematically explored. Numerous caves were found, and so far eleven caves have yielded materials from the same period as the original scrolls. Most of these materials have come from the fourth cave explored (known as cave 4 or 4Q); others of special significance come from caves 2, 5, 6, and 11.

Hundreds of MSS are represented by the fragments of cave 4 alone, about a hundred of which are biblical documents. These include fragments of every book of the Hebrew Bible except Esther. Some of the books, especially Deuteronomy, Isaiah, and Psalms, are represented in many copies. Numerous important biblical MSS have also been discovered in cave 11. In addition, fragments of deuterocanonical writings have been found, specifically Tobit and Ecclesiasticus, as well as fragments of several noncanonical writings (see APOCRYPHA; PSEUDEPIGRAPHA). Some of these latter were already known, such as *Jubilees*, *1 Enoch*, and the *Testament of Levi*; others were not previously known, such as the peculiarly Qumranian documents: the *Thanksgiving Hymns*, the *War of the Sons of Light against the Sons of Darkness*, and the commentaries on portions of Scripture. These last give us insights into the nature and beliefs of the community at Qumran.

Near the cliffs on an alluvial plateau overlooking the shore of the Dead Sea is the site of an ancient building complex often referred to as the "Monastery." This was thoroughly excavated over several seasons and has yielded important data about the nature, size, and date of the Qumran community. From coins found there, together with other remains, the community has been dated within the limits of 140 B.C. and A.D. 67. The members were almost all male, although the literature contains provisions for the admission of women and children. The number of people living there at any one time was in the neighborhood of 200 to 400 hundred. At nearby ʿAin Feshkha the remains of other buildings were found, the nature of which is not exactly clear. The fresh water of the spring probably was used for the growing of crops and other needs of the community.

From the sect's literature we know that the people of Qumran were Jews who had split off from the Jerusalem (or main) stream of Judaism, and indeed were quite critical of and even hostile toward the priests at Jerusalem. The fact that they used the name "The Sons of Zadok" has suggested to some scholars that they should be connected with the Zadokites or SADDUCEES; other scholars believe that they are rather to be identified with the ESSENES, a third sect of Judaism described by JOSEPHUS and PHILO. It is quite possible that elements of truth are to be found in both of these theories and that there was originally a split in the priestly or Sadducean line that first joined the movement known as the Hasidim, the forerunners of the PHARISEES, ultimately to split again and form a narrow separatist group, part of which located at Qumran. We must await further discoveries before

we attempt to give a final answer to this entire problem.

The community devoted itself to the study of the Bible. The life of the community was largely ascetic, and their practices included ritual bathing, sometimes referred to as baptism. This has been understood by some to be the origin of the baptism of John the Baptist. A study of John's baptism alongside that of the Qumranians shows, however, that the two practices were quite distinct: hence, even if John was associated with this community (an unproven theory), he must have developed important distinctions in his own doctrine and practice of baptism.

Some scholars believe that Zoroastrian elements from PERSIA are to be found in the Qumran writings, particularly with reference to dualism and angelology. The problem is extremely complex. Zoroastrian dualism developed greatly in post-Christian times, and therefore it is precarious to assume that the Zoroastrian beliefs as we know them represent the beliefs a century or two before the time of Christ.

The discoveries of Qumran are important for biblical studies in general. The matter of CANONICITY is not necessarily affected, since the community there was a schismatic group in the first place; and, moreover, the absence of Esther does not necessarily imply that they rejected this book from the canon. In the matter of the text of the OT, however, the DSS are of great importance. The text of the Greek OT (the SEPTUAGINT or LXX), as well

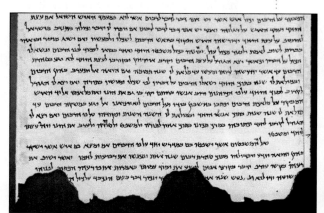

© Dr. James C. Martin. Collection of the Israel Museum, Jerusalem and courtesy of the Israel Antiquities Authority, exhibited at the Shrine of the Book the Israel Museum, Jerusalem.

The *Community Rule* (1QS) from Qumran is also referred to as the *Manual of Discipline*. Shown here is the sixth column (out of eleven).

D

as the quotations of the OT in the NT, indicate that there were other textual forms besides the one that has come down to us (the Masoretic Text or MT). The study of surviving documents suggests that at the time of the production of the DSS (i.e., about the time of the production of the Scriptures used by the NT authors) there were at least three textual forms in existence: one we might call the ancestor of the MT; the second was a text closely related to that used by the translators of the LXX; the third was a text differing from both of these other texts. The differences are usually minor, but for careful textual study of the OT it is important that we free ourselves from the notion that the MT is the only authentic text. As a matter of fact, the quotations of the OT found in the NT rather imply that it was not the MT that was most commonly in use by NT authors. These statements should be qualified by pointing out that the quality of the text varies from book to book in the OT, and that there is much more uniformity in the text of the PENTATEUCH than in some of the other portions of the Hebrew Bible. The DSS have particularly made great contributions to the study of the text of Samuel (see SAMUEL, BOOKS OF). See also TEXT AND VERSIONS (OT).

In relation to the NT, the DSS are likewise of importance. There are no NT texts among the DSS, obviously, since the earliest book of the NT were written only very shortly before the destruction of the Qumran community. Moreover, there was no reason why any of the NT writings should have reached Qumran. On the other hand, there are certain references and presuppositions found in the NT, particularly in the preaching of John the Baptist and Jesus Christ and in the writings of Paul and John, that are placed against a background now recognizably similar to that furnished by the documents from Qumran. Thus, for example, the fourth Gospel was formerly thought by many to be non-Palestinian in character, but now its alleged Greek Hellenistic features are attested in the DSS material.

A great deal has been written concerning the relationship of Jesus Christ to the Qumran community. There is no evidence in the Qumran documents that Jesus was a member of the sect, and nothing in the NT supports such a view. Rather, the outlook of Jesus with reference to the world and particularly toward his own people is diametrically opposite that of Qumran, and it can be safely asserted that he was not a member of that group at any time. He may have had some disciples who had come out of that background, particularly those who were formerly disciples of John the Baptist—though this is far from proven. The attempt to show that the Qumran Teacher of Righteousness was the pattern for the gospel portrayal of Jesus cannot be established on the basis of the DSS. The Teacher of Righteousness was a man with high ideals who apparently died young; there is, however, no clear statement that he was put to death, and certainly no indication that he was crucified or rose from the dead or that the Qumranians expected him to return. The difference between Jesus and the Teacher of Righteousness stands out clearly at several points: the Teacher of Righteousness was never referred to as the Son of God or God come in the flesh; his death was not sacrificial in its nature; the sacramental meal (if such it was indeed) was not viewed as a memorial of his death or a pledge of his return in any way connected with the forgiveness of sin. Obviously in the case of Jesus Christ, all of these things are clearly asserted, not once but repeatedly in the NT, and indeed form a necessary basis without which there is no Christian faith.

deafness. See DISEASES.

death. Both the OT and NT present death as an event belonging to our sinful existence, but also in relation to the living God as Creator and Redeemer. Death means the end of a human LIFE on earth—man is made from dust and to dust he returns (Gen. 3:19). To ponder this may cause a sense of separation from God (e.g., Ps. 6:5; 30:9; 88:5); but as death is faced the believer recognizes that total confidence should be placed in the Lord (Job 19:25-26; Ps. 73:23-24; 139:8). The hope of bodily RESURRECTION after death leading into life everlasting, which gradually emerges in the OT (Isa. 26:19; Dan. 12:2), is given prominence in the NT (esp. 1 Cor. 15).

In the NT, especially in PAUL's letters, there is teaching on the cause of death; but this is death understood theologically, not biologically—not merely the end of physical existence on earth, but also the absence of a spiritual communion with God. (This understanding of death is also found in the OT; cf. Deut. 30:15; Jer. 21:8; Ezek. 18:21-22, 31-32.) Paul declares that "the wages of sin is death" (Rom. 6:23) and "sin entered the world through one man, and death through sin" (5:12); thus he exclaims, "Who will rescue me from this body of death?" (7:24). In similar vein another writer declares that it is the devil who, in this age on this fallen earth, has power over death—until Christ takes it from him (Heb. 2:15). Thus it is not surprising that the death of Jesus for the sins of the world is greatly emphasized as is also his victory over death in bodily resurrection. As Representative and Substitute Man, Jesus tastes death for every human being so that those who believe in him and are united to him have passed from death (separation from God) into life (that triumphs over physical death). Thus the Christian can say, "Whether we live or die, we belong to the Lord" (Rom. 14:8).

The book of Revelation contains the expression "the second death" (Rev. 20:6, 14; 21:8); it is defined in symbolic terms as "the fiery lake of burning sulfur" (21:8) and is the opposite of "the crown of life" (2:10-11). It will be experienced by those whose names are not written in the Lamb's "book of life" (20:15) and means everlasting separation from God and his redeemed people.

Debir (person). dee'buhr (Heb. *dĕbîr H1809*, derivation uncertain). King of EGLON, identified as a member of the confederacy of five AMORITE rulers who opposed the town of GIBEON at the invitation of ADONI-ZEDEK, king of Jerusalem. The Gibeonites appealed to JOSHUA, and he and his army fought the Amorites in the Valley of AIJALON, where the sun stood still. The five kings fled to a cave in MAKKEDAH, but they were captured and executed (Josh. 10:1-28).

Debir (place). dee'buhr (Heb. *dĕbîr H1810*, possibly "back room [of a shrine]"). **(1)** The more frequently mentioned Debir was located in the hill country of the SHEPHELAH to the W of Jerusalem; now generally identified with modern Khirbet Rabud (8.5 mi./14 km. SSW of HEBRON). The town's original name was Kiriath Sepher ("city

of writing," Josh. 15:15), and possibly it was also known as Kiriath Sannah (v. 49, but this form may be a textual corruption). The history of the town is woven throughout the narrative of the conquest and settlement of Canaan. It is first mentioned as a Canaanite royal town whose inhabitants, the ANAKITES, were destroyed by JOSHUA (10:38; 11:21; 12:13). The particular force involved was that under the command of CALEB (15:15-17; Jdg. 1:11-15).

(2) A town or settlement near the Valley of ACHOR on the N boundary of the tribe of JUDAH (Josh. 15:7). Its precise location is unknown.

(3) A town in GILEAD located near the Jordan, within the territory of the tribe of GAD (Josh. 13:26). Its location is unknown. However, the Hebrew can be rendered "to the border of Lidbir" (so NJPS; cf. NRSV mg., "Lidebir"), and many scholars revocalize the name to read LO DEBAR (some believe that Lidbir or Lidebir is the original name of Lo Debar).

Deborah. deb'uh-ruh (Heb. *dĕbôrāh H1806*, "honey-bee"). **(1)** The nurse of REBEKAH, wife of ISAAC; she was buried under an oak at BETHEL, and the place was then named ALLON BACUTH, "The Oak of Weeping" (Gen. 35:8; cf. 24:59).

(2) The fourth and greatest (with GIDEON) of Israel's judges, identified as a prophetess and as wife of LAPPIDOTH (Jdg. 4-5). She resided near the border of Benjamin and Ephraim, probably belonging to the latter tribe, and administered justice "under the Palm of Deborah" (4:5). Like most Hebrew "judges," however, Deborah served primarily as a divinely appointed deliverer and executive leader of Israel.

After the death of the previous judge, EHUD, God's people had lapsed into apostasy, resulting in their subjection to the Canaanite king, JABIN II of HAZOR. Jabin's commander, SISERA, "had nine hundred iron chariots and had cruelly oppressed the Israelites for twenty years" (Jdg. 4:2-3). This period coincides with the unrest that followed the HITTITE collapse and the death of Egypt's RAMSES II, the treaties between which had preserved order in Palestine for eighty years (cf. 3:30). Ramses's successor, however, was the elderly Merneptah. Despite his claim to have pacified both Canaanites and Israelites, disorder became rampant: "The

D

roads were abandoned ... and not a shield or spear was seen ... in Israel" (5:6-8).

Then arose Deborah, "a mother in Israel" (Jdg. 5:7). Summoning BARAK of Naphtali, she prophesied that an offensive from Mount TABOR at the NE limit of ESDRAELON would lure Sisera and Jabin's army to annihilation on the plains below (4:6-7). Barak agreed, provided Deborah's inspiring presence should accompany the troops, though Deborah predicted Sisera's death by a woman (4:8-9). Barak and Deborah then scouted Esdraelon around KEDESH; they mustered ten thousand men of Naphtali and Zebulun; and, together with princes of Issachar (5:15), they occupied Tabor (4:12). Deborah also summoned Dan and Asher in the N (cut off by Hazor) and Reuben and Gad in TRANSJORDAN, who failed to respond (5:16-17). But Benjamin, Ephraim, and Makir (Manasseh) answered the call (5:14), probably massing at BETH HAGGAN at the SE edge of Esdraelon. Deborah thus accomplished Israel's first united action since the conquest, 175 years before.

Sisera, meanwhile, advanced from HAROSHETH HAGGOYIM in W Esdraelon, forded the Wadi KISHON southward to marshal the Canaanite kings from JOKNEAM, MEGIDDO, and TAANACH (Jdg. 5:19), and pressed inland along its southern bank. But God fought against Sisera (5:20). A providential storm (cf. 5:4), which turned the plain into a morass, rendered Sisera's chariotry unmaneuverable, and they were cut to pieces by Israel's charging foot soldiers. The routed Canaanites, cornered at the Kishon ford, were then swept away by a flash flood (5:21). Sisera fled alone and was killed by the woman JAEL at Kedesh (4:11, 17-22). Jabin was destroyed (4:24), and the land rested forty years (5:31), corresponding to the reign of Ramses III, the last great Pharaoh of Egypt's 20th dynasty. After the battle, Deborah and Barak sang a song of victory (5:2-31; cf. v. 7), the contemporaneous authenticity of which is universally recognized from its archaic language, vivid descriptions, and ringing faith (5:31).

Yet Deborah's record has occasioned manifold criticism against Scripture. (a) Confusion is alleged between Josh. 11 and Jdg. 4-5 as two garbled accounts of one actual battle against Jabin; Joshua's opponent, however, may have been a predecessor of Jabin, or "Jabin" may have been a hereditary title in Hazor. (b) Contradictions are discovered between the prose and the poem, such as fewer tribes fighting in ch. 4 and Sisera being killed in his sleep; but the poetry intentionally singles out the tribes, and Sisera's sleeping in 5:26 is apparently understood (sinking and falling in 5:27 simply describes his subsequent death agonies). (c) Regarding the prose, some surmise that an account of King Jabin in Kedesh of Naphtali and an account of King Sisera in Esdraelon were combined into one; yet the Kedesh of 4:9-11 fits Esdraelon, not Naphtali, and Scripture never designates Sisera "king," only "captain" of Jabin. (d) Morally, the charge that the scriptural account of Jael is "reprehensible ... [and] cannot be justified" is made by one modern commentary. But while we question this Gentile's treacherous methods, Deborah's insight into her fearless and unsolicited devotion to God's people renders her "most blessed of women" (Jdg. 5:24).

debt. Under the Mosaic law Jews were not allowed to exact INTEREST (usury) from other Jews (Exod. 22:25). Special laws protected the poor against usurers (22:25-27; Deut. 24:12-13). After the EXILE cruel practices arose in collecting debts (2 Ki. 4:1-7; Isa. 50:1). A debtor had to make good his obligation, so land that was pledged (mortgaged) could be seized, but had to be restored during the Year of JUBILEE (Lev. 25:28). A house so pledged could be sold, or held in perpetuity if not redeemed during a year, unless it was an unwalled town (25:29-30). In NT times the Mosaic code was often disregarded. We read of bankers, moneychangers, interest, usury (Matt. 25:16-27; Jn. 2:13-17). Debtors were often thrown into prison (Matt. 18:21-26). Jesus taught compassion toward those in debt (18:23-35). The prayer of Jesus, "forgive us our debts" (6:12), implies guilt from unpaid moral obligations to God.

Decalogue. See COMMANDMENTS, TEN.

Decapolis. di-kap′uh-lis (Gk. *Dekapolis G1279*, from *deka G1274*, "ten," and *polis G4484*, "city"). In NT times, a large area mostly E of the JORDAN constituted by ten prominent Hellenistic towns. This region had been allotted by MOSES to the

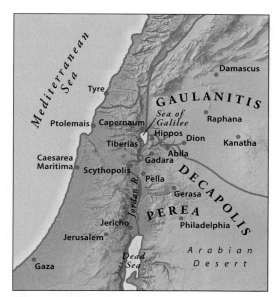

The Decapolis.

Jesus drove the demons into swine near GADARA, one of these cities (Mk. 5:1-20), and became popular in the Decapolis (Matt. 4:24-25; Mk. 7:31-37).

deceit, deception. See LIE, LYING.

decision, valley of. This phrase, which occurs in only one verse (Joel 3:14), apparently refers to the Valley of Jehoshaphat (vv. 2, 12). See JEHOSHAPHAT, VALLEY OF.

decree. This English term can be used to translate a variety of Hebrew words, some referring to God's statutes (Exod. 15:25 and frequently; see LAW), and others referring to an official edict or decision issued by a king (e.g., Esth. 9:32; similarly Gk. *dogma G1504*, Lk. 2:1 et al.). The term is also used in the theological sense of God's sovereign plans and decisions, as when JOB says, "He carries out his decree against me, / and many such plans he still has in store" (Job 23:14; cf. also Ps. 2:7; 105:10; see ELECTION; PROVIDENCE).

Dedan. dee′duhn (Heb. *dĕdān H1847*, derivation unknown; gentilic *dĕdānî H1848*, "Dedanite"). **(1)** Son of RAAMAH and descendant of HAM through CUSH; his brother was SHEBA (Gen. 10:7; 1 Chr. 1:9).

(2) Son of JOKSHAN and grandson of ABRAHAM by KETURAH; his brother also is called Sheba (Gen. 25:3; 1 Chr. 1:32). The Asshurites, the Letushites, and the Leummites are said to have descended from him. Whether there is a connection between this Dedan and #1 above is uncertain, but many scholars posit a merging of ethnic traditions. See also #3 below.

(3) As a geographical and ethnic term, Dedan is mentioned several times in the prophets. The Dedanites (prob. viewed as descendants of #2 above) are said to lodge in the thickets of ARABIA and are referred to

tribe of MANASSEH (Num. 32:33-42), but during the intertestamental period it was occupied by Greeks who had come in the wake of ALEXANDER THE GREAT's conquests. After the Romans took control of the area (65 B.C.), a league of ten cities was constituted, though later the number was increased, eventually reaching eighteen. They had their own coinage, courts, and army. Ruins of temples, theaters, and other buildings tell of the high degree of culture that developed in these cities.

© Dr. James C. Martin

The uplifted hill of the Decapolis city of Hippos located on the eastern side of the Sea of Galilee. (View to the W.)

as being in caravans (Isa. 21:13; KJV, "Dedanim"). Dedan is mentioned in company with TEMA and BUZ as the object of God's wrath (Jer. 25:23). In the context of a prophecy against EDOM, the people of Dedan are warned of God's punishment to befall them (49:8). In a similar context, God's judgment against Edom includes all the territory from TEMAN to Dedan (Ezek. 25:13). Finally, Dedan is mentioned with Sheba in a prophecy concerning GOG (38:13-14). Extrabiblical sources of antiquity indicate that Dedan also was an oasis on the trade routes of the peoples of Sheba, Tema, and Buz. It is probably to be identified with some ruins just N of modern al-ʿUla (c. 50 mi./80 km. SW of Tema in Central Arabia).

Dedanim. See DEDAN #3.

dedication. The act of setting apart or devoting to God for holy ends. The relevant Hebrew words are often used of the consecration of persons, but usually of the setting apart of things for God's use. Consecration of the TABERNACLE (Num. 7) was an elaborate ceremony, as was that of the TEMPLE (1 Ki. 8). Among various dedicated things were the city wall (Neh. 12:27), private dwellings (Deut. 20:5), the temple treasure (1 Chr. 28:12), children (Exod. 13:2), people (Exod. 19:4; 1 Sam. 16:5), and booty of war (2 Sam. 8:10-11). See also HOLINESS; NAZIRITE; SANCTIFICATION.

Dedication, Feast of. This phrase occurs once in the NT (Jn. 10:22). It refers to the Feast of Hanukkah, celebrated annually by the Jews for eight days to commemorate the cleansing of the TEMPLE in Jerusalem after it had been desecrated by the Syrians under ANTIOCHUS Epiphanes (1 Macc. 4:52-59; 2 Macc. 10:5). The restoration of the worship of God was effected by Judas MACCABEE about 165 B.C., three years after its defilement. The feast came on the twenty-fifth of Kislev (mid-December). Josephus designated it "The Feast of Lights"; it is also known as "The Feast of the Maccabees" and "The Feast of Illumination." The festival was characterized by the illumination of synagogues and homes. It was a time of joy and merriment, and no public mourning was permitted on this feast. Jewish tradition claims that Judas Maccabee found a cruse of oil that was sufficient for a day but lasted for eight. The feast is still celebrated among the Jews today. The system of lighting is one light for the first day, and an additional one for each succeeding day of the festival. The family solemnly gathers around the father as he lights the candles with a prayer of thanksgiving to God for the liberation of his people from the persecution of the oppressor. Presents and money gifts are distributed to the children.

deep, the. As an adjective, the English term *deep* can be used to translate a number of words. The chief biblical usage, however, is as a noun, referring to a lake or sea. Of particular importance is Hebrew *tĕhôm H9333*, thought by some to be used mythologically of the waters of a nether world in Gen. 1:2. This view sees a parallel to Tiamat of the Babylonian creation story—the demon of chaos from whose split body MARDUK made the earth and sky. The Hebrew term cannot be considered a direct borrowing; it is far better to assume that the old Semitic root *thm* indicated "ocean," of which the Babylonian demon Tiamat was a personification. It should be noted that *tĕhôm* is not used elsewhere in the OT of mythical subterranean waters. It is used repeatedly of the RED SEA through which Israel passed (Exod. 15:5, 8; Ps. 77:16; Isa. 51:10; Hab. 3:10). It is used also many times of the Mediterranean or the deep ocean in general (Gen. 7:11; Ps. 107:26; Jon. 2:5). The biblical cosmology does not picture any subterranean watery chaos; such terms as "the water under the earth" (Deut. 4:18 NRSV) refer only to waters below shore line, as the mention of fish in them clearly shows. The SEPTUAGINT regularly renders the Hebrew word with Greek *abyssos G12* (lit., "bottomless"), which thus about thirty times means merely the ocean and lakes. However, as the seas were the deepest things known to the ancients, the word gained a figurative sense and is used seven times in the book of Revelation of the bottomless PIT, the abode of evil spirits. See ABYSS; HADES; SHEOL.

deer. See ANIMALS.

defile. There are a number of Hebrew and Greek words that in general mean "to profane, pollute, render unclean." In the OT defilement was physical

(Cant. 5:3), sexual (Lev. 18:20), ethical (Isa. 59:3; Ezek. 37:23), ceremonial (Lev. 11:24; 17:15), and religious (Num. 35:33; Jer. 3:1). In the NT ceremonial defilement recedes into the background, so that emphasis falls on ethical or religious matters (Mk. 7:19; Acts 10:15; Rom. 14:20). In OT times God's purpose in issuing laws regarding ceremonial defilement was clearly an educative one—to impress the Israelites with his HOLINESS and the necessity of their living separate and holy lives. See UNCLEAN.

degree. This English term occurs frequently in the KJV in the older sense of "step" (2 Ki. 20:9-11). See also ASCENTS, SONG OF.

Dehavite. di-hay′vit. According to the KJV and other versions, the Dehavites were a people group listed among those who were transferred to SAMARIA by the Assyrians (Ezra 4:9). Because no satisfactory identification has been made, most scholars interpret the text differently, so that instead of the KJV's rendering, "the Susanchites, the Dehavites, and the Elamites," the NRSV translates, "the people of Susa, that is, the Elamites" (cf. NRSV; similarly NIV, "the Elamites of Susa").

Dekar. See BEN-DEKER.

Delaiah. di-lay′yuh (Heb. *dĕlāyâ H1933*, "Yahweh draws up"). **(1)** Son of Elioenai and a descendant of DAVID through SOLOMON (1 Chr. 3:24).

(2) A priest during the time of David who was the leader of the twenty-third division (1 Chr. 24:18).

(3) Son of Shemaiah; he was one of the officials in the court of JEHOIAKIM who heard BARUCH read JEREMIAH's scroll and urged the king not to burn the inspired prophecy (Jer. 36:12, 25).

(4) Ancestor of a family that returned from the EXILE but could not prove that they were Israelites (Ezra 2:60; Neh. 7:62).

(5) Son of Mehetabel and father of Shemaiah; the latter was an opponent of Nehemiah (Neh. 6:10; see SHEMAIAH #19). Some believe this Delaiah is the same as #4 above.

Delilah. di-li′luh (Heb. *dĕlîlâ H1935*, meaning disputed). A woman of pagan extraction mentioned as the temptress of the judge SAMSON (Jdg. 16:4-20). The woman was presumably a PHILISTINE. She seems to be pictured in the story as a courtesan who was hired by her countrymen to lure Samson into compromising his personal strength and his position as judge in Israel.

deliverance. See REDEMPTION; SALVATION.

deluge. See FLOOD, THE.

Demas. dee′muhs (Gk. *Dēmas G1318*; possibly a shortened form of DEMETRIUS). A companion of PAUL first mentioned in the greetings sent from Rome to COLOSSE (Col. 4:14; Phlm. 24), but later marked for his desertion of Paul in his last imprisonment (2 Tim. 4:10). Paul speaks volumes in the few words applied to Demas: he "hath forsaken me, having loved this present world" (KJV). Nothing more is known about him.

Demetrius. di-mee′tree-uhs (Gk. *Dēmētrios G1320*, "belonging to [the god] Demeter"). **(1)** The name of several SELEUCID rulers, including Demetrius I Soter, who ruled from 164 B.C. until his death c. 150 (1 Macc. 7:1—10:52; Jos. *Ant.* 12.10.1-4 et al.). His son, Demetrius II Nicator, assumed power c. 145 but lost it five years later, then ruled again 129-125 (1 Macc. 10:67—15:22; Jos. *Ant.* 13.4.3 et al.); it was this king who in the year 142 confirmed Simon MACCABEE as high priest, thereby acknowledging Jewish independence.

(2) A jeweler in EPHESUS who raised a mob against PAUL because the apostle's preaching had resulted in damage to the lucrative business of making silver shrines of the goddess ARTEMIS (Acts 19:23-27). The name of one Demetrius, a warden of the Ephesian temple, has been found by modern explorers, but the suggestion that he was the same person as the one mentioned in Acts has not been widely accepted.

(3) A disciple whom JOHN THE APOSTLE praised in his letter to GAIUS (3 Jn. 12); it has been suggested that he was the bearer of the letter.

demon. This English word is derived from the Greek *daimōn G1230*, which was used of rather anonymous influences whether of a good or bad variety. When the concept of a supernatural spirit or intelligence subsequently developed in Greek circles, the word gradually acquired a malign connotation and was used as a general designation of malevolent powers; these were commonly assigned individuality and characteristic functions. In the NT, this Greek word (which occurs only once, Matt. 8:31) and its cognate, *daimonion* G1228 (7:22 and very frequently), always have a negative connotation and are roughly synonymous with "evil spirit" (cf. Matt. 17:18 with Mk. 9:25).

The immaterial and incorporeal nature of both SATAN and his demon hosts is graphically set forth by the apostle PAUL when he describes the believer's intense conflict as being "not against flesh and blood" but against "rulers," "authorities," "powers of this dark world," and "spiritual forces of evil in the heavenly realms" (Eph. 6:12; cf. 2:2). JOHN THE APOSTLE likewise stresses their incorporeality in his reference to "spirits of demons" (Rev. 16:14); the construction is probably a genitive of apposition that defines the general term "spirits," thus "demon-spirits" (cf. NRSV, "demonic spirits").

As purely spiritual beings or personalities, demons operate above the laws of the natural realm and are invisible. The Bible presents them as such, and thus they are free from the magical rites and exorcistic rigmarole that contaminate ethnic and rabbinic demonology. The Word of God, however, does recognize the miracle whereby natural law may be temporarily transcended and residents of the spirit world glimpsed (2 Ki. 2:11; 6:17). On this principle John in apocalyptic vision *saw* the awful last-day eruption of locust-demons from the abyss (Rev. 9:1-12), as well as the three hideous frog-like spirits that emanate from the satanic trinity (the dragon, the beast, and the false prophet) in the tribulation to muster the world's armies to their predestined doom at ARMAGEDDON (16:13-16).

As spirit personalities, demons have an intellectual nature through which they possess superhuman knowledge. Scripture features their shrewdness: they know Jesus (Mk. 1:24), bow to him (5:6), describe him as "the Son of the Most High God" (5:7), entreat him (Lk. 8:31), obey him (Matt. 8:16), corrupt sound doctrine (1 Tim. 4:1-5), conceal the truth of Christ's incarnate deity and sole saviorhood (1 Jn. 4:1-3), and comprehend prophecy

Bronze sculpture of an Assyrian demon (c. 1000 B.C.).

© Dr. James C. Martin

and their inevitable doom (Matt. 8:29). Because of their superhuman knowledge, demons are consulted by spiritistic mediums, who allow themselves to get under the control of evil spirits for oracular purposes (1 Sam. 28:1-25; Acts 16:16), as is seen in both ancient and modern spiritism, erroneously called "spiritualism."

In their moral nature all demons (as fallen ANGELS) are evil and depraved, in distinction to the good spirits (the unfallen angels), who are sinless. The moral depravity of demons is everywhere evidenced in Scripture by the harmful effects they produce in their victims, deranging them mentally, morally, physically, and spiritually, and by the frequent epithet of "unclean" (NIV, "evil") which often describes them (Matt. 10:1; Mk. 1:27; Lk. 4:36; Acts 8:7; Rev. 16:13). Fleshly uncleanness and base sensual gratification are the result of demon control of the human personality (Lk. 8:27). Demons figure in the moral collapse of a people who yield to gross carnality and sexual sin (2 Tim. 3:1-9; Rev. 9:21-22).

In addition to their superhuman intelligence and moral depravity, demons possess terrible physical strength, imparting it to the human body (Lk. 8:29) and binding their victims as with chains and with physical defects and deformities (Lk. 13:11-17) such as blindness (Matt. 12:22), insanity (8:26-36), dumbness (9:32-33), and suicidal mania (Mk. 9:22).

Demons under the leadership of Satan seek to oppose God's purposes and to hinder human welfare. So intimately bound up are they with their prince leader that their work and his are identified rather than differentiated. Thus the earthly life of our Lord is said to have consisted in going about "doing good and healing all who were under the power of the devil" (Acts 10:38). Certainly much of this so-called oppression by the devil was the work of the demons, as a cursory examination of the gospel records will show.

Demons are of two classes: those who are free, with the earth and the air as their abode (Eph. 2:2; 6:11-12; Col. 1:13), and those who are imprisoned in the ABYSS (Lk. 8:31; Rev. 9:1-11; 20:1-3). The abyss is only the temporary prison house of evil spirits, which must surrender its doleful inhabitants to GEHENNA or the "lake of fire" (Matt. 25:41), the eternal abode of Satan, demons, and unsaved human beings.

den, lions'. The dwelling place of lions (see ANIMALS) is mentioned in various biblical passages (Job 38:39-40; Ps. 104:21-22; Cant. 4:8; Amos 3:4; Nah. 2:11-12). Especially well known is Dan. 6:7-24, where the Aramaic word refers to a trenched out "pit." The Babylonians and Assyrians kept lions captured in the marshlands as beasts for hunting and as pets; they are shown in the magnificent reliefs of several Neo-Assyrian rulers. The punishment described in Dan. 6 has not survived in visual representation, but the condemnation to a "trial by ordeal" has many precedents in Mesopotamian-Iranian law. When DANIEL was spared, his accusers were condemned to the same fate (6:24).

denarius. See MONEY.

deny. This term can be used in both negative contexts (such as PETER's denial or disowning of Jesus, Matt. 26:34, 70, et al.) and positive ones (we should deny ourselves, that is, set aside our self-interests, Matt. 16:24 et al.). Especially important are those passages that warn believers against denying the faith (e.g., 1 Tim. 5:8). See APOSTASY.

deposit. Since there were no banks or security houses in the ancient world, it would not be uncommon for an individual, when going on a journey, to deposit valuables with a friend or neighbor. Specific laws are spelled out in Exod. 22:7-13 and Lev. 6:1-7 concerning the protection of deposits. See PLEDGE. In the NT, the term *deposit* is sometimes used as the rendering of Greek *parathēkē G4146*, "property entrusted to another," used with reference to the GOSPEL, which has been given over to the apostles and disciples for their care, so that they might proclaim it faithfully (1 Tim. 6:20; 2 Tim. 1:12, 14). In addition, the NIV uses the phrase "a deposit, guaranteeing [what is to come]" to render Greek *arrabōn G775* (2 Cor. 1:22; 5:5; Eph. 1:14). See EARNEST.

depravity. See SIN.

deputy. One appointed to rule under a higher authority, as a regent in place of a king (e.g., 1 Ki. 22:47). The KJV uses this term also in passages where the reference is to a Roman PROCONSUL (Acts 13:7 et al.).

Derbe. duhr'bee (Gk. *Derbē G1292*). A city in the SE corner of LYCAONIA in ASIA MINOR, a region that was part of the Roman province of GALATIA. PAUL visited it on the first journey after being stoned at LYSTRA (Acts 14:20), also on his second tour (16:1), and probably on the third. A certain GAIUS, who accompanied Paul to JERUSALEM, was from this city (20:4). Derbe was approximately 65 mi. (105 km.) SE of ICONIUM.

descent into hell. The familiar Apostles' Creed affirmation that Jesus descended into HELL or HADES is based chiefly on two references by PETER (1 Pet. 3:19; 4:6), supported by implications to be taken from two other NT verses (Acts 2:27;

Rom. 10:7). The term is said to be in harmony also with the language of PAUL when he speaks of Christ's descending "into the lower parts of the earth" (Eph. 4:9 KJV), but many scholars argue that this phrase refers to the earth itself as lower than heaven (cf. NIV, "to the lower, earthly regions"). Even in the case of Peter's statements, the meaning is hotly debated by scholars. As a result, some argue that the descent into Hades is merely another way of emphasizing the depth of Christ's humiliation and his total identification with the sufferings of sinners in death. Others believe that the statement is misleading and thus exclude it in their liturgical use of the creed.

desert. This term, like *wilderness* and *wasteland*, refers to a barren, desolate area. Deserts are mentioned in numerous contexts throughout the Bible. In most places it is a mild desert receiving some RAIN during the winter season of the year. Rain falls at intervals from November to April, causing flooding at certain places because of the treeless soil, while the other six months it is extremely dry because of the *khamsin* or desert winds. Because of the lack of good natural harbors along the Palestinian coast, the desert has had a far greater influence on the life and culture of Palestine than has the SEA. There was continuous hostility between the inhabitants of the desert and those of the more fertile areas. The lure of the planted crops was more than

a hungry bedouin tribe could withstand. In other periods of time when peace was negotiated, active trade took place over the desert routes, bringing many goods from the S and E to Palestine.

Several words in the Bible are rendered "desert" or "wilderness." The most common and inclusive term in the OT is *midbār H4497*, "uninhabited land." It includes not only the barren deserts of sand and rock, but also the steppe lands that can be classified as semidesert. These would be used for the grazing of sheep and goats at certain periods of the year. The words *ṣiyyâ H7480* (e.g., Isa. 41:18; NIV, "parched ground") and *yĕšîmôn H3810* (e.g., Ps. 78:40; NIV, "wasteland") tend to be a little more narrow in meaning, referring to very dry and waterless areas. Two additional words sometimes rendered "desert" or "wilderness" are better treated as proper names: ARABAH (the barren plain located in the southern part of the Jordan valley) and NEGEV (the great southern desert tucked between the Sinai peninsula to the W and the Arabah to the E). In the NT, the standard term is Greek *erēmos G2245*, "desolate [area]." This term is used not so much to designate a dry region, but more in the sense of a solitary place. It occurs, for example, with reference to the area around BETHSAIDA on the eastern shore of the Sea of Galilee (Mk. 6:31-32), even though there was "plenty of grass in that place" (Jn. 6:10).

The desert is presented both in a positive and in a negative way in its relationship to Israel. At the beginning of the nation's history, the desert was where God showed his power and his love for Israel (Jer. 2-3; Hos. 13:5). DEBORAH sings praise to the God of SINAI and the desert (Jdg. 5:4-5), and likewise HABAKKUK as he speaks about God's deliverance of Israel (Hab. 3:2-7). The wilderness, however, also is seen as a place of sin. The golden calf scene took place in the desert (Exod. 32:23; see CALF WORSHIP). KORAH's rebellion took place there (Num. 16-17). At SHITTIM many of the Israelites identi-

© Dr. James C. Martin

Aerial view of the Desert of Paran. (View to the NE.)

fied with BAAL PEOR (Num. 25) and suffered the judgment of God.

desert creature. See ANIMALS.

desire. See COVETOUSNESS; LUST; PLANTS (under *caper*).

desire of all nations, the. This phrase is found only in Hag. 2:7, where the KJV reads, "And I will shake all nations, and the desire [NIV, desired; NRSV, treasure] of all nations shall come." The prophet predicts glory for ZERUBBABEL's temple greater in the future than in the present. The verse is often taken as a messianic prediction (cf. Zech. 3:8; 9:9; note also that Hag. 2:6 is quoted in Heb. 12:26-27). It seems from the context that the prophet was looking to the distant future, and elsewhere he apparently refers to Zerubbabel symbolically as the MESSIAH (Hag. 2:22-23; cf. Zech. 6:12). Some believe that Hag. 2:7 refers not to the arrival of the Messiah, but to the coming of the leaders of the Gentiles to join in worship in the messianic age.

desolation. See ABOMINATION OF DESOLATION.

destiny. Though this word is seldom used in English Bible versions (NIV Eccl. 9:2-3 et al.), the idea, divested of pagan implications, is frequent in the Bible. God sees the end from the beginning. He has appointed a destiny for the Christian, for the unbeliever, for Israel, and for other nations. See ELECTION; PROVIDENCE. As a proper name, the term Destiny refers to a pagan god, MENI, which is mentioned once along with GAD, "Fortune" (Isa. 65:11 [the KJV mistranslates this verse]). Pagan ideas of fate or destiny vary. In Greek mythology and in some popular forms of Islam, the hour of death is determined, and perhaps the place also, but the ordinary course of life is left to chance. The STOICS, more consistently, insisted that every event was determined. Sometimes fate is supposed to be a blind, purposeless force, rather than providence, foresight, and wise planning.

destroyer, the. In Exod. 12:23 (cf. Heb. 11:28), this term occurs in connection with the tenth plague of Egypt, the destruction of the Egyptian firstborn. Evidently the reference is to a superhuman being, used as an instrument of God's WRATH in the execution of his judgment. It is difficult to say whether this is a good ANGEL used by God as an agent of destruction, or SATAN or one of his minions. If a good angel, God could use it to bring both blessing and destruction. In 1 Cor. 10:10, PAUL warned against grumbling, as some Israelites did in the wilderness and thus "were destroyed by the destroyer" (KJV). The term "the destroyer" occurs elsewhere in a somewhat different sense (e.g., Isa. 16:4; 54:16; Jer. 6:26; 48:8, 32). With different terminology, some passages refer to the concept of an angelic destroyer. For example, the Lord sent an angel to smite the people by means of a plague because DAVID had made a census of the nation (2 Sam. 24:16). In HEZEKIAH's time in a single night an angel destroyed 185,000 men in the Assyrian camp (2 Ki. 19:35). The prophet EZEKIEL saw in a vision a number of angels executing judgment upon Jerusalem and Judah (Ezek. 9:5-7).

Destruction, City of. See CITY OF DESTRUCTION.

Deuel. doo´uhl (Heb. *děʿûʾēl H1979*, possibly "known of God"). Father of ELIASAPH; the latter was a Gadite leader (Num. 1:14, 24-25; 2:14 [MT, "Reuel"]; 7:42, 47). In all these passages the SEPTUAGINT reads *Ragouēl*, which some scholars believe reflects the correct spelling. See REUEL #2.

Deuterocanonical Books. See APOCRYPHA.

Deuteronomy. doo´tuh-ron´uh-mee. The fifth book of the Bible and traditionally one of the five books of MOSES (see PENTATEUCH). In sight of the Canaan he would not be allowed to enter, Moses gathered the hosts of Israel about him for his farewell addresses. These, set within the historical framework of several brief narrative passages, constitute the book of Deuteronomy. Since the occasion of the renewal of the COVENANT made earlier at SINAI, the appropriate documentary pattern for covenant ratification supplied the pattern for Moses' speeches and thus for the book.

The English, though not totally inappropriate, is based on the SEPTUAGINT's mistranslation of the phrase "a copy of this law" (Deut. 17:18) as *to deuteronomion touto*, "this second law," or "this repetition of the law." In Hebrew literature the book (like the other books of the Pentateuch) is known from its opening words, "These are the words," or simply, "Words" (Heb. *dĕbārîm*, pl. of *dābār H1821*). This title is well suited because it focuses attention on a clue to the peculiar literary character of the book; the treaties imposed by ancient imperial lords on their vassals began with such an expression. Deuteronomy is the text of "words" of a suzerainty covenant made by the Lord of heaven through the mediatorship of Moses with the servant people Israel beyond the Jordan.

The claims of Deuteronomy concerning its own authorship are plain. It consists almost entirely of the farewell speeches of Moses addressed to the new generation that had grown to adulthood in the wilderness. The speeches are dated in the last month of the forty years of wandering (Deut. 1:3), and it is stated that Moses wrote as well as spoke them (31:9, 24; cf. 31:22). Modern conservative scholars, therefore, join older Jewish and Christian tradition in maintaining the Mosaic authorship of Deuteronomy as well as of the first four books of the Pentateuch. Almost all such scholars, however, recognize that the account of Moses' death (Deut. 34) is exceptional and must have been recorded by some other writer; some would attribute to a compiler (perhaps the unknown author of Deut. 34)

much of the narrative framework of Deuteronomy. Whether or not the biblical testimony allows the latter latitude, even that variety of the conservative position stands in clear opposition to modern negative theories of the origin of Deuteronomy.

According to the Development Hypothesis, popular among nineteenth-century negative critics, Deuteronomy was a product of the seventh century B.C. and provided the program for the reform of JOSIAH (cf. 2 Ki. 22:3—23:25), allegedly introducing the concept of a centralized place of worship into Israelite religion at that late date. But unless a wholesale critical rewriting of the historical sources is undertaken, it is obvious that the concept of the central altar was normative during the entire life of Israel in Canaan. Moreover, it is equally apparent that, taken at face value, the covenant stipulations in Deuteronomy are directed to a unified young nation about to enter a program of conquest, not to a diminishing remnant of the divided kingdom. Indeed, many of those stipulations would be completely incongruous in a document produced in the seventh century. That dating, though still dominant, is being increasingly challenged even from the side of negative criticism. While some have suggested a postexilic origin, more have favored a date before Josiah's reign. There is a growing tendency to trace the sources of the deuteronomic legislation back to the early monarchy—if not earlier. The view that these traditions were preserved at a northern cult center, being shaped according to ritual patterns, is widespread. Some would detach Deuteronomy from the Pentateuch and treat the books of Deuteronomy, Joshua, Judges, Samuel, and Kings as a unit representing the historical-theological perspective of a distinctive school of thought, the "deuteronomic."

The unity, antiquity, and authenticity of Deuteronomy are evidenced by the conformity of its total structure to the pattern of ANE suzerainty treaties dating from the second millennium B.C. The

View from the summit of Jebel Musa looking SE up to the peaks of Jebel Katerina (St. Catherine's), the tallest mountain in Sinai.

© Dr. James C. Martin

Overview of DEUTERONOMY

Author: Although technically anonymous, most of the book consists of discourses attributed directly to Moses, who is regarded by tradition as the author of the PENTATEUCH.

Historical setting: The end of the wilderness wanderings, as a new generation of Israelites are camped E of the JORDAN ready to take possession of the Promised Land (c. 1400 or 1250 B.C., depending on the date of the EXODUS; those who reject Mosaic authorship usually date the book to the time of King JOSIAH, late in the seventh century B.C.).

Purpose: To exhort the people to renew their COVENANT with God, avoiding the sins of the previous generation, and thus becoming spiritually prepared to conquer the land before them.

Contents: Historical review of God's dealings with the Israelites (Deut. 1-4); extended exposition of the Ten Commandments and other laws (chs. 5-26); renewal of the covenant by affirming the curses and blessings (chs. 27-30); Moses' last words and death (chs. 31-34).

D

classic covenantal pattern consisted of the following sections: preamble, historical prologue, stipulations, curses and blessings, invocation of oath deities, directions for deposit of duplicate treaty documents in sanctuaries and periodic proclamation of the treaty to the vassal people.

This substantially is the outline of Deuteronomy:

I. Preamble: Covenant Mediator (Deut. 1:1-5).
II. Historical Prologue: Covenant History (1:6—4:49).
III. Stipulations: Covenant Life (chs. 5-26).
IV. Curses and Blessings: Covenant Ratification (chs. 27-30).
V. Succession Arrangements: Covenant Continuity (chs. 31-34).

In Deut. 1:1-5 the speaker is identified as Moses, as the Lord's representative. The second section (1:6—4:49 is a rehearsal of God's past covenantal dealings with Israel from Horeb to Moab and serves to awaken reverence and gratitude as motives for renewed consecration. With 5:26 it is made clear that when covenants were renewed the former obligations were repeated and brought up to

date. Thus chs. 5-11 review the Decalogue with its primary obligation of fidelity to Yahweh, while chs. 12-26 in considerable measure renew the stipulations of the Book of the Covenant (Exod. 21-33) and other Sinaitic legislation, adapting where necessary to the new conditions awaiting Israel in Canaan. In Deut. 27-30 directions are first given for the future and final act in this covenant renewal to be conducted by JOSHUA in Canaan (ch. 27). Moses then pronounces the blessings and curses as reasons for Israel's immediate ratification of the covenant, but also as a prophecy of Israel's future down to its ultimate exile and restoration (chs. 28-30). In ch. 31-34 preparations are made for the continuity of leadership through the succession of Joshua and for the continuing confrontation of Israel with the way of the covenant by periodic reading of the covenant document, which was to be deposited in the sanctuary, and by a prophetic song of covenant witness (chs. 31-32). The book ends with the final blessings and the death of Moses (chs. 33-34).

The similarity between the style of Deuteronomy and that of contemporary international suzerainty treaties is well worth noting. Also important is the overall oratorical nature of the book. The style is similar throughout, a fluent prose (chs. 32-33 are poetry) marked by majestic periods, warm eloquence, and the earnest exhortation of the preacher, calling the people to choose whom they would follow. Deuteronomy is the Bible's full-scale exposition of the covenant concept and demonstrates that, far from being a contract between two parties, God's covenant with his people is a proclamation of his sovereignty and an instrument for binding his elect to himself in a commitment of absolute allegiance.

Israel is confronted with the demands of God's governmental omnipotence, redemptive grace, and consuming jealousy. They are to show their consecration to the Lord by obeying his mandate to establish his kingdom in his land. That involves conquering the land, by which divine judgment would be visited on those who worship alien gods in God's land, and also establishing a community of brotherly love in common service to the Lord within the Promised Land. This covenant calling was not an unconditional license to national privilege and prosperity. By the covenant oath Israel came under both the curses and the blessings that were to be meted out according to God's righteous judgment. The covenant relation called for responsible decision: "This day I call heaven and earth as witnesses against you that I have set before you life and death, blessings and curses. Now choose life, so that you and your children may live and that you may love the LORD your God. ... For the LORD is your life" (Deut. 30:19-20).

devil. In the plural, this word is used by the KJV several times in the OT (Lev. 17:7 et al.) and frequently in the NT (Matt. 4:24 et al.). For these uses, see DEMON. Otherwise, the term occurs only in the NT, and only in the singular, as the rendering of Greek *diabolos* G1333, which means "slanderer" (the pl. of this Gk. word is used a few times to describe slanderous people). The devil is depicted as one inciting to evil (Matt. 4:1; 13:39; Jn. 13:2; et al.). Those under his control could be called children of the devil (1 Jn. 3:10; cf. Jn. 6:70; 8:44), and he is said to hold the power of death (Heb. 2:14). Though ruler of the world, he was defeated by the death of Christ and his resurrection (cf. Matt. 25:41; Rev. 2:10; 12:9; et al.). For discussion see SATAN.

devoted thing. The Hebrew verb *ḥāram* H3049 and its cognate noun *ḥērem* H3051, which are used of dedicating something or someone to the deity either for sacred use or for utter destruction, occur about eighty times in the OT. The verb is usually translated "utterly destroy" or the like. The translation "devote" or "devoted," though less common, is more expressive of the meaning of the root. The overwhelming usage refers to the destruction of the enemy in the total wars commanded in the conquest of CANAAN, in the campaign against the AMALEKITES, and in similar situations. The enemy was put "under the ban," as it is sometimes expressed. An example is the city of JERICHO, which was thus devoted. All was to be destroyed except metals that could be purified by fire, for the Lord's treasury. Thus ACHAN in violating the ban actually stole from God.

There is another usage observable. Some passages (Lev. 27:21, 28, 29; Num. 18:14; Ezek. 44:29) refer to offerings dedicated to holy use, which are given to the priests. Leviticus 27:21 specifies that such a field shall be the priests' in perpetuity and shall not revert to the owner in the Year of JUBILEE. We read that every devoted thing "is most holy to the LORD" (27:28). Devoted men are mentioned in the same context (27:29) as certainly condemned to death. This does not refer to those persons consecrated to the Lord by a vow and serving as slaves in the temple (these are mentioned in vv. 1-8). Nor does it refer to the firstlings of men who were redeemed when God chose the tribe of LEVI as an equivalent (Num. 3:12). There is no vestige of early human sacrifice. Rather the devoted men who must be killed as directed in Lev. 27:29 are captives from the holy wars. These captives theoretically belonged to God. Yet such foreign captives could not serve in the holy precincts. Like AGAG and the Amalekites, they must be put under the ban (1 Sam. 15:3-33). See also ACCURSED; EXCOMMUNICATION.

dew. The moisture condensed from the air that forms in drops during a still, cloudless night on the earth or any warm surface. In Syria and most of Palestine these conditions are fulfilled through the cloudless summer and early autumn, and the dew is a great blessing to the fruits of the land. The word (Heb. *ṭal* H3228) occurs thirty-five times, almost always with pleasant connotation. Dew is often used in Scripture as a symbol of BLESSING (Gen. 27:28; Mic. 5:7) and of refreshment (Deut. 32:2; Job 29:19; Ps. 133:3; Isa. 18:4).

diadem. This English term (from Gk. *diadēma G1343*, cf. NRSV Rev. 12:3 et al.), which usually refers to a CROWN as a symbol of royalty, is seldom found in Bible versions. The NIV uses it three times to translate Hebrew words that designate a headband or turban. See DRESS.

dial. Properly, a graduated arc intended to mark the time of day by the shadow of a style or shaft falling on it. In modern times the style is generally (and properly) parallel to the axis of the earth. The term is used by the KJV and other versions to render the plural of Hebrew *ma'ălāh H5092* ("ascent, step") in 2 Ki. 20:11 (also in the parallel passage, Isa. 38:8, where the text is a little different and difficult). According to this narrative, HEZEKIAH was given a sign to prove the authenticity of ISAIAH's prophecy that God would heal the king of his disease: "And Isaiah the prophet cried unto the LORD: and he brought the shadow ten degrees [*ma'ălôt*] backward, by which it had gone down in the dial [*ma'ălôt* again] of Ahaz" (so KJV; the NRSV, similarly, "and he brought the shadow back the ten intervals, by which the sun had declined on the dial of Ahaz"). The NIV translates more literally, "and the LORD made the shadow go back the ten steps it had gone down on the stairway of Ahaz," but even in this rendering it is apparent that the stairs in question functioned as a kind of sundial. One possibility is that "the device consisted of two sets of steps each facing a wall whose shadow fell upon the steps. As the sun rose, the eastern steps would be in the wall's shadow, which, as the day advanced, would grow shorter. On the other hand, during the afternoon, the steps facing west would more and more be in the shadow" (E. J. Young, *The Book of Isaiah*, 3 vols., NICOT [1965-72], 2:515n.). The miracle recorded in connection with the dial can be compared with

Joshua's "long day" (Josh. 10:12-14) and is equally inexplicable on natural grounds.

diamond. See MINERALS.

Diana. See ARTEMIS.

Diaspora. See DISPERSION.

Diblah. dib′luh (Heb. *diblâ H1812*, possibly "lump, cake [of pressed figs]"). KJV Diblath. An unknown city mentioned in a prophetic oracle of judgment (Ezek. 6:14). Because in the Hebrew alphabet the consonants *d* and *r* can be easily confused (see DALETH), many scholars emend the text to read RIBLAH (cf. NRSV).

Diblaim. dib′lay-im (Heb. *diblayim H1813*, apparently dual form of *dĕbēlâ H1811*, "lump, cake [of pressed figs]"). The father of GOMER, the unfaithful wife of the prophet HOSEA (Hos. 1:3). According to some, Diblaim was her hometown. A few scholars interpret the name allegorically (e.g., a reference to her cheap price as a prostitute or to the raisin cakes used in the worship of BAAL).

Diblath. See DIBLAH.

Dibon. di′bon (Heb. *dîbôn H1897*, derivation uncertain). **(1)** A Judean town toward the S, inhabited in the time of NEHEMIAH by members of the tribe of JUDAH (Neh. 11:25), which seems to be the same as DIMONAH (Josh. 15:22).

Excavations at this tell near modern Dibhan reveal the ruins of ancient Dibon.

© Dr. James C. Martin

(2) A city in MOAB, E of the DEAD SEA and N of the ARNON River, to which reference is first made in the OT in describing Israel's victory over SIHON of the Amorites (Num. 21:30). Dibon, together with the whole area, was given to the tribes of GAD and REUBEN (Num. 32:3, 34; Josh. 13:9), and although Dibon was built (i.e., rebuilt) by Gad (Num. 32:34) and, therefore, was sometimes called Dibon Gad (33:45-46), it was part of the territory of Reuben (Josh. 13:17). It was later taken by MOAB under King MESHA, who rebelled against Israel after the death of AHAB in 906 B.C. (2 Ki. 1:1; 3:4-5). According to 2 Ki. 3, Israel badly defeated Mesha at the ensuing battle, but Mesha set up a stele at Dibon (the famous MOABITE STONE) boasting of his defeat of Ahab.

Dibon Gad. See DIBON #2.

Dibri. dib′ri (Heb. *dibrî H1828*, possibly "talkative"). A man of the tribe of DAN whose daughter Shelomith married an Egyptian (Lev. 24:11). Shelomith's son blasphemed "the Name" (of God) and was stoned (vv. 10-23).

Didache. did′uh-kee (Gk. *Didachē G1439*, "teaching"). A writing of the early church, usually included among the APOSTOLIC FATHERS.

didrachma. See MONEY.

Didymus. did′uh-muhs (Gk. *Didymos G1441*, "twin"). This designation, another name for the apostle THOMAS, appears only in the Gospel of John (Jn. 11:16; 20:24; 21:2).

Diklah. dik′luh (Heb. *diqlâ H1989*, "date palm"). Son of JOKTAN and descendant of SHEM through EBER (Gen. 10:27; 1 Chr. 1:21). The names of Joktan's thirteen sons appear to refer to S Arabian tribes, but the places associated with them (Gen. 10:30) are difficult to identify.

Dilean. dil′ee-uhn (Heb. *dilʿān H1939*, possibly "protrusion"). A town in the Judean SHEPHELAH (Josh. 15:38). It was in the same district as LACHISH, but its precise location is not known.

dill. See PLANTS.

Dimnah. dim′nuh (Heb. *dimnâ H1962*, derivation uncertain). A town within the tribal territory of ZEBULUN, assigned to the Levites descended from MERARI (Josh. 21:35). No such place is otherwise attested, and many believe it is a scribal error for "Rimmon" or "Rimmonah" (cf. 19:13; 1 Chr. 6:77 ["Rimmono"]). See RIMMON (PLACE) #2.

Dimon. di′muhn (Heb. *dimôn H1904*, derivation unknown). A city of MOAB, mentioned only in an oracle of ISAIAH (Isa. 15:9). Because there is no other reference to such a city in Moab, many scholars follow a text from the DEAD SEA SCROLLS (1QIsaᵃ) and the Vulgate in reading DIBON (cf. NRSV), assuming either a textual corruption or a deliberate scribal play on the Hebrew word for "blood" (*dām H1947*). Dibon, however, was mentioned earlier (v. 2), and no other place is mentioned twice in the passage).

Dimonah. di-moh′nuh (Heb. *dimônâ H1905*, derivation unknown). A city of the NEGEV, near the Edomite border, belonging to the tribe of JUDAH (Josh. 15:22). It is generally thought to be the same place as the DIBON of Judah occupied by the Jews in the period of the return from EXILE under NEHEMIAH (Neh. 11:25). The exact site is not known, but some identify it with modern Khirbet edh-Dheiba, about 2 mi. (3 km.) NE of ARAD.

Dinah. di′nuh (Heb. *dînâ H1909*, possibly "justice" or "[female] judge"). The daughter of JACOB and LEAH (Gen. 30:21; 34:1-31; 46:15). During an inspection of the land and a visit with the pagan women, Dinah was criminally assaulted by SHECHEM, son of the ruler HAMOR, stated to be a HIVITE. Subsequently the brothers of the victim agreed to a marriage proposal from Shechem but insisted that the Hivite males submit to the rite of CIRCUMCISION. After the rite had been performed but while the wounds were sore and debilitating, two of Dinah's brothers, SIMEON and LEVI, took their weapons, slew all the males, and despoiled the whole village. For this act of wanton revenge the brothers Simeon and Levi were cursed in Jacob's final blessing (49:5-7). Many interpreters, both

Jewish and Christian, have suggested that Dinah was careless in her behavior or even that she was at fault in this incident, but the biblical narrative passes no judgment on her.

Dinaite. di´nay-it. According to the KJV, the Dinaites were an ethnic group that, with others, complained to the Persian monarch ARTAXERXES against the Jewish rebuilding of the TEMPLE (Ezra 4:9, following the MT). Most scholars revocalize the Aramaic word and translate it "judges."

Dinhabah. din´huh-buh (Heb. *dinhābâ H1973*, derivation disputed). The capital city of BELA, who was king of EDOM in the period before the Israelite monarchy (Gen. 36:32; 1 Chr. 1:43). Its location is unknown.

Dionysius the Areopagite. di´uh-nish´ee-uhs air´ee-op´uh-git (Gk. *Dionysios ho Areopagitēs G1477* ["of Dionysus"] + *G741* ["of the Areopagus"]). A convert of PAUL in ATHENS who was apparently a member of the council of the AREOPAGUS (Acts 17:34). He is one of a number of prominent men who are mentioned by LUKE as converts (13:12; 19:31; 26:32; 28:7). Little else is known about him except by traditions that cannot be verified, such as the claim that he was the first bishop of Athens. According to one account, Dionysius was martyred in that city under Emperor Domitian. Another indicates that he went to ROME and was then sent to Paris by Clemens I, where he was beheaded on the martyr's mount (Montmartre). He is often identified with St. Dennis, the patron of France.

Dioscuri. See CASTOR AND POLLUX.

Diotrephes. di-ot´ruh-feez (Gk. *Diotrephēs G1485*, "nourished by Zeus"). The lone biblical reference to this churchman is 3 Jn. 9, where he is reprimanded for his failure to receive the representatives sent by the author, JOHN THE APOSTLE. Evidently he had opposed a former letter from John, had maligned the apostle, and had refused to grant hospitality to the brethren, urging that all others of the congregation do likewise (v. 10). John characterizes him as someone "who loves to be first." Diotrephes probably held an office in the church

and abused his authority. In any case, he clearly tried to exercise dominance over the congregation.

Diphath. See RIPHATH.

direction. See EAST; NORTH; SOUTH; WEST.

disabilities. See DISEASES.

discerning of spirits. The ability that the HOLY SPIRIT gives to some Christians to discern between those who spoke by the Spirit of God and those who were moved by false spirits. The phrase occurs in 1 Cor. 12:10 (KJV) as one of the GIFTS of the Spirit. The NIV renders "distinguishing between spirits."

discharge. See DISEASE.

disciple, discipleship. The Greek word for "disciple," *mathētēs G3412*, occurs over 250 times in the NT. The term implies the acceptance in mind and life of the views and practices of the teacher. The Gospels refer to the disciples of JOHN THE BAPTIST (Matt. 9:14), of the PHARISEES (22:16), and of MOSES (Jn. 9:28), but the term is almost always applied to the adherents of Jesus. Although sometimes it refers to the twelve APOSTLES specifically (e.g., Matt. 10:1; 11:1), more often Christians in general are in view (Acts 6:1-2, 7; 9:36). Followers of Jesus were not called "Christians" until the founding of the church at ANTIOCH (11:26).

Jesus' teachings covered many topics, but the whole of it was summarized in one commandment, LOVE (Jn. 13:34); and although discipleship had many facets it was summed up in a single concept—obedience to this command (13:35). Many heard Jesus speak, but because his teaching was radical, and at times too difficult to accept (6:60), the majority of disciples defected (6:66). Consequently, much of what he taught about such topics as his death and resurrection (Matt. 16:21), the end of the age (Mk. 13), love, the Father, and the Holy Spirit (Jn. 14-16), was given only to the inner circle (6:68).

discipline. See CHASTISEMENT.

diseases. The diseases mentioned in Scripture appear largely to have been entities that are well known, and as a whole identical with those that now exist, especially in semitropical climates like that of Palestine. Instead of naming the disease involved, however, the Bible often simply mentions symptoms (e.g., fever, itch, sore).

I. Diseases with primary manifestations in skin. The hygienic measures outlined in Leviticus agree with modern concepts of communicable disease control, especially regarding the availability of running water and the isolation of the patient. Two kinds of skin disease are recognized in Leviticus: (1) those classified as ṣāraʿat H7669 (called "leprosy" in the KJV), which were believed to require isolation, and (2) those not requiring isolation. Leviticus 13 gives clear diagnostic distinctions and procedural guides based on the developmental characteristics of the various diseases. Some Orthodox Jews believe that human ṣāraʿat diseases include leprosy, syphilis, smallpox, boils, scabies, fungus infections (e.g., favus, tinea, actinomycosis), all of which are known to be potentially contagious, but also some that are doubtfully contagious, such as pemphigus, dermatitis herpetiformis, and skin cancer. In addition, the Hebrew term is applied to certain mold and fungus growths in houses and on cloth, conditions assuming importance from the standpoint of human allergy, often with manifestations in the form of asthma.

A. Diseases requiring isolation

1. Leprosy ("Hansen's disease"), as defined today, is the name for disease processes caused by the microorganism *Mycobacterium leprae*. It is evident that the Hebrew word ṣāraʿat includes a variety of skin diseases, and most scholars now believe

Leprosy colony near Bethany in 1905.

that it does not cover true leprosy. Hansen's disease occurs in two types: (a) The lepromatous type begins with brownish-red spots on the face, ears, forearms, thighs, and/or buttocks that later become thickened nodules and, losing their skin covering, become ulcers ("sores") with subsequent loss of tissue and then contraction and deformity. (b) The tuberculoid type is characterized by numbness of an affected area of skin and deformity such as fingers like claws resulting from paralysis and consequent muscle wasting (atrophy). Leviticus 13 and other passages dealing with skin disease make no reference to the deformity associated with true leprosy.

2. Syphilis is regarded by some Orthodox Jews as probably the disease called the "boils of Egypt" in Deut. 28:27 (KJV, "botch of Egypt"). It is a disease that from time to time throughout the ages has burst forth in virulent form with high mortality (cf. Num. 25:9). It is chiefly spread by sexual intercourse and is often associated with gonorrhea (cf. the "bodily discharge" in Lev. 22:4). Starting with a hard ulcer on the private parts, after some weeks raised spots (papular eruption) appear on the torso and extremities (almost never on the face), with no itching. Years later, syphilis of the vital organs such as heart, liver, or brain may become evident, often with fatal outcome. Some have thought that this late type of syphilis is in view in Prov. 7:22-23: "... he followed her [the harlot] like an ox going to the slaughter / ... till an arrow pierces his liver, like a bird darting into a snare, / little knowing it will cost him his life." Syphilis may be present also from birth and give rise to abnormalities such as those listed in Lev. 21:18-20.

3. Smallpox, uncontrolled, is a serious scourge of mankind, though over the last quarter of a century there has been a remarkable decrease of incidence. It consists of red spots that turn rapidly into blisterlike pustules over the entire body, including the face. A. R. Short (*The Bible and Modern Medicine* [1953]) suggested that Job's "sores" (Job. 2:7) were actually smallpox. The Hebrew word here (šĕḥin H8825), usually translated "boil," may indicate several types of diseased skin, today referred to as (a) papule (a raised red spot), (b) vesicle (a small blister containing yellow fluid; called "blain" in KJV), (c) pustule (a small blister containing pus), (d) boil (a deep, broad inflammation about

© Courtesy of Preserving Bible Times, Inc.

a hair root resulting in death of the tissues in its center, with pus formation about this core, the pus discharging through an external opening), (e) carbuncle (a large boil with multiple openings), and (f) malignant pustule (anthrax).

4. Hezekiah's "boil" (2 Ki. 20:7) which was almost fatal, may well have been a true boil or carbuncle. Another suggestion is that it was anthrax. The local application of a poultice of figs has been recognized therapy for gumboils in comparatively recent times. Its use by Hezekiah at the command of God's prophet has often been cited as divine approval of the utilization of medicinal means of therapy.

5. Festering boils are recorded among the plagues of Egypt (Exod. 9:9). This disease has provoked much speculation and two alternative explanations. (a) Since both man and beast were infected with virtually the same disease, it may have been smallpox in humans and cowpox in cattle, the germ of cowpox being originally utilized for vaccination against smallpox. (b) The "terrible" fifth plague (9:3) was anthrax of animals, later transmitted to man as malignant pustule (anthrax). Untreated, anthrax is a fatal infectious disease, chiefly of cattle and sheep, characterized by the formation of hard lumps and ulcers and symptoms of collapse. In man without modern therapy it is often fatal.

6. Scabies is called "the itch, from which you cannot be cured" (Deut. 28:27). It is caused by a tiny insect allied to spiders that burrows under the skin. The itching is intense. Infection is spread to others through close bodily contact. The ancients knew no cure for it, but it readily responds to modern medicines.

B. Diseases not requiring isolation. These probably included what today are known as eczema, psoriasis, and impetigo. Of these only impetigo is very contagious; it is of very superficial character without system manifestations. (The scurvy of modern medicine, caused by vitamin C deficiency, is not a skin disease and thus obviously different from the "scurvy" of KJV.) Inflammation, present in wounds, bruises, and sores, is aggravated by accompanying infection when the skin is broken. "Wounds" are usually due to external violence; when the skin is unbroken they are called "bruises." A "sore," more properly called an ulcer, is a wound in which the

skin and the underlying tissues are laid open, almost invariably becoming infected.

II. Diseases with primarily internal manifestations

A. Plague evidently played a major role in OT history. It begins with fever and chills that are followed by prostration, delirium, headache, vomiting, and diarrhea. Caused by the germ *Pasteurella pestis*, two forms of plague occur, both being sudden in onset and very serious.

1. Bubonic plague apparently broke out among the Philistines when they placed the captured Ark of the Covenant in an idol temple (1 Sam. 5). This disease is transmitted by rats through infected fleas that they carry on their bodies, the fleas transferring to humans for livelihood after the rat host dies of the disease. The disease causes the lymph nodes of the groin and armpits to enlarge to the size of walnuts. These enlarged nodes are known as buboes (KJV, "emerods"; NIV, "tumors"; NJPS, "hemorrhoids"). This outbreak of bubonic plague was attributed to "rats that are destroying the country" (6:5).

2. Pneumonic plague is transmitted by droplet spray from the mouth. The first case in an epidemic apparently arises from a case of bubonic plague that has been complicated by plague pneumonia. Untreated pneumonic plague is always fatal. The victim goes to bed apparently well and is found dead by morning. Very likely it was either bubonic or pneumonic plague or both that destroyed Sennacherib's army (2 Ki. 19:35) when 185,000 men were all "dead bodies" by early morning.

B. Consumption doubtless included tuberculosis, malaria, typhoid fever, typhus fever, dysentery, chronic diarrhea, and cholera. These diseases are contagious and are sometimes referred to as "pestilences," being especially prevalent under circumstances of impaired nutrition and crowding such as are encountered in the siege of a city (e.g., Deut. 28:21-22; Jer. 21:6-7, 9).

1. Tuberculosis occurs in acute or chronic form, more commonly the latter. Under the living conditions of OT days, it probably not only attacked the lungs (common form in America today), but also the bones and joints (common in underdeveloped lands today). "Crookback" (cf. the extreme hunchback of Lev. 21:20) may result from tuberculosis of the

D

spinal vertebrae or less commonly from severe back injury. Tuberculosis anywhere in the body may produce fever, defective nutrition with underweight, or discharge of infectious pus (referred to as an "issue" in Leviticus). The disease may produce chronic invalidism or death if the disease process is not arrested.

2. Typhoid fever and **typhus fever** both give rise to similar symptoms of steady fever and delirium lasting for a matter of weeks, often fatal. Typhoid fever is transmitted through contamination in water and contamination that flies carry to food and drink. Typhus fever is transmitted to humans by lice that have fed on infected human beings.

3. Malaria may have been the "great fever" with which PETER's mother-in-law was stricken (Lk. 4:38; cf. also Lev. 26:16; Deut. 28:22). Transmitted by certain species of mosquito, malaria is responsible for much chronic illness. A chill followed by fever often subsides in a few hours only to recur more severely some hours later, continuing intermittently thereafter. Death may follow if the disease is not treated.

4. Diarrhea, dysentery, and cholera, caused by microorganisms taken into the body in contaminated food or drink, were doubtless prevalent in OT times. They are characterized by frequent watery bowel movements, often by vomiting and fever, and if protracted, by weakness and prostration. PUBLIUS's father's illness (Acts 28:8) is probably rightly translated by NIV as "fever and dysentery," a diarrhea associated with painful spasms of the bowel, ulceration, and infection, either amoebic or bacillary, giving rise to blood and pus in the excreta. As to cholera, it is fatal in half of the cases when modern treatment is not utilized.

III. Diseases Caused by Worms and Snakes

A. Intestinal roundworm infection *(ascariasis)* is a common disease today in lands where sanitation is poor, and is believed to have been responsible for Herod AGRIPPA I's death (Acts 12:21-23). The pinkish yellow roundworm, *Ascaris lumbricoides,* is about 10-16 in. (26-41 cm.) long and 0.2 in. (0.5 cm.) in diameter. Aggregated worms sometimes form a tight ball with their interlocking bodies so as to obstruct the intestine, producing severe pain and copious vomiting of worms. If the obstruction is not promptly relieved by surgery, death may ensue. The roundworm does not chew and devour, but feeds on the nutrient fluids in the bowel and may work its way through diseased portions of the bowel as though it had eaten a hole through it. JOSEPHUS's account of Agrippa's death (*Ant.* 19.8.2 §§343-52) is highly suggestive of the intestinal obstruction produced by these worms.

B. The Guinea worm (*Dracunculus medinensis*), formerly called the serpent or dragon worm, has probably been known longer than any other human parasite. It is still found in interior ARABIA and the adjacent RED SEA coast. The infection enters the human body through drinking water containing *Cyclops* (an almost microscopic water insect) infected with tiny Guinea worm larvae. In about one year the female worm attains a length of 3 ft. (1 m.), being 0.07 in. (0.17 cm.) in diameter, usually maturing under the skin of the leg or arm. A blister is raised in the skin through which a huge brood of tiny larvae are extruded. This area itches and burns intensely. Death may result from internal complications or severe secondary infection, particularly if the worm is broken. The ancient and modern treatment consists in hastening the extrusion of larvae with cold water followed by gradual extraction of the worm. This is done by winding the worm around a stick of wood without breaking it, taking a turn or two of the stick each day. Complete removal takes about three weeks.

C. The snake-bite that PAUL received was doubtless inflicted by a venomous snake of the pit-viper type (Acts 28:3-6). Experts today stress that the bite of a venomous snake is not poisonous unless it is accompanied by envenomation, the latter failing to take place if the contents of the poison sac located at the base of the snake's hollow fangs have just previously been completely squeezed out, or if the sac is ineffectively squeezed when the snake strikes. Some suggest that envenomation did not take place in Paul's case, but that the snake, enraged by the fire, repeatedly struck at surrounding objects and exhausted all its venom before fastening itself to Paul's hand. This is a frequent occurrence and makes for difficulty in assessing the degree of envenomation and evaluating the efficacy of one snake-bite treatment as compared with another. When envenomation with pit-viper venom takes place, the tissues may quickly swell to three or four times their normal size in the region of the bite.

IV. Diseases of the Eyes

A. Epidemic blindness, described in 2 Ki. 6:18, when a whole army was struck with blindness, is not the rarity that some may imagine. For example, Richard H. Pousma, a medical missionary in China in the 1920s, was in close contact with an army contingent that was decimated with blindness in a few days. Gonorrhea of the sexual organs had been occurring sporadically. Suddenly this same gonorrhea germ in the midst of unsanitary conditions changed its propensities so as to produce acute blinding inflammation of the eyes in violent epidemic form, spreading from eye to eye like wildfire, which is one of the recognized potentialities of this germ. Many of the soldiers were permanently blinded. The army troops that had been the most feared for their cruel depredations were suddenly rendered powerless, and the condition of the men was pitiful as one saw them trying to grope their way about, the totally blind being led about by the partially blind.

B. Paul's illness (2 Cor. 12:7), which he described as "a thorn in my flesh," is considered by many authorities to have been *trachoma*, an infectious eye disease. Early in the disease there is often acute inflammation of the eyelids, which makes the lids feel like sandpaper. This frequently spreads on to the bulb of the eye, especially the cornea, the transparent part of the bulb, which becomes red and inflamed. At this state, infection with other germs is often added. Pus seeps out over the lid margins, forming a tough, crusting scab as it dries and unites with the greasy secretion of the glands of the lid margin. It is possible that Paul's blindness encountered on the DAMASCUS road was of this type. For three days the secretion was evidently so severe that it formed incrustations at the lid margins such as to glue and mat together the lashes of the lids, so that the eyelids could not be parted. At the end of this time we are told he saw again after scabs fell from his eyes. Later Paul may have been afflicted with chronic trachoma, for (a) he failed to recognize the high priest (Acts 23:2-5); (b) the Galatians offered their good eyes for his (Gal. 4:13-15); and (c) he wrote with "large letters" (6:11). Other scholars interpret these passages differently.

V. Nervous and Mental Diseases. While terminology and explanations of the causes of emotional and mental diseases have varied greatly through

Blind man asking for donations at the mosque in Hebron.

© Dr. James C. Martin

the centuries, there is clear insight in the Scriptures concerning the relationship between the emotional state and physical disease (psychosomatic medicine). This is exemplified in Prov. 17:22: "A cheerful heart is good medicine, / but a crushed spirit dries up the bones." The cheerful heart can resolve excessive emotional tension in a manner superior to that of any tranquilizer. In contrast, some forms of arthritis occur on an emotional basis, the outcome of a "crushed spirit," whereby the bones are seemingly dried of joint lubrication. Both ELIJAH and JONAH were men who lapsed into states of extreme nervous exhaustion, often referred to as *neurasthenia*, a common condition amid the tension of modern days. God's method of dealing with this condition as outlined in 1 Ki. 19 and in Jon. 4 is a model for modern psychiatric therapy. In the case of EPAPHRODITUS (Phil. 2:25-30) there is clear recognition then as today of the role played by *pressure* of work and *anxiety* as he endeavored to accomplish a colossal task unaided by those who should have been his helpers. No doubt there was physical illness superimposed on the emotional tension in his case, often true in modern times as well.

In addition, there are mental diseases that are recognized as disease entities just as distinctive as appendicitis or pneumonia. The general term used in KJV for those so afflicted is "lunatic," though formerly this term referred to epilepsy as well as insanity because of a supposed relationship to the phases of the moon. As today, legal responsibility for actions was regarded as tempered by proof of mental incompetence. Hence we find DAVID escaping from ACHISH by pretending "insanity" (1 Sam. 21:13-15). Perhaps he was even imitating some

D

of Saul's actions. The modern psychiatrist would diagnose Saul's state as *manic-depressive insanity*, with its periods of black melancholy, flashes of homicidal violence, and deeply rooted delusion that people were plotting against him, characteristically ending in Saul's suicide. Nebuchadnezzar (Dan. 4:24-28) is considered by Short to have been a victim of paranoia, a delusional form of insanity well known to medical science.

VI. Miscellaneous Medical Disorders and Therapy

A. The woman's **issue of blood** (NIV "bleeding") of twelve years' duration (Lk. 8:43-44) was doubtless excessive menstrual flow, a fairly common condition. In its severe form, it is commonly due to fibroid tumors in the womb encroaching on the lining of the womb. A flow of blood with large clots occurs, depleting the body of blood and causing severe anemia. The modern remedy usually used in this condition is removal of the tumor from the womb or removal of the womb (hysterectomy). This surgery obviously was not available in NT times, so it is quite understandable that all this woman's living was spent on unsuccessful medical care.

B. In connection with **Jesus' agony** in Gethsemane, we read that "his sweat was like drops of blood falling to the ground" (Lk. 22:44). Some have thought that this refers to actual blood-tinged sweat. Short tends to take this point of view despite his confession that this phenomenon must be very rare and is not well authenticated. Rather it seems that the emphasis here is to be put on the word "like," referring to the size and weight of the drops of sweat. It should be recalled that this occurred at night. Jesus' enemies carried lanterns and torches, but evidently he had neither. The color of the sweat was therefore unobservable. Some suggest that the drops of sweat sounded like blood clots falling on the ground.

C. Gangrene. Timothy was admonished to shun profane babblings because "their teaching will spread like gangrene" (2 Tim. 2:17). The term refers to local death of the tissues. Common forms of gangrene are: (a) gas gangrene, a rapidly fatal type caused by a spreading gas-forming germ in muscles after recent injury; (b) diabetic gangrene, a "dry" gangrene that spreads less rapidly caused by circulatory impairment associated with uncon-

trolled diabetes; (c) septic gangrene that spreads from the edges of infected ulcers.

D. Dropsy (Lk. 14:2), in modern medical language called edema, is a condition in which the tissues retain too much fluid. It may be caused by heart disease, kidney disease, or local infection, and may terminate fatally.

E. Dwarfism is referred to in Lev. 21:20. People may have been dwarfed through tuberculosis or injury of the spine, but deficiency of thyroid function such as is found in cretinism is also a likely cause. In the latter condition there is also usually mental deficiency, and this gives added reason for not permitting such an individual to participate in priestly service. Cretinism today responds well to thyroid extract therapy if administered early in life.

F. As to orthopedic conditions, reference is made to the **maimed** (those whose bodies are deprived of a part) and the **halt** (those who limp in walking because of lameness from a disabled lower extremity). The latter may be due to a fracture that has healed in an unfavorable position or it may be due to **atrophy** (wasting) of the muscles. Atrophy of a hand is referred to as a "shriveled" hand in Lk. 6:6 (KJV, "withered"). Atrophy usually results from palsy or **paralysis** (synonymous terms), a condition characterized by loss of control of movement of muscles through disease or destruction of nerves or nervous tissue.

G. Muteness, that is, inability to speak, may arise from deafness since one will naturally find it difficult to reproduce unheard sounds. It also may arise from hemorrhage (apoplexy) or thrombosis (clotting) in relation to the blood vessels of one or more of the speech centers of the brain. Often a marked degree of recovery takes place in these instances of so-called stroke as the clotted blood is gradually absorbed from the affected area. Such may have happened to Zechariah (Lk. 1:20-22, 64), whereas Nabal (1 Sam. 25:36-38) evidently experienced a fatal stroke.

H. Frequent instances of **unspecified sickness** occur throughout the biblical record. Some of the these cases of sickness did not experience divine healing. For example, Paul informs us, "I left Trophimus sick in Miletus" (2 Tim. 4:20). The apostle also states that three times he prayed for the removal of his thorn in the flesh; he was answered not by removal of his infirmity but by being given more grace (2 Cor. 12:8-10). Therefore, the Bible does not teach that all Christians are entitled to divine healing by virtue of being believers.

JAMES urges that the church elders be called to pray for the sick. He also directs that they "anoint him with oil in the name of the Lord" (Jas. 5:14). This directive has perhaps wrongfully been assumed to refer to a church ritual. The verb ANOINT commonly referred to rubbing oil on the skin as a household remedy. It would seem to be James's meaning that the sick one is not only to be prayed for but the commonly accepted remedies are also to be applied as an indication of compassionate concern. Jesus' disciples made similar use of the application of oil to the sick (Mk. 6:13).

dish. A receptacle for food, generally made of baked clay or else of metal. The "chargers" (NIV "silver plates") of Num. 7 were large flat dishes of beaten silver, but most of the dishes in Scripture were pottery. Orientals ate from a central platter or dish, generally using a thin piece of bread for a spoon and handling the food quite daintily (Matt. 26:23). A special courtesy consisted in picking out a good piece of meat from the central dish and handing it to a guest. See also POTTERY.

Dishan. di´shan (Heb. *dîšān H1915*, possibly "mountain goat" or "ibex"). Seventh son of SEIR and chief of a HORITE clan (Gen. 36:21, 28, 30; 1 Chr. 1:38, 42 [in the latter reference the MT reads "Dishon"]). Dishan had both a brother and a nephew called DISHON, and some argue that the two forms are variant spellings of the same name, thus reflecting some kind of confusion in the genealogies.

Dishon. di´shon (Heb. *dîšôn H1914*, possibly "mountain goat" or "ibex"). **(1)** Fifth son of SEIR and chief of a HORITE clan (Gen. 36:21, 26 [MT, "Dishan"], 30; 1 Chr. 1:38, 41b). See DISHAN.

(2) Son of ANAH and grandson of Seir the Horite (Gen. 36:25; 1 Chr. 1:41a); his sister OHOLIBAMAH became ESAU's wife.

dispensation. This English term is used by the KJV four times as the rendering of Greek *oikonomia G3873*. In three of those passages (1 Cor. 9:17;

Eph. 3:2; Col. 1:25) it refers to the commission PAUL was given so that the GOSPEL of divine GRACE might be dispensed to others. The fourth passage (Eph. 1:10, but also 3:9, where KJV translates differently) uses the term more broadly of God's plan of SALVATION (3:2 shows the conceptual connection between these two uses of the term). This Greek noun is also used in Lk 16:2-4 with regard to the "management" or "stewardship" of a business (cf. in the same passage the term *oikonomos G3874*, "manager" or "steward"), and in 1 Tim. 1:4 with the possible meaning of "training."

The modern theological use of the term as a "period of time during which man is tested in respect to obedience to some specific revelation of the will of God" (Scofield) is not found in Scripture. Nevertheless, the Scriptures do make a distinction between the way God manifested his grace in what may be called the "Old Covenant" and the way his grace has been manifested since the death of Christ in the "New Covenant," and there are accompanying differences in the requirements that God has for believers. Paul has this in mind when he speaks of God's dispensations in Ephesians and Colossians. In God's redemptive plan the era of law prepared the way, by types and shadows, for the new era of salvation through Christ, which in the NT is regarded as the climax of history (Heb. 1:2).

Dispersion. Also *Diaspora*. A term applied to the *scattering* of Jews outside of Palestine. God had warned the Jews through MOSES that dispersion among other nations would be their lot if they departed from the Mosaic Law (Deut. 4:27; 28:64-68). These prophecies were largely fulfilled in the two captivities, by Assyria and Babylonia (see EXILE), but there were other captivities by the rulers of Egypt and Syria, and by Pompey, which helped scatter the Israelites. Especially from the time of ALEXANDER THE GREAT, many thousands of Jews emigrated for the purposes of trade and commerce into the neighboring countries, particularly the chief cities. By the time of Christ the Diaspora must have been several times the population of Palestine. As early as 525 B.C. there had been a temple of the Lord in Elephantine (an island in the NILE River), in the early years of the Maccabean struggle. The synagogues in every part of the known world helped greatly in the spread of Christianity, for Paul invariably went to them in every city he visited. The Greek word *diaspora* *G1402* occurs three times in the NT (Jn. 7:35; Jas. 1:1; 1 Pet. 1:1).

dissension. See HERESY; SECT; UNITY.

dissipation. This English term, referring to intemperate conduct, is used by the NIV to render two different Greek words (Lk. 21:34; 1 Pet. 4:4). Other terms, such as *debauchery* and *licentiousness*, are used variously by English versions to indicate extreme indulgence. See also DRUNKENNESS.

distaff. A stick used to hold the wool or flax fibers in the process of spinning (Prov. 31:19).

Dives. di'veez. The name traditionally given to the rich man in the parable of the rich man and LAZARUS (Lk. 16:19-31). Actually, his name is nowhere given in the parable, but the Greek term for "rich" corresponds to Latin *dives* (cf. Vulgate), and the latter began to be used as the man's name as early as the second century.

divided kingdom. See ISRAEL; JUDAH.

divination. The practice of consulting beings (divine, human, or departed) or things (by observing objects or actions, that is, omens) in the attempt to gain information about the future and such other matters as are removed from normal knowledge. Those who practice divination assume that the gods or spirits are in possession of secret knowledge desired by humans and they can be induced to impart it. Divination was highly developed by all ancient peoples—the Babylonians, Egyptians, Greeks, Romans, etc.—and even the Hebrews practiced it, though it was severely condemned by MOSES and the prophets. Deuteronomy 18:10-11 is the classical passage on this subject. There were various modes of divination: by reading omens; dreams, both involuntary and those induced by what is called "incubation" (i.e., by sleeping in some sacred place where the god revealed his secrets to the sleeper); the use of the lot; hydromancy or foretelling from the appearance of water; astrology or the determination of the supposed influence of the heavenly bodies on the destiny of a person or nation; rhabdomancy or the use of the divining rod (Hos. 4:12; Ezek. 8:17); hepatoscopy or divination by an examination of the liver of animals; necromancy or consulting the dead; and the sacrifice of children by burning.

Diviners' Oak. The RSV rendering of *ʾēlôn mĕʿônnîm* (Jdg. 9:37; KJV, "the plain of Meonenim"; NRSV, "Elon-meonenim"; NIV, "soothsayers' tree"). This tree was evidently in a prominent place, possibly on a small rise. The translation "Diviners" is based on the Hebrew term's derivation from a verb that can mean "to practice soothsaying." The existence of a tree in Canaan used for augury is not surprising in view of the widespread practice of DIVINATION.

divinity of Christ. See CHRIST; SON OF GOD; TRINITY.

division. See HERESY; SECT; UNITY.

divorce. An act whereby a legal MARRIAGE is dissolved publicly and the participants are freed from further obligations of the matrimonial relationship. It is an ancient device that has varied procedurally over the centuries, but in the main it has been instituted on the initiative of the husband.

Among the ancient Sumerians it was easy for a man to divorce his wife, especially if she had failed to produce children. Among the Babylonians, the Code of HAMMURABI (18th cent. B.C.) provided for divorce under certain circumstances but included the return of the dowry to the wife, a situation that would give many men pause for contemplation. Where there was no dowry, the husband was required to make a payment of silver according to a schedule that was organized in terms of the social status of the wife's family. But if the wife had been negligent in her household duties, she could be sent away without payment or simply replaced and demoted to the position of a servant or a slave (Code of Hammurabi, 141, 143). Simpler and more severe was the Middle Assyrian law code, which stated that, with no fault specified, the wife could be divorced and sent away empty-handed (Middle Assyrian Laws, 37). Generally speaking, it was an

D

© Dr. James C. Martin. Israel Museum, Jerusalem. Photographed by permission.

This papyrus written in Aramaic is a *get* or "certificate of divorce," found at Wadi Murabba'at and dated to A.D. 111.

unusual and, therefore, more complex situation if a wife instituted divorce proceedings. Divorce was discouraged in the fourth century B.C. in Egypt, and later by the Hebrews, through the imposition of a substantial fine on the husband, known as "divorce money."

Although the OT seems to permit divorce for rather general reasons (Deut. 24:1), it was usually either for adultery or childlessness. The bill of divorce could be a simple repudiation, such as, "She is not my wife, and I am not her husband" (Hos. 2:2). Either party could begin the divorce proceedings (Mk. 10:11-12). Because of the strength of the family unit, divorce was in actual fact not very common among the Hebrews. Nevertheless, in the postexilic period, in order for the purity of the Hebrew faith to be maintained, wholesale divorce was required by EZRA of those Jews who had married foreign wives in Babylonia (Ezra 9:2; 10:3, 16-17).

A Greek marriage could be dissolved at any time either by mutual consent or by the husband without cause, while the wife could institute divorce pro-

ceedings against her husband where she could prove persistent adultery on his part. In the early Roman period there was little divorce, but, typically, Roman law is quite specific about the marriage contract and its dissolution. The contract could be nullified by mutual consent, or for a variety of reasons that might be considered valid by the husband. If the wife proved to be barren, suffered from a chronic illness, or showed evidence of insanity, she could be divorced on those grounds. If she had attempted to kill her husband, or if she had committed adultery, she could also be divorced. In about 17 B.C. a law was passed that made it an offense for a husband to keep a wife known to be an adulteress. By the fourth and fifth centuries A.D. there was some curtailment of the grounds for divorce, but it was still relatively easy for either party to initiate proceedings.

Jesus asserts that God had, under the Mosaic law, allowed divorce only as a concession to the hardness of the human heart (Matt. 19:8). Considerable debate has surrounded the so-called exceptive clause in Jesus' condemnation of divorce: "except for marital unfaithfulness" (5:32; 19:9; this clause does not appear in the parallels, Mk. 10:11-12; Lk. 16:18). Interpretations include: subsequent discovery of premarital unchastity, marriage in violation of the prohibited degrees (Lev. 18), extramarital sex relations, and failure to perform marital responsibility. Similarly, interpreters disagree as to whether PAUL permitted divorce and remarriage under certain circumstances (1 Cor. 7:12-15). Such differences of opinion, however, should not be allowed to minimize the clear scriptural injunctions to preserve the marriage relationship.

Dizahab. diz'uh-hab (Heb. *di zāhāb H1903*, possibly "possessor of gold"). Also Di-zahab. A locality listed along with PARAN, TOPHEL, LABAN, and HAZEROTH to specify the place where MOSES delivered the messages of the book of DEUTERONOMY to Israel (Deut. 1:1). The exact location of Dizahab has not been established. The context suggests a location in the E of the ARABAH. The other locations named provide no assistance since they are also unknown.

doctor. This English term (from Latin *doctor*, "teacher") is used by the KJV to render the Greek noun *didaskalos G1437*, "teacher" (only in Lk. 2:46; cf. also "doctor of the law" for *nomodidaskalos G3799*, Lk. 5:17; Acts 5:34). See SCRIBE. The NIV uses the term *doctor* in its modern sense of PHYSICIAN a few times (Matt. 9:12 and parallels; Col. 4:14). See OCCUPATIONS AND PROFESSIONS.

doctrine. This term is used frequently by the KJV to render the Greek terms *didaskalia G1436* (e.g., 1 Tim. 1:10) and *didachē G1439* (e.g., Acts 2:42), both of which mean "teaching," usually emphasizing the *content* of what is taught. In the Greek world, teaching implied the communication of knowledge; for the most part it had a clear intellectual character. Among the Jews, especially in the OT, teaching served not simply to communicate religious truth, but rather to bring the one taught into direct confrontation with the divine will. What is taught are the commandments; what is expected is obedience. Thus MOSES is taught what he should do (Exod. 4:15), and he in turn teaches Israel the commandments (Deut. 4:1, 5, et al.), which they likewise are to teach to their children (Deut. 6:1, 6, 7, et al.).

For the most part the NT use corresponds more to the OT idea than to the Greek. That is, teaching usually implies the content of ethical instruction and seldom the content of dogmas or the intellectual apprehension of truth. For example, in the Pastoral Epistles "sound doctrine that conforms to the glorious gospel" is contrasted with all kinds of immoral living (1 Tim. 1:9-11; cf. 6:1, 3; Tit. 1:9; 2:1-5, 9-10). This usage is strengthened by the relationship of *didachē* to *kērygma G3060*, "preaching." It was by means of the preaching that sinners were brought to faith in Christ (1 Cor. 1:21); and the content of that preaching included the essential data of the Christian message: the life, work, death, and resurrection of Jesus Christ as God's decisive act for the sinner's salvation (cf. Acts 2:14-36). Those who responded to the preaching would then be instructed in the ethical principles and obligations of the Christian life (2:42). Since ethical instruction or obedience to the divine will in the NT is so closely related to response to the preaching with its "doctrinal" content, it is not surprising that teaching itself eventually came to include the essential data of the faith. Thus *didachē* can refer to the truth of the INCARNATION, belief in which, of course, should eventuate in LOVE (2 Jn. 9-10). This latter meaning of "teaching," as including "doctrine," or the essential beliefs of the Christian faith, ultimately prevailed in the early church and continues in vogue today.

Dodai. doh´di (Heb. *dôday H1862*, "beloved") Apparently a variant of DODO. Dodai the AHOHITE, one of DAVID's military officers, was in charge of the division for the second month (1 Chr. 27:4). He was probably the same person identified as the father of Eleazar, one of David's famous warriors (2 Sam. 23:9; 1 Chr. 11:12; the KJV and other versions read "Dodo" in both verses).

Dodanim. See RODANIM.

Dodava. doh´duh-vuh. See DODAVAHU.

Dodavahu. doh´duh-vay´hyoo (Heb. *dôdāwāhû H1845*, "beloved of Yahweh"). KJV Dodavah. The father of the prophet ELIEZER of Mareshah, who condemned JEHOSHAPHAT king of Judah for his alliance with AHAZIAH of Israel and foretold the destruction of his navy (2 Chr. 20:37).

Dodo. doh´doh (Heb. *dôdô H1861*, "[his] beloved"). (**1**) Grandfather of TOLA; the latter was a judge (leader) in ISSACHAR (Jdg. 10:1).

(**2**) Father of ELEAZAR; the latter was one of DAVID's famous warriors (2 Sam. 23:9; 1 Chr. 11:12; in these verses NIV reads "Dodai"). Apparently the same as DODAI the Ahohite (1 Chr. 27:4).

(**3**) Father of ELHANAN; the latter was one of David's famous warriors (2 Sam. 23:24; 1 Chr. 11:26).

doe. See ANIMALS.

Doeg. doh´ig (Heb. *dōʾēg H1795*, possibly "anxious"). An Edomite who served King SAUL as head shepherd (1 Sam. 21:7; 22:9, 18, 22; Ps. 52 title). When DAVID, fleeing from Saul, came to NOB, Doeg was being "detained before the LORD" for some reason. He reported to Saul about the help AHIMELECH the priest had given David (1 Sam. 21:1-9). In revenge Saul gathered all the house of Ahimelech and Doeg killed them, eighty-five priests, all the women and children of the village, and even the cattle (22:11-23).

dog. See ANIMALS.

dolphin. See ANIMALS (under *badger*).

dominion. See AUTHORITY.

Domitian. duh-mish´uhn. When the popular TITUS died at the untimely age of forty-two (A.D. 81), after only two years and a few months as emperor, he was succeeded by his thirty-year-old brother Domitian (born A.D. 51), whom neither Titus nor their father VESPASIAN had expected to be called to the task. Domitian (whose full name was Titus Flavius Domitianus) was no trained soldier like his two predecessors, and he came to office, a despised younger brother, embittered by his elders' contempt, a resentment all the deeper for his keen intellect. Sensitive about his absence of military glory, Domitian ordered an attack on the Chatti of the Main Valley, and celebrated his victory in a great triumphal celebration.

Unfortunately, the pathological fears and suspicions of Domitian revived in ROME the hated cult of delation—that pernicious system of the common informer and the law of treason that so played into his hands. Among Domitian's victims were the Christians. He was heir to a policy and legislation established by NERO and sporadically pursued under Vespasian and Titus, both of whom had links with Palestine and entertained some fear of any movement initiated there. But Domitian, with a sharp eye for treason and enthusiastic for the Caesar-cult (see EMPEROR WORSHIP), justly ranks with Nero as a systematic persecutor. It is usually thought that the book of Revelation was written during the reign of Domitian and reflected the emperor's anti-Christian attitude. Domitian was murdered in the year 96, after a plot supported by his wife, who felt the insecurity of her own position.

donkey. See ANIMALS.

door. Ancient doors usually were made of wood, sometimes sheeted with metal as in the case of city gates or in large public buildings. Sometimes they were made of one slab of stone or, rarely, a single piece of metal. Hinges on doors, as known today, were unknown; instead, doors turned on pivots set in sockets above and below. The sockets were made of stone or, sometimes, of metal. In Egypt, the hinge consisted of a socket of metal with a projecting pivot, into which two corners of the door were inserted. A wide doorway had a pair of folding doors (Isa. 45:1); which could be bolted with bars of wood (Nah. 3:13) or of metal (Isa. 45:2; Ps. 107:16; NIV, "gates"). The temple doors were two-leaved (1 Ki. 6:34). Doors were provided with a bolt (2 Sam. 13:17) or with lock and key (Jdg. 3:23). The term *door* is also used metaphorically, as in Jn. 10:7, "I am the door" (NIV, "gate"); Acts 14:27, "he had opened the door of faith to the Gentiles"; and Rev. 3:20, "I stand at the door and knock." See ARCHITECTURE; GATE.

doorkeeper. A person who guarded the entrance to public buildings, temples, city walls, etc. The NIV uses this term a number of times, for example, with reference to those who guarded the ARK OF THE COVENANT (1 Chr. 15:23). To be a lowly doorkeeper of the temple is preferred to a life of wickedness (Ps. 84:10). The doorkeeper of a rich man's house is mentioned by Jesus as an example of one who watches faithfully (Mk. 13:34; NIV, "the one at the door"). A doorkeeper might guard the entrance of a sheepfold (Jn. 10:3; NIV, "watchman").

Dophkah. dof´kuh (Heb. *dopqâ H1986*, meaning disputed). A place where the children of Israel encamped on their journey from the RED SEA to SINAI (Num. 33:12-13). Some scholars identify it with Serabit el-Khadim, where the Egyptians carried on mining, and where the famous "Sinaitic Inscriptions" were found (dating from about 1525 B.C. and written in a Semitic hieroglyphic alphabet).

Dor. dor (Heb. *dôr H1888*, "generation" or "dwelling"). A fortified city on the coast of Palestine, S of Mount CARMEL, c. 8 mi. (13 km.) N of CAESAREA. The surrounding hilly area was known as NAPHOTH DOR (Josh. 11:2; 12:23; 1 Ki. 4:11; cf. Josh. 17:11). It was settled in very ancient times

D

Dor was an important harbor along the Mediterranean Sea used by Phoenicians and Israelites during the period of the Israelite monarchy. (View to the S.)

by PHOENICIA because of the abundance of shells along the coast which were the source of a rich PURPLE dye. The site is identified with modern Khirbet el-Burj (Tel Dor), N of Tanturah. The king of Dor supported JABIN king of HAZOR in his unsuccessful battle against JOSHUA at the waters of MEROM (Josh. 11:2-5; 12:23). Dor was one of the cities within the borders of Issachar and Asher that were assigned to Manasseh, although Manasseh was unable to capture it. In later years, when it was captured, its Canaanite inhabitants were subjected by Israel to forced labor (Josh. 17:11-13; Jdg. 1:27-28). Dor and the neighboring territory were made the fourth administrative district by SOLOMON (1 Ki. 4:11).

Dorcas. dor′kuhs (Gk. *Dorkas G1520*, "gazelle," corresponding to Aram. *ṭabyĕtā᾽*). A feminine name not uncommon to both Jews and Greeks, used in the NT to denote the Christian woman of JOPPA who died and was raised from the dead by PETER (Acts 9:36-43). Her ARAMAIC name was TABITHA, which has the same meaning as Dorcas. She was held in high esteem for her outstanding service to others. When she died, her friends sent for Peter. He prayed, and she was raised from the dead. As a result, many believed.

dot. This English term is used by the RSV and other versions in two passages (Matt. 5:18; Lk. 16:17; KJV, "tittle") to render Greek *keraia G3037*, which literally means "horn" but is used of any "projection." In the context of writing, it can be applied to an accent, a diacritical mark, or a small part of an individual letter. Accordingly, the NRSV renders, "one stroke of a letter"; NIV, "the least stroke of a pen."

Dothan. doh′thuhn (Heb. *dōtān H2019*, meaning uncertain). A prominent town in the boundaries between the tribes of MANASSEH and ISSACHAR, about 5 mi. (8 km.) S of the JEZREEL Valley and 11 mi. (19 km.) NNE of SAMARIA. If the doubtful suggestion is right that the name derives from an Aramaic word meaning "two wells," it adds interest to the story of JOSEPH's brothers casting him into a dry well-pit there (Gen. 37:24). Nearly a millennium after Joseph's experience, the prophet ELISHA (2 Ki. 6:13) was dwelling at Dothan when the king of SYRIA tried to capture him with an army, for he had learned that Elisha was able to tell his plans to the king of Israel, Joram (JEHORAM). When Elisha's servant informed him that a great host surrounded Dothan, Elisha prayed that the Lord would open his servant's eyes, and the servant saw angelic hosts defending his master. The site, modern Tell Dotan, was excavated by J. P. Free from A.D. 1953 onward. It showed habitation as early as c. 3000 B.C. and in the next millennium was surrounded by a thick wall. At the time of Joseph (2200-1550), it had a well-built fortress and a strong wall. Occupation continued in varying degrees of intensity until the Byzantine period.

double-minded. This English expression is used in Bible versions as a fairly literal rendering of Greek *dipsychos G1500*, which occurs twice (Jas. 1:8; 4:8). What James means by this word he makes clear with a further description: he is referring not simply to someone who experiences personal doubts, but to the one who is "unstable in all his ways." Set in context with an admonition to pray (1:5-6), it would be understood that the essence of prayer is the turning over of the entire mind to God. James's second use of the term is likewise set in an admonition to draw near to God. The answer to the double mind with its wavering loyalties, indecision, divided interests, and impurity was the rededication of the whole personality to Christ. See also DOUBLE-TONGUED.

double-tongued. An expression used by the KJV and other versions to render Greek *dilogos G1474* ("two-worded"), which occurs only once in the NT (1 Tim. 3:8). The phrase "not double-tongued" (NIV has the clearer rendering, "sincere") designates one of the qualifications of a DEACON: he must not be someone who says one thing at one time and something else at another time (or perhaps who says one thing but means another). See DOUBLE-MINDED.

dough. The soft mass of moistened flour or meal that after baking becomes bread or cake. The word may apply to the mass before it has been raised by yeast, as in Exod. 12:34, 39, but generally after raising, as in Jer. 7:18 and Hos. 7:4.

dove. See BIRDS.

dove's dung. See PLANTS.

dowry. Money (or property) given by a bride to her husband at marriage. The word is used by the KJV several times to render Hebrew *mōhar H4558*, but this term refers to the compensation a husband pays to the bride's family, that is, a sum given to the father of the bride for her economic loss to the family. It is thus better translated "marriage present" or "bride-price" (Gen. 34:12; Exod. 22:17; 1 Sam. 18:25); this compensation could be paid in service (Gen. 29:18). Other Hebrew terms may be used in a similar way (cf. Gen 30:20; 1 Ki. 9:16).

doxology. An ascription of PRAISE or GLORY to God in song or prayer (from Gk. *doxa G1518* "glory, praise, honor"). Although the word does not occur in the Bible, doxologies were uttered by angels to shepherds the night Jesus came into the world (Lk. 2:14) and by "the whole crowd of disciples" the day Jesus rode triumphantly into Jerusalem on Palm Sunday (19:37-38); the book of Revelation mentions doxologies by angels around the throne in heaven (Rev. 5:13) and by "a great multitude in heaven" (19:1-31). In the OT all five books of the Psalter end with a doxology, the last comprising a whole psalm in which "praise" appears thirteen times (Ps. 41:13; 72:18-19; 89:52; 106:48; 150:1-6). The LORD's PRAYER is traditionally concluded with the doxology: "For thine is the kingdom, and the power, and the glory, for ever. Amen" (Matt. 6:13 KJV; it does not appear in some old Greek MSS); a similar statement is found in 1 Chr. 29:11. The longest and most comprehensive doxologies in the NT, frequently used as benedictions by pastors, are in Heb. 13:20-21 and Jude 24-25.

drachma. See MONEY.

dragnet. See NET.

dragon. This English term is used in some Bible versions to render Hebrew *tannîn H9490* (NIV, "monster") in passages that speak of cosmic combat (Job 7:12; Ps 74:13; Isa. 27:1; 57:9; Ezek. 29:3; 32:2; the Heb. word can also mean "snake," Exod. 7:9 et al.). In the book of Revelation it stands for Greek *drakōn G1532* and designates SATAN (Rev. 12:3-17; 13:1-11; 16:13; 20:2).

Dragon's Spring (dragon well). See JACKAL WELL.

dram. See WEIGHTS AND MEASURES.

drawer of water. An expression used by the KJV and other versions with reference to a lowly servant class (Deut. 29:11; Josh. 9:21-27; NIV, "water carrier"). Drawing WATER from a well or spring, usually located outside the city walls, was regarded as a menial task often performed by women (Gen. 24:13; 1 Sam. 9:11). Sometimes it was assigned to young men (Ruth 2:9). It may have been customary to subject defeated enemies to this service as Israel did to the GIBEONITES (Josh. 9:21-27).

dream. In early patriarchal times, God usually appeared in theophany to godly men (cf. ABRAHAM in Gen. 18), but from the time of JACOB onward his revelations were more often in dreams (e.g., 28:10-17.) He could reveal his will in dreams today, but the written Word of God and the indwelling HOLY SPIRIT have made dreams of this sort unnecessary for added revelation. (Contrast Num. 12:6 with Jude 8.) Often in ancient times God spoke in dreams to persons outside the chosen family, such as ABIMELECH of Gerar (Gen. 20:3), LABAN (31:24), the butler and baker of PHARAOH (40:8-19), PHARAOH himself (41:36), NEBUCHADNEZZAR (Dan. 2:1-45; 4:5-33). In these dreams either the meaning was clear enough to need no interpretation, as in those of Abimelech and Laban, or else God caused one of his servants to interpret the meaning, as in the latter cases. One principle of interpretation seems quite evident: When the symbol is in the natural realm, the interpretation is in the human realm; for example, when JOSEPH dreamed of the sun, moon, and eleven stars bowing to him, his brothers immediately knew the meaning as referring to his father, mother, and brothers (Gen. 37:9-11). When the symbol is in the human realm, as in Dan. 7:8, "Eyes like the eyes of a man and a mouth that spoke boastfully," the interpretation is in the spiritual realm. Dreams may lead men astray, but God's Word declares how to deal with this situation (Deut. 13:1-3; cf. 1 Jn. 4:1-6). In the NT, God spoke to MARY, MOTHER OF JESUS, through GABRIEL (Lk. 1:26-35), whereas JOSEPH received revelation through a dream (Matt. 1:20-24).

dregs. See LEES.

dress. Our knowledge of the kind of clothing worn by the people of biblical times comes from biblical statements; from representations of the people and their clothing found on monuments, reliefs, seals, plaques, and tomb-paintings; and from graves and tomb remains. All these, coupled with the traditions and usages extant among the present bedouin Arab tribes, lead us to conclude that at a very early period people learned the art of spinning and weaving cloth of hair, wool, cotton, flax, and eventually silk (Gen. 14:23; 31:18-19; 37:3; 38:28; Job 7:6; Ezek. 16:10, 13). From these they established certain simple styles that were continued from generation to generation, then carried by ESAU and ISHMAEL and their descendants into ARABIA, where the Arab continued them through the centuries—always with a feeling that it was decidedly wrong to change. When the Arabs overran the larger part of the Bible lands in the sixth century A.D., they returned with these patterns of clothing. In general they have so nearly continued the basic forms that in unspoiled areas much the same garments are worn today as were worn by Jacob of OT times and by Jesus of NT times.

The clothing worn by the Hebrew people of biblical times was graceful, modest, and exceedingly significant. They were considered so much a part of those who wore them that they not only told who and what they were, but were intended as external symbols of the individual's innermost feelings and deepest desires, and his or her moral urge to represent God aright. With certain kinds of cloth and with astonishingly vivid colors of white, purple, scarlet, blue, yellow, and black, they represented the state of their minds and emotions. When joyful and ready to enter into festive occasions, they donned their clothing of brightest array; and when they mourned or humbled themselves, they put on sackcloth—literally cloth from which sacks were made—which was considered the very poorest kind of dress, and quite indicative of their lowly feelings (1 Ki. 20:31-32; Job 16:15; Isa. 15:3; Jer. 4:8; 6:26; Lam. 2:10; Ezek. 7:18; Dan. 9:3; Joel 1:8).

When a person's heart was torn by grief, the inner emotions were given expression by "rending" or tearing the garments (Mk. 14:63; Acts 11:14). To confirm an oath or seal a contract, a man plucked off his shoe and gave it to his neighbor (Ruth 4:8).

When JONATHAN made a covenant with DAVID, he went even farther and gave him his own garments (1 Sam. 18:3-4).

There was variety in clothing characterizing the people from the various lands adjacent to Palestine, and within the narrow confines of the country itself there was a distinctive clothing that set off the Canaanite from the Philistine. Among the Hebrews there were slight differences in dress characterizing rank, trade, and profession. Yet it was little less than amazing how similar the general patterns were. The variety for the most part was in quality and in decoration. Clothing was colored, red, brown, yellow, etc., but white was much preferred. It denoted purity, cleanliness, and joy. Princes, priests, and kings of ANE countries wore purple, except on special occasions when they often dressed in white garments. Others sometimes wore white on the occasions of joy and gladness. But in general the people wore darker colors, yet they tended toward the brighter side.

Red granite head of Pharaoh Amenophis III with double crown (from Thebes, 1390 B.C.). Headwear was used as a sign of authority and power.

© Dr. James C. Martin. The British Museum. Photographed by permission.

The basic garments used among the men of biblical times seem to have consisted of the *inner-tunic*, the *tunic-coat*, the *girdle*, and the *cloak*. Added to this was the *headdress* and the *shoes* or *sandals*.

I. The inner-tunic or undershirt, which in cooler weather the male members of the oriental family wore next to the body, was usually made of a long piece of plain cotton or linen cloth made into a short shirtlike undergarment. At times it was little more than a loincloth in length, and at other times it reached below the knees or even just above the ankles. It was not usually worn when the weather was warm. The KJV refers to such undergarments worn by priests as "breeches" (Exod. 28:42).

II. The tunic-coat, a close-fitting shirtlike garment, was the piece of clothing most frequently worn in the home and on the street. In ancient times it was often of one solid color, but at the present it is more often made of a brightly colored striped cotton material that among the Arabs is often called "the cloth of seven colors" because of the narrow vertical stripes of green, red, yellow, blue, and white that alternate. It was lined with a white cotton material and worn over the undershirts when the weather was cool, but next to the body when it was warm. This garment usually had long sleeves and extended down to the ankles when worn as a dress coat and was held in place by a girdle. Hard-working men, slaves, and prisoners wore them more abbreviated—sometimes even to their knees and without sleeves—as shown on the Behistun Inscription. On SENNACHERIB's Lachish relief (701 B.C.), the elders and important men of the city are shown wearing long dresslike white tunics that came down near the ankles. These garments were pure white, with no decorations, and no girdle to hold them. In this and other reliefs, however, the Hebrews had just been taken captive and were prisoners of war, therefore they could well have been divested of all but their basic garments.

III. The girdle was a belt made of either cloth or leather, which was worn over the loose coatlike skirt or shirt. The *cloth girdle*, ordinarily worn by village and townspeople, was a square yard of woolen, linen, or even silk cloth first made into a triangle, then folded into a sashlike belt about 5-8 in. (13-21 cm.) wide and some 36 in. (92 cm.) long. When drawn about the waist and the tapering ends

D

D

tied in the back, it not only formed a belt but its folds formed a pocket to carry a variety of articles such as nuts, loose change, and other small objects or treasures. It was worn by both men and women, and the model woman of Prov. 31 made them to sell to the merchants. The girdle is not only a picturesque article of dress but also may indicate the position and office of the wearer. It is sometimes used to signify power and strength (2 Sam. 22:40; Isa. 11:5; Jer. 13:1; Eph. 6:14).

The *leather girdle* or belt was 2-6 in. (5-15 cm.) wide and was often studded with iron, silver, or gold. It was worn by soldiers, by men of the desert, and by countrymen who tended cattle or engaged in the rougher pursuits of life. This type of girdle was sometimes supported by a shoulder strap and provided a means whereby various articles such as a scrip (a small bag or wallet for carrying small articles), sword, dagger, or other valuables could be carried. It was the kind of girdle worn by ELIJAH (2 Ki. 1:8) and by JOHN THE BAPTIST (Matt. 3:4). Today the laborer and the poorer classes use rawhide or rope for a girdle; the better classes use woolen or camel's hair sashes of different widths.

The girdle, whether made of cloth or leather, was a very useful article of clothing and often entered into many activities of everyday life. When one was to walk or run or begin any type of service he "girded himself" for the journey or for the task at hand. Girded loins became a symbol of readiness for service or endeavor. ISAIAH said of the MESSIAH that righteousness should be "his belt and faithfulness the sash around his waist" (Isa. 11:5), and PAUL spoke of the faithful Christian as having "the belt of truth buckled around your waist" (Eph. 6:14).

IV. The cloak, mantle, or robe was a large, loose-fitting garment, which for warmth and appearance was worn over all other articles of clothing as a completion of male attire. It was distinguished by its greater size and by the absence of the girdle. It existed in two varieties, which were usually known as the *mĕ῾il H5077* and the *śimlâ H8529*.

The *mĕ῾il* was a long, loose-sleeved robe or public dress worn chiefly by men of official position and by ministers, educators, and the wealthy. It was the robe of the professions, a dress of dignity, culture, and distinction—the mark of high rank and station (1 Sam. 24:11; 1 Chr. 15:27). It was rich in appearance and could well have been the "coat of many colors" that JACOB gave to JOSEPH, or the like of which HANNAH made and brought to SAMUEL from year to year as he ministered before the Lord at Shiloh (1 Sam. 2:18-19). In its finest form, it must have been the high priest's robe of the EPHOD with its fringe of bells and pomegranates swaying and swinging and tinkling as he walked (Exod. 28:31-38). It is generally understood that there were two kinds of ephods—one with its rich and elaborate insignia and paraphernalia peculiar to the office of high priest, and the other a more simple "linen ephod" worn by leaders of distinction other than the high priests (2 Sam. 6:14).

The *śimlâ* was the large sleeveless cloak or mantle that, in general pattern, corresponds to the long and flowing garment that the Arab shepherd and peasant call an *abba* or *abayeh*. They wear it by day and wrap themselves in it by night. Understandably, it was not be to taken in pledge unless it was returned by sundown (Exod. 22:26-27, which also uses the term *śalmāh H8515*).

Both of these simple yet picturesque garments were usually made of wool, goat hair, or camel hair. Men of distinction often wore more colorful cloaks called "robes," which were made of linen, wool, velvet, or silk, elaborately bordered and lined with fur. This long outer garment or topcoat was, in all probability, the "mantle" worn by ELIJAH and ELISHA (2 Ki. 2:8-14). It was the camel-hair garment worn by JOHN THE BAPTIST (Matt. 3:4). It is frequently made of alternate strips of white, red, and brown, or is formed by sewing together two lengths of cloth so that the only seams required were those along the top of the shoulders. In unusual cases, however, the cloak is woven of one broad width, with no seam. Many believe that this was the garment Christ wore, and over which, at the crucifixion, the Roman soldiers "cast lots" rather than tearing it, for it was "seamless, woven in one piece from top to bottom" (Jn. 19:23-24).

On SHALMANESER'S Black Obelisk (9th cent. B.C.), the artist shows Israelite men wearing long cloaks or mantles with elaborate fringed borders both on the cutaway fronts and along the bottom. These were in keeping with the Mosaic injunction to make blue tassels on the borders of their gar-

© Dr. James C. Martin. The British Museum. Photographed by permission.

This portrait on limewood painted with encaustic dates to c. 55-70 A.D. and depicts a woman dressed in a tunic and cloak, wearing gold ball earrings, gold necklace with a pendant, and snail curl hairdo.

ments to remind them to keep all the commandments and to be holy before God (Num. 15:38-40; Deut. 22:12).

V. The headdress was worn chiefly as a protection against the sun and as a finish to a completed costume. It varied from time to time according to rank, sex, and nationality. In the main, however, there were three known types that were worn by the male members of the Hebrew and surrounding nations. (a) The ordinary brimless cotton or woolen *cap*, corresponding somewhat to our skullcap, was sometimes worn by men of poorer circumstances. Captives are seen wearing these on the Behistun Rock. (b) The *turbans* were made of thick linen material and formed by winding a scarf or sash about the head in artistic style and neatly concealing the ends. The high priest wore a turban of fine linen (Exod. 28:39 [KJV, "mitre"]). (c) The *head-scarf*, known among the Arabs as the *kaffiyeh*, is usually made up of a square yard of white or colored cotton, wool, or silk cloth folded into a triangle and draped about the head. The apex of the triangle falls directly down the back, forming a V point, while the tapering ends are thrown back over the shoulders, or in cold weather they are wrapped about the neck. This graceful head-scarf is held in position by an *ajhal*, which is made of several soft woolen or silk twists bound by ornamental threads, and worn in coils about the head. An ornamental tassel falls to the side or down the back. When BEN-HADAD's shattered Syrian army realized the serious loss it had suffered, some of his men suggested to him that they go to the king of Israel "wearing sackcloth around their waists and ropes around their heads" (1 Ki. 20:32), hoping that he would spare their lives.

VI. Shoes and sandals were considered the lowliest articles that went to make up the wearing apparel of the people of Bible lands (Mk. 1:7). In the Bible and in secular sources, they were mentioned at a very early period and are seen in considerable variety on the Egyptian, Babylonian, Assyrian, and Persian monuments. A pair of terracotta shoes, of the modern snowshoe variety, were found in an Athenian grave of about 900 B.C. Shoes were of soft leather, while sandals were of a harder leather and were worn for rougher wear. According to some authorities, the sole was of wood, cane, or sometimes bark of the palm tree and was fastened to the leather by nails. They were tied about the feet with "thongs" (NIV), or "shoe-latchets" (Gen. 14:23 KJV). It was customary to have two pairs, especially on a journey. Shoes were usually removed at the doorway before entering a home, on approaching God (Exod. 3:5), and during mourning (2 Sam. 15:30). Property rights were secured by the seller pulling off his shoe and giving it to the purchaser (Ruth 4:7). The "clouts" referred to in Josh. 9:5 KJV are patched sandals (so NIV).

VII. Women's dress. Among the Hebrews neither sex was permitted by Mosaic law to wear the same form of clothing as was used by the other (Deut. 22:5). A few articles of female clothing carried somewhat the same name and basic pattern, yet there was always sufficient difference in embossing, embroidery, and needlework so that in appearance the line of demarcation between men and women could be readily detected. The women wore long garments reaching almost to the feet, with a girdle of silk or wool, many times having all the colors of

D

the rainbow. Often such a garment would have a fringe hanging from the waist nearly to the ankles.

The ladies' headdress, for example, usually included some kind of a *kaffiyeh* or cloth for covering the head, yet the material that was in that covering was of different quality, kind, or color from that worn by the men. Also, it was often pinned over some kind of a cap made of stiff material and set with pearls, silver, gold, or spangled ornaments common to that day. If a woman was married, these or other more significant coins covered the entire front of her cap and constituted her dowry. Her undergarments would be made of cotton, linen, or silk, as might befit her wealth or station in life. She would probably wear a long gown with long, pointed sleeves. Over this was a small rather tightly fitted jacket or "petticoat"—meaning little coat. The small jacket was made of "scarlet" or other good material and was a thing of exquisite beauty because it was covered with "tapestry" or fine needlework, wrought with multicolored threads. A woman of even moderate circumstances could have beautiful clothing, for it was "the fruit of her own hands."

In the OT many articles of women's clothing are mentioned that cannot be exactly identified. Ezekiel 13:18, 21 KJV refers to a "kerchief." The Hebrew word is *mispāḥâ H5029*, a head-covering or "veil" (so NIV) of some sort, the exact nature of which is unknown. Isaiah 3:19 KJV speaks of "mufflers," probably two-piece veils or scarves, one part covering the face below the eyes, the other the head, down over the neck (several other items in the context cannot be certainly identified).

Women often added to their adornment by an elaborate braiding of the hair. PETER found it necessary to warn Christian women against relying on such adorning to make themselves attractive (1 Pet. 3:3). In the OT there are a number of references to painting the eyes in order to enhance their beauty, but it is always spoken of as a showy and somewhat vulgar device, unworthy of good women. Jezebel painted her eyes (2 Ki. 9:30).

In ancient times women especially were much given to various kinds of ornaments. Earrings and nose-rings were especially common. On account of their drop-like shape, earrings are called "chains" (Isa. 3:19 KJV) and "pendants" (Jdg. 8:26). Men also wore such earrings (Gen. 35:4; Jdg. 8:24). The nose-ring or nose-jewel made necessary the piercing of the nostrils. Rings were worn by both men and women. All ancient Israelites wore signet rings (Gen. 38:18 KJV; NIV, "seal"). Rings were often worn on the toes, anklets (spangles) on the ankles (Isa. 3:18), bracelets on the arms and wrists (Gen. 24:22; Ezek. 16:11).

Beginning about the second century B.C., all male Jews were expected to wear at morning prayers, except on Sabbaths and festivals, two *phylacteries*, one on the forehead, called a *frontlet*, the other on the left arm. They consisted of small leather cases containing four passages of Scripture from the OT: Exod. 13:1-10, 11-16; Deut. 6:4-9; 11:13-21.

drink. The essential beverage has always been WATER. The Hebrews procured it chiefly in two ways: by means of cisterns, which were possessed by every well-appointed house (2 Sam. 17:18; Jer. 38:6), and by means of wells, which were rare and were usually the possession of a clan or community. WINE was also widely used, both in the form of new wine, called must, and fermented wine. In the heat of harvest, frequent use was made of a sour drink mixture of water and wine, and of a "strong drink"; how the latter was prepared is unknown. Wine was sometimes spiced to improve its taste. Wine was also made from pomegranates and possibly also from ripe dates and barley. Next to bread and vegetables, the most important food was milk, both of larger and smaller cattle, especially goats' milk, which was usually kept in skins. Because of the hot climate, fresh milk soon became sour, but it was very effective for quenching thirst.

drink offering. See SACRIFICE AND OFFERINGS.

dromedary. See ANIMALS.

dropsy. See DISEASES.

dross. The refuse in impure metals that is generally separated by melting, when the dross rises to the top and may be skimmed off. It is used figuratively of what is worthless (Ps. 119:119; Isa. 1:22, 25; Ezek. 22:18-19).

drought. See DESERT; RAIN.

drunkenness. The Scriptures show that drunkenness was one of the major vices of antiquity, even among the Hebrews. Well-known cases of intoxication are NOAH (Gen. 9:21); LOT (19:33, 35); NABAL (1 Sam. 25:36); URIAH (2 Sam. 11:13); AMMON (13:28); ELAH, king of Israel (1 Ki. 16:9); and BEN-HADAD, king of Syria (20:16). The prophets often denounce drunkenness as a great social evil of the wealthy. Even the women were guilty (Amos 4:1). The symptoms and effects of strong drink are vividly pictured in the Bible (Job 12:25; Ps. 107:27; Isa. 28:7; Hos. 4:11). While the writers of Scripture condemn intemperance in the strongest terms, they do not prescribe total abstinence as a formal and universal rule. Nevertheless, many believe that the principles laid down in the Bible point in that direction (cf. Mk. 9:42-43; Rom. 14:13-21; 1 Cor. 8:8-13; Eph. 5:18). In ancient times the poor could not afford to drink to excess, while the cheapening of alcoholic drinks has made drunkenness a much greater social problem in modern times.

Drusilla. droo-sil′uh (Gk. *Drousilla G1537*). The youngest of the three daughters of Herod AGRIPPA I. It was probably in A.D. 53 that Drusilla, in her sixteenth year, was married to Azizus of Emesa, a small principality in the N of SYRIA that included Palmyra (TADMOR). A year later, FELIX, who was CLAUDIUS's unprincipled freedman and that emperor's notorious appointee to the procuratorship of Palestine, persuaded the beautiful Drusilla to leave her husband. She became Felix's third wife, and in that role appears briefly in the story of PAUL's imprisonment at CAESAREA (Acts 24:24-27).

dugong. See ANIMALS (under *badger*).

duke. This English word is used by the KJV to render Hebrew ʾallûp *H477* ("head of a thousand"), applied to the tribal chiefs of EDOM until the time of MOSES (Gen. 36:15-43; Exod. 15:15; 1 Chr. 1:51-52; it also renders a word for "prince" in Josh. 13:21).

Dumah (person). doo′muh (Heb. *dûmāh H1874*, possibly "silence" or "enduring"). Sixth son of ISH-MAEL and presumed founder of an Arab community (Gen. 25:14 [cf. v. 16]; 1 Chr. 1:30). Some

scholars connect his name with that of Dumat al-Jandal, the capital of a district known as al-Jauf. The site is a large oasis in N central Saudi Arabia. Royal Assyrian and Babylonian inscriptions from the seventh and sixth centuries refer to the destruction of the Adummatu, which may be a reference to the descendants of Dumah.

Dumah (place). doo′muh (Heb. *dûmāh H1873*, possibly "silence" or "enduring"). **(1)** A town in the hills of JUDAH (Josh. 15:52). EUSEBIUS's *Onomasticon* refers to a town of this name. It is usually identified with the present Khirbet ed-Deir Domeh, located some 10 mi. (16 km.) SW of HEBRON. See also RUMAH.

(2) A place that is the subject of a prophetic oracle (Isa. 21:11). Because the next words mention SEIR, some believe that the reference is to EDOM (the reading of two Heb. MSS; cf. also LXX, *Idoumaia*). Others point to the Arabian locations in the following verses (DEDAN and TEMA) and argue that this Dumah is to be identified with #1 above.

dumbness. See DISEASES (under *muteness*).

dung. The excrement of man or beast. The NIV usually renders "offal," "refuse," "rubbish." In several of the offerings under the Levitical priesthood, the blood and the fat and the flesh were used, but the skins and the dung were discarded or burnt outside the camp (Exod. 29:14; Lev. 8:17). The ultimate disgrace was to have one's carcass treated as dung (2 Ki. 9:37 KJV; NIV, "refuse"). Dry dung was (and is) often used as fuel (see Ezek. 4:12-15). PAUL counted his natural advantages as dung (NIV "rubbish") compared with his blessings in Christ (Phil. 3:8).

dungeon. See PRISON.

Dung Gate. One of the gates of JERUSALEM in NEHEMIAH's day. From this gate Nehemiah surveyed the broken walls of Jerusalem in the night (Neh. 2:13). It was located between the VALLEY GATE and the FOUNTAIN GATE and was repaired by a certain MALKIJAH (3:13-15). It was near this gate that Nehemiah had the dedication of the wall when it was completed (12:31). Many scholars believe that the Dung Gate is to be identified with the Potsherd Gate, which apparently led to the rubbish dump in the Valley of Hinnom, S of the city (Jer. 19:2; 2 Ki. 23:10).

Dura. door′uh (Aram. *dûrā'* H10164). A plain somewhere in the province of ancient Babylon, in which King Nebuchadnezzar erected his golden image (Dan. 3:1). Its precise location is uncertain (Dura was a common geographical name in Mesopotamia).

dust. In the warm and dry climate of the ANE, dust was a reality that people had to face on a daily basis. Thus, such practices began as washing the feet on entering a home (Jn. 13:1-17). Dust, however, also had a symbolic significance for Israel and the early church. (1) Throwing dust on the head as a sign of mourning or sorrow or repentance was common (Job 2:12; Rev. 18:19). (2) Shaking off dust from the feet was a sign of having no further responsibility for the area where the dust was picked up, thus leaving that area to God's judgment (Matt. 10:14; Lk. 9:5; 10:11; Acts 13:51). (3) Paul described the first man (Adam) as a "man ... of the dust" in 1 Cor. 15:47-49, meaning that he was created from the physical elements found in the earth (into which God breathed life—see Gen. 1-2). Adam is to be contrasted with Jesus, the second Adam, for while he took his humanity from Mary he existed before his incarnation as the eternal Son of God. In referring to human beings as made of dust Paul was echoing a strong theme of the OT where man is said to be made from dust and to return to dust (Gen. 2:7; 3:19; Job 4:19; 17:17).

dwarf. See DISEASES.

dyers, dyeing. See OCCUPATIONS AND PROFESSIONS.

dysentery. See DISEASES.

E. An abbreviation for ELOHIST; it is used (along with D, J, and P) to designate one of the supposed sources of the PENTATEUCH, according to the Documentary Hypothesis.

eagle. See BIRDS.

ear. The vital organ of hearing. The Bible often refers to the ear in the physical sense. For example, we read that the tip of the right ear of the priests was touched with blood during their consecration (Lev. 8:23-14). A servant who spurned freedom to continue in the service of his master had his ear bored with an awl to signify his continual subservience (Exod. 21:6). Cutting off ears was a feared practice of the enemy (Ezek. 23:25). More frequently, however, the use of the term involves understanding and obedient response. "To incline the ear" means "to give attention" (Ps. 88:2). "To uncover someone's ear" denotes "to reveal to someone" (1 Sam. 20:2; 2 Sam. 7:27). "Uncircumcised" ears are deaf to moral and spiritual instruction, not delighting whatever in the word of God (Jer. 6:10; Acts 7:51). "Ears that hear" is an expression that indicates obedience (Prov. 20:12; 25:12), whereas one who "stops his ears" from listening to an evil plot declares that he wants no part of it (Isa. 33:15). At the hearing of disastrous news, ears tingle (1 Sam. 3:11; 2 Ki. 21:12). While idols cannot hear (Ps. 135:17), God's ears are not heavy (Isa. 59:1-2). God is said to open ears with the result that people gain understanding (Job 29:11) and display obedience (Isa. 50:4-5).

early rain. See RAIN.

earnest. As a noun, this English term is used by the KJV in the NT to render *arrabōn G775*, a word that came into Greek from a Semitic language, perhaps from the vocabulary of Phoenician traders; it is related to Hebrew *'ērābôn H6860*, "pledge" (used in Gen. 38:17-20). Right down to modern Greek, where *arrabōn* can refer to an engagement ring, the word is used for a pledge in a contract. In commercial contexts, the word was applied to a down payment. Both meanings, "pledge" and "first installment," are involved in each of the three NT uses of the word. PAUL speaks of God's gift of the HOLY SPIRIT as the pledge and foretaste of what the Christian will enjoy later (2 Cor. 1:22; the NIV renders the word with a descriptive phrase, "a deposit, guaranteeing what is to come"); significantly the word SEAL is also used in the context. Similarly, we are told that the Holy Spirit is the earnest of that fullness of life which the Christian will enjoy after the dissolution of his earthly "tent" (5:5). The promised Holy Spirit is also described as an earnest or deposit that assures our future INHERITANCE (Eph. 1:14).

earring. Earrings have been a popular ornament from the remotest antiquity, and they are mentioned frequently in the OT (Heb. *nezem H5690*, used also of nose jewels). They were often regarded as amulets or talismans (cf. Gen. 35:4). Among all ANE peoples, except the Hebrews and Egyptians, earrings were in general use by both sexes; but Exod. 32:2 shows that at least in the time of MOSES they were also worn by Israelite boys. In the W they have been largely female ornaments, but not exclusively so. The Ishmaelites customarily wore gold earrings (Jdg. 8:24-25).

earth. See WORLD.

earth, circle of the. A phrase used once in the Bible to emphasize God's greatness: "He sits enthroned above the circle of the earth, / and its people are like grasshoppers" (Isa. 40:22). The word for "circle" is combined with "heaven" in another passage, where it appears to mean "vault" or "dome" (Job 22:14). Finally, we read that God "drew a circle on the face of the deep" (Prov. 8:27 NRSV). This last reference, especially, suggests a boundary, but the sense is close to "horizon" (cf. NIV). The view that the meaning is "sphere" may be reading something into the word.

earth, four corners of the. This expression, referring figuratively to "the whole world," occurs twice in English Bible versions (Isa. 11:12 [NIV, "four quarters of the earth"]; Rev. 7:1). The Hebrew phrase is found also in Ezek. 24:16, where it refers to the country of Israel and is thus better translated "the four corners of the land." A more general phrase, "the corners [edges, ends] of the world," occurs in three other passages (Job 37:3; 38:13; Isa. 24:16). Similar expressions are found elsewhere. They generally allude to the outer limits of a vast expanse.

earth, new. See ESCHATOLOGY.

earth, pillars of the. Although the KJV and other versions use this phrase only once (1 Sam. 2:8; NIV, "the foundations of the earth"), there are two additional passages that speak of the earth as having pillars or columns (Job 9:6; Ps. 75:3). It is possible that many people in the ANE thought of the world as supported by literal columns, but this language clearly became conventional (cf. even today such expressions as "the sun rose") and was used in poetic and metaphorical texts not to describe the physical world but to exalt God's greatness.

earthen vessels, earthenware. See POTTERY.

earthquake. Four earthquakes are recorded in Scripture: (1) one occurred at Mount Horeb for ELIJAH's instruction (1 Ki. 19:11); (2) another one took place during the reign of UZZIAH (Amos 1:1; Zech. 14:5); (3) a violent earthquake is mentioned in connection with the RESURRECTION OF JESUS CHRIST (Matt. 28:2); (4) and another one freed PAUL and SILAS from prison (Acts 16:26). In addition, an earthquake is mentioned in Isa. 29:6 as a form of judgment from the Lord on the enemies of

his people, and this is in line with the steady biblical testimony that all natural phenomena—earthquake, wind, storm, rain, hail, and the rest—are under divine sovereign control and are part of his armory for ruling the world in righteousness.

east. Possibly because it is the direction in which the sun rises, the E was the point of orientation for many (but not all) ANE peoples, including the Israelites. The gate of the TABERNACLE was on the E side (Exod. 38:13-14). In the wilderness MOSES and AARON camped on the East side of the tabernacle, and this area was barred to strangers (Num. 3:38). EZEKIEL saw the glory of the Lord leave the doomed TEMPLE by the E gate (Ezek. 10:19; 11:23), but in his vision of the future temple, he saw the glory of the Lord coming from the E and entering the temple by the E gate (43:2, 4). See also NORTH; SOUTH; WEST.

east, children (people) of the. In Gen. 29:1 we are told that JACOB journeyed to the territory of the people of the E in PADDAN ARAM (N MESOPOTAMIA; see 28:2-7). The phrase is used in the book of Judges to designate Arabs who joined the Midianites and the Amalekites in fighting Israel (Jdg. 6:3, 33; 7:12; 8:10; cf. Jer. 49:28; Ezek. 25:4, 10). JOB is described as the "greatest man among all the people of the East" (Job 1:3); some think that northern ARABIA, EDOM, or MOAB provides the setting of the book, a location that fits Isa. 11:14 also.

Easter. A feast commemorating the RESURRECTION OF JESUS CHRIST. The KJV uses this term to render Greek *pascha G4247* only in Acts 12:4; in all other instances it correctly renders the word as Passover. It is held by some that the annual celebration of the Lord's resurrection was observed in apostolic times, but the earliest written evidence for such a festival appears in the "paschal controversy" over the correct date for "the feast of the Savior's passover," an issue that apparently was first discussed during the second century. The matter was settled by the Council of Nicea in A.D. 325, which ruled that Easter should be celebrated on the first Sunday after the full moon following the vernal equinox. This is the system followed today, so that the date of Easter varies between March 22 and April 25.

eastern sea. This term (lit., "the sea in front") occurs in three eschatological passages: Ezek. 47:18; Joel 2:20; Zech. 14:8. In the last two it is contrasted with "the western sea" (lit., "the sea behind"), which clearly refers to the MEDITERRA-NEAN (cf. Deut. 11:24; 34:2), and so most scholars interpret "the eastern sea" as a reference to the DEAD SEA, which could be viewed as an eastern boundary. However, some scholars suggest that these terms do not refer to geographical entities but rather reflect APOCALYPTIC language, indicating cosmic (primeval, mythological) extremes, that is, the uttermost east and west.

East Gate. Among those who helped repair the walls of JERUSALEM was a certain Shemaiah who is described as "the guard at the East Gate" (Neh. 3:29). It was situated between the HORSE GATE at its N and the MUSTER GATE at its S (3:28, 31; NIV, "Inspection Gate"), but its precise location is uncertain. Presumably, this is the same as a TEMPLE gate that existed during HEZEKIAH's reign, for a Levite named Kore is given the title, "the keeper of [the one] to the east" (2 Chr. 31:14; cf. 1 Chr. 26:14).

east wind. A scorching wind, known as the *sirocco*, which in Palestine and Egypt blows in from the desert most often in May and October. It withers vegetation (Gen. 41:6; Ezek. 17:10) and dries up fountains and springs (Hos. 13:15). Sometimes it destroys houses (Job 1:19) and ships (Ps. 48:7; Ezek. 27:26). By an E wind God drove back the waters so that the Israelites could cross the sea on dry land (Exod. 14:21). God used an E wind to bring judgment (Isa. 27:8; Jer. 4:11-12; 18:17). "God provided a scorching east wind" to afflict JONAH (Jon. 4:8).

eating and drinking. See FOOD; MEALS.

Ebal. ee′buhl (Heb. *ʿêbāl H6507*, possibly from a root meaning "stout"). **(1)** Son of Shobal and grandson of SEIR the HORITE (Gen. 36:23; 1 Chr. 1:40).

(2) Variant of OBAL (1 Chr. 1:22 KJV and other versions, following MT).

(3) The name of a mountain. See EBAL, MOUNT.

Ebal, Mount. ee′buhl (Heb. *ʿêbāl H6506*, possibly from a root meaning "stout"). A mountain 3,077 ft. (938 m.) high, one of the highest points in the land of Samaria. It stood opposite Mount GER-IZIM, across a valley through which ran an important route of travel. At its foot was JACOB'S WELL (see Jn. 4:20: "on this mountain"), and the city of SHECHEM was located nearby. When the Israelites

Looking NW toward Mt. Ebal.

© Dr. James C. Martin

first entered the land, Moses commanded them to erect on Mount Ebal a monument of stones on which the law was inscribed and a stone altar for burnt offerings and peace offerings. The law, with its blessings and curses, was recited by the people antiphonally, the blessings from Mount Gerizim and the curses from Mount Ebal (Deut. 27:4-26). JOSHUA renewed this procedure after the conquest of AI (Josh. 8:30-35). The central location of this mountain and its height made it valuable for military purposes. A ruined fortress is still visible on its summit.

Ebed. ee´bid (Heb. ʿebed *H6270*, "slave, servant"). **(1)** Father of GAAL; the latter was an Israelite who led a revolt against ABIMELECH (Jdg. 9:26-35).

(2) Son of a certain Jonathan and descendant of Adin; accompanied by fifty men, he was among those who returned from the EXILE (Ezra 8:6).

Ebed-Melech. ee´bid-mee´lik (Heb. ʿebed-melek *H6283*, "servant of the king"). TNIV Ebed-Melek. An Ethiopian (or Cushite; see CUSH) in the court of ZEDEKIAH who received permission to rescue JEREMIAH from a miry dungeon (Jer. 38:7-13). Because he risked incurring the wrath of Jeremiah's opponents, God said to him: "I will save you; you will not fall by the sword but will escape with your life, because you trust in me" (39:15-18). He is identified as a EUNUCH, probably referring to his official status.

Ebenezer. eb´uh-nee´zuhr (Heb. ʾeben hāʿēzer *H75*, "stone of help"). **(1)** The scene of two defeats of the Israelites by the PHILISTINES (1 Sam. 4:1-11). In the first battle, the Israelites lost 4,000 men, and in the second, 30,000. In the second battle, the ARK OF THE COVENANT was taken by the Philistines and taken to ASHDOD (5:1); also ELI's sons, HOPHNI and PHINEHAS, were killed. The precise location of Ebenezer is uncertain, but some identify it with ʿIzbet Ṣarṭa, about 13 mi. (21 km.) E of JOPPA.

(2) Ebenezer also was the name given by SAMUEL to the stone set up by him between MIZPAH and SHEN to commemorate a later Israelite victory over the Philistines (1 Sam. 7:12). It is not certain whether this is a place different from #1 above.

Eber. ee´buhr (Heb. ʿēber *H6299*, perhaps "traveler"; Gk. Eber *G1576*). **(1)** A descendant of SHEM (through Arphaxad and Shelah) and an ancestor of ABRAHAM (Gen. 10:21-25; 11:14-17; 1 Chr. 1:18-25); included in Luke's GENEALOGY OF JESUS CHRIST (Lk. 3:35 [KJV, "Heber"]). Practically nothing is known of him. Interest attaches to the name, which is derived from the same root as the name ʿibrî *H6303*, "Hebrew" (Gen. 14:13 et al.). See HABIRU; HEBREW PEOPLE.

(2) Son of Abihail; he was one of seven relatives from the tribe of GAD who occupied the region E of GILEAD (1 Chr. 5:13 [KJV, "Heber"]; cf. vv. 10, 14).

(3) Son of ELPAAL and descendant of BENJAMIN (1 Chr. 8:12).

(4) Son of Shashak, also a Benjamite (1 Chr. 8:22 [KJV, "Heber"]).

(5) A priest who returned from the EXILE; he was the head of Amok's family (Neh. 12:20).

(6) A place or a people group mentioned by BALAAM in one of his oracles: "Ships will come from the shores of Kittim; / they will subdue Asshur and Eber, / but they too will come to ruin" (Num. 24:24). Some scholars think that Eber here refers to N SYRIA, not far from ASSYRIA. Others prefer to see here an allusion to Abraham's ancestor (see #1 above) and thus to the Hebrews themselves.

Ebez. ee´biz (Heb. ʾebeṣ *H82*, derivation unknown). KJV Abez. A town located in the territory of ISSACHAR (Josh. 19:20), which occupied the greater part of the fertile plain of ESDRAELON. The location is unknown.

Ebiasaph. i-bi´uh-saf. Alternate form of ABIASAPH.

Ebla. eb´luh. An ancient city in N SYRIA, identified with modern Tell Mardikh, about 40 mi. (65 km.) S from the city of Aleppo. Ebla, with its surrounding towns and villages, was the largest in the region. At its height, the city reached a size of 140 acres with a population of perhaps fifteen to twenty thousand. It flourished in the middle of the third millennium B.C., but remained a center of some influence well into the second millennium. In 1975, thousands of cuneiform tablets and fragments were discovered in the royal palace near the throne room. These included some 1,757 texts that were whole or nearly complete, nearly 5,000 fragments with at least ten lines of writing, and many thousands of smaller fragments. The tablets, mostly administrative in character, date to the twenty-fourth and twenty-third centuries B.C.

Soon after the discovery of these texts, amazing claims were made regarding their relation to accounts in the Bible, such as the theory that the cities of the plain in Gen. 14 were named on one text. Similarly, earlier claims that Ebla lay at the center of a vast empire must now be rejected. It was perhaps the most significant city state of its time and is of interest in its own right. However, it had no direct or explicit relation to any events in the Bible. Ebla's role in illuminating the Bible may be more productive from the standpoint of language and vocabulary. Linked with contemporary languages found in texts elsewhere, Eblaite may form the background for the development of biblical Hebrew. Ebla itself is found in N Syria, in the general region that the Genesis records suggest that the PATRIARCHS remembered as their ancient homeland (Gen. 24:10-15; 28:1-5), a view also expressed by many of the names in Abraham's genealogy that can be associated with place names in the region (11:10-32). It should be noted also that names such as NOAH and HARAN, attested in the Ebla texts, are not found so frequently in later millennia. Therefore, they testify to the authentic antiquity of these names in the Genesis narratives and genealogies.

ebony. See PLANTS.

Ebron. ee'bruhn (Heb. ʿebrōn H6306 [not in NIV]). KJV Hebron. A town located in the territory allotted to ASHER (Josh. 19:28 NRSV). A few Hebrew MSS, however, have ABDON, and this variant has been followed by the NIV.

Ebronah. See ABRONAH.

Ecbatana. ek-bat'uh-nuh (Gk. *Ekbatana*). The Greek name of the capital of the empire of the Medes (see MEDIA), and later one of the capitals of PERSIA and of the PARTHIANS. The Old Persian name of the city was Hangmátana ("the place

of assembly"), and the Aramaic form in Ezra 6:2 is ʾaḥmĕtā ʾ H10020 (thus KJV, "Achmetha"). This biblical passage refers to it as the location of the palace in which the decree of CYRUS authorizing the building of the Jewish temple was found. The city is also mentioned a number of items in the APOCRYPHA (e.g., Tob. 3:7; 2 Macc. 9:3). The site is occupied today by Hamadan, Iran, on the plain near the NE foot of Mount Alvand, c. 175 mi. (280 m.) SW of Teheran. Ecbatana owed its importance to its strategic location on the caravan route from Mesopotamia to the Persian plateau. The pleasant summer climate accounts for its popularity as a resort city. According to the Greeks (Herodotus, *Hist.* 1.96), Ecbatana was founded by the half-legendary Deioces the Mede c. 678 B.C., who also established the Median dynasty, but scholars question the accuracy of this tradition. Cyrus captured it in 550, and ALEXANDER THE GREAT took it from the Persians in 330. The city, built on a hill, was surrounded by seven concentric walls, the inner walls rising above the outer. The citadel was also a treasure house, the city famous for its luxury and splendor. Ecbatana became the summer capital of the Parthian kings, maintaining its traditional reputation, but under the Sassanids it declined. Today very little remains of the ancient city.

Ecclesiastes, Book of. i-klee´zee-as´teez. One of the WISDOM books of the OT, though it belongs to a special genre of philosophical discourse of which there are no other extant examples in ANE literature. In the Hebrew Bible it is included among the

Flat limestone sundial with a triangular fin. "There is a time for everything" (Eccl. 3:1).

© Dr. James C. Martin

E

Overview of ECCLESIASTES

Author: "The Teacher [Preacher], son of David, king in Jerusalem" (Eccl. 1:1), apparently a reference to SOLOMON, but many (including some conservative scholars) believe that the book was written by a later, unknown sage.

Historical setting: If Ecclesiastes is the work of Solomon, it must have been composed during the last years of his life (c. 940 B.C.). Those who do not accept a Solomonic authorship date the book after the EXILE, some as late as the third century B.C.

Purpose: To show that, apart from the fear of God, life has no meaning and leads to despair.

Contents: After a prologue (Eccl. 1:1-11), the book seeks to demonstrate the meaninglessness of all earthly things (1:12—6:12), provides practical advice on various topics (7:1—12:7), and ends with an epilogue apparently written by someone other than "the Teacher" (12:8-14).

E

Five Scrolls (*Megilloth*, along with Ruth, Song of Solomon, Lamentations, and Esther) and bears the title Qoheleth (also Koheleth). The Hebrew word *qōhelet H7738*, which appears in the opening statement and elsewhere in the book (Eccl. 1:1-2, 12; 7:27; 12:8-10), has been interpreted in various ways, such as "someone who calls [or speaks in] an assembly [Heb. *qāhāl H7736*]" and "a collector of sayings," but it is often rendered "teacher" or "preacher." The SEPTUAGINT translates it with Greek *Ekklēsiastēs* (lit., "a member of the assembly"), a word that was taken over into Latin in the Vulgate translation and thence into English.

Traditionally the book has been ascribed to SOLOMON, an ascription based on several factors. The author describes the book as "The words of the Teacher, son of David, king of Jerusalem" (Eccl. 1:1). Several allusions in the book are appropriate to Solomonic authorship, such as the reference to the author's wisdom (1:16), his interest in proverbs (12:9; cf. 1 Ki. 4:32), and his building projects (Eccl. 2:4-11). From the time of Luther, however, a large number of scholars have questioned the Solomonic authorship of Ecclesiastes. The book does not actually name Solomon as its writer. The author says he *was* king of Jerusalem (1:12),

a statement difficult to apply to Solomon, and the language of the book may incline toward a later time. These observations have led many to hold that Solomon serves as a literary representation of the embodiment of wisdom.

The book presents a pessimistic view of life apart from God. The writer tells us that his observation of nature and human experience leads him to conclude that they, in and of themselves, do not impart purpose and meaning to life. He observes the endless cycles of nature (Eccl. 1:2-11) and finds in them only tedium. They do not offer satisfaction, for the "eye never has enough of seeing" (1:8). Even wisdom (1:16-18; 2:12-17), pleasure (1:1-8), and toil (1:9-11; 2:18-23) are meaningless. There is no substance or satisfaction in them. They are a "chasing after the wind" (1:17).

In the history of its interpretation the book has been characterized as hedonistic because it concludes that "a man can do nothing better than to eat and drink and find satisfaction in his work" (Eccl. 2:24). But this characterization of the book is rendered difficult by the writer's recognition that pleasure does not lead to satisfaction either (2:1). The book is understood by some to be fatalistic in its approach to life. This view is based on 3:16-22, which seems to conclude that man is not better off than the animal. Such a conclusion, however, is true only when humans are viewed in and of themselves (Heb. *hēmmâ lāhem*, 3:18), that is, apart from God.

There is a positive life view that emerges from the book that may be called a theology of contentment. In view of the lack of substance and meaning in life, Qoheleth urges his readers to enjoy life, for it is God who gives us that privilege (Eccl. 2:24-25). This satisfaction does not belong to all mankind, for the work of the sinner ends in futility (2:26). Godly contentment, however, is not the ultimate good for mankind. Qoheleth reminds us of a future time when God will bring all things into judgment. This is the conclusion of his search for meaning in life (12:14). One is reminded of the counsel of the apostle PAUL in view of the futility of life, for like Qoheleth, he looked away from life's meaninglessness to his future redemption (Rom. 8:20; cf. vv. 22-25).

Qoheleth urges us to fear God and obey him. Only when God is taken into account (Eccl. 12:1) and his will observed (12:13) does life impart purpose and satisfaction.

Ecclesiasticus. See APOCRYPHA.

eclipse. The obscuring of one celestial body by another (from an observer's perspective). For someone observing from the earth, a solar eclipse occurs when the moon passes between the sun and the earth, thus blocking sunlight; a lunar eclipse occurs when the earth passes between the sun and the moon, thus blocking moonlight. For possible references to eclipses in the Bible, see ASTRONOMY. Significant eclipses in the past aid scholars in identifying historical dates and establishing CHRONOLOGY.

eczema. See DISEASE.

Ed. ed (Heb. *ʿēd H6332*, "witness"). An altar built by the Reubenites and the Gadites (and the half-tribe of Manasseh) who settled E of the JORDAN, as a witness of their loyalty to the God of Israel and to the tribes W of the river (Josh. 22:34 KJV). The name Ed appears to be missing in the MT (but it occurs in a few Heb. MSS), therefore the KJV has "Ed" in italics on the basis of the explanation in the sec-

ond part of the verse: "And the children of Reuben and the children of Gad called the altar *Ed:* for it *shall be* a witness between us that the LORD *is* God" (the NRSV and NJPS supply "Witness" rather than "Ed"). The NIV, however, interprets the explanation as the name itself: " … gave the altar this name: A Witness Between Us that the LORD is God."

Edar. See EDER.

Eden (garden). ee´duhn (Heb. *ʿēden H6359*, prob. "delight"). The region in which the Lord God planted a garden for the newly created man, ADAM. In it grew every tree that was pleasant to see and good for food, including the tree of life and the tree of the knowledge of good and evil. A river flowed out of Eden and divided into four heads or streams: the PISHON, which went around the land of HAVILAH, where gold was found; the GIHON, which flowed around the whole land of CUSH; the HIDDEKEL (or TIGRIS), which flowed in front of ASSYRIA; and the EUPHRATES (Gen. 2:8-14). Adam and EVE lived there until they sinned by eating the forbidden fruit and were expelled from it (Gen. 2-3). Later Scripture writers mention Eden as an illustration of a delightful place (Isa. 51:3; Ezek. 28:13; 31:9, 16, 18; 36:35; Joel 2:3).

The location of Eden has been much investigated in both ancient and modern times. The data given in Genesis, however, are not sufficient to fix its site because two of the rivers, the Pishon and Gihon, were unknown even to the ancients and still are to modern scholars. Attempts have been made to locate Eden in the mountains of ARMENIA in the area where the Tigris and Euphrates and several other rivers rise. But the sources of all these streams are not together but are separated by mountain ranges. MESOPOTAMIA, where the Tigris and Euphrates rivers flow, is also within the FERTILE CRESCENT where archaeology has found the oldest civilization. Some scholars suggest the district at the head of the Persian Gulf as the likely location. It has been widely believed that the silt brought down by the rivers has added over a hundred miles of land to the head of the gulf since 3000 B.C. But recent geological examination of this land has indicated that it may not have changed much during the ages. At the site of Eridu, situated near

E

what was considered to be the ancient shoreline, clay tablets have been found that tell of a garden in the neighborhood in which grew a sacred palm tree. Further upstream, a short distance north of ancient BABYLON, the Tigris and Euphrates flow close together so that canals connect them. Some consider this area to be the proper location of Eden.

Eden (person). ee'duhn (Heb. *ʿēden H6360*, prob. "delight"). Son of Joah and a Levite from the descendants of GERSHON during the time of HEZE-KIAH (2 Chr. 29:12). He is probably the same man who faithfully assisted KORE in distributing the contributions made to the temple (31:15).

Eden (region). ee'duhn (Heb. *ʿeden H6361*). See BETH EDEN.

Eder (person). ee'duhr (Heb. *ʿēder H6374* and *ʿeder H6376*, derivation uncertain). **(1)** Son of BERIAH and descendant of BENJAMIN (1 Chr. 8:15; KJV, "Ader").

(2) Son of MUSHI and descendant of LEVI through MERARI (1 Chr. 23:23; 24:30).

Eder (place). ee'duhr (Heb. *ʿēder H6375* and *migdal-ʿēder H4468*, derivation uncertain). **(1)** The "tower of Eder" was located between BETHLEHEM and HEBRON, where JACOB pitched his tent after RACHEL's death, and where REUBEN cohabited with BILHAH (Gen. 35:21-22 NRSV; KJV, "Edar"). The NIV and others render it "Migdal Eder." Because of its proximity to Bethlehem, where DAVID was born, MICAH possibly refers to it ("watchtower of the flock") and to OPHEL ("stronghold of the Daughter of Sion," where David's palace stood in Jerusalem) as symbols of the royal house of David (Mic. 4:8).

(2) A town in the NEGEV district within the tribe of JUDAH (Josh. 15:21), identified by some with el-ʿAdar, c. 5 mi. (8 km.) S of GAZA on the right bank of the Wadi Ghazzeh. Some MSS of the SEPTUA-GINT, however, have either *Ara* or *Arad*, suggesting that ARAD is probably the correct reading.

edict. See DECREE.

edification. The Greek noun *oikodomē G3869* ("a building" or "the act of building") as well as its cognate verb *oikodomeō G3868* ("to build") occur sometimes in the NT in a literal sense (Matt 23:29; 24:1). More frequently they are used in the metaphorical sense. CHRIST spoke of building his CHURCH (Matt. 16:18), and PAUL of the building up of character in Christians (e.g., 2 Cor. 10:8; 13:10; Eph. 4:12, 16). The apostle describes the church as a building (1 Cor. 3:9; Eph. 2:21), and talks of erecting it on the proper foundation (1 Cor. 3:10, 12, 14). Paul says to the Corinthians that when they come together, each one making a contribution (hymn, instruction, revelation, etc.), all is to be done "for edification" (14:26; NIV, "for the strengthening of the church"). He is anxious that Christians mature, that they grace Christ's cause, that they become well-founded in the faith.

Edom. ee'duhm (Heb. *ʾĕdôm H121*, "red"; gentilic *ʾădômî H122*, "Edomite"). A name that can refer to ESAU (alluding to the red vegetable soup he received in exchange for his birthright, Gen. 25:30), to the land of his descendants (32:3; 36:20-21, 30), or to the Edomites collectively (Num. 20:18-21; Amos 1:6, 11; Mal. 1:4). The country was also called SEIR or Mount Seir, referring to a mountain and plateau area between the DEAD SEA and the Gulf of

Edom.

AQABAH about 100 mi. (160 km.) long and up to 40 mi. (65 km.) wide. The original inhabitants of this land were the HORITES or "cave dwellers" (Gen. 14:6). When Esau departed from Canaan to find room for his cattle and came to Mount Seir (36:5-8), the Horites had some tribal chiefs reigning in the land (36:29-30). Esau took the daughter of one of these chiefs for a wife, OHOLIBAMAH, daughter of Anah (36:2, 25). Esau's sons and grandsons were also tribal chiefs (36:15-19, 40-43). Probably the Edomites gradually absorbed the Horites until they disappeared (Deut. 2:12, 22).

Archaeological evidence suggests that the kingdom of Edom was founded during the thirteenth century B.C. In the process of about four centuries its government changed from one under tribal chiefs to a monar-

The mountains of Edom. (View to the E.)

© Dr. James C. Martin

chy. Eight of these kings reigned over Edom before the Israelites had any such ruler (Gen. 36:31-39). One of these kings was on the throne at the time of MOSES and refused to permit the Israelites to pass through his country (Num. 20:14-21). Other evidence of ancient Edom is the Papyrus Anastasi VI of Egypt, dated in the late thirteenth century, which mentions the passage of shepherd tribes from Edom to the richer pasture land of the NILE delta. The AMARNA Letter no. 256, from about 1400, mentions Edom in the form *Udumu*, one of the enemies of a Jordan Valley prince.

SAUL fought against the Edomites (1 Sam. 14:47), but DAVID conquered them and put garrisons throughout the whole land (2 Sam. 8:14). The Israelite army spent six months cutting off all the men of the kingdom (1 Ki. 11:15-16). SOLOMON made the Edomite cities EZION GEBER and ELOTH, on the Gulf of Aqabah, seaports from which his ships sailed to OPHIR (2 Chr. 8:17-18). The kingdom of Judah lost Edom in the reign of JEHORAM when the nation revolted against him about 847 B.C. (2 Ki. 8:20, 22). Some fifty years later, AMAZIAH king of Judah inflicted a severe defeat on the Edomites (14:7). About 735, REZIN

king of SYRIA went to war with Judah, captured Eloth, and drove the Jews out (16:6).

ASSYRIA came in contact with Edom as early as the seventh century B.C. When her kings began to penetrate as far S as Palestine, Edom, along with Judah and her other neighbors, paid tribute to the Assyrians for many years. She is mentioned many times in the inscription of the kings of Assyria, beginning with Adad-Nirari III (800) to Ashurbanipal (686-633). When Jerusalem was destroyed and Judah depopulated by the Babylonians in 586, the Edomites rejoiced over the affliction of the Judeans and began to take over the southern part of Palestine. Eventually they penetrated as far north as HEBRON. This action intensified the already smoldering hatred between Jews and Edomites (see Ps. 137:7; Ezek. 25:12-14; Amos 1:11; Obad. 10-13).

The Edomites were subject also to BABYLON. Under the Persian empire, Edom became a province called IDUMEA, the Greek form of Edom. In 325 B.C., an Arab tribe known as the NABATEANS conquered the eastern part of Edom's territory. During the Hasmonean period (see MACCABEES) John Hyrcanus subdued the Idumeans and forced them to accept Judaism. When the Romans took over Palestine, the Edomites also were included. From Idumea came Antipater, the father of HEROD the Great. He became procurator of JUDEA. After the destruction of Jerusalem by the Romans in A.D. 70, the Idumeans disappeared from history. Thus the rather mournful career of the Edomites

E

came to an end. Only in the early centuries of their kingdom, before the Israelites became powerful, did they enjoy freedom to any great extent.

Edom figures prominently in the prophetic Scriptures (Isa. 11:14; 34:8-15; 63:1-6; Ezek. 35:2-15; Joel 3:19; Amos 9:12; and the whole book of OBADIAH). The explanation of this often unexpected appearance of Edom finds its origin in the fact already noted that the conquest of Edom was a unique achievement of David; the overthrow of Edom therefore became a symbol of the reign of the Davidic MESSIAH.

Edrei. ed′ree-*i* (Heb. *ʾedreʿi H167*, possibly "strong"). **(1)** A residence city of OG king of BASHAN (Deut. 1:4; 3:10; Josh. 12:4; 13:12). It was built on a bluff overlooking a southern fork of the YARMUK River, along the southern boundary of Bashan near the eastern desert. MOSES defeated Og in a pitched battle outside Edrei, which was then destroyed (Num. 21:33-35; Deut. 3:1-6). The ruins were included in the allotment to the MAKIR clan of the tribe of MANASSEH (Josh. 13:31). Edrei is identified with modern Derʿa, c. 60 mi. (100 km.) S of DAMASCUS and 30 mi. (50 km.) E of the JORDAN. The site has ruins going back to Early Bronze times as well as a remarkable subterranean city of numerous streets, shops, rooms, and cisterns, probably from the Hellenistic or Roman period.

(2) A fortified city allotted to the tribe of NAPHTALI, near KEDESH in Upper GALILEE (Josh. 19:37), possibly modern Tell Khureibeh.

education. Several Hebrew verbs in the OT are used of learning and instruction, such as *ḥānak H2852*, "to train, dedicate" (Prov. 22:6), *lāmad H4340*, "to learn" (Deut. 4:10; from this root is derived the term TALMUD), and *yārāh H3723*, hiphil "to throw, direct, teach" (1 Sam. 12:23; cf. its cognate, *tôrâ H9368*, "direction, instruction, teaching, law," Deut. 1:5; Prov. 1:8). Because repetition was at the heart of learning, the verb for "repeat," *šānāh H9101*, came to be used in postbiblical Hebrew for "to study, teach" (with special reference to the Mishnah, a noun derived from the same verb). Teachers were referred to with the term *rab H8042* (which in the Bible means "commander, chief officer," from the word for "great") or derived forms, such as *rabbî* ("my mas-

ter"). This usage is reflected in the NT, where the term RABBI is translated *didaskalos G1437*, "teacher" (Jn. 1:38; "rabboni" in 20:16). Jesus is described as "teacher" about fifty times in the Gospels, and he is frequently said to have taught (e.g., Matt. 7:29). The Greek term for DISCIPLE, *mathētēs G3412* (from the verb *manthanō G3443*, "to learn," 11:28) occurs over 200 times in the Gospels. Having been taught by Jesus, his disciples were told to teach others also, making them disciples (28:19-20). See SCHOOL.

egg. The OT makes several references to eggs. The PENTATEUCH, for example, contains an injunction not to take a mother bird with her eggs or her young, but the young only (Deut. 22:6-7); and the book of JOB speaks of the ostrich leaving her eggs on the ground to be warmed by the sun (Job 39:14). Other references are found in metaphorical contexts (Isa. 10:14; 59:5; cf. also the NIV in Job 6:6; Isa. 34:15; Jer. 17:11). In the NT, Jesus refers to the absurdity of thinking that a father would give a scorpion to a son who asked for an egg (Lk. 11:12). Wild birds' eggs were first gathered for food (Deut. 22:6). By NT times eggs of domesticated fowl were a staple of diet.

Eglah. eg′luh (Heb. *ʿeglāh H6321* "heifer-calf"). A wife of DAVID who bore him his sixth son, Ithream, at HEBRON (2 Sam. 3:5; 1 Chr. 3:3).

Eglaim. eg′lay-im (Heb. *ʾeglayim H104*, possibly "[two] drops"). A town on the border of MOAB (Isa. 15:8). Its site is uncertain. See also EN EGLAIM.

Eglath Shelishiyah. eg′lath-shi-lish′uh-yuh (Heb. *ʿeglat šĕlišiyyâ H6326*, "the third Eglath [heifer-calf]"). An unidentified town near ZOAR mentioned in prophetic oracles of judgment on MOAB (Isa. 15:5; Jer. 48:34). The KJV takes the words as a metaphorical description of Zoar (and Horonaim), "an heifer of three years old."

Eglon (person). eg′lon (Heb. *ʿeglôn H6323*, "young bull"). An obese king of MOAB who early in the judges period occupied territory W of JORDAN near JERICHO. The military campaign of this king was assisted by neighboring AMMON, which attacked an area to the E of the JABBOK River

(Num. 21:24; Josh. 12:2; 13:10, 25; Jdg. 11:13, 22), and also by the desert bedouin AMALEKITES. The exploits of Eglon resulted in the occupation of the City of Palms (Jdg. 3:13), apparently a reference to the broad territory surrounding Jericho. The Israelites were dominated by the Moabites for eighteen years, after which God raised up EHUD to deliver Israel from this humiliation (3:21). Ehud brought the annual tribute to Eglon, gaining a private audience, and when the obese king stood up to receive the tribute, Ehud inflicted a fatal abdominal wound upon him.

Eglon (place). eg´lon (Heb. *ʿeglôn H6324*, "young bull"). An AMORITE town in the western SHEPHELAH, between GAZA and LACHISH; its king joined four others against GIBEON because this city had made a covenant with JOSHUA. Gibeon appealed to Joshua, who came with the Israelites and defeated and destroyed the five kings (Josh. 10:3, 5, 23). Later Joshua captured the city (10:36-37; 12:12). It was assigned to Judah (15:39). Recent work suggests that Eglon should be identified with Tell ʿAiṭun, 11 mi. (18 km.) WSW of HEBRON.

Egnatian Way. See VIA EGNATIA.

Egypt. ee´jipt. A country in the NE corner of Africa, including the NILE delta and valley, with their flanking deserts. In antiquity, it extended from the Mediterranean Sea to the first cataract of the Nile (to the second cataract in modern times). In the Table of Nations, Egypt (Heb. *miṣrayim H5213*) is listed as one of the sons of HAM and as the ancestor of seven people groups (Gen. 10:6, 13-14 = 1 Chr. 1:8, 11-12 NRSV; the NIV follows KJV in rendering "Mizraim").

I. Its Name. The Egyptians themselves had a number of names they used for their country; usually it was called "the Two Lands," which has reference to the origin of the nation in the union of Upper and Lower Egypt, just as the name "the United States of America" has historical derivation. Egypt was also Kemet, "the Black Land," the rich alluvial soil of the valley, as opposed to Desheret, "the Red Land," the barren waste of the desert. The English name *Egypt* derives from Greek *Aigyptos G131*, which in turn derives from Egyptian *ḥ(t)-kʾ-ptḥ*, "Mansion of the *ka*-spirit of [the god] Ptah," a name for MEMPHIS, the ancient capital. This term, already attested in the AMARNA letters of the 14th cent. B.C. as *Hikuptah*, shows the use of a city name for the land. Conversely, the Arabic name of the land, *Maṣr* or *Miṣr*, also stands for Cairo, successor to Memphis. This Arabic term for Egypt is that attested in the older Semitic languages, including biblical Hebrew (*miṣrayim*, which possibly means "[two] boundaries," perhaps alluding to Upper and Lower Egypt).

II. The Nile. "Egypt," said Hecateus, echoed by Herodotus, "is the gift of the Nile." This is a reflection of actual circumstances and of the Egyptian appreciation of the great river. The Nile, which courses like a living vein through the desiccated hills and deserts of NE Africa, laid down the black alluvium of the delta and the entire river valley. In view of the almost complete absence of rain, the annual overflow of the Nile was of great importance to the land, for it watered the soil and provided it with new alluvium and some organic fertilizer. Its waters were used for drinking (Exod. 7:18, 21, 24; Ps. 78:44), for bathing (Exod. 2:5), and for irrigation (Deut. 11:10). Its stream was the

The Nile River (looking W).

© Dr. James C. Martin

E

main channel of commerce and travel, with a prevailing N wind to favor southbound sailing vessels against the current.

The regularity of the inundation afforded a practical agricultural calendar, and the coincidence of the rise of the Nile and the appearance of the Dog Star (Sirius or Sothis) on the horizon at daybreak around July 19 was the basis for a chronological unit of 1,460 years, which is termed a Sothic cycle. Since the Egyptian calendar of 365 days was one-fourth of a day short of the true year, the Egyptian New Year's Day worked its way through the calendar until it again coincided with the rising of Sothis and the inundation (365 x 4 = 1,460). The recognition of this cycle and several references to it in dates of historical records make some helpful checkpoints in Egyptian chronology.

The awareness of the dependence of land and people on the resources of the Nile led to the deification of the river. The longest river in the world, the Nile covers some 4,000 mi. (6,440 km.) from its sources in equatorial Africa to its divided mouths that open into the Mediterranean. The White Nile is the principal stream, with tributaries joining it from their eastern points of origin in the Ethiopian hills. The Blue Nile enters at Khartoum. Farther N, the Atbara, the last consequential tributary, empties its periodic flow into the northbound stream. From this junction the Nile continues some 1,500 mi. (2,415 km.) without tributary to the sea. Numbered from Aswan to the S, in order of their discovery by modern explorers, are six cataracts, areas in which hard rock resisted the erosive action of the rushing stream. To varying degrees these hindered river travel and served as barriers to military movement. From Aswan to Cairo is a stretch of somewhat less than 600 mi. (960 km.). Below Cairo spreads the fan of the delta, an area about 125 x 125 mi. (200 x 200 km.).

III. Its Geography. The division of the land into Upper and Lower Egypt predates the union into one nation. Lower Egypt included the delta and a short section of the valley southward; the rest of the valley to Aswan was Upper Egypt. These areas were subdivided into administrative units that in Greek times were called "nomes," twenty in Lower Egypt and twenty-two in its southern counterpart. With the cataracts and the Nubian desert to the S

and SE, the Libyan desert and the Sahara to the W, and the Arabian desert on the E, the valley was not subject to the frequent invasions that characterized less defensible lands. The biggest threat from outside was on the delta edges; even here the passage of armies was handicapped by terrain and climate. On the NE border, fronting Asia, the Egyptians made early use of fortresses and other checkpoints to control invasion from this direction. With such protection, the country was free to develop its culture in comparative security and still to retain a free exchange of goods and ideas with other peoples.

IV. Its Climate. The climate of the land, along with the particular beliefs of the people, has been of great advantage to ARCHAEOLOGY, so that it may be said that Egypt is the archaeological area *par excellence.* Lack of rain and frost, plenty of dry sand to form a protective cover over remains, and abundant use of stone for monumental building are helpful environmental factors. The burial customs have been of much help to the cultural historian, for the relief sculpture, tomb furniture, models, and inscriptions tell much of the daily life of antiquity.

V. Its Religion. The religion of ancient Egypt is a vast and labyrinthine subject. Much of the religious literature appears as a hodgepodge of conflicting statements to the modern Western reader, to whom many of the allusions must remain obscure. In general, the religion may be described as a complex polytheism, with many local deities of varying importance. A full list of these divinities would be impractical, but these may be singled out: Osiris and Isis, who are well known from their later adoption by the mystery religions of Greece and Rome; Ra (Re), a sun-god, who came into prominence in the 5th dynasty; Horus, another sun-god, the son of Osiris and Isis; Set, the rival of Osiris and Horus; Amon-Re, who became the god of empire; Ptah, the god of Memphis; Khnum, the god of Elephantine. The attempt of Akhenaten (Amenhotep IV) to reorient Egyptian religion with a primary emphasis on Aton, the sun-disc, has been widely discussed as a tendency toward monotheism. There is no evidence of possible Israelite influence on his beliefs. His innovations did not long survive him and the priests of Amon at Thebes scored a theological-political victory. Much of the religious literature has a mortuary interest; this

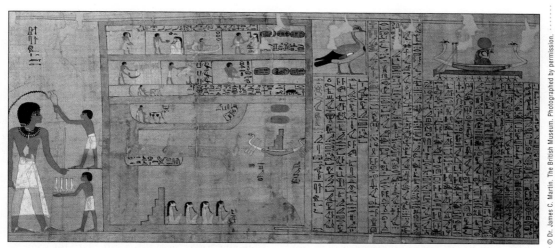

An early example of the Egyptian *Book of the Dead* on papyrus, produced by a scribe named Userhat (from Thebes, c. 1450 B.C.).

© Dr. James C. Martin. The British Museum. Photographed by permission.

preoccupation with death was a futile gesture to transfer earthly life to an eternal dimension. There are no reflections of this Egyptian concept in the Bible, and the absence of any large body of OT teaching concerning life beyond the grave may be a divine avoidance of a possible snare to the Israelites. The influence of Egyptian religion on Israelite religious practice was largely negative. In several instances the Israelites were led into apostasy to worship Egyptian gods (see below), but even these occasions were rare.

VI. Its History. Preceding the historical or dynastic period are a number of prehistoric cultures that are known in general outline. In the late predynastic epoch there is interesting evidence of cultural influence from Mesopotamia. The rudiments of hieroglyphic WRITING also appear about this time and usher in the historical period. The materials for writing the political history of Egypt are lists of kings (such as those inscribed in temples of Abydos and Karnak, that of a tomb at Saqqarah, the Turin Papyrus, and the Palermo Stone) and numerous historical records, both of kings and of lesser persons active in history-making. The dynastic scheme is a historiographical convenience inherited from the priest-historian Manetho, who divided Egyptian history from Menes to Alexander into thirty-one dynasties. Egyptologists have used a somewhat standard arrangement of these dynasties into historical periods. A highly condensed outline follows.

A. Protodynastic Period (1st-2nd dyn.; 3100-2700 B.C.). According to the tradition of Manetho, the first king of united Egypt was Menes, who came from Thinis in Upper Egypt, united the two lands, and established his capital at Memphis in about 3200-3100. Some scholars equate Menes with Narmer and/or Aha. Royal tombs of this period have been found at Saqqarah and Abydos.

B. Old Kingdom (3rd-6th dyn.; 2700-2200). This is a high point in Egyptian history. The canons of art were firmly established in this period and perhaps the bases of the applied sciences were also laid. In the 3rd dynasty, the step pyramid of Djoser, "the world's first monumental architecture in stone," was built at Saqqarah. Its architect, Imhotep, was also famed in other fields of accomplishment. The 4th dynasty was the time of the pyramid-builders *par excellence:* the pyramids of Khufu (Cheops), Khafre (Chephren), and Menkaure (Mycerions) were constructed at Giza. Kings of the 5th and 6th dynasties had their pyramids at Saqqarah; in these were inscribed the religious writings known as the Pyramid Texts. The proverbs of Ptahhotep, a vizier of the 5th dynasty, are well-known.

C. First Intermediate Period (7th-11th dyn.; 2200-2050). This was a period of weakness and confusion. The 7th-8th dynasties were at Memphis, the 9th-10th were at Herakleopolis, and the 11th was at Thebes. The literature is an outgrowth of the pessimism of the times; it includes the writings of

Ipuwer, the Dialogue of a Man Weary of Life; the Song of the Harper.

D. The Middle Kingdom (12th dyn.; 2050-1800) was another peak in Egyptian history. Art and architecture flourished. This is the time of the Eloquent Peasant and of the adventures of the courtier Sinuhe. In religious literature the Coffin Texts are found. There is a trend toward democratization of royal privileges, along with an emphasis on *ma'at,* "justice, right." The king is heralded as "the shepherd" of the people.

E. Second Intermediate Period (13th-17th dyn.; 1800-1580); another dark age for Egypt. Insignificant rulers made up the 13th-14th dynasties. The 15th-16th are the HYKSOS dynasties, which may be of greater importance than brief, derogatory Egyptian references lead us to think. The 17th dynasty was made up of Theban rulers who began the movement to expel the Hyksos.

F. The New Kingdom or Empire (18th-20th dyn.; 1580-1090) marked the height of Egyptian imperialistic ambitions, with some fluctuations. Outstanding rulers include: in the 18th dynasty, Hatshepsut, the woman-king who sponsored a voyage to Punt and built a fine mortuary temple at Deir el-Bahri; Thutmose III, the energetic warrior and capable administrator; Amenhotep III, the Magnificent, a lavish spender who neglected the empire and with his successor Akhenaten, the religious innovator, ignored the pleas for help from Palestine-Syria (AMARNA Tablets). In the 19th dynasty, the outstanding figure is Ramses II, the builder, renovator, and chiseler; in the 20th dynasty, it is Ramses III, who defeated the SEA PEOPLES.

G. The Post-Empire Period or **Period of Decline** (21st-25th dyn.; 1150-663) finds Egypt a "broken reed."

H. The Saite Period (26th dyn.; 663-525). There was a short restoration in this period, which includes Neco and Apries (biblical Hophra, Jer. 44:30).

I. Later Egypt. In 525 B.C., PERSIA (under Cambyses) took over Egypt; what followed were two centuries of Persian domination, limited independence, and Egyptian rebellions (27th-30th dyn.; 525-332). With ALEXANDER THE GREAT came the end of the dynasties and of native rule. After the death of Alexander (323), Egypt was governed by the Ptolemies until the Romans made it a province in 31.

VII. Egypt and the Bible. To the Israelites, Egypt was somewhat of an enigma, a land of contrast, a country that they hated but respected. When a psalmist looked back to the days of the EXODUS, he referred to the Egyptians as "a people of foreign tongue" (Ps. 114:1), a description to which even many moderns may assent. Egypt was the iron furnace of affliction during the bondage, but Israelites were so impressed with the might of the Pharaonic kingdom that there were elements in Judah that looked to the Egyptians for help even after Egypt had become the broken reed of Assyrian contempt (cf. 2 Ki. 18:21; Isa. 36:6). An unreliable ally, Egypt was also a sanctuary for some of Israel's individual enemies. From Egypt, too, came some of the worst occasions for apostasy in Israel. Egypt appears in the Bible as a type of the transitory, earthbound system called "the world." In one instance it is an allegorical synonym for Sodom and for rebellious Jerusalem (Rev. 11:8). Nevertheless, it was an abundant ANE breadbasket and was for centuries the ranking world power. It afforded food for many a hungry Palestinian, and heat-smitten wandering tribes were permitted to cross its borders to graze their animals in the delta. JOSEPH realized that God's providence was in his being sold into Egypt (Gen. 45:5-9), and JACOB was instructed by the Lord to go there (46:3-4).

Egypt appears early in biblical references. ABRAHAM's sojourn in Egypt is a well-known incident. It is evident from Gen. 12:10 that Egypt was the place to which Palestinians naturally looked in time of famine. The famous scene from the wall paintings of the tomb of Khnumhotep II at Beni Hasan shows a group of Asiatics in Middle Egypt for purposes of trade and illustrates several facets of Abraham's descent into Egypt. His fears concerning the king's interest in SARAH were real and perhaps well founded, but there is no certain evidence for such royal behavior in Egyptian literature. The oft-cited Tale of Two Brothers relates a quite different sort of situation, for there the wife is anxious to be rid of her husband so that she may become a wife of Pharaoh.

The closest Egyptian-biblical relationships may be seen in the narrative of Joseph and the account

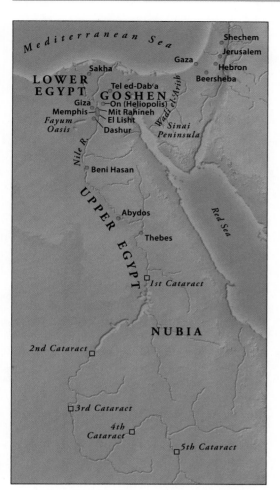

Egypt at the time of Abraham (Middle Kingdom Egypt).

In Exod. 1 there are references to brick-making, field work, and obstetrical practices that are particularly Egyptian. In ch. 2 the references to the Nile are of interest. The account of the signs and the plagues shows an intimate knowledge of Egyptian life and provides a study in the relationship of natural and miraculous phenomena. The asking for jewelry of silver and gold (11:2) is a reflection of the expert Egyptian work in metals. The Egyptian pursuit of the fleeing Israelites (14:10, 23) finds parallels in the battle reliefs of Egypt's chief monarchs. The ironic mention of graves in Egypt (14:11) reminds us of the vast necropolis that marks the desert fringe. Well into the wilderness, the refugees were outside of Egyptian concern and out of its effective reach; but, barely escaped from slavery, the Israelites were soon engrossed in worshiping the golden calf (ch. 32), a descendant of the bovine worship of Memphis and other Egyptian cities. There were also fond recollections of good eating in Egypt, with its fish, cucumbers, leeks, onions, and garlic, which the Israelites regarded as strength-giving fare (Num. 11:5-6). During the period of the judges, the hill-country of Palestine saw little likelihood of antagonistic Egyptian interference. Egyptian power had declined; in about 1100 B.C. the royal emissary Wen-Amon found little respect for the might of Egypt along the Mediterranean coast.

With this weakness, the time was ripening for the rapid growth of a young and vigorous nation in the former Asiatic empire of Egypt. When the Israelite monarchy came into existence, neither SAUL nor DAVID recorded immediate dealings with the land of the Nile. SOLOMON, however, married a daughter of the current Pharaoh, who captured and destroyed GEZER and presented it to his daughter as dowry (1 Ki. 9:16). It is stated that Solomon's wisdom excelled that of his commercial relations with Egypt (2 Chr. 1:16-17). Late in Solomon's reign, an Edomite enemy, HADAD, who as a child had found asylum in Egypt after a raid by David into Edomite territory, left Egypt to become an active adversary of Solomon. JEROBOAM fled to Egypt to escape Solomon; as first king of the northern tribes, this Jeroboam, "who made Israel to sin," set up calf images at Dan and Bethel (1 Ki. 12:26-33), a religious importation influenced by his Egyptian exile. In the fifth year of REHOBOAM

of Israelite life in Egypt to the time of their exodus (Gen. 37; 39-50; Exod. 1-15). A listing of some of the most intriguing elements includes: Joseph's coat (Gen. 37); POTIPHAR, "an Egyptian" (ch. 39); Potiphar's wife (39:6-18), with interesting parallels in the Tale of Two Brothers, a not uncommon episode in many cultures; the prison for political offenders (39:20); the duties of butler and baker; dreams in Egypt; Egyptian viticulture (ch. 40); cattle and the Nile; grain-growing (ch. 41); shaving (41:14); east wind (41:27); taxes (41:34); the gold (41:42); chariots (41:43); the priest of On (Heliopolis) (41:45); Egyptian names; Egypt as a source of food (41:57); divination (44:5); the land of GOSHEN (ch. 47); the Egyptian priesthood (47:22); embalming, mummification, and burial rites (ch. 50).

(926 B.C.) the Egyptian King Sheshonk (biblical SHISHAK) carried out an expedition into Palestine that saw the temple stripped of its treasures to meet his demands (1 Ki. 14:25, 26; 2 Chr. 12:1-9).

Egypt was a strong influence in Judean politics in the days of ISAIAH and JEREMIAH, who were aware of the weakness of Egypt against the Assyrian threat. When the Assyrian remnant was making its dying stand and Egypt marched to aid them against the rampaging Babylonians, the Judean JOSIAH made a fatal effort to stop the Egyptian forces at MEGIDDO (2 Ki. 23:29-30; 2 Chr. 35:20-27). After the fall of JERUSALEM in 586 B.C. and the subsequent murder of GEDALIAH, the Judeans again looked to Egypt as a place of refuge in spite of the prophet's warning. Here they were scattered about, with a group as far S as Elephantine maintaining a temple and keeping up correspondence with Palestine, as revealed by the Aramaic papyri found at Elephantine.

In the NT most of the references to Egypt have to do with Israel's past. One important mention had current meaning, for Joseph was divinely directed to take the infant Jesus and Mary to Egypt to escape the wrath of HEROD (Matt. 2:13-15; cf. Exod. 4:22; Hos. 11:1).

VIII. Its Significance and Future. It is remarkable that Egypt so often was a place of refuge or a means of sustaining life. Though it is regarded by some as an invariable epitome of "the world," Egypt has the scriptural prediction of a wonderful future: "In that day Israel will be the third, along with Egypt and Assyria, a blessing on the earth. The LORD Almighty will bless them, saying, 'Blessed be Egypt my people, Assyria my handiwork, and Israel my inheritance'" (Isa. 19:24-25; cf. 19:18-23).

Egypt, Brook of. See EGYPT, WADI OF.

Egypt, river of. This phrase properly renders Hebrew *nĕhar miṣrayim*, which occurs only once (Gen. 15:18); it may refer to the NILE, but more likely it is the same as "the Wadi of Egypt" (see below). The NIV uses "the river of Egypt" also as the translation of *yĕʾôr miṣrayim*, which occurs twice with reference to the Nile (Amos 8:8; 9:5 [KJV, "the flood of Egypt"; NRSV, "the Nile of Egypt"]; cf. the plural form in Isa. 7:18). In addi-

tion, the KJV uses the phrase six times to render a third Hebrew term, *nahal miṣrayim* (in Num. 34:5, *naḥālâ miṣrayim*). See also EGYPT, WADI OF.

Egypt, Wadi of. The SW border of the Promised Land (Num. 34:5; cf. Josh. 15:4, 47; 1 Ki. 8:65; 2 Ki. 24:7; 2 Chr. 7:8; Isa. 27:12). Ezekiel refers to it simply as "the wadi" (*naḥălāh H5711*; Ezek. 47:19; 48:28). In these passages the KJV has "the river of Egypt" (except Isa. 27:12, "the stream of Egypt") and the RSV, "the Brook of Egypt." The biblical evidence places this WADI or stream bed westward from GAZA (cf. Josh. 15:47) and KADESH BARNEA (cf. Num. 34:4-5). The Wadi of Egypt has usually been identified with Wadi el-ʿArish, reaching the Mediterranean at the town of el-ʿArish some 90 mi. (145 km.) E of the Suez canal and almost 50 mi. (80 km.) SW of Gaza. More recently , however, some scholars have identified it with Naḥal Besor, which is farther N. In any case, it probably should not be confused with SHIHOR, which seems to designate the old Pelusiac and easternmost arm of the Nile (never a wadi).

Egyptian, the. An unnamed individual mentioned in the context of PAUL's arrest and removal from the temple precinct (Acts 21:38). In the narrative the Roman officer asked Paul if he was not a certain Egyptian who was attempting a revolt against Rome. This man was supposed to have led his 4,000 dagger-bearers or *Sicarii* into the wilderness. JOSEPHUS (*Ant.* 20.8.6 §§168-72; cf. *War* 2.13.5 §§261-63) apparently refers to the same Egyptian, "a man who declared that he was a prophet and advised the masses of the common people to go out with him to the mountain called the Mount of Olives. ... For he asserted that he wished to demonstrate from there that at his command Jerusalem's walls would fall down, through which he promised to provide them an entrance into the city." The revolt was quelled by FELIX; 400 were killed and another two hundred taken prisoner, but the Egyptian himself escaped.

Ehi. ee′hi (Heb. *ʾēhî H305*, derivation uncertain). Sixth son of BENJAMIN and grandson of JACOB (Gen. 46:21). Some scholars regard Ehi as an abbreviated form of AHIRAM (Num. 26:38).

According to others, the Hebrew text has suffered scribal corruption.

Ehud. ee´huhd (Heb. *ʾēhûd H179* [in 1 Chr. 8:6, MT has *ʾēḥûd H287*], possibly "where is the glory?"). **(1)** Son of Gera and descendant of BENJAMIN. Ehud, a left-handed hero, led the revolt against the Moabite King EGLON, who early in the period of the judges had subjugated Israel for eighteen years (Jdg. 3:15-31; 1 Chr. 8:6). Before taking the annual tribute to Eglon, Ehud fashioned a 13-inch double-edged dagger which he carried on his right thigh for convenience, being left-handed. Having publicly paid the tribute, he seized an opportunity through a ruse to speak privately to Eglon and slew the unsuspecting king. Gaining time by locking the body in the private chamber, Ehud escaped through a window and marshaled the W Jordanian Israelites to prevent 10,000 Moabite soldiers from fleeing homeward, thus insuring peace for eighty years.

(2) Son of Bilhan and descendant of Benjamin (1 Chr. 7:10).

Eker. ee´kuhr (Heb. *ʿēqer H6831*, possibly "root" or "offspring"). Son of Ram and descendant of JUDAH (1 Chr. 2:27).

Ekron. ek´ruhn (Heb. *ʿeqrôn H6833*, possibly "barren place"; gentilic *ʿeqrônî H6834*, "Ekronite"). The most northern of the five chief cities of the PHILISTINES (see 1 Sam. 6:17). It was located on the boundary between the tribes of JUDAH and DAN (Josh. 15:11; 19:43), but was assigned to Judah (15:45). After the Philistines returned the ARK OF THE COVENANT from Ekron to escape the wrath of God (1 Sam. 6), the Israelites regained possession of the city and of neighboring towns (7:14). Following DAVID's victory over GOLIATH, the Israelites drove the Philistines back to Ekron (17:52). The god of this city was BAAL-ZEBUB (2 Ki. 1:3). The prophets mention Ekron with other Philistine cities (Jer. 25:20; Amos 1-8; Zeph. 2:4; Zech. 9:5, 7).

In the Assyrian inscriptions Ekron appears as *Amqarrūna*. SENNACHERIB assaulted it and killed its officials because they had been disloyal to ASSYRIA. ESARHADDON called on twenty-two cities that paid tribute to him (Ekron was one) to help transport building supplies for his palace.

ASHURBANIPAL included Ekron in the list of cities that paid tribute to him. The Greek form *Akkarōn* appears in the APOCRYPHA (1 Macc. 10:89) and in accounts of the Crusades. Ekron is now generally identified with Khirbet el-Muqannaᶜ (Tel Miqne), located S of the SOREK valley, about 20 mi. (32 km.) SE of JOPPA.

El. el (Heb. *ʾēl H446*, etymology disputed; ancient Semitic term for deity, cf. Assyr. *ilu*, Ugar. *il*). The generic word for God in the Semitic languages, used over 200 times in the OT. In the prose books it often has a modifying term with it, but in JOB and PSALMS it occurs alone many times. El was the chief, and somewhat vague, shadowy god of the Canaanite pantheon (see RAS SHAMRA), and the title is used in the OT to express the exalted transcendence of God. See ELOHIM. The Hebrews borrowed this word from the Canaanites. The linguistic derivation of the name is uncertain; suggestions include roots that mean "to be strong" and "to be in front of" (as a leader). The Canaanite god El was the father of human beings and of gods. He is called "father of mankind" and "father of years." He was an immoral and debased character. It is a tribute to the high morality of the OT understanding of God that a title that in Canaanite usage was so defiled could, without risk, be used to express the moral majesty of the God of Israel. Note, however, that just as the word *god* in English can be used of the true God or of false gods, so this word in Hebrew may refer to heathen gods, usually meaning idols (Exod. 15:11; 34:14; Isa. 43:10).

Ela. ee´luh (Heb. *ʾēlāʾ H452*, meaning uncertain). Father of SHIMEI; the latter was one of the twelve governors in charge of providing for King SOLOMON's household (1 Ki. 4:18; KJV, "Elah").

Eladah. See ELEADAH.

Elah. ee´luh (Heb. *ʾēlāh H462*, possibly "oak"). **(1)** One of the Edomite chiefs descended from ESAU (Gen. 36:41; 1 Chr. 1:52). Some believe that the word should be taken as a place name and identified with ELATH.

(2) Son of CALEB and descendant of JUDAH (1 Chr. 4:15).

(3) Son of BAASHA and fourth king of Israel (1 Ki. 16:8-14). He succeeded his father in the twenty-sixth year of ASA of Judah, reigned in TIRZAH, and was assassinated in the following year (vv. 10, 15). This short period was long enough for him to show his adherence to his father's religious policy, in defiance of the prophecy of JEHU son of Hanani (v. 1), but he seems to have lacked his father's energy and leadership. It is recorded that he met his death while carousing at the home of his chamberlain in Tirzah, though the army was at the time laying siege to the PHILISTINE city of GIBBETHON.

(4) Father of HOSHEA; the latter became the last king of Israel (2 Ki. 15:30; 17:1; 18:1, 9).

(5) Son of Uzzi and one of the first Benjamites to resettle in Jerusalem after the EXILE (1 Chr. 9:8).

(6) KJV form of ELA.

Elah, Valley of. ee′luh (Heb. *ʾēlāh H463*, possibly "oak"). A valley in the SHEPHELAH, generally identified with Wadi es-Sanṭ ("Valley of the Acacia"),

View looking SW through the dry streambed of the shrub-lined Wadi Elah, where David and Goliath met for battle.

© Dr. James C. Martin

about 18 mi. (29 km.) WSW of JERUSALEM. The area is rich in acacias, terebinths, and oaks. It was the scene of the combat between DAVID and GOLIATH (1 Sam. 17:2, 19; 21:9). Coursing through the valley is a watercourse (or WADI, as the Arabs call it), which runs in the period of the rains only. The bottom of the watercourse is covered with small stones, the kind David might have used for his sling.

Elam (person). ee′luhm (Heb. *ʿēlām H6521* [*H6520* for #1 below], derivation uncertain). (1) Son of SHEM, grandson of NOAH, and eponymous ancestor of the Elamites (Gen. 10:22; 1 Chr. 1:17). See ELAM (PLACE).

(2) Fifth son of Meshelemiah and descendant of LEVI through KORAH; like his father, he and his brothers were Levitical gatekeepers in the time of DAVID (1 Chr. 26:3).

(3) Son of Shahach and descendant of BENJAMIN (1 Chr. 8:24). Some identify him with #4 below.

(4) The eponym of a clan from which 1,254 persons returned to Palestine with ZERUBBABEL after the EXILE (Ezra 2:7; Neh. 7:12). An additional 70 members of this family, headed by Jeshaiah son of Athaliah, returned with EZRA (Ezra 8:7). Still another member of this family, Shecaniah son of Jehiel, suggested to Ezra that those Israelites who had married foreign women put away these wives and their children (10:2-4). Six of the men of this family put away their foreign wives (10:26).

(5) A man referred to as "the other Elam" also had a family of 1,254 who returned from the exile (Ezra 2:31; Neh. 7:34). Because the number of family members is the same as that of #4 above, some scholars identify the two individuals as one.

(6) One of the chiefs who are said to have sealed the covenant with NEHEMIAH (Neh. 10:14). Some scholars identify him with #4 above.

(7) A priest who participated in the dedication of the walls of Jerusalem in Nehemiah's time (Neh. 12:42).

Elam (place). ee′luhm (Heb. *ʿēlām H6520*; Aram. gentilic *ʿēlmāy H10551* and Gk. gentilic *Elamitēs G1780*, "Elamite"). A country situated on the east side of the TIGRIS River opposite Babylonia in a mountainous region. Its population was made up of a variety of tribes. Their language, different from the Sumerian, Semitic, and Indo-European tongues, was written in cuneiform script. It has not yet been deciphered to any great extent. Elam was one of the earliest civilizations. In Sumerian inscriptions it was called *Numma* (high mountain people), which became *Elamtu* in Akkadian texts; in classical literature it was known as *Susiana*, the Greek name for SUSA, the capital city of Elam.

Sargon (2350 B.C.) claimed conquest of Elam in his day. Later on, about 2280, an Elamite king invaded Babylonia and took back much spoil. Gudea, a ruler of the city of Lagash about 2100, mentions that the Elamites collected some of the timbers he used in constructing the temple of Ningirsu, the god of Lagash. HAMMURABI (1728-1686) subdued the Elamites. In the time of ABRAHAM, according to Gen. 14, an Elamite king, KEDORLAOMER, made a raid on Palestine.

Elam figures prominently in Babylonian and Assyrian texts because it was situated so close to them. When BABYLON became active against Assyrian supremacy, Elam became her chief ally. ASSYRIA was not able to subdue Elam completely until the time of ASHURBANIPAL (668-626 B.C.), who sacked the country thoroughly in 640. This catastrophe practically finished Elam as a nation, but part of the country was not much affected by these intrusions of Semitic powers. This district called *Anzan* was, next to the capital at Susa, the most important part of the nation. From that area, CYRUS, the conqueror of Babylon, arose.

Isaiah cites Elam as one of the nations going up with Cyrus against Babylon (Isa. 21:2) and joining the Assyrian army against Judah (22:6). Elam was one of the nations forced to drink the cup of God's wrath (Jer. 25:25) and doomed to judgment (49:34-39). Ezra 4:9-10 refers to Elamites as among the peoples brought over to SAMARIA by the Assyrians. In Acts 2:9 the Elamites are said to have been present, along with PARTHIANS, Medes (see MEDIA), and others, in Jerusalem on the day of PENTECOST.

Elasah. el′uh-suh (Heb. ʾelʿāśâ *H543*, "God has made"). **(1)** Son of SHAPHAN; he and Gemariah son of Hilkiah were entrusted with a letter from JEREMIAH to the exiles in Babylon (Jer. 29:3).

(2) One of the descendants of PASHHUR who agreed to put away their foreign wives (Ezra 10:22).

Elath, Eloth. ee′lath, ee′loth (Heb. ʾêlat *H397* and ʾêlôt *H393*, possibly "grove of [palm] trees"). The NIV renders "Elath" consistently. A town on the northern end of the Gulf of AQABAH (also known as the Gulf of Elath, the NE arm of the RED SEA). Many believe it is the same as EL PARAN (Gen. 14:6). The town is mentioned along with EZION GEBER in connection with the wilderness travels of the Israelites through MOAB (Deut. 2:8). Because of its strategic position, Elath was an asset to any nation. The first mention of the place after the EXODUS states that "King Solomon also built ships at Ezion Geber, which is near Elath in Edom, on the shore of the Red Sea" (1 Ki. 9:26; cf. 2 Chr. 8:17; David had earlier subdued the Edomites, 2 Sam. 8:14). Later, in the time of JEHOSHAPHAT, the ships were wrecked at Ezion Geber (1 Ki. 22:48; 2 Chr. 20:35-37). The Edomites apparently captured Elath when they rebelled against King JEHORAM (2 Ki. 8:20), for AMAZIAH is said to have rebuilt the city and restored it to Judah (2 Ki. 14:22). His son, King UZZIAH (Azariah), apparently completed the rebuilding (2 Chr. 26:2), but under the reign of AHAZ the Edomites reoccupied

E

Ancient Elath lay at the N end of the Gulf of Aqabah. (View to the E.)

© Dr. James C. Martin

it (2 Ki. 16:6). There is evidence that Elath continued to play an important role long after OT times. The site is thought to be a short distance SE of Tell el-Kheleifeh, which is widely identified with Ezion Geber. The modern Israeli town of Eilat shares the same general locale, but the Jordanian town of Aqabah may be covering the ancient biblical site.

El-Berith. el´bi-rith´ (Heb. *ʾēl bĕrît H451*, "God of the covenant"). A god worshiped at SHECHEM, in whose temple some of the Shechemites took refuge when ABIMELECH destroyed the city (Jdg. 9:46; KJV, "the god Berith"). It is possibly an alternate name for the god BAAL BERITH.

El Bethel. el-beth´uhl (Heb. *ʾēl bêt-ʾēl H450*, "the God [of] Bethel"). The name that JACOB, after his return from PADDAN ARAM, gave to the altar he erected at BETHEL, "because it was there that God revealed himself to him when he was fleeing from his brother" (Gen. 35:7).

Eldaah. el-day´uh (Heb. *ʾeldāʿâ H456*, possibly "God has called"). Son of MIDIAN and grandson of ABRAHAM through KETURAH (Gen. 25:4 [cf. vv. 1-2]; 1 Chr. 1:33). The names of Keturah's sons and grandsons appear to function as the clan names of various ARABIAN tribes.

Eldad. el´dad (Heb. *ʾeldād H455*, possibly "God has loved" or "God is friend"). One of the seventy elders chosen to assist MOSES in leading the Israelites (Num. 11:26-27; possibly the same person as ELIDAD, 34:21). When Moses found that the discontent of the people, on the journey from Sinai toward Canaan, was hard to bear, he was commanded to choose seventy elders who would share the burden of administration (11:16-17). The elders gathered at the TABERNACLE, and the Spirit of the Lord came upon them and they prophesied. Two of those chosen, Eldad and Medad, remained in the camp, yet they received the same Spirit of prophecy. JOSHUA was indignant because these two prophesied in the camp rather than at the tabernacle, but Moses refused to forbid them, remarking that he wished all the Lord's people were PROPHETS (11:28-29).

elder. In Israel, the elders (Heb. *zāqēn H2418*, from the word for "beard") were adult men who gathered in popular assembly, or as a kind of council in every village. They also served as local rulers. Usually they were the heads of families, but probably were selected also on the basis of age, wisdom, ability, respect, or prowess. MOSES called the elders of Israel together to announce that the Lord had heard their cries for help and had appointed him to lead them out of Egypt (Exod. 4:29). Later he called them out to institute the Passover (12:21). At SINAI, seventy of the elders went up the mountain with Moses and saw the God of Israel (24:9). In the wilderness, to relieve Moses, seventy elders shared his divine anointing (Num. 11:25). After the Israelites had settled in Canaan and had a king over them, the elders still functioned. They were a separate group from the heads of the tribes and the princes of the fathers' houses (1 Ki. 8:1). Each town had its group of elders, as BETHLEHEM did (1 Sam. 16:4), "the elders … of each town" (Ezra 10:14). After the return from exile the elders made up the SANHEDRIN, the governing council of the Jews.

This type of society continued into NT times. The elders joined the PRIESTS and SCRIBES against Jesus (Matt. 27:12). When churches came into being, elders were appointed for each congregation (Acts 14:23; Gk. *presbyteros G4565*, lit., "older person, old man," sometimes transliterated "presbyter"). The "elders" of Acts 20:17 are referred to as BISHOPS in v. 28 (NIV "overseers"). In Tit. 1:5, "elders" in the Cretan churches are mentioned; in listing qualifications for such an office, Paul calls them "bishops/overseers" in v. 7. These men were required to be blameless in their lives and obedient to the truth in their faith (1 Tim. 3:1-7; Tit. 1:6-9). Their duties involved spiritual oversight of the congregation and teaching the Word. Those who ruled well and also taught were worthy of "double honor" (1 Tim. 5:17). Before the first century A.D. had elapsed, the term *bishop* had taken on a special meaning, denoting the one leader of a church. Opinions vary regarding the twenty-four elders in heaven around the throne of God (as depicted in the book of Revelation); probably they represent the heavenly priesthood of the church associated with Christ, the Great High Priest.

Elead. el´ee-uhd (Heb. *ʾelʿād H537*, "God has testified"). Son of EPHRAIM (or possibly son of SHUTHELAH #1 and grandson of Ephraim); he and EZER (prob. his brother), while raiding the livestock in GATH, were killed by the men of the city (1 Chr. 7:21). This tragedy in the family moved Ephraim to call his next son BERIAH, an allusion to the Hebrew word for "calamity" (v. 23).

Eleadah. el´ee-ay´duh (Heb. *ʾelʿādâ H538*, "God has adorned"). KJV Eladah. Son or, more probably, descendant of EPHRAIM; it is possible that his father's (as well as his son's) name was TAHATH (1 Chr. 7:20; the referent of the repeated phrase "his son" is ambiguous).

Elealeh. el´ee-ay´luh (Heb. *ʾelʿālēh H542* and *ʾelʿālēʾ H541*, possibly "God ascends"). A city in TRANSJORDAN on the S boundary of the region known as GILEAD. It lay over a mile NNE of HESHBON, almost due E of the northern tip of the DEAD SEA. It is identified with the modern site of el-ʿAl. Elealeh and surrounding towns were given to the tribe of REUBEN (Num. 32:3). They were rebuilt and given Israelite names (32:37-38). The Moabites soon reoccupied the area, and the territory was in dispute between AMMON and MOAB (Jdg. 11:13-33). Upon the death of AHAB (c. 850 B.C.), MESHA of Moab revolted; the territory thus became Moabite and remained so throughout the prophetic period. Elealeh and Heshbon are mentioned in both Isaiah's and Jeremiah's oracles of judgment on Moab (Isa. 15:4; 16:9; Jer. 48:34).

Eleasah. el´ee-ay´suh (Heb. *ʾelʿāśâ H543*, "God has made"). **(1)** Son of Helez and descendant of JUDAH (1 Chr. 2:39-40).

(2) Son of Raphah and descendant of SAUL through JONATHAN (1 Chr. 8:37; 9:43).

Eleazar. el´ee-ay´zuhr (Heb. *ʾelʿāzār H540*, "God has helped"; Gk. *Eleazar G1789*; see also ELIEZER). **(1)** Son of AARON and ELISHEBA (Exod. 6:23). Two of Eleazar's brothers, NADAB and ABIHU, were killed when they offered "unauthorized fire before the LORD" (Lev. 10:1-11). Eleazar, the oldest remaining son, evidently had the primogeniture rather than his younger brother, ITHAMAR, and he

succeeded in the high priestly office after his father's death (Num. 20:25-28; Deut. 10:6). Eleazar supervised the Kohathites (see KOHATH), who carried the ARK OF THE COVENANT and the holy furniture upon their shoulders on the march (Num. 3:30-32). He was also charged with the oversight of the TABERNACLE and its furniture, the oil, the incense, etc. (4:16). Eleazar was prominent after the rebellion of KORAH, DATHAN, and ABIRAM (Num. 16). He was the first appointed to prepare holy water from the ashes of the red heifer (19:4), and he served as high priest to JOSHUA (27:19-21). His son PHINEHAS carried the trumpets and other articles to battle in TRANSJORDAN (31:6). With Joshua, Eleazar divided the land of Palestine by lot (34:17; Josh. 14:1; 17:4). For a time, and for reasons that are not clear, the descendants of Ithamar superseded those of Eleazar in the tabernacle of SHILOH. The priest ELI was of the house of Ithamar, but because of the wickedness of his house, his line was rejected.

(2) Son of ABINADAB; he was consecrated to keep the ARK OF THE COVENANT after it was brought back from Philistia (1 Sam. 7:1).

(3) Son of Dodo the Ahohite and one of David's first three "mighty men" (2 Sam. 23:9; 1 Chr. 11:12). See discussion under SHAMMAH #4.

(4) Son of Mahli and descendant of LEVI through MERARI; the text records twice that he died without sons (1 Chr. 23:21-22; 24:28). His daughters married the sons of his brother KISH.

(5) Son of Phinehas and a priest of the time of Ezra (Ezra 8:33; prob. the same as the temple singer mentioned in Neh. 12:42).

(6) One of the descendants of Parosh who agreed to put away their foreign wives (Ezra 10:25).

(7) Son of Eliud, included in Matthew's GENEALOGY OF JESUS CHRIST (Matt. 1:15).

election and predestination. For God to "predestine" (Gk. *proorizō G4633*) is for him to decree or foreordain the circumstances and destiny of people according to his perfect will (Rom. 8:29-30; Eph. 1:11). It is, therefore, a particular aspect of the general PROVIDENCE of God that relates to God's superintendence of the whole cosmos and everything in it. For God to "elect" (Heb. *bāḥar H1047* and Gk. *eklegomai G1721*) is for him to choose for salvation and/or service a people or a person; the

E

choice is based not on merit but on his free, sovereign LOVE (Deut. 4:37; 7:7; 14:2; Acts 13:17; 15:7; 1 Thess. 1:4). Further, since predestination and election are both presented as gracious acts of God, they cannot be based on God's knowing in advance the reactions of people to his will. Election must be choice flowing only from God's own initiative. Believers were chosen in Christ before the foundation of the world (Eph. 1:4).

Election is a prominent theme in the OT. There is the choice of ABRAHAM and his "seed" that in him the nations of the world will be blessed (Gen. 12:1-3; 22:17-18); and there is the choice of (or COVENANT with) the people ISRAEL whom God led out of bondage into liberty (Exod. 3:6-10; Deut. 6:21-23). This nation was chosen by God as those to whom he could reveal himself and his will, and through whom he could exhibit and declare to the world his purposes and salvation (Deut. 28:1-14; Isa. 43:10-12, 20, 21). Further, there was the choice, from within the chosen people, of specific individuals—e.g., AARON and DAVID—for special roles and tasks (Deut. 18:5; 1 Sam. 10:24; Ps. 105:26; 106:23).

In the NT, Jesus is the Elect One (Lk. 9:35), in whom the election of Israel and of the CHURCH of God of the new covenant find their meaning and center. Jesus is the elect "cornerstone" of the new building that God is constructing, composed of both Jewish and Gentile believers (1 Pet. 2:4-6). God destined us in love to be his children through Jesus Christ (Eph. 1:5). So the church of God is an elect race (1 Pet. 2:9), replacing the old Israel in the purposes of God. And this new race is mostly composed of poor and ordinary people (1 Cor. 1:27-29). God's election is never presented as a cause for speculation or controversy, but rather to celebrate the free GRACE of God that grants salvation and also to move believers to constant worship and lives of holiness and goodness. As in the OT there is in the NT the election of individuals for service (e.g., Acts 6:5; 15:22, 25). Further, the question as to whether the Jews are, as a people, still the elect of God is faced by Paul in Rom. 9-11 in the light of the salvation of God in and through Jesus.

elect lady. This title occurs in the salutation of 2 Jn. 1 (NIV, "To the chosen lady"). It has been understood to identify a Christian woman, the acquaintance of the Elder who wrote the letter. Her sister may have been his hostess at the time he wrote. "Lady" in Greek was sometimes a proper noun, and some have thought it should have been transliterated ("To the elect Kyria"; cf. the name of GAIUS in 3 John). It is more likely that the reference was a figure of speech referring to the church to which the letter was addressed, as also the closing reference to "sister" would be understood as a designation for a Christian community.

El Elohe Israel. el-el´oh-heh-is´ray-uhl (Heb. *ʾēl ʾĕlōhê yiśrāʾēl H449*, "God is the God of Israel"). The name of a confessional altar erected by JACOB, who appropriated the Canaanite deity name EL for use as one of the designations of the true God (Gen. 33:20). When the patriarch returned from PADDAN ARAM with his family, he purchased a portion of a field from the sons of HAMOR, on which he had camped (33:18-19) and on which he erected the altar.

El Elyon. el´el-yohn´ (Heb. *ʾēl H446*, "God," and *ʿelyôn H6610*, "high, highest"). A name of God used especially in GENESIS and PSALMS and often rendered "God Most High." When ABRAHAM paid tithes to MELCHIZEDEK, this is the name by which the latter worshiped God (Gen. 14:19-20). The name occurs exactly in this form again in Ps. 78:35, but there are other Psalms where *Elyon* is combined with *Yahweh* or *Elohim* (see 7:17; 47:2; 57:2; 78:56). Frequently, *Elyon* (the Highest) is used by itself as a name for God (Num. 24:16; Deut. 32:8; et al.).

elements, elemental spirits. These and similar English terms are used by the NRSV and other versions to render Greek *stoicheion G5122* (in the NT always pl. *stoicheia*). The NIV uses "basic principles" or "principles" (Gal. 4:3, 9; Col. 2:8, 20; TNIV, "elemental spiritual forces"), but also "elements" (2 Pet. 3:10, 12) and "elementary truths" (for a phrase in Heb. 5:12). The word meant "one of a row," that is, anything standing in a series, such as the letters of the alphabet. It aptly described the rudiments ("ABCs") of a system of knowledge or religion, which is probably its meaning in Hebrews. This "logical-pedagogical" sense also may apply to the Galatian and possibly the Colossian passages. A natural extension of the word was to the elemental substances of the world, which is its probable meaning in 2 Peter. The term also came to designate personified beings or "elemental spirits." These could be simply personifications of natural forces, or could be individualized as demons or, possibly, as angels. See ANGEL; DEMON. Recent scholarship has tended to interpret the language of Col. 2:8, 20 in this way. Some interpreters have so understood Gal. 4:3, 9 as well.

Eleph. See HAELEPH.

elephant. See ANIMALS.

Elephantine. el´uh-fan-ti´nee (Gk. *Elephantinē*, "Elephant place," translation of the older Egyptian name, *Iebew*). A settlement on an island in the NILE River, opposite ancient SYENE, with the modern name of Geziret Aswan (the "Island of Aswan"). It is best known because of certain papyri (see PAPYRUS) of the fifth century B.C. that were found there and that provide very important information about ancient ARAMAIC and about Jewish society in EGYPT.

Eleven, the. This term is used in Luke-Acts with reference to the eleven apostles of Jesus who remained after the death of JUDAS ISCARIOT (Lk. 24:9, 33; Acts 2:14; cf. Matt. 28:16; Mk. 16:14; Acts 1:26). The use of the Greek definite article sets them apart as a group who retained their continuity with the Twelve. After the choice of MATTHIAS (Acts 1:26), they became "the Twelve" again (Acts 6:2; cf. Rev. 21:14).

Elhanan. el-hay´nuhn (Heb. *'elḥānān H481*, "God has been gracious"). (1) Son of JAARE-OREGIM, from BETHLEHEM; he was a member of DAVID's army in the wars against the PHILISTINES at GOB who slew GOLIATH the Gittite, the shaft of whose spear is said to have been like a weaver's rod (2 Sam. 21:19; KJV conjecturally reads "*the brother of* Goliath"). In Chronicles, however, the father of Elhanan is said to be JAIR, and his victim is Goliath's brother, LAHMI (1 Chr. 20:5). The discrepancy may be the result of one or more scribal errors.

Other solutions include the view that there were two separate giants named Goliath (one slain by David and one by Elhanan), or that *Goliath* was a generic name for a class of giants, or that David and Elhanan are identical.

(2) Son of Dodo, from Bethlehem; he was one of David's Thirty who ranked next to the Three (2 Sam. 23:24; 1 Chr. 11:26). A few scholars have identified him with #1 above.

Eli. ee´li (Heb. *'ēlî H6603*, possibly "lofty" or "[God/Yahweh] is high"). A member of the family of ITHAMAR (fourth son of AARON) who acted as both judge and high PRIEST in Israel. He lived at SHILOH in a dwelling adjoining the TABERNACLE (1 Sam. 1-4; 14:3; 1 Ki. 2:27). Little is known about him until he was well advanced in age, when HANNAH came to pray for a son. The conduct of Eli's sons, PHINEHAS and HOPHNI, who also served as priest, gave him grief in his declining years. Their behavior shocked the people, for they "were treating the LORD's offering with contempt" (1 Sam. 2:17). While Eli warned them of their shameful ways, he did not rebuke with the severity their deeds merited. Instead, Eli mildly reasoned with his sons, saying, "Why do you do such things?" (2:23). But the sons no longer heeded their father, and he did not restrain them. An old man of ninety, almost blind, Eli waited to hear the result of the battle between the Israelites and the PHILISTINES. When the messenger came with the news of the slaughter of his sons and of the taking of the ARK OF THE COVENANT, Eli fell off his seat and died of a broken neck. Although a good and pure man, Eli was weak and indecisive.

Eli, Eli, lama sabachthani. See ELOI, ELOI, LAMA SABACHTHANI.

Eliab. i-li´uhb (Heb. *'ĕlî'āb H482*, "my God is father"). (1) Son of Helon and a leader from the tribe of ZEBULUN, heading a division of 57,400 (Num. 2:7; 10:16). He was among those who assisted MOSES in taking a census of the Israelites (1:9) and who brought offerings to the Lord for the dedication of the TABERNACLE (7:24-29).

(2) Son (or descendant) of PALLU son of REUBEN. Two of Eliab's sons (or descendants), DATHAN

and ABIRAM, were among the leaders who joined the Levite KORAH in his rebellion against Moses and Aaron in the wilderness and subsequently suffered judgment (Num. 16:1, 12; 26:8-9; Deut. 11:6).

(3) Son of Nahath and descendant of LEVI through KOHATH; he was also an ancestor of SAMUEL the prophet (1 Chr. 6:27). He is apparently the same as ELIEL (1 Chr. 6:34) and ELIHU (1 Sam. 1:1).

(4) Eldest son of JESSE whose physical appearance made him attractive to SAMUEL as a candidate for king but who at the Lord's prompting was passed in favor of his brother DAVID (1 Sam. 16:6; 1 Chr. 2:13). Eliab, who served SAUL in the Valley of Elah when Goliath challenged the army, was angry at David for coming to the battle (1 Sam. 17:13, 28). He also was the father of ABIHAIL, wife of REHOBOAM (2 Chr. 11:18). On the assumption that ELIHU is a variant name, many scholars believe Eliab was the brother of David who later became an officer over the tribe of JUDAH (1 Chr. 27:18).

(5) A warrior, third in rank among the Gadite officers, who served DAVID at ZIKLAG (1 Chr. 12:9). These Gadites "were brave warriors, ready for battle and able to handle the shield and spear. Their faces were the faces of lions, and they were as swift as gazelles in the mountains" (v. 8).

(6) A Levite, listed among those who sang and who played lyres and harps when the ARK OF THE COVENANT was transferred, as arranged by David (1 Chr. 15:18, 20; 16:5).

Eliada. i-li´uh-duh (Heb. *ʾelyādāʿ H486*, "God knows"). (1) Son of DAVID; he is listed among those children born after David took concubines and wives in Jerusalem (2 Sam. 5:16; 1 Chr. 3:8). His original name was probably BEELIADA ("Baal [= the Lord] knows," 1 Chr. 14:6) and was later changed when the term BAAL became distasteful because of its associations with IDOLATRY.

(2) Father of REZON (1 Ki. 11:23; KJV, "Eliadah"); the latter seized DAMASCUS and became SOLOMON's adversary (vv. 24-25).

(3) A skilled soldier and a commander of 200,000 archers from BENJAMIN during the reign of JEHOSHAPHAT (2 Chr. 17:17). The large numbers in this passage (well over one million soldiers residing in Jerusalem) seem impossibly high. Some argue that the word for "thousand" (*ʾelep H547*) should be "leader" (*ʾallûp H477*), in which case Eliada commanded 200 specially trained soldiers. Alternatively, the term *ʾelep* came to indicate a military unit of varying sizes. Others believe that the Chronicler deliberately uses hyperbole to indicate divine favor.

Eliah. i-li´uh. KJV form of ELIJAH (only 1 Chr. 8:27; Ezra 10:26).

Eliahba. i-li´uh-buh (Heb. *ʾelyaḥbāʾ H494*, "God hides"). A Shaalbonite (i.e., from SHAALABBIN) and one of the "Thirty," DAVID's elite guard (2 Sam. 23:32; 1 Chr. 11:33).

Eliakim. i-li´uh-kim (Heb. *ʾelyāqîm H509*, "God raises up," i.e., "may God deliver"; Gk. *Eliakim G1806*). (1) Son of HILKIAH and palace administrator under King HEZEKIAH (2 Ki. 18:18—19:7; Isa. 36:3—37:7). Eliakim, with two others (Shebna and Joah), was selected to negotiate with the besieging Assyrian army in 701 B.C. The trio objected to the Assyrian commander's use of the HEBREW LANGUAGE instead of ARAMAIC in the public conference, but to no avail. After hearing the repeated demands that Jerusalem surrender, they relayed the message to the king with great sorrow, and the king in turn sent these official to inquire of the prophet ISAIAH. Contrasted with SHEBNA, Eliakim receives very high commendation from the Lord (Isa. 22:20-24).

(2) Son of JOSIAH and one of the last kings of Judah (2 Ki. 23:34-37 et al.). See JEHOIAKIM.

(3) One of the priests who, with their trumpets, participated in the dedication of the wall of Jerusalem under the leadership of NEHEMIAH (Neh. 12:41).

(4) Son of Abiud, included in Matthew's GENEALOGY OF JESUS CHRIST (Matt. 1:13).

(5) Son of Melea, included in Luke's GENEALOGY OF JESUS CHRIST (Lk. 3:30).

Eliam. i-li´uhm (Heb. *ʾĕliʿām H500*, "God is [my] kinsman"). (1) The father of BATHSHEBA, who became DAVID's wife (2 Sam. 11:3; in 1 Chr. 3:5

he is called AMMIEL [note that the two names have the same meaning, but with the components reversed]). The fact that Bathsheba is identified first as Eliam's daughter and then as URIAH's wife may indicate that Eliam was a person of some significance. According to some scholars, this Eliam should be identified with #2 below.

(2) Son of AHITHOPHEL of Gilo and a member of DAVID's Thirty, the military élite of the nation (2 Sam. 23:34). This man is also called AHIJAH ("my brother is Yahweh") the Pelonite (1 Chr. 11:36).

Elias. i-li′uhs. The Greek form of the name of the prophet ELIJAH, used by the KJV in all occurrences of the name in the NT.

Eliasaph. i-li′uh-saf (Heb. *ʾelyāsāp H498*, "God has added"). **(1)** Son of DEUEL (or REUEL) and a leader of the tribe of GAD, heading a division of 45,650 (Num. 2:14; 10:20). He was among those who assisted MOSES in taking a census of the Israelites (1:14) and who brought offerings to the Lord for the dedication of the TABERNACLE (7:42-47).

(2) Son of Lael and the leader of the Levitical clan descended from GERSHON during the time of Moses (Num. 3:24). The Gershonites were responsible for the care of the tabernacle (vv. 25-26).

Eliashib. i-li′uh-shib (Heb. *ʾelyāšîb H513*, "God has restored"). **(1)** A priest chosen during the time of DAVID to head the eleventh of the twenty-four courses of priests who took turns serving in the sanctuary (1 Chr. 24:12).

(2) A high priest during the time of NEHEMIAH who helped to rebuild the SHEEP GATE (Neh. 3:1, 20-21). Reference is made to his son Joiada and to a grandson who married SANBALLAT's daughter (13:28). This Eliashib may be the same priest who incurred NEHEMIAH's displeasure because he made a temple storage area into special living quarters for TOBIAH (13:4-9). Some think he may also be the father (grandfather?) of a certain Jehohanan (Johanan) who provided a room for EZRA's mourning (Ezra 10:6).

(3) A singer among the Levites during the time of Ezra (Ezra 10:24). He pledged to put away his foreign wife and children when commanded to do so.

(4) One of the descendants of Zattu who agreed to put away their foreign wives (Ezra 10:27).

(5) One of the descendants of Bani who agreed to put away their foreign wives (Ezra 10:36).

(6) Son of Elioenai and descendant of DAVID through ZERUBBABEL (1 Chr. 3:24).

Eliathah. i-li′uh-thuh (Heb. *ʾelîʾātâ H484* and *ʾeliyyātâ H517*, "God has come"). Son of HEMAN, the king's seer (1 Chr. 25:4). The fourteen sons of Heman, along with the sons of ASAPH and JEDUTHUN, were set apart "for the ministry of prophesying, accompanied by harps, lyres and cymbals" (v. 1). The assignment of duty was done by lot, and the twentieth lot fell to Eliathah, his sons, and his relatives (25:27).

Elidad. i-li′dad (Heb. *ʾelîdād H485*, possibly "my God has loved" or "my God is friend"). Son of Kislon, from the tribe of BENJAMIN (Num. 34:21). He was one of the leaders chosen by God to divide the land of Canaan on the W side of the JORDAN for the inheritance of the ten tribes. Elidad is possibly the same as ELDAD, who together with MEDAD prophesied in the camp of Israel (11:26-27).

Eliehoenai. i-li′uh-hoh-ee′ni (Heb. *ʾelyĕhôʿênay H492*, "to Yahweh are my eyes [looking]"). **(1)** Son of Meshelemiah, a LEVITE (1 Chr. 26:3; KJV, "Elioenai"). Meshelemiah and his seven sons were Korahites (i.e., descendants of LEVI through KORAH) appointed as doorkeepers in the time of DAVID.

(2) Son of Zerahiah and descendant of PAHATH-MOAB; he was at the head of 200 men who returned from the EXILE with EZRA (Ezra 8:4; KJV, "Elihoenai").

Eliel. i-li′uhl (Heb. *ʾelîʾēl H483*, "my God is God"). **(1)** Son of Toah; he was a descendant of LEVI through KOHATH and an ancestor of SAMUEL the prophet and of HEMAN the musician (1 Chr. 6:34). He is probably the same as ELIAB (1 Chr. 6:27) and ELIHU (1 Sam. 1:1).

(2) One of the family heads in the eastern half of the tribe of MANASSEH (1 Chr. 5:24). He and others are described as "brave warriors, famous men, and heads of their families. But they were unfaithful to the God of their fathers and prostituted themselves to the gods of the peoples of the land" (vv. 24b-25).

(3) Son of Shimei; he was a Benjamite family head who lived in Jerusalem in David's day (1 Chr. 8:20; cf. v. 28).

(4) Son of Shashak; another Benjamite family head who lived in Jerusalem in David's day (1 Chr. 8:22; cf. v. 28).

(5) A MAHAVITE included among David's mighty warriors (1 Chr. 11:46).

(6) One of David's mighty warriors (1 Chr. 11:47, apparently different from Eliel the Mahavite, v. 46).

(7) A warrior, seventh in rank among the Gadite officers who served David at ZIKLAG (1 Chr. 12:9). These Gadites "were brave warriors, ready for battle and able to handle the shield and spear. Their faces were the faces of lions, and they were as swift as gazelles in the mountains" (v. 8). It is possible that this Eliel is the same as either #5 or #6 above.

(8) A descendant of HEBRON and one of the Levitical leaders whom David brought together when the ARK OF THE COVENANT was transferred to Jerusalem (1 Chr. 15:9, 11).

(9) One of the temple supervisors under CONANIAH, who was in charge of the contributions during the reign of HEZEKIAH (2 Chr. 31:13).

Elienai. el´ee-ee´ni (Heb. *ʾĕliʿênay H501*, short form of *ʾelyĕhôʿênay H492*, "to Yahweh are my eyes [looking]"). Son of Shimei; a Benjamite family head who lived in Jerusalem in DAVID's day (1 Chr. 8:20; cf. v. 28).

Eliezer. el´ee-ee´zuhr (Heb. *ʾĕliʿezer H499*, "my God is [my] help"; Gk. *Eliezer G1808*; see also ELEAZAR). **(1)** A servant (prob. the chief servant) in the household of ABRAHAM who was due to receive the inheritance if the latter had no sons (Gen. 15:2-3). Eliezer is described by Abraham as "the one who will inherit my estate" (the Heb. expression is difficult) and identified as "Eliezer of Damascus" (but the Heb. here is unusual too and can be translated "Dammesek Eliezer," as in NJPS). Whatever may be the precise explanation of 15:2, the following verse makes the meaning explicit, and the Lord's response is equally clear, "This man will not be your heir, but a son coming from your

own body will be your heir" (v. 4). Eliezer was most likely the unnamed servant of Gen. 24 who was sent to get a wife for ISAAC from among Abraham's people. If so, he was a devout man of faith.

(2) The second son of MOSES by ZIPPORAH (Exod. 18:4; 1 Chr. 23:15). The name was given to him by Moses with this explanation, "My father's God was my helper [Heb. *ʿezer H6469*]; he saved me from the sword of Pharaoh." Eliezer had only one son, Rehabiah, "but the sons of Rehabiah were very numerous" (23:17). One of Eliezer's descendants was in charge of all the treasuries of the gifts that DAVID and the heads of the families of Israel had dedicated to God (26:25-26).

(3) Son of BEKER and grandson of BENJAMIN (1 Chr. 7:8).

(4) One of the priests appointed to blow the trumpet when David transferred the ARK OF THE COVENANT to Jerusalem (1 Chr. 15:24).

(5) Son of Zicri and chief officer of the tribe of REUBEN in David's day (1 Chr. 27:16).

(6) Son of Dodavahu and a prophet in JEHOSHAPHAT's time (2 Chr. 20:37). He was from MARESHAH and predicted the destruction of Jehoshaphat's fleet because the king had made alliance with AHAZIAH.

(7) One of a group of leaders sent by EZRA to Iddo to get attendants for the house of God (Ezra 8:16).

(8) One the descendants of JESHUAH who agreed to put away their foreign wives (Ezra 10:18).

(9) One of the Levites who agreed to put away their foreign wives (Ezra 10:23).

(10) One of the descendants of Harim who agreed to put away their foreign wives (Ezra 10:31).

(11) Son of Jorim, included in Luke's GENEALOGY OF JESUS CHRIST (Lk. 3:29).

Elihoenai. el´ee-hoh-ee´ni. See ELIEHOENAI.

Elihoreph. el´uh-hoh´rif (Heb. *ʾĕlihōrep H495*, possibly "my God rewards"). Son of Shisha and a chief official during SOLOMON's reign; he and his brother AHIJAH functioned as secretaries (1 Ki. 4:3).

Elihu. i-li´hyoo (Heb. *ʾĕlihûʾ H491* and *ʾĕlihû H490*, "my God is he"). **(1)** Son of Tohu and ancestor of the prophet SAMUEL (1 Sam. 1:1). He is apparently the same as ELIAB (1 Chr. 6:27) and ELIEL (1 Chr. 6:34).

(2) One of the commanders from the tribe of MANASSEH who deserted SAUL to join DAVID's army (1 Chr. 12:20).

(3) Son (or relative) of Shemaiah and grandson (or descendant) of OBED-EDOM (1 Chr. 26:7). This family of Korahites (see KORAH #3) belonged to one of the divisions of gatekeepers (v. 1).

(4) A brother of David who became an officer over the tribe of JUDAH (1 Chr. 27:18). Many scholars believe he should be identified with ELIAB, David's eldest brother (1 Sam. 16:6 et al.).

(5) Son of BARAKEL the Buzite and one of the friends who reasoned with JOB (Job 32:2; see BUZ #3). He became angry with Job's arguments and the failure of his three friends to respond to those arguments. Thereupon he launched into a speech in which he insisted that suffering has a disciplinary purpose (32:6—37:24).

Elijah. i-lī´juh (Heb. *ʾēliyyāhû H489* and *ʾēliyyâ H488* [2 Ki. 1:3 et al.], "my God is Yahweh"; Gk. *Ēlias G2460*). KJV NT, Elias. **(1)** Son of JEROHAM and descendant of BENJAMIN; he is listed among the heads of families who lived in Jerusalem (1 Chr. 8:27; KJV, "Eliah").

(2) One of the descendants of Harim who agreed to put away their foreign wives (Ezra 10:21).

(3) One of the descendants of Elam who agreed to put away their foreign wives (Ezra 10:26; KJV, "Eliah").

(4) The famous ninth-century prophet who served in the northern kingdom in the reigns of AHAB and his son AHAZIAH (1 Ki. 17:1—2 Ki. 2:12). Elijah was from the town of TISHBE in GILEAD (KJV, "of the inhabitants of Gilead"), E of the JORDAN River. In our ears his first message sounds like no more than a weather forecast, a drought (1 Ki. 17:1) that would last over three years (18:1), but Ahab and all who heard knew that more was involved than a prediction of climatic hardship. The "forces of nature" are in the

Lord's hands; he uses them to bless, to warn, and to judge his people (cf. Deut. 28:1-2, 12, 15, 22-24). Elijah's commission therefore was to convey a stern message: All is not well between the Lord and his people, and they are about to suffer his judgments on their disobedience.

But, remarkably, the Lord did not leave Elijah there either to amplify the message or to seek to win the people back from the path of spiritual disaster. He took Elijah away into three hidden years of apprenticeship (1 Ki. 17:3, "hide"). First, by the Lord's word, he returned to his own home area, for even though we do not know precisely where KERITH was, it was E of Jordan (17:2-5). There Elijah was marvelously provided for. In this way he began to learn that as long as he walked in obedience he would be safe (however unlikely the means of supply might be). The next test was more demanding: he had to go to ZAREPHATH, which was only 6 mi. (10 km.) S of JEZEBEL's hometown of SIDON. Elijah not only learned once again that the Lord cared for his obedient servant, but that the Lord's power is superior to all human power (18:10). The third story from the hidden years (17:17-24) was designed by the Lord to teach Elijah specifically the power of prayer to transform situations of death—a boy was restored to life (17:22) and his mother brought to spiritual faith and testimony (17:24).

Against this background the time came for the drought to be broken. Again the word of God came (1 Ki. 18:1), and Elijah had learned in the apprentice

After confronting the prophets of Baal, Elijah fled to Horeb. The cypress trees at the bottom of the photo mark the traditional site of "Elijah's spring." (View to the SW.)

years that when the word is obeyed all must be well. He therefore went without fear to meet Ahab, but it is in fact Ahab who had to come to meet Elijah (18:2-16). Another lesson learned in the hidden years now came to fruition: knowing that the Lord answers prayer (17:20-24), Elijah proposed a prayer contest (18:24) on Mount CARMEL. The behavior of the BAAL prophets there (18:26-29) was in accord with their beliefs. According to a practice known as "imitative magic," they sought to do on earth what they desired their god to do from heaven. First they limp (literally) or dance around the altar, trying to suggest flickering and dancing flames (18:26). When that failed, they resorted to the desperate expedient of slashing and cutting their bodies, in the hope that the down-pouring blood might prompt the down-pouring of fire. But it was all to no avail. Elijah, on the contrary, began his appeal to the Lord by a deliberate disavowal of imitative magic. About to call for fire, he first demanded the pouring of water on the intended sacrifice. This was a direct denial of the whole Baal theology and tantamount to a denial of the reality of Baal. Then, with simplicity and dignity (18:36-37), he rested his case on the certainty that the Lord would answer prayer.

Why did Elijah demand the deliberate slaughter of the Baal entourage (1 Ki. 18:40)? Perhaps we are repulsed by it because we have allowed our sense of moral and spiritual outrage to atrophy: we no longer feel any deep concern at the presence and threat of false religions; we are tolerant of error and of the menace it constitutes to the souls of people; we do not face up to the exclusiveness of the person and claims of the Lord. This is not to say that we should copy the methods of Elijah in this any more than we would build altars and sacrifice animals, but we must not criticize, much less scorn or look down on him for expressing in terms appropriate to his day a decisiveness of commitment, loyalty, and concern that we are failing to express in terms appropriate to ours.

Elijah had one more matter to occupy him on Mount Carmel. James directs us to interpret Elijah's crouched attitude as one of prayer (Jas. 5:18): he was praying for the fulfillment of what the Lord had promised (1 Ki. 18:1). He was blessed with persistent faith, for seven times he sent his servant to a lookout point, and as soon as even the slightest

sign appeared, he responded in active faith to its message (18:43-45).

The collapse of Elijah (1 Ki. 19:1-4) is not at all difficult to understand. The amount of sleep the Lord insisted on giving him (19:5-6) shows the extent to which he had neglected his physical well-being. He had allowed himself to become overtired and then he became overwrought (19:3) when he was faced, not with celebrations and triumphant crowds as he had hoped, but with Jezebel's undiminished influence. It seemed as though the victory on Mount Carmel had never happened. But the Lord was not defeated. First he gave his servant rest and nourishment (19:5-7); second, he brought him into his own presence (19:8-9); third, he renewed Elijah's sense of the power of the word of God. Elijah experienced the wind, earthquake, and fire—three notable instruments of divine purpose—but he had no sense of meeting the Lord in them (19:11-12). Yet when a "gentle whisper" came (19:12b), Elijah knew he was in the very presence of the Lord. How significant then the question is: What are you doing here? (19:13). In his hidden years, he did nothing without a word (17:2-3, 8-9; 18:1-2), but the Lord had not told him to flee from Jezebel! Understandably but tragically, in the crucial moment, Elijah forgot one of the central lessons of his apprenticeship: The servant of the Lord lives by the word of the Lord, and when he does so he is provided for and kept safe. Fourth, the Lord renewed Elijah's commission and gave him a word of encouragement (19:15-18). Perhaps we ought to note as a fifth element in the restorative work of the Lord that he left Elijah's prayer unanswered (19:4). He had it in mind to grant Elijah something far better than he would dare pray for. He would never die (2 Ki. 2:11).

Elijah appears only once more in the reign of Ahab, when that weak king acquiesced in the murder of NABOTH (1 Ki. 21) and the violent seizure of his vineyard. In his response to this, Elijah is a true founder of the brilliant line of PROPHETS that was to follow him in his concern for moral and social righteousness. In the reign of Ahab's son, Ahaziah (853-852 B.C.), he vigorously resisted the king's attempt to take him by force (2 Ki. 1). Again we find ourselves affronted by the violence of Elijah's response, and we need to remind ourselves that he was acting in ways appropriate to his day with a decisiveness for God and a hatred and abhorrence of false religion that we might well covet for ourselves.

Elijah was a mighty man for God, yet the Bible does not conceal his faults, but rather selects one for special mention. Elijah was what we call a "loner." He easily felt himself isolated and solitary (1 Ki. 18:22), even when he knew that it was very far from the truth (cf. 18:13). It is true to character that when he most needed fellowship and help, he deliberately sought a solitary path (19:3-4), and when the Lord blessed him with the companionable and warm-hearted ELISHA, he was unready to share with him the great experience that he knew was to be his (2 Ki. 2:2, 4, 6). It is certain it would not have fled from Jezebel had he been willing to gather round him the supportive fellowship of OBADIAH and his large prophetic group. Nevertheless the Lord gave Elijah, that man of like nature with ourselves (Jas. 5:17), the glorious and unique honor of by-passing death and entering heaven in the whirlwind (2 Ki. 2:11).

But though Elijah thus dramatically left the earthly scene, his story was not over. His prophecy regarding Jezebel (1 Ki. 21:23) was later fulfilled (2 Ki. 9:36), and his forecast regarding the dynasty of Ahab proved true (10:10, 17). Furthermore, 2 Chr. 21:12-15 records that Elijah also had a written ministry. Beyond that, too, his ministry continued. Malachi 4:5-6 foresaw the appearance of Elijah as the forerunner of the MESSIAH, and this was fulfilled in the ministry of JOHN THE BAPTIST (e.g., Matt. 11:13-14; 17:9-13). Elijah's greatest privilege in the Bible story was to stand with the Son of God on the Mount of TRANSFIGURATION and speak with him of his coming death (Matt. 17:3-4; Mk. 9:4-5; Lk. 9:30-33).

Elika. i-li′kuh (Heb. *ʾĕliqāʾ H508*, derivation uncertain). A Harodite (see HAROD #2) included among the Thirty, DAVID's elite military force (2 Sam. 23:25; his name is omitted in the parallel list in 1 Chr. 11:27).

Elim. ee′lim (Heb. *ʾêlim H396*, "oaks" or "terebinths"). The second recorded stopping place of the Israelites on their journey from the RED SEA to SINAI (Exod. 15:27; 16:1). The EXODUS narrative recounts that they journeyed from the Red Sea to MARAH, and from there to Elim, where there were twelve springs of water and seventy palm trees (cf. Num. 33:9-10). The exact location of this oasis is not certain. If the traditional identification of Mount Sinai in the lower part of the peninsula is correct, Elim is likely to be one of the oases in the wadis along the main route into that area. The place now known as Wadi Gharandel (55 mi./88 km. SE of Suez) is frequently suggested. Another proposal is ʿAyun Musa (9 mi./14 km. SE of Suez).

E

This oasis, Wadi Gharandel, may be the location of ancient Elim. (View to the N.)

© Dr. James C. Martin

Elimelech. i-lim´uh-lek (Heb. *ʾĕlîmelek H497*, "my God is king"). TNIV Elimelek. An Ephrathite from BETHLEHEM and the husband of NAOMI (Ruth 1:2-3; 2:1, 3; 4:3, 9). Because of a famine in their homeland, Elimelech took his family to sojourn in MOAB. After the death of Elimelech and his sons, Naomi returned to Judah with her daughter-in-law RUTH. A man named BOAZ, being of the same clan as Elimelech and having the right of kinship, purchased from Naomi the land formerly belonging to Elimelech. Boaz also married Ruth, and from this marriage came DAVID and eventually the MESSIAH (Matt. 1:5; see GENEALOGY OF JESUS CHRIST).

Elioenai. el´ee-oh-ee´ni (Heb. *ʾelyô ʿênay H493*, "to Yahweh my eyes [look]"; short form of ELIEHOENAI). **(1)** Son of Neariah and postexilic descendant of DAVID through SOLOMON (1 Chr. 3:23-24).

(2) A clan leader from the tribe of SIMEON during the days of King HEZEKIAH (1 Chr. 4:36). His family and other Simeonite clans "increased greatly," and so they migrated to GEDOR "in search of pasture for their flocks." Subsequently they destroyed the Hamites and other inhabitants of the land (vv. 41-43).

(3) Son of BEKER and grandson of BENJAMIN (1 Chr. 7:8).

(4) Descendant of Pashhur; he was among the priests who put away their foreign wives (Ezra 10:22). He may be the same as #6 below.

(5) One of the descendants of Zattu who agreed to put away their foreign wives (Ezra 10:27).

(6) A postexilic priest who, with his trumpet, participated in the dedication of the wall of Jerusalem (Neh. 12:41). He may be the same as #4 above.

Eliphal. i-li´fuhl (Heb. *ʾĕlîpal H503*, "God has judged"). Son of Ur and one of the Thirty, DAVID's military elite (1 Chr. 11:35). Some scholars believe that the text has suffered scribal corruption and that his original name was ELIPHELET, as in the parallel list (2 Sam. 23:34). See also AHASBAI.

Eliphalet. See ELIPHELET.

Eliphaz. el´i-faz (Heb. *ʾĕlîpaz H502*, derivation disputed). **(1)** Firstborn of ESAU; his mother was ADAH the HITTITE, and his sons became chiefs in EDOM (Gen. 36:4, 10-12, 15-16; 1 Chr. 1:35-36).

(2) An Edomite from TEMAN (or TEMA) and one of the friends who visited JOB to "sympathize with him and comfort him" (Job 2:11). Eliphaz may have been the eldest and the leader of the three friends (cf. 42:7-9). He was the first to address Job and is marked out by the courtesy with which he spoke (chs. 4-5). Like his friends, he took for granted that Job must have committed some major sin, for only so could he explain his sufferings. But dominated, as he was, by a dream he had had of man's sinfulness before God (4:12-21), he tried to make it as easy as possible for Job to repent. In his second address (ch. 15) one senses the note of irritation caused by Job's rejection of his advice; the colors are darkened, and the applicability to Job heightened. The third address (ch. 22) is in many ways the bitterest of all: without evidence, Eliphaz accuses Job of all the worst sins according to the concepts of the time, but even then his kindliness breaks through in a final offer of hope.

Elipheleh. See ELIPHELEHU.

Eliphelehu. i-lif´uh-lee´hyoo (Heb. *ʾĕlîplēhû H504*, possibly "may God distinguish him"). KJV Elipheleh. A Levite and one of the gatekeepers assigned to be a musician when DAVID made preparation to transfer the ARK OF THE COVENANT to JERUSALEM (1 Chr. 15:18). He is called one of the brothers of the "second order" (NRSV; NIV, "next in rank") who followed HEMAN, ASAPH, and ETHAN. Eliphelehu and some others "were to play the harps, directing according to *sheminith*" (v. 21; see MUSIC AND MUSICAL INSTRUMENTS, sect. VI).

Eliphelet. i-lif´uh-let (Heb. *ʾĕlîpeleṭ H505*, "my God is deliverance"; in 1 Chr. 14:5, *ʾelpeleṭ H550*). **(1)** Son of DAVID, listed as the last of eleven (or thirteen) children born to him in Jerusalem (2 Sam. 5:16; 1 Chr. 14:7; KJV, "Eliphalet"). His mother's name is not given, but the Chronicler includes him as the last of thirteen sons who were not born of a concubine (1 Chr. 3:8; see v. 9).

(2) Son of David, listed among the thirteen children born to him in Jerusalem not from a concubine (1 Chr. 3:6); he is elsewhere called "Elpelet"

(14:5; KJV, "Elpalet"). Because his name (as well as Nogah) is not included in the parallel list in the MT (2 Sam. 5:16), some scholars doubt his existence. Others suggest scribal corruption in Samuel and speculate that this Eliphelet died at an early age and that a later child (see #1 above) was named after him.

(3) Son of AHASBAI, from MAACAH, and one of the Thirty, David's military elite (2 Sam. 23:34). Some scholars believe that he is the same as ELIPHAL son of Ur (1 Chr. 11:35).

(4) Third son of Eshek and a descendant of SAUL through JONATHAN (1 Chr. 8:39).

(5) A son or descendant of Adonikam who, with Juel, Shemaiah, and sixty other kindred, returned from Babylon with EZRA (Ezra 8:13).

(6) One of the sons or descendants of Hashum who had married foreign women (Ezra 10:33).

Elisabeth. See ELIZABETH.

Eliseus. See ELISHA.

Elisha. i-li′shuh (Heb. ʾĕlîšāʿ *H515*, "God is salvation"; Gk. *Elisaios G1811*). KJV NT Eliseus. Son of Shaphat and the prophet who succeeded ELIJAH. At Horeb, God directed Elijah to anoint Elisha to be his successor (1 Ki. 19:16-21), who was to aid HAZAEL, king of SYRIA, and JEHU, king of ISRAEL, in taking vengeance on the enemies of God. Elijah left Horeb and on his way N found Elisha at ABEL MEHOLAH (19:16) plowing with the last of twelve yoke of oxen. The number of oxen indicates the wealth of the family. Elijah cast his mantle on Elisha, who understood the significance of the act as the choice of himself to succeed the older prophet. Elisha ran after Elijah, who had not tarried to explain his action, and begged for permission to kiss his parents farewell. Elijah replied, "Go back. What have I done to you?" Elisha thus went home and made his own decision to accept the prophetic call. Elisha next appears in connection with the end of Elijah's life on earth (2 Ki. 2). He persisted in following Elijah till the latter was carried up to heaven, and a double portion of Elijah's spirit was given him. Taking the mantle of Elijah, he used it to make a dry path over the Jordan, as his master had done, and tried to dissuade the sons

of the prophets from a fruitless search for the body of Elijah.

Since Elisha thus comes into his ministry endowed with a double portion of Elijah's spirit, we are on the alert to see what his first words or deeds will be. The narrative selects two immediate acts of the prophet: the healing of the waters at JERICHO (2 Ki. 2:19-22) and the cursing of the rabble at BETHEL (2:23-25)—a curse removed and a curse invoked. Jericho had been put under a curse by JOSHUA (Josh. 6:26) at the time of its destruction. It was, in its ruin, to be a perpetual memorial to the Lord's wrath against false religion and corrupt society. In the reign of AHAB, and within the era of Elijah and Elisha, Jericho had been rebuilt. Bible history (1 Ki. 16:34) faithfully records the fulfillment of Joshua's prediction. The rebuilding of the cursed city is offered as plain evidence of the spiritually careless days of Ahab; the recording of the fulfillment of the curse is to assure us that though sinners may blithely assume power to disregard the word of God, the word remains in force. Those who had the temerity to live in the new city found this out to their cost. Every prospect was pleasing about Jericho, but nothing went right. The water was foul and the land (literally) "casts it young" (2 Ki. 2:19). Animals were miscarrying, perhaps women too, and the meaning of the phrase has even been extended to crops: nothing came to full fruitage and term. Elisha's response was not, "I could have warned you about that." He said nothing about their folly in disregarding divine wrath; rather he set about a work of grace. We see in Lev. 2:13 and Num. 18:19 that salt is linked with the covenant of God (see SALT, COVENANT OF). Elisha's requirement that the salt be brought to him in a new bowl (2 Ki. 2:20) was intended to safeguard the act as far as possible from the pollution of human use. The intention in pouring the salt into the spring was to bring the city and its life back within the covenant mercies of the Lord and (2:21-22) this is what in grace the Lord allowed to happen.

The case of Bethel was quite different. It was one of the centers of long-standing religious APOSTASY in the northern kingdom (1 Ki. 12:26-29), and the arrival there of the new prophet of the Lord was bound to be an event of special significance. What follows is related in 2 Ki. 2:23-25, which

E

View across the Harod Valley toward Mt. Moreh. To the far left is the village of Shunem (at the SW base of Mt. Moreh), where the Lord used Elisha to raise the widow's son.

states that "some youths [KJV, little children] came out of the town and jeered at him," leading Elisha to call down a severe curse on them. Some see here an irascible old man teased by playful children, losing his temper, and uttering a curse that is implemented by divine action; seemingly, the old man's God is as irascible and unattractive as he is himself. If this is the truth of the matter, then we have no recourse but to agree with those commentators who find the episode pointless and who say that it reflects no credit on either Elisha or his God. But is this what really occurred? First, Elisha was not an old man; rather, he was the young man who until recently was second in command to Elijah. Second, the Hebrew does not necessarily indicate toddlers or infants. In a suitable context the expression in v. 23 could mean youngsters of an early age (see the same expression in 2 Ki. 5:14). But in 1 Sam. 20:35 we would more naturally think of a teen-age servant in the royal household. The noun is, by itself, indeterminate regarding age. It is used of JOSEPH aged seventeen (Gen. 37:2) and of the trained men in Abram's private army (14:24). The different word in 2 Ki. 2:24 leads to the same conclusions. It is used of REHOBOAM and his contemporaries (1 Ki. 12:8, 10, 14) at a time when 1 Ki. 14:21 says Rehoboam was himself forty-one. In other words, the words derive their meaning from what suits the context, saving that the adjective "small" (2 Ki. 2:23

Heb.) means that they were less than adult. The word "kids" today is somewhat similar, covering a wide age-range short of adulthood.

The situation can be reconstructed, then, as follows. Since succeeding Elijah, Elisha has stayed near Jericho, but he must soon return to their old prophetic center at CARMEL. This road passes Bethel, and for the first time the new prophet and the old apostasy come face to face. The religious authorities at Bethel are determined not to let the chance pass; Elijah was too much for them, but they will strike at his successor before he consolidates his position. So they arrange a "reception committee" in the approved "rent-a-mob" fashion. Why they opened the proceedings with a taunt of baldness remains a mystery—though possibly, if Elisha was a Nazirite, they were mocking the uncut and abundant hair flowing out from under his head covering. At all events, they are bent on a mischief that goes beyond verbal abuse. If the victory is to remain with Elisha, it can only be so if the Lord will come to his aid. Elisha expresses his need of the Lord, not in a "will he, won't he" wish for help but in a confident commanding of divine wrath. The Lord does not desert his beleaguered servant. We might well ask if we would want it to be otherwise.

Elisha had a long ministry during the reigns of Joram (JEHORAM), JEHU, JEHOAHAZ, and JEHOASH (Joash), kings of Israel. After the death of Ahab, the country of MOAB rebelled against his son Joram (2 Ki. 3). When Joram secured the king of EDOM and Jehoshaphat, king of Judah, as allies, JEHOSHAPHAT insisted on consulting Elisha. The latter referred Joram to the prophets of his parents, but out of regard to Jehoshaphat, counseled the kings to dig trenches to channel water from Edom to relieve their army, and predicted victory over the Moabites.

Elisha saved a poor widow from financial distress by miraculous multiplication of her oil supply (2 Ki. 4:1-7). He visited the home of a "well-to-do woman" and her husband in SHUNEM so often that she had a room built for him (4:8-37). Elisha sent his servant GEHAZI to ask the woman what she would like to have him do for her in return for her hospitality. She asked for a son, and a son was given her. When the lad was old enough to go to the fields with his father, he suffered a fatal sunstroke. His mother herself went for Elisha, who, after sending Gehazi, whose efforts were fruitless, came himself, and after great effort the child came back to life. Later, during a famine at GILGAL (4:38-41), Elisha saved a company of the prophets from death because of eating poisonous vegetables. When a present of food was given him, Elisha set it before a hundred men, and the Lord increased the supply to satisfy them (4:42-44).

Elisha healed the Aramean (KJV "Syrian") captain NAAMAN of leprosy (2 Ki. 5); Gehazi proved himself an unworthy servant. Elisha rescued a young prophet's borrowed axhead (6:1-7). He gave timely warning, repeatedly saving Israel from defeat by the Arameans (6:23). The Arameans came to DOTHAN, where Elisha was living with a servant, whom Elisha showed the armies of God protecting the city. The Arameans were stricken with blindness, and Elisha led them to SAMARIA and persuaded the king of Israel to feed them and release them. The Arameans invaded Israel no more for a time. When Aram finally besieged Samaria and the city was reduced to terrible straits, the king of Israel blamed Elisha (6:24-7:20). Elisha predicted relief the next day. Four lepers, considering their case hopeless, visited the Aramean camp and found it deserted. The spoils of the Arameans relieved the inhabitants of Samaria. Elisha advised the "well-to-do woman" of 4:8 to escape a coming famine by going to PHILISTIA (8:1-6). When she returned and

sought restoration of her property, Gehazi, who had just been telling the king the deeds of Elisha, was the means by which the woman secured restitution.

Elisha visited DAMASCUS and had an innocent part in HAZAEL's succeeding BEN-HADAD as king of Aram (2 Ki. 8:7-15). Elisha sent a young prophet to anoint Jehu king of Israel (9:1-3). Before Elisha died (13:14-21), Jehoash, king of Israel, came to visit him and received an object lesson by means of arrows, with regard to his war against the Arameans. A man being hastily buried in Elisha's sepulchre touched Elisha's bones and revived (13:20-21). Elisha's ministry was filled with miracles, many dealing with private needs, some related to affairs of state. Elisha's prophetic insight and wise counsel made him a valuable though not always appreciated adviser to kings. He finished the work of Elijah, destroying the system of BAAL worship, completed the tasks assigned to Elijah of anointing Hazael and Jehu, and saw the final ruin of the house of Ahab and Jezebel. The mention of the cleansing of Naaman the Syrian from leprosy in Lk. 4:27 perhaps indicates this as the crowning achievement of his career, giving Elisha an influence with the Syrian king that enabled him to help Israel. Elisha's story is told with vigor and vivid detail, making him live as few OT characters do. The incidents are not all told in chronological order, but they bear the marks of historical truth in the simplicity of their narration.

Elishah. i-li′shuh (Heb. *ʾĕlîšâ H511*, meaning uncertain). Son or descendant of JAVAN and progenitor of a nation known by the same name (Gen. 10:4; 1 Chr. 1:7; Ezek. 27:7). Since Javan is the Hebrew word for the Greeks, Elishah is to be associated with them. Elishah and the other descendants of Javan are called "the maritime peoples" (lit., "the coasts [or islands] of the nations," Gen. 10:5), and TYRE is said to have imported blue and purple dyes "from the coasts of Elishah" (Ezek. 27:7). Its association with GREECE and KITTIM (CYPRUS) would seem to indicate a location in the area of the N Mediterranean. Some have identified Elishah with Carthage in N Africa, because of the similarity between Elishah and Elissa (a Tyrian princess said to have founded Carthage). Many identify Elishah with Alashiya, one of the islands (prob. Cyprus) affected by the invading SEA PEOPLES.

Most probably Elishah in the Bible refers generally to the inhabitants of the islands of the Aegean Sea.

Elishama. i-lish′uh-muh (Heb. *ʾĕlîšāmāʿ* H514, "my God has heard"). **(1)** Son of Ammihud of the tribe of EPHRAIM (Num. 1:10). He was selected to help MOSES as a representative from his tribe in the taking of the census. He is later described as "the leader of the people of Ephraim," with a division numbering 40,500 (2:18). In that capacity he brought his tribe's offering on the seventh day of the dedication of the altar (7:48-53). He was in command of the Ephraimite camp in the march through the wilderness (10:22). From 1 Chr. 7:26-27, one learns further that he was the father of Nun and grandfather of JOSHUA.

(2) Son of DAVID, listed among eleven (or thirteen) children born to him in Jerusalem (2 Sam. 5:16; 1 Chr. 14:7). His mother's name is not given, but the Chronicler includes him as one of the thirteen sons who were not born of a concubine (1 Chr. 3:8).

(3) Another son of David, listed among the thirteen children born to him in Jerusalem not from a concubine (1 Chr. 3:6 NRSV, following the MT); the NIV, on the basis of two Hebrew MSS and the parallels (2 Sam. 5:15; 1 Chr. 14:5), reads ELISHUA. See also ELIPHELET #2.

(4) Son of Jekamiah and descendant of JUDAH through PEREZ (1 Chr. 2:41). Jerome suggested that this Elishama is the same as #5 below.

(5) The grandfather of a certain ISHMAEL who killed GEDALIAH, the governor of Judah after the fall of Jerusalem (2 Ki. 25:25; Jer. 41:1).

(6) A royal secretary; he was one of the officials in the court of JEHOIAKIM who heard BARUCH read JEREMIAH's scroll and urged the king not to burn the inspired prophecy (Jer. 36:12). Later the scroll was put in his chamber, where it remained until it was taken to be read to the king (36:20-21).

(7) A priest sent by JEHOSHAPHAT to teach God's book of the law in Judah (2 Chr. 17:8).

Elishaphat. i-lish′uh-fat (Heb. *ʾĕlîšāpāṭ* H516, "my God has judged"). Son of Zicri and one of five commanders of units of a hundred who helped JEHOIADA depose ATHALIAH and enthrone Joash (JEHOASH, 2 Chr. 23:1).

Elisheba. i-lish′uh-buh (Heb. *ʾĕlîšebaʿ* H510, "my God is [*or* makes] an oath" or "my God is abundance"). Daughter of Amminadab and wife of AARON (Exod. 6:23). Her brother NAHSHON was leader of the tribe of JUDAH (Num. 1:7; 2:3), so Elisheba was a Judahite. She bore four sons, one of whom, ELEAZAR, succeeded Aaron as high priest (Num. 20:25-28).

Elishua. el′uh-shoo′uh (Heb. *ʾĕlîšûaʿ* H512, "God is salvation" [cf. ELISHA]). Son of DAVID, listed among eleven children born to him in Jerusalem (2 Sam. 5:16); another passage lists him as one of thirteen children born in Jerusalem (1 Chr. 14:7). Apparently the same son is called ELISHAMA in the MT of 1 Chr. 3:6, but this is probably a transcriptional error (note that "Elishama" occurs again in v. 8); thus the NIV reads "Elishua" here too on the basis of two Hebrew MSS and the parallel passages.

Eliud. i-li′uhd (Gk. *Elioud* G1809). Son of Akim, included in Matthew's GENEALOGY OF JESUS CHRIST (Matt. 1:14-15).

Elizabeth. i-liz′uh-buhth (Gk. *Elisabet* G1810, from Heb. *ʾĕlîšebaʿ* H510; see ELISHEBA). KJV Elisabeth. The wife of the priest ZECHARIAH, herself of the lineage of AARON (Lk. 1:5-57). In fulfillment of God's promise, in her old age she bore a son, JOHN THE BAPTIST. Her kinswoman (cousin), Mary of NAZARETH in GALILEE (see MARY, MOTHER OF JESUS), having learned that she was to be the virgin mother of Jesus, visited Elizabeth in the hill country of Judea. Elizabeth's Spirit-filled greeting prompted Mary to reply in a song called *Magnificat*. After Mary returned home, Elizabeth's son was born. She was a woman of unusual piety, faith, and spiritual gifts, whose witness to Mary must have been an incomparable encouragement. LUKE, who alone tells the story, appreciated the significant role of women in the history of redemption and emphasized the agency of the HOLY SPIRIT in the life of Elizabeth.

Elizaphan, Elzaphan. el′uh-zay′fan, el-zay′fan (Heb. *ʾĕlîṣāpān* H507, short form *ʾelṣāpān* H553 "[my] God has hidden [*or* treasured *or* protected]").

(1) Son of Uzziel and the leader of the Kohathites in the wilderness (Exod. 6:22 [Elzaphan]; Num. 3:30); the families descended from KOHATH "were responsible for the care of the ark" and the furniture of the TABERNACLE (v. 31). After NADAB and ABIHU offered unauthorized fire, Elizaphan and his brother MISHAEL were directed by MOSES to take their relatives away from the sanctuary (Lev. 10:4 [Elzaphan]). His descendants are mentioned during the reigns of DAVID (1 Chr. 15:8) and HEZEKIAH (2 Chr. 29:13).

(2) Son of Parnach and the leader from the tribe of ZEBULUN who assisted Moses in dividing the land into future inheritance portions for each tribe (Num. 34:25).

Elizur. i-li′zuhr (Heb. *ʾĕlîṣûr H506*, "my God is a rock"). Son of Shedeur and the leader of the tribe of REUBEN who assisted MOSES in taking a census of the Israelite community (Num. 1:5). He commanded a division numbering 46,500 (2:10; 10:18), and he brought the offering of his tribe on the fourth day of the dedication of the altar (7:30-35).

Elkanah. el-kay′nuh (Heb. *ʾelqānâ H555*, "God has taken possession" or "God has created"). A common name, especially among Levites descended from KORAH. In particular, several ancestors of the prophet SAMUEL, including his father, bore the name Elkanah. Because of ambiguities (and possible scribal corruptions) in the genealogical lists, some of the identifications are uncertain.

(1) Son or descendant of Korah and head of a Levitical clan (Exod. 6:24; see v. 25). He may be the same as #2 below.

(2) Son of Assir and grandson of Korah; father (or ancestor) of Ebiasaph (1 Chr. 6:23). He is probably the same as #3 below.

(3) Father or ancestor of Amasai and Ahimoth (1 Chr. 6:25); he is also described as the son of Joel (v. 36).

(4) Son of AHIMOTH and grandson or descendant of #3 above (1 Chr. 6:26; Ahimoth must be the same as Mahath, v. 35).

(5) Son of Jeroham, descendant of #4 above, and father of Samuel (1 Chr. 6:27, 34). Elsewhere he is described as a "man from Ramathaim, a Zuphite from the hill country of Ephraim," and thus "an Ephraimite," not by descent but by virtue of the tribal territory where he lived (1 Sam. 1:1; the KJV has "Ramathaim-zophim"; see RAMAH #3). Elkanah had two wives: the favorite HANNAH, who was barren, and PENINNAH (1:2). Aside from those who had a royal claim, Elkanah is the only man in the Samuel-Kings narrative to have more than one wife—probably an indication of his wealth and social standing. He was also a godly man who made it a habit to visit the sanctuary in SHILOH every year (1:3). Hannah, brought to tears by Peninnah's taunting, prayed to God for a son whom she would return to the Lord. God answered her petition and she bore Samuel, who after being weaned was given to ELI the priest (1:28). Later Hannah bore to Elkanah other sons and daughters (2:20-21). Elkanah's great-grandson, HEMAN, became a leading musician in DAVID's day (1 Chr. 6:33).

(6) One of the two Levites who were appointed doorkeepers for the ARK OF THE COVENANT when it was transferred by David to Jerusalem (1 Chr. 15:23).

(7) One of several Korahite warriors who joined David at ZIKLAG (1 Chr. 12:6; cf. vv. 1-2). Some argue that Korah here is the name of a locality in the tribe of BENJAMIN.

(8) A high official during the reign of AHAZ of Judah, described as second to the king in authority (2 Chr. 28:7). Because the people of Judah were unfaithful, the Lord allowed PEKAH king of Israel to inflict heavy casualties on the army of AHAZ. During the conflict Elkanah, along with a prince and another official, was killed by an Ephraimite warrior named Zicri.

(9) Grandfather or ancestor of Berekiah; the latter is listed among those Levites who first resettled in Jerusalem after the return of the Babylonian captivity (1 Chr. 9:16).

Elkosh. See ELKOSHITE.

Elkoshite. el′kosh-it (Heb. *ʾelqōšî H556*). A term used to identify NAHUM the prophet (Nah. 1:1). It presumably refers to a town named Elkosh (cf. NRSV). Various identifications have been proposed (including CAPERNAUM, which means "village of Nahum"), but there is no credible evidence to support any of these suggestions.

Ellasar. el'uh-sahr (Heb. *ʾellāsār H536*, derivation uncertain). A kingdom ruled by ARIOCH, one of the allies of KEDORLAOMER, king of ELAM, in his raid on the JORDAN Valley in the time of ABRAHAM (Gen. 14:1). Earlier scholars, who considered the identifications of these kings as reasonably firm, believed that Arioch was the same as Eri-aku, king of Larsa (an important city in S MESOPOTAMIA). Further studies weakened this confidence, and some scholars argue that Ellasar should be identified with ASSHUR.

elm. See PLANTS (under *terebinth*).

Elmadam. el-may'duhm (Gk. *Elmadam G1825*; most MSS, *Elmōdam*). KJV Elmodam. Son of Er, included in Luke's GENEALOGY OF JESUS CHRIST (Lk. 3:28).

Elmodam. See ELMADAM.

Elnaam. el-nay'uhm (Heb. *ʾelnāʿam H534*, "God is pleasantness"). The father of Jeribai and Joshaviah, two of the mighty men of DAVID's army (1 Chr. 11:46); they are mentioned in a list of sixteen warriors (vv. 41b-47) beyond the military elite known as the Thirty (vv. 10-41 = 2 Sam. 23:8-39).

Elnathan. el-nay'thuhn (Heb. *ʾelnātān H535*, "God has given"). **(1)** Father of Nehushta, who was the wife of King JEHOIAKIM and the mother of King JEHOIACHIN (2 Ki. 24:8). It is often thought that this Elnathan is the same as #2 below.

(2) Son of ACBOR and an official during the reign of Jehoiakim (this king was possibly Elnathan's son-in-law; see #1 above). Elnathan and others were sent by the king to Egypt to bring back the prophet URIAH, who was then executed (Jer. 26:22). Elnathan was also one of the officials to whom was read JEREMIAH's scroll and who urged the king not to burn it, but to no avail (36:11-26).

(3) Three men named Elnathan—two of them described as leaders and the other one as wise (NIV, "men of learning")—are said to have been part of a group of eleven sent by EZRA to search for Levites (Ezra 8:16). Because it seems unlikely that three different persons in a relatively small group

would bear a name that is otherwise not frequent, some scholars suspect textual corruption.

Elohim. el'oh-him (Heb. *ʾelōhîm H466*, prob. pl. of *ʾelôah H468* and related to *ʾēl H446*; see EL). The most frequent Hebrew word for GOD, occurring over 2,200 times in the OT. Its etymology and historical origins are debated. Elohim is plural in form, but is usually singular in construction (used with a sg. verb or adjective). When applied to the one true God, the plural is evidently due to the Hebrew idiom of a plural of magnitude or majesty. When used of heathen gods (Gen. 35:2; Exod. 18:11; 20:3; Josh. 24:20) or of angels (Job 1:6; Ps. 8:5; 97:7) or judges (Exod. 21:6; 1 Sam. 2:25) as representatives of God, Elohim is plural in sense as well as form. Elohim is the earliest name of God in the OT, and persists along with other names to the latest period. Jesus is quoted as using a form of the name on the cross (Matt. 27:46; Mk. 15:34; see ELOI, ELOI, LAMA SABACHTHANI).

Eloi, Eloi, lama sabachthani. ee'loh-*i* ee'loh-*i* lah'muh suh-bahk'thuh-n*i*. A Semitic phrase meaning, "My God, my God, why have you forsaken me?" It comes from Ps. 22:1 and was quoted by Jesus on the cross; it occurs transliterated into Greek in Matt. 27:46 and Mk. 15:34. In Matthew, according to most MSS, the divine name (including the personal possessive suffix "my") is transliterated as *ēli*, which corresponds with the Hebrew form in Ps. 22, whereas Mark (and a few important MSS of Matthew; cf. NIV) has *elōi*, which seems to reflect an Aramaic form. The interrogative pronoun "why" can be either Hebrew or Aramaic. The verb (plus suffix) *sabachthani*, however, can only be Aramaic. It is generally agreed that Jesus' mother tongue was ARAMAIC and that he naturally would have expressed himself with it at this time of suffering. The statement is of great theological significance for understanding the self-revelation of Jesus, who quoted from a messianic Psalm as his death was quickly approaching. The cry of the dying Messiah in the passion narratives highlights the mystery of Christ's two natures: the just covenant God was pouring judgment on his coeternal Son, the divine Suffering Servant. The sinless CHRIST was thus experiencing a separation from the Father that should have been the lot of sinners.

Elon (person). ee′lon (Heb. *ʾēlôn H390*, "terebinth"; gentilic *ʾēlōnî H533*). **(1)** A Hittite and father of Basemath, who married Esau (Gen. 26:34). Elsewhere (36:2) Elon's daughter is called Adah. In the latter passage the name Basemath is given to the daughter of Ishmael so that apparently two of Esau's wives were named Basemath. Perhaps the Hittite was given an alternate name to distinguish the two wives.

(2) Son of Zebulun; he was among those who came to Egypt with Jacob (Gen. 46:14). From him sprang the Elonite clan (Num. 26:26).

(3) A judge in Israel from the tribe of Zebulun; he ruled Israel ten years until his death and was buried in Aijalon (Jdg. 12:11-12).

Elon (place). ee′lon (Heb. *ʾēlôn H391*, "terebinth"). A city on the border of the inheritance of Dan between Ithlah and Timnah (Josh. 19:43). It is probably the same as Elon Bethhanan, which was part of Solomon's second administrative district (1 Ki. 4:9). The town was on the coastal plain, E of Joppa (cf. Jdg. 19:46). Its precise location is uncertain, though some have identified it with Khirbet Wadi ʿAlin (just E of Beth Shemesh).

Elon Bethhanan. ee′luhn-beth-hay′nuhn (Heb. *ʾēlôn bêt ḥānān H392*, "terebinth of the house of grace"). A town in the territory of Dan that was part of Solomon's second administrative district (1 Ki. 4:9). The Septuagint understands the passage as referring to two distinct places, and some modern scholars take the same approach. Others believe that Elon Bethhanan is an alternate name for Elon.

Elon-bezaanannim. ee′luhn-bi-zay′uh-nan′im. See Zaannannim.

Elon-meonenim. ee′luhn-mee-on′uh-nim (Heb. *ʾēlôn mĕʿônnim* [*H471* + poel ptc. of *ʿānan H6726*]). A place mentioned once in the Bible (Jdg. 9:37 NRSV, NJPS; the NIV renders the words as common nouns, "soothsayers' tree"). See Diviners' Oak.

Eloth. See Elath, Eloth.

Elpaal. el-pay′uhl (Heb. *ʾelpaʿal H551*, "God has made"). Son of Shaharaim and descendant of Benjamin (1 Chr. 8:11; five sons of Elpaal are listed in vv. 12-13). Some scholars believe that the Elpaal included later in this genealogy (v. 18, which mentions another group of sons) is a different individual. Otherwise, one of the two passages (or both) may list descendants within a large Elpaal clan.

Elpalet. See Eliphelet.

El Paran. el-pay′ruhn (Heb. *ʾēl pāʾrān H386*, "terebinth of Paran"). A place described as the southernmost point of the campaign of Kedorlaomer against the Horites in the mountains of Seir (i.e., Edom); it is said to be on the edge of the wilderness (Gen. 14:6). The name Paran refers to a wilderness area in the E central region of the Sinai peninsula whose eastern boundary was the Wadi Arabah in the N and the Gulf of Aqabah in the S. Since the mountains of Seir (the modern Jebel esh-Sharah range) extend to the SW as far as the Gulf of Aqabah, "El of Paran" on the edge of the desert (of Paran), situated at the southern limit of the mountains of Seir, exactly describes the position of Elat, the seaport on the northern tip of the gulf. It is very likely that El Paran was the ancient name of Elat.

Elpelet. See Eliphelet.

El-roi. el-roi′. The NRSV transliteration of a Hebrew phrase that the NIV renders as "the God who sees me" (Gen. 16:13). It is the name that Hagar gave to the Lord, whose protection she experienced when fleeing from Sarai (Sarah). For that reason, a spring where the angel appeared to her was named Beer Lahai Roi ("the well of the Living One who sees me").

El Shaddai. el-shad′i (Heb. *ʾēl šadday H446 + H8724*, derivation disputed). Also El Shadday. Transliteration of an epithet of God used in the patriarchal narratives and in many poetic passages of the OT. The term is usually translated "God Almighty" (Gen. 17:1; 28:3; 35:11; 43:14;

48:3; Exod. 6:3; Ezek. 10:5). In many other passages (Gen. 43:25; Num. 24:4, 16; Ruth 1:20-21; Ps. 68:14; 91:1; Joel 1:15 [cf. Isa. 13:6]; Ezek. 1:24; Job 5:17 [and thirty times more in Job]) the single element Shaddai is used and is translated "the Almighty." This rendering, which goes back to the SEPTUAGINT (Gk. *pantokratōr G4120*), is somewhat dubious. Some critics believe it refers to a tribal deity, a high god worshiped by the PATRIARCHS, who allegedly were not true monotheists. They usually point to Deut. 32:17 or Josh. 24:2, which record the fact that the Israelite ancestors served other gods "beyond the River [Euphrates]." The Genesis account, however, emphatically states that ABRAHAM turned from this false religion to worship the true and only God. See also EL.

Elteke. See ELTEKEH.

Eltekeh. el'tuh-kuh (Heb. *ʾeltĕqēʾ H558* and *ʾeltĕqēh H559*, derivation disputed). A town in the territory of DAN (Josh. 19:44). It was assigned to the Kohathite Levites (21:23; NRSV, "Elteke"). The Assyrian king SENNACHERIB destroyed the town in 701 B.C., and it was in its environs that the decisive battle between the Assyrians and Egyptians was fought. The precise location of Eltekeh is uncertain.

Eltekon. el'tuh-kon (Heb. *ʾeltĕqôn H560*, derivation uncertain). A town given in the hill country of the tribe of JUDAH (Josh. 15:59). The precise location has not been determined, but one possibility is Khirbet ed-Deir, c. 4 mi. (6 km.) W of BETHLEHEM.

Eltolad, Tolad. el-toh'lad, toh'lad (Heb. *ʾeltôlad H557*, *tôlād H9351*, possibly "[place of] request for a child"). A town in the NEGEV, part of the southernmost territory of the tribe of JUDAH (Josh. 15:30; cf. v. 21). Eltolad was later assigned to the tribe of SIMEON (19:4); the alternate name Tolad (1 Chr. 4:29) appears to be a shortened form. The precise location of the town is unknown, but presumably it was near BEERSHEBA, where an ostracon bearing the name Tolad has been found.

Elul. ee'luhl (Heb. *ʾĕlûl H469*, prob. derived from the Babylonian *Elūlu* [*Ulūlu*], the month of purification). The sixth month (August-September) in the Jewish CALENDAR (Neh. 6:15).

Eluzai. i-loo'zi (Heb. *ʾelʿûzay H539*, "God is my strength"). One of the ambidextrous Benjamite warriors who joined DAVID while he was in exile from SAUL at the PHILISTINE city of ZIKLAG (1 Chr. 12:5; cf. v. 2).

Elymas. el'uh-muhs (Gk. *Elymas G1829*, derivation disputed). Also named BAR-JESUS ("son of Joshua"); a Jewish magician and false prophet whom PAUL met on his first missionary journey (Acts 13:6-12). Elymas was in the retinue of Sergius PAULUS, the Roman proconsul of CYPRUS. He became blind following Paul's curse, causing the proconsul to believe in the Lord. The name or title Elymas has caused debate. Many believe it is to be derived from a Semitic root (cf. Arab. *ʿalim*) signifying "wise" or "one who has insight [into the future]" and thus roughly equivalent to Greek *magos G3407* ("magician"; see MAGI). The likelihood is that Bar-Jesus gave himself the name or the title Elymas because he claimed the powers of the Median priests.

Elyon. See EL ELYON.

Elzabad. el-zay'bad (Heb. *ʾelzābād H479*, "God has granted"). (1) The ninth of eleven Gadite army officers who joined DAVID while he was at ZIKLAG in exile from SAUL (1 Chr. 12:12). These men are described as "brave warriors, ready for battle and able to handle the shield and spear. Their faces were the faces of lions, and they were as swift as gazelles in the mountains" (v. 8). (2) Son of Shemaiah, grandson of OBED-EDOM, and a gatekeeper from the Korahites (1 Chr. 26:7; cf. v. 1). See KORAH. Elzabad and his brothers are described as "leaders in their father's family because they were very capable men" (v. 6).

Elzaphan. See ELIZAPHAN.

embalm. To prepare a dead body with oil and spices to preserve it from decay. Embalming was of Egyptian origin. The only clear instances of it in the Bible were in the cases of JACOB and JOSEPH, who died in EGYPT (Gen. 50:2-3, 26). The pur-

This Egyptian relief from Alexandria depicts embalming methods.

pose of the Egyptians in embalming was to preserve the body for the use of the soul in a future life. The purpose of the Hebrews was to preserve the bodies of Jacob and Joseph for a long journey to their resting place with ABRAHAM (50:13). In the case of Joseph, centuries elapsed before burial in the ancestral tomb (Exod. 13:19; Josh. 24:32). The process of embalming is not described in the Bible. Body cavities were filled with asphalt, cedar oil, or spices, or all three. The body was wrapped tightly in linen cloths, the more perishable parts being stuffed with rolls of linen to maintain the shape of the human form. The body of ASA is said to have been buried with spices, but is not said to have been embalmed (2 Chr. 16:14).

embroidery. Decoration on cloth by means of ornamental needlework. Embroidered work, chiefly using geometric patterns and stylized motifs, is well attested in sculptured and painted scenes from the ancient world. The relevant Hebrew terms are *rāqam H8387* (ptc. "embroiderer, weaver of colored fabrics," Exod. 26:36 et al.) and *riqmâ H8391* ("embroidery, many-colored fabric," Ps. 45:14; Ezek. 16:10; et al.). The latter term can also be used of the varied sheen of the eagle's feathers (Ezek. 17:3) and of multicolored stones (1 Chr. 29:2). Embroidery is well attested in the background cultures of the OT, and may be expected to appear in

Hebrew crafts also. The expressions denoting the raw materials used by the embroiderer ("blue, purple and scarlet yarn and finely twined linen," Exod. 26:36) apparently refer to thread and yarn suitable for embroidery, since they can be used of products of spinning (35:25). It should be noted, however, that some of these terms occur in contexts where they could be taken as denoting woven cloth as well as spun thread (e.g., 39:22).

Emek Keziz. ee´mik-kee´ziz (Heb. *ʿēmeq qĕṣîṣ H6681*, "valley of Keziz" or "plain of gravel"). A town on the E boundary of the tribe of BENJAMIN (Josh. 18:21; KJV, "the valley of Keziz"). The site is unidentified, but it was presumably to the SE of the tribal territory, near JERICHO.

emerald. See MINERALS.

emerod. See DISEASES (sect. II.A).

Emim. See EMITES.

Emites. ee´mits (Heb. *ʾêmîm H400*, "terrors, frightening ones"). Also Emim (KJV superfluous English pl., "Emims"). Early inhabitants of an area E of the DEAD SEA who were defeated in the time of ABRAHAM by KEDORLAOMER and his allies (Gen. 14:5). Their descriptive name was given to them by the Moabites, who subsequently occupied that territory. See Moab. The Emites are described as "a people strong and numerous"; apparently they had some connection with the Anakites and Rephaites, who were regarded as giants (Deut. 2:10-11).

Emmanuel. See Immanuel.

Emmaus. i-may´uhs (Gk. *Emmaous G1843*). The village to which two disciples were going on the day of Jesus' resurrection, when he was recognized by them as he broke bread at supper (Lk. 24:7-35). It was about 7 mi. (11 km.) from Jerusalem, in what direction is not stated, though possibly to the NW. At least half a dozen sites have been proposed as the location of Emmaus, but none can be confirmed.

Emmor. See Hamor.

emperor worship. The worship of the Roman emperor as a divine being—the cause and occasion of the tragic rift between the empire and the church—began spontaneously in the eastern provinces, was recognized by Augustus and Tiberius, and was progressively promoted by their successors as a political measure. Such a cult had manifest usefulness as a cementing and unifying force in the first century, as the principate struggled to stabilize the frontiers and establish cohesion in the Mediterranean world. From earliest times, the rulers of Egypt had been regarded as incarnations of deity and accorded divine honors and worship. When the Ptolemies, on the breakup of Alexander the Great's vast empire, took control of Egypt, they were regarded as the successors of the pharaohs, and similarly were honored by the Egyptian people. The Caesars were no more than the successors of the Ptolemies (see Caesar; Ptolemy). Nor was it difficult for similar concepts of a divine ruler to find place in Syria and Asia Minor.

An extant letter of Pliny the Younger, governor of Bithynia at the end of the first decade of the second century, showed the cult in its political operation. Pliny found his province in the grip of Christianity. Doubtless pressed hard by the temple wardens of the cult whose shrines were empty, and

the guild of butchers whose sacrificial meat was finding no purchasers, Pliny proceeded to suppression. He wrote to the current emperor, Trajan: "Those who denied they were, or had ever been, Christians, who repeated after me an invocation to the gods, and offered adoration, with wine and frankincense, to your image, which I had ordered to be brought for that purpose, together with those of the gods, and who finally cursed Christ—none of which acts, it is said, those who are really Christians can be forced into performing—these I thought it proper to discharge. Others who were named by that informer at first confessed themselves Christians, and then denied it; true, they had been of that persuasion but they had quitted it, some three years, others many years, and a few as much as twenty-five years ago. They all worshipped your statute and the images of the gods, and cursed Christ" (*Ep.* 10.96-97). The cult in no way fulfilled a religious need. It was never more than a tribute of flattery, a demonstration of gratitude, a symbol of patriotism or subjection, and as such a vastly important political force.

En. en (Heb. *ʿên*, construct form of *ʿayin H6524*, "eye" or "spring"). A word compounded with various other terms to form place names, such as En Gedi, En Rogel, etc. Note similarly the use of Arabic *ʿAin* to form numerous compounds.

Enaim. i-nay´im (Heb. *ʿênayim H6542*, possibly "[two] eyes" or "double spring"). A town "on the road to Timnah"; at its entrance Tamar, disguising herself as a prostitute, seduced her father-in-law Judah because he had not given her as a wife to his son Shelah (Gen. 38:14, 21). Enaim is widely regarded to be the same place as Enam. Some interpret the Hebrew differently (e.g., KJV, "in an open place"; NEB, "where the road forks in two directions"). See also Timnah.

Enam. ee´nuhm (Heb. *ʿênām H6543*, "[place of] the spring"). A town in the Shephelah within the tribal territory of Judah (Josh. 15:34); probably the same place as Enaim. The location is uncertain, though various sites have been suggested, including Khirbet Beith Ikka, some 5 mi. (8 km.) SE of Beth Shemesh.

Enan. ee´nuhn (Heb. *ʿēnān H6544*, possibly "spring"). Father of AHIRA; the latter was a leader in the tribe of NAPHTALI (Num. 1:15; 2:29; 7:78, 83; 10:27).

encampment. See CAMP, ENCAMPMENT.

enchanter, enchantment. See MAGIC.

Endor. en´dor (Heb. *ʿēn-dôr H6529*, perhaps "spring of habitation" or "source of generation"). Also En-dor. A town in the tribal territory of ISSACHAR allotted to MANASSEH (Josh. 17:11). Apparently, the Manassites did not drive out all the Canaanites from Endor at the time of the conquest (17:12). According to Ps. 83:9-10, the town was near the river KISHON and thus a part of the battlefield of the JEZREEL Valley; it was the scene of the defeat of JABIN and SISERA by BARAK. Endor is perhaps most famous because here King SAUL sought the help of a medium (see FAMILIAR SPIRIT) in the uncertain hours before his final battle (1 Sam. 28:7). The precise location of Endor is disputed. It was earlier identified with the historical Endur/Indur, 4 mi. (6 km.) S of Mount TABOR, but many scholars now favor Khirbet Ṣafṣafeh, about 2 mi. (3 km.) farther N.

En Eglaim. en-eg´lay-im (Heb. *ʿēn ʿeglayim H6536*, "spring of [two] heifers"). This place is mentioned only in the APOCALYPTIC vision of Ezek. 47:1-12, where the prophet describes a future river flowing from the temple to the E and emptying into the (Dead) Sea so that "the water there becomes fresh" (v. 8), making it possible for large numbers of fish to live in it. Then he adds, "Fishermen will stand along the shore; from En Gedi to En Eglaim there will be places for spreading nets" (v. 10). EN GEDI lies on the W shore of the DEAD SEA, close to the half-way point, so many scholars have sought to locate En Eglaim to its N (e.g., at ʿAin Feshka, near Qumran). Others believe that En Eglaim is viewed in this passage as opposite En Gedi, that is, on the E shore.

enemy. One who feels or behaves in a hostile manner. Enmity among human beings, resulting in murder, is one of the first recorded results of the FALL (Gen. 4:5-8), but will someday be removed (Mic. 4:3-4). Enmity is opposed to LOVE, a basic ethical principle even in the law (Lev. 19:18). The enmity of nature toward humanity is also a result of the fall (Gen. 3:17-18). The future will include reconciliation of the parts of nature with one another, as, for example, in the case of reconciling the enmity between the animals (Isa. 65:25). Those who oppose God's purposes (even among his chosen people, Lam. 2:4; Isa. 1:24-25) can become enemies of God. The Scriptures hint that their hatred of God is self-destructive (Isa. 26:11c, lit., "the fire of your enemies will consume them"). God's vengeance on his enemies is coming (Jer. 46:10), and they must be destroyed when God reigns (Ps. 97:1, 3). The NT specifically and unequivocally commands love both for the stranger (Lk. 10:29-37) and for the hostile enemy (Matt. 5:38-44). The message of Christ, however, may produce enmity (Matt. 10:34-36). Theologically, enmity with God has been universalized and used to describe fallen mankind (Rom. 5:10). RECONCILIATION, then, views salvation as making enemies of God into friends of God (cf. 2 Cor. 5:18-20). See also WRATH.

En Gannim. en-gan´im (Heb. *ʿēn gannîm H6528*, "spring of gardens"). (1) One of the towns in the second district of the tribe of JUDAH (Josh. 15:34). Beyond the fact that it was in the SHEPHELAH (lowland) and probably not far from ZANOAH and JARMUTH, there is no indication of its site.

(2) A town in the tribal territory of ISSACHAR; it was one of the Levitical cities given to the Gershonites (Josh. 19:21; 21:29). The parallel passage has ANEM, which is probably the same place (1 Chr. 6:73). The location of En Gannim is uncertain; among various proposals, a likely site is Khirbet ed-Dir, some 5 mi. (8 km.) SW of the Sea of Galilee.

En Gedi. en-ged´i (Heb. *ʿēn gedî H6527*, "spring of young goat"; cf. Arab. *ʿAin Jidi*). A spring and associated streams that issue from beneath the limestone cliffs on the W side of the DEAD SEA at a temperature of 80°F. It lies almost due E of HEBRON and apparently was also known as HAZAZON TAMAR (2 Chr. 20:2). En Gedi belonged to the territory of the tribe of JUDAH (Josh. 15:62).

E

Water springs in the canyon at En Gedi.

The "Desert of En Gedi" (1 Sam. 24:1; cf. 23:29), figuring in the story of DAVID, is one of the bleakest parts of the Wilderness of Judah (JESHIMON). When the nations of AMMON, MOAB, and EDOM tried to invade Judah through En Gedi in the time of JEHOSHAPHAT (2 Chr. 20:1-2), it was presumably because they hoped to achieve a tactical surprise by attacking one of the few weak spots on Judah's eastern flank. Once warning had been given, failure was inevitable. En Gedi is mentioned again in the prophet's vision of the transformed Dead Sea (Ezek. 47:10; see EN EGLAIM).

engine. This English term is used by the KJV twice in the OT. According to one of these passages (2 Chr. 26:15), King UZZIAH made engines (NIV, "machines") "for use on the towers and on the corner defenses to shoot arrows and hurl large stones." The reference is probably to a wooden shielding device pictured in Assyrian reliefs; part of the fortification of the walls, it protected those who were shooting arrows and throwing stones. The second passage (Ezek. 26:9) uses a Hebrew technical term for some kind of siege device; modern versions translate, "battering rams."

English Bible Versions. See BIBLE VERSIONS, ENGLISH.

engraver. See OCCUPATIONS AND PROFESSIONS.

En Haddah. en-had´uh (Heb. ʿên ḥaddâ H6532, possibly "spring of gladness"). A town in the tribal territory of ISSACHAR (Josh. 19:21). It is usually identified with the modern village of el-Ḥadatheh, about 6 mi. (10 km.) WSW of the S tip of the Sea of Galilee, or the nearby Tell el-Karm.

En Hakkore. en-hak´uh-ree (Heb. ʿên haqqôrēʾ H6530, "spring of the one who calls" or "spring of the partridge"). The spring where SAMSON drank after slaughtering the PHILISTINES at LEHI; upon drinking from it, "his strength returned and he revived" (Jdg. 15:19). Attempts to locate this site, presumably in JUDAH, have been unsuccessful.

En Hazor. en-hay´zor (Heb. ʿên ḥāṣôr H6533, "spring of Hazor [enclosure]"). A fortified city included in the assignment to the tribe of NAPHTALI (Josh. 19:37). The precise location of this town (not to be confused with the royal city of HAZOR) is unknown, although one possible site is the modern town of ʿAinitha in S Lebanon.

enlighten. True enlightenment is the intellectual and moral effect produced upon a person by the reception of the Christian REVELATION. It is not a mere intellectual illumination or understanding of divine truth, for this spiritual insight manifests itself in ethical action. Christians are "sons of light and sons of the day," as PAUL puts it (1 Thess. 5:5). The apostle prayed that the hearts of his readers "may be enlightened in order that you may know the hope to which he has called you" (Eph. 1:18; contrast SATAN's work of blinding the mind, 2 Cor. 4:4). JOHN THE BAPTIST proclaimed that the MESSIAH is the "true light that gives light to every man" (Jn. 1:9), and Jesus himself more than once claimed to be the LIGHT of the world (8:12; 9:5). In one of the most difficult passages in the NT, the author of Hebrews says, "It is impossible for those who have once been enlightened, ... if they fall away, to be brought back to repentance" (Heb. 6:4-6; cf. 10:26, 32). Ancient writers understood the language of enlightenment here as a reference to BAPTISM; modern expositors debate whether or not this statement describes REGENERATION (see also PERSEVERANCE).

En Mishpat. en-mish´pat (Heb. *ʿên mišpāṭ H6535*, "spring of judgment"). A place to which KEDORLAOMER and his allies went in the course of their military campaign; it is identified as KADESH (Gen. 14:7).

enmity. See ENEMY.

Enoch (person). ee´nuhk (Heb. *ḥănôk H2840*, possibly "dedicated" or "initiated" [see HANOCH]; Gk. *Enōch G1970*). (1) Son of CAIN and father of Irad; Cain named a city after him (Gen. 4:17-18).

(2) Son of Jared, descendant of SETH, and father of METHUSELAH (Gen. 5:18-24; 1 Chr. 1:3 [KJV, "Henoch"]). It is said of him that he "walked with God; then he was no more, because God took him away" (Gen. 5:24), clearly a reference to his being taken to heaven without dying (cf. ELIJAH's experience, 2 Ki. 2:11). His name is included in Luke's GENEALOGY OF JESUS CHRIST (Lk. 3:37). A hero of faith, he is known as a man who pleased God (Heb. 11:5), while Jude 14-15 refers to a tradition that Enoch prophesied against ungodly men (cf. ENOCH, BOOKS OF).

Enoch (place). ee´nuhk (Heb. *ḥănôk H2840*, possibly "trained" or "initiated" or "follower"; Gk.

Enōch G1970). A city that CAIN built and named after his son ENOCH (Gen. 4:17).

Enoch, Books of. A collection of APOCALYPTIC LITERATURE written by various authors and circulated under the name of ENOCH. Especially important is *1 Enoch*, regarded as a major source for the development of Jewish doctrine in the last two pre-Christian centuries. See PSEUDEPIGRAPHA.

Enos. See ENOSH.

Enosh. ee´nosh (Heb. *ʾĕnôš H633*, "man"; Gk. *Enōs G1968*). KJV Enos (except 1 Chr. 1:1). Son of SETH and grandson of ADAM; it is noted that at his birth "men began to call on the name of the LORD" (Gen. 4:26). At the age of 90 years, Enosh became the father of Kenan; he had other sons and daughters and died at 905 years (5:6-11). Because his name means "man," he may represent a new Adam, that is, a humanity revived by the birth of Seth and preserved after the FLOOD. Enosh is included in the Chronicler's genealogy (1 Chr. 1:1) and in Luke's GENEALOGY OF JESUS CHRIST (Lk. 3:38).

En Rimmon. en-rim´uhn (Heb. *ʿên rimmôn H6538*, "spring of Rimmon [pomegranate]"). A village resettled by the people of JUDAH after the EXILE (Neh. 11:29). Its identification is uncertain, but many scholars believe it is the same as RIMMON (PLACE), a city in the NEGEV (Josh. 15:32; 19:7; 1 Chr. 4:32; in these three passages, the two names "Ain" and "Rimmon" perhaps should be read as one, "En Rimmon"). It may have marked the extreme S of Judah in postexilic times (if Zech. 14:10 refers to the same town).

En Rogel. en-roh´guhl (Heb. *ʿên rōgēl H6537*, prob. "spring of the fuller"). A spring S of JERUSALEM, just below the junction of the HINNOM and KIDRON Valleys, on the boundary between the tribes of BENJAMIN and JUDAH (Josh. 15:7; 18:16). It was here that JONATHAN and AHIMAAZ, two of DAVID's spies, stayed during ABSALOM's rebellion (2 Sam. 17:17). The spring was mentioned again as the coronation site during the attempted usurpation of the kingdom by ADONIJAH, who sacrificed animals at a site near En Rogel known as the Stone of ZOHELETH

E

(1 Ki. 1:9). Today En Rogel is usually connected with Bir Ayyub ("Well of Job"). The other source of water in E Jerusalem, ʿAin Sitti Maryam ("Spring of the Lady Mary") or the Virgin's Fountain, has also been a suggested identification but is a less likely candidate (the latter is now thought to be the GIHON Spring of 1 Ki. 1:33 et al.).

enrollment. See CENSUS; QUIRINIUS.

En Shemesh. en-shem′ish (Heb. ʿ*ên šemeš H6539*, "spring of Shemesh [sun]"). A spring on the boundary between the tribes of BENJAMIN and JUDAH (Josh. 15:7; 18:17). It is usually identified with modern ʿAin Ḥod, about 2 mi. (3 km.) E of JERUSALEM on the way to JERICHO in the JORDAN Valley. It is sometimes referred to as the "Spring of the Apostles."

ensign. See BANNER.

En Tappuah. en-tap′yoo-uh (Heb. ʿ*ên tappûaḥ H6540*, "spring of Tappuah [apple tree]"). A settlement on the boundary between the tribes of EPHRAIM and MANASSEH, near the town of TAPPUAH (Josh. 17:7; cf. v. 8).

envy. A feeling of displeasure and ill will because of another's advantages or possessions. The English word usually renders Hebrew *qinʾâ H7863*, "passion," which is often used in the good sense of "zeal," less frequently in the negative sense of "envy" (e.g., Job 5:2). Both the Psalms and Proverbs warn against the temptation of becoming envious of evil persons when they seem to prosper in spite of their wrongdoing (Ps. 37:1; 73:2, 3; Prov. 3:31; 23:17; 24:1, 19). The OT abounds in examples of the evil effects of envy—among them JACOB and ESAU, RACHEL and LEAH (Gen. 30:1), JOSEPH and his brothers, HAMAN and MORDECAI. In the NT "envy" is most often the translation of Greek *phthonos G5784*, which uniformly has a negative meaning, "ill-will, envy." For example, envy is said to have led to the crucifixion of Jesus (Matt. 27:18), and it is listed by Jesus and by Paul with the worst of sins (Mk. 7:22; Rom. 1:29; Gal. 5:21). Christians are warned against it (Gal. 5:26; 1 Pet. 2:1). See also COVETOUSNESS.

Epaenetus. See EPENETUS.

Epaphras. ep′uh-fras (Gk. *Epaphras G2071*, prob. a contracted form of *Epaphroditos G2073*, "charming"). A native of COLOSSE and founder of the Colossian church, who was with PAUL when he wrote COLOSSIANS (Col. 1:7-8; 4:12-13; Phlm. 23; not to be confused with EPAPHRODITUS, a member of the Philippian church, Phil. 2:25; 4:18). Epaphras may have been Paul's convert. As Paul's representative he had evangelized Colosse (Col. 1:7) and the neighboring towns of LAODICEA and HIERAPOLIS (4:13) during Paul's Ephesian ministry (Acts 19:10). His visit to Paul in ROME and his report concerning conditions in the churches of the Lycus Valley caused Paul to write Colossians (Col. 1:7-9). Paul's high esteem for Epaphras is seen in the terms he applies to him: "our dear fellow servant," "a faithful minister of Christ on our behalf" (Col. 1:7), "a servant of Christ Jesus" (4:12), and "my fellow prisoner" (Phlm. 23).

Epaphroditus. i-paf′ruh-di′tuhs (Gk. *Epaphroditos G2073*, "handsome, charming"). A member of the church at PHILIPPI who brought an offering to PAUL when the apostle was imprisoned in ROME (Phil. 2:25-30; 4:18). His Greek name (corresponding to the Lat. *Venustus*, "belonging to Venus," called Aphrodite by the Greeks) was common and indicates a non-Jewish origin. It was also common in a contracted form, EPAPHRAS, but there is no reason to identify Epaphroditus with the Epaphras from Colosse (Col. 1:7; 4:12). Epaphroditus was an esteemed member of the Philippian church, commissioned to deliver the church's offering to Paul (Phil. 4:18) and to stay and help him (2:25, 30). He became dangerously ill "for the work of Christ." After his slow recovery, Paul felt it best to send him back home. Epaphroditus was distressed because of anxiety for him at Philippi and longed to return. Paul sent him back with the letter to the PHILIPPIANS and asked them to receive Epaphroditus "in the Lord with great joy." Some believe that the Philippians expected Epaphroditus to stay with Paul so that TIMOTHY could go to Philippi, and that the apostle was thus concerned about how the church might receive Epaphroditus; thus Paul expresses his own high esteem of him.

Epenetus. i-pee′nuh-tuhs (Gk. *Epainetos G2045*, "praised"). Also Epaenetus. A Christian in ROME affectionately greeted by PAUL as "my dear friend" and "the first convert [*lit.*, the firstfruits] to Christ in the province of Asia" (Rom. 16:5; KJV, "Achaia," reflecting an inferior variant reading). Such senior Christians naturally assumed positions of leadership in the church. That Epenetus was an accepted leader is implied in Paul's mention of him immediately after PRISCILLA AND AQUILA.

ephah (measure). See WEIGHTS AND MEASURES.

Ephah (person). ee′fuh (Heb. *ʿēpāh H6549*, "darkness"). **(1)** Son of MIDIAN and grandson of ABRAHAM and KETURAH (Gen. 25:4; 1 Chr. 1:33). Ephah was thus the eponym of a prominent Midianite tribe, apparently inhabiting NW ARABIA and famous for its camels (Isa. 60:6 [*ʿēpāh H6548*]).

(2) A concubine of CALEB who bore him three sons; she is mentioned in the genealogy of JUDAH (1 Chr. 2:46).

(3) Son of JAHDAI included in the genealogy of Judah (1 Chr. 2:47). The mention of Jahdai and his sons is abrupt, but apparently there was some connection between them and Caleb (cf. vv. 46, 48, and see #2 above).

Ephai. ee′fi (Heb. *ʿēpay H6550*, "my darkness" or "my bird"). An inhabitant of NETOPHAH (a city or group of villages near BETHLEHEM) whose sons were army officers under the authority of GEDALIAH, governor of JUDAH after the destruction of JERUSALEM by the Babylonians (Jer. 40:8; the parallel passage, 2 Ki. 25:23, reads differently; see TANHUMETH).

Epher. ee′fuhr (Heb. *ʿēper H6761*, "[kid of] gazelle"). **(1)** Son of MIDIAN and grandson of ABRAHAM and KETURAH (Gen. 25:4; 1 Chr. 1:33). Epher was thus the eponym of a Midianite tribe in NW ARABIA (cf. Gen. 25:6). There may have been more than one clan of Midian, or the name may be used broadly of different peoples.

(2) Son of EZRAH and descendant of JUDAH (1 Chr. 4:17).

(3) One of the heads of families in the half-tribe of MANASSEH during the time of TIGLATH-PILESER III (1 Chr. 5:24; cf. v. 26). These leaders are described as "brave warriors, famous men," but also "unfaithful to the God of their fathers" (v. 25).

Ephes Dammim, Pas Dammim. ee′fiz-dam′im, pas-dam′im (Heb. *ʾepes dammim H702*, "border of Dammim [blood]"; *pas dammim H7169*, perhaps a short form). A site in the territory of JUDAH between SOCOH and AZEKAH where the PHILISTINES encamped and near which DAVID defeated GOLIATH (1 Sam. 17:1; 1 Chr. 11:13; cf. 2 Sam. 23:9 NIV). Some have conjectured that the deep red color of the soil gave rise to the concept of blood, but it is more probable that the site was so named because of the number of battles fought there between Israel and the Philistines. The site was near the Valley of Elah (see ELAH, VALLEY OF), but the precise location is uncertain.

Ephesians, Letter to the. Generally acknowledged to be one of the richest and most profound of the NT letters. The depth and grandeur of its concepts, the richness and fullness of its message, and the majesty and dignity of its contents have made this letter precious to believers in all ages and in all places. Its profound truths and vivid imagery have deeply penetrated into the thought and literature of the Christian church.

Ephesians explicitly claims authorship by PAUL (Eph. 1:1; 3:1), and its entire tenor is eminently Pauline. The early Christian church uniformly received and treasured it as from Paul. Only within the modern era have critics raised doubts as to its origin. The attacks are based solely on internal arguments drawn from the style, vocabulary, and theology of the letter. These arguments are subjective and inconclusive and offer no compelling reasons for rejecting the undeviating evidence of text and tradition. If Paul's authorship is rejected, the letter must be ascribed to someone who was fully Paul's equal, but the literature of the first two centuries reveals no traces of anyone capable of producing such a writing.

Ephesians was written while Paul was a prisoner (Eph. 3:1; 4:1; 6:20). The prevailing view has been that it was written from ROME during his first Roman imprisonment (Acts 28:30-31). Some attempts have been made to shift the place

Overview of EPHESIANS

Author: The apostle PAUL, though many scholars argue that the letter consists of Pauline material brought together and edited by one or more of his disciples.

Historical setting: Probably written from ROME during the apostle's first imprisonment in that city (c. A.D. 61-63; those who believe that someone other than Paul was the author date the letter two or three decades later). Ephesians may have been addressed to several churches in and around EPHESUS in the aftermath of the problems that occasioned the writing of COLOSSIANS.

Purpose: To expound on the blessings enjoyed by the CHURCH, to stress the unity of the BODY OF CHRIST, and to encourage believers to walk in the ways of CHRIST.

Contents: A doctrinal section that focuses on our standing in Christ (Eph. 1-3), followed by a practical section on righteous Christian living (chs. 4-6).

of composition to CAESAREA (24:27) or even to EPHESUS during an unrecorded imprisonment there (19:10; 20:18-21, 31; 2 Cor. 11:23), but the traditional Roman origin firmly holds the field.

Along with COLOSSIANS and PHILEMON (Col. 4:7-8; Phlm. 9, 13, 17), the letter was transmitted to its destination by TYCHICUS (Eph. 6:21-22). Thus all three were sent to the Roman province of ASIA, but there is much scholarly disagreement as to the precise destination of Ephesians. The uncertainty arises from the fact that the words "in Ephesus" in Eph. 1:1 are not found in the three most ancient Greek MSS (P[46], Vaticanus, Sinaiticus). Passages in the writings of Origen and Basil indicate that they also knew the enigmatic reading produced by the omission of "in Ephesus." But the words are found in almost all other witnesses, and ecclesiastical tradition uniformly designates it as "to the Ephesians."

How does one explain the omission of the phrase in some MSS? One widely accepted view is that the letter was really an encyclical sent to the various churches of provincial Asia, of whom Ephesus was the most important. It is often further assumed that originally a blank was left for the insertion of the local place-name. The impersonal tone and contents of the letter are urged as

confirmation. The view is plausible, but it has its difficulties. If it was originally directed to a group of churches, would not Paul, in accordance with his known practice of including a direct address, rather have written "in Asia," or "in the churches of Asia"? In all other places where Paul uses the words "to those who are" he adds a local place-name. Then how is the uniform tradition of its Ephesian destination to be accounted for? A fair solution would seem to be that the letter was originally addressed to the saints "in Ephesus" but was intentionally cast into a form that would make it suitable to meet the needs of the Asian churches. As transcriptions of the original to the mother church were circulated, the place of destination might be omitted, though they were uniformly recognized as the letter originally addressed to the Ephesians.

Its contents offer no clear indication as to the occasion for the writing of the letter. Its affinity to Colossians in time of origin and contents suggests an occasion closely related to the writing of that letter. Ephesians seems to be the after-effect of the controversy that caused the writing of Colossians. Colossians has in it the intensity, rush, and roar of the battlefield, while Ephesians has a calm atmosphere suggestive of a survey of the field after the victory. With the theme of Colossians still fresh in mind, Paul felt it desirable to declare the positive significance of the great truths set forth in refuting the Colossian heresy. A firm grasp of the truths here stated would provide an effective antidote to such philosophical speculations.

Ephesians sets forth the wealth of the believer in union with Christ. It portrays the glories of our salvation and emphasizes the nature of the CHURCH as the BODY OF CHRIST. As indicated by the doxology in Eph. 3:20-21, its contents fall into two parts, the first doctrinal (chs. 1-3), the second practical and encouraging (chs. 4-6). An outline may suggest some of its riches.

I. Salutation (1:1-2).
II. Doctrinal: the believers' standing in Christ (1:3—3:21).
  A. The thanksgiving for our redemption (1:3-14).
  B. The prayer for spiritual illumination (1:15-23).
  C. The power of God manifested in our salvation (2:1-10).
  D. The union of Jew and Gentile in one body in Christ (2:11-22).
  E. The apostle as the messenger of this mystery (3:1-13).
  F. The prayer for the realization of these blessings (3:14-19).
  G. The doxology of praise (3:20-21).
III. Practical: the believers' life in Christ (4:1—6:20).
  A. Their walk as God's saints (4:1—5:21).
    1. The worthy walk, in inward realization of Christian unity (4:1-16).
    2. The different walk, in outward manifestation of a changed position (4:17-32).
    3. The loving walk, in upward imitation of our Father (5:1-17).
    4. The summary of the Spirit-filled life (5:18-21).
  B. Their duties as God's family (5:22—6:9).
  C. Their warfare as God's soldiers (6:10-20).
IV. Conclusion (6:21-24).

Ephesus. ef'uh-suhs (Gk. *Ephesos* G2387). A major city founded by ancient Ionians at the mouth of the Cayster River, between the Koressos Range and the sea, on the W coast of ASIA MINOR. Greek colonies that surround the Mediterranean and Black Sea were primarily trading posts. Migrant communities of Greeks did not seek to dominate the hinterlands, but to secure an *emporion* or "way in," a bridgehead for commerce and enough surrounding coast and territory to support the community. Great cities grew from such foundations from Marseilles to Alexandria, some of them royal capitals. And in all cases colonies became centers or outposts of Hellenism, distinctive and civilizing.

Ephesus displaced MILETUS as a trading port; but when its harbor, like that of Miletus, in turn silted up, SMYRNA replaced both as the outlet and *emporion* of the Maeander Valley trade route. In the heyday of Asia Minor, 230 separate communities, each proud of its individuality and wealth, issued their own coinage and managed their own affairs. The dominance of Persian despotism, wide deforestation, and the ravages of war on a natural bridge and highway between the continents slowly sapped this prosperity; but in early Roman times, as in the days of its Ionian independence, Ephesus was a proud, rich, busy port, the rival of ALEXANDRIA and Syrian ANTIOCH.

Built near the shrine of an old Anatolian fertility goddess, Ephesus became the seat of an oriental cult. The Anatolian deity had been taken over by the Greeks under the name of ARTEMIS, the Diana of the Romans. Grotesquely represented with many breasts (or clusters of fruit), the goddess and

Ephesus.

her cult found expression in the famous temple, served, like that of Aphrodite at CORINTH, by a host of priestess courtesans.

Much trade clustered round the cult. Ephesus became a place of pilgrimage for tourist-worshipers, all eager to carry away talisman and souvenir, hence the prosperous guild of the silversmiths whose livelihood was the manufacture of silver shrines and images of the meteoric stone that was

This theater in Ephesus, seating 25,000, was the site of a public hearing after the silversmith Demetrius incited the other craftsmen against Paul for opposing the worship of the idol Artemis of the Ephesians (Acts 19:29).

said to be Diana's image "fallen from heaven." Ephesus leaned more and more on the trade that followed the cult, and commerce declined in her silting harbor. A long stretch (20 mi./32 km.) of reedy marshland now separates the old harbor works from the sea, and even in Paul's day the process was under way. The historian Tacitus tells us that an attempt was made to improve the seaway in A.D. 65, but the task proved too great. Ephesus in the first century was a dying city, given to parasite pursuits, living, like ATHENS, on a reputation, a curious meeting place of old and new religions, of East and West. Acts 19 gives a peculiarly vivid picture of her unnatural life. The "lampstand" had gone from its place, for Ephesus's decline was mortal sickness, and it is possible to detect in the letter to Ephesus in the Apocalypse (Rev. 2:1-7) a touch of the lassitude that characterized the effete and declining community. The temple and part of the city have been extensively excavated.

Ephlal. ef'lal (Heb. *'eplāl H697*, derivation uncertain). Son of Zabad and descendent of JUDAH in the line of JERAHMEEL (1 Chr. 2:37).

ephod (garment). ee'fod. A sacred vestment originally worn by the high PRIEST and made of "gold, and of blue, purple and scarlet yarn, and of finely twisted linen—the work of a skilled craftsman" (cf. Exod. 28:6-14; 39:2-7). It was held together front and back by two shoulder pieces at the top and a girdle band around the waist. On each shoulderpiece was an onyx stone engraved with six names of the tribes of Israel. Attached to the ephod by chains of pure gold was a breastplate containing twelve precious stones. The blue robe of the ephod was worn underneath, having a hole for the head and extending to the feet, with a hem alternating with gold bells and pomegranates of blue, purple, and scarlet (28:31-35; 39:22-26).

Later, persons other than the high priest wore ephods. SAMUEL wore a linen ephod while ministering before the Lord (1 Sam. 2:18), which was characteristic of the ordinary priests (2:28; 14:3; 22:18). DAVID wore a linen ephod while he danced before the Lord after bringing the ARK OF THE COVENANT to Jerusalem (2 Sam. 6:14). ABIATHAR carried off from NOB an ephod that represented to David the divine presence, for of it he inquired the will of the Lord (1 Sam. 23:6, 9; 30:7-8). Earlier, the ephod was misused as an object of idolatrous worship by GIDEON (Jdg. 8:27) and associated with images by a man named MICAH (17:5; 18:14).

Ephod (person). ee'fod (Heb. *'ēpōd H681*, meaning uncertain). Father of Hanniel; the latter was a leader in the tribe of MANASSEH appointed to help distribute the land of Canaan among the tribes (Num. 34:23; cf. v. 18).

ephphatha. ef'uh-thuh (Gk. *ephphatha G2395*, Gk. transliteration of a Semitic form meaning "be opened"). This word was spoken by Jesus to a deaf mute in the DECAPOLIS (Mk. 7:34). "At this, the man's ears were opened, his tongue was loosened and he began to speak plainly" (v. 35). This passage is one of the rare occasions when a biblical author saw fit to quote from an original Semitic language the exact word Jesus used. After quoting the foreign word, Mark immediately translates it (*dianoichthēti*, "be opened," pass. impv. of *dianoigō* G1380). The use of this term (hardly a secretive word of magic), along with Jesus' touching and spitting (v. 33), may suggest the special difficulty and thus greatness of the miracle. Scholars have debated whether the Semitic word is HEBREW or ARAMAIC. Since the latter was almost surely Jesus' mother tongue and the commonly used language by Jews in GALILEE and surrounding areas, most scholars interpret *ephphatha* as representing the Aramaic form *ʾeppatah* (a contraction of *ʾetpĕtah*, 2nd masc. sing. ethpeel).

Ephraim (person and tribe). ee´fray-im (Heb. *ʾeprayim* H713, derivation uncertain, but by popular etymology, "doubly fruitful"; gentilic *ʾeprātî* H718, "Ephraimite" [the form can also mean "Ephrathite"; see EPHRATH]). The younger of two sons born to JOSEPH and ASENATH in Egypt; his older brother was MANASSEH (Gen. 41:50-52; 46:20). He was also the ancestor of the tribe that bears his name. The aged JACOB, when he blessed his grandsons Manasseh and Ephraim, adopted them as his own sons. Despite Joseph's protest, Jacob gave the preferential blessing (signified by the right hand) to Ephraim (48:1-22). When Jacob blessed his own sons, he did not mention Ephraim and Manasseh, but he did give a special blessing to their father, Joseph (49:22-26). Instead of one tribe of Joseph, the Hebrews recognized two distinct tribes among Ephraim's and Manasseh's descendants, bringing the total of tribes to thirteen, yet the original number twelve (derived from the twelve sons of Jacob) continued to be referred to. The separation of the tribe of LEVI for cultic service throughout the land,

so that they did not receive a separate territory in which to live, helped to perpetuate the concept of the "Twelve Tribes of Israel."

Ephraim together with Manasseh and Benjamin camped on the W side of the TABERNACLE in the wilderness (Num. 2:18-24). JOSHUA (Hoshea) the son of Nun, one of the spies and MOSES' successor, was an Ephraimite (13:8). Ephraim and Manasseh were mentioned as making up the Joseph group in Moses' blessing (Deut. 33:13-17). At the division of the land among the tribes, the children of Joseph (except half of Manasseh, which settled east of the JORDAN, Num. 32:33, 39-42) received the central hill country of PALESTINE (see EPHRAIM, HILL COUNTRY OF). This area is bounded on the N side by the Valley of JEZREEL, on the E by the Jordan River, on the S by a "zone of movement" that runs from JOPPA to JERICHO (a series of valleys that invite travel across Palestine) and on the west by the Mediterranean. The Joseph tribes were not able to occupy this land completely for a long time, being forced up into the heavily wooded hill country (Josh. 17:14-18) by the Canaanites and Philistines, who occupied the good bottom lands and who by their superior civilization and power (Jdg. 1:27-29) kept the Hebrews subservient until the time of DAVID.

E

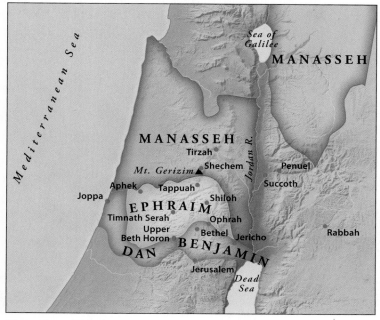

Tribal territory of Ephraim.

Ephraim and Manasseh seem to have been bitter rivals (Isa. 9:20-21), Manasseh being the larger group (Gen. 49:22), but Ephraim asserting the more vigorous leadership. Although they seem to have held their land in common for a time (Josh. 17:14-18) it was presently divided between them. Ephraim's portion was well defined and very fruitful, its soil fertile and its rainfall more plentiful than JUDAH's to the S (Deut. 33:13-16). Ephraim's inheritance is described in Josh. 16:5-10. The territory was bounded on the S by the northern borders of BENJAMIN and DAN. BETHEL was just across the line in Benjamin, the two BETH HORONS were just in Ephraim, as was GEZER toward the sea. The W boundary seems ideally to have been the Mediterranean. On the N, the brook KANAH separated Ephraim from the half of Manasseh, as did the towns of SHECHEM (in Manasseh) and TAANATH SHILOH. Then the line seems to have turned abruptly southward, through ATAROTH, passing near Jericho and thence to the Jordan. References to the towns for Ephraimites within Manasseh (16:9; 17:9) suggest that the rivalry between these two tribes had resulted in some boundary changes.

At SHILOH, in the territory of Ephraim, JOSHUA pitched the tabernacle (Josh. 18:1), and this town remained a religious center for the Hebrews (Josh. 22:12; Jdg. 18:31; 21:19; 1 Sam. 1:3, 9, 24; 2:14; 3:21) until it was destroyed by the PHILISTINES after the battle of EBENEZER (1 Sam. 4:1-11). Samuel was an Ephraimite (1:1). The Ephraimites contributed their share of the hatred and strife that divided the Hebrew tribes during the dark days of the judges (Jdg. 8:1-3; 12:1-6).

It would appear that Ephraim, in common with the rest of the central and northern tribes, was never completely reconciled to the rule of Judah that the Davidic dynasty brought (2 Sam. 2:8-9; 1 Ki. 12:16). When JEROBOAM I, an Ephraimite (1 Ki. 11:26), rebelled against SOLOMON's son REHOBOAM, no doubt his own tribe supported him completely. Ephraim became such a leader in the new northern Hebrew kingdom that in addition to its more common name ISRAEL, the kingdom is also called Ephraim (Isa. 7:2, 5, 9, 17; Hos. 9:3-16). From this time on the tribe's history is merged with that of this kingdom.

Ephraim (place). ee´fray-im (Heb. *ʾeprayim H713* [see EPHRAIM (PERSON AND TRIBE)]; Gk. *Ephraim G2394*). A town that was near BAAL HAZOR (the place where ABSALOM kept his sheepshearers, 2 Sam. 13:23). This town is often identified with OPHRAH, which in turn is usually thought to be the same as EPHRON (PLACE) and the NT village of Ephraim (modern eṭ-Ṭaiyibeh, 13 mi./21 km. NNE of JERUSALEM), where Jesus once stayed with his disciples (Jn. 11:54). It is possible, however, that 2 Sam. 13:23 refers not to a town at all but to the tribal territory of Ephraim (cf. NIV, "near the border of Ephraim").

Ephraim, forest of. The term occurs only in 2 Sam. 18:6 (KJV, "wood of Ephraim"), where it denotes the place of the decisive battle in which DAVID's soldiers defeated those of ABSALOM. Opinions differ as to whether the latter refers to the expansion by the house of JOSEPH eastward into TRANSJORDAN or to settlement in the forested sectors of the Ephraimite hill country itself. Two details in Josh. 17:15 support the first view: (1) the

Broad regional view of the topography of Ephraim.

© Dr. James C. Martin

reference to the land of the REPHAITES indicates an area in Transjordan; (2) "the forest" is placed in juxtaposition with "the hill country of Ephraim," which was clearly in Cisjordan, the area W of the Jordan. The proximity of the forest of Ephraim to MAHANAIM (2 Sam. 17:27), formerly ISH-BOSHETH's Transjordanian capital (2:8-9), firmly establishes this location. Originally this territory was granted to "the house of Joseph—to Ephraim and Manasseh" (Josh. 17:17). Ephraim later lost this woodland E of Jordan to JEPHTHAH and the Gileadites (Jdg. 12:1-15).

Ephraim, hill country of. The Hebrew phrase *har-ʾeprāyim* (KJV, "mount Ephraim"), which occurs more than thirty times in the OT (Josh. 17:15; Jdg. 3:27; 1 Sam. 1:1; et al.), denotes not a single mountain but the hill country in central PALESTINE occupied by the tribe of EPHRAIM and extending N into the territory of MANASSEH. It was more fruitful than the hill country of JUDAH, especially on its western slopes, and it was one of the few areas where the Israelites were able to establish themselves after the conquest under JOSHUA. At its highest point, the plateau rises to over 3,000 ft. (910 m.). This section is resistant to erosion, leading to extensive vegetation prior to its being deforested.

Ephraim, mount of. See EPHRAIM, HILL COUNTRY OF.

Ephraim Gate. A northward-facing gate of OT JERUSALEM (it exited to the ridge route and thus led to the hill country of Ephraim). We read that, during the reign of AMAZIAH king of Judah, JEHOASH king of Israel invaded the southern kingdom and "broke down the wall of Jerusalem from the Ephraim Gate to the Corner Gate—a section about six hundred feet [*lit.*, four hundred cubits] long" (2 Ki. 14:13; 2 Chr. 25:23). This statement has led many to infer that the Ephraim Gate was 600-650 ft. (180-200 m.) E of the CORNER GATE. The Ephraim Gate figured in postexilic celebrations (Neh. 8:16; 12:39).

Ephraimite. See EPHRAIM (PERSON AND TRIBE).

Ephrain. See EPHRON.

Ephratah. See EPHRATH, EPHRATHA.

Ephrath, Ephrathah. ef´rath, ef´ruh-thuh (Heb. *ʾeprāt H714* and *H715*, *ʾeprātāh H716* and *H717*, "fruitful"; gentilic *ʾeprātî H718*, "Ephrathite" [the form can also mean "Ephraimite"; see EPHRAIM]). KJV Ephrath, Ephratah. **(1)** A city or area associated with (and at some point absorbed into) BETHLEHEM. ELIMELECH and JESSE are identified as Ephrathites (Ruth 1:2; 1 Sam. 17:12; the KJV has Ephrathite also in 1 Sam. 1:1 and 1 Ki. 11:26, where modern versions more correctly have Ephraimite). The compound form "Bethlehem Ephrathah" occurs once (Mic. 5:2). On the way to Ephrath (the spelling used in Genesis), BENJAMIN was born and his mother RACHEL died and was buried (Gen. 35:16-20; 48:7). The burial place of Rachel is elsewhere set in the tribal territory of Benjamin (1 Sam. 10:2; cf. Jer. 31:15), whereas Bethlehem was in JUDAH (cf. also Ps. 132:6, where Ephrathah is associated with JAAR, prob. on the border between Benjamin and Judah). A plausible solution is that Ephrathah referred originally to a relatively large area extending from the Benjamin/Judah border to the S as far as TEKOA, and that Bethlehem was thus a village within this region. It has been argued further that Ephrathah was originally the name of a Judahite clan descended from #2 below.

(2) The second wife of CALEB son of HEZRON; her firstborn was HUR, whose descendants included KIRIATH JEARIM and Bethlehem (Ephrath in 1 Chr. 2:19; Ephrathah in 2:50; 4:4). There may be a reference to her also in 2:24 (cf. RSV and CALEB EPHRATHAH).

Ephron (person). ee´fron (Heb. *ʿeprôn H6766*, possibly "dust" or "fawn"). Son of Zohar; he was the HITTITE from whom ABRAHAM purchased a burial place for SARAH his wife in MACHPELAH (Gen. 23:7-20). Ephron, assuming Abraham's knowledge of propriety, offered at first to give away the land (23:11). Even when Abraham properly insisted on paying for it, Ephron did not offer to sell the land, but slyly stated the value he put on the property (23:13-15). Abraham, understanding that this was the asking price, responded by purchasing it at that price.

E

Ephron (place). ee′fron (Heb. ʿeprôn *H6767*, possibly "[place of] dust" or "fawn"). (**1**) Mount Ephron (Josh. 15:9) probably refers to a range near KIRIATH JEARIM that served to describe the N boundary of the tribe of JUDAH. The site has not been identified, but one possibility is el-Qastel, about 5 mi. (8 km.) WNW of JERUSALEM.

(**2**) A town that, along with BETHEL and JESHANAH, was taken from King JEROBOAM of Israel by King ABIJAH of Judah (2 Chr. 13:19). This Ephron, thought to be the same as OPHRAH and NT Ephraim (Jn. 11:54), is usually identified with modern eṭ-Ṭaiyibeh, about 13 mi. (21 km.) NNE of Jerusalem. See EPHRAIM (PLACE).

Epicurean. ep′i-kyoo-ree′uhn (Gk. *Epikoureios G2134*, from *Epikouros*, Epicurus, meaning "helper, ally"). A prominent philosophical school in the Greco-Roman period. The Epicureans are mentioned in Acts 17:18, along with the STOICS. Luke gives no information on their views, except that they rejected the idea of a bodily RESURRECTION. They were named after the Greek philosopher Epicurus (341-270 B.C.), who taught that nature rather than reason is the true reality; nothing exists but atoms and void, that is, matter and space. The chief purpose of human beings is to achieve happiness, and they have free will to plan and live a life of pleasure. Epicurus gave the widest scope to this matter of pleasure, interpreting it as avoidance of pain, so that the mere enjoyment of good health would be pleasure. Such stress on the good things of life, while very practical, is also very dangerous. For the philosopher the highest joy is found in mental and intellectual pursuits, but for lesser souls lower goals of sensual satisfaction fulfill the greatest pleasure. Thus the high standards of the founder were not maintained, and the philosophy gained a bad reputation. Since such teaching appealed to the common man, this natural philosophy became widespread. It was widely held at the time of Christ, and thus PAUL met it at ATHENS when he encountered the philosophers of that city.

epileptic. See DISEASES.

epiphany. This term (from Gk. *epiphaneia G2211*) can be used generally of any manifestation or even of a sudden realization. More specifically, it refers to a supernatural revelation or to the appearance of a divine being. When capitalized, it designates the Christian feast (January 6) that celebrates the visit of the MAGI because at that time the divine nature of Jesus was manifested to the Gentiles. In the Christian churches of the E, it celebrates the baptism of Jesus (when his messianic office was made manifest); this was its original significance, which can be dated to the third century.

epistle. This term (from Gk. *epistolē G2186*, "message, commission, letter") in English usage normally refers to a literary composition that is written in the form of a letter. Since the "epistles" of the NT are real pieces of correspondence (not published literary works), most modern versions translate the Greek word as LETTER. Written correspondence, whether personal or official, has been common to all ages. The OT abounds with evidence of widespread written letters, among the best known being DAVID's letter to JOAB concerning URIAH (2 Sam. 11:14-15), JEZEBEL's letter regarding NABOTH (1 Ki. 21:8-9), and SENNACHERIB's letter to HEZEKIAH (2 Ki. 19:14).

In biblical studies, however, the word *epistle* has traditionally been almost a technical term, designating twenty-one NT books written in the form of letters. Paul wrote thirteen (or fourteen, if Hebrews is by him); John, three; Peter, two; James, one; and Jude, one. According to the custom of the time, they usually began with the name or title of the writer and that of the addressee or addressees; then followed words of greeting and the body of the letter. It was Paul's usual practice to employ a secretary to write from dictation. The epistles were written to individual churches or groups of churches (almost always given by name) or to individuals. Seven are called General Epistles or CATHOLIC EPISTLES, because they were written to the church at large.

The epistles are not disguised doctrinal treatises. They were written in the way of ordinary correspondence and dealt with situations, whether doctrinal or practical, needing immediate attention. They were written in reply to letters or as the result of other information otherwise obtained. It is very apparent that the writers realized that what they wrote was authoritative and came from God.

They all dealt with some aspect of the redemptive message and experience. Although written to deal with specific local situations, they set forth fundamental principles applicable to the individual and collective life of all believers. They were received from the beginning with the OT Scriptures (2 Pet. 3:15-16). It is not to be supposed that all of the epistles of the apostles have survived. PAUL in 1 Cor. 5:9 refers to a letter he had written to the Corinthians prior to our 1 Corinthians; and in Col. 4:6 he speaks of a letter to the Laodicean church.

Er. uhr (Heb. ʿēr *H6841*, "watcher" or "protector"; Gk. Ēr *G2474*). **(1)** Firstborn son of JUDAH by his Canaanite wife, the daughter of Shua (Gen. 38:3). Er married TAMAR, but the Lord slew him for some unnamed wickedness before he had any children (Gen. 38:6-7; 46:12; Num. 26:19; 1 Chr. 2:3). Tamar was then given to his brother ONAN (Gen. 38:8).

(2) Son of Shela and grandson of JUDAH, thus nephew of #1 above (1 Chr. 4:21).

(3) Son of a certain Joshua, included in Luke's GENEALOGY OF JESUS CHRIST (Lk. 3:27).

Eran. ihr′an (Heb. ʿērān *H6896*, "watcher" or "protector"; gentilic ʿērānî *H6897*, "Eranite"). Son of SHUTHELAH and grandson of EPHRAIM; eponymous ancestor of the Eranite clan (Num. 26:36; not mentioned in the parallel passage, 1 Chr. 7:20).

Erastus. i-ras′tuhs (Gk. *Erastos*, "beloved"). A common Greek name, occurring in the NT with reference to two (or possibly three) companions of PAUL. **(1)** A helper of Paul, sent along with TIMOTHY to MACEDONIA while the apostle remained in the province of ASIA for a while longer (Acts

19:22). He is very likely the same Erastus whom Paul left behind at CORINTH (2 Tim. 4:20); some think he may be a different individual.

(2) A man described as "director of public works" in Corinth (the city from which ROMANS was written) and who sent greetings to the Christians in ROME (Rom. 16:23; NRSV, "city treasurer"). He was apparently the steward or manager (Gk. *oikonomos G3874*) of the property or financial affairs of the city. Such officials were generally slaves or freedmen, though often wealthy. It is debated whether the title reflects high social status or the humble position of a city-owned slave. In 1929, archaeologists uncovered at Corinth a 1st-cent. Latin inscription reading, "Erastus, commissioner for public works [*aedile*], laid this pavement at his own expense." That he was the Erastus of Romans is possible, but not probable. It is also unlikely that he was the same as #1 above.

Erech. ee′rik (Heb. ʾerek *H804*; Akk. *Uruk*). TNIV Uruk. The second of the cities founded by NIMROD (Gen. 10:10). In times of the Assyrian empire, Erech was one of the cities whose inhabitants were deported to SAMARIA by King ASHURBANIPAL (Ezra 4:9-10). Erech, or Uruk, was one of the oldest, largest, and most important cities of ancient SUMER. The site is located at modern Warka, c. 160 mi. (260 km.) S of Baghdad. Originally the city was on the W bank of the EUPHRATES River but the river now lies some distance to the E of the site.

Eri. ee′ri (Heb. ʿērî *H6878*, "watcher" or "protector"; gentilic ʿērî *H6879*, "Erite"). Son of GAD, grandson of JACOB, and eponymous ancestor of the Erites (Gen. 46:16; Num. 26:16).

This stone, discovered in 1929, was placed by Erastus, the commissioner for public works at Corinth, at his own expense. Some think he is the same Erastus who sent greetings to the Christians in Rome (Rom. 16:23).

© Dr. James C. Martin

Esaias. i-zay′yuhz. KJV NT form of ISAIAH.

Esarhaddon. ee′suhr-had′uhn (Heb. ʾēsar-ḥaddōn *H675*, from Akk. *Aššur-aḥ-iddin*, "Ashur has given a brother"). King of ASSYRIA 681-669 B.C. The younger son of SENNACHERIB, Esarhaddon obtained the throne of Assyria after his older brothers murdered their father (2 Ki. 19:36-37; 2 Chr. 32:21; Isa. 37:37-38). His reign saw important political developments. He restored the city of BABYLON, which his father had destroyed, and fought campaigns against the Cimmerians and other barbaric hordes from beyond the Caucasus. His main achievement was the conquest of EGYPT, Assyria's competitor for world domination.

In preparation for his Egyptian campaign, Esarhaddon subdued the Westlands. SIDON was destroyed, its inhabitants deported, its king beheaded, and a new city erected on its site. According to Ezra 4:2, Esarhaddon brought deportees into SAMARIA, which had already been colonized with pagans by SARGON when he destroyed it in 722 B.C. After Sidon's fall twelve kings along the Mediterranean seacoast submitted to the Assyrians and were forced to supply wood and stone for the king's palace in NINEVEH. Among these was "Manasi king of Yaudi," the MANASSEH of the Bible. Manasseh had little choice. The Assyrian Empire had now reached its greatest power; and it appears that most of the Judean citizenry preferred peaceful submission, even with the Assyrian pagan influences now imposed on them, to constant abortive rebellion. Manasseh's summons to appear before an Assyrian king, mentioned in 2 Chr. 33:11-13, probably took place in the reign of Esarhaddon's successor, ASHURBANIPAL.

In 671 B.C. Egypt fell to Esarhaddon. He occupied Memphis and organized Egypt into districts under princes responsible to Assyrian governors. A later Egyptian rebellion necessitated a second Assyrian campaign there, during which Esarhaddon died and Ashurbanipal his son succeeded him.

Esau. ee´saw (Heb. *ʿēśāw H6916*, derivation uncertain, but by popular etymology, "hairy"; Gk. *Ēsau G2481*). Son of ISAAC and REBEKAH, and elder twin brother of JACOB. At their birth, "The first to come out was red, and his whole body was like a hairy garment; so they named him Esau" (Gen. 25:25). He was also named EDOM, meaning "red" (25:30). Before the birth of the twins, God had told their mother that the elder should serve the younger (25:23). Esau became a man of the fields. He apparently lived only for the present. This characteristic was demonstrated when he let Jacob

have his BIRTHRIGHT for a dinner of bread and stew because he was hungry (25:30-34).

At the age of forty he married two HITTITE women (Gen. 26:34). When the time came for Isaac to give his blessing to his son, he wanted to confer it on Esau, but, through trickery, Jacob obtained the blessing instead. This loss grieved Esau very much. He begged for another blessing, and when he received it he hated it because it made him the servant of his brother. He hated Jacob for cheating him and intended to kill him (Gen. 27). When Esau saw that Jacob had been sent away to obtain a wife from his mother's relatives, he understood that Canaanite wives did not please his father, so he went out and took for himself two additional wives of the Ishmaelites (28:6-9). Years later, when he was living in Mount SEIR, Esau heard that Jacob was returning to Canaan (32:3-5). With four hundred men he set out to meet his brother warmly (32:7—33:15). They soon parted company and Esau went back to Mount Seir (33:16).

In the PROVIDENCE of God, Esau was made subservient to Jacob. In Heb. 12:16-17 he is described as a profane person. Long after Esau's death the Lord declared he had loved Jacob and hated Esau (Mal. 1:2-3). The apostle PAUL used this passage to illustrate how God carries out his purposes (Rom. 9:10-13).

eschatology. The doctrine of the last things (from Gk. *eschatos G2274*, "last," and *logos G3364*, "word, discourse, subject"). This term designates the teaching from Scripture concerning the final consummation of all things. It includes the study of such important events as the second coming (parousia) of Jesus Christ, the judgment of the world, the resurrection of the dead, and the creation of the new heaven and earth. Related topics include the kingdom of God (the saving rule of God exhibited in Jesus Christ and experienced now through the Holy Spirit in anticipation of its fullness in the new heaven and earth of the age to come), the nature of the millennium, the intermediate state, the concept of immortality, and the eternal destiny of the wicked. Only passing reference will be made to the themes of the kingdom of God and the millennium, since both of these are treated in the separate article KINGDOM OF GOD.

Because the Lord is presented in Scripture as the Creator, Preserver, Redeemer, and King, that which will bring the present age to its end and inaugurate the new age is seen as being very much under his control. Thus, the believer is to have HOPE. However, it is helpful, in order to do justice to the tension within the NT between SALVATION already (but partially) experienced and salvation not yet (wholly) experienced, to speak of "inaugurated" eschatology and "fulfilled" eschatology. The people of God are living in the last days (1 Cor. 10:11; Heb. 1:2), but the Last Day has not yet arrived. The new age broke into this present evil age when Christ rose from the dead, but the new has not yet wholly replaced the old. The Spirit of Christ brings into the present age the life of the age to come; so what he makes available is "firstfruits" (Rom. 8:23), and he is the "guarantee/guarantor" or "pledge" of the fullness of life to come (2 Cor. 1:22; 5:5; Eph. 1:14).

As the people of the new age yet living in the old world and age, the church is called to engage in mission and evangelism (Matt. 24:14; 28:19-20) until Christ's return to earth. Signs of the times—i.e., that the end is sure and near—include the evangelization of the world, the conversion of ISRAEL (Rom. 11:25-26), the great APOSTASY (2 Thess. 2:1-3), the TRIBULATION (Matt. 24:21-30), and the revelation of ANTICHRIST (2 Thess. 2:1-12). These signs are seen during the whole of the "last days," but particularly at the end of that period.

I. The second coming. Christ is now in heaven, seated at the right hand of the Father as our exalted Prophet, Priest, and King, waiting for the time appointed by the Father to return to earth. Mainly three Greek words—*parousia G4242* ("presence, arrival," e.g., Matt. 24:3), *apokalypsis G637,* ("disclosure, revelation," 2 Thess. 1:7), and *epiphaneia G2211* ("appearance, manifestation," 1 Tim. 6:14)—are used of this event in the NT. This coming will be nothing less than the personal, visible, and glorious return of the same Jesus who ascended into heaven (Matt. 24:30; Acts 1:11; 3:19-21; Phil. 3:20). It will be an event of which everyone on earth will be abruptly aware, for it will mean the end of things as they are and the universal recognition of the true identity of Jesus of Nazareth. (Some scholars hold that Christ will come in two stages: first, secretly, to gather his faithful people, and then, seven years later, openly to be seen by all. This is part of the system of pretribulational dispensationalism and is expounded, e.g., in the *Scofield Reference Bible*.)

II. The resurrection of the dead. Christ himself rose bodily from the dead. His body, though in one sense "spiritual," was a real, physical body, and he is the FIRSTBORN from the dead (Rom. 8:11, 29; Col. 1:18) and the FIRSTFRUITS of the resurrection of all believers (1 Cor. 15:20). The resurrection of each and every person who has ever lived is part of God's plan for the human race (Dan. 12:2; Jn. 5:28-29; Acts 24:15); but the resurrection of the wicked will be the beginning of God's judgment on them, while the resurrection of the righteous will be the beginning of their life in Christ in the fullness of the kingdom of God. At the second coming of Christ, the dead will appear in their resurrection bodies; those who are alive will find that their bodies are marvelously changed, even though they remain the same individual persons. Little is taught in Scripture concerning the new bodies of the wicked; but we learn that the resurrection bodies of the righteous will be incorruptible, glorious, and spiritual (1 Cor. 15:35-49) and like Christ's glorious body (Phil. 3:21). Life in the new age of the kingdom of God in the new heaven and earth will be everlasting, abundant life in an immortal body. The NT has no doctrine of the "immortality of the soul." (According to the classical tradition, there is one resurrection of the dead at Christ's coming. However, premillennialists maintain that there will be two resurrections—one of believers at the beginning of the 1,000 years and one of unbelievers at the end of the millennium. Those who adopt the dispensationalist premillennial approach specify two other groups that will be resurrected—saints from the tribulation at the end of the seven years and saints from the millennium at the end of the 1,000 years.) One should distinguish between (1) the resurrection to mortal life, that is, life that will eventually involve death, as happened to the widow's son (1 Ki. 17:17-24), the son of the Shunammite woman (2 Ki. 4:32-37), the widow of Nain's son (Lk. 7:11-17), the daughter of Jairus (Matt. 9:18-26), and Lazarus (Jn. 11:38-44); and

E

(2) the resurrection to immortality, of which Jesus is the supreme example and the "prototype."

III. The last judgment. Having returned to earth, Jesus Christ will be the judge of the nations and of every person who has ever lived. In the name of God the Father (Rom. 14:10; 1 Pet. 1:17), Jesus the Lord acts as universal judge (Acts 17:31). This JUDGMENT, however, is not to determine but to confirm the eternal destiny of human beings according to their acceptance or rejection of the gospel. Further, it is an examination of the motives and deeds of everyone, believer and unbeliever, together with judgment based on this evidence (Matt. 11:20-22; 12:36; 25:35-40; 2 Cor. 5:10) and on the human response to the known will of God (Matt. 16:27; Rom. 1:18-21; 2:12-16; Rev. 20:12; 22:12). True believers will, in this judgment, be shown to be those in whom faith has manifested itself in love and deeds of mercy (Matt. 7:21; 25:35-46; Jas. 2:18). Therefore, there are spiritual rewards in the age to come for those in this life who have faithfully served the Lord (Lk. 19:12-27; 1 Cor. 3:10-15; cf. Matt. 5:11-12; 6:19-21). Those who hold to dispensationalism often refer to several judgments—of the sins of believers (at Calvary), of the works of the believer (at the time of the rapture), of individual Gentiles (before the millennium), of the people Israel (before the millennium), of fallen angels, and of the wicked (after the millennium). After the second coming of Christ and the final judgment, those who are judged to be the righteous begin their life in the new heaven and earth, while those who are judged to be unrighteous are consigned to everlasting punishment.

IV. Eternal happiness in the new order of existence (new heaven and earth). At or following the second coming of Christ, the old universe will be marvelously regenerated (Acts 3:19-21; Rom. 8:19-21; 2 Pet. 3:2) in order to be reborn as the "new heaven and earth," the new cosmos/universe. This is described in Isa. 65:17-25; 66:22, 23; 2 Pet. 2:13; and Rev. 21:1-4. In Rev. 21-22, God himself is presented as dwelling with his people in this new order of existence, and, thus, they are supremely happy with Christ as the center and light of all. It is fitting that those with resurrection bodies should dwell with their God in a regenerated universe, from which heaven—as God's place and sphere—is not separated but is rather present. This is the force of the picture of the descent of the heavenly Jerusalem in Rev. 21:2, to be the center of the new universe.

V. Eternal misery and punishment in hell. Jesus himself had more to say about HELL than any other person whose teaching is recorded in the NT (e.g., Matt. 5:22, 29-30; 10:28; 13:41-42; 25:46). Through a variety of pictures and images, the NT presents a frightening portrayal of the everlasting suffering of those who have rejected the gospel. Since this is a difficult and hard teaching to accept, two alternatives have been proposed and remain popular. The first is universalism, which insists that God is love and that ultimately all people will receive God's salvation. This approach involves the denial of the natural interpretation of many NT passages. The second is annihilation—the wicked cease to exist after the Last Judgment. This involves the view that human beings are mortal beings (like animals) who, unless they are given the gift of immortality through grace, return to nothingness.

VI. Immortality. God alone truly possesses immortality (1 Tim. 6:16), for he is the eternal source of life. Human beings were created for immortality (rather than created with immortal souls); and this immortality, in the sense of receiving and enjoying God's life, is given to the righteous at the resurrection of the dead, in and through the gift of an imperishable and immortal new body (1 Cor. 15:53-55). This immortal/eternal life, anticipated with the gift of the Spirit in new birth in this age, is fully given at the resurrection. At all times the immortality of the redeemed sinner is dependent on the gift of God, the source of eternal life. Careless talk about the immortality of the soul can eclipse the biblical emphasis that immortality belongs to God alone and is given to believing human beings in and through a body (2 Cor. 5:1-4). The wicked retain their personal existence but away from the holy love and immortal, abundant, eternal life of God. They are never said to have immortality or to exist eternally in immortal bodies, for the NT concept of immortality denotes the immunity from death and decay that results from sharing in the divine life.

VII. The intermediate state. Those who are alive at the second coming of Christ will experience the transformation of their earthly, perishable bodies. But what of those who have died and will die before the end of the age and the resurrection of the dead? We know that their bodies return to dust. Since the emphasis of the NT is on the events that bring this age to an end and inaugurate the age of the kingdom of God, little is said about the existence of those who die before the second coming. This interim period when they await the resurrection is often called the intermediate state. The parable of the rich man and Lazarus (Lk. 16:19-31) suggests that there is conscious existence and that this can be of misery or of rest/happiness. Certainly the NT points to the comfort and security of those who die as disciples of Jesus (Lk. 23:42-43; 2 Cor. 5:6-8; Phil. 1:21-23; 1 Thess. 4:16; see also HADES; PARADISE; SHEOL).

Esdraelon. ez´druh-ee´luhn (Gk. *Esdrēlōn*, from Heb. *yizrĕʿeʾl H3476*, "God will sow"). A lowland that transects the central ranges of PALESTINE separating the hills of GALILEE and SAMARIA. It is popularly known as "the Emek" (from Heb. *ʿēmeq H6677*, "valley"). The name Esdraelon occurs only in the APOCRYPHA (Jdt. 1:8; 3:9; 4:6; 7:3), but it corresponds to the Valley of JEZREEL (Josh. 17:16;

Jdg. 6:33; cf. the "fertile valley" of Isa. 28:1, 4), and forms the setting for several passages of Scripture. In broadest usage, Esdraelon may include the whole plain from the MEDITERRANEAN SEA to the JORDAN River, but a stricter terminology excludes both the Acco plain and (less emphatically) the valley eastward from Jezreel. It thus denotes the central triangle of lowland, approximately 15 mi. (24 km.) along each side, with its apices at the KISHON Gorge, Jenin (BETH HAGGAN), and Mount TABOR.

Several passes enter into the plain, making it easy of access and important commercially and in military operations. Many cities were situated in it, one of the most important being MEGIDDO, which guarded one of the main entrances. The Canaanites were strongly established in this region before the Israelites came into Palestine. The tribes of ISSACHAR and ZEBULUN were assigned to this area, but the Israelites never gained complete control of it until the time of DAVID. Esdraelon was the scene of some of the most important battles in Bible history: The victory of BARAK over SISERA (Jdg. 4) and of the PHILISTINES over SAUL and his sons (1 Sam. 31). Here the Egyptians mortally wounded JOSIAH, king of Judah, when he went out to intercept the army of Pharaoh NECO (2 Ki. 23:29).

E

Valley of Esdraelon looking ENE toward Mt. Tabor and the Nazareth ridge.

© Dr. James C. Martin

Esdras, Books of. See Apocrypha.

Esek. ee'sik (Heb. *ʿēśeq H6922*, "dispute"). An artesian well dug by the servants of Isaac in the valley between Gerar and Beersheba (Gen. 26:20). Rather than quarrel with the native herdsmen, Isaac moved on, digging two more wells before he established an undisputed claim. The site is unknown.

Eshan. ee'shuhn (Heb. *ʾeśʿān H878*, possibly "support"). KJV Eshean. A town in the tribal territory of Judah (Josh. 15:32). It is mentioned as part of a group of towns in the hill country and presumably was not far from Hebron, but its precise location is not known.

Esh-Baal. esh-bay'uhl (Heb. *ʾešbaʿal H843*, "man of the Lord" or "the Lord exists"). An alternate form of Ish-Bosheth, son of King Saul. While this form occurs only twice (1 Chr. 8:33; 9:39), it was probably his original name, later changed by scribes when the name Baal became too closely associated with idolatry.

Eshban. esh'ban (Heb. *ʾešbān H841*, derivation uncertain). Son of Dishon and descendant of Seir the Horite (Gen. 36:26; 1 Chr. 1:41).

Eshcol (person). esh'kol (Heb. *ʾeškōl H866*, "cluster [of grapes]"). TNIV Eshkol. An Amorite, brother of Mamre and Aner, who apparently resided near Hebron (Gen. 14:13, 24). All three were allies of Abraham when Lot was rescued from Kedorlaomer. According to some scholars, the names of all three brothers refer to localities. See Eshcol (place).

Eshcol (place). esh'kol (Heb. *ʾeškōl H865*, "cluster [of grapes]"). TNIV Eshkol. The valley or wadi where the twelve spies found a cluster of grapes so huge that it required two men to carry it (Num. 13:23-24; 32:9; Deut. 1:24). The site is unknown, but some think it should be associated with ʿAin-Eshkali, a spring c. 2 mi. (3 km.) N of Hebron. The vineyards in this general area still produce delicious grapes.

Eshean. See Eshan.

Eshek. ee'shik (Heb. *ʿēśeq H6944*, possibly "strong"). Son of Eleasah and descendant of Benjamin through Saul (1 Chr. 8:39; cf. vv. 33 and 37). Some of his descendants "were brave warriors who could handle the bow" (v. 40).

Eshkalonite. See Ashkelon.

Eshkol. TNIV form of Eshcol.

Eshtaol. esh'tay-uhl (Heb. *ʾeštāʾōl H900*, "[place of] inquiry"; gentilic *ʾeštāʾulî H901*, "Eshtaolite"). A town in the Shephelah, always mentioned with Zorah; though apparently allotted to the tribe of Judah (Josh. 15:33), it is also listed as one of the cities of Dan (19:40-41). When the attempt to occupy the Shephelah region encountered stiff opposition from the Amorite cities there (Jdg. 1:34-35), the Danites of Zorah and Eshtaol played a principal role in relocating the tribe in Leshem (Josh. 19:47; Jdg. 18:2, 8, 11). Judeans from Kiriath Jearim, descendants of Hur, probably replaced the Danites in both Zorah and Eshtaol (1 Chr. 2:50-53). It was between these two towns that the Spirit of God began to stir Samson, a Danite; he was also buried there (Jdg. 13:24-25; 16:31). The site is identified with the modern village of Ishwaʿ (more precisely, the nearby site of Khirbet Deir Shubeib), about 14 mi. (23 km.) W of Jerusalem.

Eshtemoa, Eshtemoh. esh'tuh-moh'uh, esh'tuh-moh (Heb. *ʾeštĕmōaʿ H904*, *ʾeštĕmōh H903* [only in Josh. 15:50, possibly a scribal corruption], "[place of] hearing," i.e., where an oracle is heard). **(1)** Son of Ishba and descendant of Judah (1 Chr. 4:17). The genealogical connection is not stated, but he was possibly related to Caleb (cf. v. 15). Some have suggested he is the same as #2 below. Since these genealogical lists are partly personal and partly topographical, it is possible to regard Ishbah as founder or leader of the town of Eshtemoa; see #3 below.

(2) A Maacathite, described as descending from Hodiah's wife, and included in the genealogy of Judah (1 Chr. 4:19). He may have been an inhabitant of Maacah or a descendant of Caleb's concubine by the same name (cf. 2:48).

(3) A town in the hill country of Judah (Josh. 15:50); it was later ceded to the Levites (21:14;

1 Chr. 6:57). It was one of the cities where DAVID had friends who were elders of Judah and to whom he sent part of the booty taken from the AMALEKITES after his raid upon ZIKLAG (1 Sam. 30:26-28). Eshtemoa is identified with modern es-Semu', some 9 mi. (14 km.) SSW of HEBRON.

Eshtemoh. See ESHTEMOA.

Eshton. esh´ton (Heb. *'eštôn H902*, perhaps "effeminate" or "uxorious"). Son of Mehir and descendant of JUDAH (1 Chr. 4:11-12). The family is described as "the men of Recah," but their genealogical connection with other Judahite families is not stated.

Esli. es´li (Gk. *Hesli G2268*). Son of Naggai, included in Luke's GENEALOGY OF JESUS CHRIST (Lk. 3:25).

espousals. This English term, meaning "betrothal" or "wedding," is used by the KJV in two passages (Cant. 3:11; Jer. 2:2); in the second reference, "the love of thine espousals" means "your love as a bride" (so NRSV and other versions). See MARRIAGE.

Esrom. See HEZRON.

Essenes. es´eens (Gk. *Essēnoi, Essaioi*). A Jewish religious group that flourished between the second century B.C. and the first century A.D. Although not mentioned by the NT writers, the Essenes formed an important school of thought in the time of CHRIST. The meaning of the name is much debated; possibly it denotes "pious ones" or "holy ones." Our principal sources of information regarding them are the first-century writers PHILO, JOSEPHUS, and Pliny the Elder; the church father Hippolytus (c. A.D. 200) provides information based mainly on Josephus.

The Essenes lived a simple life of sharing everything in common. They practiced strict rules of conduct. They were mostly unmarried. They were reported to number 4,000. The majority of them lived together in settlements, but some resided in the cities of the Jews. Apparently they kept their ranks filled by the adoption of other people's children. They did not participate in the temple worship but had their own purification rites. They

observed the SABBATH day very strictly and greatly venerated MOSES. They would take no oaths; but new members, after going through a three-year probationary period, were required to swear a series of strong oaths that they would cooperate in every way with the organization and would never reveal to outsiders any of the affairs or beliefs of the sect.

The Essenes came into public attention in the mid-twentieth century because of the study of the DEAD SEA SCROLLS and the excavation of Khirbet Qumran, where apparently some or most of the scrolls were written. This literature and building give evidence of an organization very similar to what is known about the Essenes. The structure was occupied from the end of the second century B.C. to A.D. 135. The Essenes are known to have flourished in this period. Also, the location of the building fits the description of the elder Pliny. The literature reveals that the people of the Qumran community were avid students of the Jewish Scriptures. There appear to be a few significant differences between the Essenes and the Qumranites, and some specialists regard them as distinct groups, but many scholars are persuaded that the two groups are identical.

Esther. es´tuhr (Heb. *'estēr H676*, possibly from Akk. ISHTAR [meaning uncertain] or from Pers. *stāreh*, "star"). A Benjamite woman whose name is immortalized in the book that bears her name (see ESTHER, BOOK OF). Her Hebrew name was HADASSAH (Esth. 2:7), meaning "myrtle." Some have thought that her Persian playmates, who did not understand Hebrew, approximated a strange name to one with which they were familiar. Esther's cousin, MORDECAI, who was a minor official of the palace, reared her as his own daughter. XERXES, the Persian king, had divorced his wife. When he sought a new queen from among the maidens of the realm he chose Esther. When the Jews in the empire were faced with destruction she was able to save them. In her honor the book of Esther is read every year at the Feast of PURIM.

Esther, Additions to. See APOCRYPHA.

Esther, Book of. The last of the historical books of the OT. It was written after the death of King

Overview of ESTHER

Author: Unknown.

Historical setting: The book was probably written in PERSIA sometime between 450 and 350 B.C.

Purpose: To provide a historical-theological account of the origin of the Feast of PURIM and thus to encourage the Jewish people of the DISPERSION in the midst of their suffering.

Contents: The rejection of VASHTI and the selection of Esther (Esth. 1-2); the plot of HAMAN (chs. 3-4); the triumph of MORDECAI (chs. 5-7); the vindication of the Jews (chs. 8-10).

XERXES (Esth. 10:2; KJV, "Ahasuerus"), who reigned 486-465 B.C. Probably the book was written about 400. The author is unknown, but it is evident from the details of the record that he was well acquainted with the Persian court life. The book of Esther has always been accepted as canonical by the Jews, in spite of its outstanding peculiarities, such as the complete absence of the name of God, the lack of any direct religious teaching, and no mention of prayer. These remarkable features can have occurred only by deliberate design.

The account contains many dramatic elements. King Xerxes gave a great feast for all the officials of his realm. Queen VASHTI offended him when she refused to appear before the company at the command of the king. As a result he divorced her (Esth. 1). Later, in order to procure another queen, he ordered all the beautiful maidens of the land brought together (ch. 2). Among them was HADASSAH, who had been reared by her cousin Mordecai; it was perhaps the Persians who changed her name to Esther. This maiden was chosen by the king to be his queen, and about the same time Mordecai discovered a plot against the king's life. Subsequently, the king made HAMAN his chief minister (ch. 3). Everybody bowed down to him except Mordecai. This disrespect infuriated the high official. Knowing Mordecai was a Jew, Haman decided to destroy all the Jews in revenge for his hurt feelings. Lots (Heb. *pûr* H7052) were

cast to find an auspicious day for the destruction. The consent of the king was obtained, and an official decree was written and publicized throughout the empire, setting the date for the slaughter of the Jews. Mordecai sent word to Esther that she must plead for her people before the king (ch. 4). At the risk of her life she went in before the king. He received her favorably. Instead of pleading with him at once she invited him and Haman to a banquet. There the king asked her to state her request, but she put it off and invited them to another banquet. Haman, rejoicing in his good fortune but incensed at Mordecai, had a gallows constructed on which to hang him (ch. 5). That night, unable to sleep, the king was listening to the reading of the

© Dr. James C. Martin. Musée du Louvre; Autorisation de photographier et de filmer—LOUVRE. Paris, France. Photographed by permission.

Artistic representation of the Persian guard at the Susa palace where Esther lived.

royal chronicles. When the account of Mordecai's discovery of the assassination plot was read, the king asked what reward had been given him and was told none at all.

It was early morning and Haman had come to ask permission to hang Mordecai (Esth. 6). But the king asked him what should be done to a man he wished to honor. Being convinced that the king could have only him in mind, Haman suggested the greatest of honors he could imagine. At the king's command he was obliged to bestow those honors on Mordecai. At the second banquet Esther told the king about the scheme to destroy her people and named Haman as the one responsible for it. The king became very angry and ordered Haman to be hanged on the gallows he had made (ch. 7). Another decree was sent out that enabled the Jews to save themselves (ch. 8). In two days of fighting they were victorious everywhere. Esther and Mordecai wrote letters to the Jews instituting the commemoration of these two days in an annual Feast of PURIM (ch. 9). Mordecai, being next to the king, brought blessing to the people (ch. 10).

Etam. ee´tuhm (Heb. *ʿêṭām H6515*, possibly "place of birds of prey"). **(1)** Son (or descendant or clan) of HUR included in the genealogy of JUDAH (1 Chr. 4:3-4). The reading "These were the sons of Etam" is an emendation based mainly on the SEPTUAGINT; the Hebrew text reads, "these the father [ʾăbî] of Etam," which is obviously corrupt. Other suggestions include the conjecture "These are the families of Abi-Etam" and the view that "father" here (as elsewhere) indicates the lord or founder of a town. If the latter is correct, then it refers to #2, below. **(2)** A town near BETHLEHEM and TEKOA that REHOBOAM fortified after the secession of the ten northern tribes (2 Chr. 11:6). JOSEPHUS (*Ant.* 8.7.3) relates that Etam was a very pleasant place c. 50 furlongs (less than 6 mi./10 km.) from JERUSALEM, situated in fine gardens "and abounding in rivulets of water." According to the TALMUD, the spring of Etam supplied water for the TEMPLE at Jerusalem. This fact probably explains the ancient aqueduct that extends 7 mi. (11 km.) from Jerusalem to three large Hellenistic Roman reservoirs S of Bethlehem, now known as the "pools of Solomon." The lowest pool is fed by a stream called

ʿAin ʿAtan, and Etam is generally identified with the nearby Khirbet el-Khokh, only c. 2 mi. (3 km.) SW of Bethlehem.

(3) A village in the tribal territory of SIMEON (1 Chr. 4:32). The site is unknown today. Some identify it with #2 above, others with ʿAitum (c. 11 mi./18 km. WSW of HEBRON). It was probably located between the NW NEGEV and the Simeon-Judah boundary.

(4) The "rock of Etam" refers to a cliff somewhere in W JUDAH where SAMSON took refuge after slaughtering many PHILISTINES (Jdg. 15:8, 11). This cliff has not been identified. Some believe that it was near #2 above, but the most likely site is ʿAraq Ismaʿin in Wadi Ismaʿin, 2.5 mi. (4 km.) ESE from ZORAH.

eternal. This English word is often the rendering of Hebrew *ʿôlām H6409*, which refers to "duration," both of antiquity and futurity. The term takes color from its context. To speak of a "slave forever" (Deut. 15:17 NRSV) manifestly limits the word to the duration of a human lifetime (cf. NIV). To refer to "the everlasting hills" (Gen. 49:26 NRSV) also obviously limits the word to the geological age of a feature of the landscape (but NIV renders "age-old hills"). On the other hand, when the word is applied to God, his abiding acts, his covenants, promises, and laws, it clearly signifies the eternal and everlasting in the literal and absolute sense of the term. The word often refers simply to a long time; for example, the possession of CANAAN (Gen. 17:8); the throne of DAVID (2 Sam. 7:16; 1 Chr. 17:14); or Jewish rites and privileges (Exod. 12:14, 17; Num. 10:8).

The Greek adjective *aiōnion G173* is derived from the noun *aiōn G172* ("age") and bears the basic meaning, in consequence, of "belonging to time in its duration," that is, "constant, abiding, eternal." In the NT, its most common application is to *zōē G2437*, "life" (Matt. 19:16 et al.). The frequency of its use in Johannine contexts is notable. The significance mingles future and present, for "eternal life" in Christian belief is not only a life of endless duration, but a quality of life in which the possessor shares in God's eternal being by faith. Other NT connections with the adjective include such words as "fire" (Matt. 18:8; 25:41;

Jude 7), "punishment" (Matt. 25:46), "destruction" (2 Thess. 1:9), "sin" (Mk. 3:29), "judgment" (Heb. 6:2), "salvation" (5:9), and others. See also ESCHATOLOGY; HEAVEN; HELL; LIFE.

eternity. See ETERNAL.

Etham. ee´thuhm (Heb. *ʾētām H918*, possibly "fort"). The first encampment of the Israelites after leaving SUCCOTH at the time of the EXODUS (Exod. 13:20; Num. 33:6-7). Its precise location is unknown, but it was on the edge of the wilderness of SHUR (Exod. 15:22), a portion of which was known as the wilderness of Etham (Num. 33:8). Probably it was N of Lake Timsah and formed part of the Egyptian fortifications guarding their eastern frontier.

Ethan. ee´thuhn (Heb. *ʾêtān H420*, "long-lived"). **(1)** Son (or descendant) of ZERAH and grandson (or more distant descendant) of JUDAH (1 Chr. 2:6, 8). Because the other sons (or descendants) of Zerah included HEMAN, CALCOL, and DARDA, many scholars identify this Ethan with #2 below.

(2) A wise man described as an EZRAHITE to whom SOLOMON was compared (1 Ki. 4:31). In this verse Solomon is also said to be wiser than "Heman, Calcol and Darda, the sons of Mahol." According to many scholars, the expression "the sons of Mahol" refers to members of a musical guild and should therefore be translated "the singers" or "the musicians" (see MAHOL). In addition, Ps. 89 is attributed to "Ethan the Ezrahite" and Ps. 88 to "Heman the Ezrahite." It is possible that the term Ezrahite is equivalent to "descendant of Zerah" and that therefore this Ethan is the same as #1 above. It has also been argued, however, that the term really means "native" and was used of non-Israelite inhabitants of Canaan.

(3) Son of Zimmah, descendant of LEVI through GERSHON, and ancestor of ASAPH (1 Chr. 6:42-43; cf. v. 39).

(4) Son of Kishi (or Kushaiah), descendant of Levi through MERARI, and a musician who served at the left hand of Heman (1 Chr. 6:44; 15:17, 19). Heman, ASAPH, and Ethan had the responsibility of sounding the bronze cymbals. Some have thought that this Ethan was the same as #1 above and that both Ethan and Heman were Levites

incorporated into the Judahite family of Zerah, but the evidence for such a connection is not strong. It has also been argued by many that this Ethan is the same as JEDUTHUN (16:41-42 et al.).

Ethanim. eth´uh-nim (Heb. *ʾētānîm H923*, "ever-flowing [streams]"). The seventh month in the Hebrew religious CALENDAR (later called *Tishri*), corresponding to late September and early October (mentioned only in 1 Ki. 8:2, dating SOLOMON's transferal of the ARK OF THE COVENANT to the TEMPLE). The name was borrowed from the Canaanite calendar.

Ethbaal. eth-bay´uhl (Heb. *ʾetbaʿal H909*, "with [him is] BAAL"). The king of SIDON whose daughter JEZEBEL was married to King AHAB of Israel (1 Ki. 16:31). The Bible says nothing more about him, but the ancient historian JOSEPHUS, citing Menander of Ephesus, mentions a drought (cf. 1 Ki. 17) that occurred during the reign of Ethbaal (Jos. *Ant.* 8.13.2 §324). He states further that Ethbaal built cities in PHOENICIA and in LIBYA.

Ether. ee´thuhr (Heb. *ʿeter H6987*, perhaps "[place of] fragrance"). A town in the SHEPHELAH within the tribal territory of JUDAH (Josh. 15:42); it was later given to the tribe of SIMEON (19:7; cf. v. 1). Ether is commonly identified with Khirbet el-ʿAter, some 4 mi. (6 km.) NE of LACHISH. Because the Simeonite towns are associated with the NEGEV (19:8), some believe that there were two distinct towns and that the Ether in the latter passage should be identified with Khirbet ʿAttir (see JATTIR), about 8 mi. (13 km.) N of BEERSHEBA. Some scholars have argued that Ether (and possibly also TOKEN in the parallel, 1 Chr. 4:32) should be emended to, or is an alternate form of, ATHACH.

ethics. See COMMANDMENTS, TEN; LAW; OBEDIENCE; SANCTIFICATION.

Ethiopia. ee´thee-oh´pee-uh. A country referred to also as Nubia, located S of EGYPT, in what is now N Sudan (but modern Ethiopia, known as Abyssinia prior to the 20th cent., lies farther S and E). Ethiopia is often associated with Egypt in the Bible (e.g., Ps. 68:31; Isa. 20:3-5; Ezek. 30:4-5) and is identified as being S of Aswan (Aswan, Ezek. 29:10), the southernmost important city of Egypt. The name comes from Greek *Aithiopia* (understood to mean "[land of the] burnt-faced people"; gentilic *Aithiops G134*, "Ethiopian"), which the ancient Greeks applied generally to any

© Dr. James C. Martin. Sola Scriptura. The Van Kampen Collection on display at the Holy Land Experience in Orlando, Florida. Photographed by permission.

Ethiopian MS of the Bible (18th cent.).

region far to the S. The Septuagint uses this term to render Hebrew *kûš H3932*, and for that reason many English versions translate the Hebrew term as "Ethiopia." The NIV transliterates "Cush, Cushite," but uses "Ethiopian(s)" in two passages (Jer. 13:23; Acts 8:27) and "Nubians" once (Dan. 11:43; TNIV, "Cushites"). See Cush.

Ethiopian eunuch. A convert of the evangelist Philip (Acts 8:27-40). The ethnic term "Ethiopian" (Gk. *Aithiops G134*) was applied in Roman times to the area of E Africa, S of Egypt and beyond the mountains of the second cataract. See Ethiopia. The Acts account states that this man was "an important official" (Greek *dynastēs G1541*, "lord, ruler, vizier") of Candace, the queen of the Ethiopians. As a eunuch he could not be a full member of the Jewish community (Deut. 23:1), but he had been worshiping in Jerusalem and was reading aloud the book of Isaiah when Philip, sent by the Holy Spirit from Samaria to help him, met his chariot. From Isa. 53, Philip led the African to faith in Christ, so that he asked for and received baptism and went on his way toward Gaza rejoicing.

Eth Kazin. eth-kay´zin (Heb. *ʿēt qāṣîn H6962* [occurring only in the locative form, *ʾittâ qāṣîn*], from *ʿēt H6961*, "time," and *qāṣîn H7903*, "ruler").

KJV Ittah-kazin. A town on the NE boundary of the tribal territory of Zebulun (Josh. 19:13). Its location is unknown, but apparently it was N of Gath Hepher and S of Rimmon (place); a possible site is Kefr Kenna, some 4 mi. (6 km.) NE of Nazareth.

Ethnan. eth´nuhn (Heb. *ʾetnān H925*, possibly "gift"). Son of Asshur (by his wife Helah) and descendant of Judah (1 Chr. 4:7; cf. v. 5). Some believe Ethnan may be the name of a town, possibly Ithnan in S Judah (Josh. 15:23).

ethnarch. eth´nahrk (Gk. *ethnarchēs G1617*, "ruler of a people"). The Greek term appears after the Hellenistic expansion under Alexander the Great and has various meanings. Usually it was the title of a governor of a town or county who ruled for an overlord of a different race or culture than the subjects. In the Apocrypha (1 Macc. 14:47; 15:1-2), the title is applied to the high priest Simon as a representative of Syria. The chiefs of the seven districts of Roman Egypt bore the title, as did the princes of the Bosporus under Caesar Augustus. Moreover, after the death of Herod the Great, his son Archelaus (Matt. 2:22) was appointed ethnarch of Judea by Augustus (Jos. *Ant.* 17.11.4 §317). The term occurs only once used in the NT: Paul, in recounting his narrow escape from Damascus, uses it with reference to the city's governor under King Aretas (2 Cor. 11:32).

Ethni. eth´ni (Heb. *ʾetni H922*, "gift"). Son of Zerah, descendant of Levi through Gershon, and ancestor of Asaph (1 Chr. 6:41).

Eubulus. yoo-byoo´luhs (Gk. *Euboulos G2300*, "good counsel"). A Christian who, along with others (Claudia, Linus, and Pudens), was a friend of the apostle Paul during his second Roman imprisonment and who sent greetings to Timothy (2 Tim. 4:21).

Eucharist. yoo´kuh-rist (Gk. *eucharistia G2374*, "thankfulness, thanksgiving"). As early as the beginning of the second century, this term came to be applied to the Lord's Supper, probably because of the giving of thanks by the Lord at the time of institution, as he gave his disciples the bread and the cup (cf. Mk. 14:22; 1 Cor. 11:23-24). Early liturgies made the thanksgiving, next to the reception of the elements, the most significant part of the celebration, and this no doubt promoted the general adoption of the name.

Euergetes. yoo-uhr´juh-teez. See BENEFACTOR.

Eunice. yoo´nis (Gk. *Eunikē G2332*, "good victory"). The daughter of LOIS and mother of TIMOTHY (2 Tim. 1:5). Eunice's husband was a Gentile (Acts 16:1), but she was Jewish, as was also her mother. Timothy had not been circumcised (see CIRCUMCISION), undoubtedly because his father was a Gentile, but he was brought up by his mother and his grandmother in the Jewish faith. Paul wrote of Timothy that from a child his mother had taught him to know the holy Scriptures (2 Tim. 3:15). Eunice, her mother Lois, and Timothy were probably converted to Christianity during PAUL's first missionary journey at LYSTRA, where the apostle had been stoned and left for dead.

eunuch. A male officer in the court or household of a ruler, and often one who had been castrated. The Hebrew term, *sārîs H6247*, is probably a loanword from Akkadian *ša rēši*, indicating a courtier or confidant. The meaning "castrated one" was secondary, arising from the rulers' preference for such men in offices that involved contact with the women of their households. It is therefore improbable that all those designated with the term *sārîs* in the OT were eunuchs, but in most cases it is not possible to decide by other than the probabilities of the context whether the meaning "official" or "eunuch official" is more appropriate. There are passages in which the sense "eunuch" seems unlikely (e.g., Gen. 37:36; 40:2; 1 Ki. 22:9; 2 Ki. 8:6; 1 Chr. 28:1; Jer. 52:25), whereas in others it seems probable (Esth. 1:10; 2:3 et al.; Isa. 39:7). See also ETHIOPIAN EUNUCH.

Men who had been emasculated were not permitted to enter the assembly of the LORD (Deut. 23:1), yet ISAIAH assures eunuchs who are faithful to God's COVENANT that they will be given "a memorial and a name better than sons and daughters" (Isa. 56:4). Jesus made a distinction between those who are eunuchs (Gk. *eunouchos G2336*) in a physical sense and those who make themselves eunuchs (NIV, "have renounced marriage") for the sake of the kingdom (Matt. 19:12).

Euodia. yoo-oh´dee-uh (Gk. *Euodia G2337*, "prosperity"). KJV Euodias (wrongly interpreting it as a masculine name). A Christian woman in PHILIPPI whom PAUL asked to be reconciled to SYNTYCHE (Phil. 4:2). Clearly both were influential Christians in the Philippian church, where women were prominent from the beginning (Acts 16:12-15). The cause of their disagreement, whether doctrinal or personal, is unknown, but Paul's impartial appeal for reconciliation implies that both were responsible for the estrangement.

Euodias. See EUODIA.

Euphrates. yoo-fray´teez (Heb. *pĕrāt H7310* [from Akk. *Purattu*]; Gk. *Euphratēs G2371* [from Old Pers. *Ufrātu*]). The longest river of W Asia. It rises in the mountains of ARMENIA in modern Turkey, heads W as if to reach the MEDITERRANEAN, then swings in a wide bow in SYRIA, eventually joins the TIGRIS to become the Shatt el-Arab, and empties into the Persian Gulf. The Euphrates is some 1,780 mi. (2,865 km.) long, considerably longer than its companion stream, the Tigris, with which it is often linked in discussion of MESOPOTAMIA (a name that means, "the land between [or in the midst of] the rivers"). For approximately 1,200 mi. (1,930 km.) it is navigable for small vessels. The melting of the snows in the Armenian mountains causes the river to flood each spring. NEBUCHADNEZZAR controlled the floods by turning the water through sluices into channels for distribution over the whole country.

In the OT the Euphrates is sometimes referred to as "the River" (Isa. 8:7) or "the great river" (Gen. 15:18 et al.; cf. Rev. 9:14; 16:12), as being the largest with which Israel was acquainted, in contrast to the soon dried up torrents of PALESTINE. The promise to ABRAHAM that his seed's inheritance should reach the Euphrates (Gen. 15:18; Deut. 1:7; Josh. 1:4) received a partial fulfillment in REUBEN's

The Euphrates River in N Mesopotamia. (View to the NE.)

© Dr. James C. Martin

pastoral possessions (1 Chr. 5:9-10), and a fuller accomplishment under DAVID and SOLOMON, when an annual tribute was paid by subject petty kingdoms in that area (2 Sam. 8:3-8; 1 Ki. 4:21; 1 Chr. 18:3; 2 Chr. 9:26). The Euphrates was the boundary between Assyria and the Hittite country after Solomon's time, according to inscriptions. See also PERATH.

Eurakylon, Euraquilo. yoo-rahk′i-lon, yoo-rahk′wi-loh. See EUROCLYDON.

Euroclydon. yoo-rok′li-don (Gk. *Euroklydōn*). The KJV name for the wind that aroused a storm and caused PAUL's shipwreck at MALTA (Acts 27:14). This reading, which is based on the later Greek MSS, would refer to a SE wind that stirs up the waves. The earliest MSS, however, have *Eurakylōn G2350*, a sailor's term compounding Greek *Euros* ("E wind") with Latin *Aquilo* ("N wind"). Thus modern translations usually render it "northeaster" (some versions transliterate "Eurakylon" or "Euraquilo"). Such a word suits the local situation on the S coast of CRETE, where a southerly breeze often gives way to a NE gale.

Eutychus. yoo′tuh-kuhs (Gk. *Eutychos G2366*, "fortunate"). A young man at TROAS who fell from a window seat during a prolonged discourse by PAUL late in the evening (Acts 20:7-12). Eutychus had taken a seat in the open window, sank into a deep sleep, and "fell to the ground from the third story and was picked up dead" (v. 9). Having embraced him, Paul quieted the tumult with the assuring words, "his life is in him" (v. 10 NRSV). That Eutychus only appeared to be dead is contrary to the precise language used by LUKE, who was an eyewitness of the event ("we," v. 8; contrast 14:19, "thinking he was dead"). Paul's act of embracing the body is not the act of one investigating a case of apparent death; it clearly recalls the actions of ELIJAH (1 Ki. 17:21) and ELISHA (2 Ki. 4:34).

evangelist. A preacher of the GOSPEL (Gk. *euangelistēs G2296*, "one who announces good news," from *euangelion G2295*, "good news"). The term can be used in a general sense of anyone who proclaims the gospel of Jesus Christ. Certainly the APOSTLES did evangelistic work (Acts 8:25; 14:7; 1 Cor. 1:17), and TIMOTHY was instructed to "do the work of an evangelist" (2 Tim. 4:5). The term also designates a particular class of ministry, as in Eph. 4:11: Christ "gave some to be apostles ... prophets ... evangelists ... pastors and teachers." The evangelist founded the CHURCH; the pastor-teacher built it up in the faith. The evangelist was not confined in service to one spot but moved about in different localities, preaching the good news concerning Jesus Christ to those who had not heard the message before. Once such had put their trust in the Lord, then the work of the pastor-teacher began. He would remain with them, training them further in the things pertaining to Christ and building them up in the faith. Philip, who had been set apart as one of the seven deacons (Acts 6:5), is the typical example of an evangelist. When he went to Samaria, "he preached the good news of the kingdom of God and the name of Jesus Christ" (8:12), and subsequently he converted and baptized the Ethiopian eunuch, sending him back home with the gospel (8:26-40). Later he is specifically identified as "the evangelist" (21:8). Evangelist in the sense of "inspired writer of one of the four Gospels" was a later usage.

Eve. eev (Heb. *ḥawwāh H2558*, "life" [by popular etymology]; Gk. *Heua G2293*). The first woman, wife of Adam. Already in the summary of creation it is stated that there were two sexes ("male and female he created them," Gen. 1:27). But when Eve was brought to her husband by the Creator, Adam made the pronouncement: "she shall be called 'woman,' [*ʾiššâ H851*] / for she was taken out of man [*ʾîš H408*]" (2:23), a clever play on words (not a precise etymology, since the first term is not derived from the second). The way in which she was created and the designation "woman" emphasize also the intimacy, sacredness, and inseparability of the marital state, transcending even the relationship between children and parents (2:24). The name "Eve" originated in the experience of the fall, when God had laid disabilities on the tempter, on Adam, and on his wife. Then it became apparent to Adam that the life of mankind was tied up with his wife, and he called her *ḥawwāh* (3:20), a form that may bear some relation to *ḥāyâ H2649* ("to live"). This too is an instructive play on words, aiding the memory, not a scientific etymology. She was called "Eve" because she was to be "the mother of all the living." While the Scriptures uniformly trace the fall of the race to Adam's sin, the part Eve played in this tragedy is vividly portrayed in Gen. 3. Her susceptibility to temptation is juxtaposed with Adam's willful act of disobedience. Deceived by

Satan, she ate of the fruit. Enamored of his wife, Adam chose to leave God for the one he had given him. Paul twice refers to Eve in his letters (2 Cor. 11:3; 1 Tim. 2:13).

everlasting. See ETERNAL.

Evi. ee′vi (Heb. *ʾĕwî H209*, perhaps "desire" or "shelter"). One of the five kings of Midian slain by the Israelites (Num. 31:8). This was apparently an act of retribution, for earlier the Lord had said to Moses, "Treat the Midianites as enemies and kill them, because they treated you as enemies when they deceived you in the affair of Peor" (25:17-18). The incident is recalled in Joshua, where the kings are said to be allies of Sihon (Josh. 13:21).

evil. This English term is usually the rendering of Hebrew *raʿ H8273* in the OT. Appearing about 800 times with its cognates, it refers to what is physically undesirable and what is morally bad. For the precise meaning the context must always be consulted. Rotten figs are "evil" in the sense of "harmful," as are poisonous herbs (2 Ki. 4:41) and a "ferocious" beast (Gen. 37:20). The child prophesied by Isaiah would reject the "wrong" and choose the right (Isa. 7:15). Individuals are sometimes described as "wicked" in the sight of the Lord (Gen. 38:7; Deut. 4:25; Ps. 51:4). The same is true of the counterpart words of the NT, especially *ponēros G4505* with its cognates (e.g., Matt. 6:23; Mk. 7:23; of physical evil only twice in Matt. 7:17-18; Rev. 16:2) and *kakos G2805* and cognates (e.g., Matt. 24:48; Mk. 7:21).

The reconciliation of the existence of evil with the goodness and holiness of a God infinite in his wisdom and power is one of the great problems of theism. The Scriptures indicate that evil has been permitted by God in order that his justice might be manifested in its punishment and his grace in its forgiveness (Rom. 9:22-23). Thus the existence of evil is a reminder of the manifold perfections of God. Moral evil, or sin, is any lack of conformity to the moral law of God. According to the Bible, it is the cause of the existence of physical or natural evil in this world. Adam and Eve, the first humans, enjoyed perfect fellowship with God in the Garden of Eden. The day they ate of the fruit of the tree that was in the midst of the garden, disobeying

God, they fell under his condemnation and were banished from the Garden. The ground was then cursed for man's sake, and from that time forward man has been forced to gain his sustenance through arduous, sorrowful toil, even as woman has borne children through suffering and labor (Gen. 3:16-19). In the NT the relationship between moral and natural evil is indicated by Paul in Rom. 8:18-22.

evil eye. This phrase, as a literal rendering of the corresponding Hebrew and Greek idioms, is used by the KJV both in the OT, where it can refer to such qualities as hostility, lack of compassion, stinginess (Deut. 15:9; 28:54-56; Prov. 23:6; 28:22), and in the NT, where it refers to envy (Matt. 20:15; Mk. 7:22; cf. Matt. 6:22-23; Lk. 11:34). The expression is not used directly in the Bible in the superstitious sense of an eye that is supposed to be capable of harming, or even killing, living beings by looking at them.

Evil-Merodach. ee´vuhl-mer´uh-dak (Heb. *ĕwîl mĕrōdak H213*, from Akk. *Amēl-Marduk* [originally *Awîl-Marduk*], "man [*or* servant] of MARDUK"). Son and successor of NEBUCHADNEZZAR II as king of the Neo-Babylonian empire, c. 562-560 B.C. According to 2 Ki. 25:27-30 and Jer. 52:31-34, in the first year of his reign he released JEHOIACHIN, former king of Judah, from prison, even honoring him above all the other vassal kings in BABYLON. It is noteworthy that administrative documents found at Babylon, and containing lists of ration issues (oil), refer to a Yakukinu of Yakudu (= Jehoiachin of Judah). Some ancient sources indicate that Evil-Merodach was assassinated by his brother-in-law, Neriglissar (prob. the NERGAL-SHAREZER who appears as a Babylonian officer, Jer. 39:3, 13), who then took the throne. References to him as lawless and indecent indicate the probable reasons for the coup that cut short his reign.

evil spirits. See DEMON.

ewe. See ANIMALS.

exaltation of Christ. The term covers the sequence of events that begins with the RESURRECTION of Christ and that includes his ASCENSION and his coming again (see ESCHATOLOGY). The outcome of his humility and obedience, the "high exaltation" of Christ, will in turn lead to the bowing of every knee and the acknowledgment of his Lordship by every tongue (Phil. 2:8-11; cf. Acts 2:33). The exaltation of Christ places him "at the right hand of God" (Rom. 8:34), an expression used by Stephen (Acts 7:55-56), Paul (Eph. 1:20), Peter (1 Pet. 3:22), and the writer to the Hebrews (Heb. 1:3; 10:12; 12:2). This firmly establishes the association of Christ with God in power and glory, a glorification noted by our Lord himself (Jn. 17:5; cf. 12:32).

excellent, most. The title "most excellent" (Gk. *kratistos G3196*) is found four times in the NT. It may have been the official rendering of the Latin *vir egregius*, which meant "a man of equestrian rank," that is, one of the knights who came in order after senators in ROME. The title was applied to FELIX (Acts 23:26 [NIV, "His Excellency"]; 24:3) and to FESTUS (26:25), both of whom were governors of JUDEA. In addition, the term could be used more generally as a courtesy title in addressing one honored for his position, such as THEOPHILUS (Lk. 1:3).

excommunication. Disciplinary exclusion from church fellowship. The Jews had two forms of excommunication, perhaps alluded to by Christ: "Blessed are you ... when they exclude you [possibly the Jewish *nidduy* for thirty, sixty, or ninety days], and ... reject your name as evil [possibly the Jewish *ḥērem*, a formally pronounced, perpetual cutting off from the community], because of the Son of Man" (Lk. 6:22). Christian excommunication is commanded by Christ (Matt. 18:15-18), and apostolic practice (1 Tim. 1:20) and precept (1 Cor. 5:11; Tit. 3:10) are in agreement. "Hand this man over to Satan" (1 Cor. 5:5; 1 Tim. 1:20) seems to mean casting out of the church into the world that lies in the power of the wicked one (Eph. 6:12; 1 Jn. 5:19). The object of excommunication is the good of the offender (1 Cor. 5:5) and the moral well-being of the sound members (2 Tim. 2:17). Its subjects are those guilty of heresy or great immorality (1 Cor. 5:1-5; 1 Tim. 1:20). It is inflicted by the church and its representative ministers (1 Cor. 5:1, 3-4; Tit. 3:10). PAUL's inspired words give no

E

warrant for uninspired ministers claiming the same right to direct the church to excommunicate at will (2 Cor. 2:7-9).

execution. The OT makes a clear and precise distinction between murder—the illicit and violent killing of a human being (Exod. 20:13)—and the legal, moral act of slaying a criminal by the duly constituted authority (Gen. 9:6 et al.). Several cases of execution, or legal deprivation of life, are mentioned in the OT (2 Chr. 25:2-4 et al.). Criminals were to be either stoned (Deut. 13:10) or hanged (21:22). But strict prohibitions against vendetta were in force (24:16). Several executions at the hands of the authorities are mentioned in the NT (Matt. 14:10 et al.). The KJV uses "executioner" once (Mk. 6:27; cf. also the mg. at Gen. 37:36; Jer. 39:9; Dan. 2:14). See also CROSS; PUNISHMENT.

exegesis. See INTERPRETATION.

exile. This term usually refers to the period of time during which the southern kingdom (JUDAH) was forcibly detained in BABYLON. It began with a series of deportations during the reigns of the Judean kings JEHOIAKIM (609-598 B.C.), JEHOI-ACHIN (598), and ZEDEKIAH (598-587). After the destruction of JERUSALEM by NEBUCHADNEZZAR (587) the kingdom of Judah ceased to exist as a political entity. Although there were settlements in EGYPT, the exiles in Babylon were the ones who maintained the historic faith and provided the nucleus that returned to Judea after the decree of CYRUS (536). The northern kingdom (ISRAEL) had earlier been exiled to ASSYRIA (722). It was the policy of the Assyrian conquerors to move the populations of captured cities, with the result that Israelites were scattered in various parts of the empire and other captives were brought to the region around SAMARIA (2 Ki. 17:24). Subsequent history knows these people as the SAMARITANS. Although people from the northern kingdom doubtless returned with the Judean exiles, no organized return took place from the Assyrian captivity.

I. Causes. Both theological and political causes are mentioned in the biblical accounts of the exile. The prophets noted the tendency of both Israel and Judah to forsake the Lord and adopt the customs of their heathen neighbors. These included the licentious worship associated with the BAAL fertility cult and the MOLECH worship that required the offering of human beings in sacrifice to a heathen deity. Politically the exile was the result of an anti-Babylonian policy adopted by the later kings of Judah. Egypt, the rival of Babylon, urged the Judean kings to refuse to pay tribute to Nebuchadnezzar. Although JEREMIAH denounced this pro-Egyptian policy, it was adopted with disastrous results. Egypt proved to be a "broken reed," and the kingdom of Judah was rendered impotent before the Babylonian armies. After a siege of eighteen months Nebuchadnezzar entered Jerusalem, destroyed the TEMPLE, and took captive the inhabitants of the city.

II. Social and economic conditions. The exile worked great hardships on a people who were forcibly removed from their homeland and settled in new territory. The psalmist pictures the exiles weeping in Babylon, unable to sing the songs of Zion in a strange land (Ps. 137:4). Among other hardships, they had to endure the failure of false prophecies of an exile that would only last two years (Jer. 28:11). On the other hand, actual conditions of life in the exile were not necessarily harsh. Jeremiah, knowing that a protracted period would be spent in Babylon, urged the exiles to settle down, build homes, marry, and pray for the peace of their new land. He predicted a seventy-year captivity (29:4-14). From EZEKIEL, himself present among the exiles

Assyrian relief from the time of Tiglath-Pileser III (c. 728 B.C.) depicting captives being taken into exile. Panel from a palace in Nimrud.

© Dr. James C. Martin. The British Museum. Photographed by permission.

(Ezek. 1:1-3), we gather that the exiles were organized in their own communities under their own elders (8:1). Ezekiel's own community was situated at TEL ABIB (3:15), an otherwise unknown location on the river or canal KEBAR.

III. Religious conditions. The prophets Ezekiel and DANIEL ministered in Babylon during the exile. Jeremiah, who had urged Zedekiah to make peace with Nebuchadnezzar, was permitted to remain in Judah after the destruction of Jerusalem. The murder of GEDALIAH, who had been appointed by Nebuchadnezzar as governor of Judah, precipitated a move on the part of the remaining Judeans to migrate to Egypt. Although tradition suggests that he subsequently went to Babylon, Jeremiah's actual prophetic ministry ends among those who had fled this way to Egypt.

Ezekiel was taken to Babylon at the time of the deportation of Jehoiachin. He prophesied to the exiles at Tel Abib, warning them of the impending destruction of Jerusalem. Subsequent to the fall of the city, Ezekiel held forth the hope of a return from exile and the reestablishment of the people of God in Palestine.

Daniel was one of the youths selected to be taken to Babylon at the time of the first deportation (under Jehoiakim). God-given abilities and a spirit of faithfulness enabled Daniel to rise to a position of influence in the Babylonian court—a position that he maintained through varying political regimes to the time of Cyrus the Persian, conqueror of Babylon. Like Ezekiel, Daniel spoke of the exile as temporary in duration. He also depicted a succession of world powers, culminating in the reign of the MESSIAH as the goal of history.

Within preexilic Judaism, the center of WORSHIP was the Jerusalem temple where sacrifices were offered daily and where annual festive occasions were observed. With the destruction of the temple a new spiritual orientation took place. Jews came together for the purpose of prayer and the study of Scripture in gatherings that later were called synagogues. The emergence of the SYNAGOGUE made possible the continuation of Jewish religious life during the period of absence from the temple. The synagogue persisted after the building of the second temple (516 B.C.) and is still an important factor in Jewish life.

The sacred books of the Jews assumed great importance during the period of the exile. The LAW, which had been lost prior to JOSIAH's reign (2 Ki. 22:8), became the subject of careful study. By the time of the return from Babylon, the institution of the SCRIBE was established. Scribes not only made copies of the law, but they also served as interpreters. EZRA is regarded as the first scribe (Ezra 7:6 et al.). The SABBATH, a part of the Mosaic law, assumed a new meaning to the displaced Jews of the exile. It served as a weekly reminder of the fact that they had a definite covenant relationship to God, and became a marker to distinguish the Jew from his Babylonian neighbor. When NEHEMIAH led a group back to Palestine he insisted that the Sabbath be scrupulously observed (13:15-22).

IV. Political conditions. The exile began during the reign of the Neo-Babylonian king Nebuchadnezzar and ended with the decree of the Persian king Cyrus. Nebuchadnezzar defeated an Egyptian army that had joined forces with the Assyrians, who were retreating before the Babylonians, at CARCHEMISH on the upper EUPHRATES (605 B.C.). The campaign against Egypt was deferred when Nebuchadnezzar, on receiving news of the death of his father, Nabopolassar, returned home to insure his succession to the kingdom. Judah was among the states of W Asia that Nebuchadnezzar claimed as heir to the Assyrians whom he had defeated in battle. Babylonian armies occupied Judah during the reign of Jehoiakim (c. 603) and took captive a number of its leading citizens, leaving only "the poorest of the people" in the land. Jehoiakim was allowed to retain his throne until he rebelled (2 Ki. 24:12-16). In 598 the Babylonian king called on the vassal states (including MOAB, SYRIA, and AMMON) to support his power in Judah by force of arms (24:2). When Jehoiakim was killed in battle his eighteen-year-old son, Jehoiachin, succeeded him. After a reign of but three months, Jehoiachin was deported to Babylon with 10,000 Jews, including Ezekiel. Jehoiachin's uncle, Zedekiah, the third son of Josiah, was made a puppet king in Jerusalem (24:17-19). In spite of the warnings of Jeremiah, Zedekiah yielded to the pro-Egyptian party and refused to pay tribute to Babylon. Thereupon Nebuchadnezzar laid siege to Jerusalem and, after eighteen months, entered the

E

city, destroyed its temple, and deported its citizens (587). Following the murder of Gedaliah, whom Nebuchadnezzar had appointed to handle Judean affairs after the destruction of Jerusalem, the final deportation took place in about 581 (25:22).

Nebuchadnezzar reigned for more than forty years, but he left no able successor. Jehoiachin was given a place of honor among the exiles in Babylon by EVIL-MERODACH (561-560 B.C.), son and successor of Nebuchadnezzar. Neriglissar (559-556) and Labashi-Marduk (556) had brief, nonsignificant reigns. Nabonidus (Nabū-naʾid), with his son BELSHAZZAR, served as the last ruler of the Neo-Babylonian empire (556-539). Nabonidus had an interest in archaeology and religion but was inefficient as a ruler. He repaired the ZIGGURAT to the moon god Sin at Ur where one of his daughters served as priestess. Another daughter is said to have maintained a small museum of archaeological finds. His diversified interests caused Nabonidus to name Belshazzar, his eldest son, as prince regent. It was during the reign of Belshazzar that the Neo-Babylonian empire came to an end. Cyrus had made rapid conquests after his succession to the throne of the small Persian principality of Anshan (559). Successively unifying the Persians, conquering the neighboring Medes and the distant Lydians of Asia Minor, Cyrus marched against Babylon, which he defeated in 539. Cyrus issued the decree that permitted Jews to return to Jerusalem to rebuild the temple (Ezra 1:1-4). This may be regarded as the end of the exile, although many Jews chose to remain in Babylon.

V. Results. Although the exile ended the political independence of Judea, it served to emphasize the fact that God was in no sense confined to PALESTINE. He accompanied his people to Babylon and providentially cared for them there (cf. Ezek. 11:16). The experience of life far away from the land, city, and house where the Lord had chosen to dwell, brought to the fore the monotheism that had always been part of the faith of the people of the Lord. At the same time, the teaching of the prophets that the exile was the Lord's punishment on idolatry bore fruit. Their suffering, coupled with face-to-face contact with the realities of false religion, purged the people of idolatrous desire. Although many exiles returned to their homeland following the decree of Cyrus, others remained in the Persian empire, with the result that in due time Judaism became international in scope.

exodus. The departure of the Hebrew people from EGYPT under MOSES (from the Gk. word *exodos G2016*, "a going out"). The family of JACOB had voluntarily entered Egypt during a time of severe famine in CANAAN. JOSEPH, who had earlier been sold into slavery by his jealous brothers, was then vizier of Egypt, and his Israelite brothers were assigned suitable land in the NE section of Egypt known as GOSHEN (Gen. 42-46). When a new dynasty arose "who did not know about Joseph" (Exod. 1:8), that is, forgot what he had done for Egypt, the Israelites were reduced to the status of slaves. Afraid that they might prove sympathetic with foreign invaders, PHARAOH ordered the male children destroyed. The infant Moses, however, was placed in an ark of bulrushes where he was rescued by Pharaoh's daughter (2:1-10). Raised in the royal court, Moses chose to turn his back on the possibilities of advancement in Egypt in order to lead his oppressed people into freedom.

I. Date of the exodus. There has been a lack of unanimity among Bible students concerning the date of the exodus and thus the identity of the pharaohs who took part in the oppression of Israel. Later pharaohs are sometimes mentioned by name (e.g., Pharaoh Hophra, Pharaoh Neco), but only the title "Pharaoh" is given in the exodus account. Some biblical scholars consider that 1 Ki. 6:1 is decisive in furnishing the date of the exodus. That verse states that SOLOMON began to build the temple "in the four hundred and eightieth year after the Israelites had come out of Egypt." Since we know the approximate dates of Solomon's reign, this information can be used in calculating the date of the Exodus. The date suggested by this method of computation, about 1441 B.C., falls within the reign of Amenhotep II, son of Thutmose III, one of the great empire builders of New Kingdom Egypt. Paintings from the tomb of Rekhmire, vizier of Thutmose III, depict Semites working as slave laborers on building projects.

Adherents of this "early date" of the Exodus (1441 B.C.) also find support for their position from the AMARNA Letters (1400-1366). These cuneiform tablets discovered at the site of Akhenaten's capital contain correspondence from the kings of the city-states in Canaan, asking the help of the pharaoh against a people known as Habiru. This, it is suggested, is a description of the battles fought after the exodus by the armies of Israel when seeking to conquer Canaan.

There are, however, serious difficulties in accepting the early date. During the 18th dynasty of Egyptian history (when the early date would fall), the capital of Egypt was at THEBES, S of the NILE delta, and the building operations of Thutmose III seem to have been centered there. Later, however (during the time of the RAMSES), the pharaohs resided in the delta, where they engaged in extensive building activity. It is specifically in the delta region, adjacent to Goshen, that Moses met with Pharaoh, and it was in the city of RAMESES (also known as Avaris and Tanis) in the eastern delta that the Israelites are reported to have labored (Exod. 1:11). Advocates of the early date suggest that the name Rameses is a modernization of an older name.

Because of these problems in dating the exodus as early as the fifteenth century B.C., a number of biblical scholars have come to accept a date in the thirteenth century. Explorations in TRANSJORDAN by the archaeologist Nelson Glueck indicate a gap in the sedentary population of that region from about 1900 to 1300. The Bible, however, indicates that Israel met formidable opposition from SIHON and OG, kings in the E Jordan country, and that the Moabite king sought to bring a curse on Israel to prevent their progress into Canaan. The earlier suggestion of evidence that JERICHO fell about 1400 has been questioned by recent expeditions there under the direction of Kathleen Kenyon. The excavations at HAZOR by Yigael Yadin also tend to point toward a thirteenth-century date for the exodus, as did earlier excavations at LACHISH and DEBIR. The Stele of Merneptah (c. 1229) provides the first reference to Israel in the Egyptian monuments. Merneptah

claims a decisive victory over the Israelite people. It may be significant that the ideogram for "nation" is not used. In any event, we know that Israelites were fighting in Canaan during the reign of Merneptah. Merneptah's predecessor was Ramses II, who reigned for sixty-seven years from his capital at Tanis (or Rameses) in the delta.

Some biblical scholars suggest that Seti I, father of Ramses, began the oppression, which was continued under Ramses himself, and that the exodus took place during the latter's reign. Those who hold to this thirteenth-century date for the exodus usually suggest that the 480 years of 1 Ki. 6:1 be taken as a round number signifying twelve forty-year generations. Since generations are often much less than forty years apart, there may be a smaller time span between the exodus and the building of Solomon's temple. This view is accepted by many who hold to the full inspiration of the scriptural text. In view of the fact that the non-Israelite characters in the account of the exodus are not identified in Scripture, it is wise to avoid a dogmatic approach to the question. The evidence for the historicity of the exodus account is decisive, but the evidence for specific dates is still inconclusive.

II. Route. The biblical record (Exod. 13:17) states that Israel did not take the direct route through the PHILISTINE country to Canaan. Had

E

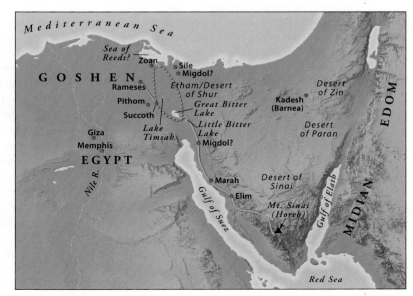

Possible routes of the Exodus.

they done so, Israel would have had to pass the Egyptian wall (biblical SHUR) that protected the NE highways out of Egypt. This wall was guarded and could be passed only with great difficulty. If they successfully crossed the border, further opposition could be anticipated from the Philistines. The discipline of the wilderness was a part of God's preparation for his people before they were to come into open conflict with formidable foes. Leaving Rameses (12:37) in the E delta, the Israelites journeyed SE to SUCCOTH (Tell el-Mashkutah).

They then moved on to ETHAM "on the edge of the desert" where they were conscious of God's guidance in the pillar of cloud and pillar of fire (Exod. 13:21-22). The Hebrew word *'ētām H918* possibly derives from an Egyptian word meaning "wall" or "fortress" and was probably part of the series of fortifications built by the Egyptians to keep out the Asiatic nomads. From Etham they turned back and camped near PI HAHIROTH, described as between MIGDOL and the sea and near BAAL ZEPHON. The location of these sites is not known with certainty. It is possible that Pi Hahiroth is Egyptian for "house of the marshes." Baal Zephon is the name of a Semitic deity who was worshiped in Egypt, doubtless at a shrine located at the town that bore his name.

After passing Pi Hahiroth, Israel arrived at the body of water designated in the English versions as the RED SEA, the *Yam Suph* of the Hebrew text. The geography of the exodus suggests that Yam Suph, or Sea of Reeds, formed a natural barrier between Egypt and the SINAI Peninsula, the destination of the Israelites. The topography of this region has been altered since the construction of the Suez Canal, but the Yam Suph was probably north of Lake Timsah. An Egyptian document from the thirteenth century B.C. mentions a Papyrus Lake not far from Tanis, whose suggested location is the southern extension of the present Lake Menzaleh. The exodus from Egypt through the Yam Suph was made possible by the direct intervention of God who "drove the sea back with a strong east wind" (Exod. 14:21). Israel was thus able to cross from Egypt to the Sinai Peninsula. When the armies of Pharaoh attempted to pursue the Israelites, the Egyptians were destroyed by the waters that returned to their normal course.

III. Miracles. The exodus period was one of the great epochs of biblical MIRACLES. The first nine PLAGUES OF EGYPT may have been related to the natural phenomena of the country, but their timing and intensification were clearly supernatural. The last plague—the death of the firstborn—signaled the beginning of the exodus. Israel ate the Passover meal in haste, ready to depart from Egypt. The opening of the Red Sea by the "strong east wind" was the means by which God brought his people out of Egypt into the wilderness where, for a period of forty years, they were miraculously sustained.

Exodus, Book of. The second book of the Bible. The title is a Latin term derived from the Greek word *exodos G2016* ("a going out"), which is the title of the book in the SEPTUAGINT. The title in the Hebrew tradition is comprised of the first several words of the book, "And these are the names" (i.e., the names of the Israelites who came out of Egypt), and it is usually referred to simply as *Shemoth*, "names." Tradition ascribes the authorship of the book to MOSES. It covers the history of the Israelites from the events surrounding the EXODUS to the giving of the LAW at SINAI.

I. The Israelites in Egypt (Exod. 1:1—12:36). The historical events recorded in this section flow logically from the last chapters of the book of GENESIS, where we are told how JACOB and his sons came to live in Egypt. The clan grew into a nation, but the lot of the Hebrew people changed when a PHARAOH arose who did not remember the contributions of Jacob's son JOSEPH, who had been elevated to prominence in the Egyptian government years before (1:8). This king forced the Hebrew people into hard servitude (1:13-14). The birth of Moses and his providential preservation, when the pharaoh ordered the death of every male child born to the Hebrews (1:22), is recorded in ch. 2.

The account of Moses' call to lead the Hebrews out of Egypt (Exod. 3:1—4:17) contains the classic statement of the Lord in which he depicts his divine character in the words, "I AM WHO I AM" (3:14). While this statement has been understood in various ways, the context emphasizes the continuity of the promise made to the forefathers (3:13, 15-16). It is probably best to understand the words as connoting the continuity of God's dealings with

Overview of EXODUS

Author: Anonymous, but comments elsewhere in the Bible seem to support the traditional view that MOSES is responsible for the PENTATEUCH as a whole.

Historical setting: The initial composition of the book must have have taken place during the wilderness wanderings (either late in the fifteenth or early in the thirteenth century B.C.; those who reject Mosaic authorship usually date the book after the EXILE, while acknowledging that much of the material is several centuries earlier).

Purpose: To provide a historical-theological account of the life of Moses, the deliverance of the Israelites from slavery in EGYPT, the establishment of the COVENANT at SINAI, and the building of the TABERNACLE.

Contents: Birth, earthly life, and calling of Moses (Exod. 1-4); confrontation with PHARAOH, leading to the plagues, the institution of the Passover, and the exodus (chs. 5-15); from the crossing of the RED SEA to the establishment of the covenant (chs. 16-24); instructions for the building and operation of the tabernacle (chs. 25-31); Israel's sin and restoration, followed by the construction of the tabernacle (chs. 26-40).

E

his people—"I am the God who is," or "I am the God who continues to be," that is, the God who appeared to Moses was the same God who gave his gracious promises to their forefathers. The God of Moses was the God of ABRAHAM. The efforts of Moses to free his people met with no success until the firstborn in Egypt were stricken by God. Only then were the Hebrews able to escape.

II. From Egypt to Sinai (Exod. 12:37—19:2). Three important Hebrew traditions were formalized just after the flight from Egypt: the Passover (12:43-49), which commemorated the fact that the Lord had passed over the houses of the Israelites (12:27); the Feast of Unleavened Bread (13:3-10); and the consecration to God of every firstborn male, "whether man or animal" (13:2). When the Israelites finally fled from Egypt, the pharaoh realized that he had lost a major source of manpower (14:5) and pursued them to the RED SEA, where God miraculously brought about their escape (14:21-31).

The period of Israelite history between the exodus and the giving of the law at Sinai was marked by frequent complaining by the people against God and their leader Moses. The complaints were often due to a lack of sustenance, but the deprivation was always met by miraculous displays of God's power. The bitter waters at MARAH were made sweet (Exod. 15:22-25), the hunger of the people was satisfied by the supply of MANNA (16:2-4) and quails (16:13), and their need for water on another occasion was met when God brought water out of a rock (17:2-7).

III. The Israelites at Sinai (Exod. 19:3—40:38). One of the most momentous events in Israelite history—the giving of the law—is recorded in this section. The law was given in three general categories: the Decalogue or the Ten Commandments (20:2-17; see COMMANDMENTS, TEN), civil and societal laws (21:1—23:11), and ceremonial laws (23:12—31:18). Moses' delay in returning from the mountain where the law was given was the cause of another period of apprehension and complaining on the part of the people. This led to the construction of a golden calf that AARON, Moses' brother, proclaimed to be Israel's god (32:4). The cult of the golden calf, which was also observed many years later in the northern kingdom of Israel (1 Ki. 12:25-30), appears not to have been an outright rejection of Yahweh, but rather a syncretistic combination of worship of Yahweh and the calf

Some think that Jebel Serbal was the Bible's Mt. Horeb (Sinai).

© Dr. James C. Martin

(see CALF WORSHIP). Verse 5 makes it clear that the worship associated with the golden calf was really directed to Yahweh. In the ancient world animal forms were often used to represent the point at which the spiritual presence of a deity was localized. For example, the storm god of MESOPOTAMIA was prefigured as a lightning bolt set on the back of a bull. This is somewhat similar to the presence of Yahweh over the CHERUBIM on the ARK OF THE COVENANT.

The remainder of the book of Exodus records the implementation of the ceremonial law in the construction of the TABERNACLE (Exod. 35:4—38:31) and the fashioning of the priests' garments (39:1-43). When the tabernacle was completed it was filled with the glory of the Lord (40:34-38).

exorcism. The act of expelling an evil spirit from a person (see DEMON). The English term derives from the Greek verb *exorkizō G2019*, "to adjure, to put someone under oath" (Matt. 26:63). Exorcism was a common practice among ancient heathen. In Acts 19:13-16 the profane use of Jesus' name as a mere spell was punished when the demon-possessed man turned on the would-be exorcists; these "vagabond Jews" were pretenders. Christ,

however, implies that some Jews actually cast out demons (Matt. 12:27)—some probably by demonical help, others (in the name of Jesus) without saving faith in him (7:22). He gave power to cast out demons to the Twelve, the Seventy, and to the other disciples after the ascension (Matt. 10:8; Mk. 16:17; Lk. 10:17-19; Acts 16:18).

expanse. See FIRMAMENT.

expiation. See PROPITIATION AND EXPIATION.

extortion. The act or crime of obtaining what belongs to another by such means as coercion, intimidation, blackmail, and fraud. Numerous passages of Holy Scripture condemning fraud and extortion of various kinds indicate that even the people of God often became guilty of exploiting others. God himself forbids all types of stealing and fraud, including extortion (Exod. 21-23). The prophet EZEKIEL warns that God will deal justly with an extortioner (Ezek. 18:18) and states that such crimes were common in his day (22:29). The psalmist preached that those who place confidence in extortion and robbery follow a vain hope (Ps. 62:10). Extortion through excessive INTEREST, or usury, is particularly hit hard to prevent the exploitation of a fellow Israelite's misfortune (Lev. 25:35-36; Deut. 23:19). One common form of extortion was to trick a man into a huge loan or pledge, then foreclose and force him to become a slave (Lev. 25:39, 47). Jesus aimed charges of extortion, fraud, and robbery against the people of his day in the sharpest terms their ears could bear (Matt. 23:25 RSV; cf. Lk. 11:39; 18:11). JOHN THE BAPTIST counseled repentant tax collectors and soldiers (Lk. 3:13-14). The final stroke is given by PAUL: "nor thieves nor the greedy nor drunkards nor slanderers nor swindlers will inherit the kingdom of God" (1 Cor. 6:10).

eye. The organ of sight. The literal sense is that which is most frequently found in the Scriptures, where the eye is recognized as among the most valued of the members of the body. In the Mosaic legislation, if a man hit a slave's eye so that it was blinded, the slave was to be released (Exod. 21:26). One of the most cruel customs of the heathen nations was that of putting out the eyes of a defeated enemy (2 Ki. 25:7). The word is also used often in figurative expressions. Frequently "eye" speaks of spiritual perception and understanding. Thus the word of God enlightens the eyes (Ps. 19:8). Growth in spiritual knowledge comes through the "eyes of the heart being enlightened" (Eph. 1:18). Other expressions speak of the eye as indicative of character. The good man has a "bountiful eye" (Prov. 22:9 KJV). High or lofty eyes (Ps. 131:1) describe the proud man. The envious man is one with an evil eye (Matt. 20:15 KJV).

eyelids of the morning. This phrase is the KJV's literal rendering of a Hebrew idiom that occurs twice in the OT (Job 3:9; 41:18; NRSV, "eyelids of the dawn"). The expression seems to refer to the gradual appearance of sunlight culminating in sunrise itself (thus NIV, "the rays of dawn").

eye of a needle. See NEEDLE.

eyes, painting of. The ancient practice of painting the eyelids in order to enhance the beauty of the feminine face (Jer. 4:30; Ezek. 23:40). JEZEBEL "painted her eyes" (2 Ki. 9:30). Oriental women still paint their eyelids with antimony or *kohl* (a black powder made of the smoke black from the burning of frankincense) to make them look full and sparkling, the blackened margin contrasting with the white of the eye.

eyesalve. This term is used by the KJV to render Greek *kollourion G3141*, which appears in the context of the address to the church at LAODICEA (Rev. 3:18; NIV simply, "salve"). Some scholars have seen a connection between the use of this term and the existence of a famous school of medicine in Laodicea. The ancient physician Galen speaks of a medicine for the eyes made from Phrygian stone and in the form of a tabloid (*De sanitate tuenda* 6.439). Since Laodicea was a well-known city in the region of PHRYGIA, some have thought that

Galen was referring to a "Phrygian powder" mentioned by Aristotle, and that this medicine came from Laodicea.

eyeservice. This term, used by the KJV and other versions, is a literal rendering of a Greek noun that appears twice in nearly identical phrases (Eph. 6:6; Col. 3:22). It vividly describes insincere service, that is, work done to impress masters (or employers) "when their eye is on you" (NIV).

eyewitness. Someone who has personally witnessed an event and can verify its truthfulness. One Greek term with this meaning (*autoptēs G898*) is used by LUKE to support and insure the authenticity of his narrative (Lk. 1:2). A close synonym (*epoptēs G2228*) is used by PETER similarly to designate himself and the other disciples who witnessed the majesty of Christ and who can testify that Christians have not followed "cleverly invented stories" (2 Pet. 1:16).

Ezar. ee′zuhr. KJV alternate form of EZER (only 1 Chr. 1:38 in some editions).

Ezbai. ez′bi (Heb. *ʾezbāy H256*, meaning uncertain). Father of NAARI; the latter is listed among the Thirty, DAVID's military elite (1 Chr. 11:37). The parallel passage at this point has "Paarai the Arbite" (2 Sam. 23:35) instead of "Naari son of Ezbai." These differences, like others in the lists, reflect scribal mistakes, but scholars do not agree regarding the original form.

Ezbon. ez′bon (Heb. *ʾeṣbōn H719*, meaning uncertain). (1) Fourth son of GAD (Gen. 46:16); apparently the same as OZNI in the parallel passage (Num. 26:16).

(2) Son of BELA and grandson of BENJAMIN (1 Chr. 7:7).

Ezekiel. i-zee′kee-uhl (Heb. *yĕḥezqēʾl H3489*, "God strengthens"). Son of Buzi, descendant of ZADOK, and a major Hebrew prophet during the EXILE (Ezek. 1:3). A play is made on this name in connection with the prophet's call (3:7-8, 14). Born of a priestly family (1:3), Ezekiel grew up in JUDAH during the last years of Hebrew independence and was deported to BABYLON with JEHOIACHIN in 597 B.C., probably early in life. He was called to be a prophet in the fifth year of his captivity (1:1-2); the last date mentioned is the twenty-seventh year (29:17); his ministry therefore lasted at least twenty-two years, from about 593 to 571 B.C. Ezekiel was a younger contemporary of the prophet JEREMIAH and probably a somewhat older contemporary of DANIEL, who also as a young man was taken to Babylon in 605. Ezekiel lived with the Jewish exiles by the irrigation canal named KEBAR (1:1, 3; 3:15) which connected the TIGRIS River with the EUPHRATES above Babylon; Daniel carried out his quite different work in the Babylonian court. We know little more about Ezekiel, except that he was married (24:18).

The "captivity" of the Jews consisted in their deportation to a foreign land. Once arrived in Babylon, however, the exiles seem to have been completely free to settle and live their lives as they pleased. At Nippur, located on the Kebar Canal, many records have been found of a Jewish business house, the Murashu Sons, indicating the possibilities open to exiles. Many of the Jews became so settled in their adopted land that they refused to leave it at the end of the exile, and from that time to this the majority of the Hebrews have lived outside of Palestine.

When Jerusalem was finally destroyed, some ten years after he arrived in Babylon, Ezekiel entered into the sufferings of his people. On the day on which the final siege began, the prophet's wife became suddenly sick and died. In this he became a sign to the people and was not allowed to go through the customary period of mourning, doubtless to emphasize to them the greater sorrow now coming on the nation.

In recent years a good deal of interest has been awakened regarding the unusual states of the prophets during the reception of their revelations. Some have diagnosed Ezekiel's condition as catalepsy, but the passages adduced (Ezek. 3:14-15, 26-27; 4:4-5; 24:27) hardly support such a theory. Rather it would seem that the occasional silence of the prophet and his lying on the ground were signs to gain the attention of the people and to act out his message. Ezekiel was a powerful preacher. Possessing a deeply introspective and religious nature, he used ALLEGORY, vivid figures, and symbolic actions to clothe his message. His favorite expression to denote the divine inspiration, "the hand of the LORD was upon me" (1:3; 3:14, 22), shows how strongly he felt impelled to communicate the message given him. His preaching was directed to his Jewish brethren in exile; and, like Jeremiah's, it was often resented, for it held out little hope for the immediate future. No doubt his message was ultimately received, for the exile became a time of religious purging. In Babylon the Jews were cured permanently of their idolatry; and Ezekiel, their major religious leader, must be given much credit for that.

The prophet's ministry was divided into two periods. The first ends with the siege of Jerusalem in 587 B.C. (Ezek. 24:1, 27). It was a message of approaching destruction for Jerusalem and of condemnation of her sin. The second period begins with the reception of the news of Jerusalem's fall, some two years later (33:21-22). Now the prophet's message emphasized comfort and looked forward to the coming of the kingdom of God. It would appear that during the two years between, Ezekiel ceased all public ministry. Frequently in this book (more than seventy times), Ezekiel is referred to as "son of man." The term means a mortal, as in Ps. 8:4, and is used here to emphasize the prophet's weakness and dependence on God for his success. Later the term came to be a messianic designation. See SON OF MAN.

© Dr. James C. Martin

Glazed brick reliefs of the lion, the sacred animal of the goddess Ishtar, from the "procession street" in Babylon (6th cent. B.C.). It was from Babylon that Ezekiel prophesied to Israel.

Overview of EZEKIEL

Author: The priest-prophet Ezekiel.

Historical setting: Ezekiel received his visions while in EXILE in BABYLON from c. 593 (seven years before the fall of JERUSALEM) to c. 571 B.C.

Purpose: To impress on the Hebrew exiles the truth that their captivity and the destruction of the nation were the result of their faithlessness; to bring them to repentance; and to assure them that God will yet restore them.

Contents: Oracles against JUDAH (Ezek. 1-24); oracles against pagan nations (chs. 25-32); promises of restoration (chs. 33-39); visions of the future temple (chs. 40-48).

Ezekiel, Book of. The third book among the Major Prophets of the OT. Until quite recently the work was universally accepted as written by the prophet EZEKIEL. Some critics have denied the unity of the book and have attributed all or parts of it to later writers. There has been, however, no agreement among these critics. The arguments for both the unity of the book and its origin with Ezekiel are very strong. The book is autobiographical, that is, the author often uses the first person singular pronoun. The arrangement of the book shows its unity—all the parts fit together and, indeed, need each other to make the whole.

The locality of Ezekiel's ministry was BABYLON, to which he had been deported in 597 B.C. Ezekiel 8-11 contains a unique vision of events that were transpiring in JERUSALEM, made possible when "the Spirit lifted me up ... and in visions of God he took me to Jerusalem" (8:3). Elsewhere in the book an intimate knowledge of events in faraway Jerusalem is implied (e.g., 24:1-2). It appears impossible that Ezekiel in Babylon could have known in such detail events in Jerusalem except by divine INSPIRATION. Therefore many scholars are now of the opinion that Ezekiel really prophesied in Jerusalem until the city fell. The clear statements of the book, however, indicate his presence with the Jews in Babylon when he "saw" (8:6, 9-10) the events taking place at Jerusalem; and one who makes a serious attempt to understand the visions should grapple with these statements rather than deny them.

The book is divided into three parts: denunciation of Judah and Israel (Ezek. 1-24, dated 593-588 B.C.); oracles against foreign nations (chs. 25-32, dated 587-571); and the future restoration of Israel (chs. 33-48, dated 585-573).

The prophecies of the first section were uttered before the fall of Jerusalem. Ezekiel's call to the prophetic work is described in Ezek. 1-3. Here occurs his vision of the divine glory—God's throne borne by an unearthly chariot of CHERUBIM and wheels (1:4-21). The prophet eats the scroll on which his sad message is written (2:8—3:3); and he is commanded to be the Lord's watchman, his own life to be forfeited if he does not cry the alarm (3:16-21; cf. 33:1-9). Ezekiel then predicts the destruction of Jerusalem by symbolic acts (4:7), such as laying siege to a replica of the city (4:1-8) and by rationing food and drink (4:9-17). Next follows the famous vision of Jerusalem's iniquity, for which Ezekiel is raptured in spirit to Jerusalem (chs. 8-11) and sees all kinds of loathsome idolatry being practiced in the temple courts. While he watches the desecration of the house of the Lord, he beholds the divine glory, which had been manifested in the Most Holy Place (8:4), leave the temple and city (9:3; 10:4, 19; 11:22-23), symbolizing God's abandonment of his apostate people. At that moment Ezekiel returns in spirit to Babylon. The

E

rest of the first section (chs. 12-24) records symbolic actions and sermons of the prophet predicting the fall of Jerusalem. He enacts the departure into exile (12:1-7), preaches against false prophets (ch. 13), and in two deeply moving oracles (chs. 16; 23) depicts the ungrateful people's apostasy. His statement of the individual's responsibility before God (ch. 18) is famous. Finally he announces the beginning of the siege of Jerusalem, and in the evening of the same day his wife dies and he becomes dumb until the fall of the city (ch. 24).

After the prophecies of judgment against foreign nations (Ezek. 25-32) comes the climax of the prophet's vision, written after the fall of Jerusalem—the restoration of Israel (chs. 33-48). God will bring back the people to their land, send the son of David to reign over them, and give them a new heart (chs. 34; 36). The vision of the valley of dry bones (ch. 37) is a figurative statement of this regathering of the nation. Then follows Israel's defeat of the Gentile powers, Gog and Magog (chs. 38-39; see MAGOG). Finally a great restored TEMPLE is pictured (chs. 40-43), its holy services (chs. 44-46), the river of life running from it (ch. 47), and the people of Israel living in their places around the city, called "The Lord is there" (ch. 48), to which the glory of the Lord has returned (43:2, 4-5; 44:4).

Ezel. ee′zuhl (Heb. *ʾezel H262*, possibly "departure"). The name of a stone, otherwise unknown, near which DAVID was supposed to wait for JONATHAN (1 Sam. 20:19). On the basis of the SEPTUAGINT, many scholars emend the Hebrew text, yielding such a rendering as "remain beside the stone there" (so NRSV).

Ezem. ee′zuhm (Heb. *ʿeṣem H6796*, "bone" [signifying "strength"]). KJV also Azem (in Joshua). One of the southernmost towns of JUDAH in the NEGEV (Josh. 15:29); it was among the towns later assigned to the tribe of SIMEON (Josh. 19:3; 1 Chr. 4:29). The location of Ezem is unknown, but a popular suggestion is Umm el-ʿAzam, 12 mi. (19 km.) SE of BEERSHEBA.

Ezer. ee′zuhr (Heb. *ʾēṣer H733*, perhaps "treasure" [only #1 below]; *ʿēzer H6470*, "help"). **(1)** Son of SEIR the HORITE in the land of EDOM; he is mentioned sixth among the chiefs of the Horites (Gen. 36:21, 27, 30; 1 Chr. 1:38 [some KJV editions, "Ezar"], 42).

(2) Father of Husha and a descendant of JUDAH (1 Chr. 4:4). His place in the genealogy is unclear.

(3) Son (or grandson) of EPHRAIM who, with his brother Elead, was killed by the men of GATH (1 Chr. 7:21). See comments under ELEAD.

(4) The chief of the mighty men of GAD, who came to DAVID in ZIKLAG when David fled from SAUL (1 Chr. 12:9). The Gadites are described as "were brave warriors, ready for battle and able to handle the shield and spear. Their faces were the faces of lions, and they were as swift as gazelles in the mountains" (v. 8).

(5) Son of JESHUA and ruler of Mizpah; he was a LEVITE who repaired a section of the walls of JERUSALEM in the days of NEHEMIAH (Neh. 3:19).

(6) A priest listed among those who assisted Nehemiah in the dedication of the rebuilt walls of Jerusalem (Neh. 12:42).

Ezion Geber. ee′zee-uhn-gee′buhr (Heb. *ʿesyôn geber H6787*, meaning uncertain). A city located on the N end of the Gulf of AQABAH, banked on the E by the hills of EDOM and on the W by those of PALESTINE. The site, Tell el-Kheleifeh, is 2.5 mi. (4 km.) NW of modern Aqabah (biblical ELATH) in Jordan, and about the same distance SE of Eilat in Israel. Some scholars, however, believe that the offshore island known as Jezirat Faraun ("Pharaoh's Island," now Coral Island) is the probable site.

Ezion Geber was the last stopping place of the Israelites in their wilderness wanderings before KADESH (Num. 33:35-36). The city's period of greatest prosperity was in the time of SOLOMON, who there built a fleet of ships that sailed between Ezion Geber and OPHIR, a source of gold (1 Ki. 9:26-28; 2 Chr. 8:17-18). Similarly, JEHOSHAPHAT joined with AHAZIAH in building ships at Ezion Geber that were designed to sail to Ophir, but the fleet was destroyed before leaving port (2 Chr. 20:35-36; 1 Ki. 22:48-49). The location was chosen to take advantage of these winds, for the city was an industrial center as well as a seaport. Archaeological work at Tell el-Kheleifeh was thought to have uncovered an extensive industrial complex centered on the smelting and refining of copper (chiefly)

Pharaoh's Island may have been the site of Ezion Geber. (View to the SE toward the border with Jordan and Saudi Arabia.)

and iron. However, the excavations failed to turn up either the clay crucibles that would have been used in smelting or the slag from the refining process. According to some, the finds and ground plans indicate that the city was a large storehouse for grain and supplies for caravans and a fortress guarding the southern approaches on both sides of the gulf.

Eznite. ez′nit. See ADINO.

Ezra. ez′ruh (Heb. *ʿezrāʾ H6474*, "help"). **(1)** KJV form of EZRAH.

(2) A leading priest who returned from BABYLON to JERUSALEM with ZERUBBABEL (Neh. 12:1); apparently the same as Azariah (10:2).

(3) The famous Jewish priest and scribe who is the main character of the book of Ezra and the coworker of NEHEMIAH. Ezra was a lineal descendant from ELEAZAR, the son of AARON the high priest, and from SERAIAH, the chief priest put to death at RIBLAH by order of NEBUCHADNEZZAR (2 Ki. 25:18-21). All that is really known of Ezra is what is told in Ezra 7-10 and Neh. 8-10. There are various traditions about him in JOSEPHUS, 2 Esdras (see APOCRYPHA), and the TALMUD, but they are discrepant, and consequently no great reliance can be put on them.

In the seventh year of the reign of ARTAXERXES Longimanus, king of PERSIA (458 B.C.), Ezra received permission from the king to return to Jerusalem to carry out a religious reform. Following the return from Babylonian captivity, the temple had been rebuilt in 516, in spite of much powerful and vexatious opposition from the SAMARITANS; but after a brief period of religious zeal, the nation drifted into apostasy once more. Many of the Jews intermarried with their heathen neighbors (Mal. 2:11); the temple services and sacrifices were neglected (1:6-14); and oppression and immorality were prevalent (3:5). Just how Ezra acquired his influence over the king does not appear, but he received a royal edict granting him authority to carry out his purpose. He was given permission to take with him as many Israelites as cared to go; he was authorized to take from the king and the Jews offerings made for the temple; to draw on the royal treasury in Syria for further necessary supplies; to purchase animals for sacrifice; to exempt the priests, Levites, and other workers in the temple from the Persian tax; to appoint magistrates in Judea to enforce the law of God, with power of life and death over all offenders. Eighteen hundred Jews left Babylon with him. Nine days later, they halted at a place called Ahava, and when it was found that no Levites were in the caravan, thirty-eight were persuaded to join them. After fasting and praying three days for a safe journey, they set out. Four months later they reached the Holy City, having made a journey of about 900 mi. (1,450 km.). The treasures were delivered into the custody of the Levites,

© Dr. James C. Martin

E

burnt offerings were offered to the Lord, the king's commissions were handed over to the governors and viceroys, and help was given to the people and the ministers of the temple.

When he had discharged the various trusts committed to him, Ezra entered on his great work of reform. The princes of the Jews came to him with the complaint that the Jewish people generally, and also the priests and Levites, but especially the rulers and princes, had not kept themselves religiously separate from the heathen around them, and had even married heathen wives. On hearing this report, Ezra expressed his horror and deep affliction of soul by tearing his garment and pulling out his hair. Those who still feared God and dreaded his wrath for the sin of the returned exiles gathered around him. At the evening sacrifice that day he made public prayer and confession of sin, entreating God not to remove his favor because of their awful guilt. The assembled congregation wept bitterly, and in the general grief, SHECANIAH came forward to propose a covenant to put away their foreign wives and children. A proclamation was issued that all Jews were to assemble in Jerusalem three days later, under pain of excommunication and forfeiture of goods. At the time appointed, the people assembled, trembling on account of their sin and promising obedience. They requested that, since it was raining hard (it was the time of the winter rains in Palestine) and the number of transgressors was great, Ezra would appoint times for the guilty to come, accompanied by the judges and elders of each city, and have each case dealt with. A divorce court, consisting of Ezra and some others, was set up to attend to the matter; and after three months, in spite of some opposition, the work of the court was finished and the foreign wives were put away.

The book of Ezra ends with this important transaction. Nothing more is heard of Ezra until thirteen years later: in the twentieth year of Artaxerxes (446 B.C.), he appears again at Jerusalem, when Nehemiah, a Babylonian Jew and the favored cupbearer of Artaxerxes, returned to Jerusalem as governor of Palestine with the king's permission to repair the ruined walls of the city. It is uncertain whether Ezra remained in Jerusalem after he had effected the above-named reformation, or whether he had returned to the king of Persia and now came back

with Nehemiah, or perhaps shortly after the arrival of the latter. Since he is not mentioned in Nehemiah's narrative until after the completion of the wall (Neh. 8:1), it is probable that Nehemiah sent for him to aid in his work. Under Nehemiah's government his functions were entirely of a priestly and ecclesiastical character. He read and interpreted the law of Moses before the assembled congregation during the eight days of the Feast of Tabernacles, assisted at the dedication of the wall, and helped Nehemiah in bringing about a religious reformation. In all this he took a chief place. His name is repeatedly coupled with Nehemiah's, while the high priest is not mentioned as taking any part in the reformation at all. Ezra is not again mentioned after Nehemiah's departure for Babylon. It may be that he himself returned to Babylon before that year.

Evidence points to Ezra's ministry taking place during the reign of Artaxerxes I (456-424 B.C.); but there are some modern critics who put Ezra after Nehemiah, holding that the sections dealing with them in the two books that bear their names have been transposed and that the Chronicler (the supposed author of the two books and of 1-2 Chronicles) blundered in the few passages that associate the two. First Esdras, a part of the OT Apocrypha, reproduces the substance of the end of 2 Chronicles, the whole of Ezra, and a part of Nehemiah, and was written somewhere near the beginning of the first century A.D. There is also an apocalyptic book known as 2 Esdras or *4 Ezra*, written about A.D. 100, describing some visions granted to Ezra in the Babylonian exile. Ezra made a lasting impression on the Jewish people. His influence shaped Jewish life and thought in a way from which they never completely departed.

Ezra, Book of. One of the historical books of the OT, included among the "Writings" (*Ketubim*) in the threefold canon of the Hebrew Bible. It is so named because EZRA is the principal person mentioned in it; possibly also because he may be its author. It does not in its entirety claim to be the work of Ezra, but Jewish tradition says it was written by him. Supporting this view is the fact that Ezra 7-10 are written in the first person singular, while events in which he did not take part are described in the third person. The trustworthiness of the book does not, however, depend on the hypothesis that Ezra is the author. Many scholars have thought that 1-2 Chronicles, Ezra, and Nehemiah constitute one large work, compiled and edited by someone designated the Chronicler, who has been dated from 400 to 300 B.C. Certainly the strong connection between Ezra and Nehemiah is established, and in Hebrew tradition they were regarded as one book; some recent scholars, however, believe that Ezra-Nehemiah should be treated independently of 1-2 Chronicles.

The book of Ezra continues the narrative after Chronicles and records the return from BABYLON and the rebuilding of the TEMPLE. The purpose of the author is to show how God fulfilled his promise given through prophets to restore his exiled people to their own land through heathen monarchs, and raised up such great men as ZERUBBABEL, HAGGAI, ZECHARIAH, and Ezra to rebuild the temple, reestablish the old forms of worship, and put a stop to compromise with heathenism. All material that does not contribute to his purpose he stringently excludes.

As sources for the writing of the book, the author used genealogical lists, letters, royal edicts, memoirs, and chronicles. Some of these were official documents found in public records. This diversity of material accounts for the varied character of the style and for the fact that it is written in both HEBREW and ARAMAIC.

The order of the Persian kings of the period is CYRUS (538-529 B.C.), DARIUS (521-486), XERXES (486-464), and ARTAXERXES I (464-424). In view of this succession, Ezra 4:7-23 departs from the chronological order of events. The reason for this is probably that the author regarded the topical order to be more important. He brings together in one passage the successful attempts of the SAMARITANS to hinder the building of the temple and the city walls.

The period covered is from 536 B.C., when the Jews returned to Jerusalem, to 458, when Ezra came to Jerusalem to carry out his religious reforms. It thus covers a period of about seventy-eight years, although the fifteen years between 535 and 520 and the fifty-eight years between 516 and 458 are practically a blank. We have a description of selected incidents, not a continuous record of the period.

For an understanding and appreciation of the book, a few historical facts must be kept in mind. The last chapter of 2 Kings records the destruction of Jerusalem by NEBUCHADNEZZAR and the

Overview of EZRA

Author: Anonymous, though Jewish tradition attributed it (as well as Chronicles and Nehemiah) to the priest EZRA.

Historical setting: The book was written possibly c. 430-400 B.C., but many date it a century later. In any case, the setting is postexilic JUDEA under Persian jurisdiction.

Purpose: To provide a historical-theological account of the restoration of Israel through the return of Hebrew exiles from BABYLON to JERUSALEM; and to encourage the people to lead a life of repentance from sin and obedience to the law.

Contents: The first part describes the return of Jewish exiles under ZERUBBABEL and JESHUA (Ezra 1-2), leading to the restoration of worship through the rebuilding of the TEMPLE (chs. 3-6); the second part details the return of additional exiles under Ezra (chs. 7-8), leading to the restoration of the community (chs. 9-10).

deportation of many of its inhabitants into Babylonia. There they were settled in colonies and were not mistreated as long as they were quiet subjects. Many of them prospered so well that when, later, they had an opportunity to return to their homeland, they chose not to do so. Since the temple was destroyed, they could not carry on their sacrificial system; but they continued such religious ordinances as the SABBATH and CIRCUMCISION, and gave great attention to the study of the LAW. The chapter concludes by noting that EVIL-MERODACH, in the year he became king (561 B.C.) released JEHOICHIN from prison and allowed him to eat from then on at the king's table (2 Ki. 25:27-30). This was about twenty-five years before the first events recorded in Ezra 1.

The EXILE was brought to a close when the Babylonian empire fell before Cyrus, king of Persia, in 538 B.C. The way in which the expectations of the Jews respecting Cyrus were fulfilled is told in the opening narrative of the book of Ezra. The return from exile did not bring with it political freedom for the Jews. They remained subjects of the Persian empire. Jerusalem and the surrounding districts were under the control of a governor, who sometimes was a Jew, but usually was not. Persian rule was in general not oppressive; but tribute was exacted for the royal treasury and the local governor. The hostile population surrounding them, especially the Samaritans, did all they could to make life miserable for them, especially by trying to bring them into disfavor with the Persian authorities. There were a few differences in the religious life of the Jews before and after the exile. Idolatry no longer tempted them—and never did again. The external features distinctive of Jewish worship and the ceremonial requirements of the laws were stressed. Prophecy became less important, scribes gradually taking the place of the prophets.

The book of Ezra consists of two parts. The first (Ezra 1-6) is a narrative of the return of the Jews from Babylonia under Zerubbabel and the restoration of worship in the rebuilt temple; the second (chs. 7-10) tells the story of a second group of exiles returning with Ezra and of Ezra's religious reforms.

Ezrah. ez′ruh (Heb. *ʿezrāh H6477*, "help"). KJV Ezra. A descendant of JUDAH who had four sons (1 Chr. 4:17). His precise place in the genealogy is not indicated.

Ezrahite. ez′ruh-hit (Heb. *ʾezrāḥi H276*). A descriptive term applied to ETHAN (1 Ki. 4:31; Ps. 89 title) and HEMAN (Ps. 88 title). The term has traditionally been understood as equivalent to "descendant of Zerah," but others believe it means "aborigine, member of a pre-Israelite family."

Ezri. ez′ri (Heb. *ʿezri H6479*, "my help"). Son of Kelub; he was an official in charge of those who farmed the royal lands during the reign of DAVID (1 Chr. 27:26).

fable. A fictitious narrative. In this general sense, the KJV uses the term to translate the Greek word *mythos G3680* ("story, legend, myth"), which occurs five times in the NT (1 Tim. 1:4; 4:7; 2 Tim. 4:4; Tit. 1:14; 2 Pet. 1:16). In a narrower sense, *fable* refers to a narrative in which animals and inanimate objects of nature are made to act and speak as if they were human beings. Two passages in the OT may be regarded as fables (Jdg. 9:7-15; 2 Ki. 14:9); some other passages employ illustrations that approach the status of fable (Isa. 5:1-7; Ezek. 17:3-10; 19:2-14).

face. This term (which renders primarily Heb. *pānîm*, pl. of *pāneh H7156*, and Gk. *prosōpon G4725*) can refer not only to the front of a human head (e.g., Gen. 4:5; Jas. 1:23) but also to that of animals (Gen. 30:40 NRSV). In a figurative sense, the Bible speaks of the face of God (Num. 6:25-26) and of Christ (2 Cor. 4:6), and the term can also refer to the surface of inanimate objects, like the waters (Gen. 1:2 NRSV), the earth (1:29), the moon (Job 26:9), and the sky (Matt. 16:3 KJV). Both the Hebrew and the Greek term can refer to the whole person (2 Sam. 17:11 [NIV, "you yourself"]; 2 Cor. 1:11). It should also be noted that the Hebrew word for "nose" (*ʾap H678*, e.g., Gen. 19:1) may stand for the whole countenance. The hidden face was the equivalent of disapproval or rejection (Ps. 13:1; 27:9). To spit in the face was an expression of contempt and aversion (Num. 12:14). To harden the face meant to harden oneself against any sort of appeal (Prov. 21:29 KJV). To have the face covered by another was a sign of doom (Esth. 7:8). Falling on the face symbolized prostration before man or God (Ruth 2:10). Setting the face signified determination (Lk. 9:51 KJV). To cover the face expressed mourning (Exod. 3:6).

fair. A word translating more than a dozen Hebrew and Greek words, none of which has the modern sense of blond or fair-skinned. It has the meaning of beautiful, attractive (Hos. 10:11; Acts 7:20 RSV; cf. NIV footnote); unspotted, free of defilement (Zech. 3:5 KJV); plausible, persuasive (Prov. 7:21 KJV); making a fine display (Gal. 6:12 KJV); good weather (Job 37:22 KJV; Matt. 16:12); honest, just (Jdg. 9:16; Prov. 1:3).

Fair Havens. A bay near Lasea on the S coast of Crete, about 5 mi. (8 km.) E of Cape Matala (Acts 27:8). Paul, in the custody of a centurion, sailed W from Cnidus on an Alexandrian grain ship. The weather forced them to sail on the S side of Crete and then to take refuge at Fair Havens. The harbor was not suitable to spend the winter in, so the captain decided to sail from there, with the hope of reaching Phoenix, a more secure harbor farther to the W. Failing, they drifted in the open sea for fourteen days until the shipwreck at Malta.

fairs. This English term (now obsolete, but related to the noun *fair*, "market, exhibition") means "wares, merchandise" and is used by the KJV to render a Hebrew word that occurs seven times, but only in one passage (Ezek. 27:12-33).

faith. The Hebrew verb meaning "to believe, trust" (*ʾāman H586* in the hiphil stem) occurs fewer than fifty times in the OT, but this comparative infrequency does not adequately reflect the importance of the place of faith in the Hebrew Scriptures. The NT draws all its examples of faith from the lives of OT believers (e.g., Rom. 4:18-25; Heb. 11; Jas. 2:20-26), and Paul rests his doctrine of faith on the word of Hab. 2:4 (Rom. 1:17). It would thus be

Distant shot of the Herodium (view to the SE). To construct this palace-fortress, Herod had to build a mountain. Referring to a different elevation, Jesus once said, "If anyone says to this mountain, 'Go, throw yourself into the sea,' and does not doubt in his heart but believes that what he says will happen, it will be done for him" (Mk. 11:23).

true to say that the OT demands faith more than it develops an explicit doctrine of faith. It looks for, and finds in its great individuals, a true commitment of self to God, an unwavering trust in his promises, and a persistent fidelity and obedience.

The foundation of Israel's faith was the Lord's REVELATION of himself to the PATRIARCHS and to MOSES, the COVENANT that he sealed at SINAI, and the conviction that God would keep his covenant promises. The observance of LAW and the life of faith were in no way incompatible because the law rested on the promises of God and obedience was motivated by a believing conviction that he would stand by what he had said. In connection, for example, with the sacrifices that the law commanded, we need to remind ourselves that OT believers did not offer their sacrifices with any thought in mind of the perfect sacrifice of Christ that was yet to come. They did not (at that point) think of themselves as doing something "pro tem" or as doing something that was allowed to be effective because the "real thing" was some day going to be done. They acted in simple faith in the promises of God. If asked how they knew their sins were forgiven, they would have replied, "Because he said so." In this way personal faith—in exactly the same terms as Paul later developed in the doctrine of JUSTIFICATION by

faith—is the presupposition behind the provisions and prescriptions of the old covenant. Obedience to the Lord's law was the way of life incumbent on those who trusted him. OT faith is never a mere assent to a set of doctrines or the outward acceptance of a legal code, but utter confidence in the faithfulness of God and a consequent loving obedience to his will.

When used with a religious application in the OT, the object of faith is sometimes a specific word or work of God (Lam. 4:12; Hab. 1:5), or in the fact of God's revelation (Exod. 4:5; Job 9:16), or in the words or commandments of God in general (Ps. 119:66), or in God himself (Gen. 15:6). Faith is put in the word of God's prophets because they speak for him, and he is absolutely trustworthy (Exod. 19:9; 2 Chr. 20:20). NT writers, especially Paul and the author of Hebrews, show that the faith manifested by OT saints was not different in kind from that expected of Christians.

In contrast with the relative infrequency of the relevant terms in the OT, the Greek word for "faith" (*pistis G4411*) and "believe" (*pisteuō G4409*) occur in the NT almost 500 times. A principal reason for this is that the NT makes the claim that the promised MESSIAH had finally come, and, to the bewilderment of many, the form of the fulfillment did not obviously correspond to the messianic promise. It required a true act of faith to believe that the humble and crucified Jesus of Nazareth was the promised Messiah. It was not long before "to believe" meant to become a Christian. In the NT, faith therefore becomes the supreme human act and experience.

In his miracles and teaching, Jesus aimed at creating in his disciples a complete trust in himself as the Messiah and Savior of sinners. He made it plain that faith is necessary for eternal life, that it is what God required in the OT, and that refusal to accept his claims will bring eternal ruin. His primary concern with his own disciples was to build up their faith in him.

The record in Acts shows that the first Christians called themselves "the believers" (Acts 2:44) and that they went everywhere persuading men and women and bringing them into obedience to the faith that is in Jesus (6:7; 17:4; 28:24). Before long, as communities of believers arose in various parts of the Mediterranean world, the apostolic leaders had to teach them more fully the meaning and implications of the Christian faith, and so the NT books appeared.

It is in Paul's letters that the meaning of faith is most clearly and fully set forth. Faith is trust in the person of Jesus, the truth of his teaching, and the redemptive work he accomplished at Calvary, and, as a result, a total submission to him and his message, which are accepted as from God. Faith in his person is faith in him as the eternal Son of God, the God-man, the second man or last Adam (1 Cor. 15:45, 47), who died in the sinner's stead, making possible justification with God, adoption into his family, sanctification, and, ultimately, glorification. His death brings REDEMPTION from sin in all its aspects. The truth of his claims is attested by God's raising him from the dead. Some day he will judge the living and the dead. Faith is not to be confused with a mere intellectual assent to the doctrinal teachings of Christianity, though that is obviously necessary. It includes a radical and total commitment to Christ as the Lord of one's life.

Unbelief, or lack of faith in the Christian gospel, appears everywhere in the NT as the supreme evil. Not to make a decisive response to God's offer in Christ means that the individual remains in sin and is eternally lost. Faith alone can save him.

faithfulness. An attribute or quality applied in the Bible to both God and human beings. When used of God, it has in the OT a twofold emphasis, referring first to his absolute reliability, firm constancy, and complete freedom from arbitrariness or fickleness, and also to his steadfast love and loyalty toward his people. God is constant and true in contrast to all that is not God. He is faithful in keeping his promises and is therefore worthy of trust. He is unchangeable in his ethical nature. God's faithfulness is usually connected with his gracious promises of salvation. Faithful men and women are dependable in fulfilling their responsibilities and in carrying out their word. In the NT there are frequent exhortations to faithfulness. It is listed as a fruit of the Spirit in Gal. 5:22.

falcon. See BIRDS.

fall, the. A term used with reference to the first SIN of ADAM and EVE, who through disobedience fell from the state of integrity in which God had created them and thus brought a curse upon themselves and their descendants. The fall is narrated in Gen. 3 as a historical fact, not as a myth. It stands in a context of historical facts. Though not directly alluded to again in the OT, it is regarded as historical by the NT writers (Rom. 5:12-13; 1 Cor. 15:22; 1 Tim. 2:14). Some philosophers and theologians think the account is an ALLEGORY describing the awakening of man from a brute state of self-consciousness and personality—a fall upward, rather than downward, but such an explanation conflicts radically with biblical teaching. There is no doubt that PAUL takes the account literally and sees in the fall the origin of sin in the human race. The scriptural view of sin and of redemption takes the fall for granted.

The Scriptures teach us that man was created in the IMAGE OF GOD, with a rational and moral nature like God's, with no inner impulse or drive to sin, and with a will free to do God's will. There was, moreover, nothing in Adam and Eve's environment to compel them to sin or to make sin excusable. In these circumstances, solicitation to sin could come only from outside. The Bible does not allow us to probe the mystery of the presence of sin in God's fair universe; as in so many other things, it faces us with the practical reality, the voice of the Tempter

F

coming from outside, the voice of the Serpent that the rest of the Bible recognizes as the voice of SATAN.

The sin that constituted the fall involved Adam and Eve in disobeying the word of God (Gen. 3:1-4) and challenging the goodness of God by imputing to him an ill motive (3:5). But chiefly it consisted in disobeying the law of God. Such was the bounty of the Creator that the whole lavish richness of the Garden of Eden was open to them with only a single condition (2:16-17). The fall was thus the breaking of the whole law of God. Equally involved in the fall was the whole of the human nature. Eve was first emotionally attracted to the forbidden fruit (3:6, "good for food and pleasing to the eye"); second, she was led into sin by a logic that contradicted the mind of God. He had said, "The tree of … knowledge … you will surely die" (2:17). Eve appears to have said to herself that a tree of knowledge was bound to make those who partake wise. It was a question of God's logic or hers. Third, the fall was an act of will: "she took … and ate it" (3:6). Emotions, mind, and will combined in the first sin. The whole law of God was broken by the whole nature of the sinner.

The effect of the fall, as Gen. 4 and the remainder of the Bible explicitly and implicitly bring out, was not merely immediate alienation from God for Adam and Eve, but guilt and depravity for all their posterity and the cursing of the earth. Redemption from the fall and its effects is accomplished through the Lord Jesus Christ (cf. Rom. 5:12-21; 1 Cor. 15:21-22, 45-49).

fallow deer. See ANIMALS.

fallow ground. Land that is left idle for a season after plowing and harrowing, so that weeds and insects are killed while the soil regains its fertility (cf. NRSV Jer. 4:3 and Hos. 10:12; NIV, "unplowed ground"). In addition, the expression "lie fallow" (NIV, "lie unplowed") is used in Exod. 23:11, which discusses the law of the sabbatical year, prescribing one year of rest every seven years for cultivated soil.

false apostle. A description used by PAUL only in 2 Cor. 11:13, applied to certain leaders who led the Corinthian Christians astray from their "sincere

and pure devotion to Christ" (v. 3) and preached "a Jesus other than the Jesus we preached" (v. 4). These false teachers boasted of their special religious prerogatives as Jews (v. 22). He also calls them "false brothers" (v. 26; Gal. 2:4). They were counterfeit apostles, but not from the circle of the apostles or apostolic men. Rather, they were members of the Judaizing party (see JUDAIZER) whose activity in the early churches gave the occasion for Paul's classic defense of his gospel and apostleship in the letter to the GALATIANS. See also FALSE PROPHET.

false brother. See FALSE APOSTLE.

false Christ. One who makes a spurious claim to be the MESSIAH. Jesus cautioned against such impostors (Matt. 24:24; Mk. 13:22). A false messiah is distinct from an ANTICHRIST. The former is an impersonator or impostor, usurping the title or allowing others to herald him as such. The latter, mentioned only by John (1 Jn. 2:18, 22; 4:3; 2 Jn. 7), indicates not impersonation as much as opposition by one who is against Christ.

false prophet. MOSES ordered the death of any PROPHET advocating the worship of another god (Deut. 13:1-4). During the monarchy, false prophets were often in the majority in the court of Israel. The 800 prophets of AHAB openly advocated the worship of BAAL and ASHERAH (1 Ki. 18:20). Later, 400 prophets, influenced by a lying spirit, assured Ahab of victory at RAMOTH GILEAD, only to be contradicted by MICAIAH, the true prophet (22:6-23). Frequently, lying prophets told the leaders what they wanted to hear (Jer. 5:31; Lk. 6:26). In the NT false prophets are often mentioned (1 Jn. 4:1) and are compared with wolves in sheep's clothing (Matt. 7:15) and false teachers (2 Pet. 2:1). The false prophet BAR-JESUS was smitten with blindness by PAUL (Acts 13:6, 11). Christ warned of false prophets whose miracles would deceive many in the end (Matt. 24:24; Mk. 13:22). In Rev. 13:12-14 and 19:20, the master false prophet is described. He will support the beast through powerful signs before his destruction.

false testimony, false witness. Bearing false testimony, particularly in court, is banned in the

OT laws (Exod. 20:16; 23:1; Deut. 5:20), and the false witness is subject to the penalty he intended to inflict on the accused (Deut. 19:16-21). Twice God is said to hate false witnesses (Prov. 6:19; Zech. 8:17). Jeremiah condemns those who swear falsely, even though they say, "As surely as the LORD lives" (Jer. 5:2). Note also the warning against taking the Lord's name in vain (Exod. 20:7). See LIE; OATH.

familiar spirit. This term is used by the KJV to render Hebrew ʾôb *H200*, which modern versions usually translate "medium." The Hebrew word appears to refer to the spirit of a dead person, which a medium, in the form of magic known as necromancy, claimed to summon to consultation (Deut. 18:11; see DIVINATION). In necromancy, in which the dead were consulted about the future, it was believed that either a spirit dwelt in the controlling medium (Lev. 20:27) or that the medium had fellowship with a spirit from whom she could receive information. The Mosaic law forbade the consulting of familiar spirits, and mediums were commanded to be put to death (Lev. 19:31; 20:6, 27; Deut. 18:11). Mediums seem to have deceived their inquirers by speaking in a thin weak voice, as though it came from the ground or from a bottle (Isa. 8:19; 29:4). King SAUL put away the mediums early in his reign, but, greatly worried about the outcome of his last battle, he consulted the witch of ENDOR and asked to speak to the prophet SAMUEL (1 Sam. 28:3, 7-9; 1 Chr. 10:13). It appears that Saul was told by the witch that she saw Samuel, and Saul himself entered into the conversation with the prophet. In the NT, Acts 16:16-18 tells of a slave girl who was a medium and brought her owners much gain by her divination.

family. The fundamental unity of human society and the center of God's COVENANT activity.

I. The general nature of the family. The Hebrew term *mišpāḥâ H5476*, having no exact equivalent in English, should be interpreted principally as "household." Another term for family, *bayit H1074* (lit., "house"), included all those living within the confines and jurisdiction of the dwelling. In a patriarchal setting the father was the head of the family, having authority over his wife, children, unmarried daughters, and sometimes married sons and their families, as well as cousins and their families and possibly grandparents and even great-grandparents (Gen. 46:8-26). Additional members of the household also included in the category of family would be concubines, servants, slaves, visitors, and occasionally prisoners of war. Some polygamy was practiced, and this also made the family unit more extensive.

In a wider sense, family could also mean clan, tribe, or village; and phrases such as "house of David" (Isa. 7:13) or "house of Israel" (Ezek. 9:9; 18:30) show that in broader terms the household could encompass the entire nation. Some families returning from EXILE in BABYLON comprised several hundred members (Ezra 8:1-14).

A common bond of blood bound together the members of the larger family or clan, who referred to each other as "brothers" (1 Sam. 20:29). Members of the clan accepted a communal responsibility for assistance, protection, the sharing of work, loyalty, and cooperation for the general well-being of the family. In places where the nomadic life gave way to a more settled existence, groups of villages (often interdependent and with intermarried members) formed a "family," as did the Danites at ZOREH and ESHTAOL (Jdg. 18:11). When arts and crafts developed, sons acquired skills from their fathers, and villages devoted to a particular type of production—such as wood or ironworking, linen or pottery (1 Chr. 4:14; cf. 4:21, 23; Neh. 11:35)—became common. With specialization, however, came a loss of the former self-sufficiency of the family and an increased interdependence on the producers of food and other goods.

In general, city life tended to fragment the family, and the size of the houses excavated indicates that in later times the family unit consisted only of father, mother, and children. During the kingdom, as family ties loosened, so the absolute authority and responsibility of the father was transferred to the king. By the eighth century B.C., the individual, instead of working primarily for the good of the larger group, worked for his immediate family and for the ultimate benefit of the king or nation. Not surprisingly, as the focus of the family unit sharpened, the sense of communal responsibility lessened, and biblical reminders concerning obligations toward widows and orphans became more

F

frequent (Isa. 1:17; Jer. 7:6). Family blood feuds declined as revenge for the honor of members of the wider family was no longer usual, though it was sometimes practiced and expected (2 Sam. 3:27; 16:8; 2 Ki. 9:26; Neh. 4:14).

By virtue of marriage, the husband and wife were regarded as being akin, and their children were legitimate family members. Close kinship was an obstacle to marriage in the clan or tribe, and Lev. 18:6-17 provided a list of degrees of relationship within which marriage was prohibited. One exception to this rule was the so-called LEVIRATE (i.e., husband's brother's) marriage (Deut. 25:5-10), in which a man was expected to marry the wife of a childless deceased brother so as to perpetuate his family name by means of children. Refusal to comply with this requirement brought shame upon the offender's house.

The family functioned as an essential unit of the religious community. The father was the spiritual head of the family and acted as the priest within the household. He was responsible for leading religious observances and for instructing the family in the religious and secular history of the Israelites, as well as in their manners and customs. The father maintained the family altar and ensured the religious observances and piety of the entire family. The religious observances and festivals were frequently family-oriented, particularly the Passover, which was observed as a religious family meal and thank offering (Exod. 12:3-4, 46). In patriarchal times, before worship was centralized in the TEMPLE, it was the fathers that offered sacrifice to God (Gen. 31:54). The supreme position of religious and secular authority that the father had helps to clarify the subsequent reverence for his grave.

In the Gospels, little reference is made to the family, except to reinforce monogamous MARRIAGE and to denounce DIVORCE (Matt. 5:27-32; 19:3-12; Mk. 10:2-12; Lk. 16:18). While a child, CHRIST set an example of obedience to parents, with whom he evidently remained until the beginning of his ministry, his brothers not understanding him (Matt. 10:36; Jn. 7:1-8). It is PAUL, however, who reinforces the duties of the family members (Eph. 5:22—6:9; Col. 3:18-22). He reiterates the financial responsibility of the members towards each other (1 Tim. 5:4, 8) and the importance of teaching religion in the home (Eph. 6:4). Also, in several of his epistles, Paul refers to the role of women in the family (1 Cor. 11:3; Eph. 5:22-24, 33; Col. 3:18; cf. also 1 Pet. 3:1-7). In Roman times, family ties loosened still further with the gradual disintegration of society. In the early church, however—where, in the absence of a church building, services took place in a private home—converts were often entire families (2 Tim. 1:5) or all the members of the household (Acts 16:15, 31-34).

II. Roles of family members

A. Father: provider, procreator of children, master, teacher, priest. In nomadic times the father, by means of his authority, held the family group together and became the symbol of their security in the encampment. His powers over the family members was awesome. His decisions could mean life or death; and as his status was unquestioned, he demanded respect and obedience. His responsibilities were extensive both within and beyond the family unit. In addition to providing for his own family security, he was expected from the time of the kingdom period to send his sons to defend the nation. Throughout biblical times the father was responsible for the economic well-being of those over whom he had authority. The entire family could be sold for falling into debt, and uncles and cousins would be expected to prevent family property from passing into outside hands (Lev. 25:25; Jer. 32:6-15). The father was also responsible for teaching his sons a trade, frequently his own, so that they would be productive members of both the family and society.

The teachings of Hebrew history, religion, law, and custom were passed on from father to son in the family setting (Exod. 10:2; 12:26; Deut. 4:9; 6:7) and reinforced by the many rites celebrated within the house, often associated with the family meal. All such occasions—whether in celebration of the Passover, some lesser feast, or an ordinary family meal—reinforced the faith, heritage, and nationalism of the family, as well as their own unity as a group. As the sons grew older it was the father's responsibility to find them suitable wives.

B. Mother: child-bearer, household manager, teacher. The list of a man's possessions included his wife, servants, slaves, goods, and animals (Exod. 20:17; Deut. 5:21). Even the phrase "to marry a wife" comes from a phrase that means "to become the master of a wife" (Deut. 21:13; 24:1). Although she would even address the husband in subservient terms, the status of the wife was higher than that of the rest of the household.

The primary responsibility of the mother was to produce children, preferably sons. A large number of sons, who became workers from an early age, ensured the future economic prosperity and security of the family. The maximum number of children was normally seven. Babies were weaned at approximately three years of age, and husband and wife did not normally have sexual relations between the child's birth and the completion of the weaning process.

Throughout her life a woman was subject to the protecting authority of a male relative—as a daughter, that of her father, and as a wife, that of her husband. If she became a widow, her nearest male relative became her protector, and under the levirate marriage provisions he could also be her "redeemer." Under such conditions the woman was subject to the man's authority.

The bride-price paid by the betrothed male to his fiancée's father, though not directly a "purchase price," was intended to compensate the father for the loss of his daughter's services. Because of the exchange of money on most occasions, the bride was left with the stigma of having been sold to her future husband (cf. Gen. 29:18, 27; Exod. 22:16-17; 1 Sam. 18:25; 2 Sam. 3:14). After the wedding the bride normally went to live with her husband's family. Thus she became part of that extended family group and was subject to its authority. Aside from the primary duty of childbearing (Gen. 1:28; 9:1), the wife's main responsibility was the organization of the household. This was her domain, and she was generally a respected manager. All aspects of food, from the collecting of olives and dates to the grinding of corn and cooking, were her responsibility, as well as the spinning and weaving of thread, the making of clothing, and the care of domestic animals.

The young children remained with their mother, and she was responsible for teaching the boys until they were about six years old, after which time they were likely to take on their own roles either as shepherds or goatherds. Some boys spent their days in the company of their father, whose skills they acquired by observation and practice. The daughters remained with their mother, who trained them in the arts of cooking, spinning, weaving, and general household management, as well as schooling them in their future roles as wives and mothers. When the wife provided a son, her position was a

Colossal statues made of hard limestone and representing the family of Pharaoh Amenophis III. From the temple of Midine, Habu (18th dynasty).

little more secure. Prior to that it was somewhat precarious. She could be divorced for any apparent offense (cf. Sir. 25:26). In early times, when polygamy was still practiced, the wife could find herself replaced by a second wife or sometimes by a CONCUBINE. Nevertheless, despite the status of the mother, her role in actual fact was not as difficult as it might seem. In many families her opinion was sought in decision making, and her ideas were respected (Exod. 20:12; Prov. 19:26; 20:20; Sir. 3:1-16).

By Persian times the status of the wife was showing definite improvement. She had her own position at games, the theaters, and religious festivals, often assisted her husband in business, and was known at times to manage her own property. In the NT one such woman, LYDIA of Thyatira (Acts 16:24), operated a textile business out of her own home.

C. Sons and daughters: status, childhood, education, and duties. The law of primogeniture provided a double portion of the inheritance as the birthright of the eldest son (Deut. 21:17). He always took precedence over his brothers and sisters (Gen. 43:33), and the elder of twins, even if only by a few minutes, could also hold this premier position with all its attendant privileges (25:24-26; 38:27-30). The right to primogeniture could be forfeited as a result of a serious offense (Gen. 35:22; 49:3-4; 1 Chr. 5:1), surrendered voluntarily, or sold, as Esau did to his brother Jacob (Gen. 25:29-34). David gave his kingdom to his youngest son, Solomon (1 Ki. 2:15), despite a law protecting the eldest son from the favoritism of a father toward a younger brother (Deut. 21:15-17). In a family that had no sons, property could be inherited by a daughter (Num. 27:8).

The inferior status of a daughter in patriarchal society is depicted clearly. She could be sold into slavery or into concubinage and then possibly resold (Exod. 21:7-11). Even her very life was at the disposition of her father. Both sons and daughters could be put to death for disobeying the head of the household. Abraham was prepared to sacrifice his son Isaac (Gen. 22:1-14). Judah ordered the burning of Tamar on suspicion that she, a widow, was having sexual relations with a man who was not of her late husband's family (Gen. 38:11-26), when she would normally have been expected to marry a relative of her husband and was, in fact, promised to his brother.

With the coming of the Mosaic law, a father could no longer put his child to death without referring the case to the authorities. Thus the elders heard accusations of disobedience, gluttony, and drunkenness, which, on conviction, were punishable with death by stoning (Deut. 21:20-21). Children, however, could no longer be held responsible for the crimes of their parents (24:16). By the time of David, there was the right of ultimate appeal to the monarch himself (2 Sam. 14:4-11).

Frequently, neither sons nor daughters were consulted when marriage partners were being selected for them. A marriage was often an alliance or contract between families, the wishes of the individual being regarded as unworthy of consideration. Although loved and valued, children were not pampered (Sir. 30:9-12). As family disciplinarian, the father spared neither the rod nor the whip (Prov. 13:24; 22:15; 29:15-17). In postexilic times, a son's more formal education took place within the precincts of the synagogue, and just prior to the time of Christ a form of general education was introduced into Palestine.

Childhood was brief, although boys and girls laughed, played, and sang. Some of them had whistles, rattles, and dolls, while the young ones sat on their mother's lap (Isa. 66:12). In later Judaism a boy's coming of age was celebrated in a manner that reinforced his position within the home and also within the religious family of the synagogue. As soon as they were old enough, both boys and girls were expected to gather fuel (Jer. 7:18), care for cattle, and tend the flocks.

Protecting sheep from wild beasts and from the danger of injuring themselves in the mountain crevices, finding them good pasture and water, and carrying them home when sick or injured, was neither a light task nor a small responsibility (Gen. 29:6; Exod. 2:16; 1 Sam. 16:11). Young boys and girls would often follow their fathers to the fields to watch and help, but more often the girls would be learning the household skills from their mothers. One of the most menial and arduous tasks was that of fetching water, often from some considerable distance, and this was the responsibility of the mother or the daughter. Young girls were by no means secluded; rather, they were free to go about unveiled and visit with friends and neighbors (Gen. 34:1).

Bearing in mind that all members of the household were subject to the strict authority of the head of the family, it is not surprising that as the household became smaller in postexilic times, it became the practice (where it was feasible practically and economically) for the married sons to move out of the patriarchal home and to set up their own family units.

III. Figurative use. The concept of family in its broadest and most figurative sense is seen in the phrase "house of Israel" (Isa. 5:7), meaning the entire nation. In the OT, the relationship between God and Israel is seen in such family terms as "bride" (Jer. 2:1), "daughter" (8:19; 31:22), "children" (3:14), or "betrothal" (Hos. 2:19-20). In the NT, the bridal imagery describing the relationship between Christ and the church is continued (2 Cor. 11:2; Eph. 5:25-33; Rev. 19:7; 21:9) and is given deep spiritual emphasis, and the CHURCH is referred to as the household of God (Gal. 6:10; Eph. 2:19; 3:15; 1 Pet. 4:17).

famine. An acute and prolonged food shortage (Heb. *rāʿāb H8280* and Gk. *limos G3350*, both of which can also be translated "hunger"). In ancient times in Palestine and Egypt, famines were not infrequent. They were produced by lack of rainfall in due season, destructive hail storms and rain out of season, destruction of crops by locusts and caterpillars, and the cutting off of food supplies by a siege. Pestilence often followed, and the suffering was great. Famines that were the result of natural causes are recorded as occurring in the time of Abraham (who left Canaan and stayed in Egypt, Gen. 12:10), Joseph (when famine "had spread over the whole country," 41:56), the judges (Ruth 1:1), David (2 Sam. 21:1), Ahab and Elijah (1 Ki. 17:1; 18:2), Elisha (2 Ki. 4:38; Lk. 4:25), and Nehemiah (Neh. 5:3). Famines were caused in Samaria and Jerusalem when these cities came under siege (2 Ki. 6:25; 25:3). The NT speaks of a famine "over the entire Roman world" (Acts 11:28) during the reign of Claudius. In the Olivet Discourse, Jesus predicted famines in various places (Matt. 24:7; Mk. 13:8; Lk. 21:11), a prophecy believed to be partly fulfilled in the siege of Jerusalem by the Roman general Titus. Famines are sometimes said to be sent as punishments, and sometimes they are threatened as such (Lev. 26:19-20; Deut. 28:49-51; 2 Ki. 8:1; Isa. 14:30; 51:19; Jer. 14:12, 15; Ezek. 5:16). To be preserved in time of famine is a special mark of God's favor and power (Job 5:20; Ps. 33:19; 37:19). Sometimes the word *famine* is used in a figurative sense, as when Amos says that God will send a famine, not of bread and water, but "a famine of hearing the words of the Lord" (Amos 8:11).

fan. See winnowing fork.

farming. The Israelites in the time of the patriarchs were a nomadic people. They first learned agriculture in Palestine after the conquest of Canaan. After that a large proportion of the people were engaged in agrarian pursuits. The pages of the Bible have much to say about agricultural occupations.

Agriculture was the background for the legislation of Israel. At the time of the conquest every family probably received a piece of land, marked off by stones that could not be removed lawfully (Deut. 19:14; 27:17; Hos. 5:10). On the year of Jubilee those who had lost their ancestral estates recovered possession of them. Terracing was necessary to make use of soil on the hillsides. Irrigation was not required, since there was usually sufficient rainfall (see rain). Aside from the Negev and other desert regions, the soil of Palestine was generally fertile. Fertilizing was almost unknown. To maintain the fertility of the land, the law required that farms, vineyards, and olive orchards were to lie fallow in the seventh year (Exod. 23:10).

Plowing to prepare the land for sowing was done in autumn, when the early rains softened the ground that had become stone-hard in the summer sun. This was done with a crude wooden plow drawn by oxen or, if the soil was thin, with a mattock. With such implements the surface of the ground was hardly more than scratched (perhaps 3-4 in./8-10 cm.). Little harrowing was done and was probably unknown in Palestine in early times.

The summer grain was sown between the end of January and the end of February. Usually the seed was scattered by hand from a basket, but careful farmers put it in furrows in rows (Isa. 28:25). Between sowing and reaping, the crops were

Modern farmer still using an ancient technique for plowing his field.

© Dr. James C. Martin

exposed to several dangers: the failure of the latter rain, which came in March and April; the hot, drying easterly winds that often came in March and April (Gen. 41:6); hail storms (Hag. 2:17); various kinds of weeds like tares and thorns (Jer. 12:13; Matt. 13:7, 25); injurious insects, especially the palmerworm, the cankerworm, the caterpillar, and the locust (Amos 7:2); the thefts of crows and sparrows (Matt. 13:4); and fungus diseases, especially mildew (Deut. 28:22). As the harvest season approached, particularly valuable crops were protected by watchmen (Jer. 4:17); but the law permitted a hungry person to pick grain when passing by (Deut. 23:25; Matt. 12:1).

The time of HARVEST varied somewhat according to the climatic condition of each region, but usually began about the middle of April with the coming of the dry season. Barley was the first grain to be cut, and this was followed a few weeks later with wheat. The grain harvest generally lasted about seven weeks, from Passover to Pentecost. Whole families moved out of their village homes to live in the fields until the harvest was over. The grain was cut with a sickle and laid in swaths behind the reaper. It was then bound into sheaves and gathered into shocks (Exod. 22:6). In the interest of the POOR, the law forbade a field to be harvested to its limits.

The grain was threshed in the open air, a custom made possible because the harvest season was free from rain (2 Ki. 13:7). During the threshing time the grain was guarded by harvesters who spent the nights on the threshing floor (Ruth 3:6). The threshing floor was constructed in an exposed position in the fields, preferably on a slight elevation, so as to get the full benefit of the winds. It consisted of a circular area 25-40 ft. (8-12 m.) in diameter, sloping slightly upward at the edges, and was usually surrounded with a border of stones to keep in the grain. The floor was level and hard. The sheaves of grain, brought in from the fields on the backs of men and animals, were heaped in the center. From this heap, sheaves were spread out on the floor; and then either several animals tied abreast were driven round and round the floor or two oxen were yoked together to a threshing machine, which they dragged in a circular path over the grain until the kernels of grain were separated from the stalks.

The threshing machines were of two kinds, a board with the bottom studded with small stones or nails, or a kind of threshing wagon. While this was going on, the partly threshed grain was turned over with a fork. After that the grain was winnowed by tossing the grain and chaff into the air with a wooden fork or shovel so that the wind might blow away the chaff. This was usually done at night, to take advantage of the night breezes. The chaff was either burned or left to be scattered by the winds. The grain was then sifted with a sieve to remove stones and other impurities, and collected into pits or barns (Lk. 12:18).

farthing. See MONEY.

fasting. The act of abstaining from food, especially for religious purposes. The only fast required by the Mosaic law was that of the Day of Atonement (Lev. 16:29, 31; 23:27-32; Num. 29:7; KJV, "afflict your souls"; NIV, "deny yourselves"). See ATONEMENT, DAY OF. Throughout the OT period, however, there are many examples of fasts on special occasions, held because of transgression or to ward off present or impending calamity. SAMUEL called for such a fast (1 Sam. 7:6); JEHOIAKIM proclaimed a fast after BARUCH had read the condemnatory word of the Lord given through JEREMIAH (Jer. 36:9); JEZEBEL hypocritically called a fast when she sought to secure NABOTH's vineyard (1 Ki. 21:9, 12). We read of individuals who were moved to fast—for example, DAVID, when his child became ill (2 Sam. 12:16, 21-23), and AHAB on hearing his doom (1 Ki. 21:27).

After the EXILE, four annual fasts were held in memory of the national calamities through which the nation had passed. They are mentioned only in Zech. 7:1-7; 8:19. These fasts, established during the captivity, were held in the fourth, fifth, seventh, and tenth months. By the time of Christ they had fallen into disuse and were not revived until after the destruction of Jerusalem by the Romans. In rabbinic times the Feast of Purim, the origin of which is explained in the book of Esther (Esth. 9:31-32), was accompanied by a fast in commemoration of the fast of ESTHER, MORDECAI, and the Jews (4:1-3, 15-17). The OT gives a number of instances of other fasts in which the whole people joined (Ezra 8:21-23; Neh. 9:1). Examples of fasts by individuals are given in Neh. 1:4 and Dan. 9:3. A fast of great strictness was proclaimed by the heathen king of Nineveh to avert the destruction threatened by the Lord through Jonah (Jon. 3:5).

DAYS OF FASTING IN THE JEWISH SACRED YEAR	
17 Tammuz (Jun-Jul)	Breaking through the walls of Jerusalem (Second Temple).
9 Ab (Jul-Aug)	Destruction of the Temple.
3 Tishri (Sept-Oct)	Fast of Gedaliah.
10 Tishri	Day of Atonement.
10 Tebeth (Dec-Jan)	Beginning of the siege on Jerusalem (Second Temple).
13 Adar (Feb-Mar)	Fast of Esther.

Fasting among the Israelites was either partial or total, depending on the length of the fast. When Daniel mourned three full weeks, he ate no "choice food; no meat or wine touched my lips" (Dan. 10:2-3). Another longer fast is mentioned in Neh. 1:4. The fast on the Day of Atonement was "from the evening … until the following evening" (Lev. 23:32); and no food or drink was taken. Other daylong fasts were from morning till evening. The fasts of Moses and Elijah for forty days were exceptional (Exod. 34:28; 1 Ki. 19:8).

Religious fasting was observed as a sign of mourning for sin, with the object of deprecating divine wrath or winning divine compassion. The prophets often condemn the abuse of the custom, for Israelites superstitiously thought that it had value even when not accompanied by purity and righteousness of life (Isa. 58:3-7; Jer. 14:10-12; Zech. 7-8). Fasts were not necessarily religious in nature. They were commonplace when someone near and dear died, as when the inhabitants of Jabesh fasted after they had buried Saul and Jonathan (1 Sam. 31:13) and after the death of Abner (2 Sam. 1:12).

There are few references to fasting in the Gospels, but what is said shows that frequent fasts were customary with those Jews who desired to lead a specially religious life. We are told that Anna "worshiped night and day, fasting and praying" (Lk. 2:37). Again, the Pharisee in the parable says, "I fast twice a week" (18:12). Jesus fasted for forty days in the wilderness, but it is not clear whether this fast was voluntary or not. There is no reason to doubt that he observed the usual prescribed public fasts, but neither by practice nor by precept did he stress fasting. Jesus was so unascetic in his ordinary mode of life that he was reproached with being "a glutton and a drunkard" (Matt. 11:19; Lk. 7:34). The references to fasting in Matt. 17:21 and Mk. 9:29 do not occur in the earliest MSS (cf. NIV mg.). Jesus did speak of fasting on two occasions recorded in the Gospels:

Matt. 6:16-18. Here voluntary fasting is presupposed as a religious exercise, but Jesus warns against making it an occasion for a parade of piety. The important thing is purity and honesty of intention. Fasting should be to God, not to impress human beings. Jesus approves of fasting if it is an expression of inner contrition and devotion. The externalism of the Pharisees had its own reward.

Matt. 9:14-17 (parallels Mk. 2:18-22; Lk. 5:33-39). In this incident the disciples of John and of the Pharisees ask Jesus, "How is it that we and the Pharisees fast, but your disciples do not fast?" Jesus replies that fasting, which is a sign of mourning, would be inconsistent with the joy that should characterize those who know that the Messiah has finally come and is now with them. The time will come, however, when he will be taken away, and then his disciples will mourn. Jesus here sanctions fasting, as he does in the Sermon on the Mount; but he refuses to force it on his disciples. In the parables of the old wineskins and the old garment he shows that fasting belongs to the body of old observances and customs and is not congruous with the liberty of the gospel. The new era that he inaugurates must have new forms of its own.

The book of Acts has a few direct references to fasting. The church at Antioch fasted and prayed before sending out Paul and Barnabas as missionaries (Acts 13:2-3). On Paul's first missionary journey, elders were appointed in every church, with prayer and fasting (14:23). The reference to the fasting of Cornelius (10:30), found in KJV and many MSS, is omitted by the NIV and other modern versions. The only other direct references

F

to fasting in the NT are found in 2 Cor. 6:5 and 11:27, where Paul describes his sufferings for Christ; and here, most likely, he has in mind involuntary fasting.

fat, fatted. The first reference to fat in the Bible is in Genesis: "Abel brought fat portions from some of the firstborn of his flock. The LORD looked with favor on Abel and his offering" (Gen. 4:4; see ABEL). According to the Mosaic law, all the fat of sacrificed animals belonged to the Lord and was burned as an offering to him, "a pleasing aroma" (Lev. 3:14-16; 7:30). The fatty portions are specified in Lev. 3-7 as the fat of the entrails, of the kidneys, and of the liver, and also the tail of the sheep. The fat had to be offered on the day the animal was sacrificed (Exod. 23:18). It is sometimes asserted that the eating of any fat was forbidden to the Israelites; however, the prohibition did not apply to animals slain solely for food, but only to specified parts of sacrificed animals (Deut. 12:15, 16, 21-24). A "fatling" (e.g., 2 Sam. 6:13 NRSV) was a young animal fattened for slaughter (cf. the references to "fatted" calves, 1 Sam. 18:24; Lk. 15:23; et al.). The word *fat* is sometimes used in a figurative sense to signify the best part of anything, for example, "the fat of the land" (Gen. 45:18), "the fat of wheat" (Ps. 81:16 lit.; NIV, "the finest of wheat"). (Note that the KJV also uses the now archaic terms *fat* and *winefat* with the meanings "vat" and "winepress"; see Joel 2:24; 3:13; Isa. 63:2; Mk. 12:1.) See SACRIFICE AND OFFERINGS.

fate. See DESTINY.

father. A male parent or ancestor (Heb. *ʾāb H3*; Gk. *patēr G4252*). In the Hebrew FAMILY the father had absolute rights over his children. He could sell them into slavery and have them put to death. Reverence and obedience by children is prescribed from the earliest times (Exod. 20:12; Lev. 19:3; Deut. 5:16). The Scriptures many times set forth the character and duties of an ideal father (e.g., Deut. 4:9; 6:7; 31:13; Prov. 22:6; Isa. 28:9). The term is used also of both immediate and remote ancestors. It may refer to a grandfather, as when ABRAHAM is called JACOB's father (Gen. 28:13). More broadly, God told Abraham that he

would be the "father of many nations" (17:4). The founders of the Hebrew race, the PATRIARCHS, are referred to as its fathers (Rom. 9:5 KJV); so also heads of clans (Exod. 6:14; 1 Chr. 27:1).

In addition, the word has many figurative and derived uses: a spiritual ancestor, whether good or bad (e.g., Abraham, "the father of all who believe," Rom. 4:11; and the devil, "You belong to your father, the devil," Jn. 8:44); the originator of a mode of life ("Jabal ... the father of those who live in tents and raise livestock," Gen. 4:20); one who exhibits paternal kindness and wisdom to another (Jdg. 17:10); a revered superior, especially a prophet and an elderly and venerable man (1 Sam. 10:12; 1 Jn. 2:13); royal advisors and prime ministers (Gen. 45:8); a source ("Does the rain have a father?" Job 38:28).

God is Father: As Creator of the universe, "the Father of the heavenly lights" (Jas. 1:17); as Creator of the human race, "Have we not all one father?" (Mal. 2:10); as one who begets and takes care of his spiritual children, "you received the Spirit of sonship. And by him we cry, 'Abba, Father'" (Rom. 8:15). See ABBA. In a special and unique sense, God is the Father of Jesus Christ (Matt. 11:26; Mk. 14:36; Lk. 22:42).

fatherless. See ORPHAN.

father's house. See HOUSE.

fathom. See WEIGHTS AND MEASURES.

fatling. See FAT.

fauna. See ANIMALS.

fawn. See ANIMALS.

fear. This word in English has two principal meanings: (1) an apprehension of evil that normally leads one either to flee or to fight and (2) awe and reverence that a person of sense feels in the presence of God and, to a less extent, in the presence of a king or other dread authority. A child feels the first of these in the presence of a cruel parent and feels the second before one who is good but who must also be just. Several Hebrew words are translated "fear" in the OT, especially the verb *yārē*ʾ *H3710* and its cognates. The corresponding Greek verb is *phobeomai G5828*; noun *phobos G5832*.

The most prevalent use of this concept in the Bible is the fear of God. The majesty and HOLINESS of God cannot but incite fear in human beings (Job 37:22-24). The phrases "the fear of God" and "the fear of the Lord" occur frequently in the Bible, particularly in the OT. The Hebrew deity was awesome, so naturally the Israelites were constantly called on to "fear the LORD your God and serve him" (Deut. 10:20; note that "serve" helps to define "fear"). The admonition was an instrument with two edges, rewards and restraints. "The fear of God" is synonymous with true religion, and therefore rewarding. It was considered so as early as ABRAHAM's day. When that patriarch misrepresented his wife SARAH to ABIMELECH, he gave as his reason, "I said to myself, 'There is surely no fear of God in this place'" (Gen. 20:11). "The fear of God" was required in the following ways: by keeping his commandments (Exod. 20:20); by serving him and keeping his statutes (Deut. 6:13, 24); by hearkening to his voice (1 Sam. 12:14); and by worshiping in his temple (Ps. 5:7).

There is also a fear that debilitates and demoralizes. The wicked person is destroyed by his fears (cf. Prov. 28:1). Fear can take its toll among good people (cf. Jn. 19:38). God said to Abraham, "Do not be afraid, Abram. I am your shield, your very great reward" (Gen. 15:1). DAVID exclaimed triumphantly, "I fear no evil, for you are with me" (Ps. 23:4). Divine visible presence, after the first startling moments, always dispelled fears (Exod. 3:6; Lk. 1:30; 2:10; Matt. 14:27; 17:6-7). Though the awesome nature of God will never diminish, his Fatherly LOVE has been manifested through Jesus. His tenderness has replaced terror. Consequently, John could give the Christian antidote for fear: "There is no fear in love. But perfect love drives out fear, because fear has to do with punishment. The one who fears is not made perfect in love" (1 Jn. 4:18). The Christian should have no fear of hunger, nakedness, sickness, suffering, wicked people, death, nor judgment. All have lost their power of fear in the love of Christ. "Do not be afraid, little flock, for your Father has been pleased to give you the kingdom" (Lk. 12:32).

Fear of Isaac. This expression appears twice in Scripture (Gen. 31:42, 53; in the latter passage, "the Fear of his father Isaac"). It is generally thought to be a name for God, pointing to his protective care and power, which inspires terror in his enemies. A few scholars have argued that in these passages the Hebrew term for "fear" (*paḥad H7065*) has a different meaning, such as "kinsman" or "thigh" (the latter sense supposedly being related to oath-making; cf. Gen. 24:2, where a different word is used).

feasts. Sacred festivals held an important place in Jewish religion. They were religious services accompanied by demonstrations of joy and gladness. In Lev. 23, where they are described most fully, they are called "sacred assemblies" (KJV, "holy convocations"). Their times, except for the two instituted after the EXILE, were fixed by divine appointment. Their purpose was to promote spiritual interests of the community. The people met in holy fellowship for acts and purposes of sacred worship. They met before God in holy assemblies.

I. The weekly Sabbath (Lev. 23:3). This celebration stood at the head of the sacred seasons. The holy meetings by which the SABBATH was distinguished were quite local. Families and other small groups assembled under the guidance of Levites or elders and engaged in common acts of devotion, the forms and manner of which were not prescribed. Little is known of where or how the people met before the captivity, but after it they met in SYNAGOGUES and were led in worship by teachers learned in the law.

II. The Passover, or the Feast of Unleavened Bread (Lev. 23:4-8). The Passover was the first of all the annual feasts, and historically and religiously it was the most important of all. It was called both the Feast of the Passover and the Feast of Unleavened Bread, the two really forming a double festival. It was celebrated on the first month of the religious year, on the fourteenth of Nisan (our April), and commemorated the deliverance of the Jews from Egypt and the establishment of Israel as a nation by God's redemptive act. The Feast of Unleavened Bread began on the day after the Passover and lasted seven days (23:5-8). This combined feast was one of the three that all male Jews who were physically able and ceremonially clean were required by the Mosaic law to attend (Exod. 23:17; Deut. 16:16). The other two were the Feast of Weeks, or Pentecost, and the Feast of Tabernacles. These were known as the pilgrimage festivals; on all of them special sacrifices were offered, varying according to the character of the festival (Num. 28-29).

A *sukkah* made from palm fronds. The Israelites built such shelters during the Feast of Tabernacles or Booths (Sukkoth).

Theologically the Passover finds its heart in the doctrine of PROPITIATION. The Lord entered Egypt bent on judgment (Exod. 12:12); but, seeing the blood, he passed over that house completely at peace with those who were sheltering there. His wrath was assuaged by the blood of the lamb.

III. The Feast of Pentecost (Lev. 23:15-21). Other names for Pentecost are the Feast of Weeks, the Day of the Firstfruits, and the Feast of Harvests. It was celebrated on the sixth day of the month of Sivan (May–June), seven weeks after the offering of the wave sheaf after the Passover. The name *Pentecost* (from a Gk. word meaning "fiftieth") originated from the fact that there was an interval of fifty days between the two feasts. The feast lasted a single day (Deut. 16:9-12) and marked the completion of the wheat HARVEST. The characteristic ritual of this feast was the offering and waving of two loaves of leavened bread, made from ripe grain that had just been harvested. This was done by the priest in the name of the congregation. In addition to these wave offerings, the people were to give the Lord an offering of the firstfruits of their produce. The amount of the offering was not designated.

IV. The Feast of Trumpets or New Moon (Lev. 23:23-25). This celebration was held on the first day of the seventh month, Tishri (Sept.–Oct.), which began the civil year of the Jews. It corresponded to our New Year's Day, and on it, from morning to evening, horns and trumpets were blown. After the exile the day was observed by the public reading of the law and by general rejoicing.

V. The Day of Atonement (Lev. 23:26-32). This sacred event was observed on the tenth day of Tishri. It was really less a feast than a fast, as the distinctive character and purpose of the day was to bring the collective sin of the whole year to remembrance so that it might earnestly be dealt with and atoned for. On this day the high priest made confession of all the sins of the community and entered on their behalf into the Most Holy Place with the blood of reconciliation. It was a solemn occasion, when God's people through godly sorrow and atonement for sin entered into the rest of God's mercy and favor. In receiving his forgiveness, they could rejoice before him and carry out his commandments.

VI. The Feast of Tabernacles (Lev. 23:33-43). Also called the Feast of Booths or Ingathering, this was the last of the sacred festivals under the old covenant in preexilic times. It began five days after the Day of Atonement (Lev. 23:34; Deut. 16:13) and lasted seven days. It marked the completion of the harvest and historically commemorated the wanderings in the wilderness. During this festival people lived in booths and tents to remind themselves of how their forefathers wandered in the wilderness and lived in booths. The sacrifices of this feast were more numerous than at any other. The last day of the feast marked the conclusion of the ecclesiastical year. The whole feast was popular and joyous in nature.

Besides the above feasts, which were all preexilic and instituted by God, the Jews after the Captivity added two others, the Feast of Lights, or Dedication, and the Feast of Purim.

F

THE JEWISH SACRED YEAR		
	MONTH	**SPECIAL DAYS**
Nisan	(Mar.–Apr.)	14—Passover 15—Unleavened Bread 21—Close of Passover
Iyar	(Apr.–May)	
Sivan	(May–June)	6—Feast of Pentecost (seven weeks after the Passover)
Tammuz	(June–July)	
Ab	(July–Aug.)	
Elul	(Aug.–Sept.)	
Tishri	(Sept.–Oct.)	1–2—The Feast of Trumpets (*Rosh Hashannah*, beginning of the civil year) 10—Day of Atonement 15–21—Feast of Tabernacles
Marchesvan	(Oct.–Nov.)	
Kislev	(Nov.–Dec.)	25—Feast of Lights (*Hanukkah*)
Tebeth	(Dec.–Jan.)	
Shebet	(Jan.–Feb.)	
Adar	(Feb.–Mar.)	14—Feast of Purim

VII. The Feast of Lights was observed for eight days beginning on the twenty-fifth day of Kislev (Nov.–Dec.). It was instituted by the MACCABEES in 164 B.C. when the temple, which had been defiled by ANTIOCHUS Epiphanes, king of Syria, was cleansed and rededicated to the service of the Lord. During these days the Israelites met in their synagogues, carrying branches of trees in their hands, and held jubilant services. The children were told the brave and stirring deeds of the Maccabees so that they might emulate them.

VIII. The Feast of Purim ("lots") is kept on the fourteenth and fifteenth days of Adar (Feb.–Mar.), the last month of the religious year. It was instituted by MORDECAI to commemorate the failure of HAMAN's plots against the Jews (Esth. 9:20-22, 26-28). On the evening of the thirteenth it became customary to read the whole book of Esther publicly in the synagogue. It was a joyous occasion. See also CALENDAR.

feet, washing of. See FOOTWASHING.

Felix. fee′liks (Gk. *Phēlix G5772*, from Lat. *fēlix*, "fruitful, fortunate"). Born Antonius Claudius, he was a freedman of the family of Emperor CLAUDIUS (A.D. 41-54). Felix and his brother Pallas were favorites of Claudius and later of NERO (54-68), and so Felix evidently thought that he could do as he pleased. The Roman historian Tacitus said of him that "he revelled in cruelty and lust, and wielded the power of a king with the mind of a slave." His very title of PROCURATOR hints at his fiscal duties of procuring funds for ROME, which he seems to have accomplished with all sorts of tyranny. He began his career as procurator of JUDEA by seducing Drusilla, the sister of AGRIPPA II and wife of the king of Emesa (modern Homs), and marrying her. Because she was Jewish (at least in part), he learned much of Jewish life and customs.

Felix appears in the biblical account only in Acts 23:24—25:14. He was susceptible to flattery, as the speech of TERTULLUS shows, and also to conviction of sin, as is shown by his terror when PAUL reasoned before him about "righteousness, self-control

© Dr. James C. Martin. The Rockefeller Museum, Jerusalem. Photographed by permission.

F

Coin minted during the procuratorship of Antonius Felix.

and the judgment to come" (24:25). His conviction faded and he procrastinated. He held Paul for about two years (c. 58-60), hoping that the apostle "would offer him a bribe" for his freedom (24:26). Felix was then replaced by FESTUS, a far better man.

felloe. Variant form of *felly*, which refers to the rim of a wheel supported by spokes. It is used by the KJV once in connection with the wheels of the ten bronze stands in the temple (1 Ki. 7:33; NIV, "spokes").

fellow. This English term (meaning "man, companion, peer") is used in Bible versions to render several words and expressions (e.g., Exod. 2:13 KJV; the NIV and NRSV clarify, "fellow Hebrew"). The term can be used in expressions of contempt (Matt. 9:3 et al.). It also occurs frequently as an adjective in combination with various nouns (e.g., "fellow worker," Rom. 16:3; "fellow servant," Col. 4:7; et al.).

fellowship. The meaningful Greek term *koinōnia* G3126 ("association, communion") and its cognates stand for one of the most powerful concepts in the Scriptures. They apply first of all to participation in a person or project and a "common" spirit. Fellowship in the family of God comes after the new birth (2 Cor. 5:17; 1 Jn. 3:9; see REGENERATION). Christians partake of Christ (Heb. 3:14), and of the HOLY SPIRIT (6:4; in Hebrews a different Gk. term is used, *metochos* G3581). True fellowship

results in mutual LOVE (Jn. 13:34). The significant KJV rendering "communicate" (for the verb *koinoneō* G3125, Gal. 6:6) touches the heart of the Christian spirit: those who are taught in the Word of God are admonished to exercise their sense of community or fellowship sharing. This was an essential strength of the early Christians. Although a minority movement, they shared the strength of belonging to each other and to God.

The notion of *koinonia* can have negative aspects as well. A Christian has no genuine "fellowship" with an unbeliever, whose nature is different (2 Cor. 6:14-16). Pagan ceremonies are not a part of true *koinonia* (1 Cor. 10:20-22). Christians should have no "fellowship" with unfruitful works of darkness (Eph. 5:11 KJV). True NT *koinonia* is rooted in a depth of fellowship with God as Father (1 Jn. 1:3, 6). Christians must continue to walk in the light to enjoy this fellowship. They are called to fellowship with the Son (1 Cor. 1:9). The Lord's SUPPER is a symbol of this inner fellowship (10:16). Fellowship with the Spirit is a blessing of Christians (2 Cor. 13:14). The true *koinonia* is not only earthly, but continues and is consummated in heaven (Rev. 21:1-4). See also COMMUNITY OF GOODS; CONTRIBUTION.

fellowship offering. See SACRIFICE AND OFFERINGS.

female. See WOMAN.

fence. This English term is used frequently by the KJV, especially in the expression "fenced city," which is better rendered "fortified city" (Num. 32:17 et al.). The NIV uses "fence" only in Ps. 62:3, where the psalmist speaks of his oppressors as a "leaning wall" and a "tottering fence," that is, ready to fall over.

ferret. See ANIMALS.

ferry boat. Term used once by the KJV to render a Hebrew noun that simply means "ford" or "crossing" (2 Sam. 19:18). Because the Hebrew expression is unusual, the KJV translators either misinterpreted the noun or rendered the clause freely, "And there went over a ferry boat to carry over the king's household" (cf. NIV, "They crossed at the ford to take the king's household over").

Fertile Crescent. This term does not occur in Scripture but is a modern description of the territory that may roughly be described as reaching NW from the Persian Gulf through MESOPOTAMIA, then W to the northern part of SYRIA, then SW through Syria and PALESTINE. In this crescent-shaped area the land is mostly rich and fertile and is watered by the TIGRIS, the EUPHRATES, the ORONTES, the JORDAN, and numerous rivers descending W in LEBANON. In most of the region irrigation has also long been employed. Various grains such as wheat and barley, and fruits such as grapes, olives, figs, oranges, lemons, and pomegranates abound. A journey in a straight line across the crescent from one end to the other would go mostly through the great Syrian desert, with only an occasional oasis. This configuration of the land explains much of Bible history.

fertility cults. Religions that promoted the fertility of humans, animals, and crops by celebrating the myth of a dying-and-rising god with rites of mourning and of later jubilation. The god was believed to typify the death and renewal of vegetation. A "sacred marriage" between the god, represented by the king, and the goddess, represented by a hierodule (temple slave or prostitute), also was believed to promote the fertility of the land. Some scholars have thought that the fertility-cult background is a key to the interpretation of a number of books of the OT. They argue that the Canaanite fertility cult was transmitted to Israel when the prophets exalted Yahweh as the god of the sacred marriage in place of BAAL. Others have compared the RESURRECTION OF JESUS CHRIST to the resurrection of such deities as Attis, Adonis, or Osiris, and have attributed some of PAUL's teachings to a dependence upon pagan mysteries. Further research, however, has tended to undermine seriously the thesis of a generically similar series of fertility cults, on the one hand, and the thesis of the dependence of Christianity upon the pagan mysteries, on the other hand.

festivals. See FEASTS.

Festus, Porcius. fes′tuhs, por′shuhs (Gk. *Phēstos G5776* [from Lat. *fēstus*, "festal, joyful"], *Porkios G4517* [a Roman clan name]). Roman governor who succeeded FELIX in the province of JUDEA (Acts 24:27). The date of his accession is uncertain. Almost nothing is known of the life of Festus before his appointment by NERO as PROCURATOR of Judea. He appears in the Bible (24:27—26:32) principally in his relationship with his prisoner, the apostle PAUL. Festus was apparently a far better and more efficient man than his predecessor. At the very beginning of his rule, he took up the case of Paul, and as King AGRIPPA II said, Paul "could have been set free if he had not appealed to Caesar" (26:32). Paul had made this appeal when Festus, at the request of the Jews, was considering bringing Paul to Jerusalem for trial. Festus evidently knew that Paul was a good man (25:25), but he was unable to understand Paul's reasoning with King Agrippa and thought that Paul had gone mad with much study (26:24). Festus died at his post and was followed about A.D. 62 by Albinus.

fetters. See SHACKLES.

fever. See DISEASES.

field. The biblical "field" was usually not enclosed, but marked off from its neighbors by stone markers at the corners and sometimes one or two along the sides. Because they were unenclosed, and because of normally unsettled conditions, a watchman was often employed, especially when the crop was nearing maturity. Besides the danger of human intruders, there might be danger from straying cattle or even of cattle driven by rustlers (Exod. 22:5), and of fire if a SAMSON (Jdg. 15:5) or an angry ABSALOM (2 Sam. 14:30) were about. The word is used also in a larger sense for "territory," as in Gen. 36:35 (KJV), where "the country of Moab" (NIV) is intended; and as in the parable of the tares (Matt. 13:38), where "the field is the world." Many of the ancient "fields" were the habitat of wild animals (Ps. 80:13).

Field of Blood. See AKELDAMA.

fiery serpent. This expression is used by the KJV with reference to the desert vipers that attacked the Hebrews in the wilderness as they journeyed around MOAB (Num. 21:6, 8; Deut. 8:15). Their bite was cured miraculously when the victim looked at the

F

bronze serpent made by MOSES on that occasion (see NEHUSHTAN). The context suggests a poisonous viper living in the desert regions near biblical Moab. In other usages, the same Hebrew term refers to legendary creatures (the flying serpents of Isa. 14:29; 30:6) or supernatural angelic beings (the SERAPHS of 6:2-7). This raises the possibility that the term is used in Num. 21:6 not because it normally designated a particular kind of snake, but rather to emphasize the supernatural, miraculous character of the plague.

fig. See PLANTS.

figure. This English term is used variously in Bible versions to render several words. Special interest attaches to the use of "figure" in the KJV to render Greek *typos G5596*, a term that has a wide range of meanings, such as "mark" (Jn. 20:25), "pattern" (Acts 7:44), and "example" (1 Tim. 4:12). The most important and characteristic usage is in the sense of an event or personage who fulfills a prophetic prefiguration. Such a connotation is involved, for example, in PAUL'S statement that ADAM "was a pattern of the one to come" (Rom. 5:14). The English cognate *type* often has been used to translated this usage (cf. NRSV). The compound form *antitypos G531*, "that which corresponds [to something else]," is also rendered "figure" by the KJV (Heb. 9:24; 1 Pet. 3:21). From such terms, along with the notion of prophetic prefiguration, the whole elaborate system of hermeneutics known as TYPOLOGY was developed. See also ALLEGORY.

figured stone. This phrase is used by the NRSV in two passages (Lev. 26:1; Num. 33:52). From contextual usage, the word probably refers to religious images carved in relief on flat surfaces (cf. NIV, "carved stone," "carved image"). These, along with other pagan cult objects, were proscribed and to be destroyed. The same Hebrew word is rendered "image" in Ezek. 8:12 (NIV, "idol"), which speaks of idolatrous pictures carved or scratched on walls (cf. v. 10). See also GRAVEN IMAGE; IDOLATRY.

figurehead. A carved figure on the prow of a ship. The term is used in connection with the Alexandrian ship on which PAUL sailed toward Rome, which had as its insignia the Dioscuri, that is, CASTOR AND POLLUX, the twin sons of ZEUS who were "good luck" deities of sailors (Acts 28:11).

filigree. Delicate ornamental work in fine wire, usually gold or silver. Archaeological finds have demonstrated that filigree work was produced throughout the ANE. Egyptian funerary jewelry provides some of the best examples, with intricate wire reproductions of divine symbols inlaid with glazed beads and semiprecious stones. Although the evidence is less than conclusive, biblical scholars generally agree that some of the settings of the high priest's garments were of gold filigree (Exod. 28:11-14 et al.).

fillet. This English term is used by the KJV with reference to the "bands" (NIV) or rings binding the pillars of the TABERNACLE, probably close to the capitals (Exod. 36:38). The fillets for the pillars of the court were overlaid with silver (38:10-12, 17, 19), while those for the door pillars were of gold (36:38).

filth. See UNCLEAN.

finances. See MONEY.

finer. KJV term for "refiner, smith" (Prov. 25:4).

finery. This English term, rarely used in Bible versions, occurs in a passage that describes the beauty of the necklaces, bracelets, and other items that adorned the upper-class women of Jerusalem (Isa. 3:18). God promises that he will replace these luxuries with articles of shame when he judges the city. The NIV uses it in another passage to render a different Hebrew word (2 Sam. 1:24; NRSV, "luxury").

fines. See PUNISHMENT.

finger. Although the fingers are an extension from the palm, they often stand for the whole hand (cf. the parallelism in Isa. 59:3). PRIESTS used a finger to sprinkle the sacrificial blood (Lev. 4:6 et al.). The fingers were used in conversation, as in most cultures, to add to the expression of the mouth (Prov. 6:13). Accusation was made, and still is, by pointing (Isa. 58:9). In addition, the finger could be used as a unit of measure (Jer. 52:21).

Several passages in the Bible use the word *finger* figuratively (e.g., 1 Ki. 12:10; Matt. 23:4). Special interest attaches to the anthropomorphic expression, "the finger of God," a striking way of referring to God's power (see ANTHROPOMORPHISM). The Egyptian magicians said, after one of the plagues of MOSES which they could not duplicate, "This is the finger of God" (Exod. 8:19), meaning, "This is beyond the power of man to do" (cf. also Deut. 9:10; Ps. 8:3). In a very important passage, Jesus is quoted as saying that he was driving out demons "by the finger of God" and that these miracles indicated the arrival of the KINGDOM OF GOD (Lk. 11:20). In the parallel passage in Matthew the words are "by the Spirit of God" (Matt. 12:28). It is possible that Luke preserved the Semitic figure and that Matthew interpreted it so as to bring out clearly the connection between this miracle and his earlier reference to the Holy Spirit (v. 18, citing Isa. 42:1). In any case, Jesus was claiming to have divine power and to inaugurate God's reign in fulfillment of the OT promises.

fining pot. KJV rendering of a Hebrew term that refers to a melting pot used for refining metals (Prov. 17:3; 27:21; NIV, "crucible").

fir. See PLANTS.

fire. The use of fire is implied in Scripture as early as Gen. 4:22, which states that TUBAL-CAIN "forged all kinds of tools out of bronze and iron." In the account of the Abrahamic COVENANT (15:17) one reads of a smoking firepot and a flaming torch. Later, God "rained upon Sodom and upon Gomorrah brimstone and fire" (19:24 KJV; NIV, "burning sulfur"). In the institution of the Aaronic priestly ceremonies, God sent fire from heaven to consume the first offering (Lev. 9:24) to show his acceptance. This fire was to be kept burning continually (6:9). When NADAB and ABIHU, the two sons of AARON, offered "unauthorized fire," probably when intoxicated (10:1, 9-10), God's fiery judgment descended on them and destroyed them. The final destiny of the enemies of God is the "fiery lake" (Rev. 19:20;

20:10, 14). This world will some day be consumed by fire (2 Pet. 3:7-12). God uses "fire" not only for judgment but also for testing, and so we learn that the works of all believers will be tested as by fire (1 Cor. 3:12-15). God's glory is accompanied by fire (Ezek. 1:27). Our Lord is pictured with eyes as a flame of fire, hinting at his work of judgment (Rev. 1:14). Fire is used to refine gold and to cleanse us (Mal. 3:2).

fire, lake of. See HELL; HINNOM, VALLEY OF.

fire, pillar of. See CLOUD, PILLAR OF.

firebrand. This English term occurs seldom in the OT, being used variously to render several Hebrew words, such as *zēq H2415*, referring to some kind of flaming missile (only Prov. 26:18; for other Hebrew words, see Job 41:19 NIV; Isa. 7:4; 50:11 NRSV).

firepan. A container for carrying live or dead coals. The Hebrew term (*maḥtâ H4746*) refers to objects that had three different functions in the SACRIFICE and WORSHIP of the OT. (1) Firepans were used to carry coals to and from the altar of burnt offering (Exod. 27:3; 38:3; Num. 4:14). (2) The containers could also be used in combination with the snuffers of the golden LAMPSTAND, probably as receptacles to catch the pieces of burned wick (Exod. 25:38; 37:23; Num. 4:9; KJV, "snuff dishes"; NIV and NRSV, "trays"). (3) Finally, the Hebrew term could refer to a CENSER (Lev. 10:1; 16:12; Num. 16:6; et al.).

firkin. See WEIGHTS AND MEASURES.

firmament. Traditional rendering for Hebrew *rāqiaʿ H8385*, a difficult word that seems to suggest beaten metal plate. The Hebrew term is used only with reference to the sky (Gen. 1:6-8 et al.), viewed apparently as an "expanse" (NIV) or "vault" (RSV) or "dome" (NRSV). While Genesis indicates that the *rāqiaʿ* was formed to separate the mass of waters and divide them into two layers, little can be inferred from that. The SEPTUAGINT rendered the term with Greek *stereōma G5106* ("solidity, foundation, firmness, steadfastness"; cf. Col. 2:5), which was in turn rendered *firmamentum* by Jerome in the Latin Vulgate, and thus "firmament" in the KJV.

The firmament is mentioned always in the context of CREATION: nine times in the Genesis account, but also in the Psalms and the Prophets (Ps. 19:1; 150:1; Ezek. 1:22-26; 10:1; Dan. 12:3). It seems probable that the Hebrew term reflects everyday experience in the human perception of nature: the firmament is thus simply the place where God put the sun, moon, and stars, and where birds fly (Gen. 1:14-17, 20).

first and last. See ALPHA AND OMEGA.

firstborn. The Hebrew word for "firstborn" (*bĕkōr H1147*) is used chiefly of human beings, but it can also be applied to animals (Exod. 11:5). From earliest times it was recognized that God had the first claim on animals (Gen. 4:4). Among the ancestors of the Hebrews, the firstborn offspring of humans and animals were sacrificed to the deity. Because the firstborn of the Israelites were preserved at the time of the first Passover, every firstborn male of man and beast became consecrated to God (Exod. 13:2; 34:19). The beasts were sacrificed, while the firstborn sons were redeemed (Exod. 13:11-15; 34:20; cf. Lev. 27:6). At Sinai the Levites were substituted for the Israelite firstborn (Num. 3:12, 41, 46; 8:13-19). On the thirtieth day after birth the father brought his firstborn son to the priest and paid five shekels to redeem him from service in the temple (cf. Lk. 2:27).

Among the Israelites the firstborn son possessed special privileges. He succeeded his father as the head of the house and received as his share of the inheritance a double portion. For that reason, sometimes the meaning of the term is figurative, denoting priority or supremacy. Israel was God's "firstborn son" (Exod. 4:22; Jer. 31:9). As the firstborn son had special priority, so Israel was privileged over other nations. Similarly, Christ is the "firstborn" of the Father (Heb. 1:6), having preeminent position over others in relation to him. He is "firstborn among many brothers" (Rom. 8:29), that is, sovereign above those related to him in the new creation. He is "the firstborn of all creation" (Col. 1:15 NRSV), a statement misunderstood by the Arians of the fourth century and modern-day Jehovah's Witnesses, who make him a created being and not God. The proper meaning is that Christ, truly God, stands in a relationship of priority or sovereignty over all creation (cf. NIV).

firstfruits. In acknowledgment of the fact that all the products of the land came from God, and to show thankfulness for his goodness, the Israelites brought as an offering a portion of the fruits that ripened first. These were looked on as a pledge of the coming HARVEST. Such an offering was made both on behalf of the nation (Lev. 23:10, 17) and by individuals (Exod. 23:19; Deut. 26:1-11). These firstfruits went for the support of the priesthood.

In a figurative use, Jesus is the firstfruits of all who die in faith; that is, the RESURRECTION of believers is made possible and is guaranteed by his resurrection (1 Cor. 15:20). Believers, in turn, are "a kind of firstfruits" of all that God created (Jas. 1:18); creation will share in the redemption of the children of God (Rom. 8:19-21).

fish. See ANIMALS.

Fish Gate. An entrance on the N wall of JERUSALEM. King MANASSEH is said to have "rebuilt the outer wall of the City of David, west of the Gihon spring, as far as the entrance of the Fish Gate and encircling the hill of Ophel" (2 Chr. 33:14; the gate was rebuilt after the EXILE, Neh. 3:3). It was apparently located between the JESHANAH GATE and the Tower of HANANEL, and one of the choirs proceeded past it at the dedication of the walls (Neh. 12:39). It presumably obtained its name from a fish market nearby (cf. 13:16). Elsewhere it is mentioned with the Mishneh or SECOND DISTRICT of the city (Zeph. 1:10). The Fish Gate was likely near the NW corner of the TEMPLE mount.

fishhook. Not only the means of catching fish as is done today, but also of keeping them, at least for a time (cf. Amos 4:2 with Job 41:1-2). Peter generally used a net, but see Matt. 17:27, where the Lord told him to cast a hook (so KJV and other versions; the NIV translates with the more idiomatic phrase, "throw out your line").

fishing. See OCCUPATIONS AND PROFESSIONS.

fitch. See PLANTS.

flag. See PLANTS.

flagon. A large vessel used for holding liquors. The NRSV uses it several times where the NIV prefers "pitcher" or "jar" (Exod. 25:29 et al.). The KJV uses it wrongly several times to translate a Hebrew word that really means "raisin cake" (2 Sam. 6:19; 1 Chr. 16:3; Cant. 2:5; Hos. 3:1).

flagstaff. Term used by the NIV and other modern versions in one passage where God warns the people that they will flee until they are left "like a flagstaff on a mountaintop, / like a banner on a hill" (Isa. 30:17). The Hebrew term apparently could refer to poles of various kinds, for in its other two occurrences it clearly means "mast [of a ship]" (Isa. 33:23; Ezek. 27:5).

flask. A small container, usually with a narrow neck. The term is occasionally used by English versions, for example, to render Hebrew *pak H7095* ("small jug, vial"), which occurs in two passages (1 Sam. 10:1; 2 Ki. 9:1, 3) or Greek *angeion G31*, used once with reference to jars of oil (Matt. 25:4 NRSV).

flat nose. The KJV translation of a Hebrew word used only once to describe one of the conditions that rendered a man unfit for priestly service (Lev. 21:18). Some believe the word refers to the condition that often accompanies a cleft palate. The NRSV renders it, "one who has a mutilated face"; NIV simply, "disfigured."

flax. See PLANTS.

flea. See ANIMALS.

fleece. The shorn wool of a sheep. The first of the shearing was to be given to the priesthood, as a part of their means of support (Deut. 18:4). GIDEON's experience as related in Jdg. 6:37-40 has given rise to the idiom "putting out a fleece" when seeking God's guidance through some observable means.

fleet. See SHIPS.

flesh. Literally, the soft part of the bodies of people and animals. However, the term (Heb. *bāśār*

H1414, Gk. *sarx G4922*) is often used figuratively in the Bible and plays a significant role in theological formulations. In many of these passages, a literal rendering can be confusing and misleading, so the NIV and other modern versions usually resort to more idiomatic translations. Thus the phrase "every living thing of all flesh" (Gen. 6:19 KJV) is rendered by the NIV simply as "all living creatures." Similarly, "the God of the spirits of all flesh" (Num. 16:22 KJV) becomes in the TNIV, "God of every human spirit."

In the NT, the term *flesh* can refer to our ordinary human constitution as opposed to our mental and moral qualities: "the spirit indeed is willing, but the flesh [NIV, body] is weak" (Matt. 26:41 KJV). Very important is the application of the word to the human nature deprived of the Spirit of God and dominated by SIN. This theological usage is difficult to translate, and the NIV uses such renderings as "unspiritual" (Col. 2:18), "world" (2 Cor. 10:2), "human effort" (Gal. 3:3), and especially "sinful nature" (Rom. 8:3-13; Gal. 5:13-24). See also HOLY SPIRIT.

fleshhook. KJV term for one of the sacrificial implements used in the TABERNACLE and the TEMPLE (Exod. 27:3; 38:3; Num. 4:14; 1 Chr. 28:17; 2 Chr. 4:16; NIV, "meat fork" or "fork"). What appears to be the same device is described as a three-pronged instrument used to remove meat from a boiling pot (1 Sam. 2:13-14).

flesh pot. This term is used by the KJV once in a passage where the Israelites complain that, when living in Egypt, they used to sit around "pots of meat" (NIV) eating whatever they wanted (Exod. 16:3). These pots were large metal kettles used not only for cooking meat (2 Ki. 4:38; Ezek. 11:3), but also for boiling water (Jer. 1:13) and for washing (Ps. 60:8).

flies. See ANIMALS.

flint. See MINERALS.

float. This English term is used by the KJV to render two Hebrew words for "raft," each of which occurs only once (1 Ki. 5:9; 2 Chr. 2:16).

F

flock. A collection of sheep under the care of a shepherd, sometimes including goats also (Gen. 27:9). The larger animals such as cattle, camels, and donkeys were counted as herds, not flocks. Israel lived in OT times in a pastoral civilization, and a man's flocks made up most of his wealth, providing clothing, food, milk, and animals for sacrifice. Figuratively, ISRAEL and the CHURCH are counted as flocks, and God is the Good Shepherd (Isa. 40:11; Matt. 26:31; Lk. 12:32; 1 Pet. 5:2-3).

flog. See SCOURGE; STRIPES.

flood, the. The great deluge that occurred during the days of NOAH, recorded in Gen. 6-9 and mentioned frequently elsewhere in the Bible.

I. Historical background of flood interpretations. The Noahic flood has been a subject for discussion among scientists and theologians for many centuries. During the Middle Ages, the church was the authority in all areas of thought. Science as we know it today did not exist, for with its theological orientation the church looked with disfavor on observations that did not have theological explanations. It was only natural then that when the early geologists observed many thousands of feet of sedimentary rocks (formed from smaller particles of rocks or chemically precipitated from solution) in the mountains of Europe and the British Isles, they turned to the church for an explanation. The easiest answer for the layers of sediments was that they were laid down by the flood.

As the sedimentary layers were studied further, problems arose when it was discovered that not all the layers were contemporaneous. It was also readily observed that some sediments had been deposited, hardened into rock, folded into mountain ranges, eroded off, and then covered with new sediments. At some places the sedimentary rock layers were cut by formerly molten rock material, which indicated volcanic activity after the sediments were deposited. Sixteenth- and seventeenth-century scientists attempted to harmonize the interpretation of field observations with church tradition.

As a result, many interpretations of the meaning and physical characteristics of the flood have been suggested, modified, abandoned, and sometimes reproposed. These interpretations have produced some highly improbable explanations of the events of the deluge and have so confused the issue that it is difficult to separate the intelligent from the fanciful. The reality of the flood can hardly be questioned, however, because of the many references to it in both the OT and NT (Gen. 6-8; 9:11, 28; 10:1, 32; Matt. 24:38-39; Lk. 17:27; 2 Pet. 2:5).

II. The purpose of the flood. An important aspect of the deluge is that God preserved some individuals, for Noah and his family were saved from destruction by going into an ark that Noah made according to God's specifications, and in which he gathered animals and birds preserved to replenish the earth.

It is apparent from Gen. 6:5-7 and other passages such as 2 Pet. 2:5-6 that the flood was brought on the earth as a judgment on the sins of the people. They had become so sinful that "the LORD was grieved that he had made man on the earth" (Gen. 6:6). The Bible refers to the flood in connection with the judgment at the second coming of the Lord (Matt. 24:39) and with the destruction of SODOM and GOMORRAH (Lk. 17:27-29; 2 Pet. 2:5-6).

The purpose of God, as stated in Gen. 6:7, indicates that the judgment was not against the

© Dr. James C. Martin. The British Museum. Photographed by permission.

Cuneiform tablet (c. 1635 B.C.) containing the *Epic of Atrahasis*, one form of the Babylonian flood story.

inanimate rocks or against plants but against "men and animals, and creatures that move along the ground, and birds of the air."

III. The phenomena of the flood. In the following passage, however (Gen. 6:11-13), the earth is included in the judgment. There is again difference of opinion as to the meaning of the statement, "I am going to put an end to all people, for the earth is filled with violence because of them. I am surely going to destroy both them and the earth." That the earth was not utterly destroyed as it will be in the last times (2 Pet. 2:10) is apparent. Some writers would interpret Gen. 6:13 to mean that great geologic catastrophes overwhelmed the earth's surface, while others point out that Gen. 6:6-7, 12-13 all stress that it was the sin of living things that was to be punished and that the effect on the inanimate rocks of the world was only incidental to punishing the human race.

Despite all attempts at scientific explanation of the minute details of the flood, there seems to be no doubt that God worked a miracle in causing it. In 2 Pet. 3:5-6 the flood is compared with the creation of the world and is a miracle of the same order. In the same passage (vv. 7-10), the final destruction of the world is given the same miraculous explanation as the Noahic flood.

IV. The source of the flood. The biblical account of the accumulation and dispersal of the waters of the flood is very brief. In Gen. 7:11 the source of the water is described as "all the springs of the great deep burst forth, and the floodgates of the heavens were opened." The Hebrew noun translated "deep" is the same used in 1:2. That this does not necessarily include all the oceans is shown by its use in Isa. 51:10, where it refers to the escape of the Israelites in "the depths of the sea" (the Red Sea). The mention of "springs" could mean that water rose from the ocean or from fresh water springs on the earth or both.

V. Suggested causes of the flood. Some would prefer to believe that the expression "the springs of the great deep burst forth" indicates that the ocean (actually the Persian Gulf, an arm of the ocean) invaded the land. Others have assumed this implies volcanic activity and that some of the water of the flood was "juvenile water," which is formed from the oxygen and hydrogen that may

occur as separate elements in the molten rock deep in the earth's crust. This school of thought would also attribute to this verse a great deal of diastrophism (movements of the solid crust that result in a relative change of position of the rock formations concerned). This could account for the sinking of the mountains of the earth so that they could be covered more easily by the waters of the deluge.

To attribute volcanic activity to Gen. 7:11 is highly speculative, for at no place in the Genesis account is any more specific description of conditions given. The fact that igneous rock (rock formed by the cooling of molten rock materials) is found between layers of sedimentary rock is not good evidence for volcanic activity at the time of the flood. Sediments that have been laid down during historic time have been cut by lava from present-day volcanoes. It has also been observed that the oldest layers are also cut by igneous rocks. It seems apparent, therefore, that volcanic activity has gone on throughout the world's history. It is not possible to designate any particular rock body as being coincident with the flood.

"The floodgates of the heavens were opened" has been accepted as a description of rain. Some have seen this as a torrential downpour greater than normally experienced on the earth today. A hypothesis has been proposed that the earth from the time of its creation was surrounded by a canopy of water in some form until the time of the flood. The canopy was supposedly made of water vapor, ice, or liquid water. It is proposed that the transfer of the canopy's water from around the earth to the earth would cause rain for many days.

The canopy idea, although firmly entrenched in literature, has doubtful biblical authority, though some cite older versions of Ezek. 1:22 in support of it. Again it should be noted that if a miraculous explanation for the flood is accepted, physical explanations are not necessary.

VI. The duration of the flood. The Hebrews used a solar calendar in contrast to the Babylonian lunar month and the Egyptian arbitrary 365-day year. Most authorities would put the number of days from the time the rain started (Gen. 7:11) to the time Noah left the ark (8:14) between 371 and 376 days.

F

VII. Traditions of the flood. Traditions regarding a disastrous flood that occurred long ago are handed down by many peoples. Isolated tribes in all parts of the world have been found to have such traditions. This is not surprising, considering the destruction caused by present-day floods as well as hurricanes and tornadoes accompanied by great rains. A tribe occupying a limited area could be destroyed completely by one storm. Any survivors would date their civilization from such an event.

The Hebrews, Assyrians, and Babylonians who lived within the area of the Tigris-Euphrates basin, all had traditions of a great flood. These narratives stated the purpose of the flood to be punishment because the world was full of violence, but the Hebrew account remained simple and credible, whereas the other accounts became complex and fanciful. Only the biblical account retained a monotheistic viewpoint. Although it is not possible to affirm dogmatically that all of these three histories had a common origin, it seems probable that they did.

VIII. The universality of the flood. One of the great differences of opinion in describing the deluge concerns its extent. Traditionally, most biblical interpreters considered the submergence to be universal; that is, it covered the entire globe including the highest mountains. The reasons mentioned in defense of this viewpoint include the fact that universal terms are used in the Genesis account. "All the high mountains under the entire heavens were covered" (Gen. 7:19), and "every living thing that moved on the earth perished" (7:21). It has been pointed out that if the flood had been local, there would have been no need for an ark to preserve Noah, for God could have directed him to move with the animals to an area that was not to be submerged.

The fact that many civilizations have flood traditions has been cited as an evidence for a universal

TABULATED CHRONOLOGY OF THE FLOOD	
1. The making of the ark (Gen 6:14)	
2. Collection of the animals (Gen 7:9)	seven days before the rain started
3. Springs of the great deep burst forth and the floodgates of heaven were opened (Gen 7:11)	second month, seventeenth day in Noah's 600th year
4. Rain (Gen 7:12)	forty days and forty nights
5. All the high hills covered (Gen 7:19)	
6. Water flooded the earth (Gen 7:24)	150 days
7. Water receded from off the earth (Gen 8:3)	150 days
8. Ark rested on the mountains of Ararat (Gen 8:4)	seventh month, seventeenth day
9. Water decreased (Gen 8:4)	
10. Tops of mountains seen (Gen 8:5)	tenth month, first day
11. Noah waited (Gen 8:6)	forty days
12. Noah sent out a raven and a dove; dove returned (Gen 8:7–9)	
13. Noah waited (Gen 8:10)	seven days
14. Noah sent forth dove again (Gen 8:10); dove returned with olive branch (Gen 8:11)	seven days
15. Noah waited (Gen 8:12)	seven days
16. Noah sent out a dove, which did not return (Gen 8:12)	seven days
17. Noah removed covering; face of the ground was dry (Gen 8:13)	first month, first day, Noah's 601st year
18. Earth dried; Noah left ark (Gen 8:14)	second month, twenty-seventh day

flood. The same evidence, however, could be used to argue for a local flood, because the accounts of floods in other parts of the world are less like the Hebrew tradition than those of the Assyrians and Babylonians, who lived in the same area as the Hebrews.

Today many conservative scholars defend a local flood. The crux of their argument seems to center in the covenant relation of God to man. He deals with certain groups, such as the children of Israel. The reasoning in regard to Noah is that Noah was not a preacher of righteousness to peoples of other areas but was concerned with the culture from which Abraham eventually came. Physical arguments have also been raised against a universal flood: origin and disposal of the amount of water necessary to make a layer 6 mi. (10 km.) thick over the whole world; the effect on plant life of being covered for a year; the effect on fresh water life of a sea that contained salt from the ocean; and the fact that many topographic features of the earth (such as cinder cones) show no evidence of erosion by a flood and are thought to be much older than the Genesis flood could possibly be.

IX. Chronology of the flood. There is not any general agreement among conservative scholars concerning the actual date of the deluge. Although Ussher in his chronology placed the flood at 2348 B.C., most scholars today hold to an earlier date. Scholars who have advocated that the earth has developed to its present condition by a series of major calamities have been called catastrophists. These consider the Noahic flood as the greatest of these catastrophes and believe that the Pleistocene ice age was related to the flood. Many catastrophists believe the flood was associated in some way with the end of the Pleistocene ice age and so accept a date of about 10,000 B.C. The lack of consensus with regard to the details of the flood should make all aware of the danger of placing so much importance on the interpretation of this event that the other lessons of the Bible are missed.

flora. See PLANTS.

flour. Fine-crushed and sifted grain, generally wheat or rye or barley (Jdg. 7:13). Eastern flour was not quite as fine or as white as ours, and thus

the bread was more wholesome. The "grain offerings" were of flour (Lev. 6:14-15).

flower. See PLANTS.

flute. See MUSIC AND MUSICAL INSTRUMENTS.

flux, bloody. KJV rendering of a Greek word referring to dysentery (Acts 28:8). See DISEASES.

fly. See ANIMALS.

foal. See ANIMALS.

fodder. The mixed food of cattle, generally from several kinds of grain sown together (Job 6:5; 24:6; Isa. 30:24).

fold. A pen in which to keep sheep or goats. Folds were used chiefly as a protection from wild beasts at night. They consisted of a walled enclosure, preferably near water, and often with a small tower inside. Sometimes flocks of more than one shepherd were kept overnight in the same fold, with one shepherd taking care of the animals. In the morning the sheep would be carefully counted when the shepherds came to reclaim their flocks. The word "fold" is used in some versions to render several Hebrew words (Jer. 23:3; Hab. 3:17; et al.) and one Greek word (Jn. 10:1, 16).

folly. See FOOLISHNESS, FOLLY.

food. Nutritive material taken into a living organism to sustain life, to promote growth and the repair of the tissues, and to give energy for the vital processes. The Bible says little about food for animals. Bible animals for the most part are herbivorous, though carnivorous ones are mentioned. Some omnivorous animals, like pigs, are mentioned, but almost always in a contemptuous way (Matt. 7:6). Pigs were forbidden as food (Isa. 65:4).

At the very beginning of human history, ADAM's food for his first day was probably some ripe fruit. Before SIN had entered the world, God possibly prescribed a vegetarian diet, both for man and beast (Gen. 1:29-30), but one must not build too much on silence here as regarding the content of diet. By

F

Almonds ready for picking.

the time that NOAH built the ark, there was a distinction between clean and unclean beasts (7:2-3), and when God made his covenant with Noah after the flood (9:3-4), flesh was expressly permitted as food. BLOOD was forbidden, and it seems that the reason for this prohibition was as much theological as sanitary (cf. Lev. 17:11). Coming down now to the time of MOSES, FAT was also prohibited as food (3:16-17), and again, the reason given is religious, not hygienic. In the time of the restoration (Neh. 8:10) NEHEMIAH encouraged the people to "enjoy choice food" (KJV "eat the fat") while celebrating a national "thanksgiving day." One might imagine here that Nehemiah had forgotten that "all the fat is the LORD's" (Lev. 3:16) until one notices that the Hebrew word in Nehemiah could just as well be rendered "dainties" and refers probably to the various rich confections of which Eastern people are so fond.

The animals most frequently mentioned in the Bible are the domestic herbivorous animals, and these are divided sharply into two classes: the clean and the unclean (see Lev. 11). The clean animals were to be used for food and for sacrifice, and the four-footed ones were distinguished by their hoofs and by whether they chewed the cud. The camel chews the cud but does not have a split hoof and so was considered unclean, though its milk was and is used by desert-dwellers. Pigs have a split hoof but do not chew the cud and so were ceremonially unclean. They were perhaps prohibited as food because of the mischievous *trichina spiralis*, a worm that has long infested pigs; from half-roasted pork it can enter the human body and create great harm. Of the seafood that was reckoned unclean the principal ones were oysters and shrimps. One can easily realize how dangerous they would be in a land where climate was hot and there was no refrigeration. In other words, sanitary reasons seem to account for many of the distinctions between "clean" and "unclean" foods.

In Palestine and Syria, fresh fruit can be obtained throughout the year. Oranges last in the spring until the very short season of apricots arrives. After the apricots come the plums, figs, pomegranates, etc., which last until the grapes appear; and they in turn remain until the oranges and lemons are again in season.

The preparation of food differs from Western custom. Generally meat is eaten not in steaks and roasts, but cut up and served with rice and often imbedded in "coosa" (a kind of squash) or wrapped in cabbage or grape leaves. The bread is not as white and fine as is ours but is far more healthful. A common laborer often takes as his lunch two hollow loaves of bread, one filled with cheese and the other with olives. There were several sorts of sweets, of which dried figs boiled in grape molasses (Gen. 43:11) was one of the best known. Near the sea, fish were very commonly eaten. Various kinds of fruit and vegetables were used: beans, lentils, millet, melons, onions, gourds; also spices: cummin, mint, mustard, and salt; and honey.

Food is a figure of spiritual sustenance. PETER tells his readers to "crave pure spiritual milk, so that by it you may grow up in your salvation" (1 Pet. 2:2). Peter was writing to young Christians, but PAUL clearly distinguishes between Scripture that can be likened to "milk for babes" and that which can be compared with "strong meat," or solid food (1 Cor. 3:1-2).

foolishness, folly. The opposite of WISDOM, with which the OT often contrasts it (Eccl. 2:13). The fool exhibits many characteristics ranging from simple stupidity (Prov. 7:7, 22) and a hot temper (14:17) to wickedness (Gen. 34:7), atheism (Ps. 14:1), and rejection of God (Job 2:9-10). In the NT it can mean thoughtlessness (Gal. 3:3) or lack of intelligence (Rom. 1:21). PAUL says that the preaching of the cross is "foolishness" to the lost (1 Cor. 1:18). In Matt. 23:17 the Lord called the SCRIBES and PHARISEES fools, not implying intel-

© Dr. James C. Martin

F

lectual stupidity but spiritual blindness. Men can be clever in mind, but at the same time be fools in spiritual matters.

foot. The lowest extremity of the leg. Because it comes in contact with the earth, the foot is thought to be less honorable than the hand or the head. But in the Christian church "the foot" (i.e., the lowest member) should not suffer a feeling of inferiority or of envy and say, "Because I am not a hand, I do not belong to the body" (1 Cor. 12:15), nor should the more prominent directing member ("the head") say to the foot, "I don't need you!" (12:21). In the East shoes are ordinarily removed when entering a house, and the lowest servant is detailed to wash the feet of the visitor. The priests, before entering the tabernacle in divine service, washed their feet as well as their hands at the laver, just outside, so that no trace of defilement would accompany their service. (For spiritual application see Jn. 13:10; Heb. 10:22.) In lands where irrigation is practiced, men use shovels to move the earth for the larger channels, but a foot will suffice for a small channel to water a furrow (Deut. 11:10). To completely humiliate an enemy, one sometimes put his foot on the captives' necks as Joshua's captains did (Josh. 10:24).

footman. This term is used by the KJV a dozen times, usually to render Hebrew *raglî* **H8081**, "foot soldier" (1 Sam. 4:10 et al.), distinguished from the soldier who rides on horseback or in a chariot. In the PENTATEUCH, however, the Hebrew word is apparently used to contrast between adult men and children (Exod. 12:37; Num 11:21). The KJV also uses the word "footman" twice to render other Hebrew expressions (1 Sam. 22:17 ["guard"]; Jer. 12:5 ["foot-runner"]).

footstool. A word used in Scripture both literally (2 Chr. 9:18) and figuratively: of the earth (Isa. 66:1; Matt. 5:35); of the temple (Lam. 2:1); of the ark (Ps. 99:5); and of subjection, especially of heathen enemies by the messianic King (Ps. 110:1; Lk. 20:43; Acts 2:35).

footwashing. Though never a major Hebrew rite, the washing of hands and feet of the PRIESTS did have a place in the Mosaic ritual (Exod. 30:17-21).

It may indeed be that all ablutions of the Bible are ritual rather than sanitary, though they rise out of assumed sanitary practices. Guests ordinarily were offered water and vessels for washing the feet (Gen. 18:4; 19:2; 24:32; 43:24; Jdg. 19:21). As a special act of affection or humility, the host or hostess might even wash a guest's feet (1 Sam. 25:41). A "sinful woman" spontaneously and gratefully served the Lord in this way (Lk. 7:36-44).

At the Last Supper the Lord, taking a towel and basin during the meal (Jn. 13:4-10), proceeded to wash the disciples' feet and to wipe them with the towel. HUMILITY was not the only, or even the main, lesson Jesus was seeking to teach. It is clear that Jesus was giving this act the symbolic significance of spiritual cleansing (v. 10). Some denominations believe footwashing to be an ordinance, citing 1 Tim. 5:10 in addition to Jn. 13. Several arguments have been advanced against this view, especially the silence of Acts and the Epistles.

forbear. See PATIENCE.

ford. A shallow place in a stream where people and animals can cross on foot. In the small streams of PALESTINE and SYRIA, fording places are quite frequent and can easily be found simply by following the main roads, which in many cases are mere bridle paths. Such probably were the fords of the JABBOK (Gen. 32:22), where Jacob halted, and of the ARNON (Isa. 16:2). The JORDAN, however, is a strong and rapid stream, and its fording places are few and far between. When Israel crossed, God miraculously stopped the waters upstream by a landslide. JOSHUA's spies (Josh. 2:7) evidently forded the Jordan, and EHUD (Jdg. 3:28) took the same place to prevent Moabites from crossing there. Farther up the river and about two hundred years after Ehud, JEPHTHAH made his famous "shibboleth test" at a ford of the Jordan (12:5-6).

forehead. Because of its prominence, appearance of the forehead often determines our opinion of the person. In Ezek. 16:12 KJV reads "I put a jewel on thy forehead," but NIV (more correctly) has "I put a ring on your nose." The forehead is used as a very dishonorable word where in the KJV we read of a "harlot's forehead" (Jer. 3:3; NIV, "brazen look of

F

a prostitute") indicating utter shamelessness. At the same time it stands for courage, as when God told Ezekiel (Ezek. 3:9) that he had made the prophet's forehead harder than flint against the foreheads of the people. The forehead is also the place for the front of a crown or mitre (Exod. 28:38), where the emblem of holiness on Aaron's forehead would make the gifts of the people acceptable before the Lord. A mark was put on the foreheads of the men of Jerusalem who mourned for its wickedness, and they were spared in a time of terrible judgment (Ezek. 9:4). Similarly in Rev. 7 God's servants were sealed by an angel, and it seems that this seal not only saved the elect ones but showed forth their godly character. In the ages of glory that are to come, the name of God will be marked on the foreheads of his own people (Rev. 22:4).

foreigner. See STRANGER.

foreknowledge; foreordination. See ELECTION AND PREDESTINATION.

forerunner. This English term occurs once in the KJV and other versions as the rendering of Greek *prodromos* G4596 (Heb. 6:20; NIV, "who went before us"). The term is applied to Jesus as having entered the Holy of Holies (cf. Exod. 26:33-35; 40:20-21) ahead of us and on our behalf. This meant that the ancient order of priests which started with Melchizedek (Gen. 14:17-20) now came to its fulfillment and completion in the last priest, the messianic priest-sacrifice. Christ is therefore the precursor of all believers, who may now enter into the presence of Yahweh himself (Rom. 8:15; Gal. 4:6).

foresail. The principal sail hung to the front mast of a SHIP (Acts 27:40).

foreskin. The prepuce, a fold of skin that covers the glans of the penis. The rite of CIRCUMCISION, which was to take place on the eighth day after birth, consisted in cutting the foreskin, an act that symbolized the COVENANT God made with ABRAHAM and his descendants (Gen. 17:11-14). Its spiritual significance is made explicit by MOSES: "Circumcise, then, the foreskin of your heart, and do not be stubborn any longer" (Deut. 10:16 NRSV; cf. Jer. 4:4; 9:25; Rom. 2:25-29; Col. 2:13). In the NT, the Greek term is used mainly in a figurative sense, meaning either "[the state of] uncircumcision" (e.g., Gal. 5:6) or "uncircumcised people" (e.g., Eph. 2:11; this usage may have originated among Greek-speaking Jews as a slur against GENTILES).

forest. A piece of land covered with trees naturally planted, as distinguished from a park where human intervention is more evident. In ancient times, most of the highlands of CANAAN and SYRIA except the tops of the high mountains were covered with forests. Several forests are mentioned by name, those of LEBANON most often, for these were famous for the cedar and the fir trees. HIRAM of TYRE (1 Ki. 5:8-10) brought down cedar and fir trees from the forest of Lebanon to the sea and floated them southward to the port that SOLOMON had constructed, from which his servants could transport the timbers to JERUSALEM. Solomon's "Palace of the Forest of Lebanon" (7:2) was apparently his own house and was so named because of the prevalence of cedar in its structure. The crucial battle of ABSALOM's rebellion was fought in a wood

The forested area on the lower flanks of Mt. Gilboa.

© Dr. James C. Martin

or forest in Ephraim (2 Sam. 18), and "the forest claimed more lives that day than the sword" (18:8). See EPHRAIM, FOREST OF.

foretell. This verb is used rarely in English Bible versions (e.g., Mk. 13:23 KJV). See PROPHETS.

forge. See MINERALS.

forgiveness. The act of pardoning or setting aside punishment and resentment for an offense. The offense may be a deprivation of a person's property, rights, or honor; or it may be a violation of moral law. The normal conditions of forgiveness are REPENTANCE and the willingness to make reparation or ATONEMENT; and the effect of forgiveness is the restoration of both parties to the former state of relationship.

God forgives sins because of the atoning death of Christ. Those forgiven by God before the INCARNATION were forgiven because of Christ, whose death was foreordained from eternity. Christ's atonement was retroactive in its effect (Heb. 11:40). The deity of Christ is evidenced by his claim to the power to forgive sins (Mk. 2:7; Lk. 5:21; 7:49). Just as God has forgiven us, so we must forgive others (Matt. 5:23-24; 6:12; Col. 1:14; 3:13). Jesus taught that forgiveness is a duty, and that no limit should be set to the extent of forgiveness (Lk. 17:4). An unforgiving spirit is one of the most serious of sins (Matt. 18:34-35; Lk. 15:28-30). The offended party is, when necessary, to go to the offender and try to bring him to repentance (Lk. 17:3).

fork. This term occurs in English Bible versions as the rendering of various words. BEZALEL, the chief architect of the TABERNACLE, was also a skillful metal artificer, and among the implements he made for it were bronze forks (Exod. 27:3; 38:3; Num. 4:14). DAVID provided gold to make implements, including forks, for the TEMPLE, and HIRAM made some of bronze (1 Chr. 28:17; 2 Chr. 4:16). What appears to be the same device is described as a three-pronged instrument used to remove meat from a boiling pot (1 Sam. 2:13-14). A WINNOWING FORK is referred to both in the OT (Jer. 15:7) and in the NT (Matt. 3:12; Lk. 3:17), used figuratively of God's JUDGMENT.

former rain. See RAIN.

fornication. This English term, which generally refers to sexual intercourse between persons not married to each other, is used by the KJV and other versions a few times in the OT (e.g., Ezek. 16:26), but primarily in the NT to render the Greek noun *porneia G4518* (usually translated "sexual immorality" in the NIV). Out of seven lists of evils in the writings of PAUL, this Greek word (or the related adjective *pornos G4521*) is included in five of them (1 Cor. 5:11; 6:9; Gal. 5:19; Eph. 5:3; Col. 3:5) and is first on the list each time. Because the term can be applied to various situations, its meaning must be determined by the context of each passage.

fort, fortification, fortress. Every major CITY in ancient times was fortified by a wall and its citadel. The KJV often speaks of such cities as "fenced," the NIV as "fortified." Even before the Israelites entered Canaan, they were terrified by the reports of cities "fortified and very large" (Num. 13; Deut. 1:28). JERUSALEM was so well fortified by the JEBUSITES that it was not until the time of DAVID that the city was captured by the Israelites. Usually the city was built on a hill, and the fortifications followed the natural contour of the hill. Many times there was both an inner and an outer wall. The walls were built of brick and stone and were many feet thick. After the Israelites entered the land they too built fortified cities (Deut. 28:52; 2 Sam. 20:6).

Fortunatus. for´chuh-nay´tuhs (Gk. *Phortounatos G5847*, from Lat. *fortunatus*, "blessed, fortunate"). A prominent member of the Corinthian church, mentioned only in 1 Cor. 16:17 (some MSS also insert it in v. 15). He is named second in a three-man delegation that brought a letter from the church to PAUL at EPHESUS (cf. 7:1). Their presence "refreshed" Paul, giving him the desired contact with that church. They may have returned with the letter that we call 1 CORINTHIANS (cf. the subscription at the end of the letter according to many MSS, followed by the KJV).

Fortune. See GAD (DEITY).

fortune-telling. See DIVINATION.

F

forty. A frequently mentioned NUMBER in the Bible, often having symbolical significance. It was used as the approximate time span of a generation and to designate an extended period of testing, repentance, vigil, or punishment. It is associated with important new developments in the unfolding drama of redemption, such as the FLOOD, the EXODUS, the united monarchy, ELIJAH and the prophetic era, the life of CHRIST, and the birth of the CHURCH (Gen. 7:4, 12, 17; 8:6; Exod. 24:18; Num. 14:33; 32:13; Deut. 9:25; 2 Sam. 5:4; 1 Ki. 11:42; Jon. 3:4; Matt. 4:2; Acts 1:3; 7:23, 29-30).

Forum Appii. See APPIUS, FORUM OF.

foundation. The basis on which something stands or is supported. The word is used of the CREATION, when God "laid the earth's foundation" (Job 38:4; Ps. 78:69). In contrast with the disappearance of the wicked, the righteous are "an everlasting foundation" (Prov. 10:25 KJV; NIV, "stand firm forever"). This heightens the description of the Lord's anger as causing the foundations of the earth to tremble (Isa. 24:18), as well as mountains (Ps. 18:7) and heaven (2 Sam. 22:8). The NT speaks of the man who built his foundation on a rock (Lk. 6:48). CHRIST is the foundation of the CHURCH (1 Cor. 3:11); the apostles and prophets are the foundation on which Christians are built, with Christ as the chief cornerstone (Eph. 2:20), and a good foundation can be built up by those "rich in this present world" by valuing more highly God's rich bounty (1 Tim. 6:17-19). And God's "solid foundation" stands firm and immovable (2 Tim. 2:19).

Foundation Gate. This name occurs only in the account of JOSIAH's coronation (2 Chr. 23:5); in the parallel passage it is called SUR (2 Ki. 11:6). The location of this gate is unknown; it was probably on an inner perimeter, close to the temple and the palace (some have thought it was the same as the HORSE GATE, where ATHALIAH was put to death, 2 Ki. 11:16; 2 Chr. 23:15).

fountain. A spring of water issuing from the earth. In a country near the desert, all sources of water, such as springs, pools, pits, cisterns, and fountains, are of great importance. Many towns and other locations are named for the springs at their sites: ENAIM, "two springs" (Gen. 38:21); EN GEDI, "spring of young goat" (Josh. 15:62); and a dozen others (cf. English "Springfield" or the French "Fontainebleau"). In the story of the FLOOD, "the fountains of the great deep" were broken up (Gen. 7:11 KJV), referring to the great convulsions of the earth's surface that, with the rain, caused the deluge; in the preparation of the earth, the Son of God (Wisdom personified) was with the Father before there were "springs abounding with water" (Prov. 8:24). The word is used both literally and figuratively, both pleasantly and unpleasantly. Figuratively, it refers in the KJV to the source of hemorrhages (Lev. 20:18; Mk. 5:29). In Proverbs, compare "a muddied spring or a polluted well" (25:26) with "a fountain of life" (13:14; 14:27). In the bridegroom's praise of his pure bride (Cant. 4:15) she is "a garden fountain." In the curse of EPHRAIM (Hos. 13:15), "his spring will fail" is a terrible punishment; but on the pleasant side, DAVID speaks (Ps. 36:9) of "the fountain of life," as being with the Lord. In the Lord's conversation with the woman at the well (Jn. 4:14), he told her of "a spring of water welling up to eternal life." Among the delights of heaven will be "the spring of the water of life" (Rev. 21:6).

Fountain Gate. One of the entrances to JERUSALEM, mentioned after the EXILE (Neh. 2:14; 3:15; 12:37). Located in the SE section of the wall restored after the return, it was apparently adjacent to "the steps of the City of David on the ascent to the wall," and near "the house of David" and "the Water Gate on the east" (12:37). A Bronze Age tower recently excavated may have been part of the Fountain Gate.

fowl. See BIRDS.

fowler. A bird-catcher. Because fowlers used snares, gins, bird-lime, etc. and caught their prey by trickery, "fowler" is used to describe those who try to ensnare the unwary and bring them to ruin (Ps. 91:3; 124:7).

fox. See ANIMALS.

frankincense. See PLANTS.

freedman. This term, referring to an emancipated SLAVE, is used by the NIV and other versions to render Greek *apeleutheros G592*, which occurs only once in a figurative sense: "For he who was a slave when he was called by the Lord is the Lord's freedman; similarly, he who was a free man [*eleutheros G1801*] when he was called is Christ's slave" (1 Cor. 7:22; cf. Gal. 4:22-23, 30; Rev. 6:15). See also FREEDMEN, SYNAGOGUE OF THE; LIBERTY.

Freedmen, Synagogue of the. When STEPHEN began to perform wonders among the people, he was opposed by "members of the Synagogue of the Freedmen (as it was called)—Jews of Cyrene and Alexandria as well as the provinces of Cilicia and Asia" (Acts 6:9; KJV, "Libertines"). In this passage, the Greek word for FREEDMAN is not *apeleutheros G592* but the Latin loanword *Libertinos G3339*. The Synagogue of the Freedmen has been linked by some to a first-century inscription that mentions the building of a SYNAGOGUE by its chief and priest Theodotus, son of Vettenus.

freedom. See LIBERTY.

freewill offering. See SACRIFICE AND OFFERINGS.

fret. This English verb, in its common intransitive meaning "to be vexed, troubled," appears rarely in modern versions (the NIV and NRSV, e.g., use it in Ps. 37:1, 7-8; Prov. 24:19). The word, however, had a broader meaning in the time of the KJV, which uses it to render various Hebrew terms. Note, for example, the expression "a fretting leprosy" (Lev. 13:51-52; NIV, "a destructive mildew"), as well as the meaning "become annoyed, angry" (Isa. 8:21).

friend, friendship. Besides references to friendship in various forms, such as HOSPITALITY, the term *friend* occurs frequently in the Bible. Although the word can be used as a simple term of familiar, kindly address (Matt. 20:13; 22:12), it usually means a well-disposed acquaintance, dependable companion, or helpful neighbor (Gen. 38:20; Jer. 6:21; Lk. 11:5-8; 14:10; 15:6, 9), a political adherent (1 Sam. 30:26; 2 Sam. 3:8; 15:37; 1 Ki. 4:5; Jn. 19:12), or a person dear as one's own soul (Deut. 13:6 KJV). There are false friends as well as true

ones (Prov. 18:24); friends who fail one (Job 6:14, 27; Lam. 1:2; Zech. 13:6) as well as friends who prove faithful (Ps. 35:14; Prov. 17:17; Jn. 15:13).

Perhaps the most notable instance of human friendship in the Bible is that of DAVID and JONATHAN (1 Sam. 18:1-4; 19:1-7; 20:1-42; 2 Sam. 1:25-26). According to some scholars, PAUL's epistle to the PHILIPPIANS exhibits the formal characteristics of Greco-Roman "letters of friendship" or "family letters." The highest friendship the Bible speaks of is friendship with God (esp. ABRAHAM's, 2 Chr. 20:7; Isa. 41:8; Jas. 2:23), whose direct opposite, enmity with God, is friendship with the world (Jas. 4:4).

fringe. See TASSEL.

frog. See ANIMALS.

frontlet. See DRESS.

frost. Usual in winter on the hills and high plains in Bible lands. Frosts in the late spring do great damage to fruit. The MANNA in the wilderness is compared to frost (Exod. 16:14). Frost is an evidence of God's power (Job 38:29).

fruit. The fruits most often mentioned in Scripture are the grape, pomegranate, fig, olive, and apple, all of which are grown today. The word *fruit* is often used metaphorically: "the fruit of your womb" (Deut. 7:13), "the fruit of their schemes" (Prov. 1:31). The fruit of the HOLY SPIRIT consists of the Christian virtues (Gal. 5:22-23).

fruits, first. See FIRSTFRUITS.

fuel. In ancient times, wood, charcoal, various kinds of thorn bushes, dried grass, and the dung of camels and cattle were used as fuel. There is no evidence that coal was used by the Hebrews as fuel; their houses had no chimneys (Isa. 9:5, 19; Ezek. 4:12; 15:4, 6; 21:32).

fulfillment. See ESCHATOLOGY; FULLNESS OF TIME; PROPHETS.

fuller. See OCCUPATIONS AND PROFESSIONS.

fuller's field. An area just outside of Jerusalem where fullers or washermen washed the cloth material they were processing. A highway and a conduit for water passed through it (Isa. 7:3; 36:2; NIV, "Washerman's Field"). It was so near the city that the Assyrian Rabshakeh, standing and speaking in the field, could be heard by those on the city wall (2 Ki. 18:17). Its exact site is uncertain.

fuller's soap. An alkali prepared from the ashes of certain plants and used for cleansing and fulling new cloth. The word is used figuratively in Mal. 3:2 (NIV, "launderer's soap").

fullness of time. This expression, used by Paul in Gal. 4:4, indicates the "right" or "proper" time for Christ's advent. The expression does not mean the "full term" of prenatal human life ("born of woman"), but rather the right time chosen by the Father ("God sent forth"). This "right time" was determined by God's plan of redemption and prepared for by historical developments: the completion of the OT era and messianic expectation, as well as cultural, political, and religious factors in the Roman world. These developments provided fertile soil for the ministry of the Messiah, the founding of the church, and the rapid spread of the gospel. Paul's language, however, calls attention to the theme of eschatological fulfillment: Jesus' coming marks "the last days" when God's promises are coming to pass. See also eschatology.

funeral. The word does not occur in the KJV, and in the NIV is found only twice, both times as an adjective (Jer. 16:5; 34:5). Funeral rites differed with the place, the religion, and the times; except for royal burials in Egypt, the elaborate ceremonies we use today were not held. Generally in Palestine there was no embalmment and the body was buried a few hours after death, sometimes in a tomb but more often in a cave. Coffins were unknown. The body was washed and often anointed with aromatic spices (Jn. 12:7; 19:39). The procession of mourners, made up of relatives and friends of the deceased, was led by professional mourning women, whose shrieks and lamentations pierced the air. It was an insult to a man's reputation to be refused proper burial (Jer. 22:19). The "Tombs of the Kings" on the east side of Jerusalem and the "garden tomb" (where some believe that our Lord's body was laid) are evidences of the two types of burial. In Egypt the bodies were embalmed so skillfully that many of them are recognizable today after the lapse of thousands of years.

furlong. See weights and measures.

furnace. This term is used to translate a variety of words, especially Hebrew *kûr H3929*, which refers to a furnace for smelting metals (Prov. 17:3; 27:21). In the Bible the word is used only in the metaphorical sense of suffering permitted by God in punishment or discipline. The deliverance of Israel from Egypt was like being taken from the midst of an iron-smelting furnace (Deut. 4:20; 1 Ki. 8:51; Jer. 11:4). God told Israel that he had refined them in the furnace of affliction (Isa. 48:10). See oven.

Furnaces, Tower of the. See Ovens, Tower of the.

furnishings, furniture. In the Bible the principal reference to furnishings is in the articles in and about the tabernacle and the temple. The main items were the large altar and the laver, outside; then the table of the bread of the Presence, the lampstand or "candlestick," and the altar of incense in the Holy Place; then in the Most Holy Place the ark of the covenant (Exod. 25-40). Generally beds were mats, spread on the floor and rolled up during the day, though Og of Bashan is said to have had a bed of iron (Deut. 3:11). The tables in OT times were generally very low and people sat on the floor to eat. Royal tables were often higher (Jdg. 1:7), as were those in NT times (Mk. 7:28).

furrow. The long trench made by a plow in its path (Job 31:38; 39:10; Ps. 65:10; et al.). The furrow was usually made with a single-handled wooden plow pulled by an animal. Iron was available after David's period, but wood continued to be used in many instances. See agriculture.

future life. See eschatology; life.

G

Gaal. gay´uhl (Heb. *ga'al H1720*, possibly "beetle" or "loathing"). Son of Ebed and leader of a revolt against Abimelech son of Gideon (Jdg. 9:26-41). Gaal and his relatives had moved into Shechem and had gained the trust of the city's inhabitants. While they were having a great banquet, Gaal and the Shechemites became drunk and scoffed at Abimelech. In the midst of their revelry, Gaal boasted that with adequate support he could overthrow Abimelech. When Zebul, the ruler of Shechem, heard this, he sent word to Abimelech urging him to quell the rebellion at once. He advised Abimelech to set an ambush around the city during the night. The next morning, as Gaal and Zebul stood in the city gate watching, they saw the troops of Abimelech arise from hiding and approach the city. Zebul challenged Gaal to make good his boast to overthrow Abimelech. Gaal and his men were defeated and driven from the field, and they were repulsed from the city by Zebul. The next day Abimelech captured Shechem, destroyed it, and sowed it with salt. This was seen by the Scripture writer as the just judgment of God on the Shechemites who supported Abimelech in the assassination of his seventy brothers (cf. vv. 56-57).

Gaash. gay´ash (Heb. *ga'aš H1724*, "quake"). A name used to identify a mountain and its ravines. Mount Gaash is described as being in the hill country of Ephraim and just S of Timnath Serah, where Joshua was buried (Josh. 24:30; Jdg. 2:9). The ravines are referred to as the area from which Hiddai, one of David's mighty men, came (2 Sam. 23:30; 1 Chr. 11:32 [Hurai]). The precise location is unknown, but it must have been approximately 20 mi. (32 km.) SW of Shechem and 15 mi. (24 km.) NW of Jerusalem.

Gaba. See Geba.

Gabbai. gab´bi (Heb. *gabbay H1480*, possibly "[tax] gatherer"). One of the leaders from Benjamin who volunteered to settle in Jerusalem after the return from the exile (Neh. 11:8). Instead of the two names "Gabbai, Sallai," some scholars emend the Hebrew text to read "men of valor" (cf. ESV).

Gabbatha. gab´uh-thuh (Gk. *Gabbatha G1119*; possibly from Aram. *gbt'*, a word of uncertain meaning). The Aramaic (KJV, "Hebrew") name

Modern reconstruction of the Herodian palace in Jerusalem. The Gabbatha or Stone Pavement where Pilate judged Jesus may have been located here.

© Dr. James C. Martin. The Holy Land Hotel, Jerusalem. Photographed by permission.

493

for "the Stone Pavement," an unknown location in JERUSALEM where PILATE judged Jesus (Jn. 19:13). The fact that Gabbatha lay outside the PRAETORIUM (governor's residence, 19:9, 13) would indicate either the palace of HEROD in the W part of Jerusalem or the fortress of ANTONIA in the E. The latter, at the NW corner of the TEMPLE area, has been favored by the identification at this spot of a large area of pavement, beneath the present church of the Dames de Sion, as belonging to the fortress. Some of the stone slabs still bear marks suggestive of Roman soldiers' games. However, more recent work indicates that this pavement was not built prior to A.D. 70, and so Gabbatha should probably be identified with a podium that apparently stood on the E side of Herod's palace.

Gabriel. gay´bree-uhl (Heb. *gabrî'ēl H1508*, "[strong] man of God" or "God is my warrior"; Gk. *Gabriēl G1120*). An ANGEL mentioned four times in Scripture, each time bringing a momentous message. He interpreted to DANIEL the vision of the ram and the goat (Dan. 8:16-17); later he explained the vision of the seventy weeks (9:21-22). Gabriel announced to ZECHARIAH the birth of JOHN THE BAPTIST, forerunner of the MESSIAH (Lk. 1:11-20); and he was sent to Mary with the unique message of Jesus' birth (1:26-38). His credentials are the ideal for every messenger of God: "I am Gabriel. I stand in the presence of God, and I have been sent to speak to you and to tell you this good news" (1:19). The Bible does not define his status as an angel, but he appears as an archangel in the PSEUDEPIGRAPHA (*1 Enoch* 9 et al.).

Gad. gad (*gād H1514*, "fortunate"). **(1)** Seventh son of JACOB; he was the firstborn of ZILPAH, LEAH's handmaid (Gen. 30:9-11). Of his personal life nothing is known except that he had seven sons at the time of the descent into EGYPT (46:16).

The tribe descended from Gad numbered 45,650 adult males at the census at SINAI (Num. 1:24-25), but at the second census their number had fallen to 40,500 (26:18). Their position on the march was S of the TABERNACLE, next to REUBEN. These two tribes and the half-tribe of MANASSEH remained shepherds like their forefathers, and because of their "very large herds and flocks" (32:1)

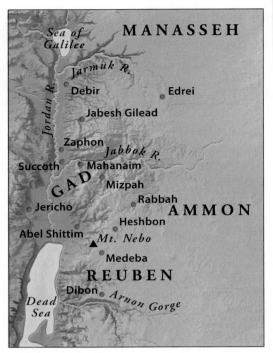

Tribal territory of Gad.

they requested of MOSES the rich pasture lands E of JORDAN for their possession. This was granted (Josh. 18:7) on the condition that they accept their responsibility and accompany the nine and a half tribes across Jordan in warfare against the Canaanites. The warriors of these two and a half tribes took the lead in the conquest of W Palestine (1:12-18; 4:12) and returned to their families with JOSHUA's blessing (22:1-9). Fearing that the Jordan would alienate their children from the fellowship and faith of the western tribes, they erected a huge altar as evidence of their unity in race and faith (22:10-34; see ED). A satisfactory explanation removed the thought of war, which seemed inevitable at first.

The territory of the Gadites, difficult to define, had formerly been ruled by SIHON, king of the AMORITES. It lay chiefly in the center of the land E of Jordan, with the half-tribe of Manasseh on the N and Reuben to the S. The northern border reached as far as the Sea of KINNERETH (Josh. 13:27); the southern border seems to have been just above HESHBON (13:26), though cities below Heshbon were built by Gad (Num. 32:34). One of these is DIBON, where the famous MOABITE STONE was found.

Jacob's words in Gen. 49:19 seem to describe the military prowess of the Gadites. MOSES said of them: "Blessed is he who enlarges Gad's domain! Gad lives there like a lion" (Deut. 33:20). Because they trusted in the Lord and cried to him for help, they totally defeated the HAGRITES (1 Chr. 5:18-22). It was natural for men of such faith and ability to extend their borders as far as GILEAD (5:16). The Gadites who joined DAVID were "brave warriors, ready for battle. … Their faces were the faces of lions, and they were as swift as gazelles in the mountains" (12:8). Other famous men of Gilead or Gad were BARZILLAI (2 Sam. 17:27; 19:31-40) and ELIJAH. The land of Gad was along the battlefield between SYRIA and ISRAEL (2 Ki. 10:33). Gad finally was carried captive by ASSYRIA (2 Ki. 15:29; 1 Chr. 5:26), and AMMON seized their land and cities (Jer. 49:1).

(2) The seer or prophet of King DAVID. He advised David to get out of the stronghold and flee from SAUL into Judah (1 Sam. 22:5). Later he gave David his choice of punishment from the Lord for his sin in numbering the soldiers of Israel (24:11-17; 1 Chr. 21:9-17) and told him to build an altar to the Lord on the threshing floor of ARAUNAH (2 Sam. 24:18). Gad assisted in arranging the musical services of the TEMPLE (2 Chr. 29:25) and recorded the acts of David in a book (1 Chr. 29:29).

Gad (deity). gad (Heb. *gad H1513*, "fortune"). A Semitic god of good fortune, mentioned with MENI (Isa. 65:11; modern versions usually render these two names respectively as "Fortune" and "Destiny"). Some scholars find a reference to this deity in LEAH's naming of GAD, her son through ZILPAH (Gen. 30:11). The popularity of the worship of this god among the Canaanites may be reflected in the place names BAAL GAD (Josh. 11:17; cf. 12:7; 13:5) and

MIGDAL GAD (15:37; cf. also the personal names GADDI and GADDIEL, Num. 13:10, 11). Gad has sometimes been equated with the Babylonian god MARDUK and with the planet Jupiter. See also DESTINY.

Gad, river (valley) of. According to the KJV, the commanders in charge of DAVID's census encamped "in Aroer, on the right side of the city that *lieth* in the midst of the river of Gad, and toward Jazer" (2 Sam. 24:5; ASV, "the Valley of Gad"). This rendering is problematic, however. Recent versions have a comma after the word "river" or "valley" (NIV, "gorge") and translate the rest of the verse, "toward Gad and on to Jazer" (NRSV; similarly NIV, "and then went through Gad and on to Jazer").

Gadara, Gadarene. gad'uh-ruh, gad'uh-reen (Gk. *Gadara* [not found in NT], *Gadarēnos G1123*). Gadara was a city of TRANSJORDAN, about 6 mi. (10 km.) SE of the southern end of the Sea of Galilee, and one of the cities of the DECAPOLIS. Its inhabitants, the Gadarenes, were predominantly non-Jewish. The only NT reference to the Gadarenes is the account of the healing of two demoniacs and the drowning of the swine in the Sea of Galilee (Matt. 8:28). The parallel passages, which mention only one demoniac, refer to the same episode, but they use the term "Gerasenes" (Mk. 5:1; Lk. 8:26; cf. v. 37). In all of these references there are textual

© Dr. James C. Martin

Gadara, one of the Decapolis cities, was a few miles SE of the Sea of Galilee (the lake is visible on the top right).

variants, reflecting some difficulty in the identification of the place. This problem is resolved if one remembers that each reference is to the *country* of the Gadarenes-Gerasenes. The geographical and historical sources suggest that the area designations probably overlapped; Gadara was the chief city of the immediate area, whereas Gerasa may have referred to a wider area. Matthew gives a specific reference to the Gadarenes, Mark and Luke a more general reference to Gerasenes. Although topographical maps show hills all along the SE shore of the Sea of Galilee, geographers who visited the area say the only place to locate the drowning swine incident is a strip of steep coastline near Gergesa, the present-day Kersa (see GERASENE). Gadara is identified today as Muqeis, or Umm Qeis, overlooking the S valley of the Yarmuk River. The ruins are extensive, including remnants of two amphitheaters, a basilica, a temple, colonnades, large residences, and an aqueduct, all showing the size, beauty, and importance of the city. Another Gadara is mentioned by JOSEPHUS as "the capital of Perea" (*War* 4.7.3), but he may have confused it with Gerasa.

Gaddi. gad´di (Heb. *gaddi* H1534, possibly "my [good] fortune" or short form of GADDIEL). Son of Susi, a leader of the tribe of MANASSEH, and one of the twelve spies whom MOSES sent from the wilderness of PARAN to spy out the land of Canaan (Num. 13:11).

Gaddiel. gad´ee-uhl (Heb. *gaddi'ēl* H1535, possibly "my fortune is God"). Son of Sodi, a leader of the tribe of ZEBULUN, and one of the twelve spies whom MOSES sent from the wilderness of PARAN to spy out the land of Canaan (Num. 13:10).

gadfly. See ANIMALS.

Gadi. gay´di (Heb. *gādi* H1533, possibly "my [good] fortune" or short form of GADDIEL). The father of MENAHEM, king of Israel (2 Ki. 15:14, 17).

Gadite. gad´it. See GAD.

Gaham. gay´ham (Heb. *gaham* H1626, possibly "bright flame"). Son of NAHOR (brother of ABRAHAM) by his concubine REUMAH (Gen. 22:24).

Gahar. gay´hahr (Heb. *gahar* H1627, derivation uncertain). The ancestor of some temple servants (NETHINIM) who returned with ZERUBBABEL from exile in BABYLON (Ezra 2:47; Neh. 7:49).

Gai. gi (Heb. *gay'* H1628, "valley"). According to some, Gai was the name of a place mentioned together with EKRON as the limit to which the Israelites chased the PHILISTINES after the victory of DAVID over GOLIATH (1 Sam. 17:52 ASV; KJV, "the valley"). On the basis of some MSS of the SEPTUAGINT, the NIV and other modern versions emend the Hebrew text to read GATH.

Gaius. gay´yuhs (Gk. *Gaios* G1127, from Lat. *Gaius* [for *Gavius*, from *gaudeo*, "rejoice"], a very common name often abbreviated *C.* for *Caius*). **(1)** A Macedonian Christian; as a travel companion of PAUL, he and ARISTARCHUS were seized by the mob during the Ephesian riot (Acts 19:29).

(2) A Christian from DERBE, listed among those waiting for Paul at TROAS (Acts 20:4). The men mentioned here were apparently the delegates assigned by the churches to go with Paul to Jerusalem with the collection (see CONTRIBUTION).

(3) A Christian in CORINTH; one of two men whom Paul names as having been baptized by him, contrary to his usual practice (1 Cor. 1:14, 17). He is doubtless the same as the Gaius who provided hospitality for Paul when he wrote ROMANS from Corinth on the third journey (Rom. 16:23). That he was host also to "the whole church" implies that the Corinthian church met in his spacious home. Tradition has made him the bishop of THESSALONICA, and some would identify him with Titius Justus (Acts 18:7).

(4) The addressee of John's third epistle (3 Jn. 1). The apostle had a deep affection for him, commended him for his hospitality, and desired his continued support for missionaries (vv. 2-8).

Galal. gay´lal (Heb. *gālāl* H1674, possibly "tortoise"). **(1)** One of the Levites who resettled in JERUSALEM after the EXILE (1 Chr. 9:15). He is not identified in any other way.

(2) Son of JEDUTHUN and grandfather of OBADIAH (Abda); the latter is listed among the Levites who resettled in Jerusalem after the exile (1 Chr.

9:16; Neh. 11:17). Since Jeduthun was a prominent temple musician (1 Chr. 16:42 et al.), it is likely that both this Galal and #1 above, as well as the other Levites mentioned in the passage, had the same profession.

Galatia. guh-lay′shuh (Gk. *Galatia G1130*). The designation in NT times of (1) a broad territory in north-central Asia Minor and (2) a Roman PROVINCE covering a smaller region in the southern part of that territory, but some additional areas as well. The name was derived from the people called *Keltoi*, that is, Celtic tribes from ancient Gallia or Gaul (roughly modern France and Belgium). After having invaded MACEDONIA and GREECE about 280 B.C., they crossed into Asia Minor on the invitation of Nikomedes I, king of BITHYNIA, to aid him in a civil war. After ravaging far and wide, they were finally confined to the north-central part of Asia Minor, where they settled as conquerors and

Paul would have traveled past Lake Egirdir in the Roman province of Galatia on his way to Pisidian Antioch. (View to the NW.)

© Dr. James C. Martin

gave their name to the territory. Their chief city-centers were Ancyra, Pessinus, and Ravium. In 189 B.C. the Galatians were subjugated by ROME and continued as a subject kingdom under their own chiefs, and after 63 B.C. under kings. On the death of King Amyntas in 25 B.C., the Galatian kingdom was converted into a Roman province called Galatia. The province included not only some of the area inhabited by the Galatians but also parts of PHRYGIA, PISIDIA, LYCAONIA, and Isauria. The term *Galatia* henceforth carried a double connotation: (1) geographically, to designate the territory inhabited by the Galatians; (2) politically, to denote the entire Roman province. The cities of ANTIOCH, ICONIUM, LYSTRA, and DERBE, evangelized by PAUL on his first missionary journey, were in the province of Galatia.

The name *Galatia* occurs in 1 Cor. 16:1; Gal. 1:2; 2 Tim. 4:10; and 1 Pet. 1:1 (in the last passage some scholars think the reference may be to the European Gaul). In Acts 16:6 and 18:23 LUKE uses the adjective in a phrase that probably means "the Phrygian-Galatian region." Although some have thought that the reference here is to the old ethnographic designations, others have argued that it means the section of Phrygian territory that was included in the new province of Galatia. Paul's general practice of using political

Cities visited by the apostle Paul in Galatia.

G

Overview of GALATIANS

Author: The apostle PAUL.

Historical setting: Disputed. According to one view, Paul was writing to churches in the northern region of GALATIA during his third journey (c. A.D. 55), probably from EPHESUS (perhaps from elsewhere during the second journey c. A.D. 51). According to others, the letter was written from Syrian ANTIOCH to communities in the Roman province of southern Galatia prior to the Jerusalem Council of Acts 15 (A.D. 49), making Galatians the earliest Pauline letter known. A third view accepts that the addressees were South Galatians, but dates the letter after the council. In any case, this epistle was motivated by the Galatians' error in accepting the JUDAIZERS' doctrine, namely, that GENTILES must be circumcised and submit to the Mosaic LAW if they want to be part of the people of God.

Purpose: To counter the message of the false teachers by demonstrating the truth of the GOSPEL of GRACE, including its implications for Christian conduct.

Contents: After an introductory paragraph (Gal. 1:1-10), the apostle defends his authority (1:11—2:21), expounds the doctrine of JUSTIFICATION by FAITH (3:1—4:31), clarifies the nature of Christian liberty (5:1—6:10), and ends with some forceful statements (6:11-18).

designations points to that usage also in Gal. 1:2 and 1 Cor. 16:1. If *Galatia* in Gal. 1:2 refers to the Roman province, then the churches addressed were those founded on the first missionary journey (Acts 13-14); those who believe it means the old ethnographic territory of Galatia have to posit a period of Pauline evangelization of that area not described by Acts.

Galatians, Letter to the. guh-lay′shuhnz. A letter addressed by the apostle PAUL to the Christian churches in GALATIA. It is a short but very important document, containing his passionate polemic against the perversion or contamination of the GOSPEL of God's GRACE. It has aptly been described as "the Magna Carta of spiritual emancipation," and it remains as the abiding monument of the liberation of Christianity from the trammels of legalism.

The contents of the letter so unmistakably reveal the traces of Paul's mind and style that its genuineness has never been seriously questioned even by the most radical NT critics. The testimony of the early church to its integrity and Pauline origin is strong and unambiguous. Written to "the churches of Galatia," it is the only letter by Paul that is specifically addressed to a group of churches. They were all founded by Paul (Gal. 1:8, 11; 4:19-20), were all the fruit of a single mission (3:1-3; 4:13-14), and were all affected by the same disturbance (1:6-7; 5:7-9). Paul had preached to them the gospel of the free grace of God through the death of Christ (1:6; 3:1-14). The Galatians warmly and affectionately received Paul and his message (4:12-15). The converts willingly endured persecution for their faith (3:4) and "were running a good race" when Paul left them (5:7).

The startling information received by Paul that a sudden and drastic change in attitude toward him and his gospel was taking place in the Galatian churches caused the writing of the letter. Certain Jewish teachers, who professed to be Christians and acknowledged Jesus as MESSIAH, were obscuring the simplicity of the gospel of free grace with their propaganda. They insisted that to faith in Christ must be added CIRCUMCISION and obedience to the Mosaic LAW (Gal. 2:16; 3:2-3; 4:10, 21; 5:2-4; 6:12). Paul realized clearly that this teaching neutralized the truth of Christ's all-sufficiency for salvation and destroyed the message of justification by faith. By means of this letter Paul sought to save his converts from this fatal mixing of law and grace.

Because of the geographical and the political connotation of Galatia in NT times, two views concerning the location of the Galatian churches are advocated. The North-Galatian theory, which interprets the term in its old ethnographic sense to denote the territory inhabited by the Galatian tribes, locates the churches in north-central Asia Minor, holding that they were founded during the second missionary journey (according to a debated interpretation of Acts 16:6). The South-Galatian theory identifies these churches with those founded on the first missionary journey (Acts 13-14), located in the Roman PROVINCE of Galatia. The former was the unanimous view of the church fathers. They naturally adopted that meaning since in the second century the province was again restricted to ethnic Galatia and the double meaning of the term disappeared. The majority of the modern commentators support the latter view for the following reasons: it was Paul's habit to use provincial names in addressing his converts; it best explains the familiar reference to Barnabas in the letter; Acts 16:6 gives no hint of such a protracted mission as the older view demands; the older view cannot explain why the Judaizers would bypass the important churches in South Galatia; known conditions in these churches fit the picture in the letter.

Views concerning the place and date of composition are even more diverse. Advocates of the North-Galatian theory generally assign the letter to Paul's third missionary journey, probably while the apostle was in EPHESUS. South-Galatian advocates vary considerably; some place it before the Jerusalem Conference (and written from Syrian ANTIOCH), others place it on the second missionary journey (perhaps during the ministry at CORINTH), and others place it as late as the third missionary journey.

The effort to date it before the Jerusalem Conference faces definite chronological difficulties. This early dating is not demanded by the silence of the letter concerning the conference decrees; the decrees were already known to the Galatians (Acts 16:4), and Paul, in writing the letter, would desire to establish his position on grounds independent of the Jerusalem church. Since he had apparently already visited the churches twice (Gal. 1:9; 4:13), a date after Paul's second visit to the churches in S Galatia seems most probable (c. A.D. 52). During that second visit Paul had sought by warning and instructions to fortify his converts against the danger (1:9; 4:16; 5:3). The impact of the Judaizers on the Galatians threatened to destroy his work. The result was this bristling letter.

The contents of Galatians make evident Paul's purpose in writing. The first two chapters show that he was compelled to vindicate his apostolic authority. The Judaizers, in order to establish their own position, which contradicted Paul's teaching, had attempted to discredit his authority. Having vindicated his apostolic call and authority, Paul next sets forth the doctrine of JUSTIFICATION to refute the teaching of the Judaizers. A reasoned, comprehensive exposition of the doctrine of justification by faith exposed the errors of legalism. Since the Judaizers asserted that to remove the believer from under the law opened the floodgates to immorality, Paul concluded his presentation with an elaboration of the true effect of liberty on the Christian life, showing that the truth of justification by faith logically leads to a life of good works. The letter may be outlined as follows:

I. The introduction (Gal. 1:1-10).
   A. The salutation (1:1-5).
   B. The rebuke (1:6-10).
II. The vindication of his apostolic authority (1:11—2:21).
   A. The reception of his gospel by revelation (1:11-24).
   B. The confirmation of his gospel by the apostles at Jerusalem (2:1-10).
   C. The illustration of his independence (2:11-21).

G

III. The exposition of justification by faith
(3:1—4:31).
    A. The elaboration of the doctrine (3:1—4:7).
        1. The nature of justification by faith (3:1-14).
        2. The limitations of the law and its relations to faith (3:15—4:7).
    B. The appeal to drop all legalism (4:8-31).
IV. The nature of the life of Christian liberty
(5:1—6:10).
    A. The call to maintain their liberty (5:1).
    B. The peril of Christian liberty (5:2-12).
    C. The life of liberty (5:13—6:10).
V. The conclusion (6:11-18).

galbanum. See PLANTS.

Galeed. gal′ee-ed (Heb. *galʿēd H1681*, "[stone] heap of witness"). The Hebrew name that JACOB gave to the heap of stones erected as a memorial to the covenant of reconciliation and nonaggression between himself and LABAN, his father-in-law (Gen. 31:47-48). Laban called the heap of stones JEGAR SAHADUTHA (Aram. for "heap of witness"), and it was also known as MITZPAH ("watchtower," v. 49). Some have identified Galeed with Khirbet Jelʿad, S of the JABBOK River, but others think the incident took place before Jacob crossed the river on his way S. This story perhaps provides the reason why this territory in TRANSJORDAN has been named GILEAD (cf. Gen. 31:25).

Galilean. gal′uh-lee′uhn (Gk. *Galilaios G1134*, from Heb. *galîl H1665*, "Galilee"). KJV Galilaean. The name applied by both Jews and Gentiles to the inhabitants of GALILEE, the portion of Syria-Palestine N of the Plain of ESDRAELON and spreading E to the shores of the Lake of Galilee and W to the Mediterranean Sea. This area was little settled by the Jews after the return from the EXILE, but later the Hasmoneans (see MACCABEES) conquered it and incorporated its mixed population of Arameans and Hellenistic peoples into the Jewish state. It was to these people that JOHN THE BAPTIST and JESUS CHRIST had preached, and from this group the first circle of our Lord's disciples were drawn and his closest apostles chosen (cf. Jn. 4:45). In the Gospels and Acts it is clear that Galileans were easily distinguishable to their fellow Jews by their speech. The classic passage is, of course, the accusation by the bystanders against Simon PETER and his denial (Mk. 14:70; Lk. 22:59; cf. also Acts 2:7). The characteristic of this speech was no doubt its vocabulary, accent, and syntax.

Galilee. gal′uh-lee (Heb. *gālîl H1665*, used with the definite article and meaning "the circuit, the district"; Gk. *Galilaia G1133*). The geographical area in PALESTINE bounded on the N by the Litani (Leontes) River, on the W by the MEDITERRANEAN Sea to Mount CARMEL, on the S by the northern edge of the Plain of ESDRAELON (though at times the plain itself is included), and on the E by the JORDAN Valley and the Sea of Galilee. This region measures approximately 50 mi. (80 km.) N to S and 30 mi. (50 km.) E to W. The Plain of Esdraelon (or JEZREEL) was a vital communications link between the coastal plain and the center of Palestine. For this reason, decisive battles were often fought here for possession of this desirable pass. The city of MEGIDDO was important for the control of the valley, and lends its name to ARMAGEDDON, where the conflict between CHRIST and the armies of the ANTICHRIST is predicted to occur (Rev. 16:16).

An imaginary E-W line from the Plain of Acco to the N end of the Sea of Galilee divided the country into Upper and Lower Galilee. "Galilee of the Gentiles" refers chiefly to Upper Galilee, which is separated from LEBANON by the Leontes River. It was the territory of ASHER and NAPHTALI, where the ruins of KEDESH Naphtali, one of the cities of refuge, can now be seen (Josh. 20:7; 21-32). In this region lay the twenty towns given by SOLOMON to HIRAM, king of TYRE, in payment for timber from Lebanon (1 Ki. 9:11). The land was luxurious and productive, a rugged mountainous country of oaks and terebinths interrupted by fertile plains. It was said that Asher in the W would eat fat for bread and yield royal dainties and dip his feet in oil (Gen. 49:20; Deut. 33:24-25). The olive OIL of Galilee has long been esteemed as of the highest quality. Lower Galilee was largely the heritage of ZEBULUN and ISSACHAR. Less hilly and of a milder climate than Upper Galilee, it included the rich Plain of Esdraelon and was a "pleasant" land (Gen. 49:15) that would yield "treasures hidden in the sand" (Deut. 33:19). The sand of these coasts was especially valuable for making glass. Important caravan trade routes carried their busy traffic through Galilee from EGYPT and S Palestine to DAMASCUS in the NE as well as E and W from the Mediterranean to the Far East.

The northern part of Naphtali was inhabited by a mixed race of Jews and pagans (Jdg. 1:33). Its Israelite population was carried away captive to ASSYRIA and was replaced by a colony of pagan immigrants (2 Ki. 15:29; 17:24), hence called "Galilee of the nations [or Gentiles]" (Isa. 9:1; Matt. 4:13, 15-16). During and after the EXILE, the predominant mixture of Gentile races impoverished the worship of Judaism. For the same reason the Galilean accent and dialect were noticeably peculiar (Matt. 26:73). This caused the southern Jews of purer blood and orthodox tradition to despise them (Jn. 7:52). NATHANAEL asked, rather contemptuously, "Nazareth! Can anything good come from there?" (1:46). Yet its very darkness was the Lord's reason for granting more of the light of his presence and ministry to Galilee than to self-satisfied and privileged Judea. He was sent for "a light for the Gentiles" (Isa. 42:6) as well as to the "lost sheep of Israel" (Matt. 15:24). Wherever he found faith and repentance, he bestowed his blessing, whereas unbelief often hindered his activity (13:58). He preached his first public sermon in the synagogue at NAZARETH in Lower Galilee, where he had been brought up (Lk. 4:16-30). His disciples came from Galilee (Matt. 4:18; Jn. 1:43-44; Acts 1:11; 2:7); in CANA of Galilee he performed his first miracle (Jn. 2:11). CAPERNAUM in Galilee, which became his new home (Matt. 4:13; 9:1), is where the first three Gospels present his major ministry. Galilee's debasement made some of its people feel their need of the Savior. This and its comparative freedom from priestly and pharisaical prejudice may have been additional reasons for its receiving the larger share of the Lord's ministry.

After the death of HEROD the Great in 4 B.C., Herod Antipas governed the tetrarchy of Galilee (Lk. 3:1) until A.D. 39. Jesus referred to him as "that fox" (13:32). Sepphoris was his capital at first, 3 mi. (5 km.) N of Nazareth, but about A.D. 20 he built a new capital on the shore of the Sea of Galilee and named it TIBERIAS, after the reign-

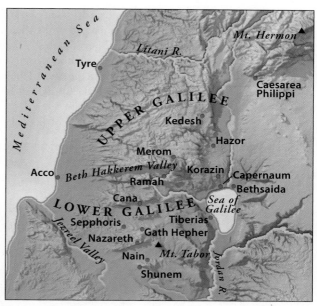

Upper and Lower Galilee.

ing emperor. Herod AGRIPPA I succeeded him and took the title of "king." After his death in 44 (Acts 12:23) Galilee was joined for a while to the Roman province of SYRIA, after which it was given to AGRIPPA II. It became the land of ZEALOTS and patriots who, in their hatred of foreign rule and in their longing for the MESSIAH, incited the populace to rebellion, and this led Rome to destroy JERUSALEM in A.D. 70. After the fall of Jerusalem, Galilee became famous for its rabbis and schools of Jewish learning. The Sanhedrin or Great Council was moved to Sepphoris and then to Tiberias on the western shore of the Sea of Galilee. This is most interesting in light of the fact that when Herod Antipas built Tiberias on top of a cemetery, strict Jews utterly abhorred the place. The Mishnah was compiled here, and the Gemara was added, forming the Palestinian TALMUD. The remains of splendid synagogues in Galilee, such as those at Capernaum and KORAZIN, still attest to the prosperity of the Jews there from the second to the seventh century.

Galilee, Sea of. So called from its location E of GALILEE, it is also called the Lake of GENNESARET (Lk. 5:1), since the fertile Plain of Gennesaret lies on the NW (Matt. 14:34). The OT calls it the Sea of KINNERETH (Heb. "harp-shaped," Num. 34:11; Josh. 13:27), from the town so named on its shore (Josh. 19:35), of which Gennesaret is probably the corruption. The Sea of TIBERIAS is another designation (Jn. 6:1; 21:10), associated with the city of Tiberias, the capital of HEROD Antipas. All its names were derived from places on the western shore.

Located some 60 mi. (100 km.) N of JERUSA-

© Dr. James C. Martin

Aerial view of the Sea of Galilee (looking N).

LEM, its bed is but a lower depression of the JORDAN Valley. The surface of the water is c. 685 ft. (210 m.) below the level of the MEDITERRANEAN and it varies in depth up to 150 ft. (45 m.). As the Jordan River plunges southward on its course from Mount HERMON to the DEAD SEA, it enters the Sea of Galilee at its N end and flows out of its S end, a distance of 13 mi. (21 km.). The greatest width of the sea is 8 mi. (13 km.), at MAGDALA. The view from the NAZARETH road to Tiberias is beautiful. The bare hills on the W, except at Khan Minyeh (present CAPERNAUM) where there is a small cliff, are recessed from the shore. From the eastern side, the western hills appear to rise out of the water to a height of c. 2,000 ft. (610 m.), while far to the N can be seen snowy Mount Hermon. The eastern hills rise from a coast of 0.5 mi. (1 km.) in width and are flat along the summit. The whole basin betrays its volcanic origin, and this accounts for the cliffs of hard porous basalt and the hot springs at Tiberias, famous for their medicinal value. The

warm climate produces tropical vegetation—the lotus thorn, palms, and indigo. The Plain of Gennesaret on the NW abounds with walnuts, figs, olives, grapes, and assorted wild flowers. The fresh water is sweet, sparkling, and transparent, with fish in abundance. The gospel accounts picture fishing as a prosperous industry here in biblical times, but today, instead of fleets of fishing vessels, only a boat or two is seen. On these shores Jesus called his first disciples, four of whom were fishermen, and made them fishers of men (Matt. 4:18; Lk. 5:1-11).

The Sea of Galilee is noted for its sudden and violent storms caused by cold air sweeping down from the vast naked plateaus of Gaulanitis, the Hauran, and Mount Hermon through the ravines and gorges and converging at the head of the lake where it meets warm air. Jesus rebuked just such a storm (Mk. 4:39). Here also Jesus walked on the tempestuous water (Matt. 14:22-34; Mk. 6:45-53; Jn. 6:15-21).

The Sea of Galilee was the focus of Galilee's wealth. Nine cities of 15,000 or more stood on its shores. To the NW was Capernaum, the home of PETER and ANDREW (Mk. 1:29) and where MATTHEW collected taxes (Matt. 9:9). It was the scene of much of Jesus' Galilean ministry. Below this, on the western side, was Magdala, home of MARY Magdalene; 3 mi. (5 km.) S was Tiberias, the magnificent capital of Galilee. On the NE corner was BETHSAIDA, the native town of PHILIP, Andrew, and Peter (Jn. 1:44) and one-time capital of Philip the Tetrarch. GERGESA lay to the south. Of these towns—once thriving with dyeing, tanning, boat building, fishing, and fish curing—two are now inhabited, namely Magdala, consisting of a few mud huts, and Tiberias.

gall. See PLANTS.

gallery. This term is used by many Bible versions to render a Hebrew architectural term of uncertain meaning referring to some sections of the TEMPLE that EZEKIEL saw in a vision (Ezek. 41:15-16; 42:3, 5). This feature is not mentioned in the description of SOLOMON's temple. Some have compared the structure of Ezekiel's building, apparently with terraces or recessed upper stories, with the design of the Babylonian ZIGGURAT or stage-tower temple. Others think the term refers to passages or streets.

galley. See SHIPS.

Gallim. gal′im (Heb. *gallim H1668*, "heaps"). A village in BENJAMIN, N of JERUSALEM, near GIBEAH of SAUL and ANATHOTH; Palti (PALTIEL) son of Laish, to whom Saul gave his daughter, was from Gallim (1 Sam. 25:44; Isa. 10:30).

Gallio. gal′ee-oh (Gk. *Galliōn G1136*). Lucius Junius Gallio Annaeanus was PROCONSUL of ACHAIA in A.D. 51-52 or 52-53, in residence at CORINTH. His brother, the well-known philosopher Seneca, said of him, "No mortal was ever so sweet to one as Gallio was to all." The book of Acts recounts that the Jews in Corinth, alarmed at the inroads that the GOSPEL was making, brought PAUL before Gallio. The Jews hoped to convince the proconsul that Paul was guilty of an offense against a lawful religion, and hence against the Roman government itself (Acts 18:12-17), but Gallio rejected their argument. The Greeks then beat the chief ruler of the SYNAGOGUE, but Gallio remained indifferent to the incident. A more stern governor might have arrested the violence at once, but in the providence of God, Gallio's action amounted to an authoritative legal decision that Paul's preaching was not subversive against ROME. This gave the apostle the protection he needed to continue his preaching there. Gallio did not become a Christian; he died by committing suicide.

gallon. See WEIGHTS AND MEASURES.

gallows. A pole for executing and exhibiting a victim by hanging or impalement. A gallows 75 ft. (23 m.) high was ordered by HAMAN to execute MORDECAI (Esth. 5:14; 6:4).

Gamad. See GAMMAD.

Gamaliel. guh-may′lee-uhl (Heb. *gamli′ēl H1697*, "God is my completion [*or* reward]"; Gk. *Gamaliēl G1137*). (**1**) Son of Pedahzur; a leader of the tribe of MANASSEH who was chosen to aid in the wilderness census and to bring the tribe's offering (Num. 1:10; 2:20; 7:54, 59; 10:23).

(**2**) A famous Jewish sage who advised moderation in the treatment of the apostles and who had earlier been PAUL's teacher (Acts 5:34; 22:3). He was one of the prominent rabbis whose rulings are mentioned in the Mishnah (see TALMUD). That document states, "When Rabban Gamaliel the Elder died, the glory of the Law ceased and purity and abstinence died" (*m. Soṭah* 9:15). He was reportedly the grandson of none other than HILLEL, but this and other similar traditions cannot be confirmed. (He is sometimes confused with his grandson, Gamaliel II, a very influential rabbi at the end of the first century.) When the enraged SANHEDRIN sought to kill the apostles for their bold testimony to Christ, Gamaliel stood up in the council and urged judicious caution on the ground that if the new doctrine was of God they could not overthrow it, and if it were of man it would fail (Acts 5:34-39). Because he was held in esteem by all the people, his counsel was valued, and God used it to give a needed respite to the infant church. Inasmuch as Gamaliel believed in God's sovereign control, his advice was sound; but also underlying it was the premise of pragmatism that what succeeds is good and what fails is evil.

game. Wild animals hunted for sport or food (Gen. 25:28; 27:3-7 et al.; KJV, "venison"). Men such as ISHMAEL (21:20) and ESAU (25:27) were renowned for their hunting skills. Game consisted chiefly of partridge, gazelle, and hart meat (Deut. 12:15), along with roebucks in the time of SOLOMON (1 Ki. 4:23).

games. Not much is known about the amusements of the ancient Israelites, partly because the earnestness of the Hebrew character did not give them prominence. Instead of public games, the great religious feasts gave them their occasions for national gatherings. There are references to DANCING (Ps. 30:11; Jer. 31:13; Lk. 15:25). The dance led by JEPHTHAH's daughter (Jdg. 11:34) and the dances of the Israelite women mentioned elsewhere (1 Sam. 18:6; 21:11; 29:5) were public celebrations of military victories. Religious dancing was engaged in by MIRIAM and the women of Israel after the crossing of the RED SEA (Exod. 15:20), by the Israelites around the golden calf at SINAI (32:19), and by DAVID before the ARK OF THE COVENANT (2 Sam. 6:14, 16; cf. also Ps. 149:3; 150:4). Of course, children of every race have their games. ZECHARIAH prophesied that "the city

© Dr. James C. Martin. The British Museum. Photographed by permission.

The Royal Game of Ur (found with other boards in graves dating to c. 2600 B.C.) was apparently one of the most popular games of the ancient world. Two players competed to race from one end of the board to the other.

streets will be filled with boys and girls playing there" (Zech. 8:5). In the NT the only children's game mentioned is that of mimicking the wedding dance and the funeral wail to the music of the flute (Matt. 11:16-17; Lk. 7:32).

The public games of GREECE and ROME were familiar to the Christians and non-Christians of the first century, providing the NT writers with rich source material to illustrate spiritual truths. Condemned criminals were thrown to lions in the arena as punishment and for sport. In 1 Cor. 15:32 PAUL alludes to fighting with beasts at EPHESUS. When a Roman general returned home victorious, he led his army in a triumphal procession, at the end of which trailed the captives who were condemned to fight with beasts. Paul felt that, in contrast to the proud Corinthians, the apostles had been put "on display, at the end of the procession, like men condemned to die in the arena" (1 Cor. 4:9). God had made them a spectacle to be gazed at and made sport of in the arena of the world. NERO used to clothe the Christians in beast skins

when he exposed them to wild beasts. (Cf. 2 Tim. 4:17, "I was delivered from the lion's mouth.")

In 1 Cor. 9:24-25 Paul alludes vividly to the Isthmian games, celebrated every two years on the Isthmus of CORINTH. Held in honor of the Greek gods, the festival consisted of foot races, horse races, chariot contests, jumping, wrestling, boxing, and throwing the discus and javelin. To the Greeks they were events of patriotic pride, a passion rather than a pastime, and thus made a suitable image of earnestness in the Christian race: "Do you not know that in a race all the runners run, but only one gets the prize? Run in such a way as to get the prize. Everyone who competes in the games goes into strict training. They do it to get a crown that will not last; but we do it to get a crown that will last forever." The coveted crown was a garland made of laurel, olive leaves, or pine needles; our crown is incorruptible (1 Pet. 1:4) and therefore demands greater fidelity. If the competitor did not strive "according to the rules," he was not crowned (2 Tim. 2:5). He had to keep to the bounds of the course, having previously trained himself for ten months with chastity, abstemious diet, the enduring of cold and heat, and extreme exercise.

As in boxing, so in the Christian race Paul beat his body and brought it under subjection, so that when he preached ("heralded"—the herald announced the name and country of each contestant and displayed the prizes) to others, he would not be rejected but receive the winner's crown (cf. Jas. 1:12). In view of the reward, Paul denied himself and became a servant of all in order to win more people to Jesus Christ. Christians do not beat the air, missing their opponent, but they fight certainly, with telling blows on the enemy (1 Cor. 9:26-27). As the runner looks intently at the goal and discards every encumbrance, so Christians run, throwing aside not only sinful lusts but even harmless and otherwise useful things that would slow them down. They must run with "perseverance" the race set before them, fixing their eyes on Jesus, "the author and perfecter" of their faith (Heb. 12:1-2).

Paul used the same figure in addressing the Ephesians (Acts 20:24) and the Philippians (3:12-14). The Colossians were urged to let God's peace *rule* in their hearts (Col. 3:15); the Greek verb here is *brabeuō G1093*, which originally meant "to judge as umpire, to award prizes in contests." Other allusions to the language of games are in Eph. 6:12, "our struggle [*palē G4097*, 'wrestling'] is not against flesh and blood," and 2 Tim. 4:7, "I have fought the good fight [*agōn G74*, 'contest, struggle'], I have finished the race." See also 1 Tim. 6:12; Rev. 2:10.

Gammad. gam'uhd (assumed name of a site, based on the gentilic *gammādim H1689*, "Gammadites"). Also Gamad. In his poetic description of TYRE, EZEKIEL says, "Men of Arvad and Helech / manned your walls on every side; / men of Gammad / were in your towers" (Ezek. 27:11; KJV, "Gammadims"). The context suggests that the reference is to a city in PHOENICIA, otherwise unknown. Proposals include Kumidi (modern Kamid el-Loz, N of Mt. HERMON), *Qmd* (a town mentioned in Egyptian sources and thought to be on or near the coast N of Byblos [GEBAL]), and others.

Gammadim. See GAMMAD.

Gamul. gay'muhl (Heb. *gāmûl H1690*, perhaps "benefit" or "weaned"). A leader of the Levites, appointed by lot as the head of the twenty-second course of priests during DAVID's time (1 Chr. 24:17). See also BETH GAMUL.

gangrene. See DISEASES.

garden. A cultivated piece of ground, planted with flowers, vegetables, shrubs, or trees, fenced with a mud or stone wall (Prov. 24:31) or thorny hedges (Isa. 5:5), often guarded by a watchman in a lodge (1:8) or tower (Mk. 12:10) to drive away wild beasts and robbers. The quince, citron, almond, and other fruits, herbs, and various vegetables and spices are mentioned as growing in gardens. A reservoir cistern, or still better a fountain of water, was essential to a good garden (cf. Cant. 4:15, "a garden fountain," i.e., a fountain sufficient to water many gardens).

The occurrence of no fewer than 250 botanical terms in the OT shows the Israelite fondness for flowers, fruits, and pleasant grounds (see PLANTS). These are still a special delight to those living in a hot, dry country. Every house court or yard generally had its shade tree. The vine that grew around the trellis or an outside staircase was the emblem of the living and fruitful wife and happy home within (Ps. 128:3). The "orchards" (KJV) or "parks" (NIV) were larger gardens especially for fruit trees (the Heb. word is *pardēs H7236*; see PARADISE). SOLOMON's gardens and fruit orchards with pools of water for irrigation (Eccl. 2:4-6) very likely suggested the imagery of Cant. 4:12-15. The "king's garden" (2 Ki. 25:4; Neh. 3:15; Jer. 39:4; 52:7) was near the pool of SILOAM.

The Hebrews used gardens as BURIAL places. The field of MACHPELAH, ABRAHAM's burial ground, was a garden with trees in and around it (Gen. 23:17). MANASSEH and AMON were buried in UZZA's garden (2 Ki. 21:18, 26). The Garden of GETHSEMANE served Jesus as a retreat for meditation and prayer (Matt. 26:36; Jn. 18:1-2). In idolatrous periods gardens were the scenes of superstition and image worship, the awful counterpart of the primitive EDEN (Isa. 1:29; 65:3; 66:17). The new paradise regained by the people of God (Rev. 22:1-5) suggests in a fuller way the old paradise planted by God but lost through sin (Gen. 2:8).

The believer is a garden watered by the HOLY SPIRIT (Jer. 2:13; 17:7-8; Jn. 4:13-14; 7:37-39). "A well-watered garden" expresses abundant happiness and prosperity (Isa. 58:11; Jer. 31:12) just as "a garden without water" (Isa. 1:30) expresses spiritual, national, and individual barrenness and misery.

garden, king's. See KING'S GARDEN.

gardener. See OCCUPATIONS AND PROFESSIONS (under *farmer*).

Gareb (person). gair'ib (Heb. *gāréb H1735*, "scabby"). An ITHRITE warrior included in DAVID's elite group, the Thirty (2 Sam. 23:38; 1 Chr. 11:40). The Ithrites were a clan from KIRIATH JEARIM (1 Chr. 2:53).

Gareb (place). gair'ib (Heb. *gāréb H1736*, "scabby"). A hill in or near JERUSALEM. JEREMIAH prophesied that God's city would be rebuilt "from

G

the Tower of Hananel to the Corner Gate. The measuring line will stretch from there straight to the hill of Gareb and then turn to Goah" (Jer. 31:38-39). Because the Tower of HANANEL was on the N wall (though its precise location is uncertain), with the CORNER GATE apparently guarding the NW approach to Jerusalem, some traditions locate Gareb on the W side of the city and GOAH farther S, but these sites have not been identified.

garland. This term, referring to a band of intertwined flowers or leaves, is used by the NIV to render a Hebrew word that occurs only twice in a metaphorical sense, indicating honor and joy (Prov. 1:9; 4:9). The NRSV uses it a few additional times as a rendering of various other words (e.g., Prov. 14:24 et al.; Acts 14:13). See also CROWN; WREATH.

garlic. See PLANTS.

garments. See DRESS.

Garmite. gahr'mit (Heb. *garmî H1753*, perhaps from *gerem H1752*, "bone"). A gentilic, used only to identify a Judahite named KEILAH, whose genealogical connection to the descendants of JUDAH is not specified (1 Chr. 4:19). Since no town by the name "Gerem" or the like is anywhere mentioned, some have speculated that the description "Garmite" may have referred to his bony or strong appearance.

garner. As a noun meaning "granary" or "barn," this term is used a few times in the KJV (Ps. 144:13; Joel 1:17; Matt. 3:12; Lk. 3:17), but not in the NIV and other modern versions. The verb *to garner* ("to gather and store") is used occasionally in recent translations (e.g., Isa. 62:9 NRSV).

garrison. A military post (or the troops assigned to it), often in a strategic frontier area, primarily for defensive purposes. Larger military units would be needed for an offensive drive. Garrisons were placed by the PHILISTINES in the Judean region of Israel (1 Sam. 14:1-15; NIV, "outpost"). Once DAVID brought these garrisons under his control, he then placed his own garrisons in ARAM and EDOM (2 Sam. 8:6, 14). See also ARMY.

Gashmu. See GESHEM.

Gaspar. gas'pahr. In late Christian tradition, the name of one of the MAGI who traveled to BETHLEHEM (Matt. 2:1-12).

Gatam. gay'tuhm (Heb. *ga'tām H1725*, derivation uncertain). Son of Eliphaz, grandson of ESAU, and head of an Edomite clan (Gen. 36:11, 16; 1 Chr. 1:36).

gate. The entrance to enclosed buildings, grounds, or cities. It was at the gates of a CITY that the people of the ANE went for legal business, conversation, bargaining, and news. The usual gateway consisted of double doors plated with metal (Ps. 107:16; Isa. 45:2), for wooden doors without iron plating were easily set on fire (Jdg. 9:52; Neh. 2:3, 17). Some gates were made of brass, as was the "gate called Beautiful" of Herod's TEMPLE (Acts 3:2), more costly than nine others of the outer court that had been "poured over" with gold and silver (Josephus, *War* 5.5.3). Still others were of solid stone (Isa. 54:12; Rev. 21:21). Massive stone doors are found in ancient towns of SYRIA, single slabs several inches thick and 10 ft. (3 m.) high, turning on pivots above and below. Gates ordinarily swung on projections that fitted into sockets on the post and were secured with bars of wood (Nah. 3:13) or of metal (1 Ki. 4:13; Ps. 107:16; Isa. 45:2).

As the weakest points in a city's walls, the gates were often the object of enemy attack (Jdg. 5:8; 1 Sam. 23:7; Ezek. 21:15, 22) and therefore were flanked by towers (2 Sam. 18:24, 33; 2 Chr. 14:7; 26:9). To "possess the gates" was to possess the city (Gen. 24:60). Gates were shut at night and opened again in the morning (Deut. 3:5; Josh. 2:5, 7).

Markets were held at the gate, and the main item sold there often gave its name to the gate; possible examples are the SHEEP GATE, FISH GATE, HORSE GATE (Neh. 3:1, 3, 28). The gate was the place where people met to hear an important announcement (2 Chr. 32:6; Jer. 7:2; 17:19-27) or the reading of the LAW (Neh. 8:1, 3), or where the elders transacted legal business (Deut. 16:18; 21:18-20; Josh. 20:4; Ruth 4:1-2, 11). The psalmist complained, "Those who sit at the gate mock me, and I am the song of the drunkards" (Ps. 69:12);

© Dr. James C. Martin. The British Museum. Photographed by permission.

The entrance to the Israelite city of Dan was guarded by a massive gate complex (dating to the Iron Age).

that is, he was an object of abusive language not only among the drunks but in the grave deliberations of the judges in the place of justice. The gate was also the king's or chief's place of audience (2 Sam. 19:8; 1 Ki. 22:10). DANIEL "sat in the gate" of King NEBUCHADNEZZAR as ruler over the province of BABYLON (Dan. 2:48-49 KJV; NIV, "remained at the royal court"). Regarded as specially sacred, the threshold in Assyrian palaces bore cuneiform inscriptions and was guarded by human-headed bulls with eagles' wings. In Israel, sentences from the law were inscribed on and above the posts and gates of private houses (Deut. 6:9). King JOSIAH destroyed the high places near the gates that were used for heathen sacrifices (2 Ki. 23:8).

Figuratively, gates refer to the glory of a city (Isa. 3:26; 14:31; Jer. 14:2) or to the city itself (Ps. 87:2; 122:2). In Matt. 16:18 the statement that the gates of HADES will not overcome the CHURCH is a reference either to the failure of the infernal powers to defeat the church or to the church's greater power to retain her members than the grave has over its victims.

Gate, Beautiful. See BEAUTIFUL GATE. Similarly, EAST GATE; GUARD, GATE OF; VALLEY GATE; etc.

gate between the two walls. This entrance is mentioned only three times in the OT (2 Ki. 25:4; Jer. 39:4; 52:7). All three references are in the same context: JERUSALEM was under siege by NEBUCHADNEZZAR's army in 587 B.C., and ZEDEKIAH and his army fled eastward by night through "the gate between the two walls" to the JORDAN Valley. This gate was near the KING'S GARDEN (which in turn was in the vicinity of the Pool of SILOAM, Neh. 3:15), and several scholars have identified it with Nehemiah's FOUNTAIN GATE. Others believe it is the same as the POTSHERD GATE (Jer. 19:2).

Gath. gath (Heb. *gat H1781*, "winepress"; gentilic *gitti H1785*, "Gittite"). One of the five great PHILISTINE cities, the others being ASHDOD, GAZA, ASHKELON, and EKRON (Josh. 13:3; 1 Sam. 6:17). Its people were the Gittites, including GOLIATH and other giants (2 Sam. 21:19-22). In harmony with this fact is the record of the ANAKITES' presence in Gath after JOSHUA had destroyed the neighboring territory (Josh. 11:22). It was one of the five cities to which the Philistines carried the ARK OF THE COVENANT and whose people God afflicted with an outbreak of tumors (1 Sam. 5:8-9).

DAVID fled from SAUL to Gath, where he feigned madness to save his life (1 Sam. 21:10-15). The second time he visited Gath, King ACHISH assigned him ZIKLAG as a residence (27:2-6). During his sixteen months there, David won the confidence of the king through subterfuge and intrigue (27:7—29:11). Some of David's 600 followers were Gittites, one of whom was his loyal friend ITTAI. They may have attached themselves to him at this time or when he defeated the Philistines (2 Sam. 8:1; 15:18-21). Although David conquered it (1 Chr. 18:1), Gath retained its own king (1 Ki. 2:39). REHOBOAM, SOLOMON's son, rebuilt and fortified the town (2 Chr. 11:8). Later, HAZAEL, king of Aram (SYRIA), captured Gath from JEHOASH, king of Judah (2 Ki. 12:17), but UZZIAH won it back (2 Chr. 26:6). In a reference to the fall of this walled

G

city, Amos sounds a warning to those at ease in Zion (Amos 6:12). The omission of Gath from the later lists of the five cities (Amos 1:6, 8; Zeph. 2:4-5; Zech. 9:5-6) indicates it had lost its place among them by that time.

The site of Gath is uncertain. It lay on the border between Judah and Philistia, between Socoh and Ekron (1 Sam. 17:1, 52). Tell eṣ-Ṣafi, c. 25 mi. (40 km.) SSE of Joppa, favors this description, lying on a hill at the foot of Judah's mountains, some 10 mi. (16 km.) SE of Ekron.

Gath Hepher. gath-hee′fuhr (Heb. *gat ḥēper H1783*, "winepress by the [water] pit"). KJV Gittah-hepher. A border town of the tribe of Zebulun, to the E, next to the territory of Naphtali (Josh. 19:13); it was the home of the prophet Jonah (2 Ki. 14:25). The town is probably to be identified with Khirbet ez-Zurra‛, about 3 mi. (5 km.) NE of Nazareth. Nearby, to the N, is the modern village of Meshhed, the traditional site of Jonah's tomb.

Gath Rimmon. gath-rim′uhn (Heb. *gat-rimmôn H1784*, "winepress by the pomegranate tree"). **(1)** A town in the territory of Dan (Josh. 19:45). It was one of four cities from this tribe allotted to the Levites descended from Kohath (Josh. 21:24; 1 Chr. 6:69), and it may have been one of the cities of refuge (see 1 Chr. 6:67 NRSV; cf. NIV note). Gath Rimmon is usually identified with Tell Jerisheh, 4.5 mi. (7 km.) NE of Joppa and just S of the Yarkon River.

(2) A town of the one-half tribe of Manasseh, W of the Jordan, and one of two cities from this tribe allotted to the Kohathite Levites (Josh. 21:25). Some have identified this Gath Rimmon with modern Rummaneh, NW of Taanach, but many scholars believe that the name here is a scribal error (repeating the name of the Danite town in the previous verse) and so emend it to Bileam, found in the parallel passage (1 Chr. 6:69).

Gaulanitis. See Golan.

Gaza. gay′zuh, gah′zuh (Heb. ‛*azzâ H6445*, "strong"; gentilic ‛*azzātî H6484*, "Gazite" [Josh. 13:3, KJV "Gazathites"; Jdg. 16:2]). KJV also

Azzah (Deut. 2:23; 1 Ki. 4:24; Jer. 25:20). The southernmost of the five chief cities of the Philistines in SW Palestine, the others being Ashdod, Ashkelon, Ekron, and Gath. Originally a seaport, the town moved to a hill 3 mi. (5 km.) inland on the great caravan route between Syria and Egypt. Here it became an important rest stop on the edge of the desert and a popular trading center. Its position and *strength* (the meaning of its name) made it the key of this line of communications.

Gaza was assigned by Joshua to the tribe of Judah (Josh. 15:47), but as the Anakites were still present (11:22; 13:3), it was not conquered until after Joshua's death (Jdg. 1:18). The Philistines soon recovered it (Jdg. 13:1), and Samson perished there while destroying his captors (16:1, 21). Solomon ruled over it (1 Ki. 4:24), but it was Hezekiah who gave the decisive blow to the Philistines (2 Ki. 18:8). God through Amos threatened Gaza with destruction by fire for her transgressions (Amos 1:6). This was fulfilled by one of the pharaohs of Egypt (Jer. 47:1). The predictions that Gaza would be forsaken (Zeph. 2:4) and that its king would perish (Zech. 9:5, referring to the Persian satrap) were fulfilled by Alexander the Great, who took the city in 332 B.C., after it had resisted his siege for two months. He bound Betis the satrap to a chariot and dragged him around the city; he killed 10,000 of Gath's inhabitants, selling the rest as slaves. The town was desolated again by fire and sword by the Maccabees in 96 B.C. In turn, Gaza passed under the control of Syria and Rome.

Philip met the Ethiopian eunuch on "the road—the desert road—that goes down from Jerusalem to Gaza" (Acts 8:26). After NT times, Gaza was for a time the seat of a Christian church and a bishop in the midst of Greek culture and temples, but most of its people turned to Islam in A.D. 634. Modern Ghuzzeh is the metropolis of the Gaza Strip; to the N lies an extensive olive grove whose fruit is used to make soap. The city's trade in corn is considerable, the corn still being ground by millstones such as Samson was forced to work at in his prison house at Gaza (Jdg. 16:21).

Gazathite. See Gaza.

gazelle. See Animals.

Looking S toward the hilltop on which the ancient site of Geba once stood.

Gazer. See GEZER.

Gazez. gay'ziz (Heb. *gāzēz H1606*, possibly "[sheep] shearer" or "born at shearing time"). **(1)** Son of CALEB by his concubine Ephah (1 Chr. 2:46). But this individual may be the same as #2 below.

(2) Son of Haran, grandson of Caleb, and nephew of #1 above (1 Chr. 2:46). Some have thought that the words "Haran was the father of [*lit.*, begat] Gazez" are an explanatory addition to the previous statement, in which case there was only one person by this name, Caleb's grandson.

Gazite. gay'zit. See GAZA.

Gazzam. gaz'uhm (Heb. *gazzām H1613*, possibly "caterpillar"). Ancestor of some temple servants (NETHINIM) who returned to Jerusalem with ZERUBBABEL (Ezra 2:48; Neh. 7:51).

Geba. gee'buh (Heb. *geba< H1494*, "hill"). KJV also Gaba. A city in the territory of the tribe of BENJAMIN (Josh. 18:24); it was assigned to the LEVITES (Josh. 21:17; 1 Chr. 6:60). SAUL and JONATHAN may have encamped there when the PHILISTINES were at MICMASH (1 Sam. 13:16; the NIV, however, regards Geba here and in Jdg. 20:10, 33 as a spelling variant of GIBEAH). It was possibly in Geba also that DAVID began to smite

the Philistines (2 Sam. 5:25; NIV, GIBEON, following LXX and 1 Chr. 14:16). ASA built a fortress in Geba with stones from RAMAH (1 Ki. 15:22; 2 Chr. 16:6). JOSIAH defiled the high places where the priests had burned incense from Geba, the N limit of JUDAH, to the S limit, BEERSHEBA (2 Ki. 23:8). Geba is coupled with Ramah in the lists of those returning from BABYLON (Ezra 2:26; Neh. 7:30), and it is one of the cities where Benjamites lived after the EXILE (Neh. 11:31) and from which singers came and sang at the dedication of the temple (12:29). It was one of the stopping points of the Assyrian army on its approach to Jerusalem (Isa. 10:29). Geba is to be identified with modern Jeba<, c. 6 mi. (10 km.) NNE of Jerusalem, and 2 mi. (3 km.) E of Ramah.

Gebal. gee'buhl (Heb. *gĕbal H1488*, "boundary"; gentilic *giblî H1490*, "Gebalite" [KJV, "Giblite"]). **(1)** A non-Israelite town or region associated with such nations as EDOM, MOAB, and AMMON (Ps. 83:7); it was probably in TRANSJORDAN, SE of the Dead Sea.

(2) A city in PHOENICIA on the Mediterranean Sea; modern Jebeil (Jubayl), 18 mi. (29 km.) NNE of Beirut. It was called Gubla by the Assyrians and Babylonians, while the Greeks and the Romans knew it as Byblos (because the city was a major exporter of writing material, the Gk. word *byblos*

G

came to mean "[papyrus] scroll"). Once a flourishing port and trading center, its most valuable export was pine and cedarwood from LEBANON. The city was also noted for shipbuilding and stonecutting. Excavations have revealed that Gebal is one of the oldest towns in the world; occupation of the site has been traced to Neolithic times. Before the end of the third millennium B.C., Canaanites in Gebal had developed a syllabic script modeled on the Egyptian hieroglyphics (see WRITING). The Gebalites were considered master builders and able seamen (1 Ki. 5:18; Ezek. 27:9). Their land is mentioned as one of those that were not conquered by the Israelites (Josh. 13:5).

Geber. gee′buhr (Heb. *geber H1506*, "man, strong one"). Son of Uri and one of the twelve district governors who supplied provisions for SOLOMON and the royal household; he was in charge of the twelfth district in GILEAD (1 Ki. 4:19). Some have thought that this passage is a duplication of the sixth district (v. 13), but Geber may have been responsible for the southern parts of Gilead; see BEN-GEBER.

Gebim. gee′bim (Heb. *gēbîm H1481*, "pits"). A village of the tribe of BENJAMIN mentioned only in the poetic listing of the conquests of ASSYRIA (Isa. 10:31). The passage mentions Gebim between MADMENAH and NOB, but none of these locations has ever been confidently identified. The context also mentions ANATHOTH, which was 2.5 mi. (4 km.) NE of JERUSALEM, so Gebim was probably in that vicinity.

gecko. See ANIMALS.

Gedaliah. ged′uh-li′uh (Heb. *gĕdalyāhû H1546*, "great is Yahweh"). **(1)** Son of JEDUTHUN and a temple musician under DAVID (1 Chr. 25:3, 9).

(2) Son of AHIKAM, grandson of SHAPHAN, and governor of Judah after the fall of JERUSALEM to the Babylonians (2 Ki. 25:22-26; Jer. 40:6—41:18). His family's political moderation, shown by his father's protection of JEREMIAH, probably made him acceptable to the Babylonians (Jer. 26:24). MIZPAH, his headquarters during his two-month rule, served as a rallying point for various groups of

Hebrew soldiers and nobility. He avoided political intrigue in rejecting the scheme of JOHANAN son of Kareah to murder ISHMAEL son of Nethaniah. He, many Jewish leaders, and the Babylonian garrison were assassinated by Ishmael. Gedaliah's partisans, fearing Babylonian reprisals, then fled to Egypt, forcing Jeremiah the prophet to go with them.

(3) Son of Pashhur; he was one of the officials who opposed Jeremiah and put him in a cistern (Jer. 38:1-6).

(4) A descendant of JESHUA son of Jozadak, listed among the priests in EZRA's time who agreed to put away their foreign wives (Ezra 10:18).

(5) Son of Amariah and grandfather of the prophet ZEPHANIAH (Zeph. 1:1).

Gedeon. See GIDEON.

Geder. gee′duhr (Heb. *geder H1554*, "stone wall"; gentilic *gĕdērî H1559*, "Gederite"). A Canaanite city conquered by the Israelites (Josh. 12:13). It is listed after DEBIR and before ARAD, which may indicate a location either in the SHEPHELAH or in the NEGEV, but the site has not been identified. One of DAVID's officials, BAAL-HANAN the Gederite (1 Chr. 27:28), was apparently from this town.

Gederah. gi-dee′ruh (Heb. *gĕdērāh H1557*, "stone-walled pen"; gentilic *gĕdērātî H1561*, "Gederathite"). **(1)** A town within the tribal territory of JUDAH located in the SHEPHELAH (Josh. 15:36; NIV regards Gederah and GEDEROTHAIM as the same place). Together with NATAIM, Gederah is listed as inhabited by clans of skilled craftsmen who served as potters for the king (1 Chr. 4:23; KJV has "plants and hedges" for "Netaim and Gederah"). Its location is unknown, although various sites have been proposed.

(2) A town in the tribal territory of BENJAMIN. We know of this village only because one of the Benjamite warriors who joined DAVID at ZIKLAG was named JOZABAD the Gederathite (1 Chr. 12:4). Some have identified this Gederah with modern Jedireh, a short distance from GIBEON.

Gederathite. gi-dee′ruh-th*it*. See GEDERAH.

Gederite. gi-dee′r*it*. See GEDER.

Gederoth. gi-dee´roth (Heb. *gĕdērôt H1558*, "stone-walled pens"). A town in the tribal territory of JUDAH located in the SHEPHELAH (Josh. 15:31). In the time of AHAZ, Gederoth was one of several towns occupied by the PHILISTINES (2 Chr. 28:18). Gederoth was no doubt located near the Judah-Philistia border, but the precise site is unknown.

Gederothaim. gi-dee´ruh-thay´im (Heb. *gĕdērôtayim H1562*, "[two] stone-walled pens"). A town in the tribal territory of JUDAH located in the SHEPHELAH (Josh. 15:36). It is the last name in a list of fifteen towns that were part of the tribe's third administrative district, but the text speaks of "fourteen towns and their villages." The NIV rendering treats Gederothaim as an alternate name for GEDERAH, thus bringing the total to fourteen. If Gederothaim is a distinct town, its location is unknown.

Gedor. gee´dor (Heb. *gĕdôr H1529* and *H1530*, "wall"). **(1)** A town in the tribal territory of JUDAH located in the hill country (Josh. 15:58). It is usually identified with Khirbet Jedur, 7.5 mi. (12 km.) NNW of HEBRON. According to many scholars, the description "Penuel was the father of Gedor" (1 Chr. 4:4) means that PENUEL founded or was an early inhabitant of this Judahite city. It is also possible that the Gedor mentioned later in the passage (v. 18) refers to the same town and that JERED was another important figure associated with it.

(2) A town in a valley settled by Simeonites (1 Chr. 4:39-40). It is described as a land very spacious and peaceful, with good pasture. The location is unknown, and some scholars, following the SEPTUAGINT, emend the name to GERAR.

(3) A town in the tribal territory of BENJAMIN and the home of JOELAH and ZEBADIAH, two of the warriors who joined DAVID at ZIKLAG (1 Chr. 12:7). Attempts have been made to identify this Gedor with #1 above or with Khirbet Gadeirah, N of el-Jib. Other scholars believe the text is corrupt.

(4) Son of Jeiel and descendant of BENJAMIN; his brother NER was the grandfather of SAUL (1 Chr. 8:31; 9:37).

Ge Harashim. gi-hair´uh-shim (Heb. *gê˒ ḥărāšîm H1629*, "valley of the craftsmen"). The genealogy of the Judahite clan of KENAZ refers to a certain JOAB as "the father [*i.e.*, founder] of Ge Harashim. It was called this because its people were craftsmen" (1 Chr. 4:14; KJV, "valley of Charashim"). The same Hebrew expression (with a slight spelling variation), referring probably to the same area, occurs in a list of places where the Benjamites resettled after the EXILE: "… in Lod and Ono, and in the Valley of the Craftsmen" (Neh. 11:35). It should probably be identified with one of the valleys bordering the Plain of SHARON.

Gehazi. gi-hay´zi (Heb. *gêḥăzî H1634*, possibly "valley of vision"). The servant of the prophet ELISHA. He first appeared when Elisha sought to reward the Shunammite woman for her hospitality (2 Ki. 4:8-37; see SHUNEM). When she declined any reward, Gehazi said, "Well, she has no son and her husband is old." Elisha promised her that she would bear a child, and within a year the child was born. When the child had grown, he died of sunstroke, and the woman went with her sorrow to the prophet. He sent Gehazi with instructions to lay the prophet's staff on the face of the child, "but there was no sound or response." Elisha then came himself and restored the child to life. Elisha had Gehazi call the woman to receive her son.

Gehazi is mentioned again in connection with the story of NAAMAN (2 Ki. 5:1-27). Elisha refused any reward from Naaman after this Aramean general was healed, but Gehazi ran after him and asked for something. Naaman gave him more than he asked. Gehazi hid his booty before he reached home, but Elisha knew what had happened and invoked on Gehazi the leprosy of which Naaman had been cured.

On a later occasion, Gehazi reported to the king "all the great things Elisha has done" (2 Ki. 8:4-6). When he told how the Shunammite woman's son was restored to life, the woman herself appeared and asked the king to restore to her the property she abandoned on the advice of Elisha during a seven-year famine. The king ordered her fully compensated. Because Gehazi appeared in the court of the king, it has been inferred that he had repented and had been healed of his leprosy, though 5:27 renders this doubtful. He showed no resentment against Elisha. Gehazi was an efficient

G

servant, but weak enough to yield to greed. He lacked his master's clear moral insight and stamina, and he had no such relation with Elisha as Elisha had with Elijah.

Gehenna. gi-hen'uh (Gk. *geenna G1147*, from Heb. *gê-hinnōm,* "Valley of Hinnom"; Aram. *gêhinnām*). In the Greek NT, this name refers to the final place of punishment of the ungodly and is usually translated HELL. The word derives from the Hebrew phrase for "the Valley of [Ben] Hinnom," identified with the Wadi er-Rababi, just S and to the W of JERUSALEM (see HINNOM, VALLEY OF). This ravine formed part of the border between the tribes of JUDAH and BENJAMIN (Josh. 15:8; cf. 18:16), and it was still recognized as the border after the EXILE (Neh. 11:30-31). Here Kings AHAZ (2 Ki. 16:3; 2 Chr. 28:3) and MANASSEH (2 Ki. 21:6; 2 Chr. 33:6) sacrificed their sons to MOLECH (Jer. 32:35). For this reason JOSIAH defiled the place (2 Ki. 23:10). After referring to these idolatrous practices (Jer. 7:31-32), Jeremiah prophesied a great slaughter of the people there and in Jerusalem (19:1-13).

After the OT period, Jewish APOCALYPTIC writers began to call the Valley of Hinnom the entrance to hell, later hell itself. In Jewish usage of the first century A.D., Gehenna referred to the intermediate state of the godless dead, but there is no trace of this sense in the NT. The NT distinguishes sharply between HADES, the intermediate, bodiless state, and Gehenna, the state of final punishment after the RESURRECTION of the body. Gehenna existed before the judgment (Matt. 25:41). The word occurs twelve times in the NT, always translated "hell" (ASV, RSV margin "Gehenna"). Eleven times it is on the lips of Jesus: as the final punishment for calling one's brother a fool (5:22); for adultery, when the severest measures have not been taken to prevent commission of this offense (5:29-30); in a warning about whom to fear (Matt. 10:28; Lk. 12:5); and others (Matt. 18:9; Mk. 9:43, 45, 47). A hypocrite is called a "son of hell" (Matt. 23:15) who cannot escape "being condemned to hell" (23:33). James 3:6 speaks of the "tongue" as "a fire ... set on fire by hell."

A fire was kept burning in the Valley of Hinnom to consume the garbage deposited there by the residents of Jerusalem. Terms parallel to Gehenna include "fiery furnace" (Matt. 13:42, 50), "fiery lake" (Rev. 19:20; 20:14-15), "lake of burning sulfur" (20:10), "eternal fire" (Jude 7); "hell" (2 Pet. 2:4; here the Greek text has Tartarus, a name for the place of punishment of the wicked dead).

Geliloth. gi-li'loth (Heb. *gĕlilôt H1667*, "circles [of stone]," thus "circuit, territory"; cf. GALILEE). **(1)** An area on the SE boundary of the tribe of BENJAMIN, near EN SHEMESH and facing the Pass of ADUMMIM (Josh. 18:17). In the corresponding description of the NE boundary of JUDAH, possibly the same place is referred to as GILGAL (15:7). The precise location is unknown. Some have thought that Geliloth refers to a general region, not a specific site. Cf. #2 below.

(2) A place "near the Jordan in the land of Canaan" where "the Reubenites, the Gadites and the half-tribe of Manasseh built an imposing altar" (Josh. 22:10-11). Many believe, however, that the Hebrew text does not give a place name but should rather be translated, "the region near the Jordan" (cf. NRSV).

gem. See MINERALS.

Gemalli. gi-mal'i (Heb. *gĕmallî H1696*, derivation uncertain). The father of AMMIEL, a Danite; the latter was one of the twelve spies sent by MOSES into the Promised Land (Num. 13:12).

Gemara. guh-mah'ruh. See TALMUD.

Gemariah. gem'uh-ri'uh (Heb. *gĕmaryâ H1701* [Jer. 29:3] and *gĕmaryāhû H1702*, "Yahweh has fulfilled"). **(1)** Son of a certain HILKIAH; he was an emissary to NEBUCHADNEZZAR from King ZEDEKIAH charged with the task of carrying JEREMIAH's message to the captive Jews (Jer. 29:3).

(2) Son of SHAPHAN the royal secretary; he was one of the officials who urged King JEHOIAKIM not to destroy the scroll of Jeremiah (Jer. 36:10-12, 25). It was from Gemariah's room, in the upper courtyard of the temple, that BARUCH read the words of Jeremiah to the people (v. 10). His brother AHIKAM was also an important functionary, and his son MICAIAH was the one who reported the reading of the scroll by Baruch (v. 13). The name "Gemariah son of Shaphan," almost certainly referring to the same individual, survives in a seal impression dated to the time of the destruction of Jerusalem.

genealogy. A list of ancestors or descendants, descent from an ancestor, or the study of lines of descent. Genealogies are compiled to show biological descent, the right of inheritance, succession to an office, or ethnological and geographical relationships. The word *genealogy* (or the adj. *genealogical*) occurs more than twenty times in English Bibles, especially in the books of Chronicles (1 Chr. 4:33 et al.; 2 Chr. 12:15 et al.; cf. also Neh. 7:5; 1 Tim. 1:4; Tit. 3:9; Heb. 7:3), but most Bible genealogies are introduced by other words, such as "the book of the generations of," or "these are the generations of," or are given without titles.

Bible genealogies are not primarily concerned with mere biological descent. The earliest, a family register of CAIN's descendants, is found in Gen. 4:17-22; by its emphasis on occupations (JABAL, cattleman; JUBAL, musician; TUBAL-CAIN, metal worker), it shows when new features of the culture were introduced. The genealogy of the line of SETH (4:25-26; 5:1-32), a list of long-lived individuals, contrasts with the genealogy in 10:1-32, which is clearly a table of nations descended from the three families of NOAH's sons, SHEM, HAM, and JAPHETH. Many of the names are Hebrew plurals (the *-im* suffix) signifying people groups rather than individuals. The scope of biblical genealogies narrows to the chosen people and their close relatives (11:10-22, Shem to ABRAHAM; 22:20-24, Abraham's near kin). Next are the children of Abraham by HAGAR (16:15; 25:12-18), by SARAH (21:1-3; 25:19-28), and by KETURAH (25:1-4); then the children of JACOB (29:31—30:24; 35:16-26) and of his brother ESAU (ch. 36).

Jacob's posterity who came into EGYPT are carefully enumerated (Gen. 46:8-27), and part of them again (Exod. 6:14-27) to bring the genealogy down to MOSES and AARON; the inclusion of brief mention of the sons of REUBEN and SIMEON before the fuller genealogy of the LEVITES may indicate that this list was taken from an earlier one. Numbers 26:1-56 records a census following genealogical relationships, for the purpose of equitable division

Cuneiform tablet containing the genealogy of the Hammurabi dynasty (prob. from Sippar, 17th cent. B.C.). It lists the names of the kings of Babylon down to Ammiditana.

of the land. The military organization of the Israelites for the wilderness journey was by genealogy (Num. 1-3); this included the priests and Levites (3:11-39) and provided for a tax and offerings (7:11-89) for the support of religion (3:40-51), as well as the order of march in peace or war (ch. 10). Many other references to persons must be taken into account in attempting a complete genealogy. Ruth 4:17-22 picks up the genealogy of JUDAH from his son PEREZ, to carry it down to DAVID, whose children are listed: those born in HEBRON (2 Sam. 3:2-5) and in JERUSALEM (5:13-16).

The major genealogical tables of the OT are in 1 Chr. 1-9. They use most of the earlier genealogical material, but show differences that are puzzling to us today. Satisfactory solutions are not available for many of these. Mistakes in copying would account for some; differences in the purpose of the recorders for others. The books of KINGS

© Dr. James C. Martin. The British Museum. Photographed by permission.

G

and CHRONICLES contain information about the family relationships of the kings of Judah and of Israel. The books of EZRA and NEHEMIAH name by families those who returned with ZERUBBABEL from Babylonian EXILE, including many whose descent could not be traced (Ezra 2:1-63; 8:1-20; Neh. 7:7-63). Ezra 7:1-6 gives Ezra's own line of descent from Aaron, and 10:18-44 names those who had married foreign women. Other lists include the names of those who helped rebuild the walls of Jerusalem (Neh. 3); those who helped Ezra proclaim the law of God (8:1-8); those who sealed the covenant to keep the law (10:1-27); the leading inhabitants in Jerusalem (11:1-10), in nearby Judah (11:20-24), and in more remote villages of Judah and Benjamin (11:25-36). An additional chapter deals with the priests who accompanied Zerubbabel (12:1-9), the succession of high priests from Jeshua to Jaddua (12:10-11), the "heads of the priestly families" in the days of Joiakim (12:12-21), Levites in this period (12:22-26), princes and priests who took part in the dedication of the wall of Jerusalem (12:31-42). The prophets usually began their books with some indication of their genealogy (Isa. 1:1; Jer. 1:1; Ezek. 1:3; Hos. 1:1; Joel 1:1; Jon. 1:1; Zeph. 1:1; Zech. 1:1).

For Jesus' lineage, see GENEALOGY OF JESUS CHRIST. Other NT persons generally appear without indication of their descent. Occasionally the father is named (e.g., "James and John, the sons of Zebedee," Lk. 5:10). PAUL cherished his pure Hebrew descent (Phil. 3:4-5). The genealogies mentioned in 1 Tim. 1:4 and Tit. 3:9 are sometimes thought to refer to a pagan Gnostic series of beings intermediate between God and the created earth (see GNOSTICISM). However, it is more likely that the rabbinic emphasis on human genealogies is meant, because the false teachers seem to be Jewish and the term *genealogies* is not used by pagan authors of the pagan Gnostic series.

It is certain that the NT shows far less concern for the genealogy of human beings than does the OT. In the OT, God was bringing together a chosen people who would be a nation peculiarly devoted to preserving his revelation until, in the fullness of time, he sent his Son, who would draw to himself a new people, united not by descent from a common human ancestry but by a genealogy of one generation only: children of God by a new and spiritual birth.

genealogy of Jesus Christ. Two genealogies of Jesus are given in the NT: Matt. 1:1-17 and Lk. 3:23-38. MATTHEW traces the descent of Jesus from ABRAHAM and DAVID, and divides it into three sets of fourteen generations each, probably to aid memorization. There are fourteen names from Abraham to (and including) David. From David to JOSIAH, and counting David a second time, there are fourteen names (David is named twice in Matt. 1:17). From Jeconiah (JEHOIACHIN) to Jesus there are fourteen names. Matthew omits three generations after Joram (JEHORAM)—namely AHAZIAH, Joash (JEHOASH), and AMAZIAH (1 Chr. 3:11-12). Such an omission in Hebrew genealogies is not peculiar to Matthew. He names ZERAH as well as PEREZ and mentions the brothers of JUDAH and of Jeconiah, which is unusual. Contrary to Hebrew practice, he names five women: TAMAR, RAHAB, RUTH, BATHSHEBA, and MARY, each name evoking associations, dark or bright, with the history of the chosen people. Matthew carefully excludes the physical paternity of JOSEPH by saying "Joseph, the husband of Mary, of whom was born Jesus" (Matt. 1:16; the word "whom" is fem. sing. in the Gk. text). The sense of "begat" (KJV) in Hebrew genealogies was not exact. It indicated immediate or remote descent, an adoptive relation, or legal heirship, as well as procreation.

LUKE's genealogy moves back in time from Jesus to ADAM. Between Abraham and Adam it is the same as in 1 Chr. 1:1-7, 24-28, or the more detailed genealogies in Genesis, making allowance for the different spelling of names in transliteration from Hebrew or Greek. From David to Abraham, Luke agrees with OT genealogies and with Matthew. Between Jesus and David, Luke's list differs from Matthew's, and there is no OT record to compare with Luke's, except for NATHAN's being one of David's sons, and for the names of SHEALTIEL and ZERUBBABEL. At this point the two genealogies crossed, through adoption or otherwise.

As Matthew gave the line of the kings from David to Jeconiah, it is probable that from Shealtiel to Joseph he named those who were heirs to the Davidic throne. Luke's record then would be that of physical descent, though crossing the royal line at one point. In Lk. 3:23—where the KJV has, "And Jesus himself began to be about thirty years of age, being (as was supposed) the son of Joseph, which was *the son* of Heli"—the question arises as to how much should be considered parenthetical. Some would include "of Joseph" in the parenthesis: "(as was supposed of Joseph)," making HELI in some sense the father of Jesus, perhaps his maternal grandfather. This construction is awkward. Another supposition is that Joseph is really the son-in-law of Heli, through his marriage to Mary, possibly Heli's daughter. If both genealogies are those of Joseph, his relationship to Heli must be different from his relationship to Jacob. Scholars have wrestled with the problems of the two genealogies from the second century, when pagan critics raised the difficulty. Many explanations have been more ingenious than convincing, involving complicated and uncertain inferences.

In a widely accepted view, Matthew gives the legal descent of heirship to the throne of David, through Joseph, while Luke gives the physical descent of Jesus through Mary. Matthew is concerned with the kingship of Jesus, Luke with his humanity. Both make plain his VIRGIN BIRTH, and therefore his deity. The agreement of Matthew and Luke on these facts is obvious, and their differences only accentuate their value as independent witnesses, whose testimony was prompted by the HOLY SPIRIT, not by collaboration with each other. Matthew's genealogy establishes the legal claim to the throne of David through his foster-father Joseph; Luke's establishes his actual descent from David through Mary. Luke 1:32 says that Mary's child "will be called the Son of the Most High. The Lord God will give him the throne of his father David." Romans 1:3-4 agrees: Jesus "as to his earthly life a descendant of David," which could only be through Mary; and he was "appointed the Son of God in power by his resurrection from the dead" (TNIV; cf. also 2 Tim. 2:8). Isaiah 11:1 indicates that the Messiah is to be physically a descendant of David's father Jesse. The genealogies must be seen in the light of this fact (see Matt. 22:41-46 and parallels with the answer in Rom. 1:4).

general. This term, referring to a high-ranking military officer, occurs rarely in Bible versions. The NRSV, for example, uses it once in the OT (Jdg. 4:7; cf. also 1 Chr. 27:34 KJV). The word is occasionally used in the NT as a translation of Greek *chiliarchos G5941*, meaning literally "commander of a thousand," but used in Roman times of military TRIBUNES who led COHORTS consisting of about 600 men, and also more generally of high-ranking officers (e.g., NIV Rev. 6:15; 19:18). See ARMY.

General Epistles. See CATHOLIC EPISTLES.

generation. A group of related persons who belong to the same stage in the line of descent. The word can also refer to a body of individuals who happened to be born about the same time, and especially to contemporaries who share social and cultural traits. The biblical words rendered "generation" correspond closely, but not fully, to the English term. The Hebrew noun *dôr H1887* has a broad range of meaning: it may refer to a period of time as well as to the individuals who live during an age. The word is used (usually in the sing.) of many generations to come (Deut. 7:9), as well as of a specific living generation, such as the one that died in the wilderness (2:14). The average length of a generation is often assumed to be forty years, for in the wilderness all Israelites over twenty died within that time. A second Hebrew term, *tôlēdôt H9352*, can refer not only to "contemporaries" (e.g., Gen. 6:9), but also of a line of "descendants" (5:1), and even of a "[family] history" or "account" (2:4; 25:19; 37:2).

In the NT, the Greek noun *genea G1155* is usually translated "generation" but can also be rendered in other ways (e.g., NIV "kind," Lk. 16:8; "time," Acts 15:21). It is used in the GENEALOGY of Matt. 1. Many times Jesus speaks of the faithless and perverse generation that opposed him (Matt. 17:17 et al.), where the reference is taken by some to be the Jewish nation. A special problem is raised by Jesus' statement, "this generation will certainly not pass away until all these things have happened" (24:34 and parallels). Some understand the term in a strictly temporal sense and claim that Christ mistakenly expected the end in his own time. Others argue for the meaning "race, clan, nation," and hold

G

that the verse predicts the continuation of the Jewish people until Christ's return. Still others believe that the statement has no temporal reference at all but rather stresses the certainty of Christ's words: "people such as these [i.e., sinful humanity] will not pass away until all these things have taken place." This assurance thus corresponds precisely to the next statement: "Heaven and earth will pass away, but my words will never pass away" (v. 35).

generosity. See CONTRIBUTION; KINDNESS.

Genesis, Book of. The first book of the Bible. In the Jewish tradition the book is named from its first word, *běrēʾšît* ("in the beginning"). The English name derives from the SEPTUAGINT (Gk. *Genesis*, "origin, beginning") and is found also in the Latin tradition. While much of the book is concerned with origins, the name Genesis does not reflect its total scope, for the larger portion of the book consists of the history of the PATRIARCHS and concludes with the record of JOSEPH's life.

I. **The authorship of Genesis.** The question of the authorship of Genesis has been the subject of debate for over two centuries. Tradition ascribes the book to MOSES, but the application of source-critical methodology has partitioned Genesis into a number of sources attributed to various authors writing at widely diverse times in Israelite history. The identification of these sources (known simply as J, E, D, P, etc.) is based on several criteria such as style, usage of the divine name, alleged contradictions, linguistic peculiarities, and development of the Israelite religion. More recent trends have tended to modify this approach, putting less emphasis on traditional historicist methodology and more on literary or canonical concerns.

The concept of Mosaic authorship does not indicate that Moses was the first to write every word of each account in the book of Genesis. It is generally understood today to mean that much of his work was compilation. Many historical accounts in Genesis predate Moses by great expanses of time. There is no reason why he could not have arranged these ancient accounts into the literary structure of the book.

Proponents of the Mosaic authorship of Genesis point to such evidence as the author's knowledge of EGYPT (Gen. 13:10) and the Egyptian language (41:43-45), archaisms in the language of Genesis (such as imprecision in the gender of certain nouns and pronouns), ancient customs recorded

Overview of GENESIS

Author: Anonymous, but comments elsewhere in the Bible seem to support the traditional view that MOSES is responsible for the PENTATEUCH as a whole.

Historical setting: The initial composition of the book must have taken place during the wilderness wanderings (either late in the 15th or early in the 13th cent. B.C.; those who reject Mosaic authorship usually date the book after the EXILE, while acknowledging that much of the material is several centuries earlier).

Purpose: To provide a historical-theological account of the long period from the CREATION to the time of JOSEPH, with emphasis on God's choosing of Abram (ABRAHAM) and his descendants; to provide those fundamental truths about God on which the rest of the Bible is built.

Contents: From the creation to Abraham's settling in HARAN (Gen. 1-11); God's COVENANT with Abraham (12:1—25:18); God's dealings with ISAAC and JACOB (25:19—36:43); God's preservation of Joseph (chs. 37-50).

in Genesis that are paralleled in other cultures of the second millennium B.C., and the orderly and purposeful arrangement of the book.

II. Archaeological background of Genesis. Excavations at a number of sites in the ANE have tended to support the antiquity and historical integrity of significant portions of the book of Genesis. For example, work at Yorgan Tepe, the site of ancient Nuzi, has yielded thousands of tablets, most of which have been dated to the fifteenth century B.C. These tablets record several legal and societal practices that are strikingly similar to customs recorded in the patriarchal narratives. For example, RACHEL's theft of the household gods of LABAN (Gen. 31:34) may be understood against the background of the Nuzi custom of determining INHERITANCE rights by the possession of the family gods. Apparently Rachel wished to insure her husband's right to the property she felt was his (cf. 31:14-16). Also, the practice of taking a concubine to produce an heir when a married couple was childless is well known, both in Genesis (16:3; 30:4, 9) and the Nuzi material. The similarity between the customs of Nuzi and those of the patriarchs gives strong support to the origin of the patriarchal accounts in a period very early in Hebrew history.

It has been asserted that the mention of camels in numerous passages in Genesis may be an anachronism, because evidence for the domestication of camels cannot be found before the end of the twelfth century B.C. However, camel bones have been discovered at Mari (25/24 cent.) and in Palestine (2000 to 1200) at various archaeological sites. Evidence for the domestication of the camel may be found in texts from the Old Babylonian period (c. 2000/1700) and a Sumerian text from Nippur.

III. Content of Genesis. The book may be divided roughly into three parts. Genesis 1-11 records events from the CREATION to the death of TERAH, the father of ABRAHAM. Chapters 12-36

View of the SW corner of the Machpelah, an imposing structure built by Herod the Great over the traditional burial cave of the patriarchs.

© Dr. James C. Martin

constitute a history of the patriarchs Abraham, ISAAC, and JACOB. Chapters 37-50 present a sustained narrative that records the account of JOSEPH.

The first section begins with the account of creation. There were other ancient cultures that produced creation accounts. For example, the Babylonian creation epic *Enuma Elish* depicts the origin of the physical phenomena. It is commonly held that the Genesis accounts are dependent on the Babylonian creation account. Linguistic evidence for such dependence has been sought in the Hebrew word *tĕhôm H9333* ("deep"), which occurs in Gen. 1:2. This word is said to find a counterpart in the word *Tiamat*, the name of a goddess in *Enuma Elish*. The evidence, however, speaks against direct dependence (see DEEP). It may also be noted that the style and content of the two accounts are vastly different. The Babylonian account depicts the Creation as taking place as a result of the sexual union of the gods Apsu and Tiamat. It is patently mythical and pagan in its orientation. After thorough examination, A. Heidel concluded that the similarities between the two accounts "are not so striking as we might expect. ... In fact, the divergences are much more far-reaching and significant than are the resemblances, most of which are not any closer than what we should expect to find in any two more or less complete creation versions" (*The Babylonian Genesis* [1963], 130).

G

The FALL of the human race is recorded in Gen. 2-3. This event had profound significance, not only for the relationship of human beings to God but also for their relationships to others as well. No longer does an intimate relationship with God exist, as it did in the garden. Murder (4:8, 23) and the lust for renown (4:17, 23-24; 6:1-4) now characterize the human race. These conditions led to the destruction of the race by a FLOOD (6:5—9:17). The question of the universality of the flood cannot be answered precisely from the biblical texts because of the ambiguity of the word "all" in the statement "all the high mountains … were covered" (7:19), which in Hebrew need not be understood in an absolute sense. Yet, it is difficult to conceive of the Noahic flood only as a local phenomenon in view of the fact that the waters apparently covered Mount ARARAT (8:3-4). The presence of a flood account in many ethnological contexts, as well as the evidence of fossils found in various sites throughout the world are often appealed to as support for a universal flood. The human race's effort to establish a name for itself culminated in the erection of the Tower of BABEL (11:1-9). The destruction of the tower by divine intervention was accompanied by the confusion of language, which led to the geographical distribution of the race (11:8).

The patriarchal accounts that begin at Gen. 12:1 are of great importance to the theology of both Testaments, for they record the first formal statement of the promise to Abraham. The promise, which later was put into the form of a COVENANT (15:12-21), guaranteed an inheritance to the people of God in all ages. It thus became a formalized statement that was invested with the authority of the divine oath. Among the elements of this covenant are the promise that Abraham's descendants would inherit the land of Canaan (12:7; 15:18-20), the promise that Abraham would be the father of a great nation (12:2; 17:2), and the promise of Gentile inclusion in the blessings of the covenant (12:3). When God gave the promise that Abraham would be the father of multitudes, that promise seemed unlikely to be fulfilled, because Abraham and his wife SARAH were well along in years (17:17-19). However, the integrity of the promise was maintained in the birth of ISAAC (17:19; cf. 21:1-7). The Genesis narratives set forth Abraham's FAITH as the central element in his relationship with God (15:6). His faith was given concrete expression in his willingness to sacrifice his son Isaac according to the word of God (22:1-9; cf. Jas. 22:22-23).

The Genesis narratives give the least attention to the patriarch Isaac. But the promise is not absent from the account of his life (Gen. 26:23-25). The narrative concerning JACOB also centers on the continuation of the promise-covenant in the patriarchal line. The elements of the promise were reiterated to him when he was forced to flee his home because he had deceived his father (27:18-45). Jacob is the progenitor of the twelve tribes of Israel (35:22-23). When his name was changed from Jacob to ISRAEL he gave a name to the Hebrew tribes (32:27-28).

A large portion of Genesis records the life of JOSEPH, Jacob's son by RACHEL. Basic to this narrative is its recounting of the way in which the Hebrews came to reside in the land of Egypt. It was due to a famine that was apparently widespread in Egypt and Canaan. Joseph had wisely provided for such emergencies, and Jacob and his sons came to Egypt to pasture their flocks. Joseph recognized his family, from whom he had been separated for many years, and settled them in the land of Egypt (Gen. 47:11-12). The narratives concerning Joseph provide the historical background for the Book of Exodus, which records the bondage of the Israelites in Egypt and their subsequent exodus from that land. These narratives also look back to the period of Egyptian bondage mentioned in the Abrahamic covenant (15:13-14).

Geneva Bible. See BIBLE VERSIONS, ENGLISH.

Gennesaret. gi-nes′uh-ret (Gk. *Gennēsaret G1166*, derivation uncertain, possibly from Heb. *kinneret H4055*). A small plain located on the NW side of the Sea of Galilee. The name should be associated primarily with an area mentioned in two NT references as the place where Jesus landed when he crossed the lake after feeding the 5,000 (Matt. 14:34; Mk. 6:53). The plain borders on the NW shore of the Sea of Galilee between CAPERNAUM and MAGDALA. It is less than 4 mi. (6 km.) long, running N and S along the shore, and about 1 mi. (less than 2 km.) wide. The land is level, rising gently from the

Sea of Galilee, which is c. 650 ft. (200 m.) below the MEDITERRANEAN. Hills rise sharply on three sides. The main road from Capernaum to TIBERIAS runs through close to the sea shore. During the time of Christ, Gennesaret was regarded as the garden spot of Palestine, producing an abundance of wild trees and flowers, as well as important crops.

Gennesaret, Lake of. See GALILEE, SEA OF.

Gentile. A non-Jewish person. This English term (derived from late Lat. *gentīlis*, "pagan"; cf. Vulg. Acts 19:10) occurs occasionally in OT versions as a rendering of Hebrew *gôy H1580*, "people, nation" (pl. *gôyim*, e.g., Isa. 42:6), but more frequently in the NT to translate Greek *ethnos G1620*, "nation, tribe" (Matt. 4:15 et al.). Sometimes it is used also to translate *Hellēn G1818*, "Hellene, Greek" (e.g., Jn. 7:35 KJV; Acts 14:1 NIV).

In times of peace, considerate treatment was accorded Gentiles under OT law (e.g., Num. 35:15; Deut. 10:19; 24:14-15; Ezek. 47:22). Men of Israel often married Gentile women, of whom RAHAB, RUTH, and BATHSHEBA are notable examples, but the practice was frowned on after the return from EXILE (Ezra 9:12; 10:2-44; Neh. 10:30; 13:23-31). Separation between Jew and Gentile became more strict, until in the NT period the hostility was complete. Persecution embittered the Jewish people, who sometimes retaliated by hatred of everything pertaining to Gentiles and by avoidance, so far as was possible, of contact with foreigners. The intensity of this feeling varied, however, and it gave way before unusual kindness (Lk. 7:4-5).

While the teachings of Jesus ultimately broke down "the middle wall of partition" between Jew and Gentile, as is seen in the writings of PAUL (Rom. 1:16; 1 Cor. 1:24; Gal. 3:28; Eph. 2:14; Col. 3:11) and in Acts, Jesus limited his ministry to Jews, with rare exceptions (the half-Jewish SAMARITANS, Jn. 4:1-42; the SYROPHOENICIAN woman, Matt. 15:21-28; Mk. 7:24-30; the Greeks in Jn. 12:20-36). He instructed his twelve disciples, "Do not go among the Gentiles or enter any town of the Samaritans" (Matt. 10:5); but he did not repeat this injunction when he sent out the Seventy (Lk. 10:1-16; NIV, "seventy-two"). Jesus' mission was first to "his own" (Jn. 1:11), the chosen people of God, but

ultimately to "all who received him" (1:12). Limitations of time held his ministry on earth within the bounds of Israel; reaching the Gentiles was left to the activity of the HOLY SPIRIT working through his disciples. Thus in the book of Acts, following the appointment of Paul as the apostle to the Gentiles (Acts 9:15), the Gentiles become increasingly prominent (cf. Paul's discussion in Rom. 11:11-36).

Gentiles, Court of the. See TEMPLE.

gentleness. See MEEKNESS.

Genubath. gi-nyoo'bath (Heb. *gĕnubat H1707*, possibly "foreigner"). Son of HADAD, an Edomite prince (1 Ki. 11:20). When the country of EDOM was invaded by DAVID's army, Hadad, who was still a boy, fled to EGYPT. In time, he married a sister of Queen TAHPANES, and out of this union Genubath was born. The child was raised by Tahpanes and lived with PHARAOH's children in the royal palace.

geography of Palestine. See PALESTINE.

Geon. gee'on. KJV Apoc. form of GIHON (Sir. 24:27).

Gera. gee'ruh (Heb. *gērā' H1733*, possibly from *gēr H1731*, "sojourner"). A name borne by several men from the tribe of BENJAMIN. Unfortunately, the genealogical lists of this tribe have suffered greatly in the course of transmission and can be correlated only partially. It is possible that "son of Gera" in some of the passages below means "belonging to the clan of Gera."

(1) Fourth son of Benjamin and grandson of JACOB (Gen. 46:21; the name is missing from the parallel list in Num. 26:38-41). See BEKER #1.

(2) Second son of BELA and grandson of Benjamin (1 Chr. 8:3; the name is missing from the parallel list in 7:7). See the next three entries.

(3) Seventh son of Bela and grandson of Benjamin (1 Chr. 8:5; the name is missing from the parallel list in 7:7). Since it is very unlikely that two sons of Bela were given the same name, some scholars believe that the text has been corrupted and that this Gera was the son of Ehud; see #4 below.

(4) Third son of Ehud (1 Chr. 8:7). This text too is emended by some scholars.

G

(5) The father of EHUD, the Israelite judge (Jdg. 3:15). This Gera may be the same as #2 above, and his son Ehud may be the same individual mentioned in ##3-4 above.

(6) The father of SHIMEI (2 Sam. 16:5; 19:16, 18; 1 Ki. 2:8). Shimei was a Benjamite from BAHURIM who belonged to the clan of SAUL and who cursed DAVID when the latter was fleeing from ABSALOM.

gerah. See WEIGHTS AND MEASURES.

Gerar. gee´rahr (Heb. *gĕrār H1761*, meaning uncertain). A town and probably also a district S of GAZA and SW of the southern border of CANAAN near the MEDITERRANEAN Sea. In its first occurrence (Gen. 10:19), Gerar is used as a reference point marking the southern end of the territory of the Canaanites. ABRAHAM and SARAH are said to have dwelt in Gerar (in the district between KADESH and SHUR), where they came in contact with its king, ABIMELECH (20:1-2). This same ruler, or possibly another in the royal line who also had the title Abimelech, is called king of the PHILISTINES in a similar encounter that ISAAC and his wife REBEKAH had with him (26:1, 6-11; cf. also 26:26). Following these experiences, Isaac encamped in the valley of Gerar (26:17), probably the present Wadi esh-Shariʿah, where Isaac dug wells and experienced difficult relations with the herdsmen of the area (26:20). Centuries later, ASA king of Judah, with the help of God, routed Ethiopian invaders and pursued them to Gerar and plundered that whole region (2 Chr. 14:13-14). The town Gerar should probably be identified with Tell Abu Hureireh (Tel Haror), about 9 mi. (15 km.) SE of Gaza and 17 mi. (27 km.) NW of BEERSHEBA. This site has been excavated and shows a long period of occupation, including that part of the Middle Bronze period when the patriarchs lived (1800-1600 B.C.).

Gerasa. See GERASENE.

Gerasene. ger´uh-seen (Gk. *Gerasēnos G1170*, gentilic of *Gerasa* [Jos. *War* 2.18.1 §458 et al.]). An inhabitant of Gerasa, a city in TRANSJORDAN, situated about 35 mi. (55 km.) SE of the S end of the Sea of Galilee (see GALILEE, SEA OF). Gerasa was one of the cities of the DECAPOLIS. The NT references (Mk. 5:1; Lk. 8:26; cf. v. 37) describe Jesus' healing of the demoniac "Legion" and the drowning of the swine in the Sea of Galilee (cf. Matt. 8:28). The Greek MSS preserve variant spellings of the name in each gospel. The best text in Matthew reads "Gadarenes" (see GADARA), but in Mark and Luke, "Gerasenes" (some MSS preserve "Gergesenes" and "Gergustenes"). The town of Gergesa, not to be confused with either Gerasa or Gadara, was probably located midway along the E bank of the Sea of Galilee; Gadara is about 6 mi. (10 km.) SE from the S end of the Sea of Galilee; and Gerasa is another 30 mi. (50 km.) to the SE.

The fact that Matthew places the healing of "Legion" in the "region of the Gadarenes," whereas Mark and Luke place it in the "country of the Gerasenes," may be explained on the historical grounds that geographical boundaries overlapped, and on the exegetical consideration that "region" embraced a wide area around the cities. Most scholars today hold that near Gergesa was the precise site for the healing of "Legion." This view agrees with the general description of the site (Mk. 5:1; Lk. 8:26). In this immediate area, steep hills come down to the shoreline and fit the story of the swine rushing headlong into the sea. No other place on the E side of the sea fits this requirement of the story. The mountainside has caves and hewn tombs where, according to Mark and Luke, the demoniac had taken shelter. The site is identified today with the town of Kursi (spelled variously), just below Wadi es-Samak.

The town of Gerasa, on the other hand, was situated near the JABBOK River about 18 mi. (29 km.) E of the JORDAN, about 20 mi. (32 km.) N of Philadelphia (OT RABBAH in AMMON). Archaeologists identify it with the modern Jerash. At this distance from the Sea of Galilee, Gerasa could not have been the site of the healing of "Legion." It is doubtful that Jesus ever visited it. Excavations at the modern Jerash clearly show that Gerasa was a large and important city already in Jesus' time. The excavations uncovered what is to date the best preserved Roman city in Palestine. These ruins date from the second to the seventh centuries and show that the city flourished during this period as a center for religion, culture, and commerce.

Gergasite. See GIRGASHITE.

Gergesa, Gergesene. See GERASA.

Gerizim. ger'uh-zim (Heb. *gĕrizîm H1748*). A mountain of SAMARIA, now known as Jebel et-Tur, 2,850 ft. (870 m.) high, SW of Mount EBAL. A main N-to-S road of Palestine runs through the valley, so that this pass is of strategic military importance. Moses commanded that when the Israelites came into the Promised Land, the blessing for keeping the law should be spoken from Mount Gerizim and the curse for not obeying it from Mount Ebal (Deut. 11:29; 27:4-26), six tribes standing on the slopes of each peak (27:11-14). It is conjectured by some that Mount Gerizim was selected for the blessing because, from the point of view of one looking eastward, it would be on the right or "fortunate" side. See BLESS, BLESSING.

From the top of Mount Gerizim, JOTHAM shouted his parable of the trees to the men of SHECHEM in the valley below, reminding them of all that his father GIDEON had done for them (Jdg. 9:7-21). After the Israelites, returning from Babylonian EXILE, refused to let the mixed races of Samaria help rebuild JERUSALEM (Ezra 4:1-4; Neh. 2:19-20; 13:28), the Samaritans built themselves a temple on Mount Gerizim. The Samaritan woman referred to it as "this mountain" (Jn. 4:20-21),

where her people worshiped in the open after their temple was destroyed by the MACCABEES. The small Samaritan community of Nablus still celebrates the Passover on Mount Gerizim. Samaritan tradition maintains that ABRAHAM attempted to sacrifice ISAAC on this mountain (Gen. 22:1-19), that at a nearby SALEM he met MELCHIZEDEK (14:17-20), and that JACOB's dream (28:10-17) occurred at Khirbet Lanzah on Mount Gerizim. A rock with a cup-shaped hollow that could have been used for libations is the traditional altar of the Samaritan temple.

Gershom. guhr'shuhm (Heb. *gērṡōm H1768*, derivation uncertain; by popular etymology, "an alien there"). **(1)** Firstborn son of MOSES. When ZIPPORAH gave birth to him in MIDIAN, "Moses named him Gershom, saying, 'I have become an alien [*gēr H1731*] in a foreign land'" (Exod. 2:22; cf. 18:3). The only other information given about him is his genealogical data and, probably, the account of his CIRCUMCISION (4:24-26; his name does not actually appear in this passage). According to the book of Judges, a descendant of Gershom named JONATHAN served as priest for the Danites. See DAN. Jonathan made use of idols, however, and his descendants continued this practice until the EXILE (Jdg. 18:30; the KJV, following the MT, has "Gershom, son of Manasseh" [see MANASSEH

Mount Gerizim rises above ancient Shechem. (View to the W.)

© Dr. James C. Martin

G

#3]). Another descendant of Gershom, SHEBUEL, was an officer in charge of the treasuries during the time of DAVID (1 Chr. 23:15-16; 26:24).

(2) A descendant, and probably clan leader, of PHINEHAS who returned from BABYLON with EZRA (Ezra 8:2).

(3) Variant form of GERSHON in 1 Chronicles.

Gershon. guhr´shuhn (Heb. *gēršôn H1767*, possibly from GERSHOM; gentilic *gēršunnî H1769*, "Gershonite"). First son of LEVI, born to him before JACOB and his family went to Egypt (Gen. 46:11). In the Hebrew text of Chronicles, this name almost always appears as Gershom (the only exceptions are 1 Chr. 6:1 [MT 5:27] and 23:6), but the NIV uses the spelling Gershon whenever the reference is to the son of Levi. Biblical references to Gershon focus on the Levitical line that descended from him. In the book NUMBERS, the Gershonites are divided into two families or clans: LIBNI (apparently called LADAN in 1 Chr. 23:7) and SHIMEI (Num. 3:18, 21). The number of male Gershonites "a month old or more who were counted was 7,500" (3:22); their leader was ELIASAPH son of Lael (3:24). They camped immediately to the W of the TABERNACLE (3:23) and "were responsible for the care of the tabernacle and tent" (3:25).

The Gershonites were assigned lands within the holdings of Issachar, Asher, and Naphtali in Palestine proper, and in the holdings of the half tribe of Manasseh in TRANSJORDAN (Josh. 21:6, 27-33; 1 Chr. 6:62, 71-76). This assignment of land placed the Gershonites in the northernmost extremes on both sides of the Jordan. Although their northern homelands were far from JERUSALEM, biblical evidences show that the Gershonites shared in the central religious life of the nation. One hundred and thirty Gershonites helped bring the ARK OF THE COVENANT to Jerusalem (1 Chr. 15:7). A Gershonite, ASAPH son of Berechiah, was the chief of the temple musicians under DAVID (16:4-5). The later prominence of the Asaphite clan of temple musicians probably originates from this office. HEMAN son of Joel was another important Gershonite official (15:17; "son of Joel" may refer to a Gershonite clan).

Geruth Kimham. gihr´ooth-kim´ham (Heb. *gērût kimhām H1745*, possibly "lodging place of Kimham"). Also Geruth Chimham. Unidentified place near BETHLEHEM (perhaps named after the son of BARZILLAI, 2 Sam. 19:37-40). After the murder of GEDALIAH, whom NEBUCHADNEZZAR had appointed governor over Judah, Hebrew forces led by JOHANAN son of Kareah fled and stayed in Geruth Kimham on their way to Egypt (Jer. 41:17).

Gerzites, Gizrites, Gerizzites. See GIRZITES.

Gesham. See GESHAN.

Geshan. gesh´uhn (Heb. *gêšān H1642*). KJV Gesham (some later editions). Son of Jahdai, from the tribe of JUDAH, possibly a descendant of CALEB, although the genealogical connection is not stated (1 Chr. 2:47).

Geshem. gesh´uhm (Heb. *gešem H1774*, possibly "[born during] rain season"; variant form *gašmû H1776* [Neh. 6:6, KJV "Gashmu"]). One of NEHEMIAH's opponents in the rebuilding of the walls of Jerusalem (Neh. 2:19; 6:1-2, 6). He was important enough to serve as witness to the Jews' alleged treason. His title, "the Arab," may identify him as the governor of EDOM, but scholars have more generally identified him with a N Arabian king referred to as "Gashm son of Shahr" in an inscription from DEDAN in ARABIA and as "Gashm king of Kedar" in an Aramaic inscription from Egypt.

Geshur. gesh´uhr (Heb. *gēšûr H1770*, possibly "bridge"; gentilic *gēšûrî H1771*, "Geshurite"). **(1)** A country just E and NE of the Sea of Galilee, corresponding to the southern part of the Golan Heights. This area, along with the land of the Maacathites, was one of the borders of the territory given to JAIR, of the tribe of MANASSEH (Deut. 3:14). The same boundary is mentioned as the limit of the area that the Israelites were able to capture (Josh. 12:5), and its inhabitants are listed as among those whom the Israelites were not able to drive out and who continued to live within Israel (13:11, 13). The Geshurites, along with the Arameans (SYRIA), took HAVVOTH JAIR (formerly possessed by Jair the Manassite) and other places from the Israelites (1 Chr. 2:23). One of DAVID's wives, MAACAH, was the daughter of TALMAI, king of Geshur (2 Sam.

3:3; 1 Chr. 3:2). When ABSALOM (son of David and Maacah) killed his half-brother AMNON, he fled to his grandfather Talmai in Geshur for protection (2 Sam. 13:37-38; cf. 14:23, 32; 15:8).

(2) The term Geshurites apparently can also refer to a people S of the PHILISTINES near SINAI, whose land was not taken originally by the Israelite forces at the time of the conquest (Josh. 13:2). When David was in exile with ACHISH king of GATH, he and his men made raids upon these Geshurites (and other peoples) and led Achish to believe that he was attacking his own people (1 Sam. 27:8).

Gether. gee´thuhr (Heb. *geter H1788*, meaning unknown). Son of ARAM and grandson of SHEM, included in the Table of Nations (Gen. 10:23). In the parallel list (1 Chr. 1:17), the phrase "the sons of Aram" is missing from the MT, making it appear that Gether was a son of Shem and thus a brother of Aram. It is possible that this passage intends to list the descendants of Shem without distinguishing generations (cf. NRSV), but many scholars believe that the phrase in question dropped out by scribal mistake at an early stage in the textual transmission of the book (cf. NIV).

Gethsemane. geth-sem´uh-nee (Gk. *Gethsēmani G1149*, prob. from Heb. *gat šĕmānî*, "oil press"). The place of Jesus' agony and arrest (Matt. 26:36-56; Mk. 14:32-52; Lk. 22:39-54; Jn. 18:1-12). Matthew and Mark refer to it simply as "a place"; Luke does not give the name but says that the place was one to which Jesus customarily went and that it was on the Mount of OLIVES. John, without naming it, explains that it was a garden across the KIDRON Valley from JERUSALEM. The traditional site, today cared for by the Franciscans, is not far from the road, near the bridge over the Kidron, and is laid out in neat gardens. Within are eight large olive trees. If Emperor Titus destroyed all the trees around Jerusalem during the siege of A.D. 70, as JOSEPHUS asserts, these trees cannot be as old as the

time of Jesus, but they are certainly ancient, and they add to the atmosphere of a place of Christian devotion. Armenian, Greek, and Russian churches claim other olive groves nearby as the correct site. It is without doubt in the vicinity. The sufferings of Christ as his hour approached—portrayed by

These ancient olive trees found in the courtyard of the Church of All Nations (possibly the site of Gethsemane) are nearly 1,500 years old.

© Dr. James C. Martin

Matthew, Mark, and Luke—and the humiliation of his arrest, told by all four evangelists, concentrate the reverent thought and feeling of believers, so that the very name Gethsemane evokes the love and adoration due the Savior who prayed there.

Geuel. gyoo´uhl (Heb. *gĕʾûʾēl H1451*, possibly "loftiness of God"). Son of Maki, from the tribe of GAD; he was one of the twelve spies sent out by MOSES to reconnoiter the Promised Land (Num. 13:15).

Gezer. gee´zuhr (Heb. *gezer H1618*, possibly "confined space"). A major city of the N SHEPHELAH, allotted to the tribe of EPHRAIM and assigned to the Levites. It is identified with modern Tell el-Jezer, about 18 mi. (29 km.) NW of JERUSALEM, between the Valley of SOREK and the Valley of AIJALON. It lies S of the main road from Jerusalem to Jaffa (Haifa) and E of the railroad. Its military importance, overlooking main routes through the country, has led to its occupation in many periods of history. The Egyptians captured Gezer about

G

1500 B.C., but their power decreased a century or so later. When Israel entered the land, Horam king of Gezer came to help Lachish (Josh. 10:33), whose king had been killed in the battle of the day on which the sun stood still. Horam and his army were completely destroyed, but Gezer was not taken. The king of Gezer is listed among those whom Joshua defeated (12:12). Gezer is on the S boundary of Ephraim, near Beth Horon (Josh. 16:3-10; 1 Chr. 7:28). The inhabitants of Gezer were not driven out (Josh. 16:10; Jdg. 1:29) but later became slave labor. Gezer was one of the cities given to the Kohathite Levites (Josh. 21:21; 1 Chr. 6:67). David defeated the Philistines as far as Gezer (2 Sam. 5:25 [KJV, "Gazer"]; 1 Chr. 14:16; 20:4), but it remained for Solomon to reduce the people of Gezer to forced labor and to rebuild the city, which the pharaoh of Egypt had taken and burned and later given to Solomon as a dowry with his daughter (1 Ki. 9:15-17).

Gezer was occupied in the Greek period. Though not mentioned in the NT, it was known in NT times as Gazara. The Crusaders fortified Gezer, and it has undergone several changes of ownership since then. Archaeological remains fully illustrate the life of the people. Excavations have revealed a stepped water tunnel 216 ft. (66 m.) long, dating to the time of Solomon. City gates were also found from the time of Solomon matching those found at Hazor (cf. 1 Ki. 9:15-16). A "high place" dating to about 1600 B.C. was found here as well as a tenth-century calendar containing a Hebrew inscription of seven lines and citing an annual cycle of agricultural activities. It is one of the oldest-known pieces of Hebrew writing. The capture of Gezer is mentioned in the stele of Pharaoh Merneptah about 1220.

Gezrite. See Girzite.

ghost. This English term, which in modern usage refers specifically to the spirit of a dead person that appears in bodily likeness, is very frequently used by the KJV to render Hebrew *rûaḥ H8120* and Greek *pneuma G4460*, which normally refer to the vital life principle of a person, or to the essence of God, or to the Holy Spirit (however, Lk. 24:37 and 39 uses *pneuma* in the sense of "ghost"; the

parallels have *phantasma G5753*, Matt. 14:26; Mk. 6:49). The NRSV also uses "ghost" a few times to render Hebrew *ʾôb H200* (e.g., Isa. 8:19; NIV, "medium"). See divination; familiar spirit.

Ghost, Holy. See Holy Spirit.

Giah. gi´uh (Heb. *gîḥa H1632*, "spring"). An unidentified site within the territory of the tribe of Benjamin, mentioned as being on the route of Abner's flight from Joab and Abishai (2 Sam. 2:24). It is said to have been E of Gibeon (emended to Geba by some scholars) and near a hill named Ammah, probably close to the edge of the wilderness.

giant. The first mention of giants in the Bible is in Gen. 6:4 (KJV), where the NIV and other modern versions have "Nephilim," a Hebrew word of uncertain etymology but possibly meaning "fallen ones" (see sons of God). Nephilim were found in Canaan when the spies went through the land (Num. 13:33). Beside these men of great stature, the spies felt like grasshoppers. The Hebrew word rendered "giant" by the KJV at Job 16:14 means simply "mighty man, warrior." For other terms alluding to giants, see Anakites and Rephaites. See also Goliath.

giants, valley of the. See Rephaim, Valley of.

Gibbar. gib´ahr (Heb. *gibbār H1507*, "[strong] man"). The ancestor of one of the families who returned with Zerubbabel from exile (Ezra 2:20). Some have argued that Gibbar here is a textual corruption of the place name Gibeon (cf. Neh. 7:25).

Gibbethon. gib´uh-thon (Heb. *gibbĕtôn H1510*, "hill, ridge"). A Philistine city allotted to the tribe of Dan (Josh. 19:44) and assigned to the Levites (21:23). It was while Nadab, son of Jeroboam, was besieging Gibbethon that Baasha murdered him and assumed the crown of Israel for himself (1 Ki. 15:27). Later, the Israelite army was again trying to wrest Gibbethon from the Philistines when word reached them that Zimri had murdered Baasha's son, Elah, and proclaimed himself king. On hearing this, the army proclaimed Omri king, and Zimri committed suicide (16:15-20). The city is identified either with Tell Melat (some 15 mi./24 km. SE of JOPPA and 3 mi./5 km. W of GEZER) or with Ras Abu Ḥumeid (a short distance farther NE; but see GITTAIM).

Gibea. gib´ee-uh (Heb. *gib‘ā’ H1495*, "hill" or possibly "highlander"). Son of Sheva and grandson of CALEB, included in the genealogy of JUDAH (1 Chr. 2:49).

Gibeah. gib´ee-uh (Heb. *gib‘āh H1497* [*gib‘at* in Josh. 18:28], "hill"; gentilic *gib‘ātî H1503*, "Gibeathite"). The name of several locations in PALESTINE. Because much of Palestine is hilly country, it is not surprising that a name meaning "hill" was widely used and that various names of similar meaning might creation confusion. GIBEON, properly the chief city of the HIVITES who tricked Israel into an alliance to avoid being massacred (Josh. 11:19), can be mistaken for Gibeah of SAUL (2 Sam. 21:6) and for GEBA (1 Chr. 14:16; cf. 2 Sam. 5:25). Again, Geba and Gibeah should properly refer to different places, but the MT reads Geba in Jdg. 20:10 and 33, where the reference is probably to Gibeah; in v. 31, on the other hand, it reads Gibeah when Geba (according to some, Gibeon) is probably intended. At least four places named Gibeah can be distinguished.

(1) A town in the hill country of the tribe of JUDAH (Josh. 15:57). It is perhaps the same city identified elsewhere as the home of MICAIAH, the mother of King ABIJAH (2 Chr. 13:2; but see #2 below). Moreover, some believe that GIBEA, described as a grandson of CALEB, refers to this town (1 Chr. 2:49). Modern el-Jeba‘ (c. 7.5 mi./12 km. WSW of BETHLEHEM) has been proposed as a possible identification of Judahite Gibeah, but this location is improbable, since the context of Josh. 15:57 suggests the area SE of HEBRON.

(2) A town (or hill) in the hill country of the tribe of EPHRAIM; it was the home of the priest PHINEHAS, grandson of AARON, and provided the burial place of Phinehas's father, ELEAZAR (Josh. 24:33). Nothing else is known about such a city, unless it was the home of King Abijah's mother (see #1 above). Some believe that the word in this passage should be understood as a common noun, "in the hill that belonged to Phinehas." If it does refer to a town, the location cannot be determined.

(3) A hill—known as Gibeath Elohim, "Gibeah [Hill] of God"—in the tribal territory of BENJAMIN where the PHILISTINES had an outpost and where SAUL met a procession of prophets (1 Sam. 10:5, 10). It has been identified with various sites, including Gibeah of Saul (see #4 below), Gibeon, and Geba.

(4) Finally, there is the Gibeah of Benjamin (1 Sam. 13:15), also known as Gibeah of Saul (11:4); it is probably the same as Gibeath (Josh. 18:28 KJV). This Gibeah was first identified with Tell el-Ful (about 3.5 mi./5 km. N of Jerusalem) in the 19th cent., a proposal later confirmed by W. F. Albright. More recently some scholars have argued that it is the same as Geba (Jeba‘, a few miles farther to the NE). It is possible that Tell el-Ful was the original site and that Saul built a fortress there (Gibeah of Saul), but that since the city itself had been destroyed, its name (Geba/Gibeah) was transferred to the neighboring site of Jeba‘. By far the most important city by this name in the biblical account, Gibeah of Benjamin first comes into prominence in the book of Judges. Here a LEVITE's concubine was raped and abused, and this event brought war between Benjamin and the rest of Israel (Jdg. 19-20). The transactions at Gibeah during the reign of Saul are recorded in 1 Sam. 10:26; 11:4; 13:2, 15-16; 14:2; 14:16; 15:34; 22:6; 23:19; 26:1. Here seven of Saul's descendants were hanged to satisfy the vengeance of the Gibeonites (21:6; NRSV has Gibeon). One of David's mighty men was from Gibeah of Benjamin (2 Sam. 23:29; 1 Chr. 11:31). The people of Gibeah fled when the Assyrians marched toward them (Isa. 10:29). Hosea called for a warning (Hos. 5:8) at Gibeah because of the sins Israel had committed "as in the days of Gibeah" (9:9; 10:9); the sins of Saul's reign had been remembered for centuries.

Gibeath. See GIBEAH #4.

Gibeath Elohim. See GIBEAH #3.

Gibeath Haaraloth. gib´ee-uhth-hay-air´uh-loth (Heb. *gib‘at hā‘ărālôt H1502*, "hill of the foreskins"). A hill in the vicinity of JERICHO where CIRCUMCISION was performed on the Israelites who were born after the EXODUS (Josh. 5:3). Presumably, the place received its name because of this event.

Gibeathite. See GIBEAH.

Gibeon. gib´ee-uhn (Heb. *gib'ôn H1500*, "hill"; gentilic *gib'ônî H1498*, "Gibeonite"). An important city in the hill country of BENJAMIN, identified with modern el-Jib, about 6 mi. (10 km.) NW of JERUSALEM (in 1 Chr. 8:29 and 9:25, "the father of Gibeon" is probably an epithet for a major figure in the early history of the city). Gibeon was one of the cities of Benjamin given to the priests (Josh. 21:17). At the time of the conquest, JOSHUA was deceived by the ambassadors of Gibeon into making a treaty with them (ch. 9), promising not to destroy them. When he discovered the deception, he spared their lives but made them woodcutters and water carriers. A coalition of Canaanite kings attacked Gibeon because they had made peace with Joshua (ch. 10). Joshua came to the aid of Gibeon, and in the battle that followed, Joshua called on the sun to stand still to give him time for more fighting (alluded to in Isa. 28:21). No other city made peace with Israel (Josh. 11:19). Gibeon was the chief of four HIVITE cities (9:17).

ABNER and JOAB met in battle at a pool at Gibeon, the remains of which may still be seen. Here, two

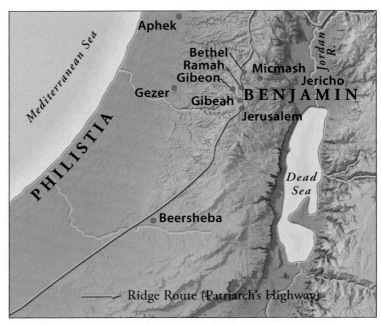

Gibeon lies at a critical internal crossroads in Palestine.

The isolated hill of el-Jib, biblical Gibeon. (View to the NE.)

© Dr. James C. Martin

groups of twelve men fought an indecisive contest, and the remaining forces joined in a disastrous battle (2 Sam. 2:8-28; 3:30), following which Abner and Joab agreed to a cessation of the fighting. At a great stone in Gibeon, Joab murdered AMASA (20:8-10). DAVID defeated the PHILISTINES from Gibeon on the N to GEZER on the S (1 Chr. 14:16). ZADOK the priest was assigned to minister at the high place in Gibeon (16:39-40; 21:29). SOLOMON, at the outset of his reign, came to Gibeon to sacrifice and there in a dream he chose wisdom above other gifts that God offered him (1 Ki. 3:3-15; 2 Chr. 1:2-13). Again Solomon received a message from the Lord here (1 Ki. 9:1-9). People from Gibeon returned to Jerusalem from the EXILE and helped rebuild the walls (Neh. 3:7; 7:25). JEREMIAH confronted a false prophet from Gibeon in the temple (Jer. 28:1). The town was the scene of a rescue of Israelites during the Assyrian occupation (41:11-16).

J. B. Pritchard excavated the site in 1957-62. All the remains are from the Iron Age (Israelite period) and later, except for a few traces of the Late Bronze Age. The main discoveries were two water tunnels, a large pool (mentioned in 2 Sam. 2:13) in which pottery vessels were found with the name Gibeon stamped on them in Hebrew, some houses, a wine cellar, and some fortifications.

Gibeonite. gib′ee-uh-n*it*. An inhabitant of GIBEON. The Gibeonites were apparently HIVITES (Josh. 9:3, 7); they are also described as AMORITES (2 Sam. 21:2). Because of the deceitful manner in which they gained the favor of JOSHUA, they were made slave laborers for menial tasks such as chopping wood and drawing water (Josh. 9). The Gibeonites and their allies, at the time of the conquest by Joshua, controlled a tetrapolis—BEEROTH, KEPHIRAH, KIRIATH BAAL, and Gibeon. Much later, during a prolonged famine, DAVID inquired of the Lord and learned that the cause was blood-guilt because SAUL had earlier massacred the Gibeonites; therefore David turned over to them seven descendants of Saul for vengeance (2 Sam. 21:1-9). A Gibeonite was leader of David's thirty mighty men (1 Chr. 12:4). Gibeonites helped repair the walls of JERUSALEM (Neh. 3:7).

Giblite. See GEBAL.

Giddalti. gi-dal′t*i* (Heb. *giddalti H1547*, "I brought up" or "I magnify [God]"). Son of HEMAN, the king's seer (1 Chr. 25:4). The fourteen sons of Heman, along with the sons of ASAPH and JEDUTHUN, were set apart "for the ministry of prophesying, accompanied by harps, lyres and cymbals" (v. 1). The assignment of duty was done by lot, and the twenty-second lot fell to Giddalti, his sons, and his relatives (25:29).

Giddel. gid′uhl (Heb. *giddēl H1543*, possibly short form of GEDALIAH). (1) Ancestor of a family of temple servants (NETHINIM) who returned with ZERUBBABEL from the EXILE (Ezra 2:47; Neh. 7:49).

(2) A servant of SOLOMON whose descendants returned with Zerubbabel from the exile (Ezra 2:56; Neh. 7:58).

Gideon. gid′ee-uhn (Heb. *gid‘ôn H1549*, "one who cuts, hewer"). KJV NT Gedeon. Son of Joash the Abiezrite, from the tribe of MANASSEH, and the fifth recorded judge of Israel (Jdg. 6-8); also called JERUB-BAAL ("let Baal contend," 6:32 et al.; JERUB-BESHETH in 2 Sam. 11:21). The family lived in OPHRAH not far from Mount GERIZIM (not the Ophrah of Benjamin listed in Josh. 18:23). Gideon had become a noted warrior (Jdg. 6:12), perhaps by waging "underground" warfare against the marauding Midianites (see MIDIAN). The extent to which the people had been enslaved is shown by the fact that Gideon had to hide in a winepress to do the threshing (6:11). A supernatural fire that consumed Gideon's sacrifice (6:17-23) attested to the fact that the messenger who called Gideon to lead Israel was from God.

Gideon responded to the call and, with the help of some friends, overthrew the altar of BAAL and cut down the sacred grove around it. He erected instead a new altar, naming it Yahweh-Shalom, "The LORD is Peace" (Jdg. 6:24). For his daring feat the followers of Baal wanted to kill him, but his father intervened. Gideon then issued a call to adjoining tribesmen to war against the Midianites. Having gathered a formidable host, he sought confirmation of his task and so put forth the famous test of the fleece (6:36-40). As further assurance, he was instructed to slip into the enemy's camp, and there he overheard one soldier tell another of a dream and interpret it to mean that Gideon's smaller army would win the battle (7:9-14). To prevent human boasting over victory, God instructed Gideon to reduce his force to three hundred picked men by (1) letting the faint-hearted go home and (2) choosing only those men who were cautious enough to lap the water with their hands to their mouths (7:1-8).

By strategy involving psychological warfare, Gideon's small band surprised the enemy in a night attack. Three groups of one hundred each attacked from three directions. At the proper time a signal was given, shields for the lights were removed, and trumpets blared. The sleeping Midianites were terrified. So complete was their rout that they killed one another in their mad flight (Jdg. 7:15-22). Gideon then called on his allies to join in the chase. Ephraim captured two of the kings (8:1-3). Gideon pursued the other two northward and captured them near the confluence of the Sea of Galilee and the Jordan (8:4-21). Thus the country was delivered all the way to the Jordan (7:22-23; 8:1-21). When his people wanted to make him king, Gideon refused and instead called for an offering of the golden trinkets that had been captured from the Midianites. With these he made an EPHOD, either an image of Yahweh or a sacred vestment worn by a priest in the sanctuary. Because of its worth and beauty, it later became an object of worship (8:24-27). Gideon's ability and statesmanship are shown in his long and fruitful ministry of forty years as judge (8:28). During his life he had seventy-one sons (8:30)—one, ABIMELECH, by a concubine of SHECHEM (8:31). After Gideon's death idolatry returned (8:32-35), Abimelech seized an opportune time, engaged mercenaries, invaded the land of Gideon, and destroyed all the seventy sons except JOTHAM, who escaped by hiding (9:1-6).

Gideoni. gid´ee-oh´ni (Heb. *gid'ōnî H1551*, in form, a gentilic of GIDEON, but meaning uncertain). Father of ABIDAN; the latter was the leader of the tribe of BENJAMIN in the wilderness wanderings (Num. 1:11; 2:22; 7:60, 65; 10:24).

Gidom. gi´duhm (Heb. *gid'ōm H1550*, possibly "cutting off, clearing"). An unknown location, probably in the E side of the territory of BENJAMIN (Jdg. 20:45). After the rape of the Levite's mistress in GIBEAH, the other tribes of Israel went to battle against the Benjamites, who "fled toward the desert to the rock of Rimmon." Along the flight, the Israelites killed 5,000 Benjamites and pressed after them "as far as Gidom," where 2,000 more died. Some scholars have thought that the Hebrew word *gid'ōm* should be understood as a verbal form and translate the text, "to their cutting down," that is, until the Benjamites were slaughtered (cf. NEB).

gier eagle. See BIRDS.

gift. This English term is used variously in Bible versions to render numerous Hebrew words, especially *minḥâ H4966* and *mattān H5508*; the most common Greek terms are *dōron G1565* and *charisma G5922* (the latter is in the NT restricted to the favors that God grants, both physical and spiritual). In Israel, gifts were presented not only to one's immediate family to mark a betrothal, marriage, birth, or death, but also to superiors in political and religious hierarchy and to the palace and temple. The ultimate gifts are those given to God as tokens of faith and dependence; however, Scripture insists upon the sincerity of the heart. See also CONTRIBUTION; CORBAN; GIFTS, SPIRITUAL; SACRIFICE AND OFFERINGS.

gifts, spiritual. The apostle PAUL uses the noun *charisma G5922* ("favor, something graciously bestowed, gift") in combination with *pneumatikos G4461* ("spiritual") only once, when writing to the Romans: "I long to see you so that I may impart to you some spiritual gift to make you strong" (Rom. 1:11). Elsewhere he uses either of these terms by itself, almost always in the plural (*charismata*, Rom. 12:6 et al.; *pneumatika*, 1 Cor. 12:1 and 14:1), to designate the special endowments that the HOLY SPIRIT bestows on believers for the benefit of the CHURCH as a whole (cf. 1 Cor. 12:4-11; cf. Rom. 12:6-8; 2 Cor. 1:11; 1 Pet. 4:10). They include the ability to speak an unlearned tongue (1 Cor. 14:1-33), the interpretation of tongues (12:30; 14:27-28), power to drive out evil spirits (Matt. 8:16; Acts 13:7-12), special ability in healing the sick (1 Cor. 12:9), prophecy (Rom. 12:6), and special wisdom and knowledge (1 Cor. 12:8). Paul told the CORINTHIANS to diligently seek these gifts (12:31), but he pointed out that "the most excellent way" (12:31) was an emphasis on FAITH, HOPE, and LOVE, among which love is the greatest gift (13:13). The fruit of the Spirit is described in Gal. 5:22-23.

Everyone is accountable for any gift given to him or her (1 Cor. 4:7; 1 Pet. 4:10). Claims of having such gifts are to be tested by doctrine (1 Cor. 12:2-3) and on moral grounds (Matt. 7:15; Rom. 8:9). The ability to preach is a spiritual gift (1 Cor. 2:4; 2 Tim. 1:6). To know the deep things of God requires spiritual insight (1 Cor. 2:11-16). The gifts are distributed by the Holy Spirit as he wills (1 Cor. 12:11; Heb. 2:4).

Gihon. gi´hon (Heb. *gîhôn H1633*, "a bursting forth, spring"). **(1)** One of the four headwaters into which the river in EDEN separated (Gen. 2:10-14). The name perhaps suggests that it arose either from a large spring or from a cataract. Because the Gihon River is described as winding through the land of CUSH (ETHIOPIA), some have argued that the reference is to the NILE, but this identification, like others, seems to overlook the fact that the TIGRIS and EUPHRATES, two of the other headwaters, do not flow out of a common source; hence the account does not literally fit today's geography.

(2) Gihon was the name also of a noted spring near JERUSALEM. SOLOMON was anointed there to succeed DAVID (1 Ki. 1:32-40). That the spring provided a good supply of water is shown by the fact that HEZEKIAH, during his prosperous reign, had its water diverted by a tunnel to serve the growing population of Jerusalem (2 Chr. 32:27-30). Recent discoveries show that this tunnel was connected with the Pool of SILOAM, where the people of the city went to draw water. Remains of an ancient canal have been found through which the water once entered and it may be of this that Isaiah wrote (8:6). This spring was originally controlled by the JEBUSITES (2 Sam. 5:6), who cut a tunnel to bring it near enough to the wall for water to be drawn without exposing their women to raiders.

Gilalai. gil´uh-li (Heb. *gilălay H1675*, meaning uncertain). A priestly musician who participated in the dedication of the rebuilt wall of JERUSALEM under EZRA (Neh. 12:36).

Gilboa, Mount. gil-boh´uh (Heb. *gilbōaʿ H1648*, prob. "hill country"). A mountain or range of mountains (today Jebel Fuquʿah), about 8 mi. (13 km.) long and 3-5 mi. (5-8 km.) wide, lying to the E of the Plain of ESDRAELON, on the border between SAMARIA and GALILEE, some 17 mi. (27 km.) SW of the Sea of Galilee. The highest peak, Sheikh Burqan, is only c. 1,700 ft. (520 m.) above sea level, but it falls off rather abruptly on the E to the JORDAN, 2,000 ft. (610 m.) below. The western slope inclines more gradually to Esdraelon, 300 ft. (90 m.) above sea level. The name Gilboa occurs in Scripture only in connection with the last battle and the death of SAUL and his three sons, which took place on this western slope (1 Sam. 31; 2 Sam. 1; 21:12; 1 Chr. 10:1-8).

Gilead. gil´ee-uhd (Heb. *gilʿād H1680*, possibly "rugged country," but see GALEED; gentilic *gilʿādî H1682*, "Gileadite"). The name of three persons and of a geographical area. **(1)** Son of MAKIR, grandson of MANASSEH, and eponymous ancestor of the Gileadite clan (Num. 26:29-30; 27:1; 36:1; Josh. 17:1; Jdg. 5:17; 1 Chr. 2:21, 23; 7:14, 17). According to one passage (Num. 32:40; cf. Josh. 17:1), MOSES gave the land of Gilead (see below, #4) to Makir, suggesting that the latter named his son after the name of the land.

(2) The father of JEPHTHAH; because Jephthah was born of a prostitute, Gilead's legitimate sons drove him away (Jdg. 11:1-2).

(3) Son of Michael and descendant of GAD (1 Chr. 5:14; the Gadites lived in Gilead and other areas, v. 16).

(4) A large mountainous region E of the JORDAN. Often mentioned in the OT, the name Gilead in its broadest sense can be applied to all of Israelite TRANSJORDAN (e.g., Josh. 22:9, where it is contrasted to the land of CANAAN, i.e., Cisjordan) or to the entire central section of that area (2 Ki. 10:33). More precisely, Gilead was located in the foothills N of the Plain of Mishor. It was bounded on the W by the Jordan River, extended near the YARMUK on the N, to the S–N branches of the JABBOK and the Arabian desert to the E, and to the ARNON on the S. Its cities included JABESH GILEAD, MAHANAIM, MIZPAH, RAMOTH GILEAD, and SUCCOTH. In NT times, as a part of the kingdom

G

The mountainous region of the Dome of Gilead, N of modern Amman. (View to the NE.)

of HEROD the Great and his son Herod Antipas, it was known as PEREA. The name is still preserved today in several locations (e.g., Jebel Jelᶜad). In OT times it was a lush region with good forests, rich grazing lands, and abundant moisture.

Beside the Jabbok in Gilead, JACOB had his reconciliation with ESAU (Gen. 32:22—33:15). When CANAAN was allocated to the Israelites, Gilead fell to the Reubenites, Gadites, and to half the tribe of Manasseh (Deut. 3:13). An account of the conquest of the region is found in Deut. 2 and 3. Moses was permitted to see the plain before his death (34:1). After the land was conquered a great altar was erected beside the JORDAN so that true worship would not be forgotten (Josh. 22:10).

JAIR, a Gileadite, served for twenty years as judge over Israel (Jdg. 10:3). JEPHTHAH, a great-grandson of MANASSEH, was also a judge. Being the son of a concubine, he was banished by his brothers, but when Gilead was in dire distress, he was recalled by the elders (11:1-3). He defeated the Ephraimites and prevented fugitives from crossing the Jordan by resorting to the noted password SHIBBOLETH (12:1-7). ABSALOM gathered his forces in Gilead when he rebelled against DAVID (2 Sam. 15:13-23). The Gileadites finally fell into gross IDOLATRY (Hos. 6:8; 12:11), were overcome by the Aramean king HAZAEL (2 Ki. 10:32-34), and were led into captivity by TIGLATH-PILESER king of Assyria (15:27-29).

Gilead became famous because of some of its products. BALM was exported to TYRE (Ezek.

27:17); JEREMIAH knew of its curative power (Jer. 8:22; 46:11; 51:8). The Ishmaelites who came from Gilead and bought Joseph carried balm to Egypt (Gen. 37:25).

Gilgal. gil′gal (Heb. *gilgāl H1652* [with def. article, except Josh. 5:9; 12:23], "circle [of stones]," thus "circuit, territory"). The name of several locations. The most important of these, JOSHUA's encampment near the JORDAN, will be treated last.

(1) A town in the tribal territory of EPHRAIM. The prophets ELIJAH and ELISHAH are said to have gone "from Gilgal" (2 Ki. 2:1) to BETHEL (v. 2) and on to JERICHO (v. 4). On the basis of such limited information, some have identified this Gilgal with the modern town of Jiljulieh, about 7 mi. (11 km.) N of Bethel, but the site cannot be confirmed. It was possibly the same place where later Elisha threw flour in the pot of death, making the stew harmless (4:38-41). In addition, Mounts EBAL and GERIZIM are elsewhere said to be "near the great trees of Moreh, in the territory of those Canaanites living in the Arabah in the vicinity of Gilgal" (Deut. 11:29-30). This description indicates a place near SHECHEM, and thus likely the same area mentioned in 2 Kings. Because the broader context of Deuteronomy speaks of the Israelites' entering the Promised Land, however, some scholars argue that this Gilgal must be the same as #4 below.

(2) A region where the Canaanite city of GOIIM (NIV, "Goyim") was located; the name is included in a list of conquered monarchs (Josh. 12:23; the KJV reads, "of the nations of Gilgal"). Because it is mentioned next to DOR (in Naphath Dor) and before TIRZAH, some think the area may have been on the eastern edge of the SHARON Plain. The SEPTUAGINT, however, has GALILEE (rather than Gilgal), a reading followed by the NRSV and other versions.

(3) A town or region on the NE boundary of the tribe of JUDAH, facing the Pass of ADUMMIM, "south of the gorge" (Josh. 15:7). Because Adummim is about 6 mi. (10 km.) SW of JERICHO, some have identified this Gilgal with #4 below, but the

latter was clearly much closer to Jericho. A similar passage (18:17, which describes the SE boundary of BENJAMIN) refers to GELILOTH as facing the Pass of Adummim, and many scholars believe that Geliloth and Gilgal are variant forms of the same name.

(4) The Gilgal most frequently mentioned in the Bible is a site "on the eastern border of Jericho" where the Israelites camped soon after entering the Promised Land (Josh. 4:19). There they built a monument of twelve stones (v. 20), the rite of CIRCUMCISION was performed (5:8), and the Passover was celebrated (5:10). From this site, the Israelites set out to march around Jericho for seven days. Apparently, Gilgal was their base camp as they made attacks on the hill country, for JOSHUA was found at Gilgal by the GIBEONITES after AI was destroyed and after he had built an altar on Mount Ebal (8:30; 9:6). From Gilgal, the Israelites left to defend Gibeon and returned to Gilgal victorious (10:15, 43). Later, Gilgal became one of three cities on SAMUEL's circuit (1 Sam. 7:16). SAUL was made king in Gilgal (11:14-15), which became a base of military operations (13:4 et al.). Here Saul sought to placate Samuel after he had disobeyed by salvaging some cattle for booty and permitting the enemy king to live (15:7-15). Gilgal is often identified with Khirbet el-Mefjir, just NE of Jericho, but another proposal is Khirbet en-Nitleh (3 mi./5 km. SE of Jericho).

Gilo. See GILOH.

Giloh. gi′loh (Heb. *gilōh H1656*, possibly "rejoicing"; gentilic *gilōnî H1639*, "Gilonite"). A town in the hill country of S JUDAH (Josh. 15:51). It was the home of DAVID's counselor, AHITHOPHEL (2 Sam. 15:12; 23:34 [RSV, "of Gilo"]). Some have identified Giloh with modern Khirbet Jala, about 5 mi. (8 km.) NNW of HEBRON, but others prefer an otherwise unknown location farther S.

Gilonite. See GILOH.

gimel. gim′uhl (Heb. *gimel* [not used in the Bible], meaning uncertain). The third letter of the Hebrew alphabet (ג), with a numerical value of three. Its sound corresponds to that of English "hard" *g* (but following a vowel, it later became a soft fricative, that is, allowing some breath to go through).

Gimzo. gim′zoh (Heb. *gimzô H1693*, perhaps "[place of] sycamore tree"). A town in the SHEPHELAH wrested from King AHAZ by the PHILISTINES (2 Chr. 28:18). Gimzo is identified with modern Jimzu, some 5 mi. (8 km.) N of GEZER and 15 mi. (24 km.) SSE of JOPPA.

gin. Term used by the KJV for SNARE (Job 18:9 et al.).

Ginath. gi′nath (Heb. *ginat H1640*, possibly "protector"). The father of TIBNI; the latter contended with OMRI for the throne of Israel after the death of ZIMRI (1 Ki. 16:21-22).

Ginnetho, Ginnethoi. See GINNETHON.

Ginnethon. gin′uh-thon (Heb. *ginnĕtôn H1715* [in Neh. 12:4, *gintôy*], perhaps "gardener"). A priest who returned from BABYLON with ZERUBBABEL and JESHUA (12:4; KJV, "Ginnetho"; NRSV, "Ginnethoi"). He was among those who affixed their seals to the covenant of NEHEMIAH (10:6). In the days of JOIAKIM, the head of his family was Meshullam (12:16).

girdle. See DRESS.

Girgashite. guhr′guh-shit (Heb. *girgāšî H1739*). A Canaanite tribe descended from HAM through his son CANAAN (Gen. 10:6) and included in various lists of peoples dispossessed by the Israelites (Gen. 15:21; Deut. 7:1; Josh. 3:10; 24:11; 1 Chr. 1:14; Neh. 9:8; in Jdt. 5:16, "Gergesites"). The Bible gives no indication of the tribe's locality. Some have suggested a connection with Karkisha, a HITTITE city in ASIA MINOR; others have identified the Girgashites with the Gergesenes (see GERASENE). These and other proposals remain unconfirmed.

girl. This English term is used in Bible versions to render primarily Hebrew *naʿărāh H5855* and Greek *korasion G3166*. It must be noted that among ancient peoples there was little in the way of a differentiation between the stages of infancy to old age. Such terms as *boy* or *girl* are therefore imprecise, and must be interpreted by the context in which they occur. See CHILD.

Girzite. guhr´zit (Heb. *girzî H1747*). A Canaanite tribe that, along with those of the Geshurites and Amalekites, was raided by DAVID while he lived in ZIKLAG (1 Sam. 27:8; see GESHUR; AMALEK). Such a tribe is otherwise unknown, and a Hebrew variant is *gizrî*, that is, "Gizrite" (cf. KJV, "Gezrite"), which would refer to an inhabitant of GEZER. Many scholars have thought, however, that Gezer was too far N for it to be involved in this account. Some have argued that the pair of names Geshurites and Girzites (or Gizrites) is the result either of a careless scribal repetition (dittography) or of a conflation of two different texts and that therefore the original reading was simply "Geshurites." While the solution to this problem remains uncertain, one must allow for the possibility that a people by the name of Girzites did indeed live "in the land extending to Shur and Egypt."

Gispa. gish´puh (Heb. *gišpāʾ H1778*). KJV Gispa. A supervisor, along with ZIHA, of the temple servants (NETHINIM) living on the hill of OPHEL (Neh. 11:21). Some have thought that he should be identified with HASUPHA, who is elsewhere mentioned next to Ziha (Ezra 2:43; Neh. 7:46).

Gittah-hepher. git´uh-hee´fuhr. KJV alternate form of GATH HEPHER (in Josh. 19:13).

Gittaim. git´ay-im (Heb. *gittayim H1786*, "[two] winepresses"). A village at the NE edge of the PHILISTINE plain, usually identified with Ras Abu Ḥumeid/Ḥamid, about 14 mi. (22 km.) SE of JOPPA and 3.5 mi. (6 km.) NW of GEZER, but there are other proposals. Gittaim became a refuge for the indigenous population of BEEROTH (2 Sam. 4:3). After the return from the EXILE in Babylon, Gittaim was settled by Benjamites (Neh. 11:33).

Gittite. git´it. An inhabitant of GATH.

gittith. git´ith (Heb. *gittît H1787*). Often capitalized. A musical term used only in the titles of three psalms (Ps. 8; 81; 84). The meaning of the term is uncertain. It may refer to a lyre or other musical instrument distinctive to the PHILISTINE city of GATH, or to a type of melody associated with that city. Others believe it is derived directly from the Hebrew word for "winepress" (*gat H1780*), thus referring to a tune sung at the grape harvest or specifically at the Feast of Tabernacles. Other suggestions have been made.

Gizonite. gi´zoh-nit (Heb. *gizônî H1604*). A descriptive term applied to a certain Hashem, one of DAVID's mighty men (1 Chr. 11:34; the parallel list in 2 Sam. 23:32 says "the sons of Jashen" instead of "Hashem the Gizonite"). The term is gentilic in form and thus appears to refer to an inhabitant of a town named "Gizo" or "Gizon," but such a place is unknown; perhaps it indicates a family name.

Gizrite. See GIRZITE.

glad tidings. See GOSPEL.

glass. See MINERALS; MIRROR.

glass, sea of. See SEA OF GLASS.

glaze. This English term is used by the NIV and other modern versions in Prov. 26:23, where the Hebrew phrase meaning "silver dross" (cf. KJV) is often emended to "like glaze," perhaps referring to a shiny metallic oxide of lead that has been used for millennia as a pigment (litharge) and as a glaze on pottery. Subsequent research, however, has challenged this emendation, and the TNIV restores the traditional rendering.

glean. This verb means "to gather the grain left behind by the reapers." The Mosaic law allowed for gleaning by the POOR (Lev. 19:9-10; 23:22), a practice beautifully illustrated in the story of RUTH and BOAZ (Ruth 2:3, 7-8, et al.). The concept is used metaphorically by the prophets (Isa. 17:5-6; Jer. 6:9; Mic. 7:1).

glede. See BIRDS (under *kite*).

glorification. See EXALTATION OF CHRIST; GLORY; RESURRECTION.

glory. Great honor or praise; used especially of God's majestic splendor. Several Hebrew words have been translated "glory," but the most frequent one is *kābôd H3883*, which has a broad range of meaning: "weight, burden, wealth, magnificence, honor." It can be used of human beings to indicate personal influence or substance. JOSEPH, for example, says to his brothers, "Tell my father about all the honor [*kābôd*] accorded me in Egypt" (Gen. 45:13; cf. 31:1). HAMAN also recounted all "the glory of his riches" (Esth. 5:11; NIV, "his vast wealth"; cf. Ps. 49:16-17; Isa. 16:14; 17:4; 61:6; 66:11).

The glory of God is the worthiness of God, more particularly, the presence of God in the fullness of his attributes in some place or everywhere. It is in this sense that ISAIAH reports the words of the SERAPHIM that "the whole earth is full of his glory" (Isa. 6:3), meaning that the Lord in his full person, deity, and majesty is present in every place. Again, when the Lord says of the TABERNACLE that it would be consecrated by his glory (Exod. 29:43), he means that without diluting or diminishing his full deity he will himself dwell in the great tent and make it holy by his presence. MOSES asked that he might see the Lord's glory (33:18), and the Lord responded that he would himself proclaim his name to him, that is, make Moses aware of all the glorious attributes and capacities that the one and only God possesses (33:19—34:8). Sometimes the Lord allowed his glory to become visible. Since the cloudy-fiery pillar was the place where he was present, there were occasions (e.g., 16:10) when there was a manifestation of his presence. Possibly the same was true in Exod. 40:34-35: either there was an awesome manifestation of the Lord's presence or an overwhelming sense that God was there so that Moses dared not come near. Later thought defined this indwelling presence of God as the SHEKINAH (or "indwelling").

In the NT, the distinctive Greek word for "glory" is *doxa G1518*. This noun means "opinion" or "reputation" in classical literature, a sense occasionally reflected in the NT (e.g., Jn. 12:43; cf. 5:41-43; 7:18). Almost always, however, the use of the word coincides with the meanings of Hebrew *kābôd*: brightness ("the glory of the Lord shone around them," Lk. 2:9; cf. 2 Cor. 3:9); outward human splendor ("Solomon in all his glory," Matt. 6:29; cf. 1 Cor. 11:15); national splendor ("all the kingdoms of the world and their glory," Matt. 4:8; cf. Rev. 21:24); honor ("you are our glory and joy," 1 Thess. 2:20). Chiefly, the word refers to the revela-

Artistic motif of Jesus' transfiguration (from the Church of Transfiguration on Mt. Tabor).

© Dr. James C. Martin

tion of God in Christ: "the Son is the radiance of God's glory" (Heb. 1:3). The apostle John declares: "We have seen his glory" (Jn. 1:14; cf. v. 18). It was seen in the MIRACLES (2:11) and in the TRANSFIGURATION (2 Pet. 1:16-17). He is "our glorious Lord" (Jas. 2:1). In his incarnate life, the Shekinah glory of God is seen. As for the saints, glory culminates in the changing of their bodies to the likeness of their glorified Lord (Phil. 3:20).

glossolalia. glos´uh-lay´lee-uh. See TONGUES, GIFT OF.

gluttony. The term *glutton* can be used to render the participle of a Hebrew verb that means "to be frivolous, profligate" (Deut. 21:20; Prov. 23:20-21). In the NT, it renders Greek *phagos G5741* (Matt. 11:19; Lk. 7:34) and *gastēr G1143* (lit., "belly," Tit. 1:12). See TEMPERANCE.

gnashing the teeth. This expression is used in Hebrew poetic passages to indicate the hatred and scorn of enemies (Job 16:9; Ps. 35:16; 37:12; 112:10; Lam. 2:16). A similar usage occurs in the NT with reference to the rage of STEPHEN's enemies (Acts 7:54). More frequently, however, the image is found repeatedly in the sayings of Jesus concerning the remorseful gnashing of teeth by those excluded from heaven (Matt. 8:12; 13:42, 50; 22:13; 24:51; 25:30; Lk. 13:28; see HELL).

gnat. See ANIMALS.

G

Gnosticism. nos´tuh-siz´uhm. Derived from Greek *gnōsis G1194*, "knowledge," this term is variously applied to certain movements within, or in relation to, early Christianity. Although some scholars use it with reference to teachings within the period when the NT was written, the word more accurately describes systems of knowledge in opposition to orthodox Christianity in the second and third centuries. It appears that some church members, embarrassed by the lowly origins of Christianity (birth in a stable, traveling teacher, death on a cross, etc.), linked aspects of traditional Christianity with attractive ideas taken from Greek philosophy and Eastern religion, magic, and astrology. We call the resulting complex systems Gnosticism.

Their main themes were as follows: The true God is pure spirit and dwells in the realm of pure light, totally separated from this dark world. This world is evil, for it is made of matter, and matter is evil. The true God will have nothing to do with it, for it was created by a lesser god and was a mistake. People in this world are normally made of body and mind, but in a few there is a spark of pure spirit. Such "spiritual" people need to be rescued from this evil world; thus there is need for a Savior. Jesus, who is pure spirit even though he appears to be body and mind, is the Savior who comes from the true God in light to bring knowledge of the spiritual realm of light. Therefore those who have the spark of spirit can receive the knowledge and be reunited with the true God.

Within the NT there are references to claims to knowledge and WISDOM (e.g., 1 Cor. 1:17-31; 8:1; 13:8) that could be the roots of the growth that led to developed Gnosticism. There was a heresy in the church of COLOSSE (Col. 2:8-23) and false teaching in the churches TIMOTHY knew (1 Tim. 1:4-7; 4:3-7; 2 Tim. 2:18; 3:5-7) that may be termed a false *gnōsis* (1 Tim. 6:20). Then in the epistles of John there are references to false teaching about the reality of the humanity of Jesus (1 Jn. 4:3; 2 Jn. 7). But there is certainly nothing in the NT of the developed kind of false doctrines that the teachers of the church had to face a century or so later.

goad. A sharp stick used for prodding cattle, particularly during plowing. It could have an iron tip (cf. 1 Sam. 13:21) and also could be utilized for cleaning PLOWS, probably with a blade on the other end. SHAMGAR used an oxgoad as a spear while killing 600 PHILISTINES (Jdg. 3:31). In a metaphorical sense, the words of the wise are compared to goads as they encourage and rebuke (Eccl. 12:11). The only NT use of the term concerns Christ's rebuke to PAUL on the DAMASCUS road for kicking against the goads (Acts 26:14), which refers not to "the prickings of an uneasy conscience over his persecuting activity but [to] the new forces which were now impelling him in the opposite direction to that which he had hitherto pursued" (F. F. Bruce, *The Acts of the Apostles: The Greek Text with Introduction and Commentary*, 3rd ed. [1990], 501, which includes parallels to this proverb in classical literature).

Goah. goh´uh (Heb. *gōʿâ* [or *gōʿet*] *H1717*, possibly from *gāʿâ H1716*, "to low, below"). KJV Goath. An area in or near JERUSALEM that would serve as one of the boundaries prophesied for the rebuilt city (Jer. 31:39; the Hebrew text has the locative form *gōʿātâ*). See GAREB (PLACE).

goat. See ANIMALS.

Goath. See GOAH.

goatskins. See SKIN.

Gob. gob (Heb. *gôb H1570*, meaning uncertain). An unknown location where DAVID's men battled the PHILISTINES on two occasions (2 Sam. 21:18-19). It was possibly a town close to GATH (mentioned in vv. 20 and 22). Because the parallel passage has GEZER (1 Chr. 20:4), some scholars believe the text in Samuel is corrupt, while others think that Gezer and Gob were alternate names for the same place. In addition, many Hebrew MSS read NOB, a variant preferred by some on the basis of the personal name ISHBI-BENOB (2 Sam. 21:16). Still other scholars identify Gob with GIBBETHON.

goblet. This English term is used variously in Bible versions to render words and expressions referring to drinking vessels. It occurs only once in the KJV (Cant. 7:2) and in the NRSV (Esth. 1:7). The NIV uses it a few other times as well (e.g., Isa. 51:17, 22).

God. The Bible does not contain a formal definition of this term, yet God's being and attributes are displayed on every page. Among Christian theological formulations, perhaps the most satisfactory is the one found in answer to the fourth question in the *Westminster Shorter Catechism*: "God is a Spirit, infinite, eternal, and unchangeable, in his being, wisdom, power, holiness, justice, goodness, and truth." It is fair to say that this description faithfully sets forth what the Bible constantly assumes and declares concerning God.

I. God is a Spirit. These words mean that God is a nonmaterial personal being, self-conscious and self-determining. The definition contains three adjectives, each modifying seven nouns. The descriptive units in which these words are combined are not logically separable but are inextricably woven together, and thus they delineate the unity and the integrated complexity of God's attributes. The analysis cannot be exhaustive but only descriptive.

II. God is infinite. The infinity of God is not an independent attribute. If we were to say, "God is the infinite," without specification, the meaning would be pantheistic, equal to saying, "God is everything." In using the word "infinite," we must always be specific, as follows:

Infinite in his being. This doctrine is intended to teach that God is everywhere. The omnipresence of God is vividly brought out in such Scriptures as Ps. 139. God is not physically, relatively, or measurably big. The word "immensity" is used by good theologians, but it conveys to some minds a false impression, as though God were partly here and partly there, like a giant, or an amorphous mass, or a fluid. The omnipresence of God means that wherever we are, even if we are like the fugitive Jacob at Bethel (Gen. 28:16), God *himself* is there. It is easier to conceive of God's omnipresence by saying, "Everything everywhere is immediately in his presence." Finite creatures can act instantaneously in a limited area. Everything within our reach or sight is immediately in our presence, in the sense that distance is no problem. So in an absolutely perfect sense, everything in the universe is immediately in the presence of God.

Infinite in his wisdom. This phrase designates God's omniscience. The Bible throughout regards God's omniscience as all-inclusive, not dependent on a step-by-step process of reasoning. God's knowledge does not increase or diminish when the temporal events of his redemptive program take place. He eternally knows what he has known in the past and what he will know in the future.

Infinite in his power. These words point to his omnipotence, his ability to do with power all that power can do, his controlling all the power that is or can be.

Infinite in his holiness, justice, and goodness. These words signify God's moral attributes. Holiness is regarded in the Bible as his central ethical character. Basic ethical principles are revealed by the will of God and derived from and based on the character of God. "Be holy because I am holy" (Lev. 11:44-45). Justice refers to his administration of rewards and punishments among the personal beings of the universe. Goodness in this context indicates his love, his common grace toward all, and his special grace in saving sinners.

Infinite in his truth. This is the attribute that designates the basis of all logic and rationality. The axioms of logic and mathematics, and all the laws of reason, are not laws apart from God to which God must be subject. They are attributes of his own character. When the Bible says that "it is impossible for God to lie" (Heb. 6:18; Tit. 1:2), it is not contradicting his omnipotence. How much power would it take to make two times two equal five? Truth is not an object of power. There is no mere tautology in the Bible, as though the multiplication tables were true by mere divine fiat. As in ethics, so in rationality, the biblical writers constantly appeal

© The Israel Museum, Jerusalem.

Within this text, written in the later Jewish script, the Tetragrammaton (YHWH, God's covenant name) occurs in paleo-Hebrew letters (first line, second word from right margin).

G

to the truth of God's immutable character. "He cannot deny himself" (2 Tim. 2:13 KJV).

Just as the adjective "infinite," in the definition we are considering, applies to all the specified attributes, so the words "eternal" and "unchangeable" similarly apply to all.

Eternal. This means without temporal beginning or ending, or in a figurative sense "eternal" may designate (as in the words "eternal life") a quality of being suitable for eternity. That God existed eternally before the creation of the finite universe does not imply a personal subject with no object, for God is triune. See TRINITY. The idea that eternity means timelessness is nowhere suggested in the Bible. This false notion doubtless came into Christian theology under the influence of Aristotle's "Unmoved Mover," the influence of which is strong in Thomas Aquinas. That the Bible does not teach that God is timeless is an objective, verifiable fact.

Unchangeable. This term points to the perfect self-consistency of God's character throughout all eternity. This is not a static concept, but dynamic, in all his relations with his creatures. That God brings to pass, in time, the events of his redemptive program is not contradictory. The notion that God's immutability is static immobility (as in Thomism) is like the notion of timelessness and is contrary to the biblical view. The God of the Bible is intimately and actively concerned in all the actions of all his creatures.

III. God is known by his acts. Supremely, "God … has spoken to us by his Son" (Heb. 1:1-2). Further, his "invisible" being, that is, his "eternal power and divine character" are "known" and "clearly seen" by "what has been made" (Rom. 1:20). "The heavens declare the glory of God" (Ps. 19; Rom. 10:18). It is customary to distinguish between "natural revelation," all that God has made, and "special revelation," the Bible. See REVELATION.

IV. God is known in fellowship. That God is known by faith, beyond the mere cognitive sense, in fellowship with his people, is one of the most prominent themes throughout the Bible. Moses, leading his people in the exodus, was assured, "My Presence will go with you, and I will give you rest." And Moses replied, "If your Presence does not go with us, do not send us up from here" (Exod. 33:13-

14). The Bible abounds in invitations to seek and find fellowship with God (e.g., Ps. 27; Isa. 55).

Other gods are referred to in the Bible as false gods (Jdg. 6:31; 1 Ki. 18:27; 1 Cor. 8:4-6) or as demonic (1 Cor. 10:19-22).

God, children of. See SONS OF GOD.

God, names of. See ELOHIM; JEHOVAH.

God, Son of. See SON OF GOD.

God, sons of. See SONS OF GOD.

God, unknown. See UNKNOWN GOD.

Godhead. A synonym of *godhood* or *divinity*, this English term is used to designate the state, dignity, condition, or quality of a deity, and in Christian theology, of the self-revealed God. The word occurs in the KJV as the rendering of two related Greek words: *theion G2521* and *theiotēs G2522* (Rom. 1:20; Col. 2:9; NIV, "divine being" and "Deity"). The first word, with the definite article, was in general Greek use for "the divine," which pagan religions saw in almost everything, and PAUL employed it in addressing a heathen audience, but in a context that urges personal faith in the living God (Acts 17:29; NIV, "divine being"). The second word was also used by non-Christians with reference, for example, to ARTEMIS; Paul uses it in association with the Creator's power upon which all creatures are dependent (Rom. 1:20; NIV, "divine being"), but also applies it to the incarnate CHRIST (Col. 2:9; NIV, "Deity").

godless. This term, referring to someone who does not acknowledge God, is most often used in the sense "wicked" or "impious." Neither it nor its cognate noun *godlessness* occurs in the KJV (which prefers *ungodly* and *ungodliness*), but the term is sometimes used in modern versions to render various Hebrew and Greek words (e.g., Job 8:13; Isa. 10:6; Rom. 1:18; Heb. 12:16). See GODLINESS; HOLINESS; RIGHTEOUSNESS.

godliness. Piety toward God, including the proper conduct that springs from a right relationship with him. It is not belief in itself, but the devotion toward God and love to others that result from that belief. Religious FAITH is empty without godliness (2 Tim. 3:5). The Greek term *eusebeia G2354* ("reverence, piety, religion") is found fifteen times in the NT, mostly in the PASTORAL LETTERS (also Acts 3:12; 1 Pet. 1:3, 6-7; 3:11). It is the sum total of religious character and actions, and it produces both a present and a future state of happiness. It is not right action that is done from a sense of duty, but is the spontaneous virtue that comes from the indwelling Christ and reflects him.

gods, pagan. See IDOLATRY.

Gog. gog (Heb. *gôg H1573*, perhaps related to Akk. *gāgu*, "costly pottery"). **(1)** Son (or descendant) of Shemaiah, from the tribe of REUBEN (1 Chr. 5:4). The names in this list may be included among the herdsmen who settled in the desert E of GILEAD (vv. 8-9).

(2) In an important prophecy, EZEKIEL speaks of "Gog, of the land of Magog, the chief prince of Meshech and Tubal" (Ezek. 38:2; see also vv. 3-23 and 39:1-16). He is viewed as the demonic and sinister leader of ungodly peoples far distant from Israel, whom he leads in a final assault against the people of God. Gog is ignominiously defeated by the intervention of Yahweh upon the mountains of Canaan. The conflict is alluded to in the NT (Rev. 20:7-9). The origin and identification of the name Gog is uncertain, though many scholars identify him as Gyges, king of Lydia (the Assyrian *Gugu*, c. 660 B.C.). See LYDIA (PLACE). MAGOG (possibly meaning "the land of Gog") was no doubt located in ASIA MINOR and may refer to Lydia. With Gog are associated many peoples: not only MESHECH and TUBAL, of whom he is prince, but also Persia, Cush, Put, Gomer, Sheba, Dedan, and Tarshish—all of whom come from widely separated parts of the earth as a mighty host, like a cloud, to do battle against Israel under

the mighty Gog. But God's judgment comes upon the enemies of Israel. Every kind of terror is summoned by Yahweh against Gog, whose defeat is so great that his vast armaments serve as fuel for Israel for seven years, and whose dead are so numerous that it takes all Israel seven months to bury them. Gog appears again in Rev. 20:7-9, where SATAN is depicted after the MILLENNIUM as gathering the godless nations of the whole earth—symbolically represented by Gog and Magog—against the saints and the beloved city, but they are destroyed and cast into the lake of fire.

Goiim, Goyim. goi´im (Heb. *gôyim H1582*, "nations"). **(1)** A territory ruled by a king named TIDAL, who joined KEDORLAOMER and other rulers in waging war against the CITIES OF THE PLAIN (Gen. 14:1, 9; NIV and most versions, "Goiim"; TNIV, "Goyim"; KJV, "Tidal king of nations"). The location of Goiim is debated. If Tidal is the HITTITE name Tudhalia (Tudkhaliyas), then the identification of Goiim with a region in SYRIA would fit the biblical references.

(2) A city in "Gilgal" whose king is included in the list of rulers defeated by JOSHUA (Josh. 12:23; NIV, "Goyim in Gilgal"; the NRSV, "Goiim in Galilee" [following LXX]; KJV, "of the nations of Gilgal"). See discussion under GILGAL #2.

Golan. goh´luhn (Heb. *gôlān H1584*, possibly "enclosure"). A city in BASHAN assigned to the tribe of MANASSEH. Chosen by MOSES as one of three CITIES OF REFUGE E of the JORDAN, it was allotted to the descendants of GERSHON as a Levitical

Prehistoric "circles" located on the Golan Heights.

© Dr. James C. Martin

G

city (Deut. 4:43; Josh. 20:8; 21:27; 1 Chr. 6:71). The name Golan/Gaulan later became attached to the adjoining country. Most probably the territory corresponds to modern Jaulan (Golan Heights), an area bounded by Mount HERMON on the NE, the Jordan and the Sea of Galilee on the W, and the Yarmuk River on the S. The ancient city of Golan is usually identified with modern Saḥm el-Jolan, some 18 mi. (29 km.) E of the Sea of Galilee, on the E bank of the river el-ʾAllan.

gold. See MINERALS.

golden calf. See CALF WORSHIP.

Golden Rule. Traditional name given to Jesus' injunction, "Do to others as you would have them do to you" (Lk. 6:31; cf. Matt. 7:12).

goldsmith. See OCCUPATIONS AND PROFESSIONS.

Golgotha. gol′guh-thuh (Gk. *Golgotha G1201*, from Aram. *gulgulṭāʾ*, "skull"). The ARAMAIC name of the "Place of the Skull," an area near JERUSALEM where CHRIST was crucified. This name appears but three times in the Bible, in parallel passages of the Gospels (Matt. 27:33; Mk. 15:22; Jn. 19:17). Luke, as usual, does not use the Semitic word but only its corresponding Greek term, *kranion G3191*, "skull" (Lk. 23:33), which the Vulgate in turn translates with Latin *calvaria*, thus KJV, "Calvary." The author of Hebrews indicates that Jesus suffered "outside the city gate" (Heb. 13:12). Therefore, Golgotha "was near the city" (Jn. 19:20), but not within the city wall in NT times. Although many places around the holy city have been suggested as the site of Calvary, only two are serious contenders for the spot of both the crucifixion and the burial. One primary claim to the site is the Church of the Holy Sepulchre, whose history goes back to the fourth century. It is within the walls of the old city today, but its supporters maintain that the NT city wall would place it outside the city. The other major contender for the site of Calvary is known today as the Garden Tomb and/or Gordon's Calvary. It is a hill or knoll and is certainly outside the city walls (both modern and NT). A garden and a tomb (in fact, several tombs) are in the immedi-

ate vicinity. The topographical feature of the hill that makes it look like a skull would not have been present in NT times. Since the Church of the Holy Sepulchre is a highly decorated building on top of a site, and the scene of much activity, a good imagination is required to see a garden tomb there, but it does have a stronger historical claim.

Goliath. guh-li′uhth (Heb. *golyāt H1669*, meaning unknown). A warrior from GATH during the reign of SAUL (late 11th cent. B.C.). Representing the PHILISTINES in the Valley of Elah (about 15 mi./24 km. W of BETHLEHEM; see ELAH, VALLEY OF), he challenged the Israelites to send an opponent. His challenge went unaccepted until DAVID visited the battleground to bring food to his brothers. David felled the giant with a stone shot from a sling and cut off his head with Goliath's own sword (1 Sam. 17). The height of Goliath was six cubits and a span (17:4), over 9 ft. (almost 3 m.). His coat of mail was 5,000 shekels, about 125 lbs. (57 kg.); his spearhead, 600 shekels, about 15 lbs. (7 kg.; 17:5, 7). His sword was kept at NOB under priestly jurisdiction and later given to David by AHIMELECH, the priest, when David fled from SAUL (21:9; 22:10). (The Goliath of 2 Sam. 21:19 may have been the son of the giant whom David killed. See discussion under ELHANAN.)

Gomer. goh′muhr (Heb. *gōmer H1699* [*H1700* in Hos. 1:3], perhaps "completion"). **(1)** First son of JAPHETH and grandson of NOAH; father of Ashkenaz, Riphath, and Togarmah (Gen. 10:2-3; 1 Chr. 1:5-6). Gomer is mentioned in Ezek. 38:6 as supporting an attack on Israel that will fail because the Lord is defending his people. The reference is probably to Gomer's offspring, the Cimmerians (Akk. *Gimirrai*, Gk. *Kimmerioi*), who were forced out of S Russia by the SCYTHIANS and settled in ASIA MINOR at the end of the eighth century B.C.

(2) Daughter of Diblaim and wife of HOSEA, the eighth-century prophet in Israel during the reign of JEROBOAM II (Hos. 1:3-8). The Lord asked Hosea to take to himself "an adulterous wife" (v. 2; NRSV, "a wife of whoredom"), so he married Gomer and by her had children to whom were given illustrative, or symbolic, names. This marriage pictured the Lord's relationship with his people, who had gone astray into IDOLATRY. Hosea is later told to marry "an adulteress" (3:1); some believe that this too is a reference to Gomer after she had left Hosea, being bought again and asked to abstain from harlotry. Whether or not this is Gomer, it illustrates that though God's people sin, he loves them and wants them to return to him, but to refrain from sin. Some argue that these are not actual marriages but simply illustrations.

Gomorrah. guh-mor′uh (Heb. *ʿămōrâ H6686*, perhaps "flooded place"; Gk. *Gomorra G1202*). A city located in the Valley of SIDDIM, probably at the S end of the DEAD SEA. Together with SODOM, it became infamous because of the circumstances of its destruction. Sodom and Gomorrah became bywords for the judgment of God (cf. Isa. 1:9-10; 13:19; Jer. 23:14; 49:18; 50:40; Amos 4:11; Zeph. 2:9). In the NT there are allusions to these ancient examples of God's retributive wrath (Matt. 10:15; Rom. 9:29; 2 Pet. 2:6; Jude 7). Gomorrah is first mentioned as the S or E extent of the Canaanite territory (Gen. 10:19). The book of Genesis also records the meeting of ABRAHAM with the angels and their warning to LOT of the imminent destruction of Sodom and Gomorrah (Gen. 18-19). Lot escaped and "the LORD rained down burning sulfur on Sodom and Gomorrah" (19:24). The location of Gomorrah is unknown. Some have argued that it was at the N end of the DEAD SEA, but the more widely accepted view is that Gomorrah and the other cities are sunken beneath the shallow waters of the Dead Sea, S of the Lisan peninsula.

gong. The expression "resounding gong" is used by PAUL to illustrate the futility of the gift of glossolalia if unaccompanied by LOVE (1 Cor. 13:1). See also TONGUES, GIFT OF.

good. This adjective, which occurs hundreds of times in the Bible, is usually the rendering of Hebrew *ṭôb H3202* (e.g., Gen. 1:2) and Greek *agathos G19* (e.g., Matt. 7:11) or *kalos G2819* (e.g., Matt. 3:10). The terms have a wide variety of related meanings that often shade off into one another, such as "kind, gracious" (of people, 1 Sam. 25:15; of God, Ps. 86:5); "befitting, appropriate" (2 Sam. 17:7; 1 Cor. 5:6); "highly esteemed" (of

a name, Eccl. 7:1); "agreeable, pleasant" (of fruit, Gen. 3:6; of a word, Prov. 15:23); "upright, righteous" (1 Sam. 12:23; Matt. 5:45).

In the Bible, God himself is the Good: he is the source of all goodness, and thus there is no good apart from him. "No one is good—except God alone" (Mk. 10:18). It follows that we cannot know the good unless we know God in a right relationship and do his expressed will. Since goodness is intrinsic to God, all that he does is necessarily good. He declared his own CREATION good (Gen. 1). The disorder, disruption, evil, and SIN that now prevail throughout his world are the result of the rebellion of moral beings originally created good. God's REVELATION of himself in history was an increasing revelation of his goodness. He made man and woman in his image for fellowship with himself. Even when they flouted him in the FALL, God's loving interest in them continued; he showed his goodness by immediately taking steps to undo the disastrous effects of the fall. His election of Israel as his people, the exodus, the giving of the law, his many deliverances of Israel, the promise and preparation for the coming of the Messiah—all these were evidences of God's goodness; as were the incarnation, the atoning death of his Son, the resurrection, Pentecost. Some day his goodness will be acknowledged by all of his creation; and he will be all in all. Because of the fall, we are by nature corrupt and capable of doing nothing that is really good (Rom. 7), but because of God's provision in Christ and the Holy Spirit, we can live a life of obedience to and fellowship with our creator.

goodman. This term is used by the KJV once in the OT (Prov. 7:19), and several times in the Gospels in the phrase "goodman of the house," to render Greek *oikodespotēs G3867*, "master of the house, householder, landowner" (Matt. 20:11 et al.). See HOUSEHOLDER.

goods, community of. See COMMUNITY OF GOODS.

gopher wood. See PLANTS.

Goshen. goh′shuhn (Heb. *gōšen H1777*, possibly "on the mountains" or "mound of earth"). **(1)** A town in the S hill country of the tribe of JUDAH (Josh. 15:51). The precise location is unknown, although some scholars have suggested Tell el-Dhahiriyeh, about 12 mi. (19 km.) SW of HEBRON.

(2) An area in S Palestine. The Israelites are said to have subdued the Canaanites "from Kadesh

The land of Goshen near Tell el-Dabᶜa. (View to the N.)

© Dr. James C. Martin

Barnea to Gaza and from the whole region of Goshen to Gibeon" (Josh. 10:41; cf. 11:16). This region was probably between the NEGEV and the hill country, and it may have received its name from the town of Goshen; see #1 above.

(3) A region in EGYPT where JACOB and his family settled (Gen. 45:10 et al.). Goshen is closely linked, and apparently to be identified, with the land and city of RAMESES (Raamses), on the eastern side of the NILE delta (47:11). At the time of the EXODUS, the Hebrews were still in Goshen (Exod. 8:22; 9:26), and they began their travel from Rameses (Exod. 12:37; Num. 33:3), which city they had helped to build (Exod. 1:11). As the Hebrews also had to work at PITHOM (Exod. 1:11), Goshen should preferably be within reasonable reach of that city. Furthermore, Goshen lay on a route from Palestine into Egypt, and near the residence of JOSEPH's pharaoh (cf. data in Gen. 45:10; 46:28, 29; 47:1-6). The region was a good place for keeping cattle (46:34; 47:6) and had room for settlers. Goshen can readily be placed in the territory

between Saft el-Henneh in the S (at the W end of Wadi Tumilat) and Qantir in the N and NE.

gospel. The Christian message, or good news, of REDEMPTION proclaimed by CHRIST and his apostles. The English term *gospel* (from Old Eng. *gōd*, "good," and *spell*, "tale, talk") renders Greek *euangelion G2295* (from *eu G2292*, "well," and *angellō G33*, "to announce"). This Greek word is used a dozen times in Matthew and Mark (where modern versions usually render it "good news," e.g., Matt. 4:23), a few times in other books (Acts 15:7; 20:24; 1 Pet. 4:17; Rev. 14:6), and most frequently in the Pauline letters (almost sixty times, e.g., Rom. 1:1).

Through the gospel, the HOLY SPIRIT works for the SALVATION of human beings (Rom. 1:15-16). In the NT the word never means a book (one of the four GOSPELS); instead, it always refers to the good tidings that Christ and the apostles announced. It is called "the gospel of God" (Rom. 1:1; 1 Thess. 2:2, 9); "the gospel about Jesus Christ" (Mk. 1:1; Rom. 15:19); "the gospel of God's grace" (Acts 20:24); "the gospel of peace" (Eph. 6:15); "the gospel of your salvation" (1:13); and "the gospel of the glory of Christ" (2 Cor. 4:4). The gospel has to do entirely with Christ. It was preached by him (Matt. 4:23; 11:5), by the apostles (Acts 16:10; Rom. 1:15), and by the evangelists (Acts 8:25). Not until the second century was the word applied to the writings concerning the message of Christ.

Gospels. The first four books of the NT, which relate the life, teachings, death, and resurrection of CHRIST. Originally, the term GOSPEL had reference to the message of salvation through Christ, and only later was the term used to designate written documents. The impact of Jesus' life compelled his disciples to present his message to the public. By repeating the significant features of his ministry and his accompanying precepts, following the general order of his biography, they formulated a body of teaching that may have varied in detail with each recital, but that maintained the same general content.

The existence of this standardized message is confirmed by the NT itself. PAUL, in the letter to the GALATIANS, mentions an early visit to JERUSALEM and says: "I went in response to a revelation and set before them the gospel that I preach among the Gentiles" (Gal. 2:2). In 1 Cor. 15:1-5 he defines that gospel clearly. A similar presentation is afforded by the report of PETER's address in the house of CORNELIUS, the Gentile centurion. After sketching the baptism, life, death, and resurrection of Jesus, Peter concluded: "[God] commanded us to preach to the people and to testify that he is the one whom God appointed as judge of the living and the dead. All the prophets testify about him that everyone who believes in him receives forgiveness of sins through his name" (Acts 10:42-43).

From such samples of apostolic preaching one may conclude that the facts of Jesus' life constituted the gospel, which was interpreted and applied to suit the occasion on which it was preached. This gospel, which was initially proclaimed in oral form, has been transmitted through the writings called the "Gospels." Although Matthew, Mark, Luke, and John differ considerably in detail, they agree on the general outline of Jesus' career, on the supernatural character of his life, and on the high quality of his moral precepts. From the earliest period of the church they have been accepted as authoritative accounts of his life and teachings.

I. Character of the Gospels. Reduced to writing, the gospel message constitutes a new type of literature. Although it is framed in history, it is not pure history, for the allusions to contemporary events are incidental, and the Gospels do not attempt to develop them. They contain biographical material, but they cannot be called biography in the modern sense of the word, since they do not present a complete summary of the life of Jesus. The Gospels are not sufficiently didactic to be called opinions of their writers. The chief purpose of the Gospels is to create faith in Christ on the part of their readers, who may or may not be believers. Nothing exactly like them can be found either in the OT, to which their writers referred frequently, or in the Greek and Roman literature contemporary with them.

Of the numerous accounts and fragments that were composed to perpetuate the ministry and teaching of Jesus, only four are accorded a place in the NT: Matthew, written by Jesus' disciple

Aerial view looking NE at Wadi Qilt along the road to Jericho, where the parable of the Good Samaritan is set. Only the Gospel of Luke reports this story from Jesus' teaching.

© Dr. James C. Martin

G

Matthew Levi, the tax-gatherer; Mark, from the pen of John Mark, an inhabitant of Jerusalem and a companion of Barnabas and Paul; Luke, the first half of a history of Christianity in two volumes (Luke and Acts) by an associate of Paul; and John, a collection of select memoirs by John, the son of Zebedee. Although the traditional authorship of all four canonical Gospels has been disputed, there are strong arguments in their favor, even if, for one or two of them, the Evangelist's relation to the finished work may have been indirect rather than direct. Other Gospels, such as *The Gospel of Peter* or *The Gospel of Thomas*, are later productions of the second and third centuries and usually represent the peculiar theological prejudices of some minor sect.

II. Origin of the Gospels. The existence of the oral gospel is attested by Papias, bishop of Hierapolis in Phrygia, one of the earliest of the church fathers (c. A.D. 80-140). A quotation from the preface to his *Interpretation of our Lord's Declarations*, preserved in a historical work by Eusebius, indicates that he still depended on the transmission of the gospel content by the living voice. "But if I met with any one who had been a follower of the elders anywhere, I made it a point to inquire what were the declarations of the elders ... for I do not think that I derived so much benefit from books as from the living voice of those that were still surviving" (quoted in Eusebius, *Ecclesiastical History* 3.39). In the time of Papias, not more than two or three of the original band of Jesus' disciples would still be living, and he would be compelled to obtain his information from those who had heard the apostles. Nevertheless, he preferred the oral testimony to written record. Irrespective of the value of Papias's judgment, his words indicate that the contents of the apostolic preaching were still being transmitted by word of mouth two generations after the crucifixion, simultaneously with the use of whatever written records existed.

A clue to the transition from oral preaching to written record is provided by explanatory statements in the Gospels of Luke and John. In the introduction to his work, Luke asserts that he was undertaking to confirm in writing what his friend THEOPHILUS had already learned by word of mouth (Lk. 1:1-4). He spoke of facts that were taken for granted among believers and indicated that there had already been numerous attempts to arrange them in orderly narratives. Since his use of the word *narrative* implies an extended account, there must have been a number of "gospels" in circulation that he considered to be either inaccessible or else unsatisfactory. If his use of language permits deductions by contrast, these rival gospels were the opposite of his own. They were partial in content, drawn from secondary sources, and perhaps were not organized by any consecutive line of thought. They may have been random collections of sayings or events that had no central theme, or they may not have contained enough biographical material to afford an adequate understanding of Jesus' life.

Luke affirms on the contrary that he had derived his facts from those who "from the first were eyewitnesses and servants of the word" (Lk. 1:2). Not only had his informants shared in the events of which they spoke, but also they had been so affected that they became propagandists of the new faith. Luke had been a contemporary of these witnesses and had investigated personally the truth of their claims, so that he might produce an orderly and accurate record of the work of Christ.

John also committed his Gospel to writing so that he might influence others to faith in Christ as the Son of God (Jn. 20:30-31). He did not profess to give an exhaustive account of Jesus' activities, but took for granted that many of them would be familiar to his readers. The selective process that he used was determined by his evangelistic purpose and theological viewpoint.

Although Matthew and Mark are less explicit concerning their origins, the same general principles apply. The introduction of Matthew, "A record of the genealogy of Jesus Christ the son of David, the son of Abraham" (Matt. 1:1), duplicates the phraseology of Genesis (Gen. 5:1) to convey the impression that, like that OT book, it is giving a significant chapter in the history of God's dealing with the human race. Mark's terse opening line, "The beginning of the gospel about Jesus Christ, the Son of God" (Mk. 1:1), is a title, labeling the following text as a summary of current preaching. Neither of these two offers any reason for its publication, but one may deduce fairly that all of the Gospels began in an attempt to preserve for posterity what had hitherto existed in the minds of the primitive witnesses and in their public addresses.

There has been some question whether the Gospels were first published in ARAMAIC (the language of Palestine, where the church began) or in GREEK. Eusebius quoted Papias's statement that Matthew composed his history in the Hebrew dialect and everyone translated it as he was able (*Eccl. Hist.* 3.39). Without the original context, these words are ambiguous. Papias does not make clear whether by "Hebrew" he meant the speech of the OT, or whether he really meant Aramaic. He does not specify whether Matthew's contribution was simply collected notes of Matthew from which others composed a gospel, or whether Matthew had already formed an organized narrative that was translated. He does imply that before the Gentile expansion had made the literature of the church Greek, there was a body of material written in Hebrew or Aramaic. Papias's statement has aroused a great deal of controversy, and some have argued that one or more of the Gospels were originally written in Aramaic. It is more likely that the Gospels originated in the evangelistic preaching to the Gentile world, and that they were written in Greek, though they contained an Aramaic background.

III. Composition of the Gospels. The personal reminiscences of the apostolic band, plus the fixed content of their preaching, constituted the materials from which the Gospels were constructed; and the purpose of the individual writers provided the method of organization. Both Luke (Lk. 1:1-4) and John (Jn. 20:30-31) pledge accuracy of historical fact before they proceed with interpretation, and the same may safely be assumed of Matthew and Mark. All the Gospels were composed for use in the growing movement of the church; they were not written solely for literary effect. Matthew obviously wished to identify Jesus with the MESSIAH of the OT by pointing out that he was the fulfillment of prophecy and that he was intimately related to the manifestation of the KINGDOM OF GOD. Mark, by his terse descriptive paragraphs, depicted the Son of God in action among men. Luke used a smoother literary style and a larger stock of parables to interest a cultured and perhaps humanistic audience. John selected episodes and discourses

that others had not used in order to promote belief in Jesus as the Son of God.

IV. Publication of the Gospels. Where and when these documents were first given to the public is uncertain. The earliest quotations from the gospel material appear in the APOSTOLIC FATHERS (the letters of Ignatius, the *Epistle of Barnabas*, the *Teaching of the Twelve Apostles*, and the *Epistle of Polycarp*). All of these quotations or allusions bear a stronger resemblance to the text of Matthew than to that of any other gospel. If, as Papias said, Matthew was first written for the Hebrew or Aramaic church in Jerusalem, it may have been the basis for a Greek edition issued from Antioch during the development of the Gentile church in that city. It would, therefore, have been put into circulation some time after A.D. 50 and before the destruction of Jerusalem in 70.

Clement of Alexandria (c. A.D. 200) described the writing of the Gospel of Mark: "When Peter had proclaimed the word publicly at Rome, and declared the gospel under the influence of the Spirit; as there was a great number present, they requested Mark, who had followed him from afar, and remembered well what he had said, to reduce these things to writing, and that after composing the Gospel he gave it to those who requested it of him. Which, when Peter understood, he directly neither hindered nor encouraged it" (Eusebius, *Eccl. Hist.* 6.14). Irenaeus, Clement's contemporary, confirmed this tradition, adding that Mark handed down Peter's preaching in writing after his death. If Mark's Gospel represents the memoirs of Peter, it is possible that its content did not become fixed in literary form until A.D. 65 or later.

The Gospel of Luke may have been a private document, sent first of all to Luke's friend and patron, Theophilus. The adjective "most excellent" (Lk. 1:3) implies that he probably belonged to the equestrian order (perhaps holding some official position; see EXCELLENT, MOST) and that the dual work Luke-Acts was calculated to remove any lingering doubts that he may have entertained concerning the historical and spiritual verities of the Christian faith. Luke can hardly have been written later than the year 62, since it must have preceded Acts, which was written about the end of Paul's first imprisonment.

G

The last chapter of John's Gospel tries to correct a rumor that he would never die. The rumor, begun by a misunderstanding of Jesus' remark to Peter about John, would have been strengthened by the fact that John had attained an advanced age at the time when the concluding chapter was written. It is possible that it can be dated before A.D. 50, but most conservative scholars place it about 85. Traditionally it has been ascribed to the apostle John, who ministered at Ephesus in the closing years of the first century.

V. The Synoptic Problem. The three Gospels of Matthew, Mark, and Luke are called *synoptic*, from a Greek word meaning "to see the whole together, to take a comprehensive view." They present similar views of the career and teaching of Christ and resemble each other closely in content and in phraseology.

The numerous agreements between these Gospels have raised the question whether the relationship between them can be traced to common literary sources. Almost the entire content of the Gospel of Mark can be found in both Matthew and Luke, while much material not found in Mark is common to the two other Gospels. On the other hand, each Gospel has a different emphasis and organization. The "Synoptic Problem," as it is called, may be stated as follows: If the three Gospels are absolutely independent of each other, how can one account for the minute verbal agreements in their text? On the other hand, if they are copied from each other, how does one explain the differences? A further question arises concerning their authority: are they, then, truly writings inspired by God, or are they merely combinations of anecdotes that may or may not be true?

Numerous theories have been propounded to account for these phenomena. The most popular has been the documentary theory, which assumes that Matthew and Luke were composed independently of each other by combining the Gospel of Mark with a hypothetical document called "Q" (from the German *Quelle*, meaning "source"), containing chiefly sayings of Jesus. Some scholars have argued for the addition of two other hypothetical sources, *M* for Matthew, *L* for Luke, embodying the private knowledge or research of the two writers.

While this hypothesis seemingly solves the problem of the verbal resemblances, it is not entirely satisfactory. The existence of "Q" is at best only a probability; no copy of it has ever been found. It has been pointed out that extant collections of the "Sayings of Jesus" dating from the second and third centuries should probably be assigned to the Gnostics, who in turn were dependent either on oral tradition or on the canonical Gospels for their text. These documents, which have been considered analogous to "Q," and therefore as justifying the hypothesis of its existence, are themselves secondary. It is more likely that the common didactic passages of Matthew and Luke are drawn from utterances that Jesus repeated until they became fixed in the minds of his disciples and were reproduced later in the Gospels.

The discipline called "form criticism" has advanced another alternative. In an attempt to ascertain the development of "the gospel before the Gospels," it has suggested that they were composed out of individual reminiscences of Jesus' deeds and bits of his teaching that were first preserved and circulated by his followers. Through repetition and selection these accounts took permanent shape and were incorporated into a general sequence that constituted the gospel narratives. Advocates of form criticism have separated the unitary sections of the Gospels into various classes: the *passion story* of Jesus' last days; the *paradigms*, accounts of Jesus' deeds that illustrate the message; *tales* of miraculous occurrences told to interest the public; morally edifying *legends* of saintly persons; *sayings* of Jesus that preserve his collected teachings in speeches or in parables.

This modification or oral tradition injects a greater uncertainty into the process of literary history. If the Synoptic Gospels are merely different arrangements of independent blocks of text, the problem of origins is multiplied. While sections of the Gospels may have been used for illustrative purposes, and while certain parts of them, like the Sermon on the Mount, might have once been a separate collection of sayings (or deeds, as the case may be), the fact that they were composed in the first century by trustworthy disciples of Jesus precludes fraud or unreliability.

Form criticism is one branch of the wider discipline of "tradition criticism" that, when applied to the Gospels, has its counterpart in "redaction criticism." Tradition criticism focuses attention on the gospel material that each evangelist received, whether it came to him orally or to some degree in written form; redaction criticism is concerned with the way in which each evangelist handled the material he received. Redaction criticism reminds us that the writers of the Gospels were no mere scissors-and-paste compilers, that each of them was an author in his own right, with his own interpretation and purpose.

Perhaps the best solution of the Synoptic Problem is to regonize that all three Gospels are dealing with the life of the same Person, whose deeds and utterances were being continually preached as a public message. Constant repetition and frequent contact between the preachers tended toward fixing the content of the message. From the Day of Pentecost, the "apostle's teaching" possessed some definite form, for it was used in instructing inquirers (Acts 2:42). As the church expanded, the written accounts were created to meet the demand for instruction, and they reproduced the phraseology and content of the oral teaching. Each gospel, however, was shaped to its own purpose and audience, so that the variations in wording reflected the differences of interest and environment. Matthew was written for Christians with a Jewish background; Mark, for active Gentiles, probably Romans; Luke, for a cultured and literary Greek. All three, however, bear united witness to the supernatural character and saving purpose of Jesus Christ.

VI. The problem of John's Gospel. The fourth gospel differs markedly in character and in content from the synoptics. Excluding the feeding of the five thousand and the passion narrative, there are few points of agreement with the others. So radical are the differences that the veracity of John has been challenged on the grounds that if it is historical, it should coincide more nearly with the Synoptics.

For this reason some have held that the fourth gospel was written in the second century as the church's reflection on the person of Christ, phrased in terms of the Greek Logos doctrine. The discovery of the Rylands Fragment—a small scrap of papyrus on which a few verses of John were written—demonstrated that by the beginning of the second century the Gospel of John was circulated as far as southern Egypt. Since the handwriting of the fragment can be dated about A.D. 130, the Gospel must have been written earlier. It could not have been a late product of church tradition.

The language of John does not necessitate a Hellenistic origin. The existence of the concepts of light and of darkness, truth and falsehood, living waters, and others in the Dead Sea Scrolls show that John need not have drawn his vocabulary from Hellenism, but that many of his terms were a part of contemporary Judaism. The Gospel of John is the account of an eyewitness writing in his later years and interpreting the person of Christ in the perspective of his Christian experience.

VII. Canonicity. The Gospels were among the first writings to be quoted as sacred and authoritative. Individual passages are quoted or alluded to in Ignatius of Antioch (c. A.D. 116), the *Epistle of Barnabas*, and the *Shepherd of Hermas*, which were written in the early part of the second century. Justin Martyr (c. 140) mentions the Gospels explicitly, calling them "Memoirs of the Apostles" (*First Apology* 66). Marcion of Sinope (c. 140) included a mutilated edition of the Gospel of Luke in the canon of Scripture that he promulgated at Rome; he may have known the other Gospels but rejected them because of the presence of what he regarded as Jewish corruptions. Tatian (c. 170), an Assyrian who was converted in Rome under the ministry of Justin and later became an Encratite, produced the first harmony of the Gospels, called the *Diatessaron*. It included only the familiar four, weaving their text together into one continuous narrative. Only a few traces of the *Diatessaron* are still available in translations or in commentaries, but the existence of this work proves that Matthew, Mark, Luke, and John were already the chief sources of information concerning the life and works of Jesus in the first half of the second century.

Growing intercommunication between the churches and the need for strengthening their defenses against heresy and the attacks of pagan critics promoted the interest of the churches in a canon of the Gospels. By 170 the four Gospels were securely established as the sole authorities. According to Irenaeus's contention, "It is not

G

possible that the Gospels can be either more or fewer in number than they are. For since there are four zones of the world in which we live and four principal winds … it is fitting that she [the church] should have four pillars, breathing out immortality on every side" (*Against Heresies* 3.11.8). Irenaeus's argument may not be cogent, but the fact that he acknowledged only four indicates the sentiment of his times. The Muratorian Canon, a fragmentary manuscript of the seventh or eighth century containing a list of accepted books earlier than 200, included in its original form the four Gospels; they were used by Tertullian of Carthage (c. 200), Clement of Alexandria (c. 200), Origen of Alexandria (c. 250), and Cyprian of Carthage (c. 250); and they appear in the manuscript texts of the Chester Beatty Papyri and of the Old Latin version, both in existence before 300. Eusebius (c. 350) and the fathers following him excluded all other Gospels from their official list, leaving these four the undisputed, supreme authorities for knowledge of the life and work of Jesus Christ. See also CANONICITY; MATTHEW, GOSPEL OF; MARK, GOSPEL OF; LUKE, GOSPEL OF; JOHN, GOSPEL OF.

gospels, apocryphal. See APOCRYPHAL NEW TESTAMENT.

gossip. Rumor or inappropriate spreading of private information; also, a person who habitually spreads such information. Gossip need not be, but often is, malicious. The English term is used occasionally by modern versions to render several words or expressions (e.g., Prov. 11:13 [KJV, "talebearer"]; Rom. 1:29 [KJV, "whisperers"]). See SLANDER.

gourd. See PLANTS.

government. The control and administration of public policy. Human sovereignty as it is exercised in the state has its source in divine sovereignty. See SOVEREIGNTY OF GOD. The starting point is the doctrine of CREATION. All that exists owes its beginning to God's creative act and to his sustaining power. Since all is dependent upon him, so everything is subject to him, whether the solar system, the world of nature, or human society. God's sovereign authority over human beings is expressed

© Dr. James C. Martin. The British Museum. Photographed by permission.

This cuneiform stone tablet from N Babylonia (c. 875-850 B.C.) illustrates ancient government. It records a land grant by King Nabu-apla-iddina (on the right) to one of his officials.

in LAW. The law of God, declared to human beings in their fallen condition, is his gracious corrective to SIN.

The ancient nation of Israel was unique in that it was organized as a THEOCRACY. Although the precise form of government varied during the nation's history, the underlying conviction was always there in the OT that the Lord is the true ruler of his people. Whoever exercised rule over the nation, the ultimate authority belonged to God. Within the CHURCH, Christ's kingship is the dominant truth. The government that is exercised by the spiritual leaders within the redeemed community is really the mediation of the royal government of Christ. To a greater degree than in Israel, the ideal of creation is realized. However, because the church is comprised of people who, although justified, are still sinful, the final realization is yet future, and the Christian still prays, "Thy kingdom come."

For most believers in NT times, the state was the Roman empire, paganistic and powerful. But it was established by divine decree. So Christ accepted the authority of CAESAR as the legal authority in civil affairs (Matt. 22:15-22), even though Caesar controlled Palestine by force of arms. PETER counseled the same attitude. Christians were to honor the emperor (1 Pet. 2:17). PAUL, in an emphatic statement (Rom. 13), insisted that all human authority is derived from God. The obvious corollary to the divinely given authority of the state is the obligation to submit to the laws of the land. Obedience to duly constituted civil authority is written into the canons of Christian conduct. To honor the emperor did not mean for Peter simply to pay lip service to the dignity of his office. It meant a readiness to obey the laws that the emperor promulgated, and to submit if need be to the penalties imposed on disobedience. The issue of disobedience for the sake of conscience will be discussed later.

God's purpose in thus ordaining the power of government is a gracious one. It is to restrain evil and punish wrongdoers. Thus the demands of the law for honesty and preservation of life reflect the demands of God. The same applies to the payment of TAX, an echo of Jesus' teaching about Caesar's rights. Since the state is divinely ordained and since obviously it requires money to carry out its divinely appointed function, the citizen must pay taxes to furnish the necessary resources. The Christian, says Paul, will pay taxes for conscience' sake.

There are, however, limits to the obedience that the state may demand. It is one thing when the state imposes repressive measures that may be very hard to accept, or even when the state acts unjustly. In such cases submission is due. It is a very different matter when the demands of the state conflict with the law of God. Where there is a conflict of loyalties the higher one must take precedence, "We must obey God rather than men!" (Acts 5:29). Although the Lord was quite insistent that one must render to Caesar the things that are Caesar's, he added an important and qualifying requirement, "and to God what is God's" (Lk. 20:25).

government, church. See CHURCH; DEACON; ELDER.

governor. An official appointed to exercise control and administer a province or territory. The English term is used in Bible versions to render a variety of Hebrew terms (1 Ki. 10:15 et al.). In the NT, "governor" usually is the rendering of Greek *hēgemōn G2450*, "leader, chief" (e.g., Matt. 10:18). During the Roman period, the various territories were constituted in different ways, and their governors were of different ranks. The rulers of senatorial PROVINCES, which were kept under control without difficulty, were appointed by the senate and given the title PROCONSUL, their term usually running for one year. Governors of imperial provinces, which were apt to cause trouble for Rome, were appointed by the emperor personally for an indefinite term of office and were called *legates*. The governor of a subdivision of an imperial province was also appointed by the emperor and given the title PREFECT (before the reign of CLAUDIUS, apparently) or PROCURATOR.

Goyim. See GOIIM.

Gozan. goh´zan (Heb. *gôzān H1579*, from Akk. *Guzana*). City and region of the upper valley of the Khabur River (biblical HABOR, a tributary of the EUPHRATES). The capital, modern Tell Halaf, lies on the river where it crosses the border between Syria and Turkey, some 200 mi. (320 km.) E of the NE tip of the MEDITERRANEAN Sea. The region was conquered by the Assyrians (2 Ki. 19:12; Isa. 37:12), and later TIGLATH-PILESER III, king of ASSYRIA, transported Israelites from TRANSJORDAN to Gozan (1 Chr. 5:26). It is also one of the areas to which Israelites were deported after SAMARIA fell to Assyria in 722 B.C. (2 Ki. 17:6; 18:11). Excavations at Tell Halaf have uncovered an ancient culture; the relics of its pottery are thought to date back to as far as 4000 B.C.

grace. A term used by the biblical writers with a considerable variety of meaning: (1) that which affords joy, pleasure, delight, charm, sweetness, loveliness; (2) good will, loving-kindness, mercy, etc.; (3) the kindness of a master toward a slave. Thus, by analogy, grace has come to signify the kindness of God to human beings (Lk. 1:30). The Greek term, *charis G5921* was common in secular

G

usage, but when taken up into the message of Christ it was to become filled out with a new and enriched content. The NT writers, at the end of their various letters, frequently invoke God's gracious favor on their readers (Rom. 16:20; Phil. 4:23; Col. 1:19; 1 Thess. 5:28). More specifically, the word *grace* is used to express the concept of kindness given to someone who does not deserve it: hence, undeserved favor, especially that kind or degree of favor bestowed on sinners through Jesus CHRIST (Eph. 2:4-5). Grace, therefore, is that unmerited favor of God toward sinners whereby, for the sake of Christ—the only begotten of the Father, full of grace and truth (Jn. 1:14)—he has provided for their redemption. He has from all eternity determined to extend favor toward all who have FAITH in Christ as Lord and Savior.

The relationship between LAW and grace is one of the major themes of PAUL's writings (Rom. 5:1, 15-17; 8:1-2; Gal. 5:4-5; Eph. 2:8-9). Grace is likewise without equivocation identified as the medium or instrument through which God has effected the SALVATION of all believers (Tit. 2:11). Grace is also regarded as the sustaining influence enabling the believer to persevere in the Christian life (Acts 11:23; 20:32; 2 Cor. 9:14). Thus, grace is not merely the initiatory act of God that secures the believers' eternal salvation, but also that which maintains it throughout all of the Christian's life. It is also used as a token or proof of salvation (2 Cor. 1:5). A special gift of grace is imparted to the humble (Jas. 4:6; 1 Pet. 5:5). Grace can also refer to the capacity for the reception of divine life (1 Pet. 1:10).

graff. KJV form (now obsolete) of GRAFT.

graft. A horticultural process by which the branches of the wild olive tree in eastern lands are cut back so that branches from a cultivated olive may be inserted and grafting take place. Paul makes use of this practice in reverse (Rom. 11:17-24): the wild branches, the GENTILES, are thought of as "grafted in" to the good stock of the parent tree, the children of Israel. This deliberate inversion, certainly not a foolish mistake, heightens rather than diminishes the picturesque figure of speech conveying the eternal truth of the rejection of Israel and the status of the church.

grain. See PLANTS.

granary. See STOREHOUSE.

grape. See PLANTS.

grass. See PLANTS.

grasshopper. See ANIMALS.

grate, grating. A grill or network of bars. The word is used to render Hebrew *mikbār H4803*, referring to the bronze lattice-work or mesh that, underneath a projecting ledge, surrounded the lower half of the ALTAR of burnt offering (Exod. 27:4-5; 35:16; 38:4-5, 30; 39:39). Various functions have been attributed to the grating itself, for example, to protect the altar and to support the ledge above it.

gratitude. The condition or quality of being grateful; an emotion or sentiment of thankfulness. No motif more adequately recalls the nature of biblical FAITH than gratitude or thanksgiving. In the OT the verb "to give thanks" is *yādāh H3344*, which can also be translated "to praise" and "to confess"; the word for "thanksgiving" is the cognate noun *tôdâ H9343*. Thanksgiving comprises the special note of the Psalter; yet Israel's gratitude to Yahweh rings throughout her history. King DAVID appointed certain Levites "to make petition, to give thanks, and to praise the LORD" (1 Chr. 16:4). This practice was continued by SOLOMON (2 Chr. 5:13; 7:6), by HEZEKIAH (31:2), and by the exiles who returned from Babylon (Neh. 11:17).

In the NT thanksgiving to God both for his work (Lk. 17:16) and for his person (2:38) is a major theme. The Greek noun *eucharistia G2374* is used fifteen times in the NT and is usually translated "thanksgiving" (1 Cor. 14:16 et al.). The cognate verb *eucharisteō G2373*, "to give thanks," occurs almost forty times. The concept abounds in PAUL's epistles (Rom. 1:8; 7:25; 2 Cor. 9:15; Col. 1:12; 1 Tim. 1:12). The NT writers urged their fellow Christians to be grateful (Eph. 5:4; Col. 3:15; Heb. 13:15; Jas. 1:2, 9; 1 Pet. 4:12-14).

Gratitude is pleasing to God (Ps. 92:1) because it is commanded (Ps. 50:14; Phil. 4:6), because

Christ set the example (Matt. 11:25; 26:27; Jn. 6:11; 11:41), and because the heavenly host is engaged in it (Rev. 4:9; 7:11-12; 11:16-17). Gratitude can be expressed for (1) the goodness and mercy of God (Ps. 106:1; 107:1; 136:1-3), (2) the gift of Christ (2 Cor. 9:15), (3) Christ's power and reign (Rev. 11:17), (4) deliverance from indwelling sin (Rom. 7:23-25), (5) the nearness of God's presence (Ps. 75:1), (6) our desire to give for God's work (1 Chr. 29:6-14), (7) the supply of our physical needs (Rom. 14:6-7; 1 Tim. 4:3, 4), (8) victory over death and the grave (1 Cor. 15:57), (9) wisdom and might (Dan. 2:23), (10) the triumph of the gospel (2 Cor. 2:14), (11) the reception of God's word (1 Thess. 2:13), (12) the conversion of souls (Rom. 6:17), (13) faith (Rom. 1:8; 2 Thess. 1:3), love (2 Thess. 1:3), and zeal (2 Cor. 8:16) manifested in others, (14) grace bestowed upon others (1 Cor. 1:4; Phil. 1:3-5; Col. 1:3-6), (15) ministers appointed by God (1 Tim. 1:12), (16) all men (1 Tim. 2:1), and (17) everything God permits (2 Cor. 9:11; Eph. 5:20).

grave. See BURIAL; SHEOL; TOMB.

graveclothes. This English term is used by the KJV once to render a Greek noun meaning "bandage" or "binding material" (Jn. 11:44; NIV, "strips of linen"). Before BURIAL the body was washed, perhaps anointed with spices, wrapped in a linen winding sheet, with hands and feet bound with grave-bands, and the face covered with a napkin.

gravel. A mix of rock fragments or pebbles. The term is used to render a Hebrew word that occurs twice in a figurative sense. In Prov. 20:17 it is used of a liar, showing the consequences of deceitfulness: "he ends up with a mouth full of gravel." In Lam. 3:16 the prophet complains, "He has broken my teeth with gravel; / he has trampled me in the dust."

graven image. An image of wood, stone, or metal, shaped with a sharp cutting instrument as distinguished from one cast in a mold (Isa. 30:22; 44:16-17; 45:20 KJV; NIV, "idols"). Images were, however, sometimes cast and then finished by the graver (40:19). Such images were used by the Canaanites (Deut. 7:5), by the Babylonians, and

by others (Jer. 50:38; 51:47, 52). The Israelites were forbidden by the Decalogue to make them (Exod. 20:4).

gray. This term occurs about a dozen times in the OT, always with reference to gray HAIR as an indication of old age (Gen. 43:38 et al.). The word does not occur in the NT.

great. This English adjective can be used to render several terms, especially Hebrew *gādôl H1524* (Gen. 1:16 et al.) and Greek *megas G3489* (Matt. 4:16 et al.). In addition, words that primarily mean "much, many" can sometimes be translated "great" (e.g., Gen. 7:11; Matt. 2:18). These and other expressions are used in a wide variety of contexts, but the Bible views greatness primarily as an attribute that should be applied to GOD (e.g., Ps. 48:1; Tit. 2:13), his qualities (such as his "great love," Ps. 17:7), and his deeds (Rev. 15:3).

Great Bible. See BIBLE VERSIONS, ENGLISH.

great lizard. See ANIMALS.

great owl. See BIRDS.

Great Sea. See MEDITERRANEAN SEA.

greaves. See ARMS AND ARMOR.

Grecia. gree´shuh. KJV alternate form of GREECE (only Dan. 8:21; 10:20; 11:2).

Grecian. gree´shuhn. A native or inhabitant of GREECE; a speaker of the GREEK LANGUAGE. The KJV uses this term once in the OT (Joel 3:6), and three times in the NT (Acts 6:1; 9:29; 11:20 [NIV, "Grecian Jews" in the first two passages, "Greeks" in the last]).

Greece. grees. A geographical area on the S Balkan Peninsula, including the islands and surrounding coasts of the Aegean Sea, and inhabited primarily by speakers of the GREEK LANGUAGE. Greece and its associated island groups form the SE end of southern Europe's mountain system, a rugged peninsula and archipelago, not rich in fertile or

G

arable land. The southward movement of the Indo-European-speaking tribes, who became the Greek people, ended here. These tribes, or their predecessors, had established ordered life in the peninsula and islands by the twelfth century B.C. Their civilization vanished before 1000 B.C., in a dark age of destruction and invasion occasioned by further waves of wandering tribes. Out of four centuries of chaos emerged the complex of peoples on island

Christianity reaches Greece.

and mainland who are called the Greeks. Their own generic name was Hellenes, but Greece was a portion of the land that, lying in the NW, naturally came first to the attention of Rome. After the common fashion of popular nomenclature, the name of the part that first became known was extended to include the whole. Mediated through ROME, the term Greece was applied to all Hellas, and all Hellenes were called Greeks by Western Europe.

Geography, as always, played a part in the history of the people. The formation of the city-state was a natural development in an isolated plain or in a river valley ringed by precipitous terrain. Seafaring naturally developed from the nearness of the sea. And from seafaring and the dearth of fertile land in a rugged peninsula, sprang colonization and the spread of Greek colonies that marked the first half of the pre-Christian millennium. As early as the eighth century B.C., Greek ports and trading posts were scattered from the Crimea to Cadiz. In these same centuries the first flowering

of Greek thought and poetry began. In Ionia the foundations of scientific and philosophical thought were laid. On Lesbos, in those same years, Sappho and Alcaeus wrote supreme lyric poetry. In short, the active, inquisitive, brilliant, inventive Greek race was visible in full promise around the eastern end of the Mediterranean Sea before the bright flowering of fifth-century ATHENS. That century was one of the great golden ages of human culture. Greece, interpreted by the dynamic people of Attica in one brief noontide of human spirit, made immortal contributions to literature, art, philosophy, and political thought. Everything Greek in all future centuries was deepened and colored by the achievement of Athens. Hellenism, which had centuries of dynamic life ahead of it, was shaped by Athens in the short years of its spiritual supremacy. The glory of Athens faded, and her strength was sapped in lamentable war with the dour and uncreative autocracy of Sparta.

On the ruins of a Greece fatally weakened from within, Philip of Macedon, in the mid-fourth century B.C., built his empire. His son ALEXANDER THE GREAT, in one of the strangest acts of conquest in all history, extended that empire to India, swept the vast state of Persia out of existence, and, as his father had unified Greece, brought under his single rule the great complex of states and kingdoms that lay between the Dardanelles and the Indus, the Caspian and the Nile. When Alexander died in Babylon at the age of thirty-three in 323 B.C., his generals divided the world; and out of the division arose the Oriental kingdoms that the Romans conquered when their empire rounded the Mediterranean Sea.

The Greek language, Greek thought, and Greek culture, in the wake of Alexander, provided a unifying element in all the Middle East. Without the vast flow of the Greek tide eastward, the NT could not have been born. Greece provided its language and fashion of thought. Hellenism was a stimulus to the human mind. To reason, question, and speculate, was a habit with the Greeks. Hence the logical mind of Greek-speaking PAUL OF TARSUS, heir of both Hellenism and Judaism. Hence the "Grecians" of the NT—STEPHEN, for example, and PHILIP—who sweep fresh, bold, and vigorous into the life of the early church, ready to reform

© Dr. James C. Martin. The British Museum. Photographed by permission.

Mycenaean artifacts from a tomb in Cyprus.

and to rethink old concepts. Paul needed his Greek education, as he needed the Judaism of GAMALIEL. Paul's synthesis of the covenants, so compelling in its logic, so fundamental in Christian theology, was the work of a Greek Jew. It was his thought, having been trained in the Hellenism of Tarsus, that solved the problem of the Testaments and brought out from the stores of Judaism the wares that Christians could recognize and use.

greed. An excessive desire to acquire more than one has (esp. wealth and material possessions), usually leading to inappropriate behavior. This English term occurs primarily as the rendering of Greek *pleonexia G4432* (Lk. 12:15 et al), but the concept is expressed in many different ways. See COVETOUSNESS.

Greek language. The language of GREECE, spoken continuously from very ancient times until the present day. As a member of the Indo-European family, Greek is related to many languages, both eastern (e.g., Persian, Sanskrit) and western (e.g., German, Russian, Latin, and esp. Armenian); but it is very clearly distinctive as well, being the only member of its own branch (contrast, e.g., the Germanic branch, consisting not only of German, but also Dutch, English, the Scandinavian languages, and so on).

The discovery and decipherment of the Mycenean tablets demonstrated that an early form of Greek was spoken in the Peloponnesus several centuries before the time once favored for the arrival in the area of the Hellenic tribes. The piecemeal nature of their southward infiltration, and the firm geographical subdivisions of the area they occupied, led to the survival into literary times of several dialects: *Attic-Ionic*, spoken in Attica and the Ionic areas of Asia Minor, with associated islands; *Achaean*, which included the Aeolic of Lesbos and the dialects of Thessaly and Boeotia, together with the undocumented dialect of the Arcado-Cyprian; and *Western Greek*, including under that name the dialects of Phocis, Locris, Elis, and Aetolia, together with the Doric of the Peloponnesus, the Peloponnesian colonies, and Magna Grecia.

Of these dialects, Attic achieved the supreme position because of the worth and greatness of the literature in which it found expression. It was the Attic dialect with which ALEXANDER THE GREAT (himself a Macedonian rather than Greek) conquered the cultures of the ancient world. Even before Alexander's time, the Attic dialect had spread to other parts of the Greek world; this process was however greatly accelerated when Alexander imposed Greek culture on eastern races. This modified Attic speech became the *lingua franca* of the ancient world, and grammarians referred to it as *hē koinē dialektos*, "the common dialect." It was characterized by some changes in phonology, especially the pronunciation of certain vowels, as well as simplification in the morphology and syntax. With regard to vocabulary, many words from Greek dialects other than Attic became common in the Koine, and contact with foreign languages resulted in numerous loanwords.

Because the Greek of the NT is, in various respects, markedly different from the language found in most Greek literature, some scholars have argued in the past that the NT language must have been a peculiar Jewish-Greek dialect or even a language specially created by the Holy Spirit to communicate the gospel. It is of course true that the NT (like any other literary corpus of related writings) includes a distinctive vocabulary; it is also true that the influence of the SEPTUAGINT (which often reflects the use of Hebrew words and expressions), as well as the Semitic background of the apostles, left a mark on the NT language. Nevertheless, the modern discovery in Egypt of many thousands of everyday documents on PAPYRUS demonstrated clearly that biblical Greek is, fundamentally, the common language of the day, that is,

G

© Dr. James C. Martin. Sola Scriptura. The Van Kampen Collection on display at the Holy Land Experience in Orlando, Florida. Photographed by permission.

An example of Greek cursive writing from a MS dealing with the Pauline epistles.

the Koine. While the level of literary sophistication varies from book to book, the NT authors wrote in the simple, colloquial language of the people while avoiding both the near-illiteracy or vulgarity sometimes found in the papyri and, at the other extreme, the artificial and archaizing forms of the Atticists. If we focus on *style*, however, we may indeed speak of biblical Greek as a coherent whole, colored by occasional Semitic idioms and enriched by a vocabulary that gave clear expression to revealed truth.

Greek versions. See SEPTUAGINT; TEXT AND VERSIONS (OT).

green. This English term is used to render a variety of words and expressions, such as Hebrew *yereq H3764*, a noun meaning "green [plant], verdure" (Gen. 1:30 et al.). The Greek adjective *chlōros G5952* can be translated "green" (e.g., Mk. 6:39), but this term covers a wide range, including "pale green" or simply "pale" (cf. Rev. 6:8), "greenish-yellow," and even "yellow" (it can be applied to honey, for example).

greet. To salute or welcome upon meeting a person or in a written communication. This English verb is found in the OT mainly as the rendering of the Hebrew expression *šāʾal lĕ-šālôm*, "to inquire about [someone's] welfare" (Exod. 19:7; Jdg. 18:15; 1 Sam. 10:4; et al.), although the verb *bārak H1385*, "to bless," can also be used in this way (e.g., 2 Ki. 4:29). The Hebrew noun *šālôm H8934* ("completeness, welfare, peace") is even today the conventional term for "Hello!" and can be used in a letter with the sense "Greetings!" (cf. Aram.

šĕlām H10720 in Ezra 4:17). This usage is reflected in our Lord's instruction to his disciples. "When you enter a house, first say, 'Peace to this house'" (Lk. 10:5), and in Paul's use of Greek *eirēnē G1645* ("peace") at the beginning of his letters (Rom. 1:7 et al.). In Hellenistic times, the conventional way of beginning a letter was to use the infinitive of the verb *chairō G5897*, "to rejoice" (e.g., Acts 15:23; Jas. 1:1). Paul's unusual formula, "Grace [*charis G5921*] and peace," combines the Hebrew greeting with a Christianized form of the Greek salutation.

greyhound. See ANIMALS.

grief. See MOURN; SORROW; TRIBULATION.

grind. A procedure by which GRAIN was reduced to flour through being pulverized between two large stones (e.g., Isa. 47:2; Lk. 17:35). Small hand mills sometimes had holes in the center of the top stone through which the grain was poured (Matt. 24:41). Larger community mills were often powered by animals (Mk. 9:42). See MILL.

grisled. An archaic term used by the KJV to render Hebrew *bārōd H1353*, meaning "spotted, mottled, dappled," and occurring in two passages that describe the appearance of goats and horses respectively (Gen. 31:10-11; Zech. 6:3, 6).

grove. This English term is found occasionally in modern versions with its usual sense of "orchard" (e.g., Deut. 6:11). In the KJV it is used (with one exception, Gen. 21:33) to render Hebrew *ʾăšērâ H895*, the name of a Canaanite goddess, ASHERAH (e.g., 1 Ki. 18:19), though the term occurs more frequently with reference to the wooden cult objects or "sacred poles" (NRSV) by which she was represented (Exod. 34:13 et al.; NIV, "Asherah poles"; the incorrect KJV rendering is based on the LXX, which has *alsos*). It is not always clear which of these two meanings is meant. See HIGH PLACE; IDOLATRY.

guarantee. See DEPOSIT; EARNEST; PLEDGE.

guard. A soldier or group of soldiers assigned to protect an important person or to keep watch over prisoners. In ancient times oriental monarchs had attached to their persons a body of picked men to protect them and carry out their wishes on important confidential matters. POTIPHAR, to whom the Midianites sold JOSEPH, was the captain of PHARAOH's guard, and NEBUZARADAN held the same position in NEBUCHADNEZZAR's bodyguard (Gen. 37:36; 41:10, 12; 2 Ki. 25:8; Jer. 52:12). The men who formed the royal bodyguard were often foreigners. DAVID had a corps of 600 foreign mercenaries, made up of KERETHITES and PELETHITES, of whom BENAIAH was the captain (2 Sam. 20:23). They accompanied DAVID on his flight from ABSALOM (2 Sam. 15:18), and formed SOLOMON's escort on the day he was crowned (1 Ki. 1:38, 44). HEROD Antipas ordered a member of his guard to bring to him the head of JOHN THE BAPTIST on a platter (Mk. 6:27; NIV, "executioner"). PILATE told the Jews to make the tomb of Jesus secure with a guard of soldiers—undoubtedly, the temple police (Matt. 27:65-66).

Guard, Gate of the. This name occurs only once, in the account of the dedication of the rebuilt wall of JERUSALEM (Neh. 12:39; not to be confused with "the gate of the guards" in the temple precincts [2 Ki. 11:19; see UPPER GATE]). Some have suggested that this entrance should be identified with the MUSTER GATE (3:31; NIV, "Inspection Gate"); others argue that it should be linked with the court (courtyard) of the guard (3:25; Jer. 32:2 et al.). In either case, the precise location of this gate is not known.

guardian. Someone who watches over or protects. This English term is used occasionally in some Bible versions to render various Hebrew and Greek words. Of special interest is the Greek noun *epitropos G2208*, which means basically "a person to whom some task or property has been entrusted." PAUL illustrated the position of Jews under the law by means of a minor in a household who was under the authority of "guardians and trustees" until a certain age (Gal. 4:2; KJV, "tutors and governors"). Under Roman law, the *epitropos* was the legal guardian of a child—potentially if his father was alive, actually if he had died. A trustee (*oikonomos G3874*) was responsible for the child's financial affairs until he was twenty-five. When he came of age, he was free and entered into his INHERITANCE.

Gudgodah. gud-goh′duh (Heb. *gudgōdâ H1516*, meaning uncertain). A station in the wilderness wanderings of the Israelites (Deut. 10:7). The name is thought to be a variant of Gidgad. See HOR HAGGIDGAD.

guest room. This expression (KJV, "guestchamber") is used of the place where Jesus and his disciples ate the PASSOVER on the eve of the CRUCIFIXION (Mk. 14:14; Lk. 22:11; the same Gk. word is translated "inn" in Lk. 2:7). It refers to a room that provided facilities for temporary lodging or for banqueting. The NIV and other versions use "guest room" also to render a different Greek word in one passage (Phlm. 22; cf. Acts 28:23).

guile. This English term, meaning "skillful deceit," occurs eleven times in the KJV, but less frequently in modern translations (not at all in the NIV). Well-known passages where the KJV uses the term include Jesus' statement regarding NATHANAEL, "Behold an Israelite indeed, in whom is no guile!" (Jn. 1:47; NIV, "in whom there is nothing false"), and PETER's affirmation that Christ "did no sin, neither was guile [NIV, deceit] found in his mouth" (1 Pet. 2:22; this passage is a quotation of Isa. 53:9, where the KJV, curiously, uses "deceit"). See LIE.

guilt. The deserving of punishment because of the violation of a law or a breach of conduct. In the OT, the concept of guilt is largely ritualistic. A person could be guiltless before both God and the nation (Num. 32:22); on the other hand, one could be guilty because of unwitting SIN (Lev. 5:17). Israel, moreover, was viewed as an organic whole: what one does affects all. There is collective responsibility for sin; when ACHAN sinned, for example, all Israel suffered (Josh. 7). The prophets stressed the ethical and personal aspects of sin and of guilt. God is less interested in ritual correctness than in moral obedience. Jesus stressed the importance of a right heart attitude in distinction from outwardly correct acts and taught that there are degrees of guilt, depending on a person's knowledge and motive (Lk. 11:29-32; 12:47-48; 23:34).

G

PAUL likewise recognized differences of degree in guilt (Acts 17:30; Eph. 4:18), though also stating that the law makes everyone guilty before God (Rom. 3:19).

guilt offering. See SACRIFICE AND OFFERING.

gull. See BIRDS.

gum. See PLANTS (under *spice*).

Guni. gyoo´ni (Heb. *gûnî H1586*, possibly "partridge"; gentilic *gûnî H1587*, "Gunite"). **(1)** Second son of NAPHTALI and grandson of JACOB (Gen. 46:24; 1 Chr. 7:13); his descendants are called Gunites (Num. 26:48).

(2) A member of the tribe of GAD who settled in GILEAD; he was grandfather of a certain Ahi who is described as head of the clan (1 Chr. 5:15). The connection between these men and the other Gadites mentioned in the context is ambiguous.

Gur. guhr (Heb. *gûr H1595*, possibly "sojourning"). An incline near IBLEAM (modern Belameh) where AHAZIAH was mortally wounded by JEHU's men as he fled from the threat of assassination after the death of Joram (2 Ki. 9:27).

Gur Baal. guhr-bay´uhl (Heb. *gûr-bāʿal H1597*, "sojourn of the lord"). A city in the NEGEV inhabited by Arabians (and possibly by PHILISTINES also), whom UZZIAH conquered with the help of God (2 Chr. 26:7). Since the verse mentions also the MEUNITES, Gur Baal was probably in or near the territory of EDOM, SE of the DEAD SEA, but its precise location is unknown.

gutter. This English term is used by the NIV in only one passage as the rendering of a Hebrew word that occurs in an architectural context with reference to the channel around the ALTAR (Ezek. 43:13-14, 17; NRSV, "base"). The KJV uses it in two passages: in one of them it refers to a water trough (Gen. 30:38, 41); in the other it renders Hebrew *ṣinnôr H7562*, probably meaning "water shaft," and referring to the tunnel that DAVID recommended to his soldiers as a way of entering Jerusalem to conquer it (2 Sam. 5:8). Dating back to pre-Israelite times, it may be "Warren's Shaft" in the SE hill that leads from the GIHON Spring to within the city wall.

gymnasium. In Greece the gymnasium (from Gk. *gymnos G1218*, "naked") was originally a place of training for the Olympic games and other ath-

The gymnasium of Sardis.

© Dr. James C. Martin

letic contests. By the fourth century B.C. it had become as well an educational and cultural center for Greek youths, and was regarded as an essential feature of a city. It derived its name from the fact that the competitors exercised naked. The gymnasium consisted of a number of large buildings, which contained not merely places for each kind of exercise—running, boxing, wrestling, discus throwing, etc.—but also baths, a covered portico for practice in bad weather and in wintertime, and outside porticos where philosophers and writers gave public lectures and held disputations. Most of the education of boys and young men was obtained in gymnasiums. In ATHENS there were three great gymnasiums, each consecrated to a particular deity. The Greek institution of the gymnasium never became popular with the Romans, and it was held in horror by orthodox Jews. Nevertheless, a gymnasium was erected in JERUSALEM by hellenizing Jews in the time of ANTIOCHUS Epiphanes, who tried to compel the Jews to give up Judaism (1 Macc. 1:10, 14; 2 Macc. 4:9, 12; 4 Macc. 4: 20). Strict Jews opposed it because it introduced heathen customs and led Jewish youths to exercise naked in public and to be ashamed of the mark of their religion, CIRCUMCISION. PAUL alluded to the exercises of the gymnasium several times: boxing (1 Cor. 9:26), wrestling (Eph. 6:12), and racing (1 Cor. 9:24; Gal. 5:7; Phil. 3:12-14). See GAMES.

G

H

H. An abbreviation used to designate the Holiness Code (the legal corpus found in Lev. 17-26). See LEVITICUS, BOOK OF.

Haahashtari, Haashtari. hay′uh-hash′tuh-ri (Heb. *hāʾăhaštārî H2028*, a gentilic form meaning "the Ahashtarite[s]"). Son of Ashhur by Naarah and a descendant of JUDAH, although the precise genealogical connection is unclear (1 Chr. 4:6). The term is probably a family name reflecting descent from an otherwise unknown person presumably named Ahashtar.

Habaiah. See HOBAIAH.

Habakkuk, Book of. huh-bak′uhk (Heb. *ḥăbaqqûq H2487*, possibly the name of a garden plant, or derived from *ḥābaq H2485*, "to clasp, embrace"). The eighth book of the Minor Prophets. Of the man Habakkuk nothing is known out-side of the book that bears his name. Legendary references to him (in the APOCRYPHA and else-where) appear to have no historical value. Tra-ditional scholars believe the book to be a unity, the work of one author, Habakkuk, produced in Judah during the Chaldean (Babylonian) period. The reasons for this view are found in the book itself. The temple still stands (Hab. 2:20; 3:19) and the rise of the Babylonian power is predicted (1:5-6). Some recent scholars emend the Hebrew word *kaśdîm H4169* ("Chaldeans") in 1:6 to read *kittiyyîm H4183* ("Cypriots," thus "Greeks"), and understand it to refer to the Macedonian Greeks under ALEXANDER THE GREAT. They therefore date the book to this much later period. There is no good reason to make this emendation.

The Neo-Babylonian or Chaldean empire first came to prominence when the Babylonian king NEBUCHADNEZZAR defeated the Egyptians at the battle of CARCHEMISH in 605 B.C. and

---

Overview of HABAKKUK

Author: The prophet Habakkuk.

Historical setting: The book was written during the final decline of the southern kingdom of Judah, probably after the rise of the Babylonian king NEBUCHADNEZZAR (605 B.C.), but before the fall of JERUSALEM (586).

Purpose: To show God's perspective in the midst of evil and suffering and thus to encourage the righteous to remain faithful.

Contents: Habakkuk's first question and God's reply (Hab. 1:1-11). Habakkuk's sec-ond question and God's reply (2:11—2:20). Habakkuk's prayer (ch. 3).

reestablished BABYLON as the seat of world power. The prophecy of Habakkuk could hardly have been given before 605. JERUSALEM fell to Nebuchadnezzar in 587. The book must be placed somewhere between these dates, probably during the reign of the Judean king JEHOIAKIM. Some date the book earlier, believing that the Chaldeans were known to Judah before Carchemish and emphasizing the unexpectedness of the attack mentioned by Habakkuk (Hab. 1:5). Still, a date soon after 605 seems to be preferred.

In modern times the unity of the book has been questioned. The psalm of Hab. 3 is certainly somewhat different in style from the rest of the book, but this is hardly a sufficient reason to deny it to Habakkuk. The theory that all psalms were postexilic in Israel is now discredited. The theme of the prose part (chs. 1-2) is the same as that of the psalm. And there are obvious similarities of language. The third chapter is specifically ascribed to Habakkuk (3:1), and there seems to be no good internal indication that he was not its author.

The first two chapters set forth Habakkuk's prophetic oracle. Twice the prophet is perplexed and asks for divine enlightenment; twice he is answered. First he is concerned over the violence and sin of his people, the Judeans. Why are these wicked men not punished (Hab. 1:2-4)? God answers that he is about to send the Babylonians to judge Judah (1:5-11). This answer plunges Habakkuk into a greater perplexity: How can a righteous God use the wicked Babylonians to punish Judah, which, though it has become apostate, is still better than the Babylonians (1:12-17)? God's answer is that the proud conquerors will themselves be punished (2:2-20). The Babylonians are puffed up with self-sufficient pride, but in this hour of national calamity the righteous will live by his faithfulness, that is, by his constancy. The prophet sees only two ways of looking at life: in faith or in unbelief. This statement naturally becomes important to the NT writers and is quoted in Rom. 1:17; Gal. 3:11; and Heb. 10:38. The second answer to Habakkuk concludes with a series of woes against the Babylonians (Hab. 2:5-20).

The third chapter is called "a prayer of Habakkuk the prophet" (Hab. 3:1). In a moving lyric poem the prophet records his final response to God's message of judgment. He describes the divine revelation in terms of a story theophany (3:2-15) but concludes that no matter what comes he will trust in God (3:16-19).

Habazziniah. hab´uh-zi-ni´uh (Heb. *ḥăbaṣṣinyâ H2484*, possibly "Yahweh has made me abundant [*or* joyful]"). KJV Habaziniah. Grandfather of JAAZANIAH, who was the leader of the RECABITES (Jer. 35:3).

habergeon. A sleeveless coat of mail. The term is used by the KJV a few times (Exod. 28:32 et al.).

Habiru, Hapiru. hah-bee´roo, hah-pee´roo. The name of a people group mentioned in the AMARNA Tablets (15th cent. B.C.) as among those who were intruders into PALESTINE. The name also appears in Babylonian, Hittite, and Hurrian texts, some as early as the eighteenth century B.C. The same name appears in Egyptian records as *Apiru* as late as the twelfth century. ABRAHAM is the first person in the Bible to bear the name HEBREW (*ʿibrî H6303*, Gen. 14:13), and some scholars infer that the Habiru are identical with the biblical Hebrews. The meaning of Habiru seems to be "wanderers" or "fugitives." It is not an ethnic designation, for the Habiru of these various texts were of mixed racial origin, including both Semites and non-Semites. The name Habiru describes more than the Hebrews, therefore, but it came to be associated with them particularly. Even so, the connection, if there is any, of the Hebrews with the Habiru remains obscure.

Habor. hay´bor (Heb. *ḥābôr H2466*). A tributary of the EUPHRATES River, flowing through the district of GOZAN, to the banks of which SHALMANESER and SARGON transported the exiled Israelites (2 Ki. 17:6; 18:11; 1 Chr. 5:26). The river originates in the mountains of SE Turkey and is now known by the name Khabur.

Hacaliah. hak´uh-li´uh (Heb. *ḥăkalyâ H2678*, perhaps "wait for Yahweh"). KJV Hachaliah; TNIV Hakaliah. Father of NEHEMIAH (Neh. 1:1; 10:1).

Hachilah. See HAKILAH.

H

Hachmoni. See HACMONI.

Hacmoni. hak′moh-n*i* (Heb. *ḥakmōnî* H2685, possibly "wise"; if gentilic, "Hacmonite"). Also Hachmoni; TNIV Hakmoni. (1) Father of JASHOBEAM; the latter was a chief officer among DAVID's mighty men (1 Chr. 11:11). However, the Hebrew expression "the son of Hacmoni" should perhaps be understood as "the Hacmonite" (cf. NIV). In the parallel passage (2 Sam. 23:8), Jashobeam is called "Josheb-Basshebeth, a Tahkemonite," probably the result of a copyist's mistake.

(2) Father of Jehiel, who was in charge of David's sons (1 Chr. 27:32); it is possible, though less likely, that here too the term should be taken as a gentilic, and the phrase rendered, "Jehiel the Hacmonite."

Hadad. hay′dad (Heb. *ḥādad* H2524 [only #1 below], possibly "sharp, fierce"; *hādad* H2060, prob. "thunderer"). (1) Son of ISHMAEL and grandson of ABRAHAM (Gen. 25:15 [KJV, "Hadar," following the Bomberg ed. of the Heb. text]; 1 Chr. 1:30 ["Hadar" in a few Heb. MSS]).

(2) Son of Bedad and a king of EDOM who is said to have defeated MIDIAN; his capital was Avith (Gen. 36:35-36; 1 Chr. 1:46-47). His dates are unknown.

(3) Another Edomite king of uncertain date; his capital was Pau, and the text includes a reference to his wife, Mehetabel daughter of MATRED (Gen. 36:39 ["Hadar" in most Heb. MSS]; 1 Chr. 1:50-51 ["Hadar" in a few Heb. MSS]).

(4) An Edomite prince who was an adversary of SOLOMON (1 Ki. 11:14-22, 25). After JOAB defeated the Edomites and occupied their country, Hadad was taken to Egypt as a young boy. There PHARAOH welcomed him and later gave him his wife's sister in marriage, so Hadad's son was brought up in the court of Egypt. After the death of DAVID, Hadad returned to Edom and attempted to stir up the Edomites against the rule of Solomon, apparently with some success.

(5) The name of an ancient Semitic deity (also known as Adad, the Akk. form). Although not directly mentioned in the Bible, this god was worshiped in PALESTINE, SYRIA, and MESOPOTAMIA from about the time of ABRAHAM on. Hadad is

Stela with representation of Baal-Hadad (from Ras Shamra, 15-13th cent. B.C.).

© Dr. James C. Martin. Musée du Louvre; Autorisation de photographier et de filmer —LOUVRE: Paris; France. Photographed by permission.

frequently mentioned in the RAS SHAMRA texts as the proper name of BAAL, a storm-god who manifests himself in thunder, lightning, and rain (the name Hadad prob. means "thunderer"). He is the dying and rising god, like TAMMUZ of Mesopotamia. He is also a warrior god and is represented as a warrior standing on a bull, carrying a mace and a thunderbolt, with the horns of a bull on his helmet. The name Hadad functions as a divine element in such compound names as BEN-HADAD, HADADEZER, and HADAD RIMMON.

Hadadezer. hay′dad-ee′zuhr (Heb. *hādad‘ezer* H2061, "Hadad is help"). KJV Hadarezer (following many Heb. MSS). Son of REHOB and king of ZOBAH in ARAM (SYRIA), whose kingdom in the time of DAVID extended as far eastward as the EUPHRATES and as far southward as AMMON. There are three accounts in the OT of conflicts between him and David (though some scholars argue that these passages refer to only one or two distinct battles). In each, Hadadezer was defeated, and finally he was made tributary (2 Sam. 8:3-8; 10:5-14; 10:15-18). After these wars, David put a garrison in DAMASCUS and received a tribute from Hadadezer.

Hadad Rimmon. hay´dad-rim´uhn (Heb. *hădad-rimmôn H2062*; Aramean and Akkadian deities, respectively, both probably meaning "thunderer"). The prophet ZECHARIAH predicted, "On that day the weeping in Jerusalem will be great, like the weeping of [*or* for] Hadad Rimmon in the plain of Megiddo" (Zech. 12:11). The name is thought by some to refer to a place, possibly alluding to the mourning that took place after the death of JOSIAH (2 Ki. 23:29-30; 2 Chr. 35:20-25). Others understand Hadad Rimmon to be a dying-and-rising vegetation god whose worship involved annual ritual mourning. See HADAD #4 and RIMMON (DEITY).

Hadar. hay´dahr (Heb. *hădar H2076* [not in NIV], "splendor"). This name, a textual variant of HADAD, occurs twice in the KJV (Gen. 25:15; 36:39; in the latter passage, NRSV has "Hadar" as well).

Hadarezer. See HADADEZER.

Hadashah. huh-dash´uh (Heb. *hădāšâ H2546*, "new"). A town in the lowland of the tribe of JUDAH (Josh. 15:37). Hadashah was in the same district as LACHISH and EGLON, but its location is unknown.

Hadassah. huh-das´uh (Heb. *hădassâ H2073*, "myrtle"). The Hebrew name of ESTHER (Esth. 2:7). Hadassah was apparently her original name, that is, given to her at birth, even though she was more commonly known by the Akkadian (or Persian) name, Esther.

Hadattah. See HAZOR HADATTAH.

Hades. hay´deez (Gk. *hadēs G87*, etymology disputed, perhaps from the negative particle *a* and the verb *idein*, "[that which is] not seen," "the invisible one"). In Greek mythology, the god of the netherworld, but the term was then applied to the underworld itself, that is, the abode of the dead. The term, as used in the NT, is contrasted with the final punishment of the wicked and reflects the OT concept of SHEOL. Although the Greek word is uniformly translated as HELL in the KJV, this latter term is properly thought of as the final destiny of the wicked and thus as the appropriate rendering of Greek *geenna G1147* (see GEHENNA).

The NT generally does not give definite light on Hades. In Matt. 11:23 (cf. Lk. 10:15) our Lord says that CAPERNAUM will go down into Hades. The preposition "down" points to the OT teaching that Sheol is inside the earth (Ps. 139:8; Amos 9:2), and the following verse (Matt. 11:24) puts the day of judgment for both SODOM and Capernaum later than the stay in Hades. In the parable of the rich man and LAZARUS (Lk. 16:19-31) the rich man is pictured as being tormented in Hades but able to see in the distance ABRAHAM with Lazarus by his side. He asks for a drop of water to cool his tongue and for a message to be sent to his five brothers who are still alive on earth, and in each case his request is denied. In the first Christian sermon (Acts 2:25-31), PETER quotes from Ps. 16:8-11, proving from it that our Lord arose from the dead and was not left in Hades. In the book of Revelation, DEATH and Hades are four times associated (Rev. 1:18; 6:8; 20:13-14), being treated as almost synonymous terms. In the last verse mentioned, death and Hades are to be cast into the lake of fire, that is, doomed to utter destruction.

Hadid. hay´did (Heb. *hādid H2531*, possibly "sharp"). A town listed with LOD and ONO as having been resettled by hundreds of Jews after the EXILE (Ezra 2:33; Neh. 7:37); those returning were "descendants of the Benjamites from Geba" (Neh. 11:31-35). Hadid is probably to be identified with ADIDA (1 Macc. 12:38; 13:13) and with the modern el-Haditheth, about 3.5 mi. (5 km.) ENE of Lod (Lydda).

Hadlai. had´li (Heb. *hadlāy H2536*, prob. "stout," fig. "successful"). Father of AMASA; the latter was a leader in the tribe of EPHRAIM during the reign of PEKAH king of Israel (2 Chr. 28:12).

H

Hadoram. huh-dor´uhm (Heb. *hădôrām H2066*, possibly "HADAD is exalted"). **(1)** Son (or descendant) of JOKTAN son of EBER (Gen. 10:27; 1 Chr. 1:21). Some scholars identify the name with Dauram, a locality in Yemen; Hadoram thus may have been the name of a S Arabian tribe.

(2) Son of Tou (Toi) king of HAMATH; he was sent by his father with presents to DAVID "to greet him and congratulate him on his victory in battle over Hadadezer, who had been at war with Tou" (1 Chr. 18:10). In the parallel passage (2 Sam. 8:10), he is called JORAM; some consider this name a textual corruption, but others interpret it as the Israelite equivalent (that is, using an abbreviated form of Yahweh rather than the pagan name Hadad).

(3) A variant form of ADONIRAM (2 Chr. 10:18).

Hadrach. had´rak (Heb. *hadrāk H2541*, meaning unknown). TNIV Hadrak. A locality N of Israel against which ZECHARIAH prophesied (Zech. 9:1). Grouped with DAMASCUS, HAMATH, TYRE, and SIDON, Hadrach is probably the same as the Hatarikka mentioned in some Assyrian inscriptions. It is identified with modern Tell Afis, about 28 mi. (45 km.) SW of Aleppo.

Hadrak. TNIV form of HADRACH.

Hadrian. hay´dree-uhn. Emperor of ROME, A.D. 117-138. Publius Aelius (Traianus) Hadrianus was born, probably in Spain, in the year 76. Before he was ten years old, his father died, and the future emperor TRAJAN (a relative) became one of his guardians. His military career began during the reign of DOMITIAN, and after Trajan became emperor, Hadrian held several posts, including the governorship of SYRIA. Shortly after Trajan's death, Hadrian was recognized as emperor. His two decades of rule were uneven. He was a cultured man, devoted to Greek literature and showing great interest in philosophy, science, and architecture. The famous Hadrian's Wall, marking the frontiers of the empire in Britain, signaled an end to Roman expansion. In the year 130 Hadrian visited JUDEA and took several steps, such as banning CIRCUMCISION, that provoked Jewish sensibilities. A revolt was inevitable, and BAR KOKHBA rose against Rome in 132. By 135 the rebellion

had been crushed, Jerusalem made into a Roman colony named Aelia Capitolina, and the nation of Israel brought to an end. Hadrian died three years later.

Haeleph. hay-ee´lif (Heb. *hāʾelep H2030*, "the ox"). A town in the tribal territory of BENJAMIN listed between ZELA and JERUSALEM (Josh. 18:28; KJV, "Eleph"). The location of the city is unknown.

Hagab. hay´gab (Heb. *hāgāb H2507*, "locust"). Ancestor of a family of temple servants (NETHINIM) who returned after the EXILE with ZERUBBABEL (Ezra 2:46; the name is absent in the parallel list, Neh. 7:48, prob. because a scribe inadvertently skipped "Akkub Hagab" after writing the similar name "Hagabah").

Hagaba, Hagabah. hag´uh-buh (Heb. *hăgābâ H2509* [*hăgābāʾ* in Bomberg ed. at Neh. 7:48], "locust"). Ancestor of a family of temple servants (NETHINIM) who returned after the EXILE with ZERUBBABEL (Ezra 2:45; Neh. 7:48). The usual English spelling "Hagaba" in Nehemiah derives from a printed edition of the Hebrew Bible published in 1524-25, but is not supported by the MSS.

Hagar. hay´gahr (Heb. *hāgār H2057*, meaning uncertain). KJV NT Agar. Concubine of Abram (ABRAHAM) and mother of ISHMAEL. Hagar was an Egyptian handmaid to Sarai (SARAH), wife of Abram. God had promised Abraham a son and heir (Gen. 15:4), but Sarai was barren. Following the marital customs of the times, she gave Hagar to her husband as her substitute (16:1-16). When Hagar saw that she had conceived, she despised her mistress, causing trouble in the household. Hagar was driven out, but the angel of the Lord appeared and sent her back to her mistress (16:7-14). When her son Ishmael was fourteen years old, his father one hundred, and Sarah ninety, ISAAC was born. At a great feast held in connection with Isaac's weaning, Ishmael scoffed at the proceedings (21:9), so Sarah insisted that Hagar and her son be cast out, and Abraham unwillingly complied. God told Abraham that Ishmael's descendants would become a nation. Hagar is last seen taking a wife for her son out of the land of Egypt, her own land (21:1-21).

Hagar was sent out into the wilderness of Beersheba. (View to the SE.)

PAUL made Hagar's experience an ALLEGORY of the difference between law and grace (Gal. 4:21-31).

Hagarene, Hagarite, Hagerite. hag´uh-reen, hag´uh-r*it*, hay´guh-r*it*. KJV forms of HAGRITE.

Haggadah. hah´gah-dah´, huh-gah´duh (Heb. *haggādâ* or *ʾaggādâ* [Aggadah], from *nāgad H5583* hiphil, "to tell, narrate"). Also Haggada, Aggada(h); pl. haggadoth, aggadoth. Traditional Jewish literature that is not legal in character; it may also refer to a specific story or lesson. Its counterpart is HALAKAH. Whereas the latter denotes authorita-tive rabbinic teaching in respect to the Mosaic law, especially as deposited in the Mishnah (see TALMUD), Haggadah is didactic discourse mainly concerned with edification. It is usually based upon homiletical exegesis and has a moral purpose in view, but the word often functions as a catch-all term to include anything nonhalakic. In modern usage, the Haggadah refers to a book that contains the story of the exodus and the Passover ritual.

Haggai, Book of. hag´*i* (Heb. *ḥaggay H2516*, "[born] on a feast day"). The tenth book of the Minor Prophets. Little is known of Haggai's personal history. He lived soon after the Babylonian EXILE and was contemporary with ZECHARIAH (cf. Hag. 1:1 with Zech. 1:1).

After their return from the captivity, the Israelites set up the altar on its base, established daily worship, and laid the foundation for the second TEMPLE; then they were compelled to cease building for some years. However, although times were hard, the people were able to build finely paneled houses for themselves (Hag. 1:4). Meanwhile kings

Overview of HAGGAI

Author: The prophet Haggai.

Historical setting: Postexilic JERUSALEM during the second year of the Persian king DARIUS I (520 B.C.), at a time when the Jewish returnees had ceased to rebuild the TEMPLE (cf. ZECHARIAH, BOOK OF).

Purpose: To admonish the Israelites for failing to construct the temple.

Contents: The book records the following four messages (delivered on four different days during a three-month period): the need to complete rebuilding the temple (Hag. 1:1-15); the promise of God's presence (2:1-9); blessings for a defiled people (2:10-19); the final victory (2:20-23).

© Dr. James C. Martin

succeeded one another in PERSIA. CYRUS, favored of God and friend of the Jews (2 Chr. 36:22; Isa. 44:28), passed away in 529 B.C.; his son Cambyses reigned 529-522, followed for only seven months in 522 by the Pseudo-Smerdis (a usurper); then arose DARIUS Hystaspes (mentioned by Ezra, Haggai, and Zechariah), who helped and encouraged the Jews to go ahead and who allowed no opposition. In the second year of Darius (520) Haggai fulfilled his brilliant mission of rebuking and encouraging the Jews. The five short messages that make up his book are identified by date and cover only three months and twenty-three days; and in those few weeks the whole situation changed from defeat and discouragement to victory. Zechariah assisted Haggai in the last month of his recorded ministry (Zech. 1:1-6).

In order to make the dates clearer to modern readers, we will give the months their approximately equivalent names in our calendar. On September 1, 520 B.C., the Lord spoke through Haggai, and instead of addressing the people at large, the prophet went straight to "headquarters," that is, to ZERUBBABEL the prince and to Joshua (JESHUA) the high priest. The people had stopped building the Lord's house though they were quite able to build their own, and God's message was, "Give careful thought to your ways." The punishment for their neglect had been futility; they labored much but produced little. God used "weather judgments" to bring them to their senses. The leaders heeded the message and, with the best of the people, began immediately to build; on September 24 God's short message was, "I am with you" (Hag. 1:13). A month later, the people were tempted to be discouraged when they contrasted their present effort with the former magnificent temple, and so God told them, "The glory of this present house will be greater than the glory of the former house" (2:9). This message was delivered on October 21, and it contained the notable statement, "The silver is mine and the gold is mine." The fourth and fifth messages came in one day, December 24, 520. In the fourth, Haggai said that holiness is not contagious, though evil is, and Israel's change in attitude would cause God to change chastening into blessing. In the last message (2:20-23), God predicted a shaking of the nations but at the same time a great reward to Zerubbabel. Perhaps his reward

was inclusion as an ancestor of our Lord in both the royal line (Matt. 1:13) and the line recorded in Luke (Lk. 3:27).

Haggedolim. hag´uh-doh´lim (Heb. *haggĕdôlim H2045*, "the great ones"). Father of ZABDIEL; the latter was a chief officer among the priests that settled in Jerusalem after the EXILE (Neh. 11:14; KJV renders, "Zabdiel, the son of *one of* the great men").

Haggeri. See HAGRI.

Haggi. hag´ee (Heb. *ḥaggî H2515*, "[born] on a feast day"; gentilic *ḥaggî H2515*, "Haggite"). Son of GAD and eponymous ancestor of the Haggite clan (Gen. 46:16; Num. 26:15).

Haggiah. ha-gi´uh (Heb. *ḥaggiyyâ H2517*, "feast of Yahweh"). Son of Shimei and a descendant of LEVI through MERARI (1 Chr. 6:30).

Haggite. See HAGGI.

Haggith. hag´ith (Heb. *ḥaggît H2518*, "[born] on a feast day"). One of DAVID's wives and the mother of ADONIJAH (2 Sam. 3:4; 1 Ki. 1:5, 11; 2:13; 1 Chr. 3:2).

Hagiographa. hag´ee-og´ruh-fuh. A term meaning "Sacred Writings" (from Gk. *hagios G41* and *graphē G1210*) and applied to the third division of the Hebrew Bible, after the Law (the PENTATEUCH) and the Prophets (which includes Joshua, Judges, Samuel, and Kings, as well as Isaiah, Jeremiah, Ezekiel, and the Minor Prophets). Also known simply as the Writings or Ketubim, this section consists of the following books: Psalms, Proverbs, Job, Song of Solomon, Ruth, Lamentations, Ecclesiastes, Esther, Daniel, Ezra, Nehemiah, and 1-2 Chronicles.

Hagri. hag´ri (Heb. *hagĕrî H2058*, perhaps "wanderer"). The father of MIBHAR, who was one of DAVID's mighty warriors (1 Chr. 11:38; KJV, "Haggeri"). The parallel passage has "Bani the Gadite" (2 Sam. 23:36), but some MSS of the SEPTUAGINT have "the son of Hagri," and this reading is adopted by the NIV. See also HAGRITE.

Hagrite. hag′rīt (Heb. *hagĕri H2058*, possibly "wanderer" or "descendant of Hagar"). The name of an Arabian tribe living in the region E of GILEAD (some think the tribe may have been ARAMEAN). In the time of King SAUL, the Israelites twice inflicted a crushing defeat upon them in war and seized their lands (1 Chr. 5:10, 19-22; KJV, "Hagarites"). DAVID appointed Jaziz the Hagrite to look after his flocks (27:30-31; KJV, "Hagerite"). A psalm of ASAPH makes mention of them along with MOAB, EDOM, and the ISHMAELITES, all of whom were enemies of Israel living in TRANSJORDAN (Ps. 83:6; KJV, "Hagarenes"). The ethnological relationship of the Hagrites with HAGAR (Gen. 16) is uncertain. The Hagrites and other Arab tribes are mentioned in an inscription of TIGLATH-PILESER III (745-727 B.C.).

Hahiroth. See PI HAHIROTH.

Hai. See AI.

hail, hailstones. Hail consists of frozen raindrops, though hailstones are often much larger than any single raindrop. When the hailstones fall, they often cohere, forming solid masses, which can do great damage to crops and even endanger life. Hailstones are not common in PALESTINE, but they are not unusual and can be very severe. Hail is often mentioned in the Bible, and always as an instrument of God's judgment. A severe hail was the seventh plague in Egypt (Exod. 9:18-34). The AMORITES were smitten by hailstones at BETH HORON, so that more died from the hailstones than were smitten with the sword by the Israelites (Josh. 10:11). The Scriptures often speak of hail as a means of punishing the wicked (Isa. 28:2, 17) and as a symbol of God's anger, both in the OT (Ezek. 38:22; Hag. 2:17) and in the NT (Rev. 8:7; 11:19; 16:21).

hair. Although all mammals have hair (e.g., goats, 1 Sam. 19:13; camels, Mk. 1:6), the term is usually applied to human beings (Heb. *śē‘ār H8552* or *śa‘ărâ H8553*; Gk. *thrix G2582*). Hair varies in length, color, and structure among the different races and seems to be intended by God for protection, for beauty, and for identification. The peoples of the Bible lands were generally black-haired,

though red-haired individuals are fairly common among the people of Israel. Hebrews and Arabs (cf. Rev. 9:8) wore their beards long as a mark of dignity, but the Egyptians were clean-shaven (Gen. 41:14). The men of Israel were not to clip off the edges of the BEARD (Lev. 19:27), and this prohibition explains the "prayer-locks" in front of the ears of Orthodox Jewish men today.

The word *hair* is used in several figurative contexts: "not a hair of his head will fall to the ground" (1 Sam. 14:45); "my sins … are more than the hairs of my head" (Ps. 40:12). Hair was a mark of beauty and sometimes of pride. ABSALOM's hair (2 Sam. 14:26; 18:9), of which he was inordinately proud, caused his death. SAMSON's uncut hair was a symbol of his NAZIRITE dedication; and when he lost his hair, his strength went with it (Jdg. 13:7; 16:17-20). In NT times the length of the hair was one mark of distinction between the sexes, and PAUL said that nature teaches that long hair is a shame for a man but a glory for a woman (1 Cor. 11:14-16).

Hakaliah. hak′uh-li′uh. TNIV form of HACALIAH.

Hakeldamah. See AKELDAMA.

Hakilah. huh-ki′luh (Heb. *hăkîlâ H2677*, meaning uncertain). A hill in the wilderness of JUDAH, S of JESHIMON, where the strongholds of HORESH were located; there DAVID took refuge when SAUL pursued him (1 Sam. 23:19; 26:1). Saul pitched his camp on the hill (26:3). It is described as being within the wilderness of ZIPH (23:19), which is a few miles SE of HEBRON, but the site has not been identified.

Hakkatan. hak′uh-tan (Heb. *haqqātān H2214*, "the little one"). Father of Johanan and descendant of Azgad; Johanan was one of the family heads who returned to Jerusalem with EZRA (Ezra 8:12).

Hakkore. See EN HAKKORE.

Hakkoz. hak′oz (Heb. *haqqôs H2212*, "the thorn"). KJV Koz (except in 1 Chr. 24:10). The head of a priestly family at the time of DAVID (1 Chr. 24:10). His descendants returned from the Babylonian captivity, but could not serve because they were unable to document their claim to priestly rank

(Ezra 2:61; Neh. 7:63). One of his descendants, MEREMOTH, was involved in repairing the wall of Jerusalem (Neh. 3:4, 21).

Hakmoni. hak´moh-ni. TNIV form of HACMONI.

Hakupha. huh-kyoo´fuh (Heb. *ḥăqûpā᾿ H2979*, "crooked"). Ancestor of a family of temple servants (NETHINIM) who returned from exile with ZERUBBABEL (Ezra 2:51; Neh. 7:53).

Halachah. See HALAKAH.

Halah. hay´luh (Heb. *ḥālaḥ H2712*). One of the places to which kings of ASSYRIA deported Israelites on the capture of SAMARIA (2 Ki. 17:6; 18:11; 1 Chr. 5:26). Halah was apparently on the way to GOZAN, but its location is uncertain. Among various proposals, one that has gained favor is Ḥalaḫḫu, the name of a town and a district NE of NINEVEH. The name Halah occurs also as a conjecture in the NRSV (Obad. 20).

Halak, Mount. hay´lak (Heb. *ḥālāq H2748*, "smooth" or "bare"). A mountain in the NEGEV described as rising toward SEIR; it formed the southern limit of the conquests of JOSHUA (Josh. 11:17; 12:7). Many scholars identify it with Jebel Halaq, on the NW side of the Wadi Marra, and some 28 mi. (45 km.) SE of BEERSHEBA.

Halakah. hah´lah-kah´ (Heb. *hălākâ*, "walk, practice, ruling, law," from *hālak H2143*, "to go, walk, behave"). Also Halacha(h), Halakhah; pl. halakot(h), halakhot(h). This term in rabbinic studies can refer either to a specific legal ruling (in which case the word is usually lowercased) or to the general literary category of legal material, contrasted with HAGGADAH. The concept thus encompasses all the laws, ordinances, and legal decisions of the rabbis that determined the Jewish way of life— religious, social, political, and civil. It was believed by the PHARISEES and their followers that God had given to MOSES on Mount SINAI not only the written law that was embodied in the PENTATEUCH, but also a large mass of oral law which he communicated to the Jewish people and which the rabbis passed on until it was written down in the Mishnah.

See TALMUD. The object of the Halakah, which involved the interpretation and the reinterpretation of the Mosaic law through a long succession of Jewish teachers from the time of EZRA onward, was to state in detail and to apply to all possible cases the principles laid down in the TORAH.

half-shekel. See MONEY.

half-tribe of Manasseh. See MANASSEH.

Halhul. hal´huhl (Heb. *ḥalḥûl H2713*, derivation uncertain). A town in the hill country of the tribe of JUDAH, listed first in a district of six towns (Josh. 15:58). It is identified with modern Ḥalḥul, 4 mi. (6 km.) N of HEBRON.

Hali. hay´li (Heb. *ḥāli H2718*, "adornment"). A town in the tribal territory of ASHER, listed between HELKATH and BETEN (Josh. 19:25). The site is now identified with Khirbet Ras ῾Ali (or a location nearby), some 11 mi. (18 km.) SSE of Acco.

hall. This English term is used variously in Bible translations to render several words and expressions. Among the buildings SOLOMON erected after the completion of the TEMPLE was "the Hall of Pillars" (NRSV, 1 Ki. 7:6; NIV, "a colonnade"), the purpose of which is not stated. Apparently, one went through it to reach "the throne hall, the Hall of Justice" (NIV), where Solomon sat in judgment on cases brought before him. The royal palace in SUSA, the winter capital of the Persian kings, included a structure called "the king's hall" (Esth. 5:1; lit., "the house of the king," which is rendered "the king's palace" earlier in the same verse). The banquet hall (Dan. 5:10) where King BELSHAZZAR saw the handwriting on the wall was in BABYLON, which for centuries was one of the great cities of antiquity. The author of the Acts of the Apostles says that when Jews in EPHESUS rejected and opposed PAUL's message, he left the synagogue where he had been teaching for three months and went to the "lecture hall" of TYRANNUS, where the apostle taught daily for two years (Acts 19:9). This hall was probably a part of some GYMNASIUM, which normally included not only areas for exercise and sports, but also gardens and

Columns in the Great Hall of Ramses II at Karnak.

© Dr. James C. Martin

halls that were made use of by teachers, poets, and philosophers for giving recitations and lectures.

Hallel. hal´el (Heb. *hallēl*, from *hālal H2146*, piel, "to praise"). Rabbinic term for several groups of psalms of praise. The expression Great Hallel usually denotes Ps. 136, though it can refer to Ps. 120-136. "Hallel" can be applied also to Ps. 146-148, but the most significant group is the Egyptian Hallel, Ps. 113-118. These psalms were recited in Jewish homes during the course of the Passover observance and in public temple and synagogue services for various FEASTS. It doubtless played its customary role in the Lord's last Passover observance with his disciples (cf. Matt. 26:30).

hallelujah. hal´uh-*loo´*yuh (Heb. *halēlû* [from *hālal H2146*, piel, "to praise"] and *yāh H3363* [short form of Yahweh]; Gk. *hallēlouia G252*). A Hebrew expression that is invariably translated "Praise the LORD"; the corresponding Greek term in the NT is transliterated "hallelujah" (KJV, "alleluia"). In the OT text, the expression consists of two words. When it was borrowed by Greek and other languages, however, it was treated as one word. *Hallelujah*, like AMEN, has practically become a universal word. It is an acclamation of PRAISE of the highest order. Its use is limited altogether to songs of praise, appearing only in Psalms and Revelation.

Hallohesh. huh-loh´hesh (Heb. *hallôḫēš H2135*, "the whisperer"). Father of SHALLUM; the latter was "ruler of a half-district of Jerusalem" in the time of NEHEMIAH and repaired a section of the walls of Jerusalem (Neh. 3:12; KJV, "Halohesh"). This Hallohesh is probably the same man listed among those who sealed the covenant with Nehemiah (10:24).

hallow. To render or treat as holy, to sanctify or consecrate. This English term is used over thirty times in the KJV but is less common in modern versions. The NIV uses it only in the context of the Lord's PRAYER (Matt. 6:9; Lk. 11:1). See CONSECRATION; DEDICATION; HOLINESS; SANCTIFICATION.

Halohesh. KJV form of HALLOHESH.

Ham (person). ham (Heb. *ḥām H2769*, possibly "warm, hot"). Also Cham (some older English versions). Second son of NOAH and brother of SHEM and JAPHETH (Gen. 5:32; 6:10; 7:13; 9:18, 22; 10:1, 6, 20; 1 Chr. 1:4, 8). Ham had four sons, CUSH, MIZRAIM (Egypt), PUT, and CANAAN (Gen. 10:6). He is identified as the ancestor of the Egyptians and of the peoples who were under the control of EGYPT in NE Africa, ARABIA, and CANAAN (with the exception of NIMROD). His name serves also as the patronymic of his descendants (Ps. 78:51; 105:23, 27; 106:22; possibly also 1 Chr. 4:40 [NIV, "Hamites," supplied also in v. 41], but this reference may allude to an otherwise unknown place). The term *Hamitic* was commonly used in the past to designate a group of languages in N Africa, including Egyptian, that are related to the Semitic languages (the label *Hamito-Semitic* is seldom used today by scholars, who prefer the term *Afroasiatic*). According to Gen. 9:20-25, Noah became intoxicated, and he lay uncovered in a drunken stupor; Ham saw him and told his brothers. When Noah awoke and learned what had happened, he cursed Ham's son Canaan

H

and said that his descendants would be the slaves of the descendants of Shem and Japheth.

Ham (place). ham (Heb. *hām H2154*). The name of a city whose inhabitants, the ZUZITES, were subdued by KEDORLAOMER and his allies in the time of ABRAHAM (Gen. 14:5). The site is usually identified with modern Tell Ham in N Jordan.

Haman. hay´muhn (Heb. *hāmān H2172*, possibly from Old Pers. *hamanā*, "illustrious"). Son of Hammedatha and prime minister of PERSIA under XERXES (Esth. 3:1 et al.). He is also called the Agagite, a name that links him with the king of the AMALEKITES that SAUL was told to destroy (1 Sam. 15). Haman became the bitter enemy of MORDECAI, the uncle of ESTHER, because Mordecai, being a Jew, would not prostrate himself before him like the other subjects of the king (Esth. 3:2). He therefore determined in revenge not only to kill Mordecai but also to exterminate all the Jews in the Persian empire, and received from Xerxes a decree to do this (3:8-9). Through the intervention of Esther, however, the people were saved, and Haman died on the very gallows he had prepared for Mordecai.

Hamath. hay´math (Heb. *hāmāt H2828*, possibly "fortress"; gentilic *hāmātî H2833*, "Hamathite"). KJV also Hemath (1 Chr. 13:5; Amos 6:14). A city of SYRIA (ARAM) c. 120 mi. (190 km.) N of DAMASCUS. One of the most ancient surviving cities on earth, Hamath was built on both banks of the ORONTES River; it was surrounded by hills and had a warm and humid climate. In the days of DAVID, Hamath had a king of its own (2 Sam. 8:9). JEROBOAM II, the last powerful king of the northern tribes (2 Ki. 14:23-28), recovered Hamath for Israel. The city has had a checkered history for thousands of years. For a time it was under the power of Assyria (18:34), later under the power of Babylonia (Jer. 39:5). Still later ANTIOCHUS Epiphanes of Syria (c. 175-164 B.C.) renamed it Epiphaneia after himself. Today it is largely Muslim but has a large admixture of Christians. The city is dominated by its citadel hill, which no doubt contains layers of many different civilizations.

Hamath, entrance of. This (or a similar) expression is used by some Bible versions to render a Hebrew phrase which is better regarded as a place name, LEBO HAMATH (Num. 13:21 et al.).

Hamathite. hay´muh-thit (Heb. *hāmātî H2833*). The Hamathites are listed as a nation descended from CANAAN (Gen. 10:18; 1 Chr. 1:16). Presumably, they were early settlers of the city of HAMATH.

Hamath Zobah. hay´math-zoh´buh (Heb. *hāmāt ṣōbâ H2832*, possibly "fortress of Zobah"). A city conquered by SOLOMON, apparently near TADMOR in the region of HAMATH (2 Chr. 8:3). Some have identified Hamath Zobah with the city of Hamath itself, while others have conjectured that it is a different city also called Hamath, but situated in the territory of ZOBAH, an ARAMEAN kingdom that Assyrian records say reached as far as the EUPHRATES. It is also possible that the double name simply indicates the extent of Solomon's conquests, that is, the combined regions of Hamath and Zobah.

Hammath (person). ham´ath (Heb. *hammat H2830*, possibly "hot [spring]"). A man included in the genealogy of CALEB and described as the father of the house of RECAB; he was the ancestor of the KENITES (1 Chr. 2:55; KJV, "Hemath"). Some scholars connect, or even identify, Hammath with the city of the same name; see HAMMATH (PLACE).

Hammath (place). ham´ath (Heb. *hammat H2829*, "hot [spring]"). A fortified city in the tribal territory of NAPHTALI (Josh. 19:35). It is probably the same as HAMMON #2 (1 Chr. 6:76) and HAM-

Hot springs at Hammath Tiberias on the W shore of the Sea of Galilee.

© Dr. James C. Martin

H

MOTH DOR (Josh. 21:32). Hammath is generally identified with the modern Ḥammam Ṭabariyeh, famous for its hot baths, c. 2 mi. (3 km.) S of TIBE-RIAS on the W shore of the Sea of Galilee.

Hammedatha. ham´uh-day´thuh (Heb. *hammĕdātā´* H2158, possibly from Pers. *amadāta*, "strongly made"). The father of HAMAN, who was the chief minister of XERXES and a bitter enemy of the Jews (Esth. 3:1, 10; 8:5; 9:10, 24).

Hammelech. ham´uh-lek. KJV transliteration of a Hebrew word that should be rendered "the king" (Jer. 36:26; 38:6).

hammer. Marks on building stones and other evidences indicate that the type of hammers available in the ancient world corresponded roughly to the types still used in the Near E today. The Hebrew term *maqqebet* H5216, refers to a relatively small tool used for driving nails and pegs (Jdg. 4:21), dressing surfaces of building stone (1 Ki. 6:7), and decorating wooden idols (Jer. 10:4; metal idols, Isa. 44:12). Another term, *paṭṭîš* H7079, is once used for the large sledge hammer used to crack boulders (Jer. 23:29) and once for a blacksmith's hammer (Isa. 41:7); it is also used figuratively of Babylon's earth-shaking role as the "hammer of the whole earth" (Jer. 50:23).

Hammolecheth. See HAMMOLEKETH.

Hammoleketh. ha-mol´uh-keth (Heb. *hammōleket* H2168, "the queen"). Also Hammolecheth. Daughter of MAKIR by his wife MAA-CAH and granddaughter of MANASSEH; she is described as the sister of GILEAD and as having given birth to three children (1 Chr. 7:18).

Hammon. ham´uhn (Heb. *hammôn* H2785, possibly "hot [spring]"). **(1)** A town included in the boundary description of the tribe of ASHER (Josh. 19:28). The location of Hammon has been debated, but most scholars identify it with modern Khirbet Umm el-ʿAwamid in Lebanon, about 14.5 mi. (23 km.) NNE of Acco.

(2) A Levitical town in the tribal territory of NAPHTALI; it was assigned to the LEVITES descended from GERSHON (1 Chr. 6:76). This Hammon is generally identified with Hammath

(Josh. 19:35) and Hammoth Dor (21:32), on the W shore of the Sea of Galilee. See further HAM-MATH (PLACE).

Hammoth Dor. ham´uhth-dor´ (Heb. *hammōt dō´r* H2831, "hot [spring] of Dor"). A Levitical town in the tribal territory of NAPHTALI; it was assigned to the LEVITES descended from GER-SHON (Josh. 21:32). Hammoth Dor is probably an alternate name for Hammath (Josh. 19:35) and Hammon (1 Chr. 6:76), on the W shore of the Sea of Galilee. See further HAMMATH (PLACE).

Hammuel. ham´yoo-uhl (Heb. *hammûʾēl* H2781, meaning uncertain). KJV Hamuel. Son of Mishma and descendant of SIMEON through Shaul (1 Chr. 4:26).

Hammurabi. ham´uh-rah´bee (Akk. *hammu* ["Sun" or "kinsman" or "nation"] + *rabi* ["great, vast"] or *rapi* ["healing"]). Also Hammurapi. This name was borne by several individuals in the ANE, but special importance attaches to the sixth king of the first dynasty of BABYLON, who brought that city to its century-and-a-half rule over S Mesopotamia, known as the Old Babylonian Kingdom. He was an AMORITE, the name given to a Semitic group that invaded the FERTILE CRESCENT about 2000 B.C., destroying its civilization and establishing their own Semitic culture. The widely accepted date for his reign is 1792-1750 B.C. (suggested alternatives include 1728-1686 and 1642-1626). Hammurabi is not mentioned in the Bible, although some earlier scholars thought that he should be identified with AMRAPHEL (Gen. 14:1, 9).

Hammurabi made Babylon one of the great cities of the ancient world. Archaeologists have discovered that its streets were laid out in straight lines that intersect approximately at right angles, an innovation that bears witness to city planning and strong central government, both little known in Babylon before this time. MARDUK, the god of Babylon, now became the head of the pantheon, and his temple, Etemenanki, became one of the wonders of the ancient world. Many letters written by Hammurabi have been found. These show his close attention to the details of his realm and enable us to call him an energetic and benevolent ruler.

H

Hammurabi began the first golden age of Babylon—the second being that of NEBUCHAD-NEZZAR, over a thousand years later. He systematically unified all of the old world of Sumer and Akkad (S Mesopotamia) under his strongly centralized government. The prologue to his famous law code describes his administration: "Anu and Enlil [the sky and storm gods] named me to promote the welfare of the people, me, Hammurabi, the devout, god-fearing prince, to cause justice to prevail in the land, to destroy the wicked and the evil, that the strong might not oppress the weak, to rise like the sun over the black-headed [people], and to light up the land. Hammurabi the shepherd, called by Enlil, am I; the one who makes affluence and plenty abound ... the one who revived Uruk, who supplied water in abundance to its people; the one who brings joy to Borsippa ... who stores up grain for mighty Urash ... the savior of his people from distress, who establishes in security their portion in the midst of Babylon ... that justice might be dealt the orphan and the widow. ... I established the law and justice in the language of the land, thereby promoting the welfare of the people."

By far Hammurabi's most famous claim to fame is his law code. The code is inscribed on a magnificent stele of black diorite, 8 ft. (2.5 m.) high, found at SUSA in 1902. Formerly it had stood in Babylon, but the Elamites carried it off when they conquered Babylon in the twelfth century B.C. It is now in the Louvre in Paris. At the top of the stele is a finely sculptured scene showing Hammurabi standing before the sun god Shamash (the patron of law and justice), who is seated and is giving the laws to Hammurabi. Beneath the scene the laws are inscribed in beautiful cuneiform characters in fifty-one columns of text.

It is now known that Hammurabi's was not the first attempt to systematize the laws of Babylonia. Fragments of several previous law codes have been found. Ur-nammu of Ur and Lipit-Ishtar of Isin both promulgated earlier codes, and another was known in Eshnunna. But Hammurabi's code is the most complete expression of early Babylonian law, and undoubtedly incorporated many laws and customs that went back to far earlier times. Hammurabi did not invent these laws; he codified them. The monument contains not only the code,

but also a prologue and an epilogue, which narrates his glory and that of the gods whom he worshiped, blessed those who would respect his inscription, and cursed future vandals who might deface it.

The law code itself included nearly three hundred paragraphs of legal provisions concerning commercial, social, domestic, and moral life. There are regulations governing such matters as liability for (and exemption from) military service, control of trade in alcoholic drinks, banking and usury, and the responsibility of a man toward his wife and children, including the liability of a husband for the payment of his wife's debts. Hammurabi's code was harsher for upper-class offenders than on a commoner committing the same offense. Death was the penalty not only for homicide but also for theft, adultery, and bearing false witness in cases involving the accused's life. But the graded penalties show a great advance on primitive laws, and contemporary legal texts show that the harsher penalties were rarely exacted.

Women's rights were safeguarded. A neglected wife could obtain a divorce. A concubine who had become a mother was entitled to the restitution of whatever she had brought with her or a pecuniary indemnity appropriate to her social position. If a house fell on its owner or a doctor injured a patient, the one who built the house or treated the patient might suffer death, mutilation, or at least a heavy fine.

Students of the Bible are especially interested in the comparison of Hammurabi's code with the Mosaic legislation of the Bible. There are many similarities. In both a false witness is to be punished with the penalty he had thought to bring on the other person. Kidnapping and breaking into another person's house were capital offenses in both. The biblical law of DIVORCE permits a man to put away his wife, but does not extend to her the same right as did Hammurabi. Both codes agree in prescribing the death penalty for ADULTERY. The principle of retaliation, on which a number of Hammurabi's laws were based, is vividly stated in Exod. 21:23-25.

How are these similarities to be explained? It is obvious that Hammurabi could not have borrowed from MOSES, for Moses lived several centuries after Hammurabi. Direct borrowing in the other direction also seems very unlikely. Most scholars today agree that the similarities are to be explained by the common background of the Hebrews and Babylonians. Both were Semitic peoples, inheriting their customs and laws from their common ancestors. At first this explanation seems to run counter to the biblical claim that Moses' law was given by divine REVELATION. A closer examination of the PENTATEUCH will show that the Hebrews, before they came to SINAI, followed many of the regulations set forth in the law (e.g., penalties against murder, adultery, fornication, Gen. 9:6 and 38:24; the levirate law, 38:8; clean and unclean animals, 8:20; Sabbath, 2:3 and Exod. 16:23, 25-29). Moses' law consisted of things both old and new. What was old (the customs the Hebrews received from their ancient Semitic ancestors) was here formally incorporated into the nation's constitution. Much is new, especially the high view of the nature of God and the idea that law is an expression of this nature (Lev. 19:2).

Hamonah. huh-moh´nuh (Heb. *hămônâ H2164*, "roaring" or "horde"). The name of a city in the symbolical valley of HAMON GOG, where the defeated armies of GOG will be buried (Ezek. 39:16). The Hebrew clause is problematic, and some scholars emend the text.

Hamon Gog. hay´-muhn-gog´ (Heb. *hămôn gôg H2163*, "horde of Gog"). The name of "the valley of those who travel east toward the Sea"; this place will be named Hamon Gog because there the forces of GOG will be destroyed and buried (Ezek. 39:11, 15). The valley is said to be "in Israel" and—if the NIV rendering "toward the Sea" is correct—probably located W of the DEAD SEA (perhaps alluding to the ESDRAELON Valley). However, the NRSV translates, "the Valley of the Travelers [Heb. *hā'ōbĕrîm*] east of the sea" (cf. also TNIV), which suggests a place in TRANSJORDAN (unless "the sea" refers to the MEDITERRANEAN). If so, the allusion may be to the ABARIM mountain range in MOAB. Given the symbolic nature of the passage, it is likely that the prophet does not intend a specific known site. See TRAVELERS, VALLEY OF.

Hamor. hay´mor (Heb. *hămôr H2791*, "[male] donkey"). The father of SHECHEM; he is called a HIVITE (Gen. 33:19; 34:2 et al.). When JACOB returned from PADDAN ARAM, he bought a piece

of ground from the sons of Hamor (this plot of land would later become the burial place of JOSEPH, Josh. 24:32; in Acts 7:16 [KJV, "Emmor"], the purchase is attributed to ABRAHAM, perhaps a telescoping of two events). DINAH, Jacob's daughter, was violated by Shechem, and in revenge the sons of Jacob slew Hamor, Shechem, and all the males of the city (Gen. 34). During the period of the judges, the inhabitants of the city of Shechem were called "men of Hamor" (Jdg. 9:28); they suffered a severe defeat from ABIMELECH, a ruler of the Israelites.

Hamran. See HEMDAN.

hamstring. To cripple by cutting the leg tendons (KJV, "hough"). This cruel treatment of animals, justified only by extreme necessity, is alluded to several times in the OT (Gen. 49:6; Josh. 11:6, 9; 2 Sam. 8:4; 1 Chr. 18:4).

Hamuel. See HAMMUEL.

Hamul. hay´muhl (Heb. *hāmûl H2783*, possibly "spared" or "pitied"; gentilic *hāmûlî H2784*, "Hamulite"). Son of PEREZ, grandson of JUDAH, and ancestral head of the Hamulite clan (Gen. 46:12; Num. 26:21; 1 Chr. 2:5).

Hamutal. huh-myoo´tuhl (Heb. *hămûṭal H2782*, possibly "my father-in-law is dew [*or* protection]"; cf. ABITAL). The mother of JEHOAHAZ and ZEDEKIAH, kings of Judah; she was the daughter of a certain Jeremiah of Libnah and the wife of King JOSIAH (2 Ki. 23:31; 24:18; Jer. 52:1).

Hanameel. See HANAMEL.

Hanamel. han´uh-mel (Heb. *hănam'ēl H2856*, "God is gracious"). KJV Hanameel. Son of Shallum and cousin of JEREMIAH the prophet (Jer. 32:7-9). Hanamel owned a field in ANATHOTH, and when Jerusalem was besieged, he asked Jeremiah, as nearest relative, to buy it (cf. Lev. 25:25).

Hanan. hay´nuhn (Heb. *hānān H2860*, prob. short form of ELHANAN or HANANEL, "God is gracious," or a similar name). **(1)** Son of Shashak and descendant of BENJAMIN; listed among the heads

H

of families who lived in JERUSALEM (1 Chr. 8:23; cf. v. 28). His genealogical connection is unclear.

(2) Son of Azel and descendant of King SAUL (1 Chr. 8:38; 9:44).

(3) Son of Maacah, included among DAVID's mighty men (1 Chr. 11:43).

(4) Son of Igdaliah; Hanan is described as "the man of God" (although this epithet perhaps applies to Igdaliah), and his sons occupied a chamber in the temple into which JEREMIAH brought the family of the RECABITES (Jer. 35:4).

(5) Ancestor of a family of temple servants (NETHINIM) who returned to Palestine after the EXILE (Ezra 2:46; Neh. 7:49).

(6) A LEVITE who helped EZRA instruct the people in the law (Neh. 8:7); he is probably the Hanan listed among the Levites who sealed the covenant (10:10). Some believe he is also the same as #9 below.

(7-8) Two leaders of the people who sealed the covenant (Neh. 10:22).

(9) Son of Zaccur; NEHEMIAH appointed him as assistant to those who were in charge of the temple storerooms (Neh. 13:13). See also #6 above.

Hananeel. See HANANEL, TOWER OF.

Hananel, Tower of. han´uh-nel (Heb. *ḥănanˀēl* H2861, "God is gracious"). KJV Hananeel. The name of a tower on the N wall of JERUSALEM, between the FISH GATE and the Tower of the HUNDRED, not far from the SHEEP GATE (Neh.

3:1; 12:39). The Tower of Hananel must have been a significant landmark, for it is mentioned in two prophetic passages that deal with the rebuilding of Jerusalem (Jer. 31:38; Zech. 14:10). Its precise location is uncertain.

Hanani. huh-nay´ni (Heb. *ḥănāni* H2862, prob. short form of HANANIAH, "Yahweh is gracious"). (1) Father of the prophet JEHU (1 Ki. 16:1, 7; 2 Chr. 19:2; 20:34). Described as "the seer," Hanani rebuked King ASA for relying on the ARAMEANS; the king "was so enraged that he put him in prison" (2 Chr. 16:7-10).

(2) Son of HEMAN, DAVID's seer (1 Chr. 25:4). Hanani and his thirteen brothers were set apart "for the ministry of prophesying, accompanied by harps, lyres and cymbal" (v. 1). When lots were cast to determine the duties of the Levitical singers, he, along with his sons and relatives, received the eighteenth lot (v. 25).

(3) One of the descendants of IMMER who agreed to put away their foreign wives in the time of EZRA (Ezra 10:20).

(4) A brother (or relative) of NEHEMIAH who brought news to SUSA of the distressing condition of the Jews in Palestine (Neh. 1:2). He was subsequently made one of the governors of Jerusalem (7:2).

(5) A musician who took part in the dedication of the walls of Jerusalem after the return from exile (Neh. 12:36). Some have suggested that this Hanani is the same as #3 or #4 above.

Hananiah. han´uh-ni´uh (Heb. *ḥănanyâ* H2863, "Yahweh is gracious"). A popular Jewish name, especially after the EXILE. It is possible that some of the references in EZRA and NEHEMIAH treated separately in this article speak of the same individual.

(1) Son of ZERUBBABEL and father of Pelatiah and Jeshaiah (1 Chr. 3:19, 21).

(2) Son of Shashak and descendant of BENJAMIN; listed among the heads of families who lived in Jerusalem (1 Chr. 8:24; cf. v. 28).

H

© Dr. James C. Martin. Holy Land Hotel, Jerusalem. Photographed by permission.

Modern reconstruction of the Antonia Fortress, possibly built on the location of the Tower of Hanael. (View to the NW from the temple court.)

(3) Son of HEMAN, DAVID's seer (1 Chr. 25:4). Hananiah and his thirteen brothers were set apart "for the ministry of prophesying, accompanied by harps, lyres and cymbal" (v. 1). When lots were cast to determine the duties of the Levitical singers, he, along with his sons and relatives, received the sixteenth lot (v. 23).

(4) A royal official under King UZZIAH of Judah; under his direction, Jeiel the secretary and Maaseiah the officer mustered the army (2 Chr. 26:11).

(5) Son of Azzur and a false prophet who opposed JEREMIAH (Jer. 28). A native of GIBEON, Hananiah prophesied that King JECONIAH and the Jewish captives in Babylon would soon return to Jerusalem, bringing with them the vessels of the temple that NEBUCHADNEZZAR had carried away. In reply, Jeremiah told him that he would die within the year because he had made the people believe a lie. Jeremiah's words were fulfilled when Hananiah died in the seventh month of that year.

(6) Father of a certain Zedekiah; the latter was one of the high officials of Judah under King JEHOIAKIM (Jer. 36:12).

(7) Father of Shelemiah and grandfather of Irijah (Jer. 37:13); the latter was captain of the guard and arrested JEREMIAH on the charge of intending to desert to the Babylonians.

(8) One of the companions of DANIEL; his name was changed to SHADRACH by the Babylonians (Dan. 1:6-7).

(9) One of the descendants of Bebai who agreed to put away their foreign wives in the time of Ezra (Ezra 10:28).

(10) A perfume-maker who helped Nehemiah rebuild the wall of Jerusalem (Neh. 3:8).

(11) Son of Shelemiah; he helped repair the wall above the HORSE GATE (Neh. 3:30). This Hananiah may be the same as #10 above.

(12) Commander of the citadel in Jerusalem. Described as "a man of integrity" who "feared God more than most men do," he was appointed joint ruler of the city along with Hanani, Nehemiah's brother (Neh. 7:2).

(13) A leader of the people who sealed the covenant with Nehemiah (Neh. 10:23).

(14) Head of the priestly family of Jeremiah in the days of JOIAKIM the high priest (Neh. 12:12). He is probably the same priest who played the trumpet at the dedication of the walls of Jerusalem (v. 41).

hand. One of the most frequently used words in Scripture, occurring over 1,600 times. Besides its literal use, it occurs in many figurative senses as well. It very often stands for power (Gen. 9:2). To put one's hand under another's thigh (24:2, 9; 47:29) meant to take a solemn oath, evidently related to covenant obligations; to put one's hand on the head meant blessing (48:14) and signified ordination (1 Tim. 4:14; 2 Tim. 1:6).

In the OT the hand is also the symbol of personal agency. When the Lord is said to stretch out his hand, it means that he is taking personal action in whatever case or situation is involved, and this usage carries over into the NT (e.g., 1 Sam. 5:11; Jn. 10:29; Acts 4:30). Correspondingly, for human beings the hand signifies a person in action (e.g., 1 Sam. 26:23); and we should understand in this light the idiom by which the Hebrew expresses the consecration of priests to their holy duties: "to consecrate" is "to fill the hand" (e.g., Exod. 29:9 Heb.; NIV, "ordain"), that is, to dedicate every capacity of personal action for the service and use of the Lord.

To be placed at the right hand of royalty is a high honor and, of course, at "the right hand" of God is incomparably higher. "The LORD says to my Lord: 'Sit at my right hand'" (Ps. 110:1), showing the supreme position of the Son of God. When he judges the nations (Matt. 25:31-46), separating "sheep" from "goats," "he will put the sheep on his right [hand] and the goats on his left," showing that the left hand is equally the place of dishonor. In a trial the accuser stood at the right hand of the accused, as is shown in Zech. 3:1, where Satan is the accuser; but our Advocate stands also at our right hand to defend us (Ps. 16:8; 109:31).

handbreadth. This term indicates a measurement of about three inches based on the width of the hand at the base of the four fingers (cf. Jer. 52:21). Three handbreadths equaled a span, and six handbreadths a cubit, but the long cubit had an extra handbreadth (Ezek. 40:5; see WEIGHTS AND MEASURES). The term is used metaphorically for the brevity of man's life (Ps. 39:5).

H

handicraft. See OCCUPATIONS AND PROFESSIONS.

handkerchief. This English term is used once to render Greek *soudarion G5051* (from Lat. *sudarium*, "face-cloth," Acts 19:12). The reference is probably to "sweat rags" tied by PAUL about his head while active as a leather worker; these were brought to sick people in EPHESUS for healing purposes. The Greek term can also refer to the cloth used as a face or head covering (Jn. 11:44; 20:7; KJV, "napkin"), and more generally of any "piece of cloth" (Lk. 19:20).

handle. This English term, as noun or verb, is used variously in Bible translations to render several words and expressions (e.g. 1 Ki. 7:34 NIV; Isa. 10:15 NRSV; Lk. 24:39 KJV). Some passages include the term "handle" as a part of an idiom (Prov. 16:20 KJV; 2 Tim. 2:15 NIV).

handmaid, handmaiden. Term used by the KJV to render words that are better translated "maidservant" (NIV) or "slave-girl" (NRSV) or simply "servant" (cf. Gen. 16:1; Jdg. 19:19; Acts 2:18). These terms are sometimes used by women with reference to themselves as an expression of humility (e.g., Ruth 2:13; 1 Sam. 1:11; Lk. 1:38). See also MAID.

hands, imposition of. See LAYING ON OF HANDS.

handwriting. See WRITING.

Hanes. hay´neez (Heb. *ḥānēs H2865*). An Egyptian city, mentioned with ZOAN (Tanis), in a passage that condemns those who look for protection from PHARAOH (Isa. 30:4). It is probably to be identified with Heracleopolis Magna, capital of the northern part of Upper EGYPT, about 50 mi. (80 km.) S of MEMPHIS and just S of the Fayum.

hanging. Death by hanging is mentioned several times in the Bible (e.g., Esth. 2:23 et al.). In the case of AHITHOPHEL (2 Sam. 17:23) and JUDAS ISCARIOT (Matt. 27:5), it was self-inflicted. In some passages, however, the terms used denote impaling, gibbeting, or crucifixion (see CROSS). This often was done to the corpse after death (Gen. 40:19, 22; 41:13; Deut. 21:22; Lam. 5:12) but not always. Ezra 6:11 indicates that a living man was to be impaled and left to die. PAUL asserts that Jesus became a curse by being hung upon a tree (Gal. 3:13, quoting from Deut. 21:23), his point being that Jesus bore the accursed death due to sin vicariously, so that those who deserved it could be set free.

hangings. See CURTAINS.

Haniel. See HANNIEL.

Hannah. han´uh (Heb. *ḥannâ H2839*, "grace, favor"). One of the two wives of ELKANAH. Peninnah, the other wife (1 Sam. 1:2), had children; but Hannah was barren for a long time and, as is common in polygamous households, "her rival kept provoking her" (1:6). The fact that Elkanah loved Hannah and gave her a double portion (1:5) only increased the hatred and jealousy in Peninnah's heart. Hannah, however, was a godly woman, and she prayed for a son and vowed to give him to the Lord as a perpetual NAZIRITE (1:11). The priest ELI saw Hannah's lips moving in silent prayer and rebuked her for what he thought was drunkenness. She replied very humbly and Eli apologized. The family returned home; Hannah conceived and became the mother of SAMUEL, the great prophet of Israel and the last of the judges. Hannah's praise (2:1-10) shows that she was a deeply spiritual woman. Mary's song, "the Magnificat," resembles Hannah's (Lk. 1:46-55). Mary, like Hannah, praised God when she was expecting a baby by miraculous conception. Each woman rejoiced in the Lord; each expressed in marvelous fashion God's way of dealing with the proud and with the humble (cf. Ps. 113:7-9).

Hannathon. han´uh-thon (Heb. *ḥannātôn H2872*, apparently from *ḥēn H2834*, "charm, favor"). A town on the N border of the tribal territory of ZEBULUN (Josh. 19:14). Located on a major highway, Hannathon is mentioned in extrabiblical sources. It is identified with modern Tell el-Bedeiwiyeh, about 2 mi. (3 km.) W of NAZARETH.

Hanniel. han´ee-uhl (Heb. *ḥannî'ēl H2848*, "God was gracious"). KJV also Haniel (1 Chr. 7:39). **(1)** Son of Ephod; he was a leader from the tribe of MANASSEH, chosen to assist in the distribution of the land (Num. 34:23).

(2) Son of Ulla and descendant of ASHER, included among the "heads of families, choice men, brave warriors and outstanding leaders" (1 Chr. 7:39-40).

Hanoch. hay′nok (Heb. *ḥănôk H2840*, possibly "dedicated" or "initiated" [see ENOCH]; gentilic *ḥănōkî H2854*, "Hanochite"). TNIV Hanok. **(1)** Son of MIDIAN and grandson of ABRAHAM by KETURAH (Gen. 25:4; 1 Chr. 1:33 [KJV, "Henoch"]). The name may be related to a location in ARABIA. **(2)** Eldest son of REUBEN, grandson of JACOB, and ancestor of the Hanochite clan (Gen. 46:9; Exod. 6:14; Num. 26:5; 1 Chr. 5:3).

Hanok. hay′nok. TNIV form of HANOCH.

Hanukkah. hah′nuh-kuh (Heb. *ḥănukkâ H2853*, "dedication"). See DEDICATION, FEAST OF.

Hanun. hay′nuhn (Heb. *ḥānûn H2842*, "favored"). **(1)** Son and successor of NAHASH, king of the Ammonites (2 Sam. 10:1-4; 1 Chr. 19:1-6; see AMMON). Upon the death of Nahash, DAVID sent a message of condolence to Hanun. This gesture was misinterpreted, and the messengers were grossly insulted and dishonored. The result was a war that David waged against Hanun, and the Ammonites lost their independence. David appointed the brother of Hanun, SHOBI, in his place (2 Sam. 17:27). **(2)** Son of Zalaph; after the return from EXILE, he assisted in repairing the VALLEY GATE in JERUSALEM and about 500 yards of the wall (Neh. 3:13, 30; according to some scholars, however, these passages refer to two different men).

Hapharaim. haf′uh-ray′im (Heb. *ḥăpārayim H2921*, "two pits"). KJV Haphraim (some editions). A town on the frontier of the tribal territory of ISSACHAR, listed after SHUNEM (Josh. 19:19). Its location is debated.

Hapiru. See HABIRU.

happiness. See JOY.

Happizzez. hap′uh-zez (Heb. *happiṣṣēṣ H2204*, apparently piel form of *pāṣaṣ H7207* [polel, "to shat-

ter"] with definite article). The leader of a priestly family whom DAVID appointed by lot as the head of the eighteenth division for temple duties (1 Chr. 24:15; KJV, "Aphses"). The name Happizzez may be a clan designation, possibly connected with the town of BETH PAZZEZ.

Hara. hair′uh (Heb. *hārā᾽ H2217*, perhaps related to *har H2215*, "mountain"). One of the places to which TIGLATH-PILESER, the king of Assyria, exiled the tribes of Reuben, Gad, and half of Manasseh in 734-732 B.C. (1 Chr. 5:26). It is mentioned along with HALAH, HABOR, and the river GOZAN—all places in N MESOPOTAMIA. Several identifications have been proposed, but the name Hara is omitted in the SEPTUAGINT, and it is also missing in the Hebrew text of the parallel passages (2 Ki. 17:6; 18:11). Many scholars believe that the text in Chronicles is corrupt, and several emendations have been suggested.

Haradah. huh-ray′duh (Heb. *ḥărādāh H3011*, "[place of] fear"). A camping station in the wilderness journeys of the Israelites (Num. 33:24-25). The name suggests that some otherwise unknown incident here may have caused anxiety among the people. It was located between Mount Shepher and Makheloth, but none of these sites can be identified.

Haran (person). hair′uhn (Heb. *hārān H2237*, possibly "mountaineer"; the place name Haran renders a different Hebrew word). **(1)** Son of TERAH, brother of ABRAHAM and NAHOR, and father of LOT and two daughters, Milcah and Iscah (Gen. 11:26-31). Haran died in UR before his father Terah set out to go to CANAAN. **(2)** Son of CALEB by his concubine Ephah, included in the genealogy of JUDAH (1 Chr. 2:46). **(3)** Son of SHIMEI and descendant of GERSHON; he was one of the Levites who headed the families of LADAN (1 Chr. 23:9).

Haran (place). hair′uhn (Heb. *hārān H3059*, from Akk. *ḥarrānu*, "road" [i.e., crossroads]; Gk. *Charran G5924*). Also Harran; KJV NT Charran. A city of MESOPOTAMIA situated c. 24 mi. (39 km.) SE of Urfa (Edessa) on the river Balikh, a tributary of

H

the EUPHRATES. It was an important commercial center because of its location on one of the main trade routes between Babylonia and the Mediterranean: CARCHEMISH lay some 50 mi. (80 km.) W, and GOZAN about the same distance E. The place name Haran is to be distinguished from HARAN (PERSON), which renders a different Hebrew word.

Terah, father of Abram (ABRAHAM) emigrated to Haran with his family (Gen. 11:31). After Terah's death, Abram left this city to go into the land of Canaan (12:4). His brother NAHOR remained in Haran, and Abraham later sent his servant there to find a wife for his son ISAAC among his relatives (24:4). Afterward JACOB, at the request of his father Isaac, came to this same area in search of a wife (29:4-5). In the time of HEZEKIAH, RABSHAKEH, an officer of SENNACHERIB, when delivering a propaganda lecture to the people of JERUSALEM, mentioned that Haran and other cities in the same area had been conquered by ASSYRIA (2 Ki. 19:12; Isa. 37:12). EZEKIEL mentions this city as one of those that carried on trade with TYRE (Ezek. 27:23).

Haran is often referred to in Assyrian and Babylonian records. The Akkadian name means "road," probably because this city was located at the intersection of the N–S trade route from DAMASCUS

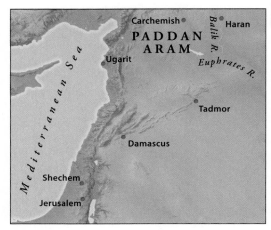

Haran.

and the E–W route between CARCHEMISH and NINEVEH. A center of worship of the moon-god Sin was established there in very early times. The city and temple were destroyed in the wars of the Assyrian kings. After the fall of Nineveh in 612 B.C., some Assyrian refugees fled to Haran and held out there until 610. Nabonidus, the king of Babylon, who delighted in restoring old temples, rebuilt the city and temple and reinstated the worship of the moon-god there about seventy-five years later.

Beehive homes from the early part of the twentieth century now cover the village of Haran, a region once inhabited by Abraham and his ancestors. (View to the S.)

© Dr. James C. Martin

H

Hararite. hair´uh-rît (Heb. *hărārî H2240*, possibly "mountain dweller"). An epithet applied to two (or three) of David's heroes. Shammah son of Agee, who was one of the Three, achieved a great victory over the Philistines (2 Sam. 23:11 [cf. vv. 32b-33a, possibly referring to a different person]; 1 Chr. 11:34 has Shagee instead of Shammah). Another Hararite included in the list of the Thirty is Ahiam son of Sharar (2 Sam. 23:33b; 1 Chr. 11:35 has "Ahiam son of Sacar"). The term Hararite may refer to a clan or, more probably, a location; if the latter, it may indicate a specific town (one suggestion is Aroer) or some general mountainous area (cf. English *hillbilly*).

Harbona. hahr-boh´nuh (Heb. *ḥarbônāʾ H3002* and *ḥarbônâ H3003*, from Pers. *kherbân*, "donkey driver"). KJV also Harbonah. One of the seven eunuchs sent by Xerxes king of Persia to bring Queen Vashti to a royal feast (Esth. 1:10). It was Harbona who later suggested that Haman be hanged on the same gallows that Haman himself had erected for Mordecai (7:9).

harbor. The sheltered part of a body of water. This noun is used twice in the NIV (Isa. 23:10, in an oracle concerning Tyre and Tarshish; Acts 27:12, with reference to Fair Havens). As a verb meaning "to hold on to a negative thought in the mind," *harbor* occurs in several passages (Deut. 15:9 et al.).

hardening, spiritual. Both the OT and the NT use a variety of terms in several combinations to express the idea of stubborn human resistance to God (e.g., Exod. 7:3; Deut. 2:30; 2 Chr. 30:8; Ezek. 2:4). Of special interest are the statements that God hardened Pharaoh's heart (Exod. 7:3; 10:1; 14:4) and that Pharaoh hardened his own heart (9:34-35; 13:15). Paul appeals to the sovereignty of God in discussing Pharaoh (Rom. 9:18), although the factor of human responsibility through repeated warnings is clearly involved (cf. 1 Sam. 6:6; Rom. 1:21-25). Hardening one's heart brings punishment (Prov. 29:1), as is evident in Israel's resistance at Meribah (Ps. 95:8). Refusal to listen, to obey, or to be thankful characterize the hardened heart, and Israel is portrayed as a prime example of this condition (2 Ki. 17:14; Neh. 9:16-

17; Heb. 3:8). The disciples' hearts were said to be hardened or dull when they failed to understand the miracle of the loaves (Mk. 6:52; 8:17). Gentile unbelievers are alienated from God because of their ignorance and hardness of heart (Eph. 4:18). With reference to Israel, Paul states that while the elect obtained salvation, "the others were hardened" (Rom. 11:7; cf. v. 25; see election). Here the individuals themselves are described as being hardened, but elsewhere he says that "their minds were made dull" (2 Cor. 3:14).

hare. See animals.

harem. This English term (from Arabic *ḥarim*, "forbidden") denotes the building assigned to the wives and concubines of one man; the word often refers to the women themselves. Modern versions use it as the rendering of a Hebrew phrase meaning literally, "house of the women" (Esth. 2:3, 9, 11, 13-14; the NIV uses it also in vv. 8 and 15, where the Heb. simply has "the women"). In addition, it is possible that a harem is in view in Eccl. 2:8 (so NIV; lit., "a mistress and mistresses").

Hareph. hair´if (Heb. *ḥārēp H3073*, possibly "sharp, shrewd"). Son of Hur, descendant of Caleb, and "father" (i.e., founder or ruler) of Beth Gader; listed in the genealogy of Judah (1 Chr. 2:51).

Hareth. See Hereth.

Harhaiah. hahr-hay´yuh (Heb. *ḥarhāyâ H3015*, derivation unknown). Father of Uzziel; the latter was one of the goldsmiths who helped to repair the walls of Jerusalem after the exile (Neh. 3:8).

Harhas. harh´has (Heb. *ḥarḥas H3030*, derivation unknown). Father of Tikvah and grandfather of Shallum; the latter was "keeper of the wardrobe" and the husband of Huldah the prophetess (2 Ki. 22:14). The name is given as Hasrah (and father of Tokhath) in the parallel passage (2 Chr. 34:22).

Har-heres. See Heres #1.

Harhur. hahr´huhr (Heb. *ḥarḥûr H3028*, possibly "raven" or "[born during mother's] fever"). Ancestor of a family of temple servants (NETHINIM) who returned after the EXILE (Ezra 2:51; Neh. 7:53).

Harim. hair´im (Heb. *ḥārim H3053*, "consecrated"). **(1)** The leader of a priestly family whom DAVID appointed by lot as the head of the third division for duties in the sanctuary (1 Chr. 24:8). He is possibly the same priest listed as the ancestor of a family of 1,017 people that returned from the Babylonian captivity with ZERUBBABEL (Ezra 2:39; Neh. 7:42), some of whom had married foreign wives and agreed to divorce them (Ezra 10:21). Perhaps this is the same priestly family (or a member of it also named Harim) that joined in sealing the covenant of NEHEMIAH (Neh. 10:5).

(2) Ancestor of a family of 320 people that returned from the Babylonian captivity with Zerubbabel (Ezra 2:32; Neh. 7:35). Because this list includes many geographic names, Harim here may refer to a town. Some members of this family had married foreign wives and agreed to divorce them (Ezra 10:31). The same family (or a member of it also named Harim) joined in sealing the covenant of NEHEMIAH (Neh. 10:27). Malkijah, a descendant of this family (or the son of the individual Harim) helped repair a section of the wall of JERUSALEM as well as the Tower of the OVENS (Neh. 3:11).

It should be noted that many scholars identify four or more different individuals (or families) by the name of Harim.

Hariph. hair´if (Heb. *ḥārip H3040*, "sharp, brisk" or "[born at] harvest-time"). Ancestor of a family of 112 members that returned from exile with ZERUBBABEL (Neh. 7:24; called "Jorah" in Ezra 2:18). The same family (or a member of it also named Hariph) joined in sealing the covenant of NEHEMIAH (Neh. 10:19).

harlot. See PROSTITUTE.

Har-magedon. See ARMAGEDDON.

Harmon. hahr´muhn (Heb. *ḥarĕmôn H2236*, meaning unknown). A city or region to which the powerful and unjust women of SAMARIA were to be exiled (Amos 4:3; KJV, "the palace"). No place with

this name is known, and the text is widely thought to be corrupt. Many emendations have been proposed (cf. NIV mg., "O mountain of oppression"), but none has been generally accepted.

harmony of the Gospels. An edition of the GOSPELS that seeks to show the agreement or coherence among them. Gospel harmonies may take two forms: (1) works that interweave material from all four Gospels into one chronological narrative, and (2) arrangements ("synopses") of the Gospels, especially the synoptics, in parallel columns according to some chronological scheme. The earliest harmony, Tatian's *Diatessaron*, was produced c. A.D. 170 and used the first method. Many modern "harmonies" are better described as *synopses*, for they do not necessarily assume agreement among the Gospels. They are an important tool for comparative study.

Harnepher. hahr´nuh-fuhr (Heb. *ḥarneper H3062*, "Horus [an Egyptian deity] is good"). Son (or descendant) of Zophah, included in the genealogy of ASHER (1 Chr. 7:36). The name Harnepher, however, may be a clan designation or even a place name (some have speculated that it was derived from an Egyptian outpost in Palestine).

harness. This English term, as noun or verb, is used a few times in Bible translations to render several Hebrew words. It can be used of hitching up chariots (1 Ki. 18:44) and yoking cows (1 Sam. 6:7). The KJV also uses this English word in its older sense of "armor" (1 Ki. 22:34; 2 Chr. 18:33).

Harod. hair´uhd (Heb. *ḥārōd H3008*, "trembling"; gentilic *ḥārōdî H3012*, "Harodite"). **(1)** A spring at which GIDEON encamped with his men while preparing for battle with the Midianites (Jdg. 7:1). Some have speculated that SAUL encamped at this spring (1 Sam. 29:1, "the spring in Jezreel") before his fatal battle with the PHILISTINES (cf. 31:1). Harod is generally identified with ʿEin Jalud, 9 mi. (14 km.) WNW of BETH SHAN.

(2) The epithet Harodite is applied to two of DAVID's mighty warriors, Shammah and Elika (2 Sam. 23:25; cf. 1 Chr. 11:27, "Shammoth the Harorite"). Some associate this name with #1 above, but many scholars believe it refers to an unrelated town also named Harod, possibly to be identified with modern Khirbet el-Ḥaredhan, c. 5 mi. (8 km.) SE of JERUSALEM.

Haroeh. huh-roh′uh (Heb. *hārōʾeh H2218*, "the seer"). Son (or descendant) of SHOBAL, included in the genealogy of CALEB (1 Chr. 2:52); probably the same as REAIAH (1 Chr. 4:2).

Harorite. hay′roh-rît (Heb. *hārôrî H2229*). Epithet applied to Shammoth, one of DAVID's mighty warriors (1 Chr. 11:27); probably the same as SHAMMAH the Harodite. See HAROD.

The Harod Spring at the base of Mt. Gilboa.

© Dr. James C. Martin

Harosheth Haggoyim. huh-roh′shith-huh-goi′im (Heb. *hărōšet haggôyim H3099*, "woodland of the nations"). A Canaanite town and the home of SISERA, from which he led his forces against DEBORAH and BARAK (Jdg. 4:13), and to which his army fled after his defeat (v. 16). Its location is uncertain, and some think it was not a town at all but, as its name suggests, a general woodland region in GALILEE of the Gentiles or in JEZREEL.

harp. See MUSIC AND MUSICAL INSTRUMENTS.

harpoon. This English term is used to render a Hebrew word that occurs only once (Job 41:7; KJV, "barbed irons"), in parallel to "fishing spears"; both weapons are said to be futile in the battle with LEVIATHAN.

Harran. See HARAN.

harrow. As a verb, this English term, meaning "to break up and smooth the soil," is a possible rendering of Hebrew *śidēd H8440*, which occurs three times (Job 39:10 KJV; Isa. 28:24 NIV, NRSV; Hos. 10:11 NRSV). The precise meaning of the Hebrew verb, however, is disputed; some scholars argue for the sense "to plow furrows [that function as boundaries]." For the use of *harrow* as a noun, see PICK.

Harsha. hahr′shuh (Heb. *ḥaršāʾ H3095*, possibly "deaf" or "mute"). Ancestor of a family of temple servants (NETHINIM) who returned from the EXILE (Ezra 2:52; Neh. 7:54).

hart. See ANIMALS.

Harum. hair′uhm (Heb. *hārûm H2227*). Father of Aharhel and a descendant of JUDAH through ASHHUR (1 Chr. 4:8; cf. v. 5).

Harumaph. huh-roo′maf (Heb. *ḥărûmap H3018*, "split nose"). Father of Jedaiah; the latter helped in repairing the walls of JERUSALEM in the time of NEHEMIAH (Neh. 3:10).

Haruphite. huh-roo′fît (Heb. *ḥărûpî H3020*; cf. HAREPH, HARIPH). Epithet applied to Shephatiah, one of the warriors from BENJAMIN who joined DAVID at ZIKLAG (1 Chr. 12:5; *Ketib*, "Hariphite"). It is not clear whether the term indicates geographic origin or connection to a clan.

Haruz. hair′uhz (Heb. *hārûṣ H3027*, possibly "gold" or "diligent"). Father of MESHULLEMETH, who was the mother of AMON, king of Judah (2 Ki. 21:19). The name may be either Phoenician or Arabic.

H

harvest. The economy of the Israelites was strictly agricultural. See AGRICULTURE. Harvest time was a very significant event for them. They had three each year. The barley reaping (Ruth 1:22) came in April-May; the wheat harvest (Gen. 30:14) was about six weeks later, in June-July; and the ingathering of the fruits of tree or vine took place in September-October.

Grain crops were reaped with sickles, and the cut stalks were laid in bunches that were carried to the THRESHING FLOOR. Some laws governed these simple harvest operations. The corners of the fields were not to be reaped, and the scatterings of the cut grain were not to be picked up. The part of the crop thus left was for the poor people to use (Lev. 23:22). The owner was required each year to present the FIRSTFRUITS of the crop as an offering to God before he could take any of it for his own use (23:10, 14). Stalks of grain that grew up without being sown were not to be harvested (25:5). With a new orchard or vineyard the fruit was not to be gathered for three years, and the fourth year's crop had to be given entirely to the Lord. So the owner had to wait until the fifth year to get any fruit for himself (19:23-25).

The Lord fitted the three main religious feasts that he prescribed for the people into this agricultural economy. The Passover came in the season of the barley harvest (Exod. 23:16). Seven weeks later at time of the wheat harvest the Feast of Pentecost occurred (34:22). The Feast of Tabernacles was observed in the seventh month, which was the period of the fruit harvest (34:22). See FEASTS.

Harvest is a picture of the blessing upon the returning captivity of Judah (Hos. 6:11). More frequently, the wielding of the sickle in harvest portrays the judgment upon the nations of the world (Joel 3:13). The NT repeats this image of judgment (Rev. 14:15). Jesus compares the harvest to the KINGDOM OF GOD, which grows by stages (Mk. 4:29). The separation of the weeds and wheat will occur at the "harvest" of the kingdom (Matt. 13:30). Christ used the harvest to represent a world of souls that is ready to be reached with the gospel. The fields are ready to be harvested, "but the workers are few" (Matt. 9:37).

Hasadiah. has´uh-di´uh (Heb. *ḥăsadyâ H2878*, "Yahweh is faithful"). Son of ZERUBBABEL and descendant of DAVID through SOLOMON (1 Chr. 3:20), possibly born in Palestine (see HASHUBAH).

Hasenuah. See HASSENUAH.

Hashabiah. hash´uh-bi´uh (Heb. *ḥăšabyâ H3116*, "Yahweh has taken account"). **(1)** Son of Amaziah, descendant of MERARI, and ancestor of ETHAN, who was a LEVITE musician in the time of DAVID (1 Chr. 6:45).

(2) Son of JEDUTHUN, father of Azrikam, ancestor of Shemaiah, and a Levite musician (1 Chr. 9:14; 25:3, 19; Neh. 11:15). This Hashabiah was the head of the twelfth company of temple musicians appointed by lot under David.

(3) A ruler from HEBRON in the time of David who, along with his relatives, was "responsible in Israel west of the Jordan for all the work of the LORD and for the king's service" (1 Chr. 26:30).

(4) Son of Kemuel and an officer over the tribe of LEVI under King David (1 Chr. 27:17).

(5) A leader of the Levites in the reign of JOSIAH who gave liberally toward the sacrifices (2 Chr. 35:9).

(6) A prominent Levite who returned from the EXILE with EZRA; he is usually associated with SHEREBIAH (Ezra 8:19; Neh. 12:24). He was also one of the priests entrusted with the temple treasures that were brought to Jerusalem (Ezra 8:24). Moreover, this Hashabiah may have been the same one who as "ruler of half the district of Keilah" helped to repair the wall (Neh. 3:17) and who affixed his seal to the covenant of NEHEMIAH (10:11).

(7) One of the descendants of PAROSH who agreed to divorce their foreign wives (Ezra 10:25 NRSV, following the LXX [MT, "Malkijah"]). See MALKIJAH ##4-6.

(8) Son of Mattaniah, descendant of ASAPH, and grandfather of Uzzi; the latter was chief officer of the Levites (Neh. 11:22).

(9) Head of the priestly house of HILKIAH in the time of JOIAKIM the high priest (Neh. 12:21).

Hashabnah. huh-shab´nuh (Heb. *ḥăšabnâ H3118*, possibly "[Yahweh] has taken account of me"). One of leaders of the Israelites who sealed the covenant under NEHEMIAH (Neh. 10:25).

Hashabneiah. hash´uhb-nee´yah (Heb. *ḥăšabnĕyâ H3119*, "Yahweh has taken account of me"). KJV Hashabniah. **(1)** Father of Hattush; the latter helped rebuild the walls of Jerusalem in the time of NEHEMIAH (Neh. 3:10).

(2) One of the LEVITES who offered prayer in the ceremonies that preceded the sealing of the covenant (Neh. 9:5). Some scholars identify him with HASHABIAH #6.

Hashabniah. See HASHABNEIAH.

Hashbaddanah. hash-bad´uh-nuh (Heb. *ḥašbaddānâ H3111*, derivation uncertain). KJV Hashbadana. One of the prominent men who stood near EZRA when the law was read at the great assembly (Neh. 8:4).

Hashem. hay´shim (Heb. *ḥāšēm H2244*). A GIZONITE whose sons are included among DAVID's mighty men (1 Chr. 11:34; however, the Heb. expression *bĕnê hāšēm* could be read as "the sons of the name," with the possible meaning, "famous men"). Many scholars emend the text by omitting "the sons of" (cf. NRSV) and changing "Hashem" to "Jashen" (cf. 2 Sam. 23:32).

Hashmonah. hash-moh´nuh (Heb. *ḥašmōnâ H3135*, derivation uncertain). A place at which the Israelites stopped during their wilderness journey (Num. 33:29-30). It was evidently located between Mithcah and Moseroth, but the site is unknown.

Hashub. See HASSHUB.

Hashubah. huh-shoo´buh (Heb. *ḥăšubâ H3112*, possibly "considered [by Yahweh]" or "[highly] esteemed"). Son of ZERUBBABEL and descendant of DAVID through SOLOMON (1 Chr. 3:20). Some scholars suggest that the word is not a name and emend the text to "after his return," indicating that the subsequent names refer to Zerubbabel's sons born in Palestine.

Hashum. hay´shuhm (Heb. *ḥāšum H3130*, "broad nose"). **(1)** Son of DAN (Gen. 46:23 NRSV, following LXX; MT, HUSHIM; see also SHUHAM).

(2) Ancestor of a family of 223 (or 328) members who returned from the EXILE (Ezra 2:19; Neh. 7:22).

Some members of this family had married foreign wives and agreed to divorce them (Ezra 10:33).

(3) One of the prominent men who stood near EZRA when the law was read at the great assembly (Neh. 8:4). He may be the same Hashum who affixed his seal to the covenant (10:18).

Hashupha. See HASUPHA.

Hasideans, Hasidim. See MACCABEE.

Hasmonean. See MACCABEE.

Hasrah. haz´ruh (Heb. *ḥasrâ H2897*, derivation uncertain). Father of Tokhath and grandfather of SHALLUM; the latter was "keeper of the wardrobe" and the husband of HULDAH the prophetess (2 Chr. 34:22). The name is given as HARHAS (and father of Tikvah) in the parallel passage (2 Ki. 22:14).

Hassenaah. has´uh-nay´uh (Heb. *hassĕnāʾâ H2189*, meaning uncertain). The father (or ancestor) of a family that rebuilt the FISH GATE (Neh. 3:3). Many believe, however, that the form *Hassenaah* should be understood as the definite article plus SENAAH (Ezra 2:35; Neh. 7:38), which may well be a place name. If so, "the sons of Hassenaah" means perhaps "the people from the [region of] Senaah." See also HASSENUAH.

Hassenuah. has´uh-noo´uh (Heb. *hassĕnuʾâ H2190*, meaning uncertain). KJV Hasenuah. Father of Hodaviah and ancestor of Sallu, from the tribe of BENJAMIN; Sallu is mentioned as one of the first to resettle in JERUSALEM (1 Chr. 9:7). In a parallel list of postexilic Benjamites, Hassenuah is mentioned as father (or ancestor) of a certain Judah who was in charge of the Second District of Jerusalem (Neh. 11:9; KJV, "Senuah"). The name is possibly a variant form of HASSENAAH and SENAAH.

Hasshub. hash´uhb (Heb. *haššûb H3121*, "considerate" or "[highly] regarded" or "one to whom has been reckoned"). KJV also Hashub (in Nehemiah). **(1)** Son (meaning prob. a descendant) of PAHATH-MOAB; along with Malkijah son of Harim, he helped repair a section of the wall of JERUSALEM as well as the Tower of the OVENS (Neh. 3:11). He is

H

probably the same Hasshub mentioned along with a certain Benjamin as having made repairs in front of their house (v. 23).

(2) One of the Israelite leaders who sealed the covenant in the time of Ezra (Neh. 10:23).

(3) Father of Shemaiah; the latter was a leader of the Merari clan among the Levites and is mentioned as having settled in Jerusalem after the return from the captivity (1 Chr. 9:14; Neh. 11:15).

Hassophereth, Sophereth. ha-sof´uh-rith, sof´uh-rith (Heb. *hassōperet H2191*, "the [office of] scribe" or "the guild of scribes"; also *sōperet H6072*). Ancestor of a family of Solomon's servants who returned after the exile ("Hassophereth" in Ezra 2:55; "Sophereth" in Neh. 7:57; KJV has "Sophereth" in both passages).

Hasupha. huh-soo´fuh (Heb. *ḥăśûpāʾ H3102*, possibly "stripped" or "prematurely born"). KJV Hashupha (in Nehemiah). Ancestor of a family of temple servants (Nethinim) who returned after the exile (Ezra 2:43; Neh. 7:46).

hat. See DRESS.

Hatach. See HATHACH.

hate, hatred. An intense aversion or active hostility that is expressed in settled opposition to a person or thing. Hatred is a response that usually comes from anger, fear, or a sense of injury, as when Esau is said to have hated Jacob (Gen. 27:41; NIV, "held a grudge against"). The apostle Paul condemned hatred, listing it as one of the works of the flesh (Gal. 5:20). Also, the OT includes a clear prohibition of hatred between kindred (Lev. 19:17).

God is said to hate IDOLATRY and false worship (Deut. 12:31; 16:22; Jer. 44:4) and even Israel's WORSHIP when it was external only (Isa. 1:14; Amos 5:21; Mal. 2:13-16). There is a special and sometimes problematic usage in the OT, where God is said to love Jacob but to hate Esau (Mal. 1:2-3), to hate evildoers (Ps. 5:5), and to hate that which was evil (Prov. 6:16). The emotional connotation we normally associate with hatred should be subtracted from such passages; God must not be understood to act on the human plane of anger and

hostility. In connection with Esau, "hate" is almost equivalent to the acknowledgement of a divine selectivity: Jacob he chose and Esau he rejected.

Jesus modified the teaching of his contemporaries by insisting that although they had heard it said they were to love their neighbors but hate their enemies, they should rather love their enemies and do good to those who hated them (Matt. 5:43; Lk. 6:27). Jesus' words of admonition to his disciples seem strange in light of another statement, "If anyone comes to me and does not hate his father and mother, his wife and children, his brothers and sisters—yes, even his own life—he cannot be my disciple" (Lk. 14:26). Clearly, however, the disciples were being instructed not that they should be hostile toward those nearest and dearest to them, but rather that even those nearest and dearest to them must be given second place to the disciples' loyalty and affection for Jesus. Nothing must be allowed to interfere with our commitment to the cause of Christ, especially not our own selfish desires or ambitions.

The antithesis of LOVE to hatred is especially emphasized in the Gospel of John, which expresses a sharp Semitic juxtaposition in the imagery of LIGHT and DARKNESS (Jn. 3:20). In the same context, it is the love of God in Jesus Christ that has become operative in the world to destroy the hatred of the light; and even though the disciples are hated by the world, they are to reveal to it the love of Christ that is stronger than hate (17:14, 20-26).

Hathach. hay´thak (Heb. *hātāk H2251*, possibly Pers., "good one" or "courtier"). KJV Hatach; TNIV Hathack. A eunuch under King Xerxes assigned to attend Queen Esther (Esth. 4:5-6, 9-10). He served as a messenger between Esther and Mordecai after Haman plotted to kill the Jews .

Hathak. hay´thak. TNIV form of HATHAK.

Hathath. hay´thath (Heb. *hātat H3171*, "dread" or "weakling"). Son of Othniel and grandson of Kenaz (Caleb's younger brother), included in the genealogy of Judah (1 Chr. 4:13).

Hatipha. huh-ti´fuh (Heb. *hătipāʾ H2640*, "captured"). Ancestor of a family of temple servants

H

(Nethinim) who returned from the captivity (Ezra 2:54; Neh. 7:56).

Hatita. huh-ti´tuh (Heb. *ḥāṭîṭāʾ H2638*, meaning uncertain). Ancestor of a family of gatekeepers who returned with Zerubbabel from the captivity (Ezra 2:42; Neh. 7:45).

hatred. See HATE, HATRED.

Hattil. hat´uhl (Heb. *ḥaṭṭil H2639*, possibly "talkative"). Ancestor of a family of Solomon's servants who returned from the captivity (Ezra 2:57; Neh. 7:59).

Hattush. hat´uhsh (Heb. *ḥaṭṭûš H2637*, meaning unknown). (1) Son of Shemaiah and descendant of David through Zerubbabel and Shecaniah; he is apparently the same Hattush mentioned among the family heads who returned from the captivity (1 Chr. 3:22; Ezra 8:2; some scholars emend these texts on the basis of 1 Esd. 8:29 ["Hattush the son of Shecaniah"]).

(2) Son of Hashabneiah; he was one of the Israelites who helped repair the wall of Jerusalem under Nehemiah (Neh. 3:10).

(3) A priest who sealed the covenant with Nehemiah (Neh. 10:4); he is probably the same man listed among those who returned with Zerubbabel and Jeshua (12:2).

Hauran. haw´ruhn (Heb. *ḥawrān H2588*, derivation uncertain). A great plain situated on a plateau 2,000 ft. (610 m.) high E of the Jordan River and N of the land of Gilead. In ancient times it was called Bashan. Its soil is of volcanic origin and is very rich, making the region famous for its wheat crops. In the Bible, the name Hauran is mentioned only by Ezekiel in his description of the boundaries of the land of Israel in the millennial age (Ezek. 47:16, 18). The Israelites never had a very great hold on this area. Its openness to the E made it a frequent prey to robbers from the desert. Under the Romans, Herod ruled over it as part of his realm, and he greatly encouraged settlement by stopping the robber raids. It was then known as Auranitis. Christianity flourished there from the second century A.D. until the seventh century, when it was overthrown by the Muslims. Today Hauran is an integral part of Syria.

haven. see Fair Havens.

Havilah. hav´uh-luh (Heb. *ḥăwîlâ H2564*, "sandy"). (1) Son of Cush and grandson of Ham (Gen. 10:7; 1 Chr. 1:9). His name is probably related to the geographical area discussed in #3 below.

(2) Son of Joktan, grandson of Eber, and descendant of Shem (Gen. 10:29; 1 Chr. 1:23). His name is probably related to the geographical area discussed in #3 below.

(3) A land described as being bounded by one of the four rivers of the Garden of Eden, the Pishon, and as being rich in gold, resin, and onyx (Gen. 2:11-12). The region—or perhaps a different place bearing the same name—is mentioned with Shur (prob. in N Sinai) as one of the limits of the territory of the Amalekites (25:18) and Saul is said to have defeated the Amalekites in this area (1 Sam. 15:7, though it is widely thought that Havilah here is a textual corruption). The location of Havilah is disputed. Many scholars connect the name with Arabic *Ḥaulan*, which refers both to an area in SW Arabia (Yemen) and to an ancient tribal federation that still lives there. Some have even suggested that the individuals mentioned in ##1 and 2 above represent two branches of this Arabian tribe. Others prefer to locate Havilah in W or NW Arabia.

Havvoth Jair. hav´oth-jay´uhr (Heb. *ḥawwōt yāʾîr H2596*, "villages of Jair"). KJV Havoth-jair (Num. 32:41; Jdg. 10:4), Bashan-havoth-jair (Deut. 3:14); "towns of Jair" (1 Chr. 2:23). A group of thirty villages captured by Jair, a descendant of Manasseh (Num. 32:41; Jdg. 10:4; 1 Chr. 2:22-23). Jair captured both Gilead and Bashan, and this latter district evidently contained thirty more towns (Deut. 3:14; Josh. 13:30; 1 Ki. 4:13; 1 Chr. 2:23). The phrase Havvoth Jair applied only to the villages in Gilead. There are, however, alternate explanations for the differences among the texts.

hawk. See Birds.

hay. See Plants (under *grass*).

Hazael. hay′zay-uhl (Heb. _ḥăzā'ēl H2599_ [also _ḥāzāh'ēl_], "God has seen"). One of the most powerful of the kings of ARAM (SYRIA), ruling from c. 843 to c. 796 B.C. He is first mentioned in 1 Ki. 19:15-17, where ELIJAH at Mount Horeb was told by God that he would anoint Hazael king over Aram. At this time he was a high officer in the court of BEN-HADAD II, king of Aram (2 Ki. 8:7-9). Subsequently, he killed Ben-Hadad by smothering him with a wet cloth, and Hazael became king in his stead (8:10-15).

Soon after, Hazael fought against the combined forces of JEHORAM and AHAZIAH at RAMOTH GILEAD (2 Ki. 8:28-29; 9:14-15). He frequently defeated JEHU in battle, devastating all his country E of the Jordan from the ARNON Rive in the S to BASHAN in the N (10:32-33). During the reign of JEHOAHAZ, Jehu's successor, he repeatedly encroached upon the territory of Israel, which was kept from complete destruction only by God's mercy (13:3, 22-23). Hazael also moved into SW Palestine, taking GATH; he compelled the king of Judah to pay a heavy bribe for sparing JERUSALEM (12:17-18; 2 Chr. 24:23, 24). It was not until the death of Hazael that Israel was able successfully to check the aggression of Aram under Ben-hadad III, the son of Hazael (2 Ki. 13:24-25).

In the Black Obelisk from CALAH, SHALMANESER III records that in 842 B.C. he joined battle with Hazael. He claims that the Aramean king was defeated, losing 6,000 warriors, 1,121 chariots, and 470 horsemen. In another inscription Shalmaneser refers to Hazael as the "son of a nobody," and mentions that Hazael had "seized the throne" and rebelled against him. Among the spoils taken from Damascus by Assyria, and found by archaeologists at Arslan Tash (Hadathah), were an ivory inlay from the side of a bed, with the words engraved on it, "Bar Ama to our Lord Hazael in the year … ," and another ivory tablet, possibly a part of the same bed, showing in relief a god or king in Phoenician-Aramean style, which some scholars believe is actually a portrait of Hazael himself.

Hazaiah. huh-zay′yuh (Heb. _ḥăzāyâ H2610_, "Yahweh has seen"). Son of Adaiah, descendant of JUDAH through Shelah, and ancestor of Maaseiah; the latter was a provincial leader who settled in Jerusalem after the EXILE (Neh. 11:5).

Hazar Addar. hay′zuhr-ad′uhr (Heb. _ḥăṣar-'addār H2960_, "settlement of Addar"). A site marking the S border of CANAAN (Num. 34:4). It was apparently between KADESH BARNEA and AZMON, but the precise location is unknown. The most common identification is modern ʿAin Qedeis (c. 51 mi./82 km. SW of BEERSHEBA). The parallel passage (Josh. 15:3) is thought by some to break up the name Hazar Addar into two, HEZRON and ADDAR; others believe that Addar and Hazar Addar are identical and to be distinguished from Hezron.

Hazar Enan. hay′zuhr-ee′nuhn (Heb. _ḥăṣar ʿênān H2966_, "settlement of Enan" [in Ezekiel, _ḥăṣar ʿênôn_]). Also Hazar Enon. A site marking the ideal NE boundary of Israel (Num. 34:9-10), apparently between DAMASCUS and HAMATH (Ezek. 47:17; 48:1). Some scholars in the past identified it with the modern Hadr at the foot of Mount HERMON, not far from DAN (PLACE) and more than 30 mi. (48 km.) SW of Damascus, but now it is generally believed to be the same as Qaryatein, a full 70 mi. (113 km.) NE of Damascus. If the latter is correct, the envisioned territory of Israel would be almost twice as large as it was during most of its history.

Hazar Gaddah. hay′zuhr-gad′uh (Heb. _ḥăṣar gaddâ H2961_, "settlement of Gad"). Also Hazar-gaddah. A town in the NEGEV, the extreme S of the tribal territory of JUDAH (Josh. 15:27). It is mentioned between Moladah and Heshmon, but its precise location is unknown.

Hazar-hatticon. See HAZER HATTICON.

Hazarmaveth. hay′zuhr-may′vith (Heb. _ḥăṣar-māwet H2975_, "village of Maveth [death]"). Son of JOKTAN, grandson of EBER, and descendant of SHEM (Gen. 10:26; 1 Chr. 1:20). His name appears to be preserved in Arabic _Ḥaḍramaut_, applied to a S Arabian tribe and to a fruitful valley running parallel to the Arabian sea coast for about 200 mi. (320 km.). In the days of its greatest glory (5th cent. B.C. and 1st–2nd cent. A.D.) it was the home of a great civilization, with its capital at Shabwa. See also Sabta, Sabtah.

Hazar Shual. hay´zuhr-shoo´uhl (Heb. *ḥăṣar šûʿāl H2967*, "fox habitat"). A village in the Negev, lying within the tribal territory of Judah, but assigned to Simeon (Josh. 15:28; 19:3; 1 Chr. 4:28). It was resettled by the Israelites after the exile (Neh. 11:27). It is always mentioned in close relationship with Beersheba, but its precise location is unknown.

Hazar Susah, Hazar Susim. hay´zuhr-soo´suh, hay´zuhr-soo´sim (Heb. *ḥăṣar sûsâ H2963* [alternate pl. form, *ḥăṣar sûsîm H2964*], "mare farm, horse enclosure"). A city in the SW part of the tribal territory of Judah, but assigned to Simeon (Josh. 19:5; called "Hazar Susim" in 1 Chr. 4:31). Some scholars believe that the town was originally called Sansannah (listed in the parallel passage, Josh. 15:31), and that it was renamed because Solomon may have kept there the horses he brought from Egypt and sold to the Hittites and Syrians (1 Ki. 4:26; 9:19; 10:29). In any case, the location is unknown.

Hazazon Tamar. haz´uh-zon-tay´muhr (Heb. *ḥăṣĕṣôn tāmār H2954*, "gravel terrain of Tamar [date-palm]"). TNIV Hazezon Tamar. After Kedorlaomer and his allies defeated the Horites in Seir, "they turned back and went to En Mishpat (that is, Kadesh), and they conquered the whole territory of the Amalekites, as well as the Amorites who were living in Hazazon Tamar" (Gen. 14:7). This description, along with the subsequent narrative, suggests that Hazazon Tamar was located S or SW of the Dead Sea, and some scholars identify it with Tamar (1 Ki. 9:18; Ezek. 47:18-19; 48:28), which is generally thought to be modern ʿAin Ḥuṣb, c. 23 mi. (37 km.) SSW of the S tip of the Dead Sea. See discussion under Tamar (place). Elsewhere, however, Hazazon Tamar is identified with En Gedi (2 Chr. 20:2), which lies on the W shore of the Dead Sea, midpoint between the N and S tips. It seems unlikely, but not impossible, that Kedorlaomer fought the Amorites in En Gedi. Perhaps the name Hazazon Tamar was applied to more than one site distinguished by palm groves.

hazel. See Plants.

Hazelelponi. See Hazzelelponi.

Hazer Hatticon. hay´zuhr-hat´uh-kon (Heb. *ḥăṣēr hattîkôn H2962*, "settlement of Hatticon" or "middle court"). Also Hazar-hatticon; TNIV Hazer Hattikon. A place said to be on the border of Hauran and named among the boundaries of ideal Israel (Ezek. 47:16). It is generally thought to be a scribal error or a variant name for Hazar Enan.

Hazerim. huh-zihr´im. The KJV transliteration of Hebrew *ḥăṣērîm*, plural form of the common noun *ḥāṣēr H2958*, "village" (Deut. 2:23).

Hazeroth. huh-zihr´oth (Heb. *ḥăṣērôt H2972*, "settlements"). A camping station of the Israelites during their wilderness wanderings (Num. 11:35; 12:16; 33:17-18; Deut. 1:1). It was here that Aaron and Miriam quarreled with Moses regarding his marriage to a Cushite woman and his claim that God spoke only through him (Num. 12:1-15). Hazeroth is generally identified with ʿAin Khadra (Ḥudrat), some 30 mi. (48 km.) NE of Jebel Musa (see Sinai), on the way to Aqabah.

Hazezon Tamar. haz´uh-zon-tay´muhr. TNIV form of Hazazon Tamar.

Haziel. hay´zee-uhl (Heb. *ḥăzîʾēl H2609*, possibly "God has seen" or "vision of God"). Son of Shimei and a Levite descended from Gershon (1 Chr. 23:9). The text is difficult and emendations have been proposed.

Hazo. hay´zoh (Heb. *ḥăzô H2605*, derivation uncertain). Son of Nahor by his wife Milcah; nephew of Abraham (Gen. 22:22). The passage as a whole seems to indicate the origins of a dozen Aramean tribes, and the name Hazo is usually associated with Assyrian *Ḥazu* (mentioned in an inscription of Esarhaddon), referring to a mountainous region in N Arabia.

Hazor. hay´zor (Heb. *ḥāṣôr H2937*, "enclosure"). (1) One of the southernmost towns within the tribal territory of Judah (Josh. 15:23). It was

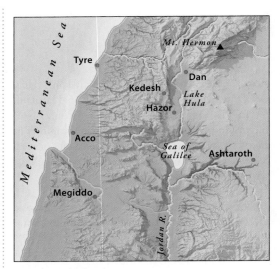

Hazor in Naphtali.

situated in the NEGEV, near the country of EDOM (v. 21), but its precise location is unknown. See also HAZOR HADATTAH.

(2) An alternate name for KERIOTH HEZRON, also included in the list of the southernmost towns of Judah (Josh. 15:25).

(3) A town within the tribal territory of BENJAMIN listed among the places settled by those who returned from the EXILE (Neh. 11:33). Its location is uncertain, though some have identified it

with Khirbet Hazzur (some 3 mi./5 km. NW of JERUSALEM).

(4) An otherwise unknown group of desert settlements against which JEREMIAH prophesied (Jer. 49:28-33). The oracle speaks of "the kingdoms of Hazor" and associates them with KEDAR (a N Arabian tribe). Although some have thought Hazor was an Arab settlement in S Palestine, most scholars believe that the name referred to associated villages inhabited by semi-nomadic peoples in W or NW ARABIA (and Kedar may have been one of the kingdoms in the league).

(5) A large and important city in N Palestine, within the tribal territory of NAPHTALI. When the Israelites entered Palestine, the land was a conglomeration of little city-states or kingdoms, and of various groups united by tribal ties (for the former, see Josh. 11:1; and for the latter, 11:3). This Hazor was reckoned as "the head of all those kingdoms" in Joshua's day, and its king, JABIN, led them against Joshua, who almost annihilated them. Nearly two centuries later, another Jabin (Jdg. 4) reigning at Hazor was reckoned as king of Canaan, but God used DEBORAH and BARAK to subdue and destroy him. Hazor, having a strategic location in the hills about 5 mi. (8 km.) W of the waters of MEROM, was fortified by SOLOMON (1 Ki. 9:15). Its Israelite inhabitants were carried away into captivity

At the height of its power, Hazor in Naphtali was the largest city of ancient Israel. (View to the E.)

H

© Dr. James C. Martin

(2 Ki. 15:29) in Assyria by Tiglath-Pileser about the middle of the eighth century B.C. The site, modern Tell el-Qedah, is located some 10 mi. (16 km.) N of the Sea of Galilee, and is 200 acres in its full extent (upper and lower areas). Hazor was the largest city ever built in Palestine during the biblical period, accommodating up to 40,000 inhabitants. It was dug first by archaeologist J. Garstang in 1928 and more extensively by Y. Yadin in 1955-58, 1968-70. Yadin discovered twenty-two strata of occupation including what he believed to be clear evidence of Joshua's destruction. A unique water tunnel was found, along with city gates similar to those at Gezer and Megiddo, dating to the time of Solomon (though some date them slightly later).

Hazor Hadattah. hay´zor-huh-dat´uh (Heb. *ḥā-ṣôr ḥădattâ H2939*, "New Hazor [enclosure]"). Also Hazor-haddattah. One of the southernmost towns within the tribal territory of Judah (Josh. 15:25; KJV reads two names, "Hazor, Haddattah"). Several towns in the Negev bore the name Hazor, but their precise locations are unknown. The second component of the name Hazor Hadattah is the Aramaic word for "new" (cf. Heb. Hadashah), which seems unusual. Some have speculated that the town was settled by residents of Hazor in Naphtali who had closer contact with Aramaic-speaking populations.

Hazzelelponi. haz´uh-lel-poh´ni (Heb. *haṣṣělelpônî H2209*, perhaps "shade my face"). KJV Hazelelponi. Daughter of Etam, included in the genealogy of Judah (1 Chr. 4:3). The name is highly unusual, however, and various emendations have been proposed (e.g., some have thought that the names of two different daughters have been merged, or that the name was simply Hazlel).

Hazzobebah. haz´oh-bee´buh (Heb. *haṣṣōbēbâ H2206*, meaning uncertain). Son of Koz, included in the genealogy of Judah (1 Chr. 4:8). The first syllable of the name appears to be the Hebrew definite article, and thus the NRSV and other versions render, "Zobebah." It may be the name of a clan.

he (letter). hay (Heb. *hē*ʾ, meaning uncertain). The fifth letter in the Hebrew alphabet (ה), with

a numerical value of five. Its sound corresponds to that of English *h* (but it is usually silent at the end of a word, where it serves to represent vowel sounds).

head. Both the brain case and the face are included in the head, considered to be the seat of life or the soul, although the Jews regarded the heart as the seat of the intellect, and often used "head" (Heb. *rōʾš H8031*) to stand for the whole person (Acts 18:6, Gk. *kephalē G3051*). The word applies to animals, such as the bull's head of the burnt offering (Lev. 1:4), and to inanimate objects in phrases like, "Lift up your heads, O you gates" (Ps. 24:7), the four heads of rivers (Gen. 2:10), and the head stone (Zech. 4:7, a concept also applied to Christ, Matt. 21:42; see cornerstone).

Injury to the head was a chief form of defeating an enemy (Ps. 68:21). Decapitation, a custom likewise practiced in Assyria and Babylonia, added insult to injury (1 Sam. 17:51). On the other hand, anointing the head was a symbol of joy and prosperity (Ps. 23:5; Heb. 1:9), and dedication to priestly service (Exod. 29:7). Leaders are heads (Isa. 9:15). Christ is the head of the church (which is his body) and of all creation (Eph. 1:22), every human being (1 Cor. 11:3), and all rule and authority (Col. 2:10). The husband is the head of the woman. Because of the Greek custom of veiling of women, as opposed to the Jewish practice, Paul urged the Corinthian women to be obedient to the local standards of decency and order, and to cover the head in worship. Men, however, pray with uncovered heads. See covering the head.

headband, headdress. See dress.

headstone. See cornerstone.

healing, health. See disease; gifts, spiritual.

heap of stones. The act of raising a heap of stones could be a symbol and reminder of a shameful act. After Achan and his family were stoned and burned, a pile of stones was heaped over their slain bodies (Josh. 7:26; cf. 8:29; 2 Sam. 18:17). A heap of stones could also symbolize a covenant made between two persons, as in the case of Jacob

H

and LABAN at MIZPAH (Gen. 31:46-52; see GAL-EED). Finally, piles of stones could indicate God's judgment upon a sinful city or family (Job 15:28; Isa. 37:26; Jer. 9:11; Hos. 12:11).

heart. Aside from some literal references to the physical organ, the term *heart* in the Bible (Heb. *lēb H4213* and *lēbāb H4222*; Gk. *kardia G2840*) usually refers to the "inner person," or the seat of mental functions (where one remembers, thinks), or the seat and center of all physical and spiritual life—the SOUL or MIND as the fountain of thoughts, passions, desires, affections, appetites, purposes, endeavors. The Hebrew terms occur almost 800 times in the OT; the Greek term occurs almost 150 times in the NT.

In ancient times, as today, different parts of the body were used figuratively as the seat of different functions of the soul; and the ancient usage often differs from the modern. In expressing sympathy, we might say, "This touches my heart," where the ancients might say, "My bowels were moved for him" (Cant. 5:4 KJV; cf. Ps. 7:9 in KJV ["the righteous God trieth the hearts and reins"] with NIV ["…who searches minds and hearts"]). This reflects a difference in common figurative usage; it is not a question of truth and error in ancient or modern psychology. The NT was written mostly by Jews and so is colored by Hebrew thinking and usage; for example, "they do always err in their heart" (Heb. 3:10 KJV) may mean that they are wrong in both their thinking and their affections. Often the word *heart* implies the whole moral nature of fallen humanity (e.g., "The heart is deceitful above all things, and beyond cure," Jer. 17:9; cf. 17:10).

hearth. In ancient times homes were heated very differently from the way they are today. In the houses of the poorer people the hearth consisted of a depression in the floor of a room in which a fire was kindled for cooking or for warmth. Chimneys were unknown; smoke escaped from the house as it could, or through a latticed opening for the purpose. The better houses were heated by means of a brazier of burning coals. The brazier was a wide, shallow pan that could also be used for cooking. (See Gen. 18:6; Ps. 102:3; Isa. 30:14; Jer. 36:22-23; Hos. 13:3; Zech. 12:6.)

heat and cold. See PALESTINE (under *climate*).

heath. See PLANTS.

heathen. This term is frequently used by the KJV to render Hebrew and Greek words that more properly mean "nation(s)" (Lev. 25:44 et al.; Acts 4:25 et al.), although many contexts do indicate the sense of "pagan, one who does not acknowledge the true God" (e.g., Matt. 6:7). See GENTILE.

heaven. (1) Cosmologically, one of the two great divisions of the universe, the earth and the heavens (Gen. 1:1; 14:19). In the visible heavens are the stars and planets (Gen. 1:14-17; Ezek. 32:7-8). Later Jews divided the heavens into seven strata, but there is no evidence for this in the Bible, though Paul spoke of being caught up into the third heaven (2 Cor. 12:2). The term "heaven of heavens" (Deut. 10:14; 1 Ki. 8:27; Ps. 148:4) is "highest heavens" in NIV.

(2) The abode of God (Gen. 28:17; Ps. 80:14; Isa. 66:1; Matt. 5:12) and of the good angels (Matt. 24:36). It is the place where the redeemed will someday be (Matt. 5:12; 6:20; Eph. 3:15), where the Redeemer has gone and intercedes for the saints, and from where he will someday come for his own (1 Thess. 4:16).

(3) The inhabitants of heaven (Lk. 15:18; Rev. 18:20).

Heaven, Queen of. See QUEEN OF HEAVEN.

heavenly. That which relates to HEAVEN. The relevant Greek adjectives (*ouranios G4039*, *epouranion G2230*) are used with reference to spiritual truths and to the divine and eternal realm. The meaning is best understood in context. Jesus contrasted "the earthly things," concerning the rebirth of men on earth, with "the heavenly things," concerning the revelation of his divine person from heaven (Jn. 3:12). In the book of HEBREWS, the TABERNACLE is characterized as a copy and shadow of the "heavenly" sanctuary (Heb. 8:5): it contains "heavenly things," which are purified by the high priestly offering of Christ (9:23). "Heavenly" here should be associated directly with "heaven itself" and "the presence of God" (9:24).

H

PAUL used the phrase in three distinguishable senses. (a) The sphere of thought is *futurist eschatology* in 1 Cor. 15, where the glorious nature of the RESURRECTION bodies of believers is seen in analogy to the heavenly bodies of the stars (vv. 40, 48-49). (b) In EPHESIANS the context is that of *"realized" eschatology:* by virtue of a present or "realized" union with Christ, the believer is the recipient of spiritual blessings "in the heavenly realms" (Eph. 1:3, 20; 2:6; 3:10; 6:12. (c) Finally, the simple idea of *locale* is present in Paul's reference to heaven (Phil. 2:10) and Christ's heavenly kingdom (2 Tim. 4:18).

heavens, new. The expression "new heaven(s) and a new earth" is a technical term in the eschatological language of the Bible to define and describe the final, perfected state of the created universe. See ESCHATOLOGY. The conception of a re-created universe has its origin in the biblical account of CREATION (Gen. 1:1, where the phrase "the heavens and the earth" is meant to embrace the whole of the created universe). "Heavens" in the primitive worldview was meant to describe all that is above the earth—the sky with its heavenly bodies—and therefore should be distinguished from HEAVEN as the dwelling place of God that is outside the realm of the created universe. The promise of a re-creation of the heavens and the earth arises not out of some inherent lack or evil in the material universe, but because of human sin and God's subsequent curse (3:17). The idea of a renewed or re-created universe is present in substance in many passages: Isa. 51:16; Matt. 19:28; 24:29-31, 35; Mk. 13:24-27, 31; Rom. 8:19-23; 2 Cor. 5:17; Heb. 12:26-28. Specific mention of "new heaven(s) and a new earth" is found in Isa. 65:17; 66:22; 2 Pet. 3:13; Rev. 21:1.

heave offering. See SACRIFICE AND OFFERINGS.

Heber. hee′buhr (Heb. *ḥeber H2491*, "associate, companion"; gentilic *ḥebrî H2499*, "Heberite"). **(1)** Son of Beriah, grandson of ASHER, and eponymous ancestor of the Heberite clan (Gen. 46:17; Num. 26:45; 1 Chr. 7:31-32).

(2) A KENITE who separated himself for a time from the main body of Kenites and settled near KEDESH, W of the Sea of Galilee (Jdg. 4:11). Heber's clan established friendly associations with JABIN king of HAZOR, who was an enemy of Israel. The king's commander, SISERA, having been defeated by BARAK, fled for refuge to Heber's settlement. Sisera went into the tent of JAEL, Heber's wife (4:17). Jael, however, betraying the alliance between Jabin and her husband, took this opportunity to kill Sisera (4:18-22; 5:24-27).

(3) Son of MERED, "father" (i.e., "ruler/founder") of SOCO, and descendant of JUDAH, although his precise genealogical connection is unclear (1 Chr. 4:18).

(4) Son of ELPAAL and descendant of BENJAMIN (1 Chr. 8:17).

(5) KJV alternate form of EBER (1 Chr. 5:13; 8:22; Lk. 3:35).

Hebrew language. With the exception of ARAMAIC in a few passages (Ezra 4:8—6:18; 7:12-26; Dan. 2:4—7:28; Jer. 10:11), Hebrew is the language of the OT. The term *Hebrew* was first used as a designation for individuals or a people and only later denoted a language. See HEBREW PEOPLE. The OT refers to the language not as "Hebrew" but as "the language of Canaan" (Isa. 19:18) or "the Jews' language" (2 Ki. 18:26 et al. KJV). With close affinity to Ugaritic, Phoenician, Moabite, and other Canaanite dialects, Hebrew is usually placed in the NW branch of the Semitic language family. Other related languages include Arabic, Akkadian, and especially Aramaic. With few exceptions, extant texts of ancient Hebrew are those of the OT and certain of the APOCRYPHA and PSEUDEPIGRAPHA. Inscriptions employing the

Contemporary display of the Ten Commandments in the paleo-Hebrew script.

language include the SILOAM Inscription from the eighth century B.C. and the Gezer Calendar from the tenth century.

In large measure, OT Hebrew is self-explanatory. However, the Ugaritic tablets from RAS SHAMRA shed much light on the meaning of the Hebrew Bible, and since the structure and vocabulary were so very similar in the various Semitic tongues, much cognate language help is available for the understanding of the language of the Israelites. The Greek translation of the OT, the SEPTUAGINT, is also of much value in interpretative study of biblical Hebrew.

Though Aramaic is itself a very ancient language, so that the presence of "Aramaisms" in the OT may indicate an early rather than a late date for the passages in which they occur, from the time of the EXILE onward Hebrew was spoken less and less and correspondingly the use of Aramaic flourished. Some of the DEAD SEA SCROLLS were written in Hebrew, which was also the vehicle for the writing of such Jewish religious literature as the Mishnah and the Midrashim in the early centuries of our era. The language was used in medieval times for biblical commentaries and philosophical and literary works. In modern Israel, Hebrew has again become a living tongue.

The historical origins of the language are somewhat obscure but go back beyond 2000 B.C. The OT literature, written over a period of more than a thousand years, reveals a minimum of stylistic changes, though loanwords and new ways of expression became more or less noticeable with the passing of years, especially after the exile. It is also true that at a given time dialectal differences existed, a fact attested by the narrative in Jdg. 12, in which Ephraimites were unable to pronounce the "sh" of their neighbors to the south.

With its short sentences and simple coordinating conjunctions, ancient Hebrew lent itself well to the vivid expression of events. These features, together with parallelism and rhythm and special meanings and constructions, made Hebrew poetry, as found in the Psalms and to a large extent in the Prophets, most expressive and strikingly effective.

Hebrew of Hebrews. A phrase used by PAUL to describe himself (Phil. 3:5). The apostle, defending his integrity and recounting his pedigree for the benefit of his readers, claims that he was of pure Hebrew stock and had retained the language and traditions of his ancestors, unlike some Jews who had adopted GREEK language and customs.

Hebrew people. Members of the nation of ISRAEL (see also JEW). The term ʿibrî H6303 has traditionally been derived from EBER (ʿēber H6299), the grandson of SHEM and ancestor of ABRAHAM (Gen. 10:24; 11:16). Others have derived the term directly from the verb ʿābar H6296, "to pass, cross over, go beyond"; thus a Hebrew would be "one from the other side," that is, beyond the JORDAN (cf. Josh. 1:2 et al.) or beyond the EUPHRATES. Jews quite uniformly have used "Israel" and "the children of Israel" (later "Jews") in referring to themselves, finding in such terminology treasured religious and national associations. Foreigners thought of them as "Hebrews" (Exod. 1:16; 2:6), and they so identified themselves in speaking to non-Jews (Gen. 40:15; Exod. 10:3; Jon. 1:9). Also, in contexts involving contrasts between Israelites and people of other nations, the same phenomenon appears (Gen. 43:32; Exod. 1:15; 2:11; 1 Sam. 13:3; 14:21).

Since the discovery of the AMARNA tablets, an effort was made to identify the nationality of the HABIRU mentioned in these documents. Some have argued that this term is not the name of a people but that it indicates wandering peoples greatly restricted as regards financial means and without citizenship and social status. Ancient records show the Habiru to be scattered over W Asia for centuries until about 1100 B.C. Nomadic peoples, mostly Semitic—sometimes raiders, sometimes skilled artisans—they frequently offered themselves as mercenaries and slaves, with individuals occasionally rising to prominence. In EGYPT, the Israelites were reduced to a lowly position and later moved about in the wilderness. Using the etymology mentioned above, some have suggested that the Hebrews were "those who crossed over" in the sense of trespassing, thus, "trespassers."

In the NT, the name Hebrews serves to differentiate between the Greeks and Hellenistic culture on the one hand and Jews and their traditional life and speech on the other (Acts 6:1). Most NT references to the "Hebrew" language in the KJV (Jn.

Overview of HEBREWS

Author: Anonymous (some parts of the early church attributed it to PAUL; suggestions include BARNABAS, APOLLOS, and others).

Historical setting: Addressed to Hebrew Christians (possibly living in or near ROME) who were suffering persecution and who were tempted to return to JUDAISM, thus abandoning the uniqueness of CHRIST and his priestly ministry. The letter was probably written shortly before A.D. 70, but some date it later.

Purpose: To prevent the apostasy of the readers by establishing the superiority of Christ over the old covenant.

Contents: The superiority of Christ over the angels (Heb. 1-2), over MOSES and JOSHUA (chs. 3-4), and over the Aaronic priesthood (chs. 5-7); the obsolescence of the old covenant (chs. 8:1—10:18); perseverance in faith (10:19—12:29); various exhortations and greetings (ch. 13).

5:2 et al.) probably refer to ARAMAIC, that is, the language normally spoken by the Hebrew people at the time (but in Rev. 9:11 and 16:16 the reference is to Hebrew proper).

Hebrews, Letter to the. The longest of the non-Pauline letters in the NT. Traditionally it follows the thirteen letters attributed to PAUL, although the order varies among the MSS (in the great uncials it comes between Paul's nine letters to churches and his four to individuals).

I. Authorship. The writer of Hebrews did not attach his name to the letter, and thus there has been much discussion since the second century as to who wrote this document. Early Christians held various opinions. Those on the eastern shore of the MEDITERRANEAN and around ALEXANDRIA associated the book with Paul. Origen (A.D. 185-254) held that the thoughts of the book were Paul's, but the language and composition were someone else's. In N Africa, Tertullian (155-225) thought that BARNABAS was the author. Although the letter was apparently first known in ROME and (*1 Clement*, dated around 95, cites Hebrews frequently), for 200 years Christians in Rome and the West were unanimous in their opinion that Paul did not write Hebrews. These early Christians did not say who wrote it.

Present-day Christians should hardly be dogmatic about an issue that from the very beginning of the church has been surrounded with uncertainty. A careful study of the letter in the Greek text discloses some important things about the author. (1) The letter has a polished Greek style, like that of a master rhetorician. The continuous use of this style is unlike Paul's. (2) The vocabulary, figures of speech, and manner of argument show an Alexandrian and Philonic influence (see PHILO). Paul, having come from TARSUS and having been educated in JERUSALEM, did not have such a background. (3) Both Paul and the writer of Hebrews quote the OT frequently. But the way they introduce their quotations is quite different. Paul's formulas—"just as it has been written" (nineteen times), "it has been written" (ten times), "the Scripture says" (six times), "the Scripture proclaims good tidings beforehand" (one time)—never occur in Hebrews. Paul's manner of introducing quotations puts the reader's attention on the content quoted. The writer of Hebrews, as an orator, puts the stress on the one who speaks. For him the Father, Christ, or the Holy Spirit is speaking.

Many present-day scholars favor APOLLOS as the possible writer of Hebrews. He was a Jew, born in Alexandria, a learned and cultured man, well-versed in the Scriptures (Acts 18:24). Being orally taught the way of the Lord, Apollos was teaching about Jesus even when he knew only the baptism of JOHN THE BAPTIST (18:25). He was a man of enthusiasm. PRISCILLA and AQUILA, Paul's friends, led Apollos to a fuller knowledge of Christ (18:26). After he received this knowledge, he was a man of courage. He left EPHESUS for ACHAIA to help the believers there (18:27). He consistently used the Scriptures in his public preaching (18:25). Paul testifies to Apollos's capability in 1 Cor. 1-4. Perhaps his polished rhetorical style was a contributing cause to the Apollos party that was found in CORINTH (1 Cor. 3:4-6). Apollos's modesty and desire to avoid friction are seen in 1 Cor. 16:12. He was still an active coworker of Paul late in Paul's ministry (see Tit. 3:13). In Apollos one can explain all of Hebrews' similarities with Paul as well as the distinct differences from Paul.

II. Original readers. As far as we can determine, the letter was first known in Rome and the West. Its first readers were Jewish Christians who spoke and wrote Greek. The brief statement "Those from Italy send you their greetings" (Heb. 13:24) certainly favors the readers' being located in Italy. If the writer had been in Italy, he would have named the precise place. A letter from any city in the United States would not say, "Those from the United States send greetings"; but if the letter came from an interior city of India or Brazil where Americans were present, such a greeting would be appropriate. Hence, it appears there were Italian Christians with the writer somewhere outside of Italy as he penned this letter. The writer knows the readers well. He refers to their spiritual dullness (5:11-14), their faithful ministering to the saints (6:9-10), and their experiences after their conversion (10:32-36). Their first leaders seem to have died (13:7), while their present leaders are continually engaged in the task of watching over the flock (13:17). To these the writer sends greetings (13:24).

Although we cannot be absolutely certain, it seems best to regard the original readers as being located somewhere in Italy. Many roads led to Rome. These believers may have been in one of the cities nearer or farther from the capital. Paul himself spent seven days with the brothers in PUTEOLI (Acts 28:13-14). They could have been in Rome or its suburbs. As the writer pens this letter, TIMOTHY has departed from him and is absent)—very likely on some tour of churches. As soon as he appears (or if he comes soon), the writer and Timothy together will visit the readers (Heb. 13:23).

III. Outline and summary of content—An outline shows the centrality of Jesus Christ in the Book of Hebrews.

A. *Prologue: course and climax of divine revelation* (Heb. 1:1-3)
B. *Preeminence of Christ himself* (1:4—4:13)
  1. Superiority of Christ to angels (1:4-14)
  2. Warning: peril of indifference to these truths (2:1-4)
  3. Reason Christ became human (2:5-18)
  4. Christ's position is greater than that of Moses (3:1-6)
  5. Warning: unbelief brings temporal and eternal effects (3:7—4:13)
C. *Priesthood of Jesus Christ* (4:14—10:18)
  1. Importance of his priesthood for the believer's conduct (4:14-16)
  2. Qualifications of a high priest (5:1-10)
  3. Warning: immaturity and apostasy are conquered only by faith, longsuffering, and hope (5:11—6:20a)
  4. Melchizedek's eternal successor (6:20b—7:28)
  5. Heavenly sanctuary and new covenant (8:1-13)
  6. Priestly service under the old covenant and the new (9:1-28)
  7. Inadequacy of the sacrifices under the law contrasted with the efficacy and finality of Christ's sacrifice (10:1-18)
D. *Perseverance of Christians* (10:19—12:29)
  1. Attitudes to be sought and attitudes to be shunned (10:19-39)
  2. Faith in action—illustrious examples from the past (11:1-40)
  3. Incentives for action in the present scene and in the future goal (12:1-29)
E. *Postscript: exhortations, personal concerns, benediction* (13:1-25)

Although God spoke to the fathers by the prophets, he has now spoken by his Son. In the prologue we see the distinctiveness of the Son.

He is before history, in history, above history, the goal of history, and the agent who brings about a cleansing of people from sins committed in history. He shares the essence of Deity and radiates the glory of Deity. He is the supreme revelation of God (Heb. 1:1-3).

The writer's first main task is to make clear the preeminence of Christ (Heb. 1:4—4:13). He is superior to ANGELS. They assist those who will be heirs of salvation. Christ, by virtue of who he is, of God's appointment, and of what he has done, stands exalted far above them. It would be tragic to be careless of the great salvation that he proclaimed. He will achieve the promise that all things will be in harmonious subjection to man. He can do this because he is fully man and has provided the expiation for sins. He is superior to MOSES, for Moses was a servant among the people of God, while Christ is a Son over the people of God. It would be tragic to cease trusting him. Unbelief kept one entire generation of Israelites from Canaan. Christians are warned of such unbelief. FAITH is emphasized as well as zeal to enter into the eternal rest of God. Both the GOSPEL of God and God himself scrutinize people.

The second major emphasis in the letter falls on the priesthood of Christ (Heb. 4:14—10:18). Qualifications, conditions, and experiences of the Aaronic priesthood are listed in comparison to Christ as a priest. Before further developing this theme, the writer warns his readers of their unpreparedness for advanced teaching. Only earnest diligence in the things of God will bring them out of immaturity. Christ as a priest, like MELCHIZEDEK, is superior to the Levitical priesthood because his life is indestructible. He is both priest and sacrifice. His priesthood is eternal. His sanctuary is in heaven and his blood establishes the validity of the new covenant, which is also an eternal covenant. His one offering on behalf of sins is final—it is for all time. Likewise he has made perfect for all time those who are in the process of being sanctified.

The last main section of Hebrews deals with the response of Christians (10:19—12:29). Perseverance on the part of Christians springs out of fellowship with God, activity for God, faith in God, and a consciousness of what lies ahead. Then, in concluding the letter, the writer puts stress on the CROSS as the Christian altar and the resurrection of the Shepherd of the sheep as the basis for God's action. Such redemptive-historical events move the believer to action (13:1-25).

IV. Teaching. Much is said about Christ. He is fully God and fully man. He is active in CREATION. The ATONEMENT of Christ, as both priest and sacrificial victim, is developed in detail. In the role of a priest, he is a leader and guide. He also is the revealer of God. Great depth is achieved in all of these teachings about Christ's person and work. The HOLY SPIRIT is mentioned only seven times—three times in reference to the inspiration of the OT, once in regard to the work of Christ, once in regard to the apostate's rejection of Christianity, and twice in regard to the believer. The old and new COVENANTS are compared and reasons for the superiority of the new or eternal covenant are given.

The doctrine of SIN in Hebrews focuses attention on unbelief and the failure to go on with God to the eternal city. Shadow and reality are carefully contrasted. Heaven is the scene of reality. Earth is concerned with both shadow and reality. Christ is the bridge between the temporary and the eternal. The people of God are looked on as migrating from a transitory setting to an abiding city. This migration involves God's Word; the matter of testing, discipline, or punishment; faithfulness; and God's activity in sanctifying or making holy. The Christian life is developed in the framework of this heavenly pilgrimage. ESCHATOLOGY or last things involves the obtaining of eternal rest, a final shaking of heaven and earth, the personal return of Christ, and glory belonging to God for ever and ever.

Hebron (person). hee´bruhn (Heb. *ḥebrôn H2497*, "associate, companion"; gentilic *ḥebrônî H2498*, "Hebronite"). **(1)** Son of KOHATH, grandson of LEVI, and uncle of MOSES (Exod. 6:18; Num. 3:19, 27; 1 Chr. 6:2, 18; 15:9; 23:12, 19; 24:23); eponymous ancestor of the Hebronite Levitical clan, which played an important role during the time of DAVID (Num. 3:27; 26:58; 1 Chr. 26:23, 30-31).

(2) Son of MARESHAH and great-grandson of CALEB (1 Chr. 2:42-43). The Hebrew text is difficult and variously emended. According to

H

the SEPTUAGINT, Mareshah (not Mesha) was the firstborn of Caleb, in which case Hebron would be Caleb's grandson; according to other reconstructions, Hebron is removed from Caleb by several generations. There may be a connection between Hebron son of Mareshah and HEBRON (PLACE).

Hebron (place). hee´bruhn (Heb. *ḥebrôn H2496*, "association"). A city located about 20 mi. (32 km.) SSW of JERUSALEM on the main road to BEERSHEBA. Hebron has one of the longest records of continuous occupation. Though lying in a shallow valley, it is about 3,000 ft. (915 m.) above sea level and 4,300 ft. (1,310 m.) above the DEAD SEA, which lies a few miles E of Hebron. The hills about the city still bear choice grapes, and the Jewish people there make a fine wine. The Valley of ESHCOL, from which the spies brought an immense cluster of grapes (Num. 13:22-24), runs quite near Hebron. The town's original name was KIRIATH ARBA (Josh. 14:15; 15:13).

Hebron is replete with historical interest. It was a camping place for Abram (ABRAHAM); here he moved his tent and lived by the "great trees of Mamre" (Gen. 13:18, mistranslated in KJV as "the plain of Mamre"). MAMRE was close to Hebron, and here Abram built an altar to the Lord. The only land that Abram owned, though God had promised him Canaan (15:18-21), was the field

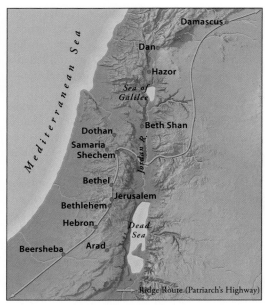

Hebron.

of MACHPELAH near Mamre, which he purchased from the HITTITES as a burial place for SARAH (Gen. 23:17-20; Heb. 11:8-10). In this cave Sarah and Abraham, later ISAAC and REBEKAH, then JACOB and LEAH, were buried. At the partition of Canaan after the partial conquest, Hebron and its environs were given to CALEB to conquer (Josh. 14:6-15), and he did so (15:14-19); but later the

The region of Hebron looking to the W.

© Dr. James C. Martin

city itself was given to the Kohathite Levites (1 Chr. 6:55-56), though Caleb's descendants kept the suburban fields and villages. When David was king over Judah, but not yet over all Israel, his capital city was Hebron for seven and a half years. There the elders of Israel anointed him king over all Israel (2 Sam. 5:3-5). Later he moved the capital to Jerusalem. When Absalom rebelled against his father, he made Hebron his headquarters and there prepared his coup d'état (2 Sam. 15:7-12). (With regard to Josh. 19:28 KJV, see Ebron.)

hedge. This noun is used by the NIV twice, in both cases with reference to thorn shrubs (Isa. 5:5; Mic. 7:4). Verbal expressions are used figuratively to refer to God's protecting care (Job 1:10) or his constraint (3:23). The KJV uses the noun in other passages, mainly in figurative contexts (e.g., Ps. 80:12; Ezek. 13:5).

hedgehog. See Animals (under *bittern*).

heel. The Hebrew word *ʿāqēb H6811* is twice used in a literal sense of Esau's heel, which Jacob grasped while still in the womb of Rebekah (Gen. 25:26; Hos. 12:3). Elsewhere, the term *heel* is use in a figurative sense. In the protevangelium (Gen. 3:15), God said that the seed of the woman would bruise the serpent's head, but the serpent would bruise his heel—clearly a reference to the conflict between Satan and the Son of God and the utter defeat Christ would administer to the foe responsible for his crucifixion at Calvary (cf. 49:17, 19; Job 18:9). The psalmist laments that the bosom friend whom he trusted and who dined at his table lifted his heel against him, that is, spurned him with brutal violence or perhaps kicked him when he was down (Ps. 41:9). Jesus referred to this statement at the Last Passover and applied it to himself; the bosom friend who ate with him and then betrayed him was Judas Iscariot (Jn. 13:18).

Hegai. heg′i (Heb. *hēgēʾ H2043* and *hēgay H2051*, derivation uncertain). Eunuch of King Xerxes in charge of the harem; he was entrusted with the women from whom the king intended to choose a queen to replace Vashti (Esth. 2:3 [KJV, "Hege"], 8, 15). Esther quickly won Hegai's favor, and he

provided her with special treatment (v. 9). Another part of the harem was the responsibility of Shaasgaz (v. 14).

Hege. See Hegai.

Heglam. heg′luhm (Heb. *heglām*, from *gālâ H1655*, hiphil "to take into exile"). Son of Ehud and father of Uzza and Ahihud (1 Chr. 8:7 NRSV). The passage is difficult, however, and it is possible that a person named Heglam did not exist. The Hebrew text rendered by the NRSV as "Gera, that is, Heglam" can be rendered "Gera, who deported them" (so NIV; cf. KJV).

heifer. See Animals.

heifer, red. See Red Heifer.

heir. See Inheritance.

Helah. hee′luh (Heb. *ḥelʾāh H2690*, "necklace"). One of the two wives of Ashhur (apparently founder of the town of Tekoa), who is included in the genealogy of Judah; she had four children (1 Chr. 4:5, 7).

Helam. hee′luhm (Heb. *ḥēlām H2663*, meaning unknown). A town in Transjordan to which the Arameans under Hadadezer retreated after Joab initially routed them; there they were subsequently defeated by David (2 Sam. 10:16-17). Some identify Helam with Alema (1 Macc. 5:26), which is modern ʿAlma in Hauran, c. 50 mi. (80 km.) S of Damascus and c. 35 mi. (56 km.) E of the Sea of Galilee.

Helbah. hel′buh (Heb. *ḥelbâ H2695*, possibly "forest" or "fruitful"). A town in the tribal territory of Asher from which Israel could not expel the Canaanites (Jdg. 1:31). Similarity in the consonants and location leads many scholars to identify Helbah with Ahlab (1:31) and Mahalab (Josh. 19:29) at modern Khirbet el-Maḥalib, 4 mi. (6 km.) NE of Tyre on the coast.

Helbon. hel′bon (Heb. *ḥelbôn H2696*, possibly "forest" or "fruitful"). A city or region mentioned

H

by Ezekiel in his lamentation over Tyre (Ezek. 27:18). From Helbon wine was imported to Tyre by traders of Damascus. It is probably to be identified with the Valley of Halbun, some 12 mi. (19 km.) N of Damascus. The area has been famous from ancient times for its fine wines, preferred even by kings.

Heldai. hel′d*i* (Heb. *ḥelday H2702*, possibly "mole"). **(1)** A descendant of Othniel from the town of Netophah who served as captain of the temple guard for the twelfth monthly course (1 Chr. 27:15). He is probably the same as Heled.

(2) One of a group of Jewish exiles who brought gold and silver from Babylon to help those who had returned under Zerubbabel; from these gifts a crown was to be made for Joshua (Jeshua) the high priest (Zech. 6:10; in v. 14 the MT has *ḥelem* [cf. KJV, "Helem"], apparently a scribal error or an alternate name for Heldai).

Heleb. See Heled.

Helech. hee′lik (Heb. *ḥelēk H2662*). TNIV Helek. A city or region that, along with Arvad (a Phoenician island town), supplied sailors and soldiers for Tyre (Ezek. 27:11). Although several identifications have been suggested, perhaps the least objectionable proposal is to equate Helech with Assyrian *Ḥilakku*, that is, Cilicia, in SE Asia Minor. The Septuagint and the KJV ("thine army") interpret the Hebrew word not as a name but as the common noun *ḥayil H2657* with suffix (2nd person fem. sing.). This view is preferred by some scholars.

Heled. hee′lid (Heb. *ḥeled H2699*, possibly "mold"; in 2 Sam. 23:29, most Heb. MSS have *ḥeleb*, possibly "fruitful"). Son of Baanah from the town of Netophah; he is included in the list of David's mighty men (23:29 [KJV, "Heleb"]; 1 Chr. 11:30).

Helek. hee′lik (Heb. *ḥeleq H2751*, "portion, lot"; gentilic *ḥelqi H2757*, "Helekite"). **(1)** Son of Gilead and great-grandson of Manasseh; eponymous ancestor of the Helekite clan (Num. 26:30). Elsewhere, however, "the sons of Helek" (Josh. 17:2, lit. trans.) are listed with other Manassite

clans as receiving an inheritance W of the Jordan, in distinction from the Gileadites, who were granted territory in Transjordan.

(2) TNIV form of Helech.

Helem. hee′lim (Heb. *ḥelem H2152*, meaning uncertain). **(1)** Son of Heber and great-grandson of Asher (1 Chr. 7:35); many scholars emend the text to Hotham (on the basis of v. 32).

(2) A variant form of Heldai (Zech. 6:14 KJV and other versions, following the MT).

Heleph. hee′lif (Heb. *ḥelep H2738*, possibly "replacement [place]" or "marsh grass [settlement]"). The (western) starting point of the southern boundary of the tribe of Naphtali (Josh. 19:33). The precise location of Heleph is uncertain, but many scholars identify it with Khirbet ʿIrbadeh, about 3 mi. (5 km.) NE of Mount Tabor.

Helez. hee′liz (Heb. *ḥeleṣ H2742*, possibly "[God/Yahweh] has rescued"). **(1)** One of David's mighty men, identified as "the Paltite" (2 Sam. 23:26), meaning probably a native of Beth Pelet or perhaps a descendant of Pelet the Calebite; in the parallel list he is called "the Pelonite" (1 Chr. 11:27), a term of unknown derivation and maybe a scribal misspelling. He is probably the same as "Helez the Pelonite, an Ephraimite," commander of the seventh division (27:10).

(2) Son of Azariah, included in the genealogy of Judah (1 Chr. 2:39).

Heli. hee′li (Gk. *Ēli G2459* [some edd. *Hēli* or *Hēlei*], from Heb. *ʿēli H6603*, possibly "lofty" or "[God/Yahweh] is high"). Son of Matthat and father of Joseph according to Luke's genealogy of Jesus Christ (Lk. 3:23). Because the parallel passage lists Matthan son of Eleazar as the father of Joseph (Matt. 1:15), some regard Heli as his grandfather, perhaps corresponding to Eleazar. Others argue that Luke gives Mary's genealogy, in which case Heli is really her father, not Joseph's.

Heliopolis. hee′lee-op′uh-lis (from *hēlios G2463*, "sun," and *polis G4484*, "city"). This name occurs in the NIV as the rendering of Hebrew *ʾāwen H225*, corresponding to Egyptian *ʾIwnw* (Ezek. 30:17;

KJV, Aven; NRSV, On); in the NRSV it is used to render *bêt šemeš*, "house of the sun" (Jer. 43:13; KJV, "Beth-shemesh"; NIV, "the temple of the sun"). Heliopolis was an ancient city in Egypt, sacred to the sun-god Re and located in Tell el-Ḥisn, near el-Matarieh, about 10 mi. (16 km.) out of Cairo to the NNE. It first attained prominence in the Old Kingdom (Pyramid Age) of Egyptian history, when the pharaohs used a solar symbol for their tombs and adopted the title "Son of Re." The main temple in Heliopolis accordingly was that of Re, or Rē-Atum, the site being marked by the remains of a great enclosure and by the sole remaining obelisk of Sesostris I (c. 1900 B.C.). This was doubtless the structure at which Joseph's father-in-law Potipherah (Potiphar) subsequently served as "priest of On" (high priest in Heliopolis?), an affiliation reflected by his name, which means "gift of Re" (Gen. 41:45, 50; 46:20).

Three OT passages appear to refer to Heliopolis. The City of Destruction in Isa. 19:18 is possibly a Hebrew pun for City of the Sun, that is, Heliopolis. Ezekiel's judgment on Egypt (Ezek. 30:17) included Aven, perhaps also a pun (*ʾāwen*, "wickedness," for *ʾôn H228*, "On" or Heliopolis). Similarly, Jeremiah threatened that Nebuchadnezzar of Babylon would ravage Egypt's temples with fire, and "break the obelisks of Heliopolis" (Jer. 43:13 NRSV).

Helkai. hel´ki (Heb. *ḥelqāy H2758*, short form of *ḥilqiyyāhû H2760*, "Yahweh is my portion" [see Hilkiah]). The head of a priestly house who returned from exile with Zerubbabel (Neh. 12:15).

Helkath. hel´kath (Heb. *ḥelqat H2762*, "smooth place" or "plot of ground"). A town that served to mark the boundary of the tribal territory of Asher (Josh. 19:25). It was one of four cities from this tribe that were assigned to the Levite family descended from Gershon (21:31; called Hukok in the parallel passage, 1 Chr. 6:75). Its precise location is uncertain, but two possible identifications are Khirbet el-Harbaj, c. 12 mi. (19 km.) S of Acco, and Tell el-Qassis, some 5 mi. (8 km.) farther S and closer to the exit of the valley of Esdraelon.

Helkath Hazzurim. hel´kath-haz´yoo-rim (Heb. *ḥelqat haṣṣurim H2763*, meaning debated). A place near the pool of Gibeon where twelve men under Joab fought to the death with an equal number from Abner's forces (2 Sam. 2:16); the precise location is unknown.

hell. This English word (from a Germanic root meaning "concealed place" or "underworld") is used by the KJV in the OT to render Hebrew *šĕʾôl H8619* (Deut. 32:22 et al.; see Sheol); in the NT it renders Greek *hadēs G87* (Matt. 11:23 et al.; see Hades) and *geenna G1147* (5:2 et al.; see Gehenna). The NIV and other modern versions use it almost exclusively as a translation of this last term, which refers to the Valley of Hinnom (Wadi er-Rababi, just SW of Jerusalem), the location of the notorious sacrificial offering by fire of children to the god Molech (2 Chr. 28:3; 33:6; cf. 2 Ki. 23:10; Jer. 7:32; 19:6). The apocalyptic book of *1 Enoch* states that there would be an abyss filled with fire S of Jerusalem into which ungodly Israelites would be thrown. Later the idea was extended so that this place was conceived to be the scene of fiery punishment for all of the ungodly. Still later, when the place of punishment was conceived of as under the earth, the idea of fiery torment was maintained. (The English term occurs also as part of a phrase used to render *tartaroō G5434*, "to send to hell," 2 Pet. 2:4. In Gk. mythology, Tartarus was the name of a deep abyss below Hades where the Titans were imprisoned, but in time the term became roughly equivalent to Hades.)

The real existence of hell is irrefutably taught in Scripture as both a *place* of the wicked dead and a *condition* of retribution for unredeemed man. The *nature* of hell is indicated by the repeated reference to eternal punishment (Matt. 25:46), eternal fire (Matt. 18:8; Jude 7), everlasting chains (Jude 6), the pit of the Abyss (Rev. 9:2, 11), outer darkness (Matt. 8:12), the wrath of God (Rom. 2:5), second death (Rev. 21:8), eternal destruction from the face of God (2 Thess. 1:9), and eternal sin (Mk. 3:29). While many of these terms are symbolic and descriptive, they connote real entities, about whose existence there can be no doubt. The *duration* is explicitly indicated in the NT. As the everlasting

H

Some ancients believed that this cave at Caesarea Philippi (modern Panias) was an entrance into the Underworld.

life of the believer is to be endless, just so the retributive aspect of hell refers to the future infinite age (Matt. 18:8; 25:41, 46; Mk. 3:29; 2 Thess. 1:9; Heb. 6:2; Jude 7).

Hell is, therefore, both a *condition* of retribution and a *place* in which the retribution occurs. In both of these aspects the three basic ideas associated with the concept of hell are reflected: absence of righteousness, separation from God, and judgment. The absence of personal righteousness, with its correlative of the presence of personal unrighteousness, renders the individual unable to enter a right relationship with the holy God (Mk. 3:29). The eternal state of the wicked, therefore, will involve a separation from the presence of God (Jn. 3:36). The concept of judgment is heightened by the note of finality in the warnings against sin (Matt. 8:12). When all else has been said about hell, however, there is still the inescapable fact taught by Scripture that it will be a retributive judgment on the *spirit* of sinners, the inner essence of their being. The severity of the judgment will be on the fixed character of a person's essential nature—the soul, which will involve eternal loss in exclusion from Christ's kingdom and fellowship with God.

Hellenism. (from *Hellēn G1818*, "Greek"). The civilization and culture of ancient GREECE; especially, the dissemination and adoption of Greek thought, customs, and lifestyle. It often implies the fusion of Greek and non-Greek culture. (Among classical scholars, the term *Hellenistic* is primarily a chronological designation, covering the period from Alexander to the beginnings of the Roman empire. In biblical scholarship, the term has a broader connotation and is roughly equivalent to *Greco-Roman*.)

ALEXANDER THE GREAT, who was taught by Aristotle, devoted his life to conquering the world for the spread of Greek culture. He was convinced of the superiority of the Greek way of life and carried with him on his campaigns copies of Homer's *Iliad* and *Odyssey*. His eleven years of conquest changed the course of history, introducing a new lifestyle that affected every nation conquered, even the Jewish nation. Alexander and his successors broke down the old national, political, cultural, and religious establishment and introduced Greek culture by establishing new colonies and cities, by rapidly spreading the Koine (see GREEK LANGUAGE), and by the intermarriages of the Greeks with the Asiatics. When the SELEUCID empire gained control of Palestine in 198 B.C., the Jewish people came under severe pressure to hellenize, and many resisted it, leading to the Maccabean War beginning in 168 (see MACCABEE). The influence of Hellenism in Palestine, however, could not be totally prevented. The entrenchment of Greek culture can more readily be seen among the Jews of the Diaspora (DISPERSION), especially in ALEXANDRIA (see PHILO JUDAEUS).

Hellenistic influence is apparent early in the church's history (in Gk. literature, the term *Hellēnistēs G1821* occurs for the first time in the NT, Acts 6:1; 9:29; 11:20; in the last passage, some early witnesses have *Hellēnas*, i.e., Greeks or Gentiles). According to Acts 6:1, there was a dispute in the Christian community at JERUSALEM between the Hebrews and the Hellenists (KJV, "Grecians"; NIV, "Grecian Jews") because the widows of the Hellenistic group were being neglected in the daily allocation from the common pool of property. Some have thought that these Hellenists were non-Jews, but most scholars believe that the passage refers to Jews who spoke Greek (in contrast to the "Hebrews," who spoke Hebrew or, more likely, Aramaic). These "Hellenists" were probably Jews from the Diaspora who had returned to Palestine. (See PAUL; STEPHEN.) In the past, some scholars

© Dr. James C. Martin

H

argued that such individuals had a liberal attitude to the adoption of Greco-Roman ways and that they would often have been in conflict with the stricter Jews native to Judea. Diaspora Jews, no doubt, were sometimes viewed with suspicion, but it is widely agreed now that the evidence does not support a sharp dichotomy between Hellenistic and "Hebraic" Jews with regard to their approach to the Mosaic law.

Hellenists. See HELLENISM.

helmet. See ARMS AND ARMOR.

Helon. hee´lon (Heb. *ḥēlōn H2735*, "strong"). Father of ELIAB; the latter was a leader of the tribe of ZEBULUN at the time of MOSES (Num. 1:9; 2:7; 7:24, 29; 10:16).

Helper. See ADVOCATE; HOLY SPIRIT.

helpmeet. This English noun, meaning "help-mate," does not occur in the Bible, but apparently was coined due to a popular misunderstanding of the KJV rendering, "I will make him an help meet [*i.e.*, a helper suitable] for him" (Gen. 2:18, 20 KJV). See ADAM; EVE.

helps. In the NT there are four lists of "gifts" that God has given to his church (Rom. 12:6-8; 1 Cor. 12:7-11, 28-31; Eph. 4:11-12; see GIFTS, SPIRITUAL), and these are not to be confused with the officers who are listed elsewhere. "Helps" are mentioned only in 1 Cor. 12:28, and the term refers to the ability to perform helpful works in a gracious manner.

hem (of a garment). The part of the outer garment (upper or lower) that would hang down loosely. The Hebrews were instructed to wear TASSELS on the four corners of the outer garment as a constant reminder of the commandments (Num. 15:38-39; Deut. 22:12). AARON's robe was to have golden bells and pomegranates on its hem (Exod. 28:33-34; 39:24-26). The hem or fringe of Jesus' garment plays an important role with the hemorrhaging woman who believed that she would be healed if she could but touch the hem of his

cloak; Jesus responded to her faith and granted her request (Lk. 8:43-48).

Hemam. hee´mam (Heb. *ḥêmām H2123*). Son of the clan chief LOTAN and grandson of SEIR the HORITE (Gen. 36:22 KJV). The NIV reads HOMAM on the basis of the parallel passage (1 Chr. 1:39), whereas the NRSV renders it HEMAN.

Heman. hee´muhn (Heb. *ḥêmān H2124*). **(1)** Son of the clan chief LOTAN and grandson of SEIR the HORITE (Gen. 36:22 NRSV, following the LXX). The KJV follows the MT, HEMAM, whereas the NIV has HOMAM (1 Chr. 1:39).

(2) Son (or descendant) of ZERAH and grandson (or more distant descendant) of JUDAH (1 Chr. 2:6). He is also listed as one of "the sons of Mahol" (meaning perhaps "members of the musical guild") who were regarded as wise men (1 Ki. 4:31). See DARDA; ETHAN; MAHOL.

(3) Son of Joel and grandson of SAMUEL; a Kohathite prophet-musician (see KOHATH) whom DAVID appointed to lead in the musical services (1 Chr. 6:33; 2 Chr. 5:12). He is usually mentioned along with ASAPH and ETHAN (JEDUTHUN): they were responsible for sounding the trumpets, the bronze cymbals, and other instruments (1 Chr. 15:17, 19; 16:41-42); and some of their sons were set apart "for the ministry of prophesying, accompanied by harps, lyres and cymbals" (25:1). Heman, also called "the king's seer," had fourteen sons and three daughters, divinely given to him "through the promises of God to exalt him" (25:4-6).

Hemath. See HAMATH; HAMMATH.

Hemdan. hem´dan (Heb. *ḥemdān H2777*, possibly "desirable"). Son of the clan chief DISHON and grandson of SEIR the HORITE (Gen. 36:26; also 1 Chr. 1:41 NIV [following a significant number of Heb. and Gk. MSS], where KJV has "Amram" and NRSV "Hamran" [MT, *ḥamrān*]).

hemlock. See PLANTS.

hemorrhage. See DISEASE.

hemorrhoids. See DISEASE.

H

hen. See BIRDS (under *chicken*).

Hen (person). hen (Heb. *ḥēn H2835*, "gracious"). Son of a certain Zephaniah; he was one of several men to whom was given the crown that was made for Joshua (JESHUA) the high priest (Zech. 6:14; NRSV, "Josiah"). Hen was apparently another name, or perhaps a descriptive title (cf. NIV mg.) for Josiah son of Zephaniah; if so, it was in his house that the crown was made (v. 10).

Hena. hen´uh (Heb. *hēnaʿ H2184*, meaning uncertain). One of several Syrian city-states vanquished by SENNACHERIB (2 Ki. 18:34; 19:13; Isa. 37:13). Because Hena is listed along with HAMATH and ARPAD (also SEPHARVAIM and IVVAH), it is thought to have been located in N SYRIA. Some scholars, noticing that Hena and Ivvah are not mentioned in similar lists (2 Ki. 17:24; Isa. 36:19), and suspecting that they are not true geographical names, have suggested that they are pagan deities or that the text is corrupt.

Henadad. hen´uh-dad (Heb. *ḥēnādād H2836*, "favor of [the god] HADAD"). Father or ancestor of a family of priests who helped rebuild the temple under ZERUBBABEL (Ezra 3:9), assisted in repairing the wall of JERUSALEM in the time of NEHEMIAH (Neh. 3:18, 24), and signed the covenant (10:9).

henna. See PLANTS.

Henoch. See ENOCH; HANOCH.

Hepher (person). hee´fuhr (Heb. *ḥēper H2918*, possibly "protector"; gentilic *ḥeprî H2920*, "Hepherite"). **(1)** Son of GILEAD, descendant of MANASSEH, father of ZELOPHEHAD, and ancestor of the Hepherite clan (Num. 26:32; 27:1; Josh. 17:2-3). His clan may be associated with HEPHER (PLACE).

(2) Son of ASHHUR (apparently founder of the town of TEKOA) by his wife Naarah; included in the genealogy of JUDAH (1 Chr. 4:6).

(3) A MEKERATHITE, included among DAVID's mighty warriors (1 Chr. 11:36; his name is missing in the parallel list in 2 Sam. 23).

Hepher (place). hee´fuhr (Heb. *ḥēper H2919*, possibly "protector" or "[water] hole"). A Canaanite royal city whose king was defeated by JOSHUA (Josh. 12:17). Presumably, it was part of the "land of Hepher," which became the third administrative district under BEN-HESED in the time of SOLOMON (1 Ki. 4:10). Possible identifications are el-Ifshar (c. 25 mi./40 km. NNE of JOPPA and only 3 mi./5 km. from the coast) and Tell el-Muhaffar in the hill country of MANASSEH (c. 2 mi./3 km. NW of DOTHAN).

Hephzibah. hef´zi-buh (Heb. *ḥepṣi-bāh H2915*, "my delight is in her"). **(1)** Wife of King HEZEKIAH and mother of King MANASSEH (2 Ki. 21:1).

(2) Symbolic name of ZION (Isa. 62:4; the NRSV translates the name, "My Delight Is in Her"). See BEULAH.

herald. A messenger who proclaims important news. The term is used occasionally in Bible versions (e.g., Dan. 3:4; 1 Tim. 2:7; 2 Tim. 1:11). A herald was usually a representative of a royal or government official having as his specific responsibility the bearing of a message. The message and whom he represented was his primary concern, and he was to remain secondary.

herb. See PLANTS.

herd. Both before and after the conquest of Canaan, the Israelites were a pastoral people for the most part. The herds consisted of the larger ANIMALS, as contrasted with the flocks of sheep, goats, etc. The cattle were used in plowing and threshing and for sacrifice but were not commonly fattened for food.

herdsman. See OCCUPATIONS AND PROFESSIONS.

Heres. hihr´iz (Heb. *ḥeres H3065*, possibly "sunny"). **(1)** "Mount Heres" (NRSV, "Har-heres") is mentioned, along with AIJALON and SHAALBIM, as one of the places from which the tribe of DAN could not drive out the AMORITES (Jdg. 1:34-35). It is usually identified with the town of IR SHEMESH ("city of the sun," Josh. 19:41) which in turn is probably the same as BETH SHEMESH ("house of the sun,"

Josh. 15:10 et al.), on the boundary between Judah and Dan. However, it would be unusual to call a village a *har H2215* ("mountain"), and some scholars prefer to identify it with a mountain range on the E side of the Valley of Aijalon.

(2) The "Pass [*or* Ascent] of Heres" was apparently a place E of the JORDAN from which GIDEON returned after defeating two kings of MIDIAN (Jdg. 8:13). The text can be interpreted differently, however (KJV translates, "before the sun was up"). If it is indeed a geographical reference, the site is unknown.

See also CITY OF DESTRUCTION.

Heresh. hihr´ish (Heb. *ḥereš H3090*, "silent, mute"). A LEVITE, listed among those who returned from the EXILE (1 Chr. 9:15; his name is omitted in the parallel, Neh. 11:15).

heresy. This English term is derived (through French and Latin) from Greek *hairesis G146*, which meant "a taking" or "choice," hence "opinion, way of thinking." In the Hellenistic period it came to mean "[political] preference," then "system, sect, faction." Not till the second century A.D. did the word come to mean specifically a position or doctrine at variance with established, orthodox church doctrine (though this was a natural development from negative uses in the NT). In the book of Acts, the word is applied to the religious "parties" of the SADDUCEES and PHARISEES (Acts 5:17; 15:5). PAUL was accused of being "a ringleader of the Nazarene sect" (24:5; cf. 24:14; 28:22). A negative element is more apparent when the apostle speaks about the "factions" present in the Corinthian church (1 Cor. 11:19 NRSV; NIV, "differences"), for in the same context he uses the stronger term *schisma G5388*, "division, split" (vv. 10, 18; cf. also Gal. 5:20). The NT use closest to the later technical, theological meaning is found in 2 Pet. 2:1, which states that false teachers "will secretly introduce destructive heresies [NRSV, opinions], even denying the sovereign Lord who bought them—bringing swift destruction on themselves." This language implies willful departure from accepted teaching.

Hereth. hihr´ith (Heb. *ḥeret H3101*, meaning uncertain). KJV Hareth. The name of a forest in the tribal territory of JUDAH where DAVID hid after he left his parents in MOAB for their safety (1 Sam. 22:5). Its location is unknown.

heritage. See INHERITANCE.

Hermas. huhr´muhs (Gk. *Hermas G2254*). One of several Christians in Rome that PAUL greets by name in his letter to the church there (Rom. 16:14b; note that the KJV, following the TR, reverses the names "Hermas" and "Hermes"). It was thought by some in the ancient church that he was the author of *Shepherd of Hermas*; this work, however, was probably composed over a period of time in the second century (see APOSTOLIC FATHERS).

hermeneutics. See INTERPRETATION.

Hermes (deity). huhr´meez (Gk. *Hermēs G2258*). In Greek mythology, the son of ZEUS and Maia (a Titan nymph), known among the Romans as Mercury. Diverse ideas were associated with him, but he was best known as the messenger of the gods; he was often represented with traveler's cap, winged sandals, and herald's staff. Preferring persuasion to violence, he could be viewed as the god of oratory (the term *hermeneutics* is derived from his name). It is this role that prompted the people of LYSTRA to identify PAUL, being "the chief speaker," with Hermes (Acts 14:12; KJV, "Mercurius"), while BARNABAS was identified with Zeus. Such a response may have as its background the story of an aged couple who lived in that general region and who entertained Jupiter and Mercury without realizing who they were.

Hermes (person). huhr´meez (Gk. *Hermēs G2258*). One of several Christians in Rome that PAUL greets by name in his letter to the church there (Rom. 16:14a; note that the KJV, following the TR, reverses the names "Hermas" and "Hermes"). This was a common name, especially among slaves, probably because Hermes was the god of good fortune.

Hermetic writings. A collection of religious and philosophical tractates, the main body of which is known as the *Corpus Hermeticum* (or simply

Hermetica), probably dating around the second or third century A.D. The title of the literature is derived from the name Hermes Trismegistus ("thrice greatest"). See HERMES (DEITY). The work, which probably originated in EGYPT though written in Greek, was a typical product of Hellenistic syncretism. The extant material is in various forms, ranging from the discourses and dialogues of the main corpus of eighteen works (the best-known treatise being the initial one, *Poimandres*) to a number of fragments, some of which are in the Gnostic library of NAG HAMMADI (see GNOSTICISM).

Hermogenes. huhr-moj′uh-neez (Gk. *Hermogenēs G2259*, "born of HERMES"). Named with PHYGELUS as among the disciples in proconsular ASIA who abandoned PAUL when he rightly expected their support (2 Tim. 1:15). Some view it as a doctrinal defection; others as a refusal to testify in Paul's behalf during the second imprisonment at Rome for fear of sharing Paul's fate.

Hermon. huhr′muhn (Heb. *ḥermôn H3056*, possibly "place of consecration [*or* of the BAN]"). The mountain that marks the southern terminus of the Antilebanon range. A line drawn from DAMASCUS to TYRE will pass through Mount Hermon at its middle point and will practically coincide with the northern boundary of PALESTINE. The ridge of Hermon is about 20 mi. (32 km.) long. It has three peaks, two of them rising over 9,000 ft. (2,740 m.). Hermon has had several names: the ancient AMORITES called it SENIR, while the people of SIDON called it SIRION (Deut. 3:9), though perhaps different peaks are in view (cf. 1 Chr. 5:23; Cant.

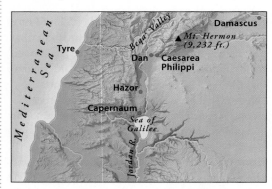

Mount Hermon, northern boundary of the Promised Land.

4:8). The Arabs call it Jebel esh-Sheikh or "Mountain of the Old Man," perhaps because of its white head, but more likely because of its dignity. (See also SIYON.) Hermon is awe-inspiring whether seen from the NE at Damascus, from the W back of Sidon, from the SW at NAZARETH, or from the SE at HAURAN. The Lord's TRANSFIGURATION almost certainly occurred on its slopes, for he was at CAESAREA PHILIPPI just S of the mountain only a week before.

Hermonites. huhr′muh-nĭts. KJV rendering of *ḥermônîm*, plural form of *ḥermôn H3056* (Ps. 42:7; NIV, "heights of Hermon"). See HERMON.

Herod. her′uhd (Gk. *Hērōdēs G2476*). The ruling dynasty in Jewish PALESTINE during the period of Roman domination. When the general Pompey organized the eastern parts of the Roman empire in 63 B.C., he appointed Hyrcanus II to be the high-priestly ruler over much of Palestine. An Idumean by the name of Antipater was Hyrcanus's senior officer. Gabinius modified Pompey's arrangement in 57 by reducing Hyrcanus's authority and dividing the ethnarchy into autonomous communities. Notable services rendered at ALEXANDRIA to Julius CAESAR in 48 led to the restoration of Hyrcanus's authority and the appointment (in 47) of Antipater to the procuratorship of Judea. Antipater had, in fact, been the leading spirit in the policy that won Caesar's favor, and Antipater used his advantage with an astuteness that foreshadowed the career of his son. He persuaded the now-aged Hyrcanus to appoint Phasael, Antipater's eldest son, to the prefecture of JERUSALEM, and Herod, his second son, to the governorship of GALILEE.

When Antipater was murdered in 43 B.C., his two sons succeeded to his position in Hyrcanus's court. It was the year after Julius Caesar's assassination. Jubilant that Caesar's plan for a decisive campaign on the vulnerable eastern frontier of Rome was shelved, the PARTHIANS, the perennial military problem of the NE, were restive. In 40 they penetrated Palestine, carried off Hyrcanus, and drove Phasael, also a captive, to suicide. Herod eluded both military action and Parthian treachery. He withdrew from Jerusalem, shook

off pursuit by clever rearguard skirmishing near
BETHLEHEM, and escaped to EGYPT. Outwitting
Cleopatra and reaching Rome through the perils of winter voyaging, Herod set his case before
Octavian and Antony. It is a remarkable tribute to
his charm, daring, political acumen, and consummate diplomacy that he won the support of both
triumvirs who were so soon to divide in disastrous
rivalry.

The thirteen years that lay between the assassination of Caesar and the emergence of Octavian
as the victorious AUGUSTUS, after Antony's defeat
at Actium in 31 B.C., were a time of paralysis and
uncertainty throughout the Roman world. Herod
saw in such confusion the opportunity for decisive
action. Landing at Acre (Acco) in 39, with only
the promise of Roman favor, Herod went to claim
his kingdom and to unseat the Parthian puppet, Antigonus. Palestine's hill country, deserts,
and walled cities called for a variety of military
strategies. Herod showed himself the able master of varied types of war. The two years of tireless activity made him, by the age of thirty-six,
the master of his inheritance and revealed all the
facets of his amazing personality. He was a ruthless fighter but at the same time a cunning nego-
tiator, a subtle diplomat, and an opportunist. He
was able to restrain his Roman helpers and simultaneously circumvent the Jews. Between 39 and
37 Herod revealed those qualities that enabled
him for thirty-four years to govern subjects who
hated him, to work within the major framework
of Roman imperial rule, to steer a safe course
through political dilemma, and to pursue a dual
policy without ruinous contradiction.

In 30 B.C. Herod succeeded in retaining the
favor of Octavian. He was confirmed in his kingdom, and for the rest of his life he never departed
from the policy of supporting the emperor and in
all ways promoting his honor. The restored town of
SAMARIA was called Sebaste, the Greek equivalent
of Augustus; CAESAREA was built to form a harbor
on the difficult open coast of Palestine, providing
Rome a base on the edge of a turbulent province,
and forming a center of Caesar-worship in the land
of the nationalistic and monotheistic Jews.

Herod followed a policy of hellenization,
establishing games at Jerusalem and adorning

The legacy of Herod the Great.

many of the Hellenistic cities of his domain (see
HELLENISM). At the same time he sought to reconcile the Jews, who hated his pro-Roman and
hellenizing policies and who never forgave him for
his Edomite blood (see EDOM). During the great
famine of 25 B.C. in Judea and Samaria, Herod
spared no trouble or private expense to import
Egyptian corn. In the eighteenth year of his reign
(20) he began to build the great Jerusalem TEM-
PLE, which was forty-three years under construction (Jn. 2:20). However, nothing he did served
to win metropolitan Jewry. It was Herod's policy
to crush the old aristocracy, even though he was
married to Mariamme, the heiress of the Jewish
Hasmonean house. He built up a nobility of service, drawing on both Jews and Greeks. He sought
subtly to channel messianic ambitions of the baser
sort in his direction by encouraging the political
party of the HERODIANS (Mk. 3:6; 12:13), whose
policy seems to have been the support of the royal
house and a hellenized society. Politically, this
royalist group was descended from the old hellenizing apostates of Maccabean times (see MACCA-
BEE and cf. the "Antiochians" of 2 Macc. 9:9-14).
They were probably Jews of the DISPERSION,
from whom Herod also recruited his subservient

H

The cliffs of Arbel, where Herod attacked the Sicarii (violent Jewish nationalists) who were hiding in the caves. (View to the NE, with the Sea of Galilee in the background.)

priesthood, and were SADDUCEES in religion. Such varied patronage and support produced checks and balances in the composite society of Herod's kingdom that made for stability of rule, but of course did nothing to reconcile the divided elements of the populace, metropolitan and Hellenistic Jews, Sadducees and PHARISEES, people and hierarchy. It was only the common challenge of Christ that could draw together such dissidents as Sadducees and Pharisees, the Romans and the priests—just as it healed, according to a surprising side remark of Luke (Lk. 23:12), a rift between Herod Antipas and Pilate.

To manage a situation so complex, and to survive, demanded uncommon ability and an ordered realm. Of Herod's ability there is no doubt, and with his foreign mercenaries, his system of fortresses, and the centralized bureaucracy that he built, he gave Palestine order and even opportunity for economic progress. At the same time Herod was a cruel and implacable tyrant. His family and private life were soiled and embittered by feuds, intrigue, and murder. The king's sister Salome and his son Antipater by Doris, his first consort, seem to have been in league against Mariamme, his favorite wife. Mariamme was put to death in

29 B.C. and her two sons, Alexander and Aristobulus, in 7 B.C. Antipater himself was put to death by Herod in the last days of Herod's reign. Herod died in 4 B.C. The murder of the innocent babies of BETHLEHEM (Matt. 2) falls within the context of his final madness. JOSEPHUS's grim picture (*War* 1.33.5) of the physical and mental degeneration of the aging king is detailed enough for diagnosis. It is the picture of an arteriosclerotic who had once been athletic and vigorous but who became increasingly prone to delusions of persecution and uncontrollable outbursts of violence, the results of hypertension and a diseased brain.

Herod's will divided the kingdom. Archelaus, son of Malthace, a Samaritan woman, took JUDEA and IDUMEA—by far the choicest share. Herod Antipas, of the same mother, received GALILEE and PEREA; and Philip, son of a Jewish woman named Cleopatra, took Iturea, Traconitis, and associated districts in the NE. Archelaus, who inherited his father's vices without his ability, took the title of king and bloodily quelled the disorders that broke out in Jerusalem. The result was a wide uprising, which required the intervention of Varus, governor of SYRIA. It was at this time that the Holy Family returned from Egypt (Matt.

2:22-23): "But when [Joseph] heard that Archelaus was reigning in Judea in place of his father Herod, he was afraid to go there ... he withdrew to the district of Galilee, and he went and lived in a town called Nazareth."

It was imperative for Archelaus to reach Rome and secure from Augustus confirmation of his position before the situation in Palestine could be presented in too lurid a light by his enemies. Archelaus's petition was opposed in person by Herod Antipas and by a Jewish embassy. Somewhat surprisingly, Augustus declared in favor of Archelaus, though he denied him the royal title. The incident may have provided the background for the parable of the pounds (Lk. 19:11-27). Archelaus was the "man of noble birth" who went "to have himself appointed king." The facts were no doubt brought to mind by the sight of the palace that Archelaus had built at JERICHO, where the story was told (Josephus, *Ant.* 17.13.1). Archelaus maintained his stupid and tyrannical reign for ten years. In A.D. 6 a Jewish embassy finally secured his deposition and banishment to Gaul. Judea fell under procuratorial rule. Coponius, a Roman knight, was appointed governor. A tax-census was the first administrative necessity, and this precipitated the revolt of Judas of Gamala and the emergence of the ZEALOTS as a sinister force in Palestinian politics. Archelaus rebuilt and restored his father's palace at Jericho, as the palace had been burned down at Herod's death. It was discovered and excavated in 1951.

Herod Antipas (the word is an abbreviation for Antipater) equaled his father in having a long reign. "That fox," Christ called the ruler of Galilee (Lk. 13:32), an epithet that has reference to the Herodian cunning, his subtle diplomacy, and his astute management of a difficult situation— qualities that enabled Antipas to retain his puppet position and petty royal power until A.D. 39. It was probably some time before 23 that Herod Antipas met the evil genius of his later years, the dynamic HERODIAS, wife of his half-brother Philip. This brother, who is not to be confused with the tetrarch of Iturea mentioned earlier, was the son of an unnamed wife of Herod I. As the daughter of Aristobulus, son of Herod I and Mariamme, Herodias was Philip's niece as well as his wife. They lived quietly in Rome, and it was here that Antipas met Herodias.

It is difficult to say who was primarily to blame for the notorious liaison that took Herodias back to Palestine as the unlawful wife and queen of Antipas. She remained loyal to him in his later misfortunes, though offered release by Caligula, and the immoral partnership of the two seems to have been cemented by genuine physical attraction and community of temperament. But trouble dogged the union. According to Josephus, Herod Antipas's rightful queen, daughter of the Nabatean king ARETAS, heard of the liaison before the couple reached Palestine and escaped first to the fortress of Machaerus and then to her father's capital of Petra, before her returning husband could detain her. Herod therefore came home to find a troublesome frontier war on his lands. He celebrated his birthday, the tragic feast described in Mk. 6:14-29, at the stronghold of Machaerus. The death of JOHN THE BAPTIST occurred here also, for after his denunciation of Herod's sin the preacher of the wilderness had been imprisoned in this fortress. The crime so dramatically contrived was the final turning point in Herod's life. Until then, according to a strange remark in the second gospel (6:20), there had been some faint aspiration for good: "Herod feared John and protected him, knowing him to be a righteous and holy man. When Herod heard John, he was greatly puzzled; yet he liked to listen to him."

Antipas's campaign against his father-in-law Aretas ended disastrously. Antipas was forced to appeal to Rome for help, and the task was assigned to Vitellius, governor of Syria. The affair dragged on until A.D. 37 when Rome's ruler TIBERIUS died. A prey to the uncertainty that was increasingly to attend changes in the Roman principate, Vitellius hesitated, and Antipas never won revenge. Two years later Antipas fell. He had been trusted by Tiberius, who appreciated his continuation of his father's pro-Roman policy, to which the foundation of TIBERIAS on Galilee was a solid monument. Tiberius, in the last year of his principate (36), had even used Herod as a mediator between Rome and Parthia. Presuming on this notable imperial favor, and incited by Herodias, Herod petitioned Caius Caligula, Tiberius's successor, for the title of king. He was, however, deposed by that incalculable prince on a suspicion of treasonable conduct, a charge leveled by Herod AGRIPPA I, his nephew. Herodias accompanied the man she had ruined morally and politically into obscure exile. SALOME her daughter, the dancer of the Machaerus feast, married her uncle Philip, tetrarch of Iturea, about 30. After Philip died in 34, she married her cousin Aristobulus, king of Chalcis, North of Abilene in the Antilebanon hill country.

Philip of Iturea seems to have been the best of Herod's three surviving sons (Josephus, *Ant.* 17.2.4). His remote province insulated him from some of the problems of Jewry, but he seems to have been a man of generous mold and notable justice. He beautified the town of CAESAREA PHILIPPI and marked his continuation of the Herodian pro-Roman policy by changing the name of the northern BETHSAIDA to Julias, after Augustus's unfortunate daughter.

The deceased Philip's vacant tetrarchy was the first foothold of the third Herod to be mentioned in the NT (Acts 12:1). Herod Agrippa I—grandson of Herod I, son of Aristobulus, and brother of Herodias—had been brought up in Rome under the protection of Tiberius's favorite son, Drusus. He had all the Herodian charm and diplomatic subtlety, and this explains how, as the boon companion of the mad Caligula, he was able to deter that prince from the final folly of setting up his statue in the temple at Jerusalem (Josephus, *Ant.* 18.8). Such an achievement demanded not only clever wits but also courage of no mean order. In A.D. 37, on Caligula's succession as emperor, Herod Agrippa was granted Philip's realm. Galilee and Perea were added when Antipas and Herodias were exiled. The malicious word in Rome had paid rich dividends. With his grandfather's subtlety, Agrippa knew how to survive a succession.

When Caligula was assassinated in 41, Agrippa, who had played his cards with remarkable astuteness, remained in the favor of CLAUDIUS, Caligula's successor, who turned over to Agrippa's control the whole area of his grandfather's kingdom. He succeeded to such power, moreover, with the consent and the favor of the Jews. The old Jewish hostility to the Idumean dynasty had vanished, and even the Pharisees were reconciled. Luke's account (Acts 12:20-23) of the king's shocking death in his royal seat of Caesarea is substantiated by Josephus's longer narrative (*Ant.* 19.8.2). Josephus looked on this Herod with admiration as the last great Jewish monarch, yet the correspondence between Josephus's and Luke's accounts is remarkable. In both accounts the pomp and circumstance of Agrippa's royal estate is notable.

Agrippa died in 44, and his reign was therefore brief. Whether it would have long survived under a less indulgent emperor or under an imperial government that had already vetoed his proposal to fortify Jerusalem, is a matter that his early death left undecided. It is possible for modern medicine to diagnose the intestinal complaint described by Luke in the accepted terminology of his day. A symptom is a visible, violent, and agonizing peristalsis. Luke uses a single adjective, translated by the English phrase "eaten of worms," for the cause of Herod's death. Agrippa was only fifty-four years of age. After his death Palestine fell wholly under Roman rule, a takeover facilitated by the consolidation under Agrippa of the old Herodian domains. There was considerable disorder over the next four years.

Agrippa left a teen-age son, whom CLAUDIUS made king of Chalcis in A.D. 48. In 53 the territory of Philip the tetrarch and Lysanias were added to this realm, together with an area on the western side of Galilee, including Tiberias. The appointment carried the title of king, so in 53 the son became AGRIPPA II, last of the Herodian line. He appears only in the brilliant account in Acts 25, where, as FESTUS's guest, he and his sister BERNICE (with whom he was thought to have an inappropriate relationship) heard the defense of PAUL. Another sister was the wife of Antonius FELIX, the procurator of Judea, whom Festus had succeeded.

In the account of the examination of Paul we see a vivid and revealing picture of the deference Rome was prepared to pay to a puppet king. Perhaps it is more accurate to say that here we see the respect that Rome undoubtedly owed to a remarkable royal house that had been a major bastion of Roman peace in the Middle East for three generations. In the king himself is seen a typical Herod of the better sort: royal, intelligent, pro-Roman, but vitally interested in Judaism, which, with unusual understanding, he saw to be the key to the history of his land.

With this event, which is difficult to date precisely, Agrippa and the Herodian line disappear from history. Festus died in A.D. 64. One brief reference in Josephus reveals that Agrippa lived on in the garrison town of Caesarea to see the vast ruin and destruction of his country in the Great Revolt of 66 to 70. So ended the Herods, an astonishingly able family, whose pro-Roman policy went far to postpone the inevitable clash between Rome and the Jews, and played, in consequence, an unwitting but significant part in holding the peace during the formative years of the Christian church in Palestine.

Herodians. hi-roh´dee-uhnz (Gk. *Hērōdianoi G2477*). A party, mentioned in the Gospels, who cooperated with the Pharisees on two different occasions in opposition to Jesus (Mk. 3:6; 12:13 [= Matt. 22:16]). Composed of the name Herod and a common suffix, the term designates partisans of Herod the Great or his dynasty. A more specific identification is a matter of conjecture, and varied suggestions concerning them have been made: soldiers of Herod; courtiers of Herod; Jews belonging to the northern tetrarchies ruled by sons of Herod; supporters of Jewish aspirations for a national kingdom who favored Herodian rule versus direct Roman rule; political supporters of Antipas. Of these, the last is most probable and receives wide support. Unlike the Pharisees, they were not a religious party but rather a political group concerned with the interests of the Herodian dynasty. Theologically, their membership doubtless cut across recognized party lines. They may have had Sadducean proclivities, but the Gospels never suggest that the Hero-

dians are to be equated with the Sadducees. That Matt. 16:6 substitutes "Sadducees" for "Herod" in Mk. 8:15 (a few MSS read "Herodians") does not establish the identity; Matthew simply omits the reference to Herod or the Herodians and names another group.

Herodias. hi-roh´dee-uhs (Gk. *Hērōdias G2478*). A wicked granddaughter of Herod the Great who married her uncle Philip; but his brother Antipas saw her at Rome, desired her, and married her. John the Baptist reproved Herod Antipas for his immoral action (Lk. 3:19-20) and was put in prison for his temerity (Matt. 14:3-12; Mk. 6:14-29). This did not satisfy Herodias, so by a sordid scheme she secured his death. Later Antipas was banished to Spain. Herodias accompanied him and died there.

Herodion. hi-roh´dee-uhn (Gk. *Hērōdiōn G2479*). A Christian at Rome to whom Paul sent greetings (Rom. 16:11). The apostle refers to him as his *syngenēs G5150* ("kinsman"), meaning that he was either Paul's blood-relative or, more likely, a fellow Jew. The name suggests that he may have been a freedman of the Herod family and perhaps a member of the household of Aristobulus (v. 10). See also Herodium.

Herodium. hi-roh´dee-uhm (Gk. *Hērōdeion*). Also Herodion. A fortress palace built by Herod

Aerial view of the Herodium hill fortress (looking SW).

© Dr. James C. Martin

the Great as a memorial to himself. It is identified as modern Jebel el Fureidis, c. 4 mi. (6 km.) SE of BETHLEHEM. It was built on a mountain that was artificially heightened and had a conical shape. It was one of a chain of palace-fortresses Herod erected to protect his kingdom. In the year 40 B.C., Herod had defeated at this spot PARTHIANS and Jews, and he built the citadel in memory of the great victory he achieved there (Jos. *War* 1.13.8). It was begun about 24 B.C. and completed by 15 B.C.

Heroes, House of the. A building somewhere in the SE area of postexilic JERUSALEM (Neh. 3:16; KJV, "house of the mighty"; NRSV, "house of the warriors"). Nothing else is known about this place, but it may have been an older structure that served as barracks for the military during the monarchy.

heron. See BIRDS.

Heshbon. hesh'bon (Heb. *ḥešbôn H3114*, perhaps "reckoning, account"). A city in TRANSJORDAN, c. 15 mi. (24 km.) ENE of the N tip of the DEAD SEA and less than 4 mi. (6 km.) NE of Mount NEBO. Originally part of MOAB, it was captured by the AMORITE king SIHON, who made it his capital. Heshbon was then taken from Sihon by the Israelites under MOSES on their way to Canaan (Num. 21:25-30; Deut. 1:4; 2:24-30; et al.). It was located within the tribal territory of REUBEN on its border with GAD, and the Reubenites rebuilt it after the conquest of Canaan (Num. 32:3, 37). Apparently absorbed by the Gadites, Heshbon was then assigned to the LEVITES descended from MERARI (Josh. 21:39; 1 Chr. 6:81). The town subsequently must have fallen again into the hands of the Moabites, for the prophets repeatedly mention it in their denunciations of Moab (Isa. 15:4; 16:8-9; Jer. 48:2, 34, 45; 49:3). The name Heshbon is apparently preserved in the modern city of Hesban in Jordan, some 12 mi. (19 km.) SW of Amman. Ruins of the city, which come chiefly from the Roman period, lie on the summit of a hill and are about a mile in circuit. Nearby there is a large ruined reservoir, which may be the "pools of Heshbon" mentioned in the Song of Solomon (Cant. 7:4). Archaeological evidence, however, has

led some scholars to believe that the OT site itself may be in nearby Jalul.

Heshmon. hesh'mon (Heb. *ḥešmôn H3132*, possibly "smooth field"). A town in the NEGEV, the extreme S of the tribal territory of JUDAH (Josh. 15:27). It was apparently near BETH PELET, but its precise location is unknown.

heth (letter). hayth (Heb. *ḥêt*). Also *het* and *cheth*. The eighth letter of the Hebrew alphabet (ח), with a numerical value of eight. Although in modern Hebrew it is pronounced as a velar fricative (ḥ, consisting of a vibration of the uvula), in biblical times it was probably a pharyngeal sound (ḥ, a constriction of the throat muscles). These two sounds were distinct phonemes in proto-Semitic (and are preserved as such in Arabic), but they merged in Hebrew and other Semitic languages.

Heth (person). heth (Heb. *ḥêt H3147*). Son of CANAAN, grandson of HAM, and eponymous ancestor of the HITTITES. The Hebrew form is rendered "Heth" by the KJV in all its occurrences (Gen. 10:15; 23:3-20; 25:10; 27:46; 49:32; 1 Chr. 1:13). The NRSV has the name "Heth" only in the Table of Nations (Gen. 10:15; 1 Chr. 1:13); elsewhere it renders the name as "Hittite(s)." The NIV uses "Hittite(s)" throughout.

Hethlon. heth'lon (Heb. *ḥetlôn H3158*, derivation uncertain). In EZEKIEL's vision, Hethlon is one of the places marking the ideal N boundary of Israel; a road passing by it leads from the MEDITERRANEAN to LEBO HAMATH (Ezek. 47:15; 48:1). The site is unknown, though some places on the Lebanese coast have been proposed, including modern Heitela, NE of Tripoli.

hewer. The expression "hewers of wood" (KJV; NIV, "woodcutters") was apparently a special social classification; it was imposed on the GIBEONITES, residents of four towns in the area of Jerusalem because they had tricked JOSHUA into a treaty (Josh. 9:21, 23, 27). This status, which is better defined as forced labor, was very low on the social ladder. Joshua also delegated the Gibeonites to be "drawers of water" (9:27 [NIV, "water carriers"]; cf.

H

Deut. 29:11), which would fit with their low class status. Some of them became the later temple servants (NETHINIM).

Hexateuch. hek´suh-ty*ook*. This term (from Gk. *hex*, "six," and *teuchos*, "book") is used by some scholars as a designation for the first six books of the Bible (cf. PENTATEUCH, "five books"). It derives from the theory that the original compilation of books pertaining to the early background and establishment of the commonwealth of Israel included the book of Joshua, rather than Deuteronomy, as its last component.

Hezeki. See HIZKI.

Hezekiah. hez´uh-ki´uh (Heb. *ḥizqiyyāhû H2625* [with several spelling variations], "Yahweh has strengthened me"; Gk. *Hezekias G1614*). **(1)** An ancestor of the prophet ZEPHANIAH (Zeph. 1:1 [KJV, "Hizkiah"]); possibly the same as #5, below.

(2) The head of a family that returned from the EXILE (Ezra 2:16; Neh. 7:21; 10:17 [KJV, "Hizkijah"]).

(3) Son of Neariah and postexilic descendant of DAVID (1 Chr. 3:23 KJV; see HIZKIAH).

(4) Son of AHAZ, descendant of David, and king of Judah; three accounts are given of his reign (2 Ki. 18-20; 2 Chr. 29:1-32; Isa. 36-39). Hezekiah probably reigned from 716/15 to 687/86 B.C. (some scholars date his reign about a decade earlier). During this period, ASSYRIA was still a mighty power; and EGYPT, though weak, was still strong enough to oppose Assyria. Judah's position, on the main road between Egypt and Assyria, was a very precarious one. Hezekiah's grandfather JOTHAM reigned at Jerusalem when Hezekiah was a child, and though he was in some ways a good king, he allowed the people to sacrifice and burn incense in the HIGH PLACES. Because of Judah's growing apostasy, the Lord permitted the ARAMEANS and the northern kingdom to trouble Jerusalem. In Hezekiah's youth and early manhood, his weak and wicked father Ahaz was king. He went so far as to follow the abominable rites of the Moabites by burning children in the fire (2 Chr. 28:3), in spite of the warnings of the prophets Hosea, Micah, and Isaiah. For a while Heze-

© Dr. James C. Martin. The Istanbul Archaeological Museum. Photographed by permission.

The Siloam Inscription, discovered in the tunnel built during the reign of Hezekiah. It describes the completion of the project, when the hewers could hear the workers on the other side.

kiah was associated in the government with his father, but because of his father's incapacitation he was made active ruler. He began his reign, at the age of twenty-five, in troubled and threatening times. Some counseled him to side with Egypt against Assyria; others favored surrender to Assyria to save themselves from Egypt. Isaiah warned against trusting in foreign alliances. One of the first acts of Hezekiah was the cleansing and reopening of the TEMPLE, which his father had left closed and desecrated. After this was accomplished, the Passover feast was celebrated (2 Chr. 30). The idolatrous altars and high places were destroyed.

From the fourth to the sixth year of Hezekiah's reign the northern kingdom was in trouble. SARGON finally destroyed SAMARIA and deported the people to Assyria. Hezekiah became ill, probably from a carbuncle, and almost died; but God granted him a fifteen-year extension of life (2 Ki. 20:1-11). After Hezekiah's recovery, MERODACH-BALADAN of BABYLON sent an embassy ostensibly to congratulate him, but actually to persuade him to join a secret confederacy against the Assyrian power. This was the great crisis for Hezekiah, and indeed for Judah. During his illness he had received from God not only the promise of recovery, but also the pledge that the Lord would deliver Jerusalem from the Assyrians (Isa. 38:6-7). The ambassadors of Merodach-Baladan were intent also on freeing Jerusalem from the Assyrians—but by force of arms and the power of a military alliance. The question facing Hezekiah was therefore whether to walk the way of FAITH

H

that the Lord would keep his promise, or to take the way of "works," setting out to liberate the city by his own abilities and clever policies. When Isaiah learned that Hezekiah had entertained the ambassadors and their suggestion, he knew that all was over for Judah and immediately predicted the Babylonian captivity (39:5-7). Hezekiah paid a high price for dabbling in rebellion. Assyria compelled Judah to pay heavy tribute; and to obtain it, Hezekiah even had to strip the plating from the doors and pillars of the temple. Shortly after (but related earlier, 2 Ki. 18:13—19:37), Assyria decided to destroy Jerusalem, but God saved the city by sending a sudden plague that in one night killed 185,000 soldiers. After Hezekiah's death, his son Manasseh succeeded him (20:21).

Hezion. hee′zee-uhn (Heb. *ḥezyôn H2611*, possibly "vision" or "lop-eared"). Father of Tabrimmon and grandfather of the Aramean king, Ben-Hadad (1 Ki. 15:18). He may be the same as Rezon (11:23).

Hezir. hee′zuhr (Heb. *ḥēzîr H2615*, "boar"). (1) A descendant of Aaron whose family in the time of David made up the eighteenth division of priests (1 Chr. 24:15).

(2) A leader of the people who signed the covenant of Nehemiah (Neh. 10:20).

Hezrai. See Hezro.

Hezro. hez′roh (Heb. *ḥeṣrô H2968*, derivation uncertain). A Carmelite included in the list of David's mighty warriors (2 Sam. 23:35 [KJV, "Hezrai," following many Heb. MSS]; 1 Chr. 11:37). On the tenuous grounds that Hezron was from the city of Carmel, some have speculated that he may have been a servant of Nabal who fled from his master to join David.

Hezron (person). hez′ruhn (Heb. *ḥeṣrôn H2969*, derivation uncertain; gentilic *ḥeṣrônî H2971*, "Hezronite"; Gk. *Hesrōm G2272*). (1) Son of Reuben, grandson of Jacob, and eponymous ancestor of the Hezronite clan (Gen. 46:9; Exod. 6:14; Num. 26:6; 1 Chr. 5:3). Some scholars argue that the

Reubenites were assimilated into the tribe of Judah and that these Hezronites became a Judahite clan; see #2 below.

(2) Son of Perez and grandson of Judah; father of Jerahmeel, Ram, Caleb (Kelubai), and Segub (the latter by the daughter of Makir, a Manassite, whom Hezron married at sixty); eponymous ancestor of the Hezronite clan within the tribe of Judah; and ancestor of David (Gen. 46:12; Num. 26:21; Ruth 4:18-19; 1 Chr. 2:5, 9, 18, 21, 24-25; 4:1). Hezron is included in the genealogy of Jesus Christ (Matt. 1:3; Lk. 3:33).

Hezron (place). hez′ruhn (Heb. *ḥeṣrôn H2970*, possibly "enclosure, settlement"). A town on the S border of the tribe of Judah (Josh. 15:3). Hezron was apparently somewhere between Kadesh Barnea and Addar, but the precise location is unknown. Regarding the parallel passage (Num. 34:4), see the discussion under Hazar Addar.

Hiddai. hid′i (Heb. *hidday H2068*, possibly "splendor [of God]"). An Ephraimite from the ravines of Gaash, included in the list of David's mighty warriors (2 Sam. 23:30; called "Hurai" in the parallel, 1 Chr. 11:32).

Hiddekel. See Tigris.

Hiel. hi′uhl (Heb. *ḥîʾēl H2647*, possibly "brother of God" or "God lives [here]"). A man of Bethel who in the days of King Ahab rebuilt the city of Jericho, and the loss of whose sons, Abiram and Segub, was interpreted as the fulfillment of a curse pronounced by Joshua upon anyone who might rebuild the city (1 Ki. 16:34; cf. Josh. 6:26). It is uncertain whether Hiel sacrificed his sons or whether they died a natural death.

Hierapolis. hi′uh-rap′uh-lis (Gk. *Hierapolis G2631*, "sacred city"). A city in the Lycus Valley, part of the region of Phrygia in W Asia Minor (its only NT mention is Col. 4:13). Hierapolis received its name from the fact that it was the seat of worship of important deities. The location was on the right bank of the Lycus River about 8 mi. (13 km.) above its confluence with the Maeander. Tradition connects the apostle Philip with the church; and Papias, notable disciple of John the apostle, was born there. Great ruins survive.

hieroglyphics. See writing.

higgaion. hi-gay´yon (Heb. *higgāyôn H2053*). A musical term of uncertain meaning, used in conjunction with *Selah* (Ps. 9:16). The Hebrew word is used three other times, once with the meaning "melody, sounding, playing" (Ps. 92:3; elsewhere "meditation, planning" (Ps. 19:14) and "murmur, talk" (Lam. 3:62).

high (higher) gate. See Upper Gate.

high places. It seems to be inherent in human nature to think of God as dwelling in the heights. From earliest times people have tended to choose high places for their worship, whether of the true God or of the false gods they have invented. The reason for this is that the so-called gods were in fact the barely personified forces of nature; they were empty of moral character and therefore one could not appeal to them in the same sense as one could appeal to the God of Israel. They had made no promises and extended no covenant to their people. All, therefore, that the worshipers could do was choose an exposed site where the "god" was likely to see what they were doing and to perform there some act comparable to what they wished their god to do for them. See Baal; idolatry.

In Canaan the high places had become the scenes of orgies and human sacrifice connected with the idolatrous worship of these imaginary gods; and so, when Israel entered the Promised Land they were told, "Drive out all the inhabitants of the land before you. Destroy all their carved images and their cast idols, and demolish all their high places" (Num. 33:52). Figured stones were covered with crude carvings, sometimes more or less like geometrical figures, or with talismans or other signs presumably understood by the priests and used to mystify or terrorize the worshipers. Israel partly obeyed the divine injunction but largely failed. In Jdg. 1:19-35 we read of the failure of eight different tribes to drive out the people of the land, and though "Israel served the Lord

throughout the lifetime of Joshua and of the elders who outlived him" (Josh. 24:31; Jdg. 2:7), they soon relapsed into idolatry, used the high places for the worship of the Baals, and "provoked the Lord to anger."

Before God would use Gideon to drive out the Midianites (Jdg. 6:25), Gideon had to throw down his father's altar to Baal and the image ("Asherah pole") that was beside it. Before Solomon built the temple, there was a mixed condition of worship. The tent of meeting (i.e., the tabernacle) with most of its furniture was at the high place at Gibeon, several miles N of Jerusalem, though David had brought the ark to Jerusalem. Solomon went to the high place at Gibeon to offer sacrifice, and there God heard his prayer and granted him surpassing wisdom (2 Chr. 1:1-13). Later some godly kings, including Hezekiah (31:1), destroyed the high places, whereas others, including his son Manasseh, relapsed and rebuilt them (33:3). After Manasseh had been punished and had repented, he was restored to his throne and resumed the temple worship; but the people "continued to sacrifice at the high places, but only to the Lord their God" (33:17). Through Manasseh's early influence, the people had gone so far into apostasy that they could not repent; but through the godliness of Josiah, the judgment was delayed until after his death. His great "housecleaning" is described in 2 Ki. 23:1-25. God's attitude toward the godly kings and toward the wicked ones like Ahab in the north and Ahaz and Manasseh in the south depended largely on their attitude toward the high places.

high priest. See priest.

Hilen. hi´luhn (Heb. *ḥilēn H2664*). A Levitical town in the hill country of the tribe of Judah, assigned to the descendants of Kohath (1 Chr. 6:58, according to many Heb. MSS; the MT reads *ḥilēz*). The parallel passage has Holon (Josh. 21:15).

Hilkiah. hil-ki´uh (Heb. *ḥilqiyyâ H2759, ḥilqiyyāhû H2760*, "Yahweh is my portion"). **(1)** Son of Amzi, descendant of Merari, and ancestor of the Levite musician Ethan (1 Chr. 6:45).

(2) Son of Hosah and descendant of Merari; he was a Levite gatekeeper during the time of David (1 Chr. 26:11).

(3) Father of Eliakim, who was palace administrator under King Hezekiah (2 Ki. 18:18, 26, 37; Isa. 22:20; 36:3).

(4) Father of Jeremiah the prophet and a priest in Anathoth (Jer. 1:1). It is often suggested that he descended from Abiathar, David's high priest, whom Solomon exiled to Anathoth for supporting Adonijah (1 Ki. 2:26-27).

(5) Father of Gemariah, who carried a message from Jeremiah to the captive Jews (Jer. 29:3).

(6) Son of Shallum (Meshullam), high priest in the time of King Josiah, and ancestor of Ezra; this is the Hilkiah who helped Josiah in his religious reforms and who found the Book of the Law in the temple (2 Ki. 22:4-14; 23:4; 1 Chr. 6:13; 9:11; 2 Chr. 34:9-22; 35:8; Ezra 7:1; Neh. 11:11).

(7) One of the leaders of the priests who returned from exile with Zerubbabel and Jeshua (Neh. 12:7); his son or descendant Hashabiah later became leader of his priestly family (v. 21).

(8) One of the prominent men who stood near Ezra when the law was read at the great assembly (Neh. 8:4). He may be the same as #7 above.

hill country. A term applied to any region of hills and valleys that could not quite be called mountainous. In Scripture it generally applies to the higher part of Judea (Lk. 1:39, 65) and in the OT to the southern part of Lebanon E of Sidon (Josh. 13:6; NIV, "mountain region"). See also Ephraim, hill country of; Palestine; Shephelah.

Hillel. hil´uhl, hi-lel´ (Heb. *hillēl H2148*, prob. "he has praised"). **(1)** Father of Abdon; the latter led Israel for eight years during the time of the judges (Jdg. 12:13, 15).

(2) A Jewish scholar (c. 60 B.C. to A.D. 20), reputed to have played a foundational role in the development of the oral law. He and his contemporary Shammai mark the beginning of the Tannaitic period in rabbinic history, although it is difficult to determine the historical value of statements attributed to them (see Talmud). According to tradition, Hillel was head of the Sanhedrin during part of the reign of King Herod. A native

of Babylon, he studied Torah in Jerusalem under the famed teachers there. The legends that are told of Hillel magnify his kindness and gentleness and contrast him with his colleague, Shammai, a native Judean, who was said to be of a harsher disposition, impatient, and irascible. The personalities of Hillel and Shammai are also reflected in their interpretation of the law, Hillel being more humanitarian and liberal, Shammai more stringent and conservative. These tendencies were later reflected in the two schools associated with their names, although in many specific cases the "House of Hillel" ruled with greater stringency than that of Shammai. Especially after A.D. 70, the generally progressive school of Hillel became preeminent, thus giving direction to the course of classical Judaism.

hill of God. See Gibeah #3.

hill of the foreskins. See Gibeath Haaraloth.

hin. See weights and measures.

hind. See animals.

hinge. This English term, referring to a device that allows a door or lid to turn, is used rarely in Bible versions (e.g., Prov. 26:14). Most of the ancient hinges were of a pivot type that would fit into a socket (cf. 1 Ki. 7:50 KJV).

Hinnom, Valley of (Ben). hin´uhm (Heb. *hinnōm H2183*, derivation uncertain). A valley running southward from the Jaffa Gate at the W side of Jerusalem, then turning eastward and running S of the city until it joined the Valley of the Kidron. It was a part of the boundary between Judah on the S (Josh. 15:8) and Benjamin on the N (18:16). Nothing is known of the "son of Hinnom" except that he lived before Joshua's time and presumably owned the valley. It seems to have been a dumping ground and a place for burning. Topheth was here (2 Ki. 23:10), where human sacrifices had been offered to Molech, and so it was later to be called "the Valley of Slaughter" (Jer. 19:6). The Hebrew for Valley of Hinnom (*gê-hinnōm*) transliterated into Greek as *geenna G1147*, which became the word for hell (see Gehenna). Jesus uses it in

Aerial view of Jerusalem (looking NE). The Hinnom Valley lies to the W and S of the Old City.

referring to the final destination of the wicked; and probably "the fiery lake of burning sulfur" (Rev. 19:20; 20:10, 14-15; 21:8) is a description of the same terrible place.

hip. This English term is used a few times in Bible versions to render Hebrew *yārēk H3751*, which properly refers to the upper THIGH. JACOB was struck on the socket of his hip (Gen. 32:25; KJV, "the hollow of his thigh") to reduce his feeling of self-sufficiency and to make him lean upon God. This Hebrew term is used alongside another word meaning "thigh" or "leg" (*šôq H8797*) when the biblical writer says that SAMSON struck the PHILISTINES *šôq ʿal-yārēk* (Jdg. 15:8), an unusual expression that the KJV and NRSV render somewhat literally, "hip and thigh," while the NIV interprets it to mean "viciously."

hippopotamus. See ANIMALS.

Hirah. hīʹruh (Heb. *ḥîrâ H2669*, derivation uncertain). A Canaanite man from the town of ADULLAM with whom JUDAH stayed after leaving his brothers (Gen. 38:1 NIV; according to the NRSV, Judah "settled near" Hirah). Subsequently Hirah is described as a friend of Judah (vv. 12, 20); he was

sent to get back the pledge that Judah had given to a woman he thought was a prostitute (in reality, TAMAR; see vv. 13-26).

Hiram, Huram. hīʹruhm, hyoorʹuhm (Heb. *ḥîrām H2671*, *ḥîrôm H2670* [1 Ki. 5:10, 18; 7:40], *ḥûrām H2586* [only in Chronicles]; from Phoen. *ʾḥrm*, "my brother is lifted up"). To avoid confusion, the NIV uses "Hiram" for #1 below and "Huram" for #2; in the Hebrew text, however, both forms are used for both individuals.

(1) The king of TYRE during the reigns of DAVID and SOLOMON, with whom they had peaceful and friendly relations. After David captured JERUSALEM and made it his capital, Hiram sent him wood, carpenters, and stonemasons to build his palace (2 Sam. 5:11). When Solomon ascended the throne, he asked Hiram for help in building a TEMPLE and a new palace, projects that took him twenty years to complete. Hiram sent him wood—cedar, pine, and algum—from the forests of LEBANON and all the gold he needed (1 Ki. 5:1-9; 2 Chr. 2:3-10), together with all the skilled workmen necessary for erecting and furnishing them. In return, Solomon sent him every year "twenty thousand cors of wheat as food for his household, in addition to twenty thousand baths of pressed olive oil"

H

(1 Ki. 5:11). He also gave Hiram twenty cities in GALILEE, but when Hiram inspected them, he told Solomon he was not well pleased with them (1 Ki. 9:10-14). When Solomon built a fleet of ships at EZION GEBER in EDOM, on the shore of the RED SEA, Hiram sent him experienced seamen to work with Solomon's men on the ships. Once every three years they brought to Solomon gold, silver, ivory, apes, and peacocks (1 Ki. 10:22; 2 Chr. 9:21).

(2) A skilled craftsman sent by King Hiram to Solomon to help him build his palace and the temple. He is also called Huram-Abi (*ḥûrām ʾābî H2587*, 2 Chr. 2:13 [KJV, "Huram my father"; cf. LXX]; *ḥûrām ʾābîw*, 4:16 [KJV, "Huram his father"]; the second element may be a title). His father was a native of Tyre of a family of craftsmen, but his mother was of the Israelite tribe of NAPHTALI (1 Ki. 14:2); according to 2 Chr. 2:13, she was of the daughters of DAN. (2 Chr. 2:13).

hire. See WAGES.

hireling. This English term, which today has a negative connotation (someone who does menial or even offensive work for pay), is used several times in the KJV (e.g., Job 7:1; Jn. 10:12-13). Modern versions prefer such renderings as "laborer" and "hired hand." See LABOR; WAGES.

hiss. To make a sharp sibilant sound (like a prolonged *s* or *sh*), an act of special meaning in many Near Eastern cultures. The English term is used by the KJV and other versions mainly to render the Hebrew verb *šāraq H9239*, "to whistle," which occurs a dozen times in the OT (Job 27:23 et al.). Because hissing is used to express derision, the NIV often renders it with "scoff" (e.g., 1 Ki. 9:8).

history. A narrative of events or the study of the past. God often has been isolated from history or too closely linked with it. Karl Marx refused even to consider divine activity in history because history is the outcome of matter in motion. Many of the theological existentialists so link God with what they call holy history that he is uninterested in the historical events resulting from human action. Others invert biblical ideas. PROVIDENCE is replaced by progress, eternity by TIME, and the

MILLENNIUM by an earthly Utopia brought about by human activity in a secular setting. The Bible, however, links the events of SALVATION with empirically verifiable history except for CREATION (Heb. 11:3) and the final consummation of history (2 Pet. 3; see ESCHATOLOGY). The historical narratives of the Bible are not neutral accounts; they involve judgment and interpretation. Nevertheless, the writers of Scripture evidently gave great importance to the truthfulness and reliability of the events described. LUKE in particular shows concern with the method of the historian: the prologue to his gospel is a summary of much of what one finds concerning historical methodology in the best modern manuals on that subject. For example, he points out in his prologue that he used several secondary narratives of the life of Christ. His use of the word "us" (Lk. 1:1-2) and "also" (v. 3) suggests that he thought these were valid documents. And like modern historians, he emphasized his use of firsthand information of eyewitnesses.

Hittite. hit´tit (Heb. *ḥittî H3153*, cf. also *běnê-ḥēt*, "the sons of HETH" [Gen. 23:3 et al.]; represented in cuneiform as *ḫatti*). The Hittites were an ancient Indo-European people who lived in ANATOLIA and N SYRIA. In the strict sense, the name applies to the Hattians, whose origins can be traced to the third millennium B.C. and who were a dominant civilization in the second. The OT employs the expressions "sons of Heth" and "Hittites" synonymously. The former expression, which has reference to HETH (Gen. 10:15; 1 Chr. 1:13), the eponymous ancestor of the "Hittites," occurs only in Genesis (Gen. 10:15; 23:3, 5, 7, 10, 16, 20; 25:10; 27:46 ["daughters of Heth"]; 49:32). It is used to designate the "Hittites" only of the patriarchal age and no others. The term *ḥittî*, on the other hand, has a much broader reference and is found not only in Genesis (15:20; 23:10; et al.), but also throughout the historical and prophetical literature of the OT. With reference to the many meanings that the term *Hittite* bears in scholarly literature, it may be noted that in the OT it denotes only two groups. There is no reference in the OT under this term to the Indo-European Hittites of Asia Minor. Nor is there any allusion to the Hattians. In the OT, the term *Hittites* refers either to an ethnic group in PALESTINE during the patri-

Basalt stela of the Hittite goddess Kubaba holding a mirror and standing beneath a winged sun-disk (9th cent. B.C., from Birecik, N of Carchemish).

archal age, the period of the exodus, and the period of the conquest, or to the "neo-Hittite" peoples and kingdoms of Syria during the first millennium B.C. Whatever the geographic origin of the "Hittites" of Palestine in the patriarchal age, it is clear that they have been thoroughly semitized, for none of their personal names can be satisfactorily interpreted as Indo-European or HURRIAN.

During the age of the Hebrew monarchy, other "Hittites" appear in the narratives, but these are foreigners rather than aboriginal inhabitants of Palestine. They are, in fact, the "neo-Hittites" of Syria. SOLOMON's Hittite wives, unlike ESAU's, were foreigners he married for political reasons, along with women from Egypt, Moab, Ammon, Edom, and Sidon (1 Ki. 11). The "kings of the Hittites" mentioned elsewhere (2 Ki. 7:6-7; 2 Chr. 1:17) were powerful monarchs from Syria. In this

category one would wish to place URIAH the Hittite, the faithful soldier in DAVID's army. The hard core of David's army consisted of foreign mercenary troops, who were undeterred by petty local allegiances from following him without question (2 Sam. 15). Since David's northern border reached all the way to the EUPHRATES (8:3), it is surely likely that among his mercenaries would be a sizable number of Syrian "Hittites."

There is evidence of Hittite influences on the literature and culture of Israel. Some have argued, for example, that the structure of the biblical COVENANT at Sinai be understood as preserving a very ancient treaty form best known from, but not originating in, the Hittite suzerainty treaties with Syrian vassal states during the second millennium B.C. Each of the elements in that form finds a striking counterpart in the OT passages relating to the Sinai covenant as well as in the book of DEUTERONOMY. Another area of possible Hittite influence is the science of historiography. From the earliest periods of Sumerian and Egyptian history, documentary records were kept of important events. The lists of such events can in a very loose sense be termed HISTORY. Historical writing in the sense in which we encounter it, as in the writings of Herodotus ("the father of history-writing") is found in only two areas of the ANE. Only in Hatti and ancient Israel is there evidence of historical writing that probes for causes, and which seeks to express a kind of moral philosophy of history. Some scholars have suggested an indirect influence here by the second millennium culture of the Hittites upon the late second millennium and early first millennium culture of the Hebrews.

Hivite. hiv′it (Heb. *ḥiwwi* H2563, derivation uncertain). One of the names appearing in the lists of peoples dispossessed by the Israelites (Exod. 3:8, 17; 13:5; 23:23, 28; 33:2; 34:11; Deut. 7:1; 20:17; Josh. 3:10; 9:1; 11:3; 12:8; 24:11; Jdg. 3:5; 1 Ki. 9:20, cf. 2 Chr. 8:7). In the Table of Nations, the Hivites are included as descendants of CANAAN (Gen. 10:17). They were located in the LEBANON hills (Jdg. 3:3) and in the HERMON range (Josh. 11:3). In the reign of DAVID they are listed after SIDON and TYRE (2 Sam. 24:7), implying their location near these cities. HAMOR, the father of

© Dr. James C. Martin. The British Museum. Photographed by permission.

SHECHEM, is called a Hivite (Gen. 34:2). The inhabitants of GIBEON to the N of JERUSALEM are also identified as Hivites (Josh. 9:7; 11:19). A certain ZIBEON is apparently identified both as a Hivite and as a Horite (Gen. 36:2, 20), and the SEPTUAGINT twice reads Horite where MT has Hivite (Josh. 9:7; Gen. 34:2). Clearly these strange ethnic designations confused the scribes. It has been maintained that, since no name that closely resembles Hivite has yet been found in extrabiblical sources, the biblical name should be viewed as a corruption of Horite, and that both Hivites and Horites should be seen as groups related culturally and linguistically to the HURRIANS.

Hizki. hiz′ki (Heb. *ḥizqî H2623*, "[Yahweh] has strengthened me"). KJV Hezeki. Son of ELPAAL and descendant of BENJAMIN (1 Chr. 8:17).

Hizkiah. hiz-ki′uh (Heb. *ḥizqiyyâ H2624*, "Yahweh has strengthened me" or "Yahweh is my strength"; see HEZEKIAH). **(1)** KJV alternate form of HEZEKIAH (Zeph. 1:1; see also Heb. text of 2 Ki. 18:1, 10, 13-16; Neh. 7:21; 10:17; Prov. 25:1).

(2) Son of Neariah and a postexilic descendant of DAVID (1 Chr. 3:23; KJV, "Hezekiah").

Hizkijah. hiz-ki′juh. KJV alternate form of HEZEKIAH (Neh. 10:17).

hoarfrost. Alternate term for FROST.

Hobab. hoh′bab (Heb. *ḥōbāb H2463*, possibly "beloved" or "crafty"). Son of REUEL the Midianite (Num. 10:29). Reuel was another name for JETHRO, father-in-law of MOSES; Hobab was therefore the sister of ZIPPORAH and Moses' brother-in-law. Because Hobab, as a native of MIDIAN, would have been very familiar with the desert regions in the SINAI peninsula, Moses invited him to guide the Israelites in their travels (vv. 29-32). Although Hobab's final response is not recorded, the text seems to imply that he consented; moreover, his descendants are later associated with the Israelites (Jdg. 1:16; 4:11). The latter passage raises a difficulty by referring to the KENITES as "descendants of Hobab the father-in-law of Moses" (NRSV). According to some scholars, Hobab was another name for Jethro/Reuel, but in this verse it may be better to translate "brother-in-law" (cf. NIV).

Hobah. hoh′buh (Heb. *ḥōbâ H2551*, meaning uncertain). A city or region N of DAMASCUS to which ABRAHAM pursued the defeated armies of KEDORLAOMER and his allies (Gen. 14:15). The location is unknown, though some have identified it with modern Ḥoba (c. 55 mi./88 km. NNW of Damascus, on the road to Palmyra/TADMOR), and others with ancient Ube/Upi, a territory of which Damascus was part.

Hobaiah. hoh-bay′yuh (Heb. *ḥōbayyâ H2469*, "Yahweh has hidden [*or* protected]"). Ancestor of a postexilic family that was unable to prove its priestly descent (Ezra 2:61 [KJV, NRSV, "Habaiah"]; Neh. 7:63 [KJV, "Habaiah"]).

Hod. hod (Heb. *hôd H2087*, "majesty, vigor"). Son of Zophah and descendant of ASHER (1 Chr. 7:37).

Hodaiah. See HODAVIAH #4.

Hodaviah. hod-uh-vi′uh (Heb. *hôdawyâ H2089* [with spelling variations], "praise Yahweh"). **(1)** A clan chief of the half-tribe of MANASSEH; he and others are described as "brave warriors, famous men, and heads of their families" (1 Chr. 5:24).

(2) Son of Hassenuah and descendant of BENJAMIN; his grandson Sallu was among those who resettled in Jerusalem after the EXILE (1 Chr. 9:7; cf. vv. 1-3; apparently called "Joed" in Neh. 11:7).

(3) Ancestor of a family of LEVITES who returned from the EXILE (Ezra 2:40; 3:9 [KJV, "Judah," following MT]; Neh. 7:43 [KJV, NRSV, "Hodevah"]).

(4) Son of Elioenai and postexilic descendant of SOLOMON (1 Chr. 3:24 [KJV, "Hodaiah"]).

Hodesh. hoh′desh (Heb. *ḥōdeš H2545*, "new [moon]"). One of the wives of SHAHARAIM, a Benjamite; she bore him seven children (1 Chr. 8:9-10). Instead of "his wife Hodesh," some render "his new wife"; apparently he married her after divorcing Hushim and Baara (v. 8).

Hodevah. See HODAVIAH #3.

Hodiah. hoh-di'uh (Heb. *hôdiyyâ H2091*, "majesty of Yahweh"). KJV Hodijah (except 1 Chr. 4:19). **(1)** Father or ancestor of KEILAH the Garmite and ESHTEMOA the Maacathite; he is included in the genealogy of JUDAH and also identified as having married the sister of a certain Naham. Hodiah's place in the genealogy is unclear, and to avoid this difficulty, the KJV interprets the verse to refer back to MERED, adds a pronoun, and renders, "the sons of *his* wife Hodiah." Others emend the text.

(2) A LEVITE who helped EZRA instruct the people in the law (Neh. 8:7). He is probably the same person mentioned among those who led the people in confession and worship (9:5) and among the Levites who signed the covenant with NEHEMIAH (10:10).

(3) Another Levite who sealed the covenant (Neh. 10:13).

(4) One of the lay leaders of the people who signed the covenant (Neh. 10:18).

Hoglah. hog'luh (Heb. *ḥoglâ H2519*, "partridge"). The third of the five daughters of ZELOPHEHAD of the tribe of MANASSEH (Num. 26:33). Since Zelophehad had no sons, Hoglah and her sisters requested ELEAZAR the priest that they be allowed to inherit their father's property, and the request was granted (27:1-11; 36:11; Josh. 17:3-4). Some see a connection between her and the town of BETH HOGLAH.

Hoham. hoh'ham (Heb. *hôhām H2097*, meaning unknown). King of HEBRON during the time of JOSHUA (Josh. 10:3). Hoham formed a league with four other AMORITE kings to make war on GIBEON because its inhabitants had signed a treaty of peace with Joshua. The five kings were decisively defeated in a battle at BETH HORON, and after being shut up in a cave at MAKKEDAH in which they had taken refuge, they were put to death (vv. 4-26).

holiday. When King XERXES chose ESTHER as his queen, he gave a great banquet and "provided a holiday throughout the provinces" (Esth. 2:18). The Hebrew term, which occurs only here, is interpreted by some in the sense of "amnesty" or "remission of taxes" (e.g., RSV, NJPS; the KJV has "release").

holiness. The state or quality of being morally pure and separate from evil. According to some scholars, holiness is the most typical concept in the OT faith. It is revealed chiefly in the Hebrew adjective *qādôš H7705* ("holy, sacred") and its various cognates. Some scholars believe that the root idea is "separateness," but the etymology of the word is disputed. In the OT the adjective *holy* is a distinctly religious term and is used exclusively in relation to God. It may refer either to God himself or to what has been sanctified by him. Primarily, however, it is God who is holy (Exod. 15:11; Isa. 6:3). There is no holiness unassociated with him.

The Hebrew word for "holy" (*qdš*) was printed on the turban of the high priest.

© Dr. James C. Martin

Holiness is not a human quality, nor is it an impersonal concept. Its divine provenance is everywhere insisted on in the OT.

The concept of holiness is expressed in the NT through various terms, but especially the adjective *hagios G41*, which recurs some 230 times, as well as several of its cognates. This adjective can be used as a substantive (e.g., of sacrificial meat, Matt. 7:6; of the sanctuary, esp. in the plural, Heb. 8:2 et al.). The expression *ho hagios*, "the Holy One," is used of God the Father in the Greek OT, but only of Christ the Son in the NT (Mk. 1:24 et al.; cf. Acts 2:27), unless 1 Jn. 2:20 is an exception. In the SEPTUAGINT, *hagios* is consistently utilized to render the Hebrew adjective *qādôš*, and the fact that this Greek term was appropriated wholly in the interests of the OT view of holiness is determinative for NT usage. Out of four or five Greek terms that could be rendered "holy," *hagios* is the least frequent in classical literature, and so the concept of holiness became filled with fresh content. What became increasingly evident in the OT is overwhelmingly explicit in the NT: that holiness means the pure, loving nature of God, separate from evil, aggressively seeking to universalize itself; that this character is inherent in places, times, and institutions intimately associated with worship; and that holiness is to characterize human beings who have entered into personal relationship with God.

The words *holiness* and *holy* do not occur in Genesis, though they are implied in the dread that the presence of God inspires (Gen. 28:16-17), but from Exod. 3:5 on, where God reveals his name and nature, holiness is constantly stressed. Only samples of the many biblical references will be given here. God is "majestic in holiness" (Exod. 15:11); he acts with "his holy arm" (Isa. 52:10); his words and promises are holy (Ps. 105:42; Jer. 23:9); his name is holy (Lev. 20:3; 1 Chr. 29:16); his Spirit is holy (Ps. 51:10; Isa. 63:10-11; see HOLY SPIRIT). Places are made holy by God's special presence: his dwelling in heaven (Deut. 26:15), his manifestation on earth (Exod. 3:5; Josh. 5:15), the tabernacle (Exod. 40:9), the temple (2 Chr. 29:5, 7), Jerusalem (Isa. 48:2), Zion (Obad. 17). Anything set apart for sacred uses was holy: the altars and other furniture of the tabernacle (Exod. 29:37; 30:10, 29), animal sacrifices (Num. 18:17), food (Lev. 21:22), the tithe (27:30), firstfruits (19:24; 23:20), anything consecrated (Exod. 28:38), the anointing oil and incense (30:23-25, 34-38). Persons connected with holy places and holy services were holy: priests (Lev. 21:1-6) and their garments (Exod. 28:2, 4), Israel as a nation (Jer. 2:3), Israel individually (Deut. 33:3), many things connected with Israel (1 Chr. 16:29). Times given to worship were holy (Exod. 12:16; 16:23; 20:8; Isa. 58:13).

In the NT the holiness of things is less prominent than that of persons. What in Isa. 6:3 was a personal revelation to the prophet is proclaimed to all from heaven in Rev. 4:8, with power and glory. God is holy and true (6:10). In one of his prayers, Jesus addressed God in this way: "Holy Father" (Jn. 17:11); and 1 Pet. 1:15 repeats the assertion of Lev. 19:2 that God is holy and his people are to be holy. Jesus' disciples are to pray that the name of God may be treated as holy (Matt. 6:9; Lk. 1:2). The holiness of Jesus Christ is specifically stressed. Evil spirits recognize him as "the Holy One of God" who has come to destroy them (Mk. 1:24; Lk. 4:34). Jesus is holy because of his wondrous birth (Lk. 1:35). The father set him apart "as his very own" and made him holy (Jn. 10:36). He is "holy and true" (Rev. 3:7). To the Jerusalem church Jesus is "the Holy and Righteous One" (Acts 3:14), the "holy servant Jesus" (4:27, 30), fulfilling the prophecy of Isa. 42:1-4, quoted in Matt. 12:16-21. In Heb. 9 Christ is the fulfillment of OT priesthood and sacrifice, in both of which capacities he had to be holy (2:11).

The holiness of the CHURCH is developed in the NT. As in the OT, Jerusalem is holy (Matt. 4:5; 27:53; Rev. 11:2), so is the temple (Matt. 24:15; Acts 6:13) and the new temple, the church, collectively (Eph. 2:21-22) and individually (1 Cor. 3:16-17). STEPHEN refers to Mount Sinai as "holy ground" (Acts 7:33) and PETER to the Mount of Transfiguration as "the holy mount" (2 Pet. 1:18 KJV; NIV, "sacred mountain"). The Scriptures are holy (Rom. 1:2; 2 Tim. 3:15). The law is holy (Rom. 7:12). Since the earthly holy place, priests, cult apparatus, sacrifices, and services were holy, much more are the heavenly (Heb. 8:5). The church is a holy nation (1 Pet. 2:9). The argument of Rom. 11:11-32 rests the holiness of Gentile Christians on their growing out of the root (11:16) of Jesse (15:12). Christ died for the church in order to make it holy (1 Cor. 1:2; sanctified in Christ Jesus, 1 Cor. 6:11; Eph. 5:26). The church as a whole, the local churches, and individual Christians are holy, "called ... saints" (Rom. 1:7; 1 Cor. 1:2; 2 Cor. 1:1; Eph. 1:1; Phil. 1:1; Col. 1:2; "saints" being a translation of *hagioi*, "holy ones"). The life of the individual Christian is to be a living, holy sacrifice (Rom. 12:1), not only through death (Phil. 2:17), but through life itself (1:21-26). In the OT the sacrifice was a *thing*, separate from the offerer; in the NT it is the *offerer himself*. Holiness is equated with purity (Matt. 5:8; 23:26; 1 Tim. 1:5; 2 Tim. 2:22; Tit. 1:15; Jas. 1:27), a purity that in Acts 18:6; 20:26 is innocence. The means of purification is the truth of the Word of God (Jn. 17:17). The "holy kiss" in the early churches was a seal of holy fellowship (1 Cor. 16:20; 2 Cor. 13:12; 1 Thess. 5:26). Holiness is prominent throughout the book of Revelation.

Holiness Code. A common designation for the legal corpus found in Lev. 17-26, thought by many to have had an independent origin; often referred to simply as *H*. See LEVITICUS, BOOK OF.

holm tree. See PLANTS.

Holon. hoh′lon (Heb. *ḥōlôn H2708*, possibly "sandy"). **(1)** A town in the hill country of the tribe of JUDAH (Josh. 15:51); it was later assigned to the LEVITES descended from KOHATH (21:15; called HILEN in the parallel passage, 1 Chr. 6:58). The site is unknown, though a location S or SW of HEBRON seems likely.

(2) A city in the plain of MOAB against which JEREMIAH pronounced judgment (Jer. 48:21). It was probably located N of the ARNON River, but the site is unknown.

holy day. God calls the SABBATH "my holy day" (Isa. 58:13; in Exod. 35:2 the word "day" is supplied by the KJV and NIV). The phrase can be used of other special ceremonial days (Neh. 10:31).

Holy Ghost. See HOLY SPIRIT.

Holy of Holies. See TABERNACLE.

Holy Place. See TABERNACLE.

Holy Spirit. In Christian theology, the third person of the TRINITY (the KJV usually renders "Holy Ghost"). The Hebrew and Greek words that are translated "spirit" are respectively *rûaḥ H8120* and *pneuma G4460*, both meaning literally "wind, breath." Both came to be used for the unseen reality of living beings, especially God and man. Therefore, breath and wind are symbols of the Holy Spirit (Gen. 2:7; Job 32:8; 33:4; Ezek. 37:9-10; Jn. 20:22). Other symbols are the dove (Matt. 3:16; Mk. 1:10; Lk. 3:22; Jn. 1:32), oil (Lk. 4:18; Acts 10:38; 1 Jn. 2:20), fire for purification (Matt. 3:11; Lk. 3:16; Acts 2:3-4), living water (Isa. 44:3; Jn. 4:14; 7:37-39) and earnest or guarantee of all

The southern steps of the temple at Jerusalem. The apostle Peter, filled with the Holy Spirit, probably preached from these steps on the day of Pentecost.

that God has in store for us (2 Cor. 1:22; Eph. 1:13-14).

There is a rich revelation of the Spirit of the Lord in the OT, running along the same lines as that in the NT and directly preparatory to it. Customarily we think of the Spirit of God in the OT as powerfully endowing chosen individuals for great tasks, but actually his work ranges much more widely.

First, we notice that the Spirit is God's agent in CREATION (e.g., Gen. 1:1; Ps. 33:6; 104:30). For animals (Isa. 34:16) and human beings (Job 27:3) alike (cf. Isa. 42:5), created life is the work of the Holy Spirit.

Second, the Spirit is the agent in the providential work of God in the moral sphere, the areas of history and ethical relationships. Though the actual translation of Gen. 6:3 is uncertain, it is by his Spirit that God senses and reacts to wickedness

© Dr. James C. Martin

H

on earth. According to Ezek. 1:14, 20, the Spirit is the power by which the sovereign God controls the complexities of life on earth (cf. Isa. 4:4; 30:1; 63:14). The godly person knows that his sin offends the Holy One and he fears quenching the Spirit (Ps. 51:11)—this is the form that the Lord's judgment on the disobedient SAUL took (1 Sam. 16:14).

Third, the Spirit is known in the OT as a personal endowment. He indwells the people of God as a whole (Hag. 2:5), just as he was among them at the exodus (Isa. 63:11). He endowed BEZALEL for artistic skill (Exod. 31:3) and many others for mighty deeds (Jdg. 3:10 and 6:34 [lit., "clothed himself with Gideon"]; 11:29; 13:25; 1 Sam. 11:6). These references correspond to what the NT speaks of as the "filling" of the Spirit, that is, a special endowment for a special task (cf. Acts 4:8); but there is also the constant endowment of individuals (Num. 11:17, 29; 27:18; 1 Sam. 16:13), especially those individuals who stood directly in the great messianic line (Isa. 11:2; 42:1; 48:16; 61:1). The OT, indeed, looks forward to the messianic day as a time of special enjoyment of the Spirit of God (Isa. 32:15; 44:3; 59:21; Ezek. 36:27; 39:29; Joel 2:28-29). The verb "to pour out" is notable in these references and points to a hitherto unknown abundance.

Fourth, the Spirit inspired the PROPHETS (Num. 11:29; 24:2; 1 Sam. 10:6, 10; 2 Sam. 23:2; 1 Ki. 22:24; Neh. 9:30; Hos. 9:7; Joel 2:28-29; Mic. 3:8; Zech. 7:12). In all these references the personality of the Spirit is notable.

Moreover, the Spirit is wise (Isa. 40:13; cf. 11:2; Dan. 4:8-9, 18), he is vexed by sin and rebellion (Isa. 63:10), and he is at rest when SIN has been dealt with (Zech. 6:8). He is holy (Ps. 51:13; Isa. 63:10) and good (Neh. 9:20; Ps. 143:10). We note that this is the same sort of evidence that we would adduce from the NT for holding that the Spirit of God is "he," not "it." But, like the NT, the OT goes further. Psalm 139:7 shows that the Spirit is the very presence of God himself in all the world. The Spirit of God is God himself actually present and in operation. In Isa. 63:10, when the people vex the Spirit, God becomes their enemy; in 63:14 the work of the Spirit giving rest is parallel to the act of God leading his people. The ascription of HOLINESS (e.g., Ps. 51:13) accords to the Spirit the character and personality of God.

That the Holy Spirit has power and influence is plain from Acts 1:8; that he is a person, the NT makes clear in detail: he dwells with us (Jn. 14:17), teaches and brings to remembrance (14:26), bears witness (15:26), convinces of sin (16:8), guides, speaks, declares (16:13, 15), inspires the Scriptures and speaks through them (Acts 1:16; 2 Pet. 1:21), speaks to his servants, (Acts 8:29), calls ministers (13:2), sends out workers (13:4), forbids certain actions (16:6-7), and intercedes (Rom. 8:26). He has the attributes of personality: love (Rom. 15:30), will (1 Cor. 12:11), mind (Rom. 8:27), thought, knowledge, words (1 Cor. 2:10-13). The Holy Spirit can be treated in certain respects as one may treat a human person: he can be lied to and tempted (Acts 5:3-4, 9), resisted (7:51), grieved (Eph. 4:30), insulted (Heb. 10:29), blasphemed against (Matt. 12:31). The Holy Spirit is God, equated with the Father and the Son (Matt. 28:19; 2 Cor. 13:14). Jesus speaks of him as of his other self (Jn. 14:16-17), whose presence with the disciples will be of greater advantage than his own (16:7). To have the Spirit of God is to have Christ (Rom. 8:9-12). God is spirit in essential nature (Jn. 4:24) and sends his Holy Spirit to live and work in people (14:26; 16:7).

In the Gospels, as in the OT, the Holy Spirit comes upon certain persons for special reasons: John the Baptist and his parents (Lk. 1:15, 41, 67), Simeon (2:25-27), and Jesus as a man (Matt. 1:18, 20; 3:16; 4:1; Mk. 1:8, 10; Lk. 1:35; 3:16, 22; 4:1, 14, 18; Jn. 1:32-33). Jesus promises the Holy Spirit in a new way to those who believe in him (Jn. 7:37-39; cf. 4:10-15); also as "what my Father has promised" in Lk. 24:49; covered in fuller detail in Acts 1:1-8. Jesus taught the nature and work of the Holy Spirit in the Upper Room Discourse (Jn. 14:16, 26; 15:26; 16:7-15). This work is to dwell in the disciples as Comforter or ADVOCATE; to teach all things; to help believers remember what Jesus said; to testify of Jesus; to reprove the world of sin, righteousness, and judgment; to guide the disciples into all truth; not to speak on his own initiative, but to speak only what he hears; to show the disciples things to come; and to glorify Jesus by showing the things of Jesus to the disciples. After his resurrection, Jesus "breathed on" the disciples (Thomas being absent) and said, "Receive the Holy Spirit"

(Jn. 20:22). This was not the complete enduement of the Holy Spirit that Jesus had taught and promised and that occurred at PENTECOST, but it was provisional and enabled the disciples to persevere in prayer until the promised day.

At Pentecost a new phase of the revelation of God to people began (Acts 2)—as new as when the Word became flesh in the birth of Jesus. With the rushing of a mighty wind and what appeared to be tongues of fire, the disciples were all filled with the Holy Spirit and spoke in foreign languages (listed in 2:9-11). The excitement drew a crowd of visitors to the feast, to whom Peter explained that the prophecy of Joel 2:28-32 was being fulfilled in accordance with the salvation that Jesus of Nazareth had accomplished by dying on the cross. Another 3,000 souls were added by baptism to the 120 disciples, and thus began the fellowship of apostolic teaching, of breaking of bread and of prayer, the fellowship that is the church. When the first crisis that threatened the extinction of the early church was passed, again "they were all filled with the Holy Spirit" (Acts 4:31), binding them more closely together. When the first Gentiles were converted, the Holy Spirit was poured out on them and they spoke in tongues (10:44-48); likewise when Paul met a group of John the Baptist's disciples, the Holy Spirit came on them (19:1-7).

The NT is full of references to the work of the Holy Spirit in the lives of believers (Rom. 8:1-27): he gives gifts (1 Cor. 12:14); our "body is a temple of the Holy Spirit" (6:19); and he works in us "the fruit of the Spirit" (Gal. 5:22-23). Being "filled with the Spirit" (Eph. 5:18) means that one experiences Christ living within (Rom. 8:9-10). As the heavenly Father is God and his Son Jesus Christ is God, so the Holy Spirit is God. The Holy Spirit as well as the Son was active in creation; he was active on certain occasions in his own person in OT times and more intensively in the Gospels; and in Acts and the Epistles he becomes the resident divine agent in the church and in its members. Teaching concerning the Holy Spirit has been both neglected and distorted, but the subject deserves careful attention as one reads the NT.

Homam. hoh′mam (Heb. *hômām H2102*, derivation uncertain). Son of the clan chief LOTAN and grandson of SEIR the HORITE (1 Chr. 1:39). The parallel passage reads HEMAM (Gen. 36:22 KJV; the NRSV has HEMAN, following LXX), though the NIV regards this form as an alternate of Homam and thus uses the latter in both passages.

home. See FAMILY; HOUSE.

homer. See WEIGHTS AND MEASURES.

homosexuality. See SEX.

honesty. See LIE; TRUTH.

honey. Early regarded as among "the best products of the land" (Gen. 43:11), honey was found in clefts of the rocks (Deut. 32:13; Ps. 81:16) and in the comb on the ground (1 Sam. 14:25-43). Job 20:17 speaks of brooks of honey and butter, indicating abundance due to the domestication of bees. Canaan was "a land flowing with milk and honey" (Exod. 3:8; Ezek. 20:15), Assyria "a land of olive trees and honey" (2 Ki. 18:32). Honey was a product of Palestine (Jer. 41:8; Ezek. 27:17). SAMSON ate wild honey found in the carcass of a lion (Jdg. 14:8-18). Honey became a common food (2 Sam. 17:29) even in times of scarcity (Isa. 7:15, 22). It was never part of a sacrifice, but it was a firstfruits offering (Lev. 2:11; 2 Chr. 31:5). Strained honey was kept in a jar or cruse (1 Ki. 14:3). Honey is a recommended food, but in moderation (Prov. 24:13; 25:16, 27; 27:7; Ezek. 16:13, 19). Honey is a standard of comparison for pleasant things, good or bad (Prov. 16:24; 5:3; Song of Songs 4:11; 5:1; Ezek. 3:3; Rev. 10:9). John the Baptist ate honey (Matt. 3:4; Mk. 1:6).

honor. In antiquity, the dual concepts of honor and SHAME played a very important role in the ordering of society, and recent scholarship has paid increasing attention to the significance of this cultural theme for biblical interpretation. In a more general sense, honor is an enviable esteem, a valuable reward for excellence in station, character, or service. It is paid in thought, word, deed, or substance (cf. Isa. 29:13; Prov. 3:9). Primarily, God is to be honored, but all people are to "honor the Son just as they honor the Father" (Jn. 5:23; cf. Mk. 6:4). All that is sacred is to be honored, such as the SABBATH (Isa.

H

58:13-14) and MARRIAGE (Heb. 13:4). PAUL told the Christians in Rome to pay "honor to whom honor is due" (Rom. 13:7 NRSV). The fifth commandment requires us to honor our parents (Exod. 20:12; Eph. 6:2-3), and Jesus rebuked the PHARISEES and SCRIBES for undermining this injunction (Matt. 15:4-6). Ancient laws pronounced the death penalty on those who dishonored parents in act or word (Exod. 21:15, 17; Lev. 20:9). PETER exhorted his readers to honor everyone, especially "the king" (i.e., the emperor, 1 Pet. 2:17), and Paul asked slaves to honor their masters (1 Tim. 6:1).

hood. See DRESS.

hook. This term occurs in English Bibles as the rendering of several words, including Hebrew *wāw* *H2260* (used of the gold and silver connectors or pegs from which various hangings were suspended in the TABERNACLE, Exod. 26:32 et al.) and *ḥāḥ* *H2626* (used, for example, of a ring put on the nose of a captive or an animal, 2 Ki. 19:28; Ezek. 19:4; et al.). In the NT, Greek *ankistron* *G45* refers to a fish-hook (Matt. 17:27).

hoopoe. See BIRDS.

hope. The most common Hebrew noun for "hope" is *tiqwāh* *H9536* (Ruth 1:12 et al.), although other terms or expressions can signify attitudes that are related to hope. According to the Bible, no one should put his trust in riches (Job 31:24; Ps. 52:7; Lk. 12:13-21; 1 Tim. 6:17), or hope in human beings rather than God (Ps. 118:8-9; 146:3-4; Jer. 17:5-6). Reliance on idols is futile (Jer. 48:13; Hab. 2:18-19), and dependence on other nations is, to say the least, uncertain (Ps. 33:10; Isa. 19:3; 20:5-6; 31:1, 3; 37:6-7; Ezek. 29:13-16). Misplaced hope may prove false, and in some cases sinful. But it should be observed that even where an

instance of hope is viewed as sinful, hope itself is nowhere in the Bible regarded as evil. Throughout the Bible, hope is considered a desirable attribute of human life. Even JOB in all his suffering does not curse hope as a cruel tantalizer, but laments the fact that his days are swifter than a weaver's shuttle and come to their end without hope (Job 7:6).

In the NT, the corresponding Greek noun *elpis* *G1828* and its cognate verb *elpizō* *G1827* occur more than eighty times. The apostle PAUL sets up ABRAHAM as an example: "Against all hope, Abraham in hope believed and so became the father of many nations" (Rom. 4:18). Elsewhere he identifies hope as a gift of the HOLY SPIRIT that, with FAITH and LOVE, is an essential characteristic of the Christian when prophecies, tongues, and knowledge pass away (1 Cor. 13:8, 13). The biblical concept of hope is not mere expectation and desire, as in Greek literature, but includes trust, confidence, refuge in the God of hope (Rom. 5:2-5; 15:13). Christ in you is the hope of glory (Col. 1:27; cf. 1 Tim. 1:1). All creation hopes for redemption (Rom. 8:19-25). PETER says that we have "a living hope through the resurrection of Jesus Christ" (1 Pet. 1:3). JOHN THE APOSTLE adds that we purify ourselves by our hope that "when he appears, we shall be like him" (1 Jn. 3:2-3).

Hophni. hof'ni (Heb. *ḥopnî* *H2909*, derivation uncertain). Son of ELI, who was the high priest

The plain N of Aphek where Hophni and Phinehas died in battle. (View to the N.)

© Dr. James C. Martin

at SHILOH (1 Sam. 1:3; 2:34; 4:4, 11, 17). Hophni and his brother PHINEHAS were greedy and rapacious when ministering as priests before the altar of Yahweh (2:12-17), and they acted immorally with the women who served at the entrance to the TABERNACLE (2:22). Not content with the share of the sacrifices assigned to them, they demanded the best part of the animal raw before the offering had been made. All this, together with their immorality, brought great discredit to their father Eli. He remonstrated with them, but not severely enough. In consequence God's judgment was pronounced against him and his house first by an unknown prophet and later through SAMUEL (2:27-36; 3:11-14). Hophni and Phinehas died in the battle against the PHILISTINES at APHEK; and Eli fell down and died when he heard of their death. This rejection of the house of Eli provides the setting for the emergence of a rightful priest, Samuel.

Hophra. hof'ruh (Heb. *ḥopraʿ H2922*, from Egyp. *ḥaʿaʿibreʿ*, meaning possibly "RE [the sun-god] is long-suffering"). Fourth king of the 26th dynasty in EGYPT. Better known as Apries (through Gk. adaptation), this PHARAOH reigned nineteen years, 589-570 B.C. When NEBUCHADNEZZAR II of Babylon besieged JERUSALEM in 589, Hophra rashly marched against him at the appeal of ZEDEKIAH of Judah. As soon as the Babylonians turned from Jerusalem to meet him, the pharaoh seems to have retreated homeward, thus affording the Hebrews no relief (Jer. 37; cf. Ezek. 17:15, 17). Hophra's end was prophesied by Jeremiah (Jer. 44:30, sole biblical reference to Hophra by name) and resulted from a military defeat in LIBYA and a consequent revolt against him in Egypt.

hopper. See ANIMALS (under *grasshopper*).

Hor. hor (Heb. *ḥōr H2216*, possibly equivalent to *har H2215*, "mountain"; the name always appears in the phrase *ḥōr hāhār*, "Hor, the mountain"). (1) A mountain on the border of the land of EDOM at the foot of which the Israelites encamped on their journey from KADESH to the Promised Land (Num. 20:22-23). It was here that God told MOSES and AARON that, because of their sin at MERIBAH,

Aaron would die on Mount Hor in the sight of the people of Israel. The two men ascended the mount with ELEAZAR, Aaron's son, and there Moses removed Aaron's high priestly garments and put them on Eleazar; then Aaron died, 123 years old. This was in the fortieth year after Israel had come out of Egypt (Num. 33:33-37; in Deut. 10:6 it is said that Aaron died at MOSERAH, possibly a neighboring area). Islamic tradition identifies Mount Hor with Jebel Nebi Harun ("Mountain of the Prophet Aaron"), which rises some 4,800 ft. (1,460 m.) and is approximately half-way between the S end of the DEAD SEA and the N end of the Gulf of AQABAH. A more likely site is Jebel Madurah, a mountain c. 15 mi. (24 km.) NE of Kadesh, on the NW border of EDOM.

(2) Another mountain peak with the same name was to mark the N boundary of Israel's promised inheritance (Num. 34:7-8). Its exact location is unknown, but it was undoubtedly a prominent peak in the LEBANON range between the MEDITERRANEAN and LEBO HAMATH.

Horam. hor'am (Heb. *hōrām H2235*, meaning unknown). King of GEZER; when LACHISH was attacked by the Israelites, Horam came to its assistance, "but Joshua defeated him and his army—until no survivors were left" (Josh. 10:33; cf. 12:12).

Horeb. hor'eb (Heb. *hōrēb H2998*, "dry, desolate"). See SINAI, MOUNT.

Horem. hor'em (Heb. *hōrēm H3054*, possibly "consecrated" or "[small] rock crevice"). A fortified town in the hill country of NAPHTALI (Josh. 19:38). It was probably in N GALILEE, but the precise site is unknown.

Horesh. hor'esh (Heb. *hōreš H3092*, found only in its locative form, *hōrēšâ*, and usually with the definite article, "the woodland"). A place in the Desert of ZIPH where DAVID took refuge from SAUL; there David and JONATHAN made a compact (1 Sam. 23:15-18). The "strongholds at Horesh" are further identified as being on the hill of HAKILAH and S of JESHIMON (v. 19). Though the precise location is uncertain, it is often identified with Khirbet Khoreisa, about 6 mi. (10 km.) S of HEBRON.

H

A few scholars, however, have thought that the word should be understood as a common noun (thus "the thicket in the Desert of Ziph") rather than as a place name.

Hor Haggidgad. hor´huh-gid´gad (Heb. *ḥōr haggidgād H2988*, "cave of Gidgad"). KJV Horhagidgad. A station of the Israelites in the wilderness, located between BENE JAAKAN and JOTBATHAH (Num. 33:31-33); apparently the same as GUDGODAH (Deut. 10:7). The site is unknown, though one proposed identification is Wadi Ghadhaghedh.

Hori. hor´i (Heb. *ḥōrî H3036*, derivation uncertain). (1) Firstborn son of LOTAN and grandson of SEIR the HORITE (Gen. 36:22; 1 Chr. 1:39). He was no doubt the ancestor of a tribal group in EDOM. The form of his name is the same as that of the gentilic "Horite," but the connection between the personal and the ethnic name is unclear. Perhaps Hori was viewed as the Horite par excellence.

(2) Father of Shaphat; the latter was the leader from the tribe of SIMEON included among the twelve spies sent by MOSES to explore the land of Canaan (Num. 13:5).

Horim. See HORITE.

Horite. hor´it (Heb. *ḥōrî H3037*, perhaps "cave dweller" or "nobleman" or "son"). Also Horim. Phonetically, this name is the OT Hebrew equivalent of extrabiblical HURRIAN, but the OT references to "Horites" do not fit what we know about the Hurrians, a non-Semitic people. The personal names of the "Horites" in Gen. 36:20-30 are inconsistent with Hurrian patterns and seem rather to be Semitic. It is moreover claimed that no archaeological evidence exists for Hurrian settlements in EDOM or TRANSJORDAN in general, whereas the OT reports "Horites" living there (Gen. 14:6; Deut. 2:12, 22). These people, whom we may refer to as E Horites, and who were driven out and destroyed by the Edomites, were apparently not Hurrians. On the other hand, it is thought by some that the name Horite originally stood in two places where the Hebrew text has HIVITE (see LXX Gen. 34:2 and Josh. 9:7; cf. also Isa. 17:9). If so, these passages would refer to a group that we may call W Horites, because they are said to reside in the region to the W of the Jordan. They are to be kept distinct from the E Horites, the predecessors of the Edomites. The W Horites, it is claimed by some, are non-Semites related to the peoples called Hurrians in extrabiblical texts of the 2nd millennium B.C.

Hormah. hor´muh (Heb. *ḥormâ H3055*, possibly "consecration, destruction" or "rock crevice"). One of the southernmost cities of the tribe of JUDAH, located in the NEGEV, toward the boundary of EDOM (Josh. 15:30; cf. v. 21); it was subsequently allotted to the tribe of SIMEON (Josh. 19:4; 1 Chr. 4:30). Hormah is first mentioned in Num. 14:45, which records that when the Israelites rashly invaded Canaan at KADESH against the will of God, the Amalekites and Canaanites defeated and pursued them as far as Hormah. On another occasion, the Israelites vowed to the Lord that if he would help them conquer the Canaanites, they would utterly destroy their cities (Num 21:1-2, using the verb *ḥāram H3049*, "to consecrate, devote [to destruction], place under the ban"; see DEVOTED THING). God answered their prayer, they conquered the Canaanite towns, and "the place" (referring either to a cluster of cities or only to the specific spot of the defeat) was named Hormah (Num. 21:3). Later, JOSHUA is said to have conquered the king of Hormah (Josh. 12:14). Moreover, the book of Judges relates that many years later "the men of Judah went with the Simeonites their brothers and attacked the Canaanites living in Zephath, and they totally destroyed the city. Therefore it was called Hormah" (Jdg. 1:17). A possible explanation is that at the time of MOSES the Israelites were satisfied with the defeat of the Canaanites of ARAD and deferred until a later time the total fulfillment of the vow. The location of Hormah/Zephath is uncertain.

horn. This term, usually the rendering of Hebrew *qeren H7967*, can refer literally to the bony structure projecting from the head of rams and other animals (e.g., Gen. 22:13), but it is also used as a symbol of power, victory, and salvation (e.g., Ps. 18:2; cf. Lk. 1:69). Musical instruments were made from rams' horns (see MUSIC AND MUSICAL INSTRUMENTS). See also HORNS OF THE ALTAR.

horned owl. See BIRDS (under *owl*).

hornet. See ANIMALS (under *bee*).

horns of the altar. The four protrusions at the corners of a hewn stone ALTAR, a feature common to the ancient world (Exod. 27:2 et al.). Blood of sacrificial animals was put on these protrusions on certain occasions (Exod. 30:10; Lev. 4:7, 18, 25, 30, 34; 16:18; cf. Ezek. 43:20). To cut off its horns rendered an altar useless for religious purposes (Amos 3:14). A person seeking sanctuary might catch hold of the horns of the altar in the temple, but this did not save ADONIJAH (1 Ki. 1:50-51; 2:28-34). In a striking figure, JEREMIAH stated that the sin of Judah was engraved "on the tablets of their hearts and on the horns of their altars" (Jer. 17:1).

Horonaim. hor'uh-nay'im (Heb. *ḥôrōnayim H2589*, prob. "twin caves"). **(1)** A place near BAAL HAZOR, mentioned in connection with the killing of AMNON by the men of ABSALOM (2 Sam. 13:34; Baal Hazor is mentioned in v. 23). The mention of Horonaim comes from the SEPTUAGINT and is accepted by the NIV and other versions (the KJV, following the MT, reads differently). If Horonaim is indeed original here, the reference is probably to "the twin Horons," that is, Upper and Lower BETH HORON (c. 12 mi./19 km. SW of Baal Hazor).

(2) A city of MOAB, mentioned in two prophetic oracles (Isa. 15:5; Jer. 48:3, 5, 34). The name Horonaim occurs also in the MOABITE STONE, where King MESHA states that he fought against it and presumably conquered it (cf. *ANET*, 322). The city was apparently near LUHITH at the foot of a descent (Jer. 48:5), but the exact location of both towns is unknown. It probably lay on one of the roads leading from the Moabite plateau to the ARABAH.

Horonite. hor'uh-n*i*t (Heb. *ḥōrōnî H3061*). An epithet applied to SANBALLAT, who opposed NEHEMIAH in his attempt to restore Jerusalem (Neh. 2:10, 19; 13:28). The name may denote a citizen of HORONAIM in MOAB or, more probably, of BETH HORON.

horse. See ANIMALS.

Horse Gate. An entrance on the E wall of JERUSALEM (Jer. 31:40). Restored by NEHEMIAH (Neh. 3:28), it was apparently N of the WATER GATE and S of the EAST GATE (vv. 26, 29), therefore near the SE corner of the TEMPLE. Queen ATHALIAH is said to have been killed "at the entrance of the Horse Gate on the palace grounds" (2 Chr. 23:15; cf. 2 Ki. 11:16), but some argue that this was a different entrance, situated between the palace and the temple, and that it led to the stables in the Palace of the Forest of Lebanon.

horse leech. See ANIMALS (under *leech*).

Hosah (person). hoh'suh (Heb. *ḥōsāh H2880*, possibly "refuge"). A LEVITE descended from MERARI whom DAVID made a gatekeeper of the tent housing the ARK OF THE COVENANT when it was brought into JERUSALEM (1 Chr. 16:38). He and his family were later part of the organization of the gatekeepers (26:10-11) and were made responsible for providing guards for the SHALLEKETH Gate on the W (26:16).

Hosah (place). hoh'suh (Heb. *ḥōsāh H2881*, possibly "refuge"). A town on the N border of the tribal territory of ASHER, near TYRE on the MEDITERRANEAN coast (Josh. 19:29). Its precise location is uncertain, though many scholars identify it with ancient Usu and modern Tell Rashidiyeh, a coastal town c. 3 mi. (5 km.) SSE of Tyre.

hosanna. hoh-zan'uh (Gk. *hōsanna G6057*, a transliteration of Heb. [or possibly Aram.] *hôsaʿ nnāʾ*, "Save, please," though this precise form is not attested). This term was originally a Hebrew invocation addressed to God (found only in Ps. 118:25 [KJV, "Save now"]), which uses the more common long form of the imperative (*hôšîʿâ nnāʾ*). Later it apparently came to be used as a joyous acclamation, an ascription of praise to God. The English transliteration *hosanna* appears in Bible versions only in connection with Jesus' triumphal entry into

H

Overview of HOSEA

Author: The prophet Hosea son of Beeri.

Historical setting: Hosea began his ministry in the northern kingdom of ISRAEL c. 750 B.C., during the last years of King JEROBOAM II, and was still active at the beginning of the reign of HEZEKIAH, king of JUDAH, c. 715. He thus witnessed the final decline of the northern kingdom, which came to an end in 722.

Purpose: To show that Israel, by repudiating the Sinaitic COVENANT, had become a faithless wife, committing spiritual adultery against her divine spouse; and to bring the nation to repentance.

Contents: Using his marriage as an illustration, Hosea depicts the relations of Israel with her God (Hos. 1-3); he then denounces the immorality and idolatry of the nation (chs. 4-8), prophesies its destruction (chs. 9-13), and urges the people to return to the Lord so that they may enjoy future blessings (ch. 14).

Jerusalem on Palm Sunday. Three of the evangelists give accounts of this incident, containing both identical and supplementary phrases (Matt. 21:9; Mk. 11:9-10; Jn. 12:13).

Hosea, Book of. hoh-zay'uh (Heb. *hôšēaʿ H2107*, "salvation," or short form of *hôšaʿyâ H2108*, "Yahweh has saved" [see HOSHAIAH]; Gk. *Hōsēe G6060*). First book of the Minor Prophets. The name in Hebrew is identical with that of HOSHEA, the last king of Israel (2 Ki. 17:1); it is also the original form of the name of JOSHUA (Num. 13:16; Deut. 32:44). Of all the prophetic material contained in the OT, the writings of Hosea were the only ones to come from the northern kingdom of Israel. This notable eighth-century B.C. prophet lived during a period of great national anxiety. He was born during the reign of JEROBOAM II (c. 786-746), the last great king of Israel, and according to the superscription of his book (Hos. 1:1) he exercised his prophetic ministry in Israel when UZZIAH (c. 783-743), JOTHAM (c. 742-735), AHAZ (c. 735-715), and HEZEKIAH (c. 715-686) reigned in Judah. While Hosea did not mention the events referred to in Isa. 7:1 and 2 Ki. 16:5, in 733 he certainly experienced the raids of the Assyrian ruler TIGLATH-PILESER III on GALILEE and TRANSJORDAN.

The time of Hosea was marked by great material prosperity. Under Jeroboam II the northern kingdom experienced a degree of economic and commercial development unknown since the early days of the united kingdom. The development of city life attracted many people from the agricultural pursuits that had formed the basis of the Israelite economy, and this presented serious problems at a later time. Characteristic of this period was the rise of successful middle-class businessmen, which was offset by the appearance of an urban proletariat or working class. The latter came into being because of the wanton demands made by the luxury-loving upper classes on the increasingly impoverished peasants and smallholders. As the latter succumbed to economic pressure, they were compelled to abandon their property and seek whatever employment was available in urban centers. Thus there resulted an ominous social gap between the upper and lower classes, a serious portent for the future of the national economy.

Nothing is known of Hosea's background, except that his father's name was Beeri. Hosea was evidently an educated person and probably came from a town in Ephraim or Manasseh. A man of profound spiritual vision, he was gifted with intellectual qualities that enabled him to comprehend

Hosea prophesied that God would "break Israel's bow in the Valley of Jezreel" (Hos. 1:5). (View to the ENE toward Mt. Moreh.)

the significance of those unhappy events that marked his domestic life and interpret them as a timely reminder of divine love toward a wayward, sinful Israel. Ever since the days of Joshua the religious life of the Israelites had been dominated by the influence of corrupt Canaanite worship, which by the time of AMOS and Hosea virtually had become the religion of the masses. The deities chiefly venerated were the fertility god BAAL and the goddess ASHERAH. Both deities were often worshiped under the form of bulls and cows, so that when Jeroboam I set up two golden calves, one at DAN and the other at BETHEL (1 Ki. 12:28), he was encouraging the people to indulge in the fertility religion of Canaan. The cultic rites were celebrated several times each year and were marked by drunkenness, ritual prostitution, acts of violence, and indulgence in pagan forms of worship at the shrines. See IDOLATRY.

Hosea saw that this form of worship was the exact opposite of what God desired of his people. The Sinaitic COVENANT emphasized the exclusive worship of the Lord by a nation holy to him. However, the religious life of the covenant people had degenerated to the point of becoming identified with the shameless immoral worship of the pagan Canaanite deities. It was Hosea's primary duty to recall wayward Israel to its obligations under the agreement made at SINAI. On that occa-

sion Israel had voluntarily made a pact with God that involved surrender, loyalty, and obedience. As a result, Israel had become God's son (Hos. 11:1; cf. Exod. 4:22) by adoption and divine grace. Of necessity the initiative had come from God, but Hosea saw that it was important to emphasize the free cooperative acceptance of that relationship by the Israelites. Hence he stressed that Israel was really God's bride (Hos. 2:7, 16, 19), and employed the marriage metaphor to demonstrate the voluntary association of the bride with her divine lover.

The catalyst of Hosea's prophetic message is his marriage to a woman named GOMER. There are two major views of this relationship. The proleptic view holds that Gomer was pure when she married Hosea but later proved unfaithful. Another major view holds that she was a harlot when the prophet married her. Either way, the shock effect of Hosea's marital difficulties would have had telling impact on the people of his community. The children born of this marriage were given symbolic names indicating divine displeasure with Israel. After Gomer had pursued her paramours, she was to be brought back and with patient love readmitted to Hosea's home, there to await in penitence and grief the time of restoration to full favor. This was a clear picture of wayward Israel in its relationship with God and showed the unending faithfulness of the Almighty.

H

The remainder of the prophecy (Hos. 4-14) is an indictment of Israel, delivered at various times from the later days of Jeroboam II to about 730 B.C. The style of this section is vigorous, though the Hebrew text has suffered in transmission, making for difficulties in translation. The first three chapters have been regarded by some as allegorical. Though the book is generally held to be a unity, critical writers have maintained that interpolations and editorial material occur throughout the work.

The book may be outlined as follows:

Hosea's unhappy marriage and its results (chs. 1-3).
The priests condone immorality (ch. 4)
Israel's sin will be punished unless she repents (ch. 5)
Israel's sin is thoroughgoing; her repentance half-hearted. (ch. 6)
Inner depravity and outward decay (ch. 7)
The nearness of judgment (ch. 8)
The impending calamity (ch. 9)
Israel's guilt and punishment (ch. 10)
God pursues Israel with love (ch. 11)
An exhortation to repentance, with promised restoration (chs.12-14)

hosen. This archaic English word is used by the KJV to render an unusual Aramaic noun that probably means "trousers" (Dan. 3:21).

Hoshaiah. hoh-shay´yuh (Heb. *hôša῾yâ H2108,* "Yahweh has saved [*or* helped]"). (1) A leader of Judah who took a prominent part in the ceremonial processions at the dedication of the walls of Jerusalem (Neh. 12:32).

(2) Father of Azariah; the latter was one of the army officers opposed to Jeremiah (Jer. 43:2). Elsewhere (42:1 [LXX 49:1]), the MT has "Jezaniah son of Hoshaiah" (see Jaazaniah), but there the NRSV follows the Septuagint in reading "Azariah son of Maaseiah." If Jezaniah/Jaazaniah is the same person as Azariah, then his father Hoshaiah was a Maacathite (2 Ki. 25:23; Jer. 40:8).

Hoshama. hosh´uh-muh (Heb. *hôšāmā῾ H2106,* prob. "Yahweh has heard"). Son of King Jeconiah (i.e., Jehoiachin), apparently born after the royal family was led away into exile in Babylon (1 Chr. 3:18).

Hoshea. hoh-shee´uh (Heb. *hôšēa῾ H2107,* "salvation," or short form of *hôša῾yâ H2108,* "Yahweh has saved"). The name in Hebrew is identical with that of Hosea the prophet.

(1) Original name of Joshua son of Nun before Moses changed it (Num. 13:8, 16; KJV, "Oshea"); apparently he was known by both names for a time (Deut. 32:44 MT).

(2) Son of Azaziah; he was an officer of David set over the tribe of Ephraim (1 Chr. 27:20).

(3) One of the leaders of the people who set their seal to the covenant of Nehemiah (Neh. 10:23).

(4) Son of Elah and last king of Israel (2 Ki. 15:30; 17:1-6; 18:1, 9-10). Hoshea ruled for nine years (732-724 B.C.) during a time of social and moral upheaval when a total of six kings came to the throne of Israel in a period of only fourteen years (746-732). Hoshea became king by forming a conspiracy against and murdering his predecessor Pekah son of Remaliah (15:30), apparently due to the utter failure of Pekah's policy of resistance to Assyria. This policy had ended in complete defeat. Hoshea reigned as the vassal king of Assyria, under heavy tribute (cf. 17:3). Nothing is known of the details of his reign except the laconic evaluation of the editor of 2 Kings: "He did evil in the eyes of the Lord, but not like the kings of Israel who preceded him" (17:2). Tiglath-Pileser III died in 727 B.C. and Shalmaneser V succeeded him. This change probably led Hoshea, apparently seeking such an opportunity, to withhold tribute and so declare independence. At the same time he sought help from Egypt, sending messengers to Pharaoh So. Shalmaneser marched against Israel in 724. Hoshea capitulated and paid tribute, but he was too badly compromised to clear himself. Shalmaneser, doubting his loyalty, imprisoned him (17:3-4). Nothing more is heard of him.

hospitality. Although the word occurs only a few times in the Bible (e.g., Rom. 12:13; 16:23; 1 Tim. 3:2; 5:10; Tit. 1:8; 1 Pet. 4:9; 3 Jn. 8), the idea appears as early as Abraham (Gen. 14:17-19). One might be entertaining angels unawares (Heb. 13:2) as Abraham did (Gen. 18), graciously inviting chance passers-by, washing their feet, preparing fresh meat and bread for them (18:1-8), and accompanying them when they left (18:16). Lot entertained the same angels (ch. 19). The extreme to which protection of a stranger might be carried is illustrated in that incident (19:4-9). REBEKAH showed kindness to Abraham's servant, giving him and his camels water and receiving various gold ornaments as a reward (24:15-28). LABAN seconded her hospitality (24:29-31); JACOB fared well in the same household (29:1-14). JOSEPH's hospitality to his brothers had a purpose (43:15-34). As a refugee, MOSES found welcome with REUEL, after helping his daughters water their flocks (Exod. 2:15-22). MANOAH entertained an angel (Jdg. 13:2-23), combining hospitality with a burnt offering. The plight of a stranger in a city where only one old man showed the ancient virtue of hospitality is told in Jdg. 19:11-28. The common people continued to be hospitable (1 Sam. 28:21-25; 2 Ki. 4:8-10).

Jesus exercised hospitality when he fed 5,000 (Matt. 14:15-21; Mk. 6:35-44; Lk. 9:12-17; Jn. 6:4-13), 4,000 (Matt. 15:32-38; Mk. 8:1-9), and, after the resurrection, his disciples (Jn. 21:4-13). He received hospitality from grudging PHARISEES (Lk. 7:36-50; 14:1-14) and loving hospitality in a home at BETHANY (Matt. 21:17; 26:6-13; Mk. 14:3-9; Lk. 10:38-42; Jn. 12:1-8). Jesus invited himself to ZACCHAEUS's house and was shown hospitality there (Lk. 19:5-10). The owner of the upper room gladly gave Jesus and his disciples use of the room for the Last Supper (Matt. 26:17-30; Mk. 14:12-26; Lk. 22:7-39; Jn. 13:1-18:1). The disciples at EMMAUS were hospitable to Jesus even when they did not recognize him (Lk. 24:29-32). Jesus taught hospitality by the parable of the Good Samaritan (Lk. 10:30-37), and he told his disciples where they would and would not find it (Matt. 10:11-15; Lk. 10:5-12). The apostles were entertained and churches begun in hospitable homes (see especially Acts of the Apostles).

host. For the sense "someone who entertains guests," see HOSPITALITY; for the sense "multitude, army," see ARMY and HOST OF HEAVEN.

hostage. This English term is used to render a Hebrew phrase that means literally, "sons of the pledges" (i.e., captives kept as surety against further political upheavals), which occurs only in the record of the victory of JEHOASH of Israel over AMAZIAH of Judah, when hostages were carried off to SAMARIA (2 Ki. 14:14 = 2 Chr. 25:24). Similar records from cuneiform sources indicate that such hostages were treated as members of a special social class and often integrated into the conquering society. Although they were in jeopardy, they were not slaves or servants.

hostility. See ENEMY.

hostility, dividing wall of. See WALL OF PARTITION.

host of heaven. This phrase is used by the KJV and other versions as a literal rendering of a Hebrew phrase that occurs eighteen times in the OT (Deut. 4:19 et al.; cf. in the NT Lk. 2:13; Acts 7:42). The NIV uses a variety of translations, such as "heavenly array" (Deut. 4:19) and "starry hosts" (2 Ki. 17:16). Although the most frequent meaning of the Hebrew noun ṣābā° *H7372* may have to do with warfare or an ARMY, it does not seem that this sense is the most fundamental. At least some passages do not bear that meaning easily (Num. 4:3). In this light, is the host of heaven to be thought of as an army of heaven, or a group of beings inhabiting heaven?

In most of the passages, the phrase probably has reference to heavenly bodies, either in general or in reference to stars in particular. These are mentioned in several different connections. For example, the host of heaven is not to receive worship (Deut. 4:19; 17:3). On the other hand, various passages show that Israel did worship the host of heaven. It is mentioned in the summary of the sins of the northern kingdom (2 Ki. 17:16 et al.; see also QUEEN OF HEAVEN). Sometimes the host of heaven is seen as the object of God's creative activity, rendering obedience to the divine will. It may be that the "host" of Gen. 2:1 (KJV) is a broader conception: the host of heaven and earth, including the whole of creation. The host of heaven was made by divine breath (Ps. 33:6), named and controlled by God (Isa. 40:26; 45:12).

Although "host of heaven" most frequently means heavenly bodies, there are a few passages where it clearly means something else. According

H

to 1 Ki. 22:19 (= 2 Chr. 18:18), the prophet MICAIAH saw the host of heaven standing beside God's throne conversing with the Lord, and in v. 21 they are called spirits. This conception of the host of heaven as angelic beings is also seen in Lk. 2:13, where the phrase must refer to ANGELS.

hosts, Lord of. See LORD OF HOSTS.

Hotham. hoh´thuhm (Heb. *ḥôtām* H2598, "signet, seal"). **(1)** Son of Heber and great-grandson of ASHER (1 Chr. 7:32; apparently called HELEM in v. 35).

(2) A man from AROER who was the father of Shama and Jeiel, two of DAVID's mighty warriors (1 Chr. 11:44; KJV, "Hothan," following LXX).

Hothan. See HOTHAM #2.

Hothir. hoh´thuhr (Heb. *ḥôtîr* H2110, possibly "abundance"). Son of HEMAN, the king's seer (1 Chr. 25:4). The fourteen sons of Heman, along with the sons of ASAPH and JEDUTHUN, were set apart "for the ministry of prophesying, accompanied by harps, lyres and cymbals" (v. 1). The assignment of duty was done by lot, and the twenty-first lot fell to Hothir, his sons, and his relatives (25:28).

hough. See HAMSTRING.

hour. The OT does not use a specific Hebrew term for "hour" (in the sense of a unit of time marking intervals during the day), for apparently the Israelites had no system of equal hours for dividing the day. In the earlier periods of OT history, the only divisions of the natural day were morning, noonday, and evening (Gen. 1:5; 43:16). The night appears under the threefold division of first, middle, and morning watches (Exod. 14:24; Jdg. 7:19; Lam. 2:19). The Babylonians must have been among the first to adopt the division of twelve equal parts for the day, for Herodotus (*Hist.* 2.109) testifies that the Greeks derived this custom from them. The sun DIAL of AHAZ (2 Ki. 20:11; Isa. 38:8) was undoubtedly introduced from Babylonia.

Although the Greek term *pēchys* G4388 ("forearm, cubit") should perhaps be rendered "hour" in one saying of Jesus (Matt. 6:27 = Lk 12:25), the standard term is *hōra* G6052, which the NT uses in different ways. (1) It may signify a brief period of time of no definite length (Matt. 26:40). (2) It is used in connection with the broad divisions of time, that is, third, sixth, and ninth hour (corresponding roughly to our 9 a.m., noon, and 3 p.m.); for example, the third and the ninth were the regular times of worship in the temple (Acts 2:15; 3:1), the times for the morning and evening sacrifice. (3) The Greek term may also refer to a definite period of time, that is, one twelfth of the day; although only one NT passage expressly mentions the twelve hours of the day (Jn. 11:9), there are references to "two hours" (Acts 19:34), the "seventh hour" (Jn. 4:52), the "tenth hour" (1:39). (4) An "hour" may be simply the point of time at which an event occurs (Matt. 8:13; 9:22 [NIV, "moment"]; 15:28). (5) The term is used of the appointed time of God's intervention in history (Matt. 24:36, 44, 50; 25:13; Mk. 13:32; Lk. 12:12, 39, 46; 22:53; Rev. 3:3, 10; 9:15; 14:7, 15; 18:10); see ESCHATOLOGY. (6) Another theological use is with reference to God's appointed time for specific events in the life of Christ. Jesus again and again made clear that the Father had a fixed time for every event in his life. This is evident especially in the Gospel of John (Jn. 2:4; 12:23, 27; 13:1; 17:1), but the other Gospels also make it clear (Matt. 26:45; Mk. 14:35; Lk. 22:53); and the disciples of Jesus were aware of it, at least in retrospect (Jn. 7:30; 8:20). There was nothing accidental in the life of Jesus; everything he did was done according to the will of his Father. See also TIME.

house. Words for "house" (mainly Heb. *bayit* H1074, Gk. *oikia* G3864 and *oikos* G3875) are very frequent throughout the Bible and include a wide variety of meanings. It is used in the OT to refer to a "household" or "family" (Exod. 2:1), the TABERNACLE (23:19; 34:26) or TEMPLE (1 Ki. 5:3-7:1) as the house of God, and a temple of heathen gods (Jdg. 16:23-30; 1 Sam. 31:9-10). It might be a nomad tent (Gen. 14:13-14; cf. 18:1; 27:15) or a building in a city (19:2-11). God contrasts tent with house in 2 Sam. 7:6. JACOB called a place outdoors marked by a stone "the house of God" (28:17-22). In the NT, *oikia* usually indicates a building; sometimes it refers to the inhabitants of a house (Matt. 12:25; Mk. 3:25; Jn. 4:53; 1 Cor. 16:15; Phil. 4:22) or even to the human BODY (2 Cor. 5:1). In 2 Cor. 5:1 (KJV), the "earthly house" is the present physical body, while the "eternal" one is the future RESURRECTION body. The related term *oikos* can also refer to a building (Matt. 9:6-7), but often to its inhabitants (Lk. 19:9; Acts 11:14) or to descendants (Matt. 10:6; Lk. 1:33) or to the temple (Matt. 12:4; 21:13; Mk. 2:26; 11:17; Lk. 6:4; 11:51; 19:46; Jn. 2:16, 17; Acts 2:47, 49).

We read of no shelters in EDEN, for probably none were needed in its mild climate; but CAIN built a CITY (Gen. 4:17), which could have been a tent-city or a cave-city. After the FLOOD, NIMROD is credited with the building of several cities (10:10-12), where archaeologists have uncovered the remains of early houses. In MESOPOTAMIA burned bricks joined with bitumen were used in place of stone (11:3). Elaborate houses in UR, of the period when ABRAHAM lived there (11:31), have been excavated. He abandoned these luxurious surroundings to live in a tent (12:8) in the Land of Promise. Abraham found houses in EGYPT (12:15), at least one for the PHARAOH. LOT, when separated from Abraham, at first moved his tent to SODOM (13:12) but later lived in a house (19:2-11). Finally Lot took refuge in a cave (19:30). The house of LABAN may well have been a tent (24:31-32, 29:13-14). When JOSEPH arrived in Egypt, there were houses there: POTIPHAR's (39:2-5), that of the captain of the guard in the prison (40:3), Joseph's own house (43:16-34; 44:14), and Pharaoh's (45:16). The law made provision in advance of the settlement in Canaan for the cleansing of a stone house in which there was leprosy (Lev. 14:33-55). Israelite spies stayed in a house in JERICHO (Josh. 2:1) with a roof where stalks of flax were dried (2:6) and with a window (2:15); the house was built into the city wall (2:15).

After the conquest under JOSHUA, the Israelites came increasingly to live in houses in the cities and towns of Canaan; though some, like the RECABITES

(Jer. 35:7, 10), continued to live in tents, and some took refuge in caves in times of uncertainty (1 Ki. 19:9). House walls were often of rough stone as much as 3 ft. (1 m.) thick and often of unburned clay brick (Job 4:19), sometimes protected with a

Partial reconstruction of an Israelite four-room house.

casing of stone slabs. In larger buildings the stones were squared, smoothed, and pointed. To enter the ordinary small house, from the street one first entered a forecourt, with a covered portion on one side. From the forecourt, doors opened into a living room, with two small bedchambers beyond. When sons married, additions were made as space permitted by using the court, complicating the design. Especially on a hilly site, a large boulder would be built into the corner to support the walls, the most necessary stone being called the CORNERSTONE (Isa. 28:16). The importance of dedicating a new house (in earliest times by sacrifices) was recognized by excusing a man from military duty until he had done so (Deut. 20:5).

The floor of a house might be a leveled surface of stone, more often beaten clay. The rich often had a stone slab floor. SOLOMON's temple had a floor of cypress boards (1 Ki. 6:15). For doors there were square openings in the wall with a stone or wood lintel, doorposts (Exod. 12:22-23; 1 Ki. 6:31), and a stone threshold. Doors might be of textiles, leather, or rushes, but wooden doors fastened by a bar were used early. Stone sill and head-sockets indicate pivot hinges, requiring sturdier construction of the door. A key is referred to as early as Jdg. 3:25. Locks (Cant. 5:5) may have been bolts.

© Dr. James C. Martin

H

Hearths were provided, but no chimney, the smoke escaping through doors and windows. Braziers or firepots were also used (Jer. 36:22). Windows were high, small openings with covers like the doors for protection; some had lattices.

Roofs had beams with transverse rafters covered with brushwood and overlaid with mud mixed with chopped straw. They were flat and were beaten and rolled. The roof was used for WORSHIP (2 Ki. 23:12; Jer. 19:13; 32:29; Acts 10:9). ABSALOM pitched his tent on the roof for publicity (2 Sam. 16:22). Three thousand PHILISTINES used the roof of their temple as a grandstand (Jdg. 16:27), illustrating its strength, while its weakness was demonstrated when SAMSON pushed apart the middle pillars on which the structure depended. There were outside stairs leading to the roof of a house and its "upper chamber." In some cases the "upper room" may have been inside the house. In the living room a raised brick platform ran across one side of the room (in the Hellenistic period at least), sometimes with ducts to heat it, and on this the family spread their bedding by night or sat by day. In cold weather the cattle might be admitted to the lower part of the living room of a poor family. PALACES were much more elaborate (1 Ki. 7:1-12). There is a sharp contrast between the humble homes of the common people and the luxurious dwellings of kings and the very rich in Egypt, Mesopotamia, Palestine under the Hebrew monarchy and after, and in Greece and Rome of the Hellenistic period.

A Christian community, many of whose members were slaves, would be familiar with the lavish contents of large houses (2 Tim. 2:20). While Christians at first continued to worship in temple and SYNAGOGUE, from the beginning they met also in private homes (Acts 1:13; 2:2, 46). Worship in homes was a well-established pattern in Paul's ministry (Rom. 16:5; 1 Cor. 16:19; Col. 4:15; Phlm. 2). Special buildings for Christian churches do not appear in the NT. The FAMILY had been the religious unit from the beginning of creation; worship centered in the house, from tent to palace. Tabernacle and temple were "the house of God." In the NT the house where a Christian family lived was open to other Christian brothers and sisters to worship together; and when the temple was destroyed and the synagogue was closed to Chris-

tians, the church in the home became the sole refuge of the believer, until special buildings were erected. Thus the sanctifying influences of corporate worship were added to the human associations that made a house a home.

household. See FAMILY.

householder. This English term (as well as "goodman of the house") is used in the KJV to render Greek *oikodespotēs G3867*, "master [*or* owner] of the house." The word, which appears only in the Synoptic Gospels, is applied to differentiate between employer and employee in Jesus' parables (Matt. 13:27 et al.). It is used also to describe Christ himself in his overlordship of the KINGDOM OF GOD (Lk. 13:25). The rendering "householder" is used consistently by the RSV (in NRSV only at Matt. 13:27), but more recent translations prefer "master of the household," "landowner," etc.

household gods. See IDOLATRY; TERAPHIM.

House (Palace) of the Forest of Lebanon. See FOREST.

House of the Heroes. See HEROES, HOUSE OF THE.

howling creatures. See ANIMALS (under *jackal*).

Hozai. hoh´zi (Heb. *ḥôzāy H2559* [not in NIV]). According to the MT (followed by NJPS), the apparent name of the author of a chronicle or history in which the prayer of MANASSEH, his sinfulness, and certain of his impious acts were recorded (2 Chr. 33:19 [KJV mg., "Hosai"]). Most versions, however, translate "the seers" (following one Hebrew MS and the SEPTUAGINT).

Hubbah. huh´buh (Heb. *ḥubbâ H2465* derivation uncertain). Son of Shomer (KJV, "Shamer"; NRSV, "Shemer") and descendant of ASHER (1 Chr. 7:34; KJV, "Jehubbah," following a textual variant.

Hukkok. huh´kok (Heb. *ḥûqōq H2982*). A town on the W border of the tribal territory of NAPHTALI (Josh. 19:34; NJPS, "Hukok"). It has often been identified with Yaquq, some 3 mi. (5 km.) NW of GENNESARET. Others, objecting that Yaquq is much too far to the E, propose Khirbet el-Jemeijmeh, 15 mi. (24 km.) W of Gennesaret. See also HUKOK.

Hukok. hyoo´kok (Heb. *ḥûqōq H2577*). A town within the tribal territory of ASHER assigned to the LEVITES descended from GERSHON (1 Chr. 6:75). Some think it may be the same as HUKKOK, but the parallel passage (Josh. 21:31) leads most scholars to identify it with HELKATH.

Hul. huhl (Heb. *ḥûl H2566*, meaning uncertain). Son of ARAM and grandson of SHEM, included in the Table of Nations (Gen. 10:23). In the parallel list (1 Chr. 1:17), the phrase "the sons of Aram" is missing from the MT, making it appear that GETHER was a son of Shem and thus a brother of Aram. It is possible that this passage intends to list the descendants of Shem without distinguishing generations (cf. NRSV), but many scholars believe that the phrase in question dropped out by scribal mistake at an early stage in the textual transmission of the book (cf. NIV).

Huldah. huhl´duh (Heb. *ḥuldâ H2701*, "mole, weasel"). A prophetess who lived during the reign of King JOSIAH (2 Ki. 22:14-20; 2 Chr. 34:22-28). Identified as the wife of SHALLUM, who was the "keeper of the wardrobe," Huldah lived in the SECOND DISTRICT of JERUSALEM (cf. Zeph. 1:10). HILKIAH the priest, SHAPHAN the scribe, and some others, having been commanded by Josiah to seek an oracle from the Lord concerning the lawbook found in the TEMPLE, came to her to fulfill the request. She then prophesied judgment and disaster upon Jerusalem and its people, but not for Josiah, since his reading of the lawbook had led to repentance. For him she relayed God's message, "I will gather you to your fathers, and you will be buried [*lit.*, be gathered to your grave] in peace. Your eyes will not see all the disaster I am going to bring on this place" (1 Ki. 22:20).

human nature, humanity. What has traditionally been called "the doctrine of man" is the biblical teaching concerning human beings in their relation to GOD and his CREATION. It includes the following truths: (1) As Creator, God made the human species, male and female (Gen. 1-2). Human beings are a part of the created order as a single species (Acts 17:26), but they are also separate from the animal world with a special relationship both to God and to the created order.

(2) God made man in the image and likeness of himself (Gen. 1:26-27; Ps. 8:5). This points to that which separates humans from the animals in terms of their moral conscience, self-knowledge, and capacity for a spiritual communion with his Creator. All human beings thus have two aspects, a bodily and a spiritual (BODY and SOUL, or body and MIND, or body and SPIRIT), and so have the capacity to relate fully both to the created order and to their Creator.

(3) This capacity has been seriously restricted, misdirected, and abused because of SIN. ADAM and EVE, the first pair of human beings, freely chose to disobey the divine command and to assert their will against that of their Creator. They lost their personal communion with God, and this had repercussions for the whole of their lives and relationships. It also had an effect on their children and their children's children (Gen. 3; Rom. 5:12-19).

(4) Whatever their historical and social context, human beings have found themselves capable, on the one hand, of great heroism, public service, personal kindness and goodness; and, on the other hand, of self-centeredness, pride, self-pity, and cruelty (Mk. 7:20-23). They show signs both of being God's special creation and of being sinful creatures (Rom. 7:14-25).

(5) The eternal Son of God became Man in order to provide salvation from sin and a new, permanent relationship with God both in this world and, more fully, in the world to come. As such, Jesus Christ is called the "last Adam" (1 Cor. 15:45; cf. Rom. 5:14-19), and the world to come is "the new heaven and earth" (Rev. 21:1).

(6) Thus in Christ human beings are restored to their right and proper relationship both with their Creator and with his created order (Col. 1:15-20).

(7) Either as unbeliever or believer, each human being is held by God to be a responsible creature, and so each person will be judged at the Last Judgment (Rom. 2:16).

H

human sacrifice. See CHEMOSH; JEPHTHAH; MOLECH.

humiliation of Christ. See INCARNATION; KENOSIS.

humility. The concept of humility shades off in various directions, but the central thought is freedom from pride—lowliness, meekness, modesty, mildness. There is a "false humility" (Col. 2:18, 23; NRSV, "self-abasement"). God humbles people to bring them to obedience (Deut. 8:2). To humble ourselves is a condition of God's favor (2 Chr. 7:14) and his supreme requirement (Mic. 6:8). God dwells with the humble (Isa. 57:15). Humility is encouraged (Prov. 15:33; 18:12; 22:4). To the Greeks humility was weak and despicable, but Jesus made it the cornerstone of character (Matt. 5:3, 5; 18:4; 23:12; Lk. 14:11; 18:14). Jesus by his humility drew people to himself (Matt. 11:28-30; Jn. 13:1-20; Rev. 3:20). PAUL emphasized the humility of Jesus (2 Cor. 8:9; Phil. 2:1-11), commanded us to be humble toward one another (Rom. 12:10; 1 Cor. 13:4-6; Phil. 2:3-4), and spoke of himself as an example (Acts 20:19). PETER exhorted humility before the brethren and before God (1 Pet. 5:5-6).

Humtah. huhm'tuh (Heb. *ḥumṭâ H2794*, "[place of] lizard"). A town in the hill country within the tribal territory of JUDAH (Josh. 15:54). It was apparently near HEBRON, but its precise location is unknown.

Hundred, Tower of the. The name of a tower on the N wall of the city of JERUSALEM, located between the Tower of HANANEL and the SHEEP GATE; it was restored by Eliashib the high priest and his fellow priests (Neh. 3:1; 12:39; KJV, "tower of Meah"). Both the Tower of the Hundred and the Tower of Hananel protected the NW approach to the TEMPLE area.

hunger. This word and the term FAMINE are both used by KJV and modern translations to represent the Hebrew word *rāʿāb H8280*, which may refer not only to an individual's hunger but also to acute and general lack of food (similarly Gk. *limos G3350*). It is not always clear in a given context which is meant. In a few passages individual hunger is meant (e.g. Deut. 28:48; Jer. 38:9), but the great majority of the uses of the word refer to famine. The cognate verbs are more often used of the individual (Prov. 19:15; Matt. 5:6 et al.), but they also can be used in the sense, "to experience famine" (Gen. 41:55).

hunter. See OCCUPATIONS AND PROFESSIONS.

Hupham. hyoo'fuhm (Heb. *ḥûpām H2573*, derivation uncertain; gentilic *ḥûpāmî H2574*, "Huphamite"). Son of BENJAMIN, grandson of JACOB, and eponymous ancestor of the Huphamite clan; the name occurs only in a census list (Num. 26:39). He is probably to be identified with HUPPIM (Gen. 46:21; 1 Chr. 7:12). See also NOHAH.

Huppah. hup'uh (Heb. *ḥuppāh H2904*, possibly "shelter"). The leader of a priestly family whom DAVID appointed by lot as the head of the thirteenth division for duties in the sanctuary (1 Chr. 24:13).

Huppim. hup'im (Heb. *ḥuppîm H2907*, derivation uncertain). Son or descendant of BENJAMIN (Gen. 46:21), usually identified with HUPHAM (Num. 26:39). Elsewhere (1 Chr. 7:12) he is called a son or descendant of Ir (presumably the same as Iri, apparently a grandson of Benjamin, v. 7), but some understand this occurrence as a gentilic, "Huppites" (cf. NIV in vv. 12 and 15, though in the latter passage many scholars suspect textual corruption). See also MUPPIM and SHEPHUPHAM.

Huppite. See HUPPIM.

Hur. huhr (Heb. *ḥûr H2581*, possibly "son," but derivation disputed). (1) A prominent Israelite who aided AARON in holding aloft the hands of MOSES at REPHIDIM so that the Israelites could win over the AMALEKITES (Exod. 17:10-13). He also assisted in the ruling of the tribes during Moses' absence on Mount SINAI (24:14).

(2) Son of CALEB (the son of Hezron), but primarily identified as the grandfather of BEZALEL (one of the craftsmen who built the TABERNACLE, Exod. 31:2; 35:30; 38:22; 1 Chr. 2:19-20, 50; 2 Chr. 1:5). He is also called a "son" (that is, descendant)

of JUDAH and "father" (i.e., founder) of BETHLE-
HEM (1 Chr. 4:1, 4).

(3) A king of MIDIAN in alliance with SIHON
the AMORITE; Hur and four other Midianite rulers, along with BALAAM, were defeated and put to
death by the Israelites (Num. 31:1-8; Josh. 13:21).

(4) According to the KJV, the father of one of
the twelve district governors who supplied provisions for SOLOMON and the royal household (1 Ki.
4:8). Modern versions, however, do not render the
Hebrew as "the son of Hur," but rather understand
the name of this officer to be BEN-HUR, who was
perhaps a descendant of #2 above.

(5) Father of a certain REPHAIAH who was
"ruler of a half-district of Jerusalem" in the time of
NEHEMIAH and who repaired a section of the wall
(Neh. 3:9). It is possible that "son of Hur" identifies
Rephaiah as belonging to a clan descended from
#2 above.

Hurai. hyoor´i (Heb. *ḥuray* H2584). See HIDDAI.

Huram. hyoor´uhm (Heb. *ḥurām* H2586, "my
brother is lifted up"). (1) Son of Bela and grandson
of BENJAMIN (1 Chr. 8:5).

(2) A king of TYRE, allied with DAVID and SOL-
OMON. See HIRAM #1.

(3) A skilled craftsman from Tyre employed by
Solomon to build his palace and the temple. See
HIRAM #2.

Huram-Abi. hyoor´uhm-ay´bi (Heb. *ḥurām ābi*
H2587). See HIRAM #2.

Huri. hyoor´i (Heb. *ḥuri* H2585, possibly "son," but
derivation disputed). Son of Jaroah and descendant
of GAD (1 Chr. 5:14).

Hurrians. hoor´ee-uhnz. A non-Semitic people
group that figured prominently in the ANE during
the second millennium B.C. Although the name
HORITE is sometimes associated with them, the
Hurrians are probably not referred to in the Bible.
Groups designating themselves as Hurrians (or
writing a language identified elsewhere with them)
have been attested all over the ANE. Appearing as
early as the middle of the third millennium B.C.,
they occupied the great half-circle of the Taurus

Mountains from N of CARCHEMISH to the country
of Namar, around Lake Van, and perhaps as far S as
the Upper Zab River. Their language, which is still
only partially understood, seems related to only
one other known language—Urartian, in which
the kings of Urartu (see ARARAT) near Lake Van
composed inscriptions c. 900-600 B.C. The greatest political achievement of the Hurrians was the
kingdom of Mitanni, whose capital was Washuk-
kanni in the Middle EUPHRATES Valley. At its
height (c. 1400), Mitanni dominated Kizzuwatna
and N SYRIA on the W, ASSYRIA in the central
region, and Nuzi in the E.

The degree of Hurrian cultural influence on the
peoples of southern and central PALESTINE was far
less than that in Syria and N MESOPOTAMIA and
ASIA MINOR. Since ABRAHAM emigrated into Palestine from the E via the HARAN region in Upper
Mesopotamia, he brought with him many customs
acquired while he lived in that city. Many hitherto
obscure aspects of the patriarchal narratives, chiefly
having to do with legal customs, have been remarkably clarified by the tablets from Nuzi, a Hurrian
settlement in northern Iraq, E of the TIGRIS. The
presence in Palestine proper of Hurrians can be
shown by Hurrian names. One of them is ARAU-
NAH, the individual from whom DAVID purchased
the site for the future TEMPLE of Yahweh (2 Sam.
24:18-25; cf. 1 Chr. 21:18-30). Clay tablets found
in TAANACH and SHECHEM in central Palestine
also contain Hurrian personal names. In the OT,
several groups that appear to be Hurrian bear the
names Jebusite, Horite, and even HIVITE (note that
in Gen. 34:2 and Josh. 9:7, the LXX has "Horite"
for MT "Hivite," possibly reflecting scribal confusion between *r* and *w*). It is possible that HAMOR
the Hivite, who is connected with the town of
Shechem, was a Hurrian. Other Hivite centers were
at GIBEON (Josh. 3-7; 11:19), and in the LEBANON
(Jdg. 3:3) and HERMON (Josh. 11:3) mountains.

husband. See FAMILY; MARRIAGE.

husbandman. See OCCUPATIONS AND PROFES-
SIONS.

Hushah. hoosh´uh (Heb. *ḥušâ* H2592, perhaps
"haste"; gentilic *ḥušātî* H3144, "Hushathite"). Son

of Ezer and descendant of JUDAH (1 Chr. 4:4). However, the word "father" in that verse probably means "founder" or "ruler," in which case Hushah was a Judean town, perhaps the same as modern Ḥusan (c. 4.5 mi./7 km. W of BETHLEHEM). The term Hushathite (that is, an inhabitant of Hushah or someone belonging to a clan that bore that name) is applied to a warrior named SIBBECAI (2 Sam. 21:18; 1 Chr. 11:29; 20:4; 27:11; apparently the same as Mebunnai in 2 Sam. 23:27).

Hushai. hoosh´i (Heb. ḥûšay *H2593*, possibly short form of HASHABIAH, "Yahweh has taken account"). **(1)** An ARKITE, from the territory W of BETHEL (Josh. 16:1-2), who was DAVID's adviser and "friend" (1 Chr. 27:33). David asked Hushai to pretend to favor ABSALOM, in order that he might defeat the counsel of AHITHOPHEL, David's former counselor, who had gone over to Absalom (2 Sam. 15:32-37). Ahithophel and Hushai both advised Absalom how to defeat David (16:15—17:4), but Absalom adopted Hushai's advice. Hushai then sent word to David to escape across the Jordan (17:15-22). When Ahithophel found that his advice was not taken, he hanged himself (17:23).

(2) Father of BAANA; the latter was one of the twelve officers commissioned to supply provisions for King SOLOMON's court (1 Ki. 4:16). Some have thought that this Hushai is the same as #1 above, but it seems improbable that the son of an Arkite (i.e., someone with roots in the tribe of BENJAMIN) would have been placed in charge of a town in ASHER.

Husham. hoosh´uhm (Heb. ḥûšām *H2595*, possibly "big-nosed"). A royal figure from TEMAN (some say TEMA) who succeeded Jobab as king of EDOM (Gen. 36:34-35; 1 Chr. 1:45-46). He lived "before any Israelite king reigned" (Gen. 36:31).

Hushathite. See HUSHAH.

Hushim. hoosh´im (Heb. ḥušîm *H3123* [with spelling variations], derivation unknown). **(1)** Son (Heb., "sons") of DAN and grandson of JACOB (Gen. 46:23). He is elsewhere called SHUHAM (Num. 26:42), and the relationship between the two names is unclear.

(2) Son (Heb., "sons") of AHER and descendant of BENJAMIN (1 Chr. 7:12; NRSV). However, the NIV takes this name as a true plural and renders, "the Hushites." Some scholars emend the genealogy and propose that the reference here is to the same person(s) as in #1 above. **(3)** One of the wives of SHAHARAIM, a Benjamite; she bore him two children (1 Chr. 8:8, 11).

Hushite. See HUSHIM #2.

husks. See PLANTS.

Huz. See UZ.

Huzzab. huh´zuhb. According to the KJV, Huzzab is the name of a city that was to be taken captive (Nah. 2:7 [Heb. 2:8]). The Hebrew word in question, however, can be understood as a common verb meaning, "It is decreed" (thus NIV and other modern versions). Several other interpretations have been proposed.

hyacinth. See MINERALS (under *jacinth*).

hyena. See ANIMALS.

Hyksos. hik´sohs (Gk. *Hyksōs* or *Hykoussōs*, from Egyptian ḥḳʾw-ḫʾswt, "rulers of foreign lands"). Term used by the Egyptian historian Manetho for the foreign rulers of the 15th and 16th dynasties in EGYPT, but wrongly interpreted by him as "shepherd kings." The 108 years of the main Hyksos 15th dynasty may be reckoned at c. 1648-1540; the "16th dynasty" consisted of petty local princelings subordinate to the main Hyksos rulers. The origins and rise to power of the Hyksos are much discussed. The JOSEPHUS version of Manetho with its sweeping invasion may be less realistic than the picture of an internal coup d'état in the E NILE delta and MEMPHIS presented in the other views. The ousted dynasty found refuge in THEBES, perhaps as vassal of the Hyksos kings. The career of JOSEPH may have fallen into the late 13th dynasty and early Hyksos period. Apparently, the Hyksos dynasty largely took over the existing Egyptian administrative machine. Its rulers adopted pharaonic style, including the title "Son of Re." The

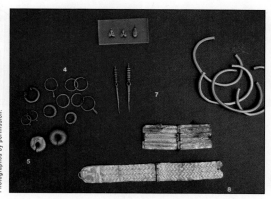

© Dr. James C. Martin. The Rockefeller Museum. Photographed by permission.

Hyksos gold jewelry from Tell el-ʿAjjul (prob. ancient Sharuhen) dating to the 17th cent. B.C.

surviving names of Hyksos rulers are usually W Semitic when not assimilated to Egyptian, such as Khayan, ʾAnat-har, etc. (according to Manetho, the Hyksos came from Phoenicia). Before the Hyksos' takeover, Semitic kings had already occasionally ruled Egypt in the 13th dynasty.

Hymenaeus. hi̇́muh-nee´uhs (Gk. *Hymenaios*, "pertaining to Hymen," the god of marriage). A heretical teacher at Ephesus who opposed Paul, mentioned with Alexander (1 Tim. 1:20) and with Philetus (2 Tim. 2:17). That he is mentioned first in both passages implies that he was the leader among these false teachers.

hymn. See Music and Musical Instruments.

hypocrisy. In the OT, the KJV uses this term to translate a Hebrew word that is better rendered "godless" (Job 8:13 et al.). In the NT, the Greek word *hypokrisis G5694* (with its cognates) is applied to human conduct that was externally religious but insincerely motivated, that is, the simulation of goodness. In classical authors, the term had no evil connotation and could be used in various contexts. It was, however, especially the part of an actor in a Greek drama represented by this term that influenced its subsequent development. By the time the OT was translated into Greek, the word had taken on negative connotations.

No sin was so sternly denounced by Jesus as that of hypocrisy. The Pharisees were guilty at this point, and Jesus both summed up the case against them and warned his disciples against such conduct by the use of this term (Lk. 12:1). Jesus did not charge all Pharisees with hypocrisy, but he did indicate that they were especially prone to this sin; it was the natural consequence of their teaching. Some of them were play actors of the first order: they had sacrificed truth to appearance and were concerned more about reputation than they were about reality (Matt. 23:27-28). The topic comes up also in the Epistles. Hypocrites are denounced because they seduce believers from the way of God in the name of religion. They persuade others to listen to them rather than to God (1 Tim. 4:2; 1 Pet. 2:1). Paul in Galatians charges Peter, Barnabas, and other Jewish Christians with dissimulation because they ate with Gentile Christians at Antioch of Syria, but only until the Judaizers came; then they refused to do so under the pressure of those strict traditionalists (Gal. 2:11-21). In this context the term *hypocrisy* need not be taken as indicating evil motives; rather, it reflects the broader sense of "play-acting."

hyssop. See Plants.

H

I am (who I am). See JEHOVAH.

ibex. See ANIMALS.

Ibhar. ib′hahr (Heb. *yibḥār H3295*, "[Yahweh] chooses [him]"). One of the sons of DAVID born at JERUSALEM (2 Sam. 5:15; 1 Chr. 3:6; 14:5). All that is known of him is that his mother was a wife, not a concubine, of David.

ibis. See BIRDS.

Ibleam. ib′lee-uhm (Heb. *yiblĕ˓ām H3300*, meaning uncertain). A Canaanite town allotted to the tribe of MANASSEH but apparently located within the territory of ISSACHAR and ASHER (Josh. 17:11). Manasseh was unable to drive the Canaanites from this city (Jdg. 1:27). AHAZIAH, king of Judah, was slain by JEHU when he fled by chariot at the ascent of GUR, which was near Ibleam (2 Ki. 9:27). The town was on the southern point of the JEZREEL Valley proper; it is identified with the Levitical city BILEAM (1 Chr. 6:70) and with modern Khirbet Bel˓ameh, about 16 mi. (26 km.) N of SHECHEM and 12 mi. (19 km.) SE of MEGIDDO.

Ibneiah. ib-nee′yah (Heb. *yibnĕyâ H3307*, "Yahweh builds up"). Son of Jehoram and descendant of BENJAMIN; listed among those who returned from the Babylonian EXILE and resettled in JERUSALEM (1 Chr. 9:8).

Ibnijah. ib-ni′juh (Heb. *yibniyyâ H3308*, "Yahweh builds up"). Descendant of BENJAMIN and ancestor of Meshullam; the latter is listed among those who returned from the Babylonian EXILE and resettled in JERUSALEM (1 Chr. 9:8).

Ibri. ib′ri (Heb. *˓ibrî H6304*, "Hebrew"). Son of Jaaziah and descendant of LEVI through MERARI (1 Chr. 24:27); listed among "the rest" of the Levites in the time of DAVID (cf. vv. 20, 31).

Ibsam. ib′sam (Heb. *yibśām H3311*, "fragrant"). KJV Jibsam. Son (or descendant) of TOLA and grandson (or more distant descendant) of ISSACHAR; he is described as head of his family, which probably means he was a military officer (1 Chr. 7:2).

Ibzan. ib′zan (Heb. *˒ibṣān H83*, prob. "swift"). One of the minor judges (Jdg. 12:8-10). All that is known about him is that he came from BETHLEHEM (prob. the town by that name in Zebulun), where he was also buried; that he led Israel for seven years; and that he had thirty sons and thirty daughters for whom he secured an equal number of husbands and wives from abroad.

ice. Because of the mildness of the climate, ice is almost never seen in PALESTINE and SYRIA except on the highest mountains. HAIL is common in the winter and is sometimes very destructive. At heights of about 4,000 ft. (1,220 m.), a little ice sometimes forms during the night in winter, but it melts in the sun the next day. Ice is mentioned in the Bible three times in connection with the power of God (Job 37:10; 38:29; Ps. 147:17). The word is used once in a figurative sense to describe treacherous friends, who are like torrents of water "darkened by thawing ice" (Job 6:16).

Ichabod. ik′uh-bod (Heb. *˒î-kābôd H376*, possibly "inglorious" or "where is the glory?"). The name given to the son of PHINEHAS (one of ELI's two evil sons) by his mother when she bore him on her deathbed. News arrived from the battle of Aphek that the Philistines had killed both Hophni and Phinehas and captured the ark of the covenant of the Lord. When their father heard this tragic news, he fell backward and broke his neck. Phinehas's wife, upon hearing that her husband and father-in-law had died and that the ark was gone, immediately went into labor. In her despondency she named the child Ichabod, saying, "The glory has departed [*lit.*, gone into exile] from Israel" (1 Sam. 4:21-22). Ichabod's nephew, Ahijah (i.e., Ahimelech), was the priest who stayed with Saul and his 600 men at Gibeah (14:3).

Iconium. *i*-koh′nee-uhm (Gk. *Ikonion G2658*). A city of Asia Minor that Paul and Barnabas visited after they had been expelled from Antioch in Pisidia (Acts 13:51—14:5). They revisited the city on their return journey to Antioch (14:21). On his second missionary journey Paul, accompanied by Silas, stopped off at Iconium to read the letter sent out by the Jerusalem Council on the Judaizing question, and at nearby Lystra he took young Timothy with him as his associate (16:1-5). In 2 Tim. 3:11 Paul alludes to persecutions endured by him at Antioch, Iconium, and Lystra.

In the first century Iconium was one of the chief cities in the southern part of the Roman province of Galatia. It was a city of immemorial antiquity and was situated near the western end of a vast, level plain, with mountains a few miles toward the W, from which streams flowed that made it a veritable oasis. Two important trade routes passed through it, and it was on the road leading to Ephesus and Rome. Its geographical position makes it the natural capital of Lycaonia. Archaeological inscriptions found there show that the Phrygian language was spoken there for two centuries after the time of Paul, though at neighboring Lystra the natives spoke "the Lycaonian language" (Acts 14:11). Emperor Hadrian made the city a Roman colony. The city has had a continuing history and is now known as Konya, still the main trading center of the Lycaonian plain.

Idalah. id′uh-luh (Heb. *yid∂ālâ H3339*, possibly from a root meaning "jackal"). A town in the tribal territory of Zebulun, named with Shimron

and Bethlehem (Josh. 19:15; not to be confused with Bethlehem of Judah). Its location is uncertain, but a possible identification is modern Khirbet el-Ḥuwarah, about 6.5 mi. (10.5 km.) W of Nazareth.

Idbash. id′bash (Heb. *yidbāš H3340*, "honeysweet" or "honey-brown"). Son of Etam, included in the genealogy of Judah (1 Chr. 4:3, following LXX; on the textual problem see Etam).

Iddo. id′oh (Heb. *ʿiddô H6333* [with many spelling variations], possibly short form of Adaiah). **(1)** Father of Abinadab, who was one of Solomon's twelve district officers (1 Ki. 4:14):

(2) Son of Joah and descendant of Levi through Gershon (1 Chr. 6:21; apparently the same as Adaiah, v. 41).

(3) Son of a certain Zechariah; he was an officer appointed by David over the half-tribe of Manasseh in Gilead (1 Chr. 27:21).

(4) A seer (also called a prophet) who received visions concerning Solomon and Jeroboam (2 Chr. 9:29), recorded genealogies associated with Rehoboam (12:15), and composed "annotations" respecting Abijah (13:22). His writings served as a source for the Chronicler's material.

(5) The leader of a group of Levites at Casiphia who provided Ezra with attendants for the temple upon their return to Jerusalem after the exile (Ezra 8:17).

(6) One of the priests and Levites who returned with Zerubbabel to Jerusalem (Neh. 12:4). Because his priestly family was headed by someone named Zechariah (v. 16), this Iddo is probably the grandfather of the prophet Zechariah (Zech. 1:1, 7; Ezra 5:1; 6:14).

idleness. The Scriptures criticize the idle person when the situation demands effort and work (e.g., Prov. 31:27; 19:15; 1 Thess. 5:14; 1 Tim. 5:13 et al.), as well as the busy person who speaks "idle words" (KJV), that is, who uses meaningless and careless language (Matt. 12:36). Idleness can be both a failure to respond to a situation calling for action and a busy loquaciousness that speaks to no purpose. The Scriptures call for purposeful work and also for purposeful rest (Exod. 20:8-11). The

I

biblically enjoined SABBATH rest is not to be confused with idleness: such rest comes after labor, and implies not laziness but an enjoyment of what has been accomplished. In biblical thought, work as mere busyness is not virtuous. The opposite of idleness is not activity, but such purposeful activity as achieves its purpose and can thereupon be entered into and enjoyed. The "busybody" is, therefore, a person who is very active but to no good purpose, and the idle man is the unproductive man, who does nothing and comes to a time of need.

idolatry. This term (Gk. *eidōlolatria G1630*, from *eidos G1626*, "that which is seen, appearance," and *latreia G3301*, "service, worship") refers to the WORSHIP of idols, though in a derived sense it can refer to blind or excessive devotion to something or someone. In biblical times, idolatry included two forms of departure from the true religion: (1) the worship of false gods, whether by means of images or otherwise; (2) the worship of the Lord by means of images. All the nations surrounding ancient ISRAEL were idolatrous, though their idolatry assumed different forms. The early Semites of MESOPOTAMIA worshiped mountains, springs, trees, and blocks of stone—things in which the deity was supposed to be in some sense incarnate. A typical example of such wooden representations is the sacred pole or Asherah pole. This was the idol of Gideon's clan; Gideon destroyed it (Jdg. 6:25-32). The religion of the Egyptians focused mostly on the veneration of the SUN and of the NILE River as sources of life. They also had a number of sacred animals: the bull, cow, cat, baboon, crocodile, etc. Some of the deities were represented with human bodies and animal heads. Among the Canaanites, religion took on a very barbarous character. The chief gods were personifications of life and fertility. The gods had no moral character whatsoever, and worship of them carried with it demoralizing practices, including child sacrifice, prostitution, and snake worship. Human and animal images of the deities were worshiped. When the Israelites conquered the land they were commanded to destroy these idols (Exod. 23:24; 34:13; Num. 33:52; Deut. 7:5).

The horror and scorn of the biblical writers toward idolatry may be gauged by the variety of terms used for "idol" or "image": *ʾāwen H224*, "trouble, sorrow" (Isa. 66:3); *ʾêmâ H399*, "terror" (Jer. 50:38; cf. NRSV); *ʾĕlîl H496*, "worthlessness" (Lev. 19:4); *gillûlîm H1658*, "rolled about, [shapeless] blocks" (Ezek. 20:31); *mipleṣet H5145*, "horrible thing, a cause of trembling" (1 Ki. 15:13); *ʿāṣāb H6773*, "shape" or "distress" (1 Sam. 31:9). All these words express the lifelessness and absence of true deity in an idol or image. Theologically, idolaters thought of their gods as spiritual beings (or forces) of cosmic significance. The OT insists, however, that the heathen worship idols and nothing more (cf. Ps. 115:2-8; Isa. 44:6-20). This is a straightforward contradiction of the theology held by the pagans and a demonstration of the rigorous MONOTHEISM of the OT.

The first clear case of idolatry in the Bible is the account of RACHEL stealing her father's TERAPHIM, which were images of household gods (Gen. 31:19). Such images were used in Babylonia. Without JACOB's knowledge, Rachel stole them from LABAN and carried them with her to Canaan. During their long sojourn in Egypt, the Israelites defiled themselves with the idols of the land (Josh. 24:14; Ezek. 20:7). MOSES defied these gods by attacking their symbols in the plagues of Egypt (Num. 33:4). In spite of the miracles of their redemption from Egypt, the Israelites insisted on having some visible shape with which to worship God; and at SINAI, while Moses was absent, they persuaded AARON to make them a golden calf, an emblem of the productive power of nature with which they had become familiar in Egypt (see CALF WORSHIP). The second commandment, forbidding people to make and bow down to images of any kind, was directed against idolatry (Exod. 20:4-5; Deut. 5:8-9). This sin seems to have been shunned until the period of the judges, when the nation was caught up in it again.

The whole of Judges tells of successive apostasies, judgments, and times of repentance. The narrative concerning MICAH (Jdg. 17-18) is an illustration of how idolatry was often combined with outward worship of God. It is significant that JONATHAN, a Levite and a grandson of Moses, assumed the office of priest to the images of Micah and that later he allowed himself to be persuaded by some Danites, who had stolen Micah's idol,

them, Ahab, to please his Sidonian queen Jezebel, built a temple and an altar to Baal in Samaria (16:31-33), while she put to death as many prophets of the Lord as she could find (18:4-13). Baal worship came to be identified with the kingdom of Israel, and no king ever rose up against it.

Things went somewhat better in the southern kingdom. Hezekiah restored the temple services, which had been abandoned during his father's reign, but the change was only outward (2 Chr. 28-29; Isa. 29:13). Not long before the destruction of Jerusalem by Babylonia, Josiah made a final effort to bring about a purer worship, but it did not last (2 Chr. 34). Not even the captivity cured the Jews of their idolatrous tendencies. When Ezra went to Jerusalem from Babylon, he found to his dismay that many Jews had married foreign wives and that the land was filled with abominations (Ezra 9:11). More than 200 years later, when Antiochus Epiphanes tried to eradicate Judaism and hellenize the Jews, many of them obeyed his command to offer sacrifices to idols, although his action led to the Maccabean war (see Maccabee).

In the ritual of idol worship the chief elements were: offering burnt sacrifices (2 Ki. 5:17), burning incense in honor of the idol (1 Ki. 11:8), pouring out libations (Isa. 57:6), presenting tithes and the firstfruits of the land (Hos. 2:8), kissing the idol (1 Ki. 19:18), stretching out the hands to it in adoration, prostrating oneself before it, and sometimes cutting oneself with knives (18:26, 28). Some of these practices were analogous to the worship of the Lord.

For an Israelite, idolatry was the most heinous of crimes. In the OT the relation between God and his covenant people is often represented as a marriage bond (Isa. 54:5; Jer. 3:14), and the worship of false gods was regarded as religious harlotry. The penalty was death (Exod. 22:20). To attempt to seduce others to false worship was a crime of equal enormity (Deut. 13:6-10). The God of Israel was a jealous God who brooked no rivals.

In the NT, references to idolatry are understandably few. The Maccabean war resulted in the Jews becoming fanatically opposed to the crass idolatry of OT times. The Jews were never again tempted to worship images or gods other than the Lord. Jesus,

© Dr. James C. Martin. On display at the University of Chicago Oriental Institute Museum.

Figurine of the Canaanite god El, made of bronze with gold leaf (from Megiddo, 1400-1200 B.C.).

to go with them as the priest of their tribe. He became the first of a line of priests to officiate at the shrine of the stolen idols all the time that the tabernacle was at Shiloh.

The prophet Samuel persuaded the people to repent of their sin and to renounce idolatry; but in Solomon's reign the king himself made compromises that affected disastrously the whole future of the kingdom. Solomon's wives brought their own heathen gods with them and openly worshiped them. Rehoboam, Solomon's son by an Ammonite mother, continued the worst features of his father's idolatry (1 Ki. 14:22-24). Jeroboam, first king of the northern kingdom, effected a great and permanent schism in the religion of Israel when he erected golden calves at Bethel and at Dan and had his people worship there instead of in Jerusalem. The kings who followed Jeroboam in the northern kingdom differed little from him. One of

however, warned that to make possessions central in life is also idolatry, and said, "You cannot serve both God and Money" (Matt. 6:24). Paul, in Rom. 1:18-25, teaches that idolatry is not the first stage of religion, from which humans by an evolutionary process emerge to monotheism, but it is the result of deliberate religious apostasy. When people sins against the light of nature and refuse to worship the Creator revealed by nature, God as a punishment withdraws the light, and they then descend into the shameful absurdities of idolatry. Christians in apostolic times, many of whom were converted from heathenism, are repeatedly warned in the letters of the NT to be on their guard against idolatry (e.g., 1 Cor. 5:10; Gal. 5:20). The OT conception of idolatry is widened to include anything that leads to the dethronement of God from the heart, as, for example, covetousness (Eph. 5:5; Col. 3:5).

A special problem arose for Christians in connection with meat offered to idols (Acts 15:29; 1 Cor. 8-10). Some of the meat sold in butcher shops had been bought from heathen temples. Should a Christian make careful inquiry about the meat he purchased, and would he countenance or indirectly support idolatry if he bought meat that had been offered to an idol? Or should a Christian invited to dinner by a friend ask before accepting the invitation whether he would be eating meat that had been offered to an idol? Many Christians had real qualms about eating such meat, while others, feeling themselves "strong" spiritually, were convinced that there was no harm in it at all. Paul urges against the latter that they should not be careless, for even though idols are nothing, they still are a tangible expression of demons who are back of them; and, moreover, Christians should never insist on their "rights," if such insistence will cause the weak to stumble. They should be governed by the law of LOVE. In the last book of the Bible the apostle JOHN THE APOSTLE predicts a time of idolatrous apostasy in the last days, when the Beast and his image will be accorded divine honors (Rev. 9:20; 13:14).

Idumea. id′yoo-mee′uh (Gk. *Idoumaia G2628*, from Heb. *ʾĕdôm H121*; the Gk. term is often used by the SEPTUAGINT with reference to EDOM). Also Idumaea. One of the regions from which crowds came to follow Jesus (Mk. 3:8). After the destruction of JERUSALEM in 586 B.C., many Edomites moved to S Palestine; the numbers of settlers increased when the NABATEANS conquered the ancient land of Edom in TRANSJORDAN. The area from BEERSHEBA in the NEGEV to BETH ZUR (not far from HEBRON) came to be known as Idumea. During the intertestamental period, the Idumeans were enemies of the Jews, but they were eventually conquered by the MACCABEES and forced to

View of Idumea (looking NW from the northern Negev to the southern Shephelah).

© Dr. James C. Martin

adopt the Jewish religion. HEROD the Great was an Idumean and thus was formally regarded as a Jew.

Iezer. i-ee′zuhr (Heb. *ʾîʿezer H404*, "help," apparently short form of ABIEZER; gentilic *ʾîʿezrî H405*, "Iezerite"). Son of GILEAD, descendant of MANASSEH, and ancestor of the Iezerite clan (Num. 26:30; KJV, "Jeezer"). He is probably the same as ABIEZER, the son of Gilead's sister (1 Chr. 7:18); if so, Gilead was considered his male progenitor for genealogical purposes.

Igal. i′gal (Heb. *yigʾāl H3319*, "[Yahweh] redeems"). **(1)** Son of Joseph and descendant of ISSACHAR; one of the twelve spies sent by MOSES to Canaan (Num. 13:7).

(2) Son of Nathan from ZOBAH; one of DAVID's mighty warriors (2 Sam. 23:36). The parallel list, which appears to have suffered textual corruption, reads "Joel the brother of Nathan" (1 Chr. 11:38).

(3) Son of Shemaiah and descendant of David in the line of ZERUBBABEL (1 Chr. 3:22; KJV, "Igeal"). According to some scholars, the phrase "and the sons of Shemaiah" (NIV has simply "and his sons") should be omitted, in which case both Shemaiah and Igal were sons of Shecaniah. See HATTUSH #1.

Igdaliah. ig′duh-li′uh (Heb. *yigdalyāhû H3323*, "Yahweh is great"). Father of a certain HANAN who is described as "the man of God" (although this epithet perhaps applies to Igdaliah), and whose "sons" (possibly a reference to a prophetic guild) occupied a chamber in the temple into which JEREMIAH brought the family of the RECABITES (Jer. 35:4).

Igeal. See IGAL.

Ignatius, Epistles of. See APOSTOLIC FATHERS.

ignorance. In some instances, ignorance in biblical usage denotes merely an innocent lack of information (Acts 23:5; 2 Cor. 1:8). In its distinctively biblical meaning, it is a specifically religious rather than an intellectual concept. Ignorance is a quality, not of the academically unschooled, but of the sinner. It is a result of SIN and refers to the lack of the KNOWLEDGE of God. Thus ignorance no

more indicates an intellectual state of poverty than WISDOM is a state of intellectual fullness. To know religious TRUTH is knowledge; to practice religious truth is wisdom; to know truth and not to practice it is FOOLISHNESS. Not to know religious truth and, consequently, to live in untruth, is ignorance.

PAUL says about the "princes of this world" who crucified Christ that they knew not the wisdom of God, "for had they known it, they would not have crucified the Lord of glory" (1 Cor. 2:8 KJV). Sins done in ignorance are of course sinful, and those who commit such sins are culpable. Nonetheless, sins done in ignorance incur less guilt than sins done in full knowledge of their sinful character and which, accordingly, incur greater guilt. Thus PILATE's guilt for the crucifixion of Christ is less than that of the Jews (Jn. 19:11); but even the Jews were not fully conscious of the nature of their act, and Jesus, therefore, invoked their forgiveness, "Father, forgive them, for they do not know what they are doing" (Lk. 23:34). The same lesser guilt and greater forgivability of sins done in ignorance appears in Paul's admission that he was a blasphemer and a persecutor of the church, and indeed the worst of sinners (1 Tim. 1:15) but that he obtained mercy because he acted "in ignorance and unbelief" (1:13 KJV).

There is, however, a willful ignorance of God's truth. There is a knowledge of God given in the things that are made that pagans sinfully suppressed (Rom. 1:18), exchanged for a lie (v. 25), and were therefore without excuse (v. 20) and were accordingly punished (vv. 24-32). Yet even such sins of willful ignorance of the truth given in general REVELATION incur less culpability than sins of willful ignorance against the economy of special revelation; the former shall perish without law but the latter shall be judged by the law. Sins done either in ignorance, or willfully against the knowledge of God given to all men in the general revelation "that enlightens every man" (Jn. 1:9), can be overlooked by God and can also be followed by REPENTANCE and FORGIVENESS (which is more than being overlooked). However, that willful ignorance which is the consequence of a conscious rejection of the knowledge of the truth revealed in Christ and made known in the gospel proclamation, God will not overlook but subject to a divine

I

judgment and fire that will devour the enemies of Christ (Heb. 10:26-27).

Iim. *i′*im (Heb. *ʿiyyîm H6517*, "[place of] ruins"). (1) One of the southernmost cities of the tribe of JUDAH, located in the NEGEV, toward the boundary of EDOM (Josh. 15:29). Although not included in the parallel passages (Josh. 19:3; 1 Chr. 4:29), Iim, like other towns in those lists, may have been allotted to SIMEON. Its location is unknown.

(2) KJV and TNIV form of IYIM.

Ije-abarim. See IYE ABARIM.

Ijon. *i′*jon (Heb. *ʿiyyôn H6510*, possibly "heap"). A town in N Israel, apparently within the tribal territory of NAPHTALI in the Huleh Valley, mentioned as having been conquered by BEN-HADAD of DAMASCUS (1 Ki. 15:20; 2 Chr. 16:4) and later by TIGLATH-PILESER of ASSYRIA (2 Ki. 15:29). The site is probably to be identified with modern Tell ed-Dibbin in Lebanon, 9 mi. (14 km.) N of ABEL BETH MAACAH.

Ikkesh. ik′ish (Heb. *ʿiqqēš H6837*, "crooked" [perhaps referring to a physical defect]). A man from TEKOA; his son Ira was one of DAVID'S thirty mighty warriors and the commander of a division of 24,000 men (2 Sam. 23:26; 1 Chr. 11:28; 27:9).

Ilai. *i′*li (Heb. *ʿilay H6519*, derivation uncertain). An AHOHITE, one of DAVID'S thirty mighty warriors (1 Chr. 11:29; called ZALMON in 2 Sam. 23:28).

Illyricum. i-lihr′i-kuhm (Gk. *Illyrikon G2665*). A Roman PROVINCE in the western portion of the Balkan peninsula N of GREECE. Now principally occupied by Yugoslavia and Albania, it was bounded in antiquity by the Adriatic, the Eastern Alps, the Danube, the Shar-Dagh and the Ceraunian mountains. The seacoast boasted of good harbors and the coastal plains were sunny and fertile, but the interior was mountainous and cold. The Greeks were first attracted to the region because of the mines, but the ferocious and piratical nature of the people prevented extensive colonization. The inhabitants were conquered by the Romans in the third century B.C. In Rom. 15:19 PAUL, emphasizing the extent of his missionary activities, says that "from Jerusalem all the way around to Illyricum, I have fully proclaimed the gospel of Christ." It is not clear whether Paul meant that Illyricum was the western boundary of the Eastern world and that he preached up to it, or that he actually preached and established churches there.

image, image worship. See IDOLATRY.

image of God. Two fundamental biblical truths about human beings is that they are created by God and that God made man, male and female, in his own image. They are God's creatures, and there is therefore an infinite qualitative difference between them and God; yet they have been made like God in a way that the rest of creation has not. The passages in which it is expressly stated that man is made in God's image are Gen. 1:26-27; 5:1, 3; 9:6; 1 Cor. 11:7; Eph. 4:24; Col. 3:10; Jas. 3:9. To these should be added Ps. 8, for the CREATION narrative as it relates to human beings is given here in poetic form. Another passage where the idea is not directly stated but is implied is Acts 17:22-31— PAUL's address on Mars' Hill. The words "image" and "likeness," used together in Gen. 1:26-27, do not differ essentially in meaning, but strengthen the idea that man uniquely reflects God. They are, moreover, used interchangeably elsewhere. The Scriptures do not define precisely the nature of the image of God, and we should be careful not to single out any individual aspect or attribute as if it were in a special sense the "image." It is rather human persons in their entirety that are to be thought of as in the image of God. The primary meaning of the words "image" and "likeness" as shown by their use throughout the OT refers to outward, visible form (e.g., 1 Sam. 6:5; 2 Ki. 16:10), an actual copy.

Throughout the Bible the Lord manifests himself in human form—so much so that he is often at first simply described as "a man" (e.g., Jdg. 13:9-10). Often this is described as an accommodation, the Lord graciously taking the form that will make it easiest for us to understand him and communicate with him. God is spirit (Isa. 31:3; Jn. 4:24) and therefore essentially invisible and, though visible form is not part of the divine nature, yet there is an outward form that suits the invisible being of God. This is the form he takes when he wills to reveal himself visibly, and in this form he created man. The human body, therefore, has its own inalienable dignity and worth.

As we proceed through the opening chapters of Genesis, we see that there are other human distinctives that are specially mentioned. The union of the man and the woman in MARRIAGE is directly related to the image of God, a unity of two different but matching beings that constituted God's image (Gen. 2:21-24; 5:1-2). Likewise, when the Creator gives to the man and the woman their joint "dominion," this too is related to possession of the image of God (1:27-28). Furthermore, we note that a clear distinction is drawn between human beings and the animal creation in that God's command to be fruitful is *imposed* on the beasts (1:22, " ... and said"), whereas the same command is *addressed* to humans (1:28, " ... and said to them"). This observation opens to us the unique spiritual nature of man: the supreme and unique creature with whom the Creator holds communion. In 2:15-17 the special moral nature of humanity is brought out. In contrast with the instinctive life of the beasts, humans have been so created that they must order their lives in terms of stated moral ends and in the light of the foreseeable good. Finally, humans are seen in contrast with the beasts in terms of their rationality (2:19-20). They have the capacity to discern both similarity and difference in the world, to frame definitions (give names) and to bring a variety of phenomena into categories and order. Here in essence is the work of both scientist and philosopher. In these six areas—physical, governmental, matrimonial, spiritual, moral, and intellectual—there is a summation of human nature and a view of this distinctive creature who alone was made in the image of God.

imagery. This English word is used once by the KJV to render Hebrew *maśkît H5381*, which more properly means "image" or "idol" (Ezek. 8:12).

imagine. This English verb, in its earlier meaning "to think," is used with some frequency by the KJV (Gen. 11:6 et al.). In modern versions it is used occasionally (e.g., Ps. 41:7; Eph. 3:20).

Imla. See IMLAH.

Imlah. im′luh (Heb. *yimlāʾ H3550* [1 Ki.] and *yimlâ H3551* [2 Chr.], possibly "[God] fills"). Father of the prophet MICAIAH, who predicted the death of King AHAB in battle (1 Ki. 22:8-9; 2 Chr. 18:7-8 [KJV, "Imla"]).

Immanuel. i-man′yoo-uhl (Heb. *ʿimmānû ʾēl H6672*, "with us [is] God"; Gk. *Emmanouēl G1842*). Also Emmanuel (NT KJV and other versions). The name given to the child born of the VIRGIN (Isa. 7:14; 8:8 [cf. v. 10]; Matt. 1:23). The birth of this child was foretold by Isaiah as a sign to King AHAZ during the Syro-Ephraimitic war (Isa. 7). At this time (c. 735 B.C.) JUDAH was threatened by the allied forces of SYRIA and ISRAEL. They were trying to compel Judah to form an alliance with

"For the Son of Man came ... to save what was lost" (Lk. 19:10). From the Church of the Annunciation in Nazareth.

them against ASSYRIA, whose king, TIGLATH-PILESER, was attempting to bring the whole of W Asia under his sway. The prophet directed Ahaz to remain confident and calm in the Lord and not to seek aid from Tiglath-Pileser. To overcome the king's incredulity, he offered him a sign of anything in heaven or earth; but when the king evasively refused the offer, Isaiah bitterly chided him for his lack of faith and gave him a sign, the sign of "Immanuel."

Isaiah's words have led to much controversy and have been variously interpreted, chiefly because of the indefinite terms of the prediction and the fact that there is no record of their fulfillment in any contemporary event. A common explanation is that the event of the birth of the child is intended as a sign to Ahaz and nothing more—the woman in question being Isaiah's own wife or one of Ahaz's wives or perhaps someone else. The traditional Christian interpretation is that the emphasis should be laid on the virgin birth of our Immanuel, Jesus Christ, as Matthew does (Matt. 1:22-23). According to this view, Isaiah has in mind Israel's MESSIAH. When the prophet learns of the king's cowardice, God for the first time gives to him a revelation of the true King, who would share the poverty and affliction of his people and whose character and work would entitle him to the great names of Isa. 9:6. In this interpretation the essential fact is that in the coming of Immanuel people will recognize the truth of the prophet's words.

Immer (person). im´uhr (Heb. *ʾimmēr H612*, "lamb"). **(1)** A descendant of AARON whose family in the time of DAVID made up the sixteenth division of priests (1 Chr. 24:14). He thus became the ancestral head of that division and gave his name to an extensive family of descendants; among the priestly clans that returned from the EXILE, his was the second largest (1 Chr. 9:12; Ezra 2:37; Neh. 7:40; 11:13). Two members of his family at that time, Hanani and Zebadiah, were among those who agreed to put away their foreign wives (Ezra 10:20).

(2) Father of PASHHUR; the latter was chief officer of the TEMPLE in the time of JEREMIAH (Jer. 20:1). It is likely, however, that "son of Immer" here is an indication of ancestry, in which case this Immer would be the same as #1 above; the phrase then distinguishes Pashhur from another priest identified as the "son [descendant] of Malkijah" (21:1; Malkijah was the head of the fifth division, 1 Chr. 24:9).

(3) Father (or ancestor) of ZADOK, who made repairs to the wall of Jerusalem opposite his house, near the HORSE GATE (Neh. 3:29). This Immer too may be the same as #1 above.

Immer (place). im´uhr (Heb. *ʾimmēr H613*, "lamb"). One of five Babylonian places from which certain Jewish exiles returned who were unable to prove their Israelite ancestry (Ezra 2:59; Neh.

7:61). On the basis of the parallel passage in the APOCRYPHA (1 Esd. 5:36), some scholars argue that the reference is to a person. If Immer here is indeed a place name, its location is unknown.

immorality. See FORNICATION.

immortality. See ESCHATOLOGY.

immutability. The perfection of God by which he is devoid of all change in essence, attributes, consciousness, will, and promises. No change is possible in God, because all change must be to better or worse, and God is absolute perfection. No cause for change in God exists, either in himself or outside of him. The immutability of God is clearly taught in Scripture (Mal. 3:6; Ps. 102:26; Jas. 1:17) and must not be confused with immobility; immutability is consistent with constant activity and perfect freedom. God creates, performs miracles, sustains the universe, etc. When the Scriptures speak of his repenting, as in Jon. 3:10, one should remember that this is only an anthropomorphic way of speaking. God adapts his treatment of people to the variation of their actions and characters. When the righteous do wickedly, his holiness requires that his treatment of them must change.

Imna. im´nuh (Heb. *yimnāʿ H3557*, "[God] holds back" or "strong"). Son of Helem, listed among the brave warriors who were heads of families of the tribe of ASHER (1 Chr. 7:35; cf. v. 40). Some scholars believe that Imna is a variant of IMNAH and (through textual corruption) of IMRAH, both of which appear in the same genealogy (vv. 30, 36).

Imnah. im´nuh (Heb. *yimnâ H3555*, "fortunate" or "[God] assigns"). Son of ASHER, grandson of JACOB, and eponymous ancestor of the Imnite clan (Gen. 46:17 [KJV, "Jimnah"]; Num. 26:44 [KJV, "Jimna," "Jimnites"]; 1 Chr. 7:30). See also IMNA.

(2) A LEVITE whose son KORE was in charge of the EAST GATE and of the free will offerings during the reign of HEZEKIAH (2 Chr. 31:14).

Imnite. im´nite. See IMNAH.

impediment. See DISEASES.

I

Imperial Regiment. See AUGUSTAN COHORT.

imperishable body. See BODY; ESCHATOLOGY; RESURRECTION.

imposition of hands. See LAYING ON OF HANDS.

imprecatory psalms. A number of OT psalms (esp. Ps. 2; 37; 69; 79; 109; 139; 143) contain expressions of an apparent vengeful attitude toward enemies. For some people, these expressions constitute one of the "moral difficulties" of the OT. We must note, however: (1) Imprecations are not confined to the OT, and, therefore, insofar as they constitute a moral problem, the problem pervades the Bible as a whole (cf. Lk. 11:37-52; Gal. 1:8-10; Rev. 6:10; 18:20; 19:1-6). We must be prepared to think, then, that what we find here is not a reprehensibly low morality but an aspect of the biblical view of the conflict between good and evil. (2) Many if not all of the imprecatory psalms contain (as well as the imprecation) theological and moral sentiments that we should wish to attain (e.g., Ps. 139). We can hardly, therefore, dismiss these psalms under some blanket condemnation as "OT morality." (3) In fact, OT morality stoutly opposed a hostile and vindictive response to opponents (e.g., Lev. 19:14-18). (4) All the imprecatory psalms except Ps. 137 are prayers. They are addressed to God about opponents, and there is no suggestion in any of them that the psalmist either said any of these things to his adversary or ever intended to take vengeance into his own hands. Even if, therefore, it should be decided that these are reprehensible as prayers, the way of the psalmist is to be preferred to the modern practice of killing, maiming, bombing, and destroying those whom we think are our enemies. (5) The imprecatory psalms are full of longing for the vindication of the Lord's good name. Over and over, the psalmist's desire is not personal relief but that the Lord should be seen in his goodness and holiness (e.g., Ps. 58:11; 83:16-18). (6) Many of the actual imprecations do no more than ask God to do what he has at any rate said that he will do in such situations (e.g., 5:10; 54:5; 79:6-7). (7) The Bible teaches that there is a "pure anger." The fact that we do not feel it and cannot express it does not mean that God's people have never risen to such heights of holiness. Our problem may well be, also, that we have so allowed our sense of moral outrage to atrophy that we are incapable of identifying with a pure WRATH.

impurity. See CLEAN; PURIFICATION; UNCLEAN.

imputation. The act of attributing something to a person. The Hebrew verb *ḥāšab H3108* ("to value, consider") and the Greek verb *logizomai G3357* ("to count, estimate, consider") can both be used in the sense of setting to one's account or reckoning something to a person. The biblical teaching on imputation applies to the doctrines of original sin, atonement, and justification.

Imputation of Adam's sin to his posterity. The record of the FALL (Gen. 2-3), taken in connection with the subsequent history of the human race as recorded in the rest of the OT, implies that ADAM's sin not only affected him but was also imputed to his posterity. This doctrine is more fully developed in the NT, especially in Rom. 5:12-21, where PAUL shows that it was by Adam's SIN that death and sin entered the world and passed to all people. All were condemned and made sinners in Adam.

Imputation of the sin of humanity to Christ. This facet of imputation is not expressly stated in the Bible but is implied in those passages that affirm that CHRIST bore our sins and died in our place. Isaiah 53 teaches that the Servant of the Lord "took up our infirmities," and God laid on him the iniquity of us all. PETER had this passage in mind when he wrote that Christ "himself bore our sins in his body on the tree" (1 Pet. 2:24). The same thought is expressed in 2 Cor. 5:21 and in Gal. 3:13. This truth is basic to the doctrine of the ATONEMENT.

Imputation of Christ's righteousness to the believer. It is said in Gen. 15:6 that God reckoned RIGHTEOUSNESS to believing ABRAHAM, that is, God regarded him as righteous, attributing or crediting to him that which he did not have in himself. In Gal. 3:6 and Rom. 4:3 the apostle PAUL quotes this passage in arguing a person's JUSTIFICATION by God through GRACE alone. Justification is a judicial act of God by which he declares righteous, on the ground of Christ's expiatory work and imputed righteousness, those who put their FAITH in Christ as their Savior. The NT stresses that justification is

I

absolutely free and unmerited so far as the sinner is concerned (Rom. 3:24; 5:15; Gal. 5:4; Tit. 3:7). Through faith, the merits of Christ's suffering and obedience are imputed to sinners, and from then on they are viewed as just in God's sight.

Imrah. im´ruh (Heb. *yimrâ H3559*, possibly "he rebels"). Son of Zophah and descendant of ASHER (1 Chr. 7:36). Some scholars emend the text to IMNAH.

Imri. im´ri (Heb. *ʾimrî H617*, prob. short form of AMARIAH). **(1)** Son of Bani and descendant of JUDAH through PEREZ (1 Chr. 9:4). Some have thought he may be the same as the Amariah mentioned in a partially parallel passage (Neh. 11:4).

(2) Father (or ancestor) of ZACCUR; the latter helped rebuild the wall of Jerusalem in NEHEMIAH's time (Neh. 3:2).

incarnation. In Christian theology, this term (Lat. *incarnatio*, from *carō* [gen. *carnis*], "flesh") refers to the event summed up in Jn. 1:14, "The Word became flesh and made his dwelling among us." The doctrine of the incarnation is taught or

The Latin inscription on this altar reads, "The Word became flesh" (Jn. 1:14). From the cave at the Church of the Annunciation in Nazareth.

assumed throughout the Bible (cf. 1 Tim. 3:16; Rom. 8:3). According to this teaching, the eternal SON OF GOD (see TRINITY) became human, and he did so without in any manner or degree diminishing his divine nature. A somewhat detailed statement of the incarnation is found in Phil. 2:5-11.

Christ Jesus, though he remained in the "form" of God (i.e., with all the essential attributes of God), took the "form" of a servant and died on the cross.

The VIRGIN BIRTH is necessary for our understanding of the incarnation. In the process of ordinary birth, a new personality begins. Jesus Christ did not begin to be when he was born. He is the eternal Son. The virgin birth was a miracle, wrought by the HOLY SPIRIT, whereby the eternal Son of God "became flesh," that is, took to himself a genuine human nature in addition to his eternal divine nature. The Holy Spirit has never been thought of as the father of Jesus. Jesus was not half man and half god like the Greek mythological heroes. He was fully God, the Second Person of the Trinity. "In Christ all the fullness of the Deity lives in bodily form" (Col. 2:9). At the same time he became genuinely a man. To deny his genuine humanity is "the spirit of the antichrist" (1 Jn. 4:2-3).

The biblical data on the incarnation came to permanent doctrinal formulation at the council of Chalcedon, A.D. 451. That council declared that Christ was "born of the virgin Mary" and is "to be acknowledged in two natures, inconfusedly, unchangeably, indivisibly, inseparably … the property of each nature being preserved, and concurring in one Person." This doctrine is concisely stated in the *Westminster Shorter Catechism*, Question 21: "The only Redeemer of God's elect is the Lord Jesus Christ, who, being the eternal Son of God, became man, and so was, and continueth to be, God and man, in two distinct natures and one Person for ever."

The creed of Chalcedon was the culmination of more than three centuries of discussion in which the main stream of Christian thought eliminated a variety of false interpretations as follows: (1) The Gnostic Docetae, condemned in 1 Jn. 4:2-3, denied the genuine humanity of Jesus and taught that he only appeared to suffer. (2) The Ebionites in the second century denied his deity. (3) The Arians, condemned at Nicea in A.D. 325, denied that his divine nature was equal with the Father's. (4) The Apollinarians, condemned at Constantinople, in 381, denied that he had a complete human nature. (5) The Nestorians, condemned at Ephesus in 431, admitted the two natures but taught that he was two personalities. (6) The Eutychians, condemned

© Dr. James C. Martin

I

at Chalcedon, in 451, taught that the two natures were so united and so changed that he was neither genuinely divine nor genuinely human. (7) The biblical doctrine of the incarnation formalized at Chalcedon, A.D. 451, as stated above, is the Christology of the true historical church.

But we need an *understanding of the words* of our doctrine, not just a formula to repeat. First, the emphasis on the unity of Christ's personality means that he was, in himself, in his *ego*, his nonmaterial self, the same numerical identity, the same person. The person who was God and with God "in the beginning" before the created universe is the same person who sat wearily at the well of Sychar, the same person who said, "Father, forgive them," on the cross. Second, the distinction of his natures means, and has always meant to the church, that Jesus is just as truly God as the Father and the Spirit are God, and at the same time, without confusion or contradiction, he is just as truly human as we are human. (His humanity as the "last Adam" is perfectly sinless, yet genuinely human, as was Adam before the fall.)

incense. Material which is burned to make a fragrant smoke; or the fragrant smoke thus produced. The most common Hebrew word for "incense," occurring almost sixty times, primarily in the Pentateuch, is *qĕṭōret H7792* (Exod. 25:6 et al.). The term *lĕbōnâ H4247*, often rendered "frankincense," occurs over twenty times (Lev. 2:1-2 et al.; cf. Gk. *libanos G3337*, only Matt. 9:4). In the NT, the Greek word for "incense" is *thymiama G2592* (only Lk. 1:10-11; Rev. 5:8; 8:3-4; 18:13).

In the OT, incense was compounded according to a definite prescription of gum resin, onycha, galbanum, and pure frankincense in equal proportions, and was tempered with salt (Exod. 30:34-35). It could not be made for ordinary purposes (Exod. 30:37; Lev. 10:1-7). Incense not properly compounded was rejected as "strange incense" (Exod. 30:9 KJV). The altar of incense was overlaid with pure gold and was set in the Holy Place of the tabernacle or temple, near the veil that concealed the Most Holy Place. Originally, to burn it was the prerogative of the high priest, and he did so each morning when he dressed the lamps (30:1-9). On the Day of Atonement he brought the incense within the veil and burned it in a censer in the Most Holy Place, so that the atonement cover of the ark was enveloped in a cloud of fragrant smoke (Lev. 16:12-13). The Korahites were punished with death for presuming to take on themselves the right to burn incense (Num. 16); the sons of Aaron died for offering it improperly (Lev. 10).

By the time of Christ, incense was offered by ordinary priests, from among whom one was chosen by lot each morning and evening (Lk. 1:9). The offering of incense was regarded as a solemn privilege. In offering incense, fire was taken from the altar of burnt offering and brought into the temple, where it was placed on the altar of incense, and then the incense was emptied from a golden vessel onto the fire. When the priest entered the Holy Place with the incense, all the people were obliged to leave the temple. A profound silence was observed by them as they prayed outside (1:9-10). When the priest placed the incense on the fire, he bowed reverently toward the Most Holy Place and retired slowly backward, lest he alarm the congregation and cause them to fear that he had been struck dead for offering unworthily (Lev. 16:13).

The use of incense in the temple may have been partly a sanitary measure, since the smell of blood from the many animal sacrifices must have polluted the atmosphere, and the air would have to be fumigated; but it is largely explained by the love for sweet odors. Incense was often offered to those one wished to honor. For example, when Alexander the Great marched against Babylon, incense was offered on altars erected to him. The offering of incense was common in the religious ceremonies of nearly all ancient nations (Egyptians, Babylonians, Assyrians, Phoenicians, etc.) and was extensively used in the ritual of Israel. Incense was symbolic of the ascending prayer of the officiating high priest. The psalmist prayed, "May my prayer be set before you like incense" (Ps. 141:2). In Rev. 8:3-5 an angel burns incense on the golden altar, and smoke ascends with the prayer of saints.

incest. See sex.

India. The name occurs only twice in the Bible (Esth. 1:1; 8:9). This was the country that marked

I

the eastern limit of the territory of Xerxes (KJV, "Ahasuerus"). The Hebrew word (*hōddû H2064*) comes from the name of the Indus, *Hondu*, and refers not to the peninsula of Hindustan, but to the country adjoining the Indus (i.e., the Punjab, and perhaps also Scinde). Some have thought that this country is the Havilah of Gen. 2:11 and that the Indus is the Pishon. Many characteristic Indian products were known to the Israelites.

inerrancy. See Inspiration.

infallibility. See Inspiration.

Infancy Gospels. See Apocryphal New Testament.

infant baptism. See Baptism.

infinite. See God.

infirmity. See Diseases.

inflammation. See Diseases.

Ingathering, Feast of. See Feasts.

inheritance. Something received from an ancestor through a legal will or Testament. In the Bible, the term (the rendering mainly of Heb. *naḥălāh H5709* and Gk. *klēronomia G3100*) is often used figuratively in a theological sense. A fundamental principle of Hebrew society was that real, as distinguished from personal, property belonged to the Family rather than to the individual. This came from the idea that the land was given by God to his children, the people of Israel, and must remain in the family. The Mosaic law directed that only the sons of a legal wife had the right of inheritance. The Firstborn son possessed the Birthright, that is, the right to a double portion of the father's possession; and to him belonged the duty of maintaining the females of the family (Deut. 21:15-17). The other sons received equal shares. If there were no sons, the property went to the daughters (Num. 27:8), on the condition that they not marry outside of their own tribe (36:6-9). If the widow

was left without children, the nearest of kin on her husband's side had the right to marry her; and if he refused, the next of kin (Ruth 3:12-13). If no one married her, the inheritance remained with her until her death, and then reverted to the next of kin (Num. 27:9-11). An estate could not pass from one tribe to another. Since the land was so strictly tied up, testamentary dispositions or wills were not needed. This strong feeling regarding family hereditary privileges was chiefly responsible for the Jews' taking such care to preserve the family genealogies.

The term *inheritance* in Scripture came to be used with a definitely theological significance. In the OT at first it refers to the inheritance promised by God to Abraham and his descendants—the land of Canaan, "the land you gave your people for an inheritance" (1 Ki. 8:36; cf. Num. 34:2; Deut. 4:21, 38; 12:9-10; 15:4; Ps. 47:4; 105:9-11). The conquest of the land under the leadership of Joshua was by God's help, not by Israel's military prowess (Josh. 21:43-45). God directed the partitioning of the land among the tribes (Num. 26:52-56; Josh. 14:1-5; 18:4-9). Israel could continue to possess the land only on condition of faithfulness to God (Deut. 4:26-31; 11:8-9). Disobedience to God would result in the loss of the land, which could be recovered only by repentance and a new wholehearted submission to God (Isa. 57:13; 58:13-14).

The idea finds a further expansion and spiritualization in two other directions. Israelites came to learn that the Lord himself was the inheritance of his people (Jer. 10:16) and of the individual believer (Ps. 16:5-6; 73:26; 142:5), and that his inheritance is his elect, brought "out of Egypt, to be the people of his inheritance" (Deut. 4:20; cf. 32:9). This conception was later broadened until the Lord's inheritance is seen to include the Gentiles also (Ps. 2:8; Isa. 19:25; 47:6; 63:17).

The conception of inheritance is very prominent in the NT too, but now it is connected with the person and work of Christ, who is the heir by virtue of being the Son (Mk. 12:7; Heb. 1:2). Through Christ's redemptive work believers are sons of God by adoption and fellow-heirs with Christ (Rom. 8:17; Gal. 4:7). As a guarantee of "the promised eternal inheritance" (Heb. 9:15),

I

Christ has given to them the HOLY SPIRIT (Eph. 1:14). The letter to the Hebrews shows that as Israel in the old covenant received her inheritance from God, so in the new covenant the new Israel receives an inheritance, only a better one. This inheritance, moreover, is not for Jews alone but for all true believers, including Gentiles (3:6). The inheritance is the KINGDOM OF GOD with all its blessings (Matt. 25:34; 1 Cor. 6:9; Gal. 5:21), both present and eschatological (Rom. 8:17-23; 1 Cor. 15:50; Heb. 11:13; 1 Pet. 1:3-4). It is wholly the gift of God's sovereign grace.

iniquity. See SIN.

ink. A writing fluid whose chief ingredient was soot or black carbon. It was mixed with gum or oil for use on parchment, or with a metallic substance for use on PAPYRUS. The early use of metallic ink in Israel is shown in the LACHISH letters (c. 586 B.C.). The DEAD SEA SCROLLS were written with ink made of carbon. The *Letter of Aristeas* says that the copy of the law sent to PTOLEMY II was written in gold. The Egyptians must have used a good quality ink, as the bright colors in some papyri

© Dr. James C. Martin. The Amman Archaeological Museum. Photographed by permission.

Copper inkpot discovered at Qumran.

show. The ingredients for making ink were kept in a writing case. The word is used once in the OT (Jer. 36:18) and three times in the NT (2 Cor. 3:3; 2 Jn. 12; 3 Jn. 13).

inkhorn. This English term (meaning a vessel made from a horn and used to hold ink) is used by the KJV in only one passage (Ezek. 9:2-3, 11). The Hebrew word refers to a writing case for reed pens and some sort of container for ink near the upper end of the case. It was carried in the belt. Monuments of all periods show the Egyptian palette, a long narrow board with grooves for pens and circular hollows for ink.

inn. The Hebrew word *mālôn H4869* (rendered "inn" by the KJV in Gen. 42:27; 43:21; Exod. 4:24) means "lodging place" or "camping ground." It may refer to the camping place of an individual (Jer. 9:2); of a family on a journey (Exod. 4:24); of a caravan (Gen. 42:27; 43:21); of an army (2 Ki. 19:23); or even of a nation (Josh. 4:3, 8). In none of these references is there any implication of a structure, with the possible exception of the one in Jeremiah. When travelers could not find lodging in private dwellings they stayed in the open (cf. Gen. 19:2; 28:11; Jdg. 19:15).

When Mary and Joseph discovered that "there was no room for them in the inn" (Gk. *katalyma G2906*, Lk. 2:7), one should not think of anything resembling a hotel. More likely they found themselves in some sort of village guest house. Indeed, the same word is used to describe the upper room where Jesus ate the Passover with his disciples (Mk. 14:14; Lk. 22:11). It is in fact possible that Mary and Joseph had to stay in the lower level of a house (perhaps the home of a distant relative), where the animals were kept, because the normal living area was full. In the story of the good Samaritan, a different term is used (*pandocheion G4106*, Lk. 10:34). An innkeeper (*pandocheus G4107*, lit., "one who receives all") is mentioned who is paid to provide food and lodging for the man who was left in his care. Something resembling a modern inn seems to be in view in this passage.

inner being. This phrase is used by the NIV and other translations to render Greek *esō anthrōpos*,

I

(lit., "man inside," Rom. 7:22 [KJV, "inward man"; NRSV, "inmost self"]; Eph. 3:16). The concept of an inner being is reflected elsewhere in the Bible. It refers to the true ego, whereas the outer person may or may not be a genuine portrayal of the inner being. In the period of the judges, for example, when Israel was clamoring for a king, SAMUEL, under divine guidance, had to make a distinction between the inner and outer person. Seven of JESSE's sons were rejected, but DAVID, the youngest, was selected for king. Samuel explained, "Man looks at the outward appearance, but the LORD looks at the heart" (1 Sam. 16:7). The inner person is the real and dominant self. PAUL was a living example of the distinction in the better way, and consequently prayed that God would strengthen the Ephesians "with power through his Spirit in your inner being" (Eph. 3:16).

innocence. Freedom from guilt. This English noun and the adjective *innocent* are used variously in Bible version to render several Hebrew and Greek terms. Especially common is the Hebrew adjective *nāqî H5929*, which occurs a number of times in legal passages (Exod. 23:7; Deut. 19:10; et al.), but in other contexts as well (Job 4:7; Ps. 10:8; et al.). The primary Greek term for "innocent" is *athōon G127* (in the NT only in Matt. 27:4, 24). In addition, a number of words that mean "clean," "good," or the like can properly be rendered "innocent" in some contexts (e.g., Gen. 20:4; Matt. 10:16).

Innocents, Massacre (Slaughter) of the. Phrase used to designate the murder by HEROD the Great of all the male children in BETHLEHEM two years old and under, when the MAGI failed to return and tell him where they found the infant Jesus (Matt. 2:16-18).

inquire. To seek information, especially to consult God with regard to his will. The people of Israel would come to MOSES to inquire of God in a dispute (Exod. 18:15 NRSV; cf. 33:7-11). The priestly EPHOD was a kind of pouch attached to the breastpiece of the high priest in which the sacred lots URIM AND THUMMIM were placed (28:28-30). JOSHUA was to come to the priest to inquire of

God and receive answer by the use of these lots to determine when Israel should move (Exod. 28:30). DAVID resorted to the ephod on occasion when he was fleeing from Saul (1 Sam. 23:9-12). SAUL used the same method to decide a vexed question (14:41). In the NT direct PRAYER is the prevailing form of inquiry, both by teaching (Jas. 1:5) and by practice, as in the case of Jesus in the Garden of GETHSEMANE (Matt. 26:39), and PAUL, when he inquired of God about his nagging thorn in the flesh (2 Cor. 12:7-9).

I.N.R.I. These letters constitute the abbreviation of the supposed Latin inscription on the cross of Jesus: *Iesus Nazarenus Rex Iudaeorum*—"Jesus of Nazareth, King of the Jews." All four Gospels mention the inscription but vary as to the contents. The traditional Latin wording of the title seems to be based on Jn. 19:19 rather than on the synoptic parallels. The abbreviation I.N.R.I. is ascribed by tradition to Helena, Emperor Constantine's mother, who claimed to have discovered it on a board.

insanity. See DISEASES.

inscription. This English term is occasionally used in Bible versions, for example, with reference to the sign that had written on it the charge laid against Jesus (Mk. 15:26 NRSV; KJV, "superscription"; NIV, "written notice"). In biblical scholarship—as in historical study more generally—the discovery of ancient inscriptions, usually engraved on stone or other hard surfaces, is of immense value. In the case of manuscripts, that is, documents written on perishable material such as PAPYRUS, we normally are dealing with copies that are many times removed from the original writing. But when an inscription such as the MOABITE STONE (9th cent. B.C.) is discovered, scholars have direct access to an ancient document in its initial form. Inscriptions thus provide important information not only regarding historical and cultural matters, but also regarding linguistic details, allowing researchers to understand ancient languages in a way not otherwise possible.

insects. See ANIMALS.

I

Inspection Gate. See MUSTER GATE.

inspiration. The supernatural work of the HOLY SPIRIT, who moves upon specially chosen individuals so that they may receive divine truth from him and communicate that truth in written form, the BIBLE. The use of the term *inspiration* for this doctrine derives from the KJV rendering of the Greek word *theopneustos* **G2535** in 2 Tim. 3:16, which literally means "God-breathed" (so NIV). The key to its meaning may be gleaned from the OT concept of the divine breathing as producing effects that God himself is immediately accomplishing by his own will and power (see Ps. 33:6). By this word, therefore, PAUL is asserting that the written documents, called Holy Scripture, are a divine product. Precisely the same idea, but with different terminology, is set forth in 2 Pet. 1:19-21. In this passage the prophetic Word (i.e., Scripture) is contrasted with mere fables devised by human cunning. Scripture is more sure and trustworthy than the testimony of any eyewitness. The explanation for its unique authority lies in its origin. It was produced not as a merely human private interpretation of the truth but by God's Spirit through the prophets.

In both 2 Tim. 3:16 and 2 Pet. 1:19-21 the fact of the divine productivity (spiration rather than *in*spiration) of the "Holy Writings" is thus explicitly asserted. This divine (in)spiration is further confirmed by a host of NT passages. The authors of Scripture wrote in or by the Spirit (Mk. 12:36). What the Scripture states is really what God has said (Acts 4:25; Heb. 3:7; and see especially the way OT quotations are introduced in Heb. 1:5-14). This is true whether or not in the particular passage cited the words are ascribed to God or are the statements of the human author. In the mind of the NT writers any passage of Scripture was really "spoken" by God. Jesus used the same type of reference, attributing directly to God the authorship of Scripture (Matt. 19:4-5).

Because of the character of the God of Truth who "inspired" (or produced) the Holy Scriptures, the result of "inspiration" is to constitute the Bible as fully trustworthy and authoritative. Indeed, this absolute divine authority of Scripture, rather than its inspiration, is the emphasis of scriptural teaching about its own nature (see Ps. 19:7-14; 119:89,

Illustration of Luke writing under divine inspiration (from a 9th-cent. Gk. MS of the Gospels).

© Dr. James C. Martin. Sola Scriptura. The Van Kampen Collection on display at the Holy Land Experience in Orlando, Florida. Photographed by permission.

97, 113, 160; Zech. 7:12; Matt. 5:17-19; Lk. 16:17; Jn. 10:34-35; 1 Thess. 2-13). Besides those passages directly teaching the authority of Scripture, such phrases as "It is written" (Matt. 21:13; Lk. 4:4, 8, 10), "it [or he] says" (Rom. 9:15; Gal. 3:16), and "Scripture says" (Rom. 9:17; Gal. 3:8) all clearly imply an absolute authority for the OT Scriptures.

These passages teaching the authority of Scripture indicate also the extent of inspiration. If the authority and trustworthiness of Scripture are complete, inspiration itself must also extend to all of Scripture. This completeness of inspiration and consequent authority of all Scripture is made explicit in such passages as Lk. 24:25: "How foolish you are, and how slow of heart to believe all that the prophets have spoken!" (see also Matt. 5:17-19; Lk. 16:17; Jn. 10:34-35). The completeness of inspiration is further established by the fact that Scripture lacks altogether any principle for distinguishing between (a) those parts of it that are inspired and thus possess binding authority and (b) supposedly uninspired parts that do not possess binding authority.

Inerrancy and *infallibility* as applied to the inspiration of Scripture, though not exactly synonymous

I

terms, are nevertheless both correctly applied to Scripture in order to indicate that inspiration and authority are complete. The word *inerrant* suggests that the Scriptures do not wander from the truth. *Infallible* is stronger, suggesting an incapability of wandering from the truth ("Are you not in error because you do not know the Scriptures?" Mk. 12:24).

The method of inspiration is never developed in the Scriptures, although the basic fact that Scripture is produced by the power of God working in and through such a writer as a prophet indicates the mutual interworking of the divine and human hand. By pointing to a human author of Scripture (e.g., "David himself, speaking by the Holy Spirit, declared," Mk. 12:36; "Moses wrote," Mk. 12:19; and "Isaiah says," Jn. 12:39), by stating his purpose in the writing of a book (e.g., Lk. 1:1-4; Jn. 20:30-31), and by acknowledging research in the preparation of the writing of Scripture (Lk. 1:2-3), the biblical authors make completely plain that the divine method of inspiration was not normally by a process of dictation.

At this point great caution should be taken not to read into the biblical idea of the origin of Scripture suggestions derived from the English word *inspiration* (or Latin *inspiratio*). The point of the biblical teaching is never a divine heightening of the human powers of the prophet (though the Bible does not deny that in certain instances such may have taken place). Rather, by all those inconceivable means at the disposal of a sovereign God, the Holy Spirit used the writers of Scripture to produce through them the message that he wished to communicate to us. God's Spirit obviously did not need in every case to "inspire" (i.e., to raise to greater heights than ordinary) a Micah or a Luke; rather, God produced the writing he wished by his sovereign preparation and control of a man who could and freely would write just what God desired to be his divinely authoritative message to his people.

In summary, biblical inspiration (as distinguished from illumination) may be defined as the work of the Holy Spirit by which, through the instrumentality of the personality and literary talents of its human authors, he constituted the words of the Bible in all of its several parts as his written word to the human race and, therefore, of divine authority and without error.

instruction. See EDUCATION; LAW; TORAH; WISDOM.

instrument. See MUSIC AND MUSICAL INSTRUMENTS.

integrity. Moral soundness; steadfast uprightness; incorruptibility. Although several Hebrew words can be translated "integrity," this English term usually renders the noun *tōm H9448*, "completeness, wholeness, perfection" (1 Ki. 9:4; Prov. 19:1 et al.). In the NT, "integrity" is used by modern versions to render Greek *aphthoria G917*, "incorruption" (Tit. 2:7), but the concept is certainly reflected in other passages (cf. Matt. 22:16 = Mk. 12:14).

intercession. The act of pleading on behalf of someone else. See PRAYER.

interest. In the OT there is no trace of any system of commercial credit. Large commercial loans were not made in ancient ISRAEL. Only the poor borrowed, and they did it to obtain the necessities of life. The LAW of MOSES forbade lending at interest to a fellow Israelite (Exod. 22:25) but permitted charging interest to a foreigner (Deut. 23:20). A needy Israelite might sell himself as a servant (Lev. 25:39; 2 Ki. 4:1). The prophets condemn the taking of interest as a heinous sin (Jer. 15:10; Ezek. 18:8, 13, 17). In the NT, references to the receiving of interest occur in two parables—of the pounds (Lk. 19:23) and of the talents (Matt. 25:27), and it is distinctly encouraged.

intermediate state. See ESCHATOLOGY.

interpretation. The correct reproduction of the thoughts of another (either a writer or speaker), often from a different language. Especially when applied to the BIBLE, interpretation is sometimes called *hermeneutics* (from the Gk. verb *hermēneuō G2257*, "to express, explain, translate, interpret"). The term *exegesis* can be used as a synonym of *interpretation*, but it usually refers to a detailed and technical analysis of the text. Many distinguish

I

between hermeneutics and exegesis by saying that the former deals with principles of interpretation (including philosophical issues) and the latter with practice and methods. The biblical material, written between 2,000 and 3,500 years ago, poses a special problem for the modern interpreter because it was formulated in environments and in languages considerably different from those that prevail in the modern world.

Biblical interpretation has a dual nature: (1) the problem of the language, and (2) the theological significance of the material. The discovery of the true meaning of all words and terms in any biblical passage is the place where interpretation begins. This is essentially an interpretation of language. It embraces such considerations as definition of words, contextual analysis, literary types and forms, historical analogy, and syntactical distinctives. In addition, biblical material is of such a nature as to demand special consideration. The doctrine of INSPIRATION holds the biblical interpreter to a proper regard for the fundamental character of Scripture. It demands a recognition of the theological significance of Scripture, resting upon the REVELATION of God that is not found in any other literature. The extraordinary character of Scripture transcends the usual and ordinary analysis of non-biblical materials.

The language of the Bible is human language and, as such, is subject to the same principles and laws that govern the interpretation of any book or writing other than the Bible. If the language of the Bible were other than a true human language subject to the usual rules of human communication, there would be no basis for human beings to interpret or come by any trustworthy knowledge of its meaning. Because the books of the Bible are records in human speech, they must be handled in view of literary structure, literary form, and literary relations as any other book or writing. There are legitimate presuppositions to be brought to Scripture that cannot be brought to other books. Because the Bible has God as its ultimate author, it must be expected that its contents will bear true and faithful relation to that fact. Every means of the historical-critical method of interpretation should claim his attention: textual criticism, literary criticism, comparative religion criticism, historical criticism, etc. Beyond all of this, however, the HOLY SPIRIT is to be acknowledged as the only infallible interpreter of God's word.

I. Words. To interpret Scripture lexically, the interpreter should have some knowledge of the historical development of words in their meaning. At the same time, one should avoid the "etymological fallacy," that is, assuming that the meaning of a word can be found in its history (diachronic approach) rather than its conventional use in its current period (synchronic approach). An example of this is reading Hebrew meanings into Greek words used in the NT. It is more important to understand the usage of words by the particular writer being interpreted. Current usage rather than history alone must determine a word's meaning. An author can refer to a past use of a word, but the context must indicate he is doing so. A good lexicon is the best source of this information. The meaning of words should be considered in light of the different periods in the development of the biblical languages. Comparison should be made between different authors of the same period where such is possible.

II. Syntax. To interpret syntactically, the grammatical principles of the language in which the text was written must be understood. A grammar of that language is the source of such information. It must always be remembered that the function of grammar is not to determine the laws of language but to explain them. Language developed first, as a means of expressing thought; grammars were written later to explain the laws and principles of language as it functioned in expressing ideas. In the interpreter's native language, these meanings of grammatical constructions are more or less sensed at once subconsciously; but when work is being done in a foreign language, it is difficult to isolate and understand the ways of expressing thought peculiar to that language, or the idioms of the language. If the interpreter wishes to get the meaning from the text, it is necessary to have the viewpoint of the writer, and follow closely the idioms that the writer used.

III. Context. To interpret contextually it is necessary to have regard for the entire composition being interpreted. The nature of the composition is of paramount importance to the interpreter,

I

whether it is a unified discourse or some other type of writing. The subject under discussion immediately surrounding the passage colors the interpretation also. Often a shade of meaning is given to words by the nature of the discussion of which they are a part. The division of the biblical text into chapters and verses has created a considerable problem for interpretation from time to time because the impression is given that the context is insignificant, that each verse stands alone. Also, the sections fail to correspond to the correct divisions of thought. A good example is Col. 2:21, which has been used not infrequently as a text for a sermon on temperance, when actually in its context it is a condemnation of asceticism.

IV. History. It is important for interpreters to discover the circumstances that surrounded and called forth the document being interpreted. The source of such information is in the introductory notes to a biblical book in some good commentary, or a special volume of introduction to the OT or the NT. The manners, customs, and psychology of the people associated with the book being studied are of tremendous importance to a correct understanding of the text. The study of the people would include their methods of recording history, figures of speech, types of literature, and their concept of time or chronology. Both general and particular historical works can supply this need for the interpreter.

V. Analogy of Scripture. One of the most important safeguards for interpreters is to do their work with a regard for the analogy of Scripture. He must use Scripture itself as a guide to understanding Scripture. Any bizarre interpretation of a passage that conflicts with the whole trend of Scripture must be judged to be wrong. Scripture confirms itself. A thorough and accurate knowledge of the biblical viewpoint is a necessity. It is hoped that interpreters seek to divest themselves of their prejudices and seek to read the text through the eyes of its author.

VI. Procedure. The hermeneutical process is not as complex as one might think. First, we must be aware of the genre or type of literature and utilize those rules of the language game that apply to each. Second, we should study the structural development of the passage and see how the various parts relate to the whole, thereby seeing how the context

develops. Third, the interpreter needs to identify the grammatical and lexical components of the sentence to determine the probable meaning of the developing text. Fourth, one must use background information to fill in the gaps between what the author expected his original readers to understand and our world today. Fifth, we should look for the theological threads that tie the passage to others in the book and in the Bible as a whole. Finally, one must take a critical realist approach to testing conclusions, evaluating their adequacy and coherence, and comparing them to the conclusions of other scholars and of the community of faith as a whole.

intertestamental period. See APOCRYPHA; MACCABEE; PSEUDEPIGRAPHA.

Iob. i′ohb (Heb. *yôb H3410* [not in NIV]). Variant of JASHUB (Gen. 46:13 RSV and other versions, following MT).

iota. i-oh′tuh (Gk. *iōta G2740*). KJV *jot*. Seventh letter of the Greek alphabet. In the Hebrew/Aramaic alphabet, the corresponding consonant (′, "yod") is the smallest letter, and Jesus alludes to it in his statement, "Till heaven and earth pass, one jot or one tittle shall in no wise pass from the law, till all be fulfilled" (Matt. 5:17 KJV). See discussion under DOT.

Iphdeiah. if-dee′yah (Heb. *yipdĕyâ H3635*, "Yahweh redeems"). KJV Iphedeiah. Son of Shashak and descendant of BENJAMIN; listed among the head of families that lived in Jerusalem (1 Chr. 8:25; cf. v. 28).

Iphedeiah. See IPHDEIAH.

Iphtah. if′tuh (Heb. *yiptāḥ H3652*, prob. "[God] opens"; see IPHTAH EL). KJV Jiphtah. A town in the SHEPHELAH, within the tribal territory of JUDAH (Josh. 15:43). Because it was in the same district as KEILAH and MARESHAH, some tentatively identify Iphtah with modern Tarqumiyeh, about 6 mi. (10 km.) NW of HEBRON.

Iphtah El. if′tuh-el′ (Heb. *yiptaḥ-ʾēl H3654*, "God opens"). KJV Jiphthah-el. A valley on the N border of the tribe of ZEBULUN and the SE border of ASHER (Josh. 19:14, 27). Its location is uncertain, but two possibilities are Wadi el-Malik and Wadi ʾAbbelin.

Ir. ihr (Heb. *ʿîr H6553*, possibly "stallion [of donkey]" or "city"). (1) Descendant of BENJAMIN and (according to NIV) ancestor of the Shupites and Huppites (1 Chr. 7:12; see HUPPIM); some scholars have suggested that he is the same as IRI (v. 7).

(2) According to some scholars, the name of an otherwise unknown city mentioned by BALAAM in one of his oracles (Num. 24:19; cf. NRSV, NJPS). Most versions understand the term here as the common noun for "city."

Ira. iʹruh (Heb. *ʿîrāʾ H6562*, possibly "stallion [of donkey]" or "city"). (1) A Jairite identified as "David's priest" (2 Sam. 20:26). Since the Jairites were probably descendants of JAIR—from the tribe of MANASSEH rather than LEVI—Ira could not have technically been a priest; perhaps the term "priest" here refers to some chief official in the service of the king (cf. the use of the same term in 2 Sam. 8:18, rendered "royal adviser" by NIV on the basis of 1 Chr. 18:17).

(2) Son of Ikkesh of TEKOA; he was one of David's thirty mighty warriors and served as commander in charge of the division for the sixth month (2 Sam. 23:26; 1 Chr. 11:28; 27:9).

(3) An ITHRITE who was also one of David's thirty mighty warriors (2 Sam. 23:38; 1 Chr. 11:40).

Irad. iʹrad (Heb. *ʿîrād H6563*, derivation uncertain). Son of ENOCH and grandson of CAIN (Gen. 4:18).

Iram. iʹram (Heb. *ʿîrām H6566*, possibly "stallion [of donkey]"). Descendant of ESAU, listed among the clan chiefs of EDOM (Gen. 36:43; 1 Chr. 1:54).

Iri. iʹri (Heb. *ʿîrî H6565*, possibly "my stallion [of a donkey]" or "my city"). Son of Bela, grandson of BENJAMIN, and family head (1 Chr. 7:7); some scholars identify him with IR (v. 12).

Irijah. i-riʹjuh (Heb. *yirʾiyyāyh H3713*, "Yahweh sees"). Son of Shelemiah; he was an officer posted at the BENJAMIN GATE in Jerusalem who arrested JEREMIAH on the charge of planning to desert to the Babylonians (Jer. 37:13-14).

Ir-moab. ihr-mohʹab (Heb. *ʿîr môʾāb*, "city of Moab"). An otherwise unknown town on the ARNON River where BALAK went to meet BALAAM (Num. 22:36, NRSV, NJPS). Most versions, however, render the Hebrew phrase as "a [or the] city of Moab."

Ir Nahash. ihr-nayʹhash (Heb. *ʿîr nāḥāš H6560*, "city of the serpent"). Son of Tehinnah and descendant of JUDAH (1 Chr. 4:12). More likely, the text should be rendered "Tehinnah the founder [or leader] of Ir [or of the city of] Nahash," in which case the reference is to a Judahite town, perhaps to be identified with Deir Naḥas (c. 7 mi./11 km. W of KEILAH) or with Khirbet en-Naḥas in the ARABAH.

iron (metal). See MINERALS.

Iron (place). iʹron (Heb. *yirʾôn H3712*, meaning uncertain). RSV Yiron. A fortified town within the tribal territory of NAPHTALI (Josh. 19:39). It is identified with modern Yarun, some 22 mi. (35 km.) NE of Acco.

Irpeel. ihrʹpee-uhl (Heb. *yirpěʾēl H3761*, "God heals"). A town allotted to the tribe of BENJAMIN (Josh. 18:27). It was in the same general area as GIBEON (v. 25) and neighboring towns, but its precise location cannot be ascertained.

irrigation. The most explicit reference to irrigation in the Bible is an assertion that the Egyptian practice is irrelevant to the Palestinian hills, where the "rain from heaven" would serve as a perpetual reminder of divine approval or disfavor (Deut. 11:10-17); but the contrast was relative, not absolute. See PALESTINE; RAIN. From Chalcolithic times, irrigation had become widespread in the FERTILE CRESCENT, and the exiles on the river or canal KEBAR were renewing contact with a system of perennial irrigation predating ABRAHAM. Larger centers of Palestine like BETH SHAN and JERICHO (with its powerful springs) long remained oases of irrigated productivity.

I

Ir Shemesh. ihr-shem′ish (Heb. *ʿîr šemeš H6561*, "city of the sun"). A town allotted to the tribe of Dan (Josh. 19:41). The Danites were unable to occupy the towns in this territory (v. 47), and Ir Shemesh apparently became part of Judah, where it was better known as Beth Shemesh.

Iru. i′roo (Heb. *ʿîrû H6564*, possibly "stallion [of donkey]" or "city"). Eldest son of Caleb, listed in the genealogy of the tribe of Judah (1 Chr. 4:15).

Isaac. i′zik (Heb. *yiṣḥāq H3663*, "he laughs"). Son of Abraham and Sarah, half-brother of Ishmael, husband of Rebekah. Isaac was born in the south country, probably Beersheba (Gen. 21:14, 31), when Abraham was a hundred and Sarah ninety years old (17:17; 21:5). He was named Isaac because both Abraham and Sarah had laughed incredulously at the thought of having a child at their age (17:17-19; 18:9-15; 21:6). His birth must be regarded as a miracle. Twenty-five years after God had promised the childless Abraham and Sarah a son, the promise was fulfilled. He is thus rightly called the child of promise, in contrast with Ishmael, who was Abraham's son through Hagar, Sarah's maid. When Isaac was eight days old, he was circumcised (21:4). Fearing future jealousy and strife between the two boys when she observed Ishmael mocking Isaac, Sarah tried to persuade Abraham to cast out Hagar and Ishmael. Abraham was loath to do this because he loved the boy and did so only when he received explicit direction from God, who said to him that his seed would be reckoned through Isaac, but he would also make a nation of Ishmael (21:9-13).

The next recorded event in the life of Isaac is connected with God's command to Abraham to offer him as a sacrifice on a mountain in the land of Moriah (Gen. 22). His exact age then is not stated, but he is described as a "lad," able to carry the wood for the burnt offering up the mountainside. In this whole experience his unquestioning submission and obedience to his father stand out almost as remarkably as his father's faith. Bound on the altar and about to die, his life was spared when an angel of the Lord interposed and substituted for him a ram, which was offered up in his place. God's purpose in this great test of Abraham's

faith is looked at in various ways, among the more important being the following: it is the last and culminating point in God's education of Abraham regarding the meaning of sacrificial obedience; it is a rebuke by God of the widespread heathen practice of sacrificing human beings; it is an object lesson to Abraham of the great sacrifice of the Messiah for the redemption of mankind.

Sarah died at Hebron when Isaac was thirty-six years old (Gen. 23:1). At the age of forty Isaac married Rebekah, a kinswoman from Mesopotamia (ch. 24); but he and his wife were childless until, in answer to prayer, twin sons, Esau and Jacob, were born to them when he was sixty (25:20, 26). At a time of famine, God admonished him not to go down into Egypt, as he had thought of doing, but to remain in the Promised Land; and he pledged his word to be with him. He went to the Philistine city of Gerar, and there, fearing for his own life, he passed his wife off as his sister, as his father had done before him. He was justly rebuked by Abimelech the king for his duplicity (26:10). Isaac then pitched his camp in the Valley of Gerar and became so prosperous as a wheat-grower and herdsman that the envious Philistines began a systematic, petty harassment by stopping up the wells that his father had dug and he had opened again. Abimelech even advised him to leave the country in the interest of peace (ch. 26). Isaac subsequently returned to Beersheba. There the Lord appeared to him at night and promised to bless him for his father's sake. Realizing that God was with Isaac, Abimelech then came from Gerar to make overtures of peace, and the two men formally entered into a covenant (26:26-31). Probably at a considerably later period, Esau, at the age of forty, brought grief to Isaac and Rebekah by marrying two women of Canaan (26:34-35).

The last prominent event in the life of Isaac is the blessing of his sons (Gen. 27). Esau, the elder, was his father's favorite, even though God had told him that the elder would serve the younger. Rebekah's favorite was Jacob (25:28). When Isaac was over a hundred years old, and dim of sight, and perhaps thinking that his end was near, he wished to bestow his last blessing on his elder son; but through Rebekah's cunning and guile Jacob the younger supplanted his brother, and the blessing of

I

the BIRTHRIGHT was given to him. To save Jacob from the murderous wrath of Esau, who determined to kill him after his father's death, Rebekah induced Isaac to send Jacob into Mesopotamia, that, after his own example, his son might take a wife among his own kindred and not imitate Esau by marrying Canaanite women. Isaac invoked another blessing on Jacob and sent him away to LABAN in PADDAN ARAM (27:1—28:5).

Isaac is mentioned only once more—twenty years later, when Jacob returned from his sojourn in Mesopotamia, having married into Laban's family. Jacob found his father at MAMRE in Hebron. There Isaac died at 180 years of age, and his two sons, Esau and Jacob, buried him (Gen. 35:27-29).

The NT refers to Isaac almost a score of times. His sacrifice by Abraham is twice mentioned, in Heb. 11:17-18 and Jas. 2:21; but while the submission of Isaac is referred to, the stress is on the triumph of Abraham's faith. Isaac is contrasted with Ishmael, as the child of promise and the progenitor of the children of promise (Rom. 9:7, 10; Gal. 4:28; Heb. 11:18). In Jesus' argument with the SADDUCEES on the matter of RESURRECTION, he represents Isaac, although dead in human terms, as still living to God (Lk. 20:37). In the SERMON ON THE MOUNT, Jesus proclaimed that many would come from the east and the west to sit down with Abraham, Isaac, and Jacob in the kingdom of heaven (Matt. 8:11).

Of the three patriarchs, Isaac was the least conspicuous, traveled the least, had the fewest extraordinary adventures, but lived the longest. He was free from violent passions; quiet, gentle, dutiful; less a man of action than of thought and suffering. His name is always joined in equal honor with Abraham and Jacob.

Isaiah, Book of. *i*-zay'yuh (Heb. *yĕšaʿyāhû H3833*, "Yahweh is salvation [*or* victorious]"). KJV NT Esaias. The first and largest of the Major Prophets; probably the most widely cherished of

Overview of ISAIAH

Author: The prophet Isaiah son of Amoz, though many scholars attribute parts of the book (esp. Isa. 40-66) to unknown authors living at the time of the EXILE.

Historical setting: Ministering in the southern kingdom of JUDAH, Isaiah began his prophetic work toward the end of the reign of King UZZIAH (c. 740 B.C.) and continued his service during the reigns of JOTHAM, AHAZ, and HEZEKIAH.

Purpose: To denounce the nation for its flagrant violations of the divine COVENANT, but also to bring hope by prophesying the coming of the MESSIAH, the SERVANT OF THE LORD.

Contents: The book begins with a harsh condemnation of Judah (Isa. 1-5), followed by an account of the prophet's commission (ch. 6) and the so-called "book of Immanuel" (chs. 7-12); it then moves to a condemnation of surrounding nations (chs. 13-23), followed by an apocalyptic vision (chs. 24-27) and by further prophecies of judgment and blessing (chs. 28-35). After a historical account of events in Hezekiah's reign (chs. 36-39), the book proclaims comfort to the exiles in Babylon (chs. 40-48), discloses God's plan for his Servant (chs. 49-55), and promises the future purification of his people (chs. 56-66).

I

the OT prophetical books. The prophet Isaiah, son of Amoz, is mentioned repeatedly in the book that bears his name and in 2 Ki. 19-20 (also 2 Chr. 26:22; 32:20, 32), but little is known about him. He was married and had two children to whom he gave significant names (Isa. 7:3; 8:3). Late tradition asserts that the prophet was martyred in the reign of MANASSEH.

I. Period. Isaiah prophesied during four reigns of kings of Judah, from UZZIAH to HEZEKIAH (Isa. 1:1). The first date given is the year of Uzziah's death (6:1), which probably occurred about 740 B.C. or several years later. The last historical event referred to is the death of SENNACHERIB (37:38), which occurred in 681. The most important events are the Syro-Ephraimitic war in the days of King AHAZ (7:1-9), which Isaiah treated, despite its devastation (2 Chr. 28:5-15), as almost insignificant compared with the far greater scourge from ASSYRIA, which was so soon to follow (Isa. 7:17-25). Assyria is the great enemy that much of chs. 7-39 deal with; and beyond it looms an even mightier foe, BABYLON, whose downfall is foretold already in chs. 13-14 and who is the great theme of ch. 40-48. Over against these terrible instruments of divine judgment Isaiah pictures the messianic hope, first in counseling unbelieving Ahaz, and repeatedly thereafter.

II. Analysis. The structure of Isaiah is, in its broad outlines, a simple one, but in its details it raises many problems. It may be briefly analyzed as follows.

A. Introduction (Isa. 1-5). The first chapter contains what has been called the "great arraignment." Like so many of Isaiah's utterances, it combines dire threatenings with urgent calls to REPENTANCE and gracious offers of FORGIVENESS and BLESSING. It is followed by the promise of world REDEMPTION (2:1-5). Then comes a series of threatening passages, including a detailed description of the finery of the women of JERUSALEM as illustrating the sinful frivolity of the people as a whole. The land is likened to an unfruitful vineyard, which will soon become desolate. It concludes with a series of six woes that end in gloom: "Even the light will be darkened by the clouds" (5:30).

B. The temple vision (Isa. 6). Whether this incident represents the initial call of Isaiah has

This famous terra-cotta prism from Nineveh describes the campaigns of Sennacherib in Israel (701 B.C.). The same events are described in Isa. 36-37.

© Dr. James C. Martin. The British Museum. Photographed by permission.

been much debated. If the woe pronounced on himself by the prophet is to be understood as the seventh woe, intended to show that the prophet was as conscious of his own sin as of the sin of his people, we may assume that this chapter stands in its proper place chronologically and that this vision came to him some time after he began to prophesy. But the question must remain unsettled. It is a vision of the Holy God; and "Holy One of Israel" becomes one of Isaiah's favorite titles for the Deity in whose name he speaks.

C. The Book of Immanuel (Isa. 7-12). This group of chapters belongs to the period of the Syro-Ephraimitic war (2 Ki. 16:1-20; 1 Chr. 28). In the midst of this time of peril, Isaiah utters the great prophecies regarding IMMANUEL (Isa. 7:14-16; 9:6-7; 11:1-10); and he concludes with a

I

song of triumphant faith that ends with the assurance, "Great is the Holy One of Israel among you" (12:6). Here again woe (10:1-4) and threatening (10:5-19) stand in vivid contrast with messianic blessing (11:1-16).

D. Prophecies against the nations (Isa. 13-23). These are ten "oracles" (weighty, solemn, and grievous utterances) against nations that either were or would be a menace to God's people: Babylon (13:1—14:27), Philistia (14:28-32), Moab (15-16), Damascus (17-18), Egypt (19-20), Babylon (21:1-10), Dumah (21:11-12), Arabia (21:13-17), Jerusalem (22), Tyre (23). Here prophecies regarding the near future (16:14; 21:16; cf. 22:20 with 37:2) appear along with others that refer to a more distant (23:17) or a quite remote time. Thus the fall of Babylon is so certain that Israel is told the taunt that will be sung on the day that Babylon falls. Compare 21:6-20, which describes it as having already taken place, with 39:6, which speaks of the Babylonian captivity as still future—a method of prophetic description frequently found in Isaiah. This group of prophecies is chiefly threatening, but it also contains wonderful promises of blessing. Israel's mightiest foes will share with her in the future blessedness (19:23-25).

E. Diverse predictions (Isa. 24-35). The first chapter in this section looks far into the future. It is world-embracing and may be called an *apocalypse* (see APOCALYPTIC LITERATURE). The world judgment will be followed by songs of thanksgiving for divine blessing (chs. 25-26). A prophecy against EGYPT follows (ch. 27). Then there are again six woes (chs. 28-34), the last being a frightful curse on EDOM. This group also closes with a beautiful prophetic picture of future blessedness (ch. 35).

F. Historical section (Isa. 36-39; cf. parallel passages in Kings and Chronicles). These chapters describe the blasphemous threats of Sennacherib against Jerusalem, Hezekiah's appeal to Isaiah, who ridicules the invader, and the flight and death of the blasphemer (chs. 36-37)—one of the most thrilling episodes in the whole Bible. Probably Hezekiah's illness and the envoy of MERODACH-BALADAN (chs. 38-39) took place during the reign of SARGON king of Assyria and father of Sennacherib. If so, the arrangement is topical and intended to prepare for the prophecies of consolation that follow.

G. The Book of Consolation (Isa. 40-66). The words "Comfort, comfort my people" at the beginning of this section are clearly intended to give Israel a hope and consolation not to be gathered from Hezekiah's words, which they immediately follow. These chapters fall into three parts as is suggested by the refrain-like words, "There is no peace for the wicked," which occur at 48:22 and 57:21, and which have their terrible echo in Isaiah's final words (66:24).

Isaiah 40-48 deal with the coming of CYRUS and the fall of Babylon as proof of the power of the God of Israel both to foretell and to fulfill, in amazing contrast to the idols of the heathen, which can do neither. The utter folly of idolatry is portrayed most vividly in 44:9-20 and 46:1-11. The last mention of Babylon, "Leave Babylon, flee from the Babylonians" (48:20), is clearly to be thought of as describing flight from a doomed city, like the flight of LOT from SODOM. In the two remaining parts of the book there is no mention of either Assyria or Babylon except by way of reminiscence (52:4).

Isaiah 49-57 form a logical and climactic sequel to the preceding group of chapters. The figure of the "servant" is common to both. The word occurs twenty times in chs. 40-53. Nine times he is called Israel, Jacob, or Jacob-Israel. Six times the Lord calls him "my servant." The title is used in three senses: of the servant as deaf and blind (42:18-19), sinful and needing redemption (44:22; cf. 43:25); of the servant as faithful and as having a mission to Israel and the Gentiles (42:1-7; 49:1-6; 50:6-9); and finally of One who, himself innocent, suffers for the sins of others (52:13—53:12). The first three of these four passages, which are often called the "Servant Songs," can refer to the pious in Israel as sharing with their Lord in his mission of salvation. The last story is one of the most precious passages in the Bible. It speaks both of the humiliation of the Savior and also of the glory that is to follow. The greatness of the salvation secured by the Servant is described in glowing terms and its worldwide scope is made clear in 53:10-12 and again and again in the chapters that follow, especially 61:1-3. See SERVANT OF THE LORD.

Isaiah 58-66 continue the same general theme and reaches its height in 66:1-3, a passage that fore-

I

tells that day of which Jesus spoke to the woman of SAMARIA, when the true worshiper will worship not in temples made with hands, but "in spirit and truth" (Jn. 4:21-24). Yet here again as constantly elsewhere, warning and denunciation alternate with offers and assurances of blessing. Thus Isa. 65:17, which speaks of the "new heavens and a new earth" (cf. 66:22), follows a denunciation of those who practice abominations. And the book closes with a reference to the torments of the reprobate.

© Dr. James C. Martin. The Israel Museum, Jerusalem. Photographed by permission.

Facsimile of the Great Isaiah Scroll (1QIsaᵃ) discovered in Qumran (2nd cent. B.C.).

III. Principal themes of Isaiah. Isaiah is preeminently the prophet of redemption. The greatness and majesty of God, his holiness and hatred of sin and the folly of idolatry, his grace and mercy and love, and the blessed rewards of obedience are constantly recurring themes. No wonder that the NT writers quote so often from Isaiah and that so much of Handel's *Messiah* is taken from it. *Redeemer* and *savior* (or *save, salvation*) are among Isaiah's favorite words. The words that describe the character of the promised Messiah (Isa. 9:6) are frequently on his lips: wonderful (25:1; 28:29; 29:14), counselor (19:17; 25:1; 28:29; 40:13-14, 16-17), mighty God (30:29; 33:13; 40:26-28; 49:20-26; 60:16), everlasting father (26:4; 40:28; 45:17; 55:3; 57:15; 60:19-20; 63:16; 64:8), prince of peace (26:12; 45:7; 52:7; 53:5; 55:12; 57:19; 66:12). Isaiah had a deep appre-

ciation of beauty and wonder of the world of nature (e.g., ch. 35). A striking figure that he uses repeatedly is the "highway" (11:16; 19:23; 33:8; 35:8; 36:2; 40:3; 49:11; 57:14; 62:10). All the barriers that separate nation from nation and delay the coming of the King to his kingdom will be removed, and "the glory of the LORD will be revealed, and all mankind together will see it" (40:5).

IV. Importance. The importance of the book is indicated by how frequently it is quoted in the NT. Isaiah is quoted by name twenty-one times, slightly more than all the other writing prophets taken together; and there are many more allusions and quotations where his name is not given. He has been called the evangelist of the OT, and many of the most precious verses in the Bible come to us from his lips. The fact that the Lord began his public ministry at NAZARETH by reading from Isa. 61 and applying its prophetic words to himself (Lk. 4:16-21) is significant of the place that this book would come to hold in the Christian church.

V. Unity. The traditional authorship and unity of this book have been vigorously assailed for two centuries. The attack is not due to any discoveries that have been made, but to the new theory regarding prophecy that is widely prevalent today and minimizes or denies prediction, declaring that the OT prophet spoke only to the people of his own time and not to future generations. This theory is refuted by the fact that the NT frequently quotes the words of the prophets, notably Isaiah, as fulfilled in the earthly life of Jesus Christ. In Jn. 12:38-40 two quotations from Isaiah are brought together, the one from Isa. 53:1, the other from 6:9-10; and as if to make it quite clear that they have one and the same source, the evangelist adds: "Isaiah said this because he saw Jesus' glory and spoke about him."

The main argument for a "Second Isaiah" is that Cyrus is referred to as one who has already entered on his career of conquest (e.g., Isa. 41:1-2, 25); and it is claimed that the writer of all or

I

part of chs. 40-66 must have lived at the close of the Babylonian captivity. We must note, therefore, that the prophets, notably Isaiah, often spoke as if they were eyewitnesses of the future events they described. The viewpoint or situation of the one who penned ch. 53 is Calvary. He describes the sufferings of the Servant as ended and depicts in glowing colors the glory that will follow, yet the prophet cannot have lived at that time. He must have lived many years, even centuries, before the advent of the One whose death he vividly portrays. Consequently, one must hold that neither in chs. 7-12 nor in ch. 53 the prophet predicted the coming and work of the Messiah; or one must hold that he could and did speak of future events, of the coming of Cyrus, of One greater than Cyrus, as if he were living in the glorious days of which he spoke. For those who accept the testimony of the Bible and hold the conception of predictive prophecy that it sets forth, the unity of Isaiah is not a discredited tradition but a well-accredited fact.

Isaiah, Martyrdom and Ascension of. See PSEUDEPIGRAPHA.

Iscah. is´kuh (Heb. *yiskâ H3576*, derivation uncertain). TNIV Iskah. Daughter of HARAN and niece of ABRAHAM (Gen. 11:29).

Iscariot. See JUDAS ISCARIOT.

Ishbaal. See ISH-BOSHETH.

Ishbah. ish´buh (Heb. *yisbāh H3786*, "[God] soothes" or "may [God's wrath] subside" or "[God] congratulates"). Son of MERED (apparently by his wife BITHIAH, Pharaoh's daughter) and father of ESHTEMOA; included in the genealogy of JUDAH (1 Chr. 4:17; note that NRSV, to clarify the sense, includes here part of v. 18).

Ishbak. ish´bak (Heb. *yisbāq H3791*, possibly from a root that in Arabic means "to anticipate, surpass"). Son of ABRAHAM and KETURAH (Gen. 25:2; 1 Chr. 1:32); no descendants are mentioned.

Ishbi-Benob. ish´bi-bee´nob (Heb. *yisbî benōb H3787*, meaning unknown). A descendant of Rapha (see REPHAITES) of GATH whose bronze spearhead weighed more than seven pounds; fighting on the side of the PHILISTINES against the Israelites, he vowed to kill DAVID but was defeated by ABISHAI (2 Sam. 21:16-17, 22). As a result of this incident, the Israelite soldiers would not allow David to fight again.

Ish-Bosheth. ish-boh´shith (Heb. *ʾiš-bōšet H410*, "man of shame"). Son of SAUL; he was made king over Israel by ABNER in repudiation of DAVID's claim to the throne (2 Sam. 2:8—4:12; NRSV, "Ishbaal"). He is also called ESH-BAAL (*ʾešbaʿal H843*), meaning "man of the Lord" or "the Lord exists," which was probably his original name (1 Chr. 8:33; 9:39). The difference between Ish-Bosheth and Esh-Baal is generally attributed to an intentional alteration of the name of BAAL because of intense hatred for that pagan deity (this word, which means "lord," could apparently be applied to Yahweh early in Israelite history). It is also possible that the name was given him as a result of his shameful demise. The appointment of Ish-Bosheth brought forth the question of the means of royal succession. David's right was charismatic, Ish-Bosheth's was hereditary, and the former prevailed. Ish-Bosheth was forty years of age when he was enthroned at MAHANAIM and reigned for only two years (2 Sam. 2:10). Abner transferred his loyalty to David as a result of an accusation by Ish-Bosheth (3:7-12; but Abner was murdered shortly thereafter, v. 27). Ish-Bosheth, lacking support, was finally assassinated (4:5-8).

Ish-hai. ish´hi (Heb. *ʾiš-hay*, "man of life"). Father of Jehoiada and grandfather of BENAIAH (one of DAVID's mighty warriors), according to 2 Sam. 23:20 KJV, following the *Ketib* ("what is written"). However, the *Qere* (the variant preferred by the MT) has *ben-ʾiš-hayil*, lit., "son of a man of power," an expression applied to Benaiah and probably meaning "valiant warrior" or the like; this reading (found in the parallel, 1 Chr. 11:22) is followed by most versions.

Ishhod. ish´hod (Heb. *ʾišhôd H412*, "man of splendor [*or* vitality]"). KJV Ishod. Son of HAMMOLEKETH, who was apparently the sister of GILEAD; included

I

in the genealogy of MANASSEH (1 Chr. 7:18). It is unclear why his father's name is not given. See discussion under ABIEZER #1.

Ishi (divine name). ish′i (Heb. *ʾišî*, from *ʾîš H408*, "man, husband," plus first person sing. pronoun). This name appears in the KJV of Hos. 2:16, "And it shall be at that day, saith the LORD, *that* thou shalt call me Ishi; and shalt call me no more Baali" (modern versions usually translate the first name with "my husband," and the second with either "my Baal" [NRSV] or "my master" [NIV]). The Hebrew word for *baʿal H1251* means "owner" or "lord," but it too can mean "husband." Because of its associations with the idolatrous worship of the pagan BAAL, the prophet declares that this name will not be used in the worship of the true God. Some have thought that this word, when it has the meaning "husband," implies a formal or legal arrangement, and that the change of name may thus indicate also a return to a closer spiritual relationship.

Ishi (person). ish′i (Heb. *yišʿî H3831*, prob. short form of ISAIAH). **(1)** Son of Appaim and descendant of JUDAH through the line of JERAHMEEL (1 Chr. 2:31).

(2) A descendant of JUDAH (1 Chr. 4:20); his genealogical connection is unclear.

(3) A member of the tribe of SIMEON whose sons led 500 Simeonites in an invasion of the hill country of SEIR (1 Chr. 4:42).

(4) A head of family in the eastern part of the tribe of MANASSEH; he and several others are described as "brave warriors, famous men" (1 Chr. 5:24).

Ishiah. i-shi′uh. TNIV form of ISSHIAH.

Ishijah. i-shi′juh (Heb. *yiššiyyâ H3807*, prob. "Yahweh forgets"). NRSV Isshijah. One of the descendants of Harim who put away their foreign wives (Ezra 10:31).

Ishma. ish′muh (Heb. *yišmāʾ H3816*, "[God] hears"; short form of ISHMAEL). Son of Etam and descendant of JUDAH (1 Chr. 4:3, NIV and other versions, following LXX). The MT is unintelligible; see discussion under ETAM #1.

Ishmael. ish′may-uhl (Heb. *yišmāʿēʾl H3817*, "God hears"; gentilic *yišmĕʿēʾlî H3818*, "Ishmaelite"). **(1)** Son of ABRAHAM by HAGAR, who was SARAH's Egyptian maid. Sarah was barren (Gen. 16:1) and, in accordance with the custom of the age, she gave to Abraham her handmaid Hagar as his CONCUBINE, hoping that he might obtain a family by her. Abraham was then eighty-six

The Wilderness of Paran, where Ishmael spent much of his life.

© Dr. James C. Martin

years old and had been in CANAAN for ten years (16:3). When Hagar saw that she had conceived, she began to despise her mistress, so that Sarah complained bitterly to Abraham, who told her that since Hagar was her slave, she could do anything she wanted with her. Sarah made things so difficult for Hagar that she fled, and somewhere on the road to Egypt the angel of the Lord met her and told her to return to her mistress and submit herself to her. He encouraged her with a promise of many descendants. Ishmael was circumcised when he was thirteen (17:25). Abraham loved him, and even after God had promised him a son by Sarah, he fervently exclaimed, "If only Ishmael might live under your blessing!" (17:18).

At the weaning of ISAAC, the customary feast was held; and Sarah saw Ishmael, now a boy of sixteen, mocking Isaac. Jealous, and probably fearing future trouble if the boys were brought up together, Sarah urged Abraham to get rid of Ishmael and his slave mother, but he was unwilling until he was encouraged to do so by God. Sent away with bread and a bottle of water, Ishmael and his mother wandered about in the wilderness of BEERSHEBA. When he became faint for thirst and was on the verge of death, she put him in the shade of a shrub and sat nearby, "for she thought, 'I cannot watch the boy die'" (Gen. 21:16). For the second time in Hagar's life, the angel of the Lord appeared to her. He directed her to some water and renewed his former promise of Ishmael's future greatness (21:19-20). Ishmael grew up and became famous as an archer in the wilderness of PARAN. His mother gave him in marriage to an Egyptian wife. When Abraham died, Ishmael returned from exile to help Isaac bury their father (25:9). He became the father of twelve sons and a daughter, whom Esau took for his wife. He died at the age of 137 (25:17). In Gal. 4:21-31 PAUL uses the lives of Ishmael and Isaac allegorically. Hagar represents the old covenant, and Sarah, the new; the rivalry between Ishmael and Isaac foreshadows the conflict in the early church between those who would cling to the ordinances of the law, which must pass away, and those who realize that through the grace of Christ there is freedom from the law.

(2) Son of Azel and descendant of BENJAMIN through SAUL (1 Chr. 8:38; 9:44).

(3) Father of a certain Zebadiah who was head of the tribe of Judah during the reign of JEHOSHAPHAT (2 Chr. 19:11).

(4) Son of Jehohanan; he was one of the commanders under JEHOIADA who took part in the revolt against ATHALIAH (2 Chr. 23:1).

(5) Son of Nethaniah, known primarily as the royal officer who assassinated GEDALIAH, the governor appointed by the Babylonians over Judah (2 Ki. 25:25; Jer. 40:7—41:18). Ishmael himself belonged to the royal family (2 Ki. 25:25; Jer. 41:1). After the destruction of JERUSALEM, he joined Gedaliah in MIZPAH. Perhaps hoping to lay a claim to the throne, Ishmael with ten of his men killed not only Gedaliah, but also the Jews who were with him in Mizpah and the Babylonian soldiers. The following day he slaughtered a large group of men who were bringing offerings to the temple. He then took the rest of the people captive and set out to join the Ammonites. The army officers, led by Johanan son of Kareah, pursued Ishmael and were able to rescue the captives, although Ishmael himself escaped.

(6) One of the descendants of Pashhur who agreed to put away their foreign wives (Ezra 10:22).

Ishmaelite. ish′may-uh-lit (Heb. *yišmĕʿēʾli H3818*). A descendant of ISHMAEL. The Bible refers to the Ishmaelites in connection with the story of JOSEPH (Gen. 37:25-28; 39:1), in the narrative of GIDEON and the Midianites (Jdg. 8:24), and in a list of enemies of Israel (Ps. 83:6). In addition, a certain JETHER the Ishmaelite is included in the genealogy of JUDAH (1 Chr. 2:17; called "Ithra the Israelite" in the MT of 2 Sam. 17:24), and the man in charge of DAVID's camels was an Ishmaelite named OBIL.

Twelve sons (or descendants) of Ishmael are listed in the Bible (Gen. 25:13-15; 1 Chr. 1:29-31), and most of these names correspond to Arabian tribes (or place names) attested in extrabiblical sources. It is clear that, no later than the eighth century B.C., the Ishmaelites formed a major tribal confederacy spread throughout most of N Arabia. Some scholars dispute that these tribes are to be linked with the biblical "sons of Ishmael," but the evidence seems to favor ethnic and political identity. In addition, there is reason to believe that the

I

name Ishmaelite functions in the Bible as a generic term for desert tribal peoples, since it can apparently include the Midianites (cf. Gen. 37:28, 36 [MT, "Medanites"]; Jdg. 8:24 [cf. v. 22]).

Ishmaiah. ish-may′yuh (Heb. *yišmaʿyâ H3819*, "Yahweh hears"). **(1)** One of the band of warriors, kinsmen of SAUL, who joined with DAVID when the latter took refuge at ZIKLAG (1 Chr. 12:4; KJV, "Ismaiah"). He was from GIBEON (as was Saul) and is described as "a mighty man among the Thirty, who was a leader of the Thirty."

(2) Son of Obadiah; he was a ruler appointed by David over the tribe of ZEBULUN (1 Chr. 27:19).

Ishmerai. ish′muh-ri (Heb. *yišmĕray H3821*, "[Yahweh] preserves"). Son of ELPAAL and descendant of BENJAMIN (1 Chr. 8:18); he is listed among the heads of families who lived in Jerusalem (cf. v. 28).

Ishod. See ISHHOD.

Ishpah. ish′puh (Heb. *yišpâ H3834*, possibly "smooth or "bald"). KJV Ispah. Son of BERIAH and descendant of BENJAMIN (1 Chr. 8:16); he is listed among the heads of families who lived in Jerusalem (cf. v. 28). His father and uncle, however, are described as "heads of families of those living in Aijalon and who drove out the inhabitants of Gath" (v. 13).

Ishpan. ish′pan (Heb. *yišpān H3836*, derivation uncertain). Son of Shashak and descendant of BENJAMIN (1 Chr. 8:22); he is listed among the heads of families who lived in JERUSALEM (cf. v. 28).

Ish-sechel. ish-see′kuhl (Heb. *ʾîš śekel*, "man of understanding"). This transliteration is used by some in Ezra 8:18 (e.g., ASV mg.) on the grounds that the context calls for a proper name. Most versions, however, take the words as common nouns (e.g., NRSV, "a man of discretion"; NIV, "a capable man").

Ishtar. ish′tahr. The Sumero-Semitic goddess of love and fertility and, mainly in ASSYRIA, goddess of war. In SUMER she was known as Inanna (or [I] nnini). Ishtar was worshiped widely throughout Babylonia and Assyria, where temples were dedicated to her in the main cities and chapels in many towns. In addition, at BABYLON alone there were 180 wayside open-air shrines, where hymns and prayers to her as goddess of fertility were frequent. As "Lady of the lands," she was revered throughout the ANE, though sometimes under other names. In the OT, Ishtar is referred to as ASHTORETH. The women of Judah were upbraided for making sacrificial cakes or incense for her under her title as QUEEN OF HEAVEN (Jer. 7:18; 44:19). According to Babylonian tradition, this goddess descended to the underworld in search of her missing lover TAMMUZ, with the result that fertility ceased and women wept (cf. Ezek. 5:14). In her various capacities, Ishtar is represented as the evening and morning star (Venus).

Ish-tob. ish′tob (Heb. *ʾîš ṭôb*, "man of Tob"). The KJV transliteration of a phrase that is better rendered "the men of Tob" (2 Sam. 10:6, 8). See TOB.

Ishuah. See ISHVAH.

Ishuai, Ishui. See ISHVI.

Ishvah. ish′vuh (Heb. *yišwâ H3796*, perhaps "[God] rules"). Son of ASHER and grandson of JACOB (Gen. 46:17 [KJV, "Ishuah"]; 1 Chr. 7:30 [KJV, "Isuah"]). Because he does not appear in the list of Asherite clans (Num. 26:44-45), some suspect that the name Ishvah is the result of textual corruption of ISHVI; others speculate that he may have died childless.

Ishvi. ish′vi (Heb. *yišwî H3798*, derivation disputed; gentilic *yišwî H3799*, "Ishvite" [KJV, "Jesuite"]). **(1)** Son of ASHER, grandson of JACOB, and ancestor of the Ishvite clan (Gen. 46:17 [KJV, "Isui"]; Num. 26:44 [KJV, "Jesui"]; 1 Chr. 7:30 [KJV, "Ishuai"]).

(2) Son of King SAUL (1 Sam. 14:49; KJV, "Ishui"). While this passage lists only three sons of Saul, 1 Chronicles includes four: Jonathan, Malki-Shua, Abinadab, and Esh-Baal (= ISH-BOSHETH, 1 Chr. 8:33; 9:39). Many believe Ishvi is the same as Esh-Baal/Ish-Bosheth; others speculate that 1 Samuel preserves an earlier list, prior to the birth of

Abinadab and Esh-Baal, and that Ishvi died before these last two sons were born.

Isis. *i´*sis. See OSIRIS.

Iskah. is´kuh. TNIV form of ISCAH.

island, isle. The Hebrew term *ʾi H362* can mean a true island (e.g., Ezek. 26:18; 27:6), dry land as distinct from wet (Isa. 42:15), and especially a coastland. Sometimes littoral regions are distinguished from interior (Esth. 10:1), and the nearby shores of PALESTINE (Isa. 20:6) and PHOENICIA (23:2, 6) are included. But more commonly distance is implied, especially where "the coastlands/islands of the nations," extending into the W MEDITER-RANEAN, are in view (Gen. 10:5 [KJV, "isles of the Gentiles"; NIV, "maritime peoples"]; Zeph. 2:11). Though references are scattered, a notable concentration appears in the Major Prophets, and a definite pattern of Israelite geographical knowledge (based partially on Phoenician and Philistine contacts) seems implied. NT references, naturally more explicit, include MALTA and specific Aegean islands, while in Rev. 6:14 and 16:20 the broader idea reappears.

Ismachiah. See ISMAKIAH.

Ismaiah. See ISHMAIAH.

Ismakiah. is´muh-ki´uh (Heb. *yismakyāhû H3577*, "Yahweh sustains"). Also Ismachiah. One of the temple supervisors under CONANIAH, who was in charge of the contributions during the reign of HEZEKIAH (2 Chr. 31:13).

Ispah. See ISHPAH.

Israel. iz´ray-uhl (Heb. *yiśrā'ēl H3776*, by popular etymology, "he struggles with God"; gentilic *yiśrĕ'ēli H3778*, "Israelite"). This name is used in Scripture to designate: (1) an individual man, the son of Isaac (see JACOB); or (2) his descendants, the twelve tribes of the Hebrews; or (3) only the ten northern tribes, led by the tribe of EPHRAIM, as opposed to the southern, under the tribe of JUDAH.

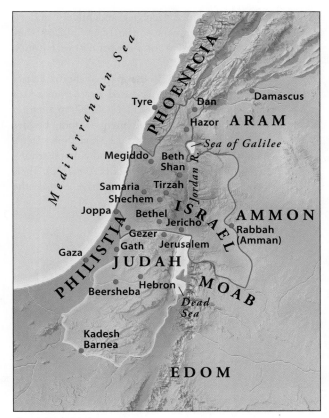

The Divided Kingdom.

When ABRAHAM was called out of UR of the Chaldees (Gen. 11:31; Neh. 9:7), the Lord's redemptive purpose was to bring Abraham and his descendants into a saving, COVENANT relationship with himself (Gen. 17:7) and also to make of Abraham's seed a nation in Palestine (17:8) and through them to some day bring salvation to the entire world (12:3; 22:18). God accordingly blessed Abraham's grandson Jacob with many children. After a long stay in HARAN, Jacob returned to Palestine and "a man" wrestled with him, bringing him to a point of total submission (32:25; Hos. 12:4). By yielding his life to God's purpose, Jacob achieved victory, and the man changed his name to Israel, saying, "because you have struggled with God and with men and have overcome" (Gen. 32:28; 35:10). Jacob's twelve sons were, literally, the "children of Israel" (42:5; 45:21), but the phrase came to signify the whole body of God's chosen and saved people (32:32;

I

34:7). It included Jacob's grandchildren and all subsequent members of the household, as they proceeded to Egypt for a stay of 430 years (46:8; Exod. 1:7).

I. Mosaic period. In the space of approximately ten generations, God increased Israel from a clan of several hundred (Gen. 14:14; 46:27) to a nation of "six hundred thousand men on foot, besides women and children" (Exod. 12:37; cf. Num. 1:46), equipped with all the material and cultural advantages of Egypt (Exod. 2:10; 12:36; Acts 7:22). Their very increase, however, seems to have aroused the

Reconstruction of the tabernacle from the time of Moses.

envy of the Egyptians (Exod. 1:8-10). Israel was thus enslaved and compelled to erect certain store-cities in the region of the eastern NILE delta (1:11; cf. Gen. 15:13) and was threatened with total national destruction under the anti-Semitic policy of the empire (Exod. 1:16). MOSES (born 1527 B.C.) was taken in by an Egyptian princess, but even he was forced to flee Egypt.

God, however, still remembered his covenant promises with Abraham (Exod. 2:24-25). At the death of the current PHARAOH (2:23), God appeared to Moses in a burning bush at Mount Sinai and commissioned him to deliver the enslaved people (3:10). Moses accordingly returned to the Egyptian court with the cry "This is what the LORD says: Israel is my firstborn son, and I told you, 'Let my son go, so he may worship me.' But you refused to let him go; so I will kill your firstborn son" (4:22-23). The new monarch, however, refused to heed the divine summons. Only after a series of ten miraculous plagues, climaxing in the death of all

the firstborn of Egypt, was the hardhearted pharaoh compelled to yield to the Lord (12:31).

Israel marched eastward from GOSHEN toward the RED SEA (see EXODUS). But when the perfidious pharaoh pursued after the seemingly entrapped Hebrews (Exod. 14:3), the Lord sent a strong E wind that blew back the waters of the sea (14:21). Israel crossed, and then the Lord caused the waters to return so that the Egyptians were destroyed to the last man (14:28; excepting pharaoh, who is not mentioned after v. 10). When the Israelites reached Mount SINAI (19:1), God extended the covenant offer of reconciliation that he had made with Abraham and Jacob (Gen. 12:1-3; 28:13-15) so as to embrace the whole nation of the sons of Israel, promising, "Now if you obey me fully and keep my covenant, then out of all nations you will be my treasured possession. Although the whole earth is mine, you will be for me a kingdom of priests and a holy nation" (Exod. 19:5-6).

Israel was required to fulfill certain subjective conditions so as to share in this testamental inheritance: "*If* you keep my covenant, then ..." Basically, they must in FAITH commit themselves to God, to be his people. As Moses proclaimed, "Hear, O Israel: ... Love the LORD your God with all your heart" (Deut. 6:4-5). God provided Israel with his fundamental moral law, the Decalogue (Exod. 20:3-17; see COMMANDMENTS, TEN), together with elaborations in the various other codes of the PENTATEUCH. God also furnished them with his ceremonial LAW, to depict Israel's reconciliation with their heavenly Father (e.g., Lev. 23:39-40) and to provide a symbolical way of FORGIVENESS, should they transgress his moral requirements (e.g., 6:1-3, 6-7). The ceremonies, however, gained their true effectiveness because they foreshadowed the ultimate redemptive work of Jesus Christ (Heb. 9:9-14, 23-24).

Eventually Israel broke up camp (Num. 10:11) and marched NE to KADESH on the southern border of the Promised Land of Canaan. But after taking forty days to spy out the land, all the tribal representatives except CALEB and JOSHUA reported unfavorably on attempting any conquest of Canaan: "But the people who live there are powerful, and the cities are fortified and very large" (13:28). Impetuous Israel then refused to advance

© Dr. James C. Martin

into the Promised Land and prayed for a return to Egypt (14:4). Moses' intercession did save them from immediate divine wrath; but the Lord still condemned them to wander for forty years in the wilderness, one year for each day of spying, until that entire generation died away (14:32-34).

Israel's route of march, after an extended stay at Kadesh (Deut. 1:46), is described in Num. 33; but the various camps cannot be identified, except that they are known to have passed through Ezion Geber at the head of the Gulf of Aqabah before a final return to Kadesh (Num. 33:35-36). This rough, nomadic existence forced the people into a life of dependence on God, who tested them and yet at the same time cared for them miraculously (Deut. 2:7; 8:2-4). This training period was still marred by repeated "murmurings" and defections, such as the revolts of Korah, Dathan, and Abiram (Num. 16-17). Even Moses, when producing water for the thirsty people, failed to credit God with the glory (20:10-11) and was therefore denied entrance into the Promised Land (20:12).

When the Hebrews resumed their advance on Canaan, the nation of Edom (a people descended from Israel's twin brother Esau) refused to allow kindred Israel to pass through their territories (Num. 20:21). The result was that the Israelites were compelled to double back to Ezion Geber on the Red Sea and go completely around the land of Edom, marching northward up the king's highway along the eastern border of Edom and Moab (21:4, 22). Opposite the midpoint of the Dead Sea, Israel reached the territory of the Canaanite kingdom of Sihon of Heshbon. Although Sihon refused to allow Israel further passage, it was actually God who had hardened the king's heart (Deut. 2:30), whose very attack provided the occasion for his total overthrow and for Israel's occupation of the land of Gilead (Num. 21:24). Similar aggression by Og, king of Bashan, resulted in Israel's acquisition of N Transjordan as well (21:35). Eventually, Israel was able to set up camp on the Plains of Moab, across the Jordan from Jericho (Deut. 1:3-5).

During the last month of Moses' life, God's great servant conducted a "numbering" or census of the people, which indicated a figure similar to what was recorded at the time of the exodus forty years before (Num. 26:51; cf. 1:46). Moses then granted the request of the tribes of Reuben, Gad, and half of Manasseh to settle in the conquered lands of Transjordan (ch. 32); and he provided for the division of W Canaan among the remaining tribes (chs. 33-34). At this time Balaam, who had been employed by the Moabites to curse Israel, uttered his famous blessings. The seer climaxed his oracles by predicting the future messianic king, whose coming constituted the purpose of Israel: "I see him, but not now; I behold him, but not near. A star will come out of Jacob; a scepter will rise out of Israel. He will crush the foreheads of Moab, the skulls of all the sons of Sheth" (24:17). Moses then anointed Joshua as his successor (27:23), spoke the final addresses that constitute most of the book of Deuteronomy, and ascended Mount Pisgah to view the Promised Land. There Moses died and was buried by God's own hand (Deut. 34:5-6). He had been the founder of the Hebrews as a nation. "Since then, no prophet has risen in Israel like Moses, whom the Lord knew face to face" (34:10).

II. The conquest. At Joshua's accession, the land of Canaan lay providentially prepared for conquest by the Hebrews (assuming the so-called "early date" for the exodus). Comprising nominally a part of the Egyptian empire, Canaan suffered the neglect of Amenhotep III (c. 1412-1376 B.C.), called "the magnificent," whose rule was one of luxury, military inactivity, and decay. Political organization within Palestine was that of many small city-states, impoverished by a century of Egyptian misrule and deficient in cooperative defense. Canaanite standards of living, however, were still superior to those of the invading Hebrews, a fact that was later to lend "cultural" appeal to their debased religion.

As the Israelites were ready to cross into W Canaan, the Jordan River was in its annual flood stage (Josh. 3:15). But Joshua anticipated a miracle of divine intervention (3:13), and the Lord did indeed open a gateway into Canaan. For "the water from upstream stopped flowing. It piled up in a heap a great distance away, at a town called Adam," some 15 mi. (24 km.) N of Jericho (3:16). Israel marched across the dry riverbed, led by the ark of God's testament (3:13).

I

Joshua's war of conquest developed in three major campaigns: in central, southern, and northern Canaan. His first objective was the city of Jericho, to his immediate W in the Jordan Valley. "At the sound of the trumpet, when the people gave a loud shout" outside Jericho's walls, the Lord caused the walls to collapse (Josh. 6:20), and Joshua proceeded to "devote" the city to God (6:21). Joshua then ascended westward into Canaan's central ridge and, after an initial setback because of sin in the camp (7:20-21), seized the post of AI. It seems to have served as an outer defense of the major city of BETHEL (8:17), which surrendered without further resistance (12:16; cf. Jdg. 1:22). Joshua was thus able to assemble Israel at SHECHEM to reaffirm the Mosaic law (Josh. 8:33; according to Deut. 27:11-26), having subdued all of central Canaan.

To the S, GIBEON next submitted and, by trickery, its inhabitants saved themselves from the destruction that God had decreed (Deut. 7:2; Josh. 9:15). Their action, however, provoked an alliance against them of five kings of the southern AMORITES, who retaliated by laying siege to Gibeon (Josh. 10:5). Joshua was informed and advanced by forced march to the relief of his clients (10:9); they surprised the enemy and with divine aid routed them westward down the AIJALON Valley. Israel then proceeded to ravage the whole of southern Palestine (10:28-42).

The northern Canaanites finally awoke to their danger and formed an offensive alliance under the leadership of JABIN king of HAZOR (Josh. 11:5). Joshua, however, attacked unexpectedly at the Waters of MEROM, in Upper GALILEE, and completely routed the allied forces (11:7-8). Only Hazor was actually destroyed (11:13), but this triumph meant that within six years of the fall of Jericho (cf. 14:10) virtually all Canaan had come to lie at Joshua's feet (11:16). "So the LORD gave Israel all the land he had sworn to give their forefathers ... every [promise] was fulfilled" (21:43, 45). The Canaanites had not yet lost their potential for resistance; and indeed, what the Lord had sworn to Israel had been a gradual occupation of the land (Exod. 23:28-30; Deut. 7:22). Much still remained to be possessed (Josh. 13:1), but at this point Joshua was compelled by advancing age to divide the land among the twelve Hebrew tribes (Josh.

13-22). He then charged his people with faithfulness to the Lord (24:15) and died.

III. Judges. Moses had ordered the "devotion" (extermination) of the Canaanites (Deut. 7:2), both because of their longstanding immoralities (9:5; cf. Gen. 9:22, 25; 15:16) and because of their debasing religious influence on God's people (Deut. 7:4; 12:31). See DEVOTED THING. In the years immediately following Joshua's death, Judah accordingly accomplished an initial capture of JERUSALEM (Jdg. 1:8; though the city was not held, 1:21); Ephraim and western Manasseh killed the men of Bethel (1:25) because the city had begun to reassert itself. But then came failure: Israel ceased to eradicate the Canaanites, no more cities were taken (1:27-34), and the tribe of DAN actually suffered eviction themselves (1:34). Israel's tolerance of evil had to be rectified by national chastening (2:3).

The next three and one-half centuries were used of God to impress on his people three major lessons: (1) The Lord's WRATH because of sin. When Israel yielded to temptation, God "sold them to their enemies all around, whom they were no longer able to resist" (Jdg. 2:14). (2) God's MERCY when people repented. The Lord would then raise "up a judge for them, he was with the judge and saved them out of the hands of their enemies" (2:18). (3) Israel's depravity. "When the judge died, the people returned to ways even more corrupt than those of their fathers" (2:19). The period of the fourteen judges or leaders (twelve mentioned in the book of Judges, plus ELI and SAMUEL in 1 Samuel) demonstrates a repeated cycle of human sin, of servitude or supplication, and then of salvation.

The chief external forces that God employed for the execution of his providential dealings were the rival empires of the HITTITES N of Palestine and of the Egyptians to the S. Neither of these powers was conscious of the way God was using them; but still, the years in which either succeeded in maintaining Palestinian law and order proved to be just the period that God had chosen for granting "rest" to Israel. Suppiluliuma, for example, who took the throne of the Hittite New Kingdom in about 1385 B.C., fomented dissension among the Palestinian states that owed nominal allegiance to Egypt's Amenhotep III and Amenhotep IV; with this international intrigue coincides Israel's first

I

oppression, by CUSHAN RISHATHAIM, an invader from Hittite-controlled MESOPOTAMIA (Jdg. 3:8). The underlying cause, however, lay in Israel's sin against the moral requirements of God's Sinaitic covenant. (Compare the sordid events of Micah and the Danites and of the Benjamite outrage, Jdg. 17-21.) When they "cried out to the LORD, he raised up for them a deliverer, Othniel son of Kenaz, Caleb's younger brother" (Jdg. 3:9). The forty years of peace that then followed probably correspond to the time of undisputed Hittite sway over Palestine, until some years after the death of Suppululiuma c. 1345.

Founded in the 1320s B.C., however, the 19th dynasty of Egypt began to reassert its territorial claims. Behind this international confusion lay the fact that "once again the Israelites did evil in the eyes of the LORD, and because they did this evil the LORD gave Eglon king of Moab power over Israel," for eighteen years (Jdg. 3:12, 14). Again the Israelites cried out to the Lord, and he gave them a deliverer—EHUD, a left-handed man, the son of Gera the Benjamite (3:15)—and granted them eighty years of peace. This may have been the time of the treaty of 1315 between Seti I of Egypt and Mursil II of Heth, who preserved order by dividing the Near East into separate spheres of influence. The treaty was then renewed in 1279, after a futile war of aggression by Rameses II, and was strictly enforced until the death of the last great Hittite king, c. 1250.

Against the oppressive Canaanite JABIN II of HAZOR (Jdg. 4:2-3), God raised up the fourth of the judges, the woman DEBORAH. Her military commander, BARAK, proceeded to muster the north-central tribes to the Valley of ESDRAELON for war with Jabin's officer, SISERA. Then "the stars fought, from their courses they fought against Sisera" (5:20; cf. v. 21): a divinely sent cloudburst immobilized the powerful Canaanite chariotry, and Sisera himself was murdered in flight by a Kenite woman. The forty-year peace that followed Deborah's victory may have coincided with the strong rule of RAMSES III at the turn of the century, the last great pharaoh of the 19th dynasty.

Next came the nomadic Midianites and Amalekites out of the eastern desert to plunder sinful Israel (Jdg. 6:2-6). In about 1175 B.C., however, the Lord answered the repentant prayers of his people and raised up GIDEON with his chosen band of 300. "A sword for the LORD and for Gideon" cleared Israel of the nomadic raiders (7:19-25; 8:10-12), as witnessed by the peaceful picture of Ruth 2-4 some twenty-five years later. The turmoil that resulted from the attempt of Gideon's son ABIMELECH to make himself king over Israel

A view of Mt. Ebal, looking N from Mt. Gerizim. Joshua gathered the Israelites in this valley to allot their tribal inheritances in the Promised Land.

© Dr. James C. Martin

I

(Jdg. 9) was rectified by the sixth and seventh judges, TOLA and JAIR (who must have overlapped, for no separate deliverance is ascribed to the latter, 10:1-5). But with their deaths in 1110 and the apostasy that subsequently arose, God delivered up his land to two simultaneous oppressions: that of the Ammonites in the east, and that of the Philistines in the west (10:7). After eighteen years, eastern Israel was freed by JEPHTHAH, the eighth judge (ch. 11), who was succeeded by three minor judges. Western Israel, however, remained subject to the rising power of the Philistines for a full forty years (13:1), until the advent of Samuel in 1070. This period must therefore embrace the activity of Eli, until about 1090 (1 Sam. 4:18), as well as the spectacular but politically ineffective exploits of SAMSON, the twelfth and last judge of the book of Judges, to about 1075 (Jdg. 13-16; see 15:20).

The PHILISTINES, by reason of their superior discipline and equipment (cf. Jdg. 3:31; 1 Sam. 13:22; 17:5-6), were able to mount three oppressions, commencing respectively in 1110, 1055, and 1010 B.C., and thereby to threaten the very existence of Israel. Their opening oppression climaxed in the first battle of EBENEZER (1 Sam. 4) and resulted in the deaths of Eli and his sons, in the capture of the ARK OF THE COVENANT, and in the destruction of the Lord's house at SHILOH (see Jer. 7:14). God in his grace, however, raised up the prophet Samuel, who ended the oppression by a God-given victory at the second battle of Ebenezer in about 1070 B.C. (1 Sam. 7). But later, as Samuel turned over many of his powers as judge to his corrupt sons (8:1-3), the Philistines returned with barbaric cruelty (cf. 31:8-10; Jdg. 16:25), seeking to crush disorganized Israel.

IV. The united kingdom. The monarchy was precipitated by the demand of the people themselves. Despite God's directive that they be holy and separate (Lev. 20:26), they still wished to be like "all the other nations" (1 Sam. 8:5), with a human king to fight their battles (8:20), rather than having God acting through a theocratic judge (8:7). They conveniently forgot that it was faithlessness that brought them under attack in the first place. Still, their rebellion served to accomplish God's purpose (see Ps. 76:10); for he had long before decreed a kingdom in Israel over which Jesus the Messiah would someday reign (Gen. 49:10; Num. 24:17). The Lord accordingly authorized Samuel to anoint a king (1 Sam. 8:22) and directed him to SAUL, from the tribe of BENJAMIN (ch. 9).

Saul's accession proceeded in three steps. He was first privately anointed by Samuel (1 Sam. 10:1) and filled with God's Spirit (10:10), then publicly selected at MIZPAH (10:24), and at last popularly confirmed at GILGAL, after having delivered the town of JABESH GILEAD from Ammonite attack (Jdg. 11). The primary concern of his forty-year reign (1050-1010 B.C., cf. Acts 13:21) was the Philistines. These oppressors had already occupied much of his territory, and open war was provoked when one of their garrisons was destroyed by Saul's son JONATHAN (1 Sam. 13:3). In the ensuing battle at MICMASH, Jonathan's personal bravery (14:14), plus the Philistines' own superstitious reaction to a heaven-sent earthquake (14:15, 20), brought about their total defeat. Saul thus terminated the second oppression but, by his failure to submit to Samuel (13:8-9), suffered the rejection of his dynasty from the throne of Israel (13:14).

From his capital in GIBEAH of Benjamin, Saul "fought valiantly" and pushed back the enemies of Israel on every hand (1 Sam. 14:47-48). In about 1025 B.C., however, having been ordered to destroy Israel's implacable enemies, the AMALEKITES (15:1-3; cf. Exod. 17:14), Saul disobeyed and spared both the king and the best of the spoils, under pretext of making offerings to God (1 Sam. 15:15). Samuel stated that "to obey is better than sacrifice" (15:22) and declared Saul's personal deposition from the kingship (15:23, 28). Samuel then privately anointed DAVID, a son of JESSE of Judah, as king over Israel (16:13). David was about fifteen at the time (cf. 2 Sam. 5:4); but by God's providence, he gained rapid promotion at court, first as a minstrel (1 Sam. 16:21-23) and then by his victory over the Philistine champion GOLIATH (ch. 17). Even Saul's growing jealousy, which removed David from court to the dangers of battle, augmented the latter's popularity (18:27-30). Saul's overt hostility finally drove David and his followers into exile, first as outlaws in Judah (20-26) and then as vassals to the Philistine king of GATH (27-30). But while Saul was diverting his resources in the futile pursuit of David, the Philistines prepared

I

for a third, all-out attack on Israel in 1010. David barely escaped engaging in war against his own people (29:4; cf. v. 8); and Saul, routed at Mount GILBOA, committed suicide rather than suffering capture (31:4). Israel's sinful demand for a king had brought about their own punishment.

Having learned of the death of Saul, David moved to HEBRON and was there proclaimed king over his own tribe of Judah (2 Sam. 2:4). But despite David's diplomacy, the supporters of Saul set up his son ISH-BOSHETH over the northern and eastern tribes (2:8-9). Civil war followed, but David increasingly gained the upper hand (3:1). Finally, after the death of Ish-Bosheth, the tribal representatives assembled to Hebron and there anointed David as king over all Israel (5:3; 1003 B.C.). The Philistines now realized that their future depended on prompt action. David, however, after an initial flight to his former outlaw retreat (5:17), rallied his devoted forces (cf. 23:13-17) and, by two brilliant victories in the vicinity of Jerusalem (5:9-25), he not only terminated the last Philistine oppression but eventually incorporated Gath into his own territory and subdued the remaining Philistine states (1 Chr. 18:1).

The time was ripe for the rise of a Hebrew empire. The Hittites had succumbed to barbarian invasion; the 21st dynasty of Egypt stagnated under the alternating rule of priests and merchants (1100 B.C. on); and ASSYRIA, after having weakened others, was itself restrained by inactive kings. With Philistia broken, Israel remained free from foreign threat for 150 years. David's first strategic move was to capture Jerusalem from the Canaanites. Militarily, Mount ZION constituted a splendid fortress (2 Sam. 5:6, 9); politically, the city afforded David a neutral capital between the recently hostile areas of Judah and northern Israel; and religiously, Zion's possession of the ark of God's testament (6:17) centered the people's spiritual hopes within its walls (Ps. 87). From about 1002 to 995 David extended his power on every side, from the EUPHRATES River on the N (2 Sam. 8:3) to the Red Sea on the S (8:14).

David sought to construct a "house," or TEMPLE, in Jerusalem that would be fitting for the Lord. This plan was denied him because of his excessive bloodshed (1 Chr. 22:8; cf. 2 Sam. 8:2);

but God's prophet did inform him, "The LORD himself will establish a house for you" (2 Sam. 7:11). He explained, "When your days are over and you rest with your fathers, I will raise up your offspring to succeed you, who will come from your own body; … he is the one who will build a house for my Name." God's promise, moreover, extended beyond SOLOMON and climaxed in that One in whom Israel's ultimate purpose would be fulfilled: "And I will establish the throne of his kingdom forever. I will be his [the Messiah's] father, and he will be my son" (7:13-14; Heb. 1:5). The eternal Christ would indeed suffer a "testator's" death (Ps. 22:16-18), but would rise in power to give everlasting life to his own (16:10-11; 22:22, 26). In the Lord's promises to him (89:3; 132:12) David experienced fundamental clarifications of God's former redemptive revelation on Mount Sinai. He exclaimed in his psalms and other inspired writings: "Is not my house right with God? / Has he not made with me an everlasting covenant, / arranged and secured in every part? / Will he not bring to fruition my salvation / and grant me my every desire?" (2 Sam. 23:5).

In his later life David became involved in sins of adultery and murder (2 Sam. 11) and of failure to control his sons (ch. 13-14), and for this he received corresponding punishments (chs. 15-16; cf. 12:10-12). The revolt of ABSALOM served also to intensify the antagonism between the northern and southern tribes (19:41-43). But at his death in 970 B.C. David was able to commit to his son Solomon an empire that marked the peak of Israel's power.

Solomon, after a bloody accession (1 Ki. 2:25, 34, 36), reigned in peace, culture, and luxury, experiencing only one military campaign in forty years (2 Chr. 8:3). He was further able to consummate an alliance with the last pharaoh of the 21st dynasty (1 Ki. 3:1). King Solomon is most famous, however, for his unexcelled wisdom (4:31), which was achieved by humility before God (3:7-12) and through which he composed the inspired Proverbs, Ecclesiastes, and Song of Songs, plus numerous other works (Ps. 72; 127; cf. 1 Ki. 4:32). His greatest undertaking was the building of the Jerusalem temple, erected from 966 to 959 B.C. (1 Ki. 6) out of materials lavishly provided by David (1 Chr. 22).

I

© Dr. James C. Martin

Ruin of the royal palace at Samaria, a city destroyed by the Assyrians in 722 B.C.

Like the tabernacle before it, the temple symbolized the abiding presence of God with his people (1 Ki. 8:11).

But Solomon also engaged in a number of luxurious building projects of his own (1 Ki. 7:1-12), so that despite his great commercial revenues (9:26-28; 10:14-15) indebtedness forced him to surrender territory (9:11-12) and to engage in excessive taxation and labor conscription. Unrest grew throughout the empire; and, while the tribute continued during his lifetime (4:21), surrounding subject countries, such as EDOM and DAMASCUS, became increasingly independent (11:14, 23). More serious was Solomon's spiritual failure, induced by wanton polygamy (11:1-8). "The LORD became angry with Solomon because his heart had turned away from the LORD. ... So the LORD said to Solomon 'Since this is your attitude and you have not kept my covenant, ... I will most certainly tear the kingdom away from you and give it to one of your subordinates. ... Yet I will not tear the whole kingdom from [your son], but will give him one tribe for the sake of David my servant and for the sake of Jerusalem, which I have chosen'" (11:9-12).

V. The divided kingdom. Early in 930 B.C. Solomon died, and his son REHOBOAM went to SHECHEM to be confirmed as king. The people, however, were led by JEROBOAM of Ephraim to demand relief from Solomon's tyranny (1 Ki. 12:4), and when Rehoboam spurned their pleas, the ten northern tribes seceded to form an independent kingdom of Israel (or Ephraim). Underlying causes for the rupture include the geographical isolation of the tribes (cf. the phrase "to your tents," 12:16) and their longstanding social tensions (2 Sam. 2:7-9; 19:43). But the basic reason lay in God's decision to punish Israel for Solomon's apostasy (1 Ki. 11:31; 12:15, 24). Furthermore, while the northern tribes possessed the advantages of size, fertility of land, and foreign-trade contacts, these very features diminished their devotion to the Lord and his word.

Ephraim's spiritual laxness became immediately apparent when Jeroboam introduced two golden calves, with sanctuaries at DAN and BETHEL to rival Jerusalem (1 Ki. 12:28; see CALF WORSHIP). He did attempt to associate these images with the historic God of the exodus; but they were still idols, "other gods" (14:9), and not mere pedestals for the Lord's invisible presence. Each succeeding king of Israel likewise "walked in all the ways of Jeroboam, ... and in his sin, which he had caused Israel to commit" (see, e.g., 15:26; 16:19, 26). The division served ultimately to separate the sinful Hebrews from the two faithful tribes of Judah and Benjamin: "For not all who are descended from Israel [Jacob] are Israel" (Rom. 9:6).

The relations between Ephraim and Judah passed through seven stages. (1) Hostility marked their course for the first two generations. Initially, both kingdoms suffered from raids by SHISHAK, the energetic founder of Egypt's 22nd dynasty (2 Chr. 12:1-9). Later, Jeroboam advanced against Rehoboam's son ABIJAH (913-910 B.C.); but God granted a great victory to outnumbered Judah (ch. 13), "because they relied on the LORD, the God of their fathers" (13:18). Pious ASA (910-869) ended Egyptian threats by routing the hosts of ZERAH the Cushite (Pharaoh Osorkon I?) at the turn of the century (14:9-15) and then led Judah in a revival of faith in God's covenant (15:12). But when faced by Ephraimite garrisons at RAMAH, only 6 mi. (10 km.) from Jerusalem, the king panicked and hired BEN-HADAD of Damascus to divert the energies of Israel (16:1-4). God's prophet condemned Asa because he "relied on the king of Aram and not on the LORD [his] God" (16:7); and the precedent of ARAMEAN intervention had serious consequences. King OMRI (885-874) founded SAMARIA as the new capital of Ephraim; but Ben-Hadad laid repeated siege to the city, and Omri's son AHAB was saved only by the grace of God (1 Ki. 20).

(2) Asa's son JEHOSHAPHAT made peace with Ahab (1 Ki. 22:44). The allies, together with Ben-Hadad, did manage to halt the westward advance of SHALMANESER III of Assyria at the bloody battle of Qarqar on the ORONTES (853 B.C.). But Jehoshaphat had given his son in marriage to ATHALIAH, the Baal-worshiping daughter of Ahab and his Phoenician queen JEZEBEL, the persecutor of ELIJAH (19:2); and such compromise could never be honored by God (2 Chr. 19:2). Jehoshaphat was almost killed at the side of Ahab at RAMOTH GILEAD (1 Ki. 22:32-35). Their joint commercial projects met with disaster (2 Chr. 20:35-37). Moab succeeded in revolting from Ephraim (2 Ki. 1:1), and Edom from Judah (8:22); and when JEHU executed God's sentence against the house of Ahab in Israel (841), he killed Judah's young king with them (9:27). Athaliah then slaughtered her princely grandchildren and seized the throne in Jerusalem (11:1).

(3) The years between 841 and 790 B.C. saw no major dealings between Israel and Judah because of Aramean domination over both kingdoms (see 2 Ki. 8:12). Thus, even though Athaliah was killed in Jerusalem, the boy-king Joash (JEHOASH) suffered humiliating submission to HAZAEL of Damascus (12:17-18). Jehu fared even worse, rendering tribute to Shalmaneser in 841 and then, after Assyria's departure, forfeiting his entire Transjordanian territory to Hazael. Only an Assyrian victory over Damascus shortly before 800 brought relief to Israel (13:5).

(4) By 790 B.C. AMAZIAH of Judah had recovered sufficiently to reconquer Edom (2 Ki. 14:7), but his success deceived him. He dared to challenge Jehoash of Israel (14:10), and Jerusalem was rendered totally subservient to Ephraim until the death of Jehoash in 782.

(5) Under the strong monarchs Jeroboam II in Israel and Uzziah in Judah the two kingdoms lived for thirty years in mutual respect and peace. It was their "Indian summer": Egypt slumbered on under the 23rd dynasty; Aram (SYRIA) was broken by Assyria; and Assyria herself, now without aggressive leadership, could be swayed even by the contemporary Hebrew prophet JONAH (2 Ki. 14:25). But beneath the outward prosperity lay moral corruption. AMOS proclaimed impending judgment on "the day of the LORD " (Amos 5:18). HOSEA, too, warned of deportation to Assyria (Hos. 10:6); but with the abolishment of God's old covenant with Israel, he anticipated a future, newer covenant in which people would "acknowledge the LORD" in truth, under "David [the Messiah] their king" (2:20; 3:5).

(6) In 752 B.C. Jeroboam II's son was murdered, and Uzziah (Azariah) of Judah assumed the leadership of the western states against the rising power of Assyria. The general Pul, that is, TIGLATH-PILESER III, was able in 743 to chronicle his defeat of "Azariah the Yaudaean"; and while Judah apparently escaped with little damage, Damascus and Israel, being farther N, were laid under heavy tribute (2 Ki. 15:19).

(7) The Arameans and Ephraimites then united in reprisals against Ahaz, Judah's new but weak and faithless ruler (2 Ki. 16:5; Isa. 7:1-2). Isaiah admonished him to trust in God and in IMMANUEL, the virgin-born Messiah (Isa. 7:3-14); but in 734 B.C. Ahaz submitted to Assyria for deliverance (2 Ki. 16:7). Edom and Philistia

I

continued to plunder Judah (2 Chr. 28:17-18) and may thus provide the background to OBADIAH (see Obad. 10) and JOEL (Joel 3:4, 19); but Ephraim's northern tribes were taken captive by Tiglath-Pileser in 733 (2 Ki. 15:29), and Damascus was destroyed (16:9). Shortly after that the energetic 25th (Cushite) dynasty rose to power in Egypt, and its pharaoh So (Shabaka?) incited Israel to a final revolt (17:4). Samaria fell to the Assyrians in 722. SARGON II (722-705) proceeded to deport 27,290 Ephraimites (17:6) and replaced them with foreign colonists, who produced the half-breed SAMARITANS (17:24-33). "They ... did not trust in the LORD their God. They rejected his decrees and the covenant. ... So the LORD removed them from his presence. Only the tribe of Judah was left" (17:14-15, 18).

HEZEKIAH (725-696 B.C.) meanwhile seized the opportunity to purify the Jerusalem temple (2 Chr. 29) and to destroy the corrupt HIGH PLACES, whether outrightly pagan or claiming the name of the Lord. His reform included even Israel, which was not helpless under Assyrian siege (31:1); and he invited Ephraimites and Judeans alike to the greatest Passover since Solomon (ch. 30). The name "Israel" came thus to be applied to God's faithful remnant, regardless of their previous citizenship (30:6; cf. Ezra 9:1; 10:5). Hezekiah was warned by both Isaiah (Isa. 30:1-7; 31:1-3) and Micah (Mic. 1:9) to take no part in Shabaka's disastrous battle against Sargon in 720; and he managed to withdraw from the equally unsuccessful revolt of Ashdod in 711, which was sponsored by Egypt and Babylon (Isa. 20 and 39; cf. 36:1). But with the accession of Sennacherib in 705, Hezekiah attempted to throw off the Assyrian yoke.

Egypt, however, proved again to be a "splintered reed" (2 Ki. 18:21); Shabaka was defeated at Eltekeh near Ekron in 701 B.C., and Sennacherib claims to have taken over two hundred thousand Jews captive (cf. Isa. 43:5, 14) and to have "shut up Hezekiah like a caged bird in Jerusalem." Hezekiah resubmitted (2 Ki. 18:14-16), but the false Sennacherib made further demands (18:17). God then rose to the defense of his chastened people (Isa. 37:6, 21-35), and, when a relief army arrived under Shabaka's brother TIRHAKA, it found the Assyrians dead, for they had been killed by the angel of the Lord (2 Ki. 19:9, 35; cf. the Egyptian legend of a plague of mice in the camp of Sennacherib [Herodotus, *Hist.* 2.141]). The event ranks with the crossing of the Red Sea as one of the greatest examples of God's deliverance. Isaiah thus had a sound basis for comforting Israel (Isa. 40:1-2) and directing their hope to that day when God would fulfill his redemptive purpose among them (53:6).

MANASSEH's reign (696-641 B.C.) was the longest and worst in Judah's history. He gave up Hezekiah's dearly bought freedom by resubmitting to Assyria. He also rebuilt the high places, served Baal with human sacrifice, and mimicked Assyrian star worship (2 Ki. 21:2-9). Through imprisonment (after the Babylonian revolts of 652-648?), he experienced personal conversion (2 Chr. 33:11-16); but it was too late to reform the people as a whole (33:17; cf. 2 Ki. 21:11, 15; 23:26). God, however, was yet to raise up JOSIAH (639-608), the greatest of Judah's reformers. While still in his teens (627), he responded to prophetic teaching such as Zephaniah's (Zeph. 1:14-17) and began actively to eliminate idolatry (2 Chr. 34:3-7). At this point the barbaric SCYTHIANS erupted over the ANE, and the terror they inspired seems to have turned men's hearts to God. The Scythians were finally driven back by the newly formed 26th dynasty in Egypt, but their devastations did serve to release Judah from foreign control for a full twenty years.

Josiah used these last precious decades to establish the covenantal faith once and for all among the pious. His reforms climaxed in 621 with the discovery of "the Book of the Law of the LORD that had been given through Moses" (2 Chr. 24:14), perhaps the chief sanctuary scroll of the Pentateuch (Deut. 31:25-26) that had been misplaced under Manasseh (cf. 2 Chr. 35:3). Josiah and his people reconsecrated themselves "to obey the words of the covenant written in this book" (34:31). He removed the high places (2 Ki. 23:8-9), including even Jeroboam's original altar at Bethel (23:15), and kept the greatest Passover since the days of the judges (2 Chr. 35). "Neither before nor after Josiah was there a king like him who turned to the LORD as he did—with all his heart and with all his soul and with all his strength, in accordance with all the Law of Moses" (2 Ki. 23:25).

In 612 B.C. NINEVEH fell to the Medes and Babylonians, just as NAHUM had prophesied (Nah. 3:18-19). The Medes then withdrew, but Egypt and Babylon arose to claim the spoils. Josiah intervened to oppose the advance of Pharaoh NECO II and was killed at MEGIDDO in 608 (2 Chr. 35:20-24). Neco, however, was decisively defeated by the Babylonians at CARCHEMISH in 605; and NEBUCHADNEZZAR appropriated the former Assyrian territories (2 Ki. 24:7). Josiah's son JEHOIAKIM (23:34) was threatened with deportation to BABYLON (cf. 2 Chr. 36:6 and 2 Ki. 24:1-6), but only a few of the nobility, such as Daniel (Dan. 1:3), were actually taken captive at this time. The date 605 marks the commencement of Judah's predicted seventy years of captivity (Jer. 25:11-12). But while the prophet Habakkuk was admonishing his people to "live by … faith" (Hab. 2:4), Jehoiakim reverted to the sins of his fathers (2 Ki. 23:37). He also rebelled against Babylon (24:1), but he died in 598, and it was his son, with 10,000 of the leaders of Judah, who suffered the second deportation when Jerusalem surrendered on March 16, 597 (24:10-16).

Finally, Jehoiakim's brother ZEDEKIAH yielded to the inducements of Pharaoh HOPHRA of the 26th dynasty and defied Nebuchadnezzar (cf. Jer. 37:11). The Babylonians advanced, Hophra withdrew, and Jerusalem fell in 586. The city and temple were burned (2 Ki. 25:9), the walls were dismantled (25:10), and most of the people were carried into EXILE in Babylon (25:11). A small, fourth deportation in 582 removed even some of the poor that were left (25:12; Jer. 52:30). Israel had "mocked God's messengers, despised his words and scoffed at his prophets until the wrath of the LORD was aroused against his people and there was no remedy" (2 Chr. 36:16). But though the external kingdom of Israel ceased to exist, it did so because it had accomplished its divine purpose. A remnant, albeit small, had been nurtured to the point of profiting from the fiery trial of Babylon so as to be ready for that ultimate day: "'The time is coming,' declares the LORD, 'when I will make a new covenant with the house of Israel. … I will put my law in their minds and write it on their hearts. I will be their God, and they will be my people. For I will forgive their wickedness and will remember their sins no more'" (Jer. 31:31-34; Heb. 8:6-13; 10:15-22).

Issachar. is'uh-kahr' (Heb. *yiśśāśkār H3779* [*Qere yiśśākār*], possibly "a man of [*or* there is] hire/reward"). **(1)** The ninth son of JACOB and the fifth of LEAH (Gen. 30:17-18; 35:23). Almost nothing is known of his personal history beyond his share in the common actions of the sons of Jacob. He had four sons, who went with him into EGYPT (46:13; Exod. 1:3). There he died and was buried.

The tribe that descended from Issachar consisted of five great tribal families (Num. 26:23-24). At SINAI they numbered 54,400 men of war over twenty years of age (1:29); at the end of the wanderings, the number had grown to 64,300 (26:25). The territory allotted to Issachar in Canaan lay S of ZEBULUN and NAPHTALI, and N of MANASSEH. On the E it was bounded by the JORDAN. Whether it ever reached the MEDITERRANEAN is uncertain (Deut. 33:18-19); it probably remained an inland tribe. Its lot included the very fertile plain of ESDRAELON, but this area for the most part remained in the possession of the Canaanites. TOLA, one of the judges, was from Issachar (Jdg. 10:10) as were two kings, BAASHA and his son ELAH (1 Ki. 15:27; 16:6). DEBORAH and BARAK belonged to this tribe as well, and in Deborah's song it is mentioned as having taken part in the battle against SISERA (Jdg. 5:15). The battle took

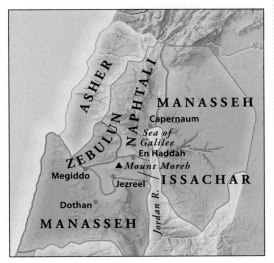

Issachar.

place on the plain of Issachar, and the victory secured free passage between the Israelites in the hill country of Ephraim and those in Galilee. In the time of DAVID, the tribe of Issachar numbered 87,000 (1 Chr. 7:5). In SOLOMON's arrangement of administrative districts, Issachar's territory formed an independent province (1 Ki. 4:17). According to the vision of Ezek. 48:25, the territory of Issachar lies between that of SIMEON and of Zebulun; these three tribes have the three gates on the S side of the new Jerusalem named after them (48:33). The tribe of Issachar is also mentioned in Rev. 7:7, where it is said that 12,000 were sealed.

(2) Seventh son of OBED-EDOM, included in the list of divisions of the Korahite doorkeepers in the reign of DAVID (1 Chr. 26:5).

issaron. See WEIGHTS AND MEASURES (sect. III).

Isshiah. i-shi′uh (Heb. *yiššiyyâ H3807*, short form of ISHIJAH). TNIV Ishiah. (1) Son of Izrahiah and descendant of ISSACHAR; a military chief (1 Chr. 7:3 [KJV, "Ishiah"]).

(2) One of several Korahite warriors who joined DAVID at ZIKLAG (1 Chr. 12:6 [KJV, "Jesiah"]; cf. vv. 1-2). These soldiers may have been LEVITES from the family of KORAH, but some argue that the reference is to a different Korah or even to a locality in the tribe of BENJAMIN.

(3) Son of Uzziel and descendant of LEVI (1 Chr. 23:20 [KJV, "Jesiah"]; 24:25).

(4) Son of Rehabiah and descendant of Levi (1 Chr. 24:21).

Isshijah. i-shi′juh. See ISHIJAH.

issue of blood. See DISEASES.

Isuah. See ISHVAH.

Isui. See ISHVI.

Italian Regiment. Also Italian Band, Italian Cohort (Gk. *speira Italikē*). A unit of the Roman army to which CORNELIUS, who was a CENTURION, belonged (Acts 10:1). It is not clear whether such a cohort was indeed stationed in CAESAREA around A.D. 40; some have thought that Cornelius (per-

Statue of Septimius Severus (emperor A.D. 193-211) in military dress. Cornelius, a member of the Italian Regiment stationed in Judea, would have worn a similar uniform.

© Dr. James C. Martin. The British Museum. Photographed by permission.

haps retired?) happened to be in this city at the time even though the unit was on duty elsewhere. See also AUGUSTAN COHORT.

Italy. it′uh-lee (*Italia G2712*). The geographical term for the country of which ROME was the capital. Originally it applied only to the extreme S of the peninsula, the region now called Calabria; but gradually the application of the name was extended, until in the first century of our era it began to be used in the current sense. It is referred to in three NT passages: (1) According to Acts 18:2 AQUILA and PRISCILLA had just come from Italy because Emperor CLAUDIUS had commanded that all Jews leave Rome. (2) Italy is mentioned in Acts 27:1, 6, as PAUL's destination when he had appealed to CAESAR. (3) In Heb. 13:24 Christians from Italy send their greetings along with those of the author of the letter.

itch. See DISEASES.

Ithai. ith´i (Heb. *ʾitay H416*, variant *ʾittay H915*, possibly "[God is] with me"; see ITHIEL). Son of Ribai, a Benjamite from GIBEAH; he was numbered among DAVID's mighty warriors (2 Sam. 23:29 [most versions, ITTAI]; 1 Chr. 11:31).

Ithamar. ith´uh-mahr (Heb. *ʾitāmār H418*, derivation uncertain). Youngest son of AARON and ELISHEBA (Exod. 6:23; Num. 3:2; 1 Chr. 6:3; 24:1). Together with his three brothers (ELEAZAR, NADAB, and ABIHU) and Aaron, Ithamar was consecrated to the priesthood (Exod. 28:1). His two elder brothers, Nadab and Abihu, were slain for offering strange fire (Lev. 10; cf. Num. 3:4; 26:61; 1 Chr. 24:2). During the wilderness wanderings he was leader over all the LEVITES (Exod. 38:21), and more specifically over the Gershonites (Num. 4:28) and the Merarites (4:33; 7:8). He founded a priestly family, to which ELI and his descendants belonged (1 Chr. 24:4-6). According to Ezra 8:2, the family of Ithamar continued after the captivity.

Ithiel. ith´ee-uhl (Heb. *ʾitîʾēl H417*, "God is with me"). **(1)** Son of Jeshaiah, descendant of BENJAMIN, and ancestor of Sallu; the latter was one of the provincial leaders who settled in JERUSALEM after the EXILE (Neh. 11:7).

(2) An otherwise unknown man to whom the words of AGUR were addressed (Prov. 30:1). Many argue, however, that instead of "to Ithiel, to Ithiel and Ucal," the text should be rendered, for example, "I am weary, O God; I am weary, O God, and I languish" (cf. NIV mg.). Other changes have been proposed (cf. NRSV), but none has received wide support. See also UCAL.

Ithlah. ith´luh (Heb. *yitlâ H3849*, derivation uncertain). KJV Jethlah. A town within the territory allotted to the tribe of DAN (Josh. 19:42). It was apparently near AIJALON, but its precise location is unknown. The Danites were unable to take possession of this territory (v. 47).

Ithmah. ith´muh (Heb. *yitmâ H3850*, perhaps "fatherless"). A Moabite, numbered among

David's mighty warriors known as the "Thirty" (1 Chr. 11:46).

Ithnan. ith´nan (Heb. *yitnān H3854*, derivation uncertain). A town in the NEGEV allotted to the tribe of JUDAH (Josh. 15:23). It was near the boundary of EDOM (v. 21), but its location is unknown.

Ithra. ith´ruh (Heb. *yitrāʾ H3859*, "abundance"). Father of AMASA, who led ABSALOM's rebel army; Ithra was married to ABIGAIL, David's sister or half-sister. In 2 Sam. 17:25 MT (cf. KJV, RSV), he is called "Ithra the Israelite," but in 1 Chr. 2:17, where the variant form JETHER occurs (cf. also 1 Ki. 2:5, 32), he is described as "the Ishmaelite." Perhaps he was an ISHMAELITE by race who had joined the nation of Israel. In the former passage, some emend "Ithra" to "Jether" (cf. NIV), or "Israelite" to "Ishmaelite" (cf. NRSV), or both.

Ithran. ith´ran (Heb. *yitrān H3864*, prob. "abundance"). **(1)** Son of DISHON and descendant of SEIR the HORITE (Gen. 36:26; 1 Chr. 1:41).

(2) Son of ZOPHAH and descendant of ASHER (1 Chr. 7:37); apparently also called Jether (v. 38).

Ithream. ith´ree-uhm (Heb. *yitrĕʿām H3865*, possibly "the Kinsman [*i.e.*, ancestral god] excels"). The sixth and last of the sons of DAVID who were born in HEBRON; his mother was Eglah (2 Sam. 3:5; 1 Chr. 3:3).

Ithrite. ith´rit (Heb. *yitrî H3863*, gentilic of *yeter H3858* [JETHER] or *yitrô H3861* [JETHRO]). A Judahite clan descended from CALEB through HUR and SHOBAL; the Ithrites made up one of several families associated with KIRIATH JEARIM (1 Chr. 2:53). Two of DAVID's mighty warriors, Ira and Gareb, are described as Ithrites (2 Sam. 23:38; 1 Chr. 11:40); however, some argue that the Hebrew here should read *yattîrî*, that is, a native of the city of JATTIR.

Ittah-kazin. See ETH KAZIN.

Ittai. it´i (Heb. *ʾittay H915*, variant *ʾitay H416*, possibly "[God is] with me"). **(1)** Son of Ribai, a Benjamite from GIBEAH; he was numbered among

I

David's mighty warriors (2 Sam. 23:29 [NIV, "Ithai"]; called Ithai in 1 Chr. 11:31).

(2) A Gittite (i.e., from Gath) who joined himself to David and commanded six hundred men and families. When Absalom rebelled against David, Ittai fled with the king and refused to return to Jerusalem. David made him commander of a third part of his army, with Joab and Abishai; he participated in the battle in the forest of Ephraim when Absalom was killed (2 Sam. 15:18-22; 18:2, 5, 12).

Ivory backrest, possibly from a couch, discovered in Nimrud (8th cent. B.C.); it depicts warriors and the fruit of the lotus tree.

© Dr. James C. Martin. The British Museum. Photographed by permission.

Iturea. it´yoor-ee´uh (Gk. *hē Itouraia chōra*, "the Iturean country," from *Itouraios G2714*). Also Ituraea. This name is found only once in Scripture, in the description of Philip's territory: "of Iturea and Traconitis" (Lk. 3:1; see Herod). It was a small principality in the northern section of Palestine that included the Lebanon and Antilebanon mountain ranges and the Lake country around Huleh with its watershed. The capital was at Chalcis. It is usually thought that the Itureans were descended from Jetur son of Ishmael (Gen. 25:15; this view goes back to the LXX of 1 Chr. 5:19). In any case, they constituted an Arab tribe that can be traced back only to the second or third century B.C. The Itureans were seminomads and famous archers, a lawless and predatory people. It is not known when they moved from the desert to the mountains in the north. In 105 B.C. Aristobulus I (see Maccabee) conquered and annexed the kingdom to Judea. In 66 Pompey defeated its king, Ptolemaeus, who purchased immunity with a large sum of money. Later Augustus gave it to Herod the Great, and after his death it passed to his son Philip.

Ivah. See Ivvah.

ivory. This hard substance, which forms the tusks of elephants, was brought from India to Palestine by both ship and caravan. Solomon's throne was made of ivory (1 Ki. 10:18), and he imported large quantities of it. Amos denounced Israel for its luxuries, among them the use of ivory (Amos 3:15; 6:4). Palaces were inlaid and decorated with ivory (1 Ki. 22:39; Ps. 45:8)

Ivvah. iv´uh (Heb. *ʿiwwâ H6394*). KJV Ivah. One of several Aramean city-states vanquished by Sennacherib (2 Ki. 18:34; 19:13; Isa. 37:13). Because Ivvah is listed along with Hamath and Arpad (also Sepharvaim and Hena), it is thought to have been located in N Syria, but the location is unknown. It is probably the same as Avvah (2 Ki. 17:24, 31). Some scholars, noticing that Hena and Ivvah are not mentioned in similar lists (2 Ki. 17:24; Isa. 36:19), and suspecting that they are not true geographical names, have suggested that they are pagan deities, or that the text is corrupt, or that the words should be rendered differently.

Iyar. ee´yahr. Also Iyyar. The second month of the Hebrew calendar, corresponding to April-May. This term, equivalent to Babylonian *Aiaru*, does not occur in the Bible, which uses rather the Canaanite name, Ziv.

Iye Abarim. i´yuh-ab´uh-rim (Heb. *ʿiyyê hāʿăbārîm H6516*, "ruins of the regions beyond"). Also called Iyim. A stopping place of the Israelites in their wilderness wanderings, near the Valley of

Zered (Num. 21:11-12; 33:44-45). It was either in Moab (33:44; NIV, "on the border of Moab") or in its vicinity (21:11), but the precise location is unknown. Possibly the place was associated with the Abarim mountain range.

Iyim. *i´yim* (Heb. *ʿiyyîm H6517*, "ruins, stone heaps"). KJV and TNIV Iim. A shortened form of Iye-Abarim (Num. 33:45). This place is not to be confused with Iim (Josh. 15:29), even though the form is identical in Hebrew.

Izehar, Izeharite. See Izhar.

Izhar. iz´hahr (Heb. *yiṣhār H3659*, "[God] shines"; gentilic *yiṣhārî H3660*, "Izharite"). KJV also Izehar, Izeharite. **(1)** Son of Kohath, grandson of Levi, father of Korah (and two other sons), uncle of Moses, and eponymous ancestor of the Izrahite clan (Exod. 6:18, 21; Num. 3:19, 27; 16:1; 1 Chr. 6:2, 18, 38; 23:12, 18). Several of his descendants were prominent Levites (1 Chr. 23:18 [cf. v. 33]; 24:22; 26:23, 29).

(2) Son of Asshur (by his wife Helah) and descendant of Judah (1 Chr. 4:7; cf. v. 5). So the NRSV, following the Ketib; the NIV and NJPS follow the Qere in reading Zohar, while the KJV's "Jezoar" is a hybrid of the two forms.

Izliah. iz-li´uh (Heb. *yizlîʾâ H3468*, "long-living" or "Yahweh delivers"). KJV Jezliah. Son of Elpaal and descendant of Benjamin (1 Chr. 8:18); he is listed among the heads of families who lived in Jerusalem (cf. v. 28).

Izrahiah. iz´ruh-hi´uh (Heb. *yizraḥyâ H3474*, "Yahweh goes forth [*or* shines]"). Son of Uzzi and great-grandson of Issachar; a military chief (1 Chr. 7:3).

Izrahite. iz´ruh-hit (Heb. *yizrāḥ H3473*). Although this term in Hebrew does not have the usual gentilic form (i.e., with the ending –*î*), it apparently refers to someone from Izrah, a place otherwise unknown. The term is applied to a certain Shamhuth, who was the commander of the fifth monthly division under David (1 Chr. 27:8). Some emend the text to read "Zerahite" (i.e., a descendant of Zerah of Judah; cf. v. 11). The problem is further complicated by the likelihood that "Shamhuth the Izrahite" is the same as "Shammah the Harodite" (2 Sam. 23:25), also called "Shammoth the Harorite" (1 Chr. 11:27). Clearly scribal activity has created confusion, and we are no longer able to identify the original form(s) of the name.

Izri. iz´ri (Heb. *yiṣrî H3673*, possibly "[Yahweh] has formed"). A Levitical musician who, with his sons and relatives, received the fourth lot (1 Chr. 25:11); the name is probably a variant of Zeri (v. 3).

Izziah. i-zi´uh (Heb. *yizziyyâ H3466*, "Yahweh sprinkles"). One of the descendants of Parosh who agreed to put away their foreign wives (Ezra 10:25; KJV, "Jeziah").

I

J

J (Jahwist). yah´wist. An abbreviation for Yahwist (German *Jahwist*); it is used (along with D, E, and P) to designate one of the supposed sources of the PENTATEUCH, according to the Documentary Hypothesis.

Jaakan. jay´uh-kan (Heb. *ya'ăqān* [not in NIV]). KJV Jakan. Son of EZER and grandson of SEIR the HORITE; he probably became the progenitor of a clan in EDOM (1 Chr. 1:42 NRSV, following MT). On the basis of some Hebrew MSS and the parallel passage (Gen. 36:37), many scholars emend *ya'ăqān* to *wa'ăqān* ("and Akan"; cf. NIV). See also BEEROTH-BENE-JAAKAN and BENE JAAKAN.

Jaakanite. jay-a´kuh-n*i*t. See BEEROTH-BENE-JAAKAN.

Jaakobah. jay-uh-koh´buh (Heb. *ya'ăqōbâ H3621*, "[God] protects"). A clan leader in the tribe of SIMEON (1 Chr. 4:36). He is listed among those whose families increased greatly during the days of King HEZEKIAH and who dispossessed the Hamites and Meunites near GEDOR (vv. 38-41).

Jaala. jay´uh-luh (Heb. *ya'ālā' H3606*, variant *ya'ălāh H3608*, "mountain goat"). Also Jaalah. A servant of SOLOMON whose descendants returned from the EXILE (Ezra 2:56; Neh. 7:58).

Jaalah. See JAALA.

Jaalam. See JALAM.

Jaanai. See JANAI.

Jaar. jay´uhr (Heb. *ya'ar H3625*, "forest"). The name of a place that, along with EPHRATHAH, was associated with the ARK OF THE COVENANT (Ps. 132:6; KJV, "the wood"). Jaar is generally regarded as a (poetic) short form of KIRIATH JEARIM (meaning "town of forests"), where the ark remained twenty years before DAVID brought it to JERUSALEM. Some believe that the name was applied to a wooded area in the environs of Kiriath Jearim.

Jaare-Oregim. jay´uh-ree-or´uh-gim (Heb. *ya'ărê 'ōrĕgîm H3629*, "forests of weavers" [but scribal error suspected]). Father of Elhanan; the latter is described as the killer of GOLIATH the Gittite (2 Sam. 21:19). Jaare-Oregim is apparently called JAIR in the parallel passage (1 Chr. 20:5). For possible solutions to the discrepancies between these two verses, see ELHANAN.

Jaareshiah. jay´uh-ree-shi´uh (Heb. *ya'ărešyâ H3631*, "Yahweh plants"). KJV Jaresiah. Son of Jeroham and descendant of BENJAMIN; he is listed among the heads of families who lived in JERUSALEM (1 Chr. 8:27).

Jaasau. See JAASU.

Jaasiel. jay-ay´see-uhl (Heb. *ya'ăśî'ēl H3634*, possibly "God makes"). KJV Jasiel. **(1)** Son of ABNER (SAUL's cousin); he was made an officer over the tribe of BENJAMIN during the reign of DAVID (1 Chr. 27:21).

(2) A MEZOBAITE, mentioned last among David's mighty warriors (1 Chr. 11:47). Some scholars emend "Mezobaite" to "from Zobah." It has also been suggested, but without good reason, that this Jaasiel is the same as #1 above.

Jaasu. jay´uh-soo (Heb. *ya'ăśû H3632* [*Qere ya'ăśāy*], possibly "[God] treats well"). KJV Jaasau.

One of the descendants of Bani who agreed to put away their foreign wives (Ezra 10:37).

Jaazaniah. jay-az´uh-ni´uh (Heb. *yaʾăzanyāhû H3280* [with spelling variations], "Yahweh listens"). (1) A military commander identified as "the son of the Maacathite"; he was among the officers who went to MIZPAH to join GEDALIAH, the governor appointed by the Babylonians after the fall of Jerusalem (2 Ki. 25:23; Jer. 40:8 [KJV, NRSV, "Jezaniah"]). It is usually thought that Jaazaniah belonged to the family that descended from MAACAH, CALEB's concubine (1 Chr. 2:48), but there are other possibilities. Some speculate that this is the Jaazaniah whose name is inscribed on a seal discovered in Mizpah.

(2) Son of Jeremiah (not the prophet), a leader of the RECABITES, whose loyalty to their ancestral precepts the prophet JEREMIAH used as a lesson to his own countrymen (Jer. 35:3).

(3) Son of Shaphan and, apparently, a prominent elder in Jerusalem at the time of the EXILE; he is the only one mentioned by name among the seventy elders of Israel whom EZEKIEL, in a vision, saw offering incense to idols (Ezek. 8:11).

(4) Son of Azzur; he and Pelatiah son of Benaiah were leaders of the people in Jerusalem at the time of the exile, and Ezekiel was commanded to prophesy against their sin (Ezek. 11:1).

Jaazer. See JAZER.

Jaaziah. jay´uh-zi´uh (Heb. *yaʿăziyyāhû H3596*, "Yahweh nourishes"). Son of MERARI and grandson of LEVI; he is not mentioned in most of the genealogies (e.g., Exod. 6:19), but only in a list of Levitical families that served during the time of DAVID (1 Chr. 24:26-27). The Hebrew text is difficult, however, and some regard it as a later gloss.

Jaaziel. jay-ay´zee-uhl (Heb. *yaʿăzîʾēl H3595*, "God nourishes"). One of the LEVITES who played the lyre when the ARK OF THE COVENANT was brought to JERUSALEM (1 Chr. 15:18; called AZIEL in v. 20; some also identify him with the first JEIEL listed in 16:5).

Jabal. jay´buhl (Heb. *yābāl H3299*, possibly "[God] leads" or "wanderer"). First son of LAMECH by ADAH; he was "the father of those who live in tents and raise livestock," meaning probably that he originated the profession of herding animals, which often required the nomadic lifestyle of constant travel in search of pasture (Gen. 4:20).

Jabbok. jab´uhk (Heb. *yabbōq H3309*, prob. "overflowing"). A river in TRANSJORDAN (Nahr ez-Zerka, "river of blue"), about 60 mi. (96 km.)

The Jabbok River valley looking W.

© Dr. James C. Martin

J

in length and, next to the YARMUK River, having the greatest drainage area in that region. The Jabbok is a perennial stream, and its average fall is c. 80 ft. (24 m.) per mile, cutting a deep valley or gorge through the E JORDAN Valley escarpment. The source lies in the vicinity of modern Amman (ancient RABBAH of AMMON), from whence it swings eastward and northward, forming a large loop before wending westward to the Jordan Valley. The lower gorge is under sea level to a point 7 mi. (11 km.) E of the rift, at an elevation of more than 2,000 ft. (610 m.) below the GILEAD Plateau to the N and the Amman Plateau to the S. Colorful oleanders line most of its banks in the hill country. After emerging into the Jordan Valley near Tell Deir ʿAlla (prob. biblical SUCCOTH), it meanders across the Ghor before joining the Jordan River near ed-Damiyeh (biblical ADAM). The loop N of Amman formed the W boundary of the Ammonites at the time of the conquest (Num. 21:24), and the contained area was settled by the tribe of GAD. The western part of the river formed a physical and political boundary between the two parts of Gilead (Deut. 3:12, 16; Josh. 12:2-6), and also divided the kingdoms of SIHON and OG. The specific ford referred to in Gen. 32:22 has not been identified.

Jabesh. jay′bish (Heb. *yābēš H3314*, "dry"). Father of King SHALLUM of Israel, who murdered King ZECHARIAH and usurped the throne (2 Ki. 15:10, 13-14). However, since the name Jabesh (*yābēš H3315*) is also a short form of JABESH GILEAD, the expression "son of Jabesh" may mean "a native of Jabesh [Gilead]."

Jabesh Gilead. jay′bish-gil′ee-uhd (Heb. *yābēš gilʿād H3316*, "dry place of Gilead"; also referred to simply as *yābēš H3315*). An important city in N TRANSJORDAN (see GILEAD). It lay a night's journey across the JORDAN from BETH SHAN (1 Sam. 31:11-12) and was located in the area given to the half-tribe of MANASSEH (Num. 32:33). When the citizens refused to attend the sacred assembly at MIZPAH, an army was sent to destroy them (Jdg. 21:8-15). The city was not destroyed and grew again in power and wealth. During SAUL's reign over Israel, NAHASH king of AMMON besieged the city. When appealed to for a treaty, Nahash proposed to

grant peace only if every able-bodied man had his right eye put out. Granted a seven-day truce, the city sought Saul's help. Saul killed a pair of oxen and sent the pieces throughout his land, indicating what would happen to those who refused to help in his battle for Jabesh. His army defeated Nahash; the city was saved and the nation reunited (1 Sam. 11:1-15). One of the purposes behind this military aid was to secure wives for Benjamites, since Israel had sworn never to allow Benjamites to marry their daughters (Jdg. 21:1). Later, when Saul's forces had been routed by the PHILISTINES and he and his sons had been killed, men of Jabesh Gilead rescued their bodies, cremated them, and buried the remains in Jabesh (1 Sam. 31:1-13). After becoming king, DAVID sent thanks for the act (2 Sam. 2:4-6) and had the remains of Saul and JONATHAN exhumed and interred in the tomb of Kish in the land of Benjamin (21:12-14). It is probable that the stream Wadi Yabis received its name from the city. Most scholars identify Jabesh Gilead with Tell el-Maqlub, c. 7 mi. (11 km.) E of the Jordan.

Jabez (person). jay′biz (Heb. *yaʿbēṣ H3584*, derivation uncertain). A man in the line of JUDAH noted for his honorable character (1 Chr. 4:9-10). In this passage, the genealogy is interrupted with the following information: "Jabez was more honorable than his brothers. His mother had named him Jabez [*yaʿbēṣ*], saying, 'I gave birth to him in pain [*bĕʿōṣeb*].' Jabez cried out to the God of Israel, 'Oh, that you would bless me and enlarge my territory! Let your hand be with me, and keep me from harm so that I will be free from pain.' And God granted his request." (The wordplay on his name requires a transposition of the consonants *b* and *ṣ*; the meaning "pain" must be regarded as a popular etymology.) This abrupt introduction of Jabez, who had not previously been mentioned, is puzzling. Some speculate that he may have been a son (or brother) of Koz (v. 8). A few scholars have further speculated that Jabez was the founder of the town by the same name. See JABEZ (PLACE).

Jabez (place). jay′biz (Heb. *yaʿbēṣ H3583*, derivation uncertain). A city in JUDAH, perhaps near BETHLEHEM, occupied by clans of scribes that were descendants of CALEB through HUR and SALMA (1 Chr. 2:55).

Jabin. jay'bin (Heb. *yābîn H3296*, possibly "perceptive"). **(1)** King of HAZOR and head of a coalition of Canaanite kings who sought to withstand the Israelites (Josh. 11:1-12). The confederacy of Canaanite princes produced an army "as numerous as the sand on the seashore" (v. 4). JOSHUA'S advance, however, took them by surprise and enabled the Israelites to defeat them. Hazor was then destroyed, and Jabin was put to death along with the other princes of the confederation (vv. 10-12).

(2) A Canaanite king who reigned in Hazor; probably a descendant of #1 above (Jdg. 4:2; some suggest that Jabin was a dynastic title). The IDOLATRY of the Israelites led to their being oppressed by him for twenty years. His armament was extensive, being described as 900 chariots of iron (v. 3). The commander of his forces was SISERA, who seemed to be more prominent in the incident than Jabin the king. The oppression of the Canaanites was overthrown by DEBORAH's plan. BARAK effected the strategy that resulted in eventual victory (vv. 23-24), which was celebrated in song (Jdg. 5; cf. Ps. 83:9).

Jabneel, Jabneh. jab'nee-uhl, jab'neh (Heb. *yabnĕʾēl H3305*, "God builds"; short form *yabnēh H3306* [2 Chr. 26:6]; Gk. *Iamneia* [1 Macc. 4:15 et al.]). **(1)** A town on the S boundary of the tribal territory of NAPHTALI (Josh. 19:33). It is identified with Tell en-Naʿam, 3.5 mi. (5.5 km.) W of the S tip of the Sea of Galilee; the modern village of Yavneel is situated nearby (the Talmudic Jabneel is identified with Kh. Yamma).

(2) A town on the W boundary of the tribal territory of JUDAH, between JOPPA and GAZA, near the coast (Josh. 15:11). It was an important station on the VIA MARIS, and was later also known as Jamnia. The modern town of Yavne (Yebna), c. 13 mi (20 km.) S of Joppa, is located on the site. The only biblical event associated with this city took place in the eighth century B.C., when King UZZIAH, campaigning against the PHILISTINES, "broke down the walls of Gath, Jabneh and Ashdod" (2 Chr. 26:6), thus gaining an access to the sea at the mouth of the Yarkon River. After the OT period, Jamnia was an important SELEUCID military base (1 Macc. 4:15; cf. 10:69; 15:40), and Judas MACCABE razed its port with fire (2 Macc. 12:8-9, 40).

In 147 B.C., the Battle of Jamnia was a signal victory for the Jews (1 Macc. 10:69-87). Jamnia is best known as the site of a gathering that supposedly made formal decisions about the canon c. A.D. 90 (see CANONICITY). Some modern scholars speculated that it was at this meeting that the OT canon was officially closed, the Hebrew text standardized, and the breach between Judaism and Christianity formalized. This hypothesis was widely accepted, but rabbinic gatherings of this sort should not be compared with the Christian ecumenical councils that reached decisions binding on the church as a whole. Moreover, there is no evidence that questions about the canon were a major concern when the rabbis met.

Jabneh. See JABNEEL.

Jacan. jay'kuhn (Heb. *yaʿkān H3602*, meaning uncertain). KJV Jachan; TNIV Jakan. Son of Abihail; he was one of seven relatives from the tribe of GAD who occupied the region E of GILEAD (1 Chr. 5:13; cf. v. 10, 14).

Jachan. See JACAN.

Jachin. See JAKIN.

jacinth. See MINERALS.

jackal. See ANIMALS.

Jackal Well. Also Jackal's Well (RSV). A well or spring in JERUSALEM, apparently between the VALLEY GATE and the DUNG GATE (Neh. 2:13 NIV). The rendering "Jackal," however, assumes that the Hebrew *tannîn H9490*, which means "serpent" or "sea monster," should be read as *tannîm* (pl. of *tan H9478*, "jackal"). Others take the word in its usual sense (thus KJV, "dragon well"; NRSV, "Dragon's Spring"). It is common to identify the Jackal (or Dragon) Well with EN ROGEL, a spring about 800 ft. (240 m.) S of the SE ridge of JERUSALEM (thus just below the junction of the HINNOM and KIDRON Valleys). It has also been argued that the reference is to the GIHON SPRING, which follows a serpentine course. Other proposals have been made. See also ZOHELETH, STONE OF.

J

Jacob. jay´kuhb (Heb. *ya‘ăqōb H3620*; possibly "[God] protects," but by popular etymology, "he takes by the heel, supplants, deceives"; (*Iakōb G2609, Iakōbos G2610* [see JAMES]). **(1)** Son of ISAAC and REBEKAH, younger twin brother of ESAU, husband of LEAH and RACHEL. He later was called ISRAEL (Gen. 32:28; 49:2) and thus, through his twelve sons, became the eponymous ancestor of the Israelites. In answer to Isaac's prayer on behalf of his barren wife, Rebekah conceived twins (25:21). An unusual prenatal incident caused her to consult the Lord, who revealed to her that her children would become the founders of two great nations (25:23). An ominous rivalry, begun in the womb, became visible during the birth of the children. Esau came first; Jacob followed at once, holding Esau by the heel, giving Jacob the name "tripper" or "supplanter" (25:25-26). Nothing is revealed about the childhood of the boys. Because of the ancient law of primogeniture (see FIRSTBORN), Isaac naturally favored the older son; but, no doubt because of the revelation from God, Rebekah was partial to Jacob (25:28). Jacob's cunning was revealed in the way he induced Esau to sell his BIRTHRIGHT (25:27-34).

Isaac became old and blind. Sensing that his end was near, he desired to impart the paternal blessing. Esau was still the favorite son, so Isaac asked him to prepare a favorite dish, saying that after eating it he would pronounce the blessing (Gen. 27:1-4). Rebekah overheard the request and took advantage of Isaac's blindness to further her plan to make Jacob first in every way. Jacob, as ambitious as his mother, joined in the plot. A dramatic scene followed (27:6-41). Jacob was dressed in his brother's robe, his mother having skillfully applied goat skins to make his hands and neck hairy like his brother's. Rebekah made a savory dish that Jacob presented to his father. He deliberately lied: (1) "I am Esau your firstborn," and, in reply to Isaac's question about how he had found the game so quickly, (2) "The Lord your God gave me success." Deceived by the odor of Esau's garments and pleased with the food, Isaac gave the firstborn's blessing to Jacob. Esau, on learning of his brother's treachery, wept and begged for another blessing, which was granted. Rebekah, knowing of Esau's vow to kill Jacob, induced Isaac to send Jacob to HARAN to choose a wife from the family of LABAN, Rebekah's brother (27:42—28:5).

On the way to Haran, Jacob camped at LUZ, where he had a vision of a ladder with angels ascending and descending. In his dream he had a promise from the Lord both to inherit the land about him and to have a numerous progeny (Gen. 28:10-15). He recognized that God had been with him, and so he named the place BETHEL, "House of God" (28:16-19), and made a vow to tithe all his further possessions (28:20-22). He met RACHEL at a well in Haran, watered her flock, revealed himself to her, and was soon at home with Laban (29:1-14). His contract to serve seven years for Rachel ended after fourteen years of indentured servitude (29:15-30).

The conflict between Jacob and Esau had its counterpart in the conflict between Rachel and her older sister LEAH, who won favor from God and bore four children: REUBEN, SIMEON, LEVI, and JUDAH (Gen. 29:31-35). Rachel was unable to conceive, and her desire for a son led her to give her maid, BILHAH, to Jacob as a CONCUBINE; Bilhah bore two sons, DAN and NAPHTALI (30:1-8). Leah in turn gave to Jacob her maid, ZILPAH, who bore GAD and ASHER (30:9-13). Later, Leah herself also bore ISSACHAR, ZEBULUN, and finally DINAH (30:17-21). Then God opened Rachel's womb and she bore a son, JOSEPH (30:22-24).

Jacob grew eager to return to his own land. After outwitting Laban in stock-breeding, he made his departure. Rachel, probably to insure her share in Laban's estate, stole the TERAPHIM or family gods (Gen. 31:19). Laban, learning of Jacob's flight, pursued and overtook him at Mount GILEAD, where they settled their differences by a covenant, sealed on a memorial heap called MIZPAH (31:25-55). At MAHANAIM Jacob met God, then sent messengers to Esau in EDOM. The messengers soon returned to report that Esau was near with a formidable force. Jacob went to the Lord in prayer and received assurance that all would be well. That night he wrestled with the angel of the Lord and secured a new name, Israel, or "Prince of God" (32:24-32). The meeting with Esau was emotion-packed (33:1-17).

Jacob then went to SHECHEM and bought land on which he erected an altar named EL ELOHE

ISRAEL, "God is the God of Israel" (Gen. 33:18-20). His daughter Dinah was raped at this place, and the men of the city were deceived into thinking that by submitting to CIRCUMCISION they would secure the marriage between Shechem and Dinah (34:1-24). While they were incapacitated by the operation, however, Simeon and Levi killed them and pillaged the city (34:25-31). Jacob fled to Bethel, and later, on the way to EPHRATH, his twelfth son, BENJAMIN, was born; but Rachel died in giving him birth (35:1-20). Jacob continued to live in Canaan, where JOSEPH incurred the ill will of his brothers, was sold to Egyptians, and became servant of Pharaoh's chief ruler (37:1—47:31). Jacob's final act was to call his twelve sons about him, prophesy regarding the future of each one's offspring, and bestow his parting blessing. When he died, he was embalmed, taken by Joseph and a troop of Egyptian soldiers to Canaan, and buried in the Cave of MACHPELAH (49:1—50:13).

(2) Son of Matthan and father of JOSEPH, Mary's husband, listed in Matthew's GENEALOGY OF JESUS CHRIST (Matt. 1:15-16; see also HELI).

Jacob's well. Modern Bir Ya'akub is generally recognized to be the well of JACOB mentioned in Jn. 4:6. The plot of ground mentioned in this passage (v. 5) had been purchased by Jacob (Gen. 33:19). The area was later wrested by force from the AMORITES (48:22). The well is near the base of Mount GERIZIM, whose bluffs are referred to by the phrase "this mountain" (Jn. 4:20-21). A narrow opening 4 ft. (1.2 m.) long led from the floor of the vault into the well, which was dug through limestone. According to the Samaritan woman's comment, the well was deep (4:11). Today it is c. 75 ft. (23 m.) deep, but it has probably been filled with much debris over the years since it was dug. There are hardly any sites that have less doubt as to their authenticity than the site of Jacob's well. All traditions agree on this as being the scene described in Jn. 4, and the biblical details fit perfectly. Through the centuries, churches have been built over the well, as various medieval pilgrims have recorded. Today the well is in a cave, or crypt, under the floor of a Greek Orthodox church that has never been finished above the exterior walls. Jacob's well is known for its soft, or light, water that is supplied in

Jacob's well.

two ways: through underground sources that make it a true well and by percolated surface water, which makes it a cistern. This detail may have prompted Jesus' remark about living water (v. 14).

Jada. jay'duh (Heb. *yādā'* H3360, possibly "[God] has known [i.e., cared]" or "skillful, shrewd"). Son of Onam, grandson of JERAHMEEL, and descendant of JUDAH (1 Chr. 2:28, 32).

Jadah. jay'duh (Heb. *yo'dâ* H3586 [MT *ya'râ*], short form of *yĕhô'addâ* H3389, possibly "Yahweh has adorned"). KJV Jarah. Son of Ahaz and descendant of King SAUL through JONATHAN (1 Chr. 9:42 NIV, following some Heb. MSS and LXX; MT, "Jarah"); called JEHOADDAH in the parallel passage (8:36).

Jadau. See JADDAI.

Jaddai. jad'i (Heb. *yadday* H3350 [*Qere yaddô*], derivation uncertain). KJV Jadau. One of the descendants of Nebo who agreed to put away their foreign wives (Ezra 10:43).

Jaddua. jad'yoo-uh (Heb. *yaddûa'* H3348, "known [by Yahweh]"). (1) One of the Israelite leaders who sealed the covenant with NEHEMIAH after the return from the Babylonian captivity (Neh. 10:21). The covenant signified the willingness of the people to abide by the Law of God.

(2) Son of Jonathan (or Johanan) and descendant of JESHUA the high priest (Neh. 12:11, 22).

J

Jadon. jay´don (Heb. *yādôn H3347*, possibly "[Yahweh] rules" or "frail one"). A man from Meronoth (see MERONOTHITE) who, along with MELATIAH of GIBEON, helped in rebuilding the walls of JERUSALEM (Neh. 3:7). These two individuals are further described as "men from Gibeon and Mizpah," suggesting that Meronoth and MIZPAH are somehow connected or even that they are two names for the same town.

Jael. jay´uhl (Heb. *yā‘ēl H3605*, "mountain goat"). The wife of HEBER the KENITE and slayer of SISERA, a Canaanite commander (Jdg. 4:17-22; 5:6, 24). The Canaanite King JABIN of HAZOR had oppressed Israel for twenty years. The Canaanites had a formidable force of 900 chariots. Under the inspiration of DEBORAH, BARAK formed a large force of Israelites at Mount TABOR to fight the Canaanite army, led by SISERA their general, along the River KISHON. The Israelite assault, probably aided by a storm (5:20-21), routed the Canaanites. Sisera ran away on foot and came to the tent of Jael, who extended him hospitality. She covered him with a rug, and in response to his request for water gave him milk. Then, as Sisera slept, Jael murdered him by hammering a tent peg through his temple into the ground. Jael's act is celebrated in the ancient Song of Deborah (ch. 5).

Jagur. jay´guhr (Heb. *yāgûr H3327*, possibly "stone heap"). A town in the NEGEV, the extreme S of the tribal territory of JUDAH, near the border of EDOM (Josh. 15:21). Its precise location is unknown.

Jah. jah (Heb. *yāh H3363*, short form of *yhwh*). This name, an abbreviation of Yahweh (JEHOVAH), is used in the KJV only once (Ps. 68:4), but the corresponding Hebrew form occurs over forty times (Exod. 15:2; 17:16; Isa. 12:2; 26:4; 38:11; the rest of the occurrences are in Psalms). In all these other passages it is translated "the LORD."

Jahath. jay´hath (Heb. *yaḥat H3511*, perhaps "[God] snatches up"). **(1)** Son of Reiah and descendant of JUDAH; Jahath's sons, Ahumai and Lahad, and possibly also other relatives, are identified as "the clans of the Zorathites" (1 Chr. 4:2). See ZORAH.

(2) Son of Libni, grandson of GERSHON, and great-grandson of LEVI (1 Chr. 6:20 [NIV, "Jehath," apparently a misprint]). He is also described as the son (descendant?) of Gershon and as the father of Shimei in a list of ASAPH's ancestors (v. 43), but this may be the result of a scribal error. See SHIMEI #1.

(3) Son of Shimei and descendant of Gershon (1 Chr. 23:10-11).

(4) Son of Shelemoth and descendant of Levi (1 Chr. 24:22).

(5) Descendant of Levi through MERARI and an overseer of the workmen who repaired the temple in the reign of King JOSIAH (2 Chr. 34:12).

Jahaz, Jahzah. jay´haz, jah´zuh (Heb. *yahaṣ H3403*, variant *yahṣâ H3404*, derivation unknown). KJV also Jahaza (Josh. 13:18) and Jahazah (21:36). A city in TRANSJORDAN where SIHON, an AMORITE king, was defeated in a great battle by the Israelites when he refused to allow them to pass through his territory (Num. 21:23; Deut. 2:32; Jdg. 11:20). MOSES assigned the city to the tribe of REUBEN (Josh. 13:18), and it was one of the cities given to the LEVITES descended from MERARI (21:36; 1 Chr. 6:78 ["Jahzah"]). According to the MOABITE STONE, the king of Israel lived in Jahaz while at war with him, but he was driven out, and MESHA took the city and added it to Moabite territory (see also ATAROTH). The Bible also refers to Jahaz as a city of MOAB (Isa. 15:4; Jer. 48:21 ["Jahzah"], 34). Its precise location is uncertain, although some tentatively identify it with Khirbet el-Medeiyineh, c. 11 mi. (17 km.) SE of MEDEBA.

Jahaziah. See JAHZEIAH.

Jahaziel. juh-hay´zee-uhl (Heb. *yaḥăzî’ēl H3487*, "God sees"). **(1)** One of the ambidextrous Benjamite warriors who joined DAVID while he was in exile from SAUL at the PHILISTINE city of ZIKLAG (1 Chr. 12:4; cf. v. 2).

(2) One of two priests appointed to blow trumpets before the ARK OF THE COVENANT when David brought it to JERUSALEM (1 Chr. 16:6).

(3) Son of Hebron and descendant of LEVI in the line of KOHATH; contemporary of David (1 Chr. 23:19; 24:23).

(4) Son of Zechariah and descendant of Levi through ASAPH; moved by the Spirit, he encouraged King JEHOSHAPHAT of Judah and his army to fight against the Moabite, Ammonite, and Edomite invaders (2 Chr. 20:14-17).

(5) Descendant of Zattu and father of Shecaniah; the latter was among the family heads that returned to Jerusalem after the EXILE (Ezra 8:5, following some LXX MSS). However, the MT does not include the name Zattu and leaves the connection between Shecaniah and Jahaziel unclear (cf. KJV).

Jahdai. jah′di (Heb. *yohdāy H3367*, prob. "Yahweh leads"). Apparently a descendant of JUDAH, included in the genealogy of CALEB (1 Chr. 2:47). The genealogical connection is unclear, although probably the reference is to a man descended from Caleb. In the light of the context (cf. vv. 46, 48), some believe however that Jahdai was one of Caleb's CONCUBINES, possibly Ephah.

Jahdiel. jah′dee-uhl (Heb. *yaḥdîʾēl H3484*, "God rejoices" or "may God give joy"). A clan chief of the half-tribe of MANASSEH; he and others are described as "brave warriors, famous men, and heads of their families" (1 Chr. 5:24).

Jahdo. jah′doh (Heb. *yaḥdô H3482*, possibly "[God] rejoices"). Son of Buz, descendant of GAD, and ancestor of Abihail; the sons of Abihail and other Gadites occupied the region E of GILEAD (1 Chr. 5:14; cf. v. 10).

Jahleel. jah′lee-uhl (Heb. *yaḥlĕʾēl H3499*, "wait for God" or "God shows himself friendly"; gentilic *yaḥlĕʾēlî H3500*, "Jahleelite"). Son of ZEBULUN and eponymous ancestor of the Jahleelite clan (Gen. 46:14; Num. 26:26).

Jahmai. jah′mi (Heb. *yaḥmay H3503*, "[God] protects"). Son (or descendant) of TOLA and grandson (or more distant descendant) of ISSACHAR; he is described as the head of his family, which probably means he was a military officer (1 Chr. 7:2).

Jahweh. See JEHOVAH.

Jahzah. See JAHAZ.

Jahzeel. jah′zee-uhl (Heb. *yaḥsĕʾēl H3505*, variant *yaḥāṣîʾēl H3507*, "God apportions" or "God favors"; gentilic *yaḥsĕʾēlî H3506*, "Jahzeelite"). Firstborn son of NAPHTALI, grandson of JACOB, and eponymous ancestor of the Jahzeelite clan (Gen. 46:24 [NIV, "Jahziel"]; Num. 26:48; called "Jahziel" in 1 Chr. 7:13).

Jahzeiah. jah-zee′yah (Heb. *yaḥzĕyâ H3488*, "Yahweh sees"). KJV Jahaziah. Son of Tikvah. When EZRA told the Israelites that those who had married foreign women should divorce their wives, Jahzeiah was one of four men who opposed him (Ezra 10:15). The Hebrew text, however, can be understood to mean that these four men supported Ezra (cf. NJPS). According to some scholars, the Hebrew expression here (lit., "stood upon this") does indicate opposition (cf. 2 Chr. 20:23 et al.), but what Jahzeiah and the others resisted was the delay proposed by the assembly (Ezra 10:12-14); in other words, the four men favored Ezra's decision and argued for swift punishment.

Jahzerah. jah′zuh-ruh (Heb. *yaḥzērâ H3492*, possibly "prudent" or "cunning"). Descendant of IMMER and grandfather (or ancestor) of a certain Maasai, who was one of the priests to resettle in JERUSALEM after the EXILE (1 Chr. 9:12); probably the same as AHZAI (Neh. 11:13).

Jahziel. See JAHZEEL.

Jair. jay′uhr (Heb. *yāʾîr H3281*, "[God] gives light"; *yāʿîr H3600* [only 1 Chr. 20:5; *Ketib yāʿûr*], "[God] stirs"). **(1)** Descendant (lit., "son") of MANASSEH who at the time of the conquest of Canaan occupied sixty villages on the border of GILEAD and BASHAN (see also ARGOB); these settlements came to be known as HAVVOTH JAIR (Num. 32:41; Deut. 3:14; Josh. 13:30; 1 Ki. 4:13). According to 1 Chr. 2:21-23, Jair's father was SEGUB, who descended from JUDAH through HEZRON, but whose mother is described as the daughter of Manasseh's son, MAKIR; thus Jair was apparently regarded as a Manassite through his mother's side.

(2) A Gileadite who judged or led Israel for twenty-two years (Jdg. 10:3-5). He is said to have had thirty sons, each of whom rode a donkey and ruled one of the towns of Havvoth Jair. The connection between this man and #1 above is unclear. It is possible that Jair of Gilead inherited the towns that had been previously under Jair of Segub.

(3) Son of Shimei, descendant of BENJAMIN, and father of MORDECAI, who was the cousin and guardian of ESTHER (Esth. 2:5).

(4) Father of Elhanan, who killed the brother of GOLIATH (1 Chr. 20:5; on the apparent discrepancies between this verse and 2 Sam. 21:19, see ELHANAN).

Jairite. jay′uh-rīt (Heb. *yāʾirî H3285*, "of Jair"). A gentilic referring apparently to someone who descended from JAIR #1. It is used to identify IRA, a priest (or royal adviser) of DAVID (2 Sam. 20:26).

Jairus. jay-i′ruhs (Gk. *Iairos G2608*, prob. from Heb. *yāʾir H3281* [see JAIR]). The name of a SYNAGOGUE official whose dead daughter Jesus raised to life (Mk. 5:22; Lk. 8:41). The incident, which took place near Lake Galilee, is recorded in all three Synoptic Gospels (Mk. 5:21-24, 35-43; Lk. 8:40-42, 49-56; Matt. 9:18-19, 23-26), but the man's name is not given by Matthew. Jairus came to Jesus and implored him to heal his daughter (Mk. 5:22-23), who was twelve years old (cf. v. 42). As they walked toward his house, some men arrived and reported that Jairus's daughter had died, but Jesus said to him, "Don't be afraid; just believe" (v. 36). When they reached the house, Jesus took the girl by the hand and said, "*Talitha koum*" (ARAMAIC for "Little girl, get up"), and at once she got up and began to walk around (vv. 39-42; see TALITHA CUM).

Jakan. See JAAKAN; JACAN.

Jakeh. jay′kuh (Heb. *yāqeh H3681*, possibly "prudent" or "[God] preserves"). Father of AGUR, who was the author of sayings recorded in the book of PROVERBS (Prov. 30:1).

Jakim. jay′kim (Heb. *yāqîm H3691*, "[God] establishes [*or* takes a stand]"). (1) Son of Shimei and Benjamite family head who lived in Jerusalem in DAVID's day (1 Chr. 8:19; cf. v. 28).

(2) A priest chosen during the time of David to head the twelfth of the twenty-four courses of

priests who took turns serving in the sanctuary (1 Chr. 24:12).

Jakin (person). jay′kin (Heb. *yākîn H3520*, "[God] establishes"; gentilic *yākînî H3522*, "Jakinite"). Also Jachin. (1) Son of SIMEON and eponymous ancestor of the Jakinite clan (Gen. 46:10; Exod. 6:15; Num. 26:12; apparently called JARIB in 1 Chr. 4:24).

(2) A leader of the LEVITES, appointed by lot as the head of the twenty-first course of priests during DAVID's time (1 Chr. 24:17).

(3) One of the priests who lived in JERUSALEM after the EXILE (1 Chr. 9:10; Neh. 11:10). It is possible, however, that the name may here be used as a family name denoting the priests in the twenty-first course, or the division of which Jakin was the head.

Jakin and Boaz. jay′kin, boh′az (Heb. *yākîn H3521*, "[God] establishes"; *bōʿaz H1245*, possibly "in him is strength"). Also Jachin and Boaz. The name of two bronze pillars SOLOMON placed in front of the TEMPLE; the one he placed on the N side was named Boaz, and the one on the S, Jakin (1 Ki. 7:21; 2 Chr. 3:17). Both pillars were beautifully adorned with capitals of lily-work, and their primary purpose appears to have been decorative and symbolic. As gateposts visible to the people (most of whom were not allowed inside), they probably indicated the entrance of the God of Israel into his earthly dwelling.

Jalam. jay′luhm (Heb. *yaʿlām H3609*, derivation uncertain). KJV Jaalam. Son of ESAU by OHOLIBAMAH; an Edomite chief (Gen. 36:5, 14, 18; 1 Chr. 1:35).

Jalon. jay′lon (Heb. *yālôn H3534*, derivation uncertain). Son of Ezrah and descendant of JUDAH (1 Chr. 4:17).

Jambres. See JANNES AND JAMBRES.

James. jaymz (Gk. *Iakōbos G2610*, hellenized form of *Iakōb G2609* [see JACOB]; English *James* derives from *Jacomus*, an alteration of Latin *Jacobus*). This name in the NT most frequently refers to James son of ZEBEDEE, one of the original twelve disciples and brother of the apostle John; his early martyrdom (c. A.D. 41) is recorded in Acts 12:1-2. Another James, the brother of Jesus, was not a believer until after the resurrection, but during the 40s he became the leader of the church in JERUSALEM (cf. Acts 15:13-21); he was probably the author of the epistle of James. A third individual named James son of ALPHAEUS, was one of the twelve disciples. A certain "James the younger" (Mk. 15:40; KJV, "the less") is sometimes identified with the son of Zebedee and more often with the son of Alphaeus, but he may be a fourth person with the same name. Finally, the father of the disciple JUDAS (not Iscariot) was named James.

(1) James son of Zebedee. He was a Galilean fisherman whose circumstances we can suppose to have been comfortable (Mk. 1:20; cf. 15:41; Lk. 8:3) and who was called to be one of the twelve disciples at the same time as his brother, JOHN THE APOSTLE (Matt. 4:21; Mk. 1:19-20). It is reasonable to assume that he was older than John, both because he is nearly always mentioned first and because John is sometimes identified as "the brother of James" (Matt. 10:2; 17:1; Mk. 3:17; 5:37). James, John, and Simon (PETER), who were part of a fishing partnership that included ANDREW, Simon's brother (Lk. 5:10), came to comprise also a trio that attained in some sense a place of primacy among the disciples. They are often found at the center of important events, such as the raising of JAIRUS's daughter (Mk. 5:37; Lk. 8:51), the TRANSFIGURATION (Matt. 17:1; Mk. 9:2; Lk. 9:28), and Jesus' agony in the Garden of Gethsemane (Matt. 26:37; Mk. 14:33). It was James and John, moreover, who had earlier accompanied Jesus to the home of Simon and Andrew (Mk. 1:29).

James and John were given by Jesus the name BOANERGES or "Sons of Thunder" (Mk. 3:17), when they were rebuked by the Lord for impetuosity and for having totally misconceived the purpose of his coming. This may have been the result of a suggestion made by them that they should pray for the destruction of a Samaritan village, whose inhabitants had repulsed Jesus' messengers (Lk. 9:54; cf. Mk. 9:38; Lk. 9:49-50). Their presumption and ill-considered thinking were obvious also when James, after asking with his brother for a place of honor in the kingdom, was told that they would drink the cup their Master was to drink

(Mk. 10:35-45; cf. Matt. 20:20-28). The wife of Zebedee was SALOME (Matt. 27:56; cf. Mk. 15:40), who appears to have been a sister of the MARY MOTHER OF JESUS (cf. Jn. 19:25). If this was so, James and John were cousins of Jesus and thus may have felt themselves in a privileged position.

The two sons of Zebedee are recorded as having been among those present when the risen Christ appeared to the disciples (Jn. 21), though it is curious to note that James's name is nowhere mentioned in the fourth gospel. We know nothing about James's career after the crucifixion until he was "put to death with the sword" by Herod

Old photo of men repairing their fishing nets on the shore of the Sea of Galilee. James son of Zebedee worked as a fisherman on these same shores.

Courtesy of the House of Anchors, Kibbutz En Gev, Sea of Galilee.

AGRIPPA I about A.D. 44 (Acts 12:2). James thus became the first of the Twelve whose martyrdom was referred to in the NT. An account attributed to Clement of Alexandria says that when James went on trial for his life, his steadfast testimony led to the conversion of his accuser, who was carried off with him to execution. A much less reliable tradition declares that he preached the gospel in Spain, of which country he is the patron saint.

(2) James, the brother of Jesus. The only two references to him in the Gospels mention him with his brothers Joses, Simon, and Judas (Matt. 13:55; Mk. 6:3). This James may have been, after Jesus, the oldest of the brothers. Some scholars have raised the question whether these were indeed full brothers of Jesus by Mary (a connection that creates difficulty for those who hold the view that Mary remained a virgin), but there seems no good reason to challenge the

J

fact from Scripture. Like the other brothers, James apparently did not accept Jesus' authority during Jesus' earthly life (Jn. 7:5). There is no specific mention of his conversion; he may have been included in the group to which Jesus appeared after the resurrection (1 Cor. 15:7). He became head of the Jewish Christian church at Jerusalem (Acts 12:17; 21:18; Gal. 2:9). Although Jesus had always taught the relative subordination of family ties (Matt. 12:48-50; Mk. 3:33-35; Lk. 8:21), it is hard to believe that James's authority was not somehow strengthened because of his relationship to the Master.

Although this James was not one of the Twelve, some believe that he was regarded as an apostle (cf. Gal. 1:19, but this passage can be interpreted differently). It has been suggested he was a replacement for the martyred son of Zebedee; others infer his apostleship by widening the scope of that term to embrace both the Twelve and "all the apostles" (see the two separate categories cited in 1 Cor. 15:5, 7). Tradition states that James was appointed the first bishop of Jerusalem by the Lord himself and the apostles. What is certain is that he presided over the first Council of Jerusalem, called to consider the terms of admission of Gentiles into the Christian church, and he may have formulated the decree that met with the approval of all his colleagues and was circulated to the churches of ANTIOCH, SYRIA, and CILICIA (Acts 15:19-29).

James evidently regarded his own special ministry as being to the Jews, and his was a mediating role in the controversy that arose in the young church around the place of the LAW for those who had become Christians from both Gentile and Jewish origins. That he continued to have strong Jewish Christian sympathies is apparent from the request made to PAUL when the latter visited Jerusalem for the last time (Acts 21:18-26). This was also the last mention in Acts of James's career. His name occurs again in the NT as the traditional author of the letter of James, where he describes himself as "a servant of God and of the Lord Jesus Christ" (Jas. 1:1; see JAMES, LETTER OF).

According to Hegesippus (c. A.D. 180), James's faithful adherence to the Jewish law and his austere lifestyle led to the designation "the just." It seems clear that he suffered martyrdom; JOSEPHUS places his death in the year 61 when there was a Jewish uprising after the death of FESTUS the procurator and before his successor had been appointed. Jerome refers to a passage in the *Gospel of the Hebrews* (the fragments of which appear in various patristic writings) that recounts the appearance of the risen Christ to James. In contrast to 1 Cor. 15:7, this apocryphal work claims that this was the first appearance of the Lord after the resurrection. The same writing is alleged to have noted James's vow to eat no bread from the time of the Last Supper until he had seen the risen Lord. This raises questions, not least about the assumption that James was present at the Last Supper.

(3) James son of Alphaeus. Another of the apostles (Matt. 10:3; Mk. 3:18; Lk. 6:15; Acts 1:13). Nothing is known for certain about him. Since Levi or MATTHEW is also described as "the son of Alphaeus" (Mk. 2:14), he and James may have been brothers. Some scholars identify him with #4 below.

(4) James "the younger." He was the son of a certain MARY (Matt. 27:56; Mk. 15:40; Lk. 24:10) who might have been the wife (or the daughter) of CLOPAS. Assuming that she was Clopas's wife, some go on to conclude from a superficial word resemblance that Clopas and Alphaeus are two forms of the same name. This in turn has led on to a suggested identification of James son of Mary with #3 above. The description "the younger" seems to have been given to distinguish him from the son of Zebedee. The word could also signify that he was smaller than his namesake (the Greek word can cover both interpretations). About this James we know nothing more.

(5) James father of Judas. This Judas (not Judas Iscariot, Jn. 14:22) is called THADDAEUS in Matthew and Mark. The elliptical text in two passages ("Judas of James"—Lk. 6:16; Acts 1:13) has been interpreted in two ways: Judas was the brother (KJV) or, more likely, the son of James.

James, Letter of. The first of the CATHOLIC EPISTLES of the NT. This letter is among the last to have become firmly established in the NT canon (see CANONICITY). While traces of it seem to be found in the writings of the APOSTOLIC FATHERS (A.D. 90-155), the oldest author to mention it by name is Origen (early 3rd cent.), who considers it canonical, although he is aware that its canonicity

Overview of JAMES

Author: James, the half-brother of Jesus.

Historical setting: The letter must have been written prior to A.D. 62, the year of James's martyrdom (some date it as early as A.D. 44, making it the first NT book to be written). It was probably addressed to Jewish Christians who lived in the DISPERSION (unless Jas. 1:1 is to be taken figuratively); they were undergoing trials as well as experiencing spiritual failures.

Purpose: To stress the need for "wisdom from above" (Jas. 3:17) and for works of obedience that demonstrate the genuineness of saving FAITH.

Contents: Wisdom amid trials and temptations (Jas. 1:1-18); being doers of the word and not merely hearers (1:19—2:26); dangers of the tongue, quarrels, and slander (3:1—4:12); depending on God and enduring with patience and prayer (4:13—5:20).

is not universally acknowledged. Eusebius (early 4th cent.) lists it among the disputed books but says it is read in most churches. In the East the church accepted it from a very early period, but in the West it was not received into the canon until the end of the fourth century.

The author of the letter refers to himself as "James, a servant of God and of the Lord Jesus Christ" (Jas. 1:1). The NT mentions five who bore the name of JAMES. Tradition attributes the authorship of the letter to James the brother of the Lord, who was probably favored with a special appearance of the risen Christ (1 Cor. 15:7) and who from a very early date occupied a leading position in the church at JERUSALEM (Acts 12:17; Gal. 1:19). PAUL names him first among the three "pillars" (Gal. 2:9). In Acts 15 he is described as the leader and chief spokesman of the Apostolic Council. All that is known of him shows that he was highly esteemed not only by Christians but also by unbelieving Jews. According to JOSEPHUS, he was put to death by the high priest in the interregnum between the death of FESTUS and the arrival of his successor Albinus in A.D. 62.

All the characteristics of the letter support the traditional attribution of it to James the brother of the Lord. The author speaks with the authority of

one who knew he did not need to justify or defend his position. There is no more Jewish book in the NT than this letter; and this is to be expected from a man whom both tradition and the rest of the NT show was distinguished by his Jewish commitments. The whole of the letter, moreover, bears a striking resemblance to the SERMON ON THE MOUNT, both in the loftiness of its morality and in the simple grandeur of its expression.

The letter is addressed to "the twelve tribes scattered among the nations." This ambiguous expression may be interpreted in a number of ways: (1) The Jews of the Diaspora (DISPERSION) in general, who were living throughout the Mediterranean world outside Palestine. This meaning is impossible, for the writer is addressing Christians (Jas. 1:18, 25; 2:1, 12; 5:7-9). (2) The Jewish Christians of the Diaspora. (3) The Christian church as the new people of God living far from their heavenly homeland. Early Christians regarded themselves as the true Israel (Gal. 6:16), the true circumcision (Phil. 3:3), and the seed of Abraham (Rom. 4:16; Gal. 3:29), so it would not be surprising if they also thought of themselves as "the twelve tribes." There is no doubt, however, that the letter is intended for Jewish Christians, although its message is applicable to all believers. Those to whom the author

J

© Dr. James C. Martin. The British Museum. Photographed by permission.

Babylonian design of a horse with a bit and bridle. James compares the power of the tongue to the power of the bit placed into the mouth of a horse to guide it (Jas. 3:3).

writes worship in synagogues (Jas. 2:2), and some have claimed that the faults he attacks were characteristic of Jews: misuse of the tongue (3:2-12; 4:2, 11), unkind judgments of one's neighbors (3:14; 4:11), the making of rash oaths (5:12), undue regard for wealth (2:1-13), etc. On the other hand, there is no mention of specifically pagan vices— e.g., idolatry, drunkenness, and impurity—against which Paul so often warns Gentile Christians. The object of the author was to rebuke and correct the error and sins into which his readers had fallen and to encourage them in the heavy trials through which they were going.

The scholars who consider this letter the work of James the brother of the Lord do not agree on the date when it was written. Two views are held, one that it was composed shortly before the death of James, in the early A.D. 60s; the other, that it appeared in the middle 40s, before the Apostolic Council. In favor of the early date are the striking simplicity of church organization and discipline, the fact that Christians still met in the synagogue (Jas. 2:2), and the general Judaic tone. All this is thought

to suggest a time before Gentiles were admitted into the church in any large numbers. Scholars who prefer the later date say that the letter gives evidence of a considerable lapse of time in the history of the church, at least enough to allow for a decline in the spiritual fervor that characterized the church in early apostolic times. The readers are obviously not recent converts. The author has a position of long-established authority. The references to persecutions, moreover, fit a later date better than an early one.

The informal character of the letter makes a logical analysis difficult. It is not a formal treatise, but a loosely related series of exhortations, warnings, and instructions, all dealing with the moral and religious life. The author rules authoritatively on questions of church life and discipline that have been brought to his attention.

After the address (Jas. 1:1), James first admonishes his readers on having a right attitude toward tribulations and temptations (1:2-18) and exhorts them to be doers and not merely hearers of the Word of God (1:19-25). He forbids them to slight the poor and favor the rich (2:1-13) and shows them the insufficiency of faith without works (2:14-26). He then warns them against the misuse of the tongue (3:1-12) and sets forth the nature of true and false wisdom (3:13-18). He rebukes them for their greed and lust (4:1-12) and for making foolhardy plans for the future in business (4:13-17). The letter closes with a warning to the godless rich (5:1-6), an exhortation to patience in suffering (5:7-12), a reminder of the power of prayer in every need (5:13-18), and a declaration of the joy of Christian service (5:19-20).

The section on FAITH and WORKS (2:14-26) is not a polemic against Paul's doctrine of JUSTIFICATION by faith, but a rebuke of the prevalent Jewish notion that saving faith is mere intellectual assent to a set of doctrinal propositions. James points out that saving faith manifests itself in works, and that if the works are not there, the genuineness of the faith may be questioned. Paul and James are in perfect harmony in their views of the relationship of faith and works to salvation.

Jamin. jay′min (Heb. *yāmîn* H3546, "valued, fortunate"; gentilic *yāmînî* H3547, "Jaminite"). **(1)** Son of SIMEON, grandson of JACOB, and eponymous ancestor of the Jaminite clan (Gen. 46:10; Exod. 6:15; Num. 26:12; 1 Chr. 4:24).

(2) Son of RAM, grandson of JERAHMEEL, and descendant of JUDAH (1 Chr. 2:27).

(3) A LEVITE who helped EZRA instruct the people in the law (Neh. 8:7).

Jamlech. jam′lik (Heb. *yamlēk H3552*, "[God] grants dominion"). A clan leader in the tribe of SIMEON (1 Chr. 4:34). He is listed among those whose families increased greatly during the days of King HEZEKIAH and who dispossessed the Hamites and Meunites near GEDOR (vv. 38-41).

Jamnia. See JABNEEL #2.

Janai. jay′ni (Heb. *ya‛nay H3614*, "[God] answers"). KJV Jaanai. A leader in the tribe of GAD in BASHAN, listed as third in importance (1 Chr. 5:12; some take the next name, "Shaphat," as a common noun, thus, "and Janai a judge in Bashan" [see SHAPHAT #4]).

Janim. jay′nim (Heb. *yānîm H3565*, derivation uncertain). KJV Janum. A town allotted to the tribe of JUDAH in the hill district of HEBRON (Josh. 15:53); the location is unknown, although one proposed identification is modern Beni Na‛im, c. 4 mi. (6 km.) E of Hebron.

Janna. See JANNAI.

Jannai. jan′i (Gk. *Iannai G2613*). KJV Janna. Son of a certain Joseph, included in Luke's GENEALOGY OF JESUS CHRIST (Lk. 3:24).

Jannes and Jambres. jan′iz, jam′briz (Gk. *Iannēs G2614* and *Iambrēs G2612*). The traditional names of Egyptian sorcerers who opposed MOSES before PHARAOH (2 Tim. 3:8, evidently a reference back to unnamed magicians mentioned in Exod. 7:11-12, 22). *Jannes and Jambres* is also the title of a pseudepigraphic work, and these names (or Jannes and Mambres) are found frequently not only in Jewish tradition, but also in pagan and early Christian literature.

Janoah. juh-noh′uh (Heb. *yānôaḥ H3562*, "resting place"). (1) A town on the E border of the tribal

territory of EPHRAIM (Josh. 16:6-7; KJV, "Janohah"); it is generally identified with Khirbet Yanun (c. 6.5 mi./10.5 km. SE of SHECHEM) or with the nearby town of Yanun.

(2) One of five cities in N Israel captured by TIGLATH-PILESER, king of Assyria (2 Ki. 15:29). Among several proposals, the most likely identifications are two places, both of which are now known as Yanuh. One of them is c. 6 mi. (10 km.) E of TYRE; the other, much farther S, is c. 11 mi. (18 km.) NE of Acco.

Janum. See JANIM.

Japheth. jay′fith (Heb. *yepet H3651*, possibly "spacious" or "[God] enlarges"). Son of NOAH. In most of the passages referring to him (Gen. 5:32; 6:10; 7:13; 9:18; 10:1; 1 Chr. 1:4), Japheth is listed as the third of Noah's sons. However, one passage (Gen. 9:24; cf. v. 22) seems to indicate that HAM was the youngest. An additional statement (Gen. 10:21) has also been construed to support the idea that Japheth was the second son rather than the third. Japheth and his wife were saved in the ark (7:7). Japheth aided his brother SHEM in covering the naked body of their drunken father (9:20-23). The blessing pronounced upon Japheth by Noah (9:27) carried with it the idea that his descendants would be greatly multiplied (enlarged) in the future. The Table of Nations recorded in ch. 10 indicates that Japheth became the ancestor of a wide-ranging family of peoples, whose homes lay to the N of PALESTINE and then W. In fact, fourteen nations of Japhethites are listed in that chapter. The area of their occupation ranged all the way from the smelting plants of TARSHISH (prob. in Spain) on the W to the Caspian Sea on the E. This included what is now the steppes of S Russia, much of ASIA MINOR, the islands of the MEDITERRANEAN, and the coasts of S Europe. Japheth is said to be the father of Gomer, Magog, Madai, Javan, Tubal, Meshech, and Tiras (Gen. 10:2; 1 Chr. 1:4). These appear to be the progenitors of the Indo-European (Caucasian) family of nations.

Japhia (person). juh-fi′uh (Heb. *yāpî‛a H3644*, possibly "high, tall" or "[God] shines forth"). (1) A king of LACHISH who formed a league with four other AMORITE kings to punish GIBEON for submitting to the Israelites (Josh. 10:3-5). Joshua defeated them in battle at Beth Horon, killed the five kings, and cast their bodies into a cave (10:6-27).

(2) One of the sons of David born at Jerusalem (2 Sam. 5:15; 1 Chr. 3:7; 14:6). All that is known of him is that his mother was a wife, not a concubine, of David.

Japhia (place). juh-fi´uh (Heb. *yāpiʿa H3643*, possibly "high, tall" or "[God] shines forth"). A town on the S border of the tribal territory of Zebulun (Josh. 19:13). It is usually identified with modern Yafa, c. 1.5 mi. (2.5 km.) SW of Nazareth, but without archaeological support.

Japhlet. jaf´lit (Heb. *yaplēṭ H3646*, "[God] delivers"). Son of Heber and descendant of Asher (1 Chr. 7:32-33). See also Japhletite.

Japhleti. See Japhletite.

Japhletite. jaf´luh-tit (Heb. *yaplēṭi H3647*, gentilic of *yaplēṭ H3646*). KJV Japhleti. A clan or larger people group whose territory, near Beth Horon, served to mark the S border of the tribe of Ephraim (Josh. 16:3). It is possible that they were descendants of Japhlet, an Asherite, but nothing is known about them.

Japho. See Joppa.

jar. See Pitcher.

Jarah. See Jadah.

Jareb. jair´ib (Heb. *yārēb H3714*, derivation disputed). According to the KJV, Jareb is the name of an Assyrian king (Hos. 5:13; 10:6). There is however no evidence, linguistically or historically, of an Assyrian king by that name. Most scholars believe that the Hebrew text parallels the common Assyrian phrase, *šarru rabū*, "the great king" (cf. NIV and other modern versions).

Jared. jair´id (Heb. *yered H3719*, derivation disputed; Gk. *Iaret G2616*). Son of Mahalalel and father of Enoch (Gen. 5:15-20; 1 Chr. 1:2 [KJV, "Jered"]); his name is included in Luke's genealogy of Jesus Christ (Lk. 3:37).

Jaresiah. See Jaareshiah.

Jarha. jahr´huh (Heb. *yarḥāʿ H3739*, meaning unknown). An Egyptian servant belonging to Sheshan (1 Chr. 2:34-35). Jarha married Sheshan's daughter (prob. Ahlai, v. 31) and thus was included in the genealogy of Jerahmeel. Some speculate that by this action Sheshan, who had no sons, made Jarha his heir (cf. Eliezer, Gen. 15:2-3).

Jarib. jair´ib (Heb. *yārib H3743*, "[Yahweh] contends [for me]"). **(1)** Son of Simeon (1 Chr. 4:24; apparently called Jakin in Gen. 46:10; Exod. 6:15; Num. 26:12).

(2) One of a group of leaders sent by Ezra to Iddo to get attendants for the house of God (Ezra 8:16).

(3) A descendant of Jeshua son of Jozadak, listed among the priests in Ezra's time who agreed to put away their foreign wives (Ezra 10:18).

Jarmuth. jahr´muhth (Heb. *yarmût H3754*, "swelling [of the ground], height"). **(1)** A city in the Shephelah whose king, Piram, entered into a conspiracy with four other Amorite kings against the Gibeonites to revenge their submission to Joshua (Josh. 10:3-5). Joshua defeated the five kings at Gibeon and slew them at Makkedah (vv. 9-26; cf. 12:11). After the conquest of Canaan, Jarmuth was assigned to the tribe of Judah (15:35). Some Jews returned there after the Babylonian exile (Neh. 11:29). Jarmuth is tentatively identified with modern Khirbet el-Yarmuk (Tell Yarmut), c. 17 mi. (27 km.) WSW of Jerusalem, even though there is no archaeological confirmation.

(2) A city within the tribal territory of Issachar allotted to the Levite clans descended from Gershon (Josh. 21:29). In other lists Jarmuth is apparently called Remeth (19:21) and Ramoth (1 Chr. 6:73). The site is tentatively identified with Kaukab el-Hawa (Hellenistic Agrippina, c. 6 mi. /10 km. NNE of Beth Shan); on this imposing location above the Jordan Valley, the Crusaders built the Belvoir castle.

Jaroah. juh-roh´uh (Heb. *yārôaḥ H3726*, "soft" or "pitied"). Son of Gilead, descendant of Gad, and ancestor of Abihail; the sons of Abihail and other

The Beth Horon ridge looking W into the Valley of Aijalon. Joshua chased the fleeing Amorite forces down this ridge, scoring a great victory for Israel (Josh. 10). The events of this memorable day, when "the sun stood still," were also summarized in the Book of Jashar.

Gadites occupied the region E of GILEAD (1 Chr. 5:14; cf. v. 10).

Jashar, Book of. jay'shuhr (Heb. *yāšār H3839*, "upright"). KJV Jasher. An ancient writing, no longer extant, mentioned twice in the OT (Josh. 10:13; 2 Sam. 1:18). On the basis of the material preserved in these passages, it has been inferred that the book was poetical in nature and that it contained songs of a national character. The references to the book imply that it was well known and respected, and consequently it may have been the source for other material found in the OT (perhaps, e.g., the songs of MIRIAM and DEBORAH in Exod. 15:21 and Jdg. 5). The origin of this document is a matter of speculation, but many scholars believe that it was the result of a gradual compilation begun in the early period of Israel's history.

Jashen. jay'shuhn (Heb. *yāšēn H3826*, possibly "sleepy"). The father of two or more unnamed warriors included among DAVID's Thirty (2 Sam. 23:32). It is widely thought, however, that the unusual MT reading here ("the sons of Jashen," without naming them) has suffered textual corruption. The parallel passage reads, "the sons of Hashem the Gizonite" (1 Chr. 11:34). Many

scholars argue that the original reading was "Jashen the Gizonite." See GIZONITE; HASHEM.

Jasher. See JASHAR, BOOK OF.

Jashobeam. juh-shoh'bee-uhm (Heb. *yāšāb'ām H3790*, "the people [*or* the father's relative] has returned"). **(1)** A Hacmonite (lit., "son of HACMONI") and chief of DAVID's officers who killed 300 men in one battle (1 Chr. 17:11). The parallel passage (2 Sam. 23:8), which has very likely suffered textual corruption, speaks of "Josheb-Basshebeth, a Tahkemonite," chief of the Three, who slew 800 men in one battle. The Hebrew words for 300 and 800 begin with the same letter, making a copyist's error possible. Many scholars, following the SEPTUAGINT, think that the original name was Ish-Baal (ISH-BOSHETH arising when the Heb. word for "shame" was substituted for the hated name BAAL) and that both Jashobeam and Josheb-Basshebeth are later scribal corruptions.

(2) One of several Korahite warriors who joined David at ZIKLAG (1 Chr. 12:6; cf. vv. 1-2). Since apparently he was a LEVITE from the family of KORAH, he probably should not be identified with #1 above. Some argue, however, that the reference is to a different Korah or even to a locality in the tribe of BENJAMIN.

J

(3) Son of Zabdiel, descendant of PEREZ, and a commander in charge of the division for the first month during the reign of David (1 Chr. 27:2-3). Because most of the other commanders listed in this chapter are also mentioned in ch. 11, many believe this Jashobeam is the same as #1 above; if so, it is unclear why one passage describes him as "son of Hacmoni" and the other as "son of Zabdiel" (possibly the former designation refers to the larger clan or is used as some kind of title).

Jashub. jay´shuhb (Heb. *yāšûb H3793*, possibly "[God] returns"; gentilic *yāšûbî H3795*, "Jashubite"). (1) Son of ISSACHAR and eponymous ancestor of the Jashubite clan (Num. 26:24; 1 Chr. 7:1). In another passage (Gen. 46:13) the MT has *yôb*, and this reading is followed by the KJV ("Job"), the RSV ("Iob"), and other versions; on the basis of some Greek MSS, the Samaritan Pentateuch, and the biblical parallels, the NIV and NRSV read "Jashub" here as well.

(2) One of the descendants of Bani who agreed to put away their foreign wives (Ezra 10:29).

Jashubi Lehem. juh-shoo´buh-lee´hem (Heb. *yāšubî leḥem H3788*). An otherwise unknown place ruled by descendants of JUDAH (1 Chr. 4:22 NIV; the KJV interprets it as the name of a person). The Hebrew text is difficult, however, and the NRSV, with a minor emendation, translates, "who married into Moab but returned to Lehem." But a place by the name of Lehem is also unknown, so other emendations have been proposed.

Jasiel. See JAASIEL.

Jason. jay´suhn (Gk. *Iasōn G2619*, "healing") (1) Son of Simon II and brother of the high priest ONIAS III; by bribery he secured the high priestly office for himself, and through his influence Greek customs became popularized (2 Macc. 4:7-26). He gave large gifts for the sacred games at TYRE honoring Hercules (4:16-20). His tenure was only three years (174-171 B.C.), for he was supplanted by MENELAUS, who offered ANTIOCHUS IV Epiphanes a greater bribe. Jason fled to the AMMONITES, but a false rumor of Antiochus's death in Egypt brought him back to JERUSALEM with a large following to overthrow Menelaus. Antiochus returned to wreak vengeance on the Jews; and Jason again fled to Ammon, then to Egypt, and later to Sparta, where he died (5:1-10).

A Jewish Christian of THESSALONICA who was probably host to the missionaries PAUL and SILAS. He and others were summoned to court on a charge of being hospitable to seditionists, but freedom was obtained by giving security for good conduct (Acts 17:5-9). See also #3, below.

(2) One of two or three "relatives" of Paul (the others being SOSIPATER and possibly LUCIUS) who sent greetings to the Christians in Rome (Rom. 16:21). According to many scholars, however, the Greek term *syngenēs G5150* here means "kinsman" (cf. RSV) and should be understood in the sense of "fellow-Jew" (cf. 9:3). In either case, this Jason is possibly the same as #1 above. Some have speculated that he became a travel companion of Paul and thus was with him in CORINTH when the letter to the ROMANS was written.

jasper. See MINERALS.

Jathniel. jath´nee-uhl (Heb. *yatnî'ēl H3853*, derivation uncertain). Fourth son of Meshelemiah and descendant of KORAH; like his father, he and his brothers were Levitical gatekeepers in the time of DAVID (1 Chr. 26:2).

Jattir. jat´uhr (Heb. *yattîr H3848*, possibly "extraordinary"). A town in the hill country within the tribal territory of JUDAH (Josh. 15:48); it was allotted to the LEVITES (21:14; 1 Chr. 6:57). DAVID sent spoil from ZIKLAG to it after his victory over the AMALEKITES (1 Sam. 30:27). It is identified with modern Khirbet ʿAttir, c. 13 mi. (21 km.) SW of HEBRON.

Javan. jay´vuhn (Heb. *yāwān H3430*, from Gk. *Iōnes*). Son of JAPHETH, grandson of NOAH, and father of ELISHAH, TARSHISH, KITTIM, and RODANIM (Gen. 10:2, 4; 1 Chr. 1:5, 7). The name corresponds etymologically to Ionia. As such it is used in the prophets to denote the descendants of Javan in Ionia proper (W coast of ASIA MINOR) but also in GREECE and MACEDONIA; thus the NIV renders the name "Greece" or "Greeks" in these books. In Isa. 66:19 Javan, in conjunction with TARSHISH, LUD, PUT, and TUBAL, is spoken of as one of the far-off nations to whom messengers will be dispatched to tell of Yahweh's glory and the restoration of Jerusalem; the nations mentioned seem to represent the far western edge of the known world in the OT. In Ezek. 27:13 Javan is included as one of the contributors to the wealth of TYRE; it is grouped with TUBAL and MESHECH as traders of slaves and bronze (cf. Joel 3:6; Zech. 9:13). The book of Daniel identifies Javan with ALEXANDER THE GREAT'S Greco-Macedonian empire (Dan. 8:21; 10:20; 11:2). Javan occurs also in the Hebrew text of Ezek. 27:19 (cf. above on v. 13), but the context seems to demand a location in ARABIA rather than in the W (the SEPTUAGINT has "wine," thought by some to represent the original Hebrew text).

javelin. See ARMS, ARMOR.

jaw. This English term is commonly the rendering of Hebrew *lĕḥî H4305*, used often of animals (e.g., the "jowls" of a bull or sheep, Deut. 18:3; a donkey's "jawbone," Jdg. 15:15-17), but also with reference to the "face" or "cheek" of people (e.g., 1 Ki. 22:24; Job 16:10). Several occurrences are figurative uses (e.g., Isa. 30:28; Ezek. 29:4). See also CHEEK.

Jazer. jay´zuhr (Heb. *yaʿzêr H3597*, "[God] helps"). KJV also Jaazer. An AMORITE city in GILEAD. There are a dozen biblical references to it, usually as a "city" (e.g., Josh. 21:39), but once as a "land" (Num. 32:1) and once as a "territory" (Josh. 13:25). Jazer was taken by MOSES (Num. 21:32), then settled and fortified by the tribe of GAD. It bordered Ammonite territory (21:24) and was one of the four towns of Gad given to the LEVITES (Josh. 21:39). Some of DAVID's most able men came from Jazer (1 Chr. 26:31), and his census takers reached it (2 Sam. 24:5). Following the death of AHAB, it was captured by the Moabites (cf. Isa. 16:9; Jer. 48:32). The identification of Jazer has been much disputed. The most likely proposals are Khirbet es-Sar (c. 6 mi./10 km. W of modern Amman) and Khirbet Jazzir (c. 7 mi./11 km. WNW of es-Sar, at the head of Wadi Shuʿeib).

Jaziz. jay´ziz (Heb. *yāzîz H3467*, meaning uncertain). A HAGRITE who was in charge of King David's flocks (1 Chr. 27:31; NRSV, v. 31).

jealousy. This English term is used in Bible versions to render several words, primarily Hebrew *qinʾâ H7863* (Num. 5:14 et al.) and Greek *zēlos G2419* (Acts 5:17 et al.). In each case it seems to indicate an ardor or zeal for something believed to belong properly to one. The term may refer both to a favorable or appropriate variety of this ardor, and to an improper form of it. When jealousy reflects concern for God's honor and glory, it is proper and good. Thus, God himself is several times described as jealous for his honor, his holy name. He desires fervently that his due status and honor be preserved, that the WORSHIP that belongs to him should be given to him. The analogy frequently used is a husband's concern for the love of his wife. This is an expression of the HOLINESS of God, which cannot endure any unfaithfulness. Just as a husband is not indulgent of adultery on the part of his wife, so no infidelity is permitted by God. It was this exclusiveness of concern that underlay the strong emphasis upon monotheistic worship among the Jews. Because Yahweh is the only true God, he alone is deserving of human worship and devotion (cf. Exod. 32; Jn. 14:6; et al.).

Another meaning or application of the word and concept of jealousy is negative in its effect and is strongly condemned by God. It is excessive concern for one's own self, and what one fancies or desires. It may also involve resentment of the good fortune of another. It is an inordinate self-centeredness or possessiveness (Gen. 37:34; 1 Sam. 18:6-9; Lk. 15:25-30). Jealousy that involves an improper inward feeling toward another person is SIN in itself, because Jesus said that thoughts and attitudes constitute sin, even without overt acts (Matt. 5:21-31). In addition, jealousy is often the motive for sinful actions. The antidote to jealousy is perfect LOVE. Because love is not self-seeking (1 Cor. 13:5), it does not go beyond its rightful claims. This love, the Scripture teaches, is of divine origin and consequently must come from above.

jealousy, water of. See BITTER WATER.

Jearim. jee´uh-rim (Heb. *yĕʿārîm H3630*, "woods"). The name of a mountain or mountain ridge on the

N border of the tribe of JUDAH (Josh. 15:10). The text identifies or associates Mount Jearim with KESALON, which was apparently the name of a border town. See also SEIR.

Jeaterai. See JEATHERAI.

Jeatherai. jee-ath´uh-ri (Heb. *yĕʾātray H3290*). KJV Jeaterai. Son of Zerah and descendant of LEVI through GERSHON (1 Chr. 6:21).

Jeberechiah. See JEBEREKIAH.

Jeberekiah. ji-ber´uh-ki´uh (Heb. *yĕberekyāhû H3310*, "Yahweh blesses"). Also Jeberechiah. Father of a certain Zechariah who was called upon by ISAIAH as a witness of his prophecy against DAMASCUS and SAMARIA (Isa. 8:2).

Jebus. jee´buhs (Heb. *yĕbûs H3293*). The name by which JERUSALEM was known while occupied by the JEBUSITES (Josh. 15:63; Jdg. 19:10; 1 Chr. 11:4). Small in area compared with the size of Jerusalem in SOLOMON's time, Jebus was taken from the Jebusites by DAVID and made the capital of ISRAEL (2 Sam. 5:1-9). Its citadel was the stronghold of ZION (1 Chr. 11:5).

Jebusite. jeb´yoo-sit (Heb. *yĕbûsî H3294*). KJV also Jebusi. The Jebusites were a Canaanite tribe descended from CANAAN and dwelling in the land before the Israelite conquest (Gen. 10:15-16; Exod. 3:8, 17; Deut. 7:1; 20:17; Josh. 3:10; 10:1-5; Jdg. 1:8). Their king, ADONI-ZEDEK, was one of the five who conspired against GIBEON and was killed by JOSHUA. The Jebusites lived many years at the site of JERUSALEM (JEBUS) and were not dislodged until DAVID sent JOAB and his men into the city (2 Sam. 5:6-7). David then bought the threshing floor of ARAUNAH (or Ornan) the Jebusite as a site for the temple (24:18-25). This large flat rock where the altar of burnt offering stood is now said to be visible in the Dome of the Rock (Mount MORIAH) at Jerusalem.

Jecamiah. See JEKAMIAH.

Jechiliah. See JECOLIAH.

Jecholiah. See JECOLIAH.

Jechoniah, Jechonias. See JECONIAH.

Jecoliah. jek´uh-li´uh (Heb. *yĕkālyāhû H3525*, *yĕkālyâ H3524*, "Yahweh is [*or* proves himself] able,

The ancient city of Jebus was located on the V-shaped ridge descending S into the valley in front of what is now known as the temple mount. (View to the NE up the Kidron Valley, with the Mt. of Olives in the background.)

© Dr. James C. Martin

powerful"). TNIV Jekoliah. Mother of King Azariah (Uzziah) of Judah (2 Ki. 15:2 [KJV, "Jecholiah"]; 2 Chr. 26:3 [ASV, "Jechiliah"]).

Jeconiah. jek uh-ni′uh (Heb. *yĕkānyāhû H3527* [only Jer. 24:1], *yĕkānyâ H3526*, "Yahweh supports" or "may Yahweh establish"; Gk. *Iechonias G2651*). Also Jechoniah; KJV NT Jechonias. Alternate name of JEHOIACHIN, king of Judah (1 Chr. 3:16-17; Esth. 2:6; Jer. 24:1; 27:20; 28:4; 29:2; Matt. 1:11-12).

Jedaiah. ji-day′yuh (Heb. *yĕdāyâ H3355* [only #1 and #5 below], "Yahweh has favored"; *yĕda‘yâ H3361*, "Yahweh has known"). **(1)** Son of Shimri and descendant of SIMEON (1 Chr. 4:37); included in the genealogy of Ziza, a clan leader.

(2) Chief of the second division of priests as appointed by DAVID (1 Chr. 24:7). Possibly the ancestor of the 973 priests (of the family of JESHUA) who returned from the EXILE (Ezra 2:36; Neh. 7:39).

(3) One of the priests who returned from the exile (1 Chr. 9:10; Neh. 11:10; 12:6); Uzzi became head of Jedaiah's priestly family (12:19). There may be a connection between this Jedaiah and #2 above.

(4) Evidently another (but less important) priest of the same name, since he is included in two of the same lists as #3 above (Neh. 12:7, 21).

(5) Son of Harumaph; he made repairs on the wall of JERUSALEM opposite his house (Neh. 3:10).

(6) One of a group of Jewish exiles who brought gold and silver from BABYLON to help those who had returned under ZERUBBABEL; from these gifts a crown was to be made for Joshua (JESHUA) the high priest (Zech. 6:10).

Jediael. ji-di′ay-uhl (Heb. *yĕdi‘ă’ēl H3356*, "known of God"). **(1)** Son (or descendant) of BENJAMIN (1 Chr. 7:6, 10-11).

(2) Son of Shimri; he and his brother Joha the Tizite were among DAVID's mighty warriors (1 Chr. 11:45).

(3) A military leader from the tribe of MANASSEH who defected from SAUL and joined David at ZIKLAG (1 Chr. 12:20); some have suggested that he may be the same as #2 above.

(4) Son of Meshelemiah and descendant of KORAH; like his father, he and his brothers were Levitical gatekeepers in the time of DAVID (1 Chr. 26:2).

Jedidah. ji-di′duh (Heb. *yĕdîdâ H3352*, "beloved [of God *or* Yahweh]"). Daughter of Adaiah and mother of JOSIAH, king of Judah (2 Ki. 22:1).

Jedidiah. jed uh-di′uh (Heb. *yĕdîdyāh H3354*, "beloved of Yahweh"). The name God gave, through the prophet NATHAN, to SOLOMON when he was born, because "the LORD loved him" (2 Sam. 12:25; lit., "for the sake of the LORD"). The giving of this second name—which appears to be related to that of DAVID and does not occur elsewhere in the Bible—has caused considerable debate. One proposal is that Jedidiah was his initial name and that Solomon was a throne name David gave to him in anticipation of the child's future rule in Jerusalem; others argue that Jedidiah was the throne name.

Jeduthun. ji-dyoo′thuhn (Heb. *yĕdûtûn H3349*, possibly derived from *yādāh H3344*, "to praise, thank"). **(1)** A Levitical musician in the time of DAVID who, with HEMAN, was "responsible for the sounding of the trumpets and cymbals and for the playing of the other instruments for sacred song" (1 Chr. 16:41-42; he is also called a royal seer, 2 Chr. 35:15). His sons, along with the sons of Heman and ASAPH, were set aside "for the ministry of prophesying, accompanied by harps, lyres and cymbals" (1 Chr. 25:1-6). He is usually thought to be the same as Ethan, which may have been an earlier name of his (6:44); see ETHAN #4. The name appears repeatedly in connection with TEMPLE music at important occasions (2 Chr. 5:12; 29:14; 35:15). The family continued to officiate after the EXILE (Neh. 11:17). The phrase "for Jeduthun" (NRSV, "according to Jeduthun") is found in the titles of Ps. 39; 62; 77. What the connection may be with David's musician is unclear; some believe it refers to an instrument or to a tune.

(2) Father of OBED-EDOM, who was a gatekeeper (1 Chr. 16:38). It is often taken for granted that he is the same as #1 above, but some argue that insofar as the Obed-Edom mentioned here was descended from KORAH (26:1, 4) and not from MERARI, this Jeduthun must be different.

J

Jeezer. See IEZER.

Jegar Sahadutha. jee´guhr-say-huh-doo´thuh (Heb. *yĕgar śāhădûtā* H3337, "heap of witness"). The Aramaic name that LABAN gave to a heap of stones set up as the sign of a covenant between him and JACOB; the latter called it by the equivalent Hebrew name, GALEED (Gen. 31:47). This passage provides the oldest evidence of the ARAMAIC LANGUAGE found in the Bible, and it is part of the evidence that ABRAHAM spoke Aramaic before adopting a Canaanite dialect (which eventually developed into the HEBREW LANGUAGE).

Jehaleleel, Jehalelel. See JEHALLELEL.

Jehallelel. ji-hal´uh-luhl (Heb. *yĕhallel°ēl* H3401, possibly "God shines forth" or "may God praise [the child]"). (1) A descendant of JUDAH (1 Chr. 4:16; KJV, "Jehaleleel"). His genealogical connection is unclear, but he may have been the eponymous ancestor of a clan related to CALEB son of Jephunneh (cf. v. 15).

(2) A descendant of LEVI through MERARI, and father of Azariah; the latter was one of the LEVITES assigned to consecrate the TEMPLE in the days of HEZEKIAH (2 Chr. 29:12; KJV, "Jehalelel").

Jehath. See JAHATH #2.

Jehdeiah. ji-dee´yah (Heb. *yeḥdĕyāhû* H3485, "Yahweh rejoices"). (1) Son or descendant of Shubael; he was a LEVITE who served in the time of King DAVID (1 Chr. 24:20).

(2) A MERONOTHITE who was in charge of David's donkeys (1 Chr. 27:30).

Jehezekel. See JEHEZKEL.

Jehezkel. ji-hez´kel (Heb. *yĕḥezqē°l* H3489, "God strengthens"). KJV Jehezekel. A priest who lived in the time of DAVID; he was head of the twentieth division (1 Chr. 24:16). The Hebrew form of this name is identical to that of Ezekiel.

Jehiah. ji-hi´uh (Heb. *yĕḥiyyâ* H3496, "Yahweh lives"). A LEVITE who, with OBED-EDOM, was appointed as a doorkeeper for the ARK OF THE COVENANT when DAVID had it brought to JERUSALEM (1 Chr. 15:24). He may be the same as JEIEL (v. 18).

Jehiel. ji-hi´uhl (Heb. *yĕḥî°ēl* H3493, "God lives"; also *yĕḥî°ēli* H3494 [gentilic in form]). (1) A LEVITE in the time of DAVID appointed among others to play the lyre (NRSV, harp) as a part of the ministrations before the ARK OF THE COVENANT (1 Chr. 15:18, 20; 16:5).

(2) Firstborn son of LADAN and descendant of LEVI through GERSHON; he was placed in charge of the TEMPLE treasury in the time of David (1 Chr. 23:8; 29:8; 26:21-22 ["Jehieli"; the Heb. text here is difficult]).

(3) Son of Hacmoni; he was an important official who took care of David's sons (1 Chr. 27:32).

(4) Son of JEHOSHAPHAT, king of Judah (1 Chr. 21:2). He and his brothers received a very generous inheritance (v. 3). Jehoshaphat's firstborn, JEHORAM, killed all his brothers when he became king (v. 4).

(5) Descendant of HEMAN the musician; he and his brother Shimei were among the Levites assigned to consecrate the temple in the days of HEZEKIAH (2 Chr. 29:14; NRSV, "Jehuel"). He is probably the same Jehiel included in the list of supervisors of the temple storerooms (31:13).

(6) One of three temple administrators during the reign of JOSIAH (2 Chr. 35:8); he is mentioned with Hilkiah and Zechariah as providing numerous offerings for the celebration of the Passover.

(7) Descendant of Joab and father of Obadiah; the latter was head of a large family who returned to Jerusalem from Babylon with EZRA (Ezra 8:9).

(8) Descendant of Elam and father of Shecaniah; the latter led a public confession concerning mixed marriages forbidden by the law (Ezra 10:2). This Jehiel is possibly the same one listed among the descendants of Elam who agreed to put away their foreign wives (10:26). If so, Shecaniah may have been the child of a mixed marriage, and thus he apparently supported the sending away of his own mother.

(9) One of the priestly descendants of Harim who agreed to put away their foreign wives (Ezra 10:21).

Jehieli. See JEHIEL #2.

Jehizkiah. jee´hiz-ki´uh (Heb. *yĕḥizqiyyāhû H3491*, "Yahweh strengthens [me]"). Son of Shallum; he was one of the princes of EPHRAIM who supported ODED the prophet in warning the Israelites not to take captives from JUDAH (2 Chr. 28:12).

Jehoadah. See JEHOADDAH.

Jehoaddah. ji-hoh´uh-duh (Heb. *yĕhô'addâ H3389*, possibly "Yahweh has adorned [me]"). KJV Jehoadah. Son of Ahaz and descendant of King SAUL through JONATHAN (1 Chr. 8:36; called Jarah or JADAH in the parallel passage, 9:42).

Jehoaddan. See JEHOADDIN.

Jehoaddin. ji-hoh´uh-din (Heb. *yĕhô'addîn H3390*, variant *yĕhô'addān H3391*, "Yahweh is delight"). KJV Jehoaddan. The mother of AMAZIAH, king of Judah; she is identified as being a native of Jerusalem (2 Ki. 14:2; 2 Chr. 25:1).

Jehoahaz. ji-hoh´uh-haz (Heb. *yĕhô'āḥāz H3370*, "Yahweh has taken hold [for protection]" or "whom Yahweh sustains," short form *yô'āḥāz H3407*). **(1)** Son of JEHU and king of ISRAEL (2 Ki. 10:35; 13:1-9; in 14:1, the NRSV has "Joahaz"). Jehoahaz became king in 814/3 B.C. (the twenty-third year of Joash of Judah) and reigned for seventeen years. His son Joash (JEHOASH) of Israel succeeded in the thirty-seventh year of Joash of Judah (13:10), and some therefore emend "seventeen" to "fifteen" in 13:1 or "thirty-seventh" to "thirty-ninth" in 13:10; others assume a shift in the reckoning system or suggest a three-year coregency of Jehu and Jehoahaz. When Jehoahaz ascended the throne, SYRIA (ARAM) controlled virtually the whole country, having penetrated down the coastal road, taken GATH, and extracted heavy tribute from Judah. Although Jehoahaz had no idea of abandoning the apostate cult of BETHEL ("the sins of Jeroboam") or removing the ASHERAH from SAMARIA (13:6, cf. 21:3), he did in desperation invoke the name of the Lord, and his prayer was answered in God's compassion for his people (13:4-5).

(2) Son of JOSIAH and king of JUDAH (2 Ki. 23:30-34; 2 Chr. 36:1-4). Also known as SHALLUM (prob. his personal name as opposed to his throne name,

1 Chr. 3:15; Jer. 22:11), Jehoahaz succeeded Josiah in the summer of 609 B.C., but he was deposed by Pharaoh NECO three months later. According to the biblical narrative, it was "the people of the land" (prob. country folk) who made him king, and this information suggests that Jehoahaz was not the natural successor (subsequently, his older brother Eliakim, renamed JEHOIAKIM, was placed on the throne by the Egyptians, 2 Ki. 23:36). If the people felt they had established their right to control the succession, the harsh realities of great power politics soon destroyed this hope. Returning that fall from his campaign in ASSYRIA, and aiming to secure his passage for the future, Neco installed Eliakim/Jehoiakim as his vassal and deported Jehoahaz to Egypt.

(3) Son of JEHORAM and king of Judah. See AHAZIAH #2.

(4) Father of JOAH; the latter was one of three officials who were sent to repair the temple in the time of Josiah (2 Chr. 34:8; rendered "Joahaz" in English versions).

Jehoash, Joash. ji-hoh´ash, joh´ash (Heb. *yĕhô'āš H3371*, short form *yô'āš H3409*, prob. "Yahweh has granted"). The short Hebrew form of this name is used for all eight individuals listed below. The longer form, which occurs only in 2 Kings (seventeen times), is used sometimes for both the son of AHAZIAH, king of Judah, and the son of JEHOAHAZ, king of Israel (note esp. 2 Ki. 14:13), but the NIV, in the interests of clarity, uses it only when referring to the king of Israel.

(1) Father of GIDEON and descendant of MANASSEH through ABIEZER (Jdg. 6:11, 29-31; 7:14; 8:13, 29, 32). Joash lived in OPHRAH, where both he and Gideon were buried. The angel of the Lord appeared to Gideon by an oak tree that belonged to Joash. Later, when the men of the town wanted to kill Gideon for breaking down the altar of BAAL and the ASHERAH pole, his father came to his defense.

(2) Son of SHELA and grandson of JUDAH; he and one (or more) of his brothers are said to have "ruled in" (or "married into") MOAB and JASHUBI LEHEM (1 Chr. 4:22). Some scholars believe that the words "and Jashubi Lehem" should be emended to either "but returned to Lehem" (so NRSV) or "and they resided in Bethlehem."

J

(3) Son of BEKER and grandson of BENJAMIN (2 Chr. 7:8).

(4) Son of Shemaah of GIBEAH; he and his brother AHIEZER are listed among the warriors, kinsmen of SAUL, who joined with DAVID when the latter took refuge at ZIKLAG (1 Chr. 12:3; cf. v. 1).

(5) An official under David who was in charge of the supplies of olive oil (1 Chr. 27:28).

(6) Son of AHAB king of Israel; he and the governor of SAMARIA were charged with the custody of the prophet MICAIAH (1 Ki. 22:26; 2 Chr. 18:25); it is however likely that the phrase "the king's son" refers to a minor royal official with police duties.

(7) Son of AHAZIAH and ninth king of JUDAH (2 Ki. 11:1—12:21; 2 Chr. 22:10—24:27). As an infant, Joash was saved from the massacre of the royal family, which ATHALIAH perpetrated on the death of her son Ahaziah. He owed his life to the courage and devotion of his aunt JEHOSHEBA, the wife of the priest JEHOIADA, who conveyed him away, concealed him, and brought him up in their own home (2 Ki. 11:1-3). When Joash was seven years old, Jehoiada took him to the temple court and crowned him before a congregation of Levites, temple guards, and elders and people from the country towns. As he was acclaimed king, his grandmother Athaliah appeared in the court and was swiftly removed to her death. With due ceremony Jehoiada inaugurated a fresh covenant of kingship, acknowledging the Lord's dominion; and the temple of BAAL was destroyed by the crowd (11:4-20). The reign of Joash probably lasted forty years from 835 to 796 B.C. (some put the death of Joash in the year 800). The reign was not very distinguished, and it ended miserably; for after Jehoiada's death, Joash was persuaded to allow the revival of pagan worship, which led to much opposition from the prophets. In the end, he was responsible for the martyrdom of ZECHARIAH son of Jehoiada; and at the end of the year, after a disastrous raid by HAZAEL of ARAM in which Joash was badly wounded and lost many of his leading men, he was assassinated by two of his servants (2 Ki. 12:20-21; 2 Chr. 24:17-27).

(8) Son of JEHOAHAZ and twelfth (thirteenth, if TIBNI is counted) king of ISRAEL (2 Ki. 13:10-25; 14:8-16; 2 Chr. 25:17-24). To distinguish him from Joash son of Ahaziah, king of Judah, this king of Israel is often referred to by his alternate name, Jehoash (cf. NIV); that practice will be followed in this article. Jehoash was the third king in the line of JEHU; he reigned sixteen years, from the thirty-seventh of Joash of Judah to the fifteenth of AMAZIAH (2 Ki. 13:10; 14:23). The dates are probably 798 to 782 B.C. Jehoash inflicted three defeats on BEN-HADAD III that marked the beginning of Israel's political revival. The story is preserved of how this event was prophesied by ELISHA as he lay dying (13:14-25). In 2 Ki. 14:8-14 is recorded the defeat of Amaziah by Jehoash at BETH SHEMESH, after which Jehoash destroyed part of the wall of Jerusalem, looted the temple, and took hostages. Nothing is said about Jehoash subsequent to this event.

Jehohanan. jee´hoh-hay´nuhn (Heb. *yĕhôḥānān H3380*, "Yahweh is gracious"). **(1)** Sixth son of Meshelemiah and descendant of KORAH; like his father, he and his brothers were Levitical gatekeepers in the time of DAVID (1 Chr. 26:3).

(2) A commander of units of one thousand in the army of JUDAH during the reign of JEHOSHAPHAT (2 Chr. 17:15).

(3) Father of Ishmael; the latter was one of the commanders of units of one hundred upon whom JEHOIADA relied in his planning to move against ATHALIAH (2 Chr. 23:1).

(4) Father of Azariah; the latter was a leader in the tribe of EPHRAIM during the reign of PEKAH king of Israel (2 Chr. 28:12; KJV and NRSV, "Johanan").

(5) Son of Eliashib; he provided a room for EZRA's mourning (Ezra 10:6; KJV, "Johanan"). The identification of this Jehohanan is disputed because of disagreements regarding the date of Ezra's mission (cf. JOHANAN in Neh. 12:22-23).

(6) One of the descendants of Bebai who agreed to put away their foreign wives (Ezra 10:28).

(7) Son of TOBIAH, who was an opponent of NEHEMIAH; Jehohanan married the daughter of Meshullam son of Berekiah (Neh. 6:18; KJV, "Johanan").

(8) Head of the priestly family of Amariah during the time of JOIAKIM the high priest (Neh. 12:13).

(9) One of the singers who participated in the purification and dedication of the wall of Jerusalem (Neh. 12:42).

Jehoiachin. ji-hoi´uh-kin (Heb. *yĕhôyākîn H3382*, short form *yôyākîn H3422* [only Ezek. 1:2], "Yahweh establishes [*or* protects]"). Son of JEHOIAKIM and last king of JUDAH before the EXILE (597 B.C.). Also known as JECONIAH and CONIAH, he reigned in JERUSALEM three months and ten days (2 Chr. 36:9). Jehoiachin was born to Jehoiakim and his wife NEHUSHTA during the reign of the godly JOSIAH, his grandfather. According to 2 Ki. 24:8, he was eighteen when he came to the throne, but 2 Chr. 36:9 (see NIV mg.) gives his age as eight. Probably an early scribe made a mistake of ten years in copying one of these two books. The evidence favors eighteen, for 2 Ki. 24:15 speaks of his wives, and he would hardly have been married at eight years of age. Jehoiakim displayed his contempt for the Word of God by cutting up and burning the prophecies of JEREMIAH (Jer. 36:23, 32), thereby adding to the curses that the Lord pronounced on Jerusalem.

In Ezek. 19:5-9, Jehoiachin is characterized as "a strong lion. He learned to tear the prey and he devoured men." The prophet announced that the "strong lion" would be taken to BABYLON, and this prediction was literally fulfilled later. Although Jeremiah was prophesying with mighty power all through the youth of Jehoiachin, the influences of the palace were stronger than those of the prophet. Jehoiakim had been rapacious, violent, and oppressive. He had "the burial of a donkey—dragged away and thrown outside the gates of Jerusalem" (Jer. 22:18-19). In these sad conditions and under the threatening shadow of Nebuchadnezzar, Jehoiachin became king; and in his three months of power "he did evil in the eyes of the LORD, just as his father had done" (2 Ki. 24:9). "In the spring King Nebuchadnezzar sent for him and brought him to Babylon" (2 Chr. 36:10), where he remained a captive the rest of his life, though apparently not under extremely hard conditions. NEBUCHADNEZZAR died in 561 B.C., and his son EVIL-MERODACH, who succeeded almost immediately, took Jehoiachin from prison and "spoke kindly to him and gave him a seat of honor higher than those of the other kings who were with him in Babylon. So Jehoiachin put aside his prison clothes," and after thirty-seven years of captivity was given a daily allowance of food the rest of his life (2 Ki. 25:27-30).

© Dr. James C. Martin. The British Museum. Photographed by permission.

The Babylonian Chronicle recounts historical events during the years 605-595 B.C., including Nebuchadnezzar's capture of Jerusalem while Jehoiachin was king.

Jehoiada. ji-hoi´uh-duh (Heb. *yĕhôyādā‹ H3381*, "Yahweh has known [*i.e.*, has been concerned]"). **(1)** Father of BENAIAH, who was a commander of DAVID's bodyguard (2 Sam. 8:18; 20:23; 23:20-22; 1 Ki. 1:8; et al.); once he is referred to as a priest (1 Chr. 27:5). See also #2 below.

(2) An Aaronite leader who joined David at HEBRON (1 Chr. 12:27). He is probably the same as #1 above.

(3) Son of a certain Benaiah and successor of AHITHOPHEL as David's counselor (1 Chr. 27:34). It has been suggested that "Jehoiada son of Benaiah" here should be emended to "Benaiah son of Jehoiada" and that therefore this Jehoiada is the same as #1 above.

(4) A very influential high priest in Jerusalem who organized the coup that ousted ATHALIAH and set Joash (JEHOASH) on the throne; he was for many years the young king's trusted adviser (2 Ki. 11-12; 2 Chr. 23-24). Jehoiada already had adult children when Athaliah massacred the royal family (2 Chr. 23:11), but his wife JEHOSHEBA, daughter

J

of King JEHORAM, must have been relatively young. Some six years after Jehosheba had rescued her infant nephew Joash from the massacre, Jehoiada ventured all when he appealed to popular loyalty to the House of David. First he secured the support of the mercenaries (CARITES), who were assigned as temple and palace guards (2 Ki. 11:4-8). The Chronicler adds that he enlisted the chiefs of the towns where the Levites resided; this tallies with references to "the people of the land" (vv. 14, 20). Upon the king's coronation, their rejoicing drew the attention of Athaliah; but Jehoiada was ready, and her death ended all opposition. Jehoiada followed up the coronation with a covenant of religious restoration in which "the people" took part (vv. 16-17; not the country folk as such, but the congregation, as representing all Judah). Jehoiada continued to guide Joash, though age doubtless weakened his administrative ability (2 Chr. 24:4-7). He was honored with a royal burial; but the nobility soon rebelled against his strict religious tradition (vv. 17-18).

(5) A priest during the time of JEREMIAH; Shemaiah the Nehelamite replaced him as chief officer of the temple with a certain Zephaniah so that the latter might arrest Jeremiah (Jer. 29:26). Some have argued, without good reason, that this Jehoiada is the same as #4 above.

(6) KJV alternate form of JOIADA (Neh. 3:6).

(7) NRSV alternate form of JOIADA (Neh. 13:28).

Jehoiakim. ji-hoi'uh-kim (Heb. *yĕhôyāqîm H3383*, "Yahweh raises up"). Throne name of ELIAKIM, son of JOSIAH, appointed king of JUDAH by Pharaoh NECO. In 607 B.C., Neco marched northward, intending to fight the king of ASSYRIA at the EUPHRATES River. Josiah imprudently intercepted him and was mortally wounded at MEGIDDO near Mount CARMEL. The people of Judah passed by Eliakim and made his youngest brother Shallum, that is, JEHOAHAZ, king after Josiah (1 Chr. 3:15; 2 Chr. 36:1). Jehoahaz reigned for three months in Jerusalem, when Neco in displeasure "put him in chains at Riblah" in the N of SYRIA, then sent him to Egypt, where he died (2 Ki. 23:33-34). The king of Egypt next took Eliakim, elder half-brother of Jehoahaz, changed his name to Jehoiakim, put the land under heavy tribute, and made Jehoiakim king over Jerusalem, where he reigned from 607

© Dr. James C. Martin. The Israel Museum, Jerusalem. Photographed by permission.

Seal of Gemaryahu son of Shaphan (c. 600 B.C.), possibly a scribe who functioned in the court of King Jehoiakim. (The top image is an enlarged reproduction.)

to 597. Jehoiakim was an oppressive and thoroughly godless king (2 Ki. 23:36—24:6; 2 Chr. 36:4-8; cf. Jer. 22-36).

The prophecies of Jer. 22:1-23 were uttered (if all at one time) soon after the death of Josiah and the taking away of Jehoahaz (22:10-12). They describe the wrongdoing and oppression by Jehoiakim (22:13-23). The prophet wrote about the dooms of Judah and the other nations at the direction of the Lord. When the princes heard these words, they let Jeremiah and his clerk BARUCH hide themselves; then when the king heard the words of the book, he cut out the passages that displeased him and burned them, with the result that the book of Jeremiah was rewritten and enlarged (ch. 36). Jehoiakim died in disgrace and had "the burial of a donkey" (22:19).

Jehoiarib. ji-hoi'uh-rib (Heb. *yĕhôyārîb H3384*, "Yahweh contends [for me]"). (1) A priest who received the first lot of the twenty-four divisions in David's time (1 Chr. 24:7). He was possibly the ancestor of #2 below.

(2) One of six priests (prob. family heads) who resettled in Jerusalem after the exile (1 Chr. 9:10). He is usually identified with a Joiarib mentioned three times in Nehemiah's lists (Neh. 11:10; 12:6, 19).

Jehonadab. See Jonadab.

Jehonathan. ji-hon´uh-thuh (Heb. *yĕhônātān* H3387, "Yahweh has given [a child]"). **(1)** Son of Uzziah; an official in the time of David who was in charge of storehouses (1 Chr. 27:25 KJV; modern versions render the name Jonathan).

(2) One of six Levites whom King Jehoshaphat sent to teach the law in the cities of Judah (2 Chr. 17:8). Appointed to the same mission were a number of princes and priests.

(3) The head of the priestly family of Shemaiah in the days when Joiakim son of Jeshua was high priest (Neh. 12:18).

Jehoram. ji-hoh´ruhm (Heb. *yĕhôrām* H3393, short form *yôrām* H3456, "Yahweh is exalted"). **(1)** One of six Levites whom King Jehoshaphat sent to teach the law in the cities of Judah (2 Chr. 17:8). Appointed to the same mission were a number of princes and priests.

(2) Son of Ahab and ninth king of the northern kingdom of Israel; mainly called Joram (2 Ki. 1:17; 3:1-13; 8:16; 9:15-24; 2 Chr. 22:5-7). The NIV consistently uses Joram to distinguish him from the son of Jehoshaphat (see #3 below), and that practice will be followed in this article. A number of stories in connection with the marvelous deeds of Elijah and Elisha refer to "the king" of Israel without mentioning his name, and it is uncertain just how many of those in which "the king" figures in some way are related to King Joram of Israel. Elijah must have survived at least until the sixth year of his reign (cf. 2 Chr. 21:12), and the many exploits of Elisha detailed in 2 Ki. 3-9 likely took place during Joram's reign (c. 852-841 B.C.). Throughout his reign the two Jewish kingdoms were allied. Upon his accession, almost at once he was joined by Judah (under Jehoshaphat) and Edom (tributary to Judah) in a war against the Moabites in an effort to recover the submission of Moab under its King Mesha. The combined expedition came to near disaster from want of water near the frontier of Edom and Moab. It was Jehoshaphat's truly pious reliance on genuine prophecy that saved them all, for Elisha was brought forward from the ranks, and through his function as prophet a life-saving miracle brought both water and military victory (3:4-27). This alliance ended with the destruction of the house of Ahab by Joram's successor, Jehu. After that, enmity between the two Hebrew kingdoms was renewed.

Though a venal and weak man, Joram was not without some good, for he at least diminished Baal worship early in his reign (2 Ki. 3:2). On occasion he gave heed to Elisha's wise and frequently friendly advice (6:20-23; 3:13). Yet when the Aramean raids diminished he seems to have begun to resent Elisha's advice and admonition (6:23) and quickly relapsed to worse idolatry. Divine judgment in the form of siege and famine were not slow to follow (6:24-25). It was at this juncture that Joram (for he is surely "the king" here), in despair, sought to kill Elisha (6:31-32). Joram was the last king of the line of Omri. His mother Jezebel and he both were killed by the rampaging Jehu, who also exterminated all members of the family and all officials of the Baal cult (chs. 9-10).

(3) Son of Jehoshaphat and fifth king of the southern kingdom of Judah; sometimes called Joram (c. 848-841 B.C., but previously regent, 853-848). Scripture portions relating to this man are chiefly an entire chapter in Chronicles (2 Chr. 21), but only four verses in Kings (2 Ki. 8:16-19). The latter passage gives an important picture of the relations familial and diplomatic between the two Jehorams: "In the fifth year of Joram son of Ahab king of Israel, when Jehoshaphat was king of Judah, Jehoram son of Jehoshaphat began his reign as king of Judah. He was thirty-two years old when he became king, and he reigned in Jerusalem eight years. He walked in the ways of the kings of Israel, as the house of Ahab had done, for he married a daughter of Ahab. He did evil in the eyes of the Lord." Except for a few months when his son Ahaziah reigned after him, Jehoram's reign corresponds with the last eight years of the reign of the northern Joram. His life and reign make up one of the saddest and most to be regretted pages of the history of the Davidic dynasty.

Jehoram's personal and domestic life were tragically wrong. His wife, ATHALIAH, brought with her the corruption of the Baalism (fertility cult religion) of her mother's Phoenician ancestors. As a result, Jehoram "walked in the ways of the kings of Israel, as the house of Ahab had done, for he married a daughter of Ahab" (2 Chr. 21:6). Soon after ascending the throne, Jehoram assassinated his six brothers and other "princes of Israel" (21:4). The direct line of the reigning family was in consequence reduced during his reign to one male descendant (AHAZIAH, 21:16-17). Everything recorded of this man indicates complete religious and moral APOSTASY, even worse than that of the Baal-worshiping heathen of his time. Chastening followed. There was first a revolt of Edom, which since David's time had been under tributary kings with only brief interruptions (2 Ki. 8:20; cf. 2 Sam. 8:14; 1 Ki. 11:14-16). Then a southwestern area with a center at LIBNAH also successfully revolted (2 Ki. 8:22). Further chastening came through successful inroads by rampaging Philistines and Arabs (2 Chr. 21:16-17). Not for generations was there significant recovery of this lost ground. The climax of these judgments to Jehoram himself was the particularly horrible manner in which he died (21:15, "disease of your bowels, until your bowels come out") after living to see God's judgment on all his sons save one, loss of his harem and all his goods.

Jehoshabeath. See JEHOSHEBA.

Jehoshaphat. ji-hosh´uh-fat (Heb. *yĕhôšāpāṭ* H3398, "Yahweh has judged"; Gk. *Iōsaphat* G2734). **(1)** Son of Ahilud and recorder in the time of DAVID and SOLOMON (2 Sam. 8:16; 20:24; 1 Ki. 4:3).

(2) One of the priests appointed to blow the trumpet when David transferred the ARK OF THE COVENANT to Jerusalem (1 Chr. 15:24 KJV; modern versions render the name JOSHAPHAT).

(3) Son of Paruah; he was one of twelve district governors of SOLOMON commissioned to supply provisions for the royal household (1 Ki. 4:17).

(4) Father of King JEHU of Samaria (2 Ki. 9:2, 14).

(5) Son of ASA and fourth king of the southern kingdom of JUDAH (1 Ki. 22; 2 Chr. 17-20;

included in Matthew's GENEALOGY OF JESUS CHRIST, Matt. 1:8 [KJV, "Josaphat"]). Jehoshaphat reigned for twenty-five years, including five years of rule with his father. He began to reign about 873 B.C. His mother was Azubah, the daughter of Shilhi. Jehoshaphat was the second of the five kings of Judah who were outstanding for godliness, the later ones being Joash (JEHOASH), HEZEKIAH, and JOSIAH. He took away the HIGH PLACES and ASHERAH poles from Judah (2 Chr. 17:6), though he apparently was not able to keep the people from using certain high places in worshiping the Lord (1 Ki. 22:43). One of the first men to sense the importance of religious education for the people, he sent out in the third year of his reign princes and PRIESTS and LEVITES to teach the people the LAW of the Lord. They went throughout the cities of Judah in doing this work (2 Chr. 17:7-9). Because of Jehoshaphat's godliness, "the fear of the LORD" fell on the surrounding nations, and even the Philistines and the Arabs brought him tribute. With all this godliness, he seems, however, to have been lacking in spiritual discernment, for he made the great and almost fatal mistake of associating with the wicked King Ahab of the northern kingdom; so much so that his son JEHORAM married ATHALIAH, who was as wicked as her mother JEZEBEL.

Ahab made a great show of hospitality to Jehoshaphat during a visit to SAMARIA and then asked him if he would be his ally in a campaign to recover RAMOTH GILEAD. Jehoshaphat suggested that they first determine the will of God. Ahab agreed and asked his prophets for their advice, and they all prophesied good success for the venture. Jehoshaphat was not satisfied and asked if there were not a real prophet of the Lord present. They sent for MICAIAH, a man of God, whom Ahab hated. He told them the truth, that God had put a spirit of delusion in the minds of all the prophets, so that Ahab might be doomed. Ahab partly believed this and arranged a trick, pretending to give Jehoshaphat the glory, but Ahab was killed. Jehoshaphat died at the age of sixty, about the year 849 B.C. His son Jehoram succeeded to the throne.

Jehoshaphat, Valley of. A valley adjacent to the city of JERUSALEM and regarded as the place of the judging of the nations (Joel 3:2, 12); it is

Looking N through the Kidron Valley, thought by many to be the same as the Valley of Jehoshaphat.

also referred to as the "valley of decision" (3:14; cf. Zech. 14:1-5). Early tradition usually identified it as the Valley of the KIDRON (the portion just E of the city), although an alternate view was the Valley of HINNOM. Some believe that JOEL was speaking of an ideal spot only; there is no clear evidence that any valley ever actually bore this name.

Jehosheba. ji-hosh′uh-buh (Heb. *yĕhôšeba*ʿ *H3394*, variant *yĕhôšabʿat H3395*, "Yahweh is abundance"). The daughter of King JEHORAM (Joram) of Judah (2 Ki. 11:2) and wife of JEHOIADA, the high priest (2 Chr. 22:11; KJV, NRSV, "Jehoshabeath"). When her brother AHAZIAH and most of the rest of the royal family were about to be murdered, she took Ahaziah's son Joash (JEHOASH), who was kept hidden for six years, until he could be made king.

Jehoshua, Jehoshuah. See JOSHUA.

Jehovah. ji-hoh′vuh. Traditional English rendering of the Tetragrammaton or divine name, *Yahweh* (Heb. *yhwh H3378*; Exod. 6:3 et al., KJV). Because Jewish tradition does not allow the pronunciation of this name, in public reading it is regularly substituted with *Adonay*, "my Lord" (ʾ*ădōnāy* from ʾ*ādôn H123*). To indicate such a reading, Hebrew copies of the Bible preserve the consonants of *Yahweh*, but

insert the vowels of *Adonay* (thus, *yĕhōwâ*, the first vowel being a short sound pronounced *ĕ*, roughly equivalent to *ă*); according to some, the inserted vowels come from Aram. *šĕmā*ʾ, "the Name" (partly on the grounds that in some MSS the Tetragrammaton is pointed simply *yĕhwâ*, that is, without the *o* vowel). This practice in the writing of the divine name misled translators (not only in English) to create the hybrid form *Jehovah*, which never existed in Hebrew. Most versions render the name with small caps as "the LORD."

According to Exod. 6:2-3, the name YHWH had not been used prior to MOSES as a meaningful understanding of the divine nature. When the PATRIARCHS used the name, it was simply as a label and had not yet become a revelation of the nature of God. This is, in fact, an accurate statement of what we find in Genesis. For example, in Gen. 17:1 Yahweh appeared to Abram (ABRAHAM), but the revelation vouchsafed was not "I am Yahweh" but "I am El Shaddai." We must return to Exod. 3:13-15 for the moment when the theological significance of Yahweh was opened to Moses. We notice the following: (1) The name is evidently related to the Hebrew verb "to be"; and it must be pointed out that while this verb can mean "to exist," its characteristic force is "to be actually present," "to be a present reality." (2) The form Yahweh, as a part of

J

the verb "to be," could be translated either "I am actively present" or "I make to be actively present." Thus "I am who I am" means either "I am actively present as and when I choose" or "I bring to pass whatever I choose."

In context Moses is made alert to the active presence of Yahweh in the coming events (the Passover REDEMPTION and the EXODUS) or to the fact that as sovereign God he is bringing these events to pass by his own determination, volition, and power. Thus, in his very nature (as summed up in his name), the Lord identifies himself with redemption, the blood of the lamb, and the choosing out of his people for himself. It is important to note, though, that Moses is not left simply to watch unfolding events and make the best interpretation of them that he can. Exodus 3-4 and 6:1-8 show that Yahweh is a God who speaks before he is a God who acts. Moses is made wise before the events, so that when they happen, they are a confirmation of the word that has preceded them, thus making the REVELATION of God doubly certain. Yahweh is thus, fundamentally, the Covenant-Redeemer, the God who brought his people out of Egypt (20:2).

Jehovah-jireh. ji-hoh´vuh-ji´ruh (Heb. *yhwh yir>ĕh*, the latter word being impf. of *rā>āh H8011*, "to see, consider, be concerned about"). The name ABRAHAM gave the place on Mount MORIAH where God substituted a ram for his son ISAAC (Gen. 22:14 KJV; NIV, "The LORD Will Provide"). Evidently, by the time of the Mosaic record, the statement had become a current proverb.

Jehovah-nissi. ji-hoh´vuh-nis´i (Heb. *yhwh nissî*, "Yahweh is my banner"). The name given the altar erected by MOSES to commemorate the defeat of the AMALEKITES in the wilderness at REPHIDIM at the hands of Israel under the leadership of JOSHUA (Exod. 17:15 KJV; NIV, "The LORD is my Banner"). The name revealed Israel's assurance that God was the One who gave them the victory and that he was the One around whom they in the future were to rally as a standard.

Jehovah-shalom. ji-hoh´vuh-shah´lohm (Heb. *yhwh šālôm*, "Yahweh is peace"). The name GIDEON gave the altar he constructed in OPHRAH to com-

memorate the visit of the ANGEL of the Lord, who assured Gideon that he would not die as a result of seeing an angel, and commissioned him to liberate Israel from the Midianites (Jdg. 6:23-24 KJV; NIV, "The LORD is Peace").

Jehovah-shammah. ji-hoh´vuh-sham´uh (Heb. *ywhw šāmmâ*, "Yahweh is there"). The name to be given the restored and beautified JERUSALEM of the MESSIAH's kingdom (Ezek. 48:35 KJV mg.). The Lord had departed from his temple and city (ch. 11); he is to return to Jerusalem (ch. 43) and remain in favor and glory among his redeemed people forever. God's name is inseparably linked with his chosen city, the place of his abode. Compare the parallel in Rev. 21.

Jehovah-tsidkenu. ji-hoh´vuh-tsid-ken´*oo* (Heb. *yhwh ṣidqqnû*, "Yahweh is our righteousness"). This name is employed, by JEREMIAH alone, in a twofold way. It is the designation of the future Davidic king, who will rule over restored Israel (Jer. 23:6 KJV mg.). RIGHTEOUSNESS is a divine attribute of the MESSIAH in providing salvation; the implication appears to be that his righteousness becomes ours (cf. the notion of imputed righteousness, 1 Cor. 1:30; 2 Cor. 5:21). In the second reference (Jer. 33:16 KJV mg.), the prophet is pointing to the capital of the king, which partakes of the nature of the righteous monarch.

Jehozabad. ji-hoh´zuh-bad (Heb. *yĕhôzābād H3379*, "Yahweh has granted"). **(1)** Son of Shomer; he was an official who, with JOZABAD (NRSV, "Jozacar," following many Heb. MSS) son of Shimeath, murdered King Joash (JEHOASH) of Judah at BETH MILLO (2 Ki. 12:21). The parallel passage identifies the officials as "Zabad, son of Shimeath an Ammonite woman, and Jehozabad, son of Shimrith a Moabite woman" (2 Chr. 24:26). Some consider Shimrith a variant form of Shomer (cf. NIV mg.); others speculate that Shomer was Shimrith's father.

(2) Son of OBED-EDOM, included in the list of divisions of the Korahite doorkeepers in the reign of DAVID (1 Chr. 26:4).

(3) A commander of units of one thousand in the army of Judah during the reign of JEHOSHAPHAT (2 Chr. 17:18).

Jehozadak. ji-hoh´zuh-dak (Heb. *yĕhôṣādāq H3392*, short form *yôṣādāq H3449* "Yahweh has been righteous"). Son of Seraiah and descendant of AARON through ELEAZAR; apparently the last high priest prior to the destruction of the temple, he was among those deported to BABYLON by NEBUCHADNEZZAR (1 Chr. 6:14-15). He is known primarily for being the father of Joshua (JESHUA) the high priest (Hag. 1:1, 12, 14; 2:2, 4; Zech. 6:11; KJV, "Josedech"). In Ezra-Nehemiah the name is shortened to Jozadak (Ezra 3:2, 8; 5:2; 10:18; Neh. 12:26);

Jehu. jee´hyoo, jay´hoo (Heb. *yēhû* H3369, "Yahweh is he" [i.e., he is the true God]). **(1)** Son of Obed and descendant of JERAHMEEL, included in the genealogy of JUDAH (1 Chr. 2:38).

(2) Son of Joshibiah, listed among clan leaders in the tribe of SIMEON whose families increased greatly during the days of King HEZEKIAH and who dispossessed the Hamites and Meunites near GEDOR (1 Chr. 4:36; cf. vv. 38-41).

(3) A man from ANATHOTH, listed among the warriors, kinsmen of SAUL, who joined with DAVID when the latter took refuge at ZIKLAG (1 Chr. 12:3).

(4) Son of HANANI; he was a prophet who warned King BAASHA (c. 909-886 B.C.) that he would be judged for following the heretical cult instituted by JEROBOAM (1 Ki. 16:1-4, 7). Much later (c. 853), Jehu had to rebuke King JEHOSHAPHAT for allying himself with AHAB in an attempt to recover RAMOTH GILEAD from the ARAMEANS (2 Chr. 19:2, where he is called "the seer"). Jehu wrote annals on the reign of Jehoshaphat that were incorporated in "the book of the kings of Israel" (1 Chr. 20:34).

(5) Tenth king of ISRAEL and founder of its fourth dynasty. Son of Jehoshaphat, but more often called "son of Nimshi," perhaps because Nimshi, his grandfather, was better known than Jehoshaphat. Jehu appears first as a soldier in the service of King AHAB (2 Ki. 9:25). Ahab and JEZEBEL were rejected for their crimes. God commanded ELIJAH to anoint Jehu king over Israel, a command that ELISHA fulfilled. He sent a young prophet to RAMOTH GILEAD, where Jehu was with his army, to carry out the command. Jehu was commissioned to conquer the house of Ahab. When Jehu told his fellow officers that he had been so anointed, they proclaimed him

king. Jehu sealed the city so that the news should not precede him, then he crossed the JORDAN and drove impetuously as was his custom (9:20) to JEZREEL, where King Joram (JEHORAM) of Israel had gone after being wounded in battle with HAZAEL of SYRIA. Jehu denounced Joram, killed him, and had his body thrown into the field of NABOTH (9:24-26); then he caused AHAZIAH king of JUDAH to be killed, and his servants carried him up to JERUSALEM for burial. He also killed Jezebel and would have had her buried, but the dogs had eaten her. He executed God's judgments on the house of Ahab and thoroughly exterminated the worship of

The famous Black Obelisk of Shalmaneser III (859-824 B.C.). This register shows King Jehu prostrate as he brings tribute to the Assyrian king.

© Dr. James C. Martin. The British Museum. Photographed by permission.

BAAL, killing all its devotees who gathered together in response to Jehu's pretended interest in worshiping Baal with them; but he did not depart from the sins of JEROBOAM. Jehu reigned in SAMARIA twenty-eight years (c. 841-814 B.C.). Because of his zeal for the Lord in the matter of Ahab's house, God allowed him to set up a dynasty that lasted just over one hundred years (Jehu, Jehoahaz, Joram, and Jeroboam II).

Jehubbah. See HUBBAH.

Jehucal. ji-hyoo´kuhl (Heb. *yĕhûkal H3385*, short form *yûkal H3426*, "Yahweh has been powerful"). TNIV Jehukal. Son of Shelemiah; he and a priest were sent by King ZEDEKIAH to JEREMIAH to ask the prophet to pray for him and the people (Jer. 37:3). He was also one of four officials who told the king to kill Jeremiah for predicting the fall of JERUSALEM (38:1; KJV and other versions, "Jucal").

J

Jehud. jee´huhd (Heb. *yĕhûd H3372*; in Heb. inscriptions and in Aram., this form corresponds to *yĕhûdâ H3373*; see JUDAH). One of the towns originally allotted to the tribe of DAN (Josh. 19:45; the Danites were unable to occupy the territory, v. 47). Mentioned between BAALATH and BENE BERAK (19:45), Jehud is identified with modern el-Yahudiyeh, 8.5 mi. (13.5 km.) ESE of JOPPAH.

Jehudi. ji-hyoo´di (Heb. *yĕhûdi H3375*, "of Judah," "Jewish"). Son of Nethaniah; an officer, probably a scribe, of King JEHOIAKIM who was sent to BARUCH so that the latter might read the prophecies of JEREMIAH to the princes of Judah, and who himself afterward read them to the king (Jer. 36:14, 21, 23). His great-grandfather's name is given as CUSHI. The tracing of Jehudi's lineage to the third generation suggests the importance of his family and thus the significance of his task.

Jehudijah. jee´huh-di´juh. KJV rendering of *yĕhudiyyâ* (fem. of *yĕhûdi H3374*, "Judean, Judahite") with reference to a wife of MERED (1 Chr. 4:18). Modern versions more accurately translate "his Judean wife" (cf. KJV mg., "the Jewess"); the word is probably used to distinguish the woman from BITHIAH, an Egyptian also mentioned in this verse.

Jehuel. See JEHIEL #5.

Jehukal. ji-hyoo´kuhl. TNIV form of JEHUCAL.

Jehush. See JEUSH #3.

Jeiel. ji-i´uhl (Heb. *yĕ⁽i⁾ēl H3599*, variant *yĕ⁽û⁾ēl H3590*, possibly "God is strong"). (1) A clan chief from the tribe of REUBEN (1 Chr. 5:7). His genealogical connection as well as the period in which he lived are unclear.

(2) Descendant of BENJAMIN, "father" (i.e., founder or leader) of GIBEON, and ancestor of King SAUL (1 Chr. 9:35; the name is missing in 8:29 MT, but NIV and NRSV insert it on the basis of some Gk. MSS). Many identify Jeiel with ABIEL.

(3) A LEVITE in the time of DAVID appointed among others to play the lyre (NRSV, harp) as a part of the ministrations before the ARK OF THE COVENANT (1 Chr. 15:18, 21; 16:5; the latter passage mentions Jeiel twice, but the first occurrence should probably be emended to JAAZIEL).

(4) Son of Hotham the Aroerite (see AROER); he and his brother Shama are included among DAVID's mighty warriors (1 Chr. 11:44).

(5) Son of Mattaniah, descendant of LEVI through ASAPH, and ancestor of a certain JAHAZIEL who prophesied in aid of King JEHOSHAPHAT just before the famous victory of BERACAH (2 Chr. 20:14).

(6) An official who held the office of secretary under King UZZIAH (2 Chr. 26:11).

(7) A Levite, descendant of ELIZAPHAN, who served during the reign of HEZEKIAH (2 Chr. 29:13; NRSV has JEUEL).

(8) A leader of the Levites in the reign of JOSIAH who gave liberally toward the sacrifices (2 Chr. 35:9).

(9) One of the descendants of Nebo who agreed to put away their foreign wives (Ezra 10:43).

(10) One of the descendants of Adonikam who returned with EZRA from BABYLON (Ezra 8:13 KJV [most other versions have "Jeuel," following the Bomberg ed.]).

Jekabzeel. See KABZEEL.

Jekameam. jek´uh-mee´uhm (Heb. *yĕqam⁽ām H3694*, possibly "the Kinsman [*i.e.*, ancestral god] establishes"). Son of HEBRON, grandson of KOHATH, and great-grandson of LEVI (1 Chr. 23:19; 24:23).

Jekamiah. jek´uh-mi´uh (Heb. *yĕqamyâ H3693*, "Yahweh establishes"). (1) Son of Shallum and descendant of JUDAH through JERAHMEEL (1 Chr. 2:41).

(2) Son of JEHOIACHIN, last king of Judah (1 Chr. 3:18; KJV "Jecamiah"); he was apparently born after the royal family was led away into EXILE in Babylon.

Jekoliah. jek´uh-li´uh. TNIV form of JECOLIAH.

Jekuthiel. ji-kyoo´thee-uhl (Heb. *yĕqûti⁽ēl H3688*, "God nourishes"). Son of MERED by his Judean wife; included in the genealogy of JUDAH (1 Chr. 4:18).

Jemima. See JEMIMAH.

Jemimah. je-mi′muh (Heb. *yĕmîmâ H3544*, possibly "dove"). KJV Jemima. The first daughter of JOB born to him after his fortunes were restored (Job 42:14).

Jemuel. jem′yoo-uhl (Heb. *yĕmû′ēl H3543*, derivation uncertain). First son of SIMEON and grandson of JACOB (Gen. 46:10; Exod. 6:15); called NEMUEL in the parallel passages (Num. 26:12; 1 Chr. 4:24).

Jephthae. jef′thee. KJV NT form of JEPHTHAH (Heb. 11:32).

Jephthah. jef′thuh (Heb. *yiptāḥ H3653*, "[God] opens [the womb?]" or "[God] frees"; Gk. *Iephthae G2650*). KJV NT Jephthae. A Gileadite warrior who as a judge delivered ISRAEL from the Ammonites (see AMMON), sacrificed his daughter to fulfill his vow to God, and defeated the Ephraimites (Jdg. 11:1—12:7). He was the son of a certain Gilead and of a woman who was a prostitute. Because of his illegitimacy, his brothers born in wedlock drove him from the paternal home and refused him any share in the inheritance. Their action was confirmed by the elders of the territory of GILEAD. He fled to the land of TOB, probably a region in the HAURAN. There he made a name for himself by his prowess and gathered about him a band of men without employment. He must not be thought of as just a captain of a band of freebooters, for he was a God-fearing man, with a high sense of justice and of the sacredness of vows made to God.

At the time of Jephthah's expulsion by his brothers, ISRAEL had been for many years under bondage to the Ammonites. In the course of time, when these oppressors of Israel were planning some new form of humiliation, the elders of Gilead offered to anyone who was willing to accept the office of captain the headship over all the inhabitants of Gilead. When no one volunteered, the elders in desperation went to Jephthah and urged him to become a captain of Israel's army. He accepted, and he and the elders made vows before the Lord to keep all promises. On assuming the headship of Gilead, Jephthah's first effort was to secure the cooperation of the tribe of EPHRAIM, one of the most influential of the tribes during the period of the judges; but they refused to help. He then sent messengers to the king of the Ammonites, asking for the grounds of his hostile action and requesting that he desist; but the king refused to listen to reason. Endued with the Spirit of the Lord, Jephthah prepared for war. Before going out to battle, he made a vow that if he was victorious

Looking W up the Jabbok River in the land of Gilead. When the Ammonites oppressed the Israelites living in Gilead, they requested the help of Jephthah.

© Dr. James C. Martin

J

he would offer to God as a burnt offering whatever first came to him out of his house. He defeated his enemies with a very great slaughter and recovered twenty cities from them. The Ephraimites then came to him with the complaint that he had slighted them in the preparation for the Ammonite campaign, but he answered their false accusation and defeated them in battle. Forty-two thousand Ephraimites were killed. Jephthah judged Israel for six years. Samuel cited him as one proof of God's faithfulness in raising up deliverers for Israel in time of need (1 Sam. 12:11). He is listed among the heroes of faith in Heb. 11 (v. 32).

The great point of interest in his history is his vow (Jdg. 11:29-40) and the way it was fulfilled. On his return home after the victory over the Ammonites, his own daughter was the first to meet him from his house. A man of the highest integrity, he knew that he could not go back on his vow to the Lord; and his daughter agreed with him. She asked only that she and her companions be allowed to go for two months to the mountains to bewail her virginity. When she returned to her father, he "did to her as he had vowed. And she was a virgin" (11:39). According to some, the meaning of the statement is that Jephthah redeemed his daughter with money and gave her up to the service of the Lord as a perpetual virgin (cf. Lev. 27:1-8; 1 Sam. 1:11). On the basis of the entire context, however, most scholars believe that Jephthah contemplated human sacrifice from the beginning. If so, the incident may be part of the revelation that the book of Judges sets out to make of the fearful deterioration of the days and the need for the perfect king.

Jephunneh. ji-fuhn´uh (Heb. *yĕpunneh H3648*, possibly "[God] turns [*i.e.*, becomes reconciled]"). (1) A Kenizzite (see KENAZ), descendant of JUDAH; always referred to as the father of CALEB (Num. 13:6; 32:12; et al.).

(2) Son of JETHER (1 Chr. 7:38), listed among the "heads of families, choice men, brave warriors and outstanding leaders" of the tribe of ASHER (v. 40).

Jerah. jihr´uh (Heb. *yerah H3733*, "month," possibly a reference to the S Arabian moon god). Son of JOKTAN, grandson of EBER, and descendant of SHEM (Gen. 10:26; 1 Chr. 1:20).

Jerahmeel. ji-rah´mee-uhl (Heb. *yĕrahmĕ᾿ēl H3737*, "God has compassion"; gentilic *yĕrahmĕ᾿ēlî H3738*, "Jerahmeelite"; see JEREMIEL). (1) Firstborn son of HEZRON, grandson of PEREZ, and great-grandson of JUDAH (1 Chr. 2:9). His brothers were RAM and CALEB, although the identity of the latter is disputed. Jerahmeel had two wives and six sons (2:25-26), and his many descendants are given prominence in this genealogy (2:27-41), suggesting that his clan played a significant role in the history of the tribe of Judah.

(2) Son of Kish (not the father of King SAUL) and descendant of LEVI through MERARI; he was among the first LEVITES to serve in the permanent sanctuary established under DAVID (1 Chr. 24:29). He apparently married a daughter of Kish's brother ELEAZAR, who had no sons (cf. 23:21-22).

(3) A royal official (the apparent meaning of the designation "a son of the king") who, with two others, was deputized by King JEHOIAKIM to arrest JEREMIAH and his assistant, BARUCH; the effort ended in failure because "the LORD had hidden them" (Jer. 36:26; the KJV understands the Heb. word for "the king" as a proper name and translates "the son of Hammelech"; cf. also 38:6 and see HAMMELECH). The same individual is apparently referred to in a seventh-century seal that bears the inscription, "Belonging to Jerahmeel, the king's son."

Jerash. See GERASENE.

Jered. jihr´id (Heb. *yered H3719*, derivation disputed). (1) Son of MERED (by the latter's Judahite wife), "father" (i.e., founder) of GEDOR, and descendant of JUDAH, although his precise genealogical connection is unclear (1 Chr. 4:18). Apparently, the town of Gedor was founded by both Jered and PENUEL (v. 4).

(2) KJV alternate form of JARED (1 Chr. 1:2).

Jeremai. jer´uh-mi (Heb. *yĕrĕmay H3757*; possibly short form of JEREMIAH or JEREMOTH). One of the descendants of Hashum who agreed to put away their foreign wives (Ezra 10:33).

Jeremiah. jer´uh-mi´uh (Heb. *yirmĕyāhû H3759*, short form *yirmĕyâ H3758*, derivation uncertain,

The cracked wall of a cistern. God said through Jeremiah, "My people have committed two sins: They have forsaken me, the spring of living water, and have dug their own cisterns, broken cisterns that cannot hold water" (Jer. 2:13).

possibly "Yahweh loosens [the womb?]" or "Yahweh raises up"; Gk. *Ieremias G2635*). KJV NT Jeremias (Matt. 16:14) and Jeremy (2:17; 27:9). **(1)** Son of Hilkiah; a prophet in the southern kingdom (JUDAH) during the last forty years of its existence (627-586 B.C.). He lived through the period of the disintegration of the kingdom, witnessed the destruction of JERUSALEM and the TEMPLE, and spent the remaining years of his life in EGYPT. See JEREMIAH, BOOK OF.

(2) One of the ambidextrous Benjamite warriors who joined DAVID while he was in exile from SAUL at the PHILISTINE city of ZIKLAG (1 Chr. 12:4; cf. v. 2).

(3-4) Two Gadite warriors who joined David at Ziklag (1 Chr. 10,;13); these Gadites are described as "brave warriors, ready for battle and able to handle the shield and spear. Their faces were the faces of lions, and they were as swift as gazelles in the mountains" (12:8).

(5) A clan chief of the half-tribe of MANASSEH; he and others are described as "brave warriors, famous men, and heads of their families" (1 Chr. 5:24). Because of their unfaithfulness, however, they and their families were taken captive by the Assyrians (vv. 25-26).

(6) Father of Hamutal, who was the mother of Kings JEJOAHAZ and ZEDEKIAH (2 Ki. 23:31; 24:18; Jer. 52:1) and thus the wife of King JOSIAH. This Jeremiah is identified as being from LIBNAH.

(7) Son of Habazziniah and father of Jaazaniah; the latter was a leader of the RECABITES, whose loyalty to their ancestral precepts the prophet Jeremiah used as a lesson to his own countrymen (Jer. 35:3).

(8) A priest who returned from the EXILE (Neh. 12:1, 12). He is probably the same who signed the covenant with NEHEMIAH (10:2), while the Jeremiah who took part in one of the choirs at the dedication of the wall may be a different individual (12:34).

Jeremiah, Book of. The second book among the Major Prophets.

I. The life of Jeremiah. JEREMIAH was one of the greatest Hebrew prophets. He was born into a priestly family of ANATHOTH, a Benjamite town 2.5 mi. (4 km.) NE of JERUSALEM. His father's name was Hilkiah (Jer. 1:1), not to be confused with the high priest HILKIAH mentioned in 2 Ki. 22-23. Because of the autobiographical nature of Jeremiah's book, it is possible to understand his life, character, and times better than those of any other Hebrew prophet.

Jeremiah was called to prophesy in the thirteenth year of King JOSIAH (c. 626 B.C.), five years after the great revival of religion described in 2 Ki. 23. This was a time of decision, a time filled with both hope and foreboding. Looking back, we can know it as the last religious awakening in a series that only slowed down the IDOLATRY and APOSTASY of the Hebrews. Their apostasy finally plunged the nation into destruction. It was the time of the revival of the Babylonian empire. After the fall of the city of NINEVEH in 612, the Assyrian Empire disintegrated; and BABYLON for a little while again ruled the world under her vigorous leader NEBUCHADNEZZAR, who sought to subdue the whole FERTILE CRESCENT to himself. Nebuchadnezzar's design on EGYPT inevitably included control of PALESTINE, and Jeremiah's lifetime saw the fall of the Hebrew commonwealth to Babylon. This fall was preceded by a generation of unrest and decline in Judah. Many solutions to her troubles were proposed, and at court pro-Egyptian and pro-Babylonian parties vied for favor with the policy makers. A knowledge of this situation of deepening crisis is necessary if we are to understand Jeremiah and his book. Jeremiah's ministry continued through the reigns of five successive Judean kings,

J

Overview of JEREMIAH

Author: The priest-prophet Jeremiah son of Hilkiah.

Historical setting: Although Jeremiah was apparently called to be a prophet in the thirteenth year of JOSIAH's reign (c. 626 B.C., Jer. 1:2), in the wake of a great revival, most of his prophecies came subsequently, during the period of decline that led to the destruction of JERUSALEM (586). The book as a whole may have been put together by Jeremiah himself near the end of his life while an exile in EGYPT (c. 580), though many argue that there is evidence of later editing and additions.

Purpose: To warn of judgment against JUDAH because of IDOLATRY, to urge REPENTANCE upon the people, and to assure them of future restoration.

Contents: Jeremiah's call (Jer. 1); denunciation of Judah's sins (chs. 2-25); reactions to the prophecies (chs. 26-29); future restoration (chs. 30-33); prediction, fulfillment, and aftermath of the fall of Jerusalem (chs. 34-45); oracles against foreign nations (chs. 46-51); summary of the fall of Jerusalem and its aftermath (ch. 52).

and Jeremiah saw the final destruction of Jerusalem in 586. The prophet died in Egypt, probably a few years after Jerusalem was destroyed.

Jeremiah's call is described in Jer. 1. The young priest pleads his youth (1:6), but God assures him that he will be given strength for his task. At this time the theme of destruction from the N (i.e., from Babylon) is already introduced (1:13-15). The prediction that Judah would inevitably fall because of its apostasy earned for the prophet the undying hostility of most of his contemporaries (even his fellow townsmen, 11:21) and led to his being charged with treason (38:1-6) and to frequent imprisonments. Jeremiah's faithfulness to his call under the most difficult circumstances makes him a prime example of devotion to God at greatest personal sacrifice.

Undoubtedly Jeremiah supported Josiah's reform (Jer. 11:1-8; 17:19-27), but as time went on he realized its inadequacy to stave off national disaster (3:10). After Josiah's unhappy death (609 B.C.) Jeremiah mourned Judah's last good king (2 Chr. 35:25), and life became more difficult for him. JEHOAHAZ, son of Josiah, reigned only three

months before he was deported to Egypt. Jeremiah said that he would not return (Jer. 22:10-12). JEHOIAKIM, the brother of Jehoahaz, succeeded him and reigned eleven years. A strong ruler and a very wicked man, he tried to do away with the prophet and, failing that, to silence him. In Jehoiakim's fourth year Jeremiah dictated the first edition of his prophecies to BARUCH, but the king promptly destroyed the scroll (ch. 36). During this reign Jeremiah preached the great temple discourse (chs. 7-10) that led to a plot to kill him; he was saved only by the intervention of friendly nobles who were a remnant of Josiah's administration (ch. 26). The battle of CARCHEMISH (46:1-12) occurred at this time; in this battle Egypt was crushed (605) by the Babylonian crown prince Nebuchadnezzar, who soon afterward became king of Babylon. Egypt's star quickly set, and Babylon entered her brief period of greatness. Judah was brought into the Babylonian orbit when Jerusalem fell to Nebuchadnezzar in 605 and a few Hebrews (DANIEL among them) were deported to Babylon. Jehoiakim later rebelled against Babylon. Jeremiah opposed the strong-willed Jehoiakim all his reign and predicted a violent death for him (22:13-19). It has been supposed that he fell in a palace coup.

JEHOIACHIN, son of Jehoiakim, succeeded him to the throne. Jeremiah called this king Coniah and Jeconiah (Jer. 24:1; 27:20; 29:2). After he had reigned only three months, the Babylonians attacked Jerusalem and carried Jehoiachin off to Babylon (597 B.C.), as Jeremiah had predicted (22:24-30), together with many artisans and other important Jews. In Jehoiachin's place Nebuchadnezzar appointed ZEDEKIAH, who maintained a precarious position on the throne for eleven years. Although a weak character, he protected Jeremiah and asked his advice, which he was never able to carry out. Jeremiah advised submission to Babylon, but, goaded by the nobles, Zedekiah rebelled and made an alliance with Egypt. Finally the Babylonians came again, determined to stamp out the rebellious Judean state. A long siege resulted, in which Jeremiah suffered greatly. He was accused of treason and thrown into a vile prison from which the king transferred him to the more pleasant court of the guard (Jer. 37:11-21). Now that the judgment had come, the prophet spoke of a hopeful future for the nation (chs. 32-33). As the siege wore on, he was cast into a slimy cistern, where he would have perished had not EBED-MELECH, a courtier, rescued him (38:6-13). He was taken again to the court of the guard until the city fell (38:28).

After a siege of a year and a half, Jerusalem was destroyed. Zedekiah was blinded and carried in chains to Babylon. For the events in Judah after the destruction of Jerusalem we are dependent almost exclusively on Jer. 40-45. The captors treated Jeremiah with kindness, giving him the choice of going to Babylon or remaining in Judah. He chose to stay behind with some of the common people who had been left in Judah when most of the Jews were deported. GEDALIAH was made puppet governor over this little group. After civil unrest, in which Gedaliah was assassinated, the Jews fled to Egypt, forcing Jeremiah to accompany them. Jeremiah died in Egypt at an old age.

II. The man and his message. Jeremiah was called to be a prophet at a most unhappy time. With the failure of Josiah's revival, the final decline of the nation was under way. When God called Jeremiah, he intimated to him that his message would

be one of condemnation rather than salvation (Jer. 1:10, 18-19). Yet he was also given a message of hope (30:1-3, 18-22; 31:1-14, 23-40). Throughout his long ministry of more than forty years his preaching reflected this theme of judgment. God had risen early and sent his servants the prophets, but Israel would not hear (7:25; 44:4). Now the fate predicted for an apostate nation in Deut. 28-30 was inevitable. Babylon would capture Judah, and it would be better for the people to surrender and so to save their lives.

This message, coming to people whose desperate nationalism was all they had to cling to, was completely rejected, and the bearer was rejected with his message. Jeremiah was regarded as a meddler and a traitor; and leaders, nobles, and kings tried to put him to death. Although he needed the love, sympathy, and encouragement of a wife, he was not permitted to marry; and in this prohibition he became a sign that normal life was soon to cease for Jerusalem (Jer. 16:1-4). Because his book is full of autobiographical sections—Jeremiah's "Confessions"—Jeremiah's personality can be understood more clearly than that of any other prophet. These outpourings of the human spirit are some of the most poignant and pathetic statements of the tension of a man under divine imperative to be found anywhere in Scripture (the most important passages are 10:23-24; 11:18—12:6; 15:10-21; 17:9-11, 14-18; 18:18-23; 20:7-18). They show us a Jeremiah who was retiring, sensitive, and afraid of people's "faces," a man we would consider singularly unfit for the work that was given him to do. That he tenaciously clung to his assigned task through the succeeding years of rejection and persecution is both a tribute to the mettle of the man and to the grace of God, without which his personality would surely have gone to pieces.

Jeremiah's penetrating understanding of the religious condition of his people is seen in his emphasis on the inner spiritual character of true religion. The external theocratic state will go, as will the temple and its ritual. Even Josiah's reform appears to have been a thing of the outward appearance—almost engineered by the king, an upsurge of nationalism more than a religious revival (Jer. 3:10). The old COVENANT had failed; a new and better one will take its place and then God's LAW will be written

J

on men's hearts (31:31-34). God will give his renewed people a heart to know him (24:7). In this doctrine of the "new heart" Jeremiah unfolds the depth of human sin and predicts the intervention of divine grace (Heb. 8:1—9:28).

III. The composition of the book. Jeremiah is a book of prophetic oracles or sermons, together with much autobiographical and historical material that gives the background of these oracles. Many modern scholars believe that the book contains substantial parts by later writers whose point of view differed markedly from the prophet's. Believing that the critics have failed to prove their case for later editors, this article takes the traditional position that the oracles are essentially Jeremiah's and that the narratives, if they were not dictated by the prophet (they are usually in the third person), were probably composed by Baruch.

Even though we may accept the fact that the book originated with Jeremiah, it is impossible to say how or when these materials were assembled in their present form. Plainly the book has gone through a number of editions, each succeeding one containing additional material. The account of the production of the first and second editions is told in Jer. 36. Baruch, the secretary of the prophet, wrote down certain judgment oracles of the prophet (we do not know the exact contents) at his dictation. This scroll was contemptuously burned by King Jehoiakim; the prophet, therefore, dictated again to Baruch "all the words of the scroll that Jehoiakim king of Judah had burned in the fire. And many similar words were added to them" (36:32); in other words, a new and enlarged edition was produced. Obviously this edition was not the same as our present book, which carries the history on for at least twenty more years. The account is of great interest in that it gives the only detailed OT description of the writing of a prophetic book. That Jeremiah should dictate to a secretary was normal for the times. Writing was a specialized skill, often restricted to a professional class. The document was probably written on a blank papyrus scroll imported from Egypt.

It has long been noted that the book of Jeremiah in the Greek translation of the OT called the Septuagint (produced in Egypt probably in the second century B.C.) is about one-eighth shorter than the Hebrew book, from which our English translations have been made. Further, the Septuagint omits many of the repetitions that are contained in the Hebrew copy and rearranges the material somewhat. Some scholars believe that the Greek Jeremiah was made from a different edition of the Hebrew text from the one on which our present text is based. It is not yet possible to arrive at any certain conclusion about the relationship of the Septuagint to the Hebrew text, nor to know how either version came to its present condition.

The material contained in Jeremiah's book is not arranged in chronological order. The outline given below indicates what seems to have been the purpose of the present arrangement: to set forth a group of oracles spoken against the Jewish nation; then to record selected events in the prophet's ministry; next to give certain discourses of Jeremiah against foreign nations; and finally to include an account of the fall of Jerusalem. The record of Jerusalem's fall had been given in Jer. 39; the somewhat different account at the end of the book (ch. 52) is practically identical to 2 Ki. 24-25 and may have been added from that source to give a climactic conclusion to Jeremiah's oracles.

IV. Outline

A. Jeremiah's oracles against the theocracy, Jer. 1:1—25:38.
  1. The prophet's call, 1:1-19.
  2. Reproofs and admonitions, mostly from the time of Josiah, 2:1—20:18.
  3. Later prophecies, 21:1—25:38.
B. Events in the life of Jeremiah, 26:1—45:5.
  1. The temple sermon and Jeremiah's arrest, 26:1-24.
  2. The yoke of Babylon, 27:1—29:32.
  3. The book of consolation, 30:1—33:26.
  4. Some of Jeremiah's experiences before Jerusalem fell, 34:1—36:32.
  5. Jeremiah during the siege and destruction of Jerusalem, 37:1—39:18.
  6. The last years of Jeremiah, 40:1—45:5.
C. Jeremiah's oracles against foreign nations, 46:1—51:64.
  1. Against Egypt, 46:1-28.
  2. Against the Philistines, 47:1-7.
  3. Against Moab, 48:1-47.
  4. Against the Ammonites, 49:1-6.

5. Against Edom, 49:7-22.
6. Against Damascus, 49:23-27.
7. Against Kedar and Hazor, 49:28-33.
8. Against Elam, 49:34-39.
9. Against Babylon, 50:1—51:64.
D. Appendix: The fall of Jerusalem and related events, 52:1-34.

V. Chronological order of the book. Although the book is not at all in chronological order, it is possible to date many of its sections because they contain chronological notations. For example, the material in Jer. 1 took place in the thirteenth year of Josiah, and chs. 2-6 later in his reign; possibly much of chs. 7-20 (except material specifically listed below) can also be dated to this period. Several passages belong early in the reign of Jehoiakim (ch. 26 and prob. 7:1—8:3; 22:1-23), while others specifically in his fourth year (chs. 25; 36; 45; 46:1-12), and one chapter later than the fourth year (ch. 35). To the reign of Jehoiachin may be dated 22:24-30 and possibly ch. 14.

Many passages belong in the reign of Zedekiah: in the beginning (ch. 24; 49:34-39); in the fourth year (chs. 27-28; 51:59-64); in unnoted years (chs. 21 and 29); during the early part of the siege (ch. 34); during the interruption of the siege (ch. 37); and during the resumption of the siege (chs. 32; 33; 38; 39:15-18). Finally, some prophecies were given in Judah after the fall of Jerusalem (39:1-4; 40:1—43:7), and others in Egypt after Jeremiah was taken there (43:8—44:30).

VI. Jeremiah and the Lachish Letters. The city of Lachish, in the Judean foothills, was one of a series of fortresses for the defense of Jerusalem against attack from the Mediterranean Plain. It was one of the last cities to fall to the Babylonians prior to the final taking and destruction of Jerusalem (Jer. 34:7). Interesting light has been shed on these last hectic days of Judah's history by a discovery in the ruins of ancient Lachish. When the city was excavated (in 1932-38), twenty-one letters written on broken pieces of pottery were found in a guard room of the outer gate. They were written in the ancient Hebrew script with carbon iron ink at the time of Jeremiah, when Lachish was undergoing its final siege.

Many of these letters were written by a certain Hoshaiah, who was a military officer at some outpost near Lachish, to Yaosh, the commander of Lachish. Their language is very much like that of the book of Jeremiah. Hoshaiah is constantly defending himself to his superior. Could it be that he was under suspicion of being ready to go over to the Babylonians? Once he describes one of the princes in words almost like those that the princes used against Jeremiah (Jer. 38:4). There is mention of "the prophet" whose message is "Beware." Is this a reference to Jeremiah? We cannot be sure. According to the book of Jeremiah, there were many prophets in that troubled time. Another letter mentions the inability of Hoshaiah to see the smoke signals of Azekah, although those of Lachish were still visible. Perhaps Azekah had already fallen (34:7). Although the specific meaning of many of the references of these letters eludes us, they do throw a vivid light on the disturbed and fearful days just prior to the fall of the Judean kingdom, the days of Jeremiah.

Jeremiah, Epistle of. See APOCRYPHA.

Jeremias. See JEREMIAH.

Jeremoth. jer'uh-moth (Heb. *yĕrēmôt H3756*, variant *yĕrîmôt H3748*, possibly "stout" or "exalted"). **(1)** Son of BEKER and grandson of BENJAMIN (1 Chr. 7:8; KJV, "Jerimoth").

(2) Son of BERIAH (or of ELPAAL; cf. NRSV), and descendant of Benjamin, listed among the heads of families living in JERUSALEM (1 Chr. 8:14; cf. v. 28). He is usually identified with JEROHAM (v. 27).

(3) Son (or descendant) of Mushi; he was one of the descendants of LEVI through MERARI appointed by DAVID to work in the temple (1 Chr. 23:23 KJV, NRSV; the NIV has "Jerimoth" on the basis of 24:30).

(4) Son of HEMAN, David's seer (1 Chr. 25:4, 22; in the former verse he is called "Jerimoth," and on that basis the NIV has "Jerimoth" in v. 22 as well). He and his thirteen brothers were set apart "for the ministry of prophesying, accompanied by harps, lyres and cymbal" (v. 1). When lots were cast to determine the duties of the Levitical singers, he, along with his sons and relatives, received the fifteenth lot (v. 22).

(5) One of the descendants of Elam who agreed to put away their foreign wives (Ezra 10:26).

J

(6) One of the descendants of Zattu who agreed to put away their foreign wives (Ezra 10:27).

(7) One of the descendants of Bani who agreed to put away their foreign wives (Ezra 10:29 [KJV, "Ramoth," following the *Qere*]).

Jeremy. See JEREMIAH.

Jeriah. ji-ri′uh (Heb. *yĕriyyāhû H3746*, short form *yĕriyyâ H3745* "Yahweh sees [me]"). Firstborn son (or most important descendant) of Hebron; he was one of the descendants of LEVI through KOHATH appointed by DAVID to work in the temple (1 Chr. 23:19; 24:23). He is also described as chief of the Hebronites; his 2,700 relatives were heads of families whom David put in charge of the tribes E of the JORDAN (26:31-32; KJV and other versions, "Jerijah"). See HEBRON (PERSON) #1.

Jeribai. jer′uh-bi (Heb. *yĕribay H3744*, "[Yahweh] contends [for me]"). Son of Elnaam; he and his brother Joshaviah are included in the Chronicler's list of DAVID's mighty warriors (1 Chr. 11:46), which adds sixteen names (vv. 41b-47) beyond the military elite known as the Thirty (vv. 10-41 = 2 Sam. 23:8-39).

Jericho. jer′uh-koh (Heb. *yĕriḥô H3735* [with variant spellings], possibly "[city of] the moon [god]"; Gk. *Ierichō G2637*).

I. The site. Jericho, also called the City of Palms (Deut. 34:3), is located 5 mi. (8 km.) W of the JORDAN and 7 mi. (11 km.) N of the DEAD SEA, some 800 ft. (245 m.) below sea level. Its climate

is tropical, with great heat during the summer. In the winter it becomes a resort for people fleeing the colder weather of the Palestinian hill country. In ancient times date palm trees flourished here; and balsam, from which medicine was extracted, was the source of great income. Today there are many banana groves here. The presence of springs of water makes the locality a green oasis in the middle of the dry Jordan rift area.

There are two sites associated with biblical Jericho. The OT city was situated on a mound now called Tell es-Sultan, on the NW outskirts of the modern town. NT or Herodian Jericho is located on a higher elevation one mile W of the modern city in the ruins on both banks of the Wadi Qelt; this site is known as Tulul Abu el-ʿAlayiq. Jericho is probably the oldest city in the world. Its strategic site by a ford of the Jordan controlled the ancient trade routes from the E. After crossing the river these branched out, one going toward BETHEL and SHECHEM in the N, another westward to JERUSALEM, and a third to HEBRON in the S. Thus Jericho controlled the access to the hill country of Palestine from TRANSJORDAN.

II. Jericho in the Bible. Jericho first enters the biblical record when it is captured by JOSHUA and the invading Hebrews as the opening wedge of their campaign to take CANAAN (Josh. 6). The city's location made its capture the key to the invasion of the central hill country. It was regarded as a formidable obstacle by the Hebrews. After the two spies had searched it (ch. 2), Joshua led the Hebrew forces against the city, marching around it daily for six days. On the seventh day they circled it seven times, then shouted and blew their trumpets, and "the wall collapsed; so every man charged straight in, and they took the city" (6:20). The city was devoted to God, totally destroyed and burned except for metal objects found in it (6:17-19). Only RAHAB and her family, who had cared for the spies, was saved (6:22-23, 25). Joshua placed a curse on the place, that it might not be rebuilt (6:26). The site seems to have remained a ruin for centuries. Jericho next became prominent when it was rebuilt by HIEL the Bethelite in the days of AHAB (c. 850 B.C.; 1 Ki. 16:34). Evidently it again became an important place during the divided kingdom era. It is mentioned in connection with ELISHA's ministry

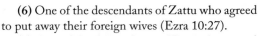

Jericho.

Looking SE across the site of OT Jericho.

(2 Ki. 2:4-5, 19; see also 25:5; 2 Chr. 28:15; Ezra 2:34; Neh. 3:2; 7:36; Jer. 39:5).

In the time of Christ, Jericho was an important place yielding a large revenue to the royal family. Here was HEROD the Great's winter palace, containing a sunken garden, two large pools, a large Roman bath, two courtyards, a reception hall, and buildings with six private mikvehs (baptistries) dating to the second century B.C. Since the road from the fords of the Jordan to Jerusalem passed through Jericho, it became a stopping place for Galilean pilgrims to Jerusalem, who came S through PEREA to avoid defilement by contact with SAMARITANS. Thus Jesus passed through it on a number of occasions. Nearby are the supposed sites of his baptism (in the Jordan) and his temptation (the hill Quarantania, W of the city). Near the city Jesus healed BARTIMAEUS (Mk. 10:46-52) and one or two other blind men (Matt. 20:29-34). The conversion of ZACCHAEUS occurred here (Lk. 19:1-10), one of the most graphic of the gospel narratives. In the parable of the Good Samaritan (10:29-37) the traveler was attacked as he was going down from Jerusalem to Jericho, a winding road, often passing between crags, going through the desolate Judean wilderness, which was frequently a hiding place of criminals.

III. The archaeology of Jericho. The earliest evidence of settlement on Tell es-Sultan is dated (by radiocarbon tests) to the seventh and sixth mil-

lennia B.C., when a prepottery Neolithic town was built there. A surprisingly strong city wall, mudbrick and stone houses, plastered floors with reed mats, and clay figurines of animals and the mother goddess show that the civilization was not crude. Of special interest from this period are several human skulls with the features modeled in clay and with shells for eyes, used possibly for cultic purposes. This is one of the oldest cities known— having existed some 5,000 years before ABRAHAM!

Of greatest interest to the Bible student is the archaeological evidence bearing on the overthrow of the city in the days of Joshua. About this Late-Bronze-Age city there has been dispute ever since John Garstang's early excavations (1930-36); and Kathleen Kenyon's reports in the 1950s, which scholars had hoped would solve the mystery, only accentuated the problem. Garstang believed that he had found ample evidence of Joshua's destruction of the Late-Bronze-Age city, which he labeled "city D" and dated to the fifteenth century B.C. He found that this city had been surrounded by a double wall that encircled the summit of the mound, the inner wall 12 ft. (almost 4 m.) thick, and the outer, 6 ft. (2 m.). These walls had been violently destroyed and had toppled down the slopes of the mound. Layers of ash and charcoal testified to the burning of the city by its captors, and great amounts of charred grain and other foodstuffs suggested the

© Dr. James C. Martin

total destruction of which the Bible speaks. Not all of Garstang's fellow archaeologists accepted his reconstructions, and the world of scholarship awaited Kenyon's findings.

After seven seasons at Jericho, Kenyon reported that virtually nothing remains of the Jericho of the period of Joshua (1500-1200 B.C.). The mound has suffered such denudation that almost all remains later than the third millennium B.C. have disappeared. According to Kenyon, the two walls that Garstang connected with his "city D" should be dated about the third millennium, hundreds of years before the EXODUS; only a bit of pottery and possibly one building remain from the Late Bronze Age. If there was once evidence of a great city of Jericho destroyed by Joshua, she believes that it has long since been eaten away by the elements. Much of the evidence on this subject that was written about prior to 1952—often written with the best intentions to "prove" the truth of the Bible—must now be reconsidered. A number of scholars now believe that the Jericho of Joshua's day was little more than a fort.

It is unlikely that the problem of Jericho will ever be solved by further archaeological work. The many successive years of digging have left the tell in a mixed-up condition, and it may be that other cities mentioned in the conquest narrative in Joshua (e.g., HAZOR) will now more readily yield their answers. In the meantime, the thoughtful Christian will not forget the mutability of scientific theories.

Jeriel. jihr´i-uhl (Heb. *yĕrî'ēl H3741*, "God sees [me]"). Son of TOLA and grandson of ISSACHAR, described as head of family (1 Chr. 7:2).

Jerijah. See JERIAH.

Jerimoth. jer´i-moth (Heb. *yĕrîmôt H3748*, variant *yĕrēmôt H3756*, possibly "stout" or "exalted"). **(1)** Son of BELA and grandson of BENJAMIN (1 Chr. 7:7).

(2) One of the ambidextrous Benjamite warriors who joined DAVID while he was in exile from SAUL at the PHILISTINE city of ZIKLAG (1 Chr. 12:5; cf. v. 2).

(3) Son (or descendant) of Mushi; he was one of the descendants of LEVI through MERARI

appointed by DAVID to work in the temple (1 Chr. 23:23 [KJV, NRSV, "Jeremoth"]; 24:30).

(4) Son of HEMAN, David's seer (1 Chr. 25:4). He and his thirteen brothers were set apart "for the ministry of prophesying, accompanied by harps, lyres and cymbal" (v. 1). When lots were cast to determine the duties of the Levitical singers, he, along with his sons and relatives, received the fifteenth lot (v. 22 [KJV and other versions, "Jeremoth"]).

(5) Son of Azriel; an officer over the tribe of NAPHTALI during the reign of David (1 Chr. 27:19 [RSV, "Jeremoth"]).

(6) Son of David and father of MAHALATH; the latter married REHOBOAM (2 Chr. 11:18). The name of Jerimoth does not appear in any of the lists of David's sons, and some scholars argue that the text is not reliable.

(7) A Levite included in the list of supervisors of the temple storerooms during the reign of HEZEKIAH (2 Chr. 31:13).

Jerioth. jer´ee-oth (Heb. *yĕrî'ôt H3750*, possibly "fearful" or "tents"). Wife of CALEB son of Hezron (1 Chr. 2:18). The MT is difficult, however, and can be interpreted in different ways: (a) Jerioth may be another name for Caleb's wife AZUBAH; (b) Azubah had been previously the wife of a man called Jerioth; (c) Jerioth was the daughter of Caleb and Azubah. Other suggestions have been made.

Jeroboam. jer´uh-boh´uhm (Heb. *yārāb'ām H3716*, "the people are great" or "my kinsman [= deity?] is great"). The name of two kings of the northern kingdom of ISRAEL.

(1) Jeroboam I. Son of Nebat, from the tribe of EPHRAIM, and of Zeruah, a widow (1 Ki. 11:26-40). Jeroboam founded the kingdom of Israel when the nation was split following the death of SOLOMON. His father was an official under Solomon and came from the village of ZEREDAH. As a young man Jeroboam showed such ability that Solomon put him in charge of the fortifications and public works at JERUSALEM and made him overseer of the levy from the house of Joseph (11:28). However, he used his position to stir up dissatisfaction against the government. This was not difficult to do, as the people were already filled with bitterness because of the enforced labor and burdensome taxation imposed on them by Solomon.

One day, as he was walking outside Jerusalem, Jeroboam was met by the prophet AHIJAH of SHILOH. Ahijah tore a new mantle into twelve pieces and gave ten of them to Jeroboam, informing him that because of the idolatrous nature of Solomon's reign the kingdom would be torn apart. Two of the tribes would remain with DAVID's dynasty, while Jeroboam would become the head of the other ten. He also told him that if as king he walked in the fear of the Lord and kept his commandments, the kingdom would be his and that of his descendants for many years. When news of these happenings reached Solomon, he tried to kill Jeroboam; but the latter escaped to EGYPT, where he was kindly received by SHISHAK (who had succeeded the PHARAOH whose daughter Solomon had married). As soon as Solomon died, Jeroboam returned from Egypt. When the people met at SHECHEM to proclaim Solomon's son REHOBOAM king, they invited Jeroboam to come and take the lead in presenting their grievances. As spokesman of the people, he urged that their burdens be alleviated, but the protest was contemptuously rejected; therefore the ten tribes revolted from the house of David and made Jeroboam their king (1 Ki. 12:1-16). In this way

Ahijah's prophecy that the ten tribes would form a separate kingdom with Jeroboam as king was fulfilled (12:15).

Although Jeroboam had been divinely set apart for his task, and although he had been raised to the throne with the full approval of the people, he failed to rise to the greatness of his opportunities. The prophet had told him the conditions of success as a ruler, but it was not long before he began to depart from the counsels of the Lord. Afraid that if his people went annually to Jerusalem to worship it would not be long before they would be won back to the house of David, he decided to establish centers of worship at the two extremities of his kingdom—DAN in the N and BETHEL in the S (1 Ki. 12:26-30). This was at variance with the LAW of MOSES, according to which there was to be but one altar of burnt offering and one place of meeting God. His disobedience became much greater when, in defiance of the commandment forbidding the worship of God by means of images, he set up a golden calf in each of the new sanctuaries and quoted to the people the words of AARON, "Here are your gods, O Israel, who brought you up out of Egypt" (12:28; cf. Exod. 32:4).

These radical decisions brought about other necessary changes. Since legitimate priests refused

Aerial view of Dan (looking NE), with the spring in the foreground and Mt. Hermon and Caesarea Philippi in the background. Jeroboam I established a golden calf worship site at Dan.

© Dr. James C. Martin

J

to serve at the new altars, Jeroboam had to find others to take their place "from all sorts of people" (1 Ki. 12:31). Furthermore, he "built shrines on high places" (12:31) and ordained that the Feast of Tabernacles, which had been held in the seventh month, should now be observed in the eighth month. He even sometimes took it on himself to minister in the priests' office (12:33). The mass of people conformed to the new religious ways. This was the sin that Jeroboam "caused Israel to commit, so that they provoked the LORD … to anger by their worthless idols" (16:26). He sacrificed the higher interests of religion to politics. To establish his throne firmly, he led the people into the immoralities of heathenism, which led eventually to the destruction of the nation. The successive kings, with one partial exception (JEHU), supported this idolatrous worship until Israel fell.

Although Jeroboam made Israel sin by introducing idolatrous religious customs, God gave him a solemn warning to give heed to his evil ways through an unnamed prophet who came to Bethel from Judah (1 Ki. 13:1-6). One day—apparently the very day the altar was consecrated—as Jeroboam stood ministering at the altar, the man of God suddenly appeared before the king and foretold that the time would come when a member of the Davidic dynasty would desecrate that altar by burning men's bones on it, a prophecy that was fulfilled in the time of JOSIAH (cf. 2 Ki. 23:15-16). When the king heard these words, he pointed to the prophet and cried out, "Seize him!" The hand that was extended instantly withered and became useless, and the altar was split in two so that the ashes spilled to the ground. The king then asked the prophet to pray that his hand might be restored. The prophet prayed, and the hand was restored. He refused the king's invitation to go home with him to dine, saying that it was against the will of God, and then left for home. In spite of this terrible warning from God, Jeroboam continued in his evil way, so that God decided to cut off and destroy his house.

At a later date, exactly when is not clear, Jeroboam's oldest son fell seriously ill. The distraught father thought of Ahijah, now old and blind, and sent his queen to him in disguise to find out whether the child would live. The prophet saw through her disguise and told her not only that the child would die, but that the house of Jeroboam would be utterly destroyed by someone whom the Lord would raise up to be king of Israel (1 Ki. 14:1-18).

There was desultory warfare between Jeroboam and Rehoboam (1 Ki. 15:6), and a great battle was fought between Jeroboam and Rehoboam's successor, ABIJAH. The army of Israel was thoroughly routed and was defeated with great slaughter, and Bethel, only a few miles from Jerusalem, was captured by Abijah (2 Chr. 13). Jeroboam reigned for twenty-two years and was succeeded to the throne by his son NADAB (2 Ki. 14:20).

For the people of Israel, the reign of Jeroboam was a supreme political and religious calamity. The warfare between the two kingdoms inevitably brought weakness to both, leaving them open to outside attack. The introduction of the golden calves led to the "baalization" of the religion of the Lord. In about 200 years the moral and religious corruption of the people had gone so far that there was no more hope for them, and God brought in a heathen power to lead them into captivity.

(2) Jeroboam II. Son and successor of JEHOASH king of ISRAEL; fourth ruler of the dynasty of JEHU. Jeroboam II became king in SAMARIA c. 790 B.C. and reigned forty-one years. He followed the example of Jeroboam I in keeping up the idolatrous worship of the golden calves (2 Ki. 14:23). In spite of this, his reign outwardly flourished. He ruled at the same time as AMAZIAH (14:23) and UZZIAH (15:1), kings of JUDAH. He continued and brought to a successful conclusion the wars that his father had undertaken against SYRIA. He took their chief cities, DAMASCUS and HAMATH, which had once been subject to DAVID, and restored to Israel territory E of the JORDAN from LEBANON to the DEAD SEA (14:25; Amos 6:14). MOAB and AMMON were reconquered (Amos 1:13; 2:1-3).

All these successful wars brought much tribute to Jeroboam and his nobles. The wealthy had both winter and summer homes; some lived in houses of ivory, others in houses of hewn stone. The prophet AMOS, contemporary with Jeroboam in the king's later years, gives us a graphic description of a banqueting scene in which the perfumed guests lay on silken cushions, eating the flesh of lambs and stall-fed calves, drinking wine from bowls, and enjoying the music of harps (Amos 6:4-6). But side by side with this luxury there was much poverty in the land. Twice the prophet says that the needy were sold for a pair of shoes (2:6; 8:6). No one was grieved for the afflictions of the poor or was distressed for the corruption that prevailed in the land. Drunkenness, licentiousness, and oppression went unchecked by the religious hierarchy.

Not that the land was devoid of religion. Worship went on not only at DAN and BETHEL, but also at subsidiary temples and altars at GILGAL and BEERSHEBA (Amos 4:4; 5:5; 8:14), places with long religious associations. Amos complained that ritual was substituted for righteousness (5:21-22), that devotees prostrated themselves before altars clothed in garments taken in cruel pledge, and that they drank sacrificial wine bought with the money of those who were condemned (2:8).

During the reign of Jeroboam not only Amos, but also the prophets HOSEA, JOEL, and JONAH ministered. In 2 Ki. 14:25 we are told that Jonah son of Amittai predicted the large extension of the territory of Israel by Jeroboam. This is the same prophet whose mission to NINEVEH forms the subject of the book of Jonah (Jon. 1:1). Amos says that he was commanded by God to go to Bethel to testify against the whole proceedings there. He was to foretell the destruction of the sanctuaries of Israel and of the house of Jeroboam (Amos 7:9). When Amaziah, the high priest of Bethel, heard this denunciation, he sent a messenger to Jeroboam with a report of a "conspiracy," claiming that Amos had declared, "Jeroboam will die by the sword" (7:10-11). There are some who regard this as a prophecy that was not fulfilled, as there is no evidence that the king died other than a natural death, for he was buried with his ancestors in state (2 Ki. 14:29). The probability, however, is that the high priest, in order to inflame Jeroboam against the prophet, gave his words an unwarranted twist.

Jeroboam was succeeded on his death by his son ZECHARIAH (2 Ki. 14:29), a weak king with whom the dynasty ended.

Jeroham. ji-roh′ham (Heb. *yĕrōḥām H3736*, derivation debated). **(1)** Son (or descendant) of Elihu, father of ELKANAH, and grandfather of SAMUEL (1 Sam. 1:1). In the Levitical genealogies of KORAH,

his immediate ancestor is given as Eliab or Eliel (1 Chr. 6:27, 34). He may have been a nonpracticing LEVITE domiciled in the tribe of EPHRAIM.

(2) A descendant of BENJAMIN whose sons are listed among the heads of families living in JERUSALEM (1 Chr. 8:27; cf. v. 28). He is usually identified with JEREMOTH (v. 14).

(3) Descendant of Benjamin and father of Ibeniah; the latter was an early settler in Jerusalem following the EXILE (1 Chr. 9:8; cf. vv. 2-3).

(4) Son (or descendant) of Passhur and father of Adaiah; the latter is included in a list of priests who were heads of families and who are described as "able men, responsible for ministering in the house of God" in postexilic Jerusalem (1 Chr. 9:12-13; in Neh. 11:12 his immediate ancestor listed is Pelaliah, with Passhur given as a more distant ancestor).

(5) A Benjamite living in GEDOR whose two sons, JOELAH and ZEBADIAH, were among the ambidextrous warriors who joined DAVID at ZIKLAG (1 Chr. 12:7).

(6) Father of AZAREL; the latter was an officer over the tribe of DAN during David's reign (1 Chr. 27:22).

(7) Father of AZARIAH; the latter was a military commander who assisted the high priest JEHOIADA in the successful overthrow of the apostate queen ATHALIAH (2 Chr. 23:1).

Jerub-Baal. ji′ruhb-bay′uhl (Heb. *yĕrubba'al H3715*, prob. "Baal contends [for me]"). Also Jerubbaal. The name given to GIDEON when he destroyed his father's BAAL altar at OPHRAH. The text says, "So that day they called Gideon 'Jerub-Baal,' saying, 'Let Baal contend with him,' because he broke down Baal's altar" (Jdg. 6:32; the name is also used in 7:1; 8:29, 35; ch. 9; and 1 Sam. 12:11). Some suggest that prior to this incident Jerub-Baal had been his name, reflecting the syncretism which then prevailed among the Israelites, but that his act of iconoclasm gave it a new significance. The Hebrew word *ba'al H1251* means "lord, owner," and in the early history of Israel was sometimes applied to the true God. Later, when the term came to be regarded as disgraceful, the name Jerub-Baal was altered to Jerub-Besheth (from *bōšet H1425*, "shame," 2 Sam. 11:21); cf. ISH-BOSHETH and MEPHIBOSHETH.

J

Jerub-Besheth. ji-rub'uh-sheth (Heb. *yĕrubbešet H3717*, deformation of *yĕrubbaʿal H3715*). Also Jerubbesheth. See JERUB-BAAL.

Jeruel. ji-roo'uhl (Heb. *yĕrûʾēl H3725*, "foundation of God"). An area in the Judean wilderness where King JEHOSHAPHAT defeated a Transjordanian coalition (2 Chr. 20:16). The exact location is not known, but it was apparently between the Pass of ZIZ (just N or NW of EN GEDI, cf. v. 2) and the Desert of TEKOA (cf. v. 20).

Jerusalem. ji-roo'suh-luhm (Heb. *yĕrûšālaim H3731* [also *yĕrûšālayim*], prob. "foundation of peace"; Aram. *yĕrûšlem H10332*; Gk. *Ierousalēm G2647* [variant *Hierosolyma*], gentilic *Hierosolymitēs G2643*). The most important city on earth in the history of God's REVELATION and REDEMPTION. It was the royal city, the capital of the only kingdom God has established on earth. Here the TEMPLE was erected, and here, during the kingdom age, sacrifices were legitimately offered. This was the city of the prophets, as well as the kings of DAVID's line. Here occurred the death, resurrection, and ascension of Jesus CHRIST, David's greatest Son. The HOLY SPIRIT descended at PENTECOST on an assembled group in this city, giving birth to the Christian CHURCH; and here the first great church council was held. Rightly did the chronicler refer to Jerusalem as "the city the LORD had chosen out of all the tribes of Israel in which to put his Name" (1 Ki. 14:21). Even the first-century Roman historian Pliny referred to Jerusalem as "by far the most famous city of the ancient Orient." This city has been the preeminent objective of the pilgrimages of devout men and women for over 2,000 years, and it was in an attempt to recover the Church of the Holy Sepulchre in Jerusalem that the Crusades were organized. No site in all Scripture receives such constant and exalted praise as Jerusalem. Concerning no place in the world have such promises been made of ultimate glory and permanent peace.

I. **Names of the city.** While the word *Jerusalem* is Semitic, it apparently was not a name given to the city for the first time by the HEBREW PEOPLE. Far back in the time of the AMARNA Letters (1400 B.C.), it was called *Urusalim*, that is, a city of Salim, generally taken to mean "city of peace." In the records of Sen-

nacherib it is called *Ursalimu*. The Romans, at the time of HADRIAN, A.D. 135, changed the name to *Aelia Capitolina*. For some centuries now the Arabs have called the city *El-Kuds el-Sharif*, which means "the Sanctuary." Some argue that SALEM is to be taken as the name of a Canaanitic deity (thus "foundation/city of the god Shalem"), but the evidence is not persuasive. Salem was probably the earlier name for the city, the name given it in the memorable interview of ABRAHAM with MELCHIZEDEK, the king of Salem (Gen. 14:18; Ps. 76:2). Because the very name of the city means "peace," we are told that in this place God himself will give PEACE (Hag. 2:9). The children of God are exhorted to pray for the peace of Jerusalem (Ps. 122:6). ISAIAH, at the end of his great series of prophecies, returns to the theme, "For this is what the Lord says: 'I will extend peace to her like a river'" (Isa. 66:12).

The name Jerusalem itself occurs about six hundred times in the OT, though it is not found in Job, Hosea, Jonah, Nahum, Habakkuk, and Haggai. In the NT, it is mentioned almost eighty times, but rather infrequently after the close of the book of Acts. The name most often used for this city, apart from Jerusalem itself, is ZION, which occurs over one hundred times in the OT, beginning as early as 2 Ki. 19:21 and found most often in the book of PSALMS and the prophecy of Isaiah (Isa. 1:8; 4:4-5; 62:11). Zion appears in the NT in some interesting passages: twice on the lips of our Lord (Matt. 21:5; Jn. 12:15), twice in Romans (9:33; 11:36), and in 1 Pet. 2:6 and Rev. 14:1. Jerusalem is often called "the city of David" (2 Sam. 5:7, 9; 6:10-16; Neh. 3:15; 12:37; Isa. 22:9). This title is later applied to BETHLEHEM (Lk. 2:4, 11).

The greatest group of titles for Jerusalem are those that identify it as *the city of God*. It is called this in the Psalms, as well as in the NT (Ps. 46:4; 48:1, 8; 87:3; Heb. 12:22; Rev. 3:12). It is also called the city of the Lord (Isa. 60:14), the mountain of the Lord (2:3; 30:29), the mountain of the Lord Almighty (Zech. 8:3), Zion of the Holy One of Israel (Isa. 60:14). The Lord himself refers to it, and to no other place, as "my city" (45:13), or more often, "my holy mountain" (11:9; 56:7; 57:13; 65:11, 25; 66:20). Because it is the city of God, where he has put his Name, it is often referred to as the Holy City (48:2; 52:1; Neh. 11:1-18), a title used twice by Matthew (4:5; 27:53), once of a future event by John (Rev. 11:2), and used also in referring to our eternal heavenly home at the close of the Scriptures (21:2; 22:19). Generally, the phrase "the holy mountain" refers to this city (e.g., Ps. 48:1; Isa. 11:9; 27:13; Dan. 11:45). Once it is given the beautiful name of HEPHZIBAH, meaning "My delight is in her" (Isa. 62:4). Isaiah in one passage calls the city ARIEL, the meaning of which is disputed (29:1, 2, 7), a word that in itself probably means "Lion of God." At the beginning of his prophecy Isaiah gives two titles to the city in most radical contrast. He designates it, because of its wickedness, as SODOM and GOMORRAH (1:10); but in the same passage he promises that the day will come when it will be accurately called "the City of Righteousness" (1:26).

II. The site. Unlike most cities that have witnessed great historical events over many centuries, Jerusalem has always remained on the same site. It is situated 34 mi. (55 km.) E of the MEDITERRANEAN and only 17 mi. (27 km.) W of the JORDAN River, at an elevation of c. 2,550 ft. (780 m.) above sea level. Geologically speaking, the city rests on three hills. The SE hill was the original city of the JEBUSITES, the city that David seized, later to be called Zion; it occupied only about 8-10 acres (3-4 hectares), and its shape was similar to that of a human footprint about 1,250 ft. (380 m.) long and 400 ft. (120 m.) wide. The area of the fortress city of MEGIDDO in contrast was 30 acres (12 hectares). The N hill was the one on which SOLOMON built the great temple and his own palace (see OPHEL). On the E and SE of these two hills was a deep valley known as the KIDRON. To the S and SW of the city was another deep valley called the HINNOM. Down through the middle of the city, running N–S, was a third depression—now built over and discernible only by careful investigation of the contours of the rock level—called the Tyropoeon Valley. These valleys today give no idea of their original depth, for debris has

filled them up in some places to a depth of 50-60 ft. (15-18 m.).

The city never occupied what could be called a large area. Even in the time of HEROD the Great, the area within the walls was not more than 1 mi. (c. 1.5 km.) in length, nor more than 0.6 mi. (1 km.) in width. The city was off the beaten path of the great caravan routes and was not, as most larger world capitals, on a navigable river or on a large body of water. Its site, therefore, had an exclusiveness about it. On the other hand, being 20 mi. (32 km.) N of HEBRON and 30 mi. (48 km.) S of SAMARIA, it was centrally located to serve as the capital of the Hebrew kingdom. Many travelers have testified to the fact that Jerusalem "from whatever direction it is approached, can be seen only when one

Aerial view of Jerusalem looking N.

© Dr. James C. Martin

J

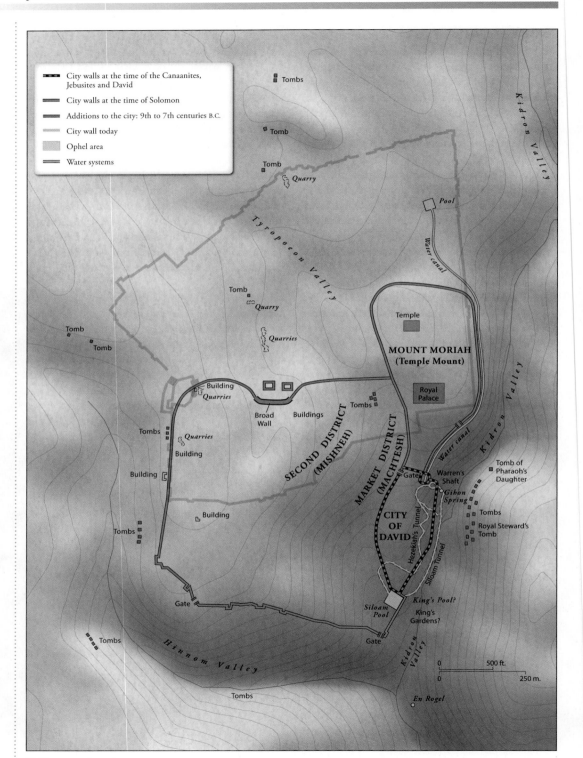

Legend:
- City walls at the time of the Canaanites, Jebusites and David
- City walls at the time of Solomon
- Additions to the city: 9th to 7th centuries B.C.
- City wall today
- Ophel area
- Water systems

Tombs

Tomb

Tomb

Quarry

Pool

Water canal

Tyropoeon Valley

Kidron Valley

Tomb

Quarry

Quarries

Temple

Tomb

Tomb

MOUNT MORIAH (Temple Mount)

Building
Quarries

Broad Wall

Buildings

Tombs

Royal Palace

Tombs

Quarries

Building

SECOND DISTRICT (MISHNEH)

MARKET DISTRICT (MACHTESH)

Gate

Warren's Shaft

Water canal

Tomb of Pharaoh's Daughter

Building

Building

Gihon Spring

Kidron Valley

Building

CITY OF DAVID

Hezekiah's Tunnel

Tombs

Royal Steward's Tomb

Siloam Tunnel

Tombs

King's Pool?

Gate

Siloam Pool

King's Gardens?

Gate

Hinnom Valley

Kidron Valley

| 0 | 500 ft. |
| 0 | 250 m. |

Tombs

Tombs

En Rogel

Old Testament Jerusalem.

J

has arrived in its immediate vicinity: a peculiarity which always brought a moment of pleasant surprise to travelers of bygone days" (J. Simons).

III. Walls and gates. The matter of Israel's gates and walls is complicated and has given rise to a great many technical disagreements; it can be discussed here only in a general way. Because of the deep valleys on the E, S, and W of the city, it was only the N side that could be easily penetrated by an invading army. The walls on the E and W were built on the ridges of these valleys. There was probably in early days a wall extending far below the present southern wall structure. The first northern wall extended from what is called the Jaffa Gate to the middle of the great temple area. The second northern wall began at the Jaffa Gate, extended northward and then curved to the E to the Tower of ANTONIA, just beyond the northern end of the temple area. The modern wall extends N and then E from the northern end of the western wall to the northern end of the present eastern wall. There was a third northern wall of which we have become aware only during the days of modern excavation.

Several ancient gates (including some that go back to biblical times) are still identifiable today. Beginning at the SE end of the early wall is the DUNG GATE; moving northward one comes to the FOUNTAIN GATE; and then, nearly in the middle of the wall of the old temple area, the famous now-closed Golden Gate. Above this is Stephen's Gate. Turning W on the northern modern wall, one comes to Herod's Gate, then the much-used Damascus Gate, and then toward the end of this northern wall, the New Gate. Turning left again at the western wall, one comes to the last of the gates now in use, the Jaffa Gate, from where the road proceeds to the Mediterranean. The present wall, though much of it is, no doubt, on the site of earlier walls, was built by Soliman II about A.D. 1540, extending for 2.5 mi. (4 km.), with an average height of 38 ft. (12 m.).

IV. History. The early history of Jerusalem is wrapped in obscurity. The first reference to Jerusalem in secular annals is in the famous AMARNA Letters of the fourteenth century, in which is found some interesting correspondence from the governor of this city, Abd-Khiba, addressed to the PHARAOH of Egypt, complaining that his city is being threat-

ened and that the Egyptians are not giving him the support he needs and expected. There is, however, a reference to the Jebusites, who are the ones who inhabited the city of JEBUS, that is, Jerusalem, as early as the great ethnological passage in Gen. 10:15-19. Actually, the first reference to Jerusalem as such is found in the account of Abraham's interview with Melchizedek, king of *Salem* (14:17-24). Here is the first occurrence of the word *priest* in the Bible, and because Melchizedek was the "priest of God Most High" we are compelled to believe that even before the nation Israel was founded, and perhaps eight hundred years before this site was taken

This excavation in the City of David (Area G) reveals a 9th-cent. B.C. stepped-stone structure, an 8th/7th cent. B.C. four-room house, and a Persian period tower.

by David, there was a witness to the true God at this place. While there is some difference of view on this point, many believe, and tradition is unanimous here, that the place where Abraham offered up ISAAC at Mount MORIAH (22:2; 2 Chr. 3:1) is the exact site on which, centuries later, the temple of Solomon was built. JOSEPHUS himself affirms that Jerusalem was in existence during the days of Abraham (*Ant.* 1.10.2; 7.11.3).

The actual name Jerusalem occurs for the first time in Josh. 10:5, where the king of the city confederated with four other kings in a futile attempt to defeat JOSHUA. In the same book it is frankly confessed that the Israelites were unable to drive out the Jebusites from the city (15:8, 63; 18:28). At the beginning of the book of Judges it is stated,

J

however, that the Israelites in an hour of victory overwhelmed a large opposing force including Adoni-Bezek and "brought him to Jerusalem," where he died (Jdg. 1:7). This seems to imply that for a brief space the Israelites held part of this city but were not able to keep it (1:21).

Nothing is known of the history of Jerusalem either from biblical or nonbiblical writings from the time of Joshua's death until the capture of this city by David (2 Sam. 5:6-10; probably 998 B.C.). No doubt the fortress that David took is that which later came to be called Zion, located on the SE hill, and outside of the present walls of the city. Kraeling estimates that the population of this city during David's time did not exceed 1,230 inhabitants. Later David purchased "the threshing floor of Araunah the Jebusite" (24:18; 1 Chr. 21:18-28) where the great temple of Solomon was later erected. After finishing the temple, Solomon built a magnificent palace to the N of it.

With the death of Solomon, the glory of Israel and so also the glory of Jerusalem began to dim. In the fifth year of REHOBOAM, 917 B.C., SHISHAK king of Egypt came up to Jerusalem and, without any struggle, "carried off the treasures of the temple of the LORD and the treasures of the royal palace. He took everything, including all the gold shields Solomon had made" (1 Ki. 14:26; 2 Chr. 12:9). This is the first of eight different plunderings of the Jerusalem temple, occurring within a little more than three hundred years. Not only must its wealth have been fabulously great, but also doubtless in times of national prosperity the more religiously inclined citizens of Judah would bestow new treasures on the temple. Only a short time later ASA (911-871) bribed BEN-HADAD king of ARAM (SYRIA) by taking "all the silver and gold that was left in the treasuries of the LORD's temple and of his own palace" and sending them to him (1 Ki. 15:18). Twice, then, within a few years after Solomon's death, Judah's kings prevented an invasion of the city only by bribing her enemies with the treasures of the Lord's house.

Again during the reign of JEHORAM (850-843 B.C.), in an episode about which we know very little, the Arabians and Philistines "carried off all the goods found in the king's palace, together with his sons and wives" (2 Chr. 21:16-17). For the fourth time within a century and a half after the death of Solomon, the temple treasures were used for bribing a threatening enemy, by Joash (JEHOASH, 837-800), who "took all the sacred objects dedicated by his fathers ... and the gifts he himself had dedicated and all the gold found in the treasuries of the temple of the LORD and of the royal palace, and he sent them to Hazael king of Aram, who then withdrew from Jerusalem" (2 Ki. 12:18). Thus far it had been foreign kings that were bribed with these treasures, but the fifth occasion involved Jehoash, king of Israel (801-786). Coming up to Jerusalem, he broke down the western wall for a length of c. 600 ft. (185 m.), and then "took all the gold and silver and all the articles found in the temple of the LORD and in the treasuries of the royal palace. He also took hostages and returned to Samaria" (2 Ki. 14:13-14; 2 Chr. 25:23).

One attack on the city of Jerusalem failed in the reign of AHAZ (733-714 B.C.), when REZIN king of Syria and REMALIAH king of Israel were repulsed in their attempt to seize the temple (2 Ki. 16:5). However, while Ahaz was still king, a mighty king of Assyria, TIGLATH-PILESER III (745-737) came up to Jerusalem. "Ahaz took some of the things from the temple of the LORD and from the royal palace and from the princes and presented them to the king of Assyria, but that did not help him" (2 Chr. 28:20-21).

In 701 B.C. occurred an event to which the OT gives more space, with greater detail, than even to the destruction of Jerusalem by NEBUCHADNEZZAR. SENNACHERIB of Assyria (704-681) threatened the city, casting one insult after another in the face of King HEZEKIAH (715-687), reminding him that he, Sennacherib, had already captured practically every city of Judah, and how could the king think Jerusalem would escape? But by divine intervention, with God's assurance that the king would this time be kept from invasion, Sennacherib's army suffered a mysterious destruction, and he returned to Assyria without fulfilling his threat (2 Ki. 18-19; 2 Chr. 32; Isa. 36).

Another century passed during which we know very little of Jerusalem's history. In 605 B.C. Nebuchadnezzar king of BABYLON forced Judah's king JEHOIAKIM into submission. After three years, the king of Judah foolishly revolted, and this brought Nebuchadnezzar back to the city in 597, leading

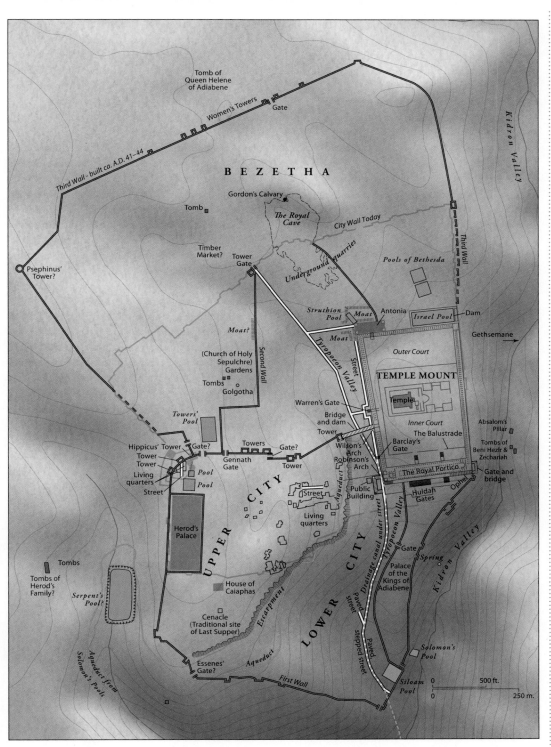

Tomb of
Queen Helene
of Adiabene

Women's Towers   Gate

Third Wall - built ca. A.D. 41–44

B E Z E T H A

Gordon's Calvary

Tomb

The Royal
Cave

City Wall Today

Psephinus'
Tower?

Timber
Market?   Tower
Gate

Underground quarries

Pools of Bethesda

Third Wall

Struthion
Pool   Moat

Antonia   Israel Pool   Dam

Moat?   Moat

Gethsemane

Second Wall

Tyropoeon Valley

Street

Outer Court

(Church of Holy
Sepulchre)
Gardens

TEMPLE MOUNT

Tombs   Golgotha

Temple

Towers'
Pool

Warren's Gate

Inner Court
The Balustrade

Absalom's
Pillar

Hippicus' Tower
Tower
Tower

Gate?

Towers   Gate?

Gennath
Gate   Tower

Bridge
and dam
Tower

Wilson's
Arch
Robinson's
Arch

Barclay's
Gate

Tombs of
Beni Hezir &
Zechariah

Living
quarters
Street

Pool

Pool

U P P E R
C I T Y

Street

Public
Building

The Royal Portico

Gate and
bridge

Aqueduct

Living
quarters

Huldah
Gates   Ophel

Drainage canal under street

Herod's
Palace

Tyropoeon Valley

Tombs

Tombs of
Herod's
Family?

L O W E R   C I T Y

Gate   Spring

Palace
of the
Kings of
Adiabene

Kidron Valley

Serpent's
Pool?

House of
Caiaphas

Escarpment

Paved
street

Paved
stepped street

Cenacle
(Traditional site
of Last Supper)

Solomon's
Pool

Aqueduct from
Solomon's Pools

Essenes'
Gate?

Aqueduct

First Wall

Siloam
Pool

Kidron Valley

0   500 ft.

0   250 m.

New Testament Jerusalem.

J

eventually to its final destruction. It is estimated that some 60,000 citizens were carried away to Babylon at this time, and the remaining treasures of the temple were also removed, to be restored again in the days of EZRA (2 Ki. 24:1—25:21; 2 Chr. 36:1-21; Jer. 52). As Jeremiah vividly reminds us, "The kings of the earth did not believe, nor did any of the world's people, that enemies and foes could enter the gates of Jerusalem" (Lam. 4:12).

Although the postexilic books of Ezra and Nehemiah are filled with details regarding Jerusalem, we mention only the two main events they record. Under ZERUBBABEL, the rebuilding of the temple by permission of DARIUS I was begun in 538 B.C., though due to many forms of opposition it was not finished until 516. Some sixty years later NEHEMIAH, cupbearer of the king of Persia, ARTAXERXES I, successfully undertook the rebuilding of the walls of the city (Neh. 1-6), followed by a great revival under the leadership of EZRA (Neh. 8-9). The condition of the city, however, even under these great leaders, was not one marked by prosperity; somehow it had lost its attractiveness for the Jews, necessitating a vigorous effort to bring people from outlying areas into the city to live (11:1). For the next hundred years, we again know very little of Jerusalem's history.

On the death of ALEXANDER THE GREAT in 323 B.C., the rulers of Egypt were known as Ptolemies, and those of Syria as the SELEUCIDS. In 320 Jerusalem came under the rule of PTOLEMY I Soter. A century later the city passed from the Ptolemies to the Seleucids. In 198 the powerful ANTIOCHUS III (the Great) took Jerusalem. He was welcomed by the Jews, who were rewarded when the Syrian king presented treasures to the temple. Any hope, however, that this would be the beginning of happier days for them was soon seen to be dashed. For in the next generation (169-168) there appeared the very type of Antichrist himself, Antiochus IV (Epiphanes), who desecrated the temple by sacrificing a pig on the altar; prohibited Jewish sacrifices, circumcision, and the observance of the Sabbath; and issued a decree that any Jew found possessing a copy of the Holy Scriptures should be killed; and great was the slaughter. See MACCABEE.

The events that followed next must be referred to only briefly. In 165 B.C. Jerusalem was delivered from its bitter yoke by Judas Maccabee on the twenty-fifth of the month of Kislev (November–December). Ever since, this time of deliverance has been celebrated by the Jews as Hanukkah, or the Feast of Lights (see DEDICATION, FEAST OF). Two years later, Antiochus V (Eupator) overthrew the walls and the temple, but soon after that the city again came into the hands of the Jewish authorities, and so it remained for almost a century.

The Romans now appeared on the scene. The city was besieged in 65 B.C. by a Roman general who, however, was ordered to desist, leaving the city open for the conquest by Pompey in 64, who destroyed Jerusalem's walls. The temple was again pillaged in 55 by Crassus. Fifteen years later the area was occupied by the PARTHIANS. The hour had struck for the rise of that cruel but gifted ruler whose name will be prominent as the NT narrative opens, HEROD the Great, made king of the Jews by AUGUSTUS in 40. He fought for the possession of the territory that had been given to him, but was not able to take Jerusalem until 37, after a siege of three months. Herod, like many other Romans, had a passion for erecting vast buildings, and out of this was born the determination to build what came to be known as Herod's temple, probably the most significant structure ever to stand on that holy site. He began its erection in 20 B.C. Herod died in 4 B.C., and not until A.D. 62 was the temple finished. In our Lord's day it presented a spectacle before which even the disciples seemed to stand in amazement (Matt. 24:1).

Entire books have been written on the single subject of Jesus and the city of Jerusalem. Here we can only summarize the relevant data. One is safe in saying that of the four gospel writers, it is LUKE who, though a GENTILE, seems to have had the greatest interest in this city. The opening events of our Lord's life occurring here are exclusively in the third gospel, and many of the concluding events are recorded only here as well. We begin with the ANNUNCIATION to ZECHARIAH, a priest in the temple (Lk. 1:5-22). When Jesus was a baby, he was taken up to Jerusalem for what is called his presentation (2:22-38). He then visited the city at the age of twelve (2:41-52). The principal episodes down to the last year of our Lord's life are given exclusively by JOHN THE APOSTLE. If we place Jesus' death in A.D. 30, then the first cleansing of the temple occurred in April of the year 27 (Jn. 2:13-25); in April in the year 28 the man at the Pool of BETHESDA was healed (5:1-47); in October of 29, Jesus went up to Jerusalem at the time of the Feast of Tabernacles (7:2); in December of 29, he was in Jerusalem for the Feast of Dedication (Lk. 10:22). Of course, the final week of Jesus' life was spent in and near the city of Jerusalem (Matt. 26:1—27:66; Mk. 11:1—15:47; Lk. 19:29—23:56; Jn. 12:12—19:42). Of the five appearances of Jesus on Easter Sunday, four are found only in Luke's gospel (Lk. 24). The sixth appearance in Jerusalem a week later is recorded only by John (Jn. 20:26-29). Jesus appeared in Jerusalem to all the disciples (Lk. 24:49; Acts 1:1-8), and from the Mount of OLIVES nearby he ascended (Lk. 24:50-53).

Our Lord made four principal statements about the city, all of them with a note of sadness. First, in stating that he must go up to Jerusalem, he declared, "Surely no prophet can die outside Jerusalem!" (Lk. 13:33). On Tuesday of Holy Week he cried out, "O Jerusalem, Jerusalem, you who kill the prophets and stone those sent to you, how often I have longed to gather your children together, as a hen gathers her chicks under her wings, but you were not willing" (Matt. 23:37). We are told by Luke that as Jesus wept over the city, he said sadly, "If you, even you, had only known on this day what would bring you peace—but now it is hidden from your eyes" (Lk. 19:42). Finally, he declared that the buildings of that city and its very walls would be thrown down, adding, "Jerusalem will be trampled on by the Gentiles until the times of the Gentiles are fulfilled" (Matt. 24:2; Mk. 13:2; Lk. 21:24).

The book of Acts opens with a group of the followers of Jesus meeting together in an upper room in Jerusalem, probably the place where the Lord's Supper was held, waiting for the fulfillment of the promise of Christ that they would be given power from on high. The church was born in Jerusalem on the Day of PENTECOST (Acts 2). The early persecutions occurred in that city toward these initial believers, and the SANHEDRIN that condemned Christ was now confronted with the phenomenon of a growing company of faithful followers of the crucified and risen Lord. In this city the first great crisis of the church was successfully faced in the first council, deciding forever the fact that salvation is wholly by

grace, apart from works (ch. 15). Years later in this same city, the apostle PAUL was arrested, mobbed in the temple, and falsely accused (chs. 21-22).

The destruction of the city after a siege of 143 days by Roman armies under the leadership of TITUS, though predicted in the Gospels, is not actually recorded anywhere in the NT. Before this dreadful event concluded, an estimated 600,000 Jews were killed and thousands more were led away into captivity. One futile and tragic attempt of the Jews to win freedom from the Romans was concentrated in the rebellion of A.D. 132, led by the false messiah BAR KOKHBA. This rebellion was overwhelmingly crushed, and what was left of the city was leveled to the ground, even the foundations being plowed

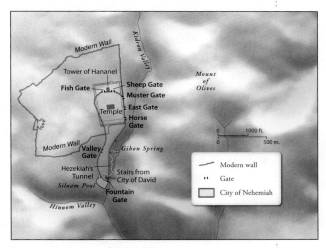

Jerusalem in the time of Nehemiah.

up. Two years later the Romans began rebuilding the city, now to be called Aelia Capitolina. All Jews were strictly excluded from this new city for two centuries, until the reign of Constantine. In the early part of the fourth century, due to the fervent devotion of Helena, the mother of the emperor, the great Church of the Holy Sepulchre called Anastasis (the Greek word for resurrection) was built. From then on, Jerusalem became increasingly the object of pilgrimages and of rich gifts. Jerome says, "It would be a long task to try to enumerate chronologically from the day of the ascension of our Lord until our own time, the bishops, martyrs, and doctors of the Church who came to Jerusalem, believing themselves to be deficient in religion, in science, and

J

to possess only an imperfect standard of virtue until they had worshiped Christ on the very spot where the Gospel first shone from the gibbet."

For Jerusalem's subsequent history, only the barest outline can be given here. In A.D. 614 a Persian general under King Chosroes II seized the city and slaughtered 60,000 Christians, taking 35,000 more into slavery. In 628 Heraclius made peace with the son of the invader Chosroes, entering Jerusalem in triumph through the Golden Gate. In 637 the city capitulated to Omar the Galiph, who entered its precincts without bloodshed. In 688 the first Dome of the Rock was erected. Muhammad, more or less acquainted with both the OT and NT, felt it was necessary to be in some way identified with this city, holy to both Jews and Christians; and Islam soon interpreted a passage in the Koran as implying that Muhammad was miraculously carried to Jerusalem and was divinely consecrated there, but there is no real evidence for this journey. In 969 Jerusalem fell under the power of the Shi'a caliph of Egypt. In 1009 the caliph Hakim, son of a Christian mother, began his devastating work in Jerusalem by ordering the destruction of the Church of the Holy Sepulchre. By 1014 some 30,000 churches in Palestine had been burned or pillaged. In 1077 a general of the Seljuk Turks drove out the Egyptians, slaughtering some 3,000 residing within the walls of the city.

A new era—pitiful, sad, and shameful—now dawned for Jerusalem. On June 7, 1099, the Christian army of the First Crusade camped before Jerusalem. The city was seized on July 14, and the awful slaughter pursued by these so-called Christian knights was something that the Muslim world has never forgotten or forgiven. For eighty years the city knew no other enemy at her gates. There then came on the stage of history the truly great Saladin who, after his overwhelming victory in his battle with the Crusaders at the Horns of Hattin, camped before the city on September 20, 1187. He entered it on October 2, enforcing strict orders that no violence or orgy of conquest should be engaged in by his soldiers such as the Christian Crusaders had participated in almost a century before. By this act of mercy he put the Christians to shame. But the city was not to know peace. In 1229, it was regained by Frederick II, through negotiations. In 1244 it fell before the Kharezmian Tartars. In 1247

it was seized again by the Egyptians. In 1260 it was recaptured by the Tartars. In 1517 it was taken by the Ottoman Turks, who held it for four centuries. On December 9, 1917, the British General Allenby entered the city on foot; on October 31, 1918, the armistice was signed, and 400 years of Turkish misrule came to an end.

On April 24, 1920, the mandate for Palestine and Transjordan was assigned to Great Britain, and for nearly thirty years she suffered one reverse after another in attempting to rule the country. On May 14, 1948, the British mandate terminated, and the National Council at Tel-Aviv proclaimed the State of Israel. There followed the bitter, often brutal war for Palestine, as a result of which nearly a million Arabs were driven from their homes. By the spring of 1949, Israel was recognized by forty-five governments. The struggle with the Arab bloc of nations has unhappily continued. One round of hostilities ended in 1967 with the end of Arab administration in the Old City, and the assumption of Israeli control over the whole city of Jerusalem.

Jerusalem, Council of. See COUNCIL.

Jerusalem, new. A name found twice in the Bible (Rev. 3:12; 21:2) where the new Jerusalem is described as coming down out of heaven from God. In Rev. 21:2 it is also called "the Holy City," and in 21:10, "the Holy City, Jerusalem." In the larger passage (21:10—22:5) the city is described in material terms, as though it were literal. It is in the form of a cube, 1,500 mi. (2,415 km.) square; its walls are of jasper; its streets, of gold; the foundations of the walls are precious stones; its twelve gates are of pearls. For light it needs neither moon nor sun. A pure river of water of life flows through it; and in the midst of it there is the tree of life, whose leaves are for the healing of the nations.

Views on the nature of the city, whether it is literal or symbolic, and on when it comes into existence are legion. Hardly any two expositors fully agree, but in general there are two main views. Some hold that the city is a symbol of the ideal CHURCH as conceived in the purpose of God and to be fully realized in his own time. The church, allegorically depicted by the city, is of course already in existence, but God's ideal for it will not be reached until the new age has been ushered in by the Lord's return. The great size of the city denotes that the church is capable of holding almost countless numbers. The fact that the city descends "out of heaven from God" means that it is the product of God's supernatural workmanship in the historic process of redemption. In support of this view it is said that in Rev. 21:9-10, when John is told that he would be shown the bride, the Lamb's wife, he is actually shown the new Jerusalem; and, moreover, as JERUSALEM and ZION often refer to the inhabitants and faithful worshipers of the Lord, so the new Jerusalem is symbolic of the church of God.

Those who consider the new Jerusalem a literal city usually regard it as the eternal dwelling place of God. Premillennialists see it as a special creation of God at the beginning of the MILLENNIUM, to be inhabited by the saints, first during the millennium and then, after the creation of the new heaven and new earth, throughout eternity. It would seem, however, that the city will not be in sight during the millennium but will be above the earthly Jerusalem. The saints in the city will have the privilege of seeing the face of God and of having his name on their foreheads. Some expositors hold that the new Jerusalem as a literal city does not appear above Jerusalem during the millennium and that the description in Revelation has reference to the eternal state.

Jerusha. ji-roo'shah (Heb. *yĕrûšā* H3729, variant *yĕrûšâ* H3730, "possession" or "inherited one"). Daughter of a certain Zadok, wife of King UZZIAH, and mother of King JOTHAM (2 Ki. 15:33; 2 Chr. 27:1 [KJV and other versions, "Jerushah"]).

Jerushah. See JERUSHA.

Jesaiah. See JESHAIAH (1 Chr. 3:21; Neh. 11:7).

Jesarelah. jes'uh-ree'luh (Heb. *yĕsarēlâ* H3777). KJV Jesharelah. See ASARELAH.

Jeshaiah. ji-shay'yuh (Heb. *yĕsayâ* H3832, short form of *yĕsayāhû* H3833, "Yahweh is salvation [*or* victorious]"; see ISAIAH). **(1)** Son of Hananiah, grandson of ZERUBBABEL, and descendant of DAVID (1 Chr. 3:21 [KJV, "Jesaiah"]).

(2) Son of JEDUTHUN; he and his brothers "prophesied, using the harp in thanking and praising the LORD" (1 Chr. 25:3). He was also the head of the eighth company of temple musicians appointed by lot under David (v. 15).

(3) Son of Rehabiah; his descendant SHELOMITH was a LEVITE who shared the supervision of David's treasury (1 Chr. 26:25).

(4) Son of Athaliah and descendant of Elam; he was head of a family that returned with EZRA to Jerusalem (Ezra 8:7).

(5) Descendant of MERARI; he was head of a Levitical family that returned with EZRA to Jerusalem (Ezra 8:19).

(6) Descendant of BENJAMIN and ancestor of Sallu; the latter is mentioned in a list of Israelites living in Jerusalem after the EXILE (Neh. 11:7 [KJV, "Jesaiah"]).

Jeshanah. jesh'uh-nuh (Heb. *yĕšānâ* H3827, "old [city]"). A town taken by ABIJAH king of Judah from JEROBOAM king of Israel (2 Chr. 13:19). It is mentioned with BETHEL and EPHRON, and was probably located on the border of Judah and Israel. The generally accepted identification is modern Burj el-Isaneh, some 5 mi. (8 km.) N of Bethel. (Some believe that SHEN in 1 Sam. 7:12 is a variant of Jeshanah; cf. NRSV.)

Jeshanah Gate. See OLD GATE.

Jesharelah. See JESARELAH.

Jeshebeab. ji-sheb'ee-ab (Heb. *yešebāb* H3784, possibly "[my] father lives" or "may [my] father stay alive"). A descendant of AARON whose family in the time of DAVID made up the fourteenth division of priests (1 Chr. 24:13).

Jesher. jesh'uhr (Heb. *yēšer* H3840, "uprightness"). Son of CALEB (apparently by AZUBAH); included in the genealogy of JUDAH (1 Chr. 2:18).

Jeshimon. ji-shi'mon (Heb. *yĕšîmôn* H3810, "wasteland"). Name given to a desolate area in the Judean wilderness, apparently S of the Desert of ZIPH and N of the Desert of MAON. This region, described as facing the hill of HAKILAH (to the N), is mentioned to

J

The wilderness area of Jeshimon.

help locate DAVID's whereabouts when he fled from SAUL and hid in the strongholds of HORESH (1 Sam. 23:19, 24; 26:1, 3). The name Jeshimon also occurs in the KJV with reference to the region of PISGAH in MOAB (Num. 21:20; 23:28), but in these passages the Hebrew word is probably used as a common noun (cf. NIV and NRSV, "the wasteland").

Jeshishai. ji-shish′i (Heb. *yĕšîšay H3814*, "aged"). Son of Jahdo, descendant of GAD, and ancestor of Abihail; the sons of Abihail and other Gadites occupied the region E of GILEAD (1 Chr. 5:14; cf. v. 10).

Jeshohaiah. jesh′uh-hay′yah (Heb. *yĕšôḥāyâ H3797*, meaning uncertain). A clan leader in the tribe of SIMEON (1 Chr. 4:36). He is listed among those whose families increased greatly during the days of King HEZEKIAH and who dispossessed the Hamites and Meunites near GEDOR (vv. 38-41).

Jeshua (person). jesh′yoo-uh (Heb. *yēšûʿa H3800*, short form of *yĕhôšuaʿ H3397*, "Yahweh is salvation [*or* help]"; see JOSHUA, JESUS). **(1)** Son of JEHOZADAK and high priest at the time of the return from Babylon and the rebuilding of the TEMPLE (Ezra 3:2). In EZRA and NEHEMIAH he is mentioned because of his official position; the only personal statement is that one or more of his sons were among those who had married foreign wives (10:18). In HAGGAI and ZECHARIAH he is called

Joshua. He and ZERUBBABEL were exhorted to further the work of rebuilding the temple (Hag. 1:14; 2:2, 4). He figures in the great prophecies regarding the "Branch" (Zech. 3; 6:11-13).

(2) A descendant of AARON whose family in the time of DAVID made up the ninth division of priests (1 Chr. 24:11 [some KJV editions, "Jeshuah"]). He was probably the ancestor of a large priestly family that returned to Jerusalem under Zerubbabel (Ezra 2:36; Neh. 7:39).

(3) A LEVITE who faithfully assisted KORE in distributing the contributions made to the temple (2 Chr. 31:15).

(4) Ancestor of a group (connected with the families of Pahath-Moab and Joab) that returned to Jerusalem under Zerubbabel (Ezra 2:6; Neh. 7:11).

(5) A Levite who, with others, "joined together in supervising those working on the house of God" (Ezra 3:9). He is probably the same Jeshua listed elsewhere among returnees (Ezra 2:40; Neh. 7:43) and named first among thirteen Levites who explained the law to the people in the days of Nehemiah (Neh. 11:26). There are several other passages that likely refer to him: he was a leader in worship (9:4-5; 12:8) and was among those who sealed the covenant (10:9, where he is identified as "son of Azaniah"; in 12:24 he is called "son of Kadmiel"). It is often thought that this Jeshua was also the father of EZER, ruler of MIZPAH, listed among those who helped to repair the wall (3:19), as well as the father of JOZABAD, a

© Dr. James C. Martin

Levite who assisted in taking inventory of the silver, gold, and sacred articles (Ezra 8:33).

(6) Alternate name for JOSHUA son of Nun (Neh. 8:17 KJV and other versions).

Jeshua (place). jesh´yoo-uh (Heb. *yēšû῾a H3801*, possibly "prosperous [town]"). A town in the S of JUDAH, listed among the settlements occupied by those who returned from the EXILE (Neh. 11:26). Its location is uncertain, but some identify it with modern Tell Jeshua, about 9 mi. (15 km.) ENE of BEERSHEBA.

Jeshuah. See JESHUA #2.

Jeshurun. jesh´uh-ruhn (Heb. *yĕšurûn H3843*, "upright"). A poetic designation for Israel as the ideal "righteous" nation. It occurs three times in Deuteronomy, both in negative and positive contexts (Deut. 32:15; 33:5, 26), and once in Isaiah: "Do not be afraid, O Jacob, my servant, / Jeshurun, whom I have chosen" (Isa. 44:2).

Jesiah. See ISSHIAH.

Jesimiel. ji-sim´ee-uhl (Heb. *yĕśîmi᾿ēl H3774*, "God sets down, establishes"). A clan leader in the tribe of SIMEON (1 Chr. 4:36). He is listed among those whose families increased greatly during the days of King HEZEKIAH and who dispossessed the Hamites and Meunites near GEDOR (vv. 38-41).

Jesse. jes´ee (Heb. *yišay H3805* [variant *᾿išay H414*], possibly short form of ISSHIAH; Gk. *Iessai G2649*). Son of Obed, grandson of BOAZ and RUTH, father of King DAVID (Ruth 4:17, 22; 1 Chr. 2:12); included in the GENEALOGY OF JESUS CHRIST (Matt. 1:5-6; Lk. 3:32). One of Jesse's ancestors was NAHSHON (Ruth 4:20), chief of the tribe of JUDAH in the days of MOSES. From such lineage and from the fact that when SAUL pursued David he entrusted his parents to the care of the king of MOAB (1 Sam. 22:3-4), we can assume that Jesse was the chief man of his village. He had eight sons, of whom the youngest was David (17:12-14), and two daughters, the latter being by a different wife from David's mother (1 Chr. 2:16; cf. 2 Sam. 17:25). Jesse lived at BETHLE-HEM and probably had land outside the town wall, as Boaz did. When SAMUEL went to Jesse to anoint

a king from among his sons, neither of them at first discerned God's choice. Jesse had not even thought it worthwhile to call his youngest son to the feast (1 Sam. 16:11). He is almost always mentioned in connection with his son David. After Saul had quarreled with David, he usually called David "the son of Jesse" (20:31; 22:7; 25:10), undoubtedly in derision. We are not told when Jesse died. The contrast between his small beginnings and future glory is brought out in Isa. 11:1, 10; and Mic. 5:2.

Jesui, Jesuite. See ISHVI.

Jesus. jee´zuhs (Gk. *Iēsous G2652*, from Heb. *yēšû῾a H3800*, short form of *yĕhôšua῾ H3397*, "Yahweh is salvation [or help]"; see also JOSHUA). (1) Jesus the Messiah. See CHRIST.

(2) Son of Sirach (named after his grandfather) and author of Ecclesiasticus. See APOCRYPHA.

(3) Son of Eliezer, included in Luke's GENEAL-OGY OF JESUS CHRIST (Lk. 3:29 NJB and other versions; KJV, "Jose"; most versions, "Joshua").

(4) Possibly the personal name of BARABBAS (Matt. 27:16-17, variant reading).

(5) A Jewish fellow worker of PAUL (Col. 4:11). See JUSTUS #3.

(6) KJV NT form of JOSHUA (Acts 7:45; Heb. 4:8).

Jesus Justus. See JUSTUS.

Jether. jee´thuhr (Heb. *yeter H3858*, "abundance"). (1) Eldest son of GIDEON. Because of his youth, he was afraid to slay the prisoners ZEBAH AND ZAL-MUNNA, kings of MIDIAN, and so Gideon killed them himself (Jdg. 8:20-21).

(2) Father of AMASA, an Israelite commander who was killed by JOAB (1 Ki. 2:5, 32). Jether is identified as an Ishmaelite in 1 Chr. 2:17, but he is called "Ithra the Israelite" in 2 Sam. 17:25 MT. See ITHRA.

(3) Son of Jada, great-grandson of JERAHMEEL, and descendant of JUDAH; he is said to have died without children (1 Chr. 2:32; cf. vv. 27-28).

(4) Son of Ezrah and descendant of Judah (1 Chr. 4:17). His precise place in the genealogy is unclear, and the verse contains some textual problems.

(5) Descendant of ASHER (1 Chr. 7:38); apparently the same as ITHRAN son of Zophah (v. 37).

Jetheth. jee´theth (Heb. *yĕtēt H3867*, derivation uncertain). Descendant of ESAU, listed among the clan chiefs of EDOM (Gen. 36:40; 1 Chr. 1:51). The name was probably applied to a territory as well.

Jethlah. See ITHLAH.

Jethro. jeth´roh (Heb. *yitrô H3861*, "abundance"). Priest of MIDIAN and father-in-law of MOSES (Exod. 3:1; 4:18; 18:1-12, 27). Jethro is called REUEL in two places (Exod. 2:18; Num. 10:29). In addition, Moses' father-in-law appears to be called HOBAB in Jdg. 4:11 (NRSV), but Hobab was the son of Jethro/Reuel (Num. 10:29), and it is possible that the Hebrew term *ḥōtēn H3162* in the Judges passage should be rendered not "father-in-law" but "brother-in-law" (so NIV). When Moses fled from Egypt to Midian, he was welcomed into the household of Jethro because of his kindness to the priest's seven daughters, whom he helped water their flocks. Moses married ZIPPORAH, one of the daughters, and kept his father-in-law's flocks for about forty years (Exod. 3:1-2). After the Lord commanded Moses to return to Egypt to deliver the enslaved Israelites, Jethro gave him permission to depart. Moses took with him his wife Zipporah and their two sons (4:18-20), but later he sent the three back to stay with Jethro temporarily.

After the deliverance from Egypt, before the Israelites reached SINAI, Jethro came to see Moses, bringing back to him his daughter and her two sons (Exod. 18:1-7). We are told that "Jethro was delighted to hear about all the good things the LORD had done for Israel," and that he offered a burnt offering to the Lord. When he saw how occupied Moses was in deciding disputes among his people, he suggested the appointment of judges of various grades to help him decide cases of minor importance. Moses acted on his advice. Jethro then returned to his own country. It is altogether possible that Jethro knew and worshiped God as Yahweh before visiting Moses' camp. When one remembers that the Midianites were descendants of ABRAHAM by KETURAH (Gen. 25:2, 4; 1 Chr. 1:32-33), it is not unlikely that at least some of the Midianite tribes, such as the KENITES (Jdg. 1:16; 4:11), may have continued to worship God as Yahweh until the time of Moses.

Jetur. jee´tuhr (Heb. *yĕṭûr H3515*, derivation uncertain). Son of ISHMAEL and eponymous ancestor of an ISHMAELITE tribe (Gen. 25:15; 1 Chr. 1:31). The two and a half Israelite tribes in TRANS-JORDAN warred with the tribe of Jetur (1 Chr. 5:19). It is possible that the inhabitants of ITUREA in NT times were descended from it.

Jeuel. ji-yoo´uhl (Heb. *yĕʿûʾēl H3590*, possibly "God is strong"). **(1)** Head of the Zerahite clan and one of the descendants of JUDAH listed among those who settled in JERUSALEM after the EXILE (1 Chr. 9:6).

(2) A LEVITE, descendant of ELIZAPHAN, who served during the reign of HEZEKIAH (2 Chr. 29:13 NRSV; the NIV has "Jeiel," following the *Qere* variant and the LXX).

(3) Descendant of Adonikam and a family head who returned with EZRA from BABYLON (Ezra 8:13; KJV, "Jeiel").

Jeush. jee´ush (Heb. *yĕʿûš H3593*, "[God] helps"). **(1)** Son of ESAU by OHOLIBAMAH; an Edomite chief (Gen. 36:5, 14, 18; 1 Chr. 1:35).

(2) Son of Bilhan and descendant of BENJAMIN (1 Chr. 7:10); he was a head of family in the clan of JEDIAEL (v. 11).

(3) Son of Eshek and descendant of King SAUL (1 Chr. 8:39; KJV, "Jehush").

(4) Son of Shimei and descendant of LEVI through GERSHON (1 Chr. 23:10); because Jeush and his brother Beriah had few sons, their two families were reckoned as one (v. 11).

(5) Son of King REHOBOAM by Mahalath (2 Chr. 11:19).

Jeuz. jee´uhz (Heb. *yĕʿûṣ H3591*, possibly "he counsels"). Son of SHAHARAIM and descendant of BENJAMIN; a family head (1 Chr. 8:10). Jeuz was one of seven children that were born to Shaharaim in MOAB by his wife HODESH after he had divorced Hushim and Baara (vv. 8-9).

Jew. joo (Heb. *yĕhûdî H3374*, "of Judah, Judahite, Judean"; Aram. *yĕhûdāy H10316*; Gk. *Ioudaios G2681* [the English form comes from Old French *giu*, an alteration of Lat. *Iūdaeus*]). This name does not occur before the period of JEREMIAH in

OT literature. Originally it denoted one belonging to the tribe of JUDAH or to the two tribes of the southern kingdom (2 Ki. 16:6; 25:25). Later its meaning was extended, and it was applied to any Hebrew who returned from the EXILE and settled in JUDEA. As these exiles were the main historical representatives of ancient ISRAEL, the term *Jew* came finally to comprehend all of the Hebrew race throughout the world (Esth. 2:5; Matt. 2:2). As early as the days of HEZEKIAH the language of Judah was called Jewish (NIV, "Hebrew"). In the OT the adjective applies only to the Jews' language or speech (2 Ki. 18:26, 28; Neh. 13:24; Isa. 36:11, 13). In the Gospels, *Jews* (always plural, except for Jn. 4:9; 18:35) is the usual term for Israelites, though in some cases it may refer specifically to someone from Judea; and in the NT, Jews (Israelites) and GENTILES are sometimes contrasted (Mk. 7:3; Jn. 2:6; Act 10:28). PAUL warns against Jewish myths (Tit. 1:14) and speaks of the Jews' religion, that is, JUDAISM (Gal. 1:13-14).

jewel, jewelry. There are many allusions to jewelry in Scripture. Among the articles of jewelry in OT times were diadems, bracelets, necklaces, anklets, rings for the fingers, gold nets for the hair, pendants, gems for head attire, amulets and pendants with magical meanings, jeweled perfume and ointment boxes, and crescents for camels. Many were acquired as booty in war. Many were personal gifts, especially at betrothals. At the court of every king there were special quarters for goldsmiths, and silversmiths were a familiar sight in the silver markets of large cities. Jewelry was used not only for personal adornment and utility, but also for religious festivals. Custom required the use of rich, festal garments and a gorgeous display of jewelry when one approached the deity. When the worship was over, these items were taken off. What became of all these jewels? Many were buried in the ground for safekeeping in time of war and were never recovered; others were carried away as booty by conquerors. A surprisingly large number have been unearthed.

Among the oldest jewels discovered in Bible lands are those found in 1927 by the archaeologist Sir Leonard Woolley in the Sumerian city of UR, the heathen city that ABRAHAM left for the Promised Land. In his excavations he found a hoard of

Gold broaches and figurines representing hawks. From the sanctuary dedicated to Artemis at Ephesus (650-600 B.C.).

© Dr. James C. Martin. The British Museum. Photographed by permission.

jeweled wealth in the royal tombs in which Queen Shubad, her husband, and her faithful court had been buried about 2500 B.C. Buried with the queen were sixty-eight court ladies, who in full regalia had walked alive into the tomb and had sat in orderly rows to die, thus showing their loyalty to her. In the royal tombs were found the queen's personal ornaments, including her diadem, a cape of polished gold and precious stones, rings, seals, earrings, amulets, and pins of gold. With the court ladies were found hair ribbons made of fine beaten gold. Ancient Sumerian artisans were capable of producing filigree work with gold at least equal in delicacy to the best done by goldsmiths today.

When the servant of Abraham went to MESOPOTAMIA to find a bride for ISAAC, he gave REBEKAH an earring and two bracelets made of gold after she had watered his camels. At her betrothal to Isaac he gave her jewels of silver and of gold, and to others in the family he also gave precious things (Gen. 24:22, 30, 53).

When the Israelites left EGYPT with MOSES, they "asked the Egyptians for articles of silver and gold" (Exod. 12:35). Not much later, while Moses was on Mount SINAI receiving the LAW, they took the golden earrings worn by men and women and gave them to AARON to make a golden calf (32:2-4). As evidence of their repentance, they were commanded by Moses to strip themselves of their ornaments (33:4-6). For the building of the first TABERNACLE, the people contributed, at Moses'

J

request, bracelets, earrings, rings, tablets, and jewels of gold (35:22).

Exodus 39 gives a description of the official garments of the Jewish high priest, worn when discharging his peculiar duties. They were gorgeous in their jeweled splendor. The robe of the EPHOD, a long, blue sleeveless garment, was adorned with a fringe of alternate pomegranates and bells of gold. Over the robe the ephod was worn, a shorter, richly embroidered vestment intended for the front and back of the body. It was made of two parts clasped together at the shoulders by onyx stones. Over the ephod there was a BREASTPIECE, described as square, made of gold thread and finely twisted linen, set with four rows of precious stones, three in a row, each inscribed with the name of a tribe of Israel. In the first row was a ruby, a topaz, and a beryl; in the second, an emerald, a sapphire, and a turquoise; in the third, a jacinth, an agate, and an amethyst; and in the fourth, a chrysolite, an onyx, and a jasper (but see NIV footnote on Exod. 39:13). Each stone was set in a gold mounting. Golden chains and rings fastened the breastpiece to the ephod of the priest at his shoulders and to the blue lacers of the woven bands. The sacred diadem was made of pure gold, on which was engraved the phrase, "Holy to the LORD" (39:30).

In the period of the judges, GIDEON, after turning down the offer of kingship, requested that every man cast into a spread garment all the gold earrings, crescents, necklaces, and camel chains captured from the Midianites. With these he made an ephod, which later became a snare to Israel when the people came to regard it idolatrously (Jdg. 8:24-27).

Until about 1000 B.C. gold and silver were not common in Palestine, and even iron was so scarce that jewelry was made of it for kings. See MINERALS. ARCHAEOLOGY has uncovered comparatively little indigenous Palestinian art. Fragments of jewelry that have been found in excavated palaces of kings is the work of imported artists. Such finds have been made at MEGIDDO, a fortress-city guarding the Plain of ESDRAELON that was destroyed in the period of the judges.

DAVID accumulated a large mass of jewels, mostly won in conquests against Syrians, Moabites, Ammonites, Amalekites, and Philistines. All these he dedicated to the Lord (2 Sam. 8:7-8) and passed on to SOLOMON for the building of the TEMPLE in JERUSALEM. When his nobles saw what he was donating, they brought for the same purpose gold, silver, brass, and iron; and the common people added what they could (1 Chr. 28). We are told that the Queen of SHEBA brought to Solomon gold and precious stones. The throne of Solomon was overlaid with gold; the steps leading to it were of gold; his footstool was of gold; his drinking cups were all of gold; and "all the household articles in the Palace of the Forest of Lebanon were pure gold" (2 Chr. 9:20). In the succeeding reigns of the kings of Judah and Israel both monarchs and people gave increasing regard to accumulations of jewelry. Repeatedly OT prophets warned the Israelites that apostasy would be punished with the loss of their gems (Ezek. 23:26).

Not a great deal is said about jewelry in the NT, and what is said is mostly condemnatory. Jesus twice mentioned jewels, in the parable of the pearl merchant (Matt. 13:45-46) and in the saying about casting pearls before swine (7:6). PAUL exhorts Christian women not to rely for adornment on "braided hair or gold or pearls or expensive clothes" (1 Tim. 2:9). JAMES warns his readers not to give preference to a man who comes into their assembly with a gold ring and fine apparel, as though he were better than a poor man (Jas. 2:2). In the book of Revelation the destruction of BABYLON is described in terms of merchants who can no longer sell "cargoes of gold, silver, precious stones, and pearls" (Rev. 18:12). The new Jerusalem is described in Rev. 21 as having a wall made of jasper, and the foundations of the walls decorated "with every kind of precious stone" (21:19)—jasper, sapphire, chalcedony, emerald, sardonyx, carnelian, chrysolite, beryl, topaz, chrysoprase, jacinth, and amethyst—a list recalling the list of precious stones in the breastpiece of the high priest.

Jezaniah. jez´uh-ni´uh (Heb. *yĕzanyâ H3470,* "Yahweh listens"). **(1)** Variant of JAAZANIAH (Jer. 40:8).

(2) Son of HOSHAIAH; he was an army officer who, with JOHANAN son of Kareah and the survivors from an attack at MIZPAH, asked JEREMIAH to pray for them (Jer. 42:1). Some scholars, on the basis of 43:2 and the SEPTUAGINT, emend the text to "Azariah" (cf. NRSV).

Jezebel. jez'uh-bel (Heb. *ʾizebel H374*, possibly from Phoen. *ʾy + zbl*, "where is the prince [i.e., Baal]?"; Gk. *Iezabel G2630*). Daughter of ETH-BAAL king of SIDON (in PHOENICIA), wife of AHAB king of ISRAEL, and mother of ATHALIAH queen of Judah (1 Ki. 16:31; 18:4, 13; 19:1-2; 21:5-25; 2 Ki. 9:7-37; Rev. 2:20). Jezebel had been brought up a zealous worshiper of BAAL, and as the wife of Ahab she not only continued her ancestral religion but tried to impose it on the people of Israel. To please her, Ahab built a temple and an altar to Baal in SAMARIA (1 Ki. 16:32). Four hundred fifty prophets of Baal ate at her table (18:19). She killed all the prophets of the Lord on whom she could lay her hands (18:4-13). When she was told of the slaughter of the prophets of Baal by ELIJAH, she threatened Elijah's life, and he was obliged to flee.

Some time later Jezebel secured NABOTH's vineyard for Ahab by having its owner unjustly executed (1 Ki. 21). When Elijah heard of this crime, he told Ahab that God's vengeance would fall on him and that dogs would eat Jezebel's body by the wall of Jezreel. The prophecy was fulfilled when, eleven years after the death of Ahab, JEHU executed pitiless vengeance on the royal household. Jezebel "painted her eyes and arranged her hair," looked out an open window, and taunted Jehu for being his master's murderer. Jehu asked those who were on his side to throw her down, and this was unhesitatingly done by some eunuchs. Jehu drove over her body with his chariot, and her blood spattered the horses and the wall. Later he gave directions that she be buried, but it was found that dogs had left nothing of her but the skull, the feet, and the hands (2 Ki. 9:7, 30-37).

Even after her death, Jezebel, through her offspring ATHALIAH (who was married to JEHORAM, the leading scion of the house of DAVID), came near to bringing the Davidic dynasty to extinction (see 2 Ki. 8:25-27; 11:1-3; 2 Chr. 21:5-7; 22:10—23:21). Jezebel's name became symbolic of APOSTASY and is used in the book of Revelation with reference to a false prophetess (prob. representing a larger group) in THYATIRA: "By her teaching she misleads my servants into sexual immorality and the eating of food sacrificed to idols. I have given her time to repent of her immorality, but she is unwilling. So I will cast her on a bed of suffering, and I will make those who commit adultery with her suffer intensely, unless they repent of her ways" (Rev. 2:20-22).

Jezer. jee'zuhr (Heb. *yēṣer H3672*, possibly "[Yahweh] has formed"; gentilic *yiṣrî H3673*, "Jezerite"). Son of NAPHTALI, grandson of JACOB, and eponymous ancestor of the Jezerite clan (Gen. 46:24; Num. 26:49; 1 Chr. 7:13).

Jeziah. See IZZIAH.

Jeziel. jee'zee-uhl (Heb. *yĕzîʾēl H3465*, possibly "sprinkled by God"). Son of Azmaveth; he and his brother Pelet are listed among the warriors, kinsmen of SAUL, who joined with DAVID when the latter took refuge at ZIKLAG (1 Chr. 12:3).

Jezliah. See IZLIAH.

Jezoar. See IZHAR #2.

Jezrahiah. jez'ruh-hi'uh (Heb. *yizraḥyâ H3474*, "Yahweh goes forth [*or* shines]"). Director of the choirs who took part in the dedication of the walls of JERUSALEM (Neh. 12:42).

Jezreel (person). jez'ree-uhl (Heb. *yizrĕʾeʾl H3475*, "God sows"). **(1)** Son of Etam and descendant of JUDAH (1 Chr. 4:3, NIV and other versions, following LXX). The MT is unintelligible; see discussion under ETAM.

(2) A symbolic name of one of the sons of HOSEA. God commanded the prophet to give his first child this name and then promptly interpreted the significance of it. "Call him Jezreel, because I will soon punish the house of Jehu for the massacre at Jezreel, and I will put an end to the kingdom of Israel. In that day I will break Israel's bow in the Valley of Jezreel" (Hos. 1:4-5). Besides the allusion to JEHU's slaughter of the house of AHAB (an act that went far beyond God's intention, 2 Ki. 10:11), there is a play on words between Jezreel (Heb. *yizrĕʾeʾl*) and ISRAEL (*yiśrāʾēl*). The reference to Jezreel in Hos. 1:11 and 2:22 has a significance opposite to that in 1:5. The place of thorough disruption and scattering will become the place that God makes fertile (as implied by the meaning of the name). See JEZREEL (PLACE).

Jezreel (place). jez′ree-uhl (Heb. *yizrĕ‘e’l H3476,* "God sows"). **(1)** A town in the hill country of the tribe of JUDAH (Josh. 15:56). Jezreel is listed as part of a group of towns 4-10 mi. (6-16 km.) S and SE of HEBRON, but its precise location is unknown. AHINOAM, one of DAVID's wives, may have been from this town (1 Sam. 25:43; 27:3; 30:5; 2 Sam. 2:2; 3:2); some think she came from Jezreel of Issachar (see below, #2).

(2) A city on the border of the tribal territory of ISSACHAR (Josh. 19:18), not far from Mount GILBOA. The Israelites made their camp near it before the battle of Gilboa (1 Sam. 29:1), its people remaining faithful to the house of SAUL. ABNER set ISH-BOSHETH over it among other places (2 Sam. 2:9). AHAB built a palace there (1 Ki. 21:2), and his son Joram (JEHORAM) also lived there (2 Ki. 8:29). NABOTH was a Jezreelite, and he was stoned outside the city for refusing to give up his vineyard to Ahab (1 Ki. 21). JEHU ordered that the heads of Ahab's seventy sons be placed in heaps at the gate of Jezreel (2 Ki. 10:1-11). Jezebel met her death by being thrown from a window of the palace in this city, and it was there that her body was eaten by dogs (9:30-35). The site of Jezreel is generally identified with the modern village of Zer‘in on the NW spur of Gilboa, approximately halfway between MEGIDDO and BETH SHAN.

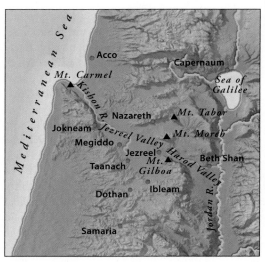

Jezreel.

(3) A valley that divides GALILEE on the N from SAMARIA on the S. See ESDRAELON.

Jibsam. See IBSAM.

Jidlaph. jid′laph (Heb. *yidlāp H3358,* possibly "he weeps" or "he is sleepless"). Son of NAHOR by his wife MILCAH; nephew of ABRAHAM (Gen. 22:22).

Jimna, Jimnah. See IMNAH.

Aerial view of Tel Yizre‘el (biblical Jezreel in Issachar) looking N across the Jezreel (Esdraelon) Valley.

© Dr. James C. Martin

Jiphtah. See IPHTAH.

Jiphthah-el. See IPHTAH EL.

Joab. joh´ab (Heb. *yôʾāb H3405*, "Yahweh is [my] father"). **(1)** Son of ZERUIAH (King DAVID's sister), brother of valiant warriors ABISHAI and ASAHEL, and commander-in-chief under David (his father's name is unknown). Joab first appears in public life in the narrative of David's war with ISH-BOSHETH for the throne left vacant by SAUL's death. He was David's captain of the army, while Abner led the forces of Ish-Bosheth. When the two armies met, a tournament took place between twelve men from each side, followed by a general engagement in which, after Joab's men were routed, Asahel was killed in his pursuit of Abner (2 Sam. 2:12-32). When Abner transferred his allegiance to David, Joab treacherously killed him, with the connivance of Abishai, thus avenging the killing of Asahel at the battle of GIBEON, though Abner had done so in self-defense. David declared himself innocent of this murder, and after composing a lament for Abner, commanded that there be a period of public mourning for the dead man (3:31). David pronounced a curse on Joab and his descendants, but he did not bring him to justice, perhaps because he was politically too weak to do so.

Joab was made the commander of all David's armies as a reward for being the first to enter the fortress on Mount ZION when that stronghold was assaulted. In the war against the Ammonites, which was declared when David's ambassadors to the king had been maltreated, Joab achieved a great victory, utterly routing the enemy (2 Sam. 10:1-14; 1 Chr. 19:1-15). After this war had been resumed, he called for David to storm the town of RABBAH, which he himself had successfully besieged, in order that David might get credit for the victory (2 Sam. 11:1; 12:26-29). It was during this war that David arranged for Joab to put URIAH in the forefront of the battle so that he might be killed and David be free to marry BATHSHEBA (11:6-27).

On a later occasion, Joab attempted to have David's son ABSALOM restored to royal favor after a three-year banishment. He arranged for a "wise woman" of TEKOA to bring to David an imaginary complaint about a son of hers who had killed his brother, and whose life was now sought, a story that paralleled David's own experience with Absalom. David saw in the story a rebuke of his own treatment of Absalom and gave his son permission to return to Jerusalem, though he was to remain in his own house and was not allowed to see his father (2 Sam. 14:1-24). Joab resisted Absalom's attempts to get him to intercede with his father for a complete restoration, until his barley field was set on fire by the prince (14:28-33). Joab then got David to receive his son back into the royal home.

When Absalom rebelled, he made AMASA, another nephew of David, general instead of Joab (2 Sam. 17:24-25). Joab remained loyal to David, and when the king fled, pursued by Absalom, he led one of the three divisions of the royal forces and defeated the rebels. Informed that Absalom was caught in a tree by his hair, he first scolded his informer for not having killed him and then himself killed the prince by thrusting three darts through his heart. When David gave vent to extravagant grief at the death of his rebel son, Joab sternly rebuked him (19:1-8).

After David returned to Jerusalem, he replaced Joab as captain of his forces with Amasa. Shortly after this, SHEBA, a Benjamite, led a revolt against David; and when Amasa took more time than was thought necessary to prepare to quell it, David asked Abishai to take the field. Joab seems to have gone with him. The two met Amasa at Gibeon, and there Joab, on pretense of kissing his rival, killed him. He then assumed command of Amasa's men, besieged Sheba in ABEL BETH MAACAH, and arranged with a woman of the city to deliver to him the head of Sheba. Thus ended the revolt (2 Sam. 20:1-22).

Joab was opposed to David's suggestion of a census but eventually carried it out, though he intentionally did the work imperfectly (2 Sam. 24:1-9; 1 Chr. 21:1-6). He supported ADONIJAH in his claim to the throne, but deserted him on hearing that SOLOMON had been proclaimed king (1 Ki. 1:7, 28-49). David on his deathbed made known that Joab should be brought to justice for the murders of Abner and of Amasa (2:5). At the order of Solomon, Joab was killed as he clung to the horns of the altar in the court of the tabernacle. His executioner was BENAIAH, chief of the bodyguard, who became

J

his successor as head of the army. He was buried in his own house in the wilderness (2:5-6, 28-34).

(2) Son of Seraiah, nephew of OTHNIEL, descendant of JUDAH through the line of KENAZ, and father (founder) of GE HARASHIM, a town inhabited by craftsmen (1 Chr. 4:14).

(3) Ancestor of a group (connected with the families of Pahath-Moab and Jeshua) that returned to Jerusalem under ZERUBBABEL (Ezra 2:6; Neh. 7:11); apparently, some of his descendants returned later with EZRA (Ezra 8:9).

(4) For the phrase "the house of Joab" in 1 Chr. 2:54 KJV, see ATROTH BETH JOAB.

Joah. joh´uh (Heb. *yô'āḥ H3406*, "Yahweh is [my] brother"). **(1)** Son of a certain Asaph; he was "recorder" (possibly the royal spokesperson) under HEZEKIAH, and member of a delegation sent by the king to deal with the Assyrian envoys during the siege of JERUSALEM (2 Ki. 18:18, 26; Isa. 36:3, 11, 22).

(2) Son of Zimnah and descendant of LEVI through the line of GERSHON (1 Chr. 6:21; 2 Chr. 29:12).

(3) Third son of OBED-EDOM, included in the list of divisions of the Korahite doorkeepers in the reign of DAVID (1 Chr. 26:4).

(4) Son of a certain Joahaz (see JEHOAHAZ #4); he was recorder (cf. #1 above) under JOSIAH, and part of a group sent to repair the temple (2 Chr. 34:8).

Joahaz. joh´uh-haz. Alternate form of JEHOAHAZ (2 Chr. 34:8; cf. also the MT at 2 Ki. 14:1 [here followed by NRSV and other versions]; 2 Chr. 36:2, 4).

Joanan. joh-ay´nuhn (Gk. *Iōanan G2720*, from Heb. *yôḥānān H3419*, "Yahweh has been gracious" [cf. JOHANAN, JOHN]). KJV Joanna. Son of Rhesa and grandson of ZERUBBABEL, included in Luke's GENEALOGY OF JESUS CHRIST (Lk. 3:27).

Joanna. joh-an´uh (Gk. *Iōanna G2721*, probably from Heb. *yôḥannâ*, "Yahweh has been gracious" [cf. HANNAH]). The wife of CUZA, who managed the household of HEROD Antipas; she was one of several women who had been healed by Jesus and who helped to support him and his disciples in their travels (Lk. 8:3). She was probably among those who witnessed the crucifixion and then returned to the city to prepare spices and ointment for the anointing of the body (23:55-56); and she is specifically mentioned as one of the women who returned to the tomb, found it empty, and brought the news to the apostles (24:10).

Joash. See JEHOASH.

Joatham. See JOTHAM.

Job, Book of. johb (Heb. *'iyyôb H373*, traditionally related to *'ōyēb H367*, "enemy" [perhaps with passive meaning, "object of ill-will, persecuted"], but more probably the same name as Akk. *Ayyabum*, "where is [my] father?"). One of the poetic books of the Bible, named after its main character. (On the reading "Job" in Gen. 46:13, see JASHUB.)

This book has a definite kinship with ANE WISDOM Literature. OT Wisdom books (esp. PROVERBS and ECCLESIASTES) applied foundational Mosaic revelation to the problems of human existence and conduct as they were being formulated in the philosophical circles of the world of that day. A figure like Job, standing outside the Abrahamic and Mosaic covenants, was an ideal vehicle for biblical wisdom doctrine, concerned as it was with the common ways and demands of God rather than with his peculiarly theocratic government of Israel.

Even an approximate date for the anonymous author is uncertain. The events he narrates belong to the early patriarchal period, as is evident from features like Job's longevity, revelation by theophany (God visibly manifesting himself), the nomadic status of the Chaldeans, and early social and economic practices. But the question is, When was the tradition of Job transformed by the inspired author into the canonical book of Job?

Modern discussions of authorship and date are perplexed by critical doubts concerning the unity of the book. Most widely suspected of being additions to an original poem are the prologue and epilogue, the wisdom hymn (Job 28), the discourse of Elihu (chs. 32-37), and at least parts of the Lord's discourses (chs. 38-41). The SEPTUAGINT text of Job is about one-fifth shorter than the Hebrew MT, but the omissions exhibit an editorial

Overview of JOB

Author: Anonymous. Possibly written by an otherwise unknown sage during the period of development of Wisdom Literature (i.e., the reign of SOLOMON or some time after).

Historical setting: The story takes place in Uz, an uncertain desert region E of PALESTINE; the time appears to be roughly contemporary to that of the Hebrew PATRI-ARCHS, that is, early in the second millennium B.C.

Purpose: To examine the value of conventional wisdom in dealing with the question, Why do the righteous suffer?

Contents: SATAN tests Job, leading to an initial lament (Job 1-3); Job's friends debate the matter in three cycles of speeches (chs. 4-14; 15-21; 22-31), followed by ELIHU's discourse (chs. 32-37); God pronounces his own verdict (chs. 38-41), resulting in Job's repentance and restoration (ch. 42).

pattern of reduction. The argument for additions to the text, therefore, leans primarily on internal considerations—language, style, alleged inconsistencies of viewpoint. Conservative scholars, however, agree that the internal evidence points compellingly to the book's integrity, though they of course allow for corruption in the transmission of textual details.

Dates have been assigned by twentieth-century critics all the way from the Mosaic to the Maccabean ages. The early extreme is eliminated by the nature of the development of the OT canon (see CANONICITY); the late extreme, by the discovery among the DEAD SEA SCROLLS of fragments of a manuscript of Job in old Hebrew script. The majority of negative critics favor an exilic or postexilic date. Conservatives favor the preexilic era, especially the age of SOLOMON, because biblical Wisdom Literature flourished then. There are close affinities in sentiment and expression between Job and parts of PSALMS (see Ps. 88-89) and Proverbs that were produced at that time. The same evidence indicates an Israelite identity for the anonymous author, conceivably one of Solomon's wisdom coterie (see 1 Ki. 4:29-34). The theory that the author was an Edomite has found little support—that he was Egyptian, still less.

The book may be outlined as follows.

I. Desolation: the trial of Job's wisdom (Job 1:1—2:10)
II. Complaint: the way of wisdom lost (2:11—3:26)
III. Judgment: the way of wisdom darkened and illuminated (4:1—41:34)
    A. Human verdicts (4:1—37:24)
        1. First cycle of debate (4:1—14:22)
        2. Second cycle of debate (15:1—21:34)
        3. Third cycle of debate (22:1—31:40)
        4. Elihu's discourse (32:1—37:24)
    B. The voice of God (38:1—41:34)
IV. Confession: the way of wisdom regained (42:1-6)
V. Restoration: the triumph of Job's wisdom (42:7-17)

Stylistic comparison of other ancient wisdom writings with Job reveals similarities, but also Job's uniqueness. The dialogue form of the book is paralleled to an extent in Egyptian and Babylonian wisdom poetry, and the various individual literary forms employed in Job (psalms of lament and thanksgiving, proverb, covenant oath, etc.) are not novelties. Nevertheless, as a masterly blend of a remarkably rich variety of forms, within a historical framework, with exquisite lyric and dramatic qualities, all devoted to didactic purpose, the book of Job creates its own literary species. Of particular significance is the bracketing of the poetic dialogue within the prose (or better, semipoetic) prologue and epilogue. This A-B-A structure is found elsewhere (e.g., Code of Hammurabi, The Eloquent Peasant) and thus supports the book's integrity.

Job proclaims the fundamental stipulation of the COVENANT, a call for perfect consecration to our covenant head, the Lord. This call is issued through a dramatization of a crisis in redemptive history. God challenges SATAN to behold in Job the triumph of divine grace. This faithful servant epitomizes the fulfillment of God's evangelical decree, which even at first took the form of an imprecatory

© Dr. James C. Martin

Bedouin man with his animals. Job's wealth was measured by the livestock he owned.

challenge to the Tempter (Gen. 3:15). By proving under fierce temptation the genuineness of his devotion to God, Job vindicates the veracity of his God as the author of redemptive promise and proves his sovereignty in putting enmity between his people and Satan. Prostrated by total grief, he praises God. While hopelessly despondent and protesting passionately against what he interprets as an unjust divine sentence on him, Job still turns and cries to no one but God. And he repentantly commits himself anew to his Lord, although the voice from the whirlwind has offered neither explanation of the mystery of his past sufferings nor promise of future restoration from his desolation. By following the covenant way, Job shows himself

ready by God's grace, and contrary to Satan's insinuations, to serve his Lord "for nothing."

The particular purpose of the book of Job as Wisdom Literature is to articulate and point the direction for a true apologetic for the faith. The doctrine of God as incomprehensible Creator and sovereign Lord is offered as the fundamental reality man must reckon with as a religious being serving God amid the historical tensions of life. It is also the presupposition with which a philosophical being bent on interpretative adventure must begin. This enterprise is illustrated by the debate of Job and his friends over the problem of theodicy (God's goodness versus evil). The folly of depending for answers on human observation and speculation is portrayed by the silencing of the trio who represent it. The book of Job identifies the way of the covenant with the way of wisdom (cf. Job 28:28) and so brings philosophy under the authority of divine revelation.

No comprehensive answer is given to the problem of suffering since theodicy is not the book's major theme; nevertheless, considerable light is given. Elihu traces the mystery to the principle of divine grace: sufferings are a sovereign gift, calling to repentance and life. Moreover, impressive assurance is given that God, as a just and omnipotent covenant Lord, will ultimately visit both the curses and blessings of the covenant on his subjects according to righteousness. Especially significant are the insights Job himself attains into the role God will play as his heavenly vindicator, redeeming his name from all slander and his life from the king of terrors. Job utters in raw faith what is later revealed in the doctrines of eschatological theophany: resurrection of the dead and the final judgment. This vision does not reveal the why of the particular sufferings of Job or any other believer, but it does present the servants of God with a framework for hope.

Jobab. joh´bab (Heb. *yôbāb H3412* [*H3411* for #1 below], derivation uncertain). **(1)** Son of JOKTAN and grandson of EBER, listed in the Table of Nations (Gen. 10:29; 1 Chr. 1:23). It may be the name of an ancient South Arabian tribe.

(2) Son of Zerah and second king of EDOM; he came from BOZRAH (Gen. 36:33-34; 1 Chr. 1:44-45).

(3) King of MADON who joined the unsuccessful coalition formed by JABIN king of HAZOR against the Israelites (Josh. 11:1); the city of Madon is listed among those conquered by JOSHUA (12:19).

(4) Son of SHAHARAIM and descendant of BENJAMIN; a family head (1 Chr. 8:9). Jobab was one of seven children that were born to Shaharaim in MOAB by his wife HODESH after he had divorced Hushim and Baara (v. 8).

(5) Son of ELPAAL, grandson of Shaharaim (see above, #4), and descendant of Benjamin (1 Chr. 8:18); he is listed among the heads of families who lived in Jerusalem (cf. v. 28).

Jochebed. jok′uh-bed (Heb. *yôkebed H3425*, "Yahweh is weighty [*or* honorable, glorious]"). Descendant of LEVI, wife (and aunt) of AMRAM, and mother of AARON, MOSES, and MIRIAM (Exod. 6:20; Num. 26:59). If the expression "daughter of Levi" (Num. 26:59) is understood literally, then she was the sister of KOHATH (Amram's father), and only a distant ancestor of Aaron, Moses, and Miriam.

jod. johd. See YOD.

Joda. joh′duh (Gk. *Iōda G2726*). Son of Joanan, included in Luke's GENEALOGY OF JESUS CHRIST (Lk. 3:26). He is apparently not mentioned in the OT, although some have identified him with a postexilic descendant of SOLOMON named HODAVIAH (1 Chr. 3:24).

Joed. joh′ed (Heb. *yô'ēd H3444*, "Yahweh is witness"). Son of Pedaiah, descendant of BENJAMIN, and grandfather of Sallu; the latter is listed among those who resettled in JERUSALEM under NEHEMIAH (Neh. 11:7; the name is not found in the parallel list, 1 Chr. 9:7).

Joel. joh′uhl (Heb. *yô'ēl H3408*, "Yahweh is God"; Gk. *Iōēl G2727*). **(1)** Joel the prophet. See JOEL, BOOK OF.

(2) Firstborn son of SAMUEL and father of the musician HEMAN (1 Sam. 8:2; 1 Chr. 6:28 [here the KJV, following the MT, has VASHNI], 33; 15:17). Joel and his brother ABIJAH served as judges in BEERSHEBA, but they were found guilty of misconduct in office (1 Sam. 8:3-5).

(3) Son of Azariah, descendant of LEVI through KOHATH, and ancestor of Samuel and the musician Heman (1 Chr. 6:36).

(4) A clan leader in the tribe of SIMEON (1 Chr. 4:35). He is listed among those whose families increased greatly during the days of King HEZEKIAH and who dispossessed the Hamites and Meunites near GEDOR (vv. 38-41).

(5) A clan chief of the tribe of REUBEN whose descendant Beerah was taken captive by TIGLATH-PILESER (1 Chr. 5:4). He may be the same Joel listed later as father of Shema and ancestor of Jeiel (vv. 7-8). His genealogical connection as well as the period in which he lived are unclear.

(6) A leader of the tribe of GAD in BASHAN, listed as first in importance (1 Chr. 5:12).

(7) Son of Izrahiah and descendant of ISSACHAR; a military chief (1 Chr. 7:3).

(8) One of DAVID's mighty warriors, identified as the brother of a certain Nathan (1 Chr. 11:38). This passage appears to have suffered textual corruption, for the parallel list has IGAL son of Nathan (2 Sam. 23:36).

(9) Head of a Levitical family descended from GERSHON, listed among those who helped to bring the ARK OF THE COVENANT to Jerusalem in the reign of David (1 Chr. 15:7, 11). He may be the same as #10 below.

(10) Son of Jehieli (see JEHIEL) and descendant of Gershon; he and his brother Zetham were temple treasurers (1 Chr. 26:22). The Hebrew text is difficult, and elsewhere Jehiel, Zetham, and Joel are identified as sons (descendants?) of Ladan (23:8). This Joel may be the same as #9 above.

(11) Son of Pedaiah and a chief officer over the half-tribe of MANASSEH during David's reign (1 Chr. 27:20).

(12) Son of Azariah and descendant of LEVI through KOHATH; listed among the Levites who purified the temple in the reform under HEZEKIAH (2 Chr. 29:12).

(13) One of the descendants of Nebo who agreed to put away their foreign wives (Ezra 10:43).

(14) Son of Zicri and chief officer over the postexilic community in Jerusalem (Neh. 11:9). He held an office perhaps similar to that of mayor, and was assisted by JUDAH son of Hassenuah (the latter was either second in command [NRSV] or in

Overview of JOEL

Author: The prophet Joel son of Pethuel.

Historical setting: Disputed, with proposals ranging from the late ninth to the third century B.C.; many recent scholars prefer dates between 600 and 400 B.C.

Purpose: To warn the nation of JUDAH about the coming DAY OF THE LORD, and to lead the people to REPENTANCE so they can enjoy the future blessings.

Contents: The Lord's judgment on Judah (Joel 1:1—2:17); the Lord's pity on his people (2:18-32); the Lord's judgment on foreign nations and future blessings on his people (3:1-21).

charge of the "Second District" [NIV]). It is not clear whether these two men were Benjamites (v. 7) or Judahites (v. 4).

Joel, Book of. Second book of the Minor Prophets (in the LXX it takes fourth place). In the MT the book consists of four chapters, but the English versions (following the LXX and Vulg.) combine Joel 2-3 MT into one chapter; thus ch. 4 MT corresponds to ch. 3 in the English Bible.

The book of Joel is without the customary dating formula used by the prophets (Hos. 1:1; Amos 1:1), and nowhere indicates the date either of the ministry of the prophet Joel or of the writing of the book. Indirect references throughout the book have been claimed in support of dates that have differed from each other by as much as half a millennium. Scholars who follow the traditional viewpoint believe the book to be preexilic, written perhaps during the reign of the boy king Joash (JEHOASH, 837-800 B.C.), for the following reasons: (1) The enemies of Judah that are mentioned—the Philistines and Phoenicians (Joel 3:4), Egypt and Edom (3:19)—are those of the preexilic period (2 Ki. 8:20-22; 2 Chr. 21:16-17) rather than the Assyrians and Babylonians, who later troubled Judah. (2) Amos, a prophet during this time, seems to have been acquainted with Joel's prophecies (Joel 3:16; cf. Amos 1:2; 3:18; cf. 9:13). (3) The fact that the elders and priests are mentioned rather than the king would seem to point to the time of Joash's

minority (2 Ki. 11:21). (4) The style of the book, quite different from that of the postexilic prophets, also argues for a preexilic date.

Many modern scholars believe the book to have been written much later, about 350 B.C. Others deny its unity and claim that the apocalyptic elements come from a time as late as 200. Thus it is claimed that Joel is the last OT prophetic book. Some arguments for the book's late date: (1) There is no reference to the northern kingdom, ISRAEL. (2) The mention of the Greeks (Joel 3:6) is believed by some to be a reference to the SELEUCID line that ruled Palestine in the second century; and even if this identification is tenuous, it is felt that the Hebrews would hardly have known about the Greek people before the exile. (3) References to the destruction of JERUSALEM are detected in 3:1-3, 17. (Certain other arguments depend on a radical reconstruction of Israel's history and hardly need to be considered here.)

The unity of the book may be taken for granted, since it is conceded by many radical critics today. The arguments for a late date are not strong. In such a short book there need be no reference to the northern kingdom, and it is quite possible that the Hebrews may have known the Greeks at a time well before the exile. It should be added that since the book makes no claim as to its date, this matter is not of primary importance. The occasion of the book was a devastating locust plague (a frequent event in the Near East). Those who have not experienced such a calamity can hardly appreciate its destruction. Descriptions of modern plagues similar to that which occasioned Joel's prophecy provide an excellent background for understanding the book. The prophet, after describing the plague and its resulting chaos, urges the nation to repent of its sins and then goes on to predict a worse visitation, the future Day of the Lord.

The book may be outlined as follows.

I. The locust plague and its removal (Joel 1:1—2:27).
   A. The plague of locusts (1:1-20).
   B. The people urged to repent (2:1-17).
   C. God pities and promises relief (2:18-27).
II. The future day of the Lord (2:28—3:21).
   A. The Spirit of God to be poured out (2:28-32).
   B. The judgment of the nations (3:1-17).
   C. Blessing on Israel following judgment (3:18-21).

The book opens with a description of the locust plague in terms of a human army. The locusts are *like* soldiers (Joel 2:7) and horses and chariots (2:4-5). Once the figures of speech are understood to be such, the description is extremely vivid and entirely in keeping with OT figurative language. The locusts are called a "northern army" (2:20). Although locust plagues in PALESTINE do not ordinarily come from the N, invasions of these insects from that direction are not unknown, one having occurred as recently as A.D. 1915. This calamity presages "the day of the LORD" (1:15; 2:1). The locust invasion provided Joel with a catalyst for his message that a greater day of judgment, known as the DAY OF THE LORD, would come if God's people did not repent. The phrase is a designation given to any intervention of God in history for the purpose of judgment (Isa. 2:12—3:5). It also designates the eschatological intervention of God when the ultimate punishment of evil will occur (Joel 2:10-11). Joel's message is that the present locust plague is a harbinger of greater woe if the people do not repent.

In the second chapter Joel continues to describe the plague and to urge repentance. The verbs in Joel 2:1-11 should be translated in the present tense (cf. NIV and other modern versions), for an event taking place in the prophet's own time is being described. Evidently the people responded to Joel's message, for a section full of comfort and promise of the renewal of the land follows (2:18-27).

The second major theme of Joel's prophecy is introduced in Joel 2:28: After the present trouble will come the future day of the Lord, a time of great trouble for the nations when Israel will be vindicated and the messianic age of peace brought in. This frequent theme of OT prophecy is here presented with emphasis on the outpouring of the Spirit of God that will begin it (2:28-29). Then terrifying portents will appear (2:30-31), and Judah and Jerusalem will be delivered and the nations judged (3:1-21).

Joel's greatest contribution to Christian thought is his teaching about the outpouring of the HOLY SPIRIT "on all people" (Joel 2:28). This prophecy is quoted by PETER in his sermon on the day of PENTECOST (Acts 2:14-21). The Holy Spirit came on people in OT times to enable them to serve God acceptably (Jdg. 6:34; 1 Sam. 16:13), and certainly he was in the world and dwelling in the saints then as now, though they had very little consciousness of this fact. But in a special way the new age was to be one of the Spirit (Isa. 32:15; Zech. 12:10; Jn.

Looking E across the Arabah into Edom. Joel prophesied that Edom would become "a desert waste because of the violence done to the people of Judah" (Joel 3:19).

© Dr. James C. Martin

J

7:39). All of God's people would now be priests and prophets, for the ideal stated when the law was given but never achieved would now become a reality (Exod. 19:5-6; 1 Pet. 2:9-10).

Joelah. joh-ee′luh (Heb. *yôʿēʾlâ H3443*, perhaps "may [God] avail, help"). Son of Jeroham from GEDOR; he and his brother Zebadiah were among the ambidextrous warriors who joined DAVID at ZIKLAG (1 Chr. 12:7).

Joezer. joh-ee′zuhr (Heb. *yôʿezer H3445*, "Yahweh is help"). One of several Korahite warriors who joined DAVID at ZIKLAG (1 Chr. 12:6; cf. vv. 1-2). These soldiers may have been LEVITES from the family of KORAH, but some argue that the reference is to a different Korah or even to a locality in the tribe of BENJAMIN.

Jogbehah. jog′buh-hah (Heb. *yogbĕhâ H3322*, "height"). A city in GILEAD fortified by the tribe of GAD near its eastern border (Num. 32:35). GIDEON made a circuit around Jogbehah in order to attack the Midianites from the rear (Jdg. 8:11). The town is usually identified with el-Jubeihat (about 7 mi./11 km. NW of RABBAH, modern Amman), where an Ammonite military tower has been found.

Jogli. jog′li (Heb. *yoglî H3332*, possibly "Yahweh reveals"). Father of Bukki; the latter was a leader from the tribe of DAN chosen to help in the distribution of Canaan W of the Jordan among the Israelites (Num. 34:22).

Joha. joh′huh (Heb. *yôḥāʾ H3418*, short form of JEHOHANAN, "Yahweh is gracious"). **(1)** Son of Beriah and descendant of BENJAMIN, listed among the heads of families living in postexilic JERUSALEM (1 Chr. 8:16; cf. v. 28). His father and uncle, however, are described as "heads of families of those living in Aijalon" and as having driven out the inhabitants of GATH (v. 13).

(2) Son of Shimri; described as "the TIZITE," he and his brother Jediael are listed among DAVID's mighty warriors (1 Chr. 11:45).

Johanan. joh-hay′nuhn (Heb. *yôḥānān H3419*, short form of JEHOHANAN, "Yahweh is gracious"). **(1)** Son of Kareah; he was one of the captains of Jewish forces in the open country during the conquest of JUDAH by NEBUCHADNEZZAR (2 Ki. 25:23). After the appointment of GEDALIAH as governor of the land, Johanan came with other captains to Gedaliah at MIZPAH (Jer. 40:8, 13). He warned Gedaliah of ISHMAEL's plan to assassinate him and asked permission to slay Ishmael, but the

Ancient Mizpah should probably be identified with this hill (Tell en-Naṣbeh). Johanan son of Kareah came to Mizpah and warned Gedaliah of an assassination attempt being plotted against him (Jer. 40:13-16).

© Dr. James C. Martin

request was denied (40:14-16). After Gedaliah's murder, Johanan led the forces against Ishmael, overtook him at the great pool of GIBEON, and rescued everyone whom Ishmael had taken away by force (41:11-14). Ishmael and eight men escaped, but the rest of the people were brought back to GERUTH KIMHAM, a place near BETHLEHEM, from where they intended to go to EGYPT because they feared a Babylonian reprisal (41:15-18). Against the advice of JEREMIAH, he and other Jewish leaders led the remnant down into Egypt, taking the prophet with them (42:1—43:7).

(2) Firstborn son of King JOSIAH (1 Chr. 3:15). Nothing else is known about him. Because he did not succeed his father on the throne, some speculate that he died at an early age.

(3) Son of Elioenai and postexilic descendant of DAVID through SOLOMON (1 Chr. 3:24).

(4) Son of Azariah, included in a genealogy of high priests (1 Chr. 6:9-10). See AZARIAH #7.

(5) One of David's ambidextrous warriors from the tribe of BENJAMIN who joined him at ZIKLAG (1 Chr. 12:4; cf. vv. 1-2).

(6) A warrior from the tribe of GAD who joined David in the wilderness; listed eighth in rank among the officers (1 Chr. 12:12).

(7) Son of Hakkatan; he was family head of the descendants of Azgad who returned to Jerusalem with EZRA (Ezra 8:12). According to some, the Hebrew words translated "Johanan son of Hakkatan" should instead be rendered "Johanan the younger."

(8) "Son" (i.e., grandson) of ELIASHIB the high priest, and high priest himself during the reign of DARIUS II (Neh. 12:22-23; cf. vv. 10-11, where "Jonathan" perhaps should be read as "Johanan"). The identification of this high priest has a bearing on the dispute regarding the date of Ezra's mission, for some argue that he is the same individual mentioned in some extrabiblical sources.

(9) Alternate KJV form of JEHOHANAN (2 Chr. 28:12; Neh. 6:18).

John. jon (Gk. *Iōannēs* G2722, from Heb. *yôḥānān* H3419, short form of JEHOHANAN, "Yahweh is gracious"). (1) JOHN THE APOSTLE. See separate article.

(2) JOHN THE BAPTIST. See separate article.

(3) John Mark. See MARK, JOHN.

(4) Father of ANDREW and PETER (Jn. 1:42; 21:15-17; the KJV has "Jona" and "Jonas" respectively, following the TR); also called JONAS (Matt. 16:17, where the Gk. text reads *Bariōna* G980, from Aram. *bar yônâ*, "son of Jonas"). Most scholars believe, on the basis of the earliest MSS, that the original text of the fourth gospel had "John," and that later scribes, influenced by the Matthean text, changed it to "Jonas." Some speculate that these were alternate forms of his name; others posit divergent traditions in the early church.

(5) A relative of the high priests ANNAS and CAIAPHAS who participated in the cross-examination of the apostles Peter and John following the healing of the lame beggar at the temple (Acts 4:6). He is otherwise unknown.

John, Gospel of. The "fourth gospel," as it is often called, probably influenced Christian thought during the first centuries of the church more decisively than any other book of the NT.

I. Authorship, date, place. Never was there a book written that made higher claim for its "hero." To the Jesus of history its author gives the most exalted titles. In fact, in the very opening verse he calls him *God*. This becomes even more remarkable when we note that the author describes himself as one who belongs to the same race, stock, and family as Jesus, in fact as an eyewitness of the scenes that he so vividly portrays. No one knew Jesus better than he did. John walked with Jesus from day to day. He reclined on his bosom. He stood by his cross. He entered his tomb (Jn. 13:25; 19:26; 20:8). Yet he does not shrink from proclaiming that this Jesus of history, whom he knew so well, was and is himself God.

Tradition holds the apostle John to be this author (see JOHN THE APOSTLE) and that the gospel was written sometime toward the close of the first century A.D. in ASIA MINOR. This tradition can be traced back from Eusebius (the church historian) at the beginning of the fourth century to Theophilus, who flourished about 170-180. The major witnesses, besides Eusebius, are Origen, Clement of Alexandria, Tertullian, Irenaeus, the writer of the Muratorian Canon, and Theophilus. Irenaeus, one of the earliest of these witnesses, was a disciple of Polycarp, who, in turn, had been

Overview of GOSPEL OF JOHN

Author: Anonymous, but traditionally attributed to JOHN THE APOSTLE, son of Zebedee.

Historical setting: Covers the life of CHRIST from his baptism to his resurrection. According to early Christian writers, the book was written c. A.D. 90 from EPHESUS.

Purpose: To evoke FAITH in Jesus as the Christ (Jn. 20:30-31); possibly also to supplement the other Gospels by providing information not found in them and by presenting a different, more theological, perspective.

Contents: After a prologue and introduction (Jn. 1), the author shows how Jesus revealed his glory to the world, only to be rejected (chs. 2-12); he then devotes the second half of the book to the last hours of Jesus' life, his death, and his resurrection (chs. 13-21).

a disciple of the apostle John. The inference seems to be legitimate that this tradition can be traced back to the disciple whom Jesus loved. Moreover, because of his wide travels, the witness of Irenaeus may be called a representative testimony, the firm conviction of the early church this Greek church father knew so well. In fact, the early writers (mentioned above) show us that in the last quarter of the second century the fourth gospel was known and read throughout Christendom—in Africa, Asia Minor, Italy, Gaul, Syria—and that it was ascribed to the well-known apostle John.

Among even earlier witnesses, Justin Martyr (*Apology* 1.61) quotes from Jn. 3:3-5. He uses a number of expressions from this gospel (see also his *Dialogue with Trypho* 105). His doctrine of the LOGOS presupposes acquaintance with the fourth gospel, which his pupil Tatian included in his *Diatessaron* (a harmony of the Gospels). Ignatius, who went to his martyrdom about the year A.D. 110, alludes to John's gospel again and again. Very significant also is the testimonial at the end of the gospel (Jn. 21:24), possibly to be traced to the elders of EPHESUS. The traditional belief regarding the authorship and date of the fourth gospel has received strong confirmation in the discovery of a very early papyrus fragment of the Gospel of John that seems to have originated in the Chris-

tian community of Middle Egypt. On the basis of solid evidence it has been established that this papyrus scrap belonged to a codex that circulated in that general region in the first part of the second century. This scrap contains part of 18:31-33 and (on the back side) part of 18:37-38. Now if this gospel was already circulating in Middle Egypt in the early part of the second century, it must have been *composed* even earlier. This means, therefore, that the traditional view with respect to the date and composition of the fourth gospel has at length been confirmed by archaeological evidence.

Internal evidence, moreover, is in line with tradition. The author was evidently a Jew, as his style (showing acquaintance with the OT) and intimate knowledge of Jewish religious beliefs and customs indicate (Jn. 2:13, 17, 23; 4:9, 25; 5:1; 6:4, 15; 7:2, 27, 37-38, 42; 10:22-23, 34-35; 11:38, 44, 49; 12:40). He was probably a Palestinian Jew, for he has a detailed knowledge of Palestinian topography (1:28; 2:1, 12; 3:23; 4:11, 20; 11:1, 54; 12:21), particularly of Jerusalem and its immediate vicinity (5:2; 9:7; 11:18; 18:1; 19:17) and of the temple (2:14, 20; 8:2, 20; 10:22-23; 18:1, 20). Having been an eyewitness, he remembered the time and place where the events occurred (1:29, 35, 39; 2:1; 3:24; 4:6, 40, 52-53; 6:22; 7:14; 11:6; 12:1; 13:1-2; 19:14, 31; 20:1, 19, 26). He knew that Jesus was weary when he sat down by the well (4:6), remembered the very words spoken by the neighbors of the man born blind (9:8-10), saw the blood and water issuing from Jesus' pierced side (19:33-35), knew the servant of the high priest by name (18:10), and was acquainted with the high priest (18:15). So intimate and full is his knowledge of the actions, words, and feelings of the other disciples that he must have been one of the Twelve (1:35-42; 2:17, 22; 4:27; 6:19; 11:16; 13:22-28; 18:15-16; 20:2; 21:20-23).

By a process of logical elimination it can easily be shown that the author was the apostle John and could not have been any one of the other twelve disciples, for though he does not mention himself by name but calls himself "the disciple whom Jesus loved," he distinguishes himself from others whom he does mention by name (Simon Peter, Jn. 1:40, 41-42, 44; Andrew, 1:40, 44; 6:8; 12:22; Philip, 1:43-46; Nathanael, 1:45-49; 21:2; Thomas, 11:16; 14:5; 20:24-29; 21:2; Judas (not Iscariot), 14:22; and Judas the Traitor, 6:71; 12:4; 13:2, 26, 29; 18:2-3, 5). Matthew's name can be eliminated for it is associated with another gospel. So also the names of obscure disciples like James the Less and Simon the Zealot can be eliminated. This leaves only the sons of Zebedee: James and John. But James died an early death (Acts 12), while this gospel's author survived even Peter (who survived James). It is clearly evident from Jn. 21:19-24 that John, "the disciple whom Jesus loved," was still alive and bearing witness when the fourth gospel first appeared (note present tense in 21:24), though Peter had already gained the martyr's crown (21:19). The reasonable conclusion would surely seem to be that the apostle John wrote the fourth gospel.

II. Purpose. The author states his purpose as follows: "Jesus did many other miraculous signs in the presence of his disciples, which are not recorded in this book. But these are written that you may believe that Jesus is the Christ, the Son of God, and that by believing you may have life in his name" (Jn. 20:30-31). The faith of believers was being undermined by the errors of men like Cerinthus, who taught that Jesus was not really God and that Christ had not actually come in the flesh (i.e., had not adopted human nature). The apostle, seeing this danger and being guided by the HOLY

SPIRIT, wrote this gospel in so that the church might abide in the true faith.

Thus, Irenaeus definitely states that John sought by the proclamation of the gospel to remove the error that Cerinthus was trying to spread (*Against Heresies* 3.11.1). According to Cerinthus, at baptism the *Christ* in the form of a dove had descended on Jesus, but this same *Christ* had left him again on the eve of his (Jesus') suffering. Hence, it was not really Christ who suffered and died and rose again but Jesus (ibid., 1.26.1; 3.3.4). Over against this, John defended the thesis that Jesus Christ is *one*, and that this one divine and human Person came not only by water (baptism) but also by blood (suffering and death). For proof see Jn. 19:34-37; cf. 1 Jn. 5:6. From the very beginning, therefore, Jesus is himself God. He adopted human nature into personal union with his divine nature and will keep it ("the Word became flesh," Jn. 1:1, 14). However, combating the error of Cerinthus was not John's *main* aim in writing this book. It was subsidiary to the aim already quoted from 20:30-31.

The readers for whom this gospel was primarily intended (though in the final analysis it was composed for the church of the entire NT period, cf. Jn. 17:20-21) were living in Ephesus and surrounding areas. They were GENTILE Christians mostly. This explains why the evangelist adds explanatory notes to some of his references to Jewish customs and conditions (2:6; 4:9; 7:2; 10:22; 18:28; 19:31,

© Dr. James C. Martin. Holy Land Hotel, Jerusalem. Photographed by permission.

John alone records the healing of an invalid by the pool of Bethesda and the subsequent words of Jesus regarding belief and witness (Jn. 5). This model of 1st-cent. Jerusalem (looking SW) shows the twin pools that are probably referred to in this passage.

41-42). It also explains the circumstantial manner in which he locates places that were situated in Palestine (4:5; 5:2; 6:1; 11:1, 18; 12:21).

III. Characteristics. In harmony with John's aim, as described above, this Gospel has the following characteristics: (1) It is emphatically the *spiritual* Gospel, whose aim is to show who Jesus is (and this with a definitely practical purpose, Jn. 20:31). Hence, much of what is found in Matthew, Mark, and Luke (the Synoptics) is here omitted. On the other hand, much material is added, the type of material that brings into clear focus the glory of the Lord, his messianic office and deity. (See 2:11; 3:16; 4:25-26, 29, 42; 5:17-18; 6:40; 7:37-38; 8:36, 46, 51; 9:38; 10:30; 11:40; 13:3; 14:6; 17:3, 5; 20:28.) The miracles here recorded also emphasize this same thought.

(2) In close connection with the above paragraph is the fact that here it is not the kingdom (as in the other gospels) but the King himself on whom the emphasis falls. This also accounts for the seven "I Ams" (Jn. 6:35; 8:12; 10:9, 11; 11:25; 14:6; 15:50).

(3) This gospel, far more than the others, records Christ's work in JUDEA.

(4) It is far more definite than are the others in indicating the time and place of the events that are related.

(5) It abounds in nonparabolic teaching.

(6) It dwells at great length on the events and discourses that belong to a period of less than twenty-four hours (chs. 13-19).

(7) It records with special emphasis the promise of the coming and work of the Holy Spirit (14:16-17, 26; 15:26; 16:13-14).

(8) Its style, especially in the prologue, is rhythmic. The manner in which the clauses are coordinated so that often a truth is stated first positively, then negatively or vice versa (1:3; 14:6; 15:5-6; 14:18; 15:16), and the careful balancing of sentences so that antithesis is followed by synthesis, pithy clauses by longer sentences—all make this gospel a very beautiful book.

IV. Contents. The arrangement of John's gospel is superb. First, we see the Word in his preincarnate glory, so that his condescending love in the salvation of sinners may be deeply appreciated. In his earthly ministry he reveals himself to ever-widening circles (to a few disciples; to his mother and friends at Cana; to Jerusalem; to Judea, Samaria, and Galilee), but he is rejected both in Jerusalem and in Galilee (Jn. 1-6; especially 5:18; 6:66). Nevertheless, he makes his tender appeal to sinners, that they may accept him (chs. 7-10; esp. 7:37-38; 8:12, 31-36; 10:7, 18, 27-28). Meanwhile opposition grows into bitter resistance (7:20, 49; 8:6, 40, 48-59, 9:22; 10:20, 31, 39).

Next, by two mighty deeds—the raising of LAZARUS and the triumphal entry into Jerusalem—Jesus manifests himself as the MESSIAH (Jn. 11-12). But though the Greeks seek him (12:20-36), the Jews repulse him (12:37-50). By way of contrast this rejection causes the anointing at BETHANY to stand out in all its beauty (12:1-8). So he turns—and this is indeed a *turning point* in the narrative—to the inner circle and tenderly instructs the Twelve in the upper room, first mainly by means of example (washing the feet of his disciples, ch. 13), and then mainly by means of his word (of comfort, ch. 14; of admonition, ch. 15; and of prediction, ch. 16). He commits himself, them, and all later generations of believers to his Father's care (ch. 17). In his very death (chs. 18-19) he overcomes the world and brings to completion the glorious work of redemption (19:30; cf. 12:30-31; 16:33). By means of his resurrection and loving manifestations (to Mary Magdalene, the eleven, the ten, the seven, particularly Peter and John), he proves his majestic claims and reveals himself as the proper object of abiding trust (chs. 20-21, especially 20:30-31).

V. Outline

A. Jesus' public ministry (Jn. 1-12)
  1. Revealing himself to ever-widening circles, *rejected* (chs. 1-6)
  2. Making his tender appeal to sinners, *bitterly resisted* (chs. 7-10)
  3. Manifesting himself as the Messiah by two mighty deeds, *repulsed* (chs. 11-12)
B. Jesus' private ministry (chs. 13-21)
  1. Issuing and illustrating his new commandment (ch. 13)
  2. Tenderly instructing his disciples and committing them to the Father's care (chs. 14-17)
  3. Dying as a substitute for his people (chs. 18-19)
  4. Triumphing gloriously (chs. 20-21)

John, Letters of. Three anonymous books from among the CATHOLIC EPISTLES in the NT that traditionally have been ascribed to JOHN THE APOSTLE.

I. The First Letter of John. Although the author does not identify himself, the early church attributed both this letter and the fourth gospel to the apostle John (see JOHN, GOSPEL OF). This attribution is supported by internal evidence of both books. The writer of the letter speaks with authority, as an apostle would (1 Jn. 1:2; 2:1; 4:6, 14). He claims to have firsthand knowledge of the facts that underlie the GOSPEL message (1:1-3; 4:14). The tone and teaching of the letter are such as we would expect from the aged apostle, writing to his disciples a last message regarding the truths he had taught throughout his life. When the gospel and the letter are compared, the conclusion is well-nigh irresistible that the two books are by the same person. There are striking resemblances in style, language, and thought. Among these resemblances are characteristic words used in a peculiar sense (e.g., *life, light, darkness,* and *world*), characteristic expressions (e.g., *eternal life, a new commandment,* and *abide in Christ*), and identical phrases (e.g., *walks in darkness* and *that your joy may be full*). The few divergencies are easily explainable on the basis of differences of purpose and of subject.

We cannot be sure whether the letter was written before or after the gospel. Tradition says that the gospel was written late in the life of John, toward the end of the first century. Evidence of a similar date for the letter is that Christianity had been so long in existence that the author can speak of its precepts as an "old commandment" (1 Jn. 2:7); moreover, the writing shows signs that an early form of GNOSTICISM was already in existence.

The purpose of the author is to warn the readers against false teachers who are trying to mislead them, and to exhort them to hold fast to the Christian faith they have received, fulfilling conscientiously the duties, especially brotherly love, that flow from it. Although he does not exactly describe the false doctrine he attacks, there is no doubt that he has in mind the heresy of Gnosticism, with its view that the person of Christ was only spiritual, not physical, and that Christians are free from moral law by virtue of grace. The false teachers are called ANTICHRISTS (1 Jn. 2:18, 22; 4:3). They claim a knowledge of God that is superior to that of ordinary Christians, but, John says, their claims are false (2:4). They deny that Jesus is the Christ (2:22), the Son of God (4:15; 5:5), and that Jesus Christ has come in the flesh (4:2). They also impugn the fundamental moral teachings of the church by their dualistic interpretation of existence, for, according to Gnosticism, sin is not moral opposition of the human personality to God, but the evil physical principle inherent in all matter.

Overview of 1 JOHN

Author: Anonymous, but traditionally attributed to JOHN THE APOSTLE, son of Zebedee.

Historical setting: Probably written toward the end of the first century, at a time when an incipient form of GNOSTICISM was influencing the Christian communities of ASIA MINOR.

Purpose: To counteract false teaching concerning CHRIST and the Christian life.

Contents: Fellowship with God (1 Jn. 1:1—2:2); obeying Jesus' commandments and loving one another (2:3—3:24); acknowledging that Jesus is the Christ who has come in the flesh (ch. 4); victory and assurance (ch. 5).

Overview of 2-3 JOHN

Author: "The elder," traditionally understood to be JOHN THE APOSTLE, son of Zebedee.

Historical setting: Probably written toward the end of the first century, and addressed respectively to an unnamed woman (2 John) and to a Christian leader named GAIUS (3 John).

Purpose: To warn against falsehood and to encourage hospitality to the true ministers of the gospel.

Contents: Walking in the truth and avoiding false teachers (2 John). Commendation of Gaius, warning about Diotrephes, and encouragement to do what is good (3 John).

Although 1 John does not have the usual characteristics of the ancient Greco-Roman letters—salutation, final greetings, messages to individuals, etc.—there is no doubt that it is a genuine letter. Most likely it is a pastoral or circular letter addressed to the churches in the province of ASIA, where the church was in danger of the errors that are warned against.

The plan of the letter is difficult to follow and has been differently understood. Some fail to recognize any regular plan at all. Thoughts that are repeated again and again throughout 1 John are the necessity of doing righteousness as an evidence of divine sonship, the necessity of love for the brethren by those who claim to love God, and believing that Jesus is the Christ come in the flesh.

II. The Second Letter of John. The letters we call 2 and 3 John are similar in words, style, ideas, and character to 1 John, and must have been written by the same author, who refers to himself simply as "the elder" (2 Jn. 1; 3 Jn. 1). Both are very brief, containing just the number of words that could conveniently be written on one sheet of papyrus. Although written to different people and for different purposes, there are striking resemblances of wording in them. The opening address is almost identical, and in both letters the writer expresses joy in the spiritual progress of those to whom he writes, and does so in almost the same

words. The conclusion of the letters is the same in both thought and words.

Second John is addressed to "the chosen lady and her children" (2 Jn. 1). Many suppose that the reference is to a church and its spiritual children, while others hold that a particular individual named Kyria (Gk. for "lady") is meant. The introductory greeting is followed by an exhortation to hold fast to the commandments they had received, especially brotherly love, a warning against false teachers who deny that Christ is come in the flesh, and a prohibition against receiving them. The author concludes with a promise to visit them soon.

III. The Third Letter of John. This epistle is addressed to GAIUS, "my dear friend" (3 Jn. 1), who is eulogized for walking in the truth and being hospitable to evangelists sent, apparently by John, to the church of which Gaius is a member. The author then censures another member of the church, the talkative, overbearing DIOTREPHES, who for some unexplained reason, probably jealousy, not only refused to receive the itinerant preachers but did all he could to get the whole church to follow his course, even to the length of threatening excommunication for those who took a different view of their duty. The author adds that he had written a letter to the church also, but apparently he has little hope that it will overcome the headstrong opposition of Diotrephes. He threatens a speedy

Roman forum and theater at Ephesus (view to the NE). Tradition says that the apostle John wrote his epistles from this city.

© Dr. James C. Martin

visit to the church, when he will call Diotrephes to account for his bad conduct. There is in this letter no suggestion of heretical tendency in the church.

John Mark. See MARK, JOHN.

John the apostle. The sources for the life of John are relatively meager. All that exists is what is found in the NT and what has been preserved by tradition. One can, therefore, give no more than a fragmentary account of his life. He was the son of ZEBEDEE and brother of JAMES the apostle, who was put to death by Herod AGRIPPA I about A.D. 44 (Matt. 4:21; Acts 12:1-2). It may be reasonably inferred that his mother was SALOME (cf. Matt. 27:56 with Mk. 15:40) and that she was the sister of MARY, MOTHER OF JESUS. Jesus and John would then have been cousins. The family lived in GALILEE, probably at BETHSAIDA. The father and the two sons were fishermen on the Sea of Galilee (Mk. 1:19-20). There are reasons for thinking that the family was not poor. They had hired servants and thus belonged to the employer class. Salome was one of the women who ministered to Jesus of her own funds (Mk. 15:40; Lk. 8:3) and was also one of the women who bought spices and came to anoint the body of Jesus (Mk. 16:1). In addition, there is good reason to believe that John is referring to himself when he speaks of the disciple who

knew the high priest (Jn. 18:15); if so, the family probably had connections not usually available to the poor.

John is first introduced as a disciple of JOHN THE BAPTIST (Jn. 1:35). He had therefore heeded the Baptist's call to REPENTANCE and baptism in preparation for the coming of the MESSIAH. How long he had been a follower of the Baptist is not known. In his gospel he tells how he first met Jesus and became his disciple (1:35-39). One day as he stood with ANDREW and John the Baptist, he heard his master say, as Jesus walked by, "Look, the Lamb of God!" The two disciples of John immediately followed Jesus, and when they were asked what they wanted, they said they wanted to know where Jesus was staying. He invited them to come and see. Their stay changed their lives and was so memorable that many years later, when John recorded the account in his gospel, he still remembered that it was about four o'clock in the afternoon. The next day he and some others accompanied Jesus to Galilee to attend a wedding feast at CANA (2:1-11). From Cana they went to CAPERNAUM and then down to JERUSALEM, where Jesus cleansed the temple and had an interview with NICODEMUS (2:13—3:21).

John was with Jesus during his seven-month sojourn in the country of JUDEA, calling the people to repentance and baptism. Since Jesus himself did

J

not baptize, he undoubtedly helped in the administration of the baptismal rite (Jn. 4:2). When Jesus heard of the Baptist's arrest, he decided to return to Galilee. A probable factor in his decision to leave Judea was his realization that the Jewish religious leaders were worried over the fact that he was acquiring an even larger following than the Baptist. On the way N, as they passed through SAMARIA, the incident with the Samaritan woman occurred, so fully described in ch. 4. For a time after Jesus returned to Galilee his disciples seem to have returned to their normal occupations, but one day Jesus appeared by the Sea of Galilee and called Peter and Andrew, James and John from their fishing to be with him constantly so that they might be trained to become fishers of men (Matt. 4:18-22; Mk. 1:16-20; Lk. 5:1-11). This was the second stage of discipleship in John's preparation for his life work. Some time later, he was chosen to the apostolate (Matt. 10:2-4; Mk. 3:13-19; Lk. 6:12-19). The list of the Twelve given in Mark's gospel states that Jesus gave James and John the surname BOANERGES, that is, Sons of Thunder, evidently because of the impetuosity of their temperament.

During the course of the Lord's ministry the experiences of John were common to all the apostles. There are, however, a few scenes in which he takes an important part. The Gospels as a whole make clear that he was one of the most prominent of the apostles, and his own work shows clear that he was greatly loved by Jesus. He was one of the three apostles who were closest to Jesus, the other two being Peter and James, John's brother. With the other two in the inner circle of the apostles, he was admitted to witness the raising of JAIRUS's daughter (Mk. 5:37; Lk. 8:51); the same three were chosen by Jesus to be present at the TRANSFIGURATION (Matt. 17:1; Mk. 9:2; Lk. 9:28); and they were nearest to Jesus during his agony in GETHSEMANE (Matt. 26:37; Mk. 14:33). It was John who told Jesus that they had seen someone casting out devils in his name and that they had forbidden him because he was not of their company (Mk. 9:38; Lk. 9:49).

The two brothers, James and John, gave evidence of their impetuosity when a Samaritan village refused to allow them to pass through on their way to Jerusalem; they said to Jesus, "Lord, do you want us to call fire down from heaven to destroy them?" (Lk. 9:54). They also showed tactlessness and presumptuous ambition when they went to Jesus with their mother and requested that in the coming kingdom they be given places of honor above the others (Mk. 10:35). On Tuesday of Passion Week, John was among those who asked Jesus on the Mount of OLIVES when his prediction about the destruction of the temple would be fulfilled (13:3). He and Peter were sent by Jesus to make preparations for the Passover (Lk. 22:8), and at the Passover feast John lay close to the breast of Jesus and asked who his betrayer would be (Jn. 13:25).

When Jesus was arrested, John fled, as did the other apostles (Matt. 26:56), but before long he recovered enough courage to be present at the trial of Jesus. Through his acquaintance with the high priest, he was able to have Peter come in too (Jn. 18:16). He stood near the cross on which Jesus was nailed and there received Jesus' commission to look after his mother (19:26). On the morning of the RESURRECTION, when he and Peter were told by Mary Magdalene about the empty grave, they went together to see for themselves (20:2-3). In the account of the appearance of the risen Lord in Galilee the sons of Zebedee received special mention, and it is John who first recognized Jesus (21:1-7). In the scene that follows, the impression is corrected that John should not die before the Lord's return. At the end of the chapter the truthfulness of the gospel record is confirmed (21:20-24).

In the rest of the NT there are only a few scattered references to John. After Jesus' ASCENSION he remained in Jerusalem with the other apostles, praying and waiting for the coming of the HOLY SPIRIT. In Acts he appears with Peter in two important scenes. Soon after PENTECOST they healed a man who had been lame from his birth, and while explaining the miracle to the astonished crowd gathered around them, they were arrested. The next day they were brought before the SANHEDRIN. After being warned not to preach about Jesus any more, they were released (Acts 4:1-22). Later, after the gospel had been preached by PHILIP to the people of Samaria, Peter and John were sent there by the apostles; and they prayed and laid hands on the new converts that they might receive the Holy Spirit (8:14-15). John's name is once mentioned in Paul's letters—in Gal. 2:9, where Paul says that on his second visit to Jerusalem after his conversion he met and consulted with James (undoubtedly the Lord's brother), Peter, and John, who were pillars of the church and who gave him the right hand of fellowship. The only other mention of John in the NT is in Rev. 1:1, 4, 9, where the authorship of the book is ascribed to him.

Five books of the NT are traditionally attributed to him—the fourth gospel, three letters, and Revelation. The only one in which his name actually appears is the last. According to tradition, he spent his last years in EPHESUS. Very likely the seven churches of ASIA enjoyed his ministry. The book of Revelation was written on the island of PATMOS, where he was exiled "because of the word of God and the testimony of Jesus" (Rev. 1:9). Tradition says that he wrote the Gospel of John in Asia at the request of Christian friends and that he agreed to do so only after the church had fasted and prayed about the matter for three days. He apparently died in Ephesus about the end of the century.

It is evident from all we know of John that he was one of the greatest of the apostles. He is described as the disciple whom Jesus loved, no doubt because of his understanding of and love for his Lord. The defects of character with which he began his career as an apostle—an undue vehemence, intolerance, and selfish ambition—were in the course of time brought under control, until he became especially known for his gentleness and kindly love.

John the Baptist. The immediate forerunner of Jesus CHRIST, sent by God to prepare the way for the coming of the MESSIAH. John was of priestly descent on the side of both his parents. His father ZECHARIAH was a priest of the course of ABIJAH, while his mother ELIZABETH belonged to the family of AARON. They are described as being "upright in the sight of God, observing all the Lord's commandments and regulations blamelessly" (Lk. 1:6). John was born in the hill country of JUDEA, about six months before the birth of Jesus. His parents were then old. His birth had been foretold by an angel to Zechariah while he was serving in the temple. The angel told him that his prayer for a child would be answered and that his wife would give birth to a son who was to be named John and who was to prepare the way for the coming of the Messiah. About his childhood and youth we know only that he lived as a NAZIRITE in the desert and that he was filled with the HOLY SPIRIT even from birth (1:15). It is thought by some that he was a member of a Jewish sect of monks called the ESSENES, but there is no clear evidence this was so.

Village of En Kerem ('Ain Karim, just W of Jerusalem), the traditional home of Zechariah, Elizabeth, and John the Baptist. (View to the S.)

© Dr. James C. Martin

J

His first public appearance is carefully dated by LUKE (Lk. 3:1-2), according to the way time was then reckoned. This was probably somewhere about A.D. 26, though some scholars argue for the year 29. His early ministry took place in the wilderness of Judea and in the JORDAN Valley. The main theme of his preaching was the near approach of the messianic age and the need for adequate spiritual preparation to be ready for it. His mission was to prepare the people for the advent of the Messiah so that when he made his appearance, they would recognize and accept him. His message did not harmonize with what many of his hearers expected, for while they looked for deliverance from and judgment on the foreign oppressor, John said that the Messiah would separate the good from the bad and would cast into the fire any tree that did not bring forth good fruit. Many of the Jews, especially the PHARISEES, seemed to think that they would enter the kingdom of God simply because they were physically descended from ABRAHAM; but John declared in no uncertain terms that this was not so at all. He called on them to repent sincerely of their sins and to be baptized. The BAPTISM by water that he administered signified a break with and cleansing from sin. His baptism was not something utterly new to the Jews; it had its roots in practices already familiar to them: in the various washings required by the Levitical law (Lev. 11-15), in the messianic cleansing foretold by the prophets (Jer. 33:8; Ezek. 36:25-26; Zech. 13:1), and in the proselyte baptism of the Jewish church. His baptism, however, differed essentially from these in that while the Levitical washings brought restoration to a former condition, his baptism prepared for a new condition.

While the multitudes of common people flocked to the Jordan, Jesus also came to be baptized. Although Jesus and John were cousins, it appears that John did not know that Jesus was the Messiah until he saw the Holy Spirit descend on him at his baptism (Jn. 1:32-34). When Jesus came to him for baptism, he saw that Jesus had no sin of which to repent, and John would have refused to baptize him, had Jesus not insisted, saying that it was necessary for him to fulfill all righteousness. Shortly after, John said to two of his disciples as they saw Jesus pass by, "Look, the Lamb of God, who takes away the sin of the world!" (1:29), and

they left him to follow Jesus. He recognized the subordinate and temporary character of his own mission. Not all of his disciples left him to follow Jesus; and when some of them came to John with the complaint that all men were coming to Jesus, he said to them, "He must become greater; I must become less" (3:30), saying also that he was not the Messiah but only the forerunner of the Messiah. Little is known about John's training of his disciples beyond the fact that it included forms of prayer (Lk. 11:1) and frequent fastings (Matt. 9:14), but he must also have taught them much concerning the Messiah and his work. Their loyalty to him is shown in their concern about Jesus' overshadowing popularity, their refusal to abandon him in his imprisonment, the reverent care they gave his body after his death, and the fact that twenty years later there were disciples of his, including APOLLOS, the learned Alexandrian Jew, in faraway EPHESUS (Acts 18:24-25; 19:1-7).

The exact time of John's imprisonment or the length of time he was in prison is not known. It is clear, however, that Jesus began his ministry in Galilee after John was arrested and that John had been in prison approximately seven months when he sent two of his disciples to Jesus to inquire whether he really was the Messiah. This inquiry seems strange in view of his previous signal testimonies and is probably to be explained either in the interest of his disciples, who needed assurance that Jesus was really the Messiah; or in some misgivings of his own because the messianic kingdom was not being ushered in as suddenly and as cataclysmically as he had expected; or perhaps because he thought he was being forgotten while others were being helped. When the two disciples returned to John, Jesus expressed the frankest appreciation of John, declaring him to be more than a prophet, and that he was indeed God's messenger sent to prepare the way for him (Matt. 11:10-19). The Gospels tell that John met his death through the vindictiveness of HERODIAS, whom John had denounced for her sin of living in adultery with HEROD Antipas (Mk. 6:18-28).

Joiada. joi′uh-duh (Heb. *yôyādāʿ H3421*, short form of JEHOIADA, "Yahweh has known"). **(1)** Son of Paseah; he and Meshullam repaired the Jeshanah Gate (see OLD GATE) under NEHEMIAH (Neh.

3:6; KJV, "Jehoiada"). They are said to have "laid its beams and put its doors and bolts and bars in place."

(2) Son of ELIASHIB and descendant of JESHUA the high PRIEST (Neh. 12:10-11, 22). A son of his married the daughter of SANBALLAT the Horonite (13:28; NRSV, "Jehoiada").

Joiakim. joi'uh-kim (Heb. *yôyāqîm H3423*, short form of JEHOIAKIM, "Yahweh raises up"). Son of JESHUA and father of ELIASHIB; all three held the office of high PRIEST after the EXILE (Neh. 12:10, 12, 26).

Joiarib. joi'uh-rib (Heb. *yôyārîb H3424*, short form of JEHOIARIB, "Yahweh contends [for me]"). (1) One of two "men of learning" who, with others, were sent by EZRA to search for LEVITES (Ezra 8:16). See comments under ELNATHAN #3.

(2) Son of Zechariah and ancestor of Maaseiah; the latter was a prominent member of the tribe of JUDAH who lived in JERUSALEM after the EXILE (Neh. 11:5).

(3) A man included among the "leaders of the priests and their associates in the days of Jeshua" (Neh. 12:6; cf. v. 7). He may be the same individual who is apparently described as the father of JEDAIAH (11:10 NRSV; the text may have suffered textual corruption, and the NIV dissociates the names of Jedaiah and Joiarib). Later, in the days of the high priest JOIAKIM, the head of Joiarib's family was Mattenai (12:19; cf. v. 12). This Joiarib is probably the same as JEHOIARIB (1 Chr. 9:10).

Jokdeam. jok'dee-uhm (Heb. *yoqdě'ām H3680*, derivation uncertain). A town in the hill country of the tribe of JUDAH (Josh. 15:56); it is usually identified with JORKEAM (1 Chr. 2:44). The precise location of Jokdeam is unknown, but it is listed with towns that lie approximately 4-10 mi. (6-16 km.) S and SE of HEBRON, so a few scholars have tentatively identified it with modern Khirbet er-Raq'ah, just N of JUTTAH.

Jokim. joh'kim (Heb. *yôqîm H3451*, short form of JEHOIAKIM, "Yahweh raises up"). Son of SHELA and grandson of JUDAH; he and one (or more) of his brothers are said to have "ruled in" (or "married into") MOAB and JASHUBI LEHEM (1 Chr. 4:22). Some scholars believe that the words "and Jashubi

Lehem" should be emended to either "but returned to Lehem" (so NRSV) or "and they resided in Bethlehem."

Jokmeam. jok'mee-uhm (Heb. *yoqmě'ām H3695*, perhaps "the Kinsman [*i.e.*, ancestral god] takes a stand"). (1) A LEVITICAL CITY within the tribal territory of EPHRAIM, allotted to the clan of KOHATH (1 Chr. 6:68; called KIBZAIM in the parallel list, Josh. 21:22); it is mentioned between GEZER and BETH HORON, which were in SW Ephraim, but its precise location is unknown.

(2) A town that marked the border of SOLOMON's fifth administrative district (1 Ki. 4:12; KJV, "Jokneam"); because it is listed after BETH SHAN and ABEL MEHOLAH, this town was probably in the JORDAN Valley, in E Ephraim, and it should possibly be identified with modern Tell es-Samadi (some 12 mi./19 km. ESE of SHECHEM) or nearby Tell el-Mazar.

Jokneam. jok'nee-uhm (Heb. *yoqně'ām H3696*, derivation uncertain). (1) A town in the tribal territory of ZEBULUN that served to mark its SW boundary (Josh. 19:11); it was assigned to the descendants of MERARI as a LEVITICAL CITY (21:34; 1 Chr. 6:77). The king of this royal Canaanite city, said to be located in CARMEL, is included in the list of kings defeated by JOSHUA on the W of the JORDAN (Josh. 12:22). Jokneam is identified with Tell Qeimun, a mound located at the NW end of the plain of ESDRAELON, 7 mi. (11 km.) NW of MEGIDDO. The town was one of the fortresses that guarded the routes across Carmel.

(2) KJV form of JOKMEAM in 1 Ki. 4:12.

Jokshan. jok'shan (Heb. *yoqšān H3705*, derivation uncertain). Son of ABRAHAM and KETURAH, and father of SHEBA and DEDAN (Gen. 25:2-3; 1 Chr. 1:32). Abraham sent the sons of Keturah to the E (Gen. 25:6), where they became the ancestors of Arabian tribes.

Joktan. jok'tan (Heb. *yoqṭān H3690*, possibly from a root meaning "vigilant"). Son of EBER and descendant of SHEM, included in the Table of Nations (Gen. 10:25-29; 1 Chr. 1:19-23). His thirteen children are said to have lived from

J

Mesha to Sephar (Gen. 10:30), probably referring to locations in SW Arabia.

Joktheel. jok'thee-uhl (Heb. *yoqtĕ'ēl H3706*, possibly "God nourishes"). **(1)** A town within the tribal territory of Judah (Josh. 15:38). Included in the S Shephelah district, it was presumably near Mizpeh and Lachish, but its precise location is unknown.

(2) Name given to the Edomite city of Sela by Amaziah, king of Judah, after he captured it (2 Ki. 14:7).

Jona. joh'nuh. According to the KJV, the father of Simon Peter (Jn. 1:42). See John #4.

Jonadab, Jehonadab. joh'nuh-dab, ji-hoh'nuh-dab (Heb. *yônādāb H3432*, short form of *yĕhônādāb H3386*, "Yahweh is willing [*or* noble *or* generous]"). **(1)** Son of Shimeah (or Shammah) and nephew of King David (2 Sam. 13:3-5, 32-35). Scripture calls him "a very shrewd man," and he used his craftiness to promote the incestuous lust of Amnon. Upon the murder of Amnon by Absalom, Jonadab reassured David that his other sons had not been killed. Some scholars identify Jonadab with Shimeah's son Jonathan, who is credited with killing a giant (2 Sam. 21:21; 1 Chr. 20:7); others believe Jonadab and Jonathan were brothers.

(2) Son (or descendant) of Recab; he encouraged Jehu in the abolition of Baal worship in Samaria (1 Ki. 10:15, 23 ["Jehonadab"]) and was the founder of a nomadic community (Jer. 35:6-19). See Recabite.

Jonah. joh'nuh (Heb. *yônāh H3434*, "dove"; Gk. *Iōnas G2731*). **(1)** Son of Amittai; Israelite prophet. See Jonah, Book of.

(2) Father of Simon Peter (Matt. 16:17). See John #4.

Jonah, Book of. Fifth book of the Minor Prophets, attributed to Jonah son of Amittai, an eighth century prophet of Israel. This little book of four chapters has been the subject of intense disagreement concerning its historicity and interpretation. The debate is occasioned primarily by the narrative's supernatural elements: the great fish, the repentance of Nineveh, and the gourd and worm.

According to 2 Ki. 14:25, Jonah son of Amittai came from the town of Gath Hepher in the tribe of Zebulun, and he predicted the restoration of the land of Israel to its ancient boundaries through the efforts of Jeroboam II. The exact words of this prediction are not given, nor are we told the specific time when the prophecy was uttered; but we may be certain that it was pronounced sometime

Overview of JONAH

Author: Anonymous, but probably composed by the main character of the book, prophet Jonah son of Amittai.

Historical setting: The events described take place during the height of the Assyrian empire, and elsewhere (2 Ki. 14:25) Jonah is identified as active in the reign of Jeroboam II (c. 750 B.C.). The book was probably written soon after the events, but critical scholars believe it was composed by someone else in the fifth century B.C. or even later.

Purpose: To point out the stubbornness and excessive nationalism of the Israelites and to stress God's compassion for those outside Israel.

Contents: Jonah flees from God's call (Jon. 1), prays in the belly of the fish (ch. 2), preaches in Nineveh (ch. 3), and sulks before God (ch. 4).

before the conquests of Jeroboam, either about the start of his reign or toward the close of the preceding reign. Jeroboam ruled for a period of forty years (c. 790-750 B.C., but the exact dates are debated). When he ascended the throne, he found the kingdom weak because ever since the time of JEHU, his great-grandfather, the people had been forced to pay continual tribute to ASSYRIA. He became the most powerful of all the monarchs who ever sat on the throne of SAMARIA, capturing HAMATH and DAMASCUS and restoring to Israel all the territory it used to have from Hamath to the DEAD SEA. The prophet HOSEA also prophesied in the time of Jeroboam, but it must have been only toward the very close of his reign, as his prophetic activity extended to the time of HEZEKIAH, sixty years later.

The identity of this prophet with the main character of the book of Jonah cannot reasonably be doubted. Jonah 1:1 reads, "The word of the Lord came to Jonah son of Amittai." It is extremely unlikely that there were two prophets with the same name. While the author of the book of Jonah does not identify himself, the likelihood is that the prophet himself wrote it (see discussion below). In all probability the book was written not long after the events took place, in the latter part of Jeroboam's reign. The spirit and teaching of the book of Jonah rank with the highest of the OT prophetical books. Not as much can be said for the prophet himself, who ranks low in the catalog of OT prophets. He was a proud, self-centered egotist: willful, pouting, jealous, bloodthirsty; a lover of Israel, but without proper respect for God or love for his enemies.

The book differs from the other Minor Prophets in that while they for the most part contain prophetic discourses, with a minimum of narrative material, Jonah is mainly occupied with a narrative, and the prophetic message in it is almost incidental. The chapter divisions mark the four natural sections of the book: Jonah's disobedience (Jon. 1); Jonah's prayer (ch. 2); Jonah's preaching to the Ninevites (ch. 3); Jonah's complaints (ch. 4). The book begins with Jonah's call to preach at NINEVEH because of its great wickedness. Instead of obeying, he took a ship in the opposite direction, to TARSHISH, probably in SW Spain. In the sequel

of the account he frankly gives his reason for refusing to obey God's command, "That is why I was so quick to flee to Tarshish. I knew that you are a gracious and compassionate God, slow to anger and abounding in love, a God who relents from sending calamity" (4:2). His disobedience thus arose from a fear that the Ninevites would heed his message and repent, and that God would forgive the city that had for many years grievously oppressed his own land. He was evidently a narrow-minded patriot who feared that Assyria would someday destroy his own people; and he did not want to do anything that might contribute to that event.

During a violent storm at sea, the heathen sailors prayed to their own gods who, they thought, must be offended with some person on board. They cast lots to discover the culprit, and when the lot fell on Jonah, he confessed that he was fleeing from the Lord and volunteered to be thrown overboard for their sakes. This was done, the storm subsided, and the sailors offered a sacrifice to God. The Lord prepared a great fish to swallow Jonah. Surprised to find himself alive in the body of the fish, the prophet gave thanks to God and expressed the confident hope that he would ultimately be delivered. After three days and three nights the fish vomited him onto the dry land.

Commanded a second time to go to Nineveh, Jonah obeyed and delivered his message, "Forty more days and Nineveh will be overturned" (Jon.

Metal relief on the door of the Church of the Annunciation (Nazareth) depicting Jonah being spewed out on dry land.

© Dr. James C. Martin

3:4). The effect of his message was undoubtedly greatly heightened by the account of his deliverance, which had either preceded him or been told by himself. The people of Nineveh repented in sackcloth and ashes, and God spared the city. When Jonah learned that Nineveh was to be spared, he broke out into loud and bitter complaint, not because he felt discredited as a prophet on account of the failure of his prediction, but because he was sure that the sparing of Nineveh sealed the doom of his own country. By the withering of a vine, the Lord taught the prophet that if a mean and perishable plant could come to have such value to him, how much greater should be the estimate put on the lives of thousands of children and cattle in the great city of Nineveh. These meant more to God than Jonah's vine could ever mean to Jonah.

The purpose of the book is primarily to teach that God's gracious purposes are not limited to Israel but extend to the GENTILE world. The author wishes to enlarge the sympathies of Israel, so that as God's missionaries they will lead the Gentiles to repentance and to God. The ready response of the Ninevites shows that the heathen are capable of genuine repentance. The book of Jonah may be regarded as a great work on foreign missions. It anticipates the catholicity of the gospel program of Jesus, and is the OT counterpart of Jn. 3:16, "For God so loved the world."

The book is anonymous, and its authorship is in dispute. The traditional view is that the prophet Jonah is the author, and his book is a record of his own experiences. A more recent view is that the book was written long after Jonah's time by some anonymous author and that it is a work of fiction (an allegory or a parable) with a moral lesson. The arguments advanced against Jonah's own authorship—e.g., that the author writes in the third person, or that the book contains late ARAMAIC features—are hardly conclusive. With regard to its historicity, proper weight must be given to the fact that from the earliest period and up to modern times, the book has been regarded as a simple and straightforward narrative. Moreover, it is apparent that Jesus agreed with his contemporaries on this matter, for on more than one occasion he treated the narrative as history and taught it as such (Matt. 12:38-41; 16:4; Lk. 11:29-32).

Jonam. joh´nuhm (Gk. *Iōnam G2729*). KJV Jonan. Son of Elikaim, included in Luke's GENEALOGY OF JESUS CHRIST (Lk. 3:30).

Jonan. See JONAM.

Jonas. joh´nuhs. (1) KJV NT form of JONAH.

(2) According to the KJV, the father of Simon PETER (Jn. 21:15-17). See JOHN #4.

Jonathan. jon´uh-thuhn (Heb. *yônātān H3440*, short form of *yĕhônātān H3387*, "Yahweh has given [a child]"; the longer form is almost twice as common, but is almost always rendered "Jonathan" in English Bibles; see also JEHONATHAN). A very common name among the Israelites in all periods.

(1) Firstborn son of King SAUL and heir apparent to the throne of Israel (1 Sam. 14:49). Jonathan comes on the scene soon after his father was crowned king. He gained an important victory over the Ammonites, who had been harassing the Israelites. Saul's army numbered 3,000 men (13:2), a third of whom he placed under the command of Jonathan at GIBEAH, while the rest he retained at his headquarters at MICMASH. In the valley midway between the two camps, at a place called GEBA, the PHILISTINES established an outpost and forced Saul to evacuate and fall back on Gibeah and GILGAL with a greatly reduced army, now numbering only 600 men (13:15), the rest having fled in fear to hide in caves or having been pressed into the enemy's service. In spite of this, Jonathan, assisted only by his armor-bearer, surprised the Philistine outpost at Geba and killed twenty men (14:1-14). The resulting panic spread to the main camp, and when Saul came to attack, he found the Philistines confusedly attacking one another, and soon the whole Philistine army was in headlong flight. In this rout, the only weapons the Israelites had were farming implements (13:22), Saul and Jonathan alone being armed with swords and spears. The victory would have been even more complete had not Saul superstitiously ordered the people to refrain from eating until the day was over (14:24). Unaware of this prohibition, Jonathan, in his hot pursuit of the enemy, refreshed himself by eating wild honey. Saul would have had him put to death, but the people intervened. They recognized

that, with the help of God, his energetic action had brought them a mighty victory.

But great as Jonathan's military qualities were, he is best remembered as the friend of DAVID. He exemplified all that is noblest in friendship—warmth of affection, unselfishness, helpfulness, and loyalty. His love for David began the day the two first met after the killing of GOLIATH (1 Sam. 18:1-4), and it remained steadfast despite Saul's suggestion that David would someday be king in their stead (20:31). When Jonathan first realized his father's animosity toward David, he interceded for his friend (19:1-7); and later, more than once, he risked his life for him. Once Saul, angered by what he regarded as unfilial conduct, threw a javelin at him, as he had done several times at David. The last meeting of the two friends took place in the desert of ZIPH, where Jonathan "helped his friend find strength in God" (23:16). He would not take part in the proceedings of his father against David, who was forced to live in hiding and from whom he was separated for many years. His disinterestedness and willingness to surrender all claims to the throne for the sake of his friend gives evidence of a character that is unsurpassed. While always holding to his own opinion of David, Jonathan conformed as much as he could to his father's views and wishes, and presents a noble example of filial piety. There was one temporary estrangement between Saul and Jonathan, provoked when Saul impugned the honor of Jonathan's mother (20:30).

Jonathan died with his father and brothers on Mount GILBOA in battle against the Philistines (1 Sam. 31:2). Their bodies were hung on the walls of BETH SHAN, but under cover of night the men of JABESH GILEAD, out of gratitude for what Saul had done for them at the beginning of his career (11:1-11), removed them and gave them honorable burial.

(2) Son of GERSHOM and grandson of MOSES (Jdg. 18:30; the MT inserts the letter *n* into the name *mōšeh*, "Moses," and vocalizes it *měnaššeh*, "Manasseh," clearly an attempt to distance the descendants of Moses from idolatry). He is apparently to be identified with the LEVITE from BETHLEHEM of Judah who traveled to the hill country of Ephraim and was installed by MICAH as his household priest (17:7-9). Jonathan was discovered by five spies from the tribe of DAN who recognized him and made use of his divinatory ability (18:2-

6). Later, when some of the Danites migrated to the N, they stopped again at the house of Micah, stole the cultic equipment accumulated by him, and talked the willing Jonathan into becoming priest for the entire tribe of Dan (18:14-20). A sanctuary was established at the city of Dan, a site formerly called Laish. There Jonathan and his descendants served as priests until the fall of Israel to the Assyrians in the eighth century B.C. (18:29-31). Perhaps the intention of the author is to indicate how far removed this worship was from the established religion of the ancestor Moses.

(3) Son of ABIATHAR the priest (2 Sam. 15:27). With AHIMAAZ the son of ZADOK, he acted as a courier for DAVID during the revolt by ABSALOM. The young men waited at EN ROGEL (17:17) for word brought by a maidservant concerning events in Jerusalem, and this word they carried to David at the fords of the Jordan. Later, when ADONIJAH proclaimed himself successor to his father David, Jonathan carried word to the celebrants at En Rogel that King David had ordered SOLOMON anointed king at GIHON (1 Ki. 1:42-45).

(4) Son of Shimei (2 Sam. 21:21 NRSV; Shimea in 1 Chr. 20:7), David's brother. This Jonathan killed a giant from GATH who had six fingers on each hand and six toes on each foot. Some identify him with JONADAB son of Shimeah, but it is more likely that they were brothers. This Jonathan should not be confused with the son of Shammah (#5, below), since this latter was not a Bethlehemite, but perhaps he may be equated with the "uncle" of David (#8).

(5) Son of Shammah the HARARITE, included among the Thirty, David's elite force (2 Sam. 23:33 [the MT lacks the words "son of"]; identified as son of Shagee in 1 Chr. 11:34).

(6) Son of Jada and descendant of JERAHMEEL, included in the genealogy of JUDAH (1 Chr. 2:32-33).

(7) Son of Uzziah and overseer of the provincial storehouses (treasuries) in the country, towns, villages, and watchtowers during the reign of David (1 Chr. 27:25).

(8) Uncle of David, described as "a counselor, a man of insight and a scribe" (1 Chr. 27:32). According to the RSV and other translations, both he and Jehiel son of Hacmoni were in charge of the king's sons, but it is likely that the Hebrew attributes that

J

responsibility only to Jehiel. Because the word for "uncle" can be used less specifically of kinship on the father's side, some have proposed that here it means "brother's son" and that therefore this Jonathan should be identified with #4 above, the son Shimei.

(9) Father of Ebed; the latter was head of the family of Adin and returned to JERUSALEM from the EXILE with fifty of his clan and EZRA the scribe (Ezra 8:6; 1 Esd. 8:32).

(10) Son of Asahel; he and "Jahzeiah son of Tikvah, supported by Meshullam and Shabbethai the Levite," apparently challenged Ezra's instruction that those who had married foreign women should divorce them (Ezra 10:15). The Hebrew text, however, can be understood differently. See comments under JAHZEIAH.

(11) Son of Joiada, descendant of JESHUA, and father of JADDUA, all of them postexilic high priests (Neh. 12:11). Some believe that the text should read "Johanan" rather than "Jonathan" (cf. v. 22). See JOHANAN #8.

(12) Head of the priestly family of Malluch (KJV, "Melicu"; NRSV, "Malluchi") during the high priesthood of Joiakim (Neh. 12:14).

(13) Son of Shemaiah, descendant of ASAPH, and father of Zechariah; the latter was one of the Levitical musicians who took part in the procession celebrating the rebuilding of the wall (Neh. 12:35).

(14) A secretary during the reign of King ZEDEKIAH of Judah; Jonathan's house was used as a prison in which JEREMIAH was confined for a time (Jer. 37:15, 20; 38:26).

(15) Son of Kareah; he and his brother JOHANAN were among those who joined GEDALIAH at MIZPAH (Jer. 40:8). The NRSV, following the SEPTUAGINT (as well as the parallel passage, 2 Ki. 25:23), omits the name of Jonathan.

(16) Son of MATTATHIAS and Maccabean leader. Surnamed Apphus (1 Macc. 2:5), Jonathan succeeded his brother Judas as head of the Judeans in 160 B.C. (9:28-31), became high PRIEST in 152 (10:18-21), and was killed in 143 (12:48). According to one interpretation, Jonathan is the "Wicked Priest" mentioned in the DEAD SEA SCROLLS. See MACCABEE.

Jonathan, Targum. See TEXT AND VERSIONS (OT).

Jonath-elem-rechokim. joh´nuth-ee´luhm-ri-koh´kim (Heb. *yônat ʾēlem rēḥōqîm*). KJV transliteration of a Hebrew phrase that probably refers to a musical tune (Ps. 56 title; NIV, "To the tune of 'A Dove on Distant Oaks'").

Joppa. jop´uh (Heb. *yāpô H3639*, *yāpôʾ* [Ezra 3:7], "beautiful [city]"; Gk. *Ioppē G2673*). KJV also Japho (Josh. 19:46). A coastal city c. 35 mi. (56 km.) NW of JERUSALEM; it served as the seaport for the Israelite capital. Joppa was the only natural harbor on the MEDITERRANEAN between EGYPT and Acco (NT Ptolemais). A rocky cape projected into the sea and, because of its elevation above the sea, it made an ideal military and commercial site. Reefs formed a rough semicircle off the shore but boats could enter from the N. Nearby were sandy beaches where shallow craft could come ashore. Two good springs supplied the city with water. The land around the city was very fertile. The site today is known as Jaffa and is a suburb of Tel Aviv.

Joppa was allotted to DAN, but there is no evidence that the Israelites ever possessed it in preexilic times. Timber from the forests of LEBANON was floated from TYRE to Joppa for the building of the TEMPLE of SOLOMON (2 Chr. 2:16), and again when the temple was being rebuilt, after the return from the Babylonian captivity (Ezra 3:7). It was then under Phoenician control. Jonah boarded a ship from Joppa when he fled from the presence of the Lord (Jon. 1:3). In Maccabean times the city was garrisoned by the SELEUCIDS, but when some 200 Jews were treacherously drowned, after being induced to go aboard ships, Judas MACCABEE in revenge set fire to the docks and the boats in the harbor and killed the fugitives. In NT times PETER raised DORCAS to life there (Acts 9:36-42), and on the roof of SIMON the tanner's house he received the famous vision that taught him the gospel was intended for Jew and GENTILE alike (9:43—11:18).

Jorah. jor´uh (Heb. *yôrâ H3454*, "[born during] autumn rains"). Ancestor of a family of 112 members that returned from EXILE with ZERUBBABEL (Ezra 2:18; called HARIPH in Neh. 7:24).

Jorai. jor´i (Heb. *yôray H3455*, perhaps "[whom] Yahweh teaches"). Son of Abihail; he was one of seven relatives from the tribe of GAD who occupied the region E of GILEAD (1 Chr. 5:13; cf. vv. 10, 14).

Joram. jor′uhm (Heb. *yôrām H3456*, short form of JEHORAM, "Yahweh is exalted"). **(1)** Son of Tou (Toi) king of HAMATH; he was sent by his father with presents to DAVID "to greet him and congratulate him on his victory in battle over Hadadezer, who had been at war with Tou" (2 Sam. 8:10). The name here is thought by some to be a corruption of HADORAM (found in the parallel passage, 1 Chr. 18:10), but Joram may be its Israelite equivalent (that is, using an abbreviated form of Yahweh rather than the pagan name HADAD).

(2) Son of AHAB and ninth king of the northern kingdom of ISRAEL (2 Ki. 1:17 et al.). See JEHORAM #2.

(3) Son of JEHOSHAPHAT and fifth king of the southern kingdom of JUDAH (2 Ki. 8:16-19; 2 Chr. 21). See JEHORAM #3.

(4) Son of Jeshaiah; his descendant Shelomith was a LEVITE who shared the supervision of DAVID's treasury (1 Chr. 26:25).

Jordan River. jor′duhn (Heb. *yardēn H3720*, derivation uncertain; Gk. *Iordanēs G2674*). The major river of PALESTINE, which begins at Mount HERMON in the N, flows through the Sea of GALILEE and ends at the DEAD SEA in the S. The most popular etymology for the name is from the Hebrew verb *yārad H3718* ("to go down"), thus, "The Descender," but other suggestions have been made. Four rivers in SYRIA are recognized as the source of what later becomes the Jordan River proper. They are (1) the Bareighit; (2) the Hasbany; (3) the Leddan; and (4) the best-known of them (though the shortest, 5.5 mi./9 km. long), the Banias, on which once stood the city of CAESAREA PHILIPPI or Paneas, site of a famous grotto of the Greek god Pan. These rivers join and pour into Lake Huleh, though in modern times this lake has been drained by Israeli settlers for farm land. The Jordan then descends for 10 mi. (16 km.) to the Sea of Galilee, a beautiful body of water.

From the place where the Jordan makes its exit from the Sea of Galilee to the place where it enters the Dead Sea is, in a straight line, a length of c. 70 mi. (110 km.). But the river itself, because of its serpentine path, is 200 mi. (320 km.) long. The surface of the Dead Sea is c. 1,290 ft. (393 m.) below sea level. The Jordan River proper varies from 90 to 100 ft. (27-30 m.) in width, and from 3 to 10 ft. (1-3 m.) in depth, but the gorge that it has cut out varies in width from 4 mi. (6 km.) at the N to 14 mi. (23 km.) near JERICHO. Because it has twenty-seven rapids between the Sea of Galilee and the Dead Sea, the

The Upper Jordan River, N of the Sea of Galilee. (View to the N, with the river cutting through Rosh Pina.)

© Dr. James C. Martin

J

Jordan carries no traffic; and because of the swampy condition of part of this valley, the terrific heat in many places, and the presence of many wild animals, especially during Israel's history, no large city was ever built directly on the banks of the Jordan.

The natural life found in the Jordan Valley has been carefully studied, some of it proving to be unique. Of the thirty species of fish found in this river, sixteen are said to be found nowhere else; of the forty-five species of birds observed in this tortuous valley, twenty-three are peculiar to this area. About 162 species of plants and trees have been identified, of which 135 are African. They include the castor oil plant, the tamarisk, willows, poplars, and, near Jericho, the oleander. Two important rivers flow into the Jordan on the E side or Transjordan (no river emptying into the Jordan on the W or Cisjordan is referred to in the OT). The first, 4 mi. (6 km.) S of the Sea of Galilee, is the Yarmuk, not mentioned in the Bible. The great modern Rutenberg electric power plant is located here. Then, about midway between the Sea of Galilee and the Dead Sea, is the Jabbok, famous as the place where Jacob wrestled with the angel (Gen. 32:22), later designated as a boundary (Num. 21:24; Josh. 12:2). At the confluence of this river with the Jordan was the site known as Adam, where the waters of the great river were held back at the time of Israel's crossing (Josh. 3:16).

By far the most significant single event relating to the Jordan River in the entire history of Israel is the crossing on the part of the Israelites after the death of Moses (Josh. 3), a crossing anticipated by him (Deut. 3:20, 25, 27). While the Jordan is usually thought of as a boundary, the tribe of Manasseh occupied a huge territory on both sides of the river. Nevertheless, Israel was told that until this river was crossed and the territory on the western side possessed, they would not be occupying the land flowing with milk and honey (Num. 35:10; Deut. 3:20; 11:31; 31:13; Josh. 1:2). The Promised Land more generally refers to the territory on the W side of the Jordan than to all of the land occupied by Israel. The account of the crossing of the Jordan is given in detail in the third and fourth chapters of Joshua.

The Jordan is important in only one particular way in the NT. It was here that John the Baptist carried on his ministry (Matt. 3:6; Mk. 1:5;

Jn. 1:28; 3:26), and thus in this river Jesus himself was baptized (Matt. 3:13; Mk. 1:9; Lk. 4:1). No other event occurs in the NT directly relating to the Jordan River. (References to the Lord's ministry on the other side of the Jordan—in Matt. 19:1 and Mk. 10:1—only imply that the Lord crossed the river.) In the statement relating to the closing days of Jesus' ministry, when escaping from those who wanted to make him king, he "went back across the Jordan to the place where John had been baptizing in the early days" (Jn. 10:40). When the early church began its great missionary work, apart from the interview of Philip with the Ethiopian eunuch near Gaza, all the ministry of the apostles and early disciples, according to the NT, proceeded neither S into Egypt nor E toward Babylon, but N into Syria and Asia Minor, and then W to Greece, to Italy, and probably Spain. Little of historic importance has actually happened at the Jordan River since the baptism of Jesus. In fact, the Jordan Valley, from the Sea of Galilee to near Jericho, was practically unexplored until the nineteenth century.

The theme of the Jordan River is frequently found in the ritual of the church and in its hymnology and poetry. Comparing death for the Christian with the crossing of the Jordan by the Israelites cannot be regarded as a very accurate interpretation of Israel's history at this point. Israel did not enter into a time of peace when she crossed the Jordan but into a series of wars, many oppressions and defeats, followed by victories for a time, and ultimately ending in disaster and expulsion from the land.

Jorim. jor'im (Gk. *Iōrim G2733*). Son of Matthat, included in Luke's genealogy of Jesus Christ (Lk. 3:29).

Jorkeam. jor'kee-uhm (Heb. *yorqŏ'ām H3767*, derivation uncertain). KJV Jorkoam. Son of Raham, included in the genealogy of Caleb (1 Chr. 2:44). It is likely, however, that "Jorkeam" is a place name and that the text should be rendered, "Raham the founder of Jorkeam"; the town referred to may be the same as Jokdeam (Josh. 15:56).

Jorkoam. See Jorkeam.

Josabad. See Jozabad.

Josaphat. See Jehoshaphat.

Jose. joh´see. KJV NT form of Joshua (only Lk. 3:29).

Josech. joh´sik (Gk. *Iōsēch G2738*). TNIV Josek. Son of Joda, included in Luke's genealogy of Jesus Christ (Lk. 3:26; KJV, "Joseph").

Josedech. See Jozadak.

Josek. joh´sik. TNIV form of Josech.

Joseph. joh´sif (Heb. *yôsēp H3441*, "may [God] add"; Gk. *Iōsēph G2737*). **(1)** Son of Jacob and Rachel. Joseph was the eleventh of Jacob's twelve sons, but the firstborn of Rachel, who said when he was born, "May the Lord add to me another son," and therefore called his name Joseph (Gen. 30:24; the Heb. verb for "add" is *yāsap H3578*). Joseph's sons were Manasseh and Ephraim, who became the ancestors of two important northern Israelite tribes. The account of Joseph's birth is told in Gen. 30:22-24, and the account of the rest of his life is found in chs. 37-50. He was born in Paddan Aram when his father was ninety years old; he was his father's favorite because he was Rachel's child and the son of his old age. The father's favoritism was shown in his getting for Joseph a special coat, which was probably a token of rank indicating that it was his intention to make Joseph the head of the tribe. This favoritism naturally aroused the envy of Joseph's older brothers. Their ill will was increased when he somewhat imprudently told them two dreams he had that were suggestive of his future greatness and their subservience to him.

When Joseph was seventeen years old, his father sent him to see how his brothers were doing at Shechem, where they were feeding their flocks; finding out that they had gone on to Dothan, Joseph followed them there. When they saw him coming, they planned to kill him, and thus make impossible the fulfillment of his dreams. Reuben, however, persuaded them not to kill him but to throw him alive into a pit, intending to rescue him later and restore him to his father. When Reuben was absent for a short time, the brothers saw a caravan of Ishmaelites making their way to Egypt

and decided that instead of allowing Joseph to die in the well, they would sell him to these merchants. They sold Joseph and then took his coat of many colors, smeared it with the blood of a goat they had killed, and took it to Jacob with the story that they had found the coat and assumed that their brother was dead, torn to pieces by some wild beast. The aged father, grief-stricken and disconsolate, mourned the loss of his son for many days.

In the meantime, Joseph was taken to Egypt by the Ishmaelites and sold in the slave market to an officer of Pharaoh, an Egyptian named Potiphar. The young slave proved himself to be so intelligent and trustworthy that his master soon entrusted to him all the affairs of his household, which prospered under Joseph's administration. But on the false accusations of Potiphar's wife, whose improper advances Joseph had rejected, he was cast into prison, where he remained for years. God was with him, however, and the providence that had previously saved his life now brought him to the favorable attention of the pharaoh. The prison keeper, finding he could put implicit confidence in Joseph, committed to his charge the other prisoners. Among these were two of the pharaoh's officers, his chief butler and chief baker, who had been imprisoned for offending the king. Joseph interpreted for them two dreams they had had; and three days later, on the king's birthday, as Joseph had foretold, the chief baker was hanged and the chief butler restored to his office (Gen. 40:5-23).

After two years, during which Joseph's circumstances remained unchanged—the chief butler had forgotten his promise to mention him to the king—Pharaoh had two dreams that no one could interpret. They had to do with fat and lean cows and full and withered heads of grain. The chief butler now remembered Joseph and told the king of Joseph's skill in interpreting dreams. Joseph was sent for, and he revealed the meaning of the dreams: seven years of plenty would be followed by seven years of famine. He then suggested that preparation be made for the years of famine by storing up the surplus produce during the seven years of plenty against the years of famine. Pharaoh immediately made Joseph head of the royal granaries and invested him with the authority necessary to carry out his proposals. As the head of the department of state, Joseph became one of the officials next in rank to the pharaoh (Gen. 41:39-44), and as a further mark of royal favor, he was given an Egyptian name and was married to the daughter of the priest of the great national temple of ON. Joseph was now thirty years old. During the seven years of plenty he amassed corn in the granaries of every city, and his wife bore him two sons, Manasseh and Ephraim.

The famine that Joseph predicted affected not only the local area, and other countries came to Egypt to buy corn. Joseph's brothers came also. They did not recognize him, but he knew them; and when they prostrated themselves before him, he saw the fulfillment of the dreams that had aroused their intense jealousy years before. The climax of the episode is reached when Joseph, after testing their character in various ways, made himself known to them, told them that he bore no ill will for the wrong they had done him, and persuaded them and their father to settle in Egypt. The pharaohs reigning in Egypt during that era were probably members of the HYKSOS dynasty and were Semites, like Joseph; and the present pharaoh consequently cordially welcomed Jacob and his family to Egypt.

In the years that followed, Joseph brought about a permanent change in the Egyptian system of land tenure because of the famine and the consequent poverty of the people, so that almost all the land became the property of the pharaoh, and the previous owners became his tenants. Jacob lived with Joseph in Egypt seventeen years. Before he died, he adopted Joseph's two sons, putting them on the same level as his own sons in the division of the inheritance. Joseph lived to the age of 110. Shortly before he died he expressed his confidence that God would some day bring the children of Israel back to Canaan, and solemnly directed that his bones be buried there. His wishes were carried out, and his bones were buried finally in Shechem, in the plot of ground bought there by Jacob (Josh. 24:32). Joseph presents a noble ideal of character, remarkable for his gentleness, faithfulness to duty, magnanimity, and forgiving spirit, so that he is often regarded as an OT type of CHRIST.

(2) Descendant of ISSACHAR and father of Igal; the latter was one of the twelve spies sent by MOSES to Canaan (Num. 13:7).

(3) One of the sons of ASAPH who assisted their father in the prophetic ministry of MUSIC; he was the head of the first company of temple musicians appointed by lot under DAVID (1 Chr. 25:2, 9).

(4) One of the descendants of Binnui who agreed to put away their foreign wives (Ezra 10:42).

(5) Head of the priestly family of Shecaniah (MT, Shebaniah) during the high priesthood of JOIAKIM (Neh. 12:14).

(6) Son of MATTATHIAS (leader of the Maccabean Revolt); he was appointed by his brother Judas MACCABEE to command a military division (2 Macc. 8:22; 10:19). The name "Joseph" here is probably a variant of "John" (1 Macc. 2:2), but some have argued that it refers to a different person, perhaps a half-brother of Judas.

(7-8) The name of two individuals included in Luke's GENEALOGY OF JESUS CHRIST: the son of Mattathias (not the leader of the Maccabean Revolt) and the son of Jonam (Lk. 3:25, 30).

(9) Son of Jacob and husband of MARY, MOTHER OF JESUS (Matt. 1:16; according to Lk. 3:23, he was the son [grandson?] of HELI; see GENEALOGY OF JESUS CHRIST). The Gospels of Matthew and Luke assert that Jesus

This canal, known as the River of Joseph, is said to have been dug during the time of Joseph to provide irrigation to agricultural fields during the Egyptian drought he predicted. (View to the NW.)

© Dr. James C. Martin

was born to Mary at a time when she was betrothed to Joseph, before their marriage was consummated (Matt. 1:18; Lk. 1:27, 35). Joseph was a carpenter (Matt. 13:55) and was known as "a righteous man" (1:19). When he learned that Mary was bearing a child, he was understandably disturbed. After he was told by an angel that she was to become the mother of Israel's MESSIAH through the instrumentality of the Holy Spirit, he proceeded with his plans, which brought him and Mary to BETHLEHEM, where the child Jesus was born. The last reference to Joseph is in connection with the Passover journey when Jesus was twelve years old (Lk. 2:41-48). Later references mention Mary and the BROTHERS OF JESUS (Mk. 3:31; 6:3), but not Joseph. Jesus asked John to treat Mary as his own mother (Jn. 19:26-27), implying that she had need of someone to care for her. References to the brothers of Jesus imply that Mary and Joseph had other children after the VIRGIN BIRTH of Jesus. Some scholars have assumed that these "brothers" were sons of Joseph by a previous marriage, or cousins of Jesus. The natural meaning of the words, however, implies that Mary and Joseph came together subsequent to the birth of Jesus (Matt. 1:25), and that they had children who grew up with Jesus and were known in the community as his "brothers."

(10) Son of Mary and thus probably a half-brother of Jesus; listed with other brothers, James, Simon, and Judas (Matt. 13:55; instead of "Joseph," some MSS have "Joses" and others have "John"). A parallel list includes James, Joses, Judas, and Simon (Mk. 6:3 NRSV; here the NIV understands JOSES as an alternate form of Joseph. See BROTHERS OF THE LORD; JAMES #2.

(11) Son of a certain Mary, possibly the wife of CLOPAS (Matt. 27:56 NRSV; NIV reads "Joses," the reading found in a majority of MSS, though probably not original). This Joseph is no doubt to be identified with Joses, the brother of James the younger (Mk. 15:40). See JAMES #3.

(12) A rich man from the town of ARIMATHEA who became a disciple of Jesus. After the crucifixion, he asked PILATE for the body of Jesus; the request being granted, he wrapped the body "in a linen cloth, and placed it in his own new tomb that he had cut out of the rock" (Matt. 27:57-60). Both Mark and Luke add the information that Joseph was a member of the Council, a term that probably refers to the SANHEDRIN, and that he "was waiting for the kingdom of God" (Mk. 15:43-46; Lk. 23:50-53). Luke also states that Joseph was "a good and upright man, who had not consented to their decision and action." John points out that Joseph was a secret disciple of Jesus "because he feared the Jews," and that NICODEMUS helped him bury the body (Jn. 19:38-40).

(13) A disciple of Jesus who also bore the surnames BARSABBAS and JUSTUS; he was one of the two men nominated to succeed JUDAS ISCARIOT in the apostolic band (Acts 1:23).

(14) An early Christian leader better known as BARNABAS (Acts 4:36).

Josephus, Flavius. joh-see′fuhs, flay′vee-uhs. First-century Jewish writer; our main source of information for Jewish history during the intertestamental and NT periods. Josephus was born in JERUSALEM, A.D. 37 or 38. His father Matthias was a priest, and his mother a descendant of the royal house of the Hasmoneans. When he grew up he joined the PHARISEES, a group that he likened to the STOICS among the Greeks. In the year 64, at age twenty-six, he went to ROME and secured the release of certain priests who were being held there on rather nebulous charges. Upon his return he found the people smarting under the high-handed administration of the procurator Florus and ready for revolt. From this he attempted to dissuade them, having seen at firsthand something of Roman power. Because of his attitude, he was sent to GALILEE to keep the peace there. Afraid that his pacification efforts would bring him under suspicion of favoring Rome, he finally pretended to concur with the views of the war party, going so far as to get them paid as mercenaries, but at the same time trying to persuade them to act on the defensive: not to attack the Romans, but let them make the first move. Thus he played a kind of double game, waiting to see the direction in which events would develop, accused by some of pro-Roman sentiment, by others of aiming at tyranny. At this juncture the Roman general VESPASIAN arrived on the scene (A.D. 67), and Josephus was captured. Later, Vespasian's son TITUS used him as a mediator. After the capture of Jerusalem, Josephus went

J

to Rome and was shown favor there. He died at about the beginning of the second century.

Three major works have come from the pen of Josephus. (a) The *Jewish War*, written between 75 and 79, in seven books. This account of the struggle between the Jews and Romans was written under Roman auspices, Titus having urged Josephus to undertake the work. The work is in the main a trustworthy account, for Josephus had firsthand materials: his own experience and the commentaries of Vespasian and Titus, the commanders involved in the struggle. (b) The *Antiquities of the Jews*, written in 93 or 94. This is a long work of twenty books, beginning with creation and extending to the outbreak of the war with the Romans. The first part of the work, to the end of the exile, follows closely the biblical narrative; the second part, dealing with the postexilic period, is compiled from miscellaneous sources. To the *Antiquities* is appended a biographical sketch (*Life*) written by Josephus as a defense against the accusations of a rival historian named Justus. (c) *Against Apion*, a defense of the Jewish religion.

Joses. joh´siz (Gk. *Iōsēs G2736*, hellenized form of *Iōsēph G2737*; see JOSEPH). **(1)** Son of MARY, MOTHER OF JESUS, and thus apparently a half-brother of Jesus (Mk. 6:3 NRSV); the NIV, on the basis of the parallel passage (Matt. 13:55), renders the name as "Joseph" (a reading attested in some MSS). See JOSEPH #10.

(2) Brother of James the younger, whose mother Mary stood by the cross of Jesus and watched his burial (Matt. 27:56 [NRSV, "Joseph," following the earliest MSS]; Mk. 15:40, 47). See JAMES 3.

(3) The original name of BARNABAS (Acts 4:36 KJV, following the TR; most modern versions read "Joseph").

Joshah. joh´shuh (Heb. *yôšâ H3459*, derivation uncertain). A clan leader in the tribe of SIMEON (1 Chr. 4:34). He is listed among those whose families increased greatly during the days of King HEZEKIAH and who dispossessed the Hamites and Meunites near GEDOR (vv. 38-41).

Joshaphat. josh´uh-fat (Heb. *yôšāpāṭ H3461*, short form of JEHOSHAPHAT, "Yahweh has judged"). **(1)**

A Mithnite who was one of DAVID's mighty warriors (1 Chr. 11:43; this list adds sixteen names beyond the military elite known as the Thirty, listed in vv. 10-41 = 2 Sam. 23:8-39). The description "Mithnite" may point to his hometown, perhaps in TRANSJORDAN.

(2) One of the priests appointed to blow the trumpet when David transferred the ARK OF THE COVENANT to JERUSALEM (1 Chr. 15:24).

Joshaviah. josh´uh-vi´uh (Heb. *yôšawyâ H3460*, possibly alternate form of JOSHIBIAH, "Yahweh makes [me] dwell"). Son of Elnaam; he and his brother Jeribai are included in the Chronicler's list of DAVID's mighty warriors (1 Chr. 11:46).

Joshbekashah. josh´bi-kay´shuh (Heb. *yošbĕqāšâ H3792*, possibly "sitting in prayer [*or* in misfortune]"). Son of HEMAN, DAVID's seer (1 Chr. 25:4). He and his thirteen brothers were set apart "for the ministry of prophesying, accompanied by harps, lyres and cymbal" (v. 1). When lots were cast to determine the duties of the Levitical singers, he, along with his sons and relatives, received the seventeenth lot (v. 26).

Josheb-Basshebeth.   joh´shib-buh-shee´bith (Heb. *yōšēb baššebet H3783*, "one sitting in the seat"). A Tahkemonite listed as chief of DAVID's three main officers (2 Sam. 23:8). See JASHOBEAM.

Joshibiah. josh´uh-bi´uh (Heb. *yôšibyâ H3458*, "Yahweh makes [me] dwell"). KJV Josibiah. Son of Seraiah and father of Jehu; the latter is listed among the clan leaders in the tribe of SIMEON whose families increased greatly during the days of King HEZEKIAH and who dispossessed the Hamites and Meunites near GEDOR (1 Chr. 4:35; cf. vv. 38-41).

Joshua. josh´yoo-uh (Heb. *yĕhôšuaʿ H3397*, short form in postexilic writings *yēšûʿa H3800* [see JESHUA], "Yahweh is salvation [*or* help]"; Gk. *Iēsous G2652* [see JESUS). **(1)** Son of Nun and commander of the Israelites during the conquest of CANAAN. Although his name appears first as Joshua (Exod. 17:9-14), one reads subsequently (Num. 13:16; cf. v. 8 and Deut. 32:44 MT) that MOSES changed his name from HOSHEA (KJV, "Oshea"), meaning

"Save," to Joshua (more accurately transliterated as Jehoshua), "Yahweh is salvation," making the name theophorous. Two months after the EXODUS, he was appointed Moses' commander and successfully repulsed an AMALEKITE attack (Exod. 17:9). Joshua attended Moses on SINAI (Exod. 24:13; 32:17) and guarded both his tent (33:11) and position (Num. 11:28). Later he represented the tribe of EPHRAIM in spying out Canaan. Joshua opposed the majority report, insisting that Israel, if faithful to God, could conquer Canaan. He almost suffered stoning for his trust in God (14:7-10). Because he "followed the LORD wholeheartedly" (32:12), however, he not only escaped destruction (14:38) but also received assurance, unique to himself and CALEB (13:30; 14:24), of entering the Promised Land (14:30; 26:65).

About forty years later, E of the JORDAN River, God designated Joshua as Moses' successor (Num. 27:18). Moses charged him to be faithful (Num. 27:23; Deut. 31:23), committed the "song of admonition" and other writings to him (Exod. 17:14; Deut. 32:44), counseled him on procedures (Num. 32:28; 34:17), and encouraged both new leader and people (Deut. 3:21; 31:3, 7). God himself warned Joshua of coming APOSTASY (31:14) but promised that Joshua would be successful in the conquest of the Promised Land (1:38; 3:28; 31:23).

After Moses' death, Joshua, as the oldest man in Israel, must have been in his nineties (Caleb was eighty-five, Josh. 13:1; 14:7-11). Yet God assured him of victory, as he relied on the inspired Book of the Law (1:6-9). From this point onward, Joshua's history is that of Israel's occupation of Canaan. His personal actions, however, include making preparations (1:10-18), sending spies against JERICHO (2:1, 23-24), and then ordering Israel's advance across Jordan (3:1). His faith in crossing the Jordan inaugurated a life of undiminishing esteem, similar even to that of Moses (3:7; 4:14). West of Jordan, Joshua superintended Israel's rituals (5:2) and the construction of monuments for building the faith of children yet to come (4:4-7). The appearance of "the commander of the army of the LORD" (5:13-15) served as a dramatic sentence on Jericho but also as a visible confirmation of Joshua's divine call, similar to the appearance of the angel of the Lord to Moses at the BURNING BUSH (Exod. 3:2-6). Joshua then executed the God-directed siege (Josh. 6:2-6). He "devoted" (destroyed) Jericho (6:17), pronounced a curse on its rebuilding (6:26; 1 Ki. 16:34), and achieved widespread recognition (Josh. 6:27).

When the disobedience of ACHAN brought defeat at AI, Joshua's prayer, his zeal for God's glory, and his enforcement of divine judgment (Josh. 7:6-9, 19, 25) compare favorably with his subsequent faithfulness to God's orders and exemplary execution of Ai's king (8:2, 29; cf. 10:24-27, 40-41). With central Palestine subdued, Joshua personally wrote Moses' law on stone at Mount EBAL and then proclaimed this law to the whole Israelite assembly (8:30-35). Though guilty of rashness with the GIBEONITES, he later condemned these pagans to bondage (9:15, 22-23, 26-27). The energy he displayed in forced marches and sudden attacks frustrated Canaanite counteroffensives in both S and N (10:9; 11:7). Basically it was the Lord who gave Israel her victories, especially evident in causing the sun to "stand still" during the battle at Beth Horon (10:12-14). In six years (14:10) Joshua took the whole land; "he left nothing undone of all that the LORD commanded Moses" (11:15, 23).

Yet Moses had anticipated a gradual occupation (Exod. 23:28-30). God had left in Canaan many nations, subdued but still powerful, to test his people (Josh. 13:2-6; Jdg. 2:21—3:4); so Joshua could not achieve Israel's final "rest" (Heb. 4:8). Thus, because of his advanced age, he divided Canaan among the tribes (Josh. 13:6-7; 14:1; 19:51). At GILGAL he confirmed Moses' Transjordanian settlement of the two and one-half tribes and assigned territory to JUDAH, including Caleb's portion at HEBRON (14:13; 15:13), and to EPHRAIM and MANASSEH (cf. 17:4), encouraging them to more effective conquest even while refusing to show them partiality (17:14-18). Later, at SHILOH, he exhorted the seven hesitant tribes, dispatched a commission on apportionment, and thus allotted the remaining lands (18:3, 8-10), including cities of refuge and Levitical assignments (20-21). He himself requested and built TIMNATH SERAH in Ephraim (19:49-51).

As death approached, Joshua first summoned Israel's leaders, urging them to faithfulness in conquest (Josh. 23), and then assembled the tribal heads to SHECHEM, charging them, "Choose for yourselves this day whom you will serve" (24:15).

J

Having renewed their COVENANT with the Lord, he inserted it in the Book of the Law (24:25-26) and died at the age of 110 (24:29-30; Jdg. 2:8-9). Throughout his days, and even afterward, his influence caused Israel to maintain faithfulness to her Lord (Josh. 24:31; Jdg. 1:1; 2:7).

(2) The owner of a field in the town of BETH SHEMESH (1 Sam. 6:14, 18). When the PHILISTINES returned the ARK OF THE COVENANT to the Israelites, the two cows pulling the cart "went straight up toward Beth Shemesh" and stopped near a large rock in Joshua's field (v. 12).

(3) A city governor in the days of King JOSIAH (2 Ki. 23:8). As part of the religious reform during his reign, Josiah "desecrated the high places, from Geba to Beersheba, where the priests had burned incense. He broke down the shrines at the gates—at the Gate of Joshua, the city governor, which is to the left of the city gate." It is usually assumed that the city in question is JERUSALEM, but an alternate view sees here a reference to BEERSHEBA.

(4) Son of Jehozadak and high PRIEST at the time of the return from BABYLON and the rebuilding of the TEMPLE (Hag. 1:1 et al.). See JESHUA #1.

(5) Son of Eliezer, included in Luke's GENEALOGY OF JESUS CHRIST (Lk. 3:29; KJV, "Jose").

Joshua, Book of. Standing sixth in Scripture, this book describes how MOSES' successor, JOSHUA, after whom the book is named, conquered Canaan (Josh. 1:1; 24:31). But while Joshua is the first of "the historical books" in the English Bible, it introduces "the prophets" in the original Hebrew canon of Law, Prophets, and Writings (see CANONICITY). These prophetic books include the "former prophets"—Joshua, Judges, Samuel, and Kings—since biblical prophets, as God's spokesmen (Exod. 7:1-2), enforced their messages using the past as well as the future. Joshua exemplifies historical "prophetic" preaching, in respect of authorship as well as of content.

Joshua's prophetic author is not named; but his statements about the death of Joshua and his colleagues (Josh. 24:29-31), plus his allusions to OTHNIEL, the migration of the Danites (15:17; 19:47), and the name HORMAH (12:14; 15:30; 19:4) indicate that the writer lived after the rise of Israel's judges, c. 1380 B.C. (Jdg. 1:12-13, 17). At the same time, his designation of JERUSALEM as JEBUSITE (Josh. 15:8, 63; 18:16, 28) and his writing before its choice as the site of God's TEMPLE (9:27), indicate that he wrote before the time of DAVID, c. 1000 (1 Chr. 11:4-6; 22:1). His references, moreover, to

Overview of JOSHUA

Author: Unknown.

Historical setting: Covers the period from the commissioning of Joshua to his death (either c. 1400-1380 or c. 1250-1230 B.C., depending on the date of the EXODUS). Some believe that the book was written by an eyewitness (perhaps AARON's grandson PHINEHAS, Josh. 24:33) within a generation after the events it relates; others date its composition centuries later.

Purpose: To provide a historical-theological account of the conquest of CANAAN and the distribution of the land among the Israelite tribes; to show the fulfillment of God's promises and to encourage faithfulness to the COVENANT.

Contents: Preparing to conquer the land (Josh. 1-5); the fall of JERICHO and AI (chs. 6-8); victory in the southern and northern territories (chs. 9-12); allotment of the land (chs. 13-22); covenant renewal and death of Joshua (chs. 23-24).

Excavation Area A of OT Jericho (looking N from the southern base of the tell). Defensive walls like these, built before the time of Joshua, may have continued to function until the time of his attack against this city.

SIDON rather than to TYRE as PHOENICIA's leading city (Josh. 11:8; 13:4-6; 19:28) suggest a date prior to 1200. Indeed, the writer must have been an eyewitness of the events he describes. He speaks, for example, of the Lord's blocking Jordan "until *we* had crossed over" (5:1); he identifies Israel's previous generation by saying, "they would not see the land that he had solemnly promised their fathers to give *us*" (5:6); he says of the prostitute RAHAB, "she lives among the Israelites to this day" (6:25); and after outlining their boundaries he addresses the tribe of JUDAH directly, "This is [your] southern boundary" (15:4). Note also his detailed narratives (2:3-22; 7:16-26) and repeated use of preconquest place-names (15:9, 49, 54). Since the writer follows Moses' Deuteronomic style and seemingly had access to Joshua himself (cf. 5:13-15), a proposed author has been PHINEHAS, the son and successor of high priest ELEAZAR son of AARON (cf. Num. 25:7-13; 31:6-8; Josh. 22:13-20; Jdg. 20:28). In any case, someone of his standing may have composed the book of Joshua about 1375 B.C.

Most modern critics, however, attribute Joshua to four mutually contradictory source documents, brought together over a millennium after the time of Phinehas—sources such as have been alleged for the Mosaic writings (see PENTATEUCH), thus making Genesis-Joshua into a "Hexateuch." In particular, the "E" and "D" records of conquest under Joshua are rejected in favor of the earlier "J" records, purportedly teaching a gradual occupation of Palestine by independent tribes (cf. Jdg. 1). But while Joshua does fulfill God's former promises (Gen. 13:14-17; 15:13-20), Scripture knows nothing of a Hexateuch. The Pentateuchal books of Moses are unique (Josh. 1:7-8; 2 Chr. 34:14; cf. Christ's own testimony, Lk. 24:44), while Joshua forms a sequel to the law (Josh. 24:26).

The prophetical character of Joshua, moreover, affects the content in the book's two divisions: conquest (Josh. 1-12) and settlement (chs. 13-24). The conquest embraces Israel's entrance into Canaan: Joshua's inauguration, the Jericho spies, crossing Jordan, and ceremonies (1:1—5:12); the conquest of the center—Jericho, Ai, and the assembly at Mount Ebal (5:13—8:35); of the south—Gibeon and the Jerusalem confederacy (chs. 9-10); and of the north—the Hazor confederacy, plus a summary (chs. 11-12). But since all of this took "a long time" (11:18; prob. 1406-1400 B.C., 14:10), the biblical content limits itself to representative instances of rewarded faithfulness. Joshua was commanded to be strong and no one would be able to stand against him (1:5-6; cf. 11:23). Israel's settlement embraces

© Dr. James C. Martin

J

Joshua's territorial apportionments at Gilgal (chs. 13-17) and Shiloh (chs. 18-19), including CITIES OF REFUGE, LEVITICAL CITIES, and Transjordan (chs. 20-22). The account demonstrates how God "gave Israel all the land he had sworn to give their forefathers" (21:43). Joshua's two farewell addresses follow, giving Israel that choice that every prophecy elicits: "We will serve the LORD our God and obey him" (24:24).

Joshua, Gate of. See JOSHUA #3.

Josiah. joh-si′uh (Heb. *yō'šiyyāhû H3288*, derivation uncertain, possibly "Yahweh heals"; Gk. *Iōsias G2739*). **(1)** Son of a certain Zephaniah; the prophet ZECHARIAH was told to go to Josiah's house and crown the high priest Joshua (JESHUA, Zech. 6:10).

(2) Son of AMON and king of JUDAH (2 Ki. 22-23; 2 Chr. 34-35). Josiah's reign on the Davidic throne for thirty-one years was the last surge of political independence and religious revival before the disintegration of the southern kingdom that ended with the destruction of JERUSALEM in 586 B.C. When palace officials murdered King Amon in 640 B.C. (2 Ki. 21:23), the eight-year-old Josiah was crowned king of Judah. While the boy-king grew to manhood, the imposing international influence of ASSYRIA declined rapidly. Insurrections and rebellions in the E and the death of ASHURBANIPAL (c. 633) provided an opportunity for a rising tide of nationalism in Judah. By 612 the coalition of MEDIA under Cyaxares and BABYLON under Nabopolassar converged on NINEVEH to destroy Assyria's famous capital. Within three years the Babylonians had routed the last of the great Assyrian army. These decades gave Josiah the political advantage not only to assert Judah's independence but also to extend its influence into the northern tribes—perhaps even kindling fond hopes of claiming the boundaries as established by DAVID and SOLOMON.

Josiah's religious leadership ranks him with JEHOSHAPHAT and HEZEKIAH (Josiah's great-grandfather) as an outstanding righteous ruler. Gross IDOLATRY—BAAL altars, ASHERAH poles, star and planetary worship, child sacrifice to MOLECH in the Valley of Ben HINNOM, astrology, occultism, altars for worshiping the host of heaven in the temple court, and the shedding of innocent blood—all these permeated the land of Judah during the reign of Josiah's grandfather MANASSEH (686-642 B.C.), whose personal penitence and reform (2 Chr. 33:13) in all likelihood did not penetrate the kingdom of Judah sufficiently to reconstruct the religious pattern. Whatever reform had

© Dr. James C. Martin

Looking SW across the Jezreel Valley toward Megiddo, near which King Josiah died in a battle with Pharaoh Neco (2 Chr. 35:20-23).

been accomplished by Manasseh after his release from captivity was countered by a reversion to idolatry under Amon. Josiah gradually reacted to these godless influences that permeated his kingdom (ch. 34). In the eighth year of his reign (c. 632) he began to seek after God and four years later initiated reforms. Images, altars, and all manner of idolatrous practices were destroyed not only in Jerusalem and Judah but in the tribal territories of Manasseh, Ephraim, Simeon, and as far N as Naphtali. At the same time offerings and contributions were collected throughout the nation for the restoration of the TEMPLE in Jerusalem, which had been neglected for a long period.

In the course of renovating the temple (622 B.C.) the Book of the Law was recovered. The reformation movement was now stimulated anew by the reading of this "Book of the Law … given through Moses" (2 Chr. 34:15). Not only had the reading and observance of the law been neglected in preceding decades, but it is possible that Manasseh even destroyed existing copies that were in circulation throughout the land of Judah. HULDAH the prophetess warned the people of impending judgment awaiting them for their neglect of the law (34:23-28). Stirred by these developments Josiah led his nation in the observance of the Passover in a manner unprecedented in Judah's history.

With the king himself leading the reformation movement, changes in personnel occurred. Priests serving by royal appointment of former kings and dedicated to idol worship were removed from office. Josiah, however, made temple revenues available for their support (2 Ki. 23:8-9). The religious climate established by Josiah must have provided favorable conditions for JEREMIAH during the first eighteen years of his ministry (627-609 B.C.), even though no references are made to the association of these great leaders in the historical records (2 Ki. 22-23 and 2 Chr. 34-35).

In 609 B.C. Josiah's leadership was abruptly ended. In an effort to interfere with Pharaoh NECO's plans to aid the Assyrians, Josiah was fatally wounded at MEGIDDO (2 Chr. 35:20-24). National and religious hopes vanished with the funeral of this thirty-nine-year-old king so that all Judah had reason to join Jeremiah in lamenting for Josiah (35:25).

Josibiah. See JOSHIBIAH.

Josiphiah. jos-i-fi'uh (Heb. *yôsipyâ H3442*, "may Yahweh add"). Descendant of BANI (so LXX; MT omits name) and father of Shelomith; the latter, head of a family of 160 men, is listed among those who returned to Palestine with EZRA (Ezra 8:10).

jot. jot. KJV transliteration of Greek *iōta G2740* (Matt. 5:18; NIV, "smallest letter"). See DOT; IOTA; YOD.

Jotbah. jot'buh (Heb. *yoṭbâ H3513*, "pleasant"). Hometown of MESHULLEMETH, wife of King MANASSEH (2 Ki. 21:19). Jotbah is usually thought to be the same as modern Khirbet Jefat (Shifat), some 9 mi. (15 km.) NNW of NAZARETH, but this identification has not been confirmed by archaeological finds.

Jotbath. See JOTBATHAH.

Jotbathah. jot'buh-thuh (Heb. *yoṭbātâ H3514*, "pleasant"). A stopping place of the Israelites in their forty years of wilderness wanderings (Num. 33:33-34). They found it to be "a land with streams of water" (Deut. 10:7; KJV, "Jotbath"). Some scholars identify it with modern Ṭabeh, c. 6.5 mi. (10.5 km.) SW of ELATH.

Jotham. joh'thuhm (Heb. *yôtām H3462*, "Yahweh is perfect" or "may Yahweh complete"). (1) Youngest son of GIDEON (Jerub-Baal). Jotham escaped the massacre of his family by the citizens of SHECHEM, who had been incited by his half-brother ABIMELECH (Jdg. 9:5). Upon hearing that Abimelech had been proclaimed king, Jotham went up to the top of Mount GERIZIM and spoke his famous fable of the trees, depicting Abimelech as a worthless bramble incapable of offering the men of Shechem security or profit. He then predicted their mutual destruction and fled to BEER (vv. 6-21). Three years later (v. 22), when Abimelech besieged THEBEZ, the curse was fulfilled (vv. 50-57).

(2) Son of JAHDAI and, apparently, a descendant of JUDAH somehow related to CALEB (1 Chr. 2:47).

(3) Son of UZZIAH (Azariah) and king of the southern kingdom of JUDAH (2 Ki. 15:32-38; 2

J

J

Chr. 26:21—27:9). Uzziah had been for the most part a good and powerful king, but his successes turned his head and he intruded into the priest's office (2 Chr. 26:16). As a result, he was struck with leprosy, and Jotham acted as coregent (c. 750 B.C.). Jotham became sole ruler upon Uzziah's death (c. 740), apparently about the time Isaiah began his great ministry (Isa. 6:1); he was probably influenced by that godly prophet. He had victory over the Ammonites, who were forced to pay him heavy tribute; he was a great builder, fortifying several places in Judah and building the Upper Gate of the temple.

joy. In the OT, joy is commonly a group expression, often associated with dancing (Ps. 96:11) or the blessings of prosperity (Isa. 60:15). God's praise is shouted or sung even in more formal public worship (Ezra 3:10-11; Ps. 100:1-2). Linked with this concept also are musical instruments, clapping, leaping, or foot-stamping. Feasting or offering sacrifice (Deut. 12:12; Isa. 56:7), celebration of harvest or victory (1 Sam. 18:6; Joel 1:16), enjoying prosperity or personal triumph (Ps. 31:7; Isa. 61:3-4) are all occasions of joy.

In the NT, the word is often found in connection with salvation (1 Pet. 1:6), but also with eating, drinking, and feasting (Lk. 12:19; Acts 7:41). Most often found in the NT, however, are the meanings "to boast, take pride, or rejoice in." Thus, Paul contrasts the human inclination to boast in oneself (Rom. 3:27) with his right to boast in Christ and his cross (Gal. 6:14; Phil. 3:3). The NT applies joy to suffering as well as to salvation. When reviled or persecuted or lied about, the Christian is to "rejoice and be glad," knowing that this is traditionally part of the believer's portion (Matt. 5:11-12). Joy comes from the Holy Spirit (Gal. 5:22).

Jozabad. joh′zuh-bad (Heb. *yôzābād H3416*, short form of Jehozabad, "Yahweh has granted"). **(1)** Son of Shimeath; an official who, with Jehozabad son of Shomer, murdered King Joash (Jehoash) of Judah at Beth Millo (2 Ki. 12:21; NRSV has Jozacar, following many Heb. MSS). The parallel passage identifies him as "Zabad, son of Shimeath an Ammonite woman" (2 Chr. 24:26).

(2) A man from Gederah who joined David at Ziklag (1 Chr. 12:4); he was among the ambidextrous warriors from the tribe of Benjamin who were kinsmen of Saul (v. 2).

(3-4) Two warriors from the tribe of Manasseh who joined David at Ziklag; they are described as "leaders of units of a thousand" (1 Chr. 12:20). Some believe that there was only one Manassite warrior named Jozabad and that the second name is a scribal mistake of dittography.

(5) A Levite included in the list of supervisors of the temple storerooms during the reign of Hezekiah (2 Chr. 31:13).

(6) A leader of the Levites in the reign of Josiah who gave liberally toward the sacrifices (2 Chr. 35:9).

(7) Son of Jeshua; he was a Levite who served in Jerusalem at the time of Ezra's return (Ezra 8:33). This is probably the same man mentioned as agreeing to put away a foreign wife (10:23), as helping the people to understand the law (Neh. 8:7), and as one who had charge over the outside work of the house of God (11:16).

(8) One of the descendants of Passhur who agreed to put away their foreign wives (Ezra 10:22).

Jozacar. joh′zuh-kahr (Heb. *yôzākār* [not in NIV], "Yahweh has remembered"). KJV Jozachar. According to many Hebrew MSS, Jozacar was the son of Shimeath; he and Jehozabad son of Shomer murdered King Joash (Jehoash) of Judah (2 Ki. 12:21 [cf. KJV, NRSV]; called "Zabad" in 2 Chr. 24:26). The NIV, following other Hebrew MSS (including Codex Leningradensis, the basis of *BHS*), has Jozabad.

Jozachar. See Jozachar.

Jozadak. See Jehozadak.

Jubal. joo′buhl (Heb. *yûbal H3415*, meaning uncertain). Son of Lamech and Adah; described as "the father of all who play the harp and flute," apparently indicating that he invented musical instruments (Gen. 4:21).

Jubilee. KJV Jubile. According to Lev. 25, every fiftieth year in Israel was to be announced as a

The beginning of the Jubilee Year was marked by the sounding of the shofar.

Jubilee Year. Three essential features characterized this year. First, liberty was proclaimed to all Israelites who were in bondage to any of their countrymen. The law provided that the price of slaves was to vary according to the proximity of the Jubilee Year. Second, there was to be a return of ancestral possessions to those who had been compelled to sell them because of poverty. This, of course, excluded the possibility of selling a piece of land permanently. This law applied to lands and houses outside of the walled cities and also to the houses owned by LEVITES, whether in walled cities or not. As in the case of the price of slaves, the law made provision that the price of real property was to vary according to the proximity of the Jubilee Year. The third feature was that it was to be a year of rest for the land. The land was to remain fallow, even though it had been so in the previous sabbatical year. The people were to live simply, on what the fields had produced in the sixth year and whatever grew spontaneously.

Jubilees, Book of. A pseudepigraphic work (see PSEUDEPIGRAPHA), claiming to be a revelation given to MOSES on Mount SINAI, and consisting of an interpretative expansion of the biblical narrative from Gen. 1 to Exod. 12. The book divides the history of the world into JUBILEE periods of forty-nine years each (cf. Lev. 25). The work presents a strict view of the LAW.

Jucal. See JEHUCAL.

Juda. See JUDAH.

Judaea. See JUDEA.

Judah. joo′duh (Heb. *yĕhûdâ H3373*, "[God/Yahweh] be praised" [by popular etymology, but possibly actual derivation]; gentilic *yĕhûdî H3374* [see JEW]; Gk. *Ioudas G2683*). KJV NT Juda, Judas. **(1)** Fourth son of JACOB; his mother was LEAH (Gen. 29:35). Few details of his life are known. He saved JOSEPH's life by persuading his brothers to sell him to the Midianites at DOTHAN (37:26-28). His disgraceful actions recorded in Gen. 38 left a stain on his memory. He gradually appears to have achieved leadership among his brothers (43:3; 46:28; 49:8-12). Through his son PEREZ, Judah became an ancestor of DAVID (Ruth 4:18-22) and of Jesus CHRIST (Matt. 1:3-16). The blessing of dying Jacob to Judah (Gen. 49:9-10) is usually understood as being a messianic prophecy: his descendants would be victorious over his enemies, and the scepter would not depart from the tribe of Judah until the coming of a promised one (for a discussion of this prophecy see SHILOH).

Indeed, Judah's progeny became a very important Hebrew tribe. In the wilderness the Judahites camped to the E of the TABERNACLE, next to the tribe of ISSACHAR (Num. 2:3-5). CALEB, a hero among the Hebrew spies and captors of Canaan, was a member of this tribe (13:6; 34:19). Judah was one of the tribes that stood on Mount GERIZIM to bless the people at the ceremony of COVENANT renewal at SHECHEM (Deut. 27:12). After JOSHUA's death, this tribe seems to have been first in occupying its allotted territory in the southern hill country of Canaan, even to occupying temporarily the city of JERUSALEM (Jdg. 1:1-20). The territory of the tribe of Judah extended from the extreme S point of the DEAD SEA westward to the MEDITERRANEAN. On the N, the boundary began at the northern end of the Dead Sea and continued westward in a crooked line, running S of JERICHO and Jerusalem (the Valley of HINNOM, which was the southern boundary of this city, was also the Judeans' northern boundary); it continued to the Mediterranean through BETH SHEMESH and TIMNAH. The Dead Sea was the eastern boundary (Josh. 15).

Judah possessed one of the largest tribal territories. From E to W it measured some 45 mi.

(72 km.). The N–S dimension of the part fit for intensive habitation was about 50 mi. (80 km.); if the NEGEV area, suited only for scattered dwelling, was included, the length was about 100 mi. (160 km.). Judah's territory consisted of three N–S belts of land: (1) the Judean hill country (Josh. 15:48), the eastern slopes of which were the wilderness of Judah; (2) the lowlands of the SHEPHELAH (15:33), that is, the low, rolling land where the hill country meets the plain; and (3) the plain near the Mediterranean Sea. The southern part, near and south of BEERSHEBA, was called the Negev. Much of the tribe's land was hilly and rocky, but apart from the wilderness of Judah and the Negev, it was well suited for pasture and for the cultivation of grapes and olives (Gen. 49:11-12). In ancient times the hills were terraced.

During the period of the rule of the judges, Judah tended to be separated from the rest of the Hebrew tribes, which were to the N, by the pagan people who lived between them (GIBEONITES, Josh. 9; JEBUSITES, Jdg. 19:10-13), and also by rough and wild land, with deep E–W valleys. The Simeonites, who lived in S Judean cities, tended to become assimilated into Judah and thus to lose their tribal identity. OTHNIEL, the judge who delivered the people from the domination of Mesopotamia, was from Judah (Jdg. 3:8-11). The PHILISTINE threat must have been especially troublesome to this tribe, for the Philistine plain, as it came to be called, was actually Judah's coastal plain land. The account of RUTH and BOAZ, which centers in BETHLEHEM, occurred during the time of the judges and first brought the country town of Bethlehem into prominence in Hebrew history. SAUL, whose reign brought the period of the judges to an end, ruled from Judah; and it was the Judeans who first anointed their fellow tribesman, DAVID, king at HEBRON (2 Sam. 2:1-4). Jesus CHRIST, as Son of David, descended from Judah (Matt. 1:2-3; Lk. 3:33; Heb. 7:14). In the book of Revelation he is called "the Lion of the tribe of Judah, the Root of David" (Rev. 5:5). See also JUDAH, KINGDOM OF.

(2) Ancestor of a family of LEVITES who returned from the EXILE (Ezra 3:9 KJV; see HODAVIAH #3).

(3) One of the Levites who agreed to put away their foreign wives (Ezra 10:23).

(4) Son of Hassenuah; a postexilic leader who had charge "over the Second District" of Jerusalem (Neh. 11:9; according to NRSV, he was "second in charge" after Joel son of Zicri).

(5) A Levite who returned from the exile and served as worship leader (Neh. 12:8).

(6) A leader who took part in the procession at the dedication of the wall (Neh. 12:34).

(7) A priest who played a musical instrument at the dedication of the wall (Neh. 12:36).

(8) Son of a certain Joseph, included in Luke's GENEALOGY OF JESUS CHRIST (Lk. 3:30).

Judah, kingdom of. One of the two kingdoms of the Hebrews into which ISRAEL was divided after the death of SOLOMON.

I. The united kingdom. SAUL, from the tribe of BENJAMIN, was Israel's first king (1 Sam. 8—2 Sam. 1). His reign was not a success, and when he died (about 1000 B.C.), a period of civil war broke out among the Hebrew tribes. Out of this chaos emerged DAVID (2 Sam. 1—1 Ki. 2), a member of the tribe of JUDAH, who founded the dynasty that ruled in JERUSALEM until the destruction of the capital city by the Babylonians (586 B.C.). David and his son Solomon (1 Ki. 2-11) succeeded in unifying the Hebrew tribes and imposing their rule on the whole nation. During their reigns the

The kingdom of Judah.

Hebrews achieved national greatness and their own empire. When Solomon died, all of this came to an end; the greater part of the nation seceded from the Judean rule to form the northern kingdom of Israel. The Davidic dynasty continued to rule at Jerusalem over a small remnant of the nation, the kingdom of Judah.

II. Background of the divided kingdom. It must not be thought that the mere ineptitude of Solomon's son REHOBOAM (1 Ki. 12) caused the split of the Hebrew kingdom. Ever since their settlement in Canaan after the EXODUS from Egypt, the Israelite tribes had manifested a fierce independence from each other and a great reluctance to give up tribal sovereignty to a national head. On several occasions during the period of the judges (Jdg. 8:1-3; 12:1-6; 20:1-48), strife and even open war broke out among the tribes. It appears that the troubled period between the death of Saul and David's move of the capital to Jerusalem (2 Sam. 2-4) produced a divided kingdom, with Judah (the southern center of power) adhering to David, and Israel (the JOSEPH tribes in central Palestine, and the northern tier of tribes) keeping aloof from David, seeking to establish Saul's son ISH-BOSHETH as their king. Evidently they felt that accepting David's claims meant giving up too much local autonomy to the central government.

After his capture of Jerusalem and the submission of all the tribes to him, David managed to keep the nation together by firm rule combined with a wise handling of explosive personalities. In the weakness of his old age, however, the centripetal forces again asserted themselves (2 Sam. 20). Solomon clamped on the nation a firm rule, assessing heavy taxes and forced labor. We infer that Judah was exempt from his most objectionable requirements, a condition hardly likely to please the ever-restless Israelite tribes. When Solomon died, there already existed an Israelite government in exile, headed by JEROBOAM son of Nebat (1 Ki. 11:26-40). He returned to Palestine to confront Solomon's son Rehoboam with an ultimatum—"Lighten the harsh labor and the heavy yoke … and we will serve you" (12:1-11). Rehoboam, stubborn and inept, tried to assert force instead of making concessions, and Jeroboam split the kingdom by organizing a secession government in Israel, which

ultimately (under OMRI) was centered in the city of SAMARIA.

III. Resources and organization of the kingdom of Judah. Rehoboam continued to reign over a small southern region, mainly equal to the territory of Judah. Most of Benjamite territory appears to have gone with the northern rebels (1 Ki. 12:20), but Jerusalem, in the extreme S of Benjamin, remained as capital of Judah because of the presence of Rehoboam's army there. Thus the boundary between Judah and Israel must have run a few miles N of Jerusalem. All of S Palestine (much of it desert) was held by Rehoboam. Even so, his territory was not more than half the size of the northern kingdom; his arable land, less than one-fourth as much as Israel's. Judah claimed suzerainty over EDOM and asserted it when they were able. Judah's population (estimated at 300,000) was probably about half that of Israel's. The northern kingdom had the best farm land and was favored with more rainfall than the south.

In spite of her small size Judah enjoyed certain advantages over Israel. She had control of Jerusalem, with its ancient heritage of the TEMPLE and its divinely ordained worship, together with the Davidic dynasty and the buildings and traditions of the strong Solomonic empire. Her location in the southern hill country removed her somewhat from the ever-increasing tempo of struggle for control of the road to Egypt by the Assyrians, a struggle that ended eventually in Israel's destruction. She tended to be a city-state (no other Judean city could begin to compete with Jerusalem) with a homogeneous population and strong centralization of authority, thus avoiding the weakness of decentralization that characterized the northern kingdom. The continuing Davidic dynasty (Israel had nine dynasties during the reigns of nineteen kings) and a Levitic priesthood (attached to the Jerusalem temple) were sources of continuing strength.

IV. The history of the kingdom of Judah. It is difficult to isolate Judah's history. In the biblical sources (the books of Kings and Chronicles) the accounts of Israel and Judah are intertwined, with Israel predominating. One gets the impression that Israel's history was dynamic and in several respects attractive, while Judah's existence (except

© Dr. James C. Martin

Looking E through the wide U-shaped valleys of the Shephelah toward the Judean hill country.

for certain great periods) was conservative—essentially a "holding operation." Judah's history from the death of Solomon to the fall of Jerusalem to the Babylonians may be divided into three periods:

A. Judah from the death of Solomon to the mid-eighth century, 922-742 B.C. During this period of nearly two centuries Judah and Israel lived side by side. For the first two generations the successive Judean kings fought against Israel, seeking to compel her to reunite with the south. Beginning with JEHOSHAPHAT, however, they saw the impossibility of success in this attempt, for Israel was, if anything, more powerful than Judah. Jehoshaphat began a tradition of friendly cooperation with Israel, which, with few exceptions, characterized the Judean kings until the fall of Samaria left the southern kingdom to carry on alone.

With the split of the kingdom, the Hebrew empire raised by David and Solomon collapsed. Judah was now a second-rate power—a city-state in the hills. As if to prove its degradation, SHISHAK, a soldier turned king of EGYPT, invaded Palestine, seeking to revive the Egyptian empire. According to the Bible he badly looted Jerusalem (1 Ki. 14:25-26); Shishak's own historical inscriptions at Karnak indicate that he sacked most of Palestine. Rehoboam's pathetic copper shields, a cheap imita-

tion of the looted gold ones (14:27-28), symbolize the condition of post-Solomonic Judah—the grandeur had departed.

Rehoboam and his son ABIJAH seem to have carried on Solomon's syncretistic tendencies; pagan rites flourished. ASA and JEHOSHAPHAT instituted reforms aimed at purifying the worship of the Lord from pagan influence. Jehoshaphat is known for the marriage of his son JEHORAM to ATHALIAH, daughter of AHAB and JEZEBEL of Israel, thus sealing his new policy of friendliness toward the northern kingdom. This policy seems to have brought great prosperity to Judah, but also the threat that the BAAL worship sponsored by Ahab in Israel might spread to the south. Jehoram's son, Ahaziah, ruled for only one year. After his death he was briefly succeeded by Athaliah, the queen mother. She sought to stamp out all the Judean royal house and to make Baalism the worship of Judah. A palace-temple coup resulted in her death (837 B.C.), the restoration of the Davidic line in the person of Joash (JEHOASH), the boy king, and the revival of the worship of Yahweh sponsored by JEHOIADA the high priest.

The next two kings, AMAZIAH and UZZIAH, reigned during a great burst of political and economic prosperity, just before the coming of the Assyrian invasions and Israel's captivity. Judah and

Israel briefly occupied much of the land they had under Solomon's reign. Increased trade brought home great wealth. Luxury (especially in Israel) was unprecedented. It was to the spiritually careless people of this time, at ease in Zion, that the great eighth-century prophets—Amos, Hosea, Jonah, Isaiah, and Micah—came.

B. Judah during the period of the Assyrian ascendancy, 742-687 B.C. In the third quarter of the eighth century an event occurred that was to influence all of succeeding history. ASSYRIA, with its capital at NINEVEH, moved westward in its effort to capture the civilized world. Ultimately Israel, located as she was on the road to Egypt, was destroyed by the Assyrians (722), and Judah was severely damaged.

King AHAZ first brought Judah into the Assyrian orbit when he called on the new empire to relieve him from the attack of the coalition formed by Israel and the ARAMEANS (SYRIA, 2 Ki. 16:7). Judah was saved, DAMASCUS destroyed, and part of Israel overrun by the Assyrians (733-732 B.C.), but at a serious cost. There naturally followed spiritual subordination of Assyria, and Ahaz introduced its pagan religious practices into Jerusalem. This problem of imported paganism was to plague Judah until its fall. Late in Ahaz's reign the city of Samaria was destroyed and Israel's national existence brought to an end. King HEZEKIAH, the pious son of Ahaz, sensing a weakening of Assyrian power, sought to throw off both the political and religious yoke of Assyria. Under him, Judah managed to survive the attacks of SENNACHERIB, although at fearful cost. Hezekiah reformed the national religion, purifying it of paganism. His treaty with the rising power of BABYLON, a threat to Assyrian domination of Mesopotamia, although condemned by ISAIAH, was another facet of his struggle to keep Judah free. The prophets Isaiah and MICAH continued their ministry into this period. Certainly much of Hezekiah's success in religious reform was due to Isaiah's support.

C. The last century of the kingdom of Judah, 687-587 B.C. During Judah's last century of national existence Palestine was the scene of intermittent warfare; empires clashed, fell, and rose around her until finally Judah fell. MANASSEH, son

of Hezekiah, through a long reign chose to submit again to Assyrian political and religious control. His grandson, JOSIAH, was the last good Hebrew king, and the last one whose reign saw anything like normal times in the Judean kingdom. Josiah's famous revival (621 B.C.), the most thoroughgoing in Judah's history, was aided by the rediscovery of the Book of the Law (probably DEUTERONOMY) in the temple (2 Ki. 22). Josiah made a great effort to rid Judah of all paganism and to centralize all the worship of the Lord at the Jerusalem temple. This meant rebellion against Assyria, which Josiah was able to carry out; in fact, it was during his reign that the Assyrian empire disintegrated. Josiah tragically lost his life trying to oppose the forces of Pharaoh NECO, who were crossing Palestine on their way to Syria to fight in the battles that marked the death throes of Assyria, with NINEVEH falling in the year 612. During Josiah's reign the young JEREMIAH began his prophetic career, which extended into the period of the captivity. A sad man with a depressing message, Jeremiah predicted the fall of the nation because of her sins. Evidently Josiah's revival had done little to stop the downward trend.

Egypt still tried to play a part in the political struggle, and her nearness to Palestine made her also a power to be reckoned with in Judah. Placed between great world powers, relying alternately on each but seldom (according to the prophets) on her God, Judah played a fateful, increasingly unsteady role. Unsettled, fearful times followed Josiah's death. King JEHOIAKIM, a puppet of Egypt, was unworthy to follow his father Josiah. Jeremiah steadily opposed his easy trust that the temple would bring security. The Babylonians raided Jerusalem during his reign (605 B.C.). Finally the proud, wicked king was killed in a coup, and his son JEHOIACHIN replaced him. After three months the Babylonians under NEBUCHADNEZZAR captured Jerusalem (597) and took captive to BABYLON many important persons, including the king. This was the beginning of the end. Babylon, having replaced Nineveh as the center of world power, would dominate Judah until she destroyed her.

ZEDEKIAH, another son of Josiah, was made regent in the place of captive Jehoiachin. He

J

rebelled against Babylon, made a league with Egypt, and so incurred the wrath of the Babylonians that they decided to destroy Jerusalem. After a bitter siege of a year and a half the city fell to Nebuchadnezzar and was destroyed, Zedekiah was blinded and carried to Babylon, and the great bulk of the population taken there with him (586 B.C.). Archaeologists have found that the cities of Judah were completely destroyed at this time. Thus ended the glorious kingdom of David and Solomon. Observers would have said that the Hebrew nation was annihilated, and indeed, the other nations conquered by the Assyrians and Babylonians did cease to exist. But the prophets proclaimed a better hope for the chosen people. "A remnant will return" Isaiah had said (Isa. 10:21), and in time this purged remnant returned and became the basis on which a new Israel would be built.

Judaism. The Greek word *Ioudaismos G2682* occurs in only one biblical passage (Gal. 1:13-14; KJV, "the Jews' religion"; cf. also 2:14). Although the term *Judaism* can be used broadly of the Hebrew culture as a whole, it often refers to the religion of the Jews subsequent to the OT period. As such, Judaism is typically contrasted to the OT, but one cannot forget that the postbiblical developments were firmly rooted in the religious attitudes and practices of the Hebrew Scriptures. See TALMUD.

The traditional tomb of King David, who holds an exalted place in Judaism.

© Dr. James C. Martin

Judaizer. The Greek verb *ioudaizō G2678*, used only once in the NT (Gal. 2:14, but found already in the LXX of Esth. 8:17), has an intransitive meaning, "live as a Jew, become a Jew, adopt the traditions of Judaism." PAUL, however, uses it in combination with the verb "to compel," and that has led to the modern use of *Judaize* in the transitive sense "to force/coerce Gentiles to become Jews." In biblical scholarship, therefore, the noun *Judaizers* is most frequently applied to early Christian Jews who opposed Paul's message of freedom from the LAW and insisted that GENTILE Christians should become circumcised and follow the Mosaic regulations (cf. Acts 15:1-2; Gal. 2:3-5). See GALATIANS, LETTER TO THE.

Judas. joo´duhs (Gk. *Ioudas G2683*, from Heb. *yĕhûdâ H3373*, "praise"). Greek form of Hebrew JUDAH, which originally was the name of one of the sons of JACOB. After the EXILE, it became one of the names most frequently used by the Jews, and it is not surprising that in the APOCRYPHA and NT it designates a considerable number of different men.

(1) Son of MATTATHIAS and leader of the Maccabean Revolt (1 Macc. 2:4 et al.; other men by the same name are mentioned in 11:17 and 16:2 et al.). See MACCABEE.

(2) Judas the Galilean, described by GAMALIEL as a man who "appeared in the days of the census and led a band of people in revolt. He too was killed, and all his followers were scattered" (Acts 5:37). The enrollment or assessment for tax purposes here in view was that under QUIRINIUS during his governorship of SYRIA in A.D. 6-7. JOSEPHUS too in a number of places (e.g., *Ant.* 18.1.6) calls this Judas a Galilean, but elsewhere, evidently referring to his place of birth, calls him a Gaulanite from the city of Gamala (18.1.1). Josephus regards Judas of Galilee as a founder of a fourth sect or school of philosophy among the Jews (18.1.6; *War* 2.8.1). Those in this party agreed with the position of the PHARISEES in all matters, he reports, except that they acknowledged God alone to be their

governor and lord and were passionately devoted to liberty. With the support of a Pharisee named Saddok, Judas vigorously opposed the enrollment under Quirinius and engendered strife, violence, and bloodshed (*Ant.* 18.1.1). From Judas's incendiary activity and teaching, the ZEALOTS and the Sicarii would seem to have sprung.

(3) Judas son of MARY, MOTHER OF JESUS, and thus probably a half-brother of the Lord; he is listed with other brothers, James, Joseph (Joses), and Simon (Matt. 13:55; Mk. 6:3). He is to be distinguished from the apostle Judas, one of the Twelve (see below, #4), because the BROTHERS OF THE LORD did not believe in him during his ministry (Jn. 7:5). The author of the epistle of Jude was in all probability this Judas (see JUDE, LETTER OF). He does not designate himself as one of the apostles, and seems to distinguish himself from them (Jude 17-18 and cf. v. 3). He identifies himself as "Jude [Gk. Judas], a servant of Jesus Christ and a brother of James" (v. 1), no doubt meaning James the Lord's brother (see JAMES #2).

(4) Judas son of James, included among the twelve apostles (Lk. 6:16; Acts 1:13). The KJV interprets the ambiguous Greek to mean "Judas *the brother* of James," but it appears that when Luke means "brother" rather than "son," he makes the designation explicit (Lk. 3:1; 6:14; Acts 12:2). In the other lists of the Twelve, THADDAEUS occurs instead of Judas of James (Matt. 10:3; Mk. 3:18); the same apostle may well have been called by both these names, but not all scholars adopt this solution. In Jn. 14:22 he is sharply distinguished from Judas Iscariot and is reported to have asked a question of Jesus: "Then Judas (not Judas Iscariot) said, 'But, Lord, why do you intend to show yourself to us and not to the world?'" In the Syriac tradition, this Judas is identified with THOMAS.

(5) JUDAS ISCARIOT (see separate article).

(6) Judas of Damascus. After the Lord had appeared to Saul (PAUL) on the road to DAMASCUS, Saul was led into the city and stayed in the house of a man named Judas, presumably a believer himself (Acts 9:11). The Lord directed ANANIAS to go to the street called STRAIGHT and inquire for Saul in Judas's house.

(7) Judas surnamed BARSABBAS. At the Council of Jerusalem, the apostles and the elders selected out of their company Judas Barsabbas and SILAS, "two men who were leaders among the brothers," to go to ANTIOCH of Syria with Paul and BARNABAS (Acts 15:22) to confirm by word of mouth the contents of the letter containing the decree of the council (15:27). The epistle from the council was delivered to the church in Antioch, and Judas and Silas, "who themselves were prophets, said much to encourage and strengthen the brothers" (15:32). Possibly this Judas was a brother of the Joseph called Barsabbas, surnamed JUSTUS, who was chosen with MATTHIAS as a candidate for the place from which Judas Iscariot fell away (1:25).

Judas Iscariot. joo´duhs is-kair´ee-uht (Gk. *Ioudas Iskariōtēs G2683 + G2697*). One of the Twelve, known primarily as the disciple who betrayed Jesus to the authorities. He and his father Simon were both surnamed "Iscariot" (Jn. 6:71), a word of uncertain meaning but thought to be a hellenized form of Hebrew *ʾîš qĕriyyôt*, "man of KERIOTH," thus serving to indicate his origin. Nothing is known of his early life. He may have joined the disciples of Jesus from pure motives and probably showed evidence of business acumen and so was appointed treasurer for the disciples (Jn. 12:6; 13:29), but perhaps after his hopes for a high place in an earthly kingdom of Jesus were dashed (cf. 6:66), he became a thief. His indignation when Jesus was anointed at BETHANY was hypocritical. His pretended zeal for the poor was really covetousness, and is so interpreted by John (12:6), though the disciples of Jesus apparently trusted him to the end (13:21-30). Jesus, however, was not deceived (cf. 6:64) but knew from the beginning who would betray him. It was only at the Last Supper that Jesus revealed that one of them "was later to betray him" (6:71). Then SATAN entered into Judas, and when Jesus dismissed him, he went out to do the dastardly deed that he had already planned (Mk. 14:10). He sold the Lord for thirty pieces of silver, betrayed him with a kiss, then in remorse threw down the money before the chief priests and elders (Matt. 27:3-10) and went out and committed suicide. Matthew says he hanged himself (Matt. 27:5), and Luke adds that "he fell headlong, his body burst open" (Acts 1:18). He is always mentioned last among the apostles.

Jude. See Judas #2; Jude, Letter of.

Jude, Letter of. The last among the Catholic Epistles. It was regarded by Origen (d. c. A.D. 253) as "of but few verses yet full of mighty words of heavenly wisdom." The opening verse describes the author as "Jude, a servant of Jesus Christ and a brother of James." This is probably the same person as Judas, brother of James and Jesus (Matt. 13:55; Mk. 6:3; see Brothers of the Lord). Nothing more is known about him or about his place of writing, nor is precise dating of the letter possible. The strong resemblance between this letter and 2 Pet. 2 has been used by some for dating purposes, but others think that this feature merely reflects dependence on a common tradition. We do know that the problems it discusses were common during the last quarter of the first century, when heresy was increasing. Concerning the purpose of the letter there is no doubt: the writer is directing to his readers an urgent appeal "to contend for the faith that was once for all entrusted to the saints" (Jude 3). The very basis of Christianity was in jeopardy.

Jude goes on to deal with the new heresy threatening the churches from within. What it was, and who its supporters were, is not clear; but we are told something about their appalling lifestyle and its baneful influence on the church. Jude reminds Christians of the inevitability of opposition, of the need for compassion toward sinners, and of the ineffable attributes of God. As he denounces those who would undermine the true faith, his voice seems to rise in righteous anger: this was a time for holy intolerance. There is no place in the church for those who divide the people of God (Jude 4-16). The Christian ranks had been infiltrated by "certain men" who held that those who became Christians were no longer under law and could behave as they wished (cf. Rom. 6:1-2; 1 Jn. 3:6). Gnostic heretics held that morals and religion were different things, but this teaching misunderstood the true nature of Christian liberty and degraded it to the level of pagan license (2 Pet. 2:2). Using the most striking images (rainless clouds, blighted trees, wandering stars), Jude warns against those who pretend to piety but are rotten at heart and leave the trace of the mire behind them. Jude reminds his readers of God's punishment in the OT (Gen. 6:1-4; 19:24; Num. 14:29, 37) against people, angels, and cities that should have known better, and he leaves them in no doubt that God still punishes sin.

Jude 17-25 exhorts to continued perseverance. There is a reminder that the apostles had foretold the coming of the "scoffers" (cf. 2 Pet. 3:3) who love worldly things and sow dissension among believers. Watchful, prayerful, expectant Christians had,

Overview of JUDE

Author: Jude, brother of James (prob. referring to the half-brother of Jesus).

Historical setting: The date, place of writing, and destination are unknown, but the addressees (possibly Jewish Christians of the Dispersion) were being challenged by heretical and immoral people. Some scholars speculate that the letter was written in the early 60s; others prefer a date near the end of the century.

Purpose: To urge the readers "to contend for the faith" (Jude 1), opposing false doctrine and immorality.

Contents: After the introduction (Jude 1-4), the bulk of this brief letter consists of a denunciation of the false teachers (vv. 5-19), followed by positive exhortations and a doxology (vv. 20-25).

however, nothing to fear from such renegades. Jude obviously knew too well the tensions and temptations, the awfulness of sin. He knew that some cases called for stern rebuke, others needed compassion and a right concern. The letter ends with a firm ascription of glory to the One to whom alone it belongs and who will bring his whole family at last, cleansed and complete, into his own presence forever.

Judea. joo-dee´uh (Gk. *Ioudaia G2677*, from Heb. *yĕhûdâ H3373*, "Judah"). Also Judaea. Name used for the southern part of PALESTINE, especially after the end of the kingdom of Judah (see JUDAH, KINGDOM OF; occasionally, however, the gentilic JUDEAN is used in the sense of "Judahite," that is, a member of the tribe of JUDAH even during the earlier periods). The corresponding Greek term occurs often (but not as often as the form *Iouda*) in the SEPTUAGINT with reference to Judah. Since most of the exiles who returned from the Babylonian exile belonged to the tribe of Judah and settled in the environs of JERUSALEM, they came to be called Judeans or JEWS, and their land Judea.

Under the Persian empire, Judea was a district administered by a governor who was usually a Jew (Hag. 1:14; 2:2). Under Rome, with the banishment of HEROD's son Archelaus, the province of Judea became annexed to the Roman province of SYRIA; but its governors were appointed by the Roman emperor. Their immediate superior was the proconsul of Syria, who ruled from ANTIOCH (Lk. 3:1). The official residence of the governors of Judea was CAESAREA. Geographically, Judea was about 55 mi. (90 km.) N to S and the same distance E to W, extending from the MEDITERRANEAN to the DEAD SEA, with its northern boundary just N of JOPPA and its southern boundary a few miles S of GAZA and the southern portion of the Dead Sea. Its exact boundary was, however, never fixed.

judge. See OCCUPATIONS AND PROFESSIONS.

Judges, Book of. The seventh book of the OT. In the Hebrew Bible, Judges is included among the Former Prophets. The book takes its name from the title of those who ruled Israel during the period from JOSHUA to SAMUEL. Although "judge" is a literal translation of Hebrew *šôpēṭ* (ptc. of the verb *šāpaṭ H9149*, "to decide, pass judgment, be in authority"), the term in this context really means "leader" or "ruler." The principal function of the Hebrew "judges" during this period was that of military deliverers.

The book makes no clear claim to authorship or date of composition. Much of it appears to be very old. The JEBUSITES are referred to as still dwelling in JERUSALEM (Jdg. 1:21). DAVID's capture of Jerusalem about 1000 B.C. (2 Sam. 5:6-10) brought this situation to an end. The Canaanites still lived in GEZER (Jdg. 1:29), a city that first came under Hebrew control at the time of SOLOMON (1 Ki. 9:16). On the other hand, there are also references that cannot be understood except as written at a time well after that of the judges. The thematic statement, "In those days Israel had no king; everyone did as he saw fit" (Jdg. 17:6; 18:1; 19:1; 21:25), could not have been written before the reign of SAUL; indeed, it would be unlikely until a time well after the institution of the monarchy, when the earlier chaotic days tended

Judea.

Overview of JUDGES

Author: Unknown.

Historical setting: Covers the period from the death of Joshua (c. 1380 or 1230 B.C., depending on the date of the Exodus) to the generation that preceded the monarchy (c. 1050 B.C.). The book itself may have been composed soon after the end of that period (a Jewish tradition attributed it to Samuel), but many scholars date it several centuries later.

Purpose: To provide a historical-theological account of the chaotic times following the Israelite occupation of Canaan, and thus to show the nation's need for the centralized rule of a king.

Contents: After a prologue (Jdg. 1:1—2:5) and a summary of the cycles of sin and deliverance (2:5—3:6), the book describes the work of twelve "judges" or leaders, with emphasis on Deborah, Gideon, Jephthah, and Samson (3:7—16:31), followed by an account of two shocking stories of religious and moral degeneration (chs. 17-21).

to be forgotten. The reference to the worship at Dan "until the time of the captivity of the land" (18:30) seems to be a reference to the conquest of Galilee by Tiglath-Pileser III in 733 B.C. It would seem, then, that the book contains very old material, which may well have been edited at a later date. It may be noted that recent critical scholarship, while holding to a later date for the final editing of the book, acknowledges the general historicity of the narrative and uses it as the major source for our understanding of the period of the judges.

It is difficult to date with precision the historical period covered by the book of Judges. It appears to have ended about a generation before Saul became king; thus we may place the end of the book at about 1020 B.C. The year of the death of Joshua, with which the book opens, depends on the date of the Exodus from Egypt, about which there is much dispute. Accordingly, some scholars date the beginning of the period of the judges at c. 1380-60; others, at c. 1230-10; still others, later. At first sight it may seem that the book itself gives the answer, for it states the duration of the judgeships of the various judges. A close examination of the

text, however, reveals that most of the judges were local, not national in their influence, and it appears likely that their periods overlapped. Further, the frequency of the number forty for the length of their office (Jdg. 3:11; 5:31; 8:28; 13:1; 1 Sam. 4:18) suggests that this figure is a round number for a generation and not to be taken exactly.

The purposes of the book of Judges are (1) to bridge in some manner the historical gap between the death of Joshua and the inauguration of the monarchy; (2) to show the moral and political degradation of a people who neglected their religious heritage and compromised their faith with the surrounding paganism; (3) to show the need of the people for the unity and leadership by a strong central government in the person of a king. The contents may be discussed under three headings, as follows.

I. Introduction (Jdg. 1:1—2:10). This section gives a description of the state of the conquest of Canaan when Joshua died. It is a record of incomplete success. The less desirable hill country had been taken, but the fertile plains and the cities were still largely in Canaanite hands. This description does not contradict the record of the conquest (found in the book of Joshua), which only claims that the Hebrew armies had "blitzkrieged" the whole land, while plainly stating that not all had been possessed (Josh. 13:1-6). It was one thing for the Hebrew armies to sweep through the land; it was quite another for the individuals and tribes of the Hebrews to dispossess the Canaanites from the land and settle there. They failed to dispossess them, and this failure meant that the Hebrews lived as neighbors with pagan Canaanites; thus, the way was prepared for the syncretism (combining worship of the Lord with worship of idols) that so characterized the Hebrews during this period. This culture and religion were often largely Canaanite and pagan. This is the reason for the moral and spiritual degradation of the Hebrew people during the period of the judges.

II. Main body of the book (Jdg. 2:11—16:31). Here occur the accounts of the judges, the cycles of failure, oppression, and relief by a judge. The cycle is set forth in the abstract in 2:11—3:6, and the accounts of the judges follow. As already noted, these "judges" were not principally civil magistrates. Rather, they were military deliverers, who led the people of Israel to freedom against their enemies. Their names are as follows:

1. OTHNIEL (3:7-11).
2. EHUD (3:12-30): Central Palestine and Transjordan.
3. SHAMGAR (3:31): Philistine plain.
4. DEBORAH and BARAK (chs. 4-5): Central Palestine and Galilee.
5. GIDEON (chs. 6-8): Central Palestine and Transjordan.
6. ABIMELECH (ch. 9): Central Palestine. Abimelech is considered by many as merely an outlaw and not a judge.
7. TOLA (10:1-2): Central Palestine.
8. JAIR (10:3-5): Transjordan.
9. JEPHTHAH (10:6—12:7): Transjordan.
10. IBZAN (12:8-10): Southern Palestine.

11. ELON (12:11-12): Northern Palestine.
12. ABDON (12:13-15): Central Palestine.
13. SAMSON (chs. 13-16): Philistine plain.

For detailed discussion of these leaders, see separate articles on each of them as well as the article JUDGES, THE.

III. Appendix (Jdg. 17-21). The events recorded here seem to have occurred, not after the

The battle between Gideon and the Midianites occurred here, in the Harod Valley. (View SE toward Mt. Gilboa.)

judges mentioned in the main part of the book, but during their judgeships. They are relegated to the appendix probably because they are narratives in their own right and if inserted in the main body would have marred the symmetry of the judge cycles there. These narratives describe life during this turbulent near-pagan period and give a frank and unvarnished description of the brutality and paganism that Israel was contaminated with because of her close association with her pagan Canaanite neighbors.

The LEVITE or Jdg. 17-18 was a priest who could follow his religious practice anywhere. He was hired as a family chaplain and soothsayer, and his presence was certain to bring "good luck" (17:13). He evidently functioned with idols (18:20) and was quite willing to change situations if the change involved a better salary (18:19-20). All of this is in direct contrast to the divine command concerning the priesthood in the Mosaic law.

J

The migration of the Danites (Jdg. 18) was necessitated by their failure to capture the territory assigned to them (Josh. 19:40-48; Jdg. 1:34-36). They then traveled to a northern valley, remote and defenseless, captured it, and settled there. Thus originated the northern DAN, known in the expression, "from Dan to Beersheba" (e.g., 1 Sam. 3:20; 2 Sam. 3:10; 1 Ki. 4:25).

The narrative of the Levite's concubine (Jdg. 19) casts a livid light on the brutality of the times and introduces the war of the tribes against the Benjamites (chs. 20-21). This is not the only intertribal war of the period (8:1-3; 12:1-6). In fact, it is clear that the loyalty of the Hebrews at this time was a merely tribal one, as is the case with the bedouin until today. There was no real Hebrew nation; Israel was at best a very loose confederation of tribes around a central sanctuary, the TABERNACLE at SHILOH (18:31).

The cruelty and paganism of the narratives of Judges are often a stumbling block to readers. It should not be imagined that the writer is approving of everything he records. Rather, the book should be viewed as a history of the tragic judgment of God on a people who failed to keep their heritage of true religious faith by assimilating far too much of their surrounding culture. The history of the judges has been called "the struggle between faith and culture." In this struggle, faith lost. And, of course, culture suffered also.

All this should not close our eyes to the beauty of the book of Judges as literature. Many of the narratives would rank high in any collection of the short stories of the world. Even in the most brutal passages there is an austere dignity. Sin is never reveled in; it is always held up to the gaze of horror. In the pungent discourse by JOTHAM (Jdg. 9:7-15), Judges has preserved almost the only fable in ancient Hebrew literature. The song of Deborah, much studied by recent scholars, has a sonorous quality and vivid narrative power. The narratives of the book are amazingly brief. The Hebrew literary artist was at his best when he used only a few sentences to describe action- and emotion-packed events.

judges, the. Two distinct functions need to be discussed under this heading.

I. The civil magistrate. In patriarchal times Hebrew life was organized around the family and the clan. Heads of families ("patriarchs") and elders of the tribes were the judges (Gen. 38:24), and their authority was based on custom. After the EXODUS from Egypt, MOSES (on the advice of JETHRO, Exod. 18:13-26), organized the nation into groups of thousands, hundreds, fifties, and tens, within each tribe. Over each unit a qualified person was placed as judge, and only the most important cases were brought before Moses (Deut. 1:12-18; 21:2). After entering CANAAN, a similar plan of local government was followed (Deut. 16:18-20; 17:2-13; 19:15-20; Josh. 8:33; 23:2; 24:1; 1 Sam. 8:1). During the period of the judges the office assumed a very different character; this will be treated below.

When the monarchy was instituted, the king himself tried important cases (2 Sam. 15:2; 1 Ki. 3:9, 28; 7:7; Prov. 20:8). DAVID assigned LEVITES to the judicial office and appointed 6,000 men as officers and judges (1 Chr. 23:4; 26:29). According to 2 Chr. 19:5-8, JEHOSHAPHAT enlarged the judicial system of Judah with a kind of supreme court at Jerusalem, made up of Levites, priests, and heads of fathers' houses. The prophets often complained bitterly that justice was corrupted by bribery and false witness (Isa. 1:23; 5:23; 10:1; Amos 5:12; 6:12; Mic. 3:11; 7:3). Kings were often unjust (1 Ki. 22:26; 2 Ki. 21:16; Jer. 36:26). The case of AHAB's seizure of NABOTH's vineyard (1 Ki. 21:1-13) shows how far a king could go in getting his own way, in flagrant contradiction of law and custom, at least in the northern kingdom of Israel.

In OT times the judges' activities were not limited to what today would be considered judicial functions. Our present division of powers among the legislative, executive, and judicial branches is a modern innovation. The word *judge* is often parallel to *king* (Ps. 2:10; 148:11; Isa. 33:22; 40:23; Amos 2:3). In several Semitic languages the term used in the Hebrew Bible for judge (*šôpēṭ*) is used for rulers of various kinds. This breadth of meaning attached to the term *judge* in ancient times leads to its extended use in the book of Judges.

II. The leaders during the period of the judges. From the time of the death of JOSHUA to the reign of SAUL, Israel's first king, the principal leaders of the people were called judges. These men and their times are described in the book of Judges and in 1 Sam. 1-7. They were charismatic leaders; that is, they were raised up to be Israel's "saviors" by a special endowment of the Spirit of God. It is clear that they were judges only in the broadest sense of that term. In reality, they were principally military deliverers, raised up to save the people of Israel from oppressing foreign powers. Much general information about the period of the judges, together with a complete list of their names and the regions in which they ruled, is given in the article, JUDGES, BOOK OF.

The discussion here will be restricted to a consideration of the careers and times of the most important of the judges. The times were most distressing. The period was cruel, barbarous, and bloody. The tribes, scattered in the hill country of Canaan, were divided into many separate enclaves. Even the TABERNACLE at SHILOH, which should have provided a religious unity, seems to have been generally neglected in favor of the local high places. Only an unusual crisis, such as the crime that brought on the Benjamite war (Jdg. 19:1-30; 20:1), could lead the tribes to united action. It appears that JUDAH in the S was unusually isolated from the other tribes.

The first judge mentioned in detail is EHUD son of Gera (Jdg. 3:12-30). A Benjamite, he is said to have been lefthanded, a serious defect in those superstitious times. Few if any of the judges are pictured as ideal individuals. The occasion of God's raising up Ehud was the oppression by EGLON king of MOAB, who with the AMMONITES and AMALEKITES (all Transjordanian herdsmen or nomads), occupied the region of JERICHO ("the City of Palms," 3:13). After eighteen years of oppression, Ehud led a revolt by killing Eglon when he presented the tribute. The gory details of the deed fit well this violent period. With Ephraimite help Eglon took the fords of the JORDAN and killed the Moabites as they sought to flee homeward. An eighty-year period of peace followed.

In the second detailed deliverance narrative (Jdg. 4-5), the scene shifts from the lower Jordan Valley to the Valley of JEZREEL and the GALILEE hill country in N Palestine. The oppressor is JABIN, who reigned in HAZOR and whose 900 chariots of iron must have struck terror into the Hebrew tribes, for they had no such machines of war (1 Sam. 13:19-22). The modern excavation of Hazor by Israeli scholars has underscored the importance of this Canaanite stronghold, probably the largest city in ancient Palestine. The deliverers were DEBORAH, "a prophetess" (Jdg. 4:4), surely the actual leader of the uprising, and BARAK son of Abinoam, a fearful man (4:8) who led the Hebrew army at Deborah's urging. The tribes of the Galilee hill country united for this battle, which was fought in the Valley of Jezreel by the Brook KISHON. Evidently a cloudburst upstream caused the Kishon to overflow onto the plains through which it flows, thus immobilizing the chariots on which the Canaanites depended (4:15; 5:20-22). When the army of Jabin was defeated, his general SISERA fled, only to be killed ignominiously by the woman JAEL (4:17-22). Deborah's warlike song of praise (ch. 5) is believed to be one of the oldest poems of the Bible and is noted for its rough, primitive vigor. A forty-year rest followed this deliverance.

The third great judge was GIDEON (Jdg. 6-8), the location of whose village of OPHRAH, in the

Courtyard of a reconstructed Philistine house at the harbor city of Tel Qasile. The Philistine presence threatened the Israelites throughout the period of the judges.

© Dr. James C. Martin. The Eretz Israel Museum. Photographed by permission.

J

tribal territory of MANASSEH, is a matter of uncertainty. It was located somewhere W of the Jordan, probably in the region between BETH SHAN and TABOR. The oppressing Midianites, desert bedouin from the TRANSJORDAN region, had crossed the Jordan and were raiding in Palestine proper. Gideon is commonly remembered for his doubt and reluctance to take action (6:15, 17, 36-40; 7:10), but it should be noted that once he assumed command he proved a steady and effective soldier (6:25-27; 7:15-24). His ruse, carried out by a mere 300 companions, frightened the disorganized bedouin from the Valley of Jezreel into full retreat across the Jordan. Gideon promptly called the Ephraimites to take the Jordan fords and thereby they destroyed the Midianites. Gideon appears to have established some form of regular rule over at least the region of the Jezreel Valley during his lifetime. His importance can be gauged by his rather large domestic establishment (8:30). Adhering to the ancient ideal of charismatic leadership, he rejected the idea of setting up a dynasty (8:22-23). His rule is said to have lasted forty years.

The account of Gideon's son ABIMELECH and his violent rule over the SHECHEM area in the central hill country is told in Jdg. 9. Abimelech is not called a judge, and he appears more as a brigand or political-military adventurer than as a deliverer of Israel from an oppressing enemy. He died as he lived—his skull was cracked by a millstone, and he was finally killed by his armorbearer. Probably his career is described solely to give a feeling of the violent, unsettled state of things during the times of the judges. If that is its purpose, it can be said to have succeeded.

JEPHTHAH, a Transjordanian chieftain, appears next (Jdg. 11-12) as the deliverer of GILEAD and Manasseh (N Transjordan) from the oppression of the Ammonites—a pastoral people who pressured Manasseh from the S. He is chiefly remembered for his thoughtless vow (11:30-31). While authorities differ as to what was involved in it, it is not unlikely that the vow involved offering his daughter as a sacrifice to God in the event of victory over the Ammonites (11:34-39). If it be objected that such an act was completely out of keeping with Hebrew religious practice, it may be answered that

this narrative only emphasized the extent of the religious degradation of the Hebrews during this turbulent period.

The last of the great judges was SAMSON (Jdg. 13-16), with whom the scene shifts to a different part of Palestine—the PHILISTINE plain. It is likely that Samson lived late in the judges period, at the time when a large invasion of the Palestinian seacoast was occurring. The invaders (SEA PEOPLES) from the Aegean area, had been repulsed in their attempt to enter Egypt (by Ramses III) and had subsequently settled in what became known as the Philistine plain. Samson lived in the SHEPHELAH area that bordered that plain. He was dedicated to a life of NAZIRITE obedience before his birth. His life was the tragedy of one whose great potential was vitiated through a lack of self-discipline. Hardly a very religious person, Samson was known for his great strength, becoming the Hebrews' champion against the Philistines. His failure to discipline his sensuous nature led him into three liaisons with Philistine women. Doubtless each was an instrument of the Philistine lords in their effort to subdue Samson. We do not read that Samson ever led a Hebrew army against the Philistines. Rather, he made single-handed exploits in Philistine territory, several of which are described (Jdg. 14:19; 15:4-5, 8, 15; 16:3). The account of Samson's being subdued at the hand of DELILAH is well known. Killing in his death more Philistines than he killed in his life (16:30), he became at the last a tragic figure. He had judged Israel twenty years.

ELI (1 Sam. 1-4) and SAMUEL (2:12) are also called judges. Although they did do some of the work of the judges described above, it would seem better to regard them as PRIEST and PROPHET respectively—transitional figures preparing the way for the monarchy.

judgment. A word found many times in Scripture, with various meanings. Sometimes it refers to the pronouncing of a formal opinion or decision by human beings, but more often it indicates either a calamity regarded as sent by God for PUNISHMENT or a sentence of God as the Judge of all. Among the more important judgments of God prior to the EXODUS are those on ADAM, EVE, and the serpent after the FALL (Gen. 3), on humanity generally at the FLOOD (6:5), on SODOM and GOMORRAH (18:20), and on BABEL (11:1-9). God brings judgment to his creatures when they rebel against his will.

In the OT, the relationship between the Lord and ISRAEL is thought of under the form of a COVENANT. Of his own will, the Lord brought first NOAH (Gen. 6:17) and then ABRAHAM and his children (15:18; 17:1-27) into a close relationship with himself. He bound himself to them by covenant and looked in return for their responsive devotion. Similarly, with Israel in the time of MOSES, grace reached out to redeem and restore (Exod. 6:4) and looked for responsive, loving obedience (ch. 20). Within the covenant, the Lord pledged blessing on obedience and judgment on disobedience (e.g., Deut. 27:1-26; 28:1-68; cf. Lev. 26:3-13). The history of Israel, beginning with the exodus, is the record of a succession of judgments on the enemies of God's people and on his covenant nation when they flouted his will. The DAY OF THE LORD becomes a day of punishment for all the unjust, even for those who boast of belonging to the people of the covenant (Isa. 2:12; Hos. 5:8; Amos 5:18). The purpose of the judgment of God's people is not their total destruction but their purification. A remnant will survive, and this will be the nucleus of the new Israel (Amos 5:15). In the later prophets there are expressions of a hope of an ultimate victory of the divine Judge, of a final or last judgment. Here God's judgment is not thought of so much in terms of his intervention in history but of a last judgment of all human beings at the end of time. Perhaps the clearest expression of this is found in Dan. 12:1-3, where the dead are described as being raised, some for everlasting life, others for shame and everlasting contempt.

In the NT the idea of judgment appears in both human and divine contexts. Jesus warns against uncharitable judgments (Matt. 7:1). PAUL says that the spiritual man cannot be judged by unbelievers (1 Cor. 2:15), and in Rom. 14 and 1 Cor. 8-10 he warns against judging those who are "weak" in the faith. Judgment is one of the aspects of the coming of the KINGDOM OF GOD. God's judgment, says JOHN THE BAPTIST, will fall on those who do not make ready the way of the Lord (Lk. 3:9). Jesus declares that someday he will come as Judge (Matt. 25:31-46).

In the NT, as in the OT, judgment is an aspect of the deliverance of believers (Lk. 18:1-8; 2 Thess. 1:5-10; Rev. 6:10). God is long-suffering in meting out judgment so that people may be able to come to REPENTANCE (Lk. 13:6-9; Rom. 2:4; 2 Pet. 3:9). The notion of judgment, when God will overthrow every resistance, both among evil spiritual powers (1 Cor. 6:2-3) and also among people (Matt. 25:31-46), will affect all individuals, because all are responsible to God according to the grace that has been granted them (Matt. 11:20-24; Lk. 12:17-21; Rom. 2:12-16). This present world will be shaken and destroyed (Matt. 24:29, 35), and a new world will replace the present one (2 Pet. 3:13; Rev. 21:2). God will entrust the administration of this final judgment to his Son at his appearance in glory (Matt. 3:11-12; Jn. 5:22; Rom. 2:16). See also ESCHATOLOGY.

judgment, last. See ESCHATOLOGY.

judgment hall. See PRAETORIUM.

judgment seat. The Greek word *bēma* G1037 (aside from Acts 7:5, where it means "step" or "length") usually refers to a "tribunal," "judicial bench," "judgment seat," or "throne," traditionally erected in public, and from which JUDGMENT and other official business was conducted. Herod AGRIPPA I thus addressed the people of TYRE and SIDON (Acts 12:21). Jesus was brought before PILATE's judgment seat (Matt. 27:19; Jn. 19:13; NIV, "judge's seat"). Jews at CORINTH accused PAUL before the tribunal of the Proconsul GALLIO, who drove them out but ignored the beating of SOSTHENES there (Acts 18:12, 16-17). Later Paul was brought before the judgment seat of FESTUS at CAESAREA (25:6, 10, 17). Ironically the roles will one day be reversed, and Jesus who was unjustly judged by men will sit in righteous judgment over them. "For we must all appear before the judgment seat of Christ, that each one may receive what is due him for the things done while in the body, whether good or bad" (2 Cor. 5:10; cf. Rom. 14:10). This includes even those who are reconciled. While they

J

In Corinth, Paul was brought before a platform known as the *bēma* ("tribunal, judgment seat," Acts 18:12) to be tried by the proconsul, Gallio. The temple prostitutes were located on the Acrocorinth seen in the background. (View to the S.)

have the righteousness of Christ, their work will be tested (2 Cor. 5:18-21; cf. 1 Cor. 3:13-15). See ESCHATOLOGY.

Judith. joo'dith (Heb. *yĕhûdît H3377*, fem. of *yĕhûdî H3374*, "of Judah, Judean, Jewish"). Daughter of Beeri the HITTITE and one of the wives of ESAU (Gen. 26:34).

Judith, Book of. See APOCRYPHA.

jug. See POTTERY.

Julia. joo'lee-uh (Gk. *Ioulia G2684*, from Lat. *Iulia*, fem. of *Iulius*). A Christian woman greeted by PAUL (Rom. 16:15). Because she appears to be linked with PHILOLOGUS, some have speculated that the two may have been related, possibly as husband and wife. Julia was a common Roman name, especially among freed slaves.

Julius. joo'lee-uhs (Gk. *Ioulios G2685*, from Lat. *Iulius*). A Roman CENTURION of the Imperial Regiment (see AUGUSTAN COHORT) stationed at CAESAREA; he was charged with the custody of PAUL for his trip to ROME and his hearing by the emperor (Acts 27:1). Although Julius did not listen to Paul's advice at one point (v. 11), the narrative suggests that there was a significant measure of mutual respect between them (cf. vv. 3, 31-32, 42-43).

Julius Caesar. See CAESAR.

Junia. See JUNIAS.

Junias. joo'nee-uhs (Gk. *Iounias G2687*, perhaps short form of Lat. *Iunianus*; because the form is elsewhere unattested, many understand it as the common fem. name *Iounia*, thus KJV, "Junia"). A Christian at Rome whom Paul greets in Rom. 16:7. Both Junias and ANDRONICUS are described as "my relatives" (KJV, "my kinsmen") and as *episēmoi en tois apostolois*; the latter phrase probably means "outstanding among the apostles," though some argue it should be rendered "well known to the apostles" (so ESV). There is debate also on whether the name should be understood as masculine or feminine; if the reference is to a woman, she was probably the wife of Andronicus.

juniper. See PLANTS.

© Dr. James C. Martin

Jupiter. See Zeus.

Jushab-Hesed. joo´shab-hee´sid (Heb. *yûšab ḥesed* H3457, "mercy will be returned"). Son of Zerub-babel and descendant of David through Solomon (1 Chr. 3:20), possibly born in Palestine (see Hashubah).

just, justice. See righteousness.

justification. In Christian theology this term may be defined as that judicial act of God by which, on the basis of the meritorious work of Christ, imputed to the sinner and received through faith, God declares the sinner absolved from sin, released from its penalty, and restored as righteous. Expressed simply, it is being placed by God in a right relationship with himself (see righteous-ness). The doctrine is found in Paul's letters, chiefly Galatians and Romans.

I. **The nature of justification.** As a reversal of God's attitude toward the sinner because of the sinner's new relation in Christ, justification is (1) a *declarative* act by which the sinner is declared to be free from guilt and the consequences of sin (Rom. 4:6-8; 5:18-19; 8:33-34; 2 Cor. 5:19-21); (2) a *judicial* act in which the idea of judgment and salvation are combined to represent Christ fulfill-ing the law on behalf of the sinner (Matt. 10:41; Rom. 3:26; 8:3; 2 Cor. 5:21; Gal. 3:13; 1 Tim. 1:9; 1 Pet. 3:18); (3) a *remissive* act in which God actu-ally remits sin in complete forgiveness (Rom. 4:5; 6:7); and (4) a *restorative* act by which the forgiven sinner is restored to favor through the imputation of Christ's righteousness (Rom. 5:11; 1 Cor. 1:30; Gal. 3:6).

The major emphasis in justification is that it is an act of God. Nevertheless, it necessarily leads in the life of the believer to a "walking in the Spirit," "bringing forth the fruit of the Spirit," and "serving righteousness," for the God who justifies also gives new birth and a call to wholehearted commitment. Saving faith leads to faithfulness to God in life, as Paul clearly shows in Galatians and Romans. See sanctification.

II. **The essentials of justification.** Four basic essentials in the act of justification are taught by Scripture.

A. **Remission of punishment,** in which the jus-tified believer is declared to be free of the demands of the law since they have been satisfied in Christ (Rom. 4:5) and is no longer exposed to the penalty of the law (6:7). It is more than a pardon from sin; it is a declaration by God that the sinner, though guilty, has had the fact of guilt remitted in Christ.

B. **Restoration to favor,** in which the justified believer is declared to be personally righteous in Christ, and therefore accepted as being in Christ's righteousness. Mere acquittal or remission would leave the sinner in the position of a discharged crim-inal. Justification goes further in that it implies that God's treatment of the sinner is as if that one had never sinned. The sinner is now regarded as being personally righteous in Christ (Gal. 3:6). In this res-toration there is not only acquittal, but also approval; not only pardon, but also promotion. Remission from sin is never separated from restoration to favor.

C. **Imputed righteousness of God,** which is granted the justified believer through Christ's presence. Salvation in Christ imparts the qual-ity and character of Christ's righteousness to the believer (Rom. 3:25-26). Christ is made the Justi-fier through whom a new life is inaugurated in the believer (1 Cor. 1:30). Paul uses the word *righteous-ness* to mean both the righteousness that acquits the sinner and the life-force that breaks the bondage of sin. Salvation can never be separated from the par-ticipational act of the believer in Christ, in which that one is now regarded judicially as having righ-teousness because the actual effect of righteousness has indeed come by faith (Rom. 3:22; Phil. 3:9).

D. **New legal standing before God,** in which, instead of being under the condemnation of sin, the justified believer stands before God in Christ. There has been an absolute interchange of posi-tion: Christ takes the place of the sinner, the place of curse (Gal. 3:15), being made sin (2 Cor. 5:21) and being judged for sin; the believer now stands in Christ's righteousness (Rom. 3:25) and is viewed as a son (Gal. 4:5).

III. **The grounds of justification.** The ground on which justification rests is the redeeming work of Christ's death. The inherent righteousness of Christ is the sole basis on which God can justify the sinner (Rom. 3:24; 5:19; 8:1; 10:4; 1 Cor. 1:8; 6:11; 2 Cor. 5:1; Phil. 3:9). It is this righteousness that, in being imputed to the justified believer, is the ground of justification. It declares the believer to have the same standing before God in personal holiness as Christ himself (Tit. 3:7).

The instrumental cause of justification is faith, as the response of the soul to God's redeeming grace (Rom. 3:28). Faith is the condition of justification not in that it is considered meritorious, but only as the condition by which the meritorious work of Christ is accepted by the sinner. The final ground of justification is the completed, finished, sufficient work of Christ atoning for the sinner in his redeeming work on the cross.

Justus. juhs´tuhs (Gk. *Ioustos G2688*, from Lat. *Iustus*, "just, righteous"). **(1)** Surname of Joseph Barsabbas, one of the two men put forward to take the place of Judas Iscariot in the apostolic band (Acts 1:23). According to an early tradition, he survived a heathen plot by drinking deadly poison without injury.

(2) Titius Justus, described as "a worshiper of God" at Corinth who, after the closing of the Jewish synagogue, opened his home next door so that Paul might continue preaching (Acts 18:7). The form of his name varies in the MSS, some of which have "Titus" (cf. KJV) instead of "Titius."

(3) "Jesus, who is called Justus," Paul's appreciated Jewish coworker who sent greetings to the church in Colosse (Col. 4:11). The apostle describes him and two others—Aristarchus and Mark (see Mark, John)—as "the only Jews among my fellow workers for the kingdom of God, and they have proved a comfort to me."

Juttah. jut´uh (Heb. *yûṭṭâ H3420*, possibly "level place" or "settlement"). A town in the hill country of the tribe of Judah (Josh. 15:55), later allotted to the Levites (21:16; the name is omitted in the MT of 1 Chr. 6:59, but see NIV and note). It is identified with modern Yaṭṭa, c. 5.5 mi. (9 km.) SSW of Hebron.

kab. See WEIGHTS AND MEASURES.

Kabbon. kab´uhn. TNIV form of CABBON.

Kabul. kay´buhl. TNIV form of CABUL.

Kabzeel. kab´zee-uhl (Heb. *qabṣĕʾēl H7696*, "God has gathered"; alternate form *yĕqabṣĕʾēl H3677*, "God will gather"). A town in the NEGEV, the extreme S of the tribal territory of JUDAH, near the border of EDOM (Josh. 15:21). Kabzeel was the native town of BENAIAH son of Jehoiada, a valiant warrior who was in charge of DAVID's bodyguard (2 Sam. 23:20; 1 Chr. 11:22). Also called Jekabzeel, it was reinhabited by the Judeans after the EXILE (Neh. 11:25). Its precise location is unknown.

Kadesh Barnea. kay´dish-bahr´nee-uh (Heb. *qādēš H7729*, "holy [city]," and *qādēš barnēaʿ H7732*, perhaps "sanctuary [at the place] of contention"). A site in the N of SINAI, often referred to simply as Kadesh (but not to be confused with KADESH ON THE ORONTES). The name Kadesh Barnea has been applied to an oasis area made up by four springs approximately 50 mi. (80 km.) SW of BEERSHEBA and about the same distance E of the MEDITER-RANEAN coast. Since the name ʿAin Qedeis pre-serves the original name of Kadesh, some scholars focused on this site, but it was only a small spring, sufficient possibly for the TABERNACLE and its staff, but no more. Kadesh Barnea is now generally identified with ʿAin el-Qudeirat, the largest of the springs between Suez and Beersheba. The ruins of a Judean fortress have been discovered at that site.

The first biblical reference to Kadesh is Gen. 14:7, where it is equated with EN MISHPAT, one of the cities singled out in connection with the invasion by the four eastern kings. When HAGAR fled from SARAH (16:7), she was met by the angel of the Lord at BEER LAHAI ROI, which was located between Kadesh and BERED (16:14). Later ABRAHAM went from MAMRE toward the NEGEV and lived between Kadesh and SHUR (20:1). The primary relationship of the Israelites to Kadesh centers in the period of time that they spent there after the EXODUS (cf. Deut. 1:46; 2:14; Num. 33:37-38). From Horeb (SINAI), via SEIR, it was an eleven-day journey to Kadesh (Deut. 1:2). Kadesh is described as being in the Desert of PARAN (Num. 13:26); it is also said to be in the Desert of ZIN (33:36; cf. 20:1); and Ps. 29:8 mentions the Desert of Kadesh. These references illustrate the overlapping of geographic territories

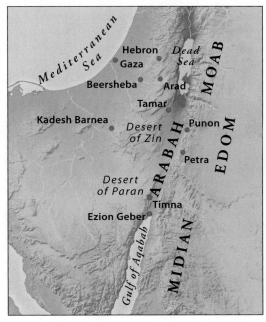

Kadesh Barnea.

whose precise limits are difficult to determine and indicate the character of Kadesh as a border location.

When the Israelites reached this place, Moses sent the twelve spies to scout S Canaan (Num. 13:1, 17, 26; 32:8; Deut. 1:19-25; Josh. 14:6-7). Encouraged by the Lord to invade the land at that time, the people rebelled (Deut. 9:23) and were sentenced to the delay in possessing the land (Num. 14:34). At Kadesh, Miriam died and was buried (20:1). It was in this area also that the waters of Meribah ("quarreling") were located (Num. 20:2-13, 24; 27:14; Deut. 32:51). Kadesh was also on the W border of Edom and it was from Kadesh that Moses sent emissaries to the king of Edom to request permission for Israel to pass through Edomite territory (Num. 20:14-16, 22; cf. Jdg. 11:16-17). The conquest of the southern section of Palestine by Joshua refers to an area from Kadesh to Gaza (Josh. 10:41). Kadesh also is named as marking the S border of Judah (15:3) and therefore the southern boundary of the land possessed by the Israelites (Num. 34:4; Ezek. 47:19; 48:28).

Kadesh on the Orontes. Also Kedesh and Qadesh. A town on the Orontes River in Syria, just S of the Lake of Humus (Ḥoms). The familiar battle between Ramses II and the Hittites took place here in 1288 B.C. It is the modern Tell Nebi Mend, about 45 mi. (72 km.) S of Hamath and 75 mi. (120 km.) N of Damascus. Some believe that the term "Desert of Kadesh" (Ps. 29:8) is a reference to this area. See also Tahtim Hodshi.

Relief of the military campaign of Ramses II against the Hittites at Kadesh on the Orontes in c. 1288 B.C.

© Dr. James C. Martin

Kadmiel. kad´mee-uhl (Heb. *qadmî'ēl H7718*, possibly "God is the ancient one" or "God is in front [*i.e.*, God leads]"). The head of a Levitical family that returned from the exile with Zerubbabel (Ezra 2:40; 3:9; Neh. 7:43; 12:8, 24). He is presumably the same Kadmiel who supervised the workmen that rebuilt the temple (Ezra 3:9), sealed the covenant of Nehemiah (Neh. 10:9), and assisted in leading worship (9:4-5; 12:24).

Kadmonite. kad´muh-nit (Heb. *qadmōnî H7720*, "easterner"). A people group whose land was promised to Abraham's descendants (Gen. 15:19). They are mentioned with other groups who lived somewhere within the region stretching between "the river of Egypt" on the S (see Egypt, River of) and the Euphrates on the N (v. 18), thus people of the "land of the east" (25:6 NIV; the Heb. word for "east" here is *qedem H7710*). Some believe that the Syrian desert E of Byblos (Gebal) is more specifically the region of the Kadmonites. Others suggest that the list in Gen. 15:19 moves from S to N; if so, the Kadmonites, along with the Kenites and Kenizzites, were Canaanites that lived in the S of Palestine and were later absorbed into the tribe of Judah.

Kain. kayn (Heb. *qayin H7805*, possibly "[place of] metal workers"). A city of the hill country in conquered territory assigned to the tribe of Judah (Josh. 15:57; KJV, "Cain"). It is tentatively identified with en-Nabi Yaqin (Khirbet Bani Dar), 3.5 mi. (5.5 km.) SE of Hebron. However, since the Septuagint omits the name and reduces the summarized number of cities from ten to nine, some scholars have proposed to read "Zanoah of Kain," that is, "of the Kenites" (the latter having been added by scribes to distinguish this Zanoah from the one mentioned in v. 34). The same Hebrew word refers to the Kenites in two other passages (Num. 24:22 [cf. v. 21]; Jdg. 4:11).

Kaiwan. ki´wuhn. Also Chiun, Kiyyun. Both this name and Sakkuth (Amos 5:26 NRSV, NIV mg.), possibly referring to one or more pagan deities associated with stars, involve a revocalization of the MT (which has *kiyyûn H3962*, apparently "pedestal," and *sikkût*, perhaps a form of *sukkâ H6109*, "tent, tabernacle" [cf. NIV, "shrine"]). The basis for the reading *Kaiwan* is Akkadian *kayamānu*, "the steady one," a term applied to Saturn. The SEPTUAGINT renders the Hebrew term with Greek *Raiphan G4818* (cf. the quotation in Acts 7:43 and see REPHAN), which perhaps refers to an Egyptian god also associated with Saturn. The rendering Kaiwan remains uncertain, however.

Kalkol. kal´kol. TNIV form of CALCOL.

Kallai. kal´i (Heb. *qallāy H7834*, derivation uncertain). Head of the priestly family of Sallu during the days of the high priest JOIAKIM (Neh. 12:20).

Kalneh, Kalno. kal´neh, kal´noh. TNIV forms of CALNEH, CALNO.

Kamon. kay´muhn (Heb. *qāmôn H7852*, derivation uncertain). KJV Camon. The town where JAIR, one of the "minor judges," was buried (Jdg. 10:3-5). Kamon was probably in GILEAD, but its location is uncertain; one possibility is modern Qamm, about 11.5 mi. (18.5 km.) SE of the Sea of Galilee.

Kanah. kay´nuh (Heb. *qānāh H7867*, "reed"). (1) A brook or ravine mentioned in the delineation of the territories of EPHRAIM and MANASSEH (Josh. 16:8; 17:9). It is generally identified with the Wadi Qana, which runs to the W, joining other wadis and then the Yarkon River before flowing into the MEDITERRANEAN Sea, just N of JOPPA.

(2) A town marking the boundary of the tribal territory of ASHER toward the N (Josh. 19:28). The village of Qanah still lives on and is about 7.5 mi. (12 km.) SE of TYRE.

Kandake. kan´duh-kee. TNIV form of CANDACE.

Kanneh. kan´uh. TNIV form of CANNEH.

kaph. kaf (from *kap H4090*, "palm [of hand], hand"). The eleventh letter of the Hebrew alphabet (כ) with a numerical value of twenty. It is named for the shape of the letter, which in its original form resembled a three-fingered hand. Later it developed an elongated diagonal stroke, and in this form was

borrowed into the Greek alphabet as *kappa*, from which the *k* in the Roman (and English) alphabet was derived.

Kareah. kuh-ree´uh (Heb. *qārēaḥ H7945*, "bald head"). Father of Johanan and Jonathan, who were among those who joined GEDALIAH at MIZPAH (2 Ki. 25:23 [KJV, "Careah"]; Jer. 40:8, 13, et al.). See JOHANAN #1.

Karka. kahr´kuh (Heb. *qarqaʿ H7978*, "floor, ground"). KJV Karkaa. A settlement that served to mark the SW border of the tribe of JUDAH (Josh. 15:3; the name is missing in the parallel, Num. 34:4). It is listed between ADDAR and AZMON, and possibly should be identified with modern ʿAin el-Qeseimeh, c. 50 mi. (80 km.) SW of BEERSHEBA, not far from KADESH BARNEA.

Karkas. kahr´kuhs. TNIV form of CARCAS.

Karkor. kahr´kor (Heb. *qarqōr H7980*, possibly "fountain"). A site in TRANSJORDAN where GIDEON defeated ZEBAH AND ZALMUNNA, kings of MIDIAN (Jdg. 8:10). Karkor was apparently not far from JOGBEHAH (v. 11), but its precise location is uncertain.

Karmi, Karmite. kahr´mi, kahr´mit. TNIV forms of CARMI, CARMITE.

Karnaim. kahr-nay´im (Heb. *qarnayim H7969*, "[two] horns"). Also Carnaim. A city in N TRANSJORDAN that was captured by the Israelites (Amos 6:13; KJV, "horns"). It is identified with modern Sheikh Saʿd, c. 23 mi. (37 km.) E of the Sea of Galilee. Karnaim eventually replaced nearby ASHTAROTH (see also ASHTEROTH KARNAIM) as the center of the region and became the capital of the Persian fifth satrapy (see SATRAP). The city had a temple dedicated to ATARGATIS that was the scene of a great and bloody slaughter by the Jews under Judas MACCABEE in 165 B.C. (1 Macc. 5:26, 44-45).

Karshena. kahr-shee´nuh. TNIV form of CARSHENA.

Kartah. kahr´tuh (Heb. *qartâ H7985*, "city"). A Levitical town within the tribal territory of ZEBULUN, allotted to the descendants of MERARI (Josh. 21:34). The location of Kartah is unknown, and the name is missing in the parallel passage (1 Chr. 6:62 MT, but see LXX, followed by NIV); many scholars think it is an inadvertent scribal repetition of "Kartan" (Josh. 21:32).

Kartan. kahr´tan (Heb. *qartān H7986*, possibly "city"). A Levitical town within the tribal territory of NAPHTALI, allotted to the descendants of GERSHON (Josh. 21:32). The parallel passage has KIRIATHAIM (1 Chr. 6:76), probably an alternate form. Some identify Kartan/Kiriathaim with modern Khirbet el-Qureiyeh in Upper GALILEE, some 12 mi. (19 km.) SE of TYRE; others believe it may be the same as RAKKATH, on the W shore of the Sea of Galilee.

Kasiphia. kuh-sif´ee-uh. TNIV form of CASIPHIA.

Kasluhim, Kasluhites. kas´luh-him, kas´luh-hits. TNIV form of CASLUHIM, CASLUHITES.

Kattah. See KATTATH.

Kattath. kat´ath (Heb. *qattāt H7793*, meaning unknown). A town allotted to the tribe of ZEBULUN (Josh. 19:15; NASB, "Kattah," apparently by mistake). It is mentioned next to NAHALAL, leading many scholars to think that Kattath is the same as KITRON (Jdg. 1:30), though the difference in form is difficult to explain. The town was probably in the N part of the JEZREEL Valley (see ESDRAELON), but the precise location is unknown.

katydid. See ANIMALS (under *grasshopper*).

Kebar. kee´bahr (Heb. *kĕbār H3894*, perhaps "large, great"). A watercourse in BABYLON; NEBUCHADNEZZAR settled a colony of Jewish exiles on its banks, and EZEKIEL saw his earlier visions as he ministered here (Ezek. 1:1, 3; 3:15, 23; 10:15, 20, 22; 43:3). Most scholars identify the "Kebar River" with the Babylonian *nāru kabari*, referring to a "great canal" that branched off from the EUPHRATES above BABYLON, flowed some 60 mi. (100 km.)

SE, through Nippur, and finally emptied back into the Euphrates near ERECH. Today, after centuries of neglect, this artificial watercourse is dry.

Kedar. kee´duhr (Heb. *qēdār H7723*, perhaps "mighty"). Son of ISHMAEL and grandson of ABRAHAM (Gen. 25:13; 1 Chr. 1:29). The OT contains no further information about him, but the name occurs ten other times as a designation of an Arabian tribe that must have been well known to the Israelites. It is used figuratively to describe the situation of one dwelling among barbarous strangers (Ps. 120:5). In Isa. 42:11 and 60:7 it indicates the future wide extension of God's kingdom. and in Jer. 2:10 it is used to point to the distant E, in parallel with KITTIM for the distant W. Isaiah also refers to the many skillful archers and mighty warriors of Kedar (Isa. 21:17). The great multitude of its flocks, camels, and tents is mentioned elsewhere (Isa. 60:7; Jer. 49:28-29; Ezek. 27:21; cf. Cant. 1:5). Isaiah predicts that God will soon remove the glory of Kedar and destroy its powerful forces (Isa. 21:16), and Jeremiah predicts a later destruction, this time at the hands of NEBUCHADNEZZAR (Jer. 49:28-29). All these comparisons show how well known distant Kedar must have been to the Israelites in the years between 1000 and 500 B.C. The account of ASHURBANIPAL's ninth campaign includes the record of an expedition against the people of Kedar (Qedar), which was evidently a powerful factor in N ARABIA. After the blows inflicted by Ashurbanipal and Nebuchadnezzar, the tribe probably dwindled rapidly and in the course of a few centuries disappeared or was assimilated into other Arabian tribes. In constructing a genealogy of Muhammad, the Islamic hagiographers traced his descent from Abraham and Ishmael through Kedar.

Kedemah. ked´uh-muh (Heb. *qēdmāh H7715*, possibly "easterner"). Son of ISHMAEL and ancestor of a tribe in N ARABIA (Gen. 25:15; 1 Chr. 1:31). In contrast to the other tribes that descended from Ishmael, Kedemah is not attested in extrabiblical literature. See also NODAB.

Kedemoth. ked´uh-moth (Heb. *qēdēmôt H7717*, "eastern [place]"). A city, probably on the upper course of the ARNON River, from which MOSES sent messengers to SIHON, king of the AMORITES, requesting a passage through his country (Deut. 2:26; Josh. 13:18). Kedemoth was assigned to the tribe of REUBEN and became one of the LEVITICAL CITIES allotted to the descendants of MERAR (Josh. 21:37; 1 Chr. 6:79). Its location is uncertain.

Kedesh. kee´dish (Heb. *qedeš H7730*, "holy place"). **(1)** The most prominent city in Scripture that bore this name was conquered by JOSHUA from a Canaanite king (Josh. 12:22; however, some scholars believe this text refers to #3 below); it later became one of the "fortified cities" in the tribal territory of NAPHTALI (19:37). Described as "Kedesh in Galilee in the hill country of Naphtali," it is listed as one of the three CITIES OF REFUGE set aside W of the JORDAN (20:7). It was also one of the LEVITICAL CITIES allotted to the descendants of GERSHON (21:32; 1 Chr. 6:76). Kedesh is listed among the cities that TIGLATH-PILESER conquered, deporting its inhabitant to ASSYRIA in the reign of PEKAH (2 Ki. 15:29). Generally identified with modern Tell Qades (c. 17 mi./27 km. NNW of the Sea of Galilee), Kedesh had a strategic location, being in a fertile plain that overlooks the Jordan Valley.

(2) BARAK is said to have come from "Kedesh in Naphtali" (Jdg. 4:6), and it was to this city that he called the representatives of ZEBULUN and Naphtali to plan the gathering of troops at Mount TABOR (vv. 9-10). We are also told that HEBER the Kenite lived near it, by a great tree in ZAANANNIM (v. 11). Some scholars have argued that this Kedesh is the same as #1 above, but the text suggests strongly that Barak's hometown must have been relatively close to Mount Tabor and Zaanannim, not in Upper Galilee. A possible identification is modern Khirbet Qedish, just W of the S tip of the Sea of Galilee. Other scholars point to Jdg. 5:19, which places the battle "at Taanach by the waters of Megiddo," and argue that the Kedesh in question should be identified with #3 below.

(3) A Levitical city within the tribal territory of ISSACHAR, allotted to the Gershonites (1 Chr. 6:72); contrast Kedesh of Naphtali, v. 76). In the parallel list (Josh. 21:28), the place occupied by Kedesh is taken by the name KISHION. Because the reference to Kedesh in Josh. 12:22 seems to point to a city in the vicinity of TAANACH, MEGIDDO, and JOKNEAM (i.e., in or near the plain of ESDRAELON), some have argued that this Kedesh is the one in Issachar, not Kedesh in Upper Galilee (see #1 above), and that it should be identified with Tell Abu Qudeis, a small mound between Taanach and Megiddo. Others argue that this site is too far W to have been included in the territory of Issachar. It has also been suggested that Kedesh in Issachar was Barak's hometown (Jdg. 4:6) and/or the place where Heber the Kenite lived (4:11; see #2 above).

(4) A town in the NEGEV, the extreme S of the tribal territory of JUDAH, near the border of EDOM (Josh. 15:23). Since there is no other mention of such a place in the Scripture, it may be a city otherwise unknown or, as some have suggested, another name for KADESH BARNEA.

Kedorlaomer. ked´or-lay´oh-muhr (Heb. *kĕdorlā ͑ōmer H3906*, prob. from Elamite *kutir* [Akk. *kudur*] and *Lagamaru*, "servant of [the goddess] Lagamar"). Also Chedorlaomer. King of ELAM and leader of a coalition with AMRAPHEL of SHINAR (Babylonia), ARIOCH of ELLASAR, and TIDAL king of GOIIM, which sacked SODOM and GOMORRAH when these cities revolted after a submission of twelve years. On their return near DAMASCUS, ABRAHAM and his band of retainers defeated them in a surprise night attack (Gen. 14:1-7). The view that this text represents an authentic historical document is in no way belittled by present uncertainty in the identification of Kedorlaomer or his associates. The commonest view is that which identifies Kedorlaomer with Kutir-naḫḫunti I of Elam (c. 1625 B.C.), but this requires an unsupported equation of *naḫḫundi* with *la ͑omar*, which is unlikely in view of the divine name given above. A more complex view, based on the so-called "Kedorlaomer" tablets in the British Museum (7th cent. B.C.), identifies him with a king of Elam named there KU.KU.KU.MAL.

keeper. This term is used over forty times in the KJV (but fewer than ten times in the NIV) to render various terms (e.g., Gen. 4:9; 1 Sam. 17:20 [NIV, "shepherd"]; Ps. 121:5 [NIV, "watches"]; Acts 5:23 [NIV, "guards"]). The expression "keeper of the wardrobe" refers to a civil servant who was apparently in charge not only of the king's personal

K

clothing, but also of robes used by others in the royal court (2 Ki. 10:22; 22:14; 2 Chr. 34:22).

Kehelathah. kee´huh-lay´thuh (Heb. *qĕhēlātâ H7739*, "assembly"). A stopping place of the Israelites between Rissah and Mount Shepher on their wilderness journey (Num. 33:22-23). The site is unknown.

Keilah. kee-*i*´luh (Heb. *qĕ῾îlâ H7881*, derivation uncertain). **(1)** A town in the SHEPHELAH allotted to the tribe of JUDAH (Josh. 15:44). It is identified with modern Khirbet Qila, c. 17 mi. (27 km.) SW of JERUSALEM and 8 mi. (13 km.) NW of HEBRON. DAVID led a daring expedition to Keilah to deliver it from attacks by the PHILISTINES who were robbing the threshing floors. Hearing of it, SAUL sent troops there to capture him and his men. David was forced to retreat again into the wilderness of ZIPH, when it became apparent after consulting the EPHOD that the men of Keilah might turn him over to Saul (1 Sam. 23:1-13). The town was inhabited by Jews returning from the EXILE and was included in the roster of those who participated in rebuilding the walls of JERUSALEM under NEHEMIAH (Neh. 3:17-18).

(2) A GARMITE included in the genealogy of Judah (1 Chr. 4:19). The passage as a whole (vv. 16-20) lists a number of persons whose connection with the descendants of Judah is not given. Keilah probably gave his name to the town (above, #1). See also ESHTEMOA; HODIAH.

Kelaiah. ki-lay´yuh (Heb. *qēlāyâ H7835*, meaning uncertain). A LEVITE who agreed to put away his foreign wife and who was also known as KELITA (Ezra 10:23).

Kelal. kee´lal (Heb. *kĕlāl H4006*, possibly "completeness, perfection"). One of the descendants of PAHATH-MOAB who agreed to put away their foreign wives (Ezra 10:30).

Kelita. ki-l*i*´tuh (Heb. *qĕliṭā᾿ H7836*, possibly "midget" or "cripple"). Also called KELAIAH (Kelita may be a nickname). A LEVITE who agreed to put away his foreign wife (Ezra 10:23). He is probably the same Levite listed among those who instructed the people (Neh. 8:7) and who signed the covenant of NEHEMIAH (10:10).

Kelub. kee´luhb (Heb. *kĕlûb H3991*, apparently from a word meaning "basket"). **(1)** A man identified as brother of Shuhah and father of Mehir (1 Chr. 4:11). These persons and others are referred to as "the men of Recah" (v. 12). They were apparently descendants of JUDAH, but their precise genealogical connection is not given.

(2) Father of Ezri; the latter was an official of DAVID charged with supervising "the field workers who farmed the land" (1 Chr. 27:26).

Kelubai. See CALEB #2.

Keluhi. kel´yoo-hi (Heb. *kĕluhî H3988*, meaning uncertain). KJV Chelluh; NRSV Cheluhi. One of the descendants of BANI who agreed to put away their foreign wives (Ezra 10:35).

Kemuel. kem´yoo-uhl (Heb. *qĕmû᾿ēl H7851*, possibly "God has arisen"). **(1)** Son of NAHOR, nephew of ABRAHAM, and father of ARAM (Gen. 22:21).

(2) Son of Shiphtan; he was a leader from the tribe of EPHRAIM, chosen to assist in the distribution of the land (Num. 34:24).

(3) Father of Hashabiah; the latter was an officer over the tribe of LEVI in the days of King DAVID (1 Chr. 27:17).

Kenaanah. ki-nay´uh-nuh (Heb. *kĕna῾ānâ H4049* [in form, fem. of *kĕna῾an H4046*; see CANAAN]). Also Chenaanah. **(1)** Son of Bilhan and descendant of BENJAMIN (1 Chr. 7:10); he and his brothers were warriors and heads of families (v. 11).

(2) Father of ZEDEKIAH; the latter was a false prophet who predicted victory for AHAB at the battle of RAMOTH GILEAD (1 Ki. 22:11, 24; 2 Chr. 18:10, 23).

Kenan. kee´nuhn (Heb. *qênān H7809*, apparently derived from CAIN; Gk. *Kainam G2783*). Son of ENOSH and grandson of SETH (Gen. 5:9-14 [KJV, "Cainan"]; 1 Chr. 1:2); included in Luke's GENEALOGY OF JESUS CHRIST (Lk. 3:37 [KJV and NRSV, "Cainan"]; in v. 36, the same Gk. form is rendered CAINAN by the NIV).

Kenani. ki-nay´ni (Heb. *kĕnānî H4039*, short form of KENANIAH, "Yahweh has strengthened"). Also Chenani. One of the LEVITES who led the people in confession and worship after EZRA read from the Book of the Law (Neh. 9:4).

Kenaniah. ken´uh-ni´uh (Heb. *kĕnanyāhû H4041* and *kĕnanyâ H4040*, "Yahweh has strengthened [*or* is firm]"). Also Chenaniah. (1) The head LEVITE who was "in charge of the singing" when the ARK OF THE COVENANT was transported to JERUSALEM (1 Chr. 15:22, 27). The Hebrew term for "singing" here (*maśśā᾿ H5362*) literally means "lifting," and some argue that Kenaniah supervised the proper handling of the ark of the covenant. Still others suggest that the word used here means "pronouncement, oracle" (*maśśā᾿ H5363*) and that Kenaniah was a leader of prophecy (cf. JB, "versed in divine oracles," v. 22).

(2) A Levite descended from IZHAR; in the time of DAVID, Kenaniah and his sons were "assigned duties away from the temple, as officials and judges over Israel" (1 Chr. 26:29; cf. Neh. 11:16).

Kenath. kee´nath (Heb. *qĕnāt H7875*, derivation unknown). A city in BASHAN, taken from the AMORITES by a Manassite leader called NOBAH, who gave it his own name (Num. 32:42; cf. Jdg. 8:11). It was later lost to the people of GESHUR and to the ARAMEANS (1 Chr. 2:23; the KJV rendering is incorrect). Kenath is usually identified with modern Qanawat in Syria (about 57 mi./92 km. E of the Sea of Galilee), where there are many impressive ruins from Greco-Roman times.

Kenaz, Kenizzite. kee´naz, ken´uh-zit (Heb. *qĕnaz H7869*, meaning uncertain; gentilic *qĕnizzî H7870*, "Kenizzite" [KJV also "Kenezite"]). (1) Son of Eliphaz and grandson of ESAU; an Edomite chief (Gen. 36:11, 15, 42; 1 Chr. 1:36, 53).

(2) Younger brother of CALEB (son of Jephunneh the Kenizzite); father of Othniel and Seraiah (Josh. 15:17: Jdg. 1:13; 3:9, 11; 1 Chr. 4:13). For the view that Othniel was Caleb's younger brother and that therefore Kenaz was Caleb's father, see comments under OTHNIEL.

(3) Son of Elah and grandson of Caleb (1 Chr. 4:15).

(4) Clan or family name. The Kenizzites are one of the S Palestinian tribes (listed between KENITES and KADMONITES) whose land God promised to ABRAHAM's descendants (Gen. 15:19). Unless predictive prophecy is involved here, these Kenizzites must be a different family from that connected with Kenaz son of Eliphaz (#1 above). Caleb is said to be the son of Jephunneh the Kenizzite (Num. 32:12; Josh. 14:6, 14), but the exact meaning of the clan name here is not clear. On the one hand, the Kenizzites are described as an alien people (Gen. 15:19), and Caleb apparently is promised a portion of the land because of faithfulness rather than birthright (Josh. 14:6-14). On the other hand, the genealogy of 1 Chr. 2 (see vv. 9, 18) speaks of Caleb son of HEZRON (the latter being a grandson of JUDAH). Many scholars believe that Caleb belonged to the Edomite clan known as the Kenizzites (which along with other non-Israelite groups living in S Palestine was absorbed into the tribe of Judah) and that the Chronicles genealogy is an attempt to give the descendants of Caleb legal status in postexilic Judaism. It is possible that the apparent discrepancy may be accounted for by duplicate names.

Kenezite. See KENAZ.

Kenite. ken´it (Heb. *qênî H7808*, gentilic of *qayin H7803*, "metal worker"; see CAIN). Clan or tribal name of seminomadic peoples of S PALESTINE and SINAI; the probable etymology of their name may indicate that they were known as metal workers. It is clear that references to the Kenites are not to a tightly knit group living in a narrowly defined area. The name rather applies to a number of loosely related groups possessing common skills or perhaps claiming a common ancestor. The land of the Kenites is promised to ABRAHAM's descendants (Gen. 15:19). This would be the territory of a certain Kenite clan, probably S of HEBRON. Similarly, it is a particular group of Kenites that is condemned in BAALAM's oracle (Num. 24:21-22), while another group is praised for having been kind to the Hebrews in the wilderness (1 Sam. 15:6). The exact cause for Baalam's condemnation is not given, but in the context it appears that these Kenites had allied themselves with the AMALEKITES against MOSES.

K

Region S of Hebron where the Kenites lived. (View to the NW.)

Moses' father-in-law is identified as a Kenite in Jdg. 1:16 (also 4:11 KJV and other versions), but his exact identity is a complex question. He seems to carry three personal names: JETHRO, REUEL, and HOBAB. And in Exodus and Numbers he is called a Midianite (Exod. 2:16-21; 18:1; Num. 10:29). One proposed solution is that Jethro belonged to a Kenite of the Reuel clan who was living in MIDIAN (well-known for its rich copper lodes) when Moses first met him. Later, during the EXODUS, Moses' *son-in-law* (*ḥātān H3163* rather than *ḥōtēn H3162*) named Hobab, also of the Reuel clan, was asked to act as guide for the Israelites (alternately, *ḥōtēn* may mean "brother-in-law"; cf. NIV at Jdg. 4:11). Whether this reconstruction of the relationship of the names is correct or not, it does appear that Kenite was the actual tribal affiliation, while the name Midianite refers to location only.

According to Jdg. 1:16, the descendants of Moses' Kenite father-in-law allied themselves with the Israelites and settled with them in the NEGEV near ARAD (at the S edge of the Judean wilderness). The nomadic character of the Kenites is clearly seen in the detail that one family (not a whole tribe), that of HEBER, had migrated northward to GALILEE (4:11). During the early monarchy a significant concentration of Kenites was located in the southern Judean territory. This is clear from 1 Sam. 15:6 and also from DAVID's relations with them. While David was a PHILISTINE vassal, he attacked the enemies of Judah in the S while telling his superiors that he was attacking Judah, the Jerahmeelites, and the Kenites (27:10). Not only was he not attacking Judah and her friends, he was sending them gifts from his spoils (30:29). In 1 Chr. 2:55 the families of scribes living at JABEZ are said to be Kenites; the same text indicates some connection between them and the RECABITES.

Kenizzite. See KENAZ.

kenosis. ki-noh´sis. The Greek noun *kenōsis* ("emptying, depletion") does not appear in the NT, but the cognate verb *kenoō G3033* (with the reflexive pronoun) occurs in Phil. 2:7, which is often translated literalistically, "[Christ] emptied himself," but which is better rendered, "made himself nothing" (cf. NIV). The term *kenosis* was used in Christian theology from very early times, usually as a synonym for the INCARNATION. It refers to a view that emphasizes CHRIST's humiliation or condescension. Support for the doctrine rests primarily on Phil. 2:6-8, with parallels having to do with his humiliation (2 Cor. 8:9) and exaltation (Jn. 17:5; see EXALTATION OF CHRIST). The theological issue is profoundly difficult, for it takes one into

© Dr. James C. Martin

the nature of the TRINITY: when divine powers are allowed in the man Christ Jesus, what, if anything, has happened to the person of God himself? Problems of interpretation are further aggravated by the fact that the other uses of the verb (Rom. 4:14; 1 Cor. 1:17; 9:15; 2 Cor. 9:3) are uniformly figurative in their context and will not bear the weight of literal usage that the Kenoticists demand of the same word in Phil. 2:7.

Solutions to the problem have moved across the spectrum of five possible interpretations. (1) In the incarnation, Christ gave up all divine attributes and thus was deprived of all cosmic functions and divine consciousness. (2) A distinction is made between essential and relative attributes in God, so that Christ in his incarnation gave up not his essential attributes but only his relative attributes. (3) In his obedience to his Father, Christ gave up no powers of the Deity but gave up their independent exercise. (4) His humanity was such that he did not exercise his divine powers at all. (5) The divine nature united itself with his humanity only gradually, and his full deity was consummated finally at the resurrection; the incarnation was process rather than act. The best interpretation of Phil. 2:6-8 focuses on the phrase, "being on an equality with God," and states that Christ did not give up his divine nature but rather divested himself of the position or prerogatives of Deity by taking on the form of a servant.

Kephar Ammoni. kee´fuhr-am´oh-ni (Heb. *kĕpar hā῾ammōnî H4112*, "village of the Ammonites"). KJV Chephar-haammonai; NRSV Chephar-ammoni. A town allotted to the tribe of BENJAMIN (Josh. 18:24). The name suggests that it was inhabited by (or perhaps captured from) the AMMONITES. The site is unknown, but like some of the other towns in the list (e.g., BETHEL, OPHRAH), it may have been N of Benjamin's boundary, within the territory of EPHRAIM.

Kephirah. ki-fi´ruh (Heb. *kĕpîrâ H4098*, "[open] village"). Also Chephirah. A city of the GIBEONITES included in the treaty they obtained from Israel by stealth (Josh. 9:17). The town was later included in the tribal territory of BENJAMIN (18:26). Inhabitants of Kephirah were among those who returned

from the EXILE with ZERUBBABEL (Ezra 2:25; Neh. 7:29). The site is modern Khirbet el-Kefireh, about 8.5 mi. (13.5 km.) WNW of JERUSALEM (on the road to Jaffa) and just N of KIRIATH JEARIM.

Kerak. kuhr´ahk (Arab. name derived from Aram. *kĕrak*, "fortified place"). **(1)** The modern name of a Transjordanian site probably to be identified with the Moabite city of KIR HARESET.

(2) Khirbet Kerak (not mentioned in the Bible) is a large and important archaeological site on the SW shore of the Sea of Galilee, just N of the present mouth of the JORDAN River. It was strategically located at the crossroads of two important caravan routes. The site covers over 54 acres, and archaeological work has revealed occupations during Late Chalcolithic through Middle Bronze II periods, with a gap until Hellenistic times. The famous Khirbet Kerak pottery ware was first identified at this site, although it evidently originated in N Anatolia and the Caucasus region. Its sudden appearance speaks of conquest from that direction.

Keran. kee´ruhn (Heb. *kĕrān H4154*). Also Cheran. Son of DISHON and grandson of SEIR the HORITE (Gen. 36:26; 1 Chr. 1:41).

kerchief. This term is used by the KJV in a passage dealing with DIVINATION, which required the head to be covered (Ezek. 13:18, 21; NIV and other versions, "veils"). It is not known what these "kerchiefs" looked like or how they were used, but apparently they were coverings that varied in length with the height of the wearer and were worn by those who consulted the seers.

Keren-Happuch. ker´uhn-hap´uhk (Heb. *qeren happûk H7968*, "horn of antimony," i.e., "container of [black] eye-paint"). The youngest of JOB's daughters, born to him after his restoration from affliction (Job 42:14). The name alludes to her beauty (cf. v. 15).

Kerethite. ker´uh-thit (Heb. *kĕrētî H4165*, possibly "Cretan"). Also Cherethite (in Ezek. 25:16, KJV has the superfluous pl., "Cherethims"). The Kerethites were a people group that apparently came from the Aegean area; DAVID chose his personal guard from the Kerethites and the PELETHITES (1 Sam. 30:14; 2 Sam. 8:18; 15:18; 20:7, 23 [*Qere*, CARITES]; 1 Ki. 1:38, 44; 1 Chr. 18:17; Ezek. 25:16; Zeph. 2:5 [cf. also v. 6 NIV]. Although some have understood the words as common nouns ("executioners" and "runners"), it is virtually certain that the words refer to people groups. The Kerethites are generally said to have been Cretans on the basis of the similarity of the two names (the name CRETE for this MEDITERRANEAN island is already attested in Homeric times) and the connection between the Kerethites and the PHILISTINES (Aegeans who invaded Palestine); but this identification is not certain. They seem to have been especially active in times of crisis for David, remaining loyal to him in all three revolts against the king. Their leader was BENAIAH son of Jehoiada (2 Sam. 8:18), who is also called the leader of David's bodyguard (23:23). It is probable that the Kerethites and Pelethites were this bodyguard.

Kerioth. ker'ee-oth (Heb. *qĕriyyôt H7954*, pl. of *qiryâ H7953*, "town, city"). **(1)** A city in MOAB declared to be under God's judgment (Jer. 48:24, 41 [NRSV, "towns"]; Amos 2:2). Kerioth is probably to be identified el-Qereiyat, about 8 mi. (13 km.) E of the DEAD SEA and 7 mi. (11 km.) NW of DIBON. **(2)** According to the KJV, a city in the extreme S of the territory of JUDAH (Josh. 15:25). See KERIOTH HEZRON.

Kerioth Hezron. ker'ee-oth-hez'ruhn (Heb. *qĕriyyôt ḥeṣrôn H7955*, "towns of HEZRON"). A town in the NEGEV, the extreme S of the tribal territory of JUDAH, near the border of EDOM; it was also known as HAZOR, a common name (Josh. 15:25; KJV, "Kerioth *and* Hezron"). Its location is uncertain, but it has been tentatively identified with modern Khirbet el-Qaryatein, about 13 mi. (21 km.) SSE of HEBRON and 4 mi. (6 km.) S of MAON.

Kerith. kihr'ith (Heb. *kĕrît H4134*, possibly "ditch" or "cutting"). Also Cherith. A brook or valley E of the JORDAN where ELIJAH fled after he had announced the coming drought to King AHAB of Israel (1 Ki. 17:3, 5). The expression "before Jordan" (KJV) is not clear as to which side of that river was meant. Since Elijah's home was in GILEAD, the E

side seems more likely, although there is a tradition that it is the Wadi Qelt near JERICHO on the W side. Any number of WADIS with their numerous caves could be the Kerith; one possibility is Wadi Yabis (Naḥal Yavesh) in Gilead, which empties into the Jordan about 22 mi. (35 km.) S of the Sea of Galilee.

Keros. kihr'os (Heb. *qêrōs H7820*, perhaps "crooked"). Ancestor of a family of temple servants (NETHINIM) who returned from the EXILE with ZERUBBABEL (Ezra 2:44; Neh. 7:47).

Kerub. kihr'uhb (Heb. *kĕrûb H4132*). Also Cherub. One of five Babylonian places from which certain Jewish exiles returned who were unable to prove their Israelite ancestry (Ezra 2:59; Neh. 7:61). If Kerub here is a place name, its location is unknown; some, however, think the name refers to a person on the basis of the parallel in the APOCRYPHA (1 Esd. 5:36 NRSV, following a generally accepted conjectural emendation).

kerygma. ki-rig'muh (Gk. *kērygma G3060*, "proclamation"). This term is used in biblical scholarship to refer to the apostolic preaching of the GOSPEL, especially its original proclamation (e.g., the sermons in the book of Acts). It is often contrasted with the *didachē G1439*, its "teaching" aspects. See DOCTRINE.

Kesalon. kes'uh-luhn (Heb. *kĕsālôn H4076*, possibly "[on the] flank, loin"). Also Chesalon. A town on the N boundary of the tribe of JUDAH (Josh. 15:10). Located between Mount SEIR and BETH SHEMESH, Kesalon is given in the text as another name for the "northern slope of Mount Jearim." The modern site is a ruin known as Kesla, about 11 mi. (18 km.) W of JERUSALEM, at an elevation of more than 1,900 ft. (580 m.). Although the region as a whole is characterized by oak forests (JEARIM means "woods"), Kesla itself is a summit on bare rock.

Kesed. kee'sid (Heb. *keśed H4168*, apparently related to *kaśdîm H4169*, "Chaldeans, Babylonians"). Also Chesed. Son of NAHOR by his wife MILCAH; nephew of ABRAHAM (Gen. 22:22). The passage as a whole seems to indicate the origins of various tribes, and possibly Kesed is presented as the ancestor of the Babylonians.

Kesil. kee´sil (Heb. *kĕsîl H4069*, "flank, side"). Also Chesil. A town in the NEGEV, the extreme S of the tribal territory of JUDAH, near the border of EDOM (Josh. 15:30). In the parallel passages the name Kesil seems to be replaced by BETHUL (Josh. 19:4) and BETHUEL (1 Chr. 4:30).

Kesulloth. ki-suhl´oth (Heb. *kĕsûlôt H4063*, possibly "[on the] loins"). Also Chesulloth. A town allotted to the tribe of ISSACHAR (Josh. 19:18). It is probably the same as KISLOTH TABOR, a town mentioned in the description of the SE border of ZEBULUN (v. 12). It has been identified with Iksal, in the foothills just SE of NAZARETH and W of Mount TABOR.

Ketib. kuh-teev´ (Heb. *kĕtîb*, "written," pass. ptc. of Aram. *kĕtab H10374*, "to write"). Also *Kethib, Ketiv*. The written, consonantal form of the Masoretic text of the Hebrew Bible. This term is used primarily in contrast to QERE, the latter indicating "what is to be read," that is, an alternate form or a textual variant preferred by the Masoretes. See TEXT AND VERSIONS (OT).

kettle. This English term is used by various Bible versions in one OT passage, referring to a deep cooking pot in which a sacrifice might be boiled (1 Sam. 2:14; the NRSV uses it also in Mic. 3:3 [NIV, "pan"]). In the NT, it occurs as the rendering of Greek *chalkion G5908*, "[copper] cauldron" (Mk. 7:4; KJV, "brasen vessel").

Ketubim, Ketuvim. ki-too´bim, kuh-*too*-veem´ (*kĕtûbîm*, "written things," from *kātab H4180*, "to write"). Also *Kethubim*. The "Writings" (also known as the HAGIOGRAPHA, "Sacred Writings"), a term applied to the third division of the OT Hebrew canon, and consisting of the poetic books (Psalms, Job, Proverbs, Song of Solomon, Ecclesiastes, Lamentations) as well as Ruth, Esther, Daniel, Ezra, Nehemiah, and Chronicles. See CANONICITY.

Keturah. ki-tyoo´ruh (Heb. *qĕṭûrâ H7778*, "one covered in incense [*i.e.*, perfumed]"). Wife of ABRAHAM (Gen. 25:1, 4; 1 Chr. 1:32-33; in the latter passage, she is referred to as a CONCUBINE). Although her name appears in the Genesis record only after the death of SARAH, it is possible that she bore sons to Abraham while Sarah was still living. To Keturah and Abraham were born six sons (Gen. 25:1-4); seven grandsons are also listed. Through these descendants a number of tribes in N ARABIA trace their lineage back to Abraham and Keturah.

Keveh. See KUE.

key. An instrument, usually of wood but sometimes of metal, for moving the bolt of a lock. In the ANE keys had nails or wooden pegs to fit corresponding holes in the bolt holding the door fast (Jdg. 3:25). Figuratively, the term is a symbol of authority, carried on the shoulder (Isa. 22:20-22). In the NT it is symbolic of the authority given to PETER (Matt. 16:19), but which Jesus still retains (Rev. 1:18; 3:7); the key that keeps destructive forces (9:1) and SATAN (20:1) in the bottomless pit.

Keys dated to the 1st or 2nd cent. A.D.

© Dr. James C. Martin. The Israel Museum, Jerusalem. Photographed by permission.

Keziah. ki-zi´uh (Heb. *qĕṣî˓āh H7905*, "cassia"). KJV Kezia. The second daughter born to JOB after his fortunes were restored (Job 42:14). The name, possibly referring to the sweet smell of cinnamon, alludes to her charm (cf. v. 15).

Kezib. kee´zib (Heb. *kĕzîb H3945*, "deceit"). Also Chezib. A town in the SHEPHELAH, near ADULLAM, where Shelah son of JUDAH was born (Gen. 38:5). Kezib is usually identified with ACZIB (#2) and COZEBA.

Keziz. See EMEK KEZIZ.

khirbet. kihr´bet. An Arabic term meaning "ruin" and often used in geographical names, such as Khirbet KERAK and Khirbet QUMRAN. The corresponding term in Hebrew is *ḥorbat* (construct of *ḥorbâ H2999*).

Kibroth Hattaavah. kib´roth-huh-tay´uh-vuh (Heb. *qibrôt hatta'ăwâ H7701*, "graves of craving"). One of the stops of the Israelites in the wilderness (Num. 11:34-35; 33:16-17; Deut. 9:22). It was probably 10-20 mi. (15-30 km.) NE of Mount SINAI (the next stop was HAZEROTH), but the exact location is unknown. Here the people, craving the foods they had left behind in Egypt, complained about the MANNA (11:4-6) and gorged themselves on the quails God sent. As they ate, God smote the people with a severe plague (11:33), so that large numbers of Israelites died and were buried there—thus the name given to the place.

Kibzaim. kib-zay´im (Heb. *qibṣayim H7698*, possibly "[twin] heaps"). A Levitical city within the tribal territory of EPHRAIM, allotted to the clan of KOHATH (Josh. 21:22). See JOKMEAM #1.

kid. See ANIMALS.

kidnapping. See PUNISHMENT.

kidney. This organ, being surrounded by pure fat, was adapted to burning in sacrifice, when the whole animal was not burned (Exod. 29:13, 22; Lev. 3:4, 10, 15; 4:9; 7:4; 8:16, 25; 9:10, 19). Slaughter in a war that was a judgment of God was a sacrifice in which the kidneys figured (Isa. 34:6). The "finest kernels of wheat" were called literally, "fat of kidneys of wheat" (Deut. 32:14 KJV). Possibly in part from their almost inaccessible location in the body, the kidneys often were thought to have many of the functions that we now know are performed by the brain, including thinking and emotional reactions. Kidneys were regarded as the seat of the emotions. This notion is possibly reflected in conventional language in the Bible, as when in the Hebrew text the kidney is linked with the HEART. For example, Ps. 7:9 says literally that God "tests kidneys [KJV, reins] and hearts" (NIV, "searches minds and hearts"; see also Ps. 26:2 and Rev. 2:23, and cf. Ps. 16:7).

Kidon. ki´duhn (Heb. *kîdōn H3961*, "javelin" or "[short] sword"). Also Chidon. The owner of a threshing floor (or possibly the name of the place itself) where UZZAH died because he touched the ARK OF THE COVENANT while it was being transported toward JERUSALEM (1 Chr. 13:9). The place is called NACON in the parallel passage (2 Sam. 6:6). Because of God's judgment here, DAVID named the field PEREZ UZZAH ("outbreak [of wrath] against Uzzah"). The location of the threshing floor is unknown, but if the procession took a direct route from KIRIATH JEARIM, the site must have been W of Jerusalem.

Kidron. kid´ruhn (Heb. *qidrôn H7724*, "turbid [stream]"; Gk. *Kedrōn G3022*). KJV NT Cedron. A valley E of JERUSALEM c. 3 mi. (5 km.) in length, lying between the walls of the city and the MOUNT OF OLIVES. Here the GIHON Spring was located, whose water was brought by an aqueduct into the pools of SILOAM within the walls. South of the city the Kidron joins the Valley of HINNOM near the pool of EN ROGEL, and the united valley, Wadi en-Nar, runs down to the DEAD SEA. Through this valley a winter torrent runs, the Brook Kidron, but the stream bed is dry much of the year. DAVID's crossing of the Kidron (2 Sam. 15:23) in his escape from his rebellious son ABSALOM marked the decisive abandonment of his throne. When SOLOMON spared SHIMEI, he warned him that to cross the Kidron would bring him death (1 Ki. 2:37). ASA burned idols at the brook (1 Ki. 15:13; 2 Chr. 15:16), as did JOSIAH (2 Ki. 23:4, 6, 12) and HEZEKIAH (2 Chr. 29:16; 30:14). It is called "the stream" (32:4) that Hezekiah stopped, to deny the attacking Assyrians a water supply. NEHEMIAH went up it by night to view the state of the walls of Jerusalem (Neh. 2:15). JEREMIAH mentions it in prophesying the permanent rebuilding of Jerusalem (Jer. 31:38-40). After the Last Supper, Jesus and his disciples crossed it on their way out of the city to reach the Garden of GETHSEMANE on the slopes of the Mount of Olives (Jn. 18:1). He must often have looked across this valley as he "was sitting on the Mount of Olives" (e.g., Matt. 24:3; Mk. 13:3), and he must have crossed it on his triumphal entry into the city of Jerusalem (Matt. 2:1-11; Mk. 11:1-10; Lk. 19:28-44; Jn. 12:12-19).

Kileab. kil´ee-ab (Heb. *kilʾāb H3976*, derivation uncertain). Also Chileab. DAVID's second son born at HEBRON, his first by ABIGAIL (2 Sam. 3:3). Many believe the Hebrew text here is corrupt and emend the name to DANIEL, as in the parallel passage (1 Chr. 3:1).

Kilion. kil´ee-uhn (Heb. *kilyôn H4002*, possibly "frailty" or "destruction"). Also Chilion. Son of ELIMELECH and NAOMI (Ruth 1:2, 5; 4:9). When the family moved to MOAB, Kilion married a woman named ORPAH, and his brother MAHLON married RUTH. Both Kilion and his brother died some years later while they were still in Moab.

Kilmad. kil´mad (Heb. *kilmad H4008*, derivation unknown). One of several places that were trading partners with TYRE (Ezek. 27:23). Nothing else is known about Kilmad, but since it is mentioned after ASSHUR, it was probably in N MESOPOTAMIA.

kiln (oven). This term is used by some versions (e.g., NRSV) to render Hebrew *kibśān H3901* in two passages (Exod. 9:8-10; 19:18; the only other occurrence of the Hebrew term is in Gen. 19:28). See FURNACE; OVEN.

Kimham. kim´ham (Heb. *kimhām H4016*, possibly "pale face"). Also Chimham. Apparently a son of BARZILLAI the Gileadite (2 Sam. 19:37-38, 40). While DAVID was in exile at MAHANAIM, Barzillai had provided him with food. After ABSALOM's rebellion had been quelled, David invited Barzillai to be his guest at Jerusalem. Barzillai declined but sent Kimham instead. Apparently David granted Kimham a royal pension (1 Ki. 2:7). See also GERUTH KIMHAM.

kin. See KINSMAN.

Kinah. ki´nuh (Heb. *qînāh H7807*, possibly "lament"). A town in the NEGEV, the extreme S of the tribal territory of JUDAH, near the border of EDOM (Josh. 15:22). Its location is unknown, but because Wadi el-Qeni may preserve the name, some have identified Kinah with nearby Khirbet Ṭaiyib (c. 3 mi./5 km. NNE of ARAD [Tell ʿArad]) and others with Khirbet Ghazzeh (on a spur of the wadi, c. 4 mi./6 km. SE of Arad).

kindness. The state or quality of being kind: generosity, humaneness, tenderness. The word can also refer to a particular instance of kind behavior: a token of friendliness, good will, affection. In the OT, it occurs primarily as the rendering of Hebrew *ḥesed H2876*, which conveys various senses, such as "loyalty," "mercy," "grace," and "love" (Gen. 19:19 and frequently). In the NT, it translates Greek *chrēstotēs G5983*, "goodness, uprightness, generosity" (Rom. 2:4; 11:22; et al.) and other expressions. Kindness is both an attribute of God (Tit. 3:4) and a characteristic of true LOVE (1 Cor. 13:4). God's kindness is great (Joel 2:13; Jon. 4:2) and everlasting (Isa. 54:8, 10). God is kind to the ignorant and wayward (Heb. 5:2), to the ungrateful and evil (Lk. 6:35). Believers are exhorted to possess this trait (Col. 3:12; 2 Pet. 1:7). God's people should be kind to fellow-believers (Deut. 22:1; Zech. 7:9, 10; Rom. 15:5; Eph. 4:32; 1 Pet. 3:8; 4:8), neighbors (Rom. 15:2), foreigners (Lev. 19:34), widows (1 Tim. 5:9, 10), orphans (Zech. 7:10), the needy (Matt. 5:7; 1 Jn. 3:17-18), the weak (Acts 20:35; Rom. 15:1), the sorrowing (12:15), the weary (Gal. 6:2), the fallen (6:1), even enemies (Lk. 6:34-35). At the final judgment, Christ will reward those who have been kind to his people (Matt. 25:34-36). See also GOOD; GRACE; MERCY.

kine. KJV plural form of "cow." See ANIMALS (under *cattle*).

king. A male ruler, usually hereditary, of a city, tribe, or nation. The Hebrew word for "king," *melek H4889*, appears over two thousand times in the OT. The SEPTUAGINT translates this term with the Greek equivalent, *basileus G995*, which occurs

K

K

some fifty times in the NT. Kings often had priestly functions in the maintenance of the religion of the group, though most of these were separated from the kingly office in the Hebrew monarchy: the king was expected to further religion but not to act as its priest. In the ANE kings came to be regarded as divine beings. This was true of EGYPT from the beginning. The idea was taken over by the Greek empire of ALEXANDER THE GREAT and his successors, later by the Romans, after their empire came to include most of the East.

The earliest king mentioned in the Bible is NIMROD (Gen. 10:8-12), whose Mesopotamian kingdom was extensive. From this region the kings who warred with kings of CANAAN came and were driven off by ABRAHAM (ch. 14). God promised Abraham (17:6) and JACOB (35:11) that kings would be among their descendants. There were city-kings such as ABIMELECH (20:2), called king of the PHILISTINES (26:1, 8), and kings in EDOM (36:31; 1 Chr. 1:43) before Israel had kings. Kings of Egypt, the PHARAOHS, figure in the Egyptian period of Israelite history (Gen. 39 to Exod. 14; Deut. 7:8; 11:3); they also appear later when Egyptian influence was strong in JUDAH. Israel contacted many kings in their wanderings (Num. 20:14—33:40; Deut. 1:4—4:47; 7:24; 29:7; 31:4; 1 Sam. 14:47; 15:8, 20, 32; 21:10, 12; 22:4). These varied in power from headmen of towns to rulers of large areas.

It is said several times that in the time of the judges there was no king in Israel (Jdg. 17:6; 18:1; 19:1; 21:25); everyone did what was right in his own eyes. MOSES had foreseen that the people would demand a king as a strong human ruler (Deut. 17:14-15; 28:36), not content with a theocracy, the direct rule of God as king over them (33:5). HANNAH looked forward to a time when there would be a king of Israel who was appointed and anointed by God (1 Sam. 2:10). Toward the end of SAMUEL's judgeship, however, Israel was unwilling to wait for a messianic king and demanded one "such as all the other nations have" (1 Sam. 8:5, 22; 19:19, 24; 12:1-25; cf. Hos. 13:10). Samuel duly warned the people what to expect of a king, then selected SAUL, whose choice they ratified. The reigns of Israelite kings are recorded as follows: Saul (1 Sam. 12-31; 1 Chr. 10); DAVID (2 Sam. 1 to 1 Ki. 1; 1 Chr. 11-29); SOLOMON (1 Ki. 1-11; 1 Chr. 28-2 Chr. 9); later kings of Israel and Judah (1 Ki. 12 to 2 Ki. 25; 2 Chr. 10-36). The books of Ezra, Nehemiah, and Esther deal with kings of PERSIA.

The prophets refer to kings of Judah and other nations. JOB reflects that in death all are equal with kings (Job 3:14); that God debases kings (12:18); ELIPHAZ observes that trouble and anguish overwhelm a man like a king prepared for attack (15:24); BILDAD says that the wicked are "marched off to the king of terrors" (18:14); Job remembers that in prosperity he was like a king (29:25); ELIHU thinks of the fear inspired by a king (34:18) and says that God sets LEVIATHAN as a "king over all that are proud" (41:34). Psalm 2 contrasts the messianic king (2:6) with kings of the earth (2:2, 10). Some references in the book of Psalms are to human kings (Ps. 20:9; 21:1, 7; 33:16; 63:11; 68:12, 14, 29; 72:10-11; 76:12; 89:27; 102:15; 105:14, 20, 30; 110:5; 119:46; 135:10-11; 136:17-20; 138:4; 144:10; 148:11; 149:8), some to God as king (Ps. 5:2; 10:16; 18:50; 145:1; 149:2). Psalm 24 acclaims the Lord as king of glory. Psalm 45 may have been a marriage song for King Solomon, but its language well suits a messianic interpretation.

Proverbs contains maxims for a king's conduct (e.g., Prov. 31:1-9). Ecclesiastes and the Song of Songs view a king's life from the inside. Isaiah develops the concept of a messianic king (Isa. 32:1; 33:17) identified with the Lord (33:22; 42:21; 43:15; 44:6). Jeremiah refers to God as king (Jer.

© Dr. James C. Martin. The British Museum. Photographed by permission.

Mosaic of a king banqueting among his friends. (Standard of Ur, c. 2600 B.C.)

8:19; 10:7, 10; 46:18; 48:15; 51:57) and to the messianic king (23:5). Ezekiel refers to the Davidic king of restored Israel whom the context shows to be messianic (Ezek. 37:22, 24). The messianic king enters Jerusalem riding on a colt (Zech. 9:9), and God is king (14:9, 16-17; Mal. 1:14). NEBUCHADNEZZAR praises the king of heaven (Dan. 4:37).

The Gospels speak of kings in general (Matt. 10:18; 11:8; 17:25; 18:23; 22:2, 7, 11, 13; Mk. 13:9; Lk. 10:24; 14:31; 21:12; 22:25) and in particular: Herod the Great (Matt. 2:1, 3, 9; Lk. 1:5); Herod Antipas (Matt. 14:9; Mk. 6:14, 22-27); David (Matt. 1:6); the messianic king of the Jews (Matt. 2:2; 21:5; 25:34, 40; 27:11, 29, 37, 42; Mk. 15:2, 9, 12, 18, 26, 32; Lk. 19:38; 23:2-3, 37-38; Jn. 1:49; 6:15; 12:13, 15; 18:37, 39; 19:3-21); and God (Matt. 5:35). References in Acts are to earthly kings, except Acts 17:7, which refers to Jesus. A few references in the Epistles are to earthly kings; one is to God (1 Tim. 1:17; cf. 6:15). In Revelation, besides earthly kings, reigning and prophesied, Jesus Christ is introduced as prince (ruler) of the kings of the earth (1:5), who made us kings (1:6; 5:10 KJV; cf. 1 Pet. 2:9). The king of the apocalyptic locusts (Rev. 9:11) is the angel of the bottomless pit. God is king (15:3) and the Lamb is king of kings (17:14).

A king sits on a throne, holds a scepter (Ps. 45:6), wears a crown (2 Ki. 11:12), lives in a palace (1 Chr. 29:1), and rides in a royal chariot (1 Sam. 8:11). From a few military and civil officers for city-kings and for Saul, the royal bureaucracy rapidly expanded (1 Sam. 8:10-18) to the dimensions of David's (2 Sam. 23:8-39; 1 Chr. 11:10, 47) and Solomon's (1 Ki. 9:22; 4:1-28; 2 Chr. 8:9-10) establishments. Yet Solomon judged comparatively trivial cases (1 Ki. 3:16-28); Ahab shared the personal oversight of his cattle (1 Ki. 18:5-6). The Persian monarchy was a vast empire (Esth. 1:1). Kings frequently met death by assassination. Among God's chosen people a rightful king was designated by God and anointed by his representative (1 Sam. 9:15-16; 16:1-13) with the approval of the people. He ruled by virtue of a COVENANT between God and his people, to which the king was a party (2 Sam. 7). This covenant was extended and renewed as the basis of the NT KINGDOM OF GOD or of heaven, of which Jesus is sovereign until

at the RESURRECTION he delivers the kingdom to his Father (1 Cor. 15:24-28).

kingdom of God (of heaven). In contemporary English, the word *kingdom* most commonly refers to the realm or territorial unit over which a monarch reigns, including the people that are under the monarch's rule. Earlier, however, the word could also mean "kingship"—that is, the reign or rule itself—and this is the predominant sense of Greek *basileia G993* in the expression "the kingdom of God."

In some passages there is indeed reference to the *realm* in which God's reign is experienced. It is a realm introduced after the ministry of JOHN THE BAPTIST; people enter it with fierce determination (Lk. 16:16). John himself did not stand within this new realm but only on its threshold; but so great are the blessings of God's kingdom that the least in it is greater than John (Matt. 11:11). Jesus offered the kingdom to ISRAEL, for they were its proper heirs (8:12); but the religious leaders, followed by most of the people, not only refused to enter its blessings but tried to prevent others from entering (23:13). Nevertheless, many tax collectors and prostitutes did enter the kingdom (21:31; see also Col. 1:13). In all of these verses, the kingdom is a present realm where people may enjoy the blessings of God's rule. Elsewhere the kingdom is a future realm inaugurated by the return of Christ. The righteous will inherit this kingdom (Matt. 25:34) and will shine like the sun in God's kingdom (13:43). Entrance into this future kingdom is synonymous with entering the eternal life of the age to come (Matt. 19:16, 23-30; Mk. 10:30). See ESCHATOLOGY. Moreover, the kingdom of God is sometimes identified with the *people* within that realm, namely, those who submit to his rule and share his reign. Thus in Rev. 1:6 and 5:10, the redeemed are called "a kingdom" (cf. Exod. 19:6).

Fundamentally, however, the kingdom of God is his sovereign activity as King in saving sinners and overcoming evil. The "abstract" meaning of the Greek word *basileia* can be seen, for example, in Rev. 17:17, which states that the ten kings of the earth (cf. v. 12) "give their kingdom unto the beast" (KJV); the NIV translates more clearly and appropriately, "give the beast their power to rule." Many

K

passages that speak of the kingdom of God clearly have this sense in view. Only those who "receive the kingdom of God," that is, accept God's rule here and now, enter into the realm of its blessings in the future (Mk. 10:15). When we seek God's kingdom and righteousness, we seek God's rule in our lives (Matt. 6:33).

God's kingdom is, of course, not merely an abstract rule, but rather a *dynamic* force manifested in Christ to destroy his (spiritual) enemies and to bring to men and women the blessings of God's reign. Christ must reign as King until he has destroyed all enemies, the last of which is death, and he will then deliver the kingdom to God (1 Cor. 15:24-26). Jesus claimed that his ability to cast out demons was evidence that the kingdom of God had come among people (Matt. 12:28). Furthermore, he said that no one could enter a strong man's house (SATAN's realm) and take away his goods (deliver demon-possessed men and women) "unless he first ties up the strong man" (12:29). By this metaphor of binding, Jesus asserts that the kingdom of God has come among human beings to break Satan's power and deliver men and women from satanic bondage.

Thus, the kingdom of God—his redemptive rule—has come into history in the person of Christ to break the power of death and Satan; it will come in power and glory with the return of Christ to complete the destruction of these enemies. Because of this present victory of God's *rule*, we may enter the *realm* of its blessings in the present, yet look forward to greater blessings when Christ comes again.

In the modern history of biblical interpretation, several differing views of the kingdom of God have been proposed. (1) *Classical Liberalism*, as formulated especially by Adolf von Harnack at the beginning of the twentieth century, viewed the kingdom as the essence of ideal religion and altogether a present subjective and spiritual reality, having to do with the individual soul and its relation to God. (2) Albert Schweitzer held to an interpretation known as *consistent (thoroughgoing) eschatology*; in his view, the kingdom of God was not a present spiritual reality. On the contrary, Jesus taught, according to Schweitzer, that (a) the kingdom was altogether a future eschatological reality that would come by a miraculous divine inbreaking to terminate human history and establish the kingdom; (b) this apocalyptic kingdom was to come immediately, so Jesus' mission was to announce the imminent end of the world and to prepare people for the impending day of judgment. (3) C. H. Dodd has reinterpreted eschatological terminology so that it no longer refers to the "last things" at the end of the age but to the "ultimate" realities experienced in Christ. The kingdom of God is then the eternal that has broken into time in Christ. This view has come to be known as *realized eschatology*. (4) *Inaugurated eschatology* is a mediating view between Schweitzer and Dodd. The kingdom of God is indeed being realized in the present, but there must also be an eschatological consummation. Many scholars follow Schweitzer in holding that Jesus expected an immediate end of the world but modify Schweitzer's view by recognizing that in some sense the kingdom was also present in the person of Jesus. They hold that Jesus was right in the basic structure but wrong in the time of the coming of the kingdom.

Most schools of interpretation—liberal and conservative—believe that God's present reign through Christ in this world has implications for the poor—both the spiritually and the materially poor. This recognition has been a cause of the rise of Liberation Theology (in various forms), which is often the expression of the belief that if God is truly king he must be concerned about the deprived and despised peoples of the world (see Lk. 4:18-19).

The importance of the gospel of the kingdom of God for evangelism and social and political service is recognized in conservative circles. There is, however, a debate as to the meaning of the millennium and its relation to the kingdom of God. (1) *Classical premillennialism* teaches that the kingdom of God has to do primarily with REDEMPTION. The kingdom was offered to Israel; but when it was rejected, its blessings were given to "a people who will produce its fruit" (Matt. 21:43), that is, the CHURCH (which is "a holy nation," 1 Pet. 2:9). The kingdom now works in the world through the church, bringing to all who will receive it the blessings of God's rule. The return of Christ is necessary for the final defeat of the enemies of God's kingdom and will involve two stages: (a) the millennium, or 1,000 year period (Rev. 20:1-6), when the glory of Christ's reign will be manifested in history and human society, and (b) the age to come with its new heavens and new earth (2 Pet. 3:12-13; Rev. 21:1). Israel, which is still a "holy people" (Rom. 11:16), is yet to be saved and brought into the blessings of the kingdom, but that will occur in terms of NT redemption rather than the OT economy. This view accepts the basic premise that the OT prophecies are to be interpreted in terms of the NT teaching.

(2) *Dispensational premillennialism* looks to the OT for its definition of the kingdom. The kingdom of God is theocratic, not soteriological. It is the earthly Davidic (millennial) kingdom destined primarily for Israel. It does not have to do chiefly with the church nor with the redemptive blessings brought into the world by Christ; rather, it concerns the earthly national blessings promised to Israel. This view believes that God has two plans that must be kept separate—an earthly national plan for Israel (theocratic) and a spiritual redemptive plan for the church (soteriological). The kingdom has to do with the former, not with the latter. Recently, however, many scholars who identify themselves as dispensationalists have modified these views in a more moderate direction.

(3) *Amillennialism* views the thousand-year reign of Rev. 20 as a reference to the church age, that is, an extended period during which Satan's power over the nations is restrained so that the gospel reaches the whole world. According to this view, the kingdom is God's redemptive rule in Christ working in the world through the church. It will come to its consummation with the second coming of Christ to inaugurate the age to come. Most amillennialists deny that Israel as a nation has any future but rather focus on the church as the new Israel, which has experienced the fulfillment of the OT prophecies in spiritual terms.

(4) *Postmillennialism* sees the millennium as a future period when revealed truth will be diffused throughout the world and accepted by the vast majority; however, it will be established through means presently operative, so that its beginning is imperceptible. Thus the kingdom is the reign of God in Christ through the church, destined to conquer all the world and to establish God's reign in all human society through the triumphant preaching of the gospel. Only after this Golden Age will Christ return for the final judgment and the resurrection of the dead to inaugurate the age to come.

kingdom of heaven. This expression occurs only in the Gospel of Matthew, which uses it more than thirty times (Matt. 3:2 et al.), in contrast to KINGDOM OF GOD, which occurs only five times in this book. Some have thought that the two phrases should be distinguished in meaning, but Matthew often uses "kingdom of heaven" in the same contexts where Mark or Luke have "kingdom of God" (e.g., Matt. 5:3 = Lk. 6:20), and so most scholars regard them as synonymous. Many believe that Matthew's use reflects the Jewish custom of avoiding the name "God" by replacing it with some other term, such as "heaven."

kingdom of Israel. See ISRAEL.

kingdom of Judah. See JUDAH, KINGDOM OF.

Kingdoms, Books of. In the SEPTUAGINT, the books of 1-2 Samuel and 1-2 Kings bear the title 1-4 Kingdoms (or Reigns; Gk. *Basileiōn*). See KINGS, BOOKS OF; SAMUEL, BOOKS OF.

King James Version. See BIBLE VERSIONS, ENGLISH.

Kings, Books of. These books cover almost 400 years of Israelite kings, from SOLOMON in the tenth century B.C. to JEHOIACHIN in the sixth. They thus provide a sequel to the books of SAMUEL, which cover the reigns of SAUL and DAVID. The title derives from the Hebrew Bible (*mĕlākîm*), where they are the last two books in the section known as the Former Prophets (Joshua, Judges, 1-2 Samuel, 1-2 Kings). Originally, the narrative formed only one book. The division between 1 and 2 Kings first appears in the SEPTUAGINT (where 1-2 Samuel and 1-2 Kings are entitled 1-4 Kingdoms or Reigns). Though regarded as "historical books" in the English Bible, the books of Samuel and Kings possess an essentially prophetic character, employing the events of past history as a vehicle for contemporary preaching (cf. Dan. 9:6). Thus, even as ISAIAH scanned the future to motivate his people's

K

obedience (Isa. 1:19-20), so the anonymous author of Kings drove home lessons, born of previous disasters, "because they had not obeyed the LORD their God" (2 Ki. 18:12).

The date of composition is not specified; but the author refers repeatedly to conditions that continued to exist in his day (e.g., the presence of the ARK OF THE COVENANT within the TEMPLE, 1 Ki. 8:8; cf. 9:21; 12:19), indicating that he wrote prior to the destruction of JUDAH in 586 B.C. (2 Ki. 8:22; 16:6; 17:41 are less definite). Even had he drawn on earlier sources (see below), an exilic writer would hardly have penned such words. References to the EXILE (1 Ki. 9:7-9; 2 Ki. 20:17-18; 21:14; 22:19-20) fail to invalidate this conclusion, for these are in fact threatening *predictions*. First Kings 4:24 indeed speaks of the western FERTILE CRESCENT as "west of the River," but this phrase had become stereotyped during Assyrian times and does not require Babylonian composition. Numerous stylistic parallels exist between the sermonic

© Dr. James C. Martin. The Israel Museum, Jerusalem. Photographed by permission.

This proto-Aeolic limestone capital, discovered in Jerusalem (Area G), may date to the time of King Solomon.

portions of 2 Ki. 17 and 21 and the writings of JEREMIAH. The whole book, moreover, breathes the spirit of JOSIAH's reform of 621 B.C. Thus, the prophet Jeremiah may well have composed 1 and 2 Kings, in his youthful enthusiasm for the Josianic reformation (Jer. 11:8; cf. Isaiah's similar authorship of a biography of UZZIAH, 2 Chr. 26:22).

Yet the climactic eulogy of Josiah speaks of the fact that the kings before or after him did not turn to the Lord in like manner (2 Ki. 23:25), and the passage goes on to assume the exile (v. 26, as does 24:3-4). Moreover, 2 Kings: 25:6-7 describes the captivity, and 25:27-30, though without awareness of the return in 538 B.C., speaks of events in BABYLON from 561 down to the death of Jehoiachin (Jer. 52:34). It would appear, therefore, that the final two and a half chapters of 2 Kings (from 23:25b on) plus the total years of Josiah's reign in 22:1 must have been added, in Babylon, over half a century after the earlier writing. Talmudic tradition attributes the entire work to Jeremiah (*b. Baba Bathra* 15a); but Jeremiah seems to have died in EGYPT, shortly after 586 (Jer. 42-44). It has been suggested that Jeremiah in old age might have been taken to Babylon by NEBUCHADNEZZAR, after his campaign against Egypt in 586. A more plausible approach, however, would be to suggest that a later Babylonian prophet, such as EZEKIEL, supplemented Jeremiah's work.

In compiling the books of Kings, the writer(s) utilized written sources: "The book of the annals of Solomon" (1 Ki. 11:41) and "the book of the annals of the kings of Israel" (14:19; 15:31) and "Judah" (14:29; 15:7). These chronicles (not to be confused with the canonical books of CHRONICLES, written in postexilic days) were probably based on court annals, but their contents went beyond what would have appeared in the official records (2 Ki. 15:15; 21:17). According to 2 Chr. 32:32, the events of Hezekiah's reign were recorded in both "the vision of the prophet Isaiah" and "the book of the kings of Judah and Israel" (cf. Isa. 36—38:8; 38:21—39:8; with 2 Ki. 18:13, 17—20:19). Other unidentified sources seemingly provided the detailed biographies of ELIJAH and ELISHA (1 Ki. 17:1—2 Ki. 8:15), plus other prophetic narratives.

Recognition of this "two-stage" composition, however, in no way supports the current negative

Overview of 1-2 KINGS

Author: Unknown.

Historical setting: Covers the period from the death of DAVID (c. 970 B.C.) to the fall of JERU-SALEM (586 B.C.). The work was probably completed during the period of Babylonian EXILE, around the middle of the sixth century B.C.

Purpose: To provide a historical-theological account of the reign of SOLOMON, the division of the kingdom, and the decline of both ISRAEL and JUDAH; to show that the exile was a righteous divine judgment; and to bring the nation back to REPENTANCE.

Contents: The transition from David to Solomon (1 Ki. 1:1—2:12); consolidation of Solomon's rule and evidence of his wisdom (1 Ki. 2:13—4:34); the building of the TEMPLE (1 Ki. 5:1—9:25); international involvements and decline of Solomon's reign (1 Ki. 9:26—11:43); division of the kingdom—REHOBOAM and JEROBOAM (1 Ki. 12-14); various kings of Judah and Israel, with emphasis on King AHAB and the prophet ELIJAH (1 Ki. 15:1—2 Ki. 1:18); decline and fall of Israel, with emphasis on the prophet ELISHA, and with attention to the kings of Judah (2 Ki. 2:1—17:41); from HEZEKIAH of Judah to the exile (2 Ki. 18:1—25:30).

criticism of Kings, divided throughout into conflicting strata similar to those of "JEDP" in the PENTATEUCH. The preexilic stratum, such views allege, was produced by the same prophetic group that "discovered" DEUTERONOMY in 621 B.C. and is said to be characterized by a tolerance of pre-Solomonic high places (1 Ki. 3:4), by faith in the unconquerability of Judah (2 Ki. 8:19), and by antagonism against northern Israel (17:21-23). The exilic stratum is then said to manifest opposite attitudes (1 Ki. 3:3; 9:6-9; 12:24). But Solomon actually conducted legitimate worship at no high place or shrine outside of JERUSALEM (1 Ki. 3:15), other than at GIBEON, where rested the Mosaic TABERNACLE (1 Chr. 16:39; 21:29); the northern kingdom obviously possessed both commendable and evil features; and the preservation of Judah never appears as more than temporary (2 Ki. 20:19; 22:20).

The teachings of the books of Kings are, however, undeniably "deuteronomistic." But since Deuteronomy-like phrases appear as often in the quoted words of David as they do in the author's own comments, an unprejudiced explanation must be sought, not in theories of wholesale Josianic forgeries, but rather in the fact of the Mosaic authenticity of Deuteronomy, on which the lives and words of Judah's pious monarchs (cf. Josh. 1:7-8) were consciously patterned. For Kings constitutes more than bare history (cf. its relative neglect of the politically significant reigns of OMRI and JEROBOAM II). A key to its theological aims appears in David's opening admonition: "... observe what the Lord your God requires ... as written in the Law of Moses, so that you may prosper in all you do" (1 Ki. 2:3; cf. 3:14; 2 Sam. 7:14). Divine retribution is then traced through the history of Solomon (1 Ki. 1-11); the divided kingdoms (treated synchronously in 1 Ki. 12—2 Ki. 17); and through the history of surviving Judah (2 Ki. 18-25). Accordingly, punishment is meted out to sinful Israel (17:7-23) and Judah (23:26-27; 24:1-4), but rewards are also given the righteous in both the northern (1 Ki. 21:29) and southern (2 Ki. 22:19-20) kingdoms.

Hope is even extended into the exile (25:27-30). Some may disparage the validity of this doctrine but, while admitting that many human acts do not find *immediate* retribution, particularly now when God deals less directly with his people, evangelical Christianity yet proclaims as fundamental to the gospel of redemption the holy theology of Kings, that "a man reaps what he sows" (Gal. 6:7).

king's dale. See KING'S VALLEY.

king's garden. When the Babylonians laid siege to JERUSALEM and broke through the city wall, King ZEDEKIAH and his army fled, leaving "the city at night by way of the king's garden, through the gate between the two walls" (Jer. 39:4; cf. 52:7 and 2 Ki. 25:4). This garden may have been watered by the overflow from the Pool of SILOAM, near which it was located (Neh. 3:15).

King's Gate. The name of a gate on the eastern side of the TEMPLE where a certain Shallum, chief of a group of postexilic gatekeepers, was stationed (1 Chr. 9:17-18; prob. the whole group was stationed there). See SHALLUM #8. Nothing else is known about this gate.

king's highway. (Often capitalized.) An important road running N–S from DAMASCUS to the Gulf of AQABAH, E of the DEAD SEA and the

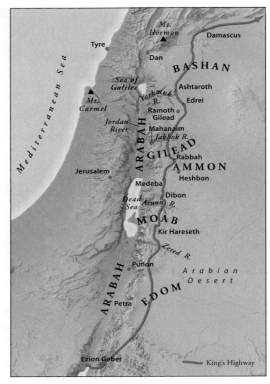

The King's Highway.

JORDAN Valley. MOSES requested permission to use this route for passing through the territory of EDOM (Num. 20:17) and of the AMORITE king SIHON (21:22; cf. Deut. 2:27), promising to keep

A modern road in the Kingdom of Jordan follows the same route taken by the king's highway through Wadi Wala. (View to the S.)

strictly to the highway. It was one of the essential caravan routes in international commerce. It ran through BASHAN (cf. Num. 21:33), GILEAD, AMMON, MOAB, and Edom, and connected with roads across the NEGEV leading into Egypt. This route of travel is known to have existed well before 2000 B.C., for a number of Bronze Age fortresses have been discovered along its line. The invasion of KEDORLAOMER and his allies apparently followed it (Gen. 14:5-6); control of this road probably lay behind the invasion.

King's Pool. A reservoir in JERUSALEM located near the FOUNTAIN GATE (Neh. 2:14). It is thought to be an alternate designation for the Pool of SILOAM, built by King HEZEKIAH.

King's Valley. KJV "king's dale." A broad valley in which the king of SODOM met ABRAHAM (Gen. 14:17). Identical with the Valley of SHAVEH, it was evidently near SALEM, the city of which MELCHIZEDEK was king. Here too ABSALOM set up a pillar or monument (2 Sam. 18:18). The location is uncertain, but it may have been S of JERUSALEM, at the juncture of the HINNON and KIDRON Valleys.

Kinnereth. kin´uh-reth (Heb. *kinneret H4055*, perhaps "lyre"; sometimes in the pl. forms *kinărôt H4054* and *kinrôt H4054*). Also Chinnereth. **(1)** A fortified town within the tribal territory of NAPHTALI (Josh. 19:35), identified with modern Khirbet el-ʿOreimeh, on the NW shore of the Sea of GALILEE. When BEN-HADAD invaded Israel, "all Kinnereth" was one of the places he conquered (1 Ki. 15:20; KJV, "Cinneroth"; NRSV, "Chinneroth"). The small plain in that area is referred to as GENNESARET in the NT (Matt. 14:34; Mk. 6:53).

(2) The Sea of Kinnereth is an old name applied to the Sea of Galilee (Num. 34:11; Josh. 12:3 [KJV, NRSV, "Chinneroth"]; 13:27). In two passages (Deut. 3:17; Josh 11:2 [KJV, NRSV, "Chinneroth"]), the name Kinnereth may be an abbreviation for Sea of Kinnereth; otherwise, it refers to the town that gave the lake its name (see above, #1) or to the general area. Some have speculated that the name (if it is related to *kinnôr H4036*, "lyre, harp") may be derived from the shape of the lake itself or from the likelihood that shepherds played lyres in that area. See also GALILEE, SEA OF.

kinship. See FAMILY.

kinsman. This English term is used sometimes in the KJV and other Bible versions in the general sense of "relative" (e.g., Lk. 14:12) or "compatriot" (e.g., Rom. 16:7). However, when it translates Hebrew *gōʾēl*, it has the more specific sense of a close relative who has a right and responsibility to redeem or avenge. In such a context, the NIV uses the rendering "kinsman-redeemer," while the TNIV has "family guardian" (e.g., Ruth 3:9). See AVENGER.

Kios. ki´os (Gk. *Chios G5944*). Also Chios, Khios. A large island in the Aegean Sea, about 30 mi. (50 km.) long N to S and varying in width from 8 to 10 mi. (13-16 km.). It is separated from the coast of ASIA MINOR by a narrow channel. The island is generally rocky and unproductive, but its wines and gum mastic have been a source of trade in ancient and modern times. Kios was the reputed home of the poet Homer and had a distinguished literary and artistic tradition. The ship on which PAUL sailed from TROAS to PATARA passed through the channel between Kios and the mainland before turning SE toward SAMOS (Acts 20:15).

Kir. kihr´ (Heb. *qîr H7817*, "wall"). **(1)** The place to which TIGLAT-PILESER, king of ASSYRIA, carried the captives of DAMASCUS (2 Ki. 16:9). AMOS had prophesied that this would happen (Amos 1:5). Apparently Kir (or Qir) had been the place of origin of the ARAMEANS in their ancient history, and their departure from Kir is compared in Scripture to God's bringing the Israelites from Egypt and the PHILISTINES from CAPHTOR (Crete; Amos 9:7). Kir is also mentioned, together with ELAM, in connection with the Valley of Vision in Isa. 22:6 (though some have doubted that this is the same place). The location of Kir is not known; it was probably in the area of the TIGRIS River in S Babylonia.

(2) A Moabite city mentioned in parallel with AR (Isa. 15:1). Often referred to as Kir of MOAB, this city is probably the same as KIR HARESETH.

K

Kir-haraseth. See KIR HARESETH.

Kir Hareseth. kihr-hair´uh-seth (Heb. *qîr ḥăreśet H7819* and *qîr-ḥeres H7818*, "wall of pottery"). Also Kir-haraseth. An important city in MOAB, apparently its capital at the time of King MESHA. When Mesha rebelled against King Joram of ISRAEL (see JEHORAM #2), JEHOSHAPHAT king of JUDAH and the king of EDOM joined Israel in attacking the Moabites and destroying their towns (2 Ki. 3). "Only Kir Hareseth was left with its stones in place, but men armed with slings surrounded it and attacked it as well" (v. 25). Years later ISAIAH, in his oracles against Moab, prophesied that Kir (prob. a reference to Kir Hareseth) would again be ruined (Isa. 15:1; 16:7, 11 [KJV, "Kir-haresh"; NRSV, "Kir-heres"]). Kir Hareseth is to be identified with el-Kerak, some 10 mi. (16 km.) E of the S part of the DEAD SEA. From ancient times it was a place of great importance in that area, easily defendable, being on a high place, with the sides of the mountain sloping steeply all around it. Located on the famous KING'S HIGHWAY from SYRIA to EGYPT, Kir Hareseth dominated the ancient caravan routes.

Kir-haresh, Kir-heres. See KIR HARESETH.

Kiriath. kihr´ee-ath (Heb. *qiryat H7956*, "city"). KJV Kirjath. A town within the tribal territory of BENJAMIN (Josh. 18:28). See KIRIATH JEARIM.

Kiriathaim. kihr´ee-uh-thay´im (Heb. *qiryātayim H7964*, "[twin] cities"). KJV also Kirjathaim. **(1)** A city built by the tribe of REUBEN in their territory (Num. 32:37; Josh. 13:19). Later it fell into the hands of MOAB, who rebuilt it (as recorded in the MOABITE STONE), and was condemned to judgment by God (Jer. 48:1, 23; Ezek. 25:9). It is possibly to be identified with Qaryat el-Mekhaiyet, about 9 mi. (14 km.) E of the DEAD SEA and the same distance N of the ARNON River.

(2) A town within the tribal territory of NAPHTALI, assigned to the LEVITES descended from GERSHON (1 Chr. 6:76). See KARTAN.

Kiriath Arba. kihr´ee-ath-ahr´buh (Heb. *qiryat ʾarbaʿ H7957* and *qiryat hāʾarbaʿ H7959*, "city of

Arba" or "fourfold city"). KJV also Kirjath-arba. Ancient name of HEBRON, used again after the EXILE. It first appears in the patriarchal narratives as the place where ABRAHAM and ISAAC stayed and where SARAH died (Gen. 23:2; 35:27). It also occurs several times in Joshua, as well as in Jdg. 1:10 and Neh. 11:25. In several passages the name is associated with a certain ARBA, said to be the ancestor of the ANAKITES (Josh. 14:15; 15:13; 21:11).

Kiriatharim. See KIRIATH JEARIM.

Kiriath Baal. kihr´ee-ath-bay´uhl (Heb. *qiryat-baʿal H7958*, "city of the lord"). KJV Kirjath-baal. Older name of KIRIATH JEARIM (Josh. 15:50; 18:14).

Kiriath Huzoth. kihr´ee-ath-hyoo´zoth (Heb. *qiryat ḥuṣôt H7960*, "city of streets" or "city of open spaces"). KJV Kirjath-huzoth. A Moabite city where BALAK and BALAAM went on their way to BAMOTH BAAL (Num. 22:39). Its location is unknown, but it was probably not far from DIBON #2.

Kiriath Jearim. kihr´ee-ath-jee´uh-rim (Heb. *qiryat yěʿārîm H7961* [*qiryat ārîm* in Ezra 2:25, prob. by scribal mistake; cf. Neh. 7:29], "city of forests"). KJV Kirjath-jearim (in Ezra 2:25, Kirjatharim; NRSV, Kiriatharim). A city of the GIBEONITES that was later on the border between the tribes of JUDAH and BENJAMIN, to which it was later assigned. It was evidently the site of a pre-Israelite shrine to BAAL, as indicated by its alternate names in the Bible: KIRIATH BAAL (Josh. 15:60; 18:14), BAALAH (Josh. 15:9), and BAALE OF JUDAH (2 Sam. 6:2; cf. 1 Chr. 13:6). The Danites, seeking a new home, encamped W of it in Judah at MAHANEH DAN (Jdg. 18:12). When the ARK OF THE COVENANT was returned by the PHILISTINES, the people of BETH SHEMESH brought it to Kiriath Jearim (1 Sam. 6:21; 7:1-2); it remained here twenty years until DAVID brought it up to JERUSALEM (1 Chr. 13:5-6; 2 Chr. 1:4). People from Kiriath Jearim were among the returning exiles (Neh. 7:29; Ezra 2:25). The town is generally identified with modern Abu Ghosh, 8.5 mi. (13.5 km.) WNW of Jerusalem, though the more precise site of the biblical period is Deir el-ʿAzar, an imposing tell or mound upon which stands the Church of the Ark of the Covenant.

Kiriath Sannah. kihr´ee-ath-san´uh (Heb. *qiryat-sannâ H7962*, "city of Sannah" [?]). Alternate name of Debir (Josh. 15:49). Possibly a textual corruption for *qiryat-sōpēr* ("city of the scribe[s]"). See DEBIR (PLACE) #1; KIRIAT SEPHER.

Kiriath Sepher. kihr´ee-ath-see´fuhr (Heb. *qiryat-sēper H7963*, "city of book[s]"). Earlier name of Debir (Josh. 15:15-16; Jdg. 1:11-12). See DEBIR (PLACE) #1; KIRIAT SANNAH.

Kirjath. kihr´jath. KJV form of KIRIATH. See also KIRIATHAIM, KIRIATH ARBA, etc.

Kish. kish (Heb. *qîš H7821*, possibly "gift"). **(1)** Son (or grandson) of ABIEL, descendant of BENJAMIN, and father of SAUL, who was the first king of ISRAEL. In 1 Sam. 9:1, Kish is identified as the son of Abiel, but in 1 Chr. 8:33 and 9:39, Kish is listed as the son of NER. The Hebrew of 1 Sam. 14:50-51, however, can be understood to mean that both Ner and Kish were sons of Abiel (cf. NIV). In that case, Ner would be the uncle of Saul (cf. v. 50 NIV), and Saul and ABNER would be cousins. This view necessitates either the altering of the text of 1 Chr. 8:33 and 9:39 or understanding Ner in those verses as a different individual, namely, a more remote ancestor of Kish. At any rate, Kish was a wealthy man (1 Sam. 9:1). One day his donkeys went astray, and Saul was sent to find them (9:3); it was through this incident that Saul met SAMUEL and was anointed by him the first king of Israel (10:1). Kish was buried in Zela in the land of Benjamin (2 Sam. 21:14). He is mentioned once in the NT (Acts 13:21).

(2) Son of JEIEL of GIBEON and descendant of Benjamin (1 Chr. 8:30; 9:36). Many believe that Jeiel is to be identified with ABIEL; if so, this Kish is the same as #1 above.

(3) Son of Mahli and descendant of LEVI through MERARI (1 Chr. 23:21-22). His sons married his brother's daughters. One of his sons was named Jerahmeel (24:29).

(4) Son of Abdi and descendant of LEVI through MERARI; he lived in the days of King HEZEKIAH

and, as one of the priests, was chosen to cleanse the house of the Lord (2 Chr. 29:12).

(5) Ancestor of MORDECAI, the cousin of ESTHER, and descendant of Benjamin (Esth. 2:5). He was among those exiled from Jerusalem by NEBUCHADNEZZAR (v. 6).

Kishi. kish´i (Heb. *qîšî H7823*, perhaps "gift"). Son of Abdi, descendant of LEVI through MERARI, and father of the musician ETHAN (1 Chr. 6:44; called KUSHAIAH in 15:17).

Kishion. kish´ee-uhn (Heb. *qišyôn H8002*, meaning uncertain). A town within the tribal territory of ISSACHAR (Josh. 19:20), assigned to the LEVITES descended from GERSHON (21:28; KJV, "Kishon"). Proposed identifications include Tell el-Muqar-qash, about 4 mi. (6 km.) SE of Mount TABOR, and el-Khirba (Khirbet Qasyun, Tel Qishyon), near the S slope of the same mountain. See also KEDESH #3.

Kishon River. ki´shon (Heb. *qîšôn H7822*, meaning unknown). A WADI that drains the ESDRAELON Valley E to NW; it is mentioned in connection with DEBORAH (Jdg. 4:7, 13; 5:21; Ps. 83:9) and ELIJAH (1 Ki. 18:40). (Note also that the KJV uses "Kishon" once as an alternate form of KISHION [Josh. 21:28].) The stream flows from sources on Mount TABOR and Mount GILBOA westward through Esdraelon and enters the Bay of Acre (Acco) N of Mount CARMEL. In winter it becomes a raging torrent, which subsides into pools that are soon drained off for irrigation, except that the last few miles are fed from the slopes of Mount Carmel and by tributaries from the north. It is treacherous to cross except at fords carefully chosen. Along the banks of the River Kishon, DEBORAH the prophetess and BARAK led Israel to victory over the Canaanite hosts of JABIN, under their commander SISERA (Jdg. 4-5). The heavily armed soldiers and chariots that were not cut down by the pursuing Israelites were swept away by the raging Kishon (Jdg. 5:21; Ps. 83:9 [KJV, "Kison"]). After his contest with the priests of BAAL on Mount Carmel, ELIJAH had the priests brought down to the brook Kishon and killed there (1 Ki. 18:40). The stream is now known as the Nahr el-Muqattaᶜ.

K

K

Kislev. kis´lev (Heb. *kislēw H4075*, from Akk. *kislimu* [*kisliwu*]). Also Chislev; KJV Chisleu. The ninth month (before the winter solstice) in the Hebrew CALENDAR, corresponding to November-December (Neh. 1:1; Zech. 7:1).

Kislon. kis´lon (Heb. *kislôn H4077*, possibly "sluggish"). Father of ELDAD; the latter was a Benjamite leader appointed to divide the land of Canaan among the tribes (Num. 34:21).

Kisloth Tabor. kis´loth-tay´buhr (Heb. *kislōt tābôr H4079*, meaning uncertain). Also Chisloth-tabor. A town mentioned in the description of the SE border of the tribe of ZEBULUN (Josh. 19:12); probably the same as KESULLOTH in ISSACHAR (v. 18).

kiss. The Hebrew verb meaning "to kiss" is *nāšaq H5975* (Gen. 27:26 and frequently; the cognate noun *nĕšîqâ H5965* occurs only twice, Prov. 27:6; Cant. 1:2). In the OT, the kiss was a common greeting among male relatives (Gen. 29:13; 33:4; 45:15; Exod. 4:27; 18:7; 2 Sam. 14:33), male and female relatives (Gen. 29:11; 31:28), in farewell (Gen. 31:55; Ruth 1:9, 14), and before death (Gen. 50:1). The kiss had a more formal character in connection with a blessing (Gen. 27:26-27; 48:10) or the anointing of a king (1 Sam. 10:1). Friends kissed (1 Sam. 20:41; 2 Sam. 19:39). The act might be a pretense (2 Sam. 15:5; 20:9; Prov. 27:6). Kissing was an act of worship toward heathen gods (1 Ki. 19:18, 20; Job 31:27; Hos. 13:2). The psalmist states that righteousness and peace will "kiss" each other, that is, will unite to bless restored Israel (Ps. 85:10). Kisses may be a lure to illicit love (Prov. 7:13). The kiss in Ps. 2:12 is one of homage to the king's son. The kiss was generally given on the cheek, forehead, or beard, though a kiss on the lips is sometimes indicated (Prov. 24:26) and is probable (in Cant. 1:2; 8:1).

In the NT, the Greek verb *phileō G5797*, which usually means "to love, have special affection for," can also mean "to kiss" (Matt. 26:48 = Mk. 14:44 = Lk. 22:47), but the latter sense is normally conveyed by the compound *kataphileō G2968* (Matt. 26:49 et al.); the cognate noun *philēma G5799* only means "kiss" (Lk. 7:45a et al.). Once Jesus' host did not give him this customary greeting, but a sinful woman kissed his feet (Lk. 7:38, 45). The father kissed the returning prodigal (15:20). JUDAS ISCARIOT kissed Jesus as a sign to the temple police (Matt. 26:48-49; Mk. 14:44-45; Lk. 22:47-48). The Ephesian elders kissed PAUL in farewell (Acts 20:37). The kiss was adopted as a formal greeting among believers, called the holy kiss (Rom. 16:16; 1 Cor. 16:20; 2 Cor. 13:12; 1 Thess. 5:26) or kiss of love (1 Pet. 5:14).

kitchen. This English term is used by modern Bible versions to render the Hebrew phrase *bêt hambaššĕlîm*, lit., "house[s] of the ones who boil" (Ezek. 46:24). It refers to four subcourts at the corners of the outer court of EZEKIEL's ideal TEMPLE where the common people could have their sacrifices boiled at the hearths provided for the purpose. The priests protected themselves from defilement through contact with unconsecrated persons by cooking their offerings in their own kitchens (vv. 19-20).

kite. See BIRDS.

Kithlish. See KITLISH.

Kitlish. kit´lish (Heb. *kitliš H4186*, derivation unknown). Also Chitlish, Chithlish, Kithlish. A town in the SHEPHELAH within the tribal territory of JUDAH (Josh. 15:40). Kitlish was in the same district as LACHISH (v. 39), but the precise site is unknown.

Kitron. kit´ron (Heb. *qiṭrôn H7790*, possibly "smoke, incense"). A Canaanite town within the tribal territory of ZEBULUN from which the Israelites could not drive out the inhabitants (Jdg. 1:30). Some believe Kitron is the same as KATTATH, but the location is unknown.

Kittim. kit´im (Heb. *kittiyyîm H4183*, gentilic of *kt* [a place name attested in Phoenician]). KJV also Chittim. **(1)** Third son of JAVAN, grandson of JAPHETH, brother of ELISHAH (associated with AEGEAN peoples), TARSHISH (Spain or N Africa?), and RODANIM (Rhodes?) (Gen. 10:4; 1 Chr. 1:7). Many interpret the name as referring to a people group descended from Javan (cf. TNIV, "the Kittites," and see below, ##2-4).

(2) The island CYPRUS. See separate article.

(3) On occasion the name Kittim, like Javan, is extended to include the W in general, but especially the seafaring western areas. Jeremiah, speaking of the whole world (Jer. 2:10), uses the isles of Kittim to symbolize the far W and KEDAR the far E. BAALAM, forecasting the coming dominance of the W over the ANE (Num. 24:24), tells that the ships of Kittim will afflict Asshur (Mesopotamia) and Eber (the Levant). Daniel apparently uses "ships of Kittim" (Dan. 11:30; NIV, "Ships of the western coastlands") to represent the Romans, who thwarted ANTIOCHUS IV (Epiphanes) in Egypt in 169 B.C.

(4) The occurrence of numerous references to the Kittim in the DEAD SEA SCROLLS has created considerable scholarly controversy over the correct interpretation. Most scholars have divided over an identification with the Greeks or with the Romans. Perhaps Kittim meant for the Dead Sea Community simply "Westerners" (as #3 above) and could be applied to any particular western people as need arose.

Kittites. kit´tits. TNIV alternate form of KITTIM (Gen. 10:4; 1 Chr. 1:7).

Kiyyun. See KAIWAN.

kneading trough. A dish or bowl in which dough was prepared to be made into BREAD (Deut. 28:5, 17). The plague of frogs infested them in Egypt (Exod. 8:3). The Israelites bound their kneeding troughs, dough and all, in the bundles of clothing on their backs, when they escaped from Egypt (12:34).

knee, kneel. The ANE custom for public PRAYER was to stand, and so kneeling was confined to acts of obedience and obeisance. The official presentation of children on the father's knee was a sign legitimizing the child's legal claim in Israel (Gen. 30:3; 50:23; Job 3:12). The Hebrew term for "knee" is *berek H1386* (Gen. 30:3 and often), and the cognate verb *bārak H1384* means "to kneel" (only Gen. 24:11; 2 Chr. 6:13; Ps. 95:6). In the NT, the common Greek term *gony G1205* (Heb. 12:12 et al.) is used without exception as the noun, and the verb *gonypeteō G1206* means specifically, "to kneel down before someone" (Matt. 17:14; 27:29; Mk. 1:40; 10:17). The verbal idea is often conveyed also by the use of the noun in combination with other verbs (Lk. 5:8 et al.). Bowing down became the traditional posture of prayer in the Christian church. It also appears as the posture of dying in the case of STEPHEN's martyrdom (Acts 7:20). PAUL and his converts prayed and said farewell on their kees (20:36), and kneeling is mentioned in Paul's epistles. The apostle uses the conception of kneeling in the figurative sense of submission to the Almighty (Eph. 3:14), where it is his own confession that is foremost, and in the magnificent prophecy of Christ's ultimate triumph when all knees shall bow before the MESSIAH (Phil. 2:10).

knife. A small single-edged or double-edged cutting instrument of stone or metal. In form the knife generally resembled the dagger or short stabbing sword, but was smaller and usually without ornamentation. The usual Hebrew word for "knife" is *ma'ăkelet H4408* (Gen. 22:6 et al.), but the word for "sword" (*ḥereb H2995*) is rendered "knife" in Josh. 5:2-3 (cf. also KJV 1 Ki. 18:28; Ezek. 5:1-2). The knife generally had a straight blade 6-10 in. (15-25 cm.) long, although knives with curved blades were known. The handles were made of one piece with the blade, or a wooden handle was fastened to the blade by a tang or by rivets. Knives were used for various purposes. JOSHUA was commanded to use flint knives to circumcise the Israelites (Josh. 5:2-3; cf. Exod. 4:25). The use of flint knives when they were no longer in common domestic use implies

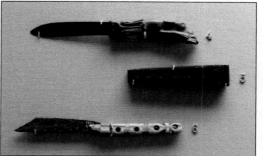

A collection of Roman knives (1st-3rd cent. A.D.).

© Dr. James C. Martin. The British Museum. Photographed by permission.

K

an ancient ritual in which their use was still appropriate. Knives or small swords were used by the frenzied priests of BAAL for self-mutilation (1 Ki. 18:28). Animals were killed and skinned with food-cutters. ABRAHAM took one along to sacrifice ISAAC (Gen. 22:6), and the Levite used one to dismember his concubine (Jdg. 19:29). The "scribe's knife" of Jer. 36:23 (NRSV, "penknife") was used for trimming and splitting the reed employed in writing.

knop. A small ornamental knob. This word is used by the KJV in Exod. 25:31-36 and 37:17-22, referring to the decorations (knobby fruits or flower buds) of the golden CANDLESTICK or lampstand in the TABERNACLE. Elsewhere it describes the decorations carved on the cedar lining of the walls of Solomon's TEMPLE (1 Ki. 6:18) and around the molten sea (7:24).

knowledge. The sum of what has been perceived or learned, that is, truth or information acquired through experience and education. The Bible frequently commends knowledge and WISDOM (1 Sam. 2:3; Ps. 14:4; 119:66; Prov. 8:10; Isa. 53:11; Jn. 8:32; 1 Cor. 13:12; Col. 1:9; 1 Jn. 5:20). Nowhere does Scripture modify the high value it places on knowledge by deprecating "mere" human reason. Reason and knowledge are integral parts of the IMAGE OF GOD in which human beings were created. Although the Hebrew and Greek verbs for knowing usually bear the most ordinary meaning (e.g., "I don't know who has done this," Gen. 21:26), they can also be used in other senses, some of which are sources of confusion in theology and philosophy. When Ps. 1:6 says that "the Lord knows the way of the righteous, but the way of the wicked will perish" (RSV), it is not reflecting on divine OMNISCIENCE. In the ordinary sense, God knows the way of the wicked as well as he knows everything else. Here the word is used in the sense of approval (cf. NIV, "watches over"). Similarly, when Amos 3:2 says, "You only have I known of all the families of the earth" (RSV), the prophet is not denying that God knew the Egyptians and Canaanites. This verse is no denial of omniscience; here the verb means "to choose, elect" (cf. NIV). See also GNOSTICISM.

knowledge, tree of. See TREE OF KNOWLEDGE.

Koa. koh´uh (Heb. *qôaʿ H7760*). An otherwise unknown place (or people) that, along with the Babylonians and others, is named as being among the enemies of JERUSALEM (Ezek. 23:23). Some scholars suggest that the name may refer to the Quti (Gutians), who lived E of the TIGRIS River. If so, the form *Koa* may be a deliberate distortion.

Kohath. koh´hath (Heb. *qĕhāt H7740* [also *qŏhāt*], meaning unknown; gentilic *qĕhātî H7741* [also *qŏhātî*], "Kohathite"). Second son of LEVI (Gen. 46:11; Exod. 6:16); he is said to have lived 133 years (6:18). He was the father of AMRAM, IZHER, HEBRON, and UZZIEL (Exod. 6:18; Num. 3:19, 27; 1 Chr. 6:2), who became Kohathite branches of the Levitical families (Num. 3:27). See LEVITE. He was the grandfather, through Amram and his wife JOCHEBED (sister of Kohath), of AARON, MOSES, and MIRIAM (Exod. 6:20; Num. 26:59; 1 Chr. 6:3). The Kohathites were, therefore, the most prominent of the Levitical families. In the wilderness they camped S of the TABERNACLE. Numbering 8,600, on duty they cared for the ark, table, lampstand, altars, and vessels of the sanctuary. These they carried on foot, no wagons being assigned them (Num. 7:8-9). JOSHUA allotted them twenty-three LEVITICAL CITIES (Josh. 21:4-5). Under the monarchy they were prominent (1 Chr. 23:13-20; 24:20-25), especially HEMAN in the service of song (6:33 et al.). They took part in the religious service the day before JEHOSHAPHAT's victory over his allied enemies (2 Chr. 20:19); and they assisted in HEZEKIAH's cleansing of the TEMPLE (29:12-19).

Koheleth. koh-hel´ith. See ECCLESIASTES.

Kolaiah. koh-lay´yuh (Heb. *qôlāyâ H7755*, possibly "Yahweh has spoken"). **(1)** Son of Maaseiah, descendant of BENJAMIN, and ancestor of Sallu; the latter was among those who settled in JERUSALEM after the EXILE (Neh. 11:7).

(2) Father of a false prophet named AHAB (Jer. 29:21).

Kol-Hozeh. kol-hoh´zuh. TNIV form of COL-HOZEH.

Konaniah. kon´uh-ni´uh. TNIV form of CONANIAH.

koph. See QOPH.

kor. Also cor. See WEIGHTS AND MEASURES.

Korah. kor´uh (Heb. *qōraḥ H7946*, "bald [head]"; gentilic *qorḥi H7948*, "Korahite" [KJV also "Korhite" and "Korathite"]; Gk. *Kore G3169*). **(1)** Son of ESAU by OHOLIBAMAH (Gen. 36:5, 14, 18; 1 Chr. 1:35).

(2) Son of ELIPHAZ and grandson of ESAU (Gen. 36:16). The parallel passages (Gen. 36:11; 1 Chr. 1:35) omit the name.

(3) Son of IZHAR, grandson of KOHATH, and great-grandson of LEVI (Exod. 6:21, 24). Korah, with 250 leaders of the congregation, rose up against MOSES and AARON, charging them with exalting themselves above the assembly of the Lord (Num. 16:1-3). At the same time, DATHAN and ABIRAM of the tribe of REUBEN rebelled against Moses' leadership, charging him with failure to bring them into the promised land and making himself a prince over the people (vv. 1, 12-14). Moses charged Korah and the LEVITES with seeking the priesthood as well as the ministry of service before the Lord (vv. 8-10). Therefore, he challenged the rebels to meet with him at the Tent of Meeting, each man taking a censer and offering incense before the Lord, that the Lord might show who was holy (vv. 4-9, 16-19). However, Dathan and Abiram refused to meet with Moses (vv. 12-14). Judgment fell against those who rebelled. The earth opened and swallowed up Korah, Dathan, Abiram, and their families, and fire from heaven consumed the 250 leaders offering their incense (vv. 23-35). In the brief account of Num. 26:9-11, it is pointed out that the line of Korah did not come to an end. The Korahites were doorkeepers and musicians in the TABERNACLE and TEMPLE (Exod. 6:24; 1 Chr. 6:22), and they are mentioned in several other passages (1 Chr. 9:19, 31, 12:6; 26:1; 2 Chr. 20:19). A dozen psalms are given the superscription as "of the Sons of Korah" (Ps. 42-49; 84-85; 87-88). It is probable that these psalms originated among this guild of singers and were perhaps sung by them in the worship of the temple.

(4) Son of HEBRON, grandson of CALEB, and descendant of JUDAH (1 Chr. 2:43). Some argue that Korah here is the name of a town.

(5) Five of the men from the tribe of BENJAMIN who joined DAVID at ZIKLAG were called Korahites (1 Chr. 12:6). While it is possible that these were Levites descended from #3 above, some scholars believe that they descended from a different (and otherwise unknown) Korah or that the reference is to a locality in the tribe of Benjamin.

Korathite. See KORAH.

Korazin. kor-ay´zin (Gk. *Chorazin G5960*). Also Chorazin. A town situated near the Sea of Galilee, denounced by Jesus, and mentioned in the Bible in only one context (Matt. 11:21 = Lk. 10:13). Little is known of Korazin. The site is probably that of Khirbet Kerazeh, on the basalt hills just N of CAPERNAUM, and evidence from the ruins indicates that it was inhabited as early as the later Stone Age. The TALMUD (*b. Menaḥot* 85a) mentions the town under the name Kerazim as being famous for its quality of wheat. A synagogue built of the black volcanic rock of the area forms part of the ruins.

Korban. See CORBAN.

Kore. kor´ee (Heb. *qōrēʾ H7927*, "one who calls out, partridge"). **(1)** Son of Ebiasaph (see ABIASAPH) and descendant of LEVI through KORAH (1 Chr. 9:19; 26:1 [here called son of Asaph]). Two of Kore's sons or descendants, SHALLUM and MESHE-LEMIAH (perhaps also OBED-EDOM, 26:4), were among the gatekeepers of the sanctuary.

(2) Son of Imnah; a LEVITE in the time of HEZEKIAH, he was keeper of the EAST GATE and "in charge of the freewill offerings given to God, distributing the contributions made to the LORD and also the consecrated gifts" (2 Chr. 31:14).

Korhite. See KORAH.

koum. See TALITHA CUM(I).

Koz. koz (Heb. *qôṣ H7766*, "thorn"). Also Coz. A man listed among the descendants of JUDAH (1 Chr. 4:8). His place in the genealogy is unclear, but the

NIV links this verse with the previous one, making Koz a son of ASHHUR by Helah (see vv. 5, 7).

Kozbi. koz´bi. TNIV form of COZBI.

Kozeba. koh-zee´buh. TNIV form of COZEBA.

Kub. kuhb. See CUB.

Kue. kyoo´ee (Heb. *qĕwēh H7750*, meaning unknown). Also Keveh. A HITTITE kingdom occupying SE ASIA MINOR, corresponding to E CILICIA. Kue is mentioned in various extrabiblical documents. An important trade route crossed this coastal plain, from the Syrian Gates in the Amanus Mountains to the Cilician Gates in the Taurus Range. Iron evidently was imported into SYRIA and BABYLON through Cilicia, but there is no evidence of its actually being mined there. The country was famous in ancient times as a source of the finest horses, many of which were imported by SOLOMON (1 Ki. 10:28; 2 Chr. 1:16; KJV says "linen yarn," following a Jewish interpretation).

kum. See TALITHA CUM(I).

Kun. koon. TNIV form of CUN.

Kushaiah. koo-shay´yuh (Heb. *qûšāyāhû H7773*, derivation uncertain). Descendant of LEVI through MERARI, and father of the musician ETHAN (1 Chr. 15:17); also called KISHI (6:44).

Kuthah. kooth´uh. TNIV form of CUTHAH.

L. The symbol used to designate material peculiar to the Gospel of Luke; for some scholars, the symbol represents an independent literary source used by Luke. See Gospels; Luke, Gospel of.

Laadah. lay´uh-dah (Heb. *la‘dâ H4355*, possibly "plump neck"). Son of Shelah and grandson of Judah (1 Chr. 4:21). He is described as the father of Mareshah (possibly meaning the founder of the town by that name) and of "the clans of the linen workers at Beth Ashbea."

Laadan. See Ladan.

Laban (person). lay´buhn (Heb. *lābān H4238*, "white" or "Moon God"). Son of Bethuel, nephew of Abraham, and brother of Rebekah (Gen. 24:29; cf. v. 15). The family is described as Arameans from Paddan Aram (25:20). Laban lived in Haran on a tributary of the Euphrates River in Mesopotamia. He belonged to that branch of the family of Terah (Abraham's father) that came from Abraham's brother Nahor and his niece Milcah (22:22-24), and is first mentioned as Rebekah's brother when she is introduced (24:29). In ancient Semitic custom, the brother was the guardian of the sister, and thus Laban takes a prominent place in the account of Rebekah's leaving for Canaan to be Isaac's bride. His grasping nature is hinted at in Gen. 24:30-31, where his invitation to Abraham's servant follows immediately after his appraisal of the servant's expensively equipped party.

Laban's later history is interwoven with Jacob's. When Jacob fled from the anger of his brother Esau, he settled in his uncle Laban's house in Haran and stayed there twenty years. The relationship between Laban and his nephew is an interesting one. Both appear to be resourceful, often grasping men, each eager to best the other in every transaction. Even in the circumstances surrounding the marriage of Jacob to Laban's daughters Rachel and Leah (Gen. 29), this competition is evident. After Jacob had served fourteen years for his brides, there followed six more years in Haran during which, according to Jacob's testimony, Laban changed his wages ten times (31:41). The famous contract involving the speckled and spotted sheep (30:31-43) was evidently one of the ten.

At the end of the twenty years, Jacob quietly stole away from Laban, taking his now-large family with him to Canaan (Gen. 31). Pursuing him, Laban overtook him in Gilead. Following mutual protestations and incriminations, uncle and nephew parted, after erecting a "witness heap"—a kind of dividing line—between them. Laban is here called "the Aramean" (31:24), and he gives the heap an Aramaic name (Jegar Sahadutha), while Jacob calls it by its Hebrew equivalent Galeed (31:47-48), both meaning "witness heap." These Aramaic references are interesting guides in the quest for better understanding of the origins of the Patriarchs. In an old confession the Hebrews were taught to say, "My father was a wandering Aramean" (Deut. 26:5). It seems likely that the patriarchal ancestors of the Hebrews sprang from a mixed Semitic stock in NE Mesopotamia, among which the Aramean was a prominent strain.

Laban (place). lay´buhn (Heb. *lābān H4239*, "white" or "Moon God"). A city in the area of encampment of Israel, across the Jordan in the Arabah (Deut. 1:1). In this area, Moses spoke to Israel the words contained in Deuteronomy, just before his death. It is perhaps the same as LIBNAH, but the location is unknown.

labor. The noun is today confined to the abstract use—the act of laboring (Gen. 31:42; Rom. 16:6). Formerly it expressed also the fruit of labor, as in Exod. 23:16, "When thou hast gathered in thy labours out of the field," or Jn. 4:38, "Ye are entered into their labours" (both KJV). The word is used also of labor in childbirth (Gen. 35:16 KJV).

In Bible times there was no class of people known as "labor" in contrast with "management." All but a favored few labored, and hard work was looked on as the common lot of man and a result of the curse (Gen. 3:17-19), a bitter servitude. Slavery was commonly practiced in the Bible world; the conscription of freemen for labor on government building projects was practiced by SOLOMON (1 Ki. 5:13-17) and ASA (15:22).

Although most workers in the simple culture of OT times were what we today would call "unskilled," there were certain skilled occupations. The potter (Jer. 18) has left behind him unnumbered examples of his skill. Some technology in the working of metals was known. Remains of smelting furnaces have been found. Stone masons, scribes (Ezek. 9:2; Jer. 36:2, 4), dyers, weavers, and workers in precious stones and ivory carried on their work. But in general life was simple, work arduous, hours long, and wages small. "Then man goes out to his work, to his labor until evening" (Ps. 104:23). "So I hated life, because the work that is done under the sun was grievous to me" (Eccl. 2:17). By NT times things had changed, and the more complex civilization of the Roman world, with its skilled and more diversified occupations and better standards of living, had come to Palestine. See also OCCUPATIONS AND PROFESSIONS.

Lachish. lay´kish (Heb. *lākîš* H4337, meaning unknown). A town within the tribal territory of JUDAH in the foothills of the SHEPHELAH, midway between JERUSALEM and GAZA, some 30 mi. (50 km.) SW of Jerusalem. Lachish had been a Canaanite royal city and later became a Judean border fortress that occupied a strategic valley, the southernmost of the five that transect the Palestinian foothills and connect Judah's central ridge and the

coastal highway leading into EGYPT. First equated with Tell el-Hesy, Lachish has now been identified by written evidence (see below) with Tell ed-Duweir, a 22-acre mound excavated by J. K. Starkey from 1932 until his death by violence in 1938.

Even before 3000 B.C. Lachish was inhabited by chalcolithic cave dwellers, but in about 2700 an Early-Bronze city was constructed on the virgin rock. Following a gap occasioned by invaders of calciform culture (c. 2300), Middle-Bronze Lachish arose, exhibiting cultural and political ties with Middle-Kingdom Egypt (2000-1780). This was succeeded by a HYKSOS-type community, which provided Lachish with its first observable fortifications, including the characteristic dry moat, or fosse. An inscribed dagger, dated about 1650, furnishes one of the earliest examples of that acrophonic writing from which all modern alphabets derive, two centuries older than the Sinaitic or the five subsequent Lachish inscriptions. After the expulsion of the Hyksos from Egypt and their defeat in Palestine (c. 1578-1573), a Late-Bronze Canaanite citadel gave at least nominal allegiance to New-Empire Egypt.

The king of Lachish, JAPHIA, joined with ADONI-ZEDEK of Jerusalem in a confederacy against JOSHUA (Josh. 10:3), only to be defeated and executed (10:23-26; 12:11). In Joshua's subsequent sweep through the SW, Israel captured Lachish (reinforced by GEZER) and annihilated its inhabitants, in accordance with MOSES' ban (Deut. 7:2; Josh. 10:31-33). Scripture contains no record, however, of its destruction (cf. Josh. 11:13); and though assigned to Judah (15:39), Lachish must have suffered rapid Canaanite reoccupation, for

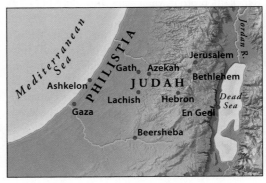

Lachish.

a Late-Bronze temple constructed in the former fosse exhibits little interruption in its use. A generation later, the AMARNA Letters criticize Lachish for furnishing supplies to the invaders and for overthrowing the Egyptian prefect Zimridi (Letters 287-288). Lachish was burned in about

© Dr. James C. Martin

Aerial view of Lachish looking E.

1230. Some interpreters have tried to associate this conflagration with Joshua's campaign, but the excavators themselves attribute the fall of Lachish to the contemporaneous raids of Pharaoh Merneptah or to attacks by immigrating PHILISTINES.

Lachish was fortified BY Rehoboam shortly after the division of the Hebrew kingdom in 930 B.C. (2 Chr. 11:9); and it was there that King AMAZIAH was murdered in 767 (25:27). The prophet MICAH condemned Lachish's chariots as "the beginning of sin to the Daughter of Zion," perhaps because the city was used as a staging point for the extravagant importation of Egyptian horses (Mic. 1:13; cf. Deut. 17:16; 1 Ki. 10:28-29). In any event, Lachish was successfully besieged by SENNACHERIB in 701 (2 Chr. 32:9); HEZEKIAH sent a message of submission there (2 Ki. 18:14); and from it Sennacherib's troops marched against Jerusalem (18:17; 19:8).

Starkey's excavations demonstrate successive destructions of Lachish in 597 and 587, corresponding to NEBUCHADNEZZAR's second and third attacks against Judah. From the final ashes twenty-one inscribed ostraca were recovered. Consisting primarily of communications from an outpost

commander named Hoshaiah to his superior, Joash, at Lachish, they constitute our first truly personal, Palestinian documents. Letter IV mentions signal fires (cf. Jer. 6:1) and establishes Jeremiah's assertion that Lachish and Azekah were the last cities, before Jerusalem, to fall to Nebuchadnezzar (34:7), and Letter VI speaks of a warning prophet (like Jeremiah himself) and of critics that "weakened the hands" of anti-Babylonian resistance (38:4). Finally, in NEHEMIAH's day, a resettled Lachish (Neh. 11:30) achieved the construction of a palace and Persian sun temple that are among the finest of the period.

Ladan. lay´duhn (Heb. *la‘dān H4356*, possibly "plump neck, double chin"). KJV Laadan. (1) Son of Tahan, descendant of EPHRAIM, and ancestor of JOSHUA (1 Chr. 7:26).

(2) Descendant of LEVI through GERSHON and ancestor of several Levitical families in charge of the temple treasuries (1 Chr. 23:7-9; 26:21). Because he is paired with SHIMEI (23:7), Ladan is usually identified with LIBNI son of Gershon (6:17), but some argue that both Ladan and the Shimei of 23:7 are more distant descendants of Gershon.

ladder. See STAIRS, STAIRWAY.

lady, chosen (elect). See ELECT LADY.

Lael. lay´uhl (Heb. *lā’ēl H4210*, "belonging to God"). Father of ELIASAPH; during the wilderness period, the latter was a leader of the LEVITES descended from GERSHON (Num. 3:24).

Lagash. lay´gash. An important city-state in SUMER during the first half of the third millennium B.C. Lagash is identified with modern Tell al-Hiba in S Iraq, but it included the urban centers of Girsu and Nina-Sirara (modern Tello and Zurghul). Large temple complexes have been

L

excavated. The *Lagash Kinglist* (early second millennium), purportedly a record of the city's ancient rulers, includes a flood narrative.

Lahad. lay´had (Heb. *lāhad H4262*, possibly "slow, lazy"). Son of Jahath, descendant of JUDAH, and ancestor of a Zorathite clan (1 Chr. 4:2; see ZORAH).

Lahmam. See LAHMAS.

Lahmas. lah´mahs (Heb. *laḥmās H4314* [many MSS *laḥmām*], meaning uncertain). Also Lahmam. A town of JUDAH in the SHEPHELAH district of LACHISH (Josh. 15:40). The location is unknown, although some have suggested modern Khirbet el-Laḥm, about 3 mi. (5 km.) E of Lachish.

Lahmi. lah´mi (Heb. *laḥmî H4313*, in form a gentilic from the word meaning "bread"). A PHILISTINE who is described as the brother of GOLIATH the Gittite and who was killed by Elhanan son of Jair (1 Chr. 20:5). The parallel passage (2 Sam. 21:19) reads differently. See comments under ELHANAN #1.

Laish (city). lay´ish (Heb. *layiš H4332*, "lion"). **(1)** A Canaanite town in N PALESTINE captured by the Danites and renamed by them DAN (Jdg. 18:7, 14, 27, 29); earlier called LESHEM (in Josh. 19:47).
   (2) KJV form of LAISHAH (Isa. 10:30).

Laish (person). lay´ish (Heb. *layiš H4331*, "lion"). Father of PALTIEL, to whom SAUL gave MICHAL, DAVID's wife (1 Sam. 25:44; 2 Sam. 3:15).

Laishah. lay´i-shah (Heb. *layšâ H4333*, "lion"). KJV Laish. A village probably in BENJAMIN, named with GALLIM and ANATHOTH as lying along the usual invasion route of armies coming from the N (Isa. 10:30). The location is unknown, but it must have been a relatively short distance NNE of JERUSALEM.

lake. The Greek word for "lake," *limnē G3349*, is used only by Luke with reference to the Lake of GENNESARET—that is, the Sea of Galilee—and by the book of Revelation with reference to the LAKE OF FIRE (Lk. 5:1-2; 8:22-23, 33; Rev. 19:20;

20:10, 14-15; 21:8). To prevent misunderstanding, the NIV also employs "lake" frequently to render Greek *thalassa G2498*, "sea," whenever this term (in imitation of the corresponding Heb. and Aram. terms) is used by itself with reference to the Sea of Galilee (Matt. 4:18 et al.). See also GALILEE, SEA OF. There are not many lakes in SYRIA and PALESTINE. Among the most important are the following: the DEAD SEA; the Waters of MEROM (Josh. 11:5, 7); Yammuneh (in the LEBANON, W of BAALBEK); and some small lakes E of DAMASCUS into which the rivers of Damascus flow and are evaporated.

lake of fire. This phrase occurs several times in the book of Revelation (Rev. 19:20; 20:10, 14-15; cf. 21:8). All the enemies of God—the beast and the false prophet (19:20), the devil (20:10), death and HADES (20:14), all whose names are not found written in the BOOK OF LIFE (20:15), the cowardly, the faithless, the murderers, etc. (21:8)—are to be consigned at the end of this age (in the case of the beast and the false prophet), or after the 1,000 years, to the lake of fire. This is said to be the second death (20:14)—the first being presumably physical death—and consists in eternal exclusion from the new heaven and the new earth, and the new Jerusalem (21:2). See GEHENNA; HELL.

Lake of Gennesaret. See GALILEE, SEA OF.

Lakkum. lak´uhm (Heb. *laqqûm H4373*, derivation uncertain). KJV Lakum. A town on the SE border of the tribal territory of NAPHTALI, named between JABNEEL and the JORDAN River (Josh. 19:33). Its precise location is uncertain, but some scholars identify it with modern Khirbet el-Mansurah, just SW of the S tip of the Sea of Galilee, at the head of Wadi Fejjas.

Lakum. See LAKKUM.

lamb. The principal words in Hebrew for "lamb," that is, the young of sheep, are *keśeb H4166* (Gen. 30:33 et al.) and *śeh H8445* (Gen. 22:7-8 et al.). The common term in Greek is *amnos G303*, but *arnion G768* is used almost thirty times Revelation (Rev. 5:6-13 et al.; elsewhere only in John 21:15).

See ANIMALS. The lamb was the principal animal of SACRIFICE among the Jews, being the offering each morning and each evening in the Mosaic system (Exod. 29:38-42), and especially on the SABBATH. Also the lamb was sacrificed on special days of religious significance. To the Jews the lamb represented innocence and gentleness. The prophets portrayed the tender compassion of God for his people under the figure of the shepherd and the lamb (Isa. 40:11), and the lamb was an important symbol of the ultimate intention of God for his people (11:6). The psalmist carried the imagery of the shepherd and the lamb to its most beautiful expression in Ps. 23. Likewise the lamb was the climax of prophetic symbolism of the suffering of God's people, the servant nation, which the NT found to be a prefiguring of Jesus (Isa. 53:7; Acts 8:32). See LAMB OF GOD.

Lamb of God. Jesus was called the Lamb of God by JOHN THE BAPTIST (Jn. 1:29, 36). Some have regarded that pronouncement to be a thematic statement of the contents of the fourth gospel, Jesus being presented throughout the document as the lamb of SACRIFICE to take away the sins of the world. Much speculation has centered on the OT reference believed to have been in the mind of John when he thus spoke of Jesus. The Mosaic lamb of the Passover has been suggested frequently because Jesus is thus identified by PAUL (1 Cor. 5:7). Naturally many have found the suffering lamb (Isa. 53) to have been foremost in his mind. Still others have sought to avoid any particular reference and have considered the lamb simply as the principal animal of sacrifice in the worship of God.

Two things about this designation as applied to Jesus were most notable: he was declared to be the lamb of God and his sacrifice was for the world. All other lambs in the sacrificial system had been offered by human beings under the commandment of God; but just as God had substituted his own provision of a lamb instead of ISAAC who was under ABRAHAM's hand, so God in Jesus provided his own Lamb. All other sacrifices of a lamb had been limited to the nation or to the individual; but the sacrifice of Jesus was worldwide, embracing all humanity in its scope. He was to take away the sins of the world. The lamb was a worthy symbol of Jesus, who in innocence patiently endured suffering as a substitute (Acts 8:32; 1 Pet. 1:19).

Of special interest is the use of the term *lamb* in Revelation, where it occurs twenty-eight times in symbolic reference to Christ. The introductory reference in Rev. 5:1-14 is to the Lamb triumphant; the description clearly identifies him as the Christ. He stood as "one slain," as if his throat had been cut in sacrifice; yet he was alive forevermore. He had seven horns, which probably were symbolic of his great power. He had seven eyes that represented his ceaseless vigilance for the people of God; thus the eyes were reinterpreted as the seven spirits of God, the fullness of God's Spirit working in behalf of his people. His attributes were those of God—OMNIPOTENCE and OMNISCIENCE.

lame. See DISEASES.

Lamech. lay´mik (Heb. *lemek H4347*, possibly "strong man"; Gk. *Lamech G3285*). **(1)** Son of METHUSHAEL and descendant of CAIN; the first polygamist (Gen. 4:18-24). Lamech was married to ADAH and ZILLAH. By Adah he produced JABAL, the first tent dweller and herder, and JUBAL, who invented the harp and flute, indicative of leisure time. By Zillah he begat TUBAL-CAIN, the first artificer in metals, and a daughter, NAAMAH. Lamech's poem in Gen. 4:23-24 is an example of early Hebrew poetry, with perfect parallelism. Lamech, drunk with self-confidence and self-sufficiency, was not willing to wait for God's justice to operate. He did not trust in God, but rather his weapons became his gods—a phenomenon paralleled in Mesopotamian religion. In Lamech, Cain's trend toward obstinate estrangement from God reached its climax.

(2) Son of METHUSELAH, descendant of SETH, and father of NOAH (Gen. 5:25-31; 1 Chr. 1:3; Lk. 3:36). This Lamech, weary because of the toil spent on the unfruitful land, expected the birth of his son (Noah) to remove the curse of ADAM (Gen. 5:29; cf. 3:17-19). Since the number ten represented completion or conclusion, Lamech hoped that the tenth generation from Adam would bring fulfillment of the Edenic promise. He had lived 182 years when Noah was born, and died at the age of 777.

lamed. lah´mid (Heb. *lāmed*, traditionally "ox-goad"). Also *lamedh*. The twelfth letter of the Hebrew alphabet (ל), with a numerical value of thirty. It is possibly named for the shape of the letter, which in its older form resembled a pointed stick. Its pronunciation corresponds approximately to that of English *l*.

lamentation. See MOURNING.

Lamentations, Book of. The third book among the five MEGILLOTH (Scrolls) in the Hebrew Bible; found after JEREMIAH in English Bibles. Its title in Hebrew is taken from the first word in the book, *ʾêkâ H377* ("How!"), and may express a deep sense of lament over the tragic reversal of events. In the SEPTUAGINT, the title is *Thrēnoi*, "funeral songs, dirges, laments," reflecting the Hebrew term *qînôt* (pl. of *qînāh H7806*), which is also used as a title for the book in the rabbinic writings. This Hebrew word designates a formal composition of grief arising from tragic misfortune (2 Sam. 1:17-27; Amos 5:1). Because of its position in the Megilloth, the book of Lamentations is read in synagogue worship on the fast of the ninth of AB, during the evening and morning services. This particular occasion commemorates the destruction of JERUSALEM by Babylonian forces in 586 B.C., and again by the Roman armies under Titus in A.D. 70.

The book comprises five poems lamenting the desolation that had overtaken the Holy City in 586 B.C. The first four compositions consist of acrostics: each verse of Lam. 1 and 2 commences with a word whose initial consonant is successively one of the twenty-two letters of the Hebrew alphabet (a slight variation of the regular order occurs in 2:16-17; 3:47-48; and 4:16-17). The third chapter is peculiar in that a triple alphabetical arrangement is followed, so that all three lines in each stanza commence with the same letter. The fifth chapter is not an acrostic, although like the others it contains twenty-two stanzas, and is a prayer rather than an elegy. Alphabetical forms of this kind probably served as a useful stimulus to memory at a time when MSS were rare and costly.

Some writers have regarded the mechanical structure of most of the book as incompatible with the grief and sincere penitence of the writer. These two ideas need not be inconsistent, however, particularly if the book was composed with a view to consistent liturgical usage. Judging from the manner in which it has survived among the Jews we may well believe that this was the intention of the author. The elegiac meter that characterizes the poems was occasionally employed in the writings of the prophets (e.g., Jer. 9:19-20; Ezek. 19) and some psalms (e.g., Ps. 84; 119).

Although in the Hebrew no name was attached to the book, the authorship was uniformly ascribed

Overview of LAMENTATIONS

Author: Anonymous, though traditionally attributed to the prophet JEREMIAH.

Historical setting: Probably written during the Babylonian EXILE, thus sometime between the fall of JERUSALEM (586 B.C.) and the fall of BABYLON to the Persians (538 B.C.).

Purpose: To express deep sorrow over the end of the theocracy and the destruction of Jerusalem and the TEMPLE; to urge confession for sin and REPENTANCE.

Contents: The book consists of five poems: Zion's devastation (Lam. 1); the anger of the Lord (ch. 2); despair and consolation (ch. 3); horrors of the destruction (ch. 4); prayer for restoration (ch. 5).

by ancient authorities to Jeremiah. The LXX added an introductory note stating that "Jeremiah lamented this lamentation over Jerusalem," but the traditional view of the authorship appears to be rooted in the elegy composed for the mourning period of the deceased Josiah (c. 609 B.C.). Many modern critics have envisaged several authors at work in the book, or else have assumed that Baruch, Jeremiah's secretary, was responsible for the work in its final form. The reasons adduced include the fact that the physical circumstances of the prophet would make the work of composition rather difficult, that there are certain implicit contradictions between the prophecy of Jeremiah and the book of Lamentations, and that some literary expressions characteristic of Jeremiah are lacking in Lamentations. Thus the thought of Lam. 2:9 that God no longer reveals himself in his prophets is held to be inconsistent with the thought of Jeremiah. Similarly the reference in Lam. 4:17 to the possibility of Egypt as a deliverer ill accords with the patriotism expressed by the prophet (Jer. 42:15-17; 43:12-13).

On the other hand, most of the poems appear intimately connected with the calamity of the exile. Lamentations 2 and 4 indicate that the author personally witnessed the tragedy of 586 B.C., while the remainder of the book may have been written in Babylonia in the early captivity. It seems improbable that the final chapter was written in Jerusalem after the return from exile, perhaps about 525 B.C., as has been suggested by some writers. The arguments for diversity of authorship do not seem particularly strong, though the possibility that the poems were recast in mnemonic form at a time subsequent to their original composition must not be overlooked. Until more decisive evidence is forthcoming, there seems little reason for questioning the substantial unity and traditional authorship of Lamentations.

The book bewails the siege and destruction of Jerusalem and sorrows over the sufferings of the inhabitants during this time. It makes poignant confession of sin on behalf of the people and their leaders, acknowledges complete submission to the divine will, and prays that God will once again favor and restore his people. The book may be outlined as follows:

I. The fallen city admits its sin and the justice of divine judgment (Lam. 1-2).

II. Lamentation; reassertion of divine mercy and judgment; prayer for divine intervention (chs. 3-4).

III. Further confession and prayers for mercy (ch. 5).

lamp. An instrument used for artificial lighting. Lamps are often mentioned in Scripture, but no description of their form and structure is given. Archaeology has recovered many specimens in a great variety of forms, from the early simple, shallow, saucerlike bowl (with one side slightly pointed for the lighted wick) to the later closed bowl (with only a hole on top to pour in the oil, a spout for the wick, and a handle to carry it). Lamps for domestic use were generally of terra-cotta or of bronze.

The use of lamps is mentioned in connection with the golden lamps in the tabernacle and the ten golden lamps in the temple (Exod. 25:37; 1 Ki. 7:49; 2 Chr. 4:20; 13:11; Zech. 4:2). As shown from their usage, the "lamps" of Gideon's soldiers (Jdg. 7:16 KJV) were doubtless torches (so NIV). The common NT mention of lamps is in connection with their household usage (Matt. 5:15; Mk. 4:21; Lk. 8:16; 11:33; 15:8). Such lamps were generally placed on a lampstand, usually a niche built into the wall. It appears that the Hebrews were accustomed to burning lamps overnight in their chambers, perhaps because of a dread of darkness, more likely to keep away prowlers. The use of oil-fed lamps in a marriage procession is mentioned in Matt. 25:1. Since such lamps contained only a few spoonfuls of oil, a reserve supply would be a necessity. The lighted lamp is also mentioned metaphorically to symbolize (1) God's word (Ps. 119:105), (2) God's guidance (2 Sam. 22:29; Ps. 18:28), (3) salvation (Isa. 62:1 KJV), (4) the human spirit

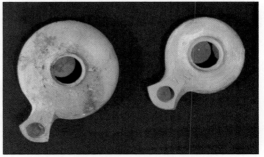

Herodian oil lamps discovered at Masada.

© Dr. James C. Martin

(Prov. 20:27), (5) outward prosperity (Prov. 13:9), (6) a son as successor (1 Ki. 11:36; 15:4).

lampstand. The Hebrew word *mĕnôrâ H4963*, always rendered "candlestick" in KJV, occurs forty-three times in the OT, and is more accurately rendered "lampstand" in NIV, because the "lights" were not candles at all, but olive-oil lamps. In the TABERNACLE, as constructed in the wilderness, the lampstand (described in Exod. 25:31-40) with its seven branches holding seven lamps of gold stood at the left as the priest entered the Holy Place. In the TEMPLE that SOLOMON built, there were ten lampstands of gold (2 Chr. 4:7), but they were placed in front of the Most Holy Place (1 Ki. 7:49; 2 Chr. 4:7). The term *mĕnôrâ* is rendered by the SEPTUAGINT with Greek *lychnia G3393*, which in turn is used in the NT both for the tabernacle lampstand (Heb. 9:2) and for the seven lampstands that represent the seven churches (Rev. 1:20 et al.).

lance. See ARMS AND ARMOR.

Land, Holy. See PALESTINE.

land crocodile. See ANIMALS (under *lizard*).

landmark. An object used to mark the boundary of a field. Landmarks were often such movable objects as a stone or a post. Since a cunning and unscrupulous individual could take advantage of his neighbor by shifting the location of such boundary marks, thus robbing him of part of his means of support, such removal of landmarks was prohibited by the Mosaic law (Deut. 19:14; 27:17; NIV, "boundary stone"). Hebrew piety denounced the act (Prov. 22:28; 23:10), and it was considered equal to theft (Job 24:2).

lane. This English term is used by the KJV once (Lk. 14:21; NIV, "alleys") to render a Greek noun that elsewhere is translated "street" (Matt. 6:2; Acts 9:11; 12:10).

languages. The first language spoken by the invading Israelite tribes in PALESTINE was HEBREW, a Semitic tongue related to Akkadian (the language of ASSYRIA and BABYLON), Arabic, Aramaic, and

This cuneiform tablet lists numerous foreign names with their Akkadian equivalents.

© Dr. James C. Martin. The British Museum. Photographed by permission.

other important ANE languages. Hebrew was especially close to the language of PHOENICIA, to the CANAANITE dialects of the tribes they dispossessed, and to the speech of MOAB. Hebrew, over the first centuries of the occupation of Palestine, was both the literary and colloquial language. It remained the literary language permanently. In colloquial use it was replaced by ARAMAIC. The date of this change is difficult to determine with precision. ELIAKIM's request to SENNACHERIB's field commander (2 Ki. 18:26) to speak not "in Hebrew in the hearing of the people" but in Aramaic—which as a common eastern language of diplomacy the leaders understood—shows that Hebrew was still the Jewish vernacular in 713 B.C. Such was still the case as late as NEHEMIAH, two centuries later.

The next evidence is from the NT, where phrases quoted in the Palestinian vernacular (e.g., TALITHA CUM in Mk. 5:41) are undoubtedly Aramaic. Before Aramaic replaced Hebrew, it had, of course, infiltrated its vocabulary. The other colloquial dialect of NT times was GREEK, which also provided the literary language for the NT writings. It is the Koine or common dialect of Greek that is thus represented—a simplified form that descended from Attic and became an alternative language in most of the Mediterranean basin, and especially in the kingdoms of ALEXANDER THE GREAT's successors. CHRIST spoke Aramaic, but undoubtedly understood Greek, and read the Scriptures in classical Hebrew. PAUL probably knew all three languages and used them with equal facility, with the likely addition of Latin.

lantern. This English term is used in Bible versions once to render Greek *phanos G5749*, which occurs only in Jn. 18:3. In that passage we are told that the soldiers and officials who went to arrest Jesus were carrying lanterns and torches (*lampas G3286*, usually translated "lamp"). In contrast to other versions, the NIV seems to regard *phanos* as meaning "torch" (which in fact was the earlier meaning of the term) and *lampas* as "lantern." It is possible that either or both of these terms refer to some kind of torch, although Romans in the time of Christ did have lanterns of cylindrical shape with translucent sides.

Laodicea. lay-od´i-see´uh (Gk. *Laodikeia G3293*; gentilic *Laodikeus G3294*, "Laodicean"). A wealthy city in Asia Minor founded by the Seleucid ruler Antiochus II (261-246 B.C.), and head of the "circuit" of "the seven churches in the province of Asia" (Rev. 1:4). The church in this city evidently had a close connection with the Christian community in Colosse (Col. 2:1; 4:13-16). Laodicea lay on one of the great Asian trade routes, and this insured its commercial prosperity. The city was a leading banking center, and it was no doubt the rich banking firms that in A.D. 60 financed the reconstruction after the great earthquake that destroyed it. Laodicea refused the Senate's earthquake relief. She was "rich and increased with goods" and had "need of

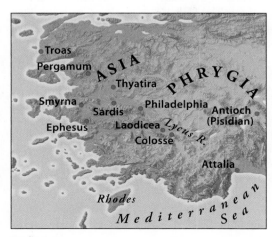

Laodicea.

nothing" (3:17 KJV). The Lycus Valley produced a glossy black wool, the source of black cloaks and carpets, for which the city was famous. Laodicea was also the home of a medical school and the manufacture of collyrium, a famous eye salve. The scornful imagery of the apocalyptic letter to Laodicea is obviously based on these activities. It also has reference to the emetic qualities of the soda-laden warm water from nearby Hierapolis, whose thermal springs ran into the Maeander. Laodicea's water supply also came from Hierapolis, and its vulnerability, together with the city's exposed position and its easy wealth, possibly caused the growth in the community of that spirit of compromise and worldly mindedness castigated in the Revelation.

Laodiceans, Epistle to the. In Col. 4:16 Paul urges the Colossians to exchange letters with the Laodiceans. A letter written by the Laodiceans to Paul is ruled out by the context ("from" here denotes present locality, not origin). There are three views of its identity: (1) The spurious *Epistle to the Laodiceans* found among Paul's letters in some Latin MSS from the sixth to the fifteenth centuries. Its twenty verses, being phrases strung together from Philippians and Galatians, are a forgery with no heretical motive. (2) A Pauline letter to the Laodiceans now lost. This is not improbable, though opponents hold it multiplies epistles unnecessarily. (3) Our Ephesians. This view is very probable if Ephesians is accepted as being encyclical, and it accounts for Marcion's title of Ephesians as "the epistle to the Laodiceans."

Lapidoth. See Lappidoth.

lapis lazuli. See minerals.

Lappidoth. lap´i-doth (Heb. *lappîdôt H4366*, possibly "flames, lightning strikes"). KJV Lapidoth. Husband of Deborah, the prophetess and leader of Israel (Jdg. 4:4). Some have speculated that there may be a connection between Lappidoth and Deborah's military associate, Barak (v. 6; the latter's name means "lightning"); in any case, the text clearly distinguishes between the two.

lapwing. See birds.

lasciviousness. This English term, meaning "lust, overt sexual desire," is used by the KJV to render Greek *aselgeia G816* in a number of passages (e.g., 2 Cor. 12:21; NIV, "debauchery"; NRSV, "licentiousness"). The Greek noun occurs eight times in the NT (Mk. 7:22; Rom. 13:13; 2 Cor. 12:21; Gal. 5:19; Eph. 4:19; 1 Pet. 4:3; 2 Pet. 2:2, 7, 18; Jude 4), and the reference is always to sensuality, particularly that which outraged public decency. There could be no place for such behavior in the Christian life.

Lasea. luh-see´uh (Gk. *Lasaia G3297*). A city of CRETE near FAIR HAVENS, the bay that the ship on which PAUL was being taken to Italy had reached with difficulty (Acts 27:8). Quite possibly ruins about 5 mi. (8 km.) E of Fair Havens are those of Lasea. Not much is known about this city, which has received little notice in surviving literature.

lash. See SCOURGE.

Lasha. lay´shuh (Heb. *lešaʿ H4388*, meaning unknown). A place marking one of the boundary points of the land of the CANAANITES, mentioned after SODOM, GOMORRAH, ADMAH, and ZEBOIIM (Gen. 10:19). Its location is unknown, although a number of identifications have been suggested, among them LAISH (surely too far N) and Callirrhoe (or Kallirhoe, a ravine E of the DEAD SEA to which HEROD the Great went for his health during his last illness; see ZERETH SHAHAR).

Lasharon. luh-shair´uhn (Heb. *laššārôn H4389*, "belonging to Sharon [the plain]"). A Canaanite royal city whose king was defeated by JOSHUA (Josh. 12:18). On the basis of a SEPTUAGINT reading, many scholars believe that the word is not the name of a city, but part of a phrase, distinguishing APHEK of SHARON from other cities of the same name.

last days, last judgment, last times. See ESCHATOLOGY.

Last Supper. See LORD'S SUPPER.

Latin. One of the Indo-European languages, Latin was the official medium of communication in the Roman empire (see ROME), and it was used in the provinces, such as JUDEA, in official acts and at the Roman courts. GREEK was the language of commerce; in PALESTINE itself, ARAMAIC was the language spoken in the rural districts and more remote towns, while in the cities both Aramaic and Greek were used. That is why the inscription on the CROSS of Christ was written in those three languages (Jn. 19:20). Hellenistic Greek borrowed many words from Latin and was otherwise influenced by this language, especially in the area of government. Many Latin names, such as PAUL (*Paulus*), are found in the NT.

Latin versions. See TEXT AND VERSIONS.

latter days. See ESCHATOLOGY.

latter rain. See RAIN.

lattice. A window covering made of crossed strips or bars of wood or metal and used as a screen. Latticework served a threefold purpose: (1) privacy, so that one might look out without being seen; (2) ventilation, so that a breeze might flow in and the sun's hot rays be kept out; and (3) decoration, so that a house or public building might be architecturally more attractive (Jdg. 5:28; 2 Ki. 1:2; Prov. 7:6 [KJV, "casement"]; Cant. 2:9).

laughter. Although sometimes associated with genuine JOY (Ps. 126:2; Eccl. 10:19; Lk. 6:21), laughter in the Bible more often denotes derision and mockery. Unbelievers laugh at Christ (Ps. 22:7; Matt. 9:24), at the righteous (Neh. 2:19; Job 12:4; Ps. 80:6), and at God's ordinances (2 Chr. 30:10); but their laughter will vanish (Prov. 1:26; Lk. 6:25; Jas. 4:9). God himself laughs at his enemies (Ps. 2:4; 37:13; 59:8). Believers sometimes laugh incredulously (Gen. 17:17; 18:12-15; 21:6), but they also are said to laugh in derision of the wicked (Job 22:19; Ps. 52:6; Isa. 37:22).

launderer's soap. See FULLER'S SOAP.

laver. See BASIN.

law. This English term most commonly means "a rule of conduct prescribed by a recognized authority"; in that sense it it roughly synonymous with such words as *commandment, ordinance, precept, statute*. In the Bible, the term very often refers specifically to the Mosaic law, that is, the COVENANT established by God through MOSES at SINAI. More generally, it can refer to the PENTATEUCH, the first five books of the OT. But in fact the primary Hebrew word for "law," *tôrâ H9368*, has an even broader meaning, namely, "guidance, instruction, teaching," whether human (Prov. 1:8b) or divine (Isa. 1:10; cf. TNIV and NRSV). This factor needs to be kept in mind when seeking to understand the notion of law in Scripture. The SEPTUAGINT's choice of Greek *nomos G3795* as the rendering of *tôrâ* is thought by some to have injected an extraneous legal element into the concept, but the NT use of this Greek term corresponds closely with OT teaching.

I. The moral law. It is plain from the Decalogue (Exod. 20:3-17; Deut. 5:7-21; see COMMANDMENTS, TEN) that morality is not to be derived from human standards and the verdict of society but from God and his declarations and one's relationship of subordination to him. Right and wrong are not determined by the voice of society but by the voice of God. The Ten Commandments declare the broad principles of God's moral law. We can find positive teaching as to the will of God for our lives in those commandments that are couched in the negative, and we can find admonition and prohibition in those framed as positive exhortations. The Decalogue constitutes the regulative core of REVELATION as to acceptable lines of human conduct. The first tablet of the law was considered to express our duty toward God (Exod. 20:3-11), and the second our duty toward other human beings (20:12-17). The NT seems to follow this division in summarizing the law, for Jesus said that it demands LOVE for God and love for one's neighbor comparable to the love that one has for oneself (Matt. 22:35-40).

The NT, rather than setting aside the moral law, reiterates its commands, develops more fully the germinal truths contained in it, and focuses attention on the spirit of the law as over against merely the letter. So it is that PAUL affirms there is but one God (Eph. 4:6) and cautions against IDOLATRY both directly and indirectly (Rom. 1:21-23;

1 Cor. 10:14). While the NT suggests an attitude toward the SABBATH somewhat different from that of Jewish legalism (Mk. 2:23-28) and comes to recognize the time of observance as the first day of the week (Acts 20:7; 1 Cor. 16:2), it preserves the observance as of divine institution and enriches its significance by associating with it Christ's RESURRECTION. So also, the NT emphasizes the law of love (Rom. 13:8-10; Gal. 5:14; Jas. 2:8) and selflessness and humility as representative of the mind of Christ (Phil. 2:3-8). Although the NT commandments are for the most part positive exhortations rather than warnings and prohibitions, the underlying principles are the same.

Scripture makes clear the function of the moral law. As the expression of the character and will of God, it sets forth the only standard of righteousness acceptable to him; but humans were without power to conform to that perfect standard. The law made them aware of their sinfulness (Rom. 7:7, 13), condemned them as unrighteous (7:9-11; Gal. 3:13; Jas. 2:9), and, having removed any hope of salvation through their own RIGHTEOUSNESS, brought them to the place where they would cast themselves on the grace of God and trust only in the righteousness and merit of the atoning Savior, Jesus Christ (Gal. 3:24).

Christians are free from the condemnation of the law (Rom. 8:2) since the righteousness of him who kept the law perfectly and who vicariously paid the penalty for the transgression of the law on the part of his people has been imputed to them. More than that, Christians are declared righteous by God (Rom. 4:5-6), renewed in righteousness and progressively sanctified as the HOLY SPIRIT applies the Word in their lives (2 Cor. 5:21; Gal. 5:16-26; 1 Thess. 5:23). The goal of the Christian is conformity to the moral image of God as manifested to them by the Incarnate Son (Eph. 4:13). So it is that Christians are under obligation to keep the moral law (cf. Matt. 5:19-48; Eph. 4:28; 5:3; 6:2; Col. 3:9; 1 Pet. 4:15), not as a condition of salvation, but that they may become more and more like their Father in heaven (Rom. 8:1-9; Eph. 4:13), and this because of love for the One who redeemed them (Rom. 13:8-10; 1 Jn. 5:2-3).

II. Social legislation. In the giving of the law at Sinai, Moses first communicated to the people

L

the body of principles, the Ten Words, and then the applicatory precepts. Careful study of the individual statutes shows the specific commands to be rooted in the basic principles set out in the Decalogue. OT laws of judicial, civil, or political nature are to be found in the block of legislative material known as the Book of the Covenant (Exod. 20:23—23:33), in the so-called Holiness Code (Lev. 17-26), and throughout most of the book of DEUTERONOMY (esp. Deut. 21-25).

Since human beings are inherently sinful and lawless, social life must come under regulations. So it was that in the OT times both Jews and Gentiles found themselves subject to law. Nor was the civil legislation binding on Israel much different from that of the heathen nations. The Code of HAMMURABI has much in common with the laws promulgated under Moses, and other ancient statutes are found among non-Jews as well as in Israel. Basic principles of right and wrong are the same everywhere and for all people, reflecting the work of the Holy Spirit in the realm of common grace. The difference was that in the Israelite theocracy the

laws regulating society were recognized as declared through God's prophets and with divine authority, whereas in other nations the authority behind the codes was the voice of tradition or the voice of the state.

A basic institution ordained of God, the FAMILY, was necessarily governed in its many relationships by various regulations that it might be preserved from corruption and dissolution. There were many prescriptions regarding MARRIAGE itself (Exod. 21-22; 34; Lev. 18; 21; Num. 5; 25; Deut. 7; 21-22; 24-25; 27). Within the family, children were to honor and obey their parents (Exod. 20:12; Deut. 5:16; 21:18-21; 27:16). And since the family circle might include servants, slaves, and strangers, there were laws pertaining to them also (Exod. 12; 21-22; Lev. 19; 22; 24-25; Num. 9; 15; 35; Deut. 1; 12; 14-16; 23-24; 27).

As might be expected, crimes against society were to be punished according to law. These might be of a moral nature, such as sexual violations or perversions (Exod. 20-22; Lev. 18-20; Num. 5; Deut. 5:22-25, 27). Again, they might be crimes against individuals, either their persons (Gen. 9; Exod. 20-23; Lev. 19; 24; Num. 35; Deut. 5; 19; 21-22; 24; 27) or their property (Exod. 20; 22; Lev. 6; 19; Deut. 5; 19; 23; 25; 27). Or the offenses might be against the state (Exod. 20; 23; Lev. 19; Deut. 5; 16; 19; 27). In addition to the laws already mentioned, other regulations governing property are to be found in Exod. 21-23; Lev. 6; 24-25; Num. 27; 36; and Deut. 21-22; 25.

OT legislation contained numerous stipulations about the operation of the state. Certain aspects of political organization were outlined (Exod. 22; Num. 1; 3-4; 26; 33; Deut. 17; 23). Specifications were made regarding the army (Num. 1-2; 10; 26; 31; Deut. 7; 11; 20-21; 23-24). Judicial prescriptions were set forth (Exod. 18; 20-21; 23; Lev. 5; 19; Num. 35; Deut. 1; 4-5; 16-17; 19; 25; 27), and provision was made for bringing to the people a knowledge of the law (Deut. 6; 11; 27; 31; Josh. 8).

Many Israelite laws were laws of kindness. Even the treatment of animals was subject to regulation (Exod. 23; 34; Lev. 22; 25; Deut. 22; 25). The general commandment of love, whether for friends or strangers, was invoked (Exod. 23; Lev. 19; Deut. 10). The poor, unfortunate, lowly, defenseless, and

© Dr. James C. Martin

Torah scroll.

needy were to be treated humanely (Exod. 21-23; Lev. 19; 23; 25; Deut. 14-16; 21-27).

The prescriptions of the law were to the end that there might be peace and order, whether in the operations of the state or the family or in other spheres of human interrelations. The dignity of the individual was to be preserved. A high premium was set on selflessness and consideration of others. God's wisdom and grace were manifest in the legislation given the Israelites through his servant Moses.

III. Religious legislation. Embodied in the OT are many laws governing the WORSHIP of God. Some are very general in nature, having to do with purity of worship. Large numbers of the laws concern the sanctuary, its priesthood, and the rites and ceremonies connected with it and the covenant relationship between the Israelites and their God. Some consist of prescriptions pertaining to special occasions of the religious year.

Basic principles of worship are outlined in the first table of the Decalogue (Exod. 20:3-11). They are then worked out into detailed applicatory legislation. Because the Lord is the only true God, exalted and holy, other so-called gods are not to be worshiped (Exod. 22-23; 34; Deut. 5-6; 8; 11; 17; 30), apostasy is a sin (Deut. 4:25-31; 27; 31:16; cf. Lev. 19; 26), and such occult arts as witchcraft, sorcery, and divination are not to be practiced (Exod. 22; Lev. 18-20; Deut. 18). So also, blasphemy is not to be tolerated (Exod. 22; Lev. 18-19; 24), and God's Sabbath Day is to be kept inviolate (Exod. 23; 31; 34-35; Lev. 19; 26; Num. 15).

Since the Lord is the only true God, his people are to study and keep his law (Lev. 18-20; 25; Num. 15; Deut. 4-8; 10-11; 22; 26-27; 30), as well as to separate themselves from the heathen and their religious practices (Exod. 22-23; 34; Lev. 18-20; Deut. 6-7; 12; 14; 18). They are to be a holy nation (Exod. 19; 22; Lev. 19; 26; Deut. 7; 14; 18; 26; 28), and they are to give to God the allegiance, love, gratitude, and obedient service due him (Exod. 23; 34; Lev. 19; 25; Deut. 4-6; 8; 10-11; 13-14; 17; 30-31).

When Moses was on Mount Sinai, God delineated in detail the pattern for the sanctuary (Exod. 25-27), and the TABERNACLE was built in conformity to that pattern (Exod. 35-38). Later its essential features were reproduced in the TEMPLE built by SOLOMON (2 Chr. 3-4). The sanctuary was in a special sense God's dwelling place among his people and spoke silently of his fellowship with them (Exod. 25:8, 22). As the place where God drew nigh to the people and they to him, it was designed to remind them of him—his splendor, his magnificence, his glory, his transcendence, his holiness, his presence, his mercy and forgiveness, his requirements of Israel, and his covenant headship. Through its structure and the regulations as to who might enter each part, God's holiness was emphasized.

The brazen ALTAR was for SACRIFICE and therefore implied the necessity of worship and ATONEMENT. As one approached the holy God, the laver was mute evidence of the fact that cleansing from defilement must first take place. The altar of INCENSE pointed to the importance of adoration and praise (Ps. 141:2; Isa. 6:3-4). The table of showbread suggested the need for dedication, and the golden LAMPSTAND perhaps indicated that the worshiper should reflect in his life the light that comes from God and which is ever to be linked with him. These conclusions rest on the assumption that the sanctuary furnishings in the outer court and in the Holy Place were for the purpose of instructing OT worshipers how they should draw near to God in adoration.

On the other hand, the symbolism of the Most Holy Place may be thought of as speaking of God in his approach to people. Through the tablets of the law in the ARK OF THE COVENANT, through the ark's cover, and through the CHERUBIM symbolizing the presence of God, the Lord said to his people, "I, God, am a spiritual Being here in your midst. My law accuses and condemns. Who can keep it? But I have provided a covering, a propitiation, an atonement. Despite sin, it is still possible for you to look forward to dwelling in my immediate presence." The veil testified that the time had not come, but the typology was unmistakable. The worshiper might come only as far as the court. The ordinary priest could enter the Holy Place. Only the high priest might enter the Most Holy Place, and that but once a year. The symbolism was plain: it was not a light thing to seek acceptance in the presence of the holy God, but there was indeed a way of approach.

L

L

The OT worshiper learned that through the offering of sacrifice God dealt with sin and granted forgiveness (Lev. 4:20), that through the shedding of blood there was atonement of sin (16:15-16), that the animal of the ceremony was reckoned as a substitute for the worshiper (16:20-22), that the sacrifices were perhaps not the full and final answer to the sin problem (since they must continue to be offered), that sacrifice without obedience to God's revelation was of no value (Isa. 1:10-17), and that God's Suffering Servant was to be a guilt offering (53:10). The Mosaic legislation prescribes the kinds of sacrifices and the details governing them: the whole burnt offering (Exod. 20; Lev. 1; 6; Deut. 12:27), the sin offering (Lev. 4-6; 8-10; Num. 15), the guilt offering (Lev. 5-7; 19; Num. 5), and the peace offering (Lev. 3; 7; 19; 22). Also the law had much to say about other offerings and sacrificial dues (Exod. 10; 13; 18; 22-23; 29-30; 34; Lev. 2-3; 6; 14; 19; 22-23; 27; Num. 3; 5-6; 8; 15; 18-19; 28; 30-31; Deut. 12; 14-18; 23; 26).

Through the priesthood, people came to understand that the transcendent, holy God cannot be approached in a casual way by sinful people but only by a mediator representing both God and human beings, that the mediator must be emblematic of HOLINESS and perfection, and that God deals with sin through the representative acts of the mediator. As to the concept of the priesthood, the focus of attention was narrowed from the whole nation (Exod. 19:6) to the PRIESTS and LEVITES and finally to one man, the high priest, whose acts on behalf of the people brought reconciliation. Many passages contain laws pertaining to the priesthood (Exod. 28-30; 39-40; Lev. 2:5-8, 10, 16; 21-24; 27; Num. 3-6; 15; 18; 31). The law codes regulated ceremonial cleanliness not only for the priests but also in reference to food (Exod. 12; 22-23; 34; Lev. 3; 7; 11; 17; 19-20; 22; Deut. 12; 14-15) and purification (Lev. 5:11—15:22; Num. 6; 19; 31; Deut. 21; 24).

The rite of CIRCUMCISION symbolized the taking away of defilement that the individual might be rightly related to God and a partaker of the covenant of grace. The FEASTS and festivals had significance that was partly historical, partly merely symbolical, partly typical. The Passover was a reminder of physical deliverance from bondage in Egypt (Exod. 12:17; Deut. 16:1). Sacred history

and prophecy often blend, and so the observance of the Passover might well have had this message: As God delivered, so he *will* deliver. The central sacrifice in this festival as in others pointed to a need for atonement just as did the daily and weekly sacrifices did, and the unleavened bread and the meat and drink offerings pointed to the importance of a holy, fruitful life before God. As a harvest festival, Pentecost signified rejoicing and the place of thanksgiving to God in the life of the covenant participant (Deut. 16:9-10), especially in the light of deliverance from Egypt (16:12). Except for the significance of the extra sacrifices, the Feast of Tabernacles (Exod. 23; Lev. 23; Num. 29; Deut. 16) may have been to the Jews little more than a reminder of God's love and care during the period of the nation's youth when the Jews wandered in the wilderness and were tested by deprivation that they might learn to trust in God and his provision. On the other hand, the Day of Atonement emphasized the need for the expiation of sin, the atoning nature of the blood sacrifice, and the idea of substitution in relation to atonement.

IV. NT teaching. The writers of the NT spell out the antitypes involved. As God's dwelling among his people was symbolized in the OT through the Garden of Eden, the tabernacle, and the temple, so the new covenant tells us that God as the Son "lived for a while among us" (Jn. 1:14), that he indwells the individual believer (1 Cor. 6:19) and the church (2 Cor. 6:16), and that the final and everlasting dwelling place of God will be heaven itself (Heb. 9:24; Rev. 21:3). In the new dispensation, that which was symbolized by the Passover celebration and circumcision came to be represented and defined more clearly in the LORD'S SUPPER and Christian BAPTISM. The types and shadows of the ceremonial law gave way to antitypes.

The cross replaced the brazen altar. There was no longer a sanctuary laver but a laver of regeneration, "a washing of rebirth" (Tit. 3:5). "The prayers of the saints" (Rev. 5:8) took the place of the altar of incense. Dedicated lives came to be offered (Rom. 12:1-2) rather than symbolic showbread, and good works produced by children of the light made unnecessary the golden lampstand. Instead of the mercy seat as a "propitiatory covering," Christ became the PROPITIATION for the sins of his people (Rom. 3:25; 1 Jn. 2:2; 4:10); and sinners redeemed and in fellowship with God became the prophetic fulfillment of the symbolic cherubim, which were basically human in form (Ezek. 1:5; 10:21) and always associated with the presence of the Lord (Gen. 3:24; Ps. 18:10; Ezek. 1; 10; 28). The Lord Jesus was seen to be God's Passover LAMB (1 Cor. 5:7), a perfect, all-sufficient sacrifice (Eph. 5:2; Heb. 7:27; 9:11-14). As *the* High Priest, Christ made RECONCILIATION (Heb. 2:17) and lives to make intercession for his people (7:25).

As a covenant child, our Lord was related to the ceremonial law as shown by his circumcision (Lk. 2:21) and his presence at the temple at the Passover feast (2:42). He instructed lepers to carry out the provisions of the law (17:14). He drove from the temple those who defiled it (Matt. 21:12-13). He and his disciples were accustomed to go to Jerusalem at feast time (Jn. 7:37; 13:1, 29). Christ spoke negatively regarding the traditions of the Jews but not of the ceremonial law as set forth in the OT. Yet he indicated that the time was coming when the ritual of the law would give place to spiritual worship (Jn. 4:24).

The apostolic view of the law, especially in relation to the doctrine of grace, has always caused much debate, and modern scholarship has intensified the disagreements. Some general observations may be made, however. In the transitional period after the cross, the resurrection, and the ascension, conditions in each case determined whether the stipulations of the law should be observed. PAUL might circumcise TIMOTHY (Acts 16:3) but not TITUS (Gal. 2:3-4). He could assure the CORINTHIANS that circumcision in the flesh was not essential for salvation (1 Cor. 2:2; 7:18-19); and, in writing to the GALATIANS, he could argue strongly against the contentions of the JUDAIZERS (Gal. 2:4-5; 5:1-12) in line with the decisions of the Jerusalem Council (Acts 15). The argument of the book of Hebrews is that the types and shadows of the ceremonial law have passed away with the coming of Christ, the perfect High Priest, who as the Lamb of God offered himself on GOLGOTHA that he might satisfy every demand of the law and purchase salvation for his people.

By means of the ceremonial law, God spoke in picture language of the salvation he was to effect through the life and death of the Incarnate Son. Therefore, it was necessarily imperfect and temporary. The social legislation governing Israel was designed for a particular culture at a given period of history, and so it, too, was only for a time; yet its principles are timeless and applicable to all generations. God's moral law is in force everywhere and at all times, for it is a reflection of his very being. It has never been abrogated, nor indeed can be.

law, oral. See TALMUD.

lawgiver. The KJV uses this term in several passages where a more appropriate rendering is "staff, scepter" (Gen. 49:10; Num. 21:18; Ps. 60:7; 108:8) or "leader, ruler" (Deut. 33:21). The meaning "lawgiver" is possible in Isa. 33:22 (so NIV, but NRSV has "ruler," NJPS "prince") and certainly correct in Jas. 4:12; both of these passages reflect the view that God is the only absolute lawgiver. Insofar as God used MOSES to proclaim the divine law to the Israelites (Jn. 1:17; 7:19; cf. Gal. 3:19), this Hebrew leader may be regarded as a "lawgiver," but the term is not explicitly applied to him.

lawlessness, man of. See ANTICHRIST.

lawyer. See OCCUPATIONS AND PROFESSIONS.

laying on of hands. A ceremony of ancient origin with different meanings, depending upon its occurrence in various contexts. In the OT this act symbolizes (1) the parental bestowal of inheritance rights (Gen. 48:14-20); (2) the gifts and rights of an office (Num. 27:18, 23; Deut. 34:9); and (3) substitution. The latter involves three categories: (a) substitution of an animal for one's guilt (Exod. 29:10, 15, 19; Lev. 1:4; 3:2, 8, 13; 4:4, 15, 24, 29, 33; 8:14, 18, 22; 16:21; cf. Gen. 22:9-13); (b) substitution of the LEVITES for the FIRSTBORN of the other tribes (Num. 8:10-19); and (c) substitution of one's innocence for another's guilt (Lev. 24:13-16; Deut. 13:9; 17:7).

In the NT the laying on of hands can indicate (1) the bestowal of blessings and benediction (Matt. 19:13, 15; cf. Lk. 24:50); (2) the restoration of health (Matt. 9:18; Acts 9:12, 17); (3) the reception of the HOLY SPIRIT in BAPTISM (Acts 8:17,

19; 19:6); and (4) the gifts and rights of an office (Acts 6:6; 13:3; 1 Tim. 4:14; 2 Tim. 1:6).

Lazarus. laz´uh-ruhs (Gk. *Lazaros G3276*, from Heb. *laꜤzār*, abbreviated form of *ꜢelꜤāzār H540*, "God has helped"). (1) Brother of MARTHA and MARY, who lived in BETHANY. Lazarus, during Christ's absence, became sick and died; Christ, after some delay, returned and raised him from death (Jn. 11:1—12:19). The following factors enhance the importance of this miracle: (a) the number of days (four) between death and resurrection (11:39), (b) the number of witnesses involved (11:45; 12:17-18), (c) the evident health of Lazarus after the event (12:1, 2, 9), and (d) the significance of the event among the Jews (11:53; 12:10-11).

This miracle (a) illustrates Christ's sympathy (Jn. 11:5, 11, 34-35) and power (11:40-45), (b) manifests the purposiveness of his MIRACLES (11:4, 40; 20:31), (c) gives concrete backing to the truth of Lk. 16:30-31, (d) affords opportunity for eschatological teaching (Jn. 11:23-25), and (e) precipitates the crucifixion (11:45-53; 12:9-19).

The silence of the Synoptic Gospels regarding this event is explainable: (a) the miracle was outside their scope; (b) it was not the leading accusation brought against Christ (cf. Matt. 26:61-66); (c) it was indirectly confirmed by the "envy" they attribute to the Jews (27:18); and (d) it did not fit their purpose for writing as it did John's (Jn. 20:31).

(2) In a parable of Jesus, Lazarus was the name of a beggar who died and went to ABRAHAM's BOSOM (Lk. 16:19-31). The passage illustrates these truths: (a) destiny is settled at death; (b) no purgatory awaits the righteous; and (c) sinners have sufficient warning now.

laziness. See IDLENESS.

lead (metal). See MINERALS.

leaf. Although this term is sometimes used literally in the Bible (e.g., Gen. 3:7), it more often occurs in figurative contexts illustrating a variety of concepts: (1) a distressed and nervous spirit (Lev. 26:36; Job 13:25), (2) the spiritual productivity of the righteous (Ps. 1:3; Prov. 11:28; Jer. 17:8), (3) the spiritual unproductivity of the wicked (Isa. 1:30),

(4) the completeness of God's judgment (Isa. 34:4; Jer. 8:13), (5) the frailty and evanescence of man (Isa. 64:6), (6) the blessings of messianic times (Ezek. 47:12), (7) the unfruitfulness of Israel (Ezek. 17:9 KJV; Matt. 21:19; Mk. 11:13), (8) the nearness of the eschatological judgment (Matt. 24:32; Mk. 13:28), (9) the glory of an earthly kingdom (Dan. 4:12, 14, 21), and (10) the glory and fruitfulness of the heavenly kingdom (Rev. 22:2).

Leah. lee´uh (Heb. *lēꜢâ H4207*, possibly "wild cow" [but not in a pejorative sense; cf. RACHEL, "ewe"]). Eldest daughter of LABAN, granddaughter of BETHUEL, and first wife of JACOB (Gen. 29:16). Leah is described as "tender eyed" (29:17 KJV), which may mean that she did not have a positive appearance (cf. NIV, "weak"; but NRSV, "lovely"). Leah became the mother of REUBEN, SIMEON, LEVI, JUDAH, ISSACHAR, ZEBULUN, and DINAH (29:31-35; 30:17-21). Loyal to Jacob (31:14-16), she returned with him to CANAAN, where, at her death, she was buried in MACHPELAH (49:31). Two of her sons (Levi and Judah) became progenitors of prominent tribes in Israel, and through Judah, Jesus Christ came (49:10; Mic. 5:2; Matt. 2:6; Heb. 7:14; Rev. 5:5; cf. Ruth 4:11).

leather. The skin of certain animals after it has been specially treated. Those who performed this work as a trade were called tanners (Acts 10:32). Leather was an article of clothing (Lev. 13:48; Heb. 11:37). However, JOHN THE BAPTIST (Matt. 3:4) and his prototype, ELIJAH (2 Ki. 1:8), are the only ones specifically mentioned as wearing "a leather belt." Leather was used also for armor, shoes, containers, and writing material.

leaven. A general term for agents that produce fermentation and cause dough to rise. It usually refers to yeast (the term used consistently by the NIV), which is a specific fungus of the genus *Saccharomyces*. BREAD was made to rise by putting a piece of sour dough (from a previous batch of dough) in the flour, bringing on fermentation of the whole. Leavened bread was a regular part of the diet of ancient Israel (Hos. 7:4). Bread made in haste without allowing it to rise is the UNLEAVENED BREAD often mentioned in Scripture (Gen. 19:3;

Exod. 12:15; Jdg. 6:19; 1 Sam. 28:24; et al.). The haste to depart from Egypt left no time for bread to rise, therefore the people carried with them dough and kneading troughs (Exod. 12:34, 39). In memorial of the EXODUS and its hurried flight (Exod. 12:11, 39; Deut. 16:3), Israel was commanded to cast out leaven from the house annually and to eat unleavened bread for seven days.

The significant thing about leaven is its power, which may become a symbol of either good or evil. Jesus, in the parable of the leaven (Matt. 13:33; Lk. 13:21), used the working of yeast to teach the pervasiveness of the KINGDOM OF GOD, which eventually transforms the world. The small bit of leaven—the Word—has power to accomplish this great result. On the other hand, some, insisting that leaven in Scripture is always a symbol of evil, attempt to make the parable a picture of the true teaching being mingled with corrupt and corrupting false doctrine, resulting in the final apostasy of the professing church. One's approach to this issue is ordinarily determined by a prior decision on the question of whether the NT outlook for the kingdom is optimistic or pessimistic.

Jesus did use leaven as a symbol of undesirable teaching when he warned against "the yeast of the Pharisees and Sadducees" (Matt. 16:6, 11-12; cf. Mk. 8:15; Lk. 12:1). PAUL also employed the term negatively as a symbol of the pervasiveness of evil

(1 Cor. 5:6). Here malice and evil are the leaven that need to be replaced by sincerity and truth so that the true Passover may be celebrated (vv. 7-8; cf. also Gal. 5:9 RSV).

Lebana. See LEBANAH.

Lebanah. li-bay´nuh (Heb. *lĕbānāh H4245* [one Hebrew ed. has *lĕbānāʾ* in Neh. 7:38], "white" or "full moon"). Ancestor of a family of temple servants (NETHINIM) who returned from BABYLON (Ezra 2:45; Neh. 7:48 [most versions, "Lebana"]).

Lebanon. leb´uh-nuhn (Heb. *lĕbānôn H4248*, "white [mountain]"). The name of a mountainous region in PHOENICIA just inland from the coast (called simply "Mount Lebanon," in Jdg. 3:3; NIV, "the Lebanon mountains"). Its area corresponds roughly to that of the modern state of Lebanon (but the latter includes also the strip of land on the coast as well as the Beqaᶜ Valley and the western slopes of the Antilebanon mountains). The snow-clad range extends in a NE direction for 100 mi. (160 km.) from TYRE to ARVAD. Its name alludes to the whiteness either of the fossil-bearing limestone cliffs or the snowy crests of this mountain system. Rising precipitously from the MEDITERRANEAN (cf. Josh. 9:1), Lebanon proper averages c. 6,000 ft. (1,830 m.) above sea level (cf. the steep grades on

Looking NE through the Beqaᶜ Valley with the lower ridges of the Antilebanon mountains in the background.

© Dr. James C. Martin

L

the present Beirut-Damascus highway), with peaks rising to c. 10,200 ft. (3,110 m.); but the elevation then drops to 2,300 ft. (700 m.) for 10 mi. (16 km.) across the ORONTES River Valley. East of this "Valley of Lebanon" (Josh. 11:17; 12:7), however, rises the Antilebanon range, the southernmost promontory of which is Mount HERMON, whose peak at 9,383 ft. (2,860 m.) remains visible as far S as JERICHO. The melting snow of these watersheds (Cant. 4:15; Jer. 18:14) creates the Orontes, flowing northward; the ABANA, watering DAMASCUS to the east; the westward-flowing Leontes or Litany; and the JORDAN, meandering southward through PALESTINE to the DEAD SEA. Yet these same peaks desicate the moisture-laden western winds, causing desert farther east.

Lebanon's southern slopes grade into the foothills of GALILEE, and the gorge of the Litany marks out a natural NW boundary for Israel (Deut. 11:24; 2 Ki. 19:23). Strictly speaking, Lebanon lies outside Palestine and, though included in God's promise, it was never totally occupied (Josh. 13:5; though cf. its eschatological possession, Ezek. 47:15-16). Its isolated crags, however, supported watchtowers (Cant. 7:4) and refuge points (Jer. 22:20, 23) and came to symbolize the exalted status of Judah's royal house (Jer. 22:6; Ezek. 17:3).

Ancient Lebanon was heavily forested with varieties of budding foliage (Ps. 72:16; Isa. 29:17; Nah. 1:4), including the Phoenician juniper, which resembles the cypress (1 Ki. 5:8; 2 Ki. 19:23), but above all the great cedars of Lebanon (1 Ki. 4:33). Biblical poetry praises the fragrance of their wood (Cant. 3:6-9; cf. 4:11 and Hos. 14:6 where Lebanon means trees, per Isa. 10:34; 40:16), their height as symbolic of dignity or pride (Cant. 5:15; Isa. 2:13), and their growth and resistance to decay (Ps. 92:12). The psalmist's inspired thought thus advances to the corresponding greatness of the Creator, who both plants the cedars (104:16) and shatters them by his voice (29:5). The Lebanons were famous also for choice wine (Hos. 14:7), for thorny plants, and for beasts such as the lion and leopard (2 Ki. 14:9; Isa. 40:16; Cant. 4:8). "The glory of Lebanon" climaxes Isaiah's prophetic descriptions (Isa. 35:2; 60:13).

Coastal Lebanon was early inhabited by Phoenicians (Josh. 13:5-6), skilled in the employment of its cedars for civil and marine construction

(Ezek. 27:4-5), while its sparser inland population was HIVITE (Josh. 11:3; Jdg. 3:3). Lebanon is cited in JOTHAM's fable against SHECHEM (Jdg. 9:15; cf. the reference to fire hazard), as well as in JEHOASH's fable against AMAZIAH over three centuries later (2 Ki. 14:9; 2 Chr. 25:18). King SOLOMON contracted with HIRAM of Tyre for the use of Lebanon's cedars in the Jerusalem TEMPLE (1 Ki. 5:6-18; cf. Ezra 3:7, concerning the second temple also), 10,000 workers per month hewing the timbers and floating them in great rafts along the Mediterranean coast. Solomon likewise erected government buildings and palaces in his capital, including a hall and armory called "the Palace of the Forest of Lebanon" from its rows of cedar pillars and paneling (1 Ki. 7:2-7; 10:17, 21; Isa. 22:8). The king's Lebanese building projects (cf. 1 Ki. 10:27) led him to construction work in Lebanon itself, at least portions of which came within his widespread domains (1 Ki. 9:19; Cant. 4:8).

Subsequent advances by the pagan empires of antiquity furthered both the conquest and the ruthless exploitation of Lebanon's resources (Isa. 33:9). Egyptians, Assyrians, and Greeks left their successive inscriptions at the mouth of the Dog River (Nahr el-Kelb); and Ezekiel compares the destruction of ASSYRIA's king with the felling of cedars of Lebanon (Ezek. 31:3, 15-16; cf. Zech. 11:1). Habakkuk bewails the violence done also by BABYLON in cutting down these forest giants (Hab. 2:17; cf. Isa. 14:8). By the days of Justinian (A.D. 527-565) the once-extensive groves had suffered heavy depletion, and most of the remainder were destroyed early in the twentieth century to supply fuel for the Beirut-Damascus railway. Conservation projects, however, have in recent times attempted reforestation.

Lebanon, House (Palace) of the Forest of. See FOREST.

Lebaoth. li-bay'oth (Heb. *lĕbāʾôt H4219*, "lionesses"). One of the "southernmost towns of the tribe of Judah in the Negev toward the boundary of Edom" (Josh. 15:32; cf. v. 21). The site is unknown. Lebaoth is thought to be the same as BETH LEBAOTH (19:6), apparently later known as BETH BIRI (1 Chr. 4:31).

Lebbaeus. li-bee´uhs (Gk. *Lebbaios G3304* [not in NIV], corresponding to the Heb. or Aram. name *libay*, "heart"). According to the KJV (following the majority of Greek MSS and some ancient versional evidence), one of the twelve disciples was "Lebbaeus, whose surname was Thaddaeus" (Matt. 10:3; both in this passage and in Mk. 3:18, some MSS read Lebbaeus only instead of Thaddaeus). See THADDAEUS.

Leb Kamai. leb´kuh-mi´ (Heb. *lēb qāmāy H4214*, "heart of my adversaries"). NRSV Leb-qamai. In an oracle against BABYLON, God announces that he will stir up a destroying spirit (or wind) against "the people of Leb Kamai" (Jer. 51:1; KJV, "them that dwell in the midst of them that rise up against me"). It is generally thought, however, that the term is a code name for CHALDEA. See also SHESHAK.

Lebo Hamath. lee´boh-hay´muhth (Heb. *lēbōʾ ḥāmāt H4217*, "entrance of Hamath"). A place on the S border of the territory controlled by HAMATH, regarded in the OT as the ideal N border of the Promised Land of Israel. However, it was only under DAVID and SOLOMON, and later under JEROBOAM II, that the territory of Israel extended so far (Num. 13:21; 34:8; Josh. 13:5; Jdg. 3:3; 1 Ki. 8:65; 2 Ki. 14:25; 1 Chr. 13:5; 2 Chr. 7:8; Amos 6:14). EZEKIEL prophesied that some day it would be the boundary of the ideally restored Israel (Ezek. 47:15-20). The KJV and other versions, taking the term as a general description, render it "the entrance of Hamath" or the like, but it is now generally thought to be the actual name of a particular region or city. The precise location of Lebo Hamath has been debated. It is now generally identified with modern Lebweh, a town about 45 mi. (72 km.) N of DAMASCUS.

Lebonah. li-boh´nah (Heb. *lēbônāh H4228*, "frankincense"). A town in the hill country of EPHRAIM, mentioned only once when the writer of Judges gives the location of SHILOH, which is said to be "east of the road that goes from Bethel to Shechem, and to the south of Lebonah" (Jdg. 21:19). Lebonah is probably to be identified with modern el-Lubban, about 3 mi. (5 km.) WNW of Shiloh and 10 mi. (16 km.) SSW of SHECHEM.

Lecah. lee´kuh (Heb. *lēkâ H4336*, meaning unknown). TNIV Lekah. Son of Er and great-grandson of JUDAH (1 Chr. 4:21). Many believe, however, that Lecah is the name of an otherwise unknown town founded by Er (according to the view that "father" here and in some other genealogical passages means "founder" or "chief citizen").

lectionary. A book of biblical lections (i.e., lessons, readings) used for worship services. The term is used especially of Greek MSS in which Scripture portions are written, not in the order in which they appear in the Bible, but according to the schedule set for the church calendar. They are of great value in NT textual studies. See TEXT AND VERSIONS (NT).

ledge. This English term is used to render several Hebrew words referring, for example, to a rim half way between the base and the top of the ALTAR in the TABERNACLE (Exod. 27:5; 38:4), or to two projections forming part of the altar described in Ezekiel's vision of a future TEMPLE (Ezek. 43:14, 17, 20; 45:19).

leech. See ANIMALS.

leeks. See PLANTS.

lees. A term used by the KJV and other versions for the dregs that settle at the bottom of wine jars and wineskins. It renders Hebrew *šĕmārîm* (pl. of *šemer H9069*), which occurs in four passages (Ps. 75:8 [here the KJV has "dregs"]; Isa. 25:6 [NIV, "aged wine"]; Jer. 48:11; Zeph. 1:12). WINE gained strength and flavor by being allowed to remain on the lees, and such wine was regarded as superior to the newly fermented product. The word is used in the OT only in a figurative sense.

left-handed. This description is used only regarding warriors from the tribe of BENJAMIN. They include EHUD, one of the judges (Jdg. 3:15); 700 soldiers who "could sling a stone at a hair and not miss" (20:16); and a group of ambidextrous relatives of SAUL who joined DAVID in ZIKLAG (1 Chr. 12:2).

leg. Several Hebrew terms may be rendered "leg," such as *keraʿ H4157*, found in OT passages dealing

L

with sacrificial rituals and referring to the shank or splint-bone (Exod. 12:9; Lev. 1:9, 13; et al.). It is also used of the bending hind legs of locusts that were permitted for food (Lev. 11:21), and it formed the basis for an illustration of divine judgment (Amos 3:12). The narrow part of the THIGH was considered one of the choicest pieces of the sacrificial animal, and was reserved for the use of the priests. Animal bones from the upper portion of the right foreleg have been recovered from the debris of a Canaanite temple at LACHISH. These bones evidently comprised the remains of the priestly perquisites, suggesting that the rest of the sacrifice had been eaten by the worshipers outside the sanctuary or in some adjoining room. There was little to indicate that the bones had been burned, and presumably the meat had been cooked by boiling (cf. 1 Sam. 2:15). This evidence provides an authentic historical background for the ritual prescriptions (Lev. 7:32 et al.).

legion. The major unit in the Roman army, consisting of several thousand soldiers. In the NT the word, representing a vast number, is used only in the Gospels and with reference to angels and demons (Matt. 26:53; Mk. 5:9, 15; Lk. 8:30). A division of infantry at full strength consisted of about 6,000 Roman soldiers. Each division was divided into ten COHORTS, and each cohort was further divided into six centuries (see CENTURION). Each subdivision, as well as the large whole, had its own officers and its own standards.

Lehabim. See LEHABITES.

Lehabites. li-hay´bits (Heb. *lĕhābîm H4260*). Also Lehabim. One of the people groups descended from MIZRAIM (Egypt), son of HAM (Gen. 10:13; 1 Chr. 1:11). Nothing is known about them, but many scholars suggest that the word is either a textual corruption or an alternate form of *lûbîm*, "Libyans." See LIBYA.

Lehi. lee´hi (Heb. *lĕḥî H4306*, "cheek, jawbone," possibly in the fig. sense of "border"). A site in JUDAH where SAMSON slew 1,000 PHILISTINES with the jawbone of a donkey (Jdg. 15:9, 14, 19; cf. v. 17, "Ramath Lehi"). There has been much debate

regarding the identification of Lehi. One popular proposal is Khirbet eṣ-Ṣiyyaj, which lies some 4 mi. (6 km.) E of TIMNAH (cf. 14:1-2). The evidence for this and other identifications, however, is very ambiguous. It has also been suggested that Lehi is a general term denoting the entire borderline between Judah and Philistia.

Lekah. lee´kuh. TNIV form of LECAH.

Lemuel. lem´yoo-uhl (Heb. *lĕmûʾēl H4345*, "belonging to God"). The reputed author of Prov. 31, who repeats his mother's teachings about good government, the dangers of sex and wine, and (if his sayings include vv. 9-29) the virtues of a noble wife. Rabbinic tradition equates Lemuel with SOLOMON, but modern scholars reject this view. Some translations, such as RSV and NJPS, understand the Hebrew term *maśśāʾ H5363* ("oracle," v. 1) as a proper name, making Lemuel king of MASSA.

lend. See BORROW.

length. See WEIGHTS AND MEASURES.

lentil. See PLANTS.

leopard. See ANIMALS.

leper, leprosy. See DISEASES.

Leshem. lee´shem (Heb. *lešem H4386*). An alternate form of LAISH (only in Josh. 19:47).

lethech, lethek. lee´thik. See WEIGHTS AND MEASURES.

letter. This English word is used in various senses to translate several different terms in both Testaments. For example, Hebrew *ʾiggeret H115* (2 Chr. 30:1, 6; Neh. 2:7-9; 6:5, 17, 19; Esth. 9:26, 29), meaning an official or commercial communication, refers to a tablet of a specific small size with a clay envelope upon which the sender and addressee were noted and on occasion some of the contents were indicated. In the NT, Greek *gramma G1207* can refer to a written communication (e.g., Acts 28:21), but more common is the meaning "letter

This small clay tablet is one of the famous Tell el-Amarna letters (c. 1350 B.C.). In it, Burna-Buriash II writes to Amenhotep III of Egypt, requesting more gold with the next exchange of presents.

[of the alphabet], written character" (cf. 2 Cor. 3:6-7; Gal. 6:11). Paul uses it in the sense of "written code," contrasted with *pneuma G4460*, "Spirit/spirit" (Rom. 2:27, 29; 7:6). Another Greek term is the familiar *epistolē G2186*, which occurs more than twenty times. See EPISTLE.

Letushim. See LETUSHITES.

Letushites. li-too´shits (Heb. *lĕṭûšîm H4322*, possibly "sharpened ones"). Also Letushim. A people group descended from DEDAN, grandson of ABRAHAM and KETURAH (Gen. 25:3). Neither this tribe nor the related ASSHURITES and LEUMMITES have been identified, but they probably inhabited parts of N ARABIA.

Leummim. lee-uh´mim. See LEUMMITES.

Leummites. lee-uh´mits (Heb. *lĕʾummîm H4212*, possibly "hordes" or "tribesmen"). Also Leummim. A people group descended from DEDAN, grandson of ABRAHAM and KETURAH (Gen. 25:3). See LETUSHITES.

Levant. luh-vant´. A modern name applied to the countries that border the E end of the MEDITERRANEAN Sea: Turkey, Syria, Lebanon, Israel, and Egypt.

Levi. lee´vi (Heb. *lēwî H4290*, by popular etymology related to *lāwāh H4277*, "to join, attach" [Gen. 29:34], but actual derivation disputed; gentilic *lēwî H4291*, "Levite"). (1) Third son of JACOB and LEAH, and ancestor of the tribe bearing his name (Gen. 29:34; 35:23; Exod. 1:2; 1 Chr. 2:1). When SHECHEM the HIVITE assaulted DINAH, her brothers Levi and SIMEON led in executing vengeance by killing all the males and pillaging the city of Shechem (Gen. 34:25-31; cf. Jacob's disapproval in 49:5-7). Levi's three sons, GERSHON, KOHATH, and MERARI, were born before the EXODUS from EGYPT. The descendants of Levi are called LEVITES, but because they were especially chosen to assist the PRIESTS, this term took on the sense of a religious office, almost meaning "ministers." Although AARON was a descendant of Levi (through Kohath), he and his progeny were granted the office of the priesthood and thus were distinguished from the Levites. The tribe of Levi did not receive a share of the territory in Canaan, for the Lord himself was their inheritance (Num. 18:20). See LEVITICAL CITIES.

(2) Son of Melki, included in the GENEALOGY OF JESUS CHRIST (Lk. 3:24).

(3) Son of Simeon, included in the GENEALOGY OF JESUS CHRIST (Lk. 3:29).

(4) Son of ALPHAEUS; he was a TAX COLLECTOR (publican) who later became one of the twelve apostles (Mk. 2:14-17; Lk. 5:27-32). In the Gospel of Matthew he is always called MATTHEW instead of Levi (Matt. 9:9-13). The name does not appear in any of the formal lists as a variant of Matthew.

Leviathan. li-vi´uh-thuhn (Heb. *liwyātān H4293*, possibly "twisting one"). There can be no doubt that this name is basically the same as that found

L

in Ugaritic documents for Lotan (Litan), the sea-monster killed by Baal and called "the crooked serpent" (cf. Isa. 27:1). All five occurrences of the term in the OT (Job 3:8; 41:1; Ps. 74:14; 104:26; Isa. 27:1) are in poetic passages and belong to "dead mythology," that is, old mythic concepts employed without suggestion that they are still believed. Because Leviathan is merely poetic imagery, there is no absolute consistency in the OT use of the term. For example, the use in Isa. 27:1 is part of an eschatological section (chs. 24-27) where the term refers to the future forces of lawlessness in terms of past chaos. In Job 41:1 Leviathan seems to be the crocodile. See animals (under *crocodile* and *Leviathan*), and cf. the use of Rahab (monster), another mythological figure (26:12).

levirate marriage. A law of Moses which states that if two brothers live together, and one of them dies without leaving a male heir, his brother shall marry his widow, and the first son of the union shall take the name of the brother who died (the term derives from Latin *lēvir*, "husband's brother"). If the brother refuses to marry the widow, she shall bring him before the elders of the city, and in their presence remove a sandal from his foot and spit in his face. The purpose of the law obviously was to provide an heir for the dead brother (Deut. 25:5-10; cf. also Gen. 38:1-11; Ruth 4:1-12). This practice underlies the argument of the Sadducees in Matt. 22:23-33.

Levite. lee´vit (Heb. *lēwî H4291*). The name given to the descendants of Levi son of Jacob. Because they were chosen to administer the religious life of the nation of Israel, the name *Levite* took on a specialized sense roughly equivalent to "minister."

I. **Their origin.** Levi was the third son of Jacob by Leah (Gen. 29:34; 35:22-26). The Genesis record gives no intimation regarding the later greatness of the tribe bearing Levi's name. Such silence bears indirect testimony to the fact that the Genesis account must have been written prior to the noble event that took place at Mount Sinai (Exod. 32:25-29) causing Levi's descendants to receive special status in Israel. The Genesis record is thus free of any bias or hint of Levi's future greatness as a tribe in Israel. Furthermore, if the Genesis

account had been written after the event on Mount Sinai, as claimed by many, it is difficult to understand why the record of Levi's notorious deed at Shechem (Gen. 34:25-31) was still retained, especially if, as also claimed by modern criticism, the early "history" was written, subjectively, to reflect the later greatness of Israel. Let us remember also that Genesis closes with a curse on Levi for his participation in the crime at Shechem (49:5-7). This curse, pronounced by the dying Jacob, would be utterly inconsistent with the view that Genesis, written by multiple writers late in Israel's history, reflects the national prestige of later times.

II. **Their appointment.** Several discernible factors undoubtedly influenced the selection of Levi's descendants for their special place in Israel's religion. (1) The divine selection of Moses and Aaron, who were descendants of Kohath, one of Levi's three sons (Exod. 2:1-10; 6:14-27; Num. 26:59), obviously conferred on the Levites an honor that was recognized by the other tribes. (2) However, an event of transcending importance at Mount Sinai (Exod. 32:25-29) gave to the Levites as a tribe their place of privilege and responsibility in God's plan. The event just referred to transmuted the curse of Jacob's prophecy (Gen. 49:5-7) into the blessing of Moses' prophecy (Deut. 33:8-11). (3) Moreover, this choice was undoubtedly confirmed by a very similar event when an individual Levite, Phinehas by name, stayed the plague that was about to decimate the Israelites (Num. 25:1-13). Thus the true record of history shows how the curse on Levi the ancestor became, by the wonders of God's providence, a blessing to his descendants.

Let us consider here some of the purposes served in the divine plan by the selection of the Levites for their special ministry in the worship of God's ancient people. (1) As just recounted, their selection and appointment were rewards for their faithfulness to the Lord in a time of moral declension (Exod. 32:25-29). (2) The doctrine of substitution was illustrated by the selection of this tribe, for, although God claimed the firstborn males of all the tribes on the basis of the death of the firstborn among the Egyptians (13:11-16), God graciously allowed the Levites to become substitutes for their fellow tribesmen (Num. 3:9, 11-13,

40-41, 45-51; 8:14-19). (3) The simplification of service would surely result from the selection of one tribe, for one such tribe closely knit by blood and by ancestral prestige would be more manageable than uncertain detachments from many tribes. (4) The law of the TITHE enhanced the selection of the Levites, for, in a sense, this tribe was a tithe of all the tribes; and it was to this tribe that the tithe was paid (Num. 18:20-21; Deut. 18:1-8; Neh. 10:37-39; Heb. 7:5, 9). (5) Israel's separation from the nations was further intensified by the selection of one tribe that was separated from all the other tribes and separated and purified to the Lord (Num. 8:5-22). (6) Life as a sojourner without an inheritance here is illustrated by the fact that the Levites had no INHERITANCE in Israel; the Lord alone was their inheritance (Num. 18:20-24; 26:62; Deut. 10:9; 12:12; 14:27). Nevertheless it is clear, in the light of Exod. 19:4-5, that humanly speaking the appointment of Levi as the priestly tribe to act on behalf of the whole people was an expedient arising from the fact that the people of God in their entirety could not yet attain to their privilege as priests of the Lord. This, however, has now been secured for us by CHRIST (cf. 1 Pet. 2:9).

III. Their organization. A threefold organization is discernible: (1) The top echelon was occupied by Aaron and his sons; these alone were priests in the restricted sense. The priests belonged to the family of Kohath. (2) The middle echelon included all the other Kohathites who were not of Aaron's family; to them were given certain privileges in carrying the most sacred parts of the TABERNACLE (Num. 3:27-32; 4:4-15; 7:9). (3) The bottom echelon comprised all members of the families of GERSHON and MERARI; to them lesser duties were prescribed (3:21-26, 33-37).

IV. Priests and Levites. The Mosaic legislation made a sharp distinction between the PRIESTS and nonpriests or ordinary Levites. (1) The priests must belong to Aaron's family; the Levites belonged to the larger family of Levi. A priest was a Levite (a descendant of Levi); but a Levite was not necessarily a priest. (2) Priests were consecrated (Exod. 29:1-37; Lev. 8); Levites were purified (Num. 8:5-22). (3) Levites were considered a gift to Aaron and his sons (3:5-13; 8:19; 18:1-7). (4) The fundamental difference consisted of this: only the priest had

the right to minister at the altar and to enter the sanctuary (Exod. 28:1; 29:9; Num. 3:10, 38; 4:15, 19-20; 18:1-7; 25:10-13). The rebellion of KORAH, a Kohathite (Num. 16:1) against the uniqueness of Aaron's priesthood illustrated, in the way the rebellion was subdued, the heinous nature of attempting to enter the priesthood without the necessary prerequisites (ch. 16). The choice of Aaron was further confirmed by the budding of his staff (Num. 17:1-11; Heb. 9:4).

V. Post-Mosaic changes. NT TYPOLOGY (cf. Heb. 8-10) considers the Sinaitic legislation the standard form. The post-Sinaitic activity of the Levites may be succinctly summarized in the following way: (1) In the settlement in Canaan the Levites were necessarily relieved of some of their duties, since the tabernacle no longer needed transportation; also, it is doubtful if the Levites ever fully occupied all the forty-eight cities assigned to them and the priests. (2) In DAVID's time the neglect of the provision of Num. 7:1-9 brought death to a Levite (1 Chr. 13:7-10; 15:12-15); David introduced innovations in the age and service of the Levites (23:26), some of whom, particularly ASAPH, became musicians and probably wrote some of the Psalms (1 Chr. 6:39, 43; 15:16-22; 16:4-6; 25:1-9; Ps. 50; 73-83). (3) In the disruption of the united kingdom many Levites from the northern kingdom sought political and religious asylum in JUDAH (2 Chr. 11:13-16; 13:9-12; 15:9), but some Levites were evidently involved in the APOSTASY of the northern kingdom (Ezek. 44:10-15); the Levites during this period were still considered teachers (2 Chr. 17:8-9; 19:8; cf. Deut. 33:10). (4) The exilic period brings before us the symbolism of Ezekiel: only the true Levites, sons of ZADOK, ministered in the TEMPLE (Ezek. 43:19; 44:10-16; 48:11-12). (5) In the postexilic period Levites did not return from BABYLON in the same proportion as the priests (Ezra 2:36-42; Neh. 7:39-45), though later a special effort was required to get the Levites to return (Ezra 8:15-19); they were still considered to be teachers (8:16) and musicians (2:40-41; 3:10-11; Neh. 7:43-44). (6) Only a few references to the Levites are found in the NT (Lk. 10:32; Jn. 1:19; Acts 4:36; Heb. 7:11).

Two points merit a final word: first, Levi, through his ancestor ABRAHAM, paid tithes to

MELCHIZEDEK (Gen. 14:17-20), thus proving the superiority of Melchizedek's (i.e., Christ's) priesthood to Aaron's (Heb. 7:4-10); second, since the Levitical priesthood could not bring perfection, it was required that another priest, from a different tribe and a different order, arise (Heb. 7:11-17; cf. Gen. 49:10; Ps. 110).

Levitical cities. Forty-eight cities were allotted to the LEVITES by MOSES and JOSHUA (Num. 35:1-8; Josh. 21; the parallel passage in 1 Chr. 6:54-81 [Heb. 6:39-66] has a smaller list with many differences, some reflecting spelling or textual variations, and others perhaps indicating new cities in later historical periods). The tribe of LEVI did not receive any part of the land of CANAAN as an INHERITANCE (Num. 18:20-24; 26:62; Deut. 10:9; 18:1-2; Josh. 18:7). As compensation, they received

THE LEVITICAL CITIES (acc. to Josh. 21)	
Abdon (Asher)	Helkath (Asher)
Aijalon (Dan)	Heshbon (Gad)
Ain (Judah)	Holon (Judah)
Almon (Ben.)	Jahaz (Reuben)
Anathoth (Ben.)	Jarmuth (Man.)
Be Eshtarah (Man.)	Jattir (Judah)
Beth Horon (Ephraim)	Jazer (Gad)
Beth Shemesh (Judah)	Jokneam (Zeb.)
Bezer (Reuben)	Juttah (Judah)
Daberath (Iss.)	Kartah (Zeb.)
Debir (Judah)	Kartan (Naph.)
Dimnah (Zeb.)	Kedemoth (Reuben)
Eltekeh (Dan)	Kedesh (Naph.)
En Gannim (Iss.)	Kibzaim (Ephraim)
Eshtemoa (Judah)	Kishion (Iss.)
Gath Rimmon (Dan)	Libnah (Judah)
Gath Rimmon (Man.)	Mahanaim (Gad)
Geba (Ben.)	Mephaath (Reuben)
Gezer (Ephraim)	Mishal (Asher)
Gibbethon (Dan)	Nahalal (Zeb.)
Gibeon (Ben.)	Ramoth Gilead (Gad)
Golan (Man.)	Rehob (Asher)
Hammoth Dor (Naph.)	Shechem (Ephraim)
Hebron (Judah)	Taanach (Man.)

the TITHES of Israelites for their support (Num. 18:21), and cities were allotted to them out of the inheritance of the other tribes. Of these cities, the priests received thirteen, all of which were within the tribe of JUDAH (Josh. 21:4); and six were CITIES OF REFUGE, to which a person who had accidentally killed someone could go for protection (Num. 35:9-34; Deut. 4:41-43).

The Levitical cities were made up by taking four cities from each of the twelve tribes. The apparent purpose of thus dispersing the Levites throughout the land was to enable them, as the official representatives of the Hebrew faith, to instruct the people throughout the land in the law and in the worship of Yahweh. The Levites were not the sole possessors or occupiers of these cities. They were simply allowed to live in them and have fields for the pasture of their herds. These cities did not cease to belong to the tribes within which they were located. The Levites did not live only in Levitical cities. They appear to have been regarded, in some respects at least, as belonging to the tribe within which they resided, even if it did not happen to be a Levitical city (cf. Jdg. 17:7; 1 Sam. 1:1). The Levites are never regarded as a thirteenth tribe.

Leviticus, Book of. li-vit´i-kuhs. The third book of the Bible and traditionally one of the five books of MOSES (the PENTATEUCH or TORAH). Its Hebrew title is the first word, *wayyiqrāʾ*, "and he called." The English title is derived from the VULGATE's *Leviticus* (in turn derived from the SEPTUAGINT). Although the material of the book focuses on the duties of PRIESTS and nowhere refers to the special functions of the LEVITES, its title is not inappropriate, since the priests were chosen only from the tribe of LEVI. Leviticus is closely associated with Exodus and Numbers in historical continuity, but differs from them in that the purely historical element is subordinate to legal and ritual considerations.

Leviticus enshrines the laws by which the religious and civil organization of the primitive THEOCRACY in CANAAN was to be regulated. At SINAI the Israelites had been incorporated into a special relationship with God, had been given the covenant laws, and had been provided with a TABERNACLE for WORSHIP. Leviticus contains much that

Overview of LEVITICUS

Author: Anonymous, but comments elsewhere in the Bible seem to support the traditional view that Moses is responsible for the Pentateuch as a whole.

Historical setting: The initial composition of the book must have taken place during the wilderness wanderings (either late in the fifteenth or early in the thirteenth cent. B.C.; those who reject Mosaic authorship usually date the book after the exile, while acknowledging that much of the material is several centuries earlier).

Purpose: To provide details of the laws that were to govern God's people, with emphasis on sacrificial requirements and ritual cleanness; to impress upon the people the need for holiness.

Contents: The laws of sacrifice (Lev. 1-7); the consecration of the priests (chs. 8-10); ceremonial purity (chs. 11-16); the ways of holiness (chs. 17-27).

L

is technical in nature and meant for the direction of the priesthood in the conduct of worship and the regulating of social life. Thus it is distinct from Deuteronomy, which in effect provides a popular exposition of the law.

The composition of the book was universally ascribed by ancient tradition, both Jewish and Christian, to Moses the lawgiver of Israel, and it was only during the eighteenth century that literary criticism seriously challenged this view. The movement grew in the following century and reached its classic formulation under Julius Wellhausen in 1887. Using a background of Hegelian evolutionary philosophy, he reconstructed Israelite history, and on the basis of a documentary hypothesis for Pentateuchal origins he assigned Leviticus to a postexilic date along with other elements of the so-called Priestly Code. Later criticism held that Leviticus was compiled by temple priests between 500 and 450 B.C., using earlier legislation such as the Holiness Code (Lev. 17-26), which is regarded as dating from about 650. Most critical writers, however, concede that Leviticus contains much older material, such as the Azazel or scapegoat ritual in ch. 16 and traditional historical narratives including the punishment of Aaron's sons (10:1-7) and the stoning of the blasphemer (24:10-14).

The literary criteria used in assigning a late date to the bulk of Leviticus have been criticized continuously since the time of Wellhausen, and the number of scholars who find them very difficult to sustain is increasing gradually. This arises in part from a wider knowledge of the media of communication in antiquity and also from historical and archaeological considerations. It is now known that if the techniques of compilation alleged by Wellhausen had actually been employed in the composition of Leviticus and the rest of the Pentateuch, it would have been unique in the literary annals of the ANE. Archaeological discoveries have shown that in actual fact the Hebrews used much the same literary methods as their neighbors, and that significant areas of biblical literature are closely related in language and style to other writings of that day.

The first seven chapters of Leviticus give the detailed sacrificial procedures showing how the various kinds of burnt offerings, the meal offering, the sin and guilt offerings, and other sacrifices avail for the removal of sin and defilement under the covenant. A subsequent liturgical section (Lev. 8:1—10:20) describes the consecration of Aaron and the priesthood, followed by the designation of clean and unclean beasts and certain rules of hygiene (11:1—15:33). The ritual of the Day of

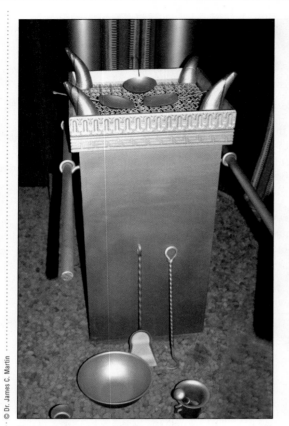

Reconstruction of the altar of incense.

lewdness. Sexual licentiousness. The English term and equivalents such as "lewd conduct" are used a dozen times in Ezekiel (and occasionally elsewhere) to translate *zimmâh H2365*. In general contexts this Hebrew word means "scheme, [evil] intent" (e.g., Prov. 21:27), but it apparently can function as a semi-technical term for shameful behavior, especially of a sexual nature (Ezek. 23:21 et al.; cf. also Jdg. 20:6; Jer 13:27 [KJV]).

lex talionis. leks′tal-ee-oh′nis. Also *ius talionis*. This Latin phrase (meaning literally "the law of that [same] kind") refers to a principle of retaliation whereby a person suffers the same harm that he or she has inflicted on someone else. The concept is expressed in the Bible as early as Gen. 9:6, "Whoever sheds the blood of man, by man shall his blood be shed," but especially in Exod. 21:23-25, "But if there is serious injury, you are to take life for life, eye for eye, tooth for tooth, hand for hand, foot for foot, burn for burn, wound for wound, bruise for bruise" (cf. Matt. 5:38). The principle expresses not only the validity of legal retaliation but also, and perhaps primarily, the requirement of equity and proportionality in the administration of punishment. The *lex talionis* therefore does not justify personal VENGEANCE or excessive retaliation.

libation. Usually referred to as a "drink offering"; the pouring out of liquids, such as wine, water, oil, etc., but generally wine, as an offering to a deity. Libations were common among the heathen nations (Deut. 32:38). Drink offerings accompanied many OT SACRIFICES (Exod. 29:40-41; Lev. 23:13, 18, 37; Num. 15:4-10, 24; 28:7-10). In 2 Tim. 4:6 and Phil. 2:17, PAUL pictures his death as a drink offering.

liberalism. In a religious sense, this term (or better, Classical Liberalism, also known as Modernism) refers to a movement that arose in Protestant circles in the middle of the nineteenth century and was prominent through the first decades of the twentieth. It was characterized by an emphasis on free intellectual inquiry, suspicion (or rejection) of orthodox theology, and confidence in the natural goodness of human beings. The label *liberalism* is often used more broadly to describe any depar-

Atonement is found in ch. 16, followed by a section (17:1—20:27) treating sacrificial blood, ethical laws, and penalties for transgressors. The theme of 21:1—24:23 is priestly holiness and the consecration of seasons, while the following chapter deals with the legislation surrounding the sabbatical and jubilee years. A concluding chapter outlines promises and threats (26:1-46), and an appendix (27:1-34) covers vows. Human SIN, substitutionary ATONEMENT, and divine HOLINESS are prominent throughout Leviticus.

levy. A TAX or TRIBUTE, often to be rendered in service. It is used by the KJV in reference to the 30,000 free Israelites conscripted by SOLOMON for four months' service a year in Lebanon (1 Ki. 5:13-14) and to the tribute labor imposed on the surviving Canaanites (9:21). The NIV uses this term for the tribute of gold and silver imposed by Pharaoh NECO on Judah (2 Ki. 23:33; 2 Chr. 36:3).

© Dr. James C. Martin

ture from historical Christian thought, especially with regard to the INSPIRATION and authority of the Bible. In a less careful sense, the term *liberal* is sometimes applied loosely to scholars who use the methods of "higher criticism" or who otherwise do not appear to follow traditional views.

libertine. A person who emphasizes liberty in moral questions and acts without ethical restraints; also, a freethinker who rejects religious authority. The term is used by the KJV with reference to freedmen who composed a synagogue in NT times (Acts 6:9). See FREEDMEN, SYNAGOGUE OF THE.

liberty. Freedom, the opposite of servitude or bondage, whether physical, moral, or spiritual. The term is used of SLAVES or captives being set free from physical servitude or imprisonment (Lev. 25:10; Jer. 34:8, 15-17; Acts 26:23; Heb. 13:23), or the granting of certain privileges while imprisoned (Acts 24:23; 27:3). In Ezek. 46:17 reference is made to "the year of freedom," which is the Year of JUBILEE. The term has a legal and moral tone in 1 Cor. 7:39 in asserting the right of a widow to remarry. The special concern of Christianity is the spiritual liberty of believers in Christ. Found in union with Christ, it carries with it freedom from the ceremonial law (Gal. 5:1; cf. 2:4) and must be valued and guarded. The essence of Christian liberty lies not in external freedom but in deliverance from the bondage of sin and its consequent inner corruption (Jn. 8:34-36; Rom. 6:20-22).

Spiritual liberty is the result of the Spirit's regenerating work, for his presence and work within produces liberty (2 Cor. 3:17), giving a sense of freedom through a filial relation with God (Rom. 8:15-16). Godly people in OT times knew a measure of this spiritual liberty (Ps. 119:45), but the GOSPEL reveals and offers it in its fullness. Using the picture of Isa. 61:1, CHRIST proclaimed this liberty to be the goal of his mission (Lk. 4:18). Intimately related to practical HOLINESS of life (Rom. 6:18-22), spiritual liberty never condones license. Believers are warned against abuse of this liberty in sinful indulgence (Gal. 5:13; 1 Pet. 2:16; 2 Pet. 2:19); and speech and conduct are to be judged by "the law of liberty" (Jas. 2:12), which has taken the place of the ancient LAW. In regard to things

not expressly commanded or forbidden, Christian liberty must be granted, allowing for the exercise of individual judgment and Christian conscience before God (1 Cor. 10:29-31); but its use must be limited by considerations of love, expediency, and self-preservation, lest that liberty become a stumbling block to the weak (8:9). Romans 8:21 points to creation's future "liberation" from decay and imperfection when God's children are glorified.

Libnah. lib´nuh (Heb. *libnâ H4243*, possibly "white[ness]" or "poplar" or "storax tree"). **(1)** A stopping place of the Israelites between Rimmon Perez and Rissah on their wilderness journey (Num. 33:20-21; it is thought by some to be identical with LABAN, Deut. 1:1). The site is unknown.

(2) A Canaanite city located in the SHEPHELAH, conquered by the Israelites under JOSHUA (Josh. 10:29-32; 12:15). Libnah was one of the cities included in the territory allotted to the tribe of JUDAH (15:42) and later became one of the LEVITICAL CITIES (21:13; 1 Chr. 6:57). The town successfully revolted against Judah in the reign of JEHORAM, indicating the weakening hold of Judah on her outlying cities (2 Ki. 8:22; 2 Chr. 21:10). Later during the reign of HEZEKIAH, it was one of the fortified cities attacked by SENNACHERIB in his campaign against Judah (2 Ki. 19:8; Isa. 37:8). Libnah was the home of Hamutal, the mother of ZEDEKIAH (2 Ki. 23:31; 24:18; Jer. 52:1). The identification of ancient Libnah is debated, but a widely accepted suggestion is Tell Bornaṭ, about 5 mi. (8 km.) NE of LACHISH.

Libni. lib´ni (Heb. *libnî H4249*, "white"; gentilic *libnî H4250*, "Libnite"). **(1)** Son of GERSHON, grandson of LEVI, and ancestor of the Libnite clan (Exod. 6:17; Num. 3:18, 21; 26:58; 1 Chr. 6:17, 20). Some believe that the name Libnite is derived from the town of LIBNAH. See also LADAN #2.

(2) Son of MAHLI, grandson of MERARI, and great-grandson of Levi (1 Chr. 6:29).

library. A collection of books purposely brought together by, and in the possession of, an individual or an institution. While BOOKS frequently are mentioned in the Bible, nowhere is there a reference to a *library* existing in Israel. SOLOMON, however, did complain, "Of making many books there is no end" (Eccl. 12:12), indicating that he was well acquainted with an existing body of literature. There is also a remarkable reference in the OT to a library in PERSIA. When the enemies of Israel complained to DARIUS about the Jews, they asked that a search be made in BABYLON concerning the decree of CYRUS permitting the building of the second TEMPLE (Ezra 5:17). Then "King Darius issued an order, and they searched in the archives [*lit.*, the house of the books] stored in the treasury at Babylon" (6:1; see also 4:15). Moreover, ARCHAEOLOGY has uncovered extensive libraries of cuneiform tablets in MESOPOTAMIA and SYRIA, and there is much evidence of literary collections in ancient EGYPT and elsewhere. See also WRITING.

Libya. lib´ee-uh (Heb. *lûb H4275*, occurring only in the pl. *lûbim*, "Libyans"; Gk. *Libyē G3340*). A country in N AFRICA, the immediate western neighbor of EGYPT. Greek writers often identified Libya with Cyrenaica (see CYRENE); sometimes the name was used more broadly of the whole N African coastal zone. Many believe that the LEHABITES listed in the Table of Nations (Gen. 10:13; 1 Chr. 1:11) are to be identified with the Libyans. In the OT, the "Lubim" appropriately feature in the forces of Pharaoh SHISHAK (himself of Libyan extraction) when he invaded PALESTINE (2 Chr. 12:3), and also in those of ZERAH defeated by ASA (cf. 2 Chr. 16:8). Along with PUT, the Lubim were reckoned as part of the strength of THEBES by Nahum (Nah. 3:9). Libya and CUSH are also subordinate to Egypt

Relief in Hatshepsut's temple at Karnak reflecting her conquest of Libya.

(Dan. 11:43), as happened so often in their history. The MT reading *kûb* (see CUB) in Ezek. 30:5 is often emended to *lûb* on the basis of the SEPTUAGINT and the Syriac (cf. NIV and NRSV, "Libya," but see TNIV). In the NT, we read that visitors from "the parts of Libya near Cyrene" were present in JERUSALEM at PENTECOST (Acts 2:10).

lice. See ANIMALS.

licentiousness. Disregard of accepted moral rules and standards; lack of moral restraint, especially in sexual conduct. The term is used by the NRSV and other versions to render Greek *aselgeia G816* (e.g., Rom. 13:13, where NIV has "debauchery"). See LASCIVIOUSNESS.

Lidbir, Lidebir. See DEBIR (PLACE) #3; LO DEBAR.

lie, lying. Since God is TRUTH and truthful, he cannot lie as humans do (Num. 23:19). When Israel was not in a harmonious relation to God and the people rejected his truth, they fell prey to a lie—a false view of life often including IDOLATRY. They are "the fruit of lies" (Hos. 10:13 KJV; NIV, "deception"), allowed a lie to become their refuge (Isa. 28:15), and been led astray by lies (Amos 2:4 KJV; NIV, "false gods"). But God will make an end of all liars (Ps. 5:6). In contrast to those who live a life of lies, the righteous remnant of Israel "do no wrong … speak no lies" (Zeph. 3:13). In the LAW of Moses there are laws against bearing false witness (Exod. 20:16) and perjury (Lev. 19:12), and there is the general command, "Do not lie" (19:11).

The NT also presents the picture of people of the world who "exchanged the truth of God for a lie" (Rom. 1:25). Within the churches there are those who make God a liar by claiming they are not sinners (1 Jn. 1:10) and those who preach a lie— that Jesus is not the CHRIST (1 Jn. 2:22; Rev. 2:2). The source of lies is the DEVIL (Jn. 8:44; Acts 5:3). Christians must not lie to one another (Eph. 4:25; Col. 3:9), for Christ is the truth and those who lie are not one with him. Therefore those who are redeemed by the LAMB are those with no lie on their lips (Rev. 14:5). Connected with the idea of a lie are those who live a lie or convey a lie—a false brother (2 Cor. 11:26), a false apostle (11:13), a false

© Dr. James C. Martin

teacher (2 Pet. 2:1), a false witness (Matt. 26:60), a false prophet (7:15), and a false Christ (24:24).

lieutenant. This English term is used by the KJV to render a Hebrew word that refers to a SATRAP (Ezra 8:36; Esth. 3:12; 8:9; 9:3; in the Aram. sections of Daniel, the KJV has "prince," Dan. 3:2-3, 27; 6:1-7).

life. A complex concept with varied shades of meaning, rendering several Hebrew and Greek terms. It may denote *physical* or natural life, whether animal (Gen. 1:20; 6:17; Rev. 8:9) or human (Lev. 17:14; Matt. 2:20; Lk. 12:22). It is the vital principle or breath of life, which God imparted to ADAM, making him a living soul (Gen. 2:7). This life is a precious gift, and the taking of life is prohibited (Gen. 9:5; Exod. 20:13; Lev. 24:17). It is propagated through physical generation and is subject to physical DEATH. The term may signify the period of one's earthly existence, one's lifetime (Gen. 23:1; 25:7; Lk. 16:25), or the relations, activities, and experiences that make up life (Exod. 1:14; Deut. 32:47; Job 10:1; Lk. 12:15). Occasionally it means one's manner of life (1 Tim. 2:2; 1 Jn. 2:16) or the means for sustaining life (Deut. 24:6; 1 Jn. 3:17).

But the primary concern of the Scriptures is *spiritual* or *eternal* life for the human race. It is the gift of God, mediated through FAITH in Jesus CHRIST (Jn. 3:36; 5:24; Rom. 5:10; 6:23; 1 Jn. 5:12). It is not synonymous with endless existence, which is also true of the unsaved. It is qualitative, involving the impartation of a new nature (2 Pet. 1:3-4). It is communicated to the believer in this life, resulting in fellowship with God in Christ, and is not interrupted by physical death (1 Thess. 5:10). It will find its perfection and full reality of blessedness with God in the life to come (Rom. 2:7; 2 Cor. 5:4). As "the living God" (Deut. 5:26; Ps. 42:2; 1 Thess. 1:9; 1 Tim. 3:15), the eternal and self-existent One, God has *absolute* life in himself (Jn. 5:26) and is the source of all life (Ps. 36:9; Jn. 1:4; 17:3; 1 Jn. 1:1-2; 5:20).

life, author of. See AUTHOR.

life, book of. This figurative NT expression (Rev. 13:8; 17:8; 20:12; 21:27; cf. also Phil. 4:3; Rev. 3:5;

20:15) is based on OT references to God's book in which were written the names of the righteous (Ps. 69:28; Exod. 32:32). This notion, in turn, is related to the ancient custom of keeping genealogies and national registers in Israel (Neh. 7:5, 64; 12:12; Ps. 87:6; Jer. 22:30; Ezek. 13:9). Just as these latter records were carefully inscribed and preserved, so God knows his people. The NT uses the phrase to stress the ASSURANCE of salvation. Anchored in eternity, that salvation is certain for all those whose names are written in "the book of life belonging to the Lamb that was slain from the creation of the world" (Rev. 13:8). They may rejoice because their names are written in heaven (Lk. 10:20). To be in the book of life is ground for the certainty of salvation. Not to be found in God's book, or to be blotted out of it (Exod. 32:32-33; Ps. 69:28), or not to be found in the book of life (Rev. 17:8; 20:15) means separation from God and perdition.

life, tree of. See TREE OF LIFE.

light. The first recorded utterance of God in the Bible is "Let there be light" (Gen. 1:3), the first sign of divine operation in the world of chaos and DARKNESS. Dawn indicates the sure dispelling of darkness, the essence of all God's gifts. God is the creator of both light and darkness (Isa. 45:6-7) and watches over their orderly succession (Ps. 104:20; Amos 4:13), yet light is superior (Eccl. 2:13). It is often very difficult to distinguish between natural and metaphorical uses of light in the Bible. Light is above all the source of life (11:7). The word is used in parallel with expressions for being alive (Job 3:20) or being born (3:16) or for the pleasures of life (Ps. 97:11) or for good days for the righteous (112:4) or for an essential in man's happiness (36:9).

Light brings order to the world. Light and TRUTH are coupled biblically (Ps. 43:3; cf. Ps. 19; Prov. 6:23; Isa. 51:4). Truth and LAW give the light of knowledge (Ps. 19:8; 139:11-12). The recipients of light themselves become light, shining outwardly (Ps. 34:5; Eccl. 8:1) and inwardly (Prov. 20:27; Dan. 5:11). God is described as "the Father of the heavenly lights" (Jas. 1:17), he who dwells in light (Exod. 13:21; Ps. 104:2; 1 Tim. 6:16) and who imparts light as a divine gift. The OT concept of Scripture as a LAMP or a light is taken over in the NT (2 Pet. 1:19). Conversion is spoken of as illumination (Heb. 6:4; 10:32). Believers are "people of the light" (Lk. 16:8; 1 Thess. 5:5) and the "light of the world" (Matt. 5:14). Because the gift may be lost through inactivity (Jn. 5:35; 1 Thess. 5:5-6), the heavenly light must be used as armor or a weapon (Eph. 6:12; Rom. 13:12) in the fight against darkness. The light is permanently present in Christ (Jn. 1:7-9; Heb. 1:3) and in the GOSPEL (Acts 26:23; 2 Cor. 4:4). In the new age there will be no more night (Rev. 21:23). John stresses that "God is light" (1 Jn. 1:5), and he who hates his brother is in darkness (2:11).

lightning. A visible electric discharge between rain clouds or between a rain cloud and the earth, producing a thunderclap. In PALESTINE and SYRIA lightning is common during the heavy fall and spring rains. Lightning is generally accompanied by heavy rain, and at times by hail (Exod. 9:23-24). The Scriptures mention lightning as a manifestation of God's power, symbolizing his command of the forces of nature (Job 28:26; 38:35; Ps. 135:7; Zech. 10:1). Lightnings are his instruments in bringing about the destruction of his opponents (Ps. 18:14; 144:6; Zech. 9:14-15). Lightning is a symbol of speed (Ezek. 1:14; Nah. 2:4; Zech. 9:14) and of dazzling brightness (Dan. 10:6; Matt. 28:3). In Matt. 24:27 and Lk. 17:24 Jesus uses the figure of lightning to indicate the unmistakable certainty of the fact that he will come again. In Lk. 10:18 Jesus speaks of beholding Satan fallen as lightning, symbolic of a definite and terrific defeat.

Lights, Feast of. See FEASTS.

lign aloes. See PLANTS (under *aloe*).

ligure. A precious stone. The term is used by the KJV to render a Hebrew word that probably refers to the jacinth (Exod. 28:19; 39:12). See MINERALS.

Likhi. lik´hi (Heb. *liqhî H4376*, perhaps "[Yahweh] takes"). Son of SHEMIDA and descendant of MANASSEH (1 Chr. 7:19). The precise genealogical connection is not specified in 1 Chronicles, but elsewhere (Num. 26:32) Shemida seems to be regarded as a son of GILEAD.

Lilith. lil´ith (Heb. *lilit H4327*, derivation uncertain). This name is used by the NRSV and some other versions as a transliteration of a Hebrew word that occurs only once in a passage describing the terrible desolation that will befall EDOM (Isa. 34:14). The term is associated, probably by popular etymology, with Hebrew *laylâ H4326*, "night." Because most (or perhaps all) of the other creatures mentioned in the context are real animals or birds thought to inhabit waste solitudes, this word has been rendered variously as "screech owl" (KJV), "night hag" (RSV), "night-jar" (NEB), "night creatures" (NIV). Its rendering as a proper name, "Lilith," reflects a derivation from Akkadian *lilîtu*, the name of a female demon or lesser deity about whom little is known. It must not be assumed that the prophet himself believed in the existence of Lilith. More likely, in a highly imaginative passage in which he describes the awful desolation of Edom, he simply mentions some creatures, real and unreal, which in the popular imagination are said to inhabit unpeopled solitudes.

lily. See PLANTS.

lily-work. This term is used by several Bible versions with reference to the architectural ornamentation on the tops of the free-standing pillars, JAKIN AND BOAZ, at the vestibule of Solomon's TEMPLE (1 Ki. 7:19, 22 [NIV, "in the shape of lilies"]; note also the description of the molten sea, 2 Chr. 4:5). It is thought likely that this lily-work was modeled after the Egyptian lotus, which was the staple ornament not only in Egyptian art, but also was widely used, as archaeological remains show, in Assyria, Persia, and Palestine.

lime, limestone. See MINERALS (under *marble*) and MORTAR.

line. This English term, with its different senses, is used variously to render a number of Hebrew words, especially *qāw H7742*, referring to a "measuring line," such as builders use (2 Ki. 21:13; Jer. 31:39; Ezek. 47:3; Zech. 1:16; sometimes used figuratively, as in Isa. 28:10, 17; 28:1; 34:11). The Greek word *kanōn G2834*, "[measuring] rod, ruler," is rendered "line" by the KJV in a passage where

Paul refers to a person's sphere of work or "territory" marked out by God (2 Cor. 10:16).

linen. Thread or cloth, prepared from the fiber of flax (see plants). The use of flax fiber for cloth and other purposes is very ancient, being traceable as far back as the Stone Age. Flax was cultivated in Mesopotamia, Assyria, and Egypt, and linen was well known in the ancient biblical world. Ancient Egypt was noted for its fine linen and carried on a thriving export with neighboring nations. Flax was being cultivated in the tropical climate around Jericho at the time of the conquest (Josh. 2:6). Having learned the art in Egypt (Exod. 35:25), Hebrew women practiced the spinning and weaving of flax (Prov. 31:13, 19). The clans of Beth Ashbea attained eminence as workers in linen (1 Chr. 4:21).

Linen is the translation of several different Hebrew and Greek words. In some contexts these terms can be differentiated, but they often are used interchangeably. The term "fine linen" in the Bible refers to sheer, often almost translucent material of the expensive finely woven linen worn by royal and wealthy people or the priests of the temple. The biblical references show varied uses of linen. For clothing it was preferred to cotton material in warm climates because of the sensation of coolness given by linen garments. Its use is frequently mentioned in connection with the garments of the Aaronic priests (Exod. 28:42; Lev. 6:10; 1 Sam. 22:18), their tunics, undergarments, and headdresses being exclusively of linen, and the girdle largely of it (Exod. 28:39; 39:27-29). It was also preferred by others for dress in religious services; it was worn by the child Samuel (1 Sam. 2:18), by the Levitical singers in the temple (2 Chr. 5:12), and even by royal personages (2 Sam. 6:14; 1 Chr. 15:27).

Angels are described as dressed in linen (Ezek. 9:2; 10:2; Dan. 10:5; 12:6), as also the host of the redeemed returning with Christ from heaven (Rev. 19:14). In Rev. 19:8 linen is used figuratively of the moral purity of the saints. Linen was used also for garments of distinction (Gen. 41:41; Esth. 8:15). Apparently linen garments of a coarser material were worn by men (Jdg. 14:12-13) and women (Prov. 31:22). But the use of fine linen for ordinary purposes was apparently a sign of luxury and extravagance (Isa. 3:23; Ezek. 16:10; Lk. 16:19; Rev. 18:12, 16). Linen was used also for nets (Isa. 19:9), measuring lines (Ezek. 40:3), girdles (Jer. 13:1), and for fine hangings (Esth. 1:6). In NT times at least, linen was extensively used by the Jews for burial shrouds, as at the burial of Jesus (Matt. 27:59; Mk. 15:46; Lk. 23:53; Jn. 19:40; 20:5ff.). Egyptian mummies were wrapped exclusively in linen sheets of vast proportions. See also dress.

lintel. The head-piece of a door, carrying the weight of the structure above it. The term is used by some Bible versions to render Hebrew *mašqôp H5485* (Exod. 12:22-23). The Israelites were commanded to mark the top as well as the sides of the doorframe with the blood of the paschal lamb when the Passover was instituted.

Linus. lī′nuhs (Grk. *Linos G3352*). A Christian who, along with others, was a friend of the apostle Paul during his second Roman imprisonment and who sent greetings to Timothy (2 Tim. 4:21). According to early church tradition, this Linus was given the office of the episcopate of the church in Rome by the apostles Peter and Paul, serving there as bishop for twelve years.

lion. See animals.

lip. The fold of flesh that surrounds the opening of the mouth. The diverse usage of the Hebrew and Greek terms for "lip" illustrates the manner in which a primary organ of the body was employed to describe a number of widely variant phenomena.

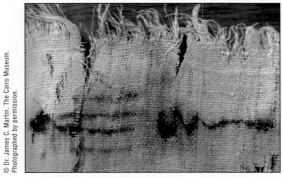

© Dr. James C. Martin. The Cairo Museum. Photographed by permission.

Egyptian linen with fringes (from Saqqara, latter part of 2nd millennium B.C.).

By metonymy, for example, the Hebrew word *śāpâ H8557* came to mean language or manner of speaking of individuals and nations alike (Gen. 11:1; Prov. 17:7), as well as the gossip of casual conversationalists (Prov. 17:4; Ezek. 36:3). The extension of the term by metaphorical usage naturally suggested the brink or shore of the sea or the bank of a river (Gen. 22:17; 41:3; Dan. 12:5; et al.). By further derivation the word was used to designate the border or edge of something, as with a garment or curtain (Exod. 26:4, 10; 28:26; et al.). The ancients also could assign emotional and ethical qualities to bodily organs, including the lips. The lips not merely spoke but rejoiced (Ps. 71:23), quivered fearfully (Hab. 3:16), preserved knowledge (Prov. 5:2), offered praise (Ps. 63:3); and besides being righteous (Prov. 16:13) they could be lying (Ps. 120:2), uncircumcised (Exod. 6:12, 30), perverse (Prov. 4:24), and so on. Literary parallelism with the tongue or mouth was common in poetry (Ps. 34:13; 51:15). In the NT the Greek word *cheilos G5927* was used both literally and metaphorically in the same sense as in the OT, almost always in quotations from the SEPTUAGINT (Matt. 15:8; Mk. 7:6; Rom. 3:13; 2 Cor. 14:21; 1 Pet. 3:10; cf. also Heb. 11:12; 13:15).

literature. See BOOK; WRITING.

litter. This English term, in its meaning of an enclosed BED or COUCH used to carry a person, is used by some Bible versions to render the common Hebrew word *miṭṭâ H4753*, "bed," in Cant. 3:7 (NIV, "carriage"), and the rare term *ṣāb H7369*, "covered cart or wagon," in Isa. 66:20 (NIV, "wagons").

Little Apocalypse. A term applied sometimes to Isa. 24-27, but more frequently to Jesus' eschatological discourse recorded in Mk. 13 and parallels. See ESCHATOLOGY.

little owl. See BIRDS.

liver. The heaviest of the viscera, both in weight and importance, mentioned over a dozen times in the OT. Usually the reference is to the bodily organ in connection with SACRIFICES (e.g., Exod. 29:13, 22; Lev. 3:4, 10, 15; 4:9; 7:4). Its use for purposes of DIVINATION was common among heathen nations (Ezek. 21:21), but the practice is not verified among the Jews. Being closely identified with the source and center of life, it is mentioned in depicting profound sorrow (Lam. 2:11 KJV), and piercing it was fatal (Prov. 7:22-23).

living creature. The usual translation of Hebrew *nepeš ḥayyâ* (*H5883* plus the adjective *ḥay H2645*, thus "alive soul, alive being") or simply the noun *ḥayyâ H2651* ("animal"). In Genesis and Leviticus, it is a nontechnical expression referring to ANIMALS (Gen. 1:21 et al.; Lev. 11:10, 14). By using it technically, Ezekiel referred to the CHERUBIM (Ezek. 1:5, 13-15, 19-22). The four living creatures in his vision each had four faces (man, lion, ox, eagle). In the NT, the corresponding Greek term, *zōon G2442* ("living being, animal"), refers simply to animals a few times (Heb. 13:11; 2 Pet. 2:12; Jude 10), but the special sense occurs only in Revelation, where it is applied to the four living creatures in the heavenly scene, always present in and around the throne of the Lamb (Rev. 4:6-9 et al.). Each had six wings (four in Ezekiel) and further differed from the OT description where the ox was replaced by an eagle, each creature having a single identity.

lizard. See ANIMALS.

loaf. See BREAD.

Lo-Ammi. loh-am´i (Heb. *lōˀ ˁammî H4204*, "not my people"). A symbolical name given by the prophet HOSEA to his second son and third child by his wife GOMER (Hos. 1:9). His firstborn son was called Jezreel, which means "Yahweh sows," an allusion to scattering or destruction (vv. 4-5); see JEZREEL (PERSON) #2. A previous daughter was given the name LO-RUHAMAH, meaning "not pitied/loved" (v. 6). The names given to the children were symbolic of the fact that Israel, because of its disobedience, had forfeited the compassion and protection of Yahweh. Nevertheless, the passage immediately promises a reversal of this judgment (1:10; 2:1 [Heb. 2:1, 3]).

loan. See BORROW.

L

lock. In the sense of a device for securing doors, see DOOR; KEY. In the sense of a length of hair, see HAIR.

locust. See ANIMALS.

Lod, Lydda. lod, lid´uh (Heb. *lōd H4254*; Gk. *Lydda G3375* [LXX, *Lod*]). A town said to have been built, along with ONO, by a Benjamite named SHEMED (1 Chr. 8:12); it is listed with Ono and HADID among the towns to which the Jews returned after the EXILE (Ezra 2:33; Neh. 7:37; 11:35). Lod is identified with modern el-Ludd, some 11 mi. (18 km.) SE of JOPPA. Its strategic position—on the two highways that led from EGYPT to BABYLON and from Joppa to JERUSALEM—made it a prize of war throughout the centuries. In the Hellenistic period it came to be known as Lydda. PETER cured a man with palsy there (Acts 9:32-35, the only NT reference to the town). After the destruction of Jerusalem in A.D. 70, it became a center of Christian activity in N Palestine. It had been a center of rabbinic studies for a period even before the Roman overthrow of the rebellion. The town became known as Diospolis by the third Christian century and was the center of a trade in purple dye. It was the site of the death of St. George, who was martyred there in 303.

Lo Debar. loh-dee´buhr (Heb. *lô dĕbār H4274* [with variant spellings], by popular etymology, "nothing"). A town or city-state in TRANSJORDAN that was the home of MAKIR son of Ammiel (2 Sam. 9:4-5; 17:27). JONATHAN's lame son, MEPHIBOSHETH, lived in Makir's house, and from that place DAVID summoned him to the palace (9:1-13). AMOS plays on the sound of the name Lo Debar (Amos 6:13). Some scholars think its original name was Lidbir (Lidebir), which may have been a town on the N boundary of the tribe of GAD in GILEAD (Josh. 19:26 NJPS; cf. NRSV mg.). See DEBIR (PLACE) #3. In any case, the location of Lo Debar is uncertain.

lodge. This English verb is used often by the KJV, mainly as the rendering of Hebrew *lîn H4328*, "remain [through the night]" (Gen. 24:23 et al.), and Greek *aulizomai G887*, "to lie in the courtyard, to pass the night" (Matt. 21:17 et al.). The term is found less frequently in modern versions, which prefer such expressions as "stay" and "spend the night." As a noun, "lodge" occurs in the KJV as the rendering of *mĕlûnâ H4870* (Isa. 1:8; NIV, "hut").

log. A Hebrew term used of the smallest liquid measure of capacity, about two-thirds of a pint. See WEIGHTS AND MEASURES.

logia. loh´jee-ah. This Greek term (pl. of *logion G3359*) is used in nonbiblical literature for the utterances of deities. Such usage is also found in the SEPTUAGINT (e.g., Ps. 12:6 [Heb. 12:7, LXX 11:7]) and occasionally in the NT (Acts 7:38; Rom. 3:2; cf. Heb. 5:13; 1 Pet. 4:11). In the church fathers the term begins to be used for the sayings of Jesus, and in the present day it is generally restricted to this usage. The existence and circulation of collections of Logia may be the source of possibly two AGRAPHA (sayings ascribed to Jesus in the NT, but not found in the Gospels)—Acts 20:35 and 1 Thess. 4:16-17. Luke may also have used such collections in his research in the preparation of his gospel (Lk. 1:1-3). In modern times, actual collections of sayings dating from the early church have been discovered. For example, a PAPYRUS fragment dated about the middle of the third century and designated POxy 1 (from ancient Oxyrhynchus on the NILE) contains seven sayings attributed to Jesus; it seems to be a part of a large collection of sayings. The phenomenal discovery of Gnostic papyri in 1945 near modern Nag Hammadi in Egypt included two documents entitled *Gospel of Thomas* and *Gospel of Philip*. These are collections of sayings of Jesus in Coptic. The *Gospel of Thomas* contains 114 sayings; in comparison with the canonical sayings, this book shows some of the heretical tendencies of the Gnostic community where it circulated (see GNOSTICISM). The *Gospel of Philip*, a collection of 127 sayings purported to be revelations imparted by Jesus to a group (Hebrews) including Philip and dated about A.D. 400, is more heretical and esoteric than the *Gospel of Thomas*.

Logos. loh´gohs. A transliteration of the Greek term *logos G3364*, which has a wide range of meanings, including "word, statement, conversation, speech," as well as "thought, opinion, reason," etc.

As a philosophical term, the concept goes back to the Ionian philosopher Heraclitus (c. 500 B.C.), to whom Logos meant the universal reason permeating the world and finding self-consciousness in the mind of the philosophers. The STOICS adopted the term for a dynamic principle of reason operating in the world and forming a medium of communion between God and human beings. The latter function becomes prominent in PHILO, with whom the Logos is at once the Stoics' active and intelligent world-principle, the thought in the divine mind, which was identical with the sum total of Plato's "Forms" or "Ideas," and a mediator between God and the matter of his creation. For Philo, as indeed for his predecessors, the Logos is neither personal nor impersonal. It was vaguely equated with God's utterance (Gen. 1:3; Ps. 33:9), his "word" in such passages as Ps. 107:20; 147:15, 18, and such expressions as "the angel of the covenant," and equated with "wisdom" in the personification of Prov. 8. It is possible that the Qumran community (see DEAD SEA SCROLLS) fused the same Hebrew and Hellenistic concepts into their doctrine of the spirit of truth, which, like the spirit of error, was a creature of God (the relevant passages in the *Rule of the Community* document do not admit of dogmatism).

In the NT the Logos appears in John's writings (Jn. 1:1-3, 14; 1 Jn. 1:1; Rev. 19:13), though allusions in Paul's writings and the epistle to the Hebrews might be added. Logos is imperfectly translated "Word," and it is not easy to comprehend the full context of the idea in its Judeo-Hellenistic context. There can be no doubt that John saw value in expressing Christian thought in the terminology of the day, a point appreciated by the early church fathers in their sometimes perilous development of the Logos doctrine. Significantly enough, John wrote his prologues at the end of the first century, when the first signs of Gnostic error were discernible (see GNOSTICISM). In John's use of Logos we must certainly see that blending of Judaic and Hellenistic concepts that appeared in Philo's use of the term. From its Greek ancestry, etymological and philosophical, the Johannine Word would contain not only the notion of reason, but also the active expression of reason on a divine and perfect plane. Hence the conception of the visible universe as an expression of God's reason, that reason being the force and agency of creation, the Word who said: "Let there be ..." But John becomes entirely original and creative when he boldly equates this reason with God himself, and simultaneously sees its INCARNATION in CHRIST. It seems likely that John, in this bold thought, brought to firmer expression in the terminology of Hellenistic thought a concept already expressed in 1 Cor. 8:6; Col. 1:15-17; and Heb. 1:2-3. In view of the Colossian heresy of angelic mediatorship the last context is significant.

loins. Used in the KJV to describe the part of the body between the ribs and the hip bones. It is the place where the girdle was worn (Exod. 12:11; 2 Ki. 1:8; Jer. 13:1; Matt. 3:4) and the sword was fastened (2 Sam. 20:8). Pain and terror were reflected in weakness and shaking of the loins (Ps. 38:7; 66:11; 69:23; Jer. 30:6). Girding the loins with sackcloth was a sign of mourning (1 Ki. 20:32; Isa. 32:11; Jer. 48:37). As the place of the reproductive organs the loins are euphemistically named for the generative function (Gen. 35:11; 1 Ki. 8:19; Acts 2:30; Heb. 7:5). Since garments were worn ungirded about the house, to gird up the loins signified preparation for vigorous action (Exod. 12:11; 1 Ki. 18:46; Job 38:3; Prov. 31:17; Lk. 12:35; 1 Pet. 1:13). To have the loins girded with truth signified strength in attachment to truth (Eph. 6:14; cf. Isa. 11:5).

Lois. loh´is (Gk. *Lōis G3396*). The grandmother of TIMOTHY; she was probably the mother of Timothy's mother, EUNICE (2 Tim. 1:5). The family lived at LYSTRA (Acts 16:1). Lois, a devout Jewish believer, likely was converted to Christianity during PAUL's first missionary journey (Acts 14). Paul speaks of the unpretending faith of Timothy, and adds that this faith first dwelt in his grandmother Lois and his mother Eunice.

longsuffering. The term preferred by KJV to account for the delay of the Lord in inflicting punishment or exercising his WRATH (modern versions prefer "slow to anger, forbearance, patience"). The idea is that God delays his exercise of WRATH to give time for repentance and amendment of life (Exod. 34:6; Num. 14:18; Ps. 86:15; Jer. 15:15; Rom. 2:4; 2 Pet. 3:9). In a similar manner, CHRIST is said to be longsuffering (1 Tim. 1:16; 2 Pet. 3:15). The KJV uses the term also to describe human beings. As so used, it refers to being patient especially when facing evil. It is one of the aspects of the fruit of the Spirit (Gal. 5:22), for the Lord's servants must be longsuffering (2 Tim. 2:24). The relation between divine and human longsuffering is conveyed by the parable of the unforgiving servant told by Jesus in Matt. 18:21-35.

loom. An apparatus for weaving thread or yarn into cloth (Jdg. 16:14; Isa. 38:12). In Bible times three types of looms were in use. One was the horizontal loom, also called the ground loom, because it was laid out horizontally on the ground. The other two types of loom were upright and were operated from a sitting or a standing position. See WEAVING.

Turkish woman working at a wooden loom.

loop. The TABERNACLE was covered with two sets of five linen curtains, and along one side of each set fifty loops of blue thread were sewn. Fifty gold clasps were attached to one side of the other set of curtains, and thus the two halves of the curtain were joined. The outer covering was made of goatskin in the same way, also with clasps and loops (Exod. 26:4-5, 10-11; 36:11-12, 17).

lord. The English word *lord* (or capitalized, *Lord*) is used to translate various terms in the OT. As a title of men, it can designate governmental, religious, and military officials. The common Hebrew word *baʿal H1251* ("owner, husband," etc.) can be used in this sense (e.g., Isa. 16:8 NRSV; NIV, "rulers"), as can *ʾādôn H123* (Gen. 42:20 et al.) and other nouns. When applied to deity, the title *baʿal* came to be identified directly with a specific Canaanite god (see BAAL). In contrast, *ʾādôn* is used of the true God (e.g., Josh. 3:11), esp. in the form *ʾādōnāy H151* (lit., "my lords"; Gen. 15:2 et al.). Most English Bible versions use the form LORD (i.e., in small caps) to render God's special covenant name, Yahweh. See JEHOVAH.

The Greek word *kyrios G3261*, which can also refer to human beings in positions of authority, is used by the SEPTUAGINT to render the Hebrew words applied to the true God. In the NT it occurs as a designation of the sovereign God in relationship to his CREATION (Matt. 1:20; 11:25; Lk. 4:18). But it is also the supreme title given to CHRIST. "Jesus is Lord" was perhaps the earliest creedal statement formulated and recited (prob. chiefly at BAPTISM, Acts 8:16; 19:5) by the early Christians. In its infancy, the CHURCH had worshiped Jesus as Lord, and its ARAMAIC prayer, MARANATHA, "Our Lord, come," still stands in the text as witness to this fact (1 Cor. 16:22). Indeed, if Phil. 2:6-11 is a primitive Christian hymn, as some have claimed, then PAUL was the recipient of an earlier tradition about the Lordship of Jesus rather than the originator of a new title to describe his own understanding of him. This title stood also in the tradition Paul had received concerning the LORD's SUPPER (1 Cor. 11:23). By referring to Jesus as Lord, the early church declared him as standing above the human level—an object of prayer (Acts 7:59, 60; 1 Cor. 12:8; 16:22) and trust (Acts 5:14; 9:42; 11:24; cf. also the fourth gospel), sharing with God in his sovereign rule (2:34), and ultimately sharing with God in his nature. For being conscious that the Greek OT regularly used *kyrios* to designate Yahweh, early Christians, even Jewish

© Dr. James C. Martin

L

Christians, chose that term as the supreme title to convey their understanding of Jesus. By it, therefore, they intended to identify him with the God of the OT. This intent is seen most clearly in those NT passages where OT texts originally referring to Yahweh are now boldly quoted as referring to Jesus (Rom. 10:13; Heb. 1:10; 1 Pet. 2:3; 3:15).

Lord, day of the. See DAY OF THE LORD; LORD'S DAY.

Lord of hosts. The phrase "LORD of hosts" is used by the KJV and other Bible translations as a literal rendering of Hebrew *yhwh ṣĕbā'ôt*, which occurs well over 200 times in the OT as a designation of the true God (it is esp. frequent in Isaiah, Jeremiah, Zechariah, and Malachi). The first word in the phrase is the divine name *Yahweh* (see JEHOVAH). The second word is the plural form of the Hebrew noun *ṣābā' H7372*, which means "army" but also is applied to the stars (e.g., 2 Ki. 17:16) and to the heavenly attendants (1 Ki. 22:19). See HOST OF HEAVEN. In many instances (mostly in Isaiah) the SEPTUAGINT renders the phrase with a transliteration, *kyrios sabaōth* (used twice in the NT, Rom. 9:29 [a LXX quotation]; Jas. 5:4), but in over one hundred passages it renders the phrase, with minor variations, as *kyrios pantokratōr*, "Lord Almighty," and this understanding has been followed by the NIV. The precise reference of the Hebrew phrase is debated. A military allusion is clear in some contexts, as when DAVID exclaimed that he was coming against GOLIATH "in the name of the LORD of hosts, the God of the armies of Israel" (1 Sam. 17:45 NRSV; cf. also Isa. 13:4; 31:4). But many other passages are more general in character. The initial use of the concept of the "hosts" is found in Gen. 2:1, where it refers back to the totality of created beings in the "heaven and the earth" (cf. also Isa. 45:12-13).

Lord's Day. This expression (Gk. *hē kyriakē hēmera*) is found in the Bible only in Rev. 1:10, where John states, "On the Lord's Day I was in the Spirit," when he received a divine commission to write the book of Revelation. The adjective *kyriakos G3258* (which also occurs in 1 Cor. 11:20 in the expression, "the Lord's Supper") can also be trans-

lated "belonging to the Lord" and so the expression denotes a day consecrated to CHRIST. Some would equate it with the OT prophetic DAY OF THE LORD, but clearly John is not speaking of that prophetic day. The form of his expression marks a distinction between the prophetic "day of the Lord" (1 Cor. 5:5; 2 Cor. 1:14; 1 Thess. 5:2) and the first day of the week, on which Christ arose. It was the RESURRECTION victory on that day that marked it as distinct and sacred to the Christian CHURCH. The gospel emphasis on "the first day of the week" as the day of resurrection stresses its distinctiveness. On that day the risen Christ repeatedly appeared to his disciples (Lk. 24:13-49; Jn. 20:1-25), and again a week later (Jn. 20:26). The Pentecostal outpouring apparently also came on that day. Acts 20:7 and 1 Cor. 16:1-2 show that the early church consecrated the day to WORSHIP and almsgiving (but not to earning).

Sunday (this name is of pagan origin) as the day of special worship is a Christian institution, and some believe that it must be sharply distinguished from the SABBATH. Others would argue that there are important continuities, as well as differences, between the two. Certainly the detailed OT regulations regarding the Sabbath were not necessarily transferred to the Lord's Day as a "Christian Sabbath." However, the fourth commandment was not expressed in terms of "legalistic ceremonialism"; rather, it was grounded in God's own pattern of rest at CREATION (Exod. 20:8-11; Heb. 4:4) and in his work of REDEMPTION (Deut. 5:12-15). The NT clearly views the Jewish calendar as something that must not be imposed on GENTILES (Gal. 4:10; Col. 2:16-17), and PAUL states that observance of special days is a matter of Christian liberty (Rom. 14:5-6). But Christians continue to differ on whether the Decalogue's injunction of a weekly rest has been abrogated.

Lord's Prayer. The traditional name given to the prayer Jesus taught his disciples, as recorded in Matt. 6:9-13 and, more briefly, in Lk. 11:2-4. The fuller form, part of the SERMON ON THE MOUNT, is the one commonly used. As a pattern prayer it is unsurpassed for conciseness and fullness, delineating the proper approach and order in prayer. It directs the disciples, as members of God's family,

The Lord's Prayer written in Bariba, Cherokee, and Moore languages. From the Pater Noster Church in Jerusalem.

reverently to pray to a personal heavenly Father. The petitions are divided into two parts, the first three relating to God's interests. They are arranged in a descending scale, from himself, through the manifestation of himself in his kingdom (the coming messianic kingdom), to the complete doing of his will by his subjects. Placing God's interest first, the disciples can pray for their own needs. The petitions, whether counted as three or four, are arranged in an ascending scale—from the supply of daily material needs to the ultimate deliverance from all evil. The doxology in Matthew, which constitutes an affirmation of faith, is lacking in the leading MSS and is generally regarded as a scribal addition derived from ancient liturgical usage.

Lord's Supper. This expression is found only once in the NT (Gk. *kyriakon deipnon*, 1 Cor. 11:20), where it refers not only to the special Christian rite of breaking the bread and drinking the cup, but also to the love feast that accompanied it (see AGAPE). Elsewhere PAUL uses the related phrase, "Lord's table" (1 Cor. 10:21), while the expression "breaking of bread," which occurs several times in Acts, probably also refers to the Lord's Supper. The institution of this ceremony is described in four passages (Matt. 26:26-29; Mk. 14:22-25; Lk.

22:15-20; 1 Cor. 11:23-25). On the night before the crucifixion, Jesus adopted the position of head of a household and ate the Passover meal with his disciples in a room within the city limits of JERUSALEM. It is interesting to note that he did not give new and special significance to the special parts of that meal (e.g., lamb and bitter herbs) but to the bread and wine, common to many meals. Distributing the bread he had broken for his disciples, he said, "I am myself this bread." Later in the meal, he said of the wine, "This is my blood of the covenant, which is poured out for many." Then at the end of the meal Jesus declared that he would not drink again of the fruit of the vine until he drank it anew in the KINGDOM OF GOD.

There are two important themes in the words of Jesus. First he was telling them that the cup of red wine represented his own blood, shed to inaugurate a new COVENANT between God and "the many" (see Isa. 52:15; 53:12). He was to offer himself to God as a sacrifice for sin so that a new relationship could be created by God between himself and the redeemed community of believers. Second, he was pointing toward the full realization and consummation of the kingdom of God at the end of the age, when the meal would be resumed in the "messianic banquet." Thus, it may be said that

L

the Lord's Supper is eaten in remembrance of his atoning death by which comes redemption and in expectation of the arrival of the kingdom of God in its fullness.

Paul's teaching is found in 1 Cor. 10-11. He stressed the spiritual communion between Christ and his body (disciples) and within the body (see BODY OF CHRIST). Even as the Israelites were miraculously fed by MANNA and water in the wilderness, so in communion with Christ believers are spiritually nourished by heavenly food. Therefore, those who eat the body and drink the blood of Christ are not to participate in Jewish or pagan sacrifices (10:16-22), and they are to ensure that when they partake of the Lord's Supper, they partake worthily, being in genuine fellowship with fellow believers.

The actual services of the Lord's Supper began in the church after the coming of the HOLY SPIRIT on the Day of PENTECOST: Acts 2:42 refers to the table fellowship as "breaking of bread" (cf. Acts 20:7). These acts of WORSHIP and FELLOWSHIP are to be seen as the result of the fusion of various strands of experience enjoyed by the disciples with Jesus. They had fellowship with Jesus in eating (Matt. 14:13-21; 15:23-39—and note that according to Jn. 6:33-34, when he fed the 5,000 Jesus taught that he was the true heavenly food). These times of miraculous feeding and the Last Supper itself (within the Passover meal) belong to the time before the crucifixion; then the table fellowship with the risen Lord (Lk. 24:30-35; Jn. 21:13; Acts 10:41) in the "forty days" belongs to the postresurrection period. Thus, when the disciples came together on that Day of Pentecost and on subsequent occasions, their breaking of bread was the continuation of a rich tradition of fellowship already established by Jesus and into which they incorporated the actual Lord's Supper. At first the ceremony was a part of a larger meal (see 1 Cor. 11:17-22); but, being a special part, it could be separated. As the years went by, it was in fact separated and became the second half of the Sunday worship of the local church, the first part being the ministry of the Word, prayers, singing of psalms, and intercessions.

Nowhere in the NT is the Lord's Supper called a SACRIFICE. However, the believers are said to be offering spiritual sacrifices to God when God is worshiped, served, and obeyed (Rom. 12:1; Heb. 13:15-16; 1 Pet. 2:5). The Lord's Supper as a part of the worship and service offered to God is thus a sacrifice of praise and thanksgiving. Regrettably the EUCHARIST (ministry of Word and Lord's Supper as one service) has often been referred to in sacrificial terms as though it were a sacrifice in a unique sense—an unbloody sacrifice. While the Lord's Supper is the memorial of a sacrifice, and is a sacrifice of praise offered to God, it is neither a repetition of the sacrifice of Christ made at Calvary nor a participation in the self-offering that Christ is perpetually making to the Father in heaven as the heavenly Priest. It is a proclamation of the Lord's death sacramentally until he returns to earth.

Lo-Ruhamah. lo′roo-hah′muh (Heb. *lō' ruḥāmâ H4205*, "she has not received compassion" or "she has not been loved"). A symbolical name given by the prophet HOSEA to his daughter and second child by his wife GOMER (Hos. 1:6). See LO-AMMI.

Lot. lot (Heb. *lôṭ H4288*, derivation uncertain; Gk. *Lōt G3397*). Son of HARAN and nephew of Abram (ABRAHAM; Gen. 11:27). His life may be summarized under the following heads. (1) *Departure and dependence.* Born in UR of the Chaldees, Lot, whose father had died (11:28), migrated to the city of Haran with his grandfather, TERAH, and Abram and Sarai (11:31). After Terah's death (11:32), Lot followed Abraham in his journeys from MESOPOTAMIA to CANAAN, thence to EGYPT, and back again to Canaan (12:5, 10; 13:1). During this period there was unity and fellowship between uncle and nephew.

(2) *Decision and destiny.* Because of a conflict between their herdsmen, Abraham suggested that his nephew choose another place. Lot, apparently prompted by selfishness, chose the country in the environs of SODOM, a city that had already become notorious because of its wickedness (Gen. 13:5-13). This fatal choice determined his subsequent destiny. It was Abraham now who maintained the greater spiritual status (13:14-18).

(3) *Devastation and deportation.* Lot, then in Sodom, was taken captive when KEDORLAOMER

and his confederates conquered the king of Sodom and his four allies (Gen. 14:1-12). Abraham, the separated and faithful servant, pursued the enemies and rescued his nephew (14:13-16).

(4) *Depravity and degeneration.* Angels then visited Lot in Sodom to hasten his departure from the imminent doom decreed on the wicked city. Although originally only a sojourner (Gen. 19:9), Lot acted like a citizen; he had imbibed the Canaanites' mores and standards. Look at his willingness to sacrifice his daughters' chastity (19:8), his utter ineffectiveness in dealing with his sons-in-law (19:14), his hesitation in leaving the doomed city (19:15-16), and his unwillingness to leave the comforts of a city (19:17-22). In spite of all these adverse things, Lot was, as the NT plainly declares, "a righteous man" (2 Pet. 2:7-8); and, furthermore, his righteous soul was daily vexed with the lawless deeds (2:8) of Sodom's inhabitants. By implication, it seems that the term "godly" is also applied to Lot (2:9).

(5) *Dénouement and disgrace.* Lot, because of fear, left ZOAR and lived in a cave with his two daughters (Gen. 19:30), his wife already having become, because of unbelief, "a pillar of salt" (19:17, 26; Lk. 17:29). In this cave one of the most unseemly scenes recorded in the Bible took place (Gen. 19:31-38). Made drunk by his daughters, Lot became the unwitting father of their sons, MOAB and BEN-AMMI, the progenitors of the Moabites

© Dr. James C. Martin

Byzantine chapel built over the "cave of Lot," on the SE side of the Dead Sea (view to the SW). Lot associated himself with the cities of the plain traditionally located in this area.

and the Ammonites (Deut. 2:9, 19; Ps. 83:8). The almost buried faith of Lot reappeared in RUTH, a Moabitess, the great-grandmother of DAVID and thus a member of the messianic line (Ruth 1:16-18; 4:13-21).

Lotan. loh´tan (Heb. *lôṭān H4289*). First son of SEIR the HORITE; he was a clan chief of EDOM (Gen. 36:20-22, 29; 1 Chr. 1:38-39).

lots. Objects used for DIVINATION or for making a choice. In the history of the Bible, the casting of lots was used to determine the will of God. The method is not clearly defined. Some scholars believe that the URIM AND THUMMIM (Exod. 28:30; Deut. 33:8; Ezra 2:63) were objects, possibly two small round pebbles signifying "yes" or "no," that were placed in the EPHOD of the high priest. When the priest reached blindly into the ephod and took out one stone, the question was answered either affirmatively or negatively by the stone he found in his hand. There were, however, many instances recorded where lots were cast without the use of the Urim and Thummim.

Numerous passages in the OT indicate that the casting of lots was customarily employed for making important decisions (Lev. 16:7-10, 21-22; Josh. 7:14; 14:2; 1 Sam. 14:42; 1 Chr. 25:7-8; Neh. 10:34). The principle underlying this usage is stated in Prov. 16:33: "The lot is cast into the lap, / but its every decision is from the LORD." (Regarding the Feast of Lots, see PURIM.) The same usage persisted in NT times. The soldiers at the foot of the cross cast lots for the clothing of Jesus (Matt. 27:35), thus fulfilling an OT prophecy (Ps. 22:18). Within the CHURCH, the successor of JUDAS ISCARIOT among the apostles was selected by lot (Acts 1:26). In the latter instance the choice was preceded by PRAYER. There is no explicit indication that this procedure was approved by God, and it never appears

L

in the later activities of the church. The guidance of the HOLY SPIRIT seems to have been manifested in other ways.

lotus. See PLANTS.

love. Love is presented in Scripture as the very nature of God (1 Jn. 4:8, 16) and the greatest of the Christian virtues (1 Cor. 13:13). It receives definition in Scripture only by a listing of its attributes (13:4-7). It lies at the very heart of Christianity, being essential in our relationship to God and to others (Matt. 22:37-40; Mk. 12:28-31; Jn. 13:34-35). Jesus taught that on it hang all the Law and the Prophets (Matt. 22:40). It is the fulfillment of the LAW, for its sense of obligation and desire for the welfare of the one loved impels it to carry out the demands of the law (Rom. 13:8-10). Love found its supreme expression in the self-sacrifice on Calvary (1 Jn. 4:10).

The Bible makes the unique revelation that God in his very nature and essence is love (1 Jn. 4:8, 16), Christianity being the only religion thus to present the Supreme Being. God not only loves, he *is* love. In this supreme attribute all the other attributes are harmonized. His own Son, Jesus Christ, is the unique object of this eternal love (Isa. 42:1; Matt. 3:17; 17:5; Jn. 17:24). God loves the world as a whole (Jn. 3:16), as well as individuals in it (Gal. 2:20), in spite of the sinfulness and corruption of the human race (Rom. 5:8-10; Eph. 2:4-5). God's love for his creatures manifests itself not only in supplying all their needs (Acts 14:17) but supremely in the REDEMPTION wrought for sinners (Rom. 5:8; 1 Jn. 4:9-10). Believers in Christ are the objects of his special love (Jn. 16:27; 17:23), causing him to deal in chastisement with them (Heb. 12:6-11), but they are assured that nothing can separate them from his unfathomable love in Christ (Rom. 8:31-39).

All human love, whether Godward or manward, has its source in God. Love in its true reality and power is seen only in the light of Calvary (1 Jn. 4:7-10). It is created in believers by the HOLY SPIRIT (Rom. 5:5; Gal. 5:22), prompting them to love both God and other believers (2 Cor. 5:14-15; 1 Jn. 4:20-21). Love finds its expression in service to our neighbor (Matt. 22:37-39; Gal. 5:13)

and is the chief test of Christian discipleship (Lk. 14:26; Jn. 13:35; 1 Jn. 3:14). Love is vitally related to FAITH; faith is basic (Jn. 6:29; Heb. 11:6), but a faith that does not manifest itself in love is dead and worthless (Gal. 5:6, 13; Jas. 2:17-26). Christians must love even their enemies (Matt. 5:43-48; Rom. 12:19-20; 1 Jn. 3:14). Our love "must be sincere" (Rom. 12:9) and should manifest itself "with actions and in truth" (1 Jn. 3:18). Love is the bond uniting all the Christian virtues (Col. 3:14).

love feast. See AGAPE.

lovingkindness. This term, rarely found in modern versions, is used by the KJV almost thirty times to render Hebrew *ḥesed H2876*, a theologically significant word that has a broad range of meaning. It signifies an attitude—either divine or human—born out of mutual relationship, for example, between relatives, friends, master/subject, host/guest. Primarily it is not a disposition but a helpful action; it corresponds to a relationship of trust. As exercised by a sovereign, it protects his dominion; it gives people security in their mutual dealings. The Hebrew term also denotes "kindness" or "help" received from a superior. The meaning fluctuates: "obligation," "loyalty," "love," "grace." Frequently it is associated with FORGIVENESS and is almost equal to MERCY (Exod. 20:6; 34:6, 7; Mic. 7:18). Many scholars believe that the principal connotation is "loyal love"—a love that is associated with the COVENANT (Deut. 7:12; 1 Sam. 20:8). When the term refers to God, it indicates in general the divine LOVE flowing out to sinners in unmerited kindness. On the divine side it comes to designate particularly his FAITHFULNESS and GRACE (Ps. 25:6; 36:7; 136:1-26).

low country. See SHEPHELAH.

loyalty. See FAITHFULNESS; LOVINGKINDNESS.

Lubim. See LIBYA.

Lucas. loo´kuhs. KJV alternate form of LUKE (Phlm. 24).

Lucifer. loo´si-fuhr. KJV rendering of Hebrew *hêlēl H2122* ("shining one"), which occurs only once, in an oracle against the king of BABYLON (Isa. 14:12). The name comes from the Vulgate (Latin *lucifer*, "light-bringing"; cf. LXX, *eōsphoros*) and is applied to the MORNING STAR, that is, Venus. Some Latin church fathers, associating this passage with Lk. 10:18 (cf. also 2 Cor. 11:14), applied the name to SATAN, and this usage became common.

Lucius. loo´shuhs (Gk. *Loukios G3372*, Lat. *Lucius*, from *lux*, "light"). **(1)** A Roman CONSUL who, in response to an embassy sent to ROME by Simon MACCABEE, wrote a letter to PTOLEMY Euergetes of Egypt (1 Macc. 15:16-21) and other ANE rulers (15:22-23) supporting Simon in his struggles with the SELEUCIDS. His identification is problematic.

(2) A man from CYRENE, named third among the five "prophets and teachers" in the church at ANTIOCH OF SYRIA (Acts 13:1). This Lucius was apparently one of the Hellenistic Jewish Christians who had boldly preached to the Greeks in this city (11:20-21), where he remained to minister in the church.

(3) One of three "relatives" of PAUL (the others being JASON and SOSIPATER) who sent greetings to the Christians in Rome (Rom. 16:21). According to many scholars, however, the Greek term *syngenēs G5150* here means "kinsman" (cf. RSV) and should be understood in the sense of "fellow-Jew" (cf. 9:3). It is possible, however, that this description applies only to Jason and Sosipater. The Lucius mentioned here is thought by some to be the same as #2 above, but that identification is not probable. Inscriptional evidence shows that *Loukas* (LUKE) was used as an alternative form for Lucius or Lucanus, and this fact has been used to support a proposed identification of the author of the third gospel and Acts with either of the above companions of Paul. Many believe that such identifications are ruled out by Col. 4:12-14, which indicates that Luke was a GENTILE rather than a Jew; in response, some point out that Rom. 16:21 is ambiguous regarding the ethnic identity of Lucius #3.

lucre. This English term is used by the KJV once in the OT in a passage where the term has a negative connotation (1 Sam. 8:3; NIV, "dishonest gain"; NRSV, "bribe"). In the KJV NT it is always qualified by "filthy" as the rendering of Greek

aischrokerdēs G153 ("shameful gain") or a cognate expression (1 Tim. 3:3 [TR], 8; Tit. 1:7; 1 Pet. 5:2). The term *lucre* can mean simply "profit," but the rendering "filthy lucre," which goes back to Tyndale's translation, has given the word itself a bad name.

Lud. luhd (Heb. *lûd H4276*). Son of SHEM and grandson of NOAH (Gen. 10:22; 1 Chr. 1:17). Earlier in the Table of Nations, however, the Ludites (KJV "Ludim") are said to be descendants of MIZRAIM or EGYPT (Gen. 10:13; 1 Chr. 1:11). Since the passage is basically ethnographic in character and concerned chiefly with the origin and classification of certain of the nations of the ancient world, Lud and Ludim are to be regarded as eponymous ancestors of two different nations (one Semitic and the other Hamitic) that continued to bear their names. (1) The identification of Ludim/ Ludites with Lydia is ruled out on the basis of the close geographical and ethnic association of Ludim with Egypt. It is probably better to regard it as a nation now unknown. (2) Lud, on the other hand, is almost certainly Lydia in at least one passage where it appears in association with TARSHISH, TUBAL, and GREECE (Isa. 66:19), nations that were located along the N shores of the MEDITERRANEAN Sea. See LYDIA (PLACE). The NIV also translates "Lydia" elsewhere (Jer. 46:9; Ezek. 27:20; 30:5; in this last passage, however, the association with ETHIOPIA and LIBYA suggests an African nation).

Ludim, Ludites. See LUD; LYDIA (PLACE).

Luhith. loo´hith (Heb. *lûḥît H4284*, "platform, terrace, shelf"). A city of MOAB, associated with HORONAIM (Isa. 15:5; Jer. 48:5). Refugees from ruined Moab are described as fleeing to ZOAR by the ascent of Luhith and in the way to Horonaim. Luhith may therefore have been on a hill a few miles SE of the DEAD SEA, but the precise location is uncertain.

Luke. look (Gk. *Loukas G3371*, a name used in inscriptions as an affectionate form of *Loukios* [see LUCIUS], but some believe it should be connected with *Lucanus* or *Lucianus*). According to very ancient tradition, Luke was the writer of the third gospel (see Luke, Gospel of) and of the Acts of the Apostles. From the latter book his association with Paul is established. In four passages of varying length the author of Acts writes in the first person (Acts 16:10-17; 20:5-15; 21:1-18; 27:1—28:16). These so-called "we sections" constitute the major portion of the extant biographical material on Luke. Apart from this he is mentioned three times in the NT (Col. 4:14; Phlm. 24; 2 Tim. 4:11). From the first reference it is evident that Luke was a physician; from the last, that he was with Paul some time after he disappears from view at the end of the Acts of the Apostles. The context of the Colossians reference (see Col. 4:11) also suggests that Luke was a Gentile.

It appears from Luke's own writings that he was a man of education and culture. He begins his gospel with an elaborate paragraph, showing that he could write in the sophisticated tradition of the Hellenistic historians, and then lapses into a polished vernacular. He uses this speech with vigor and effectiveness. He is an accurate and able historian and has left some of the most powerful descriptive writing in the NT. His medical knowledge and his interest in seafaring are apparent from his writings. Whatever is said beyond this is tradition and conjecture. There is no solid support for the conjectures that Luke was Lucius of Cyrene (Acts 13:1), or one of "the Seventy" (Lk. 10:1; NIV, "seventy-two"), one of the Greeks of Jn. 12:20, or one of the two disciples of Emmaus (Lk. 24:13).

Some evidence supports other conjectures and traditions. That he knew Mary, mother of Jesus is fairly clear from the earlier chapters of his Gospel, and the period of acquaintance may have been during Paul's incarceration at Caesarea. Eusebius and Jerome say that Luke was a Syrian of Antioch, and he does seem to have a close knowledge of the church there. On the other hand, certain features of the account of Paul's visit to Philippi suggest that Luke had an intimate knowledge of that city and no little loyalty toward it. Here, too, on two occasions, he appears to have joined Paul's party. This has given grounds for the contention that Luke was a Macedonian (perhaps even the one who appeared to Paul in a vision, Acts 16:9). Tradition and conjecture could be reconciled if Luke was an Antiochene of Macedonian origin who had studied at the medical school of Philippi and spent significant years in Macedonia. Luke must have been a person of singular sweetness of character to earn the apostle's adjective "beloved" (Col. 4:14 KJV; NIV, "dear"). He was obviously a man of outstanding loyalty, of unusual capacity for research, and with the scholar's ability to strip away the irrelevant and dispensable detail. A bare tradition states that he suffered martyrdom in Greece.

Luke, Gospel of. The third account of the gospel of Jesus Christ, according to the present common order of listing in the NT canon.

I. Authenticity. References to this gospel are frequent in the second century A.D. (Justin, Polycarp, Papias, Hegesippus, Marcion, Heracleon, the Clementine Homilies, Theophilus of Antioch). It is probable that Clement alludes to it (95). It is mentioned as the work of Luke by the Muratorian Fragment (170) and by Irenaeus (180). This

Latin MS of Luke with glosses or brief explanations (12th cent.).

© Dr. James C. Martin. Sola Scriptura. The Van Kampen Collection on display at the Holy Land Experience in Orlando, Florida. Photographed by permission.

Overview of LUKE

Author: Anonymous, but traditionally attributed to Luke the physician.

Historical setting: Covers the period from the annunciation of John the Baptist to the ascension of Christ. The book was probably written in Rome c. A.D. 60, but some date it to the 70s or even later.

Purpose: To provide a full and orderly historical-theological account of the life of Christ that will reassure the reader concerning the certainty of the gospel (Lk. 1:3-4), focusing on such themes as the universality of salvation (offered even to Gentiles and tax collectors), the Holy Spirit, and prayer.

Contents: The nativity stories and Jesus' childhood (Lk. 1-2); the baptism and temptation, leading to ministry in Galilee (3:1—9:50); journey to Jerusalem, with much unique material, especially a number of parables found only in this gospel (9:51—19:27); ministry in Jerusalem, leading to Jesus' death, resurrection, and ascension (19:28—24:53).

testimony continues into the third century (Clement of Alexandria, Tertullian, Origen). Such a mass of evidence is quite decisive.

II. Date. Although uncertain, the date can be confined to fairly narrow limits. The abrupt termination of the Acts of the Apostles suggests that the author did not long survive his friend and associate Paul. Nor is it likely to have been written after the fall of Jerusalem in A.D. 70. The period of Paul's imprisonment in Caesarea saw Luke in Palestine, and this period (conjecturally 58-59) would presumably give abundant opportunity for the research that is evident in the record. Luke's Gospel is thus probably the latest of the Synoptic Gospels.

III. Historiography. W. M. Ramsay's work on the Acts of the Apostles has established the right of Luke to rank as a first-rate historian in his own capacity. He was demonstrated to have maintained a consistent level of accuracy wherever detail could be objectively tested, and the vividness of narration so evident in the second work is visible also in the gospel.

IV. Style. Luke's preface is in the elaborate style of ancient historians and demonstrates that Luke could write with facility in the literary tradition of his time. At Lk. 1:5 he moves into an easy ver-

nacular, which he employs for his whole narrative. His language is the common dialect, but used with grace and vigor and with an educated man's skill in composition.

V. Unique features. Many incidents and much teaching are found only in Luke's Gospel. (1) The nativity section is fresh and different and seems to point to direct contact with Mary herself; the record of the birth of John the Baptist is especially noteworthy, as are the four psalms (Lk. 1:46-55, 68-79; 2:14, 29-32) that form a striking link between the hymnology of the OT and that of the NT. (2) The human genealogy (3:23-38) of Christ, traced to Adam, is chosen in accordance with the cosmopolitan flavor of the gospel and the writer's conception of his writing as the first movement of the great historical process that took the faith from Bethlehem to Rome. (3) The childhood of Jesus is recorded in Jesus' visit to the temple (2:41-52); found only in Luke, this account also points to the probability that Mary was the chief authority. (4) Some of Jesus' discourses and sayings, together with their associated incidents, Luke alone records, especially those contained in the unique section from 9:51 to 18:14 (e.g., the rejection by the Samaritans, the sending out of the Seventy, etc.).

L

(5) Parables and illustrative anecdotes that only Luke records are those of the two debtors (7:41-43), the good Samaritan (10:30-37), the persistent friend at night (11:5-8), the rich fool (12:16-21), the barren fig tree (13:6-9), the lost coin and the prodigal son (15:3-32), the unrighteous steward and the rich fool and Lazarus (16:1-12, 19-31), the wicked judge and the Pharisee and the tax collector (18:2-14), the ten minas (19:13-27). (6) Only Luke records the following miracles: the large catch of fish (5:1-11), the widow's son (7:11-14), the sick woman (13:11-13), the sick man (14:2-6), the ten lepers (17:12-19), the healing of Malchus in Gethsemane (22:51). (7) In the closing chapters of the gospel, the prayer on the cross (23:34), the penitent thief (23:39-43), the walk to Emmaus (24:13-35), and much of the ascension narrative are recorded only by Luke.

VI. Special characteristics. Apart from material content there are special characteristics of Luke's approach that should be noted. (1) As in the Acts of the Apostles, he exalts womanhood; apart from the nativity narratives, see, for example, Lk. 7:11-17; 8:1-3, 48; 10:38-42; 13:16; 23:28. (2) It is perhaps part of the universality of Luke's conception of the Christian message that he stresses the Lord's attitude toward the poor; see 6:20-25; 8:2-3; 12:16-21; 14:12-15; 16:13; 18:25. (3) The same notion of a universal evangel, natural in an associate of Paul, is found as vividly in Luke's completion of John's Isian quotation ("And all mankind will see God's salvation," 3:6), as in Acts 17:27; note in the same connection the strain of racial tolerance illustrated by the tale of the good Samaritan, the word of praise for the grateful Samaritan leper, and the rebukes of Lk. 9:49-56. (4) Luke also gives prominence to prayer: he speaks of the Lord's prayer at his baptism, after cleansing the leper, before calling the Twelve, on the Mount of Transfiguration, on the cross, and at death; see also 11:8; 18:1; 21:36 and the parables in 11:5-13 and 18:1-8. (5) A kindliness of judgment pervades Luke's gospel as was proper in one who was not himself an associate of the Twelve: he gives a milder version of Peter's denial, touches the faults of the apostles with gentle hand, and omits the conversation on the leaven of the Pharisees and the ambitious request of James and John.

VII. Sources. Beyond the writer's own statement that he collected his material from eyewitnesses (Lk. 1:2), it is impossible to be dogmatic. From the first words of the Gospel it is evident that Luke had both written accounts and living witnesses to draw from. In parts he appears to have followed Mark or Mark's authorities and tradition. Mary could have supplied information regarding the nativity, and the unique material on the passion and resurrection had apostolic authority.

lunatic. See DISEASES.

lust. This term (as a noun or verb), referring to an intense desire, most often has a negative connotation, being used especially of unrestrained sexual craving. English Bible translations use the term variously to render a number of words and expressions, in particular Greek *epithymia G2123*. This Greek noun (as well as the cognate verb *epithymeō G2121*) can refer to desire in a neutral or even positive context (e.g., Lk. 22:15; Phil. 1:23; 1 Thess. 2:17), but in the NT it is so frequently joined with such terms as "evil" (e.g., Col. 3:5) that the word by itself takes on a negative nuance ("covetousness, sinful passion," etc.). The consequences of evil lust are not only privation of good, but also enslavement, suffering, and death.

lustration. A SACRIFICE or ceremony for the purpose of PURIFICATION. The word is not found in the English Bible, but other terms referring to purification are found in both Testaments often. See CLEAN; UNCLEAN

lute. See MUSICAL INSTRUMENTS.

Luz. luhz (Heb. *lûz H4281*, "almond tree"). (1) The earlier Canaanite name of the city better known as BETHEL (Gen. 28:19; 35:6). It was changed to the latter (meaning "house of God") by JACOB after the Lord appeared to him in a dream during his flight from home, and it became a holy place in the later history of Israel. The book of Joshua, in delineating the territories of EPHRAIM and MANASSEH, speaks of the boundary as going out "from Bethel to Luz" (Josh. 16:2), apparently regarding the two as distinct locations. The reference here is probably not to the city of Bethel but to a mountain range closely associated with the city which is mentioned as the previous boundary point (v. 1) and from which the line went out to Luz, that is, the city of Bethel (in 18:13, Bethel and Luz are regarded as identical).

(2) A town built in the land of the HITTITES by a former inhabitant of Luz #1, apparently named after the Canaanite city (Jdg. 1:26). The expression "land of the Hittites" probably refers to SYRIA, but the term *Hittite* is ambiguous, and some think that the phrase may designate the hill country W of Bethel (cf. Num. 13:29). The location of this town is unknown.

LXX. Abbreviation for SEPTUAGINT.

Lycaonia. lik´uh-oh´nee-uh (Gk. *Lykaonia G3377*; cf. *Lykaonisti G3378*, "in Lycaonian [language]"). A region in south central ASIA MINOR. Although its borders are not well defined, Lycaonia had GALATIA to the N, CAPPADOCIA to the E, CILICIA to the S, and PISIDIA to the W. It consisted for the most part of a high, treeless plateau, the land being fertile enough and productive where there was water, but good mainly for raising sheep and goats. The people who inhabited the region have been described as warlike and energetic. In NT times the region was administered by the Romans as part of their settlement in Asia, and from 25 B.C. onward became part of Galatia or Galatia-Cappadocia. The leading cities of Lycaonia were LYSTRA and DERBE. ICONIUM was evidently a Phrygian city (see PHRYGIA), for when the Jews stirred up trouble for PAUL and BARNABAS there, they fled to the Lycaonian cities for safety (Acts 14:5-6). As everywhere else in the Seleucid realm, the process of hellenization went on (see HELLENISM), but slowly in Lycaonia, for the people are described as being backward. The GREEK LANGUAGE was no doubt understood in the cities, but the people still retained their own speech, which they used in response to the miracle Paul worked upon the cripple in Lystra (Acts 14:11). They then proceeded to get ready to sacrifice to Paul and Barnabas as though they were gods, an act from which Paul barely restrained them. This whole incident indicates the strong hold of pagan religion upon the populace of the region.

Lycia. lish´uh (Gk. *Lykia G3379*). A mountainous country in SW ASIA MINOR. This territory of about 3,500 sq. mi. (9,000 sq. km.) protrudes southward into the MEDITERRANEAN Sea bounded on the NW by CARIA, on the N by PHRYGIA and PISIDIA, and on the NE by PAMPHYLIA. Lycia was shut in by rugged mountain ranges, and since the land jutted out into the sea, it would not have any important trade routes. Its climate rapidly fluctuated between the extremes of temperature. Its mountainous slopes afforded much excellent timber for the building of houses and ships, and were also suitable for grazing and for vineyards and olive farms. The valleys provided space for the cultivated grains.

Its main contact to the outside world was through its seaports, the main two being PATARA and MYRA. On the return of the third missionary journey, PAUL's ship stopped at Patara (Acts 21:1) and then sailed to PHOENICIA. On his journey to ROME, Paul's ship went along the coast of CILICIA and Pamphylia, and at Myra he and the other prisoners were put on another ship that had come from ALEXANDRIA and was sailing for Italy. Due to prevailing W winds, it was common for Alexandrian grain ships to travel N along the Syrian coast and then move slowly E along the coasts of Cilicia and Pamphylia. Myra was a natural place for the grain ships (cf. Acts 27:38) to harbor and to be serviced before their journey to Italy; and hence it would not be unusual for the centurion to find one here for Paul and the other prisoners.

Lydda. lid´uh (Gk. *Lydda G3375*). A town about 11 mi. (18 km.) SE of JOPPA where the apostle PETER healed a paralytic named AENEAS (Acts 9:32-35, 38). See LOD.

Lydia (person) lid´ee-uh (Gk. *Lydia G3376*). A business woman from THYATIRA; she lived in PHILIPPI and was PAUL's first convert there (Acts 16:12-15, 40). Her name, while common for women, may be an adjectival form, "the Lydian [woman]," as indicating her origin, since Thyatira was in the region of Lydia. See LYDIA (PLACE). She is identified as "a dealer in purple cloth." Her trade implies that she was a woman of some means. If a widow, she may have been carrying on the business of her deceased husband. Lydia is further described as "a worshiper of God," the usual designation for a Jewish PROSELYTE. She probably had accepted the Jewish faith in her native city, for it had a strong Jewish colony. At Philippi she faithfully participated in the SABBATH services at the place of prayer by the riverside. After listening to Paul's message there she was converted. After Lydia and her household (presumably her servants and their dependents) were baptized, she urged Paul and his coworkers to make her home their headquarters. Her home apparently became the meeting place of the local church (Acts 16:40). Lydia's own hospitality doubtless did much to foster the unique financial relations between Paul and the Philippian church (Phil. 4:15-16).

Lydia (place). lid´ee-uh (Gk. *Lydia*). A large territory in NW ASIA MINOR, bounded on the N by MYSIA, on the S by CARIA, on the E by PHRYGIA, and on the W by the AEGEAN SEA. It is a land mostly of fertile river valleys. SARDIS served as Lydia's capital. The earliest reference to Lydia is in Gen. 10:22 (cf. also 1 Chr. 1:17), where it refers to LUD as a son of SHEM; expounding on that passage, JOSEPHUS refers to the Lydians as Lud's descendants (*Ant.* 1.6.4. §144). In Isa. 66:19 Lud is listed with TUBAL (in Asia Minor), GREECE, and "the distant islands" (or "coastlands"), a context that would fit with the location of Lydia. In Ezek. 27:10 and 30:5 Lud is listed as an ally with TYRE and with EGYPT respectively. Lydia is mentioned also in the Neo-Babylonian annals. In NT times, Lydia formed a part of the Roman province of ASIA and remained so until it became a separate entity in Diocletian's reign (c. A.D. 316). The region was rich in natural resources, and its best-known industry was the manufacture of textile fabrics; along with this THYATIRA was well known for its dyeing processes. One of those in the industry was the Thyatiran woman who was converted to Christianity at PHILIPPI by PAUL (Acts 16:14). See LYDIA (PERSON). Also in Lydia was EPHESUS, the place where Paul spent nearly three years (Acts 19). Moreover, out of seven churches addressed by John in Rev. 2-3, five of them were in Lydia (see EPHESUS, SMYRNA, THYATIRA, SARDIS, PHILADELPHIA). However, the NT writers never address the above churches as being in Lydia, but rather in Asia, in accordance with the Roman provincial classification.

lye. KJV, "nitre." An alkaline substance used for cleansing purposes; it refers either to sodium carbonate, found in certain places as an incrustation on the ground or in certain saline lakes, or to potassium carbonate, which was obtained by leaching wood ashes or other vegetable matter. Both possess excellent detergent qualities. The term is used by the NRSV several times (Jer. 2:22 [NIV, "soda"]; Job. 9:30 [NIV, "soap"]; Isa. 1:25 [NIV differently]). See SOAP.

lying. See LIE, LYING.

lyre. See MUSIC AND MUSICAL INSTRUMENTS.

Lysanias. li-say´nee-uhs (Gk. *Lysanias G3384*). The TETRARCH of ABILENE at the beginning of JOHN THE BAPTIST's ministry (Lk. 3:1), probably in A.D. 26. There is no satisfactory explanation of the inclusion of this obscure non-Jewish ruler in the dating list, but epigraphical evidence frees the historian from the old allegation that he confused the tetrarch with an earlier ruler.

Lysias. lis´ee-uhs (Gk. *Lysias G3385*). (1) A prominent Syrian general and official who served under ANTIOCHUS IV Epiphanes and Antiochus V Eupator. He is given considerable attention in 1 and 2 Maccabees and in JOSEPHUS (e.g., 1 Macc. 3:32-38; 6:17; 7:1-4; 2 Macc. 10-11; Jos. *Ant.* 12 §§295-98, 313-15, 361, 367).
(2) See CLAUDIUS LYSIAS.

Lystra. lis´truh (Gk. *Lystra G3388*, construed both as fem. sg. and neut. pl.). A town in the central region of S ASIA MINOR (Acts 14:6, 8, 21; 16:1-2; 2 Tim. 3:11). Lystra is an ancient village of the district of LYCAONIA that was c. 24 mi. (39 km.) S of ICONIUM (in PHRYGIA). Lystra was built upon a small hill suddenly rising above the surrounding plain located on the E of the mountain ranges that form the Pisidian triangle (see PISIDIA). It is probable that the territory of Lystra was bounded in the N by Iconium, in the W by the mountains, and

The region of Lystra as seen from the city acropolis. (View to the S.)

in the S by Isauria Vetus. The plain surrounding Lystra was fertile, with two small rivers passing by the village's mound. On the first missionary journey, PAUL and BARNABAS arrived at Lystra (c. A.D. 49), having fled the hostility of the Jews at Iconium (Acts 14:6). Upon arrival, Paul healed a man who had been lame from birth and the crowd concluded that the apostles were the gods HERMES and ZEUS (vv. 6-18; on an earlier occasion, the same two gods, as the local legend relates, had come to that region to visit an aged and pious couple). Afterward the Jews from ANTIOCH of Pisidia and Iconium came and influenced the people against Paul and consequently stoned the apostle dragging him out of the city as dead. Probably it was this visit of Paul during which TIMOTHY was converted and undoubtedly helped to establish the infant church at Lystra (2 Tim. 3:10-11). Paul and Barnabas went on to DERBE but later on their return visited Lystra (Acts 14:19-23). On his second missionary journey Paul traveled through SYRIA and CILICIA (c. A.D. 50) and revisited the churches of Derbe and Lystra (Acts 15:41—16:2). A visit to Lystra on the third journey (c. A.D. 53) is implied in Acts 18:23.

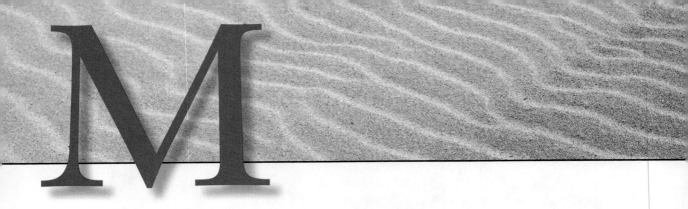

M

M. The symbol used to designate material peculiar to Matthew; for some scholars, the symbol represents an independent literary source used by this evangelist. See GOSPELS; MATTHEW, GOSPEL OF.

Maacah (person). may´uh-kuh (Heb. *maʿăkāh H5082*, perhaps "dull" or "oppression"). KJV also Maachah; TNIV Maakah. At least nine OT figures, both male and female, have this name. **(1)** Son of NAHOR by his concubine Reumah; nephew of ABRAHAM (Gen. 22:24). He may have been the ancestor of the people who inhabited a region by the same name. See MAACAH (PLACE). Some have thought that this Maacah was a daughter, not a son, of Nahor.

(2) Sister or wife of MAKIR son of MANASSEH (1 Chr. 7:15-16). The passage appears to speak of two different women named Maacah, one of whom was Makir's sister (v. 15) and another one his wife (v. 16). Some interpret (cf. KJV) or emend the Hebrew text so that it refers to only one woman named Maacah, Makir's wife, who bore him two sons, Peresh and Sheresh.

(3) Second concubine of CALEB son of Hezron (1 Chr. 2:48). His first concubine was EPHAH (v. 46).

(4) Wife of JEIEL, who was a descendant of BENJAMIN and the "father" (i.e., founder or a civic leader) of GIBEON (1 Chr. 9:35; the name Jeiel is missing from the MT of the parallel passage, 8:29, but most versions insert it).

(5) Daughter of TALMAI king of GESHUR; she became a wife of DAVID and bore ABSALOM during David's reign at HEBRON (2 Sam. 3:3; 1 Chr. 3:2). Absalom fled for safety to his mother's homeland after he killed his half-brother AMMON (2 Sam. 13:37-38).

(6) Father of Hanan; the latter was one of David's mighty warriors (1 Chr. 11:43).

(7) Father of Shephatiah; the latter was an officer over the tribe of SIMEON during the reign of David (1 Chr. 27:16).

(8) Father of the PHILISTINE king ACHISH (1 Ki. 2:39). Many believe this Maacah is the same as MAOCH (1 Sam. 27:2; the two forms may be variant spellings of the same name); others question this identification, since it would mean that the reign of Achish lasted at least forty years.

(9) Daughter of Abishalom (ABSALOM), favorite wife of REHOBOAM, and mother of Abijam (ABIJAH; 1 Ki. 15:2; 2 Chr. 11:20-22). Elsewhere she is called "Micaiah daughter of Uriel of Gibeah" (2 Chr. 13:2 NRSV), but the name MICAIAH may be a scribal error or an alternate form of Maacah (cf. NIV), while the word "daughter" here may mean "granddaughter" (cf. NIV mg.). Another difficulty is raised by 1 Ki. 15:10, which says with respect to ASA, Abijah's son, that "his mother's name was Maacah daughter of Abishalom" (NRSV; cf. also v. 13). Perhaps a different Maacah is involved, but more likely "mother" here means "grandmother" (cf. NIV). In any case, the biblical writer tells us that Asa deposed his grandmother (or mother!) Maacah from her royal position because of her IDOLATRY (v. 13).

Maacah (place). may´uh-kuh (Heb. *maʿăkāh H5081* [*maʿăkāt* in Josh. 13:13b], perhaps "dull" or "oppression"; gentilic *maʿăkāti H5084*, "Maacathite" [KJV, "Maachathi" and "Maachathite"]). KJV Maachah; TNIV Maakah; NRSV also Maacath (only Josh 13:13b). A small ARAMEAN state SE of Mount HERMON. It bordered GESHUR on the S and may have crossed the JORDAN to ABEL BETH MAACAH on the W. JAIR son of Manasseh made conquest of the land (Deut. 3:14; Josh. 12:5), and it was assigned to the half tribe of MANASSEH (Josh. 13:29-30). However, both the original Maacathites and the neighboring Geshurites remained in occupancy of their lands after Jair's conquest (Josh. 13:13; 2 Sam. 10:6-8; 1 Chr. 19:6-7). Maacathites are mentioned elsewhere (2 Sam. 23:34; 2 Ki. 25:23 = Jer. 40:8; 1 Chr. 4:19).

Maacath, Maacathite. See MAACAH (PLACE).

Maachah, Maachathi, Maachathite. See MAACAH (PERSON) and MAACAH (PLACE).

Maadai. may´uh-d*i* (Heb. *ma῾ăday H5049*, short form of MOADIAH, "ornament of Yahweh"). One of the sons of Bani who gave up their foreign wives in the time of EZRA (Ezra 10:34).

Maadiah. may´uh-d*i*´uh. See MOADIAH.

Maai. may´*i* (Heb. *mā῾ay H5076*, derivation uncertain). A priestly musician who participated in the dedication of the rebuilt wall of JERUSALEM under EZRA (Neh. 12:36).

Maakah. may´uh-kuh. TNIV form of MAACAH.

Maaleh-acrabbim. may´uh-leh-uh-krab´im. See AKRABBIM.

Maarath. may´uh-rath (Heb. *ma῾ărāt H5125*, possibly "barren [field]"). A town in the hill country of the tribe of JUDAH (Josh. 15:59). Maarath is listed between GEDOR and BETH ANOTH, so it was probably a few miles N of HEBRON, but its precise location is unknown. Some have thought it is the same as MAROTH (Mic. 1:12), but the context seems to place this town too far W.

Maareh-geba. may´uh-ri-gee´buh. Transliteration used by some versions (e.g., NJPS) to render the difficult Hebrew phrase *ma῾ăreh-gāba῾*, referring to a place where the men of Israel lay in ambush and from which they rushed forth to attack the Benjamites (Jdg. 20:33; KJV, "the meadows of Gibeah"). On the basis of the SEPTUAGINT and the VULGATE, the NIV and other versions read *ma῾ărab-gāba῾*, "west of Gibeah."

Maasai. may´uh-s*i* (Heb. *ma῾śay H5127*, short form of MAASEIAH, "work of Yahweh"). KJV Maasiai. Son of Adiel, listed among the first priests that returned from the EXILE and resettled in Jerusalem (1 Chr. 9:12). Because Maasai seems to correspond to AMASHSAI in a parallel passage (Neh. 11:13), some have argued that they are the same person and that the latter form is the result of scribal error.

Maaseiah. may´uh-see´yah (Heb. *ma῾ăśêāhû H5129* [in 1-2 Chr.] and *ma῾ăśêâ H5128* [in Ezra, Neh., and Jer., except Jer. 35:4], "work of Yahweh"). **(1)** One of the LEVITES who played the lyre when the ARK OF THE COVENANT was brought to JERUSALEM (1 Chr. 15:18, 20). **(2)** Son of Adaiah; he was one of the commanders under JEHOIADA who took part in the revolt against ATHALIAH (2 Chr. 23:1). **(3)** An officer under King UZZIAH who took part in mustering the army (2 Chr. 26:11). **(4)** Son of King AHAZ; all that is known about him is that he and two royal officials were assassinated by an Ephraimite warrior named Zicri (2 Chr. 28:7). **(5)** The ruler of Jerusalem at the time of King JOSIAH; he was among those sent to repair the TEMPLE (2 Chr. 34:8). **(6)** Father of the priest ZEPHANIAH; the latter figures in the ministry of JEREMIAH (Jer. 21:1; 29:25; 37:3). This Maaseiah is perhaps the same as the son of Shallum, a doorkeeper who had a room in the temple (35:4). **(7)** Father of the false prophet ZEDEKIAH (Jer. 29:21). **(8-11)** Four different men by the name of Maaseiah are listed among those who agreed to put away their foreign wives. Three of them—descendants of Jeshua, Harim, and Passhur respectively—were priests (Ezra 10:18-22); the fourth was a descendant of Pahath-Moab (10:30). **(12)** Father of a certain Azariah who made repairs to the wall of Jerusalem in NEHEMIAH's time (Neh. 3:23). **(13)** One of the prominent men who stood near EZRA when the law was read at the great assembly (Neh. 8:4); he is possibly the same as #11 above. **(14)** A Levite who helped EZRA instruct the people in the law (Neh. 8:7).

M

(15) One of the leaders of the people who signed the covenant of Nehemiah (Neh. 10:25); he is possibly the same as #11 or #13 above.

(16) Son of Baruch and descendant of JUDAH through SHELAH; he was an inhabitant of Judah resident in Jerusalem in postexilic times (Neh. 11:5 [KJV has "Shiloni" instead of "Shelah"; NRSV, "the Shilonite"]; apparently the same as ASAIAH in 1 Chr. 9:5). See SHILONITE.

(17) Son of Ithiel and an ancestor of Sallu; the latter was a Benjamite who lived in postexilic Jerusalem (Neh. 11:7).

(18-19) Two priests who participated in the choirs at the dedication of the walls of Jerusalem (Neh. 12:41-42); the first of these played the trumpet. Either or both of these men are possibly to be identified with one or more of the priests mentioned above (##8-10).

(20) KJV form of MAHSEIAH (Jer. 32:12; 51:59).

Maath. may´ath (Gk. *Maath G3399*, possibly from Heb. *maḥat H4744*; see MAHATH). Son of Mattathias, included in the GENEALOGY OF JESUS CHRIST (Lk. 3:26).

Maaz. may´az (Heb. *maʿaṣ H5106*, perhaps "angry"). Son of RAM, grandson of JERAHMEEL, and descendant of JUDAH (1 Chr. 2:27).

Maaziah. may´uh-zi´uh (Heb. *maʿazyāhû H5069* and *maʿazyâ H5068*, "Yahweh is [my] refuge"). **(1)** A priest during the time of DAVID who was the leader of the twenty-third division (1 Chr. 24:18). Some scholars believe that Maaziah here is the family name of a later priestly group. See #2 below.

(2) One of the priests (or priestly families) who signed the covenant of NEHEMIAH (Neh. 10:8).

Macbannai. mak´buh-i (Heb. *makbannay H4801*, perhaps from a root meaning "wrap around"). KJV Machbanai, NRSV Machbannai; TNIV Makbannai. A Gadite who joined DAVID's forces at ZIKLAG (1 Chr. 12:13).

Macbenah. mak-bee´nuh (Heb. *makbēnâ H4800*, perhaps from a root meaning "wrap around"). Also Machbenah; TNIV Makbenah. Son of Sheva and grandson of CALEB, included in the genealogi-

cal list of JUDAH (1 Chr. 2:49). However, it may be the name of a town, and the expression "Sheva the father of Macbenah and Gibea" probably indicates that Sheva was the founder of those two cities. Some identify Macbenah with CABBON (Josh. 15:40); others think it was a Calebite settlement in an unknown location S of HEBRON.

Maccabaean, Maccabaeus. See MACCABEE.

Maccabee. mak´uh-bee. The name given to a Jewish family that initiated the revolt against ANTIOCHUS Epiphanes, the SELEUCID Syrian king who was forcing his hellenizing policies on Palestine. The term *Makkabaios* was a surname given to Judas son of Mattathias (1 Macc. 2:4 et al.); it was later applied to his brothers and, more generally, to the Hasmonean dynasty that followed. The name Maccabee is probably related to Aramaic *maqqābāʾ*, "hammer," referring either to Judas's crushing military exploits or to a physical characteristic. The story, as outlined below, is told in two independent narratives written by authors of different emphases and abilities, the First and Second Books of the Maccabees. The first book is an honest piece of historical writing, detailing with little adornment the events of a stirring struggle for freedom, though written to glorify the Maccabean heroes. The second book covers much of the same material but slants the account in the direction of religious instruction and admonition, focusing on the superiority of JUDAISM over pagan culture.

The uprising began in 168 B.C., when Mattathias, an aged priest in the village of MODEIN, struck down a royal commissioner and an apostate Jew who were about to offer pagan sacrifice in the town. Mattathias leveled the altar and fled to the hills with his sons. To his standard rallied the Hasidim or Hasideans ("the Pious"). The old priest died after a few months of guerrilla warfare, and the same early fighting claimed two of his sons, Eleazar and John. The remaining three sons—Judas, Jonathan, and Simon—each in turn led the insurrection; and all left a deep mark on Jewish history.

Judas was a fine soldier and patriot, with a clear policy of Jewish independence and religious reconstruction. Raising and organizing a fighting force of Galileans, he defeated major military expeditions sent against him in 166 and 165 B.C. In December of the latter year, Judas formally cleansed the TEMPLE of Syrian pollution and celebrated the occasion with a great festival. This festival (Hanukkah) became a permanent fixture, falling on December 25 and lasting eight days (1 Macc. 4:52-59; 2 Macc. 10:6; Jn. 10:22). See DEDICATION, FEAST OF.

For the next eighteen months, Judas campaigned E of JORDAN, while his brother Simon collected the Jews who were scattered through GALILEE into the comparative safety of JUDEA. Judas at this point lost some of the support of the Hasidim, whose ambitions were largely fulfilled by the reestablishment of the temple service. Religious division, the perennial problem of all the Jewish struggles for independence, was thus responsible for a weakening of Judas's position. Lysias, the Syrian general whom Judas had signally defeated at Beth Zur in the autumn of 165 B.C., gained his revenge at Beth Zacharias. Judas was routed, and the Syrian garrison still holding out in the citadel of Jerusalem was relieved. Lysias was in control of Syria during the brief reign of Antiochus Eupator, a minor who succeeded Epiphanes in 163, and he was sensible enough to abandon Epiphanes' attack on the religion of the Jews for the much more effective political policy of patronage. He set up a puppet high priest, Alcimus, who was accepted by the Hasidim. Judas was thus isolated but, on Lysias's withdrawal, marched against Alcimus.

Demetrius I, the able and decisive ruler who succeeded Eupator in 162, sent a force under Nicanor to put down this new rebellion. Defeated by Judas, Nicanor retired to Jerusalem, but foolishly drove "the Pious" into renewed support of Judas by threatening reprisals against the temple. With the country again behind him, Judas defeated the Syrians at Adasa. Judas was now in control of the land and negotiated a treaty with ROME, in the terms of which Rome ordered Demetrius I to withdraw from Palestine. Judas's move was a shrewd one, for since the Peace of Apamea (188) Syria had existed by Rome's sufferance, and Demetrius had spent his youth as a hostage in Rome. Time was against Judas, for before the senate's prohibition was delivered to the king, Judas was defeated and killed by the general BACCHIDES at Elasa (1 Macc. 3—9:22). The international policy, illustrated by the approach to Rome, had again alienated the fickle Hasidim; and the withdrawal of support fatally weakened Judas's power of resistance and led directly to his military defeat.

Jonathan succeeded his brother in 161 B.C., and the Maccabean revolt reverted to the guerrilla warfare with which it had begun. Dynastic troubles in Syria, however, played into Jonathan's hands. Alexander Balas, supported by PERGAMUM and EGYPT, aspired to the Syrian throne; and both Demetrius and Alexander thought it expedient to secure the support of so determined a fighter as the second Maccabee. Demetrius offered the control of all military forces in Palestine and the governorship of Jerusalem. Alexander added an offer of the high priesthood. Jonathan chose Alexander and thus became the founder of the Hasmonean priesthood. By skillful support of Demetrius II, who dethroned Alexander, Jonathan maintained and strengthened his position. The difficulties of the later Seleucid empire served his purposes well. Jonathan was even able to extend his power over the maritime plain, to fortify Jerusalem and other strong points in Judea, and to enter into treaty relationships with Rome.

The high desert butte of Masada was once fortified by Jonathan Maccabee. (In this aerial view, looking N, the excavations reveal structures from the time of Herod.)

© Dr. James C. Martin

M

An army revolt in 143 unseated Demetrius II, and the young son of Alexander was enthroned as Antiochus VI. Power was in the hands of the generals, one of whom, Tryphon, laid hold of Jonathan by treachery and executed him (1 Macc. 9:23—12:54).

Simon, the third brother, inherited this critical situation. Simon was an able diplomat who carried on his brother's policy of profiting with some success by Syria's internal troubles. In 143 and 142 B.C. he succeeded in establishing the virtual political independence of Judea. In 141, at a great assembly of princes, priests, and elders of the land, Simon was elected to be high priest, military commander, and civil governor of the Jews, "for ever until there should arise a faithful prophet." The high priesthood was thus rendered hereditary in the family of Simon. He reestablished the treaty with Rome, which had proved a useful diplomatic advantage over Syria, whom Rome watched with some care and was not sorry to see embarrassed by her petty imperialism. Simon was murdered by his son-in-law at a banquet (1 Macc. 13:1—16:16).

Simon's son, the celebrated John Hyrcanus, inherited the political authority and held it for thirty years, during which time he achieved considerable territorial expansion. In 104 B.C. Hyrcanus was succeeded by his son Aristobulus, who assumed the royal title, but he died within a year. Aristobulus's brother, Alexander Jannaeus, ascended the throne and ruled as a tyrant for over thirty years. He was succeeded by his widow, Salome Alexandra, whose reign was characterized by peace and prosperity (76-67 B.C.). Upon her death, however, civil war broke between her two sons (Hyrcanus II and Aristobulus II), and the resulting instability provided ROME with the opportunity to intervene. In 63 B.C., POMPEY took Palestine. Although the heirs of the Hasmoneans continued to serve under the Romans for a few decades, Pompey's invasion brought the dynasty to a close. (For subsequent developments, see HEROD.)

Maccabees, Books of. See APOCRYPHA.

Maccabeus. See MACCABEE.

Macedonia. mas´uh-doh´nee-uh (Gk. *Makedonia* G3423; gentilic *Makedōn* G3424, "Macedonian").

Macedonia.

Also Macedon. In NT times a Roman senatorial PROVINCE encompassing much of what is now northern GREECE. Lying geographically between the Balkan highlands and the Greek peninsula, Macedonia was initially a Greek kingdom; it occupied a quadrangle of territory that formed only the eastern half of the Roman provincial unit. The province extended from the Aegean to the Adriatic, with ILLYRICUM to the NW, THRACE to the NE, and ACHAIA to the S. Culturally, Macedonia came under strong Athenian influence (see ATHENS) in the latter years of the fifth century before Christ and in the first half of the fourth century, the period between Euripides, who emigrated to Macedonia in 408 or 407 B.C., and Aristotle, who came to Macedonia as tutor to Alexander in 343 or 342 after the death of Plato. The population was Indo-European but of mixed tribal elements, of which the Dorian stock was probably a strong ingredient.

The history of the early kingdom is confused, and the tradition that Perdiccas I conquered the Macedonian plain in 640 B.C. probably marks the emergence of one dominant clan among an agglomeration of mountain tribes striving for the mastery of a significant area on an ancient invasion route. Until the reign of Philip II (359 to 336 B.C.), the kingdom was insignificant in Aegean history and was preoccupied with the continual tension of tribal war. By consolidation, conquest, pacification, and an enlightened policy of hellenization, carried out with the speed, precision, ruthlessness, and clear-headed determination that marked the man,

Philip unified Macedonia and finally conquered all Greece. The orations of Demosthenes, directed against the Macedonian menace, are poignant documents of this day of the democratic decadence of Athens and the upsurge of Macedonian power that was to extend Greek rule to the east. It was the army created by Philip that followed ALEXANDER THE GREAT, his son, to the Ganges and overthrew the Persian empire.

The history of Macedonia from Hellenistic times to the Roman conquest and annexation (167 B.C.) is undistinguished. Macedonia was the first part of Europe to receive Christianity (Phil. 4:15). The "man from Macedonia" of Paul's dream may have been LUKE, who, if not a native of PHILIPPI in Macedonia, was certainly long a resident there (Acts 16:9-12). PAUL was more than once in the province (Acts 19:21; 20:1-3; 1 Cor. 16:5; 2 Cor. 1:16). Some Macedonian believers were evidently close to the apostle; for example, Gaius and Aristarchus, Secundus, Sopater, and Epaphroditus (Acts 17:11; 20:4; Phil. 4:10-19; 1 Thess. 2:8, 17-20; 3:10).

Machaerus. muh-kihr´uhs (Gk. *Machairous*). The name Machaerus does not occur in the NT, but JOSEPHUS (*Ant.* 13.5.2 §119) reports that JOHN THE BAPTIST was imprisoned and beheaded at this fortress. According to the account in the Gospels (Matt. 14:3-12; Mk. 6:17-29; Lk. 3:19-20), it was during the birthday celebration of HEROD Antipas that this ruler ordered the death of John. Machaerus (modern Mukawir) is located E of the DEAD SEA on a high mountain overlooking the sea. Antipas's father, Herod the Great, constructed an impressive palace on a hill opposite the fortification, and Antipas was given control of it when he received the territory of PEREA. The attractive view of the Dead Sea, the commanding position with HERODIUM and Alexandrium visible on the W bank, and the presence of hot springs nearby no doubt made this a delightful residence for the healthy and ailing Herods.

Machbanai. See MACBANNAI.

Machbenah. See MACBENAH.

Machi. See MAKI.

Machir. See MAKIR.

Machnadebai. See MACNADEBAI.

Machpelah. mak-pee´luh (Heb. *makpēlâ H4834*, always with the definite article, meaning "the double [cave]"). The burial place that ABRAHAM purchased of EPHRON, the HITTITE of HEBRON, now located under the Ḥaram el-Khalil in Hebron. The name does not occur outside GENESIS and always designates the sepulchres of the PATRIARCHS (Gen. 23:9 et al.; 25:9; 49:30; 50:13).

Macnadebai. mak-nad´uh-b*i* (Heb. *maknadbay H4827*, meaning unknown). Also Machnadebai; TNIV Maknadebai. One of the descendants of Binnui who agreed to put away their foreign wives (Ezra 10:40).

Madaba. See MADEBA MAP; MEDEBA.

Madai. may´d*i* (Heb. *māday H4512*, meaning unknown). Son (or descendant) of JAPHETH and grandson (or more distant descendant) of NOAH (Gen. 10:2;

Herod the Great built a prison and fortress at Machaerus (view to the W). It was probably here that his son Herod Antipas executed John the Baptist.

© Dr. James C. Martin

M

1 Chr. 1:5). The Hebrew term is elsewhere rendered "Medes" (e.g., 2 Ki. 17:6) or "Media" (e.g., Esth. 1:3). See MEDIA.

Madeba map. mad´uh-buh. An early Christian mosaic, set into the floor of a sixth century Greek Orthodox church in the town of Madeba, Jordan (see MEDEBA). Almost 40 ft. (12 m.) long, it is the earliest known map of the Holy Land.

Madmannah. mad-man´uh (Heb. *madmannāh H4526*, "dung place"). One of the "southernmost towns of the tribe of Judah in the Negev toward the boundary of Edom" (Josh. 15:31; cf. v. 21). Elsewhere a man named SHAAPH, one of the sons of CALEB, is described as "the father of Madmannah" (1 Chr. 2:49), which probably means that he was the founder or civic leader of the town. Many scholars believe that Madmannah is the same as BETH MARCABOTH, a city taken from JUDAH's allotment and transferred to the tribe of SIMEON. The town is identified by some with modern Khirbet Umm ed-Deimneh, and by others with nearby Khirbet Tatrit, both about 9 mi. (15 km.) NE of BEERSHEBA.

Madmen. mad´muhn (Heb. *madmēn H4522*, "dung place"). A town in MOAB against which JEREMIAH prophesied (Jer. 48:2). It is often identified with modern Khirbet Dimneh, some 10 mi. (16 km.) E of the DEAD SEA and 7.5 mi. (12 km.) N of KIR HARESETH. It is possible that the original reading was DIMON, corrupted either as a result of scribal error or for literary reasons (altering the spelling to mock the Moabites).

Madmenah. mad-mee´nuh (Heb. *madmēnāh H4524*, "dung place"). An unidentified place, apparently near ANATHOTH, mentioned in Isaiah's description of the Assyrian advance upon JERUSALEM (Isa. 10:31).

madness. Insanity. See DISEASES.

Madon. may´don (Heb. *mādôn H4507*, "[place of] contention"). A royal city of the Canaanites in GALILEE whose king, JOBAB, joined JABIN king of HAZOR in his unsuccessful alliance against ISRAEL

(Josh. 11:1 [LXX *Marrōn*]; 12:19 [cf. LXX in v. 20]). The proposal that Madon should be identified with modern Khirbet Madin (c. 10 mi./16 km. ENE of NAZARETH) has little in its favor other than name similarity. On the basis of the SEPTUAGINT (cf. also 11:5, 7), many scholars suspect textual corruption and identify Madon with MEROM (prob. some 20 mi./32 km. farther N), near which the battle took place. See also SHIMRON (PLACE).

Magadan. mag´uh-dan (Gk. *Magadan G3400*). A locality on the W shore of the Sea of Galilee to which Jesus came after feeding the 4,000. The name appears only in Matt. 15:39 (KJV, "Magdala," following the Majority text), while the parallel passage reads DALMANUTHA (Mk. 8:10). Magadan and Dalmanutha may have been contiguous; and possibly Magadan was identical with, or at least included in, MAGDALA, the home of MARY Magdalene.

Magbish. mag´bish (Heb. *magbîš H4455*, possibly from a root meaning "to pile up" or "to be massive"). Either the ancestor of some Israelites who returned from EXILE or, more likely, a town in JUDAH resettled by them (Ezra 2:30; the name is omitted in the parallel list, Neh. 7:33). If it is a town, its location is unknown.

Magdala, Magdalene. mag´duh-luh, -leen (Gk. *Magdala G3401* [not in NIV], prob. from Heb. *migdāl H4463*, "tower"; gentilic *Magdalēnē G3402*). The town of Magdala was apparently the home of MARY Magdalene, who is mentioned a number of times in the Gospels (Matt. 27:56 et al.). The name Magdala itself does not occur in any textually secure passage, although it is found in a few MSS at Mk. 8:10 (where the original reading is no doubt DALMANUTHA); it also occurs in many MSS, followed by the KJV, at Matt. 15:39 (where the earliest texts, as well as most modern versions, read MAGADAN). Magdala is sometimes linked with *migdāl nûnayyāʾ*, "Fish Tower," a place mentioned in the TALMUD as being close to TIBERIAS. It is also thought to be the same as *Taricheas* (Tarichea or Tarich[a]eae), "Fish-Salting," an important town mentioned several times by JOSEPHUS (*War* 1.8.8 §180 et al.) and usually identified with modern Majdal, 3 mi. (5 km.)

NW of Tiberias. Majdal (also Mejdel) stands at a strategic road junction, and so perhaps justifies the name—a tower or fortification, some strong point, perhaps, on a vital crossroad.

Magdiel. mag´dee-uhl (Heb. *magdî˒ēl H4462*, "gift of God"). Descendant of Esau, listed among the clan chiefs of Edom (Gen. 36:43; 1 Chr. 1:54).

maggot. See ANIMALS.

Magi. may´ji (pl. form of Latin *magus*, from Gk. *magos G3407*, in turn a borrowing of Old Pers. *maguš*; cf. Heb. *māg H4454*, "official"). Originally a religious caste among the Persians. Their devotion to astrology, divination, and the interpretation of dreams led to an extension in the meaning of the word, and by the first century B.C. the terms "magi" and "Chaldean" were applied generally to fortune tellers and the exponents of esoteric religious cults throughout the Mediterranean world. Magus or "sorcerer" is the name given to Simon in Acts 8:9 and to Bar-Jesus in 13:6 (Elymas, 13:8). The Magi of Matt. 2:1-12 (KJV, "wise men") may have come from Arabia Felix (S Arabia). Astrology was practiced there, and a tradition of Israelite messianic expectation may have survived in the region since the days of the Queen of Sheba. Much early legend connects S Arabia with Solomon's Israel. Ancient report, linked to later astrological study, may have prompted the famous journey. This, of course, can be no more than speculation. The legend of "the Three Kings" is late and medieval. The old Arabian caravan routes entered Palestine "from the East."

magic. Originally the word meant the science or art of the Magi, the Persian priestly caste, who, like the Levites, were devoted to the practice of religion. In time, however, the Greek term *magos G3407* (Lat. *magus*) acquired broader significance. Thus *magic* came to mean all occult rituals or processes designed to influence or control the course of nature; to dominate people or circumstances by the alliance, aid, or use of supernatural powers; and generally to tap and to employ the forces of an unseen world. Divination, the art of forecasting the future with a view to avoiding its perils and pit-

falls, might be included under the same classification. Its methods were frequently "magic." In lands ethnologically stratified, magic was often associated with the religion of a conquered or depressed class, or with imported faiths. Therefore magic was found frequently in the hands of foreign elements, was secret in its practice, and was often under official ban as antisocial and illicit. For this reason the Bible gives stern prohibitions against all forms of "wizardry" and "sorcery" (Exod. 22:18; Lev. 19:26; 20:27; Deut. 18:10-11), causing security precautions like those surrounding the royal visit to "the witch of Endor" (1 Sam. 28).

In the Mosaic law, contact with magic and its practitioners was strictly forbidden (e.g., Deut. 18:9-14). This is not only because it was typical of the abominations of the heathen that the people of God were to avoid and, indeed, destroy, but more particularly because it was a denial of the true function of prophecy and therefore of the way of faith. In a word, magic is an attempt to make the future secure, whether by trying to find out about it in advance or by casting spells so as to make things happen in a predetermined and favorable way. The Lord's desire for his people is that they should recognize that his sovereignty has planned the future already, and that their part is, therefore, to walk trustfully into it. Furthermore, the voice of prophecy brings them all the immediate guidance and future knowledge that God thinks they need, and their task is to trust his trustworthiness.

Magic was widely practiced in Egypt (Exod. 7:11; 8:7, 18-19; 9:11) and in Babylon (Dan. 1:20; 2:2). In both empires the craft and ritual of magic came long before the Persian religious caste whose practices provided the later name. Nonetheless, both before and after Moses, the intrusion of such unhealthy beliefs may be detected in Hebrew history. The incident of the mandrakes found by Reuben (Gen. 30:14) is a clear example, and perhaps also the obscure incident of Jacob's trickery with the rods at the waterhole (30:37). It is fairly evident that Jacob believed his knowledge of animal genetics was determining the breeding trend, but God revealed to him in a dream that it was the Lord, not his own manipulations, that caused the favorable results (30:10-12). Jacob's family was remote from the lofty MONOTHEISM of Abraham,

M

© Dr. James C. Martin. The British Museum. Photographed by permission.

M

Babylonian astrological tablet in cuneiform script, giving omens regarding lunar eclipses.

and the EUPHRATES Valley towns were devoted to magic, hence the TERAPHIM mentioned later in the account (Gen. 31:19; see also Jdg. 17:5; 1 Sam. 19:13; Ezek. 21:21-26; Zech. 10:2). These were household deities, crudely carved, like the Roman Lares and Penates. In popular religion their worship was a base addition to, or substitute for, the worship of the Lord. Similar in concept was the cult of the BAALS of the fields, whose corrupt worship in fertility rituals and sympathetic magic was fiercely castigated by the prophets for the obscene thing it was. In every revival of pure worship the teraphim were swept away with other forms of vicious paganism (e.g., 2 Ki. 23:24).

Magic practices are mentioned also in the NT. The reference to the pagans' "vain repetitions" (Matt. 6:7 KJV; e.g., see 1 Ki. 18:26 and Acts 19:28) may allude to the belief in the magic value of set formulas. Simon (Acts 8:9) and Elymas (13:8) are spoken of as practicing "sorcery." There is evidence that this tribe of charlatans was wide-

spread and often Jewish in origin (e.g., "the Sons of Sceva" in Ephesus, 19:14). Emperor TIBERIUS had given much encouragement to "the Chaldeans and soothsayers" by his belief in magic. Juvenal pictures the old prince in retirement on Capri "with his wizard mob" (*cum grege Chaldaeo*). The senate, indeed, had more than once banished them, but a Roman weakness for the caster of horoscopes and the purveyors of superstition always ensured the return of the magicians, whom Tacitus bitterly describes as "a tribe faithless to the powerful, deceitful to those who hope, which will ever be banned among us— and ever tolerated." Sergius PAULUS, the governor of CYPRUS, seems to have held his Jewish soothsayer with a light hand and to have been quite convinced by the apostle's exposure of him. The record of the first Christian impact on the city of EPHESUS reveals the tremendous influence of magic among the populace at large. With the spread of Christian doctrine, those who practiced "curious arts" brought their books of incantations of magic formulas to burn. The early church in general did not dismiss magic as a delusion, but attributed its results to the work of malign and evil beings who were without power against a Christian.

magistrate. This English term, referring to an official entrusted with the administration of laws, is used to render two Aramaic terms in the OT (Ezra 7:25; Dan. 3:2-3). In the NT it renders Greek *archōn G807*, "ruler" (only Lk. 12:58), and especially *stratēgos G5130* (Acts 16:20-38). The latter was a common term in classical Greek literature for a high military officer and is usually translated "general" or "captain" (e.g., 4:1). In the context in Acts 16, *stratēgos* is used as the title of the Roman official of the colony of PHILIPPI and probably stands for the Latin *duumviri* (also *duoviri*), referring to the magistrates of the colony. This Greek term, however, was used also of the much higher Roman official, the *praetor*. In the provincial colonial seats of the Roman empire there often were several of these officials whose power included paramilitary and police affairs as well as administrative and political functions. There were usually three to five such officials who levied taxes, commanded the Roman garrison, tried criminal cases, and kept civil order.

Magnificat. mag-nif′uh-kat. The title given to Mary's psalm of praise (Lk. 1:46-55), drawn from the first line of the Latin VULGATE, "Magnificat anima mea Dominum" ("My soul magnifies the Lord"). The passage is similar to the prayer or song of HANNAH (1 Sam. 2:1-10) and contains allusions to it. It is one of the three psalms in Hebrew poetic style in this narrative of the birth of our Lord. The text makes a most fitting ending to the expectations of the OT COVENANT which looked forward to the consummation of the promised blessing to ABRAHAM through the MESSIAH. The utter humility of the means by which God is pleased to bring this grace to his people is glorified as a singular instance of his sovereign power.

Magog. may′gog (Heb. *māgôg H4470*, possibly from Akk. *māt gugi*, "land of Gyges"; Gk. *Magōg G3408*). In Ezek. 38:2 and 39:6, Magog is described as a land in which (or people over which) GOG acts as chief ruler. The name appears first in the Table of Nations for one of the sons (or descendants) of JAPHETH (Gen. 10:2; 1 Chr. 1:5), who are eponymous ancestors of national groups. JOSEPHUS (*Ant.* 1.6.1) identifies Magog with the SCYTHIANS of the far N. Resemblance of names has caused some to identify Gog with Gyges (Gugu) of LYDIA, and so Magog with Lydia. Ezekiel's association of Gog and Magog with peoples at the extremities of the then known world (Ezek. 38:2) suggests that they might be interpreted in a representative and eschatological sense rather than identified particularly (Rev. 20:8 uses the terms this way). Ezekiel sees them as representing northern nations (Ezek. 38:14-16), who in the "latter days" come against Israel in battle and experience God's wrath in defeat.

Magor-Missabib. may′gor-mis′uh-bib (Heb. *māgôr missābîb H4474*, "terror all around"). The name that JEREMIAH gave to PASHHUR, the priest who beat him and put him in stocks (Jer. 20:3-4). The TNIV renders, "Terror on Every Side." In describing the coming of the Babylonian army, Jeremiah used the same phrase on a number of occasions to press home that terrible truth (6:25; 20:10; 46:5; 49:29; cf. Lam. 2:22). The phrase appears also in Ps. 31:13.

Magpiash. mag′pee-ash (Heb. *magpî'āš H4488*, derivation uncertain). An Israelite leader who sealed the covenant of NEHEMIAH (Neh. 10:20). Some think that the personal name Magpiash may have been derived from MAGBISH (Ezra 2:30) if the latter was the village settled by the family.

Magus. may′guhs. See MAGI; SIMON #8.

Mahalab. may′huh-lab (from a conjectured place name, *mĕhallēb*). A border town within the tribal territory of ASHER, near Aczib and the MEDITERRANEAN Sea (Josh. 19:29 NRSV). The MT, however, reads *mēhebel*, "from the territory" (cf. KJV, "from the coast to Achzib"; NIV, "in the region of Aczib"). If the conjecture Mahalab is correct, it may be the same as a town called Maḥalliba (in an inscription of SENNACHERIB) and probably should be identified with AHLAB (Jdg. 1:31), which in turn may be the same as modern Khirbet el-Maḥalib, some 4 mi. (6 km.) NE of TYRE.

Mahalah. See MAHLAH.

Mahalaleel. See MAHALALEL.

Mahalalel. may-hal′uh-luhl (Heb. *mahălal'ēl H4546*, "praise of God" or "God shines"; Gk. *Maleleēl G3435*). KJV Mahalaleel; KJV NT, Maleleel. **(1)** Son of Kenan and grandson of ENOSH in the line of SETH (Gen. 5:12-17; 1 Chr. 1:2); included in the GENEALOGY OF JESUS CHRIST (Lk. 3:37; NRSV, "Mahalaleel").

(2) Descendant of PEREZ and ancestor of ATHAIAH, a postexilic Judahite who settled in JERUSALEM (Neh. 11:4).

mahalath, mahalath leannoth. may′huh-lath, may′huh-lath-lee-an′oth (Heb. *māhălat H4714* and *lĕ'annôt H4361*). Musical terms of uncertain meaning found, respectively, in the titles of Ps. 53 and 88. The first term is often interpreted as referring to a musical instrument, such as the flute; if so, the phrase could mean "[upon] a flute for singing." According to a different analysis, the phrase indicates a tune perhaps entitled "The Suffering of Affliction" (so NIV mg.)

M

Mahalath (person). may´huh-lath (Heb. *māḥălat H4715*, meaning unknown). **(1)** Daughter of ISHMAEL (Gen. 28:9). ESAU married her because his previous marriages to Canaanite women had displeased ISAAC (v. 8). Mahalath may be the same as the BASEMATH mentioned in 36:3, but some scholars argue that the two passages preserve conflicting traditions.

(2) Daughter of JERIMOTH and ABIHAIL, granddaughter of DAVID, and wife of REHOBOAM (2 Chr. 11:18). She gave birth to three sons (v. 19).

Mahali. See MAHLI.

Mahanaim. may´huh-nay´im (Heb. *maḥănayim H4724*, "double camp"). A city in N TRANSJORDAN, important especially in the time of the monarchy. Mahanaim, according to Gen. 32:2, was named by JACOB after he left LABAN, his father-in-law, and met God's angels on the way back to CANAAN. This town was appointed as one of the CITIES OF REFUGE and was assigned to the LEVITES (Josh. 21:38; 1 Chr. 6:80). It was situated in GILEAD, on the boundary between the tribes of GAD and MANASSEH (Josh. 13:26, 30). After the death of SAUL, Mahanaim was made the capital of Israel for a short time (2 Sam. 2:8). DAVID, fleeing from ABSALOM, came to this place (19:32). SOLOMON's officer ABINADAB was stationed in this city (1 Ki. 4:14). There may be a mention of Mahanaim in Cant. 6:13 (NIV, "the dance of Mahanaim"; NRSV, "a dance before two armies"). The Bible gives little information to identify the site, apart from the deduction in Gen. 32:22 that it was N of the JABBOK River. Various proposals have been made, but the most likely site is Tell edh-Dhahab el-Gharbi, on the N bank of the Jabbok and some 7 mi. (11 km.) E of the JORDAN.

Mahaneh Dan. may´hun-uh-dan´ (Heb. *maḥănēh-dān H4723*, "camp of Dan"). A place between ZORAH and ESHTAOL (therefore c. 15 mi./24 km. W of JERUSALEM) where "the Spirit of the LORD began to stir" SAMSON (Jdg. 13:25; KJV, "the camp of Dan"). The area received its name because 600 Danites camped there before attacking the Ephraimites (18:12). The latter passage describes the place as being "west" (lit., "behind") KIRIATH JEARIM, which seems inconsistent with 13:25. Some scholars suspect textual corruption in 13:25; others speculate that two different places had the same name; still others interpret "west of Kiriath Jearim" loosely. In any case, the precise location of Mahaneh Dan is unknown.

Maharai. may´huh-ri (Heb. *mahray H4560*, possibly "impetuous"). A warrior from the town of NETOPHAH who became one of DAVID's Thirty (2 Sam. 23:28; 1 Chr. 11:30). Elsewhere he is identified as a descendant of ZERAH and as an army commander in charge of the division for the tenth month (1 Chr. 27:13).

Mahath. may´hath (Heb. *mahat H4744*, perhaps "harsh"). **(1)** Son of AMASAI, descendant of KOHATH, and ancestor of the musician HEMAN (1 Chr. 6:35).

(2) Son of Amasai (prob. different from #1 above); this Mahath was a Kohathite LEVITE who assisted in the reforms of King HEZEKIAH (2 Chr. 29:12) and is probably also to be identified with the Mahath who was one of the supervisors of the temple offerings (31:13).

Mahavite. may´huh-vit (Heb. *maḥăwim H4687*, derivation unknown). Epithet applied to ELIEL, one of DAVID's mighty warriors (1 Chr. 11:46); it serves to distinguish him from the Eliel in the following verse. The term, which occurs only here, appears to be a gentilic, but its reference is unknown (many scholars emend the text to "Mahanite" [see MAHANAIM], or to "Maonite" [see BAAL MEON and MAON], but these forms too are unattested).

Mahazioth. muh-hay´zee-oth (Heb. *maḥăzî'ôt H4692*, prob. from a root meaning "vision"). Son of HEMAN, the king's seer (1 Chr. 25:4). The fourteen sons of Heman, along with the sons of ASAPH and JEDUTHUN, were set apart "for the ministry of prophesying, accompanied by harps, lyres and cymbals" (v. 1). The assignment of duty was done by lot, and the twenty-third lot fell to Mahazioth, his sons, and his relatives (25:30).

Maher-Shalal-Hash-Baz. may´huhr-shal´al-hash´baz (Heb. *maḥēr šālāl ḥāš baz H4561*, prob. "hurry [to seize] plunder, hasten [to seize] spoil").

A symbolic name given to one of the sons of Isa-iah to signify the speedy destruction of Rezin and Pekah by the king of Assyria (Isa. 8:1, 3). In this phrase, the two verbs are usually understood as imperatives, but it is possible to take them as participles ("the one who hurries … who hastens").

Mahlah. mah'luh (Heb. *maḥlâ H4702*, possibly "weak"). **(1)** The eldest of the five daughters of Zelophehad of the tribe of Manasseh (Num. 26:33). Since Zelophehad had no sons, his daughters requested Eleazar the priest that they be allowed to inherit their father's property, and the request was granted on condition that they marry into their father's tribe (27:1-11; 36:11; Josh. 17:3-4). This decision was very important and became a precedent.

(2) Son (or daughter) of Hammoleketh, who was apparently the sister of Gilead; included in the genealogy of Manasseh (1 Chr. 7:18). It is unclear why the name of Mahlah's father is not given. See Abiezer #1.

Mahli. mah'li (Heb. *maḥli H4706*, derivation uncertain; gentilic *maḥli H4707*, "Mahlite"). **(1)** Son of Merari and grandson of Levi (Exod. 6:19; Num. 3:19; 1 Chr. 6:19, 29; 23:21; 24:26, 28; Ezra 8:18). His offspring, the Mahlites (Num. 3:33; 26:58), along with their brothers, the Mushites (see Mushi), were responsible for carrying the frames of the tabernacle with its bars, pillars, bases, and all the accessories attached to these things (Num. 4:31-33). (There are some unexplained differences in the various lists.)

(2) Son of Mushi, grandson of Merari, and thus nephew of #1 above (1 Chr. 6:47; 23:23; 24:30). He is listed as an ancestor of Ethan, one of the Levites that David put in charge of the temple music (cf. 6:31, 44).

Mahlon. mah'lon (Heb. *maḥlôn H4705*, possibly "sickly"). Son of Elimelech and Naomi; first husband of Ruth (Ruth 1:2, 5; 4:10). He and his brother Kilion, as well as their father, died in Moab.

Mahol. may'hol (Heb. *māḥôl H4689*, "[round or circle] dance"). A term used to designate the father of four sages who are compared with Solomon for wisdom (1 Ki. 4:31). Elsewhere, however, their father is said to be Zerah (1 Chr. 2:6). Since the name means "dance," and two of these sages, Heman and Ethan, are ascribed authorship of one psalm each (Heman, Ps. 88; Ethan, Ps. 89), it is likely that "sons of Mahol" is an appellative expression indicating membership in a musical guild. These men apparently were dancers whose activity played an important role in religious exercises (cf. Ps. 149:3; 150:4).

Mahseiah. mah-see'yah (Heb. *maḥsêâ H4729*, "Yahweh is [my] refuge"). KJV Maaseiah. Father of Neriah and grandfather of Baruch and Seraiah; the latter two men assisted the prophet Jeremiah (Jer. 32:12; 51:59).

maid, maiden. The English term *maid* is a short form of *maiden*, both of which mean "unmarried young woman," usually applied to virgins. The shorter form, however, often has the more specific meaning of "female servant," its most common modern use. The KJV uses *maid* (in both the general and the specific meaning) over forty times to render several Hebrew and Greek words. Modern versions as a rule apply this term only to servants and thus employ it less frequently (similar terms used include *maidservant* and *slave-girl*; cf. also *handmaid* and *handmaiden* in the KJV).

The fuller term, *maiden*, occurs twenty-six times in the KJV as the translation of such words as Hebrew *na'ărāh H5855*, "girl," and *bĕtûlâ H1435*,

Young Palestinian maiden.

M

"virgin" (cf. both terms in Gen. 24:16). In the NIV, *maiden* occurs sixteen times, usually as the translation of *bĕtûlâ* (e.g., Ps. 78:63), but a few times it renders *'almâ H6625* (Gen. 24:43; Ps. 68:25; Prov. 30:19; Cant. 1:3). The latter Hebrew term has proven controversial because of its use in Isa. 7:14. Following the SEPTUAGINT (which uses *parthenos G4221* here [also in Gen. 24:43]), the KJV translates "virgin," as does the NIV. Many scholars, however, argue that it should be rendered "young woman" (cf. NRSV). It is true that Hebrew *'almâ* does not fully correspond to English *virgin*, but it may well indicate a marriageable young woman, who in that culture would have been presumed to be a virgin. In this respect, English *maiden* may be a close equivalent of this Hebrew word. See discussion under VIRGIN.

mail, coat of. See ARMS AND ARMOR.

maimed. See DISEASES.

Makaz. may´kaz (Heb. *māqaṣ H5242*, derivation uncertain). One of four towns within the second of the twelve districts that supplied provisions for SOLOMON and the royal household (1 Ki. 4:9); governed by BEN-DEKER, this district was apparently in the N SHEPHELAH, but the precise location of Makaz is unknown.

Makbannai. mak´bu-ni. TNIV form of MACBANNAI.

Makbenah. mak-bee´nuh. TNIV form of MACBENAH.

Makheloth. mak-hee´loth (Heb. *maqhēlôt H5221*, "places of assembly"). A stopping place of the Israelites, between Haradah and Tahath, during their forty years of wilderness wanderings (Num. 33:25-26). The location is unknown.

Maki. may´ki (Heb. *mākî H4809*, possibly short form of MAKIR). Also Machi. Father of Geuel, who was one of the twelve spies sent out to reconnoiter the Promised Land; he represented the tribe of GAD (Num. 13:15).

Makir. may´kihr (Heb. *mākir H4810*, prob. "bought"; gentilic *mākîrî H4811*, "Makirite"). **(1)** Son of MANASSEH (through an ARAMEAN concubine, 1 Chr. 7:14) and grandson of JOSEPH. Makir may have married a woman "from among the Huppites and Shuppites" (so NIV, v. 15, but NRSV has, "Machir took a wife for Huppim and for Shuppim" [similarly NJPS]). In any case, his wife MAACAH bore him two sons (Pesher and Sheresh, v. 16); his son GILEAD may have been borne by another wife. We read that the children of Makir "were placed at birth on Joseph's knees," apparently an adoption ritual (Gen. 50:23). A daughter of Makir married the Judahite HEZRON and bore him SEGUB, who became the father of JAIR (1 Chr. 2:21-23). Makir's descendants, the Makirites, are at the head of the list of Israelites who came out of Egypt (Num. 26:29). Makir's son Gilead gave his name to (or was named for?) the area in TRANSJORDAN that his family inhabited (Num. 27:1; 32:39-40). In addition, BASHAN was allotted to the Makirites because they were "great soldiers" (Josh. 17:1). Makir's great-grandson, ZELOPHEHAD, had no sons and thus his daughters claimed the inheritance (Num. 27 and 31; cf. Josh. 13:29-31).

(2) Son of Ammiel and probably a descendant of #1 above. This Makir is identified as a citizen of LO-DEBAR in whose house MEPHIBOSHETH the son of JONATHAN stayed (2 Sam. 9:4-5). He subsequently helped DAVID when the latter went into exile (17:27-29).

Makkedah. muh-kee´duh (Heb. *maqqēdâ H5218*, possibly related to a root that in Aram. means "to be clean"). A Canaanite royal city taken by JOSHUA in his battle with the southern confederacy of five kings (Josh. 10:10-29). These kings, having been defeated at GIBEON, fled first eastward toward BETH HORON and then southward toward AZEKAH and Makkedah. The kings sought refuge, under pressure of Joshua's attack and God's rain of "stones," in a cave near Makkedah. There Joshua killed them in the presence of his men. Then Joshua took the city of Makkedah nearby, killing the king (10:28). The town was in the SHEPHELAH and was later incorporated into the tribe of JUDAH, in the same district as LACHISH (15:41). Its precise location is uncertain, however.

Malachi, Book of. mal´uh-ki (Heb. *maPāki* H4858, "my messenger"). The last book among the twelve Minor Prophets. The traditional ascription of the prophecy to an individual named Malachi was derived from the opening words in Mal. 1:1. Some have thought that *maPāki* is a common noun, and indeed it is so rendered in 3:1 (cf. also the LXX at 1:1); but since the other prophetic books of the OT always begin by stating the prophet's name, it seems more likely that here, too, the name of the prophet is given. It is not unusual to have word-plays on the names of real people (Ezek. 3:8-9). Nothing more is known about the author of this book.

Malachi is believed to be one of the latest of the OT books. Since no statement as to its date is made in the book, one must seek to determine this by the nature of its contents. It is clearly postexilic. The TEMPLE had been completed and sacrifices were being offered (Mal. 1:7-10; 3:8). A Persian governor was ruling in JERUSALEM (the word for governor in 1:8 is a borrowed word, used for the Persian governors in Palestine in postexilic times). This indicates a date later than that of HAGGAI and ZECHARIAH.

It is also clear that the early zeal for the rebuilding of the temple had died out, and a situation of moral and religious declension had set in. Mixed marriages (Mal. 2:10-12), the failure to pay tithes (3:8-10), and the offering of blemished sacrifices (1:6-14) are conditions not unlike those referred to in the times of EZRA and NEHEMIAH (cf. Ezra 7; Neh. 13); and it would seem that Malachi's prophecy was given at about that time, or possibly shortly thereafter—about the middle or end of the fifth century B.C.

There are two principal themes in the book: the sin and apostasy of the people of Israel, emphasized in Mal. 1-2; and the judgment that will come on the faithless and the blessing in store for those who repent, predominating in chs. 3-4. A more detailed analysis follows:

(1) Title, 1:1.

(2) An argument for the love of God toward Israel as shown in the contrasted experiences of Edom and Israel, 1:2-5.

(3) A protest against the negligence of the priests in worship, 1:6—2:9.

(4) A condemnation of those who divorce their wives and marry foreign women, 2:10-16.

(5) An answer to those who complain that God is indifferent to injustice: a day of judgment is at hand, 2:17—3:5.

(6) A rebuke for the neglect of tithes and offerings, 3:6-12.

(7) A reply to doubters and a promise to the faithful, 3:13—4:3.

(8) A recall to the law and prophecy of the coming of Elijah, 4:4-6.

The book of Malachi is characterized by several unique features. First, it uses the rhetorical

Overview of MALACHI

Author: The prophet Malachi.

Historical setting: The postexilic period in JERUSALEM, after the rebuilding of the TEMPLE (516 B.C.). Most scholars date the book c. 450 B.C.

Purpose: To condemn the negligence of the priests and the faithlessness of the people, and to announce "the great and dreadful day of the Lord" (Mal. 4:5).

Contents: After reminding the Israelites of their privileges (Mal. 1:1-5), God denounces the failures of the priests (1:6—2:9) and the unfaithfulness of the people (2:10—3:18), concluding with a warning about the coming of the DAY OF THE LORD (ch. 4).

question and answer as a method of communication. This device begins most of the eight sections referred to above. It anticipates the later catechetical method of teaching.

Second, Malachi evinces prophetic and priestly interests. It has been called "prophecy within the law." Generally the prophets exhibit little interest in sacrifices and ceremonial laws, preferring to stress the more inward aspects of religious life. Malachi, however, sees the people's apostasy manifested by their carelessness in the sacrificial offerings (Mal. 1:6-14), the priests' neglect of their duties (2:1-9), and the failure of the people to pay their tithes and other offerings (3:7-12). This book is thus an antidote to the view commonly held today that the prophets did not believe in the necessity of the ritual law. Rather, they accepted the sacrificial system but often protested against its abuse that resulted from the people's failure to apprehend the necessity of inward faith and outward moral righteousness in addition to ritual cleanness.

Finally, the growing OT messianic expectation is witnessed to in the announcement of God's "messenger of the covenant," by whose coming Israel will be purified and judged (Mal. 3:1-5; cf. Matt. 11:10); and of the prophet ELIJAH who will announce the DAY OF THE LORD (Mal. 4:5-6; cf. Matt. 17:9-13).

Malcam. mal´kam (Heb. *malkām H4903*, from a root meaning "king"). KJV Malcham; TNIV Malkam. **(1)** Son of SHAHARAIM and descendant of BENJAMIN; a family head (1 Chr. 8:9). Malcam was one of seven children that were born to Shaharaim in MOAB by his wife HODESH after he had divorced Hushim and Baara (v. 8).

(2) The same Hebrew form occurs in the last phrase of Zeph. 1:5, which speaks of idolaters who swear both by Yahweh and by *malkām*. The SEPTUAGINT (Old Greek) translators, reading the same vowels as does the MT, analyzed the form as the noun *melek H4889* plus the third masculine plural pronominal suffix, and rendered it *tou basileōs autōn*, "their king." These and other early translators, however, were working with an unvocalized Hebrew text (thus simply *mlkm*). The Lucianic recension of the Greek version, analyzing it as *milkōm* (*H4904*), transliterates the word as *Melchom* (similarly the

Syriac Peshitta and the Latin Vulgate). Most modern versions take this second approach (as they do also in Jer. 49:1, 3; and cf. 2 Sam. 12:30 = 1 Chr. 20:2; Amos 1:15). Many believe that MILCOM is an alternate name for MOLEK.

Malcham. See MALCAM.

Malchiah. See MALKIJAH.

Malchiel, Malchielite. See MALKIEL.

Malchijah. See MALKIJAH.

Malchiram. See MALKIRAM.

Malchi-shua. See MALKI-SHUA.

Malchus. mal´kuhs (Gk. *Malchos G3438*, prob. from an Arabic name meaning "king"). A servant of the high priest (CAIAPHAS); according to John, Simon PETER struck him with a sword and cut off his right ear when Jesus was arrested (Jn. 18:10). Although this incident is also recorded in the Synoptic Gospels (Matt. 26:51; Mk. 14:47; Lk. 22:50-51 [Luke adds the information that Jesus healed his ear]), John alone reports that his name was Malchus and that it was Peter who struck him.

Maleleel. See MAHALALEL.

malice. An evil desire to do harm to or act wickedly toward someone. This English term is used variously in Bible versions to render several terms for EVIL, such as Hebrew *ra^c H8273* (Ps. 41:5 et al.) and Greek *kakia G2798* (1 Cor. 5:8 et al.). It is obviously an internal feeling or attitude that Christians must put away (Eph. 4:31; 1 Pet. 2:1), for it is wholly opposed to the life in, and the fruit of, the indwelling Spirit of God. It belongs to the old nature, the FLESH that is under the domination of sin. The NIV uses the semi-technical English expression "malice aforethought" in several legal contexts to translate Hebrew *śin[,]â H8534*, "hatred" (Num. 35:20 et al.).

Malkam. mal´kam. TNIV form of MALCAM.

Malkiel. mal´kee-uhl (Heb. *malkî[,]ēl H4896*, "God is [my] king"; gentilic *malkî[,]ēlî H4897*, "Malkielite").

Also Malchiel. Son of BERIAH, grandson of ASHER, and eponymous ancestor of the Malkielite clan (Gen. 46:17; Num. 26:45; 1 Chr. 7:31).

Malkijah. mal-ki′juh (Heb. *malkiyyâ H4898* and *malkiyyāhû H4899* [only Jer. 38:6], "Yahweh is [my] king"). Also Malchiah (nine times in KJV and three times in NRSV), Malchijah (six times in KJV, twelve times in NRSV), Melchiah (KJV only Jer. 21:1). The inconsistency in the English spelling has no textual basis; the NIV uses "Malkijah" throughout.

(1) Son of Ethni, descendant of LEVI, and ancestor of the musician ASAPH (1 Chr. 6:40).

(2) A priest who received the fifth lot of the twenty-four divisions in DAVID's time (1 Chr. 24:9).

(3) A man identified as "the king's son" (which prob. indicates that he was a royal official with police duties); he was owner of the cistern into which JEREMIAH's enemies cast him while King ZEDEKIAH pretended to be powerless to stop them (Jer. 38:6). Some believe that this Malkijah is the same man identified elsewhere in Jeremiah as the father of PASHHUR (21:1; 38:1). It is also possible that he is the same Malkijah listed as an ancestor of ADAIAH, the head of a priestly family who resettled in Jerusalem after the EXILE (1 Chr. 9:12; a fuller genealogy is given in Neh. 11:12).

(4-6) In a list of Israelites who pledged themselves to put away their foreign wives, three are named Malkijah, two of whom were descendants of Parosh (Ezra 10:25, but NRSV emends the second to HASHABIAH on the basis of the SEPTUAGINT), and the third a descendant of Harim (10:31). This third Malkijah may be the same as the son of Harim who helped repair the wall of Jerusalem (Neh. 3:11).

(7) Son of Recab and ruler of BETH HAK-KEREM; he was in charge of repairing the DUNG GATE (Neh. 3:14).

(8) A goldsmith who "made repairs as far as the house of the temple servants and the merchants, opposite the Inspection Gate, and as far as the room above the corner" (Neh. 3:31).

(9) One of the prominent men (not identified as priests) who stood near EZRA when the law was read at the great assembly (Neh. 8:4). If this Malkijah was a priest, he may be the same as #10 or #11 below.

(10) A priest who sealed the covenant of NEHEMIAH (Neh. 10:3). He may be the same as #11 below.

(11) A priest or LEVITE listed among those who assisted Nehemiah in the dedication of the rebuilt walls of Jerusalem (Neh. 12:42).

Malkiram. mal-ki′ruhm (Heb. *malkirām H4901*, "[my] king is exalted"). Son (or descendant) of King Jeconiah, that is, JEHOIACHIN (1 Chr. 3:18).

Malki-Shua. mal′ki-shoo′uh (Heb. *malki-šûaʿ H4902*, "[my] king is salvation"). KJV Melchi-shua (in 1 Sam.) and Malchi-shua (in 1 Chr.); NRSV, Malchishua. The third son of King SAUL (1 Sam. 14:49; 1 Chr. 8:33; 9:39). The PHILISTINES killed him at the battle of GILBOA (1 Sam. 31:2; 1 Chr. 10:2).

Mallothi. mal′uh-thi (Heb. *mallôtî H4871*, from *mālal H4910*, "to speak"). Son of HEMAN, the king's seer (1 Chr. 25:4). The fourteen sons of Heman, along with the sons of ASAPH and JEDU-THUN, were set apart "for the ministry of proph-esying, accompanied by harps, lyres and cymbals" (v. 1). The assignment of duty was done by lot, and the nineteenth lot fell to Mallothi, his sons, and his relatives (25:30).

mallow. See PLANTS.

Malluch. mal′uhk (Heb. *mallûk H4866*, variant *mallûkî H4868* [Neh. 12:14], from a root meaning "king"). TNIV Malluk. (1) Son of Hashabiah, descendant of LEVI through MERARI, and ancestor of the musician ETHAN (1 Chr. 6:44).

(2) One of the descendants of BANI who agreed to put away their foreign wives (Ezra 10:29).

(3) One of the descendants of HARIM who agreed to put away their foreign wives (Ezra 10:32).

(4) One of the priests who signed the covenant of NEHEMIAH (Neh. 10:4).

(5) One of the leaders of the people who signed the covenant of NEHEMIAH (Neh. 10:27). Possibly the same as #2 or #3 above.

(6) One of the priests (or priestly families) who returned from the EXILE with ZERUBBABEL (Neh. 12:2). He is probably the same person mentioned

later, when a certain Jonathan is listed as the head of the family of Malluch (v. 14; KJV, "Melicu"; NRSV, "Malluchi").

Malluchi. See MALLUCH #6.

Malluk. mal´uhk. TNIV form of MALLUCH.

Malta. mawl´tuh (Gk. *Melitē G3514*). A Mediterranean island lying between Sicily and Africa. The name occurs once in the NT as the place where PAUL was shipwrecked on his journey to ROME (Acts 28:1; KJV, "Melita"). The apostle and his fellow-travelers stayed in Malta three months (28:11). Its inhabitants treated the survivors with "unusual kindness" (v. 1; cf. v. 10). Soon after reaching the island, Paul was bitten by a snake, but nothing happened to him, so the islanders thought he was a god (vv. 3-6). The chief official, PUBLIUS, welcomed Paul and the others in his home. Publius's father was sick and Paul healed him; as a result, "the rest of the sick on the island" came to the apostle, and they too were healed (vv. 7-9).

Located 90 mi. (145 km.) from Syracuse, the great commercial center of the W Mediterranean, Malta occupied a strategic position in the ancient world. Endowed with good harbors safe from the stormy waters of the sea, it offered a convenient haven for commercial traffic moving both E-W and N-S. Some 18 mi. long and 8 mi. wide (29 x 13 km.), it was barren and arid, with few natural resources other than building stone. The eastern half, however, was somewhat productive; olive oil, wool, and lapdogs are mentioned as commodities that were profitable. During the third century B.C., Carthage and ROME engaged in a series of wars for mastery of the W Mediterranean, and in the course of the struggle Malta passed into Roman hands (218 B.C.), though Carthaginian and Greek elements remained strong for a long time afterward. The Romans granted Malta the status of a municipium, which allowed them to control their own domestic affairs. Cicero and others speak of the beauty and elegance of the houses on Malta, and of the prosperity of the island, indicating a high degree of civilization and wealth. Under AUGUSTUS, the island was seemingly administered by an official who was known by the people of Malta as "chief" or

"first man" of the island (Gk. *ho prōtos*, Acts 28:7). Tradition has it that Publius, who held this position when Paul was shipwrecked there, was the first Christian convert in Malta, and that from this time there developed a Christian community. Catacombs from the fourth and fifth centuries A.D. give evidence of Christian influence on the island.

mammon. mam´uhn. This term, derived from Greek *mamōnas G3440* (via the Latin VULGATE) comes ultimately from ARAMAIC *māmôn*, "wealth," the etymology of which is disputed (the equivalent Hebrew term appears in various postbiblical writings). In Matt. 6:24 and Lk. 16:13, the term is personified, and the NIV translates, "You cannot serve both God and Money" (NRSV, "wealth"). In Lk. 16:9, Jesus speaks of "the mammon of unrighteousness" (equivalent to "the unrighteous mammon," v. 11), which the NIV renders as "worldly wealth" (more negative is the NRSV rendering, "dishonest wealth"). There has been much discussion of the implications of unrighteousness in connection with WEALTH, but the simplest explanation seems to be that material riches are a resource open to misuse and characteristically employed by unscrupulous people for wicked purposes. Yet it is possible for the true servants of God to use wealth for good and salutary purposes, and thus procure for themselves treasure in heaven such as money cannot buy.

Mamre (person). mam´ree (Heb. *mamrēʾ H4935*, derivation uncertain). An AMORITE, brother of ESHCOL and ANER, who apparently resided near HEBRON (Gen. 14:13, 24). All three were allies of ABRAHAM when LOT was rescued from KEDORLAOMER. The expression "the great trees of Mamre the Amorite" (v. 13; cf. 13:18) suggests that he owned the place that came to be known by his name. See MAMRE (PLACE). However, some scholars believe that there is confusion in the text and that the names of all three brothers refer to localities.

Mamre (place). mam´ree (Heb. *mamrēʾ H4934*, derivation uncertain). After LOT separated from Abram (ABRAHAM), the latter "moved his tents and went to live near the great trees of Mamre at Hebron, where he built an altar to the LORD" (Gen. 13:18). Abraham was still living there when

© Dr. James C. Martin

Traditional tomb of Isaac in the Machpelah (Hebron), near Mamre.

he entertained the three heavenly visitors (ch. 18). It was in Mamre that he prayed for the deliverance of SODOM and GOMORRAH. After SARAH died, he bought a burial plot from EPHRON the HITTITE; thus Abraham came into possession of the field of MACHPELAH, which is E of Mamre, and there he buried his wife (23:17-20; cf. 23:19; 25:9; 49:30; 50:13). Through the centuries there have been several places vying for the site of Mamre and Abraham's oaks. The most widely accepted site today is Ramat el-Khalil, "The high place of the friend (of God)," which is c. 2.5 mi. (4 km.) N of HEBRON. An enclosure of huge proportions built by HEROD is there; it may have marked where the site was thought to be in NT times. Chalcolithic and Early Bronze remains found in the vicinity show at least that it is an ancient site.

man. See ADAM; HUMAN NATURE; WOMAN.

man, new. The words *eis hena kainon anthrōpon*, literally rendered "into one new man," occur in Eph. 2:15 with reference to the unity that Jews and GENTILES enjoy in Christ. In Eph. 4:24, *ho kainos anthrōpos* ("the new man") is contrasted with *ho palaios anthrōpos* ("the old man," v. 22). In Col. 3:10, instead of the adjective *kainos G2785*, PAUL uses the synonym *neos G3742* (with *anthrōpos G476* understood), also contrasted with *palaios G4094* (v. 9). The NIV and the NRSV render both con-

structions as "the new self." The phrase, in general terms, refers to human beings as changed by the HOLY SPIRIT through FAITH in Jesus CHRIST. Some believe that *neos* points to the idea in respect to its historical context, while *kainos* in respect to its quality of perennial newness. The distinction is blurred, however, by the fact that in these two passages the one idea is qualified by the other. See REGENERATION; SANCTIFICATION.

man, old. The expression *ho palaios anthrōpos*, literally rendered "the old man," occurs three times in the NT and refers to the unregenerate nature and activities that characterized a person prior to new life "in Christ." It is frequently translated "the old self" or "the old nature." PAUL states in Rom. 6:6 that "our old self" was crucified with Christ, and exhorts Christians to live conscious of this fact. In Eph. 4:22 he urges his converts to "put off your old self, which is being corrupted by its deceitful desires," and in Col. 3:9, similarly, he pleads for honesty on the basis of having "taken off your old self with its practices." In this period in redemptive history between the finished work of Christ in the past and the consummation of God's plan in the future, Christians live as citizens of two worlds who are constantly conscious of (1) the crucified nature of "the old self," and yet (2) the need to deaden the effects of that depravity in their lives which will be eradicated finally when Christ comes again. This tension, experienced by all believers, provides the context for almost all of the exhortations in the NT. See MAN, NEW.

Man, Son of. See SON OF MAN.

Manaen. man´ee-uhn (Gk. *Manaēn G3441*, from Heb. *mĕnaḥēm H4968*, "comforter" [see MENAHEM]). One of the five "prophets and teachers" listed as ministering in the church at ANTIOCH of Syria (Acts 13:1). The others were BARNABAS, Simeon NIGER, LUCIUS of Cyrene, and Saul (PAUL). Manaen's position indicates a man of spiritual power and influence. Nothing further is known about Manaen beyond Luke's designation of him as one "who had been brought up with Herod the tetrarch" (NRSV, "a member of the court of Herod the ruler").

M

Manahath (person). man´uh-hath (Heb. *mānaḥat H4969*, prob. "resting [place]"). Son of Shobal and grandson of Seir the Horite (Gen. 36:23; 1 Chr. 1:40); he was a chieftain living in Edom (Gen. 36:21). See also Manahathite.

Manahath (place). man´uh-hath (Heb. *mānaḥat H4970*, prob. "resting [place]") A city to which certain sons or descendants of Ehud—described as heads of families among the Benjamites who lived in Geba—were deported (1 Chr. 8:6). The town is usually identified with modern el-Malḥah, about 4 mi. (6 km.) SW of Jerusalem. It has also been argued, however, that Manahath should be sought in Gilead and identified with modern Maḥnah, about 8 mi. (13 km.) SE of Jabesh Gilead.

Manahathite. man´uh-ha´thit (Heb. *mānaḥtî H4971*, gentilic of *mānaḥat H4969*). KJV Manahethite. A clan descended from Caleb through Hur. According to 1 Chr. 2:54, the descendants of Salma (son of Hur) included "half the Manahathites," while v. 52 says that the descendants of Shobal (another son of Hur) included "half of the Menuhoth" (NRSV, following the MT). Many scholars believe that in v. 52 "Menuhoth" must be a variant (or textual corruption) of "Manahathites" (so NIV; cf. KJV). It is uncertain whether this gentilic is derived from Manahath (person) or from Manahath (place).

Manahethite. See Manahathite.

Manasseh (person). muh-nas´uh (Heb. *mĕnaššeh H4985*, "one who causes to forget"; gentilic *mĕnaššî H4986*, "Manassite"; Gk. *Manassēs G3442*). KJV NT Manasses. **(1)** The older of two sons born to Joseph and his Egyptian wife Asenath (Gen. 41:50-51; 46:20). Joseph interpreted Manasseh's name by the statement, "God has made me forget all my trouble and all my father's household" (41:51). When Joseph brought his sons Ephraim and Manasseh to his father for his blessing, Jacob adopted them as his own, placing them on an equality with his own sons as progenitors of separate tribes (48:1-5). In blessing the two boys, Jacob subordinated Manasseh the elder to Ephraim the younger, who thus inherited the position of privilege, the blessing of the firstborn (48:13-14). Nevertheless, Manasseh was to be blessed by the Angel who had delivered Jacob from all harm (48:16) and was to become a great people (48:19). It was Manasseh's Aramean concubine who gave birth to Makir, whose descendants became the tribe of Manasseh (1 Chr. 7:14). See Manasseh (tribe).

(2) Son of Hezekiah and king of Judah from c. 696 to 641 B.C. (2 Ki. 21:1; 2 Chr. 33:1). Manasseh was only twelve years of age when he succeeded his father as king (according to a different system of chronology, Manasseh was coregent with his father for ten years). His reign of fifty-five years was the longest in Judah's history, and its events are recorded in 2 Ki. 21:1-18 and 2 Chr. 33:1-20. Judah, during practically the entire reign of Manasseh, was a tribute-paying province of the Assyrians. Second Chronicles describes the arrest of Manasseh and his deportation to Babylon in chains by "the army commanders of the king of Assyria." The Chronicler declares that from the prophetic point of view Manasseh's arrest and deportation was the result of the judgment of God upon the king's wickedness (2 Chr. 33:9-11). In the course of his imprisonment, Manasseh repented of his sins and was restored to his kingdom (33:12-13). A penitential psalm attributed to Manasseh is included in the apocryphal Prayer of Manasseh, probably from the Maccabean period. It is an attempt to give expression to Manasseh's repentance and faith at the time of his arrest by the Assyrians. His religious reforms when he was restored were superficial, for he did not remove the high places of paganism (33:17). Upon his return from Babylon, Manasseh gave himself to a program of building, measures of defense, and administration besides the religious reforms. His reign was a period of great material prosperity due to his cooperation with the Assyrians. Assyrian records list Manasseh along with other subjects who paid tribute (33:12-19).

The reign of Manasseh is distinguished by his personal responsibility for the religious syncretism of his time, which gained him the reputation of being the typical evil king of Judah. According to the account in 2 Ki. 23:26-27, his was the most immoral reign of all the kings and was the reason for the ultimate collapse of the southern kingdom. The record in 21:1-18 and 24:3-4 emphasizes three degrading aspects of the regime of Manasseh: upon his accession to the throne he led in a reaction against the reforms instituted by his father Hezekiah; he accelerated the development of heathenism in the country; he instituted a bitter persecution of the prophetic party that opposed the popular syncretism led by the king. He "filled Jerusalem with innocent blood" (24:4), and the prophets were put to the sword (Jer. 2:30). Rabbinical literature places emphasis upon the idea that Manasseh was even more evil than Ahaz, and that he killed ISAIAH, who had fled and hidden in a tree, by sawing him asunder. When Manasseh's immediate successor, JOSIAH, came to the throne, the supreme need was religious revival (2 Ki. 23:26). Jeremiah said that Manasseh's sin had yet to be expiated (Jer. 15:4; cf. 2 Ki. 23:26). Manasseh is included in the GENEALOGY OF JESUS CHRIST (Matt. 1:10).

(3) Father of Gershom and grandfather of JONATHAN; the latter was a priest for the tribe of DAN (Jdg. 18:30 KJV, following the MT). The NIV and other versions, however, read MOSES instead of Manasseh. It is generally presumed that the reading in the MT is an intentional misspelling, since the Jonathan referred to is said to be a priest of the idolatrous shrine of MICAH. Thus Jonathan's grandfather was probably Moses, but his name was changed to Manasseh to avoid stigmatizing the revered name and sparing Moses the humiliation of having an idolatrous descendant. The change was accomplished by merely inserting the small Hebrew letter *nun* between the first two letters of the name for Moses. This not only removed the stigma but also gave to the man a name familiar to the Hebrews as an idolater.

(4) One of the descendants of PAHATH-MOAB who agreed to put away their foreign wives (Ezra 10:30).

(5) One of the descendants of HASHUM who agreed to put away their foreign wives (Ezra 10:33).

Manasseh (tribe). One of the twelve tribes of Israel descending from MANASSEH (PERSON), the grandson of JACOB through JOSEPH; the other Joseph tribe was EPHRAIM. At the time of the EXODUS, Manasseh numbered 32,200 (Num. 1:35; 2:21) while Ephraim had 40,500 (1:32, 33; 2:19). At the time of Israel's conquest of CANAAN forty years later, Manasseh had increased to 52,700 (26:34), while Ephraim had fallen to 32,500 (26:37). During the wilderness wanderings, each tribe through its leader presented an offering at the TABERNACLE. Gamaliel, the son of Pedahzur, offered on the eighth day for Manasseh (7:54). In the order of march Manasseh came in the eleventh place (10:23). In the layout of the camp Manasseh was on the W side in the third division (2:20).

Before the Israelites crossed over the JORDAN River into Canaan, half the tribe of Manasseh, along with the tribes of REUBEN and GAD, chose land E of the river, and MOSES assigned it to them (Num. 32:33). The descendants of MAKIR, son of Manasseh, conquered GILEAD and lived there. JAIR also captured other towns (32:39-41). The half-tribe of Manasseh was given the N half of Gilead, all of BASHAN, and the region of ARGOB (Deut. 3:13). This territory included sixty cities (Josh. 13:30). The rest of the tribe was given ten portions of land W of the Jordan, including areas for ZELOPHEHAD's daughters (17:1-6). This territory was situated between Ephraim on the S and ASHER, ZEBULUN, and ISSACHAR on the N. Its eastern border was the Jordan River and on the W

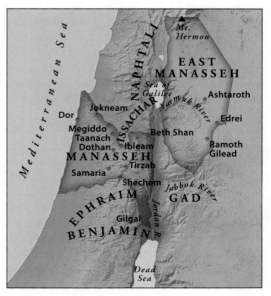

The tribal territories of Manasseh.

M

© Dr. James C. Martin

View E across the tribal territory of Manasseh at the Jezreel Valley with Jokneam in the foreground.

was the MEDITERRANEAN Sea (17:7-10). GOLAN, in the territory of the half-tribe E of the Jordan, was selected as one of the CITIES OF REFUGE (20:8). Thirteen cities of E Manasseh were assigned to the Gershonite clan of the LEVITES, and W Manasseh furnished ten cities to the Kohathites of the Levites (21:5-6). West Manasseh failed to drive the Canaanites out of the towns (Jdg. 1:27). GIDEON was of the tribe of Manasseh (6:15), so was Jair the Gileadite, who judged Israel twenty-two years (10:3). JEPHTHAH came from Gilead in E Manasseh (11:1). This half-tribe, with Reuben and Gad, fell into idolatry and was later carried away into captivity by ASSYRIA (1 Chr. 5:25-26) during PEKAH's reign over ISRAEL (2 Ki. 15:29).

    The tribe of Manasseh joined DAVID while he was a fugitive from SAUL (1 Chr. 12:19-22). When David was made king at HEBRON, W Manasseh furnished 18,000 soldiers, and E Manasseh with Reuben and Gad provided 120,000 (12:31, 37). People from Manasseh and Ephraim joined with JUDAH in making a covenant to seek the Lord during the reign of ASA king of Judah (15:9-15). Certain pious souls from W Manasseh joined in the Passover during HEZEKIAH's reign (2 Chr. 30:10-22). When JOSIAH was king, he destroyed idols and purged altars in Manasseh's territory as

well as elsewhere (34:6). The people of Manasseh contributed to an offering for the repairing of the TEMPLE in Josiah's time (34:9).

Manasseh, Prayer of. See APOCRYPHA.

Manasses. See MANASSEH (PERSON).

Manassite. See MANASSEH (tribe).

Mandaic. See MANDEAN.

Mandean. man-dee´uhn. Also Mandaean. This term (from an Aram. word meaning "knowledge") refers to a member of Mand(a)eism, a religious community that claims to have originated in Palestine, with JOHN THE BAPTIST regarded as one of its prophets; its earliest extant writings (bowls with magical texts) are from fourth century MESOPOTAMIA. A number of Mandean villages still survive today, mainly in S Iraq. The Mandean religion is a form of GNOSTICISM, with complex myths based on a strong dualism between light (life, goodness, spirit) and darkness (death, evil, matter); it is also characterized by intricate rituals. The Mandean language, usually referred to as Mandaic, is a form of E ARAMAIC. See also MANICHEAN.

mandrake. See PLANTS.

maneh. See WEIGHTS AND MEASURES.

manger. A receptacle for feeding livestock. The NIV uses this term as the rendering of Hebrew *ʾēbûs H17*, "feeding trough" (Job 39:9; Prov. 14:4; Isa. 1:3; KJV and NRSV have "crib"), and most versions use it to translate Greek *phatnē G5764* in the nativity story (Lk. 2:7, 12, 16). This Greek term sometimes has the broader meaning of "stall" or "stable" (cf. possibly 13:15). In the ANE, animals might be kept in outdoor enclosures with lean-to roofing, or in permanent shelters made of stone and mud-wall, or in cave stalls. When Joseph and Mary were unable to find room in the INN (prob. a private home or a public shelter), they sought refuge in some kind of stable, perhaps next to the inn, though it is not possible to ascertain what type of animal shelter this was.

Manichean. man´uh-kee´uhn. Also Manichaean, Manichee. A follower of the teachings of Mani (also Manes). The term is sometimes applied more broadly to a believer in *dualism*. Born of PARTHIAN princely blood in A.D. 216, probably in Babylonia, Mani was under MANDEAN influence as a child, and claimed to have received his first revelation at the age of twelve. He first preached in India, but later, during the long and tolerant reign of Shapur (c. 242-273), he made numerous converts in Babylonia, Media, and Parthia. Upon the accession of Bahram I in 273, Zoroastrianism gained the upper hand; the Manicheans were persecuted, and Mani died in prison (prob. 276). Mani taught that Buddha, Zoroaster, and Jesus were great prophets, but that he was the last and greatest. His system was a dualism in which God opposed matter. See GNOSTICISM. The elect among his followers abstained from meat, all killing of animals and plants, and sexual relations. The influence of this teaching lasted over a millennium.

Manichee. See MANICHEAN.

manna. man´uh. This term is a transliteration of Greek *manna G3445*, which is the usual SEPTUAGINT rendering of Hebrew *mān H4942*. When the Israelites saw the "thin flakes like frost" that God had miraculously provided as food (lit., "bread") for them, they asked, *mān hûʾ*, "What is it?" (Exod. 16:15), and so they called the substance *mān* (v. 31). This food is also described as "white like coriander seed," and we read that it "tasted like wafers made with honey" (v. 31). According to Num. 11:7-8, "The manna was like coriander seed and looked like resin. The people went around gathering it, and then ground it in a handmill or crushed it in a mortar. They cooked it in a pot or made it into cakes. And it tasted like something made with olive oil." In Exod. 16:13-14, the manna is associated with the dew (cf. also Ps. 78:24-25). Some believe that the manna was a gum-resin, which exuded from trees such as *Alhagi maurorum* (called the prickly alhagi and sometimes the Sinai manna).

God provided the manna on a daily basis to the Israelites through all the years of their wanderings (Exod. 16:35; Josh. 5:12). They were told to take only one *omer* (about two liters) per person, but on the sixth day they were to take twice as much so that it would last them through the SABBATH (Exod. 16:16-30). Following the Lord's command, MOSES instructed AARON to put some manna in a jar that was to be kept in the TABERNACLE as a memorial for future generations (vv. 32-34; cf. Heb. 9:4). Near the end of the Israelites' wandering, Moses explained to them that the manna was part of God's testing (Deut. 8:3; cf. v. 16; Neh. 9:20). The Lord Jesus alluded to the manna at the time of his TEMPTATION in the wilderness (Matt. 4:4; Lk. 4:4). Later in his ministry he claimed to be "bread from heaven" (Jn. 6:31-35, 41, 48-51, 58). And in the book of Revelation, the glorified Lord says to the church in PERGAMUM: "To him who overcomes, I will give some of the hidden manna" (Rev. 2:17), which probably refers to the eschatological fellowship believers will enjoy with Christ at the MESSIANIC BANQUET (cf. 19:9).

Manoah. muh-noh´uh (Heb. *mānôḥa H4956*, "[place of] rest"). The father of SAMSON. Manoah lived in ZORAH, a town in the tribal territory of DAN before the Danites moved N to take the city of LAISH. Manoah's wife, who was sterile, received a message from the angel of the Lord, announcing the birth of a son, who was to be a NAZIRITE

(Jdg. 13:2-21). Manoah responded with fear, but his wife, who remains nameless, seemed to have a better understanding of the divine will (vv. 22-23).

man of lawlessness, man of sin. See ANTI-CHRIST.

mansion. This term, which in present English usually refers to an imposing house, is used by the NIV a few times (e.g., for the expression "great houses," Amos 3:15). The KJV uses it only once in the well-known words of Jesus, "In my Father's house are many mansions" (Jn. 14:2), but the meaning here is certainly not "palatial residence." The English term *mansion* used to mean simply "dwelling," and thus in the seventeenth century it was an appropriate rendering of the Greek term here, *monē* G3665 (derived from the verb *menō* G3531, "to remain, dwell," which is used frequently in Jn. 14-15). This noun occurs in only one other place in the NT—in this same chapter, where Jesus says, "If anyone loves me, he will obey my teaching. My Father will love him, and we will come to him and make our home [*monē*] with him" (14:23; here the KJV renders it "abode"). On this basis it has been argued that v. 2 does not refer (at least not exclusively) to HEAVEN, but to the presence of Christ in the believer's heart.

mantle. See DRESS.

manuscript. A handwritten document (from Latin *manus*, "hand," and *scriptus*, "written"). Prior to the invention of printing, any document, whether a work of literature or a private writing, was written by hand and was thus a "manuscript" (although in present-day English the term is also used of typewritten compositions). See TEXT AND VERSIONS; WRITING.

Maoch. may´ok (Heb. *māʿôk* H5059, derivation uncertain). TNIV Maok. Father of ACHISH, who was the PHILISTINE king of GATH with whom DAVID and his men took refuge when they were fleeing SAUL (1 Sam. 27:2; cf. 1 Ki. 2:39). See MAACAH #8.

Maok. may´ok. TNIV form of MAOCH.

Maon (person). may´on (Heb. *māʿôn* H5062, "dwelling"). Son of Shammai, descendant of CALEB, and "father" of BETH ZUR (1 Chr. 2:45). The latter description means either that he was the ancestor of the people of Beth Zur or the founder of that city. It is also possible that the name in this passage is a collective for the people of the town of Maon, and that they were the ones who founded the city of Beth Zur. See MAON (PLACE); MAONITES.

Maon (place). may´on (Heb. *māʿôn* H5063, "dwelling"). A town in the hill-country of JUDAH, in the same district as CARMEL and ZIPH (Josh. 15:55). It is identified with modern Khirbet Maʿin, situated on a hilltop about 8 mi. (13 km.) SSE of HEBRON. Hiding from SAUL, DAVID and his men took refuge in the Desert of Maon (1 Sam. 23:24-25), which was a wilderness area E and SE of the town. Maon was the residence of NABAL, whose widow ABIGAIL became the wife of David (25:1-2).

Maonites. may´uh-nīts (Heb. *māʿôn* H5062, "dwelling"). Name given to a group of people who were hostile to Israel (Jdg. 10:12; lit., "Maon"). They are probably not to be connected with the town of Maon; see MAON (PLACE). Perhaps these people are the same as the MEUNITES (1 Chr. 4:41; 2 Chr. 20:1; 26:7), but this identification is by no means established.

Mara. mair´uh (Heb. *mārāʾ* H5259, "bitter"). The name that NAOMI chose for herself when she returned from MOAB to her native country, bereaved of her husband and sons. Earlier, Naomi had said to her daughters-in-law, "It is more bitter [*mar* H5253] for me than for you" (Ruth 1:13). When she arrived in BETHLEHEM, she asked the women of the town not to call her Naomi: "Call me Mara, because the Almighty has made my life very bitter [*mārar* H5352]" (v. 20).

Marah. mair´uh (Heb. *mārâ* H5288, "bitter"). The name that the Israelites gave to a place (between ETHAM and ELIM) where they found water that was brackish and undrinkable (Exod. 15:23; Num. 33:8-9). When the people came to the spring and were unable to drink from it, they murmured

This oasis may be the site of biblical Marah.

against MOSES. Then the Lord showed Moses a piece of wood, which he threw into the water, thereby miraculously sweetening the spring (Exod. 15:24-25). The location of Marah is uncertain, but proposals include modern ʿAin Hawarah (some 47 mi./76 km. SE of Suez) and Bir Mara (much farther N, only 10 mi./16 km. E of Suez).

Maralah. mahrʹuh-luh (Heb. *marʿālâ H5339*, possibly "mountain ledge"). A town on the W border of the tribal territory of ZEBULUN between SARID and DABBESHETH (Josh. 19:11; RSV, "Mareal"). Maralah was in the Valley of JEZREEL, but its precise location is uncertain. Possible identifications are modern Tell el-Ghaltah (about 7 mi./11 km. NNW of MEGIDDO) and, more likely, Tell Thorah (2 mi./3 km. closer to Megiddo).

maranatha. mairʹuh-nathʹuh (Gk. *marana tha G3448*, from Aram. *māranāʾ tāʾ*, "our Lord, come!" or *māran ʾaĕtāʾ*, "our Lord has come"). This term, which is a transliteration of two ARAMAIC words, occurs once in the NT (1 Cor. 16:22, after an ANATHEMA against anyone who does not love the Lord) and once in the APOSTOLIC FATHERS (*Didache* 10.6). Its precise meaning is disputed. The rendering "Our Lord has come" makes good sense, especially if a eucharistic background is assumed (the context in *Didache* 10.6 definitely centers on the Lord's table). If so, the reference is either to the INCARNATION or to his presence at the EUCHARIST. Most scholars, however, prefer the meaning "Our Lord, come!" in view of the parallel expression, "Come, Lord Jesus" (Rev. 22:20). This rendering too is fitting to the LORD'S SUPPER, at which time Jesus' death is proclaimed "until he comes" (1 Cor. 11:26), but a reference to the Eucharist remains speculative. If the imperative is preferred, the term *maranatha* would be a very early evidence of a prayer addressed to Jesus as Lord. The Aramaic form *maran(a)* bears witness in any case to the fact of a Palestinian recognition of Christ as LORD.

marble. See MINERALS.

Marcheshvan. (*marḥešwān*, not found in the OT; prob. of Persian origin). The postbiblical name for the eighth month (October-November), corresponding to Canaanite BUL and Babylonian *Arahsamna* ("eighth month"). It is also known as Heshvan.

Marcion. mahrʹshuhn (Gk. *Markiōn*). A native of Sinope in PONTUS, Marcion moved to ROME c. A.D. 140 and joined the church there but in 144 was excommunicated for his heretical opinions. The sect he founded spread widely and was for a time a serious menace to the church. Strongly anti-Jewish, he distinguished the merely just God of the OT from the loving God and Father of Jesus revealed in the NT, and accordingly rejected the OT altogether. He believed that only PAUL had truly grasped the contrast of law and gospel, so the Pauline letters (purged of what he considered Jewish accretions) formed the basis of his canon. See CANONICITY. Marcion's *Gospel* was not an independent work, but an expurgated version of Luke, adapted to Marcion's own doctrinal theories. Because Marcion's edition of Luke and Paul is quoted extensively by other writers, these citations are an important source for the work of NT textual criticism. See TEXT AND VERSIONS (NT).

Marcus. See MARK, JOHN.

Marduk. mahr´dyook (Heb. *mĕrōdāk H5281*, from Akk. *Mar(u)duk*). A Babylonian deity (Jer. 50:2; KJV and other versions, MERODACH; cf. also the personal names EVIL-MERODACH, MERODACH-BALADAN, MORDECAI). Already known in SUMER in the third millennium B.C., Marduk became chief god of the Babylonian pantheon at the time of HAMMURABI. To him were transferred the functions and exploits of the storm-god and creator Enli. His principal temple was the Esagila ("the house that lifts up its head") in BABYLON. In the myth and ritual of the Babylonian New Year Festival each spring, his victory as champion of the gods was celebrated. Marduk was given the title BEL ("Lord") and eventually became known primarily by that name (cf. Isa. 46:1; Jer. 50:2; 51:44).

Marduk-Baladan.   mahr´dyook-bal´uh-duhn. TNIV form of MERODACH-BALADAN.

Mareal. See MARALAH.

Mareshah (person). muh-ree´shuh (Heb. *mārēšāh H5359*, possibly "head place"). **(1)** Son of Mesha (or of Ziph), grandson (or great-grandson) of CALEB, and father of Hebron (1 Chr. 2:42 NIV). The MT appears to have suffered scribal corruption, and it is possible that "Mesha" in the first part of the verse should be "Mareshah" also (so LXX), in which case Mareshah was the firstborn of Caleb and the father of Ziph (cf. NRSV mg.). See HEBRON (PERSON) #2.

(2) Son of LAADAH and descendant of JUDAH (1 Chr. 4:21). However, in the phrase "Laadah the father of Mareshah," *father* could mean "founder" or "civic head," in which case the reference would be to MARESHAH (PLACE).

Mareshah (place). muh-ree´shuh (Heb. *mārēšāh H5358*, "head place, summit"). A town in the SHEPHELAH of JUDAH, in the same district as LIBNAH (Josh. 15:44). Mareshah is identified with modern Tell Sandaḥannah, about 3 mi. (5 km.) NE of LACHISCH. The town was strengthened by REHOBOAM in the early ninth century B.C. (2 Chr. 11:8). ASA met a threateningly large Ethiopian army under ZERAH nearby in the Valley of ZEPHATHAH. Victorious by divine aid, Asa drove the enemy back to GERAR, c. 30 mi. (50 km.) SW of Mareshah (2 Chr. 14:9-15). A prophet from Mareshah, ELIEZER son of Dodavahu, foretold the failure of JEHOSHAPHAT's naval expedition bound for TARSHISH, because of the unholy alliance with AHAZIAH of Israel (20:35-37). In a play on words, MICAH speaks of a conqueror (*yōrēš*) who will be brought against Mareshah (Mic. 1:15). During the EXILE, the Edomites infiltrated S Judah, and Mareshah—thereafter commonly known as Marisa—became a capital city.

Mari. mah´ree. An important ancient city of W MESOPOTAMIA, c. 7 mi. (11 km.) NW of modern Abu-Kemal at Tell Hariri. Its importance and its prosperity were due to its strategic location at the intersection of two caravan roads: one beginning on the MEDITERRANEAN coast and passing across the Syrian desert to the EUPHRATES, and the other beginning in N Mesopotamia and passing southward through the valleys of the Khabur and Euphrates Rivers. This strategic location is reflected not only in the fabulous wealth of the city but also in the truly international character of its population. It was the center of an influential AMORITE kingdom c. 1800-1700 B.C.

Excavations at Mari have yielded significant discoveries. The chief buildings were: (1) a temple dedicated to the goddess ISHTAR, (2) a ZIGGURAT or stage-tower, and (3) a 300-room palace at the center of the mound. In the palace area the excavators found c. 20,000 cuneiform tablets, most of which date from the reigns of Yasmakh-Adad (c. 1796-1780), under whose reign the palace was begun, and Zimri-Lim (c. 1779-1761), under whom it was finished. Both of these kings were contemporaries of HAMMURABI of Babylon (c. 1792-1750). Most of the documents were written in Akkadian, the E Semitic language spoken in BABYLON and ASSYRIA. Several rooms contained chiefly texts of an economic, administrative, or judicial nature, while others contained the royal correspondence.

Several letters addressed to King Zimri-Lim concern prophetic utterances; these are instructive in their similarities and differences with biblical prophecy.

From a linguistic point of view the Mari texts have aided OT study in the wealth of Amorite personal names, many of which resemble those in the Hebrew Bible. Also of interest to OT students are the so-called "Yahweh names" of Mari. These names (Yawi-Addu and Yawi-El) are not only reminiscent of OT personal names like JOEL (= Yawi-El), but have raised the question of whether Yawi was a divine name at Mari. Opinions differ, but it seems unlikely in view of the fact that the word Yawi never occurs with the determinative for deity (i.e., ^DYawi). More likely *yawi* is a verb telling what the gods Addu and El had done or were expected to do. The OT name of Israel's God, Yahweh, may indeed contain that same verb as a description of the unnamed God (cf. Exod. 3:14; see JEHOVAH). Another aid to OT study afforded by the Mari texts lies in the description of the customs of the nomadic peoples surrounding Mari, including a group known as "Benjaminites." Even if that is a correct understanding of the Akkadian name (DUMU.MEŠ *Yamina*), the view that they were related to the OT tribe of BENJAMIN is very unlikely. Nevertheless, the customs held by all these nomadic groups provide interesting insights into certain OT practices of the Israelites.

Mariamme. (*Mariammē*, from Heb. *miryām H5319*; see MIRIAM). Traditionally spelled Mariamne. A Hasmonean princess (see MACCABEE), famous for her beauty, who became the second wife of HEROD the Great. This marriage strengthened the position of Herod (a foreigner from IDUMEA) as ruler of the Jews. Mariamme bore him four children, but she was accused of unfaithfulness, and Herod, who was exceedingly jealous, had her executed (Jos. *Ant*. 15.2.5 §23; 15.2.9 §§81-87; 15.7.5 §§232-36). The name Mariamme was borne by another wife of Herod the Great, by Herod's son Archelaus, and by others in the Herodian family.

mark. This English noun is used variously to translate a number of Hebrew and Greek words in the Bible. For example, Hebrew *ʾôt H253* (more frequently translated SIGN) occurs with reference to the mark that God placed "on Cain so that no one who found him would kill him" (Gen. 4:15; the nature of the mark is not known). In the NT, PAUL uses Greek *stigma G5116* when he refers to the scars he bears in his body as a result of his suffering for the sake of Jesus (Gal. 6:17). When the book of Revelation speaks of the "mark of the beast" (Rev. 16:2 et al.), which the ANTICHRIST will require of all people during his reign of terror in the tribulation period, the term used is *charagma G5916*.

Mark, Gospel of. The second account of the gospel of Jesus Christ, according to the present common order of listing in the NT canon. Being the shortest of the four Gospels, Mark contains relatively little of the teachings of Jesus and nothing at all about his birth and childhood. Starting with the ministry of JOHN THE BAPTIST, it moves immediately to the public ministry of CHRIST, ending with his death and resurrection.

I. Authorship. On two points the tradition of the early church is unanimous: the second gospel was written by John Mark (see MARK, JOHN) and presents the preaching of PETER. Papias (c. A.D. 140) is quoted by Eusebius as saying, "And John the presbyter also said this, Mark being the interpreter of Peter, whatsoever he recorded he wrote with great accuracy ... he was in company with Peter, who gave him such instruction as was necessary, but not to give a history of our Lord's discourses" (*Eccl. Hist.* 3.39). This suggests that Mark has given us a summary of the message of Peter. Justin Martyr (c. A.D. 150) quotes Mk. 3:17

© Dr. James C. Martin. The British Museum. Photographed by permission.

Roman coin of the 1st/2nd cent. depicting the running boar, mascot of the Tenth Legion. Mark appears to have written his gospel with a Roman audience in view.

Overview of MARK

Author: Anonymous, but traditionally attributed to John Mark.

Historical setting: Covers the period from the baptism to the resurrection of CHRIST. The book was probably written in ROME, and if it served as a literary source for Matthew and Luke, it may have been completed in the 50s, but many date it to the 60s or even later.

Purpose: To provide a brief historical-theological account of the ministry of CHRIST that focuses on his activity as evidence that he is the SON OF GOD.

Contents: After a short introduction (Mk. 1:1-13), the book focuses on Jesus' Galilean ministry, characterized by both popularity and growing opposition (1:14— 9:50), followed by the briefer period in Perea and Judea (ch. 10), and then by passion week (chs. 11-15) and the resurrection (ch. 16).

as from "Peter's Memoirs." Irenaeus (c. 185) writes that after the "departure" (prob. meaning "death") of Peter and PAUL from Rome, "Mark the disciple and interpreter of Peter, also transmitted to us in writing what had been preached by Peter" (Eusebius, *Eccl. Hist.* 5.8). Clement of Alexandria, however, affirms that the Gospel was written during Peter's lifetime. In spite of this minor confusion, the early church fathers, including specifically Tertullian (c. 200) and Origen (c. 230), unite in affirming that Mark's gospel gives us the preaching of Peter. Such strong tradition can hardly be discounted, though some recent scholars have sought to do so. The traditional authorship of the second gospel is accepted more generally today than is the case with any of the other three Gospels.

II. Date. Most scholars today believe that Mark is the earliest of the Gospels, and conservatives commonly hold to a date in the 50s. Mainstream scholarship places the writing of Mark between A.D. 65 and 70, and if one accepts the tradition that Mark wrote after Peter's death, the later date would have to be adopted.

III. Place of writing. About this there is little question. From the early church to the present it has been generally held that Mark's gospel was written at ROME. Several distinctive features point in this direction. Mark uses ten Latin words, some

of which do not occur elsewhere in the NT. He explains Jewish customs because he is writing to GENTILES. To his Roman readers he presents Jesus as the mighty conqueror and the suffering servant of the Lord. Because of this purpose no genealogy nor infancy narratives are given. These are found only in Matthew and Luke.

IV. Character. In addition to those just mentioned, there are three main characteristics of this gospel. The first is *rapidity of action*: the narrative moves quickly from one event to the next; this probably reflects the impulsive personality of Peter. The second characteristic is *vividness of detail*: Mark often includes details omitted by the other Synoptics that make the narrative more alive; he gives special attention to the looks and gestures of Jesus. The third characteristic is *picturesqueness of description*: he describes, for instance, the 5,000 sitting "in groups on the green grass" (Mk. 6:39); perhaps Peter was impressed with the striking scene of the groups of people in brightly colored garments sitting on the green hillside, and Mark has preserved the picture for us.

Mark's is the Gospel of action. Only one long message of Jesus is recorded, the Olivet Discourse (Mk. 13). Mark includes eighteen MIRACLES of Jesus, about the same number as Matthew or Luke. In contrast he has only four of the PARABLES, compared with eighteen in Matthew and nineteen in Luke.

V. Content. The period of preparation (Mk. 1:1-13) for Jesus' public ministry is described very briefly. It consists of three items: the ministry of John the Baptist (1:1-8), the baptism of Jesus (1:9-11), and the temptation of Jesus (1:12-13). After an introduction of only 13 verses—in contrast to 76 in Matthew and 183 in Luke—Mark plunges immediately into the public ministry of the Master.

First comes the great Galilean ministry (Mk. 1:14—9:50). This is commonly thought to have lasted about a year and a half. It may be divided into three sections. The first period (1:14—3:12) was a time of immense popularity. Jesus called four fishermen to follow him—and later Levi—and engaged in a vigorous healing ministry. This was the time when large crowds thronged about him.

In the second period (Mk. 3:13—7:23) he appointed the twelve apostles, and opposition began to show itself. The PHARISEES clashed with Jesus over questions about SABBATH observance and ceremonial cleansing. He healed the Gerasene demoniac and the woman with the issue of blood and raised Jairus's daughter. He sent out the Twelve and fed the 5,000.

In the third period (Mk. 7:24—9:50) Jesus gave more attention to his disciples. Three times he is described as withdrawing from the crowd to teach the disciples. After Peter's confession at CAESAREA PHILIPPI he began a new phase of teaching: predicting his passion.

The great Galilean ministry was followed by the briefer Perean ministry (Mk. 10), and then by passion week (chs. 11-15) and the resurrection (ch. 16).

VI. Evaluation. In the early church the Gospel of Mark received the least attention of any of the four. This is not true today. The importance of Mark as giving us the basic message of the primitive church (cf. Acts 1:22; 2:22-24, 36) is increasingly recognized. The theological as well as historical value of this Gospel is widely appreciated. It is the logical place to start one's study of the four Gospels.

Mark, John. mahrk, jon (Gk. *Markos G3453*, from Lat. *Marcus*, "[large] hammer"; *Iōannēs G2722* [see

JOHN]). Son of a Christian woman named Mary (see MARY #2), cousin of BARNABAS, assistant to PAUL and Barnabas, and traditionally the author of the second gospel (see MARK, GOSPEL OF). John was his Jewish name, Mark (Marcus) his Roman. In Acts he is twice referred to simply as John (Acts 13:5, 13), once as Mark (15:39), and three times as "John, also called Mark" (12:12, 25; 15:37). In the Epistles he is uniformly (four times) called simply Mark (KJV calling him Marcus three times).

The first allusion to John Mark may be in Mk. 14:51-52. The most reasonable explanation for the passing mention of this incident is that it was a vivid personal memory in the mind of the author of the second gospel. The first definite reference to John Mark is Acts 12:12. Peter, when delivered from prison, went to the home of John Mark's mother, where many believers were praying for him. When Barnabas and Saul returned to ANTIOCH from their famine visit at JERUSALEM (11:27-30), they took along John Mark (12:25). This opened the opportunity for him to accompany them on their missionary journey as "their helper" (13:5).

The missionaries first evangelized the island of CYPRUS. When they reached PERGA in PAMPHYLIA, John returned home to Jerusalem. Some have thought that this decision was due to homesickness or fear of perils in the mountainous country ahead. However, Paul must have regarded Mark's action as desertion, for when the time came for the second journey and Barnabas desired that his younger cousin should accompany them again, Paul steadfastly refused (Acts 15:37-38). So sharp was the contention between the two elder missionaries that, in the end, Paul departed with SILAS while Barnabas took Mark and set sail for his native Cyprus. Paul's firmness on this matter has led some scholars to believe that Mark may have earlier objected to the fact that the apostle became the leader of the expedition (13:13, "Paul and his companions"); due to Jewish scruples, he may have disapproved of the apostle's distinctive mission to the Gentiles, that is, his gospel of freedom without the intermediary role of JUDAISM.

Mark next appears in ROME, where he is a fellow worker with Paul (Phlm. 24). Paul recommended him to the church at COLOSSE (Col. 4:10). Here he was called "the cousin of Barnabas." That John Mark

M

had fully reinstated himself with Paul is shown by the latter's statement in 2 Tim. 4:11. Peter refers to him as "my son Mark" (1 Pet. 5:13). This may be a mere expression of affection, or it may indicate that Mark was converted under Peter's ministry. An early tradition says that Mark founded the church in Alexandria, Egypt, but this is uncertain.

Mark, Secret Gospel of. In 1958, the well-known scholar Morton Smith (1915-1991) discovered a letter that purports to have been written by Clement of Alexandria (c. A.D. 150-215). This document refers to a "secret" and "more spiritual" gospel written by Mark intended only for "those who are being initiated into the great mysteries." Although some have dismissed this letter as a forgery (no scholar other than Smith has seen it), many believe it is genuine. However, controversy has raged about the authenticity and significance of the gospel to which it refers. A few writers have accepted and developed Smith's hypothesis that the *Secret Gospel* predates the canonical Gospel of Mark, but others are convinced that the work, if it existed at all, consisted of second-century apocryphal material.

market, market place. There is little mention of market places in the OT (cf. 1 Ki. 20:34 NIV; Ps. 55:11 NRSV). In the NT, however, the Greek term *agora G59* occurs eleven times, mainly in the Gospels, where the reference is to typically Eastern (rather than Greek) marketplaces, much like the bazaars of present-day oriental towns. Not only were they used for buying and selling of goods, but a variety of other activities centered there (Matt. 11:16; 20:3; 23:7; et al.). On the other hand, the two market places mentioned in Acts were in Greek cities and were typically Hellenic: surrounded by colonnades, temples, and public buildings, and adorned with statues, they were centers of public life, lending themselves to such uses as the holding of trials (Acts 16:19) and as centers for public disputation (17:17).

Maroth. mair´oth (Heb. *mārôt H5300*, prob. "bitter [things]"). An otherwise unknown town mentioned in a difficult passage that contains a number of wordplays (Mic. 1:11). The imprecations in the

context are against the enemies of JUDAH and refer to places mostly in the SHEPHELAH, but the location of Maroth cannot be determined. Some have suggested it is the same as MAARATH, an unlikely identification.

marriage. The formalization and sanctification of the union of man and woman. Historically, as Hebrew society developed from nomadic to village settlement, complex customs and feasts became associated with the ceremony of marriage, and in the Christian era it became regarded as a SACRAMENT. Normally the bride left her family at marriage, and from that time she, and subsequently her children, became part of her husband's family or clan (Gen. 24:58-61) and, as such, part of their responsibility also. There are some well-known instances in the OT of the bride continuing to live with her own family. After JACOB had worked for the agreed period of fourteen years in order to pay his father-in-law LABAN the required bride price for his daughters LEAH and RACHEL, he remained voluntarily with Laban for a further six years (Gen. 31:41). Laban considered that the children of the union belonged to him and were a part of his family (31:43). Similarly, GIDEON's CONCUBINE and her son lived with her family (Jdg. 14:8; 15:1-2). These examples, however, are few, and neither Gideon, visiting a concubine rather than a wife, nor SAMSON, whose bride was a foreigner, was ever considered a part of the woman's family.

Marriage contracts appear to have originated in SUMER and soon became common features of life in MESOPOTAMIA and beyond. Indeed, according to the Code of HAMMURABI (§128), they were essential to a marriage, since they constituted the public attestation of the event. From Ugarit (RAS SHAMRA), evidence contained in contracts shows that marriages could be temporary or permanent, while tablets from NUZI mention a childless wife forced to secure a concubine for her husband, in order to safeguard the future of the family (cf. Code of Hammurabi §146). Egyptian marriages were often documented by means of contracts, and some contracts recovered from Elephantine, near Aswan, stated the terms of the union and made provision for divorce and the disposal of property in the event of the death of either partner.

Marriage was often a means of strengthening and promoting the fortunes of the family, quite aside from the prospect of producing children. A bride was more likely to be chosen because of the desirability of union with her family, or for her healthy physique and suitability for family life, rather than for other considerations. The father was responsible for finding a suitable bride for his son, and the wishes and feelings of the young people were largely irrelevant to this decision. On some occasions the bride's consent was asked for after the actual marriage arrangements had been made. Thus ISAAC's marriage was arranged between his father's servant and his future wife's brother. She was then consulted (Gen. 24:33-53, 57-58), though perhaps only because her father was no longer living. On rare occasions, parental advice was either ignored, rejected, or not sought (26:34-35), and, in a most unusual initiative, MICHAL, daughter of SAUL, expressed her love for DAVID (1 Sam. 18:20).

In general, marriages were arranged with relatives or with those of the same clan. One might marry a member of the same tribe or possibly move outside this circle to marry within another Israelite tribe. Marriage to a foreigner was generally discouraged, though some Hebrews took wives from among those women captured in war, while others, such as Samson, received permission from their parents to marry a PHILISTINE woman (Jdg. 14:2-3). Concern was always expressed that marriage with a non-Israelite would dilute the covenantal faith by the introduction of ideas and practices concerning strange gods (1 Ki. 11:4).

Because marriages with close relatives were common, limits of consanguinity are recorded for the Israelites to follow (Lev. 18:6-18). Formerly, a man could marry his half-sister on his father's side (Gen. 20:12; cf. 2 Sam. 13:13), though this is forbidden in Lev. 20:17. Cousins—such as Isaac and Rebekah, as well as Jacob, Rachel, and Leah—frequently married, though a simultaneous marriage with two sisters was specifically forbidden (Lev. 18:18). The union between an aunt and her nephew produced MOSES (Exod. 6:20; Num. 26:59), though a marriage between such relatives was subsequently forbidden by the Mosaic law.

In the ancient world the primary purpose of marriage was procreation rather than companionship, and, as a result, large numbers of offspring were regarded as an asset. But an important secondary objective of marriage was the maintaining or increasing of family property, and in royal circles many marriages constituted the seal to what in fact were really political alliances. From the time of the PATRIARCHS, wealthy and powerful people were able to indulge in polygamy, but because of the bride-price there were comparatively few men who could afford more than two wives. One way of circumventing this problem, however, was for a man to have several concubines, and this custom seems to have had quasi-legal sanction in cases where the legitimate wife was barren. Thus the childless SARAH provided her handmaid HAGAR for her husband ABRAHAM (Gen. 16:3), as a woman in these circumstances would also have been required to do under the law Code of Hammurabi (§146). Jacob, already married to the two sisters Rachel and Leah, was also provided with the maid of each of his wives (Gen. 30:3-9), while his brother ESAU had three wives (26:34; 28:9; 36:1-5).

Less mention is made of polygamy after the patriarchal period ended, though Gideon is described as having "many wives" (Jdg. 8:30-31), and the practice was still popular in royal circles, where vast polygamous marriages for political reasons were common. SOLOMON is described as having had "seven hundred wives of royal birth and three hundred concubines" (1 Ki. 11:1-3). Individual preferences gave rise to strong rivalries between wives and children in such polygamous households (1 Sam. 1:6). Nevertheless, the law codes

© The Israel Museum, Jerusalem.

Medieval (11th cent.) *ketubah* or marriage contract from Palestine.

M

of ASSYRIA (about 2000 B.C.) and Hammurabi (about 1760 B.C.) both protected the rights of the wife, concubine, and children, and this precedent continued to be followed by the Israelites.

Despite these examples of polygamy, the most general and acceptable form of marriage was monogamy, which received the sanction of the Mosaic law (cf. Exod. 20:17; 21:5; Deut. 5:21; et al.). This followed the tradition of the instruction to ADAM and his descendants that "a man ... shall cleave to his wife" (Gen. 2:24), and Adam's fidelity to the one mate. In the postexilic period the emphasis that EZRA laid on the purity and integrity of the Jewish national stock reinforced the ideals of monogamy, against which the marital encounters of HEROD the Great stood out as a glaring exception. The teaching of Jesus on marriage stressed the lifetime nature of the commitment, and while recognizing that Moses had regularized an already existing practice of divorce "because of the hardness of your hearts" (Mk. 10:4-5), he taught the traditional Hebrew monogamy and added that the remarriage of a divorced person while the spouse was still alive constituted adultery (10:11-12).

The importance of maintaining and protecting the family name and property led to the institution of LEVIRATE MARRIAGE (from the Latin *lēvir*, "husband's brother"). Where a man died without issue, it was the responsibility of the closest male relative, usually his brother, to marry the widow. The first baby born of this union would then be regarded as the child of the dead man and would be entitled to his name and the entire rights of his property. Even if the widow already had children, the male relative would still be expected to marry and support her on the theory that women needed to live under a protector all their lives. Before marriage, a woman was a member of her father's household, and as such she was subject to his authority. At marriage, her husband became her protector, and on his death, through her levirate marriage, she found her new "redeemer." Like many other Hebrew traditions, the levirate marriage was also known to the Canaanites, Assyrians, and Hittites. The best-known levirate marriage in the OT is that of RUTH the Moabitess, who married BOAZ after the next of kin refused to undertake the responsibility (Deut. 25:5-10; Ruth 4:1-12). See also KINSMAN.

In addition to finding a bride who was healthy and suitable for the family alliance, parents also had to be aware of the bride price that was payable to the girl's father. However this is viewed, whether as a payment for the loss of her services to her own parents or simply as a gift, it still retains something of a stigma by implying that the exchange of gifts or money meant that, in fact, the bride had been sold by the father to her future husband. Under the Mosaic law a man's wife, children, slaves, and animals were listed as his possessions (Exod. 20:17).

The sum of money payable for the bride price varied according to the "value" of the bride and the social position of the family (1 Sam. 18:23-25). Where it was thought desirable, jewelry, animals, goods, or service could be substituted for gold or silver (Gen. 34:12; 1 Sam. 18:25). In Lev. 27:4-5, ten to thirty shekels is mentioned as a price when people made special vows to the Lord, but whether the thirty shekels mentioned in connection with a woman was the same as the bride price is unknown. There is some reason for thinking that by the time of the second TEMPLE a sum of about fifty shekels was more usual as a bride price for a virgin, whereas a widow or a divorced woman was worth only half that amount. It was during this period that a marriage with a virgin bride normally took place in the middle of the week, so that if she were found not to be a virgin, her husband had time to take proof to court the following day, which was still prior to the SABBATH.

Traditions concerning the bride price show some variation. Often the bride price came to the daughter on the death of her father. Under Assyrian law it was paid directly to the bride, while the Code of Hammurabi specified that the sum had to be paid to the bride's parents, with a penalty clause of double the amount if the engagement was broken off (§§160-61). The Babylonian tradition was for the bride's father to bring gifts to the husband, similar to a dowry, for his use but not his ownership, since they reverted to the bride on the death of her husband. It was customary for the Hebrew groom to bring gifts for other members of the bride's family, but these would rarely have been as valuable as those that Rebekah and her family received (Gen. 24:53).

The betrothal (Deut. 28:30; 2 Sam. 3:14) had a particular legal status attached to it that made it almost identical to marriage. The law required that a man committing adultery with a betrothed virgin should be stoned for violating his neighbor's wife (Deut. 22:23-24). A one-year betrothal was considered normal, and it constituted a part of the permanent marriage relationship (Matt. 1:18; Lk. 1:27; 2:5). For one year after being married the groom was exempt from military service (Deut. 24:5) so that the marriage might be established on a proper footing. The bride's father already used the term "son-in-law" from the time of the betrothal (Gen. 19:14), a custom that enhanced the concept of family solidarity.

There remained a distinction between betrothal and marriage, however, especially in the later periods of Jewish history; and although Mary and Joseph were betrothed, and in all other respects she was considered his wife, intercourse would not have taken place until after the marriage, and in this particular situation not until after the birth of Jesus. Following common practice in various cultures, sexual relations probably were not resumed until after the baby was weaned, at approximately three years of age.

Circumcision as an initiation rite before marriage was practiced from about 1500 B.C. in Palestine and Syria. The Hebrew tradition of circumcision was of an independent kind, however, since it signified the admission of the baby to the fellowship of the covenant nation. It was in this connection that God legislated for that event to occur for male children on the eighth day (Lev. 12:3). The events in Gen. 34:14-19 and Exod. 4:24-26 are of a different category, however, the former relating to adult males who, as uncircumcised persons, wished to enter the Hebrew community by marriage, while in the latter the child was uncircumcised, perhaps according to local custom.

The wedding ceremony itself was usually brief, but from early days it became surrounded by an elaborate tradition of ceremony and feasting that was very much in vogue in the time of Christ. Both bride and groom were attired in the finest, colorful clothing, the bride being especially resplendent in an elaborate dress. She had previously been washed, perfumed, and decked out with the gold and jewels of her family, together with any personal gifts that she had received. Toward sunset of the marriage day the groom would set out in procession with his friends, attendants, and musicians for the home of the bride's parents, where she would be waiting with her procession of friends and handmaidens. Then the marriage procession, with the attendant torchbearers, would pass through the village or town streets, to the accompaniment of shouts and singing. At the house where the groom's family lived the feasting, dancing, and entertainment would normally last for seven days, or occasionally for fourteen (Gen. 29:27; Jdg. 14:12; Tob. 8:20). The crowning of the bride and groom as king and queen of the nuptials dates from the Solomonic period and, with other accretions, also became part of the wedding tradition.

In the pre-Christian period, DIVORCE was an option that was always available to the husband and sometimes also to the wife. After the return from EXILE, wholesale divorce was required of those Hebrews who had married foreign wives. This provision was to ensure that the purity of the Hebrew religion would not be tainted by the influence of those who had grown up with the tradition of strange gods and idolatrous practices. Normally, however, there was a distinct tendency in Jewish tradition to discourage divorce, and, following Egyptian custom, a substantial fine of "divorce money" was levied as a deterrent. The status of the wife was not very high, however, and the bill of divorce could take the form of a simple repudiation by the husband. The role of the wife was always subservient to that of her husband. He was the provider, decision-maker, protector, and master. The wife was the legal mother of his sons and manager of his household. She obeyed his instructions, was his helper, and became his confidante. By Roman times the status of the wife had improved, particularly at the higher levels of society. In those households where menial tasks were performed by SLAVES, the Roman matron occupied a position of respect and was able to indulge in her own special way of life.

marrow. The soft tissue in the cavities of bones (Job 21:24; Heb. 4:12). The Hebrew term is used figuratively of richness (Ps. 63:5 KJV) and good things (Isa. 25:6 KJV).

Marsena. mahr-see´nuh (Heb. *marsĕnā* *H5333*). One of "the seven nobles of Persia and Media who had special access to the king and were highest in the kingdom" (Esth. 1:14). Queen Vashti was banished by Ahasuerus (Xerxes) on their advice.

marsh. Because of the dryness of the climate, there are very few marshes in Palestine, except along the Dead Sea. In Ezek. 47:11 the prophet foretells future blessings for Israel and writes that

Marshes near Lake Timsah in Egypt.

© Dr. James C. Martin

the marshes around the sea (prob. the Dead Sea) shall not be sweetened, but left as beds for digging salt. The references in Job 8:11 and 40:21 are probably to marshes in Egypt, since there are many in the Nile delta.

marshal. A commanding officer. The term is used occasionally by the NRSV and other versions (e.g., Jdg. 5:14; Jer. 51:27). See captain.

Mars' Hill. See Areopagus.

Martha. mahr´thuh (Gk. *Martha* *G3450*, from Aram. *mārĕtā*, "lady, mistress, hostess" [fem. of *mar*, "lord, master"]). The sister of Mary and Lazarus, all three being among the special friends of Jesus (Jn. 11:5). Their home is clearly stated by John to be in Bethany in Judea (Jn. 11:1), but Luke does not name the village (Lk. 10:38). Martha appears three times in the gospel narratives (Lk. 10:38-42;

Jn. 11:1-44; 12:2). The historical accuracy of the accounts in Luke and John is supported by the consistent characterization in these two independent records. In both, Martha is busy serving at table and tends to be outspoken, in contrast to Mary's quieter devotion to Jesus. Luke's statement that Martha received Jesus into her house (Lk. 10:38) implies that she was mistress of the house, probably being the elder sister. Jesus' affectionate rebuke (10:41-42) was evoked by Martha's failure to recognize the primary importance of his teaching. Her activity was not out of place but out of proportion. Jesus did not condemn Martha's work, but her excessive attention to material provision, which disturbed her peace of mind, prompted criticism of both Mary and Jesus, and robbed her of the benefit of receiving the Lord's instruction. Both Martha and Mary expressed the same faith in Jesus' power to save Lazarus from dying (Jn. 11:21, 32). The Lord would not have spoken to her the profound truth of 11:25-26 did he not know that she was sufficiently receptive to hear it. Her declaration of belief rose to the highest level (11:27), but her hesitancy of faith (v. 39) shows that she did not yet realize its full implications.

martyr. This English term derives (through Latin) from Greek *martys* *G3459*, meaning "a witness," that is, someone who can assert what he or she has seen and heard. Because in the early church those who witnessed to Christ often gave their lives for their faith (cf. Acts. 22:20; Rev. 2:13), the sense of the term became specialized to mean "a person who suffers death for refusing to renounce a religion." See also testimony.

marvel, marvelous. These English terms are used frequently in the KJV (where the adjective is spelled "marvellous"), almost always with reference to divinity. OT writers extolled God's "marvelous works," including his creation and his salvation

(1 Chr. 16:24; Job 5:9 [NIV, "miracles"]; Ps. 96:3; 98:1; cf. 1 Pet. 2:9 [NIV, "wonderful"]). Prophets predicted his marvelous work of REDEMPTION through the MESSIAH (Ps. 118:23; Isa. 29:14 [NIV, "wonder"]; Zech. 8:6). Significantly, Jesus himself, his message, and his works were marvelous. "The child's father and mother marveled at what was said about him" by SIMEON (Lk. 2:33). NICODEMUS, the Jews, and all the people marveled at his teaching (Jn. 3:7; 5:20, 28; 7:15, 21). Jesus' works repeatedly made the crowds marvel (Matt. 8:27; Mk. 5:20; Lk. 8:25; 11:14). Jesus, in turn, marveled at the great faith of the centurion (Matt. 8:10), and at the unbelief of the Nazarene citizens (Mk. 6:6). In most of these NT passages the NIV uses various synonyms.

Mary. mair´ee (Gk. *Maria* G3451 [frequently in the form *Mariam*], from Heb. *miryām H5319*; see MIRIAM). The name was made famous by the sister of MOSES. Possibly its prevalence in NT times was due to the popularity of MARIAMME, the last of the Hasmoneans and wife of HEROD the Great. Six (or seven) women of this name are mentioned in the NT.

(1) MARY, MOTHER OF JESUS. See separate article.

(2) Mother of John Mark (see MARK, JOHN). Though mentioned only once by name in the NT (Acts 12:12), this Mary must have been prominent in the JERUSALEM church. She was related to BARNABAS (Col. 4:10), and her large home was used by the apostolic church for assembly (Acts 12:12; mention is made of servants, v. 13).

(3) Sister of LAZARUS and MARTHA, from BETHANY (Jn. 11:1). Jesus appreciated Mary of Bethany as a special friend and devoted follower. Jesus probably was entertained frequently in this home just outside Jerusalem, especially during the feast seasons. Three events reveal what is known of Mary. In the first one (Lk. 10:38-42) she appears as the contemplative type, sitting at Jesus' feet and feeding on his words. Martha, in her frustration, objected to doing all the work, but Jesus complimented Mary's sense of values. The second cluster of reactions relates to the death and restoration to life of Lazarus (Jn. 11:1-46). Mary and Martha first sent word to Jesus in PEREA of the illness of

Lazarus (v. 3). When Jesus delayed his coming and Lazarus died, Mary was deeply affected. She sat still in the house among the comforters when Martha went to meet Jesus (v. 20). When Jesus sent for her, she came quickly (vv. 28-29). Faith and sorrow mingled in her words, "Lord, if you had been here, my brother would not have died" (v. 32). Throughout, Martha was still the manager and Mary was the sensitive, contemplative soul. The third event was a dinner, perhaps in gratitude for Jesus' raising Lazarus (Jn. 12:1-8; cf. Matt. 26:6-10 and Mk. 14:3-9, where Mary is not named, and where the event is said to take place in the home of SIMON the leper). On this occasion contemplative Mary burst forth with an impulse that has been growing in her heart. Forgetting her reserve in the intensity of her act, she pushed past the reclining forms, broke an expensive jar and poured the oil on the head of Jesus. Recoiling from the gaze of the guests, no doubt, she pulled back from the center of attention, stopping at Jesus' feet with the remainder of the perfume, dripping it on his feet and lovingly wiping the feet with her hair. To "practical" men, it was a stupid waste, but Jesus considered it a most beautiful tribute paid to him.

(4) Mother of James the younger and of Joseph/Joses (Matt. 27:56; 28:1 ["the other Mary"]; Mk. 15:40, 47). See JAMES #3 and JOSEPH #12. A problem arises in relation to the husband of this Mary. Most English versions mention "Mary the wife of Clopas" as present at the cross (Jn. 19:25; the Gk. reads simply, "Mary of Clopas"). But James the younger is regularly designated "son of Alphaeus" (Matt. 10:3; Mk. 3:18; Lk. 6:15). Is the same Mary wife of CLOPAS (to be distinguished from CLEOPAS) and of ALPHAEUS? That would be possible if Clopas and Alphaeus are names of the same person or if there was a second marriage. In any case, it is quite unlikely that this Mary should be identified with the sister of Mary in Jn. 19:25, since two sisters would not normally bear the same name. According to some scholars, "Mary of Clopas" (a description found only in Jn. 19:5) is not the same as the mother of James and Joseph/Joses, but altogether a different person, about whom nothing else is known. We do know that Mary the mother of James the younger and of Joseph/Joses was one of the Galilean women who, having been healed of evil spirits and infirmities, followed Jesus and supported him financially (Mk. 15:40; Lk. 8:2-3). It is interesting to note that two mothers with their sons thus joined the group and at least three of the four sons became apostles. According to the records, this Mary accompanied Jesus to Jerusalem (Matt. 27:56; Mk. 15:41), witnessed the crucifixion (Matt. 27:55, 56; Mk. 15:40; Lk. 23:49), observed the entombment (Matt. 27:61; Mk. 15:47; Lk. 23:55), joined in the securing of spices for anointing Jesus' body (Mk. 16:1; Lk. 23:56), saw the empty tomb and heard the angelic announcement of Jesus' resurrection (Matt. 28:1-7; Mk. 16:2-7; Lk. 24:1-7), reported to the apostles what she had seen and heard (Matt. 28:8; Lk. 24:9-11), and even saw the resurrected Jesus (Matt. 28:9-10).

(5) Mary Magdalene, so called after the name of her native city, MAGDALA, on the W bank of the Sea of Galilee, 3 mi. (5 km.) NW of TIBERIAS. Jesus had driven seven demons out of Mary Magdalene (Lk. 8:2; cf. Mk. 16:9). This obviously meant that she was a healed invalid, not a rescued social derelict. There is no evidence that she was promiscuous, much less a harlot for hire. That she was a person of means is evident from her ability to support Jesus from her means. She is mentioned more often than most of the other believing women, and usually first. A dozen references show her as healed of evil spirits or infirmities (Lk. 8:2), following Jesus from Galilee and ministering to him (Matt. 27:56), beholding the crucifixion from afar (Mk. 15:40), standing by the cross (Jn. 19:25), locating the tomb (Matt. 28:1; Mk. 15:47), watching the tomb (Matt. 27:61), coming early to the tomb with spices (Mk. 16:1; Jn. 20:1), being first to see the risen Lord (Mk. 16:9), and reporting the resurrection to the disciples (Lk. 24:10; Jn. 20:18).

(6) An early Christian who "worked very hard" for the church in Rome (Rom. 16:6). It is not possible to determine whether this Mary was a Jewish Christian or a Gentile (the Latin *Maria*, not as the Hebrew name but as the feminine form of *Marius*, was common in Rome).

Mary, mother of Jesus. mair´ee (Gk. *Maria G3451* [frequently in the form *Mariam*], from Heb. *miryām H5319*; see MIRIAM). In the opinion of many Mary, like her husband JOSEPH, was descended from DAVID, because she was told that her son would receive the throne of his father David, also because Christ "as to his human nature was a descendant of David" (Rom. 1:3; Acts 2:30; 2 Tim. 2:8); in addition, it is possible that Luke's GENEALOGY OF JESUS CHRIST is through his mother.

I. Mary in the infancy narratives (Matt. 1-2; Lk. 1-2). The source of these narratives is not known, but it is more than likely that LUKE's account came from Mary herself, since she and her relatives figure so prominently in it, with special attention given to her personal reactions (Lk. 1:29; 2:19, 34, 48, 51). She was probably a cousin of ELIZABETH, the mother of JOHN THE BAPTIST (1:36), but the exact nature of their relationship is uncertain. Luke writes about Jesus' birth from Mary's standpoint, describing her maidenly fears (1:26-27), her humble submission to the will of God (1:38), and her hymn of praise to God for the favor accorded her in being the mother of the MESSIAH (1:39-55; see MAGNIFICAT). MATTHEW, on the other hand, writes from the standpoint of Joseph, describing his reaction when he found she was with child, his determination to protect her from shame and insult as much as possible, his obedience to God's command that he marry Mary, and his taking her and Jesus to Egypt to escape the wrath of Herod. The two accounts harmonize and dovetail perfectly. In any case, Mary shows herself to be a woman with a quiet spirit, humble piety, self-control, and knowledge of the OT. It is apparent that neither she nor Joseph fully understood her son (2:50-51).

II. Mary at Cana in Galilee (Jn. 2:1-11). In this episode Mary seems to have some intimation that Jesus had more than natural powers. She may have needed some correction from him regarding her notion about the use of those powers, but it is wrong to think that Jesus sharply rebuked her. It must be kept in mind that he actually did exercise his power by relieving an embarrassing situation, as she had suggested. And his addressing her as "woman" (2:4) does not imply disrespect; he did the same from the cross when he tenderly commended her to the beloved disciple (19:26). His words to her were a gentle suggestion that it was not for her or any other human being to determine the course of action, for that was entirely in the Father's hands.

III. Mary seeking Jesus (Matt. 12:46-50; Mk. 3:21, 31-35; Lk. 8:19-21).

In this incident Jesus is informed, while teaching the multitudes, that his mother and brothers desire to see him. The reason for this desire is not stated; but it appears from the context in Mark's account that they were concerned for his safety because of the bitter opposition of the authorities, who were accusing him of casting out demons in the power of BEELZEBUB; and they wanted to induce him to go into retirement for a time, until it was safe to teach in public again. Jesus' words, "For whoever does the will of my Father in heaven is my brother and sister and mother," are meant to teach that physical relationship to him conveys no special privilege, no right of interference with him—the same lesson he taught on a later occasion (Lk. 11:27).

IV. Mary at the cross (Jn. 19:25-27).

In this incident we find Mary, who had come to Jerusalem for the Passover, watching the crucifixion with agony. Jesus shows his appreciation of the earthly filial relation by committing her to the trustworthy keeping of the apostle who was closest to him.

V. The scene in the upper room (Acts 1:14).

After the RESURRECTION and ASCENSION of Jesus, Mary appears in the midst of the Christian community, engaged with them in prayer for the baptism of the HOLY SPIRIT, but without any discernible preeminence among them. This is the last mention of her in Scripture. It is not known how or when she died.

After Mary's death, many legends grew up around her name, but none of them are trustworthy. The keen desire to know further particulars about her was partly satisfied by the writers of apocryphal gospels (see APOCRYPHAL NEW TESTAMENT). There is no direct evidence of prayer being offered to Mary during the first four centuries. Augustine was among the earliest of the church fathers who thought it possible that she had never committed actual sins, though he agreed that she shared the common corruption of humanity (this view led eventually to the promulgation of the Roman Catholic dogma of the Immaculate Conception of Mary in 1854). In the early centuries, with the development of the idea that the celibate and virgin state is morally superior to the married state, it was suggested that she was a perpetual virgin and that the "brothers" and "sisters" of Jesus mentioned in the Gospels were not her children at all, but were either Joseph's children by a prior marriage or were the cousins of Jesus (see BROTHERS OF THE LORD). In 1950 Pope Pius XII declared the dogma of the Assumption of Mary; that is, that Mary's body did not decompose in the grave but was reunited by God to her soul soon after she died.

Masada. muh-sah´duh (Gk. *Masada*, from Aram. *mĕṣādā᾽* [cf. Heb. *mĕṣād H5171*], "stronghold"). A natural fortress in the eastern Judean Desert on the western shore of the DEAD SEA, located some 50 mi. (80 km.) S of Khirbet Qumran (see DEAD SEA SCROLLS). The upper plateau of the boat-shaped rock covers 20 acres (8 hectares) and rises abruptly, almost perpendicularly 1,320 ft. (400 m.) above its surroundings. The natural advantages of this remote mountain were first recognized during the Maccabean period (see MACCABEE), when several structures and buildings were constructed, including four small palaces at the center. HEROD the Great kept his family at Masada during the years of his struggle for power in JUDEA. Subsequently he rebuilt it with casemate walls, towers, a palace, cisterns, and storerooms.

At the beginning of the first war against the Romans (A.D. 66), Masada was taken by a group

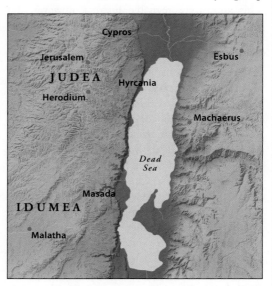

King Herod fortified the southern portion of his kingdom with various outposts including Masada.

Northern portion of the Masada plateau, with a view of Herod's palaces.

of Zealots (Jos. *War* 2.17.2). Herod's armories there were broken into and large quantities of weapons were taken to Jerusalem and distributed to the insurgents (*War* 2.17.8). For the six following years the community on Masada seems to have practiced a normal way of life without being seriously involved in the war with the Romans. This almost impregnable fortress, however, did not escape the fate that fell upon other parts of the country. Two years after the fall of Jerusalem (A.D. 70) this last stronghold to survive the war with the Romans had to defend itself against a vast army. Eight Roman camps and a circumvallation wall were put up around the fortress. Access to the fortifications of Masada for heavy siege machines was provided by an extensive rampart erected on the western side of the rock (*War* 7.8.5). Masada was besieged and attacked for seven months during the autumn of A.D. 72 and the winter and spring of the following year. It was then that the Romans succeeded in creating a breach in the wall. Several attempts by the defenders to check the breach failed, and hopes to survive the Roman attack consequently faded. Their leader, Elazar Ben Yaiʾr, persuaded his 960 followers—men, women, and children—to take their own lives, and to die as free people rather than to be enslaved by the Romans.

When the Romans entered the fortress the next day they encountered only seven survivors—two women and five children. All the others had taken their own lives after having burned their belongings (*War* 7.9.1-2).

maschil. See Maskil.

Mash. mash (Heb. *maš H5390* [not in NIV]). Son of Aram and grandson of Shem, listed in the Table of Nations (Gen. 10:23 KJV and most versions). On the basis of the parallel passage (1 Chr. 1:17), as well as the Septuagint reading in both passages, the NIV reads Meshech (TNIV, Meshek).

Mashal. may´shuhl (Heb. *māšāl H5443*). See Mishal (1 Chr. 6:74).

maskil. mas´kil. Transliteration of Hebrew *maśkîl H5380* (in the title of fourteen psalms, beginning with Ps. 32). It derives from the common verb *śākal H8505* (hiphil, "to understand," but also "act devoutly"), and suggested meanings include "meditation" and "skillful poem."

mason. See Occupations and Professions.

Masorah. muh-sor´uh (postbiblical *māsôrâ* or *massôrâ*, from *māsar H5034*, "to select," later "hand over, transmit"). Also Masora and Massora(h). A systematic collection of textual notes made by medieval Hebrew scholars, called the *Masoretes*. In their production of biblical MSS, they would place a small circle (later called a *circellus*) above or between the words that required comment. Placed usually to the side on the margin, the comment might give statistical information on the word (e.g., that it appears nowhere else in the Hebrew Bible), or indicate that a different word should be read (often the equivalent of a textual variant; see KETIB). Other types of information were also included. In order to preserve accurately the traditional pronunciation, the Masoretes also developed a very sophisticated system for indicating vowels (the Hebrew alphabet originally had only consonants) and cantillation ("accents"). At least two major Masoretic schools, the Eastern or Babylonian and the Western or Palestinian (Tiberian), can be traced back to about A.D. 500. Prior to the discovery of the DEAD SEA SCROLLS, all available copies of the Hebrew Bible were those produced by the Masoretes (thus the standard Masoretic text). See TEXT AND VERSIONS (OT).

Masoretic text. See MASORAH; TEXT AND VERSIONS (OT).

Masrekah. mas´ruh-kuh (Heb. *maśrēqâ H5388*, possibly "red" or "vineyard"). The royal city of SAMLAH king of EDOM (Gen. 36:36; 1 Chr. 1:47). The site is unknown, though some have proposed Jebel el-Musraq, about 20 mi. (32 km.) SW of Maʿan in TRANSJORDAN.

Massa. mas´uh (Heb. *maśśāʾ H5364*, "burden"). Son of ISHMAEL and grandson of ABRAHAM (Gen. 25:14; 1 Chr. 1:30). Extrabiblical evidence supports the view that Ishmael's descendants, including those of Massa, settled in NW ARABIA, not far from the homeland of their ancestor. Some scholars further identify or otherwise associate Massa with MESHA, a place "in the east country" (prob. Arabia) that, along with SEPHAR, served to delimit the territory occupied by the sons of JOKTAN, a descendant of SHEM through EBER (Gen. 10:30). According to

the RSV (cf. also NJPS), both AGUR and LEMUEL were from Massa (Prov. 30:1; 31:1; the NIV and other versions understand *maśśāʾ H5363* here as a common noun, "burden, oracle"). If this rendering is correct, the two men may well have descended from the son of Ishmael; or perhaps they lived in an area associated with the Ishmaelite tribe.

Massah. mas´uh (Heb. *massāh H5001*, "testing, trial"). An unidentified place near REPHIDIM in the Desert of SINAI where the Israelites quarreled and tested God because of their thirst (Exod. 17:1-7). A very similar event (Num. 20:1-13) evidently took place some forty years later and in a different geographical location (KADESH BARNEA, in S Palestine). The place was also called MERIBAH ("contention"). The two names occur in combination once (Exod. 17:7) and in parallelism twice (Deut. 33:8; Ps. 95:8). The name Massah is mentioned by itself in two other passages (Deut. 6:16; 9:22), and "the waters of Meribah" more frequently (Num. 20:13, 24; Ps. 81:7; 106:32; Meribah Kadesh in Num. 27:14; Deut. 32:51; Ezek. 47:19; 48:28).

massebah. mas´uh-buh. Sometimes *mazzebah*. A transliteration of Hebrew *maṣṣēbâ H5167*, "[cultic] stone" (Gen. 35:20 et al.), used especially by archaeologists with reference to a sacred PILLAR, that is, a stone monument set up as a memorial or as an object of worship.

Massorah, Massorete, Massoretic. See MASORAH.

master. This English term, meaning "lord, owner," is used very frequently to translate a number of biblical words, especially Hebrew *ʾādôn H123* (Gen. 18:12 et al.) and Greek *kyrios G3261* (Matt. 6:24 et al.). See LORD. Other relevant terms include Greek *despotēs G1305* (1 Tim. 6:1-2 et al.) and *epistatēs G2181* (only in Luke, e.g., Lk. 5:5). The KJV uses *master* also in the sense of "teacher" to render Greek *didaskalos* (Matt. 8:19 et al.).

Mathusala. See METHUSELAH.

Matred. may´trid (Heb. *maṭrēd H4765*, possibly from a root meaning "to pursue, drive away").

Daughter of a certain Edomite named Me-Zahab (Gen. 36:39; 1 Chr. 1:50). Matrel's daughter, Mehetabel, married Hadad (Hadar), king of Edom; see Hadad (person) #3. There is some versional support for the reading "son" instead of "daughter."

Matri. may´tri (Heb. *maṭrî H4767*, lit., "Matrite," the gentilic form of an unattested name related to the noun *māṭār H4764* ["rain"] and possibly meaning "[born during] the rainy season"). Presumably, the head of a Benjamite family. When Samuel proceeded to choose a king for Israel, the lot fell on the tribe of Benjamin, then on "the Matrite family" (lit. rendering), and from within that clan, on Saul (1 Sam. 10:21; KJV, "the family of Matri"; NIV, "Matri's clan"). Nothing more is known about Matri or his family.

Mattan. mat´uhn (Heb. *mattān H5509*, possibly short form of Mattaniah, "gift of Yahweh"). **(1)** A priest (perhaps the chief priest) of Baal during the rule of Athaliah. At the time of the overthrow of her reign, the Israelites under the leadership of Jehoiada the priest destroyed the temple of Baal with its altars and idols, and they also killed Mattan "in front of the altars" (2 Ki. 11:18; 2 Chr. 23:17). **(2)** Father of Shephatiah (Jer. 38:1); the latter was one of the officials who heard Jeremiah preach and recommended that he be put to death (v. 4).

Mattanah. mat´uh-nuh (Heb. *mattānāh H5511*; a common word with the same form means "gift"). A camping place of the Israelites in Transjordan, near the end of their wilderness wanderings (Num. 21:18-19). Mattanah was evidently between Beer (v. 16) and Nahaliel (possibly a tributary of the Arnon), but the precise location is unknown.

Mattaniah. mat´uh-ni´uh (Heb. *mattanyâ H5514* and *mattanyāhû H5515*). A very common name, also attested (in full or abbreviated form) in various nonbiblical sources. **(1)** Son of Heman, David's seer (1 Chr. 25:4). He and his thirteen brothers were set apart "for the ministry of prophesying, accompanied by harps, lyres and cymbal" (v. 1). When lots were cast to determine the duties of the Levitical singers, he, along with his sons and relatives, received the ninth lot (v. 16).

(2) A Levite, descendant of Asaph and ancestor of Jahaziel son of Zechariah; Jahaziel was apparently a prophet in the court of King Jehoshaphat (2 Chr. 20:14).

(3) A Levite, descendant of Asaph, who served during the reign of Hezekiah in the work of consecrating the temple (2 Chr. 29:13).

(4) Son of Josiah and last king of Judah (2 Ki. 24:17). See Zedekiah.

(5-8) The name of four postexilic Israelites who agreed to put away their foreign wives. They were respectively descendants of Elam (Ezra 10:26), Zattu (10:27), Pahath-Moab (10:30), and Bani (10:37).

(9) Son of Mica and descendant of Asaph; he was one of the Levites who resettled in Jerusalem (1 Chr. 9:15). When the temple was restored, Mattaniah became "the director who led in thanksgiving and prayer" (Neh. 11:17; 12:8). He may be the same person listed among the "gatekeepers who guarded the storerooms at the gates" (12:25). One of Mattaniah's descendants, Uzzi son of Bani, became chief officer of the Levites (11:22).

(10) Son of Micaiah, descendant of Asaph, and ancestor of Zechariah; the latter was a Levite who played the trumpet in the procession when the walls of Jerusalem were rededicated (Neh. 12:35).

(11) Grandfather of a certain Hanan who assisted in the distribution of supplies for priests and Levites (Neh. 13:13).

Mattatha. mat´uh-thuh (Gk. *Mattatha G3477*, from Heb. *mattatâ* [prob. short form of Mattithiah]). Son of Nathan and grandson or descendant of David (not mentioned in the OT); included in Luke's genealogy of Jesus Christ (Lk. 3:31).

Mattathah. See Mattattah.

Mattathias. mat´uh-thi´uhs (Gk. *Mattathias G3478*, from Heb. *mattityāhû H5525*; see Mattithiah). **(1)** The priestly father of the famous Maccabean line (see Maccabee), whose five sons carried on the fight for law and liberty after the father's death (1 Macc. 2:1 et al.). He descended from the clan of Joarib (prob. the same as Jehoiarib, 1 Chr. 24:7). It was at Modein, W of

Jerusalem, that the revolt against Antiochus Epiphanes began. Determined to eradicate Judaism, Antiochus abolished sacrifices, erected pagan altars, even one to Zeus in the temple, and executed any who possessed the law. Mattathias defied the king, the climax coming when Greek officers under Apelles set up an altar at Modein, demanding sacrifice to heathen gods. Mattathias, refusing, killed the Jew who volunteered, and also the Greek officer, destroyed the altar, and fled to the hills with his followers. He conducted a guerrilla campaign, reversing his early refusal to fight on the Sabbath. At the end of one year (166 B.C.), he died (1 Macc. 2:14-70). In special Hanukkah prayers (see Dedication, Feast of), this patriot is remembered as the spearhead of the warfare for religious freedom.

(2-3) Two men included in Luke's genealogy of Jesus Christ; one is identified as the son of Amos (Lk. 3:25), and the other one as the son of Semein (v. 26).

Mattattah. mat´uh-tuh (Heb. *mattattâ H5523*, prob. short form of Mattithiah, "gift of Yahweh"). KJV Mattathah. One of the descendants of Hashum who agreed to put away their foreign wives (Ezra 10:33).

Mattenai. mat´uh-ni (Heb. *mattĕnay H5513*, short form of Mattaniah, "gift of Yahweh"). **(1-2)** The name of two Israelites who agreed to put away their foreign wives. One was a descendant of Hashum (Ezra 10:33); the other one a descendant of Bani (10:37). **(3)** Head of the priestly family of Joiarib in the days of the high priest Joiakim (Neh. 12:19).

Matthan. math´an (Gk. *Matthan G3474*, from Heb. *mattān H5509* [possibly short form of Mattaniah]). Son of Eleazar, father of Jacob, and grandfather of Joseph, included in Matthew's genealogy of Jesus (Matt. 1:15; cf. Matthat in Lk. 3:24).

Matthat. math´at (Gk. *Maththat G3415*, from Heb. *mattat H5522*, "gift"). **(1)** Son of Levi, father of Heli, and grandfather of Joseph, included in Luke's genealogy of Jesus Christ (Lk. 3:24). In Matthew's genealogy, Joseph's grandfather has

the very similar name Matthan (Matt. 1:15), and many scholars have thought that both names refer to the same person, with various solutions (e.g., levirate marriage) offered to the problem that Joseph's father in Matthew is called Jacob, not Heli. Others argue that Matthan and Matthat are two different people. **(2)** Son of a certain Levi, also mentioned in Luke's genealogy of Jesus (Lk. 3:29).

Matthew. math´yoo (Gk. *Maththaios G3414*, prob. from Heb. *matta'y*, short form of Mattithiah, "gift of Yahweh"). A Jewish tax collector (see occupations and professions) or revenue officer of Capernaum, called to be a disciple of Jesus (Matt. 9:9; 10:3; Mk. 3:18; Lk. 6:15; Acts 1:13), identified with Levi son of Alphaeus (Mk. 2:14; Lk. 5:27-29), and traditionally thought to be the author of the first gospel. See Matthew, Gospel of. Since double names were common among the Jews, there can be little doubt that Levi and Matthew were one and the same person. Levi possibly changed his name to Matthew when he became a disciple of Jesus.

The readiness with which Matthew answered Jesus' call seems to indicate that he had previously come into contact with the Lord and responded positively to his teachings. That Jesus should have chosen as his disciple a Jewish tax collector who was in the employ of the Roman government is indeed remarkable. Tax collectors were bitterly hated by their own countrymen and regarded as little more than traitors. However, Matthew's background and talents must have been of great value to Jesus. As a tax collector he was skilled at writing and keeping records. In addition, he must have been a man of deep spiritual convictions. This is revealed by his concern for his former colleagues whom he invited to a dinner at his own house (Lk. 5:29-32 makes it clear that it was Matthew's house), Jesus being the honored guest. No doubt Matthew's purpose was to win these men to Christ. Apart from the mention of Matthew in the lists of the apostles (Matt. 10:3; Mk. 3:18; Acts 1:13), no further notices of him are found in the NT.

Matthew, Gospel of. The first book of the NT. In the early church Matthew was the most highly

M

M

View from the Mt. of Beatitudes toward the tree-covered hill of Gennesaret (looking W, with the Plain of Gennesaret, Arbel, and the Horns of Hattin in the background). Jesus called Matthew to ministry from his tax collection station, which may have been located on this hill.

valued and widely read of the four Gospels. This is revealed both by its position in the canon (it is found in first place in almost all the known lists) and by its widespread citation, for it is by far the most often quoted of the Gospels in the Christian literature before A.D. 180. Among the reasons for this popularity two are particularly important: (1) its apostolic authority and (2) its emphasis on Christ's teaching. A growing church needed the authoritative word of CHRIST both to instruct converts and to refute heresy.

I. Authorship. The first gospel, as is the case with the other three, is anonymous. Nevertheless, the church, from the early second century until the rise of modern critical studies, unanimously ascribed it to Matthew, one of the Twelve (Matt. 9:9; 10:3; Mk. 3:18; Acts 1:13), also called Levi (Mk. 2:14; Lk. 5:27), a tax collector by occupation. The results of source criticism, in particular the evident dependence of Matthew on Mark's gospel, have led many, but by no means all, biblical scholars to abandon Matthew's authorship. Why would an eyewitness to the life of Christ, as Matthew most certainly was, depend so heavily on Mark's account? On the other hand, how does one account for the early and unanimous tradition of Mat-

thew's authorship? The answer of the consensus of modern biblical scholarship is that the first gospel was ascribed to Matthew, not because he wrote it, but because he was the author of one of its sources, namely, a sayings source, usually referred to as Q (from the German *Quelle*, "source").

Despite the results of source criticism, however, strong arguments persist for the traditional view: (1) Matthew's occupation as a tax collector qualified him to be the official recorder of the words and works of Jesus. His job accustomed him to notetaking and the keeping of records. Since shorthand was widely known in the ancient Hellenistic world, perhaps he kept a shorthand notebook record of Jesus' activities and teachings.

(2) There is a good historical tradition that Matthew actually wrote gospel material. This comes from Papias of Hierapolis as quoted by the church historian Eusebius: "Matthew wrote down the Logia in the Hebrew [i.e., Aramaic] language and everyone translated them as best he could" (*Eccl. Hist.* 3.39.16). Much uncertainty exists as to the meaning of this famous statement, but one of two explanations seems most likely: (a) the reference is to an ARAMAIC gospel, written by Matthew prior to the Greek gospel, for the Jewish-Christian

community in Palestine, or (b) Papias's statement refers to an Aramaic compilation of the sayings of our Lord made by Matthew for the instruction of Jewish converts. In either case, the authorship by Matthew of our present Greek gospel is not excluded. If an Aramaic gospel preceded our Matthew, the publication of the Greek edition completely superseded the Aramaic, since no fragment of an Aramaic Matthew remains. A Greek edition is more likely than a Greek translation, since the Greek gospel does not, on the whole, give evidence of being a translation. If the second alternative is accepted—namely, that the Logia were a collection of our Lord's sayings—then it is possible that Matthew expanded these into a Greek gospel. It is a significant fact that the so-called Q material, with which Matthew's Logia is most often associated, shows signs of being a translation from Aramaic.

(3) It is more likely that the gospel would have taken its name from the person who put it in its Greek dress than from the author of one of its sources. The Greeks were not interested so much in who was the authority behind the sources of a book as in who made the book available in the Greek language. In this respect it is significant that although Peter is certainly the source of Mark's Gospel, it was not called the Gospel of Peter but of Mark.

Although certainty eludes us, there are cogent reasons for holding the traditional view that Matthew, the apostle and eyewitness to the events of Christ's life, wrote the first gospel. If he used other sources, in particular Mark, he added his own apostolic witness to that of Peter's, and by so doing may have contributed to the alleviation of tensions between Gentile and Jewish Christianity.

II. Date and place of origin. We do not know precisely when Matthew was written. Its dependence on Mark and its failure to mention the destruction of Jerusalem (especially in connection with Jesus' prediction of that event in Matt. 24) suggest a date shortly before A.D. 70. Antioch of Syria is the most likely place of origin. Early in the second century Ignatius of that city refers to Matthew as "the Gospel." Also, the Gentile-Jewish

Overview of MATTHEW

Author: Anonymous, but traditionally attributed to the apostle Matthew/Levi.

Historical setting: Covers the period from the baptism to the resurrection of Christ. The book was probably written in Antioch of Syria in the late 60s, but some date it to the 70s or even later.

Purpose: To provide a full historical-theological account of the ministry of Christ that focuses on his discourses; to show that Jesus is the fulfillment of the OT; to encourage Jewish Christians who are suffering persecution and are tempted to be lax in their discipleship.

Contents: Genealogy and nativity story (Matt. 1-2); the beginning of the Galilean ministry, followed by the Sermon on the Mount (chs. 3-7); the miracles of Jesus, followed by a discourse on mission (chs. 8-10); growing opposition, followed by the parables of the kingdom (chs. 11-13); final stage of the Galilean ministry, followed by a discourse on humility (chs. 14-18); ministry in Perea and Judea, followed by a denunciation of Jewish leaders and by the Olivet Discourse (chs. 19-25); Jesus' passion, death, and resurrection (chs. 26-28).

character of the Antioch church accords well with the contents of the book.

III. Characteristics. Several features make the Gospel of Matthew distinctive. (1) Matthew is the *teaching* gospel par excellence. In this respect it greatly supplements Mark, which is more interested in what Jesus did than in what he said.

(2) Matthew is the gospel of the *church*. Matthew is the only evangelist who uses the word CHURCH at all (Matt. 16:18; 18:17). The first occurrence is in Jesus' response to Peter's confession. Here its use is clearly anticipatory. In 18:17 the context is church discipline and seems to indicate not only the existence of a church, but also the emergence of problems within it.

(3) Matthew is the gospel of *fulfillment*. It is especially concerned with showing that Christianity is the fulfillment of the OT revelation. The many OT proof texts cited by the use of the formula "that it might be fulfilled," the emphasis on the messiahship of Jesus, and the presentation of Christianity as a new "law," all reveal this basic concern of the author. It has been noted that Matthew sometimes suggests that events in the life of Jesus recapitulate the experiences of the Israelites (cf. Matt. 2:15).

(4) Matthew is the gospel of the *King*. The genealogy of Matt. 1 traces Jesus' lineage back to DAVID. At his birth the MAGI come asking, "Where is the one who has been born king of the Jews?" (2:2). Eight times the regal title "Son of David" is ascribed to Christ (1:1; 9:27; 12:23; 15:22; 20:30-31; 21:9, 15). The triumphal entry clearly has kingly significance (21:1-11). In the Olivet Discourse Jesus prophesied his future kingly reign (25:31). To PILATE's question, "Are you the king of the Jews?" Jesus gave the tacit answer, "Yes, it is as you say" (27:11). And over the CROSS were written these words: "This is Jesus the king of the Jews" (27:37). The climax comes at the very end of the gospel, where Jesus in the Great Commission declared: "All authority in heaven and on earth has been given to me" (28:18). There can be no doubt that the author of this gospel deliberately presents Jesus as the King.

IV. Structure. The arrangement of the material reveals an artistic touch. The whole of the Gospel is woven around five great discourses: (1) Matt. 5-7;

(2) Matt. 10; (3) Matt. 13; (4) Matt. 18; (5) Matt. 24-25, each of which concludes with the refrain, "And it came to pass when Jesus ended these sayings … " In each case the narrative portions appropriately lead up to the discourses. The gospel has a fitting prologue (Matt. 1-2) and a challenging epilogue (28:16-20). The resulting outline is as follows:

Prologue: the birth of the King (chs. 1-2).

Narrative: the preparation of the King (chs. 3-4).

First discourse: the law of the kingdom (chs. 5-7).

Narrative: the power of the King (chs. 8-9).

Second discourse: the proclamation of the kingdom (ch. 10).

Narrative: the rejection of the King (chs. 11-12).

Third discourse: the growth of the kingdom (ch. 13).

Narrative: the mission of the King (chs. 14-17).

Fourth discourse: the fellowship of the kingdom (ch. 18).

Narrative: the King goes to Jerusalem (chs. 19-23).

Fifth discourse: the consummation of the kingdom (chs. 24-25).

Narrative: the death and resurrection of the King (26:1—28:15).

Epilogue: the great challenge of the King (28:16-20).

Matthew's Bible. See BIBLE VERSIONS, ENGLISH.

Matthias. muh-thi´uhs (Gk. *Maththias G3416*, short from of MATTATHIAS, "gift of Yahweh"). The name of the "twelfth apostle," chosen to take the place of JUDAS ISCARIOT, the traitor (Acts 1:23-26). Following PETER's proposal (vv. 20-22), two men were put forward who were considered to have the necessary qualifications for apostleship, for they had been followers of Jesus since the time he was baptized by John. To make divine selection clear, the sacred LOTS were cast after prayer, as had been done frequently in OT days (e.g., 1 Sam. 14:42). Matthias is never mentioned again in the NT. Rival traditions say that he was either martyred in Judea or that he evangelized the Ethiopians. As usual with such shadowy figures, a "Gospel" and "Traditions" were later fathered on him.

Mattithiah. mat´uh-thi´uh (Heb. *mattityāhû H5525* and *mattityâ H5524*, "gift of Yahweh"). **(1)** Son of JEDUTHUN; he and his brothers "prophesied, using the harp in thanking and praising the LORD" (1 Chr. 25:3). He was one of the LEVITE gatekeepers who played the harp when the ARK OF THE COVENANT was brought to JERUSALEM (15:18, 20; 16:5). Later he became the head of the fourteenth company of temple musicians appointed by lot under DAVID (25:1).

(2) Firstborn son of Shallum and descendant of LEVI through KORAH; he was a postexilic Levite responsible for baking the offering bread (1 Chr. 9:31).

(3) One of the descendants of Nebo who agreed to put away their foreign wives (Ezra 10:43).

(4) One of the prominent men (not identified as priests) who stood near EZRA when the law was read at the great assembly (Neh. 8:4). If he was a priest, he may be the same as #2 above.

mattock. A farming implement, with a blade at one end and usually a pick at the other, used to break up the soil. It was especially used on hills, where vines were often grown. The English term is used by modern versions in one passage (1 Sam. 13:20-21; KJV has "coulter," but it uses "matlock" for a different Heb. word in this same passage, and for still other words in 2 Chr. 34:6 and Isa. 7:25).

maul. Originally a hammer such as used by coppersmiths. Today it refers to any smashing weapon like those carried by shepherds (Prov. 25:18 KJV; NIV, "club").

maw. This English term is used by the KJV once with reference to the stomach of sacrificial animals (Deut. 18:3; NIV, "inner parts"). The Hebrew term (*qēbâ H7687*) occurs in one other passage, where it refers to a woman's belly (Num. 25:8).

Mazzaroth. maz´uh-roth (Heb. *mazzārôt H4666*). Transliteration used by the KJV and other versions to render a Hebrew word that occurs only once (Job 38:32). The context (vv. 31-33) clearly has to do with the stars, and this term is used in parallel with a Hebrew word that probably refers to a constellation (either the Bear [Ursa Major] or the Lion [Leo]). If Mazzaroth is not a general term for "constellations" (cf. NIV), it may refer to a specific constellation or star cluster (one possibility is the Hyades). See ASTRONOMY III.

mazzebah. See MASSEBAH.

meadow. Defined as moist, low-lying grasslands, and associated with lush pastures, meadows are scarcely characteristic of hot, dry PALESTINE. Grassy meadows do occur, however, in rainier uplands as in GALILEE and LEBANON, and in damp patches near springs, wells, streams, and irrigation channels. The presence of the latter often is indicated by the occurrence of *ʾābēl H64* in place names (e.g., ABEL MEHOLAH, "meadow of the dance," Jdg. 7:22). English versions use the rendering "meadow" occasionally for other Hebrew words (e.g., NIV at Ps. 65:13 and Jer. 25:37).

Meah. See HUNDRED, TOWER OF THE.

meal. This English term has two distinct meanings, both of which are found in Bible versions. It most commonly refers to the time or act of eating, or more specifically to the portion of food eaten at such a time. For this sense, see MEALS. The second meaning is its reference to the coarsely ground grains of cereal grass. The KJV uses it in a number of passages where modern versions commonly have "[fine] flour" (Gen. 18:6 et al.). The NIV sometimes uses "ground meal" where other versions have "dough" (e.g., Num. 15:20-21). See also BREAD.

meal offering. See SACRIFICE AND OFFERINGS.

meals. In Bible times meals varied greatly in terms of eating, diet, and table customs. Two meals were generally served daily, though three were not uncommon. The time of these meals was not set as ours are today. The first meal of the day could be served at any time from early morning until noon (Prov. 31:15; Jn. 21:12, 15). The rank and occupation of a person caused the time of the noon meal to vary. It came after the work of the morning was completed (Mk. 7:4) or when the noonday heat made work too difficult (Ruth 2:14). The evening meal was not served at any set time, but came

M

when the day's work ended. This was usually the principal meal of the Hebrews (3:7), whereas the Egyptians served their main meal at noon (Gen. 43:16). Jesus fed the multitudes at the end of the day (Matt. 14:15; Mk. 6:35; Lk. 9:12).

The food of the Eastern peoples generally may be classified into four groups: grains, vegetables, fruits, and animal foods. Wheat, barley, millet, spelt, lentils, beans, cucumbers, onions, leeks, garlic, saltwort, pods of the carob tree referred to as "husks," and wild gourds were all eaten. See PLANTS. The grain was often picked in the field, rubbed in the hands to separate it from the chaff, and eaten raw (Lk. 6:1). Sometimes it was crushed with mortar and pestle and made into a porridge or cakes (Num. 11:8; Prov. 27:22). More often the grain was ground between two stones. The grinding was usually done by women (Matt. 24:41) or by servants (Exod. 11:5; Jdg. 16:21).

No meal was considered complete without BREAD, which was prepared both leavened and unleavened. Sometimes honey and oil were mixed into the dough as it was being made in the kneading troughs or wooden bowls. In times of poverty bread was made from beans, millet, and spelt (Ezek. 4:9). Bread was usually eaten warm and seldom by itself, but was served with sour wine or meat gravy (Jn. 13:26; 21:13). Spices, used freely as flavors, consisted of cummin or dill, mustard or mint. Salt also became an important item in the diet of people in the biblical period.

Fruits grew in great abundance in Palestine and consisted of grapes, figs, olives, mulberries, pomegranates, oranges, lemons, melons, dates, almonds, and walnuts. Grapes were eaten as fresh food and dried as raisins. They were the chief source of the wines, which were used both sweet and fermented. Olives were eaten as food as well as used to make olive oil. There were two kinds of figs, early (Isa. 28:4) and late (Jer. 8:13). The late figs were dried and pressed into cakes. Dates were used both raw and dried.

The bulk of the meat came from sheep, lambs, kids, and fatted calves. Pork was eaten, but not by the Hebrews. Some game such as the hart, gazelle, goat, antelope, and deer, as well as doves, turtle-doves, and quails, formed part of the meat diet. Some eggs were used for food (Isa. 10:14). Locusts

A single bowl located in the center of a mat served as the common dish from which those at the meal would take their portions.

© Dr. James C. Martin

and fish were also eaten. The Hebrews used milk from cattle and goats for drinking. From this they made cheese and butter. Arabs drank camels' milk. Cheese was made from curdled milk, and after being salted and formed into small units was placed in the sun to dry. Some of this was later mixed with water to make a sour but cooling drink.

Knives, forks, and spoons were not used in eating. The hands were usually washed and a prayer was offered before the meal. Meat was cooked and placed with its gravy in a large dish on the table. The contents were taken either with the fingers or placed on bread and carried to the mouth. The Egyptians sat at a small round table for their meals. The early Hebrews sat, knelt, or squatted as they ate, but later they evidently reclined at meals, often using a couch that extended three sides around a table (*triclinium*), leaving the fourth side free to use in serving.

Mearah. mee-air´uh (Heb. *mĕˁārâ* [not in NIV]; cf. the noun *mĕˁārāh H5117*, "cave"). A Sidonian city, listed among the territories that the Israelites had not occupied (Josh. 13:4 KJV, NRSV). The site is unknown, and several emendations of the text have been proposed. The NIV, understanding the first consonant as a preposition, translates, "from Arah" (see ARAH).

measure. See WEIGHTS AND MEASURES.

measuring line. This expression is used in many English versions as a rendering of two Hebrew phrases (Jer. 31:3; Zeph. 2:5). The word *qāw H7742*, "cord, line," by itself can be rendered "measuring line" (cf. NIV, 2 Ki. 21:13; Job 38:5; et al.), and several passages speak of allotting or dividing up land with its synonym, *ḥebel H2475* (Ps. 78:55; Amos 7:17; cf. also the beautiful metaphorical expression in Ps. 16:6). The use of a cord of definite length for measuring was common (cf. 2 Sam. 8:2; Isa. 44:13). See also MEASURING REED.

measuring reed (rod). This expression occurs six times in EZEKIEL as the prophet gives the dimensions of the future TEMPLE (Ezek. 40:3, 5; 42:16-18), and this use no doubt influenced the writer of Revelation (see Rev. 11:1; 21:15-16). Reeds were commonly used in the ANE as instruments of measurement. The length of such rods would have varied over any given period of time. See MEASURING LINE; WEIGHTS AND MEASURES.

meat. See FOOD.

meat offering. See SACRIFICE AND OFFERINGS III.D.2.

Mebunnai. mi-buhn´i (Heb. *mĕbunnay H4446*, apparently from *bānâ H1215*, "to build"). A Hushathite (i.e., from HUSHAH) and one of the Thirty, DAVID's elite guard (2 Sam. 23:27); because he is called SIBBECAI in the parallel passages (2 Sam. 21:18; 1 Chr. 11:29; 20:4; 27:11), some scholars suspect that the name Mebunnai is the result of textual corruption.

Mecherathite. See MEKERATHITE.

Meconah. mi-koh´nuh (Heb. *mĕkōnâ H4828*, "foundation, abode"). KJV and TNIV Mekonah. A town in JUDAH, listed between ZIKLAG and EN RIMMON in a list of cities settled after the EXILE (Neh. 11:28). It was probably in the NEGEV, but the site is unknown.

Medad. mee´dad (Heb. *mêdād H4773*, "beloved"). An Israelite elder upon whom the Spirit of the Lord came, enabling him to prophesy (Num. 11:26-27). See ELDAD.

Medan. mee´dan (Heb. *mĕdān H4527*, "strife"). Son of ABRAHAM and KETURAH and the founder of an Arabian tribe (Gen. 25:2; 1 Chr. 1:32). Medan is not mentioned anywhere else in the Bible or in any extrabiblical document and therefore remains unidentified.

Medanite. mee´duh-nit. According to the MT, the Medanites (Heb. *mĕdānîm*) sold JOSEPH in Egypt (Gen. 37:36). This name is regarded as an alternate form or a misspelling of *midyānîm*, "Midianites" (cf. v. 28). See MIDIAN.

Mede. See MEDIA.

Medeba. med´uh-buh (Heb. *mêdĕbāʾ H4772*, perhaps "waters of strength"). An ancient town in MOAB, identified with modern Madeba in Jordan, on a tableland c. 16 mi. (26 km.) SE of the mouth of the JORDAN River and 6 mi. (10 km.) S of HESHBON. The first biblical reference to Medeba is found in a victory song over Moab (Num. 21:30), where Medeba is mentioned as one of the cities taken from SIHON, king of the AMORITES; afterwards, Medeba was assigned to the tribe of REUBEN (Josh. 13:9, 16). The claim to this land often

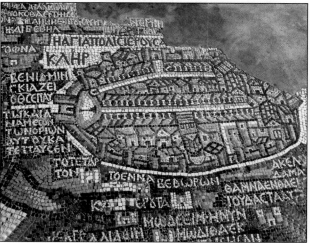

The Medeba (or Madeba) map, a mosaic that depicts the Holy Land, including a detailed representation of Jerusalem.

© Dr. James C. Martin

was disputed. The AMMONITES, after the disgraceful treatment of DAVID's messengers, united with the ARAMEANS in a campaign against JOAB and ABISHAI near Medeba, but they were defeated (1 Chr. 19:6-15). According to the MOABITE STONE, Medeba had belonged to OMRI and AHAB, but MESHA king of Moab captured it and had it rebuilt (*ANET*, 320, lines 8, 30). The prophet ISAIAH names Medeba in an oracle against Moab (Isa. 15:2). In the Byzantine period Medeba was apparently a wealthy city, for several of the mosaic pavements dating from this time are still partially preserved here. Today the fame of Medeba rests upon its mosaic map of the Holy Land, dating from the late sixth century, but first discovered in 1884. The Medeba (Madeba) Map in its original form is said to have been comprised of some 2 million mosaic pieces, stretching almost 40 ft. (12 m.) from N to S, having an E orientation, and featuring the JORDAN River and a very detailed JERUSALEM near its center. Unfortunately, large portions were damaged or destroyed during the construction of a new church on the old site.

Media. mee´dee-uh (Heb. *māday H4512*; this form, as well as *mādî H4513* [only Dan. 11:1], is also used as a gentilic, "Mede[s]"; Aram. *māday H10404*; Gk. *Mēdos G3597*). The home of the Medes, an ancient Indo-European people of NW Iran who were absorbed by the rise of PERSIA in the seventh century B.C. The Hebrew name appears as MADAI, one of the sons of JAPHETH (Gen. 10:2; 1 Chr. 1:5); Madai is evidently regarded as the ancestor of the Medes.

The boundaries of Media have varied from time to time, but generally it was regarded as that land to the W and S of the Caspian Sea. It was bounded on the West by the Zagros Mountains, on the North by the Araxes and Cyrus rivers, on the E by Hyrcania and the great Salt Desert, and on the South by Susiana or Elam. It is shaped like a parallelogram with its longest portion extending about 600 mi. (960 km.) and its greatest width about 250 mi. (400 km.), thus making it a territory of some 150,000 sq. mi. (400,000 sq. km.). It had many natural barriers, making its defense easy. Its water supply was scant, and thus much of the land proved arid and sterile, though some

of its valleys were abundantly productive. Irrigation for the most part was impractical, for some of its rivers were salty while others had worn such deep canyons as to make their waters useless for this purpose. Its few towns were scattered, since its people preferred to live in small groups. Its climate was varied, with some extreme temperatures in both directions. Minerals were many and animals and birds were plentiful. Eventually these factors led to luxurious living, spelling the downfall of the empire. It became famous for its horses, and at one time paid yearly tribute of 3,000 horses, plus 4,000 mules and almost 100,000 sheep.

The people of Media were warlike and skilled in their use of the bow. They were linked very closely in their background, linguistically and religiously, to the Persians, whom they antedate by several centuries and with whom they eventually united. While their early worship was polytheistic, there were some monotheistic leanings that were very significant. Their worship was conducted by priests and consisted of hymns, sacrifices—bloody and unbloody—and a ceremony in which the priests offered an intoxicating liquor to the gods and then consumed it until they were drunken. Their religion was a revolt against the nature worship about them. They believed in real spiritual intelligence divided into good and bad. At the head of the good beings was one supreme intelligence who was worshiped as supreme creator, preserver, and governor of the universe. He was called Ahura-Mazda and was the source of all good. Later, along with Zoroastrian dualism, there developed a worship of heavenly bodies.

The people were for a long period a strong power. SHALMANESER plundered several of their more important cities, evidently with the sole purpose of exacting tribute. They continued strong and were a menace to ASSYRIA's last king, ASHURBANIPAL, after whose death the Median king Cyaxares carried on an extensive campaign.

The more than twenty references to these people or their land in the Scriptures show their importance. Their cities are referred to in 2 Ki. 17:8; 18:11. Esther tells of the binding character of their laws (Esth. 1:19); Isaiah and Daniel speak of their power against Babylon (Isa. 13:17; Dan. 5:28). The last scriptural reference to them is in

Acts 2:9, where Luke says that Medes were among those to whom PETER preached on PENTECOST.

mediator. One who acts as intermediary between parties to reconcile them. In a general sense it means one who interposes and, in so doing, gives some kind of guarantee. The word *mediator* occurs in the English OT once as the rendering of Hebrew *mēlîṣ H4885* (Job 33:23; this Heb. word occurs also in Gen. 42:33; 2 Chr. 32:31; Isa. 43:27). In the NT it renders Greek *mesitēs G3542*, which is found six times, twice in connection with MOSES as the mediator of the LAW (Gal. 3:19 and 20), and four times regarding CHRIST (1 Tim. 2:5; Heb. 8:6; 9:15; 12:24; cf. also LXX Job 9:33 and note the verb *mesiteuō G3541* in Heb. 6:17). Three facts regarding this divine ministry should be noted:

I. **The grounds of mediation.** Throughout the Bible the estrangement between the sinner and God is repeatedly set forth. God is the moral ruler; human beings, as his natural subjects, have violated his laws, hence have gone away from God. All people are thus alienated (Rom. 3:23) because they refuse to be led by the REVELATION that God made of himself (1:18-26). Since a person cannot keep the law perfectly from birth until death, it is evident that the law cannot save anyone from the curse of SIN (Jn. 7:19; Acts 13:39; Rom. 3:20; 8:3). The law, therefore, is the pedagogue, the servant of God, who, by making sinners aware of their estrangement from God, causes them to turn to Christ as mediator (Gal. 3:24-25).

II. **Examples of mediatorial work.** These can be found in the OT. JONATHAN was intercessor for DAVID before SAUL (1 Sam. 19:4). ABRAHAM made intercession on behalf of ABIMELECH (Gen. 20) and SODOM (18:23-33). MOSES was mediator on behalf of PHARAOH (Exod. 8:8-13; 9:28-33) and for ISRAEL (33:12-17). SAMUEL was middleman when Israel was given a king (1 Sam. 9:15-27) and when the nation became wicked (12:19).

III. **Other agents of mediation.** In addition to the intercessory work of such individuals as Moses, God dealt with Israel through other agents. There were ANGELS who acted as media through whom God's will was made known to human beings (Gen. 22:15; 24:40; 32:1; Jdg. 6:11). Because of the tendency of unthinking worshipers to put the mediating angel in the place of the promised MESSIAH, later Jewish scholars refused to recognize angels as mediators. At times God appeared in human form (Gen. 12:7; 17:1; 35:7, 9; Dan. 8:17). In some cases the "angel of the Lord" seems to have been a manifestation of God, perhaps a temporary appearance of Messiah (Gen. 16:7-13). As the revelation from God came to be more fully understood and the results of it more clearly seen, there came the priestly class between human beings and God (Lev. 1-7). With the development of this class there arose the elaborate ritualistic rules for WORSHIP whereby God set forth the requirements for making ATONEMENT. From this ceremonial system developed a set of rules that tended to separate the people from God and made them feel wholly dependent on the prelates for contact with God. So, as the priests degenerated, the people likewise became more wicked. During days of captivity, when priests were not always at hand to serve, the longing of the people for the Promised One increased. And when Jesus did come, he broke down the middle wall of partition between sinners and the offended God (Eph. 2:14).

medicine. See DISEASES.

meditation. This English noun occurs a few times in the OT (Ps. 19:14; 104:34). More common is the verb *meditate* (Josh. 20:47; Ps 1:2; esp. in Ps. 119, e.g., vv. 15, 23, et al.). The KJV uses the verb in the NT as a translation of Gk. *meletaō G3509*, "to attend to, practice" (only in 1 Tim. 4:15; cf. also Lk. 21:14 KJV and RSV). To judge by the use of the terms, meditation seems to have been more a Hebrew than Christian practice. It is a most rewarding act of WORSHIP, of spiritual renewal, of mental refreshing, and of divine communion (see Job 15:4; Ps. 77:3, 6). The most familiar passage is Ps. 19:14, "May the words of my mouth and the meditation of my heart / be pleasing in your sight, / O LORD, my Rock and my Redeemer." Also well known is the command given to JOSHUA to meditate on the Book of the Law "day and night" (Josh. 1:8, echoed in Ps. 1:2; cf. 119:97). The godly meditate also on God's CREATION (Ps. 77:12; cf. 119:27; 145:5).

M

Mediterranean Sea. Because this body of water was the largest known to the Hebrews, it became known as *the Sea*. The Canaanites occupied the land from JORDAN to the Sea (Num. 13:29). It marked the end of the Promised Land (34:5). JOSHUA located it as "the Great Sea on the west" (Josh. 1:4). It was the utmost sea (Deut. 11:24) or western sea (34:2). It was known also as the Sea of the Philistines (Exod. 23:31). Cedar for the TEMPLE was shipped on the Mediterranean from TYRE to JOPPA (2 Chr. 2:16). This sea played a big part in NT days. PAUL's missionary tours took him across the eastern half. If he did set foot in Spain, he saw most of this inland sea.

The sea was known and used by many early civilized people, and they had commercial dealings across PALESTINE with civilizations of the TIGRIS-EUPHRATES Valley. At one time it had been an open channel to the RED SEA. Drifting sands from the African desert and silt from the NILE River closed this and made a land route from Asia to Africa. The sea is 2,300 mi. (3,700 km.) long and more than 1,000 mi. (1,600 km.) across at its widest point. An elevated underwater area once reached from upper Tunisia in Africa east to Sicily. This now shallow area divides the sea into the eastern and western Mediterranean. Its northern shore is broken by the Greek and Italian peninsulas. The islands of CRETE and CYPRUS served as havens for shippers of ancient times. Paul was on both islands during his journeys (Acts 13:4; 27:7).

medium. See DIVINATION; FAMILIAR SPIRIT.

meekness. Mildness and gentleness of character; a quality often commended in Scripture. The word does not imply a weak, vacillating, or supine nature. Jesus pronounced a blessing on the meek, "for they will inherit the earth" (Matt. 5:5). Meekness is a fruit of the HOLY SPIRIT (Gal. 5:23). It is characteristic of Jesus (Matt. 11:29; 2 Cor. 10:1). Believers are commanded to be meek and to show a lowly spirit one to another (Eph. 4:2; Col. 3:12; Tit. 3:2). A teacher should be meek (2 Tim. 2:25). Meekness is a mark of true discipleship (1 Pet. 3:15).

Megiddo. mi-gid´oh (Heb. *mĕgiddô H4459* and *mĕgiddôn H4461* [only Zech. 12:11], derivation uncertain). A major Bronze Age and Israelite city in the JEZREEL Plain. It commands the entrance to the Wadi ʿArah, which served in antiquity as the main pass on the VIA MARIS between the SHARON Plain and the Valley of Jezreel. Near the foot of Megiddo, that route branches out in three main directions: (1) NW past JOKNEAM to the Phoenician coast; (2) NE via HAZOR and thence to DAMASCUS; (3) E to BETH SHAN and from there to TRANSJORDAN. Throughout the three millennia of its existence, Megiddo was one of the most strategic points in Palestine: the pass it controlled was the channel for the flow of peaceful commerce and also the route by which the armies of antiquity marched. One of the best recorded and

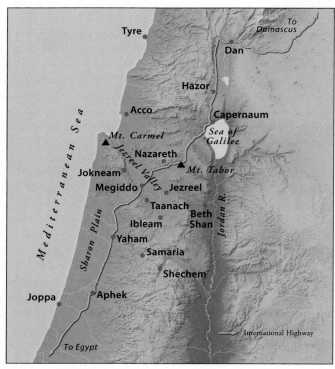

Megiddo and the Jezreel Valley.

Megiddo lies at a key crossroads on what served as an international highway. (View to the NE.)

most interesting military operations of ancient times took place at Megiddo when THUTMOSE III defeated an Asiatic coalition headed by the king of KADESH ON THE ORONTES. The importance of the city is reflected in the statement of the Egyptian king that the capture of Megiddo was the capture of a thousand towns.

The first mention of Megiddo in the Bible is in the list of kings defeated by JOSHUA W of the JORDAN (Josh. 12:21). In the tribal allotments, Megiddo was in the territory of MANASSEH, but this tribe was unable to conquer Megiddo and the other fortress cities that rimmed the plain of ESDRAELON (Josh. 17:11; Jdg. 1:27). During the period of the judges, Israelite forces under DEBORAH and BARAK annihilated the army of SISERA in a battle that raged in part "by the waters of Megiddo" (Jdg. 5:19), the sources of the KISHON (see MEGIDDO, WATERS OF). Though the biblical record does not relate the circumstances under which Israel finally took the city, there are indications of the greatness of Megiddo during the Solomonic period. Megiddo is listed among the cities in the charge of BAANA, one of the twelve officers responsible in rotation for the monthly provisions of the king and his court (1 Ki. 4:12). It is also singled out as one of the cities to which

SOLOMON assigned forced labor for construction (9:15); the text speaks of store cities and cities for chariots and horsemen (1 Ki. 9:19; cf. 2 Chr. 1:14; see below). The hard-driving JEHU killed King Joram (JEHORAM) with an arrow as that king fled in his chariot; Jehu also ordered the shooting of the Judean AHAZIAH, who was attempting to escape. Mortally wounded, Ahaziah went as far as Megiddo and died there (2 Ki. 9:27). In 609 B.C. NECO of Egypt marched N to aid the Assyrian remnant at CARCHEMISH; on his way he was opposed by JOSIAH king of Judah. In the brief battle that ensued in the Plain of Megiddo, Josiah was hit by Egyptian archers and soon died (2 Ki. 23:29-30; 2 Chr. 35:20-27).

The OT has only one reference to Megiddo in the prophetical writings: Zechariah mentions a heathen mourning that took place in the Plain of Esdraelon: "On that day the weeping in Jerusalem will be great, like the weeping of Hadad Rimmon in the plain of Megiddo" (Zech. 12:11). The single NT allusion is in the name ARMAGEDDON (prob. from a Heb. phrase meaning "mountain of Megiddo"), where "the battle on the great day of God Almighty" will be fought (Rev. 16:14, 16).

The modern name for the site of Megiddo is Tell el-Mutesellim. Excavations have provided much information about the history and culture of the city and considerable illumination of the biblical text. The more important discoveries include the city gate and wall, the governor's residence, and the stables of Stratum IV; the water system, the temples and palaces of earlier levels; and a remarkable find of ivories (early twelfth century B.C., Stratum VII). Stratum IV has been usually assigned to Solomonic times, though some recent scholars have argued that it should be dated to the time of Ahab. The stables for at least 450 horses do illustrate the statements of 1 Ki. 9:15-19 and 2 Chr. 1:14. Evidence of similar structures had been previously found elsewhere. An interesting feature of Stratum IV is the use of the three courses of hewn stone and a course of cedar beams, as described in the building process of Solomon at Jerusalem (7:12). The temples and shrines of the earlier levels and numerous cult objects from various periods shed light on the religious life of the city. Inscriptional material includes some Egyptian cartouches and titles, as well as seals with Hebrew inscriptions, one reading "[Belonging] to Shema, servant of Jeroboam." Innumerable small objects also contribute to the knowledge of the art, daily life, and commercial relations of Megiddo.

Megiddo, waters of. A place mentioned in the victory song of Deborah (Jdg. 5:19). The allusion is probably to the wadi draining the basin behind Megiddo, between it and the hills to the S. Thutmose III encamped beside that brook, which was called Qina, before attacking Megiddo. The biblical passage suggests that instead of dividing the spoil and receiving a reward for their services, which would have been done on the southern side of the Jezreel Valley in front of Taanach and Megiddo, the Canaanite kings were swept away by the torrent Kishon in the center of the plain.

Megilloth. mi-gil´oth. The plural form of Hebrew *mĕgillâ H4479*, meaning "scroll" or "roll" (Jer. 36:28-29; Ezek. 3:1-3). The name Megilloth is given to a set of five short OT books, each brief enough to be read publicly at an annual religious festival. The order in some MSS and in editions of the Hebrew Bible follows that of the feasts throughout the year: Song of Songs (Passover), Ruth (Pentecost),

Lamentations (the ninth of Ab, commemorating the destruction of the temple), Ecclesiastes (Tabernacles), and Esther (Purim).

Mehetabeel. See Mehetabel.

Mehetabel. mi-het´uh-bel (Heb. *mĕhêṭabʾēl H4541*, "God does good"). (1) Daughter of Matred and wife of Hadad (Hadar) king of Edom (Gen. 36:39; 1 Chr. 1:50). See Hadad (person) #3.

(2) Grandfather or ancestor of the false prophet Shemaiah (Neh. 6:10; KJV, "Mehetabeel"). See Shemaiah #19.

Mehida. mi-hi´duh (Heb. *mĕḥîdāʾ H4694*, meaning unknown). Ancestor of a family of temple servants (Nethinim) who returned from the exile with Zerubbabel (Ezra 2:52; Neh. 7:54).

Mehir. mee´huhr (Heb. *mĕḥîr H4698*, "bought [as slave]"). Son (or descendant) of Kelub, included in the genealogy of Judah (1 Chr. 4:11). His place in the genealogy is unclear.

Meholah. See Abel Meholah.

Meholathite. mi-hoh´luh-thit (Heb. *mĕḥōlātî H4716*, prob. gentilic of *mĕḥôlâ*, "dancing"). A descriptive adjective given to Adriel son of Barzillai, who married Saul's daughter, Merab (1 Sam. 18:19 [NIV, "of Meholah"]; 2 Sam. 21:8). He was probably an inhabitant of Abel Meholah, but some scholars, vocalizing the Hebrew word differently, read Mahlathite, that is, a descendant of Mahlah, from the tribe of Manasseh.

Mehujael. mi-hyoo´jay-uhl (Heb. *mĕḥûyāʾēl H4686*, prob. "smitten by God"). Son of Irad and descendant of Cain (Gen. 4:18).

Mehuman. mi-hyoo´muhn (Heb. *mĕhûmān H4540*, possibly from Old Pers. *vahumanah*, "intelligent"). One of the seven eunuchs sent by Ahasuerus, king of Persia (i.e., Xerxes, who reigned 486-465 B.C.), to bring Queen Vashti to a royal feast (Esth. 1:10). Some have speculated that the name is a variant of Memucan (see v. 14).

Mehunim. See MEUNIM.

Me Jarkon. mi-jahr´kon (Heb. *mê hayyarqôn H4770*, "waters of the Jarkon" or "pale waters"). A town (or river?) within the tribal territory of DAN (Josh. 19:46). The text is difficult, and some writers emend the text. Most scholars, however, associate the name with a stream called Nahr el-ʿAuja, which flows into the MEDITERRANEAN a few miles N of JOPPA. The ancient Hebrew name "pale waters" may well reflect the considerable quantity of organic soil the river carries at certain times, giving it its greenish appearance. See also RAKKON.

Mekerathite. mi-ker´uh-th*i*t (Heb. *mĕkērātî H4841*, gentilic of an otherwise unattested name, *mĕkērâ*, meaning "plan"). A descriptive title given to HEPHER, one of DAVID's mighty warriors (1 Chr. 11:36). It is not clear whether Mekerah was a place or an ancestor.

Mekonah. mi-koh´nuh. KJV and TNIV form of MECONAH.

Melatiah. mel´uh-ti´uh (Heb. *mĕlatyâ H4882*, "Yahweh has delivered"). A man from GIBEON who helped rebuild the wall of Jerusalem under NEHEMIAH (Neh. 3:7). See comments under JADON.

Melchi. See MELKI.

Melchiah. See MALKIJAH.

Melchior. mel´kee-or. According to late Christian tradition, the name of one of the MAGI who traveled to BETHLEHEM (Matt. 2:1-12).

Melchisedec. See MELCHIZEDEK.

Melchi-shua. See MALKI-SHUA.

Melchizedek. mel-kiz´uh-dek (Heb. *malkî-ṣedeq H4900*, "king of righteousness"; Gk. *Melchisedek G3519*). KJV NT Melchisedec. A priest-king mentioned in three biblical books (Gen. 14:18-20; Ps. 110:4; Heb. 5:6-11; 6:20—7:28) and in several nonbiblical documents (e.g., in the DEAD SEA SCROLLS and in the writings of PHILO JUDAEUS). According to Genesis, Melchizedek went out to meet Abram (ABRAHAM) after the latter's return from the slaughter of KEDORLAOMER and the kings who were with him in the Valley of SIDDIM. He presented Abram with bread and wine and blessed him in the name of "God Most High, Creator of heaven and earth." Abram gave him "a tenth of everything." Melchizedek was evidently a monotheist and worshiped essentially the same God as Abram, who recognized him as a priest.

The reference in Ps. 110:4 reads, "You are a priest forever, / in the order of Melchizedek." This psalm is of special interest because Jesus referred to it (Matt. 22:41-42; Mk. 12:35-36; Lk. 20:41-42), and it is regarded as one of the messianic psalms. The ideal ruler of the Hebrew nation would be one who combined in his person the role of both priest and king.

The author of the letter to the HEBREWS uses Melchizedek (Heb. 5-7) in his great argument showing Jesus Christ as the final and perfect revelation of God because in his person he is Son and in his work he is Priest. The author cites Ps. 110:4, indicating that Jesus' priesthood is of a different

M

View of the Kidron Valley (looking S, with modern Silwan to left). This is probably the location of the Valley of Shaveh, where Melchizedek went out to meet Abram (Gen. 14:17-18).

© Dr. James C. Martin

order from the Levitical: it is "in the order of Melchizedek." Looking back on the history of his people, he comes to the conclusion that the Levitical priesthood proved to be a failure. It was incapable of securing victory over sin and full communion with God. Thus the ideal priest must belong to "the order of Melchizedek." To the author, Christ was the fulfillment of this prophecy, for he came out of JUDAH, a tribe with no connection to the Levitical priesthood. While the claims of the old priesthood were based on genealogy, Christ's were displayed in his power of an endless life. The claim of Jesus to be the real fulfillment of the psalmist's prophecy rested on the fact of his resurrection and the proof it gave that his life was indestructible. The psalmist had declared that the ideal high priest would be forever—and only one whose life could not be destroyed by death could be said to answer to the psalmist's ideal, a priest "in the order of Melchizedek."

Melea. mee´lee-uh (Gk. *Melea G3507*, perhaps from *mĕlēʾâ H4852*, "fullness"). Son of Menna, included in Luke's GENEALOGY OF JESUS CHRIST (Lk. 3:31).

Melech. mee´lik (Heb. *melek H4890*, "king," possibly short form of MALKIJAH, "Yahweh is [my] king"). TNIV Melek. Son of Micah and descendant of SAUL through JONATHAN and MERIB-BAAL, included in the genealogy of BENJAMIN (1 Chr. 8:35; also 9:41).

Melek. mee´lik. TNIV form of MELECH.

Melicu. See MALLUCH #6.

Melita. See MALTA.

Melki. mel´ki (Gk. *Melchi G3518*, from Heb. *malki*, possibly short form of MALKIJAH, "Yahweh is [my] king"). The name of two men included in Luke's GENEALOGY OF JESUS CHRIST: Melki son of Jannai and Melki son of Addi (Lk. 3:14, 28).

melon. See PLANTS.

Melzar. mel´zahr (Heb. *melṣar H4915*). According to the KJV, Melzar was the name of the Babylo-

nian official in charge of DANIEL and his friends (Dan. 1:11, 16). In fact, however, the term is a common noun (from Akk. *maṣṣāru*) meaning "guard" or "warden."

mem. maym (from *mayim H4784*, "water[s]"). The thirteenth letter of the Hebrew alphabet (מ), with a numerical value of forty. It is named for the shape of the letter, which in its older form seems to be a stylized picture of running water. Its sound corresponds to that of English *m*.

member. A body part; also, one of the persons that compose a group. In the NT, the term usually has a derived sense. The parts of the body are not to be an instrument of wickedness but of righteousness (Rom. 6:13, 19; cf. 7:5, 23; Jas. 4:1). The "members that are upon the earth" (NIV, "whatever in you is earthly") are to be put to death (Col. 3:5). Even the tongue, though a "small member," can be "a world of evil" (Jas. 3:5-6). A different metaphor is that of Christians viewed as members of the BODY OF CHRIST (cf. 1 Cor. 6:15; Eph. 4:25; et al.).

memorial. An object or a ceremony that commemorates an event or keeps its remembrance alive. That which qualifies for memorial is the worthily unusual—persons, incidents, or things, usually epoch-making. Memorials are direction markers in history, indicating trends in the course of events. When the Hebrews discovered that there was one living God who participated in human affairs, and with whom COVENANT could be made, his name became a memorial. An apocalyptic psalmist said, "O LORD, we wait for thee; thy memorial name [NIV, your name and renown] is the desire of our soul" (Isa. 26:8 RSV). Also, "the law of the LORD" was to be memorialized (Exod. 13:9). Great acts of God are preserved in memorials: the CREATION (20:11); the deliverance from Egyptian bondage (13:8); and Christ's death on the cross (1 Cor. 11:24-26). True worship and good deeds were objects of memorials: Israelite worship (Lev. 2:2; Num. 31:54); MARY's anointing Jesus (Matt. 26:13; Mk. 14:9); and CORNELIUS's worship and neighborly service (Acts 10:4). These and others are recalled by the various memorials that perpetuate them.

Memphis. mem´fis (from Gk. *Memphis*; Heb. *nōp H5862* and *mōp H5132* [only Hos. 9:6]). KJV Noph (except. Hos. 9:6). A city of EGYPT, on the W bank of the NILE, some 13 mi. (21 km.) S of Cairo, in an area including the modern village of Mit Rahineh. Legend ascribes the founding of the city to Menes, the traditional first king. The original name of the city was "The White Wall." Later it was called Men-nefer-Pepi, after the name of the pyramid of Pepi I of the 6th dynasty; it is from this name that "Memphis" is derived. The chief god of Memphis was Ptah; also prominent at Memphis was the worship of the Apis bull, whose famous burial place, the Serapeum, is located just to the W in the necropolis of Saqqarah. All of the biblical references to Memphis are in the Prophets. Hosea foretold a return of Israelites to Egypt and specifically to Memphis (Hos. 9:6). After the murder of GEDALIAH, a number of Jews fled from Palestine to Egypt (cf. Jer. 41:16-18), and Memphis is mentioned as a place of their residence (44:1). Both Isaiah and Jeremiah had seen the results of an Egyptian-Judean alliance and refer to Memphis (Isa. 19:13; Jer. 2:16). Jeremiah prophesied that Memphis would become a ruin (cf. Jer. 46:14, 19). Ezekiel declared that the Lord would "destroy the idols and put an end to the images in Memphis" (Ezek. 30:13) and spoke of coming distresses in that city (30:16). Today there is little for the casual visitor to see in the ruins of Memphis, and only the colossus of RAMSES II and the alabaster sphinx attract tourist attention.

Memucan. mi-myoo´kuhn (Heb. *mĕmûkān H4925*, derivation uncertain). TNIV Mamukan. One of "the seven nobles of Persia and Media who had special access to the king and were highest in the kingdom" (Esth. 1:14, 16, 21). Memucan served as their spokesman, and Queen VASHTI was banished by Ahasuerus (XERXES) on their advice.

Menahem. men´uh-hem (Heb. *mĕnaḥēm H4968*, "comforter"). Son of GADI; he usurped the throne and became one of the last kings of Israel (2 Ki. 15:14-22). He began his reign of ten years by killing his predecessor SHALLUM. The biblical historian states, "He did evil in the eyes of the Lord" (v. 18). Through gifts collected from his subjects, he bribed

Panel depicting Tiglath-Pileser III (from Nimrud, c. 728 B.C.). Menahem king of Judah was forced to pay tribute to this Assyrian conqueror.

© Dr. James C. Martin. The British Museum. Photographed by permission.

the Assyrian king Pul (TIGLATH-PILESER III) and was thereby able to retain his throne. In this restless period of the northern kingdom, with sinful men usurping the throne time and again, Menahem was the only king who died a natural death. His son PEKAHIAH inherited the kingdom.

Menan. See MENNA.

mene, mene, tekel, parsin (upharsin). mee´nee, mee´nee, tek´uhl, pahr´sin, yoo-fahr´sin (Aram. *mĕnê mĕnê tĕqēl ûparsin*, from *mĕnēʾ H10428*, *tĕqēl H10770*, *pĕrēs H10593*). An inscription that appeared on the wall of the palace of BELSHAZZAR at BABYLON (Dan. 5:25-28). Belshazzar "gave a great banquet for a thousand of his nobles and drank wine with them" (5:1) out of the golden vessels taken by NEBUCHADNEZZAR from the temple at JERUSALEM after its capture in 586 B.C. (2 Ki. 25:14-15). The king became terrified when he saw the writing. "All the king's wise men" failed to interpret the words, and DANIEL, at the suggestion of the queen, was called in to decipher the message.

There has been much discussion about the original form of the inscription and about its interpretation. The text could be understood as meaning, "Mina, mina, shekel, and half-shekels." This series of WEIGHTS was approximately equivalent

M

to our "pound, pound, ounce, half-ounce." Such a reading must have offered many speculative possibilities to the Babylonians versed in arithmetical, algebraic, and astronomical methods, especially as numbers or words were sometimes used as symbols in certain types of omen texts. The "Peres" (*pĕrēs*, Dan. 5:28) is attested as a "half-shekel" both at Babylon and in the Alalakh tablets from SYRIA in the fourteenth century B.C. The form *parsin* could be a plural (or even dual) referring to two half-shekels. (The *u*- represents the conjunction "and.") Another reading would be, "Counted, counted, weighed, and assessed." These words might be a popular proverbial saying involving wordplay on the former reading or even a technical legal phrase denoting the completion of a contract and the final demand for fulfilling its terms.

What Daniel had to deliver as the message by the mysterious writer was the fact that "God had numbered" the days of the kingdom; the king had "been weighed on the scales and found wanting"; his "kingdom is divided and given to the Medes and Persians." There was not much time between interpretation and fulfillment, for "that very night Belshazzar, king of the Babylonians, was slain."

Menelaus. men'uh-lay'uhs (Gk. *Menelaos*). A brother of Simon the Benjamite (2 Macc. 4:23) who usurped the high priesthood in the Maccabean era. See MACCABEE. In the reign of ANTIOCHUS Epiphanes, Menelaus was sent by the high priest Jason (who had himself undermined Onias) to ANTIOCH of Syria (171 B.C.) to carry promised tribute to the king; instead of executing his commission, however, he offered a higher bid for the high priesthood and was authorized to supplant Jason (2 Macc. 4:23-24.). Upon Menelaus's return to JERUSALEM, Jason fled (4:25-26), but Menelaus, failing to pay Antiochus the money, was called to account (vv. 27-28). Reporting to Antioch, he did more bribing. Some time later, the reported death of Antiochus in Egypt brought back the fugitive Jason with allies who forced Menelaus to flee. When the king returned, he massacred Jerusalem's citizens and plundered the temple with the aid of the scoundrel Menelaus (2 Macc. 5:5-23). Menelaus is later mentioned in a letter from Antiochus's son and successor, Eupator (11:29, 32). In 162

B.C., apparently no longer high priest, he was condemned by Eupator. The death of Menelaus was as unique as his career was notorious: he was flung from the top of a tower into some ashes below (13:1-7).

Meni. muh-nee´ (Heb. *mĕnî H4972*, from *mānāh H4948*, "to count, consign"). The name of a pagan deity mentioned in Isa. 65:11, "But as for you who forsake the LORD / and forget my holy mountain, / who spread a table for Fortune [Gad] / and fill bowls of mixed wine for Destiny [Meni]." (The KJV renders the names as common nouns, respectively "troop" and "number.") See GAD (DEITY). In the rites referred to in this verse a table was spread, furnished with food as a meal for the gods. With a wordplay, the next verse says, "I will destine [Heb. *mānîtî*] you for the sword." Gad and Meni were worshiped by apostate Jews. It is possible that they were Babylonian deities, but the evidence points to W Asia as the natural environment of this cult.

Menna. men´uh (Gk. *Menna G3527*). Son of Mattatha, included in Luke's GENEALOGY OF JESUS CHRIST (Lk. 3:31; KJV, "Menan").

menorah. muh-nor´uh. See LAMPSTAND.

Menuchah, Menuhah. See NOHAH #2.

Menuhoth. min-yoo´hoth (Heb. *mĕnuḥôt*, "resting places"). A clan descended from CALEB through HUR (1 Chr. 2:52 NRSV). The name is probably a variant of MANAHATHITES (v. 54).

Meonenim, plain of. mee-on´uh-nim (Heb. *mĕʿōnnîm*, from *ʿānan H6726*, "to practice soothsaying"). A place mentioned once in the KJV (Jdg. 9:37). However, the reference is probably to a tree. See DIVINERS' OAK.

Meonothai. mee-on´oh-thi (Heb. *mĕʿōnōtay H5065*, "my dwellings"). Son of OTHNIEL, nephew of CALEB, descendant of JUDAH, and father of OPHRAH (1 Chr. 4:13-14). The MT lacks the name Meonothai in v. 13, but the context seems to require it, and most versions supply it on the basis of the Lucianic recension of the SEPTUAGINT as well as the VULGATE.

Mephaath. mi-fay´ath (Heb. *mêpa'at H4789*, possibly "shining, radiant"). A town within the tribal territory of REUBEN, listed between KEDEMOTH and KIRIATHAIM (Josh. 13:18); it became one of the LEVITICAL CITIES assigned to the descendants of MERAR (Josh. 21:37; 1 Chr. 6:79). Apparently it was later conquered by MOAB (Jer. 48:21). The location of Mephaath is uncertain.

Mephibosheth. mi-fib´oh-sheth (Heb. *mĕpibōšet H5136*, "from the mouth of shame"). (1) Son of SAUL by his concubine RIZPAH (2 Sam. 21:8). Saul had tried to exterminate the GIBEONITES (21:2), who had tricked JOSHUA into a pledge of protection when Israel had invaded Palestine (Josh. 9). In answer to DAVID's offer to atone for Saul's bloody deed in order to secure the Gibeonites' blessing on Israel, they demanded the hanging of seven of Saul's sons (2 Sam. 21:3-6). This Mephibosheth was one of the seven (21:8). Possibly his original name was Mephibaal; see #2 below.

(2) Son of JONATHAN and grandson of Saul (2 Sam. 4:4). In the Chronicler's genealogies he is called MERIB-BAAL (1 Chr. 8:34; 9:40), probably his original name (and perhaps also the original name of #1 above). When the name BAAL (meaning "lord") took on pagan associations, the scribes apparently substituted it with the word *bōšet H1425*, meaning "shame" (see ISH-BOSHETH); but the change in the first element of the name is unexplained. After the disaster at Mount GILBOA, where both Saul and Jonathan were killed in the battle against the PHILISTINES (2 Sam. 1:4; 1 Chr. 10:1-8), Mephibosheth as a child of five was carried by his nurse to LO DEBAR in TRANSJORDAN, where they took refuge in the house of MAKIR son of Ammiel (2 Sam. 9:4). On David's accession to the throne, Mephibosheth was called back to JERUSALEM, given his father's inheritance, and allowed to eat at the king's table for the rest of his life. Saul's servant ZIBA was commanded to serve him. The servant, however, tried to ingratiate himself with David at the expense of his master by representing Mephibosheth as a traitor (16:1-4).

David did not fully believe the servant's story, for later he received Mephibosheth in a friendly manner (19:24-30).

Merab. mee´rab (Heb. *mērab H5266*, possibly "abundance" or "chief"). Older daughter of king SAUL (1 Sam. 14:49). Merab was promised to DAVID (18:17), but when the time came for David to marry the girl, for some unknown reason she was given to ADRIEL the Meholathite (v. 19). Merab bore five sons to Adriel (2 Sam. 21:8, where the MT, surely by mistake, has MICHAL, the name of Saul's younger daughter; most modern versions read Merab, following some Heb. and Gk. MSS).

Meraiah. mi-ray´yuh (Heb. *mĕrāyâ H5316*, perhaps short form of AMARIAH, "Yahweh has said"). The head of the priestly family of Seraiah in the time of the high priest JOIAKIM (Neh. 12:12). EZRA belonged to the same family (Ezra 7:1).

Meraioth. mi-ray´yoth (Heb. *mĕrāyôt H5318*; possibly "obstinate"). (1) Son of Zerahiah, descendant of LEVI through ELEAZAR, and ancestor of ZADOK and EZRA (1 Chr. 6:6-7, 52; Ezra 7:3).

(2) Son of AHITUB and ancestor of Azariah and Seraiah; the latter two had supervisory responsibilities in "the house of God" (1 Chr. 9:11; Neh. 11:11).

(3) A priestly family in the days of the high priest JOIAKIM (Neh. 12:15 KJV and other versions, following MT; the NIV, on the basis of some Gk. MSS, reads MEREMOTH, as in v. 3).

Merari. mi-rah´ri (Heb. *mĕrārî H5356*, "bitter" or "strong" or "blessing"; the same form [*mĕrārî H5357*] is used as a gentilic, "Merarite," in Num. 26:57 and perhaps elsewhere). Third son of LEVI and eponymous ancestor of the Merarites, an important Levitical family (Gen. 46:11; Exod. 6:16; 1 Chr. 6:16). He had two sons, MAHLI and MUSHI (Exod. 6:19; 1 Chr. 6:19; 23:21). The clans of the Mahlites and Mushites (Num. 3:20; 33; 26:58) were charged with carrying the frames, the bars, pillars, bases, and accessories of the TABERNACLE (Num. 3:36-37; 4:31-33; 7:8; 10:17; Josh. 21:7, 34, 40). After the conquest, the Merarites were allotted twelve LEVITICAL CITIES from the tribes of Reuben, Gad, and Zebulun (Josh. 21:7, 34-40; 1 Chr. 6:63, 77-81). Numerous references to Merari's family in the Chronicles show their importance as workers in the TEMPLE in late OT times (1 Chr. 6; 9; 15; 23; 24; 26; 2 Chr. 29; 34; cf. also Ezra 8:19).

Merathaim. mer´uh-thay´im (Heb. *mĕrātayim H5361*, dual [emphatic?] form derived from *mārāh H5286*, "to be obstinate"). A symbolic name for BABYLON in Jer. 50:21. Meaning something like "doubly bitter" or "twice rebellious," the name appears to be a wordplay on *nār marratum* ("bitter river"), a large lagoon or marshy area formed by the convergence of the TIGRIS and EUPHRATES in S Babylonia. See also PEKOD.

merchandise. The goods or wares that are bought and sold in business. This term is used variously in the English versions to render a variety of Hebrew terms (Neh. 13:16; Ezek. 27:9-34). The KJV uses the term a few times in the NT to render, for example, Greek *emporia G1865*, "business" (Matt. 22:5) and *gomos G1203*, "cargo" (Rev. 18:11-12). See also MERCHANT; TRADE AND TRAVEL.

merchant. A trader; someone who buys and sells commodities for profit. The participle of the Hebrew verb *sāḥar H6086* is used fifteen times, chiefly of international merchants (e.g., Gen. 37:28; Prov. 31:14), whereas the participle of *rākal H8217*, which occurs with similar frequency, seems to be a more general term (Neh. 3:31; Ezek. 17:4; Nah. 3:16). The term *kĕnaʿănî H4050* means "Canaanite," but a different word with the same form (*kĕnaʿănî H4051*) clearly refers to traders in at least two passages (Job 41:6; Prov. 31:24; possibly also Zech. 14:21; note also *kĕnaʿan H4047* in Ezek. 16:29; 17:4; Hos. 12:7; Zeph. 1:11; *kinʿān H4048* in Isa. 23:8). The Canaanites, and in particular the Phoenicians, were so famous for their trading that the name for the inhabitants of Canaan took on this additional meaning (see CANAAN; PHOENICIA). In NEHEMIAH's time different classes of merchants had their own quarters in JERUSALEM; thus goldsmiths and grocers had one location, and fishmongers another (Neh. 3:32; 13:16). The NT makes reference to merchants in

a parable of Jesus and several times in Revelation (Matt. 13:45; Rev. 18:3 et al.). See also TRADE AND TRAVEL.

Mercurius. muhr-kyoor´ee-uhs. That is, Mercury. KJV rendering of Greek *Hermēs G2259* (Acts 14:12). See HERMES (DEITY).

mercy. Compassion or leniency shown to another, especially an offender. In this sense, mercy has special reference to God's act of FORGIVENESS by means of ATONEMENT. In a more general sense, mercy is the compassion that causes one to help the weak, the sick, or the poor. Showing mercy is one of the cardinal virtues of a true Christian (Jas. 2:1-13) and is one of the determinants of God's treatment of us. Christian mercy is a "fruit of the Spirit" (Gal. 5:22-23), made up in part of love, longsuffering, kindness, gentleness, and goodness. God's mercy toward sinners was shown most clearly and fully in his giving of his beloved Son to die in our stead; and our Lord's mercy enabled him to make willingly the awful sacrifice (Rom. 5:8). See also LOVE; LOVINGKINDNESS.

mercy seat. See TABERNACLE.

Mered. mee´rid (Heb. *mered H5279*, "rebellious" or "daring"). Son of Ezrah, included in the genealogy of JUDAH (1 Chr. 4:17-18). Mered had two wives, one of them an unnamed Judean woman, and the other an Egyptian named BITHIAH, who is described as "Pharaoh's daughter." Each of his wives bore him three children.

Meremoth. mer´uh-moth (Heb. *mĕrēmôt H5329*, derivation uncertain). **(1)** Son of Uriah; he was a priest commissioned to handle "the silver and gold and the sacred articles" that EZRA brought to JERUSALEM (Ezra 8:33). He may be the same Meremoth—also described as son of Uriah (and grandson of Hakkoz), but not called a priest—who repaired a section of the wall adjacent to the house of Eliashib and a section next to the Fish Gate (Neh. 3:4, 21). This identification, however, seems to be at odds with the information that the descendants of Hakkoz were unable to find their names in the genealogical records and thus were excluded from the priesthood (Ezra 2:61-62; Neh. 7:63-64), and thus some scholars argue that the Meremoth who helped repair the wall was a different person, possibly a layman.

(2) A priest (or priestly family) who returned from Babylon with ZERUBBABEL (Neh. 12:3). Later, in the days of the high priest JOIAKIM, the head of Meremoth's family was Helkai (v. 15 NIV, following some Gk. MSS; the MT has MERAIOTH).

(3) One of the priests who sealed Nehemiah's covenant (Neh. 10:5); he is probably to be identified with #1 or #2 above.

(4) One of the descendants of BANI who agreed to put away their foreign wives (Ezra 10:36).

Merenptah. muhr′enp-tah′. Variant form of MERNEPTAH.

Meres. mee′reez (Heb. *meres H5332*, meaning uncertain). One of "the seven nobles of Persia and Media who had special access to the king and were highest in the kingdom" (Esth. 1:14). Queen VASHTI was banished by Ahasuerus (XERXES) on their advice.

Meribah. mer′i-bah (Heb. *mĕrîbâ H5313*, "contention"). A name applied to two different places where water was brought miraculously from rock to satisfy thirsty Israelites in the wilderness. The first place, which bears the double name "Massah and Meribah," was near REPHIDIM and Mount HOREB in the Desert of SINAI, and the incident took place when Israel was less than two months out of Egypt (Exod. 17:7; the names Massah ["testing"] and Meribah ["contention"] are used in parallelism in Deut. 33:8 and Ps. 95:8). Another incident took place in S Palestine at KADESH BARNEA nearly thirty-nine years later; this place is referred to as "the waters of Meribah" (Num. 20:13, 24; Ps. 81:7; 106:32) or "the waters of Meribah Kadesh" (Num. 27:14; Deut. 32:51; Ezek. 47:19; 48:28; NRSV, "Meribath-kadesh"). See also MASSAH.

Meribath-kadesh. mer′i-buhth-kay′dish. See MERIBAH.

Merib-Baal. mer′ib-bay′uhl (Heb. *mĕrib baʿal H5311*, possibly "Baal is [my] contender [or advo-cate]"). Son of JONATHAN and grandson of SAUL (1 Chr. 8:34; 9:40). See MEPHIBOSHETH #2.

Merneptah. muhr′nep-tah′. Also Merenptah (and other spellings). Son and successor of RAMSES II. Although not mentioned in the OT, Merneptah is of significance for biblical studies. He ascended the throne of EGYPT when he was around sixty years old, c. 1224 (or 1213) B.C., and ruled ten years. Accordingly, some scholars who adopt a very late date for the Israelite EXODUS have regarded Merneptah as the PHARAOH who ruled Egypt at the time of this event. Among the items discovered in his mortuary temple, on the W bank at THEBES,

The Merneptah Stela, also known as the "Israel Stela" (from Thebes, c. 1230 B.C.). The inscription is a poetic eulogy of Merneptah's victories and includes the statement, "Israel is laid waste; his seed is not."

© Dr. James C. Martin. The Cairo Museum. Photographed by permission.

is a large granite stela dated to his fifth year. This monument is often referred to as the Israel Stela because it refers to several victories in Canaan, including the claim: "Israel is laid waste; his seed is not" (*ANET*, 376-78). According to most scholars, this statement requires that the Israelites had occupied Palestine prior to the accession of Merneptah.

Merodach. mi-roh´dak (Heb. *mĕrōdak H5281*). Hebrew form of Akkadian MARDUK, the Babylonian god (Jer. 50:2 KJV and other versions). Merodach is the divine element in the names EVIL-MERODACH (2 Ki. 25:27; Jer. 52:31), MERODACH-BALADAN (2 Ki. 20:12; Isa. 39:1), and possibly MORDECAI (Ezra 2:2 et al.).

Merodach-Baladan. mi-roh´dak-bal´uh-duhn (Heb. *mĕrōdak-bal'ădān H5282*, from Akk. *Marduk-apla-iddin[na]*, "Marduk has given a son"). TNIV Marduk-Baladan. A Babylonian king at the time of King HEZEKIAH of JUDAH (2 Ki. 20:12 [KJV, "Berodach-baladan"]; Isa. 39:1). According to the biblical record, Merodach-Baladan sent an embassy to Hezekiah when the latter was sick, although probably his real motive was to encourage revolt against ASSYRIA. Merodach-Baladan claimed descent from Eriba-Marduk, king of BABYLON c. 800 B.C., and was first mentioned in the inscriptions of TIGLATH-PILESER III, king of Assyria. When the latter entered Babylon in 731, Merodach-Baladan brought gifts to him and supported the Assyrians. In 721, under the rule of another Assyrian king, SARGON II, Merodach-Baladan usurped the Babylonian throne. Although the Assyrians reacted, Merodach-Baladan stayed on the throne until 710, when Sargon entered Babylon unopposed. Even then, he remained as local ruler and did not oppose Sargon during the rest of his reign. After the death of Sargon, Merodach-Baladan again revolted and ruled for a short period in 703, but when SENNACHERIB seized Babylon, he retreated to his homeland. Sennacherib defeated the rebels and entered Babylon, where he placed Bel-ibni on the throne. Eventually this throne was occupied by Sennacherib's son, Ashur-nadin-shumi. When Sennacherib attacked the coastal cities of ELAM, where Merodach-Baladan had fled, no mention was made of him, but his son

Nabushumishkun was taken prisoner by Sennacherib in the battle of Halulê. Merodach-Baladan died in ELAM before Sennacherib entered the area in 694. This Babylonian king is remembered as a clever and ambitious ruler who bitterly opposed the influence of Assyria in Babylon.

Merom, Waters of. mee´rom (Heb. *mĕrôm H5295*, "high place"). A place near which the Israelites defeated the combined forces of the kings of GALILEE (Josh. 11:5, 7). Merom was most certainly a town in Upper Galilee, as evidenced by ancient extrabiblical sources, but the precise location is debated. The frequent identification of Merom with the village of Meirun at the foot of the Jebel Jarmaq is problematic. More likely is Tell el-Khirbeh, an impressive site S of Jebel Marun on the Israel-Lebanon border; in this case, the Waters of Merom may be identified either with the perennial spring at the foot of the tell or, what is more likely, with the numerous wells in the several branches of the Wadi Far῾ah. Another proposal is Qarn Ḥaṭṭin, 10 mi. (16 km.) ENE of NAZARETH. See also MADON.

Meronoth. mi-ron´oth. See MERONOTHITE.

Meronothite. mi-ron´oh-thit (Heb. *mĕrōnōtî H5331*, gentilic of the unattested name *mĕrōnōt*). The designation of two men in the OT: JEHDEIAH, a member of DAVID's household (1 Chr. 27:30), and JADON, who helped NEHEMIAH repair the wall of Jerusalem (Neh. 3:7; NIV, "of Meronoth"). The latter passage suggests that Meronoth was near GIBEON and that it was closely connected (or perhaps even an alternate name for) MIZPAH, but the exact location is unconfirmed.

Meroz. mee´roz (Heb. *mĕrôz H5292*, derivation uncertain). A place in or near the Valley of ESDRAELON. DEBORAH in her song of victory called a curse upon the town of Meroz for not sending help in the battle against SISERA (Jdg. 5:23). Because a Hebrew city would probably not have been cursed, since that implies extermination, some have suggested that it was a Canaanite town allied with one of the Israelite tribes. Although several identifications have been proposed, the location of Meroz is unknown; however, it must have been very near the scene of battle by the KISHON River.

Mesech. See MESHECH.

Mesha. mee′shuh (Heb. *mêšā* H5392 [Gen. 10:30] and *mêšā* H4791 [1 Chr. 8:9], derivation uncertain; *mêša* H4795 [2 Ki. 3:4] and *mêšā* H4796 [1 Chr. 2:42], "helper, savior"). **(1)** A place "in the east country" (prob. ARABIA) that, along with SEPHAR, served to delimit the territory occupied by the sons of JOKTAN, a descendant of SHEM through EBER (Gen. 10:30). Some have identified it with the MASSA of the Ishmaelite group (25:14).

(2) Firstborn son of CALEB and descendant of JUDAH (1 Chr. 2:42). The Hebrew text is difficult. See MARESHAH (PERSON).

(3) Son of SHAHARAIM and descendant of BENJAMIN; a family head (1 Chr. 8:9). Mesha was one of seven children that were born to Shaharaim in MOAB by his wife HODESH after he had divorced Hushim and Baara (v. 8).

(4) King of MOAB during the days of AHAB and his sons (2 Ki. 3:4, which also describes Mesha as a sheep breeder). In the famous MOABITE STONE, Mesha identifies himself as a Dibonite (see DIBON) and as the son of Chemosh[-yat], and says that his father had reigned thirty years before him (*ANET*, 320; the component -*yat* is restored from a fragmentary inscription found in KERAK). See CHEMOSH. From the time of DAVID (2 Sam. 8:2), Moab was subject to ISRAEL until the divided kingdom, when several peoples including Moab rebelled. But the mighty OMRI of the northern kingdom brought Moab again into subjection. After the country had been tributary to Israel for some forty years, the forceful King Mesha sought independence. The biblical record indicates that the tribute laid upon Mesha's people was exorbitant—an annual levy of 100,000 lambs and the wool of 100,000 rams (2 Ki. 3:4). According to the Moabite Stone, deliverance was effected after forty years of subjection to Israel, in the middle of the reign of Omri's son, meaning either AHAB or perhaps one of Omri's grandsons, AHAZIAH or Joram (JEHORAM). Whatever the exact date of Mesha's rebellion, it was during the reign of Ahab's second son, Joram, that the attempt was made to recover Moab to Israel (see 2 Ki. 1:17;

3:5). Joram secured the aid of JEHOSHAPHAT of Judah, and the king of EDOM joined the two. The Moabites rushed to battle, but were repulsed with heavy loss, and took refuge in the strong city of KIR HARESETH. In desperate extremity, Mesha, having failed to break through the besiegers' lines, sacrificed his firstborn son. For an unrevealed reason, perhaps fearful for having occasioned human sacrifice, the allies retired, losing the fruits of victory (3:6-27).

Meshach. mee′shak (Heb. *mêšak* H4794 [Aram. H10415], derivation uncertain). A pagan name given to MISHAEL, one of DANIEL's companions taken by NEBUCHADNEZZAR to be trained in his palace as counselors to the king (Dan. 1:3-7 et al.). See ABEDNEGO.

Meshech. mee′shek (Heb. *mešek* H5434, meaning unknown; cf. Akk. *Mušku*). TNIV Meshek. **(1)** Son of JAPHETH and grandson of NOAH, included in the Table of Nations (Gen. 10:2; 1 Chr. 1:5); he became the eponymous ancestor of a people group in ASIA MINOR (Ps. 120:5; Ezek. 27:13; 32:26; 38:2-3; 39:1). Meshech is listed as the sixth son of Japheth, after TUBAL, and he is always associated with the latter in the book of EZEKIEL. The descendants of Meshech are identified with the *Muškaya* mentioned in Assyrian records (sometimes in association with the *Tabalu*) and with the *Moschoi* of the Greek tradition. They lived for several centuries in central Asia Minor, but were eventually pushed by their enemies into the mountainous area SE of the Black Sea. In Ezek. 38 and 39 the references to Meshech are especially interesting. Meshech and Tubal, now one people whose chief prince is GOG, seem to serve as some sort of symbol. As the dominant provinces in the land of MAGOG, they represent all the anti-God forces in the world who are maliciously bent on destroying God's people. In apocalyptic fashion Ezekiel seems to be describing something that is to take place in the end time (Rev. 20:8).

(2) Son of ARAM and grandson of SHEM, included in the Table of Nations (Gen. 10:23 [so NIV, following LXX]; 1 Chr. 1:17). Many scholars, however, accept the MT reading (*maš*) in Genesis and emend 1 Chronicles accordingly. See MASH.

M

Meshek. mee´shek. TNIV form of Meshech.

Meshelemiah. mi-shel´uh-mi´uh (Heb. *měšelemyâ H5452*, "Yahweh repays [*or* replaces]"). Son of Kore, descendant of Levi through Korah and Asaph, and head of a family of gatekeepers consisting of eighteen sons and relatives who are described as "able men" (1 Chr. 26:1-2, 9). Meshelemiah's firstborn, Zechariah, had the distinction of being "the gatekeeper at the entrance to the Tent of Meeting" (9:21). Meshelemiah is elsewhere called Shelemiah (26:14) and probably also Shallum (9:19, apparently to be distinguished from the Shallum in vv. 17 and 31).

Meshezabeel. See Meshezabel.

Meshezabel. mi-shez´uh-bel (Heb. *měšêzab'ēl H5430*, "God delivers"). KJV Meshezabeel. (1) Father of Berekiah and grandfather of Meshullam; the latter is listed among those who made repairs to the wall of Jerusalem (Neh. 3:4; cf. v. 30).
(2) One of the Israelite leaders who sealed the covenant with Nehemiah (Neh. 10:21). He may be the same as #1 (note that the name of Zadok is also mentioned in both passages).
(3) Descendant of Judah through Zerah; his son Pethahiah "was the king's agent in all affairs relating to the people" in the days of Nehemiah (Neh. 11:24).

Meshillemith, Meshillemoth. mi-shil´uh-mith, -moth (Heb. *měšillēmît H5454* and *měšillēmôt H5451*, "restitution"). (1) Son of Immer and ancestor of Maasai; the latter (apparently the same as Amashsai) was among the priests who resettled in Jerusalem after the exile (1 Chr. 9:12; Neh. 11:13).
(2) Father of Berekiah; the latter was a leader in Ephraim during the reign of Pekah who opposed the bringing of Judahite captives into Samaria (2 Chr. 28:12).

Meshobab. mi-shoh´bab (Heb. *měšôbāb H5411*, prob. "brought back, restored"). A clan leader in the tribe of Simeon (1 Chr. 4:34). He is listed first among those whose families increased greatly during the days of King Hezekiah and who dis-

possessed the Hamites and Meunites near Gedor (vv. 38-41).

Meshullam. mi-shool´uhm (Heb. *měšullām H5450*, "given as repayment" or "recompensed [by Yahweh]"). A very common name, especially after the exile. (1) Father of Azaliah and grandfather of Shaphan; the latter was secretary to King Josiah and brought to his attention the book of the law that Hilkiah the high priest had found in the temple (2 Ki. 22:3).
(2) Son of Zerubbabel and scion of the house of David (1 Chr. 3:19).
(3) Son of Abihail; he was one of seven relatives from the tribe of Gad who occupied the region E of Gilead (1 Chr. 5:13; cf. vv. 10, 14).
(4) Son of Elpaal, included in the genealogy of Benjamin (1 Chr. 8:17).
(5) Son (or descendant) of Hodaviah and father of Sallu; the latter is mentioned in a list of Benjamites who resettled in Jerusalem after the exile (1 Chr. 9:7). Elsewhere, in a similar list of Benjamites who apparently resettled in Jerusalem at a later time, Meshullam father of Sallu is identified as son (or descendant) of Joed (Neh. 11:7). It is possible that different people are meant; more likely, Sallu could be understood as an eponym or family name.
(6) Son of Shephatiah, listed among the Benjamites who resettled in Jerusalem (1 Chr. 9:8).
(7) Son of Zadok and grandfather of Azariah; the latter is listed among the priests who resettled in Jerusalem and is described as "the official in charge of the house of God" (1 Chr. 9:11; Neh. 11:11 [the latter has Seraiah instead of Azariah]). This Meshullam is probably the same as Shullam in the parallel lists (1 Chr. 6:12-13; Ezra 7:2).
(8) Son of Meshillemith and ancestor of Maasai; the latter is listed among the priests who resettled in Jerusalem (1 Chr. 9:12).
(9) A Levite descended from Kohath who served as one of the overseers in repairing the house of the Lord during the reign of Josiah (2 Chr. 34:12).
(10) One of a group of leaders sent by Ezra to Iddo to get attendants for the house of God (Ezra 8:16).
(11) One of the men who apparently challenged Ezra's instruction that those who had married

foreign women should divorce them (Ezra 10:15). The Hebrew text, however, can be understood differently. See comments under JAHZEIAH.

(12) One of the descendants of BANI who agreed to put away their foreign wives (Ezra 10:29).

(13) Son of Berekiah; he is mentioned as having made repairs to two sections of the wall of Jerusalem (Neh. 3:4, 30). Meshullam's daughter was given in marriage to Jehohanan son of TOBIAH, NEHEMIAH's opponent (6:18).

(14) Son of Besodiah; he and JOIADA son of Paseah repaired the Jeshanah Gate (Neh. 3:6). See OLD GATE.

(15) One of the prominent men who stood near EZRA when the law was read at the great assembly (Neh. 8:4).

(16-17) The name of one of the priests and of one of the lay Israelite leaders who signed the covenant of Nehemiah (Neh. 10:7, 20). Perhaps either of these men should be identified with one of the individuals mentioned above.

(18-19) The name of two heads of priestly families (respectively the family of Ezra and the family of Ginnethon) in the time of the high priest JOIAKIM (Neh. 12:13, 16).

(20) One of the Levitical "gatekeepers who guarded the storerooms at the gates" (Neh. 12:25).

(21) A leader of Judah who took part in the procession at the dedication of the wall (Neh. 12:34). Perhaps he should be identified with #17 above.

Meshullemeth. mi-shool´uh-mith (Heb. *měšullemet H5455*, fem. of MESHULLAM). Daughter of HARUZ, from JOTBAH; she was married to King MANASSEH and gave birth to AMON (2 Ki. 21:19).

Mesobaite. See MEZOBAITE.

Mesopotamia. mes´uh-puh-tay´mee-uh (Gk. *Mesopotamia G3544*, "between rivers," used by the LXX to render *aram nahărayim H808*, "Aram of the [two] rivers," and *paddan ʾărām H7020*, possibly "open country of Aram"). The land around and

between the TIGRIS and EUPHRATES Rivers. This term is used in most English versions to render the name ARAM NAHARAIM (Gen. 24:10; Deut. 23:4; Jdg. 3:8; 1 Chr. 19:6; Ps. 60 [title]). It occurs also in the KJV and RSV at Jdg. 3:10, where the Hebrew has only the name ARAM; the context makes it clear, however, that this is the same place mentioned in v. 8. Mesopotamia could refer to anything from modern E Turkey to the Persian Gulf. When it is used in the Bible, usually the northern parts are understood.

According to Gen. 24:10, ABRAHAM's servant went to Mesopotamia to find a wife for ISAAC and came to the town of Nahor, a place mentioned in the MARI texts and located near the Balikh tributary of the Euphrates (see NAHOR #3). BALAAM's home town of PETHOR of Mesopotamia (Deut. 23:4) is in the same vicinity. The judgeship of OTHNIEL was occasioned by the aggression and oppression of CUSHAN-RISHATHAIM, a king of Mesopotamia (Jdg. 3:8). The king's name has not yet been attested nor is any definition of his realm certain. Mesopotamia was the Ammonites' source of chariots and horsemen when they battled with DAVID (1 Chr. 19:6-7). The context of the name Aram Naharaim in the title of Ps. 60 connects this passage with 2 Sam. 8:5.

Mesopotamia has gone under various names throughout its long history. In the beginning it was mostly SUMER in the extreme S, AKKAD in

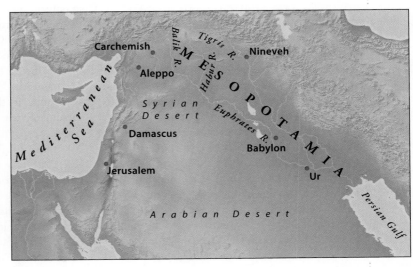

Mesopotamia.

© Dr. James C. Martin

Aerial view of the northern Euphrates River (looking E).

the middle, and Subartu in the NW. In the second millennium B.C., BABYLON was the power in the lower half and Mitanni in the N. With the turn of the millennium, ASSYRIA in the N gained control of the whole but lost it again to Neo-Babylonia in 587 B.C. This was followed by the Persian, Hellenistic, and Roman rules. The Greek name occurs twice in the NT (Acts 2:9; 7:2). Today most of Mesopotamia is in Iraq, with small parts in Syria and Turkey.

messenger. This English term is usually the rendering of Hebrew *malʾāk H4855* and Greek *angelos G34* or *apostolos G693* (see ANGEL; APOSTLE). It may refer to a bearer of news, as when JOB was told of the disasters that fell on his property and family (Job 1:13-19) or when DAVID was notified of ABSALOM's rebellion (2 Sam. 15:13). A messenger may be a bringer of requests, as from MOSES to the king of EDOM (Num. 20:14) or to SIHON (Num. 21:21; Deut. 2:26) to go through their country, or from David when his men asked toll from NABAL for having protected him (1 Sam. 25:14). A messenger of God might be a teaching priest (Mal. 2:7). He is synonymous with a prophet in the summary of the divine appeal (2 Chr. 6:15-16), as was JOHN THE BAPTIST (Mal. 3:1 quoted in Matt. 11:10), though Christ is the messenger of

the COVENANT (Mal. 3:1). A messenger might be an appointee of the churches, as in the collection for the Jerusalem saints (2 Cor. 8:23) or a church gift to the apostle (Phil. 4:18).

Messiah. muh-si´uh (Heb. *māšîaḥ H5431*, "anointed one"; almost always rendered by the LXX with *christos G5986*, same meaning; the Gk. NT, in addition, uses twice the transliteration *Messias G3549* [Jn. 1:41; 4:25]). The KJV uses this term in only one passage in the OT (Dan. 9:25-26), and the variant form "Messias" in two NT passages that have the Greek transliteration *Messias* (Jn. 1:41; 4:25); the RSV and the NIV use "Messiah" only in the two verses in John. By contrast, such versions as the NRSV and TNIV use the term over sixty times in the NT to render Greek *Christos*, presumably when the translators believe that this Greek word functions as a title (e.g., Matt. 1:1; Mk. 14:61; Lk. 2:11; Jn. 1:20; Acts 2:31; Rom. 9:5; Rev. 11:15); the rendering "Christ" is then reserved for the many passages where it functions as a name. Drawing the distinction between these two senses is sometimes difficult. It is sometimes argued that even the combination Jesus Christ should always be rendered "Jesus the Messiah."

In ancient ISRAEL both persons and things consecrated to sacred purposes were anointed by having OIL poured over them. See ANOINT. When the TABERNACLE was dedicated, the building, its various parts, and the holy vessels were anointed (Exod. 30:26-30; 40:9-11). Official persons were consecrated with oil. Sometimes PROPHETS were anointed when they were consecrated (1 Ki. 19:16). The statement in Isa. 61:1 "The LORD has anointed me to preach good news to the poor" is an allusion to this practice. PRIESTS were also anointed with oil for their office (Exod. 29:21; Lev. 8:30). The KINGS apparently were anointed regularly (1 Sam. 9:16; 16:3; 2 Sam. 12:7; 1 Ki. 1:34). The king was "the Lord's anointed" in a special sense, and in the OT the primary significance of this expression refers to the earthly king who is reigning over the Lord's people. It is a reference to the king's close relationship to the Lord and to the sacral character of his position and person. The Israelites did not think of crowning a king but of anointing him when he was enthroned. The fact that he was anointed was the essential characteristic of the ruler.

Where such expressions as "the Lord's anointed," "my anointed," "your anointed," occur in the OT, the reference is not used as a technical designation of the Messiah, but refers to the king of the line of DAVID, ruling in JERUSALEM, and anointed by the Lord through the priest. ISAIAH uses the term only once, and then of the Persian CYRUS (Isa. 45:1). Later the expression "Son of David" was a synonym for "Messiah" (Matt. 21:9; Mk. 10:47-48). It is obvious that there must be some historical connection between the designation "the Lord's anointed" (and similar expressions) and the title "Messiah." The latter term apparently is a later expression and is an abbreviation of the fuller title "the Lord's anointed." It shows that the Messiah of Israel's messianic hope derived his name from the sacral title of the kings of David's line. With the possible exception of Dan. 9:25-26, the title "Messiah" as a reference to Israel's eschatological king does not occur in the OT. It appears in this sense later in the NT and in the literature of JUDAISM. In the NT the Messiah is "the Christ," its Greek equivalent.

Closely related to the eschatological character of the Messiah is his political significance. He will destroy the world powers in an act of judgment, deliver Israel from her enemies, and restore her as a nation. The Messiah is the king of this future kingdom to whose political and religious domination the other nations will yield. See KINGDOM OF GOD. His mission is the redemption of Israel and his dominion is universal. This is the clear picture of the Messiah in practically all of the OT passages that refer to him. The Messiah will put an end to war, for he is the Prince of Peace, and he will rule righteously over his people. He himself is righteous and is called the righteous Messiah or the Messiah of righteousness (Jer. 23:6). But this implies more than just a judgment and government of his people. The term RIGHTEOUSNESS when used in connection with the Messiah is inseparably related to SALVATION. The Messiah will establish the right of his people against any foe from without or within. He will establish this salvation and maintain it in the face of all opposing forces. Righteousness

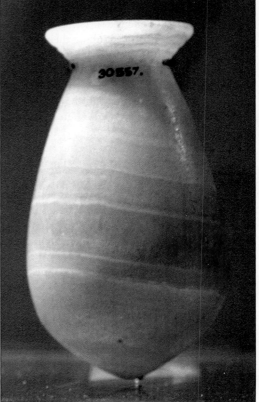

An alabaster oil jar for holding special ointments of the Egyptian 18th dynasty (c. 1500 B.C.). Refined oil was used to anoint leaders set aside for special assignments.

© Dr. James C. Martin

M

M

and salvation are the same because the Messiah's righteousness is declared in his saving acts. Jewish writers have made much of this with reference to Mal. 4:2. At the same time it is often emphasized that by his righteousness the Messiah will establish justice and righteousness, in the ethical sense, in the land. Sin will be rooted out, and Israel will become a holy people.

Perhaps the most profound spiritual work of the Messiah is seen in his position as the intermediary between God and the people by interceding for them. This is the Aramaic Targum's interpretation of Isa. 53, but this chapter is much more profound than the Jewish exegetes seemed to realize. It is true that the Targum on Isaiah identifies the SERVANT OF THE LORD with the Messiah and that it uses this expression as a title of the Messiah, but his suffering is interpreted merely as the danger and anxiety that are his lot in the war with the ungodly. There is no real distinction here between the suffering of the Servant and the suffering the prophets of Israel experienced in fulfilling their mission. But what Isaiah said of the suffering of the Servant of the Lord is infinitely more significant than this. In the Suffering Servant the Messiah is seen making vicarious atonement through his passion and death, which has a positive purpose in the plan of God for the salvation of sinful men. The Messiah as the Suffering Servant sums up the entire prophetic movement and constitutes a climax in OT prophecy.

The progress of prophetic revelation in history leads up to the idea of the innocent Suffering Servant of God, who in the redemptive purpose of his death reconciles sinners to God. In the Messiah's SACRIFICE of himself as an expiation for sin his priestly office is revealed and combined with his work as prophet and king. The redemptive work of the Messiah includes the restoration of the paradise that existed in the beginning but was lost through the fall of ADAM. Through the Messiah the kingdom of the end time will be established, the kingdom of God on earth, the restoration of Israel. As the Messiah was present from the first in the creation so he is also present as the central figure of the last events. He is declared to be the firstborn of creation and also the end and goal of creation (Jn. 1:1; Col. 1:15-17; Rev. 3:14).

The NT conception of the Messiah is developed directly from the teaching of the OT. The essential features of the OT picture of the Messiah are in the person of Jesus. The suffering, dying, and glorified Servant of the Lord of the OT is that same NT SON OF MAN who will return on the clouds of heaven. The Messiah, as the Son of Man, will suffer, die, and rise again on the third day, "according to the Scriptures." But even though Jesus was victorious over death in his resurrection and ascension, he did not yet reign in his full messiahship in his righteous kingdom. His ultimate victory is revealed to be in the future, and consequently he must come again in power to establish his messianic throne and kingdom. Jesus often used the phrase "the Son of Man" to express his interpretation of his nature and his part in the coming of God's kingdom. It seems that Jesus preferred this title in referring to himself. He did not use it primarily to express his humanity; on the contrary, it was a proclamation of the paradox that he, who appeared as an ordinary man, was at the same time the One in whom there are supernatural powers of the kingdom of God. He who took on himself the form of a man will some day be revealed as "the Son of Man" with power and glory. The title, then, is an expression for the triumphant Messiah who comes on the clouds in the majesty of his exaltation.

The expression "the Son of Man" used of the Messiah reflects the general picture in the NT of a more profound view of his person. The Messiah as the Son of Man is a preexistent heavenly being. Long before Abraham, Jesus said, the Son of Man *was* (Jn. 8:58; cf. Jn. 17:5; Col. 1:17). The origin of creation is linked with the Messiah Jesus in various Scriptures (1 Cor. 8:6; 2 Cor. 8:9; Col. 1:15-17). It is also as preexistent that Jesus is called "elect" (1 Pet. 2:6; NIV, "chosen"). God has prepared him to carry out his purpose in redemption and eschatological judgment. Furthermore, the Messiah is revealed to be the Son of Man in a unique sense (Jn. 1:1; Rom. 1:4). Jesus affirmed this in his conversation with the priests and elders. Jesus was asked to declare if he was "the Messiah, the Son of God" (Matt. 26:63-64; Mk. 14:61; Lk. 22:67-70), and his claim is clear. As the SON OF GOD, the Messiah possesses the power of God's authority. It is as the Son of God that the divine nature of the Messiah is supremely revealed.

Messianic Banquet. A term used sometimes to refer to "the wedding supper of the Lamb" (Rev. 19:9) or more generally to the festivities of the end time, which are often symbolized by means of a meal. In the ANE, it was not uncommon for kings to celebrate a military victory by providing a great banquet (cf. 1 Chr. 12:38-40; 3 Macc. 6:30-41), and this notion was transferred to the gods in some myths. It was only natural that the symbol should be used to depict Yahweh's eschatological celebration (Isa. 25:6, 8; cf. Rev. 21:4). The theme becomes prominent in APOCALYPTIC LITERATURE and is picked up in the NT. Jesus promises that those "who hunger now ... will be satisfied" (Lk. 6:21); he also compares the kingdom of heaven to "a king who prepared a wedding banquet for his son" (Matt. 22:1; cf. Lk. 14:16). The imagery is especially prominent in the book of Revelation (see Rev. 19:6-7).

messianic secret. A term used in biblical scholarship to refer to those passages in the Gospels where Jesus tells his followers not to publicize his miracles (or other extraordinary details). This feature is especially prominent in Mark (e.g., Mk. 1:43-44; 5:43; 7:36; 8:30; 9:9), and it has led to considerable debate regarding its significance. The phrase is especially associated with Wilhelm Wrede, who in 1901 argued that the element of secrecy was invented and added to the tradition in order to account for the lack of evidence that Jesus had proclaimed himself as the MESSIAH. Although this theory was generally rejected in its original form, it has exerted profound influence in NT scholarship, mainly because it showed that the secrecy motif required some kind of theological explanation.

Messias. See MESSIAH.

metals. See MINERALS.

Metheg Ammah. mee´thig-am´uh (Heb. *meteg hā᾽ammâ H5497*, possibly "bridle of the forearm [*or* cubit]"). An otherwise unknown town that DAVID took from the control of the PHILISTINES (2 Sam. 8:1). Instead of this name, the parallel passage has "Gath and its surrounding villages" (1 Chr. 18:1), leading some to speculate that GATH was considered the "mother city" of the Philistines (cf. ASV, but the form *᾽ammâ* never means "mother" in the OT). Some argue that the words should be translated as common nouns, referring to one cubit's length of a bridle and symbolizing either friendship or surrender.

Methusael. See METHUSHAEL.

Methuselah. mi-thoo´suh-luh (Heb. *mĕtûšelaḥ H5500*, possibly "man of the javelin"; Gk. *Mathousala G3417*). Son of ENOCH, descendant of SETH, and grandfather of NOAH (Gen. 5:21-22, 25-27; 1 Chr. 1:3; included in Luke's GENEALOGY OF JESUS CHRIST, Lk. 3:37). In the ANTEDELUVIAN age of unusual longevity, Methuselah lived 969 years, longer than any other (Gen. 5:27). Some believe that the second element in his name (*šelaḥ*) is a divine proper name indicating idolatry. In later APOCALYPTIC LITERATURE, Methuselah plays an important role.

Methushael. mi-thoo´shay-uhl (Heb. *mĕtûšā᾽ēl H5499*, possibly "man of God"). KJV Methusael. Son of MEHUJAEL, descendant of CAIN, and father of LAMECH (Gen. 4:18). Some have speculated that Methushael and METHUSELAH represent different traditions arising from the same name.

Meunim. mi-yoo´nim (Heb. *mĕ῾ûnîm H5064*, apparently the gentilic pl. of a name such as *mā῾ôn H5062*; see MAON). In the NIV, the Hebrew term is rendered "Meunim" only twice, namely, in parallel passages that list the descendants of temple servants (NETHINIM) who returned from the EXILE (Ezra 2:50 [KJV, "Mehunim"]; Neh. 7:52). Apparently, the NIV regards Meunim here as a personal name referring to the ancestor of that family. It is possible, however, that in these passages, as elsewhere, the name is that of a non-Israelite people group. See MEUNITES.

Meunites. mi-yoo´nits (Heb. *mĕ῾ûnîm H5064*, apparently the gentilic pl. of a name such as *mā῾ôn H5062*; see MAON). Also MEUNIM (for no obvious

M

reason, the NRSV has "Meunim" in 1 Chr. 4:41, but "Meunites" in 2 Chr. 20:1; 26:7). A minor desert tribe of uncertain origin. This people group occupied an area SE of the DEAD SEA on the eastern border of EDOM whose chief city was Maʿan (about 12 mi./19 km. SE of PETRA). The Meunites were not Edomites, but apparently had such close relations with the people of Mount SEIR that they were in danger of being identified with them. It is possible, but disputed by some, that the Meunites were the same as the MAONITES who oppressed the Israelites in the time of the judges (Jdg. 10:12).

The Simeonites seem to have dispossessed one group of the Meunites and occupied their territory (1 Chr. 4:41; the KJV here understands the name as a common noun, *hammĕʿônîm*, "the habitations"). On another occasion some of the Meunites joined forces with the Moabites and Ammonites to attack Judah (2 Chr. 20:1, where the MT reads "Ammonites" [cf. KJV], which seems redundant in context; most scholars emend to "Meunites" on the basis of the LXX and of 26:7 [KJV, "Mehunims"]). In the reign of King UZZIAH (c. 783-742 B.C.) the Meunites are mentioned, along with the PHILISTINES and ARABIANS, as being troublesome to Judah again (26:7). The passage records that Uzziah was successful in his campaign against them, and it is thought that he may have taken a number of them prisoners and given them to the temple priests as servants (cf. Num. 31:30; Josh. 9:27; Ezra 8:20; and see NETHINIM). This assumption would help to explain the presence of descendants from the Meunites among the temple servants who returned after the EXILE (Ezra 2:50; Neh. 7:52), although some think that the reference here is to descendants of CALEB associated with the town of Maon. See MAON (PLACE). In these passages, however, the NIV and the NRSV have "Meunim," as though it were the name of an ancestor.

Me-Zahab. mee´zuh-hab (Heb. *mê zāhāb H4771*, "waters of gold"). Grandfather of MEHETABEL, who was the wife of Hadad (Hadar) king of EDOM (Gen. 36:39; 1 Chr. 1:50). See HADAD (PERSON). The name, however, would seem to refer to a place. The description of MATRED as the daughter of Me-Zahab might mean that the latter was Matred's native city.

Mezobaite. mi-zoh´bay-it (Heb. *mĕṣōbāyâ H5168*, derivation uncertain). KJV Mesobaite. A descriptive title identifying JAAZIEL, one of David's mighty warriors (1 Chr. 11:47). If the adjective is a gentilic of *ṣôbâ H7420*, the form is anomalous, so many scholars conjecture that the original was *miṣṣōbah*, "from Zobah" (cf. 2 Sam. 23:36). Several of David's warriors in the latter part of the list seem to have come from TRANSJORDAN, so it is indeed possible that Jaaziel was an ARAMEAN from the kingdom of ZOBAH.

mezuzah. muh-zoo´zuh. Plural *mezuzot*. This term does not occur in English versions of the Bible. It is a transliteration of Hebrew *mĕzûzâ H4647* ("doorpost"), used, for example, for the doorframes of ordinary houses where the blood of the Passover sacrifice was sprinkled (Exod. 12:7, 22-23), or where the law was to be written (Deut. 6:9; 11:20; cf. Prov. 8:34; Ezek. 43:12). The doorposts of a building, like the THRESHOLD, evidently had a special significance, bordering on sacredness. In the course of time the term *mezuzah* came to mean the small container of portions of Scripture which orthodox Jews still attach to the doorposts of their home (Deut. 6:9; 11:20).

Miamin. See MIJAMIN.

Mibhar. mib´hahr (Heb. *mibḥār H4437*, "choice, special"). Son of Hagri; he is included in the list of DAVID's mighty warriors (1 Chr. 11:38). The name does not appear in the parallel passage (2 Sam. 23:36; see HAGRI).

Mibsam. mib´sam (Heb. *mibśām H4452*, "fragrant"). **(1)** Son of ISHMAEL and grandson of ABRAHAM (Gen. 25:13; 1 Chr. 1:29). The twelve sons of Ishmael became the eponymous ancestors of tribes in N ARABIA. See also below, #2.

(2) Son of SHAUL or, more likely, of SHALLUM; included in the genealogy of SIMEON (1 Chr. 4:25). Because the name MISHMA occurs in connection with both this Mibsam and #1 above, some scholars speculate that #1 and #2 refer to the same clan. According to this view, the Ishmaelite or Arabian clans of Mibsam and Mishma inhabited the NEGEV; when the tribe of Simeon occupied this region, these clans somehow became integrated into the Simeonite genealogy.

Mibzar. mib´zahr (Heb. *mibṣār H4449*, possibly "fortress"). Descendant of ESAU, listed among the clan chiefs of EDOM (Gen. 36:42; 1 Chr. 1:53). His name may have been preserved in an ancient locality known as Mabsara (a large village subject to PETRA); others have suggested BOZRA.

Mica. mi´kuh (Heb. *mikā> H4775*, short form of *mikāyāhû H4780*, "who is like Yahweh?"). KJV also Micha; TNIV Mika. (1) Son of MEPHIBOSHETH (2 Sam. 9:12). See MICAH #2.

(2) Son of Zicri (or Zabdi), descendant of ASAPH, and father of MATTANIAH; the latter is listed among the LEVITES who resettled in Jerusalem after the EXILE and is described as being responsible for leading in thanksgiving and prayer (1 Chr. 9:15 [KJV, "Micah"]; Neh. 11:17; in the latter reference, the name is spelled *mikâ*). One of his descendants, UZZI son of Bani, became chief officer of the Levites (11:22). This Mica is probably the same as MICAIAH son of Zaccur, whose descendant, ZECHARIAH son of Jonathan, participated in the procession at the dedication of the wall (Neh. 12:35).

(3) A Levite who affixed his seal to the covenant of NEHEMIAH (Neh. 10:11). Because of the chronological differences, this Mica cannot be the same as #2 above.

Micah. mi´kuh (Heb. *mikâ H4777*, short form of *mikāyāhû H4780*, "who is like Yahweh?"). KJV also Michah. (1) An Ephraimite who set up an idolatrous shrine, and whose idols were used by the Danites when they resettled in LAISH (Jdg. 17-18). Micah had stolen 1,100 pieces of silver from his mother, who pronounced a curse on the thief. He then returned the money to her, and she used 200 pieces of the silver to make "a carved image and a cast idol" (17:3), which were put in Micah's house. Micah also made an EPHOD and some TERAPHIM, and even made one of his sons priest of this shrine. Some time later, a Levite from BETHLEHEM became Micah's priest. When five Danites in search of a new home for their tribe obtained a favorable oracle from the Levite, they returned with 600 armed

men and offered him employment as priest in their new tribal territory. They took with them Micah's ephod, teraphim, and the carved image. Micah was helpless to prevent this action. He pursued after them, but was warned that interference would cost him his goods and his life. Micah's idols became a shrine in the city of Laish. See DAN.

(2) Son of MERIB-BAAL (MEPHIBOSHETH) and descendant of King SAUL through JONATHAN; he had four sons (1 Chr. 8:34-35; 9:40-41). He is also called MICA (2 Sam. 9:12).

(3) Son of Shimei, descendant of REUBEN through Joel, and ancestor of Beerah; the latter was a Reubenite leader who was taken into exile by the Assyrians under TIGLATH-PILESER (1 Chr. 5:4-6).

(4) Son of Uzziel and descendant of LEVI; he served during the latter part of DAVID's reign (1 Chr. 23:20; 24:24-25).

(5) Son of Imlah (2 Chr. 18:14 Heb.); see MICAIAH #2.

(6) Father of Abdon; the latter was one of JOSIAH's messengers to HULDAH (2 Chr. 34:20; also called MICAIAH, 2 Ki. 22:12).

(7) Son of Zicri (or Zabdi) and father of Mattaniah (1 Chr. 9:15 KJV; Neh. 11:17 Heb.); see MICA #2.

(8) Micah the MORASTHITE, prophet (Jer. 26:18; Mic. 1:1). See MICAH, BOOK OF.

Micah, Book of. Sixth book of the Minor Prophets, dating from the late eighth century B.C. The book predicts the fall of SAMARIA, which occurred in 722, but concerns more especially the sins and dangers of JERUSALEM in the days of HEZEKIAH around 700. As the following outline shows, the message varies between condemnation for the present sins and God's purpose of ultimate blessing for his people.

I. Predicted desolation of Samaria and Jerusalem (Mic. 1:1—3:12)

II. Eventual blessings for Zion (4:1-8)

III. Invasion and deliverance by Davidic ruler (4:9—5:15)

IV. Condemnations for sins (6:1—7:6)

V. Eventual help from God (7:7-20)

In the opening portion of the book, Mic. 1:1—3:12, God's judgment is first announced on Samaria for her IDOLATRY. Micah's interest seems to lie chiefly in Jerusalem, however, whose desolation is announced in 3:12 in very similar terms. Chapters 2 and 3 are a catalogue of Judah's sins. Oppression of the poor was a characteristic, but another basic factor was the refusal to hear God's prophets. As in JEREMIAH's day, they preferred prophets who predicted peace (cf. 3:5 with Jer. 8:10-11; Ezek. 13:10). It is not improbable that Jeremiah and EZEKIEL took their texts on this subject from Micah. At least Micah's warnings of Mic. 3:12 were well known in Jeremiah's day (Jer. 26:18). Jeremiah's friends quote these words verbatim, ascribing them to the Micah of Hezekiah's time. Some critics point out that Jeremiah quotes Micah as a prophet of *doom,* and they conclude that no prediction of hope in Micah is genuine. The conclusion seems far-fetched. Jeremiah's friends quoted only that part of the book that was applicable to their situation. This argument need not be extended to the rest of the book.

The second section, Mic. 4:1-8, includes a passage that is practically identical with Isa. 2:1-4. Many have questioned whether Micah quoted Isaiah or vice versa, or whether both quoted a common oracle. But Isa. 2:1 calls this passage the word of Isaiah, which should decide the matter. Micah evidently uses Isaiah's promise and skillfully weaves it into his own composition.

The third section, Mic. 4:9—5:15, comes against the background of the wars of Hezekiah's day. The Assyrians had captured the fortified cities of JUDAH and received tribute from Hezekiah (2 Ki. 18:13-16), but God delivered Jerusalem (18:35). The "seven shepherds, even eight leaders of men" of Mic. 5:5 probably is merely a symbolic numerical way of saying "one great deliverer"—a numerical device that can be paralleled in old Canaanite literature. Yet in this section the EXILE and return from BABYLON are also predicted. Some scholars insist that similar passages in Isaiah (e.g., Isa. 48:20) are late and actually written after the events described. In their denial of supernatural prediction, they must also say that Mic. 4:10 is late. But according to Isa. 39:6 and also by Assyrian testimony, Babylon was a menace in Micah's own day; so these verses are quite appropriate. Against these dangers to Judah, God holds out that messianic hope of Mic. 5:2. The mention of BETHLEHEM Ephrathah identifies the MESSIAH as of DAVID's line (cf. Isa. 11:1; Jer. 23:5; Ezek. 37:24).

The condemnations of the fourth section (Mic. 6:1—7:6) include several references to the PENTATEUCH and other historical books (6:4-5, 16; cf. also 5:6 with Gen. 10:8-9). The response of Mic. 6:8 is famous. Some have argued that it teaches SALVATION apart from SACRIFICE. Actually, it alludes to

© Dr. James C. Martin

A general view of the region around Bethlehem, where Micah prophesied that Messiah would be born (Mic. 5:2).

Overview of MICAH

Author: The prophet Micah from the Judahite town of MORESHETH GATH.

Historical setting: A contemporary of ISAIAH, Micah received his revelations during the last decades of the eighth century B.C. and the early years of the seventh. Thus he lived through the decline and fall of the northern kingdom of ISRAEL, and prophesied during the reigns of JOTHAM, AHAZ, and HEZEKIAH, kings of JUDAH (Mic. 1:1). The composition of the book should probably be dated prior to the death of Hezekiah (c. 687 B.C. or perhaps ten years earlier).

Purpose: To denounce the sin and predict the destruction of both Israel and Judah, but also to announce the hope of messianic salvation.

Contents: Condemnation of SAMARIA and JERUSALEM (Mic. 1-3), followed by promises of restoration (chs. 4-5); God's complaints against Israel (6:1—7:7), followed by a psalm of hope and praise (7:8-20).

M

Deut. 10:12 and involves Israel's duty to obey *all* the Mosaic injunctions. Christ probably refers to this verse in his condemnation of the PHARISEES (Matt. 23:23).

The book closes (Mic. 7:7-20) with the prophet's declaration of faith in the ultimate fulfillment of God's covenant of blessing for Abraham.

Micaiah. mi-kay′yuh (Heb. *mîkāyâ H4779* [2 Ki. 22:12; Neh. 12:35, 41], *mîkāyāhû H4780* [2 Chr. 17:7], elsewhere *mîkāyhû H4781*, "who is like Yahweh?"). KJV also Michaiah. **(1)** An Ephraimite (Jdg. 17:1, 4, Heb.); see MICAH #1.

(2) Son of Imlah, prophet (1 Ki. 22:8-26; 2 Chr. 18:7-25 [in v. 14 the Heb. has the short form *mîkâ*]). This man performed a deed which took great courage and unwavering faith in the Lord as God. King JEHOSHAPHAT, though a man of God, had made the mistake of associating with AHAB, the worst of all the kings of ISRAEL. (Contrast 2 Chr. 17:3-6 with 1 Ki. 16:30-33.) Ahab took advantage of Jehoshaphat's visit by asking his assistance in taking RAMOTH GILEAD from the ARAMEANS, whose king BEN-HADAD I had captured it from Ahab's father OMRI. Jehoshaphat, letting his courtesy overcome his good judgment, consented, asking only that the prophets be consulted. Four hundred of Ahab's false

prophets said, "Go, for the Lord will give it into the king's hand" (1 Ki. 22:6). When Jehoshaphat showed his distrust in the prophets and asked if there was not a prophet of the Lord also, Ahab replied, "There is still one man through whom we can inquire of the LORD, but I hate him because he never prophesies anything good about me, but always bad. He is Micaiah son of Imlah" (22:8). A messenger was sent to bring Micaiah, who was told to prophesy favorably, but Micaiah replied that he could speak only what God would give him. At first Micaiah responded frivolously to Ahab's question (22:15), but when the king demanded the truth, Micaiah told him how the hosts of heaven had planned to ruin Ahab by putting a false spirit in the mouth of all his prophets. Micaiah, after being insulted by the false prophet Zedekiah, was sent back to the city to be imprisoned and fed only bread and water until the king returned to deal with him. Micaiah boldly replied, "If you ever return safely, the LORD has not spoken through me" (22:28). Since Ahab partly believed this prophecy, he contrived a clever trick to get Jehoshaphat killed in his place. With a show of generosity he proposed that Jehoshaphat wear his kingly robes in the battle, but Ahab would disguise himself like a common soldier. The outcome was that Jehoshaphat cried out and escaped, but an Aramean drew his bow at random and the arrow killed Ahab (22:34-35).

(3) Mother of King ABIJAH of Judah (2 Chr. 13:2 NRSV; KJV, "Michaiah"; NIV, "Maacah," following some versional evidence). See MAACAH #9.

(4) One of five officials sent by King JEHOSHAPHAT "to teach in the towns of Judah" (2 Chr. 17:7).

(5) Son of Zaccur and father of Mattaniah; his descendant, ZECHARIAH son of Jonathan, participated in the procession at the dedication of the wall (Neh. 12:35). See MICA #2.

(6) A priest who played the trumpet at the dedication of the wall (Neh. 12:41).

(7) Father of Acbor; the latter was one of JOSIAH's messengers to HULDAH (2 Ki. 22:12); also called MICAH (2 Chr. 34:20).

(8) Son of GEMARIAH, grandson of SHAPHAN, and a contemporary of JEREMIAH (Jer. 36:11, 13). Micaiah carried Jeremiah's message to the princes gathered at the palace of King JEHOIAKIM. The princes then called for the sermon to be read to them. Some have proposed that this Micaiah is the same as #7 above.

mice. See ANIMALS (under *rat*). See MOUSE.

Micha. mi´kuh. KJV alternate form of MICAH.

Michael. mi´kay-uhl, mi´kuhl (Heb. *mikā'ēl H4776*, "who is like God?"; Gk. *Michaēl G3640*). **(1)** Father of Sethur, who was one of the twelve spies sent out to reconnoiter the Promised Land; he represented the tribe of ASHER (Num. 13:13).

(2) Son of Abihail; he was one of seven relatives from the tribe of GAD who occupied the region E of GILEAD (1 Chr. 5:13; cf. vv. 10, 14).

(3) Son of Jeshishai and ancestor of #2 above (1 Chr. 5:14).

(4) Son of Baaseiah, descendant of LEVI through GERSHON, and great-grandfather of ASAPH the singer (1 Chr. 6:40).

(5) Son of Izrahiah and descendant of ISSA-CHAR; a military chief (1 Chr. 7:3).

(6) Son of Beriah and descendant of BENJAMIN, listed among the heads of families living in postexilic Jerusalem (1 Chr. 8:16; cf. v. 28). His father and uncle, however, are described as "heads of families

of those living in Aijalon and who drove out the inhabitants of Gath" (v. 13).

(7) One of several warriors from the tribe of MANASSEH who joined DAVID at ZIKLAG; they are described as "leaders of units of a thousand" (1 Chr. 12:20).

(8) Father of Omri; the latter was an officer over the tribe of ISSACHAR during the reign of David (1 Chr. 27:18).

(9) Son of JEHOSHAPHAT, king of Judah (1 Chr. 21:2). He and his brothers received a very generous inheritance (v. 3). Jehoshaphat's firstborn, JEHORAM, killed all his brothers when he became king (v. 4).

(10) Descendant of Shephatiah; his son Zebadiah was one of the family heads who returned to Jerusalem with EZRA (Ezra 8:8).

(11) An angel. The book of DANIEL refers to Michael as a (great) prince (Dan. 10:13, 21; 12:1). The NT refers to him as "the archangel Michael" (Jude 9) and elsewhere speaks of "Michael and his angels" (Rev. 12:7). See ANGEL. PAUL does not expressly mention Michael but makes reference to "the archangel" (1 Thess. 4:16; the Bible never uses the pl. "archangels"). The Bible also names GABRIEL as an important angel (Dan. 8:16; 9:21; Lk. 1:19, 26). During Israel's unprecedented "time of distress" (Dan. 12:1; cf. Jer. 30:7; Matt. 24:21), Michael will be active for her welfare when SATAN is seeking to destroy her (Rev. 12:7-9). Jude 9 speaks of Michael resisting the devil, but committing the judgment of him to the Lord. The dispute involved the body of MOSES, an incident nowhere mentioned in the OT.

Michah. See MICAH.

Michaiah. See MICAIAH.

Michal. mi´kuhl (Heb. *mikal H4783*, "who is like God?"). Younger daughter of King SAUL (1 Sam. 14:49). Saul, insanely jealous of DAVID, desired to kill him but, finding it impossible to do so by his own hands (18:11), he tried trickery. He offered David his elder daughter MERAB for his service against the PHILISTINES, but changed his mind and gave her to another; then he learned that Michal loved David, so he offered her to David if he would give evidence of having killed a hundred Philistines. David killed two hundred and married Michal; but Saul hated him all the more. Once, when Saul sent some men to kill David, Michal helped him to escape (19:11-17), deceiving Saul's officers by putting an idol in his bed. Though Michal truly loved David, she could not comprehend him, and so scoffed at him for rejoicing before the Lord (2 Sam. 6:16-23). As a result, she never had a child.

Michmas, Michmash. mik´mas, mik´mash. See MICMASH.

Michmethah, Michmethath. See MICMETHATH.

Michri. See MICRI.

michtam. See MIKTAM.

Micmash. mik´mash (Heb. *mikmās H4820* [only Ezra 2:27; Neh.7:31] and *mikmās H4825*, possibly "hidden place"). TNIV Mikmash; other versions have Michmas or Michmash (the final consonant in both Hebrew forms is properly represented in English with *s* and not with *sh*, but the latter has become traditional). The name of a town and of a pass c. 6 mi. (10 km.) SE of BETHEL within the tribal territory of BENJAMIN. The town apparently was not a large enough town to warrant mention in the list of Benjamite cities. Its only real claim to fame is in the battle that was fought there by SAUL and JONATHAN against the PHILISTINES (1 Sam. 13:1—14:35). The town does receive brief mention elsewhere (Isa. 10:28-29; Ezra 2:27; Neh. 7:31; 11:31). Biblical Micmash is modern Khirbet el-Hara el-Fawqa, just N of the Arab town of Mukhmas. On the S side of Mukhmas is the narrow canyon of the Wadi es-Suweiniṭ, a deep ravine that joins the Wadi Qelt and empties into the JORDAN near JERICHO. To the SW of Micmash is GEBA, situated on another hill. A knowledge of this geography is helpful in understanding the battle of Micmash, when Jonathan took his armor-bearer, made his way across the pass, and scaled the precipitous N wall in front of the town. The two of them made a surprise attack on the garrison and killed twenty men (14:14). This threw the whole Philistine army into panic and they raced westward to escape. It was then that Saul and his men joined in the chase and "the LORD rescued Israel that day, and the battle moved on beyond Beth Aven" (14:23). There were Philistine casualties all the way from Micmash to AIJALON (14:31).

Jonathan, creeping through the canyon of Wadi es-Suweiniṭ in the distance (view to the ESE), surprised the Philistine outpost at Micmash (foreground).

© Dr. James C. Martin

Micmethath. mik´mu-thath (Heb. *mikmĕtāt H4826* [used with the definite article], meaning unknown). KJV Michmetha; NRSV Michmethath. A town or geographical feature that served to define the boundary between the tribes of EPHRAIM and MANASSEH (Josh. 16:6; 17:7). The latter passage locates Micmethath E of SHECHEM, but its location is uncertain.

Micri. mik´ri (Heb. *mikrî H4840*, perhaps "recompense"). Also Michri; TNIV Mikri. Descendant of BENJAMIN and grandfather (or more distant ancestor) of Elah; the latter is listed among the first Benjamites who resettled in Jerusalem (1 Chr. 9:8).

Middin. mid´uhn (Heb. *middîn H4516*, meaning unknown). A town allotted to the tribe of JUDAH in the desert (Josh. 15:61). It was apparently between BETH ARABAH and SECACAH, but its location is uncertain. Many identify it with modern Khirbet Abu Tabaq, some 10.5 mi. (17 km.) ESE of JERUSALEM, in el-Buqeᶜah (the Valley of ACHOR). See SALT, CITY OF.

Middle Gate. A gate in JERUSALEM where the officials of NEBUCHADNEZZAR gathered after they had captured the city (Jer. 39:3; the LXX reads "Middle Gate" also in 2 Chr. 23:5, where the Heb. has FOUNDATION GATE). Nothing else is known about the Middle Gate, although its name possibly suggests that it was located at some point between the upper and lower sections of Jerusalem.

middle wall of partition. See WALL OF PARTITION.

Midian. mid´ee-uhn (Heb. *midyān H4518*, derivation unknown; gentilic *midyānî H4520*, "Midianite"). Son of ABRAHAM and KETURAH (Gen. 25:1-2; 1 Chr. 1:32), and eponymous ancestor of a people group that lived E and SE of CANAAN (cf. Gen. 25:6). Nothing else is known about the person Midian (see also MEDAN). The land claimed by the Midianites lay mostly E of the JORDAN and the DEAD SEA, then southward through the ARABAH and (in the time of MOSES) including the southern and eastern parts of the SINAI peninsula. Traders in the caravan that bought JOSEPH

are called "Ishmaelites" (37:25) either because they descended from ISHMAEL or because the term could be used generally of desert people; the same traders are subsequently called "Midianites" (37:36) either because they descended from Midian or because they lived in the land known as Midian. When Moses fled from Egypt forty years before the EXODUS (Exod. 2:15-21), he helped the daughters of REUEL (or JETHRO) the priest of Midian, was invited to their encampment, and married ZIPPORAH, the priest's daughter. Thus the descendants of Moses had Midianite as well as LEVITE ancestry. Jethro, though priest of Midian, acknowledged the God of Israel as supreme (18:11); but neither he nor his son HOBAB, though very friendly to Moses, could bring himself to join Israel (Num. 10:29).

Toward the end of the life of Moses, Midian had apparently become confederate with MOAB (Num. 22:4). Through the counsel of BALAAM, the Midianite women wrought much harm in Israel, and God commanded Moses to conquer the nation (25:16-18). Two hundred years later, in the days of GIDEON, God delivered Israel into the hand of Midian for seven years (Jdg. 6:1-6). They allowed the Israelites to plow and to sow the seed, but they (the Midianites) did the reaping. Gideon defeated them and killed their two kings ZEBAH AND ZALMUNNA (8:21) as well as two leaders, OREB AND ZEEB (7:25). Though the Midianites were nomads, they had great wealth in the time of Moses. They had not only 675,000 sheep, 72,000 oxen, and 61,000 donkeys, but also gold, silver, brass, iron, tin, and lead; all of which are mentioned in the booty taken by the men of Israel (Num. 31:22, 32-34). The Midianites have long since disappeared from the earth.

midrash. mid´rash. Plural *midrashim*. The Hebrew term *midrāš H4535* ("study, writing, story") occurs only twice in the OT. Reference is made to the midrash (NIV, "annotations") of the prophet IDDO for additional information concerning ABIJAH (2 Chr. 13:22; NRSV, "story") and to the midrash on "the book of the kings" (24:27; NRSV, "Commentary"). These midrashim may have been historical records themselves or commentaries on the historical narratives, but the precise meaning is debated. The term is very common, however, in rabbinic literature, where it refers to the elucidation and exposition of the Bible. The term *midrash* (esp. when capitalized) can also refer more specifically to a type of literature consisting of biblical exposition. Thus the Midrashim are rabbinic commentaries on the Bible. These works sometimes address detailed issues of exegesis, but their primary purpose is religious edification. See JUDAISM; TALMUD.

midwife. A woman who helps in childbirth. A midwife may often have been an older relative or friend of the family. Some of her duties included cutting the umbilical cord, washing the baby with water, rubbing it with salt, and wrapping it in swaddling clothes (cf. Ezek. 16:4). A midwife was with RACHEL at the birth of BENJAMIN (Gen. 35:17-18). When twins were born to TAMAR, the midwife put a scarlet thread on the firstborn so that it might be known which was the older (38:28). The pharaoh of Egypt ordered the midwives, Shiphrah and Puah, to kill the Hebrew boy babies, but to let the girls live (Exod. 1:15-16). The midwives disobeyed the king, however. Midwives probably are referred to also in 1 Sam. 4:20 and Ruth 4:14-15.

Migdal Eder. mig´duhl-ee´duhr. See EDER (PLACE) #1.

Migdal El. mig´duhl-el´ (Heb. *migdal-ʾēl H4466*, "tower of God"). A fortified city within the tribal territory of NAPHTALI (Josh. 19:38). It was apparently in the vicinity of IRON in N GALILEE, but its precise location is unknown.

Migdal Gad. mig´duhl-gad´ (Heb. *migdal-gad H4467*, "tower of Gad [fortune]"). A town in the SHEPHELAH, within the tribal territory of JUDAH (Josh. 15:37). It is tentatively identified with Khirbet el-Mejdeleh, about 4 mi. (6 km.) SE of LACHISCH.

Migdol. mig´dol (Heb. *migdōl H4465*, "tower, fort"). A place name in the NE part of the NILE delta. Twice in Jeremiah, Migdol heads a short list of places in Egypt where Jews sought refuge (Jer. 44:1; 46:14); and twice in Ezekiel, Migdol is the N or NE extremity of Egypt, while Aswan (SYENE) marks its S limit (Ezek. 29:10; 30:6; KJV,

"tower of Syene"), true to conditions in the 26th dynasty. This Migdol is the Magdolo of the Antonine Itinerary, being generally identified with Tell el Ḥer, some 12.5 mi. (20 km.) NE of Qantara on the ancient road from Egypt to Palestine. In the PENTATEUCH, however, we read that the Israelites, after turning back from the wilderness, encamped "between Migdol and the sea" (Exod. 14:2; cf. Num. 33:7), and then crossed the latter from W to E into the wilderness again. This seems to require a Migdol differently sited from Tell el Ḥer (which is E of all likely candidates for the RED SEA). It is, therefore, probable that Migdol here is simply another fort—*migdāl H4463* is a common word—SE of Daphnai and W of the Red Sea (Lake Ballaḥ region?). If so, it has not yet been identified in Egyptian sources. See also EXODUS.

mighty men. This expression is often used to render Hebrew *gibbôrîm* (pl. of *gibbôr H1475*, "strong, valiant; man, warrior, champion"). The word first appears in Gen. 6:4 with reference to the NEPHILIM (NIV and NRSV, "heroes"). It can be used of fighting men in general (e.g., 2 Sam. 10:7), but also more especially of warriors notable for their valor (17:8). The names and exploits of three such men and those of DAVID's "Thirty" are recorded in 2 Sam. 23:8-39 and 1 Chr. 11:10-47.

Migron. mig´ron (Heb. *migrôn H4491*, prob. "threshing floor"). A locality in the outskirts of GIBEAH where SAUL at one time camped under a pomegranate tree (1 Sam. 14:2). The Gibeah referred to in this passage is either the modern Tell el-Full (3 mi./5 km. N of the temple terrace in JERUSALEM) or Jebaʿ (an additional 2 mi./3 km. NE). A place by the name of Migron is mentioned also in Isa. 10:28 as being in the line of march of the Assyrian army, suggesting it is N of MICMASH. An unresolved question is whether these two Migrons are the same place; in any case, the precise location of Migron is unknown.

Mijamin. mij´uh-min (Heb. *miyyāmîn H4785*, "from the right" [i.e., "favored"] or perhaps "from the south"). KJV also Miamin. **(1)** A priest who received the sixth lot of the twenty-four divisions in DAVID's time (1 Chr. 24:9).

M

(2) One of the descendants of Parosh who agreed to put away their foreign wives (Ezra 10:25).

(3) A priest who affixed his seal to the covenant of NEHEMIAH (Neh. 10:7).

(4) One of the priestly leaders who had returned from the EXILE with ZERUBBABEL (Neh. 12:5). He was possibly an ancestor of #3 above, and both of these priests may have belonged to the priestly order of #1 above.

Mika. mi´kuh. TNIV form of MICA.

Mikloth. mik´loth (Heb. *miqlôt H5235*, derivation uncertain). **(1)** Son of JEIEL and descendant of BENJAMIN; his brother NER was the grandfather of SAUL (1 Chr. 8:31; 9:37-38).

(2) The leader of a division in the army of DAVID (1 Chr. 27:4). On the basis of the SEPTUAGINT, and in conformity with the pattern in this passage, many scholars omit the reference to Mikloth (e.g., RSV, "Dodai the Ahohite was in charge of the division of the second month; in his division were twenty-four thousand").

Mikmash. mik´mash. TNIV form of MICMASH.

Mikneiah. mik-nee´yah (Heb. *miqnêāhû H5240*, "possession of Yahweh"). A LEVITE and one of the gatekeepers assigned to be a musician when DAVID made preparation to transfer the ARK OF THE COVENANT to Jerusalem (1 Chr. 15:18). He is called one of the brothers of the "second order" (NRSV; NIV, "next in rank") who followed HEMAN, ASAPH, and ETHAN. Mikneiah and some others "were to play the harps, directing according to *sheminith*" (v. 21; see MUSIC AND MUSICAL INSTRUMENTS, VI).

Mikri. mik´ri. TNIV form of MICRI.

miktam. mik´tam (Heb. *miktām H4846*). Also *michtam* (sometimes capitalized). Apparently a musical (or liturgical) term found in the superscription of six psalms (Ps. 16 and 56-60). Some think it means nothing more than "inscription" or "epigram"; others relate it to a Semitic root meaning "to cover" and deduce that these psalms deal with ATONEMENT for sin. An ancient proposal is that the term derives from a word meaning "gold"

and that it refers either to a golden inscription or, figuratively, to the precious quality of the poem.

Milalai. mil´uh-li (Heb. *milālay H4912*, perhaps "Yahweh has spoken"). A priestly musician who participated in the dedication of the rebuilt wall of JERUSALEM under EZRA (Neh. 12:36).

Milcah. mil´kuh (Heb. *milkâ H4894*, "queen, princess"). TNIV Milkah. **(1)** Daughter of HARAN, sister of LOT (and ISCAH), and wife of NAHOR, who was her uncle (Gen. 11:29; cf. v. 27). ABRAHAM was also Milcah's uncle. Her offspring are mentioned in Gen. 22:20-23; one of them was BETHUEL, the father of REBEKAH and LABAN (22:22-23; 24:15, 24, 29, 47).

(2) One of five daughters of ZELOPHEHAD of the tribe of MANASSEH (Num. 26:33). Since Zelophehad had no sons, his daughters requested ELEAZAR the priest that they be allowed to inherit their father's property, and the request was granted on condition that they marry into their father's tribe (27:1-11; 36:11; Josh. 17:3-4). This decision was very important and became a precedent.

Milcom. mil´kuhm (Heb. *milkōm H4904*, "king"). The national god of the AMMONITES. Most scholars believe he is to be identified with MOLECH (cf. 1 Ki. 11:5 with v. 7). The Hebrew form *milkōm* occurs only three times (always rendered "Molech" by the NIV): (1) Milcom was one of the foreign gods for whom SOLOMON built a high place on the MOUNT OF OLIVES (1 Ki. 11:5); (2) he was worshiped by many Israelites (v. 33); (3) he was later desecrated by JOSIAH (2 Ki. 23:13). In addition, the form *malkām* ("their king") occurs in the MT in some passages where most scholars believe that the context requires a reference to Milcom (2 Sam. 12:30 = 1 Chr. 20:2; Jer. 49:1, 3; Zeph. 1:5). See MALCAM #2.

mildew. A common species of fungus that attacked the crops of Palestine; it is produced by dampness. The Hebrew term *yērāqôn H3766*, in its meaning "rust" or "mildew," always occurs in combination with *šiddāpôn H8730*, "blight, scorching." These conditions were interpreted as God's punishment upon the disobedient (Deut. 28:22;

Amos 4:9; Hag. 2:17), and SOLOMON prayed for deliverance from them (1 Ki. 8:37; 2 Chr. 6:28). The NIV uses "mildew" also as the rendering of Hebrew *ṣāraʿat H7669* (which refers to a variety of skin diseases), when this word occurs in connection with objects, such as clothing (Lev. 13:47-59) and walls (14:34-57).

mile. See WEIGHTS AND MEASURES.

Miletum. See MILETUS.

Miletus. mi-lee´tuhs (Gk. *Milētos G3626*). Also Miletos. Ancient and important Ionian city in ASIA MINOR, in the region of CARIA, on the shore of the MEDITERRANEAN near the mouth of the river Maeander. It was colonized first by Cretans, and later by Greeks (see CRETE; GREECE). During the great period of colonization (750-550 B.C.), Miletus was most active, being credited with the establishment of about ninety colonies and leading the way in the Greek penetration of Egypt. Situated favorably, with four good harbors, Miletus became a great sea power and dominated the Black Sea trade, from which it became exceedingly wealthy. The city was distinguished also for its literary and scientific accomplishments; for example, it was the home of the first Greek philosopher, Thales, and of his successors, Anaximander and Anaximenes. In the fifth century B.C. Miletus fell under PERSIA, but later it was conquered and rebuilt by ALEXANDER THE GREAT. Under the Hellenistic kings it retained some importance as a commercial town, and some great buildings were raised by these rulers. In 133 B.C. the city passed into Roman hands as part of the province of ASIA. The apostle PAUL stopped at Miletus on his journey from Greece to JERUSALEM, and spoke to the elders of the Ephesian church whom he asked to meet him there (Acts 20:15, 17). In 2 Tim. 4:20 (KJV, "Miletum") he mentions leaving TROPHIMUS in Miletus to recover from an illness. The city, however, played little part in the history of Christianity, though it had a bishopric in the fifth century.

milk. See FOOD.

Milkah. mil´kuh. TNIV form of MILCAH.

Milkom. mil´kuhm. TNIV form of MILCOM.

mill, millstone. An apparatus used to grind any edible grain—wheat, barley, oats, rye, etc.—into flour. It consists of two circular stones, the lower one having a slightly convex upper surface to help the drifting of the broken grain toward the outer edge from which it drops. It is made of a hard stone, which after being shaped is scratched with curved furrows so as to multiply the cutting and grinding effect. The lower stone has a stout stick standing at its center, and the upper one (called the rider) has a hole at its center so that it can rotate around the stick, and a handle 8-10 in. (20-25 cm.) from the center by which it is turned. Generally it is worked by two women, facing each other, and each grasping the handle to turn the rider. One woman feeds the grain in at the center of the rider and the other guides and brushes the products into a little pile. The process is very ancient, for we read of "the slave girl, who is at her hand mill" in the days of MOSES (Exod. 11:5), and the process was no doubt already old at that remote time. Even the MANNA that fell

© Dr. James C. Martin

A basalt millstone typical of those found throughout the Holy Land.

in the wilderness was hard enough or tough enough so that the people used to grind it in mills or beat it in mortars before cooking it (Num. 11:7-8).

It is altogether probable that people pounded grain before they thought of grinding it, and so the mortar is probably more ancient even than the mill. Because people depended on flour as their "staff of life" and because they generally ground it only as needed, it was forbidden to take a millstone

M

in pledge (Deut. 24:6). In Jer. 25:10 "the sound of millstones" is mentioned as a sign of happy prosperous life, but in Isa. 47:2 the prophet taunted the proud and delicate women of Babylon with the thought that they would have to become slaves and labor at the mill. When the Philistines blinded Samson (Jdg. 16:21), he had to grind in the prison, and this mill was probably a large one ordinarily turned by a blinded ox or donkey. Abimelech, usurping "king" of Israel, was killed by a woman who dropped a millstone on his head (9:53). Our Lord prophesied that at his coming "two women will be grinding with a hand mill; one will be taken and the other left" (Matt. 24:41). A millstone cast into the sea is a symbol of absolute destruction (Rev. 18:21).

millennium. See ESCHATOLOGY; KINGDOM OF GOD.

millet. See PLANTS.

Millo. mil´oh (Heb. *millô* H4864, "filling, mound"). **(1)** A fortification or citadel near JERUSALEM, constructed by SOLOMON with forced labor (1 Ki. 9:15, 24; 11:27). The NIV translates the Hebrew term as a common noun, "supporting terraces" (TNIV simply "terraces"). Apparently Solomon added to an existing Millo, for DAVID is said to have built the city of Jerusalem "around from the Millo inward" (2 Sam. 5:9 NRSV; cf. 1 Chr. 11:8). The Millo formed a prominent part of the works of defense set up by King HEZEKIAH for the protection of the city (2 Chr. 32:5). The BETH MILLO where King Joash (JEHOASH) was assassinated (2 Ki. 12:20; KJV and other versions have "the house of Millo") is thought to have been some well-known building in this area.

(2) The place where ABIMELECH was crowned king is called "the house of Millo" in the KJV (Jdg. 9:6, 20). See BETH MILLO #1.

mina. See WEIGHTS AND MEASURES.

mind. The seat of the mental faculties; the part of the individual that thinks, reasons, and feels. Both OT and NT focus attention on the human being's concrete and total relationship to God, and where psychological terms do appear their intention seems to be emphasis rather than a concern to divide or compartmentalize human activity. For this reason, no consistent pattern of terminology can be determined in the Bible. In some cases, our English versions idiomatically render the Hebrew text with the word "mind" even in passages where no Hebrew equivalent is found (cf. Gen. 37:11). Otherwise, it is used in the OT to render a variety of terms, such as Hebrew *yēṣer H3671*, "thought, tendency" (Isa. 26:3), *rûaḥ H8120*, "spirit" (Num. 16:28 NIV), and especially *lēb H4213* and *lēbāb H4222*, "heart" (Deut. 28:65; Ezek. 38:10). In the NT, the faculty of cognition or thought is variously referred to by such terms as *nous G3808*, "mind, intellect" (Rom. 7:25); *kardia G2840*, "heart" (in imitation of the Heb.; cf. Matt. 13:15, citing Isa. 6:10 LXX); *psychē G6034*, "soul" (Phil. 1:27); *dianoia G1379*, "thought, understanding" (2 Pet. 3:1); and others. See also HEART; SOUL; SPIRIT.

minerals. Mineralogists find it somewhat difficult to define the word *mineral*, but its scientific meaning can be clarified by the use of specific examples. A granite boulder belongs to the mineral kingdom as contrasted to the animal or vegetable kingdoms, but it is a rock and not a mineral. It is composed of a number of minerals most of which are of microscopic size. The minerals in granite, visible to the naked eye, are the clear, glassy particles of quartz, one or more of the white or pink feldspars, and the darker biotite or hornblende. Quartz is classified as a mineral for a number of reasons: it is formed in nature, it is not formed by plant or animal, it has a uniform composition throughout the particle, and it always crystallizes in a hexagonal system of crystals. Quartz is always composed of 46.7 percent silicon and 53.3 percent oxygen. The chemist may make silicon dioxide in the laboratory, which has the same percentage of silicon and oxygen as that of natural quartz, but it is not a mineral. It does not pass the test of having been formed in nature unattended by humans. It is referred to as a synthetic.

The present science of mineralogy with its names and exact terminology is a young discipline, younger even than physics, chemistry, astronomy, or mathematics. Mineralogy as a science certainly did not exist at the time the Bible was written. In many cases, minerals mentioned in Scripture cannot be identified with certainty. It is possible, however, to survey biblical minerals under three groups: precious stones, metals, and common minerals.

I. Precious stones. The reaction of the human race to beauty and to the things that endure does not change. We share certain criteria with the ancients for evaluating precious stones. There must be beauty of color, transparency, luster, and brilliance. There must be some degree of durability, at least if the gem is to be worn or handled. Selenite, a clear crystalline variety of gypsum, may be beautiful, but it is so soft that it can easily be scratched by the thumbnail. We now use a scale of hardness called the Mohs scale which rates the hardness of gems on the basis of the ease or difficulty of scratching. On this scale the hardness of thumbnail is 2.5.

The Mohs Scale of Hardness (H)

1. Talc
2. Gypsum
3. Calcite
4. Fluorite
5. Apatite
6. Orthoclase
7. Quartz
8. Topaz
9. Corundum
10. Diamond

The most precious stones are those that have a hardness of 7 or greater. All of these could easily scratch glass, which has a hardness of 5.5 to 6. Many of the precious stones of the Bible belong to the quartz or chalcedony family with a hardness of 7. Emerald is a green beryl (H 7.5 to 8); topaz has a hardness of 8; the ruby and sapphire, both forms of the mineral corundum, have a hardness of 9.

There are four principal lists of minerals recorded in the Scriptures. They are as follows: (1) the twelve precious stones of AARON's breastplate, each stone representing one of the tribes of Israel (Exod. 28:17-20; 39:10-13); (2) the stones that are unfavorably compared to WISDOM (Job 28:16-19); (3) the gems of the king of TYRE (Ezek. 28:13); (4) the precious stones of the Holy City, one for each of the twelve foundations (Rev. 21:18-21). Many other passages mention individual precious stones.

A. Agate (Exod. 28:19; 39:12). This member of the chalcedony family, described below under *chalcedony*, was the second stone in the third row of the priest's breastplate.

B. Amethyst (Exod. 28:19; 39:12; Rev. 21:20). A purple to blue-violet form of quartz. This is one of the loveliest forms of quartz. Natural cubic crystals of fluorite in transparent blues and purples match amethyst for beauty, but this mineral has a hardness of only 4 and is easily split by the tap of a knife blade. Amethyst was the third stone of the third row of the priest's breastplate and will be the twelfth of the foundation stones of the Holy City.

C. Beryl (Exod. 28:17; 39:10; Ezek. 28:13; Rev. 21:20). A beryllium aluminum silicate. It is now mined and valued as a source of beryllium, a light metal unknown until A.D. 1828. A single crystal taken from the Black Hills of South Dakota weighed as much as 75 tons. Gem varieties include yellow or golden beryl; emerald, which is a highly prized translucent to transparent sea-green stone; aquamarine, which is blue; and morganite, a rose-red variety. Beryl was the third stone in the top row of the priest's breastplate, and will be the eighth of the foundation stones of the Holy City.

D. Carnelian (Rev. 4:3; 21:20). The sixth foundation stone of the Holy City. See below under *chalcedony*.

E. Chalcedony (Rev. 21:19). The third foundation stone of the Holy City. Quartz and chalcedony

M

Entrances to horizontal mineshafts in Timnah. Copper was mined from these hills in the Desert of Paran.

© Dr. James C. Martin

are both composed of silicon dioxide, but chalcedony does not crystallize into the bold hexagonal forms taken by quartz. Any crystalline character that the various forms of chalcedony have is of microscopic size. The lighter colored varieties are named chalcedony in contrast to such names as carnelian and jasper. The following are some of the varieties of chalcedony.

1. Agate. This stone is chalcedony with colors unevenly distributed, often banded, with the bands curved. Petrified wood is often a form of agate in which the silicon dioxide has replaced the original wood. Agates are very common and many varieties exist. They have become one of the most popular minerals for cutting and polishing. The moss agates found along the Yellowstone River from Glendive, Montana, to Yellowstone Park are particularly well known. The "thunder eggs" of Idaho and Oregon may look like drab gray stones, but when sawed in two with a diamond saw, they may reveal a center of lovely agate.

2. Carnelian (sard, sardius, sardine). Chalcedony with colors usually clear red to brownish red; iron oxide imparts the color.

3. Chrysoprase. An apple-green variety of chalcedony, sometimes called green jasper; a small percentage of nickel may account for the green color. Beads of genuine chrysoprase dating to 1500 B.C. have been taken from an Egyptian grave.

4. Flint. Usually a dull gray to black form, not valued or classified as a precious stone, but highly prized by primitive peoples for arrowheads, spear points, skinning knives, etc.

5. Jasper. Jasper pebbles may be found in many gravel deposits (the petrified wood of Arizona is largely jasper). This mineral is hard, opaque, and takes a beautiful polish. It is sufficiently abundant so that it must have been used by ancient peoples as a gem stone. Although this gem has many shades, the chief colors are red, yellow, brown, and green. Green jasper is also known as chrysoprase. The colors largely result from the presence of iron oxide.

6. Onyx. This stone is similar to banded agates, except that the bands are flat. Specimens are usually cut and polished parallel to the layers, enabling cameo production. (Objects of Mexican onyx, beautifully cut and polished and available in a number of Mexican border cities, are really not onyx at all: the composition is calcium carbonate instead of silicon dioxide.)

7. Sardonyx. Merely onyx that includes layers of carnelian or sard.

F. Chrysolyte (Exod. 28:20; 39:13; Cant. 5:14; Ezek. 1:16; 10:9; 28:13; Dan. 10:6; Rev. 21:20). A yellow to greenish-yellow form of olivine; green olivine is known as peridot. The mineral is a silicate of magnesium and iron. In Rev. 21:20 it is the seventh foundation stone of the Holy City, and in Exodus it is the first gem in the fourth row of the priest's breastpiece.

G. Chrysoprase (Rev. 21:20). The tenth foundation stone of the Holy City. See above under *chalcedony*.

H. Coral (Job 28:18; Ezek. 27:16). When the writer of Job speaks of the priceless value of wisdom, he compares it to a number of precious stones and metals, one of them being coral; and in Ezekiel, coral is associated with turquoise and ruby. The inclusion of coral, which has its origin in the animal world and grows in the sea, is difficult to understand on the basis of modern classifications of precious stones. This indicates that in the ancient world other factors were taken into account in the classification of gem stones. Factors that contributed to the value of coral probably included its beauty; its use in the production of jewelry, creating an economic demand for it; and its workability.

I. Crystal (Job 28:17; Rev. 4:6; 21:11; 22:1). The term *crystal* in these passages is generally understood to refer to glass or clear quartz. This type of quartz is remarkably brilliant and beautifully shaped, even as it is found in nature. However, the word could connote other brilliant colorless minerals. The book of Job says that wisdom cannot compare with it. It is used in Revelation to depict the brilliance of the objects with which it is compared, such as the "sea" of glass (Rev. 4:6), the Holy City (21:11), and the water of life (22:1).

J. Emerald (Exod. 28:18; 39:11; Ezek. 28:13; Rev. 4:3; 21:19). The emerald is a transparent to translucent deep green form of beryl (beryllium aluminum silicate). The meaning of the Hebrew word is uncertain. It is probably derived from a root that means "to hammer" and may refer to the hardness of this gem. The Greek word connotes a light green gem and is almost certainly the emerald. The emerald was the last stone in the second row of the priest's breastplate and is listed as the fourth foundation stone of the Holy City.

K. Flint (Exod. 4:25; Josh. 5:2-3; Isa. 5:28; 50:7; Jer. 17:1; Ezek. 3:9; Zech. 7:12). See above under *chalcedony*. In all the occurrences of flint in the Bible the emphasis is on its hardness and its ability to hold a sharp edge.

L. Jacinth (Exod. 28:19; 39:12; Rev. 21:20). Also *hyacinth*. In modern mineralogy the jacinth is the transparent red, yellow, orange, or brown form of the mineral zircon (zirconium orthosilicate). The meaning of the word in Hebrew is uncertain; it refers to the first stone in the third row of the priest's breastplate. Because the Greek word seems to indicate a dark blue stone, some believe the reference is to the sapphire. It will be the eleventh foundation stone of the Holy City.

M. Jasper (Exod. 28:20; 39:13; Job 28:18; Ezek. 28:13; Rev. 4:3; 21:11, 18-19). Third stone in the fourth row of the priest's breastplate and first foundation stone of the Holy City. See above under *chalcedony*.

N. Lapis lazuli. A gem of deep azure-blue; it is a soft stone composed of sodium aluminum silicate and was fashioned by the ancients into various types of ornaments. See below under *sapphire*.

O. Onyx (Gen. 2:12; Exod. 25:7; 28:9, 20; 35:9, 27; 39:6, 13; 1 Chr. 29:2; Job 28:16; Ezek. 28:13). Second stone in the fourth row of the priest's breastplate. See above under *chalcedony*.

P. Pearl (Gen. 2:12 mg.; Matt. 7:6; 13:45; 1 Tim. 2:9; Rev. 17:4; 18:12, 16; 21:21). Pearls, like coral, develop in the sea by the abstraction of calcium carbonate from sea water. The pearl develops around a bit of foreign matter within the shell of oysters or mussels. Like coral, it cannot be classed with the hard enduring precious stones. It is easily destroyed. A small amount of acid would convert it to nearly worthless calcium chloride, a water-soluble salt, and the gas carbon dioxide. The reference in Matt. 7:6 implies a fragile structure. Swine might step on rubies without harming them, but pearls would be crushed. They are not much harder than a fingernail. The references to pearls are found almost exclusively in the NT, and there is no reason to doubt the identity of this precious stone.

Q. Ruby (Exod. 28:17; 39:10; Job 28:18; Prov. 3:15; 8:11; 20:15; 31:10; Isa. 54:12; Lam. 4:7; Ezek. 27:16; 28:13). Corundum as a mineral usually occurs as a dull, unattractive but hard form of aluminum oxide, often crystallized in hexagonal forms. Corundum of a rich, clear, red variety is the ruby, whereas the other colors of gem-quality corundum account for the sapphires. The best source for the good rubies is Burma. The ruby was the first stone in the priest's breastplate.

R. Sapphire (Exod. 24:10; 28:18; 39:11; Job 28:6, 16; Cant. 5:14; Isa. 54:11; Lam. 4:7; Ezek. 1:26; 10:1; 28:13; Rev. 21:19). In these references, the TNIV translates "lapis lazuli." Sapphires, like rubies, belong to the corundum or aluminum-oxide family, with a hardness of 9, or next to diamond. True sapphires are blue; others are colorless, yellow, or pink. The sapphire is listed as the second of the foundation stones of the Holy City, and the second stone in the second row of the priest's breastplate. It is generally agreed that our modern lazurite (lapis lazuli) was called sapphire by the ancients. But we must remember that it is entirely possible that a variety of blue stones were termed sapphire. Lazurite does not seem to belong to the elite company of the most precious stones. For the greater part these most precious stones are noted for a rich purity of color, which lazurite does not have. Lazurite is beautiful but usually consists of a considerable mixture of minerals, including pyrite, calcite, muscovite, and pyroxene. In hardness it is softer than glass (H 5 to 5.5) In three of the references given above, there is a strong implication that the mineral referred to was blue (Exod. 24:10; Ezek. 1:26; 10:1). In Lamentations sapphire is linked to ruby, the other highly prized form of corundum.

S. Sardonyx (Rev. 21:20). The sardonyx is an onyx layered with red sard or carnelian. It is the fifth foundation stone in the Holy City.

T. Topaz (Exod. 28:17; 39:10; Job 28:19; Ezek. 28:13; Rev. 21:20). The modern topaz is an aluminum fluoro hydroxy silicate with a hardness of 8, thus harder than the quartz and chalcedony groups. The most highly prized is the yellow topaz; but colorless, pink, blue, and green varieties occur as well. The topaz was the second stone of the first row of the priest's breastplate and is listed as the ninth foundation stone of the Holy City.

M

U. Turquoise (Exod. 28:18; 39:11; 1 Chr. 29:2; Isa. 54:11; Ezek. 27:16; 28:13). A blue to bluish-green mineral which is a hydrous phosphate of aluminum and copper. It has a hardness of 5 to 6. The stone polishes well and is commonly fashioned into beads. It was the first stone in the second row of the priest's breastplate.

II. Metals. Of the more than 115 elements known today, over 90 are considered metals. Of these only gold, silver, iron, copper, lead, tin, and mercury were known to the ancients. A metal is an element with a metallic luster; it is usually a good conductor of heat and electricity. Metals such as gold, silver, and copper may occur in nature as the free recognizable metal; most metals, however, occur in compound form, chemically united with other elements in such a way that the ore appears dull and nonmetallic. Metallurgy is the science of separating the metal from its ore and the subsequent refining and treating for adapting it to its many and varied uses. The earliest reference to someone skilled in iron and bronze work is to TUBAL-CAIN (Gen. 4:22). Human progress in metal working has provided anthropologists and archaeologists with a chronological structure for dating various periods in ancient history. This structure includes the Chalcolithic or Copper Age (4000-3000 B.C.), the Bronze Age (3000-1200), and the Iron Age (1200-586). There is, of course, much overlapping, and none of these ages has really ended. In fact, when one considers the tonnages used, it should

© Dr. James C. Martin

The upper register of this tomb painting from Egypt shows men smelting metal during the New Kingdom period (Tomb of Rekhmine near the Valley of the Kings, c. 1500 B.C.).

be apparent that we are still living in the Iron or Steel Age. The metals mentioned in the Bible are as follows.

A. Bronze. A metal alloy composed of varying amounts of copper and tin. It is generally believed that bronze had its origin in MESOPOTAMIA. The discovery and production of bronze marked a turning point in human history because of its degree of hardness. The softer copper, which continued to be used for some purposes, was replaced to a great extent by bronze in the production of utilitarian objects. However, nails, knives, statuettes, and other objects continued to be made of pure copper far into the Bronze Age. CYPRUS bronze usually contained from 2 to 4 percent tin, while a cup from NINEVEH, dated about 1000 B.C., tested over 18 percent tin. In the Bible bronze was used in ornamental construction (Exod. 25:3; 26:11; 27:2), and the manufacture of such utilitarian objects as pots (Lev. 6:28) and mirrors (Job 37:18). Cymbals of bronze were used in the temple for worship (1 Chr. 15:19). The use of bronze weaponry is found in the reference to the armament of the Philistine warrior GOLIATH (1 Sam. 17:5-38) and the shields made under the direction of REHOBOAM (2 Chr. 12:10). However, the latter appear to have been primarily objects of decoration or value rather than weapons of war. Job 20:24 speaks of arrows tipped with bronze. The KJV uses the word *brass*, which at the time of its writing denoted any alloy of copper.

B. Copper. A heavy, reddish-yellow metal, copper is frequently found on or near the surface of the ground. Its malleability and accessibility account for its being one of the first metals to be used by early humans. In the Bible the presence of copper ore in Canaan is cited as one of the benefits of that land (Deut. 8:9). The process of smelting copper and other metals is used illustratively in its other references in the OT (Job 28:2; Ezek. 22:18, 20; 24:11). In the NT reference is made to the use of copper only in coinage (Matt. 10:9; Mk. 12:42; Lk. 21:2).

C. Gold. This precious metal was used freely and skillfully in the oldest of civilizations. A multitude of gold ornaments in the museums of the world verify this. The earliest evidence of gold mining (at least 2500 B.C.) may be found in rock carvings of Egypt, depicting the washing of gold sands and the melting of gold in a small furnace. The Greek historian Strabo describes the country of the Iberians (Spain) as full of metal such as gold, silver, copper, and iron. He tells of mining gold by digging for it in the usual way and also by washing for it (hydraulic mining). Pliny the Elder accurately described the occurrence of placer gold in stream beds, including the finding of nuggets. He also described the process of hydraulic mining. He claimed that a river was brought from a distance and from the heights, with enough fall to wash away whole mountain sides, leaving the gold in sluice baffles. Most surprising of all, Pliny described in some detail the use of mercury to capture the gold from the ore by amalgamation.

Why is gold so highly valued? Gold is good and highly prized because it is warmly beautiful. It is enduring, for it never rusts or dissolves away. It retains its beauty. Of the common acids, only a mixture of concentrated nitric and hydrochloric acids (*aqua regia*) will dissolve it. Strong acid alone will have no effect. Gold is good also because it is so adaptable to shaping. It can be melted without harm; it can be hammered into thin leaves because it is extremely malleable. It may easily overlay large objects thus imparting beauty and protection to the whole. It may readily be alloyed with other metals with an improvement of the degree of hardness while still retaining the beauty of gold. In fact Pliny noted correctly that gold comes naturally alloyed with silver. Finally gold has been valued because of its scarcity. It seems reasonable to presume that if the core of the earth is largely iron, the free metals such as gold, platinum, and even cobalt and nickel have been depleted to a great extent because they have dissolved in this core.

Gold is mentioned very early in the Bible (Gen. 2:11-12). We are told that in the land of HAVILAH, in the vicinity of the Garden of EDEN, there was gold, and that the gold was good. Gold is also mentioned at the end of the Bible in Rev. 21:15, 18, 21. Here the most precious of metals is envisioned as constituting the Holy City and its streets. The rod used to measure the city was made of gold. There are numerous other references to this metal in the Bible. Exodus 37 describes the construction of the ARK OF THE COVENANT and other appointments of the TABERNACLE, all made of gold or overlaid with

gold. When the writer of Job asks where wisdom can be found (Job 28:12), he responds by observing that wisdom is so priceless that gold, silver, and precious stones cannot buy it (28:15-19). It is worthy of note that gold is mentioned five times in this passage, whereas each of the other precious items is mentioned only once.

D. Iron. In spite of advances in the use of light metals such as aluminum, magnesium, and beryllium, we are still living in the Iron Age. No other metal rivals iron in the amount produced. The reason for this is that iron ores, chiefly the oxides and carbonates, are abundant in concentrated deposits, the metal is easily won from the ore and varies over a wide range in its properties. By removing impurities, by heat treatment, and by alloying, the strength, hardness, ductility, malleability, resistance to corrosion, appearance, and retention of temper may be varied. Iron does not occur free in nature. When it is so found it is on such a minute scale that it may be considered a curiosity. Terrestrial free iron is very likely secondary, having been formed from regular ores by hot carbon or carbon-containing materials, a process that is carried out in blast furnaces today.

It is clear that the ancients found meteoric iron and shaped it for utilitarian purposes. Iron beds taken from a grave in Egypt dating from about 4000 B.C. contain a nickel analysis corresponding favorably to that of meteorites. In fact, the Egyptians and people of other cultures referred to iron as the metal from heaven. In ancient religious literature the Egyptians claimed that the firmament of heaven was made of iron. An iron object dating to about 3000 was blasted out of the masonry at the top of the Great Pyramid of Giza and is now in the British Museum. No one knows who first discovered the way to reduce iron from ore in a furnace. Evidently the discovery was made in the undetermined past. Egyptian frescoes dated at about 1500 depict small furnaces with men operating bellows or mouth blowpipes. This is the essential principle of the modern blast furnace.

The first reference to iron in the Bible is found in Gen. 4:22 where Tubal-Cain is cited as a worker of iron. In other passages (Deut. 4:20; 1 Ki. 8:51; Jer. 11:4) there is evidence that the Hebrews were familiar with furnaces for the making of iron. As

M

slaves in Egypt they probably had to work at these furnaces. Their lot must have been difficult. The smith and his forge were well known to Isaiah (Isa. 44:12; 54:16). The Philistines hindered the Hebrew occupation of the whole of Canaan because they were skilled in iron working. They prevented the Hebrews from making and maintaining their own tools and weapons by refusing to allow a single smith in all the land. The Israelites were forced to go to the Philistines to sharpen their plowshares, mattocks, axes, and sickles (1 Sam. 13:19-20). But the great victories of David ended all this. When David came to power, iron was used freely by the Israelites.

Additional items of iron not previously mentioned are as follows: (1) the huge bed of OG, the AMORITE king of BASHAN, was made of iron (Deut. 3:11); (2) the Israelites feared the Canaanites because they had iron chariots (Josh. 17:16, 18); (3) the spear shaft of Goliath weighed 600 shekels (roughly 15 lbs./ 7 kg., 1 Sam. 17:7); (4) there is ample evidence that many types of fetters and other implements for binding captives and slaves were made of iron. In addition to these references the term is used in a figurative sense (Ps. 2:9; 107:10; Jer. 28:13-14).

E. Lead. Free metallic lead is extremely rare. The chief ore is lead sulfide (galena), which often occurs as bright glistening clusters of cubic crystals. The metal is readily obtained from the ore and was known long before it came into common usage. The British Museum had a lead figure of Egyptian origin dated at about 3000 B.C. Lead plates and statuettes have been found in Egyptian tombs of 1200. The high density of lead is noted in Exod. 15:10. In Num. 31:22 lead is listed along with gold, silver, bronze, iron, and tin. Its use for lettering in rock is noted in Job 19:24. Jeremiah speaks of the use of bellows in the processing of the metal (Jer. 6:29). Lead is listed with copper, tin, and iron as metals melted in a furnace (Ezek. 22:18, 20), and again with silver, iron, and tin as metals used for monetary exchange (Ezek. 27:12; see also Zech. 5:7-8)

F. Silver. At the present time much more silver is obtained as a by-product of the refining of copper and lead than by mining native silver or silver ore. The methods used in this refining were

Sumerian silver lyre from Ur (c. 2600 B.C.). Silver covers the lyre itself and the bull's head.

© Dr. James C. Martin. The British Museum. Photographed by permission.

not available to the Hebrews, since it requires the extensive use of electricity, cyanide, zinc, and aluminum. However, silver is ten times as abundant in the crust of the earth as is gold, and much of it was mined by the ancients. Pliny says, "Silver is only found in deep shafts, and raises no hopes of its existence by any signs, giving off no shining sparkles such as are seen in the case of gold." He describes its use for making mirrors and notes that "the property of reflecting is marvelous; it is generally agreed that it takes place owing to the repercussion of the air which is thrown back into the eyes."

The shekel and talent of silver were used as mediums of exchange. At first this was done by weighing out the silver pieces. This is apparent in Job 28:15: " ... nor can its price be weighed in silver." Silver was used in conjunction with gold because of its beauty. A great many references to silver and gold are found in the Bible. Only occasionally are the terms reversed, as in Esth. 1:6, which refers to couches made of gold and silver. When Christ sent out the Twelve, he commanded them to carry neither gold nor silver nor brass in their purses (Matt. 10:9). Many objects made of silver are referred to in the Scriptures. The cup that JOSEPH had hidden in BENJAMIN's sack of food was a silver cup (Gen. 44:2). DEMETRIUS, the silversmith of EPHESUS, made silver shrines for ARTEMIS (Acts 19:24).

III. The common minerals. Several of these are mentioned in Scripture.

A. Alabaster (Matt. 26:7; Mk. 14:3; Lk. 7:37). These passages refer to an alabaster box or jar used to contain a precious ointment. Modern alabaster is a form of gypsum (hydrated calcium sulfate). It is soft, with a hardness of 2, and may be scratched by the thumbnail. It is easily carved and many larger decorative articles like book ends, vases, and paper weights are made of this material. It is usually very light in color, but may be mottled or veined with various colors. The ancients may have used a calcite or aragonite mineral resembling our modern alabaster in its general appearance. A simple test with the thumbnail will distinguish between the two varieties. Calcite has a hardness of 3 and cannot be scratched with the thumbnail. Alabaster is usually formed by the process of water deposition in caves.

B. Glass (Rev. 4:6; 15:2; 21:18, 21). Glass is a product of the fusion of silicates, borates, or phosphates. Although its use appears to have been widespread in the ancient world, its place of origin is unknown. The ancient Egyptians were, to the best of our knowledge, the first to make small vessels of glass. It appears in the Bible only in the book of Revelation, which describes the appearance of the "sea" before the throne, and the purity and transparency of the gold of which the street and wall of the Holy City are made.

C. Marble (1 Chr. 29:2; Esth. 1:6; Cant. 5:15; Rev. 18:12). Marble is recrystallized limestone, capable of receiving a high polish. Limestone is somewhat impure calcium carbonate. Dolomitic marble contains a considerable amount of magnesium carbonate as well as the calcium compound. Marble is used for decorative purposes such as statuary, pillars, and walls of buildings. There is no reason to think that the marble of the Bible was different from the marble of modern times, except in the sense that marble from different quarries varies in color and texture.

D. Salt. An extremely abundant mineral. The evaporation of one cubic mile (4 cubic km.) of sea water would leave approximately 140 million tons of salts, most of which would be sodium chloride or common salt. The "Salt Sea" of the Bible (Gen. 14:3 et al.) was no doubt the DEAD SEA. In most of the many references to salt, either the preservative property or else the savor it adds to food is the point of interest. Jesus states that the children of the kingdom are the salt of the earth (Matt. 5:13). He uses the analogy of salt losing its "saltiness." The implication is that Christians must not lose that which makes them distinctive. How could salt lose its "saltiness"? It has been suggested by some that as salt was stored it would eventually react chemically and be salt no more. Under any conditions salt would remain salt. But if stored salt was contaminated with other salts, such as magnesium chloride or sulfate, these salts would attract moisture. In due time enough salt might leach away to leave behind the less soluble contaminants, and this would result in a salt of much poorer quality. The container might then be emptied on a foot path to inhibit the growth of weeds.

E. Soda (Job 9:30; Prov. 25:20; Jer. 2:22). Soda is a term applied today to several forms of sodium. In the Bible it probably refers only to sodium carbonate, which forms a gas with vinegar and effervesces freely. It thus fits the description of the process described in Prov. 25:20. In Job 9:30 and Jer. 2:22 it is associated with SOAP. Sodium carbonate would be useful in washing with soap because it acts as a softener of water. It is used today in the making of soap. It is found either in solution in salty seas or in the mud that surrounds such seas.

F. Sulfur (Gen. 19:24; Deut. 29:23; Job 18:15; Ps. 11:6; Isa. 30:33; 34:9; Ezek. 38:22; Lk. 17:29; Rev. 9:17-18; 14:10; 19:20; 20:10; 21:8). In modern times most sulfur comes from deep deposits and is brought to the surface by hot water and compressed air. Sulfur deposits also may be found in the vicinity of volcanoes. Hot gases such as sulfur dioxide and hydrogen sulfide are emitted and deposit sulfur in the surrounding rock by chemical reaction. Sulfur deposits may also be found in the vicinity of some hot springs that are the relics of previous volcanic action. When sulfur is burned, it gives off a blue flame that forms a gas (sulfur dioxide). This gas is used as a bleaching agent. In the Bible sulfur is nearly always associated with fire and metaphorically with punishment or devastation. No natural product readily available to the ancients would so completely symbolize the awful punishment to be meted out to the wicked. The flame of burning sulfur is very hot, and the sulfur dioxide gas has a suffocating stench. Hot sulfur eventually turns to a bubbling, dark red, sticky liquid.

G. Water. This is the most marvelous and exciting mineral of the Bible. Every modern textbook of mineralogy includes a section on the oxides of nature such as those of silicon, copper, iron, aluminum, etc., but hydrogen oxide heads the list. This extremely abundant mineral is found either in liquid or in solid forms, such as snow and ice. As a chemical it is an unusual compound with unusual properties. When it freezes to ice it expands so that it floats. The chemist accounts for most of its odd properties by explaining that hydrogen bonds form between oxygen atoms holding particles together in a framework. Were it not for these hydrogen bonds water would boil away at 150 degrees Fahrenheit *below* zero.

There are more references to this mineral in the Bible than to any other. See WATER. In Genesis the condition that existed before God formed the earth is described as a watery mass. Water was important for various ceremonies of washing found in Leviticus. Elaborate cisterns and water systems may be found at the sites of certain ancient cities in Israel. The importance of water for LIFE is reflected in its metaphorical usage, such as the water of life in Rev. 21:6. Cleansing with water is also used to depict the process of REGENERATION (Eph. 5:26).

mines, mining. The extraction of MINERALS from the earth is an ancient human occupation. We read in the account of the antedeluvian Cainite patriarchs that TUBAL-CAIN "forged all kinds of tools out of bronze and iron" (Gen. 4:22). In Job 28:1-11 there is mention of "a mine for silver and place where gold is refined. Iron is taken from the earth, and copper is smelted from ore." This is followed by a poetic account of a man digging a mine. In SINAI are very ancient copper mines, worked by the Egyptians as early as the 4th dynasty (the great pyramid builders); and, at the head of the Gulf of AQABAH, at ELATH, are the remains of SOLOMON's blast furnaces for copper. At this locality there is a constant strong N wind, and through openings and conduits this wind was used to form a draft for the furnaces. The great development of metalworking in Israel must have come between the

time of SAUL and the time of Solomon. Compare 1 Sam. 13:19-22, where the PHILISTINES are in the Iron Age, which the Israelites had not yet reached, with the accomplishments of Solomon's time (1 Ki. 7:13-50) only about a century later.

The Greeks and the Romans considered mining and metalworking as very ancient, for they pictured Hephaestus or Vulcan, son of ZEUS or Jupiter, as a metalworker. In the time of MOSES, the Midianites (see MIDIAN) had gold, silver, brass, iron, tin, and lead (Num. 31:22); and the Israelites knew how to cleanse them by fire. Moses described the Promised Land as "a land where the rocks are iron and you can dig copper out of the hills" (Deut. 8:9). Although shafts have been found in the "valley of the cave" in Sinai, they do not penetrate far, the reason probably being the inability of the ancients to ventilate their mines.

mingled people. See MIXED MULTITUDE.

Miniamin. min'yuh-min (Heb. *minyāmîn H4975*, "from the right" [i.e., "favored"] or perhaps "from the south"). **(1)** A LEVITE who faithfully assisted KORE in distributing the contributions made to the TEMPLE during the reign of HEZEKIAH (2 Chr. 31:15).

(2) The ancestor of a priestly family in the days of JOAKIM; both this family and that of MOADIAH were headed by Piltai (Neh. 12:17)

(3) A priest who played the trumpet at the dedication of the wall (Neh. 12:41).

minister. In modern religious usage, this noun refers to a member of the clergy, although the verb *to minister* can mean both "to officiate in religious service" and more generally "to provide service, give aid." The KJV uses the noun in its older sense of "attendant, assistant," for example, with reference to JOSHUA (Exod. 24:13; NIV, "aide"). The queen of SHEBA, visiting SOLOMON, was amazed at "the attendance of his ministers" (1 Ki. 10:5; NIV, "the attending servants"). In the NT certain governmental offices are called "God's ministers" (Rom. 13:6; NIV, "God's servants"). John Mark (see MARK, JOHN) is described as the minister of PAUL and BARNABAS (Acts 13:5; NIV, "helper"). In Christian thought, a more distinctive sense emerges.

For example, Paul refers to himself as "a minister of Christ Jesus" (Rom. 15:16), using the Greek term *leitourgos* **G3313**, which has a cultic connotation (cf. Heb. 8:2 KJV). More frequent is the noun *diakonos* **G1356** (from which the term DEACON derives), properly translated "minister" in several passages (e.g., Col. 1:7; 4:7; 1 Tim. 4:6). The cognate verb *diakoneō* **G1354** ("to serve, render assistance") is very frequent in the NT, and the functions implied by it are incumbent not only on those who hold special church offices but on all believers. The basic principle was stated by Christ himself, "For even the Son of Man did not come to be served, but to serve, and to give his life as a ransom for many" (Mk. 10:45). See also BISHOP; CHURCH; ELDER; WORSHIP.

Minni. min´i (Heb. *minnî* **H4973**, meaning unknown). A kingdom that, along with ARARAT (Urartians) and ASHKENAZ (prob. SCYTHIANS), was summoned by God to attack BABYLON (Jer. 51:27). Its people, identified as the Manneans (Mannaeans, Assyrian *Mannai*), occupied the area to the S of Lake Urmia in W Iran from the ninth to the seventh centuries B.C. They are mentioned as a warlike people in various Assyrian and Urartian inscriptions. According to the Babylonian Chronicle they sided with the Assyrians when the Babylonians attacked in 616 B.C. Four years later, when NINEVEH fell to the Babylonians, Medes, and possibly the Scythians, their territory became part of the Median dominion (see MEDIA), and they disappear from the record.

Minnith. min´ith (Heb. *minnit* **H4976**, meaning unknown). Apparently one of the "twenty towns" of the AMMONITES which JEPHTHAH conquered (Jdg. 11:33). According to the description of Jephthah's campaign, which took him from AROER "to the vicinity of [*lit.*, till you come to] Minnith," this city must have been the easternmost limit of his victories. Minnith was presumably not far from HESHBON, but the location is unknown. Ezekiel mentions the "wheat from Minnith," suggesting its exceptional quality (Ezek. 27:17; cf. 2 Chr. 27:5).

minstrel. A term for "musician" used by the KJV in two passages (2 Ki. 3:15 [NIV, "harpist"]; Matt. 9:23 [NIV, "flute players"; TNIV, "people playing pipes"]).

mint. See PLANTS.

minuscule. A cursive writing style. The term is also applied to medieval MSS that use this type of writing. See TEXT AND VERSIONS (NT).

Miphkad. See MUSTER GATE.

miracles. A term commonly applied to extraordinary events that manifest God's intervention in nature and in human affairs. It can be useful to describe miracles negatively as follows.

(1) Miracles should be distinguished from works of PROVIDENCE. We must recognize that in good use *miracle* has a metaphorical or hyperbolical meaning, such as when we say that every sunrise, every tree, every blade of grass is a "miracle." But works of providence are, for Christians, the ordinary works of God through secondary causes. Unbelievers generally deny the supernatural cause of such events. However, in the biblical events strictly regarded as miracles, the adversaries of faith acknowledged the supernatural character of what took place. After the healing of the lame man at the temple, the Jewish leaders, "since they could see the man who had been healed standing there with them, there was nothing they could say" in response to Peter and John (Acts 4:14). But they later admitted to each other, "Everybody living in Jerusalem knows they have done an outstanding miracle [TNIV, a notable sign], and we cannot deny it" (4:16). In the case of the miracle at LYSTRA (14:8-23) the pagans said, "The gods have come down to us in human form!" With reference to the RESURRECTION OF JESUS CHRIST, Paul could ask a Roman court of law to take cognizance of an indisputable, publicly attested fact, for, he said, "it was not done in a corner" (26:26).

(2) Miracles are further to be distinguished from the type of answers to PRAYER that do not constitute "signs" or demonstrative evidence for unbelievers. When ELIJAH prayed for fire on the altar of the Lord (1 Ki. 18:17-46), God answered with a demonstrative miracle that convicted the priests of BAAL. In the experience of Christians,

however, there are numberless events, constantly recurring, in which those who know the Lord can see the hand of God at work, but in which there is not the demonstrative "sign" element. It is a great mistake for Christians to distort their reports of answered prayer so as to make out "sign" miracles where nothing comparable to the biblical "signs" has occurred. God gives abundant evidence of his love and care without any exaggeration on our part.

(3) Miracles of God should also be distinguished from works of MAGIC. In magic the wonder-worker himself possesses a formula that causes the result. The alleged supernatural power is controlled by the performer (cf. Exod. 7:11; 8:7). In miracles of God the results depend wholly on the divine will, and the one who works the miracle is simply an agent for the Lord.

(4) Miracles of God must be distinguished from miracles of Satanic or demonic origin. Christ warned in his Olivet Discourse: "For false Christs and false prophets will appear and perform great signs and miracles to deceive even the elect—if that were possible" (Matt. 24:24). Paul foretells of the Man of Sin "in accordance with the work of SATAN displayed in all kinds of counterfeit miracles, signs and wonders" (2 Thess. 2:9; cf. Rev. 13:14; 16:14; 19:20).

(5) Miracles must also be distinguished from mere exotic occurrences. There are many events in nature that excite wonder, but such matters are evidences of nothing but oddity. Genuine miracles are always "signs" that teach a lesson. Every miracle of God is a part of God's great integrated system of revealed truth.

I. Epochs. The majority of the miracles recorded in the Bible fall into three great epochs. First came the miracles associated with the EXODUS, including the BURNING BUSH, the ten PLAGUES OF EGYPT, the numerous miracles between the parting of the RED SEA and the crossing of the JORDAN, the fall of JERICHO, and the battle of GIBEON. This *first epoch of miracles* came at a time of great spiritual depression. The people in slavery in EGYPT had forgotten the name of the Lord their God. Wholly by his grace God brought them out, amalgamated them into a nation at SINAI, and brought them into the Promised Land. In all subsequent history, God's people have looked back to the miracles of the exodus as a type of divine salvation.

There followed, after the first epoch of miracles, a long period of decline under the judges (see JUDGES, THE), and then a revival of godly faith under DAVID and SOLOMON. During all this time miracles were very few. God did not leave himself

© Dr. James C. Martin

A view of the Bitter Lakes region in Egypt. The miraculous dividing of the water at the time of the exodus probably took place near this location.

without a witness, but the working of miracles was not his chosen method. Then came a period of idolatrous compromise and "inclusive" religion. The names of the Lord and BAAL were brought together, and even the good king JEHOSHAPHAT was badly mixed up with idolatrous AHAB (1 Ki. 21:25-26; 22:1-50). So God gave the *second epoch of miracles*, centering in the ministry of ELIJAH and ELISHA. By mighty "signs" and works of his grace, God restored and confirmed his pure worship. The miracle of JONAH and two notable miracles at the time of ISAIAH (2 Ki. 19:35; 20:9-11) were of outstanding significance, as were two or three special miracles in the experience of DANIEL. But from the epoch of miracles in the time of Elijah and Elisha until the time of Christ and the apostles, miracles were again very few. God worked through the prophets, through the providential discipline of the Babylonian EXILE, and in other ways. Enough REVELATION had been given by the time of MALACHI for the spiritual life of God's people until the time of the coming of Christ. God's faithful servants were sustained without demonstrative "sign" miracles.

The *third epoch of miracles*, the greatest in all recorded history, occurred in the ministry of CHRIST and his APOSTLES. It was, in a way, a time of low spirituality. The Jewish people read the Torah diligently, but they read with a dark veil of hardness over their eyes and hearts. They were so "religious" in their pride that they crucified the Lord of glory. It was to this kind of world that God sent his Son. Nearly forty demonstrative "sign" miracles wrought by Christ are recorded in the Gospels; but these are selected by the writers from among a much larger number. John says, "Jesus did many other miraculous signs in the presence of his disciples, which are not recorded in this book" (Jn. 20:30).

The ministry of the apostles after Christ's ascension began with the miracle of "languages" on the day of PENTECOST. This miracle recurred until the CHURCH organization for this age was well established, and probably until the NT books were all put into circulation. There were numerous other demonstrative miracles. As the author of the letter to the Hebrews puts it, this "salvation, which was first announced by the Lord, was confirmed to us by those who heard him. God also testified to it

by signs, wonders and various miracles, and gifts of the Holy Spirit distributed according to his will" (Heb. 2:3-4).

II. Purpose. The purpose of miracles is revelation and edification. After saying that there were many unrecorded miracles of Christ, John adds, "But these are written that you may believe that Jesus is the Christ, the son of God, and that by believing you may have life in his name" (Jn. 20:31). Christ several times expressed his purpose in working miracles. He rebuffed those who had only a desire to see the spectacular. "A wicked and adulterous generation asks for a miraculous sign!" This was not a complete rejection even of idle curiosity, for he followed his rebuke with a powerful reference to Jonah as a type of his own resurrection (Matt. 12:39-40; cf. also Lk. 23:8). To seek to see miracles is better than merely to seek free food (Jn. 6:26). His miracles were evidence of the genuineness of his message. "For the very work that the Father has given me to finish, and which I am doing, testifies that the Father has sent me" (5:36). He preferred that people would accept his message for its intrinsic worth, but to believe him because of his miracles was not wrong. "Do not believe me unless I do what my Father does. But if I do it, even though you do not believe me, believe the miracles, that you may know and understand that the Father is in me, and I in the Father (10:37-38).

III. The question of miracles today. This is a disturbing question to many. In the ancient church the Montanist party insisted that miracles and predictive prophecy must be perpetual gifts. Christ pointed out that miracles do not occur with any uniform regularity (Lk. 4:25-27). In fact, if miracles were regular occurrences, they would cease to be regarded as miracles. Paul's rules for the restriction of the use of foreign languages (1 Cor. 14) might be applied by analogy to all miracles. Evidently the miracle of language that occurred on the day of Pentecost had been confused, in the minds of devout people in CORINTH, with mere ecstatic meaningless utterances. Paul points out, "Tongues, then, are a sign, not for believers but for unbelievers" (14:22). And he commands that in Christian assemblies not more than two or, at the most, three, in turn, should be allowed to speak in a foreign language, and "if there is no interpreter, the speaker

M

M

should keep quiet in the church and speak to himself and God" (14:27-28). If analogous methods were used in examining reports of alleged miracles, genuine miracles would never be hindered, but would be the better attested. At the same time delusions and exaggerations would be prevented.

Some have sought to account for the occurrence or nonoccurrence of miracles on "dispensational" grounds. Accordingly, God's dealings with and his gifts to his people have varied throughout history. Thus, perhaps God used miracles to initiate the present "age of grace" but has withdrawn any such special "gift" that some early believers possessed. It must be recalled, however, that the period of time between Sinai and Calvary is recognized by dispensationalists as one uniform age of "law." Yet this "dispensation" included the epoch of miracles under Elijah and Elisha, as well as long periods during which no miracles were recorded.

From Bible history, and history since Bible times, the fact stands out that God does not choose to reveal himself by demonstrative miracles at all times. On the contrary, there have been long periods of history, even in Bible times, when God did not use miracles (except the "miracle of grace") in his dealings with his people. The Bible does not specifically say that God cannot or that God will not work demonstrative "sign" miracles in our day. It is, however, a reasonable opinion, not controvertible by any clearly attested facts, that God generally ceased to work through "sign" miracles when the NT was finished; and that it is his will that the "miracle of grace," the witness of the Spirit, answered prayer, and, supremely, the written Word shall be the chief sources of knowledge of himself for his people during this age. It should be clear to all that, except on extremely rare occasions, even the most godly, sacrificial, competent ministers, missionaries, and laymen today do not experience demonstrative "sign" miracles.

A healthy mind, full of faith in God's power and in God's wisdom, without denying that "sign" miracles may occur when God chooses to use them, expects to learn foreign languages by regular processes of study and hard work. A healthy Christian mind expects to observe the ordinary principles of bodily health and sanitation, using such physical provisions of food, shelter, and medicine as divine providence may make available. In spreading the gospel one does expect the convicting ministry of the Spirit and the evidence of transformed lives, but one does not expect, unless God should so choose, that the sudden healing of a man born with twisted feet and ankle bones will gather a crowd to hear the Word preached. One is prepared to serve the Lord, to experience wonderful answers to prayer, and to find that the Word does not return void, regardless of "signs and wonders."

IV. Essential to Christianity. Miracles are an absolutely essential element in Christianity. If Jesus Christ is not God manifest in the flesh, our faith is a silly myth. If he did not arise from the dead in bodily form, the grave being empty and his appearance being recognizable, then we are yet in our sins and of all people most miserable. If the miracle of grace is not verifiable in the transformation of the life of the one who puts his faith in Jesus as his Lord and Savior, then our Christian gospel is a miserable fraud.

V. Rational. The rational nature of miracles has been misconstrued by the British philosopher David Hume and those who follow his positivistic methods. Miracles are not violations of natural law as Hume supposed; they are intelligent acts of a personal God. They are not erratic or exotic occurrences; they are reasonable parts and phases of a cosmic program of revelation and redemption. There is no greater logical problem in the act of God in raising the dead than there is in the act of a person in lifting his hand. We speak or signal to our children and our neighbors with appropriate gestures, and God reveals himself and his plan for us by "signs" or by other means according to his will.

Christianity is indeed a "supernatural" faith, but the distinction between the natural and the supernatural is only a convenient classification of events. From the point of view of the biblical writers it was perfectly natural for God to wrestle with Jacob or to roll back the Red Sea or to raise his Son from the dead. Consistent, miracle-believing, Christian theism is just as unified in rational thought, just as scientific in its attitude toward evidence and verification, as any laboratory technician who believes that natural law does not exclude intelligent, purposeful, personal causation.

Miriam. mihr´ee-uhm (Heb. *miryām H5319*, derivation disputed). **(1)** Daughter of AMRAM and JOCHEBED, and sister of MOSES and AARON (Num. 26:59; 1 Chr. 6:3). Miriam showed concern and wisdom in behalf of her infant brother Moses when he was discovered in the NILE by the Egyptian princess (Exod. 2:4, 7-8). Miriam first appears by name in Exod. 15:20, where she is called a prophetess and is identified as the sister of Aaron. After passing through the RED SEA, she led the Israelite women in dancing and instrumental accompaniment while she sang the song of praise and victory (15:20-21). In Num. 12:1 Miriam and Aaron criticized Moses for his marriage to a Cushite woman. Because of this criticism, Miriam was punished by the Lord with leprosy (12:9), but on the protest of Aaron and the prayer of Moses (12:11, 13) she was restored after a period of seven days, during which she was isolated from the camp and the march was delayed. Her case of leprosy is cited in Deut. 24:9. Miriam died at Kadesh and was buried there (Num. 20:1). Micah refers to her along with her brothers as leaders whom the Lord provided to bring Israel out of the Egyptian bondage (Mic. 6:4).

(2) Son of MERED (apparently by his wife BITHIAH, Pharaoh's daughter) and descendant of JUDAH through CALEB (1 Chr. 4:17; note that NRSV, to clarify the sense, includes here part of v. 18). Some leave open the possibility that this Miriam too was a woman.

Mirma. See MIRMAH.

Mirmah. mihr´muh (Heb. *mirmāh H5328*, possibly "deceit"). KJV Mirma. Son of SHAHARAIM and descendant of BENJAMIN; a family head (1 Chr. 8:10). Mirmah was one of seven children that were born to Shaharaim in MOAB by his wife HODESH after he had divorced Hushim and Baara (vv. 8-9).

mirror. Any smooth or polished surface as of glass or of metal that forms images by reflecting light. The Israelite women who served at the entrance of the TABERNACLE used mirrors made of bronze (Exod. 38:8) and so could be used as material for the laver. ELIHU speaks of the sky as resembling "a mirror of cast bronze" (Job 37:18). He was, no

Collection of copper mirrors from Egypt.

© Dr. James C. Martin. The Cairo Museum. Photographed by permission.

doubt, thinking of the brightness of the sky as like that of polished metal. Of the inadequacy of these ancient mirrors PAUL says that "now we see but a poor reflection" (1 Cor. 13:12). JAMES compares a hearer of the word who is not also a doer to "a man who looks at his face in a mirror" (Jas. 1:23-24) and then forgets what he looks like. "Mirror" is a better translation than "glass" or "looking glass," because the material was metal, not glass.

mischief. This English term occurs about fifty times in the KJV as a rendering of several Hebrew words (Gen. 42:4 et al.; in the NT only once, Acts. 13:10). It occurs much less frequently in the NRSV, and not at all in the NIV. Modern versions prefer such renderings as "harm, evil, injury, trouble," and others.

Misgab. mis´gab. The KJV transliteration of Hebrew *miśgāb H5369*, treating it as the name of a place in MOAB (Jer. 48:1). It is more likely to be taken as a common noun meaning "stronghold" or "fortress."

Mishael. mish´ay-uhl (Heb. *mîšā'ēl H4792*, "who is like God?" or "who belongs to God?"). **(1)** Son of Uzziel and descendant of LEVI through KOHATH (Exod. 6:22). One of Uzziel's brothers was AMRAM (father of MOSES), so Mishael was Moses' first cousin. Mishael and his brother ELZAPHAN were called by Moses to carry out the bodies of NADAB and ABIHU after their sin and death (Lev. 10:4-5).

(2) One of the prominent men (not identified as priests) who stood near EZRA when the law was read at the great assembly (Neh. 8:4).

M

M

(3) The Jewish name of Meshach, one of Daniel's three companions in Babylon (Dan. 1:6-7 et al.).

Mishal. mi´shuhl (Heb. *miš'āl H5398*, possibly "[place of] request, inquiry"). A town within the tribal territory of Asher (Josh. 19:26 KJV, "Misheal"); it was one of the four towns allotted to the Levites descended from Gershon (21:30-31). The town is called Mashal in the parallel passage (1 Chr. 6:74). The site has not been positively identified, but one possibility is modern Tell Kisan, about 5 mi. (8 km.) SE of Acco.

Misham. mi´shuhm (Heb. *miš'ām H5471*, derivation unknown). Son of Elpaal and descendant of Benjamin (1 Chr. 8:12).

Misheal. See Mishal.

Mishma. mish´muh (Heb. *mišmā' H5462*, possibly "hearing," i.e., "obedient"). (1) Son of Ishmael and grandson of Abraham (Gen. 25:14; 1 Chr. 1:30). See also Mibsam.
(2) Son of Shaul or, more likely, of Mibsam; included in the genealogy of Simeon (1 Chr. 4:25).

Mishmannah. mish-man´uh (Heb. *mišmannâ H5459*, possibly "fat" or "noble"). A Gadite who joined David's forces at Ziklag (1 Chr. 12:10). The Gadites are described as "brave warriors, ready for battle and able to handle the shield and spear. Their faces were the faces of lions, and they were as swift as gazelles in the mountains" (v. 8).

Mishnah. See Talmud.

Mishneh. See Second District, Second Quarter.

Mishraite. mish´ray-it (Heb. *mišrā' H5490*, gentilic form of the unattested name *mišrā'*). The Mishraites were a Judahite clan descended from Caleb through Hur and Shobal; they made up one of several families associated with Kiriath Jearim (1 Chr. 2:53). Their name apparently derives from an otherwise unknown ancestor or place called Mishra.

Mispar. mis´pahr (Heb. *mispār H5032*, possibly from a word of the same form meaning "number"). An Israelite mentioned among leading individuals who returned from Babylon with Zerubbabel (Ezra 2:2; called "Mispereth" in Neh. 7:7).

Mispereth. mis-pee´rith (Heb. *misperet H5033*). See Mispar.

Misrephoth Maim. mis´ruh-foth-may´im (Heb. *miśrepôt mayim H5387*, "burnings [i.e., limekilns] at the water"). A place in the vicinity of Sidon, mentioned in Josh. 11:8 in connection with Israel's defeat of the kings of N Canaan, and in 13:6 as one of the places still in the hands of the Canaanites. These passages suggest that Misrephoth Maim was on or near the S border of Sidon, but its location is uncertain. It is often identified with Khirbet el-Musheirefeh, just S of the promontory known as the Ladder of Tyre (Ras en-Naqura), though some have preferred a nearby collection of warm springs known as 'Ain Mesherfi. It has also been suggested, however, that Misrephoth Maim is the same as the Litani River, which flows into the Mediterranean about 6 mi. (10 km.) NNE of Tyre.

mission. See Acts of the Apostles; apostle; evangelist; gospel.

mist. Water particles in the atmosphere near the earth. Mist is caused by water vapor filling the air until it is only partially transparent. Mist or fog is not common in Palestine and Syria at sea level, but occurs almost daily in the mountain valleys, coming up at night and disappearing with the morning sun. The rare Hebrew word *'ēd H116*, which apparently means "stream" (Gen. 2:6), perhaps can also be rendered "mist" (Job 36:27 NRSV, NIV mg.). The usual word for "cloud," *'ānān H6727*, may in some contexts refer to the morning mist or fog (Hos. 13:3 et al.). In Acts 13:11, the Greek word for "mist," *achlys G944*, describes incipient blindness, and has been so used since Homer. Human life is compared to a mist or vapor "that appears for a little while and then vanishes" (Jas. 4:14; Gk. *atmis G874*), while false prophets are compared to mists or clouds driven by the storm because of the confusion they bring to unwary believers (2 Pet. 2:17; Gk. *homichlē G3920*).

Mitanni. mi-tan´ee. An important kingdom in N Mesopotamia that flourished during the period c. 1500-1340 B.C. The ruling class of this kingdom seems to have been Indo-Iranian; its capital, the ruins of which have not yet been identified, bore the name Washshukanni (some think it may have been located in what is now Tell el-Fakhariyeh near Gozan). They are thought to have introduced into the ANE at this time techniques for the training of chariot horses. The rank and file of Mitanni's citizenry, on the other hand, were not Indo-Iranians, but Hurrians, and it is the Hurrian and Akkadian languages that the Mitannian kings employ for official correspondence. At the height of Mitanni's power it controlled Mesopotamia, SE Asia Minor (Kizzuwatna), all of N Syria, and most of S Syria. Mitannian princesses entered the harems of the pharaohs of Egypt and became quite influential in the Egyptian court. An end was put to the Mitannian kingdom as an independent state by the Hittite emperor Suppiluliuma I (c. 1345 B.C.). The name Mitanni does not occur in the OT, but the Hurrians, who made up the majority of Mitanni's citizens, also constituted a significant minority group in pre-Israelite Palestine.

mite. See money.

Mithcah. mith´kuh (Heb. *mitqâ H5520*, "sweet [place]"). Also Mithkah. A stopping place of the Israelites during their wilderness journeys (Num. 33:28-29). It was between Terah and Hashmonah, but the location of these sites is unknown.

Mithkah. See Mithcah.

Mithnite. mith´nit (Heb. *mitni H5512*, gentilic form of an unattested name such as *meten*). A descriptive title applied only to a certain Joshaphat, one of David's mighty warriors (1 Chr. 11:43). It is not known whether the form Mithnite derives from an ancestor or a place name.

Mithradates. mith´ruh-day´teez. See Mithredath.

Mithraism. mith´ruh-iz´uhm. The cult of Mithras, a Persian sun-god, the worship of which reached Rome in or about A.D. 69, by the agency of the eastern legions who set up Vespasian as emperor. It is possible that the cult was known in the capital a century before, but it was the latter half of the first century of the Christian era that saw its strong dissemination in the West, and indeed its notable challenge to Christianity. Based on the trials, sufferings, and exploits of Mithras, the cult appealed to soldiers; and two shrines of Mithraism on Hadrian's wall, one excavated in 1948 at Carrawburgh, and another still covered at Housesteads, reveal the popularity of Mithraism with the British legions. There is a place of ordeal under the altar, for the initiate advanced through various grades by way of physical suffering and endurance. Archaeologists were able to establish the fact that chickens and geese were eaten at the ritual feasts and that pine cones provided aromatic altar fuel. December 25 was the chief feast of Mithras, and in fixing on that date for Christmas, the early church sought to overlay both the Mithraic festival and the Saturnalia. Christianity triumphed over Mithraism because of its written records of a historic Christ, and its associated body of doctrine adapted for preaching, evangelism, and the needs of every day.

Mithras. mith´ruhs. See Mithraism.

Mithredath. mith´ruh-dath (Heb. *mitrĕdāt H5521*, from Pers., "gift of Mithras" [see Mithraism]). **(1)** The treasurer of King Cyrus (Ezra 1:8).

(2) One of three Persian officials who wrote a letter of complaint against the Jews to King Artaxerxes (Ezra 4:7).

(3) Mithradates (from the Gk. form of Mithredath) was the name of seven Parthian kings of the Arsacid dynasty. The Romans fought a series of three wars against Mithradates VI Eupator, called "the Great," between 88-64 B.C. This war prohibited the Romans from taking effective control over Palestine until 63 B.C. Although Persian, the Mithradatid rulers were Hellenistic in outlook and preserved this way of life in Syria-Palestine for a century after the other Hellenistic kingdoms had fallen to Rome. See Hellenism.

M

mitre. See DRESS; PRIEST, PRIESTHOOD.

Mitylene. mit´uh-lee´nee (Gk. *Mitylēnē G3639*). Also Mytilene. Chief city of the island of Lesbos, a splendid port with a double harbor (Acts 20:14), and a center of Greek culture. It was the home of Sappho and Alcaeus, the early lyric poets, and a considerable maritime and colonizing power. Sigeum and Assos were Mitylene's foundations. The city's history forms the usual checkered story of a Greek state too weak for independence and torn between the demands of rival imperialists—PERSIA, ATHENS, and ROME.

mixed multitude. This phrase (also "mixt multitude") is used by the KJV to render the Hebrew word ʿēreb *H6850* in two passages: in Exod. 12:38 (NIV, "other people") it refers to the heterogeneous camp followers who escaped with the Israelites from Egypt but were not descended from JACOB; similarly, in Neh. 13:3 it refers to people "of foreign descent" (NIV, NRSV) who were excluded from Israel after the return from exile. The Hebrew word is also used of foreigners in Jeremiah, where the KJV renders it as "mingled people" (Jer. 25:20, 24; 50:37). In addition, the KJV uses the phrase "mixed multitude" to translate Hebrew ʾăsapsup *H671*, "rabble," with reference to a group (apparently the same non-Israelites who left Egypt) that "began to crave other food" in the wilderness (Num. 11:4).

Mizar. mi´zahr (Heb. *miṣʿār H5204*, "small"). The name of a mountain in the HERMON range (Ps. 46:2); alternatively, the word may be a common adjective, used to contrast the mighty Hermon with a small mountain. In either case, the precise site is not known.

Mizpah, Mizpeh. miz´puh, miz´peh (Heb. *miṣpâ H5207* and *miṣpeh H5206*, "watchtower"). The KJV uses the form Mizpeh twenty-three times, whereas the NRSV uses it only when the Hebrew is *miṣpeh*; for consistency, the NIV uses Mizpah throughout. See also RAMATH MIZPEH.

(1) One of three names given to the covenant heap of stones erected by JACOB and LABAN (Gen. 31:49; see GALEED). It was so named because

Laban called on the Lord to watch between him and Jacob. Some believe that this place is the same as #2 below.

(2) A town in GILEAD where JEPHTHAH the judge lived (Jdg. 10:17; 11:11, 29, 34; cf. Hos. 5:1). Its location is uncertain, but some identify it with modern Khirbet Jalʿad, some 14 mi. (22 km.) S of the JABBOK River.

(3) A town in MOAB (1 Sam. 22:3). When DAVID was being pursued by SAUL, he took his parents there and left them with the king of Moab, while he returned to his followers in Judah. Since KIR HARESETH (modern Kerak) was at one time the capital of Moab, some have thought that Mizpeh is another name for Kir. Most scholars regard this place as unidentified.

(4) An area in the extreme N of GALILEE is called "the region [*lit*., land] of Mizpah" and "the Valley of Mizpah" (Josh. 11:3, 8). The precise identification is uncertain since the descriptive phrases are too vague. The first passage indicates that the HIVITES "below Hermon" lived there, while the second refers to it as the eastward terminus of JOSHUA's pursuit of the Canaanites after his victory over them in the battle at the Waters of MEROM. It is not clear whether in these passages Mizpah might have been a town or only the name of a general area.

(5) A town in the SHEPHELAH of JUDAH (Josh. 15:38). It was in the same district as LACHISH, but its location is unknown.

(6) The most important place bearing the name Mizpah was a town allotted to the tribe of BENJAMIN (Josh. 18:26). Scholars differ in its identification. Some favor Nebi Samwil, about 5 mi. (8 km.) WNW of JERUSALEM, though most scholars today prefer Tell en-Naṣbeh, 7.5 mi. (12 km.) NNW of Jerusalem. At Mizpah the Israelites gathered to consider the steps to be taken against GIBEAH in the case of the atrocity related in Jdg. 19 (cf. 20:1, 3; 21:1, 5, 8). Mizpah was one of the cities closely associated with SAMUEL, for he made the circuit of BETHEL, GILGAL, and Mizpah and judged Israel in those places (1 Sam. 7:16). At Mizpah, Israel came to meet with Samuel in repentance (7:5-16) and from there they went out to meet the attacking PHILISTINES and to gain the victory that was celebrated by the setting up of the EBENEZER

Tell en-Naṣbeh, a widely favored identification of biblical Mizpah in the territory of Benjamin.

memorial "between Mizpah and Shen." Asa king of Judah fortified Mizpah with stones transported from the building venture of Baasha king of Israel at Ramah (1 Ki. 15:22; 2 Chr. 16:6).

After the destruction of Jerusalem by Nebuchadnezzar in 586 B.C., Gedaliah was appointed governor of Judah. He located his headquarters at Mizpah (2 Ki. 25:22-23; Jer. 40:5-12), and the Jews who remained in the land gathered to him there. Johanan son of Kareah and the other military leaders came to Mizpah and warned Gedaliah of a plot against his life by Ishmael son of Nethaniah. Johanan volunteered to kill Ishmael, but Gedaliah rejected the offer (Jer. 40:16) and ignored the warning. Ishmael carried out his plot successfully, killing not only Gedaliah but also other Jews and Babylonian soldiers who were there (2 Ki. 25:25; Jer. 41:1-3). The following day a group of eighty men on a religious pilgrimage arrived from Shechem, Shiloh, and Samaria. Ishmael deceived the men, killed them, and threw them into a cistern, except for ten men who were able to buy their lives. Ishmael took captive the remainder of the people of Mizpah, but the captives made their escape when Johanan and others gave pursuit. The survivors then went to Egypt, contrary to the command of the Lord

(41:17—42:22). Mizpah also appears in the lists of rebuilders of the walls of Jerusalem (Neh. 3:7, 15, 19) and is mentioned by Hosea in his rebuke of Israel (Hos. 5:1).

Mizpar. See Mispar.

Mizpeh. See Mizpah.

Mizraim. miz-ray´im (Heb. miṣrayim H5213, possibly "[two] boundaries"). This English transliteration is used by the KJV and the NIV only with reference to one of the sons of Ham (Gen. 10:6, 13; 1 Chr. 1:8, 11; NJPS uses it also in 1 Ki. 10:28-29 and 2 Ki. 7:6, but the form does not occur at all in NRSV or TNIV). In the Hebrew Bible, however, miṣrayim occurs very frequently as the name for Egypt and its people. Thus the man Mizraim is regarded as the eponymous ancestor of the Egyptians. The descendants of Mizraim, moreover, included several other important people groups, such as the Philistines (Gen. 10:14; 1 Chr. 1:12).

Mizzah. miz´uh (Heb. mizzâ H4645, derivation uncertain). Son of Reuel and grandson of Esau by Basemath; an Edomite clan chief (Gen. 36:13, 17; 1 Chr. 1:37).

M

Mnason. nay´suhn (Gk. *Mnasōn G3643*). A friend of PAUL mentioned only in Acts 21:16. Mnason was from CYPRUS, like BARNABAS, and probably a Jew, though bearing a common Greek name. Described as "one of the early disciples," he may have been converted at PENTECOST or soon afterward. Mnason was evidently a hospitable person, welcoming Paul and his companions to his house.

Moab. moh´ab (Heb. *mô᾽āb H4565* and *H4566*, derivation uncertain; gentilic *mô᾽ābî H4567*, "Moabite"). A Transjordanian state, lying E of the DEAD SEA and occupying the plateau between the Wadis ARNON and ZERED. It was bounded on the S by EDOM. The area is about 3,200 ft. (975 m.) above sea level and is chiefly rolling country, well adapted for pasturage.

The ancestor of the Moabites was Moab, product of an incestuous union between LOT and his eldest daughter (Gen. 19:30-38); he is mentioned nowhere else in the Bible. The Moabites settled first at AR, just E of the southern part of the Dead Sea and quite close to the site of the destroyed cities of the plain. The Lord commanded MOSES not to vex them when ISRAEL passed through their vicinity on their way to the Promised Land. However, when Israel had almost reached their destination and were camped in the plains of Moab (Num. 22-24), BALAK, sensing that he could not save himself from Israel by force of arms, hired BALAAM to come and curse Israel. Balaam went to do so; but after being rebuked by the voice of a donkey for his sin, God permitted him to proceed on the condition that he would speak only the words God gave him to speak. As a result he prophetically gave blessing to Israel four times. However, he evidently suggested to the Moabites that though they could not conquer Israel by force of arms, they could seduce the nation (cf. Num. 31:16), for the Moabite women entered the camp of Israel and seduced the men (25:1-9). As a result God sent a plague that killed 24,000 men.

Shortly before the Israelites entered CANAAN, Moses died on Mount Pisgah in the land of Moab. Nearly a century later, Israel was "subject to Eglon king of Moab for eighteen years" (Jdg. 3:12-14). Moab was able to gather the AMMONITES and the AMALEKITES against Israel, but when the children

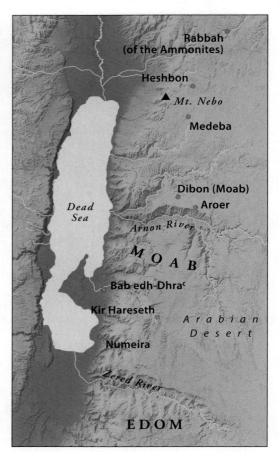

Moab.

of Israel repented and prayed, God raised up EHUD, who killed EGLON and so subdued Moab (3:30). There seems to have been considerable travel between Moab and JUDAH, for in the days of the judges ELIMELECH of BETHLEHEM took his family to Moab to stay during a famine; there his two sons married and died, and RUTH the Moabitess returned with NAOMI, married BOAZ, and became an ancestress of DAVID. David, when in difficulty with King SAUL, took his father and mother to the king of Moab for their protection (1 Sam. 22:3-4). Later MESHA king of Moab paid heavy tribute to AHAB king of Israel (2 Ki. 3:4). After the death of Ahab, he rebelled, but Joram (JEHORAM) king of Israel with JEHOSHAPHAT of Judah thoroughly defeated him and, so far as possible, ruined his land.

From that time on, Moab gradually declined in accordance with the word of the Lord through his prophets. Amos 2:1-3 pronounces the death sentence on Moab; Isa. 15-16, "the prophecy against Moab," gives in much detail the coming destruction of Moab, and this was fulfilled by SHALMANESER of ASSYRIA or by his successor SARGON. Isaiah points out the prevailing sin of Moab aside from their idolatry: "We have heard of Moab's pride— her overweening pride and conceit, her pride and her insolence" (16:6); and Ezekiel and Jeremiah, a century and a half later, completed the picture. Moab and SEIR were to be punished for likening the house of Judah to the other nations (Ezek. 25:8-11). Jeremiah 48 depicts both past and future judgments on Moab, and Zeph. 2:8-11 foretells utter destruction on Moab for their wicked pride.

Moabite Stone. An inscribed monument found in MOAB and recording Moabite history. In 1868 F. A. Klein, a German missionary employed by the Church Missionary Society (Church of England), while traveling through the territory formerly occupied by the tribe of REUBEN E of the DEAD SEA, was informed by an Arab sheik of a remarkable stone inscribed with writing and lying at DIBON, near Klein's route. The stone was bluish basalt, neatly cut into a monument about 4 by 2 ft. (120 x 60 cm.), with its upper end curved and a raised rim enclosing an inscription. Klein informed the authorities of the Berlin Museum, and meanwhile M. Ganneau of the French Consulate at Jerusalem and a Captain Warren made "squeezes" on the writing so as to secure roughly the text of the inscription. While the French and the Germans were bargaining with the Turks for the stone, the Arabs argued that if the stone as a whole was of value it would be far more valuable if cut to pieces, so they built a fire around it, poured cold water over it, and well-nigh destroyed it. However, their purpose was largely thwarted because the inscription had already been ascertained. The fragments of the stone were purchased and pieced together and are now in the Louvre in Paris.

The writing consisted of thirty-four lines, in the Moabite language (very closely related to HEBREW), and it was authored by MESHA, king of the Moabites in the time of AHAZIAH and Joram (JEHORAM), the sons of AHAB. It gives his side of the account found in 2 Ki. 3. It reads, in

The famous Moabite Stone mentions conflict between Mesha of Moab and the dynasty of Omri of Israel.

© Dr. James C. Martin. Musée du Louvre; Autorisation de photographer et de filmer— LOUVRE. Paris, France. Photographed by permission.

M

part: "I, Mesha, king of Moab, made this monument to Chemosh to commemorate deliverance from Israel. My father reigned over Moab thirty years, and I reigned after my father. Omri, king of Israel, oppressed Moab many days and his son after him. But I warred against the king of Israel, and drove him out, and took his cities, Medeba, Ataroth, Nebo and Jahaz, which he built while he waged war against me. I destroyed his cities, and devoted the spoil to Chemosh, and the women and girls to Ashtar. I built Qorhah with prisoners from Israel. In Beth-Diblathaim, I placed sheep-raisers." It seems strange that though Mesha names Omri who had long since died, he does not name his son Ahab, who reigned almost twice as long, and to whom Mesha had paid heavy tribute (2 Ki. 3:4). Perhaps he hated his very name. Neither does he mention the sons of Ahab, Ahaziah and Joram, though he warred against them. Probably he had the monument made before the time of his defeat by Joram and JEHOSHAPHAT.

Moadiah. moh´uh-di´uh (Heb. *ma'adyâ H5050* [Neh. 12:5], "ornament of Yahweh"; the alternate form *mô'adyâ H4598* [12:17], if genuine, perhaps means "assembly of Yahweh"). One of the priestly leaders who returned from the EXILE with ZERUBBABEL (Neh. 12:5 NIV; the KJV and other versions have "Maadiah"). Both his family and that of MINIAMIN were headed by Piltai (12:17). Some believe that Maadiah and Moadiah are two different individuals; if only one person is involved, the reason for the spelling variation is uncertain.

mocking. This English term and its cognates are used to render a variety of Hebrew and Greek words. Mocking may be harmless teasing, as the boy ISHMAEL with baby ISAAC (Gen. 21:9; the Heb. verb here is *ṣāḥaq H7464*, a play on Issac's name). Or it may be a lover's complaint, as of DELILAH with SAMSON (Jdg. 16:10, 13 KJV; NIV, "you have made a fool of me"). SANBALLAT and others "mocked and ridiculed" the Jews for rebuilding JERUSALEM (Neh. 4:1; cf. Ps. 80:6). Mocking may be biting sarcasm, as of ELIJAH against the prophets of the fertility god (1 Ki. 18:27 KJV; NIV, "taunt"). JEREMIAH felt scorn directed at him (Jer. 20:7; cf. Ps. 119:51). The psalmist says God holds all nations in derision (59:8), especially when they rebel against him (Ps. 2:4). God "mocks proud mockers" (Prov. 3:34).

In the NT, mocking may be public laughter at a failure, as in the parable of the unfinished tower (Lk. 14:29). Jesus foretold his own mockery by the Romans (Matt. 20:19), and it came to pass (27:29). Jesus also was mocked in the Jewish trial (Lk. 22:63), and it was repeated with the men of Herod Antipas (23:11) and by the soldiers at the cross (23:36). When the apostolic band spoke in tongues at PENTECOST, unbelievers mocked saying the disciples were drunk (Acts 2:13; NIV, "made fun of"). The members of the AREOPAGUS likewise mocked by gesture and word the message of the resurrection that PAUL brought (17:32). Dedicated Christians will constantly meet scoffers (Jude 18), especially when they speak of the second coming (2 Pet. 3:3). Sinners, thinking they can "get away"

with their sins, turn up their noses at God and his laws, but they cannot outwit him (Gal. 6:7).

Modein. moh´deen (Gk. *Modein*). A town where MATTATHIAS and his sons initiated the Maccabean Revolt (1 Macc. 2:15 et al.). It is identified with modern Midyah (more specifically, el-Arba'in), about 17 mi. (27 km.) NW of JERUSALEM. See MACCABEE.

modernism. An approach that accommodates the Bible and theology to contemporary thought, devaluing traditional views of biblical authority and supernaturalism.

Moladah. moh´luh-duh (Heb. *môlādâ H4579*, from *yālad H3528*, "to give birth"). One of "the southernmost towns of the tribe of Judah in the Negev toward the boundary of Edom" (Josh. 15:26); also listed in the allotment to the Simeonites (Josh. 19:2; 1 Chr. 4:28). In the postexilic period Moladah was one of the villages where "the people of Judah" settled (Neh. 11:26). The town was evidently close to BEERSHEBA, but the precise location is uncertain. Many recent scholars identify Moladah with Khereibet el-Waṭen, some 5.5 mi. (9 km.) E of Beersheba. Since one of the descendants of JERAHMEEL bore the name MOLID (1 Chr. 2:29), some have speculated that Moladah was a part of the Jerahmeelite settlement, which is known to have been in the S of Judah (1 Sam. 27:10).

molding. This English term is used to render a Hebrew term that occurs with reference to a shaped rim around the ARK OF THE COVENANT (Exod. 25:11, 24-25; 37:2), a similar rim around the altar of INCENSE (30:3-4; 37:26-27), and still another one around the table for the showbread (37:11-12; see TABERNACLE). In all three cases the molding was of pure gold and was ornamental, giving a finished appearance to the objects.

mole. See ANIMALS.

Molech. moh´lek (Heb. *mōlek H4891*, prob. *melek H4889*, "king," with the vowels of *bōšet H1425*, "shame"; Gk. *Moloch G3661*). Also Moloch (Amos 5:26 KJV; Acts 7:43 KJV, NRSV); TNIV Molek.

A heathen god, especially of the AMMONITES, who apparently was worshiped with gruesome orgies in which children were sacrificed (although some scholars think that the relevant texts should be translated differently). The worship of Molech was known to Israel before they entered CANAAN, for MOSES very sternly forbade its worship (Lev. 18:21; 20:1-5). In spite of this prohibition, King SOLOMON, to please his numerous heathen wives, set up high places for CHEMOSH and for Molech on the MOUNT OF OLIVES (1 Ki. 11:7), though Molech's principal place of worship in and after MANASSEH's time was the Valley of Ben HINNOM (2 Chr. 33:6), a place of such ill repute that it became a type for hell (Matt. 5:29-30; see GEHENNA). Later Jews, after making sacrifices to Molech, would often go to worship in the house of the Lord (Ezek. 23:37-39), and this impiety was particularly offensive to the Lord (see Jer. 7:9-11; 19:4-13). Because of this heathen worship by Israel, God allowed her enemies to rule over her for many years (Ps. 106:35-42). See also MILCOM.

Molek. moh'lek. TNIV form of MOLECH.

Molid. moh'lid (Heb. *môlîd H4582*, "descendant" or "begetter"). Son of Abishur and descendant of JUDAH through PEREZ and JERAHMEEL; his mother's name was Abihail (1 Chr. 2:29).

Moloch. See MOLECH.

molten image. This phrase is used by the KJV and other versions to render the Hebrew word *massēkāh H5011* (from *nāsak H5818*, "to pour"); it is usually rendered "cast idol" by the NIV. The word refers first of all to an image of a god cut from stone, shaped from clay, or carved from wood, but it also includes images cast from metal (Lev. 19:4; Deut. 27:15). Such an image was made by pouring molten metal, gold, silver, iron, or bronze, over a prepared form or into a mold (Isa. 40:18-20). The term is used of the golden calf made by AARON (Exod. 32:4) and of the two calves set up at BETHEL and DAN by JEROBOAM (1 Ki. 14:9). See CALF WORSHIP; GRAVEN IMAGE; IDOLATRY.

molten sea. See TEMPLE.

money. Translators of the Bible have always had difficulty finding terms for the various kinds of money in the Bible that indicate their value or purchasing power in Bible times. Therefore, a knowledge of the nature and value of ancient money is very helpful to the Bible reader in understanding the Word today.

I. General. Money in the sense of stamped coins did not exist in ISRAEL, so far as is known, until after the EXILE. Before this time exchange of values took place by bartering, that is, trading one thing for another without the exchange of money. This method was followed by the WEIGHT system, later by minted coins and still later by paper money, until today we have the credit system by which one may live, buy, and sell without the physical transfer of money at all. WEALTH is first mentioned in the Bible in connection with ABRAHAM (Gen. 12:5, 16, 20; 13:2). Among the Romans the word for money was *pecunia*, which is derived from *pecus*, the Latin word for cow or cattle. Perfumes and ointments also had great value. Besides gold, the MAGI brought frankincense and myrrh to worship the newborn King.

II. The shekel. The first metal exchange was crude, often shapeless, and heavy so as to approximate the value of the item purchased in actual weight. The buyer usually weighed his "money" to the seller. The Jewish shekel was such a weight (the Heb. term *šeqel H9203* is derived from the verb *šāqal H9202*, which means "to weigh"). It was based on the Babylonian weight of exchange, generally of gold, silver, bronze, and even iron. Among the Jews

Replica of stone carving on a funerary stela (Hungary, late 2nd cent. A.D.), depicting a money changer and his servant counting daily income.

the shekel was used for the temple tax, the poll tax, and redemption from the priesthood (Exod. 30:11-16; 13:13; Num. 3:44-51). A piece believed to be from the days of the MACCABEES (2nd cent. B.C.), has on the obverse (front) a pot of manna (Exod. 16:33) with the inscription, "Shekel Israel." On the reverse is Aaron's budding rod (Num. 17:8) with the legend in Hebrew letters, "Jerusalem the Holy." In NT times the value of a shekel was approximately a day's wage for a laborer. It required 3,000 shekels to equal one talent of silver, which reveals that the 10,000 talents the unmerciful servant owed his master (Matt. 18:23-25) was an unpayable debt. The mina (Lk. 19:13; KJV, "pound") was equivalent to fifty shekels, and sixty minas equaled one talent.

III. Beginning of the coin system. Most historians believe that the earliest money pieces were struck about 700 B.C. in the small kingdom of LYDIA in ASIA MINOR. These early Lydian "coins" were simply crude pieces of metal cut into small lumps of a standard weight and stamped with official marks to guarantee the value. The Egyptians also developed such a system. Later the quality of the metal and the image on the coin indicated the worth in buying power, much like today. It is believed that the Jews first became acquainted with the coinage of the Babylonians and Persians during the captivity and that they carried these coins with them when they returned to Palestine. Except for a few brief periods of independence, they were compelled to use the coinage of their pagan conquerors.

IV. The drachma. After 330 B.C. the world-conquering Greeks developed the Persian and Babylonian coinage, and their own, into something of a fixed world system. Animals, natural objects,

© Dr. James C. Martin. The British Museum. Photographed by permission.

Silver shekels minted during the first Jewish revolt against Rome (A.D. 66-70).

and the Greek gods were used as symbols on the coins. Each coin was made individually with hammer, punch, and die. The Greeks called these coins *drachmas*, of which there was a variety with about the same value. Later the terms *drachma* and *shekel* were used more or less interchangeably. The "lost coin" (Lk. 15:8) was a silver drachma equivalent to a Roman *denarius*, a day's wages. The temple or half-shekel tax (Matt. 17:24) was a *didrachma*. Another drachma was the *tridrachma* of CORINTH, a silver coin about the size of our quarter with the head of Athena on one side and the winged horse Pegasus on the other. No doubt PAUL earned it making tents and used it for payment of passage on ships during his journeys. A Greek coin Paul also may have "spent" is the now-famous "bee coin," a silver *tetradrachma* of EPHESUS dating back to 350 B.C. All these drachmas were about equal in value to the Jewish shekel.

V. The stater. The coin PETER found in the fish's mouth was the Greek *stater* (Matt. 17:27). Since the temple tax was a half-shekel, the stater would pay for two. Many authorities believe that the stater really was the tetradrachma of ANTIOCH or TYRE since these coins were accepted at the temple. It is believed that the thirty pieces of silver (Matt. 26:15; 27:3-5) that bought the greatest betrayal in history were these large silver coins, tetradrachmas of either Tyre or Antioch from about 125 B.C. In Exod. 21:32 we read that thirty shekels was the price of a slave.

VI. The assarion. The Greek *assarion* is mentioned twice in the NT (Matt. 10:29; Lk. 12:6). In the Roman empire this Greek coin was small in both size and value, and translators usually render the term with "penny" (KJV, "farthing") as a similar small coin with which English-speaking people would be familiar.

VII. Lepton and kodrantes (widow's mite). During pre-Roman times under the Maccabees, the Jews for the first time were allowed to issue money of their own. One such piece, as we have seen, was the shekel. Another piece was the *lepton*, a tiny bronze or copper coin, which we know as the "widow's mite," from the famous incident in Mk. 12:42 and Lk. 21:2 (NIV, "two very small copper coins"). The KJV uses the rendering "mites" because it was the coin of least value, as is clearly implied in Lk. 12:59 (here the NIV has "penny"). Even the metal was inferior and deteriorated easily. The coins, in contrast to those of pagan rulers, had pictures from their religious history and agriculture instead of gods and men, obeying the command, "You shall not make for yourself an idol in the form of anything" (Exod. 20:4). Mark specifies that two *lepta* were worth the same as one *kodrantes* (Mk. 12:42 [KJV, "farthing"]; cf. also Matt. 5:26).

VIII. The denarius. The most interesting coin of the Bible is the Roman *denarius*, known by collectors as the "penny" of the Bible because of this misleading translation in the KJV. Made of silver and resembling our modern dime in size, the denarius was the most common Roman coin during the days of Jesus and the apostles. Collectors have been able to obtain originals of all twelve Roman emperors (Augustus to Nerva) who reigned during the NT period. There were also gold denarii, but these were generally special issues and not nearly so numerous. The Romans as well as the Greeks struck mainly silver coins (alloys) and kept large government-owned silver mines throughout the empire (e.g., at Antioch and Ephesus).

The true value of the denarius may be seen in our Lord's parable of the laborers in the vineyard: "He agreed to pay them a denarius for the day and sent them into his vineyard" (Matt. 20:2, 10). This was the normal rate, the equivalent of what a Roman soldier also received (cf. Rev. 6:6, where the NIV translates, "a day's wages"). When the Samaritan (Lk. 10:35) gave the innkeeper two days' wages and was willing to pay anything more above that amount to aid an unknown stranger, he showed how great his love for his neighbor was. The denarius is mentioned also in the miracle of feeding the 5,000 when PHILIP declared that it would take 200 denarii to give everyone in the crowd even a small amount (Jn. 6:7; NIV, "Eight months' wages would not buy enough bread for each one to have a bite!"). Similar light is thrown on the generous act of MARY, who anointed Jesus with perfume that, according to Judas, could have been sold for 300 denarii (12:5; NIV, "It was worth a year's wages"). See also the reference in Rev. 6:6.

The denarius was also the "tribute money" imposed by the Romans on the Jewish people.

The "image" on the denarius handed our Lord in Matt. 22:19 was the head of either Caesar AUGUSTUS (43 B.C. to A.D. 14) or, more likely, that of TIBERIUS Caesar (A.D. 14–39). On it Caesar's name was spelled out entirely to the right of the head, as in the case of a coin that has survived: CAESARAVGVSTVS. To the left of the head are the following Latin abbreviations, all run together: DIVIMPPATERPATRIAE. The abbreviation DIV means "divine," IMP is "imperator," PATER PATRIAE is Latin for "father of his country." On the reverse one sees the figures of two Caesars, and above and around the figures this inscription: AVGVSPONCOSTRPGER. The abbreviation AVGVS is "Augustus"; PON is "pontifex maximus" (religious ruler or "highest priest"); COS is "consulship"; TRP is "tribuncia potestate," tribune power, civil head of the state. Below the images is the word CAESARES, Latin for "Caesars." From this coin alone one can discern that the Roman emperor was an absolute monarch, head of both state and religion.

To study and handle these coins, some over 2,000 years old, makes one feel close to the people who lived in Bible days, and helps us understand the times in which they lived. A study of the denarius reveals that this coin was not only a medium of exchange, but also a disseminator of information and propaganda for the emperor. This was an age without newspapers! The Roman emperors believed the people read the legends on the coins and went to much trouble to change them often, sometimes every year. The coins also yield much historical data, such as the dates of the emperors, and help to establish the historical setting of the Bible.

The value of coins fluctuated much in ancient times, making it difficult to state the exact value of each coin. The government issued money through moneychangers, and often the rate of exchange varied according to what a changer was willing to give on a certain day. The denarius became much less valuable after the second century of our era. To give the value of Bible coins in modern terms can be misleading. Many modern translators simply transliterate the Greek and Latin names (denarius, shekel, assarion, etc.), and allow Bible readers to interpret for themselves the value of the coins.

M

M

moneychanger. See CHANGERS OF MONEY.

monkey. See ANIMALS (under *ape* and *baboon*).

monotheism. The doctrine or belief that there is but one God. Atheism is the belief that there is no god; polytheism, that there is more than one god; monolatry, the worship of one god as supreme, without denying there are other gods; henotheism, belief in one god, though not to the exclusion of belief in others; pantheism, belief in a god that is identified with nature. There are three great monotheistic religions: Judaism, Christianity, and Islam, the latter two having their origin in the first. According to the Bible, humans were originally monotheistic. This has been denied by the school of comparative religion, which teaches that monotheism was a late development in human religious experience. It holds that the religion of ISRAEL was not originally monotheistic but that it gradually became so through the influence of the prophets. Others have shown, on the contrary, that polytheism was a late development. The Christian doctrine of the TRINITY does not conflict with the monotheism of the OT. Rather, the manifold revelation of God contained in the OT is crystallized in the NT into the supreme doctrine of the Three Persons. See also JEHOVAH.

monsters. See ANIMALS (under *dragon*).

month. See CALENDAR.

monument. A MEMORIAL stone. Kings in the ANE often set up stelae with inscriptions boasting of their accomplishments. SAUL set up a memorial after his victory over the AMALEKITES (1 Sam. 15:12), and ABSALOM set up a PILLAR, which he called "Absalom's Monument," as a memorial for himself (2 Sam. 18:18). Stelae, some of them memorials, have been found in Canaanite sanctuaries, including one at HAZOR on which two arms with upraised hands are carved. A hand is carved also on many Carthaginian funerary stelae.

moon. See ASTRONOMY.

moon, new. See CALENDAR; FEASTS.

Morasthite. moh´ruhs-thit (Heb. *môraštî H4629*, gentilic of *môrešet*). A descriptive title applied to MICAH the prophet, according to the KJV and some other versions (Jer. 26:18; Mic. 1:1; the NIV and NRSV render "of Moresheth"). See MORESHETH GATH.

Mordecai. mor´duh-ki (Heb. *mordŏkay H5283*, apparently based on the Babylonian name MARDUK). **(1)** An Israelite mentioned among leading individuals who returned from BABYLON with ZERUBBABEL (Ezra 2:2; Neh. 7:7).

(2) Son of Jair and descendant of BENJAMIN who lived in SUSA during the rule of the Persians (Esth. 2:5); his great-grandfather Kish was among those who had been deported from JERUSALEM to BABYLON by NEBUCHADNEZZAR (v. 6). Mordecai brought up his cousin ESTHER, whose parents had died (2:7). When Esther was taken into the royal harem, Mordecai forbade her to reveal her nationality (2:20); yet he remained in close connection with her. Mordecai discovered at the palace gate a plot against the king. By informing Esther of the plot, he secured the execution of the two eunuchs responsible (2:19-23). When HAMAN was made chief minister, Mordecai aroused his wrath by refusing to bow before him. To avenge the slight, Haman procured from the king a decree to destroy the Jews (ch. 3). Mordecai then sent Esther to the king to seek protection for her people (ch. 4). Haman meanwhile prepared a high gallows on which he planned to hang Mordecai (ch. 5). By a singular, highly dramatic series of events, Haman fell from favor and was hanged on the gallows he had prepared for Mordecai (ch. 7). Mordecai succeeded him as chief minister of the king (ch. 8). Thus the Persian officials everywhere assisted the Jews, who killed their enemies and instituted the feast of Purim to celebrate their deliverance (ch. 9). The book of Esther ends with an account of the fame and dignity of Mordecai (ch. 10). In the apocryphal additions to Esther, Mordecai is glorified still more. He is a favorite character in the rabbinical literature also.

Moreh. mor´eh (Heb. *môreh H4622*, "teacher"). **(1)** A place near SHECHEM. When Abram (ABRAHAM) first entered CANAAN, he "traveled through

The hill of Moreh. (View to the N from Mt. Tabor.)

the land as far as the site of the great tree of Moreh at Shechem" (Gen. 12:6; NRSV, "the oak of Moreh"; KJV incorrectly, "the plain of Moreh"). There God revealed himself to Abraham with the promise to give Canaan to his descendants, whereupon Abraham responded by building his first altar to the Lord in Canaan. The phrase "the great tree of Moreh" may also be translated "the teacher's [*or* diviner's] tree" (prob. different from the DIVINERS' OAK, or "soothsayers' tree," of Jdg. 9:37). It must have been a "holy" tree, and the place an old Canaanite sanctuary. Although it is difficult to understand Abraham's motives for visiting this place, there is no reason to suggest that he recognized the sacred character of the place and willfully adapted himself to it. The reference merely serves to indicate the place where Abraham camped and built his own altar. Elsewhere, the expression "the great trees of Moreh" serves to indicate the general location of Mounts EBAL and GERIZIM (Deut. 11:30). Some have thought that there is a connection with "the oak at Shechem" (Gen. 35:4; cf. Jdg. 9:6).

(2) The "hill of Moreh" was a place near which the Midianites were camping when they were attacked by GIDEON (Jdg. 7:1). This hill was at the E end of the Valley of JEZREEL (6:33) and is generally identified with Jebel Nabi Dahi, about 8 mi. (13 km.) NNW of Mount GILBOA, and just S of NAIN.

Moresheth. See MORESHETH GATH.

Moresheth Gath. mor´uh-sheth-gath´ (Heb. *môrešet gat H4628*, "possession of Gath"). One of several towns in the SHEPHELAH of JUDAH that were going to be conquered (Mic. 1:14). The passage is full of wordplays, and some believe that this name alludes to a Hebrew word meaning "betroth"; if so, the figure is that of Judah having to part with one of its towns and giving a dowry besides. It is generally thought that the prophet MICAH's gentilic, "the Morasthite" (KJV in 1:1 and Jer. 26:28, where the NIV and other versions say "of Moresheth"), refers to Moresheth Gath. The addition "Gath" is to define more precisely Moresheth's situation as in the vicinity of, or as belonging to, GATH. Some scholars have thought that it is the same as the better known city of MARESHAH (Mic. 1:15; Josh. 15:44; et al.), but most believe it was a distinct village and tentatively identify it with the modern Tell el-Judeideh, about 7 mi. (11 km.) SE of Gath.

Moriah. muh-ri´uh (Heb. *môriyyâ H5317*, derivation uncertain; by popular etymology, "the place where Yahweh provides [*or* appears]," Gen. 22:14). (1) The region to which God instructed ABRAHAM to go so that he might offer up ISAAC on one of its mountains (22:2). The district may have received its name from the incident in which Yahweh *provided* a sacrifice and *appeared* to Abraham (22:8, 14). The SAMARITANS connected Moriah with MOREH (in the vicinity of SHECHEM) so as to identify it with GERIZIM. The precise location of the mountain is not given in Genesis beyond the statement that it was a three days' journey from BEERSHEBA (22:4).

(2) The rocky hilltop of JERUSALEM N of the City of David (see ZION) where Yahweh appeared to DAVID when he presented offerings on the threshing floor of ARAUNAH the Jebusite (2 Chr. 3:1). Some argue that the author of Chronicles is indirectly identifying this hill with the place where Abraham offered Isaac. Such an identification was widely accepted in ancient times. The Muslim mosque known as the Dome of the Rock presently sits on the site. Many modern scholars, however, regard this identification as unlikely or even impossible, and explain the connection between the two passages in other ways.

morning sacrifice. See SACRIFICE AND OFFERINGS.

morning star. This term is applied to Venus (occasionally to other bright planets) because it is often visible in the eastern sky before sunrise, heralding the appearance of the sun. The expression is used by the NIV to render Hebrew *hêlēl H2122* ("shining one"), which occurs only once, in an oracle against the king of BABYLON (Isa. 14:12; NRSV, "Day Star"). See LUCIFER; SHAHAR. In the NT the phrase once renders Greek *phōsphoros G5892* (lit., "light-bringer," but a common term for Venus in Greek literature), which PETER uses as a symbol of Christ's second coming (2 Pet. 1:19; KJV, "day star"). It also appears twice in Revelation as a literal rendering of the corresponding Greek phrase (Rev. 2:28; 22:16); in the second of these the reference to Jesus is explicit. All three NT passages seem to allude to the prophecy of BALAAM, "A star will come out of Jacob" (Num. 24:17).

morsel. This term is used a number of times in the KJV in the OT, especially in the expression "a morsel of bread" (e.g., Gen. 18:5, where the NIV has "something to eat"), and once in the NT (Heb. 12:16, where the Greek really means "one meal," not "one piece of food"). The NIV uses the word only twice in the expression "choice morsels" (Prov. 18:8; 26:22; NRSV, "delicious morsels," but KJV wrongly, "wounds").

mortal. As an adjective ("subject to death"), this English term is used by the KJV once in the OT (Job 4:17) and several times in the NT (Rom. 6:12 et al.). See DEATH. As a noun meaning "human being," the term *mortal* does not occur in the KJV, but is so used a number of times in the NIV, especially in Job (Job 4:17; 9:2; 10:4-5), and very frequently in other modern versions, including the TNIV.

mortal sin. This precise expression is not found in the Bible, though it is clear that SIN in itself, and therefore every manifestation of a depraved nature, issues unto DEATH (Rom. 6:23 et al.). In Roman Catholic theology, however, mortal sin is contrasted with "venial" sin, which is seen as less aggravated and therefore much less damaging to the soul than mortal sin. This distinction is not explicitly asserted in Scripture. In 1 Jn. 5:16-17, the apostle distinguishes between "sin unto death" and "sin not unto death" (the NIV renders, "sin that leads to death"). Inasmuch as he directs that no prayer should be offered for the former, this passage has been quite naturally related to Matt. 12:31-32 (and parallels); Heb. 6:4-6; 10:26-31 (sometimes also 2 Pet. 2:20-22). It is not certain that all of these passages refer to the same kind of transgression; but if this be so, the sin in view would appear to be the hardening of the heart against the offer of the divine light in its most unmistakable form.

mortar. This English term has two distinct meanings, both of which occur in the Bible. In the sense of "a utensil for pounding material," especially for the purpose of crushing grain, it renders two different Hebrew words (Num. 11:8; Prov. 27:22). The second sense is "a substance used for uniting brick or stone in construction." According to Gen. 11:3, the builders of the Tower of BABEL used "tar" in place of "mortar." The use of BITUMEN (or asphalt) for mortar is attested in Babylonia by archaeological evidence; and its occurrence in the Valley of SIDDIM (14:10 NRSV) beside the JORDAN, near the DEAD SEA, renders its use in Palestine possible.

mortgage. This English term occurs just once in the Bible, in the context of a time of drought and want (Neh. 5:3). Although a specific reference to mortgaging real estate occurs nowhere else, there can be no question that mortgaging was a much-practiced mode of securing loans from the time of the Hebrew conquest and onward. According to the Pentateuch, one of the duties of the kinsman-redeemer was to purchase the mortgaged property of his indigent relative. This was one of the services performed by Boaz for Naomi, his dead kinsman's widow (in addition to his levirate marriage with Ruth). See also borrow.

mosaic. This English term refers to a surface ornamentation of designs or pictures, and sometimes inscriptions, made by inlaying in patterns small pieces of colored stone, glass, shell, or other material. (The word derives from Medieval Latin *mūsāicum*, "of the Muses"; it is therefore to be distinguished from *Mosaic* as an adjective derived from the name Moses.) Although no Hebrew term in the OT specifically means "mosaic," in Esth. 1:6 a pavement in the palace at Susa is described as made of porphyry, marble, mother-of-pearl, and precious stones (the NIV and other versions regard this as a "mosaic pavement"). Mosaics were very ancient in Mesopotamia; they are one of the most durable parts of ancient structures and often are the only surviving part. Mosaics have survived from ancient Sumer from as early as 2900 B.C. They were widely used in the early Christian and Byzantine buildings in Palestine, and remaining examples throw considerable light on ancient biblical customs and afford insight into early Christian beliefs and symbols. Very famous is the fine mosaic picture-map of Jerusalem from the floor of a church in Medeba, probably from the sixth century A.D. This is one of the earliest maps known from Palestine. The mosaics from the Arab palace at Khirbet al-Mafjar (near Jericho) are among the most beautiful known.

Moserah, Moseroth. moh-see´ruh, -ruhth (Heb. *môsērāh H4594*, "bond," also in the pl. form *môsērôt H5035*). A place where the Israelites encamped on their journey from Egypt to Canaan (Num. 33:30-31), and where Aaron was said to have died

(Deut. 10:6). The site is unknown, but it must have been near Mount Hor, by the border of Edom. Some scholars regard the latter passage as a variant tradition, because elsewhere Aaron is said to have died at Mount Hor itself (Num. 33:38; cf. 20:22). One possible solution is to relate the two passages to different journeys.

Moses. moh´zis (Heb. *mōšeh H5407*, derivation uncertain, but by popular etymology, "drawn out [of the water]"; Gk. *Mōysēs G3707*). The national hero who delivered the Israelites from Egyptian slavery, established them as an independent nation, and prepared them for entrance into Canaan. Exact dates for the life of Moses are dependent on the date of the Exodus: he may have been born as early as 1520 B.C. or as late as 1225 B.C. According to Exod. 2:10, Moses received his name from Pharaoh's daughter, who said, "I drew him out of the water" (the Heb. verb for "draw out" here is *māšâ H5406*). It is often thought, however, that the name is Egyptian, derived from the root *mśy*, "to bear," a common component in theophoric names (e.g., Thutmose or Thutmosis, "[the god] Thoth is born"). Alternatively, if Moses was originally a Hebrew name, perhaps it was Pharaoh's daughter who assimilated it to the Egyptian form. In any case, while the name occurs more than 750 times in the OT, no further explanation is given; and like the names of some other prominent OT characters, it is given to only one person, the great leader and lawgiver of Israel.

Moses was born of Israelite parents in the land of Egypt (Exod. 2:1-10). Perilous times prevailed. Not only were the Israelites enslaved, but a royal edict designed to keep them in subjection ordered the execution of all Israelite male children at birth. Hidden among the reeds near the river's bank, Moses was discovered by Pharaoh's daughter. So favorably was she disposed toward this Hebrew babe that she requested Moses' mother to nurse him until he was old enough to be taken to the royal court, where he spent the first forty years of his life.

Little is narrated in the book of Exodus regarding the early period of the life of Moses. Stephen in his address to the Sanhedrin (Acts 7:22) asserts that Moses was not only instructed in the

M

© Dr. James C. Martin. The Cairo Museum.
Photographed by permission.

Basket coffin (Egypt, 1st-3rd dynasties). Moses' mother may have placed her son in a basket coffin like this one.

science and learning of the Egyptians but also was endowed with oratorical ability and distinctive leadership qualities. The court of Egypt provided educational facilities for royal heirs of tributary princes from city-states of the Syro-Palestinian territory subject to the Egyptian rulers. Consequently Moses may have had classmates from as far N as the EUPHRATES River in his educational experiences in the Egyptian court.

Moses' first valiant attempt to aid his own people ended in failure. While trying to pacify two fellow Israelites, he was reminded that he had killed an Egyptian (Exod. 2:11-25). Fearing the vengeful hand of Pharaoh, Moses escaped to MIDIAN, where he spent a forty-year period in seclusion. In this land Moses found favor in the home of a priest named JETHRO (also known as REUEL). In the course of time he married Jethro's daughter ZIPPORAH. As shepherd of his father-in-law's flocks Moses gained firsthand geographical knowledge of the territory surrounding the Gulf of AQABAH. Little did he realize that through this area he would one day lead the great nation of Israel!

The call of Moses was indeed significant. Confronted with a BURNING BUSH, he was given a revelation from God, who commissioned him to deliver his people Israel from Egyptian bondage (Exod. 3). Fully acquainted with Pharaoh's power, Moses was assured of divine support in contesting the authority of the ruler of Egypt. He furthermore anticipated the lack of confidence and the reluctance of the Israelites to accept him as a leader. To counter this, God assured him that the great "I AM" was about to fulfill his promise made to the PATRIARCHS to redeem Israel from bondage and settle them in the land of Canaan (Gen. 15:12-21). In addition two miraculous signs were provided as evidence for the verification of divine authority: Moses' staff changed to a serpent and his hand became leprous and later was healed (Exod. 4:1-17). Finally, Moses was assured of Aaron's support in his divine commission to deliver the Israelites from the powerful clutch of Pharaoh. Accompanied by his wife Zipporah and their two sons, Moses returned to the land of Egypt.

In a series of ten plagues Moses and Aaron countered Pharaoh's attempt to retain Israel in bondage (Exod. 7-11). See PLAGUES OF EGYPT. As a whole these plagues were directed against the gods of Egypt, demonstrating God's power to the Egyptians as well as to the Israelites. Pharaoh immediately expressed his attitude of resistance, retorting, "Who is the LORD, that I should obey him and let Israel go? I do not know the LORD, and I will not let Israel go" (5:2). As Pharaoh continued to resist, his heart hardened. Finally the last plague brought judgment on all the gods of Egypt, as the FIRSTBORN sons were killed throughout the land. Then Pharaoh complied with Moses' demand and allowed the Israelites to leave.

On the eve of Israel's dramatic departure the Passover feast was initially observed (Exod. 12). Each family unit that followed the simple instructions—killing a year-old male lamb or goat and applying the blood to the doorposts and lintel of their home—was passed by in the execution of divine judgment. The directions given (12:3-4) for the choice of the Passover lamb stressed the equivalence that was to be made between the lambs and the people who would find shelter beneath the shed blood. This accords with the word spoken to Moses even before he entered Egypt: "Israel is my firstborn son" (4:22). Passover night saw the climax of the context of the firstborn sons. All the firstborn of Egypt died (12:29), but the Lord's firstborn was redeemed by the blood of the lamb. In a special sense it was the actual firstborn of every Israelite household that was spared this dreadful but still only token divine judgment. Therefore, the firstborn son of every Israelite family belonged to God. Immediately after the partaking of this Passover

M

meal consisting of meat, unleavened bread, and bitter herbs, the Israelites left Egypt. The annual observance of the Passover on the fourteenth day of ABIB (later known as Nisan) was to remind each Israelite of the miraculous deliverance under Moses.

The exact route by which Moses led the Israelites, who numbered some 600,000 men, plus women and children, is difficult to ascertain. Succoth, Etham, Pi Hahiroth, Migdol, and Baal Zephon are place-names with imprecise meanings and whose geographical identifications are uncertain. When the Israelites reached the RED SEA (Sea of Reeds) they were threatened by the Egyptian armies from the rear (Exod. 14). As they appealed to Moses, divine protection was provided in the pillar of cloud that barred the Egyptians from overtaking them. In due time a strong east wind parted the waters for Israel's passage. When the Egyptian forces attempted to follow they were engulfed in a watery grave. MIRIAM, Moses' sister, led the Israelites in a song of victory (15:1-21).

Under divine direction Moses led Israel southward through the Desert of SHUR (Exod. 15:22-27). At MARAH bitter waters were sweetened, at ELIM the Israelites were refreshed by twelve springs of water and seventy palm trees, and in the Desert of SIN daily MANNA was supplied, solving the food problem for this great multitude throughout their years of desert wanderings until they reached the land of Canaan (ch. 16). At REPHIDIM Moses was commanded to strike the rock, which brought forth a gushing water supply for his people (17:1-7). Confronted by an AMALEKITE attack, Moses prevailed in intercessory prayer with the support of AARON and HUR, while JOSHUA led the armies of Israel in a victorious battle (17:8-16). In his administrative duties Moses appointed seventy elders to serve under him in accordance with Jethro's advice. In less than a three months' journey from Egypt the Israelites settled in the environs of Mount SINAI (Horeb), where they remained for approximately one year (chs. 18-19).

In this wilderness encampment Moses became the great lawgiver through whom Israel's religion was revealed. As a representative for his people Moses received the LAW from God. This law constituted God's COVENANT with his newly delivered nation. In turn the congregation ratified this covenant (Exod. 20-24), which included the Ten Commandments, also known as the Decalogue (see COMMANDMENTS, TEN). To enable the Israelites to WORSHIP their God properly Moses was given detailed instructions for the building and erection of the TABERNACLE. These plans were carefully executed under Moses' supervision. At the same time the Aaronic family, supported by the LEVITES, was designated for their priestly service and carefully equipped for their ministration (chs. 25-40). Details concerning various sacrifices, laws for holy living, and the observance of feasts and seasons were set forth through Moses as God's prescription for his people Israel (Lev. 1-27). In this manner the Israelites were distinctively set apart from the religious and cultural pattern of Egypt and Canaan.

Moses also supervised the military census and organization of the Israelites during this encampment in the Sinaitic peninsula. The tabernacle with its court occupied the central position. The Levites were placed immediately around the court, with Moses and the Aaronic family located at the E end before the entrance to the tabernacle. The other tribes were divided into four camps—each camp composed of three tribes—with the camp of Judah taking the place of leadership ahead of the priestly family.

Guidance and protection were provided for Moses and his people throughout this wilderness journey in the PILLAR OF CLOUD AND FIRE that was visible day and night. Representing the presence of God with his people, this cloud first made its appearance in preventing the Egyptians from overtaking them (Exod. 13:21-22; 14:19-20). During Israel's encampment the cloud hovered over the tabernacle. Efficient human organization and responsible leadership provided the counterpart to the divine guidance conveyed by the cloud. Silver trumpets were used to assemble the leaders as well as to alert the people whenever divine indication was given en route. An efficient organization was in evidence whether Israel was encamped or journeying. Law and order prevailed throughout (Num. 1:1—10:10).

In an eleven-day march northward from the Sinaitic peninsula to KADESH BARNEA, which was only about 50 mi. (80 km.) SW of BEERSHEBA, Moses not only encountered the murmurings of

M

the multitude but was also severely criticized by Miriam and Aaron (Num. 11-12). The grumbling crowds who hungered for the meat they had eaten in Egypt were satiated to the point of sickness when quails were supplied in excessive abundance. Aaron and Miriam were likewise humiliated when the latter was temporarily subjected to leprosy. While at Kadesh, Moses sent out twelve representatives to spy out the land of Canaan (chs. 13-14). The majority report, given by ten spies, influenced the Israelites to demonstrate their unbelief. In open rebellion they threatened to stone JOSHUA and CALEB, the two spies who exercised faith and recommended that they should conquer and occupy the land promised to them. When God proposed to destroy the rebellious and unbelieving Israelites, Moses magnanimously responded with intercession in behalf of his people. The final verdict involved all of the people who had been twenty years of age and older at the time of the exodus: they were doomed to die in the wilderness. Joshua and Caleb were the only exceptions.

Relatively little is recorded about Moses' leadership during the thirty-eight years of wilderness wandering (Num. 15-20). Not only was the political leadership of Moses challenged by DATHAN and ABIRAM, but also Korah and his supporters contested the position of Aaron and his family. In the course of these rebellions 14,000 people perished in divine judgment. Furthermore all Israel was given a miraculous sign when, among the twelve staffs representing the tribes of Israel, Levi's produced buds, blossoms, and almonds. With Aaron's name inscribed on this staff, the Aaronic priesthood was securely established.

The Israelites, denied permission to use the highway through the land of EDOM, were led from Kadesh to the Plains of MOAB by way of the Gulf of Aqabah. En route Moses himself forfeited entrance into the Promised Land when he struck the rock that he should have commanded to supply water for his people (Exod. 20). When a scourge of serpents caused many murmuring Israelites to die, Moses erected a bronze snake, which offered healing to all who turned to it in obedience (21:4-9). This incident was used by Jesus in explaining his own death on the cross and the simple principle of salvation involved (Jn. 3:14-16).

When Moses bypassed Moab and led the Israelites into the ARNON Valley, he was confronted by two rulers—SIHON, king of the AMORITES, and OG, king of BASHAN. Israel defeated both kings and as a result claimed the territory E of the JORDAN River, which was later allotted to REUBEN, GAD, and half of the tribe of MANASSEH. With this Amorite threat removed, the Israelites settled temporarily in the Plains of Moab, N of the Arnon River (Exod. 21:10-35).

BALAK king of Moab was so disturbed about Israel's encampment near his people that he chose a subtle way to bring about the ruin of God's covenant nation (Num. 22-25). He enticed BALAAM, a prophet from MESOPOTAMIA, with rewards of riches and honor, to curse Israel. Balaam accepted Balak's invitation. While en route he was vividly reminded by his donkey that he was limited in his oracles to speak only God's message. Although the Moabite leaders prepared offerings to provide

Aerial view of the Wilderness of Sinai. It was in desert terrain like this that the Israelites murmured against God and Moses.

© Dr. James C. Martin

an atmosphere for cursing, Balaam was restricted to pronounce blessings for Israel each time he spoke. God did not allow his chosen people to be cursed. When Balaam was dismissed, his parting advice to the Moabites and Midianites was to seduce the Israelites into immorality and idolatry. Incurring divine wrath by accepting invitations to these heathen festivities, thousands of Israelites died in a plague and many guilty leaders were executed. Moses led his people in a punitive war against the Midianites. In this battle Balaam was killed (31:16).

Moses once more ordered a military census. This was supervised by ELEAZER, Aaron's son, who had served as high priest since his father's death. The total count of Israel's military manpower was actually somewhat lower than it had been when they left Egypt (Num. 26). Joshua was appointed and consecrated as the successor to Moses. Inheritance problems and additional instructions for regular offerings, festivals, and vows were carefully delineated (chs. 27-30). Reluctantly Moses granted permission to the Reubenites, Gadites, and some of the Manasseh tribe to settle E of the Jordan, exacting from them the promise to aid the rest of the nation in the conquest of the land beyond the river (ch. 32).

Anticipating Israel's successful occupation of the land of Canaan, Moses admonished them to destroy the idolatrous inhabitants. He appointed twelve tribal leaders to divide the land among the tribes and instructed them to provide forty-eight cities throughout Canaan for the Levites with adequate pasture area adjoining each city. Six of these LEVITICAL CITIES were to be designed as cities of refuge where people might flee for safety in case of accidental bloodshed (Num. 34-35). Moses also provided solutions to inheritance problems when daughters inherited the family possessions (ch. 36).

The magnitude of Moses' character is clearly set forth in his farewell speeches to his beloved people. Even though he himself was denied participation in the conquest and occupation of the land, he coveted the best for the Israelites as they entered Canaan. His admonition to them is summed up in his addresses as given in the book of DEUTERONOMY. He reviewed the journey, beginning from Mount Horeb, where God had made a covenant with Israel. He pointed out especially the places where the Israelites had murmured, reminding them of their disobedience. Because of this attitude the generation that Moses had led out of Egypt had been denied entrance into the land that God had promised them for a possession. With that as the background Moses warned them to be obedient. For their encouragement he pointed to the recent victories God had given them over the Amorites. This experience provided a reasonable basis for the hope of victory under the leadership of Joshua as they actually entered the land of Canaan (Deut. 1:1—4:43).

In his second speech (Deut. 4:44—28:68) Moses emphasized that love as well as obedience is essential for a wholesome relationship with God. The Decalogue at Mount Sinai was repeated. Wholehearted love for God in daily life represented the basis for maintaining this covenant relationship in such a way that they could enjoy God's blessing. Consequently each generation was responsible for teaching the fear of the Lord their God to the next generation by precept and obedience. In this pattern of living they would be God's holy people in practice. Faithfully Moses delineated many of the laws already given, admonishing the people to be true to God, warning them against IDOLATRY, advising them in the administration of justice, and adding various civil and religious regulations. He concluded this speech with a list of curses and blessings that were to be read publicly to the entire congregation after they crossed the Jordan. In this manner he set before the Israelites the way of life and death. Moses provided a written record of the law as a guide for Israel.

At the close of Moses' career, Joshua, who had already been designated as Israel's leader, was ordained as successor to Moses. In a song (Deut. 32) Moses expressed his praise to God, recounting how God had delivered Israel and provided for them through the wilderness journey. Then, with the pronouncement of the blessing on each tribe, Moses departed for Mount Nebo (see NEBO, MOUNT), where he was privileged to view the Promised Land before he died.

Moses, Assumption of. See APOCALYPTIC LITERATURE.

M

Moses' seat. See SEAT, MOSES'.

Most High. See EL ELYON.

Most Holy Place. See TABERNACLE.

Mot. The god of death in the Canaanite pantheon (cf. Heb. *māwet H4638*, construct form *môt*). He is regarded as the son (or the beloved) of EL and as the adversary of BAAL. Some biblical passages personify DEATH (e.g., Job 18:13; Hab. 2:5), but it is not certain whether these allude to the Canaanite deity.

mote. This English term, meaning "small particle," is used by the KJV to render Greek *karphos G2847* ("chip [of wood], piece [of straw], bit [of wool]" etc.), which occurs only in two passages in the metaphorical sense of a minor fault (Matt. 7:3-5; Lk. 6:41-42; modern versions typically use the term "speck").

moth. See ANIMALS.

mother. See FAMILY; MARRIAGE.

mount, mountain. These terms, along with *hill*, are roughly synonymous in the English Bible. Much of PALESTINE is hilly or mountainous. These elevations are not dramatically high but are old worn-down hills. A central hill country stretches N–S in Palestine, attaining its greatest elevations in GALILEE (nearly 4,000 ft./1,220 m. above sea level) and finally ending in the NEGEV. Much of TRANSJORDAN is high plateau land, although in SYRIA, N of Palestine, this section reaches a great height in Mount HERMON (c. 9,000 ft./2,740 m. above sea level), which is snow-covered throughout the year. Many ancient peoples considered mountains holy places. Mount SINAI (Deut. 33:2; Jdg. 5:4-5) and Mount ZION (Ps. 68:16) were specially honored by the Hebrews as the places of God's revelation and abode. Mountains in Scripture are symbolic of eternity (Gen. 49:26) and of strength and stability, but God is infinitely strong and stable (Ps. 97:5; 121:1-2 RSV; Isa. 40:12). They also portray the difficult obstacles of life, but God will overcome these mountains for his people (Isa. 49:11; Matt. 21:21).

Mount, Sermon on the. See SERMON ON THE MOUNT.

mountain goat, mountain sheep. See ANIMALS (under *ibex* and *sheep*).

Mount Hermon. See HERMON. Similarly for other mountains that have proper names.

mount of assembly. See CONGREGATION, MOUNT OF THE.

Mount of Beatitudes. A slope on the NW shore of the Sea of Galilee where Jesus delivered the SERMON ON THE MOUNT, part of which consisted of the BEATITUDES (Matt. 5:3-12; Lk. 6:20-23). Apart from Matthew's statements that Jesus was on a mountain (Matt. 5:1; 8:1) and Luke's account that the sermon was on a level place (Lk. 6:17), the only other help in locating the site is the record that Jesus went from there directly to CAPERNAUM. The older suggested location was the Horns of Hattin (Qarn Ḥaṭṭin), 7 mi. (11 km.) W of TIBERIAS.

Church on Mount of Beatitudes.

Now the more popular site is the slope up from the Sea of Galilee SW of Capernaum. There is a Catholic church in this place.

Mount of Olives. See OLIVES, MOUNT OF.

mount of the congregation. See CONGREGATION, MOUNT OF THE.

mourning. The ancient Hebrews placed a much greater emphasis on external symbolic acts than do modern Western people; people in the East today still carry on this respect for symbolic actions. Ceremonies for expressing grief at the death of a relative or on any unhappy occasion are referred to frequently in the Bible. One reared in the modern West must be careful not to view these public expressions as hypocritical; they were a natural valid manifestation of grief in that culture.

When bad news was received or when sudden calamity came, it was customary to tear the clothes (2 Sam. 1:2) and to sprinkle earth or ashes on the head (Josh. 7:6). Hair cloth ("sackcloth") was adopted as clothing in times of grief (Isa. 22:12). We read of covering the head in mourning (Jer. 14:3), and also the lower part of the face (Ezek. 24:17, 22). Among those who habitually wore some covering on the head it was a sign of mourning to let the hair go loose (Lev. 10:6), which normally (like that of a Greek Orthodox priest in the Near East) would be coiled up.

A death in the household set in motion an elaborate ceremony of mourning that lasted a week or more. The members of the family and their friends gathered around the corpse and indulged in lamentations bordering on hysteria. The rites mentioned above were observed, but in a more abandoned form than for other mourning. During the last century, W. M. Thomson saw a ceremony of mourning carried out by the Arabs of Palestine. He described the three concentric circles of mourners, slowly marching, clapping their hands, and chanting a funeral dirge. At times they stopped and, flinging their arms and handkerchiefs about in wild frenzy, screamed and wailed like maniacs.

Professional mourners were often called in for a funeral (Jer. 9:17-22; Amos 5:16; Matt. 9:23). In the earliest times these were probably to protect the living from the spirits of the departed, who were greatly feared. By Bible times, however, the mourning women served merely as another manifestation of grief for the departed. The OT contains warnings against pagan mourning rites (Lev. 19:27-28; Deut. 14:1-2). Israelite priests were not allowed to take part in any mourning or other funeral ceremonies (Lev. 21:1-4, 10-11).

JEREMIAH, the weeping prophet, made many references to mourning. He taught the mourning women their dirge (Jer. 9:17-22), heard the land lament because of the destruction by the Babylonians (9:10; 12:4, 11; 14:2; 23:10), and mentioned RACHEL's mourning (31:15-16). He urged Israel to mourn for its sins (4:8; 6:26; 7:29) and secretly mourned for the nation himself (9:1; 13:17).

mouse. See ANIMALS.

mouth. Both Hebrew *peh H7023* and Greek *stoma G5125* are used literally (1 Sam. 1:12; Acts 23:2; et al.) as well as figuratively. Among the latter uses, the word "mouth" can refer to an entrance, such as of a cave (Josh. 10:27), the grave (Ps. 141:7), a sack (Gen. 42:27), and a well (29:10). It is used metaphorically to refer to the absolute sovereignty of God in the fiat of his words in judgment, as in the phrases "rod of his mouth" (Isa. 11:4) and "out of his mouth comes a sharp sword" (Rev. 19:15). Jesus taught that "the things that come out of the mouth come from the heart, and these make a man 'unclean'" (Matt. 15:18 and parallels; cf. also Rom. 3:14).

mow. To cut down the standing grass or other herbage. The Hebrew noun *gēz H1600* (which twice refers to wool or fleece, Deut. 31:20; Job 31:20), is used of mown grass or a mown field in two passages (Ps. 72:6; Amos 7:1). In the latter, the phrase "the king's mowings" (NIV, "the king's share") refers to the first cut of spring herbage, which was to be given as tribute to the kings of Israel to feed their horses; after that the owner of the field could have his portion. The word occurs in the NT once as the rendering of Greek *amaō G286* (Jas. 5:4).

Moza. moh´zuh (Heb. *môṣāʾ H4605*, "[act or place of] going out"). Some scholars believe that this is a place name, rather than a personal name, and that

M

it possibly should be related to Mozah. **(1)** Son of Caleb by Ephah his concubine, included in the genealogy of Judah (1 Chr. 2:46).

(2) Son of Zimri and descendant of Saul through Jonathan (1 Chr. 8:36-37; 9:42-43). Several of the names in this section of the genealogy correspond to towns within the tribal territory of Benjamin.

Mozah. moh´zuh (Heb. *mōṣâ H5173*, perhaps "[water] source" or "[oil] press"). A town within the tribal territory of Benjamin (Josh. 18:26). Because the name is stamped on the handles of vessels excavated at Jericho and Tell en-Naṣbeh (Mizpah), it is thought that Mozah was a center for the manufacture of pottery. The town was evidently near such W Benjamite cities as Mizpah and Kephirah, but its precise location is uncertain. Many scholars believe that the site is at or near the Arab village of Qaloniyeh (Qalunyah), about 5 mi. (8 km.) WNW of Jerusalem on the road to Tel Aviv.

muffler. See dress.

mulberry tree. See plants.

mule. See animals.

Muppim. muh´pim (Heb. *muppîm H5137*, derivation unknown). Son of Benjamin and grandson of Jacob (Gen. 46:21). This name does not occur in the other genealogies of Benjamin, although many scholars identify Muppim with Shephupham (Num. 26:39 MT; KJV and NIV, "Shupham"), Shuppim (1 Chr. 7:12, 15; NIV, "Shuppites"), and Shephuphan (8:5). See also Huppim.

Muratorian Canon. myoor´uh-tor´ee-uhn. Also known as the Muratorian Fragment, this seventh/eighth-century Latin document provides a very early list of accepted NT books. It was discovered by L. A. Muratori (1672-1750) in the Ambrosian Library of Milan and published by him in 1740. Although some recent scholars have argued that the original Greek work from which it was translated may have been produced in Syria or Palestine as late as the fourth century, it is widely believed that the Muratorian Canon is the earliest existing list of its kind, composed originally c. A.D. 180-190 in or near Rome. For a discussion of its significance, see canonicity II.A.

murder. From the days of Noah the biblical penalty for murder was death: "Whoever sheds the blood of man, by man shall his blood be shed" (Gen. 9:6). Throughout OT times, the ancient Semitic custom of the avenger of blood was followed: a murdered person's nearest relative (the *goel*) had the duty to pursue the murderer and kill him (Num. 35:19). Since in the practice of avenging blood in this fashion people failed to distinguish between murder and manslaughter, and vicious blood feuds would frequently arise, the Mosaic law provided for cities of refuge (ch. 35). To these cities a person pursued by the avenger of blood could flee. He would be admitted and tried; if judged guilty of murder, he would be turned over to the avenger; if judged innocent, he was afforded protection in this city from the avenger. It appears likely that the advent of the monarchy began a trend away from the ancient *goel* custom, for we find the king putting a murderer to death (1 Ki. 2:34) and pardoning another (2 Sam. 14:6-8).

In a murder trial, the agreeing testimony of at least two persons was necessary for conviction (Num. 35:30; Deut. 17:6). An animal known to be vicious had to be confined, and if it caused the death of anyone, it was destroyed and the owner held guilty of murder (Exod. 21:29, 31). The right of asylum in a holy place was not granted a murderer; he was dragged away even from the horns of the altar (Exod. 21:14; 1 Ki. 2:28-34). No ransom could be accepted for a murderer (Num. 35:21). When a murder had been committed and the killer could not be found, the people of the community nearest the place where the corpse was found were reckoned guilty. To clear them of guilt, the elders of that community would kill a heifer, wash their hands over it, state their innocence, and thus be judged clean (Deut. 21:1-9).

murrain. This English term, meaning "pestilence" or "plague," is used once by the KJV to render the common Hebrew word *deber H1822* (Exod. 9:3). See also plagues of Egypt.

Mushi. myoo´sh*i* (Heb. *mûšî H4633*, derivation uncertain; the same form [*mûšî H4634*] is used as a gentilic, "Mushite"). Son of MERARI and grandson of LEVI (Exod. 6:19; Num. 3:20; 1 Chr. 6:19, 47; 23:21, 23; 24:26, 30); eponymous ancestor of the Mushite clan of Levites (Num. 3:33; 26:58). It has been argued that the name is derived from *mōšeh H5407* (MOSES), and some speculate that the Mushites constituted an early priesthood competing with that of AARON.

music and musical instruments.

I. Musical instruments

A. The bell. In Exod. 28:33-35, where the Lord prescribes the high priest's garments, he states: "Make pomegranates of blue, purple and scarlet yarn around the hem of the robe, with gold bells between them. The gold bells and the pomegranates are to alternate around the hem of the robe. Aaron must wear it when he ministers. The sound of the bells will be heard when he enters the Holy Place before the LORD and when he comes out, so that he will not die." This custom typifies the ringing of the bell during the Roman Mass to call the attention of the worshipers to the sacred function in the sanctuary. Bells and jingles on the hem of garments not only were found in Israel but also are used by many primitive tribes in worship.

B. The cymbals. The only permanent percussive instrument in the TEMPLE orchestra was the cymbal. In the Holy Scriptures, the use of cymbals is solely confined to religious ceremonies: at the time when the ARK OF THE COVENANT was brought back from KIRIATH JEARIM (1 Chr. 15:16, 19, 28); at the dedication of SOLOMON's temple (2 Chr. 5:13); at the restoration of worship by HEZEKIAH (29:25); at the laying of the foundation of the second temple (Ezra 3:10); and the dedication of the wall of JERUSALEM (Neh. 12:27). In Ps. 150:5 reference is made to cymbals "of sound" and cymbals "of shout" (NIV, "clash of cymbals" and "resounding cymbals"). If two different types are meant, one possible distinction is between small cymbals that perhaps were held vertically, and large ones held horizontally. In the time of DAVID, much stress was laid on the cymbal and percussive instruments. His chief singer, ASAPH, was a cymbal player (1 Chr. 16:5). However, in the last century of the second

temple the percussive instruments apparently were restricted to one cymbal, which was used to mark pauses only, not to be played while the singing and the playing were going on.

C. The harp and the lyre. Harps have the neck at an angle to the body, either arched (of the same piece as the body) or angular (neck fastened to body at near right angle), whereas lyres have a body with two arms joined by a crossbar, the strings going from body to crossbar. It is difficult to determine which Hebrew words refer to which of these stringed instruments. The NIV usually has "harp" for *kinnôr H4036* and "lyre" for *nēbel H5575*, terms that are often found in the same context (e.g., 2 Sam. 6:5; 1 Ki. 10:12; et al.). Other translations, however, reverse these two words (e.g., TNIV, NRSV, NJPS). In the historical books, the SEPTUAGINT renders them by means of unhelpful loanwords, but in the poetic and prophetic literature it uses respectively *kithara* (a triangular lyre or lute with seven strings) and *psaltērion* (psaltery or a type of harp). The reference to a ten-string lyre or harp (Ps. 33:2; 144:9) probably indicates that normally a different number of strings was employed. It has

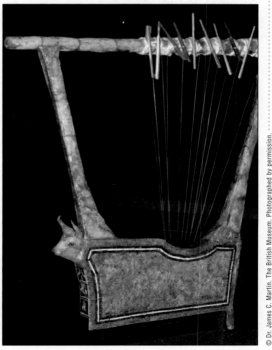

A silver lyre from c. 2600 B.C.

© Dr. James C. Martin. The British Museum. Photographed by permission.

M

been suggested that *kinnôr* refers to a "thin" lyre, consisting of no more than eight strings, whereas *nēbel* refers to a "thick" lyre, which can have as many as thirteen. In any case, these two instruments were the most important ones in the temple orchestra, without which no public religious ceremony could be held (cf. 1 Chr. 25:3). They also were used at secular festivities (cf. Isa. 5:12).

D. The lute. Lutes have strings stretched along a neck attached to a resonating body as in guitar-like and violin-like instruments. Although lutes are represented in Egyptian, Mesopotamian, and Hittite art, it is uncertain whether they are mentioned in the Bible. The English term is used by the NIV twice to render two different Hebrew words (1 Sam. 18:6; 2 Chr. 20:28), while the NRSV also uses it twice, but other Hebrew words occur (Ps. 92:3; 150:3; cf. also 1 Macc. 4:54). The simplicity of the lute (possibly originating from the hunting bow being plucked) should caution one against assuming that it did not exist in Israel.

E. The pipe and the flute. Reed pipes have either one or two reeds (as in the present-day clarinet and oboe, respectively) into which air is blown, while with flutes the air is blown against one edge of the mouth-hole. Flutes can be end-blown (vertical), cross-blown (hole in side, held transversely like the modern flute), or whistle flutes. Certain Hebrew terms designate instruments belonging to the general class of pipes, but it is difficult to be more specific. The *ḥālîl H2720*, translated "flute" in modern English versions ("pipe" in KJV), was probably a reed pipe, an interpretation that fits the context of lament in Jer. 48:36. Since in antiquity two reed pipes often were played simultaneously by the same person, this might also have been true of the *ḥālîl* (some believe that the word refers specifically to the double-pipe; the *nĕḥîlôt H5704*, mentioned only in the title of Ps. 5, may have been another form of this instrument). Of the four occurrences of Hebrew *ʿûgāb H6385*, two passages indicate only that it is a musical instrument (Gen. 4:21; Ps. 150:4), and the other two imply that it is normally used to express rejoicing (Job 21:12; 30:31); the NIV renders this term "flute," but the TNIV and other modern versions have "pipe" (KJV, "organ," which is misleading).

F. The sistrum or rattle. The Hebrew word *mĕnaʿanʿîm H4983* (from the root *nûaʿ H5675*, "to

quiver") occurs only in 2 Sam. 6:5 and apparently denotes an instrument that was shaken. The reference could be either to a rattle (e.g., beads in a hollow gourd; cf. NRSV, "castanets") or to a sistrum (so Vulg.; cf. NIV). The latter, consisting of a small frame with metal pieces loosely attached, was more common, especially in Egypt.

G. The tambourine or timbrel. This instrument (Heb. *tōp H9512*) was evidently a small drum made of a wooden hoop and probably two skins, without any jingling contrivance like the modern tambourine. It was a rhythm-indicator and was used for dances and joyous occasions as well as religious celebrations. It was one of the instruments employed at the installation of the ark in Jerusalem (2 Sam. 6:5). It is not listed among the musical instruments either of the first or second temple, despite its being mentioned three times in the Psalms (Ps. 81:2; 149:3; 150:4). It appears that the instrument was played primarily by women (Exod. 15:20; Jdg. 11:34; 1 Sam. 18:6).

H. The trumpet. The Hebrew term *šôpār H8795*, usually translated "trumpet," refers specifically to a "ram's horn" used as a sound instrument for communicating signals and announcing important events (e.g., 1 Ki. 1:34). The characteristic of this animal horn is its curved shape and relatively wide, conical bore. The same instrument can be referred to with the word *yôbēl H3413* ("ram" or "ram's horn"), used either by itself (Exod. 19:13) or in combination with *šôpār* or *qeren H7967* (Josh. 6:4-8, 13). On the other hand, the common term *ḥăṣōṣĕrâ H2956* (Num. 10:2 et al.), also translated "trumpet," designates a tube of straight, narrow bore. The main difference between the two types

Jewish man blowing the shofar or ram's horn trumpet.

© Dr. James C. Martin

of instrument was one of tone quality, but it is likely that a secondary difference was the often metallic construction of the *ḥăṣōṣĕrâ*. For either instrument only a limited number of pitches (two or three) could be produced, so that they are far removed from the modern trumpet.

I. **Nebuchadnezzar's orchestral instruments.** Finally, a word about the orchestral instruments of Nebuchadnezzar king of Babylon, as described by Daniel: "As soon as you hear the sound of the horn, flute, zither, lyre, harp, pipes and all kinds of music, you must fall down and worship the image of gold that King Nebuchadnezzar has set up" (Dan. 3:5; cf. vv. 10, 15). Some of the Aramaic terms used in this verse are of uncertain meaning. For example, it has been suggested that the last item, *sûmpōnĕyâ H10507*, reflects Greek *tympanon* and thus designates a drum (cf. NRSV), but the word must rather represent *symphōnia G5246*, which can simply mean "music" (Lk. 15:25) or "in unison" or "musical band," though here it may refer to a kind of bagpipe (thus NIV "pipes") or to the double-flute. The second item in the list is *mašrôqî H10446*, which probably signifies some type of flute or whistle (the NRSV and other versions have "pipe"). Zithers have many strings stretched across a body, either struck (dulcimer) or plucked (psaltery); it is problematic whether such instruments are mentioned in the Bible, although both NIV and NJPS use "zither" in this verse to render Aramaic *qîtrōs H10630* (from Gk. *kithara*). The fourth term here, *śabbĕkā' H10676*, is rendered "lyre" by the NIV, but "trigon" by the NRSV and NJPS (the KJV's "sackbut," referring to a medieval trombone, is wrongly based on the similarity of sound between the Aram. and Eng. words).

II. **Music**

A. **The history of Hebrew music.** The history of Israel's higher civilization in general and the organization of the musical service in the temple began with King David's reign. To him has been ascribed not only the creation and singing of the psalms, but also the provision (invention?) of musical instruments (1 Chr. 23:5; 2 Chr. 7:6). King David chose the Levites to supply musicians for the holy temple. Out of the 30,000 who were employed at this time, the impressive number of 4,000 was selected for the musical service. Years later, when

King Solomon had finished all work for the temple and brought in all the things David his father had dedicated, the priest and the congregation of Israel assembled before the ark, and the musical service was begun by the Levites. The number of them who were instructed in the songs of the Lord was 288, divided into twenty-four classes (1 Chr. 25:6-7). On the day of the dedication of the temple, "all the Levites who were musicians—Asaph, Heman, Jeduthun and their sons and relatives—stood on the east side of the altar, dressed in fine linen and playing cymbals, harps and lyres. They were accompanied by 120 priests sounding trumpets. The trumpeters and singers joined in unison, as with one voice, to give praise and thanks to the Lord. Accompanied by trumpets, cymbals and other instruments, they raised their voices in praise to the Lord and sang: 'He is good; his love endures forever.' Then the temple of the Lord was filled with a cloud, and the priests could not perform their service because of the cloud, for the glory of the Lord filled the temple of God" (2 Chr. 5:12-14). When the king and the people had offered their sacrifices, the Levites began to play, "the priests blew their trumpets, and all the Israelites were standing" (7:6).

In Solomon's temple the choir formed a distinct body. They were furnished homes and were on salary. Ezekiel says they had chambers between the walls and windows with southern views (Ezek. 40:44). The choir numbered 2,000 singers and was divided into two choirs. The Psalms, according to the Mishnah (see Talmud), were sung antiphonally. The first examples in the Bible of antiphonal or responsive singing are the songs of Moses and Miriam after the passage through the Red Sea (Exod. 15). There were three forms after which the Psalms and the prayers were rendered in the temple. First, the leader intoned the first half verse, whereupon the congregation repeated it. Then the leader sang each succeeding half line, the congregation always repeating the same first half line, which thus became a refrain throughout the entire psalm. Second, the leader sang a half line at a time, and the congregation repeated what he had last sung. The third form was responsive in the real sense of the word—the leader would sing the whole first line, whereupon the congregation would respond with the second line of the verse.

M

M

The orchestra and the choir personnel were greatly reduced in the second temple. The orchestra consisted of a minimum of two harps and a maximum of six; a minimum of nine lyres, maximum limitless; a minimum of two oboes and a maximum of twelve; and one cymbal. The second temple choir consisted of a minimum of twelve adult singers, maximum limitless. The singers, all male, were between thirty and fifty years of age. Five years of musical training was a prerequisite to membership in the second temple choir. In addition to the male adults, sons of the Levites were permitted to participate in the choir "in order to add sweetness to the song."

The musical service in the temple at the time of Christ was essentially the same as that in King Solomon's temple, with the exception of a few minor changes in certain forms of singing. There were two daily services in the temple—the morning and evening sacrifices. After the sacrificial acts, the trumpet was sounded, which was the signal for the priests to prostrate themselves, but for the Levites it marked the beginning of the musical service. Two priests would now take their stand at the right and left of the altar and blow their silver trumpets. After this, these two priests would approach the cymbal player and take their stand beside him, one on the right and one on the left. When given a sign with a flag by the president, this Levite sounded his cymbal, and this was the sign for the Levites to begin singing a part of the daily psalm accompanied by instrumental music. Whenever they stopped singing, the priests would again blow their trumpets, and the people would prostrate themselves. Not only psalms were sung but also parts of the Pentateuch. The psalm of the day was sung in three sections and at the close of each the priests would blow three fanfares on their silver trumpets, a signal for the congregation to bow down and to worship the Lord.

B. Music in the Psalms. The order of the Psalms in the daily service of the temple was as follows: On the first day of the week, Ps. 24: "The earth is the Lord's" in commemoration of the first day of creation. On the second day they sang Ps. 48: "Great is the Lord, and most worthy of praise." On the third day, Ps. 82: "God presides in the great assembly." On the fourth day, Ps. 94: "O Lord,

the God who avenges." On the fifth day, Ps. 81: "Sing for joy to God our strength." On the sixth day, Ps. 93: "The Lord reigns." On the seventh day they sang Ps. 92: "It is good to praise the Lord." With the singing of the daily psalm, the morning sacrifice came to a close. The evening sacrifice was identical to the morning sacrifice, with the exception that the incense offering followed the evening sacrifice, at sunset. Thus they began and ended the day with prayer and praise, of which the burning of incense was symbolical.

The real meaning of the headings of the various psalms is still veiled in darkness. Whether they indicate the names of the instruments employed in accompanying the psalms, or whether they refer to the tune to which they were sung, is still a problem for the musicologist. The word SELAH, which is found so frequently in the Psalms, is another expression that has not been satisfactorily explained. Whether it means an interlude, a pause, or a cadence, is not known. Many scholars believe it indicates a musical interlude by the temple orchestra.

C. The dance. This element was considered an integral part of the religious ceremonies in ancient Israel. Examples include the Israelite women led by Miriam after the crossing of the Red Sea (Exod. 15:20), Jephthah's daughter (Jdg. 11:34), and David himself (2 Sam. 6:14). Religious dancing is mentioned only twice in Psalms (Ps. 149:3; 150:4). On the Feast of Tabernacles, at the celebration of "water libation," prominent men would dance, displaying their artistic skill in throwing and catching burning torches. See also DANCING.

mustard. See PLANTS.

Muster Gate. A gate in JERUSALEM, not far from the TEMPLE. The Hebrew name ša'ar hammipqād, which occurs only once in connection with NEHEMIAH's rebuilding of the wall of JERUSALEM (Neh. 3:31), is rendered "the gate Miphkad" by the KJV, "the Muster Gate" by the NRSV, and "the Inspection Gate" by the NIV. The Hebrew word mipqād H5152 can mean both "regulation, appointment" (cf. 2 Chr. 31:13) and "counting" (as when mustering troops, 2 Sam. 24:9 = 1 Chr. 21:5). The exact location of the Muster Gate is uncertain, but it was apparently opposite the temple on the NE part of the city, between the EAST GATE and the SHEEP GATE (Neh. 3:29, 32), and some identify it with the BENJAMIN GATE.

mute. See DISEASES.

Muth-labben. my*oo*th-lab´uhn. The Hebrew musical term ʿalmût labbēn (in the superscription of Ps. 9) is rendered by the KJV and other versions as "upon [NRSV, according to] Muth-labben" (the NJPS has "almuth labben"). The meaning is obscure. Interpreting the phrase as a reference to a particular melody, the NIV renders, "To the tune of 'The Death of the Son.'"

muzzle. The Israelites were commanded not to muzzle the ox when it was treading out the grain, that is, THRESHING (Deut. 25:4). The muzzle was a guard placed on the mouth of the oxen to prevent them from biting or eating. The threshing ox was to have ample opportunity of feeding, thus making the labor more agreeable. The injunction is in harmony with the spirit of the Deuteronomic exposition of the Mosaic law throughout. PAUL quotes this injunction to illustrate, with an appropriate light touch of humor, his view that it is proper to pay the minister for his work in the gospel (1 Cor. 9:8-11; 1 Tim. 5:17-18).

Myra. mi´ruh (Gk. *Myra G3688*, meaning uncertain). A city of LYCIA, in SW ASIA MINOR; modern Dembre. The apostle PAUL visited the town on his journey to ROME, and the fact that he changed ships there indicates its importance as a port (Acts 27:5). The origins of Myra are lost in antiquity; it was known as an ancient town, achieved some importance as the chief city of the Lycian district, and actually was called a metropolis. It is described by ancient writers as the "best and most sparkling" city of Lycia. Its public buildings were distinguished, and included a GYMNASIUM with an arcade furnished with recesses and seats, a theater, a bath, a stoa or roofed colonnade, a temple of Peace, and during the Christian era several churches.

myrrh. See PLANTS.

myrtle. See PLANTS.

Mysia. mis´ee-uh (Gk. *Mysia G3695*). A region in NW ASIA MINOR bounded by the Aegean, the Hellespont, the Propontis, BITHYNIA, PHRYGIA, and LYDIA; it includes the historic TROAS and the areas of Aeolian Greek settlement on the Aegean coast. In Greek times it shared the fortunes of the W stub of the peninsula, fell to the Romans in 133 B.C. as part of the royal legacy of Attalus III, and in Roman days was part of the province of ASIA. This is why Mysia, never itself an independent political entity, lacks precise boundaries. It was a mountainous and, in early times, well-forested region, traversed by some of the main trade routes. PERGAMUM lay within its somewhat vague boundaries. The early inhabitants of Mysia were probably of Thracian origin. Like the Trojans, who held their strategic foothold in Mysia near the entrance to the Hellespont, and the HITTITES, whose great empire at times held dominance this far, they probably were an Indo-European stock, an early wave of the great invasions of the peoples who, with their kindred dialects, were to settle all Europe. Mysia was traversed by PAUL in the course of his second journey (Acts 16:7-8), but no pause was made there save at Troas. There is evidence, however, of church foundations of a very early date.

mystery. In the NT, the Greek word *mystērion G3696* refers to the counsel of God, unknown to human beings except by REVELATION, especially concerning his saving works and ultimate purposes in history. Among the Greeks, *mystery* meant not something obscure or incomprehensible, but a secret imparted only to the initiated, what is unknown until it is revealed. This word is connected with the MYSTERY RELIGIONS of Hellenistic times. The mysteries appealed to the emotions rather than the intellect and offered to their devotees a mystical union with the deity, through death to life, thus securing for them a blessed immortality. Great symbolism characterized their secret ritual, climaxing in the initiation into the full secret of the cult.

The chief use of the concept in the NT is by PAUL. As an educated man of his day, he knew well the thought world of the pagans and accepted this term to indicate the fact that "his gospel" had been revealed to him by the risen Christ. This fact could best be made clear to his contemporaries by adopting

M

the pagan term they all understood, pouring into it a special Christian meaning. In a few passages the term refers to a symbol, allegory, or parable, which conceals its meaning from those who look only at the literal sense, but is the medium of revelation to those who have the key to its interpretation (cf. Mk. 4:11 [NIV, "secret"]; Eph. 5:32; Rev. 1:20; 17:5, 7).

The more common meaning of mystery in the NT, Paul's usual use of the word, is that of a divine truth once hidden but now revealed in the GOSPEL. A characteristic usage is Rom. 16:25-26: " … my gospel and the proclamation of Jesus Christ, according to the revelation of the mystery hidden for long ages past, but now revealed and made known through the prophetic writings by the command of the eternal God, so that all nations might believe and obey him" (cf. Col. 1:26; Eph. 3:3-6). A mystery is thus *now* a revelation: Christian mysteries are revealed doctrines (Rom. 16:26; Eph. 1:9; 3:3, 5, 10; 6:19; Col. 4:3-4; 1 Tim. 3:16). Christianity, therefore, has no secret doctrines, as did the ancient mystery religions. To the worldly wise and prudent the gospel is foolishness (Matt. 11:25; 1 Cor. 2:6-9); although it is communicated to them, they do not have the capacity to understand it (2 Cor. 4:2-4). The Christian mystery, then, is God's world-embracing purpose of REDEMPTION through Christ (Rom. 16:25).

mystery religions. A term applied in the Greek, the Hellenistic, and the Roman world to the cult of certain deities that involved a private initiation ceremony and a reserved and secret ritual. They were probably vestiges of earlier religions, maintaining themselves as secret societies after the introduction of the Olympian and other Indo-European deities, and ending after what seems a common social pattern, by winning their way with the conquering people. The deities with whose worship the Greek "mysteries" were principally connected were Demeter, whose cult was organized into the ceremonials of Eleusis, and Dionysus, a predominantly female cult. The worship of Demeter and Dionysus appears to have been in origin a nature worship, with a ritual symbolizing death and resurrection in a seasonal sequence, and a spiritual reference of this natural pattern to the experience of the soul.

Little is known about the rites of worship and initiation, for the initiates seem to have been faithful in the keeping of their vows of secrecy; but it is fairly certain that the worship had to do with notions of sin, ritual uncleanness, purification, regeneration, and spiritual preparation for another life. It is probable that their influence was widespread, and, on the whole, salutary in tranquility of spirit and uprightness of conduct. Besides the worship of the goddess and the god already named in connection with metropolitan Greece, there were other ancient deities whose cults can be properly named "mystery religions," for example, the worship of Orpheus, Adonis or Tammuz, Isis, and especially Mithras. The triumph of Christianity over the powerful rivalry of the mystery cults, and especially MITHRAISM, was due principally to its possession of a historic Person as the center of its faith. PAUL adapted some of the vocabulary of the mystery cults to a Christian purpose, and his use of the word MYSTERY for a truth revealed but comprehended only by the "initiated," is a clear allusion to them.

myth. This term (from Gk. *mythos* G3680, "story, fable") is usually applied to traditional stories about gods, narrated in a communal setting and regarded as occurrences of permanent significance. The word occurs only in the Pastoral Epistles and in 2 Peter (1 Tim. 1:4; 4:7; 2 Tim. 4:4; Tit. 1:14; 2 Pet. 1:16). In every case myths are repudiated as profitless, but each passage adds particular characterizations or contrasts. Discussions about these allusions generally turn on (1) whether all have some connection with JUDAISM, or only the reference in Titus; (2) whether they can be directly associated with Gnostic speculations; (3) whether they might indicate a sincere but misguided attempt by Christians (or Jews) to allegorize pagan myths for homiletical purposes. Some think it probable that the Pastorals refer to an early form of GNOSTICISM that flourished on the soil of Hellenistic Jewish Christianity, in some ways comparable with what is reflected in COLOSSIANS. There is insufficient data, however, to allow firm conclusions

Mytilene. See MITYLENE.

Naam. nay´uhm (Heb. *na'am H5839*, possibly short form of ELNAAM, "God is pleasantness"). Son of CALEB and descendant of JUDAH (1 Chr. 4:15).

Naamah (person). nay´uh-muh (Heb. *na'ămāh H5841*, possibly "pleasantness"). (1) Daughter of LAMECH and ZILLAH, sister of TUBAL-CAIN, and descendant of CAIN (Gen. 4:22). She is the only daughter named in the lineage of either Cain or ABEL (4:17—5:32).

(2) AMMONITE wife of SOLOMON and mother of REHOBOAM (1 Ki. 14:21, 31; 2 Chr. 12:13). It is often assumed that Naamah was one of the many foreign women that Solomon married when his heart was turned away from God (cf. 1 Ki. 11:1-8), but Rehoboam's age suggests that this marriage had taken place when Solomon was relatively young, and some have speculated that it was a diplomatic arrangement on the part of DAVID. It remains possible, however, that Naamah played a role in Judah's apostasy under Rehoboam (14:22-24).

Naamah (place). nay´uh-muh (Heb. *na'ămāh H5842*, possibly "pleasantness"). A city in the SHEPHELAH allotted to the tribe of JUDAH (Josh. 15:41). It was apparently near MAKKEDAH, but its precise location is unknown. See also NAAMATHITE.

Naaman. nay´uh-muhn (Heb. *na'ămān H5845*, "pleasantness"; gentilic *na'ămî H5844*, "Naamite" or "Naamanite"). (1) Listed among the "sons" of BENJAMIN in Gen. 46:21, but elsewhere identified more specifically as a son of BELA and therefore as Benjamin's grandson (Num. 26:40; 1 Chr. 8:4, 7 [the Heb. syntax in vv. 6-7 is ambiguous]). He became the eponymous ancestor of the Naamites (Num. 26:40; NJPS, "Naamanites").

(2) The ARAMEAN commander who was cured of a skin disease by ELISHA (2 Ki. 5). Prior to this incident, the king of ARAM (SYRIA), probably BEN-HADAD II, had credited Naaman's victories to his military genius (v. 1). To the successful record of his life, the Scriptures, however, add the pathetic phrase, "but he had leprosy" (a feared affliction of the skin, but apparently not the DISEASE called leprosy in modern times). A young girl, who had been taken captive in one of the Aramean raids into Israelite territory, served Naaman's wife. One day she said to her mistress, "If only my master would see the prophet who is in Samaria! He would cure him of his leprosy" (5:3).

After a fruitless visit at the court of the king of Israel, Naaman finally went to the prophet Elisha and was told to wash himself seven times in the river JORDAN, a suggestion that Naaman met with anger and contempt as he recalled the clear waters of the rivers of DAMASCUS (2 Ki. 5:12). Prevailed on, however, by his servants to heed the prophet, Naaman followed the prophet's instructions, "and

Elisha directed Naaman to wash in the Jordan River in order to be healed from his leprosy.

© Dr. James C. Martin

his flesh was restored and became clean like that of a young boy" (5:14). Naaman's cure led to his acceptance of the God of Israel as the only God "in all the world." In Lk. 4:27 Jesus referred to this incident "in the time of Elisha the prophet" when he spoke in the synagogue at Nazareth.

The rest of the account (as told in 2 Ki. 5:15-19) shows how the people believed in henotheism—the view that nations had their individual gods. Naaman wanted some of Israel's soil to take home so that he could worship Israel's God even if it was in "the temple of Rimmon" where his official duties required him to be with his king. (RIMMON was the thunder-god of the Assyrians.) The great Omaiyid Mosque at Damascus, today the city's most magnificent structure is, according to tradition, built on the site of the temple of Rimmon where Naaman deposited his load of soil from Israel.

Naamathite. nay´uh-muh-th*i*t (Heb. *na‘āmātî H5847*, "of Naamah"). Descriptive title of ZOPHAR, one of JOB's three friends (Job 2:11; 11:1; 20:1; 42:9). It evidently refers to his place of origin. The Judahite town of NAAMAH (Josh. 15:41) is almost certainly not in view. Since the other two friends (ELIPHAZ and BILDAD) apparently came from the Arabian desert, the term Naamathite may point to a place or clan in NW ARABIA.

Naamite. nay´uh-m*i*t. See NAAMAN #1.

Naarah (person). nay´uh-ruh (Heb. *na‘ărāh H5856*, "young woman"). One of the two wives of ASHHUR, a descendant of JUDAH; she bore him four sons (1 Chr. 4:5-6).

Naarah, Naaran (place). nay´uh-ruh, -ruhn (Heb. *na‘ărāh H5857*, "watermill"; also *na‘ărān H5860*). A city listed as marking part of the SE border of the tribe of EPHRAIM (Josh. 16:7 [KJV, "Naarath"]; called Naaran in 1 Chr. 7:28). It is mentioned between ATAROTH and JERICHO. A note from JOSEPHUS (*Ant.* 17.13.1) says that Archelaus (see HEROD), after rebuilding JERICHO, "diverted half the water with which the village of Neara used to be watered," thus locating Neara (Naarah) near Jericho and associating it with a good water supply. Most scholars identify Naarah with Tell el-Jisr, just

below the springs ‘Ain Duq and ‘Ain Nu‘eimeh at the foot of the Judean hills, less than 2 mi. (3 km.) NW of Jericho.

Naarai. nay´uh-r*i* (Heb. *na‘āray H5858*, possibly "young man [*or* attendant] of Yahweh"). Son of EZBAI, listed among DAVID's mighty warriors (1 Chr. 11:37); in the parallel passage he is called "Paarai the Arbite" (2 Sam. 23:35). It is uncertain which of the two passages preserves the original name.

Naaran. nay´uh-ruhn. See NAARAH, NAARAN (PLACE).

Naarath. See NAARAH.

Naashon, Naasson. See NAHSHON.

Nabal. nay´buhl (Heb. *nābāl H5573*, "foolish," possibly by popular etymology; the name originally may have derived from a root meaning "noble"). A wealthy descendant of CALEB who lived in MAON, some 8 mi. (13 km.) SSE of HEBRON (1 Sam. 25:2-3). He owned 3,000 sheep and 1,000 goats which he pastured in the vicinity of CARMEL (just N of Maon). He is described as "surly and mean" (v. 3). DAVID, a fugitive from SAUL, had been giving protection to Nabal's flocks from marauding bedouins (vv. 15-16) and so sent ten of his men now to extend good wishes to Nabal, remind him of his service to him, and request a gift in return. Nabal showed his ungrateful character in not only refusing the reasonable request but also returning insulting remarks. Immediately David prepared with 400 men to bring retaliation, but Nabal's wife ABIGAIL, described as "intelligent and beautiful" (v. 3), came quickly to David to make amends, bringing a bountiful gift of food and making humble apology for her husband's conduct. When Abigail later told her husband of his narrow escape, "his heart failed him" (v. 37), and ten days later he died. David then made Abigail one of his wives.

Nabateans. nab´uh-tee´uhnz (Gk. *Nabataioi*). Also Nabataeans. Although this name does not occur in the OT or NT (but see 1 Macc. 5:25; 9:35), the Nabateans were an influential, ARAMAIC-speaking people who were active in the NW part of

Aerial view near Ein Avdat along the Nabatean trade route from Petra to Gaza. In the foreground are stone walls located in the valley floor to slow the flow of water over the agricultural fields.

ARABIA and TRANSJORDAN from about the fourth century B.C. to the beginning of the second century A.D. In Hellenistic times they were a formidable foe to the Greek successors of ALEXANDER THE GREAT, their capital, PETRA, being inaccessible and impregnable. While their king Aretas I befriended the early MACCABEES, they were in conflict with the later Jewish rulers. By NT times their political domain extended at times W of Petra to the NEGEV and N as far as DAMASCUS. They lost Damascus when the Romans came to the aid of the Jews against them, but later recovered it, so that their king ARETAS IV controlled it when PAUL was there (2 Cor. 11:32). Aretas IV fought with the Romans against the Jews and was victorious over HEROD Antipas, who had divorced Aretas's daughter to marry HERODIAS. Nabatea was absorbed into the Roman province of Arabia in A.D. 106.

The Nabateans, a nomadic people, influenced by Aramean, Hellenistic, and Roman culture, developed skill in pottery, fine specimens of which have been recovered. The architecture of Petra, "the rose-red city," is remarkable; its religious high places, pillars, and figures carved out of sandstone cliffs of a canyon are accessible only on foot or muleback. By 100 B.C. the Nabateans developed water storage and irrigation systems in the highlands of Transjordan, the remains of which are still impressive. Yet the Nabateans in the SINAI peninsula and other outlying districts remained nomadic. They were traders between Egypt and Mesopotamia, dealing also in wares from India and China, both by caravan overland and by sea from a port on the AQABAH.

Nabonidus. nab′uh-ni′duhs (from Akk. *Nabūna'id*, "[the god Nabu] is to be revered"). The last king of Chaldean Babylonia, 556-539 B.C. See BABYLON. Nabonidus possibly was related to NEBUCHADNEZZAR through marriage so that Nabonidus's son and coregent Bēl-šar-uṣur (BELSHAZZAR) could claim to be a descendant of that illustrious monarch (so Dan. 5:11, 18). Nebuchadnezzar had been succeeded by a period of family strife during which the rulers were his son EVIL-MERODACH (for two years), his son-in-law Neriglissar (for four years), and another son, Labashi-Marduk, who was recognized as king only for two months, May-June 556 B.C., in part of Babylonia. Nabonidus, who was supported by other cities, was accepted as sole ruler by the end of June. Two years later Nabonidus entrusted the rule of Babylon to his son Belshazzar. He himself moved to Haran, where restoration work on the temple of the moon-god Sin, Ehulhul, was begun after its ruin by the Medes, as indicated to him in a dream. See HARAN (PLACE). From there he moved S to attack Adummu (EDOM) and the sheikh of Teima² (TEMA) in NW ARABIA, who was killed.

In 545 B.C. Nabonidus returned to Babylon, where he carried out work on various shrines, including that of the sun-god Shamash at Sippar. The weakness of the state was evident in both its economy and defense. The Medes overran the zone E of the Tigris River, and the Elamites parts of S Babylonia. The Persians moved on Babylon in 539. The city was entered by a stratagem and without a battle on October 12. On that night Belshazzar was put to death (Dan. 5:30). Nabonidus, who had fled to Borsippa, reentered the city and was taken prisoner. According to one tradition, he died in exile in Carmania. Seventeen days later Cyrus himself entered the city and took over the throne. The political power at Babylon now passed from Semitic into Persian hands.

Nabopolassar. nab´uh-puh-las´uhr (Akk. *Nabū-apla-uṣur*, "may [the god] Nabu protect the son!"). First king (626-605 B.C.) of the Neo-Babylonian ("Chaldean") Dynasty, and the father of NEBUCHADNEZZAR II. See BABYLON. Nabopolassar was originally a petty chieftain in S Babylonia, but at the death of King ASHURBANIPAL of ASSYRIA in 626 B.C., he became king of BABYLON and in a few years had control of all Babylonia. To bind a treaty made between Nabopolassar and Cyaxares, king of the Medes (see MEDIA), the latter gave his daughter Amytis in marriage to Nabopolassar's son, Nebuchadnezzar. Nabopolassar's army was well-trained in Assyrian methods of fighting, and eventually in 612 he and his ally took NINEVEH. This conquest meant that the Assyrian empire was divided, with the southern part falling to Nabopolassar. In 609 Haran, the last Assyrian stronghold, fell to the Babylonians. See HARAN (PLACE).

In 606 Nabopolassar took up the EUPHRATES front, where the Egyptian hold on CARCHEMISH posed a threat to the entire western part of his newly won empire. Pharaoh NECO II of Egypt had invaded PALESTINE and SYRIA in order to get his share of the fallen Assyrian empire, and it was Nebuchadnezzar, the crown prince, acting for his ailing father, who achieved the conquest of Carchemish and drove the Egyptian army back

home in 605. King Nabopolassar had returned to Babylon in the spring of the same year, and died there on 15 August. Although Nabopolassar is not mentioned in the Bible, JOSIAH of Judah may have been friendly with him (as HEZEKIAH had been an ally of the Babylonians), for Josiah lost his life at MEGIDDO in a futile attempt to stop Pharaoh Neco II from going to the aid of the Assyrians (2 Ki. 23:29; 2 Chr. 35:20-27).

Naboth. nay´both (Heb. *nābôt H5559*, "growth, sprout," possibly short form of a theophoric name, such as "scion of Yahweh"). The owner of a vineyard desired by King AHAB because it lay near his alternate royal palace in JEZREEL (1 Ki. 21:1-29), probably on the E side of the city (2 Ki. 9:25-26). Ahab offered Naboth either money or the exchange of a better vineyard. Naboth refused on the valid ground that it was part of his paternal INHERITANCE. Patrimonies belonged to families, not individuals, and Naboth would have wronged his descendants by selling it, as well as having broken God's law (Lev. 25:23-28; Num. 36:7-9). Ahab himself, though angry and sullen, did not force the issue, but his wife JEZEBEL did by having Naboth falsely accused of blasphemy and stoned to death. When Ahab went to take possession of the vineyard, ELIJAH met him and pronounced judgment on him and his family. Ahab repented and a temporary stay was granted (21:27-29), but after further warning by MICAIAH the prophet, punishment fell on Ahab (22:24-40) as well as on Jezebel and their son Joram (JEHORAM, 2 Ki. 9:25-37).

Nabu. See NEBO (DEITY).

Nachon. See NACON.

Nachor. See NAHOR.

Nacon. nay´kon (Heb. *nākôn H5789*, possibly "established"). KJV Nachon; TNIV Nakon. The owner of a threshing floor next to which UZZAH died because he touched the ARK OF THE COVENANT while it was being transported toward JERUSALEM (2 Sam. 6:6; the parallel passage in 1 Chr. 13:9 reads KIDON). Some have speculated that the form here is not a proper name and that the phrase should be rendered "a certain threshing floor" or "the threshing floor of striking" (i.e., destruction).

Nadab. nay´dab (Heb. *nādāb H5606*, possibly short form NEDABIAH, "Yahweh is willing"). **(1)** Eldest son of AARON and ELISHEBA (Exod. 6:23; Num. 3:2; 26:60; 1 Chr. 6:3; 24:1). He and his next younger brother, ABIHU, were permitted to accompany Aaron and seventy Israelite elders while ascending Mount SINAI to see a representation of God and to eat and drink in God's presence (Exod. 24:1, 9-11). Nadab and his brothers, Abihu, ELEAZAR, and ITHAMAR, were admitted to priestly office with their father, Aaron (Exod. 28:1; Lev. 8:1-36). After several days of consecration, on the eighth day when official service began, Nadab and Abihu sinned in offering "unholy" (NIV, "unauthorized") fire before the Lord, but the exact nature of the sin is not clear. They were immediately consumed in death by fire from the Lord (Lev. 10:1-2; Num. 3:4). To emphasize the seriousness of the sin, MOSES forbade Aaron and the two living sons to observe customary mourning ceremonies for them (Lev. 10:6). Both men died without offspring (Num. 3:4; 1 Chr. 24:2).

(2) Son of Shammai and descendant of JUDAH through JERAHMEEL (1 Chr. 2:28, 30).

(3) Son of JEIEL and descendant of BENJAMIN; apparently a great-uncle of King SAUL (1 Chr. 8:30-33; 9:35-39).

(4) Son of JEROBOAM I and king of ISRAEL about 910-909 B.C. (1 Ki. 15:25-31). His two years of rule (v. 25) were really only parts of two years (cf. vv. 25, 28, 33). While besieging the town of GIBBETHON, Nadab was killed by his successor, BAASHA, who exterminated the whole house of Jeroboam, thus fulfilling AHIJAH's prophecy (14:10-11).

Naggai. nag´i (Gk. *Nangai G3710*). KJV Nagge. Son of Maath, included in Luke's GENEALOGY OF JESUS CHRIST (Lk. 3:25).

Nagge. See NAGGAI.

Nag Hammadi Library. nahg´huh-mah´dee. In 1945, a dozen Coptic MSS (plus part of a thirteenth) were accidentally discovered near the modern Egyptian town of Nag Hammadi. These leather codices were acquired by the Coptic Museum in Old Cairo. The significance of these MSS soon became clear when they were shown to date to the fourth century A.D. and to contain more than fifty tractates that give expression to what may be called Gnostic Christianity (see GNOSTICISM). It appears that these writings had originally been composed in Greek a century or two earlier. Prior to this discovery, our knowledge of Gnostic ideas in early Christianity had been largely limited to partial (and hostile) descriptions in the patristic literature. Now, however, it became possible to read firsthand, and in context, the writings associated with that movement. The various tractates are quite diverse in character: some have a strong tie to Jewish traditions, others reproduce non-Christian philosophical treatises, still others consist of HERMETIC texts. Many of the documents contain obscure myths, made even more difficult by their fragmentary nature and by the fact that in the course of transmission numerous copying and translation errors were introduced. Still, these writings have opened up a new world to students of early heterodox Christianity, shedding considerable light on religious developments after the apostolic period. In addition, some scholars have argued that a few of the texts provide a direct and independent link to the teachings of Jesus (see LOGIA; THOMAS, GOSPEL OF).

Nahalal. nay´huh-lal (Heb. *nahălāl H5634*, also *nahălōl H5636* [Jdg. 1:30], "water place"). A city allotted to the tribe of ZEBULUN (Josh. 19:15; KJV, "Nahallal"), later given to the LEVITES descended from MERARI (21:35). Zebulun was unable to expel the Canaanite inhabitants who dwelt among them, but the latter became subject to forced labor (Jdg. 1:30; here the name occurs in the form "Nahalol"). Nahalal was evidently close to SHIMRON, but the precise location is uncertain.

Nahaliel. nuh-hay´lee-uhl (Heb. *nahăliʾēl H5712*, "river [*or* palm-grove] of God"). A stopping place of the Israelites in TRANSJORDAN toward the end of their wanderings (Num. 21:19). Nahaliel was evidently between MATTANAH and BAMOTH, but the precise location of these sites is unknown. If the name alludes to a wadi, it might be one of the northern tributaries of the ARNON.

N

Nahallal. See NAHALAL.

Nahalol. See NAHALAL.

Naham. nay´ham (Heb. *naḥam H5715*, "comfort"). Brother of HODIAH's wife, included in the genealogy of JUDAH (1 Chr. 4:19).

Nahamani. nay´huh-may´ni (Heb. *naḥămānî H5720*, "comfort," possibly a form of NEHEMIAH, "Yahweh has comforted"). An Israelite mentioned among leading individuals who returned from BABYLON with ZERUBBABEL (Neh. 7:7; the name is omitted in the parallel in Ezra 2:2).

Naharai. nay´huh-ri (Heb. *naḥray H5726*, perhaps "diligent" or "gaunt"). A man from BEEROTH who served as armor-bearer for JOAB and who was included among DAVID's mighty warriors (2 Sam. 23:37 [some eds. of KJV, "Nahari"]; 1 Chr. 11:39).

Nahari. See NAHARAI.

Nahash. nay´hash (Heb. *nāḥāš H5731*, "serpent," or related to Akk. *naḥāšu*, "to be luxuriant"). **(1)** King of AMMON in the late eleventh century B.C. Soon after SAUL became king of Israel, Nahash besieged JABESH GILEAD and agreed to make a treaty with its inhabitants "only on the condition that I gouge out the right eye of everyone of you and so bring disgrace on all Israel" (1 Sam. 11:1-2). This incident caused Saul to prove himself as king in the way he rallied Israel against Nahash and defeated him (11:4-11; cf. 12:12). One of the DEAD SEA SCROLLS (4QSam^a) precedes this story with a paragraph that many scholars consider original; it indicates that the siege of Jabesh Gilead was only one (the last) in a series of repressive acts by Nahash against the Transjordanian tribes of GAD and REUBEN (see the NRSV, which includes the passage). According to 2 Sam. 10:1-2 (= 1 Chr. 19:1-2), after "the king of the Ammonites died," DAVID said to himself, "I will show kindness to Hanun son of Nahash, just as his father showed kindness to me." Many scholars assume that Nahash must have aided David when the latter was fleeing from Saul, their mutual enemy. The chronology is prob-

lematic, however; in addition, some have thought that the Nahash in the latter passage is a different individual altogether. It has also been suggested that the Nahash referred to in 2 Sam. 10:2 was a descendant of the one mentioned in 11:1, though the biblical text gives no indication that two different people are meant. See also #2 below.

(2) Father of ABIGAIL, the sister of ZERUIAH (2 Sam. 17:25). Both women are called sisters of David (1 Chr. 2:16), even though David's father was named JESSE, not Nahash. Perhaps the best explanation is that Nahash was the first husband of David's mother; if so, these two women were half-sisters of David and stepdaughters of Jesse. Some have argued that this Nahash is the same as #1 above, in which case David would have had a connection with the Ammonite royal family even before the conflicts between Saul and Nahash.

(3) Possibly the name of a town in Judah. See IR NAHASH.

Nahath. na´hath (Heb. *naḥat H5740*, possibly "rest" or "pure"). **(1)** Son of Reuel and grandson of ESAU by BASEMATH; an Edomite clan chief (Gen. 36:13, 17; 1 Chr. 1:37).

(2) Son of Zophai, descendant of LEVI through KOHATH, and ancestor of SAMUEL (1 Chr. 6:26; possibly the same as TOAH in v. 34 and TOHU in 1 Sam. 1:1, both of whom are identified as being a son of ZUPH).

(3) A Levite who, in the time of King HEZEKIAH, was a supervisor of the temple offerings (2 Chr. 31:13).

Nahbi. nah´bi (Heb. *naḥbî H5696*, possibly "timid"). Son of Vophsi, from the tribe of NAPHTALI; he was one of the twelve spies sent out by MOSES to reconnoiter the Promised Land (Num. 13:14).

Nahor. nay´hor (Heb. *nāḥôr H5701*, meaning uncertain; Gk. *Nachōr G3732*). KJV also Nachor (only Josh. 24:2; Lk. 3:34). **(1)** Son of Serug, descendant of SHEM, father of TERAH, and grandfather of ABRAHAM (Gen. 11:22-25; 1 Chr. 1:26); included in Luke's GENEALOGY OF JESUS CHRIST (Lk. 3:34). After the birth of Terah in his twenty-ninth year, Nahor "lived 119 years and had other sons and daughters" (Gen. 11:25).

(2) Second son of Terah, and brother of Abraham and HARAN (Gen. 11:26-29; Josh. 24:2). A list is given of the twelve children of Nahor (Gen. 22:20-24), eight by his wife MILCAH, who was the daughter of his brother Haran (11:29; 24:15, 24, 47), and four by his concubine REUMAH. The contention that these "children" of Nahor must have represented the names of twelve Aramean tribes or places does not necessarily follow from the text. LABAN is once called the "son" of Nahor (29:5 NRSV) but the Hebrew word *bēn H1201* can refer to a descendant, thus a grandson (cf. NIV). In concluding the covenant at MIZPAH, Laban called upon "the God of Abraham and the God of Nahor" (31:53).

(3) A city mentioned in Gen. 24:10. The reference may be either to a city called Nahor, or else it may be understood as the personal name, referring to #2 above; in the latter case, the passage may be rendered, "the city where Nahor lived," that is, Haran. See HARAN (PLACE). The Akkadian name *Naḫur*, however, occurs frequently in the MARI texts, referring to a location in N MESOPOTAMIA. It must have been near to Haran (Gen. 27:43; 28:10; 29:4-5).

Nahshon. nah´shon (Heb. *naḫšôn H5732*, "little snake"; Gk. *Naassōn G3709*). KJV also Naashon (Exod. 6:23) and Naasson (Matt. 1:4; Lk. 3:32). Son of Amminadab, descendant of JUDAH, grandfather (or ancestor) of BOAZ, and ancestor of DAVID; included in the GENEALOGY OF JESUS CHRIST (Ruth 4:20; 1 Chr. 2:10-11; Matt. 1:4; Lk. 3:32). Nahshon was the leader of the tribe of Judah as they camped in the wilderness (Num. 2:3). As such, he assisted MOSES in taking a census of the Israelites (1:7) and brought offerings to the Lord on the first day of the dedication of the TABERNACLE (7:12-17). Since this tribe led the way when the whole nation moved, Nahshon was an important man (10:14). His sister ELISHEBA married AARON (Exod. 6:23).

Nahum. nay´huhm (Heb. *naḫum H5699*, possibly "[God] comforts" or "comforter"; Gk. *Naoum G3725*). **(1)** An ELKOSHITE, author of a prophetic book (Nah. 1:1). See NAHUM, BOOK OF.

(2) Son of Esli, included in Luke's GENEALOGY OF JESUS CHRIST (Lk. 3:25; KJV, "Naum").

Nahum, Book of. The seventh book among the Minor Prophets. This short book is largely a poem, a literary masterpiece, predicting the downfall of NINEVEH, the capital of ASSYRIA. Nineveh was conquered by the Babylonians and their allies in 612 B.C. Nahum declared that Nineveh would fall as did THEBES, which the Assyrians themselves had conquered in 663. The book therefore was written between 663 and 612—in turbulent times. In 633 ASHURBANIPAL, the last great king of Assyria, died. Soon BABYLON rebelled, and the Assyrian power rapidly dwindled. In JUDAH the wicked MANASSEH reigned until about 641, followed by AMON's two-year reign and then the long reign of the good king JOSIAH (639-608). Perhaps it was in Josiah's day that Nahum prophesied the overthrow of the mighty nation that had so oppressed the Jews. ZEPHANIAH also predicted in Josiah's time the overthrow of Nineveh (Zeph. 1:1; 2:13).

The book of Nahum is in two parts: first, a poem concerning the greatness of God (Nah. 1:2-15), then another and longer poem detailing the overthrow of Nineveh (2:1—3:19). The impassioned expressions of Nahum can be better understood when we remember how Assyria had overthrown the northern kingdom of Israel in 722 B.C. and had later taken forty cities of Judah captive, deporting over 200,000 people—according to SENNACHERIB's own boast in his royal annals (cf. 2 Ki. 18:13). The cruelty of the Assyrians is almost beyond belief. Their policy seems to have been one of calculated terror. Their own pictures show captives staked to the ground and being skinned alive. No wonder

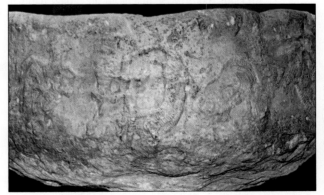

© Dr. James C. Martin. The British Museum. Photographed by permission.

A pedestal from Nineveh with mythological creatures (c. 2250 B.C.). Nahum prophesied against Nineveh, capital of the Assyrian empire.

Overview of NAHUM

Author: The prophet Nahum, an ELKOSHITE.

Historical setting: The focus of Nahum's prophecy is the nation of ASSYRIA prior to its fall (612 B.C.). The book was probably written sometime between 650 and 630 B.C.

Purpose: To announce the coming destruction of NINEVEH and thus to bring comfort to God's people.

Contents: After a psalm of praise to God (Nah. 1:1-11), the book promises deliverance to JUDAH (1:12-15) and proclaims judgments on Nineveh (chs. 2-3).

Nahum exulted at the overthrow of the proud, rich, cruel empire of Assyria.

Some modern critics take issue with Nahum's theology, saying that such vengeful expressions are far from the spirit of the gospel. Such views are usually based on a one-sided conception of NT teaching. In truth, Nahum declares, God is merciful, a statement similar to that found in Exod. 34:6 (Nah. 1:3). Nahum also quotes from ISAIAH the promise of good tidings of peace for his own (Nah. 1:15; cf. Isa. 52:7). But for Nineveh the cup of iniquity was full. A century and a quarter earlier, Nineveh had repented at the preaching of JONAH. But the repentance was temporary, and now a hundred years of savage cruelty and oppression of God's people must be paid for. Assyria, the pride of TIGLATH-PILESER, SARGON, Sennacherib, and Ashurbanipal, must be laid in the graveyard of nations.

The poem of Nineveh's doom (Nah. 2:1—3:19) is really quite remarkable. The figures of speech are bold and depict in staccato fashion the strokes of war. The glamour of the attack with whip and prancing horses and flashing swords suddenly gives way to the picture of the innumerable corpses that mark Nineveh's defeat (3:2-3). If it was wrong for Nahum to rejoice at Nineveh's fall, what shall be said of the heavenly throng of Rev. 19:1-6? Inveterate sin must at last bring well-deserved punishment. The death knell of all opposition to the gospel is here: "'I am against you,' declares the LORD Almighty" (Nah. 2:13; 3:5).

nail. The nails of the carpenter and cabinet maker were widely used from ancient times and differed little in size and shape from those used today. Made usually of bronze or iron (cf. 1 Chr. 22:3), they were hand-forged and tapered more gradually than the machined nails of today. Decorative nails with heads of gold (cf. 2 Chr. 3:9) or silver have been found. In the sense of the heath that protects the human finger, the term *nail* occurs only once: the end of mourning was marked by dressing the hair and cutting the nails (Deut. 21:12).

Nain. nayn (Gk. *Nain G3723*). During his great Galilean ministry, following the healing of the Roman CENTURION's slave in CAPERNAUM, Jesus journeyed about 25 mi. (40 km.) S to a city called Nain (Lk. 7:11-17). As he approached the city, he met the funeral procession of a widow's son, apparently a well-known person, since the procession consisted of a large crowd from the city. Touched by the desolate state of the widow, Jesus miraculously restored the young man to life to the astonishment and gratitude of the whole city and neighboring territory. Luke is the only evangelist to report this episode. Nain is identified with the modern village of Nein (c. 6.5 mi./10.5 km. SE of NAZARETH), which lies at the foot of the lower N slope of Mount MOREH. It is intriguing that on the S side of the same hill lies the OT town of SHUNEM, where ELISHA also restored a child to life (2 Ki. 4:8-37).

Naioth. nay´yoth (Heb. *nāyôt H5766*; in 1 Sam. 20:1 many MSS have the common noun *nāwôt*, "grazing place, township," and this is the form preferred by some scholars). A place in RAMAH to which DAVID fled from SAUL (1 Sam. 19:18—20:1). When Saul went to this location, "the Spirit of God came even upon him, and he walked along prophesying until he came to Naioth. He stripped off his robes and also prophesied in Samuel's presence" (19:23-24a). The site is unknown, however, and many believe that the word is not a proper name, but rather a common noun to be rendered "camps" or the like. Since SAMUEL lived in Ramah (c. 5 mi./8 km. N of JERUSALEM), some think that "the camps/dwellings at Ramah" described the domicile of Samuel and his school of prophets (v. 20).

nakedness. The first use of the word *naked* in the Bible gives insight into the meaning in many other contexts: "The man and his wife were both naked, and they felt no shame" (Gen. 2:25). In the unfallen state the exposure of the body would not provoke TEMPTATION. The sense of SHAME at nakedness is illustrated graphically in the account of NOAH's drunkenness and the reaction of his sons to his consequent exposure (9:20-23). The expression "to uncover nakedness" is used to describe forbidden degrees of cohabitation (Lev. 18:6 et al.). The terms *naked* and *nakedness* are used figuratively in many ways. "To be naked" may mean to be without full covering (Jn. 21:7) or destitute (Job 22:6) or impoverished (Gen. 42:9). JOB used the word to indicate the transcience of earthly possessions (Job 1:21). The expression "nakedness of the land" (Gen. 42:9 NRSV) indicates exposure and helplessness. The spiritual state of the church in LAODICEA was "wretched, pitiful, poor, blind and naked" (Rev. 3:17)—a vivid characterization of its utter bankruptcy.

Nakon. nay´kon. TNIV form of NACON.

name. In Bible times names had greater significance than they usually have today. A name was given only by a person in a position of authority (Gen. 2:19; 2 Ki. 23:34) and could signify that the person named was appointed to a particular position, function, or relationship (Gen. 35:18; 2 Sam. 12:25). The name given was often determined by some circumstance at the time of birth (Gen. 19:22); sometimes the name expressed a hope or a prophecy (Isa. 8:1-4; Hos. 1:4). When a person gave his own name to another, it signified the joining of the two in very close unity, as when God gave his name to Israel (Deut. 28:9-10). To be baptized into someone's name therefore meant to pass into new ownership (Matt. 28:19; Acts 8:16; 1 Cor. 1:13, 15). In the Scriptures there is the closest possible relationship between a person and his name, the two being practically equivalent, so that to remove the name was to extinguish the person (Num. 27:4; Deut. 7:24). To forget God's name is to depart from him (Jer. 23:27). The expression "the name of the LORD" could signify not simply the word by which he is called (see JEHOVAH), but more importantly the Lord himself in the attributes he had manifested—holiness, power, love, etc. Often in the Bible the name signified the presence of the person in the character revealed (1 Ki. 18:24). To be sent or to speak in someone's name meant to carry that person's authority (Jer. 11:21; 2 Cor. 5:20). To pray in the name of Jesus is to pray as his representatives on earth—in his Spirit and with his aim—and implies the closest union with Christ.

names. When God named what he had made, he described the essence of the thing (Gen. 1:5, 8, 10; 2:11-14). By allowing ADAM to give names, God enabled him to express relationships to his fellow creatures: Adam named the beasts (2:19-20) and woman (2:23). EVE's personal name is from her function as mother of all living (human) beings (3:20). CAIN's name is a play on two Hebrew words (4:1). SETH is a reminder that God "appointed" him instead of ABEL (4:25). "Men began to call on the name of the LORD" (4:26); did they possibly already at this time begin to recognize him by his revealed name, JEHOVAH (Yahweh)? God changed the name of Abram to ABRAHAM in view of his destiny (17:5). Names in Gen. 10 are of individuals (e.g., Nimrod) or nations (e.g., Egypt [=Mizraim], Jebusites, Canaanites), or eponymous ancestors or tribes descended from them. People were named for animals (Caleb, dog; Tabitha and Dorcas, gazelle), plants (Tamar, palm tree), precious things (Peninnah, coral or pearl), qualities (Hannah,

N

grace; Ikkesh, perverse; Ira, watchful), historical circumstances (Ichabod, inglorious), or for relatives (Absalom named a daughter after his sister Tamar).

The significance of the names of the tribes of Israel is brought out in Gen. 48-49. Names compounded with EL (God) or Jeho- and -iah (Yahweh) became common. JACOB (supplanter) received the name ISRAEL (prince of God) and recognized God without learning his secret name (32:24-32). Prophets gave their children symbolic names (Isa. 8:1-4; Hos. 1:4-11). The MESSIAH was given significant names: IMMANUEL (God with us, Isa. 7:14; Matt. 1:23), JESUS (Yahweh saves, Matt. 1:21; Lk. 1:31). In his name (Acts 3:16) miracles were wrought, as he promised (Jn. 14:13-14). When we act in Jesus' name, we represent him (Matt. 10:42). Place-names are for natural features (Lebanon, white, because it is snow-capped; Bethsaida and Sidon from their fishing; Tirzah, pleasantness, for its beauty). By NT times both personal and family names were common (Bartimaeus) or descriptive phrases were added, as for the several Marys. Hybrid or duplicate names occur in a bilingual culture (e.g., Cephas/Peter). Patriarchal times saw names as indicators of character, function, or destiny. Soon names began to be given more hopefully than discriminatingly, until finally we are not sure whether the name tells us anything about the nature: Was Philip truly a "lover of horses"? The many genealogical tables in the Bible follow the practice of ancient historians, showing the importance of descent and of the relations thus established between individuals.

Naomi. nay-oh´mee (Heb. *nā ͑ŏmî H5843*, "pleasant[ness]"). Wife of ELIMELECH and mother-in-law of RUTH. Naomi and her husband, who were originally from BETHLEHEM, had two sons, MAHLON and KILION (Ruth 1:1-3). Because of a famine in JUDAH they moved to MOAB, and when Naomi was widowed, her sons married Moabite wives, namely ORPAH and Ruth (v. 4). When the two sons died, she returned to Bethlehem with Ruth. In her depression she said she should no longer be called Naomi, "pleasant," but now more appropriately MARA, "bitter." She advised Ruth in the steps that led to Ruth's marriage to BOAZ (Ruth 3:1-6), and she nursed Ruth's child (4:16-17).

Naphath, Naphath-dor. See NAPHOTH DOR.

Naphish. nay´fish (Heb. *nāpîš H5874*, derivation uncertain). Son of ISHMAEL and grandson of ABRAHAM (Gen. 25:15; 1 Chr. 1:31). His descendants became an Arabian tribe living in TRANSJORDAN and were among those defeated by the Reubenites, the Gadites, and the Manassites (1 Chr. 5:19; KJV, "Nephish"). Some scholars believe that the NEPHUSSIM, listed among postexilic temple servants (Ezra 2:50; Neh. 7:52; see NETHINIM), were descendants of prisoners of war from this tribe.

Naphoth. See NAPHOTH DOR.

Naphoth Dor. nay´foth-dor´ (Heb. *nāpôt dôr H5869* [with variant spellings], possibly "heights of Dor"). Also Naphath-dor. A hilly region surrounding the city of DOR. The first element occurs in the plural form *nāpôt H5868* only once (Josh. 11:2), while the singular construct *nāpat* is found twice (12:23; 1 Ki. 4:11). In addition, the word *nepet* by itself occurs once (in the pausal form *hannāpet*, Josh. 17:11); it is treated as a proper name by some versions (NIV, "Naphoth"; NRSV, "Naphath"), but as a common noun by others (KJV, "countries"; NJPS, "regions").

Naphtali. naf´tuh-li (Heb. *naptālî H5889*, "[my] struggle"; Gk. *Nephthalim G3750*). KJV NT Nephthalim. Sixth son of JACOB, and his second by

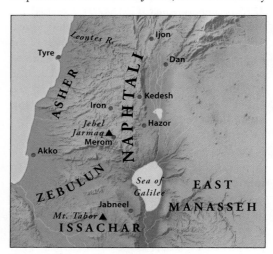

The tribal territory of Naphtali.

Part of the tribal territory of Naphtali in Galilee (looking N from the Arbel cliffs toward Wadi ʻAmmud).

BILHAH, the handmaid of RACHEL (Gen. 29:29). Naphtali and DAN (Bilhah's older son) usually are mentioned together in OT contexts. Of Naphtali himself practically nothing is known, and Jacob's blessing for Naphtali was brief and noncommittal (49:21). He had four sons, and his descendants became one of the Israelite tribes.

The tribe of Naphtali appears in the lists of the book of NUMBERS as a tribe of moderate size. It furnished 53,400 soldiers at KADESH BARNEA (Num. 1:43) and 45,000 at the mustering of the troops across from JERICHO (26:50). In the wilderness organization, Naphtali was supposed to camp on the N side of the TABERNACLE under the standard of Dan, and this group of tribes brought up the rear in marching. Interestingly, they settled together in CANAAN. Naphtali's prince Ahira gave the last offering for the dedication of the altar (7:78). Naphtali received the next to the last lot in the final division of the land (Josh. 19:32-39), but in many ways its inheritance was the best.

The territory of Naphtali, as nearly as we can tell, included the fertile scenic area just W of the Sea of Galilee and the sources of the JORDAN. It reached from the lower limits of the Sea of Galilee almost up to a point opposite Mount HERMON. On the W it reached halfway to the MEDITERRANEAN, being bounded by the tribe of ASHER. The chief cities of Naphtali were HAZOR, KINNERETH, and

KEDESH. The latter was the northernmost of the CITIES OF REFUGE in W Palestine; it was also the home of BARAK. Naphtali figured largely in DEBORAH's conquest of Hazor (Jdg. 5:18). Men from this tribe also assisted GIDEON (7:23). Naphtali is mentioned as one of SOLOMON's revenue districts (1 Ki. 4:15), and the collector was a son-in-law of the king.

Lying exposed in the N, the territory of Naphtali proved vulnerable. It was conquered by BEN-HADAD (1 Ki. 15:20), and the tribe was later deported after the first invasion of TIGLATH-PILESER about 733 B.C. (2 Ki. 15:29), who settled Gentiles in the territory. This event is mentioned in Isa. 9:1 with a prediction of the MESSIAH, who preached, as Matthew reminds us (Matt. 4:12-16), in this same region of Galilee of the Gentiles in fulfillment of the ancient prophecy.

Naphtuhim. See NAPHTUHITES.

Naphtuhites. nafʹtuh-hits (Heb. *naptuḥim H5888*, derivation uncertain). A people group that descended from MIZRAIM (NRSV, "Egypt"), the son of HAM (Gen. 10:13; 1 Chr. 1:11). Their identity is unknown, but because they are listed just before the PATHRUSITES, who lived in Upper (i.e., southern) EGYPT, some scholars have proposed that the Naphtuhites were associated with Lower

N

Egypt, in particular the NILE delta. An alternate suggestion links the name with the Egyptian god Ptah and thus with the city of MEMPHIS in Middle Egypt.

napkin. See HANDKERCHIEF.

Narcissus. nahr-sis´uhs (Gk. *Narkissos G3727*). When writing to the church in ROME, PAUL sends greetings to "those in the household of Narcissus who are in the Lord" (Rom. 16:11). Evidently, the reference is to Christians among the slaves (or possibly freedmen) in this household. Why Narcissus himself is not greeted has been the subject of speculation. Had he died? Or did Paul know that he was absent from Rome at the time? Or perhaps Narcissus was not a believer?

nard. See PLANTS.

Nathan. nay´thuhn (Heb. *nātān H5990*, "gift," or short form of a name such as ELNATHAN, "God has given"; Gk. *Natham G3718*). **(1)** Son of DAVID and BATHSHEBA (2 Sam. 5:14; 1 Chr. 3:5; 14:4). This Nathan was an older brother of SOLOMON, and his family is pictured as having a part in Israel's future eschatological events (Zech. 12:12; some believe that the reference here is to #2 below, Nathan the prophet). He is also included in Luke's GENEALOGY OF JESUS CHRIST (Lk. 3:31; in Matt. 1:6, the genealogy is traced through Solomon).

(2) A prophet at the royal court in JERUSALEM during the reign of David and the early years of Solomon. David consulted him regarding the building of the TEMPLE (2 Sam. 7; 1 Chr. 17). Nathan at first approved, but that same night he had a vision directing him to advise David to leave the building of the temple to the son who would succeed him. David humbly obeyed, expressing gratitude to God for blessings bestowed and others promised. Later Nathan rebuked David for adultery with Bathsheba (2 Sam. 12:1-25). David earnestly repented. The title of Ps. 51 links it with this incident. When ADONIJAH sought to supplant his aged father David as king, Nathan intervened through Bathsheba to secure the succession for her son Solomon (1 Ki. 1:8-53). Nathan wrote chronicles of the reign of David (1 Chr. 29:29) and

shared in writing the history of the reign of Solomon (2 Chr. 9:29). He was associated with David and GAD the seer in arranging the musical services for the house of God (29:25).

(3) Father of IGAL, who was one of David's mighty warriors (2 Sam. 23:36); the parallel passage, apparently as a result of later scribal corruption, identifies Nathan as brother of Joel (1 Chr. 11:38).

(4) The list of Solomon's "chief officials" (1 Ki. 4:2) includes the following: "Azariah son of Nathan—in charge of the district officers; Zabud son of Nathan—a priest and personal adviser to the king" (4:5). It is often assumed that both Azariah and Zabud were sons of the same man. Many have thought that this Nathan should be identified with Solomon's brother (#1 above); others have proposed Nathan the prophet (#2). In addition, some have wondered if there is a connection between Nathan father of Zabud and Nathan father of Zabad (see #5 below). None of these suggestions can be confirmed.

(5) Son of ATTAI, descendant of JUDAH through JERAHMEEL, and father of Zabad (1 Chr. 2:36).

(6) One of a group of leaders sent by EZRA to IDDO to get attendants for the house of God (Ezra 8:16). He is usually thought to be the same Nathan as the descendant of Binnui who agreed to put away his foreign wife (10:39).

Nathanael. nuh-than´ay-uhl (Gk. *Nathanaēl G3720*, from Heb. *nĕtan´ēl H5991*, "God has given"). A disciple of Jesus, mentioned only in Jn. 1:45-51; 21:2. His home was in CANA of GALILEE (21:2) and he heard of Jesus from PHILIP (1:45). The circumstances surrounding his calling are somewhat striking, since Christ praises his integrity at their initial encounter and demonstrates to Nathanael his own foreknowledge by reference to the fig tree. Evidently Nathanael's knowledge of the Scripture was considerable because of the remarkable theological repartee that occurred between Christ and him (1:47-51). Because Nathanael is not mentioned in the Synoptic Gospels, efforts have been made to identify him with one of the apostles listed in Matt. 10:2-4 and parallels. A widely accepted suggestion since antiquity is that Nathanael was the same as BARTHOLOMEW. Though it is true that double names (even double Semitic names) were sometimes used, this proposal remains only a conjecture.

Nathan-Melech. nay'thuhn-mee'lik (Heb. *nĕtan-melek H5994*, "Melech [= king] has given," possibly in reference to Yahweh or to MOLECH). TNIV Nathan-Melek. An official or chamberlain near whose quarters were kept "the horses that the kings of Judah had dedicated to the sun"; these horses were removed by King JOSIAH (2 Ki. 23:11).

nations. See GENTILE.

nature, natural. Both the OT and NT CREATION primarily as a backdrop to REDEMPTION. The closest one gets in Scripture to nature as a distinct entity is in three passages: the wording "all the host of them" in reference to the totality of God's creation (Gen. 2:1); PAUL's statement regarding the ungodly changing the course of "nature" (Gk. *physis G5882*, Rom. 1:26); and the apostle's appeal, "Does not the very nature of things teach you ... ?" (1 Cor. 11:14).

The emphasis in Scripture is on the following facts: (a) God the Father is Creator, Sustainer, and Ruler of all (Gen. 1-2; Isa. 44:24; Amos 4:13); (b) God is omnipresent in all he has created (Ps. 139:7-12); (c) Christ the Son also must be spoken of in terms of Creator, Sustainer, and Ruler (Jn. 1:3; Col. 1:16-17; Heb. 1:10-12); (d) the order and beauty of the universe reflect and proclaim the existence, wisdom, and power of God (Job 38:4—39:30; Ps. 8:1-4; 19:1-6; 104:1-32; 136:6-9; Prov. 8:22-31; Rom. 1:19-20); and (e) one may learn from God's bounty and care in nature regarding God's provision and concern for human beings (Matt. 6:25-34; Lk. 12:22-31).

The Greek noun *physis* denotes (a) a condition, endowment, or status inherited from one's ancestors, as in reference to those who "by nature" are Jews (Gal. 2:15), heathen (Rom. 2:27), "children of wrath" (Eph. 2:3 NRSV), or the "natural" and "wild" branches of the olive tree (Rom. 11:21, 24); (b) innate characteristics and instinctive dispositions, as of false gods (Gal. 4:8), men (Rom. 2:14; Jas. 3:7b), or even God (2 Pet. 1:4); (c) the established order within nature, as of sexual relations (Rom. 1:26b) or decorum (1 Cor. 11:14); and (d) a creature or product of nature (Jas. 3:7a). The

cognate adjective *physikos G5879* is employed with reference to natural human instincts (Rom. 1:26-27), and in a deprecatory sense of only the natural instincts (2 Pet. 2:12). The adjective *psychikos G6035* (see SOUL) signifies the life of the natural world and whatever belongs to it, always to be contrasted with the supernatural world and that which may be characterized as belonging to the HOLY SPIRIT (1 Cor. 2:14; 15:44-46; Jas. 3:15; Jude 19; see also SENSUAL). It is in this latter theological and ethical sense that the word comes to its distinctive expression in the Bible, identifying the state of human beings as they are "in Adam" and serving as a backdrop to God's complete redemption "in Christ."

Naum. See NAHUM.

nave. This English term is used by the NRSV and other versions to render Hebrew *hêkāl H2121* (which usually means "palace" or "temple") in passages where the word refers to the larger room (NIV, "main hall") of the TEMPLE (e.g., 1 Ki. 6:3, 5; Ezek. 41:1-2; cf. also *habbayit haggādôl*, lit., "the big house," 2 Chr. 3:5).

navel. The Hebrew term *šōr H9219* is used once in the sense "navel" (Cant. 7:2), once with reference to the navel cord (Ezek. 16:4), and once by synecdoche for the whole body (Prov. 3:8). (A similar word, *šārîr H9235*, which occurs only in Job 40:16, is rendered "navel" by the KJV, but its meaning is "muscle.") Another word for "navel" is *ṭabbûr H3179*, and in both of its occurrences it is constructed with *ʾereṣ H824*, yielding the metaphorical meaning of "the center of the land" (Jdg. 9:37; Ezek. 38:12).

navy. See SHIPS.

Nazarene. naz'uh-reen (Gk. *Nazarēnos G3716* and *Nazōraios G3717*, "of Nazareth"). In almost every occurrence, this name identifies Jesus on the basis of his long residence in NAZARETH; in one passage it serves to identify his followers (Acts 24:5). Used by friends, the term had a friendly meaning (Acts 2:22; 3:6; 10:38), and Jesus applied the title to himself (22:8). Used by his enemies, it was a title of scorn (Matt. 26:71; Mk. 14:67). It is not altogether certain what Matthew intended in

N

the words, "So was fulfilled what was said through the prophets: 'He will be called a Nazarene'" (Matt. 2:23). Most interpreters have thought that Matthew had in mind Isa. 11:1, in which the MESSIAH is referred to as a "branch" or "shoot" (Heb. *nēṣer H5916*) out of the roots of JESSE. Others have said that Matthew meant only that the MESSIAH would be a despised person (ch. 53) and not a prominent or accepted individual (Nazarenes apparently were despised by their neighbors in the first century; cf. Jn. 1:46). Still others have understood the verse only as a positive statement that pointed to a negative truth, namely that the Messiah would not be called a Bethlehemite, the place of his nativity, in order to avoid hostility. He, therefore, would be called something else, in fact, a Nazarene. In any case, Matthew sees a fulfillment of Isaiah's prophecy when Jesus' parents took up their residence in Nazareth.

Nazareth. naz´uh-rith (Gk. *Nazareth G3714* [also *Nazaret* and *Nazara*]; meaning uncertain). A city in GALILEE, the home of Mary and Joseph, the human parents of Jesus (Lk. 1:26; 2:4). After their flight into EGYPT to escape the ruthless hands of HEROD the Great, the holy family contemplated returning to BETHLEHEM of JUDEA; but hearing that Herod's son Archelaus was now reigning in Judea, they withdrew to Nazareth in Galilee (Matt. 2:13-23). Important as it may seem to have been in the NT, the town is not mentioned in the OT, the TALMUD, or the writings of JOSEPHUS. There is reason to believe that Nazareth was a rather insignificant town in Jesus' day, overshadowed by the larger city to the N, SEPPHORIS. Nazareth is about halfway between the S end of the Sea of Galilee and Mount CARMEL. Situated in the hills to the N of the Plain of ESDRAELON, the site (modern en-Naṣira) commands a good view of the ancient battlegrounds. To the N one also can see Mount HERMON; to the W, the MEDITERRANEAN; and to the E, BASHAN.

Upon reaching the age of thirty and the beginning of his ministry, our Lord went from Nazareth to Judea to be baptized by JOHN THE BAPTIST. An interesting comment on Nazareth from the mouth of NATHANAEL appears in Jn. 1:46: "Nazareth! Can anything good come from there?" This question has been understood in many ways, but the most common is that Nathanael was casting an aspersion on the smallness of the town, perhaps viewing it as a rival to his own village of CANA (cf. 21:2). Luke records that Jesus was rejected by the people of Nazareth when he read from Isa. 61:1-2 at the synagogue and told the congregation that he was the fulfillment of that prophecy. Then he proceeded to illustrate from the lives of ELIJAH and ELISHA that prophets are rejected by their own people. In their anger the citizenry led him to the brow of the hill

The Nazareth ridge as seen from the floor of the Jezreel Valley. (View to the NW.)

© Dr. James C. Martin

Nazareth.

on which the city was built, that they might throw him over; but he escaped in the crowd (Lk. 4:16-30). Some see a second and later rejection of Jesus at Nazareth in the parallel accounts of Matthew and Mark (Matt. 13:54-58; Mk. 6:1-6a). Again, the people were offended at him when he read in the synagogue. Mark comments: "He could not do any miracles there, except lay his hands on a few sick people and heal them. And he was amazed at their lack of faith" (Mk. 6:5-6).

Nazareth Decree. An inscription cut on a slab of white marble, sent in 1878 from NAZARETH for the private collection of a German antiquarian named Froehner. It was not until 1930, when, on Froehner's death, the inscription found a place in the Cabinet de Medailles of the Louvre, that the historian Michel Rostovtzeff noticed its significance. The decree states: "Ordinance of Caesar. It is my pleasure that graves and tombs remain undisturbed in perpetuity for those who have made them for the cult of their ancestors, or children or members of their house. If, however, any may lay information that another has either demolished them, or has in any other way extracted the buried, or has maliciously transferred them to other places in order to wrong them, or has displaced the sealing or other stones, against such a one I order that a trial be instituted, as in respect of the gods, so in regard to the cult of mortals. For it shall be much more obligatory to honor the buried. Let it be absolutely forbidden for anyone to disturb them. In the case of contravention I desire that the offender be sentenced to capital punishment on the charge of violation of sepulchre."

Evidence suggests that the inscription falls within the decade that closed in A.D. 50. The central Roman government did not take over the administration of GALILEE until the death of AGRIPPA I in 44. This limits the date, in the opinion of competent scholarship, to five years under CLAUDIUS. This emperor's interest in continuing the religious policy of AUGUSTUS led to a wide knowledge of the religions of the empire and prompted investigation in the courts of any case involving cults or religious beliefs. Nazareth having recently fallen under central control, Claudius proceeds to deal with the trouble on the spot. Inquiries are made in Palestine, and the local authority asks for directions. The result is a "rescript" or imperial ruling. Claudius wrote more than one long letter on religious matters (e.g., a notable letter to the Jews of Alexandria in A.D. 41). The decree set up at Nazareth may have been part of such a communication. If this hypothetical reconstruction is correct, it is in the words of an emperor that the twentieth century read the first secular comment on the Easter story, and legal testimony to its central fact.

Nazarite. See NAZIRITE.

Nazirite. naz'uh-rit (Heb. *nāzîr* H5687, "dedicated, withheld"). KJV Nazarite. A member of a Hebrew religious class, specially dedicated to God. The authorization for Nazirites appears in Num. 6:1-21 and was divinely revealed, through MOSES, shortly before Israel's departure from Mount SINAI (Num. 10:11; cf. Exod. 40:17). It would appear that the practice of separation for religious purposes is very ancient and was shared by a number of peoples. In Israel, however, it assumed unique proportions. There were two different types of Naziritism, the temporary and the perpetual, of which the first type was far more common. In fact, we know of only three of the latter class: SAMSON, SAMUEL, and JOHN THE BAPTIST.

The three principal marks that distinguished the Nazirite were (1) a renunciation of all products of the vine, including grapes; (2) prohibition of the use of the razor; and (3) avoidance of contact with a dead body. The OT nowhere explains why these three areas of prohibition were chosen as giving expression to the Nazirites' positive "separation to

N

N

the LORD" (Num. 6:2), but there are some fairly obvious, even if speculative, lines of thought. Abstention from the fruit of the vine could point to the renunciation of earthly joys in order to find all joy in the Lord. Allowing the hair to grow must surely symbolize the dedication of personal strength and vitality to the Lord (at the end of the period of the vow the hair was shaved and cast into the fire of sacrifice, 6:18). The avoidance of contact with the dead symbolizes the primacy of the Nazirite's relationship to the Lord: no duty to others can take its place. It should be noted that Nazirites were not expected to withdraw from society, that is, to live a monastic type of life, nor to become celibate. The question has been raised whether the RECABITES of Jer. 35 were included within the Nazirite classification. It appears, however, that the Recabites had more the status of a (Hebrew) nomadic group, since they were not merely forbidden to drink wine but also to refrain from owning real estate (they lived in tents, Jer. 35:7, 10).

John the Baptist, the forerunner of Christ, was a Nazirite from birth (Lk. 1:15). The connection between John the Baptist and the Qumran community is rather tenuous, nor can it be proved that the men of Qumran were all Nazirites (see DEAD SEA SCROLLS). The case of PAUL and Naziritism has frequently elicited discussion. Although it cannot be established that the apostle assumed such vow, it is certain that he did assume the expenses of those who did (Acts 21:23-24). The court of Herod AGRIPPA supported a large number of Nazirites, according to JOSEPHUS.

The reasons for taking a Nazirite vow were numerous. A vow might be assumed by a parent before the birth of a child; by one in some sort of distress or trouble; or by a woman suspected by her husband of unfaithfulness in their marriage relationship until the suspicion could be removed. Women and slaves could take vows only if sanctioned by their husbands or masters. The period of time for the Nazirite vow was anywhere from thirty days to a whole lifetime.

There is only one clear-cut mention of the Nazirites by the prophets. The prophet AMOS voices a complaint of the Lord against the children of Israel that he had given to Israel the prophets and the Nazirites as spiritual instructors and examples, but that the people had given wine to the Nazirites and had offered inducements to the prophets to refrain from prophesying (2:11-12).

Neah. nee´uh (Heb. *nēʿâ H5828*, derivation unknown). A town on the N border of the tribal territory of ZEBULUN (Josh. 19:13). Neah was located between RIMMON (PLACE) and HANNATHON, but the site has not been identified.

Neapolis. nee-ap´uh-lis (Gk. *Nea polis* or *Neapolis G3735*, "new city"). A town on the N shore of the Aegean Sea (to be distinguished from Neapolis, modern Naples, in Italy). The best evidence places its site at the present Greek town of Kavala. The city belonged first to Thrace (see THRACIA), then became part of both the first and second Athenian Confederacy, during which time it was commended for its loyalty. It finally fell within the Roman province of MACEDONIA. Neapolis was the first point in Europe touched by PAUL and his companions when they came from TROAS (Acts 16:11). From here it was an easy journey to PHILIPPI (about 10 mi./16 km. inland). It is possible that the apostle

A general view of modern Kavala, ancient Neapolis. (View to the W.)

© Dr. James C. Martin

passed through the town again when he revisited Macedonia (20:1); and it is almost certain that he embarked from Neapolis on his journey back to Troas (20:6).

Neariah. nee´uh-ri´uh (Heb. *nĕʿaryâ H5859* "young man [*or* servant] of Yahweh"). **(1)** Son of Ishi and descendant of SIMEON during the reign of HEZEKIAH; Neariah and his brothers led 500 Simeonites in an invasion of SEIR and wiped out the AMALEKITES (1 Chr. 4:42-43).

(2) Son of Shemaiah and postexilic descendant of DAVID through SOLOMON and ZERUBBABEL (1 Chr. 3:22-23). Some scholars believe he was the son of Shecaniah; see HATTUSH #1.

Nebai. nee´bi (Heb. *nēbāy H5763*, derivation uncertain). One of the leaders of the people who signed the covenant of NEHEMIAH (Neh. 10:19; the LXX and some modern versions follow the *Ketib*, "Nobai").

Nebaioth. ni-bay´yoth (Heb. *nĕbāyôt H5568*, meaning unknown). Firstborn son of ISHMAEL and grandson of ABRAHAM and HAGAR (Gen. 25:13; 28:9; 36:3; 1 Chr. 1:29). The name is used also of his descendants (Isa. 60:7), an E Semitic tribal people of ARABIA. The Nebaiothites (Nabaiateans) are mentioned in Assyrian records in connection with KEDAR (as in Isaiah). Moreover, the form *nbyt* occurs in N Arabian inscriptions with reference to a tribe hostile to Teimaʾ (TEMA). Attempts to equate Nebaioth with the historical NABATEANS have been widely rejected both on philological and historical grounds.

Neballat. ni-bal´uht (Heb. *nĕballāṭ H5579*, possibly from a root *blṭ*, attested in Akk. *balāṭu*, "life"). A town overlooking the Plain of SHARON; along with HADID, ZEBOIM, LOD, and ONO, Neballat was settled by Benjamites after the EXILE (Neh. 11:34). It is identified with the modern Beit Nabala, c. 13 mi. (21 km.) ESE of JOPPA and less than 2 mi. (3 km.) NNE of Hadid.

Nebat. nee´bat (Heb. *nĕbāṭ H5565*, possibly "[God] has looked at [*i.e.*, approvingly]"). Father of JEROBOAM I, who was the first king of ISRAEL

after the division of the kingdom (1 Ki. 11:26 et al.). Because Jeroboam's mother is described as a widow, many infer that Nebat died while Jeroboam was still a child.

Nebiim, Neviʾim. nuh-bee´im, nuh-vi-eem´ (Heb. *nĕbîʾim*, pl. of *nābîʾ H5566*, "prophet"). A term applied to the second division of the OT Hebrew canon, and consisting of the Former Prophets (Joshua, Judges, Samuel, Kings) and the Latter Prophets (Isaiah, Jeremiah, Ezekiel, and the Twelve). See CANONICITY.

Nebo (deity). nee´boh (Heb. *nĕbô H5550*, from Akk. *Nabū*, prob. "one called [by god]"). Also Nabu. Name of a Babylonian deity mentioned only in Isaiah's taunt song on the downfall of BABYLON (Isa. 46:1). Nebo was the god of wisdom and writing, and (alongside MARDUK) the patron-god of the Babylonian rulers. His center of worship was at Borsippa, SW of Babylon. The cult continued to flourish until the end of the neo-Babylonian period (612-538 B.C.) and survived in SYRIA for several more centuries. The name Nabu was commonly used as a component of personal names (NABONIDUS, NEBUCHADNEZZAR, and others; possibly also ABEDNEGO).

Nebo (person). nee´boh (Heb. *nĕbô H5551*, "height"). Ancestor of some Israelites who agreed to put away their foreign wives (Ezra 10:43). Some believe that the name refers to the town from which the family came. See NEBO (PLACE) #2.

Nebo (place). nee´boh (Heb. *nĕbô H5550*, "height"). **(1)** A town in MOAB near Mount Nebo (see NEBO, MOUNT), requested by the tribes of REUBEN and GAD (Num. 32:3). It was rebuilt by the Reubenites (Num. 32:38; 33:47; cf. 1 Chr. 5:8). The town was later retaken by MESHA, king of Moab, who recorded his victory on the MOABITE STONE. Nebo is mentioned also in prophetic oracles of judgment (Isa. 15:2; Jer. 48:1, 22). Its precise location is uncertain.

(2) A postexilic town in JUDAH, mentioned in a list just after BETHEL and AI (Ezra 2:29; called "the other Nebo" [prob. a scribal error] in Neh. 7:33). It is often, but tentatively, identified with

Nuba, c. 7 mi. (11 km.) NW of HEBRON; some, however, think this Nebo is the same as #1 above. See also NEBO (PERSON).

(3) Traditional burial place of MOSES. See NEBO, MOUNT.

Nebo, Mount. nee´boh (Heb. *har nĕbô H2215* and *H5549,* "high mountain"). A mountain in TRANS-JORDAN from which MOSES viewed the Promised Land. Mount Nebo is mentioned only twice (Deut. 32:49; 34:1). Some rather specific indications of its location are given in each passage. The first one records God's command to Moses, "Go up into the Abarim Range to Mount Nebo in Moab, across from Jericho, and view Canaan, the land I am giving the Israelites as their own possession." The second states that "Moses climbed Mount Nebo from the plains of Moab to the top of Pisgah, across from Jericho." Today known as Jebel en-Neba (or Nabba), Mount Nebo is a spur of the plain of Moab, some 6 mi. (10 km.) NW of MEDEBA. It is almost opposite the N end of the DEAD SEA and therefore not due E of Jericho. It rises c. 4,000 ft. (1,220 m.) above the Dead Sea or c. 2,700 ft. (820 m.) above sea level. PISGAH, which is associated with Nebo in Deut. 34:1, may be another name for the same peak, or Nebo may be a part of Pisgah. Since several elevations in that same vicinity afford the same view, it is not certain whether the one bearing the name *Neba* is necessarily the one Moses climbed. A saddle connects it to Ras es-Siyaghah, which was revered by early Christians and is the site preferred by many scholars.

Nebo-Sarsekim. nee´boh-shar´suh-kim (Heb. *nĕbû śar-sĕkim H5552*). One of NEBUCHADNEZ-ZAR's officials who participated in the siege of JERUSALEM (Jer. 39:3 NIV; other versions translate differently). See comments under SARSECHIM.

Nebuchadnezzar, Nebuchadrezzar. neb´uh-kuhd-nez´uhr, neb´uh-kuh-drez´uhr (Heb. *nĕbûkadne˒ṣṣar H5556* and *nĕbûkadre˒ṣṣar H5557* [in Jeremiah and Ezekiel], with some spelling variations; from Akk. *Nabū-kudurru-uṣur,* "may [the god] Nabu protect [my] heir"; LXX, *Nabouchodono-sor;* the spelling with *n* instead of *r* is often explained as the result of dissimilation). Son of NABOPOLAS-SAR and King of BABYLON, 605-562 B.C. Often referred to as Nebuchadnezzar II (to distinguish him from a king of the same name who ruled at the end of the twelfth century B.C.), it was he who carried away the people of JUDAH in the seventy-year Babylonian captivity. He figures prominently in the books of Jeremiah, Ezekiel, Daniel, and the later chapters of Kings and Chronicles.

Nebuchadnezzar's father, Nabopolassar, seems to have been a general appointed by the Assyrian king. However, in the later years of ASSYRIA he rebelled and established himself as king of Babylon in 626 B.C. The rebellion increased and finally Nabopolassar with the Medes (see MEDIA) and SCYTHIANS conquered NINEVEH, the Assyrian capital, in 612. The Medes and Babylonians divided the Assyrian empire, and a treaty was probably sealed by the marriage of the Median princess to the Babylonian prince, Nebuchadnezzar. In 607 the crown prince Nebuchadnezzar joined his father in the battle against the remnants of the Assyrian power and their allies, the Egyptians. In 605, when his father was in his last illness, he decisively defeated the Egyptians at CARCHEMISH and was able to take over all SYRIA and PALESTINE. Apparently JEHOIAKIM, king of Judah, who had been vassal to EGYPT, quickly did homage to Babylon and gave hostages (Dan. 1:1).

Nebuchadnezzar at this time got news of his father's death, and with a picked bodyguard he hastened home to secure his throne. On repeated occasions thereafter he struck toward the west. In about 602 B.C. Jehoiakim revolted (2 Ki. 24:1), probably with promise of Egyptian help, but was forced to submit. In 601 Nebuchadnezzar attacked Egypt itself but was defeated, as he frankly admits. Later, Pharaoh HOPHRA submitted to him. In 597 Jehoiakim rebelled again, and Nebuchadnezzar called out his troops for another western expedition. Jehoiakim died either in a siege or by treachery (Jer. 22:18-19), and his son JEHOIACHIN ascended the throne. But he lasted only three months until the campaign was over; he was taken as a hostage to Babylon, where he lived and finally was given relative freedom. Here the biblical account (2 Ki. 25:27-30) is confirmed by discovery of the Weidner Tablets.

Nebuchadnezzar installed Jehoiachin's uncle as puppet king, taking heavy tribute from Jerusalem.

EZEKIEL was among the captives of that expedition. Nebuchadnezzar's chronicle agrees with the biblical account, telling how (in 597 B.C.) he "encamped against the city of Judah and on the second day of the month Adar [Mar. 15/16] he seized the city and captured the king. He appointed there a king of his own choice, received its heavy tribute and sent them to Babylon" (D. Wiseman, *Chronicles of the Chaldean Kings* [1956], 73). This discovery gives about the best authenticated date in the OT. The Chronicle tells of subsequent repeated expeditions of Nebuchadnezzar toward the W to collect tribute and keep the satellite kingdoms in line. Unfortunately, the present tablets do not go beyond 593, so they give no record of the final and brutal devastation of Jerusalem in 586 when ZEDEKIAH revolted.

Nebuchadnezzar is celebrated by the historians of antiquity for the splendor of his building operations as well as for the brilliance of his military exploits. The archaeological excavations in Babylon illustrate the histories. Still impressive are the remains of the Ishtar Gate and the processional street lined with facades of enameled brick bearing pictures of griffins (fabled monsters with eagle head and wings and lion body). The temple of Esagila was famous, as were also the ZIGGURAT, or temple tower, and the hanging gardens. These were regarded by the Greeks as one of the wonders of the world, though nothing certain of them has been excavated. According to legend, they were built for Nebuchadnezzar's wife, the Median princess Amytis, who was homesick for her mountains.

Historical records are brief and could hardly be expected to mention the incidents of Nebuchadnezzar's life detailed by DANIEL. As to the king's madness (Dan. 4), there is no historical account remaining for us, but it must be remembered that much of Nebuchadnezzar's reign is a historical blank. Among the DEAD SEA SCROLLS a fragment has been found, the *Prayer of Nabonidus*, that refers to an illness of King NABONIDUS for seven years that was healed by God after the testimony of a Jewish magician. Some now say that this is the source of the legend that in Daniel is misapplied to Nebuchadnezzar. This can hardly be proved or denied from historical evidence. It seems equally possible that the canonical record was duplicated and applied to the later king. Indeed, more than

one king suffered from illness and from mental distress (Ashurbanipal and Cambyses may be mentioned). If truth is stranger than fiction, both Nebuchadnezzar and Nabonidus may have suffered in a somewhat similar way—the similarities being emphasized in the latter's prayer. There is perhaps a bare possibility that the names are confused.

Of the death of Nebuchadnezzar we have no knowledge. He was succeeded by his son EVIL-MERODACH (Amil-Marduk), then by his son-in-law NERGAL-SHAREZER (Neriglissar), for brief reigns. Nabonidus, who followed after the short reign of Labashi-Marduk, was perhaps related. There is some evidence that Nabonidus's mother was the daughter of Nebuchadnezzar by a second wife, Nitocris. With the passing of the brilliant Nebuchadnezzar, however, the Neo-Babylonian empire soon crumbled and fell an easy prey to the Persians under CYRUS.

Nebushasban. See NEBUSHAZBAN.

Nebushazban. neb´uh-shaz´ban (Heb. *nĕbûšazbān H5558*, prob. from an unattested Akk. name, *Nabū-šezibanni*, "may [the god] Nabu deliver me"). KJV Nebushasban. An important official (see RABSARIS) of the Babylonian army; he was among those ordered to provide for the safety of JEREMIAH after the Babylonians took JERUSALEM (Jer. 39:13; on the basis of this verse, some scholars emend v. 3 so that it too refers to NERGAL-SHAREZER as Rabmag and to Nebushazban as Rabsaris).

Nebuzaradan. neb´uh-zuh-ray´duhn (Heb. *nĕbûzar'ădān H5555*, from Akk. *Nabū-zēr-iddin*, "[the god] Nabu has given offspring"). NEBUCHADNEZZAR's officer in charge of the destruction of JERUSALEM after its capture. He carried out the burning and destruction of the city a month after its fall (2 Ki. 25:8-9), the deportation of the Jews to Babylonia (2 Ki. 25:11; Jer. 39:9; 52:15, 30), and the sending of the leading Jewish rebels to Nebuchadnezzar at RIBLAH for execution (2 Ki. 25:18-21; Jer. 52:24-27). He acted kindly toward JEREMIAH, entrusting him, together with royal princesses and other innocent people, to GEDALIAH, the Jewish noble he appointed as governor (Jer. 39:13-14; 41:10; 43:6).

N

Necho, Nechoh. See NECO.

neck. There are almost twenty passages in the Bible where people, usually the children of Israel, are called "stiff-necked" (e.g., Exod. 32:9; Deut. 9:6; Jer. 7:26; cf. Acts 7:51). In these contexts the word always is used to signify determination in an evil direction. This image is very apt, because when a person shows determination the muscles of not only the jaw but also the neck become tense. God says to the Israelites, "For I knew how stubborn you were; / the sinews of your neck were iron, / your forehead was bronze" (Isa. 48:4). The neck is used frequently as the part of the body bearing a yoke or burden (e.g., Gen. 27:40; Deut. 28:48; Isa. 10:27; Jer. 27:2, 8; 30:8; Acts 15:10). To fall on someone else's neck was to put one's arms about the neck or embrace (e.g., Gen. 33:4; 45:14; 46:29; Lk. 15:20; Acts 20:37).

necklace. See CHAIN.

Neco. nee′koh (Heb. *nĕkōh H5785* [in 2 Ki.] and *nĕkô H5786* [in 2 Chr. and Jer.], from Egyp. *nkʾw*). Also Necho(h). Son of Psammetichus (Psamtik) I and the second king of the 26th, or Saite, dynasty of EGYPT (ruled 610-595 B.C.). Neco began his rule at a propitious time: the Assyrian empire was falling, and the Neo-Babylonian empire was emerging. He thus was able to gain and retain control over SYRIA for a number of years. Of particular interest to the reader of the Bible is JOSIAH's defeat by Neco at the battle of MEGIDDO (2 Ki. 23:29; 2 Chr. 35:20-24). When Josiah died, JEHOAHAZ was made king, but Neco dethroned him and set up in his stead Jehoahaz's brother JEHOIAKIM (2 Ki. 23:29-34; 2 Chr. 35:20-36:4). In 605 he was badly defeated by NEBUCHADNEZZAR at the battle of CARCHEMISH and lost all of his Asiatic possessions (2 Ki. 24:7).

necromancy. The practice of conjuring the spirits of the dead to inquire about the future. The Mosaic law sternly forbade such a practice (Deut. 18:10-11). The most familiar case in the Bible is that of King SAUL and the medium of ENDOR (1 Sam. 28:7-25). There are several quite legitimate interpretations of this admittedly difficult passage; perhaps the most feasible view is that God for his own purpose allowed Saul to converse with the deceased Samuel. See also DIVINATION.

nectar. The sweetish liquid of plants that is used by bees in making HONEY. This English term is used by the NIV once to render a Hebrew word that usually refers to grape juice (Cant. 8:2); it is also used once by the NRSV as the translation of a word that means "honey" (4:11).

© Dr. James C. Martin

King Josiah challenged the advancing army of Pharaoh Neco as it advanced northward near the Aruna Pass, seen here. (View to the N through the pass up Nahal Iron.)

Nedabiah. ned´uh-bi´uh (Heb. *nĕdabyâ H5608*, prob. "Yahweh is willing [*or* shows himself generous]"). Son of Jeconiah (JEHOIACHIN) and descendant of DAVID (1 Chr. 3:18).

needle. The use of needles and the art of sewing seem to have been among the earliest human accomplishments. ADAM and EVE sewed fig leaves together to cover their nakedness (Gen. 3:7). The basic design of needles has not changed at all through the millennia. Needles made from sharp pierced bones have been found dating as far back as the sixth millennium B.C. In the days of Israel's history, needles were commonly made of BRONZE, either pierced or with a loop to form the "eye." They have been found by archaeologists in the dust of ancient cities, made from ivory, bone, bronze, and iron, from 1.5 to 5.5 inches (4-14 cm.) in length. The only place in the Bible a needle is actually mentioned is in Jesus' proverb that "it is easier for a camel to go through the eye of a needle than for a rich man to enter the kingdom of God" (Matt. 19:24; Mk. 10:25; Lk. 18:25). Some have speculated that Jesus was referring to a small gateway through which a large animal would have difficulty passing, but this and other explanations ignore the shock value of Jesus' words. The expression is hyperbolic and refers to the impossibility of entering God's kingdom by mere human effort. The disciples understood the point, for their reaction was to express doubt that *anyone* could be saved (Matt. 19:25). And Jesus responded, "With man [not just a rich man] this is impossible, but with God all things are possible" (v. 26).

needlework. See EMBROIDERY.

neesing. An archaic English word meaning "sneezing," used once by the KJV (Job 41:18; NIV, "snorting"). As published in 1611, and for a century and a half after that, the KJV also had "neesed" in 2 Ki. 4:35, but this was changed to "sneezed" in 1762.

Negeb. See NEGEV.

Negev. neg´ev (Heb. *negeb H5582*, meaning apparently "dry land"). Also Negeb. The name of the southern, desert region of PALESTINE (Gen. 12:9;

Num. 13:17; Deut. 1:7; et al.); thus the term acquired the additional meaning "south" (e.g., Gen. 13:14; the Heb. term is usually so rendered in the KJV). The physical characteristics of the Negeb are the rolling hills that abruptly terminate in the desert region. This region is bounded on the E by the DEAD SEA and on the W by the MEDITERRANEAN. It is a land where the water supply is scarce because of a very meager amount of rainfall in the summer months. At other seasons of the year, however, it is used by the nomads for pasturage. In this territory the PATRIARCHS lived (Gen. 20:1; 24:62; 37:1), though for a period it was also inhabited by AMALEKITES (Num. 13:29). The Negev was considered to be the tribal territory of JUDAH, but some of it was allotted to SIMEON (Josh. 15:20-32; 19:1-9). Many of DAVID's exploits during the reign of SAUL are described as happening in the Negev, centering on ZIKLAG and its environments (1 Sam. 27:5-10). After NEBUCHADNEZZAR sacked JERUSALEM in 586-585 B.C., a group of Jews retreated to the Negev, where they were harassed by the Edomites (see EDOM) who sided with the Babylonians. Much of the area came to be known as IDUMEA.

Neginah, Neginoth. neg´i-nuh, -noth (Heb. *nĕgînâ H5593*, pl. *nĕgînôt*). KJV transliteration of a Hebrew musical term referring probably to string instruments (Ps. 4 title, et al.).

Nehelamite. ni-hel´uh-mit (Heb. *nehĕlāmî H5713*, apparently the gentilic form of an unattested name, *nehĕlām*, meaning unknown). An epithet applied to SHEMAIAH, one of the false prophets who opposed JEREMIAH and whom he rebuked (Jer. 29:24, 31-32). The NRSV renders "of Nehelam," but no such place name is found in the OT. It could be a family name.

Nehemiah. nee´huh-mi´uh (Heb. *nĕhemyâ H5718*, "Yahweh has comforted"). **(1)** An Israelite mentioned among leading individuals who returned from BABYLON with ZERUBBABEL (Ezra 2:2; Neh. 7:7).

(2) Son of Abzuk; he ruled part of BETH ZUR and helped repair the wall of JERUSALEM (Neh. 3:16).

(3) Son of Hacaliah (Neh. 1:1) and governor of the Persian province of JUDAH after 444 B.C.;

known primarily as the rebuilder of Jerusalem after the EXILE. Virtually all that is known of him comes from the biblical book that bears his name (see NEHEMIAH, BOOK OF). His times, however, are illuminated by the rather considerable material found among the Elephantine papyri from EGYPT, which were written in the fifth century B.C. These documents come from a military colony of Jews residing on an island far up the NILE, opposite Aswan. They include copies of letters to and from Jerusalem and SAMARIA. They name several men who are also mentioned in the book of Nehemiah.

Nehemiah was a "cupbearer" to King ARTAXERXES (Neh. 1:11; 2:1). Inasmuch as some of the Elephantine papyri that are contemporary with Nehemiah are dated, we know that the king in question is Artaxerxes I, called Longimanus, who ruled 465-423 B.C. The title "cupbearer" clearly indicates a responsible office—not merely a servile position—for the king speaks to Nehemiah as an intimate and also indicates that he regards Nehemiah's journey to Jerusalem only as a temporary leave from official duties (2:6). Furthermore, the credentials given Nehemiah by the king and also the office of governor entrusted to him show that the king looked on him as a man of ability. That a captive Jew should attain to such an office need not surprise us when we remember the examples of DANIEL, ESTHER, and others. Indeed some ancient courts made it a practice to train captive noble youths for service in the government (Dan. 1:4-5).

Nehemiah was an officer of the palace at SUSA, but his heart was in Jerusalem. Word came to him from Hanani, one of his brothers, of the ruined condition of Jerusalem. (It has been suggested that this Hanani is the same man mentioned in the Elephantine papyri as an official who seems to have gone into Egypt on a government mission.) Overcome with grief, Nehemiah sought the refuge of prayer—and God answered abundantly. Only about twelve years earlier, in Artaxerxes's seventh year (457 B.C.), EZRA had gone back to Jerusalem with about 1,750 men, besides women and children (Ezra 8:1-20) and treasure worth a king's ransom (8:26-27). But if we refer 4:6-23 to the days of Ezra himself, it appears that his adversaries had persuaded the king to stop Ezra's efforts at rebuilding. The city, therefore, lay unrepaired, needing a

© Dr. James C. Martin. The British Museum. Photographed by permission.

The Cyrus Cylinder, recording the conquest of Babylon by this Medo-Persian king in 539 B.C. Here Cyrus claims to have restored to their homes the gods and peoples of many towns. This text may provide the context for the return of the Jewish exiles to rebuild Jerusalem.

new decree from the king. This permission Nehemiah providentially secured, thanks to his position at the court. Nehemiah therefore appeared at Jerusalem with a royal commission to continue the work that Ezra had begun.

Nehemiah was a man of ability, courage, and action. Arriving at Jerusalem, he first privately surveyed the scene of rubble (Neh. 2:1-16), and he encouraged the rulers at Jerusalem with his report of answered prayer and the granting of the king's new decree (2:18). Then he organized the community to carry out the effort of rebuilding the broken-down wall. Courageously and squarely he met the opposition of men like SANBALLAT, TOBIAH, and GESHEM (who are all now known from nonbiblical documents); and at last he saw the wall completed in the brief span of fifty-two days (6:15). Nehemiah cooperated with Ezra in numerous reforms and especially in the public instruction in the law (ch. 8). However, he left for Persia, probably on official business, in 431 B.C. (13:6). Later he returned to Jerusalem, but for how long we do not know. Of the end of his life we know nothing. The Elephantine papyri indicate that a different man, Bagohi, was governor by 407 B.C.

Nehemiah, Book of. One of the last historical books of the OT, recounting the history and reforms of NEHEMIAH the governor from 444 to about 420 B.C. In the Hebrew Bible, EZRA and Nehemiah are considered two parts of one book. Nehemiah may be outlined as follows.

I. Nehemiah travels to Jerusalem (Neh. 1:1—2:20).

N

II. Building despite opposition (3:1—7:4).

III. Genealogy of the first returning exiles (7:5-73 [= Ezra 2:2-70]).

IV. The revival and covenant sealing (8:1—10:39).

V. Dwellers at Jerusalem and genealogies (11:1—12:26).

VI. Final reforms (13:1-31).

Nehemiah's great work of restoring the wall of JERUSALEM depended basically on securing permission from the king. Ezra had returned to Jerusalem with a sizable group of people and much gold and silver only a dozen years previously, but had been hindered in his work by adverse royal decrees secured by his enemies. In God's providence Nehemiah secured the restoration of royal favor.

The actual building of the wall was parceled out among different leaders. Various cities of the province of Judea sent contingents of workers, and we can here learn something of the extent of Nehemiah's domain. The rapidity of building may have been due to preliminary work that Ezra might have accomplished. Most of the gates and sections of the wall mentioned in Neh. 3 cannot be identified with certainty. Perhaps the wall enclosed only the eastern hill of Jerusalem.

The opposition to Nehemiah by SANBALLAT and others combined ridicule, threat, and craft. Sanballat is called the governor of Samaria in the Elephantine papyri. He was apparently not anxious to see a rival province strengthened, and there was religious antagonism as well to Nehemiah's strict reform program. Internal difficulties also developed. The rich charged interest of 1 percent (per month, apparently, Neh. 5:10), whereas the Mosaic law required outright charity to the poor. But against all opposition the wall was built by Israelites who used both sword and trowel in the work of the Lord.

The genealogy of Neh. 7, which is a duplicate of the list in Ezra 2, is of interest. There are unimportant differences between the lists such as might be expected in the copying of detailed data like this. It is instructive to note that the record of ZERUBBABEL's returnees that Nehemiah used was a *written* record—not preserved by oral tradition as many have suggested was the method used for the passing on of Israel's histories.

Nehemiah's reform involved the teaching of Moses' law by Ezra and others at the Feast of Tabernacles (as commanded in Deut. 31:10). This led to the great prayer of confession of Neh. 9, redolent

Overview of NEHEMIAH

Author: Most of the narrative is written in the first person by Nehemiah himself, but Jewish tradition attributed the composition of the book as a whole (as well as Chronicles and Ezra) to the priest EZRA, while many modern scholars ascribe final authorship to a later, unknown editor.

Historical setting: The book was written possibly c. 430-400 B.C., but many date it a century later. In any case, the setting is postexilic JUDEA under Persian jurisdiction.

Purpose: To recount the reforms of Nehemiah as governor in JERUSALEM, particularly in rebuilding the wall of the city, and thus to encourage the returnees to continue the work of restoration.

Contents: Nehemiah secures permission to travel to Jerusalem (Neh. 1:1—2:8); the wall of the city is rebuilt, and more exiles return (2:9—7:73a); the COVENANT is renewed and the wall is dedicated (7:73b—12:47); Nehemiah brings reforms to the community (ch. 13).

with quotations from and allusions to the PENTA-TEUCH. A covenant was solemnly sealed to walk in the Law of the Lord as given by Moses (10:29). Nehemiah's final reform included the removal of TOBIAH from the temple precincts. Tobiah had entered through friendship with ELIASHIB the high priest while Nehemiah was back in PERSIA. Also a grandson of Eliashib had married Sanballat's daughter (13:28).

Nehiloth. nee´huh-loth (Heb. *nĕḥîlôt H5704*, meaning uncertain). KJV transliteration of a Hebrew musical term referring possibly to a type of flute (only in Ps. 5 title).

Nehum. nee´huhm (Heb. *nĕḥûm H5700*, "[God] comforts" or "comforter"). An Israelite mentioned among leading individuals who returned from BABYLON with ZERUBBABEL (Neh. 7:7); this name is likely a scribal error for REHUM, the form found in the parallel passage (Ezra 2:2).

Nehushta. ni-hoosh´tuh (Heb. *nĕḥuštāʾ H5735*, possibly "abundant, luxuriant" or "bronze"). Daughter of Elnathan, wife of King JEHOIAKIM, and mother of King JEHOIACHIN; she was a native of JERUSALEM (2 Ki. 24:8). NEBUCHADNEZZAR deported her, Jehoiachin, and other members of the royal family and court to BABYLON in 597 B.C. (24:12, 15).

Nehushtan. ni-hoosh´tuhn (Heb. *nĕḥuštān H5736*, "bronze [statue]," apparently a play on the words *nāḥāš H5729*, "serpent," and *nĕḥōšet H5733*, "bronze, copper"). Name given to the bronze snake that MOSES had made in the wilderness (2 Ki. 18:4). The origin of this statue is described in Num. 21:4-9. It was made out of copper or bronze and elevated upon a standard; and anyone who had been bitten would live by looking at it. To its contemporaries, the bronze serpent therefore symbolized a looking to God in faith for salvation; and into the future it typified Christ's being lifted up on the cross, "that everyone who believes in him may have eternal life" (Jn. 3:15; cf. Lk. 23:42-43). With the passage of time, however, Israel lost sight of the symbolical and typical function of the statue. By the later eighth century, the Israelites were burning INCENSE to it,

as if it were in itself a deity (2 Ki. 18:4). As a part, therefore, of HEZEKIAH's overall campaign against the HIGH PLACES and their idolatrous objects, begun in the first year of his reign (2 Chr. 29:1), the king broke the serpent into pieces (2 Ki. 18:4). It was apparently at this time that the name Nehushtan was assigned to it, probably in disparagement: it was not "the serpent," but simply "the bronze thing."

Neiel. ni-i´uhl (Heb. *nĕʿîʾēl H5832*, derivation unknown). A town that served to mark the SE border of the tribal territory of ASHER (Josh. 19:27). It is generally identified with modern Khirbet Yaʿnin, about 8.5 mi. (14 km.) ESE of Acco.

neighbor. The duties and responsibilities towards one's neighbor are varied. In the OT, injunctions are given more in the negative than in the positive. The tenth commandment (see COMMANDMENTS, TEN) is directed toward the protection of the neighbor's property (Exod. 20:17); the commandment immediately preceding, toward the protection of a neighbor's reputation (20:16). CITIES OF REFUGE were appointed for one who killed his neighbor accidentally (Deut. 19:4). The book of Proverbs is replete with admonitions concerning one's neighbor, of which the following may be regarded as the epitome: "He who despises his neighbor sins" (Prov. 14:21). Due regard for one's neighbor is expressed in the great OT and NT precept, "Love your neighbor as yourself" (Lev. 19:18; Matt. 19:19). The parable of the Good Samaritan (Lk. 10:30-37) was given in answer to the question, "And who is my neighbor?" (10:29). From the lips of the questioner, *neighbor* excluded all Gentiles, but Christ's corrective expanded the meaning by criticizing the wording of the question. The proper emphasis would be, "To whom am I neighbor? Whose claim on neighborly help do I recognize?" It is not a question of how narrowly we can restrict our neighborhood, but rather how broadly we can enlarge our devotion to others.

Nekeb. See ADAMI NEKEB.

Nekoda. ni-koh´duh (Heb. *nĕqôdāʾ H5928*, "speckled"). **(1)** Ancestor of a family of temple servants (NETHINIM) who returned to JERUSALEM after the Babylonian captivity (Ezra 2:48; Neh. 7:50).

(2) Ancestor of a family of returned exiles who were unable to prove their Israelite descent (Ezra 2:60; Neh. 7:62).

Nemuel. nem´yoo-uhl (Heb. *nĕmûʾēl H5803*, derivation uncertain; gentilic *nĕmûʾēlî H5804*, "Nemuelite"). **(1)** Son of SIMEON, grandson of JACOB, and eponymous ancestor of the Nemuelite clan (Num. 26:12; 1 Chr. 4:24); called JEMUEL in the parallel passages (Gen. 46:10; Exod. 6:15).

(2) Son of Eliab and descendant of REUBEN (Num. 26:9). Nemuel's brothers, DATHAN and ABIRAM, were among the leaders who joined the Levite KORAH in his rebellion against MOSES and AARON in the wilderness and subsequently suffered judgment (Num. 16).

Nepheg. nee´fig (Heb. *nepeg H5863*, meaning uncertain). **(1)** Son of IZHAR and great-grandson of LEVI through KOHATH (Exod. 6:21).

(2) Son of DAVID, listed among the children born to him in JERUSALEM (2 Sam. 5:15; 1 Chr. 3:7; 14:6).

nephew. No Hebrew word in the OT or Greek word in the NT means specifically "nephew" (the KJV uses this English term in its obsolete sense of "descendant" several times: Jdg. 12:14; Job 18:19; Isa. 14:22; 1 Tim. 5:4). In some OT passages, however, one finds the expression "brother's son" or the like, which may be properly rendered "nephew" (Gen. 12:5; 14:12; Ezra 8:19).

Nephilim. See GIANT.

Nephish. See NAPHISH.

Nephishesim. See NEPHUSSIM.

Nephisim. See NEPHUSSIM.

Nephthalim. See NAPHTALI.

Nephtoah. nef-toh´uh (Heb. *neptôaḥ H5886*, perhaps "opening"). In the descriptions of the N boundary of JUDAH and the S boundary of BENJAMIN, reference is made to "the spring of the waters of Nephtoah" (Josh. 15:9; 18:15). The place is generally identified with modern Lifta, c. 3 mi. (5 km.)

NW of JERUSALEM. Some believe that the MT reading should be modified slightly so that it reads, "the spring of [Pharaoh] MERNEPTAH," referring to a site mentioned also in Egyptian documents.

Nephushesim. See NEPHUSSIM.

Nephusim. See NEPHUSSIM.

Nephussim. ni-fyoo´sim (Heb. *nĕpûsîm H5866* [Ezra 2:50; *Ketib, nĕpîsîm*] and *nĕpûssîm H5867* [Neh. 7:52; *Ketib, nĕpîšsîm*], derivation uncertain). KJV, TNIV, and other versions, Nephusim. Ancestor or clan name of a family of temple servants (NETHINIM) who returned from the Babylonian exile (Ezra 2:50 [NRSV, "Nephisim"]; Neh. 7:42 [KJV, "Nephishesim"; NRSV, "Nephushesim"]). Some believe that the Nephussim were descendants of prisoners of war related to the Ishmaelite tribe of NAPHISH.

Ner. nuhr (Heb. *nēr H5945*, "light, lamp," possibly short form of *nēriyyāhû H5950*, "Yahweh is [my] light"). **(1)** Son of JEIEL, descendant of BENJAMIN, father of KISH, and grandfather of King SAUL (1 Chr. 8:30 [NIV, following LXX], 33; 9:36, 39). Some believe that the genealogy here is not accurate and that this Ner should be identified with #2 below.

(2) Son of ABIEL, descendant of Benjamin, uncle of Saul, and father of ABNER (1 Sam. 14:50-51 NIV; the Heb. can be understood to mean that Saul's uncle was Abner rather than Ner). Elsewhere his name occurs only in the phrase "Abner son of Ner" (26:5 et al.). See also comments under KISH.

Nereus. nee´ri-yoos (Gk. *Nēreus G3759*, in Gk. mythology the name of a sea-god). A Roman Christian who, along with his unnamed sister, was greeted by PAUL (Rom. 16:15). His name, common among slaves, suggests that Nereus was a Gentile freedman.

Nergal. nuhr´gal (Heb. *nērgal H5946*, from Akk. *Nergal*). A Mesopotamian god of the underworld worshiped in CUTHAH; when some of the inhabitants of that city-state were resettled by the Assyrian empire, they brought their cult to the province of SAMARIA (2 Ki. 17:30). According to Babylonian tradition, he was the consort of Ereshkigal, queen of the underworld. Nergal was regarded also as a god of pestilence, disease, and various calamities, but he could be appeased by incantations. Nergal became a theophoric element found in personal names, such as NERGAL-SHAREZER.

Nergal-Sharezer. nuhr´gal-shu-ree´zuhr (Heb. *nērgal śar-ʾeṣer H5947*, from Akk. *Nergal-śar-uṣur*, "may [the god] NERGAL protect the king"). Name of a senior official (see RABMAG) with the Babylonian army at JERUSALEM in 587 B.C. (Jer. 39:3). Because the name occurs twice in this verse, some believe that the first mention refers to a different person who was ruler of SAMGAR (Sinmagir), but the Hebrew text is difficult: the NIV has "Nergal-Sharezer of Samgar, Nebo-Sarsekim," whereas the NRSV renders, "Nergal-sharezer, Samgar-nebo, Sarsechim." In any case, when a breach was made in the city's defenses, he was among the officials who occupied the MIDDLE GATE. Later, he and other officers had JEREMIAH taken out of prison and entrusted to GEDALIAH (39:13-14). Nergal-Sharezer has often been identified with Neriglissar, a private citizen who was, according to Berossus, a son-in-law of NEBUCHADNEZZAR; after disposing of his brother-in-law, EVIL-MERODACH, Neriglissar ruled BABYLON for a few years (560-556).

Neri. nee´ri (Gk. *Nēri G3760*, from Heb. *nēr H5945*; see NER). Son of Melki, included in Luke's GENEALOGY OF JESUS CHRIST (Lk. 3:27). In this passage, Neri appears as the father of SHEALTIEL, but elsewhere Shealtiel's father is said to be Jeconiah, that is, JEHOIACHIN (1 Chr. 3:17; Matt. 1:12). Attempts to explain the discrepancy are often tied to Jer. 22:30. Some think, for example, that Luke omits Jeconiah as legally unfit to be part of the messianic line.

Neriah. ni-ri´uh (Heb. *nēriyyâ H5949* and *nēriyyāhû H5950*, "Yahweh is [my] light"). Son of Mahseiah; he was the father of BARUCH (Jer. 32:12 et al.) and SERAIAH (51:59-64). Baruch was JEREMIAH's friend and scribe, while Seraiah served as staff officer for King ZEDEKIAH and on one occasion acted as messenger for Jeremiah. It is likely that Neriah himself held a significant position in society or at the court.

Neriglissar. See NERGAL-SHAREZER.

Nero. nihr´oh. Nero Claudius CAESAR Drusus Germanicus was the fifth emperor of ROME (A.D. 54-68). He was a son of the first marriage of Julia Agrippina, daughter of Germanicus; Nero's father was Cnaeus Domitius Ahenobarbus, who had been consul in the year 32. Named L. Domitius Ahenobarbus at birth in the year 37, he acquired the name Nero at the age of twelve, when he was adopted by CLAUDIUS. His mother was Agrippina, who cared little for her son's morals but was interested only in his temporal advancement.

The first years of Nero's reign were quite peaceful and gave promise of good things to come. Nero himself could boast that not a single person had been unjustly executed throughout his extensive empire. During these "rational years," the apostle PAUL, in compliance with his own expressed appeal (Acts 25:10-11), was brought before Nero as the reigning CAESAR (c. A.D. 63). We can hardly do otherwise than infer that Paul was freed of all charges to continue his labors of evangelization.

Nero's marriage to Poppaea opened the second period of his reign. He killed his mother, his chief advisers Seneca and Burrus, and many of the nobility to secure their fortunes. In A.D. 64 a large part of ROME was destroyed by fire. Whether or not Nero actually ordered the burning of the city is very controversial. However, justly or not, the finger of suspicion was pointed in Nero's direction. A scapegoat was provided in the Christians. Even the Roman historian Tacitus, who certainly cannot be given the name "Christian," bears testimony as to the severity of the sufferings inflicted on them. "Their death was made a matter of sport; they were covered in wild beast's skins and torn to pieces by dogs or were fastened to crosses and set on fire in order to serve as torches by night … . Nero had offered his gardens for the spectacle and gave an exhibition in his circus, mingling with the crowd in the guise of a charioteer or mounted on his chariot. Hence, … there arose a feeling of pity, because it was felt that they were being sacrificed not for the common good, but to gratify the savagery of one man" (Tacitus, *Annals* 15, 44).

Nero's private life was a scandal. Surrendering himself to the basest of appetites, he indulged him-

Marble bust of Emperor Nero.

self in the most evil forms of pleasure. Conspiracies and plots dogged his latter years. He was advised to destroy himself, but could not find the courage to do so. Learning that the senate had decreed his death, Nero's last cruel act was to put many of the senators to death. He finally died by his own hand in the summer of A.D. 68. Thus perished the last of the line of Julius Caesar. Both Paul and PETER suffered martyrdom under Nero.

Nerva. nuhr´vuh. Emperor of ROME, A.D. 96-98. Marcus Cocceius Nerva was born c. A.D. 35. He became a confidant of NERO and was subsequently appointed CONSUL on two occasions: by VESPASIAN in 71 and by DOMITIAN in 90. After the assassination of Domitian, the conspirators placed Nerva on the throne. The new emperor was genuinely interested in freedom and justice, but he was unable to restore political stability, and in any case his health quickly failed. Some months before his death he adopted TRAJAN, who succeeded him as emperor in 98.

nest. The nests of birds differ from species to species (Ps. 104:17; Jer. 22:23; 48:28; Ezek. 31:6). Many are built high (Job 39:27; Jer. 49:16; Obad.

4; Hab. 2:9). Mosaic law forbade one who found a bird's nest with the mother and her brood from harming the mother bird (Deut. 22:6). Semite people in general view with extreme disfavor anyone who willfully disturbs a bird in the nest. Isaiah compares the despoiling of Israel by the Assyrians to the robbing of a bird's nest (Isa. 10:14). Jesus contrasts birds having nests with his having no home (Matt. 8:20; Lk. 9:58).

net. This term can refer to a lattice utilized in furniture and architectural design (e.g., Exod. 27:4-5; 38:4; see NETWORK). But it is mostly in contexts of hunting and fishing that nets are mentioned in the OT. These activities were pursued not so much for sport as for livelihood. Nets were particularly needed in fishing, because sufficient quantities for commercial purposes could not be caught in any other way. Fishing was limited to the inland bodies of water in Bible history, since the Mediterranean did not offer convenient opportunities. The casting net (Matt. 4:18), when thrown out over the water, assumed a circular shape as it fell upon the surface of the water. Immediately the weighted perimeter would sink rapidly to the bottom, causing the net to assume a shape variously described as conical, bell-like, or pear-shaped. Thus would be trapped all the fish below the net. The dragnet, in contrast, was supported on one side at the water's surface by floats, while the other side was kept at the lake's bottom by weights. Thus was formed a vertical wall of netting between its two ends. If one end of the net were secured at the shore, a boat would carry the other in a great semicircular arc and drag along all underwater life in its path, until all was swept ashore. On the other hand, if both ends were secured to boats, the boats would be maneuvered so as to form a circular shape with the net, which would then be dragged ashore with the catch. Dragnets often were immense in size, and the term could be used figuratively of vastness and all-inclusiveness. They retrieved all types of fish, large and small, choice and worthless, living and dead. How appropriate that the Lord should choose this method to describe a gathering for judgment in the kingdom of heaven (Matt. 13:47).

Netaim. ni-tay´im (Heb. *nĕṭā'îm H5751*, "plantings"). An otherwise unknown place, probably in

N

© Dr. James C. Martin

the SHEPHELAH of JUDAH, where some royal potters lived (1 Chr. 4:23; KJV has "plants and hedges" for "Netaim and Gederah"). See also GEDERAH.

Nethaneel. See NETHANEL.

Nethanel. ni-than´uhl (Heb. *nĕtan'ēl H5991*, "God has given"; cf. NATHANAEL). KJV Nethaneel. **(1)** Son of Zuar; he was a leader from the tribe of ISSACHAR, heading a division of 54,500 (Num. 2:5-6; 10:15). Nethanel was among those who assisted MOSES in taking a census of the Israelites (1:8) and who brought offerings to the Lord for the dedication of the TABERNACLE (7:18-23).

(2) Fourth son of JESSE and older brother of DAVID (1 Chr. 2:14).

(3) One of the priests appointed to blow the trumpet when David transferred the ARK OF THE COVENANT to Jerusalem (1 Chr. 15:24).

(4) Father of Shemaiah; the latter was a LEVITE and scribe in David's organization of the priestly service (1 Chr. 24:6).

(5) Third son of OBED-EDOM, included in the list of divisions of the Korahite doorkeepers in the reign of David (1 Chr. 26:4).

(6) One of five officials sent by King JEHOSHAPHAT "to teach in the towns of Judah" (2 Chr. 17:7).

(7) A leader of the Levites during the reign of King JOSIAH; along with his brothers CONANIAH and SHEMAIAH, Nethanel provided 5,000 offerings (lambs) and five head of cattle for the renewed celebration of the PASSOVER (2 Chr. 35:9).

(8) One of the descendants of PASHHUR who agreed to put away their foreign wives (Ezra 10:22). Some think he may be the same as #10 below.

(9) The head of the priestly family of JEDAIAH in the time of the high priest JOIAKIM (Neh. 12:12).

(10) A priestly musician who participated in the dedication of the rebuilt wall of Jerusalem under EZRA (Neh. 12:36).

Nethaniah. neth´uh-ni´uh (Heb. *nĕtanyâ H5992* and *nĕtanyāhû H5993*, "Yahweh has given"). **(1)** Son of Elishama and father of ISHMAEL; the latter murdered GEDALIAH, who had been made governor by NEBUCHADNEZZAR (2 Ki. 25:23, 25; Jer. 41:1-2; et al.). The family was of royal blood.

(2) One of the sons of ASAPH who assisted their father in the prophetic ministry of MUSIC; he was the head of the fifth company of TEMPLE musicians appointed by lot under DAVID (1 Chr. 25:2, 12).

(3) One of five officials sent by King JEHOSHAPHAT "to teach in the towns of Judah" (2 Chr. 17:8).

(4) Son of Shelemiah and father of JEHUDI; the latter was an official under King JEHOIAKIM who was sent to BARUCH so that the latter might read the prophecies of JEREMIAH to the princes of Judah (Jer. 36:14).

Nethinim. neth´in-im (Heb. *nĕtînim*, pl. of *nātîn H5987*, "given, donated"). The KJV uses the improper transliteration *Nethinims* (*Nethinim* itself is a plural form) to represent a postexilic Hebrew term that modern versions render with "temple servants" (1 Chr. 9:2; Ezra 2:43 et al.; Neh. 3:26 et al.). Ezra 8:20 gives the most specific clue to the origin of the Nethinim. That DAVID should have given them to assist the LEVITES is in keeping with the general account of David's organization (1 Chr. 23-24) in preparation for the TEMPLE. Nethinim means "those who are given." Just as the Levites as a whole were "wholly given" to the Lord from among the people of Israel (Num. 8:16), so the Levites were given as "gifts" to AARON and his sons (v. 19). David appears to have followed this pattern in assigning another group to assist the Levites. The order listed in 1 Chr. 9:2 and Neh 11:3 is, "Israel, priests, Levites, and Nethinim" (the latter passage adds, "descendants of Solomon's servants"; the singling out of such a hereditary group makes a natural parallel to the group originating with David). Some have thought that the GIBEONITES were the original Nethinim (Josh. 9:27). After the killing of the Gibeonites by SAUL (2 Sam. 21:1), additional Nethinim were given by David for special service. Perhaps they were slaves acquired in war.

Netophah. ni-toh´fuh (Heb. *nĕṭōpâ H5756*, from *nāṭap H5752*, "to drip, pour"; gentilic *nĕṭōpātî H5743*, "Netophathite"). A town of JUDAH, mentioned after BETHLEHEM in a postexilic list (Ezra 2:22); the parallel combines the inhabitants of Netophah and Bethlehem (Neh. 7:26). The actual town plays no part in the biblical narrative, but individual Netophathites are mentioned in a number of OT passages. Two were among DAVID's elite group of mighty warriors (2 Sam. 23:28-29; 1 Chr. 11:30); two others were included among his twelve monthly divisional army commanders (1 Chr. 27:13, 15); another one was an army officer named SERAIAH who supported GEDALIAH in 586 B.C. (2 Ki. 25:23; but see Jer. 40:8); finally, one was the grandfather of a leading LEVITE who resettled in Jerusalem (9:16). In addition, there were fifty-six people from Netophah who returned to Palestine with ZERUBBABEL in 537 (Ezra 2:22; cf. Neh. 7:26); and the Levitical singers who participated in the dedication of the walls of Jerusalem in 444 are said to have come "from the villages of the Netophathites" (Neh. 12:28). The precise location of Netophah remains uncertain, but a probable location is Khirbet Bedd Faluḥ, 3 mi. (5 km.) SE of Bethlehem, where the biblical name is still preserved in the nearby spring, ʿAin en-Naṭuf.

nettle. See PLANTS.

network. This English term is used in most Bible versions primarily to render Hebrew *śĕbākâ H8422*, which serves to describe the network of bronze that hung upon the capitals of the two great bronze pillars, JAKIN AND BOAZ, in front of the TEMPLE of SOLOMON (1 Ki. 7:17-20, 41-42; 2 Chr. 4:12-13; Jer. 52:22-23). The same word is used for the lattice of the upper room of AHAZIAH through which he fell and was mortally hurt (2 Ki. 1:2). A different term, *reśet H8407*, is used with reference to the grating of the ALTAR of burnt offering (Exod. 27:4-5; 38:4). This is conceived by some to be a grate running through the altar, and by others a step running around the altar, faced with a grille of bronze. (The KJV use of "network" in Isa. 19:9 reflects a misunderstanding of an unusual Heb. word that probably refers to white cloth or linen.)

new, newness. The common OT Hebrew word for "new" is *ḥādāš H2543*, which has the sense of "recent" or "fresh"; this adjective may connote newness in both qualitative and chronological aspects. It occurs in such expressions as new king (Exod. 1:8), offering of new grain (Lev. 23:16), new house (Deut. 20:5), new heavens and new earth (65:17;

66:22); new COVENANT (Jer. 31:31), and so on. From these examples, the difficulty of making a distinction between quality and time is apparent; for often, if something is new in kind, it is also recent in appearance.

In the NT, the two common Greek words are *kainos G2785* and *neos G3742*. It has often been thought that the first of these is used regularly to emphasize qualitative newness, and that the latter indicates chronological newness in the sense of modernity or youthfulness. Others deny the distinction based on the seemingly interchangeable use of the two words in the NT. Matthew speaks of new wine with *neos* (Matt. 9:17), while in a different context he refers to new wine as *kainos* (26:29). PAUL in Eph. 4:24 commands the Christian to put on the *kainos* man, while in Col. 3:10 he speaks of the *neos* man. The writer to the Hebrews refers to "the new covenant" but uses both adjectives (Heb. 9:15; 12:24). Furthermore, the papyri seem to use the two words practically synonymously. See also NEW COMMANDMENT; REGENERATION.

new birth. See REGENERATION.

new commandment. This phrase first appears in words attributed to Jesus in the upper room discourse reported by the fourth evangelist (Jn. 13:34). In an apparent reference to the Decalogue (see TEN COMMANDMENTS) Jesus said, "A new command I give you: Love one another." Of course, the commandment to LOVE God and one's neighbor was not new, for it is emphasized in the PENTATEUCH and the Prophets (esp. Hosea), and restated by Jesus as a summation of the TORAH (Deut. 6:5; Hos. 11:4; Matt. 22:37; cf. Rom. 13:9; Gal. 5:14; Jas. 2:8). Jesus did however give this command fresh emphasis, bringing it into sharper perspective: a discriminating love resulting from choice. The newness consists in the source and nature of this love; it is the supreme criterion of one's relationship to God (1 Jn. 5:3; cf. Lk. 10:27).

New Gate. The book of JEREMIAH speaks twice of "the New Gate of [the house of] Yahweh" (Jer. 36:10; 26:10). The entrance of this gate was the setting for a royal inquiry into the preaching of Jeremiah (26:7-16). Here also was the room

N

belonging to the secretary GEMARIAH son of Shaphan (36:10). This verse also indicates that the gate was in the upper (inner) courtyard of the TEMPLE, leading some to infer that "New Gate" was the name given to the UPPER GATE after it was rebuilt by King JOTHAM (2 Ki. 15:35; 2 Chr. 27:3). It may have been S of the inner court, but its precise location is unknown (it is not to be confused with the New Gate built in modern times on the NW wall of Jerusalem).

new heavens. See ESCHATOLOGY; HEAVENS, NEW.

new Jerusalem. See JERUSALEM, NEW.

new man, new self. See MAN, NEW.

new moon. See CALENDAR; FEASTS.

New Quarter. See SECOND DISTRICT, SECOND QUARTER.

New Testament. A collection of twenty-seven documents, the second part of the sacred Scriptures of the Christian church, the first part being called by contrast the OLD TESTAMENT. In the name "New Testament," apparently first given to the collection in the latter half of the second century, the word "testament" represents Greek *diathēkē* G1347, variously translated "testament," "settlement," "covenant" (the last of these being on the whole the most satisfactory equivalent). The new COVENANT is the new order or dispensation inaugurated by the death of Jesus (compare his own designation: "the new covenant in my blood" in Lk. 22:20; 1 Cor. 11:25). It was so called because it fulfilled the promise made by God to his people in Jer. 31:31-34 that he would "make a new covenant" with them whereby the desire and power to do his will would be implanted within them and all their past sins would be wiped out (cf. Heb. 8:6-12). By contrast, the earlier covenant established by God with Israel in MOSES' day came to be known as the "old covenant" (cf. 2 Cor. 3:14; Heb. 8:13). The foundation documents of the covenant instituted by Jesus are accordingly known as "the books of the new covenant (testament)," while the earlier Scriptures, which trace the course of the old dispensation, were known as "the books of the old covenant

[testament]" from the time of Melito of Sardis (A.D. 170) onward.

I. Contents. In speaking of the books of the NT we must be clear whether we refer to the individual documents or to the whole collection as such. The individual documents naturally existed before the collection, and some of them were grouped in smaller collections before they were ultimately gathered together in the complete NT. All, or nearly all, of the individual documents belong to the first century A.D.; the NT as a collection makes its appearance in the second century.

The order in which these documents appear in our NT today is based on subject matter rather than chronology. First come the four GOSPELS—or rather the four records of the one and only GOSPEL—narrating Jesus' ministry, death, and resurrection. These are followed by the ACTS OF THE APOSTLES, which begins by mentioning Jesus' appearances to the disciples following the resurrection; from then on we are told how, over the next thirty years, Christianity spread along the road from JERUSALEM to ROME. This book was originally written as the continuation of the Gospel of Luke. These five constitute the narrative section of the NT.

The next twenty-one documents take the form of LETTERS written to communities or individuals.

Facsimile of Codex Bezae (Acts 1:1-8).

© Dr. James C. Martin. Sola Scriptura. The Van Kampen Collection on display at the Holy Land Experience in Orlando, Florida. Photographed by permission.

Thirteen of these bear the name of PAUL as writer, one the name of JAMES, two of PETER, and one of JUDE (Judas). The others are anonymous. One of these, the letter to the HEBREWS, is more properly described as a homily with an epistolary ending; its authorship remains a matter of conjecture to this day. The three that we know as the letters of JOHN THE APOSTLE are so called, not because they bear John's name, but because it is plain from their contents that they are closely associated with the fourth gospel (which, though itself anonymous, has from early times been known as John's). First John is an exhortation in which the writer impresses on his readers (whom he calls his "dear children") the practical implications of some of the leading themes of John's gospel. In 2 and 3 John the writer refers to himself as "the elder."

The last book of the NT bears some features of the epistolary style in that it is introduced by seven covering letters addressed to churches in the Roman province of Asia; but for the most part it belongs to the class of literature to which it has given its own name ("apocalyptic," from "Apocalypse" or "Revelation"). In APOCALYPTIC LITERATURE the outworking of God's purpose on earth is disclosed in the form of symbolical visions. Written probably between A.D. 69 and 96, when the Flavian dynasty ruled the Roman empire, Revelation aims to encourage persecuted Christians with the assurance that they are on the winning side; that Jesus, and not the Roman emperor, has won the victory that entitles him to exercise sovereignty over the world and control its destiny. See REVELATION, BOOK OF.

II. Order of writing. Although the four Gospels deal with events of the first thirty years of the Christian era and the NT letters belong to the remaining two-thirds of the first century, several of the letters were in existence before even the earliest of the Gospels. With the possible exception of James, the earliest NT documents are those letters that Paul composed before his two years' detention in Rome (A.D. 60-62). Therefore, when one of Paul's earlier letters mentions an action or saying of Jesus, that mention is our first written account of it. For example, Paul's account of the institution of the LORD'S SUPPER (1 Cor. 11:23-25) is earlier by several years than the account of it given in our oldest gospel (Mk. 14:22-25).

Jesus himself wrote no book, but he gave his teaching to his disciples in forms that could be easily memorized and enjoined them to teach others what they had learned from him. There is good reason to believe that one of the earliest Christian writings was a compilation of his teaching, arranged according to the chief subjects he treated, though this document has not been preserved in its original form but has been incorporated into some of the existing NT books.

The necessity for a written account of the life of Jesus was not felt acutely in the earlier years of the Christian mission. In those years, when there were so many eyewitnesses of the saving events who could testify to what they had seen and heard, their testimony was regarded as sufficient, and the gospel material circulated far and wide by word of mouth. But even in those early years the necessity arose for an apostle to give instruction in writing to people from whom he was separated at the time. While ministering in EPHESUS, Paul heard disturbing news of the state of affairs in the church he had founded three or four years previously in CORINTH. He was unable just then to visit Corinth in person but sent his converts in that city a letter conveying much the same message as he would have given them orally had he been with them. Again, a few years later, he proposed to visit Rome and thought it wise, during a brief stay in Corinth, to prepare the Roman Christians for his coming, especially as he had never been in their city before. So he sent them a letter in which he took the opportunity of making a full-length statement of the gospel as he understood and preached it. In such "occasional" circumstances the NT letters were first written. Yet Paul and the other writers were conscious of the fact that they expressed the mind of Christ, under the guidance of his Spirit. Their letters are therefore full of teaching, imparted to the first readers by apostolic authority, which retains its validity to the present day, and have by divine providence been preserved for our instruction.

The Gospels began to appear about the end of the first generation following the death and resurrection of Jesus. By that time the eyewitnesses were being removed by death, one by one, and before long none of them would be left. It was desirable, therefore, that their testimony should be placed on

N

permanent record, so that those who came after would not be at a disadvantage as compared with Christians of the first generation. About the middle sixties, then, we find gospel writing first undertaken. Mark provided the Roman church with an account of Jesus' ministry, from his baptism to his resurrection, which is said by Papias and other second-century writers to have been based in large measure on the preaching of Peter.

In the following years Matthew provided the Christians of ANTIOCH and the neighborhood with an expanded version of the life of Jesus, including a systematic presentation of his teaching. Luke, Paul's companion and dear physician, having traced the course of events accurately from the beginning, set himself to supply the "most excellent Theophilus" with an ordered narrative of Christian origins that not only related "all that Jesus began to do and to teach until the day he was taken up" (Acts 1:1-2), but went on to tell what he continued to do after that, working by his Spirit in his apostles. Then, toward the end of the century, John recorded Jesus' life in a different way, bringing out its abiding and universal significance, so that his readers might apprehend the glory of Jesus as the Word that became flesh, and by believing in him might have life in his name. These four records are not biographies in the ordinary sense of the term; they are concerned rather to perpetuate the apostolic witness to Jesus as Son of God and Savior of the world.

III. Early collections of writings. For some time these four evangelic records circulated independently and locally, being valued, no doubt, by those for whom they were primarily written. But by the early years of the second century they were gathered together and began to circulate as a fourfold record throughout the Christian world. When this happened, Acts was detached from Luke's gospel, to which it originally formed the sequel, and set out on a new, but not insignificant, career of its own.

Paul's letters were preserved at first by those to whom they were sent. At least, all that have come down to us were so preserved, for here and there in his surviving correspondence we find reference to a letter that may have been lost at a very early date (cf. 1 Cor. 5:9; Col. 4:16). But by the last decade of the first century there is evidence of a move to bring his available letters together and

circulate them as a collection among the churches. Thus Clement of Rome, writing as foreign secretary of his church to the church of Corinth about A.D. 96, was able to quote freely, not only from Paul's letter to the Romans (which would naturally be accessible to him) but also from 1 Corinthians and possibly from one or two of his other letters. What provided the stimulus for this move to collect Paul's letters, or who began to collect them, can only be a matter of speculation. Paul himself had encouraged some interchange of his letters (cf. Col. 4:16), and one or two of them may have been from the start general or circular letters, not to be confined to one single group of recipients. By the first or second decade of the second century, at any rate, a Pauline collection was in circulation—first a shorter collection of ten letters, and then a longer collection of thirteen (including the three "pastoral letters," those addressed to Timothy and Titus).

From the time when the first collection of Paul's letters began to circulate, the letters appear to have been arranged mainly in descending order of length. That principle is still apparent in the arrangement most familiar today: Paul's letters to churches come before his letters to individuals, but within these two groups the letters are arranged so that the longest comes first and the shortest comes last. (There is one inconspicuous exception to this rule: Galatians, which is slightly shorter than Ephesians, comes before it, and has had this position since the second century. There may have been some special reason for this.)

IV. Canon of the NT. The circulation of two collections—the fourfold gospel and the Pauline corpus—did not constitute a NT, but it marked a stage toward that goal. About A.D. 140 the Gnostic leader Valentinus, according to Tertullian, accepted practically the whole NT as it was recognized toward the end of the second century. It is not certain, however, whether Valentinus knew the NT as a closed canon or simply quoted as authoritative most of the documents that Tertullian acknowledged as making up the NT.

The church was stimulated to define the NT limits more precisely, not by the main Gnostic groups, but by MARCION. Marcion came to Rome about A.D. 140 from Asia Minor, where he had tried unsuccessfully to press his views on leading churchmen. He rejected the OT altogether, as reflecting the worship of a different God from the God whom Jesus revealed as Father, and he held that the writings of all the apostles except Paul had been corrupted by an admixture of Judaism. He promulgated a Christian canon comprising (1) "The Gospel" (an edition of Luke's Gospel edited in accordance with his own viewpoint) and (2) "The Apostle" (ten letters of Paul, excluding the Pastorals, similarly edited). Paul, in Marcion's eyes, was the only faithful apostle of Christ, all the others having Judaized; but even Paul's letters had been tampered with by Judaizing scribes or editors and required correction back to their original form.

The publication of Marcion's NT, with its restricted number of documents, was a challenge to the leaders of Christian orthodoxy. If they refused Marcion's canon, it was incumbent on them to define the canon they accepted. They replied to his challenge by saying, in effect, that they did not reject the OT. They accepted it as Holy Scripture, following the example of Christ and the apostles. Along with it they accepted the NT writings—not one Gospel only, but four (one of the four being the authentic text of the Gospel that Marcion issued in a mutilated form); not ten letters only of Paul, but thirteen; not letters of Paul only, but of other apostolic men as well.

They also accepted the Acts of the Apostles and appreciated as never before its crucial importance as the "hinge" of the NT. Acts links the fourfold Gospel with the apostolic letters because it provides the sequel to the former and supplies a historical background for much of the latter. Moreover, it provides irrefutable independent evidence of the sound basis for the authority that Paul claims in his letters. Tertullian and others were not slow to expose the folly of those Marcionites who asserted the exclusive authority of Paul while rejecting the one document that supplied objective testimony to his authority. The Marcionites, indeed, had no option but to reject Acts, as it also bore witness to the authority of Peter and the other apostles, whom they repudiated. But the very fact that Acts attested the authority both of Paul and of Peter and his colleagues gave it all the greater value in the eyes of orthodox churchmen. From this time on it was called "The Acts of the Apostles." Indeed,

Reconstruction of a lead bulla (with the seal impression of a menorah) used to secure a scroll that had valuable content.

toward the end of the second century one zealously anti-Marcionite work, the Muratorian list, goes so far as to call it "The Acts of *All* the Apostles." That was a great exaggeration, but Acts does at least record something about most of the apostles or apostolic men to whom are ascribed the letters the catholic church came to acknowledge as canonical.

Another factor that made it advisable to define what was, and what was not, the Word of God was the rise of the Montanists from the mid-second century onward. They claimed to announce further revelations by the Spirit of prophecy; it was helpful, therefore, to appeal to a recognized standard by which such claims might be evaluated; and such a standard was provided by the canon of Scripture.

From the second half of the second century, then, the church came to acknowledge a NT of the same general dimensions as ours. For a considerable time there was some questioning about a few of the books at the end of our NT, and arguments were occasionally put forward for the recognition of books that did not ultimately maintain their place

N

© Dr. James C. Martin

within the collection. But after some generations of debate about the few "disputed" books in relation to the majority of "acknowledged" books, we find the twenty-seven books that make up our NT today listed by Athanasius of Alexandria in A.D. 367, and not long after by Jerome and Augustine in the West. These leaders did not impose decisions of their own but published what was generally recognized. It is unhistorical to represent the limits of the NT as being fixed by the verdict of any church council. When first a church council did make a pronouncement on this subject (A.D. 393), it did no more than record the consensus of the church in East and West.

The invention of the codex, or leaf-form of book, made it a practicable matter to bind the NT writings, or indeed the whole Bible, together in one volume—something that could not have been done with the older scroll-form of book. The earliest comprehensive codices known to us belong to the fourth century, but already in the third century, and possibly even in the second, groups of NT books were bound together in smaller codices. The Chester Beatty biblical papyri (early 3rd cent.) include one codex of the four Gospels and Acts, one of ten Pauline letters and Hebrews.

V. Authority of the NT. The authority of the NT is not based on archaeological evidence or on any other line of comparative study. By such means we can confirm the historical setting of the record in the first century and provide ourselves with an illuminating commentary on it. The value of this should not be underestimated, but the essential authority of the NT derives from the authority of Christ, whether exercised in his own person or delegated to his apostles. The NT documents are the written deposit of the apostles' witness to Christ and of the teaching they imparted in his name. When we emerge from the "tunnel" period, which separates the apostolic age from the last quarter of the second century, we find the church still attaching high importance to apostolic authority. The apostles are no longer there, but the apostolic faith is confessed, the apostolic fellowship is maintained, and apostolic church order is observed. We find too, that the apostolic writings, whether penned directly by apostles or indirectly by their associates ("apostolic men"), are available in the NT canon

to serve as the church's rule of faith and life—the criterion by which it may be determined whether doctrine or fellowship or anything else that claims to be apostolic really is so. And from those days to our own, it is the NT that, from time to time, has called Christians back to the ways of apostolic purity, to the truth as it is in Jesus. Reformation is not something that the church needed once for all in the sixteenth century; true "reformation according to the word of God" is an abiding need of the church. And where the NT is given its proper place in the church's belief and practice, true reformation goes on continually.

Not only in his works and words during his earthly ministry, but also in the continuing ministry that he has exercised since his exaltation, Jesus reveals God to human beings. Therefore not only the Gospels, which record the revelation given in the days of his flesh, but also the other NT books, which record the further outworking of that revelation, are accepted by the church as her normative documents. The HOLY SPIRIT, who came to make the significance of Jesus plain to his followers and to lead them into all the truth, still performs these services for his people; and the NT writings are his primary instrument for their performance. How else could the Spirit take the things of Christ and declare them to men and women today if these writings were not available as a basis for him to work on? The Spirit who was imparted in fullness to Jesus and who worked through the apostles is the Spirit under whose direction the Christians of the earliest centuries were enabled to distinguish so clearly the documents that bore authoritative witness to Jesus. He is also the Spirit by whose illumination we today may appropriate that witness for our own and others' good.

In all this the place of the OT as an integral part of the Christian Scriptures is not ignored. The two Testaments are so organically interwoven that the authority of the one carries with it the authority of the other. If the OT records the divine promise, the NT records its fulfillment; if the OT tells how preparation was made over many centuries for the coming of Christ, the NT tells how he came and what his coming brought about. If even the OT writings are able to make the readers "wise for salvation through faith in Christ Jesus" and equip them thoroughly for the service of God (2 Tim. 3:15-17), how much more is this true of the NT writings! Our Lord's statement of the highest function of the earlier Scriptures applies with at least equal force to those of the NT: "These are the Scriptures that testify about me" (Jn. 5:39).

new year. See FEASTS.

Neziah. ni-zi´uh (Heb. *nĕṣîaḥ H5909*, possibly "faithful" or "famous"). Ancestor of a family of temple servants (NETHINIM) who returned from the EXILE in Babylon (Ezra 2:54; Neh. 7:56).

Nezib. nee´zib (Heb. *nĕṣîb H5908*, "pillar[s]" or "garrison"). A town in the SHEPHELAH allotted to the tribe of JUDAH (Josh. 15:43). It is identified with modern Khirbet Beit Neṣib esh-Sharqiyeh, some 7 mi. (11 km.) NW of HEBRON and 9 mi. (15 km.) ENE of LACHISH.

Nibhaz. nib´haz (Heb. *nibḥaz H5563*, derivation uncertain). An idol of the Avvites (see IVVAH); Nibhaz, along with TARTAK, was introduced by them into SAMARIA when they were relocated there by SARGON after 722 B.C. (2 Ki. 17:31). The names Nibhaz and Tartak are not attested elsewhere, and various explanations have been proposed, such as the view that they refer to Ibnahaza and Dirtak, gods worshiped in ELAM. None of the suggestions can be verified.

Nibshan. nib´shan (Heb. *nibšān H5581*, derivation uncertain). A city in the wilderness of JUDAH listed between SECACAH and the City of Salt (Josh. 15:62; see SALT, CITY OF). It is tentatively identified with Khirbet el-Maqari (in the Buqeiʿah Valley), some 10 mi. (16 km.) SE of JERUSALEM.

Nicanor. ni-kay´nuhr (Gk. *Nikanōr G3770*, "conqueror"). **(1)** Son of Patroclus (2 Macc. 8:9); he was a general of the SELEUCID army who warred against Judas MACCABEE (1 Macc. 3:38-39 et al.). He is described as an able man "among the Friends" of ANTIOCHUS Epiphanes (3:38). In 166-165 B.C. Nicanor, along with two other generals, was assigned by Antiochus's regent, LYSIAS, to destroy Judah and Jerusalem (3:38-42). They took up their

positions at EMMAUS, just a few miles from Jerusalem, but were badly routed by Judas and his forces (4:3-14), forcing the Syrian generals and their army to flee into PHILISTINE towns nearby (4:15). A few years later Nicanor was sent on a similar mission, but Judas won a decisive victory and Nicanor was slain. After mutilating his body, the Jews displayed it in Jerusalem (1 Macc. 7:47; 2 Macc. 15:33), and set aside the thirteenth of ADAR as "Nicanor's Day" in honor of their great victory over him on that day (1 Macc. 7:48-49; 2 Macc. 15:36).

(2) One of the seven men appointed by the early church to serve tables and thereby relieve the apostles for other duties (Acts 6:5). See also DEACON; STEPHEN.

Nicanor Gate. See BEAUTIFUL GATE.

Nicodemus. nik´uh-dee´muhs (Gk. *Nikodēmos G3773*, "conqueror over the people"). A leading PHARISEE, "a ruler of the Jews," and a member of the SANHEDRIN. Perhaps from curiosity, and possibly under conviction, but certainly led of God, he came to Jesus by night (Jn. 3:1-14). He must have thought of himself as quite condescending to address Jesus, the young man from GALILEE, as RABBI, but Jesus, instead of being puffed up by the recognition, quickly made Nicodemus aware of his need by announcing the necessity of a new birth (see REGENERATION) in order "to see the kingdom of God." Nicodemus did not then understand but was deeply touched, though he had not yet the courage to stand out for the Lord. Later, when at the Feast of Tabernacles (7:25-44) the Jewish leaders were planning to kill Jesus, Nicodemus spoke up, though timidly, in the Sanhedrin, suggesting their injustice in condemning a man without a fair trial (7:50-51). After the death of Jesus, however, Nicodemus came boldly with JOSEPH of Arimathea (19:38-42), provided a rich store of spices for the embalmment, and assisted in the burial of the body. After that he is not mentioned in Scripture.

Nicolaitan. nik´uh-lay´uh-tuhn (Gk. *Nikolaitēs G3774*). Name given to a heretical group in the early church, mentioned only twice in the book of Revelation, in the messages to the churches of EPHESUS and PERGAMUM (Rev. 2:6, 15-16). In

N

the latter passage the Nicolaitans are associated closely with certain people who held the teaching of BALAAM (2:14), and some scholars have argued that Nicolas and Balaam would then be regarded as Greek-Hebrew equivalents, alluding in each instance to an evil teacher who had influence over the people and brought them into bondage to heresy. These people apparently used Christian liberty as an occasion for the flesh (cf. Paul's warning in Gal. 5:13). The enticement to such a course of action was the pagan and often immoral society in which Christians lived. The Nicolaitans were judged by the author of Revelation to be most dangerous, because the result of their teaching would have conformed Christianity to the world rather than have Christianity change the world. According to some ancient Christian writers, the Nicolaitans were (or claimed to be) disciples of NICOLAS of Antioch, a proselyte who was among the seven men chosen to serve the Jerusalem congregation (Acts 6:5) and who allegedly had forsaken true Christian doctrine. There is, however, no concrete evidence for this claim.

Nicolas. nik´uh-luhs (Gk. *Nikolaos G3775*, "conqueror of the people"). Also Nicolaus. A PROSELYTE from ANTIOCH OF SYRIA chosen as one of the seven men to serve the church in Jerusalem (Acts 6:5; see DEACON). Evidently he was a GENTILE who had become a convert to JUDAISM and subsequently to Christianity. Nothing more is known about Nicolas, though he was thought by some church fathers to have been the founder of the heretical sect known as the NICOLAITANS (Rev. 2:6, 15). Clement of Alexandria (*Miscellanies* 2.20.118) excused him from responsibility for this by indicating that it was a perversion of his teaching that had produced the Nicolaitans.

Nicolaus. See NICOLAS.

Nicopolis. ni-kop´uh-lis (Gk. *Nikopolis G3776*, "city of victory"). A city selected by Octavian (later AUGUSTUS) and built as the capital of Epirus, an area in NW GREECE. He built the city on a promontory of the Ambracian Gulf (Gulf of Arta) to celebrate his decisive victory over Mark Antony. It is likely that this Nicopolis was the rendezvous that the apostle PAUL planned to use as a base from which to evangelize in Epirus (Tit. 3:12). Although there are other towns that bear the same name, none of them would have warranted Paul's intention to spend a whole winter in it. Nicopolis has extensive ruins (just N of modern Preveza), including two theaters.

Niger. ni´guhr (Gk. *Niger*, from Lat. *niger*, "black"). The surname of Simeon, one of the five "prophets and teachers" listed as ministering in the church at ANTIOCH of Syria (Acts 13:1). Because the name may suggest that he was African in origin (though this inference is hardly necessary), some have speculated that he was the same as SIMON of CYRENE (Lk. 23:26 and parallels), but the latter need not have been dark-skinned, and in any case this identification is unlikely, since Luke himself says nothing about it.

night. See TIME.

night creatures, night hag. See LILITH.

nighthawk. See BIRDS.

Nile. nil. The main river, not only of EGYPT, but of AFRICA as well. In terms of length of the main stream, it is the longest of all rivers, covering some 4,160 mi. (6,700 km.) from its sources in equatorial Africa to its delta on the MEDITERRANEAN. Rising in a region of mountains, lakes, and seasonal rains, it traverses marshy and tropical areas and eventually threads its way through rocky desert wastes, where its waters have afforded the sole basis for the existence of living things. It is in the latter reaches that the Nile fostered in Egypt one of the oldest and most long-lived civilizations of the world. To the ancient Egyptians the Nile was *Hapi*, which was also the name of the river-god. It was also simply *itrw*, "river," from which the Hebrews apparently derived the term *yĕʾōr H3284*, "river," the name for the Nile in the Hebrew Bible (to be distinguished from "the river of Egypt"; see EGYPT, RIVER OF). The ultimate origin and meaning of the name *Nile* (from Gk. *Neilos*; Lat. *Nilus*) are unknown.

The "White" Nile, flowing N from Lake Victoria on the equator, has a fairly even flow northward till it is joined by the "Blue" Nile at modern Khartoum in the Sudan. This stream and the other affluents that join the Nile from the E, rise in the mountains of ETHIOPIA and are fed by the torrential rains of the springtime. They fluctuate greatly and provide the annual inundation that for thousands of years has flooded and fertilized Lower (northern) Egypt. The ancient mythological belief was that the goddess Isis annually shed a tear into the Upper (southern) Nile, and the resulting flood that is so great a blessing that Egypt has been called, from the time of Herodotus onward, "the Gift of the Nile."

Near the end of June the water at Cairo and onward takes on a greenish tinge and an unpleasant taste because of the vast multiplication of the algae; then about the beginning of July the life-giving inundation begins so that the delta region overflows and the stream deposits the rich gift of sediment brought down from the mountains. During an average year, the vast delta seems almost like a sea with islands protruding here and there. If the inundation is unusually deep, many houses are destroyed and loss ensues, while if it is much below the average level, famine follows. A failure of this inundation for seven successive years (Gen. 41) was used by God to work a great but peaceful revolution in Egypt in which JOSEPH bought up for the PHARAOH practically all private property except

that of the priests and brought the Israelites into Egypt for a stay of several hundred years.

From the days of ABRAHAM, who as Abram went down into Egypt (Gen. 12:10), until the infancy of our Lord Jesus Christ (Matt. 2:14), Egypt and the Nile were well known by the Hebrews and exerted a strong effect on the civilization of ISRAEL. In describing the Promised Land, MOSES (Deut. 11:10-12) emphasized its difference from Egypt "where you planted your seed and irrigated it by foot" (i.e., by irrigating furrows manipulated, and then altered from time to time, by foot power); and the prosperity or poverty of Egypt at various periods was in proportion to the ingenuity and faithfulness of the people in spreading the water of the Nile on their plants. The rise and fall of the Nile is very regular, but there have been times (e.g., A.D. 1877) when an unusually feeble flood led to widespread famine and many deaths. It was, no doubt, a series of these dry years in the days of Joseph that caused the seven years of famine (Gen. 41) and that led, under God, to the descent of Israel into Egypt.

When the Egyptians later feared the resident Israelites, it was commanded that every Israelite male child that was born should be thrown into the river (Exod. 1:22). JOCHEBED, the mother of MOSES, saved her son by placing him in a water-proofed basket of bulrushes and concealing him

A view of the Nile River. (Near the Valley of the Kings, looking W.)

© Dr. James C. Martin

in the reeds along the water's edge (2:3), where the king's daughter discovered the child when she came to the river to bathe (v. 5). When the Lord commissioned Moses, one of the signs he gave to confirm his appointment was the turning of the Nile water into blood (Exod. 4:9; cf. also 7:15, 17-24; 8:3-11, 20; 17:5; Ps. 78:44). In the prophecy of Amos there are references to the Nile and its rising and falling (Amos 8:8; 9:5). The river is mentioned elsewhere in other prophetic writings (Isa. 19:7 et al.; Jer. 46:7-8; Ezek. 29:3, 9; Zech. 10:11). The biblical writers were well aware of the importance of the Nile to Egypt and they practically identified the country with its river.

Nimrah. See Beth Nimrah.

Nimrim. nim´rim (Heb. *nimrîm H5810*, derivation uncertain). A locality in Moab. Both Isaiah and Jeremiah declared, "The waters of Nimrim are dried up" (Isa. 15:6; Jer. 48:34). The former passage (Isa. 15:5-7) seems to trace the Moabites' flight downstream from Horonaim, and then S across the Ravine of the Poplars (i.e., the Zered). If so, then Nimrim would probably be Wadi (Seil) en-Numerah, a stream-oasis near the SE tip of the Dead Sea.

Nimrod. nim´rod (Heb. *nimrôd H5808*, derivation uncertain). Son of Cush and grandson of Ham; an early warrior and hunter who founded a kingdom in Mesopotamia (Gen. 10:12; 1 Chr. 1:10). That he was "a mighty hunter before the Lord" may be a way of expressing "a renowned hunter." His rule included such great cities as Babel (Babylon) and Erech (Warka) in the land of Shinar. From that land he went out to Assyria and built Nineveh and other cities; this area is called "the land of Nimrod" by Micah (Mic. 5:6). Archaeological support for the presence of southerners in prehistoric and Sumerian times is found in the lower levels of these sites. Various attempts have been made to identify Nimrod with figures mentioned in extrabiblical documents (e.g., the Akkadian god Ninurta, the Babylonian hero Gilgamesh, the Assyrian king Tukulti-Ninurta I of Assyria [c. 1244-1208 B.C.], and so on), but none of these proposals is convincing.

Nimrud. nim´rood. See Calah.

Nimshi. nim´shi (Heb. *nimšî H5811*, derivation uncertain). Grandfather of King Jehu (2 Ki. 9:2, 14). Elsewhere Jehu is identified as "son of Nimshi" (1 Ki. 19:16; 2 Ki. 9:20; 2 Chr. 22:7), but in these passages the Hebrew word for "son" (*bēn H1201*) probably means "descendant."

Nineve. See Nineveh.

Nineveh. nin´uh-vuh (Heb. *ninwēh H5770*, from Akk. *Ninu(w)a*; in the NT, gentilic *Nineuitēs G3780*, "Ninevite"). KJV NT Nineve. One of the most ancient cities of the world, founded by Nimrod (Gen. 10:11-12) and enduring till 612 B.C. Nineveh lay on the banks of the Tigris above its confluence with the Greater Zab, one of its chief tributaries, and nearly opposite the site of the modern Mosul in Iraq. It was for many years the capital of Assyria, and its fortunes ebbed and flowed with the long strife between this empire and Babylon. Of the two kingdoms, or empires, Babylonia was the more cultured, but Assyria the more warlike. The kingdom over which Nineveh and its kings long ruled was N of Babylon and in the hills, and these facts made more for warlikeness than the more sedentary culture of a warmer climate. Babylon was the more important from Abraham's time to David's; then from David's time to that of Hezekiah and Manasseh, Nineveh and its kings were paramount; then still later, from the time of King Josiah to that of Daniel, Babylon was again at the head.

Among the great rulers of Assyria may be mentioned Tiglath-Pileser I, who made conquests about 1100 B.C., and Ashurnasirpal and Shalmaneser III, who inaugurated a system of ruthless conquest and deportation of whole populations, which greatly increased the power of Assyria and the influence of Nineveh. It was this latter king who defeated Hazael of Syria and boasted of receiving tribute from Jehu of Israel. The Assyrians, instead of numbering their years, named them from certain rulers; and lists of these "eponyms" have been found, but with a gap of fifty-one years around the beginning of the eighth century, due no doubt to some great calamity and/or the weakness of her kings. It was in this space of time that JONAH was sent of the Lord to warn the people of Nineveh: "Forty more days and Nineveh will be overturned" (Jon. 3:4), but God gave Nineveh a respite for nearly two hundred years.

ESARHADDON, the great king of Assyria from 680-668 B.C., united Babylonia to Assyria and conquered lands as far away as EGYPT (Isa. 19:4) and N ARABIA. He was succeeded by his greater son ASHURBANIPAL, who presided over Assyria in its brief climax of power and culture; but NABOPO-LASSAR of Babylon, who reigned from 625 to 605, freed it from Assyria and helped to bring about the destruction of Nineveh in 612. About 623 Cyaxares, king of the Medes (see MEDIA), made his first attack on Nineveh, and this was probably the occasion of NAHUM's prophecy.

For many centuries the very location of Nineveh was forgotten, but it was discovered in the nineteenth century, and among its buried ruins the great palace of SARGON, with its wonderful library of cuneiform inscriptions and its still-striking wall ornamentation, has been exhumed.

Nippur. ni-poor´. An ancient city in MESOPO-TAMIA, known today as Nuffar, about 100 mi. (160 km.) S of Baghdad or 50 mi. (80 km.) SE of Babylon. It was founded by the Ubaid people c. 4000 B.C. Although the city wielded no political power, it was the undisputed religious and cultural center from the early third millennium until the days of HAMMURABI, when it yielded to BABYLON as a religious and cultural center—though it continued to be an important city down to Parthian times. Nippur was the seat of the cult of ENLIL, and the ancient renown of this god insured his city the continued care on the part of the Babylonian kings. Excavators found some 50,000 tablets and fragments at Nippur, and about one tenth of these are inscribed with Sumerian works. Various temples and other important buildings have also been unearthed.

Nisan. ni´san, nee´sahn (Heb. *nîsān H5772*, from Akk. *Nisannu*). The first month in the Jewish religious CALENDAR (corresponding to March-April), during which the Passover took place. This name appears twice in the Bible, and only in postexilic

writings (Neh. 2:1; Esth. 3:7); it was earlier known as ABIB.

Nisroch. nis´rok (Heb. *nisrōk H5827*, derivation uncertain). TNIV Nisrok. An Assyrian deity worshiped at NINEVEH. After SENNACHERIB, the Assyrian king, returned from his loss near JERU-SALEM, he was murdered by his two sons ADRAM-MELECH and SHAREZER while he was worshiping in the house of Nisroch, his god. Sennacherib was apparently "smashed with statues of protective deities" (*ANET*, 288) as well as being slain "with the sword" (2 Ki. 19:37; Isa. 37:38). Since the name Nisroch is completely unknown in the source material for Mesopotamian religion, a textual corruption or an intentional scribal modification is suspected. Perhaps the reference is to some well-known deity (such as MARDUK or Nusku), but the problem remains unexplained.

Nisrok. nis´rok. TNIV form of NISROCH.

nitre. See LYE.

No. noh (Heb. *nō H5530*, from Egyp. *nwt*). KJV transliteration of the Hebrew name for the city of THEBES (Jer. 46:25; Ezek. 30:14-16; Nah. 3:8).

Noadiah. noh´uh-di´uh (Heb. *nôʿadyâ H5676*, possibly "Yahweh has met"). (1) Son of Binnui; he was a LEVITE and one of four men designated as final custodians of the treasure that EZRA brought back from EXILE (Ezra 8:33).

(2) A prophetess who allied herself with TOBIAH and SANBALLAT against NEHEMIAH at the time of the rebuilding of the walls of JERUSALEM (Neh. 6:14). Nothing else is known about her.

Noah (man). noh´uh (Heb. *nōaḥ H5695*, possibly from *nûḥa H5663*, "to rest," but in Gen. 5:29 explained [by popular etymology?] with reference to *nāḥam H5714*, "to comfort"; Gk. *Nōe G3820*). KJV NT Noe. Son of LAMECH and descendant of SETH; the last of the ten ANTEDILUVIAN patriarchs listed in Genesis (5:28-29). He received this name because Lamech foresaw that through him God would comfort the race and partially alleviate the effects of the Edenic curse. Noah was uniquely righteous (6:1-13). When he was 480 years old, 120 years before the FLOOD (6:3), he was warned of God that the world would be destroyed by water (Heb. 11:7). He was then given exact instructions for building the ark (Gen. 6:14-16). While engaged in this colossal task, he warned his contemporaries of the coming catastrophe, as a "preacher of righteousness" (2 Pet. 2:5), while God in longsuffering waited for them to repent (1 Pet. 3:20). Noah's three sons—SHEM, HAM, and JAPHETH—were not born until he was 500 years old (Gen. 5:32). One week before the flood, God led Noah and his family into the ark and supernaturally directed the animals also to enter. When all were safely inside, God shut the door (7:16).

The flood came in Noah's 600th year, increased steadily for 40 days, maintained its mountain-covering depth for 110 more days, and then subsided sufficiently for Noah to disembark in the mountains of ARARAT after another 221 days. During all this time, "God remembered Noah and all the wild animals … in the ark" (Gen. 8:1), implying that the Lord did not leave the task of caring for these creatures entirely to Noah. To determine whether it was safe to disembark, Noah sent forth first a raven and then a dove at regular intervals (8:6-10). The freshly plucked olive leaf proved to him that such sturdy plants had already begun to grow on the mountain heights. God commanded him to disembark, and Noah built an altar and offered clean beasts as burnt offerings to God. The Lord then promised never to send another universal flood, confirming it with the RAINBOW

A mosaic from the Church of the Holy Sepulchre in Jerusalem showing a representation of Noah's ark.

© Dr. James C. Martin

sign (8:21-22; 9:9-17). God blessed Noah and his family and commanded them to multiply and fill the earth (9:1).

Among the things preserved in the ark was sinful human nature. Noah became a husbandman, planted a vineyard, drank himself into a drunken stupor, and shamefully exposed himself in his tent (Gen. 9:20-21). Ham, presumably led by his son CANAAN, made fun of Noah. For this foul deed, Canaan was cursed and Ham received no blessing (9:25-27). On the other hand, Shem and Japheth showed due respect to their father (9:23) and received rich blessings for their descendants. Noah lived 350 years after the flood, dying at the age of 950 (9:29).

In the Babylonian flood account (the *Gilgamesh Epic*), Noah's counterpart is Utnapishtim. He likewise received divine warnings of the flood, built a huge ark, preserved human and animal life, sent out birds, and offered sacrifices. However, the gross polytheism and absurdities of the Babylonian account demonstrate that it suffered from a long oral transmission and that it did not influence Genesis in any way.

Noah (woman). noh´uh (Heb. *nō ʿâ H5829*, derivation uncertain). One of five daughters of ZELOPHEHAD of the tribe of MANASSEH (Num. 26:33). Since Zelophehad had no sons, his daughters requested ELEAZAR the priest that they be allowed to inherit their father's property, and the request was granted on condition that they marry into their father's tribe (27:1-11; 36:11; Josh. 17:3-4). This decision was very important and became a precedent.

No-Amon. noh-am´uhn. See THEBES.

Nob. nob (Heb. *nōb H5546*, derivation unknown). A town NE of JERUSALEM. Nob is described as "the town of the priests" (1 Sam. 22:19), near SAUL's capital of GIBEAH, to which the TABERNACLE came to be transferred after the destruction of SHILOH (14:2-3; cf. Jer. 7:14). At the time of DAVID's flight from Saul, c. 1015 B.C., the high priest AHIMELECH provided David at Nob with SHOWBREAD and the sword of GOLIATH (1 Sam. 21:1-9). Vengefully, Saul subsequently slew eighty-five of the priests and put the city to the sword (22:11-19). Three centuries later the town was described as a halting place for the Assyrians as they arrived from the NE; from Nob they could "shake their fist at the mount of the Daughter of Zion" (Isa. 10:32). It suggests the identification of Nob with Ras Umm eṭ-Ṭalaʿ (the eastern slope of Mount Scopus, on the N part of the Olivet ridge) or some other nearby site. Such a general location for Nob is confirmed by 2 Sam. 15:32, which speaks of David's coming to the top of the ascent of the Mount of OLIVES "where people used to worship God," and by Neh. 11:31-32, which lists Nob as a Benjamite town between ANATHOTH and ANANIAH (= NT BETHANY, modern el-ʿAzariyeh).

Nobah (person). noh´buh (Heb. *nōbaḥ H5561*, apparently from *nābaḥ H5560*, "to bark"). One of the descendants of MANASSEH who conquered GILEAD and drove the AMORITES from the area; he "captured Kenath and its surrounding settlements and called it Nobah after himself" (Num. 32:42). See JAIR; KENATH; NOBAH (PLACE).

Nobah (place). noh´buh (Heb. *nōbaḥ H5562*, apparently from *nābaḥ H5560*, "to bark"). A town in GILEAD that was in the neighborhood of JOGBEHAH, W of a Transjordanian caravan route (Jdg. 8:11). It was on that route, in the city of KARKOR (v. 10), that GIDEON fell upon a Midianite army and captured the kings ZEBAH AND ZALMUNNA (v. 12). This Nobah is probably the town that was originally known as KENATH and later renamed by a Manassite (Num. 32:42); see NOBAH (PERSON). Some, however, argue that a different Nobah is in view and that it should be identified with modern Tell Ṣafut, a short distance NW of Jogbehah.

Nobai. See NEBAI.

noble, nobleman. The Hebrew term *ḥōr H2985*, indicating free or noble birth, is used as a noun, occurs only in the plural, and is especially frequent in the book of Nehemiah (1 Ki. 21:8, 11; Neh. 2:16; 4:14; et al.). The adjective *ʾaddîr H129*, "majestic, splendid," can also be used as a noun with reference to nobles and chieftains (Jdg. 5:13; 2 Chr. 23:20; et al.). Another adjective, *nādîb H5618*, means "will-

ing," but when applied to someone who is willing or generous, it too can be rendered "noble [one]" or even "prince" (Num. 21:18; 1 Sam. 2:8; et al.). Several other Hebrew words can occasionally be used in this sense in particular contexts (e.g., Esth. 1:3; Job 29:10; Jon. 3:7).

In the NT, the Greek adjective *eugenēs G2302* indicates nobility in the sense of being "well-born" or "of noble race" (Lk. 19:12; 1 Cor. 1:26), but it can also refer to nobility of mind (e.g., the Bereans in Acts 17:11). Another adjective, *kalos G2819*, "good," can be properly rendered "noble" in certain contexts (e.g., 1 Tim. 3:1). The same is true of some other terms (cf. Rom. 9:21 NIV; Acts 24:3 KJV; et al.).

Nod. nod (Heb. *nôd H5655*, apparently from *nûd H5653*, "to wander"). A district E of EDEN to which CAIN went to live after he had killed his brother ABEL (Gen. 4:16). The location of Nod is unknown, and some argued that the name is symbolic of Cain's judgment as a fugitive.

Nodab. noh´dab (Heb. *nôdāb H5656*, perhaps "[God] has incited"). The name of an Arabian (less likely, Aramean) tribe in TRANSJORDAN, mentioned with JETUR and NAPHISH as allies of the HAGRITES (1 Chr. 5:19). This coalition was defeated and dispossessed by the tribes of REUBEN and GAD and the half-tribe of MANASSEH (vv. 18, 20-22), apparently during the time of SAUL (v. 10).

Noe. See NOAH.

Nogah. noh´guh (Heb. *nōgahh H5587*, "brightness, splendor"). Son of DAVID, listed among the children born to him in Jerusalem (1 Chr. 3:7; 14:6). This name, like that of ELIPHELET #2, is missing in the parallel list (2 Sam. 5:14-15).

Nohah. noh´hah (Heb. *nôḥâ H5666*, "rest"). **(1)** Third son of BENJAMIN (1 Chr. 8:2). This name, which curiously is feminine in form, does not appear in the other lists of Benjamin's sons (Gen. 46:21; Num. 26:38-40; 1 Chr. 7:6). Some have thought that Noah and RAPHAH in 1 Chr. 8:2 were alternate names of SHUPHAM (SHEPHUPHAM) and HUPHAM (who occupy the same places on the list at Num. 26:39). Other views have been proposed. See also comments under Ahiram.

(2) According to Codex Vaticanus (LXX^B), followed by the NRSV and other versions, Nohah was also the name of a place from which the Israelites pursued the men of Benjamin (Jdg. 20:43, where the MT has *mĕnûḥâ*, of uncertain meaning).

noise. This English term is used by the KJV almost ninety times, but it occurs with much less frequency in modern versions, which often use synonyms (e.g., "sound," as in Isa. 24:18) or alternate expressions (e.g., "the noise of the shout" in 1 Sam. 4:6 KJV becomes simply "the uproar" in NIV). Many references to noise occur in the context of God's predicted judgment, either direct or indirect, against the earth's inhabitants (Isa. 29:6; 33:3; Jer. 4:29; 47:3; 50:22; Ezek. 26:10; Rev. 6:1; 8:5; 9:9; 11:19; 16:18). The psalmist's admonition to "make a joyful noise" to God is rendered by the NIV, "shout with joy" or the like (Ps. 66:1; 95:1; 98:4, 6; 100:1). A roaring noise is associated with a jubilant throng (Isa. 24:8), enemy hordes in their attack on Israel (25:5), and the waves of the sea (Jer. 51:55).

nomad. Nomads are wandering groups of individuals who change area of residence, usually according to a seasonal pattern, within a larger area that is their home territory. Some nomads are characterized by hunting and collecting its immediate needs, with little concern for surplus or organized divisions of labor. Other groups are pastoral in nature and are characterized by following a consistent pattern of grazing, regulated by the seasons and nature of the herd or flock. A third type is characterized by agricultural ties; they stay in one spot until the crop is exhausted, then move on to new land.

Certain values arise from the demands of nomadic life. The need for mobility results in reduction of property—the wealth of the group being often largely limited to livestock. The mutual dependence of members of the tribe, together with consciousness of common descent, leads to solidarity and to such concomitant practices as blood revenge. Most present-day nomads are camel nomads who also possess the horse. The donkey played a significant role in the patriarchal narrative

(Gen. 22:3; 24:35; 30:43; 32:5). When Abraham undertook his travels he began a nomadic life that continued for Isaac and Jacob before the children of Israel settled in Egypt. The prophecy of Ishmael's future suggests a nomadic life (16:11-12), and later references reflect this nomadic state (37:25). The Kenites and Midianites (see Midian) seemed to be tent-dwelling nomads (Jdg. 5:24; 6:4-5). In the wilderness wandering, Israel was again a seminomadic people moving with their cattle from oasis to oasis (Num. 10:31; 33:1). The tabernacle was especially suitable for a people with such a nomadic tradition.

Non. See Nun.

noon. See Time.

Noph. See Memphis.

Nophah. noh´fuh (Heb. *nōpaḥ H5871*, perhaps related to *nāpaḥ H5870*, "to blow"). An unknown city of Moab, mentioned only in a poem: "We have demolished them as far as Nophah, / which extends to Medeba" (Num. 21:30). The Hebrew text, however, presents textual problems, and other renderings are possible. For example, the ESV translates, "we laid waste as far as Nophah; fire spread as far as Medeba"; the RSV and NRSV, in addition to accepting the reading "fire," delete the reference to Nophah and translate simply, "we laid waste until fire spread to Medeba."

north. The Hebrew term *ṣāpôn H7600* designates one of the four cardinal points of the compass and is often so used in the OT (Gen. 13:14 et al.). The prophets also use this term to refer generally to identifiable countries lying NE, or even due E of Palestine. Usually these are references to foes who, because of the sea on the W and the Arabian desert on the E, were forced to enter Palestine from the N. As a result, even Babylon, lying due E of Palestine, was spoken of as being N (Jer. 1:14-15; 6:1, 22; et al.). The many references in Dan. 11 to "the king of the North" probably are references to the Seleucid kings of Syria as opposed to "the king of the South" (i.e., Ptolemies of Egypt). The Greek term *borras G1080* appears twice in the NT and in both instances means "north" as the cardinal compass point (Lk. 13:29; Rev. 21:13). See also EAST; SOUTH; WEST.

northeast, southeast. See NORTHWEST, SOUTHWEST.

northwest, southwest. These words occur only in Acts 27:12, which says that Phoenix was "a harbor in Crete, facing both southwest and northwest." The RSV, however, translates "looking northeast and southeast." See discussion under PHOENIX.

nose, nostrils. It is not hard to see why the nose (Heb. *ʾappayim*, dual of *ʾap H678*, "face") should be regarded as the organ of ANGER in the body. DAVID, in telling of God's power and in particular his anger, says, "Smoke rose from his nostrils; / consuming fire came from his mouth, / burning coals blazed out of it" (2 Sam. 22:9; cf. Job 41:20 [Heb. v. 12], where a different term is used). The Hebrews did not consider the respiratory system any further than its entrance, and so the nose (rather than the lungs) was regarded as containing the breath of life (Gen. 2:7; 7:22). The term can thus be used to indicate passion (e.g., Job 27:3). See also FLAT NOSE.

nose jewel. See DRESS.

Not my people, Not pitied. See LO-AMMI; LO-RUHAMAH.

novice. This English term is used by the KJV to render Greek *neophytos G3745* (lit., "newly planted"), which occurs only once (1 Tim. 3:6; NIV and NRSV, "recent convert"). In his instruction to TIMOTHY, PAUL wrote that if any man desires the office of a BISHOP, he must not be new to the Christian faith, "or he may become conceited and fall under the same judgment as the devil."

Nubian. See ETHIOPIA.

number. Before the EXILE, the Hebrew spelled the numbers out in full, as is seen in the present text of the Hebrew Scriptures, in the SILOAM inscrip-

tion, and on the MOABITE STONE. Subsequently, some of the Jews employed such signs as were used among the Egyptians, the Arameans, and the Phoenicians—an upright line for 1, two such lines for 2, and so on; there were also special signs for 10, 20, 100. At least as far back as the reign of Simon MACCABEE (143-135 B.C.), the consonants of the Hebrew alphabet began to be used as numbers (ALEPH for 1, BETH for 2, etc.); the letters of the Greek alphabet were used in the same way.

Numbers were used conventionally and symbolically. Certain numbers and their multiples had sacred or symbolic significance: 3, 4, 7, 10, 12, 40, 70. For example, three expressed emphasis, as in "A ruin! A ruin! I will make it a ruin!" (Ezek. 21:27). From early times seven was a sacred number among the Semites (Gen. 2:2; 4:24; 21:28). Ten was regarded as a complete number. Forty was often used as a round number with special significance (Exod. 24:18; 1 Ki. 19:8; Jon. 3:4). Some of the higher numbers also seem sometimes to have been used as round numbers: 100 (e.g., Gen. 26:12; Lev. 26:8; 2 Sam. 24:3), 10,000 (e.g., Lev. 26:8; Deut. 32:30).

Some later rabbis developed the theory that all numbers have secret meanings and all objects their fundamental numbers, and elaborate mathematical rules were devised to carry out these concepts. The system came to be known as *gematria* (from Gk. *geōmetria*). It is often thought that an example of this approach is found in Rev. 13:18, which gives the number of the Beast as 666 ("Nero Caesar" in Heb. can be spelled *qsr nrwn*, and the numerical values are: $q = 100$, $s = 60$, $r = 200$, $n = 50$, $r = 200$, $w = 6$, $n = 50$). See also SYMBOL.

Numbers, Book of. The fourth book of the Bible and traditionally one of the five books of MOSES (the PENTATEUCH or TORAH). The English title is a literal translation of the title in the SEPTUAGINT and reflects the censuses of Num. 4 and 26. Some have proposed that this title was chosen by someone with a superficial knowledge of the book, since the censuses appear to have so little to do with its major thrusts. The usual Hebrew title, *běmidbar*, "in the wilderness" (based on the fifth word of 1:1), seems much more apt. However, the two censuses do relate directly to the overall themes of the book.

N

The first represents the organization of the people for the impending journey and the occupation of the land that was intended to follow shortly. The second census and its accompanying reorganization was necessitated by the people's failure to obey God at KADESH BARNEA, the resulting death of that generation in the wilderness, and the preparation of the new generation to possess the land at last.

Exception has been taken to the large number of Israelites—totaling an estimated two million or more. Some say the territory could not sustain so many people. This is true if the Israelites traveled as a closely knit group seeking forage in a limited radius. But if they fanned out with their flocks over a wide area, they could sustain themselves as did the large NABATEAN kingdom in the same area in Roman times. Furthermore, God specially and miraculously fed and sustained Israel. The size of the Israelite nation was surely great or JOSHUA would never have been able to conquer and occupy the land of Palestine as he clearly did. Large and well-fortified cities were conquered in the area from LACHISH in the S to HAZOR in the N, as well as the territory in TRANSJORDAN. Six hundred thousand men, not all active, would not have been too large a force to accomplish such a feat. David in later days of prosperity called up an army of 1,300,000 (2 Sam. 24:9). (Because such large figures seem disproportionate to what is otherwise known of populations in the ANE, alternate interpretations have been suggested, such as the view that the Heb. word translated "thousand" may refer to one military unit of undetermined size.)

The body of Numbers up to Num. 10:11 gives additional legislation and the organization of the host. From 10:11 to 12:16 is recorded the march from Sinai to Kadesh Barnea. Then comes the debacle at Kadesh recorded in chs. 13 and 14. The three leaders of this occasion—Joshua and Caleb, the believing spies, and Moses the intercessor—are forever memorialized as among God's great men. The next section (15:1—21:11) records the repeated faithlessness on the part of the people.

Overview of NUMBERS

Author: Anonymous, but comments elsewhere in the Bible seem to support the traditional view that MOSES is responsible for the PENTATEUCH as a whole.

Historical setting: The initial composition of the book must have taken place at the end of the wilderness wanderings (either late in the 15th or early in the 13th cent. B.C.; those who reject Mosaic authorship usually date the book after the EXILE, while acknowledging that much of the material is several centuries earlier).

Purpose: To provide a historical-theological account of the Israelite wanderings, beginning with their departure from SINAI, stressing their unfaithfulness in the wilderness, and ending with their arrival in the plains of MOAB; to encourage the new generation to remain faithful to God and thus to prepare themselves to conquer the Promised Land.

Contents: Organization of the people for their march into the wilderness (Num. 1-4); sanctification of the people and beginning of their march (chs. 5-10); complaints and rebellion of the people (chs. 11-19); events during the last stage of the wanderings (chs. 20-25); preparation of the new generation to possess the Promised Land (chs. 26-36).

An aerial view of the Desert of Zin. The Israelites lived for thirty-eight years around this wilderness.

Apparently during much of the forty years, according to Amos 5:25-26 and Josh. 5:2-7, the people wandered far away from God, and even their national unity may have lapsed temporarily. The forty years are treated very briefly.

From Num. 21:11 on, the accounts of the conquest of Transjordan and the preparations to enter the land are given. SIHON and OG of the northern territory were conquered in swift moves detailed more extensively in DEUTERONOMY. Then Numbers portrays the very interesting activity of BALAAM, the hireling prophet who was supernaturally restrained from cursing Israel (chs. 22-24). These chapters are now studied with new interest because they appear to show a very early type of Hebrew. Final material includes Joshua's installation (ch. 27), the summary of the journeys (ch. 33), and the provision of cities of refuge (ch. 35).

nun (letter). nuhn (from *nûn* [attested in the Bible only as a personal name], "fish"). The fourteenth letter of the Hebrew alphabet (נ), with a numerical value of fifty. It is named for the shape of the letter, which in its older form was thought to be a stylized picture of a fish; more likely, however, the letter originally depicted a snake. Its sound corresponds to that of English *n*.

Nun (person). nuhn (Heb. *nûn H5673* [variant *nôn* only 1 Chr. 7:27], "fish"). KJV also Non (1 Chr. 7:27). The father of JOSHUA (Hoshea, Jeshua), and therefore an Ephraimite (Exod. 33:11; Num. 11:28; 13:8; et al.). Nothing more is said about him.

Nunc Dimittis. noonk´di-mit´is. The title given to SIMEON's prayer (Lk. 2:29-32), drawn from the first line of the Latin VULGATE, "Nunc dimittis servum tuum, Domine" ("Now, O Lord, let your servant go"). The poem declares that God's promises, as prophesied by ZECHARIAH in his BENEDICTUS (1:68-79), have "now" been fulfilled. The description of Jesus as "a light of revelation to the Gentiles and for glory to your people Israel" (2:32) is a clear allusion to Isaiah's prophecies concerning the SERVANT OF THE LORD (cf. esp. Isa. 42:6; 46:13; 49:6).

nurse. See OCCUPATIONS AND PROFESSIONS.

nut. See PLANTS.

Nuzi. noo´zee. A town occupied by HURRIANS in the second millennium B.C. The importance of Nuzi for the Bible student results from the fact that the 4,000 clay tablets found there probably give a fuller picture of the life of the individual citizens

N

than can be gained for any other town in the ANE, with the possible exception of MARI. However, at Mari most of the tablets deal mainly with the royal family and its political activities, while at Nuzi there were found records of the life and activity of hundreds of ordinary citizens. Still more important to the Bible student is the fact that at many points the customs evidenced in these tablets show a remarkable similarity to those described in the book of GENESIS. Thus the Nuzi material is valuable for corroborating the accuracy of Genesis and also for giving a better understanding of its meaning. This article will pass over the many references to features of life that probably were common in most parts of the ANE at that time, but will note particularly a few that are valuable for throwing special light on the book of Genesis.

For example, dozens of adoption tablets have been found at Nuzi. Israelite law, so detailed on many subjects, contains no regulations for ADOPTION, and the history of the Hebrews in Palestine after the conquest, as recorded in the OT, contains no evidence of such a practice. But at Nuzi it was customary for a man, if he had no children, to adopt someone to carry on his name and inherit his property. This seems to be reflected in the statement of ABRAHAM, before ISAAC was born, that unless the Lord should give him a child, ELIEZER of Damascus would be his heir (Gen. 15:2).

Similarly, the incident of the TERAPHIM (31:17-35) was extremely puzzling before the discovery of the Nuzi documents. When JACOB determined to leave his uncle LABAN, RACHEL stole Laban's teraphim. Laban became anxious not simply because his daughters and his son-in-law had left without notice, nor because of the great amount of property that they had taken with them, but primarily because of the loss of the household gods. Why such concern? The tablets from Nuzi show that according to Hurrian custom at that early time, if a man desired to appoint a son-in-law as his principal heir he would turn over to him his household gods. Rachel was trying to secure all of Laban's property for her husband, and Jacob was rightfully indignant at being accused of attempting such an underhanded trick. The whole incident becomes understandable in the light of these facts, and it becomes clear why Laban, still suspicious, desired that a boundary stone be put up at MIZPAH, and that Jacob should swear that he would not pass over this boundary in order to do him harm (Gen. 31:44-53, esp. v. 52). The Nuzi tablets make it clear that a great part of Laban's reason for this was his desire that at his death the remainder of his property should go to his own sons and not be taken away from them by Jacob.

Nympha. nim´fuh (Gk. *Nympha G3809*, "bride, young woman, nymph"; possibly masc. *Nymphas*, short form of *Nymphodōros*, "gift of the nymphs"). KJV Nymphas. A Christian woman (or man?) in whose house the believers had meetings, and to whom PAUL sent greetings (Col. 4:15). Apparently she lived in LAODICEA, although some have argued that the language is ambiguous and that her home may have been either in COLOSSE or in HIERAPOLIS. Nympha must have been a woman of means, possibly a widow. Many have inferred that she did not merely host the Christian assembly, but that she was also a leader in the local church. It is not certain, however, whether a man or a woman is referred to (the accusative form found in the text can be accented either as a feminine, *Nymphan*, or as a masculine, *Nymphan*, and according to some MSS, the personal pronoun in the context is "his" rather than "her").

Nymphas. nim´fuhs. KJV form of NYMPHA.

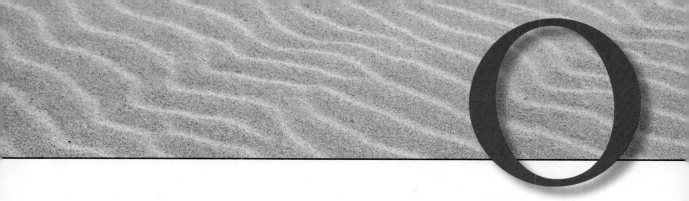

oak. See PLANTS.

oar. See SHIPS.

oath. An appeal to God to witness the truth of a statement or of the binding character of a promise (Gen. 21:23; 31:53; Gal. 1:20; Heb. 6:16). Two varieties of the oath are found in the OT—a simple one for common use and a more solemn one for cases of greater solemnity. Oaths played a very important part not only in legal and state affairs, but in the dealings of everyday life. A number of formulas were used in taking an oath, such as "the LORD is witness between you and me forever" (1 Sam. 20:23) and "as the LORD who rescues Israel lives" (14:39). Certain ceremonies were observed in taking an oath—in ordinary cases the raising of the hand toward heaven (Gen. 14:22; Deut. 32:40), and in some cases the putting of the hand under the thigh of the one to whom the oath was made (Gen. 24:2; 47:29). Sometimes one taking an oath killed an animal, divided it into two parts, and passed between the pieces (15:8-18). Swearing was done by the life of the person addressed (1 Sam. 1:26), by the life of the king (17:55), by one's own head (Matt. 5:36), by the angels, by the temple (23:16), by Jerusalem (5:35), and by God. It was forbidden to swear by a false god (Josh. 23:7). A virgin could take an oath if her father did not disallow it; and a married woman, if her husband permitted it (Num. 30:3-15). By the time of Christ the OT law regarding oaths (Exod. 22:11) was much perverted by the scribes, and our Lord therefore condemned indiscriminate and light taking of oaths, saying that people should be so transparently honest that oaths between them are unnecessary. The lawfulness of oaths is recognized by the apostles, who called on God to witness to the truth of what they said (2 Cor. 11:31; Gal. 1:20).

Obadiah. oh´buh-di´uh (Heb. *ʿōbadyāhû H6282* and *ʿōbadyâ H6281*, "servant [*i.e.*, worshiper] of Yahweh"). **(1)** Son of Izrahiah and descendant of ISSACHAR; a military chief (1 Chr. 7:3).

(2) A Gadite who joined DAVID's forces at ZIKLAG (1 Chr. 12:10). The Gadites are described as "brave warriors, ready for battle and able to handle the shield and spear. Their faces were the faces of lions, and they were as swift as gazelles in the mountains" (v. 8).

(3) Father of Ishmaiah; the latter was an officer over the tribe of ZEBULUN during the reign of David (1 Chr. 27:18).

(4) Son of Azel and descendant of SAUL through JONATHAN (1 Chr. 8:38; 9:44).

(5) An official of King AHAB who was in charge of the palace and who risked his life to save a hundred of the prophets when they were being hunted by JEZEBEL. During a time of famine, he was instructed by the king to go through the land and find grass for the animals. As he was walking, the prophet ELIJAH met him and gave him a message for the king (1 Ki. 18:3-16). Jewish tradition identifies him with the prophet Obadiah, but there is no evidence to support this suggestion.

(6) One of five officials sent by King JEHOSHAPHAT "to teach in the towns of Judah" (2 Chr. 17:7).

(7) Descendant of LEVI through MERARI and an overseer of the workmen who repaired the temple in the reign of King JOSIAH (2 Chr. 34:12).

(8) A prophet (Obad. 1). See OBADIAH, BOOK OF.

(9) Postexilic descendant of David in the line of ZERUBBABEL (1 Chr. 3:21). His place in the

1033

Overview of OBADIAH

Author: The prophet Obadiah.

Historical setting: Uncertain. The prophecy may have taken place as early as the ninth century B.C. or as late as the sixth.

Purpose: To denounce the nation of Edom, predicting its destruction, and thus to reassure the nation of Judah that God will bring deliverance.

Contents: The book consists of a series of condemnatory statements against the Edomites (Obad. 1-16), followed by a promise that the Hebrew nation will experience triumph (vv. 17-21).

genealogy is uncertain. The NRSV and other versions, following the Septuagint, understand Obadiah to be the son of Arnan and the grandson of Rephaiah (see comments under Rephaiah #1).

(10) Son of Shemaiah; a postexilic Levite (1 Chr. 9:16). He is commonly identified with Abda son Shammua (Neh. 11:17).

(11) Son of Jehiel and descendant of Joab; he was head of a large family who returned to Jerusalem from Babylon with Ezra (Ezra 8:9). Some believe he is the same as #12 below.

(12) One of the priests who signed the covenant with Nehemiah (Neh. 10:5).

(13) A Levitical gatekeeper in charge of the storerooms in the time of Nehemiah (Neh. 12:25).

Obadiah, Book of. The shortest OT book, fourth among the Minor Prophets. It is directed against Edom; from time immemorial the Edomites were hostile to Israel. The principal clue to the date of its writing is in Obad. 11, 14. If "the day you stood aloof" alludes to the events of 2 Ki. 8:20-22 and 2 Chr. 21:16-18, when the Edomites and others rebelled against King Jehoram in the ninth century B.C., the book probably would be dated quite early; but if the reference is to other events (cf. Ps. 137:7;

2 Chr. 36:20; Ezek. 25:13-14), the prophecy would be late, subsequent to 586 B.C. Most scholars date the book after the exile, but the more likely view is that 2 Chr. 28:16-18 is the apposite reference and that the time was late in the eighth century, during the reign of Ahaz of Judah. At that time Edom and the Philistines were associated in warfare against Judah, and the names of the two nations are again coupled in Obad. 19.

Obadiah 1-9 is very similar to Jer. 49:7-22 in pronouncing punishment on Edom. Apparently either Jeremiah or Obadiah made use of the other, or both made use of a common source that is no longer available. In Obad. 10-14 Edom is arraigned for its guilt in standing with the enemies of Israel

Not even these inaccessible mountains in Edom could save its inhabitants from the judgment announced by Obadiah.

© Dr. James C. Martin

in the time when Judah and Jerusalem were in deep distress. In vv. 12-14 the prophet exhorts Edom to quit its evil association with the enemies of Jerusalem. In vv. 15-16 the DAY OF THE LORD, that is, a time of awful judgment, is proclaimed as being "near for all nations," and national annihilation is predicted for those peoples who fight against the Lord—they will "be as if they had never been." To this point in Obadiah, the Lord has been addressing Edom in the second person singular, but in the closing paragraph, he speaks of a coming restoration of Israel when Zion will be holy and God will use Israel as a flame to destroy Esau. The people of the NEGEV (the southern part of Judah) are to possess the land of Edom; Israel will greatly enlarge its borders (vv. 19-21). The principal message of Obadiah to the peoples of today seems to be the proclamation, not only of the danger of fighting against God, but also of the peril of fighting his people.

Obal. oh´buhl (Heb. ʿōbāl *H6382*, derivation uncertain). Also EBAL. Son of JOKTAN and descendant of SHEM (Gen. 10:28). In the parallel passage (1 Chr. 1:22), the MT has "Ebal" (cf. NRSV and other English versions), but some Hebrew and Greek MSS, as well as the Syriac, read "Obal" (cf. NIV). Obal/Ebal was presumably the eponymous ancestor of a S Arabian tribe, perhaps to be identified with the *Banū ʿUbal* in Yemen.

Obed. oh´bid (Heb. ʿōbēd *H6381*, possibly short form of OBADIAH, "servant [*i.e.*, worshiper] of Yahweh"; Gk. *Iōbēd G2725*). (1) Son of BOAZ and RUTH (Ruth 4:17, 21-22; 1 Chr. 2:12); included in the GENEALOGY OF JESUS CHRIST (Matt. 1:5; Lk. 3:32).

(2) Son of Ephlal and descendent of JUDAH in the line of JERAHMEEL (1 Chr. 2:37-38).

(3) A member of DAVID's elite corps of mighty warriors (1 Chr. 11:47).

(4) Son of Shemaiah, grandson of OBED-EDOM, and a gatekeeper from the Korahites (1 Chr. 26:7; cf. v. 1). See KORAH. Obed and his brothers are described as "leaders in their father's family because they were very capable men" (v. 6).

(5) Father of Azariah; the latter was a military commander who assisted the high priest JEHOIADA

in the successful overthrow of the apostate queen ATHALIAH (2 Chr. 23:1).

Obed-Edom. oh´bid-ee´duhm (Heb. ʿōbēd-ʾĕdôm *H6273*, "servant [*or* worshiper] of Edom," where *Edom* may refer to a Canaanite deity). (1) A "Gittite" in whose house King DAVID deposited the ARK OF THE COVENANT after the death of UZZAH (2 Sam. 6:10). Obed-Edom guarded the ark for three months, and the Lord blessed him and his household (vv. 11-12; cf. 1 Chr. 13:13-14; 15:25). Because the term *Gittite* normally refers to an inhabitant of GATH (2 Sam. 15:18; 21:19), many scholars believe that Obed-Edom was a PHILISTINE living in Israel, presumably a convert to Yahweh. Others argue that *Gittite* could refer to a native of some Israelite town (such as GATH HEPHER and GATH RIMMON), that Obed-Edom was a name borne by several LEVITES (see below), and that the narrative in Chronicles suggests that Obed-Edom the Gittite was a Levitical gatekeeper and musician (1 Chr. 15:18-25; 26:4-8, 15; but see below, ##2 and 3).

(2) Son of JEDUTHUN #2 (1 Chr. 16:38). He was a Levite who may have served both as a gatekeeper for the ark (15:18, 24) and as a musician (15:21; 16:5). He may be the same as #1 above. According to some, however, a distinction is intended between the Obed-Edom mentioned in 16:38a (presumably the musician) and the Obed-Edom mentioned in 16:38b (the gatekeeper, here identified as son of Jeduthun and thus distinguished from the previous one; cf. the renderings in the NRSV and NJPS). Similarly, it may be that the Chronicler distinguishes between the Obed-Edom in 15:21 and the one in 15:24.

(3) A descendant of KORAH who is listed, along with his sons and descendants, as belonging to a division of gatekeepers (1 Chr. 26:4-8). He was responsible for the South Gate, and his sons for the storehouse (v. 15). This Obed-Edom may have been a son of Kore (cf. v. 1). Because we are told that "God had blessed Obed-Edom" (v. 5), he is probably being identified with #1 above.

(4) A Levite who was in charge of "all the gold and silver and all the articles found in the temple of God" during the reign of AMAZIAH king of Judah (2 Chr. 25:24). When JEHOASH king of Israel

sacked the temple, Obed-Edom may have been one of the hostages he took to Samaria.

obedience. The Bible, by exhortation and commandment, requires submission and obedience to six principal authorities: (1) parents (Eph. 6:1; Col. 3:20; 1 Tim. 3:4), (2) teachers (Prov. 5:12-13), (3) husbands (Eph. 5:21-22, 24; Col. 3:18; Tit. 2:5; 1 Pet. 3:1, 5-6), (4) masters—today, employers— (Eph. 6:4; Col. 3:22; Tit. 2:9; 1 Pet. 2:18), (5) government (Rom. 13:1-2, 5; Tit. 3:1; 1 Pet. 2:13), and (6) God (Gen. 26:5; Eph. 5:24; Heb. 5:9; 12:9; Jas. 4:7). When there is a clear conflict regarding obedience to authority, Christians are to obey God, not human beings (Acts 5:29). The supreme test of faith in God is obedience (1 Sam. 28:18); the Bible often links obedience to faith (Gen. 22:18; Rom. 1:5; 1 Pet. 1:14). Jesus' obedience to the Father (Phil. 2:8) is the supreme example for Christians, who are to be "obedient children" (1 Pet. 1:14).

obeisance. This English term, indicating a bow as a token of respect or reverence to a superior, is used occasionally (in the phrase "do/make obeisance") by the KJV and other versions to translate selected instances of the frequent Hebrew verb *ḥāwâ H2556* (Gen. 37:7 et al.), which is often rendered "to bow down." When used of homage given God, it is commonly rendered "to worship" (22:5 et al.). See WORSHIP.

obelisk. An obelisk is a monumental stone PILLAR, often associated with the worship of the sun and sometimes commemorative. It consists of a tapering, four-sided shaft, about square in cross-section, with a pyramidal top. Such monuments were a feature of the religion of the Egyptians, and obelisks of various sizes are known from ancient times, with the smaller ones often of funerary character. Jeremiah predicted that the obelisks of HELIOPOLIS would be destroyed (Jer. 43:13 NRSV). Obelisks commemorating military victories and the like were common in the ANE.

Obil. oh´bil (Heb. *ʾôbîl H201*, "camel-driver"). An ISHMAELITE who was the overseer of the camels in the court of King DAVID (1 Chr. 27:30). *Obil* may have been a nickname based on his occupation.

oblation. See SACRIFICE AND OFFERINGS.

Oboth. oh´both (Heb. *ʾōbōt H95*, possibly "skin bottles"). A stopping-place of the Israelites on their wilderness journeys, between PUNON and IYE ABARIM in MOAB (Num. 21:10-11; 33:43-44). Its precise location is uncertain.

occupations and professions.

apothecary. See *perfumer.*

artificer. See *craftsman.*

author. The composer of a literary production; an authority on a statement or fact. Agur and Lemuel, for example, are referred to as having recorded "words" or "sayings" in the form of prophecy and wisdom (Prov. 30:1; 31:1). For a different meaning of the term, see separate article AUTHOR.

baker. A trade that occupied a special street in JERUSALEM (Jer. 37:21). The baking of BREAD is one of the chief household duties. But in the towns and principal villages, the larger OVEN of the regular baker is required (1 Sam. 8:13). In addition to the home and public bakers, there was the royal baker, who baked for the king (Gen. 40:1-22; 41:10). The Hebrews used large stone jars, open at the mouth, about 3 ft. (1 m.) high, with a fire inside for baking bread and cakes. As soon as the sides were sufficiently heated, the thin dough was applied to the outside, and the opening at the top was closed. Sometimes wood was used for heating, but more often thorns and occasionally dry dung were used (Ezek. 4:12). See also FOOD; MEALS.

barber. One whose trade possibly originated in connection with the shaving of the head as part of a vow (Num. 6:18-19). The instruments of his work were probably the razor, the basin, the mirror, and perhaps the scissors. He usually plied his trade in the open, on the street. The word *barber* occurs only once in Scripture (Ezek. 5:1). However, great attention was paid to the HAIR and BEARD among the ancients. The barber must have been a well-known tradesman.

beggar. The beggar as a professional class was unknown during Mosaic times. The law of Moses made ample provision for the poor of the land. In imprecatory fashion, Ps. 109:10 sets forth begging as the fate and punishment of the children of the wicked. As cities developed, begging became more prevalent. In the NT beggars appear with some frequency: the blind beggar (Jn. 9:8-9); blind BARTIMAEUS (Mk. 10:46-52); the beggar by the BEAUTIFUL GATE of the temple (Acts 3:1-11); and perhaps most famous of all, LAZARUS, who is presented in opposition to the ungodly rich man (Lk. 16:19-31).

blacksmith. See *smith*.

butler. See *cupbearer*.

carpenter. A worker in wood. The work of carpenters is often mentioned in the Bible (Gen. 6:14; Exod. 37; Isa. 44:13). DAVID employed Phoenician carpenters in building his palace (2 Sam. 5:11; 1 Chr. 14:1). Some of the tools used by the ancient Egyptians were the adze, saw, square, awl, hammer, and glue-pot (Exod. 21:6; Jer. 10:4). The adze was their favorite implement. In ripping a board with the saw, the carpenter sat on the board and sawed away from himself (Isa. 44:13). In the NT, JOSEPH, the legal or foster father of Jesus, is described as a carpenter (Matt. 13:55); so also is Jesus (Mk. 6:3). The Greek word *tektōn G5454*, however, can be applied to various building professions, and it is likely that Joseph and Jesus were in the construction business, including masonry and similar activities.

chamberlain. This English term is used by the KJV in 2 Ki. 23:11 and throughout the book of Esther (Esth. 1:12 et al.) as a rendering of Hebrew *sārîs H6247* (lit., EUNUCH), which is used of important functionaries, including military officers (e.g., Jer. 52:25). In the NT, the KJV uses it twice (Rom. 16:23 [NIV, "director of public works"]; Acts 12:20 [NIV, "a trusted personal servant"]).

clerk. The "city clerk" at EPHESUS was an official who dispersed the mob gathered at the theater to attack PAUL (Acts 19:35; Gk. *grammateus G1208*). In the Greco-Roman world, such a clerk occupied a position of considerable importance in urban administration. His initial duties consisted of keeping the records of the city, taking the minutes of the council and assembly, caring for official correspondence, receiving the edicts of emperors and governors, plus a great mass of miscellaneous documents, then filing and publishing these, as required. He publicly read decrees, put up temporary notices for the people to read, and those of permanent importance were inscribed on stone.

confectioner. See *perfumer*.

coppersmith. This English term is used by a number of Bible versions in 2 Tim. 4:14 to translate a term that was applied generally to metalworkers. See article on MINERALS.

counselor. An adviser in any matter, particularly as the king's state adviser (2 Sam. 15:12; 1 Chr. 27:33). His position usually ranked him among the chief men of the government (Ezra 4:5; Job 3:14; 12:17; Isa. 19:11).

craftsman. Also called artisans and artificers (KJV), craftsmen were skilled in metals, carving wood and plating it with gold, setting precious stones, and designing embroideries (2 Ki. 24:14, 16; Jer. 24:1; Acts 19:24). From "artificers" comes "artifacts," an archaeological term, meaning anything that was made or modified by human art or workmanship. SOLOMON procured many craftsmen from HIRAM, king of TYRE, when building the TEMPLE (1 Chr. 29:5; 2 Chr. 34:11).

cupbearer. An important official who served wine to the king. Due to the ever-present possibility of intrigue, the position was one of great responsibility and trust. The officer's chief duty was to guard the king's person. The first mention of a cupbearer is in the JOSEPH story (Gen. 40:2); since the man there is designated as "chief cupbearer," several must have held a similar position under him. Under SOLOMON, this office was apparently very important, for his cupbearers highly impressed the queen of SHEBA (1 Ki. 10:5; 2 Chr. 9:4). NEHEMIAH was cupbearer to the Persian king ARTAXERXES I Longimanus (Neh. 1:11), and he tells us that after he "took the wine and gave it to the king" (2:1), the two had a conversation involving new political action. The office of cupbearer was thus a highly influential one.

diviner. One who obtains or seems to obtain secret knowledge, particularly of the future. Diviners stood in contrast to the prophets of the Lord (Zech. 10:2). Although in some passages the diviner is classed with the prophet, the contexts are always negative (e.g., 1 Sam. 6:2; Jer. 27:9). See article on DIVINATION.

doctor of the law. See *teacher of the law*.

dyer. The practice of dyeing textiles was in existence even before the time of ABRAHAM. Vats and clay looms that were used as weights have been found in LACHISH. The dyer obtained his dye from

O

various sources. The crimson was obtained from a worm or grub that fed on the oak or other plants. Indigo was made from the rind of the pomegranate. Purple was made from the murex shellfish found on the beach at the city of Acre (Acco). It was also found along the Phoenician coast N of Acre. Luke tells of Lydia, "a dealer in purple cloth from the city of Thyatira" (Acts 16:14). Excavations have revealed that "a guild of dyers" existed in the vicinity of Thyatira.

elder. The elders in Israel were adult men who served as rulers. See separate article on ELDER.

engraver. The OT and ARCHAEOLOGY reveal a knowledge of engraving or carving among the Israelites. However, the practice was not developed as extensively nor as skillfully as among some of the neighboring countries, perhaps because of the command against worshiping graven images (Exod. 20:4). Signet rings, engraved with a man's seal or sign, were common (Gen. 38:18; Esth. 3:12; Jer. 22:24). Each of the two onyx stones on the high priest's shoulders was engraved with the names of six tribes, and his breastplate bore twelve stones, each engraved with the name of a tribe (Exod. 28:9-21). BEZALEEL and OHOLIAB were craftsmen in gold, silver, brass, stones, and wood (31:1-9; 38:22-23). God gave them the skills to make the furnishings of the tabernacle. Not only did they carve and engrave, but they also taught these skills to others (35:30-35).

farmer. Farming had its beginning with the first man, ADAM. CAIN tilled the soil, and ABEL was a livestock farmer, perhaps a shepherd (Gen. 4). The early farm implements were very crude. The plow was a simple affair, being made of wood and having an iron share, small and shaped like a sword. Donkeys and oxen were used to pull the light plow, which had only one handle, except in cases where human beings were used in place of oxen. When Israel entered the land of Canaan, farming took on a new aspect. Every seventh year, the farmers allowed the ground to remain idle. Whatever grew of itself was left to the poor, the stranger, and the beasts of the field (Lev. 25:1-7). See the article on AGRICULTURE.

fisher. The frequent allusions to the art of fishing in Scripture are in connection with the Sea of Galilee (Matt. 4:18; 13:48; Mk. 1:16; Lk. 5:2).

Several methods of fishing were practiced. (1) The casting net was a common method used. The fisherman stood on the bank or waded breast-deep into the water, and skillfully threw the net, which he had arranged on his arm, into the water in front of him. It fell in the shape of a ring, and as the weights dragged it down, the net took the shape of a dome or cone and enclosed the fish. (2) The dragnet was used in herring and salmon fishing, with floats marking the location of the submerged nets. It was usually operated from boats. (3) Hooks or angles were occasionally used. Fish were speared on the Mediterranean coast, being attracted to the surface by a moving torch. Night fishing was very common, especially on the Sea of Galilee.

fuller. One who washes or bleaches clothing. This is one of the oldest arts and at an early period was comparatively perfect. Both men and women engaged in cleaning clothes and other materials. The cleansing was done by treading or stamping the garments with the feet or with rods or sticks in containers of water. The fullers discovered a singular art of bleaching cloth white by the aid of alkali, soap, putrid urine, fumes of sulfur, and the ashes of certain desert plants. Therefore, the fuller's shop was located usually outside the city where offensive odors could be avoided, the cloth could be trampled clean in a running stream, and then spread out for drying. In Jerusalem the FULLER'S FIELD was located near the conduit of the upper pool, which was in all probability in the KIDRON Valley between the GIHON Spring and the well EN ROGEL (2 Ki. 18:17; Isa. 7:3; 36:2).

gatekeeper. The biblical "porter" (KJV) was a gatekeeper and not a burden-bearer (2 Sam. 18:26; 1 Chr. 9:22). The LEVITES who had charge of the various entrances to the temple were called gatekeepers or doorkeepers (1 Chr. 9:17; 15:18, 23-24; 2 Chr. 23:19). A gatekeeper was stationed at the city gates and among the shepherds, where he was responsible for guarding the doors of the sheepfold. In David's time, the gatekeepers of the temple, who were also guards, numbered 4,000 (23:5).

goldsmith. An artisan who works in gold. The furnishings of the TABERNACLE and the TEMPLE that were constructed of gold or overlaid with gold required skilled workmen (see, e.g., Exod. 25). Goldsmiths were not above helping out in the reconstruction of the wall of Jerusalem after the EXILE (Neh. 3:8, 31-32). Most often the word "goldsmith" in the NIV is used of those who craft idols from gold (Isa. 40:19; 41:7; 46:6; Jer. 10:9 et al.).

herdsman. A tender of oxen, sheep, goats, and camels. The PATRIARCHS were great herdsmen. The occupation was not inconsistent with state honors. David's herdsmen were among his chief officers of state. In general, however, the herdsman was seldom the owner of the flock or herd that he tended (Gen. 13:7; 26:20; 1 Sam. 21:7; Amos 1:1; 7:14). His duty was to protect the herd from wild beasts, to keep them from straying, and to lead them to suitable pasture. The herdsmen usually carried a sharpened or metal-pointed goad and a small bag, or scrip, for provisions. Their dress consisted of a long cloak. Their food was very simple, and they usually lived on what they could find. Their wages were given them in products taken from the herd.

hunter. The work of hunter or fowler was one of the earliest occupations. It was originally a means of support, but later became a source of recreation. It was held in very high repute and was engaged in by all classes, but more often by royalty (Gen. 10:9; 27:3, 5; 1 Sam. 26:20; Job 38:39; Prov. 6:5). Three principal methods of hunting are mentioned in the Bible: (1) Shooting with bow and arrows (Exod. 27:3). (2) Snaring by spring net and cage, especially for birds such as quail, partridge, and duck (Jer. 5:27; Amos 3:5). (3) Pits covered with a net and brushwood for deer, foxes, wolves, bears, lions, etc. (Ps. 35:7; Isa. 24:18; 42:22).

husbandman. See *farmer.*

judge. The head of the house was considered the judge over his own household. With the enlargement of the human family, this power quite naturally passed to the heads of tribes and clans. After Israel came into the wilderness beyond Sinai, MOSES found the responsibility of handling all the judicial matters too great. Taking the advice of his father-in-law JETHRO, he was advised to choose "men who fear God, trustworthy men who hate dishonest gain" to handle these matters. There were to be judges over thousands and hundreds and fifties (Exod. 18:19-26; Deut. 1:16). After coming into Canaan, judges sat at the gates of the cities (Deut. 16:18).

lawyer. One who is conversant with the LAW. There were court lawyers and SYNAGOGUE lawyers (Matt. 22:35; Lk. 7:30; 10:25; 11:45-46, 52; 14:3; Tit. 3:13). The SCRIBE functioned in the capacity of a lawyer in the pronouncement of legal decisions. (See also *teacher of the law,* below.)

magician. One who practices superstitious ceremonies to hurt or to benefit mankind. The Hebrews were forbidden to consult magicians (Gen. 41:8; Exod. 7:11, 22; Dan. 1:20; 2:2; 5:11; Acts 13:6, 8). See article on MAGIC. So-called *natural* magic attributes its power to a deep, practical acquaintance with the power of nature. *Supernatural* (or spiritual) magic attributes its power to an acquaintance with celestial or infernal agencies. There are many accounts of the use of magical art in the Scriptures. Before Israel left Egypt the magicians were called by PHARAOH to duplicate the works of God in changing a rod into a serpent and turning water into blood. They were sometimes classified with the "wise men." In the interpretation of dreams and visions, the magicians and soothsayers were called. The Chaldeans were particularly famous as magicians.

mason. A worker in stone. Certain villages were famous for their masons. The farmers were usually skillful in building low terrace walls of undressed stone for the fields and vineyards, but most buildings required a master mason. The work required acquaintance with the proper kind of foundation. Masons knew how to lay the cornerstone and how to select and lay the stones in the wall. Their equipment consisted of the plumb line, the measuring

Egyptian stone mason chiseling stone.

© Dr. James C. Martin

reed, the leveling line, the hammer with the toothed edge for shaping stones, and a small basket for carrying off earth (2 Ki. 12:12; 22:6; 1 Chr. 22:15; 2 Chr. 24:12; Ezra 3:7).

medium. See *witch*.

merchant. A dealer in MERCHANDISE. Merchants bought goods from distant lands or from caravans and sold them to traders in the marketplaces. Many became wealthy. Sometimes merchants are spoken of appreciatively (2 Chr. 9:13-14; Cant. 3:6), but sometimes they were dishonest (Hos. 12:7), and, especially in the book of Revelation, they are condemned for seeking only material gain (Rev. 18:3, 11, 13, 15). See also separate article on MERCHANT.

musician. Since MUSIC was a very prominent art in biblical, especially OT, times and played such an important part in the life of Israel and in their religious exercises and festivities, there was a demand for those who were adept at playing instruments and in singing hymns and psalms (Ps. 68:25). Hebrew music was primarily vocal, yet many of the psalms have signs indicating that they were to be accompanied by musical instruments (1 Ki. 10:12; 2 Chr. 9:11; Rev. 18:12). The "chief musician" occurs in the titles of fifty-four psalms. ASAPH and his brothers were apparently the first to hold this position, and the office was probably hereditary in the family (1 Chr. 15:19; 2 Chr. 35:15). Among the instruments used by the Hebrews were the cymbal, harp, organ, pipe, psaltery, and trumpet.

nurse. One who looks after, tutors, or guides another, as in a period of inexperience or sickness. In ancient times the nurse had an honored position in a home, often as a nursemaid, or nanny (2 Sam. 4:4; 2 Ki. 11:2). Most patriarchal families had a nurse or nurses. REBEKAH's nurse went with her to Canaan and was buried with great mourning (Gen. 24:59; 35:8). Foster fathers or mothers were sometimes referred to as nurses (Ruth 4:16; Isa. 49:23).

perfumer. A compounder of drugs, oils, and perfumes. (The KJV uses the terms "apothecary" and "confectionary.") All large oriental towns had their perfumers' street. Their stock included anything fragrant in the form of loose powder, compressed cake, or essences in spirit, oil, or fat, as well as seeds, leaves, and bark. Perfumes were used in connection with the holy OIL and INCENSE of the tabernacle

(Exod. 30:25, 33, 35; 37:29; 2 Chr. 16:14; Neh. 3:8). The ritual of BAAL-worshipers (Isa. 57:9) and the embalming of the dead and rites of burial (2 Chr. 16:14; Mk. 16:1; Lk. 23:56) all used perfume. The apothecary compounded and sold these sweet spices and anointing oils (Eccl. 10:1). The frequent references in the OT to physicians and perfumers indicate the high esteem in which the professions were held (Gen. 50:2; Jer. 8:22; Lk. 4:23).

physician. One who understands and practices medicine in the art of healing. The priests and prophets were expected to have some knowledge of medicine. In the days of Moses there were midwives and regular physicians who attended the Israelites (Exod. 1:19). They brought some knowledge of medicine with them from Egypt, whose physicians were renowned for their healing arts. In the early stages of medical practice, attention was more often confined to surgical aid and external applications. Even down to a comparatively late period, outward maladies appear to have been the chief subjects of medical treatment among the Hebrews, though they were not entirely without remedies for internal and even mental disorders. The medicines prescribed were salves, particular balms, plaster and poultices, oil baths, mineral baths, etc. In Egypt the physicians also aided in carrying out the elaborate preparations connected with embalming a body (Gen. 50:2). See also the article on DISEASES.

Collection of ancient medical tools found at Ephesus.

© Dr. James C. Martin. The Ephesus Museum. Photographed by permission.

plowman. See *farmer.*

porter. See *gatekeeper.*

potter. Although regarded as an inferior trade, the work of POTTERY making supplied a universal need. In antiquity, potters lived in settlements in the lower city of Jerusalem (Jer. 18:2-4), in the neighborhood of Hebron and Beit Jibrin, where clay was plentiful and where the royal potteries probably were situated (1 Chr. 4:23). There is a great demand for potters in the Middle East because copper vessels are expensive and leather bottles are not suitable for some purposes. The maker of earthenware was one of the first manufacturers. The potter found the right kind of clay, prepared it by removing stones and other rough substances, shaped and made it into the vessel desired, baked it, and marketed it. If the vessel became marred in the shaping process, it was made over again into another vessel. When one broke after baking, it was discarded and thrown into the "potter's field" (Matt. 27:7, 10). The Hebrew potter, sitting at his work, turned the clay, which had first been kneaded with his feet, into various kinds of vessels on his potting wheels, which were generally made of wood (Lam. 4:2).

preacher. One who heralds or proclaims, usually by delivering a discourse on a text of Scripture. This method of presenting messages from God to man is as old as the human family. NOAH is referred to as "a preacher of righteousness" (2 Pet. 2:5). The prophets were given the responsibility of delivering messages of truth in song and action, in accusation and rebuke, with pleading and exhortation, by prophecy and promise. The temple, the synagogue, and the church were designed chiefly as places where the profession of preaching was practiced, where human beings became the conveyors of God's message. Since the completion of the Bible, preaching has come to mean the exposition of the Word of God to believers or the declaration of the gospel message to unbelievers.

priest. See separate article on PRIEST, PRIESTHOOD.

publican. See *tax collector.*

rabbi. A title given by the Jews to the teachers of their law. It was also applied to Christ by his disciples and others (Matt. 23:7-8; Jn. 1:38, 49; 20:16). See separate article RABBI.

recorder. An officer of high rank in the Jewish state, exercising the functions not simply of an annalist, but of chancellor or president of the privy council (Isa. 36:3, 22). He was not only the grand custodian of the public records, but he also kept the responsible registry of the current transactions of government (2 Sam. 8:16; 20:24; 2 Ki. 18:18). In David's court, the recorder appears among the high officers of his household (2 Sam. 8:16; 20:24). In Solomon's court, the recorder is associated with the three secretaries and is mentioned last, probably as being their president (1 Ki. 4:3).

robber. One who engages in theft and plunder. Among the nomad tribes of the Middle East, it was considered a most worthy profession. The Mosaic law strictly forbids robbery; it is denounced in Proverbs and by the prophets. The prophet Hosea compares the apostate priests to robbers, bandits, and marauders (Hos. 6:9; 7:1). Robbery is often mentioned in the Bible, but never is it commended (Isa. 61:8; Ezek. 22:29; Lk. 18:16; Jn. 10:8).

ruler. One who governs or assists in carrying on government. An honor often bestowed by kings on their subjects. DANIEL was made ruler over the whole province of BABYLON by NEBUCHADNEZZAR for interpreting a dream, and again made third ruler of the kingdom after interpreting the writing on the wall at the time of BELSHAZZAR's great feast (Dan. 2:10, 38; 5:7, 16, 29). There were such positions as the "synagogue ruler" (Lk. 8:49) and the "ruler of the treasures" (1 Chr. 26:24 KJV); and the high priest was considered the "ruler of the house of God" (1 Chr. 9:11).

sailor. One whose occupation is navigation, or the operation of SHIPS, particularly one who manipulates a ship with sails (1 Ki. 9:27; Jn. 1:5, 7; Rev. 18:17).

schoolmaster. This term is used by the KJV to translate a Greek word that more accurately refers to a well-educated slave who was given constant supervision of a boy between the ages of six and sixteen (Gal. 3:24 KJV). See the article on CUSTODIAN.

scribe. A person employed to handle correspondence and to keep accounts. They were given a high place alongside the high priest. HEZEKIAH set up a body of men whose work it was to transcribe old records, or to put in writing what had been handed down orally (Prov. 25:1). After the EXILE,

O

Stela of a scribe named Dedu-Sobek and his family (from the period of the 12th dynasty in Egypt). The duties of a scribe included teaching.

© Dr. James C. Martin. The Cairo Museum. Photographed by permission.

the term was applied to those responsible for the preservation and interpretation of the LAW (Neh. 8:1-13; Jer. 36:26). See separate article on SCRIBE.

seer. One who is considered able to foresee things or events; a PROPHET (1 Sam. 9:9). SAMUEL identified himself as a seer (10:19). Often kings and rulers had their own personal seers to assist them in decision making, especially when the future seemed unclear (2 Sam. 24:11; 2 Chr. 29:25; 35:15).

sergeant. A Roman lictor or officer who attended the chief magistrates when they appeared in public, and who inflicted the punishment that had been pronounced (Acts 16:35, 38 KJV; NIV, "officers").

servant. Applied to anyone under the authority of another, implying that not all servants were domestics or slaves. In some passages of Scripture, the word properly means "young man" or "minister." It is applied to the relation of men to others occupying high position, as ELIEZER, whose place

in the household of ABRAHAM compared with that of a prime minister (Gen. 15:2; 24:2; Prov. 14:35; Jn. 18:20).

sheepmaster. One who is both a shepherd and the owner of the sheep (2 Ki. 3:4 KJV). In some areas, the sheepmaster is one who owns a superior kind of sheep.

sheepshearer. When the wool of the sheep is long and ready to "harvest," a sheep-shearing time is announced, and it is a great time of rejoicing (Gen. 38:12; 2 Sam. 13:23-24). This festival is usually marked by revelry and merry-making (Gen. 31:19).

shepherd. One employed in tending, feeding, and guarding the sheep. Abel, Rachel, and David were all keepers of sheep. The shepherd's equipment consisted of a bag made of goats' skin with legs tied, in which food and other articles were placed; a sling for protection against wild animals; a rod (stick) with a knob on one end; a staff, usually with a crook on one end; a flute made of reeds for entertainment and for calming the sheep; and a cloak to use as bedding at night. Sheep would learn to recognize the voice of their master (Gen. 46:32; 1 Sam. 17:20; Jn. 10:3-4). Metaphorically, God is pictured as the shepherd of his flock (Gen. 48:15; Jn. 10; Rev. 7:17).

silversmith. A worker in silver, the most famous example of which was DEMETRIUS the silversmith, whose business was interfered with by the evangelistic work of the apostle PAUL (Jdg. 17:4; Prov. 25:4; Acts 19:24).

singer. A trained or professional vocalist. Hebrew MUSIC was primarily vocal. BARZILLAI mentioned the "voices of men and women singers" (2 Sam. 19:35). Solomon was a composer of songs (1 Ki. 4:32). David's trained choir numbered 288 members (1 Chr. 25:7).

slave. A person held in bondage to another, having no freedom of action, his person and service being wholly under the control of his master or owner. Jewish slaves were of two classes—Hebrew and non-Hebrew—and both were protected by law. Hebrew slaves became such through poverty or debt, through theft and inability to repay, or in case of females, through being sold by their parents as maidservants. The slavery of Hebrews was the mildest form of bondservice (Exod. 21:20-32; Deut. 21:14; Jer. 34:8-16). At the time of Christ, slavery was established throughout the world and considered even by the wisest people as a normal state of society. But Christianity, by teaching the common creation and redemption of mankind and enjoining the law of kindness and love to all, instructed believers how to live under slavery and then provided principles that have been used as the basis for emancipation and the ultimate extinction of the whole institution (1 Cor. 12:13; Gal. 3:28; Col. 3:11; Rev. 19:18). See separate article on SLAVE, SLAVERY.

slave driver, slave master. One whose duty is to assign tasks; an overseer or bond master. Pharaoh appointed slave drivers over the Hebrews to make their work hard and wearisome. He hoped by such oppression to break down their physical strength and thereby to reduce their numerical growth and also to crush their hope of ever gaining their liberty (Exod. 1:11; 3:7; 5:6, 10, 13-14).

smith, blacksmith. A workman in stone, wood, or metal. The first smith mentioned in Scripture is TUBAL-CAIN, though the term is not applied to him (Gen. 4:22). So necessary was the trade of the smith in ancient warfare that conquerors removed the smiths from a vanquished nation to more certainly disable it (Isa. 44:12; 54:16; Jer. 24:1).

soldier. One who engages in military service and receives pay for his services. In the earlier times, every man above the age of twenty was a soldier (Num. 1:3); and each tribe formed a regiment, with its own banner and its own leader (2:2; 10:14). Up until the time of David, the army consisted entirely of infantry (1 Sam. 4:10; 15:4), the use of horses having been restrained by divine command (Deut. 17:16). The Jews had experienced the great advantages found in the use of chariots, both in their contests with the Canaanites and at a later period with the Arameans, and hence they eventually attached much importance to them (1 Ki. 22; 2 Ki. 9; 1 Chr. 19:6-7). See also article on ARMY.

soothsayer. See *magician*.

sorcerer. One who practices the arts of the magicians and astrologers, by which he pretends to foretell events with the assistance of evil spirits (Isa. 47:9, 12; Acts 8:9, 11). In its broader sense, a sorcerer is one who practices in the whole field of divinatory occultism (Exod. 7:11; 22:18; Jer. 27:9). See article on DIVINATION.

spinner. A person who uses the distaff and the spindle in the making of thread from wool, flax, or cotton (Prov. 31:19; Matt. 6:28).

steward. One to whose care is committed the management of the household (Gen. 43:19; Lk. 16:1). The term is also applied to ministers (1 Cor. 4:1 KJV) and to Christians (1 Pet. 4:10 KJV). The meaning of the word is different in Gen. 15:2, where NIV has this description: "the one who will inherit my estate."

tanner. One who is skilled in dressing and preserving hides or skins of animals. Among the ancient Jews, ceremonial uncleanness was attached to the occupation of the tanner, and hence he was obliged to do his work outside the town. The tanneries of JOPPA are now on the shore S of the city, where possibly the "house of Simon" was located (Acts 9:43; 10:6, 32).

taskmaster. See *slave driver*.

tax collector. The *publicans* (KJV) or tax collectors were hated for being the instruments through which the subjection of the Jews to the Roman emperor was perpetuated. They looked at the paying of tribute as a virtual acknowledgment of the emperor's sovereignty. Tax collectors were noted for imposing more taxes than were required so that they might more quickly enrich themselves. The publicans of the NT were regarded as traitors and apostates, defiled by their frequent contacts with pagans, and willing tools of the oppressor. Hence, they were classed with sinners, harlots, and pagans (Matt. 9:11; 21:31; Mk. 2:16; Lk. 5:27-30).

teacher. One who imparts instruction and communicates knowledge of religious truth or other matters. "Teachers" are mentioned among those having divine gifts in Eph. 4:11. "Teacher" doubtlessly refers to the well-informed persons to whom inquiring Christian converts might have recourse for removing their doubts and difficulties concerning Christian observances, the sacraments, and other rituals, and for receiving from Scripture and demonstration that "this is the very Christ," that the things relating to the MESSIAH have been accomplished in Jesus (Ezra 7; Matt. 23; Heb. 5:12).

teacher of the law. A term used in the NT with reference to those learned in the LAW of Moses, both written and oral, of which they were the official interpreters. GAMALIEL was such a person

(Acts 5:34). The title is often used synonymously with that of *scribe*.

tentmaker. One skilled in making tents from hair, wool, or skins. The early patriarchs largely lived in tents and were skilled in the art of tentmaking. In NT times it was the custom to teach every Jewish boy some trade. Jesus was a carpenter or builder, and Paul was a tentmaker. Paul practiced his trade in company with Aquila at Corinth (Acts 18:1-3).

tetrarch. A ruler over a fourth part of a kingdom or province in the Roman empire. Locally, his authority was similar to that of a king, and the title of king was often given to him (Matt. 14:1; Lk. 3:1; Acts 13:1).

tiller. See *farmer*.

treasurer. An important officer in Middle East courts, probably having charge of the receipts and disbursements of the public treasury (Ezra 1:8; 7:21; Isa. 22:15; Dan. 3:2-3). This title was given to the officer of state, was considered superior to all others, and was sometimes filled by the heir to the throne (2 Chr. 26:21).

watchman. One whose duty was to stand in the tower on the walls or at the gates of the city. He also patrolled the streets, and, besides protecting the city and its inhabitants from violence, he was required to call out the hours of the night (2 Sam. 18:24-27; Cant. 5:7; Isa. 21:11-12). God's prophets were also his "watchmen" to warn his people (Isa. 21:6 KJV; NIV "lookout").

weaver. One who is skilled in the making of cloth or rugs from spun thread or string. The Israelites probably perfected the art of weaving while in Egypt, though they no doubt made progress in it from their own resources, even before they entered Egypt. Weaving, for the most part, was done by women. The fibrous materials woven were usually linen, flax, and wool (Exod. 35:35; Lev. 13:48; 1 Chr. 11:23; Isa. 38:12).

witch. A "knowing or wise one." Witch was the name given to the woman and wizard the name given to the man who practiced "witchcraft." There was an apparent communication with demons and a pretended conversation with the spirits of the dead by means of which future events were revealed, diseases cured, and evil spirits driven away. The woman of Endor to whom Saul went

for help is called a "medium" in the NIV (1 Sam. 28). Witchcraft was severely denounced (Lev. 20:6; 2 Ki. 9:22; Gal. 5:20). See also *sorcerer*.

writer. The knowledge of writing was possessed by the Hebrews at a very early period. The materials on which they wrote were of various kinds. Tables of stone, metal, plaster, skins, paper made from bulrushes, and fine parchment were used. The pens were also different, to correspond with the writing material (Jdg. 5:14; Ps. 45:1; Ezek. 9:2). The prophets were often told by the Lord to write and may be considered writers (Rev. 1:11; 21:5). See article on WRITING

Ochran. See OCRAN.

Ocran. ok´ruhn (Heb. *ʿokrān* H6581, prob. "sorrowful"). Also Ochran; TNIV Okran. Father of Pagiel, who was the leader of the tribe of Asher during the wilderness wanderings (Num. 1:13; 2:27; 7:72, 77; 10:26).

Oded. oh´did (Heb. *ʿôdēd* H6389, possibly "[Yahweh] has helped"). **(1)** Father of Azariah; the latter was a prophet who urged King Asa to reform worship (2 Chr. 15:1; in v. 8 the KJV, following the MT, makes Oded himself the prophet; the NIV and most modern versions restore "Azariah son of," following the ancient versions). Some have thought that *ʿôdēd* was originally a common noun meaning "prophet," later misinterpreted as a name.

(2) A prophet who successfully challenged King Pekah of Israel for attempting to enslave many people from Judah (2 Chr. 28:9).

odor. This English term is used by the NRSV and other versions primarily to render Hebrew *rêaḥ* H8194 (KJV, "savour"; NIV usually, "aroma"), which occurs mostly with reference to the sacrificial scent that is pleasing to God (Gen. 8:21 et al.; it is esp. frequent in Leviticus and Numbers). The Septuagint renders this term with Greek *osmē* G4011, which also occurs in the NT (e.g., Eph. 5:2). See SACRIFICE AND OFFERINGS.

offal. See DUNG.

offence. This noun, which in Elizabethan English could mean "stumbling," is used by the KJV to render several terms, especially *skandalon* **G4998**. The Greek word originally referred to the bait stick on a snare or trap, but later to the trap or snare itself, and in the NT figuratively to that which causes someone to stumble morally (Matt. 16:23 et al.). Similarly, the cognate verb *skandalizō* **G4997** is translated "offend" or "make to offend" in the KJV. The Master warned his disciples solemnly: "If your right eye causes you to sin [KJV, offend thee], gouge it out and throw it away" (Matt. 5:29; cf. Mk. 9:43-47). Believers should also avoid being a STUMBLING BLOCK to others (Matt. 18:6; Rom. 14:13; 1 Cor. 8:13). Modern English versions use the noun *offense* in the more common sense of "affront."

Offence, Mount of. See CORRUPTION, HILL (MOUNT) OF.

offerings. See CONTRIBUTION; SACRIFICE AND OFFERINGS.

officer, official. One who holds a position of authority in civil, military, or religious matters. Hebrew words that can be so rendered include *niṣṣāb* (niphal ptc. of *nāṣab* **H5893**, "to [take a] stand, be stationed"), which can designate "overseers" of both religious and military groups (1 Ki. 4:5; 2 Chr. 8:10), and *sārîs* **H6247**, which can certainly mean EUNUCH (Isa. 39:7), but usually refers to a male court official who may or may not have been castrated (Gen. 37:36 et al.). Among NT terms that may be rendered "officer," the Greek word *praktōr* **G4551** is found only in Lk. 12:58; apparently it is used here in distinction to the judge of the court, so it must refer to some sort of constable who follows the court's direction. The noun *hypēretēs* **G5677** ("assistant, administrator") can be rendered "officer" or "guard" (Matt. 5:25, parallel to Lk. 12:58).

offices of Christ. A phrase traditionally used to describe the various facets of the redeeming work of CHRIST. The principle that underlies this terminology is simply that the work that Christ accomplished is the perfect fulfillment of certain basic functions or offices in which the essential relationship between God and human beings is expressed. These offices often are classified as prophetic, priestly, and kingly. While these categories are not fully exhaustive of all that Christ accomplished, and while some overlapping may be occasionally observed between them, there are good reasons why these may continue to be used. One of the most significant (and common) designations of Jesus is MESSIAH (the Anointed One). Now in the OT three offices were commonly inaugurated by a ceremony of unction as indicative of God's sanction: the offices of PRIEST (Exod. 30:30; 40:13, 15; and many other references), of KING (1 Sam. 10:1; 15:1, 17; 16:3, 12-13; 1 Ki. 1:34; 19:15-16; et al.), and of PROPHET (1 Ki. 19:16; Isa. 61:1; cf. Ps. 105:15). A development of the nature of Christ's work along this structure is therefore particularly well suited to exhibit the correspondence between OT and NT, between the expectation of the old COVENANT and the fulfillment of the new.

offscouring. This English term, referring to something that is rubbed off, and figuratively to the scum or castoffs of society, is used twice by the KJV and RSV. In one passage it is used metaphorically of Jerusalem's being "scrapings" in the midst of her enemies (Lam. 3:45; NIV, "scum"). In the NT it is used of the apostles, whose low estate is contrasted by PAUL with the pride and self-satisfaction of the Corinthian church (2 Cor. 4:13; NIV, "refuse").

Og. og (Heb. *ʿôg* **H6384**, meaning unknown). King of BASHAN whose territory in TRANSJORDAN evidently included not only Bashan proper (from near Mt. HERMON in the extreme N to the River YARMUK in the S) but also part of GILEAD (from the Yarmuk to the JABBOK). The kingdom had two royal cities, EDREI and ASHTAROTH (Josh. 13:12), corresponding to the two sections, and there were sixty strongly fortified towns (Deut. 3:4). He was an AMORITE (3:8) and was described as the last of the remnant of the REPHAITES (v. 11). The account of his war with Israel, after the defeat of SIHON, is given in Num. 21:33-35 and Deut. 3:1-12. It would appear that he prepared to attack before Israel could take the initiative, but was defeated and killed near his capital, Edrei (Deut. 3:1). His territory was given to the half tribe of MANASSEH. Sihon and Og are mentioned frequently together as reminders of God's victory over the enemies of Israel (e.g., Deut. 31:4; Josh. 2:10; Neh. 9:2; Ps. 135:11).

Ohad. oh´had (Heb. *ʾōhad H176*, derivation uncertain). Son of SIMEON and grandson of JACOB (Gen. 46:10; Exod. 6:15). The name is not found in the parallel lists (Num. 26:12-14; 1 Chr. 4:24-25), leading some to suspect corruption in the text.

Ohel. oh´hel (Heb. *ʾōhel H186*, "tent"). Son of ZERUBBABEL and descendant of King DAVID through SOLOMON (1 Chr. 3:20), possibly born in Palestine (see HASHUBAH).

Oholah and Oholibah. oh-hoh´luh, oh-hoh´li-buh (Heb. *ʾohōlâ H188*, "her tent," and *ʾohōlîbâ H191*, "my tent is in her"). KJV Aholah, Aholibah. Two symbolic names employed by the prophet EZEKIEL to designate idolatrous SAMARIA and JERUSALEM respectively (Ezek. 23). They are described as "daughters of the same mother. They became prostitutes in Egypt, engaging in prostitution from their youth" (vv. 2b-3a). The Lord, however, adopted them and they bore sons and daughters, but they continued their IDOLATRY, doting on the Assyrians, Babylonians, and others. As punishment the Lord delivered them into the hands of these nations. The allegory was yet another means used by God to bring his people to repentance and to warn them of impending judgment.

Oholiab. oh-hoh´lee-ab (Heb. *ʾohōlîʾāb H190*, possibly "[the divine] father is my tent [*i.e.*, protection]"). KJV Aholiab. Son of Ahisamach and descendant of DAN; he assisted BEZALEL in the building of the TABERNACLE and its furniture (Exod. 31:6; 35:34; 36:1-2; 38:23). The skill in craftsmanship of these men is traced to the Spirit of God.

Oholibah. See OHOLAH.

Oholibamah. oh-hoh´li-bah´muh (Heb. *ʾohōlîbāmâ H192*, possibly "my tent [*i.e.*, protection] is a high place" or "my tent is with them"). KJV Aholibamah. (1) One of the wives of ESAU (Gen. 36:2, 5, 14, 18, 25). The MT describes her as "the daughter of Anah the daughter of Zibeon the Hivite" (cf. KJV), meaning possibly that ANAH was a woman. However, the

NIV translates the second instance of Hebrew *bat H1426* as "granddaughter" (i.e., referring to Oholibamah rather than Anah), and this rendering leaves open the question whether Anah was Oholibama's father or mother. Others emend the word to *bēn H1201*, "son" (cf. NRSV), on the reasonable assumption that this Anah is the same as the HORITE (rather than HIVITE) mentioned elsewhere in this chapter (36:24). See also #2 below.

(2) A clan chief of EDOM (Gen. 36:41; 1 Chr. 1:52). Some believe, however, that this Oholibamah is the same as #1 above, Esau's wife. Because she had three sons who were chiefs (Gen. 36:18), she was considered a tribal mother, and it is possible that the tribe was known by her name.

oil. In the Bible the reference is almost always to olive oil, perhaps the only exception being Esth. 2:12, where it is oil of myrrh. The olives were sometimes beaten (Lev. 24:2), sometimes trodden (Mic. 6:15), but generally crushed in a mill designed for that purpose. The upper stone, instead of rubbing against the lower as in a flour mill, rolled on it and so pressed out the oil. The wheel usually was turned by an ox or donkey, the animal being blindfolded. Olive oil was not only a prime article of food, bread being dipped in it, but it was also used for cooking, for anointing, and for lighting. Oil was one of the principal ingredients in making soap (Jer. 2:22).

Anointing with oil was for three diverse purposes: wounded animals were anointed for the soothing and curative effects of the oil (Ps. 23:5); people anointed themselves with oil for its cosmetic value (104:15); but most notably, some were anointed as an official inauguration into high office,

Reproduction of a beam press at Hazor. Such devices were used to extract oil from olives.

© Dr. James C. Martin

including the priesthood. See ANOINT. Anointing the head of a guest with oil was a mark of high courtesy (Lk. 7:46). Oil is used also as a symbol for the HOLY SPIRIT. Jesus' messiahship was not bestowed with the use of literal oil but was confirmed when the Holy Spirit came down on him in the form of a dove at his baptism (3:22). Oil was also the prime source of light in homes and in the tabernacle. Home lamps were little clay vessels having a wick lying in the oil and supported at one end, where the oil burned and furnished just about "one candlepower" of light. See also OINTMENTS AND PERFUMES.

oil tree. See PLANTS.

ointments and perfumes. The use of perfume in the form of ointment or impregnated oil was a Middle Eastern practice long before it spread to the Mediterranean world. In all probability it was originally used for ceremonial purposes, first religious then secular, and became a personal habit with the growing sophistication of society and the need for deodorants in hot lands (Esth. 2:12; Prov. 7:17; 27:9; Isa. 57:9). So universal was the practice that its suspension was an accepted sign of MOURNING (Deut. 28:40; Ruth 3:3; 2 Sam. 14:2; Dan. 10:3; Amos 6:6; Mic. 6:15). The skin as well as the hair was perfumed and anointed (Ps. 104:15); and, especially on high occasions, the scented unguent was used with profusion (133:2). Anointing an honored guest was a courtesy a host performed (Lk. 7:46). Among the directions listed for the service of the tabernacle are two prescribed "recipes," possibly Egyptian in form (Exod. 30:23-25, 34-36). One recipe prescribes 750 ounces of solids in 6 quarts of oil. It is possible that the oil was pressed off when the scent of the aromatic gums was absorbed. The liquid would then be used as anointing oil, while the solid residue provided an incense. The process of manufacture is not clear, and the account takes for granted that "the work of a perfumer" is commonly familiar to the reader (Exod. 30:25, 35; Neh. 3:8; Eccl. 10:1). It is clear, however, that the compound was based on the aromatic gum of Arabian plants (indigenous especially in Arabia Felix in the south of the peninsula) and that the medium or base was some form of

fat or oil (probably calves' fat and olive oil). In its later trade form perfume was sometimes packed in alabaster boxes or flasks (Lk. 7:37). Such ointment was heavily scented (Jn. 12:3) and costly (12:5).

Okran. ok´ruhn. TNIV form of OCRAN.

Old Gate. A city gate in postexilic JERUSALEM (Neh. 3:6; 12:39; so KJV and other versions). In the first passage, which describes the rebuilding of the wall, this gate is mentioned after the FISH GATE (3:3), which was on the N wall near the NW corner, and before the BROAD WALL (3:8), which jutted out of the W wall. In the second passage, which traces the procession of the choirs at the dedication of the wall, it is mentioned between the EPHRAIM GATE, whose location is uncertain, and the Fish Gate (the choir in view marched N then turned E). The gate in question must have been either on the N wall very close to the NW corner or, more likely, on the W wall below the NW corner. Some have argued, however, that the Hebrew term *yĕšānâ* is a proper name (cf. NIV and NJPS), and that it was so named because it led to the village of JESHANAH.

old man, old self. See MAN, OLD.

Old Testament. This name, in Christian terminology, refers to the collection of books that constitute the Hebrew Bible. In the English versions it consists of thirty-nine books: the five books of MOSES (PENTATEUCH), twelve historical books, five poetical books, and seventeen prophetical books. In the Hebrew Bible, the books are organized differently, and some of them are combined, so that the total number of books is twenty-four. Neither of these classifications exhibits the fact that much of the Pentateuch is history, nor do they show the chronological relation of the books. A logical survey of the OT literature may approach the subject chronologically.

I. **Before Abraham**. The first eleven chapters of GENESIS give a brief outline of major events from the CREATION to the origin of the Jewish people in Abraham. Genesis 1 is a majestic revelation of God creating all the material and organic universe, climaxing in human beings. This picture is not given in the categories of modern science, but neither should it be thought to contradict contemporary scientific theory. The creation of plants, animals, and human beings is spread over six "days" and is left undated. Chapters 2-3 detail the special creation of the man and the woman and God's dealing with them in EDEN. ADAM and EVE on probation fell into SIN, and the race was involved in misery. God, however, promised a Redeemer (3:15) and instituted SACRIFICE as a type of that redemption. As people multiplied, sin increased, and God sent a FLOOD to destroy all mankind (chs. 6-8). Many widely separated cultures, including the old Babylonian, preserve legends of a great flood. The genealogies given in the early chapters of Genesis seem to be schematic and incomplete, as are other biblical genealogies. If 11:10-26 has no gaps, SHEM must have outlived Abraham, but no other hint of this is given in the biblical picture.

II. Abraham and the patriarchs. As sin again increased, God chose Abraham to found a new nation, which God would protect and isolate to a degree, and through whom he would reveal himself at last as Savior. Abraham left polytheistic MESOPOTAMIA and settled in CANAAN, where God instructed and blessed him, his son ISAAC, and grandson JACOB. From Jacob came the twelve sons who fathered the tribes of Israel. The midpoint of Genesis (Gen. 25) records the death of Abraham, who lived in the Middle Bronze Age, about 1900 B.C. His main characteristic was FAITH. To the sacrifices God now added CIRCUMCISION as a sign of his covenant. Although circumcision was practiced elsewhere in antiquity, infant circumcision seems to have been unique. It was to be a sign both of the material and spiritual aspects of the COVENANT.

III. Bondage and exodus (Exod. 1-19). Through providential circumstances of famine and through JOSEPH's exaltation, God took Jacob's family to Egypt for a period of growth. At first it was sheltered under Joseph's viziership, but later Israel was enslaved. God saw their bitter bondage and through Moses delivered Israel by an outstretched hand. Ever since, Israel has remembered the deliverance from PHARAOH's army when the Lord brought them through the RED SEA (probably referring to one of the lakes through which the Suez Canal now passes). God led Israel to Mount SINAI, where the company of slaves became a nation under Moses, the great lawgiver, and where the Ten Commandments and other legislation were received. The date of the exodus has been much discussed. The biblical data (1 Ki. 6:1; Jdg. 11:26; Acts 13:20) appear to favor a date of 1440 B.C. The archaeological evidence for the conquest of Palestine is ambiguous, but some is interpreted to favor an invasion much later, at about 1230. See EXODUS I.

IV. Israel's law (Exod. 20-Num. 10). At Sinai Israel encamped for one year (see EXODUS, BOOK OF). Here God revealed himself and his LAW in majestic miracles. The Ten Commandments of Exod. 20 and Deut. 5 summarize the eternal principles of duty to God and to others (see COMMANDMENTS, TEN). The last twenty chapters of the book of Exodus, except for the apostasy of the golden calf (see CALF WORSHIP), which took place while Moses was on the mount, concern the building of the TABERNACLE. Leviticus mainly concerns the ceremonial WORSHIP of Israel—the offerings, feasts, and cleansings. The section Lev. 18-22, however, also includes regulations for civil conduct of the nation, as does Exod. 21-23.

V. The wilderness (Num. 11-36). The book of NUMBERS adds some laws to Leviticus but mainly records the abortive attempt to invade Canaan from the S and the experiences during the forty years of wilderness wanderings. The first numbering is not a mere census but a mustering of the ranks for the invasion. In Num. 14 Israel at KADESH BARNEA hears the reports of the spies and, in little faith, fails to conquer. Condemned to wander, they live as nomads at the edge of the arable land in Sinai until the "generation of wrath" dies. Several of the rebellions of these years are given in Numbers. At the end of the book a new mustering of the people provides 600,000 fighting men for Joshua's army.

VI. Deuteronomy. The book of DEUTERONOMY recounts portions of the history detailed in the previous books, restates the regulations given to the nation, and describes the renewal of the covenant by a new generation. The end of the book preserves the last words of Moses and tells of his death.

VII. Job. The date of the book of JOB is uncertain. As it seems to speak of a time before the Levitical legislation and names descendants of Uz, Buz, and others of Abraham's kin, many scholars have placed it in the general time of Moses and in the area E of Palestine. It poses the problem of the suffering of the righteous and answers that the sovereign God has his own purposes, for which he is not answerable to people. It suggests a further answer that apparent injustices in this world are to be adjusted in a future life.

VIII. The conquest. JOSHUA's invasion of Canaan is detailed in the first half of the book that bears his name (Josh. 1-12). In a whirlwind campaign, after the miracles of the crossing of JORDAN and the fall of JERICHO, he gained possession of the middle of the country. At Aijalon he conquered the army of the southern confederacy and, thanks to the extended day of the battle, demolished the enemy before it took refuge in its cities. The deserted cities were then easily taken. Soon after, he turned N to HAZOR and its confederates and won a signal victory, burning it to the ground. But Israel did not at once effectively occupy the area. The Canaanites reestablished themselves in many cities. Key fortresses like BETH SHAN, MEGIDDO, and JERUSALEM were not subdued. The land was allocated to the tribes (chs. 13-22), but the period of the judges witnessed various battles, with the Israelites restricted mainly to the central mountain section.

IX. Judges and Ruth. For some 350 years the Israelites lived disorganized and to an extent disunited. Frequently falling into APOSTASY, they were punished by God. Each time a leader arose for military deliverance and often for spiritual reviving as well. Sketches of six of these twelve judgeships are given. The rest are barely named. See JUDGES, BOOK OF. The beautiful account of RUTH, the Moabite convert, belongs in this time.

X. The early monarchy. The last judge was SAMUEL. In his early days PHILISTINE expansion became a great threat to Israel. The sanctuary at SHILOH was destroyed, as excavations also attest, at about 1050 B.C. The nation was laid low. Yet under the leadership of four great men—Samuel himself, Saul, David, and Solomon—Israel in one hundred years attained its peak of greatness. Samuel was a prophet of power. His preaching, prayers, and policies led to a revival that was the basis for much of Israel's later successes. He was followed by SAUL, who was capable but not good. Condemned in the records for his disobedience, he nevertheless seems to have made a real military contribution to Israel's unity. His army numbered 330,000 men. He gained important victories in the S and E and had some limited successes against the Philistines. His strength was sapped by disobedience to God and insane jealousy of David. He made a pitiable spectacle at the house of the medium at ENDOR before his final failure, in which he dragged down his fine son JONATHAN and all Israel with him to defeat.

XI. The golden age. DAVID's history as king begins in 2 Samuel, which parallels 1 Chronicles after the first nine chapters of genealogies in the latter book. God had schooled David the hard way. Highly emotional, and consecrated to God as a very young man, he had gone through deep waters. Military lessons had been learned in repeated dangers when he was exiled by Saul. Faith was begotten and tested in adversity. Eventually God used this background to make David Israel's greatest conqueror and best-loved poet, the founder of the royal house and reestablisher of the Lord's worship. Family troubles resulting from David's grievous sin with BATHSHEBA marred his later days, but the greatness of the man was shown in the depth of his REPENTANCE. He was a man after God's own heart.

In David's day people would probably have honored him mostly for his military successes, his power, and his wealth; but actually, his greatest blessing to mankind has doubtless been his work in the establishing of psalmody. David composed at least half of the psalms and arranged for the temple choirs and for Israel's liturgy. First Chronicles 15-16 and 25 tell something of this work. David's psalms of praise have lifted up the hearts of millions in godly worship. His psalms of trust in the midst of trouble have for centuries comforted those in sorrow and in despair. Psalm 23 is perhaps the best-loved poem of the OT. In the hour of death and in times of deliverance alike, it has expressed the faith of untold multitudes of God's people. Associated with David in song were the prophets ASAPH, HEMAN, JEDUTHUN, and others.

SOLOMON inherited David's vast kingdom, which reached from the EUPHRATES in SYRIA to the border of Egypt and from the desert to the sea. To these large possessions Solomon added the natural resources of the copper mines S of the DEAD SEA. He built a famous foundry at EZION

O

GEBER, using the force of the prevailing winds to increase the temperature of his fires. For the first time people had harnessed the forces of nature in industrial processes. The products of his industry he exported in lucrative trade that drenched Jerusalem in opulence. His building program was extensive and is illustrated by many excavations, especially at MEGIDDO. It is best remembered in his construction of the TEMPLE, described in 1 Kings and 2 Chronicles. This remarkable building was so engineered that the stones were cut at a distance and the sound of a hammer was not heard on the spot (1 Ki. 6:7). It was double the dimensions of the wilderness tabernacle and more lavishly adorned. The building was about 30 ft. (9 m.) high and wide, and 90 ft. (27 m.) long. The building was flanked on each side with three stories of rooms for priests' quarters and storage. In the front court was the great altar where Israel declared its faith that there is remission of sin through the blood of a substitute. Near the end of his reign Solomon and his kingdom decayed. Solomon probably did not marry his many women because of lust, but because of his extensive political alliances. They proved his undoing, however, because they brought to Israel their heathen worship. For this compromise he was rejected.

XII. Divided monarchy to Hezekiah. Solomon's sins bore bitter fruit. REHOBOAM attempted to maintain the old glory without returning to the old sources of power. God punished him and all Israel by allowing division. JEROBOAM I took ten tribes and established the northern kingdom (see ISRAEL) about 920 B.C. AHIJAH promised him God's blessing if he would do God's will, but for political reasons he at once broke with the worship of the Lord at Jerusalem. He set up golden calves at DAN and BETHEL, the N and S of his realm, and instituted a new priesthood and counterfeit feasts. He thus sealed his doom. The following kings did not depart from Jeroboam's sins. In the next 200 years of its existence the northern kingdom had nine dynasties and many revolutions, and they sank deeply into IDOLATRY. The southern kingdom, Judah, had its troubles, but many of its kings, such as ASA, JEHOSHAPHAT, HEZEKIAH, and JOSIAH were godly men. See JUDAH, KINGDOM OF.

The northern kingdom of Israel fell most deeply into the worship of BAAL of PHOENICIA in the reign of Ahab. He was faced with the threat of the Assyrian empire expanding to the W. His policy was to form a western coalition. Thus he married JEZEBEL, daughter of the king of TYRE. He united with Jehoshaphat of Judah, marrying his daughter to Jehoshaphat's son. Politically he was successful, and his coalition at the battle of Qarqar in 854 B.C. stopped the Assyrians. The Assyrian records tells us that Ahab was their principal opponent.

Religiously, Ahab was a failure. The Bible, being more interested in character than in conquest, shows the unvarnished sins of Ahab and his queen, Jezebel. At this time the great prophets ELIJAH and ELISHA ministered in the north. Their deeds are graphically told (1 Ki. 17–2 Ki. 13). Only a passing reference is made to them in Chronicles, which is a book more interested in Judah. Elijah, the fearless prophet who stood alone on Mount CARMEL, was one of two men in all history taken to heaven without death (the other being ENOCH). Encouraged by Elisha, JEHU revolted, exterminated the dynasty of Ahab, slaughtered the devotees of Baal, and even killed Ahaziah of Jerusalem who was in Samaria at the time.

The dynasty of Jehu began about 840 B.C. and lasted a century, its chief king being Jeroboam II, 793 to 753. The kings of Judah included some good men, but from about 740 to 722 both kingdoms were evil and felt the scourge of the great Assyrian monarchs—TIGLATH-PILESER, SHALMANESER, SARGON, and SENNACHERIB. This was the time of ISAIAH and the first six minor prophets. Their messages in the N went unheeded, and SAMARIA was destroyed in 722. In Judah there was a revival under HEZEKIAH, and God wonderfully delivered him.

XIII. Isaiah and his contemporaries. HOSEA, Amos, and MICAH prophesied especially to Israel; OBADIAH and JOEL preached to the southern kingdom; JONAH, the disobedient prophet, finally ministered in NINEVEH. The repentance of the Ninevites may well have delayed their invasion of Israel for a generation. However, their repentance did not have lasting results in the Assyrian empire. Amos and Micah forthrightly denounced the sins of the court and of the rich people of Israel. At the same time, Amos and Hosea, especially, denounced the idolatry of BETHEL and of Samaria. Against the background of rebuke, these prophets announced

Israel's and Judah's hope—the coming of the child from David's city, BETHLEHEM, and the reestablishing of the fallen tabernacle of David. To Isaiah, the evangelical prophet, it was given to condemn AHAZ for his idolatry, to encourage Hezekiah in his reforms, and to see beyond his day the threat

Medieval Hebrew scroll of the book of Isaiah in Hebrew (1350).

of BABYLON, the liberation of the exiles by CYRUS, and the coming of the MESSIAH in future suffering and glory.

XIV. Judah's fall. The reforms of Hezekiah were engulfed in the long and wicked reign of his son MANASSEH. Further decline followed in AMON's two years. Then in 640 B.C. the good king JOSIAH came to the throne. In Josiah's thirteenth year, JEREMIAH began his ministry; and in five more years Josiah, in a real revival, invited all Judah and the remnant of Israel to a great Passover. But, as a reading of Jeremiah shows, the mass of the people were not changed. Josiah's successors again did evil.

In 612 B.C. Babylon conquered Nineveh, but Egypt assisted Assyria, attempting to keep the old balance of power. On Egypt's first march N against Babylon, Josiah attempted to prevent Pharaoh NECO's passage at Megiddo and was killed. His son JEHOAHAZ succeeded him, but when Neco returned southward in three months, he took Jehoahaz to Egypt as a hostage and set his brother JEHOIAKIM on the throne. In 605 NEBUCHADNEZZAR in his first year conquered the Assyrian and Egyptian forces at CARCHEMISH on the Euphrates and proceeded S to Judah. He received Jehoiakim's submission and

carried DANIEL and many others into captivity. In 597 Jehoiakim died, perhaps by assassination, and his son JEHOIACHIN took the throne, revolting against Babylon. Subsequently Nebuchadnezzar destroyed Jerusalem and took EZEKIEL and others captive. He put a third son of Josiah, ZEDEKIAH, on the throne. Zedekiah continued the wicked policies of the others. In 586 he too rebelled, and Nebuchadnezzar returned in a final thrust, devastating Jerusalem and the cities of Judah. Palestine never fully recovered.

NAHUM, HABAKKUK, and ZEPHANIAH were early contemporaries of Jeremiah. Nahum predicted the downfall of Nineveh. Habakkuk is famous for contrasting the wicked Babylonian invader with the just person who lives by faith. In Jeremiah's ministry to his people, he rebuked them for sin and idolatry. The Assyrian and Babylonian gods had filtered into the southern kingdom until Judah's idols were as numerous as the streets in Jerusalem. When some Jews had gone to Babylon, Jeremiah counseled the later kings to submit. Resistance was futile and would make it hard for those Jews already in exile. God would care for Israel in captivity and in seventy years would bring them back (Jer. 25:11-12).

XV. The exile. For seventy years, from about 605 B.C. to about 538, the Jews were slaves in Babylon. See EXILE. Some Jews were left in Judah, and Jeremiah at first ministered to them. Many Jews had fled to Egypt, and finally Jeremiah was taken to that country by some of these men. In Babylon God blessed the Jews and kept them in the faith through the witness of Ezekiel, Daniel, and others. Ezekiel prophesied to his people in exile, being still greatly concerned with Jerusalem before its final fall. Like Jeremiah, he used many object lessons in his preaching. Finally came the word that the city had fallen (Ezek. 33). Thereafter Ezekiel emphasized more the coming of the Davidic king, the Messiah. His final chapters picture in schematic form the reestablishment of the temple, a prophecy held by many to apply to millennial times.

© Dr. James C. Martin. Sola Scriptura. The Van Kampen Collection on display at the Holy Land Experience in Orlando, Florida. Photographed by permission.

O

Daniel was a towering figure of those days. Beloved of God and granted many remarkable visions of the future times, he maintained his faith while he held an important position at court. His prophecies accurately depict the future kingdoms of Medo-Persia, Greece, and Rome and tell of both Christ's first coming and his return. Christ's own designation for himself, SON OF MAN, likely comes from Dan. 7:13. The book has been heavily attacked by criticism, but there is no good reason to deny the authorship by Daniel (see DANIEL, BOOK OF).

XVI. Postexilic times. When Cyrus the Persian conquered Babylon, his policy was to allow captive peoples to go home. Thus he befriended the Jews. EZRA and NEHEMIAH tell about these returns. HAGGAI, ZECHARIAH, and MALACHI prophesied in this period. ZERUBBABEL led back the first contingent of about 50,000 people shortly after Cyrus gave them permission. His work is detailed in Ezra 1-6. He laid the foundation of the temple at once, but did not finish the building until 516 B.C. under the ministry of Haggai and Zechariah. A second contingent returned in 456 under Ezra, as is related in Ezra 7-10. Nehemiah returned with various royal pledges in 444, and these two together did much work in restoring Jerusalem. Nehemiah organized the work and carried through the rebuilding of the wall. Ezra, a knowledgeable scribe in the law of Moses, instructed the people in the faith. Malachi, the final book of the OT, was written around 400. It reveals the problems of the day caused by insincerity among some of the priests themselves. But it also, like so many of the other prophets, pointed forward to messianic times. The OT closes with the annunciation of the rise of a new and greater prophet in the spirit and power of Elijah who would precede the Messiah of Israel.

olive. See PLANTS.

Olives, Mount of. Also known as Olivet (cf. KJV at 2 Sam. 15:30; Acts 1:12), this mount is a N-S, flattened, and rounded ridge with four identifiable summits. Its name is derived from the olive groves that covered it in ancient times. It is of cretaceous limestone formation, something over a mile (almost 2 km.) in length, and forms the highest level of the range of hills to the E of JERUSALEM (Ezek. 11:23; Zech. 14:4), rising c. 250 ft. (75 m.) higher than the temple mount, and 2,600 ft. (790 m.) above sea level. Hence the supreme tactical significance of the Mount of Olives, demonstrated in the Roman siege of Jerusalem under TITUS in A.D. 70. The Romans seem to have named the northern extension of the ridge "the Lookout," or Mount Scopus, for this very reason. It gave "a plain view of the great temple," according to JOSEPHUS (*War* 5.2.2; but some doubt that he is referring to Mt. Scopus). The legions had a large camp on the mount itself, which, as Josephus says in the same context, "lies over against the city on the east side, and is parted from it by a deep valley interposed between them." The valley, through which flows the KIDRON stream, encompasses the city before turning SE to flow down the long valley to the DEAD SEA.

Near the foot of the Mount of Olives, on the W slope above the Kidron, is the likely site of the Garden of GETHSEMANE. In NT times the whole area seems to have been a place of resort for those who sought relief from the heat of the crowded city streets. Dean Stanley called it the "park" of Jerusalem. In much earlier times it must have been heavily wooded, for when the Feast of the Tabernacles was restored in 445 B.C., NEHEMIAH commanded the people to "go out into the hill country and bring back branches from olive and wild olive trees, and from myrtles, palms and shade trees, to make booths" (Neh. 8:15). The palm fronds of Palm Sunday were also gathered there. Four summits are traditionally distinguished. Scopus has already been mentioned. Second, there is the "Viri Galilaei," the Latin invocation of Acts 1:11 ("Men of Galilee"), and the reputed site of the ASCENSION OF CHRIST. To the S, above the village of Silwan (old Siloam) is the so-called Mount of Offense (see CORRUPTION, HILL (MOUNT) OF). This vantage-point is separated from the rest of the mount by a deep cleft. It faces W along the line of Jerusalem's second valley, the Valley of the Sons of HINNOM (GEHENNA). The eminence derives its name from the tradition that SOLOMON here built his altars to CHEMOSH, "the detestable god of Moab," and to MOLECH, "the detestable god of the Ammonites" (1 Ki. 11:7). The "offense" of this blatant paganism was purged by JOSIAH four and a half centuries

The Mount of Olives (ridge with the 3 towers) rises above the Kidron Valley. (View to the E, with the temple mount visible in the middle far right.)

© Dr. James C. Martin

later (2 Ki. 23:13). The Josian context adds Ash-toreth to the "abominations" on the site.

The ridge, besides being a tactical vantage point in war, was a peacetime highway into Jerusalem. It was the route of David's flight from Absalom in the time of the palace rebellion (2 Sam. 15:30; 16:1, 13) and, significantly, was the route of Christ's approach for the triumphal entry on Palm Sunday, for it was there that the acclaiming multitude met him. Hence, too, the prominence of the mount in Josephus's account of the "Egyptian false prophet" and his 30,000 dupes (*War* 2.13.5). "These he led round from the wilderness," the account runs, "to the mount which is called the Mount of Olives, and was ready to break into Jerusalem by force from that place." Here, it would appear, Felix met the rebels with his legionary force and broke the revolt. The remaining OT reference to the Mount of Olives is the scene of the theophany of Zech. 14:4, an obscure apocalyptic portion that awaits a clear explanation.

Historically the Mount of Olives finds its chief interest in NT times, where it is a locality intimately connected with the Jerusalem ministry of Christ. It is important here to distinguish authentic history from the thick accretions of legend and tradition. As Jesus approached Jerusalem for the last time, his first sight of the city was from the summit of the Mount of Olives (Lk. 19:37), and his visits to the home of Mary, Martha, and Lazarus in Bethany must have frequently taken him that way (21:37). The barren fig tree of his striking object lesson on fruitless profession was probably on the Olivet slopes (Matt. 21:19). The mount was also the scene of his apocalyptic utterance, inspired no doubt by the prospect of doomed Jerusalem from the mountainside (chs. 24-25). Gethsemane has already been mentioned as a place somewhere on the Mount of Olives.

The rest is wavering ecclesiastical tradition. Spurious sites include the Tomb of the Virgin; the Grotto of the Agony; one or both of the sites of the garden, admitted though it is that it was somewhere on the mount; the "footprint of Christ" in the Chapel of the Ascension; the Tomb of Huldah, the impossible site for Christ's lament over Jerusalem; the place where he taught the Lord's Prayer, and where the Apostles' Creed was composed. This does not exhaust the list of legends. It has been the fate of Jerusalem to suffer thus from the pious but not too scrupulous imagination of men. More authentic are a few archaeological remains, some Jewish and Christian tombs, and an interesting catacomb known as "the Tombs of the Prophets."

Olivet, Mount. Alternate designation of the MOUNT OF OLIVES.

Olivet Discourse. Name given to Jesus' eschatological discourse, addressed to the disciples on the MOUNT OF OLIVES (Matt. 24-25; Mk. 13; Lk. 21). See ESCHATOLOGY.

Olympas. oh-lim´puhs (Gk. *Olympas G3912*). A Roman Christian to whom PAUL sent greetings (Rom. 16:15). The name, which is not common, is probably a shortened form (cf. Olympianus, Olympiodorus, etc.).

Omar. oh´mahr (Heb. *ʾômār H223*, possibly "[God] has spoken"). Son of ELIPHAZ, grandson of ESAU, and head of an Edomite clan (Gen. 36:11, 15; 1 Chr. 1:36).

omega. oh-meg´uh. The last letter of the Greek ALPHABET. See ALPHA AND OMEGA.

omen. See DIVINATION.

omer. See WEIGHTS AND MEASURES.

omnipotence. The attribute of God that describes his ability to do whatever he wills. God's will is "limited" by his nature, and he therefore cannot do anything contrary to his nature as God, such as to ignore sin, to sin, or to do something absurd or self-contradictory. God is not controlled by his power, but has complete control over it: otherwise he would not be a free being. Some believe that, to a certain extent, he has voluntarily limited himself by the free will of his rational creatures. Although the word *omnipotence* is not found in the Bible, the Scriptures clearly teach this doctrine (e.g., Job 42:2; Jer. 32:17; Matt. 19:26; Lk. 1:37; Rev. 19:6).

omnipresence. The attribute of God by virtue of which he fills the universe in all its parts and is present everywhere at once. Not a part but the whole of God is present in every place. The Bible teaches the omnipresence of God (Ps. 139:7-12; Jer. 23:23-24; Acts 17:27-28). This is true of all three members of the TRINITY. They are so closely related that where one is the others can be said to be also (Jn. 14:9-11).

omniscience. The attribute by which God perfectly and eternally knows all things that can be known—past, present, and future. God knows how best to attain to his desired ends. God's omniscience is clearly taught in Scripture (Ps. 147:5; Prov. 15:11; Isa. 46:10).

Omri. om´ri (Heb. *ʿomri H6687*, perhaps "pilgrim of Yahweh"). (1) The sixth king of ISRAEL and founder of an important dynasty (1 Ki. 16:16-28). His reign may be tentatively dated from 885 to 874 B.C. Omri, an able if unscrupulous soldier, is the first Hebrew monarch to be mentioned in nonbiblical records, and the fact may be some measure of his contemporary importance. MESHA king of MOAB included Omri's name in the inscription known as the MOABITE STONE, and it is especially significant that the Assyrian records after Omri's day frequently refer to northern Palestine as "the land of Humri."

Omri had been commander-in-chief under ELAH son of BAASHA. When Elah was murdered by ZIMRI, Omri was proclaimed king by the army in the field. The army was engaged at the time in siege of the stronghold of GIBBETHON, one of the LEVITICAL CITIES (Josh. 21:23) in the tribal territory of Dan (19:44), which the PHILISTINES appear to have held for a considerable period (1 Ki. 15:27; 16:15). Omri immediately raised the siege, marched on the royal capital of TIRZAH, which does not appear to have been vigorously defended against him. Zimri committed suicide by burning the palace over his head. There was some opposition to the dominance of the military, for four years of civil war ensued, with half the populace supporting TIBNI son of Ginath. Omri prevailed, and after a six-year reign at Tirzah, he transferred the capital to SAMARIA, an eminently sensible move from the point of view of military security. Here Omri reigned for at least another six years. Samaria was named after SHEMER, from whom Omri bought the hill site (1 Ki. 16:24).

Omri is dismissed by the Hebrew historian as an evil influence (1 Ki. 16:25-26). Indeed, the marriage of his son AHAB to JEZEBEL, princess of TYRE, probably to cement a trade alliance, was fraught with most disastrous consequences, even though it was a continuation of SOLOMON and DAVID'S Tyrian policy. The CALF WORSHIP that had been established by Jeroboam (12:32) was continued at Bethel throughout Omri's reign; and 140 years after Omri's death, Micah is found denouncing "the statutes of Omri" (Mic. 6:16). The palace of Omri has been excavated at Samaria, a series of open courts with rooms ranged round them. Omri died opportunely, one year before the first tentative thrust of the Assyrians toward the Mediterranean and Palestine—the preface to much misery.

(2) Son of Beker and grandson of Benjamin (1 Chr. 7:8).

(3) Son of Imri and descendant of Judah; listed among the first to resettle in Jerusalem after the exile (1 Chr. 9:4; cf. v. 2).

(4) Son of Michael and a chief officer over the tribe of Issachar during the reign of David (1 Chr. 27:18).

On (person). on (Heb. *'ôn* H227, "strong"). Son of Peleth and descendant of Reuben; he and two other Reubenite leaders—Dathan and Abiram, sons of Eliab—joined Korah in his rebellion against Moses (Num. 16:1). Dathan and Abiram are mentioned again in the actual account of the rebellion (vv. 12-27; cf. also 26:9; Deut. 11:6; et al.), but On is not. For that reason, some scholars omit the name or otherwise emend the text.

On (place). on (Heb. *'ôn* H228, from Egyp. *Yunu* ['*Iwnw*], "pillar city"; cf. also *'āwen* H225). The city where Potiphera (Joseph's father-in-law) served as priest (Gen. 41:45, 50; 46:20). The name "On" is also used by the NRSV to render Aven (only Ezek. 30:17). In all these passages, the reference is to Heliopolis (see separate article).

onager. See animals (under *wild ass*).

Onam. oh´nuhm (Heb. *'ônām* H231, "strong").

(1) Son of Shobal and grandson of Seir the Horite (Gen. 36:23; 1 Chr. 1:40); he was a chieftain living in Edom (Gen. 36:21).

(2) Son of Jerahmeel (by his second wife Atarah) and descendant of Judah through Perez and Hezron (1 Chr. 2:26, 28).

Onan. oh´nuhn (Heb. *'ônān* H232, "strong"). The second son born to Judah by his Canaanite wife,

the daughter of Shua (Gen. 38:4; 46:12; Num. 26:19; 1 Chr. 2:3). After the death of his older brother Er, whom the Lord slew for his wickedness, Onan was commanded by his father Judah to enter into a levirate marriage with his brother's wife Tamar, but he refused to produce offspring for his brother. For this sin the Lord punished him with death (Gen. 38:8-10).

Onesimus. oh-nes´uh-muhs (Gk. *Onēsimos* G3946, "profitable"; cf. the wordplay on this name in Phlm. 11, 20). A plain reading of the letters to Philemon and to the Colossians leads to the conclusion that Onesimus was a slave of Philemon in the city of Colosse. He robbed his master and made his way to Rome, the frequent goal of such fugitives. Some Ephesian or Colossian person in Rome, perhaps Aristarchus (Acts 27:2; Col. 4:10-14; Phlm. 24), or Epaphras (Col. 1:7; 4:12-13; Phlm. 23) seems to have recognized the man and brought him to Paul in his captivity. Onesimus became a Christian and was persuaded to return to his master. From that incident came the exquisite letter of Paul to Philemon, which demonstrates so vividly the social solvent that Christianity had brought into the world. It appears that Onesimus left Rome in company with Tychicus, carrying the letter to Philemon and also Paul's letters to the Ephesian and Colossian churches. Nothing more is known about Onesimus.

Onesiphorus. on´uh-sif´uh-ruhs (Gk. *Onēsiphoros* G3947, "bringer of profit [*or* of usefulness]"). An Ephesian believer whose fearless ministry to Paul during his second Roman imprisonment was held up as a model of Christian kindness (2 Tim. 1:16-18; 4:19). His courageous conduct stands in contrast to the desertion of Phygelus and Hermogenes (1:15). Whether Onesiphorus was asked to come or went on personal business, as soon as he arrived in Rome he began a diligent and successful search for Paul. He repeatedly "refreshed" Paul in his dungeon, apparently by his means as well as by his unashamed friendship. His conduct was in keeping with his previous well-known services at Ephesus. That Paul did not greet Onesiphorus personally but rather sent greetings to his household (4:19) and uttered a prayer for the household (1:16) has led some commentators to conclude that he was no longer alive; but it is just as likely that Onesiphorus was simply absent from home. That Paul should think of his family is natural, since they too were involved in the risk he took.

Onias. oh-ni´uhs (Gk. *Onias*, prob. short form of *yĕhôḥānān H3380*, "Yahweh is [*or* has been] gracious"). The name of three persons who were high priests during the intertestamental period. Special significance attaches to Onias III, son of Simon II. Having assumed office c. 198 B.C., he was high priest mainly during the reign of the Syrian King Seleucus IV (187-175; see SELEUCID). He was noted for his piety and hatred of wickedness and commanded the respect of Seleucus (cf. 2 Macc. 3:1-3). A dispute between him and a man named Simon, a captain of the temple, led to a break between Onias and the king. Seleucus then commissioned Heliodorus to confiscate the treasury. With the strong backing of his people Onias refused to yield. According to the account in 2 Macc. 3:8, Heliodorus was supernaturally repulsed. After the assassination of Seleucus, to whom Onias had gone to plead his cause, ANTIOCHUS Epiphanes deposed him and put his brother JASON in his place. Onias later was murdered (4:33-38).

onion. See PLANTS.

only begotten. The word *monogenēs G3666* (with variations) occurs throughout Greek literature with more than one meaning, but especially with the sense, "peerless, matchless, of singular excellence, unique, the only one of his/her kind," that is, expressions denoting quality more than descent. This sense, among others, is also present in the SEPTUAGINT (e.g., Gen. 22:2, 12, 16). The NT employs *monogenēs* nine times, and only by three writers. In Luke, it denotes an only son or daughter (Lk. 7:12; 8:42; 9:38). In Hebrews, it is used with reference to Abraham's "favored, chosen, unique" son (Heb. 11:17). And this qualitative idea is uppermost

in John's use of the term in regard to Jesus (Jn. 1:14, 18; 3:16, 18; 1 Jn. 4:9). Jesus is not only God's Son, which connotes derivation, relationship, and loving obedience, but the Father's "unique" Son, which is John's way of expressing the Lord's qualitatively superior sonship. See also SON OF GOD.

Ono. oh´noh (Heb. *ʾônô H229*, "strong"). A town built (or rebuilt) by a descendant of BENJAMIN named Shemed son of Elpaal (1 Chr. 8:12); the area around it could be referred to as "the plain of Ono" (Neh. 6:2). To Ono, and also to neighboring LOD and HADID, hundreds of exiles returned from the Babylonian captivity (Ezra 2:33; Neh. 7:37). These towns were located in or near the Valley of the Craftsmen (Neh. 11:35), which possibly should be identified with "the plain of Ono" (see GE HARASHIM). The town is identified with modern Kafr ʿAna, 7.5 mi. (12 km.) ESE of JOPPA.

onycha. See PLANTS.

onyx. See MINERALS.

Ophel. oh´fel (Heb. *ʿōpel H6755*, "swelling, mound"). A projecting area in the original SE hill of JERUSALEM (2 Chr. 27:3; 33:14; Neh. 3:26-27; 11:21; the word, however, is also used more generally in the sense of "hill" or "citadel," 2 Ki. 5:24; Isa. 32:14; Mic. 4:8). While precise identification for the Ophel at Jerusalem remains uncertain, it

Looking NW toward the Ophel in Jerusalem. The southern wall of the temple mount is visible to the right.

© Dr. James C. Martin

appears to be that narrower part of the city's E ridge that expands NE from DAVID's initial town (the original Mt. ZION) toward the TEMPLE on Mount MORIAH. The walls of Jerusalem's Ophel were strengthened by JOTHAM (2 Chr. 27:3) and MANASSEH (33:14), but ISAIAH predicted the subsequent destruction of this "citadel" (Isa. 32:14). In Nehemiah's day the temple servants (NETHINIM) resided in Ophel and restored its walls (Neh. 3:26; 11:21). Micah visualized the messianic era as one in which God's eternal kingdom would be established on the "stronghold [ʿōpel] of the Daughter of Zion" (Mic. 4:8).

Ophir. oh´fuhr (Heb. ʾōpîr H234, meaning unknown). **(1)** Son of JOKTAN and descendant of SHEM, mentioned in the Table of Nations (Gen. 10:26-29; 1 Chr. 1:23). Ophir was presumably the eponymous ancestor of a S Arabian tribe, and his name may be the origin of #2 below.

(2) A region, probably a maritime nation in the Arabian peninsula, known for its export of fine woods, precious stones, and especially gold (1 Ki. 9:28; 10:11), although it is not clear whether these products originated in Ophir itself. The expression "gold of Ophir" appears to be less a reference to the origin of the metal than a way of indicating its high quality. Many theories concerning the actual location of the place have been proposed over the centuries, including parts of ARABIA and INDIA, but none that can be confirmed. Of special interest is the association of the queen of SHEBA with Ophir (1 Ki. 10:10-12). This connection might be made even more certain if indeed she ruled over the SABEANS, as is usually supposed. The earliest mention of the location Ophir is Job 22:24; 28:16. It is next noted as the origin of David's gifts to the temple (1 Chr. 29:4) and the destination of SOLOMON's expedition (1 Ki. 9:28; 10:11; 2 Chr. 8:18; 9:10). It is used in poetic passages by Isaiah and the psalmist (Isa. 13:12; Ps 45:9). An expedition to Ophir sent by JEHOSHAPHAT was wrecked near EZION GEBER in the Gulf of AQABAH (1 Ki. 22:48).

Ophni. of´ni (Heb. ʿopnî H6756, derivation uncertain). A town within the tribal territory of BENJAMIN (Josh. 18:24). Ophni was apparently near GEBA, but the precise site is unknown. It has been suggested that the place is the same as Gophna, a town referred to by JOSEPHUS (e.g., *War* 3.3.5 §55), usually identified with modern Jifna, about 3 mi. (5 km.) NW of BETHEL.

Ophrah (person). of´ruh (Heb. ʿoprāh H6763, "fawn"). Son of Meonothai, grandson of OTHNIEL, and descendant of JUDAH (1 Chr. 4:14).

Ophrah (place). of´ruh (Heb. ʿoprāh H6764, possibly "[place of] dust" or "fawn"). **(1)** A town within the tribal territory of BENJAMIN (Josh. 18:23). It must have been in the area of MICMASH, for from there one of three raiding parties of PHILISTINES, prior to battle with SAUL, headed toward Ophrah (1 Sam. 13:17). Since the other two parties went W and E respectively (v. 18), and Saul was S at GIBEAH, it is likely that Ophrah lay to the N. Ophrah is commonly identified with EPHRON, which in turn is associated with BETHEL (2 Chr. 13:19). Moreover, Eusebius identifies Ophrah with the NT city of EPHRAIM (Jn. 11:54). These data point to modern eṭ-Ṭaiyibeh, a conical hill some 4 mi. (6 km.) NE of Beitin (Bethel). Some argue, however, that this site is too far N to have been included in Benjamite territory.

(2) A town within the tribal territory of MANASSEH, the home of GIDEON son of Joash, of the family of ABIEZER (Jdg. 6:11 et al.). Here God called Gideon to lead in war against annually invading Midianites; at God's command, he destroyed a local BAAL high-place (6:25-27). Gideon first assembled his own Abiezrite family in Ophrah for his army before requesting aid from others (6:34-35). Later, unwisely, he made a gold EPHOD from the spoils of victory over MIDIAN and placed it in Ophrah (8:27); here he died and was buried in the grave of his father (8:32). In Ophrah, ABIMELECH son of Gideon slew seventy of his brothers, possible rivals to his claim of kingship (9:5).

oracle. This English term, in the sense of a message or answer given by the deity or by a wise man, is used in the NIV and other Bible versions to render such various Hebrew terms, especially *maśśāʾ* H5363 (Isa. 13:1; KJV, "burden," which is the meaning of the homonym *maśśāʾ* H5362). In the NT, the term is used sometimes by the KJV and other versions to render Greek *logion* G3359, "saying, announcement" (Acts 7:38; Rom. 3:2; Heb. 5:12; 1 Pet. 4:11). Because the English word can refer to the shrine where divine messages are given, the KJV uses it also to render Hebrew *dĕbîr* H1808, designating the "inner sanctuary" of the TEMPLE, that is, the Holy of Holies (1 Ki. 6:5 et al.).

oral law. See TALMUD.

orator. This English term, referring to a skillful public speaker, is used by the KJV twice. In Isa. 3:3, the expression "eloquent orator" renders a Hebrew phrase that means literally "intelligent in whispering," referring to someone who has expertise in the use of charms (cf. NIV, "clever enchanter"). In Acts 24:1, "orator" renders Greek *rhētōr* G4842, which does indeed mean "public speaker," but often, as here, with specific reference to someone who uses his skills to plead a case, so that the translation "advocate, attorney, lawyer," is preferred. See TERTULLUS.

orchard. See GARDEN.

ordain. This English verb, in its several meanings (such as "appoint," "establish," "issue an order") is used variously in Bible versions to render a large number of Hebrew and Greek terms (e.g., 2 Sam. 17:14 NRSV; 2 Ki. 19:25 NIV; Ps. 132:17 KJV). More significant is the use of this term in the special religious sense, "to invest officially with ministerial or priestly authority," that is, installing or elevating a special officer of the congregation. In the OT, the peculiar Hebrew phrase *fill the hands* is applied to such an installation of priests, and so modern versions translate this idiom with "ordain" (Exod. 28:41 et al.). Ordination of church officers for a certain work by the LAYING ON OF HANDS was practiced in apostolic times (1 Tim. 4:14; 2 Tim. 1:6).

ordinance. An authoritative decree. The Passover, for example, is described as a "lasting ordinance" (Exod. 12:14 et al.; Heb. *ḥuqqâ* H2978). Of special interest is the rich term *mišpāṭ* H5477, which in legal contexts can mean "ruling, judgment," or "claim, demand," or "justice"; more generally it

denotes "what is fitting, proper." In the Book of the Covenant (Exod. 20:22—23:33) the term "judgments" or "ordinances" denotes civil, as contrasted with ritual, enactments. See LAW. In Christian theology, the term *ordinance* also has a specialized meaning referring to BAPTISM and the LORD'S SUPPER. See SACRAMENTS.

ordination. See ORDAIN.

Oreb and Zeeb. or´eb, zee´uhb (Heb. *ʿōrēb* H6855, "raven," and *zĕʾēb* H2270, "wolf"). Two Midianite leaders (see MIDIAN) active in battle against GIDEON and killed by Ephraimites (Jdg. 7:25; 8:3). The main battle had occurred in the valley of JEZREEL, between the spring of HAROD and the hill of MOREH (7:1), after which Gideon quickly sent messengers to the Ephraimites to cut off the retreat of the foe (7:24). The Ephraimites responded, and Oreb was slain at "the rock of Oreb" and Zeeb at "the winepress of Zeeb" (both places likely named as a result of this occasion). These two sites are unknown, and it is not clear whether they were located W or E of the JORDAN. Subsequent references use the occasion as illustrative of a time of great destruction (Ps. 83:11 and Isa. 10:26) and thus suggest that a major slaughter of Midianites took place.

Oren. or´en (Heb. *ʾōren* H816, possibly "fir"). Son of JERAHMEEL and descendant of JUDAH through PEREZ and HEZRON (1 Chr. 2:25).

organ. See MUSIC AND MUSICAL INSTRUMENTS I.E.

Orion. See ASTRONOMY.

ornament. See DRESS.

Ornan. See ARAUNAH.

Orontes. or-on´teez (Gk. *Orontēs*). Known today as Nahr el-ʿAsi, the Orontes was the chief river of SYRIA, about 170 mi. (275 km.) long. Its sources are E of the foothills of the Qurnet es-Sauda, the highest mountain of the LEBANON range. Then it flows northward through the Beqaʿ valley until it enters

Lake Homs, an artificial lake created by damming the river. Near HAMATH (modern Hama), it turns to the NW, and eventually follows the Amq Valley westward to the MEDITERRANEAN Sea, passing through ANTIOCH (Antakya in modern Turkey) on the way. The well-watered Orontes valley played a crucial role in history. It was a natural N-S route

The Orontes River in SE Turkey. (View from Antakya to the NE.)

for traders and conquerors. Traders either followed it to BAALBEK, from which they crossed the Antilebanon range to DAMASCUS, or they went S to the Litani Gorge, where they turned W to TYRE or SIDON. In ancient times it was both a target of, and a route for, Egyptian conquests in Asia. KADESH ON THE ORONTES (Tell Nebi Mindu) was a victim of THUTMOSE III. RAMSES II fought the HITTITES near this same city. Hittite, Hebrew, and Assyrian empires all extended into this valley. Much later, the Roman satirist Juvenal, writing of the undesirable Syrian immigrants in Rome, used the river as a metaphor for the whole province: "Long since has Syrian Orontes been a tributary of the Tiber."

Orpah. or′puh (Heb. ʿorpâ H6905, possibly "obstinate"). A Moabite woman who married KILION, one of two sons of ELIMELECH and NAOMI, after the family had migrated to MOAB from JUDAH in time of famine during the period of the judges (Ruth 1:1-4). RUTH married the other son, MAHLON (1:4; 4:10). Naomi, after the death of her husband and two sons, departed for her homeland accompanied by her two widowed daughters-in-

law. Upon urging by Naomi, Orpah returned to her own people and gods (1:15; Jdg. 11:24), in contrast to Ruth who would not leave Naomi.

orphan. The Hebrew word *yātôm H3846* apparently refers specifically to a child left "fatherless." Along with LEVITES, aliens, and widows, the fatherless were to be provided with special three-year TITHES (Deut. 26:12). A further provision was the special plots of "gleanings" left in fields for such individuals (14:29 et al.). The OT repeatedly pleads the case of the two states, the WIDOW and the fatherless (Exod. 22:22). Since INHERITANCE was through the male heir, the plight of a widow without sons, as in the case of NAOMI (and RUTH), was especially tragic. Daughters inherited only in the extreme case of no male heirs surviving (Num. 27:7-11). In the NT the term Greek *orphanos G4003*, "orphaned," appears twice, once used figuratively (Jn. 14:18), and once with reference to the ministry of mercy (Jas. 1:27).

Oshea. See HOSHEA.

Osiris. oh-si′ruhs. One of the principal gods of ancient EGYPT. According to Egyptian mythology, Osiris's brother Seth cut up his body and scattered the pieces. Isis, wife of Osiris, assembled his body and restored him to life. Osiris was connected with vegetation and the life-giving water of the NILE. His annual festival celebrated the sprouting of the grain. Osiris was also king of the dead. He judged each person after death according to truth and moral laws. Later the worship of Osiris became popular outside of Egypt as a MYSTERY RELIGION that mourned his death and celebrated his revival. In Ptolemaic times he was combined with the bull-god Apis as Serapis (Osiris + Apis), who was widely worshiped. Isis also was a popular goddess throughout the Greco-Roman world, and many shrines and statues in her honor have been preserved.

O

Osnappar, Osnapper. See Ashurbanipal.

osprey. See birds.

ossifrage. See birds.

ossuary. os´yoo-er´ee. Ossuaries are small boxes of varying size usually made of limestone or baked clay, and often decorated with carved geometrical patterns. The bones of the dead were placed in these after the flesh had decayed, and they were then deposited in special tombs, often large enough for a family or even several families. Here a series of shelves (*loculi*) cut into the walls of the excavated rock chamber housed the ossuaries. Although the term (from Lat. *ossuarium*, "bone container") does not occur in the English Bible, such boxes were used widely in biblical times. Generally, ossuaries date from the early Roman period. Many hundreds have been found in Palestine both Jewish and Christian in origin. Of particular value are ossuaries inscribed with Hebrew, Aramaic, or Greek, giving the name of the departed and sometimes a brief additional sentence.

Ostia. os´tee-uh (Lat. *ostia*, mouth). Although not mentioned in the Bible, this town, located at the mouth of the Tiber River, was of vital significance to the city of Rome. For reasons of security and trade, Rome was built on the banks of this river, approximately 16 mi. (26 km.) from the seacoast. As the city grew, the need for access to the sea became apparent, and Ostia was settled at the mouth of the river sometime between 350 and 300 B.C. During the second Punic War (218-201 B.C.) it served as a naval base, and upon the conclusion of peace developed into an important commercial center. During the first century A.D. the city developed steadily as trade increased, and various emperors improved it by building a new harbor and other public facilities. Rome's alternate port, much farther away, was Puteoli (Acts 28:13).

ostraca. os´truh-kuh. Plural form of the Greek noun *ostrakon*, which means "fragment of an earthen vessel," "potsherd" (e.g., LXX Ps. 21:16 [22:15]). In ancient Greece it referred to the potsherds used in voting on the banishment of a public official

© Dr. James C. Martin. The British Museum. Photographed by permission.

This ostracon is one of the series of "Eliashib letters" discovered at Arad.

(whence the English word *ostracize*). More generally, the term refers to pieces of broken pottery on which people wrote, especially in ancient Palestine, where many have been found in archaeological excavations. The abundance of potsherds made them a cheap and readily available form of writing material. Chiefly they were employed for documents requiring only small space, such as letters, brief memoranda, receipts, short lists, and notes. Although unsuitable for longer documents, such as biblical books, ostraca may have been used for recording brief prophetic oracles and proverbs that later were incorporated into books. Because the material is virtually imperishable, some of the oldest surviving documents in Palestine are ostraca and inscriptions. Especially noteworthy discoveries are (1) over seventy ostraca found in a storehouse in one of the palaces of Samaria, consisting of receipts for oil and wine paid as taxes to the king, and dating to the early eighth century B.C.; (2) twenty-one Hebrew ostraca found in the excavations of ancient Lachish, consisting mainly of letters written by a commanding officer at Lachish shortly before the capture of the city by the Babylonians in 589-588 B.C.; (3) more than 170 Hebrew and Aramaic uncovered in ARAD that date as far back as the tenth century B.C.

ostrich. See BIRDS.

Othni. oth′ni (Heb. *ʿotni H6978*, prob. short form of OTHNIEL). Son of Shemaiah, grandson of OBED-EDOM, and a gatekeeper from the Korahites (1 Chr. 26:7; cf. v. 1). See KORAH. Othni and his brothers are described as "leaders in their father's family because they were very capable men" (v. 6).

Othniel. oth′nee-uhl (Heb. *ʿotniʾel H6979*, possibly "God is my strength" or "God has exalted me"). Son of KENAZ and first deliverer or judge of the Israelites (Josh. 15:17-18; Jdg. 1:13-14; 3:9-11; 1 Chr. 4:13). The expression "son of Kenaz, Caleb's younger brother" (Jdg. 1:13; 3:9) is ambiguous. Since CALEB (the spy who with Joshua had brought back a good report of the land of Canaan) is sometimes called the "Kenizzite" (Num. 32:12; Josh. 14:6, 14), some hold that he was the son of Kenaz and thus the older brother of Othniel. The evidence as a whole, however, supports the view that Caleb should be regarded as the younger brother of Kenaz; thus Othniel was Caleb's nephew. Caleb, in his old age at the division of the land, offered his daughter to any one who would take DEBIR, about 8.5 mi. (13.5 km.) SSW of HEBRON. His nephew Othniel took Debir and so acquired ACSAH as wife. Within fifteen years after the death of Joshua, Israel fell into apostasy, and God delivered them into the hand of CUSHAN-RISHATHAIM (Jdg. 3:8-11), king of MESOPOTAMIA. In their distress they prayed to the Lord who raised up Othniel to deliver them. He was thus the first of the seven "judges" to deliver Israel from foreign oppression. He so restored Israel that a period of forty years of peace set in. His son was Hathath (1 Chr. 4:13). See JUDGES, THE.

ouches. This English term, which refers to the settings where precious stones are mounted, is used by the KJV a number of times (Exod. 28:11, 13, 14, 25; 39:6, 13, 16, 18; NJPS, "frames"). The Hebrew word in question probably refers to a filigree setting—woven gold thread or wire (cf. NIV,

NRSV). In the OT it refers most often to the gold settings of the engraved stones in the BREASTPIECE of the high priest.

outpost. See GARRISON.

oven. A chamber that is heated so as to roast or bake the food materials placed inside. There were three principal types. In EGYPT there was in nearly every house a structure of clay built on the house floor. In this, or on it, baking was done. In PALESTINE and SYRIA, a barrel-shaped hole in the ground was coated with clay and a quick hot fire of brambles or dry dung mixed with straw heated it. The dough, beaten very thin, was spread on the inside and almost immediately taken out, fully baked. In some places, a curved plate of iron is put over the sunken oven; but in cities the oven is a chamber of stone, from which the fire is raked when the oven is very hot and into which the unbaked loaves are then placed (Hos. 7:4-7). See also BREAD.

Ovens, Tower of the. A tower in the western wall of postexilic JERUSALEM, restored by NEHEMIAH (Neh. 3:11). When the walls were rededicated, one of the processions, starting presumably from the VALLEY GATE, went N "past the Tower of the Ovens to the Broad Wall" (12:38). Archaeological excavations have uncovered the BROAD WALL, which intersected the western wall; thus the general location of the Tower of the Ovens can be determined (i.e., a relatively short distance S of the Broad Wall), though the precise site is unknown. Earlier attempts to associate this tower with the CORNER GATE were misleading.

overlay. Archaeology reveals that the process of overlaying was known quite early among the Egyptians, and the offspring of JACOB may have learned it during their stay in EGYPT. By far, gilding was the most prominent type of overlaying practiced by Israel. Gold plates covered parts of the TABERNACLE structure: the pillars that supported the veil and the side frames of the tabernacle with their bars. Gold-plated items of tabernacle furniture were the ARK OF THE COVENANT (inside and out; cf. Heb. 9:4) with its carrying bars, the table of SHOWBREAD with its bars, and the altar of INCENSE

O

with its bars (Exod. 25-26; 36-37). Even more extensive was the amount of gold used in this way in Solomon's TEMPLE: the cherubim, the floor, the two doors to the Holy of Holies, and the doors at the entrance to the temple were overlaid with gold. Overlaying with SILVER was done only sparingly, being limited to the capitals of the pillars in the court of the tabernacle (38:17, 19, 28). The altar of burnt offering with its carrying poles and the doors to the court of the temple were coated with bronze (Exod. 27:2, 6; 38:2, 6; 2 Chr. 4:9).

overseer. This English term or related words occur frequently in the OT. Overseers had charge of the workmen in the construction of Solomon's TEMPLE (2 Chr. 2:18; NIV, "foremen") and of those involved with repairing the temple under Josiah's auspices (34:12-13, 17). JOSEPH was given oversight of POTIPHAR's house (Gen. 39:4-5; NIV, "put him in charge") and suggested to PHARAOH the appointment of overseers throughout Egypt (41:34; NIV, "commissioners"). Various other OT passages refer to overseers (e.g., 2 Chr. 31:13; Neh. 11:9, 14, 22; Isa. 60:17). In the NT, the KJV gives "overseer" only once as the rendering of *episkopos G2176*, which is descriptive of the function of ELDERS in the Ephesian church (Acts 20:28). In the other passages where this Greek noun appears, the KJV has "bishop," but the NIV translates it consistently as "overseer" (Phil. 1:1; 1 Tim. 3:2; Tit. 1:7; 1 Pet. 2:25). See BISHOP.

owl. See BIRDS.

ox. See ANIMALS.

oxgoad. See GOAD.

Ozem. oh´zuhm (Heb. *ʾōṣem H730*, possibly "hot-tempered"). (1) Sixth son of JESSE and older brother of DAVID (1 Chr. 2:15).

(2) Son of JERAHMEEL and descendant of JUDAH through PEREZ and HEZRON (1 Chr. 2:25).

Ozias. See UZZIAH.

Ozni. oz´ni (Heb. *ʾozni H269*, prob. short form of AZANIAH, "Yahweh has heard"; the gentilic has the same form, *ʾozni H270*, "Oznite"). Son of GAD and eponymous ancestor of the Oznite clan (Num. 26:16); called EZBON in the parallel list (Gen. 46:16).

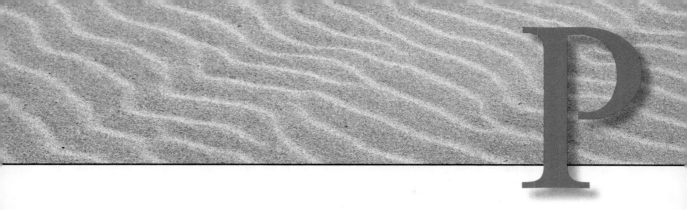

P (Priestly). An abbreviation used (along with D, E, and J) to designate one of the supposed sources of the PENTATEUCH, according to the Documentary Hypothesis. This priestly document is dated after the EXILE, when the professional priesthood is thought to have elaborated the ritual practices of the Jews and made them binding upon all the Jews. See also PRIEST.

Paarai. pay´uh-r*i* (Heb. *pa‘ăray H7197*, apparently from *pā‘ar H7196*, "to open [the mouth wide]"). An ARBITE, listed among DAVID's mighty warriors (2 Sam. 23:35); in the parallel passage he is called "Naarai son of Ezbai" (1 Chr. 11:37). See comments under EZBAI.

Pacatania. pak´uh-tan´ee-uh. See PACATIANA.

Pacatiana. pak´uh-ti-ay´nuh (Gk. *Pakatianos*, "peaceful"). Sometimes Pacatania. A province in ASIA MINOR whose capital was LAODICEA. At the end of 1 Timothy, the KJV includes this subscription on the margin: "The first to Timothy was written from Laodicea, which is the chiefest city of Phrygia Pacatiana." This is the reading of the TR and of most Greek MSS, but none earlier than the eighth century. The name Pacatiana was first applied to a section of PHRYGIA in the fourth century A.D.

Paddan, Paddan Aram. pad´uhn, pad´uhn-air´uhm (Heb. *paddān H7019* [only Gen. 48:7], prob. "plain"; *paddan ’ārām H7020*). KJV Padan, Padan-aram. The area of Upper MESOPOTAMIA around HARAN, upstream of the confluence of the rivers EUPHRATES and HABOR (Gen. 25:20; 28:2-7; 31:18; et al.). The name occurs only in Genesis and is usually thought to be equivalent to ARAM NAHARAIM. The strategic importance of this sector of the FERTILE CRESCENT is reflected in the patriarchal narratives. Here ABRAHAM dwelt before his emigration to Canaan. He sent his servant to it to procure a bride for his son, ISAAC. And to the same area JACOB fled and dwelt with LABAN. See also ARAM.

The Plain of Haran, where this photo of an old beehive home was taken, is in the region that the Bible calls Paddan Aram.

paddle. This word, which in Middle English referred specifically to a spade-shaped tool used for cleaning a plow, is used once by the KJV in a passage where the corresponding Hebrew word refers to a wooden spade (Deut. 23:13; NRSV, "trowel"; NIV, "something to dig with").

Padon. pay´duhn (Heb. *pādôn H7013*, "ransom," possibly short PEDAIAH, "Yahweh has redeemed"). Ancestor of a family of temple servants (NETHINIM) who returned from the EXILE with ZERUBBABEL (Ezra 2:44; Neh. 7:47).

pagan. See GENTILE.

© Dr. James C. Martin

Pagiel. pay´gee-uhl (Heb. *pagʿîʾēl H7005*, perhaps "one who intercedes with God" or "God has entreated [*or* met]"). Son of Ocran; he was the leader from the tribe of Asher, heading a division of 41,500 (Num. 2:27-28; 10:26). Pagiel was among those who assisted Moses in taking a census of the Israelites (1:13) and who brought offerings to the Lord for the dedication of the Tabernacle (7:72-77).

Pahath-Moab. pay´hath-moh´ab (Heb. *paḥat môʾāb H7075*, "governor of Moab"). This name (apparently derived from a title) is attributed to an Israelite who may have held some office in Moab, perhaps at the time that David subjugated that nation (cf. 2 Sam. 8:2). We know nothing about him, but he had more than 2,800 descendants (through two distinct lines, it seems) who returned from the exile under Zerubbabel (Ezra 2:6; Neh. 7:11). Another group of 200 of his descendants returned later with Ezra (Ezra 8:4). Some of these descendants are mentioned elsewhere (Ezra 10:30; Neh. 3:11; 10:14).

Pai. See Pau.

paint. Biblical references to paint and painting are comparatively few, in spite of the fact that the people of the ANE have always been fond of bright colors. Black paint was used to enlarge the eyes (2 Ki. 9:30; Jer. 4:30; Ezek. 23:40). In Jer. 22:14, mention is made of painting a house in red; in Ezek. 23:14, of drawing pictures on the wall with the same pigment (the Heb. word is *šāšar H9266*, referring prob. to the bright red pigment *vermilion*, either *cinnabar*, red mercuric sulphide, or *minium*, red oxide of lead).

palace. The dwelling place of an important official. Palaces are found all over the biblical world. The science of archaeology has given much light on these ancient structures. Israel built many palaces, and one finds frequent mention of them in Scripture. At Gezer the remains of a palace belonging to the period of Joshua's conquest have been found. It is thought to be the palace of Horam king of Gezer, whom Joshua conquered (Josh. 10:33). This building belongs to the group of structures known as fortress palaces. Many of these old palaces were made of stone. They were sometimes the entrances to great tunnels. Some were constructed over important wells or springs of water, which they controlled. The ruins of another palace at this site stem from a much later period. It is the Maccabean palace (see Maccabee) and is thought to be the private headquarters of John Hyrcanus, the military governor.

David had two palaces at different times in his reign. The first was a simple one located at Hebron, but the second one was much more elaborate, built of cedar trees furnished by Hiram of Tyre and erected by workmen that this Phoenician king supplied (2 Sam. 5:11). Solomon's palace, which was built later, was a much more lavish structure, judging from its description given in 1 Ki. 7. It was about 150 x 75 ft. (45 x 22.5 m.) in size, constructed mostly of cedar in the interior and of hand-hewn stones for the exterior. Some of the foundation stones were 15 ft. (4.5 m.) long. Solomon's wealth and the skill of the Phoenician craftsmen must have produced a magnificent building. Nothing remains of this building today.

Remains of a palace have been found at Megiddo. Another palace has been discovered at Samaria, possibly built by Omri. The foundation of this palace is in the bedrock common in that area. Most of these palaces are similar in style—a series of open courts with rooms grouped around them. An ivory palace belonging to Ahab is mentioned in 1 Ki. 22:39. For a long time scholars denied the truthfulness of this record, but archaeologists have confirmed the report. It was a large edifice about 300 ft. (90 m.) long from N to S. Many of its walls were faced with white marble. Wall paneling, plaques, and furniture made of or adorned with ivory have been uncovered.

Besides these palaces of Palestine, there were many splendid structures in Mesopotamia in the Assyrian and Babylonian period. The remains of the great temple of Sargon II have been found at Khorsabad, 12 mi. (19 km.) N of the site of old Nineveh. It was a mammoth structure covering 25 acres (10 hectares). Some of its walls were from 9 to 16 ft. (3-5 m.) thick. In the Oriental Institute Museum in Chicago one may see one of the stone bulls that once stood at the entrance of this palace. It is 16 ft. (5 m.) high, weighing c. 40 tons. An elaborately decorated palace was built by NEBUCHADNEZZAR at BABYLON. Another has been found on the EUPHRATES at MARI, dating to the early centuries of the second millennium B.C. This one is quite well preserved and reveals paintings, offices, apartments, and even a scribal school. Its discovery was important for many reasons, but especially because of the light it shed on the early development of ANE art. In addition, many famous palaces belonging to the PHARAOHS have also been found in EGYPT. Perhaps the best known of these is the palace of MERNEPTAH, from about 1230 B.C. Many of these were very elaborate structures.

palaeography. See PALEOGRAPHY.

Palal. pay´lal (Heb. *pālāl* H7138, prob. short form of PELALAIAH, "Yahweh has intervened"). Son of Uzai; he assisted NEHEMIAH in repairing the wall of JERUSALEM, working "opposite the angle and the tower projecting from the upper palace near the court of the guard" (Neh. 3:25).

palanquin. This English term, referring to an enclosed litter carried with poles, is used by the NRSV to render a Hebrew word that occurs only once (Cant. 3:9; KJV, "chariot"; NIV, "carriage"). The precise meaning of the word is uncertain, but it probably refers to a sedan, that is, a portable, covered chair designed to carry one person.

paleography. Also *palaeography*. The study of ancient writings. In biblical studies, the term is applied especially to the examination of Hebrew, Aramaic, and Greek MSS, focusing on the form, materials, and dates of ancient books, as well as on scribal practices. See TEXT AND VERSIONS (OT); TEXT AND VERSIONS (NT).

Palestina. pal´uh-sti´nuh. KJV alternate name for PHILISTIA (Exod. 15:14; Isa. 14:29, 31; in Joel 3:4, "Palestine"). See also PALESTINE.

Palestine. pal´uh-stin. This name (derived from Heb. *pĕlešet* H7148 ["Philistia"] through Lat. *Palaestina*) refers to an ancient region of SW Asia

lying between the E coast of the MEDITERRANEAN Sea and the JORDAN River (but sometimes considered to include TRANSJORDAN). Often called "the Holy Land" or "the land of the Bible."

I. Name. The term *Palestine* is not used in the NIV; it occurs four times in the KJV (Exod. 15:14; Isa. 14:29, 31; Joel 3:4), where the reference is to PHILISTIA, the SE coastal strip of the Mediterranean occupied by the PHILISTINES. JOSEPHUS used the Greek word *Palaistinē* in the same restricted geographical sense (e.g., *Antiq.* 1.6.2; 13.5.10). It is in Herodotus, the fifth-century Greek historian, that the extension of the term to cover a wider area is first seen (*Hist.* 2.104; 3.5; 91.7.89). The name Palestine is therefore another example of the common phenomenon whereby a land or a people is named after the part or the division with which first contact is made (e.g., the French name for Germany, *Allemagne*, derives from the trans-Rhenane federation of the Allemanni). The older Semitic name was CANAAN.

II. Locality and area. The limits of Palestine in ancient times lack precise definition, save in the case of the second-century Roman province of that name, whose boundaries may be fairly certainly drawn. The Leontes River (modern Litani) in PHOENICIA is commonly regarded as the logical N boundary, and the Wadi el-ʿArish in the S as the natural frontier with EGYPT. Political frontiers, ancient and modern, have not always respected these boundaries. Even the limits of Israel poetically marked in the phrase "from Dan to Beersheba" do not correspond (Jdg. 20:1). DAN was ancient Laish, some 30 mi. (50 km.) due E of TYRE on the sources of the Jordan. BEERSHEBA lay about 150 mi. (240 km.) to the S, as the crow flies, where Palestine merges into the desert of the NEGEV.

The description of the promised territory in Josh. 1:4 is geographically much more inclusive. The seacoast formed a definite enough W boundary, though alien powers, from ancient Philistine to modern Egyptian, have always disputed the possession of these fertile lowlands behind the coast. The deepening desert made a firm, though changing boundary line to the E. To the W of a line drawn down the Jordan Valley, Palestine measures about 6,000 sq. mi. (15,500 sq. km.). If areas E of the Jordan, from time to time counted part of Palestine, are

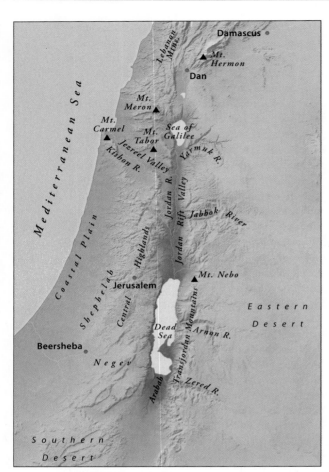

The physical geography of Palestine.

tions. At JERICHO, 15 mi. (24 km.) to the E, and 3,300 ft. (1,000 m.) below Jerusalem or 700 ft. (210 m.) below sea level, tropical climate prevails with intense and enervating summer heat. A similar contrast marks the temperate climate around the Sea of Galilee and the tropical heat around the Dead Sea.

Prevailing winds are W or SW and precipitate their moisture on the western slopes of the high country in a rainy season extending roughly from October to April. An occasional sirocco, or E wind, brings burning air from the great deserts of the hinterland (Job 1:19; Jer. 18:17; Ezek. 17:10; 27:26). The southern desert, S of Beersheba, is a parched wilderness, at present the scene of some of the world's major experiments in "dry-farming." The chief climatic advantage is a heavy fall of dew. The "former rain" of the biblical phrase (Jer. 5:24; Joel 2:23 KJV; NIV, "autumn rain") was the early part of the rainy season. The period is commonly followed by a time of heavy falls alternating with fine clear weather, until March or April, when the "latter rain" (NIV, "spring rain") falls with immense advantage to the maturing crops before the dry season, the ripening, and the harvest.

IV. Geography

A. The coast. The coast of Palestine is a line that sweeps S, with a slight curve to the W, without break or indentation. North of CARMEL lies Phoenicia, where a great maritime nation found the means to use and tame the sea; in this area, significantly, the coast is more hospitable, and offers hope of haven for ships. Those who lived behind the stern, flat coast of Palestine necessarily found the sea a barrier (Josh. 1:4) and an image of violence and restlessness (Isa. 17:12-13). By the same token, they were agricultural rather than maritime. From Carmel S to the Nile delta, the coastline is built of sandhills and low cliffs, without a sheltering offshore island to form a roadstead, or a river mouth to give minimum protection from the sea. The currents are parallel with the coast, and still bear the silt of the Nile. The prevailing wind beats on the shore with ceaseless surf. No intruder, with the possible exception of the Philistines themselves, has ever landed there. Palestine's invaders have followed the open roads of her N−S plains and valleys.

For the same reason, artificial harbors anciently built on the coast, even HEROD's fine port of CAE-

also included, the total area is nearer 10,000 sq. mi. (26,000 sq. km.). It is thus a little larger than the state of Vermont. As mentioned above, the distance from Dan to Beersheba is 150 mi. (240 km.). From W to E the distances are smaller still: in the N, from Acco to the Sea of Galilee (see GALILEE, SEA OF), the distance is 28 mi. (45 km.); in the S, from GAZA to the DEAD SEA, the distance is about 55 mi. (90 km.).

III. Climate. In spite of its narrow limits, the varied configuration of Palestine produces a great variety of climates. Thanks to the adjacent sea, the coastal plain, lying between latitudes 31 and 33, is temperate, with an average annual temperature of 57°F at JOPPA. Inland 34 mi. (55 km.), JERUSALEM, thanks to its height of c. 2,600 ft. (790 m.), registers an annual average of 63°, though with wider varia-

SAREA, have always been difficult to maintain: on the first relaxation of human effort, the sea has overwhelmed them. The makeshift or artificial ports on the Mediterranean coast may be listed as follows. DOR was used as a port, but it was an open roadstead, and never in firm control of the Israelite authorities. JOPPA was little better, save that some offshore reefs broke the force of the Mediterranean swell and offered a fair-weather port. First under Philistine and later under Syrian control, Joppa fell to the Jews as a conquest of Simon MACCABEE in 148 B.C. "To add to his reputation," runs the account, "he took Joppa for a harbor, and provided an access for the islands of the sea" (1 Macc. 14:5). Simon found a considerable Greek population in the port and had some trouble in occupying and fortifying it. After eighty-five years, during which the Syrians twice reoccupied the port, Pompey allotted it to SYRIA in his political organization of the area (63 B.C.). It was later returned to the Jews, and AUGUSTUS made it part of the domains of Herod the Great. These historical vicissitudes illustrate the disadvantages of a coastline that is geographically so disadvantageous. ASHKELON, the only Philistine city actually on the coast, and a foundation old enough to find mention in the Tell el-AMARNA Letters, served also as a port, and underwater archaeology has established the presence of harbor works. Caesarea, Herod's ambitious foundation 20 mi. (32 km.) S of modern Haifa, was an efficient port. Herod spent twelve years building, not only a harbor, but also a city of some magnificence. Enormous blocks of stone formed a breakwater, about 200 ft. (60 m.) wide in 120 ft. (35 m.) of water, and made the only real harbor on the coast. Associated harbor buildings, navigational aids, and a well-equipped town made Caesarea the natural seat for Roman authority in Palestine.

B. The maritime plain. A coastal plain shaped like a long spear point, with its tip where Carmel thrusts to the sea, is the main western geographical feature of Palestine. North of Carmel, the small plain of Acco or Acre, a detached section of the coastal plain, should be mentioned. South of Carmel, widening from 8 to 12 mi. (13-19 km.) and extending for 44 mi. (71 km.), is the Plain of SHARON, once an extensive oak forest, well-watered,

and bounded to the S by low hills. South again of this inconsiderable barrier, and similarly widening over the course of its 40 mi. (65 km.) to the borders of Egypt, is the famous Plain of Philistia, after which the entire land was named. Unhealthy marshes were found at the S end of the Philistine plain, but in spite of that, the coastal plain has always been a highway of commerce or aggression. By this path traveled the Egyptian conquerors THUTMOSE III, RAMSES II, and SETI I, seeking out their northern foes, the HITTITES. By this same path, and thence into the Plain of ESDRAELON, traveled Cambyses, Alexander, Pompey, Saladin, Napoleon, and Allenby. The plain forms the western blade of the FERTILE CRESCENT, the grand highway between Africa, Asia, and Europe.

C. The uplands. The tumbled hill-country that forms the core or backbone of the land, is a continuation of the more clearly defined Lebanon ranges N of Palestine. This extended mountain chain breaks up into confused hills in the desert of the S. Three divisions are to be distinguished: GALILEE, SAMARIA, and JUDAH. Galilee is rugged, especially to the N, where a height of c. 4,000 ft. (1,220 m.) above sea level is reached near MEROM. The S portion is less hilly and might even be described as rolling land, arable, fertile, and temperate in climate. South of Galilee, the Valley of JEZREEL, or the Plain of Esdraelon, cuts the range, the location of many important ancient towns and an open highway to the N. The town of MEGIDDO controlled the pass into the Plain of Sharon. Since Mount Carmel dominated the road along the coast, Megiddo was a place of paramount strategic importance. From the strife that, through the centuries, necessarily gathered around it, ARMAGEDDON, or "the Hill of Megiddo" became a symbol of the struggle of nations (Rev. 16:16). Two valleys from Esdraelon give access to the Jordan. One passes between TABOR and MOREH, the other between Moreh and GILBOA. Here lay the best E–W travel routes of the land.

The Samaria hill-country forms the geographical heart of Palestine. The uplands rise in the N to about 1,640 ft. (500 m.) in Mount Gilboa, and cast up two conspicuous peaks: EBAL (3,077 ft./938 m. above sea level) and GERIZIM, a lower eminence. Fertile valleys intersect these high masses, and

P

Aerial view of the Jezreel Valley looking N toward the western section of the Nazareth Ridge. This area provided an important transportation route across ancient Palestine.

© Dr. James C. Martin

since the valley floors are themselves of considerable altitude, the higher country has not the visible height or prominence that the sea level figures appear to indicate.

The third division of the hill country is Judah. Here the summits are lower than in the region of Samaria, falling to about 2,600 ft. (800 m.) in Jerusalem and touching their highest point, 3,370 ft. (1,030 m.), near Hebron. This country forms a watershed that strains the moisture from the Mediterranean sea breezes. The eastern slopes, in consequence, deteriorate into the barren "wilderness of Judah," deeply intersected by the arid ravines that converge on the Dead Sea. This barren wasteland was the refuge of DAVID in his outlaw days.

Ordered life and agriculture was concentrated on the W in the so-called SHEPHELAH, the sloping foothills and valley tongues that led up from the coastal plain into the Judean hills. In sheltered folds of the hills, agriculture flourished, and fertility seeped down from the higher land. The Shephelah was disputed territory. In days of strength the Hebrew highlanders pressed down toward the plain. When their strength flagged, the Philistine lowlanders thrust up into the foothills. The Shephelah saw a pressure front between the

Semitic claimants from the desert and the E, and those from the W. Fortresses such as LACHISH, DEBIR, LIBNAH, AZEKAH, and BETH SHEMESH were located in the Shephelah. To the S the Judean hill-country breaks up into the arid wilderness of the Negev. There is strong archaeological evidence for a considerable population in this area in the early centuries of the Christian era, made possible by efficient water conservation, irrigation systems, and the effective use, through rock-mulching, of the heavy fall of dew.

D. The Jordan Valley. This depression, which contains the Jordan River and its associated bodies of water, is part of a huge split in the crust of the globe, a geological fault that extends N to form the valley between the two Lebanon ranges, and S to form the arid valley of the ARABAH, the Gulf of AQABAH, and the African chain of lakes. The Jordan rises from multiple sources on the W slopes of Mount HERMON and becomes a distinctive stream a few miles N of the shallow reedy lake called Huleh today. The Canaanite stronghold of HAZOR lay a few miles to the SW. From its sources to Huleh, the Jordan drops 1,000 ft. (300 m.) over a distance of 12 mi. (19 km.), and enters the lake 7 ft. (2 m.) above sea level. Over the 11 mi. (18 km.)

to the Sea of Galilee, it drops to 682 ft. (208 m.) below sea level. From Galilee to the Dead Sea there is a further drop of c. 600 ft. (180 m.).

Some of Palestine's most fertile soil is found around the shores of the Sea of Galilee, and the lake itself was the center of an extensive and vigorous fishing industry. CAPERNAUM, BETHSAIDA, and perhaps KORAZIN, were lakeside towns, with a strong fishing industry. It is clear that the first disciples, who were firshermen, were called from an active and prosperous stratum of Galilean society. Flowing S from Galilee, through a wide-floored valley walled by cliffs, the Jordan follows a fantastically meandering course, taking 200 mi. (320 km.) of winding stream to cover 65 mi. (105 km.) measured in a straight line. Much of the valley floor is tangled vegetation, fed lushly by the periodic floodwaters of the river. It is this wilderness that JEREMIAH calls "the swelling" (KJV) or "the thickets" (NIV) of Jordan (Jer. 12:5; 49:19). Fords are numerous.

The river enters the Dead Sea near Jericho. This lake has no outflow and its water is therefore 25 percent salt deposits, the raw material of a flourishing chemical industry recently established in the region of the lake. Two-thirds of the way down the eastern coast, W of KIR HARESETH in MOAB, an irregular peninsula known as "the Tongue" projects into the sea. South of this peninsula the water is only a few feet deep, forming a large bay known anciently as "the Valley of Siddim" (Gen. 14:3). Here, it is thought, were situated the CITIES OF THE PLAIN, namely, SODOM, GOMORRAH, ADMAH, ZEBOIIM, and ZOAR. About 2000 B.C. a great catastrophe overwhelmed the area and depressed the ground level. Underwater archaeological exploration seems to confirm that Sodom and its associated towns perished in this cataclysm.

E. The plateau of Transjordan. This is not part of modern Palestine and was alien territory over much of ancient history. It was, however, intimately connected with biblical history, and its geography is relevant in con-

sequence. North of the YARMUK, a tributary of the Jordan, is BASHAN. Through this region in NT times curved the eastern members of the federation of ten cities known as the DECAPOLIS. In its eastern quarter lay the TRACONITIS of the Greeks (Lk. 3:1), a tumbled waste of ancient volcanic stone, a natural defensive area, and part of the principality of OG of Bashan (Deut. 3:4).

South of Bashan, and extending to the river, is GILEAD. The JABBOK, whose banks were the scene of JACOB's contest (Gen. 33), rose near RABBAH of the Ammonites (the Philadelphia of the Decapolis) and irrigated a considerable territory. In the tribal settlement recorded in Num. 32 and Josh. 12, MANASSEH was allotted all Bashan in the N, REUBEN the Moabite highlands in the S, and GAD the central land of Gilead. Hence the identification of Gad with Gilead in Jdg. 5:17. In Gilead was the brook KERITH, scene of ELIJAH's retreat, and David's refuge of MAHANAIM. It was well watered and wooded.

South of Jabbok, down to the ARNON, which joins the Dead Sea halfway down its eastern coast, the plateau becomes increasingly arid and desolate. This area contains the height of NEBO, the old land of AMMON. South of Arnon is MOAB, a high plateau seldom controlled by Israel; and farther S still is EDOM, a region valuable for its mineral deposits and first controlled and exploited by David and Solomon. It was possibly the iron of Edom, smelted in the considerable industrial district just

The Maktesh Ramon, the world's largest karst crater (c. 24 mi./39 km. long), lies in the southern portion of Palestine. (View to the SW.)

© Dr. James C. Martin

P

N of the Gulf of Aqabah, that enabled Israel to emerge from the Bronze Age and meet the iron-using Philistines on their own terms. PETRA, the strange rock of the desert trade routes, was originally an Edomite stronghold.

V. Animal life. Besides the common domesticated animals of the ANE (horse, ox, sheep, goat, camel, ass, mule), Palestine was the habitat of numerous predatory beasts, principally the lion, leopard, wolf, jackal, and fox. The hare, the coney (a species of rabbit), the wild boar, and the deer were also found. A concordance, under any of these heads, will show the variety of metaphor and imagery based on animal life, both tame animals and the "beasts of the field." The dog was considered almost a wild creature and provided a term for uncleanness, treachery, and contempt. The dog of Palestine was a pariah and scavenger; no mention is made of its being used in hunting nor shepherding, except Job 30:1. Song birds are rare, but scavenger and predatory fowl included the eagle, vulture, owl, hawk, and kite. The heron, bittern, osprey, partridge, peacock, dove, pigeon, quail, raven, stork, and sparrow were common and find frequent reference in both Testaments. Fish were plentiful, especially in Galilee, where the shoals were dense. The chief edible fish seem to have been carp. Bees, grasshoppers, and locusts were among the insects. Palestine lies in the belt of territory subject to locust invasion, and the book of JOEL is striking evidence for the destructive visitation of such insect swarms. See also ANIMALS; BIRDS.

VI. Plant life. Flowers are abundant in spring, giving brilliant display for a brief period only; hence their use as a symbol of the ephemeral nature of life (Job 14:2; Ps. 103:15). The "lilies of the field" (Matt. 6:28) may have been a comprehensive term covering anemones, irises, and other blooms. The rose was probably the crocus (Cant. 2:1; Isa. 35:1). Trees grow vigorously in Palestine under proper cultivation, but the forest coverage in ancient times is a matter for conjecture. It may be safely assumed that parts of Palestine must have been more heavily wooded in ancient times than today. Invasion and the Turkish tax on trees combined over the centuries to destroy the arboreal flora of Palestine. On the other hand, Palestine is not an ideal region for major forest growth. The

chief kinds of trees were the oak, including the evergreen ilex, the terebinth, the carob, and the box; some pines; cypresses; and plane trees by the water. The plane is probably the tree of Ps. 1, "planted by streams of water." Josephus mentions the walnut, and the sycamore-fig is mentioned in Amos (Amos 7:14), Isaiah (Isa. 9:9-10; NIV "fig"), and Luke (Lk. 19:4). Smaller growth is formed of dwarf or scrub oak, dwarf wild olive, wild vine, juniper, and thorn. Such scrub often marks the abandoned sites of ancient cultivation. Oleanders sometimes line riverbeds. The olive, the vine, the fig, and the date palm were the chief fruit-bearing trees or plants of ancient Palestine, and balsam groves were farmed at Jericho. Grain crops were barley, wheat, and millet. Wheat grew in the broader valleys and plains, the best areas for its cultivation being Philistia and Esdraelon. Barley grew on the higher slopes, a less-valued crop. Beans and lentils were the chief vegetables. Jacob's "red stew" (Gen. 25:30) was probably a variety of red beans or lentil. The land was poor in grass; pasturage, as Western countries know it, was unknown. Hence the imagery of grass in reference to the brevity of life (Ps. 90:5-7; 103:15; Isa. 40:6). See also PLANTS.

palimpsest. A writing material (esp. a PARCHMENT MS) that has had its text scraped off and replaced with new writing. Many biblical MSS are palimpsests, including an important parchment from the fifth century known as CODEX EPHRAEMI: its biblical text was erased in the Middle Ages and replaced with patristic writings. Through the use of chemical reagents and other means, much of the original text can often be recovered. See TEXT AND VERSIONS (NT).

pallet. This English term, referring to a small and portable bed or mattress, is used by some versions to render Greek *krabatton G3187* (Mk. 2:4 et al.; NIV, "mat").

Pallu. pal´yoo (Heb. *pallû* H7112, perhaps short form of PELAIAH, "Yahweh is wonderful"; gentilic *pallu'i H7101*, "Palluite"). Son of REUBEN, grandson of JACOB, and eponymous ancestor of the Palluite clan (Gen. 46:9 [KJV, "Phallu"]; Exod. 6:14; Num. 26:5, 8; 1 Chr. 5:3). His "son" or descendant

ELIAB was the father (or ancestor) of DATHAN and ABIRAM, who joined KORAH in his rebellion against MOSES (Num. 16:1; in this verse, some emend PELETH to Pallu).

palm (of the hand). See WEIGHTS AND MEASURES.

palmerworm. See ANIMALS (under *grasshopper*).

Palms, City of. A designation used with reference to JERICHO (Deut. 34:3; 2 Chr. 28:15). In the book of Judges, however (Jdg. 1:16 [note the reference to ARAD]; 3:13), the context has suggested to some scholars that the name originally designated a site S of the DEAD SEA, such as TAMAR (PLACE) or ZOAR.

palm tree. See PLANTS.

Palmyra. See TADMOR.

palsy. See DISEASES.

Palti. pal'ti (Heb. *palṭî H7120*, prob. short form of *palṭî᾽ēl H7123*, "God is my deliverance"). (1) Son of Raphu, from the tribe of BENJAMIN, and one of the twelve spies sent out by MOSES to reconnoiter the Promised Land (Num. 13:9).

(2) Alternate form of PALTIEL #2.

Paltiel. pal'tee-uhl (*palṭî᾽ēl H7123*, "God is my deliverance"). (1) Son of Azzan; he was a leader from the tribe of ISSACHAR, chosen to assist in the distribution of the land (Num. 34:26).

(2) Son of Laish, from the Benjamite village of GALLIM; for a time he was the husband of SAUL's daughter, MICHAL (1 Sam. 25:44 [KJV, "Phalti," and NRSV, "Palti," both following MT]; 2 Sam. 3:15 [KJV, "Phaltiel"]). Michal had been married to DAVID, but when he lost favor with Saul, she was given to Paltiel. After the death of Saul, David demanded of ISH-BOSHETH that Michal be restored to him; as she was taken back to David, Paltiel followed her weeping (2 Sam. 3:16).

Paltite. pal'tit (Heb. *palṭî H7121*, gentilic of *peleṭ H7118*, "deliverance"). A designation applied to Helez, one of David's mighty warriors (2 Sam. 23:26). See comments under HELEZ #1.

Pamphylia. pam-fil'ee-uh (Gk. *Pamphylia G4103*, "[land of] all tribes"). A lowland district situated halfway along the S coast of ASIA MINOR. At the time of the apostle PAUL, Pamphylia was a small Roman PROVINCE, extending some 75 mi. (120 km.) along the coast and 30 mi. (50 km.) inland, following the lower course of the valley of the Cestrus to the Taurus mountains in the interior. It was surrounded by CILICIA to the E, LYCIA to the SW, and PISIDIA to the N. The region was subject to numerous invasions of peoples throughout its history.

Pamphylia is first mentioned in the NT in Acts 2:10, where it is said that some of the pilgrims in Jerusalem at PENTECOST were from that province. Later, Paul visited the territory on his first missionary journey when he preached at PERGA, the chief center of the territory (13:13; 14:24). Here John Mark left the party and returned to Jerusalem (13:13; 15:38; see MARK, JOHN). Later, when Paul as a prisoner sailed near Pamphylia (27:5), he evidently crossed the Pamphylian Gulf. Christianity appears to have been slow in becoming established here, in an area characterized by its amalgam of ethnic groups. Besides Perga, the chief cities of Pamphylia were Attalia (c. 12 mi./19 km. SW of the chief city), Side (over 30 mi./50 km. to the SE, founded by Aeolian settlers), Aspendus (a Persian naval base), and Attaleia. It was probably at Attaleia where the apostle Paul began his journey through the province.

pan. This English term is used variously in Bible translations to render several Hebrew terms, such as *kiyyôr H3963* (1 Sam. 2:14, where it is distinguished from "kettle," "caldron," and "pot"). See also POTTERY; VESSEL.

panel. The NIV and other versions use this noun to translate, for example, Hebrew *misgeret H4995* with reference to the rims or sides of the wheeled laver stands in the TEMPLE (1 Ki. 7:28-29 et al.; KJV and NRSV, "borders"; NJPS, "insets"). These lavers were box-shaped, with the sides formed of ornamented stile and rails. As a verb, *panel* sometimes translates *sāpan H6211*, "to cover," used of the labor that Shallum (i.e., JEHOAHAZ), king of JUDAH, foolishly lavished on the walls and ceiling

P

of his palace in the face of impending doom (Jer. 22:14); it was also invidious that the repatriates of Haggai's day paneled their houses, but left God's house in ruins (Hag. 1:4).

Pannag. pan´ag (Heb. *pannag H7154*). KJV transliteration of a Hebrew term that occurs only once, with reference to the items that Judah and Israel traded with Tyre: "wheat of Minnith, and Pannag, and honey, and oil, and balm" (Ezek. 27:17; similarly NJPS). If the word is indeed a place name, the town or region is not known. Most modern versions interpret it as a type of food, though what that might be can only be conjectured (NRSV, following the Syriac, has "millet"; NIV, more generally, "confections"). See also Minnith; plants.

pantheism. The view that God should be identified with the forces and laws of nature. See monotheism.

pap. KJV term for "breast, chest" (Ezek. 23:21; Lk. 11:27; 23:29; Rev. 1:13), now obsolete in this sense.

paper. See papyrus; writing.

Paphos. pay´fos (Gk. *Paphos G4265*). The capital city of Cyprus, located at the extreme western end of this large island. The Paphos of the NT is really Nea (New) Paphos, a Roman city rebuilt by Augustus; the old Greek city of Paphos, dedicated to the worship of Aphrodite, lay 10 mi. (16 km.) to the south. In Nea Paphos, Paul and Barnabas

encountered the wiles of the Jewish sorcerer Elymas in the court of Sergius Paulus, the Roman governor. Paul's miracle of blinding the magician led to the conversion of Paulus (Acts 13:6-13). New Paphos is now known as Baffa.

papyrus. A reed or rush that grows in swamps and along rivers or lakes, often to the height of 12 ft. (c. 3.5 m.) with beautiful flowers at the top. The stalk is triangular in shape, something like a giant celery stalk. In ancient times it was found mainly along the Nile in Egypt but was also known in Palestine. For commercial use the stalk was cut into sections about 12 in. (30 cm.) long, and these pieces were then sliced lengthwise into thin strips, which were shaped and squared and laid edge to edge to form a larger piece. Other strips were laid horizontally over these strips and both were pressed together, dried in the sun, scraped, and rubbed until there emerged a smooth yellowish sheet much like our heavy wrapping paper, only thicker and heavier. The juice of the pith served as the glue, but sometimes other paste was added.

The manufacture of papyrus was a flourishing business in Egypt, where baskets, sandals, boats, and other articles were made of it. It was not unknown among the Hebrews (Job 8:11), and many believe that the ark of bulrushes that held baby Moses was made of papyrus (Exod. 2:3). But the most common use of the product was for writing material, so much so that *papyrus* became the name for writing paper. The art of making papyrus goes back to 2000 B.C., and it was the common writing material in the Greek and Roman worlds from 500 B.C. until A.D. 400, when vellum (see parchment) largely replaced it. There is little doubt that the NT books were written on papyrus (pl. *papyri*). The material was also called *chartēs G5925* in Greek, and John no doubt wrote his second letter on such paper (2 Jn. 12).

For long books (rolls or scrolls) many pieces of papyrus were glued together and rolled up. Such a roll was called *mĕgillâ H4479* in Hebrew and *biblion G1046* in Greek (cf. Ezek. 2:9-10; 2 Tim. 4:13; Rev. 10:2, 8, 9-10). The width of the roll varied from 3 to 12 in. (8-30 cm.), and sometimes the roll got to be very long. Luke's gospel is estimated to have been about 30 ft. (9 m.) long, 2 Thessalonians

© Dr. James C. Martin

This mosaic, depicting a boxing scene, is from the floor of a Roman house in the city of Paphos.

P

may have been only 18 in. (46 cm.), and short letters like Jude or Philemon were perhaps written on a single small sheet. The writer wrote in columns evenly spaced along the length of the roll, and the reader read one column at a time, unrolling with one hand and rolling up with the other.

Papyrus, however, becomes brittle with age and easily decays, especially when damp. This is why the autographs of the NT writings have perished. They may also have been literally read to pieces and during persecution were deliberately destroyed. But thousands of ancient papyri, both biblical and secular, have been found in the dry sands of Egypt and elsewhere. Many of these documents the ancient inhabitants themselves regarded as useless: outdated commercial transactions, brief private letters, contracts of marriage and divorce, memoranda. Yet it was precisely these insignificant materials that revealed how the common folk of Hellenistic times actually lived and spoke. The discovery revolutionized our understanding of NT GREEK, for it soon became clear that the apostles had written in the language of the common people. In addition, extremely important MSS of the NT itself have been discovered, some of them dating back to the second century; examples are the Rylands Papyrus, the Chester Beatty Papyri, and the Bodmer Papyrus of the Gospel of John. They have added much to our knowledge of the Greek language and the text of the NT. See TEXT AND VERSIONS (NT).

parable. In classical Greek, the noun *parabolē G4130* meant "juxtaposition, comparison, illustration" (from the verb *paraballō*, which had several senses, including "to lay [one thing] beside [another], to compare"). In the NT, the word is applied to a saying or story that seeks to drive home a point the speaker wishes to emphasize by illustrating it from a familiar situation of common life. In the SEPTUAGINT, this term is used frequently as the equivalent of Hebrew *māšāl H5442*, in which the idea of comparison can also be present (e.g., Ezek. 17:2; 24:3).

When the subject of parables is discussed it is preeminently the stories told by JESUS CHRIST that come to mind. Whether in his instruction of the disciples or his preaching to the crowds that flocked to hear him or his debates with the scribes

and PHARISEES, he regularly used this method: "he did not say anything to them without using a parable" (Matt. 13:34). When his disciples asked him why he did this, he replied that it was an effective method of revealing truth to the spiritual and ready mind and at the same time of concealing it from others (13:11). Christ came as Israel's King and only after they had rejected him did he employ this form of imparting spiritual truth. Those who had rejected him were not to know the "secrets of the kingdom of heaven."

The parables of Jesus are not allegories, even though sometimes they include allegorical elements. The details of the stories make them more vivid and effective, but each parable is told to drive home one major point. The most distinctive parables of Jesus are parables of the KINGDOM OF GOD, designed to embody some aspect of his preaching. They were not mere illustrations, but integral to the whole ministry of Jesus. In the parables the kingdom of God itself comes to expression and Jesus bears testimony to his own person and mission, albeit in veiled form, so that the hearers' response to the parable is their response to the kingdom of God and to Jesus himself.

The following classification of parables is adapted from A. B. Bruce, *The Parabolic Teaching of Christ* (1904), pp. 8ff.

I. Didactic parables

A. Nature and development of the kingdom
1. The sower (Matt. 13:3-8; Mk. 4:4-8; Lk. 8:5-8)
2. The tares (Matt. 13:24-30)
3. The mustard seed (Matt. 13:31-32; Mk. 4:30-32; Lk. 13:18-19)
4. The leaven (Matt. 13:33; Lk. 13:20-21)
5. The hidden treasure (Matt. 13:44)
6. The pearl of great price (Matt. 13:45-46)
7. The drag net (Matt. 13:47-50)
8. The blade, the ear, and the full corn (Mk. 4:26-29)

B. Service and rewards
1. The laborers in the vineyard (Matt. 20:1-16)
2. The talents (Matt. 25:14-30)
3. The pounds (Lk. 19:11-27)
4. The unprofitable servants (Lk. 17:7-10)

C. Prayer
  1. The friend at midnight (Lk. 11:5-8)
  2. The unjust judge (Lk. 18:1-8)

D. Love for neighbor: the Good Samaritan (Lk. 10:30-37)

E. Humility
  1. The lowest seat at the feast (Lk. 14:7-11)
  2. The Pharisee and the publican (Lk. 18:9-14)

F. Worldly wealth
  1. The unjust steward (Lk. 16:1-9)
  2. The rich fool (Lk. 12:16-21)
  3. The great supper (Lk. 14:15-24)

II. Evangelic parables

A. God's love for the lost
  1. The lost sheep (Matt. 18:12-14; Lk. 15:3-7)
  2. The lost coin (Lk. 15:8-10)
  3. The lost son (Lk. 15:11-32)

B. Gratitude of the redeemed: the two debtors (Lk. 7:41-43)

III. Prophetic and judicial parables

A. Watchfulness for Christ's return
  1. The ten virgins (Matt. 25:1-13)
  2. The faithful and unfaithful servants (Matt. 24:45-51; Lk. 12:42-48)
  3. The watchful porter (Mk. 13:34-37)

B. Judgment on Israel and within the kingdom
  1. The two sons (Matt. 21:28-32)
  2. The wicked husbandmen (Matt. 21:33-34; Mk. 12:1-12; Lk. 20:9-18)
  3. The barren fig tree (Lk. 13:6-9)
  4. The marriage feast of the king's son (Matt. 22:1-14)
  5. The unforgiving servant (Matt. 18:23-25)

Paraclete. See ADVOCATE; HOLY SPIRIT.

paradise. This term derives from Greek *paradeisos G4137*, "park, garden" (itself borrowed from Persian; cf. also Heb. *pardēs H7236* [only Neh. 2:8; Eccl. 2:5; Cant. 4:13]). Its common English meaning is "a place [or state] of bliss," but in biblical usage it has a specialized sense. The Greek transla-tion of the OT (see SEPTUAGINT) uses this term most frequently with reference to EDEN (Gen. 2:8-10 et al.). The word begins to take on an escha-tological nuance in some prophetic passages (e.g., Isa. 51:3 LXX), and this idea becomes more promi-nent in the PSEUDEPIGRAPHA (e.g., *2 En.* 8.1-3). The term occurs three times in the NT, always with reference to the ultimate place of spiritual bliss (Lk. 23:43; 2 Cor. 12:4; Rev. 2:7).

paraenesis. pair´uh-nee´sis. Also *parenesis* (adj. *paraenetic* or *parenetic*). This technical term (from a common Gk. noun, *parainesis*, "exhortation"; cf. the cognate verb *paraineō G4147*, "to exhort, recom-mend, advise, warn") is used in biblical scholarship with reference to passages characterized by instruc-tions and commands. It occurs most frequently in discussions of hortatory sections in the NT letters.

Parah. pay´ruh (Heb. *pārāh H7240*, possibly from the verb *pārāh H7238*, "to be fruitful"). A town within the tribal territory of BENJAMIN (Josh. 18:23). It is generally identified with Khirbet ʿAin Farah, c. 4.5 mi. (6.5 km.) NE of JERUSALEM, although some believe it should be located farther N, near BETHEL and OPHRAH, with which it is grouped.

parallelism. See POETRY.

paralysis, paralytic. See DISEASES.

paramour. This term, meaning "an illicit lover," is used once by the KJV and other versions (Ezek. 23:20; NIV, "lovers"). In this passage, where the symbolic women OHOLAH AND OHOLIBAH rep-resent adulterous (i.e., idolatrous) SAMARIA and JERUSALEM, the Hebrew word refers to males, but elsewhere it is properly rendered CONCUBINE (Gen. 22:24; Jdg. 8:31; et al.).

Paran. pay´ruhn (Heb. *pāʾrān H7000*, meaning uncertain). A broad central area of desert in the SINAI Peninsula. It is to be distinguished from three smaller deserts that are peripheral districts: SHUR in the NW, bordering EGYPT; Sinai itself, in the southern tip of the peninsula; and ZIN, in the NE between KADESH BARNEA and the ARABAH

The Desert of Paran.

trough. Consequently, there is some overlap in the rather vaguely defined boundaries of Paran. The whole area is some 23,000 sq. mi. (60,000 sq. km.), divisible into three main topographical sections. In the wilderness of Shur, to the N, lie wide open sandy plains and the dune-fringed coast. Paran is bordered to the S by ranges of hills or isolated groups of hills. The central area consists of elevated sedimentary tablelands, collectively called the Jebel at-Tih. This is the great "desert of the wanderings," rising from 3,900 to 5,290 ft. (c. 1200-1610 m.) above sea level, terminating in the S in the high plateau of Egma. All this area, over half of the total drainage area of the Sinai Peninsula, is drained by the Wadi el-ʿArish and its seasonal tributaries into the MEDITERRANEAN. To the S of these tablelands are the crystalline mountains of southern Sinai, a deeply dissected landscape of gorges and mountain blocks. The eastern edge of the Sinai Peninsula is intensely broken up into dissected hills, trough faults, and wadi floors—a wild assortment of landforms impossible to describe in detail.

Paran thus has been associated with wild desert conditions of both relief and climate, astride the trade routes, and also as an inhospitable refuge to those seeking isolation. It was the district settled by ISHMAEL (Gen. 21:21) and crossed by the Israelites at the EXODUS (Num. 10:12; 12:16; 13:3-26).

From it the Israelites sent their spies into Palestine (13:26). DAVID fled into Paran after the death of SAMUEL (1 Sam. 25:1), possibly to the N sector of the area. Mount Paran (Deut. 33:2 and Hab. 3:3) could refer to any one of a number of prominent peaks in the mountains in the southern Sinai Peninsula.

parapet. This English word, referring to a structure that protects the edge of a platform or roof, is used especially to render a Hebrew word that occurs only once (Deut. 22:8; KJV, "battlement"). Houses in Palestine were built generally with flat roofs, which frequently were used as porches, so parapets were needed to prevent persons from falling off. Negligent homicide was to be avoided by the builder and owner. The English term is also used by the NIV in another context (Ezek. 40:13, 16).

Parbar. pahr´bahr. KJV transliteration of a Hebrew word that occurs only in a verse indicating one of the stations of temple gatekeepers: "At Parbar westward, four at the causeway, *and* two at Parbar" (1 Chr. 26:18; cf. also what may be the pl. form in 2 Ki. 23:11). The precise meaning of this term is uncertain, but it may be derived from a Persian word meaning "outer court, vestibule," so the rendering "court" (cf. NIV) is probably the most satisfactory.

© Dr. James C. Martin

parchment. The skin of a sheep (or goat) prepared in such a way that makes it suitable for writing; also, a MS made of this material. This term (derived from the name PERGAMUM, because this city had a reputation for manufacturing the product) is often interchangeable with *vellum*, although the latter refers more specifically to the fine-grained skin of a young animal. Because parchment was more durable and expensive than PAPYRUS, it was used for particularly important or valuable documents. When PAUL asked TIMOTHY to bring him his SCROLLS, he added the comment, "especially the parchments" (2 Tim. 4:13, Gk. *membrana G3521*), which many think is a reference to the apostle's personal copies of the OT Scriptures. See TEXT AND VERSIONS (OT); TEXT AND VERSIONS (NT).

pardon. See FORGIVENESS.

parenesis, parenetic. See PARAENESIS.

parent. See FAMILY; FATHER.

Parmashta. pahr-mash´tuh (Heb. *parmaštā⁾ H7269*, possibly from Old Pers. *fara-ma-ištha*, "preeminent"). One of the ten sons of HAMAN who were put to death by the Jews (Esth. 9:9).

Parmenas. pahr´muh-nuhs (Gk. *Parmenas G4226*, "steadfast," prob. short form of *Parmenidēs* or a similar name). One of the seven men appointed by the early church to serve tables and thereby relieve the apostles for other duties (Acts 6:5).

Parnach. pahr´nak (Heb. *parnāk H7270*, perhaps from Pers. *farnaces*, "success"). TNIV Parnak. Father of ELIZAPHAN; the latter was a leader from the tribe of ZEBULUN appointed to assist in dividing the land of CANAAN among the tribes (Num. 34:25).

Parnak. pahr´nak. TNIV form of PARNACH.

Parosh. pay´rosh (Heb. *par⁽ōš H7283*, "flea"). Ancestor of a family of 2,172 people who returned from the EXILE with ZERUBBABEL (Ezra 2:3; Neh. 7:8). Subsequently, a leader of the same family

named Zechariah, along with 150 other men, came up from BABYLON with EZRA (Ezra 8:3). Some of his descendants are mentioned elsewhere (Ezra 10:25; Neh. 3:25; 10:14).

parousia. See ESCHATOLOGY.

Parshandatha. pahr-shan´duh-thuh (Heb. *paršandātā⁾ H7309*, a Persian name of uncertain meaning). One of the ten sons of HAMAN who were put to death by the Jews (Esth. 9:7).

parsin. See MENE, MENE, TEKEL, PARSIN.

Parthians. pahr´thee-uhnz (Gk. *Parthoi G4222*). On the day of PENTECOST, some of the people who heard the apostles speak in foreign languages were Parthians (Acts 2:9). Parthia was the name of a Persian satrapy (see PERSIA) lying to the SE of the Caspian Sea and corresponding to the NE section of modern Iran. Originally, its inhabitants were the Parni, but in the middle of the third century B.C. they successfully rebelled against the SELEUCIDS and formed what came to be known as the Parthian empire. During the next century, under Mithradates I and II, their territory expanded greatly, from the Indus River to as far W as the EUPHRATES. The Parthians became a constant threat to the ROMAN EMPIRE and were not subdued until the time of TRAJAN (c. A.D. 116). Some have thought that the vision of the two hundred million mounted troops in Rev. 9:13-19 alludes to the dreaded Parthian cavalry.

partition, middle wall of. In Eph. 2:14 PAUL asserts that Christ has broken down the "middle wall of partition" (KJV; NIV, "dividing wall of hostility") that divided JEWS and GENTILES, and has made of the two one new people. Paul probably alludes here to a literal wall as a tangible symbol of the division between Jews and Gentiles—the wall in the TEMPLE area in JERUSALEM separating the court of the Gentiles from the courts into which only Jews might enter. On this wall was a notice in Greek and Latin, warning Gentiles to keep out on pain of death. In A.D. 1871 archaeologists who were excavating the site of the temple found a pillar with this inscription, "No man of another nation is to enter within the fence and enclosure around the temple, and whoever is caught will have himself to blame that his death ensues." Paul himself almost lost his life in the temple enclosure when at the end of his third missionary journey his Jewish enemies accused him of bringing TROPHIMUS the Ephesian past this barrier in the temple (Acts 21:29).

partridge. See BIRDS.

party. This English term, in the sense of an organized group taking one side of a dispute, is used a few times by the NIV and other versions to render Greek *hairesis G146* ("choice," but also "sect"). It occurs, for example, with reference to the SADDUCEES (Acts 5:17) and the PHARISEES (5:17). See SECT. The Greek term sometimes has a negative connotation, such as "faction" (1 Cor. 11:19 [NRSV]; Gal. 5:20) or even HERESY (2 Pet. 2:1).

Paruah. puh-roo´uh (Heb. *pārûaḥ H7245*, "happy"). Father of Jehoshaphat, who was one of SOLOMON's twelve district officers; ISSACHAR was the territory assigned to him (1 Ki. 4:17).

Parvaim. pahr-vay´im (Heb. *parwayim H7246*, meaning unknown). The place from which SOLOMON obtained gold for the TEMPLE (2 Chr. 3:6). The name is unknown elsewhere, but it is generally thought that it refers to some place in the Arabian peninsula, such as Saq el-Farwein (NE ARABIA) or Farwa (Yemen). It has moreover been suggested that Parvaim is an alternate form for SEPHAR (Gen. 10:30), which also is unknown, though it was probably in Arabia as well. (Cf. comments on OPHIR.)

Pasach. pay´sak (Heb. *pāsak H7179*, derivation uncertain). TNIV Pasak. Son of Japhlet and descendant of ASHER (1 Chr. 7:33).

Pasak. pay´sak. TNIV form of PASACH.

paschal. pas´kuhl. Adjectival form of Pasch (or Pascha), which in turn is derived from Greek *pascha G4247*, meaning "Passover." The NRSV and other versions render this Greek word with the phrase "paschal lamb" (NIV, "Passover lamb") in a passage

where PAUL says that Christ is "our Passover" (lit. trans.) that has been sacrificed (1 Cor. 5:7).

Pas Dammim. pas-dam´im. See EPHES DAMMIM.

Paseah. puh-see´uh (Heb. *pāsēaḥ H7176*, "one who hobbles, lame"). (1) Son of Eshton and apparently a descendant of JUDAH, though the precise genealogical connection is not given (1 Chr. 4:12).

(2) Ancestor of a family of temple servants (NETHINIM) who returned from the EXILE with ZERUBBABEL (Ezra 2:49; Neh. 7:51 [KJV, "Phaseah"]).

(3) Father of JOIADA; the latter was one of those responsible for repairing the Jeshanah Gate (OLD GATE) when NEHEMIAH rebuilt the walls of JERUSALEM (Neh. 3:6). Some have speculated that this Paseah may be one of the descendants of #2 above.

Pashhur. pash´huhr (Heb. *pašḥûr H7319*, possibly an Egyp. name meaning "son of [the god] Horus"). KJV Pashur. (1) Son (or descendant) of IMMER; he was a priest and the chief officer of the TEMPLE in the time of JEREMIAH (Jer. 20:1-6). When Pashhur heard about Jeremiah's predictions of the destruction of Jerusalem, he struck the prophet and had him put in the stocks for a day. Upon being released, Jeremiah strongly rebuked him and said that the Lord would give Pashhur a new name, MAGOR-MISSABIB, meaning "terror all around." He further announced that Pashhur and his friends would be carried into captivity to BABYLON and would die there.

(2) Son of Malkijah; he was one of the men that King ZEDEKIAH sent to inquire from Jeremiah as to the ultimate fate of the city (Jer. 21:1-2). This Pashhur was also one of a group—including GEDALIAH son of Pashhur, thus probably his own son—who complained to Zedekiah about the unfavorable predictions of Jeremiah (38:1-4); upon receiving the king's permission, they put the prophet in a dungeon (vv. 5-6). These incidents probably took place more than fifteen years after the events described above, under #1 (though some have speculated that the same man is in view and that Immer may have been an ancestor rather than the immediate father). Pashhur son of Malkijah is probably the same one who is included in the genealogy of ADAIAH son of

P

Jehoram, a priest who resettled in Jerusalem after the EXILE (1 Chr. 9:12; Neh. 11:12).

(3) Ancestor of a family of 1,247 priests who returned from Babylon with ZERUBBABEL (Ezra 2:38; Neh. 7:41). Some of his descendants are mentioned elsewhere (Ezra 10:22; Neh. 10:3). Some think he is the same as #2.

Pashur. See PASHHUR.

pass, passage. These English terms are used variously in the Bible versions to render a large number of Hebrew and Greek words, including the very common verbs *ʿābar H6296*, "to cross over" (e.g., Gen. 32:10 KJV) and *ginomai G1181*, "to become, happen" (esp. in the expression "it came to pass"; e.g., Matt. 7:28 KJV). Other examples are Hebrew *pāsaḥ H7173*, "to pass over" (Exod. 12:13 et al.) and Greek *parerchomai G4216*, "to go by" (Matt. 8:28 et al.). The KJV uses "passage" to render, for example, Hebrew *maʿbārâ H5045*, "a crossing," with reference to the fords of the JORDAN River (e.g., Jdg. 12:6).

passengers, valley of the. See TRAVELERS, VALLEY OF THE.

passion. This English term—which in modern usage means primarily "emotion, ardent affection," and the like—used to have other senses, including "suffering." The word is derived from Latin *patior*, "to experience, undergo, suffer" (pf. pass. *passus*). Similarly, the related Greek verb *paschō G4248* (aor. inf. *pathein*) communicates primarily the notion "to receive an impression, to undergo," so that depending on the context it can refer to good or evil happenings; in the absence of a modifying term, however, in the NT it consistently refers to a bad experience, thus, "to suffer." The most important and far-reaching expression is a phrase in the prologue to Acts that describes Jesus as presenting himself "alive after his passion" (Acts 1:3 KJV). Consequently the English word, especially when capitalized, can refer specifically to the last sufferings and death of CHRIST—the betrayal, arrest, trial, scourging, journey to GOLGOTHA, and crucifixion (see CROSS). The fact that the passion is mentioned in the opening of the Acts shows that it was the central core of the message taught throughout the apostolic period. In the patristic writers the concept of the passion became a central theme, and throughout the Middle Ages the art from the passion, the passion plays, and the Passionist Fathers expanded the importance of the concept as annunciated in Acts.

Passover. See FEASTS.

pastor. This English term (from Lat. *pastor*, "herdsman, shepherd"; cf. Vulg. Gen. 4:2 and often) is used by the KJV several times in Jeremiah (e.g., Jer. 2:8) and once in the NT (Eph 4:11). In all of these instances the reference is not to shepherds in the literal sense but to rulers or spiritual leaders. Modern English versions usually retain the term *pastor* only in Eph. 4:11, and this word has come to be one of the most common and preferred designations of Protestant clergymen. See ELDER.

Pastoral Letters. A common designation applied to three letters written by the apostle PAUL in the early 60s. Two of these epistles were addressed to TIMOTHY and one to TITUS, who were Paul's special envoys sent by him on specific missions and entrusted with concrete assignments.

I. **Authorship**. The author of these letters calls himself "Paul," using the identification, "an apostle" (1 Tim. 1:1; 2 Tim. 1:1; Tit. 1:1); in addition, he speaks of himself in a way that is consistent with the description of Paul found in Acts. In the nineteenth century, however, F. Schleiermacher rejected the authorship by Paul of one of these letters (1 Timothy), and F. C. Baur of all three. Baur had many followers, and today this rejection is rather common. The grounds on which it is based are as follows.

A. **Vocabulary**. Difference in vocabulary between the Pastorals and the letters generally recognized as Pauline must be admitted, but it has often been exaggerated. Of words found in 1-2 Timothy and Titus but not found in the other letters, only nine are common to the three Pastorals. Detailed study, moreover, has shown that the Pastoral Letters contain not one single word that was foreign to the age in which Paul lived and could not have been used by him. Besides, vocabulary always varies with the specific subject that is being discussed. Thus, in addressing Timothy and Titus, who were in need of good counsel with respect to their own task of imparting instruction, the frequent use of words belonging to the word-family of *teaching* is certainly not surprising. Other factors that may have influenced the choice of words are the character of the addressees, the apostle's age and environment, the progress of the church with its expanding vocabulary, and the not improbable use of secretaries.

B. Style. This argument is self-defeating, for candid examination of the actual facts clearly points to Paul as the author of the Pastorals. These three picture the same kind of person reflected in the others: one who is deeply interested in those whom he addresses, ascribing to God's sovereign grace whatever is good in himself and/or in the addressees, and showing wonderful tact in counseling. Again, they were written by a person who is fond of litotes or understatements (2 Tim. 1:8 ["do not be ashamed"]; cf. Rom. 1:16), of enumerations (1 Tim. 3:1-12; cf. Rom. 1:29-32), of plays on words (1 Tim. 6:17; cf. Phlm. 10-11), of appositional phrases (1 Tim. 1:17; cf. Rom. 12:1), of expressions of personal unworthiness (1 Tim. 1:13, 15; cf. 1 Cor. 15:9), and of doxologies (1 Tim. 1:17; cf. Rom. 11:36). It is clear that much of their style is definitely Pauline. Hence, many critics now grant that Paul may be the source of some, though not all, of their contents. But this theory does not go far enough in the right direction, for those who hold it are unable to show where the genuine material begins and the spurious ends. The acceptance of Paul's authorship for the entire contents is the only theory that fits the facts.

C. Theology. It is claimed that GRACE is no longer in the center, and that there is here an overemphasis on good works. The facts contradict this judgment. Is not grace the heart and center of such passages as 1 Tim. 1:14; 2 Tim. 1:9; Tit. 2:11-14; 3:5? It is true that in these three letters the fruit

Remains of a gate on the acropolis of Lystra, Timothy's hometown.

© Dr. James C. Martin

(good works) of faith is emphasized, but the reason is that the nature of faith and its necessity over against law-works had been fully set forth in the letters that preceded. The tree is first; then comes the fruit.

D. Marcionism. It is said that the Pastorals controvert second-century Marcionism (see MARCION), hence they cannot have been written by first-century Paul. The question is asked, "Does not 1 Tim. 6:20 refer to the very title of Marcion's book *Antitheses*?" This is shallow reasoning. Surely a merely verbal coincidence cannot prove any relationship between Marcion and the author of this verse. What the author has in mind is not Marcion's contrast between Christianity and Judaism but the conflicting opinions of those who speculated in Jewish genealogies. Other supposed allusions to second-century "-isms" are equally far-fetched.

E. Ecclesiastical organization. Do not the Pastorals reveal a marked advance in CHURCH government, far beyond the time of Paul? Some critics reason that the three letters evidence the beginning of pyramidal organization, where one BISHOP (1 Tim. 3:1-2; Tit. 1:7) rules over several presbyters (Tit. 1:5). In the Pastorals the terms *bishop* (overseer) and *presbyter* (ELDER) refer to the same individual, as is proved by 1 Tim. 1:5-7 (cf. 3:1-7; Phil. 1:1; 1 Pet. 5:1-2). With respect to age and dignity these men were called presbyters; with respect to the nature of their task they were called

P

Overview of 1 TIMOTHY

Author: The apostle PAUL (though many scholars consider the work pseudonymous).

Historical setting: Probably written after the apostle's first Roman imprisonment (thus c. A.D. 63, perhaps from MACEDONIA) to his spiritual son TIMOTHY, who was ministering in EPHESUS. (Those who deny Pauline authorship date the letter as late as the first decades of the second century.)

Purpose: To encourage and instruct Timothy in his pastoral responsibilities, especially with regard to sound teaching and matters of church organization and worship.

Contents: Warnings against heresy (1 Tim. 1); prayer and worship (ch. 2); church leadership (ch. 3); further warnings about false teaching (ch. 4); pastoring different groups within the church (ch. 5); final instructions (ch. 6).

overseers. From very early times the church had its elders (Acts 11:30; 14:23; cf. 1 Thess. 5:12-13). It is also very natural that Paul, about to depart from the earth, should specify certain qualifications for office, so that the church might be guarded against the ravages of error, both doctrinal and moral.

F. Chronology. It is maintained that the book of Acts, which records Paul's life from his conversion to a Roman imprisonment that terminated in the apostle's execution, leaves no room for the Pastorals, which presuppose journeys not recorded in Acts. However, Acts points toward Paul's release, not his execution (Acts 23:12-35; 28:21, 30-31); so do Paul's Prison Letters (Phil. 1:25-27; 2:24; Phlm. 22). There are strong arguments in favor of the view that the apostle experienced two Roman imprisonments, with ample room for the writings of the Pastorals after the first of these two.

II. Background and purpose. The biblical text itself helps us to identify the historical situation that led to the writing of these letters.

A. Common to Timothy and Titus. Released from his first Roman imprisonment, Paul, perhaps while on his way to ASIA MINOR, left Titus on the island of CRETE to bring to completion the organization of its church(es) (Acts 2:11; Tit. 1:5). At EPHESUS, Paul was joined by Timothy (possibly back from PHILIPPI; cf. Phil. 2:19-23). On leav-

ing for MACEDONIA, Paul instructed Timothy to remain in Ephesus, which was sorely in need of his ministry (1 Tim. 1:3-4). From Macedonia Paul wrote a letter to Timothy in Ephesus (1 Tim.) and one to Titus in Crete (Titus).

B. Further background and purpose of 1 Timothy. At Ephesus JUDAIZERS were spreading strange and dangerous doctrines (1 Tim. 1:4, 7; 4:7). Both men and women attended WORSHIP spiritually unprepared (ch. 2). To cope with that situation there was Timothy—*timid* Timothy. The letter's aims may be listed as follows: (1) to impart guidance against error (cf. 1:3-11, 18-20; chs. 4 and 6), including the need for proper organization and the right kind of leaders (chs. 3 and 5); (2) to stress the need of proper preparation and conduct (for both men and women) with respect to public worship (ch. 2); (3) to bolster Timothy's spirit (4:14; 6:12, 20).

C. Further background and purpose of Titus. The reputation of the Cretans was poor. True sanctification was needed (Tit. 2:11-14; 3:10). Gospel workers (such as ZENAS and APOLLOS, whose itinerary included Crete and who probably carried with them Paul's letter) had to receive every assistance. As to Paul himself, having recently met with Timothy, and the situation in Crete being critical, it is natural that he wished to have a face-to-face

Overview of 2 TIMOTHY

Author: The apostle PAUL (though many scholars consider the work pseudonymous).

Historical setting: Written during the apostle's final imprisonment in ROME (c. A.D. 66) to timid TIMOTHY, whose spirit may have been waning in the face of difficulties. (Those who deny Pauline authorship date the letter as late as the first decades of the second century.)

Purpose: To encourage Timothy as he experienced conflict and suffering in EPHESUS; to warn him regarding heresy; to ask him to come quickly to Paul, whose martyrdom is near.

Contents: Timothy's faith and responsibilities (2 Tim. 1); the nature of the pastoral ministry (ch. 2); opposing heresy and teaching sound doctrine (3:1—4:5); Paul's approaching death (4:6-22).

---

conference with Titus also. The purpose of his letter to Titus was (1) to stress the need of thorough sanctification; (2) to speed on their way Zenas the law-expert and Apollos the evangelist (3:13); (3) to urge Titus to meet Paul at NICOPOLIS (3:12).

D. Background and purpose of 2 Timothy. Emperor NERO, blamed for ROME's fearful conflagration (July, A.D. 64), in turn blamed Christians, who suffered frightful persecution. Paul was now imprisoned there a second time and he faced death (2 Tim. 1:16-17; 2:9). Luke alone was with him; others had left him, either on legitimate missions (CRESCENS, Titus) or because they had become enamored of the present world (DEMAS; 4:6-11). Meanwhile, soul-destroying error continued in Timothy's Ephesus (1:8; 2:3, 12, 14-18, 23; 3:8-13). The letter's purpose was, accordingly, (1) to urge Timothy to come to Rome as soon as possible in view of the apostle's impending departure from this life, and to bring Mark (see MARK, JOHN) with him, as well as Paul's cloak and books (4:6-22); to admonish Timothy to cling to sound doctrine, defending it against all error (ch. 2; 4:1-5).

III. Contents
A. 1 Timothy
Chapter 1: Timothy should remain at Ephesus to combat the error of those who refuse to see their own sinful condition in the light of God's holy law, while pretending to be law experts; by contrast, Paul thanks God for having made him, who regards himself as "chief of sinners," a minister of the gospel.

Chapter 2: Directions with respect to public worship; prayers must be made in behalf of all. Both the men and the women must come spiritually prepared.

Chapter 3: Directions with respect to the offices and functions in the church.

Chapter 4: Warning against apostasy; instructions on how to deal with it.

Chapters 5 and 6: Directions with respect to certain definite groups and individuals: older and younger men, older and younger women, etc.

B. Titus
Chapter 1: Well-qualified elders must be appointed in every town, for Crete is not lacking in disreputable people who must be sternly rebuked.

Chapter 2: All classes of individuals who compose the home-circle must conduct themselves so that by their life they adorn their doctrine.

Chapter 3: Believers should be obedient to the authorities and kind to all people, whereas foolish questions should be shunned and persistently factious people should be rejected; concluding directions are given with respect to kingdom travelers and believers in general.

P

Overview of TITUS

Author: The apostle Paul (though many scholars consider the work pseudonymous).

Historical setting: Written from Nicopolis (a city in W Greece), probably after the apostle's first Roman imprisonment (thus c. A.D. 63), to his spiritual son Titus, who was ministering on the island of Crete. (Those who deny Pauline authorship date the letter as late as the first decades of the second century.)

Purpose: To instruct Titus to complete the appointment of elders over the various congregations in Crete; to warn him of false teaching; to give instructions about Christian conduct.

Contents: Church organization (Titus 1:1-9); false teaching (1:10-16); pastoring different groups within the church (ch. 2); final instructions (ch. 3).

C. 2 Timothy

Chapter 1: Timothy must hold on to sound doctrine, as did Lois and Eunice, as well as Paul himself and Onesiphorus.

Chapter 2: Timothy must teach sound doctrine, which brings great reward, for the gospel is glorious in its contents; vain disputes serve no useful purpose.

Chapter 3: Timothy must abide in sound doctrine, knowing that enemies will arise, and that the Christian faith is based on the sacred writings.

Chapter 4: Timothy must preach sound doctrine, in season and out of season; he must remain faithful in view of the fact that Paul is about to depart.

pastureland. See SUBURBS.

Patara. pat´uh-ruh (Gk. *Patara G4249*). A port city of Lycia in SW Asia Minor, near the mouth of the river Xanthus. Because of its fine harbor, its maritime commerce, and its inland trade, Patara was a large city. Its importance may be judged by the fact that it issued its own coinage as early as the fourth century B.C. The city was said to have been founded by Patarus, the son of Apollo, and its temple and oracle of the god were famous. Modern Patara is a beach town in a national park, but many ancient remains can still be seen, such as the walls, baths, and a theater. (According to tradition, St. Nicholas was born in Patara.) The apostle Paul

reached Patara, via Cos and Rhodes, coming from Miletus on his final trip to Jerusalem. There he transferred to another ship, bound for Tyre (Acts 21:1-2).

path. The various words that may be rendered "path" or "way" (e.g., Heb. *ʾōraḥ H784* and Gk. *hodos G3847*) are used in the Bible not only with reference to a literal stretch of ground that has been trodden solid, but also figuratively to describe the course of human life and conduct. There are paths requested by Yahweh (Gen. 18:19; Deut. 9:16; 1 Ki. 2:3), but corrupted by sinners (Gen. 6:12). Samuel instructed the people in the good and the right way (1 Sam. 12:23). The iniquities of the Israelites are referred to as corrupted roads and paths (Isa. 59:7b-8a). Some passages speak of God's "paths" (Ps. 17:5; Isa. 2:3), but also of the "ways" of nations (Acts 14:16) and of individuals (e.g., 1 Ki. 13:33; 2 Ki. 8:27; 2 Chr. 11:17; 1 Cor. 4:17). Jesus contrasted the two "roads" (Matt. 7:13-14; cf. also Jn. 14:6; Acts 9:2; et al.). See also WAY.

Pathros. path´ros (Heb. *patrôs H7356*, from Egyp. *pʾ-tʾ-rśy*, "land of the south"; gentilic *patrusim H7357*, "Pathrusim" or "Pathrusites"). A geographical term referring to Upper (i.e., southern) Egypt, roughly the Nile Valley between Cairo and Aswan. This area, whose main city was Thebes, suffered isolation from the royal Egyptian dynasty in MEM-PHIS and the Nile delta beginning in the eleventh century B.C. Pathros is listed between Egypt and ETHIOPIA in Isa. 11:11 (the NIV renders, "Lower Egypt . . . Upper Egypt . . . Cush"). The term occurs elsewhere in juxtaposition to (Lower) Egypt (Jer. 44:1, 15; Ezek. 30:13-14), and it is further described as the Egyptians' land of origin (Ezek. 29:14). The Pathrusites are included in the Table of Nations as descendants of MIZRAIM (Gen. 10:14; 1 Chr. 1:12).

Pathrusim, Pathrusite. puh-throo´sim, puh-throo´sit. See PATHROS.

patience. In the OT, the notion of patience is expressed through certain idioms, especially *'erek 'appayim*, "long [i.e., slow] of anger," which is most often applied to God (Exod. 34:6 et al.), but occasionally also to human beings (Prov. 14:29 et al.). In the NT, the common word for "patience" is *makrothymia G3429*, "longsuffering" (e.g., Rom. 2:4; cognate verb *makrothymeō G3428*), but notice also the common noun *hypomonē G5705*, "patient endurance, perseverance" (e.g., 2 Cor. 1:6; cognate verb *hypomenō G5702*).

God's patient endurance of human rebellion extends to all humankind, and is evident today in that he still withholds his final judgment, "not wanting anyone to perish, but everyone to come to repentance" (2 Pet. 3:9; cf. Ps. 86:15). Since patience is exemplified in God, so it is expected in his children. Thus believers are exhorted "to live a life worthy of [their] calling" and to "be patient, bearing with one another in love" (Eph. 4:1b-2; Col. 1:11; 3:12). This is possible only as a result of the Spirit-filled life (Gal. 5:22; cf. Rom. 8:3-4). Christ's own endurance is the Christian's model (Heb. 12:1-2). One trial of the believer is living among sinful people and seeing them prosper in spite of their wickedness (cf. Ps. 37:1; 73:1-10; Prov. 3:31; 23:17; 24:1; Jer. 12). In addition, however, God chastens and tests those he loves to develop their faith and character (Heb. 12:5-13). This is for the believer's profit and is a part of the "all things" that work for his good (Rom. 8:28). The faith and patience entailed in bearing trials deepens the believer's experience, and the trials themselves are therefore to be received and borne with joy (Jas. 1:2-4). See also LONGSUFFERING.

Patmos. pat´muhs (Gk. *Patmos G4253*). An island off the SW coast of ASIA MINOR, about 35 mi. (65 km.) SW of MILETUS. Patmos is a mountainous island of irregular outline, measuring approximately 6 by 10 mi. (10 by 16 km.). The early history of

The harbor and modern town of Patmos. It was on this island that John wrote the book of Revelation.

© Dr. James C. Martin

the island is obscure, in spite of some topographical remarks in ancient authors. Not until the Christian era did Patmos assume an important historical role, especially in the religious sphere. It was to this place that JOHN THE APOSTLE was banished by the emperor DOMITIAN, and here he received his vision and wrote the Apocalypse (Rev. 1:9-11). See REVELATION, BOOK OF. Because of this, there rested upon the island a sort of religious aura throughout late Roman and Byzantine times, despite the fact that it was attacked and depopulated by pirates. The cave or grotto near Scala in which John supposedly lived is still pointed out to travelers, as well as the Monastery of St. John above the city.

patriarch. The father or head of a family, tribe, or clan. In the NT, the Greek word *patriarchēs G4256* occurs with reference to the most ancient ancestors of the people of Israel, primarily ABRAHAM (Heb. 7:4; in Acts 7:8-9 it refers to the twelve sons of JACOB), but in one passage is is used of King DAVID (Acts 2:29). The NIV and other English versions also use "patriarch" to render Greek *patēr G4252*, "father," when the reference is clearly to the earliest ancestors (Jn. 7:22; Rom. 9:5; 11:28; 15:8). While past scholars often tended to regard the Genesis accounts of the patriarchs as legendary, archaeological discoveries have confirmed the authenticity of many details in the narratives and have thrown much light on puzzling customs of the time, such as Abraham's taking SARAH's slave HAGAR as a CONCUBINE, his making his steward ELIEZER his heir, and RACHEL's carrying away her father's household gods (see TERAPHIM). Excavations at UR, where Abraham lived, reveal it to have been a rich commercial center, whose inhabitants were people of education and culture.

Patriarchs, Testaments of the Twelve. See PSEUDEPIGRAPHA.

Patrobas. pat´ruh-buhs (Gk. *Patrobas G4259*, prob. short form of *Patrobios* [cf. Lat. *Patrobius*]). One of several Christians in Rome that PAUL greets by name in his letter to the church there (Rom. 16:14). It has been suggested that possibly all five men mentioned in this verse were, or had been, slaves. The group apparently formed a household

church. It has also been suggested that Patrobas may have been a dependent of an influential freedman under NERO who was named Patrobius, but there is no evidence to confirm this connection.

Pau. pou (Heb. *pāʿû H7185* [in 1 Chr. 1:50, *pāʿî*], meaning unknown). Capital city of HADAD king of EDOM (Gen. 36:39; in 1 Chr. 1:50, the KJV and other versions, following MT, have "Pai"). Some have thought that the name is preserved in Wadi Faʿi, near the SW tip of the DEAD SEA, but the precise location is unknown.

Paul. pawl (*Paulos G4263*, from Lat. *Paulus*, meaning "small"; also known by his Heb. name, *Saulos G4930*, hellenized form of *Saoul G4910*, from *šāʾûl H8620*, "one asked for"). A leading apostle in the early church whose ministry was principally to the GENTILES. The main biblical source for information on the life of Paul is the ACTS OF THE APOSTLES, with important supplemental information from Paul's own letters. Allusions in the letters make it clear that many events in his checkered and stirring career are unrecorded (cf. 2 Cor. 11:24-28).

I. Names. Paul's Hebrew name was SAUL, and he is always so designated in Acts until his clash with BAR-JESUS at PAPHOS, where Luke writes, "Then Saul, who was also called Paul ... " (Acts 13:9). Thereafter in Acts he is always called Paul, the name the apostle himself uses in all his letters. As a Roman citizen he doubtless bore both names from his youth; having both a Hebrew and a Greek or Roman name was a common practice among Jews of the DISPERSION. The change to the use of the Greek name was particularly appropriate when the apostle began his position of leadership in bringing the gospel to the Gentile world (cf. the order "Paul and his companions" in 13:13 instead of "Barnabas and Saul" in vv. 2 and 7).

II. Background. Providentially, three crucial elements in the world of that day—Greek culture, Roman citizenship, and Hebrew religion—met in the apostle to the Gentiles. Paul was born near the beginning of the first century in the busy Greco-Roman city of TARSUS, located at the NE corner of the MEDITERRANEAN Sea. A noted trading center, it was known for its manufacture of goats' hair cloth, and here the young Saul learned his trade of tentmaking (Acts 18:3). Tarsus had a famous university; although there is no evidence that Paul attended it, its influence must have made a definite impact on him, enabling him to better understand prevailing life and views in the Roman Empire. He had the further privilege of being born a Roman citizen (22:28), though how his father had come to possess the coveted status is not known (see

A Roman street in Paul's hometown of Tarsus.

CITIZENSHIP). Proud of the distinction and advantages thus conferred on him, Paul knew how to use that citizenship as a shield against injustice from local magistrates and to enhance the status of the Christian faith. His Gentile connections greatly aided him in bridging the chasm between the Gentile and the Jew.

But of central significance was his strong Jewish heritage, which was fundamental to all he was and became. He was never ashamed to acknowledge himself a Jew (Acts 21:39; 22:3), was justly proud of his Jewish background (2 Cor. 11:22), and retained a deep and abiding love for his compatriots (Rom. 9:1-2; 10:1). Becoming a Christian meant no conscious departure on his part from the religious hopes of his people as embodied in the OT Scriptures (Acts 24:14-16; 26:6-7). This racial affinity with the Jews enabled Paul with great profit to begin his missionary labors in each city in the SYNAGOGUE, for there he had the best-prepared audience.

Born of purest Jewish blood (Phil. 3:5), the son of a PHARISEE (Acts 23:6), Saul was cradled in orthodox JUDAISM. At the proper age, perhaps thirteen, he was sent to JERUSALEM and completed his studies under the famous GAMALIEL (22:3; 26:4-5). Being a superior, zealous student (Gal. 1:14), he absorbed not only the teaching of the OT but also the rabbinical learning of the scholars. At his first appearance in Acts as "a young man" (Acts 7:58, probably around thirty years old), he was already an acknowledged leader in Judaism. His active opposition to Christianity marked him as the natural leader of the persecution that arose after the death of STEPHEN (7:58—8:3; 9:1-2). The persecutions described in 26:10-11 indicate his fanatical devotion to Judaism. He was convinced that Christians were heretics and that the honor of the Lord demanded their extermination (26:9). He acted in confirmed unbelief (1 Tim. 1:13).

III. Conversion. The persecution was doubtless repugnant to his finer inner sensitivities, but Saul did not doubt the rightness of his course. The spread of Christians to foreign cities only increased his fury against them, causing him to extend the scope of his activities. As he approached DAMASCUS, armed with authority from the high priest, the transforming crisis in his life occurred. Only an acknowledgment of divine intervention can explain it. Repeatedly in his letters Paul refers to it as the work of divine grace and power, transforming him and commissioning him as Christ's messenger (1 Cor. 9:16-17; 15:10; Gal. 1:15-16; Eph. 3:7-9; 1 Tim. 1:12-16). In Acts, LUKE provides three accounts of this experience, and these vary according to the immediate purpose of the narrator and supplement each other. Luke's own version (Acts 9) relates the event objectively, while the two passages in which Luke quotes Paul's account (chs. 22 and 26) stress those aspects appropriate to the apostle's immediate endeavor.

When the supernatural Being arresting him identified himself as "Jesus, whom you are persecuting," Saul at once saw the error of his way and surrendered instantaneously and completely. The

P

three days of fasting in blindness were days of agonizing heart-searching and further dealing with the Lord. The ministry of Ananias of Damascus consummated the conversion experience, unfolded to Saul the divine commission, and opened the door to him to the Christian fellowship at Damascus. Later, in reviewing his former life, Paul clearly recognized how God had been preparing him for his future work (Gal. 1:15-16).

IV. Early activities. The new convert at once proclaimed the deity and messiahship of Jesus in the Jewish synagogues of Damascus, truths that had seized his soul (Acts 9:20-22). Since the purpose of his coming was no secret, this action caused consternation among the Jews. Paul's visit to Arabia, mentioned in Gal. 1:17, seems best placed between Acts 9:22 and 23, which suggests that during this period Paul was ministering in the environments of Damascus (under Nabatean rule). Many speculate, however, that Paul felt it necessary to retire to rethink his beliefs in the light of the new revelation that had come to him; if so, the apostle came out of Arabia with the essentials of his theology fixed.

After returning to Damascus, his aggressive preaching forced him to flee the murderous fury of the Jews (Acts 9:23-25; Gal. 1:17; 2 Cor. 11:32-33). Three years after his conversion Saul returned to Jerusalem with the intention of becoming acquainted with Peter (Gal. 1:18). The Jerusalem believers regarded him with cold suspicion, but with the help of Barnabas became accepted among them (Acts 9:26-28). His bold witness to the Hellenistic Jews aroused bitter hostility and cut the visit to fifteen days (Gal. 1:18). Instructed by the Lord in a vision to leave (Acts 22:17-21), he agreed to be sent home to Tarsus (9:30), where he remained in obscurity for some years. Galatians 1:21-23 indicates that he did evangelistic work there, but we have no further details. Some think that many of the events of 2 Cor. 11:24-26 must be placed here.

After the opening of the door of the gospel to the Gentiles in the house of Cornelius, a Gentile church was soon established in Syrian Antioch. Barnabas, who had been sent to superintend the revival, saw the need for assistance, remembered Saul's commission to the Gentiles, and brought him to Antioch. An aggressive teaching ministry

"for a whole year" produced a profound impact on the city, resulting in the designation of the disciples as "Christians" (Acts 11:20-26). Informed by visiting prophets of an impending famine, the Antioch church raised a collection and sent it to the Jerusalem elders by Barnabas and Saul (11:27-30), marking Saul's second visit to Jerusalem since his conversion. Some scholars equate this visit with that described by Paul in Gal. 2:1-10, but Acts 11-12 reveals no traces as yet of such a serious conflict in the church about circumcision as the apostle relates in Galatians.

V. Missionary journeys. The work of Gentile foreign missions was inaugurated by the church at Antioch under the direction of the Holy Spirit in the sending forth of "Barnabas and Saul" (Acts 13:1-3). What is usually known as the "first missionary journey" began apparently in the spring of A.D. 48 with work among the Jews on the island of Cyprus. Efforts at Paphos to gain the attention of the proconsul Sergius Paulus encountered the determined opposition of the sorcerer Elymas. Saul publicly exposed Elymas's diabolical character, and the swift judgment that fell on the sorcerer caused the amazed proconsul to believe (13:4-12). It was a signal victory of the gospel.

After the events at Paphos, Saul, henceforth called Paul in Acts, emerged as the recognized leader of the missionary party. Steps to carry the gospel to new regions were taken when the party sailed to Perga in Pamphylia on the southern shores of Asia Minor. Here their attendant, John Mark, cousin of Barnabas (Col. 4:10), deserted them and returned to Jerusalem, an act that Paul regarded as unjustified (see Mark, John). Arriving at Pisidian Antioch, located in the province of Galatia, the missionaries found a ready opening in the Jewish synagogue. Paul's address to an audience composed of Jews and God-fearing Gentiles, his first recorded address in Acts, is reported at length by Luke as representative of his synagogue ministry (Acts 13:16-41). The message made a deep impression, and the people requested that he preach again the next Sabbath. The large crowd, mainly of Gentiles, who flocked to the synagogue the following Sabbath aroused the jealousy and fierce opposition of the Jewish leaders. In consequence Paul announced a turning to the Gentiles with their message. Gentiles formed the core of the church established in Pisidian Antioch (13:42-52).

Jewish-inspired opposition forced the missionaries to depart for ICONIUM, SE of Antioch, where the results were duplicated and a flourishing church begun. Compelled to flee a threatened stoning at Iconium, the missionaries crossed into the ethnographic territory of LYCAONIA, still within the

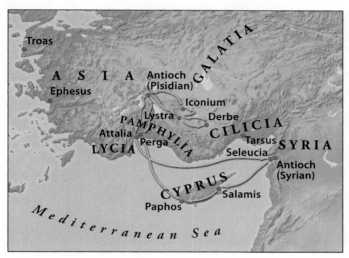

Paul's first missionary journey.

province of Galatia, and began work at LYSTRA, which was apparently without a synagogue. The healing of a congenital cripple caused a pagan attempt to offer sacrifices to the missionaries as gods in human form. Paul's horrified protest (Acts 14:15-17), arresting the attempt, reveals his dealings with pagans who did not have the OT revelation. TIMOTHY apparently was converted at this time. Fanatical agitators from Antioch and Iconium turned the disillusioned pagans against the missionaries, and in the uproar Paul was stoned. Dragged out of the city, the unconscious apostle was left for dead, but as the disciples stood around him, he regained consciousness, and reentered the city. The next day he was able to go on to neighboring DERBE. After a fruitful and unmolested ministry there, the missionaries retraced their steps to instruct their converts and organize them into churches with responsible leaders (14:1-23). They returned to Syrian Antioch and reported how God "had opened the door of faith to the Gentiles"

(14:27). That is a summary of Paul's message to the Gentiles: salvation is solely through FAITH in Christ.

The Jerusalem Council (Acts 15; Gal. 2:1-10) arose out of the tension produced by the mass influx of Gentiles into the church. This movement evoked the anxiety and opposition of the Pharisaic party in the church. Certain men from JUDEA came to Antioch and taught the believers there that unless they received CIRCUMCISION they could not be saved. This demand, contrary to Paul's doctrine of JUSTIFICATION by faith, aroused sharp controversy and resulted in the sending of Paul, Barnabas, and certain others to Jerusalem concerning this matter. Although some scholars reject the identification, it seems best to equate Gal. 2:1-10 with Acts 15. The differences are due to the differing standpoint of the two writers, Luke's account being historical, whereas Paul's was personal. In Acts there are apparently two public sessions (Acts 15:4 and 15:5-6), while Paul speaks of a private meeting with the Jerusalem leaders. After ample discussion of the problem, the conference repudiated the view of the Judaizers and refused to impose the law on Gentile believers, only requesting them to abstain from specific offensive practices. The decision was formulated in a letter and was sent to Antioch through JUDAS and SILAS as official delegates.

Their position vindicated, Paul and Barnabas continued their ministry at Syrian Antioch. Apparently during this time the incident of Gal. 2:11-21 occurred. The Jerusalem conference had left unmentioned the problem of the relation of *Jewish* believers to the LAW. As represented by JAMES, Judaic Christians continued to observe the Mosaic law, not for salvation, but as a way of life, simply because they were Jewish believers. PETER's decision to withdraw from table fellowship with Gentiles, lest he offend those of the circumcision, led him into inconsistency, which Paul recognized as undermining the status of the Gentile believer.

P

Paul's second missionary journey.

For the second missionary journey Paul and Barnabas separated because of their "sharp disagreement" concerning John Mark. Barnabas sailed to Cyprus with Mark, while Paul chose Silas and revisited the churches in Galatia (Acts 15:36-41). At Lystra, Paul added young Timothy to the missionary party, having circumcised him to make him acceptable for work among the Jews. Negative leadings closed the door to missionary work in ASIA and BITHYNIA, but at TROAS Paul received the positive call to MACEDONIA (16:1-9). The use of "we" (16:10) reveals Luke's presence with the group that sailed for Macedonia. The accounts of LYDIA's conversion, the deliverance of the demon-possessed slave girl, the subtle charges against and imprisonment of Paul and Silas, and the startling events that followed (16:11-40) are so vivid they must be the work of an eyewitness. Paul's demands of the magistrates the next morning established the dignity of the preachers and safeguarded the status of the young church.

Leaving Luke at PHILIPPI, the missionaries next began an expository ministry in the synagogue at THESSALONICA. With the synagogue soon closed to him, Paul apparently carried on a successful Gentile ministry in this city. A Jewish-instigated riot forced the missionaries to flee to BEREA, where a fruitful ministry resulted among the "noble" Bereans. When the work there was interrupted by agitators from Thessalonica, Silas and Timothy remained, but Paul, the leader of the work, was brought to ATHENS by some brothers (Acts 17:1-15). From 1 Thess. 3:1-2 it appears that Timothy came to Athens, but after a short time Paul sent him back to Thessalonica.

Distressed by the Athenian idolatry, Paul preached in the synagogue and daily in the marketplace. Drawing the attention of the Athenian philosophers, he was requested to give a formal exposition of his teaching. His appearance at the AREOPAGUS was not a formal trial. His memorable speech before the pagan philosophers (Acts 17:22-31) is a masterpiece of tact, insight, and condensation; but the people's contemptuous interruption at the mention of the RESURRECTION kept him from elaborating the essentials of the gospel. A few converts were made, but Paul must have regarded the mission at cultured, philosophical, sophisticated Athens with keen disappointment.

By contrast, the work at CORINTH—a city of commerce, wealth, squalor, and gross immorality— proved to be a definite success, lasting eighteen months (Acts 18:1-17). After finding employment at his trade with AQUILA and PRISCILLA, recently expelled from ROME, Paul preached in the Corinthian synagogue. Apparently he was depressed from his experience at Athens, but the arrival of Silas and Timothy lifted his spirits and a vigorous witness was begun (18:5). Timothy's report concerning the Thessalonians caused the writing of 1 THESSALONIANS. A few months later, because of further information about them, 2 Thessalonians was written. Unable to return to Thessalonica, Paul wrote both letters to meet the needs of his converts. Some would also place the writing of GALATIANS at Corinth, but Galatians is capable of a wide range of dating within the Acts framework. A successful work among the Gentiles resulted in the formation of a large church, the majority of the members being from the lower levels of society (1 Cor. 1:26). With the arrival of the new proconsul, GALLIO, perhaps in May A.D. 52, the Jews accused Paul of teaching an illegal religion, but the governor, declaring a religious controversy outside his jurisdiction, refused to judge the matter. His action in effect gave tacit governmental recognition to Christianity.

When he left Corinth, Paul took Aquila and Priscilla with him as far as EPHESUS, intending on his return to continue the profitable partnership with them there. Refusing an invitation for further ministry in the Ephesian synagogue, Paul hurried to Judea. He apparently visited Jerusalem and then spent some time at Syrian Antioch (Acts 18:18-22). Paul's subsequent departure from Antioch traditionally marks the beginning of the third missionary journey. It is convenient to retain this designation, but we should remember that with the second journey Antioch had ceased to be the center for Paul's activities.

Having strengthened the disciples in "the region of Galatia and Phrygia," Paul commenced a fruitful ministry at Ephesus that lasted nearly three years

Painting of the apostle Paul discovered in a monastic cave in Ephesus (c. A.D. 300).

© Dr. James C. Martin

(Acts 19:1-41; 20:31). His work in this city, one of the most influential cities of the east, placed Paul at the heart of Greco-Roman civilization. After three months of work in the synagogue, Paul launched an independent Gentile work, centering his daily preaching in the school of TYRANNUS for a two-year period. The Ephesian ministry was marked by systematic teaching (20:18-21), extraordinary miracles (19:11-12), a signal victory over the magical arts (19:13-19), and devastating inroads on the worship of ARTEMIS (19:23-27). Streams of people came to Ephesus for purposes of commerce, religion, or pleasure. Many of them came into contact with the gospel, were converted, and spread the message throughout the province (19:10). But the work was marked by constant and fierce opposition (20:19; 1 Cor. 15:32). The financially prompted riot led by DEMETRIUS brought the work of Paul at Ephesus to a close (Acts 19:23—20:1). At Ephesus Paul had inaugurated a collection among the Gentile churches for the saints in Judea (1 Cor. 16:1-4). Since its delivery was to mark the close of his work in the east, Paul was making plans to visit ROME (Acts 19:21), intending to go from there to SPAIN (Rom. 15:22-29).

While at Ephesus Paul experienced anxieties because of difficulties in the Corinthian church. In

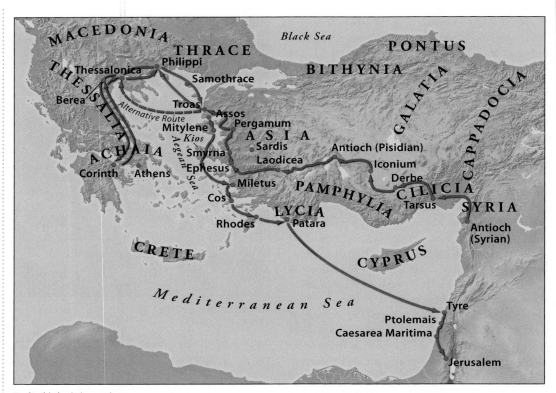

Paul's third missionary journey.

a letter, now lost (1 Cor. 5:9), he counseled them about their relations to pagan society. Apparently he also made a brief visit to Corinth (2 Cor. 12:14). The arrival of a delegation from Corinth with a letter from the church was the immediate occasion for the writing of 1 CORINTHIANS (1 Cor. 16:17-18; 7:1), in which Paul dealt with the evils plaguing that church. TITUS was sent to Corinth with plans for him to come to Paul at Troas. Paul found an open door at Troas, but anxiety because of the continued absence of Titus caused him to leave for Macedonia. The report of Titus, whom he met in Macedonia, relieved Paul's anxiety, and it was the immediate occasion for his writing of 2 Corinthians (2 Cor. 2:12-13; 7:5-16), which he sent back to Corinth with Titus (8:6, 16-18). After speaking "many words of encouragement" in Macedonia, Paul spent the three winter months in Corinth (Acts 20:2-3), where he wrote the letter to the ROMANS to prepare them for his coming visit and to secure their support for his contemplated work in Spain (Rom. 15:22-29; 16:1, 23).

Paul's plan to take the collection to Jerusalem directly from Corinth was canceled because of a plot on his life; instead he went by way of Macedonia, leaving Philippi with Luke after the Passover (Acts 20:3-6). Their church-elected travel companions waited for them at Troas, where they spent a busy and eventful night (20:7-12). Hoping to reach Jerusalem for Pentecost, Paul called the Ephesian elders to meet him at MILETUS. His farewell to them is marked by tender memories, earnest instructions, and searching premonitions concerning the future (20:17-35). The journey to Jerusalem was marked by repeated warnings to Paul of what awaited him there (21:1-16). Some interpreters hold that Paul blundered in persisting on going to Jerusalem in the face of these clear warnings, thus cutting short his missionary labors. The apostle, however, apparently interpreted the warnings not as prohibitions but as tests of his willingness to suffer for the cause of his Lord and the church.

VI. Paul the prisoner. Although cordially received at Jerusalem by James and the elders, Paul's presence created tension in the church because of reports that he taught Jews in the Dispersion to forsake Moses. To neutralize these reports, the elders suggested to Paul a plan to prove that he had no aversion to a voluntary keeping of the law (Acts 21:17-25). Always anxious to avoid offense, Paul agreed to their proposal. The act of conciliation apparently satisfied the Judean believers, but it caused Paul's arrest. Certain Jews from Asia, seeing him in the temple, created a tumult by falsely charging him with defiling the temple. Rescued from the Jewish mob by the Roman commander and some soldiers, Paul secured permission to address the Jews from the steps of the barracks. They gave silent attention until he mentioned his commission to the Gentiles, when the riot broke out anew (21:37—22:29). A scourging, ordered to force information out of him, was avoided by Paul's mention of his Roman citizenship. The commander's efforts the next day before the SANHEDRIN to gain further information about Paul proved futile. That night the Lord appeared to the discouraged apostle, commended his efforts at witnessing, and assured him that he would go to Rome. Informed of a plot to murder Paul, the commander sent Paul to CAESAREA under a large protective guard (23:17-35).

The trial before FELIX at Caesarea made it clear to this governor that the charges against Paul were spurious, but, unwilling to antagonize the Jews, he simply postponed a decision. Asked to expound the Christian faith before Felix and his Jewish wife DRUSILLA, Paul courageously probed their consciences by preaching "on righteousness, self-control and the judgment to come." Terrified, Felix dismissed the preacher but later sent for him frequently, hoping Paul would try to use bribery to secure his release. After two years Felix was summoned to Rome and left Paul an uncondemned prisoner (Acts 24:1-27).

With the coming of the new governor, FESTUS, the Jewish leaders renewed their efforts to have Paul condemned. When it became clear to Paul that he could not expect justice from the new governor, he used his right as a Roman citizen and appealed his case to CAESAR, thereby removing it from the jurisdiction of the lower courts (Acts 25:1-12). When Herod AGRIPPA II and his sister BERNICE came to visit the new governor, Festus discussed Paul's case with Agrippa, an acknowledged expert in Jewish affairs. The next day before his royal audience Paul delivered a masterly exposition of his position and used the occasion to seek to win Agrippa to Christ. Uncomfortable under Paul's efforts, Agrippa terminated the meeting but frankly declared Paul's innocence to the governor (25:13—26:32).

Paul was sent to Rome, perhaps in the autumn of A.D. 60, under the escort of a CENTURION named JULIUS. Luke and ARISTARCHUS accompanied him. Luke's detailed account of the voyage has the minuteness, picturesqueness, and accuracy of an alert eyewitness. Adverse weather delayed the progress of the ship. At MYRA they transferred to an Alexandrian grain ship bound for Italy. Futile efforts to reach commodious winter quarters at PHOENIX caused the ship to be caught in a hurricane-force storm for fourteen days, ending in shipwreck on the island of MALTA. After spending three months on Malta, the travelers journeyed to Rome in another Alexandrian grain ship. Paul's treatment in Rome was lenient; he lived in his own hired house with a soldier guarding him. Permitted to receive all who came, he was able

© Dr. James C. Martin

Road at Ephesus leading toward the harbor. Pillars indicate the traditional site of the school of Tyrannus, where Paul had discussions about the gospel (Acts 19:9).

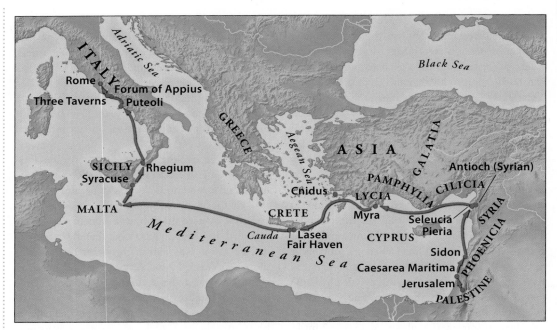

Paul's journey to Rome.

to exercise an important ministry in Rome (Acts 27-28). The Prison Letters—COLOSSIANS, PHILEMON, EPHESIANS, and PHILIPPIANS—are lasting fruit of this period, which afforded him opportunity to meditate and to write. (Not all scholars date these letters to the Roman imprisonment.)

VII. **Closing years.** Acts leaves the question of Paul's legal status unanswered, but there is strong evidence for believing that he was released at the end of two years. The amicable attitude of the Roman government in Acts favors it, the Prison Letters expect it, the Pastoral Letters require it, and tradition asserts it. Paul's subsequent activities must be inferred from scant references in the Pastorals. From their contents it seems clear that 1 Timothy and Titus were written before the outbreak of the persecution under NERO. After his release, perhaps in the spring of A.D. 63, Paul may have visited Spain, but eventually he traveled back to the east, visited Ephesus, stationing Timothy there when he left for Macedonia (1 Tim. 1:3). He left Titus to complete the missionary work on CRETE, and in writing to him mentions plans to spend the winter at NICOPOLIS (Tit. 1:5; 3:12). Some place the visit to Spain at this stage; if so, he may have been working there at the outbreak of the persecution by

Nero in the autumn of 64. Second Timothy makes it clear that Paul is again a prisoner in Rome, kept in close confinement as a malefactor (2 Tim. 1:16-17; 2:9). At his first appearance before the court he escaped immediate condemnation (4:16-18), but to Timothy he writes of no hope for release (4:6-8). He was executed at Rome probably in late 66 or early 67. Tradition says he was beheaded on the Ostian Way.

VIII. **Achievement and character.** Paul's achievements proclaim him an unexcelled missionary statesman. His labors firmly planted churches in the strategic centers of Galatia, Asia, Macedonia, and Achaia, while his plans for work at Rome and in Spain reveal his imperial missionary strategy. His foresight led him to select and train strong young workers to carry on the work after him. Paul was supremely the interpreter of the gospel of Jesus Christ, interpreted to the Gentile world through his labors and letters. It was primarily through his work that the worldwide destiny of Christianity was established and liberated from the yoke of legalism. His letters to various churches—formulating, interpreting, and applying the essence of Christianity—are vital to Christian theology and practice. His theology was rooted in his own revolutionary experience in Christ. Paul saw the human race's inability to attain to righteousness through their own efforts, but realized that God had provided a way of salvation, wholly out of grace and love, in Christ Jesus, available through faith alone. He also saw that the gospel made strenuous ethical demands on the life and conduct of the believer. The essence of the Christian life for Paul was union with Christ, whom he loved and served and for whose imminent return he yearned.

Physically, Paul did not present an imposing appearance, as is evident from 2 Cor. 10:10. Tradition pictures him as small of stature, having a decidedly Jewish physiognomy. That he had a rugged physical constitution seems plain from all the hardships and sufferings he underwent (11:23-27) and from his ability, amid his spiritual anxieties, to earn his own living through manual labor. He endured more than most men could endure, yet he keenly felt the frailty of his body. He was especially afflicted by "a thorn in [his] flesh" (12:7). The exact nature of the affliction can only be conjectured; attempts at identification have varied widely. Whatever its precise nature, his feelings of weakness made him constantly dependent on divine empowerment (2 Cor. 12:10; Phil. 4:12-13).

The many-sided personality of Paul is difficult to gather into one picture. He seems to embody polar extremes: bodily weakness and tremendous power, a keen intellect and profound mysticism, strongly attracting and furiously repelling people. Intellectually he was a man of outstanding ability, one of the world's great thinkers. He grasped truth at its full value and logically worked out its implications. But his subtlety of intellect was combined with practical good sense. He was a man of strict integrity, ever careful to maintain a good conscience. His life was characterized by a love of the truth that allowed no temporizing for the sake of expediency. Having understood his duty, he followed it unflinchingly, undeterred by possible consequences to himself. He was characterized by native zeal and ardor, giving himself wholly to his work. He was warm-hearted and affectionate, longing for and making strong friendships. He was humble, sincere, and sympathetic. He was by nature a religious man, and, already as a Jew but much more as a Christian, his faith dominated his life and activities. The secret of his unique career lay in his fervent nature as possessed and empowered by the living Christ.

Paulus, Sergius. paw´luhs, suhr´jee-uhs (Gk. *Sergios Paulos G4950 + G4263*). When PAUL and BARNABAS visited PAPHOS, the capital of CYPRUS, on their first missionary journey, they were called before Sergius Paulus, the Roman PROCONSUL, because this man of understanding "wanted to hear the word of God" (Acts 13:6-12). When ELYMAS, his court magician, attempted to turn him against the gospel, Paul through a miracle struck him with blindness. The incident so affected Sergius Paulus that he "believed, for he was amazed at the teaching about the Lord" (13:12; many have thought that Paul, then known as Saul of Tarsus, took his name from this first Gentile convert, but it is more likely that as a Jew of the DISPERSION he had always borne both a Hebrew and a Roman name). Sergius was an old Roman senatorial name, and it is possible that this proconsul of Cyprus was the Sergius Paulus mentioned in various extrabiblical sources.

pavement. See GABBATHA.

pavilion. This English word, referring to a large canopy, tent, or the like, occurs seven times in the KJV (2 Sam. 22:12), but rarely in modern versions (e.g., Job 36:29). It usually renders Hebrew *sukkâ H6109*, which most frequently refers to a "hut" or "booth."

pe. pay´ (from *peh H7023*, "mouth"). Also *peh*. The seventeenth letter of the Hebrew alphabet (פ), with a numerical value of 80. It is named for the shape of the letter, which in its older form resembles a mouth. Its sound corresponds to that of English *p* (following a vowel, it is spirantized, with a sound similar to that of English *f*).

peace. The word used in the OT (Heb. *šālôm H8934*) basically means "completeness" or "soundness." It can denote neighborliness (Ps. 28:3; NIV, "cordially") or well-being and security (Eccl. 3:8) or the reward of a mind stayed on God (Isa. 26:3). It is linked with honest dealing and true justice (Zech. 8:16; NIV, "sound"), and is a prominent feature of the coming MESSIAH (Isa. 9:6).

P

According to the NT, peace (Gk. *eirēnē G1645*) results from God's FORGIVENESS (Phil. 4:7) and is the ideal relation among believers (2 Cor. 13:11; cf. Matt. 5:23-24). Peace is a mark of serenity (Jn. 14:27) to be sought after (Heb. 12:14), and it summarizes the gospel message (Acts 10:36). It is a fruit of the Spirit (Gal. 5:22), will benefit those who practice it both now (Jas. 3:18) and at the second coming (Rom. 2:10), and is the opposite of disorder or confusion (1 Cor. 14:33). Peace is the presence of God, not the absence of conflict. The Christian who knows peace is charged to tell others so that it may come for them, too, through Christ, who brought, preached, and is our peace (Eph. 2:14-17).

peacemaker. One of Jesus' well-known BEATITUDES is, "Blessed are the peacemakers, for they will be called sons of God" (Matt. 5:9). Believers are to function as such, finding their example in CHRIST. Christ reconciled sinners to God in offering himself as a sacrifice to satisfy God's divine justice (Rom. 5:1; Col. 1:20; cf. Eph. 2:14-17). Through the proclamation of the GOSPEL, sinners are restored to harmony with God and act as peacemakers (2 Cor. 5:18-19). The ministry of RECONCILIATION that Christ started (Matt. 5:24; 18:15-17) and that he committed to his followers (2 Cor. 5:18), he will complete when he returns in his kingdom (Isa. 9:6-7; 14:7; 66:12; Ezek. 34:25; 37:26; Zech. 9:10). See PEACE.

peace-offering. See SACRIFICE AND OFFERINGS.

peacock. See BIRDS.

pearl. See MINERALS.

Pedahel. ped'uh-hel (Heb. *pĕdah°ēl H7010*, "God has redeemed"). Son of Ammihud; he was a leader from the tribe of NAPHTALI, chosen to assist in the distribution of the land (Num. 34:28).

Pedahzur. pi-dah'zuhr (Heb. *pĕdāhṣûr* or *pĕdâ-ṣûr H7011*, "the Rock has redeemed [*or* delivered]"). Father of GAMALIEL; the latter was the head of the tribe of MANASSEH during the wilderness wanderings (Num. 1:10; 2:20; 7:54, 59; 10:23).

Pedaiah. pi-day'yuh (Heb. *pĕdāyâ H7015* and *pĕdāyāhû H7016* [1 Chr. 27:20], "Yahweh has redeemed"). (1) Father of ZEBIDAH, who was the mother of King JEHOIAKIM (2 Ki. 23:36).

(2) Son of King JEHOIACHIN and father of ZERUBBABEL (1 Chr. 3:18-19). However, Zerubbabel is elsewhere identified as son of SHEALTIEL (Ezra 3:2; Hag. 1:1).

(3) Father of JOEL; the latter was an officer over W MANASSEH during the reign of DAVID (1 Chr. 27:20).

(4) Son of Parosh; along with "the temple servants living on the hill of Ophel," he helped repair the Jerusalem wall "up to a point opposite the Water Gate toward the east and the projecting tower" (Neh. 3:25). Some have thought that he may be the same as #5 or #7 below.

(5) One of the prominent men (not identified as priests) who stood near EZRA when the law was read at the great assembly (Neh. 8:4).

(6) Son of Kolaiah and ancestor of Sallu; the latter was one of the leaders from BENJAMIN who volunteered to settle in Jerusalem after the return from the EXILE (Neh. 11:7).

(7) A Levite who was one of the men appointed by NEHEMIAH as treasurers in charge of the temple storerooms (Neh. 13:13).

peddle. This English verb, meaning "to go from place to place selling wares," renders Greek *kapēleuō G2836*, which occurs only once in the NT (2 Cor. 2:17). The Greek verb originally meant simply "to drive a trade, sell by retail," but deceitful practices gave the term a pejorative sense, and so the KJV renders it with the English verb "corrupt." The NIV preserves the metaphor: "we do not peddle the word of God for profit" (NIV; similarly NRSV and other modern versions). In a parallel passage (4:2), Paul says, "nor do we distort [*doloō G1516*] the word of God." Both expressions convey the idea of falsifying, but the former includes the additional idea of deceit for worldly advantage. Peddlers often sold short measure or adulterated their wine with water. Paul distinguishes himself from religious hucksters of the word of God. He gave full measure of the whole counsel of God without ulterior motive.

peg. See PIN.

Pekah. pee´kuh (Heb. *peqaḥ H7220*, short form of PEKAHIAH, "Yahweh has opened"). Son of Remaliah and one of the last kings of Israel (2 Ki. 15:25-31). In the fifty-second year of the reign of UZZIAH, Pekah usurped the throne by murdering his predecessor, PEKAHIAH, and reigned twenty years (15:27). Incensed by the weakening of Israel under the leadership before him, caused by internal trouble and the heavy tribute paid to ASSYRIA, he formed a league with the Gileadites to resist the encroachments of Assyria. To strengthen his position further and accomplish his purposes, he allied himself with REZIN of DAMASCUS against JOTHAM king of JUDAH (15:37-38). The godly character of Jotham (2 Chr. 27) probably delayed the realization of this plot until Jotham's son AHAZ was on the throne. The details of this campaign are recorded in two places in the OT (2 Ki. 16; 2 Chr. 28). Perhaps the most important thing about this struggle was that it occasioned the important prophecies of Isa. 7-9. Finally Pekah became subject to the Assyrians (2 Ki. 15:29) and a short time later was murdered by HOSHEA. His sad epitaph is summarized in 2 Ki. 15:28: "He did evil in the eyes of the LORD."

Pekahiah. pek´uh-hi´uh (Heb. *pĕqaḥyâ H7222*, "Yahweh has opened," meaning possibly that he has opened his own eyes in compassion, or that he has opened a person's eyes [in the sense of either revealing truth to a person or bringing a child to life], or that he has opened the womb). Son of MENAHEM and one of the last kings of Israel, reigning c. 741-740 B.C. (2 Ki. 15:22-26). The character of his two-year reign is described in these terms: "Pekahiah did evil in the eyes of the LORD. He did not turn away from the sins of Jeroboam son of Nebat, which he had caused Israel to commit" (v. 24). In other words, Pekahiah continued the CALF WORSHIP instituted by JEROBOAM. During Pekahiah's reign, one of his officers, PEKAH son of Remaliah, was apparently active in GILEAD, and it is possible that the Israelites there and elsewhere in TRANSJORDAN opposed Pekahiah's rule. Pekah took fifty Gileadite warriors with him and assassinated Pekahiah (15:25). One may assume that Pekahiah had continued his father Menahem's policy of submission to ASSYRIA, and that anti-Assyrian parties in Israel had been looking for a suitable opportunity to gain control.

Pekod. pee´kod (Heb. *pĕqôd H7216*, from Assyr. *Puqūdu*). A place in SE Babylonia. Its inhabitants, known as the Puqudu in Assyrian and Babylonian sources, were an ARAMEAN tribe that had settled E of the TIGRIS River. They were conquered (at least temporarily) by the Assyrian kings TIGLATH-PILESER III, SARGON II, and SENNACHERIB. JEREMIAH mentions the lands of MERATHAIM and Pekod in his prophecy against BABYLON (Jer. 50:21). Ezekiel includes Pekod along with the Babylonians and others among the lovers of Oholibah (i.e., Jerusalem; see OHOLAH AND OHOLIBAH) who will turn and come against her (Ezek. 23:22).

Pelaiah. pi-lay´yuh (Heb. *pĕlā’yâ H7102* and *pĕlāyâ H7126*, "Yahweh has done a wondrous thing"). (1) Son of Elioenai and postexilic descendant of DAVID (1 Chr. 3:24).

(2) One of the LEVITES who assisted EZRA in instructing the people concerning the law (Neh. 8:7) and who affixed their seals to NEHEMIAH's covenant (10:10).

Pelaliah. pel´uh-li´uh (Heb. *pĕlalyâ H7139*, "Yahweh has intervened [*or* interceded]"). Son of Amzi and grandfather of a priest named Adaiah; the latter was a priest and head of family who returned to Jerusalem after the EXILE (Neh. 11:12).

Pelatiah. pel´uh-ti´uh (Heb. *pĕlatyāhû H7125* and *pĕlatyâ H7124*, "Yahweh has delivered"). (1) Son of Hananiah, grandson of ZERUBBABEL, and descendant of SOLOMON (1 Chr. 3:21).

(2) Son of Ishi and descendant of SIMEON during the reign of HEZEKIAH; Pelatiah and his brothers led 500 Simeonites in an invasion of SEIR and wiped out the AMALEKITES (1 Chr. 4:42-43).

(3) One of the leaders of the people who sealed the covenant under NEHEMIAH (Neh. 10:22).

(4) Son of Benaiah; he and Jaazaniah son of Azzur were leaders of the people in JERUSALEM at the time of the EXILE, and EZEKIEL was commanded to prophesy against their sin (Ezek. 11:1). While the prophet was speaking, Pelatiah died (v. 13).

P

Peleg. pee´lig (Heb. *peleg H7105*, derivation disputed, but by popular etymology, "division"; Gk. *Phalek G5744*). Son of EBER and descendant of SHEM (Gen. 10:25; 11:16-19; 1 Chr. 1:19, 25); included in Luke's GENEALOGY OF JESUS CHRIST (Lk. 3:35 [KJV, "Phalec"]). According to the biblical text, Peleg received his name "because in his time the earth was divided [verb *pālag H7103* niphal, 'to be separated']" (Gen. 10:25; 1 Chr. 1:19), apparently a reference to the dispersion of the peoples on the earth when the Tower of BABEL was built (Gen. 11:1-9). The text also seems to suggest that with the sons of Eber there is a dividing line among the descendants of Shem: the line of Peleg leads to ABRAHAM, whereas the line of JOKTAN (10:26-30) is the last group mentioned before the story of Babel.

Pelet. pee´lit (Heb. *peleṭ H7118*, "deliverance, escape"). (1) Son of Jahdai, included in the genealogy of CALEB (1 Chr. 2:47). See comments under JAHDAI.

(2) Son of Azmaveth; he and his brother Jeziel are listed among the warriors, kinsmen of SAUL, who joined with DAVID when the latter took refuge at ZIKLAG (1 Chr. 12:3).

Peleth. pee´lith (Heb. *peleth H7150*, meaning unknown, but possibly derived from an Egyptian place name). (1) Descendant of REUBEN and father of ON; the latter was one of the Reubenites who joined KORAH in his rebellion against MOSES (Num. 16:1). On the basis of other data (e.g., 26:8), some scholars emend "Eliab, and On son of Peleth" to read "Eliab son of Pallu" (or the like); PALLU was a son of Reuben.

(2) Son of Jonathan and descendant of JUDAH through JERAHMEEL (1 Chr. 2:33).

Pelethite. pel´uh-thit (Heb. *pĕlēti H7152*, derivation uncertain, perhaps related to *pĕlišti H7149*, "Philistine"). The Pelethites were a people group that possibly should be identified with the PHILISTINES or perhaps with a particular subgroup within this nationality. See further discussion under KERETHITE.

pelican. See BIRDS.

Pella. pel´uh (Gk. *Pella*). A city of the DECAPOLIS in TRANSJORDAN (modern Ṭabaqat Faḥil). Although not mentioned in either the OT or the NT, the city had a long history and is of significance for biblical studies. Pella lies among rugged hills and sharp valleys, about 2.5 mi. (4 km.) E of the JORDAN River and 17 mi. (27 km.) S of the Sea of Galilee. Pella stood on two mounds, separated by Wadi Jirm; the large oval mound to the N of the wadi is the location of the majority of ancient habitation and archaeological investigation. A spring, which supported the ancient civilizations in the area, still flows into the wadi. The town had a number of names but became *Pella*, after ALEXANDER THE GREAT's birthplace and the capital of MACEDONIA, when Alexander conquered the area about 332 B.C. In 63 B.C. it came under the control of ROME with the conquests of Pompey, who made it one of ten semi-independent Hellenistic cities that constituted the DECAPOLIS; as such, it may have been visited by Jesus (Mk. 7:31). Several writers indicate that Jerusalem Christians, apparently remembering Jesus' warning (13:14-16), fled to Pella during the war with Rome in A.D. 66-70. Although some writers have questioned the historicity of the flight to Pella, the city evidently maintained a role in ancient Christianity. An early Christian era sarcophagus found in a church in the W part of Pella may be a relic of the first Christians' stay in the city. Remains of Byzantine churches and monasteries throughout the general area, including a large church complex in Pella itself, indicate an on-going Christian presence there.

Pelonite. pel´uh-nit (Heb. *pĕlônî H7113*, gentilic form apparently related to *pĕlōnî H7141*, meaning "a certain one"). A designation applied to two of DAVID's mighty warriors, Helez (1 Chr. 11:27; 27:10) and Ahijah (27:10). Because no family or place is known to have the name Pelon, these passages are problematic. See comments under HELEZ #1 and AHIJAH #2.

Pelusium. pi-loo´see-uhm (Lat. name from Gk. *Pēlousion*; known in the Heb. OT as *sîn H6096*, from the Egyptian name, prob. *śwn* or *śyn*). KJV Sin. A city at the NE extremity of the NILE delta, very close to the MEDITERRANEAN (modern Tell el-Farama). Though noted in antiquity for its flax and wine, the city acquired military importance as a frontier fortress facing PALESTINE. EZEKIEL called it the "stronghold of Egypt," but prophesied that it would "writhe in agony" (Ezek. 30:15-16). It was the site of numerous battles. In 525 B.C. Cambyses defeated the Egyptians nearby and made Egypt a Persian province. In 343 it was held by ARTAXERXES, and a decade later by ALEXANDER THE GREAT. In 169 it was seized by ANTIOCHUS IV, and a century later Gabinius and Marc Antony captured it for the Romans. In 30 B.C. it was occupied by the young Octavian (see AUGUSTUS) in his campaign against Antony. During the ROMAN EMPIRE the city was an important station on the route to the RED SEA.

pen. In the sense "implement for writing," the term *pen* is the translation of Hebrew ʿēṭ *H6485*, referring to a stylus with a hard point (e.g., Ps. 45:1; Jer. 17:1), and of Greek *kalamos G2812* (only 3 Jn. 13 in this sense). See WRITING. For the meaning "enclosure," see FOLD.

pence. Plural of *penny*, which is used in the KJV with reference to a denarius. See MONEY.

pendant. See DRESS.

Peniel. pen´ee-uhl. See PENUEL (PLACE).

Peninnah. pi-nin´uh (Heb. *pĕninnâ H7166*, possibly "ruby" or other reddish jewel). Wife of ELKANAH the Ephraimite, and rival of his other wife, HANNAH (1 Sam. 1:2, 4). Peninnah taunted Hannah because the latter had no children (vv. 6-7). Hannah prayed for a child, and the Lord answered her prayer by giving her SAMUEL (vv. 10-20).

penknife. See KNIFE.

penny. See MONEY.

Pentateuch. pen´tuh-tyook (Gk. *Pentateuchos*, from *pente*, "five," and *teuchos*, "book, volume"). A term applied to the first five books of the Bible—Genesis, Exodus, Leviticus, Numbers, and Deuteronomy. It corresponds to one of the meanings of the Hebrew word TORAH (Law). These five books, whose canonicity has never been called into ques-

tion by the Jews, Protestants, or Catholics, head the list of the OT canon (see CANONICITY). As a literary unit they provide the background for the OT as well as the NT. Chronologically the Pentateuch covers the period of time from the CREATION to the end of the Mosaic era.

The book of GENESIS begins with an account of creation but soon narrows its interest to the human race. ADAM and EVE were entrusted with the responsibility of caring for the world about them, but forfeited their privilege through disobedience and fell into SIN. Subsequent generations became so wicked that the entire human race, except NOAH and his family, was destroyed (see FLOOD, THE). When the new civilization degenerated, God chose to fulfill his promises of redemption through ABRAHAM. From Adam to Abraham represents a long period of time, for which the genealogical lists in Gen. 5 and 10 hardly serve as a timetable (see ANTEDELUVIANS; GENEALOGY).

The era of the PATRIARCHS (Gen. 12-50) covers the events of approximately four generations—namely, those of Abraham, ISAAC, JACOB, and JOSEPH. Scholars generally agree that Abraham lived during the nineteenth or eighteenth century B.C., though some date him a century earlier and some considerably later. The contemporary culture of this period is much better known to us today through recent archaeological discoveries. In A.D. 1933 a French archaeologist, André Parrot, discovered the ruins of MARI, a city located on the EUPHRATES River. Here he found numerous temples, palaces, and statues and some 20,000 tablets—all of which reflected the culture of the patriarchal era. NUZI, a site E of NINEVEH, excavated beginning in 1925, yielded several thousand documents that likewise provide numerous illustrations of customs that reflect the patriarchal pattern of living as portrayed in the Genesis record.

After the opening verses of Exodus (see EXODUS, BOOK OF), the rest of the Pentateuch is chronologically confined to the lifetime of MOSES. Consequently the deliverance of Israel from Egypt and their preparation for entrance into the land of Canaan is the prevailing theme. The historical core of these books may be briefly outlined as follows: (1) Exod. 1-19, from EGYPT to Mount SINAI; (2) Exod. 19–Num. 10, encampment at Mount

P

The mountains of Sinai, with Jebel Katarina in the background (tallest peak). It was probably in this general region that Moses received the law.

© Dr. James C. Martin

Sinai, approximately one year; (3) Num. 10-21, wilderness wanderings, approximately thirty-eight years; (4) Num. 22–Deut. 34, encampment before CANAAN, approximately one year.

The Mosaic LAW was given at Mount Sinai. As God's COVENANT people the Israelites were not to conform to the idolatrous practices of the Egyptians nor to the customs of the Canaanites whose land they were to conquer and possess. Israel's religion was a revealed religion. For nearly a year they were carefully instructed in the law and the covenant. A TABERNACLE was erected as the central place for the WORSHIP of God. Offerings and SACRIFICES were instituted to make ATONEMENT for their sins and for expression of their gratitude and devotion to God. The Aaronic family (see AARON), supported by the LEVITES, was ordained to serve at the tabernacle in the ministration of divine worship. FEASTS and seasons likewise were carefully prescribed for the Israelites so that they might worship and serve God as his distinctive people. After the entrance into Canaan was delayed for almost forty years because of the unbelief of the Israelites, Moses reviewed the law for the younger generation. This review, plus timely instructions for the occupation of Palestine, is summarized in the book of DEUTERONOMY.

For study purposes the Pentateuch lends itself to the following analysis:

I. The era of beginnings (Gen. 1:1—11:32)
   A. The account of creation (1:1—2:25)
   B. The fall and its consequences (3:1—6:10)
   C. The flood: God's judgment on the human race (6:11—8:19)
   D. New beginning (8:20—11:32)

II. The patriarchal period (Gen. 12:1—50:26)
   A. The life of Abraham (12:1—25:18)
   B. Isaac and Jacob (25:19—36:43)
   C. Joseph (37:1—50:26)

III. Emancipation of Israel (Exod. 1:1—19:2)
   A. Israel freed from slavery (1:1—13:19)
   B. From Egypt to Mount Sinai (13:20—19:2)

IV. The religion of Israel (Exod. 19:3—Lev. 27:34)
   A. God's covenant with Israel (Exod. 19:3—24:8)
   B. The place of worship (Exod. 24:9—40:38)
   C. Instructions for holy living (Lev. 1:1—27:34)
     1. The offerings (1:1—7:38)
     2. The priesthood (8:1—10:20)
     3. Laws of purification (11:1—15:33)
     4. Day of atonement (16:1-34)

P

5. Heathen customs forbidden (17:1—18:30)
6. Laws of holiness (19:1—22:33)
7. Feasts and seasons (23:1—25:55)
8. Conditions of God's blessings (26:1—27:34)

V. Organization of Israel (Num. 1:1—10:10)
   A. The numbering of Israel (1:1—4:49)
   B. Camp regulations (5:1—6:21)
   C. Religious life of Israel (6:22—9:14)
   D. Provisions for guidance (9:15—10:10)

VI. Wilderness wanderings (Num. 10:11—22:1)
   A. From Mount Sinai to Kadesh (10:11—12:16)
   B. The Kadesh crisis (13:1—14:45)
   C. The years of wandering (15:1—19:22)
   D. From Kadesh to the Plains of Moab (20:1—22:1)

VII. Instructions for entering Canaan (Num. 22:2—36:13)
   A. Preservation of God's chosen people (22:2—25:18)
   B. Preparation for conquest (26:1—33:49)
   C. Anticipation of occupation (33:50—36:13)

VIII. Retrospect and prospect (Deut. 1:1—34:12)
   A. History and its significance (1:1—4:43)
   B. The law and its significance (4:44—28:68)
   C. Final preparation and farewell (29:1—34:12)

The authorship of the Pentateuch has been a major concern of OT scholars for more than two centuries. According to the consensus of mainstream scholarship, the Pentateuch was composed of four major documents, which actually reflected the historical conditions between Davidic and exilic times. These documents were then combined into one literary unit about 400 B.C. or even later. This Documentary Hypothesis originated in the observation that Exod. 6:2-3 appears to teach that the divine name, Yahweh (see JEHOVAH), was not revealed until the time of Moses, whereas the book of Genesis as we have it allows the knowledge of the name from Gen. 4:26 onward. Since it is unreasonable that a single author would use the name virtually from the start and then say that it was not known until much later, it became fashionable to divide sections of Genesis and Exodus into originally separate documents depending on whether the divine name was used or not. This process of

sifting out original documents was then extended to the rest of the Pentateuch.

In its classical form the Documentary Hypothesis held to four basic documents, for convenience named J (a document using the divine name Yahweh, also spelled Jahweh), E (a document using ELOHIM to refer to God), P (a document specializing in priestly material, genealogies, sacrifices, etc.), and D (Deuteronomy). Of these, J and E were the earliest (900 B.C. onward), D was the product of the reform of King JOSIAH (650 onward), and P was postexilic (400 onward). Some features of the text have been attributed to one or more sets of redactors. Individual scholars, moreover, proposed additional sources. The theory as a whole has been greatly modified in specialist circles based on the results of further archaeological, linguistic, literary, and theological research. While scholars continue to refer to J E D P, today it has become more fashionable to think of streams of tradition, many of them reaching back to Mosaic times.

The Pentateuch itself, from Exodus to Deuteronomy, registers a pervasive claim to be Mosaic, not necessarily indicating that Moses wrote every word of it, but in the sense that by far most of the material claims to come directly from him, however it was written down. Like all leaders of the ancient world, Moses must have had his own secretary, and it would be taken for granted that written records would be kept. Moses was himself a highly educated man, brought up in the most advanced and sophisticated society of his day. The book of Genesis, unlike Exodus-Deuteronomy, registers no authorship claim, though it should be considered a reasonable understanding of the evidence that whoever is responsible for Exodus onward is also responsible for Genesis. Genesis gives evidence of quoting source documents, and Moses would have been better placed than anyone else to have access to the archives of his people.

Pentateuch, Samaritan. See TEXT AND VERSIONS (OT).

Pentecost. pen'ti-kost (Gk. *pentēkostē G4300*, "fiftieth [day]"). The Greek equivalent for the OT Feast of Weeks (Exod. 34:22; Deut. 16:9-11), variously called the Feast of Harvest (Exod. 23:16) or the Day of Firstfruits (Num. 28:26), which fell on the fiftieth day after the Feast of the Passover. The exact method by which the date was computed is a matter of some controversy.

Originally, the festival was the time when, with appropriate ritual and ceremony, the FIRSTFRUITS of the grain harvest, the last Palestinian crop to ripen, were formally dedicated. The festival cannot therefore have antedated the settlement in Palestine. Leviticus 23 prescribes the sacred nature of the holiday and lists the appropriate sacrifices. Numbers 28 appears to be a supplementary list, prescribing offerings apart from those connected with the preservation of the ritual loaves. In later Jewish times, the feast developed into a commemoration of the giving of the Mosaic law. To reinforce this function, the rabbis taught that the law was given fifty days after the EXODUS, a tradition of which there is no trace in the OT nor in PHILO and JOSEPHUS.

It was the events of Acts 2 that transformed the Jewish festival into a Christian one. Some have seen a symbolic connection between the firstfruits of the ancient festival and the firstfruits of the Christian dispensation. In any case, the primary reference to Pentecost in the NT is in connection with the outpouring of the HOLY SPIRIT to dwell in the CHURCH (Acts 2:1). This event was in answer to the explicit promise of Christ (Jn. 16:7, 13; Acts 1:4, 14). Of the events of Pentecost recorded in Acts 2, much interest attaches to the manifestation of glossolalia (see TONGUES, GIFT OF). In his sermon on that day, PETER stressed that the bestowal of the Spirit was in fulfillment of Joel's prophecy (2:16-21, quoting Joel 2:28-32).

Penuel (person). peh-ny*oo*´uhl (Heb. *pĕnû´ēl* H7158, "the face of God"; cf. PHANUEL). **(1)** Son (or descendant) of HUR, descendant of JUDAH, and "father" (i.e., founder) of GEDOR (1 Chr. 4:4). Apparently, the town of Gedor was founded by both Penuel and JERED (v. 18).

(2) Son of Shashak and descendant of BENJAMIN (1 Chr. 8:25).

Penuel (place). peh-ny*oo*´uhl (Heb. *pĕnû´ēl* H7159 and *pĕnî´ēl* H7161 [only Gen. 32:30], "the face of God"). Also Peniel. A place on the JABBOK River E of the JORDAN where JACOB wrestled with the angel. Penuel is identified with modern Tell edh-Dhahab esh-Sherqiyeh, 8 mi. (13 km.) E of the Jordan on the Nahr ez-Zerqa (the biblical Jabbok). The NIV uses the variant form *Peniel* consistently to distinguish this place from PENUEL (PERSON).

Ancient Penuel was located in this area along the Jabbok River. (View to the E.)

© Dr. James C. Martin

Genesis 32:22-32 records what happened when Jacob stayed at the ford of the Jabbok on his way back from PADDAN ARAM. That night he wrestled with "a man" (v. 24; "the angel," according to Hos. 12:4) who finally blessed him and changed his name to Israel. "So Jacob called the place Peniel, saying, 'It is because I saw God face to face, and yet my life was spared'" (v. 31). A town was evidently built on the site, for the name appears again in connection with the judgeship of GIDEON (Jdg. 8). In his pursuit of the Midianite kings ZEBAH AND ZALMUNNA, Gideon sought help from SUCCOTH and Peniel, but these towns refused. Whereupon, when he captured the two enemy kings, he punished both towns. "He also pulled down the tower of Peniel and killed the men of the town" (8:17). Whether Peniel fell into ruin and was vacated at this time is not certain, but we are told that many years later King JEROBOAM "built up" the town (1 Ki. 12:25).

people. See GENTILE.

people of the east. See EAST, PEOPLE (CHILDREN) OF.

Peor. pee´or (Heb. *pĕ῾ôr H7186*, derivation uncertain). (1) A mountain in MOAB in the vicinity of NEBO (Num. 23:28), associated with #2 below. Here BALAK brought BALAAM to curse Israel. The precise location of this high point is unknown.

(2) The name of a Moabite deity (Num. 25:18). See BAAL PEOR.

Peraea. See PEREA.

Perath. pee´rath (Heb. *pĕrāt H7310*). According to the NIV and a few other versions, Perath was a place where JEREMIAH was instructed to hide a linen belt (Jer. 13:4-7). Most versions, however, understand the name as a reference to the EUPHRATES, which is the rendering of the Hebrew word elsewhere.

Perazim. pi-ray´zim (Heb. *pĕrāṣîm H7292*, "breaches" or "the ones that break through"). A mountain mentioned by Isaiah to illustrate God's rising against the scoffers in Jerusalem (Isa. 28:21). See BAAL PERAZIM.

perdition. This English term is used eight times in the KJV as the rendering of Greek *apōleia G724*, "destruction, ruin," but it is seldom used in modern versions (not at all in the NIV). The Greek term occurs almost twenty times in the NT, but it is used literally in only one context (Matt. 26:8 = Mk. 14:4, with reference to the waste of the ointment). Otherwise it is used in the NT in a metaphorical sense of the doom of the enemies of God. The beast of Revelation is described as going "to his destruction" (Rev. 17:8, 11; cf. Matt. 7:13; Rom. 9:22). Elsewhere, the perdition that awaits persecutors of the church is contrasted with the SALVATION of believers (Phil. 1:28; cf. 3:19). From the foregoing, it appears that the meaning is not annihilation, but the state of being lost—outside the enjoyment of God's salvation and eternal life, and under God's WRATH and JUDGMENT. See also PERDITION, SON OF.

perdition, son of. A phrase used to designate two men in the NT. CHRIST uses it in referring to JUDAS ISCARIOT (Jn. 17:12 KJV; NIV, "the one doomed to destruction"). PAUL uses it in 2 Thess. 2:3, applying it to the "man of lawlessness" (the ANTICHRIST). The phrase comes from the Hebrew custom of noting a certain trait or characteristic in a person and then referring to that person as the son of that trait. The term therefore would designate these two men as being the complete devotees of all that PERDITION signified.

Perea. puh-ree´uh (Gk. *Peraia*, from *peran G4305*, "beyond, on the other side"). The Greek term for TRANSJORDAN, that is, the land E of the JORDAN River. This name never occurs in the Bible (except in a textual variant at Lk. 6:17), but it is regularly used by JOSEPHUS and others to describe not only that general area, but more specifically the political district known as Perea. Thus in the statement that large crowds followed Jesus "from Galilee, the Decapolis, Jerusalem, Judea and the region across the Jordan" (Matt. 4:25), the last area mentioned refers to Perea.

Before the Israelite conquest, Transjordan was occupied by Moabites, Ammonites, and others. Reuben, Gad, and the half tribe of Manasseh inherited it in the original allotment. Being on the eastern frontier of the Promised Land, this area often was the first to suffer as a result of invasions from the E. During the intertestamental period, the Jewish (Hasmonean) ruler Alexander Jannaeus conquered and forcibly converted the Pereans to JUDAISM. After the death of HEROD the Great in 4 B.C., and during the life of CHRIST, Perea was controlled by HEROD Antipas. Its northern boundary was S of PELLA, while the southern boundary was MACHAERUS, a Herodian fortress halfway down the E shore of the DEAD SEA. AGRIPPA II, under Emperor NERO, ruled Perea until his death in A.D. 100.

NT scholars often speak of a "Perean ministry" during the last few months of Christ's life. It is said to begin with his departure from GALILEE (Matt. 19:1; Mk. 10:1), ending with the anointing by MARY in BETHANY (Matt. 26:6-13; Mk. 14:3-9). However, very few of the incidents recorded for that period of our Lord's ministry actually took place beyond the Jordan, so the designation

"Perean ministry" is somewhat of a misnomer. The BETHANY of Jn. 1:28 where Jesus was baptized is described as being "beyond the Jordan." Jesus certainly passed through Perea on his many journeys from NAZARETH to JERUSALEM in the years before his public ministry.

peres. pee´res. See MENE, MENE, TEKEL, PARSIN.

Peresh. pee´rish (Heb. *pereš H7303*, derivation uncertain). Son of MAKIR (by his wife MAACAH) and grandson of MANASSEH (1 Chr. 7:16).

Perez. pee´riz (Heb. *pereṣ H7289*, "breach," but original meaning of name disputed; gentilic *parṣi H7291*, "Perezite" [KJV, "Pharzite"]; Gk. *Phares G5756*). KJV Pharez (OT except 1 Chr. 27:3; Neh. 11:4, 6) and Phares (NT). Son of JUDAH by his daughter-in-law TAMAR; his twin brother was ZERAH. Popular etymology attributes his name to the manner of his birth (Gen. 38:28-30). In the genealogies Perez and his progeny (Hezron and Hamul) take precedence over Zerah (Gen. 46:12; Num. 26:20-21; 1 Chr. 2:4-5), and some leading families of Judah traced their lineage to him (1 Chr. 9:4; 27:3; Neh. 11:4, 6). Perhaps his real prominence derives from the fact that he was an ancestor of DAVID (Ruth 4:18-22). Perez is included in the GENEALOGY OF JESUS CHRIST (Matt. 1:3; Lk. 3:33). (See also PEREZ UZZAH; RIMMON PEREZ.)

Perez-uzza. See PEREZ UZZAH.

Perez Uzzah. pee´riz-uh´zuh (Heb. *pereṣ ʿuzzâ H7290* and *pereṣ ʿuzzāʾ H7290*, "the breach of Uzzah"). Also Perez-uzza. The name given to the place where God struck UZZAH dead for touching the ARK OF THE COVENANT. Both 2 Sam. 6:6-11 and 1 Chr. 13:9-14 record the sin of Uzzah. The ark was being transported on an oxcart, and as the procession reached "the threshing floor of Nacon" (or Kidon), Uzzah touched the ark to stop it from tipping. God killed him for that, and DAVID reacted in anger. The place was named Perez Uzzah "because the LORD's wrath had broken out [*pāraṣ pereṣ*, lit., breached a breach] against Uzzah." The site is unknown, but it must have been a short distance W of JERUSALEM (see comments under KIDON).

perfection, perfect. In the Bible, God alone, who lacks nothing in terms of goodness or excellence, is presented as truly perfect. Everything he is, thinks, and does has the character of perfection (Deut. 32:4; 2 Sam. 22:31; Job 37:16; Ps. 18:30; 19:7; Matt. 5:48). In the OT, the primary relevant words are the adjectives *šālēm H8969* (1 Ki. 8:61 et al.) and *tām H9447* (Cant. 6:9 et al.), as well as their cognates. The meaning is that of wholeness or completeness, and this quality often is ascribed to a person (Job 1:1, 8; 2:3; Ps. 37:37; 64:4). The words are used to describe the hearts of individuals (1 Ki. 8:61; 11:4; 15:3, 14; 2 Ki. 20:3; 1 Chr. 12:38; 28:9; 29:19; 2 Chr. 16:9; 25:2; Isa. 38:3), the quality of offerings (Lev. 22:21), God's way (2 Sam. 22:31; Ps. 18:30), the way of the righteous (Ps. 18:32; 101:6), the law of the Lord (19:7), and so forth. The main adjective employed in the NT is *teleios G5455* (e.g., Jas. 1:4). This term is employed to describe God himself (Matt. 5:48), God's will (Rom. 12:2), the function of spiritual discipline (Jas. 1:4), God's gifts (1:17), the "law of liberty" (1:25), the quality of love (1 Jn. 4:18), and persons (Matt. 19:21; Eph. 4:13; Phil. 3:15; Col. 1:28; 4:12; Jas. 3:2). In some passages the idea is clearly that of reaching the point of full growth or maturity (e.g., 1 Cor. 14:20; Heb. 5:14). It is almost universally recognized that the Bible does not support the notion of absolute ethical perfection, or sinlessness, in the present life. See SANCTIFICATION.

The theme of perfection is especially prominent in the letter to the HEBREWS. God is said to have made Jesus, the author of our salvation, "perfect through suffering" (Heb. 2:10). Again, "Although he was a son, he learned obedience from what he suffered and, once made perfect, he became the source of eternal salvation for all who obey him" (5:8-9). As a result, Jesus is "the author and perfecter of our faith" (12:2). This line of thought is evidently connected to the EXALTATION OF CHRIST (cf. 2:9), to the lack of perfection of the old COVENANT (7:11; 9:9; 10:1), to the perfection of the new covenant (9:11; cf. 8:13), and to the perfecting of believers (11:40). By his death and resurrection, Jesus brings in perfection, that is, eschatological fulfillment, which is even now experienced by his "brothers" (2:11).

perfume. See OINTMENTS AND PERFUMES.

perfumer. See OCCUPATIONS AND PROFESSIONS.

Perga. puhr´guh (Gk. *Pergē G4308*). Also Perge. The chief city of PAMPHYLIA. PAUL and BARNABAS passed through Perga twice on their first penetration of ASIA MINOR, both on the way into the territory and on the way out (Acts 13:13-14; 14:24-25). Perga stood some 8 mi. (13 km.) inland from the coast, a situation frequently found with cities in the E Mediterranean, where the Cilician pirates were a recurrent danger. The intervening tract of land formed a glacis and served as protection against a surprise attack by night. Not much is known about the early history of Perga, though archaeology has revealed its ancient prosperity and standing. The ruins are well known, standing as they do near the modern Murtana, some 11 mi. (18 km.) to the E of Antalya (ATTALIA), in the province of Konia. There is an acropolis, naturally formed by a rocky eminence, a position of vantage and defensive strength that must have attracted the first colonists. Surviving remnants of the lower city are chiefly Hellenistic. Surrounding fortifications and a fine city gate are visible, the whole complex elaborated and adorned by the benefactions of a noble Roman matron, Plancia Magna, to whom considerable epigraphic tribute is found. Curbed and channeled Roman shopping streets, over a chain wide and lined with Ionic columns, are characteristic of this period of city building. Outside is a Roman stadium and a theater cleverly built into a hillside. The seating capacity, some 12,000, is an indication of the population of the city in imperial times.

Pergamos. See PERGAMUM.

Pergamum. puhr´guh-muhm (Gk. *Pergamos G4307*). Also Pergamon, Pergamos (KJV), Pergamus. A city in the region of MYSIA, located 15 mi. (24 km.) from the Aegean Sea, with the hills around SMYRNA and the island of Lesbos in distant view, on a great humped hill that dominates the plain of the Caicus River. This eminence formed Pergamum's first acropolis (an upper, fortified part of the city). The name is also applied to a kingdom that had this city as its capital and that for a time covered most of ASIA MINOR. Pergamum was an ancient seat of culture and possessed a library

that rivaled ALEXANDRIA'S. PARCHMENT (*charta Pergamena*) was invented at Pergamum to free the library from Egypt's jealous ban on the export of PAPYRUS. When the last of the Pergamenian kings bequeathed his realm to Rome in 133 B.C., Pergamum became the chief town of the new Roman province of ASIA and was the site of the first temple of the CAESAR cult, erected to ROME and AUGUSTUS in 29 B.C. One of the seven letters in the book of Revelation is addressed to the Christian community in Pergamum (Rev. 1:11; 2:12-17).

An altar dedicated to Zeus at Pergamum. (View to the E, with modern Bergama in the background.)

© Dr. James C. Martin

In addition to EMPEROR WORSHIP, the cults to Asclepius and ZEUS were also endemic. The symbol of the former was a serpent, and Pausanias describes his cult image "with a staff in one hand and the other on the head of a serpent." Pergamenian coins illustrate the importance that the community attached to this cult. Caracalla is shown on one coin, saluting a serpent twined round a bending sapling. On the crag above Pergamum was a thronelike altar to Zeus (cf. Rev. 2:13), now in the Berlin Museum. It commemorated a defeat of a Gallic inroad and was decorated with a representation of the conflict of the gods and the giants, the latter shown as monsters with snakelike tails. To deepen Christian horror at Pergamum's obsession with the serpent-image, Zeus was called in this context "Zeus the Savior." It is natural that "Nicolaitanism" should flourish in a place where politics and paganism were so closely allied (2:15; see NICOLAITAN), and where pressure on Christians to compromise must have been heavy.

P

Perge. See PERGA.

Perida. See PERUDA.

Perizzite. per´i-zit (Heb. *pĕrizzî H7254*, possibly "of the open country," but perhaps a non-Semitic name). A collective term for one of the older population groups of PALESTINE that lived in the hill country of JUDAH. The name is frequently coupled with those of other peoples living in Palestine before the conquest under JOSHUA; for example, Perizzites and Canaanites (Gen. 13:7; 34:30; Exod. 23:23; et al.); Perizzites, Hivites, and Jebusites (Josh. 9:1; 12:8; Jdg. 3:5; et al.); Perizzites and Hittites (Exod. 3:8, 17; Josh. 24:11; et al.). The Perizzites are included among the groups that the Israelites were unable to exterminate, and whose descendants were made slaves by SOLOMON (1 Ki. 8:20; 2 Chr. 8:7; cf. also Jdg. 3:5). The older view that assumed the term to mean simply "villager" as distinguished from other nomadic peoples is now unacceptable. There is little question that a specific group or tribe is meant in the various biblical lists, but the origin of the term is uncertain (some think that it is an equivalent to AMORITE; others have suggested that the name is HURRIAN). To date the Perizzites are unknown in any but the biblical citations.

perjury. See OATH.

persecution. In its most common sense, this signifies a particular course or period of systematic infliction of punishment or penalty for adherence to a particular religious belief. Oppression is to be distinguished from it. PHARAOH oppressed the Hebrews; so did NEBUCHADNEZZAR. DANIEL and JEREMIAH were persecuted. Systematic persecution began with the Roman imperial government. Notably tolerant toward alien religious beliefs in general, the Romans clashed with the Christians over the formalities of EMPEROR WORSHIP. In that fact, according to some, lies the prime significance of the persecutions. Persecution began as a social reaction and became political later, a process that can be detected in the surviving documents. The state's policy of repression was intermittent and was visibly daunted by the growing numbers of the Christians.

A considerable body of literature has gathered around the difficult theme of the legal basis on which the authorities pursued their policy and on the incidence and severity of the persecutions themselves. Disregarding CLAUDIUS's anti-Semitism of A.D. 49 (Acts 18:2), in which the Christians were not distinguished from Jews, NERO must be regarded as the first persecutor. In 64 (Tacitus, *Annals* 15.38-44) this emperor used the small Christian community as a scapegoat for a disastrous fire in ROME, placing on the Christians the charge of arson that was popularly leveled against him. DOMITIAN's execution of Glabrio and Flavius Clemens in 95 and the exile of Domitilla for "atheism" and "going astray after the customs of the Jews" (Dio Cassius, *Roman History* 67.44) was probably anti-Christian action, incidents that strikingly reveal the spread of Christianity to prominent Roman citizens by the end of the first century. Pliny's famous correspondence with TRAJAN in 112 (Pliny, *Epistles* 10.96-97) reveals the state more moderate but still uncompromising in its action against Christians. Trajan's policy, laid down for Pliny in BITHYNIA, was followed by HADRIAN and Antonius Pius (117-161). At the close of the second century, with the death of Septimius Severus, a long period of relative peace followed that continued until 303, when Diocletian initiated the last short but savage period of persecution, described by Lactantius and Eusebius.

perseverance. This English term is used a number of times in the NIV to render Greek *hypomonē G5705*, "patience, endurance" (Rom. 5:3-4 et al.). The KJV uses it to render *proskarterēsis G4675*, which occurs only once (Eph. 6:18). See PATIENCE. The Christian doctrine of perseverance, however, is based not on particular uses of such terms but on explicit declarations of Scripture. In Jn. 10:29, for example, in a continuation of the passage on Jesus as the great shepherd, the Lord said: "My Father, who has given them to me, is greater than all; no one can snatch them out of my Father's hand." Paul wrote that "God's gifts and his call are irrevocable" (Rom. 11:29). And again he gave assurance to the Philippians: "being confident of this, that he who began a good work in you will carry it on to completion until the day of Christ Jesus" (Phil. 1:6; cf. 2 Thess. 3:3; 2 Tim. 1:12; 4:18). On the basis

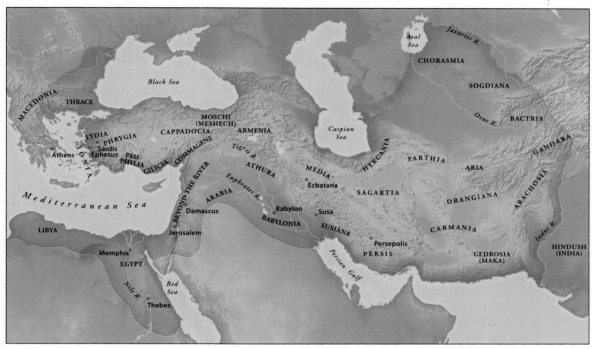

The Persian Empire.

of such promises, a strong position has been taken historically by those of the Reformed and Calvinistic tradition, which maintains that those whom God has elected and upon whom he has poured out his Spirit effectually will persevere to the end. Others object that some passages seem to allow for the possibility that believers may fall away (esp. Heb. 6:4-6; 10:26-27). See also APOSTASY; ELECTION; SANCTIFICATION.

Persia. puhr´zhuh (Heb. *pāras H7273*, gentilic *porsî H7275*, "Persian"; from Old Pers. *Pārsa*, later *Pārs* and *Fārs*). A country of SW Asia, to the E of Babylonia. In 1935 its name was changed to Iran (from the Avestan term *Airyana*; cf. English *Arian*). As a geographical term Persia may be taken to mean the Iranian plateau, bounded by the TIGRIS Valley on the W and S, the Indus Valley on the E, and the Armenian ranges and the Caspian Sea on the N, comprising in all something near one million sq. mi. (2.6 million sq. km.). The plateau is high and saucer-shaped, rimmed by mountains rich in mineral wealth, but with wide tracts of arid desert in the interior. The land lies across the old road

communications of Europe and Asia, a fact that has done much to determine Persia's ethnology and history.

It is seldom possible to separate history and geography, and the term Persia has signified both less and more than the geographical and general meaning just given. The original Persia was a small area N of the Persian Gulf, known as Persis, the modern Fars. It was a rugged area with desert on its maritime borders, its chief town known to the Greeks as Persepolis. The Medes lay to the N, Elam was on the W, and Carmania to the E. This small province was the original home of the Iranian tribe that finally dominated the whole country and founded the vast Persian empire, which at the time of its widest extent stretched from the Aegean Sea to the Indus River, and from N to S extended from the Black Sea, the Caucasus, the Caspian Sea, the Oxus, and the Jaxartes to the Persian Gulf, the Indian Ocean, and the cataracts of the Nile. This was the imperial power, described by Herodotus, that clashed with the Greeks at the beginning of the fifth century B.C. and that ALEXANDER THE GREAT overthrew a century and a half later. This,

P

too, was the imperial Persia of the OT, which rose on the ruins of BABYLON, which is seen in the life of ESTHER, and which formed the background of the events described in the books of EZRA and NEHEMIAH.

The Persians belonged to the people groups known as Indo-European (so called because most of the languages of Europe together with the Persian and Indic languages clearly descended from a common source). Migrations during the third and second millennia B.C. appear to have spread tribal groups who spoke a common language through the European peninsulas, into India, and into the northern Middle East. The picture is complex, but the Persians emerged to dominate the whole complex of the Iranian tribes. A ninth-century B.C. Assyrian inscription mentions Parsua as a northern country adjoining MEDIA. This may be the first historical reference to the Persians before their movement S into Anshan and Parsa, the Persis mentioned above. The Assyrian reference may catch the Iranian tribe in the process of its migration. In Persis, the Persians were at first subject to the power of their northern neighbors, the Medes, although ELAM, encroaching from the W, tended to form a buffer state between them. If reasons are sought for historical processes, it could have been the stimulus of Elam that caused Persian expansion.

Through Elam, Persis had contact with the developed civilizations of the EUPHRATES Valley. On the other hand, it may have needed no more than the emergence of a masterful personality to initiate the process. Such a person was CYRUS, second of that name from the ruling family of the Achaemenids. According to tradition, Cyrus was related to Astyages, king of Media. Rising against his relative, Cyrus threw off the Median hegemony and established the Persians as the dominant tribe in 549 B.C. Some form of governmental partnership appears to have been established, for Medes held privileged posts in the new administration. Cyrus then moved W to defeat the Lydian empire of Croesus in 545, and S to defeat Nabonidus of Babylon in 538. The conquest of Lydia gave Cyrus Asia Minor; the overthrow of Babylon made him master of the Euphrates River plain, Assyria, Syria, and Palestine. Thus arose the greatest W Asian empire of ancient times. It was indeed the first of the world's great imperial organizations, a foreshadowing of the system of ROME, beneficent and

Colorful depiction of a row of guards on the E gate of the Achaemenid palace at Susa (6th cent. B.C.).

© Dr. James C. Martin. Musée du Louvre; Autorisation de photographier et de filmer—LOUVRE: Paris, France. Photographed by permission.

humane when compared with the Assyrian empire, but too loosely held and geographically divided to survive. The conflict between SAMARIA and JERUSALEM, depicted in the life of NEHEMIAH, is an illustration of the indiscipline that could reign in remoter corners. Nehemiah was working by royal decree and yet found his work hampered by armed interference. EZRA's fear (Ezra 8:22) suggests similar pockets of anarchy.

Cyrus's great empire was organized by him and by DARIUS (521-486 B.C.), who succeeded him, after a period of revolt and dynastic trouble. Coming to terms with geography, Cyrus and Darius sought to combine a measure of local autonomy with centralization in a supreme controlling power, a difficult task even where communications are swift and efficient. The empire was cut into provinces, each under the rule of a satrap, who might be a local ruler or a Persian noble. With the satrap were military and civil officials directly responsible to the king, who was also kept informed on local matters by means of his "eyes," or his itinerant inspectors. This was an attempt to check maladministration in the satrapies and to anticipate challenges to the royal power. All provinces were assessed for monetary and manpower contributions to the central treasury and armed forces. An attempt was wisely made to preserve efficient forms of local government, and Greek city-states on the Ionian seaboard still functioned, with religion, language, and civic government intact. Inscriptions suggest that there were three official languages—Persian, Elamitic, and Babylonian. Darius further unified his empire by an efficient gold coinage, state highways, and a postal system, arrangements that became famous for their usefulness. The four books of the OT in which Persia forms a background (Ezra, Esther, Ezekiel, and Daniel) all illustrate the royal tendency to delegate special authority to individuals for specific tasks.

Cyrus and the Achaemenid kings were Zoroastrians, worshipers of Ahura Mazda, "the Wise Lord." The MAGI of the Medes appear to have been reorganized by Cyrus into a Mazdaist priesthood. Zoroaster taught that Ahura Mazda, together with his holy spirit, warred against an evil spirit, Ahriman. There was an element of messianism in the cult, for it taught that after the earthly life of a future savior, God will finally triumph over evil, and that all souls pass over the "bridge of decision" and enjoy eternal bliss, though some must first go through a purgatory of fire. Zoroaster stressed truth and mercy. Isaiah 45:7 is supposed by some to be a reference to Zoroastrian religion. The context is a tribute to Cyrus, and in contrast with the crude paganism of other peoples, the Persian monotheism may have appeared to the Hebrews to contain elements of divine insight. The notable favor shown to the religion of the Lord in the books of Ezra and Nehemiah may illustrate the same affinity from the other side. It will be useful in conclusion to list the Persian kings whose reigns have significance in OT history:

Cyrus, 538-529 B.C. 2 Chr. 36:22-23; Ezra 1 to 5 passim; Isa. 44:28; 45:1; Dan. 1:21; 6:28; 10:1.

Cambyses, 529-522 B.C. Some have suggested that Cambyses is the mysterious Darius the Mede of Dan. 5:31; 6:9, 25; 9:1; 11:1; others think this obscure person was Gobryas, governor of Media, who exercised authority for Cyrus in Babylon.

Gaumata, a usurper, who held brief royal authority until put down by Darius, 522-521 B.C.

Darius I (Hystaspis), 521-486 B.C., the great imperialist, whose seaborne attack on GREECE was defeated at Marathon in 490. He is known for his trilingual inscription at Behistun, famous in linguistic studies. This is the Darius mentioned by Ezra under whose protection permission was given for the temple to be built.

Xerxes I (Ahasuerus), 486-465 B.C. This is the mad king who in a mighty combined operation sought to avenge Marathon and whom the Greeks defeated at Salamis (480) and Plataea (479). Xerxes I is the monarch featured in the book of Esther.

Artaxerxes I (Longimanus), 464-424 B.C. It was this monarch who permitted Ezra to go to Jerusalem to restore the affairs of the Jewish community (Ezra 7-8), and who promoted the mission of his cupbearer Nehemiah, thirteen years later. See also Neh. 2:1; 5:14; 13:6.

Darius II (Ochus), 423-404 B.C. This king, who ruled over a period of disintegration, is possibly mentioned in Neh. 12:22 (cf. 13:6-11); according to some, the reference is to Darius III (Codomannus), the last king of Persia, overthrown by Alexander in 330.

Persis. puhr´sis (Gk. *Persis G4372*, "Persian"; names alluding to geographical areas were borne esp. by slaves). A woman member of the Christian church at ROME, to whom PAUL sent greetings (Rom. 16:12). The apostle thought highly of Persis, referring to her as "my dear friend … who has worked very hard in the Lord."

Peruda. pi-roo´duh (Heb. *pĕrûdāʾ H7243* and *pĕrîdāʾ H7263*, possibly "separate, solitary"). A servant of SOLOMON whose descendants returned from the EXILE (Ezra 2:55; Neh. 7:57 ["Perida"]).

pesharim. pesh´uh-rim. See PESHER.

pesher. pesh´uhr (Heb. *pēšer H7323*, "explanation, interpretation"). Plural *pesharim* (sometimes, less accurately, *pesherim*). This Hebrew term appears frequently in sectarian documents among the DEAD SEA SCROLLS, where it is almost always used in formulas such as *pšrw ʿl* ("its interpretation concerns … "), which serve to introduce the interpretation of the biblical text just cited. This kind

P

of language is characteristic of a number of biblical expositions, especially the Habakkuk Commentary (1QpHab), and modern scholars now use the term *pesher* with reference to the literary genre of, or the hermeneutical techniques found in, these documents. Often the term is used loosely of any Jewish interpretation that focuses on the fulfillment of biblical passages in contemporary events. See also MIDRASH.

Peshitta. puh-shee´tuh. The standard Syriac version of the Bible. See TEXT AND VERSIONS (OT); TEXT AND VERSIONS (NT).

pest. See ANIMALS.

pestilence. This English term, referring to a virulent epidemic or plague, is used frequently by the KJV and other versions primarily to render Hebrew *deber H1822*, which occurs almost fifty times in the OT (Exod. 5:3 et al.; the NIV usually prefers the rendering "plague"). It is often found in company with *famine* and other terms indicating judgment. Pestilence was so feared by the people that SOLOMON prayed for relief from it before it should come on Israel (1 Ki. 8:37). Relief could come only when the people repented, humbled themselves, and sought God's face (2 Chr. 7:13-14). Thus pestilence was viewed as a punishment on Israel for her disobedience and rebellion against God (cf. Hab. 3:5). The word is especially frequent in the prophecies of Jeremiah (17 times, e.g., Jer. 14:12) and Ezekiel (12 times, e.g., Ezek. 5:12), where pestilence is repeatedly referred to as a punishment threatened on Israel and Judah for their sin against God.

pestle. A rounded hand tool of wood or stone to pound or grind substances in a MORTAR (only Prov. 27:22).

Peter. pee´tuhr (Gk. *Petros G4377*, "stone"). An apostle who figures generally as the leader of the twelve disciples in the NT. The name Peter was given to him by Jesus (Mk. 3:16; Lk. 6:14; Jn. 1:42). He was earlier called SIMON, a common name among Greeks and Jews. Occasionally in the Gospels the two names are used together (Matt. 16:16; Lk. 5:8; Jn. 1:40; et al.). Twice, the more exact Semitic form SIMEON occurs (Acts 15:14; 2 Pet. 1:1). The Aramaic equivalent of Peter is Cephas (*kêpā'*, "rock," transliterated into Greek as *Kêphas G3064*). Aside from Jn. 1:42, the only occurrences of Cephas in the NT are in the Pauline letters (1 Cor. 1:12; 3:22; 9:5; 15:5; Gal. 1:18; 2:9, 11, 14; Paul apparently calls him Peter only in Gal. 2:7-8, although there is some variation in the MSS).

I. Background. Peter was a native of BETHSAIDA (Jn. 1:44), the son of a certain John (1:42; 21:15-17; called Jonah in Matt. 16:17). As a Jewish lad he would have received a normal elementary education. As a native of "Galilee of the Gentiles" he was able to converse in GREEK, while his native ARAMAIC was marked with provincialisms of pronunciation and diction (Matt. 26:73). The evaluation by the SANHEDRIN of Peter and John (see JOHN THE APOSTLE) as "unschooled, ordinary men" (Acts 4:13) simply meant that they were unschooled in official rabbinical lore and were laymen. He and his brother ANDREW followed the hardy occupation of fishermen on the Sea of Galilee, being partners with ZEBEDEE's sons, JAMES and John (Lk. 5:7). He was a married man (Mk. 1:30; 1 Cor. 9:5) and at the time of Christ's Galilean ministry lived in CAPERNAUM (Mk. 1:21, 29).

II. Training under Jesus. Of the second period of his life, from his first encounter with Jesus until the ASCENSION, the Gospels give a vivid picture. Simon attended the preaching ministry of JOHN THE BAPTIST at the JORDAN and, like Andrew, probably became a personal disciple of John. When he was personally introduced to Jesus by his brother Andrew, Jesus remarked, "You are Simon son of John. You will be called Cephas" (Jn. 1:42). This designation, like *Peter*, means "rock"; afterward more fully explained in its prophetic import (Matt. 16:18; Mk. 3:16), it came to be regarded as his personal name. (No other man in the NT bears the name Peter.) After a period of companionship with Jesus during his early Judean ministry (Jn. 1:42—4:43), Peter resumed his ordinary occupation.

With the commencement of Christ's Galilean ministry, Peter and Andrew, with James and John, were called by Jesus to full-time association with him to be trained as "fishers of men" (Mk. 1:16-20; Lk. 5:1-11). With the growth of the work, Jesus selected twelve of his followers to be his nearest companions for special training (Mk. 3:13-19; Lk. 6:12-16). In the lists of these twelve designated apostles (Lk. 6:13), Peter is always named first (Matt. 10:2-4; Mk. 3:16-19; Lk. 6:14-16; Acts 1:13-14). His eminence among them was due to his being among the first chosen as well as his native aggressiveness as a natural leader. But the other disciples did not concede to Peter any authority over them, as is evident from their repeated arguments about greatness (Matt. 20:20-28; Mk. 9:33-34; Lk. 22:24-27). While he was with them, Jesus alone was recognized as their leader.

The development of an inner circle among the disciples is first seen when Jesus took Peter, James, and John with him into the house of JAIRUS (Mk. 5:37; Lk. 8:51). The three were further privileged to witness the TRANSFIGURATION (Matt. 17:1; Mk. 9:2; Lk. 9:28) and the agony in GETHSEMANE (Matt. 26:37; Mk. 14:33). Even in this inner circle Peter usually stands in the foreground, but the fourth gospel indicates that his position of eminence was not exclusive.

Peter was the natural spokesman of the twelve. When Christ's sermon on the Bread of Life produced a general defection among his followers, Peter spoke for the twelve in asserting their loyalty to him (Jn. 6:66-69). Again, at CAESAREA PHILIPPI, when Jesus asked the twelve their view of him, Peter promptly replied, "You are the Christ, the Son of the living God" (Matt. 16:16). His confession of the messiahship and deity of our Lord expressed a divinely given insight higher than the current view, which regarded the Messiah only as a man exalted to the messianic office (cf. 22:41-46). His confession elicited Christ's prompt commendation and the further assertion, "You are Peter, and on this rock I will build my church" (16:18). By his believing confession Peter identified himself with Christ the true Rock (Isa. 28:16; 1 Cor. 3:11; 1 Pet. 2:4-5), thus fulfilling Christ's prediction concerning him (Jn. 1:42). He thus became a rock (*Petros*); and on "this rock" (*petra G4376*), composed of Peter and the other confessing apostles, joined by faith in Christ the chief cornerstone (Eph. 2:20), Jesus announces that he will build his triumphant CHURCH.

The account in Acts historically interprets Peter's use of the keys in opening the doors of Christian opportunity at PENTECOST (Acts 2), in SAMARIA

Peter's great confession of faith took place at Caesarea Philippi, in the vicinity of the Cave of Pan, regarded as the entrance to Hades.

© Dr. James C. Martin

(ch. 8), and to the GENTILES (ch. 10). The power of binding and loosing was not limited to Peter (Matt. 18:18; Jn. 20:3). But Peter was also the spokesman in attempting to dissuade Jesus from his announced path of suffering, thus proving himself a "stumbling block" (Matt. 16:23; Mk. 8:33).

Peter came into prominence in the Gospels also in connection with the matter of the payment of the temple tax (Matt. 17:24-27), his inquiry as to the limits on forgiveness (18:21), and his reminder to Jesus that they had left all to follow him (Matt. 19:27; Mk. 10:28). During Passion Week his activities were prominent. He called Jesus' attention to the withered fig tree (Mk. 11:21), and with three others he asked Jesus concerning his prediction about the temple (13:3). With John he was commissioned to prepare for the Passover (Lk. 22:8). Peter objected to the Lord's washing his feet in the upper room, but impulsively swung to the opposite extreme when informed of the implications of his

P

denial (Jn. 13:1-11). He beckoned to John to ask the identity of the betrayer (13:23-24) and stoutly contradicted Jesus when warned of his impending denials (Matt. 26:33-35; Mk. 14:29-31; Lk. 22:31-34; Jn. 13:37-38). In the Garden of Gethsemane, when chosen with James and John to watch with Jesus, he slept (Matt. 26:37-46; Mk. 14:33-42). Later, in fleshly zeal he sought to defend Jesus, and Jesus rebuked him for it (Jn. 18:10-11). He fled with the other disciples when Jesus was bound; but, anxious to see the end, he followed afar, was admitted (through John's action) into the court of the high priest, and there shamefully denied his Lord three times (Matt. 26:58, 69-75; Mk. 14:66-72; Lk. 22:54-62; Jn. 18:15-18, 25-27). The look of Jesus broke his heart, and he went out and wept bitterly (Lk. 22:61-62). That Peter witnessed the crucifixion is not stated (but cf. 1 Pet. 5:1).

On the resurrection morning he and John ran to the tomb of Jesus to investigate the report of MARY Magdalene (Jn. 20:1-10). Somewhere during that day the risen Lord appeared to Peter (1 Cor. 15:5). At his postresurrection manifestation to seven at the Sea of Galilee, John was the first to recognize the Lord; but, typically, Peter was the first to act. Following the group breakfast, Christ tested Peter's love and formally restored him by the threefold commission to feed his sheep (Jn. 21:1-23).

III. The early church. The third period in Peter's life began with the ASCENSION OF CHRIST. In the early days of the church (Acts 1-12), Peter appeared as the spokesman of the apostolic group, but there is no hint that he assumed any authority not also exercised by the other apostles. He suggested the choice of another to fill the place of JUDAS ISCARIOT (1:15-26), preached the Spirit-empowered sermon on Pentecost to the assembled Jews (2:14-40), and with John healed the lame man, the first apostolic miracle to arouse persecution (3:1—4:21). He was used to expose the sin of ANANIAS and SAPPHIRA (5:1-12), was held in high esteem by the people during the miracle ministry in the church that followed (5:12-16), and spoke for the Twelve when arraigned before the SANHEDRIN (5:27-41).

With John he was sent to Samaria, where, through the laying on of hands, the Holy Spirit fell on the Samaritan believers and Peter exposed the unworthy motives of SIMON the sorcerer (Acts 8:14-24). While on a tour through Judea, Peter healed AENEAS and raised DORCAS from the dead (9:32-43). Through a divinely given vision at JOPPA, Peter was prepared and commissioned to preach the gospel to CORNELIUS at CAESAREA, thus opening the door to the Gentiles (10:1-48). This brought on him the criticism of the circumcision party in Jerusalem (11:1-18). During the persecution of the church by AGRIPPA I in A.D. 44, Peter escaped death by a miraculous deliverance from prison (12:1-19).

IV. His later life. With the opening of the door to the Gentiles and the spread of Christianity, Peter receded into the background and PAUL became prominent as the apostle to the Gentiles. In the Acts narrative Peter is last mentioned in connection with the Jerusalem conference, where he championed the liberty of the Gentiles (Acts 15:6-11, 14). The remaining NT references to Peter are scanty. Paul records a visit to Syrian Antioch, where his inconsistent conduct evoked a public rebuke (Gal. 2:11-21). From 1 Cor. 9:5 it appears that Peter traveled widely, taking his wife with him, doubtless in Jewish evangelism (cf. Gal. 2:9).

Nothing further is heard of Peter until the writing of the two letters that bear his name, apparently written from ROME. In the first letter, addressed to believers in five provinces in Asia Minor, the shepherd-heart of Peter sought to fortify the saints in their sufferings for Christ (see PETER, FIRST LETTER OF), while in the second he warns against dangers from within (see PETER, SECOND LETTER OF). A final NT reference to the closing years of Peter's life is found in Jn. 21:18-19. John's interpretation of Christ's prediction makes it clear that the reference is to Peter's violent death. Beyond this the NT is silent about him.

Tradition uniformly asserts that Peter went to Rome, that he labored there, and that in his old age suffered martyrdom under NERO. The embellished tradition that he was bishop of Rome for twenty-five years is contrary to all NT evidence. He apparently came to Rome shortly after Paul's release from his first imprisonment there, but the evidence is ambiguous.

V. His character. The personality of Peter is one of the most vividly drawn and charming in the NT. His sheer humanness has made him one of the most beloved and winsome members of the apostolic band. He was eager, impulsive, energetic, self-confident, aggressive, and daring, but also unstable, fickle, weak, and cowardly. He was guided more by quick impulse than logical reasoning, and he readily swayed from one extreme to the other. He was preeminently a man of action. His life exhibits the defects of his character as well as his tremendous capacities for good. He was forward and often rash, liable to instability and inconsistency, but his love for and associations with Christ molded him into a man of stability, humility, and courageous service for God. In the power of the Holy Spirit he became one of the noble pillars of the church (Gal. 2:9).

Peter, First Letter of. One of the CATHOLIC EPISTLES, addressed to Christians scattered throughout much of ASIA MINOR. The keynote of this letter is suffering and the Christian method of meeting it. The writer endeavored to convey a message of hope to Christians who had been undergoing PERSECUTION and who were succumbing to discouragement because they could find no redress. He brings an exhortation of Christian truth calculated to strengthen believers.

I. **Authorship.** Of the two letters that bear the name of PETER, the first is better attested. Echoes of its phraseology appear as early as the letter of Polycarp to the Philippians (c. A.D. 125), the let-

ter of Barnabas (c. 135), and the writings of Justin Martyr (c. 150). The second letter of Peter refers to a former letter, probably meaning this one (2 Pet. 3:1). It was unanimously accepted as a letter of Peter by all of the church fathers, who mention it by name, beginning with Irenaeus (c. 170).

The internal structure reflects Peter's mind and life. The first main paragraph, "Praise be to the God and Father of our Lord Jesus Christ! In his great mercy he has given us new birth into a living hope through the resurrection of Jesus Christ from the dead" (1 Pet. 1:3), expresses the joy that Peter felt after the risen Christ forgave him for his denial. The injunction to "be shepherds of God's flock" (5:2) is almost identical in language with Jesus' commission to him at the lake of Galilee (Jn. 21:16). "Clothe yourselves with humility" may be a reminiscence of the Last Supper, when Jesus wrapped a towel around his waist and washed the disciples' feet (13:4-5).

There are also some remarkable agreements between the vocabulary of 1 Peter and the speeches of Peter in Acts (1 Pet. 1:17 and Acts 10:34; 1 Pet. 1:21 and Acts 2:32; 10:40-41; 1 Pet. 2:7-8 and Acts 4:10-11).

II. **Destination.** The letter was directed to members of the DISPERSION located in the Roman provinces of N Asia Minor, which Paul did not visit and which may have been evangelized by Peter between

Overview of 1 PETER

Author: The apostle Simon Peter (though some believe the work is pseudonymous).

Historical setting: Probably written from ROME (the "Babylon" of 1 Pet. 5:13) in the late A.D. 50s or early 60s, but an earlier date is not impossible (those who reject Petrine authorship date it c. 80 or even later). Addressed to Christians in various regions of ASIA MINOR who were undergoing severe PERSECUTION.

Purpose: To encourage holy conduct in the face of suffering by assuring the readers of their coming reward.

Contents: The greatness of our SALVATION (1 Pet. 1:1-12); the call to SANCTIFICATION (1:13—2:12); the need for submission (2:13—3:12); the proper response to suffering (3:13—5:14).

P

the Council of Jerusalem (A.D. 48) and the Neronian persecution at Rome (64). There is some question whether the "Dispersion" should be taken literally as applying strictly to Jews or whether it may be used figuratively of Gentile Christians who were scattered abroad. In favor of the former conclusion are one or two passages that seemingly indicate that the recipients were Jews (1 Pet. 2:12; 3:6); on the other hand, the references to the ungodly past of these people (1:14; 4:3) do not seem to agree with the hypothesis that they were of Jewish descent. If Peter wrote this letter from Rome, he may have been writing to refugees from the Neronian persecution who were converts from Judaism or proselytes who turned from Judaism to Christianity.

III. Date and place. If Silas (KJV Silvanus, 1 Pet. 5:12) and Mark (5:13; see Mark, John) were the same persons mentioned in Paul's letters (2 Cor. 1:19; 1 Thess. 1:1; Col. 4:10; 2 Tim. 4:11), 1 Peter must have been written subsequent to Silas's departure from Paul and prior to Mark's rejoining him. Silas was with Paul in Corinth in the early A.D. 50s, and Mark probably rejoined him just before his death, which took place about 65-67. Furthermore, 1 Peter bears traces of the influence of Paul's letters to the Romans and to the Ephesians in its structure and thought (compare the following: 1 Pet. 2:13 and Rom. 13:1-4; 1 Pet. 2:18 and Eph. 6:5; 1 Pet. 3:9 and Rom. 12:17; 1 Pet. 5:5 and Eph. 5:21), implying that it was written after 60. Probably 1 Peter was written about the year 64, when the status of Christians in the empire was very uncertain and when persecution had already begun in Rome.

The place of writing is closely connected with the date. Babylon (1 Pet. 5:13) may refer to the ancient city on the Euphrates, where there was a large Jewish settlement in Peter's day, or to a town in Egypt near Alexandria, where Mark traditionally ministered, or figuratively to Rome as the center of the pagan world (Rev. 17:5; 18:10). The second alternative need not be considered seriously, for the Egyptian Babylon was only a border fort. Opinion among commentators is divided between the other two opinions. In the absence of any strong tradition that Peter ever visited the literal Babylon, it seems more likely that he wrote this letter from Rome shortly before his martyrdom. He would have had opportunity to find some

of Paul's writings there and to have met Silas and Mark, both of whom were familiar to Paul.

Those who deny Peter's authorship place the letter in the early second century under the reign of Trajan (A.D. 96-117). Some have assigned it to the time of Domitian (87-96), conceding that Peter might have been executed in the time of Vespasian or Domitian (c. 80).

IV. Structure and content. In general arrangement 1 Peter closely resembles the letters of Paul, with a salutation, body, and conclusion. Its main subject is the Christian's behavior under the pressure of suffering. Its key is the salvation that is to be revealed at the last time (1 Pet. 1:5). The letter may be outlined as follows:

I. Introduction (1:1-2)

II. The nature of salvation (1:3-12)

III. The experience of salvation (1:13-25)

IV. The obligations of salvation (2:1-10)

V. The ethics of salvation (2:11—3:12)

VI. The confidence of salvation (3:13—4:11)

VII. The behavior of the saved under suffering (4:12—5:11)

VIII. Concluding salutations (5:12-14)

Peter, Second Letter of. One of the Catholic Epistles, written by the apostle Peter as he was about to finish his career. It is a general treatise, written to warn its readers of threatening apostasy.

I. Authorship. Second Peter has the poorest external attestation of any book in the canon of the NT (see canonicity). It is not quoted directly by any of the church fathers before Origen (c. A.D. 250), who affirms Peter's authorship of the first letter, but who seemed uncertain about the second, although he did not repudiate it. Eusebius, to whom we are indebted for quoting Origen's testimony, placed 2 Peter in the list of writings that were disputed by some ancient Christian churches. Its literary style and vocabulary differ from that of 1 Peter, and its close resemblance to the book of Jude has led some scholars to believe that it is a late copy or adaptation of that work. Numerous scholars have pronounced it spurious, dating it to the middle of the second century.

On the other hand, the internal evidence favors authorship by Peter. If a forger knew 1 Peter, it seems he could have been more careful to follow its

The striking topography of Cappadocia. Among the Christians addressed by Peter were residents of this country.

style exactly. The allusions to Peter's career agree with the existing records and can best be explained as the testimony of an eyewitness. These allusions include the TRANSFIGURATION (2 Pet. 1:17-18), at which Peter was present (Matt. 17:1-18), and the Lord's prediction of his death (2 Pet. 1:14; Jn. 21:18-19). The Greek of the second letter is more labored than that of the first, but if Peter did not have the aid of SILAS in this work, as he apparently did in the first letter (1 Pet. 5:12), he may have been forced to rely on his own writing. Doubtlessly he knew Greek, as most Galileans did, but he may not have been able to write it easily.

The allusion to the writings of "our dear brother Paul" (2 Pet. 3:15) confirms the impression that 2 Peter was written by someone who knew PAUL personally and who treated him as an equal. A writer of the second century would have been more likely to say "the blessed apostle" or the like, for he would have regarded Paul with a greater veneration and would thus have used a more elevated title.

Reasons exist, therefore, for accepting the letter as Peter's. The relative silence of the early church may be explained by the brevity of the letter, which could have made it more susceptible to being overlooked or lost.

II. Date and place. Second Peter must have been written subsequent to the publication of at least some of Paul's letters, if not of the entire collection. It cannot, therefore, have been written before A.D. 60; but if Paul was living and was still well known to the existing generation, it could not have been later than 70. Probably 67 is as satisfactory a date as can be established. The writer was anticipating a speedy death (2 Pet. 1:14), and this may mean that the letter was sent from ROME during the tense days of the persecution under NERO. There is no indication, however, that Peter had spent a long time in Rome. He may have labored there only at the conclusion of Paul's life (between 63 and 67).

III. Destination and occasion. The reference to a previous letter sent to the same group (2 Pet. 3:1) connects the document with 1 Peter, which was written to the Christians of N ASIA MINOR. Whereas the first letter was an attempt to encourage a church threatened with official persecution and repression, the second letter dealt with the peril of APOSTASY, which was an even greater threat. An influx of conscienceless agitators who repudiated the lordship of Christ (2:1) and whose attitude was haughty (2:10), licentious (2:13), adulterous (2:14), greedy (2:14), bombastic (2:18), and libertine (2:19) seemed imminent. Knowing that he would not be spared to keep control of the situation, Peter was writing to forestall this calamity and to warn the church of its danger.

P

Overview of 2 PETER

Author: The apostle Simon Peter (though many believe the work is pseudonymous).

Historical setting: Since the writer views his death as imminent (cf. 2 Pet. 1:13-15), the letter must have been written shortly before Peter's martyrdom (c. A.D. 65-67), probably from ROME. (Those who reject Petrine authorship date it to the end of the first century or even as late as the middle of the second.) The letter was addressed to Christian communities (possibly in ASIA MINOR, if 2 Pet. 3:1 is an allusion to the epistle we call 1 Peter) that were being threatened by false teaching.

Purpose: To warn the readers against APOSTASY by stressing true KNOWLEDGE over against the message of the false teachers.

Contents: Spiritual growth and true knowledge (2 Pet. 1); denunciation of false teachers (ch. 2); the coming of the DAY OF THE LORD (ch. 3).

IV. Content and outline. The key to this letter is the word *know* (or *knowledge*), which occurs frequently in the three chapters, often referring to the knowledge of Christ. This knowledge is not primarily academic, but spiritual, arising from a growing experience of Christ (2 Pet. 3:18). It produces peace and grace (1:2) and fruitfulness (1:8), is the secret of freedom from defilement (2:20), and is the sphere of Christian growth (3:18). It may be that the false teachers were Gnostics (see GNOSTICISM), who stressed knowledge as the means to salvation, and that Peter sought to counteract their falsehoods by a positive presentation of true knowledge.

Second Peter teaches definitely the INSPIRATION of Scripture (2 Pet. 1:19-21) and stresses the doctrine of the personal return of Christ, which was ridiculed by the false teachers (3:1-7). It concludes with an appeal for holy living and with the promise of the new heavens and the new earth.

The following is a brief outline of the epistle:
I. Salutation (1:1)
II. The character of spiritual knowledge (1:2-21)
III. The nature and perils of apostasy (2:1-22)
IV. The doom of the ungodly (3:1-7)
V. The hope of believers (3:8-13)
VI. Concluding exhortation (3:14-18)

Pethahiah. peth´uh-hi´uh (Heb. *pĕtaḥyâ* H7342, "Yahweh has opened," meaning possibly that he has opened his own eyes in compassion, or that he has opened a person's eyes [in the sense of either revealing truth to a person or bringing a child to life], or that he has opened the womb). **(1)** A priest during the time of DAVID who was the leader of the nineteenth division (1 Chr. 24:16). Some scholars believe that Pethahiah here is the family name of a later priestly group. See below, #2.

(2) One of the LEVITES who agreed to put away their foreign wives (Ezra 10:23). He is probably the same Pethahiah who, along with others, offered prayer in the ceremonies that preceded the sealing of the covenant (Neh. 9:5).

(3) Son of Meshezabel and descendant of JUDAH through ZERAH; he was one of the Israelites who resettled in JERUSALEM after the EXILE and is described as being "the king's agent in all affairs relating to the people" (Neh. 11:24). He may have been a local official who advised the king through regional governors.

Pethor. pee´thor (Heb. *pĕtôr* H7335, from Hittite *Pitru*). A city of N MESOPOTAMIA, evidently located on the W banks of the Upper EUPHRATES near the point where it is joined by the river Sagura (now Sajur), a short distance S of CARCHEMISH. It was the home of BALAAM son of Beor, who was summoned by King BALAK of MOAB to curse the Israelites who were entering the land (Num. 22:5; Deut. 23:4). Pethor is mentioned in various extra-biblical sources

Pethuel. pi-thyoo´uhl (Heb. *pĕtûʾēl H7333*, meaning uncertain, perhaps "young man of God"). The father of the prophet JOEL (Joel 1:1).

Petra. pee´truh (Gk. *Petra*, "rock"). Ancient capital of the NABATEANS, on the E edge of the ARABAH rift, some 50 mi. (80 km.) SSE of the DEAD SEA. Petra is not mentioned in the Bible, but it has commonly been identified with OT SELA (Heb. *selaʿ H6153*, "rock, cliffs"), a major fortified city in EDOM. According to JOSEPHUS, the Arabians (Nabateans)

© Direct Design

View from a hewn chamber into the rock-cut city of Petra.

regarded it as their "metropolis" and called it *Arkē* after the name of one of their kings, but the Greeks renamed it Petra (*Ant.* 4.4.7 §82). The ruins of Petra were discovered in 1812. Their setting is impressive, reached by descending Wadi Musa and passing through a magnificent gorge (the Siq) with high and frequent walls that nearly touch each other. This gorge is over 1 mi. (almost 2 km.) in length, which provided an excellent defense for the city. Petra was situated in an open basin, approximately 1 mi. in length by three-fourths mi. in width (1.6 x 1 km.). The craggy mountains surrounding the area are formed of sandstone, in beautifully variegated shades of red color. Perpendicular cliffs are covered with tombs and other facades carved into the native rock. These date primarily from the times of the Nabateans, as Petra was their capital from about the close of the fourth century B.C. to A.D. 105, when it was incorporated into Roman territory.

Peullethai. pi-ool´uh-thi (Heb. *pĕʿullĕtay H7191*, possibly "reward"). KJV Peulthai. Seventh son of OBED-EDOM, included in the list of divisions of the Korahite doorkeepers (see KORAH) in the reign of DAVID (1 Chr. 26:5).

Peulthai. See PEULLETHAI.

Phalec. See PELEG.

Phallu. See PALLU.

Phalti. See PALTIEL.

Phaltiel. See PALTIEL.

Phanuel. fuh-nyoo´uhl (Gk. *Phanouēl G5750*, from Heb. *pĕnûʾēl H7158*, "the face of God"; see PENUEL). The father of ANNA the prophetess (Lk. 2:36).

pharaoh. fair´oh (Heb. *parʿōh H7281*, from Egyp. *par-ʿəʾo* [vocalization uncertain], meaning "great house"; Gk. *Pharaō G5755*). Title of the kings of ancient EGYPT. The recorded rulers of this country, constituting twenty-six separate dynasties, extend from Menes, c. 3400 B.C., to Psamtik III, deposed at the Persian conquest in 525 B.C. The term

P

pharaoh can be traced back to the 22nd dynasty (945-745), when it became commonly attached to the monarch's name. Thus "Pharaoh Neco" and "Pharaoh Hophra" are exact Hebrew translations of the Egyptian title. Pharaohs of Egypt are mentioned in various OT contexts, as follows.

(1) Genesis 12:10-20. The date of Abram's descent into Egypt was probably in the early years of the second millennium B.C. (see ABRAHAM). Amenemhet I, according to one dating, was pharaoh from 2000 to 1970. There is no strong evidence that N Egypt was already under the power of the HYKSOS intruders at this time, plausible though it may seem to connect the patriarch's sojourn with the presence of racially related rulers. On the tomb of Khnumhotep at Beni Hasan, dating from the twentieth century B.C., the visit of such a Semitic party is vividly portrayed.

(2) Genesis 39-50. It is reasonable to place the period of JOSEPH's (and ISRAEL's) favor in Egypt in the times of the Hyksos invaders. These foreigners, who included Canaanite and Semitic elements from Palestine, supplanted the weak rulers of the 13th and 14th dynasties and settled in the NILE delta and Lower (i.e., northern) Egypt, where they maintained their power for some two centuries. They were driven out in 1580 B.C.

(3) Exod. 1-15. Controversy surrounds the identity of the pharaoh of the oppression and the date of the Hebrew EXODUS. One, to some extent, depends on the other. John Garstang's excavations at Jericho in the early 1930s seemed to establish a date for the Hebrew storming of the city around the turn of the fourteenth century B.C. This would postulate a date for the exodus around 1440, and would identify THUTMOSE III as the pharaoh of the oppression and the famous princess Hatshepsut as MOSES' protectress. The theory produces a neat pattern of dates, and the events of the oppression through to the infiltration of the tribes into Palestine correspond very well with events of Egyptian history during the years 1580 to 1350, the period of the great 18th dynasty. Ahmose I would thus be the pharaoh "who did not know about Joseph" (Exod. 1:8). Indeed, as the first native ruler after the expulsion of the hated Hyksos, he would be naturally hostile to the shepherd protégés of the old regime. The breakdown of Egyptian control in Palestine under Amenhotep IV (Akhenaten) would also account for the comparative ease of the Hebrew conquest and explain the HABIRU references of the Tell el-AMARNA Letters.

Many scholars, however, argue for a later date, under which Seti I (1313-1292 B.C.) is regarded as the pharaoh of Exod. 1:8. RAMSES II (1292-1225), in whose reign the store cities of PITHAM and RAMESES were completed, would thus fill the role of pharaoh of the oppression, and perhaps of the exodus (1:11; 12:40). Rameses was the fort from which the great militarist Ramses II sought to control his Asiatic empire, and the war base from which he marched to his great battle with the HITTITES at KADESH ON THE ORONTES, the conflict depicted on the walls of the Ramesseum at THEBES. Those who thus identify the pharaoh of the oppression point out that the Egyptian hold over Palestine slackened after Ramses' treaty with the Hittites, and that this weakening of policy allowed the fragmentation of the country from which the Hebrew incursion profited. Some more precisely date the exodus in the reign of Ramses' son, MERNEPTAH, mainly on the strength of the "Israel Stele," discovered by Flinders Petrie in 1896. This inscription, self-dated in "the third year of Merneptah" (1223 B.C.), tells of the pharaoh's victories in Canaan. One line runs: "Israel is devastated. Her seed is not" (or "Her crops are destroyed"). A natural reference from this statement might, however, be that Israel was already in settled possession of large tracts of Palestine. At this point the matter must be left.

(4) First Chronicles 4:18 speaks of "the children of Pharaoh's daughter Bithia, whom Mered had married." No identification of this pharaoh is possible, and the name of the princess appears to be hebraized.

(5) First Kings 3:1; 9:16, 24; 11:1. SOLOMON's reign may be reliably dated 961 to 922 B.C., a period that corresponds with the reign of Pharaoh Sheshonk I (SHISHAK, 945 to 924), the founder of the 22nd dynasty. Under this ruler, Egypt's foreign policy again took on an aggressive character, and at all such times it was Egypt's custom to establish the safety of the northern approaches, virtually her only invasion route. Hence the policy of Thutmose III, Ramses II, Seti I, and Sheshonk. The dynastic alliance with Solomon and the handing of the city

of GEZER to his authority were part of the recurrent Egyptian plan to create a defensive buffer in Palestine. The ruler who acted with such foresight and energy can hardly have been one of the feeble monarchs of the earlier dynasty. A further facet of the same policy is revealed by Pharaoh's befriending of HADAD of EDOM (1 Ki. 11:14-22). Hadad was a useful weapon for possible employment against a recalcitrant Solomon or against a hostile Palestine.

(6) Second Kings 18:21 and Isa. 36:6 both mention the pharaoh of SENNACHERIB's day. He is "that splintered reed of a staff, which pierces a man's hand and wounds him if he leans on it," says the field commander to the people of Jerusalem. The date is 701 B.C. Egypt was in the state of political disintegration and weakness pictured in Isa. 19. Shabaka was pharaoh, the first monarch of the feeble 26th dynasty. The army scraped together to face the Assyrian threat was a motley horde of mercenaries and ill-armed levies. Egyptian contingents had served in the past against ASSYRIA, but this was the first time the two empires, that of the Tigris and that of the Nile, actually confronted each other. Sennacherib led in person. Shabaka entrusted his force to his nephew Taharka who, some thirteen or fourteen years later, became king of ETHIOPIA. Hence the title given in 2 Ki. 19:9 by anticipation of events. The Assyrian rapidly dealt with Taharka's force, and was proceeding to overthrow Palestine and the strong pocket of resistance in Jerusalem, when the famous plague that decimated his army fell on him. This overwhelming catastrophe was the cause of the Assyrian retreat and deliverance for both Palestine and Egypt.

(7) Second Kings 23:20-35. Pharaoh NECO was the last king to endeavor to reestablish Egyptian authority in the northern approaches. He succeeded Psametik I, founder of the 26th dynasty, in 609 B.C., and reigned until 593. Immediately after his accession, taking advantage of the collapse of NINEVEH, Neco drove N into PHILISTIA. On the Plain of MEGIDDO, where Egypt had won control of the land 900 years before, Neco routed and killed King JOSIAH of JUDAH. He moved on to the Euphrates, unopposed by Nineveh, but not feeling strong enough to go against that stronghold. From RIBLAH on the Orontes, three months after the battle at Megiddo, Neco deposed JEHOAHAZ and sent him to die in Egypt. He placed JEHOIAKIM on the throne of Judah and fixed a tribute for the conquered land. Two years later Neco's new empire fell before the attack of BABYLON. JEREMIAH refers to the event (Jer. 37:7; 46:2).

(8) Ezekiel 29:1. The date is 587 B.C., and the pharaoh referred to must therefore be HOPHRA (Apries), in the first year of his rule. He reigned from 588 to 569. This was the pharaoh whose troops failed to relieve Jerusalem in 586 and whose weak action against NEBUCHADNEZZAR's Babylon vindicated the advice of Jeremiah. Egypt escaped the calamity that befell Palestine by prudent modification of her challenge. Preoccupied with TYRE, Nebuchadnezzar did not press the war against Egypt, and Hophra brought his country its last flourish of prosperity before the land fell in the Persian conquest. Jeremiah prophesied his end (Jer. 44:30, the sole biblical reference to Hophra by name).

Phares, Pharez. See PEREZ.

Pharisee. fair′uh-see (Gk. *Pharisaios G5757*, prob. from Heb. *pārûš*, "separated" [pass. ptc. of *pāraš H7300*]). Of the three prominent parties of JUDAISM at the time of CHRIST—Pharisees, SADDUCEES, and ESSENES—the Pharisees were by far the most influential. The origin of this most strict sect of the Jews (Acts 26:5) is shrouded in some obscurity, but it is believed the organization came out of the *Hasidim* ("faithful ones"), a broad movement in the second century B.C. that sought to preserve ancient Jewish traditions in the face of HELLENISM and that fueled the Maccabean revolt (165 B.C.; see MACCABEE). The name *Pharisee* itself, however, first appears during the reign of John Hyrcanus (135 B.C.). In NT times, Pharisees were found everywhere in Palestine, not only in JERUSALEM, and even wore a distinguishing garb so as to be easily recognized. According to JOSEPHUS, their number at the zenith of their popularity was more than 6,000. Because of the significant role the Pharisees played in the life of the Lord and the apostles, knowledge of the character and teachings of this group is of great importance for the understanding of the NT. They are mentioned dozens of times, especially in the Gospels, and often form the background for the works and words of Jesus.

P

Pharisaism is usually associated with *legalism*, although this term has a strong negative connotation that can lead to an inadequate understanding of the movement. After the destruction of Jerusalem in 586 B.C., much of the nation was taken into EXILE in BABYLON, where Judaism had to develop in a radically new setting. Even in the case of those

© Dr. James C. Martin. Collection of the Israel Museum, Jerusalem and courtesy of the Israel Antiquities Authority. Exhibited at the Rockefeller Museum, Jerusalem.

Two coins (a prutah and a half prutah, c. 67 B.C.) from the time of Hyrcanus II, who had the support of the Pharisees.

who eventually returned to Judea, there was a need to interpret and apply the TORAH or law in a context that was very different from that of the earlier Hebrew THEOCRACY. These circumstances gave rise to the scribal movement, with its focus on the preservation of both the text and the relevance of Scripture. The scribes (NIV, "teachers of the law") became the legal experts and developed an extensive exegetical tradition that came to be known as the *oral law*. The precise connection between scribes (who were professional religious leaders) and Pharisees (who apparently were regarded as laymen) is disputed, but there was obviously a very close association between the two—as indicated by the fact that in the Gospels they are mentioned together some twenty times (e.g, Matt. 5:20; Mk. 2:15; Lk. 5:21; Jn. 8:3). This collaboration lies behind the development of rabbinic or mainstream Judaism (see TALMUD). At times this focus on the law did become legalism in the negative sense—either because the concern for legal obedience overshadowed other important issues (cf. Matt. 23:23) or because such obedience made people "confident of their own righteousness" (Lk. 18:9)—but it must not be thought that all (or even most?) Pharisees failed to recognize the fundamental importance of divine GRACE.

Pharisaism was also strongly committed to Jewish nationalism. They opposed the secularization of Judaism by the pagan Greek thought that penetrated Jewish life after the Alexandrian conquest. Their pride in Jewish traditions and law often developed into a feeling of superiority over the other nations and people, especially evident in their extreme separatism from the SAMARITANS (Jn. 4:9). The Pharisees became a closely organized group, very loyal to the society and to each other, but separate from others, even their own people. They pledged themselves to obey all facets of the traditions to the minutest detail and were sticklers for ceremonial purity. In truth, they often made life difficult for themselves and bitter for others. In extreme cases, some were haughty and arrogant because they believed they were the only interpreters of God and his Word. It is only natural that ultimately such an attitude could lead to a religion of externals and not of the heart, and that God's grace was sometimes thought to come only from doing the law. As a whole, however, the Pharisees were perceived by most other Jews as paragons of virtues and were regarded highly as religious leaders.

The doctrines of the Pharisees included predestination, or, as some have termed it, a teaching of special divine providence. They also laid much stress on the immortality of the soul and had a fundamental belief in spirit life, teachings that usually caused much controversy when they met the Sadducees, who just as emphatically denied them (Acts 23:6-9). Being people of the law, they believed in final reward for good works and that the souls of the wicked were detained forever under the earth, while those of the virtuous rose again and even migrated into other bodies (Josephus, *Ant.* 18.1.3; Acts 23:8). They accepted the OT Scriptures and fostered the usual Jewish messianic hope, to which they gave a material and nationalistic twist.

It was inevitable, in view of these factors, that many Pharisees bitterly opposed Jesus and his teachings. If they despised the Herods and the Romans, they hated Jesus' doctrine of equality and claims of messiahship with equal fervor (Jn. 9:16, 22). He in turn condemned both their theology and life of legalism. They often became a fertile background against which he taught God's free salvation by grace through his own death and resurrection. Clashes between Jesus and the Pharisees were frequent and bitter, as examples in the Gospels reveal: he called them a generation of vipers and condemned them for impenitence (Matt. 3:7), criticized their view of righteousness (5:20), upbraided their pride against others (Matt. 9:12; Lk. 19:10), scorned their lovelessness on the Sabbath (Lk. 12:2), rebuked them for not being baptized (7:30), taught them regarding divorce (Matt. 19:3) and taxes (Mk. 12:17), and condemned them for their covetousness (Lk. 16:14). The Pharisees, in turn, accused Jesus of blasphemy (5:21), of being in league with the devil (Matt. 9:34), and of breaking the law (12:2). They often planned to destroy him (12:14). Jesus' longest and most scathing rebuke of the Pharisees is found in Matt. 23: "Woe to you, teachers of the law and Pharisees, you hypocrites! You are like whitewashed tombs, which look beautiful on the outside but on the inside are full of dead men's bones and everything unclean" (23:27).

The picture of the Pharisees painted by the NT is thus almost entirely negative. Many modern scholars point out that rabbinic literature, when taken as a whole, provides a rather different perspective. Moreover, some of the Pharisees became adherents of the Christian movement (cf. Acts 15:5), including NICODEMUS (Jn. 3:1) and the apostle PAUL (Acts 26:5; Phil. 3:5). Indeed, Paul does not speak the name *Pharisee* with great reproach but as a title of honor, for the Pharisees were highly respected by the masses of the Jewish people. In identifying himself as a former Pharisee, he did not think of himself as having been an arrogant fraud; rather, he was claiming the highest degree of faithfulness to the law. Evaluating Pharisaism therefore requires some balance: it is inaccurate and unjust to paint the whole movement with the broad brush of haughtiness and hypocrisy, but it would be even more erroneous to suggest that the criticisms Jesus directed against those who opposed him were without foundation.

Pharosh. See PAROSH.

Pharpar. fahr´pahr (Heb. *parpar H7286*, meaning unknown). One of two rivers in DAMASCUS that NAAMAN considered superior to the JORDAN (2 Ki. 5:12). It seems likely that the reference is to the two major rivers of the whole Damascus plain, Nahr el-Barada itself and Nahr el-Awaj; the former would then be identified with the ABANA, and the latter with the Pharpar (this ancient name is apparently preserved in the river's offshoot, Wadi Barbara). El-Awaj originates in the eastern foothills of Mount HERMON and flows E, passing some 10 mi. (16 km.) S of Damascus (during its early course it is known by the name Sabirany). Much of the productivity of the southern Damascus plain is due to its waters; and its cool, fresh waters, particularly in the early spring, could provide a favorable contrast to the frequently sluggish waters of the lower Jordan.

Pharzite. See PEREZ.

Phaseah. See PASEAH.

Phebe. See PHOEBE.

Phenice, Phenicia. See PHOENICIA and PHOENIX.

Phichol. See PHICOL.

Phicol. fi´kol (Heb. *pikōl H7087*, meaning unknown). KJV Phichol. The captain of ABIMELECH's army in the conflicts with ABRAHAM and ISAAC (Gen. 21:22, 32; 26:26). Phicol may be a title or a family name.

Philadelphia. fil´uh-del´fee-uh (Gk. *Philadelpheia G5788*, "brotherly love"). A city of LYDIA in ASIA MINOR, the recipient of one of the letters in the book of Revelation (Rev. 1:11; 3:7); this city is not to be confused with another one of the same name in TRANSJORDAN, for which see RABBAH (AMMON). Philadelphia was founded by Attalus II Philadelphus (159-138 B.C.), the king of PERGAMUM. It lay in the valley of the Cogamus, near the pass that carries the main trade route from the Maeander to the Hermus valley, a wide vale beneath Mount Tmolus. It was an outpost of Greek culture in Anatolia, and came violently into Roman history with the shocking earthquake that devastated the SW end of Asia Minor in A.D. 17. The city on its low hill was strategically valuable. It lay on a frontier of civilizations, the gateway to central

Asia Minor with its non-Greek, non-Roman patterns of life. Some allusions in the apocalyptic letter are explained by the presence in Philadelphia of an active synagogue of Jews who were bitterly nationalistic, fighting the Christian secessionists with every refinement of persecution. The author of Revelation insisted that the true Jew was rather one who interpreted aright his international privilege and responsibility (Rev. 3:9).

Philemon, Letter to. fi-lee´muhn (Gk. *Philēmōn G5800*, "affectionate"). A letter written by the apostle PAUL to an early Christian, and secondarily to APPHIA and ARCHIPPUS (prob. members of the household), and to the church that met in Philemon's house. This document dates, in all probability, from the period of Paul's (first) Roman imprisonment. Pauline authorship is not seriously disputed. Apphia is usually thought to have been Philemon's wife, and Archippus may have been his son. Archippus appears to have been a person of some standing, but perhaps not notable for stability of character (Col. 4:17). The Christian community was organized around a home, a practice of the early church. Many ancient churches were no doubt founded on the sites of homes where early Christians met. There is no evidence of church building of any sort before the third century.

The occasion of the letter was the return of the runaway slave ONESIMUS to his master. Paul founds all he has to say on Christian fellowship. He writes with exquisite tact and with words of praise before referring to obligation. The word "brother" comes like a friendly handclasp at the end of Phlm. 7; "for my son Onesimus" adds a curiously poignant appeal at the end of v. 10. He is Paul the ambassador and as such might speak of duty. An imperial legate had a right to speak for the emperor, and the analogy would not be lost on Philemon. Paul reminds Philemon that, in respect to bondage, his own position did not vary from that of the man for whom he pleaded. Onesimus was a fellow bondsman and a son. His name means "useful," and the writer makes a play on the word in v. 11, proceeding immediately to point to the sacrifice he himself was making. Onesimus was "briefly" parted from Philemon, says Paul, and he proceeds strongly to hint that manumission might be the truest mark of brotherliness. With what may be a closing touch of humor, Paul offers to pay Philemon back for anything the runaway owes, discounting, as he returns to seriousness, Philemon's own deep debt.

"I do wish, brother," Paul concludes, "that I may have some benefit from you in the Lord." He puns once more on Onesimus's name (the Gk. verb is *oninēmi G3949*). The remark is a further appeal for Onesimus's freedom. The approach is characteristic of early Christianity. SLAVERY is never directly attacked as such, but principles that must prove fatal to the institution are steadily inculcated. To speak of brotherly love between master and slave ultimately renders slavery meaningless.

Overview of PHILEMON

Author: The apostle PAUL.

Historical setting: Probably written from ROME during the apostle's first imprisonment in that city (c. A.D. 61-63), but some scholars prefer an earlier date and alternate places (EPHESUS or CAESAREA). The letter was motivated by the conversion of ONESIMUS, a runaway slave.

Purpose: To persuade Philemon to forgive Onesimus and receive him back.

Contents: After introductory comments (Phlm. 1-7), Paul makes his case (vv. 8-21) and adds concluding remarks (vv. 22-25).

The letter ends on notes of intimacy. There was something truly Greek about Paul. The great Greek orators seldom placed the climax of their speech in the closing words, ending on a minor note designed to bring the excited audience back to normalcy and rest. So Paul ends here.

Philetus. fi-lee´tuhs (Gk. *Philētos G5801*, "beloved" or "worthy of love"). A man named with Hymenaeus as a teacher of false doctrine, doubtless akin to Gnosticism, which undermined the Christian faith (2 Tim. 2:17-18). Paul warned Timothy to avoid such teaching, which spreads destructively "like gangrene." Their basic doctrinal error was the claim that "the resurrection has already taken place." They must have denied a bodily resurrection and allegorized the doctrine, holding probably that the resurrection takes place in the lives of believers when they arise from ignorance and sin to a knowledge of God.

Philip. fil´ip (Gk. *Philippos G5805*, "fond of horses"). **(1)** The name of several kings of Macedonia, including Philip II, father of Alexander the Great (1 Macc. 1:1; 6:2). Philip V is mentioned (along with his son Perseus, the last Macedonian king) as an example of those who rose against the Romans and were "crushed in battle" (8:5).

(2) Son of Herod the Great and his fifth wife (Cleopatra of Jerusalem), identified by Luke as tetrarch of Iturea and Traconitis (Lk. 3:1). Two of the Gospels (Matt. 14:3; Mk. 6:17) refer to a brother of Herod Antipas who bore the name Philip. Presumably, the latter is a different individual, namely, a son of Herod the Great (by his wife Mariamme) who is however called Herod rather than Philip by Josephus (*Ant.* 18.5.1 §109); some scholars refer to this man as Herod Philip, while others argue that the Gospels are incorrect in calling him Philip.

(3) One of the original twelve apostles. In the lists of disciples his name invariably occurs fifth (Matt. 10:3; Mk. 3:18; Lk. 6:14; Acts 1:13). Philip was from Bethsaida (Jn. 12:21), a village on the N shore of the Sea of Galilee, home of Andrew and Peter (1:44). He was probably first a disciple of John the Baptist (1:43). In the synoptics, Philip is merely mentioned, but in the fourth gospel he

(a) is one of the first to be called (1:43); (b) is instrumental in bringing Nathanael to Jesus (1:45-49); and (c) is mentioned personally in connection with the feeding of the 5,000 (6:5-7), as also in one of Jesus' major discourses (14:8). He is often characterized as being timid and retiring; others suggest that he was reluctant to believe wholeheartedly in the kingdom. At times he seems to have had difficulty in grasping its meaning (14:8-14). Possibly this is the reason Jesus asked him the unusual question to arouse and test his faith before feeding the 5,000: "Where shall we buy bread for these people to eat?" (6:5-6). He served as something of a contact man for the Greeks and is familiarly known for bringing Gentiles to Jesus (12:20-23). The last information regarding Philip in the NT is found in Acts 1:13, where we are told that he was among the number of disciples in the upper chamber before Pentecost. His days after this event are shrouded in legend and mystery, but the best tradition says he did mission work in Asia Minor. The historian Eusebius says that he was a "great light of Asia," and that he was buried at Hierapolis.

(4) Philip the evangelist and deacon is not mentioned in the Gospels. His name first appears in the list of seven deacons chosen by the Jerusalem church (Acts 6:5). These men were ordained by the apostles and described as "known to be full of the Spirit and wisdom" (6:3). Their duty was to care for the neglected widows (and the poor in general) in the mother church. Philip was a Greek-speaking Jew and was apparently well known. The persecution instigated by Saul of Tarsus (Paul) resulted in the martyrdom of Stephen (Philip's colleague) and the scattering of Christians abroad from Jerusalem (8:1). Philip fled to Samaria (modern Sebaste), where he became an evangelist or missionary. His preaching, accompanied by miracles of healing and the casting out of demons, turned the allegiance of the entire city from Simon the sorcerer to Christ (8:5-13). After this unusual revival, the church at Jerusalem sent Peter and John (see John the apostle) to Samaria that the new Christians might receive the gift of the Holy Spirit (8:15). Philip's converts included not only Simon Magus (8:9-13) but also the Ethiopian eunuch, treasurer to Queen Candace (8:26-40). Thus Philip was instrumental in introducing Christianity into

NE Africa. This conversion story implies trustful obedience to divine guidance plus rare insight into the process of personal evangelism; LUKE probably heard the account from the lips of the great evangelist himself (cf. the pronoun "we" in 21:8). Philip preached in every port city from ASHDOD (Azotus) to CAESAREA on the sea (8:40). Apparently he settled there, since about twenty years later Paul (on his last journey to Jerusalem) was a guest in Philip's home in this city (21:8-9). Philip had four unmarried daughters living at home who had the gift of prophecy. Nothing certain is known of his later life.

Philippi. fi-lip´i, fil´i-pi (Gk. *Philippoi G5804*, "[city of] Philip"; gentilic *Philippēsios G5803*, "Philippian"). A city of MACEDONIA, visited by the apostle PAUL (Acts 16:1, 12-40; 20:6; Phil. 1:1; 1 Thess. 2:2). Situated in the plain E of Mount Pangaeus. Philippi was a strategic foundation of PHILIP II, father of ALEXANDER THE GREAT, in 358/7 B.C. The position dominated the road system of N GREECE; hence it became the center for the battle of 42 B.C.

Excavations at Philippi, S of the agora.

in which Antony defeated Brutus and Cassius. After the battle of Actium (31 B.C.), Octavian (the future AUGUSTUS) constituted the place a Roman colony, housing partisans of Antony whose presence was undesirable in Italy. Philippi had a school of medicine connected with one of those guilds of physicians that the followers of early Greek medicine scattered through the Hellenistic world. This adds point to the suggestion that LUKE was a Philippian.

There may be a touch of pride in Luke's description of Philippi as "the leading city of that district" (Acts 16:12), though AMPHIPOLIS was the capital.

Philippi was the first European city to hear a Christian missionary, as far as the records go. Paul's choice of the locality throws light on the strategy of his evangelism. He came there from TROY by way of NEAPOLIS on the second missionary journey. He went to a place of prayer beside the river on the Sabbath where he sat down with a group of women, among them LYDIA, a seller of purple dye from THYATIRA. On the way there he exorcized a girl that had a spirit of divination. Her owners, displeased, dragged Paul and Silas before the magistrates of the city and accused them of disturbing the peace. The two missionaries were then scourged and put in stocks in the inner prison. At midnight an earthquake shook the prison to its foundation. Fearful that his prisoners had escaped, the jailer contemplated suicide. Paul indicated to him that he and Silas were still there. As a result of Paul's witness, the man believed, and he and his family were baptized. The next day the authorities learned that Paul and Silas were Roman citizens, apologized to them, and asked them to leave the city. They then visited Lydia and other believers before departing for Thessalonica (Acts 16:12-40).

At this point in the narrative of Acts the pronoun of the first person is dropped until Paul returned to Macedonia on the third missionary journey (Acts 20:5). Many conjecture that Luke, probably a native of Philippi, was left behind to work among the churches of Macedonia. Paul would later express a deep affection for the PHILIPPIANS in a letter written to it while he was in prison. The letter was written to thank the church for the gifts of funds and clothing that EPAPHRODITUS had brought to him. After his (first) Roman imprisonment, Paul may again have visited Philippi (cf. 1 Tim. 1:3). In the second century, both Ignatius and Polycarp wrote letters to the Philippians (see APOSTOLIC FATHERS).

Overview of PHILIPPIANS

Author: The apostle PAUL.

Historical setting: Probably written from ROME during the apostle's first imprisonment in that city (c. A.D. 61-63), but some scholars prefer an earlier date and alternate places (EPHESUS or CAESAREA). The letter was occasioned by Paul's receipt of an offering from the church at PHILIPPI and by news of discontent and divisions within that community.

Purpose: To thank the Philippians for their moral and financial support and to update them concerning his situation; to impress upon them the need for humility and unity within the church; to relieve their anxieties and urge contentment whatever their needs.

Contents: After a thanksgiving and prayer (Phil. 1:1-11), the apostle reports on his imprisonment and prospects (1:12-26), issues a call for SANCTIFICATION (1:27—2:30), deals with doctrinal problems (ch. 3), and gives final admonishments (ch. 4).

Philippians, Letter to the. fi-lip´ee-unz. A letter written by the apostle PAUL to the church in the city of PHILIPPI, the first Christian church in the province of MACEDONIA. The events leading to the founding of the congregation are related in Acts 16:9-40. The great apostle, accompanied by his coworkers SILAS, TIMOTHY, and LUKE, was on his second missionary journey through ASIA MINOR. Forbidden by the HOLY SPIRIT to preach in the provinces of ASIA and BITHYNIA, they made their way to TROAS, farthest port of Asia Minor on the Aegean Sea. In Troas Paul received a vision from the Lord to take the gospel to Europe. A man stood before him, a Greek of Macedonia, begging him, "Come over to Macedonia and help us" (16:9). Paul and his companions immediately answered this divine call and set sail for the nearest Macedonian port, NEAPOLIS; from there, it was a short distance to the important city of Philippi.

Philippi had been thoroughly colonized by the Romans after 30 B.C., but the city was still more Greek in culture than Roman. Also the city was the first station on the Egnatian Way (see VIA EGNATIA) and was the gateway to the East. Luke describes the city as follows: "From there we trav-eled to Philippi, a Roman colony and the leading city of that district of Macedonia. And we stayed there several days" (Acts 16:12). It is not unusual, therefore, that Paul's first convert there was a merchant woman named LYDIA, a seller of purple. Her whole household was baptized and became the nucleus of the new church (16:15). The remarkable conversion of the jailer with its accompanying miraculous events also took place in Philippi (16:25-34). There was, therefore, a very intimate relationship between the apostle and this church. No doubt this was true also because the congregation consisted mainly of GENTILES and Paul saw in them the real future of the church. They were poor, but the fruits of faith were abundant. On several occasions they collected funds for Paul and also aided him while he was in prison (Phil. 4:10-16). He had visited this favorite congregation whenever possible. The letter to the Philippians reflects deep affection for the recipients; they were Paul's "joy and crown" (4:1).

Before 1900 it was universally accepted that this document was written at ROME, where Paul was in prison. Since then, however, scholars have developed the hypothesis that it was written during

P

Paul's imprisonment in either CAESAREA or EPHESUS. The matter cannot be solved definitively. Pauline authorship is generally recognized, although some have argued the letter is made up of two or three smaller letters of Paul. Most recent commentators affirm the unity of the document.

The letter was occasioned by the gift of funds and clothing that EPAPHRODITUS brought to Paul in prison. Paul took the opportunity to thank the Philippians for this and other favors. In doing so, as was his custom, Paul added practical Christian admonition. He urged harmony and unity in aim and work (Phil. 1:27-29), humility as exemplified by Christ (2:1-11), the cultivation of joy and gladness amid difficulties (3:1; 4:1, 4-7), the pursuit of noble virtues (4:8-9), and settlement of disagreements among them (4:2-3). He strongly warned them against the Judaizers, gently rebuked a "perfectionist" element among them, and censured sensualists and materialists (3:18-21). The letter may be outlined as follows.

I. Chapter 1

Greetings and thanksgiving (1:1-11).
Progress of the gospel (1:11-20).
On remaining in the world and working and suffering for Christ (1:21-30).

II. Chapter 2

Exhortation to humility based on the humiliation and exaltation of Christ (2:1-13).
Exhortation to the Christian life (2:14-18).
Personal remarks involving Timothy and Epaphroditus (2:19-30).

III. Chapter 3

Warning against false teachers (3:1-3).
Paul's mighty confession of his faith (3:4-14).
The Christian's hope of heaven (3:15-21).

IV. Chapter 4

"Rejoice in the Lord always" (4:1-7).
Admonition to Christian virtues (4:8-13).
Paul's confidence in divine providence (4:14-19).
Final greeting (4:20-22).

Philistia. fi-lis´tee-uh (Heb. *pĕlešet H7148*, derivation uncertain; gentilic *pĕlišti H7149*, "Philistine").

Name given to a territory on the coastal plain of CANAAN, extending approximately from GAZA in the S to JOPPA in the N. The name PALESTINE derives from the Greek form of Philistia, *Palaistinē*, applied to the whole of Canaan. See PHILISTINE.

Philistim. See PHILISTINE.

Philistine. fi-lis´teen (Heb. *pĕlišti H7149*, derivation uncertain). KJV also Philistim (only Gen. 10:14). A warlike people of Aegean origin who occupied a territory in SW PALESTINE known as PHILISTIA. Their period of greatest importance was 1200-1000 B.C., when they were the principal enemy of ancient ISRAEL. The five large cities of the Philistines were ASHDOD, GAZA, ASHKELON, GATH, and EKRON (Josh. 13:3; 1 Sam. 6:17). They were situated in the broad coastal plain, except for Gath, which is in the SHEPHELAH or hill country. Our word *Palestine* is derived from Greek *Palaistinē*, which referred originally to the land of the Philistines.

I. Origins. The origin of the Philistines is not completely known. They are said to have come from CAPHTOR (Jer. 47:4; Amos 9:7), which is believed to be a name for CRETE, or perhaps more generally for the island world of the Aegean area. It is clear that they had migrated to CANAAN within historical times and that this migration was remembered by the Hebrews.

Most authorities connect the coming of the Philistines with certain political and ethnic movements in the E Mediterranean area in the late thirteenth and early twelfth centuries B.C. Five groups of SEA PEOPLES left their homeland and moved southeastward at this time. They destroyed Ugarit (an ancient city-state in what is now Syria; see RAS SHAMRA) and sought to invade EGYPT, where they were repulsed by RAMSES III in a great naval and land battle about 1191. On his monuments Ramses pictures these peoples as Europeans. Their pottery indicates that they came from the Greek islands, particularly Crete. The Philistines were one of these groups, and the Thekels another. After their repulse by the Egyptians, they invaded Canaan, the Philistines settling in what is now called the Philistine Plain, and the Thekels settling farther North, in the SHARON Plain.

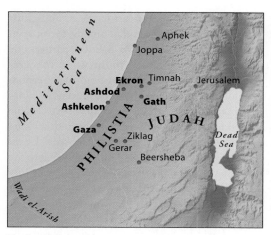

The five Philistine cities.

domination of the Hebrews so evident toward the end of the period of the judges and in SAUL's reign.

While the Philistines seem to have taught the Hebrews technology, the Hebrews and other inhabitants of Canaan influenced their Philistine neighbors in other ways. Soon after migrating to Canaan the Philistines seem to have adopted the Canaanite language and Semitic names. The Philistines worshiped the Semitic gods DAGON (Jdg. 16:23; 1 Sam. 5:1-7), ASHTORETH (1 Sam. 31:10), and BAAL-ZEBUB (2 Ki. 1:2, 6, 16). On the other hand, their non-Semitic origin is recalled in the epithet "uncircumcised" (Jdg. 14:3), so frequently used of them in the Bible.

III. History. The book of Judges mentions the Philistines as a major contender against the Hebrews for the possession of Palestine. No doubt the tribes of JUDAH, SIMEON, and DAN felt the pressure most, for their lands were adjacent to the Philistines. The judge SHAMGAR fought them (Jdg. 3:31). A Philistine oppression is briefly mentioned in 10:6-7. The life of SAMSON, the last of the deliverers mentioned in the book of Judges, is set in a violent struggle with the Philistines (chs. 13-16; note 14:4c; 15:11). Samson, a man of great strength but little self-discipline, was finally snared by a Philistine spy, DELILAH (16:4-21). No doubt the Danite migration (ch. 18) was occasioned by the Philistine pressure that kept the tribe of Dan from occupying the territory assigned them and forced them to seek a more easily taken area.

The book of 1 Samuel opens with the theme of Philistine oppression with which Judges closes. ELI's judgeship seems to have been characterized by Philistine domination (1 Sam. 4-6). SAMUEL was able to see a measure of victory when he defeated them at the battle of MIZPAH and forced them to return certain cities they had taken from Israel (7:7-14). Saul's reign, although it began well, ended in complete defeat for the Hebrews; and the Philistines seem to have overrun most of Palestine W of the JORDAN, even occupying BETH SHAN at the E end of the Valley of JEZREEL (13:5; 14:1-52; 17:1-58; 31:1-13).

During the latter part of the reign of Saul, David, the contender for the throne, fled for safety to the Philistines (1 Sam. 21:10-15; 27:1—28:2; 29:1-11), who gladly protected him, thinking thus

What caused these people to leave their Aegean homeland and come to Canaan? There appears to have taken place at this time a great torrent of migration out of Europe, which swept through the Aegean world, Anatolia (ASIA MINOR), and N SYRIA, destroying the HITTITE empire and creating a situation of movement and folk wandering that was destined to change the ethnic make-up of the E Mediterranean world.

II. Civilization. The Philistines had a unique political organization. Their cities were ruled by five "lords" or "rulers" (Josh. 13:3; Jdg. 16:5), one for each city. The Hebrew word is *seren H6249* (always used in the plural), a non-Semitic term that possibly corresponds to Greek *tyrannos*, used of absolute sovereigns. The Philistine city-states were certainly united in some sort of a confederation forming a pentapolis.

It is clear that the Philistines were more wealthy and more advanced in technology than their Hebrew neighbors. According to 1 Sam. 13:19-22 they knew how to forge iron, whereas the Hebrews did not. This monopoly the Philistines jealously guarded, forcing the Hebrews to come to them even for agricultural implements, which they repaired at exorbitant cost (13:21). This situation has been confirmed by ARCHAEOLOGY; the Philistines were in the Iron Age when they came to Palestine, but the Hebrews did not attain to this level of advance until the time of DAVID. This technological superiority (the Philistines even had chariots, 13:5) is the reason for the Philistines' military

P

Philistine pottery.

to contribute to the weakness of the Hebrews. No doubt David learned from the Philistines many things he later used to advantage when he became king, including perhaps the technique for working iron.

Probably David remained a Philistine vassal during the seven and a half years he reigned at HEBRON (2 Sam. 2:1-4). When at the end of this time he asserted his independence and united all Israel under his rule, he was immediately opposed by them, but he decisively defeated them in two battles (5:17-25). From this time on, the Philistine grip was broken. In later campaigns (21:15-22; 23:9-17) David consistently bested them, and it seems clear that from this time on the Philistines were confined to their own territory and were no longer a threat. David must have had peaceful relations with them at times, for his bodyguards, the KERETHITES and PELETHITES, appear to have been recruited from them (8:18; 15:18).

After the death of SOLOMON and the division of the Hebrew kingdom, the Philistines reasserted the independence they had lost to David and Solomon. Their cities appear to have engaged in commerce, for which their location certainly was ideal (Joel 3:4-8; Amos 1:6-8). Some of them paid tribute to JEHOSHAPHAT, after whose death they raided JUDAH (2 Chr. 17:11; 21:16-17). When the Assyrians later sought to control the road to Egypt, it is quite natural that the Philistines were frequently mentioned in their inscriptions, along with Israel and the other "Westlands" countries. SARGON (722-705 B.C.) captured the Philistine cities, deported some of the inhabitants, and set an Assyrian governor over them. In the days of HEZEKIAH the Philistines played a great part in the revolt against SENNACHERIB. It appears that among them, as in JERUSALEM, there were two political parties, one recommending submission to the world conquerors, the other urging a stubborn fight for freedom in union with their neighbors the Judeans.

ESARHADDON and ASHURBANIPAL name Philistine tributaries as well as the Judean king MANASSEH. The later struggles between Egypt and Assyria were the cause of great suffering to the Philistine cities, and practically close their history as strictly Philistinian. The cities did continue as predominantly non-Jewish centers, becoming Hellenistic cities in the Greek period.

IV. Early biblical mention. Long before the times of the judges certain Philistines and their land are mentioned in the Bible (Gen. 10:14; 21:32-34; 26:14). ABIMELECH king of GERAR is called "king of the Philistines" (26:1; cf. 26:14-15). These references have often been regarded as anachronisms, since the Philistines appear not to have entered Canaan before the period of the judges. A more generous judgment has seen here a later revision of the text, bringing the proper names up to date. It is possible that a later editor, perhaps during the Hebrew kingdom, may have revised the proper names to make them meaningful in his time, thus introducing the name Philistine into Genesis (cf. also Exod. 13:17; 23:31; Josh. 13:2-3).

On the other hand, recent studies of the problem suggest another approach. Folk movements are never completed in one generation. It is not impossible that the great Philistine movement that entered Canaan during the judges period may have had a small precursor as early as the patriarchal age. The army of Ramses III, which repulsed the invading Philistines in 1191 B.C., itself contained soldiers who are portrayed on the Egyptian monuments as Philistines. Evidently these had joined the Egyptian army as mercenaries at an earlier date. Further, pottery identified as Philistine has turned up in Palestinian excavations recently in layers earlier than those of the judges period. It also seems that the Sea Peoples invading Egypt came from land as well as sea, and Ramses III refers to "The Peleset [i.e., Philistines] who are hung up in their towns," implying that some of these troublesome people had already settled nearby.

It therefore seems possible that some Philistines were settled in Gerar by the time of Isaac. They were not a large hostile group (as later), but a small settlement with which the patriarch had more or less friendly relations.

Philo Judaeus. fī´loh joo-dee´uhs (Gk. *Philōn*, "beloved" or "loving, friendly"). Also known as Philo (or Philon) of Alexandria. A 1st-cent. Hellenistic Jewish philosopher born in ALEXANDRIA about 20 B.C. Alexandria had an old tradition of Jewish scholarship, and Philo sprang from a rich and priestly family. Few details are known of his life, save that in A.D. 39 he took part in an embassy to ROME to plead the case of the Jews whose religious privileges, previously wisely recognized by Rome, were menaced by the mad CALIGULA. He died about the year 50.

Philo was a prolific author. His writings include philosophical works, commentaries on the PENTATEUCH, and historical and apologetic works in the cosmopolitan tradition of Alexandrian Jewry, which had long sought to commend its literature to the GENTILE world. These concerns led him to develop an allegorical interpretation of the OT (see ALLEGORY). His aim was to show that much of the philosophy of the Greeks had been anticipated by the Jews. He was also, like PAUL of Tarsus, a citizen of two worlds and sought to synthesize his own Hellenistic and Hebraic traditions. His doctrine of God most notably reveals this synthesis. The LOGOS, in Philo's rendering of the Greek doctrine, was simultaneously the creative power that orders the universe and also a species of mediator through whom people know God. JOHN THE APOSTLE possibly had Philo's philosophy in mind when he wrote the first eighteen verses of the fourth gospel, sharply personal though John's own interpretation is. Others, too, were influenced by Philo's mysticism and principles of exegesis. Clement and Origen used his works; and the Latin fathers, generally following his methods of allegorical interpretation, established a tradition of exegesis that still finds favor in some quarters.

Philologus. fil-ol´uh-guhs (Gk. *Philologos G5807*, "lover of learning, scholar"). A Christian in ROME to whom PAUL sent greetings (Rom. 16:15). He is listed first in a group of five, and it is possible that he was the leader of a house church (cf. vv. 5, 10, 11, 15). In the Greek text, his name seems to be coupled with that of JULIA, and some have speculated that she was his wife (or possibly his sister).

philosophy. This term (from Gk. *philosophia G5814*, lit., "the love of wisdom") is used in a derogatory sense in the Bible. It is not a genuine love of wisdom that PAUL deprecates in Col. 2:8, but "hollow and deceptive philosophy, which depends on human tradition and the basic principles of this world rather than on Christ." The same thought is expressed in the discussion of WISDOM in 1 Corinthians (1 Cor. 1:18—2:16; 3:18-21), where Paul not only emphasizes the inadequacy of worldly wisdom, but says, "We ... speak a message of wisdom among the mature" (2:6), a wisdom based on REVELATION. This is similar to the "wisdom" doctrine of Job, Ecclesiastes, certain psalms, and especially Proverbs. The book of Ecclesiastes, which teaches that "all is vanity under the sun," may be regarded as an answer to modern philosophical naturalism. For the "philosophers" of Acts 17:18, see EPICUREAN and STOIC.

Phinehas. fin´ee-huhs (Heb. *pinḥās H7090*, prob. from Egyp. *p'-nḥsy*, "the southerner," referring mainly to Nubians, hence "dark-skinned"). **(1)** Son of ELEAZAR and grandson of AARON (Exod. 6:25; 1 Chr. 6:4, 50; 9:20). He was once superintendent of certain Korahite gate keepers (1 Chr. 9:20; see KORAH). He is noted as ancestor of EZRA (Ezra 7:5; cf. also 8:2). The number of occasions that called Phinehas into special activity indicates that he was a man of integrity and dependability, one in whom flamed deep moral passion. The first of these was at SHITTIM, at the end of the wilderness journey before crossing the JORDAN (Num. 25:1), when the incident involving BALAAM led to licentiousness with Moabite women (Num. 25:3; 31:16; Mic. 6:5). A plague broke out, but it was stayed following Phinehas's exploit in transfixing ZIMRI and COZBI, his paramour, with one spear-thrust, because of which he was given the covenant of an everlasting priesthood (Num. 25:7-15; Ps. 106:30). It was Phinehas who accompanied the 1,000 from each tribe in the move to avenge Israel, when he

P

carried certain "articles from the sanctuary and the trumpets for signaling" (Num. 31:6). Again Phinehas was commissioned to inquire into the apparent violation of divine law by the E Jordan tribes, which were exonerated and praised when it was found that the altar raised was simply for reminder in times to come (Josh. 22:9-34). Once more, following the outrage of the concubine of the sojourning Levite at GIBEAH of Benjamin, it was Phinehas who at that time ministered before the ARK OF THE COVENANT, and who gave divine endorsement and promise of success for the third attempt in avenging the crime (Jdg. 20:28).

(2) Son of ELI the priest who, along with his brother HOPHNI, demanded reversal of sacrificial regulations, engaged in gross immorality, and was condemned by a "man of God" (1 Sam. 2:11-36). The brothers connived at taking the ark into battle, but they were killed, and the ark was taken by the PHILISTINES (ch. 4).

(3) Father of Eleazar, a postexilic priest who with others made accounting for certain valuables that the returnees brought from BABYLON (Ezra 8:33).

(Phinehas was also the name of the last high priest before the destruction of Jerusalem in A.D. 70 and of the last treasurer of the temple, who when the city fell handed the Romans some of its treasures [Jos. *War* 4.3.8; 6.8.3].)

Phlegon. fleg´uhn (Gk. *Phlegōn G5823*, "burning, blazer"). A Christian in ROME to whom PAUL sent greetings (Rom. 16:14). He is named in a group of five believers who possibly formed a household church.

Phoebe. fee´bee (Gk. *Phoibē G5833*, "bright, pure," orig. the name of a Greek mythological figure). KJV Phebe. A woman from the church in CENCHREA (a harbor village to the E of CORINTH) whom PAUL commended to the church in ROME. The apostle describes her as (1) "our sister," (2) a "servant" or "deacon" or "deaconess," (3) a person who "has been a great help to many people, including me" (Rom. 16:1-2; it is generally assumed that she acted as courier, delivering the Romans epistle to its destination). Whether the Greek term *diakonos G1356* (a form that is both masc. and fem.)

bears in this passage the general sense of "servant, assistant" (Matt. 20:26 et al.) or denotes an ecclesiastical office has been a matter of considerable dispute. Some argue that elsewhere in the NT and other early Christian literature there is no clear evidence that women held the position of DEACON and that a distinct office of "deaconess" did not arise until the third century. Others respond that Paul's description of Phoebe suggests more than general service and that she must have held a position of ministerial leadership. Moreover, the apostle applies to her the term *prostatis G4706* (NIV, "great help"), which could be used in the sense of "benefactor" or "patron," implying some leadership role. The matter cannot be resolved with certainty.

Phoenicia. fi-nish´uh (Gk. *Phoinikē G5834*). KJV Phenicia (Acts 21:2) and Phenice (11:19; 15:3). An ancient country on the E coast of the MEDITERRANEAN. Its two main cities were TYRE and SIDON. The name is applied to a strip of seacoast stretching about 120 mi. (190 km.) N from Mount CARMEL, in what is now Lebanon and Syria. Exact definition of boundaries is not possible, for the Phoenicians were associated with their cities rather than with their hinterland, after the fashion of the Greek colonies. It can be said, however, that to the N Phoenicia never extended beyond Arvad or Arados on the modern island of Ruad, 80 mi. (130 km.) N of Sidon. The Semitic name for the

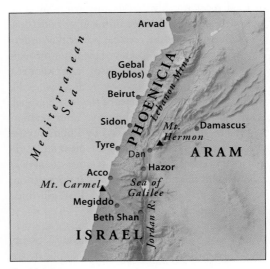

Phoenicia.

land was CANAAN, a name of doubtful significance. The name Phoenicia possibly derives from a Greek word meaning "(dark) red," but if so, it is unclear whether the Phoenicians were so designated because of their purple industry or their dark skin or their copper trade or their date palms (the latter is another meaning of Gk. *phoinix*).

The Phoenicians were Semites who came to the Mediterranean as one ripple of the series of Semitic migrations that moved W and S round the FERTILE CRESCENT during the second millennium B.C. ABRAHAM was part of this historical process, but the movement brought major tribal elements—the AMORITES, for example, to PALESTINE, the Kassite dynasty to BABYLON, and the HYKSOS to EGYPT. The tribes who occupied the coastal strip turned their attention to the sea because of the pressure on the agricultural lands in the narrow lowland strip, never more than 20 mi. (32 km.) wide, behind them. A tradition of seafaring may have accompanied the immigrants from the Persian Gulf, itself the first scene of human navigation and seaborne trade. Such was the challenge and stimulus that made the Phoenicians the most notable sailors of the ancient world and led to their feats of colonization, which spread their trading posts around the African coast from Carthage westward and established them in Spain and Sicily.

It is not known whether they built the towns that formed the centers of their power and trade, or whether, descending to the sea, they found the towns awaiting their occupation. Like that of the Greeks, the Phoenician civilization was organized around the city. That is why Phoenicia had no place in history as a political unit. It is Tyre and Sidon, and less frequently other cities, such as Acco and DOR, that appear in the record as units. Sidon was the most powerful and influential of the Phoenician cities. To the Greek poet Homer, Phoenicians were commonly Sidonians; the OT uses the same nomenclature. "The gods of Sidon," BAAL and ASHTORETH (Jdg. 10:6), were the gods of the Phoenicians generally (also Jdg. 18:7; 1 Ki. 5:6; 11:5, 33; 16:31; 2 Ki. 23:13). The reference to "Jezebel daughter of Ethbaal king of the Sidonians" (1 Ki. 16:31) is at first sight strange, for ETHBAAL was king of Tyre. As stated above, however, "Sidonian" had become a generic term for "Phoenician."

Woman at the balustrade window. This popular theme in Phoenician art is often associated with Astarte (Ashtoreth) and ritual prostitution.

© Dr. James C. Martin. The British Museum. Photographed by permission.

Phoenicia first appears in recorded history in the Egyptian account of the northern campaigns of THUTMOSE III. In his campaign against the Hittites of 1471 B.C., the pharaoh found it necessary to secure the Phoenician coastal strip as an essential avenue of communications. He punished severely the revolt of Arvad, the northernmost town of the Phoenicians, and went to considerable pains to organize the series of Phoenician ports as supply depots. Sporadically, as with the rest of the lands to the N, Egypt asserted or relaxed her authority. The AMARNA Letters show Phoenicia in the same state of disunity and internal rivalry as Palestine during the weak reign of the mystic Amenhotep IV. Seti I (1373-1292) pushed his conquests as far as Acco and Tyre, RAMSES II (1292-1225) as far as Biruta (modern Beirut). The whole coast revolted in the reign of MERNEPTAH (1225-1215), including Philistia, for this pharaoh boasts, "Plundered is Canaan with every evil."

Egyptian influence fluctuated over the next century, and when Ramses XII (1118-1090 B.C.) sent the priest Wen-Amon to buy cedar for his funeral barge, the Egyptian envoy was treated with the scantest courtesy in Dor and Tyre. An entertaining

P

papyrus tells his story. A century later found HIRAM, king of Tyre, in alliance with DAVID, a partnership that developed into a trade alliance in the days of SOLOMON. Solomon's fleet of "ships of Tarshish" at EZION GEBER on the Gulf of AQABAH seems to have been part of a combined trading venture whereby the Phoenicians used Solomon's port and piloted Solomon's ships to southern Arabia and India (1 Ki. 10:22; 2 Chr. 9:21).

With the division of ISRAEL, Phoenicia became the neighbor and partner of the northern kingdom, while JUDAH lay along the communication route with the Gulf of Aqabah and the Red Sea. Hence AHAB's alliance with JEZEBEL, the prosperity of the N, and the sequence of events that led to ELIJAH's protest and the contest on Carmel. The Assyrians had dealings with Phoenicia. Ashurnasirpal (884-860 B.C.) imposed tribute on Tyre and Sidon after his thrust to the sea. Shalmaneser II added Arvad. TIGLATH-PILESER III (745-727) reasserted the Assyrian authority, which had lapsed. SHALMANESER V (726-722) unsuccessfully besieged Tyre for five years. SENNACHERIB (705-681) besieged Sidon, took tribute from Sidon and Acco, but left Tyre undisturbed. Tyre was a formidable task for a besieger. ASHURBANIPAL (668-626) claimed to have reduced Tyre and Arvad, but by the end of his reign Phoenicia was free again, as Assyria lapsed into one of her phases of fatigue.

NEBUCHADNEZZAR (605-562) besieged Tyre for thirteen years and seems to have captured the city (Ezek. 26-29) or received its surrender on terms. Hence, probably, the preeminence of Sidon in Persian times. According to historians Diodorus and Herodotus, Sidon provided XERXES with his best ships for the great raid on GREECE. All the Phoenician cities submitted to ALEXANDER THE GREAT after Issus (333), except Tyre, which Alexander took after a vigorous siege of seven months. Under the successors, the power of the Ptolemies of Egypt (see PTOLEMY) first extended far up the Phoenician coast, but after 197 the SELEUCIDS of SYRIA controlled the land, until the whole area passed into Roman hands in 65. The reference to a woman "born in Syrian Phoenicia" in Mk. 7:26 reflects the fact of the century and a half of Syrian rule.

The Phoenician stock must by this time have been heavily diluted by immigrant blood, principally Greek. The whole area figured largely in the early evangelism of the church (Acts 11:19; 15:3; 21:2). Phoenicia's achievement was principally in the realm of trade and in her simplification and diffusion of the alphabet, as a tool and means, no doubt, of commerce. Ezekiel 27 and 28 give some notion of the extent and variety of Phoenician trade, but the Phoenicians did nothing to spread or communicate the knowledge, geographical and social, that their voyaging won. Tyre's colony at Carthage blockaded the Straits of Gibraltar for many generations in an attempt to guard the western and Atlantic trade routes, and this secrecy was a Phoenician principle. The land made no contribution to art and literature, and its religious influence, heavily infected with the cruder fertility cults, was pernicious.

Phoenix. fee´niks (Gk. *Phoinix G5837*, a term that had several meanings, such as "purple" and "date palm"; in Gk. literature it was the name attributed to the eponymous founder of the Phoenicians and other figures, but the term also refers to a mythological bird believed to arise from the corpse of its parent). KJV Phenice. A harbor in CRETE on the W end of its S shore. According to Acts 27:12, it provided a safer shelter in winter than FAIR HAVENS, the place where the Alexandrian grain ship carrying PAUL had anchored. The location of Phoenix has caused some debate. Available information suggests a site in the neighborhood of the small rocky peninsula of Cape Mouros. On the E side lies the village of Loutro (Loutron) with a deep harbor, and on the W is a larger and more open bay. Evidence seems to favor the western bay, which still retains the name of Phineka. The description of its aspect in Acts, "facing both southwest and northwest," supports this view (27:12; the RSV rendering, "northeast and southeast," is rejected by most scholars). Nevertheless, some commentators favor the E harbor.

Phrygia. frij´ee-uh (Gk. *Phrygia G5867*). A tract of territory of indeterminate and wavering boundaries, lying on the W watershed of the Anatolian plateau, and comprising in earliest times, apparently, the major part of W ASIA MINOR. It may be said that Phrygia was simply the area occupied by the Phrygians, with its W limits at one time on the Aegean Sea, and its N boundaries on the upper valley of the

Sangarius River (modern Sakarya), thus adjacent to BITHYNIA; to the S and E, Phrygian occupation seems not to have penetrated beyond the basin of the Maeander River or the areas around ANTIOCH of Pisidia and ICONIUM. Its tablelands, which rose to c. 4,000 ft. (1,220 m.), contained many cities and towns considerable in size and wealth. In NT times "Phrygia" certainly meant an extensive territory, which at times contributed area to a number of different Roman provinces. It is thought to have this broader meaning in Acts 2:10, which speaks of devout Jews from Phrygia at PENTECOST.

Whatever the exact extent of the province, it receives its renown mainly from PAUL's missionary journeys. He and his coworkers visited the fertile territory, which contained rich pastures for cattle and sheep and a heavy population in need of the gospel, during all three missionary journeys. If Phrygia is understood in its broader sense, Paul and BARNABAS introduced Christianity into the province during the first journey (Acts 13:13; 14:24). Acts 16:6 briefly describes the visit on the second journey in these words: "Paul and his companions traveled throughout the region of Phrygia and Galatia, having been kept by the Holy Spirit from preaching the word in the province of Asia." On his third journey Paul quickly revisited the province on his way to EPHESUS and CORINTH (18:23): "After spending some time in Antioch, Paul set out from there and traveled from place to place throughout the region of Galatia and Phrygia, strengthening all the disciples." Although a great deal of Christian activity took place in ancient Phrygia, with this reference it passes from the biblical record.

Phurah. See PURAH.

Phut. See PUT.

Phuvah. See PUAH.

Phygellus. See PHYGELUS.

Phygelus. fi´juh-luhs (Gk. *Phygelos G5869*). KJV Phygellus. A Christian named with HERMOGENES as among those in the Roman province of ASIA who deserted PAUL in his hour of need (2 Tim. 1:15). It may be that Phygelus, being in ROME,

forsook Paul's personal cause in the Roman courts at a crucial time when his testimony could have meant much for the future of the church (cf. 4:16). Some scholars speculate that Phygelus may also have been one of the leaders of a group of wayward Christians in Rome (Phil. 1:15-16).

phylactery. fi-lak´tuh-ree. This term is a transliteration of Greek *phylaktērion*, which in classical literature meant "safeguard, means of protection, amulet" (the Latin VULGATE took over the Greek word and it was accepted by English translations). The term occurs only once in the NT (Matt. 23:5), which records Jesus' accusation against the SCRIBES and PHARISEES, "Everything they do is done for men to see: They make their phylacteries wide and the tassels on their garments long." This was not necessarily a condemnation of the custom of wearing phylacteries, but only of ostentation that prostituted an ancient custom full of symbolism in the interests of outward display. Most scholars regard the "phylacteries" as identical with the *tefillin* that every male Israelite over the age of thirteen was required to "wear at daily morning prayer." Modern Jewish usage follows essentially the practice described in the Mishnah (see TALMUD) and is based ultimately on the biblical injunctions (Exod. 13:9, 16; Deut. 6:8; 11:18) that the people of Israel were to bind God's law as frontlets between the eyes and as a sign upon the hand. (Christian exegesis has taken these passages figuratively.) The four passages where this command occurs (Exod. 13:1-10; 13:11-16; Deut. 6:4-9; 11:13-21) were written out on parchment and placed in small cubic boxes made of the skin of clean animals. Leather flaps were left on the top of the cube through which passed long leather straps for binding the phylacteries to the head and the left arm. Both the boxes and the straps were black. Fragments of phylacteries have been found in the Qumran caves (see DEAD SEA SCROLLS), but here the TEN COMMANDMENTS were included among the texts, which shows that the form was not absolutely standard before the fall of Jerusalem in A.D. 70.

physician. See OCCUPATIONS AND PROFESSIONS.

Pi Beseth. pi-bee´sith (Heb. *pi-beset H7083*, from Egyp. *pr-bᵓstt*, "house of [the goddess] Bastet";

class. Gk. *Boubastis*, LXX *Boubastos*). Capital of the 18th nome (province) of Lower (northern) Egypt, and capital of EGYPT under the 22nd dynasty. It is modern Tell Baṣteh on the Tanitic branch of the NILE, near modern Zagazig. The city was important throughout Egyptian history, but its greatest glory came when SHISHAK made it second only to THEBES in prestige and glory under the 22nd dynasty. The city's original name, Bast, and that of its goddess, Bastet, were related. Later it was known by its sacred name, House of Bastet (Bubastis). The goddess usually was depicted as a woman with the head of a cat or a lioness. She was one of the lesser deities whose popularity greatly increased after the Assyrians sacked Thebes and caused a readjustment in Egyptian religion. This new religious importance may have helped turn EZEKIEL's attention to the city, for the prophet predicts that its young men, as well as those of HELIOPOLIS, would fall by the sword, and the inhabitants would be taken captive (Ezek. 30:17; NIV, "Bubastis").

pick. This English noun is used to render a Hebrew word that refers to a sharp iron instrument. The word occurs only when it is stated that DAVID consigned the Ammonites "to labor with saws and with iron picks and axes" (2 Sam. 12:31; 1 Chr. 20:3; KJV, "harrow").

picture. The KJV uses "picture" on three occasions to render two different Hebrew terms (Num. 33:52 [NIV, "carved images"]; Prov. 25:11 [NIV, "settings"]; Isa. 2:16 [NIV, "vessel," referring to a ship]). The NRSV and NJPS use the term once to render the common Hebrew word for "likeness," *dĕmût H1952* (Ezek. 23:15).

piety. See GODLINESS.

pig. See ANIMALS.

pigeon. See BIRDS.

Pi Hahiroth. pi´huh-hi´roth (Heb. *pi haḥîrôt H7084*, probably an Egyp. name otherwise unknown). A place near BAAL ZEPHON, between MIGDOL and the RED SEA (Sea of Reeds), where PHARAOH was miraculously defeated (Exod. 14:2, 9; Num. 33:7-

8). Its identification is dependent upon the route taken by the Israelites when they left Egypt. See EXODUS, THE. One view would identify the Sea of Reeds with Lake Sirbonis and place Pi Hahiroth near the MEDITERRANEAN Sea. A second theory, keeping the Hebrews in the S to avoid the way of the PHILISTINES (Exod. 13:17), places Pi Hahiroth just N of modern Suez. At present, this view attracts relatively little support. Third, it may be placed near modern Tell Defneh (Defenneh, classical Daphne) on the assumption that Baal Zephon is TAHPANHES; the evidence is less than conclusive, but this view seems more compatible with contemporary identifications of RAMESES and PITHOM. Another suggestion is the low ground near the Bitter Lakes, W of the Suez Canal.

Pilate, Pontius. pi´luht, pon´shuhs (Gk. *Pilatos G4397*, meaning uncertain; his *nomen* or tribal name was *Pontios G4508*, "Pontius," which occurs only three times in the NT [Lk. 3:1; Acts 4:27; 1 Tim. 6:13]). Roman governor of JUDEA who held office A.D. 26 to 36 and who sentenced CHRIST to death by crucifixion (Matt. 27:2-65; Mk. 15:1-44; Lk. 3:1; 13:1; 23:1-52; Jn. 18:29—19:38; Acts 3:13; 4:27; 13:28; 1 Tim. 6:13). Whether it be considered an honor or a disgrace, he is the one man of all Roman officialdom who is named in the Apostles' Creed—"suffered under Pontius Pilate."

Little is known of Pilate's early or later years, since most of the secular references may be only legend and tradition, such as the story that he was an illegitimate son of Tyrus, king of Mayence, who sent him to ROME as a hostage. In Rome, so a story goes, he committed murder and was then sent to PONTUS of ASIA MINOR where he subdued a rebellious people, regained favor with Rome, and was awarded the governorship of Judea. It is more probable that, like the sons of many prominent Romans, he was trained for governmental service; and either because of his political astuteness or as a political plum the Emperor TIBERIUS gave him the hard task of governing the troublesome Jews. The Romans had many such governors throughout the provinces, which was part of their success in local government. Judea had a succession of these smaller rulers before and after Pilate. Generally they were in charge of tax and financial matters, but

© Dr. James C. Martin. The Israel Museum, Jerusalem. Photographed by permission.

This inscription, which dedicates a temple to Emperor Tiberius, contains the only known extrabiblical reference to Pontius Pilate.

governing Palestine was so difficult that the procurator there was directly responsible to the emperor and also had supreme judicial authority such as Pilate used regarding Christ. In addition to Judea, his territory included SAMARIA and old IDUMEA.

Most governors disliked being stationed in a distant, difficult, dry outpost such as Judea. Pilate, however, seemed to enjoy tormenting the Jews, although, as it turned out, he was seldom a match for them. He never really understood them, as his frequent rash and capricious acts reveal. The Jewish historian JOSEPHUS tells us that he immediately offended the Jews by bringing the "outrageous" Roman standards into the Holy City. At another time he hung golden shields inscribed with the names and images of Roman deities in the temple itself. Once he even appropriated some of the temple tax to build an aqueduct. To this must be added the horrible incident mentioned in Lk. 13:1 about "the Galileans whose blood Pilate had mixed with their sacrifices," meaning no doubt that Roman soldiers killed these men while they were sacrificing in the Holy Place. These fearful events seem to disagree with the role Pilate played in the trial of Jesus, where he was as clay in the hands of the Jews, but this may be explained by the fact that his

fear of the Jewish people increased because of their frequent complaints to Rome.

According to his custom, Pilate was in JERUSALEM at the time to keep order during the Passover Feast. His usual headquarters were in Caesarea. After the Jews had condemned Jesus in their own courts, they brought him early in the morning to Pilate, who was no doubt residing in HEROD's palace near the temple. It is surprising he gave them a hearing so early in the day (Jn. 18:28). From the beginning of the hearing he was torn between offending the Jews and condemning an innocent person, and, apart from simply acquitting him, he tried every device to set Jesus free. He declared Jesus innocent after private interrogation; he sent him to Herod Antipas; he had Jesus scourged, hoping this would suffice; finally he offered the Jews a choice between Jesus and a coarse insurrectionist. When he heard the words, "If you let this man go, you are no friend of Caesar," and "We have no king but Caesar!" he thought of politics rather than justice and condemned an innocent man to crucifixion. Washing his hands only enhanced his guilt. Pilate is to be judged in the light of his times when one lived by the philosophy of self-aggrandizement and expediency.

Scripture is silent regarding the end of Pilate. According to Josephus, his political career came to an end six years later when he sent soldiers to Samaria to suppress a small harmless religious rebellion, and in that suppression innocent men were killed. The Samaritans complained to Vitellius, legate of SYRIA, who sent Pilate to Rome. His friend Tiberius the emperor died while Pilate was on his way to Rome, and Pilate's name disappears from the official history of Rome. The Christian historian Eusebius says that soon afterward, "wearied with misfortunes," he took his own life. Various traditions conflict as to how and where Pilate killed himself. One familiar legend states that he was banished to Vienna; another that he sought solitude from politics on the mountain by Lake Lucerne, now known at Mount Pilatus. After some years of despair and depression, he is said to have plunged into the lake from a precipice.

Pildash. pil´dash (Heb. *pildāš H7109*, derivation uncertain). Son of NAHOR by his wife MILCAH;

P

nephew of ABRAHAM (Gen. 22:22). The passage as a whole seems to indicate the origins of various tribes; the descendants of Pildash may have inhabited N ARABIA.

Pileha. See PILHA.

pilgrim, pilgrimage. The KJV uses the term *pilgrimage* in three OT passages (Gen. 47:9 [also NIV]; Exod. 6:4; Ps. 119:54; cf. also the NIV's contextual translation in Ps. 84:5). In addition, it uses *pilgrim* twice to render Greek *parepidēmos G4215*, "stranger, foreigner," describing Christians whose final citizenship is in heaven and who are regarded as temporary dwellers on earth (Heb. 11:13; 1 Pet. 2:11; in the only other passage where this Greek word occurs, 1 Pet. 1:1, the KJV uses "strangers"). A whole group of Psalms, the so-called "Songs of Ascent" or "Pilgrim Songs" (Ps. 120-134), may have been used by pilgrims on their way to JERUSALEM. The NT makes reference to Jews going to the Holy City for Passover and Pentecost (Lk. 2:41; Jn. 5:1; 7:2; Acts 2:1-11; et al.) after "the manner of pilgrims."

Pilha. pil´hah (Heb. *pilḥāʾ H7116*, possibly "millstone"). KJV Pileha. One of the Israelite leaders who sealed the covenant with NEHEMIAH (Neh. 10:21).

pillar. There is usually a religious element in the purpose and use of pillars: stones were set erect as memorials of a divine appearance in connection with the WORSHIP of the one true God (Gen. 28:18-22; 31:13; 35:14; Exod. 24:4; Isa. 19:19; Hos. 3:4; 10:1-2). LOT's wife, looking back at the ruin of SODOM, became a pillar of salt (Gen. 19:26). In addition to heaping up stones, people set up stone pillars to signify an agreement with religious conditions between them (31:43-52). RACHEL's grave was marked by a pillar (35:20). ABSALOM in his lifetime erected a pillar to be his memorial (2 Sam. 18:18). Standing stones used in idolatrous worship are frequently mentioned (Exod. 23:24; 34:13; Lev. 26:1; Deut. 7:5; 12:3; 16:22; 1 Ki. 14:23; 2 Ki. 17:10; 18:4; 23:14; 2 Chr. 14:3; 31:1; Mic. 5:13).

The term *pillar*, however, occurs also in other contexts, referring to (1) the pillar of cloud and fire (see next article) that guided Israel in the wilderness, (2) tabernacle pillars either of acacia wood or of bronze or material not named (Exod. 26:32, 37; 27:10-17; 36:36, 38; 38:10-17, 28; 39:33, 40; 40:18; Num. 3:36-37; 4:31-32), (3) the pillars of Solomon's TEMPLE (1 Ki. 7:2-42; 2 Ki. 25:13-17; 1 Chr. 18:8; 2 Chr. 3:15, 17; 4:12-13; Jer. 27:19; 52:17-22), (4) the pillars of the new temple that EZEKIEL saw in a vision (Ezek. 40:49; 42:6), (5) the supporting pillars that SAMSON pushed apart in the PHILISTINE temple (Jdg. 16:25-29), and (6) the marble pillars of the Persian king's palace (Esth. 1:6).

God promised to make Jeremiah an iron pillar (Jer. 1:18). A man's legs are compared to pillars of marble (Cant. 5:15). The seven pillars of wisdom are mentioned but not defined (Prov. 9:1). The pillars of the earth (Job 9:6; Ps. 75:3) and of heaven (Job 26:11) refer to the fixed order in the heavens; God "suspends the earth over nothing" (Job 26:7). The four NT uses are figurative: a victorious Christian (Rev. 3:12), the church (1 Tim. 3:15), apostles (Gal. 2:9), and an angel (Rev. 10:1).

pillar of cloud and fire. God guided ISRAEL out of EGYPT and through the wilderness by a pillar of cloud by day. In darkness, it became a pillar of fire that they might travel by night in escaping from the Egyptian army (Exod. 13:21-22). When the Egyptians overtook the Israelites, the angel of the Lord removed this cloudy, fiery pillar from before them and placed it behind them as an effective barrier (14:19-20, 24). The pillar of cloud stood over the tent of meeting outside the camp whenever the Lord met MOSES there (33:7-11). The Lord came down for judgment in the cloud (Num. 12; 14:13-35), and God met Moses and JOSHUA in the cloud at the tent to make arrangements for the succession when Moses was near death (Deut. 31:14-23). Psalm 99:7 reminds the people that God spoke to them in the pillar of cloud. When EZRA prayed in the presence of the returning exiles at JERUSALEM, he reviewed the way God had led the people by the pillar of cloud and fire (Neh. 9:12, 19). PAUL speaks of the Israelite forefathers being under the cloud, baptized into Moses in the cloud (1 Cor. 10:1-2). No natural phenomenon fits the biblical description. The cloud and fire were divine manifestations, in a form sufficiently well-defined to be called a pillar.

pillow. This English term is used by the KJV to translate several Hebrew words that most modern versions render differently (Gen. 28:11, 18; 1 Sam. 19:13, 16; Ezek. 13:18, 20). In addition, it is used to translate Greek *proskephalaion G4676*, which does mean "pillow" or "cushion" (only Mk. 4:38).

Piltai. pil′ti (Heb. *piltāy H7122*, prob. short form of PELATIAH, "Yahweh has delivered"). Head of the priestly families of Miniamin and Moadiah in the days of the high priest JOIAKIM (Neh. 12:17).

pim. See WEIGHTS AND MEASURES.

pin. This English term is used by the KJV mainly to render Hebrew *yātēd H3845*, referring to the tent pegs of the TABERNACLE (Exod. 27:19 et al.); they were probably sharpened at one end and so shaped at the other end as to allow chords to be attached (38:18). Modern versions render this Hebrew word as "pin" in other contexts, for example, with reference to the objects used in a loom to tighten the weave (Jdg. 16:13-14).

pine. See PLANTS.

pinnacle. Traditional rendering of Greek *pterygion G4762* (lit., "small wing," but applied to any "tip" or "edge"), referring to the part of the TEMPLE in Jerusalem to which Satan took Jesus and from which he tempted him to cast himself down (Matt. 4:5; Lk. 4:9; NIV, "highest point"). The exact location is unknown. The two places suggested most frequently are a high point on the SE corner, overlooking the valley of the KIDRON, or some part of the roof of the temple.

Pinon. pi′non (Heb. *pînōn H7091*, meaning unknown). Descendant of Esau, listed among the clan chiefs of EDOM (Gen. 36:41; 1 Chr. 1:52). His name may be preserved in PUNON, an Edomite copper-mining center.

pipes. See MUSIC AND MUSICAL INSTRUMENTS.

Piram. pi′ruhm (Heb. *pir'ām H7231*, possibly from the Heb. word for "wild donkey"). A king of JARMUTH (a city-state SW of Jerusalem) who formed a league with four other AMORITE kings to punish GIBEON for submitting to the Israelites (Josh. 10:3-5). JOSHUA defeated them in battle at BETH HORON, killed the five kings, and cast their bodies into a cave (10:6-27).

Pirathon. pihr′uh-thon (Heb. *pir'ātôn H7284*, meaning uncertain; gentilic *pir'ātônî H7285*, "Pirathonite"). A town in EPHRAIM, "in the hill country of the Amalekites," that was the home of the Israelite judge ABDON (Jdg. 12:15). Both Abdon and BENAIAH, one of DAVID's mighty warriors, are called "Pirathonites" (Jdg. 12:13; 2 Sam. 23:30; 1 Chr. 27:14). Pirathon is identified with modern Far'ata, some 7 mi. (11 km.) WSW of SHECHEM.

Pisgah. piz′guh (Heb. *pisgâ H7171*, perhaps "cleft"). A height in the mountains of ABARIM, NE of the DEAD SEA. The name Pisgah never occurs apart from the phrases "the top of Pisgah" (Num. 21:20; 23:14; Deut. 3:27; 34:1) and "the slopes of Pisgah" (Deut. 3:17; 4:49; Josh. 12:3; 13:20; the KJV, following LXX, transliterates the Heb. word for "slope" with "Ashdoth" [except Deut. 4:49, "springs of Pisgah"]). The first occurrence of the name is in the account relating the progress of the wandering Israelites. They came "to the valley in Moab where the top of Pisgah overlooks the wasteland [KJV,

North shoulder of Mt. Nebo; many scholars believe this to be Pisgah. (View to the SW toward the N end of the Dead Sea.)

© Dr. James C. Martin

Jeshimon]" (Num. 21:20). It was to "the top of Pisgah" that BALAAM was taken to curse Israel (23:14). Not only does this height overlook the plains of MOAB where the Israelites were, but to the W it looks over the Dead Sea (Deut. 3:17; 4:49; Josh. 12:3). The slopes of Pisgah later became part of the tribe of REUBEN (Josh. 13:15-20). God told MOSES to go there to look in all directions (Deut. 3:27). Many scholars identify Jebel en-Neba with Mount Nebo and Ras es-Siyaghah with Pisgah (but see NEBO, MOUNT). These two peaks, approximately 5 mi. (8 km.) NW of MEDEBA, are connected by a saddle. Pisgah commands a magnificent view of the JORDAN Valley and even to Mount HERMON on clear days.

Pishon River. pi´shon (Heb. *pîšôn H7093*, derivation uncertain). KJV Pison. One of the four headwaters into which the river flowing from EDEN divided (Gen. 2:11; cf. Sir. 24:25). It is described as winding "through the entire land of Havilah, where there is gold" (see HAVILAH). Suggested identifications of the Pishon include Wadi Baish and nearby Wadi Bisha, in SW ARABIA. It must be kept in mind, however, that the TIGRIS and EUPHRATES, two of the other headwaters, do not flow out of a common source; hence the account does not literally fit today's geography.

Pisidia. pi-sid´ee-uh (Gk. *Pisidia G4407*; adj. *Pisidios G4408*, "Pisidian"). One of the small Roman PROVINCES in S ASIA MINOR, just N of PAMPHYLIA and lying along the coast. Pisidia is a mountainous district, some 120 mi. long by 50 wide (190 x 80 km.), at the W end of the Taurus range, forming a hinterland to Pamphylia. The nature of the terrain, where the Taurus breaks into a tangle of ridges and valleys, made it the natural home of independent and predatory mountain tribesmen, who resisted successfully the attempts of the Persians, during their occupancy of Asia Minor, to subdue them. Pisidia, however, was more densely populated than the rough coastal areas, especially because it contained the important city of ANTIOCH. PAUL and BARNABAS visited the city twice. On their first visit (Acts 13:14-50) Paul preached a lengthy sermon in the synagogue, testifying of Christ. A week later "almost the whole city gathered to hear the word

of the Lord" (13:44). Then the jealous Jews stirred up both the honorable women and the chief men of the city (13:50), and Paul and Barnabas were forced out of this greatest Pisidian city. On their return journey they revisited Pisidia and Antioch, "strengthening the disciples and encouraging them to remain true to faith" (14:21-24).

Pison. See PISHON.

Pispa. See PISPAH.

Pispah. pis´puh (Heb. *pispâ H7183*, derivation unknown). Also Pispa. Son of JETHER (1 Chr. 7:38), listed among the "heads of families, choice men, brave warriors and outstanding leaders" of the tribe of ASHER (v. 40).

pistachio. See PLANTS.

pit. This English term is used frequently in Bible versions to render a variety of Hebrew words. For example, the noun *bôr H1014*, which occurs more than sixty times, conveys the idea of a hole especially dug for water, but is also used where water is not present. It can often refer to a CISTERN (e.g., Lev. 11:36), and sometimes to a dungeon (Exod. 12:29; see PRISON). The word may be used to describe the place of physical BURIAL, a hole with graves dug into the sides. By a natural transition it refers to calamity (e.g., Ps. 40:2). Probably by analogy to the burial crypt, the expression "go down to the pit," means more than dying without hope, being a reference to the nether world of departed spirits (Ps. 28:1). In the NT, the Greek word *bothynos G1073* ("hole, pit") occurs three times (Matt. 12:11; 15:14; Lk. 6:39). In Lk. 14:5 (parallel to Matt. 12:11), the term *phrear G5853* is used; this word often means a "well" purposely dug (Jn. 4:11-12), but in Revelation it refers to the "shaft" of the ABYSS (Rev. 9:1-2; KJV and other versions, "bottomless pit"), where mention of a key indicates that the pit was considered a type of dungeon.

pitch. As a verb meaning "to erect, raise" (esp. with reference to a TENT), this English word is usually the rendering of Hebrew *nāṭâ H5742* (Gen. 12:8

et al.), although the KJV uses it frequently to translate other words (Gen. 26:17 et al.). For its use as a noun, see BITUMEN.

pitcher. This English term, referring to a container used for holding and pouring liquids, is used seventeen times by the KJV, mainly as the rendering of Hebrew *kad H3902* (nine times in Gen. 24:14-46 alone; modern versions prefer the rendering "jar"). GIDEON's attacking force was equipped with pitchers that served to hide the torches until the moment of attack (Jdg. 7:16-20). The NIV uses "pitcher" also to render Hebrew *qaśwâ H7987* (Exod. 25:29). In the NT, the KJV has "pitcher" for Greek *keramion G3040*, referring to an earthenware vessel (Mk. 14:13; Lk. 22:10; the English word *ceramics* is derived from this Gk. term). The NIV uses it for *xestēs G3829* (Mk. 7:4; the KJV and NRSV, less precisely, "pots").

Pithom. pi´thom (Heb. *pitōm H7351*, from Egyp. *pr-ʾitm*, "house [*i.e.*, temple] of Atum"). A store city in EGYPT that the Hebrews were forced to build (Exod. 1:11). Although Pithom is securely attested as a proper name in Egyptian sources from the 13th cent. B.C. onward, its precise identification and localization present some problems, especially in its relation with Tjeku (modern Tell el-Maskhuta), called SUCCOTH in the OT (Exod. 12:37 et al.). The Egyptian name Per-Atum (or Pi-Tum) seems to be identified with Tjeku in some texts, thus Tjeku-Succoth has been advocated as the site of biblical Pithom: Tjeku would be the ordinary name of the town, fort, and immediate neighborhood, and Per-Atum its religious name. Some, however, prefer to identify Per-Atum/Pithom with modern Tell er-Retabe (some 9 mi./14 km. W of Tell el-Maskhuta), which would place it closer to the land of GOSHEN. Still a third proposal identifies Pithom with HELIOPOLIS (Tell el-Ḥisn, c. 10 mi./16 km. NNE of Cairo) on the grounds that Per-Atum would be naturally understood as the national shrine located in that major city, but this location is too far from Succoth (more than 40 mi./65 km. to the SW).

Pithon. pi´thon (Heb. *pitôn H7094*, derivation uncertain). Son of Micah and descendant of SAUL through JONATHAN and MERIB-BAAL, included in the genealogy of BENJAMIN (1 Chr. 8:35; also 9:41).

pity. A tender, considerate feeling for others, ranging from judicial clemency (Deut. 7:16) through kindness (Job 6:14; Prov. 19:17; 28:8) and mercy (Matt. 18:33) to compassion (Lam. 4:10). Pity may be mere concern for a thing (Jon. 4:10) or for a thing deeply desired (Ezek. 24:21). It may also be the concern of God for his holy name (36:21). Pity for one's children is of the essence of fatherhood, human or divine (Ps. 103:13 KJV), inherent in the redemptive activity of God (72:13). The several Hebrew and Greek words are translated variously in all versions, the translators being guided by the meaning in context rather than by the particular word used, for each has a wide range of connotation. See also MERCY.

plague. See DISEASES.

plagues of Egypt. A series of ten penal miracles performed against the people of EGYPT, and the means by which God induced PHARAOH to let the Israelites leave (Exod. 7-12). Although chiefly related to natural phenomena, their miraculous character is clear from the following factors: (1) extraordinary severity, (2) the occurrence of so many disasters within a relatively short span of time, (3) accurate timing, (4) GOSHEN and its people were spared some of them, and (5) evidence of God's control over them. The plagues overcame the opposition of Pharaoh, discredited the gods of Egypt (the NILE and the SUN), and defiled their temples.

I. **Water turned into blood** (Exod. 7:14-25). When the Nile is at flood in June, its water turns reddish from soil brought down from ETHIOPIA, but it is still fit to drink, and fish do not die. But when the river is at its lowest, in May, the water is sometimes red, not fit to drink, and fish die. The Egyptians had to dig wells, into which river water would filter through sand. God directed MOSES to lift up his rod at the right time. Once the time was disclosed, the Egyptian magicians could do likewise.

II. **Frogs** (Exod. 8:1-15). When the flood waters recede, frogs spawn in the marshes and invade the

P

dry land. God directed Moses to lift up his rod at such a time. This sign the Egyptian magicians also claimed to produce.

III. Lice (Exod. 8:16-19). What insect is meant is uncertain; the NIV and other modern versions have "gnats." So many biting, stinging pests abound in Egypt that people might not be discriminating in naming them. The magicians failed, by their own admission, to reproduce this plague and recognized in it "the finger of God"; but Pharaoh would not listen to them.

IV. Flies (Exod. 8:20-31). The rod is no longer mentioned. Swarms of flies came over Egypt in unusual density to feed on dead frogs. God directed Moses as to the time. The magicians no longer competed with Moses. Now there was a differentiation between Goshen and the rest of Egypt. Pharaoh tentatively offered to let the people go to sacrifice to their God, only in the land of Egypt (8:25). Moses insisted that they must go three days' journey into the wilderness. Pharaoh assented, provided they did not go far, and the plague was stayed at the intercession of Moses. When the plague was removed, Pharaoh again refused to let Israel go.

V. The plague on cattle (Exod. 9:1-7; KJV, "murrain"). This punishment was announced with a set time ("tomorrow") for its occurrence. There is no record of its removal. Presumably it wore itself out. The Israelite cattle were spared, evidence of God's favor and power.

VI. Boils (Exod. 9:8-12). Moses was told to take soot from a furnace and sprinkle it in the air. The air over Egypt was filled with dust, and it became boils breaking out on both people and animals. The magicians, still watching Moses, could not stand because of the boils. From the specific mention that the plague was on "all the Egyptians" we may infer that the Israelites were not attacked. This plague was not recalled. Presumably it also wore itself out.

VII. Hail (Exod. 9:13-35). God directed Moses to stretch forth his hand, and hail (which rarely occurs in Egypt) descended in unusual violence. Egyptians who feared the word of the Lord—and after such displays of power there may have been many—brought in their cattle out of the coming storm. Those who did not, lost them to the violent hail. Only in Goshen was there no hail. The hand

of God directed its local incidence. The season must have been January or February, for the flax was in the ear and the barley in bud or bloom.

VIII. Locusts (Exod. 10:1-20). After seven plagues, even a frequently recurring one such as locusts was so dreaded that Pharaoh's servants used bold language in advising that the Israelites be let go (10:7). Goshen was not spared the locusts' visitation. Still Pharaoh was obdurate.

IX. Darkness (Exod. 10:21-29). A sandstorm, accentuated by the dust-bowl condition of the land and borne on the W wind that drove off the locusts, brought a tawny, choking darkness. The patience of God was at an end: Pharaoh would see the face of Moses no more. The darkness lasted three days, but the children of Israel had light where they lived.

X. Death of the firstborn (Exod. 11:1—12:36). This final and convincing demonstration of God's power broke down the resistance of Pharaoh long enough for the Israelites to escape. The Israelites were directed to protect their FIRSTBORN with the blood of the Passover lamb, that they might not be killed along with the firstborn of the Egyptians. They "borrowed" valuables of the Egyptians and, amid the lamentations of the latter, were allowed to leave. Egypt had had enough. Even if the deaths were due to bubonic plague, as many think, the incidence on the firstborn alone is not thereby explained. Bubonic plague is said to take the strongest, but this does not explain why all the firstborn and only the firstborn died. The character of this plague is clearly that of divine judgment on incurable obstinacy.

The memory of the plagues was cultivated as a warning to Israel for generations to come (Ps. 78:43-51; 105:26-36; 135:8-9; Acts 7:36; 13:17; Heb. 11:28).

plain. An extensive level (or rolling) area. Various Hebrew words may be rendered "plain," but in their original context some of these referred to a specific area, that is, they possessed a topographic meaning to the users. Modern versions often pick these out and render them as place names. For example, the term *ʿărābâh H6858* in Deut. 1:7 is translated "plain" by the KJV, but most modern versions use the name ARABAH (the great Rift Valley, from the point where its floor becomes dry and barren S of

Lake GALILEE to its exit into the Gulf of AQABAH). The mountains of S PALESTINE are surrounded by plains: on the E by the valley of the JORDAN and the Arabah; on the W by the SHEPHELAH ("lowland") and the coastal plain; and on the N by the Plain of ESDRAELON. The notion held by the ARAMEANS that Israel's God was a God of the hills and not of the plains (1 Ki. 20:23) may well serve as a commentary on the fact that, throughout the nation's history, her people seldom, and only after great efforts, secured a firm grip on the lowland areas of Palestine, although these formed part of the land of promise. Israel remained a hill people, the plains around their home more often than not occupied by their enemies.

plaiting. See DRESS.

plane. This English term, referring to a carpenter's tool used for smoothing or carving wood, is used by the KJV and other versions to render a Hebrew word that occurs only once (Isa. 44:13; NIV, "chisels").

plane tree. See PLANTS.

plank. See BEAM.

plants. Plants mentioned in the Bible present a fascinating study of various shrubs, herbs, trees, and vines that far outweighs the perplexing problems that have arisen. Such difficulties surfaced because of a lack of information about the botany of ancient PALESTINE, exegetical obstacles, and faulty translations. Better translations, along with more accurate botanical analyses, have helped to remove some of the confusion regarding the identification of plant names included in such categories, for example, as spices, gums, fruits, and thorns. The names of most plants growing in the Holy Land during Bible times present little or no difficulty for the translator, for they clearly refer to the plants or the close relatives of species that are growing in our own day; however, the origins of some are lost in antiquity.

acacia. A genus of trees and shrubs of the mimosa family native to warmer climates. The gnarled, rough-barked, thorny acacia or shittah

trees (Isa. 41:19) of the OT are most likely the *Acacia seyal*. The acacia or shittim wood is a durable, close-grained wood, orange when cut, turning darker with age. The TABERNACLE and the ARK OF THE COVENANT were constructed from this sturdy wood (Exod. 25-27, 35-38; Deut. 10:3). The acacia tree yields gum arabic and gum senegal used in adhesives, pharmaceuticals, dyes, and confections. Thorny acacia bushes, such as the *Acacia nilotica*, thickly covered the land of Palestine in early times.

Acacia tree located in the barren region of N Sinai.

algum (almug) tree. A type of wood mentioned in 1 Ki. 10:11-12 ("almug") as an import from OPHIR. It is thought by some to be the red sandalwood (*Pterocarpus santalinus*), an Indian wood that accepts a high polish; it is red-colored, smooth, and expensive to use. Others believe it is the *Juniperus phoenicia excelsa*, native to Lebanon. In 2 Chr. 2:8 and 9:10-11 the word appears as "algum," probably a spelling variant, although some think it may be a different species growing in Lebanon.

almond. The almond tree (*Prunus amygdalus communis*) was common in Palestine in JACOB's days (Heb. *šāqēd H9196*, Gen. 43:11), probably introduced into EGYPT when JOSEPH was governor. This is how the children of Israel were able to use almonds as models for the cups of the golden lamps (Exod. 25:33-36). AARON's STAFF that budded and produced almonds (Num. 17:1-8) was probably brought from Egypt in the EXODUS. There is a play on the Hebrew word in Jer. 1:11-12, based on the fact that the flowers of the almond appear long before the leaves. The blossoming of the almond tree pictures old age in Eccl. 12:5 because the flowers, which appear in midwinter in Palestine, look white from a distance. The Hebrew word *lûz* *H4280* (Gen. 30:37; KJV, "hazel") also refers to the almond tree, which gave its name to the city of Luz (later Bethel).

In the biblical world an almond tree in blossom was a reminder of the white hair that comes with old age.

almug. See *algum tree.*

aloe. A genus of the lily family (*Aloë succatrina*) with thick fleshy basal leaves containing a substance called *aloin.* The OT references to aloes (Num. 24:6 [KJV, "lign aloes"]; Ps. 45:8; Prov. 7:17; Cant. 4:14) are more likely referring to a large and spreading tree known as the eaglewood (*Aquilaria agallocha*). When decaying, the inner wood gives off a fragrant resin used in making perfumes. John 19:39 is probably the only biblical reference to true aloe, a shrubby succulent plant containing juices that were used by the ancients for embalming and as a purgative.

anise. See *dill.*

apple. See *apricot.*

apricot. A shade tree that reaches nearly 30 ft. (9 m.) in height. It yields orange-colored fruit and grows abundantly in Palestine. Traditionally the Hebrew word *tappûaḥ* *H9515* has been translated "apple" (Cant. 2:3, 5; 7:8; 8:5; Joel 1:12; Zech. 2:8). However, the western apple, introduced recently into Palestine, does not grow well in its soils. Existing in Mesopotamia prior to the patriarchal period, the apricot (*Prunus armeniaca*) meets all the requirements of the OT contexts.

ash. See *pine tree.*

aspen. See *willow.*

balm. An aromatic resin. The "balm in Gilead" (Jer. 8:22; cf. 46:11; Gen. 37:25) may be the *Commiphora (Balsamodendron) opobalsamum.* This shrub is not truly native to Palestine, but is known and grown in Arabia. The tree is evergreen—a straggly grower with few trifoliate leaves. The white flowers are borne three to a cluster. When a cut is made in the trunk or branches of the tree, the sap exudes. The small, sticky globules harden, and then may easily be removed from the bark. One can get this gum from the root as well as from the trunk. Some think (on the basis of Jer. 8:22) that the balm had a medicinal value and that the plant may be the turpentine tree, *Silphium terebinthinaceum.*

balsam tree. In one of the battles with the Philistines in the Valley of Rephaim, God instructed David to circle the enemy "and attack them in front of the balsam trees" (Heb. *bākāʾ* *H1132*). He was to wait until he heard "the sound of marching in the tops of the balsam trees" as an indication that God had "gone out in front … to strike the Philistine army" (2 Sam 5:23-24; 1 Chr. 14:14-15; KJV, "mulberry trees"). This plant is often referred to as the baka-shrub. It is probably the *Populus euphratica,* which makes a rustling sound when the wind blows through it. The tree grows readily in the Jordan Valley and may be the same as the poplar or willow mentioned in Ps. 137:2.

barley. A grain cultivated in ancient Mesopotamia as early as 3500 B.C. Common barley (*Hordeum distichon*) was the main staple bread plant of the Hebrews (Deut. 8:8) and the main food of the poor (Ruth 1:22; 2 Ki. 4:42; Jn. 6:9, 13). Its adaptability to a variety of climate conditions and its short growing season make it an excellent foodstuff. Barley straw served also for bedding and feed for livestock.

bay tree. The *Laurus nobilis,* sometimes called the "bay laurel" or "sweet-bay," is a dark evergreen tree that in Europe grows to a height of 30 ft. (9 m.) but in Palestine may reach 60 ft. (18 m.). The small flowers are greenish-white and the small berries are black. The fragrant leaves are dark green and glossy, and often are used in cooking with fish, like mackerel. The only biblical reference to a bay tree is in the KJV of Ps. 37:35, where, however, the Hebrew term really means "native" (cf. NIV).

bean. The broad bean, *Faba vulgaris*, is extensively cultivated in Palestine. The bean is sown in the fall and harvested after barley and wheat in the spring. A staple article of diet for the poor of Palestine (2 Sam. 17:28), the dried ground beans were mixed in with grain flour to make bread (Ezek. 4:9).

bitter herb. See *Herb*.

bramble. A fast-growing, rough, prickly shrub (*Rubus ulmifolius*) of the rose family, usually associated with thorns or nettles (Isa. 34:13; Lk. 6:44 KJV; NIV, "thorns") or representing the rabble of society (Jdg. 9:14-15 KJV; NIV, "thornbush").

brier (briar). A plant with a woody or prickly stem (Jdg. 8:7, 16; Ezek. 28:24). A sure identification of the exact Hebrew and Greek words that mean "brier" is next to impossible. Fifteen Hebrew and four Greek terms are interchangeably translated as bramble, brier, thistle, or thorn, among the different English translations.

broom. A small flowering shrub or tree, reaching a height of 12 ft. (c. 3.5 m.), with long slender branches and small leaves. The OT passages refer to the white broom, *Retama raetam*. The white broom's scant foliage provides little relief from the desert sun (1 Ki. 19:4); its burning quality makes good firewood (Ps. 120:4); and its mildly poisonous roots supply little gratification to hungry people (Job 30:4).

bulrush. A tall, slender reedlike plant that formerly grew prolifically in and along the banks of the NILE (Exod. 2:3; KJV "ark of bulrushes"; NIV "papyrus basket"). PAPYRUS (*Cyperus papyrus*) provided the earliest known material for the making of paper, which receives its name from the plant (Exod. 2:3; Job 8:11; Isa. 18:2). Flag, of the iris family, is a generic term used for a variety of marshal plants (KJV at Exod. 2:3, 5; Job 8:11). An orderly alignment of the six Hebrew words referring to marsh plants with their English translations is difficult since they are interchangeably translated as bulrush, flag, papyrus, reed, and rush. See ARK OF BULRUSHES.

bush, burning. See separate article, BURNING BUSH.

calamus. A fragrant ginger-grass (*Andropogon aromaticus*) from NW and central India. Its bruised leaves give off a strong, spicy, aromatic scent and their pungent taste is like ginger. The sweet calamus is a valuable import item in Palestine (Cant. 4:14; Jer. 6:20; Ezek. 27:19). In some translations (e.g., KJV and NRSV) the calamus of Isa. 43:24 is rendered "sweet cane" (*Saccharum officinarum*), a stout perennial, growing to a height of 15 ft. (4.5 m.). The juice of the sugar cane, though not used at that time for sugar making, was highly esteemed for sweetening foods and drinks, and the pithy sweet stalks for chewing. Calamus was an ingredient mixed in the sacred ointment used in the tabernacle (Exod. 30:23 KJV, TNIV).

camphire. See *henna*.

cane. See *calamus*.

caper, caperberry. A small prickly shrub (*Capparis spinosa*), common to the Mediterranean (Eccl. 12:5 NASB, NJPS). The context is a graphic description of old age in which various natural associations are used for figurative effect. This text apparently uses the term in the sense of its enhancement of sexual desire, which in the declining years of life fails. Since this meaning would not be conveyed by a literal translation, the KJV and many modern versions render the term as "desire."

caraway. See *dill*.

carob. *Ceratonia siliqua*, a member of the pea family, native to the E Mediterranean, about 50 ft. (15 m.) tall, with shiny evergreen leaves and red flowers. These red flowers form into pods in which seeds are embedded in a flavorful, sweet, and nutritious pulp. Called "St. John's bread" from a belief that carob pods rather than insects were the locusts that JOHN THE BAPTIST ate (Matt. 3:4; Mk. 1:6). Doubtless the pods of the carob tree were the "pods" (KJV, "husks") eaten by the prodigal son in Jesus' parable (Lk. 15:16).

cassia. An aromatic bark of the *Cinnamomum cassia*, related to cinnamon, though its bark is less delicate in taste and perfume. Its buds are used as a substitute for cloves in cooking. Cassia was mixed into the holy anointing oil of the tabernacle (Exod. 30:24) and was a valuable trade product (Ezek. 27:19).

cedar. Derived from an old Arabic root meaning a firmly rooted, strong tree, the word denotes a magnificent evergreen, often 120 ft. (36 m.) high and 40 ft. (12 m.) wide. It exudes a fragrant gum or balsam used as a preservative for fabric and parchment. The wood does not quickly decay and is

P

insect-repellent. Cedarwood is of a warm red tone, durable, light, and free from knots. The stately *Cedrus libani* is the cedar of LEBANON to which the OT often refers (1 Ki. 6:9; Job 40:17; Ps. 92:12; Ezek. 27:5). Though the cedar of Lebanon was once abundant in the Mediterranean region, it is now scarce.

chestnut. See *plane tree.*

cinnamon. A bushy evergreen tree (*Cinnamomum zeylanicum*), about 30 ft. (9 m.) high, with spreading branches, native to Sri Lanka (Ceylon). Commercial cinnamon is obtained from the inner bark of the young branches. A cinnamon oil is also distilled from the branches for use in food, perfume, and drugs. The sweet, light brown aromatic spice was as precious as gold to the ancients. It was used for embalming and witchcraft in Egypt, the anointing oil of the tabernacle (Exod. 30:23), perfume (Prov. 7:17), spice (Cant. 4:14), and trade merchandise (Rev. 18:13).

citron. This term (not to be confused with *citrus*) is properly used by the NIV to render Greek *thyinos* G2591 (Rev. 18:12; KJV transliterates "thyine"; NRSV, "scented"). The citron tree is the *Tetraclinis articulata*, or the sandarac tree—a conifer of the cypress family found in N Africa and on the Barbary Coast. The fragrant citron wood was highly prized and much used in biblical days for cabinet making.

cockle. An annual sturdy noxious weed (*Agrostemma githago*) with purplish red flowers found in abundance in Palestinian grain fields. The KJV uses this English term once (Job 31:40; NIV, "weeds"; TNIV, "stinkweed").

coriander. A herb (*Coriandrum sativum*) of the carrot family, native to the Mediterranean region; it bears small yellowish-brown fruit that gives off a mild, fragrant aroma. The coriander seed is used for culinary and medicinal purposes. In the OT it was comparable in color and size to MANNA (Exod. 16:31; Num. 11:7).

corn. See *grain.*

cotton. *Gossypium herbaceum* was imported into Palestine from PERSIA shortly after the EXILE. The Egyptians spun cotton into a fabric in which they wrapped their mummies. The NRSV translation of "cotton" in Esth. 1:6 is perhaps more accurately "linen" (so NIV).

crocus. A perennial herb with variously colored flowers. The word is used by some modern versions, such as the NIV and the NRSV, in Isa. 35:1 (the Heb. term here also occurs in Cant. 2:1, where it is traditionally rendered "rose [of Sharon]"). Other proposed renderings include "asphodel" (in the lily family), "narcissus," and "red tulip." There were fifteen different types of crocuses known in Palestine, such as the gray-blue *Crocus canclelatus damascenus* and the pale blue *C. zonatus.*

cucumber. A succulent vegetable cultivated from an annual vine plant with rough trailing stems and hairy leaves. Several varieties were known to the ancient Egyptians, but *Cucumis sativus* was probably the most common. The refreshing fruit of the cucumber vine was one delicacy the children of Israel longed for in the hot wilderness after leaving Egypt (Num. 11:5). The "lodge in a garden of cucumbers," mentioned in Isa. 1:8 (KJV and other versions; NIV, "hut in a field of melons"), was a frail temporary construction of four poles and walls of woven leaves, meant to house the watchman who guarded the garden during the growing season.

cummin (cumin). This small, slender plant (*Cuminum cyminum*) is not found wild. It is the only species of its genus and is native to W Asia. The strong-smelling, warm-tasting cummin seeds were used as culinary spices and served medicinal functions (Matt. 23:23). The seeds are still threshed with a rod as described in Isa. 28:25-27.

cypress. This term occurs only once in the KJV as a rendering of *tirzâ* H9560, which seems to refer to a conifer (Isa. 44:14; NIV also "cypress," but NRSV has "holm tree"). In addition, the NIV uses the term to render *gōper* H1729, also of uncertain meaning (Gen. 6:14), as well as *tēʾaššûr* H9309, which occurs two or three times (Isa. 41:19; 60:13 [prob. also Ezek. 27:6]; NRSV, "pine"). Another and more frequent word, *bĕrôš* H1360, is usually rendered "cypress" by the NRSV (1 Ki. 5:8 et al.; NIV, "pine"). There were certainly cypress forests in ancient Palestine. This evergreen (*Cupressus sempervirens horizontalis*), usually 30-40 ft. (9-12 m.) high, has spreading branches, and its durable wood was used for building purposes and coffins. See also *pine.*

date palm. See *palm.*

desire. See *caper.*

dill. An annual or biennial weedy umbellifer that grows like parsley and fennel. Native to Mediterranean countries, dill (*Anethum graveolens*) is used as a culinary seasoning and for medicinal purposes. This plant was cultivated for its aromatic seeds, which were subject to the TITHE (Matt. 23:23; KJV, "anise"). Some versions use "dill" also in one OT passage (Isa. 28:25, 27), but here the NIV has "caraway" (*Carum carvi*), which faintly resembles dill.

dove's dung. This phrase is used by some versions in 2 Ki. 6:25: "As the siege continued, famine in Samaria became so great that a donkey's head was sold for eighty shekels of silver, and one-fourth of a kab of dove's dung for five shekels of silver" (NRSV). Some scholars interpret the phrase literally, assuming that the material was used either as food or as fuel. Others, however, argue that the term refers to a cheap vegetable. According to one tradition, it designates the bulb *Ornithogalum umbellatum*: also known as "bird's milk" or "bird's dung," the plant is known today as Star of Bethlehem; the bulbs have to be roasted or boiled before eating. There is some Akkadian evidence, however, that the phrase "dove's dung" was used of the seeds of the *carob* and that it was thus a colloquial way of referring to inedible husks.

ebony. A hard, heavy, durable, close-grained wood (*Diospyros ebenum* or *D. ebenaster*) that takes a glistening polish. Because of its excellent woodworking qualities, this black heartwood, native to Sri Lanka (Ceylon) and southern India, has long been a valuable trade item (Ezek. 27:15).

eelgrass. A type of marine eelgrass from the *Zosteraceae* family, it thrives in tidal waters and may grow out to a depth of 35 ft. (11 m.). Its slimy, ribbonlike leaves, 3-4 ft. (c. 1 m.) long, lie in submerged masses, a menace to the offshore diver who may become fouled in their coils. The "seaweed" of Jon. 2:5 is most likely a reference to some type of marine eelgrass.

elm. See *terebinth*.

fig. A versatile, bushlike tree (*Ficus carica*), producing pear-shaped fruit, excellent for eating (1 Sam. 25:18). Because of its natural abundance in most Mediterranean countries and its good food qualities, it has become known as "the poor man's food." The fig was the first plant to be mentioned in

Fig tree.

© Dr. James C. Martin

the Bible (Gen. 3:7); it represented peace and prosperity (1 Ki. 4:25; Mic. 4:4; Zech. 3:10). A fig tree was the object of Jesus' curse (Matt. 21; Mk. 11).

fir. This English term (which refers to various evergreen trees of the genus *Abies*) can be used to render several Hebrew words. In the KJV it is normally the translation of *bĕrôš H1360* (e.g., 1 Ki. 5:8; NIV, "pine"; NRSV, "cypress"). The NIV uses it to render *bĕrôt H1361*, which occurs only once (Cant. 1:17; NRSV, "pine"), and *tidhār H9329*, which occurs twice (Isa. 41:19; 60:13; NRSV, "plane"). Some believe that one or more of these terms refer to the Aleppo pine (*Pinus halepensis*), a tree that grows to a height of 60 ft. (18 m.), bearing short, stalked cones. Able to withstand considerable periods of drought, it is certainly abundant in the hilly areas of Palestine, where its wood is considered almost as valuable as cedar. Other possibilities are *Pinus tinaster* (which grows to a height of 120 ft. [36 m.] and is an important resin-producing tree), *Pinus brutia* (with dark and whorled branches), *Juniperus phoenicea*, and *Cupressus sempervirens*. See *cypress*; *juniper*; *pine*.

fitches. This English term (which in modern usage refers to the polecat, a mammal of the weasel family) is used by the KJV in the sense of "vetch," an herb (Isa. 28:25, 27; Ezek. 4:9). In the first passage the Hebrew possibly refers to the caraway (see *dill*); in the second it mistakenly renders a word that refers to a grain.

P

flag. See *bulrush*.

flax. A slender-stalked, blue flowering plant (*Linum usitatissimum*), cultivated to make linen and linseed oil. The fibers from the stem of the plant are the most ancient of the textile fibers (Exod. 9:31; Josh. 2:6), manufactured into various grades of linen for clothing and other articles where material requiring strength and resistance to moisture is necessary (Prov. 31:13; Isa. 19:9). The cooling effect that linen has on the wearer makes it a useful garment to be worn under the hot Mediterranean sun.

frankincense. A clear yellow resin obtained from certain trees of the *Boswellia* genus, family Burseraceae, native to northern India and Arabia. To obtain frankincense, an incision is made through the bark of the tree deep into the trunk, from which flows a milklike juice that hardens in the air. When sold, frankincense is in the form of teardrops or irregular lumps. It is used in perfumes, as a medicine, and as INCENSE in religious rites. Incense is spoken of as coming from SHEBA (Isa. 60:6; Jer. 6:20; Matt. 2:11, 15). It was an ingredient in the perfume used in the Most Holy Place (Exod. 30:34-38). Frankincense (NIV, "incense") was mingled with the flour in the meal offering (Lev. 2:1, 15-16) but was excluded from the sin offering (5:11), which was far from being an offering of a sweet savor. Soon after the birth of Jesus, the MAGI presented to him gifts of gold, frankincense (NIV, "incense"), and myrrh; and these precious gifts, presented in worship, may well have helped to finance his family's sojourn in Egypt (Matt. 2:11, 15).

galbanum. A brownish-yellow, aromatic, bitter gum excreted from the incised lower part of the stem of the Persian *Ferula galbaniflua*. It has a pungent, disagreeable odor, but when mixed with other ingredients in the sacred incense the fragrance of the incense was increased and lasted longer (cf. Exod. 30:34). Galbanum also functions as an antispasmodic.

gall. The Hebrew word *rōʾš* *H8032*, which modern versions usually translate "poison" or the like (e.g., Deut. 29:18; Ps. 69:21; Jer. 8:14), perhaps refers to the inner pulp of the *Colocynth*, possibly the same as the "vine of Sodom" (Deut. 32:32). The belief that the gall comes from the poppy, whose juice is certainly bitter, is also feasible. In addition, most translations use "gall" to render Greek *cholē* *G5958* in Matt. 27:34, referring to the substance that was mixed with the wine given to the Lord; this Greek term probably means nothing more than "something bitter" (cf. Acts 8:23; see also Job 16:13). See also *wormwood*.

garlic. A bulbous perennial plant (*Allium sativum*) with a strong, onionlike aroma used for flavoring foods and as an ingredient of many medicines. Small edible bulblets grow within the main bulb. Garlic grew in great abundance in Egypt. The only reference to it in the Bible (Num. 11:5) mentions Israel's longing for the garlic of Egypt while they were traveling through the wilderness.

gopher wood. See *cypress*.

gourd. A generic term applied to various trailing or climbing plants (such as the pumpkin and the cucumber). Gourds have very broad leaves; they grow quickly in the E, lengthening themselves by as much as 12-18 in. (30-45 cm.) a day. They wither and die quickly when attacked at their base by insects like wireworms. The term is properly used to render Hebrew *paqquʿōt* *H7226*, which occurs only once, referring probably to the *Citrullus colocynthis*, a cucumber-like plant with purgative qualities (2 Ki. 4:39). The cognate *pĕqāʿîm* *H7225* refers to ornaments shaped like gourds (1 Ki. 6:18; 7:24). The carving of little gourds alternated with open flowers would have been very attractive. The term *gourd* is also used by the KJV and other versions to render Hebrew *qîqāyôn* *H7813* (Jon. 4:6-10; NRSV, "bush"; NIV, "vine"). Although some have identified this plant as the pumpkin (*Cucurbita pepo*), most specialists believe it is the castor oil tree (*Ricimum communis*, also known as *Palma Christi*). This plant has huge leaves, which provide excellent shade.

grain. Edible, starchy, kerneled fruits from the grasses, including corn, wheat, and rice varieties. Grain is a staple food in most diets, providing calorie and protein content. Fifteen Hebrew words and four Greek terms are variously translated as grain in the Bible, suggesting the importance of it in ancient times. The most common kinds of grain were *barley*, *millet*, *spelt*, and *wheat*. The rendering "corn" in the KJV (Gen. 27:28 and frequently) is a generic term for grain and does not refer to American maize, which was unknown in the ancient world.

grape. The grape plant is a small, climbing, woody VINE (or an erect shrub) from the genus *Vitis*; it produces leaves and small green flowers that mature into grapes. Grapes may be eaten fresh or dried as raisins or drunk as grape juice or WINE. The grapevine is the first plant to be recorded as cultivated in biblical history (Gen. 9:20). The grape, its origin lost in antiquity, grew first on the ground, over walls, or on crude supports. Later it was trained on a trellis and finally cultivated in vineyards. It was a symbol of fruitfulness, and the grape harvest was a time of joyous festivity (Gen. 40:9-11; Deut. 8:8; Ps. 105:33; Zech. 3:10). The wild grape mentioned in Isa. 5:2-4 and Jer. 2:21 refers to a wild variety of grapes that closely resembles the cultivated grape; it could deceive the owner of the vineyard.

grass. A low, green, nonwoody plant serving a multitude of functions for the soil, beasts, and humans. There are a great many species of grasses in Palestine, but actual turf is virtually unknown. In English the word *grass* is used in a more comprehensive sense and is the rendering of eight Hebrew terms and one Greek word. In the Bible, grass is used figuratively to portray the brevity of life (Ps. 103:15-16; Matt. 6:30; Lk. 12:28), to represent abundance (Job 5:25; Ps. 72:16), and as a barometer for OT Israel's spiritual condition (Jer. 12:4). Hay, which is grass mowed and cured for animal fodder and bedding, represented useless or inferior work built on the foundation of Jesus Christ (1 Cor. 3:12).

gum. See *spice*.

hay. See *grass*.

hazel. See *almond*.

heath. A low-growing shrub with evergreen leaves (also known as *heather*). The term is used by the KJV twice (Jer. 17:6; 48:6; NIV, "bush"). Since the true heath does not grow in Palestine, the Hebrew word probably refers to the *juniper*, a small tree with very small scale-like leaves and round cones; it grows on the W side of the mountains of EDOM.

hemlock. The KJV translation of two Hebrew words that allude to a poisonous substance (Hos. 10:4; Amos 6:12). According to some scholars, the first passage does refer to the poison hemlock (*Conium maculatum*), which grows throughout Palestine. See also *gall*; *wormwood*.

henna. Rendered "camphire" in the KJV, this is a small thorny shrub (*Lawsonia inermis*) with fragrant white flowers. The dried leaves of the henna, crushed and made into a paste, provided a gaudy yellow stain for the hair and beard. This use of it, common among the Egyptians, was cautioned against in Deut. 21:11-14. King Solomon lauded its fragrance (Cant. 1:14; 4:13). Henna still grows by the Dead Sea at EN GEDI.

herb. A seed-producing plant that does not develop woody fibers and dries up after its growing season (2 Ki. 4:39; Lk. 11:42). Bitter herbs were gathered fresh and eaten as a salad at the time of the Passover (Exod. 12:8; Num. 9:11). These include endive, common chicory, garden lettuce, watercress, sorrel, and dandelion. At the Passover the bitter herbs were symbolic of the bitterness of Israel's servitude to the Egyptians.

holm tree. This term is used by the NRSV and other English versions to render a Hebrew word that occurs only once (Isa. 44:14). The holm oak, also known as the holly oak (*Quercus ilex*), is a beautiful Mediterranean evergreen that reaches a height of 40-50 ft. (12-15 m.). The meaning of the Hebrew word is uncertain, however, and the NIV follows the KJV in interpreting it as a reference to the *cypress*.

husks. See *carob*.

hyssop. Probably *Origanum maru*, of Syrian origin, or *Origanum aegyptiacum*, from Egypt. This plant is a member of the mint family. The hairy stem of the multibranched inflorescence holds water externally very well; thus it was a suitable instrument for sprinkling blood during the Passover rites (Exod. 12:22; Lev. 14; Heb. 9:19). Some think that in Jn. 19:29 the reference is to the sorghum cane (*Sorghum vulgare*), which reaches a height of over 6 ft. (2 m.). The seed is ground for meal and is known in Palestine as "Jerusalem corn." In any case, the hyssop grown today (*Hyssopus officinalis*, which produces blue flowers from June to September, plus aromatic leaves) does not grow in Palestine or Egypt and so cannot be the plant mentioned in Scripture.

incense. A combination of gums and spices used to emit a fragrant odor when burned. See separate article, INCENSE.

juniper. An evergreen tree (or shrub) with leaves like needles or scales; their seed-bearing cones are aromatic. The KJV uses "juniper" to render

P

Hebrew *rōtem H8413* (1 Ki. 19:4-5; Job 30:4; Ps. 120:4), but this word appears to refer to the *broom tree*. According to some scholars, another Hebrew term, *bĕrôš H1360*, designates the *Juniperus phoenicia* (e.g., 1 Ki. 5:8; NIV, "pine logs"). The rare word *ʿarʿār H6899* (Jer. 17:6) is identified by some with *J. phoenicia* or *J. oxycedrus*.

leek. A robust, bulbous biennial plant (*Alium porrum*) of the lily family, with succulent broad leaves, the bases of which are edible. Its much-desired small bulbs, growing above ground, native to the Mediterranean region, were used in seasoning along with onions and garlic (Num. 11:5).

lentil. A small, trailing leguminous plant (*Lens esculenta*) of the pea family. When soaked and cooked, its seeds make a nourishing meal known as "pottage," and the rest of the plant serves as fodder for the animals. The red pottage or stew for which Esau exchanged his birthright was probably the red Egyptian lentil (Gen. 25:30-34). A favorite food in antiquity, lentils still appear on many tables in the East (2 Sam. 17:28; Ezek. 4:9).

lign. See *aloe*.

lily. A standing, leafy-stemmed bulbous perennial. Blooming from a bulb after the spring rains, the "lilies of the field" (Matt. 6:28; Lk. 12:27) carpeted the plains and roadsides of Palestine with their colorful blossoms. It is uncertain whether the reference here and in several OT passages is to the white "madonna lily" (*Lilium candidum*) or to other

© Dr. James C. Martin

The red anemone is one of the flowers linked to the biblical "lily."

species (e.g., the deep-blue *Hyacinthus orientalis* or the red *Lilium chalcedonicum*).

lotus. In modern Bible versions this word is used in Job 40:21-22 in a description of the behemoth. The plant in view is apparently *Zizyphus lotus*, a deciduous small tree, bearing three-veined leaves and tiny flowers, followed by yellow, roundish fruits. The tree gives good shade (cf. KJV, "shady trees") and is well known in Palestine.

mallow. Because the Hebrew word *mallûaḥ H4865* is related to the term for "salt" (*melaḥ H4875*), many believe that this plant is a species of salty herb or saltwort known as the "sea orache" (*Atriplex halimus*), a robust bushy shrub eaten as a vegetable but supplying little nutritional value. Mallows are mentioned only once in Scripture, where it is seen as a food of the poor (Job 30:4 KJV and other versions; NIV, "salt herbs").

mandrake. A member of the nightshade family, native to the Mediterranean, with ovate (egg-shaped) leaves, white or purple flowers, and a forked root. Its root is large, sometimes resembling the human body in shape. The mandrake (*Mandragora offinarum* or possibly *Atropa mandragora*), also called the "love apple," was believed to possess magical powers. Although insipid tasting and a slightly poisonous narcotic, it was used for medicinal purposes, as a charm against the evil spirits, and, as indicated by the account of Rachel and Leah, it was credited with aphrodisiac qualities (Gen. 30:14-16; Cant. 7:13). It is no longer used in medicine.

melon. A generic term referring to annual vine-trailing watermelons (*Citrullus vulgaris*) and muskmelons (*Cucumis melo*), both of which were familiar to ancient Palestinian and Egyptian cultures. The muskmelon varieties include the casuba, honeydew, and cantaloupe. Watermelons originated in Africa, while muskmelons began in Asia. These luscious fruits grew in abundance in Egypt and were used by rich and poor alike for food, drink, and medicine. Their seeds were roasted and eaten. Traveling under a hot desert sun, the weary Israelites remembered with longing the melons of Egypt (Num. 11:5; Isa. 1:8; Jer. 10:5).

millet. Various grasses bearing small edible seeds from which a good grade of flour can be made. One stalk may carry 1,000 grains. Millet

(*Panicum miliaceum*) is still a main food staple in Asia. The common people ate a mixture of wheat, barley, beans, lentils, and millet moistened with camel's milk and oil (Ezek. 4:9).

mint. An aromatic plant (*Mentha longifolia*) with hairy leaves and dense white or pink flower spikes, extensively cultivated in the eastern Mediterranean for its food-flavoring value. This pungent garden mint (along with the sharp-scented pennyroyal mint and peppermint) was used to make the meat dishes of the Jews more palatable. Mint was a tithable herb according to Jewish tradition (Matt. 23:23; Lk. 11:42) and one of the bitter herbs used in the paschal supper of the Passover.

mulberry tree. A fruit-bearing ornamental, genus *Morus*, indigenous to Palestine and western Asia. The "mulberry tree" of KJV (2 Sam. 5:23-24; 1 Chr. 14:14-15) is better explained as *balsam* (NIV) or "baka shrub" (NASB mg). The black mulberry or sycamine tree (*Morus nigra*) was cultivated throughout Palestine for its delectable fruit (Lk. 17:6).

mustard. Thick-stemmed plants, reaching a height of 15 ft. (4.5 m.) under suitable growing conditions, native to the Mediterranean region. For over 2,000 years the mustard plant has been an important economic plant of the Holy Land. Its seeds were either powdered or made into paste for medicinal and culinary purposes. The mustard tree and seed were used by Jesus to illustrate and explain faith (Matt. 13:31; 17:20; Mk. 4:31; Lk. 13:19; 17:6). The reference in these passages is probably to the black mustard (*Brassica nigra*), but others species are possible.

myrrh. A yellow to reddish-brown gum resin obtained from a number of small, thorny trees. One of the most valuable of these gum resins is collected from the shrub-like tree *Commiphora myrrha* (or *Balsamodendron myrrha*). The pale yellow liquid gradually solidifies and turns dark red or even black, and is marketed as a spice, medicine, or cosmetic (e.g., Cant. 5:5; Matt. 2:11; Mk. 15:23; Jn. 19:39). The Hebrew word *lōṭ H4320* (only in Gen. 37:25; 43:11) has often been translated "myrrh," but it is questionable whether *Commiphora myrrha*, native to Arabia and E Africa, was known in Palestine during the patriarchal period. Some think it is the resin or mastic of the *Pistacia mutica* (cf. NRSV) or

else ladanum (the gum of the rockrose *Cistus salvifolius*; cf. NJPS).

myrtle. A small, evergreen shrub (*Myrtus comminis*) with fragrant flowers, blackberries, and spicy-sweet scented leaves. This aromatic plant was considered a symbol of peace and prosperity (Isa. 55:13). Highly valued by the Jews, myrtle boughs were used in constructing the booths for the Feast of Tabernacles (Neh. 8:15; Zech. 1:7-8).

nard. See *spikenard*.

nettle. A little scrubby plant of the *Urticaceae* family, covered with tiny prickly hairs containing poison that when touched produce a painful, stinging sensation. The nettle and its companions—such as briers, thorns, thistles, brambles, underbrush, and weeds—form the low, scrubby rabble of plant life in Palestine that thrive in neglected areas. The KJV uses it five times (Job 30:7; Prov. 24:31; Isa. 34:13 [also NIV]; Hos. 9:6; Zeph. 2:9), but it is difficult to determine whether the Hebrew words refer to a specific plant.

nut. See *pistachio; walnut*.

oak. This English term, referring to a tree of the birch family (genus *Quercus*) that produces acorns, is used variously by different Bible versions to render several Hebrew words. According to some scholars, "oak" is properly the translation of *ʾēlôn H471* (Gen. 12:6 and nine other times) and *ʾallôn H473* (Gen. 35:8 and seven other times), whereas the terms *ʾēlāh H461* (Gen. 35:4 and eleven other times) and *ʾallâ H464* (only Josh. 24:26) refer properly to the *terebinth*. Other scholars, however, doubt that the terms can be clearly differentiated, or even that they refer to specific trees. It may be that some or all of them denote, in general, "stately, mighty tree" (cf. the rendering "great/large tree" in the NIV for *ʾēlôn* at Gen. 12:6; Josh. 19:33; Jdg. 4:11; 9:6; 1 Sam. 10:3; and for *ʾēlāh* at 1 Chr. 10:12). At least one passage, though, appears to make a distinction among the terms (Hos. 4:13; cf. also Isa. 6:13). In any case, it is generally acknowledged that many or most of the passages involved do refer to some type of oak. Just as the *cedar* was considered the most important evergreen tree, the oak was viewed as the most important deciduous tree. At least three of the prophets compared cedars and oaks for their strength (Isa. 2:13; Amos 2:9; Zech. 11:2). It is uncertain whether the biblical passages refer to

P

only one or to several of the species of oak found in Palestine. Suggestions include *Quercus ilex* (the beautiful evergreen oak or holm tree), *Q. (pseudo) coccifera* (or kermes oak), *Q. aegilops* (or valonian oak), and *Q. ithaburensis* (the Tabor oak, which can live for over 300 years).

oil tree. This term occurs only once in the KJV (Isa. 41:19), but the Hebrew phrase it renders occurs elsewhere. In one passage (1 Ki. 6:23, 31-33) it is used of the wood used in parts of the TEMPLE, and in another one (Neh. 8:15) it is explicitly distinguished from the olive tree. The identification of the "oil tree" is uncertain, but many believe it is the oleaster (cf. NJPS), that is, *Elaeagnus angustifolia.*

olive tree. A broad-leaved evergreen tree (*Olea europaea*), ranging from 10 to 40 ft. (3-12 m.) in height, yielding edible fruit from which OIL is obtained. Indigenous to the Near Eastern area, the olive tree was cultivated by Semitic groups as early as 3000 B.C. The olive tree is named or alluded to nearly eighty times throughout the Bible in reference to the tree itself (Isa. 24:13; Rom. 11), its wood (1 Ki. 6:23-33), its oil (Exod. 30:24; Rev. 18:13), or a geographical location named for its olive groves (Matt. 24:3; see OLIVES, MOUNT OF). It flourishes near the sea and under proper cultivation. The olives were beaten down with poles when ripe (black) and crushed by an upright stone wheel. The oil thus obtained was stored in vats. Olive oil

was used for the lights of the temple (Exod. 27:20). Heated in lye to remove the bitter taste and soaked in brine, green olives were eaten with coarse brown bread (Hos. 14:6). The oil tree, sometimes called "Jerusalem willow," or "Oleaster," produces a fruit like a small olive from which an inferior grade of medicinal oil may be pressed. Its fruits are edible but slightly bitter. Translated "oil tree" by KJV (Isa. 41:19), it is "olive" in NASB and NIV (NASB mg "Oleaster").

onion. A bulbous plant (*Allium cepa*), originating in the E Mediterranean and parts of Asia. Both its inflated leaves and its bulbous underground base were universally used for culinary purposes. The onion has been cultivated since time immemorial. Mentioned only in Num. 11:5, the onion was one of a list of foods in Egypt, regrettably unavailable to the disgruntled journeying Israelites.

onycha. This term is found in most English Bible versions as the rendering of Hebrew *šĕḥēlet H8829*, which occurs only once in a list of spices used to make incense (Exod. 30:34; here the LXX has *onycha*, from *onyx*, meaning "nail, claw," or "something in the shape of a nail"; the Vulg. transliterated *onycha*, which was chosen in English perhaps to avoid confusion with the precious stone onyx). The word probably refers to the *operculum*, that is, the horn-shaped plate that closes the shell of many marine mollusks. When burnt, the operculum produces a penetrating aroma (thus NEB, "aromatic shell"). It is usually thought that the mollusk in view is one of several species in the Strombus family. The RED SEA, an isolated warm water pocket of the Indian Ocean, is noted for its peculiar subspecies of mollusks.

palm tree. The Hebrew term *tāmār H9469* refers specifically to the date palm (*Phoenix dactylifera*) and occurs a dozen times in the OT (Exod. 15:27 et al.; cf. the name TAMAR). The crown of the date palm may reach 75 ft. (23 m.) above the ground. Its cultivation goes back at least 5,000 years. The fruit hangs in clusters below the leaves. Every part of the palm has some economic

© Dr. James C. Martin

An olive tree in Israel.

use. The leaves are woven into mats and the fibers provide thread and rigging for boats. Syrup, vinegar, and liquor are derived from its sap. Its trunk provides timber, and its seeds can be ground into a grain meal for livestock. This ornamental palm was a welcome sight to the travel-weary Israelites (Exod. 15:27; Num. 33:9). Palm branches were used in the Jewish celebration of the Feast of Tabernacles (Lev. 23:40; Neh. 8:15); were laid at Jesus' feet on his triumphal entry into Jerusalem, which Christians celebrate as Palm Sunday (Jn. 12:13); and came to signify victory (Rev. 7:9).

pannag. See separate article PANNAG.

papyrus. See *bulrush*.

pine. A coniferous evergreen tree with elongated needles. The term occurs seldom in most Bible versions, but the NIV uses it regularly to render Hebrew *bĕrôš H1360* (1 Ki. 5:8 et al.; KJV, "fir"; NRSV, "cypress"; others, "juniper"; the use of "pine" by the KJV in Neh. 8:15 is inaccurate). A Palestinian conifer is the Jerusalem pine, also known as the Aleppo pine (*Pinus halepensis*), which can grow 60 ft. (18 m.) high and has irregularly arranged, slender branches. The cones are short-stalked.

pistachio. An oval nut containing two green edible halves covered by a reddish outer shell; it comes from a small but wide-spreading tree with pinnate (featherlike) leaflets. Also known as the green almond, the pistachio nut has been cultivated in Palestine for nearly 4,000 years. It is used for food and food coloring. Considered a good product of the land, it was carried by Jacob's sons to Egypt (Gen. 43:11). The species may be *Pistacia vera*.

plane tree. A deciduous tree, known as the eastern or oriental plane, *Pla(n)tanus orientalis*. It grows in Palestine and Mount Lebanon, bearing flowers in clusters of rounded balls on a common stalk. The leaves are large and resemble those of the *sycamore*. This tree was held sacred in the E and was very much valued for its shade by the Greeks. The plane is probably referred to in the OT with Hebrew *ʿermôn H6895*, though the KJV translators thought it was the chestnut (Gen. 30:37; Ezek. 31:8; cf. Sir. 24:14). In addition, the NRSV and others use "plane" to render Hebrew *tidhār H9329*, a term of uncertain meaning that may refer to a type of *pine* (Isa. 41:19 and 60:13; NIV, "fir"; NJPS, "Box tree").

A pomegranate.

pomegranate. A small bush or tree (*Punica granatum*, originally called *Malum granatum*), common to Palestine, yielding leathery-skinned fruit. Its hard, orange-shaped fruits with thin rinds contain many seeds, each in a pulp sack filled with a tangy, sweet amethyst-colored juice. Although a small tree giving little shade, its refreshing fruit more than compensated the tired traveler who rested under it (1 Sam. 14:2). The fruit of the pomegranate was used as a decorative model in building (1 Ki. 7:18, 20, 42) and as an ornament on the vestment of the high priest (Exod. 28:33-34). The tree grew in the hanging gardens of BABYLON, and King Solomon possessed an orchard of them (Cant. 4:13).

poplar. This English term refers to a number of deciduous trees of the *willow* family, with catkins that hang. Most versions use the term to render Hebrew *libneh H4242*, which occurs twice (Gen. 30:37; Hos. 4:13). The reference is probably to the white poplar (*Populus alba*), which can grow to a height of 60 ft. (18 m.) and produces very thick shade. The leaves are a pretty shiny green above, and a showy-white below. The flower buds as they open produce a pleasant fragrance in the spring. Because of the shade and privacy the poplars afforded, they were widely used as groves in which heathen worship took place. Some scholars, however, argue that *libneh* refers to the storax tree (*Styrax officinalis*), whose leaves are also white below; this tree bears white flowers as well. The NIV uses "poplar" also as the rendering of Hebrew *ʿărābāh H6857* (Lev. 23:40 et al.; most versions translate with "willow"); the reference could be to the Euphrates poplar

P

© Dr. James C. Martin

(*Populus euphratica*), a large tree frequently seen on the banks of rivers in the Middle East.

poppy. See *gall*.

reed. A number of Hebrew words can be rendered "reed," an English term that is applied to various tall grasses growing primarily in wet areas. The *Arundo donax*, also known as the "giant reed" and the "Persian reed" (used for the manufacture of woodwind instruments) is found in the Jordan Valley and around the Dead Sea. Sometimes confused with bamboo, it can grow to the height of 18 ft. (5.5 m.), carrying at its tip a white plume. Its unusually hard stem may have a diameter of 3 in. (8 cm.). These thick, strong stems were used as canes or walking sticks, hence the reference in Ezek. 29:6 and 2 Ki. 18:21, where King Sennacherib referred to Egypt as the staff of a bruised reed. Pens in biblical days were made from reeds (cf. 3 Jn. 13). Reed pens can be made from the tall grass, *Phragmites communis* (a perennial allied to the *Arundo*). See also *bulrush*.

resin, gum resin. See *stacte*.

rolling thing. See *tumbleweed*.

rose. This term is used by the KJV to render Hebrew *ḥăbaṣṣelet H2483*, which occurs twice: in Cant. 2:1 ("the rose of Sharon") and in Isa. 35:1 ("the desert shall rejoice and blossom as the rose"). The identification of the plant is disputed, however. Although it cannot be what we normally mean by "rose," the NIV and other modern versions follow this traditional rendering in the former passage; they use a different term, *crocus*, in the latter. The plant should not be confused with what is today called the "rose of Sharon" (*Hibiscus syriacus*, an Asian shrub that produces bell-shaped flowers of different colors). The reference in Cant. 2:1 could be to *Hypericum calycinum* (sometimes called "Aaron's beard"), which is not sweet-smelling; known to grow in W Asia Minor and in the Plain of Sharon, it is more or less evergreen, and its golden, powder-puff flowers are seen for four long months. This plant will grow almost anywhere, even under trees. It could therefore have succeeded in the Plain of Sharon, even if it had to grow among different vegetation. Other suggestions include the following: *Tulipa montana*, which, as its name suggests, is a tulip that grows happily in the mountains; *Tulipa sharonensis*, a red flower found growing abundantly

around Sharon; *Narcissus tazetta*, a scented plant of the *lily* family that grows plentifully in Palestine, bearing on one stem clusters of cream-colored flowers with a yellow cup; and *Asphodelus*, also a kind of lily. It is uncertain whether Isa. 35:1 refers to the same plant.

rue. A small, woody, perennial shrub (prob. *Ruta graveolens*), noted for its pungent, bitter leaves and yellow flowers. Of the four varieties grown, the species *graveolens*, meaning "strong smelling," is the most common, indigenous to the E Mediterranean coast. It was relished for its peculiar strong taste and used as a culinary spice and for medicinal reasons. It was a customary tithable garden plant (Lk. 11:42).

rush. A cylindrical, hollow-stalked plant of the *Juneus* genus. There are twenty varieties of this grasslike plant growing in and along the water courses of Palestine. Where NASB and KJV have "rush" (Job 8:11; 41:20; Isa. 19:6; 35:7), NIV has "papyrus" or "reed." See also *bulrush*.

rye (rie). See *spelt*.

saffron. An aromatic plant used for producing condiments and perfume, and for other purposes. The Hebrew term used in the Song of Solomon to describe the bride (Cant. 4:14) could be Indian saffron (*Curcuma longa*) or crocus saffron (*Crocus sativus*), the latter name indicating the plant from which the flavoring powder is derived. Saffron comes from the upper end of the style of the flower. Over 4,000 crocus flowers are needed to produce 1 oz. of saffron.

seaweed. See *eelgrass*.

shittah, shittim. See *acacia*.

spelt. This English term, referring to a coarse *wheat*, is used by the NIV and other versions in three passages (Exod. 9:32; Isa. 28:25; Ezek. 4:9; the KJV has "rie" in the first two passages and "fitches" in the last). The Hebrew word may refer to the so-called one-grained wheat, *Triticum monococcum* (or *T. monoccum*, a diploid wheat also known as "einkorn" or "small spelt"), though most scholars believe it designates a hexaploid wheat that was introduced from Egypt, *T. spelta* (synonym *T. aestivum spelta*, also known as "big spelt"). This spelt is a very hard-grained wheat with loose ears.

spice. A generic term pertaining to aromatic substances, usually of plant extract, used to flavor and season food. Various Hebrew and Greek words can be translated "spice." Spices were mixed together to form the sacred anointing oil and the fragrant incense used in the tabernacle (Exod. 25:6; 30:23-25; 35:8). Spices were a precious trade commodity (1 Ki. 10; Rev. 18:13), part of the palace treasury (2 Ki. 20:13; Isa. 39:2), valued for their aromatic fragrance (Cant. 4:10, 14), and used in preparing Jesus' body for burial (Lk. 23:56; Jn. 19:40).

spikenard, nard. A costly perennial herb (*Nardostachys jatamansi*), with an aromatic root, native to E India and presently cultivated on the Himalayas. The rose-red fragrant ointment made from its dried roots and woolly stems was a favorite perfume of the ancients (Cant. 1:12 [NIV, "perfume"]; 4:13-14). The ointment is stored in an alabaster jar to preserve its fragrance. Mary's anointing of Jesus with the precious nard was an act of real sacrifice (Mk. 14:3; Jn. 12:3).

stacte. This English term is found in the KJV and other versions at Exod. 30:34, referring to one of the fragrant spices used to produce incense. The precise meaning of the Hebrew term is uncertain, but it evidently refers to the secretion of some aromatic plant, such as *Commiphora opobalsamum* or *Pistacia lentiscus*. Another possibility is *Styrax officinalis*, a small tree found throughout Palestine that bears snowdrop-shaped, pendulous pure white flowers; if an incision is made in the bark, the fragrant resin is easily obtained. The NIV, appropriately, uses a generic rendering, "gum resin."

sweet cane. See *calamus*.

sycamine. See *mulberry tree*.

sycamore. A large spreading tree, producing sweet, edible fruit, native-grown in Egypt and Asia Minor. The sycamore-fig tree, often called the fig-mulberry (*Ficus sycomorus*), bears fruit, like the ordinary fig (*Ficus carica*), directly on the stem, but its fruit is of inferior quality. Its wood is light, durable, and good for carpentry. The Egyptians made their mummy cases of this wood (1 Ki. 10:27; Amos 7:14; Lk. 19:4). The tree in question should be distinguished from what is today referred to as "sycamore" (either *Acer pseudoplatanus*, a Eurasian maple, or *Platanus occidentalis*, the buttonwood).

tamarisk. A desert tree with tiny, scale-like leaves that hardly transpire at all (thus suited for hot, dry places). The Hebrew word *ʾēšel H869*, which occurs three times in the OT (Gen. 21:33; 1 Sam. 22:6; 31:13), probably refers to the *Tamarix aphylla*, also known as the athel tree (other suggestions include *T. syriaca* and *T. gallica* [= *T. mannifera*]).

tares. An annual weedy grass, probably the bearded darnel (*Lolium temulentum*), that flourishes in grain fields (Matt. 13:24-30, 36-43 KJV; NIV, "weeds"). It is difficult to distinguish domesticated grains from the wild darnel until their heads mature. At harvest time the grain is fanned and put through a sieve. The smaller darnel seeds left after fanning pass through the sieve, leaving behind the desired fruit. The darnel is host to an ergot-like smut fungus, which infects the seeds and is poisonous to man and herbivorous animals but not to poultry.

teil tree. See *terebinth*.

terebinth. Also known as the turpentine tree, the terebinth (*Pistacia terebinthus*, including the subspecies *P. terebinthus palaestina*) is a deciduous and long-lived tree native to the Mediterranean region. The NIV and other versions use "terebinth" to render *ʾēlāh H461* in two passages where this Hebrew term is distinguished from *ʾallôn H473*, "oak" (Isa. 6:13 [KJV, "teil tree"]; Hos. 4:13 [KJV, "elms"]; the NRSV uses "terebinth" also in the title of Ps. 56, and the NJPS uses it some twenty times to render more than one term). See also *oak*.

thistle. A prickly plant, often with pink or purple-flowered heads. Generic in character, it is represented by about twenty Hebrew and Greek words interchangeably translated "bramble," "brier," "thistle," and "thorn" (e.g., 2 Ki. 14:9; 2 Chr. 25:18; Hos. 10:8; Matt. 7:16; 13:7; Heb. 6:8). Of the more than a hundred species of thistles that grow in Palestine, "Mary's thistle" (*Silybum marianum*) and the red star thistle (*Centaurea calcitrapa*) are the most common. Thistles originated at the time of God's curse on ADAM because of his sin (Gen. 3:18) and are found in every part of Palestine.

thorn. This generic term includes small, spiny shrubs and vines. The *Zizyphus spina Christi* and the Palestine buckthorn, *Rhamnus palaestine*, are the two thorny shrubs most widespread and well known in biblical times in Palestine. Both were planted as hedges and the latter was used as firewood (Jdg. 9:14-15; Prov. 26:9; Isa. 55:13; Matt. 7:16; Lk. 6:44). The crown of thorns placed on Jesus'

P

head at the time of his crucifixion might have been the "Christ Thorn" (*Paliurus spina Christi*), a straggling shrub, growing from 3 to 9 ft. (1-3 m.) tall. Its pliable branches, with their uneven stiff thorns, lent themselves to the braiding of the "crown" or "wreath" made by the soldiers (Matt. 27:29; Mk. 15:17; Jn. 19:2, 5). However, since this species was not readily accessible in Jerusalem, the *Zizyphus* or *Rhamnus* might have been the thornbush used.

thyine. See *citron*.

tumbleweed. This English term—referring to various plants that, breaking from their roots, roll about driven by the wind—is used by the NIV to render Hebrew *galgal H1650*, which occurs only twice (Ps. 83:13 [KJV, "wheel"]; Isa. 17:13 [KJV, "rolling thing"; NRSV uses "whirling dust" in both passages]). The plant referred to is thought by some to be *Gundelia tournefortii*, a member of the *thistle* family whose dried calyx has the shape of a wheel. Others identify it as *Anastatica hierochuntica*, the "resurrection plant," also called "the rose of Jericho" (it is found abundantly about that town). This annual loses its leaves after flowering; the stems become incurved and hard, forming a hollow ball. This ball breaks off at ground level in the wind, and then rolls away as light as a feather, distributing the ripened seeds on the surface of the soil as it travels.

turpentine. See *terebinth*.

vine. See *grape*.

vine of Sodom. Mentioned in Deut. 32:32, this plant cannot be clearly identified. Possible fruit plants have been suggested, but each one has problems in fully satisfying the requirements of the text. It is generally accepted that the vine of Sodom is an example of Hebrew poetry, epitomizing the utter wickedness of SODOM, from which comes toxic fruit and fatal drink.

walnut. A large, ornamental, spreading shade tree (*Juglans regia*), with long leaves and woody edible fruit, native to Iran. Also named the "English walnut" or the "Persian walnut," this tree provides edible fruit; dark, close-grained hardwood for woodworking; and dye. The "nut trees" of Cant. 6:11 are most likely walnut trees.

weed. See *cockle*; *eelgrass*; *tares*.

wheat. A common cereal grain that yields fine flour (*Triticum aestivum*, the ordinary summer or winter wheat, or *T. compositum*, the bearded wheat,

with several ears on one stalk). Wheat is sown in the winter and harvested in late spring or early summer in Palestine. Egypt, Babylonia, Syria, and Palestine were renowned for their quality wheat. Wheat is first noted in Gen. 30:14. Certain varieties of wheat still yield 60 to 100 grains per head as they did in Jesus' day (Matt. 13:3-8). Heads roasted over fire constituted the "parched corn" (KJV) of the OT (Lev. 23:14; Ruth 2:14; 1 Sam. 17:17; 25:18). Straw and stubble are the dried stalks and remnants of wheat and other cereal grains (Exod. 5:12; 1 Cor. 3:12).

wild gourd. See *gourd*.

willow. Any of various trees and shrubs of the genus *Salix*, bearing flowers without petals arranged in the form of spikes (catkins). It is found in moist places and on the margins of rivers and shallow streams. The Hebrew word *'ărābāh H6857* (Lev. 23:40; Job 40:22; Ps. 137:2; Isa. 15:7; 44:4) is rendered "willow" by the KJV and other versions, but "poplar" (a related tree) by the NIV. Botanists know over twenty kinds of willows growing in Paletine, including *Salix alba, S. acmophylla, S. fragilis,* and *S. safsaf*, all of which grow well in the region. If *'ărābāh* refers to a tree of the *Salix* genus rather than to the poplar (genus *Populus*), the particular species is difficult to determine. Many have thought that the tree mentioned in Ps. 137:2 is the *Salix babylonica*, whose appearance may have evoked the picture of weeping.

wormwood. In the KJV OT (Deut. 29:18 et al.), "wormwood" may refer to *Artemisia judaica*, a bitter, aromatic herb with clusters of small, greenish yellow flowers and alternating greenish gray leaves, growing in desert areas (another possibility is *Artemisia herba-alba*, which has a camphor scent and is extremely bitter). In Rev. 8:11, the reference is evidently to *Artemisia absinthium*, a herbaceous perennial with silky leaves that bears masses of small yellow flowers; it yields a bitter dark oil that is one of the ingredients used to produce a green liqueur known as *absinthe*. This drink has a most objectionable taste to the uninitiated. The wormwood has come to be used symbolically to describe sorrow, calamity, and even cruelty. See also *gall*.

plaster. A mixture that hardens as it dries and is used to coat walls and ceilings. Plaster was widely used, and variously made, in the ancient world. The higher quality material was produced by heating broken limestone or gypsum. Simple CLAY with straw binder was also used, but was practical only where rainfall was slight. The Israelites were commanded, "When you have crossed the Jordan into the land the LORD your God is giving you, set up some large stones and coat them with plaster" (Deut. 27:2; cf. v. 4). They were also to engrave the words of the law (v. 3), a process that probably took place while the plaster was soft (cf. also Lev. 14:42-43, 48; Dan. 5:5).

plate. This English term is used mainly to translate the Hebrew word *qěʿārâ H7883*, referring to the gold and silver dishes used in the TABERNACLE (Exod. 25:29; 37:16; Num. 4:7; 7:13-85). See also BOWL; DISH; POTTERY.

platter. The KJV uses this term in two NT passages: one of them has Greek *paropsis G4243* (Matt. 23:25-26) and the other one has *pinax G4402* (Lk. 11:39). Modern versions usually render these passages with DISH or PLATE; on the other hand, they typically use "platter" to render *pinax* with reference to the dish on which the head of JOHN THE BAPTIST was placed (Matt. 14:8, 11; Mk. 6:25, 28; KJV, "charger").

pleasure. For the sense "gratification," see the article on LUST. The English expression *good pleasure*, however, is often used with reference to choice or PURPOSE, especially the divine "goodwill" or "favor." This expression sometimes renders the Hebrew word *rāṣôn H8356* (e.g., Ps. 51:18), which itself has a wide semantic range but is frequently used of God's gracious will. In the NT, the Greek word *eudokia G2306* occurs nine times, sometimes with reference to human desire or goodwill (Rom. 10:1; Phil. 1:15; 2 Thess. 1:11), but more often to the divine purpose (Matt. 11:26; Lk. 2:14; 10:21; Eph. 1:5, 9; Phil. 2:13).

pledge. Personal property of a debtor held to secure a payment (Gen. 38:17-18, 20). This English term is used to translate several Hebrew words. The Mosaic law protected the POOR. An outer garment, taken as a pledge, had to be restored at sunset for a bed covering (Exod. 22:26-27; Deut. 24:12-13). The creditor was forbidden to enter his neighbor's house to take the pledge (24:10-11). A handmill or its upper millstone might not be taken (24:6), nor a widow's clothing (24:17-18). Abuses of the pledge were censured (Job 22:6; 24:3, 9; Amos 2:8; Hab. 2:6 [NRSV]). The person who puts up security for strangers ought to be taken in pledge (Prov. 20:16; 27:13). The pledge DAVID was to take from his brothers in exchange for cheeses may be a prearranged token or assurance (NIV) of their welfare (1 Sam. 17:18). The pledge in 1 Tim. 5:12 is the marriage vow. See also DEPOSIT; EARNEST.

Pleiades. See ASTRONOMY.

plowman. See OCCUPATIONS AND PROFESSIONS (under *farmer*).

plow, plowshare. Also *plough* (British). A farming tool used to break up the ground for sowing. An ancient plow scratched the surface but did not turn over the soil. It consisted of a branched stick, the larger branch, usually the trunk of a small tree, hitched to the animals that pulled it, the branch braced and terminating in the plowshare, which was at first simply the sharpened end of the branch, later a metal point. It was ordinarily drawn by a yoke of oxen (Job 1:14; Amos 6:12). Plowing with an ox and a donkey yoked together was forbidden (Deut. 22:10). A man guided the plow with his left hand, goading the oxen and from time to time cleaning the share with the goad in his right, keeping his eyes forward in order to make the furrow straight (Lk. 9:62). Plowing done, the farmer sowed (Isa. 28:24-26). He who does not plow in autumn will have no HARVEST (Prov. 20:4). Amos 9:13 foretells a time when the soil will be so fertile that there will not need to be a fallow interval between harvest and the next plowing. Then foreigners will plow for Israel (Isa. 61:5). Plowing may indicate destruction (Jer. 26:18; Mic. 3:12). Hosea 10:11-13 contrasts plowing for righteous and for evil ends (Job 4:8; Ps. 129:3). Servants plowed (Lk. 17:7). The plowman should plow in hope of a share of the crop (1 Cor. 9:10). ELISHA plowing with twelve yoke of oxen indicates his ability and the magnitude of his farming operations (1 Ki. 19:19).

P

To beat swords into plowshares was symbolic of an age of peace (Isa. 2:4; Mic. 4:3); to beat plowshares into swords portended coming war (Joel 3:10).

plumb line. A cord with a stone or metal weight, the plummet, tied to one end; used by builders to keep a wall perpendicular. Plumb line and plummet are used figuratively of God's action in testing the uprightness of his people (2 Ki. 21:13; Isa. 28:17; Amos 7:7-9).

plunder. See BOOTY; SPOIL.

Pochereth. See POKERETH-HAZZEBAIM.

poet. This English term is derived from Greek *poiētēs G4475*, which often has the general meaning "maker, doer" (cf. Rom. 2:13; Jas. 1:22-25; 4:11), but which can refer as well to "a maker of a writing" and more specifically to someone who composes poems (it is so used in Acts 17:28). The NIV has "poets" in one OT passage (Num. 21:27; NRSV, "ballad singers"). See also POETRY.

poetry. Many modern versions of the Bible happily try to differentiate poetry from prose in the OT by formatting the text of the former according to assumed poetic lines. Interpreters, however, do not always agree whether specific passages are poetic in character. Hebrew poetry is very different from its Greek, Latin, or English counterparts. While it is certainly not lacking in rhythm, assonance, and other literary features such as we accept in classical and English poetry, in OT poetry everything is subservient to meaning. Thus lines of Hebrew poetry are not to be "scanned" by marking off long and short syllables (as though the "form" were the primary consideration), but marking off significant words or groups of words (because the message is primary). Thus (as, for example, in the so-called "dirge" rhythm) a line of three significant words is followed by a line with two, usually written 3:2. Another frequent "rhythm" in Hebrew poetry is 3:3.

But the most familiar feature of Hebrew poetry arises from the balance between successive lines. This feature is called *parallelism*. Several varieties have been distinguished, of which the three principal ones are *synonymous*, in which the meaning of both lines is similar, although the second member usually advances the thought (e.g., 1 Sam. 18:7; Ps. 15:1; 24:1-3); *antithetic*, in which the meanings of the members are opposed (Ps. 37:9; Prov. 10:1; 11:3); and *synthetic*, in which the sense was developed in a continuous manner to reach its logical conclusion (Ps. 1:1-2). Strictly speaking, however, this last category does not involve parallelism.

In addition, quite a number of poems are alphabetical acrostics; that is to say, successive lines begin with the successive letters of the Hebrew alphabet (e.g., Ps. 34; 37; Lam. 1-4). In Ps. 119 each group of eight verses begins with the same letter. This literary device may have been chosen for mnemonic reasons (i.e., to assist in memorization) or to suggest comprehensiveness (just as we say, "From A to Z"), so that in Ps. 119, for example, we have a total statement about the Word of God.

Short poems (usually so printed in NIV) are embedded in the historical books as follows: Adam to Eve (Gen. 2:23); God to the serpent, Adam, and Eve (3:14-19); Lamech to his wives (4:23-24); Noah about his sons (9:25-27); Melchizedek's blessing (14:19-20); God to Rebekah (25:23); Isaac's blessing on Jacob (27:27-29) and Esau (27:39-40); Jacob in blessing Joseph (48:15-16) and in prophecies concerning his sons (49:2-27); the victory song of Moses (Exod. 15:1-18, 21); the priestly blessing (Num. 6:24-26); a quotation from the Book of the Wars of the Lord (21:14-15); the song of the well (21:17-18); a ballad (21:27-30); Balaam's prophecies (23:7-10, 18-24; 24:3-9, 15-24); Moses' song (Deut. 32:1-43) and blessing of the people (33:2-29); the curse on a future rebuilder of Jericho (Josh. 6:26b); a quotation from the Book of Jasher (1:12b-13a); the song of Deborah and Barak (Jdg. 5); Samson's riddle, solution, and answer (14:14, 18); his victory song (15:16); Hannah's song (1 Sam. 2:1-10); a poem by Samuel (15:22-23); a women's song (18:7); David's lament over Jonathan (2 Sam. 1:19-27) and over Abner (3:33-34); his psalm (Ps. 18:2-50; 22:5-31); his last words (2 Sam. 23:1-7); a quatrain by Solomon (1 Ki. 8:12-13); a popular song (12:16; 2 Chr. 10:16); a prophetic poem by Isaiah (2 Ki. 19:21-28); a soldiers' song (1 Chr. 12:18); a refrain (2 Chr. 5:13; 7:3b, "He is good; his love endures for ever"); a snatch of song by Solomon (6:1b-2, 41-42).

In the NT, easily recognizable poems are all in Luke: the MAGNIFICAT of Mary (1:46b-55), adapted from Hannah's song (1 Sam. 2:1-10); the prophecy of Zachariah (Lk. 1:68-79); the angels' Gloria in Excelsis (2:14); and the NUNC DIMITTIS of Simeon (2:29-32). All these are echoes of Hebrew poetry, sung by Hebrews. Snatches of Christian hymns are thought to be found in some of the letters (Eph. 5:14; Phil. 2:6-11; 1 Tim. 1:17; 3:16; 6:16; 2 Tim. 4:18). Paul rises to heights of poetic eloquence (e.g., Rom. 8; 11:33-12:2; 1 Cor. 13; 15:25-57). James's letter is lyrical. The language of Jesus is poetic in the highest degree. The NT contains many quotations of OT poetry. But it is the elevated thought of the NT as of the OT, and not the technical form, that gives us the feeling of poetry. Thus Bible language has lent itself admirably to the use of hymn writers, in many languages and to their own native poetic forms.

poison. Any substance that, on contact with or upon being absorbed into the body, is capable of exerting a deleterious effect. It often refers to the venom of reptiles (Deut. 32:24, 33; Job 20:16; Ps. 58:4; Rom. 3:13). Job 6:4 refers to poisoned arrows. Vegetable poisons also were known (Hos. 10:4; 2 Ki. 4:39-40). See HEMLOCK.

Pokereth-Hazzebaim.   pok´uh-rith-haz-uh-bay´im (Heb. *pōkeret haṣṣĕbāyim H7097*, possibly "hunter of gazelles"). Also Pochereth-hazzebaim; KJV Pochereth of Zebaim. A servant (official) of SOLOMON whose descendants returned from Babylon (Ezra 2:57; Neh. 7:59). The name originally may have been a title designating this person's occupation as being in charge of the king's gazelles. Because the form *pōkeret* is feminine, some have thought the reference is to a woman.

pollution. This English term, referring to ceremonial or moral impurity, is used rarely in Bible versions. The verb *pollute* and the adjective *polluted* are more frequent (e.g., Num. 35:33; Prov. 25:26). The KJV uses the verb repeatedly in Ezekiel (Ezek. 7:21-22 et al.). The terms are less common in the NT, but "pollution" or "polluted thing" can be used, for example, to render Greek *alisgēma G246* (Acts 15:20). See PURIFICATION; UNCLEAN.

Pollux. See CASTOR AND POLLUX.

Polycarp. See APOSTOLIC FATHERS.

polygamy. See MARRIAGE.

pomegranate. See PLANTS.

pommel. This English term, meaning "knob," is used by the KJV in one passage where the reference is to ornaments on top of the two pillars of the TEMPLE (2 Chr. 4:12-13).

Pompey. pom´pee. A Roman general who intervened in JUDEA in 63 B.C., effectively ending the period of independence under Hasmonean rule (see MACCABEE). Born Gnaeus Pompeius in 106 B.C., he served as a young man under the dictator Sulla. His career rose rapidly and, in spite of his youth, was made consul in 70 B.C. A few years later his military campaigns in the Middle E, particularly against the PARTHIAN king Mithridates VI, made him famous. Toward the end of these campaigns, Pompey founded several colonies and also succeeded in annexing SYRIA. At the time, a civil war was raging in Judea between Hyrcanus II and his brother Aristobulus II. In 63 B.C., Pompey marched against JERUSALEM and, after a three-month siege, captured the temple. Although he did not plunder the treasures, he did enter the Holy of Holies, a great sacrilege in Jewish eyes. In 59 he formed a coalition with Julius CAESAR and Crassus, but when the latter died in 53, serious tensions developed between Pompey and Caesar. Five years later they met in battle in MACEDONIA and, soon after, Pompey fled to EGYPT, where he was stabbed to death (September of the year 48).

pond. See POOL.

Pontius Pilate. See PILATE.

Pontus. pon´tuhs (Gk. *Pontos G4510*, "sea"). A large PROVINCE of N ASIA MINOR that lay along the Black Sea (Pontus Euxinius). All the references to Pontus in the NT indicate that there were many Jews in the province. Jews from Pontus were in JERUSALEM on the day of PENTECOST (Acts 2:9).

P

LUKE mentions in Acts 18:2 that a certain Christian Jew named AQUILA was born in Pontus. So far as we know, Pontus and the other northern provinces were not evangelized by PAUL. The HOLY SPIRIT did not permit him to preach in BITHYNIA (16:7), which was just W of Pontus. However, Peter addresses his first letter to "strangers in the world, scattered throughout Pontus" and other regions (1 Pet. 1:1), lending credence to the tradition that PETER preached in northern Asia Minor rather than in Rome after Pentecost. In secular history, Pontus is noted for the dynasty of kings, headed by the great Mithridates, that ruled from 337 to 63 B.C.

pool. A pocket of water, natural or artificial. The characteristic Hebrew term for "pool" or "pond" is *bĕrēkâ H1391*, which generally seems to refer to an artificial body of water (2 Sam. 2:13; 4:12; 1 Ki. 22:38; 2 Ki. 18:17). Of special significance is the Pool of SILOAM, built by King HEZEKIAH (2 Ki. 20:20; Neh. 3:15). The word *ʾăgam H106*, on the other hand, is normally used of standing water or marsh (see esp. Isa. 14:23; Jer. 51:32). In the NT, the Greek word for "pool" is *kolymbēthra G3148*, used by John with reference to the pools of BETHESDA (Jn. 5:2, 7) and Siloam (9:7). The conservation of WATER was crucial to the people of PALESTINE, since RAIN does not fall for extended periods. Natural terrain was utilized to store water where possible, and where nature was not so obliging, toiling hands carved out a substitute. Large pools were made by damming streams. Smaller ones were rectangular, wider than they were deep, to collect rain from the roofs or from the surface of the ground. Water from springs was collected in masonry pools. If the sources of water happened to be outside the walls of the city, the people often would construct tunnels to bring in the precious commodity so that it would be available in time of siege. Hezekiah's tunnel is an instance of this (2 Ki. 20:20), and similar arrangements have been uncovered at GEZER and MEGIDDO. Because of the cruciality of water, disputes often broke out in the vicinity of its sources (Gen. 26:15-22).

poor. God's LOVE and care for the poor are central to his PROVIDENCE (Ps. 34:6; 68:10; Eccl. 5:8).

He encourages us to do the same (Exod. 22:23). The Mosaic law has specific provisions for the benefit of the poor (Exod. 22:25-27; 23:11; Lev. 19:9-10, 13, 15; 25:6, 25-30; Deut. 14:28-29; 15:12-13; 16:11-14; Ruth 2:1-7; Neh. 8:10). Israel as a nation was born out of deep poverty (Exod. 1:8-14; 2:7-10) and was never allowed to forget it (e.g., 1 Ki. 8:50-53). If Israel met the conditions of God's COVENANT, there would be no poor among them; but God knew this would never be realized (Deut. 15:4-11). Willful neglect leading to poverty is not condoned (Prov. 13:4-18). National disasters caused the poor to rely on God and thus they become almost synonymous with the pious (e.g., Ps. 68:10; Isa. 41:17). Even in the early nomadic and later agricultural economy there were slaves and poor freemen, but there were many more in the urban and commercial economy of the monarchy. The wrongs done to the poor concerned the prophets (e.g., Isa. 1:23; 10:1-2; Ezek. 34; Amos 2:6; 5:7; 8:6; Mic. 2:1-2; Hab. 3:14; Mal. 3:5).

At the outset of his ministry, Jesus, taking for his text Isa. 61:1-2, presents as his first aim, "to preach good news to the poor." That physical poverty is meant is shown by the contrasts in Lk. 6:20-26, but the parallel passage in Matt. 5:3 ("poor in spirit") suggests that the mere lack of possession is not what calls the divine benediction. Rather, Jesus has in mind the one "who is humble [KJV poor] and contrite in spirit, and trembles at my word" (Isa. 66:2), that is, the person who in the midst of oppression turns to God for deliverance. Jesus moved among the poor and humble. He associated himself with them in his manner of living and his freedom from the encumbering cares of property (8:20). He understood and appreciated the sacrificial giving of a poor widow (Mk. 12:41-44). He recognized the continuing obligation toward the poor and at the same time appreciated a unique expression of love toward himself (14:7). The early church moved among the poor, who were not too poor to be concerned for one another's welfare (2 Cor. 8:2-5, 9-15), drawing inspiration from Christ's leaving heavenly riches for earthly poverty. The origin of the diaconate is linked with a special need (Acts 6:1-6). Those with property contributed to the common fund (2:45; 4:32-37). The

Jerusalem Council asked PAUL and BARNABAS to remember the poor (Gal. 2:10). JAMES has some sharp words about the relations of rich and poor (Jas. 1:9-11; 2:1-13; 5:1-6).

poplar. See PLANTS.

Poplars, Ravine of the. See WILLOWS, BROOK (WADI) OF THE.

Poratha. por-ay´thuh (Heb. *pôrātā* H7054, meaning uncertain). One of the ten sons of HAMAN who were put to death by the Jews (Esth. 9:8).

porch. This English term is used frequently by the KJV to render several words, especially Hebrew *'êlām H395* (1 Ki. 6:3 et al.). Modern versions prefer such renderings as "portico" (NIV) and "vestibule" (NRSV), although in one passage "hall" is more appropriate (1 Ki. 7:7-8). The most widespread form of porch was the *bît ḫilāni* of SYRIA of the 11th cent. B.C. that served as the grand entry of the palace. It was partially open on the front side and enclosed on the other three sides, the rear opening into the main hall or others beyond. The facade usually had decorative columns that were also structural to support the roof above. In the NT, the KJV uses "porch" once for *pylōn G4784* (Matt. 26:71; the term more commonly means "gateway"), but it also occurs in the parallel passage for *proaulion G4580*, "forecourt" (Mk. 14:68). Finally, the KJV uses it four times for *stoa G5119*,

© Dr. James C. Martin. The Holy Land Hotel, Jerusalem. Photographed by permission.

Reconstruction of the colonnaded porch in the 1st-cent. Jerusalem temple.

which refers to a roofed colonnade (Jn. 5:2; 10:23; Acts 3:11; 5:12). See also ARCHITECTURE; HALL; HOUSE; SOLOMON'S COLONNADE.

Porcius. See FESTUS, PORCIUS.

porcupine. See ANIMALS (under *bittern*).

porphyry. See MINERALS.

porpoise. See ANIMALS (under *badger*).

port. See HARBOR. The KJV uses this term in the sense "gate" (only Neh. 2:13).

porter. See OCCUPATIONS AND PROFESSIONS.

portico. See PORCH.

portion. A part—that is, less than the whole; a share (Num. 31:30, 47 KJV), of food served to one person (Neh. 8:10, 12; Dan. 1:5-16; 11:26 KJV; NIV, "amount, provision"; Deut. 18:8 KJV) or of property acquired by gift (1 Sam. 1:4-5) or by inheritance (Gen. 31:14 KJV; Josh. 17:14). It can also refer to a plot of ground (2 Ki. 9:10, 36-37 KJV) or one's destiny (Job 20:29 KJV; Ps. 142:5; Lam. 3:24). Several Hebrew and Greek words are translated "portion" in the KJV, though modern versions often use different terms appropriate to the context. The most significant sense appears in passages like Ps. 119:57, where one's relation to God and eternal well-being are involved. See INHERITANCE.

possession, demoniacal. See DEMON.

post. This English word, in its several senses as noun or verb, is used variously in the Bible versions to render a number of Hebrew terms. For example, it occurs often in the KJV as the rendering of *mĕzûzâ H4647*, "doorpost, doorframe" (Exod. 12:22 et al.; see DOOR), while the NIV uses it sometimes to translate *ʿammûd H6647*, "column, pillar" (Exod. 38:17 et al.; see PILLAR). As a verb in the sense "to station," the word can render *ʿāmad H6641* (Isa. 21:6 et al.). The KJV uses it also to translate the participle of *rûṣ H8132* ("to run") with reference to "runners," that is, "messengers" or "couriers" (2 Chr. 3:7; the Hebrew term can be applied to messengers mounted on horses, Esth. 8:10).

postmillennialism. See KINGDOM OF GOD.

pot. The translation of more than a dozen Hebrew and Greek words. Most of them referred to utensils for holding liquids and solid substances such as grain or ashes. The Hebrew *sîr H6105* was the most common pot used in cooking (2 Ki. 4:38; Jer. 1:13). It was also the VESSEL that held ashes (Exod. 27:3). Some of these vessels were made of metal and others of clay, and there were a great variety of sizes and shapes. Their chief NT use was for water or wine (Mk. 7:4; Jn. 2:6 KJV; NIV, "pitchers, jars"). See PITCHER; POTTERY.

potentate. This English term, meaning "ruler, sovereign," is used by the KJV once with reference to God (1 Tim. 6:15). The Greek word here is *dynastēs G1541* ("powerful one, master, ruler"), which occurs also in two other NT passages (Lk. 1:52; Acts 8:27).

Potiphar. pot´uh-fuhr (Heb. *pôṭîpar H7035*, prob. short form of POTIPHERA, "whom [the god] Ra has given"). The Egyptian official who purchased JOSEPH and placed him in charge of his household (Gen. 37:36; 39:1, 4-5). Potiphar is described as "the captain of the guard," which in Middle Egyptian would refer to a leader of the bodyguard.

Potiphera. puh-ti´fuh-ruh (Heb. *pôṭî peraʿ H7036*, from Egyp. *pʾdy pʾrʿ*, "whom [the god] Ra has given"). The father-in-law of JOSEPH (Gen. 41:45, 50; 46:20). He is referred to as a priest of ON (i.e., HELIOPOLIS), the center of the worship of the sun-god, Ra (RE). Because of his apparent prominence, some have thought that Potiphera may have been the high priest and thus one of the most influential figures of his time. The PHARAOH chose Potiphera's daughter, ASENATH, to be Joseph's wife.

potsherd. A fragment of any broken pottery jar (cf. Job 2:8 [KJV]; 41:30; Ps. 22:15; Isa. 45:9). Large ones were used to carry coals from one house to another or to dip up water from a spring or cistern (Isa. 30:14). They were also used as lids for storage jars or cooking pots. Potsherds were ground fine and added to the waterproof plaster used in lining cisterns. Finally, sherds from large storage jars were used for writing material (see OSTRACA).

Potsherd Gate. A place near the Valley of Ben HINNOM where JEREMIAH was told to prophesy (Jer. 19:2; KJV renders incorrectly, "east gate"). In view of its name and location, most scholars identify it with the DUNG GATE, where refuse and broken pottery were probably discarded.

pottage. A thick broth or porridge made by boiling vegetables, sometimes with meat or suet, usually in water. This English word is used by the KJV to render Hebrew *nāzîd H5686* ("boiled food, stew"), which occurs in connection with the red lentil stew that induced ESAU to give up his birthright (Gen. 25:29, 34), and the food poisoned with wild gourds and eaten by the company of prophets (2 Ki. 4:38-40). It is also mentioned in Hag. 2:12 with bread, wine, and oil.

potter. See OCCUPATIONS AND PROFESSIONS.

potter's field. See AKELDAMA.

pottery. Earthenware, that is, ware made from clay. Pottery making is one of the oldest crafts in Bible lands. This artificial substance—thought to be the first synthetic discovered by humans—is produced by heating clay to such high temperatures that its chemical properties change, resulting in a new substance similar to stone. References, both literal and figurative, to the potter and his products occur throughout the Scriptures.

I. Pottery production in Palestine. Let us follow JEREMIAH down to the potter's house (Jer. 18:1-6). This "factory" was in the Valley of HINNOM near the POTSHERD GATE (19:2). In addition to his workshop the potter needed a field (Matt. 27:7) for weathering the dry native clay-dust or wet stream-bank clay (Nah. 3:14) and for mixing it with water and treading it by foot into potter's clay, as in Isa. 41:25. For cooking vessels, sand or crushed stone was added to temper the clay. In his house the potter kneaded the clay for several hours to remove all air bubbles. He could either build up a large vessel freehand, using long sausagelike rolls of clay; or he could "throw" a ball of soft clay on the center of a pivoted disc or dual stone wheel that was spun counterclockwise by his hand or by his apprentice. By thrusting his forearm into the mass of wet clay, he hollowed out the interior. The centrifugal force imparted to the spinning lump enabled the potter in a matter of minutes to form a vessel with only light pressure from his fingers. In mass production he pinched off the completed jug from the cone of clay spinning on the wheel. Impurities in the clay or insufficient treading could mar the vessel on the wheel. The potter easily remedied this by reshaping the clay into a ball and making a less elegant object out of the former discard (Jer. 18:3-4).

After drying to a leathery consistency the vessel was replaced on the wheel for "turning," cutting and paring off excess clay as on a lathe. To fill the pores and beautify the vessel the potter could coat the pot with "slip," clay of the consistency of cream, often with a mineral color added. Next he might burnish or rub the surface with a smooth stone to produce a sheen, or he might paint on a design. Finally, the jar was "fired" by heating it, usually between 700 and 1,050 degrees Celsius in an open fire or in a kiln. Firing was the most difficult art for the apprentice to master, and this skill was probably passed on from father to son as a trade secret. Such potters' installations have been found in a cave at LACHISH (c. 1500 B.C.), within the ESSENE community center at Qumran, and by the NABATEAN city of Avdat (Eboda) in the NEGEV.

God, who formed (Heb. *yāṣar H3670*) ADAM from the dust or soil (Gen. 2:7), is likened to a potter (*yôṣēr H3450*), who fashions us according to his will (Job 10:8-9; 33:6; Isa. 29:16; 45:9; 64:8; Lam. 4:2; Rom. 9:20-23; 2 Tim. 2:20-21). He will conquer the wicked as one smashes a piece of pottery (Ps. 2:9; Jer. 19:10-11; Rev. 2:27).

II. Historical development of pottery styles in Palestine. Ceramic vessels, like clothing and automobiles, have been changing in fashion down through the centuries of human existence. Recog-

nizing this fact, the Egyptologist Flinders Petrie in 1890 catalogued the sequence of broken pottery according to the varying shapes and decorations at Tell el-Ḥesi in SW PALESTINE. He succeeded in assigning dates to several of his pottery periods by identifying certain wares with wares previously discovered in datable Egyptian tombs. Today when an archaeologist uncovers no more precise evidence (e.g., inscriptions on clay tablets, monuments, or coins), he depends on dominant pottery styles from an occupation level of an ancient city to furnish the clue to the date. On the second day of excavation in 1953, the Wheaton Archaeological Expedition verified that Dothan was settled in Joseph's time (Gen. 37:17) by unearthing orange and black burnished juglets and a double-handled juglet, of the same style as the Hyksos-Age juglets found in the 1930s at MEGIDDO.

A. Neolithic Age (?–c. 4300 B.C.). Depending on the accuracy of dating methods and assumptions, pottery—all handmade—can be dated to around 4500 B.C. But scores of generations before the first pottery appeared at JERICHO, people who practiced irrigation and constructed massive city fortifications settled the town. The vessels were either exceedingly coarse or else made with much finer clay, usually with painted decorations, and well-fired.

B. Chalcolithic Age (4300-3300 B.C.). When copper came into use, the peculiar pottery styles included swinging butter churns; jars with small "cord-eye" handles; cups with a long, tapering, spikelike "cornet" base; and ossuaries for human bones, made of pottery in the shape of miniature houses.

C. Early Bronze Age (3300-2300 B.C.). In this millennium potters began to use the stone disc tournette or turntable, predecessor of the potter's wheel. Characteristic features of the pottery of this age are flat bottoms, hole-mouth pots, spouts on jars, inward-projecting bowl rims, ledge handles on water jugs, and bands of parallel, wavy, or crisscross lines painted over the jar's surface.

D. Middle Bronze Age I (2300-2000 B.C.). A transition period in pottery styles, these centuries saw the coming of ABRAHAM to Palestine and an irruption of seminomadic AMORITES from SYRIA, who destroyed many towns and depopulated much of Canaan.

P

© Dr. James C. Martin. The Israel Museum, Jerusalem. Photographed by permission.

A pithos (wide-mouth earthenware storage jar) from the Chalcolithic Period (ca. 3200 B.C.) decorated with rope-like bands.

E. Middle Bronze Age II (2000-1550 B.C.). The Hyksos, descendants of the Amorites and native Canaanites, dominated Palestine in this era. Hazor was their chief city. They were already entering Egypt as merchants or Egyptian slaves in the nineteenth century when Jacob settled in Goshen. Later they ruled in Egypt, 1730-1570. In the nineteenth century the fast-spinning potter's wheel revolutionized the industry in the ANE. Virtually all Middle Bronze II pottery was wheel-made. Distinctively Hyksos were the pear-shaped juglets with "button" base, double- or triple-strand handles, chalk-filled pinprick designs, and highly burnished vessels with orange or black coating. Bowls and jars with ring or disc bases were introduced in Palestine, as well as dipper flasks and chalices. Hyksos cities in S Palestine fell before the pursuing Egyptians about 1550, whereas cities in northern Palestine remained in Hyksos hands until the campaigns of Thutmose III (c. 1480).

F. Late Bronze Age (1550-1200 B.C.). With the Hyksos' power broken, numerous petty kings ruled in Canaan. The native pottery declined in gracefulness and technique as the prosperity slumped. Thus, imported vessels from Cyprus are all the more striking: milk bowls with wishbone handles, and "bilbils," jugs with a metallic ring when tapped. From 1400 to 1230 Mycenean pottery imports were common: stirrup vases, squat pyxis (cylinder-shaped) jars, and large craters with horizontal loop handles. While the nomadic Israelites invaded Canaan (prob. c. 1400), they continued using wooden bowls, goatskins, and cloth sacks (Lev. 11:32) and produced little pottery until they could conquer a town and discard tents for more permanent houses.

G. Iron Age I (1200-1000 B.C.). In the latter time of the judges Israel was more settled, and iron came into common use. Typical pottery objects were the traveler's water canteen, many-handled wine craters, and lamps with a thick, disclike base. The decorative features are the most distinctive: hand burnishing and gaudy, painted designs, even on rims and handles. After 1150 Philistine painted-ware, very similar to late Mycenean pottery elsewhere, is outstanding with its designs of swans pluming themselves, dolphins, spirals, loops, and maltese crosses. In Israel the period ended when Pharaoh Shishak destroyed many towns on his Palestinian campaign.

H. Iron Age II (1000-586 B.C.). During the divided monarchy the cities of Israel prospered materially, and their potters excelled. Most helpful for dating a town to this period are the ring-burnished water decanters; wheel burnishing on banquet bowls; twisted, ridged handles on storage jars; black perfume juglets; and the beautiful red, highly burnished Samaria ware. Archaeologists have unearthed Hebrew writings in ink on potsherds, such as the seventy-odd Samaria ostraca from the palace of Jeroboam II and the twenty-one Lachish letters dated to 589/8. From Isaiah's time onward in Judah appear many inscribed handles of jars for wine, olive oil, or grain. In some cases, as on those found at Gibeon, the name of the owner of a vineyard was inscribed. On others the letters lmlk ("belonging to the king") appear together with the name of one of four cities, probably where royal potteries were established to make jars of the correct capacity for the payment of taxes

© Dr. James C. Martin. The British Museum. Photographed by permission.

Iron Age II pottery from Lachish. These red burnished juglets, possibly imported from Cyprus, are representative of pottery found in Judah more generally.

in produce (cf. 1 Chr. 4:23). NEBUCHADNEZZAR's devastating invasion produced a cultural void in Palestine for fifty years.

I. Persian Age (538-333 B.C.). During this period locally made storage jars had pointed bases rather than the earlier rounded style. The lip of the lamp evolved into an elongated spout. The most distinctive pottery in the sixth century was imported Greek black-figured ware, and in the fifth, Greek red-figured ware. Coins, which began to appear in Palestine in the fifth century, aid the archaeologist in dating.

J. Hellenistic Age (333-63 B.C.). The conquests of ALEXANDER THE GREAT began the hellenization of Palestine (see HELLENISM). The double potter's wheel, with a large footpower wheel to turn the thrower's wheel (Sir. 38:29-30), was a Greek improvement. The ubiquitous Rhodian wine-jar handles, each stamped with the name of the potter or of the annual magistrate in RHODES, immediately classify a stratum of an ancient town as Hellenistic.

K. Roman Age (63 B.C.–A.D. 325). POMPEY's capture of JERUSALEM in 63 B.C. brought Palestine under Roman domination. Significant pottery styles are the beautiful red-glazed (*terra sigillata*) bowls and plates, jugs and pots with horizontally corrugated surfaces, and the exquisitely painted, extremely thin Nabatean pottery from about 50 B.C. to A.D. 150.

III. Identification of biblical terms for pottery objects. The Hebrew and Greek words, about which there is some degree of understanding, are classified under several main groups.

A. Bowls, basins, and cups. The "cups" of biblical times were usually small bowls without handles. Flat dinner plates were unknown, shallow bowls serving as platters and dishes.

1. The Hebrew word *kôs H3926* and the Greek word *potērion G4539* are regularly translated "cup," a small individual drinking bowl for water (2 Sam. 12:3; Ps. 23:5; Matt. 10:42) or for wine (Prov. 23:31; Jer. 35:5; Matt. 26:27). Figuratively a cup might be symbolic of one's destiny, whether it be of salvation (Ps. 16:5; 116:13) or of judgment and suffering (Isa. 51:17, 22; Jer. 49:12; Matt. 20:22; 26:39; Rev. 14:10).

2. The *sĕlōḥit H7504*, mentioned only in 2 Ki. 2:20 (KJV, "cruse") must have been an open, shallow bowl to hold salt, for salt would cake up in a cruse.

3. A vessel similar to no. 2 was the *ṣallaḥat H7505*, which must have been the well-known ring-burnished bowl of Iron Age II. It had no handles to hang it up, hence it was turned over to dry (2 Ki. 21:13). It could be used by a sluggard both for cooking and to contain his food (Prov. 19:24; 26:15).

4. Another Hebrew term, *ʾaggān H110*, refers to a banquet bowl, ring- or spiral-burnished on the interior, with two or four handles, similar in size and purpose to our punch bowls (Cant. 7:2; but KJV and NIV, "goblet"). The "lesser vessels" in Isa. 22:24 were hung from a nail or peg on the tent-pole but were large enough to sometimes cause the peg to give way.

5. Probably an earlier style of no. 4 was the *sēpel H6210*, since the Arabic word for a large four-handled bowl in Palestinian villages today is *sifl*. Since it was called a "bowl fit for nobles," JAEL may have offered SISERA curdled milk (Jdg. 5:25) in one imported from Mycenae or Cyprus, decorated with painted designs and having pushed-up horizontal loop handles, holding from 4 to 10 pints (about 2-5 liters). Or it may have been smaller and of the variety known as the Cypriote milk bowl with a wishbone handle, typical of the Late Bronze Age, and holding 1-3 pints (0.5-2 liters). GIDEON squeezed the dew from his fleece into a similar bowl (6:38).

6. The Greek term *tryblion G5581* refers to a large deep dish or bowl, either of metal or fine Roman sigillata pottery, from which all could take out food (Matt. 26:23).

P

7. The *niptēr G3781* was a basin or vessel for washing the hands and feet (Jn. 13:5). In Iron Age II the Israelites had oval ceramic footbaths, about 2 ft. (60 cm.) long, with a raised footrest in the middle and drain hole at the bottom of one side.

B. Cooking pots. Sherds of these common vessels are very numerous in excavated cities since every household needed several pots. Because these vessels broke or cracked easily, they were often "despised," considered the lowliest type of pottery; hence they are seldom found in tombs.

1. The Hebrew word *sîr H6105* refers to a wide-mouth, broad, round-bottom cooking pot; in Iron Age I it was handleless, but in Iron Age II and later it is found with two handles. The large diameter of its mouth permitted it to be used as a washbasin (Ps. 60:8). It could be of great size, large enough to boil vegetables for all the sons of the prophets at Gilgal (2 Ki. 4:38). It was used by the Israelite slaves in Egypt (Exod. 16:3) and by the poor family whose only fuel was the thorn bush (Eccl. 7:6; the word for "thorns" is *sîrîm* [pl. of *sîrâ H6106*], thus a play on words).

2. A one-handled or two-handled cooking pot, deeper and with a narrower mouth than no. 1, was the *pārûr H7248*. With one hand Gideon carried such a pot containing broth, in the other hand a basket containing bread and meat (Jdg. 6:19). The Israelites boiled manna in this type of vessel (Num. 11:8).

3. The *marḥešet H5306* was a ceramic kettle used for deep-fat frying (Lev. 2:7; 7:9); the meal-offering cakes made in this "pan" would be of the texture of our doughnuts.

4. The term *ʿeṣeb H6775* occurs only once (Jer. 22:28) and its precise meaning is uncertain (KJV wrongly, "idol"). The reference is probably to a cooking pot; thus Coniah (Jehoiachin) is likened to a large pot that is broken and despised.

C. Jars. These would include large stationary (apparently not mentioned in the Bible) as well as the smaller jars for carrying water from well to house and for the storage of grain, of olive oil, and of wine.

1. Hebrew *kad H3902* and Greek *hydria G5620* probably refer to jars that were 13-20 in. (33-51 cm.) tall, with two handles, an egg-shaped bottom, and a small mouth used for carrying water on one's shoulder (1 Ki. 18:33; Eccl. 12:6; Jn. 4:28).

In Rebekah's day the flat-bottom, folded ledge-handle jar was in use in Palestine (Gen. 24:15). When the purpose was to store grain or meal, the jar was often more cylindrical, with or without handles (1 Ki. 17:12, 14, 16). The Late-Bronze jars used by Gideon's 300 to conceal their torches (Jdg. 7:16-20) must have had handles and must have been common and easily obtainable.

2. It seems probable that the Hebrew word *nēbel H5574* originally referred to a wineskin (1 Sam. 1:24; 10:3; 25:18; 2 Sam. 16:1; Jer. 13:12), that is, a prepared goatskin that could hold 5-10 gallons (about 20-40 liters). The term could also be applied to a ceramic storage jar used especially for wine, olive oil, and grain. It held approximately a *bath*, or about 6 gallons (23 liters) and stood about 2 ft. (60 cm.) high. Since this vessel had two handles, it could be hung from a peg, but its weight might break the peg (Isa. 22:24). The men of Judah, recipients and containers of the Lord's blessings as well as of his judgments, are likened to the *nēbel*: the breaking of a storage jar with its valued contents would be a household disaster (Isa. 30:14; Jer. 13:12; 48:12; Lam. 4:2).

3. Another Hebrew term, *ʾāsûk H655*, occurs only once (2 Ki. 4:2), where the phrase "a jar of oil" is rendered by the NIV as "a little oil." The vessel in view is probably the typical Iron Age II jar for olive oil. It had three handles arranged at ninety degrees around the mouth; the fourth quadrant had a funnel or spout that probably held a juglet used for taking oil from the jar (the drippings of oil from the juglet would thus go back into the jar). Various sizes stand from 6 to 16 in. (15-40 cm.) in height.

D. Decanters, flasks, and juglets.

1. Hebrew *baqbuq H1318* evidently refers to the handsome ring-burnished water decanter of Iron II. Its narrow neck caused a gurgling sound when the water was poured; hence its name. It came in graduated sizes from 4 to 10 in. (10-25 cm.) high. Jeremiah uses this pitcher to typify the city of Jerusalem (Jer. 19:1-15), a fitting illustration, considering its beauty and expense, as well as the fact that its neck could never be repaired (19:11). Jeroboam I sent to the prophet Ahijah a gift of honey in such a vessel (1 Ki. 14:3).

2. The *ṣappaḥat H7608* was a two-handled traveler's flask or canteen, very popular from the

Late Bronze Age until the middle of Iron Age II (1 Sam. 26:11-12; 1 Ki. 19:6). Made of a lightly baked clay, its resulting porosity allowed for evaporation that cooled the water within. In 1 Ki. 17:12-16 this word is used for the oil jar of the widow of Zarephath. While the porous clay of the canteen is ill-suited to contain oil, the widow was very poor and may have had to put her few vessels to unwonted uses; probably also she never had had a large supply of oil before this incident.

3. Another Hebrew term, *pak H7095*, refers to a small juglet used for holding perfumed anointing oil (1 Sam. 10:1; 2 Ki. 9:1, 3). In one or both of the biblical references it may have been a lovely Cypro-Phoenician flask. Or it may have been the local blue-black hand-burnished juglet found in great quantities at Megiddo and Tell Beit Mirsim.

4. Greek *keramion G3040* designates a one-handled ribbed water jug, 8-12 in. (20-30 cm.) high, by which Jesus' disciples were to identify the owner of the house where they were to celebrate the Passover (Mk. 14:13; Lk. 22:10). Ordinarily only a woman would be seen carrying a jug of water into the city from the fountain.

E. Other objects

1. The common pottery LAMP that burned olive oil was called *nēr H5944* in Hebrew. In OT times it was basically a small bowl or saucer; while the molded clay was still soft, the potter pinched in the rim at one section to hold the linen or flax wick (Isa. 42:3). Never more than a few inches in diameter, the lamp was suitable for carrying in the palm of the hand when walking (Ps. 119:105; Zeph. 1:12) or for placing in a niche in the wall of the house or cave-home. Fearing darkness, people would leave a lamp burning all night (Prov. 31:18); thus it was just as essential as the millstones for grinding grain (Jer. 25:10). The presence of a burning lamp with its light symbolized joy and peace (2 Sam. 22:29), whereas the extinguishing of the lamp suggested utter gloom and desolation (Job 18:5-6; 21:17; Prov. 13:9; 20:20; 24:20). Since the ancient considered his life to be continued through his sons, his "light" was not put out if he had a son; thus the lamp also symbolized posterity (1 Ki. 11:36; 15:4; 2 Ki. 8:19). In patriarchal times (Middle Bronze I) the lamp sometimes had its rim pinched in four places. Some Israelite lamps had seven such

pinched "wick-holders," undoubtedly reminiscent of the seven-branched golden candlestick or lampstand of the tabernacle and temple.

2. Greek *lampas G3286* refers also to a hand-sized clay lamp but with considerable change in shape from the OT lamps. By the first century A.D. the pinched rim had given way to a nozzle for the wick. This type was carried by the ten virgins (Matt. 25:1-8), by the band led by Judas Iscariot (Jn. 18:3; NIV, "lanterns"), and by the Christians congregating in an upper room in Troas (Acts 20:8).

3. The lamp placed on a lampstand was the *lychnon G3394* (Matt. 5:15; Lk. 11:33-36).

4. Hebrew *měnôrâ H4963* usually refers to the golden lampstand in the tabernacle and temple. But in 2 Ki. 4:10 it probably refers to a pottery lamp of a different style from no. 1. Often discovered in Palestinian sites are "cup-and-saucer" lamps, consisting of a high cup in the center of a small bowl, all made in one piece by the potter. Sometimes this style has been found in connection with shrines, serving a ritual purpose. Since the Shunammite couple considered Elisha a holy man of God, they chose a type of lamp appropriate for him.

5. Hebrew *tannûr H9486* and Greek *klibanon G3106* are used chiefly of the common oven in every home, for baking flat bread (Lev. 2:4; 7:9a; Hos. 7:4-8). Like a hollow truncated cone, it was made of clay nearly an inch (2.5 cm.) thick. The household oven varied from 1.5 to 2.5 ft. (45-65 cm.) in diameter, and often was plastered over with additional mud and potsherds on the outer surface. Placed over a depression in the courtyard floor, the oven was preheated by a smoky fire of grass, thorns, twigs, or stubble kindled inside it (Mal. 4:1; Matt. 6:30). The soot was then wiped off (Lam. 5:10), and the thin sheets of dough were slapped onto the concave inner surface of the oven and baked in a few seconds. A large cooking pot could be placed over the top opening, making the oven serve also as a stove (Lev. 11:35). When ten women could bake their pitifully small loaves in a single oven, then there was severe famine in the land (26:26).

6. The *'aḥ H279* was a small brazier for holding burning coals. King Jehoiakim's winter house may have had a metal or a ceramic brazier or firepot (Jer. 36:22-23).

P

7. The *maḥăbat H4679* was probably the nearly flat disclike baking tray or griddle (Lev. 2:5; 6:14; 7:9; 1 Chr. 23:29). Such pans, 12-14 in. (30-35 cm.) in diameter, had holes punched or notched on the concave surface, which was placed over the fire.

8. Greek *paropsis G4243* was a side dish for relishes and other delicacies. Jesus accused the scribes and Pharisees of cleaning the outside of this dish but filling the inside with greed and self-indulgence (Matt. 23:25-26).

poultry. See BIRDS (under *fowl*).

pound. See WEIGHTS AND MEASURES.

poverty. See POOR.

powders. The KJV rendering of Hebrew *ʾăbāqâ H86*, which occurs only once in a description of SOLOMON's carriage (Cant. 3:6). Because the reference is obviously to a scented mixture (NRSV, "fragrant powders"), the NIV renders it "spices" ("perfumed with myrrh and incense / made from all the spices of the merchant").

power. See AUTHORITY.

power of the keys. A phrase whose origin lies in the words of CHRIST to PETER, "I will give you the keys of the kingdom of heaven; whatever you bind on earth will be bound in heaven, and whatever you loose on earth will be loosed in heaven" (Matt. 16:19). It has also been connected with the BINDING AND LOOSING of Matt. 18:18 and the authority to forgive or not to forgive of Jn. 20:22-23. Moreover, Jesus is presented in Rev. 3:7 as having the key to open and shut the door into the CHURCH and the KINGDOM OF GOD. The possession of keys—not as a doorkeeper but as chief steward in a household—was a symbol of rule and authority conferred by the master. So the Father conferred such authority on the MESSIAH, and the Messiah conferred that authority on Peter and the other apostles. They had authority to preach the GOSPEL and perform the deeds of the gospel, and in so doing to admit into God's household those who responded in REPENTANCE and FAITH. They were not to be like the PHARISEES, whose word and example actually only

shut the kingdom of heaven (Matt. 23:13). The "power of the keys" has also been understood as the authority to make binding rules for the young and developing church in the earliest period and/or as the power to exercise discipline within the church through the use of the power of excommunication. Further, the words of Jesus to Peter (16:17-19) seem to establish a particular role for Peter in the creation and early growth of the church. To claim that this role is repeated in the bishops of Rome is hardly a legitimate deduction from the text.

praetor. pree´tuhr. Also *pretor*. A MAGISTRATE of ancient ROME. The usual Greek equivalent was *stratēgos G5130* (Acts 16:20 et al.; in a military context, the Gk. term means "commander, captain"). In the earliest Roman republic the highest magistrate was called the *praetor*. Later the name CONSUL designated the chief magistrate and the term *praetor* was used for secondary office. Beginning about the middle of the fourth century B.C., the praetors were associated with the administration of justices in Rome, a function which the office retained. In keeping with the original purpose of the office, the praetors in the second century B.C. acted chiefly in the administration of justice. Developments in judicial procedure under the emperors rendered the office obsolete, and it was reduced to a merely honorary appointment. See also PRAETORIAN; PRAETORIUM.

praetorian. pri-tor´ee-uhn. Also *pretorian*. An adjective formed from PRAETOR (itself from *praeire*, "to go before"). *Praetor* was originally the name for Rome's highest magistrate, later called *consul*. The adjective was used in certain special contexts. The *cohors praetoria*, for example, was the general's special bodyguard. Out of this grew the praetorian guard of the ROMAN EMPIRE. Originally this force of "household troops" consisted of nine cohorts constituted by AUGUSTUS at the time of his alleged reconstitution of the republic in 27 B.C. At first, to avoid the appearance of despotism, this *corps élite* was stationed outside the city and in scattered billets and barracks. Sejanus, TIBERIUS's minister, concentrated the force in A.D. 23, when he was appointed sole PREFECT. From this time dated the political importance of the praetorians and the sinister role that they assumed in the setting up and pulling down of emperors.

The praetorians were a pampered unit, paid three times the ordinary legionary pay, and granted service and retirement conditions beyond the common army practice. The Greek term *praitōrion G4550* (see PRAETORIUM) probably refers to this force in Phil. 1:13 (KJV, "palace"), for political prisoners under house arrest would be in the control of the prefect and guarded personally by soldiers of the corps. This is certainly the case if the epistle to the PHILIPPIANS was written from ROME, and the evidence seems to be in favor of that supposition.

praetorium. pri-tor´ee-uhm. Also *pretorium*. This Latin term (transliterated into Gk. as *praitōrion G4550*) denoted initially the general's tent or military headquarters, reflecting the original meaning of the word PRAETOR. The praetorium in a permanent camp (e.g., on Hadrian's Wall in Northumberland) was the headquarters building; like the rest of the cantonment, it was in stone, and a residence of some consequence. The term thus found ready extension in Roman usage to the residence of a provincial governor.

In the NT, the word occurs seven times, five of them in the passion narrative (Matt. 27:27; Mk. 15:16; Jn. 18:28, 33; 19:9). There it apparently refers to PILATE's headquarters in JERUSALEM. But is the location in view the palace that HEROD the Great had built in the W part of the city, which may have been placed at the governor's disposal? Or the Tower of ANTONIA, contiguous to the outer court of the temple? Or some special residence or "barracks" (Matt. 27:27)? The NIV renders "Praetorium" in Matthew and Mark, but "palace of the Roman governor" (or simply "palace") in John, although it is not clear whether a distinction is intended. Most scholars incline toward the first option, Herod's palace. In Acts 23:35 the word undoubtedly refers to Herod's palace at CAESAREA. In a controversial passage, PAUL states that his Christian testimony had become evident "throughout the whole praetorium" (Phil. 1:13). The most probable meaning is the PRAETORIAN corps at Rome. The usage is attested in Latin. Some scholars, however, argue that it refers to a governor's palace in some other city, such as EPHESUS. Other suggestions include "the praetorians' camp," "the palace of Nero," and "the judicial authorities."

praise. A general term for words or deeds that exalt or honor men (Prov. 27:21), women (31:30), heathen gods (Jdg. 16:24), or God, especially in song (Exod. 15:11 KJV). Some of the Hebrew and Greek words mean "thanksgiving," "blessing," or "glory," and are often so translated (2 Chr. 7:3, 6; Lk. 1:64; Jn. 9:24). We are to be the praise of God's GLORY (Eph. 1:6, 12, 14). The book of PSALMS is filled with praise, increasing in intensity toward the end (Ps. 145-50). Psalms 113-18 are called the HALLEL, the praises. Praise for redemption dominates the NT (Lk. 2:13-14; Rev. 19:5-7).

prayer. In the Bible prayer is the spiritual response (spoken and unspoken) to God, who is known not merely to exist but to have revealed himself and to have invited his creatures into communion with himself. Thus prayer covers a wide spectrum of addressing and hearing God, interceding with and waiting for the Lord, and contemplating and petitioning our Father in heaven. What prayer is may best be seen in the example and teaching of

© Dr. James C. Martin. The Holy Land Hotel, Jerusalem. Photographed by permission.

Modern reproduction of the palace complex built by Herod the Great on the NW corner of the temple mount. This structure, called the Tower of Antonia, may be what the Gospels refer to as the Praetorium.

P

Jesus. This information can then be supplemented by the apostolic practice of, and teaching on, prayer as well as examples of prayer from the OT.

I. Jesus at prayer. In the Gospels there are seventeen references to Jesus at prayer. These may be divided into four groupings. (1) Prayers at critical moments in his life: (a) his BAPTISM (Lk. 3:21), (b) the choice of the APOSTLES (6:12-13), (c) the confession of his being the MESSIAH (9:18), (d) his TRANSFIGURATION (9:29), (e) before the cross in GETHSEMANE (22:39-40), and (f) on the CROSS (23:46). (2) Prayers during his ministry: (a) before the conflict with the Jewish leaders (5:16), (b) before providing the LORD'S PRAYER (11:1), (c) when Greeks came to him (Jn. 12:7-8), and (d) after feeding the 5,000 (Mk. 6:46). (3) Prayers at his MIRACLES: (a) healing the multitudes (1:35), (b) before feeding the 5,000 (6:41), (c) healing a deaf-mute (7:34), and (d) raising LAZARUS from death (Jn. 11:41). (4) Prayers for others: (a) for the Eleven (17:6-19), (b) for the whole CHURCH (17:20-26), (c) for those who nailed him to the cross (Lk. 23:34), and (d) for PETER (22:32). We are to understand these as pointing to a rich prayer life rather than considering them the only times when Jesus prayed. As the letter to the Hebrews put it, "In the days of Jesus' life on earth, he offered up prayers and petitions with loud cries and tears ... and he was heard because of his reverent submission" (Heb. 5:7).

II. Jesus' teaching on prayer. It was seeing the prayer life of Jesus (so different from the usual way of prayer in JUDAISM) that led the disciples to say, "Lord, teach us to pray" (Lk. 11:1). In response, Jesus provided them with what we now call the LORD'S PRAYER (11:2-4; Matt. 6:9-13), which includes six requests—for God's name to be hallowed, for God's kingdom to come, for God's will to be done, for daily bread to be provided, for forgiveness of our debts (sins), and for deliverance from temptation/testing and evil (or the evil one).

Elsewhere Jesus taught that prayer may be characterized by (1) importunity (Lk. 11:5-8)—a laying hold of God's willingness to bless; (2) tenacity (18:1-8)—a persistence and certainty in praying; (3) humility (18:10-14)—penitence and a sense of unworthiness; (4) compassion (Matt. 18:21-35); (5) simplicity (6:5-6; 23:14; Mk. 12:38-40); (6) intensity and watchfulness (Mk. 13:33; 14:38); (7) unity of heart and mind in the community of prayer (Matt. 18:19-20); and (8) expectancy (Mk. 11:24).

Jesus also indicated some of the themes for intercession in prayer. (1) The casting out of evil forces from the hearts of those in darkness and despair (Mk. 9:14-29). (2) The extension of the KINGDOM OF GOD in the hearts and minds of people everywhere (Matt. 9:35-38; Lk. 10:2). (3) Our enemies (Matt. 5:44; Lk. 6:28).

A major new departure in the method of prayer introduced by Jesus was that disciples should ask the Father in the name of Jesus (Jn. 14:13; 16:23-24). To pray in this manner is not to use a magic formula but rather represents the new ground on which the worshiper stands, a new plea for the success of his petitions, and a new mind within which the prayer is conceived. Thus the aim of prayer is not to make God change his will but to enable disciples of Jesus to change their minds and dispositions as they are molded by his Spirit.

III. The apostles' teaching on prayer. The letters of PAUL are saturated with references to prayer; these range from praise to petition, from celebration of God's grace and benevolence to urgent requests for the needs of the churches. Conscious at all times that the exalted Jesus is making intercession for his church (Rom. 8:34), Paul saw prayer as arising through the presence and activity of the HOLY SPIRIT (sent from Christ) within the body of Christ and within the individual believer (8:15-16), and being offered to the Father in and through the Lord Jesus.

A variety of verbs are used to cover the spectrum of prayer: (1) glorify God the Father (Rom. 15:6, 9); (2) praise God the Father (Eph. 1:6, 12, 14); (3) bless (or give thanks to) God (1 Cor. 14:16; 2 Cor. 1:3); (4) worship God the Father (Jn. 4:20-24; 1 Cor. 14:25); (5) offer thanksgiving to God the Father (Phil. 1:3; Col. 1:3); (6) ask or petition God for personal things (Rom. 1:10; 1 Cor. 14:13; 2 Cor. 12:8) and on behalf of others (Gal. 1:3; 6:16; 1 Thess. 3:10-13; 5:23). The most obvious feature of Paul's prayers and references to prayer is that they arise within and are motivated by the gospel concerning Jesus Christ.

JAMES also saw the Christian life as a life of prayer. "Is any one of you in trouble? He should pray. Is anyone happy? Let him sing songs of praise. Is any one of you sick? He should call the elders of the church to pray over him ... and pray for each other" (Jas. 5:13-16). Then James pointed to the example of ELIJAH, "who prayed earnestly ..." (5:17-18). He was well aware that the Hebrew Scriptures supply many examples of prayer and provide guidelines (especially in the PSALMS) on the content and nature of prayer.

IV. Examples of prayers and ways to pray. Most of the recorded prayers of leaders of Israel are intercessions; see the prayers of MOSES (Exod. 32:11-13, 31-32; 33:12-16; Num. 11:11-15; 14:13-19; Deut. 9:18-21), AARON (Num. 6:22-27), SAMUEL (1 Sam. 7:5-13), SOLOMON (1 Ki. 8:22-53), and HEZEKIAH (2 Ki. 19:14-19). God always answered the prayers of his people, but sometimes his answer was no (Exod. 32:30-35). Once JEREMIAH was commanded not to intercede (Jer. 7:16; 11:14; 14:11). We are to assume that the prophets were constantly engaged in prayer in order to be the recipients of the word of the Lord (see Isa. 6; Dan. 9:20-23; Hab. 2:1-3).

In the five books of the Psalter many types of prayers are found. There are communal hymns (Ps. 33; 145-150), communal laments (Ps. 44; 74; 79), royal psalms (Ps. 2; 18; 20; 21), laments of the individual Israelite (Ps. 3; 5-7; 13), thanksgivings of the individual Israelite (Ps. 30; 32; 138), songs for pilgrimage (Ps. 84; 122), thanksgivings of the community (Ps. 67; 124), wisdom poems (Ps. 1; 37; 73; 112), and liturgies (Ps. 15; 24; 60; 75).

Obviously the emphasis in the whole Bible is not on the right posture or the correct position, but on the right attitude in prayer. Thus people pray kneeling (1 Ki. 8:54; Ezra 9:5; Dan. 6:10; Acts 20:36), standing (Jer. 18:20), sitting (2 Sam. 7:18), or even lying prostrate (Matt. 26:39). They pray sometimes with hands uplifted (1 Ki. 8:22; Ps. 28:2; 134:2; 1 Tim. 2:8). They pray silently (1 Sam. 1:13); they pray aloud (Ezek. 11:13); they pray alone (Matt. 6:6; Mk. 1:35); they pray together (Ps. 35:18; Matt. 18:19; Acts 4:31); they pray at fixed times (Ps. 55:17; Dan. 6:10) or at any time (Lk. 18:1). They pray everywhere (1 Tim. 2:8)—in bed (Ps. 63:6), in an open field (Gen. 24:11-12), in the temple (2 Ki. 19:14), at the riverside (Acts 16:13), on the seashore (21:5), on the battlefield (1 Sam. 7:5). They pray spontaneously (Matt. 6:7);

they pray liturgically (e.g., Ps. 120-126); they pray, as we have observed, quite literally for everything (Gen. 24:12-14; Phil. 4:6; 1 Tim. 2:1-4).

Prayer, Lord's. See LORD'S PRAYER.

prayer, place of. This phrase is used in Acts 16:13 and 16 to translate the Greek noun *proseuchē G4666*, which properly means "prayer." When used with reference to a place, this term in Jewish contexts normally refers to a SYNAGOGUE, but probably not in the present passage, for a synagogue required as a congregation a minimum of ten Jewish men, and at PHILIPPI only women are mentioned as gathering for WORSHIP at the river bank. PAUL and his companions used this occasion to proclaim the gospel to the women who were there.

Prayer of Azariah. See APOCRYPHA.

preacher. See OCCUPATIONS AND PROFESSIONS.

preaching. The proclamation of the word of God as found in the Bible and centered in the redemptive work of Jesus Christ, summoning sinners to repentance, faith, and obedience. It is God's appointed means for communicating the GOSPEL of salvation to the unbelieving world and for strengthening the spiritual life of his people. Of the various NT terms for preaching, the most characteristic is the Greek verb *kēryssō G3062*, which occurs about sixty times (e.g., Matt. 3:1; Mk. 1:14; Acts 10:42; 1 Cor. 1:23; 2 Tim. 4:2). Also common is *euangelizō G2294* ("to announce the good news"), used over fifty times (e.g., Lk. 3:18; 4:18; Acts 5:42; Rom. 10:15; 1 Cor. 1:17). The combination *kēryssein to euangelion* ("to proclaim the gospel") is also found (e.g., Matt. 4:23; Gal. 2:2). In the OT, the comparable function of the PROPHETS is usually described with the verb *prophesy* (Heb. *nābā> H5547*, niph. and hithp.), but other terms can be used (e.g., *qārā> H7924*, "to call out, proclaim," which the SEPTUAGINT renders with *kēryssō* in Isa. 61:1b; Jon. 1:2; et al.). The Hebrew verb *bāśar H1413* (piel) means "to bear good tidings" and thus is properly rendered with Greek *euangelizomai* (e.g. Isa. 40:9; 61:1a).

The Synoptic Gospels summarize Jesus' public ministry as one of preaching, teaching, and healing

P

(Matt. 4:23; Mk. 1:39; Lk. 4:44). His message was the good news of the KINGDOM OF GOD, with its imperious demand that the hearers repent and believe in the gospel (Matt. 9:35; Mk. 1:14, 15; Lk. 4:43). The preaching of the apostles reported in Acts and gleaned from scattered fragments in the Pauline epistles seems at first glance to strike a somewhat different note. Although the apostles are still said to preach the kingdom of God (Acts 28:31), the genius of their message is CHRIST himself as divine Lord and Redeemer (2:22-36; 5:42; 11:20; 17:3; 1 Cor. 1:23-24; 2 Cor. 1:19; 4:5). This difference, however, represents not a contradiction, but a progression. The kingdom of God that Jesus proclaimed achieved its triumph over the forces of evil and unleashed its creative power in the world through his own death and resurrection.

The apostolic message, in its essential substance and general outline, can be reconstructed in these terms. In fulfillment of OT prophecy, the new age of salvation has dawned through the ministry, death, and resurrection of Jesus, now exalted as LORD and MESSIAH. The presence of the HOLY SPIRIT in the CHURCH testifies to Christ's present power and glory. The messianic age will reach its consummation at the return of Christ in judgment. God's action in Christ promises forgiveness of sins, the gift of the Holy Spirit, and eternal salvation to all who repent and believe in Jesus. On the basis of this reconstruction, the following observations can be made about the Christian message: (1) it consists of a definite body of facts; (2) it is essentially neither a doctrinal nor philosophical system, still less an ethic, but a proclamation of those mighty acts in history whereby God has accomplished the salvation of his people; (3) it is centered in the person and work of Christ, especially his cross and resurrection; (4) it is organically related to the OT; (5) it imposes a stern ethical demand on the hearers; and (6) it has an eschatological dimension, looking forward to a final fulfillment yet to be. Only the preaching that strikes all of these chords stands in the apostolic tradition.

precious stones. See MINERALS.

predestination. See ELECTION.

preexistence of Christ. See CHRIST.

prefect. This term (from Lat. *praefectus*, "placed at the head of") refers primarily to a high official or magistrate of ancient ROME. Officials with various functions and ranks could bear this title. It was often applied to commanders of cavalry and infantry (see COHORT), as well as to the head of the PRAETORIAN guard. Prior to the emperorship of CLAUDIUS, governors of imperial provinces were called *prefects* (see PILATE, PONTIUS). In a more general sense, English Bible versions use "prefect" as the rendering of the Aramaic word *sĕgan H10505*, "governor" (Dan. 2:48; 3:2-3, 27; 6:7).

premillennialism. See KINGDOM OF GOD.

Preparation Day. Also, "the day of Preparation." This phrase is used to translate the single Greek word for "preparation," *paraskeuē G4187* (Matt. 27:62 [here with the definite article]; Mk. 15:42; Jn. 19:31) and the fuller expression *hēmera ... paraskeuēs* (Lk. 23:54). John also uses the phrases *tēn paraskeuēn tōn Ioudaiōn*, "the Preparation [Day] of the Jews" (Jn. 19:42) and *paraskeuē tou pascha*, "[day of] Preparation of the Passover" (v. 14). As observed in JUDAISM, the day in question was Friday, when everything had to be made ready to observe the day on which no work was permitted, the SABBATH. That Preparation was a reference to the sixth day is a point made explicitly by Mark ("that is, the day before the Sabbath") and less directly by Luke ("and the Sabbath was about to begin"). All of the biblical references mentioned above have to do with the last week of Jesus' life, during Passover Week, and the question arises whether John's expression, *paraskeuē tou pascha* (Jn. 19:14), might be a reference not to Friday but to the eve of Passover Day. In view of the parallel passages in the synoptics, it has been argued that John's phrase means "the Friday during the week of Passover" (cf. NIV; TNIV differently).

presbyter. See ELDER.

presbytery. This term is used by the KJV to render Greek *presbyterion G4564* with reference to the body of church ELDERS who formally recognized TIMOTHY's spiritual gift (1 Tim. 4:14). The same Greek word occurs in Lk. 22:66 and Acts 22:5 for the Sanhedrin, the organized council of Jewish elders in Jerusalem.

Presence, bread of the. See SHOWBREAD.

president. This English term is used by the KJV and other versions to render the Aramaic word *sārak H10518*, denoting a high official and referring specifically to three "administrators" (NIV) or "ministers" (NJPS) appointed by the king of PERSIA to be rulers over the 150 SATRAPS of the empire (Dan. 6:2-7). DANIEL was one of these officials, but the other two, as well as the satraps, conspired to condemn him.

press. A device used for extracting liquids from certain fruits from which WINE and OIL were made (Isa. 16:10 et al.). See WINEPRESS.

Wooden screw press used to extract oil from olives.

© Dr. James C. Martin

prevent. This English term, which now means "to hinder, to keep from happening," is used by the KJV in the archaic sense "to come or go before, to anticipate," a rendering that can be confusing in a number of passages (e.g., Ps. 119:147; Matt. 17:25; 1 Thess. 4:15).

prick. See GOAD.

pride. One of the worst forms of sin, regarded, indeed, by many as the basis of all sin. The various Hebrew words reflect the deep-seated and far-reaching nature of pride, for they are associated with terms such as presumption, vanity, vain boasting, haughtiness, and arrogance. Pride makes impossible a right perspective toward both God and neighbor. It deceives the heart (Jer. 49:16) and hardens it (Dan. 5:20). It brings contention (Prov. 13:10; 28:25) and destruction (16:18). It was a fundamental fault of the wandering Israelites that brought a stern warning from God (Lev. 26:19) and was associated with the punishment on King UZZIAH (2 Chr. 26:16-21), the nation of MOAB (Isa. 25:11), JUDAH and JERUSALEM (Jer. 13:9), JACOB (Amos 6:8), and the country of EDOM (Obad. 3), among others. NEBUCHADNEZZAR testified of the "King of heaven" that "those who walk in pride he is able to humble" (Dan. 4:37). The Greek words used in the NT also convey the idea of empty display, glorying, and arrogance. James quotes Prov. 3:34 in pointing out God's opposition to the proud (Jas. 4:6). Paul made it clear that no one has any grounds for boasting in God's sight, but he does also speak of "pride" as a legitimate attribute (e.g., 2 Cor. 5:12; 7:4).

Priestly Code (Source). See LEVITICUS, BOOK OF.

priest, priesthood. The customary Hebrew word for "priest," occurring about 650 times in the OT, is *kōhēn H3913* (of uncertain etymology). The term is applied primarily to those authorized to perform the rites of Israelite religion, but it can also be used with reference to pagan priests (2 Ki. 10:19 et al.). In the NT, the relevant Greek term is *hiereus G2636*.

I. The history of the formal priesthood. The formal priesthood in Israel began with the time of the EXODUS. In the patriarchal times the heads of families offered sacrifices and intercessory prayers and performed general religious functions, but there seems to have been no specialization and no separate priestly office, as there was among the Egyptians (Gen. 47:22, 26) and in the instance of MELCHIZEDEK (14:18-20).

We read in Exod. 24:5 that MOSES sent young men of Israel to offer the burnt offerings at the covenant ceremony at Mount SINAI. Presumably

P

these must be linked with the command in 13:1 that the Lord's claim to all the FIRSTBORN males among the people be honored. Was it, then, the divine intention at this point that the priestly officiants should be taken from all the people, in this way reflecting the Lord's desire that his people should be a kingdom of priests? (19:4-5). Note too that AARON is described in 4:14 as "the Levite." Was there, even then, some particular significance attaching to the tribe of LEVI? Furthermore, the appointment of Aaron and his sons as priests (chs. 28-29) precedes the events at Sinai (ch. 32) that led to the special appointment of the tribe of Levi to officiate before the Lord, and to do so instead of the firstborn (Num. 8:16). It looks, therefore, as if the Lord intended a "priestly people" who would exercise their priesthood through their firstborn sons under the rule of the house of Aaron, but that this became, through the failure of the people, the Aaronic-Levitical system familiar throughout the OT period. Yet, in the background, the vision of the priest-people remains, waiting to become the "priesthood of all believers" under the one and only new covenant priest, the Lord Jesus Christ.

In Exod. 28-29 and Lev. 8 is the record of the founding of the Aaronic order of priests. The choice of the tribe of Levi as the priestly tribe to serve as assistants to the Aaronic priests is recorded in Num. 3 (cf. Exod. 32:26-29; Num. 8:16-26). See LEVITE. It is not possible in this article to go into technical historical and critical questions related to the OT priesthood. Major attention must here be confined to the theological, devotional, and ethical implications of the biblical idea of the priest and the priesthood.

II. Christ's priesthood. Traditionally, Christian theology has spoken of the three OFFICES OF CHRIST: prophet, priest, and king (though the distinction is not to be made rigidly). The priesthood of Christ is the principal theme of the letter to the HEBREWS. That Christ combines in himself the three offices is a matter of special significance. After the establishment of the Aaronic priesthood, it was considered an offense in Israel for anyone not officially consecrated as a priest to offer formal ritual sacrifices. The rebellion of KORAH (Num. 16) involved intrusion into the priesthood, even though he and his associates were Levites (16:8-9). King

SAUL was most severely rebuked for a similar intrusion (1 Sam. 13:8-14), and King UZZIAH was struck with leprosy for this offense (2 Chr. 26:16-21).

The offices of prophet and priest might be combined in one person (Jn. 11:49-52). JEREMIAH was a member of a priestly family (Jer. 1:1). The offices of king and prophet might also be combined (Acts 2:29-31), but the kingly line of DAVID was of the nonpriestly tribe of JUDAH, and therefore no king of David's line could have been also a priest according to the Levitical law.

The NT writers made much of the fact that Jesus belonged to the house and line of David (Lk. 2:4-5; cf. Matt. 21:9; Mk. 11:10). How then could he be also a priest? The author of the letter to the Hebrews finds the scriptural answer in the priestly order of Melchizedek (Heb. 6:10, 20-7:17), who was Abraham's superior and both king and priest. This amplifies ZECHARIAH's prophecy that "the Branch" will be "a priest on his throne" (Zech. 6:13; cf. Isa. 4:2; Jer. 23:5-6).

A. The atonement of Christ was just as effective before the event as afterward. See ATONEMENT. The high priestly office of Christ did not begin at his INCARNATION; it was a fact known to David (Ps. 110:4) along with his sovereign lordship (110:1). His priesthood with reference to fallen humanity was established in the eternal decrees of God and has been exercised in every age on behalf of God's elect. The Bible presents Christ, our prophet, priest, and king, as a figure of cosmic proportions, whose work as our redeemer has "neither beginning of day nor end of life."

B. The priestly ministry of Christ is introduced in Heb. 1:3 in the words "after he had provided purification for sins." This is, of course, a reference to his death on the CROSS, regarded as an atoning SACRIFICE. But this act of sacrifice was not a mere symbol, as were all of the Aaronic priestly acts; it was of infinite intrinsic worth. He was "crowned with glory and honor because he suffered death, so that by the grace of God he might taste death [sufficiently for the offer of salvation] for everyone" (Heb. 2:9).

Christ's priesthood was in no sense contrary to the Aaronic order. It fulfilled all the soteriological significance of it. But the priesthood of Christ furnished the *substance* of which the Aaronic priesthood was only the shadow (Col. 2:17; Heb. 8:5) and symbol. Examination of the wealth of detail in which the priesthood of Christ is said to complete and supersede the Aaronic priesthood, especially in Heb. 5-10, would require an elaborate and extended thesis. All that is possible here is an attempt to clarify certain points of misunderstanding.

C. The tabernacle of which Christ is the High Priest is the entire cosmic scene of the redemption of God's elect. This was the "pattern" that Moses saw (Heb. 8:5)—God's plan of salvation. It includes all the spiritual and temporal furniture of heaven and earth. The cross of Christ was the altar of sacrifice on which he offered himself. When he gave up his life on the cross, the atonement was "finished" (Jn. 19:30) once and for all (Heb. 7:27; 9:26) with absolutely nothing more for God or man to add to it. The meaning of Rom. 4:25 is not that his RESURRECTION added anything to our JUSTIFICATION but that, having died "for our sins," which we had committed, he was raised from the dead "for our justification," which he had fully accomplished in his death. His resurrection does not add to the atonement, but of course death could not keep him, and for us it is a proof that his death was a victory.

On the Day of Atonement in Levitical ritual (Lev. 16), the high priest had to go in and out past the curtain that separated the Most Holy Place from the Holy Place. By this symbolism the HOLY SPIRIT signified that "the way into the Most Holy Place had not yet been disclosed" (Heb. 9:8-9) while the Levitical mode of WORSHIP still had its proper standing. But when Jesus' body was broken on the cross, this symbolized the tearing of the curtain (10:19-22) and the clear revealing of the way

Reproduction of the table of showbread, one of the furnishings of the tabernacle.

into the very presence of God (Matt. 27:51; Mk. 15:38; Lk. 23:45).

The notion that the atonement was not finished until Jesus presented his blood in some far-distant sanctuary is entirely unscriptural. The atonement was finished on the cross in the immediate presence of God the Father. The "way of the sanctuaries" is now fully revealed. The curtain has been torn from top to bottom and no longer hides the "place of mercy." True, the curtain is once spoken of as though it still cuts off our view (Heb. 6:18-20; see also 4:14), but this is a different metaphor. It is not the "mercy seat" that is hidden in Heb. 6:18-20, but the "hope offered to us," the "kingdom that cannot be shaken" (9:28; 12:14-29).

D. The present intercession of Christ is taught in Rom. 8:34; Heb. 7:25. (Cf. Rom. 8:26-27 for the intercession of the Holy Spirit.) But there is nothing in the Scripture to indicate an unfinished atonement or an unfinished case in court. The NT word for "intercession" does not necessarily indicate any plea being offered. It suggests conferring over, or brooding over. Similarly the word "advocate" in 1 Jn. 2:1 (KJV) does not mean that our case is not completely settled. "Who will bring any charge against those whom God has chosen?" (Rom. 8:33). SATAN accuses, but he has no standing in court. The case is settled, the verdict has been given. We are justified in Christ. Now our "Advocate," our great High Priest, broods over us and counsels and guides.

The comparisons of different priesthoods in the letter to the Hebrews are *not* between the religion of the OT and the "Churchianity" of this age. The comparisons are between the *outward form* of Judaism and the *reality* in Christ. Every argument against Judaism could be turned with equal logic against the outward forms of the church, if Christ is not the center of it all.

III. The priesthood of believers. This can be but briefly mentioned. Our church SACRAMENTS conducted by ordained ministers are analogous to those of the OT. They are but shadows, as worthless as "the blood of goats and bulls and the ashes of a heifer sprinkled on those who are ceremonially unclean" (Heb. 9:13), unless they are received by genuine faith in the atonement of Christ. No act of any human being in any age could do more than shadow the atonement of Christ. "No man can

© Dr. James C. Martin

redeem the life of another or give to God a ransom for him" (Ps. 49:7).

The nation of Israel was called a "a kingdom of priests" (Exod. 19:6), and the church (1 Pet. 2:5, 9; Rev. 1:6; 5:10) and all who have part in the first resurrection (Rev. 20:6) are called priests. PAUL uses symbols of priestly ritual with reference to his own ministry (Rom. 15:16; Phil. 2:17; 2 Tim. 4:6). Neither the apostles (Matt. 19:28; Lk. 22:18, 28-30) nor believers in general (Rev. 20:6; cf. 1 Cor. 4:8) reign with Christ—i.e., are "kings"—until he comes to reign; but we are priests as we bring the gospel to human beings and human beings to Christ. It is significant that the priestly function of believers continues through the millennial reign of Christ (Rev. 20:6) but is not mentioned as being part of the perfection of the new heavens and new earth, when mortality will have ended, and sin will have been completely eliminated. There will be no need for the priesthood of believers after the Great White Throne judgment; "today" is the day of salvation (Heb. 3:13).

prince. This English term occurs about 280 times in the KJV as the rendering of more than a dozen Hebrew words and three Greek words, almost all of which refer to a person who holds significant authority. Because in modern English the term is normally restricted to a monarch or to the son of a sovereign, it occurs much less frequently in contemporary Bible versions. For example, the Hebrew noun *nāśî²* H5954 (perhaps meaning originally "one lifted up") may properly be rendered "prince" in a variety of contexts (e.g., Ezek. 7:27), but the KJV uses it also in numerous passages where "leader" is more appropriate (e.g., Num. 1:16 and frequently in this book). Similarly, the term *śar* H8569, which is often translated "prince" even in modern versions (Eccl. 10:16-17; Isa. 9:6), may at times have a different meaning, such as "official" (e.g., Gen. 12:15) and "commander" (e.g., 1 Sam. 18:30). In the NT, "prince" is used by the KJV, and sometimes by modern versions, primarily to render Greek *archōn* G807, "ruler" (Jn. 12:31 et al.).

principality. This English term, in the sense of "authority," is used eight times by the KJV in the NT to render Greek *archē* G794, mostly in the plural (Rom. 8:38; Eph. 1:21; 3:10; 6:12; Col. 1:16; 2:10, 15; Tit. 3:1 [the KJV uses it also one time in the OT, Jer. 13:18]). This Greek word, which occurs more than fifty times in the NT, means "beginning" (Mk. 1:1 et al.), but in a derived sense "first place," thus "sovereignty, dominion," then "someone who holds authority," that is, "ruler." In the passages listed above (with the exception of Tit. 3:1, where the reference is to earthly rulers), PAUL uses the word to signify the organization of supernatural and angelic powers (so also in 1 Cor. 15:23, where KJV has "rule"). In almost all these verses, the apostle pairs *archē* with *exousia* G2026, "control, authority"; several times the term *dynamis* G1539, "power," occurs as well. See ANGEL; DEMON.

principles. See ELEMENTS, ELEMENTAL SPIRITS.

Prisca. See PRISCILLA.

Priscilla. pri-sil´uh (Gk. *Priskilla*, diminutive of *Priska* G4571 [the latter is the form always used by Paul], "of a former time"). The wife of the Jewish Christian, AQUILA, with whom she is always mentioned in the NT. They were tentmakers who seem to have migrated about the MEDITERRANEAN world, teaching the GOSPEL wherever they went. PAUL met them in CORINTH (Acts 18:2); they instructed APOLLOS in EPHESUS (18:24-26); Paul sent them greetings when he wrote his letter to the church in ROME (Rom. 16:3); and in 1 Cor. 16:19 Paul spoke of their being in Ephesus again, where they had a church in their house. In Rom. 16:3-4 Paul lauded not only their service but also their courage ("they risked their lives for me"), and plainly stated that all the churches owed them a debt of gratitude. From all the scriptural references one may easily see that Priscilla was a well-known and effective worker in the early church.

prison. A place where persons suspected, accused, or convicted of crime are kept. Most Hebrew and Greek words used have the idea of restraint. JOSEPH was thrown into a pit while his brothers decided how to dispose of him (Gen. 37:22-28), and into the Egyptian king's prison, in the house of the captain of the guard (39:20-40:7). SAMSON was confined in a PHILISTINE prison at GAZA (Jdg. 16:21, 25). Prisoners taken in war were usually killed or enslaved (Num. 21:1; Isa. 20:4). Under the monarchy Mic-AIAH the prophet was put into prison (1 Ki. 22:27; 2 Chr. 18:26), where his food was bread and water. JEREMIAH was threatened with prison (Jer. 29:26), including the stocks and shackles or neck irons, and subjected to long imprisonment (32:2; 33:1) in the court of the guard in the king's house. He was also kept in a dungeon before being transferred to the house of JONATHAN the scribe, which had been made a prison (37:14-21); then he was held in a dungeon or cistern in the prison (38:2-28), from which EBED-MELECH rescued him. He was restored to the court of the guard and finally released (39:14). Kings were imprisoned by conquerors (2 Ki. 17:4; 25:27, 29; Eccl. 4:14; Jer. 52:11, 33).

The pitiable state of those in prison is spoken of (Ps. 79:11; Isa. 14:17; 42:22; Lam. 3:34; Zech. 9:11), and sometimes their hope in God is declared (Ps. 69:33; 102:20; 142:7; 146:7; Isa. 42:7). JOHN THE BAPTIST was imprisoned for criticizing a king's marriage (Matt. 4:12; 11:2; 14:3, 10), PETER and JOHN THE APOSTLE were imprisoned for preaching about Jesus (Acts 4:3; 5:18-25); Peter was delivered by an angel (12:3-19). PAUL, before his conversion, led Christians to prison (8:3; 22:4; 26:10) and later was himself often in prison (2 Cor. 11:23): with SILAS at PHILIPPI (Acts 16:23-40), in JERUSALEM (23:18), in CAESAREA (25:27), and on shipboard (27:1, 42). He was under house arrest in ROME in his own rented dwelling (28:16-17, 30). He refers to his imprisonment as for the Lord (Eph. 3:1; 4:1; Phil. 1:14; 17; 2 Tim. 1:8; Phlm. 9), and he mentions his fellow prisoners (Rom. 16:7; Col. 4:10). Jesus spoke about visiting those in prison (Matt. 25:36, 39, 43-44). He predicted that his followers would be put in prison during PERSECUTION (Lk. 21:12; Rev. 2:10). Peter expresses willingness to go to prison with Jesus (Lk. 22:33). Disobedient spirits are now in prison (1 Pet. 3:19-20); SATAN will be imprisoned during the millennium (Rev. 20:1-7).

Prison Epistles. Term used to refer to a group of letters traditionally thought to have been written by the apostle PAUL during his first Roman imprisonment: EPHESIANS, PHILIPPIANS, COLOSSIANS, and PHILEMON. In all of these letters Paul makes some allusion to his being in chains or in prison,

but not all scholars agree regarding the time and place of writing.

Prochorus. See PROCORUS.

proconsul. The title given to a MAGISTRATE functioning outside ROME "in place of a consul" (Lat. *pro consule*); it was applied to the governor of a Roman PROVINCE. Under the Roman system of provincial administration, the authority of a CONSUL might be extended after the expiration of his term of office, usually to allow him to serve as the governor of a province. Under the emperors, the title was used generally to designate provincial governors regardless of whether they were ex-consuls or ex-praetors. Acts (using the equivalent Gk. term *anthypatos G478*) mentions two proconsuls: Sergius PAULUS (Acts 13:7) and GALLIO (Acts 18:12). See also PRAETOR; PREFECT; PROCURATOR.

Procorus. prok´uh-ruhs (Gk. *Prochoros G4743*). Also Prochorus. One of the seven men appointed by the early church to serve tables and thereby relieve the apostles for other duties (Acts 6:5; see DEACON).

procurator. An agent or manager, that is, someone appointed "to care on behalf of" (Lat. *pro curare*) someone else. In preimperial ROME, this term was used in a general way to designate an administrator and was applied also to the manager of an estate, such as a bailiff or steward. Later, however, the term was used as the title of more prominent officials who acted as personal agents for the emperor; most of them belonged to the equestrian rank (Romans of the second highest social class). Some procurators governed a minor province, such as THRACIA and JUDEA, in which case they had the power of life and death as any other governor; most often they were semidependent on the governors of larger provinces. The Roman historian Tacitus (in *Annals* 15.44) used the term *procurator* with reference to Pontius PILATE, but it is now recognized that prior to the emperorship of CLAUDIUS, provincial governors bore the title PREFECT. Subsequent to the reign of AGRIPPA I (A.D. 37-44), Judea was again ruled by Roman representatives, two of whom are named in the NT, FELIX (c. 52-58) and FESTUS (c. 58-62).

These are properly called *procurators*, although Luke uses the general term for "governor," *hēgemōn* G2450 (Acts 23:24; this is also the title used by the Gospels with reference to Pilate).

profane. This verb (from Latin *profānus*, "outside the sanctuary," that is, "ordinary, not sacred") is used frequently in English Bible versions, primarily as the translation of Hebrew *ḥālal H2725* (piel stem), which can also be rendered "defile," "desecrate," and so on. The word occurs especially in LEVITICUS and EZEKIEL, where the issue of ritual PURITY is prominent (Lev. 20:3; Ezek. 7:21-22 et al.). The English verb can be used also to render Greek *bebēloō G1014* (cf. KJV in Matt. 12:5; Acts 24:6), a term derived from the earlier adjective *bebēlos G1013* ("allowable to be trodden, unhallowed, godless"), which also occurs in the NT and is usually rendered "profane" by the KJV and NRSV (1 Tim. 1:9 et al.). Moreover, the NRSV in some passages gives "profane" as the rendering of Greek *koinos G3123*, "common" (Acts 10:14-15 et al.; NIV, "impure"). See also HOLINESS; UNCLEAN.

professions. See OCCUPATIONS AND PROFESSIONS.

promise. In the OT there is no separate Hebrew word corresponding precisely to "promise"; such terms as "word," "speak," and "say" are used instead. In the NT, however, the word "promise" (Gk. *epangelia G2039*) is often used, usually in the technical sense of God's design to visit his people redemptively in the person of his Son. This promise was first given in the *protevangelium* (Gen. 3:15) and was repeated to ABRAHAM (12:2, 7). It was given also to DAVID when he was told that his house would continue on his throne (2 Sam. 7:12-13, 28). It is found repeatedly in the OT (Isa. 2:2-5; 4:2; 55:5). In the NT all these promises are regarded as having their fulfillment in Christ and his disciples (2 Cor. 1:20; Eph. 3:6). Jesus' promise of the Spirit was fulfilled at PENTECOST. PAUL makes clear that God's promises to Abraham's seed were meant not only for the circumcision but for all who have Abraham's faith (Rom. 4:13-16). In the NT there are many promises of blessing to believers, among them the kingdom (Jas. 2:5), eternal life (1 Tim. 4:8), and Christ's coming (2 Pet. 3:9).

prophecy. See PROPHET.

prophet. Three Hebrew words are used in the OT to designate the prophets, namely, *nābîʾ H5566*, *rōʾeh H8014*, and *ḥōzeh H2602*. The last two words are participles and may be rendered "seer." They are practically synonymous in meaning. The first term is difficult to explain etymologically, although various attempts have been made. The significance of these words, however, may be learned from their usage.

Each of the words designates one who is spokesman for God. The usage of *nābîʾ* is illustrated by Exod. 4:15-16 and 7:1. In these passages it is clearly taught that MOSES stood as God in relation to the PHARAOH. Between them was an intermediary, AARON, who was to speak to the pharaoh the words that Moses gave to him. "He [Aaron] will speak to the people for you, and it will be as if he were your mouth and as if you were God to him" (Exod. 4:16). The man who can be designated a *nābîʾ*, then, is one who speaks forth for God.

The two words *rōʾeh* and *ḥōzeh* perhaps have primary reference to the fact that the person so designated sees the message God gives him. This seeing may mean that the message first came through a vision and in some instances it did, but overall the use of these two words is as broad as the English words *perceive* and *perception*. They may refer to sight, but they usually refer to insight. Thus the words designate one who, whether by vision or otherwise, is given insight into the mind of God, and who declares what he has "seen" as a message to the people. The biblical emphasis throughout is practical. It is not the mysterious mode of reception of the prophetic revelation that is emphasized, but rather the deliverance of the message itself for God.

The biblical prophet must be distinguished from the *prophētēs G4737* of the Greeks. The latter really acted as an *interpreter* for the muses and the oracles of the gods. The biblical prophets, however, were not merely interpreters—they uttered the actual words that God had given to them, without any modification on their part. The Bible itself gives an accurate description of the function of the true prophet: "I will put my words in his mouth, and he will tell them everything I command him" (Deut. 18:18). The words were placed in the prophet's mouth by God; that is, they were revealed to the prophet, and then the prophet spoke to the nation precisely what God had commanded him.

I. The position of the prophet in the OT administration. The establishment of the prophetic institution was necessitated by the settlement of the nation ISRAEL in the Land of Promise. Israel entered CANAAN with the precious possession of the LAW. This law, revealed by God at Mount SINAI, laid the broad basis on which the life of the people of God was to be built. The basic principles of divinely revealed ethics and morality are found in the Ten Commandments (see COMMANDMENTS, TEN), and sundry rules for particular situations are expressed in the other laws. On this basis the life of the people of God was to be conducted.

At the same time this law was not adequate to meet all the situations that would arise when the period of Israel's nomadic wanderings came to an end. This inadequacy was not due to any inherent weakness in the law itself, but simply to the fact that the law did not speak in detail on every possible situation that could arise in Israel's life. There would be occasions when a specific revelation of God would be needed in order to show the nation the course it should pursue. This needed revelation God would give to the people by means of his servants, the prophets.

When Israel entered Canaan, it would find a people that sought to learn the future and the will of the gods by the practice of various superstitions, which the Bible calls "abominations" or "detestable ways" (Deut. 18:9). These abominations were being regularly and continually practiced by the inhabitants of Canaan, and there was a danger that the Israelites would be influenced by such customs and would themselves learn to do them. To offset this danger the Lord declared that he would raise up the prophets and that the Israelites were to listen to the prophets and to obey them (18:15). In this passage, Scripture points both to a great individual prophet, one who would be as significant and central to the people as was Moses at Sinai, and also to what we, with hindsight, would call the successive line of prophets. Note that in vv. 21-22 a test was given whereby the true might be distinguished from the false. Just as later the people would wonder if the next Davidic king in line would be the

promised Greater David, so also from the time of Moses onward there was expectation of the coming Mosaic prophet (cf. Deut. 34:10), and each prophet who arose would be scrutinized (cf. Jn. 1:21) to see if he were the one Moses predicted. By the order of prophets, the Lord enabled his people to walk into the unknown future with faith and obedience, trusting in the sovereign God, not, as the pagan, trying to secure and control the future by MAGIC rites.

The prophet whom the Lord would raise was to be like Moses; just as Moses was a mediator between God and the nation, so that prophet would serve as a mediator. At Horeb, when God appeared to the nation, the people trembled and asked that Moses alone should speak to them. God commended Israel for their request and announced that there would be a mediator, even the prophets. The prophets, then, served as mediators between God and the nation. Just as the priests represented the people before God, so the prophets represented God to the people.

In ancient GREECE we have the god, the oracle, the prophet, and the people. The same seems to have been the case in the Mesopotamian countries. In Israel, however, there was only one intermediary between God and the people, namely, the prophet. This arrangement was truly unique. One who heard the words of the prophet heard the very words of God himself, and these words required implicit obedience.

In many nations of antiquity there were soothsayers or people who had visions. They represented a part of that web of superstition that covered the ancient world. The prophetic institution of Israel, however, according to the testimony of the Bible, was of divine origination. God himself raised up this institution (Deut. 18:15-18), and it is this fact that distinguished the prophets from the soothsayers of the Homeric world and from the so-called prophets of antiquity.

II. The relation of the prophets to Moses. Unique as was the prophetical body, it can properly be understood only as having served under Moses, who occupied a position of preeminence in the OT economy. He was faithful *in* all God's house as a servant, and so pointed forward to CHRIST, who as a Son is faithful *over* God's house (Heb. 3:1-6). To the prophets God made himself known in dreams

P

and visions and probably also in dark, enigmatic sayings. To Moses, however, God spoke clearly and distinctly, mouth to mouth, as a man speaks to his friend (Num. 12:1-8). A distinction in the method or manner of REVELATION thus appears with respect to Moses and the prophets. Moses was the leading figure of the OT administration, and the prophets served under him. The revelations made to them were sometimes obscure and ambiguous, in that they were given in dreams and visions. It would follow, therefore, that when the prophets spoke, they spoke in terms and forms of thought that were current in and that characterized the OT dispensation.

The entire Mosaic administration must be understood as a witness of the later-to-be-revealed NT administration. Moses and the prophets therefore were types of Christ and of his blessings. They witnessed not to themselves but to the "things to be spoken of" (Heb. 3:1-6). In speaking of the future salvation under Christ, the prophets spoke sometimes in language that was not free of ambiguity, and the interpretation of their prophecies depended on a further revelation and in particular on the NT.

It is sometimes said that the prophets were "forthtellers" and not foretellers. Such a disjunction, however, is not warranted. It is true that the prophets were forthtellers, speaking forth the message of the Lord. That message, however, sometimes had to do with past occurrences, as when the prophets often reminded the people of how God had brought them out of the land of Egypt and given them Canaan for a possession. They also spoke of contemporary events, as witness the words of ISAIAH with respect to the situation that confronted AHAZ (Isa. 7). At the same time it must not be forgotten that the prophets also spoke of the future. They predicted future calamity to come on the nation because of the people's refusal to repent of their sins, and they spoke also in language beautiful and mysterious of the coming of One who would save his people from their sins. The prophets truly were forthtellers, but they were foretellers as well; and the predictive element is extremely important for a proper understanding of the true nature of the prophets.

III. Classification of the prophets. In the arrangement of the books of the Hebrew OT there are three parts—the Law, the Prophets, and the Writings. The division known as the Prophets is further subdivided into the Former and the Latter Prophets. Under the first heading are included the historical books of Joshua, Judges, 1-2 Samuel, and 1-2 Kings. These books are rightly classified as prophets because the history they contain conforms to the biblical definition of prophecy as a declaration of the wonderful works of God (Acts 2:11, 18). This does not mean they are less than true history, but that the process of selection of events to record was performed to show how God was at work in and for his people and how the moral principles of divine PROVIDENCE worked out over the centuries. Against this background of interpretative history we are to understand the work of the great prophets. The former prophets cover the period from Israel's entrance into the Land of Promise until the destruction of the THEOCRACY under NEBUCHADNEZZAR.

The Latter Prophets are also called "writing prophets." They are the prophets who exercised so great a ministry in Israel—Isaiah, Jeremiah, Ezekiel, and the Twelve. The designation "latter" does not necessarily have reference to historical chronology, but is simply a designation of those prophetical books that follow the "former" prophets in the Hebrew arrangement of the OT. Note, however, that the Former and the Latter Prophets complemented one another. The Former Prophets set forth the history of a particular period in Israel's life; the Latter Prophets interpreted particular phases of that history. The one is necessary for the proper understanding of the other.

The Scripture does not say much as to the methods used by the great "writing" prophets in preparing their messages. The theory has been advanced by Herman Gunkel that the prophets were first of all oral preachers, and that they did not write their messages. The written books that we now possess, Gunkel argued, were the work of disciples of the prophets. From the example of JEREMIAH, however, it appears that the prophets did write down their messages. It may be impossible for us fully to know what is the precise relationship between their spoken word and their written messages. It could very well be that the prophets often spoke far more than they have written down. It could be that in many instances they enlarged on their messages when they were delivering them orally and that they made digests of these messages for writing.

With respect to the last twenty-seven chapters of the book of ISAIAH, for example, it may well be that these messages were never delivered orally. It is quite likely that the prophet, after retirement from active preaching and prophesying, went into solitude during the latter days of HEZEKIAH and wrote down the wondrous messages that concern the future destinies of the people of God and their deliverance from sin by the SERVANT OF THE LORD. It is quite possible also that some of the prophecies of Jeremiah are the results of intense polishing and reworking. These written messages need not in every instance have been identical with what had been delivered orally. What we have in the Scriptures is what the Spirit of God intended us to have.

IV. Schools of the prophets. After the people had entered the Promised Land, there came a time when "everyone did as he saw fit" (Jdg. 21:25). It was evident that the nation had to have a king, but the first requests for a king were made in a spirit and for a purpose that conflicted with what God intended the theocracy to be. The first king was not a man after God's own heart, but one who often did his own desires. This was a time when

there was danger not only from the IDOLATRY of Canaan but also from the incursions of the PHILISTINES. For the encouragement and spiritual welfare of the nation, "companies" (KJV) or "bands" (NRSV) of prophets were raised up (1 Sam. 10:5 et al.). Whether the groups of prophets so designated had a formal organization or not, one cannot tell. It may be that such groups were more or less loosely knit together, and that they served under SAMUEL.

Following Samuel's death these prophetical bodies seem to have disbanded. We hear no more of them until the times of ELIJAH and ELISHA. During the days of these men groups of prophets again appear, though most likely they are not to be thought of as hereditary descendants of the bodies that existed under Samuel. The reason for this is that in Elijah's day they appear only in the northern kingdom. The theocracy had become divided because of the schism introduced by JEROBOAM son of Nebat. There was now need for support against the worship of the Tyrian BAAL as well as the CALF WORSHIP at DAN and BETHEL. Both Elijah and Elisha exercised a vigorous ministry in the north, but the government was opposed to them. They needed particular assistance, and this was found in the companies that now bear the designation "sons

Aerial view of Nebi Samwil, a few miles WNW of Jerusalem. The mosque on the mound marks the traditional site of the burial of Samuel the prophet.

P

of the prophets" (2 Ki. 4:1 et al.; NIV, "company of the prophets"). The phrase reveals the close and intimate association in which these men stood to the great prophets Elijah and Elisha. After this period, however, they seem to die out, and we hear no more of them.

V. The prophets and the temple. The regular WORSHIP by ancient Israel after the establishment of the monarchy was conducted in the TEMPLE located in JERUSALEM. This worship was in the hands of priests, men who represented the nation before God. What was the relation in which the prophets stood to the temple worship? It used to be held, particularly by the school of Wellhausen, that the prophets and the priests were working in opposition to one another, that the priests represented a sacrificial type of worship, whereas the prophets were more concerned about ethics and behavior. It was even held that the prophets denied that God had ever required SACRIFICES. This supposition was used to support the position of Wellhausen that the books of the PENTATEUCH in which sacrifices were commanded were not composed until late in Israel's history, when the priestly religion had triumphed over the prophetical.

This reconstruction of Israel's history, once so dominant, is more and more losing ground. It is now widely recognized that there was not, after all, such an antagonism between prophet and priest. In fact, some of the prophets, such as JEREMIAH and EZEKIEL, were themselves priests. Indeed, what the prophets were condemning, as a more careful and sober exegesis has shown, was not the sacrifices themselves, but the manner in which the sacrifices were offered (cf. Isa. 1:9-15). The sacrifices were truly an approach to God, but the worshiper must come with clean hands and a pure heart. Otherwise the sacrifices in themselves, divorced from a proper attitude of humility and repentance on the part of the worshiper, were nothing but vain oblations and were not acceptable to the Lord.

If, then, the prophets were not condemning sacrifice in itself, what was the relation in which they actually stood to the worship in the temple? In recent years the opinion has become more and more widespread that the prophets were servants of the temple, and that they may even have received a salary and been in the employ of the temple. It is perhaps safest to say that this question cannot be answered positively one way or the other. The prophets at times may have been officially connected with the temple; at times they may have been more or less "on their own" in being special spokesmen of the Lord. It is difficult to say how they did earn their livelihood. The servant of Saul had suggested the giving of a small gift to Samuel in return for information as to the whereabouts of the lost donkeys of Saul's father (1 Sam. 9:8). Possibly the prophets at times were dependent on such small gifts and on donations they obtained for services rendered. That they were actually officials in the employ of the temple is a matter on which it is wisest not to speak dogmatically.

VI. True and false prophets. True religion has always been plagued by imitators. Alongside the faithful and true prophets of the Lord there were others, men who had not received a revelation from God. Jeremiah refused to have anything to do with these men. They were not true prophets, but men who deceived. There were those who claimed to have received messages from God, but who as a matter of fact had not received such messages.

In the OT there were three tests the people could apply in order to discern between the true and the false prophet. First, the theological test (Deut. 13). Through Moses there had been a revelation of the Lord who brought his people out of Egypt. Even if the prophet performed some sign to give validation to what he was saying, if his message contradicted Mosaic theology—the truth known about the Lord who brought his people out—the prophet was false. Second, the practical test (18:20-22). The prediction that is not fulfilled has not come from the Lord. We ought to notice that this is a negative test. It does not say that fulfillment is proof that the Lord has spoken, for that might in fact be the evidence offered by a false prophet to validate his word; rather, what is not fulfilled is not from the Lord. Third, the moral test (Jer. 23:9-40). This is a test first to be applied to the lives of the prophets themselves (23:13-14) and then to the tendency of the message they preach. Do they in fact strengthen the hands of evildoers, assuring them that they need not fear judgment to come (23:17)? This is a sure sign they have not stood before the Lord to hear his word (23:18-19). The prophet who comes

The modern village of Tekoa. This area was the home of Amos the prophet.

fresh from the Lord's presence has a message turning people from evil (23:22).

VII. Messianic prophecy. Any proper estimation of the prophetic movement must take into account the following three factors. Prophecy was a continuous movement, extending over several centuries in Israel's history. There was nothing essentially similar to it anywhere in the ancient world. The prophets, during so many centuries, all claimed to be recipients of messages from Yahweh, the God of Israel, and to speak the messages that he had given to them. Lastly, in all these messages there ran a teleological element: the prophets spoke of future deliverance to be wrought by the MESSIAH. It is this element of prophecy that we call "messianic prophecy."

The word *Messiah* is itself not frequently used in the OT. It means "one who is anointed," and this anointing possesses an abiding character. The Messiah is a human individual who came to earth to perform a work of deliverance for God. He is also himself a divine person, as appears from passages such as Isa. 9:5-6. His coming to earth reveals the coming of the Lord, and so it was a supernatural coming. Furthermore, his coming represents the end of the age. It occurred in the "last days," and hence was eschatological (see ESCHATOLOGY). He came as a king, a descendant of David, and is to

reign on David's throne. Lastly, the purpose of his coming is to save his people from their sins. He is a Savior and is to bear the sins of his own that they may stand in right relation with God.

Messianic prophecy must be understood against the dark background of human SIN. ADAM's disobedience in the Garden of EDEN had involved humanity in corruption of the heart and also in guilt before God. Sinners could not of their own efforts make themselves right with God, and hence it was necessary that God take the initiative. This God did in announcing that he would place enmity between the woman EVE and the serpent. God also announced the outcome of that enmity, in that the seed (NIV, "offspring") of the woman would bruise the serpent's head (Gen. 3:15). Though the point is debated, this seems to be the first definite announcement that the Messiah would come and that his work would be victorious.

All subsequent messianic prophecy is based on this Edenic prediction. To NOAH it was announced that the blessing of God would be with SHEM, and hence among the descendants of Shem one must look for the Messiah. The promise is then narrowed down to ABRAHAM and after him to ISAAC. For a time it seemed that Abraham would have no son, and then ISHMAEL was born to Abraham's concubine, HAGAR. Yet the promise was not to be fulfilled through Ishmael, but through ISAAC. After Isaac had been born, however, Abraham was commanded to sacrifice him. Finally, when Abraham's faith was sufficiently tested, it was made clear that Isaac was after all the one through whom the Messiah was to come.

Of Isaac's two sons, JACOB was chosen and ESAU rejected. Finally, Jacob called his twelve sons about him and announced to them what would take place in the "days to come" (Gen. 49:1). In his prophecy he clearly pointed to the fact that REDEMPTION would come in JUDAH. Later BALAAM, a heathen soothsayer, also prophesied, "A star will come out of Jacob; a scepter will rise out of Israel" (Num. 24:17). In Deuteronomy, in the passage in which the divine origin of the prophetic movement is revealed, we learn also of the prophet to come, who was to be like Moses. Whereas in a certain sense the entire prophetic body was like Moses, there was really only one who followed Moses, and that one was the Messiah.

In the books of Samuel it is revealed that the throne of David was to be established permanently, and that a ruler on that throne would rule over an eternal kingdom (2 Sam. 7). On the basis of this prophecy we are to understand many of the Psalms that speak of a king (e.g., Ps. 2; 45; 72; 110) and also many of the prophecies. The Messiah was to be the king of a kingdom that will never perish. This is taught by Isaiah, for example, who announced the supernatural birth of the Messiah and the government over which he is to rule. He was to be born of a virgin, and his supernatural birth was to be a sign to the people that God was truly with them. They did not have to fear before the growing power of ASSYRIA. The Assyrian king would not destroy them nor render void the promises of God. They were to look to the king whom God would present to them. This king is the Messiah. His kingdom is to be eternal; it is to be built up in righteousness and justice and is to be the hope of the people.

Daniel also spoke of this kingdom as eternal. He contrasted it with the kingdoms of this world, which are both temporal and local. These kingdoms, great and powerful as they are, would nevertheless pass away; and there would be erected a kingdom that would belong to a heavenly figure, the one like a SON OF MAN. His kingdom alone would be universal and eternal, for he is the true Messiah. Stressing, as they do, the kingly work of the Messiah, many of these prophecies do not lay their emphasis on the actual saving work the Messiah was to perform.

There was a danger that the eyes of the people would be so attracted to the Messiah as a king that they might tend to think of him only as a political figure. This danger became very real, and the Jews more and more conceived of him as merely one who was political, who would deliver them from the yoke of foreign oppressors.

To offset this danger it was necessary that the people know full well that the Messiah's work was truly to be spiritual in nature. Hence, in the latter portion of his book, Isaiah with remarkable lucidity speaks of what the Messiah would do to save his people. It is in these great "Servant" passages that we learn that the Messiah was to be a Savior. He is set forth as one laden with griefs and sorrows, but they were not his own. They belonged to his people, and he bore them in order that people might be free and have the peace of God. The Messiah suffers and dies vicariously; that is the nature of his saving work, and Isaiah presents it with great vividness.

All the prophets were under Moses, and just as Moses was a type of Christ, so it may be said that the prophetical body as such, being under Moses, was also typical of the great prophet to come. Although they did not understand the full depth of their messages, yet they were speaking of the coming salvation and so of Jesus Christ. Through them God spoke in "various ways" (Heb. 1:1) to the children of Israel. What is so remarkable is that, when their messages are taken as a whole and in their entirety, they form such a unified picture of the work of the Messiah.

We must guard against the view that there is merely a correspondence between what the prophets said and what occurred in the life of Jesus Christ. There was of course a correspondence, but to say no more than this is not to do justice to the situation. Jesus Christ did not merely find a correspondence between the utterances of prophets and the events of his own life. Rather, the events of his life constituted the fulfillment of what the prophets had declared. It is this point on which we must insist if we are to understand them properly. As was said of Isaiah, so we may say of the entire prophetic body: they saw Christ's day and spoke of him.

prophetess. Both Hebrew and Greek have specific terms referring to a female prophet. In the OT, the word *nĕbîʾâ H5567* (fem. form of *nābîʾ H5566*) is applied to several women: MIRIAM, the sister of MOSES (Exod. 15:20); the charismatic leader DEBORAH (Jdg. 4:4); HULDAH (2 Ki. 22:14; 2 Chr. 34:22). NEHEMIAH was opposed by a prophetess named NOADIAH (Neh. 6:14); her stature is suggested by the merely anonymous mention of the prophets associated with her. The wife of ISAIAH is called a prophetess, perhaps because of her relation to him (Isa. 8:3). In the NT, the Greek word *prophētis G4739* occurs only twice, once with reference to the venerable ANNA, who shared in the prophetic revelation concerning the coming Messiah (Lk. 2:36), and once as a term arrogantly assumed by "that woman Jezebel," evidently a false prophetess in THYATIRA (Rev. 2:20). There is, however, ample evidence of prophetic activity among women in the apostolic period (Acts 2:17; 1 Cor. 11:5; cf. the general language of 12:10, 28-29, et al.). The four daughters of PHILIP prophesied (Acts 21:9), though they are not designated as prophetesses. See PROPHET.

propitiation and expiation. The verb *propitiate* means "to (re)gain someone's favor, to appease," and thus the noun *propitiation* refers either to "the act of pacifying a person or deity" or to "something, such as a sacrifice, that brings about conciliation." The noun is used by the KJV and other versions (e.g., NASB, ESV) to render the Greek word *hilastērion G2663* in one passage (Rom. 3:25, where both the NIV and the NRSV have "sacrifice of atonement"), and in two other passages to render *hilasmos G2662* (1 Jn. 2:2 and 4:10, where both NIV and NRSV have "atoning sacrifice"). In all three passages, the RSV and other versions have "expiation."

Although the terms *propitiation* and *expiation* are related, they need to be distinguished. Propitiation is something done with reference to a person: Christ propitiated God in the sense that he turned God's WRATH away from guilty sinners by enduring that wrath himself in the isolation of Calvary. Expiation is done with reference to crimes or evil deeds: Jesus expiated sins, that is, he removed them

or wiped them away. Certainly Jesus' death provided an expiation for the sins of the world; the NT clearly affirms this. But was it necessary for Jesus to provide a propitiation (to avert the wrath of God against guilty sinners) in order to provide expiation (cleansing, forgiveness, and pardon)? Those scholars who take the biblical portrayal of the wrath of God as the description of a real, perfect attitude of God toward SIN (of which genuine human righteous indignation would be an imperfect analogy) recognize that propitiation was necessary and that Christ's death was such. Those scholars who believe that the wrath of God is not the personal attitude of God toward sin and sinners but rather only a way of describing the results of evil and sin in the world, prefer to think of Christ's death as only an expiation. However, even when it is accepted that the Greek terms point to the genuine active anger of God toward sin being appeased by the death of Jesus, the translation "propitiation" is not always thought to be clear or appropriate.

proselyte. The Greek term *prosēlytos G4670* ("one who has come, sojourner, visitor") is the usual SEPTUAGINT rendering of the Hebrew noun *gēr H1731*, "one who lives in a foreign community, alien" (e.g., Exod. 12:48). By NT times, however, the term had come to be applied to GENTILES who wholly or partially joined themselves to the religious life of Israel, thus "converts." The Greek word occurs only four times in the NT (Matt. 23:15; Acts 2:10; 6:5; 13:43).

There has been much scholarly debate over whether all proselytes were fully initiated Jews or whether the term included also Gentile believers in God who had not accepted the initiatory rites, but who were associated with SYNAGOGUE worship in varying degrees of fellowship. The probability is that the first-century Jews had no very fixed or rigid use of the term and that they differed among themselves. JUDAISM up to the time of Christ was not the narrow racial national religion it is sometimes made out to be. There were evidently many Gentiles in the synagogue at Pisidian ANTIOCH (Acts 13:16, 26, 43, 50). See also the references to those who "worshiped" or "feared" God (10:2, 7; 16:14; 18:7), and note the instance of CORNELIUS (10:1-11:18) as well as Jesus' relations with the Roman CENTURION (Matt. 8:5-13; Lk. 7:1-10).

P

prostitute. The Bible uses several words to denote the prostitute or harlot. The most common OT word is *zōnâ H2390* (Gen. 34:31 et al.). It describes the secular prostitute who offers herself for money. In certain instances it appears to be a more general term encompassing the cult prostitute as well. There appears to be, however, a distinct term for the cult or religious prostitute, male or female: *qādēš H7728* (Deut. 23:17 et al., where KJV has "sodomite"). In addition, the term for "dog," *keleb H3978*, is possibly used with reference to cultic sodomites (v. 18); and some have thought that the words for "strange woman" and "stranger" in Proverbs may refer to prostitutes (e.g., Prov. 5:20, though "adulteress" or "immoral woman" may be more accurate). The NT word for "prostitute" is Greek *pornē G4520* (Matt. 21:31 et al.); in 1 Cor. 6:9, the NIV and NRSV use the debatable rendering "male prostitute" for *malakos G3434*, a word that means "soft," but also "effeminate," possibly referring to a catamite (i.e., a man or boy used by a pederast).

In ISRAEL, legal measures were in force concerning prostitutes. Parents were not to force their daughters into the practice (Lev. 19:29; 21:14), priests were not to marry harlots (21:7), and the wages of prostitution were not to be brought into the temple to pay a vow (Deut. 23:18). These prohibitions were necessary to keep the WORSHIP of the Lord free from the impurities of the sin of harlotry. The actual punishment of prostitutes was severe when enforced. According to Gen. 38:24, JUDAH ordered TAMAR to be burned for being a prostitute (until he came to see his own sin as worse than hers, v. 26). A priest's daughter who became a prostitute was to be executed by burning (Lev. 21:9).

Such a common sin needed to be guarded against. The book of PROVERBS teaches about and warns against prostitutes by admonition and illustrations. The situation in the Corinthian church was such that Paul had to give the Christians there special warnings against fornication with prostitutes (1 Cor. 6:15-16).

The words for prostitution and ADULTERY are used very often, especially in the prophetic books, to describe IDOLATRY. This figurative use was evidently based on the idea that the Lord was the husband of the nation of Israel (Jer. 3:20). When the people took their allegiance from God and gave it to idols instead, he called it "prostituting themselves to their gods" (NIV). This expression occurs often in the prophetic books in this or similar forms, a few times in other books, and several times in Rev. 17.

protevangelium. proh´ti-van-jel´ee-uhm. Also *protoevangelium*. This Latin term (from Gk. *prōtos G4755*, "first," and *euangelion G2295*, "gospel") is sometimes used to refer to Gen. 3:15 as the initial promise of a MESSIAH.

proto-. This prefix (from Gk. *prōtos G4755*, "first") is frequently used to refer to a conjectured early form, or to the supposed original source of a document or language. For example, the term *Proto-Luke* refers to a theoretical first draft of a document that later became the canonical Gospel of Luke. Similarly, the label *Proto-Semitic* is applied to a reconstructed language (or language group) from which the Semitic languages are thought to have derived. Sometimes the equivalent German word *Ur* is used instead; thus, *Ur-Markus* refers to an early version of the Gospel of Mark that supposedly was used by Matthew and Luke.

© Dr. James C. Martin

The cult prostitutes of Corinth lived on top of this mountain, the Acrocorinth.

provender. Dried grains and grasses used to feed domestic animals. It is used a few times by the KJV and the RSV, but more recent versions prefer the terms *fodder* and *feed* (Gen. 24:25 et al.). The simple provender was chopped straw or chaff, as used extensively in Palestine even today. Often grasses and grains (barley, wheat) were mixed into a type of dry roughage or hay.

proverb. A pithy saying, comparison, or question (usually Heb. *māšāl H5442*, from a root meaning "represent" or "be like"); notably of SOLOMON's proverbs (1 Ki. 4:32; Prov. 1:1, 6; 10:1; 25:1; Eccl. 12:9) and others (1 Sam. 10:12; 24:13; Ezek. 12:22-23; 16:44; 18:2-3). A person or a nation might become a proverb or a byword (Deut. 28:37; 1 Ki. 9:7; 2 Chr. 7:20). The term can also be translated "parable." Another Hebrew word, *ḥîdâ H2648* ("riddle, question"), is rendered "parable" in some contexts (Ps. 49:4 et al.). The relevant NT words are Greek *parabolē G4130* and *paroimia G4231*. The former occurs frequently in the synoptics as the regular term for Jesus' parabolic teaching and is regularly translated "parable," but in Lk. 4:23 the meaning is clearly "proverb" (cf. also 6:39; in Heb. 9:9 and 11:19 it means "figure, illustration"). As for *paroimia*, it occurs several times in John with the meaning "figure of speech" (Jn. 10:6; 16:25, 29), but it means "proverb" in 2 Pet. 2:22. A proverb is thought of as a short saying, a parable a somewhat longer saying, but the distinction is relative. A proverb may be a snatch of poetry with parallel structure, a sharp question, a pithy sentence, or a very brief story. Felicity of expression insures its long preservation and wide currency through oral transmission, even after it is fixed in literary, written form. See further PROVERBS, BOOK OF.

Proverbs, Book of. One of the poetic books of the OT, consisting of admonitions and sayings about WISDOM. Its title in the Hebrew Bible, taken from the first two words of the book, is *mišlê šĕlōmōh*, "The Sayings of Solomon." The best representative of the so-called Wisdom Literature of ancient Israel, the book of Proverbs comprises thirty-one chapters of pithy statements on moral matters (see also PROVERB). Its central text is, "The fear of the LORD is the beginning of knowledge" (Prov. 1:7).

Overview of PROVERBS

Author: King SOLOMON is represented as the source for most of the book (Prov. 1:1; 10:1; 25:1), but some sections are attributed to others ("the wise," 22:17; 24:23; AGUR, 30:1; King LEMUEL, 31:1), and much of the material has no certain attribution.

Historical setting: The earliest sayings go back to the Solomonic period, c. 950 B.C., but the book could not have taken final form prior to the reign of HEZEKIAH, c. 700 (Prov. 25:1).

Purpose: To impart true WISDOM, especially to the young.

Contents: After a preamble that identifies the fear of the Lord as the beginning of wisdom (Prov. 1:1-7), the first major sections consist of discourses on wisdom from a father to his son(s) (1:8—9:18), followed by sayings specifically attributed to Solomon (10:1—22:16), anonymous sayings (22:17—24:34), sayings of Solomon transcribed by "the men of Hezekiah" (chs. 25-29), and sayings of Agur and Lemuel (chs. 30-31, although the poem about the noble wife in 31:10-31 may be anonymous).

P

The headings in Prov. 1:1 and 10:1 claim a Solomonic authorship for the bulk of the book; and this claim, though often denied in modern times, has no objective evidence against it. Chapters 25-29 are said to be by Solomon, copied by the men of Hezekiah. This obscure reference may refer to later collecting or editing of other Solomonic material. Of the authors Agur (ch. 30) and King Lemuel (ch. 31) we know nothing. They may be poetic references to Solomon himself. Proverbs is mentioned in the apocryphal book of Ecclesiasticus (Sir. 47:17), written about 180 B.C. Although the canonicity of Proverbs, as well as Ezekiel and a few other books, was questioned by some individual rabbis, it had long been accepted as authoritative Scripture, as the quotation in the Zadokite Document shows (CD XI, 19-21). It is quoted and alluded to several times in the NT.

An outline of the book should accord with the material and style of the composition. Damage has been done by some who find in the book merely a collection of ancient maxims for success—a kind of *Poor Richard's Almanac.* Actually the book is a compendium of moral instruction. It deals with sin and holiness. And the vehicle of instruction is a favorite Semitic device—teaching by contrast. The style of Proverbs with its trenchant contrasts or more extended climactic poems can be paralleled in ancient literature in Egypt and Mesopotamia. The Hebrew author, however, has given instruction on life and holiness in proverbial form. The case is similar in Christian hymnody. There are countless examples of secular poetry and melody combined in ordinary song. But Christian hymns use the vehicles of poetry and song to express distinctively Christian thought and experience. The book of Proverbs may be outlined as follows.

I. Introduction (Prov. 1:1-9)

II. Sin and righteousness personified and contrasted (1:10—9:18)

III. Single-verse contrasts of sin and righteousness (10:1—22:16)

IV. Miscellaneous and longer contrasts (22:17—29:27)

V. Righteousness in poems of climax (30:1—33:31)

Both the introduction (Prov. 1:7) and the second section (9:10) include the statement that "the

Funerary mask of Amenemope, an Egyptian sage of the early 10th cent. B.C. The work known as the *Wisdom of Amenemope* is thought by many scholars to have influenced the style of writing found in Proverbs.

© Dr. James C. Martin. The Cairo Museum. Photographed by permission.

fear of the Lord is the beginning of knowledge" and "wisdom." Thus the wisdom extolled in Proverbs is not just a high degree of intelligence but a moral virtue. This is made plain in the first section by the contrasts involved. Wisdom is personified as a righteous woman (8:1). The foolish woman is depicted as using words similar to those of wisdom, to invite men into her house (9:4, 16), but she invites them to sin. The prostitute, who is given prominence in this section, represents all sin. Murder and theft are the opposite of wisdom in ch. 1, but usually the harlot or the adulteress, also called the strange woman, the simple woman, or the foolish woman, is held up as the opposite of personified righteousness. Some find Christ personified in the wisdom cited in 8:22, but this is not certain.

In the major section, Prov. 10:1—22:16, the same contrast appears in single-verse aphorisms. Here the personification of sin and righteousness does not appear, but the same synonyms for virtue and vice are repeatedly used and should be understood as such. Perhaps the greatest error in interpreting the book comes from the tendency to quote these Proverbs as mere secular maxims instead of godly instruction. "Folly" here does not mean stupidity, just as "the woman of folly" (9:13) does not refer to an ignoramus. Both terms refer to sin. Through this whole section the terms *wisdom, understanding, integrity*, and *knowledge* are synonymous terms referring to holiness. Their opposites, *fool, folly, simple, mocker, quarrelsome*, etc., refer to wickedness. In short, a "foolish son" is not a dullard, but a scoundrel. A "mocker" is not just supercilious, but is a rebel against wisdom. The lack of context sometimes clouds the interpretation. But occasionally a verse is partially repeated elsewhere, where the variant form clarifies the meaning (cf. 27:15 with 21:19).

Section IV, Prov. 22:19—29:27, is more general but uses the same vocabulary of morality. In this part are some special parallels with an Egyptian work entitled *The Wisdom of Amenemope* (or *Amenemapet*). The correspondence, however, does not invalidate the above claim that the author of Proverbs gives distinctive treatment to his theme.

The last section, Prov. 30:1—31:31, includes several climactic proverbs that apparently emphasize the last point in a series of four. For example, "There are three things that are too amazing for me, / four that I do not understand: / the way of an eagle in the sky, / the way of a snake on a rock, / the way of a ship on the high seas, / and the way of a man with a maiden" (30:18-19; cf. 6:16-19, where among seven things the seventh is the climax). Here also is the famous final poem—an alphabetical poem—extolling the wife of noble character.

providence. God's support, care, and supervision of all CREATION, from its beginning to all eternity. The term comes from Latin *providentia*, which in turn derives from the verb *provideo*, "to foresee," but far more is meant than foresight or foreknowledge; the meaning is "prearrangement" (cf. Gk. *problepō G4587* in Heb. 11:40, which the RSV renders "foreseen," but the KJV and NRSV have "provided," and the NIV, "planned"). As used historically the theological term *providence* means nothing short of "the universal sovereign rule of God." The definition in the *Westminster Shorter Catechism* (Q. 11)

expresses the view of all Bible-believing Christians: "God's works of providence are his most holy, wise and powerful preserving and governing all his creatures, and all their actions." Divine providence is the outworking of the divine decrees, which are "the plan of him who works out everything in conformity with the purpose of his will" (Eph. 1:11).

The biblical doctrine of divine providence does not imply a mechanistic or fatalistic view of the processes of the world or of human life. In a more extended treatise on this subject, secondary causes, as well as the relation between human responsibility and divine sovereignty, would have to be canvassed. For the present purposes it must suffice to acknowledge that God's providence includes his decision to permit sin. One of the clearest biblical illustrations of this principle is found in Joseph's words to his brothers, who had sold him into slavery: "You intended to harm me, but God intended it for good to accomplish what is now being done, the saving of many lives" (Gen. 50:20).

It is customary to distinguish *special* providence from *general* providence. The former term refers to God's particular care over the life and activity of the believer. "We know that, in reference to those who love God, God works all things together for good" (Rom. 8:28, author's trans.). "If the LORD delights in a man's way, he makes his steps firm" (Ps. 37:23; see Phil. 1:28). "But seek first his kingdom and his righteousness, and all these things [daily needs] will be given to you as well" (Matt. 6:33). The entire book of JOB is devoted to the temporal sufferings of a godly man under divine providence. Hebrews 11:40 teaches that providence, for people of faith, includes something far better than experiences of this life.

General providence encompasses the government of the entire universe, but especially of human beings. "To the LORD your God belong the heavens, even the highest heavens, the earth and everything in it" (Deut. 10:14). "The Most High gave the nations their inheritance, when he divided all mankind, he set up boundaries for the peoples ... " (Deut. 32:8; see also Neh. 9:6; Dan. 4:35). God by his providence is revealed as "sustaining all things by his powerful word" (Heb. 1:3). "He causes his sun to rise on the evil and the good, and sends the rain on the righteous and the unrighteous" (Matt. 5:45, see Ps. 68:9; Acts 14:15-17; Rom. 1:20).

P

Although God's grace is always offered to all people (Acts 10:34-35), yet the *main stream* of historical revelation and blessing for the world, through the instrumentality of Israel and the church, is a principal theme of all Scripture (see Acts 7:1-60; 13:16-43; Rom. 3:1-2; 9:3-6; 11:1; 1 Tim. 3:15; cf. Heb. 11:38a). To this end God sometimes moves in unrecognized events and processes (Isa. 40:1-5; 44:28-45:4).

Not only is the general course of nature sustained by God's providence, but the moral order and its logical consequences are as well: "A man reaps what he sows. The one who sows to please his sinful nature, from that nature will reap destruction; the one who sows to please the Spirit, from the Spirit will reap eternal life" (Gal. 6:7-8). Divine providence sustaining the moral order is the principal theme of the book of PROVERBS.

The distinction between God's immanent or natural action and his transcendent or supernatural action is of supreme importance in the understanding of the doctrine of providence. See the article on MIRACLES. The case of Christianity depends entirely on the miracles of the INCARNATION and the RESURRECTION of Christ. Nevertheless, as the article on miracles shows, godly faith has always existed in a world in which there are long periods of time, even in Bible history, in which God does not choose to give "signs" or display miracles as evidences. It is imperative that we learn to see the glory of God in the regular works of providence as well as in the miraculous. The genuinely miraculous in Christianity is not dimmed but rather magnified by recognition of God's providential faithfulness in the regular processes of nature.

province. An administrative district of government. The Latin term *provincia* originally designated the sphere in which a magistrate functioned and was used especially with reference to the administration of conquered territory. With the ROMAN EMPIRE's gradual acquisition of new lands, spheres of magisterial duty signified increasingly the defense, organization, and government of distant territories; and the word *province* acquired the geographical significance that became its prime Latin meaning and its exclusive derived meaning. The provinces of ROME in this sense of the word

were acquired over a period of more than three centuries. The first was Sicily (241 B.C.). The last were Britain, organized by CLAUDIUS, and Dacia, acquired by TRAJAN. Under the settlement of 27 B.C., all provinces were divided into two categories. First there were the imperial provinces, those that required a frontier army and that, in consequence, were kept under the control of the emperor, who was commander-in-chief of all armed forces. Second there were the senatorial provinces, those that presented no major problems of military occupation or defense and that were left in the control of the Senate. Imperial provinces were governed by the emperor's *legati* or, in the case of smaller units like JUDEA or Thrace (THRACIA), by PREFECTS, later by PROCURATORS. The senatorial provinces were under a PROCONSUL.

provocation. This English term occurs relatively few times in the Bible versions, but the verb *to provoke* ("to incite, stir up," from Lat. *provocare*, "to call forth to someone, to challenge") is used often, especially as the rendering of Hebrew *kāʿas H4087* (hiphil, "to incite to anger," Deut. 4:25 et al.). In the NT, the KJV uses the expression "provoke to jealousy" to render Greek *parazēloō G4143*, "to make envious" (Rom. 10:19 et al.). The verb *prokaleō G4614* (lit., "to call out to someone") is often translated "provoke" in its only occurrence in the NT (Gal. 5:26). The KJV occasionally uses the English term in a positive sense, as in Heb. 10:24, "Let us consider one another to provoke unto love and to good works" (NIV, "spur one another on toward love and good deeds"). Special interest attaches to Heb. 3:8, 15, where the writer quotes from Ps. 95:8-9, warning his readers against that "provocation" (KJV) where the Israelites had suffered the judgment of God. The Greek term is *parapikrasmos G4177* (lit., "bitterness"; NIV and other modern versions, "rebellion"). The reference is to the events at MERIBAH (place of contention) and MASSAH (place of testing), where the Israelites tested God by their rebellion against MOSES (Exod. 17:1-7). Thus provoked, God condemned them to the forty years of wanderings. The writer to the Hebrews implies from God's response in the wilderness the possibility of a similar judgment against his readers.

prudence. See WISDOM.

pruning hook. This English term, referring to a pole that has a curved blade used for pruning plants, is used to render Hebrew *mazmērâ H4661*, which occurs in four passages. Two of these occurrences contain the familiar phrase about beating "spears into pruning hooks" (Isa. 2:4 and Mic. 4:3; in Joel 3:10 the terms are reversed; the fourth passage is Isa. 18:5, where NIV has, "pruning knives"). Pruning was necessary to remove superfluous twigs and shoots that would impair proper growth and maximum productivity. The exact shape of the pruning hook is not known. Pruning and the use of the pruning hook are signs of peace and prosperity (cf. Isa. 5:6, where lack of pruning describes desolation).

Psalms, Book of. The longest book in the Bible follows "the Law" and "the Prophets" in the Hebrew OT (Lk. 24:44) and inaugurates the final division of the OT, called "the Writings" (see CANONICITY). This book is more often quoted by the NT and more revered by Christians than any other OT writing, and the reason is found in its inspiring subject matter. Both for public WORSHIP—"the hymnbook of Solomon's temple"—and for individual devotional guidance, its 150 poems constitute the height of God-given literature.

I. Name. The Hebrew designation of Psalms is *tĕhillîm*, "praises" (masc. pl. of *tĕhillâ H9335*, a fem. noun that is actually used as the title of Ps. 145; its normal pl. form is *tĕhillôt*, and the masc. pl. occurs only as the title of the book). Two other Hebrew nouns that identify the formal literary types of most of the psalms are *šîr H8877* (for twenty-nine psalms) and *mizmôr H4660* (for fifty-seven psalms), both of which can be rendered "song." The term *psalm* derives from Latin *psalmus*, which in turn was a borrowing of Greek *psalmos G6011* (the verb *psallō G6010* originally meant "to pluck [a stringed instrument]," but later "to sing to the accompaniment of an instrument," and then simply "to sing"). The Greek-speaking church sometimes used the alternate title *psaltērion* ("string instrument," then "a collection of harp songs"), from which comes the English term *Psalter*.

II. Authorship. The individual psalms, naturally enough, make no attempt within their respective poetic framework to reveal the circumstances under which they were written. But, as might be expected, many of them do prefix explanatory titles in prose, indicating their authorship and occasion for writing, often giving poetic and musical direction as well (see below, sections V and VI). Most commonly appears the phrase *mizmôr lĕdāwid*, "a psalm of David" (Ps. 3 et al; sometimes "of Asaph," etc.). The Hebrew preposition *lĕ-* may indicate several ideas, such as possession (e.g., "The earth is the LORD's," Ps. 24:1) or the one to whom a psalm is dedicated or assigned (e.g., *For* the director of music," Ps. 4 title). Thus the phrase "a psalm of David" has sometimes been interpreted to mean merely "of Davidic character" or "belonging to a collection entitled *David*." But the preposition can clearly express authorship (e.g., "A prayer *of* Habakkuk the prophet," Hab. 3:1), and the actual usage of the phrase in the book of Psalms strongly supports Davidic authorship (see esp. the title of Ps. 18). The book of Psalms thus assigns seventy-three of its chapters to DAVID, two to SOLOMON (Ps. 72; 127), one each to the wise men HEMAN and ETHAN (Ps. 88; 89; cf. 1 Ki. 4:31), one to MOSES (Ps. 90), and twenty-three to Levitical singing clans of ASAPH (Ps. 50; 73-83) and KORAH (Ps. 42-49; 84-85; 87-88). Forty-nine remain anonymous.

Modern biblical criticism consistently rejects the psalm titles as of little value. Admittedly, these titles must have been inserted subsequent to the original composition of the poems, but from the viewpoint of lower criticism there is no reason for denying their authenticity within the text of the OT: all Hebrew manuscripts contain these titles, and the earliest versions (such as the LXX) not only exhibit their translation but even misrepresent certain of their meanings, which had been lost in antiquity. Moreover, various scholars have demonstrated the compatibility of David's authorship with the content of each psalm attributed to him (cf. Ps. 44, once considered Maccabean, but equally comprehensible as from David's era, under military duress). Archaeological research in Babylonia and Egypt has brought to light advanced hymnody centuries before Abraham; and the recovery of Canaanite literature at Ugarit has furnished significant parallels to the Psalms, from the time of Moses. David himself is known to have had

P

certain musical and literary endowments (1 Sam. 16:16-18; Amos 6:5; cf. his acknowledged composition of 2 Sam. 1:19-27), exercised leadership in the development of Israel's liturgy (2 Sam. 6:5, 13; 1 Chr. 15-16, 25; 2 Chr. 7:6; 29:30), and realized Spirit-born empowerment as "Israel's singer of songs" (2 Sam. 23:1-2; Mk. 12:36; Acts 1:16; 2:30-31; 4:25).

The NT repeatedly authenticates ascriptions to David: Ps. 16 (Acts 2:25); Ps. 32 (Rom. 4:6); Ps. 69 (Acts 1:16; Rom. 11:9); Ps. 110 (Lk. 20:42; Acts 2:34). Some of the anonymously titled psalms are also recognized as of Davidic composition: Ps. 2 (Acts 4:25); Ps. 95 (Heb. 4:7). It is significant that no psalm that claims *other* authorship, or contains later historical allusions (as Ps. 137, exilic) is ever attributed in Scripture to David.

III. Occasions. The titles of fourteen of the Davidic psalms designate specific occasions of composition and contribute to a historical understanding of Scripture as follows (chronologically):

Ps. 59 sheds light on David's envious associates (cf. 1 Sam. 19:11).

Ps. 56 shows how David's fear at Gath led to faith (1 Sam. 21:11).

Ps. 34 illuminates God's subsequent goodness (1 Sam. 21:13).

Ps. 142 depicts David at Adullam, persecuted (1 Sam. 22:1).

Ps. 52 emphasizes Saul's wickedness (1 Sam. 22:9).

Ps. 54 judges the Ziphites (1 Sam. 23:19).

Ps. 57 concerns En Gedi, when Saul was caught in his own trap (1 Sam. 24:3).

Ps. 7 introduces slanderous Cush (1 Sam. 24:9-12).

Ps. 18 is repeated in 2 Sam. 22.

Ps. 60 illumines the dangerous Edomitic campaign (2 Sam. 8:13-14).

Ps. 51 elaborates on David's guilt with Bathsheba (2 Sam. 12:13-14).

Ps. 3 depicts David's faith versus Absalom's treachery (2 Sam. 15:16).

Ps. 63 illumines the king's eastward flight (2 Sam. 16:2).

Ps. 30 reviews David's sin prior to his dedication of the temple area (2 Sam. 24:25; 1 Chr. 22:1).

Among the remaining psalms that ascribe authorship, the twenty-three composed by Israel's singers exhibit widely separated backgrounds, since these Levitical clans continued active in postexilic times (Ezra 2:41). Most of them concern the Davidic or Solomonic periods. Psalm 83, however, suits the ministry of the Asaphite Jahaziel in

A family pausing by one of the fresh water springs at En Gedi, with the Dead Sea and the mountains of Moab in the distance (view to the E). David spent time in this region and drew upon its scenes when composing his psalms.

© Dr. James C. Martin

P

852 B.C. (cf. vv. 5-8 with 2 Chr. 20:1-2, 14), while Ps. 74, Ps. 79, and the concluding strophe of Ps. 88-89 were produced by Asaphites and Korahites who survived the destruction of Jerusalem in 586. (Ps. 74:3, 8-9; 79:1; 89:44). A few anonymous psalms stem from the EXILE (Ps. 137), from the return to Judah in 537 (Ps. 107:2-3; 126:1), or from NEHEMIAH's rebuilding of Jerusalem's walls in 444 (147:13). Yet others that depict tragedy could as easily relate to the disorders of ABSALOM's revolt or to similar Davidic calamities (cf. Ps. 102:13-22; 106:41-47). Some scholars once spoke confidently of numerous Maccabean psalms (2nd cent. B.C.); but the discovery of the DEAD SEA SCROLLS, which date from this very period and contain manuscripts of both the canonical psalms and secondary psalmodic compositions, establishes the Persian era as the latest possible point for inspired psalmody. It reinforces the hypothesis of EZRA as the writer of 1-2 Chronicles (the last book in the Hebrew Bible) and as compiler of the entire Jewish canon, shortly after 424 (Darius II, mentioned in Neh. 12:22).

IV. Compilation. Psalms is organized into five books: Ps. 1-41; 42-72; 73-89; 90-106; and 107-150. Since certain psalms appear in more than one collection—e.g., Ps. 14 and part of Ps. 40 (Book I) as Ps. 53 and Ps. 70 (Book II), and the latter halves of Ps. 57 and Ps. 60 (Book II) as Ps. 108 (Book V)—it seems likely that each compilation originally experienced independent existence. Furthermore, since the last psalm of each collection was composed with terminal ascriptions that were designed for the book as a whole (41:13; 72:18-20; 89:52; 106:48; and the entire Ps. 150 for Book V), it appears that the origins of these five concluding psalms provide clues for the compilation of their respective books.

Psalm 41 was written by David; and, since the remaining psalms of Book I are also attributed to him (except for Ps. 1, which constitutes the book's introduction; Ps. 10, which combines with Ps. 9 to form one continuous acrostic; and Ps. 33, which has no title), it may be that David himself brought together this first collection. He further composed Ps. 106 (cf. 1 Chr. 16:34-36), so that Book IV, with its liturgical nature (contrast the more personal character of Ps. 1-41), must likewise be traced to David's own hand, prior to 970 B.C., the year of his death.

Books II-III exhibit more of a national interest (cf. their stress on Elohim, God transcendent, rather than on the Lord's personal name, Yahweh). King Solomon (died 930), who was responsible for the doxology of Ps. 72:18-20, thus becomes the historical compiler of Book II (his reference to "the prayers of David," v. 20, seems to be due to his father's having composed over half of the chapters that make up Ps. 42-72). Book III, however, was completed and collected by unnamed Korahites soon after 586 (see above); for though the body of Ps. 88-89 was written by Solomon's Ezrahites, the title that is prefixed to both designates the sons of Korah as its ultimate compilers (cf. its terminal strophe, 89:38-52, which they seem to have suffixed in the spirit of Ps. 88). Indeed, this third book includes several post-Solomonic and sixth-century compositions; and, when combined with Books I-II, it constituted Israel's psalter of the exile.

Finally Book V, which parallels David's Book IV in liturgical interest but includes several postexilic (as well as early Davidic) psalms, came into being shortly after 537. It then remained for a Spirit-led scribe to bring Books IV and V into union with I-III, adding his own inspired composition of Ps. 146-150 as a grand hallelujah for the entire Psalter. Since this last writing occurred in 444 (Ps. 147:13) at the time of Ezra's proclamation of the written law and reform of the temple worship (Neh. 8-10), it may well be that Ezra himself executed the final compilation of the book (cf. Ezra 7:10).

V. Contents. Each of the 150 psalms exhibits the formal character of Hebrew POETRY. This consists not primarily in rhyme, or even rhythmic balance, but rather in a parallelism of thought, whereby succeeding phrases either restate or in some way elaborate the previous line. The poems vary in content. Hermann Gunkel has proposed a number of categories, not all of which appear valid (see Section VI); but the following psalm-types do distinguish themselves, by subject or by their Hebrew titles. Certain portions (e.g., Ps. 34:11-16) exhibit a marked gnomic or wisdom character, much akin to Proverbs (cf. Ps. 37; 49; 73; 128; 133; and especially Solomon's Ps. 127). The title *maśkil* H5380 (possibly meaning "instruction"), which suggests a didactic or at least meditative quality, appears in thirteen of the superscriptions. Included

P

Overview of PSALMS

Author: More than half of the psalms, primarily in Books I and II (Ps. 1-72), are attributed to King DAVID; one to MOSES (Ps. 90); two to SOLOMON (Ps. 72; 127); a dozen to ASAPH (Ps. 50; 73-83); one to ETHAN (Ps. 89). Many have no ascription.

Historical setting: Aside from Ps. 90 (attributed to Moses, either 15th or 13th cent. B.C.), the poems were composed over several centuries, from the Davidic period (c. 1000 B.C.) to postexilic times (c. 400 B.C., though some scholars have argued that various psalms are as late as the 2nd cent. B.C.).

Purpose: To provide God's people with a collection of poems appropriate for WORSHIP, expressing praise, thanks, confession, lament, and confidence, as well as encouraging obedience and faith.

Contents: The collection consists of five parts (alluding to the PENTATEUCH), each of which concludes with a doxology: Book I (Ps. 1-41), Book II (Ps. 42-72), Book III (Ps. 73-89), Book IV (Ps. 90-106), Book V (Ps. 107-150).

is the historical 78th Psalm (cf. the recited histories of Ps. 81; 105; 106). The title *miktām H4846* (perhaps meaning "atonement"), introduces Ps. 16 and Ps. 56-60, perhaps because of reference to covered sins; and among David's most famous penitential psalms are Ps. 32 and Ps. 51 (cf. Ps. 38; 130; 143).

Most of the poems possess a lyric, singing quality. Their praises may be general (Ps. 145) or specific (e.g., Ps. 19; 119, concerning God's revelation). The term *šiggāyôn H8710* (Ps. 7; Hab. 3:1), possibly meaning "dirge," suggests the emotion of grief and validates Gunkel's categories of both national and individual laments. Of related character are the IMPRECATORY PSALMS. Particularly significant are the seventeen specifically messianic psalms, in the whole or in parts of which Christ either is referred to in the third person (Ps. 8:4-8; 72:6-17; 89:3-4, 28-29, 34-36; 109:6-19; 118:22; 132:11-12), is addressed in the second person (45:6-7; 68:18; 102:25-27; 110), or speaks himself in the first person (2; 16:10, 22; 40:6-8; 41:9; 69:4, 21, 25; 78:2).

VI. Use. Psalm titles in Books I-III contain a number of musical terms in Hebrew. Some of these designate ancient melodies, to which the poems may have been sung: "The Doe of the Morning" (Ps. 22); "Do Not Destroy," probably a vintage song (Ps. 57-59; 75; cf. Isa. 65:8); "A Dove on Distant Oaks" (Ps. 56); "The Death of the Son" (Ps. 9); "Lilies" (Ps. 45; 69); and "The Lily of the Covenant" (Ps. 60; 80). The psalm titles also preserve certain other musical directions, much of the original significance of which is now uncertain; but they suggest various methods of performance. For example, "according to *alamoth*" (Ps. 46; cf. 1 Chr. 15:20) uses the plural form of the Hebrew word for "maiden" (*ʿalmâ H6625*) and thus may indicate a high-pitched voice or a treble register. The term is perhaps contrasted with *sheminith* (Ps. 6; 12; cf. 1 Chr. 15:21), feminine form of *šĕmînî H9029*, "eighth," which some take as a reference to a lower octave, though there is some doubt whether the concept of an "octave" existed among the Hebrews; more likely it refers to a particular mode or rhythm or to an instrument with eight strings. Other terms include *gittith*, perhaps referring to an instrument associated with the city of GATH (Ps. 8; 81; 84); *mahalath*, possibly "song, dance" (Ps. 53); and words that probably refer to musical instruments (Ps. 4; 5; et al.). See MUSIC AND MUSICAL INSTRUMENTS.

The term *selâ H6138*, which most versions simply transliterate as "Selah," occurs seventy-one times in thirty-nine psalms (also Hab. 3:3, 9, 13); it is found not in the titles, but at the end of strophes (cf. Ps. 3:2, 4, 8). Various meanings have been proposed. It possibly indicates a dramatic pause for musical effect or the place where the benediction was sung.

A number of Israel's psalms had specific liturgical usage. The "songs of ascents" (Ps. 120-134) may have been chanted by pilgrims ascending to Jerusalem (cf. 121:1; 122:4). Psalm 92 was composed for SABBATH use. The "Hallel" ("praise") psalms (Ps. 113-118) accompanied the Passover (cf. Matt. 26:30), and the psalms that begin with "The Lord reigns" (Ps. 93-100) constitute a liturgical series magnifying God's sovereignty. Gunkel, accordingly, proposes a category of "psalms for the enthronement of Yahweh." Sigmund Mowinckel even postulates an elaborate Hebrew new year's festival based on Babylonian analogies: the king, as the Lord's "son," is said to have participated in various cult-dramas and processions, with a climactic reestablishment of God's kingship for another season. But while verses such as Ps. 24:7, "Lift up your heads, O you gates … that the King of glory may come in," probably do preserve references to David's historic procession to bring the ARK OF THE COVENANT into Jerusalem (2 Sam. 6; cf. 1 Ki. 8:6), Mowinckel's enthronement theory is both theologically unacceptable and historically unsupported.

Paralleling Mowinckel's stress on cultic origins is a modern emphasis on a collective rather than individualistic understanding and use of Psalms. Yet while certain of its poems do exhibit group expression (particularly among the pilgrim songs, Ps. 124; 126), others manifest distinctly individualistic consciousness (Ps. 1; 21; 112; 127). The compilation embraces not simply the congregational hymnbook of Solomon's temple, but also the devotional heartbeat of men like David, who "found strength in the LORD his God" (1 Sam. 30:6). The richest blessings of the Psalms flow from their affirmations of personal faith—"The LORD is my shepherd, I shall not be in want" (Ps. 23:1).

Psalmody, Psalter. See PSALMS, BOOK OF.

psaltery. An ancient stringed instrument. The term is used by the KJV where modern versions usually have "harp" or "lyre." See MUSIC, MUSICAL INSTRUMENTS.

Pseudepigrapha. soo´duh-pig´ruh-fuh (sg. *pseudepigraphon*, from *pseudēs G6014*, "false," and *epigraphō G2108*, "to inscribe"). This modern title is given to a large body of ancient Jewish writings that are not included either in the Hebrew canon (see CANONICITY) or in the collection that Protestants refer to as the APOCRYPHA. They were written originally in Hebrew, Aramaic, and Greek from c. 200 B.C. to c. A.D. 150. Especially significant are such works as *(Martyrdom and) Ascension of Isaiah, Assumption of Moses, Book of Enoch, Book of Jubilees, Greek Apocalypse of Baruch, Letter of Aristeas, 3 and 4 Maccabees, Psalms of Solomon, Secrets of Enoch, Sibylline Oracles, Syriac Apocalypse of Baruch, Epistle of Baruch, Testaments of the Twelve Patriarchs*. These writings are important for their disclosure of Jewish thought during the Second Temple ("Intertestamental") Period.

Ptolemais. See Acco.

Ptolemy. tol´uh-mee (Gk. *Ptolemaios*). The dynastic name of the Macedonian Hellenistic kings who ruled EGYPT after ALEXANDER THE GREAT until the Roman conquest. Some of these kings are mentioned in the APOCRYPHA, and their conflicts with their SELEUCID rivals in SYRIA appear to be shadowed in the book of DANIEL (see ANTIOCHUS).

The first Ptolemy, surnamed Soter, 367 to 282, was a distinguished officer of Alexander. He became SATRAP of Egypt in 323, but converted his command into a kingdom in 305. As a successor of the pharaohs, Ptolemy I took over the ancient administration of Egypt and the ownership of the land. His vast and highly centralized bureaucracy, which became a permanent feature of Ptolemaic rule, prepared the way for the Roman imperial administration of Egypt and contrasted with the Hellenistic policies of the rival Seleucid regime in Syria.

The second Ptolemy, surnamed Philadelphus, 308 to 246 B.C., consolidated the organization of the land. He was responsible for much of his

P

Limestone relief of Ptolemy II (from Tanis, c. 260 B.C.).

© Dr. James C. Martin

government's remarkable financial system, including the most highly developed banking system of ancient times; a rigid machinery of control in commerce and industry; and a nationalized, planned, and budgeted economy. In the reign of Ptolemy II there first erupted the long rivalry with the Seleucids of Syria over the Palestinian frontier. Ptolemy II also instituted the cult of the divine ruler, a simple enough graft on old indigenous beliefs, a preparatory factor for EMPEROR WORSHIP. The great city of ALEXANDRIA grew apace during this reign. Ptolemy II built the amazing Pharos lighthouse outside the twin harbors, and the museum, the most notable center of culture and literature in the ancient world. He established the famous library of Alexandria and cut a canal from the RED SEA to the NILE. This was the Golden Age of Ptolemaic Egypt.

The next reign, that of Ptolemy III, surnamed Euergetes I, 288 to 222 B.C., saw the high tide of expansion and the first symptoms of decline. These symptoms were in full view under the fourth Ptolemy, surnamed Philopator, 244 to 205, whose reign saw some significant native uprisings and the loss of Nubia for a generation. There followed a century of dynastic strife, palace intrigue, anarchic minorities, and decline, during which Egypt survived through the strength of its natural defenses and its strategic isolation rather than through the worth and enlightenment of its leadership. Ptolemy XI, surnamed Alexander II, 100 to 80 B.C., was the last of the male line of Ptolemy I. He was killed by rioting Alexandrians, notoriously an unruly populace.

Ptolemy XII, surnamed Auletes or the Flute-player, 116 to 51 B.C., fled to Rome in the face of Alexandrian lawlessness. His restoration to his tottering throne by Gabinius, at the senate's orders, was ROME's first significant intervention in the land, which the republic (no less than Napoleon nearly nineteen centuries later) saw to be the strategic key to the Middle East. The wife of Ptolemy XIII was Cleopatra VII, the famous bearer of the name. Domestic, and consequently political and dynastic, strife between husband and wife led to CAESAR's intervention, after his rival POMPEY had met his death in Egypt. Ptolemy XIV was an insignificant brother of Cleopatra, and Ptolemy XV was her ill-fated son by Caesar.

The great achievement of the Ptolemies was Alexandria, with all that its immense cultural institutions signified in the ancient world. Alexandria was creative and conservative. It preserved much of the literature of Greece, produced great writers and scientists, and fathered the SEPTUAGINT. Alexandria always stood apart from Egypt. It was a Greek city, and its peculiar contribution to HELLENISM was the gift to history and civilization of the first Ptolemies.

Pua. See PUAH (MAN).

Puah (man). pyoo'uh (Heb. *pûʾâ H7025* and *puûʾâ H7026*, possibly "[red] dye"; gentilic *pûnî*, "Punite" [Num 26:23, but NIV emends to *pûʾî H7027*, "Puite," while others emend to *puwwānî*, "Puvanite"]). (1) Son of ISSACHAR (Gen. 46:13 [KJV, "Phuvah"; NRSV, "Puvah"]; Num. 26:23 [KJV, "Pua"; NRSV, "Puvah"]). His descendants are referred to as "the clan of the Punites" (Num 26:23 NRSV, following MT; NIV, "the Puite clan").

(2) Son of Dodo and father of TOLA; the latter was a judge in the tribe of Issachar (Jdg. 10:1).

Puah (woman). pyoo'uh (Heb. *pûʿâ H7045*, prob. "girl"). One of the two Hebrew midwives who were commanded by the king of Egypt to kill all Hebrew male children at birth (Exod. 1:15). See MIDWIFE.

publican. See OCCUPATIONS AND PROFESSIONS.

Publius. puhb´lee-uhs (Gk. *Poplios G4511*, from Lat. *Publius*, a common *praenomen*). The "chief official" (*ho prōtos*) on the island of MALTA who for three days hospitably entertained PAUL and members of the shipwrecked party (Acts 28:7). His father, sick with fever and dysentery, was healed by Paul (v. 8). The epithet *ho prōtos* (lit., "the first one") has been confirmed by two Maltese inscriptions as an official title. It is unclear whether he was a Roman official or a local officer.

Pudens. pyoo´dinz (Gk. *Poudēs G4545*, from Lat. *Pudens*, "modest, bashful"). A Christian who, along with others (CLAUDIA, EUBULUS, and LINUS), was a friend of the apostle PAUL during his second Roman imprisonment and who sent greetings to TIMOTHY (2 Tim. 4:21). The Latin poet Martial in his *Epigrams* (1.31; 4.13, 29; et al.) mentions a friend named Pudens with his wife Claudia who was of British birth. Much learned labor has been expended to establish their identity with the Pudens and Claudia of 2 Timothy, but the identification is very doubtful.

Puhite. See PUTHITE.

Puite. See PUAH (MAN).

Pul (person). puhl (Heb. *pûl H7040*, from Akk. *Pūlu*). A name used twice with reference to the Assyrian king TIGLATH-PILESER III (745-727 B.C.). It may be that Pul was his original name, and that when he ascended the throne he assumed the name Tiglath-Pileser, which had been borne by a great king of the past. He is mentioned in 2 Ki. 15:19 and 1 Chr. 5:26.

Pul (place). puhl (Heb. *pûl H7039* [not in NIV]). According to the KJV (following MT), the name of a place mentioned along with TARSHISH, LUD, and others to which God would send survivors (Isa. 66:19). It is generally regarded as a scribal error for PUT (cf. NRSV; the NIV has "Libyans").

pulpit. This English term is used by the KJV once (Neh. 8:4) to render Hebrew *migdāl H4463*, a common word for "tower." In this passage the reference is evidently to some kind of raised wooden platform, probably reached by steps.

pulse. This term, referring to the edible seeds of various legumes, is used by the KJV in two passages. In one of them the English term is supplied (2 Sam. 17:28, where the MT simply has the word for "parched" or "roasted"); in the other (Dan. 1:12, 16), the reference is to the vegetables that DANIEL and his friends requested to eat so that they might not defile themselves with the rich food and wine of the king.

punishment. In the OT THEOCRACY, death was the punishment for the following sins: striking or even reviling a parent (Exod. 21:15-17), blasphemy (Lev. 24:14, 16, 23), Sabbath-breaking (Num. 15:32-36), witchcraft (Exod. 22:18), adultery (Lev. 20:10), rape (Deut. 22:25), incestuous or unnatural connection (Lev. 20:11, 14, 16), kidnapping (Exod. 21:16), and idolatry (Lev. 20:2). Being cut off from the people was ipso facto excommunication or outlawry; it meant forfeiture of the privileges of the COVENANT people (18:29). The hand of God executed the sentence in some cases (Gen. 17:14; Lev. 23:30; 20:3; Num. 4:15, 18, 20). Capital punishment was by stoning (Deut. 22:24), burning (Lev. 20:14), the sword (Exod. 32:27), hanging (the hanged were accounted accursed, so were buried at evening, as the hanging body defiled the land [2 Sam. 21:6, 9; Gal. 3:13]), and strangulation (not in Scripture, but in rabbinical writings).

There is record of much cruel treatment, including torturous methods of killing, such as sawing people in two (Heb. 11:37) or throwing them from a cliff (2 Chr. 25:12; Lk. 4:29). In the case of flogging, only forty lashes were allowed (Deut. 25:2-3), but in later JUDAISM, out of fear of transgressing this limit, only thirty-nine were given (2 Cor. 11:24). The convict who was to be flogged was stripped to the waist and received lashes from a three-thonged whip, either lying on the ground (Deut. 25:2) or tied to a pillar in a bent position. If the one flogging exceeded the allowed or prescribed number of lashes, he was punished. People

P

who committed crimes against others were often punished in kind (LEX TALIONIS—Exod. 21:23-25), including also the recompense of time or restitution of an article or its equivalent (21:19, 30). Slander of a wife's honor was punished by a fine and flogging (Deut. 22:18-19). Crucifixion was not practiced until Roman times. Punishment for sin is widely recognized in the Bible and is in the hands of God (directly, Gen. 4:1-16; Lam. 3:37-39; 4:6; Zech. 14:19; indirectly, 1 Pet. 2:14; in everlasting punishment, Matt. 25:46).

punishment, everlasting. See ESCHATOLOGY.

Punite. See PUAH (MAN).

Punon. pyoo´non (Heb. *pûnōn H7044*, meaning unknown). A town in EDOM that served as a desert stop in Israel's wilderness sojourn (Num. 33:42-43), shortly after leaving Mount HOR (v. 41) and before arrival at MOAB (v. 44). *Punon* may be a secondary form of PINON, which was the name of an Edomite chieftain (Gen. 36:41). The place is usually identified with modern Feinan (c. 32 mi./52 km. S of the DEAD SEA), called *Phainō* in Greek sources; it is a large well-watered city about 5 mi. (8 km.) from the mining and smelting at Khirbet en-Nahas and Khirbet Nqieb Aseimer. The site at the juncture of two wadis has great copper slag heaps.

Pur. See PURIM.

Purah. poor´uh, pyoo´ruh (Heb. *purâ H7242*, derivation uncertain). The servant that accompanied GIDEON in a reconnaissance of the Midianite camp (Jdg. 7:10-11; KJV "Phurah").

pure. See CLEAN.

purification. That the conception of purity was deep within the religio-social structure of the children of Israel since very early times is well known to the student of the Bible. The attitude of the Jews as a whole, and of the PHARISEES as a class, is expressed in Mk. 7:3-4. Religious purity was both ceremonial and ethical. Under the Mosaic law, ceremonial purification was required for four acts: (1) the birth of a child, removed through circumcision (if male) and through the isolation of

the mother for a varying period (Lev. 12:2-8); (2) contact with a corpse, the offering of a red heifer being prescribed for sacrifice of purification (Num. 19:1-10); (3) certain diseases, such as leprosy (Lev. 13:8); and (4) uncleanness due to a running sore (Lev. 15). Family purity was guarded through strict regulations concerning sex (Lev. 20:1-21; Deut. 22:20-21). In the NT, though there is a transference from the outward to the inner, there is no relaxing of the basic requirements for purity itself (Matt. 5:27-28; 19:3-9; Mk. 10:2-11; 1 Cor. 5:9-13; 6:18-20). See also UNCLEAN.

Purim. poor´im, pyoo´rim (Heb. *pûrîm*, pl. of *pûr H7052*, from Akk. *pûru*, "lot"). The Jewish festival observed on the 14th and 15th days of the month Adar, the last month in the Hebrew calendar,

A Jewish child in costume celebrating Purim.

© Dr. James C. Martin

answering to February-March. Although the festival is not prescribed in the law of Moses or elsewhere in the OT, its origin is fully recorded in the book of ESTHER (Esth. 3:7; 9:24-32). It commemorates the deliverance of the Hebrews from the murderous plans of the wicked HAMAN in the postexilic period. This festival is named from the casting of the LOTS to determine the most expeditious time for the mass murder of the Jews.

purity. See CLEAN; PURIFICATION.

purple. A very costly dye extracted from the marine mollusk *murex trunculus*. The manufacture of this dye was developed by the Phoenicians (the meaning of both CANAAN and PHOENICIA may reflect this industry). The shell was broken so that a small gland in the neck of the mollusk might be removed and crushed. The crushed gland gave out a milklike fluid that turned purple or scarlet on contact with the air. The shells of the mollusk from which purple is obtained can still be seen strewn along the shore of TYRE and near the ancient dyeworks of ATHENS and Pompeii. The book of Exodus lists extensive use of purple in the TABERNACLE and for the priests' garments (Exod. 25:4; 26:36; 28:15). Because of its extreme costliness, it became a mark of distinction to wear a robe of purple. In later times ecclesiastical officials arrayed themselves in purple robes. In early times royalty was so dressed (Jdg. 8:26 et al.). In very ancient times the common people of Sumerian civilization were forbidden on pain of punishment to wear purple. The Savior was dressed in mockery at his trial in a robe of purple (Mk. 15:17). LYDIA, PAUL's first European convert, was a seller of purple (Acts 16:14), that is, of the purple dye.

purpose. According to the Bible, God has plans, or intentions, or purposes, and they are sure to triumph, at least finally (Prov. 19:21). In the first place, God created the world out of nothing ("Let there be," Gen. 1:3, etc.) through his *will*, so that the world did not emanate from his nature. Thus there is purpose in the CREATION of the world: "God saw that it was good" (1:12, 18, 21, 25). There is also purpose in the creation of man, male and female, made in the IMAGE OF GOD and instructed to fill

and subdue the earth (vv. 27-28). After the FALL, God purposed human REDEMPTION. There was a foregleam of this purpose in the PROTEVANGELIUM (3:15). God's redemptive purposes were clear in his intention to "bless" ABRAHAM: "I will make you into a great nation" (12:2). The rest of the OT develops this notion, while the NT proclaims its fulfillment (e.g., Lk. 24:27).

Theologians in the Reformed or Calvinist tradition have tended to call the purposes of God *decrees* and to affirm a predestination of individuals that precedes the human response to God's offer of salvation (see ELECTION). Arminians often have avoided the term *decrees* and have interpreted the predestination taught in such passages as Rom. 9-11 and Eph. 1-2 as speaking of God's purpose to save the ones that he knows will repent and believe on Christ. All would agree, however, that God does have purpose, for he "made known to us the mystery of his will according to his good pleasure [Gk. *eudokia G2306*], which he purposed [*protithēmi G4729*] in Christ, to be put into effect when the times will have reached their fulfillment—to bring all things in heaven and on earth together under one head, even Christ. In him we were also chosen, having been predestined [*proorizō G4633*] according to the plan [*prothesis G4606*] of him who works out everything in conformity with the purpose [*boulē G1087*] of his will [*thelēma G2525*]" (Eph. 1:9-11). See also PLEASURE.

purse. This English term can be used to translate several words, including Hebrew *kîs H3967* (Prov. 1:14 et al.) and Greek *ballantion G964* (Lk. 10:4 et al.). Depending on the context, these terms can just as easily be rendered "bag." It is probable that all types of purses were baglike, drawn together at the neck with leather straps or strong cords made of other material, and hung from the shoulder. The belt also served as a purse (Mk. 6:8); the money was inserted in the folds or in a pouch attached to the belt, functioning very much like a present-day money belt.

purtenance. This rarely used English term, referring to the viscera or entrails of an animal, occurs once in the KJV (Exod. 12:9, where it is applied to the "inner parts" of the Passover lamb).

P

Put. poot´ (Heb. *pûṭ H7033*, derivation uncertain). KJV also Phut (Gen. 10:6; Ezek. 27:10). Son of HAM, listed in the Table of Nations (Gen. 10:6; 1 Chr. 1:8). No descendants are listed for him, but JOSEPHUS (*Ant.* 1.6.2) says he was the founder of LIBYA, whose inhabitants were called Putites. As a geographical area, however, the identity of Put is debated. Jeremiah lists Put between CUSH (roughly ETHIOPIA) and the "Ludim" (see LUD) as nations whose warriors would be used in the conquest of EGYPT by NEBUCHADNEZZAR (Jer. 46:9); he describes its soldiers as men "who carry the shield." Ezekiel says that the armies of PERSIA, Lud, and Put were once numbered among the armies of TYRE and contributed to her splendor (Ezek. 27:10). Elsewhere he includes Put with Egypt, Cush, Lud, ARABIA, and Libya (the latter by emendation) as nations that shall fall by the sword (30:5), and with GOG, Persia, and Cush as objects of God's wrath (38:5). Nahum associates Put with Ethiopia, Egypt, and Libya (Nah. 3:9). Finally, it is probable that Isaiah places Put (the MT reads "Pul") between TARSHISH and Lud as nations that will one day hear of the glory of God (Isa. 66:19). None of these passages yields sufficient information to locate Put with certainty, but the linking with African countries makes clear that Put was also located in the same area, and Libya appears to be the most likely choice.

Puteoli. pyoo-tee´oh-lee (Gk. *Potioloi G4541*, from Lat. *Puteoli*). A well-known seaport of ITALY located in the Bay of Naples; it was the nearest harbor to ROME. Puteoli was the natural landing place for travelers from the E to Rome. In Acts 28:13-14 LUKE reports that PAUL landed there with the other prisoners when he was taken to Rome for trial. Paul and Luke and their party found Christian brothers there and enjoyed their hospitality for seven days before going on to Rome. The old ruins may still be seen in the northern part of the bay, including part of a pier Paul is supposed to have used. The modern name is Pozzuoli.

Puthite. pyoo´thit (Heb. *pûtî H7057*, gentilic form of a presumed ancestor or place named *pût*). KJV Puhite. The Puthites were a Judahite clan descended from CALEB through HUR and SHOBAL;

they made up one of several families associated with KIRIATH JEARIM (1 Chr. 2:53).

Putiel. pyoo´tee-uhl (Heb. *pûṭî²ēl H7034*, possibly from Egyp. *p²-dy* plus Heb. *²ēl H446*, meaning perhaps "whom God has given"). Father-in-law of AARON's son ELEAZAR; grandfather of PHINEHAS (Exod. 6:25).

Puvah, Puvite. See PUAH (MAN).

pygarg. See ANIMALS (under *ibex*).

pyramid. An architectural form of triangular profile built upon a square or rectangular base, used for (or over) tombs in ancient EGYPT, especially of royalty. The oldest pyramids rose in stages (e.g., that of Djoser, 3rd dynasty); then came the true pyramid (4th dynasty onward) so typical of the Old and Middle Kingdoms, best exemplified by

The pyramid of Titi (c. 2500 B.C.), located near the Saqqara pyramid.

© Dr. James C. Martin

P

those of the kings Kheops, Khephren, and Mycerinus at Giza, opposite modern Cairo. The step pyramids may have embodied the idea of a "stairway" to heaven for the king to join the circumpolar stars. The true pyramids imitated the sacred *benben* stone of the sun-god RE at HELIOPOLIS, and so are a symbol derived from the solar cult. It has also been suggested that they were conceptually a ramp up to heaven for the king, like the rays of the sun slanting down upon the earth (and so corresponding to the "stairway" function of step pyramids).

Pyrrhus. pihr´uhs (Gk. *Pyrros G4795*, "[red] like fire"). Father of SOPATER the Berean (Acts 20:4). The name is missing in the TR (prob. by scribal oversight) and thus in the KJV as well; its early textual support is overwhelming.

Python. p*i*´thon (Gk. *Pythōn G4780*, from *Pythō*, the name of a geographical region). The giant mythical serpent that came to be named Python was said to have been produced from the mud left after the deluge of Deucalion and to live in caves of Mount Parnassus. It was killed by Apollo, who then received the surname Pythius. In later times the word came to mean "a spirit of divination" (as in Acts 16:16) that possessed certain persons and made them prophesy, unconsciously and usually with the mouth closed; thus the term was applied to ventriloquists who were thought to be possessed. The chief oracle was at Delphi, which stressed the idea of Apollo as a god of prophecy. (Without connection to these Greek beliefs, the word was applied in modern times to a genus of giant snakes.)

P

Q

Q. The symbol used to designate a hypothetical source of sayings of Jesus and other discursive materials found in Matthew and Luke but not in Mark (or John). This abbreviation is thought to be derived from the German word for "source," *Quelle.* According to the Two-Source Theory of gospel origins, both Matthew and Luke used the Gospel of Mark for their basic narrative framework, and both also had access to a collection of dominical sayings (Q) that apparently was unknown to Mark. For many scholars, Q was a written document (possibly composed in Aramaic originally); for others, Q designates a body of oral tradition or is simply a convenient way of referring to the material that is shared by Matthew and Luke but missing in Mark; still others deny the validity of this concept.

Qadesh. See KADESH ON THE ORONTES.

Qere. kuh-ray´ (Heb. *qěrê,* either impv. ["read!"] or, more prob., pass. ptc. ["what is read"] of Aram. *qěrā᾽ H10637* "to call, read"). This term is applied to Hebrew or Aramaic readings preferred by the Masoretes over the written, consonantal text of the OT. Rules prohibited changing the authoritative, consonantal text; but the Masoretes sometimes attached the vowels of a preferred reading to the unchanged consonants (called the KETIB, "what is written") and then indicated the appropriate consonants of the amended word in the margin.

More than 1,300 such marginal notes are said to be found in the MT. See TEXT AND VERSIONS (OT).

Qoheleth. See ECCLESIASTES, BOOK OF.

qoph. kohf (Heb. *qôp H7761,* "monkey"). The nineteenth letter of the Hebrew alphabet (ק), with a numerical value of 100. It was one of several "emphatic" consonants, the exact pronunciation of which is uncertain. The sound may have been similar to that of the consonant *k,* but articulated toward the back of the mouth, near the soft palate (as in Arabic).

quail. See BIRDS.

Quarantania. kwah´ruhn-tay´nee-uh. Also Quarantana. The name given by Christians to a high mountain near JERICHO where, according to a late

A late tradition regards this mountain, called Quarantania, as the site of Jesus' temptation.

© Dr. James C. Martin

tradition, Jesus was tempted by Satan (Matt. 4:8-10). The name alludes to the forty days of the TEMPTATION; in Arabic it is known as Jebel Kuruntul.

quarry. An excavation made by removing stone for building purposes. This term is used by the KJV twice to render *pĕsîlîm* (pl. of *pāsîl H7178*) in a difficult passage (Jdg. 3:19, 26). The Hebrew word elsewhere refers to an image carved for religious purposes (Deut. 7:5 et al.), thus the NIV here translates "idols," but some think such a reference makes little sense in the context. The NRSV renders it "sculptured stones," whereas the NJPS treats it as a place name, "Pesilim." Modern versions use *quarry* occasionally to render other Hebrew terms (e.g. Isa. 51:1). See also SHEBARIM.

Stone quarries abound in Palestine (see STONE). Suitable ROCK is plentiful. The limestone used is easily worked and hardens when exposed to air. Stones yet in their quarries, only partially extracted, illustrate methods employed in biblical days. A narrow-bladed pick was used to cut around the sides of the projected stone. The cut was wide enough only for the workman's arm and pick. Sometimes wedges, inserted in pre-cut holes in a line, were driven deep with a heavy hammer to split the rock. Other times wooden strips were inserted in pre-cut cracks and then made to swell with water. Once loose, the stone was moved with crowbars and then transported by sledges or rollers.

quart. See WEIGHTS AND MEASURES.

Quarter, Second (New). See SECOND DISTRICT.

quartermaster. This term, referring to an army officer responsible for the subsistence of a group of soldiers, is used by the NRSV and other versions to render the expression *śar mĕnûḥâ* (lit., "chief of resting"; cf. KJV, "a quiet prince"), which occurs only once (Jer. 51:59; NIV, "staff officer").

Quartus. kwor'tuhs (Gk. *Kouartos G3181*, from Latin *Quartus*, "fourth"). An early Christian who sent greetings to the Christians in ROME (Rom. 16:23). PAUL refers to him as "our [*lit.*, the] brother," and some have speculated that Quartus was the physical brother of a previously mentioned

individual in the list. Most scholars believe that the expression is simply equivalent to "Brother Quartus," indicating spiritual kinship, though it is possible that he was an associate of the apostle.

quaternion. kwah-tuhr'nee-uhn. See SQUAD.

queen. Of the several Hebrew words that can be translated "queen," *malkâ H4893* (fem. of *melek H4889*, "king") is the most common. It is the term used for the queen of SHEBA (1 Ki. 10:1 et al.), for VASHTI and ESTHER (Esth. 1:9; 2:22; et al.), and for the wife of the Babylonian monarch BELSHAZZAR (Dan. 5:10). The second most common word for "queen," *gĕbîrâ H1485* (lit., "mighty woman, mistress," fem. of *gĕbîr H1484*, "lord, master"), is used of TAHPENES, Pharaoh's wife (1 Ki. 11:19); of MAACAH, the queen mother of King ASA (1 Ki. 15:13; 2 Chr. 15:16); of JEZEBEL (2 Ki. 10:13); and of NEHUSHTA, the mother of JEHOIACHIN (Jer. 29:2; cf. 2 Ki. 24:8). In the NT, the Greek word *basilissa G999* is applied to the Queen of the South (i.e., of Sheba, Matt. 12:42; Lk. 11:31) and to the Ethiopian queen, CANDACE (Acts 8:27); the title is also assumed by the prostitute Babylon (Rev. 18:7).

The only ruling queen the Hebrews ever had was ATHALIAH, who had been queen mother until her son AHAZIAH died; she reigned for seven years, until JEHOIADA the priest overthrew her (2 Ki. 11:1-20). The wives of the Hebrew kings were understood to be queens. The queen mother was generally the widow of the former king and mother of the reigning one. Certain obligations devolved upon her and she received appropriate respect. SOLOMON bowed to his mother, BATHSHEBA (1 Ki. 2:19). ASA, however, removed his heretical mother, MAACAH, for unbecoming religious behavior (1 Ki. 15:13).

Queen of Heaven. An object of Jewish worship in the time of JEREMIAH. Most of the information regarding this cult comes from outside the Bible. The only biblical clues available are in Jer. 7:18 and 44:17-19, 25. The problem is compounded by the use of the unusual MT form of the word "queen," *mĕleket H4906*. Some consider this an erroneous writing of the normal *malkâ H4893* (see QUEEN). It is well accepted that this was a borrowed deity. Several of Israel's neighbors had consorts for their

Q

male deities—goddesses and a queen of heaven. In ASSYRIA, the goddess ISHTAR was called the "lady of heaven," whereas in the literature from Ugarit (see RAS SHAMRA) she is "queen of heaven." The Canaanite Astarte, or ASHTORETH, was a well-known FERTILITY goddess. This seems to be the domain of the Queen of Heaven mentioned in Jer. 44, since the people were rejoicing in her for their general welfare and freedom from famine. The people of Ugarit also had ANATH, a kind of mother goddess. This name appears in the texts from Elephantine, Egypt, where Anat-Yaho is represented as the consort of Yaho (Yahweh). Perhaps this was a recurrence of the Queen of Heaven cult against which Jeremiah preached.

queen of Sheba. See SHEBA.

quick, quicken. The adjective *quick* in modern usage refers most often to speed, but the KJV translators used it in its older sense, "alive": " ... and they go down quick into the pit" (Num. 16:30); "Then they had swallowed us up quick" (Ps. 124:3); " ... who shall judge the quick and the dead" (2 Tim. 4:1); "For the word of God is quick, and powerful" (Heb. 4:12). Similarly, the verb *quicken* is used in the KJV with the meaning "revive, make alive" (Ps. 119:50 et al.). This verb is found in contexts that speak of REGENERATION (e.g., Eph. 2:5) and RESURRECTION (e.g., Rom. 4:17).

quicksands. This term is used by the KJV to render Greek *Syrtis G5358*, which refers to an area of the Libyan coast known for its shifting sandbars (Acts 27:17). See SYRTIS.

quiet, quietness. These and related words, as well as "silence" and "silent," are found in Scripture (mostly in the OT) as the translation of about thirty different Hebrew and Greek words. Most uses are in the prophetic (e.g., Isa. 53:7) or historical (e.g., Matt. 26:63) portions of Scripture, but several are involved with apostolic instructions to Christians. Followers of Christ are encouraged to live (1 Thess. 4:11) and work quietly (2 Thess. 3:12); those who speak in tongues should remain silent if there is no interpreter present (1 Cor. 14:28); a prophet speaking in church is to stop speaking if another prophet

gets a revelation (1 Cor. 14:30); and women are to have a quiet spirit (1 Pet. 3:4) and to remain silent in church (1 Cor. 14:34; 1 Tim. 2:11, 12).

Quirinius. kwi-rin′ee-uhs (Gk. *Kyrēnios G3256*). KJV Cyrenius. Publius Sulpicius Quirinius held a Roman consulship (12 B.C.) and various provincial governorships. The reference to him in Lk. 2:2 has raised some historical difficulties. LUKE, a historian of proved accuracy, is not likely to have made a major mistake. The task falls on the commentator to sort out the facts with due consciousness of the gaps in our historical material. It is known that Quirinius was governor of SYRIA A.D. 6-9, that JUDEA was incorporated at the time, and that a census was taken that caused the rebellion of a certain JUDAS (Acts 5:37). Abundant papyrological evidence from Egypt has established the fourteen-year cycle of the census in that province and fixes A.D. 20 as a census year. This date in turn fixes Quirinius's census in A.D. 6, that is, about ten years later than the time indicated in Lk. 2:2. If we assume that Luke is giving reliable information, he must be referring to a different, earlier census, which would have taken place in 9 or 8 B.C., or at least 7 or 6 B.C., if account be taken of political and practical impediments not apparent today. The difficulty then arises that Sentius Saturninus, and not Quirinius, was governing Syria from 9 to 7 B.C., and Quinctilius Varus from 6 to 4 B.C. Several solutions have been suggested, but probably the best proposal is that Quirinius may well have been in control of the foreign relations of Syria during the war with the Cilician hill tribe of the Homonadenses in 6 B.C. and that therefore an enrollment in HEROD's kingdom would have been supervised by him. The census could have taken place in the autumn of 5 B.C., postponed by the dying Herod's devices of obstruction and procrastination.

quiver. As a case for carrying arrows, a quiver was used by soldiers (Job 39:23; Isa. 22:6; Jer. 5:16; Lam. 3:13) and by hunters (Gen. 27:3). The man who has many children is like the quiver that is full of arrows (Ps. 127:4-5).

quotations in the New Testament. Most of the quotations in the NT are drawn from the OT.

The bulk of these occur in the Synoptic Gospels, the epistles of Paul, Hebrews, and Revelation. The number of explicit OT quotations has been variously estimated in the range of 150-300, allusive quotations over 1,000. The explicit citations are easy to identify; quotation formulas often introduce them. Allusive quotations are clauses, phrases, and sometimes single words that may easily escape notice. For example, the unattentive reader might well miss that the words from the cloud at Jesus' TRANSFIGURATION (Matt. 17:5) came from three separate passages in the OT: "This is my Son [Ps. 2:7]...; with him I am well pleased [Isa. 42:1]. Listen to him [Deut. 18:15]!" More easily overlooked is Matthew's changing the description of Joseph of Arimathea (see JOSEPH #12) as "a prominent member of the Council" in Mk. 15:43 to "a rich man" (Matt. 27:57) to conform with a prediction by Isaiah that the Suffering Servant would have "his grave ... with *a rich man* in his death" (Isa. 53:9 RSV).

In his book *According to the Scriptures* (1952), C. H. Dodd showed that most of the NT quotation material relating to Jesus and the church comes from fairly restricted text plots in the OT. These he outlined as follows: (1) *Apocalyptic-Eschatological Scriptures*—Joel 2-3; Zech. 9-14; Dan. 7; 12; Mal. 3:1-6. (2) *Scriptures of the New Israel*—Hos. 1-14; Isa. 6:1—9:7; 11:1-10; 28:16; 40:1-11; Jer. 31:10-34; Isa. 29:9-14; Jer. 7:1-15; Hab. 1-2. (3) *Scriptures of the Servant of the Lord and the Righteous Sufferer*—Isa. 42:1-44:5; 49:1-13; 50:4-11; 52:13—53:12; 61; Ps. 69; 22; 31; 38; 88; 34; 118; 41; 42-43; 80; Isa. 58; 6-10. (4) *Unclassified Scriptures*—Ps. 8; 110; 2; Gen. 12:3; 22:18; Deut. 18:15, 19; Ps. 132; 16; 2 Sam. 7:13, 14; Isa. 55:3; Amos 9:11-12. To the list may be added vari-ous others references (e.g., Exod. 1-4; 24; 34; Num. 23-24; 2 Ki. 1; Ps. 78; Dan. 2; Mic. 4-5; 7; Zech. 1-6). Since the church recognized these OT passages as specially relevant to the new dispensation, an individual quotation became a pointer to the text-plot as a whole.

The motif of fulfillment in OT quotations is very strong. The main themes are as follows: Jesus acts as Yahweh himself; he is the foretold Messianic King, the Isaianic Servant of Yahweh, and the Danielic Son of Man; he culminates the prophetic line, the succession of OT righteous sufferers, and the Davidic dynasty; he reverses the work of ADAM, fulfills the divine promise to ABRAHAM, and recapitulates the history of Israel. The priesthood of MELCHIZEDEK and AARON both prefigure (the latter sometimes contrastingly) the priesthood of Christ. The paschal lamb and other sacrifices represented the sacrificial, redemptive death of Jesus, and also Christian service. Jesus is life-giving bread like the manna, the rock source of living water, the serpent lifted up in the wilderness, and the tabernacle-temple abode of God among his people.

Underlying the fulfillment quotations is the concept of *Heilsgeschichte* (salvation-history). God directs history according to his redemptive purpose. He reveals what he will do through his PROPHETS. Their predictive word has a potency to bring about its own fulfillment, for it comes from the Lord of history. Thus, when the fulfillment takes place, confirmation results. Confirmation also comes when, looking back, one sees predictive symbolism in the pattern of OT events, persons, and institutions—that is, TYPOLOGY—not within the purview of the OT writers, but divinely intended.

Qumran. See DEAD SEA SCROLLS.

Q

R

Ra. See RE.

Raamah. ray′uh-mah (Heb. *ra'māh H8311* and *ra'mā' H8309* [1 Chr. 1:9], derivation uncertain). Son of CUSH, grandson of HAM, and father of SHEBA and DEDAN (Gen. 10:7; 1 Chr. 1:9). Raamah thus appears as the eponymous ancestor of a tribe in ARABIA. The traders of both Raamah and Sheba brought to the markets of TYRE their best of all kinds of spices, precious stones, and gold (Ezek. 27:22). Its location has not yet been fixed.

Raamiah. ray′uh-mi′uh (Heb. *ra'amyâ H8313*, perhaps "Yahweh has thundered"). An Israelite mentioned among leading individuals who returned from Babylon with ZERUBBABEL (Neh. 7:7; called "Reelaiah" in Ezra 2:2).

Raamses. See RAMESES.

Rabbah (Ammon). rab′uh (Heb. *rabbâ H8051*, "great [city]"). The capital city of AMMON, also known as Rabbath-Ammon (cf. "Rabbath of the sons of Ammon," i.e., "Rabbah of the Ammonites," Deut. 3:11; Ezek. 21:20). Its modern name is Amman, the capital of the Hashemite Kingdom of Jordan. Rabbah seems to be the only Ammonite city that is mentioned by name in the Bible. It is located about 23 mi. (37 km.) E of the JORDAN River and lies at the headwaters of the Wadi Amman, which soon becomes the JABBOK River. This very strong spring on the edge of the desert was the reason for the city's existence. Ammon, or a fortified sector within it, was called "the city of waters" (2 Sam. 12:27 KJV; NIV, "its water supply").

Rabbah is first mentioned in connection with the "bed" or sarcophagus of OG king of BASHAN (Deut. 3:11). It is mentioned in passing in the book of JOSHUA (Josh. 13:25), but then disappears from biblical history until the days of DAVID, who sent an embassage of consolation to HANUN king of the Ammonites because of the death of his father. The Ammonite monarch, unfortunately, grossly insulted the messengers of David (2 Sam. 10:13), and the next spring Rabbah was besieged by the army of David. The city capitulated when JOAB captured its water supply (12:26-31). The prophetic utterances against Rabbah of the Ammonites are of interest. JEREMIAH utters imprecatory judgment against MOLECH, the chief Ammonite deity (Jer. 49:2-3). EZEKIEL pictures NEBUCHADNEZZAR as pausing at Rabbah to decide his further course of action (Ezek. 21:20-21). AMOS predicts, "I will set fire to the walls of Rabbah" (Amos 1:14). It seems to have been at Rabbah that BAALIS, king of the Ammonites, concocted the plot that was to cost GEDALIAH, the provisional governor for the Babylonians, his life (Jer. 40:14-15). Subsequently, Rabbah was captured by PTOLEMY Philadelphus

Typical pottery from the Ammonite culture in Transjordan dating to the Late Bronze Age (c. 1550-1200 B.C.).

© Dr. James C. Martin. The Amman Archaeological Museum. Photographed by permission.

(285-247 B.C.), who changed its name to Philadelphia. It later became the seat of Christian bishops.

Excavations by J. B. Hennessy revealed a Late-Bronze (1550-1200 B.C.) temple. Remains exist from the Roman period on the citadel above Philadelphia (the name of the city in the Roman times) and in the city below. These include a beautifully preserved, 6,000-seat theater, a smaller odeum (music hall), and a nymphaeum. These all date to the second century A.D. The principal remains are on the citadel hill, which contained all the public buildings, temples, churches, etc.

Rabbah (Judah). rab′uh (Heb. *rabbâ H8051*, with the definite article attached, "the great [city]"). A town in the hill country of the tribe of JUDAH (Josh. 15:60). Rabbah and KIRIATH JEARIM are the only towns included in the last district listed in this passage; apparently, they were intended to guard the western approach to JERUSALEM. It is generally agreed that Rabbah is the same as *Rbt* (vocalized Rubute or Robbotu), a town mentioned in Egyptian sources. The identification of Rabbah is uncertain.

Rabbath. See RABBAH (AMMON).

rabbi. rab′i (Gk. *rabbi G4806*, from Heb. *rab H8042* [Aram. *rab H10647*], with 1st person pronominal suffix, "my master, my teacher"). A term used by the Jews after the OT period in designation of their religious teachers. First employed as a term of respect, particularly in reference to scribes trained in the LAW (Matt. 23:2-7), it came to be used during the first century as a title (the pronominal suffix losing its significance). It was translated into the Greek by the word *didaskalos G1437*, meaning "teacher" (Matt. 23:8; Jn. 1:38). Due to its significance (the adjective *rab H8041* means "great"), Jesus forbade his disciples to accept it in self-designation (Matt. 23:8). Christ was so addressed (Matt. 26:25, 49; Mk. 9:5; et al.), as was JOHN THE BAPTIST (Jn. 3:26). In some of these passages, the use of the term appears to be a form of address corresponding roughly with English *sir*. The title "Rabboni" (Gk. *rhabbouni G4808*, Mk. 10:51; Jn. 20:16) derives from a heightened form of the word in ARAMAIC (*rabbān* or *rabbôn*).

rabbinic literature. See TALMUD.

rabbit. See ANIMALS.

Rabbith. rab′ith (Heb. *rabbît H8056*, with the definite article attached, meaning possibly "the great [city]"). A town within the tribal territory of ISSACHAR (Josh. 19:20). Rabbith is listed between ANAHARATH (prob. a site some 7 mi./11 km. SE of Mount TABOR) and KISHION (prob. near the S slope of the mountain), and many think it is the same town as DABERATH (on the N side of the mountain), but this identification is disputed.

rabboni. ra-boh′ni. See RABBI.

Rabmag. rab′mag (Heb. *rab H8041*, "great, chief," and *māg H4454*, possibly from Akk. *maḫḫu*, "soothsayer"; the whole phrase is prob. a loan from Akk. *rab-mu[n]gi*, a title applied to high military officials). Also Rab-mag. The Babylonian title borne by NERGAL-SHAREZER (Jer. 39:3). Most English versions simply transliterate the term, but the NIV renders it as "a high official." The title was apparently given to special royal envoys. See also RABSARIS; RABSHAKEH.

Rabsaris. rab′suh-ris (Heb. *rab H8041*, "great, chief," and *sārîs H6247*, "eunuch, official"; the phrase corresponds to Akk. *rab-ša-rēši*, lit., "chief of the one at the head"). Also Rab-saris. Title applied to one of three officials sent by SENNACHERIB, king of ASSYRIA, to HEZEKIAH (2 Ki. 18:17 NRSV and most versions); the other two were the TARTAN and the RABSHAKEH. The title is applied also to Nebo-Sarsekim (Jer. 39:3; see SARSECHIM) and to NEBUSHAZBAN (v. 13), both of whom were Babylonian senior officials. In every instance, the NIV renders this phrase "chief officer." See also RABMAG.

Rabshakeh. rab′shuh-kuh (Heb. *rab-šāqēh H8072*, from Akk. *rab-šāqê*, "chief cupbearer"). Title applied to high-ranking Assyrian officials. When SENNACHERIB attacked LACHISH, he sent the Rabshakeh, along with the TARTAN and the RABSARIS, to deliver an ultimatum to HEZEKIAH (2 Ki. 18:17 et al.; cf. Isa. 36:2 et al.). The Rabshakeh, however, acted as the chief spokesman. The NIV, instead

R

of transliterating the term, renders it "field commander." See also RABMAG.

raca. ray'kah (Gk. *rhaka G4819*, prob. from Aram. *rêqā*, "empty"). A term of reproach or insult. In the Bible the word occurs only in Matt. 5:22, where Jesus warns that "anyone who says to his brother, 'Raca,' is answerable to the Sanhedrin" (NRSV, "if you insult a brother or sister, you will be liable to the council"). The Aramaic word *rêqā* is used figuratively in rabbinic literature as a term of contempt, meaning "worthless, good for nothing, stupid." For example, the MIDRASH on Eccl. 9:15 states that NOAH said to his contemporaries, "Woe, ye foolish ones [*rqyy*]! Tomorrow a flood will come, so repent" (*Qoh. Rab.* 9.17). Note also that a Greek papyrus letter dating from the 3rd cent. B.C. already uses the similar form *rhacha* as an insult.

Racal. ray'kuhl (Heb. *rākāl H8218*, perhaps from a root meaning "to trade"). KJV Rachal; TNIV Rakal. A place in S JUDAH to which DAVID sent some of the plunder he took from ZIKLAG (1 Sam. 30:29). On the basis of some SEPTUAGINT MSS, many scholars emend the text to CARMEL, referring to a town not far from ESHTEMOA, the previous place mentioned on the list (v. 28).

race. See GAMES.

Rachab. See RAHAB.

Rachal. See RACAL.

Rachel. ray'chuhl (Heb. *rāḥēl H8162*, "ewe"; Gk. *Rhachēl G4830*). Wife of JACOB and mother of JOSEPH and BENJAMIN (Gen. 29:6-28; 30:22-25; 35:16-19; cf. Jer. 31:15; Matt. 2:18). Rachel was the younger daughter of LABAN (brother of REBEKAH, Jacob's mother, Gen. 28:2); thus Jacob and Rachel were full cousins. The circumstances under which Jacob met Rachel are interesting. Jacob had quarreled bitterly with his brother ESAU over the stolen blessing (27:35-42). Accordingly, Rebekah told her son Jacob that he should leave for a time, which she hopefully imagined would be brief, and go to the house of her brother Laban in HARAN (PADDAN ARAM, 27:43-45). On his arrival, struck by Rachel's beauty, Jacob immediately fell in love with her (29:17-18). He signed a contract with Laban for seven years of labor (the usual period of indentured servants), at the expiration of which Rachel was to be his wife.

In the light of the NUZI tablets, many of the transactions between the two men become easier to understand, if not entirely justifiable by Christian mores. It appears that according to contemporary customs, Jacob became male heir, Laban at this time having no male heir of his own. He thus adopted Jacob as his son, giving him both LEAH and her sister Rachel as his wives. After becoming prosperous, Jacob took his departure from the house of Laban (Gen. 31:21). One reason "Laban's attitude toward him was not what it had been" is that Laban by now apparently had sons, and they regarded Jacob as an interloper (31:1). Thus arose the dispute over the right of the possession of the TERAPHIM, the household gods that Rachel concealed in the baggage as she, together with Jacob her husband, fled away (31:30-31). These household deities, about the size of miniature dolls, were regarded as indisputable evidence of the rights and privileges of family ownership and inheritance. Cf. Laban's indignant query, "But why did you steal my gods?" (31:30).

For some time, Rachel remained barren, bearing no children. The two children that Rachel finally had were Joseph (Gen. 30:22), while yet in the house of Laban, and Benjamin after the return home. Rachel, however, died in childbirth with Benjamin (35:16-19). This may partially show why Jacob favored the sons of his beloved Rachel above the sons of Leah. The character of Rachel varies between very attractive and unattractive. She inherited her family's traits of scheming and duplicity (31:34). A believer in monotheism, she yet clung to the forms of polytheism. JEREMIAH pictures her as rising from her grave to weep over the children who are being carried to BABYLON, never to return (Jer. 31:15). MATTHEW cites this passage in connection with HEROD's murder of the children in BETHLEHEM (Matt. 2:18).

Raddai. rad'i (Heb. *radday H8099*, "[Yahweh] rules"). Fifth son of JESSE and brother of DAVID (1 Chr. 2:14).

raft. See SHIPS.

Ragau. ray′gaw. See REU.

Raguel. ruh-gyoo′uhl (Heb. *rĕʿûʾēl H8294*, "friend of God"; LXX *Ragouēl*). KJV alternate form of REUEL (Num. 10:29).

Rahab. ray′hab (Heb. *rāḥāb H8147*, meaning uncertain; Gk. *Rhachab G4829* [Matt. 1:5] and *Rhaab G4805* [LXX; Heb. 11:31; Jas. 2:25]). A prostitute of JERICHO, at whose house two spies stayed just prior to the conquest of Palestine by JOSHUA (Josh. 2:1-21). Terrified by the approach of the Israelites, she made an agreement with the spies to protect them if they would guarantee the safety of her family and herself. She concealed them from the agents of the king of Jericho and helped them to escape through her window on the city wall. At the fall of Jericho, Joshua spared Rahab and her relatives (Josh. 6:17,

A partially reconstructed house built over a wall of ancient Jericho (c. 2200-1500 B.C.). Rahab lived in a house that was part of the city walls.

22, 25). According to Matthew's GENEALOGY OF JESUS CHRIST, Rahab became the wife of Salmon (see SALMA) and the mother of BOAZ (Matt. 1:5). The author of Hebrews cites her as an example of FAITH (Heb. 11:31), and James refers to her demonstration of faith by good works (Jas. 2:25). Jewish tradition has held Rahab in high honor, one tradition making her the wife of Joshua himself.

Rahab (monster). ray′hab (Heb. *rahab H8105*, "assault, violence"). In the poetical books of the OT the name is applied to a monster or demonic power. The allusions occur in the context of God's power in nature: he overcomes Rahab in a contest of force (Job 9:13; 26:12 [in parallel with "serpent," v. 13]; Ps. 89:10 [in parallel with "enemies"]; Isa. 51:9 [in parallel with DRAGON]). Each of these passages is connected with the providential act of God in restraining the sea, and as a demonstration of his supreme power. (See also LEVIATHAN.) The concept was applied to the deliverance of Israel from EGYPT, when God opened the waters of the sea to provide a safe passage for his people (Isa. 51:10). Possibly because of this association with the EXODUS, Rahab became a symbolic name for Egypt. It is included in the list of hostile nations cited in Ps. 87:4, and it is specifically identified with Egypt in Isa. 30:7.

Raham. ray′hum (Heb. *raham H8165*, possibly "[God has shown] mercy," but this derivation is uncertain). Son of Shema and descendant of CALEB (1 Chr. 2:44). Some believe that Raham was the name of a town (understanding "father" in the sense of "founder").

Rahel. See RACHEL.

raiment. See DRESS.

rain. The amount of rainfall in biblical countries varies greatly. In EGYPT, for example, there is very little rainfall, the land being dependent on the river NILE for water. In much of SYRIA and ISRAEL, however, the rainfall normally is abundant. The contrast between Egypt and PALESTINE in rainfall is brought out in Deut. 11:10-12. Since the summer is very dry in Israel, the rainy seasons come in the spring (the "latter rains") and in the fall (the "former rains"). One can be almost certain that from about May 1 to about October 15, no measurable rain will fall. "The winter is past; the rains are over and gone" (Cant. 2:11). Many people thus sleep on the roofs of the houses to escape the heat and to enjoy the cooling night breezes. The greatest amount of rain falls between November and February, tapering off until the coming of summer, and beginning again the next autumn.

The latter or spring rains are considered such a natural blessing that they assume an eschatological significance (Joel 2:23; Zech. 10:1). The withholding of the rain at the proper season, particularly in the spring, was regarded as a most severe punishment (Deut. 28:23-24; 1 Ki. 17:1-16; 18:18), and conversely, the abundance of rain denoted the rich blessing of the Lord on his people (Deut. 28:12). FAMINE, one of the more tragic effects of the lack of rain, was therefore seen as an indication of divine displeasure (2 Sam. 21:1-14). In pagan concepts, BAAL was conceived of as the god of storm and rain. This aids in explaining the immoral practices of the FERTILITY CULTS, which believed that their sexual orgies would induce Baal to send rain. ELIJAH's contest on Mount CARMEL was to prove the superiority of the God of Israel in the realm of the forces of nature.

rainbow. The biblical interpretation of the rainbow is found in the record of NOAH's life. God's COVENANT with Noah declared that he would never again send a universal FLOOD to destroy the whole inhabited earth (Gen. 9:8-17). This feature of the flood account is unique in that none of the accounts from BABYLON, such as the well-known *Gilgamesh Epic*, makes mention of the rainbow as the covenantal sign. In the Bible the rainbow is the first of the covenant signs and provides the key to understanding all of them, including the signs of BAPTISM and the LORD'S SUPPER in the new covenant. The rainbow in the clouds speaks to human beings from God. God allowed Noah to understand what the bow means to him: a visible declaration that the Lord will never again destroy the earth by flood. The rainbow is the Lord's promise made visible. Thus covenant signs express covenant promises to covenant people. Ezekiel compares the glory of God to that of a rainbow (Ezek. 1:28). John, as a prisoner on PATMOS, beheld the throne of God encircled by the rainbow (Rev. 4:3).

raisin. See PLANTS (under *grape*).

raisin cake. The Hebrew term *ʾăšîšâ H862* (mistakenly rendered "flagon" by the KJV) refers to cakes that were formed after the grapes had completely dried; when coated, they were imperishable. More often than not such desiccated plant stuffs were soaked in water or broth and mixed with gruel made from some cereal grain for consumption. They often were compounded with other fruits, such as figs and dates, and seasoned with salts or spices. Raisin cakes were used as cultic offerings by many ancient peoples (cf. Hos. 3:1) and appear in lists of commodities from various sea ports. They are mentioned as part of an offering meal for travelers and soldiers (2 Sam. 6:19; 1 Chr. 16:3). Another Hebrew word, *ṣimmûqîm H7540*, which occurs four times (1 Sam. 25:18; 30:12; 2 Sam. 16:1; 1 Chr. 12:40), is translated as "clusters of raisins" by the KJV and other versions, but it too probably refers to raisin cakes (so NIV, NJPS).

Rakal. ray′kuhl. TNIV form of RACAL.

Rakem. ray′kim. See REKEM (PERSON) #3.

Rakkath. rak′uhth (Heb. *raqqat H8395*, possibly "marshy bank"). A fortified city within the tribal territory of NAPHTALI (Josh. 19:35). According to Jewish tradition, it was the place where later TIBERIAS was built, but modern scholars usually locate Rakkath a short distance NNW of Tiberias, identifying it with Khirbet el-Quneiṭireh (Tell Eqlatiyeh), a small ancient site on the W shore of the Sea of Galilee. Some believe that Rakkath and KARTAN are the same place.

Rakkon. rak′on (Heb. *raqqôn H8378*, with definite article attached, meaning possibly "the narrow place" or "the shore" or "the marshy bank"). Apparently a town near JOPPA within the territory allotted to the tribe of DAN (Josh. 19:46). The location of such a town is unknown, although one proposal is Tell er-Reqqeit, c. 6 mi. (10 km.) N of Joppa. Some think that "the Rakkon" is a river; others emend the text, omitting this name altogether (cf. LXX). See also ME JARKON.

ram (animal). See ANIMALS.

Ram (person). ram (Heb. *rām H8226*, prob. "[God] is exalted"; Gk. *Aram G730*). (1) Son of HEZRON, descendant of JUDAH through PEREZ, and ancestor of King DAVID (Ruth 4:19; 1 Chr. 2:9-10). Ram is included in the GENEALOGY OF JESUS CHRIST (Matt. 1:3-4 [KJV and other versions, "Aram"]; Lk. 3:33 [NRSV, "Arni," following some ancient MSS]).

(2) Firstborn son of JERAHMEEL and descendant of Judah (1 Chr. 2:25, 27). This Ram is apparently the nephew of #1, above (i.e., Jerahmeel's brother, 1 Chr. 2:9).

(3) Apparently the head of a clan; ELIHU, the last speaker in the book of JOB, is described as belonging to "the family of Ram" (Job 32:2).

ram, battering. See WAR.

Rama. See RAMAH.

Ramah. ray´muh (Heb. *rāmāh H8230* [usually with the definite article], "the height" or "the hill"). **(1)** In NAPHTALI. This city is mentioned once (Josh. 19:36). The name is preserved in that of the village er-Rameh, about 8 mi. (13 km.) WSW of Safad (present-day Zefat) and 9 mi. (14 km.) E of Acco; it lies on the natural dividing line between Lower GALILEE on the S and Upper Galilee on the N. In the village of er-Rameh, the ancient remains date to the Roman and Hellenistic periods. As for the biblical Ramah, its actual site was at Khirbet Zeitun er-Rameh, also known as Khirbet Jul, an ancient mound about 2 mi. (3 km.) E of er-Rameh. It is a typical tell of Iron Ages I and II, located on a rocky outcrop in the valley. The exact limits of the ancient settlement are hard to determine today since the whole area is covered by the famous olive orchards of this region.

(2) In ASHER. The boundary description of the Asher tribe, the exact line of which is difficult to follow, apparently places the town of Ramah somewhere between Great SIDON and "the fortified city of Tyre" (Josh. 19:29). Therefore, this Ramah should most likely be sought in the area NW of modern TYRE, but the precise location is unknown. The oft-proposed identification with the small village of er-Ramiyeh seems out of the question because it is too far S.

(3) In BENJAMIN (Josh. 18:25). The evidence for the identification of this town is some of the most conclusive for any site in Israel. It is clearly to

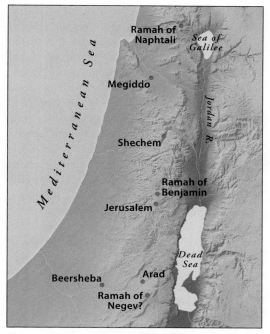

Cities named Ramah in the Promised Land.

be located close to BETHEL (Jdg. 4:5), the modern Beitin, on the ancient trunk road leading N from BETHLEHEM and passing to the W of JERUSALEM (19:13). The prophetess DEBORAH exercised her authority as a judge in Israel at a place between Bethel and Ramah (Jdg. 4:5). Instead of turning in to spend the night at GIBEAH, the Levite from the hill country of Ephraim could have gone on a little way farther to Ramah (19:13). In addition to standing on the N–S highway, er-Ram is also within striking distance of the E–W road from JERUSALEM via GIBEON and the descent of BETH HORON to GEZER. During the monarchy, the hostile act of BAASHA consisted in the establishment of a strong point at Ramah that could effectively block traffic to and from Jerusalem along this vital route (1 Ki. 15:17; 2 Chr. 16:1). In retaliation, ASA persuaded the Syrians to attack Israel from the N; by thus relieving pressure on the front with Judah, he was able to dismantle the fortification at Ramah and to use the building blocks for constructing two new forts of his own at GEBA and MIZPAH.

Thus the boundary between JUDAH and ISRAEL was fixed at a line dissecting the former tribal inheritance of Benjamin in half (1 Ki. 15:17-22;

R

2 Chr. 16:2-6). The partition of Benjamin in this manner is reminiscent of the division reflected in Josh. 18:21-28, where Ramah belongs to the southernmost district. A brief oracle by Hosea against Gibeah, Ramah, and BETH AVEN is apparently directed at Benjamin, perhaps with particular reference to this "Judahite" half of the tribe (Hos. 5:8). When one column of SENNACHERIB's army was evidently storming southward from Samaria toward Jerusalem, Ramah stood in the direct line of the Assyrian advance (Isa. 10:29). Jeremiah describes Ramah as the scene of RACHEL's weeping for her children (Jer. 31:15; cf. Matt. 2:18 [KJV, "Rama"]). Some of Ramah's former residents were among the postexilic returnees (Ezra 2:26; Neh. 7:30); the town is also mentioned in the list of settlements (11:33).

It is most likely that Ramah of Benjamin was the birthplace of SAMUEL the prophet. The home of ELKANAH and HANNAH is called *hārāmātayim ṣôpîm* (1 Sam. 1:1), but the Hebrew construction is somewhat awkward. Since Elkanah was a descendant of ZUPH (a LEVITE of the Kohathites who settled in N Benjamin (1 Sam. 9:5; 1 Chr. 6:35; cf. Josh. 21:5; 1 Chr. 6:22-26, 35, 66-70), it would appear that the correct understanding of the name in 1 Sam. 1:1 is "Ramathaim of the Zuphite(s)." The identity of Ramathaim Zophim with Ramah is confirmed by a comparison of 1 Sam. 1:1 with 1:19 and 2:11. Although Samuel was born there, he grew up at SHILOH but returned to his home when the latter was abandoned as the religious center of Israel. At Ramah he made his headquarters, and from there he went on his annual circuit to Bethel, Gilgal, and Mizpah (1 Sam. 7:15-17). The elders of Israel came to him at Ramah when making their request for a king (1 Sam. 8:4). It was doubtless at Ramah in "the land of Zuph" that SAUL first encountered Samuel and was secretly anointed king (1 Sam. 9:5—10:10). Samuel continued to dwell at Ramah, where he died and was buried (15:34; 16:13; 25:1; 28:3). Here DAVID sought refuge from Saul, whose attempts to have the renegade prince arrested were brought to naught (19:18-24).

(4) In the NEGEV. A town mentioned in the description of SIMEON's tribal inheritance (Josh. 19:8). The MT states that the towns of Simeon and their respective villages extended "as far as Baalath

This minaret tower in the modern village of er-Ram identifies the ancient site of Ramah of Benjamin, the prophet Samuel's hometown.

Beer, Ramath Negev" (KJV, "Ramath of the south"; NIV, "Ramah in the Negev" within parentheses). It is likely that the Hebrew *rāʾmat negeb* stands as an adverbial accusative of direction. The verse may thus be rendered: "as far as Baalath Beer (in the direction of) Ramath Negev." Such an interpretation obviates two conjectures previously proposed, namely, that the reference is to the S boundary of Simeon's settlement, or that Ramath Negev should be equated with Baalath Beer (cf. NIV). In the parallel passage (1 Chr. 4:33), the MT has simply "as far as Baal"; and Ramath Negev is also missing from the roster of settlements in the Negev of JUDAH (Josh. 15:21-32), which included Simeon. On the other hand, it seems likely that this town appears as Ramoth Negev (1 Sam. 30:27), one of the places to whose elders DAVID sent some of his spoil from the Amalekites. There is no indication of its locale. Current speculation about its identification centers on Khirbet Ghazzeh (Ḥorvat ʿUza) at the eastern edge of the Negev of Judah, some 20 (32 km.) ESE of BEERSHEBA, guarding a major route from EDOM; but the lofty commanding position of Khirbet Gharreh (Tel ʿIra) and its location in the center of the Negev of Judah (i.e., on the fringe of Simeon's inheritance) are strong arguments in favor of the latter.

(5) In GILEAD. The name Ramah occurs as the short form of RAMOTH GILEAD in one context (2 Ki. 8:29 = 2 Chr. 22:6; the NIV reads "Ramoth").

Ramath. See RAMAH #4; RAMATH LEHI; RAMATH MIZPAH.

Ramathaim, Ramathaim-zophim. See RAMAH #3.

Ramathite. ray′muh-th*i*t (Heb. *rāmātî H8258*, gentilic of *rāmāh H8230*). A native of RAMAH. DAVID's vine-dresser was known as "Shimei the Ramathite" (1 Chr. 27:27), but which is meant of the several towns that bore this name cannot be determined.

Ramath Lehi. ray′muhth-lee′h*i* (Heb. *rāmat lĕḥî H8257*, "jawbone hill"). The scene of SAMSON's rout of the PHILISTINES with the jawbone of a donkey for a weapon (Jdg. 15:17). See LEHI.

Ramath Mizpeh. ray′muhth-miz′puh (Heb. *rāmat hammiṣpeh H8256*, "hill of the watchtower"). A town assigned to the tribe of GAD in the division of PALESTINE (Josh. 13:26). It is mentioned between HESHBON and BETONIM when delineating the Gadite territory E of the JORDAN, but its location is unknown.

Ramath of the south. See RAMAH #4.

Rameses. ram′uh-seez (Heb. *ra`mĕsēs H8314* [*ra`amsēs* in Exod. 1:11], from Egyp. *R`mśś*, short form of *Pr-R`mśśw*, "[house of] Ramses"). KJV and other versions have Raamses once (Exod. 1:11). The usual orthographic distinction in English between the name of the city (Rameses or Raamses) and the name of some pharaohs (Ramesses or RAMSES) has no basis in the Egyptian language. According to Gen 47:11, JACOB and his sons were given "property in the best part of the land, the district of Rameses," apparently a term equivalent to "the region of Goshen" (45:10 et al.; see GOSHEN), where the city of Rameses was located. Rameses and PITHOM are named as the store cities that the Hebrews built (Exod. 1:11), and it was from Rameses that they began their journey out of Egypt

(12:37; Num. 33:3, 5). Rameses (Pi-Ramessē or Per-Ramessē) was the residence city of the 19th and 20th Egyptian dynasties in the NE NILE delta. Its location has been much debated: some place it at Tanis (ZOAN, S of Lake Menzaleh) and others c. 17 mi. (27 km.) farther S near Qantir (Tell el-Dab`a, site of the earlier HYKSOS capital, Avaris). Several factors clearly favor Qantir as the probable site of Rameses, and this identification is now generally accepted.

Ramesses. ram′uh-seez. See RAMSES.

Ramiah. ruh-mi′uh (Heb. *ramyâ H8243*, "Yahweh is exalted"). One of the descendants of PAROSH who agreed to put away their foreign wives (Ezra 10:25).

Ramoth (person). ray′moth (Heb. *rāmôt H8238* [not in NIV], possibly "heights"). One of the descendants of BANI who agreed to put away their foreign wives (Ezra 10:29 KJV, following the *Qere*; NIV and other versions follow the *Ketib*, JERAMOTH).

Ramoth (place). ray′moth (Heb. *rā'môt H8030*, "heights"). **(1)** Short form of RAMOTH GILEAD (Deut. 4:43; Josh. 20:8; 21:38; 1 Chr. 6:80 [Heb. 6:65]).

(2) A city in the NEGEV to which DAVID sent gifts after his devastating attack upon the camp of the Amalekites (1 Sam. 30:27).

(3) A town within the tribal territory of ISSACHAR designated as one of the LEVITICAL CITIES for the descendants of GERSHON (Gershom, 1 Chr. 6:73). It is doubtless the same as JARMUTH (Josh. 21:29) because it occupies the same position in the list of Levitical cities and there are many other comparable differences between the two rosters. Moreover, Ramoth is probably the same as REMETH (Josh. 19:21). A stela of Seti I (1309-1290) states that the `Apiru (see HABIRU) from Mount Yarmuta had attacked the Asiatics; Mount Yarmuta is doubtless to be associated with Jarmuth-Remeth-Ramoth of Issachar, that is, in the elevated region NW of BETH SHAN. Thus the form Jarmuth is probably more original than Ramoth. The site is possibly modern Kaukab el-Hawa, the Crusading Belvoir, located some 6 mi. (10 km.) NNE of Beth

R

Shan on a plateau almost 1000 ft. (c. 300 m.) above sea level in a region of springs.

Ramoth Gilead. ray´muhth-gil´ee-uhd (Heb. *rāmôt gilʿād H8240*, "heights of GILEAD"). Under Solomon's administration Ramoth Gilead was designated as the center of the district that was E of the Jordan and extended N of the Yarmuk (1 Ki. 4:13). This town was one of the CITIES OF REFUGE (Deut. 4:43; Josh. 20:8) assigned to the LEVITES descended from MERARI in the tribal territory of GAD (Josh. 21:38; 1 Chr. 6:80). A frontier town, Ramoth Gilead was a key military outpost in the wars between ARAM and Israel; AHAB was killed in battle there (1 Ki. 22:3-40; 2 Chr. 18). Some time later, Ahab's son Joram (JEHORAM) was wounded in a battle at Ramoth Gilead, then JEHU was anointed king there by one of ELISHA's young prophets (2 Ki. 8:28—9:14). The location of Ramoth Gilead has been disputed, but most scholars today identify the town with modern Tell Ramith (er-Rumeith), c. 17 mi. (27 km.) NE of JABESH GILEAD.

rampart. This English term is used in some Bible versions of the bulwarks surrounding ZION (Ps. 48:13), and figuratively of the sea as a physical barrier protecting THEBES (Nah. 3:8 NRSV; NIV, "defense"). It is used also of a moat referring to both the walls and the water-filled ditch at BETH MAACAH (2 Sam. 20:15 NRSV; NIV, "fortifications"). The northern side of ancient JERUSALEM above the Valley of HINNON was protected by such a wall (Lam. 2:8). Most of these walls, as at JERICHO, were built up of tamped earth and in later periods faced with stone blocks.

Ramses. ram´seez (Egyptian *Rᶜ-mś-św*, meaning "Re is the one who created him"). Also Ramesses. The name of eleven PHARAOHS of EGYPT; it was also the epithet of two others. Ramses I was the founder of the 19th dynasty, but the most illustrious of the bearers of this name was his grandson,

Ramses II (reigned c. 1290-1224 B.C.). He was ambitious and imperious. He made a determined effort to recover the Asiatic empire, but his errors in judgment in the HITTITE encounter at KADESH ON THE ORONTES brought about a stalemate, which later produced an Egyptian-Hittite treaty. Ramses established his capital at Tanis, in the NILE delta, but his building and rebuilding activities extended throughout the land and even beyond Egypt proper. Among his impressive constructions are the completion of the hypostyle hall at Karnak, his father's funerary temple at Abydos, his own temple at Abydos, the forecourt and pylon of the Luxor temple, the Ramesseum at the Theban necropolis, and Abu Simbel in Nubia. Extensive building operations were supplemented by his usurpations of monuments of his predecessors, a practice that enhanced his reputation beyond his merits. This, plus the presence in the OT of the name RAMESES for a city and district in the delta, brought about the opinion that Ramses II was the pharaoh of the Israelite oppression, in spite of chronological complications with OT data. Among the varying interpretations of the EXODUS, this identification of Ramses II is not widely held at present.

Ramses III (c. 1184-1153 B.C.) was the second king of the 20th dynasty; perhaps his most outstanding accomplishment was the repelling of an invasion of the delta by the SEA PEOPLES. His

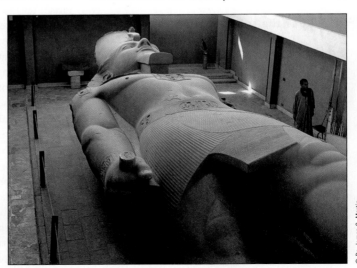

This limestone colossus of Ramses II at the Memphis museum in Egypt is over 40 ft. (12 m.) long.

© Dr. James C. Martin

R

best-known construction is his mortuary temple at Medinet Habu, not far from the Ramesseum. At the end of his reign a serious harem conspiracy occurred. The other eight kings of this name, all members of the 20th dynasty, are relatively unimportant, though documents relating to the tomb robberies in the Theban necropolis in the reign of Ramses IX are of interest. Although certain of these kings, such as Ramses II and III, must have had at least indirect influence on Israelite life, none of them is mentioned in the OT.

rams' horns. See MUSIC AND MUSICAL INSTRUMENTS.

ram skins. The skins of the sheep tanned with oil used for outer clothing by the shepherds of the ANE. They were also used as the exterior covering for the TABERNACLE (Exod. 25:5 et al.).

ransom. As a verb, this English term means "to free someone by paying a price," and it is used in modern Bible versions primarily to render Hebrew *pādâ H7009*, "to buy out, deliver" (Lev. 19:20 et al.; KJV, "redeem"). As a noun, *ransom* refers to "that which is paid for someone's release," and it translates both Hebrew *kōper H4111* (Exod. 30:12 et al.) and Greek *lytron G3389* (Matt. 20:2; Mk. 10:4; cf. cognates in 1 Tim. 2:6; Heb. 9:15). See ATONEMENT; REDEMPTION.

rape. See SEX.

Rapha. ray′fuh (Heb. *rāpā° H8325*, prob. "[God] has healed"). **(1)** Fifth son of BENJAMIN and grandson of JACOB (1 Chr. 8:2). However, the parallel lists of Benjamin's sons (Gen. 46:21; Num. 26:38-40; 1 Chr. 7:6) omit mention of Rapha altogether. See comments under NOHAH #1.

(2) See BETH RAPHA.

(3) A different form of the Hebrew word (*rāpāh H8335*, always with the definite article attached, 2 Sam. 21:16-22; 1 Chr. 20:6, 8) is rendered "Rapha" in the NIV (NJPS, "the Rapha"), but "giants" in the NRSV and other versions. See REPHAITES.

Raphah. ray′fuh (Heb. *rāpāh H8334*, prob. "[Yahweh] has healed"). Son of Binea and descendant of SAUL through JONATHAN (1 Chr. 8:37); called REPHAIAH in the parallel genealogy (9:43).

Raphu. ray′fyoo (Heb. *rāpû° H8336*, "healed"). Father of PALTI; the latter was one of the spies sent out by MOSES (Num. 13:9).

rapture. See TRIBULATION, THE GREAT.

Ras Shamra. rahs-shahm′ruh. The modern name of the mound that marks the site of the ancient city of Ugarit, located on the Syrian coast opposite the island of CYPRUS. The city, with its port Minet el-Beida (White Harbor), was an important commercial center through which passed the trade of SYRIA and MESOPOTAMIA with EGYPT, Cyprus, and the Aegean area. Occasionally antiquities had been found here by local people, but in 1928 a peasant struck the roof of a buried tomb with his plow and made a discovery that attracted the attention of the authorities. In 1929 the French archaeologist C. F. A. Schaeffer began a series of excavations that have revealed much of the history of the site. Test shafts showed that there were five major strata, the earliest dating to the Neolithic period.

Ugarit was swept from the historical scene in about 1200 B.C., when the SEA PEOPLES overran the area. The city is mentioned in Egyptian historical inscriptions, in the AMARNA Tablets (Akkadian), and in HITTITE records. Its relations with Egypt were quite close during the 12th dynasty and again in the time of RAMSES II. Ugarit was at the peak of its prosperity in the fifteenth-fourteenth centuries B.C. but was destroyed by an earthquake in the mid-fourteenth century. It recovered from this catastrophe but was under Hittite and then Egyptian domination. Although the excavation of the mound has resulted in many significant finds, the most striking was that of a scribal school and library of clay tablets, adjoining the temple of BAAL and dating from the Amarna Age. Various ANE languages and scripts appeared at Ugarit, but the majority of the tablets used an unknown cuneiform script, which study showed to have an alphabet of some thirty signs. The language, now called Ugaritic, was found to be of the Semitic family and closely related to HEBREW. The texts contain various types of writings: syllabaries and vocabularies;

R

personal and diplomatic correspondence; business, legal, and governmental records; veterinary texts dealing with diagnosis and treatment of ailments of horses; and, most important, religious literature.

The myths and legends of Ugarit have provided valuable primary sources for the knowledge of Canaanite religion. These stories have been given modern titles, such as "The Loves and Wars of Baal and Anat," "The Birth of the Gods," "The Wedding of Nikkal and the Moon," "The Legend of Keret," and "The Legend of Aqhat." At the head of the Ugaritic pantheon was EL, who was also known as Father of Man, Creator of Creators, Bull El. His consort was ASHERAH, a fertility goddess who was a stumbling block to ISRAEL. AHAB (1 Ki. 16:33) and JEZEBEL (18:19) promoted her worship, and MANASSEH even put her image in the temple (2 Ki. 21:7).

Among the many offspring of El and Asherah was DAGON (Jdg. 16:23; 1 Sam. 5), a grain god, whose son BAAL was of great prominence. A god of rain and storm, Baal, whose proper name was HADAD (Thunderer), also figured in the fertility cycle. Baal was also called Aliyan Baal, Dagon's Son, Servant of El, Rider of Clouds, and BAAL-ZEBUB (cf. 2 Ki. 1; Matt. 12:24). In Israel the priests of Baal lost an important contest with the prophet of God on Mount CARMEL (1 Ki. 18). Baal's sister and wife, the virgin Anat, goddess of love and fertility and goddess of war, is known in the OT as Astarte or ASHTORETH. In addition to these, numerous lesser divinities are named. The deities of Ugarit are often quite ungodly: El ordinarily is easygoing and easily influenced, but sometimes is rash and even immoral, as in his seduction and expulsion of two women. Baal mates with his sister and also with a heifer. Anat slaughters people and wades in blood and gore. This aspect of Canaanite religion occasioned the stern warning of the Lord to Israel concerning such worship.

The texts provide information concerning ritual and sacrifice and the temple plan, and recovered objects also contribute to an understanding of the religion and culture. The tablets and the OT elucidate each other; the Ugaritic texts have been used extensively in the analysis of the Hebrew text. Many interesting suggested relationships may be cited. Ugaritic practice illuminates the biblical pro-hibition against boiling a kid in its mother's milk (Exod. 23:19; 34:26; Deut. 14:21). A veterinary text refers to a poultice that has been cited as a parallel to Isaiah's prescription for King HEZEKIAH (2 Ki. 20:7; Isa. 38:21). The legend of Aqhat tells of a good and just king named Dan'el, whom some have sought to equate with the DANIEL of Ezekiel (Ezek. 14:14, 20; 12:3). The system of weights used at Ugarit was like that of Israel. These examples illustrate the type of information provided and discussion aroused by the investigation of the remains of this long-dead city.

rat. See ANIMALS.

raven. See BIRDS.

ravenous bird. See BIRDS.

razor. A sharp-edged cutting instrument for cutting and shaving the hair or beard; referred to in the OT especially in connection with the NAZIRITE vow (Num. 6:5; et al.). The word is also used metaphorically of the tongue (Ps. 52:2). Razors were made of metal, and were simply or elaborately made. Many specimens have survived from antiquity. See also KNIFE.

Re. ray (Egyp. *Rē*, meaning "sun"). Also *Ra*. The principal SUN god of ancient EGYPT, shown as a man with a falcon's head, wearing the sun's disc. In very early times, Re was identified with the creator god Atum of HELIOPOLIS and became chief deity there. He is commonly referred to as Re-Harakhte, "Re-Horus of the Horizon," as the morning sun in the eastern horizon. Re first had royal patronage in the 2nd dynasty, and reached greatest prominence with the pyramid builders of the 4th and 5th dynasties (c. 2600-2400 B.C.), when the kings first called themselves "Son of Re"; thereafter, the funerary god OSIRIS grew in prominence. The universal claims of Re and influence of Heliopolitan theology led to combinations with other deities: Amen-Re, Sobk-Re, etc. In the 18th dynasty, AKHENATEN made the sun god—manifest in the solar disc as Aten—sole god of Egypt, but thereafter (19th and 20th dynasties) Amun of THEBES (see AMON #4), Re, and Ptah of MEMPHIS formed

R

© Dr. James C. Martin. The Cairo Museum. Photographed by permission.

This bronze statue of Sekhmet, Egyptian goddess of war, depicts her with the head of a lioness; the sun disk on top symbolizes the god Re.

a trio and could be conceived of as three aspects of a single deity. Re appears in the OT only in the name of Joseph's father-in-law, Potiphera the priest of On (Heliopolis).

Reaia. See Reaiah #2.

Reaiah. ree-ay'yuh (Heb. *rĕʾāyâ H8025*, "Yahweh has seen"). (1) Son of Shobal and descendant of Judah (1 Chr. 4:2).

(2) Son of Micah and descendant of Reuben (1 Chr. 5:5; KJV, "Reaia").

(3) Ancestor of a family of temple servants (Nethinim) who returned with Zerubbabel from exile in Babylon (Ezra 2:47; Neh. 7:50).

reaping. The act of cutting or gathering the produce of the fields, usually in the late summer. In Bible times, as in primitive areas today, reapers cut the grain with a sickle or pulled it up by the roots. In Leviticus, there is legislation regarding reaping. The people were to leave the corners of the field for the poor to reap (Lev. 19:9; 23:22). In the seventh and fiftieth years, they were to reap none at all. Sowing and reaping served to illustrate investment and reward. As an example, Prov. 22:8 has, "He who sows wickedness reaps trouble." Somewhat the opposite is in Ps. 126:5, "Those who sow in tears reap with songs of joy." A different figure is used in the book of Revelation, "So the one who was seated on the cloud swung his sickle over the earth, and the earth was reaped" (Rev. 14:16). See agriculture; harvest.

Reba. ree'buh (Heb. *rebaʿ H8064*, perhaps "fourth one"). One of five kings of Midian killed by the Israelites in a battle on the plains of Moab (Num. 31:8). Moses was commanded by God to exact vengeance on the Midianites because they had enticed Israel with their gods. In another passage (Josh. 13:21) the kings are said to be princes of (NIV, "allied with") Sihon, the Amorite ruler, possibly indicating that they were his vassals. Apparently Sihon had taken possession of the area of Moab and made the Midianite tribes residing there subject to him.

Rebecca. See Rebekah.

R

Rebekah. ri-bek′uh (Heb. *ribqâ H8071*, possibly "cow" [if so, an affectionate term, comparable to Rachel, "ewe"]; Gk. *Rhebekka G4831*). KJV NT Rebecca (a spelling followed by other versions). Daughter of Bethuel, who was nephew to Abraham (Gen. 22:23) and lived in the Aramean country near the Euphrates. Rebekah was Laban's sister. She became the wife of Isaac and the mother of Esau and Jacob.

Rebekah's encounter with Abraham's steward (prob. Eliezer) is remembered as a classic example of divine providence and guidance (Gen. 24). She met this aged traveler with his camels outside her city as she returned one evening from the well. When he asked her for a drink, she readily gave it, but she also offered to draw for his camels, and did so with good will, little knowing that the man had just prayed for this very sign. Finding that she was a relative of his master, and realizing that she was also beautiful, he recognized the abundant answer to his prayer. When Rebekah's father and brother heard what the steward had to say, they could only acknowledge the Lord's leading. They wanted her, however, to delay for a few days of leave-taking; asked to decide, she preferred to go immediately. So Rebekah was brought to Isaac, "and he loved her; and Isaac was comforted after his mother's death" (v. 67).

For twenty years of her marriage Rebekah had no children (see barrenness); then in answer to Isaac's prayer, God gave her twins (Gen. 25:20-26). Her experience while carrying them foreshadowed conflict between her descendants, and she was told that God had chosen the younger twin for his blessing. Malachi cites the evidence of it in Israel's experience (Mal. 1:2-3), and Paul shows that God was establishing and typifying the principle of electing grace (Rom. 9:10-13). Jacob, the younger son, unadventurous, always in camp, became Rebekah's favorite (Gen. 25:28); and she plotted the deception by which he gained his father's formal blessing (ch. 27). Esau then would have murdered Jacob, but God overruled in this also. Esau had married Hittite women to the disappointment of his parents; Rebekah induced Isaac to send Jacob back to Haran to find a wife. According to Gen. 49:31, Rebekah was buried in the family tomb at Machpelah near Hebron.

Recab. ree′kab (Heb. *rēkāb H8209*, from a root meaning "chariot" or possibly "rider"). Also Rechab, Rekab. **(1)** Son of Rimmon, from the tribe of Benjamin; he and his brother treacherously murdered Ish-Bosheth, their king, and met with the due reward of their deed at David's hands (2 Sam. 4:2-12). See comments under Baanah #1.

(2) Father (or ancestor) of Jehonadab/Jonadab (2 Ki. 10:15, 23; 1 Chr. 2:55; Jer. 35:6-8, 14-19). See Recabite.

(3) Father of Malkijah; the latter was a postexilic ruler of Beth Hakkerem who repaired the Dung Gate in Jerusalem (Neh. 3:14). Some speculate that he may have been a descendant of #2 above.

Recabite. rek′uh-b*i*t (Heb. *rēkābî H8211* [always in the phrase *bêt hārēkābîm*, "house of the Recabites"], gentilic of *rēkāb H8209*). Also Rechabite, Rekabite. Name applied to a nomadic family that descended from Recab (#2) and Jonadab; they were famous for their rules to abstain from wine, build no houses, sow no seed, and plant no vineyard (Jer. 35). According to 1 Chr. 2:55 certain Kenites "came from

Modern-day bedouin tent in Jordan. The Recabites used similar dwellings and refused to build houses (Jer. 35:7-10).

© Dr. James C. Martin

R

Hammath, the father of the house of Recab." HAM-
MATH, like various other names in this genealogy,
may refer to a place as well as to a person, and the
preposition "from" seems to imply that the Kenites
in view came from a place Hammath. Moreover, we
are told elsewhere that a Kenite named HEBER separated from the rest of the Kenites (who descended
from HOBAB) and settled in KEDESH of NAPHTALI
(Jdg. 4:11, 17), in the same general region as Hammath (cf. Josh. 19:35-37). As for the term "father" in
1 Chr. 2:55, it may indicate either that the Recabites
had a blood relationship with the Kenites or that
Hammath was the founder of the Recabites as a
professional guild; in either case the text is of interest
because some of the Kenites gained their livelihood
in metallurgy, possibly the trade of the Recabites.

The founder of the Recabite discipline was
Jehonadab/Jonadab (2 Ki. 10:15, 23; Jer. 35:6, 14).
Some scholars have viewed him as a naive nomad,
but others see him as a member of a guild with
high social standing. The designation "the son of
Recab" (2 Ki. 10:15) possibly does not indicate a
true father-son relationship or even a descendant
of one Recab. Rather the term "son" could indicate that he was a member of a guild named *rekab*;
that is, an occupational group associated in some
way with chariotry (Heb. *rekeb* H8207, "chariot"),
a specialty group well attested in the ANE. "Son
of Recab" could also indicate that Jehonadab was
a native of a place named Recab, possibly so called
because of its association with chariotry. According
to either of these last interpretations, it may not
be coincidental that JEHU took Jehonadab into his
chariot for the trip to SAMARIA.

Regarding Jehonadab's religious position there
is no ambiguity. Like ELIJAH and ELISHA, he was
a radical supporter of Yahwism in the face of the
increasing threat of Baalism under the Omrides.
The statement that Jehonadab "was on his way to
meet" Jehu (2 Ki. 10:15) shows that Jehonadab
took the initiative. Scholars have differed also in
their understanding of the object of the rules formulated by Jehonadab for his descendants. Some
have argued that the object of the regulations was
the preservation of primitive simplicity, that is, the
maintenance of nomadism because civilization and
settled life inevitably leads to apostasy from Yahweh. Others have suggested that the Rechabites'

rules can be interpreted as belonging to a guild of
metal-workers involved in the making of chariots and other weaponry. This much is sure: the
Recabites are not commended by Yahweh for their
rules as such but rather for their faithfulness to the
rules. And because of their steadfastness, these few
Recabites—who were able to fit into one chamber
of the TEMPLE and all of whose names mentioned
in the text contain Yahweh as a theophoric element
(Jer. 35:3)—are promised that they will never fail
to have a descendant to represent them (v. 19).

Recah. ree′kuh (Heb. *rēkâ* H8212, meaning uncertain). KJV Rechah; TNIV Rekah. Apparently a
town inhabited by some descendants of JUDAH
(1 Chr. 4:12). Nothing is known about such a
place, and some scholars, following a variant SEP-
TUAGINT reading, emend the text to RECAB.

receipt of custom. See CUSTOM, RECEIPT OF.

Rechab, Rechabite. See RECAB; RECABITE.

Rechah. See RECAH.

recompense. See RETRIBUTION; REWARD.

reconciliation. The act of restoring harmony,
bringing again into unity or agreement what has
been alienated. According to biblical teaching,
there is need for reconciliation between God and
human beings because of the alienation between
them, which has its source in SIN and the righteous
aversion to it on the part of God. The Bible teaches
that God himself has provided the means of reconciliation through the death of his Son Jesus Christ.

The Greek verb *katallassō* G2904, when applied
to persons, suggests an "exchange" from enmity to
fellowship. Reconciliation is, therefore, God's exercise of GRACE toward the person who is in enmity
because of sin, establishing in Christ's redemptive work the basis of this changed relationship
(2 Cor. 5:19). That this reconciliation comes about
through the initiative and work of God is shown
by Rom. 5:10, where PAUL asserts that even while
we were enemies, God reconciled *us* to himself
through the death of his son. This changed relationship, however, is possible only because of the

changed status of the sinner, not of God. God is never said to be reconciled to the sinner, but the sinner to God, since it is the person's sinfulness that creates the enmity (Rom. 8:7; Col. 1:21). This enmity precipitates God's WRATH (Eph. 2:3, 5) and JUDGMENT (2 Cor. 5:10), which is allayed only through the reconciliation brought about through the death of Christ (Rom. 5:10), who knew no sin but became sin for us that we might receive his RIGHTEOUSNESS as the basis of reconciliation. See ATONEMENT.

Reconciliation also involves a change of condition so that all basis of the enmity relationship is removed and a complete basis of fellowship is established (2 Cor. 5:18-20; Eph. 2:16). Sinners are out of their condition of unrighteousness and thus reconciled to God in this new relationship. The grace of God assures the reconciled person that the grace basis replaces the sin basis and that he or she is established before God in a new relationship. Moreover, sinners are reconciled not merely because a relationship has changed, but because God has changed them through Christ so that they can be reconciled (Rom. 5:11; 11:15; 2 Cor. 5:18; Eph. 2:5). Reconciliation arises, therefore, out of God, through Christ, to the sinner. In this way, not only are the barriers to fellowship existing in the sinful person removed, but also the positive basis for fellowship is established through the righteousness of Christ imputed to the sinner.

The definitive basis for reconciliation rests both in what God does in annulling the effects of sin in a person so that no enmity exists and in what he does in creating a redeemed nature in that person so that there can be fellowship between God and the redeemed one. Reconciliation is always preeminently God working in human beings to change the basis of relationship. Yet people are (1) given the ministry of reconciliation (2 Cor. 5:18) and (2) invited to be reconciled to God (5:20). Even though the sufficient ground of reconciliation is established in the completed redemptive work of Christ, reconciliation is the basis on which the continued fellowship is established, "For if, when we were God's enemies, we were reconciled to him through the death of his Son, how much more, having been reconciled, shall we be saved through his life!" (Rom. 5:10).

recorder. See OCCUPATIONS AND PROFESSIONS.

red. Out of several Hebrew words that may be translated "red," the most common root is ʾdm (e.g., verb ʾādēm H131, "to be red"; adjectives ʾādōm H137, ʾadmônî H145). This root is related to the noun ʾădāmāh H141, "earth, land," indicating a connection with the color of the soil in the Middle East. The root appears also in the name of the first man, ADAM, who was formed "from the dust of the [red] ground" (again, ʾădāmāh, Gen. 2:7). The name of the nation EDOM has the same origin: not only does that nation come from the "red" man ESAU, but also the color of much of its landscape is red (cf. PETRA, "the red Rose City"). When the reference is to the color of human skin, English prefers the term *ruddy* (1 Sam. 16:12; 17:42; Cant. 5:10; Lam. 4:7). The well-known verse Isa. 1:18 uses three parallel words for "red" to describe SIN (in addition to the verb ʾādēm, it includes the nouns šānî H9106, usually rendered "scarlet," and tôlāʿ H9355, "crimson"). The Greek NT uses the adjective *pyrros* G4794 (Rev. 6:4) and the verb *pyrrazō* G4793 (Matt. 16:2-3), both from the noun *pyr* G4786, "fire."

red heifer. The ashes of the red heifer were used for the removal of certain types of ceremonial uncleanness, such as purification of the leper, or defilement incurred through contact with the dead (Num. 19:2-13). See also ANIMALS; SACRIFICE AND OFFERINGS.

Red Sea. In modern usage, this name refers to the NW arm of the Indian Ocean, separating Africa from the Arabian Peninsula; at the end it splits into the Gulf of Suez on the W and the Gulf of Aqabah on the E. In the OT, the name is a translation of the Hebrew phrase *yam-sûp* (H3542 + H6068), meaning literally "Sea of Reeds." The SEPTUAGINT renders it with *erythra thalassa* (G2261 + G2498), "Red Sea," a term that had earlier been used by Herodotus (though he applied it more generally to include even the Indian Ocean). As used in the Bible, the name appears to refer to three distinct places.

I. **The waters of the exodus.** From comparison of Exod. 14 with 15:22, and by noting the poetic parallelism within 15:4, it is clear that the "sea" crossed by the Hebrews in ch. 14 was the Sea of Reeds. The word *sûp* corresponds precisely to Egyptian *ṯwf(y)*, "papyrus," and the *yam-sûp* to the Egyptian *p̄-ṯwf*, "papyrus-marshes," particularly in the NE delta of the NILE (see PAPYRUS). In an ancient Egyptian document, the products of *p̄-ṯwf* are said to come to Pi-Ramessē (or Per-Ramesses; see RAMESES), and the phrase is set in parallel

Some identify the Bitter Lakes, pictured here, with the Red (or Reed) Sea, which the Israelites crossed during the exodus out of Egypt.

© Dr. James C. Martin

with SHIHOR. Shihor is indubitably the northeasternmost stretch of the Pelusiac arm of the Nile, running from just W of the present Suez Canal (roughly the latitude of Tineh) to the MEDITERRANEAN coast in antiquity, but not extant today. Thus, *p̄-ṯwf* would be associated with the ancient lakes and marshes corresponding approximately to the SE corner of present Lake Menzaleh and to the region S of it, such as Lake Ballah and its environs southward to the Bitter Lakes. (Some scholars, however, have a different view of the relationship between the Hebrew and Egyptian terms.)

This general location on a N–S line due E of the probable site of Rameses near Qantir agrees well with Exod. 10:13, 19. A strong E wind was the means of bringing locusts into Egypt and troubling the PHARAOH at his residence; conversely, after his appeal to MOSES, a strong W wind bore them back eastward into the Sea of Reeds, implying that the latter was E from Rameses. This geographical factor thus supports an identification of

the Sea of Reeds of the EXODUS with the area of lakes and marsh already mentioned, and not with the present-day Gulf of Suez. The very name "Sea of Reeds" would suggest waters that bordered on fresh-water marshes, etc., where papyrus and reeds might grow, again not true of the Gulf of Suez and the modern Red Sea.

In any case, the wilderness through which the Hebrews were to go near the *yam-sûp* (Exod. 13:18) was that of SHUR (15:22), this being roughly the N SINAI desert E of the Suez Canal and between the Mediterranean coast and about the latitude of Lake Timsah. This agrees with a Sea of Reeds in the Lake Ballah area, and both locations are, in turn, readily compatible with a possible route of the exodus from Rameses (at Qantir) to SUCCOTH (prob. Tell el-Maskhuta) and then to the wilderness edge, turning back up to Lake Ballah and so across a Sea of Reeds (alternatively, the crossing may have been farther S, such as at the junction of the Great and Little Bitter Lakes). Thence, the Hebrews went S through Shur/Etham toward the W coast of the Sinai peninsula.

II. Gulf of Suez. After reaching the wilderness of Shur/Etham (Exod. 15:22; Num. 33:8), the Hebrews in three days (prob. on the third day, our mode of reckoning) reached MARAH, went on to ELIM, and thereafter encamped by the *yam-sûp* (Num. 33:10-11) before proceeding into the Desert of Sin (Exod. 16:1; Num. 33:11) en route to Sinai, which they reached after three more stops (Exod. 17; 19:1-2; cf. Num. 33:12-15). On this reckoning, the *yam-sûp* (of Num. 33:10-11) would be somewhere on the Gulf of Suez coast of Sinai, if Mount Sinai/Horeb be located in the S of that peninsula. Such an application of the name *yam-sûp* to the Gulf of Suez may perhaps be considered as simply an extended use of terminology to include the gulf adjoining the lakes region to the S. (There seems to be no warrant for identifying this *yam-sûp* with the Mediterranean Sea, as this would

The Red Sea.

After dwelling by KADESH BARNEA (Num. 13:26) in the wilderness of Paran (12:16), the Hebrews were commanded to go to the wilderness by the way of the *yam-sûp* (14:25; Deut. 1:40). Thereafter occurred the incident of KORAH, DATHAN, and ABIRAM, who were swallowed up by the earth with their tents (Num. 16), an incident that may have occurred among the mudflats of the Arabah, not so far from the Gulf of Aqabah. Similarly, after the burial of AARON at Mount HOR consequent upon a further sojourn around Kadesh Barnea (20:22—21:3), Israel again went by the way of the *yam-sûp* "to go around Edom" (21:4; cf. Deut. 2:1; Jdg. 11:16), a route that would appear to take them S from Kadesh Barnea to the head of the Gulf of Aqabah as if to go past the southern extremity of Edom and then to by-pass that land northward along its eastern border, and on past MOAB (both nations refusing Israel entry, Num. 20:14-21; Jdg. 11:17).

redeemer. See REDEMPTION.

redemption. A metaphor used in both OT and NT to describe God's merciful and costly action on behalf of his people (sinful human beings). The basic concept is that of release or freedom on payment of a price, deliverance by a costly method. When used of God's action, however, the term does not suggest that he paid a price to anyone, but rather that his mercy required his almighty power and involved the greatest possible depth of suffering. Thus God redeemed ISRAEL from EGYPT by delivering the people from bondage and placing them in a new land (Exod. 6:6; 15:13; Ps. 77:14-15), and he did this by his "mighty hand." See EXODUS.

Two virtually synonymous verbs are used in the OT doctrine of redemption: *gāʾal H1457* and *pādâ H7009*. The basic meaning of the former is fixed in the secular example of BOAZ: NAOMI and RUTH were in need, and it was the right of the next-of-kin to take their needs on himself. The dramatic tension in the book of Ruth centers on the desire of Boaz to play the part of the *gōʾēl* (participle of the verb *gāʾal*), "one who acts as redeemer." When this word group is used of the Lord, it is pervasively with reference to the exodus (cf. Exod. 6:6; 15:3; Ps. 77:15; Isa. 43:1; 51:10-11). The exodus was

bring the Hebrews along the forbidden way of the land of the PHILISTINES. To identify it with the Gulf of Aqabah would probably require a Mount Sinai located in MIDIAN to the E of that Gulf, possible but perhaps improbable because it would take the Hebrews across the howling wilderness of et-Tih instead of the wadis of south-central Sinai.)

III. Gulf of Aqabah. From periods in Hebrew history subsequent to the exodus, it is clear that the term *yam-sûp* could also be applied to the present-day Gulf of AQABAH, along the E coast of the Sinai peninsula. First Kings explicitly locates EZION GEBER—SOLOMON's seaport settlement—beside Eloth (ELATH) on the shore of the *yam-sûp* in the land of EDOM (1 Ki. 9:26), a location which fits the Gulf of Aqabah but neither that of Suez nor of Lake Ballah. Jeremiah 49:21 alludes to the *yam-sûp* in an oracle on Edom, again probably the Gulf of Aqabah. From this basis, one may work back to occasional references in the Pentateuch. Deuteronomy 1:1 locates the words of Moses "in the desert east of the Jordan—that is, in the Arabah—opposite Suph, between Paran and Tophel, Laban, Hazeroth and Dizahab." PARAN is the wilderness in the vicinity of KADESH BARNEA (Num. 10:12; 13:26; et al.), and the ARABAH is the S end of the JORDAN Rift Valley, between the Dead Sea and the Gulf of Aqabah. Hence, SUPH is some place in this vicinity, if it is not merely an abbreviation for *yam-sûp*, the Gulf of Aqabah itself.

R

itself an act of redemption (e.g., Ps. 74:2; 106:10) and a model for such acts, as well as the basis on which appeal is made to the Lord to redeem (Isa. 43:14-16; 48:20; 63:16; Jer. 31:11). Isaiah 43:3 brings to the fore the price-paying concept: at the exodus the Lord redeemed Israel at the expense of Egypt. Since it was a case either that Israel perish at Egypt's hand or that Egypt perish in order that Israel go free, the Lord did not hesitate, nor, says Isaiah, would he ever hesitate to pay whatever price Israel's redemption demanded: *at all costs* he will redeem a people for himself.

The verb *pādâ* is virtually synonymous. In its secular use it is entirely given over to express ransom-price (e.g., Lev. 27:27; Num. 18:15-17; Ps. 49:7). When it is used of the Lord's ransoming work, thirteen out of the thirty-nine references allude to the exodus (e.g., Deut. 9:26; 2 Sam. 7:23; Neh. 1:10). Three references speak specifically of the FORGIVENESS of sins (Deut. 21:8; Ps. 130:8; Isa. 1:27). Insofar, then, as the two verbs cover the same area of meaning, it is that redemption demands the payment of an equivalent price; insofar as they differ, perhaps it can be said that *pādâ* concentrates on price and payment, while *gāʾal* also points with emphasis to the person of the redeemer as the closest of kin.

To appreciate the NT theme of redemption, the position of human beings as slaves of SIN must be assumed (Jn. 8:33-34). Thus they must be set free in order to become the liberated servants of the Lord. "For even the Son of Man did not come to be served, but to serve, and to give his life as a ransom for many" (Mk. 10:45). Here again the use of the metaphor of ransom does not require that the question, "To whom was the ransom paid?" be answered. The emphasis is on costly sacrifice, the giving of a life.

PAUL wrote of "the redemption that came by Christ Jesus" (Rom. 3:24) and claimed that in Christ "we have redemption through his blood" (Eph. 1:7). PETER wrote that "it was not with perishable things ... that you were redeemed ... but with the precious blood of Christ" (1 Pet. 1:18-19; cf. Heb. 9:12, 15; Rev. 5:9-10). This redemption paid for by the costly sacrifice of the life of Jesus is a completed act as far as God is concerned. But the results of the redemption as far as we are con-

cerned are experienced in part now and in full at the beginning of the new age, following the Last Judgment. There is real freedom from the guilt and power of sin now as well as a freedom to love and serve God (Gal. 5:1, 13); but the final freedom from this mortal body and the principle of sin within it will only be known at the resurrection of the dead (Lk. 21:27-28; Rom. 8:23; Eph. 4:30).

reed. See PLANTS; WEIGHTS AND MEASURES.

Reeds, Sea of. See RED SEA.

Reelaiah. ree´uh-lay´uh (Heb. *rĕʿēlāyâ H8305*, derivation uncertain). An Israelite mentioned among leading individuals who returned from BABYLON with ZERUBBABEL (Ezra 2:2; called "Raamiah" in Neh. 7:7).

refiner. See OCCUPATIONS AND PROFESSIONS (under *coppersmith, craftsman, goldsmith, silversmith*).

refuge. This English term, which is especially common in the book of Psalms, is used to render a variety of Hebrew words (Ps. 14:6 et al.). These terms express security from danger, such as is found in a shelter during a storm. God is the shelter of the pious (Ps. 104:18; Isa. 4:6). Some nouns that mean "tower," "stronghold," and so on are used figuratively for "refuge" (e.g., Ps. 9:9). See also CITIES OF REFUGE.

Regem. ree´guhm (Heb. *regem H8084*, perhaps "friend" "voice" [i.e., of God]). Son of Jahdai and apparently a descendant of JUDAH in the line of CALEB (1 Chon 2:47). See comments under JAHDAI.

Regem-Melech. ree´guhm-mee´lik (Heb. *regem melek H8085*, perhaps "friend of the king" or "[the god] Milk has spoken"). TNIV Regem-Melek. An Israelite leader who, with SHAREZER, was sent by the people of BETHEL to the temple priests to inquire regarding the propriety of continuing to fast in commemoration of the destruction of the TEMPLE (Zech. 7:2). There is uncertainty as to whether a personal name or a title ("the king's friend" applied to Sharezer?) is intended. Some scholars emend the text.

R

regeneration. The biblical doctrine of the new birth, referring to a radical spiritual renewal. Though the Greek word *palingenesia G4098* is actually used only twice in the NT (Matt. 19:28 [here referring to the eschatological renewal of the world]; Tit. 3:5), various other passages refer to the same concept. Related expressions are "to be born again" (Jn. 3:3, 5, 7), "to be born of God" (1:13; 1 Jn. 3:9), "to make alive" (Eph. 2:1, 5), and "renewal" (Rom. 12:2; Tit. 3:5).

This *mikveh*, uncovered at the S end of the temple mount, was used for purification rites in Jewish ceremonies. Ceremonial cleansing or washing, a key symbolic act in the ritual of the OT, formed part of the background for the theological idea of regeneration in the NT.

Regeneration is, therefore, the spiritual change wrought in people's hearts by an act of God in which their inherently sinful nature is changed and by which they are enabled to respond to God in FAITH. This definition grows out of the nature of human sinfulness. As long as people are in sin, they cannot believe in God. If they are to believe, they will do so only after God has initiated a change by which they may be released from the bondage of their will to sin. Regeneration is that act of God by which a person is thus released and by which he or she may exercise the dispositions of a freed nature.

Regeneration is, therefore, an act of God through the immediate agency of the HOLY SPIRIT operative in human beings (Col. 2:13), originating in them a new dimension of moral life, a resurrection to new life in Christ. This new life is not merely a neutral state arising out of FORGIVENESS of sin, but a positive implantation of Christ's righteousness by which a sinner is quickened (Jn. 5:21), begotten (1 Jn. 5:1), made a new creation (2 Cor. 5:17), and given a new life (Rom. 6:4).

Regeneration involves an illumination of the mind, a change in the will, and a renewed nature. It extends to the total human nature, irrevocably altering our governing disposition, and restoring us to a true experiential knowledge in Christ. It is a partaking of the divine nature (2 Pet. 1:4), a principle of spiritual life having been implanted in the heart. The efficient cause of regeneration is God himself (1 Jn. 3:9) acting in love through mercy (Eph. 2:4-5) to secure new life in the sinner through the instrument of his Word (1 Pet. 1:23). In regeneration, the soul is both passive and active: passive while it is still in bondage to sin and active when it is released. The regenerating work of the Holy Spirit is not conditioned by a prior acquiescence of the soul, but when the soul is released from sin, regenerated, it voluntarily and spontaneously turns toward God in fellowship.

Rehabiah. ree´huh-bi´uh (Heb. *rĕḥabyâ H8152* and *rĕḥabyāhû H8153*, "Yahweh has made wide" [i.e., has been generous]). Son of ELIEZER, grandson of MOSES, and ancestor of a leading LEVITE family (1 Chr. 23:17; 24:21; 26:25).

Rehob (person). ree´hob (Heb. *rĕḥōb H8150*, possibly related to a root meaning "to be wide"). (1) Father of HADADEZER king of ZOBAH, whom DAVID defeated at the EUPHRATES (2 Sam. 8:3, 12). Some have taken the expression "son of Rehob" to indicate that Hadadezer was from BETH REHOB (cf. 10:6), suggesting that he united this town and Zobah under his rule. See also REHOB (PLACE) #1.

(2) One of the LEVITES who signed the covenant of NEHEMIAH (Neh. 10:11).

Rehob (place). ree´hob (Heb. *rĕḥōb H8149*, "broad place, open plaza"). (1) A town or district at the N end of the JORDAN Valley marking the limit of the journey of the Israelite spies (Num. 13:21). During the reign of DAVID it was one of the ARAMEAN strongholds that sent forces to the aid of AMMON (2 Sam. 10:8; called BETH REHOB in v. 6; cf. Jdg. 18:28). Its exact location is unknown.

© Dr. James C. Martin

R

(2) A town on the N border of ASHER, listed between ABDON and HAMMON (Josh. 19:28). Its location is uncertain, but some identify it with Tell el-Balaṭ, some 12 mi. (19 km.) SE of TYRE; another possibility is Tell el-Raḥb, 4 mi. (6 km.) farther to the SE. Other scholars believe that this Rehob is the same as #3 below.

(3) A town on the S border of Asher, listed after APHEK (Josh. 19:30); it was one of the LEVITICAL CITIES assigned to the descendants of GERSHON (21:31; 1 Chr. 6:75 [Heb. 6:60]). However, the people of Asher were unable to drive the Canaanite inhabitants out of the city (Jdg. 1:31). A town by the name of Rahabu is mentioned beside DOR in a list of RAMSES II, and therefore many believe this Rehob should be located in the southern plain of Acco. It is probably to be identified with Tell el-Bir el-Gharbi (also T. Berweh and T. Bira), some 6 mi. (10 km.) ESE of Acco.

Rehoboam. ree´huh-boh´uhm (Heb. *rĕḥabʿām H8154*, possibly "the people have become extended" or "the [divine] kinsman has been generous"; Gk. *Rhoboam G4850*). KJV NT Roboam. Son of SOLOMON and first king of JUDAH after the division of the kingdom (1 Ki. 11:43—12:27; 14:21—15:6; 2 Chr. 9:31—12:16). Rehoboam's mother was NAAMAH, an Ammonitess (1 Ki. 14:21; see AMMON). He was forty-one when he began to reign (c. 930 B.C.). He chose SHECHEM as the site of his inauguration.

Solomon's wild extravagances and his vain ambition to make ISRAEL the world power of his day had led him to set up a tremendously expensive capital and a very elaborate harem. The importation of so many pagan women for his HAREM resulted in a spiritual debacle in Israel. The luxuries of his palace and the expenses of his diplomatic corps and of his vast building program resulted in burdensome taxation. The northern tribes turned for leadership to JEROBOAM, to whom God had revealed that he was to rule ten of the tribes (1 Ki. 11:26-40). When the coronation had been set, Jeroboam was called home from Egypt, and through him an appeal was made to Rehoboam for easier taxes. The latter, however, heeding the advice of young men, refused to heed the appeal, with the result that Israel rebelled against him. When ADORAM was sent to collect the tribute, he was killed, and Rehoboam

fled to JERUSALEM (12:16-19). Jeroboam was then made king of the ten northern tribes. Rehoboam raised an army from JUDAH and BENJAMIN, but was forbidden by God to attack (12:20-24). Jeroboam then fortified Shechem and Peniel, instituted pagan rites, and waged a relentless struggle against Rehoboam (12:25-28; 14:29-30).

Rehoboam set to work to make his realm strong. Pagan high places were set up and shrines throughout the land allowed abominable practices to be observed among the people (1 Ki. 14:22-24). After being dissuaded from attacking Israel, Rehoboam began to strengthen his land. He fortified BETHLEHEM, GATH, LACHISH, HEBRON, and other cities and made them ready to endure a siege by enemy forces. He gave refuge to priests and Levites whom Jeroboam had driven from Israel, and they brought wisdom and strength to his realm (2 Chr. 11:5-17). The fortified cities were captured by King SHISHAK of Egypt. It is possible that Shishak's invasion resulted from Jeroboam's influence in Egypt, where he had fled to escape Solomon's wrath (1 Ki. 11:40). Inscriptions in the temple at Karnak name 180 towns captured by Shishak, many of them in the northern kingdom.

Rehoboam seems to have inherited his father's love for luxury and show, for he gathered a substantial harem and reared a large family (2 Chr. 11:18-23). He had eighteen wives and sixty concubines. He was not content with fortifying his land but spent large sums on ornate places of worship. When Rehoboam died (c. 913 B.C.), he was succeeded by his son ABIJAH.

Rehoboth. ri-hoh´both (Heb. *rĕḥōbôt H8151*, "broad places"). **(1)** A well dug by ISAAC after his troubles with ABIMELECH and the herdsmen of GERAR (Gen. 26:22). The PHILISTINES had filled in the old well so that Isaac's servants had to dig new ones. But the herdsmen of Gerar claimed the first two for themselves (vv. 20-21). When a third one was uncontested, Isaac named it "Rehoboth," saying, "Now the LORD has given us room and we will flourish in the land" (v. 22). This Rehoboth has often been identified with modern Ruḥaibeh, c. 22 mi. (35 km.) SW of BEERSHEBA, though the narrative suggests a site farther N, between Gerar and Beersheba.

R

(2) The hometown of SHAUL, an early Edomite king (Gen. 36:37; 1 Chr. 1:48). The text names it *rĕḥōbôt hannāhār*, "Rehoboth of the river," and since EUPHRATES is sometimes referred to as "the River" (e.g., Deut. 11:24; Josh. 24:3), the phrase can be translated "Rehoboth on the Euphrates" (cf. NRSV). If this is correct, the place in view may be modern Raḥba, S of the mouth of the Khabur (HABOR), a tributary of the Euphrates in N SYRIA. More likely, however, the site should be looked for in EDOM, in which case the river in question may be Wadi er-Riḥab (just S of the Edom-Moab border), leading to a possible identification of Rehoboth with modern Khirbet ʿAin Riḥab.

Rehoboth Ir. ri-hoh´both-ihr´ (Heb. *rĕḥōbôt ʿîr H8155*, "broad places of the city," i.e., city squares or plazas). A city built by NIMROD in ASSYRIA (Gen. 10:11). Alternatively, it may have been built by ASSHUR, as indicated by the KJV rendering, "Out of that land went forth Asshur, and builded Nineveh, and the city Rehoboth" (cf. also NJPS). Because no such place is known from Assyrian sources, most interpreters believe the reference is to an area within (or in the environs of) NINEVEH. Thus, instead of "Nineveh and Rehoboth Ir," the words should probably be translated, "Nineveh with its city squares" (NIV mg.) or the like. It has also been suggested that *rĕḥōbôt ʿîr* is an epithet, so that the words should possibly be rendered, "Nineveh, the broad [*or* broadest] city," or "Nineveh, the city of open streets."

Rehum. ree´huhm (Heb. *rĕḥûm H8156*, possibly "[God has been] compassionate"). **(1)** An Israelite mentioned among leading individuals who returned from BABYLON with ZERUBBABEL (Ezra 2:2; called NEHUM in Neh. 7:7). See also #4 below. **(2)** A Persian officer who coauthored a letter to King ARTAXERXES opposing the rebuilding of the Jerusalem TEMPLE (Ezra 4:7-16). When a favorable reply came (vv. 17-22), Rehum, Shimshai, and their associates "went immediately to the Jews in Jerusalem and compelled them by force to stop" (v. 23). The NIV refers to him as "commanding officer," but the Aramaic phrase probably indicates a civil rather than military position; some think he may have been the governor of SAMARIA.

(3) Son of Bani; he was in charge of some of the LEVITES who helped NEHEMIAH repair the wall of JERUSALEM (Neh. 3:17). **(4)** One of the leaders of the people who sealed the covenant of Nehemiah (Neh. 10:25). Some connect this Rehum with #1 above. **(5)** One of the priestly leaders who returned with Zerubbabel (Neh. 12:3). Some scholars believe that here the name should be emended to HARIM (cf. v. 15).

Rei. ree´i (Heb. *rēʿî H8298*, possibly "friendly"). One of the supporters of SOLOMON at the time ADONIJAH attempted to secure the throne of DAVID (1 Ki. 1:8). He may have been an officer in the royal guard. Some scholars emend the text to read "Shimei and his friends" (following the Lucianic recension of the SEPTUAGINT).

reins. See KIDNEY.

Rekab, Rekabite. TNIV forms of RECAB, RECABITE.

Rekah. TNIV form of RECAH.

Rekem (person). ree´kuhm (Heb. *reqem H8390*, meaning uncertain). **(1)** One of five kings of MIDIAN killed by the Israelites in a battle on the plains of MOAB (Num. 31:8; Josh. 13:21). See REBA. Some scholars think that the name Rekem may indicate a place rather than (or in addition to) a person, and JOSEPHUS says that it was in fact the ancient name of PETRA in Edomite territory (*Ant.* 4.7.1 §161). **(2)** Son of HEBRON and descendant of JUDAH in the line of CALEB (1 Chr. 2:43-44). **(3)** Son of Peresh (or of Sheresh), grandson of MAKIR, and great-grandson of MANASSEH (1 Chr. 7:16 NRSV, NJPS). The KJV, NIV, and other translations, without good reason, render this name according to its pausal form, "Rakem."

Rekem (place). ree´kuhm (Heb. *reqem H8389*, meaning uncertain). A town within the tribal territory of BENJAMIN (Josh. 18:27). It was probably a short distance NW of JERUSALEM, but its location is unknown. This town is to be distinguished from Rekem in EDOM; see REKEM (PERSON) #1.

R

religion. The Latin verb *religare* means "to hold back, restrain." It came to be applied to the services and ritual and rules by which faith in and devotion to deity were expressed. In the OT there is no word that corresponds precisely to English "religion." FEAR (Ps. 2:11; Prov. 1:7) and WORSHIP (Deut. 4:19; 29:26; Ps. 5:7; 29:2) of God refer primarily to attitudes of the mind and acts of adoration, rather than to a ritual. In the NT, "religion" renders Greek *thrēskeia G2579* (adj. *thrēskos G2580*, "religious"), referring to the outward expression as well as the content of faith. JAMES makes a distinction between the sham and the reality of religious expression (Jas. 1:26-27). PAUL was loyal to his Hebrew religion before being converted (Acts 26:1-5). The KJV uses "the Jews' religion" for Greek *Ioudaismos G2682*, "Judaism" (Gal. 1:13-14), and "religious" for a word better rendered "devout" (middle ptc. of *sebō G4936*, Acts 13:43).

Remaliah. rem´uh-li´uh (Heb. *rĕmalyāhû H8248*, perhaps "Yahweh has adorned" or "Yahweh, be exalted!"). Father of PEKAH, who was one of the last kings of Israel (2 Ki. 15:25 et al.).

Remeth. ree´mith (Heb. *remet H8255*, possibly variant of *rā'môt H8030*, "heights"). A border town in the tribal territory of ISSACHAR (Josh. 19:21). It is probably identical with Ramoth (1 Chr. 6:73) and Jarmuth (Josh. 21:29). See RAMOTH (PLACE) #3.

remission (of sins). See FORGIVENESS.

Remmon. Remmon. See RIMMON (PLACE) #1.

Remmon-methoar. See RIMMON (PLACE) #2.

remnant. The common notion of "something left over" occurs in the Bible with some frequency in a variety of contexts, including its application to political divisions and social groupings within Israel (e.g., "the rest of the populace" who were left in the city of Jerusalem after the capture of the city by NEBUCHADNEZZAR, 2 Ki. 25:11). The shift from these uses to the theological meaning is easy to understand. Such a concept is of prime interest. The judgment of God upon a remnant, or, contrariwise, the manifestation of grace to them,

shows how history and theology are intertwined. An example of a pertinent text is Mic. 5:3, which states: "Therefore Israel will be abandoned / until the time when she who is in labor gives birth / and the rest [Heb. *yeter H3856*] of his brothers return / to join the Israelites." Thus the term came to be applied specifically to the spiritual kernel of the nation who would survive God's judgment and become the germ of the new people of God. Thus MICAH saw the returning glory of Israel (Mic. 2:12; 5:7). ZEPHANIAH saw the triumph of this remnant (Zeph. 2:4-7), and so did ZECHARIAH (Zech. 8:1-8). Isaiah named a son SHEAR-JASHUB, which means "a remnant returns" (Isa. 7:3). The apostle PAUL highlighted this concept to explain that the true Israel consists of those who believe (Rom. 9:23-30; 11:5).

Remphan. See REPHAN.

rending of garments. See MOURNING.

repentance. The act or process of changing one's mind, of turning the course of one's life (esp. toward God) is encountered repeatedly in both OT and NT. It is expressed in Hebrew primarily by the verbs *nāḥam H5714* (niphal), "to regret, be sorry," and *šûb H8740*, "to return." In Greek it is represented almost always by the verb *metanoeō G3566*, "to change one's mind," and its cognate noun *metanoia G3567*. In the KJV OT, God himself is described as repenting (Exod. 32:14; 1 Sam. 15:11; Jon. 3:9-10; 4:2), but in the sense that he changed his attitude toward people because of a change within the people. God as perfect Deity does not change in his essential nature; but because he is in relationship with people who do change, he himself changes his relation and attitude from WRATH to MERCY and from blessing to judgment, as the occasion requires. There is of course no suggestion of change from worse to better or bad to good. In contrast, human repentance is a change for the better and is a conscious turning from evil or disobedience or sin or idolatry to the living God (2 Ki. 17:13; Isa. 19:22; Jer. 3:12, 14, 22; Jon. 3:10).

In the NT repentance and FAITH are the two sides of one coin (Acts 20:21). They are a response to GRACE. Jesus preached the need for the Jews to repent (Matt. 4:17), and required his apostles/disciples to preach repentance to Jews and Gentiles (Lk. 24:47; Acts 2:38; 17:30). Repentance is a profound change of mind involving the changing of the direction of life from that of self-centeredness or sin-centeredness to God- or Christ-centeredness. God's forgiveness is available only to those who are repentant, for only they can receive it. The positive side of repentance is CONVERSION, the actual turning to God for grace.

Rephael. ref´ay-uhl (Heb. *rĕpā´ēl H8330*, "God has healed"). Son of Shemaiah, grandson of OBED-EDOM, and a gatekeeper from the Korahites (1 Chr. 26:7; cf. v. 1). See KORAH. Rephael and his brothers are described as "leaders in their father's family because they were very capable men" (v. 6).

Rephah. ree´fuh (Heb. *repaḥ H8338*, perhaps "abundance"). Son (or descendant) of EPHRAIM (1 Chr. 7:25). His precise place in the genealogy is not clear, and the name Rephah does not occur in the parallel list (Num. 26:35-36).

Rephaiah. ri-fay´yuh (Heb. *rĕpāyâ H8341*, "Yahweh has healed"). **(1)** A descendant of DAVID through JEHOIACHIN and ZERUBBABEL (1 Chr. 3:21). The Hebrew text is difficult. Some believe that Rephaiah

was the son of Hananiah; others, the son of Jeshaiah (cf. NRSV and NJPS, following the LXX).

(2) Son of Ishi and descendant of SIMEON during the reign of HEZEKIAH; Rephaiah and his brothers led 500 Simeonites in an invasion of "the hill country of Seir" (1 Chr. 4:42).

(3) Son of Tola and grandson of ISSACHAR, described as head of family (1 Chr. 7:2).

(4) Son of Binea and descendant of King SAUL through JONATHAN (1 Chr. 9:43); the shorter form RAPHAH is used in the parallel genealogy (9:43).

(5) Son of Hur; he ruled "a half-district of Jerusalem" and was in charge of repairing a section of the city wall near the BROAD WALL (Neh. 3:9).

Rephaim. See REPHAITES.

Rephaim, Valley of. ref´ay-im (Heb. *rĕpā´îm H8329*; for meaning, see REPHAITE). A basin SW of JERUSALEM whose N end marked the N boundary of the tribe of JUDAH and the S boundary of the tribe of BENJAMIN (Josh. 15:8; 18:16). This area is today called simply the *Baqʿa* or "valley" and constitutes a suburb of Jerusalem. After DAVID captured Jerusalem and the PHILISTINES heard about his being anointed king, they camped in the Valley of Rephaim anticipating an attack on the new capital of Israel (2 Sam. 5:17-21). David took up

General view of the Valley of Rephaim (looking SW). David defended his kingship against the Philistines who came up this valley twice after the death of King Saul.

© Dr. James C. Martin

the challenge and defeated the Philistines at BAAL PERAZIM. The Philistines prepared a second attack, but this time David routed them with an attack from the E on their rear guard (2 Sam. 5:22-25; the account of these two episodes is expanded in 1 Chr. 11:15-19 and 14:10-17). The seventh and last mention of the Valley of Rephaim is in Isa. 17:5. The Bible records no reason that this valley should be named after the early inhabitants of CANAAN whom the Israelites thought to be GIANTS (cf. Gen. 14:5; 15:20; Josh. 17:15). One can only guess that the people called "Rephaim" (REPHAITES) lived in the vicinity of this valley.

Rephaites. ref′ay-*i*ts (Heb. *rěpā'îm H8328*, often with the definite article, meaning possibly "the healers" or "the weak"). The Hebrew form *rěpā'îm*, evidently the plural of *rāpā'* or perhaps *rāpâ* (see RAPHA #3), is transliterated by the KJV as "Rephaim" when it refers to the valley of that name (see REPHAIM, VALLEY OF) but as the superfluous plural "Rephaims" on two occasions (Gen. 14:5; 15:20); elsewhere, the KJV translates "giants." The NRSV and other versions transliterate "Rephaim" throughout. The NIV uses the more natural English form "Rephaites" when the term designates a people group, but preserves "Rephaim" when the reference is to the valley.

There is a term that has the same form (*rěpā'îm H8327*, possibly "shades") but that probably should be regarded as a distinct word (these terms may be related, though the etymology is disputed). This second word denotes the inhabitants of the netherworld in the OT (esp. in poetic and wisdom literature) and in some extrabiblical texts. The most that can be said with certainty about this use of *Rephaim* is that the Israelites applied the term to people who were dead and gone (cf. Ps. 88:10; Prov. 2:18; Isa. 26:14; et al.).

Whatever the connection between these terms, the people group known as Rephaites were inhabitants of TRANSJORDAN in pre-Israelite times. The Moabites called them EMITES, while the Ammonites referred to them as ZAMZUMMITES (Deut. 2:11, 20). They were subdued by KEDORLAOMER c. 2000 B.C. in ASHTEROTH KARNAIM (Gen. 14:5). The Rephaites were one of ten ethnic groups whose lands God promised to ABRAHAM (Gen. 15:20).

This promise, apparently, was later qualified to exclude that portion of their land that had been taken over by MOAB and AMMON (Deut. 2:9-12, 19-21), and thus it came to designate specifically the Rephaite holdings in GILEAD and the whole of Bashan (Deut. 3:13), but also the forest of Ephraim (Josh. 17:15). OG, king of Bashan, who reigned in Ashtaroth and Edrei and who was defeated by MOSES, was the last survivor of the remnant of the Rephaites (Josh. 12:4; 13:12).

According to Deut. 2:10-11, the Rephaites were "strong and numerous, and as tall as the Anakites" (see ANAK). The name is also applied to GIANTS among the PHILISTINES who fought against DAVID and his mighty warriors along their disputed border at both GEZER (1 Chr. 20:4) and GATH (vv. 6, 8). In the latter two verses (as in 2 Sam. 21:16-22), they are described as descendants of "the Raphah" (so NJPS; the NIV has "Rapha"; KJV, "the giant"; NRSV, "the giants"). The relationship between the ethnic Rephaites and these Philistine warriors is debated; perhaps the latter were not precisely "descendants" but rather "devotees" of a deity named Rapha.

Rephan. ref′uhn (Gk. *Rhaiphan G4818*, variants *Rhemphan, Rhompham*, etc., meaning uncertain). KJV Remphan; NASB Rompha. The name of an astral deity mentioned in Acts 7:43, which cites the SEPTUAGINT translation of Amos 5:26. In the latter, the MT has *kiyyûn H3962*, which may represent the Akkadian word *kayamānu*, a term applied to Saturn (see KAIWAN). Some have speculated that the Hebrew scribes substituted the vowels of *šiqqûṣ H9199* ("a detested thing") for those of the Akkadian word to reflect the detestability of the pagan god. How the LXX came to have the unexpected *Rhaiphan* is uncertain. It may be the result of a mistaken transliteration of the Hebrew or it may be a form of Repa, a late Egyptian name for the god of the planet Saturn.

Rephidim. ref′i-dim (Heb. *rěpîdim H8340*, prob. "camping [places]"). A stop in the wilderness wanderings of the Israelites (Exod. 17:1, 8; 19:2; Num. 33:14-15). On the basis of the traditional Mount SINAI, near the S end of the peninsula formed by the gulfs of Suez and Aqabah, Rephidim might be

R

the Wadi Feiran (cf. PARAN) or the Wadi Rufaid. At Rephidim the Israelites rebelled against MOSES because there was no water to drink. God instructed Moses to strike the rock. He did, and water came forth (v. 6). Because of the attitude of the people, Moses named the place MASSAH and MERIBAH, meaning "testing" and "contention" (17:7). It was also at Rephidim that AMALEK fought with Israel (Exod. 17:8-15).

reprobate. This adjective, meaning "corrupt" or "depraved," is seldom if ever used in modern Bible versions. The KJV uses it once in the OT (but in the archaic sense "rejected," with reference to silver, Jer. 6:30), and three times in the NT (Rom. 1:28; 2 Tim. 3:8; Tit. 1:16); the noun "reprobates" occurs three times in one passage (2 Cor. 13:5-7). In all the NT passages, the Greek word is *adokimos G99* (which also appears in 1 Cor. 9:27 and Heb. 6:8, the latter passage referring to "worthless" land). Its basic meaning seems to be "not standing the test, and so rejected."

reptile. See ANIMALS.

Resen. ree´suhn (Heb. *resen H8271*, possibly from Assyrian *rēš ēni*, "head of spring"). A city in ASSYRIA said to have been "between Nineveh and Calah" and to have been built by NIMROD (Gen. 10:11-12; the Hebrew text can be understood to mean that the builder was ASSHUR [cf. KJV and NJPS]). It is unclear whether the description "that is the great city" (v. 12b) refers to Resen, or to NINEVEH, or (most likely) to CALAH. No city of suitable prominence has been identified in this area, and some scholars have thought Resen corresponds to one of several Assyrian places referred to as Resh-eni ("fountain head"). Others have identified Resen with modern Selamiyeh, less than 3 mi. (5 km.) NW of Nimrud, which seems more plausible. Still others consider Resen not a place name as such, but rather a parenthetical description of some impressive water installation or military construction.

reservoir. A place for the storage of WATER. This English term is used occasionally by modern versions (e.g., Isa. 22:11). The general climate of PALESTINE made it necessary to devise ways of pre-serving the water supply through the dry months from May through September. The rocky terrain provided convenient opportunity for water storage with minimal effort. The rain or spring water was channeled into these storage facilities (see CISTERN), and with care it could be kept palatable for a considerable time. An adequate supply of water was vital at all times, especially during siege (cf. 2 Chr. 32:3, 4). See also POOL.

resh. reysh (from late Heb. *rêš*, "head"). The twentieth letter of the Hebrew alphabet (ר), with a numerical value of 200. It is named for the shape of the letter, which in its older form resembled a human head. Its sound corresponds roughly to that of English *r*, although in some traditions it has a uvular pronunciation.

Resheph (deity). ree´shif. Also Rashaph, Rasaph. A deity worshiped through most of the ANE and associated with pestilence, death, and the underworld. The very ancient documents discovered in EBLA show that Resheph was a prominent deity as early as the third millennium B.C., for one of the city gates was given his name. Much pertinent information comes from EGYPT, where Rephesh was a minor deity related to war and healing. In Ugarit (RAS SHAMRA), Resheph was more prominent and was represented both as a god of plague and as a benevolent deity. The Hebrew word *rešep H8404*, meaning "flame" or the like (Job 5:7; Ps. 76:3; 78:48; Cant. 8:6), and possibly by extension "pestilence" (Deut. 32:24; Hab. 3:5), possibly derives from the name of this god.

Resheph (person). ree´shif (Heb. *rešep H8405*, possibly "flame"). Son of Rephah and descendant of EPHRAIM (1 Chr. 7:25). The MT (lit., "and Rephah his son and Resheph and Telah his son") could be interpreted to mean that both Rephah and Resheph were sons of BERIAH, the son of Ephraim (vv. 23-24), but most modern versions insert "his son" after "Resheph" (following a few Heb. MSS and the Lucianic recension of the LXX). In any case, the specific connection of the names in v. 25 to the Ephraimite genealogy is unclear.

resin, gum resin. See PLANTS.

rest. A word of frequent occurrence in the Bible, in both Testaments. It is used of God, who "rested from all his work" (Gen. 2:2). God commanded that the seventh day, the SABBATH, was to be one of rest (Exod. 16:23; 31:15) and that the land was to have its rest every seventh year (Lev. 25:4). God promised rest to the Israelites in the land of Canaan (Deut. 12:9). The word is sometimes used in the sense of trust and reliance (2 Chr. 14:11). Christ offers rest of soul to those who come to him (Matt. 11:28). Hebrews 4 says that God offers to his people a rest not enjoyed by those who died in the wilderness.

restoration. The act of bringing back to a former state. This term is especially applied to the period of Hebrew history following the EXILE. The time covered by the restoration of the Israelites may be said to begin about 515 B.C. and end with the time of MALACHI, about 450 B.C. Once the edict of CYRUS, proclaimed in 538, had given official permission for expatriate groups in BABYLON to return to their homelands and renew the pattern of their former ways of life, those members of the captive Jewish population who had caught the vision of a new existence in JUDEA along theocratic lines, as indicated by EZEKIEL, were not slow to begin the arduous journey back to the desolated homeland. As the prophecies of HAGGAI and ZECHARIAH make plain, the initial enthusiasm which the returned exiles had manifested for the rebuilding of the ruined TEMPLE became dissipated at a comparatively early period. The most that the inhabitants of Jerusalem were apparently willing or able to do was the reconstruction of their own houses in the city. However, the situation was remedied by the timely intervention of Haggai and Zechariah in the year 520, and five years later the successor to the temple of Solomon was dedicated amid scenes of great rejoicing.

resurrection. The divine miracle of restoring a deceased person to life in BODY and SOUL, either to temporal life, as was the case with LAZARUS (Jn. 11), or more properly to eternal, glorified life, to which CHRIST was raised and to which those who are his will be raised at his return. Scripture also teaches a resurrection to eternal punishment in body and soul of those who lived and died without Christ (Matt. 10:28; Jn. 5:28-29; Acts 24:15; see ESCHATOLOGY). When the word *resurrection* is qualified, as a rule the expression "the resurrection of [*or* from] the dead" is used (Matt. 22:31; Lk. 20:37; Acts 4:2; 17:32; 23:6; 24:21; 26:23; 1 Cor. 15:12-13). The resurrection of believers is sometimes called "the resurrection of the righteous" (Lk. 14:14; Acts 24:15) or "the resurrection of life" (Jn. 5:29 NRSV); that of the unbelievers, "the resurrection of condemnation" (Jn. 5:29 NRSV) or "of the unrighteous" (Acts 24:15 NRSV). The expression "resurrection of the body," frequently used in the church creeds, is based on Scripture (cf. Matt. 27:52; Rom. 8:11; 1 Cor. 15:35, 42-44; Phil. 3:21). The Bible does not speak of an abstract "immortality of the soul," but rather of the REDEMPTION of human beings in their whole complex personality, both body and soul.

In the OT the most explicit passage on the resurrection is Dan. 12:2, which clearly predicts the resurrection and eternal judgment of those who have died. Almost equally explicit is Isa. 26:19. In its context, this verse is parallel to vv. 11-15. In them the voice of God's people is heard, repeating his promises and looking forward to their fulfillment; in v. 19 the voice of the Lord responds, affirming the hope that lies before his distressed people, confirming the conviction that they will rise again. The reference to "dew" is added by way of explanation: dew had a wide metaphorical use, picturing the heavenly contribution to earthly well-being. The dead wait in the dust until God's life-giving, reviving dew falls on them and brings them to life. Again, Isa. 25:8 is explicit in its affirmation that in the DAY OF THE LORD, even DEATH itself will disappear to be seen no more. The meaning of Job 19:23-27 is much disputed and the Hebrew text is not at all easy to translate, yet a case can undoubtedly be made out for an interpretative translation along the following lines: "Though, after my skin (i.e., my present life, wasting away with disease), they destroy this (body), yet from (the vantage point of) my flesh I shall see God."

In the PROVIDENCE of God, revelation is a matter of progress rather than full clarity all at once. The Lord educated his people from truth to truth, as any careful teacher does. Each age was given sufficient light for its own needs so as to enjoy spiritual life and fellowship with God. The full revelation of immortality awaited the advent of our Lord and Savior who "brought life and immortality to light through the gospel" (2 Tim. 1:10).

In the NT the word for "resurrection," *anastasis* G414, signifies the arising to life of a dead body. In secular Greek the word may refer to any act of rising up or sitting up; but the theological interpretation of the word in the NT does not depend only on its literal meaning but also on the contexts in which it is found. The doctrine of resurrection is stated clearly in its simplest form in PAUL's words before the Roman law court presided over by FELIX: "There will be a resurrection of both the righteous and the wicked" (Acts 24:15). The most detailed statement of the doctrine of twofold resurrection is found in Rev. 20:4-15.

In the words of Jesus, the only clear allusion to a twofold resurrection is found in Jn. 5:25, 28-29. It must be remembered that John shares the cosmic perspective according to which the eschatological complex began with the INCARNATION (see 1 Jn. 2:18). In Jn. 5:25 Jesus refers to the fact that he "now" exercises his power to raise the dead selectively, "those who hear will live." (Compare the resurrection of LAZARUS, Jn. 11, and of the son of the widow of NAIN, Lk. 7:11-17, as well as Matt. 27:50-53.) John 5:28-29 refers to the future and alludes to the distinction made in Dan. 12:2, which John develops in Rev. 20:4-15.

Some see in 1 Thess. 4:16-17 an implication that the dead who are not "in Christ" will not be raised at the same time as the redeemed. This is possibly also the implication of 1 Cor. 15:20-28. John 5:28-29 bases the resurrection of the dead firmly on the power of Christ as exhibited in his own resurrection (see RESURRECTION OF JESUS CHRIST), and states the substance of the later pronouncement before Felix (Acts 24:15). By the power of Christ all the dead will be raised.

With 1 Cor. 15:23-24 Paul gives an enumeration of three "orders" of resurrection, one of which, the resurrection of Christ, is past. (1) Christ the firstfruits. (2) "Those who belong to him." This second "order" of resurrection is said to take place "when he comes." (3) "Then the end will come." The "end" in this context follows the resurrection of those who are Christ's. It includes the time

when Christ "reigns" and subdues all his enemies. The last enemy, death itself, is to be subdued. This must be regarded as taking place when all the rest of the dead without exception stand before the Great White Throne (Rev. 20:12-15). This final subduing of death is Paul's third "order" of resurrection. Since Paul's first "order" is the resurrection of Christ, it is obvious that Paul's second and third "orders" of resurrection coincide with John's future "first resurrection" and his resurrection of "the rest of the dead" (Rev. 20:4-15).

resurrection of Jesus Christ. Although no one was present at the moment of the resurrection of Jesus of Nazareth, the disciples witnessed the appearance of the resurrected Jesus, and they also saw the empty tomb. In the NT there are six accounts of these events. Each of the four Gospels contains an account (Matt. 28; Mk. 16; Lk. 24; Jn. 20-21), and there are two others (Acts 1:1-11; 1 Cor. 15:1-11).

I. The narratives. The brief accounts of the resurrection appearances contrast with the lengthy narratives of the passion and death of Jesus. The reason for this is as follows. Concerning the death of Jesus, Jews asked, "How could Jesus be the true Messiah and die on a cross when the law of Moses teaches that to die such a death is to be under God's curse?" And Gentiles asked, "If Jesus was the true King of the Jews, why was he rejected by his own people?" Thus long accounts were necessary to provide answers. But the questions concerning the resurrection were basically concerning proof. So the six accounts provide the testimony of eyewitnesses who claimed to have seen not only the empty tomb but also the resurrected Jesus. There was no need for lengthy descriptions.

II. Within and beyond history. On the basis of the NT, Christians usually make two parallel claims concerning the resurrection of Jesus. First, it was a definite historical event and as such is open to historical investigation. Second, it was more than a historical event, for it involved a major dimension that is not open to historical investigation. The evidence for the Resurrection as an event within history may be listed as follows:

(1) *The tomb of Jesus found empty some thirty-six hours after his burial.* Despite efforts by Jews

to prove that the body was stolen and buried elsewhere, the body was never located or produced by those who allegedly stole it or by anyone else. Further, the suggestion that Jesus only swooned on the cross and then revived in the cool tomb is impossible to substantiate.

(2) *The disciples claiming that Jesus actually appeared.* They saw Jesus when they were fully

Tombs (*kokhim*) at the Church of the Holy Sepulchre in Jerusalem. The resurrection of Jesus occurred in the newly hewn tomb of Joseph of Arimathea.

awake and when they doubted that he was alive. What they saw was neither a subjective vision (in their imagination, a kind of hallucination) nor an objective vision (provided by God to show that the true and essential *spirit* of Jesus was alive). They actually saw Jesus on earth; they were witnesses of resurrection.

(3) *The sober nature of the narratives describing the resurrection appearances.* There is no attempt to describe the resurrection itself, and there is no obvious collusion between the various writers to doctor or adorn their material. The most amazing event in human history is described with reverential reserve.

(4) *The transformation of the disciples and the existence of the church.* Men who were cowards became fearless preachers and founded the church for one reason and one alone—they believed with all their hearts that Jesus had risen from the dead and was alive forevermore. And when they preached the GOSPEL that Jesus who was crucified now lives as

Lord and Savior, they saw lives changed by that living Lord.

In modern times there has been a readiness within the church to discount or hold loosely to the fact of the resurrection of Jesus as an event within history. This tendency must be resisted, for if his resurrection is not an event within history (within the same physical universe and space and time in which we live), then what the NT claims that God accomplished in Jesus Christ on the cross for SALVATION is not applicable to us in history. The bodily resurrection of Jesus (as Paul insists in 1 Cor. 15) is of fundamental importance and cannot be ignored or set aside.

As a real event in history, the resurrection cannot, however, be wholly explained in terms of historical causation. There is both continuity and discontinuity with history. The continuity is seen in the kind of information listed above as evidence. The discontinuity is in terms of what the believing church receives and accepts concerning that resurrection: that it is the disclosure of the KINGDOM OF GOD; that it is the incursion of the new creation into the old creation; and that it is the foundation of a new humanity in Jesus, the second and last ADAM. These "theological truths" are beyond historical investigation, for they are claims that can be verified only at the end of the age.

III. What kind of body? There were both differences and similarities in the pre- and postresurrection body of Jesus. Yet there was a basic identity so that one may speak of "identity-in-transformation." For Jesus, bodily resurrection meant resuscitation with transformation—that is, not only resuscitation (as with Lazarus in Jn. 11), but also the metamorphosis of the body so that what was a mortal body became a spiritual and immortal body, transformed by the power of God, Creator of life and bodies. Apart from isolated incidents (e.g., walking on the water), the pre-Easter Jesus was subject to material, physical, and spatial

R

limitations. He walked from one place to another, passed through doors to enter rooms, and climbed steps to get onto the roofs of houses. Yet after his resurrection he was no longer bound by these limitations. He passed through a sealed tomb, through locked doors, and appeared and disappeared without notice. He became visible here and there and from time to time. This suggests that his true or essential state as a transformed person was that of invisibility and immateriality, with the ability to be localized at will.

IV. A theology of resurrection. There are various ways of stating a theology of resurrection, but perhaps that which best reflects the NT evidence is the theme of vindication.

(1) *God raised Jesus from the dead and thereby vindicated him as the true Messiah.* The manner of Jesus' death gave the impression that God had rejected him, for to hang on a tree was to be under the divine curse (Deut. 21:23; Gal. 3:13). In resurrection, Jesus was vindicated. He was no longer implicitly claiming to be the MESSIAH by his teaching and deeds: he was now demonstrated to be Messiah in fact and in truth. PETER, over a year before the crucifixion, had asserted, "You are the Christ" (Matt. 16:16), and fifty days after the resurrection he told the crowd in Jerusalem: "Therefore, let all Israel be assured of this: God has made this Jesus, whom you crucified, both Lord and Christ" (Acts 2:36). Later, by means of a quotation from Ps. 118, Peter explained to the Jewish leaders the vindication of Jesus; he claimed that Jesus is "the stone you builders rejected, which has become the capstone" (Acts 4:11). Then PAUL wrote that Jesus "as to his human nature was a descendant of David, and who through the Spirit of holiness was declared with power to be the Son of God by his resurrection from the dead" (Rom. 1:3-4); Jesus was always SON OF GOD, but the resurrection was the actual vindication of this Sonship (however, see the TNIV rendering).

(2) *God raised Jesus from the dead and thereby vindicated his teaching and work of atonement.* The resurrection is God's "Amen" to the cry of Jesus, "It is finished." The resurrection is God's "Yes" to the ministry and teaching of Jesus. Jesus was "delivered over to death for our sins and was raised to life for our justification" (Rom. 4:25). In the light of the resurrection Paul could "boast ... in the cross of our Lord Jesus Christ" (Gal. 6:14) because it revealed the eternal love of God for human sinners.

(3) *God caused the new age to dawn in the resurrection.* With the raising of Jesus from death and the transformation of his body, there began a new order of existence. What belongs to the future kingdom of God, the glorious age to come, has made its appearance in this present evil age. Paul deliberately spoke of the resurrected Jesus as the FIRSTFRUITS of the harvest of the age to come (1 Cor. 15:20, 23).

In the NT the theology of the resurrection cannot be separated from the theology of the ASCENSION or the theology of EXALTATION. Often in the NT the word *resurrection* includes the idea of ascension, while the word *exaltation* takes in both resurrection and ascension.

retribution. The act of paying back to someone according to that person's just deserts. Retribution is usually, although not exclusively, considered in terms of punishment for wrongdoing. In systematic theology, the distinction is sometimes made between God's *remunerative justice*, in which he distributes REWARDS, and his *retributive justice*, in which he expresses his hatred of sin by inflicting penalties. The word *retribution* is not found in Scripture, but the idea is expressed in reference to the divine WRATH, vengeance, punishment, and judgment when God "will give to each person according to what he has done" (Rom. 2:6). The concept reminds us not to misinterpret the GRACE of the GOSPEL in such a way that we overlook God's judgment on the impenitent sinner (1:18). Retribution is the natural outcome of SIN (Gal. 6:7-8), the thought of which was reflected in JOHN THE BAPTIST's warning to "flee from the coming wrath" (Matt. 3:7; Lk. 3:7; cf. 1 Thess. 1:10). One of the NT's most terrible references is to "the wrath of the Lamb" (Rev. 6:16).

return of Christ. See ESCHATOLOGY.

Reu. ree´yoo (Heb. *rĕʿû H8293*, possibly short form of REUEL, "friend of God"; Gk. *Rhagau G4814*). Son of PELEG and descendant of SHEM (Gen. 11:18-21; 1 Chr. 1:25); included in Luke's GENEALOGY OF JESUS CHRIST (Lk. 3:35; KJV, "Ragau").

R

Reuben. roo′bin (Heb. *rĕʾûbēn H8017*, "See! A son!"; gentilic *rĕʾûbēni H8018*, "Reubenite"; Gk. *Rhoubēn G4857*). Firstborn son of JACOB and LEAH; the name is also applied to the Israelite tribe that descended from him. According to the biblical text, Jacob loved RACHEL more than Leah, but "the LORD saw that Leah was not loved," and thus "he opened her womb" (Gen. 29:30-31). When her son was born, she named him Reuben "because the LORD has seen [*rāʾâ*] my misery [*bĕʿonyî*]" (v. 32; thus her explanation involves a wordplay). Nothing is known about Reuben's early life, except that on one occasion he brought his mother mandrakes, which she used in getting Jacob to give her another son (30:14-15). As an adult, Reuben committed incest at Eder (35:22), and because of this sin Jacob later predicted, "Turbulent as the waters, you will no longer excel" (49:4). He delivered JOSEPH from death by warning his brothers (37:19-22; 42:22) and later offered his sons as surety for BENJAMIN (42:37). He took four sons into Egypt (46:9).

Some centuries later, when ISRAEL went out from Egypt, his tribe numbered 46,500 men of military age (Num. 1:21; 2:10); near the end of the wilderness wanderings, the number was 43,730 (26:7). The Reubenites made a covenant with MOSES in order to occupy the rich grazing lands of GILEAD (32:1-33). That they kept the covenant is

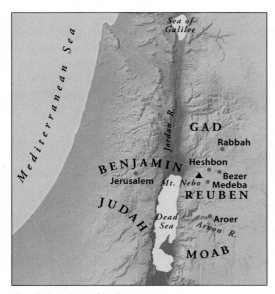

The tribal territory of Reuben.

attested by the monument to BOHAN, a descendant of Reuben (Josh. 15:6). When the other tribes were settled in Canaan, Reuben, along with GAD and half of MANASSEH, returned to Gilead and set up a great monument as a reminder of the unity of the Israelites (Josh. 22). In protecting their flocks against marauding nomads they became a bold and skilled warlike people (1 Chr. 5:1-19). Along with Gad and the half-tribe of Manasseh, they sent 120,000 men to support King DAVID (12:37). During JEHU's reign, these tribes were oppressed by HAZAEL (2 Ki. 10:32-33). Because of their unfaithfulness, they were eventually taken into captivity by TIGLATH-PILESER of ASSYRIA (1 Chr. 5:25-26).

Reuel. roo′uhl (Heb. *rĕʿûʾēl H8294*, "friend of God"). KJV also Raguel (only Num. 10:29). **(1)** Son of ESAU by BASEMATH daughter of ISHMAEL (Gen. 36:3-4, 10; 1 Chr. 1:35). His four sons became clan chiefs in EDOM (Gen. 36:13, 17; 1 Chr. 1:37).

(2) Priest of MIDIAN and father-in-law of MOSES (Exod. 2:18; Num. 10:29), usually referred to as JETHRO (see separate article). Some scholars connect the use of the name Reuel with the Edomite tribe (above, #1).

(3) Father of ELIASAPH; at the time of the census in SINAI, Eliasaph was appointed leader of the tribe of GAD (Num. 2:14 KJV and most versions, following MT). Instead of Reuel, the NIV reads DEUEL because that is the form used in every other reference to this individual (Heb. *dĕʿûʾēl H1979*, Num. 1:14; 7:42, 47; 10:20). The difference no doubt resulted from the common scribal error of confusing the consonants *d* and *r*, which look very similar in Hebrew. The SEPTUAGINT reads *Ragouēl* in all five passages, and on that basis some scholars argue that Reuel is the original form.

(4) Son of Ibnijah, descendant of BENJAMIN, and ancestor of Meshullam; the latter is listed among the Benjamites who resettled in JERUSALEM (1 Chr. 9:8).

Reumah. roo′muh (Heb. *rĕʾûmâ H8020*, derivation uncertain). The concubine of NAHOR, brother of ABRAHAM (Gen. 22:24). Her four sons probably became ancestors of ARAMEAN tribes who lived in the environs of DAMASCUS.

revelation. In Christian theology, this term refers to God's disclosure of himself in nature (general revelation) and in Scripture (special revelation). The phrase *general revelation*, which includes CREATION, CONSCIENCE, and HISTORY, focuses on the fact that God exists and must be honored as sovereign—a truth that is known, and has always been known, by all human beings everywhere, rendering them without excuse when they ignore him and do what is evil (Ps. 19:1-6 [cf. 14:1]; Rom. 1:18-20). *Special revelation* focuses on SALVATION—truths about SIN, GRACE, ATONEMENT, FAITH, and so on; these were disclosed in both word (verbal communication) and deed (redemptive history) to the chosen line of ABRAHAM and then more extensively through the GOSPEL. To call the BIBLE the Word of God is to claim that it is the unique and faithful statement of God's self-revelation to human beings. When used in this way, it usually is coordinated with the concept of INSPIRATION (the work of the HOLY SPIRIT in guiding the writers of the Bible to put down what God wanted them to write). The equation of the Bible with revelation derives from such texts as Jn. 10:34-35; 2 Tim. 3:15-16; Heb. 3:7-11; 2 Pet. 1:19-21. Revelation may also be studied, however, as an actual theme within the Bible by noticing how the cluster of words that convey the idea of God's self-disclosure in word and deed are used. This article will deal with the latter theme.

The common Hebrew verb *gālâ H1655* ("to uncover") is frequently used of God's self-disclosure (Gen. 35:7 et al.). In the Greek NT such words as the noun *apokalypsis G637* ("unveiling, disclosure") and the verbs *apokalyptō G636* ("to disclose, bring to light") and *phaneroō G5746* ("to show, make known") are often employed in a strong theological sense. These and other terms convey the whole spectrum of ways and means through which God discloses himself, his will, and his purposes to his people. And God reveals himself in order that his people might know, love, trust, serve, and obey him as Lord.

At the center of God's self-unveiling or revelation is Jesus, the MESSIAH and Incarnate Son. In the past God spoke to the patriarchs and prophets in many and varied ways, but his complete and final word is given in and through Jesus, the LOGOS (Jn. 1:1; Heb. 1:1). The presence, words, deeds, and exaltation of Jesus constitute revelation. He is the Light for rev-

elation to the Gentiles (Lk. 2:32), and it is he who reveals the Father to the disciples (Matt. 11:27). The incarnate Son is the embodiment of revelation: "The grace of God that brings salvation has appeared to all men" (Tit. 2:11); and with the incarnation "the kindness and love of God our Savior appeared" for men to see (3:4; in these two passages the Gk. verb meaning "to appear" is *epiphainō G2210*).

Before the ASCENSION of Jesus the apostles were the recipients of revelation, even though their hearts and minds were not always open or able to receive it. After the sending of the Holy Spirit—who came from the Father through the exalted, incarnate Son, and who came to represent the Son within the apostolic group and within the church they created—the apostles were very conscious of having witnessed revelation in and by Jesus before his ascension, and of receiving revelation from the exalted Jesus through the Spirit since PENTECOST. In fact, the Spirit shared with them the mind of the exalted Christ so that they were able to see his ministry, death, resurrection, and exaltation in the way in which he, as Messiah, saw them (Jn. 14:26; 15:26; 16:13). Thus to hear them preach the Good News was the same as hearing Jesus himself proclaim the KINGDOM OF GOD (Matt. 10:40; Lk. 10:16; Jn. 12:44). PAUL was conscious that Christ was working and speaking through him (Rom. 15:18; 2 Cor. 13:3). Therefore what the apostles preached and taught, and what eventually they wrote in the books of the NT, constitutes God's revelation given to and through them. In fact they refer to the receiving of revelation not only in terms of the central realities of the faith, but also in the form of personal instructions and guidance for their own lives and ministry (e.g., 2 Cor. 12:1-10; Gal. 2:2).

Christ revealed God in ancient Galilee and Judea, and Christ will reveal God when he returns to earth to judge the living and the dead. The last book of the Bible, which tells of the last days, is called Revelation (see REVELATION, BOOK OF). Paul taught that Christians should look for the glorious appearing of their Savior (2 Thess. 2:8; 1 Tim. 6:14; 2 Tim. 4:1).

Revelation, Book of the. The last book of the NT, frequently called *The Apocalypse of John* from the use of the Greek word *apokalypsis G637* ("unveiling") in Rev. 1:1. This is the only book of the NT that is exclusively prophetic in character. It belongs to the class of APOCALYPTIC LITERATURE in which the divine message is conveyed by visions and dreams. According to the initial statement in the book, it consists of the REVELATION that God gave to Jesus Christ so that he might "show his servants what must soon take place."

I. The Author. Unlike many apocalyptic books that are either anonymous or published under a false name, Revelation is ascribed to a man named John, evidently a well-known person among the churches of ASIA MINOR. He described himself as a brother of those who were suffering persecution (Rev. 1:9), and traditionally he has been identified as JOHN THE APOSTLE, son of ZEBEDEE.

The earliest definite historical reference to this Apocalypse appears in the works of Justin Martyr (c. A.D. 135), who, in alluding to the twentieth chapter, said that John, one of the apostles of Christ, prophesied that those who believed in Christ would dwell in Jerusalem a thousand years. Irenaeus (180) quoted Revelation five times and named John as the author. Clement of Alexandria (c. 200) received the book as authentic Scripture, and the Muratorian Fragment (c. 170) lists it as a part of the accepted canon by the end of the second century.

Its relation to John son of Zebedee was questioned by Dionysius of Alexandria (A.D. 231-265) on the grounds that the writer unhesitatingly declared his name, whereas the author of the fourth gospel did not do so, and that the vocabulary and style were utterly different from John's gospel and letters. He admitted that the Apocalypse was undoubtedly written by a man called John, but not by the beloved disciple. Eusebius, who quotes Dionysius at length, mentions both in the quotation and in a discussion of his own that there were hints of two Johns in EPHESUS, and intimates that one wrote the Gospel of John and the other wrote Revelation. This view is not generally supported by the church fathers, nor does the internal evidence make it necessary. The second "John" is a shadowy figure and cannot be identified with any of the known disciples of Jesus mentioned in the Gospels.

The so-called grammatical mistakes in Revelation are chiefly unidiomatic translations of Hebrew or Aramaic expressions, which would be impossible to render literally into Greek. The very nature of the visions made smooth writing difficult, for the seer was attempting to describe the indescribable. There are some positive likenesses to the accepted writings of John, such as the application of the term "Word of God" to Christ (Rev. 19:13), the reference to the "water of life" (22:17), and the concept of the "Lamb" (5:6). It is possible that John had the aid of a secretary in writing the gospel and his letters, but that he was forced to transcribe

© Dr. James C. Martin

The island of Patmos as it looks today. It was here that John received his visions and wrote the book of Revelation

immediately the visions without the opportunity to reflect on them or to polish his expression.

II. Date and place. There are two prevailing views regarding the date of the Apocalypse. The earlier date in the reign of NERO is favored by some because of the allusion to the temple in Rev. 11:1-2, which obviously refers to an early structure. Had the Apocalypse been written after A.D. 70, the temple in Jerusalem would not have been standing. The number 666 in Rev. 13:18 has also been applied to Nero, for that is the total numerical value of the consonants of his name as spelled in Hebrew. In ch. 18 the allusion to the five kings that are fallen, one existing, and one yet to come, could refer to the fact that five emperors—AUGUSTUS, TIBERIUS, CALIGULA, CLAUDIUS, and Nero—had already passed away; another, perhaps Galba, was reigning, and would be followed shortly by still another (17:9-11). By this reasoning the Revelation would have been written at the end of Nero's reign, when his mysterious suicide had given rise to the belief that he had merely quit the empire to join the PARTHIANS, with whom he would come to resume his throne later.

A second view, better substantiated by the early interpreters of the book, places it in the reign of DOMITIAN (A.D. 81-96), almost at the close of the first century. Irenaeus (c. 180), Victorinus (c. 270), Eusebius (c. 328), and Jerome (c. 370) all agree on this date. It allows time for the decline that is presupposed by the letters to the churches, and it fits better with the historical conditions of the ROMAN EMPIRE depicted in the symbolism.

The place of writing was the island of PATMOS, where John had been exiled for his faith. Patmos was the site of a penal colony, where political prisoners were condemned to hard labor in the mines.

III. Destination. Revelation was addressed to seven churches of the Roman province of ASIA, which occupied roughly the western third of what is now Turkey. The cities where these churches were located were on the main roads running N and S, so that a messenger carrying these letters could move in a direct circuit from one to the other. There were other churches in Asia at the time when Revelation was written, but these seven seem to have been selected because they were representative of various types of need and of Christian experience.

They have been interpreted (1) as representing successive periods in the life of the church or (2) as seven aspects of the total character of the church. Undoubtedly they were actual historical groups known to the author.

IV. Occasion. Revelation was written for the express purpose of declaring "what must soon take place" (Rev. 1:1), in order that the evils in the churches might be corrected and that they might be prepared for the events that were about to confront them. The moral and social conditions of the empire were deteriorating, and Christians had already begun to feel the increasing pressure of paganism and the threat of persecution. The book of Revelation provided a new perspective on history by showing that the kingdom of Christ was eternal and that it would ultimately be victorious over the kingdoms of the world.

V. Methods of interpretation. There are four main schools of interpretation. The *preterist* holds that Revelation is simply a picture of the conditions prevalent in the Roman empire in the late first century, cast in the form of vision and prophecy to conceal its meaning from hostile pagans. The *historical* view contends that the book represents in symbolic form the entire course of church history from the time of its writing to the final consummation, and that the mystical figures and actions described in it can be identified with human events

The seven churches of Revelation 2 and 3.

Overview of REVELATION

Author: An early Christian named John, probably to be identified with JOHN THE APOSTLE.

Historical setting: Written from prison on the island of PATMOS. The earliest Christian traditions date the book to the time of PERSECUTION under Emperor DOMITIAN c. A.D. 95, but some scholars prefer a date during the reign of NERO c. A.D. 65.

Purpose: To encourage Christians in the midst of opposition and suffering by assuring them that CHRIST will be victorious over the forces of evil.

Contents: After an introduction that includes a vision of Christ (Rev. 1), the book conveys messages to seven specific churches in ASIA MINOR (chs. 2-3), followed by a series of visions: the heavenly court, the scroll, and its seven seals of judgment (4:1—8:1); seven angels with seven trumpets (8:2—11:19); a woman and a dragon, two beasts, and other figures (chs. 12-14); seven bowls of wrath (chs. 15-16); the fall of Babylon and the final battle (chs. 17-19); the reign of Christ and the new Jerusalem (chs. 20-22)

in history. The *futurist*, on the basis of the threefold division given in Rev. 1:19, suggests that "what you have seen" refers to the immediate environment of the seer and the vision of Christ (1:9-19), "what is now" denotes the churches of Asia or the church age they symbolize (2:1—3:22), and "what will take place later" (most of the book) relates to those events that will attend the return of Christ and the establishment of the city of God. The *idealist* or *symbolic* school treats Revelation as purely a dramatic picture of the conflict of good and evil, which persists in every age but which cannot be applied exclusively to any particular historical period.

VI. Structure and content. Revelation contains four great visions, each of which is introduced by the phrase "in the Spirit" (Rev. 1:10; 4:2; 17:3; 21:10). Each of these visions locates the seer in a different place, each contains a distinctive picture of Christ, and each advances the action significantly toward its goal. The first vision (1:9—3:22) pictures Christ as the critic of the churches, who commends their virtues and condemns their vices in the light of his virtues. The second vision (4:1—16:21) deals with the progressive series of seals, trumpets, and bowls,

which mark the judgment of God on a world dominated by evil. The third vision (17:21—21:8) depicts the overthrow of evil society, religion, and government in the destruction of Babylon and the defeat of the beast and his armies by this victorious Christ. The last vision (21:9—22:5) is the establishment of the city of God, the eternal destiny of his people. The book closes with an exhortation to readiness for the return of Christ. Thus the document may be outlined as follows:

I. Introduction: the return of Christ (1:1-8)
II. Christ, the critic of the churches (1:9—3:22)
III. Christ, the controller of destiny (4:1—16:21)
IV. Christ, the conqueror of evil (17:1—21:8)
V. Christ, the consummator of hope (21:9—22:5)
VI. Epilogue: appeal and invitation (22:6-21)

revenge. See AVENGER OF BLOOD; VENGEANCE.

reverence. Profound respect felt and shown to someone, especially God. The English term is used a number of times in Bible versions to render several Hebrew and Greek terms. Reverence consists

R

of fear, awe, and deference in worshipful tribute paid to God (or some other deity) and to things sacred. Various OT references are related to contrasts between the WORSHIP of Yahweh and that of other gods (e.g., Lev. 19:30; 26:2). PAUL said to the Ephesian Christians, "Submit to one another out of reverence for Christ" (Eph. 5:21). See FEAR.

revellings. This English term, referring to extreme intemperance and lustful indulgence, is used by the KJV in two passages. PAUL lists it with murder as barring the way into the kingdom of God (Gal. 5:21), and PETER denounces it (1 Pet. 4:3). The NIV renders "orgies" in both instances.

revile. To address with abusive or insulting language, to reproach. Israelites were forbidden to revile their parents on pain of death (Exod. 21:17 KJV; NIV, "curses"). Israel was reviled by MOAB and AMMON (Zeph. 2:8 KJV; NIV, "taunts"). Jesus endured reviling on the cross (Mk. 15:32 KJV). Revilers will have no part in the kingdom of God (1 Cor. 6:10 KJV). The NIV uses the word when speaking of those who insult or blaspheme God (Ps. 10:13; 44:16; 74:10, 18).

revised versions. See BIBLE VERSIONS, ENGLISH.

reward. Something given in return for an action, whether good or evil; recompense, requital. In the preponderance of biblical citations, it is the reward of good for good deeds that is in evidence. In the OT the OBEDIENCE of the people of God to their COVENANT obligations resulted in both spiritual and physical benefits. The OT threefold blessing of (1) the continuance of the descendants of ABRAHAM, (2) the settlement in Canaan, and (3) the final culmination of the covenant in the MESSIAH—all were included as aspects of the reward for the faithfulness of Israel. Spiritual blessings were uppermost, while, as in all God's providential dealings with his people, obedience to the law and its structure of the spheres of life brought about material well-being. Similarly, the NT presents two separate levels of reward: the spiritual, which results only from faith in Christ, and the physical, which accrues to all who follow God's creation ordinances.

The fundamental principle, however, is made clear by PAUL: "It does not, therefore, depend on human desire or effort, but on God's mercy" (Rom. 9:16 TNIV). The Scripture does teach degrees of rewards dependent upon the individual's faithfulness to God's commands (e.g., Matt. 25:14-30; 1 Cor. 3:12-15). Such rewards are like all others in Scripture, promised both for the present life and for the glorification of the believer in the world to come. "As the outcome of your faith you obtain the salvation of your souls" (1 Pet. 1:9 RSV). The rich meaning of the reward of faith as it is promised throughout Scripture can be seen in the beginning of the covenant of grace when God said to Abram: "I am your … very great reward" (Gen. 15:1), and in the final chapter of Revelation, when Jesus says, "Behold, I am coming soon! My reward is with me, and I will give to everyone according to what he has done" (Rev. 22:12).

Rezeph. ree´zif (Heb. *reṣep H8364*, meaning uncertain). A city in MESOPOTAMIA conquered by the Assyrians (2 Ki. 19:12 = Isa. 37:12). When SENNACHERIB was threatening to crush Jerusalem, he sent a message to HEZEKIAH in which he asked, "Did the gods of the nations that were destroyed by my forefathers deliver them: the gods of Gozan, Haran, Rezeph and the people of Eden who were in Tel Assar?" The identification of Rezeph is uncertain because several places in the general area bear a similar name. One likely candidate is the Raṣappa of Assyrian records, identified with modern Reṣafeh (several variant spellings), some 80 mi. (130 km.) NNE of Palmyra (TADMOR) and 15 mi. (24 km.) S of the EUPHRATES.

Rezia. See RIZIA.

Rezin. ree´zin (Heb. *rĕṣin H8360*, possibly "delight" or "[God] is pleased"). **(1)** King of ARAM (SYRIA) who supported PEKAH king of ISRAEL in his fight against JUDAH (2 Ki. 5:37; 16:5; Isa. 7:1). Rezin is also credited with recovering ELATH (2 Ki. 16:6). He was the last Aramean king to rule DAMASCUS, for in 732 B.C. TIGLATH-PILESER III conquered the city and put him to death (16:9). The first clear knowledge of his position is that he, along with MENAHEM, paid tribute to Tiglath-Pileser in 740.

Some years later, Rezin and Pekah—the latter having usurped the throne of Israel—made an alliance, seeking to organize a coalition against ASSYRIA. When AHAZ of Judah refused to be drawn in, these "two smoldering stubs of firewood" (Isa. 7:4) tried to bring Judah into line by military pressure and to set up a puppet king identified as "the son of Tabeel." Rezin drove S to the RED SEA, always a direction of Syrian interest, and captured the port Elath, which he handed over to the Edomites (2 Ki. 16:6, emending MT *ʾrm* to *ʾdm*). The northern allies had to be content with the knowledge that Judah, beaten into her defenses and beset by Edomites and Philistines (2 Chr. 28:18), was powerless to interfere. In 734 the Assyrian answered his vassal's call for help. He struck through GALILEE at PHILISTIA, returned to mop up N Israel, and extracted tribute from TYRE. Rezin was thus isolated in Damascus and was killed when the city fell after a two-year siege; so the Aramean empire of Damascus came to an end.

(2) Ancestor of a family of temple servants (NETHINIM) who returned from the EXILE (Ezra 2:48; Neh. 7:50).

Rezon. ree´zuhn (Heb. *rĕzôn* H8139, "dignitary, ruler"). Son of Eliadah and king of ARAM (1 Ki. 11:23-25). Rezon began his career in the service of HADADEZER, Aramean king of ZOBAH. Probably at the time when DAVID defeated Hadadezer (2 Sam. 8:3), Rezon forsook his master, gathered men about him, and became a captain of freebooters. It was possibly years later, during the reign of SOLOMON, that he occupied DAMASCUS and founded there the dynasty which created the most powerful of the Aramean kingdoms. This ordering of events is necessary to allow time for David's establishment of garrisons among the Arameans from Damascus and his putting them under tribute after his victory over Hadadezer c. 984 B.C. (2 Sam. 8:5-6). After Rezon's seizure of Damascus he became an adversary against Solomon (1 Ki. 11:23). Many scholars identify him with HEZION, grandfather of BEN-HADAD I (1 Ki. 15:18), and suggest that "Rezon" was a title.

Rhegium. ree´jee-uhm (Gk. *Rhēgion G4836*). A town on the toe of the Italian peninsula; modern Reggio di Calabria. Opposite Messana in Sicily, where the strait is only 6 mi. (10 km.) wide, Rhegium was an important strategic point. As such it was the special object of ROME's care, and in consequence a loyal ally. The port was also a haven in extremely difficult water. The captain of the ship PAUL was on, having tacked widely to make Rhegium, waited in the protection of the port for a favorable southerly wind to drive his ship through the currents of the strait on the course to PUTEOLI (Acts 28:13).

Rheims Version. See BIBLE VERSIONS, ENGLISH.

Rhesa. ree´suh (Gk. *Rhēsa G4840*). Son of ZERUBBABEL, included in Luke's GENEALOGY OF JESUS CHRIST (Lk. 3:27). Because this person is otherwise unknown, some have proposed that the name reflects the ARAMAIC word for "the prince" (*rēʾšāʾ* or *rêšāʾ*) and that in an earlier form of the genealogy it was intended as the title of Zerubbabel.

Rhoda. roh´duh (Gk. *Rhodē G4851*, "rose"). The name of a slave girl in the house of MARY, the mother of John Mark (see MARK, JOHN), who came to answer the door when PETER arrived there after his miraculous deliverance from prison (Acts 12:13). She recognized Peter's voice and joyfully announced to the company gathered there for prayer that Peter was at the door; she was accused of being mad but persisted in her claim (vv. 14-15). Nothing more is known of her. The name was common, especially among slave girls.

Rhodes. rohdz´ (Gk. *Rhodos G4852*, "rose"). Modern Rodhos, a large island of the Dodecanese group, about 540 sq. mi. (1400 sq. km.) area, 12 mi. (19 km.) off the coast of ancient CARIA in SW ASIA MINOR (modern Turkey). Rhodes is hilly, but cut by fertile and productive valleys. Three city-states originally shared the island, but after internal tension and conflict with ATHENS, which lasted from 411 to 407 B.C., a federal capital with the same name as the island was founded. Rhodes controlled a rich carrying trade, and after the opening of the E by ALEXANDER THE GREAT, became the richest of all Greek communities. It was able to maintain its independence under the Diadochi, or "Successors," of Alexander. Rhodes, over this period,

R

© Dr. James C. Martin

Aerial view of the harbor in Rhodes.

became a center of exchange and capital and successfully policed the seas. Coming to terms with the rising power of ROME, Rhodes cooperated with the republic against Philip V of Macedon and ANTIOCHUS of Syria (201-197). In the third Macedonian war Rhodes adopted a less helpful attitude and was punished by economic reprisals. Rome in fact was seeking an excuse to cripple a rival to her growing eastern trade. The amputation of Rhodes's Carian and Lycian dependents, and the declaration of Delos as a free port ruined the community (166 B.C.). Loyalty to Rome in the war with Mithridates won back some of the mainland possessions, but Rhodes's glory was past.

It is generally thought that the inhabitants of Rhodes are meant by the term RODANIM (Gen. 10:4; 1 Chr. 1:7). The island is probably mentioned by EZEKIEL as one of the places that had commercial dealings with TYRE (Ezek. 27:15; here the MT has DEDAN, but LXX reads *Rhodiōn*). When PAUL passed that way, traveling from TROAS to CAESAREA (Acts 21:1), Rhodes was little more than a port of call with a degree of prosperity and distinction as a beautiful city, but no more than that. It is still a beautiful city, full of ancient and Crusader remains, on a lovely island.

Ribai. ri'bi (Heb. *ribay H8192*, possibly short form of JERIBAI, "[Yahweh] contends [for me]"). Father

of ITHAI, one of DAVID's mighty warriors (2 Sam. 23:29 [MT "Ittai"]; 1 Chr. 11:31).

Riblah. rib'luh (Heb. *riblâ H8058*, meaning uncertain). **(1)** A town some 50 mi. (80 km.) SSW of HAMATH and less than 7 mi. (11 km.) S of KADESH ON THE ORONTES; its ruins are just ENE of the modern village of Ribleh (near the border between Syria and Lebanon). Topographically and geographically, it is well situated, and one can understand why military monarchs like Pharaoh NECO (2 Ki. 23:33) and the Babylonian NEBUCHADNEZZAR would have chosen it for a base of operations (25:1-7, 18-21; cf. Jer. 39:1-7; 52:1-11, 24-27). The town is probably mentioned also in a prophetic oracle where God says he will make the land desolate "from the wilderness to Riblah" (Ezek. 6:14 NRSV; the NIV, following the MT, has DIBLAH).

(2) An unidentified place somewhere E or NE of the Sea of Galilee, included in a description of the boundaries of the Promised Land (Num. 34:11, here used with the definite article, "the Riblah"). The view that this Riblah is the same as #1 above creates confusion in the text. The town was evidently a short distance E of AIN, which also is unidentified, though some think it is the modern Khirbet ʿAyyun, c. 3 mi. (5 km.) E of the S tip of the Sea of Galilee.

riches. See WEALTH.

riddle. A question or problem intended to puzzle the hearer. The relevant Hebrew word is *ḥîdâ H2648*, which occurs seventeen times in the OT (eight of these in one passage, Jdg. 14:12-19). Although it is usually translated "riddle," occasionally one finds such renderings as "dark sayings" (Ps. 78:2 KJV, NRSV; "hidden things," NIV) and "hard questions" (1 Ki. 10:1 = 2 Chr. 9:1). MOSES is stated to have communed with God "face to face," and this is contrasted with "dark speech" (Num. 12:8 KJV). SAMSON's riddle (Jdg. 14:12-19) is the most notable example in the OT. In alluding to experiences of killing a lion and later finding honey in its carcass, Samson said, "Out of the eater, something to eat; / out of the strong, something sweet" (Jdg. 14:14). The QUEEN OF SHEBA came to SOLOMON "to test him with hard questions" (1 Ki. 10:1). A true riddle is found in Rev. 13:18, where the number 666 is apparently an obscure reference to some individual. Some of Jesus' sayings qualify as enigmas, statements difficult to understand (Lk. 22:36; Jn. 3:1-3; 4:10-15; 6:53-59).

rie. KJV spelling of "rye"; see PLANTS (under *spelt*).

righteousness. Morally right behavior or character. In the Bible and theology, this term has broad and profound significance. The Hebrew word translated "righteousness" is *ṣĕdāqâ H7407* (Gen. 15:6 et al.), which can also be rendered "justice, honesty, loyalty." The NT uses Greek *dikaiosynē G1466* (Matt. 3:15 et al.), sometimes rendered "justification." In its general use, *righteousness* represents any conformity to a standard, whether that standard has to do with the inner character of a person or the objective standard of accepted law. The Lord God always acts in righteousness (Ps. 89:4; Jer. 9:24). That is, he always has a right relationship with people, and his action is to maintain that relationship. As regards ISRAEL, God's righteousness involved treating the people according to the terms of the COVENANT that he had graciously made with them. This involved acting both in judgment (chastisement) and in deliverance (Ps. 68; 103:6; Lam. 1:18). The latter activity is often therefore equated with SALVATION (see Isa. 46:12-13; 51:5). The picture behind the word "righteousness" is from the law court (forensic). This comes to the surface in passages from the Prophets (e.g., Isa. 1:2-9; Jer. 2:4-13; Mic. 6:1-8); there the Lord is presented as the Judge, and Israel as the accused party, with the covenant supplying the terms of reference.

As God acts in righteousness (because he is righteous), so he called Israel to be righteous as his chosen people. They were placed in his covenant, in right relationship with him through faith (Gen. 15:6; Hab. 2:4), and were expected to live in right relationship with others. The king as the head and representative of the people was called by God to be righteous—to be in a right relationship with God, his people, and the surrounding nations (Ps. 72:1-4; 146:7-9). So we see that righteousness begins as a forensic term but easily becomes an ethical term in the OT.

In the teaching of CHRIST, similarly, righteousness means a right relationship with God (see

the parable of the Pharisee and tax collector, Lk. 18:14), as well as the quality of life that involved a right relationship both with God and one's fellow human beings (Matt. 5:6, 17-20). But it is PAUL who uses the word to the greatest effect in the NT with his formulation of the doctrine of JUSTIFICATION by FAITH (that is, being placed by God in a right relationship with himself in and through Christ by faith). His great statement is found in Rom. 1:16-17. The gospel is the power of God for salvation because "a righteousness from God is revealed, a righteousness that is by faith from first to last." That is, the gospel is effective because, along with the proclamation, a righteousness goes forth—a righteousness that God delights to see and accept. This righteousness is the provision of a right relationship with himself through the saving work of Jesus, substitute and representative Man. To receive this gift of righteousness is to be justified by faith. And those who receive the gift then are to live as righteous people, devoted to the service of what God declares to be right.

Rimmon (deity). rim´uhn (Heb. *rimmôn H8235*, "pomegranate," possibly an alteration of Akk. *Rammānu*, "the thunderer"). An ARAMEAN representation of HADAD, the god of storm, rain, and thunder. In SYRIA (ARAM) this god is called BAAL that is, the lord par excellence, and to the Assyrians he was known as Rammānu, "the thunderer." NAAMAN, the commander of the Aramean army, worshiped in the temple of this deity at DAMASCUS (2 Ki. 5:17-19). See also HADAD RIMMON.

Rimmon (person). rim´uhn (Heb. *rimmôn H8233*, "pomegranate"). A Benjamite of BEEROTH whose two sons, BAANAH and RECAB, guerrilla captains, assassinated SAUL's son, ISH-BOSHETH (2 Sam. 4:2-9).

Rimmon (place). rim´uhn (Heb. *rimmôn H8234*, "pomegranate"). A common place name that presumably reflects the existence of pomegranate trees in the respective locations. The name is also used as a compound (see EN RIMMON; GATH RIMMON; RIMMON PEREZ).

(1) A town in the NEGEV by the border of EDOM at first assigned to the tribe of JUDAH (Josh. 15:32)

R

The area around "the rock of Rimmon," usually identified with the modern-day village of Rammun.

and later given to SIMEON (Josh. 19:7 [KJV, "Remmon"]; 1 Chr. 4:32). In these texts Rimmon is preceded by AIN, and some believe these two names should be read as one; the reference is probably to EN RIMMON, a village resettled after the EXILE (Neh. 11:29). According to Zech. 14:10, Rimmon marked the S extremity of the land, to be turned into a plain with JERUSALEM towering over it when Yahweh comes. Its location is uncertain, but some scholars identify it with modern Tell Khuweilifeh (Tel Halif), some 9.5 mi. (15 km.) NNE of BEERSHEBA.

(2) A town on the NE border of the tribe of ZEBULUN (Josh. 19:13; KJV, "Remmon-methoar," understanding the difficult word *hammĕtōʾār* ["which curved"?] as part of the name). This city was assigned to the LEVITES descended from MERARI (1 Chr. 6:77, where it is called "Rimono"; see also DIMNAH). This Rimmon is located on the S edge of the Valley of Bet Netofa, at modern Rummaneh, a village 6 mi. (10 km.) NNE of NAZARETH.

(3) Six hundred survivors of the Benjamites took refuge for four months at "the rock of Rimmon" when pursued after the slaughter at GIBEAH (Jdg. 20:45, 47; 21:13); this Gibeah is thought by some to be the same as GEBA (modern Jebaᶜ, which is c. 3 mi./5 km. NE of the site usually thought to

be Gibeah of Benjamin/Saul, namely, Tell el-Ful). Most scholars have identified the rock of Rimmon with modern Rammun, which is located on a lofty, conical chalk hill c. 6 mi. (10 km.) NNE of Jebaᶜ and 3 mi. (5 km.) E of BETHEL. This hill is visible in all directions, protected by ravines on most sides, and contains many caves. Some have argued, however, that the narrative suggests a location in a wilderness area closer to Gibeah and that the hill where Rammun sits would probably not be described as a "rock." (A few scholars have thought that the word for "pomegranate tree" in 1 Sam. 14:2 is in fact a reference to the rock of Rimmon. In addition, the NRSV, following an old conjecture, reads "He has gone up from Rimmon" in Isa. 10:27.)

Rimmon, rock of. See RIMMON (PLACE) #3.

Rimmono. ri-moh´nuh (Heb. *rimmônô H8237,* "pomegranate"). A city within the tribal territory of ZEBULUN that was assigned to the LEVITES descended from MERARI (1 Chr. 6:77). See RIMMON (PLACE) #2.

Rimmon Perez. rim´uhn-pee´riz (Heb. *rimmôn pereṣ H8236,* "pomegranate breach"). KJV Rimmonparez. One of the stopping places of the Israelites in their wilderness journey (Num. 33:19-20). It was located between Rithmah and Libnah, but the precise location of all these places (prob. somewhere in the general area of PARAN) is unknown.

ring. A circular ornament worn mainly on the finger. Rings were used in great antiquity, as archaeologists have discovered among Assyrian, Babylonian, and Egyptian artifacts. The PATRIARCHS probably wore them. Rings for costume were usually of silver or gold, but BRONZE rings were added to these in furniture. The signet ring, probably the earliest form, may have been used first to replace the neck cord in bearing the SEAL (Gen. 38:18). PHARAOH gave his signet ring to JOSEPH as a symbol of authority (Gen. 41:42). Ahasuerus (XERXES) gave his to HAMAN to seal a royal decree (Esth. 3:10, 12; later it was taken from him and given to MORDECAI, 8:2, 8, 10). A costly ring was of special importance to royalty, nobility, and social station (Jas. 2:2). The returning prodigal received a ring from his father as a symbol of dignity (Lk. 15:22). Besides finger rings, EARRINGS also were worn by women and children (Gen. 35:4; Exod. 32:2), as discovered at GEZER, MEGIDDO, and TAANACH. Nose rings were also quite popular among feminine paraphernalia (Gen. 24:22, 30, 47; Isa. 3:21).

ringleader. An accusatory term that occurs once in the NT; the lawyer TERTULLUS argued that PAUL was "a ringleader of the Nazarene sect" (Acts 24:5).

ringstraked. An archaic English term meaning "marked with circular stripes." It is used by the KJV to describe the marks on the livestock that became JACOB's while working for his uncle LABAN (Gen. 30:35, 39, 40; 31:8, 10, 12). Modern versions have "streaked" or "striped."

Rinnah. rin′uh (Heb. *rinnāh H8263*, prob. "jubilation"). Son of Shimon and descendant of JUDAH (1 Chr. 4:20).

Riphath. ri′fath (Heb. *ripat H8196*, meaning unknown). Son of GOMER and grandson of JAPHETH (Gen. 10:3; in 1 Chr. 1:6 the MT has "Diphath," evidently a scribal error due to the similarity between the Heb. consonants *d* and *r*). His name, like those of his brothers ASHKENAZ and TOGARMAH, appears to be non-Semitic and probably Anatolian (see ASIA MINOR). Some have attempted to identify Riphath with various place names in the area.

Rissah. ris′uh (Heb. *rissâ H8267*, derivation uncertain). A stopping place in the wilderness wanderings of the Israelites (Num. 33:21-22). It was between Libnah and Kehelathah, but the location of these places is unknown.

Rithmah. rith′muh (Heb. *ritmâ H8414*, possibly "[place of the] broom trees"). A stopping place in the wilderness wanderings of the Israelites (Num. 33:18-19). It was located between HAZEROTH (possibly ʿAin Khadra, c. 30 mi./50 km. NE of Jebel Musa) and RIMMON PEREZ (unknown). Proposals for the identification of Rithmah include a valley E of AQABAH named er-Retame and a wadi S of KADESH BARNEA named Abu Retemat.

ritual. See LAW; PURIFICATION; SACRIFICE AND OFFERINGS; WORSHIP.

river. The lands of the Bible include the two great areas of riverine civilization of the ancient world—those of the NILE and the EUPHRATES. In these regions, where the river was the life-giver and was worshiped as such, it formed the main geographical feature in the consciousness of the people. It is not surprising that the Bible sometimes refers to the Euphrates simply as "the River" (Josh. 24:3; Ps. 72:8; et al.). Hence the basic image of the river as a source of LIFE, and consequently of comfort and PEACE, which is so frequently encountered in Scripture (e.g., Isa. 48:18; 66:12).

PALESTINE never possessed a riverine civilization comparable to those of the great valleys to the N and S of it. The JORDAN is too small in volume, and too entrenched in its deep valley, to provide the kind of irrigation AGRICULTURE that supported EGYPT or MESOPOTAMIA. Indeed, in biblical times the valley of the Jordan was sparsely inhabited, filled with dense vegetation, and the home of wild animals. Only in Ezekiel's vision does there appear a river large enough to flow down into the Jordan rift and support widespread cultivation (Ezek. 47): a river of life entering the DEAD SEA at the precise

R

point where the Jordan—so often the Bible's symbolic river of death—enters it in reality, at a point due E of the temple in Jerusalem. The same visionary image reappears in the NT (Rev. 22). See also BROOK; VALLEY.

river of Egypt. See EGYPT, RIVER OF.

Rizia. ri-zi'uh (Heb. *riṣyāʾ H8359*, possibly "pleasing"). Son of Ulla and descendant of ASHER, included among the "heads of families, choice men, brave warriors and outstanding leaders" (1 Chr. 7:39-40).

Rizpah. riz'puh (Heb. *riṣpāh H8366*, "glowing coal"). Daughter of Aiah and a concubine of SAUL (2 Sam. 3:7). After the death of Saul, his son ISH-BOSHETH, now king in name only, accused ABNER of sleeping with Rizpah. If true, this act would have amounted to a claim to the throne (cf. 2 Sam. 16:20-22; 1 Ki. 2:22). In response to this probably false accusation, Abner promptly proffered the northern kingdom to DAVID (c. 997 B.C.). Some years later, when the Gibeonites demanded, in compensation for Saul's slaughter of their people, the execution of seven of Saul's sons, the king gave them two of Rizpah's sons and five of MERAB's (2 Sam. 21:7-8; the MT has MICHAL instead of Merab). Then Rizpah began her heroic vigil by the bodies, keeping off the birds and beasts of prey (cf. Ps. 79:2) from the beginning of barley harvest (c. April) until the anger of Yahweh relented and "the rain poured down from the heavens" (2 Sam. 21:10; cf. v. 1). For her devotion David had their bones buried with the bones of Saul and JONATHAN in the tomb of Saul's father, Kish (vv. 11-14).

roads. In PALESTINE the chief S-to-N traverse is the road via Pelusium, Rafia, and GAZA, up the Maritime Plain, the ancient invasion route used by THUTMOSE, RAMSES, SENNACHERIB, Cambyses, ALEXANDER THE GREAT, POMPEY, TITUS, Saladin, Napoleon, and Allenby. Mount CARMEL closes the northern end. Passage was possible by a rough and exposed route on the seaward side, a path known as *Les Detroits* by the Crusaders. On the landward side ESDRAELON and PHOENICIA were reached by several low passes, chiefly those that run through

MEGIDDO, and the route through the Valley of DOTHAN (Gen. 37:35). The latter route was used by those traveling to the JORDAN and DAMASCUS.

A more easterly route from Damascus to the S lay through the arid deserts and mountains east of the Jordan Valley, through the tribal territories of MANASSEH, REUBEN, and GAD, into MOAB, and down the desert valley of the ARABAH (Deut. 8:15). This was the so-called KING'S HIGHWAY.

Lateral roads from the high country joined the N–S communications of the Maritime Plain and provided alternative routes across Palestine to Syria and Damascus. One road ran from Gaza to HEBRON. Another from JERUSALEM ran through Lydda (LOD) to JOPPA, with a loop to EMMAUS, if that town may be properly located W of Jerusalem (Lk. 24). This road was probably PAUL's route to CAESAREA (Acts 23), branching N at Lydda and passing through ANTIPATRIS.

The N–S routes inland were naturally not so numerous as those on the easy Maritime Plain. However, a road ran up to Jerusalem from Hebron through Bethlehem and continued north from Jerusalem to SAMARIA, forking at SYCHAR (Jn. 4).

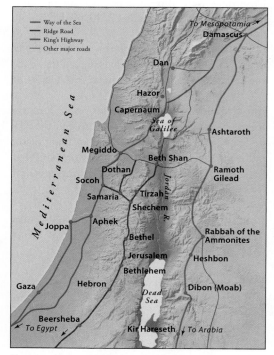

Three key roadways in the Promised Land.

A key international road in ancient times, often referred to as the Via Maris (Way of the Sea), came along the NW shore of the Sea of Galilee through the plain N of Magdala. (View to the N, with Mt. Hermon at the top left; Magdala is off to the bottom right.)

The roads from the E into JUDEA crossed miles of arid and difficult wilderness. There were roads from JERICHO NW to AI and BETHEL, SW to Jerusalem, and SSW to the lower KIDRON and Bethlehem. The first was Israel's invasion route, the second the road of Jesus' last journey to Jerusalem, the third probably the route of NAOMI and RUTH. There were numerous minor roads W from EN GEDI and MASADA.

The NEGEV desert lies across the southern approaches to Palestine and thrusts the highways, as indicated above, either W toward the level seacoast or E into the Wadi ARABAH. SOLOMON's cargoes from OPHIR came, no doubt, by the Arabah route from EZION GEBER on the Gulf of AQABAH, cutting the corner of the Negev S and W of the DEAD SEA and reaching Jerusalem by way of Hebron.

robbery. Illegal seizure of another's property (see also COMMANDMENTS, TEN; THIEF). Early in Israel's history such a crime was forbidden by law (Lev. 19:13). In the days of the judges it was unsafe to travel the highways because of robberies by highwaymen (Jdg. 5:6; 9:25). Houses were built to resist robbers, who were often base enough to seize the money of orphans and widows (Isa. 10:2).

Honor did not exist among thieves (Ezek. 39:10). So depraved had Israel become by HOSEA's day that companies of priests had turned to pillage (Hos. 6:9).

DAVID warned against the lust for riches that resulted in robbery (Ps. 62:10). ISAIAH wrote of God's hatred for this means of getting a burnt offering (Isa. 61:8). Among the vices of God's people listed by EZEKIEL is robbery (Ezek. 22:29). NAHUM accused NINEVEH of being a center of numerous robberies (Nah. 3:1). Withholding TITHES and offerings from God's storehouse was a kind of robbery (Mal. 3:8).

The prevalence of theft during NT times is attested by the account of the Good Samaritan (Lk. 10:30-37). Jesus warned against robbers who will enter the Christian fold (Jn. 10:1). Heaven is the secure depository for those who wish to store treasures for the future (Matt. 6:19-20). PAUL, who knew his world as few men of his day knew it, was familiar with violent seizure by thieves (2 Cor. 11:26). (The KJV use of the term *robbery* in Phil. 2:6 is misleading; cf. TNIV, "something to be used to his own advantage.")

robe. See DRESS.

Roboam. See Rehoboam.

rock. The two Hebrew terms for "rock" are not easy to distinguish, but *selaᶜ H6152* often refers to a high, cliff-like feature, while *ṣûr H7446* seems to indicate a crag or slab of rock. Both types of features abound in the Bible lands, where centuries of forest destruction and soil erosion have removed the vegetation cover even from those areas that originally possessed any. As a result, the rocks of Palestine repeatedly play a part in the Bible story, which is also rich in metaphors that follow from references to God as "the Rock" (e.g., Deut. 32:4). In the unsettled state of this region in OT times, it was a sensible precaution to use the natural defensive quality of rocky sites to build fortress cities. Rocks also offered shelter from storms, and they could even serve as a source of water (Exod. 17:6; Num. 20:11). It is a well-known feature of limestone terrain that water seeps down through crevices to break out at unexpected points in the form of springs; God evidently guided Moses to points where this could take place.

The NT transfers the symbolic image of the OT to make Christ "the spiritual rock" from which his people drank (1 Cor. 10:4). Various rabbinic sources refer to a movable well in the form of a rock that followed the Israelites in the wilderness, although interpreters are divided regarding the relevance of this tradition for Paul. Some commentators have also suggested that when John reports the piercing of "Jesus' side with a spear, bringing a sudden flow of blood and water" (Jn. 19:34), he is alluding to Moses' act of striking the rock on which God stood (Exod. 17:6). Just as in the wilderness that act caused physical water to flow and thus met the needs of God's people, so at the crucifixion the striking of God who had come in the flesh made possible the granting of living water—that is, the Holy Spirit—to believers (cf. Jn. 1:1, 14; 4:10-14; 7:38-39).

rock badger. See animals (under *badger*).

Rock of Escape (of Separation). See Sela Hammahlekoth.

rod, staff. Originally a piece of tree limb used as a support or as a weapon. The rod had varying uses in ancient times. Jacob used rods to change, as he supposed, the color of Laban's goats and sheep (Gen. 30:37-41; cf. 31:10-12). Staffs became symbols of authority (Jer. 48:17). Moses carried one when he returned to Egypt (Exod. 4:2, 17, 20; 7:9-20). Aaron's staff was used to bring gnats on Egypt (8:16-17). Moses' rod, upheld, brought hail and lightning (9:23) and locusts (10:13). It caused the sea to divide (14:16). He struck the rock at Horeb (Sinai) with a rod (17:5-7), and also at Kadesh (Num. 20). It was held aloft in Rephidim (17:9-13). The rod, used at first as a weapon, came to be a sign of authority, hence a scepter. To kill a servant with the rod was illegal (21:20). The shepherd's rod was used in counting sheep (Lev. 27:32). God's anger was for Job a rod (Job 9:34). Chastisement was symbolized by the rod (Ps. 89:32; 125:3; Prov. 13:24; 22:15; 29:15). The coming of Christ was to be preceded by the rod (Mic. 5:1). Paul would use a rod of judgment if forced to do so (1 Cor. 4:21). Aaron's budding rod was symbolic of Christ's eternal reign (Heb. 9:1-28). The victorious believer will rule with a scepter or rod (Rev. 2:27).

Rodanim. roh′duh-nim (Heb. *rôdānîm*, pl. of the unattested form *rôdan H8102*). TNIV "the Rodanites." Son of Javan and grandson of Japheth (Gen. 10:4 [KJV, "Dodanim," following most Heb. MSS]; 1 Chr. 1:7). However, since the name is in the plural form, the reference is evidently to a people group descended from Javan (who is associated with Greece and surrounding areas). The Septuagint reads *Rhodioi* ("Rhodians"), and most scholars believe that indeed the Rodanim were thought to be inhabitants of the island of Rhodes. On the other hand, some have argued that the spelling "Dodanim" is original.

Rodanites. roh′duh-nits. TNIV form of Rodanim.

rodent. See animals.

roe, roebuck. See animals.

Rogelim. roh′guh-lim, (*rōgĕlîm H8082*, prob. "[place of] those who tread," referring to fullers who cleaned textiles). A town in Transjordan identified as the home of Barzillai (2 Sam. 17:27;

19:31), who along with others befriended DAVID when the latter arrived in MAHANAIM in his flight from ABSALOM; he later escorted David back over the Jordan. The location of Rogelim is unknown. The description of Barzillai as "the Gileadite from Rogelim" may suggest a place in GILEAD, but even this is uncertain.

Rohgah. roh′guh (Heb. *rohgâ H8108*, meaning unknown). Son of Shomer (KJV, "Shamer"; NRSV, "Shemer") and descendant of ASHER (1 Chr. 7:34).

roll. See SCROLL.

rolling thing. See PLANTS (under *tumbleweed*).

Romamti-Ezer. roh-mam′ti-ee′zuhr (Heb. *rōmamtî ʿezer H8251*, "I have lifted help" or "I have exalted [my] helper"). Son of HEMAN, the king's seer (1 Chr. 25:4). The fourteen sons of Heman, along with the sons of ASAPH and JEDUTHUN, were set apart "for the ministry of prophesying, accompanied by harps, lyres and cymbals" (v. 1). The assignment of duty was done by lot, and the twenty-fourth lot fell to Romamti-Ezer, his sons, and his relatives (25:29).

Roman empire. The word *empire* requires definition, for it is used in two distinct senses, geographical and political, and both are applicable to the Roman empire. Geographically, an empire is an aggregation of territories under a single absolute command. The term *empire* is used most commonly, however, in a political sense to distinguish between the republic and the principate, between the rule of the senate and the rule of the constitutional autocrats who were called, in view of their exercise of supreme military command, by the term *imperator* (whence *emperor*). The Roman empire, in this sense of the word, is that period of Roman history that begins with the final victory of Octavian in the republic's last civil war and ends with the collapse of all Roman authority.

I. **Geographical.** Considered as a territorial phenomenon, the Roman empire was the result of a process of expansion that began in the sixth and seventh centuries before Christ. The process was initiated by the pressure of a rapidly filling and not overfertile peninsula on a Latin-speaking community that occupied a strategically advantageous position on some low hills by the major ford over the river Tiber. The main fortress and federation of this group of associated settlements was called ROME, probably an Etruscan name. The origin of the population was an amalgam of tribal elements welded into a dynamic unity by the pressure of the Etruscans to the N and the Italic hill-tribes of the hinterland. Casting off the domination of Etruria in 509 B.C., Rome early began the search for a stable frontier that was to form the guiding motive of her history. That quest took her step by step to the subjugation of the Italian peninsula and the domination of its peoples: (a) the Etruscans, whose culture and empire, Asiatic in origin, opportunely decayed in the fourth century before Christ; (b) the Italic tribes who occupied the highland spine of the peninsula with its associated plains; (c) the Greeks, whose colonies, since the eighth century, had dotted the coastline from Cumae to Tarentum; and finally (d) the Celtic Gauls of N Italy and the Po Plain.

Italy was Roman as far as the Alps by the middle of the third century before Christ. This metropolitan empire was no sooner achieved than Rome clashed with Carthage, the great Phoenician commercial empire of the N African coast. The island of Sicily, half Greek, half Carthaginian, lay between the continents and became the scene of the first collision between two powers, for whom the W Mediterranean was proving too small a common sphere. Sixty years of intermittent war followed, from which Rome emerged victorious with her first provinces, Sicily, Sardinia, and Spain. An overseas empire thus visibly began, but defense and security were still the motives as Rome moved into the sister peninsulas, first Spain and then Greece. Despite such later leaders as CAESAR and POMPEY, originally and generally Roman imperialism owed no inspiration to an ALEXANDER THE GREAT seeking conquest for motives of personal glory and mysticism, no SENNACHERIB or NEBUCHADNEZZAR systematically building empires and concentrating the world's wealth in mighty capitals, no Cortés or Pizarro in frank search of loot. Even in the second and first centuries before Christ, when the material advantages of the empire were corrupting the republic's ruling class, expansion and

Aerial view of the remains of ancient Rome. (View to the NNE.)

© Dr. James C. Martin

conquest were still associated with the search for a defensible frontier and military security.

The eastward movement through Greece, Asia Minor, and the ANE began because of Macedon's support of Carthage in the Second Punic War. It continued in the clash with imperial Syria and found uneasy pause with Pompey's pacification and organization of the E Mediterranean, completed in 63 B.C. The historic process of expansion was associated with the emergence of successive perils, and Rome's attempts to meet them. The northward expansion through Gaul, which paused finally on the Rhine and the fortification lines of N Britain, was a process similarly motivated. If Pompey was the architect of the eastern empire, Julius Caesar was the builder of the western. Although the personal ambitions of army commanders is an element the historian cannot discount, it remains a fact that it was the uneasy memory in Italy of barbarian inroads from the unpacified northern hinterlands that provided the stimulus for the conquest of Gaul and the associated islands across the English Channel.

By the beginning of the Christian era the Roman empire was reaching the limits of its expan-

sion. It was the policy of AUGUSTUS to consolidate, but that policy was based on a shrewd realization that the physical limit of Roman expansion was in sight. It is true that the stable frontier long sought for was still elusive. A major military disaster in A.D. 9 caused Augustus to choose the Rhine as a northern frontier. The Danube formed its logical eastward continuation. The Rhine-Danube line in general remained the limit of the empire. Extensions beyond it were never completely integrated, and safer and more defensible alternatives were beyond physical reach. History was to demonstrate how difficult the Rhine-Danube line was to defend. Spain, Gaul, and Britain formed stable enough buttresses in the W, while the southern marches rested on the Sahara, a desert frontier, and strategically the most stable of all. The E was never totally secured, and some of the imagery of the Apocalypse reflects the fear felt in the ANE of the archer cavalry from over the EUPHRATES.

The NT came into being and the early church was established in an empire that had organized and pacified a deep belt of territory around the Mediterranean basin and W Europe. That area owed its security to Rome, a security achieved against notable dangers and grave disadvantages and destined to endure for a vital three centuries. The same complex of territories owed to Rome a more stable government than much of it had ever known, and a community of life that went far to produce the fusion of Greece, Rome, and Palestine that formed the background and climate for the NT and subsequent Christendom.

II. Political. In a political sense, the term *Roman empire* must be distinguished from the *Roman republic*. The empire describes the system of rule and government known as the principate. The year 31 B.C., the date of the Battle of Actium, is arbitrarily chosen as the dividing line when republic became empire. The observer of that day was conscious of no change or transition. Such an observer saw the passing of danger and the prospect of peace after another violent bout of civil strife and constitutional crises. Octavian, Julius Caesar's adoptive nephew, had defeated Antony. When the victor drew into his hands the powers of the republican magistrates and the ancient constitutional executives, adding the marks of prestige that accompanied the titles of *princeps, imperator*, and Augustus, no one at the time who observed merely the surface of events saw anything but a continuation and an intensification of a policy that for fifty years had made a mockery of constitutional government. Extraordinary commands and special powers had long since prepared the way for the autocracy that emerged full-fledged with Octavian/Augustus.

The constitutional breakdown from which the principate arose can be traced back for over a century. The senate had ruled Rome, more by prestige than by a clearly defined legal right to do so, in the great days of Rome's struggle with Carthage. A tight oligarchy, the great families whose members gave Rome her generals and administrators ruled with a strength and a decisiveness the times demanded, and the land had no reason to regret their leadership. Rome emerged from the wars with Carthage, shaken but victorious, at the beginning of the second century before Christ. At the end of that century the ills that broke the republic and led to the principate were in full view.

The senate, whose leadership had sufficed for a compact city-state and for Italy, proved unequal to the task of governing an empire. Three problems were beyond their solution: (a) the city mob, tool and instrument of a new breed of demagogues; (b) the corruption arising from the temptations of rule in conquered lands; and (c) the power of the generals. All three were problems of empire. The urban working class had been built out of a decayed farming class ruined by changes in Italian land utilization when vast amounts of capital from subjugated territories began to come in. The generals owed their power to the needs of distant defense and the military forces that new frontiers demanded. Commander and soldier alike had a vested interest in these new frontiers. Rome, throughout the next four centuries, was never to hear the last of it. The only answer would have been the creation of a strong, free middle class, which the early acceptance of Christianity would have provided.

Julius Caesar was the most notable of the military dynasts, and he died under the daggers of a frustrated senate because he drove too ruthlessly toward the autocratic solution of the senate's corruption and the republic's breakdown. His adoptive nephew, Octavius, was a more suitable person. By a mixture of good fortune, astute diplomacy, and a flair for picking colleagues, Octavius won power; but it was always power with a flavor of constitutional legality. Octavius, later called by the honorary title Augustus, was emperor only in the sense that, as supreme commander, he alone had the right to the title *imperator*, with which victorious generals had ever been saluted by their troops. To most men he was simply *princeps*, or "prince," which meant simply "first citizen." His varied powers, functions, and privileges nevertheless added up to autocracy. The system gave peace, and the world, especially the provinces, was prepared to barter a pretense of liberty for peace.

The Roman empire, using the word in the political sense of the term, was the governmental framework of the *Pax Romana*, that era of centralized government that kept comparative peace in the Mediterranean world for significant centuries. No wonder the eastern provinces, accustomed since ancient days to the deification of rulers, early established the custom of worshiping the emperor (see EMPEROR WORSHIP). The notion gained currency through the writings of poets such as Horace and Vergil, who genuinely believed in the divine

R

call of Augustus and who, without a higher view of deity, saw no incongruity in ascribing divine attributes to a mere man of destiny. Such were the sinister beginnings of a cult that Rome chose as a cement of empire, and which led to the clash with the church, the early acceptance of which might have provided a more noble and effective bond.

Romans, Letter to the. The longest of the thirteen NT epistles bearing the name of PAUL, and the first letter in the long-established canonical order. The genuineness of the letter has never been seriously questioned by competent critics familiar with first-century history. Although other NT letters have been wrongly attacked as forgeries not written by the alleged authors, this letter stands with Galatians and 1 and 2 Corinthians as one of the unassailable documents of early church history.

There can be no doubt that the author, Paul, formerly Saul of TARSUS (Acts 13:9), was a highly intellectual, rabbinically educated Jew (Acts 22:3; Gal. 1:14) who had been intensely hostile to the Christian movement and had sought to destroy it (Acts 8:1-3; 9:1-2; 1 Cor. 15:9; Gal. 1:13). Even the critics who reject the supernatural cannot deny the extraordinary nature of the fact that this able enemy became the greatest exponent of the Christian faith and wrote the most powerful statements of Christian doctrine. The accounts of his conversion are given in LUKE's historical work (Acts 9:3-19; 22:1-16; 26:9-18), and the event is alluded to in his writings (1 Cor. 15:8-10; Gal. 1:15).

I. Literary unity. The literary unity of Romans has been questioned with regard to the last two chapters of the letter. There are manuscripts that have the doxology of Rom. 16:25-27 at the end of ch. 14; some have it in both places. Yet none of the manuscripts lacks chs. 15-16, and there is no evidence that the letter was ever circulated without that material. It is not difficult for anyone

Overview of ROMANS

Author: The apostle PAUL.

Historical setting: Written from CORINTH during the third missionary journey (prob. the winter of A.D. 56-57) to the Christian church in ROME, which was facing challenges related to Jewish-Gentile issues. The apostle was about to travel to JERUSALEM to deliver a contribution from the GENTILES for the poor Jewish churches in JUDEA, after which he planned to visit Rome on his way to SPAIN (Rom. 15:23-33).

Purpose: In preparation for his visit, Paul needed to clarify the nature of his message of grace to the GENTILES over against the objections of the JUDAIZERS; he also wanted to deal with doctrinal and practical problems faced by the Roman church.

Contents: After an introduction that summarizes his GOSPEL and ministry (Rom. 1:1-17), the apostle demonstrates the universal need for God's RIGHTEOUSNESS in view of the SIN of both Gentiles and Jews (1:18—3:20), expounds and defends his message of JUSTIFICATION by FAITH (3:21—5:21), develops the doctrine of Christian SANCTIFICATION (chs. 6-8), and deals with the difficult problem of Israel's unbelief (chs. 9-11); he then addresses specific issues involving the Christian life (12:1—15:13) and concludes with a summary of his plans, greetings, and final exhortations (15:14—16:27).

R

who is familiar with letters of a theological and missionary nature to imagine how this inspiring doxology might occur out of its intended place in some copies.

This is a letter, not a treatise. It was not intended to be a formal literary product. In the midst of greetings from friends who were with the author as he wrote (Rom. 16:21-23), TERTIUS, the scribe to whom the letter was dictated, puts in his own personal greeting (16:22). One can speculate that Paul was interrupted at v. 21. As he stepped away, he may have said, "Tertius, put in your greeting while I attend to so and so." He returned in a moment and resumed his dictating. The people of the Bible were human beings under human circumstances, and the letter means more to us because this is so. Perhaps Paul composed vv. 25-27 at the end of his discussion of "judging and scandalizing" (ch. 14). This little doxology is a compact paragraph, a unit in itself. It would fit appropriately in a number of places. The opening verses of ch. 15, on "the strong and the weak," are obviously related to the material in ch. 14. One can picture Paul resuming his work at 15:1 after an interruption. Tertius takes up his pen, and Paul says, "I must say more about the treatment of the weaker brother. The little paragraph of praise to God that we did last, is to go at the very end, after we have finished everything else." Tertius draws a line through it, and later faithfully copies it at the end.

The prayer at the end of Rom. 15 is not to be taken as the conclusion of a letter. It is only the appropriate conclusion of a particular topic. Paul had been telling of his itinerary. He was deeply moved as he contemplated the perils of his impending visit to JERUSALEM, and he strongly implored the prayers of the saints in ROME in respect to this matter (15:30-32). Quite naturally and spontaneously at this point he broke into a prayer for them. The conclusions of Paul's letters always contain some striking use of the word *grace* (see 2 Thess. 3:17-18), a term not found here. Therefore the prayer of 15:33 should not be construed as a conclusion of a letter. The main body of the letter ends at 16:20 with the words, "The grace of our Lord Jesus be with you." Verses 21-24 are intentionally a postscript. He has finished the personal greetings to people in Rome. PHOEBE,

who is to take the letter to Rome, is nearly ready to begin her journey. Greetings from friends in CORINTH, who may have assembled for a farewell, belong by themselves in a postscript, followed by another benediction (16:24). Then finally comes the exalted doxology (16:25-27).

Opening of Paul's letter to the Romans in a parallel Greek/Latin edition published in 1835.

© Dr. James C. Martin

The peculiarities that have caused some to question the literary unity of the last two chapters with the main body of the letter give no ground whatever for questioning the letter's genuineness. No forger or redactor would have left such matters open to question. The only reasonable explanation of the data is that the letter is exactly what it purports to be, a personal letter from the apostle Paul to the church at Rome, which he was planning to visit.

II. The time and place of writing. The personal information included in Rom. 15:23-29 clearly places the letter in the three-month period that Paul spent in GREECE, undoubtedly at CORINTH, just before going to Jerusalem (Acts 20:3). The reference is probably to the winter of A.D. 56-57.

III. The reason for writing. It is not difficult to know why this epistle was written. In the first place Paul was emphatic in his claim to be "the apostle of the Gentiles" (Rom. 11:13; 15:16; see also Acts 9:15; 22:15-21; 26:17-20, 23; Gal. 2:7-9; Eph. 3:2-8), and Rome was the capital of the GENTILE world. Paul was a Roman citizen, and a visit to Rome was consistent with his regular mode of operation, namely, the establishing of churches in strategic centers and major cities. There was this difference, however. A church already existed in Rome, probably founded by local people who had heard the gospel in their travels. It was Paul's distinctive policy to preach in hitherto unevangelized areas (Rom. 15:17-24; cf. also 2 Cor. 10:14-16). His proposed visit to Rome was not inconsistent, however, for (1) he had a contribution to make to their spiritual welfare (Rom. 1:11-13) and (2) he planned to visit Rome on his way to evangelize SPAIN (15:24). He was asking the church in Rome to help him in this project. The structure of the letter is built around Paul's travel plans.

There was also a great theological reason for composing this letter—a problem that had demanded the writing of a letter to the GALATIANS at an earlier juncture in Paul's ministry. It concerned the relation among (1) the OT Scriptures, (2) contemporaneous JUDAISM, and (3) the GOSPEL implemented by the earthly work of Christ. The problem in the Galatian churches focused on whether Gentile Christians were obligated to fulfill the Mosaic LAW, and in particular whether they should submit to CIRCUMCISION (Gal. 2:1-11). It has been said that if Galatians is the "Magna Charta" of the gospel, Romans is the "Constitution." The theological substance of this letter had to be presented to the NT church, whether addressed to Rome or not, but there were circumstances in Rome that made it appropriate for Paul—in a relatively calm frame of mind, with time for fuller elaboration, and without having become personally involved in local affairs, as he had in Galatia—to expand the central doctrine of the letter to the Galatians. Thus he explained his purpose in coming to Rome and the main purpose of his life ministry and message. There was friction and misunderstanding between Jewish and Gentile Christians in the Roman church. We know from the personal greetings at the end that it was a mixed church. The problem is reflected in almost every section of the document, but especially in Rom. 3-4 and 9-11. Both sides were stubborn. A clarification of the gospel and its implications was needed.

IV. The content and outline. These must be understood from the point of view of Paul's total ministry and his particular travel plans. True, the greatest theme in the work is JUSTIFICATION by FAITH. But this is not an essay on that subject. Much of the material simply does not fall under any subheading of that theme. This is a letter from the apostle to the Gentiles of the church in Rome, and the subject is, "Why I am coming to visit you." Outlines that fail to see this viewpoint and seek to force the material into formal divisions as though this were an essay are very likely to assign subtopics and secondary subheadings that do not fit. Some outlines are almost like "zoning" laws, forbidding the reader to find in certain sections material that certainly is there. The following very simple outline is suggested.

A. Introduction (Rom. 1:1-17)
B. The world is lost (1:18—3:20)
  1. The Gentile world is wretchedly lost (1:18-32) in spite of God's justice for attempted morality (2:1-16).
  2. The Jewish world is equally lost, in spite of all their privileges (2:17—3:20).
C. Justification by faith (3:21—5:21).
D. Holy living in principle (6:1—8:39).
E. God has not forgotten the Jews (9:1—11:36).
F. Details of Christian conduct (12:1—15:13).
G. Miscellaneous notes (15:14—16:27).
  1. Travel plans (15:14-33).
  2. Personal messages to people in Rome (16:1-20).
  3. Personal messages from people in Corinth (16:21-23).
  4. Doxology (16:24-27).

Rome. (Gk. *Rhōmē G4873*; *Rhōmaios G4871*, "Roman"; cf. *Rhōmaisti G4872*, "Roman [i.e., Latin] language" [Jn. 19:20]). A city-state in the Italian peninsula (see ITALY); located on the Tiber River some 15 mi. (24 km.) from the W MEDITERRANEAN, Rome eventually became the capital of the ROMAN EMPIRE. Of the Indo-European tribes who entered Italy, the Latins formed a separate branch, occupying an enclave round the mouth of the Tiber and the Latium Plain. They were surrounded, and indeed constricted, by the Etruscan empire in the N, by the Greek maritime colonies in the S, and by related but hostile Italic tribes who held the rest of the peninsula and the arc of hill-country that fenced off the plain. Therefore, a sense of unity arose in the Latin-speaking communities, and their scattered groups were linked into leagues and confederacies. The lowlanders built defendable stockaded retreats to which the plainsmen could retire with flocks and families, and located such forts on hills and outcrops of higher land. In this way Rome came into being. Virgil's idyllic picture of primitive Rome in the eighth book of his *Aeneid* is not far from the truth. The most ancient acropolis could have been the Palatine hill, where the stockade of one shepherd community was built.

But the Palatine was not the only hill of Rome. The Tiber River cut into the soft limestone of the area, and the valley thus formed was further eroded by tributary streams, forming the famous group of hills with which the future city of Rome was always associated. They were the Capitol, the Palatine, and the Aventine, with the Caelian, Oppian, Esquiline, Viminal, and Quirinal as flat-topped spurs. Through the area the river forms an S-shaped curve. In the course of this curve the river grows shallow and forms an island. This point is the one practicable ford on the river between the sea and a very distant locality upstream. The Tiber tends to run narrow and deep. Geography thus played a dominant role in history. The group of hills and spurs were ultimately occupied by separate communities such as those whose ninth-century B.C. traces have been discovered on the Esquiline and the Quirinal. The old habit of Latin federation gave them a sense of unity, which was finally translated into common institutions and defense. Traffic across the Tiber ford necessarily concentrated at this point. Indeed all the trade between the Etruscan north and the Greek and Italian south had to cross the river here. The river valley was also a highway of commerce between the sea and the hills. Salt may have been the principal commodity carried on that route. The group of hill settlements thus straddled central Italy's main communications, and those who have held such positions of advantage have always grown rich and powerful. Perhaps a faint memory of the significance of the Tiber ford is embedded in the Latin name *pontifex*, which appears to mean etymologically "bridgemaker."

Archaeological evidence suggests that the settlements had joined to form the original city of Rome by the sixth century B.C., for burials from the Palatine and Capitoline cemeteries on the edge of the marshy bottom (which was to be the Forum) cease at that time. The Cloaca Maxima, which drained these hollows, may have been built about this date.

Aerial view of the city of Rome (looking W), with St. Peter's Basilica (background, center top) and the Forum (left foreground).

© Dr. James C. Martin

R

Synoecism (the amalgamation of small settlements into one powerful city-state) took place under the kings whose rule in early Rome, encrusted though it is with legend, is established fact. The Wall of Servius made Rome into a considerable fortress. Over the period of the kings, and especially the Etruscan kings, whose rule closes the regal period of early Roman history, the city built the Pons Sublicius to replace the Tiber ford, developed the Campus Martius as a training-ground, concentrated business activities in the Forum, and began to crowd the hills and hollows with houses and temples. Rome was probably a large populous city by the fourth century B.C. Valleys formed an irregular pattern for roads—a pattern that remained a feature through all history, and by the third century there is evidence of the great *insulae* or tenement houses that were to become another characteristic feature of Rome and that suggest the overcrowding, squalor, and slums of the early capital.

It is difficult to obtain a clear picture of a city that has always been occupied, and whose accumulated buildings have limited archaeological investigation. Aqueducts, bridges, quays, temples, porticoes, the monuments of civic and of family pride, followed over the centuries. It is possible to trace great bursts of building activity at certain periods. At the end of the second century B.C., the influx of capital from the beginnings of provincial exploitation promoted expansion. Sulla endeavored to bring order to some of the central urban tangle, POMPEY did much to adorn the city, and AUGUSTUS boasted that he had "found the city built of brick and left it built of marble." Augustus set the fashion for two imperial centuries, and it is from the first and second centuries after Christ that most of the surviving ruins date: the great baths of Caracalla, Diocletian, and Constantine, for example, and, most famous of all, the Flavian Amphitheater, called still by the medieval name of Colosseum.

A vivid picture of the perils and inconveniences of life in the great city at the turn of the first century of our era is found in the *Third Satire of Juvenal*, a rhetorical poem. In population the city of Rome probably passed the million mark at the beginning of the Christian era, and during the first century may have risen somewhat above this figure. It was a motley and cosmopolitan population. Early in the second century Juvenal numbers the foreign rabble as one of the chief annoyances of urban life, to be ranked with traffic dangers, fire, and falling houses. In the third and fourth centuries, a time of urban decay all over the empire, the city declined, and the population probably fell to something near half a million by the last days of the western empire.

It is possible roughly to estimate the proportion of Christians over the imperial centuries. In the catacombs, ten generations of Christians are buried. It is difficult to reach an accurate estimate of the extent of these galleries in the limestone rock or of the number of graves they contain. The lowest estimate of the length is c. 350 mi. (560 km.), the highest 600 mi. (960 km.). The lowest estimate of the burials is 1,175,000, the highest 4,000,000. Given a population averaging one million over the ten generations of the church's witness, and this is rather high in view of the third- and fourth-century decline, we have on the first figure a Christian population averaging 175,000 per generation, and on the higher figure one averaging 400,000 per generation. Such averaging is obviously inaccurate, for the number of the Christian population would be smaller in the earlier and larger in the later centuries. But if the figure of 175,000 is taken to represent a middle point in the period, say about the middle of the third century after Christ, it becomes clear that Gibbon's well-known estimate is hopelessly awry. Gibbon suggested that, at this time, probably one-twentieth of the population of the city consisted of Christians. The most conservative estimate from the evidence of the Catacomb burials is that at least one-fifth were Christians, and that probably the proportion was much larger.

The catacombs also provide evidence of the vertical spread of Christianity in the imperial society of the capital, and Gibbon is incorrect also in saying that the church was "almost entirely composed of the dregs of the populace." The case of Pomponia Graecina, for example, reported by Tacitus (*Ann.* 13.32), may be traced to the catacombs. Some evidence suggests that she faced a domestic tribunal because of a Christian faith. If Pomponia was, in fact, a Christian, since she lived on into the principate of DOMITIAN, she may have had part in two aristocratic conversions of which there is evidence—those of Flavius Clemens the consul and of Domitilla, his wife. The former was the cousin and the latter was the niece of Domitian himself. Dio Cassius (*Rom. Hist.* 67.44) informs us that these two were accused of "atheism," a common allegation against Christians, and of "going astray after the custom of the Jews." Flavius Clemens was put to death and his wife banished. Next to Domitian, this illustrious and evidently Christian pair held the highest rank in the empire.

Rome, like BABYLON, became a symbol of organized paganism and opposition to Christianity in the Bible. In the lurid imagery of the Apocalypse, John mingles empire and city in his symbolism of sin. Revelation 17-18 envisages the fall of Rome. Passionate, indeed shocking in its imagery, the first of these chapters shows Rome like a woman of sin astride the seven hills, polluting the world with her vice. The second reads like a Hebrew "taunt-song." It pictures, in imagery reminiscent of EZEKIEL on TYRE, the galleys loading for Rome in some eastern port. There were "cargoes of gold, silver, precious stones, and pearls; fine linen, purple, silk and scarlet cloth, ... ivory, costly wood, bronze, iron and marble, ... cinnamon and spice, ... cattle and sheep; horses and carriages; and bodies and souls of men." The climax is bitter, as John pictures Rome under the smoke of her burning, the voice of gladness stilled.

The city appears several times in a historical context, the most notable being PAUL's enforced stay there. The apostle landed at PUTEOLI; and alerted by the little church there (Acts 28:14-15), members of Rome's Christian community met Paul at two stopping-places. A group of believers had been established in Rome possibly as early as the principate of CLAUDIUS in the late forties of the first century. Paul probably entered Rome by the Capena Gate. His "rented house" (28:30) would be in some block of flats, an *insula*.

Rompha. See REPHAN.

roof. The top of a HOUSE or other building, accessible by outside stairs. Occasionally pitched roofs were used, but most were flat, usually formed of clay packed with stone rollers, supported by mats of rushes or branches across wood beams or palm tree trunks. The roof was commonly occupied

(Deut. 22:8), used for storage (Josh. 2:6), for rest in the evening (2 Sam. 11:2), and was even used in idolatrous worship (Jer. 19:13). An uncommon Hebrew word for "beam" or the like (*qôrâ H7771*) is used in Gen. 19:8 with reference to a roof structure, describing the latter in terms of one supporting member. In this passage the term is idiomatic for "house" or "home," a use reflected also in the phrase "under my roof" (Gk. *stegē G5094*, Matt. 8:8). The roof was not a hindrance to securing healing for the paralytic (Mk. 2:4).

room. See ARCHITECTURE; HOUSE; UPPER ROOM.

rooster. See BIRDS.

root. That part of the plant which penetrates the soil and draws up sap and nourishment for the plant. The numerous references to roots in the Bible are mostly figurative, drawn from the important relation which the root bears to the plant. Roots near water symbolize prosperity (Job 29:19; Ezek. 31:7); the opposite is a "withered" root (Hos. 9:16). A root growing old in the ground (Job 14:8) signifies loss of vitality, while "to take root" or "be rooted" denotes becoming or being firmly established (2 Ki. 19:30; Eph. 3:17). Judgment upon sinners is pictured as rottenness of root (Isa. 5:24), roots drying up (Job 18:16; Isa. 14:30), or being uprooted in destruction (Ezek. 17:9; Lk. 17:6; Jude 12). The ax lying at the root of the tree indicates impending judgment (Matt. 3:10). The root is the source of a moral or spiritual condition. Thus the love of money is pictured as "a root of all kinds of evil" (1 Tim. 6:10), while a "bitter root" causes the defilement of apostasy (Heb. 12:15; cf. Deut. 29:18). The root of a family or nation is its progenitor (Rom. 11:16). MESSIAH as "the Root of Jesse" (Isa. 11:10) is not a mere shoot from the root but himself the origin and strength of the messianic line; "the Root and the Offspring of David" (Rev. 22:16; cf. 5:5) denotes Christ's divine-human nature as the source and descendant of DAVID. The messianic Servant's appearance as a "root out of dry ground" (Isa. 53:2) depicts his lowly surroundings in contrast to his inner vigor.

rope. See CORD.

R

rose. See PLANTS.

Rosetta stone. A bilingual stela of basalt inscribed in Egyptian and Greek, with Egyptian written in both the hieroglyphic and demotic scripts (see WRITING). The text is a decree promulgated by the Egyptian priesthoods in honor of PTOLEMY V Epiphanes in his ninth year, 196 B.C. The monument was unearthed in 1799 by Lieutenant Bouchard of Napoleon's army, but terms of the French surrender to the British gave the French finds to the victors, and the stone reached the British Museum in 1802. The stone's bilingual text played a vital role in the decipherment of the ancient Egyptian writing systems, accomplished primarily by Jean François Champollion in 1822. The way was thus opened into the entire written patrimony of ancient EGYPT, covering 3000 years of history and civilization of the utmost value for the humanities in general, and for biblical backgrounds in particular.

Rosh. rosh (Heb. *rōʾš H8033*, "head, chief"). Son of BENJAMIN and grandson of JACOB (Gen. 46:21). The name does not appear in the parallel lists (Num. 26:38-39; 1 Chr. 8:1-5; see BEKER #1), and the SEPTUAGINT of Genesis lists Rosh as son of BELA and grandson of Benjamin. It has also been conjectured that the names "Ehi and Rosh, Muppim and Huppim" in the Genesis passage are a textual corruption of "Ahiram and Shupham and Hupham" (cf. Num. 26:38-39).

(2) According to some scholars, the Hebrew words describing GOG as "chief prince [*nĕśyʾ rōʾš*] of Meshech and Tubal" (Ezek. 38:2-3; 39:1) should rather be translated "prince of Rosh, Meshech, and Tubal" (cf. ASV; also NIV mg.). A people or country named *Rosh* is impossible to identify, although Russia and Rasu (in ASSYRIA) have been suggested. Russians are mentioned for the first time in the tenth century A.D. by Byzantine writers; it is therefore unlikely that the prophet could be referring to them.

row, rowers. See SHIPS.

ruby. See MINERALS.

rudder. See SHIPS.

ruddy. See RED.

rude. This English term, in the sense "untrained, unskilled," is used by the KJV in 2 Cor. 11:6, where PAUL concedes that he was inexpert and lacking in technical training. The NIV and other versions use the same term, but in the sense "discourteous," in 1 Cor. 13:5, where the apostle states that LOVE "is not rude" (KJV, "doth not behave itself unseemly").

rudiments. The KJV rendering of Greek *stoicheia* in a controversial passage, Col. 2:8, 20. See discussion under ELEMENTS, ELEMENTAL SPIRITS.

rue. See PLANTS.

Rufus. roo´fuhs (Gk. *Rhouphos G4859*, hellenized form of the common Latin name *Rufus*, "red"). (1) Son of SIMON of Cyrene (who was forced to carry Jesus' cross) and brother of ALEXANDER (Mk. 15:21). Mark's mention of Alexander and Rufus suggests that these brothers may have been known to his readers; and since his gospel is usually thought to have a Roman origin, it is possible that this Rufus is the same as #2 below.

(2) A Christian in ROME to whom PAUL sent greetings (Rom. 16:13). The apostle refers to him as "chosen in the Lord" (prob. suggesting, "a genuine believer" or the like) and states that his mother "has been a mother to me, too." We may infer that this family was originally from the eastern part of the empire and had there hosted or otherwise helped Paul.

rug. See CARPET.

Ruhamah. roo-hay´muh (Heb. *ruḥāmâ* [from *rāḥam H8163*], "pitied, loved"). A symbolic name given to Israel to indicate the return of God's mercy (Hos. 2:1; NIV, "My loved one"). There is a play on words involved, for the second child of GOMER, Hosea's wife, was called Lo-RUHAMAH, "not pitied" (Hos. 1:6, 8), to indicate that God had turned his back on Israel because of her apostasy. See also AMMI; LO-AMMI.

ruler. See OCCUPATIONS AND PROFESSIONS.

R

ruler of the synagogue. This phrase, or the simpler "synagogue ruler," is used to render Greek *archisynagōgos G801*, referring to the person chosen to care for the physical arrangements of the SYNAGOGUE services ("president of the synagogue" would be the equivalent designation today). Several serving in this capacity are mentioned in the NT: JAIRUS (Mk. 5:22-43; cf. Matt. 9:18-26; Lk. 8:40-56); some who are unnamed (Lk. 13:10-17; Acts 13:15); and two men from CORINTH named SOSTHENES and CRISPUS (Acts 18:7-8; cf. 1 Cor. 1:1). See also ELDER.

Rumah. roo′muh (Heb. *rûmâ H8126*, "height"). The hometown of a certain Pedaiah and/or his daughter Zebidah, who was the wife of JOSIAH and the mother of JEHOIAKIM (2 Ki. 23:36). The site has been variously located. Some suggest that it is identical with DUMAH (#1), one of the towns in the mountains of JUDAH, near HEBRON (Josh. 15:52). Others suggest that it is to be identified with ARUMAH, a place mentioned in the vicinity of SHECHEM (Jdg. 9:41). A more likely proposal is modern Khirbet er-Rameh in the Valley of Bet Netofa, near RIMMON in Galilee.

run. See RACE.

rush. See PLANTS.

rust. A brittle coating that tarnishes the surface of metals, especially iron, due to oxidation or corrosion. The few biblical references to rust are all figurative. In one of EZEKIEL's parables, the thick rust or deposit in a cooking pot of bronze became symbolic of the unpurged wickedness of the inhabitants of Jerusalem (Ezek. 24:6-13). In two NT passages a similar type of indictment, using the symbolism of the rusting of silver and gold, is pronounced against those who accumulate WEALTH (Matt. 6:19-20; Jas. 5:3 [NIV, "corroded" and "corrosion"]). In both cases the question arises whether the rust testifies to the impermanence of the wealth or whether it witnesses against the rich who prefer to hoard the wealth and let it rot rather than use it for benefiting others. The latter may better suit the context, for in the apocalyptic imagery rust is almost a living avenging force.

Ruth, Book of. (*rût H8134*, possibly "refreshment"). One of the historical books of the OT in the English Bible. In the Hebrew Bible, it is found among the Writings (HAGIOGRAPHA or KETUBIM) and grouped with the Five MEGILLOTH (Scrolls). Each of the Megilloth was associated with one of Israel's principal feasts, and Ruth was read at the Feast of Weeks (PENTECOST). The author of this book is unknown. The historical setting is the period of the judges (Ruth 1:1; see JUDGES, THE),

The fields E of Bethlehem to which Naomi returned with her daughter-in-law, Ruth. (View to the N.)

© Dr. James C. Martin

R

Overview of RUTH

Author: Unknown (the rabbinic view that Samuel wrote the book is discounted by most modern scholars).

Historical setting: The story takes place in the time of the judges (Ruth 1:1; see JUDGES, THE sect. II), probably c. 1100 B.C. The book may have been written during the reign of DAVID or shortly after (though some scholars date it centuries later).

Purpose: To demonstrate God's PROVIDENCE in the lives of ordinary people; to show that the Moabite ancestry of DAVID was divinely overseen and thus does not invalidate his kingship; to inculcate filial devotion.

Contents: NAOMI's bitterness and Ruth's devotion (Ruth 1); Ruth gleans grain in BOAZ's fields (ch. 2); Ruth requests kinsman-redemption from Boaz (ch. 3); Boaz becomes Ruth's kinsman-redeemer (ch. 4).

but there are certain indications that it was composed, or at least worked into its final form, at a much later time. For example, the opening words, "In the days when the judges ruled," appear to look back to that period; the explanatory comment in 4:7 refers to the period as "in earlier times"; and 4:22 mentions DAVID. Thus the final editorial process could not have ended before the Davidic era. It is best to place its final shaping in, or immediately following, David's reign.

The book records the circumstances that led to the marriage of Ruth, a Moabitess, to BOAZ, an Israelite. A famine forced NAOMI and her husband to move to MOAB, where her sons married Moabite women, one of whom was Ruth. Naomi and her daughters-in-law became widows, and when Naomi returned to BETHLEHEM, Ruth accompanied her. In the course of providing food for herself and her mother-in-law, Ruth met Boaz, a prosper-

ous farmer and a relative of Naomi. With Naomi's encouragement, Ruth tenderly reminded Boaz of the LEVIRATE obligation (Ruth 3:1-9), a Deuteronomic law that required a man to marry his brother's widow if she was childless, the purpose being that the dead man have an heir (Deut. 25:5-10). However, Boaz was not the nearest of kin. When the closest relative learned that there was a levirate obligation attached to the redemption of Naomi's land, he rejected it (Ruth 4:1-6), and Boaz was free to marry Ruth.

The book of Ruth demonstrates the providence of God at work in the life of an individual, and it exalts family loyalty. It shows how a GENTILE became part of the Davidic ancestry (4:17-21); thus Ruth is cited in Matthew's GENEALOGY OF JESUS CHRIST (Matt. 1:5).

rye. See PLANTS (under *spelt*).

R

S. In Septuagint studies, a symbol used to designate Codex Sinaiticus. See also TEXT AND VERSIONS (NT).

Saba, Sabaean, Sabaite. See SABEAN; SHEBA.

sabachthani. See ELI, ELI, LAMA SABACHTHANI.

Sabaoth. sab´ay-oth. See LORD OF HOSTS.

Sabbath. sab´uhth (Heb. *šabbāt H8701*, possibly "cessation, rest";Gk. *sabbaton G4879*). The Hebrew weekly day of REST and WORSHIP, which was observed on the seventh day of the week, beginning at sundown on Friday and ending at sundown on Saturday. The Sabbath was instituted at CREATION: "By the seventh day God had finished the work he had been doing; so on the seventh day he rested from all his work. And God blessed the seventh day and made it holy, because on it he rested from all the work of creating that he had done" (Gen. 2:2-3). There is no distinct mention of the word *Sabbath* in Genesis, but a seven-day period is mentioned several times in connection with the FLOOD (7:4, 10; 8:10, 12) and once in connection with JACOB's years at HARAN (29:27-28), showing that the division of time into sevens must have been known then.

There is in fact no express mention of the Sabbath before Exod. 16:21-30. In the Desert of Sin (see SIN, DESERT OF), before the Israelites reached Mount SINAI, God gave them MANNA, a double supply being given on the sixth day of the week, in order that the seventh day might be kept as a day of rest from labor. MOSES said to the people, "This is what the LORD commanded: 'Tomorrow is to be a day of rest, a holy Sabbath to the LORD. So bake what you want to bake. ... Save whatever is left and keep it until morning'" (Exod. 16:23). Shortly afterward the Ten Commandments were given by the Lord at Sinai (20:1-17; see COMMANDMENTS, TEN). The fourth commandment enjoined ISRAEL to observe the seventh day as a holy day on which no work should be done. Everyone, including even the stranger within the gates and the animals, was to desist from all work and to keep the day holy. The reason given is that the Lord rested on the seventh day and blessed and hallowed it. It is clear that God intended the day to be a blessing to the people, both physically and spiritually. The Sabbath is frequently mentioned in the Levitical legislation. It was to be kept holy for the worship of the Lord (Lev. 23:3) and was to remind the Israelites that God had sanctified them (Exod. 31:13). Forty years later, Moses rehearsed the Decalogue and reminded the Israelites of God's command to observe the Sabbath, specifying that they were under special obligation to keep it because God had delivered them from bondage in Egypt (Deut. 5:15).

Various attempts have been made by OT critics to find a Babylonian origin for the Jewish Sabbath. There is evidence that among the Babylonians certain things were to be avoided on the seventh, fourteenth, nineteenth, twenty-first, and twenty-eighth days of the month; but the nineteenth day breaks the sequence of sevens; and there is no question that the Hebrew Sabbath has much older historical attestation than this Babylonian observance. Among the Hebrews, moreover, the Sabbath was associated with the idea of rest, worship, and divine favor, not certain taboos.

After the time of Moses the Sabbath is mentioned sometimes in connection with the festival of the new moon (2 Ki. 4:23; Isa. 1:13; Ezek. 46:3;

Hos. 2:11; Amos 8:5). See FEASTS. The prophets always exalted the Sabbath and found fault with the Israelites for the perfunctory observance of it. They made confession of Israel's sin in profaning the Sabbath (Isa. 56:2, 4; 58:13; Jer. 17:21-27; Ezek. 20:12-24).

The sanctity of the Sabbath is shown by the offering on it of two lambs, in addition to the regular burnt offering (Num. 28:9-10). The twelve loaves of showbread were also presented on that day (Lev. 24:5-9; 1 Chr. 9:32). A willful Sabbath-breaker was put to death (Num. 15:32-36). The Israelite was not permitted even to light a fire in his home on the Sabbath. Psalm 92, expressing delight in the worship and works of the Lord, was composed for the Sabbath day. In the Persian period NEHEMIAH rebuked and took strong measures against those who disregarded the law of the Sabbath by doing business on it (Neh. 10:31; 13:15-22).

With the development of the SYNAGOGUE during the EXILE, the Sabbath became a day for worship and the study of the LAW, as well as a day of rest. There are not many references to the Sabbath in the apocryphal books. ANTIOCHUS Epiphanes tried to abolish it, along with other distinctively Jewish institutions (168 B.C.) . At the beginning of the Maccabean war (see MACCABEE), Jewish soldiers allowed themselves to be massacred rather than profane the Sabbath by fighting, even in self-defense. After 1,000 Jews were slaughtered in this way, they decided that in the future it would be permissible to defend themselves if attacked on the sacred day, but not to engage in offensive operations (1 Macc. 2:31-41). It was not, however, considered allowable to destroy siege-works on the Sabbath; and so POMPEY was permitted to raise his mound and mount his battering rams against JERUSALEM without interference from the Jews (Josephus, *Ant.* 14.4.2-3).

During the period between EZRA and the Christian era the SCRIBES formulated innumerable legal restrictions for the conduct of life under the law. Two whole tractates of the Mishnah (see TALMUD) are devoted to the details of Sabbath observance. One of these enumerates the following thirty-nine principal classes of prohibited actions: sowing, plowing, reaping, gathering into sheaves, threshing, winnowing, cleansing, grinding, sifting, kneading, baking; shearing wool, washing it, beating it, dyeing it, spinning it, making a warp of it; making two cords, weaving two threads, separating two threads, making a knot, untying a knot, sewing two stitches, tearing to sew two stitches; catching a deer, killing, skinning, salting it, preparing its hide, scraping off its hair, cutting it up; writing two letters, blotting out for the purpose of writing two letters, building, pulling down, extinguishing, lighting a fire, beating with a hammer, and carrying from one property to another (*Shabbat* 7:2).

Each of these chief enactments was further discussed and elaborated, so that actually there were several hundred things a conscientious, law-abiding Jew could not do on the Sabbath. For example, the prohibition regarding writing on the Sabbath was further defined as follows: "He who writes two letters with his right or his left hand, whether of one kind or of two kinds, as also if they are written with different ink or are of different languages, is guilty. He even who should from forgetfulness write two letters is guilty, whether he has

© Dr. James C. Martin.

Reconstruction of a first-century synagogue in Capernaum. This may have been the site where Jesus was criticized for healing on the Sabbath (Mk. 3:1-6).

written them with ink or with paint, red chalk, India rubber, vitriol, or anything which makes permanent marks. Also he who writes on two walls which form an angle, or on the two tablets of his account book, so that they can be read together, is guilty. He who writes upon his body is guilty. If any one writes with dark fluid, with fruit juice, or in the dust on the road, in sand, or in anything in which writing does not remain, he is free. If any one writes with the wrong hand, with the foot, with the mouth, with the elbow; also if any one writes upon a letter of another piece of writing, or covers other writing" (*Shabbat* 12:3-5). Although it is uncertain how many of these details go back to the NT period, Jesus must have had such things in mind when he said that the experts of the law were loading "people down with burdens they can hardly carry" (Lk. 11:46).

Jesus came into conflict with the religious leaders of the Jews especially on two points: his claim to be the MESSIAH, and on the matter of Sabbath observance. The rabbis regarded the Sabbath as an end in itself, whereas Jesus taught that the Sabbath was made for the benefit of human beings and that human needs must take precedence over the law of the Sabbath (Matt. 12:1-14; Mk. 2:23-3:6; Lk. 6:1-11; Jn. 5:1-18). He himself regularly attended worship in the synagogue on the Sabbath (Lk. 4:16).

The early Christians, most of whom were Jews, kept the seventh day as a Sabbath, but since the RESURRECTION of their Lord was the most blessed day in their lives, they soon began to meet for worship also on the first day of the week (Acts 2:1) and designated it as the Lord's Day (Rev. 1:10). PAUL directed the Corinthians to bring their weekly offering to the charities of the church on the first day of the week (1 Cor. 16:1-2), and eventually Sunday came to be viewed as the proper day of Christian worship. There is considerable difference among Christians, however, whether Sunday worship should be viewed as fulfilling the Sabbath commandment or as a different observance altogether.

Sabbath canopy. According to 2 Ki. 16:17-18, King AHAZ removed certain items from the TEMPLE, apparently in fear of, or to be sent as tribute to, TIGLATH-PILESER III. One of these items is described as *mûsak haššabbāt*, an architectural term of uncertain meaning usually rendered with such phrases as "covert for the sabbath" (KJV), "covered portal for use on the sabbath" (NRSV), and "Sabbath canopy" (NIV). Since Ezek. 46:1 speaks of a gate in the temple that was to be kept closed except on the Sabbath and on the day of the New Moon, some think the item in question may have been a barrier or grille (cf. NJPS, "sabbath passage"). Other proposals have been made.

Sabbath day's walk (journey). This expression occurs in the NT only once referring to the distance from the MOUNT OF OLIVES to JERUSALEM (Acts 1:12). This unit of measure (somewhat similar to the Egyptian unit of 1000 double steps) evidently served to indicate the limit of travel on the SABBATH, but the phrase became a common expression for a relatively short distance. From the Eastern Gate of Jerusalem to the present site of the Church of the Ascension on Mount Olivet, the distance is slightly over half a mile (almost 1 km.), and indeed a Sabbath day's journey was reckoned by the rabbis as 2000 cubits (c. 3000 ft./900 m.). It is assumed that the regulation had its origin in the Mosaic period in the injunction to the Israelite not to leave camp to collect MANNA on the Sabbath (Exod. 16:29). There are other regulations to which appeal is made in an effort to locate the origin of this practice or precept. One is the provision that the area belonging to the Levitical cities included land that extended from the wall 2000 cubits on every side (Num. 35:5). Another is the supposed distance that separated the ARK OF THE COVENANT and the people both on the march and at camp (Josh. 3:4). The original intent of the provision was to insure a quiet, leisurely Sabbath and to keep it from becoming a harried and busy day (Exod. 16:29). It was also designed to keep the Israelite worshiper in the area of the center of his worship. The motive was noble but, unfortunately, it often led to a barren legalism and to casuistic schemes to circumvent it. One such method was to go out on Friday and establish a residence somewhere by depositing at least two meals there; from that site, the person was allowed to travel an additional 2000 cubits on the Sabbath.

sabbatical year. See FEASTS.

Sabean. suh-bee′uhn. Also Sabaean. This name occurs three (possibly four) times in the Bible as the rendering of three Hebrew forms. In Isa. 45:14, the term *sĕbā*ʾ*î H6014* is used with reference to a tall people in a context that also speaks of EGYPT and CUSH, suggesting that these Sabeans were from SE AFRICA. It is possible that the same form occurs in Ezek. 23:42 with reference to certain people "from the desert," but the meaning of this text is very uncertain. In Job 1:15, we read that JOB's oxen and donkeys were carried off by the Sabeans; here the name *sĕbā*ʾ *H8644* is used, and the context of the story appears to be N ARABIA. Finally, in Joel 3:8 the Phoenicians (see PHOENICIA) and PHILISTINES are told: "I will sell your sons and daughters to the people of Judah, and they will sell them to the Sabeans, a nation far away"; in this ambiguous reference, the form used is *sĕbā*ʾ*îm H8645* (a gentilic from *sĕbā*ʾ).

The matter is further complicated by the fact that the Bible distinguishes between a son of Cush named SEBA and a grandson of Cush named SHEBA (Gen. 10:7; 1 Chr. 1:9; the names Cush and Seba occur together in Isa. 43:3, while Seba and Sheba are associated in Ps. 72:10). Moreover, there were two additional people by the name of Sheba who were descended not from HAM (father of Cush) but from SHEM, namely, Sheba son of JOKTAN (Gen. 10:28) and Sheba son of JOKSHAN (25:3); the latter was a grandson of ABRAHAM and brother of DEDAN. According to some scholars, a genetic distinction should be made between northern Sabeans (descended from a Semitic Sheba) and southern Sabeans (descended from a Hamitic Sheba or Seba). Others argue for a common progenitor. The possibility must be left open either (a) that at some point the southern Sabeans colonized some regions of N Arabia or (b) that the Sabean state began in N Arabia, with a movement toward, and settlement of, the southern part of the country during the middle of the second millennium B.C.

Be that as it may, the name Sabeans normally refers to the people of Saba (Sheba), a kingdom in S Arabia in the area presently known as Yemen and Ḥadramaut; its capital was Marib. Their position at the end of the Arabian peninsula was of twofold

advantage: (1) they were remote from the powers to the N, and so relatively secure; and (2) they were centrally located with respect to merchandising goods from nearby Africa and India. These included gold, incense, gem stones, probably ivory, etc. (Ps. 72:15; Isa. 60:6; Jer. 6:20; Ezek. 27:22; 38:13), giving rise to a great caravan industry (cf. Job 6:19). Evidently trading in slaves was also carried on (Joel 3:8; cf. Job 1:15). Fertile land and an extensive irrigation system, illustrated by the dam and sluices seen at Marib, made the country fairly self-sustaining. The history of Saba is extensive, including a strong pre-Islamic tradition. The biblical narrative suggests that the Sabeans were established prior to the tenth century, for their queen journeyed to Jerusalem to visit SOLOMON (1 Ki. 10:1-13; 2 Chr. 9:1-12). From the third century B.C. there appear references to these people in the works of historians and geographers, and in some Syriac and Ethiopic religious texts.

Sabta, Sabtah. sab′tuh (Heb. *sabtā*ʾ *H6029* and *sabtâ H6030*, derivation unknown). Son of CUSH and grandson of HAM, included in the Table of Nations (Gen. 10:7; 1 Chr. 1:9). The view that the text should be emended so that the name corresponds with that of Shabako, an Egyptian PHARAOH who ruled in the eighth century B.C. has not been widely accepted (see also SABTECA). Presumably, Sabta(h) is also a place name. If the Cushites settled in the area occupied by ETHIOPIA, the name may correspond to one of several places mentioned by Greek authors. It is possible, however, that the Cushites extended across the RED SEA from Nubia northeastward over the Arabian peninsula, and some scholars prefer a location in S ARABIA, in particular Ḥadramaut (HAZARMAVETH), which Strabo refers to as *Sabata* (*Geogr.* 16.4.2).

Sabteca. sab′tuh-kuh (Heb. *sabtĕkā*ʾ *H6031*, derivation unknown). KJV Sabtecha; TNIV Sabteka. Son of CUSH and grandson of HAM, included in the Table of Nations (Gen. 10:7; 1 Chr. 1:9). Sabteca is also very likely the name of a place in ARABIA, although its identification is uncertain. Some scholars identify Sabteca with Shabataka, an Egyptian PHARAOH from ETHIOPIA at the beginning of the seventh century B.C. (see SABTA).

Sabtecha. sab´tuh-kuh. KJV form of Sabteca.

Sabteka. sab´tuh-kuh. TNIV form of Sabteca.

Sacar. say´kahr (Heb. *śākār H8511*, "reward"). NRSV Sachar; TNIV Sakar. **(1)** A Hararite who was the father of Ahiam, one of David's mighty warriors (1 Chr. 11:35; called Sharar in the parallel, 2 Sam. 23:33).

(2) Fourth son of Obed-Edom, included in the list of divisions of the Korahite doorkeepers (see Korah) in the reign of David (1 Chr. 26:4).

Sachar. See Sacar.

Sachia. See Sakia.

sackbut. See music, musical instruments.

sackcloth. Strong, rough cloth woven from the long, dark hair of the oriental goat or the camel. The Hebrew word *śaq H8566* (as well as the loan-word in Greek, *sakkos G4884*) can refer both to the cloth itself and to a bag (sack) made from it. When large, such a bag was used at times as a container for grain (Gen. 42:25). On some occasions it was utilized for saddlebags (Josh. 9:4) and provided a common bedding material (2 Sam. 21:10). Its main use, however, was as an article of clothing: made of cheap and durable material, it served the purpose of an ordinary item of garb. At times it seems to have served as the distinctive garb of the prophets (Isa. 20:2; Zech. 13:4), but gradually it came to bear a primarily symbolical meaning. The wearing of sackcloth was regarded as proper garb for serious and sober occasions. Since it was dark in texture, it was deemed fitting in times of grief and sadness. Jacob clothed himself in it at the report of the death of his favorite son Joseph (Gen. 37:34), and David commanded Joab and the other mourners to wear it upon the death of Abner (2 Sam. 3:31). Sackcloth was also a mark of abject penitence (Neh. 9:1; Jer. 6:26; Matt. 11:21; et al.).

sacrament. The Latin noun *sacramentum* (from the verb *sacrō*, "to set apart as sacred") was originally used in a variety of secular contexts with such meanings as "guarantee" and "oath." In a religious context, however, the term would refer to something sacred or consecrated, and in the Vulgate it translates the Greek word *mystērion G3696*, "mystery" (cf. Eph. 1:9; 3:2-3, 9; 5:32; Col. 1:26-27; 1 Tim. 3:16; Rev. 1:20; 17:7). In a wide sense it came to designate any sign which possessed a hidden meaning. Religious rites and ceremonies such as the sign of the cross, anointing with oil, preaching, confirmation, prayer, aid to the sick, etc., were equally called sacraments.

Because of the absence of any defined sacramental concept in the early history of the church, the number of sacraments was not regarded as fixed. Baptism and the Lord's Supper were the chief. In the twelfth century Hugo of St. Victor listed thirty sacraments that had been recognized by the church, while Gregory of Bergamo and Peter Lombard listed only seven: baptism, confirmation, the Eucharist, penance, extreme unction, orders, and matrimony—a list adopted by Thomas Aquinas and later by the Council of Trent. The number seven, viewed as sacred, was supported by many fanciful arguments. There is no NT authority for it, and it is a purely arbitrary figure. It is hard to see on what principle baptism and the Lord's Supper, which were instituted by Christ, can be put in the same category with marriage, which is as old as the human race.

The Reformers saw in baptism and the Lord's Supper three distinguishing marks: (1) they were instituted by Christ; (2) Christ commanded that they be observed by his followers; and (3) they are visible symbols of divine acts. Since there are no other rites for which such marks can be claimed, only two sacraments exist. There is justification for classifying them under a common name because they are associated together in the NT (Acts 2:41-42; 1 Cor. 10:1-4).

Some modern critics challenge the claim that baptism and the Lord's Supper owe their origin to Christ, but a fair reading of the NT shows that these sacramental rites were universal in the apostolic church and that the apostles observed them because they were convinced that Christ had instituted them. They taught the church to observe the things that Christ commanded (Matt. 28:20). Circumstances of great solemnity surrounded the institution of the sacraments by Christ. He

S

appointed the Lord's Supper on the eve of his redemptive sacrifice and commanded baptism in the Great Commission at the time of his ascension.

These rites were regarded as ritual acts of faith and obedience toward God (Matt. 28:19-20; Acts 2:38; Rom. 6:3-5; 1 Cor. 11:23-27; Col. 2:11-12). They are symbolic rites setting forth the central truths of the Christian faith: death and resurrection with Christ and participation in the redemptive benefits of Christ's mediatorial death. They are visible enactments of the gospel message that Christ lived, died, was raised from the dead, ascended to heaven, and will some day return, and that all this is for our salvation. In the NT the idea of baptism is intimately connected with the following: the FORGIVENESS of sin (Acts 2:38; 22:16; Eph. 5:26; Tit. 3:5), the gift of the HOLY SPIRIT (Acts 2:38; 1 Cor. 12:13), UNION WITH CHRIST in his death and resurrection (Rom. 6:3-6; Col. 2:12), REGENERATION (Jn. 3:5; Tit. 3:5), entering into the relationship of sonship with God (Gal. 3:26-27), belonging to the CHURCH (Acts 2:41), and the gift of SALVATION (Mk. 16:16). The Lord's Supper symbolizes Christ's death for the remission of sins (Matt. 26:28). It is a seal of the new covenant in Christ's blood, an assurance of eternal life now, a promise of the second coming, and a pledge of the eventual messianic triumph.

sacrifice and offerings. A religious act belonging to WORSHIP in which offering is made to God of some material object belonging to the offerer—this offering being consumed in the ceremony, in order to attain, restore, maintain, or celebrate friendly relations with the deity. The motives actuating the offerer may vary, worthy or unworthy, and may express faith, repentance, adoration, or all of these together; but the main purpose of the sacrifice is to please the deity and to secure his favor.

I. Origin of sacrifice. Did sacrifice arise from the natural religious instinct of human beings, whether guided by the Spirit of God or not, or did it originate in a distinct divine appointment? Genesis records the first instances of sacrifice, by CAIN and ABEL, but gives no account of the origin of the idea. The custom is clearly approved by God, and in the Mosaic law it is adopted and elaborately developed. The view that the rite was initiated by an express command of God is based mainly on Gen. 4:4-5, which states that Abel offered to God an acceptable sacrifice, and on Heb. 11:4, where it is said that Abel's sacrifice was acceptable to God because of his FAITH. It is argued that Abel's faith was based on a specific command of God in the past and that without such a divine command his sacrifice would have been mere superstition. Many who hold this view also say that the garments provided by God to hide the nakedness of Adam and Eve must have come from an animal that had been sacrificed and that in this sacrifice we have a type of the sacrifice of Christ to cover the sinner's spiritual nakedness before God. While all this possibly may be deduced from Scripture, it is not a necessary deduction.

Those who hold that sacrifice was devised by human beings, with or without direction by God's Spirit, as a means of satisfying the wants of their spiritual nature, have advanced several theories. (1) The *gift* theory holds that sacrifices were originally presents to God that the offerer hoped would be received with pleasure and gratitude by the deity, who would then grant him favors. (2) The *table-bond* theory suggests that sacrifices were originally meals shared by the worshipers and the deity, with the purpose of knitting them together in a firmer bond of fellowship. (3) The *sacramental-communion* theory is a modification of the table-bond theory. The basis of it is the belief among some primitive peoples that animals share along with humans in the divine nature. The worshiper actually eats the god, thus acquiring the physical, intellectual, and moral qualities that characterized the animal. (4) The *homage* theory holds that sacrifice originates not in a sense of guilt, but in the desire to express homage to and dependence on the deity. (5) The *expiatory* theory says that sacrifices are fundamentally piacular or atoning for sin. Conscious of their sin and of the punishment that it deserves, people substitute an animal to endure the penalty due to themselves and so make their peace with the deity. See ATONEMENT.

II. Classification of sacrifices. Sacrifices have been classified in a variety of ways, chiefly the following: (1) Those on behalf of the whole congregation and those on behalf of the individual. (2) Animal or bleeding sacrifices and bloodless offerings. (3) Sacrifices assuming an undisturbed cov-

Altar found in Megiddo, most likely used for burning incense or as a stand for a grain or meal offerings.

enant relationship and those intended to restore a relationship that has been disturbed. (4) Animal sacrifices, vegetable sacrifices, liquid and incense offerings. (5) Sacrifices made without the help of a priest, those made by a priest alone, and those made by a layman with the help of a priest. (6) Sacrifices that express homage to the deity; those designed to make atonement for sin; and peace offerings, to express or promote peaceful relations with the deity. (7) Self-dedicatory sacrifices, eucharistic sacrifices, and expiatory sacrifices. (8) Sacrifices in which the offering was wholly devoted to God, and sacrifices in which God received a portion and the worshiper feasted on the remainder.

III. History of sacrifice in OT times. The sacrifices of Cain and Abel (Gen. 4:4-5) show that the rite goes back almost to the beginnings of the human race. No PRIEST was needed in their sacrifices, which were eucharistic and possibly expiatory. The sacrifice of NOAH after the FLOOD (8:20-21) is called a burnt offering and is closely connected with the COVENANT of God described in Gen. 9:8-17. In the sacrifices of ABRAHAM, several of which are mentioned (12:7-8; 13:4, 18; 15:9-10), he acted as his own priest and made offerings to express his

adoration of God and probably to atone for sin. In Gen. 22 God reveals to him that he does not desire human sacrifices, a common practice in those days. The patriarchs ISAAC and JACOB regularly offered sacrifices (26:25; 28:18; 31:54; 33:20; 35:7; 46:1). JOB and his friends offered sacrifices (Job 1:5; 42:7-9), probably to atone for sin. The Israelites during their sojourn in EGYPT no doubt were accustomed to animal sacrifices. It was to some such feast that MOSES asked the PHARAOH for permission to go into the wilderness (Exod. 3:18; 5:3; 7:16); and he requested herds and flocks for the feast to offer burnt offerings and sacrifices (10:24-25). The sacrifice of the Passover (12:3-11) brings out forcibly the idea of salvation from death. JETHRO, Moses' father-in-law, a priest, offered sacrifices on meeting Moses and the people (18:12).

The establishment of the covenant between Israel and the Lord was accompanied by solemn sacrifices. The foundation principle of this covenant was *obedience*, not sacrifices (Exod. 19:4-8). Sacrifices were incidental—aids to obedience, but valueless without it. The common altars were not abolished with the giving of the covenant code but continued to be used for centuries by Joshua, Gideon, Jephthah, Samuel, Saul, David, Elijah, and many others. They were perfectly legitimate and even necessary at least until the building of the TEMPLE in JERUSALEM.

At the division of the kingdom in 931 B.C. CALF WORSHIP was established at DAN and BETHEL, with priests, altars, and ritual (1 Ki. 12:27-28). HIGH PLACES, most of them very corrupt, were in use in both kingdoms until the time of the EXILE, although occasionally attempts were made in the southern kingdom to remove them. With the destruction of the temple in Jerusalem in 586 B.C. the entire cultus was suspended, but on the return from the captivity an altar was built and sacrifices resumed. At the time of NEHEMIAH there existed a temple at Elephantine in Egypt, built by Jews, where a system of sacrifices was observed. Sacrifices were made in the temple in Jerusalem until its destruction by the Romans in A.D. 70. The Jews have offered none since then.

IV. The Mosaic sacrifices. Every offering had to be the honestly acquired property of the offerer (2 Sam. 24:24). Sacrifices had value in the eyes of

S

S

the Lord only when they were made in acknowledgment of his sovereign majesty, expressed in obedience to him, and with a sincere desire to enjoy his favor. The only animals allowed for sacrifice were oxen, sheep, goats, and pigeons. Wild animals and fish could not be offered. The produce of the field allowed for offerings was wine, oil, grain, either in the ear or in the form of meal, dough, or cakes. Sacrifices were of two kinds: animal (with the shedding of blood) and vegetable or bloodless.

A. Animal sacrifices. Both male and female animals were accepted for sacrifice, although for some sacrifices the male was prescribed. With one exception (Lev. 22:23), no animal with any sort of wound or defect could be offered (22:21-24). The law commanded that animals be at least eight days old (22:27); and in some cases the age of the animal is specified (9:3; 12:6; Num. 28:3, 9, 11). According to the later rabbis, animals more than three years old could not be sacrificed. There was no prescription of age or sex with regard to pigeons or turtle doves, but they were offered only by the poor as substitutes for other animals.

1. The sin offering (Lev. 4:1-35; 6:24-30). This was for sins unconsciously or unintentionally committed; sins committed intentionally, but with mitigating circumstances (5:2-3; 12:6-8); certain kinds of ceremonial defilements (5:2-3; 12:6-8); and sins deliberately committed but afterwards voluntarily confessed. For conscious and deliberate violations of the law no atonement was possible, with some exceptions, for which provision was made in the guilt offerings. Capital crimes: the breaking of the law of the Sabbath (Num. 15:32), adultery (Deut. 22:22-23), murder (Exod. 21:12), and sacrilege (Josh. 7:15) were punished with death. Sin offerings were made for the whole congregation on all the feast days and especially on the Day of Atonement. They were also offered on the occasion of the consecration of priests and Levites (Exod. 29:10-14, 36). Every year, on the great Day of Atonement, sin offerings were brought for the high priest. With the exception of these important national occasions, the sin offerings were presented only when special circumstances demanded expiation of sin.

The costliness of the offering and the procedure to be followed depended on the theocratic importance of the offender. For the high priest a young bullock was the appointed offering (Lev. 4:3); for a prince it was a male goat (4:23); in ordinary cases a female goat or a sheep was sufficient. The poor could offer two pigeons, and where even these were too much, a small portion of fine flour was substituted (5:7, 11).

In all other blood sacrifices the blood was simply poured around the altar; in this one the blood was sprinkled. If a member of the congregation made the offering, the blood was smeared on the horns of the altar in the forecourt (Lev. 4:7, 18, 25, 30). When a sin offering was for a priest or the whole congregation, the officiating priest took some of the blood of the sacrifice into the Holy Place and sprinkled it seven times before the veil of the sanctuary and then smeared it on the horns of the altar of incense. The blood that was left had to be poured out at the base of the altar. After the blood was sprinkled, the fat portions of the animal were burned on the altar. The remainder of the flesh was disposed of in two ways: in the case of sin offerings of any of the congregation the flesh was eaten in the forecourt by the officiating priest and his sons; in the case of sin offerings for a priest or for the whole congregation, the whole animal was burned outside the camp in a clean place.

2. The guilt offering (Lev. 5:14-6:7; KJV, "trespass offering"). This was a special kind of sin offering for transgressions where restitution or other legal satisfaction could be made or was made. When the rights of God or neighbor were violated, the wrong had to be righted, the broken law honored, and the sin expiated by a guilt offering. The offering, which was always a lamb, with one exception (14:12), was given after the required satisfaction had been made. The ritual was the same as in the sin offering, except that the blood was not sprinkled but poured over the surface of the altar. Its main purpose was to make expiation for dues withheld from God, like neglect to pay at the proper time what was due to the sanctuary; and from man, like robbery, failure to return a deposit, swearing falsely regarding anything lost, and seduction of a betrothed slave girl. The sin offering of a lamb made atonement to God. Restitution, with an additional one-fifth, made reparation to man.

3. The burnt offering (Lev. 1). The distinguishing mark of this offering was that it was wholly consumed on the altar, while in other animal sacrifices only the fat portions were burned. The purpose of the offering was PROPITIATION; but with this idea was united another, the entire consecration of the worshiper to the Lord. Because of the regularity and frequency with which it was offered, it was called the "continual" burnt offering (Exod. 29:42); and because no part was left for human consumption, it was also called the "whole burnt offering" (Ps. 51:19). This was the normal sacrifice of the Israelite in proper covenant relationship with God and was the only sacrifice regularly appointed for the sanctuary service. It was offered every day, in the morning and in the evening. On ordinary days a yearling lamb was sacrificed; on the Sabbath day two lambs were offered at morning and evening sacrifice (Num. 28:9-10). On other special feast days a larger number of animals was offered. There were also private burnt offerings when a NAZIRITE fulfilled his vow or defiled himself (Num. 6), at the consecration of priests (Exod. 29:15), at the cleansing of lepers (Lev. 14:9), at the purification of women (12:6), and for other ceremonial uncleanness (15:15, 30). This was the only sacrifice that a non-Israelite was permitted to offer (17:8; 22:18, 25).

4. The fellowship offering (Lev. 3; KJV, "peace offering"). These were called fellowship offerings because they were offered by those who were at peace with God, to express gratitude and obligation to God, and fellowship with him. They were not commanded to be offered at any set time except PENTECOST (23:20); they were presented spontaneously as the feelings of the worshiper prompted (19:5).

The ritual was the same as for the sin offering, except that the blood was wholly poured on the altar, as in the guilt offering and burnt offering. The fat was burned; the breast and thigh were kept by the priests; and the rest of the flesh was eaten at the sanctuary by the sacrificer and his friends (Lev. 7:15-16, 30-34; Deut. 12:1, 17-18). A meat and drink offering always accompanied this sacrifice. This meal denoted the fellowship that existed between the worshiper and God and was a symbol and pledge of friendship and peace with him. There were three kinds of fellowship offerings: praise offerings, votive offerings, and freewill offerings. For all three classes oxen, sheep, and goats of either sex could be offered (Lev. 3:1, 6, 12). The animals had to be without blemish, except for the freewill offerings, where animals with too short or too long a limb were allowed (22:23). Fellowship offerings were also offered on occasions of great public solemnity or rejoicing.

B. Vegetable or bloodless sacrifices. These were of two kinds, the grain offerings (called "meat offerings" in the KJV) and the drink offerings. They were offered on the altar of the forecourt.

1. The grain offerings (Lev. 2:1-16; 6:14-18) were not animal offerings as the name in the KJV suggests, but offerings of fine flour or of unleavened bread, cakes, wafers, or of ears of grain toasted, always with salt and, except in the sin offering, with olive oil (2:1, 4, 13-14; 5:11). They were sometimes accompanied by frankincense. Only a portion was consumed by fire on the altar; the rest was kept by the priests, who ate it in a holy place (6:16; 10:12-13). The grain offering accompanied the other offerings, except the sin offering, on all important occasions (7:11-14; Num. 15). It always followed the morning and evening burnt offerings. The idea behind the grain offering seems to have been that since people would not ordinarily eat meals consisting only of flesh, it would be wrong to offer only flesh to God.

2. The drink offerings were not independent offerings under the law but were made only in connection with the grain offering that accompanied all burnt offerings and all fellowship offerings that were Nazirite, votive, or freewill (Num. 6:17; 15:1-2). They did not accompany sin and guilt offerings. The drink offering consisted of wine, which was poured out on the altar, probably on the flesh of the sacrifice.

Besides the above, three offerings were regularly made in the Holy Place: the twelve loaves of SHOWBREAD, renewed every SABBATH; the oil for the seven-branched LAMPSTAND, which was filled every morning; and the incense for the altar of INCENSE, which was renewed every morning and evening.

sacrifice, human. See CHEMOSH; JEPHTHAH; MOLECH.

sacrilege. The KJV uses the expression "commit sacrilege" once to render the Greek verb *hierosyleō G2644*, which more probably means "to rob temples" (Rom. 2:22). In Roman law the term *sacrilegium* was applied to the removal of a sacred object from a sacred place, and carried severe penalties. The NRSV uses "sacrilege" to render *bdelygma G1007* ("detestable thing"), but only in the expression "desolating sacrilege" (Matt. 24:15; Mk. 13:14); see ABOMINATION OF DESOLATION.

saddle. A seat for riding an animal. Perhaps an early invention of the Persians, the saddle served both as a carriage for riders and as a covering to prevent the animal's back from chafing. Ordinarily, as is indicated in the record of ABRAHAM's going up to Mount MORIAH with ISAAC (Gen. 22:3) and of BALAAM's setting out to curse Israel (Num. 22:21), it was the donkey that was saddled. In one instance (Gen. 31:34), reference is made to the saddle of a camel, probably a basket-like seat.

Sadducee. sad´joo-see (Gk. *Saddoukaios G4881*, derivation uncertain). A member of an important Jewish sect, more political than religious, which arose among the priestly aristocracy of the Hasmonean period (see MACCABEE), but which ceased to exist with the demise of the aristocracy after the destruction of JERUSALEM (A.D. 70). The Sadducees are perhaps today best known for their opposition to the popular party of the PHARISEES, with whom they differed on various doctrinal and political questions.

The derivation of the name *Sadducee* has been the subject of considerable discussion but has not been established with any certainty. The more significant possibilities are the following: (1) Since in Hebrew the name consists of the same three radicals (*ṣdq*) as the word for "righteousness," it has been argued that *Sadducees* means "righteous ones." This account, however, leaves unexplained the presence of the vowel *u* in the name; moreover, it is not at all clear in what sense "righteousness" could be attributed to, or even claimed by, the Sadducees as their distinguishing characteristic. (2) An explanation that has gained popularity in modern times and is held by the majority of contemporary scholars, traces the word back to the proper noun *ṣādôq H7401* (Gk. *Sadōk G4882*, sometimes spelled *Saddouk* in the LXX). *Sadducee* thereby becomes the

Stone weight inscribed in Aramaic, found in the so-called Burnt House of Jerusalem, and bearing the name Bar Kathros. The Babylonian Talmud refers to "the house of Kathros" as a priestly family who probably belonged to the Sadducean party (*b. Pesaḥim* 57a).

equivalent of *Zadokite* ("descendant of Zadok"), the ZADOK in question being the descendant of AARON who became a leading priest under DAVID (2 Sam. 8:17; 15:24-29), and chief priest under SOLOMON (1 Ki. 1:32; 2:35). However, although the priestly line begun by Zadok continued through NT times, the Jerusalem priesthood of the Hasmonean period was manifestly not of Zadokite lineage. Some have therefore argued that a different Zadok is in view. (3) Another suggestion is that the Aramaic/Hebrew word is a transliteration of Greek *syndikoi*, meaning "syndics, judges, fiscal controllers," and that *Sadducee* was used also to refer to members of the Jewish senate, the SANHEDRIN. Even if this third proposal is sound, however, there is no evidence that such a derivation played a role in people's understanding of who the Sadducees were. It would seem safe to say that soon after the word achieved currency and its referent (a particular sect) was established, its real etymology became unimportant (and may even have been forgotten), and that alternative etymological possibilities sprang readily to mind.

© Dr. James C. Martin

The chief authorities for our knowledge of this sect are the Jewish historian Josephus, the NT, and the Talmud. Josephus lays great stress on the aristocratic nature of the Sadducees. He says, "They only gain the well-to-do; they have not the people on their side." They were the political party of the Jewish aristocratic priesthood from the time of the Maccabees to the final fall of the Jewish state. The Sadducees were priests, but not all priests were Sadducees. Josephus himself, for example, was a priest and a Pharisee. The likelihood is that the priestly party only gradually crystallized into the sect of the Sadducees. From the time of the exile, the priesthood in general constituted the nobility of the Jewish people, and the high priest became an increasingly powerful figure. The priestly aristocracy became leaders in the hellenizing movement that began with Alexander the Great. Because of their sympathy with the policy of Antiochus Epiphanes, they took no part in the Maccabean struggle, which was supported mainly by the Pharisees, a group of religious enthusiasts who opposed what they regarded as the religious deterioration of the Jewish nation.

In the Hasmonean dynasty, high priesthood and civic rule were united in a single person. This centralization of power led to various reactions, especially from the Pharisees. Probably not a theological party at first, the Sadducees had to address theological issues in order to defend their policies against the attacks of the Pharisees. Under the Romans they became the party favorable to the government. As aristocrats they were naturally very conservative and were more interested in maintaining the political status quo than in the religious purity of the nation. Since they were satisfied with the present, they did not look forward to a future messianic age. Not popular with the people, they sometimes found it necessary to adopt the pharisaic policy in order to win the popular support.

The Sadducees had a number of distinctive beliefs, contrasting strongly with those of the Pharisees. (1) They held only to the written law and rejected the "traditions of the elders" (cf. Mk. 7:3-5; Gal. 1:14). Josephus says, "The Pharisees have delivered to the people a great many observances by succession from their fathers, which are not written in the law of Moses; and for that reason it is that Sadducees reject them, and say that we are to esteem those observances to be obligatory which are in the written Word, but are not to observe what are derived from the tradition of our forefathers. And concerning these things it is that great disputes and differences have risen among them" (*Ant.* 13.10.6). Some have thought that the Sadducees viewed the Pentateuch as alone canonical, but that inference seems unnecessary. The primary point of contention was rather the *oral law*, which the Pharisees traced to Moses himself and regarded as on a par with the written law.

(2) A second distinctive belief of the Sadducees was their denial of the resurrection of the body. "The doctrine of the Sadducees," says Josephus, "is this, that souls die with the bodies" (*Ant.* 18.1.4); and again, "They also take away the belief of the immortal duration of the soul, and the punishments and rewards in Hades" (*War* 2.1.14). According to the NT, the Sadducees denied the resurrection of the body (Matt. 22:23; Mk. 12:18; Lk. 20:27; Acts 23:8; cf. Acts 4:1-2), but the NT says nothing about their denial of personal immortality and future retribution.

According to Acts 23:8, the Sadducees denied the existence of angels and spirits. Seeing that they accepted the OT, in which spirits often appear, it is hard to understand their position on this subject. Perhaps they were reacting to developments in the intertestamental period: the idea of a spiritual world containing elaborate hierarchies of angels and demons flourished particularly in the intertestamental period.

(4) The Sadducees differed from both the Pharisees and the Essenes on the matter of divine predestination and the freedom of the human will. According to Josephus, the Essenes held that all things are fixed by God's unalterable decree; the Pharisees tried to combine predestination and free will; and the Sadducees threw aside all ideas of divine interposition in the government of the world. "They take away fate," says Josephus, "and say there is no such thing, and that events of human affairs are not at its disposal, but they suppose that all our actions are in our own power, so that we are ourselves the causes of what is good, and receive what is evil from our own folly" (*Ant.* 13.5.9; cf. also *War* 2.8.14). If this description is

accurate, they apparently felt no need of a divine PROVIDENCE to order their lives but rather thought human beings were entirely the master of their own destinies and that the doing of good or evil was entirely a matter of free choice.

The Sadducees are mentioned by name in the NT only about a dozen times (Matt. 3:7; 16:1, 6, 11-12; 22:23, 34; Mk. 12:18; Lk. 20:27; Acts 4:1; 5:17; 23:6-8); but it must be remembered that when mention is made of the chief priests, practically the same persons are referred to. They seem mostly to have ignored Jesus, at least in the early part of his ministry. Jesus directed his criticism against the Pharisees, although once he warned his disciples against the "yeast" of the Sadducees (Matt. 16:6, 11). With the Pharisees, the Sadducees asked Jesus to show them a sign from heaven (16:1). They resented his action in cleansing the temple (Matt. 21:12; Mk. 11:15-16; Lk. 19:45-46) and were filled with indignation at his claim of the messianic title "son of David" (Matt. 21:15-16). They tried to discredit him in the eyes of the people and get him into trouble with the Roman power by their questions about his authority (21:23), the resurrection (22:23), and the lawfulness of paying tribute to Caesar (Lk. 20:22). They joined the scribes and Pharisees in their attempt to destroy him (Mk. 11:18; Lk. 19:47). They sat in the Sanhedrin, which condemned him; and the chief priest who presided was a member of their party. In their opposition they were probably most influenced by their fear that a messianic movement led by him would bring political ruin (Jn. 11:49).

After the Day of PENTECOST the Sadducees were very active against the infant church. Along with the priests and the captain of the temple they arrested Peter and John and put them in prison. A little later they arrested all the apostles and made plans to kill them (Acts 5:17, 33). Their hostile attitude persisted throughout the apostolic times. According to Josephus (*Ant.* 20.9.1), they were responsible for the death of JAMES, the brother of the Lord. With the destruction of Jerusalem in A.D. 70, the Sadducean party disappeared.

sadhe. sah´day. See TSADHE.

Sadoc. See ZADOK.

saffron. See PLANTS.

Sahidic version. See TEXT AND VERSIONS (NT).

sail. See SHIPS.

sailor. See OCCUPATIONS AND PROFESSIONS; SHIPS.

saint. A person sacred to God. In the OT, this English word is used primarily to render the Hebrew adjective *qādôš H7705*, which means "set apart, consecrated, holy." When the plural is used substantivally, it is translated "holy ones" or "saints" (Ps. 16:3 et al.). The focus of this term is on the CONSECRATION of the subject involved, but all people consecrated to God are ideally to be free from moral and ceremonial defilement. See HOLINESS. In the NT the adjective *hagios G41*, when used as a noun, usually refers to members of the Christian church. It is used once in the Gospels (Matt. 27:52) of the saints of the former age. The other references are in Acts, the Epistles, and Revelation. *All* believers are called "saints," even when their character is dubiously holy. The term is applied usually to the group of Christians constituting a CHURCH, rather than to one individual Christian (e.g., Acts 9:13; Rom. 8:27; Rev. 5:8). The reference is to those who belong to God as his own. In some instances, however, their saintly character becomes prominent (e.g., Rom. 16:2; Eph. 5:3).

It is easy to see how the term *saints* would inevitably take on an ethical and moral meaning. If a person belonged to Christ, showed Christian character by an exemplary life, and made notable progress in SANCTIFICATION, so that his or her reputation as a good, moral, and spiritual Christian became widely spread among the churches, people would begin to speak of that person's exceptional "saintly" character. In that way the term would gradually be used only of such persons who were outstanding in spirituality. That is probably the origin of the Roman Catholic custom of restricting the usage of the term to notable persons like the apostles and those whom the church selected and honored officially as "saints." Such a practice, however, does not correspond to the biblical usage of the term.

Sakar. say´kahr. TNIV form of SACAR.

Sakia. suh-ki′uh (Heb. *śokyâ H8499*, possibly "Yahweh has fenced in"). KJV Shachiah; NRSV Sachia; NJPS Sachiah. Son of SHAHARAIM and descendant of BENJAMIN; a family head (1 Chr. 8:10). He was one of seven children that were born to Shaharaim in MOAB by his wife HODESH after he had divorced Hushim and Baara (vv. 8-9).

Sakkuth. sak′uhth. Also Sikkuth. This name is used by some versions to represent the Hebrew word *sikkût* in Amos 5:26: "You shall take up Sakkuth your king, and Kaiwan your star-god" (NRSV). Such a rendering assumes that the Hebrew term is a loanword from Akkadian *sakkud*, and it is often thought that both this name and KAIWAN are references to the planet Saturn as a deity. The evidence for this interpretation, however, is not strong. Accordingly, the NIV understands the word as a form of *sukkâ H6109*, "tent, tabernacle" (cf. also *skēnē G5008* in LXX, quoted in Acts 7:43), yielding the translation, "You have lifted up the shrine of your king, the pedestal of your idols." See also REPHAN.

Sala, Salah. See SALMA, SALMON; SHELAH.

Salamis. sal′uh-mis (Gk. *Salamis G4887*). A harbor on the W coast of the island of CYPRUS. The ancient site, N of modern Famagusta, has been completely silted in by the River Pedias. Salamis traded actively with PHOENICIA, EGYPT, and other countries of the ANE. The sources of commerce were grain, wine, olive oil, and salt. The Romans annexed the island in 58 B.C. in repayment for loans made to PTOLEMY Auletes. At first, Cyprus was part of the province of CILICIA, but in 31 B.C. it became a separate imperial province. In 22 B.C. it became a senatorial province; hence, Sergius PAULUS is correctly identified as PROCONSUL (Acts 13:7). PAUL and BARNABAS, assisted by John Mark (see MARK, JOHN), preached in the synagogues there on the first missionary journey (13:5). From Salamis they proceeded across the island to PAPHOS.

Salathiel, Salatiel. See SHEALTIEL.

Salcah, Salchah. See SALECAH.

Salecah. sal′kuh (Heb. *salkâ H6146*, derivation unknown). KJV Salcah and Salchah; TNIV Salekah. A town that defined the eastward extent of BASHAN (Deut. 3:10; Josh. 12:5; 13:11; 1 Chr. 5:11). Taken from King OG, Salecah was apparently assigned to the eastern part of MANASSEH (Josh. 13:29-31), but was later inhabited by the

The civic center of the Roman city of Salamis. On the left is the wrestling ground of the gymnasium, with the theater on the right.

© Courtesy of The British Museum. Photo: Sonia Halliday and Laura Lushington.

S

tribe of GAD (1 Chr. 5:11). Its identification is not certain. A suitable site with a similar name is modern Salkhad, located on an extinct volcanic cone 8 mi. (13 km.) S of Jebel ed-Druze. Its strategic importance makes it the proper eastern extremity of Bashan.

Salem. say′luhm (Heb. *šālēm H8970*, "complete, safe"). An abbreviated form of JERUSALEM. Though occurring only four times in Scripture, Salem is the city's first designation (Gen. 14:18) and, along with ZION, identifies the place of God's dwelling (Ps. 76:2). The title given to MELCHIZEDEK, king of Salem (Heb. 7:1), is understood by the writer of Hebrews as "king of peace" (v. 2), in its sense of security, prosperity, and well-being (see PEACE). The name Salem/Shalem may also have connoted to Jerusalem's original Jebusite inhabitants (see JEBUS) a "prospering" Canaanite deity of that name.

Salim. say′lim (Gk. *Salim G4890*, also *Saleim*, prob. from Heb. *šālēm H8970* [see SALEM]). A place used to specify the location of AENEON, where JOHN THE BAPTIST was baptizing (Jn. 3:23). Salim must have been a well-known site, but it has not been identified with certainty. Suggestions include (1) Hellenistic Salumias, modern Tell er-Radghah, c. 7.5 mi. (12 km.) SSE of Scythopolis (BETH SHAN); (2) modern Salim, a few miles E of Nablus (ancient SHECHEM), the town nearest to the springs of Wadi Fariʿa (Farah), though some have argued that John was unlikely to minister in SAMARIA; (3) Wadi Saleim, only about 6 mi. (10 km.) NE of JERUSALEM.

Sallai. sal′i (Heb. *sallay H6144*, meaning uncertain). **(1)** One of the leaders from BENJAMIN who volunteered to settle in JERUSALEM after the return from the EXILE (Neh. 11:8). Instead of the two names "Gabbai, Sallai," some scholars emend the Hebrew text to read "men of valor" (cf. ESV). **(2)** See SALLU #2.

Sallu. sal′oo (Heb. *sallu H6132*, *sallû H6139*, possibly "[God] has returned [*or* restored]"). **(1)** Son of MESHULLAM; mentioned in a list of Benjamites who resettled in Jerusalem after the EXILE (1 Chr.

9:7; Neh. 11:7). It is possible that Sallu was a family name rather than the name of an individual.

(2) A priest who returned with ZERUBBABEL from the exile (Neh. 12:7). Later, in the days of the high priest JOIAKIM, the head of Sallu's family was Kallai (v. 20, where most versions, following the MT, read "Sallai," an alternate form or a textual corruption).

Salma, Salmon. sal′muh, sal′muhn (Heb. *salmāʾ H8514* [1 Chr. 2:11, 51, 54], *salmâ* [Ruth 4:20], *salmôn H8517* [Ruth 4:21], all of these alternate spellings possibly meaning "mantle" or "spark"; Gk. *Salmōn G4891* [Matt. 1:4-5], *Sala* [Lk. 3:32]). **(1)** Son of HUR, grandson of CALEB, and descendant of JUDAH; he is described as the "father" (i.e., founder) of BETHLEHEM and as the ancestor of several important clans (1 Chr. 2:51, 54).

(2) Son of Nahshon and father of BOAZ (Ruth 4:20-21); included in the GENEALOGY OF JESUS CHRIST (Matt. 1:4-5; Lk. 3:32 [NRSV, "Sala"]).

Salmai. See SHALMAI.

Salmon. See SALMA, SALMON.

Salmone. sal-moh′nee (Gk. *Salmōnē G4892*). A promontory, now called Cape Sidero, constituting the most easterly portion of CRETE. When PAUL and his companions boarded ship at MYRA in LYCIA, they had to cope with strong northwesterly winds. Hugging the shore, they reached CNIDUS in SW ASIA MINOR with some difficulty. There the land protection ceased. It would have been possible to lie at anchor in that harbor awaiting a fair wind, but because of their urgent desire to reach ROME the only course was to tack to the S and sail "to the lee of Crete, opposite Salmone" (Acts 27:7).

Salome. suh-loh′mee (Gk. *Salōmē G4897*, possibly "peaceful"). **(1)** One of the women who followed and ministered to Jesus in GALILEE, were witnesses to the crucifixion, and afterwards went to the tomb to anoint his body (Mk. 15:40-41; 16:1). A comparison between these passages and Matt. 27:56 identifies her as the wife of ZEBEDEE, and therefore mother of James and John (see JAMES I; JOHN THE APOSTLE). Her request for prominence for her sons in the kingdom was rebuked by the Lord and drew the indignation of the other disciples (Matt. 20:20-24; Mk. 10:35-41). Many infer from Jn. 19:25 that she was the sister of MARY, MOTHER OF JESUS, but others take the phrase "his mother's sister" as a reference to "Mary the wife of Clopas" which follows.

(2) The daughter of HERODIAS and HEROD Philip (Jos. *Ant.* 18.5.4 §§136-37); her name is not given in the Gospels. Because her dancing before Herod Antipas, her father's half-brother, pleased him so much, he promised to grant her whatever request she might make. Prompted by her mother, she asked for the head of JOHN THE BAPTIST, who had rebuked the marriage of Herodias and Antipas (Matt. 14:3-11; Mk. 6:16-28). Salome became wife first to her uncle Philip, tetrarch of Traconitis (Lk. 3:1, not to be confused with Herod Philip), and then to her cousin Aristobulus, son of Herod king of Chalcis.

salt. See MINERALS.

Salt, City of. (*ʿir-hammelaḥ H6551 + H4875*). One of six cities allotted to JUDAH in the desert (Josh. 15:62). Four of these—MIDDIN, SECACAH, NIBSHAN, and the City of Salt—are often identified with four Iron II settlements in el-Buqeʿah, a valley SW of JERICHO (see ACHOR), and many have thought that the City of Salt in particular is the same as Khirbet Qumran (see DEAD SEA SCROLLS). Alternate proposals include ʿAin el-Ghuweir (c. 9 mi./14 km. S of Qumran) and even Tell el-Milḥ (much farther away, c. 14 mi./23 km. SE of BEERSHEBA; but see MOLADAH).

salt, covenant of. An expression used in OT times for a perpetual covenant. The ceremonial law called for the use of salt in all cereal offerings and perhaps in other offerings as well, according to the Mosaic instruction (Lev. 2:13). Being a necessary part of human diet, it is not surprising that it should be included in the prescribed offerings to God. While some of these offerings were consumed on the altar, the greater part was for use by the priests, for they had no inheritance among their brethren by which to obtain food. Therefore, all the holy offerings the people presented to God

were given to the priests and their families "as a perpetual due; it is a covenant of salt for ever before the LORD for you [the priests] and your descendants as well" (Num. 18:19 NRSV). From this Levitical concept there evidently arose the expression among the Hebrews that any perpetual covenant is a covenant of salt. Thus JEROBOAM son of Nebat, who split Israel from the Davidic line, is reminded by King ABIJAH that God gave the kingship to DAVID and his sons by a covenant of salt, that is, forever (2 Chr. 13:5).

Salt, Valley of. (*gê*-*melaḥ H1628 + H4875*). The scene of two important victories of the Israelite armies over EDOM (2 Sam. 8:3 = 1 Chr. 18:12; 2 Ki. 14:7 = 2 Chr. 25:11). The exact location of the Valley of Salt is disputed. Wadi el-Milḥ (salt), to the S of BEERSHEBA, which flows by the foot of Tell el-Milḥ, has been suggested because of the similarity of names. Because that area lay outside Edomite territory, others have proposed es-Sebkha, S of the DEAD SEA, a barren saline area. Still another proposal is GE HARASHIM, but the location of this valley is also uncertain.

Salt Sea. See DEAD SEA.

Salu. say'loo (Heb. *sālûʾ H6140*, possibly "[God] has returned [*or* restored]"). Father of ZIMRI; the latter was a leader in the tribe of SIMEON who took a Midianite woman and was killed by PHINEHAS (Num. 25:14).

salutation. This English term is used by the KJV seven times to render the Greek noun *aspasmos G833*, "greeting" (Mk. 12:38 et al.; in the three other passages where this Gk. word occurs [Matt. 23:7; Lk. 11:43; 20:46], the KJV has "greetings"). See GREET. In biblical studies, the English word is used primarily to designate the opening greeting in an EPISTLE.

salvation. What God in mercy does for his sinful, finite human creatures is presented in the Bible through a variety of metaphors, images, and models (e.g., REDEMPTION and JUSTIFICATION). Of these, none is more important or significant than salvation: thus God is called "Savior" (Hos. 13:4;

Lk. 1:47) and portrayed as the "God of salvation" (Ps. 68:19-20; Lk. 3:6; Acts 28:28).

In the OT, salvation refers both to everyday, regular types of deliverance—as from enemies, disease, and danger (see 1 Sam. 10:24 KJV; Ps. 72:4)—and to those major deliverances that are specifically interpreted as being a definite part of God's unique and special involvement in human history as well as special revelations of his character and will. The supreme example of the latter is the EXODUS (Exod. 14:13, 30-31; 15:1-2, 13; 18:8), which involved deliverance from the bondage of EGYPT, safe travel to the Land of Promise, and settlement there as a new people in a new relationship with God (Deut. 6:21-23; 26:2-10; 33:29).

There are two further aspects to salvation in the OT. First, salvation refers to the future action of God when he will deliver Israel from all her enemies and ills and create a new order of existence ("a new heaven and a new earth") in which she and all people will worship the Lord and live in peace and harmony (see Isa. 49:5-13; 65:17-25; 66:22-23; Hag. 2:4-9; Zech. 2:7-13). Second, intimately related to the future salvation of God is the hope of the MESSIAH, who will deliver his people from their sins, and will act for the Lord, who alone is Savior (Isa. 43:11; 52:13; 53:12).

Further, in the OT the theme of salvation is closely related to the themes of God's RIGHTEOUSNESS and God's CREATION. God is righteous when he acts to preserve his side of the COVENANT he made with the people of ISRAEL. Thus when he acts to deliver his people, he acts in righteousness, and his act is also one of salvation (Isa. 45:21; 46:12-13). God's future salvation involves a new creation, the remaking and renewing of the old created order (9:2-7; 11:1-9; 65:17-25).

In the NT, Jesus is portrayed as the Savior of sinners (Lk. 2:11; Jn. 4:42; Acts 5:31; 13:23; Phil. 3:20; 2 Pet. 1:1, 11; 1 Jn. 4:14). The title reserved for God in the OT is transferred to Jesus as Incarnate Son in the NT. He is the Savior or Deliverer from sin and its consequences as well as from SATAN and his power. Jesus preached the arrival of the KINGDOM OF GOD—the kingly, fatherly rule of God in human lives. When a person repented and believed, that person received salvation: "Today salvation has come to this house" (Lk. 19:9-10),

said Jesus to ZACCHAEUS. To others who believed and received God's kingdom/salvation Jesus said, "Your sins are forgiven" or "Your faith has saved you" (Mk. 2:5; Lk. 7:50). And since healing of the body was not separated by Jesus from healing of the person, to be healed by Jesus was to receive God's salvation. In fact the Greek verb *sōzō* G5392 means both "to heal" and "to save" (Mk. 1:40-45; 5:33-34).

PETER preached that "salvation is found in no one else, for there is no other name under heaven given to men by which we must be saved" (Acts 4:12). PAUL wrote, "Now is the day of salvation" (2 Cor. 6:2). The writer of HEBREWS asked, "How shall we escape if we ignore such a great salvation?" (Heb. 2:3). Because of the life, death, and exaltation of Jesus, salvation is a present reality, and the GOSPEL is the declaration that salvation is now accomplished and available in and through Jesus. It is deliverance from the dominion of sin and Satan; it is freedom to love and serve God now. Salvation is also, however, a future HOPE, for we will "be saved from God's wrath through him" at the Last Judgment (Rom. 5:9), and Peter wrote of the salvation "that is ready to be revealed in the last time" (1 Pet. 1:5). Salvation, which belongs to our God (Rev. 19:1), includes everything that God will do for and to his people as he brings them to fullness of life in the new heaven and the new earth of the age to come.

salve. See EYESALVE.

Samaria (city). suh-mair'ee-uh (Heb. *šōmĕrôn* H9076, possibly "guarding [place], observation [point]," derived from the personal name *šemer* H9070, "guardian" [1 Ki. 6:24]; Aram. *šomrayin* H10726; Gk. *Samareia* G4899). The capital of the northern kingdom of Israel. See also SAMARIA (TERRITORY) and SAMARITAN. The city of Samaria had an excellent hilltop location c. 40 mi. (65 km.) N of JERUSALEM and c. 25 mi. (40 km.) from the MEDITERRANEAN. In the spring, when the wild flowers are in blossom, the setting is exquisite. The king could see the Mediterranean Sea from his palace windows as he looked W down the fertile "valley of barley," leading to the Plain of SHARON and the sea. Samaria was located on the main N-S ridge ROAD of PALESTINE, and almost directly W across the mountain ridge from the preceding capital, TIRZAH. It was c. 6.5 mi. (10.5 km.) NW of SHECHEM, the kingdom's first capital.

Although lower than some surrounding hills, Samaria was beyond artillery (catapult) range from them. The city withstood several sieges by the ARAMEANS, and one of three years' duration by ASSYRIA, before it fell (2 Ki. 17:5). When HEROD the Great rebuilt the city, he named it Sebaste in honor of his patron AUGUSTUS (Gk. *sebastos* *G4935*, "revered," corresponds to Lat. *augustus*; cf. Acts 25:25). The present Arab village at the E end of the site still carries the Herodian name, Sebastiyeh. The OT population of the city can only be conjectured, but SARGON deported 27,290 of its population. Its maximum population even in NT times was probably not more than 40,000. The size of the hilltop, of course, determined the city's size, c. 20 acres (8 hectares).

The city of Samaria is referred to over a hundred times in the OT, although it was not built until some fifty years after the death of SOLOMON. It was founded c. 875 B.C. by OMRI. "He bought the hill of Samaria from Shemer for two talents of silver and built a city on the hill, calling it Samaria, after Shemer, the name of the former owner of the hill" (1 Ki. 16:24; see SHEMER). Omri died before completing the new city and it was finished by his son, AHAB. The new capital was in every way an improvement on the former one, Tirzah.

Archaeological excavations have revealed occupation on the hilltop in the Early Bronze Age, and the evidence from a later period could be interpreted as the remains of Shemer's estate. The city built by Omri and Ahab was largely replaced by later constructions; the portions of the original city found by the archaeologists show that it was well designed and excellently constructed. The palace was called an ivory house (1 Ki. 22:39; Amos 3:15). There are three theories of interpretation. One considers the polished white limestone of the buildings as "ivory colored." Another thinks the reference is to wooden wall panels inlaid with ivory. The third, and most likely, is to apply it to the ivory inlay furniture used. Since the inlays are small, they fit the pattern of furniture better than large wall panels. Over 500 of the ivory plaques or

fragments of them have been found. Other interesting palace finds were numerous clay sealings with imprints showing. These were the seals with which papyrus rolls were closed and made official by the seal imprint of a government official.

Samaria was well fortified with both an outer and an inner city wall. The former averaged c. 20 ft. (6 m.), with the greatest width 32 ft. (10 m.). It was the casemate type and was provided with towers and bastions. The casemates were narrow rectangular rooms with the length of the casemate being the width of the wall. They were filled with earth. The inner wall was solid stone c. 5 ft. (1.5 m.) in thickness. There also seems to have been a third defensive wall on the hillside just below the outer wall, but the evidence is not conclusive. The city's main gate was naturally at the E end of the city, where the hill joined the main mountain mass. Near the gateway a fragment of a large stone stela was found, but only three letters remained and they gave no clue to the inscription The script would date it about the time of JEROBOAM II, who was Samaria's greatest king. Such memorial stelae were common at the gates of capital cities. Limestone pilasters with proto-Ionic capitals were found nearby, showing that an important public building had stood there. These are similar to those used by Solomon's architects.

Samaria has been rebuilt so often in the areas excavated by archaeologists that only fragments of buildings are left. The first major reconstructions seem to have come about the time of JEHU. The reason for this work is unknown. Perhaps destruction by an earthquake made rebuilding necessary, as earthquakes were frequent in the history of Palestine. At any rate the new work was very inferior to that of Omri and Ahab. The next building phases came about the time of Joash (JEHOASH) and Jeroboam II, when wealth flowed into Samaria from all directions. Although there were several building phases, they were inferior to the earliest work. The excellent masonry has been replaced and the newer more crude work has its deficiencies concealed under heavy coats of plaster. The most important objects found in this period were sixty-five OSTRACA from the time of Jeroboam II. These were business documents written on pieces of broken pottery (one of the most common writing

S

materials used in ordinary business). Scholars differ concerning their exact nature, but they seem to be receipts for produce (wine and oil) given to the government at Samaria as taxes. They list the name and city of the taxpayer and also the name of the tax collector. They seem to show that the federal departments set up by Solomon were still intact at this time in the northern kingdom. Twenty-two cities or towns are mentioned.

Although Samaria was at the peak of her glory under Jeroboam II, the city was to be destroyed within twenty-five years. The whole of its last period was chaotic, and it fell to the Assyrian king, SARGON II, in 721 B.C. Sargon's records state that he rebuilt Samaria and made it greater than it had been under the Israelite monarchs. The land was resettled with refugees from other Assyrian conquests (2 Ki. 17:24), but it is uncertain whether Samaria in this text refers to the territory of Samaria or to the capital city itself. More deportees came in under ESARHADDON (Ezra 4:2) and ASHURBANIPAL (Osnappar, 4:9-10). Loyal Yahweh worshipers continued to come to JERUSALEM from the city of Samaria even after NEBUCHADNEZZAR's conquest of the city and TEMPLE (Jer. 41:5). When the Babylonians seized world power from the Assyrians, they continued to have Samaria as the capital of the province of Samaria, now called Samerina; but they also added to it the territory around Jerusalem. When the Persians took over the world empire, Samaria was continued as the capital of the province of Samerina. Although SANBALLAT, the governor of that province, plays a large part in the postexilic period, his capital city Samaria is mentioned only in Ezra 4:17.

With the coming of ALEXANDER THE GREAT to Palestine, the city of Samaria assumed a new character. It became the most important Greek city in central Palestine; and the Samaritan influence in what was the old province of Samaria was now only religious. (Shechem from this time became the important city of the Samaritans. Its significance was climaxed by the building of a temple on nearby Mount GERIZIM.) After the death of Alexander, the city belonged to the Ptolemies (see PTOLEMY) most of the time up to 198 B.C., when it became the permanent property of the Seleucids (see SELEUCUS). After the Maccabean war (see MAC-

CABEE), the Jewish Hasmonean ruler John Hyrcanus captured Shechem and then moved against Samaria, which he besieged and conquered (c. 107 B.C.). The city was occupied at least in part by the time POMPEY conquered Palestine, and he added it to the Roman empire in 63 B.C. Samaria was annexed to the province of SYRIA by the Romans.

The greatest builder in the history of Palestine was not Solomon, but HEROD the Great. Samaria was a city he loved, and he embellished it in every way. He began the reconstruction of the city in 30 B.C. and spent at least ten years at the task. As mentioned above, he renamed it Sebaste in honor of his patron, Emperor Augustus. On the site of Omri's palace, the highest point in the city, he erected a large beautiful temple for the worship of Augustus as a god! Herod built a new city wall, strengthened with towers. The wall was more than 2 mi. (3 km.) in length.

Herod the Great willed Samaria to his son Archelaus, but he was such a poor ruler that Rome removed him. Samaria was then placed under the jurisdiction of the Roman governor, whose headquarters were at CAESAREA. This Herodian city was the Samaria of the NT. It is not specifically mentioned in the Gospels. In Acts, Samaria is mentioned as a place where PHILIP went to preach and as the center for the work of SIMON Magus (Acts 8:5, 9), but it is uncertain whether the city or the territory is meant (in v. 5 the earliest MSS have "the city of Samaria," but most witnesses omit the definite article, thus, "a city of Samaria"). In v. 14, a reference to the city seems likely, as the apostles did their crucial doctrinal work in urban areas. There is a strong tradition that JOHN THE BAPTIST was buried at Samaria, but there is no proof. Two early churches here honor him.

Samaria (territory). A name applied to the general region in which the city of Samaria was located; see SAMARIA (CITY). This use of the term, however, is attested only after the fall of the city. There is very little definite data on the boundaries of the territory of Samaria. Usually it is considered as the land occupied by the tribes of EPHRAIM and W MANASSEH. Geographically, the S boundary is the road that goes from JERICHO to BETHEL and then descends via the valley of AIJALON to

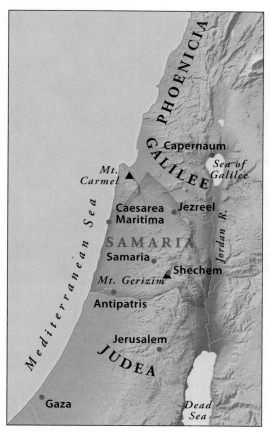

The region of Samaria.

way had a much better grade through a natural pass at Shechem between Mounts GERIZIM and EBAL. The N road was a continuation of the coastal road, where it cut across the plain of DOTHAN to modern Jenin and down through the vale of JEZREEL to the Jordan River at BETH SHAN (later called Scythopolis). Most of the land commerce between EGYPT and SYRIA went through the district of Samaria.

The use of SAMARITAN as a political term came only after the conquest of Samaria by the Assyrian SARGON II in 721 B.C. (see 2 Ki. 17:29, which has the only OT occurrence of Heb. *šōměrônî H9085*, "Samaritan"). Sargon made it into the province of Samerena. His records specifically speak of 27,290 persons being deported from the capital city of Samaria. He apparently took prisoners from other cities, since he settled large numbers of deportees in the province of Samaria, taking them from Babylon, Cuthah, Avva, Hamath, and Sepharvaim (2 Ki. 17:24). Later deportees were also settled in the province by ESARHADDON and his son ASHURBANIPAL (Osnappar, Ezra 4:2, 10). The basic population of the land, however, remained essentially Israelite, for not a single permanent feature of any of the religions practiced by the colonists influenced the Samaritan faith.

When the Assyrian empire weakened, JOSIAH tried to annex the Samaritan territory but he lost it to his military rival Pharaoh NECO. The latter, however, soon lost it in turn to NEBUCHADNEZZAR, who seems to have incorporated this old Assyrian province into his own Babylonian empire in 612 B.C. At that time the province reached as far S as Bethel, for that city was spared when Nebuchadnezzar destroyed Jerusalem in 586. Apparently he then added this new area around Jerusalem to the old Samaritan province. The Persians seemed to have continued the same provincial policy as the Babylonians, for SANBALLAT was politically in charge of this area until NEHEMIAH reduced its size slightly by making the Jerusalem section into a semi-independent political unit under the high priests.

Historical evidence concerning the province of Samaria between the RESTORATION under NEHEMIAH and the era of ALEXANDER THE GREAT is scanty. It is known, however, that Alexander pensioned off some of his soldiers from the TYRE

the Mediterranean. The N boundary consists of Mount CARMEL and Mount GILBOA and the hills that connect these two bastions. The MEDITERRANEAN is the W boundary with the JORDAN on the E. Both SHECHEM and the city of Samaria are near the center of the area, with Samaria more to the N and W. The area made its wealth from its productive farm lands and its international trade routes.

The natural produce included grains and olives and the fruit of vineyards and orchards, plus flocks and herds. Samaria always had a good produce market in nearby commercial PHOENICIA. Note the economic-political marriage between AHAB and JEZEBEL. It was to the benefit of commerce that both the N-S ROADS, one along the coast and one along the high ridge, went through the territory of Samaria. There were three roads running E and W. The S road, as mentioned above, went from Jericho to Bethel to the Mediterranean. The center high-

Topography of the hill country of Samaria. (View to the NE.)

© Dr. James C. Martin

campaign at the city of Samaria. Shechem became the only major Samaritan city. The southern half of the province of Samaria seems always to have continued in the Samaritan faith. Paganism apparently prevailed in the northern half of the province around the capital city itself. The Ptolemies (see PTOLEMY) carried prisoners to ALEXANDRIA from both the Jews and the Samaritans. The province of Samaria first appears in the Maccabean story (see MACCABEE) when the SELEUCID Demetrius rewarded Jonathan for lifting the siege of the Acra in Jerusalem by giving him three districts of Samaria: Ephraim, Lydda, and Ramathaim. By 128 B.C. John Hyrcanus was strong enough to capture Shechem and Gerizim and to destroy the Samaritan temple there. As the capital city of Samaria was a strong Greek fortress, it was able to hold off the Jewish forces for a year before it fell. Scythopolis was the next city to be captured, and with its fall the entire province of Samaria was in Jewish hands. When POMPEY captured Palestine, he annexed the city of Samaria to the province of SYRIA, and the Samaritans again became the local power in the district. In NT times Samaria extended from the free cities of Scythopolis and Jenin on the N to a line c. 15 mi. (24 km.) S of Shechem. The history of Samaria in NT times is treated under the article SAMARITAN.

Samaritan. suh-mair′uh-tuhn (Heb. *šōměrōnî H9085*, gentilic of *šōměrôn H9076*; Gk. *Samaritēs G4901*). An inhabitant of SAMARIA (TERRITORY); the term may also signify the religious sect associated with that region. Racially, the Samaritans are difficult to identify. In 721 B.C. SARGON of ASSYRIA destroyed Samaria. He recorded the fact on the walls of the royal palace at Dur-Sarraku (Khorsabad), as well as his subsequent policy of depopulation, deportation, and reestablishment: "In my first year of reign … the people of Samaria … to the number of 27,290 I carried away … .The city I rebuilt—I made it greater than it was before. People of the lands which I had conquered I settled therein. My tartan I place over them as governor." It seems that the policy of deportation applied particularly to the city of Samaria rather than to the region. See SAMARIA (CITY). Jeremiah 41:5, for example, seems to imply that a remnant of true Israelites remained in SHECHEM, SHILOH, and Samaria a century later; so a substratum, or admixture of the Hebrew stock in the later total population must be assumed. The newcomers from the N may be presumed to have intermarried with the Israelite remnant, and ultimately the population took the general name of Samaritans.

The completeness of the devastation left by the Assyrian invasion is evident from the infestation by wild beasts of which the immigrants complained (2 Ki. 17). Superstitiously, the intruders concluded that "the god of the land" was angry at their presence and their ignorance of his propitiatory rites. They sent to the Assyrian monarch and asked him to select a priest from among the deportees to instruct them in the necessary ritual of worship. The king (ESARHADDON) acceded to the request, and some instruction in the faith of the true God penetrated the stricken district. A mixed religion resulted. "They worshiped the LORD," we read, "but they also served their own gods" (17:33). The reforms of JOSIAH, king of JUDAH, crossed the border at BETHEL and seem to have extended into the northern districts. There was little, indeed, to prevent their infiltration. Religious revival was not the sort of military penetration that invited Assyrian attention (2 Ki. 23:15; 2 Chr. 34:6-7). The measure of purification, which may be presumed to have taken place in the Samaritan religion about this time, did not, however, reconcile the Samaritan and the Jew racially.

After the return from EXILE, enmity became inveterate between the Samaritans and the Jewish remnant of EZRA and NEHEMIAH. On the strength of their worship of the LORD "since the time of Esarhaddon" (Ezra 4:2), the Samaritans sought a share in the rebuilding of the TEMPLE in JERUSALEM, but they were firmly rebuffed; hence the policy of obstruction from SANBALLAT of Samaria, which was a serious hindrance to Nehemiah's work (Neh. 2:10, 19; 4:6-7). Both Sanballat and his partner TOBIAH the Ammonite were Yahweh worshipers. The struggle, therefore, was primarily political rather than religious. It may, however, have ended as a religious schism, if one follows the reasoning of the historians who date the Samaritan break to this feud. In any case, the rift led to the establishment of the sect of the Samaritans through the building of a schismatic temple on Mount GERIZIM. In 109 B.C., the Jewish Hasmonean ruler John Hyrcanus destroyed the temple; and when Herod provided another temple in 25 B.C., the Samaritans refused to use it, continuing to worship on the mount (Jn. 4:20-21).

Founded as it was before the rise of the great prophetic tradition, the religion of the Samaritans was based on the PENTATEUCH alone. Their position was held with some firmness, and JOSE-

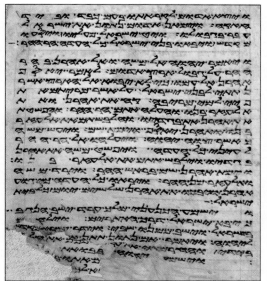

A MS of the Samaritan Pentateuch (13th cent. A.D.).

PHUS (*Ant.* 13.3.4 §§74-79) mentions a disputation before PTOLEMY Philometor on the question that the Samaritan woman poses in Jn. 4:20, the answer to which resulted in the death, according to the rules of the debate, of the defeated Samaritan advocates. CHRIST's firm answer (4:21-23) stressed the incompleteness of the Samaritan tradition, its inadequate revelation, and the common transience of the cherished beliefs of both Samaritan and Jew. The greatness of Christ is shown in the passage, for at no time had the bitterness between the two groups been greater. At one Passover during the governorship of Coponius (A.D. 6-9), when, according to annual custom, the gates of the temple were opened at midnight, some Samaritans had intruded and polluted the Holy Place by scattering human bones in the porches. Samaritans were thereafter excluded from the services (Josephus, *Ant.* 18.2.2 §§29-30). They were cursed in the temple. Their food was considered unclean, even as swine's flesh. The whole situation narrated in Jn. 4 is therefore remarkable: the buying of food in SYCHAR, the conversation at JACOB's WELL, and the subsequent evangelization of the area. (See also Acts 8:5-25.) It is a magnificent illustration of the emancipation that Christianity was to bring to those grown immobile in the bondage of Judaistic prejudice.

© Dr. James C. Martin, Sola Scriptura. The Van Kampen Collection on display at the Holy Land Experience in Orlando, Florida. Photographed by permission.

Samaritan Pentateuch. See TEXT AND VERSIONS (OT).

Samaritan Targum. See TEXT AND VERSIONS (OT).

samech. sah´mek (Heb. *sāmek*, "support," from *sāmak H6164*, "to support, help"). The fifteenth letter of the Hebrew alphabet (ס), with a numerical value of 60 (the reason for its name is uncertain). Its sound corresponds to that of English *s*.

Samgar. sam´gahr (Heb. *samgar H6161*, meaning uncertain). According to some scholars, Samgar (Jer. 39:3) is a place name corresponding to Babylonian *Sinmagir*, a province N of BABYLON ruled by NERGAL-SHAREZER (Neriglissar), one of NEBUCHADNEZZAR's officials who participated in the siege of Jerusalem. This view is adopted by the NIV, which identifies three officials in the text: (1) Nergal-Sharezer of Samgar, (2) a chief officer (RABSARIS) by the name of Nebo-Sarsekim, and (3) a high official (RABMAG) who was also called Nergal-Sharezer, but who may be the same as (1). The NRSV and other versions, following the MT more closely, identify four individuals: (1) "Nergal-sharezer," (2) "Samgar-nebo," (3) "Sarsechim the Rabsaris," and (4) "Nergal-sharezer the Rabmag" (the KJV, failing to understand that "Rabsaris" and "Rabmag" are titles, identifies six officials; see also SARSECHIM).

Samgar-nebo. sam´gahr-nee´boh (Heb. *samgar-nĕbû*). A Babylonian army officer who participated in the siege of Jerusalem (Jer. 39:3 KJV and other versions). See SAMGAR.

Samlah. sam´luh (Heb. *śamlâ H8528*, possibly an alternate form of SALMA). An early king of EDOM who ruled in MASREKAH (Gen. 36:36-37; 1 Chr. 1:47-48). Nothing else is known about him.

Samos. say´mos (Gk. *Samos G4904*, "height"). An island in the Aegean Sea off the W coast of ASIA MINOR, opposite the headlands of Mycale and the city of EPHESUS. Samos is 27 mi. long and 14 mi. wide (43 x 23 km.), and it is separated from the mainland by a strait of 1 mi. (1.6 km.). The entire island is mountainous, but the terraced land is remarkably fertile. It produced olives, unusually fine wine, and abundant timber for native shipbuilders in antiquity. Settled by Ionian immigrants from Epidaurus, the island enjoyed great prosperity throughout antiquity, but particularly in the sixth century. Later it passed into the hands of PERSIA, EGYPT, and then PERGAMUM. It was bequeathed to ROME by Pergamum in 133 B.C. and became part of the province of ASIA. In the first century A.D. it became an autonomous city-state. Samos is mentioned in the NT in connection with PAUL's sea voyage from TROAS to MILETUS as he returned to JERUSALEM at the end of his third missionary journey (Acts 20:15). The verb used in this text (*paraballō G4125*) leaves unclear whether the ship only passed by the island or actually stopped there. Possibly a scribe, understanding the verb to mean that the traveling party did not reach Samos, and thinking that an alternate port of call was needed, added the clause "and tarried to Trogyllium" (so KJV, following most MSS). See TROGYLLIUM.

Samothrace. sam´uh-thrays (Gk. *Samothrakē G4903*, "Thracian height"). An island in the NE Aegean Sea, about 20 mi. (32 km.) off the coast of THRACE. Samothrace is very mountainous, and its central peak, Mount Fengari (5,577 ft./1,700 m.), is the most conspicuous landmark of the N Aegean. From it the god Poseidon was said to have surveyed the plains of TROY. The island became an anchorage for ships plying the N Aegean because they had to anchor somewhere due to the hazards of sailing at night. The FERTILITY CULT of the great mother Cybele, as well as the MYSTERY RELIGION associated with the twin gods Cabeiri (or Cabiri), flourished on the island. The apostle PAUL and his companions, on their way from TROAS to NEAPOLIS, anchored on Samothrace for a night (Acts 16:11).

Samson. sam´suhn (Heb. *šimšôn H9088*, possibly "sunny"; Gk. *Sampsōn G4907*). Son of MANOAH, of the tribe of DAN; a leader and hero of Israel, famous for his prodigious strength displayed against the PHILISTINES (Jdg. 13-16). He may have been the last of the judges of ISRAEL prior to SAMUEL (see JUDGES, THE). ZORAH, where

S

Samson was born, was about halfway between JERUSALEM and the MEDITERRANEAN, along the coast of which the Philistines lived. His birth was announced by the angel of the Lord beforehand to his mother, who was barren. The angel told her that she would have a son, that this son should be a NAZIRITE from his birth, and that the Lord would begin to use him to deliver Israel out of the hand of the Philistines. Nazirites were under a special vow to God to restrain their carnal nature, thus showing the people generally that if they would receive God's blessing, they must deny and govern themselves and be faithful to their vows of consecration as God's covenant people. The preternatural strength that Samson exhibited at various times in his career was not his because he was a natural giant, but because the Spirit of the Lord came on him to accomplish great deeds.

At the time of his birth the Israelites had been in bondage to the Philistines for forty years because they had done evil in the sight of the Lord. After his birth "he grew and the LORD blessed him, and the Spirit of the LORD began to stir him while he was in Mahaneh Dan, between Zorah and Eshtaol" (Jdg. 13:24-25). But almost from the beginning of his career he showed one conspicuous weakness, which was ultimately to wreck him: he was a slave to passion. He insisted, against the objections of his parents, on marrying a Philistine woman of TIMNATH, which was not far from Zorah. At the wedding feast he challenged the guests with a riddle, making a wager with them for thirty changes of clothing. By threatening the life of his bride, the Philistines compelled her to obtain the answer from him. When he found he had been tricked, he killed thirty Philistines of ASHKELON in revenge and gave his guests their garments, thus fulfilling his wager. He went home without his wife, giving the impression that he had forsaken her. When he returned later, he found that her father had given her in marriage to someone else, and he was offered her sister in her stead. In revenge Samson caught 300 foxes and sent them into the Philistine grain fields in pairs, with burning torches tied between their tails. The Philistines retaliated by burning his wife and her father to death.

This act of vengeance only provoked another and a greater vengeance from Samson. He "attacked them viciously and slaughtered many of them" and went to a cave in a rock called ETAM. The Philistines invaded JUDAH and demanded the surrender of their archenemy. Samson agreed to allow the Israelites to deliver him into the hands of the Philistines; but on the way he broke the cords that bound him and, seizing the jawbone of a donkey, killed 1,000 men with it. With this great feat Samson clearly established his title to the position of a judge in Israel. The historian says in this connection, "Samson led Israel for twenty years in the days of the Philistines" (Jdg. 15:20). The last clause in this statement implies that the ascendancy of the Philistines was not destroyed but only kept in check by the prowess of Samson.

Samson next went down to GAZA, a Philistine stronghold, and yielded to the solicitations of a PROSTITUTE. When it became known that he was in the city, the Philistines laid a trap for him; but at midnight Samson got up, took the doors of the gate of the city and the two posts, and carried them a quarter of a mile to the top of the hill before HEBRON. God in his mercy continued to give him supernatural strength in spite of his evil actions.

Continuing his life of self-indulgence, Samson before long became enamored of a non-Israelite woman named DELILAH, through whom he lost his physical power. The Philistine leaders bribed her with a large sum of money to betray him into their hands. By their direction she begged him to tell her in what his great strength lay. Three times he gave her deceitful answers, but at last he gave in to her importunities and revealed that if only his hair were cut he would be like other men. She lulled him into a profound sleep, his hair was cut, and when he awoke and heard her derisive cry, "Samson, the Philistines are upon you!" he found that not merely his strength but also God had departed from him. Now at the mercy of his enemies, he was bound with chains, his eyes were put out, and he was sent to grind in the prison of Gaza.

How long Samson continued in this state of shameful bondage is unknown—perhaps some weeks or even months. On the occasion of a great feast to the god DAGON, his captors resolved to make sport of him before the assembled multitude. The temple of Dagon was filled with people—with 3,000 on the roof to watch the sport.

S

Meanwhile, his hair had grown again, and with his returning strength he longed for revenge on his enemies for his two blinded eyes (Jdg. 16:28). He asked the servant who attended him to allow him to rest between the two pillars on which the building was supported. Taking hold of them, he prayed that God would help him once more; and with a mighty effort he moved the pillars from their position and brought down the roof, burying with himself a large number of Philistines in its ruins. In dying he killed more than he had killed in his life.

With all of his failings he is listed with the heroes of faith in Heb. 11:32. By faith in God's gift and calling, he received strength to do the wonders he performed. Too often animal passion ruled him. He was without real self-control, and accordingly he wrought no permanent deliverance for Israel.

Samuel. sam'yoo-uhl (Heb. *šěmû'ēl H9017*, derivation uncertain [see also SHEMUEL, rendered "Samuel" by NIV in 2 Chr. 7:2]; Gk. *Samouēl G4905*). The last Israelite leader prior to the monarchy (see JUDGES, THE). In his ministry Samuel served as judge, priest, and prophet. The first nineteen chapters of 1 Samuel provide the basic source material for his life. The Hebrew form *šěmû'ēl* possibly means "his name is God," but by a wordplay on the verb *šāma' H9048* ("to hear"; note the consonant *'ayin* rather than *'aleph*) it can be understood as "heard by God" (1 Sam. 1:20; the explanation here also evokes the name *šā'ûl H8620*, "one asked for"; see SAUL).

Samuel is often called the last of the judges (cf. 1 Sam. 7:6, 15-17) and the first of the prophets (3:20; Acts 3:24; 13:20). His parents were ELKANAH and HANNAH. By lineage Elkanah was a LEVITE, a descendant of KOHATH but not of the Aaronic line (1 Chr. 6:26, 33 [KJV, "Shemuel"]). Geographically Elkanah was identified as an Ephraimite, since he lived in the mountainous territory of EPHRAIM in the city of Ramah, more specifically identified as Ramathaim (1 Sam. 1:1; see RAMAH #3). The account of the events associated with the birth of Samuel indicates that his parents were a devoted and devout couple. Hannah's childlessness led her to pour out her complaint and supplication to God in bitterness of heart; but she

trusted God to provide the answer and promised to give to the Lord the son she had requested. When Samuel was born, she kept her promise; as soon as the child was weaned she took him to SHILOH and presented him to ELI the priest. Then she praised the Lord in prayer (usually called her "Song," 2:1-10).

Samuel grew up in the Lord's house and ministered before the Lord (1 Sam. 2:11; 3:1), and each year when his parents came to sacrifice at Shiloh, his mother brought a little robe for him (2:19). Spiritually and morally, the times were bad. The sons of Eli were unworthy representatives of the priestly office. In their greed they violated the laws of offering (2:12-17); they also engaged in immoral acts with the women who served at the entrance to the tent of meeting (2:22). Though Eli remonstrated with them, he was not firm enough, and the Lord declared that he would punish him (2:27-36).

Under such circumstances there was little communion with God, but the Lord called to Samuel in the night and revealed to him the impending doom of Eli's house. The Lord blessed Samuel and "let none of his words fall to the ground" (1 Sam. 3:19), so that all Israel knew that Samuel was a prophet of the Lord. Eli died when he received the news of the death of his sons and the capture of the ARK OF THE COVENANT in a PHILISTINE victory over ISRAEL. Some time after the return of the ark to Israel, Samuel challenged the people to put away foreign gods and to serve the Lord only (7:3). When the Philistines threatened the Israelite gathering at MIZPAH, Samuel interceded for Israel and the Lord answered with thunder against the enemy. The Philistines were routed and Samuel set up a memorial stone, which he called EBENEZER ("stone of help," 7:12).

Samuel, judge and priest, made his home at Ramah, where he administered justice and also built an altar. He went on circuit to BETHEL, GILGAL, and MIZPAH (1 Sam. 7:15). In his old age he appointed his sons, Joel and Abijah (cf. 1 Chr. 6:28), as judges in BEERSHEBA, but the people protested that his sons did not walk in his ways but took bribes and perverted justice. The people requested a king to rule them, "such as all the other nations have" (1 Sam. 8:5-6). Samuel was displeased by their demand, but the Lord told him to grant their request and to warn them concerning the ways of a king. Samuel was now brought into acquaintance with SAUL the son of Kish, who was searching for his father's lost donkeys. About to give up, Saul was encouraged by his servant to confer with Samuel, of whom he said, "Look, in this town there is a man of God; he is highly respected, and everything he says comes true" (9:6; cf. v. 9, "the prophet of today used to be called a seer"). God had revealed to Samuel that Saul was to come to see him, and at the conclusion of this first meeting, Samuel secretly anointed Saul as king (10:1) and foretold some confirmatory signs, which came to pass as predicted (10:1-13).

Samuel then called an assembly of Israel at Mizpah, and the choice of Saul was confirmed by lot. Samuel related to the people the rights and duties of a king and wrote these in a scroll, which was placed in the sanctuary "before the LORD" (10:25). After Saul's victory over the Ammonites, Samuel again convened Israel and Saul's kingship was confirmed at Gilgal. Samuel was now advanced in years and retired from public life in favor of the king. In his address to Israel he reviewed the Lord's dealings with them and reminded them of their duty to serve God. He called on the Lord to give witness to the words of his prophet by sending a thunderstorm, though it was the season of wheat harvest. The Lord sent the storm, and "all the people stood in awe of the LORD and of Samuel" (12:18). They requested Samuel to intercede for them, and he replied with a significant statement on responsibility and intercession (12:19-25).

Samuel next appears in conflict with Saul; a national crisis had arisen with a Philistine threat and Saul summoned the people to Gilgal. When Samuel was late in coming to make offerings, Saul presumed to make them himself. Samuel accused Saul of foolishness and disobedience and said that Saul's kingdom would not continue. Samuel then went to GIBEAH and Saul engaged in a victorious battle with the Philistines. After Saul's success, Samuel commissioned him to annihilate the AMALEKITES (1 Sam. 15). In this expedition Saul again showed incomplete obedience; Samuel reminded him of the necessity of absolute obedi-

ence and told him God had rejected him as king. This was the last official meeting of Samuel and Saul (15:35). Samuel returned to Ramah and grieved over Saul.

The Lord appointed Samuel to serve again as "kingmaker" and sent him to BETHLEHEM to anoint the young shepherd DAVID as Saul's successor (cf. 1 Chr. 11:3). Later, in flight from Saul, David took refuge on one occasion with Samuel in NAIOTH of Ramah (1 Sam. 19:18), where Samuel was head of a group of prophets. When Saul set out to pursue David, the Spirit of God came on Saul, and he prophesied before Samuel (19:23-24). Second Chronicles provides additional information concerning Samuel's part in the organization and conduct of the service of God. David and Samuel installed the gatekeepers of the tabernacle (1 Chr. 9:22). Samuel also dedicated gifts for the house of the Lord (26:28). Samuel was diligent in the Lord's service and kept the Passover faithfully (2 Chr. 35:18). Samuel was also a writer (cf. 1 Sam. 10:25); he is credited with "the records of Samuel the seer" (1 Chr. 29:29). Jewish tradition also ascribed to him the writing of the biblical books that bear his name. Samuel died while Saul was still king; he was buried by solemn assembly of the people at Ramah (1 Sam. 25:1).

Samuel's last message to Saul—that the king and his sons were about to die—came when the latter consulted the medium of ENDOR (2 Sam. 28:7-19, although some scholars argue the apparition of Samuel here was the result of trickery). Samuel is mentioned in several other OT books and is recognized as a man of prayer. In Ps. 99:6 it is said that he was "among those who called on [God's] name." The intercession of Samuel is cited in Jer. 15:1. In the NT he is referred to by PETER (Acts 3:24) as one who foretold the events of NT times. PAUL mentions him in a sermon at ANTIOCH of Pisidia (Acts 13:20). In Heb. 11:32 he is listed among those whose faith pleased God.

Samuel, Books of. Two historical books of the OT that cover a period of more than one hundred years, from the birth of SAMUEL to shortly before the death of DAVID. In the Hebrew Bible, they are regarded as one book and are ranked among the

Overview of 1-2 SAMUEL

Author: Unknown.

Historical setting: Covers the period from the end of the era of the judges (c. 1050 B.C.; see JUDGES, THE) to the end of the Davidic period (c. 970). The work must have been composed sometime after the division of the kingdom (c. 930), and possibly as late as the period of EXILE (c. 550).

Purpose: To provide a historical-theological account of the Hebrew nation during the judgeship of SAMUEL and during the reigns of SAUL and DAVID; to give an account of the rise of the Israelite monarchy; to stress the importance of faithfulness to the COVENANT.

Contents: Birth and judgeship of Samuel (1 Sam. 1-7); Saul's rise, triumphs, and failures (1 Sam. 8-15); David's rise, his years as fugitive, and the death of Saul (1 Sam. 16-31); the establishment and successes of David's reign (2 Sam. 1-10); David's sin and its consequences (2 Sam. 11-20); other events during David's reign (2 Sam. 21-24).

Former PROPHETS. In the SEPTUAGINT the books of Samuel are called 1-2 Kingdoms (or Reigns), and 1-2 Kings are then designated 3-4 Kingdoms.

I. **Authorship and date.** There is little external or internal evidence about the authorship of the books of Samuel. Jewish tradition ascribes the work to the prophet Samuel, but all of the events after 1 Sam. 24 occurred after Samuel's death. The statement of 27:6, "Ziklag ... has belonged to the kings of Judah ever since," is taken by some to refer to a date in the divided kingdom; others insist that this need not be later than the end of the reign of David. Samuel was a writer (1 Chr. 29:29), and certainly his writing was used in the composition of these books. Since David's death is not included in our books of Samuel, it has been thought probable that they were written before that event. Another suggestion is that some Judean prophet wrote the books shortly after the division of the kingdom, writing by INSPIRATION and using sources such as those mentioned above.

Some critical scholars regard Samuel as a composite of at least two sources, early and late, similar to the so-called J and E sources of the PENTATEUCH. The earlier is dated to Solomonic times and focuses on Saul and David; the later, dated to the eighth century B.C., deals with Samuel; their union is assigned to a date about a century after that. Others isolate three sources. Such divisions are based on alleged duplicates, contradictions, and differences in style and viewpoint. For detailed discussion, one must refer to the commentaries. In general it may be noted that the "duplicates" may be records of separate but similar events, or of the same incident from different viewpoints, or of references to previously recorded happenings. Supposed contradictions may often be harmonized by close examination of the text and context. Differences in style and point of view need not indicate multiple authorship but may reflect various purposes in the writing of a single author. As usual in theories of composite authorship, the redactor or editor must bear a heavy load of mixed credit and blame. Positively, the unity of Samuel is attested by the following: (1) the orderly and consistent plan of the work; (2) the interrelations of parts of the books; and (3) uniformity of language throughout. The unity of 2 Samuel is generally recognized.

II. **Contents.** The narrative may be outlined as follows (following the outline of R. H. Pfeiffer):

A. Shiloh and Samuel (1 Sam. 1:1—7:1)
B. Samuel and Saul (1 Sam. 7:2—15:35)
C. Saul and David (1 Sam. 16-31; 2 Sam. 1)
D. David as king of Judah (2 Sam. 2-4)
E. David as king of all Israel (2 Sam. 5-24)

A. The book begins with HANNAH's distress, her supplication, and the answer in the form of Samuel's birth. Samuel's childhood was spent at SHILOH; here the Lord spoke to him and revealed the future of the priestly line of ELI. The battle with the PHILISTINES resulted in a Philistine victory, the capture of the ARK OF THE COVENANT, and the death of Eli. A source of trouble in Philistia, the ark was sent back to Israel.

B. When the people requested a king, Samuel remonstrated with them but was directed by the Lord to grant their request. SAUL was brought to Samuel and was privately anointed as king. This selection was later confirmed by lot at an assembly of all Israel at MIZPAH. Saul's first impressive act, the rescue of JABESH GILEAD from the besieging Ammonites, led to his confirmation as king at GILGAL. Samuel now retired from active public life (1 Sam. 12), though he continued to serve as adviser to the king. Saul's incomplete obedience brought about his rejection from the kingship.

C. God designated the youthful David as Saul's successor and Samuel secretly anointed him. David became Saul's court musician and later served king and country well by killing GOLIATH in single combat. On this occasion Saul inquired concerning David's family, so that JESSE too could be rewarded (cf. 1 Sam. 17:24). David now became a close friend of JONATHAN, Saul's son, but Saul was now both jealous and afraid of David, and his hostility soon produced open attempts on David's life. David was forced to flee, and the pursuit by Saul, though intermittent, was not concluded until the Philistines swept the Israelites before them on Mount GILBOA, leading to the death of Saul and his sons. David mourned their passing in an eloquent elegy (2 Sam. 1).

D. David reigned as king of JUDAH in HEBRON for seven and a half years. Overtures were made to unite all Israel under his leadership.

E. These efforts were crowned with success, and David wisely took JERUSALEM and made it

his new capital, for since the time it had been in JEBUSITE hands it had had no definite affiliation with Judah or the northern tribes. David continued to build the kingdom and the Lord announced to him the perpetuity of his dynasty (2 Sam. 7). Though David conquered his enemies and was gracious to Jonathan's son, he was overcome by temptation in the idleness of semiretirement. The affair with BATHSHEBA led to bitter heartache and also to sincere REPENTANCE on the part of the king. Circumstances in the royal family brought about the rebellion of ABSALOM, which again saw David in flight for his life. The killing of Absalom ended the revolt but increased David's sorrow. Restored to Jerusalem, David had to deal promptly with the short-lived revolt of SHEBA. Second Samuel ends with a summary of battles with the Philistines, David's praise of the Lord (1 Sam. 22; 23:2-7), the listing of his mighty men, and the catastrophe of the census (ch. 24).

III. Purpose. The purpose of all OT history is clearly stated in the NT (Rom. 15:4; 1 Cor. 10:11): to serve as warning, instruction, and encouragement. More specifically, the books of Samuel present the establishment of the kingship in Israel. In

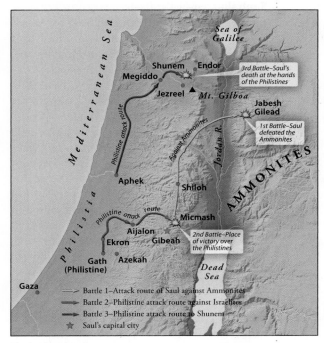

The battles of Saul.

Saul's reign and life came to a close on the heights of Mt. Gilboa (1 Sam. 31), pictured here looking E from the Jezreel Valley.

preserving the account of Samuel, the judge and prophet, the books mark the transition from judgeship to monarchy, since Samuel filled the prophetic office and administered the divine induction into office of Israel's first two kings.

Sanballat. san-bal′at (Heb. *sanballaṭ H6172*, from Akk. *Sin-uballiṭ*, "Sin [the moon god] has saved" or "may Sin give life"). A man identified as a HORONITE (prob. a native of BETH-HORON) who, along with TOBIAH and GESHEM, opposed NEHEMIAH's efforts to rebuild JERUSALEM (Neh. 2:10, 19; 4:1-9; 6:1-14). A grandson of ELIASHIB the high priest married Sanballat's daughter (13:28). Among the Elephantine papyri from Egypt (407 B.C.), a document mentions "Delaiah and Shelemiah, the sons of Sanballat the governor of Samaria" (*ANET*, 492b). See SAMARIA (TERRITORY). This wording suggests that Sanballat was then very old and that the effective control was in the hands of his sons. In the time of Nehemiah he may already have been governor of Samaria. This would account for his influence, and he had probably hoped to become joint governor of both Samaria and JUDAH if Nehemiah had not come. (Other possible motives for Sanballat's opposition have been suggested.) In spite of his foreign name, Sanballat gave his sons names with a Yahweh ending, but he may well have been descended

from the mixed races who had been brought into the northern kingdom and who had a syncretistic worship with a preference for Yahweh (2 Ki. 18:23). JOSEPHUS makes Sanballat the founder of the SAMARITAN temple on Mount GERIZIM, with his son-in-law Manasseh as high priest, Manasseh being brother to the Jewish high priest, Jaddua (*Ant.* 11.8.4 §324). The situation Josephus describes is not unlike that of Neh. 13:28-29, but he dates it in the time of ALEXANDER THE GREAT about a century later. He may have mistaken the name (or the period), but it is possible that he is referring to a different man of the same name.

sanctification. The process or result of being made holy. The notion of HOLINESS, when applied to things, places, and people, means that they are consecrated and set apart for the use of God, who is utterly pure and apart from all imperfection and evil. See CONSECRATION. When used of people, it can refer also to the practical realization within them of consecration to God: that is, it can have a moral dimension. Thus in the NT, believers are described as already (objectively) sanctified in Christ. PAUL refers to the Corinthians believers as "those sanctified in Christ Jesus" (1 Cor. 1:2), and says to them, "[God] is the source of your life in Christ Jesus, who became for us wisdom from God, and righteousness and sanctification and redemption" (1:30 NRSV). Also, though set apart in Christ for God and seen as holy by God because they are in Christ, believers are called to show that consecration in their lives. "It is God's will that you should be sanctified" (1 Thess. 4:3). "May … the God of peace sanctify you" (5:23). The same emphasis is found in HEBREWS (Heb. 2:11; 9:13; 10:10, 14, 29; 13:12). Because believers are holy in Christ (set apart for God by his sacrificial, atoning blood), they are to be holy in practice in the power of the HOLY SPIRIT. They are to be sanctified because they are already sanctified.

sanctuary. A holy place set apart from profane use for the purpose of WORSHIP of, or communion with, a deity. The forerunners to Israel's sanctuaries were the patriarchal worship places, usually designated by a theophany or some other special revelation of God (e.g., Gen. 12:7; 26:24-25; 28:16-17). The Hebrew term term *miqdāš H5219* is most frequently used of the TABERNACLE, but also of the TEMPLE and of pagan holy places (Isa. 16:12 [NIV, "shrine"]; Ezek. 28:18). The first reference to a sanctuary (Exod. 15:17) speaks of the abode of God to which he brings his redeemed people to reign over them as King. This eschatological sanctuary (cf. Heb. 8:2) forms the reality of which the earthly sanctuaries of God are but the foreshadowing. The sanctuary is a place for the Lord to dwell in the midst of his people (Exod. 25:8), and since the presence of God is the important factor, the establishment of the right relationship with God ultimately renders the special holy place unnecessary (Ezek. 11:16; Rev. 21:22; see also Jn. 4:21, 23).

sand. A rock material made up of loose grains of small size formed as the result of weathering and decomposition of various kinds of rocks. It is found in abundance in deserts, in the sea, and on the shores of large bodies of water. The writers of the Bible were very familiar with it, and they often referred to it as a symbol of (1) numberlessness or vastness, (2) weight, (3) instability. The descendants of ABRAHAM were numberless (Gen. 22:17; Jer. 33:22; Rom. 9:27; Heb. 11:12); as were also the enemies of Israel (Josh. 11:4; Jdg. 7:12; 1 Sam. 13:5). JOSEPH accumulated grain as measureless as the sand of the sea (Gen. 41:49). God gave to SOLOMON understanding and largeness of heart as the sand on the seashore (1 Ki. 4:29). The thoughts of God, says the psalmist, "outnumber the grains of sand" (Ps. 139:18). JOB says that if his grief were weighed, it would be heavier than the sand of the sea (Job 6:3). A house built on sand symbolizes a life not built on hearing the teachings of Jesus (Matt. 7:26).

sandal. See DRESS.

sand lizard, sand reptile. See ANIMALS (under *lizard*).

Sanhedrin. san-hee′druhn (Gk. *synedrion G5284*, "a sitting together, a council-board"; transliterated into Mishnaic Heb. as *sanhedrîn*). The council or governing body that met in JERUSALEM in NT times and that constituted the highest Jewish authority in PALESTINE prior to A.D. 70. It must be distinguished from lesser, local courts of law to which the name *sanhedrin* was also regularly applied. The TALMUD connects the Sanhedrin with MOSES' seventy elders, then with the alleged Great Synagogue of EZRA's time; but the truth is that the origin of the Sanhedrin is unknown, and there is no historical evidence for its existence before the Greek period.

During the reign of the Hellenistic kings, Palestine was practically under home rule and was governed by a *gerousia G1172*, an aristocratic "council of elders" or "senate" that was presided over by the hereditary high priest (the term occurs once in the NT [Acts 5:21]; another word used to refer to the Sanhedrin is *presbyterion G4564*, "council of elders" [Lk. 22:66; Acts 22:5]). It was this body that later developed into the Sanhedrin. During most of the Roman period the internal government of the country was practically in its hands, and its influence was recognized even in the DISPERSION (Acts 9:2; 22:5; 26:12). After the death of HEROD the Great, however, during the reign of Archelaus and the Roman PROCURATORS, the civil authority of the Sanhedrin was probably restricted to JUDEA, and this is very likely the reason why it had no judicial authority over the Lord so long as he remained in GALILEE. The Sanhedrin was abolished after the destruction of Jerusalem (A.D. 70). A new court

S

was established bearing the name "Sanhedrin," but it differed in essential features from the older body: it had no political authority and was composed exclusively of RABBIS, whose decisions had only a theoretical importance.

The Sanhedrin was composed of seventy members plus the president, who was the high priest. Nothing is known as to the way in which vacancies were filled. The members probably held office for life, and successors were likely appointed either by the existing members themselves or by the supreme political authorities (Herod and the Romans). Since only pure-blooded Jews were eligible for the office of judge in a criminal court, the same principle was probably followed in the case of the Sanhedrin. New members were formally admitted by the ceremony of the laying on of hands.

The members of the Sanhedrin were drawn from the three classes named in the Gospels: "the elders, the chief priests and the teachers of the law" (Matt. 16:21; 27:41; Mk. 8:31; 11:27; 14:43, 53; 15:1; Lk. 9:22; 22:26). By "chief priests" is meant the acting high priest, those who had been high priests, and members of the privileged families from which the high priests were taken. The priestly aristocracy comprised the leading persons in the community,

and they were the chief members of the Sanhedrin. The teachers of the law (SCRIBES) formed the Pharisaic element in the Sanhedrin, though not all PHARISEES were professional scribes. The ELDERS were the tribal and family heads of the people and priesthood. They were, for the most part, the secular nobility of Jerusalem. The president bore the honorable title of "prince." Besides the president, there were also a vice-president, called the "head or father of the house of judgment," and another important official, whose business it was, in all probability, to assist in the declaration of the law. There were also two or three secretaries and other subordinate officials, of which "officer" (Matt. 5:25) and "servant of the high priest" (Matt. 26:51; Mk. 14:47; Jn. 18:10) are mentioned in the NT. According to JOSEPHUS, in the time of Christ the Sanhedrin was formally led by the Sadducean high priests (see SADDUCEE), but practically ruled by the Pharisees, who were immensely popular with the people (*Ant.* 18.1.4). The Pharisees were more and more represented in the Sanhedrin as they grew in importance.

In the time of Christ the Sanhedrin exercised not only civil jurisdiction, according to Jewish law, but also, in some degree, criminal. It could deal with all those judicial matters and measures of an administrative character that could not be competently handled by lower courts, or that the Roman procurator had not specially reserved for himself. It was the final court of appeal for all questions connected with the Mosaic LAW. It could order arrests by its own officers of justice (Matt. 26:47; Mk. 14:43; Acts 4:3; 5:17-18; 9:2). It was also the final court of appeal from all inferior courts. It alone had the right of judging in matters affecting a whole tribe, of determining questions of peace or war, of trying the high priest or one of its own body. It pronounced on the claims of prophets and on charges of blasphemy. The king himself could be summoned to its bar; and Josephus relates that even Herod did not dare to disobey its summons (*Ant.* 14.9.4).

The Sanhedrin enjoyed the right of capital punishment until about forty years before the destruction of Jerusalem. After that it could still pass, but not execute, a sentence of death without the confirmation of the Roman procurator. That is why

© Garo Nalbandian

Interior of the Huldah Gates, located at the S end of the temple mount. The members of the Sanhedrin would have frequently used this entrance to the temple.

Jesus had to be tried not only before the Sanhedrin but also before PILATE (Jn. 18:31-32). But for this requirement, Jesus would have been put to death in some other way than by crucifixion, for crucifixion was not a Jewish mode of punishment. The stoning of STEPHEN (Acts 7:57-58) without the approval of the procurator was an illegal act—a lynching. In the case of one specific offense the Sanhedrin could put to death, on its own authority, even a Roman citizen, namely, when a GENTILE passed the gate of the temple that divided the court of the Jews from that of the Gentiles (cf. 21:28), but even this case was subject to the procurator's revision of the capital sentence. The Roman authority was, however, always absolute, and the procurator or the tribune of the garrison could direct the Sanhedrin to investigate some matter and could remove a prisoner from its jurisdiction, as was done in the case of PAUL (22:30; 23:23-24).

The Sanhedrin at first met in "the hall of hewn stones," one of the buildings connected with the temple. Later, the place of meeting was somewhere in the Court of the Gentiles, although they were not confined to it. They could meet on any day except the Sabbath and holy days, and they met from the time of the offering of the daily morning sacrifice until that of the evening sacrifice. The meetings were conducted according to strict rules and were enlivened by stirring debates. Twenty-three members formed a quorum. While a bare majority might acquit, a majority of two was necessary to secure condemnation, although if all seventy-one members were present, a majority of one was decisive on either side. To avoid any hasty condemnation where life was involved, judgment was passed the same day only when it was a judgment of acquittal. If it was a judgment of condemnation, it could not be passed until the day after. For this reason, cases involving capital punishment were not tried on a Friday or on any day before a feast.

Sansannah. san-san'uh (Heb. *sansannâ H6179*, prob. "stalk of the date palm"). One of the "southernmost towns of the tribe of Judah in the Negev toward the boundary of Edom" (Josh. 15:31; cf. v. 21). It is probably the same as modern Khirbet esh-Shamsaniyat, some 8 mi. (13 km.) NE of BEERSHEBA. A comparison with the parallel lists

(Josh. 19:5; 1 Chr. 4:31) has led some to equate Sansannah with HAZAR SUSAH (Hazar Susim), but this identification remains uncertain.

Saph. saf (Heb. *sap H6198*, meaning unknown). A descendant of Rapha (see REPHAITES) who was killed by SIBBECAI the Hushathite in a fight with the PHILISTINES at Gob (2 Sam. 21:18). In the parallel passage, he is called "Sippai" (evidently an alternate form of the name), and the battle is said to have taken place in GEZER (1 Chr. 20:4). See comments under GOB.

Saphir. See SHAPHIR.

Sapphira. suh-fi'ruh (Gk. *Sapphira G4912*, from Aram. *šappîrā᾽*, "beautiful"). Wife of ANANIAS. The couple sold a piece of property and pretended to bring the money to the apostles. For their hypocrisy in pretending not to have kept any of the money for themselves, and lying to the HOLY SPIRIT, they both died suddenly within three hours of each other, much to the fear of the early church and of all who heard about it (Acts 5:1-11).

sapphire. See MINERALS.

Sara. See SARAH.

Sarah, Sarai. sair'uh, say'ri (Heb. *šārāh H8577* [from Gen. 17:15 on], alternate form *šāray H8584* [Gen. 11:29—17:5], "princess"; Gk. *Sarra G4925*). KJV NT Sara. **(1)** The wife of ABRAHAM (Gen. 11:29-30), and also his half-sister on his father TERAH's side (20:12). She was ten years younger than Abraham and was married to him in UR of the Chaldeans (cf. 11:31). Her name was originally Sarai. She was about sixty-five years old when Abraham left Ur for HARAN. Later she accompanied Abraham into EGYPT and was there passed off by him as his sister because she was still so beautiful and he feared the Egyptians might kill him if they knew she was his wife. Years later Abraham did the same thing at the court of ABIMELECH king of GERAR (20:1-18). In each instance, grievous wrong was averted only by God's intervention, and Abraham was rebuked by the pagan rulers for his lack of candor.

S

Still childless at the age of seventy-five, Sarah induced Abraham to take her handmaid HAGAR as a CONCUBINE. According to the laws of the time, a son born of this woman would be regarded as the son and heir of Abraham and Sarah. When Hagar conceived, she treated her mistress with such insolence that Sarah drove her from the house. Hagar, however, returned at God's direction, submitted herself to her mistress, and gave birth to ISHMAEL. Afterward, when Sarah was about ninety, God promised her a son; her name was changed, and a year later ISAAC, the child of promise, was born (17:15-27; 21:1-3). A few years later, at a great feast celebrating the weaning of Isaac, Sarah observed Ishmael mocking her son, and demanded the expulsion of Hagar and Ishmael (ch. 21). Abraham reluctantly acceded, after God had instructed him to do so. Sarah died at Kiriath Arba (HEBRON) at the age of 127 and was buried in the cave of MACHPELAH, which Abraham purchased as a family sepulcher (23:1-2). Sarah is mentioned again in the OT only in Isa. 51:2, as the mother of the chosen race. She is mentioned several times in the NT (Rom. 4:19; 9:9; Gal. 4:21-5:1; Heb. 11:11; 1 Pet. 3:6).

(2) KJV alternate form of SERAH (Num. 26:46).

Saraph. sair´uhf (Heb. *śārāp H8598*, "burning one"). Son of SHELA and grandson of JUDAH; he and one (or more) of his brothers are said to have ruled in MOAB and JASHUBI LEHEM (1 Chr. 4:22; the NRSV emends the text and renders, "who married into Moab but returned to Lehem").

sardine. See MINERALS (under *carnelian*).

Sardis. sahr´dis (Gk. *Sardeis G4915*). The chief city of LYDIA, under a fortified spur of Mount Tmolus in the Hermus Valley; near the junction of the roads from central ASIA MINOR, EPHESUS, SMYRNA, and PERGAMUM. Sardis was the capital of Lydia under the ancient ruler Croesus; it became seat of the governor after the Persian conquest. Sardis was famous for arts and crafts and was the first center to mint gold and silver coins. So wealthy were the Lydian kings that Croesus became a legend for riches, and it was said that the sands of the Pactolus were golden. Croesus also became a legend for pride and presumptuous arro-

gance, when his attack on PERSIA led to the fall of Sardis and the eclipse of his kingdom. The capture of the great citadel by surprise attack by CYRUS and his Persians in 549 B.C., and three centuries later by the Romans, may have provided the imagery for John's warning in Rev. 3:3. The great earthquake of A.D. 17 ruined Sardis physically and financially. The Romans contributed ten million sesterces in relief, an indication of the damage done, but the city never recovered.

Sardite. See SERED.

sardius. See MINERALS (under *carnelian*).

sardonyx. See MINERALS.

Sarepta. See ZAREPHATH.

Sargon. sahr´gon (Heb. *sargôn H6236*, from Ass. *šarrukēn*, "the king is legitimate"). The name of three Mesopotamian kings: Sargon of AKKAD (c. 2300 B.C.) and the Assyrian Sargon I (c. 1900) and Sargon II (721-705). The name is found only once in the Bible, where it refers to Sargon II of ASSYRIA (Isa. 20:1). This Sargon was the son of

This relief of Sargon II from the palace of Khorsabad (c. 710 B.C.) pictures the king wearing the royal tiara and holding a staff as he faces a high official or crowned prince.

© Dr. James C. Martin. The British Museum. Photographed by permission.

TIGLATH-PILESER III, successor to his brother SHALMANESER V, and father of SENNACHERIB. His reign is amply known from his inscriptions at Khorsabad and from letters and historical texts found at NINEVEH and Nimrud (CALAH). Although he is named only once in the OT, his campaigns are of importance for understanding the historical background of the prophecies of ISAIAH.

During the siege of SAMARIA, Shalmaneser died (722 B.C.), and a year later the city fell to Sargon. It is strange that the Bible does not mention him in the record of Samaria's fall (2 Ki. 17:1-6). Some authorities believe that Sargon did not become king until after the city fell. However, Sargon claims to have captured Samaria, and a certain ambiguity in 2 Ki. 17:6 allows for a new, although unnamed, Assyrian monarch there. Soon after Sargon came to the throne, the Babylonians, assisted by the Elamites, revolted against him and were subdued with difficulty. According to Sargon's inscriptions the remnant of the Israelites at Samaria, who had been put under an Assyrian governor, revolted, along with other Syrian and Palestinian provinces (720 B.C.). This revolt Sargon quickly suppressed. At this time he also defeated the Egyptian ruler So, who had come to the aid of rebelling GAZA (2 Ki. 17:4). Later Sargon captured CARCHEMISH, the great HITTITE city (717 B.C.), thus precipitating the fall of the Hittite empire. He also mentions placing Arab tribes as colonists in Samaria. Sargon claims on his inscriptions to have subdued JUDAH. Evidently Judah became more or less involved in a rebellion against Assyria, led by ASHDOD. This PHILISTINE city was captured by the Assyrians and reorganized as an Assyrian province (711; cf. Isa. 20:1), and Judah was subdued but not harmed.

In 717 B.C. he laid the foundations of "Sargon's fortress," *Dur-Sharrukin*, a hitherto virgin site 12 mi. (19 km.) NE of NINEVEH, near the modern village of Khorsabad. Ten years later the workmen completed a town that was square in plan, each side measuring about one mile. The palace itself stood on a 60-ft. (18-m.) high platform overriding the city wall and comprised more than 200 rooms and thirty courtyards. The royal abode was richly decorated and the gates of the town were guarded by colossal bull-men. Evidence, however, indicates that the city was scarcely inhabited and almost immediately abandoned at the king's death. One year after Dur-Sharrukin was officially inaugurated, Sargon was killed (705 B.C.). His successors preferred Nineveh, and Khorsabad, deserted, fell slowly to ruins.

Sarid. sair′id (Heb. *śārîd H8587*, possibly "survivor"). A border town within the tribal territory of ZEBULUN (Josh. 19:10, 12). If the MT is correct, perhaps the name of the town is related to SERED, one of the sons of Zebulun, but the site is unknown. However, on the basis of some Greek MSS and other versional evidence, many scholars believe that the original Hebrew reading was *śādûd* and that the site should be identified with modern Tell Shadud on the northern edge of the Plain of ESDRAELON c. 5 mi. (8 km.) SW of NAZARETH and 6 mi. (10 km.) NE of MEGIDDO.

Saron. See SHARON.

Sarsechim. sahr′suh-kim (Heb. *śar-sĕkîm*). A Babylonian army officer who held the title of RABSARIS and who participated in the siege of JERUSALEM (Jer. 39:3 NRSV and other versions). Some scholars analyze the text differently and, joining this name with the previous one, read NEBO-SARSEKIM (cf. NIV). Others, on the basis of v. 13, emend the text to read NEBUSHAZBAN. See also SAMGAR.

Saruch. See SERUG.

Satan. say′tuhn (Heb. *śāṭān H8477*, "adversary" or "accuser"; Gk. *satanas G4928* [from Aram. *sāṭānāʾ*], usually with the definite article [*satan* in 1 Ki. 11:14 LXX]). The grand adversary of God and human beings, identified with the DEVIL (Rev. 12:9; 20:2). Without the article, the Hebrew word is used in a general sense to denote someone who is an opponent, an adversary; for example, the angel who stood in BALAAM's way (Num. 22:22), DAVID as a possible opponent in battle (1 Sam. 29:4), and a political adversary (1 Ki. 11:14). With the definite article prefixed, it is a proper noun (Job 1-2; Zech. 3:1-2), designating Satan as a personality. In Ps. 109:6 the article is lacking, and reference may be to a human adversary (cf. NIV, "an accuser"),

S

but it is generally conceded that in 1 Chr. 21:1 the word is a proper name without the article.

The teaching concerning evil and a personal devil finds its full presentation only in the NT. There the term always designates the personal Satan (but cf. Matt. 16:23; Mk. 8:33). This malignant foe is known in the NT by a number of other names and descriptive designations. He is often called "the devil," meaning "the slanderer" (Matt. 4:1; Lk. 4:2; Jn. 8:44; Eph. 6:11; Rev. 12:12). Other titles or descriptive designations applied to him are ABADDON ("Apollyon," Rev. 9:11); "accuser of our brothers" (12:10); "enemy" (1 Pet. 5:8); BEELZEBUB (Matt. 12:24); BELIAL (2 Cor. 6:15); the one who "leads the whole world astray" (Rev. 12:9); "the evil one" (Matt. 13:19, 38; 1 Jn. 2:13; 5:19); "the father of lies" (Jn. 8:44); "the god of this age" (2 Cor. 4:4); "a murderer" (Jn. 8:44); "that ancient serpent" (Rev. 12:9); "the prince of this world" (Jn. 12:31; 14:30); "the ruler of the kingdom of the air" (Eph. 2:2); "the tempter" (Matt. 4:5; 1 Thess. 3:5).

These varied designations indicate the dignity and character of Satan. In the book of JOB he is pictured as mixing with the sons of God (ANGELS) in their appearing before God, though by his moral nature not one of them. Jude 9 pictures him as a formidable foe to MICHAEL the archangel. While clearly very powerful and clever, he is not an independent rival of God but is definitely subordinate, able to go only as far as God permits (Job 1:12; 2:6; Lk. 22:31). Christ gives a fundamental description of his moral nature in calling him the evil one (Matt. 13:19, 38). Moral evil is his basic attribute; he is the very embodiment of evil. Christ's words in Jn. 8:44 give the fullest statement of Satan's moral character: "He was a murderer from the beginning, not holding to the truth, for there is no truth in him. When he lies, he speaks his native language, for he is a liar and the father of lies." John asserts that "the devil has been sinning from the beginning" (1 Jn. 3:8). Because he is a murderer, liar, and sinner, evil is the very environment and inherent nature of the devil.

The origin of Satan is not explicitly asserted in Scripture, but the statement that he did not hold to the truth (Jn. 8:44) implies that he is a fallen being, while 1 Tim. 3:6 indicates that he fell under God's condemnation because of ambitious pride.

While many theologians refuse to apply the far-reaching prophecies in Isa. 14:12-14 and Ezek. 28:12-15 to Satan, contending that these passages are strictly addressed to the kings of BABYLON and TYRE, other scholars hold that they contain a clear revelation of Satan's origin. These profound prophecies are thought to go much beyond any earthly ruler and harmonize with the scriptural picture of Satan's close relations with world governments (Dan. 10:13; Jn. 12:31; Eph. 6:12). These passages picture Satan's prefall splendor as well as his apostasy through pride and self-exaltation against God. A consuming passion of Satan is to be worshiped (Isa. 14:14; Matt. 4:9; 1 Cor. 10:20; Rev. 13:4, 15). In his fall Satan drew a vast number of lesser celestial creatures with him (Rev. 12:4).

Satan is the ruler of a powerful kingdom standing in opposition to the KINGDOM OF GOD (Matt. 12:26; Lk. 11:18). He exercises authority in two different realms. He is the head of a vast, compact organization of spirit-beings, "his angels" (Matt. 25:41). As "the ruler of the kingdom of the air" (Eph. 2:2), he skillfully directs an organized host of wicked spirits who do his bidding (6:12). Acts 10:38 makes it clear that the outburst of demonic activities during the ministry of Jesus was Satan-inspired. Satan is not omnipresent, but through his subordinates he makes his influence practically worldwide. He also exercises domination over the world of lost humanity. He is "the prince of this world" (Jn. 12:31, 14:30, 16:11), the evil world system that he has organized on his own principles (2 Cor. 4:3-4; Col. 1:13; 1 Jn. 2:15-17). That "the whole world is under the control of the evil one" (1 Jn. 5:19) indicates that the world is in the grip of and passively yielded to the power of the devil. This power over people he holds by virtue of usurpation.

Animated by an unrelenting hatred against God and all goodness, Satan is engaged in a worldwide and agelong struggle against God, ever seeking to defeat the divine plans of grace and to seduce people to evil and ruin. As he who "leads the whole world astray" (Rev. 12:9), his primary method is that of deception—about himself, his purpose, his activities, and his coming defeat. Satan was the seducer of ADAM and EVE (Gen. 3:1-7; 2 Cor. 11:3); he insinuated to God that Job served him only for what he got out of it (Job 1:9); and he stood up against Israel (1 Chr. 21:1) and God's high priest (Zech. 3:1-2). Under divinely imposed limitations he may be instrumental in causing physical affliction or financial loss (Job 1:11-22; 2:4-7; Lk. 13:16; 2 Cor. 12:7). He snatches away the Word of God sown in the hearts of the unsaved (Matt. 13:19), sows his counterfeit Christians among the children of the kingdom (13:25, 38-39), blinds the minds of people to the gospel (2 Cor. 4:3-4), and induces them to accept his lie (2 Thess. 2:9-10). Often he transforms himself into "an angel of light" by presenting his apostles of falsehood as messengers of truth (2 Cor. 11:13-15). He clashes in fierce conflict with the saints (Eph. 6:11-18), is ever alert to try to destroy them (1 Pet. 5:8), and hinders the work of God's servants (1 Thess. 2:18). Certain members of the church who were expelled are said to have been delivered to Satan, but with the design to produce their reformation, not their destruction (1 Cor. 5:5; 1 Tim. 1:20).

Although Satan was judged in the CROSS (Jn. 13:31-33), he is still permitted to carry on the conflict, often with startling success. But his revealed doom is sure. He now has a sphere of activities in the heavenly realms (Eph. 6:12); he will be cast down to the earth and will cause great woe because of his wrath, which he will exercise through "the dragon" (2 Thess. 2:9; Rev. 12:7-12; 13:2-8). The book of Revelation describes his incarceration in the bottomless pit for 1,000 years (Rev. 20:1-3, a passage whose meaning is debated). When again released for a season, he will again attempt to deceive the nations but will be cast into "the eternal fire" prepared for him and his angels (20:7-10; Matt. 25:41).

satrap. A ruling official in the far-flung Persian empire (Ezra 8:36; Esth. 3:12 et al.; Dan. 3:2-3 et al.). The satrap's jurisdiction extended over several provinces; his office was virtually that of a vassal king. The satrap held extensive power but was checked by the presence of a royal scribe who had regularly to render a report to the sovereign of the realm; moreover, the military forces were under the command of a general who held independent status. In Ezra 8:36 ("They also delivered the king's orders to the royal satraps and to the governors of Trans-Euphrates") the term seems to be used loosely, since the only satrap whom Ezra's commission would really concern was the one ruling in Trans-Euphrates itself (cf. 5:3).

satyr. The Greek term *satyros* referred to a mythological god, half human and half beast (with pointed ears and goat's tail and legs), which inhabited the woods and engaged in the revelries of Dionysus. For lack of a better term, the KJV chose *satyr* to render Hebrew *śāʿîr* in Isa. 13:21 and 34:14, understanding the word to refer to demonic creatures that gambol in desolate areas. This rendering was followed by the RSV and other versions not only here, but also in Lev. 17:7 and 2 Chr. 11:15 (where the KJV has "devils"). The NRSV, while accepting the same interpretation, translates "goat-demon." The NIV interprets the term in Isaiah as the usual noun for "goat" or "wild goat" (*śāʿîr* II *H8538*), but acknowledges the sense "goat idol" or "goat demon" (*śāʿîr* III *H8539*) in the other two references. It does seem likely that in some or all of these passages there is a reference to one of the demonically inspired pagan gods of CANAAN, in the image of a goat, having a brutal and lustful nature, which was an object of worship for Israel and became a snare to them (cf. Deut. 32:17; Ps. 106:37).

Saul. sawl (Heb. *šāʾûl H8620*, "one who has been begged for"; Gk. *Saoul G4910* [LXX, also Acts 9:4; 13:21; 22:7, 13; 26:14] and *Saulos G4930*, the common hellenized form in NT). Son of KISH, descendant of BENJAMIN, and first king of ISRAEL. (In the NT, the name is applied only once to the Israelite king [Acts 13:21], elsewhere to Saul of Tarsus; see PAUL. The KJV uses the form *Saul* also in reference to the Edomite king SHAUL [Gen. 36:37-38].) A handsome man who was a head taller than his fellow Israelites, Saul is introduced in 1 Sam. 9, after the people had asked SAMUEL for a king (ch. 8). Saul and Samuel met for the first time when Saul was searching for some lost donkeys of his father. Greeted by Samuel with compliments, Saul replied with becoming humility (9:21; cf. Jdg. 6:15), but, sadly, before the record of Saul's life is concluded we are to find that he suffered, to a chronic degree, the disability that matches his virtue: he was diffident and personally insecure more than most, making him both attractively unassuming and also (in later

S

days) pathologically defensive and highly overreactive. Before Saul left, Samuel secretly anointed him as king of Israel, as the Lord had directed. God gave Saul a changed heart (1 Sam. 10:9), and Saul prophesied among a group of prophets who met him on his way home.

The choice of Saul as king was confirmed by lot at an assembly of Israel convened by Samuel at MIZPAH, but the bashful young man was in hiding and had to be brought before the people. In spite of his manly appearance he was ridiculed by some riffraff, "but Saul kept silent" (1 Sam. 10:27). His forbearance was supplemented by compassion and decision in his rescue of JABESH GILEAD from the threat of the Ammonites (ch. 11). The lowly nature of the young kingdom is demonstrated by the fact that the king earned his livelihood as a farmer. When the message arrived from the besieged city, Saul was returning from the field behind his oxen (11:5). The king's summons to the people, in the form of pieces of a dismembered yoke of oxen, galvanized Israel into a unified response (11:7; cf. Jdg. 19:29).

After the deliverance of the city, Saul showed his generosity by insisting that his earlier detractors should not be punished. A military crisis with the PHILISTINES revealed flaws in the character of Saul. When Samuel delayed in coming to make offering before battle, Saul presumed to present the offering himself. He found himself in the sort of situation that imposed the severest pressures on a man of his temperament. No leader easily accepts the criticism of inaction nor is any leader always aware when the moment of action has come. Those who, like Saul, are temperamentally hesitant, are often betrayed into hasty responses to crises lest they be thought inadequate. For such, as for Saul, the solution is a resolute determination to obey such commands of God as touch the situation. Saul had a command (cf. 1 Sam. 10:8), and his sin was that he listened to the voice of his own insecurity rather than to the plain word of God. For this the privilege of founding a dynasty was withdrawn from him (13:13-14).

On the human side we are reminded of the pressure of the situation: the great superiority of the Philistines in number (1 Sam. 13:5), attitude (13:6-7), and equipment (13:19-23). The Philistines had a monopoly on the metal industry; they limited smiths to their own territory and charged the Israelites high rates for the sharpening of tools. At the time of battle only Saul and JONATHAN among the Israelites had sword or spear. The Philistines were routed in spite of Saul's

© Dr. James C. Martin

Aerial view of ancient Beth Shan (looking SE), where the bodies of Saul and Jonathan were hung after they were killed by the Philistines.

S

bad judgment in denying food to his soldiers at a time when they most needed strength. Saul fought valiantly and successfully against all the enemies of Israel (14:47-48); though he was a brave leader he was not a good soldier, for he was not aware of the necessity of absolute obedience. The affair of the AMALEKITES, though a military success, was a spiritual failure. We have no ground for accepting the excuse Saul made for his incomplete obedience (15:21). It is consistent with Saul's deep-seated inner insecurity that popular pressure, coupled with his genuine religious feeling, made him a compromiser in such a situation: the people were bent on a religious festival that would have been as much a party for them as a thanksgiving to the Lord. We can share Saul's tossings and turnings until he gives way. Once more obedience has been sacrificed on the altar of temperament, and this time (15:27-28) the continuance of his own period of reign and indeed the validity of his kingship itself comes under judgment.

DAVID enters the narrative in 1 Sam. 16; he was anointed by Samuel as future king and was introduced to court life by appointment as court musician to play the lyre for Saul when the king was tormented by an evil spirit. After David defeated GOLIATH, he was again presented before Saul and was heralded by the women of Israel as a greater hero than Saul. Jealousy, hatred, and fear led Saul to direct and indirect attempts against David's life (18:10-11, 21; 19:1, 11) and resulted in the hide-and-seek chase that twice drove David into Philistine territory (21:10; 27:1-3). The unsuspecting aid given to David by the priests of NOB moved Saul to slaughter the priests and to annihilate the city (22:17-19). Saul's life was spared by David on two occasions—at EN GEDI (24:1-7) and in the Desert of ZIPH (26:6-12).

The eve of what proved to be Saul's final battle brought the king under desperate pressure. He was so far gone in the disintegration of his personality that he did not know how to get right with God, and in a final and tragic way his temperamental insecurity again triumphed. He yielded to advice that affronted all that his life had held dear and all that his considerably successful period as king had achieved—he turned to the forces of darkness, those same forces he had earlier banished from the land (1 Sam. 28:3). The heartrending tragedy of his life reached its climax in the darkened room of a spiritist medium. Samuel could give him no earthly comfort, but some believe there was a word of compassionate divine grace in the prophet's message: "Tomorrow you and your sons will be with me" (28:19). The next day Saul and his sons died in the battle on Mount GILBOA. The Philistines decapitated Saul and took his remains to BETH SHAN, where they placed his armor in the temple of the ASHTORETHS (31:10), his head in the temple of DAGON (1 Chr. 10:10), and his body on the city wall. The men of Jabesh Gilead remembered Saul's concern for them; in gratitude they recovered his body and the bodies of his sons from the walls of Beth Shan, gave them honorable burial at Jabesh, and fasted in mourning. David also, when he heard the report, went into mourning and expressed his grief in the elegy of 2 Sam. 1:19-27.

savior. One who saves, delivers, or preserves from any evil or danger, whether physical or spiritual, temporal, or eternal. A basic OT concept is that God is the Deliverer of his people; it is emphatically declared that human beings cannot save themselves and that the Lord alone is the Savior (Ps. 44:3, 7; Isa. 43:11; 45:21; 60:16; Jer. 14:8; Hos. 13:4). The Hebrew word for "savior" is a participle (*môšiaʿ H4635*, from the verb *yāšaʿ H3828*), which may suggest that in the thought of the OT this term is not so much a title as it is a description of God's activity in behalf of his people. In the OT the term is not applied to the MESSIAH; he received salvation from God (2 Sam. 22:51; Ps. 28:8; 144:10); but he came to offer salvation to all (Isa. 49:6, 8; Zech. 9:9). The term is also applied to people who are used as the instruments of God's deliverance (Jdg. 3:9, 15 ASV; 2 Ki. 13:5; Neh. 9:27; Obad. 21).

The Greeks applied the title *sōtēr G5400* to their gods; it was also used of philosophers (e.g., Epicurus; see EPICUREAN) or rulers (e.g., PTOLEMY I, NERO) or men who had brought notable benefits on their country. But in the NT it is a strictly religious term and is never applied to a mere person. It is used of both GOD the Father and CHRIST the Son. God the Father is Savior, for he is the author of our salvation, which he provided through Christ

S

(Lk. 1:47; 1 Tim. 1:1; 2:3; 4:10; Tit. 1:3; 2:10; 3:4; Jude 25). Savior is preeminently the title of the Son (2 Tim. 1:10; Tit. 1:4; 2:13; 3:6; 2 Pet. 1:1, 11; 2:20; 3:2, 18; 1 Jn. 4:10). At his birth the angel announced him as "a Savior ... he is Christ the Lord" (Lk. 2:11). His mission to save his people from their sins was announced before his birth (Matt. 1:21) and was stated by Jesus as the aim of his coming (Lk. 19:10). He is twice described as "the Savior of the world" (Jn. 4:42; 1 Jn. 4:14). Those who are saved are brought into a spiritual union with Christ as members of his body; hence he is called "the Savior" of "the body [the CHURCH]" (Eph. 5:23). In Tit. 2:10 it is implied that Christian salvation extends also to the ethical sphere, since "the teaching about God our Savior" is urged as an incentive to holy living. Believers await a future work of Christ as Savior when he will come again to consummate our salvation in the transformation of our bodies (Phil. 3:20).

savour. See ODOR.

saw. A tool with notched blade or teeth used for cutting hard material. Probably the earliest saws were made of flint, with serrated edges, mounted in a frame. Other saws were like knives, of bronze or iron. Small handsaws were like ours today, but the teeth were shaped in the other direction, so that the worker did not shove but pulled against the wood. Large handsaws were unknown in Bible times. Palestinian carpenters probably sat on the floor and held the wood between their toes, which became as skillful as extra hands. Stone was sawed as well as wood (1 Ki. 7:9). Saws used in the construction of the PYRAMIDS and other great buildings of Egypt were made of bronze and had one handle. The Assyrians used a double-handled

saw. Hebrews 11:37 speaks of martyrs who were sawn in two. Jewish tradition (in the *Martyrdom of Isaiah*, a pseudepigraphical book) states that the prophet ISAIAH was sawn asunder with a wooden saw by King MANASSEH; perhaps the reference in Hebrews is to this event.

sayings of Jesus. See LOGIA.

Scab. See DISEASES.

scaffold. This English term is used by the KJV once with reference to a bronze structure on which SOLOMON knelt when he dedicated the temple (2 Chr. 6:13). Modern versions properly render the Hebrew term as "platform."

scale. See BALANCE; WEIGHTS AND MEASURES.

scales, fish. The rough exterior surface of a fish, removable by scraping. Only those aquatic animals that had scales and dorsal fins were permissible for the Israelites to eat (Lev. 11:9-12; Deut. 14:9-10). In a figurative use, EZEKIEL speaks of the scales of a crocodile (Ezek. 29:4). The Hebrew term, like the English, can be used with reference to a military coat of mail (scale armor, 1 Sam. 17:5) because its small overlapping pieces resemble fish scales. The Greek term is used once to describe recovery from temporary blindness—"something like scales fell from Saul's eyes, and he could see again" (Acts 9:18).

scall. See DISEASES.

scapegoat. Three times in the ritual of the Day of Atonement reference is made to one of two goats being consigned to "Azazel" (Heb. *ʿăzāʾzēl H6439*),

© Dr. James C. Martin. The British Museum. Photographed by permission.

Iron saw used by the Assyrians for cutting stone (from Nimrud, 9th–7th cent. B.C.).

which the KJV and NIV render as "the scapegoat" (Lev. 16:8, 10, 26; see ATONEMENT, DAY OF). Uncertainty still attaches to its origin and significance. Several interpretations have been advanced: (1) The name describes the animal itself as "the goat that departs" (from ʿēz H6436 and ʾāzal H261, thus the traditional rendering of (e)scapegoat, though the English term has come to mean something else); this etymology is inadmissible, since the goat was released *to* or *for* Azazel. (2) The name is derived from a Semitic root ʿzl ("to remove" in Arabic) and refers to the "entire removal" of sin. (3) The common rabbinic view was that it designated the area to which the goat was released as a rugged or desolate place; the main difficulty with this and the previous view is that the parallelism of v. 8 virtually demands a personal name in apposition to "the Lord." (4) Most scholars (some of whom derive the name from ʿāzaz H6451 + ʾēl H446, "fierce god") accept that Azazel is the leader of the evil spirits of the wilderness, possibly to be identified with DEMONS (Deut. 32:17; Ps. 106:37; 2 Chr. 11:15; in *1 Enoch* Azazel appears at the head of the rebel angels). The consigning of a goat to Azazel was probably one of many features adapted from contemporary cultic life in the Mosaic period and incorporated into the Israelite cultus, receiving an entirely different significance in the process. Leviticus 17:7 precludes the view that the goat provided a sacrifice for Azazel; in all likelihood this custom meant no more than a symbolic transfer of sin from the realm of society into that of death.

scarlet. A term applied to various bright red colors. This English word is used by the KJV and NIV to render Hebrew šānî H9106 (Gen. 38:28 and frequently), though the NRSV and NJPS prefer to translate with CRIMSON (a deeper, purplish red). In the NT, "scarlet" is the standard rendering of the Greek term kokkinos G3132 (Matt. 27:28 et al.). The dye used for coloring the wool and thread a scarlet color undoubtedly came from the insect *Coccus ilicis*. This is an insect pest that attacks the species of oak called *Quercus coccifera*, commonly called the kermes oak. The actual preparation of the dyes was probably done by the Phoenicians (see PHOENICIA), though it is agreed that the Egyptians taught the Israelites the actual application. It is obvious that this scarlet dye was known as far back as the first half of the second millennium B.C., for TAMAR's midwife put a scarlet thread around the hand of ZERAH in order to make sure that he was known as the firstborn (Gen. 38:27-30). Scarlet clothing suggested luxury (2 Sam. 1:24; Prov. 31:21; Rev. 17:4), and the color is used to describe the beauty of a woman's lips (Cant. 4:3). In an important figurative use, however, both scarlet and crimson represent sin in contrast to the white purity of snow and wool (Isa. 1:18).

scented wood. See PLANTS (under *citron*).

scepter. A staff (see ROD, STAFF) representing the authority of a king or other sovereign. The rendering "scepter" may be viewed as a specialized meaning of various biblical words that commonly denote an ordinary rod or may have some other meaning in particular contexts. Hebrew šēbeṭ H8657, for example, can be used of a shepherd's staff (Mic. 7:14), of instruments for administering discipline (Prov. 22:15), including clubs studded with iron (Ps. 2:9), and so on. Similarly, maṭṭeh H4751 may refer simply to a stick used for support (Gen. 38:28) or to a branch (Ezek. 19:12). Both terms, however, can refer specifically to the scepters of rulers (cf. Jer. 48:17). In the NT, Greek rhabdos G4811 also has a variety of uses (e.g., traveler's staff, Matt. 10:10; discipline stick, 1 Cor. 4:21; measuring rod, Rev. 11:1), but it can be used in particular of the Son's kingly scepter (Heb. 1:8, citing Ps. 45:6).

Scepters were associated mainly with kings, but lesser officials sometimes carried a staff of office. In the OT, reference is made to the scepters of the rulers of Israel, Egypt, Moab, Damascus, Ashkelon, and Judah (Ps. 60:7; 108:8; Jer. 48:17; Ezek. 19:11; Amos 1:5, 8; Zech. 10:11). Two passages often regarded as messianic associate a scepter with Israel's future rulers (Gen. 49:10; Num. 24:17). The Roman soldiers had the royal scepter in mind when they mockingly placed a reed in the hand of Jesus to represent it (Matt. 27:29). Several passages in Esther illustrate a special use made of the scepter by the Persian kings (Esth. 4:11; 5:2; 8:4). In these passages it is described as golden, meaning either that it was of solid gold or that it was gold-studded, like the scepters of the Homeric kings.

Sceva. see´vuh (*Skeuas G5005*, possibly the Greek form of Latin *Scaeva* [from *scaevus*, "left"]). A Jewish chief priest living in EPHESUS (Acts 19:14-17). Since he would not have been able to function as such in the synagogues of ASIA MINOR, he may have exercised the office at JERUSALEM (some think he may have simply been a member of a high-priestly family or the chief of one of the twenty-four courses of priests). Sceva's seven sons traveled from place to place attempting to exorcise demons by using the name of Jesus, but on one occasion the evil spirit denied knowing them with these famous words: "Jesus I know, and I know about Paul, but who are you?" (Acts 19:15). Lacking the authority of PAUL and Jesus, they were attacked by the demon-possessed man and had to flee "naked and bleeding" (v. 16). The incident was widely reported, with the result that awe and reverence for the name of the Lord Jesus came upon all the Ephesians.

schin. See SHIN.

schism. This English term, meaning "division," is used once by the KJV (1 Cor. 12:25), referring to dissensions that threaten disruption, but not necessarily involving doctrinal HERESY (the more usual meaning in modern religious contexts). The same Greek word is rendered "division" by the KJV with reference to the dissensions in the Corinthian church (1 Cor. 1:10; 11:18).

school. A place or institution devoted to teaching and learning. The word *school* occurs only once in the KJV (Acts 19:9, referring to the "lecture hall" of TYRANNUS, apparently a Greek teacher of rhetoric or philosophy). But the references to teachers and teaching are numerous in both Testaments. The OT stresses the duty and importance of religious teaching and training. Hebrew appreciation of the nature and value of the teaching function is evident from the fact that ten different Hebrew verbs are translated "teach" in KJV. Yet significantly the Mosaic legislation contains no commands requiring the establishment of schools for formal religious instruction. Hebrew education was mainly domestic and continued to be so until after the return from the Babylonian captivity.

The home (see FAMILY) was the first and most effective agency for religious training. During the nomadic life of the PATRIARCHS, education was purely a domestic activity, and the parents were the teachers. God called ABRAHAM as the father of the chosen people and put on him the responsibility to train his children and his household to walk in the ways of the Lord (Gen. 18:19; cf. Ps. 78:5-7). The varied commands in DEUTERONOMY to teach the children, clearly imply domestic education (Deut. 4:9; 6:7-9; 11:19; 32:46). Proverbs 22:6 is an exhortation extolling the importance of parental instruction. The training was imparted primarily through conversation, example, and imitation; it utilized effectively the interest aroused by actual life situations, such as the Passover, the redemption of the firstborn, and family rites (Exod. 12:26-27; 13:14-16). The well-known talent of the Middle East for storytelling would also be used in the vital transmission of religious truth and faith to the children. Although all teaching was religiously oriented, reading, writing, and elementary arithmetic were taught. The command to the Israelites to write the precepts of the LAW on their doorposts and gates (Deut. 6:9; 11:20) and on great plastered stones in the land (27:2-8) implies a general ability among the people at the time to read and write.

The older people had opportunity to receive religious instruction from the PRIESTS and LEVITES (Lev. 10:10-11), who could be found at the sanctuary or in LEVITICAL CITIES. Every seventh year, at the Feast of Tabernacles, the law was read publicly for the instruction of the assembled people (Deut. 31:10-13). The priests and Levites, supported by the offerings of the people, were to be the religious teachers of the nation, but it seems clear that this aspect of their work was not consistently maintained. Only during the revival under King JEHOSHAPHAT does one read of the priests and Levites fulfilling their calling to teach the people all the ordinances of the law (2 Chr. 17:7-9).

The ineffective teaching ministry of a corrupt priesthood was supplemented by the service of the PROPHETS, beginning with SAMUEL. To make his reform permanent and effective, Samuel instituted a school of the prophets at RAMAH (1 Sam. 19:19-20). Later such schools flourished at BETHEL (2 Ki. 2:3), JERICHO (2:5), GILGAL (4:38), and elsewhere

(6:1). Living in colonies under a leader, these "sons of the prophets" formed a religious training center, their chief study being the law and its interpretation. They became teachers and preachers who denounced national, family, and personal sins (1 Ki. 20:35-42; 2 Ki. 17:13). Not all the students in these schools possessed the predictive gift, nor were all the prophets of Israel students in such schools (Amos 7:14-15). The preaching of God's prophets—rebuking, instructing, and announcing the future purposes of God—spread religious knowledge and stimulated spiritual life. Professional teachers were employed in the homes of the wealthy (2 Sam. 12:25; 2 Ki. 10:5; Isa. 49:23). The sages, or "men of wisdom," were apparently informal, self-appointed teachers, instructors in practical philosophy, the spiritual descendants of the great SOLOMON (Ps. 119:99; Prov. 5:13; 13:20). But there is no positive evidence that special rooms or buildings for school purposes were yet used, although the thought is not excluded.

With the return of the Jews from Babylonian captivity there came a renewed emphasis on religious instruction. Regular teaching was carried out during the days of EZRA and NEHEMIAH, the Levites being the teachers of the people (Ezra 7:10; Neh. 8:7-9). Ezra the priest, described as "a teacher well versed in the Law of Moses" (Ezra 7:6), made the study and teaching of the law his chief concern. With the cessation of prophecy in Israel the study of the law became a matter of scholastic learning. Gradually there arose a class of men who came to be known as the SCRIBES or teachers of the law, men whose chief employment was the study and interpretation of the law and its application to the practical duties of life. At first the scribes restricted their educational activities to adults, and the education of the children remained in the home.

The SYNAGOGUE, which has a prominent place in postexilic Jewish life, apparently had its origin during the Babylonian captivity. When the exiled people were deprived of their TEMPLE and its services, they found it helpful to gather for the reading of the Scriptures and prayer. On their return to the Land of Promise the synagogue spread rapidly and developed into an important education agency. The synagogue services with their readings from "the Law and the Prophets" and the sermonic "exhortation" (Lk. 4:17-21; Acts 13:15-16; 15:21) made their educational contribution to the religious life of the people. Regarded chiefly as places of teaching (never of sacrifice), they became associated with the development of an elementary school system among the Jews. Even before the days of Jesus, synagogues with schools for the young were to be found in every important Jewish community.

The synagogue "attendant" (Lk. 4:20) generally served as teacher, but assistants were sometimes provided. Reading, writing, and arithmetic were taught as a means to an end. Since the primary aim of education was religious, the OT furnished the subject matter of instruction. Memorization had a prominent place, with emphasis on catechizing, drill, and review. Discipline was strict, and the cane was kept available, but undue severity was not condoned. Students seeking training beyond that given in the synagogue schools turned to eminent scribes for further instruction. This was given partly in their homes and partly in the synagogues or the temple porticoes. The instruction was

One of the few synagogues that date to the period of the Gospels is this one at Gamla (NE of the Sea of Galilee; view to the SW). The small room at the bottom left of the photo may have been used as a Bet Midrash (school) where the rabbis would have taught the Torah to their disciples.

© Dr. James C. Martin

S

devoted to the rabbinical interpretation of the law and its applications to life. Such advanced theological training Saul of Tarsus (see PAUL) received in JERUSALEM under GAMALIEL (Acts 22:3).

Jesus was much more than a teacher, but he was first of all a teacher and was recognized as such by his contemporaries. Although unauthorized by the Jewish authorities, as a God-sent teacher he was constantly engaged in teaching the people. He generally used the methods of the RABBIS but poured into his teachings an authority that challenged and held his audiences. In selecting and training the Twelve he became a teacher of teachers. He commissioned his followers to carry out a worldwide teaching ministry (Matt. 28:19-20). Teaching was an important phase of the work of the early CHURCH in Jerusalem (Acts 2:42; 4:1-2; 5:21, 28). The work of BARNABAS and Saul at ANTIOCH was essentially a teaching ministry (11:26). Paul the apostle, preeminent as missionary and evangelist, was an itinerant teacher, teaching in public assemblies, by personal contact, and by his letters. He thought of himself as "a teacher of the true faith to the Gentiles" (1 Tim. 2:7).

The NT places emphasis on the teaching function in the Christian church. "Pastors and teachers" (Eph. 4:11) were recognized as Christ's gift to his church. Teaching, or discipleship training, was regarded as an essential function of the pastor (1 Tim. 3:2). Unofficial or volunteer teachers also had an important part in the work of the church (Rom. 12:7; Jas. 3:1). The author of Hebrews insisted that all believers should mature spiritually so that they could become teachers (Heb. 5:12). Much unofficial Christian teaching was carried on by members in their homes (Acts 18:26; Tit. 2:3-4). In NT times the Christian churches assembled in the homes of members (Rom. 16:3-5; 1 Cor. 16:19; Col. 4:15; Phlm. 2). By the end of the first century the educational work of the church came to be systematically developed. The church fathers were foremost in all educational matters and did much to develop and promote education, the chief handmaid of the church.

schoolmaster. See CUSTODIAN.

science. This English term, in its older general sense of "knowledge," occurs twice in the KJV

(Dan. 1:4; 1 Tim. 6:20). In the second passage the reference is to that professed knowledge that sets itself up in contradiction to the truth of the GOSPEL. As used here the word does not have its modern connotation.

scoff. The Hebrew verb *lîṣ H4329*, "to scoff, brag, deride" (the participle *lēṣ H4370* functions as a noun, "scoffer"), is used in the Bible specifically as the opposite of wise behavior. To scoff is to willfully refuse to learn the way of the Lord and to mock those who do. In PROVERBS the scoffer is characterized by his refusal to learn the way of WISDOM, the basis of true happiness. Since wisdom is more than an intellectual achievement, but is also an ethical-religious attitude of commitment to God, scoffing is more than a matter of naive ignorance; it is sinful, foolish PRIDE (Prov. 9:7-10; 21:24; 24:9). See FOOLISHNESS, FOLLY; MOCKING.

scorn. See MOCKING.

scorpion. See ANIMALS.

Scorpion Pass. See AKRABBIM.

scourge. A whip used for flogging, especially to inflict PUNISHMENT. Scourging was common among ancient peoples, but most instances in the OT are metaphorical. The figure is used for the tongue (Job 5:21), for a disaster that slays suddenly (9:23), and for divine judgment (Isa. 28:15, 18). The Lord is said to lash his enemies with a scourge (10:26). Israel was warned that the Canaanites might become a scourge on the nation (Josh. 23:13). The only references to the scourge as an instrument of punishment are in 1 Ki. 12:11, 14 (= 2 Chr. 10:11, 14). It is not certain whether the word "scorpions" here is merely a vivid figure or implies a weighted scourge. Mosaic LAW permitted a person found guilty in court to be beaten. The sentence was executed upon the prostrate man in the presence of the judge. The number of strokes was no doubt proportioned to the offense but might not exceed forty (Deut. 25:1-3). Later the Jews used a three-thonged whip, but kept to the stated limit, indicating one stroke short for fear of miscounting (cf. 2 Cor. 11:24). Local SYNAGOGUE authorities and the SANHEDRIN administered scourging for offenses against the law (Matt. 10:17).

The Mishnah (see TALMUD) describes the method employed (*m. Makkot* 3:11-12). When the physical fitness of the offender had been ascertained, his hands were bound to a pillar and his back and chest bared. Thirteen strokes were administered on the chest and thirteen on each shoulder. If the victim died, no blame was attached to those inflicting punishment. The Roman Porcian law forbade scourging a Roman citizen, but slaves and non-Romans might be examined by scourging (cf. Acts 22:24-25). The Romans commonly used a scourge weighted by pieces of bone or metal, but the Greek verb *rhabdizō G4810* (Acts 16:22; 2 Cor. 11:25) may imply that lictors' rods were employed on the occasions mentioned. Scourging usually preceded crucifixion (Matt. 27:26; Mk. 15:15; Lk. 23:16, 22; Jn. 19:1).

screech owl. See BIRDS.

scribe. This English noun (derived from Latin *scriba*, "[official] writer, secretary") is used to translate Hebrew *sōpēr H6221* (also rendered "secretary" and the like, 2 Sam. 8:17 et al.; Aram. *sāpar H10516*) and Greek *grammateus G1208* (Matt. 2:4 and frequently). In the ancient world, relatively few people received the training necessary to gain skill in the art of writing, and those who followed the scribal profession were usually regarded as scholars (cf. the NIV translation of 1 Cor. 1:20) and could hold high civic offices. Especially after the EXILE, Jewish scribes were involved not only in clerical activities, such as the copying of biblical MSS, but also in religious instruction. Accordingly, the NIV sometimes uses the rendering "teacher" in the OT (e.g., Ezra 7:6), and in the NT it consistently uses "teacher of the law." See also AMANUENSIS.

In ancient ISRAEL the scribal craft was principally confined to certain clans who doubtless preserved the trade as a family guild profession, passing the knowledge of this essential skill from father to son. During the united and later Judean monarchies a substantial number of scribes came from the LEVITES. A Levite recorded the priestly assignments (1 Chr. 24:6), and the royal scribe helped in counting the public funds collected for

the repair of the temple (2 Ki. 12:10-11; 2 Chr. 14:11). Since the furnishing of written copies of the LAW was a (scribal) Levitical responsibility (Deut. 17:18), the reforms of JEHOSHAPHAT (cf. 2 Chr. 17) cannot be disassociated from the scribal function.

The scribes who served in the government played a very important role. They may have served as counselors (e.g., 1 Chr. 27:32) or borne the responsibility for mustering the army (2 Ki. 25:19). The highest ranking government scribe was that of the king. If the members of DAVID's cabinet are listed in sequence in 2 Sam. 8:16-18 (cf. 1 Chr. 18:15-17, but differences in 2 Sam. 20:23-26), the royal scribe ranked below the top military commander, the recorder, and the two chief priests, but above the commander over special forces and the "royal advisers" (so NIV; lit., "priests"). The list of SOLOMON's officers may then be given in ascending order (1 Ki. 4:2-6). The hierarchy may have been different during the divided monarchies, since the scribe is twice listed between the recorder and the palace administrator (2 Ki. 18:18, 37; cf. Isa. 36:3, 22).

EZRA marked the watershed for the later development of the understanding of the term *scribe*. Indeed, the transition is already suggested in the book of Ezra: the term is used in an administrative sense in ARTAXERXES' royal decree (Ezra 7:12-26), but in the narrative (7:6, 11) the term already refers to Ezra as a scribe who, by reason of his learning, is capable of interpreting the law for the common people. Moreover, by his priestly lineage (7:6) he symbolized the close connection between the

© Dr. James C. Martin. Sola Scriptura. The Van Kampen Collection on display at the Holy Land Experience in Orlando, Florida. Photographed by permission.

Among the duties of the scribes was the copying of the Hebrew Scriptures.

S

priesthood and this official interpretation of the law. See PRIEST. By Persian royal decree, the law of Moses was made civilly binding on Jews living in Trans-Euphrates (i.e., W of the EUPHRATES, 7:25). The essential task of interpreting Moses' law so that it could function in this new civil capacity was given to the priesthood (Ezra) and the Levites (cf. Neh. 8:6-9).

The precise role of the "scribe" during the postexilic period is somewhat difficult to assess for lack of source material. According to one rabbinic tradition recorded in the Mishnah (*m. ʾAbot* 1:1), the oral law (which allegedly was also given to Moses on Sinai) was mediated from the prophets to the generation of Simeon "the Just" by "the Great Assembly." It seems quite probable that the "scribes" of the Persian and Ptolemaic periods were identical with (or at least participant in) this body of formulators of the oral law. The rules and practices established by the scribes acquired a binding authority, particularly with the specially orthodox of later (NT) times. One tradition ascribes greater stringency to their teachings than to the written law (*m. Sanh.* 11:3), and a proselyte was required to follow the scribal traditions as well as the simply interpreted written law (*Sipra* on Lev. 19:34). The scribes were essentially biblical interpreters, for occasional scribal rules not based on Scripture caused later rabbis considerable consternation (*m. Kelim* 13:7). This situation fits very well with the enactments of a body or class of interpreters functioning during the Persian and Ptolemaic periods.

The Wisdom of Ben Sira (ECCLESIASTICUS), written in the second century B.C., includes an "ode" to the "perfect scribe" (Sir. 38:24—39:11). This ode confirms the picture of a scribe as one schooled in the law and religious WISDOM, understanding the implications of both the written law and oral traditions. As a result of his learning, he enjoyed a prominence in public assemblies, and both understood and exercised justice among the people. Moreover, he was considered particularly pious by virtue of his knowledge of the revealed will of God, a feature of rabbinic understanding of piety.

In the GOSPELS, scribes are found in connection with both the priestly (Sadducean) party (e.g., Matt. 2:4; 21:15; see SADDUCEE) and the Pharisaic

party (cf. Matt. 23; see PHARISEE). The scholars of this latter group were the leaders of what was to become rabbinic JUDAISM, known subsequently, however, as "sages" (or "wise") and still later as RABBIS. But the scribes (scholars) of both parties challenged Jesus principally on his disobedience to traditional practice under the law (e.g., eating with those obviously unobservant of these traditions [Mk. 2:16], and eating without ritually cleansing the hands, referring to the disciples [Matt. 15:2; Mk. 7:5]). Matthew 23 (which parallels Lk. 11) is a classic condemnation of the scribal approach to the will of God. The scholars of both parties in all probability took part in whatever Jewish legal proceedings were initiated against Jesus during the week of his passion, but the very complex questions of the legality of such proceedings (under Roman rule) makes further conclusions very tenuous. PAUL clearly understood the scribe as a dialectician (1 Cor. 1:20-25) who was a scholar on the written and oral law; in Paul's view such dialectics were foolishness in the face of God's saving work in Christ. After the period of the NT, *scribe* came to describe a teacher of children and composer of legal documents, the terms *sage* and then *rabbi* being used for the scholar of the law.

scrip. See DRESS.

scripts. See WRITING.

Scripture. See BIBLE; NEW TESTAMENT; OLD TESTAMENT.

scroll. Sheets of PAPYRUS, LEATHER, or PARCHMENT joined together in long rolls, usually 10-12 in. (25-30 cm.) wide and up to 35 ft. (10.5 m.) long, and used for various kinds of documents in ancient times. Prior to the invention of the CODEX, BOOKS were commonly produced in the form of scrolls. The material could be rolled from left to right between two wooden rollers, with part of the roller projecting as a handle. Rarely were both sides written on (but see Ezek. 2:10; Rev. 5:1). The writing was in short vertical columns a few inches wide, side by side, separated by a narrow space. The scroll was read by uncovering one column, then rolling it up on the other roller as the reading continued.

The use of the standard-length papyrus scrolls necessitated the division of the Hebrew PENTATEUCH into five books. One scroll was sufficient for a book the length of ISAIAH. The Egyptians used some scrolls of enormous lengths, such as the Papyrus Harris (133 ft. x 17 in. [40 m. x 43 cm.]) and a Book of the Dead (123 ft. x 19 in. [37 m. x 48 cm.]). The more convenient book form (codex) was popularized by the early Christians, though its origins are unclear. There is little evidence of its use by the Jews prior to the 3rd cent. A.D. Most of the DEAD SEA SCROLLS were of leather, and Talmudic law required that copies of the Torah intended for public reading be written on scrolls made of leather of clean animals, for papyrus was a great deal more perishable than leather. Scrolls were often stored in pottery jars, such as those found in the caves of Qumran.

The most familiar reference to a scroll is found in Jer. 36, where BARUCH wrote down at JEREMIAH's dictation all that God had spoken to the prophet over a twenty-three year period. In this passage, the SEPTUAGINT takes it for granted that the scroll was made of papyrus, for it renders Hebrew *mĕgillâ H4479* with *chartion* ("papyrus sheet"). It was surely papyrus and not leather that JEHOIAKIM cut in strips and burned, for the odor of burning leather would have been unbearable (Jer. 36:22-23). In EZEKIEL's inaugural vision, he was ordered to eat the scroll on which God's words had been written (Ezek. 2:9—3:3; cf. Rev. 10:8-10 [Gk. *biblion G1046* and *biblaridion G1044*]). There was a flying scroll in ZECHARIAH's vision (Zech. 5:1-2). DAVID refers to a scroll in a statement that the NT interprets as messianic (Ps. 40:7, cited in Heb. 10:7). Most of the NT references to books have a roll in view (cf. esp. Lk. 4:17, 20). See also TEXT AND VERSIONS (OT); TEXT AND VERSIONS (NT).

Scrolls, Dead Sea. See DEAD SEA SCROLLS.

sculpture. See ART.

scum. See OFFSCOURING.

scurvy. See DISEASES.

Scythian. sith´ee-uhn (Gk. *Skythēs G5033*). A name designating primarily a nomadic people that inhabited the Caucasus, E and NE of the Black Sea. The term came to be applied more generally to horse-riders who raised livestock in that region and farther N and who were viewed as uncivilized (Col. 3:11). The Scythians were one of several Indo-Iranian groups that appeared in the ANE around the eighth century B.C. They were initially opposed by King ESARHADDON of ASSYRIA, but eventually the Scythians and Assyrians became allies. After the fall of NINEVEH (612 B.C.), the Scythians were defeated and destroyed by the Medes, who expelled the remnants of them to the N. Many identify the Scythians with the name ASHKENAZ, who in Gen. 10:3 and 1 Chr. 1:6 is said to be one of the sons of GOMER (Cimmerians), along with RIPHATH and TOGARMAH. Gomer in turn was one of the sons of JAPHETH. In Jer. 51:27, in a prophecy against BABYLON, God threatened to raise up against her the kingdoms of ARARAT (Urartu), MINNI (Manneans), and Ashkenaz (Scythians). Herodotus devotes considerable attention to the Scythians' history and culture (*Hist.* 4.1-142). The memory of them persisted in the Holy Land in the popular Greek name of the city of BETH SHAN, namely, *Scythopolis*, "city of the Scythians."

sea. In the Hebrew Bible, the term for "sea," *yām H3542*, is used by extension in the sense WEST, for that was the direction in which the Great Sea, the MEDITERRANEAN, lay to an observer in PALESTINE. The NT writers frequently use the common Greek term *thalassa G2498*, while *pelagos G4283* ("high sea, open sea") occurs once in reference to the Mediterranean (Acts 27:5).

Four "seas" form the background to biblical events, and each appears in the record under a variety of names. (1) The RED SEA, often referred to as "the sea" (Exod. 14:2 et al.; cf. "Egyptian Sea" in Isa. 11:15). (2) The MEDITERRANEAN, first mentioned in Exod. 23:31 as "the Sea of the Philistines," since its coastlands were held, then and for long afterward, by this people group. In Num. 34:6-7, it is called the Great Sea, and this is its designation all through the topographic descriptions concerned with Israel's settlement in the land (Josh. 1:4 et al.; Ezek. 47:10 et al.). In Joel 2:20 and Zech. 14:8 it is called the "western" sea (lit., "at the back"), contrasted with the "eastern" sea (lit., "former"), that is, the Dead Sea on the other flank of the mountains of JUDEA. (3) The DEAD SEA, also called the "Salt Sea" (Num. 34:12 et al.), "the sea of the Arabah" (Deut. 3:17; KJV, "the sea of the plain"), and "the eastern sea" (Ezek. 47:18; Joel 2:20; Zech. 14:8). As with the Sea of Galilee (see below), the name *sea* is here given to what is in reality only a lake (cf. also Caspian Sea); unlike that body of water, however, the Dead Sea has no outlet—its level is maintained by a very high rate of evaporation from its surface. This same phenomenon is responsible for its extremely salty waters, and it is contrasted frequently with the Mediterranean for the fact that no fish can live in it (cf. Ezek. 47:10). (4) The Sea of Galilee (see GALILEE, SEA OF) appears in the OT as the Sea of KINNERETH (Num. 34:11 et al.), and in the NT occasionally as the Sea of TIBERIAS (after the town of that name built on its shore by HEROD Antipas), or the Lake of GEN-NESARET (Lk. 5:1; this name is thought by some to be derived from Kinnereth).

In the OT there are really only three naval episodes, the first when HIRAM, king of TYRE, floated rafts of timber S along the Mediterranean coast to supply SOLOMON with materials for the TEMPLE (1 Ki. 5:9), the second when Solomon built his Red Sea fleet (1 Ki. 9:26-28), and the third when JONAH fled from the Lord (Jon. 1). The Israelites seem to have had little contact with the sea and no maritime tradition; with the Phoenicians as their near neighbors they would, in any case, probably have been outclassed. This lack of maritime interest may have been due, at least in part, to geographical reasons: S of PHOENICIA, the coastline of Palestine offers no good natural harbors and only a few unimportant ones; the straight, dune-fringed coast provides no shelter. Perhaps more important, Israel seldom occupied the coastline politically: without assured access to the sea along the Philistine coast, they had little opportunity to become seafarers.

The sea is a source of much symbolic imagery. Some of the references are positive: "If only you had paid attention to my commands, / your peace would have been like a river, / your righteousness like the waves of the sea" (Isa. 48:18). On the whole, however, the Bible views the sea as a hostile and dangerous element (e.g., Job 26:12; Ps. 89:9). It is a part of the anticipated glories of the new

heaven and earth that the sea has been eliminated (Rev. 21:1; cf. 12:18—13:1). See DEEP (THE).

sea, brazen (bronze). See BRONZE SEA.

Sea, Great. See MEDITERRANEAN SEA.

sea, molten. See BRONZE SEA.

sea cow. See ANIMALS (under *badger*).

sea gull. See BIRDS (under *gull*).

seah. See WEIGHTS AND MEASURES.

seal. A device bearing a design or a name made so that it can impart an impression in relief on a soft substance like clay or wax. When the clay or wax hardens, it permanently bears the impression of the seal. The discovery by archaeologists of thousands of seals reveals that their use goes back to the fourth millennium B.C. and that they were used throughout the ancient civilized world from MESOPOTA-MIA to ROME. They were made of a variety of hard substances like limestone, metal, and all kinds of precious stones. Originally they took the form of a cylinder with a hole from end to end for a cord to pass through, but this was gradually superseded by the scarab (beetle-shaped object). Some were carried by cords hung from the neck or waist; many were cone-shaped and were kept in boxes; but most were made into finger rings. Every person of any standing had a seal. The best ones were engraved by skilled seal cutters and were works of art. The

© Dr. James C. Martin. The British Museum. Photographed by permission.

These scarabs (seals in the form of a beetle), made of amethyst, were discovered in Lachish and date to the middle of the 2nd millennium B.C.

designs were of a great variety of objects—deities, people, animals, birds, fish, plants, and combinations of these. Many of the seals bore inscriptions giving the name of the owner or of his overlord and his profession or office. Many seals with biblical names have been found—among them Hananiah, Azariah, Menahem, Micaiah, Jotham, Nehemiah, and Gedaliah. Excavations in PALESTINE have produced hundreds of jar handles bearing seal impressions, some with the place of manufacture and personal names (perhaps of the potter).

Seals were used for a various purposes: (1) as a mark of authenticity and authority to letters, royal commands, etc. (1 Ki. 21:8; Esth. 3:12; 8:8, 10); (2) as a mark of the formal ratification of a transaction or covenant, as when JEREMIAH's friends witnessed his purchase of a piece of property (Jer. 32:11-14) or when the chief men of JERUSALEM set their seal to a written covenant to keep its laws (Neh. 9:38; 10:1); (3) as a means of protecting books and other documents so that they would not be tampered with (Jer. 32:14; Rev. 5:2, 5, 9; 6:1, 3); (4) as a proof of delegated authority and power (Gen. 41:42; Esth. 3:10; 8:2); (5) as a means of sealing closed doors so as to keep out unauthorized persons (Dan. 6:17; Matt. 27:66; Rev. 20:3)—usually by stretching a cord across them and then sealing the cord; and (6) as an official mark of ownership, as, for example, on jar handles and jar stoppers.

Scripture often uses the term *seal* metaphorically to indicate authentication, confirmation, ownership, evidence, or security. God does not forget sin, but stores it up against the sinner, under a seal (Deut. 32:34; Job 14:17). Prophecies that are intended to be kept secret for a time are bound with a seal (Dan. 12:4, 9; Rev. 5:1-2; 10:4). PAUL speaks of having sealed the offering of the GENTILES for the saints in Jerusalem (Rom. 15:28 KJV). This may have been literal, thus guaranteeing his honesty, or it may denote Paul's approval of the Gentile gift, or his assurance that it would be delivered (cf. NIV). The word has the sense of authentication in 1 Cor. 9:2, where Paul describes his converts at Corinth as the "seal" placed by Christ on his work—the proof or vindication of his apostleship. The CIRCUMCISION of ABRAHAM is described as a seal or outward ratification by God of the righteousness of faith

© Dr. James C. Martin. The Israel Museum, Jerusalem. Photographed by permission.

Seal of "Elishama son of Semaḥyah(u)" (bottom, with enlarged replica on top). Numerous bullae, or clay impressions made from seals, were found at the excavations in the City of David Area G (7th-6th cent. B.C.).

that he had already received before he was circumcised (Rom. 4:11). Believers are said to be "marked in him with a seal, the promised Holy Spirit" (Eph. 1:13), as an owner sets his seal on his property; and the same thought is conveyed in the words, "with whom you were sealed for the day of redemption" (4:30). God marks off his own by putting his seal on their foreheads (Rev. 7:2-4).

sea monster. The NRSV and other versions use this phrase to render the Hebrew noun *tannîn H9490* in two passages (Gen. 1:21 [NIV, "creatures of the sea"]; Ps. 148:7 [NIV, "sea creatures"]; the RSV also uses it in Job 7:12, and the KJV in Lam. 4:3 [in the latter passage, the more likely reading is *tannîm*, pl. of *tan H9478*, "jackal"]). For other uses of the Hebrew term, see DRAGON. The NRSV uses "sea monster" also to render Greek *kētos G3063*, which occurs only once (Matt. 12:40 [KJV, "whale"; NIV, "huge fish"]).

sea of glass. In his description of the heavenly council chamber, JOHN THE APOSTLE says that "before the throne there was what looked like a sea of glass, clear as crystal" (Rev. 4:6). In a different

S

vision he says, "I saw what looked like a sea of glass mixed with fire and, standing beside the sea, those who had been victorious over the beast and his image and over the number of his name" (15:2). These references have been interpreted in numerous ways. Some have considered this glassy sea to be the counterpart of the lavers or BASINS in Solomon's TEMPLE, which stood there as a symbol of the purity that was required of any person who would approach God (1 Ki. 7:38). Others point to the BRONZE SEA in the temple (1 Ki. 7:23-26), which possibly alluded to the water above the skies (Gen. 1:7; Ps. 184:4; cf. Ezek. 1:22). The symbolism may have indicated the vastness and transcendence that separate God from his creation.

Sea of Kinnereth (Chinnereth). See GALILEE, SEA OF.

Sea of the Arabah. See ARABAH; DEAD SEA.

Sea of Tiberias. See GALILEE, SEA OF.

Sea Peoples. Documentary sources from EGYPT and elsewhere attest to the existence of various people groups that began to reach the Syrian coast around 1300 B.C. (although there is sporadic evidence for an even earlier presence). These seafaring invaders caused considerable havoc in the ANE over an extended period of time. Their precise origins cannot be established, but it seems likely that their migration was caused by disturbances in the Aegean. See PHILISTINES.

seasons. See CALENDAR; TIME.

seat. In the OT, the Hebrew word *kissēʾ H4058* often refers to any seat occupied by an important person, whether king, minister, or priest (Jdg. 3:20; 1 Sam. 1:9; 4:13, 18; 1 Ki. 2:19; Esth. 3:1). In NT times, special seats of importance were a part of the furniture of the SYNAGOGUE. Jesus rebuked the leaders of his day for seeking the "most important seats" there (Matt. 23:6; Mk. 12:39; Lk. 11:43; 20:46). In the synagogues of PALESTINE, the back seats were occupied by children and unimportant people; the closer the seat was to the front, the greater the honor of the person who occupied it.

The most honored seats of all were the seats of the ELDERS, which faced the congregation. The Greek noun *kathedra G2756* is applied to the seats or benches of the merchants who were selling doves in the TEMPLE (Matt. 21:12; Mk. 11:15). This word is also used in the expression "Moses' seat" (Matt. 23:2; see SEAT, MOSES'). In some instances in the NT, the word *bēma G1037* is used to designate a JUDGMENT SEAT (Matt. 27:19; Jn. 19:13; Acts 18:12, 16-17; 25:6, 10, 17), referring to the place occupied by a governor or other official who was sitting in function as a judge. Twice it is used of Christ's sitting in judgment (Rom. 14:10; 2 Cor. 5:10), and some have thereby distinguished between the judgment of Christ and the judgment of God from his THRONE.

seat, Moses'. Matthew reports Jesus as saying, "The teachers of the law and the Pharisees sit in Moses' seat. So you must obey them and do everything they tell you. But do not do what they do, for they do not practice what they preach" (Matt. 23:2). Archaeological evidence confirms that in the front of the SYNAGOGUES there was a stone seat where the authoritative SCRIBE (teacher of the law) sat and taught. The phrase "sit in Moses' seat" may suggest that the scribes viewed themselves as successors of MOSES.

Seba. see'buh (Heb. *sĕbāʾ H6013*, meaning unknown). Son of CUSH and grandson of HAM (Gen. 10:7; 1 Chr. 1:9). The term is also applied to his descendants, a people group that inhabited the eastern part of ETHIOPIA or possibly a region in S ARABIA (Isa. 43:3). One passage associates Seba with SHEBA (Ps. 72:10). For discussion see SABEAN.

Sebam. See SIBMAH.

Sebat. See SHEBAT.

Secacah. si-kay'kuh (Heb. *sĕkākâ H6117*, prob. "covering" or "protection"). TNIV Sekakah. One of six towns allotted to the tribe of JUDAH in the desert (Josh. 15:61). Some settlements in el-Buqeʿah (i.e., ACHOR, a valley SW of JERICHO) dating to Iron II are thought to correspond with four of these towns, including Secacah. Assuming that the list of cities in this passage runs from N to S, Secacah would then be identified with Khirbet es-Samrah, about 4 mi. (6 km.) SW of Qumran (see Dead Sea Scrolls). Some scholars, however, prefer to identify Secacah with Qumran itself.

Sechu. See Secu.

second Adam. This title, which does not occur in Scripture, results from a conflation of "the last Adam" (1 Cor. 15:45) and "the second man" (v. 47), and it incorporates a concept that is prominent in both 1 Cor. 15:45-49 and Rom. 5:12-21. Paul proclaimed a dynamic redemption for real people on earth and a fulfillment in history by the "spiritual" and "heavenly" man Jesus Christ (1 Cor. 15:46-49). In contradistinction to the first man's sin, which brought death and condemnation, the second man's "act of righteousness" and "obedience" results in an "abundant provision of grace" bringing justification, righteousness, and eternal life (Rom. 5:15-19). See Adam.

second coming. See eschatology.

second death. See death.

Second District, Second Quarter. The district of Jerusalem in which Huldah the prophetess lived is referred to as the *mišneh H5467* (2 Ki. 22:14 = 2 Chr. 34:22). This Hebrew term, which means "second," could simply be transliterated as "Mishneh" (cf. NJPS), but most versions prefer to translate it with such renderings as "Second Quarter" (NRSV), "Second District" (NIV), and "New Quarter" (TNIV). (The KJV understood it to mean "college," apparently following the Targum, which has "house of instruction.") This area is mentioned also in Zeph. 1:10 (NIV and TNIV, "New Quarter"; here the KJV has "second [gate]") and possibly in Neh. 11:9 (but this text can be understood in more than one way). The name evidently referred to an expansion of Jerusalem toward the W (opposite the Tyropoeon Valley) that probably took place during the reign of Hezekiah. Archaeological excavations during the 1970s uncovered a portion of the Broad Wall that may have protected this new area, as well as evidence of Israelite occupation there c. 700 B.C. (cf. N. Avigad, *Discovering Jerusalem* [1983], 46-54).

Second Temple Period. A label commonly employed (and preferred by many contemporary scholars) to designate the interval of time that has traditionally been called "intertestamental," that is, from the rebuilding of the Jerusalem temple after the exile (c. 520 B.C.) until its destruction by the Romans (A.D. 70). Thus this period begins near the end of the OT period and extends to NT times. See Maccabee; restoration.

secret. See mystery.

secretary. See amanuensis; scribe.

sect. This English term, referring to a dissenting religious group or faction, is used in Bible versions to render the Greek term *hairesis G146*, which literally means "a choosing," but by extension, "that which is taken or chosen" in a religious or political sense, thus a party or sect. Although the English term heresy derives from this Greek word, the latter does not have that later and specialized ecclesiastical sense, but it simply refers to a body of people distinguishing themselves from others by choice (however, see 2 Pet. 2:1 NIV). On three occasions in the NT, the term is used in reference to the Christian movement, and with a suggestion of reproach (Acts 24:5, 14; 28:22). Elsewhere, the term is applied to the Sadducees (5:17) and to the Pharisees (15:5; 26:5). In his epistles, Paul used it in the negative sense of "division, dissension" (1 Cor. 11:19; Gal. 5:20), while Peter possibly meant by it something like "[false] opinion" (2 Pet. 2:1).

Secu. see´kyoo (Heb. *šekû H8497*, perhaps "lookout point"). KJV Sechu; TNIV Seku. A place known for its great cistern and apparently located between Gibeah and Ramah (#3); it was visited by Saul when seeking information to search out David and Samuel (1 Sam. 19:22). The proposed identification with Khirbet Shuweikeh, 3 mi. (5 km.) N of Ramah, has not been accepted, so the location of Secu remains unknown.

S

Secundus. si-koon'duhs (Gk. *Sekoundos G4941*, from Lat. *Secundus*, "second"). A Thessalonian Christian who with others accompanied Paul through Greece on his return to Antioch of Syria from his third missionary journey. If he was one of the delegates entrusted with the offerings of the churches to the Jewish Christians, he may have accompanied Paul to Jerusalem (Acts 20:4; Rom. 15:25-26; 2 Cor. 8:23). See Aristarchus.

security of the believer. See Assurance; Perseverance.

seed. The primary biblical words for "seed" (Heb. *zera' H2446* and Gk. *sperma G5065*) are used to indicate both agricultural and human seed, the latter both in a narrow physical sense and as a description of the descendants of a common ancestor. Seedtime to the farmer in Palestine occurred in late October or November. After the dry, hot summer it was impossible to plow and plant until the early rains had softened the ground and made it workable. Sowing then took place; the Israelite was commanded not to mix his seed in any field or vineyard, but to plant only one crop (Lev. 19:19; Deut. 22:9), a stricture parallel to that regarding the mixture of human seed by intermarriage with other nations. See Agriculture; Calendar. Our Lord gave the word *seed* a new dimension of meaning when he said "the seed is the word of God" (Lk. 8:11). Thereafter the NT combines the agricultural and physical concepts of the seed in its presentation of spiritual truth; the word of God is sown, takes root in the hearts of men, who are then born as children into the family of God (1 Pet. 1:23), and become a spiritual seed or nation.

seedtime. See Agriculture.

seer. See Prophets.

Segub. see'guhb (Heb. *segûb H8437*, possibly "[God] is exalted"). (1) The youngest son of Hiel of Bethel. During Ahab's reign, Hiel rebuilt Jericho "at the cost of" his sons Abiram and Segub (1 Ki. 16:34). The Aramaic Targum indicates that Hiel actually killed his sons, suggesting that he offered them as "foundation" or "threshold" sacri-fices, a rite apparently practiced by the pagans of the area. Other scholars question this theory. In any case, the writer of Kings considered the death of Hiel's sons as a fulfillment of Joshua's curse upon anyone who tried to rebuild Jericho (Josh. 6:26).

(2) Son of Hezron and descendant of Judah (1 Chr. 2:21-22). Three of Hezron's sons had been mentioned earlier in the genealogy (v. 9). The reintroduction of Hezron in v. 21 is unusual, apparently motivated by the desire to note a connection between the tribes of Judah and Manasseh: Segub was born when Hezron, at sixty years of age, married the daughter of Makir (son of Gilead); and Segub's son, Jair, became a powerful Manassite.

Seir. see'uhr (Heb. *se'îr H8541*, "hairy, shaggy," possibly indicating a thicket or wooded area). Aside from one reference to a Mount Seir in Judah N of Kesalon (Josh. 15:10, prob. a ridge W of Kiriath Jearim) and two references to a Horite whose descendants were chieftains in Edom (Gen. 36:20-21; 1 Chr. 1:38), all other occurrences of the name Seir, including "Mount Seir" (Deut. 1:2; 2 Chr. 20:10, 22-23; Ezek. 35:2-3, 7, 15) and "land of Seir" (Gen. 32:3; 36:30), designate the mountain range of Edom lying E of the rift valley known as the Arabah and roughly parallel to it. The range extends from Wadi Arnon southward to the vicinity of modern Aqabah. Petra and Mount Hor are among its chief features. The rugged cliffs of this range mark the W boundary of Edom while its eastern foothills extend as far as Edom's E boundary, above sea level. The region was important to the Hebrews because of its command of the routes to Ezion Geber.

This area apparently derived its name from "Seir the Horite," founder of a line of rulers who lived there (Gen. 36:20-30). Subsequently, the descendants of Esau (Edom) dispossessed and destroyed the Horites in a manner comparable to the Hebrew conquest of Canaan (Deut. 2:12). The precise geographical distinction between Seir and Edom is a matter of some dispute, but after the Edomite conquest the two names became virtual synonyms. At the time of Hezekiah, a group of Simeonites massacred a colony of Amalekites somewhere in the range and settled the site themselves (1 Chr. 4:42-43).

Seirah. see´uh-ruh (Heb. *śĕˁîrāh H8545*, "female goat" or "wooded"). KJV Seirath. A town or wooded region, apparently in the hill country of Ephraim W of Jericho, where Ehud sought refuge after killing Eglon (Jdg. 3:26; cf. v. 27). No suitable identification has been offered. Some have thought that the term simply designates a topographical feature in the Jordan Valley; if so, the sense of the text may be that Ehud escaped to "the woody hills" of Ephraim (cf. Josh. 17:15, 18). See Ephraim, forest of; Ephraim, hill country of.

Seirath. see´uh-rath. KJV form of Seirah.

Sekakah. si-kay´kuh. TNIV form of Secacah.

Seku. see´kyoo. TNIV form of Secu.

Sela. see´luh (Heb. *selaˁ H6153*, "rock, cliff"). A fortified city that served as the capital of ancient Edom; early in the eighth century, King Amaziah of Judah captured it and renamed it Joktheel (2 Ki. 14:7). At least one prophecy refers to this city (Isa. 42:11), but it is uncertain whether it is named elsewhere in the Bible. The name Sela is possibly applied once to a site in Amorite territory that is otherwise unidentified (Jdg. 1:36). In several passages, it is disputed whether the term should be interpreted as a name-place or as the common word for "rock" (2 Chr. 25:12; Isa. 16:1; Jer. 49:16; Obad. 3). Ancient Sela has commonly been thought to be the same as Petra, the later capital of the Nabateans. This site, however, lies about 50 mi. (80 km.) SSE of the Dead Sea, and some scholars prefer to identify Sela with modern es-Selaˁ (almost 30 mi./50 km. closer to the Dead Sea).

selah. see´luh. See Psalms, Book of (sect. VI).

Sela Hammahlekoth. see´luh-huh-mah´luh-koth (Heb. *selaˁ hammaḥlĕqôt H6154*, possibly "rock of divisions" or "slippery rock"). A well-known crag in the Desert of Maon where Saul almost captured David (1 Sam. 23:28; cf. v. 25). If the second element of the name is derived from a verb meaning "to divide," the rock may have been so named because it seemed to mark the parting of the ways between these two men (cf. NJPS, "Rock of Separation"). Others derive the noun from a different verb meaning "to be smooth, slippery," perhaps suggesting that David was able to "slip away" from Saul (cf. NRSV, "Rock of Escape"). The location of Sela Hammahlekoth is unknown, although some have proposed Wadi el-Malaqi, some 12 mi. (19 km.) ESE of Hebron. The popular idea that it may be the rock later known as Masada does not take into account that Masada is too distant from Maon to be identified with the biblical site.

Seled. see´lid (Heb. *seled H6135*, possibly from *sālad H6134*, "to jump [for joy]"). Son of Nadab and descendant of Judah through Jerahmeel; the text notes that he had no children (1 Chr. 2:30).

Seleucia. si-loo´shuh (Gk. *Seleukeia G4942*). A city on the coast of Syria in the NE corner of the Mediterranean, some 5 mi. (8 km.) N of the mouth of the Orontes River. Antioch, the capital of Syria, royal seat of the Seleucid kings, was a few miles inland, near the point where the Orontes, after its northern course between the Lebanon ranges, turns sharply W to the sea. The city was founded in 300 B.C. by Seleucus I Nicator, to provide a seaport for Antioch. Seleucia was the port of departure for Paul and Barnabas on their first journey (Acts 13:4). (This city is to be

The area of Syrian Seleucia (Pereia), with remains from its harbor.

© Dr. James C. Martin

distinguished from the Seleucia on the TIGRIS founded by the same monarch twelve years earlier.)

Seleucid. si-loo′sid. An adjective derived from the name Seleucus. As a noun, *Seleucid* refers to a member of the dynasty founded by Seleucus I, one of the Diadochi ("Successors"), the title given to those remarkable military personalities who successfully divided the empire of ALEXANDER THE GREAT after his death. By 312 B.C. Seleucus had established himself in command of Babylonia, Susiana, and Media, and from this date his dynasty and era can be conveniently reckoned. By 301 he was master of SYRIA, founding ANTIOCH and SELEUCIA to express the westward expansion of his kingdom and to balance Seleucia on the TIGRIS, its eastern bastion. Some of the more important Seleucid rulers bore the name ANTIOCHUS.

The Seleucids were the true heirs of the kingdom of Alexander. Their borders fluctuated, but for over two centuries of independent rule the Seleucids held the major portion of Alexander's realms. Their empire was frequently called Syria from their holdings on the NE corner of the MEDITERRANEAN, where their major centers were located and where they sought to establish an eastern Macedonia. In many ways they followed Alexander's policies. They sought to hellenize their domains (see HELLENISM), to mingle immigrant Greeks with Asiatics. In so doing they set the stage for PAUL of Tarsus, heir of two cultures, and for the Greek NT. The clash between the Seleucids and the Jews that brought on the Maccabean revolt (see MACCABEE), inhibited to a great extent hellenizing influences in Israel. The Greek cities, which the Seleucids founded all over their empire, were in general a civilizing force that prepared the way for the fruitful mingling of PALESTINE, GREECE, and ROME, and hence for the development of Europe in the West. Greek life and thought took root in the Middle East and penetrated far into Asia. Royal authority, in spite of its Greek democratic foundations, was shaped by the Seleucids on the autocratic model favored by Alexander. The Seleucid monarchy, therefore, prepared the eastern half of the ROMAN empire for the later deification of the emperor. This imperial cult helped to precipitate the damaging contest between the Christians and the Roman state in NT times.

self-control. See TEMPERANCE.

self-denial. See DENY.

self-righteousness. Confidence in one's own RIGHTEOUSNESS. In popular usage, a self-righteous person is one who views himself or herself as morally upright in contrast to others; it often implies adherence to the letter of legal requirements (legalism) without regard to their spirit. In a theological sense, the term *self-righteousness* is applied to the belief, attitude, or behavior of persons who seek God's acceptance by their own efforts, that is, by doing good works and keeping the divine statutes. Although the term *self-righteousness* itself does not appear in the Bible, the concept is clearly indicated in various passages. For example, LUKE informs us that CHRIST related the parable of the PHARISEE and the tax collector to "some who were confident of their own righteousness and looked down on everybody else" (Lk. 18:8). Similarly, PAUL says of the unsaved Israelites that "they did not know the righteousness that comes from God and sought to establish their own" (Rom. 10:1-3). The apostle further testifies that he wishes to gain Christ, "not having a righteousness of my own that comes from the law, but that which is through faith in Christ" (Phil. 3:9). The self-righteous person is righteous neither in the religious nor the moral sense. Those who trust in themselves do not have right standing with God through self-effort or adherence to the law; nor are they morally upright, since only their external conduct is affected and not their attitudes. See also JUSTIFICATION.

selvedge. This English term, referring to the border of a fabric, is used by the KJV twice to render a Hebrew term that literally means "end, edge" (Exod. 26:4; 36:11). Both passages have to do with the manufacture of curtains for the TABERNACLE.

Sem. See SHEM.

Semachiah. See SEMAKIAH.

Semakiah. sem′uh-ki′uh (Heb. *sĕmakyāhû H6165*, "Yahweh has sustained"). Son (or relative) of Shemaiah and grandson (or descendant) of OBED-

EDOM (1 Chr. 26:7). This family of Korahites (see KORAH #3) belonged to one of the divisions of gatekeepers (v. 1).

Semei. See SEMEIN.

Semein. sem′ee-uhn (Gk. *Semein G4946*, from Heb. *šim‛i H9059* [see SHIMEI]). KJV Semei. Son of Josech, included in Luke's GENEALOGY OF JESUS CHRIST (Lk. 3:26).

Semite. This term is derived from NOAH's son SHEM (Gen. 9:18-19; 10:21-31) and is used to identify a diverse group of ancient peoples whose languages are related, belonging to the Semitic family of languages. The descendants of Shem, however, do not correspond entirely to the Semitic-speaking peoples. ELAM, for example (10:22), was not a nation that spoke a Semitic language, while the Canaanites, who were certainly Semitic, are listed among the descendants of HAM (10:15; see CANAAN). There is however a clear connection between Egyptian (and other "Hamitic" languages) and Semitic, and modern scholars posit a large family called Afro-Asiatic; perhaps there was a very primitive Semitic-Hamitic community in the vicinity of ARABIA and EGYPT. Such facts indicate that the Table of Nations in Gen. 10 was not entirely ethnological, but at least partly geographical. Since it is impossible now to gain a more accurate knowledge of the relationship of ancient peoples, the obvious connection in language is of some use.

The world of the Semites, in ancient historical times, was the FERTILE CRESCENT, the green land that begins in S Babylonia in the E and includes MESOPOTAMIA, SYRIA, and PALESTINE, ending at the border of Egypt in the W. It is hemmed in by mountains, seas, and deserts. Strangely enough, one of the latter, the great Arabian desert, appears to have been the original homeland of the Semites. From earliest times there have been irruptions from this desert into the Fertile Crescent, bringing new strength to the Semitic civilizations. We can name some of the principal invasions: the AMORITES, the Canaanites, the ARAMEANS, the NABATEANS, and the Arabs. The last of these, under Muhammad's leadership, brought a new religion and later a great empire to a large part of the Asia-Africa-Europe continent.

I. The Akkadians. The Babylonians and Assyrians who lived in Mesopotamia spoke a common language. From c. 2350 B.C. to 538 these gifted, vigorous people dominated Mesopotamia. Several times they produced empires that ruled the ancient world. Their Akkadian language, written on clay by means of cuneiform signs, was for more than a millennium the lingua franca of the world of that time. The cities of UR, BABYLON, and NINEVEH, and many rulers such as HAMMURABI the law codifier (who though an Amorite ruled a Babylonian empire) and Ashurbanipal the library builder, testify to the greatness of the Akkadian civilization. See ASSYRIA.

II. The Arameans. Principally traders and catalysts of culture rather than its creators, the Aramean-speaking people lived in Syria from c. 1700 B.C. to the time of Christ, though their political power ceased some centuries earlier. DAMASCUS and HAMATH were among their cities. Their language, ARAMAIC, supplanted Akkadian as the world language and was adopted by the Jews after their return from EXILE. Parts of the books of EZRA and DANIEL, and later much of the TALMUD, was written in Aramaic. It was through this language that the Semitic civilization was given to the Greeks and Romans. Syriac (a form of Aramaic) was an important language in the early church. Today there are still a few Aramaic-speaking islands of culture in the Middle East.

III. The Canaanites. This term is used to designate a number of peoples who lived in S Syria (including Palestine) in ancient times. Even the Hebrews can be considered a Canaanite group. Although we still know very little about the Canaanites before the coming of the Hebrews, the modern finds at Ugarit (see RAS SHAMRA) are shedding light on their culture. The inhabitants of EDOM, MOAB, and AMMON were Canaanites. The earliest use of the alphabet is traceable to the people of Canaan, and some believe the Canaanites should be credited with its invention. The Hebrews seem to have borrowed the Canaanite language and culture and made it their own. The Phoenicians were a Canaanite people who took to the sea and became the first people to dominate the

S

Mediterranean and make it their common highway (1200-400 B.C.).

IV. The Arabs. Little is known about the inhabitants of Arabia prior to Muhammad. The great contributions of the Arabs after the coming of Islam lie beyond the scope of this work. See ARABIA.

V. The Ethiopians. Across the RED SEA from S Arabia, the Ethiopians had a flourishing Semitic civilization as early as 500 B.C. See ETHIOPIA.

Semitic. See SEMITE.

Semitism. Also *Semiticism.* A feature that is characteristic of one or more Semitic languages and that has been adopted by a non-Semitic language. In biblical studies, the term is applied specifically to the presence of Hebrew or Aramaic distinctives in the Greek of the SEPTUAGINT and the NT. Semitisms include various kinds of lexical borrowing (loanwords, loan translations, semantic loans), syntactical and stylistic features, and alleged mistranslations. See also GREEK LANGUAGE.

Senaah. suh-nay´uh (Heb. *sĕnāʾâ H6171*, possibly "hated [woman]"). Either the ancestor of some Israelites who returned from EXILE or, more likely, a town in JUDAH resettled by them (Ezra 2:35; Neh. 7:38). Because the number of returnees seems rather large, some have interpreted the phrase *bĕnê sĕnāʾâ* to mean "sons of the rejected woman," referring to the poorer classes of JERUSALEM or to some other group that was regarded with contempt. The matter is complicated by references to the son(s) of HASSENAAH (Neh. 3:3) and HASSENUAH (1 Chr. 9:7; Neh. 11:9), both of which could be understood as designating people from (the) Senaah. Some scholars suspect textual error.

senate. An authoritative assembly possessing legislative powers. The English term derives from Latin *senatus,* meaning "an assembly of elders" (from *senex,* "old man"). The KJV uses "senator" once in the OT to render the Hebrew word for "elder" (Ps. 105:22), and "senate" once in the NT to render the Greek word for "council of elders," probably referring to the SANHEDRIN (Acts 5:21). Among the Romans, the state council or senate

was very ancient. It first consisted of 100 men, but later the number was increased to 300, and plebeians as well as patricians were made eligible. Under the ROMAN EMPIRE, the number was increased to 900 by Julius CAESAR but was reduced to 600 by AUGUSTUS, who added age and property requirements. Under the empire, the principal duties of the senate consisted of (1) the maintenance of state religion, (2) supervision of government property and finances, (3) control of the senatorial provinces, (4) legislative ratification of the emperor's decisions, (5) jurisdiction over breach of contract, cases of high treason, and offenses of senators, and (6) exercise of the right to nominate all magistrates except consuls.

Seneca. sen´uh-kuh. Latin orator, writer, philosopher, and statesman. Lucius Annaeus Seneca (the Younger) was born in southern Spain c. 4 B.C. (possibly as late as A.D. 1), but a relative took him to ROME while he was still a child. Trained in rhetoric, Seneca was attracted to STOIC philosophy and became a brilliant orator. In 49 he was appointed tutor to the young NERO, and when the latter became emperor five years later, Seneca (alongside Afranius Burrus) served as his minister and confidant. He eventually retired from public life, and in the year 65, accused of conspiracy, was forced to commit suicide. Seneca wrote a number of ethical treatises and other prose works that are a major source for our understanding of Stoicism. His poetic writings consist primarily of tragedies, and these proved influential during the Renaissance. An apocryphal document known as *Epistles of Paul and Seneca*—composed in the third century or later, and popular in the late Middle Ages—purports to preserve mutually admiring correspondence between these two figures. These letters were no doubt composed with the purpose of commending Christianity to pagan society, which was strongly influenced by Stoicism; the unknown author(s) may also have wished to enhance Seneca's reputation among Christians.

Seneh. see´nuh (Heb. *senneh H6175,* possibly "thorny"). A notable rock or crag which, together with BOZEZ, commanded the pass at MICMASH (1 Sam. 14:4). This important access route to the Judean highlands follows the Wadi Qelt in its lower stages. In the vicinity of Micmash the route becomes narrower and passes through these two crags, thus forming one of the strategic locations for governing access to the Judean highlands. This accounts for its importance to the PHILISTINES. Suitable rock formations are found along Wadi es-Suweinit in the immediate vicinity of ancient Micmash (c. 7 mi./11 km. NE of JERUSALEM).

Senir. see´nuhr (Heb. *sĕnir H8536*, meaning unknown; cf. Akk. *Saniru*). KJV also Shenir. The AMORITE name for Mount HERMON (Deut. 3:9). At times the name has been used for larger portions of the Antilebanon range (as perhaps in Ezek. 27:5). However, Hebrew usage also distinguished between Hermon and Senir (Cant. 4:8), and between those and BAAL HERMON as well (1 Chr. 5:23). It is tempting to suppose that such usage distinguishes the three individual peaks of Mount Hermon.

Sennacherib. suh-nak´uh-rib (Heb. *sanḥērib H6178*, from Akk. *Sin-aḥḥē-erība*, "Sin [the moon god] has replaced the [lost] brothers"). King of ASSYRIA, 705-681 B.C. As his name implies, Sennacherib was not the eldest son of SARGON II, but he was chosen as crown prince and made military governor of the troublesome northern frontier. He restored the capital to NINEVEH, on the east bank of the TIGRIS, opposite the present city of Mosul. He constructed palaces, temples, city walls, and a water system, including the aqueduct of Jerwan.

Sennacherib was an able soldier, and it is in this capacity that he is best remembered. On his succession to the throne he found it necessary to deal with revolts throughout the empire. Exasperated by the repeated intrigues of BABYLON and its king, MERODACH-BALADAN, he finally reduced the city to ruins in 689 B.C. In the W there was also rebellion; among the rebels was HEZEKIAH of JUDAH, and on his third campaign in 701, Sennacherib marched to settle those difficulties. The accounts of his campaigns were recorded on clay prisms that include the Assyrian version of the conflict with Hezekiah. Sennacherib took SIDON and moved S, receiving tribute and capturing ASHKELON, BETH DAGON, JOPPA, and other Palestinian cities. At ELTEKEH (cf. Josh. 19:44; 21:23) he defeated a coalition of Palestinians, plus some Egyptian forces.

Hezekiah had captured Padi king of EKRON, who was allied with Sennacherib, and made him a captive. Sennacherib now seized Ekron and restored Padi to his throne. He did not take JERUSALEM, but he boasted that he shut up Hezekiah "like a bird in a cage." The OT gives three records of this invasion and its results (2 Ki. 18:13-19:17; 2 Chr. 32:1-22; Isa. 36:1-37:38).

It was in the fourteenth year of Hezekiah that Sennacherib came against Judah and took all of its fortified cities. Hezekiah offered to pay tribute and had to strip the TEMPLE of its treasures to make payment. The Assyrian sent his officers to Jerusalem to deliver an ultimatum concerning capitulation. At this time Sennacherib was besieging LACHISH; after taking it, he moved against LIBNAH. The reliefs of the palace of Sennacherib depict the capture of Lachish. When Sennacherib heard that TIRHAKAH king of EGYPT was coming against him, he sent a second message to Hezekiah. Hezekiah made this a matter for prayer, and the prophet ISAIAH brought him God's assurance of deliverance. Tirhakah was involved in the coalition defeated by Sennacherib; Egypt of that period was correctly evaluated by the Assyrian spokesman as "that splintered reed" (2 Ki. 18:21; Isa. 36:6). The Bible relates that Jerusalem was delivered by the Lord, who sent his angel to strike the Assyrian armies and force Sennacherib to retire to his homeland (2 Ki. 19:35-36; 2 Chr. 32:21; Isa. 37:36-37). Various naturalistic explanations of this incident have been attempted.

© Dr. James C. Martin. The British Museum. Photographed by permission.

Relief of Sennacherib on a magnificent throne watching prisoners being brought before him from the capture of the city of Lachish during the time of Hezekiah (from Nineveh, 7th cent. B.C.).

S

Herodotus preserves a story of an Assyrian defeat occasioned by a plague of mice, which consumed the equipment of the armies and left them helpless before their enemies; some have associated the mice with the carrying of some disease or plague. Back in Nineveh, Sennacherib was assassinated by two of his sons in 681 B.C. (2 Ki. 19:37; Isa. 37:38) in an effort to upset the succession that he had decreed for ESARHADDON, but Esarhaddon was equal to the situation and gained the throne.

sensual. The KJV uses this English adjective twice to render the Greek word *psychikos G6035* (Jas. 3:15; Jude 19). This Greek term occurs in three other passages where the KJV uses the rendering "natural" (1 Cor. 2:14; 15:44, 46). In one of the references (Jas. 3:15), the term is applied to a wisdom that is "earthly" in contrast with "the wisdom that comes from heaven" (v. 17). In the other passages, the term is applied to people and contrasted with *pneumatikos G4461* ("spiritual") and/or with (having the) *pneuma G4460* ("Spirit"). Thus the person characterized as *psychikos* is one who does not have, or whose conduct is not controlled, by the HOLY SPIRIT (cf. the various renderings used by modern versions). (For the specific meaning, "preoccupied with bodily/sexual pleasures," see LUST.)

Senuah. See HASSENUAH.

Seorim. see-or´im (Heb. *sĕ'ōrîm H8556*, possibly from *śā'îr H8537*, "hairy"). A priest who received the fourth lot of the twenty-four divisions in DAVID's time (1 Chr. 24:8).

separation. See CONSECRATION; HOLINESS; SANCTIFICATION.

Sephar. see´fuhr (Heb. *sĕpār H6223*, meaning uncertain). A place "in the east country" (prob. ARABIA) that, along with MESHA, served to delimit the territory occupied by the sons of JOKTAN, a descendant of SHEM through EBER (Gen. 10:30). The location of Sephar is unknown, although many scholars believe it was somewhere in S ARABIA.

Sepharad. sef´uh-rad (Heb. *sĕpārad H6224*, meaning unknown). A place mentioned by OBA-DIAH as the site of the exile of certain captives from Jerusalem (Obad. 20). A rabbinic tradition preserved understood the name as a reference to SPAIN (cf. the term *Sefardi*, applied to Jews who first settled in Spain and Portugal). Some modern scholars identify Sepharad with Saparda, a country that appears in the Assyrian Annals of SARGON II as a district of SW MEDIA (though other documents suggest a location near ASIA MINOR). More likely, however, Sepharad should be identified with SARDIS, the capital of LYDIA. If this view is correct, the biblical reference is of historical significance, for it attests to the existence of a Jewish colony in SW Asia Minor at a rather early date.

Sepharvaim. sef´uhr-vay´im (Heb. *sĕparwayim H6226*, meaning unknown; gentilic *sĕparwîm H6227*, "Sepharvites"). A city conquered in the eighth century B.C. by the Assyrians; SHALMANESER V resettled its inhabitants in SAMARIA (2 Ki. 17:24). The deities of the Sepharvites included ADRAMMELECH and ANAMMELECH (v. 31). Subsequently, SENNACHERIB's envoy mentioned Sepharvaim as a place whose gods were helpless against the Assyrians (2 Ki. 18:34; 19:13; Isa. 36:19; 37:13). The location of Sepharvaim is uncertain. Some identify it with biblical SIBRAIM, which EZEKIEL locates between DAMASCUS and HAMATH (Ezek. 47:16). Another proposal is ancient Sippar (modern Abu Habba) in MESOPOTAMIA.

Sepharvite. sef´uhr-vit. See SEPHARVAIM.

Sepphoris. sef´uh-ris (*Sepphōris*, with various spellings; apparently from Heb. *ṣippôr H7606*, "bird"). A strongly fortified city c. 4 mi. (6 km.) NW of NAZARETH. Although not mentioned in the Bible, Sepphoris was famous as a military, political, and cultural center and as one of the chief cities of Hellenistic GALILEE. HEROD Antipas did much to rebuild and enhance the importance of the city. Sepphoris figures prominently in the writings of JOSEPHUS and in rabbinic literature, and Jesus must have often visited it.

Septuagint. sep´too-uh-jint. This term, derived from Latin *Septuaginta* ("Seventy," reflecting the view that seventy or seventy-two translators pro-

S

duced the Pentateuch) and commonly abbreviated with the corresponding Roman numeral LXX, is the traditional but imprecise name given to the primary Greek version of the Hebrew Bible. The LXX appears to have been the first translation made of the OT or of any literary work of comparable size into another language, and it thus marks a milestone in human culture.

The story of the origin of the LXX is told in the *Letter of Aristeas*, a pseudepigraphical book written in the second half of the third century B.C. It states that PTOLEMY II (called Philadelphus, king of Egypt, 285-247) wished to have a translation of the Jewish law for his famous library in Alexandria. At his request the high priest Eleazer of Jerusalem sent seventy-two men, six from each tribe, to Egypt with a scroll of the TORAH (the five books of MOSES). In seventy-two days they translated one section each from this scroll and afterward decided on the wording together. Later writers elaborated on this story to the effect that the seventy-two had translated the whole OT (not the PENTATEUCH only), each independently of the other, in seclusion. The exact agreement of the seventy-two copies proved the work's inspiration.

What is the truth of this story? It is generally agreed that the Pentateuch was translated from Hebrew into Greek in Egypt around the time of Ptolemy II, ca. 280 B.C. The rest of the OT was done by various scholars in various places during the next two centuries. It seems most likely that the LXX originated not by the desire of Ptolemy II (although the project may have had his approval), but out of the need of the Alexandrian Jews. ALEXANDRIA of the third century B.C. was a large city with a great Jewish population that spoke GREEK rather than Hebrew. The vigorous Jewish intellectual life of Alexandria (exemplified by PHILO JUDAEUS in a later century) would require that the Torah be available in Greek.

The fact that the LXX was not made all at once is plain by the unevenness of its character. Some parts, such as the Pentateuch, present a moderately literal and reliable translation of a Hebrew text very similar to the Masoretic text (the Hebrew Bible preserved in Judaism). Other books, such as Job and Proverbs, are rather free translations, at times paraphrastic. In the books of 1 and 2 Samuel,

the Greek text differs greatly from the Masoretic text, and moreover the character of the translation of Samuel and Kings is not homogeneous (thus the Greek version of 1 Sam. 1:1 to the end of 2 Sam. 10, and then again of 1 Ki. 2:12 to the end of 1 Ki. 21, is quite different from the Greek version of the rest of these books). The LXX of Jeremiah is one-seventh shorter than the Hebrew form of Jeremiah preserved by the Masoretes. And so on. The LXX, then, is not one book, but a collection of translations of the OT produced by Jews of the DISPERSION. Moreover, some biblical books (e.g., Judges, Daniel, the Minor Prophets) have been preserved in more than one Greek translation. Because of the potential for confusion, some scholars reserve the term *Septuagint* (or LXX) for the original Greek version of the Pentateuch, while using *Old Greek* for the original Greek version of the other books ("original" serves to distinguish these versions from later revisions or new translations, but it is not always certain which of two competing Greek versions may have been produced first).

The LXX came to have great authority among the non-Palestinian Jews. Its use in the SYNAGOGUES of the Dispersion made it one of the most important missionary aids, for now the Greeks could read the divine revelation in their own tongue. When the NT quotes from the OT, as it frequently does, the form of the quotation often follows the LXX. Indeed, the early Christian CHURCH, built largely on converts from the synagogues of the Greek-speaking world, took over the LXX as their Bible. Their use of this version to prove that Jesus was the MESSIAH, however, caused a change in the Jews' attitude toward it. Even prior to the coming of Christ, there had been competing Greek versions of parts of the Hebrew Bible, but by the second century A.D. the Jews completely gave up the LXX, which thus became a Christian book. The Jews sponsored new Greek translations or revisions of the OT, those by Aquila, Symmachus, and Theodotion being best known.

Our oldest complete or nearly complete copies of the LXX available today are the three great Greek MSS of the Bible from the fourth and fifth centuries A.D.—Sinaiticus, Vaticanus, and Alexandrinus. It is quite plain that these represent a LXX that has had a long textual history, and that it

S

is now impossible to say to what extent these copies agree with the original translation made some six or seven hundred years before. Origen (died c. A.D. 250) sensed the problem of many divergent readings in the MSS in his day and sought to produce a resultant text in his *Hexapla* (a "six-columned" work that contained the Hebrew text in Hebrew characters, the Hebrew text in Greek characters, Aquila, the LXX, Symmachus, and Theodotion). In addition to this "Hexaplaric" recension of the LXX, there is at least another systematic revision known as the "Antiochene" or "Lucianic" recension (attributed to Lucian of Samosata).

The Greek versions of the Hebrew Bible are of value for two primary reasons. First, they provide an important witness to the *interpretation* of the OT in pre-Christian days. The Greek translators were also interpreters who came to the text with the theological and political prejudices of their time and thus had to deal with hermeneutical issues similar to those we face today. Their work was no doubt influenced, whether deliberately or subconsciously, by what they believed the Hebrew meant in light of their contemporary situation. Because the LXX reflects the theological, social, and political interests of the translators, it provides valuable information about how the Hebrew Bible was understood and interpreted at the time the translators were working. It should be noted that in many difficult passages the renderings in our English versions can be traced back to the LXX. Moreover, the Greek version played a significant role in the Christian church. The writers of the Greek NT naturally read and used the LXX in giving expression to the gospel. They drew on its vocabulary, often using expressions found in the LXX to draw the reader's mind to specific passages and themes of OT Scripture, and in hundreds of passages they quoted the Greek OT directly.

In the second place, the LXX is a very important tool for the *textual criticism* of the Hebrew Bible. In quite a few cases the Masoretic text and the LXX do not agree. A person knowing neither of the original languages can sense the difference by comparing Amos 9:11-12 with Acts 15:16-17. JAMES quotes AMOS, and his quotation agrees in general with the LXX, which is quite different from the Masoretic text. Of course, the great majority of the differences between the two are insignificant, but in some cases, such as this one, the discrepancy is of consequence for the meaning of the passage. Another example is Ps. 22:16, where the Masoretic text has the strange reading, "like a lion my hands and my feet"; most English Bibles, following the LXX, emend the Hebrew text to read, "they pierced my hands and my feet." The use of the Greek versions for this purpose is beset with dangers, and some scholars have assumed too quickly that the LXX preserves the original text in difficult passages. Nevertheless, it would be foolish to deny that the Greek versions provide essential data for the establishment of the Hebrew text.

sepulcher. See TOMB.

Serah. sihr-uh´ (Heb. *śeraḥ H8580*, possibly "abundance, prospering"). Daughter of ASHER and granddaughter of JACOB (Gen. 46:17; Num. 26:46 [KJV, "Sarah"]; 1 Chr. 7:30). Aside from DINAH (Gen. 46:15), Serah is the only daughter mentioned in any of these lists, and Jewish tradition has attempted to explain this peculiarity in various ways. The biblical text itself gives no explanation, although one of the references (Num. 26:46) may hint that one of the Asherite clans was descended from her.

Seraiah. si-ray´yuh (Heb. *śĕrāyâ H8588* and *śĕrāyāhû H8589* [only Jer. 36:26], "Yahweh has persevered" or "Yahweh has shown himself ruler"). **(1)** A royal secretary (see SCRIBE) in DAVID's court (2 Sam. 8:17). For the variations on his name and further discussion, see SHAVSHA.

(2) Son of Azariah, descendant of ZADOK, and chief priest at the time of the fall of JERUSALEM; he was seized and put to death at RIBLAH by NEBUCHADNEZZAR, probably not for anything he had done, but because he was a symbol of Hebrew autonomy (2 Ki. 25:18-21; 1 Chr. 6:14; Jer. 52:24-27). Seraiah was the father of JEHOZADAK, who was taken into exile by NEBUCHADNEZZAR (1 Chr. 6:14-15); the grandfather of JESHUA, postexilic high priest (cf. Hag. 1:1 et al.); and an ancestor of EZRA (Ezra 7:1, where "son" means "descendant").

(3) Son of TANHUMETH from NETOPHAH and one of the military officers who supported

GEDALIAH at MIZPAH (2 Ki. 25:23; in Jer. 40:8 the descriptive "Neophatite" is applied not to Tanhumeth but to EPHAI). Gedaliah, who had been made governor by Nebuchadnezzar, advised them to accept Babylonian rule and promised to treat them fairly (2 Ki. 25:24; Jer. 40:9-10).

(4) Son of KENAZ and brother of OTHNIEL, listed in the genealogy of JUDAH (1 Chr. 4:13-14).

(5) Son of Asiel and grandfather of Jehu; the latter is listed among the clan leaders in the tribe of SIMEON whose families increased greatly during the days of King HEZEKIAH and who dispossessed the Hamites and Meunites near GEDOR (1 Chr. 4:35; cf. vv. 38-41).

(6) An Israelite mentioned among leading individuals who returned from Babylon with ZERUBBABEL (Ezra 2:2; apparently called AZARIAH in Neh. 7:7). Perhaps he is the same Seraiah as a priest mentioned elsewhere (Neh. 12:1, 12).

(7) A priest who signed the covenant of NEHEMIAH (Neh. 10:2). Some identify him with #6 above.

(8) Son of Hilkiah; he is listed among the priests who settled in Jerusalem and is described as "supervisor in the house of God" (Neh. 11:11; apparently called Azariah in 1 Chr. 9:11).

(9) Son of Azriel; he was one of the officials of king JEHOIAKIM who were commanded to arrest JEREMIAH and his scribe BARUCH because of Jeremiah's prophecies that had been read to the king (Jer. 36:26).

(10) Son of Neriah (thus brother of Baruch, Jer. 32:12); he was a staff officer to whom Jeremiah gave a scroll so that he might read its prophecy to ZEDEKIAH in Babylon (Jer. 51:59-64). The name "Seraiah [ben] Neriah" occurs in a seal impression dated to the seventh century B.C. and is thought to refer to the individual mentioned in Jeremiah.

seraph. ser´uf, ser´uh-fim (Heb. *śārāp* H8597 [pl. *śĕrāpîm*], possibly "glowing, burning," or "noble"). KJV "seraphims" (superfluous English pl. form). There are only two references in the Bible to the seraphs (Isa. 6:2, 6). The number of these creatures is not given. Each seraph is said to have six wings, a face, hands, and feet (many scholars regard the latter as a euphemism for the genitalia). Two wings covered the face, two covered the feet, displaying

humility before God, and with two they flew. They expressed themselves in words that human ears comprehended (6:3, 7). The description seems to suggest a six-winged, humanoid figure.

Seraphs are described by some scholars as winged demons or as guardian-griffins. Others make a connection with the snake cults of the ANE, pointing both to the FIERY SERPENTS (KJV) that afflicted the Israelites in the wilderness and to the bronze serpent (see NEHUSHTAN), which later was destroyed because it had become an object of worship (Num. 21:6-9; 2 Ki. 18:4). According to this view, the term for "fiery [serpent]" (cf. also Deut. 8:15; Isa. 14:29; 30:6), which possibly alludes to the "burning" sting of the snakes' fatal bite or to their bright "glowing" color, is the same term used for "seraph." However, the seraphs as described by Isaiah are more like men than snakes. Moreover, although they handled hot coals from the altar (Isa. 6:6-7) or may have had fiery countenances, it is not certain that their name is derived from the verb meaning "to burn" (*śārap* H8596). More likely, the seraphs or seraphim were an order of supernatural or angelic beings (see ANGEL) similar to the CHERUBS, possibly related to the living creatures of Rev. 4:6-8. They stood beside or hovered above the heavenly throne of God as functionaries and attendants. They acted as agents and spokesmen for God (Isa. 6:6-7). A chief duty was that of praising God (6:3).

Sered. sihr´id (Heb. *sered* H6237, derivation uncertain; gentilic *sardî* H6238, "Seredite" [KJV, "Sardite"]). Son of ZEBULUN, grandson of JACOB, and ancestral head of the Seredite clan (Gen. 46:14; Num. 26:26).

sergeant. See OCCUPATIONS AND PROFESSIONS.

Sergius Paulus. See PAULUS, SERGIUS.

serjeant. KJV form of "sergeant." See OCCUPATIONS AND PROFESSIONS.

Sermon on the Mount. Traditional title given to Jesus' discourse recorded in Matt. 5-7. This and several other extended discourses of Jesus included in the Gospel of MATTHEW are given in Mark and Luke in the same situations as in Matthew, but always in shorter form. Moreover, much of the teaching material that Matthew gives in these long discourses is given also by Mark and Luke, with close verbal similarity, but in fragments in other settings than Matthew's.

These facts have caused critical students to question, in greater or lesser degree, the integrity of Matthew's record of the Lord's teaching ministry.

The Church of Beatitudes.

Some conservative scholars have held that Matthew presents the material reliably but that he has gathered it in topical form. It should be remembered, however, that the nature of Jesus' itinerant ministry to shifting crowds was such that he must have repeated similar material a great many times under a great variety of circumstances. Moreover, in any one extended session of his teaching, there were interruptions, questions, arguments, digressions.

The word *sermon* is misleading to the modern mind. Matthew does not say that Jesus arose, entered the pulpit, and delivered a sermon that he had formally prepared in a quiet library. The crowds were following him (Matt. 5:1; Lk. 6:17) to see his MIRACLES. He went up the mountain a little way so that his immediate followers would be nearer than the rest (Matt. 5:1); and then he came down with them to a level place (Lk. 6:17), still in "the mountain." Presently he sat down and began to teach, with special attention to the disciples who were near.

The biblical writers, of course, used no quotation marks, and the modern reader must understand that they do not claim to give quotations word for word. Neither do they claim to give all that was said on any occasion. They do claim that their words are a true presentation of the substance quoted. We can allow our imagination to picture, for example, the giving of the first beatitude. Jesus says, "Blessed are you poor people." A dull person interrupts, "How can that be? We're in want." Jesus replies, "God's kingdom is yours [if you will have it], but more important, Blessed are they who feel their spiritual poverty, for the kingdom of heaven is theirs" (Matt. 5:3; Lk. 6:20). The "sermon," then, is a student's (Matthew's) report of a class lecture and discussion and should be studied in that light. Luke's account is to be understood as based on another student's notebook (see Lk. 1:1-4 for Luke's sources of information). The fact that there are digressions from a formal outline (Matt. 5:25-26, 29-30) is evidence of the genuineness of the record. What teacher in touch with the minds of his class is ever able to avoid digressions from his basic outline?

It is remarkable what unity and order of thought is evident in the Sermon on the Mount. There is no space for a detailed analytical outline, which careful readers can profitably make for themselves. Is the teaching of Jesus literally applicable to human beings in this world? The meek do not now inherit the earth (Matt. 5:5), and public or national nonresistance leads to slavery.

If we take the teaching of Jesus in the same reasonably flexible way that it seems he interpreted the Ten Commandments (Matt. 12:4-5, 11-12), the way of the heart rather than of mere outward conduct (5:22, 28), there is not a word that we need not heed today. We should be willing to take a slap in the face. This is not to say that we must stand by and see the innocent suffer lawless injury. Jesus did not contradict the principle that those responsible for law enforcement must bear "the sword" (Rom. 13:1-5) and that "not for nothing." The Sermon on the Mount is Christ's instruction to us for godly living in the present world.

© Dr. James C. Martin

Sermon on the Plain. Common title given to Jesus' discourse recorded in Lk. 6:17-49. See SERMON ON THE MOUNT.

serpent. See ANIMALS.

serpent, bronze (brasen). See NEHUSHTAN.

Serpent's Stone. See ZOHELETH.

Serug. sihr′uhg (Heb. *sĕrûg H8578*, meaning unknown; gk. *Serouch G4952*). Son of Reu and descendant of SHEM (Gen. 11:20-23; 1 Chr. 1:26); included in Luke's GENEALOGY OF JESUS CHRIST (Lk. 3:35; KJV, "Saruch").

servant. See OCCUPATIONS AND PROFESSIONS; SERVICE.

Servant of the Lord. The Hebrew expression *ʿebed yhwh*, "the servant of Yahweh," occurs frequently in the OT with reference to various individuals, especially MOSES (e.g., Josh. 1:1 and often in this book). In biblical scholarship, however, the phrase "the Servant of the Lord" refers primarily to a messianic figure mentioned repeatedly in Isa. 42-53 whom God calls "my servant" (though the specific phrase *ʿebed yhwh* occurs only in Isa. 42:19). Modern scholarship distinguishes in this section four passages that are often referred to as the "Servant Songs." They are Isa. 42:1-4; 49:1-6; 50:4-9; 52:13—53:12. The limits of the individual "Songs" are not clear; many would add 42:5-7; 49:7; 50:10-11; and others would see a fifth Servant Song in ch. 61:1.

The interpretation of these passages has been contested. Some contend that the prophet was speaking of himself, a view that can sustain itself only by the unwarranted removal of Isa. 49:3 (in whole or part) from the text of Isaiah and by the most tortuous and unlikely interpretation of ch. 53. A much more prevalent view is that Isaiah was speaking of the mission, suffering, and marvelous continuance of ISRAEL, the nation. This view accords with 49:3 but makes difficult an explanation of ch. 53 in credible terms; for in what possible sense can the national sufferings be understood as vicarious when the prophet himself says (e.g.,

42:18-25) that it was all their own fault? Besides, though Israel is spoken of as the servant (e.g., 43:10), the portrait of the servant-nation outside the key passages and of the Servant in the passages is dramatically different. The only interpretation capable of sustaining itself through all the details of the four passages is that which sees Isaiah as looking forward to the perfect Servant and his perfect act of service.

On this understanding the passages fit perfectly into their context and offer a developing portrait of the Lord Jesus Christ. The plight of the GENTILE world (Isa. 41:28-29) prepares for the Servant, who will bring "judgment," that is, the revelation of the Lord and of his will, to the Gentiles (42:1-4). Following this, Isaiah becomes increasingly aware of the plight of national Israel (e.g., 42:18-20) until, by ch. 48, he is ready to say that the people no longer have any right to their privileged name as "Israel" (48:1) and that, though mercy may redeem them from slavery in BABYLON (48:20-21), yet they know nothing of peace with God (48:22). This prepares us for the lesson that the Servant's task (49:1-6) is first to Israel and then to the whole world and that he is himself the only one deserving the name Israel (49:3). Unlike the nation (49:13-50:4), the Servant is obedient, resolute, and filled with buoyant faith, notwithstanding that his obedience will involve him in dreadful suffering (50:4-9), but as we obey the call to "behold" (52:13 KJV) we see that these sufferings, arising from perfect obedience, are in fact the sufferings of a holy sin-bearer (53:1-12), and that as soon as he has suffered, the call to enter and enjoy a free salvation can go out alike to Israel (ch. 54) and to the whole world (ch. 55).

The NT applies Isaiah's Servant passages to Christ (Isa. 42:1-4 is quoted as fulfilled in Matt. 12:18-21; and parts of Isa. 52:13—53:12 are quoted in Matt. 8:17; Lk. 22:37; Jn. 12:38; Acts 8:32-33; Rom. 10:16; cf. also Jn. 1:29; Rom. 8:34; Heb. 9:28; 1 Pet. 2:21-25). The Servant's mission is fulfilled only in Christ: election (Isa. 42:1; 49:7; 1 Pet. 2:4, 6), birth (Isa. 49:1; 53:2; Lk. 1:31-35), anointing (Isa. 42:1; 48:16; 59:21; 61:1; Matt. 3:16; Lk. 4:18-19), ministry (Isa. 49:8-13; Acts 3:13-18), obedience (Isa. 50:4-7; Phil. 2:7-8), new covenant (Isa. 42:6; 49:8; 55:3; Matt. 26:26-29), vicarious death

S

(Isa. 53:4-12; 1 Pet. 2:22-25), resurrection (Isa. 53:10-12; Acts 2:24-36), offer of salvation (Isa. 49:8; 6:1-2; Lk. 24:46-49), mission to Gentiles (Isa. 42:1, 6-7; 49:6, 12; 60:3, 9; Matt. 28:18-20), and glorification and intercession (Isa. 49:3; 53:12; Acts 2:33-36; Phil. 2:6-11; Heb. 7:24-25).

service. The first biblical occurrences of the Hebrew noun *ʿăbōdâ H6275* ("work, service") concern JACOB's service to LABAN (Gen. 29:27; 30:26).

© Dr. James C. Martin. The British Museum. Photographed by permission.

Gilded shabti of the Egyptian priest of Amun (from Iwy, c. 1700 B.C.). Shabtis were small, mummy-shaped figurines that came to represent servants for the deceased in the afterlife.

A different expression (lit., "to stand before") is used with reference to JOSEPH's entering "the service of Pharaoh" (Gen. 41:46). Religious service in the OT is closely associated with WORSHIP rituals in the TABERNACLE and the TEMPLE (Exod. 27:19 et al.). The PRIESTS and LEVITES were responsible "for the service of the temple of the LORD" (1 Chr. 23:32; cf. Num. 8:11 et al.). As revelation progressed, service acquired a broader meaning. "The Son of Man did not come to be served, but to serve [Gk. *diakoneō G1354*]" (Matt. 20:28), and thereby Jesus set an example for his followers (cf. the FOOTWASHING incident, Jn. 13:3-17). He said, "Whoever serves me must follow me. ... My Father will honor the one who serves me" (12:26). Early Christians soon grasped Jesus' concept of total religious service, including evangelism and missions. Paul said, "There are different kinds of service [*diakonia G1355*]" (1 Cor. 12:5), and he thanked Jesus Christ for "appointing me to his service" (1 Tim. 1:12). In a more general sense, all believers are to "serve [*douleuō G1526*] one another in love" (Gal. 6:13).

Seth. seth´ (Heb. *šēt H9269*, possibly "provision, restitution"; Gk. *Sēth G4953*). KJV also Sheth (only 1 Chr. 1:1). Third son of ADAM and EVE, father of ENOSH, and ancestor of the godly messianic line that descends from him to NOAH (Gen. 4:25-26; 5:3-8; 1 Chr. 1:1; Sir. 49:16; included in Luke's GENEALOGY OF JESUS CHRIST, Lk. 3:38). He is reported to have lived 912 years (Gen. 5:8). When Eve named him Seth, she said, "God has granted [*šāt*] me another child in place of Abel, since Cain killed him" (Gen. 4:25). It is uncertain whether the name originally derives from the verb *šît H8883* ("to place, set, appoint"); the statement may reflect a popular etymology or it may be simply a play on words. See also SHETH.

Sethur. see´thuhr (Heb. *sĕtûr H6256*, possibly "hidden [by God]"). Son of Michael, from the tribe of ASHER, and one of the twelve spies sent out by MOSES to reconnoiter the Promised Land (Num. 13:13).

seven. See NUMBER.

Seveneh. See SYENE.

seventy disciples. According to Lk. 10:1 and 17 (KJV and other versions), Jesus sent out seventy disciples to minister as a part of his extended journey to JERUSALEM (the NIV, following some important MSS, has "seventy-two"). The number seventy was symbolic to the Jews. It alluded to the group of ELDERS that MOSES had chosen to help with the task of leading Israel in the wilderness (Num. 11:16-17, 24-25). Apparently on the basis of that group, the number of the members of the SANHEDRIN, the supreme council of the Jews, was set at seventy-one (i.e., seventy plus a leader). It was also the "number" of the nations in the world (see Gen. 10, where the LXX has seventy-two), and of the members of JACOB's family in Egypt (Gen. 46:27). Some have supposed that Jesus, by his choice of this number, was foreshadowing the preaching of the GOSPEL to all nations. Others have argued that the original number of disciples was seventy-two, and that later scribes altered it to seventy because the latter number had greater significance.

seventy weeks. According to Dan. 9:24, seventy weeks (lit., "seventy sevens") were decreed for ISRAEL and JERUSALEM "to finish transgression, to put an end to sin, to atone for wickedness, to bring in everlasting righteousness, to seal up vision and prophecy and to anoint the most holy." The period is said to begin with "the issuing of the decree to restore and rebuild Jerusalem" and ends with the time of "the Anointed One, the ruler" (v. 25). The seventy weeks are subdivided into seven weeks, sixty-two weeks, and one week. After the sixty-two weeks have been accomplished, the Anointed One is to be cut off, a period marked by desolation and war when the city and sanctuary are destroyed (v. 26). It is also stated that either the Anointed One or, more likely, the ruler or prince mentioned in v. 26b makes a firm covenant with many for one week, in the midst of which "he will put an end to sacrifice and offering. And on a wing of the temple he will set up an abomination that causes desolation, until the end that is decreed is poured out on him" (v. 27). This passage has received three basic interpretations, all of which agree that each week represents seven years so that in round figures the seventy weeks equal 490 years.

(1) According to the traditional view, the end of the seventy weeks represents the time of the accomplished work of CHRIST on the CROSS. The 490 years are thus the period of time from the edict to rebuild Jerusalem until Jesus' death. The question of when that edict was given is however greatly disputed. It is most often identified with the time of ARTAXERXES' decree to send EZRA back to Jerusalem (c. 458 B.C.). This would put the seventieth week approximately in the time of Christ's earthly ministry. Usually the seventieth week is considered to have begun with Christ's baptism, and the "cutting off" is identified with his death about three and one-half years later. Others date the seventy weeks from the time of the decree issued by CYRUS (538 B.C.).

(2) Many modern scholars hold that the prophecy was written in the second century B.C. and that the writer of DANIEL is not predicting but telling what has already happened. The seventy weeks began in 538 B.C. with Cyrus's decree and ended with the deposition of the high priest ONIAS III in 175 B.C. and his assassination in 172. In this interpretation, Dan. 9:26-27 describes the attack on the city by ANTIOCHUS Epiphanes.

(3) The dispensational view considers the seventy weeks to have begun with Artaxerxes' decree and the sixty-ninth week to have ended with Christ's death. But the great "parenthesis" or unreckoned period from Christ's death until the second coming of Christ for his saints (more specifically, the "rapture") is the period of the Gentiles. Finally, the seventieth week is that period of the ANTICHRIST in Jerusalem until Christ comes again to deliver his church, a period covering seven years.

seven words from the cross. These sayings of CHRIST were probably uttered in the following order: (a) Before the darkness: "Father, forgive them ... " (Lk. 23:34); "Today you will be with me ... " (23:43); "Dear woman, here is your son ... " (Jn. 19:26). (b) During the darkness: "My God, my God ... " (Matt. 27:46; Mk. 15:34). (c) After the darkness: "I am thirsty" (Jn. 19:28, fulfilling Ps. 69:21); "It is finished" (19:30); "Father, into your hands ... " (Lk. 23:46, quoting Ps. 31:5). Theologically, these words, in the order given above, illustrate (1) divine forgiveness, (2) assurance of immortality,

S

(3) good works, (4) the awfulness of Christ's death, (5) the true humanity of Christ, (6) the perfection of Christ's atonement, and (7) the divine will.

sewing. The origin of the skill of sewing is lost in the antiquity of the race. The book of Genesis, however, relates that ADAM and EVE sewed fig leaves to make aprons for themselves (Gen. 3:7). Sewing was done by both men and women in the MEDITERRANEAN world. The only explicit reference to sewing in the NT is Jesus' saying, "No one sews a patch of unshrunk cloth on an old garment" (Mk. 2:21 and parallels). It is very likely, however, that PAUL practiced the craft in tent-making, which was his trade.

sex. The OT contains the major portion of the biblical teaching concerning sex. Reference is made to distinctions between the sexes in the CREATION account in Genesis; and the PENTATEUCH contains numerous commandments related to sex and sexual acts. The narrative portions of the OT contain references to normal and abnormal sexual activities. Portions of the WISDOM Literature deal with sex in relation to such diverse themes as married love (SONG OF SOLOMON) and the dangers of promiscuity (PROVERBS). The Bible states that OT teachings were included in the Scriptures not only for the purpose of conveying redemptive truth but also for the "instruction" of believers through the centuries (1 Cor. 10:11). The OT references to sex seem to fall largely under the latter category.

Sexual intercourse is not referred to directly, but rather by expressions such as "becoming one flesh with" (Gen. 2:24), "knowing" (4:1, 17, 25; Jdg. 19:25), and "lying with" someone (Gen. 34:7; Num. 31:17, 18; Deut. 22:22). This language tends to emphasize the intimate nature of the sex act. The concept of "knowing" someone may have a relationship to the FALL and the knowledge of good and evil with its possible sexual overtones (Gen. 2:17 and 3:7). The Scriptures manifest a clear awareness of the emotional and intimate nature of sexual intercourse along with the companionship involved between two lovers (Song of Solomon). Sexual intercourse outside of MARRIAGE is condemned along with prostitution (see PROSTITUTE) and other types of sexual activity, such as homo-

sexuality, incest, rape, and bestiality (Exod. 20:14, 17; 22:16; Lev. 18:6-18, 23; 19:20; 20:15-16).

For the most part, the early church seemed to rely upon the teachings of the OT with respect to sex and the sex role. However, the NT is not silent on the topic. When the topic is mentioned, it usually is dealt with in relation to the spiritual life of the CHURCH, and the total message of redemption as it related to the family and the individual. Sexual intercourse between marriage partners is considered appropriate and expected (Heb. 13:4); but married couples may forego, at times, natural sex relations in order to give themselves to prayer (1 Cor. 7:5). Refraining from sexual intercourse is referred to as "depriving each other," and uncontrolled sexual desire of the unmarried and widows is spoken of as "burning" (v. 9). Polygamy was condemned by the early church and monogamy was the expected practice (1 Cor. 7:1-2; 1 Tim. 3:2). Homosexuality (Rom. 1:26-28), prostitution, adultery, and fornication (Gal. 5:19; Jude 7) were condemned along with other vices prevalent in the early Christian era. It was stated that indulgence in such vices would keep a person from entering the kingdom of God (1 Cor. 6:9-10).

Shaalabbin, Shaalbim. shay′uh-lab′uhn, shay-al′bim (Heb. *šaʿălabbîn H9125* and *šaʿalbîm H9124*, prob. "[place of] foxes"; gentilic *šaʿalbônî H9126*, "Shaalbonite"). The form Shaalabbin occurs in a list of towns allotted to the tribe of DAN; it is included between Ir Shemesh (see BETH SHEMESH #3) and AIJALON (Josh. 19:41-42). It must be the same as Shaalbim , which is associated with Mount HERES and Aijalon as places from which the Danites could not drive out the AMORITES (Jdg. 1:34-35; cf. also 1 Ki. 4:9). The descriptive "Shaalbonite," used of Eliahba, one of DAVID's mighty warriors (2 Sam. 23:32; 1 Chr. 11:33), very probably is a gentilic adjective of Shaalbim, and some argue that Shaalbon (which does not occur in the OT) may have been the original form of the place name. See also SHAALIM. Shaalabbin/Shaalbim is generally identified with modern Selbit, c. 3 mi. (5 km.) NW of Aijalon.

Shaalbon, Shaalbonite. See SHAALABIN, SHAALBIM.

Shaalim. shay'uh-lim (Heb. *ša'ălîm H9127*, "hollows"). KJV Shalim. A region near SHALISHA, between the hill country of Ephraim (see EPHRAIM, HILL COUNTRY OF) and the tribal territory of BENJAMIN, where SAUL went looking for his father's donkeys (1 Sam. 9:4). Shaalim has often been identified with the Danite town of Shaalbim (see SHAALABBIN), some 16 mi. (26 km.) W of JERUSALEM. However, an area around BETHEL, N of Jerusalem, would fit the context better; accordingly, Shaalim may be the same as SHUAL, a region close to OPHRAH (1 Sam. 13:17), a few miles N of MICMASH.

Shaaph. shay'af (Heb. *ša'ap H9131*, prob. "balm"). **(1)** Son of Jahdai (1 Chr. 2:47) and apparently a descendant of JUDAH in the line of CALEB (1 Chon 2:47). See comments under JAHDAI.

(2) Son of CALEB by his concubine MAACAH; he is described as the "father" (i.e., founder) of MADMANNAH (1 Chr. 2:49). Some emend the text so that this Shaaph can be identified with #1 above.

Shaaraim. shay'uh-ray'im (Heb. *ša'ărayim H9139*, "[pair of] gates"). **(1)** A town within the tribal territory of JUDAH located in the SHEPHELAH (Josh. 15:36; KJV, "Sharaim"). The way from the Valley of Elah (see ELAH, VALLEY OF) to GATH and EKRON is identified as "the Shaaraim road" (1 Sam. 17:52). The site has not been positively identified, but an attractive proposal is modern Khirbet Sairah, very near AZEKAH.

(2) One of the Simeonite towns where the clan of SHIMEI son of Zaccur lived (1 Chr. 4:31). Its location is uncertain, but some scholars regard Shaaraim here as a textual error for SHARUHEN (Josh. 19:6).

Shaashgaz. shay-ash'gaz (Heb. *ša'ašgaz H9140*, meaning uncertain). A EUNUCH in the court of Ahasuerus (XERXES), king of PERSIA (Esth. 2:14). He is described as being "in charge of the concubines," who resided in "the second house of the women" (KJV; NIV, "another part of the harem"). Initially, the young women who were candidates to become queen spent time in the part of the HAREM reserved for virgins, which was supervised by HEGAI (v. 8); after spending a night with the king, they became CONCUBINES (lesser wives) under the custody of Shaashgaz. ESTHER, however, won the king's approval and was made queen rather than a lesser wife (v. 17).

Shabbethai. shab'uh-thi (Heb. *šabbĕtay H8703*, prob. "[born on] the Sabbath"). A LEVITE who apparently challenged EZRA's instruction that those who had married foreign women should divorce them (Ezra 10:15). The Hebrew text, however, can be understood differently. See comments under JAHZEIAH. He is probably the same Shabbethai listed among the Levites who "instructed the people in the Law" (Neh. 8:7). Elsewhere, he and a certain JOZABAD are described as "two of the heads of the Levites, who had charge of the outside work of the house of God" (Neh. 11:16).

Shachia. See SAKIA.

shackles. Bonds, chains, or fetters, generally for the feet of prisoners, and made of bronze or of iron (Jdg. 16:21; Ps. 105:18; 149:8). The NT word (Mk. 5:4; Lk. 8:29) indicates that the shackles were for the feet.

Shaddai, Shadday. See EL SHADDAI.

shade, shadow. A word used literally, figuratively, and theologically. Literally, a shadow of a mountain (Jdg. 9:36), of a tree (Hos. 4:13; Mk. 4:32), of a dial (2 Ki. 20:9-11), of a booth (Jon. 4:5), of a gourd (4:6), of a person (Acts 5:15). Figuratively, it signifies life's shortness (1 Chr. 29:15; Job 8:9; Ps. 102:11), protection (either good, as in Ps. 17:8; 36:7; 91:1; or evil, as in Isa. 30:3; Jer. 48:45), the Messiah's

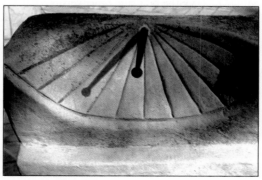

Shadow cast on sundial.

© Dr. James C. Martin. The Eretz Israel Museum. Photographed by permission.

S

blessings (Isa. 4:6; 32:2; 49:2; 51:16), death (either physical, as in Job 10:21-22; Ps. 23:4; or spiritual as in Isa. 9:2; Matt. 4:16; Lk. 1:79), and changeableness (contrasted with God's unchangeableness, Jas. 1:17). Theologically, it is used of the typical nature of the OT (Col. 2:17; Heb. 8:5; 10:1), illustrated in these facts: the OT prefigures in outline the NT substance; the OT represents externally (in rites and ceremonies) what the NT fulfills internally; the OT saints, nevertheless, could by faith comprehend the inner reality of the shadow; the NT, therefore, fulfills and abolishes the OT shadow; the NT saints, however, can still draw spiritual instruction from the shadow; and, finally, even NT saints, with the shadow and the substance, await the full day of spiritual understanding (1 Cor. 13:12).

Shadrach. shad′rak (Heb. *šadrak H8731* [Aram. *H10701*], perhaps from Akk. *šadurāku*, "I have been made to feel afraid"). The Babylonian name given to HANANIAH, one of DANIEL's companions taken by NEBUCHADNEZZAR to be trained in his palace as counselors to the king (Dan. 1:3-7 et al.).

Shadud. See SARID.

shaft. See WATER SHAFT.

Shage. See SHAGEE.

Shagee. shay′gee (Heb. *šāgēh H8707*, derivation uncertain). KJV Shage. A Hararite and the father of Jonathan; the latter was one of DAVID's mighty warriors (1 Chr. 11:34). In the parallel passage the MT reads "Jonathan, Shammah the Hararite" (2 Sam. 23:32-33; the NIV and other versions emend to "Jonathan son of Shammah the Hararite"), and Shammah is also identified as "son of Agee the Hararite" (2 Sam. 23:11). Evidently there has been textual corruption in one or more of these passages. According to one view, the name Shagee in Chronicles is original, and 2 Sam. 23:32-33 should be emended accordingly. Others believe Shagee is a false form, resulting from a confusion of the names Shammah and Agee. See also HARARITE.

Shahar. shay′hahr (Heb. *šahar H8840*, "dawn," referring prob. to the reddish morning twilight).

In English Bible versions, this name appears only in the title of Ps. 22 (KJV, "Aijeleth Shahar"; NIV, "The Doe of the Morning") and in the place name ZERET SHAHAR (Josh. 13:19). The Hebrew word, however, occurs over twenty times in the OT, and some scholars believe that at least in a few passages it alludes to the AMORITE god Shahar (the Morning Star, referring to Venus at dawn). Ugaritic mythology describes the birth of Shahar and his twin Shalem (deity of the dusk or evening) to the Canaanite god EL. Such expressions as "the rays of dawn" (Job 3:9; 41:18) and "the wings of the dawn" (Ps. 139:9) are sometimes thought to reflect this Canaanite myth, without necessarily suggesting that the biblical writers themselves held to it. Similarly, the description of the king of BABYLON as "morning star, son of the dawn" (Isa. 14:12; see MORNING STAR) has been interpreted as suggesting a divine being.

Shaharaim. shay′huh-ray′im (Heb. *šaharayim H8844*, "[two] dawns"). A descendant of BENJAMIN, although his place in the genealogy is unclear (1 Chr. 8:8). The passage contains some difficult textual problems, but it appears to say that Shaharaim divorced two wives, HUSHIM (who had given birth to two sons, v. 11) and BAARA, and that afterwards his third wife Hodesh gave birth to seven sons in MOAB (vv. 9-10; it is not clear whether he had always lived in Moab or only after his divorces). Shaharaim had an extensive progeny, especially through ELPAAL (born to Hushim).

Shahazimah. See SHAHAZUMAH.

Shahazumah. shay′huh-zoo′muh (Heb. *šahaṣûmâ H8833*, meaning uncertain). KJV Shahazimah. A site on the northern boundary of ISSACHAR between Mount TABOR and BETH SHEMESH (Josh. 19:22). Its location is unknown, though several proposals have been made, including modern el-Kerm (SE of Tabor), which appears to lie on the divide between the watersheds of Issachar and NAPHTALI.

Shalem. shay′luhm (Heb. *šālēm H8970*, "complete"). A city of SHECHEM where JACOB went after he left PADDAN ARAM (Gen. 33:18 KJV; cf. also NIV mg.). Most scholars, however, believe that the Hebrew word here is the common adjective *šālēm H8969* ("complete, whole, safe"), yielding the translation, "he arrived safely at the city of Shechem" (NIV). The Hebrew form is identical with the name usually rendered SALEM (Gen. 14:18; Ps. 76:2).

Shalim. See SHAALIM.

Shalisha. shuh-li´shuh (Heb. *šālišâ H8995*, possibly "third [part]"). Also Shalishah. A region near SHAALIM, between the hill country of Ephraim (see EPHRAIM, HILL COUNTRY OF) and the tribal territory of BENJAMIN, where SAUL went looking for his father's donkeys (1 Sam. 9:4). Unfortunately, the topographical information in this text is difficult to sort out. Shalisha was probably a district in SE Ephraim, but the precise location is unknown; it is usually thought that the town of BAAL SHALISHAH (2 Ki. 4:42) was found in the same area.

Shalishah. See SHALISHA.

Shallecheth. See SHALLEKETH.

Shalleketh. shal´uh-kith (Heb. *šalleket H8962*, meaning uncertain). Also Shallecheth. The name of a gate on the upper road in the W part of the TEMPLE enclosure in JERUSALEM; the gatekeepers assigned to it were SHUPPIM and HOSAH (1 Chr. 26:16). Nothing else is known about this gate, although on the assumption that the name might mean "casting forth," the improbable suggestion has been made that the ashes and offal from the sacrifices were discarded there. Also doubtful is the view that the name means "departing" and that therefore the reference is to the gate elsewhere called SUR (2 Ki. 11:5). Some scholars, on the basis of the SEPTUAGINT, emend the Hebrew text and translate, "the chamber gate."

Shallum. shal´uhm (Heb. *šallûm H8935*, possibly short form of SHELEMIAH, "Yahweh has repaid [*or* replaced]"). **(1)** Son of JABESH and one of the last kings of the northern kingdom of ISRAEL (2 Ki. 15:10-15). Shallum reigned over the ten tribes after having murdered ZECHARIAH, who was the son of JEROBOAM II and the last king of JEHU's dynasty. Within a month this usurper was himself assassinated by MENAHEM, c. 745 B.C.

(2) Son of TIKVAH and husband of the prophetess HULDAH; he had charge of the royal wardrobe (2 Ki. 22:14; 2 Chr. 34:22 ["son of Tokhath"]). Some identify him with #13 below.

(3) Son of Sismai and descendant of JUDAH in the line of JERAHMEEL (1 Chr. 2:40). He descended from Jerahmeel's son, SHESHAN, who gave his daughter in marriage to an Egyptian slave (vv. 34-35).

(4) Son of JOSIAH and king of Judah (1 Chr. 3:15; Jer. 22:11). See JEHOAHAZ #2.

(5) Son of SHAUL and grandson of SIMEON (1 Chr. 4:25).

(6) Son of the high priest ZADOK and ancestor of EZRA (1 Chr. 6:12-13; Ezra 7:2); probably the same as MESHULLAM in the parallel lists (1 Chr. 9:11; Neh. 11:11).

(7) Son of NAPHTALI and grandson of JACOB (1 Chr. 7:13 MT, followed by most versions); the NIV, on the basis of some MSS and the parallel passages (Gen. 46:24; Num. 26:49), has SHILLEM.

(8) Son of KORE and descendant of KORAH; after the EXILE, he was the chief gatekeeper, stationed at the KING'S GATE (1 Chr. 9:17-19 [although some think that v. 19 refers to a different person]; see also Ezra 2:42; Neh. 7:45). His firstborn, MATTITHIAH, "was entrusted with the responsibility for baking the offering bread" (1 Chr. 9:31). This Shallum is often identified with MESHELEMIAH (v. 21), SHELEMIAH (26:14), and MESHULLAM (Neh. 12:25). He is probably the same person listed among the gatekeepers who agreed to put away their foreign wives (Ezra 10:24).

(9) Father of JEHIZKIAH, an Ephraimite leader (2 Chr. 28:12).

(10) One of the descendants of Binnui who agreed to put away their foreign wives (Ezra 10:42).

(11) Son of Hallohesh; he was "ruler of a half-district of Jerusalem" and, with his daughters, repaired a section of the walls of Jerusalem (Neh. 3:12).

(12) Son of Col-Hozeh (Neh. 3:15 NRSV). See SHALLUN.

(13) Father of HANAMEL and uncle of JEREMIAH (Jer. 32:7). Some identify him with #2 above.

(14) Father of Maaseiah; the latter was a doorkeeper (NJPS, "guardian of the threshold") who had a room in the temple (Jer. 35:4).

Shallun. shal'uhnm (Heb. *šallûn H8937*, possibly "carefree" or else a variant of SHALLUM). Son of Col-Hozeh; he was a postexilic "ruler of the district of Mizpah" who rebuilt the FOUNTAIN GATE, "roofing it over and putting its doors and bolts and bars in place." Shallun was responsible also for repairing the wall of the Pool of SILOAM (see SHELAH, POOL OF), which was apparently used to irrigate the KING'S GARDEN (Neh. 3:15; NRSV, "Shallum").

Shalmai. shal'mi (Heb. *šalmay H8978*, derivation uncertain). Ancestor of a family of temple servants (NETHINIM) who returned after the EXILE with ZERUBBABEL (Ezra 2:46 [NRSV, "Shamlai," following the *Qere*]; Neh. 7:48).

Shalman. shal'muhn (Heb. *šalman H8986*, meaning uncertain). An otherwise unknown person who "devastated Beth Arbel on the day of battle, / when mothers were dashed to the ground with their children" (Hos. 10:14; see BETH ARBEL). Evidently this event was well known to the Israelites, but the identification of Shalman is difficult. Many think the reference is to SHALMANESER V; various other proposals have been made.

Shalmaneser.   shal'muh-nee'zuhr   (Heb. *šalmanʾeser H8987*, from Ass. *šulmānu-ašarēd*, "[the god] Shulman is chief"). The name of several Assyrian kings, though only the last one is mentioned in the OT. **(1)** Shalmaneser I (1274-1245 B.C.), son of Adad-nirari I and the greatest warrior of the Middle Assyrian period, is known for having defeated the people of Urartu and Guti, and in the W, the HURRIANS, HITTITES, and ARAMEANS. By his capture of CARCHEMISH he was the first to bring ASSYRIA into direct clash with the Egyptians in SW Asia.

(2) Little is known about Shalmaneser II (1030-1020 B.C.), who took action to strengthen Assyria after a period of domination by Aramean tribes.

(3) Shalmaneser III (859-824 B.C.), son of Ashurnasirpal II, was the first Assyrian king to come into direct contact with ISRAEL. By a long series of raids he sought to contain the pressure of the hill-tribesmen in Urartu (see ARARAT) and the Medes and Persians in the Urmia region, but this did not prevent his main thrust to the W in thirty-one years of campaigning. Three expeditions were needed to neutralize Bīt-Adini (Beth-Eden) and thus gain a hold of the EUPHRATES crossing. In 853 the main march was directed toward DAMASCUS; the army advanced to Qarqar on the ORONTES, where it was faced by a powerful alliance led by Irhuleni of HAMATH backed by Adad-ʾidri (Hadadezer, the biblical BEN-HADAD II). AHAB the Israelite supplied 2,000 chariots and 10,000 men. Contingents from twelve other kings brought the total muster to 62,900 men, 1,900 cav-

Basalt statue of Shalmaneser III (from Ashur, 9th cent. B.C.). On the robe is a cuneiform inscription in which Shalmaneser describes himself as "the great king, king of all the four regions, the powerful and the mighty rival of the princes of the whole universe."

© Dr. James C. Martin. The Istanbul Archaeological Museum. Photographed by permission.

alry, and 3,900 chariots. Shalmaneser claimed the victory in a bloody contest in which 20,500 died. It is, however, significant that neither Hamath nor Damascus was taken, and that the Assyrians did not reappear in the W for three years (1 Ki. 16:29; 20:20; 22:1).

In 849 Shalmaneser again marched westward. CARCHEMISH, the last nominally independent state in the Upper Euphrates Valley, was incorporated into the growing provincial system under direct Assyrian control. By 841 the alliance had broken up and HAZAEL was ruling in Damascus in place of the murdered Adad-ʾidri (2 Ki. 8:15). He now had to face the Assyrians alone, and to do this he made a vigorous stand on Mount SENIR (HERMON, cf. Deut. 3:9), losing 16,000 men and some territory. However, the line of attack was diverted to the MEDITERRANEAN via the HAURAN. At Baʿal-rasi (N of Beirut) Shalmaneser received tribute from TYRE and SIDON brought in by ship, and from "Jehu, son of Omri"; according to the inscription and reliefs on the Black Obelisk set up in CALAH to commemorate the event, the tribute was carried by Israelite porters. Although this incident is not mentioned in the OT, it accords with the policy of the usurper JEHU, who may well have sought unsuccessfully for help against Hazael's raids on N Israel (2 Ki. 10:31-32). It explains the subsequent need for Assyrian intervention when SAMARIA made its bid for independence. After one further unsuccessful attempt to capture Damascus in 838, Sennacherib appears to have left the W alone, probably because of increasing internal disorders at home.

Toward the end of his reign, Shalmaneser seems to have stayed at Calah, the city rebuilt by his father. Here he built himself a new palace and armory, an action perhaps necessitated by the revolt of one of his sons. Another son, Shamshi-Adad V, was taking action against the rebels when his aged father died and he claimed the throne.

(4) The reign of Shalmaneser IV (782-772 B.C.), son of Adad-nirari III who had taken tribute from Samaria (Rimah stela), was spent mostly in attempting to suppress local disturbances.

(5) Shalmaneser V (726-722 B.C.) son of TIGLATH-PILESER III (who died in 727); the only Assyrian king named Shalmaneser in the OT history (unless SHALMAN, in Hos. 10:14, is a contraction of Shalmaneser). There are two references to him. One of these (2 Ki. 17:3-5) recounts how Shalmaneser received tribute from HOSHEA, the last king of the northern kingdom; then, after Hoshea had formed an alliance with So king of Egypt, Shalmaneser returned to Palestine in a more extensive campaign, imprisoned Hoshea, and besieged the city of Samaria for three years. The prophet Hosea, a contemporary of Hoshea's turbulent reign, speaks out against entanglements with either Assyria or Egypt (Hos. 5:13; 7:11; 8:9; 12:1). The second reference (2 Ki. 18:9-11) synchronizes the siege and fall of Samaria with the ruling house of Jerusalem (HEZEKIAH). Since not Shalmaneser, but SARGON II, was, according to his own testimony, the conqueror of Samaria (in 722/721), the biblical record can be understood to agree, for it says that (a) "the king of Assyria took Samaria" (2 Ki. 17:6) and (b) "the Assyrians took it" (2 Ki. 18:10)—in neither case actually affirming that Shalmaneser was the one who captured the city. There is a possible allusion to Shalmaneser V in "King Jareb" (KJV; NIV, "the great king"), which Hosea uses as a humorous or sarcastic reference to some Assyrian king (Hos. 5:13; 10:6).

Shama. shay′muh (Heb. *šāmāʿ H9052*, prob. "[God] has listened"). Son of Hotham the Aroerite (see AROER); he and his brother Jeiel were among DAVID's mighty warriors noted as the "Thirty" (1 Chr. 11:44).

Shamariah. See SHEMARIAH.

shambles. This English term, in its archaic sense of "meat market," is used by the KJV once (1 Cor. 10:25). The Greek word it renders could refer to a food market more generally.

shame. This subject has many aspects: subjective (Gen. 2:25; 3:7) and objective (Jer. 11:13; Hos. 9:10); positive (Prov. 19:26; 28:7) and negative (Prov. 10:5; Rom. 1:16; 1 Jn. 2:28); literal (Exod. 32:25) and figurative (Rev. 3:18; 16:15); individual (Gen. 38:23) and national (Jdg. 18:7; Isa. 30:3-5); removable (Isa. 54:4) and unremovable (Jer. 23:40); loved (Hos. 4:18 ASV) and hated

S

(Eph. 5:12); punitive (Isa. 47:3; Ezek. 16:51-54; 44:12) and commendatory (1 Sam. 20:30-34; 2 Sam. 6:20; 13:11-14); now (Heb. 6:6) and future (Ezek. 32:24-25; Dan. 12:2); human (Ps. 119:31) and divine (Ps. 69:7-9; 89:45; Isa. 50:6; Heb. 12:2); due to something natural (2 Sam. 19:1-5; 1 Cor. 11:6, 14) and due to something unnatural (2 Sam. 13:11-14; Phil. 3:19).

Shamed. See SHEMED.

Shamer. See SHEMER.

Shamgar. sham′gahr (Heb. *šamgar H9011*, apparently from Hurrian *šimigari*, "[the god] Shimig has given"). One of the Israelite leaders during the period of the judges (Jdg. 3:31; 5:6; see JUDGES, THE). Shamgar is identified as "son of Anath," but some believe that here the Hebrew expression may have originally meant something like "warrior of [the goddess] Anath" and that subsequently it came to be used as a military title. Shamgar is noted for having made a successful raid on the PHILISTINES with an oxgoad, a metal-tipped instrument which needed sharpening repeatedly. Although Shamgar may have been a Canaanite, he is listed among those who delivered the Israelites from oppression. Very likely this was the earliest oppression by the Philistines, who interfered with Israel's trade and restricted travel. Shamgar was successful in bringing relief to the Israelites before the Canaanite oppression in the days of DEBORAH and BARAK.

Shamhuth. sham′huhth (Heb. *šamhût H9016*, derivation uncertain). An IZRAHITE who served as commander in charge of the division for the sixth month under DAVID (1 Chr. 27:8). Shamhuth is usually thought to be the same as SHAMMAH the Harodite, one of the Thirty (2 Sam. 23:25; called SHAMMOTH the Harorite in 1 Chr. 11:27).

Shamir (person). shay′muhr (Heb. *šāmîr H9033*, "thorn" or "diamond"). Son of Micah and descendant of LEVI (1 Chr. 24:24).

Shamir (place). shay′muhr (Heb. *šāmîr H9034*, "thorn" or "diamond"). (1) A town in the hill country of the tribe of JUDAH (Josh. 15:48). Shamir

was part of a district that included such towns as JATTIR and SOCOH, but its precise location is unknown. Although some think that its name is preserved in modern Khirbet es-Sumara (c. 12 mi./19 km. SW of HEBRON), the identification cannot be confirmed.

(2) A town in the Ephraimite hill country (see EPHRAIM, HILL COUNTRY OF), and the home and burial place of TOLA, one of the judges (Jdg. 10:1-2). The site is unidentified (there is little to commend the suggestion that Shamir may be connected with SAMARIA). Why Tola, who came from the tribe of ISSACHAR, was living in Ephraim is a matter of speculation.

Shamlai. See SHALMAI.

Shamma. sham′uh (Heb. *šammā᾽ H9007*, derivation uncertain). Son of Zophah and descendant of AHER (1 Chr. 7:37).

Shammah. sham′uh (Heb. *šammāh H9015* and *šammā᾽ H9007* [only 2 Sam. 23:11], derivation uncertain). (1) Son of Reuel and grandson of ESAU; a chief in EDOM (Gen. 36:13, 17; 1 Chr. 1:37).

(2) Third son of JESSE and older brother of DAVID. He was present when SAMUEL anointed David as future king of Israel (1 Sam. 16:9; cf. v. 13). He fought, with two older brothers, in the campaign against the PHILISTINES under SAUL and was with the Israelite forces in the Valley of Elah when David killed GOLIATH (1 Sam. 17:13, 19). Shammah apparently had two sons: the crafty JONADAB (2 Sam. 13:3, 32 [here he is called SHIMEAH]; 1 Chr. 2:13; 20:7 [SHIMEA]) and a warrior named JONATHAN (2 Sam. 21:21; here the *Ketib* has SHIMEI).

(3) A Harodite (see HAROD) who was one of David's mighty warriors (2 Sam. 23:25; called SHAMMOTH the Harorite in 1 Chr. 11:27). He is usually thought to be the same as SHAMHUTH the Izrahite (1 Chr. 27:8).

(4) Son of Agee the HARARITE (2 Sam. 23:11-12). This Shammah, regarded as one of David's three chief warriors (cf. v. 8), is said to have defended, successfully and alone, after the other troops had fled, "a field full of lentils" from a band of Philistines. (The parallel, 1 Chr. 11:12-14, appears

to attribute this incident to ELEAZAR son of Dodo, but it is generally acknowledged that in this passage the reference to Shammah, with surrounding text, accidentally dropped out at some point in the textual transmission.) Shammah is apparently mentioned again in the list of the Thirty, but only as the father of the warrior Jonathan (2 Sam. 23:33, if the NIV's emendation is correct; however, see comments on 1 Chr. 11:34 under SHAGEE). Some scholars also believe that this Shammah is the same as #3 above (with confusion of the descriptives Harodite and Hararite).

Shammai. sham′*i* (Heb. *šammay H9025*, derivation uncertain). **(1)** Son of Onam and descendant of JUDAH in the line of JERAHMEEL (1 Chr. 2:28).

(2) Son of Rekem and descendant of Judah in the line of Jerahmeel's brother, CALEB (1 Chr. 2:44-45). The statement that Shammai's "son" was MAON may indicate that Shammai was the founder of the town by that name or that he was the ancestor of the people who settled there.

(3) Son of MERED (by BITHIA), included in the genealogy of Judah (1 Chr. 4:17).

(4) A Jewish scholar who lived at the end of the first century B.C. and the beginning of the first century A.D. See discussion under HILLEL.

Shammoth. sham′oth (Heb. *šammôt H9021*, derivation uncertain). A Harorite (see HAROD), listed among DAVID's mighty warriors (1 Chr. 11:27); probably the same as SHAMMAH the Harodite (2 Sam. 23:25) and SHAMHUTH the Izrahite (1 Chr. 27:8).

Shammua. sha-myoo′uh (Heb. *šammûaᶜ H9018*, prob. "heard [by God]"). Also Shammuah (2 Sam. 5:14 some KJV editions). **(1)** Son of Zaccur and descendant of REUBEN; one of the twelve spies sent by MOSES to Canaan (Num. 13:4).

(2) Son of DAVID and BATHSHEBA, born after David moved from HEBRON to JERUSALEM (2 Sam. 5:14; 1 Chr. 14:4; called SHIMEA in 1 Chr. 3:5 MT).

(3) Son of Galal and descendant of the musician JEDUTHUN; one of the LEVITES who resettled in JERUSALEM after the EXILE (Neh. 11:17; called SHEMAIAH in 1 Chr. 9:16).

(4) Head of the priestly family of BILGAH in the days of JOIAKIM the high priest (Neh. 12:18).

Shammuah. See SHAMMUA.

Shamsherai. sham′shuh-r*i* (Heb. *šamšĕray H9091*, derivation uncertain). Son of Jehoram and descendant of BENJAMIN; he is listed among the heads of families who lived in JERUSALEM (1 Chr. 8:26).

Shapham. shay′fuhm (Heb. *šāpām H9171*, derivation unknown). A leader of the tribe of GAD in BASHAN, listed as second in importance (1 Chr. 5:12). He lived "during the reigns of Jotham king of Judah and Jeroboam king of Israel" (v. 17).

Shaphan. shay′fuhn (Heb. *šāpān H9177*, "coney, rock badger"). **(1)** Son of Azaliah and royal secretary (see SCRIBE) under JOSIAH king of JUDAH (2 Ki. 22:3-20; 2 Chr. 34:8-20). It was Shaphan to whom HILKIAH the high priest gave the Book of the Law, which was discovered when the TEMPLE was being repaired in 621 B.C. Shaphan read from this law to Josiah, who then sent him with Hilkiah the priest and others to confer with HULDAH the prophetess. As a result, the king's reform movement gained impetus. Shaphan was an important leader in those reforms, and this must have brought him into close contact with the prophet JEREMIAH and his work. Shaphan's family for two generations participated as lay leaders in the religious life of Judah and supported the work of Jeremiah. His sons were AHIKAM, ELASAH, and GEMARIAH (#2); two grandsons mentioned are GEDALIAH (#2) and MICAIAH (#8).

(2) Father of JAAZANIAH (#3); the latter was one of seventy idolaters that EZEKIEL saw in the temple (Ezek. 8:11). Some believe this Shaphan is the same as #1, above.

Shaphat. shay′fat (Heb. *šāpāṭ H9151*, prob. short form of SHEPHATIAH, "Yahweh has judged"). **(1)** Son of Hori and descendant of SIMEON; one of the twelve spies sent by MOSES to Canaan (Num. 13:5).

(2) Father of the prophet ELISHA (1 Ki. 19:16, 19; 2 Ki. 3:11; 6:31).

(3) Son of Shemaiah and postexilic descendant of DAVID through SOLOMON and ZERUBBABEL (1

S

Chr. 3:22). Some scholars believe he was the son of Shecaniah; see HATTUSH #1.

(4) A leader of the tribe of GAD in BASHAN (1 Chr. 5:12). Some scholars, following the SEPTUAGINT and the Targum, interpret the Hebrew *špṭ* as a common noun rather than a name and translate, "Janai a judge in Bashan."

(5) Son of Adlai; he was an official under King DAVID in charge of the herds in the valleys (1 Chr. 27:29).

Shapher. See SHEPHER.

Shaphir. shay′fuhr (Heb. *šāpîr H9160*, "beautiful, fair"). KJV Saphir. A geographic area, probably a town, against which MICAH prophesied (Mic. 1:11). Its location is unknown. Because of the association with GATH (v. 10), some have looked for a site in PHILISTINE territory (e.g., modern Tell es-Sawafir, 4 mi./6 km. SE of ASHDOD); others believe the context demands a Judean site and have suggested Khirbet el-Kom (or el-Qom, c. 7 mi./11 km. W of HEBRON; this site is on Wadi es-Saffar, which possibly preserves the biblical name).

Sharai. shair′i (Heb. *šāray H9232*, perhaps "Yahweh has delivered"). One of the descendants of Binnui who agreed to put away their foreign wives (Ezra 10:40).

Sharaim. See SHAARAIM #1.

Sharar. shair′ahr (Heb. *šārār H9243*, possibly "firm, healthy"). A HARARITE who was the father of Ahiam, one of DAVID's mighty warriors (2 Sam. 23:33; called SHACAR in the parallel, 1 Chr. 11:35).

share. This term, in its meaning PLOWSHARE, is used once by the KJV (1 Sam. 13:20).

Sharezer. shuh-ree′zuhr (Heb. *śar'eṣer H8570*, possibly short form of Akk. *Nabu-šar-uṣur*, "may [the god] Nebo protect the king"). (1) Son of SENNACHERIB; he and his brother, Adrammelech, joined in murdering their father in the temple of NISROCH (2 Ki. 19:37; Isa. 37:38). See comments under ADRAMMELECH. No extrabiblical sources attest to the name Sharezer for one of Sennach-

erib's sons. Since the Greek historian Abydenus refers to the two brothers as Adramelus and Nergilus, some have thought that the full name of the latter was Nergal-šar-uṣur (NERGAL-SHAREZER). It could equally well be a rendering of Šar-eṭir-aššur, the name of a known son of Sennacherib.

(2) An Israelite leader sent by the inhabitants of BETHEL to inquire concerning the propriety of keeping the anniversary feast which commemorated the destruction of JERUSALEM (Zech. 7:2; KJV, "Sherezer"). The text is difficult, however, and some argue that it should be rendered, "Bethel-Sharezer and Regem-Melech and his men sent to entreat the favor of the LORD" (cf. NJPS); if so, the name may be equivalent to Bel-šar-uṣur (i.e., BELSHAZZAR, "may Bel protect the king"). Another possible rendering is, "Bethel—that is, Sharezer and Regem-Melech and his men—sent … " See also REGEM-MELECH.

Sharon. shair′uhn (Heb. *šārôn H9227*, "flat land" or "wet land"; gentilic *šārônî H9228*, "Sharonite"; Gk. *Sarōn G4926*). KJV NT Saron. (1) When used with the definite article (*haššārôn*, prob. meaning "the plain"), this term refers to the largest of the coastal plains of N PALESTINE, extending from the Crocodile River in the N to the Valley of AIJALON and JOPPA in the S, a distance of about 50 mi. (80 km.), with a variable width of 9-10 mi. (14-16 km.). The relief is of Quaternary and Pleistocene origin, largely determined by ancient shorelines, sand-dune deposits, and the weathering of red sands that give a brilliant hue to much of its soil cover. The sand dunes, some of fossil character, tend to choke or divert the lower courses of the rivers, so that swampy conditions have tended to prevail in the past along the coast and valleys. It was here that SHITRAI the Sharonite supervised the flocks of King DAVID (1 Chr. 27:29). The "splendor" of Sharon (Isa. 35:2) suggests the dense vegetation originally associated with the whole plain. Its rich soil, now utilized extensively under irrigation for citrus groves and other commercial farming, formerly yielded beautiful covers of wild flowers. The "rose of Sharon" (Cant. 2:1) has been identified with various bulbous PLANTS. In Canaanite times, the chief town of Sharon was DOR (Josh. 11:2; 12:23; 1 Ki. 4:11). Sharon

Aerial view of the Sharon Plain, SW of Mt. Carmel, looking E.

is mentioned alongside LYDDA in the NT (Acts 9:35). See also LASHARON.

(2) Sharon was also the name of a pasture district E of the JORDAN (1 Chr. 5:16). It is referred to as among the possessions of GAD, along with GILEAD and BASHAN, but its precise location is unknown. Some think Sharon here may be a corruption of SIRION, the pasture lands of HERMON. Others believe it may be the "plateau" of Gilead between HESHBON and the ARNON Valley (Deut. 3:10). It is possible that the MOABITE STONE refers to this place.

Sharonite. shair'uh-nit. A description applied only to SHITRAI, DAVID's chief herdsman in the Plain of SHARON (1 Chr. 27:29).

Sharuhen. shuh-roo'huhn (Heb. *šārûḥen H9226*, from Egyp. *š-ra-ḥu-na*). One of the cities within the territory of JUDAH allotted to the tribe of SIMEON (Josh. 19:6). A comparison of the Simeonite list (19:1-9) with the Judahite list (ch. 15) indicates that Sharuhen may be identical with SHILHIM (15:32; see also SHAARAIM). The city was located in the extreme SW corner of Canaan. and is mentioned in various Egyptian texts. The identification of Sharuhen is debated. Modern Tell el-Farʿah (c. 12 mi./19 km. SE of GAZA) has been a popular proposal in the past, but many scholars

prefer a site closer to the coast, such as Tell el-ʿAjjul (c. 4 mi./6 km. SW of Gaza).

Shashai. shay'shi (Heb. *šāšay H9258*, derivation uncertain). One of the descendants of Binnui who agreed to put away their foreign wives (Ezra 10:40).

Shashak. shay'shak (Heb. *šāšāq H9265*, possibly an Egyp. name). Son of BERIAH (or of ELPAAL; cf. NRSV) and descendant of BENJAMIN, listed among the heads of families living in JERUSALEM (1 Chr. 8:14, 25; cf. v. 28). See also AHIO #2.

Shaul. shawl (Heb. *šāʾûl H8620*, "one who has been begged for" [cf. SAUL]; gentilic *šāʾûlî H8621*, "Shaulite"). **(1)** Son of Samlah; he was an early king of EDOM who lived in "Rehoboth on the river" (Gen. 36:37-38 [KJV, "Saul"]; 1 Chr. 1:48-49). See REHOBOTH #2.

(2) Son of SIMEON (by a Canaanite woman), grandson of JACOB, and ancestor of the Shaulite clan (Gen. 46:10; Exod. 6:15; Num. 26:13; 1 Chr. 4:24).

(3) Son of Uzziah, descendant of LEVI through KOHATH, and ancestor of SAMUEL (1 Chr. 6:24).

Shaveh. shay'vuh (Heb. *šāwēh H8753*, possibly "level [place]" or "wasteland"). A plain or valley near SALEM (Gen. 14:17). See discussion under KING'S VALLEY.

Shaveh Kiriathaim. shay´vuh-kihr-ee-uh-thay´im (Heb. *šāweh qiryātayim H8754*, prob. "plain of the [twin] cities"). The place where KEDORLAOMER defeated the EMITES (Gen. 14:5). Apparently it was a plain in the environs of KIRIATHAIM, a city in TRANSJORDAN.

shaving. Probably most Israelites, like ABSALOM, generally allowed their hair to grow for a considerable time before cutting it (2 Sam. 14:26). A BEARD was regarded as a natural accompaniment of manhood. The ceremonial law forbade priests to shave their heads on account of mourning (Lev. 21:5) or to adopt long flowing hair for the same reason (Ezek. 44:20). A NAZIRITE was not allowed to shave his head until the time covered by his vow expired (Num. 6:5) unless because of accidental defilement (6:9). In regard to the vows of SAMSON and SAMUEL, lifelong consecration was intended (Jdg. 13:5; 1 Sam. 1:11). The main biblical implications of shaving were (1) *cleansing* (e.g., Gen. 41:14; Lev. 14:8-9; Num. 8:7); (2) *mourning* (Deut. 21:12; Job 1:20; Jer. 7:29); (3) *vows* (Num. 6:18; Acts 18:18; 21:24); (4) *contempt* (2 Sam. 10:4; 1 Chr. 19:4); (5) *dishonor* (1 Cor. 11:5-6).

Shavsha. shav´shuh (Heb. *šawšā› H8807*, meaning uncertain, but possibly an Egyp. word). A royal secretary (see SCRIBE) in DAVID's court (1 Chr. 18:16). The need for such an office reflects the development of governmental affairs both domestic and foreign. There are variations of this man's name: SHEVA (2 Sam. 20:25), SERAIAH (2 Sam. 8:17), and SHISHA (1 Ki. 4:3). Many have thought that the spelling Shavsha is the original one. Others suggest that the man's true name was Seraiah and that the form Shisha (with its variants) reflects an Egyptian title. In SOLOMON's reign, two of this man's sons occupied the same office (1 Ki. 4:3).

sheaf. A handful of grain left behind the reaper (Jer. 9:22 NRSV), gathered and bound usually by children or women (Ruth 2:7, 15) in a joyous mood (Ps. 126:6; 129:7-8). Thus stacked the sheaves became dry and inflammable (Zech. 12:6; cf. Jdg. 15:1-5), but they made a beautiful sight (Song of Songs 7:2). A donkey (Neh. 13:15) or a heavily loaded cart (Amos 2:13) bore these bundles to the threshing floor (Ruth 3:6-7; Mic. 4:12). Some sheaves, however, were left behind for the poor (Deut. 24:19; cf. Ruth 2:7, 15; Job 24:10). The sheaf of the FIRSTFRUIT (Lev. 23:10-15; cf. 2 Chr. 31:5-10) typically represents (1) Christians, as representatives of a larger harvest (Rom. 16:5; 1 Cor. 16:15; Jas. 1:18), possessed by the Spirit (Rom. 8:23), and dedicated to God (Rev. 14:1-5) or (2) Christ, as an evidence of believers' later RESURRECTION (1 Cor. 15:20, 23).

Sheal. shee´uhl (Heb. *šě›āl H8627*, possibly "he has asked [*i.e.*, for a child]"). One of the descendants of Bani who agreed to put way their foreign wives in the time of EZRA (Ezra 10:29).

Shealtiel. shee-al´tee-uhl (Heb. *šě›altî›ēl H8630* and *šaltî›ēl H9003*, possibly "I have requested [a child] from God"; Gk. *Salathiēl G4886*). Also Salathiel (KJV in 1 Chr. 3:17 and NT; NRSV in Matt. 1:12). Eldest son of King JEHOIACHIN (Jeconiah) of Judah and father of ZERUBBABEL, the leader of the first group that returned from the Babylonian captivity (1 Chr. 3:17; Ezra 3:2 et al.; Neh. 12:1; Hag. 1:1 et al.). Shealtiel is included in the GENEALOGY OF JESUS CHRIST (Matt. 1:12; Lk. 3:27; on the latter passage, see NERI).

Sheariah. shee´uh-ri´uh (Heb. *šě›aryâ H9138*, perhaps "Yahweh has acknowledged"). Son of Azel and descendant of BENJAMIN in the line of SAUL (1 Chr. 8:38; 9:44).

shearing house. See BETH EKED.

Shear-Jashub. shee´uhr-jay´shuhb (Heb. *šě›ār yāšûb H8639*, "a remnant will return"). Son of the prophet ISAIAH (Isa. 7:3; cf. 10:21-22). Shear-Jashub was present when Isaiah confronted King AHAZ, and his name is symbolical of the message the prophet delivered. Judgment in the form of the EXILE was an essential aspect of Isaiah's message, but there was also the promise of restoration for a purified REMNANT.

Sheba. shee´buh (Heb. *šěbā› H8644*, meaning uncertain; for ##5-7 below, the form is *šeba‹ H8680* [2 Sam. 20:1-22; 1 Chr. 5:13; *H8681* in Josh. 19:2],

S

"seven," possibly suggesting "completeness"). **(1)** Son of Raamah, descendant of CUSH, and brother of DEDAN (Gen. 10:7; 1 Chr. 1:9). See #3, below.

(2) Son of JOKTAN and descendant of SHEM (Gen. 10:28; 1 Chr. 1:22). See #3, below.

(3) Son of JOKSHAN, descendant of ABRAHAM and KETURAH, and brother of Dedan (Gen. 25:3; 1 Chr. 1:32). Many have argued that this must be the same person as #1 and/or #2 above because (a) all three are associated with names connected with ARABIA, (b) the first and third have Dedan as a brother, and (c) the second and third are in the line of Shem. That the first one is in the line of Cush and HAM may indicate the close relationship between the S Arabians and Africans (Hamites). It is widely thought that the name Sheba is primarily a geographical term, as follows.

(4) A country in S Arabia, now Yemen, the most mountainous and fertile part of Arabia. The biblical writers probably regarded the person Sheba (#3?) as the source of this country's name and the progenitor of its people, the SABEANS. This country gained wealth through control of the trade in perfumes and incense, which were important in the life and religion of the ancient world. Camel caravans from Sheba (Job 6:19) carried northward to the MEDITERRANEAN countries the gold, precious stones, and frankincense of S Arabia (Isa. 60:6; Jer. 6:20; Ezek. 27:22). The capital of Sheba was first Sirwaḥ and then Marib. In the tenth century B.C. the queen of Sheba visited SOLOMON (1 Ki. 10:1-13; 2 Chr. 9:1-12). Her camel caravan brought typical products of Sheba: gold, precious stones, and spices, which she exchanged with Solomon. The country also played a role in Israel's expectations for the future. It was hoped that Sheba would give gifts to the king of Israel (Ps. 72:10, 15) and praise to the God of Israel (Isa. 60:6).

(5) A town within the tribal territory of SIMEON (Josh. 19:2). Sheba is missing in the parallel list (1 Chr. 4:28); moreover, if it is included in Joshua, the total comes to fourteen towns instead of thirteen (as stated in Josh. 19:6). Thus the NIV and other versions translate "or Sheba," indicating that this is an alternate name for BEERSHEBA. A few have thought that Sheba and Beersheba were parts of the same city. Still others emend Sheba to Shema (on the basis of the similar list in Josh. 15:26). See SHEMA (PLACE).

(6) Son of BICRI; he is known for having revolted against DAVID (2 Sam. 20:1-22). Sheba's revolt appealed to followers of SAUL's family, since he was from the tribe of BENJAMIN and perhaps a relative of Saul. Also he appealed to all northern Israelites with his rallying cry, "We have no share in David, / no part in Jesse's son! / Every man to his tents, O Israel!" (2 Sam. 20:1), a cry that was repeated later in JEROBOAM's rebellion (1 Ki. 12:16). JOAB and the royal bodyguard pursued Sheba until he took refuge in ABEL BETH MAACAH in the northernmost part of Israel. Joab besieged the city until the inhabitants decapitated Sheba and threw his head over the city wall to Joab.

(7) Son of Abihail; he was one of seven relatives from the tribe of GAD who occupied the region E of GILEAD (1 Chr. 5:13; cf. vv. 10, 14).

Shebah. See SHIBAH.

Shebam. See SIBMAH.

Shebaniah. sheb´uh-ni´uh (Heb. *šĕbanyāhû* H8677 [only 1 Chr. 15:24] and *šĕbanyâ* H8676, perhaps "Yahweh has drawn near"). **(1)** One of the priests appointed to blow the trumpet when DAVID transferred the ARK OF THE COVENANT to JERUSALEM (1 Chr. 15:24).

(2) One of the postexilic LEVITES who led worship when the Feast of Tabernacles was celebrated (Neh. 9:4-5). He is probably the same as either #4 or #5 below.

(3) A priest who signed the covenant with NEHEMIAH (Neh. 10:4). In the days of the high priest JOIAKIM, the head of Shebaniah's family was a man named Joseph (12:14 KJV and most versions, following MT); here the NIV, following some Heb. MSS and ancient versions, has SHECANIAH (which harmonizes with v. 3).

(4-5) Two Levites who signed the covenant with Nehemiah (Neh. 10:10, 12). One of them should probably be identified with #2 above.

Shebarim. sheb´uh-rim (Heb. *šĕbārîm* H8696, prob. pl. of *šeber* H8691, "fracture, crushing"). A place cited in connection with the retreat of the Israelites from AI (Josh. 7:5 KJV and other versions). It evidently lay somewhere between Ai and JERICHO, but the location is unknown. Some ancient versions understood *šĕbārîm* not as a name but as a common term, indicating that the men of Ai pursued the Israelites "until they broke [*i.e.*, vanquished] them" (cf. NAB, "until they broke ranks"). Similarly, modern scholars have suggested such renderings as "to the broken city walls" and "as far as the stone quarries" (the latter adopted by NIV).

Shebat. shee'bat (Heb. *šĕbāṭ H8658*, from Akk. *šabāṭu*). The eleventh month in the Hebrew CALENDAR, corresponding to January-February (Zech. 1:7; KJV, "Sebat").

Sheber. shee'buhr (Heb. *šeber H8693*, meaning uncertain). Son of CALEB (by his concubine MAACAH), included in the genealogy of JUDAH (1 Chr. 2:48).

Shebna, Shebnah. sheb'nuh (Heb. *šebnâ H8675*, also *šebnāʾ H8674* [2 Ki. 18:26, 37], possibly short form of SHEBANIAH, "Yahweh has drawn near"). In one passage (Isa. 22:15) Shebna is described as a "steward" and as being "in charge of the palace," evidently a very high and influential position that may have included authority over the standing army. In this passage, the Lord accuses him of pride and predicts his fall (vv. 16-19). Elsewhere, however, ELIAKIM son of Hilkiah is said to be the palace administrator, while Shebna appears as royal secretary (see SCRIBE); the two of them were part of the delegation sent by King HEZEKIAH to meet the emissaries of SENNACHERIB (2 Ki. 18:18, 26, 37; 19:2 = Isa. 36:3, 11, 22; 37:2). It appears that Shebna was demoted from his high position and that Eliakim replaced him (cf. Isa. 8:20-22). Given his unusual name, as well as the fact that his father's name is not mentioned, it is possible that Shebna was a foreigner. (According to some scholars, the Shebna of Isa. 22 should be distinguished from the one mentioned in the other passages, but it is most improbable that there were two officials of the same name, both without any "pedigree," holding one or other of the two most responsible state offices, in the same general period.)

Shebuel. See SHUBAEL.

Shecaniah. shek'uh-ni'uh (Heb. *šĕkanyāhû H8909* [only 2 Chr. 24:11; 31:15] and *šĕkanyâ H8908*, "Yahweh dwells"). TNIV Shekaniah. **(1)** Postexilic descendant of DAVID in the line of ZERUBBABEL (1 Chr. 3:21-22). The NRSV and other versions, following the SEPTUAGINT, understand Shecaniah to be the son of Obadiah (see REPHAIAH #1). This Shecaniah is to be identified with the father (or ancestor) of HATTUSH (Ezra 8:3) and of SHEMAIAH (Neh. 3:29).

(2) A descendant of AARON whose family in the time of DAVID made up the tenth division of priests (1 Chr. 24:11).

(3) A LEVITE who faithfully assisted KORE in distributing the contributions made to the TEMPLE during the reign of HEZEKIAH (2 Chr. 31:15).

(4) Son of Jahaziel; he and 300 members of his family returned with EZRA from Babylonia to Jerusalem in the reign of ARTAXERXES (Ezra 8:5; according to 1 Esd. 8:32 [KJV, "Sechenias"], the family descended from ZATTU, and this reading is adopted in Ezra 8:5 by the NIV and other versions).

(5) Son of Jehiel and descendant of Elam (Ezra 10:2). He acted as spokesman for the large congregation whose conscience on the subject of mixed marriages had been stirred by Ezra. Shecaniah confessed the national sin, expressed the nation's hope, suggested that a covenant be made before the Lord to eliminate the evil of intermarriage, and encouraged Ezra to take the lead in this reform. Since his name does not appear in the list of Ezra 10:18-44, it is possible that he was not personally guilty.

(6) Son of Arah and father-in-law of TOBIAH the Ammonite, NEHEMIAH's sworn adversary (Neh. 6:18).

(7) One of the priests and Levites who returned from exile with ZERUBBABEL (Neh. 12:3). Later, in the days of the high priest JOIAKIM, a certain Joseph was the head of his family (v. 14 NIV, following some ancient witnesses; see SHEBANIAH #3).

Shechem (person). shek'uhm (Heb. *šĕkem H8902* and *šekem H8903* [Num. 26:31; Josh. 17:2; 1 Chr. 7:19], probably from the corresponding place name meaning "shoulder, ridge"; gentilic *šikmî H8904*, "Shechemite"). **(1)** Son of HAMOR the HIVITE; Shechem raped DINAH, the daughter of JACOB, and was killed by SIMEON and LEVI

(Gen. 34:2-26; Josh. 24:32; Jdg. 9:28). See further SHECHEM (PLACE).

(2) Son of GILEAD, great-grandson of MANASSEH, and eponymous ancestor of the Shechemite clan (Num. 26:31). Elsewhere, however, "the sons of Shechem" (Josh. 17:2 Heb.) are listed with other Manassite clans as receiving an inheritance W of the JORDAN, in distinction from the Gileadites, who were granted territory in TRANSJORDAN. See also #3 below.

(3) Son of SHEMIDA and descendant of Manasseh (1 Chr. 7:19). Some argue that this Shechem is really Shemida's brother (cf. Num. 26:31-32) and therefore the same as #2 above.

Shechem (place). shek´uhm (Heb. *šĕkem H8901*, "shoulder, ridge"; Gk. *Sychem G5374*). KJV also Sichem (Gen. 12:6; Sir. 50:26) and Sychem (Acts 7:16). An ancient Canaanite town in the hill country of Ephraim (Josh. 20:7; see EPHRAIM, HILL COUNTRY OF) in the neighborhood of Mount GERIZIM (Jdg. 9:7), being about 30 mi. (50 km.) N of JERUSALEM, just E of modern Nablus. It became an important Israelite political and religious center. The site is known today as Tell Balaṭah.

The city of Shechem makes its initial appearance in biblical history as the first place in CANAAN to be mentioned in connection with the arrival of Abram (ABRAHAM) in the land. Here the Lord appeared to Abram and promised the land to his descendants; Abram responded by building an altar (Gen. 12:6-7). When JACOB returned from PADDAN ARAM, he settled down at Shechem and purchased land from the sons of Hamor (33:18-19; Josh. 24:32). In Gen. 33-34 it is seen that Shechem was the name of the city and also of the prince of the city. It appears that the names Shechem and HAMOR are hereditary names or perhaps a kind of title (cf. Jdg. 9:28). While Jacob was at Shechem the unfortunate incident of DINAH occurred; and SIMEON and LEVI, her full brothers, exacted drastic revenge on the city (Gen. 34). Later the brothers of Joseph were herding Jacob's flock at Shechem when JOSEPH was sent to check on their welfare (37:12-14). The city is not referred to again until the listing of the tribal divisions of the land after the conquest (Josh. 17:7); Shechem was in the territory allotted to Ephraim. It was selected by JOSHUA as

one of the cities of refuge (Josh. 20:7; 21:21; 1 Chr. 6:67). Joshua gave his farewell address here (Josh. 24:1) and made a covenant with the people (24:25). Joseph was buried in the plot of ground that his father Jacob had purchased here (Josh. 24:32).

One of the interesting personages in the kaleidoscopic history of Judges, ABIMELECH, the son of GIDEON and a CONCUBINE, is closely associated with Shechem. Abimelech conspired with his mother's relatives to kill all the other sons of Gideon and to have himself made king of Shechem (Jdg. 9:6). Trouble developed between Abimelech and the inhabitants of the city; a conspiracy against Abimelech was revealed to him by the ruler of the city. In the fighting that followed, Abimelech took the city and completely destroyed it. When a number of people took final refuge in the stronghold of the temple of BAAL-BERITH (or EL-BERITH), Abimelech gathered fuel and fired the stronghold, so that about 1,000 persons perished in the conflagration (9:46-49).

After the death of SOLOMON, his son REHOBOAM went to Shechem to be made king by all ISRAEL (1 Ki. 12:1; 2 Chr. 10:1); when the principles of his prospective administration were challenged by JEROBOAM, Rehoboam followed the disastrous

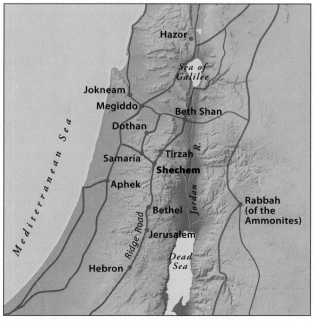

Shechem's importance is closely linked to its position on the central Ridge Road in Palestine.

Excavation remains of ancient Shechem (Tell Balaṭah) with Mt. Gerizim in the background.

advice of his impetuous, youthful counselors and thus caused the rupture of the kingdom. Jeroboam became king of ten tribes and "fortified Shechem in the hill country of Ephraim" (1 Ki. 12:25) as his capital. The city is mentioned in parallel passages in the Psalms (Ps. 60:6; 108:7) and is named in a list of prophetic condemnations against Israel (Hos. 6:9). After the destruction of Jerusalem, men from Shechem and other cities came to MIZPAH to be under the protection of GEDALIAH and there were deceived and murdered by ISHMAEL (Jer. 41:5). The city is not certainly mentioned again in the Bible, but the conversation of Jesus and the Samaritan woman (Jn. 4) occurred in this vicinity (see SYCHAR). In A.D. 72 the city was rebuilt as Flavia Neapolis, from which the name of the present village of Nablus is derived.

The name Shechem occurs in historical records and other sources outside PALESTINE. It is mentioned as a city captured by Senusert III of Egypt (19th cent. B.C.) and appears in the Egyptian cursing texts of about the same time. "The mountain of Shechem" is referred to incidentally in a satirical letter of the 19th dynasty of EGYPT. Shechem also figures in the AMARNA Letters; its ruler, Labʾayu, and his sons are accused of acting against Egypt, though the ruler protests that he is devotedly loyal to the pharaoh.

Archaeological work at Tell Balaṭah has produced some important results. In the first campaign a triple gate of Middle Bronze date was found in the NW section of the city; nearby, unearthed in 1926, was a large temple that has been identified as the temple of Baal-Berith. Also in 1926 the eastern gate of the city was found, along with part of the city wall. Middle Bronze Shechem had a fine battered (sloping) wall of large, undressed stones, found standing to a maximum height of 32 ft. (10 m.), with some of its stones over 6.5 ft. (2 m.) long. HYKSOS-type fortifications also occur at Shechem, with ramparts of beaten earth. Several cuneiform tablets of the Amarna Age add to the store of written materials from Palestine. In 1934 a limestone plaque bearing a representation of a serpent goddess and an inscription in alphabetic script was found. Additional archaeological work was done from 1956 to 1973. It is of great interest that the excavators conclude that the temple of Baal-Berith (Jdg. 9:4), "Beth Millo" (v. 6), and the "tower" (v. 46) are designations of the same temple-citadel structure.

Shechinah. See SHEKINAH.

Shedeur. shed´ee-uhr (Heb. *šĕdêʾûr H8725*, prob. "SHADDAI is light"). Father of ELIZUR; the latter was a leader of the tribe of Reuben at the time of Moses (Num. 1:5; 2:10; 7:30, 35; 10:18).

sheep. See animals.

sheepcote, sheepfold. See sheep pen.

Sheep Gate. The easternmost entrance into the N side of the ancient city of Jerusalem (Neh. 12:39; Jn. 5:2). The Sheep Gate marked the terminus in the circuit of the walls, as rebuilt in 444 B.C. and as recorded by Nehemiah (Neh. 3:1, 32). Almost five centuries later Christ healed the man who had been lame for thirty-eight years at the neighboring pool of Bethesda (or Beth-zatha, Jn. 5:2-9). This in turn confirms the location of the Sheep Gate. Pilgrim reports of the fourth Christian century, the mosaic map from Medeba, and modern excavation of the large double pools by the Church of St. Anne unite to confirm the NE location of Bethesda and hence of the gate.

sheepmaster. See occupations and professions.

sheep pen, sheepfold. An enclosure intended for the protection of sheep and also to keep them from wandering out and getting lost. These folds were simple walled enclosures, usually without roofs, with the walls covered with thorns to keep out robbers. Several flocks would usually pass the night in one fold under the care of a shepherd who guarded the door. Each shepherd knew his own sheep and was known by them. (See Jn. 10:1-6.)

sheepshearer. See occupations and professions.

sheepskin. A simple garment made from the tanned pelt of sheep. It may well be that the sheepskin, still an ordinary article of dress in the E, was the initial covering of Adam and Eve in the Garden of Eden (Gen. 3:21). It was the common dress of the prophets of Israel, and this "hairy mantle" (Zech. 13:4 NRSV) was one of their distinctive marks. The Lord warned his followers against impostors who borrowed this dress when he said: "Watch out for false prophets. They come to you in sheep's clothing" (Matt. 7:15). The material was also used as covering for the tabernacle (Num. 4:25). See skin.

Sheerah. shee´uh-ruh (Heb. *šeʾĕrâ H8641*, perhaps "relative, descendant"). KJV Sherah. Daughter of Ephraim (according to some, of Beriah); she is credited with having built Lower and Upper Beth Horon as well as an otherwise unknown town

Sheepfold located in the hills near Nazareth.

© Dr. James C. Martin

S

called UZZEN SHEERAH (1 Chr. 7:24). No other woman in the Bible is said to have founded a town.

sheet. A large piece of linen (Acts 10:11; 11:5). In Jdg. 14:12-13 "sheets" in KJV probably means "linen undergarments," though NIV has merely "linen garments" (cf. Prov. 31:24).

Shehariah. shee´huh-ri´uh (Heb. *šĕḥaryâ H8843*, possibly "Yahweh is dawning" [cf. Isa. 60:2 and see SHAHAR]). Son of Jehoram and descendant of BENJAMIN; he is listed among the heads of families who lived in Jerusalem (1 Chr. 8:26).

Shekaniah. shek´uh-ni´uh. TNIV form of SHECANIAH.

shekel. See MONEY; WEIGHTS AND MEASURES.

Shekinah. shuh-ki´nuh (Heb. *šĕkinâ* [from *šākan H8905*, "to dwell"], "dwelling, residence"; in Aram. the word appears also in the form *šĕkîntāʾ*). A postbiblical term applied especially to the divine presence. The concept is alluded to in passages that refer to God's GLORY (Isa. 60:2; Rom. 9:4). MOSES calls this the "cloud" in Exod. 14:19. Its first appearance occurred for a twofold purpose when ISRAEL was being led by Moses out of EGYPT. It hid the Israelites from the pursuing Egyptians and lighted the way at night for Israel (Exod. 13:21; 14:19-20). To the Egyptians it was a cloud of darkness, but to Israel a cloud of light. It later covered SINAI when God spoke with Moses (24:15-18), filled the TABERNACLE (40:34-35), guided Israel (40:36-38), filled Solomon's TEMPLE (2 Chr. 7:1), and was seen in connection with Christ's ministry in the NT (Matt. 17:5; Acts 1:9).

Shelah (person). shee´luh (Heb. *šelaḥ H8941*, possibly "offshoot"; gentilic *šēlānî H8989*, "Shelanite"; Gk. *Sala G4885*). KJV also Salah, NT Sala. (1) Son (or descendant) of ARPHAXAD and more distant descendant of SHEM (Gen. 10:24; 11:12-15; 1 Chr. 1:18, 24); included in Luke's GENEALOGY OF JESUS CHRIST (Lk. 3:35, where Shelah is listed as son of CAINAN, following the LXX). (2) Son of JUDAH (by his Canaanite wife), grandson of JACOB, and ancestor of the Shelanite

clan (Gen. 38:5; 46:12; Num. 26:20; 1 Chr. 2:3; 4:21; the gentilic SHILONITE in 1 Chr. 9:5 and Neh. 11:5 is widely thought to be a textual corruption of "Shelanite"). Shelah was promised in marriage to Judah's widowed daughter-in-law, TAMAR, but Judah failed to keep his promise (vv. 11, 14, 26).

Shelah, Pool of. shee´luh (Heb. *šelaḥ H8940*, perhaps "canal"). A reservoir in JERUSALEM, near the FOUNTAIN GATE and the KING'S GARDEN; its wall was repaired by the ruler of the district of Mizpah, SHALLUN son of Col-Hozeh (Neh. 3:15 NRSV). It is thought by many to be identical with the King's Pool (2:14) and with the Lower Pool (Isa. 22:9). While some identify it with the Pool of SILOAM (so NIV; similarly KJV ["Siloah"; cf. Isa. 8:6, "Shiloah"]), others regard it as a separate reservoir in the complex water system of JERUSALEM that was fed by the Spring of GIHON. The NJPS interprets the word not as a name but as a common noun and renders, "the irrigation pool."

Shelanite. See SHELAH.

Shelemiah. shel´uh-mi´uh (Heb. *šelemyāhû H8983* and *šelemyâ H8982*, "Yahweh has repaid [*or* replaced]"). (1) A LEVITE who was responsible for the EAST GATE (1 Chr. 26:14). His full name was MESHELEMIAH (1 Chr. 9:21; 26:1-2, 9).

(2-3) Two of the descendants of Binnui who agreed to put away their foreign wives (Ezra 10:39, 41).

(4) Father of Hananiah; the latter, along with Hanun son of Zalaph, was in charge of repairing the portion of the JERUSALEM wall above the HORSE GATE (Neh. 3:30).

(5) A priest who, along with others, was appointed by NEHEMIAH to oversee the collection and distribution of tithes for the support of the Levites (Neh. 13:13).

(6) Son of CUSHI and grandfather of JEHUDI; the latter was the official sent to BARUCH, instructing him to bring to the court the scroll on which were written the prophecies of JEREMIAH (Jer. 36:14).

(7) Son of Abdeel; he was one of three men commanded by King JEHOIAKIM to seize Baruch and Jeremiah, a mission that proved unsuccessful (Jer. 36:26).

(8) Father of JEHUCAL; the latter and a priest were sent by King ZEDEKIAH to Jeremiah to ask the prophet to pray for him and the people (Jer. 37:3; subsequently Jehucal [Jucal] joined others in recommending the death sentence for Jeremiah, 38:1-4).

(9) Father of Irijah; the latter was a sentry who seized Jeremiah on suspicion of deserting to the Babylonians during a temporary lifting of the siege (Jer. 37:13).

Sheleph. shee'lif (Heb. *šelep H8991*, meaning uncertain). Son of JOKTAN and grandson of EBER, listed in the Table of Nations (Gen. 10:26; 1 Chr. 1:20). Many think Sheleph is a tribal name, referring to a group in S ARABIA otherwise known by the name of as-Salif (or as-Sulaf).

Shelesh. shee'lish (Heb. *šēleš H8994*, possibly "gentle"). Son of Helem; listed among the brave warriors who were heads of families of the tribe of ASHER (1 Chr. 7:35; cf. v. 40).

Shelomi. shi-loh'mi (Heb. *šēlōmî H8979*, possibly "my peace"). Father of Ahihud, from the tribe of ASHER; the latter was among the leaders appointed to divide the land of CANAAN among the tribes (Num. 34:27).

Shelomith. shi-loh'mith (Heb. *šēlōmît H8984* [male] and *šēlōmît H8985* [female], possibly "at peace" or "complete"). Sometimes confused with SHELOMOTH, which according to some scholars is the original male form of the name. **(1)** Daughter of Dibri, from the tribe of DAN. Shelomith's unnamed son (by an Egyptian father), following a quarrel with another Israelite, blasphemed the divine name and was subsequently stoned to death (Lev. 24:11).

(2) Daughter of ZERUBBABEL and descendant of DAVID (1 Chr. 3:19); she is the only woman listed in this genealogy.

(3) Son of Shimei and descendant of LEVI through GERSHON (1 Chr. 23:9 KJV and NJPS, following the *Qere*; NIV and NRSV, "Shelomoth").

(4) Son of Izhar and also a Gershonite (1 Chr. 23:18; called "Shelomoth" in 24:22).

(5) Son of Zicri and descendant of MOSES; he was in charge of all the spoils of war and other gifts dedi-

cated to the maintenance of the sanctuary (1 Chr. 26:25-28, following the *Qere*; NRSV, "Shelomoth").

(6) Son of REHOBOAM (by his favorite wife MAACAH) and descendant of DAVID (2 Chr. 11:20).

(7) Son of Josiphiah; he was family head of the descendants of BANI who returned with EZRA from EXILE (Ezra 8:10 NIV and NRSV, following LXX and 1 Esd. 8:36). The MT omits the name Bani, yielding the translation, "of the descendants of Shelomith: the son of Josiphiah, and with him 160 men" (cf. KJV and NJPS).

Shelomoth. shi-loh'moth (Heb. *šēlōmôt H8977*, possibly "at peace" or "complete"). Sometimes confused with SHELOMITH. **(1)** Son of Shimei and descendant of LEVI through GERSHON (1 Chr. 23:9 NIV and NRSV, following the *Ketib*; KJV and NJPS, "Shelomith").

(2) Son of Izhar and also a Gershonite (1 Chr. 24:22; called "Shelomith" in 23:18).

(3) Son of Zicri and descendant of MOSES; he was in charge of all the spoils of war and other gifts dedicated to the maintenance of the sanctuary (1 Chr. 26:25-28 NRSV, following the *Ketib*; KJV and NIV, "Shelomith").

Shelumiel. shi-loo'mee-uhl (Heb. *šēlumî>ēl H8981*, "God is my peace [*i.e.*, salvation]"). Son of Zurishaddai; he was a leader from the tribe of SIMEON, heading a division of 59,300 (Num. 2:12; 10:19). Shelumiel was among those who assisted MOSES in taking a census of the Israelites (1:6) and who brought offerings to the Lord for the dedication of the TABERNACLE (7:36-41). See also SALAMIEL.

Shem. shem (Heb. *šēm H9006*, possibly "name [*i.e.*, esteemed]" or, like Akk. *šummum*, "son, offspring" [perhaps short form of a theophoric name such as SHEMUEL]; Gk. *Sēm G4954*). Son of NOAH, possibly his firstborn (Gen. 5:32 et al.; 1 Chr. 1:4 et al.); included in Luke's GENEALOGY OF JESUS CHRIST (Lk. 3:36; KJV, "Sem"). Shem evidently was born ninety-eight years before the FLOOD and lived to the age of 600 (Gen. 11:10-11). In the prophecy that Noah made after the episode of his drunkenness (9:25-27), he mentioned "the LORD, the God of Shem," and added that Japheth's descendants would "live in the tents of Shem," suggesting that

S

the Aryan peoples to a large extent have derived their civilization from the Semites. Shem is considered the ancestor of the peoples known as the SEMITES. The Table of Nations gives additional details concerning Shem's descendants (Gen. 10:21-31; 1 Chr. 1:17-27). His sons ELAM, ASSHUR, ARPHAXAD, LUD, and ARAM are identified in the earlier Bible geographies as ancestral to the lands of PERSIA, ASSYRIA, CHALDEA (prob.), LYDIA, and SYRIA, respectively. (The MT at 1 Chr. 1:17 adds four additional sons of Shem, but the NIV, following some Gk. MSS and Gen. 10:23, identifies them as sons of Aram.) This genealogical information corresponds generally, but not fully, to known historical affinities among the peoples of the ANE.

Shema (person). shee′muh (Heb. *šemaʿ H9050*, prob. short form of SHEMAIAH, "Yahweh has heard"). **(1)** Son of HEBRON and descendant of CALEB, included in the genealogy of JUDAH (1 Chr. 2:43-44). Many of the names in this passage refer to places, and Shema could be the name of a Judahite settlement; see SHEMA (PLACE).

(2) Son of Joel and descendant of REUBEN (1 Chr. 5:8); it is possible that Shema in this verse should be identified with SHEMAIAH, or perhaps with SHIMEI, both of whom are mentioned as descendants of Joel earlier in the passage (v. 4). See also JOEL #5.

(3) Son of ELPAAL and descendant of BENJAMIN; he and his brother BERIAH, heads of families in AIJALON, put to flight the inhabitants of GATH (1 Chr. 8:13). This Shema is apparently the same as the Shimei mentioned later in this genealogy (v. 21).

(4) One of the prominent men who stood near EZRA when the law was read at the great assembly (Neh. 8:4).

Shema (place). shee′muh (Heb. *šěmaʿ H9054*, meaning uncertain). One of "the southernmost towns of the tribe of Judah in the Negev toward the boundary of Edom" (Josh. 15:26). Some scholars emend Shema to Sheba on the basis of a partially parallel passage that includes the latter name among Simeonite towns within Judahite territory (Josh. 19:2); see SHEBA #5. Others identify Shema with the "son" of Hebron (1 Chr. 2:43); see SHEMA

(PERSON) #1. In any case, the location of this town is not known.

Shema, the. shuh-mah′. Name give to the confession found in Deut. 6:4-9 (followed in SYNAGOGUE services by 11:13-21 and Num. 15:37-41). This designation derives from the first word of the passage, *šěmaʿ*, "Hear!" (imperative form of the verb *šāmaʿ H9048*).

Shemaah. shi-may′uh (Heb. *šěmāʿâ H9057*, occurring with the definite article, *haššěmāʿâ*, suggesting that the form should be emended to *yěhôšāmāʿ*, "Yahweh has heard"). A man from GIBEAH whose two sons, AHIEZER and Joash (JEHOASH), were among the ambidextrous relatives of SAUL who joined DAVID's forces at ZIKLAG (1 Chr. 12:3; cf. v. 1). On the basis of the primary SEPTUAGINT witnesses and a few Hebrew MSS, the plural "sons" is often emended to "son"; if the singular reading is original, then Shamaah was the father only of Joash.

Shemaiah. shi-may′yuh (Heb. *šěmaʿyāhû H9062* and *šěmaʿyâ H9061*, "Yahweh has heard"). One of the most common biblical names, borne especially by PRIESTS and LEVITES; in some cases it is difficult to distinguish between them. **(1)** Son of Shecaniah and descendant of DAVID in the line of ZERUBBABEL (1 Chr. 3:22).

(2) Descendant of SIMEON and ancestor of Ziza; the latter was one of the clan leaders in the time of HEZEKIAH who invaded the land of the Hamites and the Meunites (1 Chr. 4:37; cf. vv. 38-41).

(3) Son of Joel and descendant of REUBEN (1 Chr. 5:4; possibly the same as SHEMA in v. 8).

(4) Son of Hasshub and descendant of LEVI through MERARI; listed among those who resettled in JERUSALEM after the EXILE (1 Chr. 9:14) and among the heads of the Levites "who had charge of the outside work of the house of God" (Neh. 11:15).

(5) Son of Galal, also a Merarite, whose son Obadiah is included among those who resettled in Jerusalem (1 Chr. 9:16); he is evidently the same as SHAMMUA father of Abda (Neh. 11:17).

(6) Head of a Levitical family descended from ELIZAPHAN, listed among those who helped to bring the ARK OF THE COVENANT to Jerusalem in the reign of DAVID (1 Chr. 15:8, 11).

(7) Son of Nethanel; he was a Levitical scribe who recorded the results of King David's choice by lot of those who would serve in the twenty-four priestly divisions (1 Chr. 24:6).

(8) Firstborn son of OBED-EDOM; he and his brothers belonged to the division of the gatekeepers, and Shamaiah's sons "were leaders in their father's family because they were very capable men" (1 Chr. 26:4, 6-7).

(9) A "man of God" or prophet who advised REHOBOAM not to take military action against JEROBOAM and the ten northern tribes that seceded (1 Ki. 12:22-24 = 2 Chr. 11:2-4). Rehoboam was later the subject of another word from the Lord through Shemaiah, who predicted the king's defeat at the hand of SHISHAK, pharaoh of Egypt (2 Chr. 12:5-8). Along with IDDO the seer, Shemaiah was also a chronicler of the life of Rehoboam (12:15).

(10) One of six Levites whom King JEHOSHAPHAT sent to teach the law in the cities of JUDAH (2 Chr. 17:8). Appointed to the same mission were a number of princes and priests.

(11) Descendant of JEDUTHUN the musician; he and his brother UZZIEL were among the Levites assigned to consecrate the temple in the days of HEZEKIAH (2 Chr. 29:14).

(12) A Levite who faithfully assisted KORE in distributing the contributions made to the TEMPLE during the reign of HEZEKIAH (2 Chr. 31:15).

(13) A leader of the Levites during the reign of King JOSIAH; along with his brothers CONANIAH and NETHANEL, Shemaiah provided 5,000 offerings (lambs) and five head of cattle for the renewed celebration of the Passover (2 Chr. 35:9).

(14) Descendant of Adonikam and and a family head who returned with EZRA from BABYLON (Ezra 8:13).

(15) One of a group of leaders sent by EZRA to Iddo to get attendants for the house of God (Ezra 8:16).

(16) One of the priests descended from Harim who agreed to put away their foreign wives (Ezra 10:21).

(17) Another man in the line of Harim, evidently not the same as #16 above, but an ordinary Israelite, who had also married a foreign wife (Ezra 10:31).

(18) Son of Shecaniah; he was a priest who guarded the EAST GATE and who made repairs to the wall in front of his house (Neh. 3:29).

(19) Son of Delaiah; he was a hired prophet sent by TOBIAH and SANBALLAT to intimidate NEHEMIAH and so hinder progress on the rebuilding of the wall (Neh. 6:10). The fear of assassination was calculated to cause Nehemiah to flee into the temple, a forbidden act, and so bring reproach upon him in the eyes of the people, and perhaps divine wrath as well. Nehemiah wisely refused this ploy (vv. 11-13).

(20) One of the priests who participated with Nehemiah in the sealing of the covenant at the dedication of the wall (Neh. 10:8). He is probably the same Shemaiah mentioned in connection with the coming of Zerubbabel to Jerusalem (12:6). In the days of the high priest JOIAKIM, Jehonathan was the head of Shemaiah's priestly family (12:18).

(21) A priest who took part in one of the choirs at the dedication of the wall (Neh. 12:34).

(22) Descendant of ASAPH and grandfather of Zechariah; the latter was a musician who participated in the dedication of the wall (Neh. 12:35).

(23) Another musician who participated in the dedication of the wall (Neh. 12:36).

(24) A priest or Levite who participated in the choir at the dedication of the wall (Neh. 12:42).

(25) Father of a prophet named URIAH, from KIRIATH JEARIM. He prophesied against Jerusalem in the time of King JEHOIAKIM, who sought his life. Uriah, however, escaped to Egypt, but he was brought back and executed by Jehoiakim (Jer. 26:20-23).

(26) A NEHELAMITE who was a false prophet; JEREMIAH pronounced judgment upon him and predicted the extinction of his family (Jer. 29:24-32).

(27) Father of Delaiah; the latter was one of the officials who witnessed Jehoiakim's burning of the scroll containing the words of Jeremiah (Jer. 36:12).

Shemariah. shem´uh-ri´uh (Heb. *šĕmaryāhû* *H9080* [only 1 Chr. 12:5, MT 12:6] and *šĕmaryâ* *H9079*, "Yahweh has watched over"). **(1)** One of the ambidextrous Benjamite warriors who joined DAVID while he was in exile from SAUL at the PHILISTINE city of ZIKLAG (1 Chr. 12:5; cf. v. 2).

S

(2) Son of King REHOBOAM by his first wife MAHALATH (2 Chr. 11:19; KJV, "Shamariah").

(3) One of the descendants of Harim who agreed to put away their foreign wives in the time of EZRA (Ezra 10:32).

(4) One of the descendants of Binnui who agreed to put away their foreign wives (Ezra 10:41).

Shemeber. shem-ee´buhr (Heb. *šem²ēber H9008*, meaning uncertain). The king of ZEBOIIM (Gen. 14:2); he and four other kings were defeated in the Valley of Siddim by KEDORLAOMER and his allies.

Shemed. shee´mid (Heb. *šemed H9013*, derivation uncertain). Son of ELPAAL and descendant of BENJAMIN; he is credited with having built ONO and LOD (1 Chr. 8:12; KJV, "Shamed").

Shemer. shee´muhr (Heb. *šemer H9070*, possibly short form of SHEMARIAH, "Yahweh has watched over"). **(1)** Owner of a hill purchased by King OMRI as the site for a city; the king called it SAMARIA (Heb. *šōmĕrôn H9076*) after Shemer (1 Ki. 16:24).

(2) Son of Mahli, descendant of LEVI through MERARI, and ancestor of the musician ETHAN (1 Chr. 6:46).

(3) An Asherite (1 Chr. 7:34 NRSV). See SHOMER.

Shemida. shi-mi´duh (Heb. *šemîdāᶜ H9026*, possibly "the Name [*i.e.*, God] has understood"; gentilic *šemîdāᶜî H9027*, "Shemidaite"). Son of GILEAD, grandson of MANASSEH, and ancestor of the Shemidaite clan (Num. 26:32; Josh. 17:2; 1 Chr. 7:19 [some KJV editions, "Shemidah"]).

sheminith. See MUSIC AND MUSICAL INSTRUMENTS (sect. VI).

Shemiramoth. shi-mihr´uh-moth (Heb. *šemîrāmôt H9035*, meaning unknown). **(1)** A LEVITE; one of the gatekeepers assigned to be a musician when DAVID made preparation to transfer the ARK OF THE COVENANT to JERUSALEM (1 Chr. 15:18). He is called one of the brothers of the "second order" (NRSV; NIV, "next in rank") who followed HEMAN, ASAPH, and ETHAN. Shemiramoth and some others "were to play the lyres according

to *alamoth*" (v. 20; see MUSIC AND MUSICAL INSTRUMENTS sect. VI). Later, he was one of the Levites appointed "to minister before the ark of the LORD, to make petition, to give thanks, and to praise the LORD, the God of Israel" (16:4-5).

(2) One of six Levites whom King JEHOSHAPHAT sent to teach the law in the cities of JUDAH (2 Chr. 17:8). Appointed to the same mission were a number of princes and priests.

Shemuel. shem´yoo-uhl (Heb. *šemûʾēl H9017*, possibly "his name is God"; see details under SAMUEL). **(1)** Son of Ammihud; he was a leader from the tribe of SIMEON, chosen to assist in the distribution of the land (Num. 34:20).

(2) Son of Tola and grandson of ISSACHAR, described as head of family (1 Chr. 7:2; NIV, "Samuel").

(3) KJV alternate form of Samuel (only 1 Chr. 6:33).

Shen. shen (Heb. *šēn H9095*, with the definite article, *haššēn*, "the tooth" [possibly alluding to the shape of a topographical formation]). A place near which the stone named EBENEZER was set up by SAMUEL (1 Sam. 7:12). Shen was evidently not far from MIZPAH, but its location is unknown. On the basis of Greek and Syriac evidence, the NRSV emends the text to JESHANAH, a town some 5 mi. (8 km.) N of BETHEL.

Shenazar. See SHENAZZAR.

Shenazzar. shi-naz´uhr (Heb. *šenʾaṣṣar H9100*, prob. from Akk. *Sin-uṣur*, "may [the god] Sin protect"). KJV Shenazar. Son of the exiled King JEHOIACHIN (1 Chr. 3:18). See also SHESHBAZZAR.

Shenir. See SENIR.

Sheol. shee´ohl (Heb. *šeʾôl H8619*, derivation disputed; suggestions include "place of inquiry," alluding to necromancy [from *šāʾal H8626*, "to ask"], and "desolation, destruction" [from *šāʾāh H8615*, "to be desolate"]). The place where the DEAD were believed to dwell. The Hebrew term is used sixty-five times in the OT, and more than half of its occurrences are found in the WISDOM Literature.

The KJV translates it as "the grave" or "hell" ("the pit" three times). The NIV usually renders it "the grave" (Gen. 37:35 et al.), but occasionally gives such contextual renderings as "the realm of death" (Deut. 32:22; TNIV, "of the dead"), "death" (Job 17:16 et al.), and "depths" (Ps. 139:8). The NRSV and other modern versions use the transliteration *Sheol*.

The Hebrews evidently shared with their contemporaries the belief that there was a region occupied by the dead as a shadowy underworld existence. A number of obvious parallels exist between the biblical descriptions and references in extrabiblical literature. According to the OT, the realm of the dead was a place of darkness (Job 10:21-22; cf. Ps. 143:3). It was also viewed as a place of silence whose inhabitants cannot praise God (Ps. 6:5; 94:17; 99:10-12; 115:17; Eccl. 9:5, 10). The inhabitants of Sheol are but a shadow of their former selves; in fact, they are called by a term that may mean "shades" (*rĕpā'îm H8327*; see REPHAITE). Sheol is a place of continued existence rather than annihilation, and it does not lie beyond the reach of God (Ps. 139:8; Job 26:6).

An important question regarding Sheol is this: At death, did the OT believers go to such a place of gloom or did they go to be with the Lord immediately? The former view was prevalent in the early church, which also held that CHRIST at his death descended into Sheol (HADES) to bring the OT believers to heaven with him. The latter view is held by those who believe that the Sheol concept was held by the Israelites in common with their pagan neighbors until God gradually revealed more and more information about the life after death, climaxing his revelation in Christ who brought life and immortality to light. Both views contain considerable difficulties.

Shepham. shee'fuhm (Heb. *šĕpām H9172*, meaning uncertain). One of the sites in NE CANAAN which served to delineate the E boundary of the Promised Land (Num. 34:10-11). It is mentioned between HAZAR ENAN (prob. modern Qaryatein, c. 70 mi./110 km. NE of DAMASCUS) and RIBLAH (an unknown location apparently not too far to the E or NE of the Sea of Galilee), but the site is unknown.

Shephatiah. shef-uh-thi'uh (Heb. *šĕpaṭyāhû H9153* [only 1 Chr. 12:5; 27:16; 2 Chr. 21:2] and *šĕpaṭyâ H9152*, "Yahweh has judged [i.e., obtained justice for the innocent]"). (1) Son of DAVID by his wife Abital; he was among David's children who were born in HEBRON (2 Sam. 3:4; 1 Chr. 3:3).

(2) Son of Reuel, descendant of BENJAMIN, and father of MESHULLAM; the latter was a family head who returned to JERUSALEM from the Babylonian EXILE (1 Chr. 9:8).

(3) A HARUPHITE from the tribe of Benjamin who joined David's band while the latter dwelt at ZIKLAG to escape SAUL's attempt to take him (12:5).

(4) Son of Maacah and chief officer of the tribe of SIMEON while David was king (27:16). He belonged to one of the divisions responsible for the affairs of the kingdom, serving a month at a time (v. 1).

(5) Son of JEHOSHAPHAT king of JUDAH (1 Chr. 21:2). He and his brothers received a very generous inheritance (v. 3). Jehoshaphat's firstborn, JEHORAM, killed all his brothers when he became king (v. 4).

(6) Ancestor of an Israelite family, 372 of whom returned to Jerusalem from Babylon with ZERUBBABEL (Ezra 2:4; Neh. 7:9). Later, 80 more members of this family, plus their head Zebadiah, returned to Jerusalem with EZRA (Ezra 8:8).

(7) Ancestor of a family of SOLOMON's servants who returned to Jerusalem with Zerubbabel (Ezra 2:57; Neh. 7:59).

(8) Son of Mahalalel, descendant of JUDAH, and ancestor of Athaiah; the latter was a postexilic provincial leader listed among those who lived in Jerusalem at the time of NEHEMIAH (Neh. 11:4).

(9) Son of Mattan; he was one of the officials who complained to ZEDEKIAH about the unfavorable predictions of JEREMIAH (Jer. 38:1-4).

Shephelah. shi-fee'luh, shef'uh-luh (Heb. *šĕpēlâ H9169*, "lowland"). This name occurs a dozen times in the NRSV, which however does not use it consistently to translate the Hebrew term (it is rendered "lowland" in Joshua and Judges). The KJV uses a variety of renderings (e.g., "valley," "vale," "plain"), while the NIV has "western foothills" (Deut. 1:7 et al.) or simply "foothills" (1 Ki. 10:27 et al.). The term refers to a well-known

S

The low hills of the Judean Shephelah, looking E through the Elah Valley.

feature of the landforms of PALESTINE, namely, the low hill tract between the coastal plain and the high central hills of JUDEA and SAMARIA. It consists of hard Eocene limestones that form low, rocky plateaus and hilly swells that rise from the coastal plain to elevations of some 1,500 ft. (460 m.) above sea level. The word derives from *šāpēl H9164*, "to become low," and topographically it is accurate, suggesting the foothills below the main limestone dorsal of Judea-Samaria. As a buffer zone between the coastal plain of PHILISTIA and the Israelite highlands to the interior, the geopolitical character of the Shephelah was given clear identity in the OT (e.g., 2 Chr. 26:10; 28:18).

Shepher. shee´fuhr (Heb. *šeper H9184*, possibly "beauty"). KJV Shapher. The name of a mountain at which the Israelites camped in the period of the wilderness wandering (Num. 33:23-24). It is listed between Kehelathah and Haradah, but none of these sites can be identified.

shepherd. See OCCUPATIONS AND PROFESSIONS.

Shephi. See SHEPHO.

Shepho. shee´foh (Heb. *šepô H9143* [*šepy* in 1 Chr. 1:40], derivation uncertain). Son of SHOBAL and

grandson of SEIR the HORITE (Gen. 36:23; in 1 Chr. 1:40 the KJV and other versions have "Shephi," following MT); he was a chieftain living in EDOM (Gen. 36:21).

Shephupham. shi-fyoo´fuhm (Heb. *šĕpûpām H9145* [not in NIV], prob. a textual corruption of *šûpām H8792*, meaning unknown). Son of BENJAMIN, grandson of JACOB, and eponymous ancestor of the Shuphamite clan (Num. 26:39 NRSV and other modern versions, following the MT). Both the KJV and the NIV have SHUPHAM, which is the reading of a few Hebrew MSS and several ancient versions. In the several genealogical lists of Benjamin there seems to be a tendency toward the use of pairs of names of similar sound with some variations occurring. For example, in the present passage Shephupham/Shupham is paired with HUPHAM and Huphamites, whereas a parallel passage has SHUPPIM and HUPPIM (1 Chr. 7:12). Huppim occurs also in the initial list of Benjamin's sons, but instead of Shuppim that list has MUPPIM (Gen. 46:21). See also SHEPHUPHAN. There seems to have been a trend toward stylization and simplification of names.

Shephuphan. shi-fyoo´fuhn (Heb. *šĕpûpān H9146*, meaning unknown). Son of BELA and grandson of

© Dr. James C. Martin

BENJAMIN (1 Chr. 8:5). Some Hebrew MSS and the Aramaic Targum read SHEPHUPHAM.

Sherah. See SHEERAH.

sherd. See POTSHERD.

Sherebiah. sher´uh-bi´uh (Heb. *šērēbyâ H9221*, meaning uncertain). **(1)** A LEVITE who, with his extended family, joined EZRA at a river encampment in BABYLON in preparation for journeying to PALESTINE (Ezra 8:18, 24). Mentioned alongside HASHABIAH, he is described as "a capable man" to whom were committed funds and vessels for the TEMPLE treasury at JERUSALEM. Although opinions differ, this Sherebiah is probably the same Levite who assisted in Ezra's public reading and exposition of the law (Neh. 8:7), shared in leading worship (9:4-5), and joined in sealing the covenant with NEHEMIAH (10:12). See also #2 below.

(2) A Levite who returned from exile in company with ZERUBBABEL and "who, together with his associates, was in charge of the songs of thanksgiving" (Neh. 12:8, 24). Some believe that he is the same as #1 above, but that presents chronological problems. It is also possible that "Sherebiah" was a family name.

Sheresh. shihr´ish (Heb. *šereš H9246*, perhaps "offshoot" or "clever"). Son of MAKIR and grandson of MANASSEH (1 Chr. 7:16).

Sherezer. See SHAREZER.

Sheshach. shee´shak (Heb. *šēšak H9263*). TNIV Sheshak. This name, which occurs twice (Jer. 25:26; 51:41), is evidently a reference to "Babel" (BABYLON), using a cryptic device whereby the first letter of the Hebrew alphabet was substituted for the last letter, the second letter for the next-to-last letter, and so on. See also LEB KAMAI.

Sheshai. shee´shi (Heb. *šēšay H9259*, derivation uncertain). One of three descendants of ANAK who lived in HEBRON when the Israelites spied out the land and who were defeated by the invading Israelites (Num. 13:22; Josh. 15:14; Jdg. 1:10). See AHIMAN.

Sheshak. shee´shak. TNIV form of SHESHACH.

Sheshan. shee´shan (Heb. *šēšān H9264*, meaning unknown). Son of Ishi and descendant of JUDAH through the line of JERAHMEEL (1 Chr. 2:31). He is said to have had a son named AHLAI, but subsequently the text states that he only had daughters, that he gave an unnamed daughter in marriage to his Egyptian servant JARHA, and that this daughter gave birth to a son named ATTAI (vv. 34-35). Some have argued that Ahlai was the name of Sheshan's daughter (in which case the introductory phrase in the Hebrew of v. 31, "the sons of Sheshan," is a general reference to progeny). Other proposals have been made; for example, that Ahlai and Attai were one and the same person, or that Ahlai was the name given to Jarha when he was adopted.

Sheshbazzar. shesh-baz´uhr (Heb. *šēšbaṣṣar H9256* [Aram. *H10746*], an Akk. theophoric name [cf. SHENAZZAR], though the precise derivation is disputed). A postexilic Israelite referred to as the "prince" of JUDAH who brought the TEMPLE treasures from BABYLON to JERUSALEM (Ezra 1:8, 11). Elsewhere we are told that, having been appointed "governor" by CYRUS, Sheshbazzar "laid the foundations of the house of God in Jerusalem" (Ezra 5:14, 16). The identity of Sheshbazzar is disputed. If the designation "prince" indicates royalty, he may well have been the son of JEHOIACHIN (Jeconiah), king of Judah from 598 to 597 B.C., who was carried into captivity by NEBUCHADNEZZAR. Among the sons of Jehoicahin was one named SHENAZZAR (1 Chr. 3:18), which some scholars have considered a variant form of Sheshbazzar. Others have proposed that Sheshbazzar should be identified with Zerubbabel. In any case, Sheshbazzar holds an important place in the continuation of the Davidic royal line, which after the return and restoration of the city of David and the other covenant sites of his once glorious kingdom, should produce the MESSIAH. The hope of Cyrus, called God's "anointed" (Isa. 45:1), was that the divine temple of the Jews be rebuilt and that the core of Israel's heritage be preserved; both were accomplished through Sheshbazzar.

Sheshonk. See SHISHAK.

Sheth. sheth (Heb. *šēt H9269*, possibly "provision, restitution"). **(1)** The expression "the sons of Sheth" is used in one of BALAAM's oracles with reference to the people of MOAB (Num. 24:17). The Hebrew form of the name is identical to that of SETH (Gen. 4:25-26 et al.), but since it is very unlikely that Seth could have been viewed as the ancestor of the Moabites—or of any other nation, for that matter—perhaps the Shethites were a people group living in or near Moab. The Hebrew text is difficult, however, and many scholars (on the basis of Jer. 48:45, which seems to be a quotation of Num. 21:28a plus 24:17b) emend it to "the people of tumult" (cf. NIV mg., "the noisy boasters").

(2) KJV alternate form of SETH (only 1 Chr. 1:1).

Shethar. shee´thahr (Heb. *šētār H9285*, meaning uncertain). One of "the seven nobles of Persia and Media who had special access to the king and were highest in the kingdom" (Esth. 1:14). Queen VASHTI was banished by Ahasuerus (XERXES) on their advice.

Shethar-Bozenai. shee´thahr-boz´uh-n*i* (Heb. *šētar bôznay H10750*, meaning uncertain). KJV Shethar-boznai. A Persian official who joined TATTENAI, the governor of the province of Trans-Euphrates, in complaining to King DARIUS about the Jewish rebuilding of the TEMPLE (Ezra 5:3, 6; 6:6, 13). Darius returned a decree requiring them to refrain from hindering the work and to assist completion of the building, and its continuing services, in every way possible.

Shethar-boznai. See SHETHAR-BOZENAI.

Sheva. shee´vuh (Heb. *šēwāʾ H8737*, prob. an Aram. name meaning perhaps "similar [to his father]"). **(1)** A royal secretary (see SCRIBE) in DAVID's court (2 Sam. 8:17). For the variations on his name and further discussion, see SHAVSHA.

(2) Son of CALEB (by his concubine MAACAH) and descendant of JUDAH (1 Chr. 2:49). He is identified as "the father of Macbenah and Gibea," meaning probably that he was the founder of the two cities bearing those names.

shewbread. See TABERNACLE.

Shibah. shi´buh (Heb. *šibʿâ H8683*, "oath" or "abundance"). The name that ISAAC gave to a well dug by his servants (Gen. 26:33). See discussion under BEERSHEBA.

shibboleth. shib´uh-lith (Heb. *šibbōlet H8672*, "[head of] grain," or *H8673*, "flood"; contrasted in pronunciation with *sibbōlet H6027*). The password used by the Gileadites at the JORDAN to detect the fleeing Ephraimites (Jdg. 12:6). Because the point to the story is not the meaning of the word but its pronunciation, the English versions transliterate (rather than translate) it as *shibboleth*; similarly, the Ephraimites' pronunciation is given as *sibboleth*. What the difference was, however, has been a matter of considerable debate. It has been argued that some Israelites pronounced *š* (*sh*) as *s*, but this view lacks evidence. Others suggest that the Israelites in TRANSJORDAN (where GILEAD is located) preserved an earlier sound that those W of the Jordan (Cisjordan) were unable to imitate precisely.

Shibmah. See SIBMAH.

Shicron. See SHIKKERON.

shield. See ARMS AND ARMOR.

shiggaion. shuh-gay´on (Heb. *šiggāyôn H8710*). The meaning of this term (found only in the title of Ps. 7, and the plural *shigionoth* in Hab. 3:1) is obscure, and Bible versions simply transliterate it. It probably derives from the verb *šāgâ H8706* ("to go astray, stagger"), so some have suggested the meaning "dithyramb" (i.e., a song with rapidly changing mood or with sporadic rhythm); others appeal to Akkadian *šegû* and translate "dirge, lament," characterized by a wandering style.

shigionoth. See SHIGGAION.

Shihon. See SHION.

Shihor. shi´hor (Heb. *šîḥôr H8865*, prob. from Egyp. *š(y)-ḥr*, "waters of [the god] Horus"). KJV also Sihor. A river described as lying "on the east of [*lit.*, before] Egypt" and cited as the southern extremity of the land that remained to be conquered

S

in JOSHUA's old age (Josh. 13:3). Shihor appears to have been an extremity of one of the arms of the NILE, perhaps the Pelusiac or the Bubastite. This identification agrees with the occurrence of Shihor in Isa. 23:3, where it is in parallelism with "the River" (i.e., the Nile), and in Jer. 2:18, where it parallels the EUPHRATES, the chief river of ASSYRIA. Some have thought that the occurrence of Shihor in Josh. 13:3 and 1 Chr. 13:5 (where it is cited as the S extremity of the Davidic empire) would seem to warrant an identification of Shihor with the Wadi el-ʿArish, c. 100 mi. (160 km.) E of the Nile (see EGYPT, WADI OF). Since, however, the area of the SINAI S of this wadi was for the most part uninhabited, it may be that these passages simply indicate the extreme limits of Israelite influence.

Shihor Libnath. shiʹhor-libʹnath (Heb. *šiḥôr libnāt H8866*, possibly "the waters of Libnath" [see SHIHOR]). A town or stream that served to mark the SW boundary of the territory apportioned to the tribe of ASHER (Josh. 19:26). It was evidently in the area of Mount CARMEL, but its identification is uncertain. Some scholars have suggested locations S of Carmel; others believe the name refers to the mouth of the River KISHON.

Shikkeron. shikʹuh-ron (Heb. *šikkārôn H8914*, meaning uncertain). KJV Shicron. A town on the NW border of the tribal territory of JUDAH, between the PHILISTINE city of EKRON and Mount BAALAH, toward the sea (Josh. 15:11). Shikkeron is probably to be identified with modern Tell el-Ful, some 4 mi. (6 km.) NW of Ekron and a little N of the Valley of SOREK.

Shilhi. shilʹhi (Heb. *šilḥi H8944*, meaning uncertain). The father of Azubah, who was King ASA's wife and mother of King JEHOSHAPHAT (1 Ki. 22:42; 2 Chr. 20:31). Because the name is otherwise unattested, some emend the text to read "Azubah from Shilhim" or understand the term as a gentilic, "Azubah daughter of a Shilhite" (see SHILHIM).

Shilhim. shilʹhim (Heb. *šilḥim H8946*, meaning uncertain). A town in the NEGEV within the tribal territory of JUDAH (Josh. 15:32). It is probably to

be identified with SHARUHEN, as suggested by the parallel list (19:6).

Shillem. shilʹuhm (Heb. *šillēm H8973*, prob. short form of SHELEMIAH, "Yahweh has repaid"; gentilic *šillēmî H8980*, "Shillemite"). Son of NAPHTALI, grandson of JACOB, and eponymous ancestor of the Shillemite clan (Gen. 46:24; Num. 26:49; in 1 Chr. 7:13 most versions, following the MT, have SHALLUM).

Shiloah. shi-lohʹuh (Heb. *šilōaḥ H8942*, from *šalaḥ H8938*, "to send"; possibly alternate form of *šelaḥ H8940*, which may mean "canal" [see SHELAH]). The prophet ISAIAH, in the days of King AHAZ, accused his people of rejecting "the gently flowing waters of Shiloah" (Isa. 8:6). The SEPTUAGINT renders this name as *Silōam G4978*, but one should not assume that the passage refers specifically to the Pool of Siloam mentioned in Jn. 9:7; more likely it has in view an aqueduct connecting the GIHON Spring to the southern side of JERUSALEM. See comments under SILOAM.

Shiloh. shiʹloh (usually *šilōh H8926*, but also *šilô H8931* [Jdg. 21:19 et al.] and *šilô H8870* [only Jdg. 21:21; Jer. 7:12], meaning uncertain; the original form was prob. *šilōn*, for the gentilic is *šilōni H8872* [see SHILONITE]). A city in the territory of EPHRAIM, located by the biblical text as N of BETHEL, S of LEBONAH, and to the E of a road that connected Bethel to SHECHEM (Jdg. 21:19). It is identified with modern Khirbet Seilun, 20 mi. (32 km.) NNE of JERUSALEM. The ARK OF THE COVENANT and the TABERNACLE were there from the time of JOSHUA through that of SAMUEL. Shiloh was thus an important religious center for the Israelites. Its location was well suited to be a quiet place of worship. The town was surrounded by hills on all sides except the SW, and pasture lands and a water supply were nearby. The position is not strategic, however, and did not lend itself to defense nor to control of highways and land areas.

It was from Shiloh that the men of BENJAMIN, by Israel's permission, kidnapped wives after the Benjamite war under the priesthood of PHINEHAS, the grandson of AARON (Jdg. 21). The godly

Remains of ancient Shiloh in the hill country of Ephraim. (View to the E.)

ELKANAH and his family went to Shiloh before the birth of Samuel (1 Sam. 1:3). Here the boy Samuel received his call from God (3:20-21). From the time of the removal of the ark, however, Shiloh gradually lost its importance, especially when DAVID made JERUSALEM the capital of the kingdom of ISRAEL. This loss of importance was principally because God "abandoned the tabernacle of Shiloh, the tent he had set up among men" (Ps. 78:60). During the reign of King SAUL and especially during his war with the PHILISTINES, AHIJAH, great-grandson of Eli, was high priest of Israel, wearing the sacred EPHOD at Shiloh (1 Sam. 14:3). After the division of the kingdom, though the ark and the TEMPLE were at Jerusalem, and though JEROBOAM, the apostate king, had set up centers of worship at Dan and at Bethel, another Ahijah, prophet of the Lord, was still at Shiloh, representing God before the true people of God in the northern kingdom. To him Jeroboam sent to inquire about his sick son (1 Ki. 14), and here Ahijah pronounced the doom of Jeroboam's house (14:13). In the days of Jeremiah, Shiloh was a ruin (Jer. 7:12, 14), though there were some men there after the destruction of Jerusalem (41:5).

In Gen. 49:10, part of JACOB's blessing to his son JUDAH, we find the Hebrew phrase ʿad kî-yābōʾ šîlōh (Qere šîlô). Rendered "until Shiloh come" by the KJV, these words have been the occasion of a great deal of discussion and difficulty. (1) Shiloh in this passage has been taken traditionally as a name designating the MESSIAH. The name in this case might be derived from the verb šālāh *H8922*, "to be at ease," and would mean something like "the peace-giver," but this derivation is linguistically difficult. Shiloh is not found elsewhere in the Bible as a personal name, and the passage is not cited in the NT (as it likely would be if it had been regarded as a prediction of the Messiah). (2) A second interpretation suggests that Shiloh does refer to the city mentioned above, and the passage indicates that Judah or Judean rule was to continue until it extended as far as Shiloh (or until the Messiah came to Shiloh). (3) Another suggestion, which involves a minor textual change, is based on the ancient versions. According to this view, the word should be read as šellô, "what belongs to him" (i.e., the particle ša- *H8611*, "which," plus lô, "to him"). In support of this rendering, appeal can be made to Ezek. 21:27 ("until he comes to whom it rightfully belongs," probably an echo of Gen. 49:10). Thus the NIV renders the Genesis passage, "until he comes to whom it belongs" (so also the Syriac version). (4) Alternatively, some scholars understand the first element of the word to be šay *H8856*, "gift," and translate, "until tribute comes to him" (NRSV; similarly, NJPS). (5) Among various emendations proposed, a popular suggestion is *mōšĕlōh*, "his ruler." Interestingly, the Akkadian word for "prince" or "ruler" is *šêlu* (*šîlu*), and "his ruler" would appear as *šayyālô*.

Shiloni. See SHILONITE #2.

Shilonite. shi′luh-nit (Heb. *šílōnî H8872* [in 1 Chr. 9:5, *šílônî*], gentilic of *šílōh H8926*; see SHILOH). (1) Descriptive term applied to AHIJAH the prophet, who tore the garment of JEROBOAM into twelve pieces and prophesied that ten tribes would be given him (1 Ki. 11:29 [NIV, "of Shiloh"]; 12:15; 15:29; 2 Chr. 9:29; 10:15).

(2) A clan descended from JUDAH, mentioned in two lists of those who returned from the Babylonian EXILE (1 Chr. 9:5 [TNIV, "Shelanites"]; Neh. 11:5 [NIV and TNIV, "of Shelah"; KJV, "Shiloni"]). If the Masoretic vocalization is correct, these may have been persons who traced their relationship and ancestry to the city of Shiloh and who after the exile resettled in Jerusalem. The NIV/TNIV renderings are based on the view that one or both of these passages should read *šēlānî H8989*, "Shelanite," that is, descendants of SHELAH son of Judah (cf. Gen. 38:5; Num. 26:20).

Shilshah. shil′shah (Heb. *šílšâ H8996*, perhaps "gentle"). Son of Zophah and descendant of ASHER (1 Chr. 7:37); some emend the text to "Shelesh" (v. 35).

Shimea. shim′ee-uh (Heb. *šim⁽â⁾ H9055*, prob. short form of a name such as SHEMAIAH, "Yahweh has heard"). (1) Son of JESSE (1 Chr. 2:13 [KJV, "Shimma"]; 20:7). See SHAMMAH #2.

(2) Son of DAVID (1 Chr. 3:5). See SHAMMUA #2.

(3) Son of Uzzah and descendant of LEVI through MERARI (1 Chr. 6:30 [Heb. text, v. 15]).

(4) Son of Michael, descendant of Levi through GERSHOM, and grandfather of ASAPH the musician (1 Chr. 6:39 [Heb. text, v. 24]).

Shimeah. shim′ee-uh (Heb. *šim⁽â⁾ H9009* [1 Chr. 8:32], derivation uncertain; *šim⁽â⁾ H9056* [2 Sam. 13:3 et al.], prob. short form of a name such as SHEMAIAH, "Yahweh has heard"). (1) Son of JESSE (2 Sam. 13:3, 32; 21:21). See SHAMMAH #2.

(2) Son of Mikloth, descendant of BENJAMIN, and relative of King SAUL (1 Chr. 8:32; called "Shimeam" in 9:38).

Shimeam. shim′ee-uhm (Heb. *šim⁾ām H9010*, derivation uncertain). See SHIMEAH #2.

Shimeath. shim′ee-ath (Heb. *šim⁽āt H9064*, prob. short form of a name such as SHEMAIAH, "Yahweh has heard"). An "Ammonite woman" who was the mother of ZABAD, one of the murderers of King Joash (JEHOASH) of JUDAH (2 Chr. 24:26). In the parallel passage (which has JOZABAD, 2 Ki. 12:21), Shimeath is not identified as a woman; the name could be masculine (in spite of the apparently feminine ending), and some scholars argue that Shimeath was in fact the father of Zabad/Jozabad. See also SHIMRITH.

Shimeathite. shim′ee-uh-thit (Heb. *šim⁽ātî H9065*, prob. gentilic of a place name such as *šĕma⁽ H9054*). Among the descendants of CALEB (through his son HUR and grandson SALMA) are listed three "clans of scribes who lived at Jabez: the Tirathites, Shimeathites and Sucathites. These are the Kenites who came from Hammath, the father of the house of Recab" (1 Chr. 2:55). Nothing else is known about these clans, and their names cannot be traced to a particular person or place. See also KENITE.

Shimei. shim′ee-i (Heb. *šim⁽i H9059*, "my listening" or short form of a name such as SHEMAIAH, "Yahweh has heard"; gentilic *šim⁽i H9060*, "Shimeite" [KJV, "Shimite"]). (1) Son of GERSHON, grandson of LEVI, and eponymous ancestor of the Shimeite clan; usually paired with his brother LIBNI (Exod. 6:17 [KJV, "Shimi"]; Num. 3:18, 21; 1 Chr. 6:17). In one passage (1 Chr. 6:42-43) Shimei is identified as son of Jahath and *grandson* of Gershon. Elsewhere (23:7-11) Shimei is paired with LADAN, while Jahath is listed as first son of Shimei. Some scholars posit two different descendants of Gershon named Shimei; others believe that the genealogies have suffered textual corruption. The descendants of Shimei are mentioned unexpectedly in Zechariah's prophecy of future mourning, which focuses on the Levites in general and on the Shimeite clan in particular (Zech. 12:13).

S

(2) Son of Gera, descendant of BENJAMIN, and relative of SAUL (2 Sam. 16:5). When DAVID was seeking to escape from his son ABSALOM, Shimei met the fleeing party at BAHURIM and began hurling stones as well as ugly words at the king (vv. 6-8). David's men offered to silence the insolent Benjamite but the king refused, believing that Yahweh would take note of the affliction he suffered under the tormenting tongue of Saul's house (16:11-12). With the turn of events that brought deliverance to David and his faithful followers, Shimei found it necessary to reverse his former behavior. As David returned to Jerusalem, Shimei met him again, but this time at the JORDAN River with 1,000 Benjamites; in great humility and penance, he pleaded for mercy (19:16-23). The king restrained his men from seeking vengeance and assured the trembling Benjamite that he would not be executed. Later, however, as David saw his death approaching, he instructed SOLOMON to see to it that Shimei receive the punishment befitting his deeds (1 Ki. 2:8-9). Solomon brought Shimei to Jerusalem and warned him that he would be put to death if he ever left the city (vv. 36-37). Things went well for Shimei for three years, but when his slaves ran away he left the city to retrieve them. Upon his return, Solomon carried out the threatened penalty; Shimei was slain (vv. 38-46).

(3) Son of JESSE (2 Sam. 21:21 NRSV). See SHAMMAH #2.

(4) Son of Ela; he was appointed by Solomon from the tribe of BENJAMIN to provide food for the royal household (1 Ki. 4:18). Shimei was one of the twelve officers whose task it was to provide supplies one month of the year. If this appointment was a reward for faithful service under David, this Shimei may be the same man who with Rei remained faithful to David in ADONIJAH's attempt to usurp the throne (1:8).

(5) Son of Pedaiah, descendant of David, and brother of ZERUBBABEL (1 Chr. 3:19).

(6) Son of Zaccur and descendant of SIMEON; the text notes that he had twenty-two children (1 Chr. 4:26-27). Some interpret the Hebrew to mean that Shimei, Zaccur, and Hammuel were all sons of MISHMA.

(7) Son of Gog and descendant of REUBEN (1 Chr. 5:4).

(8) Son of LIBNI and descendant of Levi through MERARI (1 Chr. 6:29).

(9) A head of family in the tribe of BENJAMIN (1 Chr. 8:21; KJV, "Shimhi"). He is probably the same as Shema son of Elpaal (v. 13). See SHEMA #4.

(10) Son of the musician JEDUTHUN; he and his brothers, under their father's supervision, "prophesied, using the harp in thanking and praising the LORD" (1 Chr. 25:3 NIV; the name "Shimei" is omitted by the KJV following the MT). He was also the head of the tenth company of temple musicians appointed by lot under DAVID (v. 17).

(11) A RAMATHITE whom David placed in charge of his vineyards (1 Chr. 27:27).

(12) Descendant of HEMAN the musician; he and his brother Jehiel were among the LEVITES assigned to consecrate the TEMPLE in the days of HEZEKIAH (2 Chr. 29:14). This may be the same Shimei who is later identified as brother of CONANIAH; the latter was in charge of the contributions brought to the temple, and Shimei assisted him (31:12-13).

(13) One of the Levites who agreed to put away their foreign wives in the time of EZRA (Ezra 10:23).

(14) One of the sons of Hashum who agreed to put away their foreign wives (Ezra 10:33).

(15) One of the sons of Binnui who agreed to put away their foreign wives (Ezra 10:38).

(16) Son of Kish, descendant of Benjamin, and grandfather of MORDECAI (Esth. 2:5).

Shimeon. shim´ee-uhn (Heb. *šim'ôn* H9058, possibly "[God] has heard"; see SIMEON). One of the sons of Harim who agreed to put away their foreign wives (Ezra 10:31). The distinction in English between "Shimeon" and "Simeon" has no basis in the Hebrew.

Shimhi. See SHIMEI #9.

Shimi. See SHIMEI #1.

Shimite. KJV form of "Shimeite"; see SHIMEI.

Shimma. See SHIMEA #1.

Shimon. shi´muhn (Heb. *šîmôn* H8873, derivation uncertain). A descendant of JUDAH (1 Chr. 4:20);

his place in the genealogy is unclear, but he was probably the head of a clan.

Shimrath. shim´rath (Heb. *šimrāt H9086*, possibly short form of SHEMARIAH, "Yahweh has watched over"). Son of SHIMEI (#9) and descendant of BENJAMIN (1 Chr. 8:21).

Shimri. shim´ri (Heb. *šimrî H9078*, "my protection" or short form of SHEMARIAH, "Yahweh has watched over"). **(1)** Son of Shemaiah, descendant of SIMEON, and ancestor of Ziza; the latter was one of the clan leaders in the time of HEZEKIAH who invaded the land of the Hamites and the Meunites (1 Chr. 4:37; cf. vv. 38-41).

(2) Father of Jediael and of Joha the Tizite; both of his sons were among DAVID's mighty warriors (1 Chr. 11:45).

(3) Son of Hosah and descendant of LEVI through MERARI; listed among the gatekeepers appointed by David (1 Chr. 26:10; KJV, "Simri"). Although Shimri was not the firstborn, he was designated by Hosah as first in rank.

(4) Descendant of Levi through ELIZAPHAN; he was among the Levites who assisted in the TEMPLE reforms under HEZEKIAH (2 Chr. 29:13).

Shimrith. shim´rith (Heb. *šimrît H9083*, possibly "guardian"). A "Moabite woman" who was the mother of JEHOZABAD, one of the murderers of King Joash (JEHOASH) of Judah (2 Chr. 24:26). In the parallel passage (2 Ki. 12:21), the name is given as the masculine SHOMER, which is not likely to have been applied to a woman. Possibly the final Hebrew consonant (transliterated *th*) dropped out by a scribal mistake. Some have argued that Shomer was the father of Shimrith (in which case the latter passage could be rendered "Jehozabad grandson of Shomer"); others consider such a solution to be artificial and argue that, for theological reasons, the two Israelite fathers mentioned in 2 Kings were deliberately turned by the Chronicler into non-Israelite mothers. See also SHIMEATH.

Shimrom. See SHIMRON (PERSON).

Shimron (person). shim´ron (Heb. *šimrôn H9075*, possibly "[God] has watched over"; gentilic

šimrōnî H9084, "Shimronite"). Son of ISSACHAR, grandson of JACOB, and eponymous ancestor of the Shimronite clan (Gen. 46:13; Num. 26:24; 1 Chr. 7:1 [here some editions of KJV have "Shimrom"]).

Shimron (place). shim´ron (Heb. *šimrôn H9074*, derivation disputed). A Canaanite city whose king was included in a military alliance initiated by JABIN of HAZOR, the purpose of which was to resist the Israelite invasion under JOSHUA (Josh. 11:1). It was later included in the territory assigned to the tribe of ZEBULUN (19:15). Shimron is usually thought to be the same as the "Shimron Meron" mentioned in 12:20 (though the SEPTUAGINT may be correct in listing Shimron and Meron as two distinct towns; see MADON). However, because the name appears as *Symoōn* in the LXX (Codex B), many scholars believe that the original name of the town was "Simeon" (*šim῾ôn*) and that it should be identified with modern Khirbet Sammuniyeh, some 5 mi. (8 km.) W of NAZARETH.

Shimron Meron. shim´ron-mee´ron (Heb. *šimrôn mĕr᾽ôn H9077*). See SHIMRON (PLACE).

Shimshai. shim´shi (Heb. *šimšay H10729*, possibly "child of the sun" or "my [little] sun"). A Persian secretary (see SCRIBE) who, with another official, REHUM, wrote a letter to ARTAXERXES asking him to prohibit the rebuilding of the TEMPLE by the Jews (Ezra 4:8-16). They succeeded in their purpose; work on the temple was halted (vv. 17-24).

shin. shin (from *šēn H9094*, "tooth"). KJV *schin*. The twenty-first letter of the Hebrew alphabet (שׁ), with a numerical value of 300. It is named for the shape of the letter, which in its older form resembled the outline of sharp teeth. Its sound corresponds to that of English *sh*. Originally, the Hebrew alphabet made no distinction between *shin* (transliterated *š*) and *sin* (*ś*, transliterated *ś*); the pronunciation of the latter is uncertain, but it was probably an intermediate sound between *š* and *s*.

Shinab. shi´nab (Heb. *šin᾽āb H9098*, prob. from Akk. *Sin-abum*, "[the god] Sin is his father"). The king of ADMAH, who joined four other S

Palestinian rulers in a failed rebellion against KEDORLAOMER (Gen. 14:2).

Shinar. shi′nahr (Heb. *šin*ʿ*ār* H9114, derivation debated). A designation for the land of Babylonia. In Genesis the name Shinar is used early to describe the land that included the cities of BABYLON, ERECH, and AKKAD (possibly also CALNEH) within the kingdom of NIMROD (Gen. 10:10). This was the place where migrants from the E settled and built the city and tower of BABEL (11:2). A king of Shinar (AMRAPHEL) took part in the coalition that raided SODOM and GOMORRAH (14:1) and was defeated by ABRAHAM. A fine garment looted by ACHAN near JERICHO was described as a "fine Shinar mantle" (Josh. 7:21 NJPS; NIV, "beautiful robe from Babylonia"). It was to this land that NEBUCHADNEZZAR took the captives from JERUSALEM (Dan. 1:2; cf. also Isa. 11:11; Zech. 5:11). The references to known Babylonian cities within Shinar (Gen. 10:10; 11:2) and the mention of Shinar as the place of EXILE make the identification with Babylonia almost certain. However, no undisputed equivalent of this name has yet been found in early texts from Babylonia itself.

© Dr. James C. Martin. The British Museum. Photographed by permission.

An example of a Sumerian text, typical of the early cuneiform writing style of the region of Shinar.

Shion. shi′uhn (Heb. *šîʾōn* H8858, meaning unknown). KJV Shihon (some editions). A town within the tribal territory of ISSACHAR (Josh. 19:19). Its location is uncertain; possible identifications include two sites near NAZARETH.

Shiphi. shi′fi (Heb. *šipʿî* H9181, "my abundance" or "[Yahweh] is fullness"). Son of Allon, descendant of SIMEON, and father of Ziza; the latter was one of the clan leaders in the time of HEZEKIAH who invaded the land of the Hamites and the Meunites (1 Chr. 4:37; cf. vv. 38–41).

Shiphmite. shif′mit (Heb. *šipmî* H9175, possibly gentilic of *šĕpām* H9172). Descriptive applied to ZABDI, an official under DAVID (1 Chr. 27:27). The reference of this term is uncertain, but some scholars have suggested that it designates a native of SHEPHAM.

Shiphrah. shif′ruh (Heb. *šiprāh* H9186, "fair, beautiful"). One of the two Hebrew midwives who were ordered by the king of Egypt to kill all male children born to the Israelites (Exod. 1:15). See MIDWIFE.

Shiphtan. shif′tan (Heb. *šipṭān* H9154, prob. from *šepeṭ* H9150, "judgment"). Father of KENUEL; the latter was a leader from the tribe of EPHRAIM appointed to assist in dividing the land of CANAAN among the tribes (Num. 34:24).

ships. Seafaring finds only a small place in the OT. The Hebrews were an agricultural people, and PHOENICIA and PHILISTIA, over long periods, separated them from a coastline that was itself harborless and difficult. In Jdg. 5:17 there is cryptic reference to some experience of ships in the case of the two tribes of ASHER and DAN, but Hebrew seafaring in general was secondhand. The Phoenicians, confined to their coastal strip, and with the timber resources of the Lebanon range in their hinterland, were prompted by geography to exploit the sea, and became, in the process, the great navigators of the ancient world; hence the symbolic vessel with ivory benches and embroidered purple sails of EZEKIEL's metaphor in his denunciation of TYRE (Ezek. 27:4–11). Solomon's fleet at EZION

GEBER (1 Ki. 9-10) consisted of Phoenician ships manned by Phoenicians. JEHOSHAPHAT's later attempt to revive the trade ended in shipwreck, due, no doubt, to the Hebrews' inexperienced handling of the ships. The ships of TARSHISH mentioned in this connection and elsewhere (e.g., Isa. 2:16; NIV, "trading ship") were probably sturdy vessels, built at first for commerce with Tartessus in Spain, the term later being applied, like "China clipper" and "East Indiamen," to vessels generally used for arduous and distant voyaging. SOLOMON's southern fleet, for example, traded to OPHIR, and, if the cargoes are an indication, to southern INDIA as well (1 Ki. 10:22).

It is certain that the Phoenicians penetrated to Cornwall for tin and to the Canary Islands. They probably used the trireme, the useful vessel with three banks of oars, which was a Phoenician invention. Remaining OT references are few and commonly poetic. Psalm 107:23-27 speaks of the terrors of a storm at sea, and 104:26 briefly mentions ships. Isaiah 18:2 speaks of the boats or rafts built of bound bundles of PAPYRUS; these are sometimes depicted in Egyptian murals. Daniel 11:30 refers to warships from the western coastlands or CYPRUS (Chittim or Kittim). In NT times the shipping of the MEDITERRANEAN was principally Greek and Roman. The Romans maintained war fleets of triremes and quinqueremes. How the rowers on these vessels were arranged has been much debated, and the view that there were three (or five) banks of benches is now generally rejected. It is probable that the benches had a forward slant, and that each rower pulled an individual oar sitting three (or five) to a bench. The warship (or "long ship," as it was sometimes called) was not designed for heavy loads but for speed and maneuverability. Hence the frequency of shipwreck, and sometimes mass disaster, in Roman naval history. The great artists in the naval use of the trireme were the Athenians, whose admiral Phormion (c. 440-428 B.C.) developed the tactics that kept ATHENS supreme at sea until the Syracusans invented the ramming device, which struck Athenian naval power a fatal blow in the Great Harbor (413 B.C.). Merchant ships were more heavily built and were designed to stay at sea for long periods in all weathers, carrying considerable cargoes.

Relief from Corinth showing a sailing vessel with sailor.

© Dr. James C. Martin

The classic passage is Acts 27, which contains LUKE's brilliant account of the voyage and wreck of the Alexandrian grain ship. These vessels were of considerable size. There were 276 people aboard the ship on which PAUL and Luke traveled (27:37). JOSEPHUS (*Life* 3) states that he traveled to ROME on a ship with no fewer than 600 aboard. The Alexandrian grain ship, Isis, of the second century A.D., measured 140 by 36 ft. (43 by 11 m.), and would be rated at 3,250 tons burden. No doubt these were exceptional vessels, and the average merchant ship was probably in the vicinity of 100 tons. Paul's ship may have been on a northern route because of the lateness of the season (27:6), though some have thought that this was the regular route from Egypt to Rome. According to Vegetius, from mid-September to mid-November was a particularly dangerous period for autumn navigation. Paul's voyage fell within this period.

The account illustrates the difficulty of handling the ancient sailing ship in adverse winds. From MYRA, on the extreme S point of ASIA MINOR, the ship was proceeding W to CNIDUS, a port at the SW extremity of Asia Minor. A wind off the shore drove the vessel S, and the shipmaster was compelled to seek shelter under the lee of the island of Crete (27:7), which was 140 mi. (225 km.) long. FAIR HAVENS, where the ship found refuge was (and is) a little more than halfway along this coast, just E of the part where the island rises into a group of lofty mountains. Funneled down from these highlands (27:14), the NE wind drove them S from the "more commodious" harbor of PHENICE, over 23 mi. (37 km.) of turbulent sea, to the off-shore island of CLAUDA. The

S

brief advantage of the island's protection was used to haul in the waterlogged boat, which was being towed behind (27:16). To the S lay the Syrtis, ancient graveyard of ships, as modern underwater archaeology has strikingly revealed. Hence the battle to maintain a westerly course, aided by a veering of the wind to the E, as the cyclonic disturbance shifted its center.

At this point they "passed ropes under the ship itself" (Acts 27:17) These tautened cables, used to bind the straining timbers against the stress of the sea and the leverage of the loaded mast, are mentioned elsewhere in ancient literature. "See you not," says Horace, writing metaphorically of the laboring ship of state (*Odes* 1.14), "that the side is stripped of oars, the masts crippled by the rushing southwest wind, the yard-arms groaning, and that without ropes the hull can scarcely bear the too peremptory sea." (See also Plato, *Republic* 10.616c.) It is possible that the hull was "undergirded" by strong ropes, but that an extension of the cables above deck formed a network that could be twisted to tautness. It is probable that the "tackling," which was thrown overboard, was the rigging and the long spar on which the mainsail depended, a device likely to become unmanageable during a storm.

The ship on which Paul continued his voyage from Malta to the grain port of Puteoli had "the sign" of Castor and Pollux (Acts 28:11). In

Greek mythology, the Great Twin Brethren were the patrons of shipmen and had special charge of storm-bound ships (Horace, *Odes* 1.12:27-32). The account in Acts also tells of soundings for depth (27:28) and the bracing of the ship by a system of compensatory anchors (27:29). This is the purport of the metaphor in Heb. 6:19. James 3:4 refers to the rudder paddles.

The boats of the Sea of Galilee, mentioned in the Gospels, were sturdy fishermen's craft or the barges of local lakeside trade. See Galilee, Sea of. They comfortably held a dozen men, but even two of them could not hold all that Jesus' miracle produced (Lk. 5:7). It is not known what wood was used for these boats, but Theophrastus says that seagoing ships were made of larch, cypress, and fir.

Shisha. shiʹshuh (Heb. *šîšāʾ* H8881, meaning uncertain, but possibly an Egyp. word). A royal secretary (see scribe) in Solomon's court (1 Ki. 4:3). For the variations on his name and further comments, see Shavsha.

Shishak. shiʹshak (Heb. *šîšaq* H8882, a Libyan name of unknown meaning; the form *šûšaq* [1 Ki. 14:25, *Ketib*] is considered the more correct vocalization, for it appears in Akk. as *Susinqu* and *šusanqu*). Also Sheshonk, Shishonk, Shoshenq. King of Egypt (c. 945-924 B.C., but dated a decade later by some) who founded the 22nd (or Bubastite) dynasty. Several of his less important successors bore the same name. Shishak's ancestors were among the Libyan lords of the Meshwesh who entered Egypt as mercenary soldiers (see Libya). In Egypt, the Meshwesh became the dominant members of a militaristic, land-holding aristocracy. At the same time, they attempted to become completely Egyptian, that is, to adopt the language and culture of Egypt. Within several generations, they succeeded in establishing a small feudal principality. When the last ruler of the 21st dynasty died, Shishak's power was such that he was able to assume royal power in Bubastis (see Pi Beseth). He gained legitimacy for his dynasty by marrying his son to a princess of the former dynasty.

Shishak's predecessors had maintained an interest in Asia. Hadad of Edom had taken refuge in Egypt, probably with Siamun of the 21st

This mosaic of a Galilean sailboat was discovered at Magdala, on the NW shore of the Sea of Galilee.

© Dr. James C. Martin

dynasty (c. 978-959 B.C.; cf. 1 Ki. 11:14-22). With JEROBOAM's flight to Egypt (11:40) Shishak's personal role is clearly attested. He continued the policy of sheltering enemies of the Jewish kings while keeping an eye on Palestinian affairs. In the fifth year of REHOBOAM, about Shishak's twentieth year, the latter raided JUDAH and ISRAEL. The Bible reports only the plundering of JERUSALEM (1 Ki. 14:25-26; 2 Chr. 12:2-12), but Egyptian records reveal the true scope of the raid. This record is found on a huge relief in the classical Egyptian stela at Karnak. The god Amun (see AMON #4) and a goddess are shown presenting ten lines of Asiatic captives to Shishak. Each of the 156 captives bore the name of a site captured by Shishak. From these names one learns that his raid extended N as far as the Sea of Galilee; thus he had plundered Israel as well. About half the names are legible and include the following: Taanach, Beth Shan, Gibeon, Beth Horon, Aijalon, and Socoh. There is little doubt that Jerusalem was originally included in the list. The raid was not a conquest; Egypt no longer had sufficient strength for permanent rule. However, Shishak still may have aimed at more than the plunder which helped to finance his building program. He also may have desired to intercept the profitable trade routes from the RED SEA to the MEDITERRANEAN, and to divert them from Hebrew territory to Egypt by destroying the cities located along the routes through Israel.

Shitrai. shit′ri (Heb. *šiṭray H8855*, meaning uncertain). A Sharonite who was DAVID's chief shepherd of the herds that pastured in SHARON (1 Chr. 27:29).

shittah tree. See PLANTS (under *acacia*).

Shittim. shi′tim (Heb. *šiṭṭim H8850*, "acacia trees"). A region in the plains of MOAB just NE of the DEAD SEA. Shittim was the scene of the final events before the crossing of the JORDAN (Num. 25:1). It is probably an abbreviation of ABEL SHIT-TIM, listed as the last encampment site in the record of the journey from EGYPT to the Jordan (33:49). While the modern Tell-el Kefrein (c. 5 mi./8 km. NNE of the DEAD SEA) was previously regarded as the location of the site of ancient Shittim, most

scholars today favor Tell el-Ḥammam (c. 5 mi./8 km. farther E). Shittim figures prominently in the history of the Hebrews. Here the people fell into grave error, for many Israelites took wives from among the Moabites (25:1-3). This was apparently done at the instigation of BALAAM, who otherwise failed in his attempts to aid the Moabites in driving out the Hebrews (Num. 31:16). A plague in which 24,000 died was the punishment for their intermarriage and idolatry (25:9). It was here also that a census was taken of those twenty years of age and over. Apparently it was a military conscription, but it was done with a view toward the eventual settlement of the people in Canaan (26:2; cf. v. 53).

MOSES learned in Shittim that he would not see the Promised Land and that JOSHUA was to succeed him as the leader of the people (Num. 27:13-23). A successful military campaign against the Midianites was conducted by the Israelites during the encampment, which resulted in the gain of much booty. Moses delivered his farewell address here, then viewed the Promised Land from Mount Nebo just before his death (see NEBO, MOUNT). Later, it was from Shittim that Joshua sent two spies to scout the city of JERICHO (Josh. 2:1), and from here the Israelites departed for the passage of the Jordan (3:1). MICAH refers to "what happened from Shittim to Gilgal" (Mic. 6:5), evidently reminding the Israelites of the grace of God revealed in the Jordan crossing. JOEL speaks of a fountain that will "water the valley of Shittim" (Joel 3:18 RSV; NIV, "the valley of acacias"), but this reference probably has in view a different location, such as the Wadi en-Nar, a section of the KIDRON as it runs toward the Dead Sea.

shittim wood. See PLANTS (under *acacia*).

Shiza. shi′zuh (Heb. *šizāʾ H8862*, derivation uncertain). Father of ADINA; the latter is described as "chief of the Reubenites" and included among DAVID's mighty warriors (1 Chr. 11:42).

Shoa. shoh′uh (Heb. *šôʿa H8778*, derivation uncertain). A people group who, along with the Babylonians and others, would be brought by God against Judah (Ezek. 23:23). They have not been identified with certainty, but the name is probably

S

a deliberate distortion of *Sutu*, an Akkadian word referring to a nomadic people who for a time lived E of the TIGRIS and also in the Syrian desert. They were often at war with the Assyrians, but were never completely conquered. See KOA; PEKOD.

Shobab. shoh′bab (Heb. *šôbāb H8744*, prob. short form of MESHOBAB, "brought back"). **(1)** Son of CALEB (apparently by AZUBAH) and descendant of JUDAH (1 Chr. 2:18).

(2) Son of DAVID, listed among the children born to him in JERUSALEM (2 Sam. 5:14; 1 Chr. 3:5; 14:4).

Shobach. shoh′bak (Heb. *šôbak H8747* and *šôpak H8791* [in Chronicles], an Aram. name of uncertain meaning). TNIV Shobak. A general of the ARAMEAN forces under HADADEZER who battled DAVID at HELAM (2 Sam. 10:16, 18; called "Shophach" [TNIV Shophak] in 1 Chr. 19:16, 18). The attack was an Aramean attempt to reverse two previous defeats at the hands of ISRAEL (2 Sam. 8:3-8; 10:6-14). David's men were victorious again, however; Shobach was struck down and died.

Shobai. shoh′bi (Heb. *šōbay H8662*, meaning uncertain). Ancestor of a family of gatekeepers who returned with ZERUBBABEL from the EXILE (Ezra 2:42; Neh. 7:45).

Shobak. shoh′bak. TNIV form of SHOBACH.

Shobal. shoh′buhl (Heb. *šôbāl H8748*, perhaps "lion"). **(1)** Son of SEIR the HORITE; he was a clan chief of EDOM (Gen. 36:20, 23, 29; 1 Chr. 1:38, 40).

(2) Son of HUR and descendant of CALEB, included in the genealogy of JUDAH as the "father" (i.e., founder) of KIRIATH JEARIM (1 Chr. 2:50, 52). This Shobal is evidently the same that is later called a "son" (i.e., descendant) of Judah (4:1-2). Some believe that the inclusion of Shobal in these genealogies reflects an immigration into Judahite territory by the Edomite clan referred to in #1 above.

Shobek. shoh′bek (Heb. *šōbēq H8749*, possibly "leader"). One of the leaders of the people who sealed the covenant with NEHEMIAH (Neh. 10:24).

Shobi. shoh′bi (Heb. *šōbî H8661*, meaning uncertain). Son of NAHASH king of AMMON. Shobi and two companions, MAKIR son of Ammiel and BARZILLAI the Gileadite, brought provisions to DAVID and his men as they fled from ABSALOM and his supporters (2 Sam. 17:27-29).

Shocho, Shochoh, Shoco. See SOCO and SOCOH.

shoe. See DRESS.

shoe-latchet. See DRESS.

shofar, shophar. A ram's horn used as a trumpet. See MUSIC AND MUSICAL INSTRUMENTS (sect. I.H).

Shoham. shoh′ham (Heb. *šōham H8733*, "jewel"). Son of Jaaziah and descendant of LEVI through MERARI (1 Chr. 24:27).

Shomer. shoh′muhr (Heb. *šōmēr H9071*, "guardian"). **(1)** Father of JEHOZABAD, one of the murderers of King Joash (JEHOASH) of JUDAH (2 Ki. 12:21). In the parallel passage, however, Jehozabad is described as "son of Shimrith a Moabite woman" (2 Chr. 24:26). See comments under SHIMRITH.

(2) Son of Hemer and descendant of ASHER (1 Chr. 7:32); two verses later he is called SHEMER (v. 34 NRSV, following MT, which has the pausal form *šāmer*, thus KJV, "Shamer"). It is difficult to determine which form is original. Moreover, some scholars have suggested that Shomer and Shemer in this genealogy are two different individuals.

Shophach, Shophak. See SHOBACH.

Shophan. See ATROTH SHOPHAN.

shophar. See MUSIC AND MUSICAL INSTRUMENTS (sect. I.H).

shore. The meaning "shore" or "seashore" is usually represented in Hebrew by the noun *śāpâ H8557* (lit., "lip," Gen. 22:17 et al.). As in Hebrew, so also in Greek the word for "lip," *cheilos G5927*, can be used metaphorically of the shore (Heb. 11:12), but more frequent is *aigialos G129* (Matt. 13:2 et al.). The seashore plays little part in the Bible narrative,

S

mainly because the Israelites were not a seafaring nation, nor was their grip upon the MEDITERRANEAN coastlands ever secure for long periods (see SEA; SHIPS). The frequent NT references to shores relate to the Sea of Galilee (see GALILEE, SEA OF). With these the Galileans were, of course, entirely familiar, since so much of their livelihood originated at the lake shore. In the almost continuous circle of shoreline towns that surrounded the lake in biblical times, not only lake fishing but all kinds of cross-lake transport (such as wheat from the rich arable lands E of the lake) formed the basis of employment. Consequently, Jesus might be said to have chosen the focal point of the region's life and activity for his pulpit when he went down to the lake shore to fulfill his ministry.

Shoshannim, Shoshannim-eduth, Shushan-eduth. shoh-shan´im, shoh-shan´im-ee´duhth, shoo´shan-ee´duhth. KJV transliterations of terms found in the titles of various psalms (Ps. 45; 60; 69; 80). The Hebrew word *šûšan H8808* (pl. *šôšannîm*) means "lily," and *ʿēdût H6343* means "covenant." It is uncertain whether the reference is to lily-shaped musical instruments, or to the mood or content of the poem, or (more likely) to the name of a melody.

Shoshenq. See SHISHAK.

shoulder. This word is used in the Bible both literally and figuratively. In both cases the shoulder is usually shown as the part of the body bearing a burden. The ancients carried heavy objects such as water jars on the shoulder (Gen. 21:14). The shepherd who found his lost sheep is depicted as carrying it back upon his shoulders (Lk. 15:5). There is an echo here of Yahweh's dealings with his children: "the one the LORD loves rests between his shoulders" (Deut. 33:12). Both passages illustrate human helplessness and total dependence on God in dealing with personal sin. Figuratively, the shoulder usually indicates submission, whether it be to an unwelcome burden or to an accepted responsibility. Matthew, in reference to the unnecessary laws imposed by the PHARISEES, quotes Jesus as saying, "They tie up heavy loads and put them on men's shoulders" (Matt. 23:4). Isaiah relates the Lord's promise to break the Assyrians'

yoke upon his people and remove the burden from their shoulders (Isa. 14:25). The same prophet, predicting the coming of CHRIST, refers to the responsibility of judgment: "the government will be upon his shoulders" (9:6).

shoulder piece. That part of the EPHOD where the front and the back were joined together, making the garment to be of one piece (Exod. 28:7-8).

shovel. This English term usually renders Hebrew *yāʿ H3582*, which refers to a ceremonial implement used in removing the debris from the altars of the TABERNACLE and TEMPLE (Exod. 27:3; 38:3; Num. 4:14; 1 Ki. 7:40, 45; 2 Ki. 25:14; 2 Chr. 4:11, 16; Jer. 52:18). In one other passage (Isa. 30:24) two uncommon words are paired with reference to winnowing implements; the NIV translates "fork and shovel," whereas the NRSV has "shovel and fork" (KJV and NJPS, "shovel … fan").

showbread. See TABERNACLE.

shrine. This English term (from Lat. *scrinium*), meaning originally "case, receptacle," refers in particular to a box where sacred relics or objects of WORSHIP are deposited, and by metonymy to a small building where such objects are kept or more generally to any place where devotion to a deity or saint is paid—thus a "sanctuary." The word is used by the KJV only once (Acts 19:24), referring to certain small idol houses made by the silversmith DEMETRIUS. Modern versions use "shrine" not only here but also with some frequency in the OT; for example, in passages where the Hebrew word for "house" is used in a similar sense (Jdg. 17:5; 1 Ki. 12:31; Isa. 44:13; et al.).

shroud. This English noun is used once by the KJV in the archaic meaning, "shelter" (Ezek. 31:3). Modern versions use it occasionally either in the general sense of "a covering" (Isa. 25:7) or more specifically of the winding sheet with which the dead were covered (see RSV at Matt. 27:59; Mk. 15:46; Lk. 23:53; Gk. *sindōn G4984*, meaning "[fine *or* linen] cloth").

shrub. See PLANTS.

Shua. shoo´uh (Heb. *šûʿa H8781*, "salvation, prosperity"; also *šûʿāʾ H8783* [only 1 Chr. 7:32], but the derivation of the latter is uncertain). **(1)** A Canaanite man whose daughter married JUDAH (Gen. 38:2, 12 [KJV, "Shuah"]; 1 Chr. 2:3); she gave birth to three sons, ER, ONAN, and SHELAH. In the Chronicles passage, the words *bat-šûaʿ* ("the daughter of Shua"; cf. KJV and NIV) are rendered as the name BATH-SHUA by the NRSV and other versions (but the same Hebrew expression occurs in Gen. 32:12).

(2) Daughter of Heber and descendant of ASHER (1 Chr. 7:32).

Shuah. shoo´uh (Heb. *šûaḥ H8756*, meaning uncertain; gentilic *šûḥî H8760*, "Shuhite"). **(1)** Son of ABRAHAM and KETURAH (Gen. 25:2; 1 Chr. 1:32). Some scholars link Shuah with the Akkadian place name *šūḫu*, which refers to a region near the confluence of the rivers EUPHRATES and HABOR. One of JOB's friends, BILDAD, is identified as "the Shuhite" (Job 2:11 et al.), but his connection with either Abraham's son or the Akkadian toponym is uncertain.

(2) KJV alternate form of SHUA (Gen. 38:2, 12).

(3) KJV form of SHUHAH (1 Chr. 4:11).

Shual (person). shoo´uhl (Heb. *šûʿāl H8786*, "fox, jackal"). Son of Zophah and descendant of ASHER (1 Chr. 7:36). Some scholars link him with SHUAL (PLACE) and infer that the Asherite clan of Shual had settled not within the tribal territory of Asher but rather in the southern hill country of EPHRAIM.

Shual (place). shoo´uhl (Heb. *šûʿāl H8787*, "fox, jackal"). A region in the vicinity of OPHRAH to which one of three detachments of PHILISTINES went while encamped at MICMASH (1 Sam. 13:17). Two of the detachments went W and E, while the third headed N of Micmash in the direction of Ophrah. Shual is possibly an alternate form of SHAALIM, the country through which SAUL passed in seeking the lost donkeys of his father KISH (1 Sam. 9:4). The precise location is uncertain. See also SHUAL (PERSON).

Shubael. shoo´bay-uhl (Heb. *šûbāʾēl H8742* and *šĕbûʾēl H8649*, possibly "Return, O God!"). Also Shebuel. **(1)** Descendant of LEVI through AMRAM,

MOSES, and GERSHOM (1 Chr. 23:16 [KJV and other versions, "Shebuel"]; 24:20). On the basis of the first passage listed, Shubael is usually thought to be a son of Gershom, but if so, he must then be distinguished from the Shubael who was in charge of the temple treasuries at the time of DAVID (26:24 [KJV and other versions, "Shebuel"]).

(2) Son of HEMAN, the king's seer (1 Chr. 25:4 [KJV and other versions, "Shebuel"]). The fourteen sons of Heman, along with the sons of ASAPH and JEDUTHUN, were set apart "for the ministry of prophesying, accompanied by harps, lyres and cymbals" (v. 1). The assignment of duty was done by lot, and the thirteenth lot fell to Shubael, his sons, and his relatives (25:20).

Shuhah. shoo´huh (Heb. *šûḥāh H8758*, meaning unknown). KJV Shuah. Brother of Kelub and descendant of JUDAH (1 Chr. 4:11). His place in the genealogy is unclear.

Shuham. shoo´ham (Heb. *šûḥām H8761*, meaning unknown; gentilic *šûḥāmî H8762*, "Shuhamite"). Son of DAN and eponymous ancestor of the Shuhamite clan (Num. 26:42); elsewhere called HUSHIM (Gen. 46:23).

Shuhite. See SHUAH.

Shulammite. shoo´luh-mit (Heb. *šûlammît H8769*, derivation uncertain). The name of, or a designation given to, the bride in SONG OF SOLOMON (Cant. 6:13). The Hebrew form suggests that this term is the gentilic of an otherwise unknown place (or clan) named Shulam. Many scholars, however, suspect that the name should be read as *Shunammite*, referring to someone from the town of SHUNEM (cf. 2 Ki. 4:12 et al.). In this light it has been suggested that since ABISHAG was a "Shunammite" taken to minister to DAVID in his old age (1 Ki. 1:1-4, 15; 2:17-22), she was perhaps the "Shulammite" of SOLOMON's Song. It was common in ancient times for a conquering or succeeding king to take over the former king's HAREM (cf. 2 Sam. 16:22). Solomon, as David's successor, may have acquired Abishag along with other women of David's harem. Several other interpretations of the term have been proposed.

Shumathite. shoo'muh-thit (Heb. *šumātî* H9092, gentilic form of a presumed ancestor or place named *šumâ*). The Shumathites were a Judahite clan descended from CALEB through HUR and SHOBAL; they made up one of several families associated with KIRIATH JEARIM (1 Chr. 2:53).

Shunammite. See SHUNEM.

Shunem. shoo'nuhm (Heb. *šûnēm* H8773, meaning unknown; gentilic *šûnammî* H8774, "Shunammite"). A town in the territory allotted to the tribe of ISSACHAR (Josh. 19:18). Shunem is identified with modern Solem, about 3 mi. (5 km.) N of JEZREEL and just S of Mount MOREH. The town is mentioned in several extrabiblical sources. The PHILISTINES encamped here in preparation for battle against the Israelites (1 Sam. 28:4); this maneuver led SAUL to occupy Mount GILBOA, about 8 mi. (13 km.) SSE of Shunem (the resultant conflict led to Saul's death on the slopes of the mountain). ABISHAG, DAVID's nurse who cared for him shortly before his death, was a Shunammite; ADONIJAH sought unsuccessfully to marry her, evidently in an attempt to strengthen his weak claim to the throne (1 Ki. 2:13-18, 22). The prophet ELISHA lodged frequently at Shunem in the home of a benefactress, the birth of whose son he accurately predicted; he later restored the child to life (2 Ki. 4:8-37; cf. Jesus' raising of the widow's son at NAIN, which is on the N side of Mount Moreh and thus very close to Shunem). Elisha's use of Shunem as a stopping place on his way from SAMARIA indicates that the prophet ministered in an extensive circuit. See also SHULAMMITE.

Shuni. shoo'ni (Heb. *šûnî* H8771, meaning unknown; gentilic *šûnî* H8772, "Shunite"). Son of GAD, grandson of JACOB, and eponymous ancestor of the Shunite clan (Gen. 46:16; Num. 26:15).

Shupham. shoo'fuhm (Heb. *šûpām* H8792, meaning unknown; gentilic *šûpāmî* H8793). Son of BENJAMIN, grandson of JACOB, and eponymous ancestor of the Shuphamite clan (Num. 26:39 KJV and NIV; other versions, "Shephupham," following MT). See comments under SHEPHUPHAM.

Shuppim. shuh'pim (Heb. *šuppim* H9173 [not in NIV], meaning unknown). **(1)** Son of Ir and descendant of BENJAMIN (1 Chr. 7:12, 15 KJV and other versions; NIV, "Shuppites"). See HUPPIM; HUSHIM #2; SHEPHUPHAM.

(2) A doorkeeper who, along with HOSAH, was responsible for the SHALLEKETH Gate on the W side of JERUSALEM (1 Chr. 26:16). Many scholars, however, believe that the name Shuppim here is the result of a scribal mistake (dittography due to *hā'ăsuppîm* at the end of v. 15) and delete the name.

The village of Shunem, located on the SW side of Mt. Moreh in the Jezreel Valley. (View to the E.)

© Dr. James C. Martin

S

Shuppites. shuh´pits (Heb. *šuppîm H9157*, meaning unknown). A clan descended from BENJAMIN through Ir (1 Chr. 7:12, 15 NIV; the KJV and other versions have "Shuppim"). See discussion under HUPPIM.

Shur. shoor (Heb. *šûr H8804*, "wall"). A desert region along the eastern border of EGYPT (Gen. 16:7). Because the name means "wall," some have argued that the reference is to a line of fortifications attested in extrabiblical sources. It is more likely, however, that the ancient fortifications gave their name to the region E of it, and it is to the latter that the instances of Shur may refer. In Exod. 15:22 such is obviously the case, for Moses led "from the Red Sea and they went into the Desert of Shur" (this wilderness area, or possibly part of it, was also identified as the Desert of ETHAM, Num. 33:8). The same region is probably also intended when it is said that ABRAHAM "dwelt between Kadesh and Shur" (Gen. 20:1). The possibility must be left open, however, that Shur could refer to a more specific locality not yet identified. In the account of HAGAR's flight from SARAH, mention is made of "the spring that is beside the road to Shur" (16:7). Such a road was probably an ancient caravan route, the last segment of the northern route of the KING'S HIGHWAY, which came out of EDOM, passed through the wilderness of ZIN to KADESH BARNEA, and reached Egypt via "the Desert of Shur" (Exod. 15:22).

Shushan. See SUSA.

Shushan-eduth. See SHOSHANNIM.

Shuthalhite. See SHUTHELAH.

Shuthelah. shoo´thuh-luh (Heb. *šûtelaḥ H8811*, meaning uncertain; gentilic *šutalḥi H9279*, "Shuthelahite"). **(1)** Son of EPHRAIM, grandson of JOSEPH, and eponymous ancestor of the Shuthelahite clan (Num. 26:35-36 [KJV, "Shuthalhites"]; 1 Chr. 7:20). There are some unexplained differences between the genealogies in these two passages.

(2) Son of Zaba and descendant of Ephraim (1 Chr. 7:21). Some suspect textual corruption and delete Shuthelah here as a repetition from the pre-

vious verse. Others insert Shuthelah in v. 25; see RESHEPH (PERSON).

shuttle. A device containing a reel or spool; it is used in WEAVING to carry the woof thread back and forth between the warp threads. The word occurs in the Bible as a figure of the quick passing of life (Job 7:6; the Heb. word apparently refers to the LOOM in its only other occurrence, Jdg. 16:14).

Sia, Siaha. si´uh (Heb. *sîʿāʾ H6103* [Neh. 7:47] and *sîʿāhāʾ H6104* [Ezra 2:44]). A descendant of temple servants (NETHINIM) who returned from the EXILE with ZERUBBABEL (Ezra 2:44; Neh. 7:47).

Sibbecai. sib´uh-ki (Heb. *sibbĕkay H6021*, derivation uncertain). KJV Sibbechai; TNIV Sibbekai. A Hushathite (see HUSHAH) who was among DAVID's mighty warriors and who slew a GIANT named Saph or Sippai during a battle with the PHILISTINES at GOB (2 Sam. 21:18; 1 Chr. 11:29; 20:4; called MEBUNNAI in 2 Sam. 23:27). Sibbecai was the commander heading the eighth division (1 Chr. 27:11, where he is also referred to as a Zerahite; see ZERAH).

Sibbechai. sib´uh-ki. KJV form of SIBBECAI.

Sibbekai. sib´uh-ki. TNIV form of SIBBECAI.

sibboleth. sib´uh-lith. See SHIBBOLETH.

Sibmah. sib´muh (Heb. *śibmâ H8424* and *śĕbām H8423* [only Num. 32:3], possibly "cold"). A city in the territory allotted to the tribe of REUBEN (Num. 32:3 [where it is called "Sebam"; KJV, "Shebam"], 38 [KJV, "Shibmah"]; Josh. 13:19). Sibmah was apparently known for its vines and grapes: both Isaiah and Jeremiah predicted that its vines were to languish under the judgment of God (Isa. 16:8-9; Jer. 48:32). The town, usually mentioned in connection with such other places as HESHBON and KIRIATHAIM, was located in the pastoral plateau area of MOAB acquired by conquest from SIHON king of the AMORITES. The oracles of Isaiah and Jeremiah indicate that Sibmah must have fallen back into Moabite hands. Some have identified it with modern Qarn el-Qibsh (c. 3 mi./5 km. WSW of Heshbon), but there is no archaeological evidence to support this proposal.

Sibraim. sib´ray-im (Heb. *sibrayim H6028*, derivation uncertain). A place between DAMASCUS and HAMATH, mentioned in EZEKIEL'S prophecy as part of the N border of Israel (Ezek. 47:16). Some have suggested that that Sibraim is the same as SEPHARVAIM. In any case, its exact location is unknown.

Sibylline Oracles. sib´uh-leen. A Jewish collection of prophecies, with many Christian additions, written in imitation of pagan oracles attributed to the sibyl (originally the term *sibyl* may have been a proper name, but it was applied to some ten prophetesses from various countries). The work consists of books that date as early as c. 150 B.C. and as late as the 7th century A.D. See APOCALYPTIC LITERATURE; PSEUDEPIGRAPHA.

Sicarii. See ZEALOT.

Sichem. See SHECHEM.

Sicily. The triangular island lying off the toe of ITALY was colonized by a tribe closely related to those from the region of the Tiber who became the Roman people. The W and S of the island was colonized from the eighth century B.C. onward by the Carthaginians (themselves Phoenician colonists from TYRE), and the E and N by the Greeks. Colonization in both cases was by the building of *emporia*, or seacoast towns, designed to exploit the hinterland. Centuries of tension and strife between the Greeks and Carthaginians ended with the intervention of ROME in the middle of the third century B.C. The W MEDITERRANEAN was too small for two first-class powers, and Rome and Carthage both looked on Sicily as a bridgehead. Hence the firmness with which Rome took advantage of factional strife at Messana to invade the island. The end of the Punic wars saw Sicily a Roman PROVINCE.

sick, sickness. See DISEASES.

sickle. A curved cutting tool for harvesting grain (Deut. 16:9; 23:25; 1 Sam. 13:20 [MT, "plow-share"]; Jer. 50:16; Joel 3:13; Mk. 4:29; Rev. 14:14-19). The earlier sickles seem to have been constructed of wood. They resembled our modern scythes, though smaller, and the cutting edge was made of flint. Later sickles were constructed of metal. These were used mostly for cutting grain, but on occasion they were used for pruning. In usage the NT follows the Joel passage in presenting the sickle as the instrument of divine WRATH and JUDGMENT.

Siddim, Valley of. sid´im (Heb. *siddim H8443*, derivation uncertain). A place identified with the "Salt Sea" where KEDORLAOMER and his allies defeated the kings of SODOM, GOMORRAH, and the other cities of the JORDAN pentapolis (Gen. 14:3, 8, 10). The armies apparently followed the KING'S HIGHWAY in TRANSJORDAN to the field of battle somewhere in the locality of the DEAD SEA. Some believe that Siddim was the plain S of el-Lisan, which has been down-faulted and submerged beneath the lake. Certainly, the lake terrain around the shores of the Dead Sea indicate that as a consequence of climatic oscillations, drainage evolution, and faulting, possibly twenty-five distinct lake levels have occurred in the trough since Pleistocene times. The exact locale of the Valley of Siddim remains speculative.

Sidon. si´duhn (Heb. *ṣîdôn H7477*, possibly "fishing town"; gentilic *ṣîdōnî H7479*, "Sidonian"). KJV Zidon (Sidon in Gen. 10:15, 19, and NT). The first biblical occurrence of this name is in reference to the firstborn son of CANAAN (Gen. 10:15 = 1 Chr. 1:13), but elsewhere it designates an important coastal city-state of PHOENICIA. As a geographical term, it first occurs in Gen. 10:19 in a description of the territory of the Canaanites, which is said to have extended from Sidon to the S as far as GAZA. JACOB prophesied that the territory of ZEBULUN would reach all the way to Sidon (49:13; cf. Josh. 19:28). The city is mentioned at various points in the historical books of the OT (Josh. 11:8; Jdg. 1:31; 10:6; 18:28; 2 Sam. 24:6; 1 Ki. 17:9; Ezra 3:7) and figures in a number of prophetic oracles (Isa. 23:2-12; Ezek. 28:21-22; et al.). The modern Lebanese city of Sidon is built over the ruins of the ancient city, also known as Saida. It is located

S

© Dr. James C. Martin. The Istanbul Archaeological Museum. Photographed by permission.

Limestone foundation inscription from the Eshmun temple in Sidon (6th cent. B.C.). The Phoenician text reads: "Bodastarte, the son of Eshmunazar, the king of Sidon, has ordered this temple to be built for the god Eshmun."

about 28 mi. (45 km.) SSW of Beirut and about 25 mi. (40 km.) N of Tyre. On the N side of the city there was a good harbor, protected by a low line of rocks joining the promontory and the mainland. To the S of the city there was a large bay.

Sometimes in the OT (Jer. 25:22 et al.), and often in the NT, Sidon is combined with Tyre, almost as a formula. One visit by Jesus to the region of Tyre and Sidon is recorded in the Gospels, at which time he had the encounter with the Syrophoenician woman (Matt. 15:21-28). In his invectives upon the cities of Galilee, Jesus compared Korazin and Bethsaida to Tyre and Sidon and declared that the latter cities would have responded more quickly than the former (Matt. 11:21-22; Lk. 10:13-14). The people of Tyre and Sidon were involved in difficulties with Herod Agrippa at the time of his death (Acts 12:20). On Paul's shipwreck voyage to Rome a port call was made at Sidon (Acts 27:3).

The skill of the artisans of Sidon is well attested in ancient times. The carving of ivory to decorate furniture, architecture, and small objects was a flourishing industry in Sidon. The Assyrian documents record great quantities of ivory articles sent to the Assyrian kings as gifts and tribute. Homer lists one of the prizes at the funeral games of Patrocles as a beautiful Sidonian silver bowl (*Iliad* 23.741ff.). Such trade in ancient times reflects an extensive Sidonian influence in E and W. The chief god of the Sidonians was Eshmun, and of the Tyrians, Melqart. These two were part of the

familiar ANE fertility cult and harvest myth, represented in Babylonia as Ishtar and Tammuz, in Egypt as Isis and Osiris. Eshmun also became the chief god of Carthage.

siege. See war.

sieve. A utensil used to sift grains. Some of the Egyptian sieves were made of strings or reeds. Those constructed of string were used for finer work whereas those made from reeds were used for sifting coarser material. The word is used in the Bible in a figurative sense in both passages where it occurs (Isa. 30:28; Amos 9:9).

sign. In Scripture this word generally refers to something addressed to the senses to attest the existence of a divine power. Miracles in the OT were often signs (Exod. 4:8; 8:23). Several specific things were given as signs, such as the rainbow (Gen. 9:12-13), some of the feasts (Exod. 13:9), the Sabbath (Exod. 31:13), and circumcision (Rom. 4:11). Often extraordinary events were given as a sign to insure faith or demonstrate authority. When Moses would not believe God, his rod was turned into a serpent and his hand became leprous as signs of God's divine commission (Exod. 4:1-8). Sometimes future events were given as signs, as in the case of Isaiah's prophecy to Ahaz (Isa. 7:14). When Christ was born, the place of his birth and his dress were to be signs of his identity to the shepherds. When the scribes and the Pharisees asked Jesus for a sign, he assured them that no sign was to be given them except the sign of Jonah, whose experience in the fish portrayed Christ's burial and resurrection. Revelation tells that before Christ returns there will be signs in the heavens, in the stars, moon, and sun.

signal. The standard method for communicating in times of war and peace in antiquity was by signal fires. Such are mentioned in the OT (e.g., Jer. 6:1) and in the records from Tell el-Amarna and Lachish. However, banners or flags are also mentioned (e.g., Isa. 5:26).

signature. This term is used by the NRSV once (Job 31:35) to render *tāw* H9338, the name of the last letter of the Hebrew alphabet, which in its earlier form resembled the English letter *X* (see TAU). The same Hebrew word is translated "mark" elsewhere (Ezek. 9:4, 6). In sealing documents, individuals would have used their own recognizable signs, thought to correspond with the fingernail impressions made on clay tablets.

signet. See SEAL.

Sihon. si'hon (Heb. *siḥôn H6095*, meaning unknown). A king of the AMORITES defeated by the Israelites on their way to CANAAN (Num. 21:21-30). MOSES had sent messengers to Sihon, hoping to obtain permission to lead the Israelites through his land. The king refused to grant this permission; rather he went out against ISRAEL with his army, but was defeated and slain. Israel then claimed Sihon's land as its first conquered area. HESHBON had been his capital city; his S boundary was the river ARNON; and his N boundary was the river JABBOK (Num. 21:24). Further, his country was a land of many villages and cities (21:25); it became a part of the Transjordanian territory claimed and settled by the tribes of REUBEN, GAD, and part of MANASSEH.

Moses used the defeat of Sihon as a meaningful reference to the past (Deut. 1:3-4; 2:24-37; 3:1-11; 29:7; 31:4). It is of interest to observe that other peoples told about this incident and spread the news, causing dread among the inhabitants on the W side of the Jordan (Josh. 2:10; 9:10). JOSHUA referred to it as he recounted great victories and apportioned the conquered land to certain tribes (Josh. 12:2, 5; 13:10, 21, 27). Later writers mentioned this Israelite victory as a reminder of what God had done for his people (Jdg. 11:19-20; 1 Ki. 4:19; Neh. 9:22; Ps. 135:11; 136:19; Jer. 48:45).

Sihor. See SHIHOR.

Sikkuth. See SAKKUTH.

Silas. si'luhs (Gk. *Silas G4976* [in Acts], apparently from Aram. *šĕʾîlāʾ* [= Heb. *šāʾûl H8620*, SAUL]; the form *Silouanos G4977* [2 Cor. 1:19; 1 Thess. 1:1; 2 Thess. 1:1; 1 Pet. 5:12] is thought to be either a surname [cognomen from Lat. *silva*, "wood, for-

est"] or a latinized form of *Silas*, though some have suggested that the latter was rather a shortened form of what may have been his original name, *Silvanus*). A prominent member of the JERUSALEM church and companion of the apostle PAUL on most of his second missionary journey. When the Council of Jerusalem decided that GENTILE believers were not obligated to be circumcised, Silas was one of two delegates appointed to accompany Paul and BARNABAS to ANTIOCH with the letter announcing the council's decision (Acts 15:22-23). The sentiments of the council were orally expressed as well (v. 27), together with strengthening words of exhortation by Silas and Judas Barsabbas (see JUDAS #7), who are referred to as "prophets" (v. 32). After some time in Antioch, their mission accomplished, they returned to "those who had sent them" (v. 33; according to v. 34 in the KJV, Silas remained in Antioch, but this verse is omitted by most witnesses, including the earliest MSS).

Paul chose Silas as his companion for the second missionary journey after the apostle and Barnabas had a falling out over the John Mark incident (Acts 15:36-40; see MARK, JOHN). Not much is said directly of Silas until the incident at PHILIPPI when he and Paul were beaten and imprisoned, accused of causing a breach of the peace and preaching false doctrine (16:12-40). Undaunted, the two prisoners prayed and sang praises to God at midnight until an earthquake secured their miraculous release. After the conversion of the jailer and his family, and the realization by the magistrates that Paul and Silas were Roman citizens (see CITIZENSHIP), they took leave of Philippi and the brethren there for THESSALONICA (17:1-9). Later, in BEREA, Silas was left with TIMOTHY while Paul went to ATHENS to escape the riots (17:1-15). The apostle had asked his companions to join him when they could, but it was not until he had left Athens and arrived at CORINTH that they caught up with their leader (18:5).

The person who is invariably called Silas in Acts and the one who is invariably called Silvanus in the NT epistles are undoubtedly one and the same. Paul always mentions him together with Timothy (2 Cor. 1:19; 1 Thess. 1:1; 2 Thess. 1:1). PETER, at the end of his first letter, gives the following information: "With the help of Silas [Silvanus], whom I regard as a faithful brother, I have written to you

S

briefly" (1 Pet. 5:12). While the full meaning of this remark is uncertain, it has been taken to mean that he was not simply bearer of the epistle, but also its AMANUENSIS, responsible for much of the style and arrangement of the letter.

silence. See QUIET, QUIETNESS.

silk. This English term is used by the KJV in two passages where modern versions usually have "fine linen" (Prov. 31:22; Ezek. 16:10, 13). It is doubtful that the woven thread of the Chinese silkworm (*Bombyx mori*) was known in the ANE in OT times. The Greek term for "silk" (*sirikos G4986*) appears only in Rev. 18:12. It is derived from a Hellenistic term (*Sēres*) that referred to people from China; certainly by the first century B.C. Chinese silk was known in ASIA MINOR.

Silla. sil'uh (Heb. *sillā' H6133*, meaning unknown). An unidentified place cited in connection with the murder of King Joash (JEHOASH), an event that is said to have taken place "at Beth Millo, on the road down to Silla" (2 Ki. 12:20). Its association with BETH MILLO (KJV and other versions, "the house of Millo") suggests that it may have been a sector of JERUSALEM or a place within its environs. See MILLO.

Siloam. si-loh'uhm (Gk. *Silōam G4978*, from Heb. *šilōaḥ H8942*; see SHILOAH). A pool and tower in biblical JERUSALEM; the term is also currently applied to the water tunnel that empties into the pool. As a defense against the attacks by ASSYRIA, which culminated in SENNACHERIB's campaign of 701 B.C. (cf. 2 Chr. 32:4), King HEZEKIAH of JUDAH constructed the Siloam water tunnel from the GIHON, southwestward through the rocky core of Mount ZION, and out into the central Tyropoeon Valley of Jerusalem (v. 30). The American traveler and scholar Edward Robinson and his missionary friend Eli Smith discovered this tunnel in 1838. They first attempted to crawl through it from the Siloam end, but soon found that they were not suitably dressed to crawl through the narrow passage. Three days later, dressed only in a wide pair of Arab drawers, they entered the tunnel from the Spring of Gihon and, advancing much of the way on their hands and knees and sometimes flat on their stomachs, went the full distance. They measured the tunnel and found it to be about 1,750 ft. (533 m.) in length. The tunnel has many twists and turns, however; a direct line would be less than 1,100 ft. (335 m.)

In 1867 Captain Charles Warren also explored the tunnel, but neither he nor Robinson and Smith before him noticed the inscription on the wall of the tunnel near the Siloam end. This was discovered in 1880 by a native boy who, while wading in the tunnel, slipped and fell into the water. When he looked he noticed the inscription. The boy reported his discovery to his teacher, Herr Conrad Schick, who made the information available to scholars. The inscription consists of six lines written in the older Hebrew alphabet with pronglike characters. The first half of the inscription is missing, but what remains reads as follows: "The boring through [is completed]. And this is the story of the boring through: while yet [they plied] the drill, each toward his fellow, and while yet there were three cubits to be bored through; there was heard the voice of one calling unto another, for there was a crevice in the rock on the right hand. On the day of the boring through the stonecutters struck, each to meet his fellow, drill

Staircase leading to the depression which once functioned as the Pool of Siloam. The excavation remains here have been dated as early as the first century B.C.

© Dr. James C. Martin

upon drill; and the water flowed from the source to the pool for 1,200 cubits, and a hundred cubits was the height of the rock above the head of the stone cutters." The importance this inscription can scarcely be overestimated. Not only does it give a fascinating account of the building of the tunnel, but has also provided a crucial point of reference for understanding the development of the Hebrew script and thus for dating other inscriptions. (In 1890 a vandal entered the tunnel and cut the inscription out of the rock. It was subsequently found in several pieces in the possession of a Greek in Jerusalem who claimed he had purchased it from an Arab. The Turkish officials seized the pieces and removed them to Istanbul, where they are today.)

ISAIAH appears to speak of Hezekiah's project when he mentions "a reservoir between the two walls for the water of the Old Pool" (Isa. 22:11). The "Old Pool" may refer to an original Upper Pool (7:3) near the Gihon Spring. The Lower Pool (22:9), possibly modern Birket el-Hamra, at the S tip of the pre-Hezekian city is known to have received water from it by a surface conduit. The course of its upper 200 ft. (60 m.), with a minimal drop along the E side of Mount ZION—"gently flowing waters"—is still traceable. Thus it appears that the original Siloam Pool predated Hezekiah. However, by postexilic times, at least, the Lower Pool itself came to be called SHELAH (Neh. 3:15), since it seems to have continued in use for overflow from Hezekiah's newer pool. By Christian times the name Siloam had, understandably, become transferred to the newer pool. The NT thus designates this pool, to which Jesus sent the man who had been born blind, as the Pool of Siloam and appropriately interprets it to signify "Sent" (Jn. 9:7). Traces remain of a Herodian reservoir and bath structure, c. 70 sq. ft. (6.5 sq. m.), with steps on the W side. Here the man would have washed, miraculously receiving his sight (vv. 8, 10).

Siloam, tower in. A structure that was probably part of the ancient system of fortifications on the walls of the city of JERUSALEM near the Pool of SILOAM. The collapse of this tower and the resulting death of eighteen persons is cited by Jesus (Lk. 13:4). Apparently the accident was well known to his hearers, but it is not mentioned elsewhere.

Siloam, village of. There is no mention of a village by this name in the Bible. However, across the valley E of the Spring of GIHON is a rocky slope on which is situated the modern village of Silwan (Siloam). At this site an inscription over the door of a tomb, discovered at the end of the nineteenth century, indicates that the tomb may have belonged to Shebna, an official during HEZEKIAH's time (cf. Isa. 22:15-16).

Silvanus. sil-vay′nuhs. See SILAS.

silver. See MINERALS.

silverling. This archaic term, meaning "small silver coin," is used once by the KJV (Isa. 7:23, where modern versions have "shekels").

silversmith. See OCCUPATIONS AND PROFESSIONS.

Simeon. sim′ee-uhn (Heb. *šim'ôn H9058*, possibly "[God] has heard" [cf. SHIMEON and SIMON]; gentilic *šim'ōnî H9063*, "Simeonite"; Gk. *Symeōn G5208*). Also Symeon (some versions in the NT). **(1)** Son of JACOB and ancestor of the Israelite tribe that bears his name. According to the book of Genesis, Jacob loved RACHEL more than he loved his other wife, LEAH (Gen. 29:30). Because of this, God opened Leah's womb and she bore first REUBEN and then Simeon; the latter received that

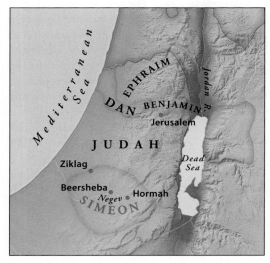

The tribal territory of Simeon.

S

name because God had "heard" Leah's grief (vv. 31-33). It was Simeon and his younger brother LEVI who used deception to avenge themselves upon SHECHEM the HIVITE after that prince violated their sister DINAH (34:25-31). The act made Jacob persona non grata in the area and aroused his anger upon the two brothers (34:30; Jacob's last testament indicates that his anger did not abate through the years, for he predicted that because of the violent nature of the two, their descendants would be scattered throughout the land, 49:5-7). Simeon was the brother whom JOSEPH held hostage until BENJAMIN should be brought to him (42:24).

Simeon and his five sons (including SHAUL, the son of a Canaanite woman) settled in EGYPT with the rest of Jacob's family and by the time of the EXODUS had developed into a tribe (Gen. 46:10; Exod. 1:2; 6:15). In those sections of Numbers that deal with the organization of the Israelite camp, the tribe of Simeon is mentioned several times in its appropriate position, the second (Num. 1:6, 22, 23; 2:12; 7:36; 10:19). However, a comparison of the census figures in chs. 1 and 26 shows that while the nation as a whole lost only 2,000 during the wilderness sojourn (603,000 to 601,000), the tribe of Simeon lost more than 27,000. This represents a decline of more than fifty percent, from 59,300 to 22,100. There were no smaller tribes than Simeon. Apparently, then, the tribe of Simeon was hard hit during the wandering. The man whom PHINEHAS killed at BAAL PEOR (25:14) was the head of a Simeonite clan. If the Simeonites were leaders in this apostasy, the resulting plague may have rested upon that tribe especially heavily and may partially account for the decline. At any rate, it was perhaps because of the weakness of the Simeonite tribe that it seems to have lost its independent status at an early stage, for the Simeonites were not accorded a separate inheritance in the land (Josh. 19:1-9). Simeon alone, of all the tribes, was rather given certain villages within the boundaries of another tribe, JUDAH (19:2-9; cf. 15:20-63); these villages were located in the southern area of Judah, the NEGEV.

Simeon's special situation within Judah meant that the two groups were more and more melted into one, with Judah taking the lead (Josh. 21:9;

Jdg. 1:3, 17-19). This is especially plain in that Simeon is not mentioned in the numerous tribal lists of Judges. Its absence from the books of Samuel and Kings is also noteworthy. During the reign of HEZEKIAH, a group of Simeonites migrated to GEDOR (prob. modern Khirbet Judur, c. 8 mi./13 km. SW of BETHLEHEM), while another group migrated S into EDOM (1 Chr. 4:39-43). If the identification of Gedor is correct, this may indicate that the Simeonites, deposed from their cities, spread both northward and southward in the area of Judah during the monarchy.

The treatment of Simeon in 2 Chr. 15:9 and 34:6 is difficult to interpret. In both instances, the tribe appears to be grouped with EPHRAIM and MANASSEH as typifying the northern kingdom versus Judah and BENJAMIN. This seems impossible unless one presumes that a majority of the Simeonites had migrated into the northern area. Perhaps the statements intend to say only that peoples from both N (Ephraim and Manasseh) and S (Simeon) were drawn into Judah and Benjamin at this time. Further complicating this question is the issue of the tribal make-up of the kingdoms of Judah and ISRAEL. If Judah was composed of Judah and Benjamin (1 Ki. 12:21; 2 Chr. 15:9), then Simeon would have had to be counted as one of the ten (northern) tribes of Israel. Only in the unlikely circumstance that LEVI was counted as one of the northern tribes would it then be possible to argue that Simeon was simply dropped from the enumeration. Some scholars have argued that SOLOMON so effectively broke the separate identities of the tribes that the idea of ten northern tribes was not literally carried out. The final reference to the tribe of Simeon occurs in Rev. 7:7, which states that 12,000 Simeonites, along with representatives of the other eleven tribes, were sealed against the coming doom.

(2) Grandfather of MATTATHIAS (#2) and thus great-grandfather of the Maccabean leaders (1 Macc. 2:1). See MACCABEE.

(3) Son of a certain Judah, included in Luke's GENEALOGY OF JESUS CHRIST (Lk. 3:30). This Simeon had a son named Levi, but nothing else is known about him.

(4) A devout man of JERUSALEM who had been promised by God that he would see the MESSIAH

before he died (Lk. 2:25-26). When Jesus was taken by his parents to the temple for the performance of the purification rites, Simeon was prompted by the HOLY SPIRIT. Recognizing the baby Jesus as the MESSIAH, Simeon took him in his arms and uttered the famous prayer known by its first two Latin words, NUNC DIMITTIS (2:29-32). He further predicted the necessity of suffering involved in Jesus' redemptive work, especially as it would affect Mary. This incident is apparently related by Luke as a part of his program of locating independent witnesses to Christ's messiahship.

(5) One of the prophets and teachers of the church at ANTIOCH (Acts 13:1). See NIGER.

(6) The name used by JAMES with reference to Simon PETER (Acts 15:14 most versions; NIV, "Simon"). This use of Peter's Hebrew name may well have been intended to remind troubled Jews in the group that it was through a faithful Jew like Peter that God had inaugurated the Gentile mission.

similitude. This English term, meaning "corresponding likeness," is used a number of times in the KJV, mostly in the OT (Num. 12:8 et al.). In the KJV NT it translates *homoiōma G3930* (Rom. 5:14; cognate nouns in Heb. 7:15 and Jas. 3:9). The apostle PAUL can use this Greek term to express the reality of the INCARNATION. God has sent "his own Son in the likeness of sinful humanity" (Rom. 8:3 TNIV); Jesus was born "in human likeness" (Phil. 2:7; conversely, believers are united with Christ "in the likeness" [KJV] of his death and resurrection, Rom. 6:5). Using the cognate verb (*homoioō G3929*), the epistle to the Hebrews states that Jesus "had to be made like his brothers in every way" (Heb. 2:17; cf. 4:15). Though many have taken the "likeness" to point to some remaining "unlikeness," surely the intent of these passages is to teach the agreement of Christ's nature with true humanity. These passages underline the reality of Christ's work, including his continuing care and intercession for his people. On the concept that we "have been made in God's likeness" (Jas. 3:9), see IMAGE OF GOD.

Simon. si′muhn (Gk. *Simōn G4981*, from Heb. *šim‘ôn H9058*; see SIMEON). (1) One of the twelve disciples of Jesus. See PETER.

(2) Another of the twelve disciples of Jesus, called "the Zealot" (Matt. 10:4; Mk. 3:18; Lk. 6:15; Acts 1:13). See CANANAEAN.

(3) A brother of Jesus (Matt. 13:55; Mk. 6:3).

(4) A leper of BETHANY in whose house a woman anointed Jesus' head with expensive ointment (Mk. 14:3-9; cf. Jn. 12:1-8).

(5) A PHARISEE in whose house a sinful woman anointed the feet of Jesus with her tears

Remains of the Roman forum at Samaria (Sebaste), city of Simon Magus. (View to the NE.)

© Dr. James C. Martin

S

and ointment. Simon's criticism of the act by an unclean woman of such low reputation drew forth from Jesus a parable which taught Simon the relation between forgiveness and appreciation (Lk. 7:36-50). Jesus commended the woman for her love and faith.

(6) A man from CYRENE in N Africa who was compelled to carry the CROSS of Christ (Matt. 27:32; Mk. 15:21; Lk. 23:26). Mark calls him "the father of Alexander and Rufus," who must have been well known to Mark's readers (prob. in the church at ROME, cf. Rom. 16:13 and see RUFUS). Simon was likely one of many Jews living in Cyrene, now visiting Jerusalem.

(7) The father of JUDAS ISCARIOT (Jn. 6:71; 12:4 [KJV, following the TR]; 13:2, 26).

(8) A man who practiced sorcery in SAMARIA (Acts. 8:9-24), often referred to as Simon Magus. The deacon/evangelist PHILIP encountered him in a town, probably Sebaste, the capital of the province. The magician himself became a convert (8:13, "believed," which is the normal term in Acts), was baptized with many others, and was amazed at the miracles of Philip, which apparently surpassed his own. How genuine was his conversion can only be judged by the sequel. This remarkable response in Samaria caused the apostles to dispatch PETER and John (see JOHN THE APOSTLE), their most prominent members. Their special function was to lay hands on the converts so that they might receive the HOLY SPIRIT. It was these visible acts of the Jerusalem leaders which aroused Simon to an intense interest in their "craft." Perhaps the gift of tongues was evident, if one follows the analogies of Acts 10:44-46 and 19:6. The externality of Simon's faith seems indicated by his bold attempt to bribe the apostles into imparting their "power." Peter's severe rebuke (8:20-23; the last verse echoes Deut. 29:18 and Isa. 58:6) implies Simon's basic misconception about the gifts of God, which are inward in their nature. Yet there remained the possibility of his seeking in penitence the forgiveness of God. His final plea (Acts 8:24) does not make it clear whether he had penetrated beyond the "signs" and the fear of retribution to any real faith, but his subsequent heretical reputation and the doubts raised by Luke himself make it safer to regard him as a nominal convert only. The story closes with a reference to a preaching tour that may have been partly designed to counter the cult of Simon. (The name of Simon Magus occurs frequently in the early history of "Christian" GNOSTICISM, and there has been much debate as to whether the Simoniani, a sect that lasted well into the 3rd cent., had its origins in the magician of Acts 8. Some traditions view him as the heretic par excellence of the subapostolic age.)

(9) A tanner of JOPPA in whose house PETER stayed "for some time" (Acts 9:43; 10:6, 17, 32). His house was by the seaside outside the city wall, because the handling of dead bodies made tanning ceremonially unclean to a Jew.

(10-11) The name of two high priests during the intertestamental period. Simon I ("the Just"), who lived in the first half of the third century B.C., was the son of ONIAS I and the father of Onias II. Toward the end of the century, Onias II was succeeded by his son Simon II. The ancient sources (e.g., Sir. 50:1-21; Jos. *Ant.* 12.2.5 §43) are sometimes ambiguous regarding which Simon is being referred to.

(12) A man from the tribe of BENJAMIN who was captain of the temple early in the second century B.C. (2 Macc. 3:4 et al.).

(13) One of the Maccabean brothers. See MACCABEE.

(14) Simon ben Kosiba. See BAR KOKHBA.

Simon Maccabeus. See MACCABEE.

Simon Magus. See SIMON #8.

Simon Peter. See PETER.

Simon the Canaanite. See CANANAEAN.

simple. This English term occurs primarily in the book of PROVERBS. Those who are simple hate knowledge and the fear of the Lord (Prov. 1:29; cf. vv. 22, 32); they are fools (8:5) who shall inherit folly (14:18). While the prudent foresee, the simple just go on their way and are punished (21:11), as when they visit the harlot (7:7). Since the simple can still learn, they are invited to the dinner prepared for them by WISDOM (9:4), and the book of Proverbs itself is written to give wisdom to the simple and the young (1:4; cf. also Ps. 19:7; 119:130). The NT usage is somewhat different. The KJV uses "simple" in one passage (Rom. 16:18-19) to render two Greek words that can mean "innocent" or "guileless"; the reference is to those who are unsuspecting and can be easily deceived.

Simri. See SHIMRI.

sin. The biblical writers portray sin with a great variety of terms because they have such a powerful sense of the living Lord, who is utterly pure and holy. For sin is that condition and activity of human beings that is offensive to God, their Creator. However, it is only as they are conscious of his HOLINESS that they are truly aware of their sin (1 Ki. 17:18; Ps. 51:4-6; Isa. 6).

The first book of the OT reveals how human beings were created by God without sin but chose to act contrary to his revealed will and thereby caused sin to become an endemic feature of human existence (Gen. 3; Ps. 14:1-3). Sin is revolt against the holiness and sovereign will of God. Therefore, it is both a condition of the heart/mind/will/affections (Isa. 29:13; Jer. 17:9) and the practical outworking of that condition in thoughts, words, and deeds that offend God and transgress his holy LAW (Gen. 6:5; Isa. 59:12-13). For ISRAEL, sin was a failure to keep the conditions of the COVENANT that the Lord graciously made with the people at SINAI (Exod. 19-23).

There is no person in Israel or the whole world who is not a sinner. However, those who have a right relationship with God receive his FORGIVENESS and who walk in his ways are sometimes described as righteous (Gen. 6:9) and blameless (Job 1:1; Ps. 18:20-24). This is not because they are free from sin, but because the true direction of their lives is to serve and please God in the way he requires.

The sins of the fathers have repercussions for their children and their children's children (Isa. 1:4; Lam. 5:7). Yet it is also true that individual Israelites are personally responsible to God for their own sins (Jer. 31:19-20; Ezek. 18; 33:10-20). Sin was punished by God in various ways (e.g., EXILE), but the final punishment for individual sin and wickedness was DEATH (Gen. 2:17; Ps. 73:27; Ezek. 18:4). This is certainly physical death but is also spiritual death, being cut off from communion with the living God.

The reality of sin and the need for CONFESSION and ATONEMENT are clearly presupposed by the SACRIFICES offered to God in the TEMPLE, especially the regular guilt (or trespass) offering and sin offering, as well as the special annual sacrifice of the Day of Atonement (Lev. 4; 6:24-30; 7:1-7; 16). They are also presupposed in the prophecy of the vicarious suffering of the SERVANT OF THE LORD who acts as a "guilt offering" and bears the sin of many (Isa. 53:10, 12).

The NT strengthens the OT portrayal of sin by viewing it in the light of CHRIST and his atonement, which is a victory over sin. Jesus was sinless and taught that the root of sin is in the human heart: "For from within, out of men's hearts, come ... evils" (Mk. 7:20-23). The outward life is determined by the inner (Matt. 7:15-17), and thus an outward conformity to laws and rules is not in itself a true righteousness if the heart is impure. The law of God, rightly understood, requires inner as well as outer conformity to its standards. But sin is more than failure to keep the law: it is also the rejection of the MESSIAH and the kingdom he proclaims and personifies. The work of the HOLY SPIRIT, said Jesus, is to convict "the world of ... sin ... because men do not believe in me" (Jn. 16:8-9; 15:22). Further, to live without the light of God from Jesus, the Messiah, is to live in darkness and to be in the grip of evil forces (1:5; 3:19-21; 8:31-34). And to call the light darkness and the Spirit of the Messiah unclean is to commit the unforgivable sin (Matt. 12:24, 31).

PAUL has much to say about sin. He believed that sin is revealed by the law of God, but it is only as the Holy Spirit enlightens the mind that a person truly sees what righteousness the law demands (Rom. 3:20; 5:20; 7:7-20; Gal. 3:19-24). Thus for Paul a person could be a devout keeper of the law (externally) and yet be a slave of sin (internally) because he knew, as Jesus also said, that sin begins in the heart (or flesh; see Rom. 6:15-23). The origin of sin can be traced back to the first human beings, ADAM and EVE, and to their revolt against the Lord (Rom. 5:12-19; 2 Cor. 11:3; 1 Tim. 2:14).

There is a positive message in all this. In a dream JOSEPH was told that MARY's baby "will save

S

his people from their sins" (Matt. 1:21), and JOHN THE BAPTIST proclaimed that Jesus was the Lamb of God who takes away the sin of the world (Jn. 1:29)—referring to Jesus as the fulfillment of the atoning sacrifices of the temple. Paul declared that God sent his only Son to be a sin offering (Rom. 8:3). Jesus made himself to be the friend of sinners (Lk. 7:34), and he understood that his ministry leading to death was the fulfillment of the ministry of the Suffering Servant who gives his life as a ransom for many (Mk. 10:45).

Sin (city). See PELUSIUM.

sin (letter). See SHIN.

Sin, Desert of. (*sîn H6097*, derivation uncertain). This desert region—not to be confused with the Desert of ZIN in the northern NEGEV—was on the route followed by the Hebrews when they left EGYPT, somewhere between ELIM and Mount SINAI (Exod. 16:1; 17:1; Num. 33:11-12 locates it more narrowly between the RED SEA and DOPHKAH). It was here that God provided both MANNA and QUAIL for the Israelites. Assuming that Mount Sinai should be identified with Jebel Musa or another mountain in its vicinity, some have suggested that the Wilderness of Sin is Debbet er-Ramleh, a sandy tract of desert at the foot of Jebel et-Tih, in the SW of the Sinai peninsula. Others believe it refers to the plain of el-Merkha on the W coast, half-way between the head of the Red Sea and the tip of the peninsula. Scholars who argue that the Israelites took a northerly route have proposed various other sites. The location remains unknown. See also EXODUS.

sin, man of. See ANTICHRIST.

Sinai, Mount. si´ni (Heb. *sînay H6099*, perhaps from Akk. *Sin*, name of the moon god; Gk. *Sina* or *Sinā G4982* [the mountain is also called Horeb, *ḥōrēb H2998*, "dry, desolate"]). The

name of the sacred mountain before which Israel encamped and upon which MOSES communicated with Yahweh. In the Bible, the name occurs almost exclusively in the PENTATEUCH. The Israelites reached Mount Sinai in the third month after their departure from Egypt and camped at its foot where they could view the summit (Exod. 19:1, 16, 18, 20). Yahweh revealed himself to Moses here and communicated the Ten Commandments and other laws to the people through him (see COMMANDMENTS, TEN; LAW). God established his COVENANT with the people through Moses as mediator, and this covenant has been remembered throughout Israel's history (e.g., Jdg. 5:5; Neh. 9:13; Ps. 68:8, 17; Mal. 4:4; Acts 7:30, 38). ELIJAH later visited Sinai (Horeb) in a time of particular discouragement and depression (1 Ki. 19:4-8). In the allegory of Gal. 4:24-25, Mount Sinai is representative of the bondage of the law in contrast to the JERUSALEM above, which is free. (The name Sinai is also applied to the large peninsula lying to the S of the Wilderness of PARAN between the Gulf of AQABAH on the E and Suez on the W; it has a triangular shape and is c. 150 mi./240 km. wide at the N and 250 mi./400 km. long. In addition the "Desert of Sinai" [Exod. 19:1] is the place where Israel came in the third month after they left Egypt; it may be used loosely as a synonym for the Sinaitic Peninsula but technically does not embrace as much territory.)

There has been much debate over the exact location of Mount Sinai. Possible sites include the

Pinnacle of Jebel Musa, traditional site of Mt. Sinai. (View to the S.)

© Dr. James C. Martin

following: (1) Mount Serbal, on Wadi Feiran; a serious objection to this identification, however, is that there is no plain large enough in the neighborhood to offer camping ground for a large group of people. (2) The traditional site is Jebel Musa (Arabic for "Mountain of Moses"), with an altitude of 7,363 ft. (2,244 m.; the well-known St. Catherine's Monastery is located at the foot of Jebel Musa); another peak in the same ridge, Ras Safsaf (6,540 ft./almost 2,000 m.) is often identified specifically with Horeb. (3) Jebel Hellal, a 2,000-ft. (610-m.) elevation that is 30 mi. (50 km.) south of el-ᶜArish. (4) Mount Seir, on the edge of the ARABAH. The identification of Mount Sinai depends primarily on the route of the EXODUS, a hotly disputed problem.

Sinaiticus, Codex. sin´i-it´uh-kuhs. See SEPTUAGINT; TEXT AND VERSIONS (NT).

sincere. This term and its cognates *sincerity* and *sincerely* appear rarely in English versions of the OT. In the NT, the Greek adjective *eilikrinēs G1637* ("unmixed, pure, sincere") and similar terms occur a handful of times. According to the NT, sincerity is an all-embracing attitude, not just one virtue among many. In Phil. 1:9 (where *eilikrinēs* is often rendered "pure") it is a quality required at the judgment, and requires growth in both love and knowledge, fitting one to discern that which is truly excellent (v. 10). The eschatological perspective is in view also in 2 Pet. 3:11; the sincere mind believes God's promises of Christ's return, over against the attitude of the scoffers that covers up God's promises with proud self-evaluation of the future. In 1 Cor. 5:8, sincerity is the (unmixed, plain) unleavened bread that rejects immorality in the church and the pride which condones it.

sinew. A tough fibrous band connecting muscle to bone; synonymous with *tendon*. Sinews are depicted as holding the bones of the body together (Job 10:11; 40:17; Ezek. 37:6, 8). JACOB's experience at PENUEL (Gen. 32:32; cf. v. 25) may have involved a mighty contraction of the muscle and tendon that tore muscle fibers and left Jacob limping at dawn. "Out of joint" would refer to any injury of the hip region; taken literally, it would imply a dislocation of the hip, a major injury making walking impos-

sible (see THIGH). In the NT, PAUL uses the Greek noun *syndesmos G5278* ("bond, ligament") figuratively when he compares the relationship between Christ and the CHURCH to the human body (Col. 2:19; see BODY OF CHRIST).

singer. See OCCUPATIONS AND PROFESSIONS.

singing. See MUSIC AND MUSICAL INSTRUMENTS; SONG.

single eye. The KJV rendering of a Greek phrase (Matt. 6:22; Lk. 11:34) that has been interpreted variously, for example, "honest," "generous," "healthy."

Sinim, land of. si´nim. See SINITE; SYENE.

Sinites. sin´its (*sînî H6098*, meaning unknown). A people group descended from CANAAN and mentioned in the Table of Nations (Gen. 10:17; 1 Chr. 1:15; it is possible, but unlikely, that the same people are referred to by the name *sînim* in the MT of Isa. 49:12, for which see SYENE). Some believe the Sinites should be connected to a coastal city-state named *syn*, located S of RAS SHAMRA (possibly modern Siyano, c. 2 mi./3 km. E of Jeble-Gabala).

sin offering. See SACRIFICE AND OFFERINGS.

Sion. si´uhn. (1) KJV form of SIYON (Deut. 4:48).
(2) KJV alternate form of ZION (Ps. 65:1 and NT).

Siphmoth. sif´moth (Heb. *śipmôt H8560*, meaning unknown). One of the cities of JUDAH with which DAVID shared the spoils taken from ZIKLAG (1 Sam. 30:28). It was visited by David during the time in which he was a fugitive from King SAUL. Siphmoth was evidently in the southern part of Judah's territory, but its location is unknown.

Sippai. sip´i (Heb. *sippay H6205*, meaning unknown). A descendant of the REPHAITES who was killed by SIBBECAI the Hushathite (1 Chr. 20:4). See SAPH.

Sirach. si´ruhk. See APOCRYPHA (under *Ecclesiasticus*).

S

Sirah. si′ruh (Heb. *sirâ H6241*, "thorn bush"). The name of a cistern or well from which JOAB summoned ABNER in order to put him to death (2 Sam. 3:26). Proposed identifications of Sirah include a spring named ʿAin Sarah (1.5 mi./2.5 km. NW of HEBRON) and a site called Ṣiret el-Bellaʿ (farther E).

Sirion. sihr′ee-uhn (Heb. *śiryôn H8590*, possibly "armor"). The Phoenician name that the people of SIDON used for Mount HERMON (Deut. 3:9). This mountain served to indicate the northern limit of the territory held by AMORITE kings (4:48 NRSV, following the Syriac version [but see SIYON]). The name occurs in poetic parallelism with LEBANON (Ps. 29:6).

Sisamai. See SISMAI.

Sisera. sis′uh-ruh (Heb. *sîsrāʾ H6102*, derivation uncertain; prob. not a Semitic name). **(1)** Commander of the army under JABIN, the Canaanite king of HAZOR (Jdg. 4:2-22). Sisera oppressed Israel for twenty years, waging war against them with 900 iron chariots (4:2-3). Finally, DEBORAH the prophetess, who judged Israel at that time, urged BARAK under the direction of God to unite his forces and go against Sisera. She assured Barak that God would deliver Sisera into his hands. He agreed, if Deborah would go with him, and she gave her consent. These two armies met in battle on the plain at the foot of Mount TABOR (4:14). The forces of Sisera were killed or scattered, and Sisera fled on foot, taking refuge in the tent of JAEL, the wife of HEBER the KENITE. Here he was killed by Jael while he slept in her tent. The remarkable victory was celebrated by the Song of Deborah (ch. 5).

(2) The ancestor of a family of temple servants who returned from the EXILE with ZERUBBABEL (Ezra 2:53; Neh. 7:55). Because the temple servants were apparently non-Israelites (see NETHINIM), some have speculated that this family descended from #1, above.

Sismai. sis′mi (Heb. *sismay H6183*, meaning unknown). KJV Sisamai. Son of Eleasah and descendant of JUDAH through the line of JERAHMEEL (1 Chr. 2:40).

sister. A word used in both Hebrew and Greek with varying ideas. In the OT it is used of females having the same parents, having but one parent in common, a female relative, or a woman of the same country (Gen. 20:12; Lev. 18:18; Num. 25:18; Job

The Kishon River, a wadi that flows through the Jezreel Valley, was the scene of Sisera's defeat at the hands of Deborah and Barak. (View to the E.)

© Dr. James C. Martin

42:11). In the NT it is used of girls belonging to the same family or just to blood relatives (Matt. 13:56; Mk. 6:3; Lk. 10:39). It is also used figuratively (Ezek. 16:45; 23:11; Rom. 16:1; 2 Jn. 13).

sistrums. See MUSIC AND MUSICAL INSTRUMENTS (sect. I.F).

Sithri. sith´ri (Heb. *sitrî H6262*, "[God is] my hiding place"). KJV Zithri. Son of Uzziel and descendant of LEVI through KOHATH (Exod. 6:22). One of Uzziel's brothers was AMRAM (father of MOSES, AARON, and MIRIAM), so Sithri was Moses' first cousin.

Sitnah. sit´nuh (Heb. *śiṭnāh H8479*, possibly "enmity, contention"). The name of the second well dug by the servants of ISAAC in the vicinity of GERAR (Gen. 26:21). The name reflects the conflict that ensued when the herdsmen of Gerar disputed with Isaac's herdsmen concerning the water rights. Although the exact location is uncertain, it was in the vicinity of REHOBOTH (v. 22).

Sivan. si´van (Heb. *sîwān H6094*, meaning uncertain). The third month in the Jewish religious CALENDAR, corresponding to May–June (Esth. 8:9).

six hundred sixty-sixty. See NUMBER.

Siyon. si´yuhn (Heb. *śî'ôn H8481*, perhaps "small height"). Alternate name of Mount HERMON, possibly referring to a specific part of the range (Deut. 4:48; KJV and NJPS, "Sion"). However, some scholars suspect textual corruption and, following the Syriac Peshitta, emend to *śiryôn H8590* (see SIRION), which was the Phoenician name for the mountain (cf. NRSV and TNIV; see also 3:9).

skin. Biblical references to animal skins used for clothing go back to the narrative of ADAM and EVE (Gen. 3:21). See DRESS; LEATHER. REBEKAH put the skins of kids on JACOB's hands and neck so that he would feel rough, like ESAU, to his blind father (Gen. 27:16). Animal skins were used also to manufacture leather bags for WINE (Josh. 9:4 et al.). Jesus, in response to complaints that his disciples were not fasting, commented that people do not "pour new wine into old wineskins. If they do,

the skins will burst, the wine will run out and the wineskins will be ruined. No, they pour new wine into new wineskins, and both are preserved" (Matt. 9:17; cf. Mk. 2:22; Lk. 5:37-38). New wine was still fermenting, and the expansion caused by the resulting gases was easily accommodated by a new stretchable bottle. As skin bottles grew old, however, they lost their elasticity, becoming hard and brittle; new wine would cause them to burst.

There are some references to human DISEASES of the skin. That JOB in his affliction suffered from smallpox is a good possibility. He was afflicted with sores from head to toe, to the extent that his friends could not recognize him (Job 2). The condition was very itchy, for he scraped himself with a piece of broken pottery. He commented, "my skin hardens, then breaks out again" (Job 7:5 NRSV). All this fits smallpox, although there are other possibilities. Israelite law addressed the problem of skin disorders (e.g., Lev. 13).

skink. See ANIMALS (under *lizard*).

skirt. See DRESS.

Skull, Place of the. See GOLGOTHA.

sky. In the OT, the KJV uses "skies" seven times and only as the rendering of *šĕḥāqîm* (pl. of *šaḥaq H8836*, Deut. 33:26 et al.); this Hebrew term, however, normally means "clouds." The KJV also uses the singular "sky" in three NT passages to translate Greek *ouranos G4041* (Matt. 16:2-3; Lk. 12:56; Heb. 11:12), a word usually rendered "heaven." The NIV and other modern versions use the English term much more frequently to translate the words for "heaven" (both Gk. *ouranos* and Heb. *šāmayim H9028*) when these refer to the physical space above the earth that has the appearance of a vault (Gen. 1:8 et al.; Matt. 24:29 et al.).

slander. A false accusation that defames a person's reputation. The basic character of this sin is shown by its inclusion in the Decalogue (Exod. 20:16; see COMMANDMENTS, TEN), and also in the immediate context from which CHRIST quotes the second and great commandment (Lev. 19:16; cf. v. 18 and see Matt. 19:19; 22:39; Jas. 2:8). There, LOVE for one's

S

neighbor is characterized by not slandering him. That slander is against God's wisdom is stressed by Proverbs (e.g., Prov. 10:18). When it is against God's messengers, it is against God himself and is so punished (Num. 14:36; Rom. 3:8). It is placing human standards over God's judgment, and is implicit BLASPHEMY (cf. Jas. 4:11-12). It belongs in the category of those ultimate sins to which God delivers men and women (Rom. 1:30; 2 Tim. 3:3 for its eschatological character). The great slanderer is SATAN himself (Gk. *diabolos G1333*, "accuser, slanderer"). He attempts to alienate JOB from his God. The Apocalypse describes him as the one who continually accuses the brethren (Rev. 12:10). The deliberate false witness against Christ, particularly at his trial, must be seen in this context (Matt. 26:59). It is on Christ's account that his followers are falsely accused (Matt. 5:11), but when God has pronounced his judgment on the elect (justification), who dares bring any charge against them (Rom. 8:33)?

slave, slavery. While Hebrew *'ebed H6269* and Greek *doulos G1528* are very common words in the Bible, these are usually rendered "servant" by the KJV, which uses the English term *slave* only twice (Jer. 2:14; Rev. 18:13), and *slavery* not at all. The NIV and other modern versions frequently use these English words if the context so indicates. Among the Hebrews, slaves could be acquired in a number of ways: as prisoners of war (Num. 31:7-9), by purchase (Lev. 25:44), by gift (Gen. 29:24), by accepting a person in lieu of a debt (Lev. 25:39), by birth from slaves already possessed (Exod. 21:4), by arrest if the thief had nothing to pay for the object stolen (22:2-3), and by the voluntary decision of the person wanting to be a slave (21:6). Slaves among the Hebrews were more kindly treated than slaves among other nations, since the Mosaic law laid down rules governing their treatment. They could gain their freedom in a number of ways (Exod. 21:2-27; Deut. 15:12-23). Slavery continued in NT times, but the love of Christ seemed to militate against its continued existence (Gal. 3:28; Eph. 6:5-9; Phlm. 15-16).

sleep. There is nothing unusual about most biblical uses of this word in its literal or physical sense. After JACOB dreamed about the ladder he simply woke from his sleep (Gen. 28:16); when EUTYCHUS fell down during PAUL's long sermon it was due to a typical human loss of concentration in weariness (Acts 20:9). In a few cases natural sleep was, for supernatural reasons, deepened. This is recorded in the account of the creation of EVE (Gen. 2:21-22). The men around SAUL were in a similar deepened sleep while DAVID and ABISHAI took the spear and jar of water from his head (1 Sam. 26:12). The Bible refers to sleep also in a figurative sense; for example, to indicate spiritual indolence (Prov. 24:33-34; cf. 6:9). Similarly CHRIST, in talking to his followers about his second coming, exhorted them to be faithful and watchful: "If he comes suddenly, do not let him find you sleeping" (Mk. 13:36). PAUL, in exhorting Christians in everyday living and in warning them of the enormity of their task, stressed that "it is full time now for you to wake from sleep" (Rom. 13:11 RSV; cf. 1 Thess. 5:6-7). Where sleep is used to indicate physical DEATH, the picture is of a temporary state pending a final consummation (1 Cor. 15:51; cf. 1 Thess. 4:13-18). It is clear that this reference to death as sleep is figurative, and does not refer to sleep of the soul (cf. Lk. 16:24; 23:43; 2 Cor. 5:8; Rev. 6:9-10).

sleeves. See DRESS.

slime. See BITUMEN.

sling. See ARMS AND ARMOR.

slothfulness. See IDLENESS; SLUGGARD.

slow of anger. See LONGSUFFERING.

slug. See ANIMALS.

sluggard. See IDLENESS.

smell. See ODOR.

smith. See OCCUPATIONS AND PROFESSIONS.

smoke. Literal references to smoke in the Bible are relatively few (e.g., Josh. 8:20-21; Jdg. 20:38-40). The offering of INCENSE produced a cloud of smoke that represented the prayers of God's people (Lev. 16:13; Ezek. 8:11; Rev. 8:4). The most significant references to smoke indicate a visible concomitant of the presence of God in divine self-manifestations. In the instance of the Abrahamic covenant, while ABRAHAM slept "he saw a smoking fire pot with a flaming torch" passing between the pieces of the sacrifices he had divided (Gen. 15:17). When MOSES met with God on Mount SINAI, the mountain was "covered with smoke" (Exod. 19:18). The TEMPLE was filled with smoke when ISAIAH saw the Lord (Isa. 6:4); he also prophesied that God would "create over all of Mount Zion ... a cloud of smoke by day and a glow of flaming fire by night" (4:5). In John's vision, the heavenly temple "was filled with smoke from the glory of God and from his power" (Rev. 15:8). Though not explicitly stated, one can assume that other references to the divine self-manifestation (e.g., Exod. 3:2; 13:21; Num. 10:34; 14:14) include also the presence of smoke. See PILLAR OF FIRE AND OF CLOUD.

There are other figurative uses. The fire of God's anger is accompanied by "smoke ... from his nostrils" (Ps. 18:8; cf. Job 41:20). MOSES warned that the WRATH of God would "burn" against idolaters (Deut. 29:20). The psalmist cried out, "Why does your anger smolder against the sheep of your pasture?" (Ps. 74:1). Smoke also symbolizes the transient: enemies (Ps. 37:20; 68:2), idolaters (Hos. 13:3), the days of one's life (Ps. 102:3), and the heavens (Isa. 51:6).

Smyrna. smuhr′nuh (Gk. *Smyrna* G5044, "myrrh"). A port on the W coast of ASIA MINOR at the head of the gulf into which the Hermus River flows, a well-protected harbor and the natural terminal of a great inland trade-route up the Hermus Valley. Smyrna's early history was checkered. It was destroyed by the Lydians in 627 B.C. and for three centuries was little more than a village. It was refounded in the middle of the fourth century B.C., after ALEXANDER THE GREAT's capture of Sardis, and rapidly became the chief city of Asia. Smyrna was shrewd enough to mark the rising star of ROME. A common danger, the aggression

of ANTIOCHUS the Great of SYRIA, united Smyrna with Rome at the end of the third century B.C., and the bond formed remained unbroken. Smyrna was, indeed, the handiest of the bridgeheads, balancing the naval power of RHODES in the Aegean Sea. Smyrna referred to their ancient alliance with Rome when, in A.D. 26, they petitioned Emperor TIBERIUS to allow the community to build a temple to his deity. The permission was granted, and Smyrna built the second Asian temple to

Excavations at ancient Smyrna.

© Dr. James C. Martin

the emperor. The city had worshiped Rome as a spiritual power since 195 B.C., hence Smyrna's historical pride in her Caesar cult (see EMPEROR WORSHIP). Smyrna was famous for science, medicine, and the majesty of its buildings.

One of the letters in the book of Revelation was addressed to the Christian church in Smyrna (Rev. 2:8-17). It refers to "a synagogue of Satan" in the city (v. 9), undoubtedly indicating a Jewish community that was scornful of Christianity. The exhortation to endure and win a "crown of life" (v. 10) is probably a piece of imagery caught from a diadem of porticoes surrounding her hilltop, and described by Apollonius of Tyana (1st cent. A.D.): "For though their city is the most beautiful of all cities under the sun, and makes the sea its own, and holds the fountains of Zephyrus, yet it is a greater charm to wear a crown of men than a crown of porticoes, for buildings are seen only in their one place, but men are seen everywhere, and spoken about everywhere, and make their city as vast as the range of countries which they visit" (Philostratus, *Life of Apollonius* 4.7). Early in the second century, Ignatius wrote a letter to the Smyrneans; and in the middle of the century, Polycarp, who had been a disciple of JOHN THE APOSTLE, became a martyr in that city.

snail. See ANIMALS (under *slug*).

snake. See ANIMALS.

snake charming. Various kinds of serpents were numerous in Palestine, and the art of snake charming was practiced in the country. Some snakes were susceptible to such influence (Eccl. 10:11) and others resisted the techniques of the charmer. In Jer. 8:17 serpent charming is used metaphorically to describe the enemies of Judah who are "vipers that cannot be charmed"; and in Ps. 58:4-5 it characterizes the wicked who are "a cobra that has stopped its ears, / that will not heed the tune of the charmer."

snare. A device used to entangle and capture animals. Several Hebrew nouns can be rendered "snare," especially *môqēš H4613*, which probably refers to a wooden contrivance for catching birds (cf. Amos 3:5). The near synonyms *paḥ H7062* and *rešet H8407* seem to indicate trapping nets (all three words are used together in Ps. 140:5). These and other words are almost always used in metaphorical contexts. For example, IDOLATRY is often described as a snare to God's people (Exod. 23:33). For further comments see TRAP.

sneeze. The verb *sneeze* occurs once to indicate that the SHUNNAMITE's son had returned to life as a result of ELISHA's work (2 Ki. 4:35). The noun *sneeze* (or *sneezing*) is used by most versions in the description of the LEVIATHAN (Job 41:18; KJV, "neesings"); the Hebrew term in this passage probably refers to the animal's snorting (cf. NIV).

snow. The Hebrew words for "snow" occur nearly twenty times in the Bible (the corresponding Gk. word occurs only twice in the NT, Matt. 28:3; Rev. 1:14). Almost all the references, however, are figurative, indicating healing (Exod. 4:6 et al.), purity

(Ps. 51:7; Isa. 1:18; et al.), refreshment (Prov. 25:13), and the like. In the historical record, snow is mentioned only once, when it is said concerning BENAIAH son of Jehoiada: "He also went down into a pit on a snowy day and killed a lion" (2 Sam. 23:20; 1 Chr. 11:22). Mention in this context presumably indicates that the event was exceptional, not only as a feat of arms but also as a fact of climate, for the lion's home would be in the JORDAN Valley, where snow does not occur. In the Judean hills snow is rare, but no means unknown. JERUSALEM has a mean January temperature of 48°F, with a daily range of some 13°. But there are two areas where snowfalls are both heavy and regular: (1) on the Lebanese mountains in the N, where Mount HERMON rises to 9,100 ft. (c. 2,770 m.) and snow patches lie throughout the year (cf. Jer. 18:14)—it was the distant view of these snows from the hot Galilean trench that prompted so much biblical imagery; and (2) on the mountains of EDOM, E of the Jordan, where the land rises to over 5,000 ft. (1,525 m.). For many Israelites, therefore, snow was better known to them as a distant prospect than as a common experience. See also PALESTINE; RAIN.

snuffers. This English term, referring to a device used for cropping the snuff of a candle, occurs in the KJV and other versions as the rendering of two Hebrew words, both of which are applied to instruments made of gold used in tending fires and lamps in the TABERNACLE and the TEMPLE. One of the words, *mĕzammeret H4662*, was probably a type of knife used for shearing a wick (1 Ki. 7:50; 2 Ki. 12:13; 25:14; Jer. 52:18; 2 Chr. 4:22); the NIV renders it "wick trimmers." The precise meaning of the second term, *melqāḥayim H4920*, is less certain. According to Isa. 6:6, this tool could be used to handle live coals, and thus most versions render it "tongs" not only here but also in 1 Ki. 7:49 and 2 Chr. 4:21 (where *mĕzammeret* occurs in the same context). It is possible, however, that this instrument was also used as a wick trimmer (cf. Exod. 25:38; 37:23; Num. 4:9).

So. soh (Heb. *sô' H6046*, derivation disputed). According to 2 Ki. 17:4, King HOSHEA of JUDAH betrayed the Assyrians by sending envoys to So king of EGYPT. There have been numerous attempts to identify this Egyptian king. An older proposal that the person in question was Sib²e, an Egyptian general at the Battle of Raphia (c. 720 B.C.), has been discredited. Also unlikely is the view that the biblical text refers to Shabaka, who ruled Egypt at the very end of the eighth century; Hoshea's contemporary would have been an earlier pharaoh, Tefnakht I, whose capital was Sais. An intriguing suggestion is that the name So is an abbreviated form of Osorkon IV (c. 730-715), a competing pharaoh at Tanis and Bubastis. These and other identifications have not won wide acceptance, however, and thus alternative interpretations of the text have been put forward. According to some scholars, *So* should be understood not as a proper name but rather as an Egyptian title. More widely accepted, but not without problems, is the view that the reference is to the city of Sais; in this case, the text should be rendered, "he had sent envoys to Sais, [to] the king of Egypt," and the king in question would be Tefnakht.

soap. Soap in a modern sense was unknown in OT times. Even until recent time it was not used in some parts of the Middle East. Clothes, cooking utensils, and even the body were cleansed with the ashes of certain plants containing alkali (e.g., soapwort, glasswort, and saltwort). This cleansing material is referred to in Jer. 2:22 and Mal. 3:2.

Socho, Sochoh. See Soco.

socket. The base into which the pintle of a DOOR was set to act as a pivot for swinging. The socket in Solomon's TEMPLE was a recess cut in the stone sill (1 Ki. 7:50). The KJV and other versions use "socket" also in reference to the base supporting the posts of the TABERNACLE curtains and walls (Exod. 26:19 et al.), some of silver, others of bronze, formed to mortise or tenon the elements supported.

Soco, Socoh. soh′koh (Heb. *śôkô H8459* and *śôkōh H8458*, probably "thorny [place]"). TNIV Soko, Sokoh; KJV variously (Socoh, Sochoh, Socho, Shochoh, Shoco). **(1)** A town in the SHEPHELAH of JUDAH, listed between ADULLAM and AZEKAH (Josh. 15:35). It was here that the PHILISTINES assembled prior to the confrontation between DAVID and GOLIATH (1 Sam. 17:1). Soco was one of the cities that REHOBOAM repossessed and fortified after the revolt of the northern tribes (2 Chr. 11:7; however, this passage may refer to #2 below). It was retaken by the Philistines in the reign of AHAZ (2 Chr. 28:18). The town is identified with modern Khirbet ʿAbbad, some 17 mi. (27 km.) WSW of JERUSALEM.

(2) A town in the southern hill country of JUDAH, listed between DANNAH and JATTIR (Josh. 15:48; perhaps mentioned in 2 Chr. 11:7, but see

The foreground mound of ancient Soco in the Shephelah.

© Dr. James C. Martin

#1 above). This site is identified with another Khirbet Shuweikeh, E of modern Dahariyeh and about 10 mi. (16 km.) SW of HEBRON.

(3) A city in the SHARON Plain that was under the administration of Ben-Hesed in the time of Solomon (1 Ki. 4:10). It has been identified with modern Khirbet Shuweiket er-Ras (a little N of modern Tul-Karem), some 11 mi. (18 km.) NW of SAMARIA and about the same distance from the MEDITERRANEAN coast.

(4) In 1 Chr. 4:18 it is difficult to know whether Soco is the name of a person or place. It occurs in a genealogy of the descendants of Judah, yet some of the other names listed are place names (cf. Josh. 15:48-58). Either the person took his name from the town (possibly #2 above) or a clansman is mentioned along with the clan's settlement indicating that he is the "father" of the town (i.e., HEBER was the founder or settler of Soco).

soda. See MINERALS.

Sodi. soh′d*i* (Heb. *sôdî H6052*, possibly "[God is] my confidant"). Father of GADDIEL, from the tribe of ZEBULUN; the latter was one of the ten spies sent by MOSES into the Promised Land (Num. 13:10).

Soko, Sokoh. soh′koh. TNIV forms of SOCO, SOCOH.

Sodom. sod′uhm (Heb. *sĕdōm H6042*, meaning uncertain; Gk. *Sodoma G5047*). KJV also Sodoma (only Rom. 9:29). One of the CITIES OF THE PLAIN destroyed by God because of their sin, along with ADMAH, GOMORRAH, ZEBOIIM, and ZOAR. The site of "the plain" has been variously conjectured, but many believe that it is the shallow S end of the DEAD SEA, and that the waters cover the remains. An area around the N end of the Dead Sea has been favored by others, mainly on the grounds that only this region is fully within the range of vision from BETHEL, from which vantage point LOT made his fatal choice (cf. Gen. 13:3, 10-11). The S end is shut off by the high country around EN GEDI. ABRAHAM's field of view from a point E of Hebron, from which he looked in the morning toward Sodom and Gomorrah (19:28), may lead to the same conclusion. But what the patriarch saw

was the column of smoke from whatever form of catastrophe destroyed the whole area.

Attempts have been made to pinpoint the site by a reconstruction of the invasion route of the raid described in Gen. 14. According to 2 Chr. 20:2, HAZAZON TAMAR is En Gedi, halfway up the W shore of the Dead Sea. If the invaders, circling the sea from the S, clashed with the AMORITES here, they must then have continued N to capture Sodom, and not returned on their tracks. But could not the Hazazon Tamar of Gen. 14 be the Tamar of Ezek. 47:19 to the SW of the water? Zoar can be located on the Moabite shore from Isa. 15:5 and Jer. 48:34 and at the S end of the sea from JOSEPHUS (*War* 4.8.4), but Deut. 34:3 assumes that the town was visible from PISGAH. Perhaps there were two towns of the name. Failing conclusive archaeological evidence, the cities of the plain must be listed as lost. Sodom, because of the episode of Gen. 19, became a name for vice, infamy, and judgment (Isa. 1:9-10; 3:9; Jer. 23:14; Lam. 4:6; Ezek. 16:46; Amos 4:11; Zeph. 2:9; Matt. 10:15; Lk. 17:29; Rom. 9:29; 2 Pet. 2:6; Jude 7; Rev. 11:8).

Sodom, Vine of. See PLANTS.

sodomite, sodomy. Historically, the English term *sodomy* (derived from the story of SODOM and GOMORRAH in Gen. 18-19) has referred to any kind of nonprocreative sexual act, although it is usually applied specifically to homosexuality. The KJV uses the term *sodomite* to translate Hebrew *qādēš H7728* ("set apart [for the use of the deity]"; Deut. 23:17; 1 Ki. 14:24; 15:12; 22:46; 2 Ki. 23:7), which evidently refers to a male shrine PROSTITUTE. In the NT the NRSV uses the same word to translate Greek *arsenokoitēs G780* (1 Cor. 6:9; 1 Tim. 1:10), probably meaning "pederast," a man who assumes the dominant role in homosexual activity.

sojourner. See STRANGER.

soldier. See OCCUPATIONS AND PROFESSIONS; WAR.

solemn assembly. This phrase is used by the KJV and other versions to render the Hebrew term *ʿăṣārâ H6809* (NIV simply "assembly"). It refers to the gathering and sanctifying of the community of

Israel for a solemn occasion (in one passage it is used simply in a nonreligious sense, Jer 9:2). The term is used in a technical sense as the eighth day of the Feast of Booths (Lev. 23:36; Num. 29:35; Neh. 8:18; see FEASTS) and the seventh day of Passover (Deut. 16:8). In both instances the people were instructed to do no work for they were in a state of ritual HOLINESS. At the dedication of the TEMPLE, SOLOMON proclaimed a solemn assembly (2 Chr. 7:9). For quite a different purpose, JEHU ordered the people, "Sanctify a solemn assembly for Baal" (2 Ki. 10:20 NRSV); he was then able to complete his purge of BAAL worshipers from the land of Israel through the massacre of those who gathered in that assembly. The solemn assembly also was convened for special days of fasting, as when a locust plague threatened the land (Joel 1:14; 2:15). Amos and Isaiah disparaged these solemn assemblies (among other things) as that which God could not endure (Isa. 1:13; Amos 5:21) because the people did not do justice in the land.

Solomon. sol'uh-muhn (Heb. *šĕlōmōh H8976*, prob. "peaceable"; Gk. *Solomōn G5048*). Son of DAVID and third king of Israel (c. 970-930 B.C.). Shortly after his birth, the boy received the additional name JEDIDIAH, "beloved of Yahweh," from NATHAN the prophet, who had himself received the name from God (2 Sam. 12:24-25). In another passage, the name Solomon (which apparently derives from *šālôm H8934*, "peace") is connected with God's promise that he would "grant Israel peace and quiet during his [Solomon's] reign" (1 Chr. 22:9; some believe that the name derives from the verb *šālēm H8966* [piel, "to recompense, restore"] and that BATHSHEBA regarded Solomon as compensation for the loss of her first child). It is probable that either Jedidiah or Solomon was a throne name.

Solomon built the kingdom of ISRAEL to its greatest geographical extension and material prosperity. Though a very intelligent man, in his later years he lost his spiritual discernment and for the sake of political advantage and voluptuous living succumbed to apostasy. His policies of oppression and luxury brought the kingdom to the verge of dissolution, and when his son REHOBOAM came to the throne the actual split of the kingdom occurred.

Solomon did not enter the history of Israel until David's old age, when a conspiracy attempted to crown as king ADONIJAH, the son of David and HAGGITH. Nathan and Bathsheba quickly collaborated to persuade David of the seriousness of the situation, and David had Solomon anointed king at GIHON by ZADOK the priest while the conspirators were still gathered at EN ROGEL. As David's death drew near, he gave Solomon practical advice regarding faithfulness to God, the building of the TEMPLE, and the stability of the dynasty. Solomon had to deal harshly with Adonijah and his followers when they continued to plot against him. Adonijah and JOAB were put to death, and ABIATHAR the priest was expelled from the priesthood. Solomon made BENAIAH head of the army, and Zadok became priest in Abiathar's stead. David had also told Solomon to kill SHIMEI, who had cursed David at the time of ABSALOM's revolt; this was done after Shimei violated the probation Solomon had ordered.

Solomon then began a series of marriage alliances that were his eventual undoing. He married the daughter of the king of EGYPT, who had sufficient power to capture GEZER and to present it as a dowry to his daughter. Early in Solomon's reign he loved the Lord; he sacrificed at the great high place of GIBEON, where the TABERNACLE was located; here he offered a thousand burnt offerings. The night he was at Gibeon the Lord appeared to him in a dream and told him to request of him whatever he desired. Solomon chose above all else understanding and discernment. God was pleased with this choice, granted his request, and also gave him riches and honor. A demonstration of this gift came when he returned to JERUSALEM, where his decision in the case of two prostitutes caused the people to see that God's WISDOM was in the king. He was an efficient administrator: each department had its appointed officers and the country was divided into twelve districts, different from the tribal divisions, each responsible for the provisions of the royal household for a month of the year. With taxation and conscription Israel began to see some of the evils of monarchy against which Samuel had warned (1 Sam. 8:11-18), though during the reign of Solomon "Judah and Israel were as numerous as the sand on the seashore; they ate, they drank and they were happy" (1 Ki. 4:20). The

S

kingdom extended from the Euphrates in the north to the border of Egypt in the SW.

Solomon was a wise and learned man; it is stated that his wisdom was greater than that of the wise men of the E and of Egypt. Expert in botany and zoology, he was also a writer, credited with three thousand proverbs and one thousand songs (1 Ki. 4:32) and named the author of two psalms (titles, Ps. 72; 127) and of the books of Proverbs (Prov. 1:1), Ecclesiastes (Eccl. 1:1, 12), and Song of Solomon, his greatest song (Cant. 1:1). His fame was widespread, and people came from afar to hear him.

He made an alliance with Hiram king of Tyre, who had been a friend of David. This relationship was of great advantage to Solomon, as he undertook an immense building program, particularly that of the temple in Jerusalem on Mount Moriah. He contracted with Hiram for the supply of cedar and cypress wood and arranged for Phoenician builders to supplement the Israelite conscription of workers. A chronological reference is supplied in 1 Ki. 6:1, which states that the year that construction of the temple was begun numbered the 4th year of Solomon and the 480th year after the exodus from Egypt. David had wanted to build the temple, but the Lord reserved that privilege for Solomon (2 Sam. 7:13; 1 Chr. 17:4-6, 12; 22:6-11; 28:6); nevertheless, Solomon got the complete plan of the structure from his father (1 Chr. 28:11-19). David had also gathered much building material, especially precious metals and other costly commodities, and had taken freewill offerings for the

building of the temple (1 Ki. 7:51; 1 Chr. 22:2-5; 29:1-19). A description of the temple is given in some detail (1 Ki. 6:2-36).

The temple was finished in seven years, and Solomon's palace was thirteen years in building. The latter consisted of various houses or halls: the House of the Forest of Lebanon, the Hall of Pillars, the Hall of the Throne (also the Hall of Judgment), his royal quarters, and a palace for his Egyptian wife. A great amount of bronze was used for ornamental work, for architectural features such as the two large pillars of the temple vestibule, and for decorative and functional articles, such as the altar, the molten sea, and all sorts of utensils and implements used in the temple service. This part of the project was the responsibility of a craftsman, Huram of Tyre (1 Ki. 7:14; cf. 2 Chr. 2:13-14). See Hiram #2. Much of the copper used for these purposes probably came from mines worked by the Israelites. It is only in comparatively recent years that the great mining and smelting enterprises of Solomon have become known, for they are not referred to in the Bible. Explorations in the Negev have revealed that the area was of much importance in Solomonic times. Many towns were built and fortified, a number of copper mines were worked, and the preliminary processing done nearby. Exploration led to the identification (not accepted by all) of Tell el-Kheleifeh as Ezion Geber; excavation here brought to light the remains of an industrial town, with blast furnaces utilizing the prevailing winds to operate on the modern principle of the Bessemer forced-air draft.

When the temple was completed, an impressive dedication service was held. The ark of the covenant was brought up from Zion by the priests and was placed in the Most Holy Place (1 Ki. 8). Solomon blessed the people and made a heartfelt prayer of dedication. Sacrifices were made, and fire from heaven consumed them. Finally, a great feast was held. The Lord appeared to Solomon again, as at Gibeon; he had heard his supplication and now promised to establish his heirs as he had promised to do for David, if he and his descendants would remain faithful to the Lord. After the celebration of the dedication, Solomon settled accounts with Hiram king of Tyre. Solomon gave him twenty cities in the land of Galilee, but when Hiram

Remains of the northern palace at Megiddo, dated by some to the period of Solomon.

© Dr. James C. Martin

inspected them and was not satisfied, he also paid him 120 talents of gold. Solomon's work of building extended throughout the land, with labor provided by a forced levy of the descendants of the people Israel did not annihilate at the time of the conquest. He built at Gezer, Hazor, Megiddo, Upper Beth Horon, Lower Beth Horon, Baalath, Tadmor in the desert, and in Lebanon. He did additional building at Jerusalem. He made store cities throughout the domain.

And now Israel no longer had a lack of armaments. Solomon had 1,400 chariots and 12,000 horsemen (2 Chr. 1:14); he also had 4,000 stalls for horses (9:25). He built cities for his chariots and cavalry. Stables for at least 450 horses were found at MEGIDDO. Similar stables were excavated at Gezer, Taanach, Tell el-Hesi, and Tell el-Farʿah. He also engaged in a profitable trade in chariots and horses between Egypt and the HITTITES. His commercial interests led him to the sea; since the Mediterranean coast afforded no good harborage in the area held by him, he made his port at Ezion Geber near Eloth on the Gulf of Aqabah of the Red Sea. Again he was assisted by Hiram, who provided Phoenician seamen (8:18).

The rulers were enriched by this trade with the East. OPHIR was a source of gold, almugwood (algumwood), and precious stones. Solomon's ships also went to TARSHISH with the Phoenician fleet and brought back all sorts of exotic things. Immense wealth thus came to Solomon by commerce, mining, tribute (1 Ki. 4:21), and gifts from visitors (10:25). Among the most distinguished of these visitors was the queen of SHEBA. Women were a serious weakness of Solomon; not only did he make many political alliances through marriage, but he "loved many foreign women" (11:1) and "held fast to them in love" (11:2). God had warned that such marriages would lead to apostasy. The HAREM of Solomon held a collection of some seven hundred wives and three hundred concubines; and "his wives turned his heart after other gods, and his heart was not fully devoted to the LORD his God" (11:4). He built places of worship for the false gods to satisfy his heathen wives. The Lord was angered at Solomon's failure to keep his explicit commands and announced to him the rift in the kingdom that was to take place in the reign of his son.

The rule of Solomon had been quite peaceful, but trouble was brewing. HADAD the Edomite, who as a child had survived a raid by David and had escaped to Egypt, now returned to plague him. In SYRIA, REZON was made king at DAMASCUS and became an enemy of Israel. In Israel a capable young man, JEROBOAM son of Nebat, was informed by the prophet AHIJAH that he would become ruler of ten tribes of Israel. Solomon attempted to kill Jeroboam, but Jeroboam took refuge in Egypt until the death of Solomon. The signs of the impending division of the kingdom were evident; when he died in 930 B.C. and his son Rehoboam became king, the break soon became a reality. Other historical records of Solomon's reign cited in the Bible include "the book of the annals of Solomon" (1 Ki. 11:41), "the records of Nathan the prophet," "the prophecy of Ahijah the Shilonite," and "the visions of Iddo the seer concerning Jeroboam the son of Nebat" (2 Chr. 9:29). A great temporal ruler, possessing every natural advantage, almost inconceivably wealthy in material splendor, learning, and experience, Solomon was nevertheless a disappointment. Although he began extremely well, the tragedy of his gradual apostasy had more disastrous results than the infamous scandal of his father, who sincerely repented and was a man after the Lord's own heart.

Solomon, Pools of. Name given (cf. Eccl. 2:6) to three POOLS located in the valley of ETHAM, just S of BETHLEHEM and 10 mi. (16 km.) from JERUSALEM. For centuries they have been an important part of the water supply for Jerusalem. The pools are fed by springs and surface water, and a twisting AQUEDUCT, at least as old as Roman times, conveyed the water ultimately to Jerusalem and to Bethlehem en route. Lacking pumping facilities, the ancients had to plan and engineer with skill to take full advantage of the gravity. The pools were hewn out of rock and in part artificially constructed with masonry. They have been repaired many times through the years. The pools are arranged at successive levels with conduit connections between them. The E wall of the lowest one forms a dam across the valley. The pools were roughly rectangular in shape and varied in depth from about 25 ft. in the upper pool to 50 ft. in the lower pool

S

(c. 7-15 m.). The lower pool is the largest, being about 582 ft. (177 m.) long with a width varying from 148 to 207 ft. (45-63 m.).

Solomon, Psalms of. See PSEUDEPIGRAPHA.

Solomon, Song of. See SONG OF SOLOMON.

Solomon, Wisdom of. See APOCRYPHA.

Solomon's Colonnade (Porch). What the KJV calls "Solomon's porch" (NRSV, "the portico of Solomon") was a roofed colonnade in the temple built by HEROD the Great. It bordered on the E side of the outer court of the TEMPLE, resting on a massive Herodian retaining wall (still largely visible as the lower courses of the present temple-area wall) built out over the KIDRON Valley. It may have been so named because of a tradition that SOLOMON had once constructed a similar E wall and cloister. It was here that Christ walked and talked during the Feast of Dedication (Jn. 10:23); here also his disciples seem later to have gathered regularly (Acts 5:12; cf. 3:11).

Solomon's servants. A class of state SLAVES in Israel instituted by King SOLOMON. Of course, all subordinates of a king might be considered his servants, but the specific Hebrew phrase usually translated "Solomon's servants" does not refer generally to all those who served the king in any capacity. Rather, it is a technical term designating a slave class that was common in the ANE, where prisoners of war were made servants for big commercial or industrial enterprises carried out by the king. Not until the time of DAVID was ISRAEL strong enough to have any state slaves (cf. 2 Sam. 12:31), but the extensive building projects of Solomon called for state slavery on a vast scale. It was thus Solomon who reduced the native Canaanites to slavery (1 Ki. 9:20-21), and the new class of slaves was appropriately called ʿabdê šĕlōmōh (1 Ki. 9:27; 2 Chr. 8:18; 9:10; in these three passages the NIV [but not the TNIV] renders "Solomon's men" or "men of Solomon"). The descendants of Solomon's servants after the EXILE are noted as having been merged with the NETHINIM or temple servants (Ezra 2:55-58; Neh. 7:57-60; 11:3). It is

doubtful that at this time these two groups were regarded as slaves in the strict sense of the term.

Solomon's temple. See TEMPLE.

son. See BEN (PREFIX AND IDIOM); CHILD; SON OF GOD; SON OF MAN.

song. See MUSIC AND MUSICAL INSTRUMENTS.

Song of Solomon. One of the poetical books of the OT and the first of the five MEGILLOTH ("scrolls") that were read at Jewish FEASTS. It is unique among biblical books, for it centers in the joys and distresses of the love relationship between a man and a woman.

I. Name. The book is generally known as "Song of Songs" (Heb. šîr haššîrîm), the phrase with which it begins (Cant. 1:1). This use of the Hebrew superlative declares the book the best of the 1,005 songs of Solomon (1 Ki. 4:32), or perhaps the greatest of all songs. In the VULGATE the work was entitled *Canticum canticorum*, hence the alternative English title of *Canticles*.

II. Authorship and date. Although the work is attributed to SOLOMON (Cant. 1:1), there is considerable range of opinion as to its authorship and date. On the basis of its language—various Aramaic forms and words, the presence of names of foreign products, a Persian word, and a Greek word—some have concluded that the book is a collection of erotic poems dating to about 250 B.C. On the other hand, it has been pointed out that these usages are not inconsistent with authorship by Solomon. In view of the extensive commerce and widespread diplomatic relations of Solomon, the presence of foreign terms, especially for articles imported or imitated from foreign sources, is to be expected. The use of ARAMAIC is not a valid indication of date and may be accounted for by the northern origin of the SHULAMMITE (Cant. 6:13). There are lines of evidence that agree with the ascription of the book to Solomon. The work has affinities with other writings attributed to him. The author's acquaintance with plants and animals is reminiscent of Solomon (1 Ki. 4:33). The mention of "a mare harnessed to one of the chariots of Pharaoh" (Cant. 1:9) accords with Solomon's

Overview of SONG OF SONGS

Author: The work appears to be attributed directly to King SOLOMON (Cant. 1:1, though the Hebrew can be understood to mean, "The Song of Songs which is for [*or* concerns] Solomon"). Some scholars are uncertain about this attribution, and others argue against it.

Historical setting: The subject matter is the life of Solomon (c. 950 B.C.). The date of the composition of the book, if not written by Solomon himself, is uncertain.

Purpose: To celebrate human LOVE, probably as a reflection of the love between God and his people.

Contents: The lovers praise each other (Cant. 1:1—2:7); (2) deepening of their affection (2:8—3:5); (3) arrival of Solomon and marriage (3:6—5:1); (4) the wife's longing for the return of her husband (5:2—6:9); (5) the beauty of the bride (6:10—8:4); (6) the wonder and permanence of love (8:5-14).

involvement in horse trading with EGYPT and with his being married to a daughter of the PHARAOH. The lover is called "the king" (1:4), and there are other indications of his royal interests, in addition to references to Solomon by name. The place-names range throughout PALESTINE and thus fit well with an origin predating the divided kingdom.

III. Content. Though the book is difficult to analyze, a common outline is as follows: (1) the mutual admiration of the lovers (Cant. 1:2—2:7); (2) growth in love (2:8—3:5); (3) the marriage (3:6—5:1); (4) longing of the wife for her absent husband (5:2—6:9); (5) the beauty of the Shulammite bride (6:10—8:4); (6) the wonder of love (8:5-14).

IV. Interpretation. There is great diversity and much overlapping among interpretations of the Song of Songs. (1) The *allegorical* view regards the Song as descriptive of the LOVE of God and his people ISRAEL or of the love of CHRIST and the CHURCH. Usually this view denies or ignores the historicity of the events described. Hippolytus and Origen introduced this interpretation into the ancient church, and it has been the popular or prevailing position. There are two major arguments in its favor: (a) it explains the inclusion of the book in the canon; (b) it harmonizes with the biblical use of

MARRIAGE as an illustration of the Lord's relationship to his people. Opposing arguments include the following: (a) other reasons may be advanced for its presence among the canonical books; (b) elsewhere the figure of the marriage relationship is made the basis for specific teaching; (c) nothing in the book itself invalidates its historicity; (d) the necessity of interpreting details leads to fanciful and absurd interpretations.

(2) The *typical* interpretation combines literal and allegorical views, maintaining both the historicity and the spiritualizing of the book. In support of this view: (a) the superlative of the title connotes spiritual meaning; (b) Solomon is a type of Christ; (c) marriage also is a type. Against this view: (a) spiritual value does not demand typology; (b) the definition and application of the concept of "type" are debatable.

(3) The *literal* view is that the book presents actual history and nothing more.

(4) The *dramatic* interpretation regards the Song as a drama based on the marriage of Solomon to a Shulammite girl. Here may be included the so-called shepherd hypothesis, which proposes a triangle of Solomon, the girl, and her shepherd-betrothed. On this hypothesis, the girl refuses the blandishments of the king and remains true to her

S

shepherd. The book is not labeled drama, which was not a widely used Hebrew literary form. If the book were merely a drama, its presence in the canon is not explained.

(5) The *erotic-literary* view is that the book is simply a collection of love songs.

(6) The *liturgical* view regards the Song as borrowed pagan liturgy associated with FERTILITY CULTS. It is inconceivable that a work of such an origin should be in the canon.

(7) The *didactic-moral* interpretation holds that the book presents the purity and wonder of true love. It regards the book as history and also agrees that the love portrayed does direct us to the greater love of Christ, in accordance with the history of Christian interpretation. The purpose of the Song of Songs, therefore, is to teach the holiness and beauty of the marriage-love relationship that God ordained.

Song of Songs. See SONG OF SOLOMON.

Song of the Three Young Men (Children). See APOCRYPHA.

songs of degrees. See ASCENTS, SONG OF.

Son of God. One of the primary titles of CHRIST in the NT. His claim to this title was the principal charge that the Jewish leaders made against him. "Tell us if you are the Christ, the Son of God," the

Medieval mosaic in the church of Hagia Sophia (Istanbul) depicting Christ, the Son of God, on his throne.

high priest taunted (Matt. 26:63-64; Mk. 14:61-62; cf. Jn. 5:17-18; 19:7). Further, the confession that Jesus is the Son of God was basic to the teaching of the apostles and the faith of the early church (2 Cor. 1:19; Gal. 2:20; 1 Jn. 4:15; 5:5, 13). The title is to be understood both as a synonym for MESSIAH (Ps. 2:7; Matt. 16:16; 26:63; 27:40) and as implying deity through a unique relation with the Father (Jn. 5:18). Sometimes the latter implication is obvious (as in the Gospel of John), and sometimes it is hidden (as often in the three other Gospels).

Jesus became conscious of his special relation with the Father as a boy and expressed it when he was twelve years old (Lk. 2:49). At his baptism, the voice from heaven confirmed what he already knew—that he had a unique spiritual and moral union with the Father and that he was called to be the Messiah and to do the work of God's Chosen Servant (Matt. 3:13-17; Mk. 1:9-12; Lk. 3:21-22). This consciousness was severely tested in the temptations (Matt. 4; Lk. 4). Throughout his ministry Jesus was sustained and inspired by the knowledge that he was the Father's Son, doing his will (Matt. 17:5; 21:33-44). In GETHSEMANE and on the CROSS this consciousness remained his possession (Matt. 26:36-42; Lk. 22:39-44; 23:46).

The filial consciousness of Jesus and his unique relationship with the Father are particularly emphasized in John's Gospel. Jesus is God's only Son (Jn. 1:18), one with the Father (10:30), always doing the Father's will (4:34; 5:30; 6:38), and being in the Father as the Father is in him (10:38). He speaks what he hears from the Father (12:50), has unique knowledge of the Father (10:15; cf. Matt. 11:27), and possesses the authority of the Father (Jn. 3:35; 5:22; 13:3; 16:15). Thus, only in and through the Son is God's salvation given (3:36; 5:26; 6:40). However, as *incarnate* Son there are things that the Son does not know and cannot do—"the Father is greater than I" (Mk. 13:32; Jn. 14:28). See INCARNATION.

Outside the Gospels we find the expression "the God and Father of our Lord Jesus Christ," suggesting a particular intimacy between Father and Son (Rom. 15:6; 2 Cor. 1:3; Eph. 1:3; Col. 1:3; 1 Pet. 1:3; cf. Rev. 1:6). By his RESURRECTION and ASCENSION Jesus is designated Son of God (Rom. 1:3)

© Dr. James C. Martin

and preached to be so (Acts 8:37; 9:20; 13:33; 2 Cor. 1:19). The distinction and difference between Jesus and the great prophets of Israel is that Jesus is the unique Son of God (Heb. 1; 3:6). True unity in the church and true spiritual maturity involves growing into "the knowledge of the Son of God" (Eph. 4:13). The people of God wait for the Son to return to earth from heaven (1 Thess. 1:10).See also SONS OF GOD.

Son of Man. An expression found in the OT and used as a self-description of Jesus in the NT. In Hebrew, "son of man" means an individual human being (Num. 23:19; Ps. 8:4-5; ADAM is "humankind"). This phrase was used once by the Lord in addressing DANIEL (Dan. 8:17) and over eighty times in addressing EZEKIEL (Ezek. 2:1 et al.). There must have been a special reason for its use with them. Both of them were privileged to see visions of God. Probably the Lord wanted to emphasize to them that they were, after all, only men of the earth, in spite of this privilege of receiving the divine word. In Ps. 80:17 the king of Israel is called "the son of man" whom God has raised up for himself.

Daniel used this phrase to describe a personage whom he saw in a night vision. He saw one "like a son of man" (that is, a member of the genus man) coming with the clouds of heaven and approaching God (the "Ancient of Days") to be given authority, glory, and an everlasting kingdom (Dan. 7:13-14). While opinions differ about the interpretation of this vision, and many hold the "son of man" to be a personification of "the saints of the Most High" (see 7:22) to whom the dominion is given, it is on the whole entirely in accord with the evidence to see here a messianic figure predictive of the Lord Jesus Christ. In the extrabiblical *Similitudes of Enoch* the presentation of the Son of Man in the terms found in Daniel's prophecy is continued.

Why Jesus decided to call himself "Son of Man" (eighty-two times in the Gospels; see also Acts 7:56; Rev. 1:13; 14:14) is not known, despite much scholarly study of the question. Often he put his statements about himself in the third person to give his teachings more force. Whenever he did this he used this phrase as a name for himself. No doubt he took it from Daniel's prophecy. The Jews must have been familiar with this prophecy. Jesus, in assuming this title, was saying to the Jews, "I am the Son of Man in that prophecy." This title emphasized his union with mankind. It was also a name no one would criticize. If Jesus called himself the Son of God or the Messiah, the Jews would not accept him as such. But they did not object to the term, the Son of Man. But no one else ever called him by that name.

Jesus certainly used the title in a variety of contexts: (1) As a substitute for "I" (e.g., Matt. 11:19; 16:13; Lk. 9:58). (2) When making his important declarations and claims (e.g., Matt. 20:28; Mk. 10:45; Lk. 9:56; 11:30; 19:10); these relate to his saving role. (3) Once in the Gospels this phrase occurs without the definite article: "a son of man" (Jn. 5:27 ASV); although most versions understand it in the usual sense as "the Son of Man," possibly Jesus made the statement that he had been given authority to execute judgment because he was a son of man, that is, he was qualified to judge human beings because of his experience as man, living among men. (4) Concerning his resurrection: "Don't tell anyone what you have seen, until the Son of Man has been raised from the dead" (Matt. 17:9). (5) Concerning the glorious state into which as the exalted Son of Man he would enter (Matt. 19:28; 24:30; 26:64; Mk. 13:26; 14:62; Lk. 17:2, 30; 22:69). These verses relate to his reign with the Father in and from heaven. (6) Concerning the return to earth in a glorious manner (Matt. 24:27, 30, 44; Lk. 17:24; 18:8). (7) Concerning his role in judgment (Matt. 13:41; 25:31-32; Lk. 9:56; 21:36). (8) Most important of all, concerning his passion and violent death (Matt. 17:12, 22; 26:2, 24, 45; Mk. 9:12, 31; 10:33; 14:21, 41; Lk. 9:44; 18:31-32; 22:22, 48). In view of the usage of "son of man" in Dan. 7:13, this emphasis by Jesus that he as Son of Man must, of necessity, suffer, is quite remarkable.

sons of God, children of God. A description of those who are in a special or intimate relationship with God. In the OT the Lord chose the people ISRAEL and made a holy COVENANT with them. As a result, the people as a unit (and thus each member) were described as the son(s) of God. MOSES told PHARAOH that the Israelite nation was God's "firstborn son," and that this "son" must be released in

S

order to offer WORSHIP to his "Father" (Exod. 4:22-23). Later the description was "children of God" and "a people holy to the Lord" (Deut. 14:1). Further, the Davidic King-Messiah was described as the Son of God (see 2 Sam. 7:14; 23:5; Ps. 2:7; 89:27-28). This usage is continued in the NT, where the ancient people of Israel are said to possess the "sonship" (Rom. 9:4) and be God's children (Jn. 11:52), and the Messiah is seen as God's "Son" (Heb. 1:5; citing Ps. 2:7 and 2 Sam. 7:14). See SON OF GOD.

Building on this OT usage, members of the new covenant are also described as sons/children of God. PAUL declared that "you are all sons of God through faith in Christ Jesus" (Gal. 3:26), and he used the image of adoption to convey the idea of being taken into God's family, of receiving forgiveness and the gift of the indwelling Spirit (Rom. 8:13-17). JOHN THE APOSTLE taught that by spiritual birth (see REGENERATION) believers become the children of God and are thereby in an intimate spiritual/moral union with God their heavenly Father (1 Jn. 3:1). Both Paul and John insisted that to be called son or child meant living in a way that reflects this relationship (Rom. 8:17, 29; 1 Jn. 3:9). Jesus himself made a similar point (Matt. 5:9, 44-45; 12:48-50). Again this continues the OT emphasis that to be the son or child of God means being godlike in behavior (Deut. 32:6; Isa. 1:2; Hos. 1:10).

A special problem attaches to the use of the phrase "sons of God" (Heb. *běnê hā'ĕlōhîm*) in Gen. 6:1-4. (1) Some argue that this passage reflects mythological stories of the ANE, depicting deities that engage in illicit relations among themselves and in some instances with humans. Although most biblical scholars admit that erotic mythology is not a normal feature of the OT literature, it is alleged that the writer of Genesis altered an ancient myth and, with embarrassment, set it forth as a basis for God's judgment in the form of a FLOOD. This method of analysis, however, is contrary to procedure elsewhere in the OT.

(2) According to an old Jewish interpretation, the "sons of God" were pagan royalty or members of the nobility who, out of lust, married women from the general population. A variation of this view is that the term refers to ANE kings who were honored as divine rulers and who were characterized by tyrannical and polygamous behavior.

The main difficulty with this approach is that the Hebrew phrase is not used in this particular sense elsewhere in the OT.

(3) The term does occur in several OT passages in reference to ANGELS or "heavenly beings" (Job 1:6; 2:1; 38:7; Aram. *bar-'ĕlāhîn* in Dan. 3:25; cf. also Ps. 29:1; 89:6). Thus a common interpretation is that fallen angels married women and begat children, and that this unnatural union explains the appearance of the Nephilim (Gen. 6:4). Many object to this approach on the basis of Jesus' comment that a married state does not apply to angels (Matt. 22:30).

(4) Conservative interpreters have often identified the "sons of God" with the descendants of SETH. Earlier in the Genesis narrative, in connection with the births of Seth and of his son ENOSH, the comment is made, "At that time men began to call on the name of the LORD" (Gen. 4:24). Thus the context, by identifying the Sethites as worshipers of God, seems to provide a referent for the otherwise ambiguous phrase, "sons of God." If so, the passage views the intermarriage of such worshipers with the ungodly as the immediate cause of the flood. The primary objection to this view is that the contrasting phrase in Gen. 6:2, "daughters of men [Heb. *hā'ādām H132*]," seems to be a general human designation rather than a way of describing a specific (ungodly) part of the population.

(5) Still another approach argues that the passage should not be understood negatively as an explanation for the flood but simply as a conclusion to Gen. 5. According to this view, the phrases "sons of God" and "daughters of man/Adam" simply refer to men and women in general, alluding respectively to Adam's divine origin and Eve's origin from Adam.

sons of the prophets. The Hebrew phrase *běnê-hannĕbî'îm*, which the NIV renders as "company of the prophets," occurs almost always in connection with ELISHA (2 Ki. 2:3 et al.; the only exception is 1 Ki. 20:35). The term is a technical one referring to the members of a prophetic order or guild, and has no reference to physical descent from a PROPHET. There were several different guilds or branches of the same guild located at various places: (1) BETHEL (2 Ki. 2:3), (2) JERICHO (2:5),

(3) GILGAL (4:38), (4) the hill country of Ephraim (5:22; see EPHRAIM, HILL COUNTRY OF). Yet it appears that they were all under the authority of one prophet whom they called "master" (2:3, 5). When the master died or was taken, as ELIJAH was, one of the guild members took his place as the new master. The promotion had to be recognized by the guild members, and the test was whether the new master had the powers of the old master (2:8, 14) and whether the spirit of the old leader rested on the new one (2:15). The guild may have lived in a monastic community. They erected community buildings (6:1-2) and shared a common table (4:38-44). Yet some were married (4:1). Some of their work was done at the command of the master (4:38; 9:1), and often they sought his approval before doing something (2:16-18; 6:1-2). Yet they could act on their own (1 Ki. 20:35). It is possible that other passages where the phrase does not occur reflect the existence of prophetic guilds (see 1 Sam. 10:5-12; 19:20; 1 Ki. 18:4, 19; 22:6; 2 Ki. 23:2; Jer. 26:7-8, 11; cf. also Amos 7:14).

soothsayer. See OCCUPATIONS AND PROFESSIONS (under *magician* and *sorcerer*).

sop. This English term is used by the KJV to render *psōmion G6040*, which occurs in only one passage (Jn. 13:26-27, 30). The Greek word (diminutive in form) refers to a small, wafer-like piece of bread dipped into the common dish as a kind of improvised spoon. Knives and forks were unknown at table; therefore the more liquid parts of a meal were secured by dipping a morsel of bread into them.

Sopater. soh´puh-tuhr (Gk. *Sōpatros G5396*, prob. short form of *Sōsipatros G5399*, "saving the father"). Son of Pyrrhus; a Christian from BEREA who, along with others, accompanied PAUL on his way back from GREECE (Acts 20:4). The group may have served as representatives when the apostle conveyed the offering from the Gentiles to the needy in JERUSALEM (24:17). Sopater is usually thought to be the same as SOSIPATER (Rom. 16:21).

Sophereth. See HASSOPHERETH.

sorcerer, sorcery. See DIVINATION; MAGIC; OCCUPATIONS AND PROFESSIONS.

sore. See DISEASES.

Sorek. sor´ik (Heb. *śōrēq H8604*, "vine"). The valley where DELILAH, the lover of SAMSON, lived (Jdg. 16:4). This region was one of three parallel narrow E-W valleys that crossed the SHEPHELAH (a rocky plateau stretching from AIJALON to GAZA).

The Sorek Valley. (View to the W.)

© Dr. James C. Martin

EshtaoL and ZorAH were on the N of the valley, while Timnah, where Samson sought a wife (Jdg. 14:1), is located farther SW, near the mouth of the valley. The Valley of Sorek is known today as Wadi eṣ-Ṣarar, beginning about 13 mi. (21 km.) SW of Jerusalem and running in a NW direction for about 20 mi. (32 km.) toward the Mediterranean.

sorrel. This English term, referring to a brownish color, is used by the NRSV and other versions to render Hebrew *śārōq H8601*, which occurs only once (Zech. 1:8; NIV, "brown"). The Hebrew word may indicate a reddish color.

sorrow. The Bible speaks of sorrow in various contexts. For example, Christ's suffering and departure brings sorrow to his disciples' hearts (Jn. 16:6; cf. Matt. 9:15), but it was good that he go away, for then the Comforter (of the sorrowful) would come (see Holy Spirit). As the woman in childbirth has sorrow but also joy at birth, so the disciples' sorrow will be turned into joy at his return (Jn. 16:21-22); when they ask and receive, their joy will then be made full. Elsewhere Jesus says that the mourners will be comforted (Matt. 5:4).

If Christ brings joy, so sin should bring sorrow and mourning. Those who laugh now should mourn and weep (Lk. 6:25); sinners should be wretched and mourn (Jas. 4:9). Not only should there be mourning over one's own sins, but also over those of others in the church (1 Cor. 5:2). Second Corinthians is practically a treatise on the necessary sorrow that Christians must inflict on each other as they admonish and correct sin. Paul did not desire to make another painful visit to Corinth (2 Cor. 2:1), nor was his purpose ever just to bring sorrow (2:4). Instead his goal was godly grief, the sort that produces repentance, salvation, zeal, and finally Paul's own comfort and joy (7:8-13). Hebrews teaches that the Father's disciplining of his own sons indeed yields the fruit of repentance even though painful at the time (Heb. 12:11). Peter makes the similar statement that our rejoicing is in our imperishable inheritance, even though its genuineness is tested by various trials for a short time (1 Pet. 1:6). We shall be approved if we suffer unjustly (2:19-20). So the inheritance of comfort enables us to sorrow with hope.

Sosipater. soh´sip´uh-tuhr (*Sōsipatros G5399*, "saving the father"). One of two or three "relatives" of Paul (the others being Jason and possibly Lucius) who sent greetings to the Christians in Rome (Rom. 16:21). According to many scholars, however, the Greek term *syngenēs G5150* here means "kinsman" (cf. RSV) and should be understood in the sense of "fellow-Jew" (cf. 9:3). Sosipater is usually identified with Sopater (Acts 20:4).

Sosthenes. sos´thuh-neez (Gk. *Sōsthenēs G5398*). (1) Ruler of the synagogue at Corinth during Paul's first visit there (Acts 18:17; see ruler of the synagogue). It is possible that Sosthenes succeeded Crispus in this office when the latter became a Christian (v. 8). For some unclear reason, Sosthenes was seized and beaten by a crowd after Gallio, proconsul of Achaia, had dismissed a Jewish prosecution of Paul. Possibly Sosthenes was the victim of an anti-Semitic demonstration by Greeks (cf. KJV following many MSS) or of Jewish spite against an unsuccessful spokesman. See also #2, below.

(2) An early Christian whom Paul refers to as "our [*lit.*, the] brother" (1 Cor. 1:1). The fact that the apostle includes the name of Sosthenes with his own in the salutation suggests that this individual was well known to the Corinthians. Thus many have thought that this Sosthenes should be identified with #1, above. If so, he probably became a Christian during Paul's ministry in the city.

Sotai. soh´ti (Heb. *sôṭay H6055*, derivation uncertain). Ancestor of a family of Solomon's servants that returned from the Babylonian exile with Zerubbabel (Ezra 2:55; Neh. 7:57).

soul. This English term, which most often refers to the immaterial essence, or more specifically the moral and emotional nature, of human beings, is used to translate mainly Hebrew *nepeš H5883* and Greek *psychē G6034*. Both of these words may indicate "breath," "life," and the like (in this sense even beasts have a soul or spirit, Gen. 1:20; 7:15; Eccl. 3:21), but they can be used with a wide range of connotations. The term *soul* is one of a number of psychological nouns, all designating

General view of the Negev terrain in southern Israel.

the same nonmaterial self, but each in a different functional relationship. Thus, the MIND is the self in its rational functions. HEART is the self as manifesting a complex of attitudes. Will is the self as choosing and deciding. SPIRIT is the self when thought of apart from earthly connections. When the blessed dead in heaven are spoken of as having been put to a martyr's death, they are called "souls" (Rev. 6:9). When there is no reference to their former bodily experience, they are called "spirits" (Heb. 12:23). But these functional names of the ego are not used with technical discrimination; they often overlap. See also NATURE, NATURAL.

The above remarks assume dichotomy, that is, that there are only two substantive entities that make up the whole person: (1) the BODY, which at death returns to dust, awaiting the RESURRECTION; and (2) the nonmaterial self, which if regenerate goes to paradise or heaven; if not, to the abode of the wicked dead. There are many, however, who hold to a trichotomous view, arguing that *soul* and *spirit* are two distinct substantive entities, with the *body* as a third (they cite mainly 1 Thess. 5:23 and Heb. 4:12 for evidence; dichotomists respond that no one would interpret passages such as Lk. 10:27 ["heart ... soul ... strength ... mind"] to mean that there are more than three substantive entities).

south. The problem of defining directions in a community that did not possess the compass must always have been a difficult one. *East* and *west* could be related to sunrise and sunset, but the intermediate direction of *south* produced a number of different Hebrew concepts. For example, the term *yāmîn H3545*, "right [side]," could be used in the sense "south" because by convention a person was normally thought of as facing the sunrise (Josh. 17:7 et al.). Most commonly, however, the Hebrew adopts *negeb H5582*, which probably means "parched," describing the region of semidesert and desert lying in a southerly direction, when viewed from the Israelite heartland. This term NEGEV has now become firmly attached, as a regional name, to the southern extension of the modern Israeli state. The NT uses the common Greek term *notos G3803* (Lk. 13:29 et al.).

sovereignty of God. The word *sovereign*, although it does not occur in any form in the English Bible, conveys the oft-repeated scriptural thought of the supreme authority of God. He is referred to by the Greek word *pantokratōr G4120*, "Almighty" (2 Cor. 6:18 and nine times in Revelation), and is described as "the blessed and only Ruler, the King of kings and Lord of lords" (1 Tim. 6:15). He "works out everything in conformity

S

with the purpose of his will" (Eph. 1:11). His sovereignty follows logically from the doctrine that he is God, Creator, and Ruler of the universe.

The sovereignty of God is sometimes presented in the Bible as an unanalyzed ultimate. "But who are you, O man, to talk back to God? Shall what is formed say to him who formed it, 'Why did you make me like this?' Does not the potter have the right to make out of the same lump of clay some pottery for noble purposes and some for common use?" (Rom. 9:20-21; see Isa. 45:9; cf. Ps. 115:3; Dan. 4:35; and many similar passages). God is not subject to any power or any abstract rule or law that could be conceived as superior to or other than himself. Yet the Scripture is equally emphatic that God's character is immutably holy and just and good. "He cannot disown himself" (2 Tim. 2:13). "It is impossible for God to lie" (Heb. 6:18; cf. Tit. 1:2). A believer may rightly stand before the Lord and plead, "Will not the Judge of all the earth do right?" (Gen. 18:25). "His love endures forever" is an oft-recurring phrase (Ps. 136). He assures his people of his eternal self-consistency: "I the LORD do not change. So you, O descendants of Jacob, are not destroyed" (Mal. 3:6).

The inscrutable sovereignty of God is manifested not so much in the punishment of the reprobate as in the SALVATION of his people. In his holy character he must logically punish moral evil (see SIN). But his sovereignty is most marvelously revealed in that he has graciously elected to save a people from their sin and from its consequences (see ELECTION).

sower, sowing. See AGRICULTURE.

Spain. spayn (Gk. *Spania G5056*). The westernmost of the European peninsulas was called variously, in reference to its primitive inhabitants, Iberia, Liguria, and Celtica. In historic times the name Hispania, the origin of which is unknown, prevailed. The area was populated basically by an Indo-European stock allied to the Celts. The land was early noticed by the Phoenicians, who established a major center of trade at Tartessus (in the southern part of the peninsula). The Carthaginians inherited the Phoenician interest in Spain, and New Carthage (Cartagena) was developed by

Hannibal as his base against Italy in the Second Punic War. Spain, in consequence, became a theater of conflict in this clash of nations, and with the victory of ROME remained in Roman hands. It was not until the time of AUGUSTUS that the peninsula was finally pacified and organized. It was rapidly romanized. TRAJAN, HADRIAN, and Theodosius I, among the emperors, were Spaniards; among men of letters the two Senecas, Lucan, Columella, Quintillian, Martial, and Prudentius came from Spain. PAUL's projected visit to Spain (Rom. 15:23-28) was clearly in line with his evident policy to capture for the church the principal centers of the empire. Whether he achieved his ambition is not known for certain. According to Clement of Rome, writing some thirty years after Paul's death, the apostle went to "the limits of the West" (*1 Clem.* 1.5), but it would be dangerous to build too weighty an assumption on a phrase so vague.

span. See WEIGHTS AND MEASURES.

sparrow. See BIRDS.

spear. See ARMS AND ARMOR.

speckled. A word used to denote varied colors of beasts. The most familiar example of its use is in Gen. 30:25-43, where JACOB is said to have applied his knowledge of selective breeding of livestock in order to collect from LABAN what he considered a fair wage (cf. 31:6-12). The word is also used by the KJV and NIV to render a Hebrew word that occurs only once (Jer. 12:9); the term literally means "colored [with stripes]," and some scholars have argued that it refers to the striped hyena (cf. NRSV).

speech. See TONGUE.

spelt. See PLANTS.

spice. See PLANTS.

spider. See ANIMALS.

spies. The custom of sending secret agents to discover facts about an enemy is age-old. JOSEPH accused his brothers of being spies (Gen. 42).

S

Joshua sent spies to Jericho (Josh. 6:23). David sent them to see if Saul was with his army at Hakilah (1 Sam. 26:1-4). Absalom put secret agents throughout Israel to seize power when they were notified he had become king (2 Sam. 15:7-10). Priests and scribes sent spies to entrap Jesus (Lk. 20:20).

spikenard. See PLANTS.

spindle. An implement, 8-12 in. (20-30 cm.) long, used in spinning. The rope of carded fiber or wool was attached to one end and the spindle rotated by hand. Thus the thread was twisted. In Egypt both men and women did spinning, but among the Hebrews it may be that only women did the work (Exod. 35:25; Prov. 31:19).

spinning. The art of drawing out and twisting natural fibers into a continuous thread. Its origins are lost in deep antiquity. The earliest premechanical devices were the hooked stick used as a SPINDLE and the receiving stick or DISTAFF. Such were usually made of wood and few have survived from antiquity except as illustrated on tombs. The other type of spinning device, the spindle whorl, a small torus of stone not much larger than a spool, is often found in Palestinian sites. The Hebrew verb meaning "to spin" appears only in the context of the Israelite offerings of material and labor for the TABERNACLE (Exod. 35:25-26). In the NT the word is used only in the illustration of the lilies of the field (Matt. 6:28; Lk. 12:27).

spirit. This English term (from Latin *spiritus*, "breath") is usually the rendering of Hebrew *rûaḥ H8120* and Greek *pneuma G4460*; both of these nouns can also mean "air, blowing, breath, wind" (e.g., Job 41:16 [Heb. text v. 8]; Ps. 18:15 [Heb. text v. 16]; Jn. 3:8; 2 Thess. 2:8). When used with reference to human psychology, *spirit* is one of several nouns denoting the nonmaterial ego in special relationships (see SOUL). The self is generally called "spirit" in contexts where its bodily, emotional, and intellectual aspects are not prominent, but where the direct relationship of the individual to God is the point of emphasis. A typical instance is Rom. 8:16, "The Spirit himself testifies with our spirit

that we are God's children." The martyrs in heaven are called "souls" when there is special reference to the brutal form of their death (Rev. 6:9). But in the exalted description of the heavenly goal that lies before the CHURCH (Heb. 12:22-24), the blessed dead are referred to as "the spirits of righteous men made perfect." See also HOLY SPIRIT.

Spirit, Holy. See HOLY SPIRIT.

spirits in prison. This phrase occurs in only one passage: "For Christ died for sins once for all, the righteous for the unrighteous, to bring you to God. He was put to death in the body but made alive by the Spirit, through whom also he went and preached to the spirits in prison who disobeyed long ago when God waited patiently in the days of Noah while the ark was being built" (1 Pet. 3:18-20a). These verses have proven to be among the most difficult in the whole NT, and at least three major interpretations have been proposed.

(1) The traditional understanding has been that "the spirits in prison" were people from the time of NOAH who had gone to HADES, and that Jesus, after his death but before his resurrection, went to this abode of the dead and preached to them (cf. 1 Pet. 4:6). Some who hold this view believe that these individuals were given another opportunity to be saved; others insist that Jesus was only proclaiming the victory of the gospel; still others suggest that Jesus was announcing the gospel to people who had already been saved.

(2) Another popular interpretation agrees that the phrase refers to people at the time of the FLOOD, but argues that PETER has in view Noah's own witness to his contemporaries before they died. In other words, the preincarnate Jesus may be said to have preached in the spirit through Noah.

(3) Most modern scholars believe that Peter's words should be understood against the background of *1 Enoch* (esp. chs. 12-16), a Jewish pseudepigraphic work that speaks of fallen angels who intermarried with human beings in the period before the flood (Gen. 6:1-4; see discussion under SONS OF GOD) and whom God imprisoned inside the earth. While some scholars argue that Peter accepted the mythology itself, this is not a necessary inference; he may well have appealed to his reader's

S

familiarity with the story to make a different point, namely, Jesus' condemnation of the spirits.

spiritual body. See BODY; RESURRECTION.

spiritual gifts. See GIFTS, SPIRITUAL.

spit, spittle. In the OT the action of spitting usually indicates a purposeful deed with an added notion of ritual defilement or legal rejection (Lev. 15:8; Num. 12:14; Deut. 25:9). The notion of defilement or rejection occurs also in the accounts of Christ's PASSION (Matt. 26:67; 27:30; Mk. 10:34; 14:65; 15:19; Lk. 18:32). The action of spitting is mentioned in connection with several healing accounts (Mk. 7:33; 8:23; Jn. 9:6). In addition, modern English versions usually have "spit" as the rendering of Greek *emeō G1840* in Rev. 3:16, but this verb properly means "to vomit."

spoils. The plunder taken from the enemy in war—pillage, booty, loot. The spoils of war were divided equally between those who went into battle and those who were left behind in camp (Num. 31:27; Josh. 22:8; 1 Sam. 30:24). Parts were given to the LEVITES and to the Lord (Num. 31:28, 30). Under the monarchy, the king received part of the spoils (2 Ki. 14:14; 1 Chr. 18:7, 11).

spokes. Rods connecting the rim of a wheel with the hub. In the temple there were ten lavers or basins made of bronze (1 Ki. 7:27-33), apparently for the washing of sacrifices. They were set on bases of elaborate design moving on wheels. The spokes were part of these wheels.

sponge. See ANIMALS.

spot. This term is used with reference to skin lesions that might indicate DISEASE (Lev. 13:2 et al.). The KJV uses it of a blemish (Cant. 4:7; NIV, "flaw") and of the taint of sin ("without spot," 2 Pet. 3:14; Jude 23; NIV, "spotless").

spouse. See MARRIAGE.

spread. To scatter, strew, or disperse, as in "spread abroad" (Isa. 21:5; Matt. 21:8; Mk. 1:28).

spring. See FOUNTAIN.

spring rain. See RAIN.

sprinkling. The sprinkling of blood, water, and oil formed a very important part of the act of sacrifice. In the account of the forming of the COVENANT between the Lord and Israel (Exod. 24:6-8), half of the blood was sprinkled on the altar and the rest on the people. When AARON and his sons were consecrated, some blood was sprinkled on the altar and some on Aaron and his sons and on their garments. In the various offerings—burnt, peace, sin—blood was always sprinkled. Sprinkling was sometimes done in handfuls, sometimes with the finger, and sometimes with a sprinkler (a bunch of hyssop fastened to a cedar rod).

spy. See SPIES.

squad. This English term, referring to a small military group, is used in modern Bible versions to render Greek *tetradion G5482*, which occurs once with reference to the detachments assigned by Herod AGRIPPA I to guard PETER as a prisoner (Acts 12:4). The Greek term, meaning "foursome," corresponds to Latin *quaterni* (thus KJV, "quaternions"), indicating a detachment of four soldiers; Peter was assigned four such groups, one for each watch of the night (thus NIV, "four squads of four soldiers each"). In the Acts account the disposition of the squad is given. Peter was sleeping chained to two soldiers (v. 6) while the other two stood guard at the doors where Peter and the angel passed them on leaving (v. 10).

stable. See STALL.

Stachys. stay'kis (Gk. *Stachys G5093*, "head of grain"). A Christian in ROME to whom PAUL sent greetings, calling him "my beloved" (Rom. 16:9; NIV, "my dear friend," Gk. *agapētos G28*).

stacte. See PLANTS.

stadia. See WEIGHTS AND MEASURES.

staff, staves. See ROD.

stag. See ANIMALS (under *deer*).

stair, stairway, steps. In the ANE, one-story houses might have a stair outside, usually of stone and without a railing. Two-story houses had the stair frequently inside, but with an exterior stair from balcony to roof. To provide access to deep wells, steps were cut into the sides. A common Hebrew word that can be translated "stairs" or "steps" is *maʿălāh H5092* (more generally meaning "ascent"). It is used, for example, of the six steps that were part of the throne of King SOLOMON (1 Ki. 10:19-20), and of a stairway that went down from the City of David (Neh. 3:15; 12:37). The latter, which has been excavated, descended about 35 ft. (11 m.) to the end of the hill S of the TEMPLE area near the FOUNTAIN GATE. The "stairway" or "ladder" that JACOB saw in his dream (Gen. 28:12; Heb. *sullām H6150*) may have been a ramp of rising stones. (On 2 Ki. 20:11 = Isa. 38:8, see DIAL.) In the NT, Greek *anabathmos G325* is used of the steps from which PAUL addressed the mob in JERUSALEM (Acts 20:35, 40); the reference is to a stairway that led from the temple area to the ANTONIA fortress.

stake. A tent pin or tent peg (Exod. 27:19; Isa. 33:20; 54:2).

stall. Thousands of stalls were built by SOLOMON for securing his chariots and horses (1 Ki. 4:26 = 2 Chr. 9:25). Reference is made also to the "stalls for various kinds of cattle, and pens for the flocks" in the time of HEZEKIAH (2 Chr. 32:28). In two-story homes, cattle were usually housed in the ground level where there were stalls and MANGERS. The stables of MEGIDDO were arranged on either side of an aisle, each stall separated by posts and provided with a manger, paved with cobblestones. The Hebrew term *marbēq H5272* is usually rendered "stall" in two passages (Amos 6:4; Mal. 4:2), but the connotation is "stall-fed," that is, "fattened" (thus 1 Sam. 28:24; Jer. 46:21; cf. also Prov. 15:17 KJV). In the NT, "stall" or "manger" translates Greek *phatnē G5764* (Lk. 13:15).

stallion. See ANIMALS (under *horse*).

standard. See BANNER; WEIGHTS AND MEASURES.

star. See ASTRONOMY.

star, day (morning). See MORNING STAR.

Star of Bethlehem, Star of the Wise Men. See ASTRONOMY.

state. See GOVERNMENT.

stature. This English term, usually referring to a person's height, occurs seventeen times in the KJV, but seldom in modern versions, which prefer "size" or other expressions (e.g., Num. 13:32). In the NT the meaning "stature" is conveyed by Greek *hēlikia G2461*, and this meaning is clear in Lk. 19:3, where ZACCHAEUS is described as being a short person. The Greek word, however, often has the sense "age" (see esp. Jn. 9:21, 23; Heb. 11:11), which produces some ambiguity in several passages. For example, when Luke describes the boy Jesus as having grown in wisdom and *hēlikia* (Lk. 2:52), is he referring to Jesus' physical size or to his age (cf. NRSV, "increased in wisdom and in years") or to his maturity? In the SERMON ON THE MOUNT Jesus asked the rhetorical question, "Which of you by taking thought can add one cubit unto his stature?" (Matt. 6:27 KJV; cf. Lk. 12:25). Some interpreters, understanding the word for "cubit" (Gk. *pēchys G4388*) figuratively of a small measure of time, translate, "Who of you by worrying can add a single hour to his life?" (so NIV; similarly, NRSV). The transition between these two senses of the word may be illustrated by Eph. 4:13, where PAUL speaks of believers attaining "the measure of the full stature of Christ" (NRSV). Even this literal rendering is understandable to an English reader, who naturally interprets *stature* (physical height) in the figurative sense of "maturity."

staves. A form used by the KJV consistently as the plural of *staff*. See ROD.

steadfast. This adjective and its cognates (which the KJV spells *stedfast, stedfastly, stedfastness*) indicate firmness, determination, loyalty; they are used variously to render several Hebrew and Greek terms. The adverb is used a number of times in the KJV to translate verbs that have an intensive

S

meaning, such as Greek *atenizō G867* (as in Acts 1:10, "they looked stedfastly toward heaven"). In the NIV the adjective occurs relatively few times (e.g., Ps. 51:10), but the NRSV uses the phrase "steadfast love" with great frequency as the translation of the noun *ḥesed H2876* (Gen. 24:12 et al.); see comments under LOVINGKINDNESS. See also FAITHFULNESS; PATIENCE.

stealing. See COMMANDMENTS, TEN.

stedfast. KJV form of STEADFAST.

steed. See ANIMALS (under *horse*).

steel. See MINERALS.

steer. See ANIMALS (under *cattle*).

stela, stele. A stone slab (Lat. *stela*, Gk. *stēlē*), usually oblong, not forming part of a structure but set up in a vertical position, used for votive purposes or as a memorial to some person or event.

Basalt stele from the late Hittite period (Maras, 9th cent. B.C.) depicting a banquet scene.

© Dr. James C. Martin. The Istanbul Archaeological Museum. Photographed by permission.

Upon these slabs were carved INSCRIPTIONS often accompanied by ornamental designs or reliefs of particular significance. Such stelae have been found throughout Mesopotamia, Syria, Egypt, Asia Minor, and the Greco-Roman world. Some of them have important connections with events narrated in the Bible. The stela was essentially of a secular character even though it may have been erected at a sanctuary and have had religious images carved on it. No Israelite stela has ever been discovered, although such a MONUMENT may be indicated in 1 Sam. 15:12 (cf. 2 Sam. 18:18). See also PILLAR.

Stephanas. stef'uh-nuhs (Gk. *Stephanas G5107*, "crown"). A Corinthian Christian who, with his household, was one of the few persons baptized personally by the apostle PAUL in CORINTH (1 Cor. 1:16). The household of Stephanas were the FIRST-FRUITS of the GOSPEL in ACHAIA (1 Cor. 16:15-16; although individuals had earlier been converted in ATHENS [Acts 17:34], this family must have been the foundation for the first Christian community in the region). Paul commends them for devoted "service"—which probably included both Christian teaching and hospitality—to God's people and urges the Corinthian believers to be subject to such leaders. This instruction suggests that the Corinthians had failed to show proper esteem to Stephanas and his family. Paul also states that he rejoiced and that his spirit was lifted by the visit of Stephanas, FORTUNATUS, and ACHAICUS while he was in EPHESUS, and asked that recognition be given them (1 Cor. 16:17-18). These three men are said to "have supplied what was lacking from" the Corinthians. Most interpreters understand this comment to mean that the apostle missed the company of the Corinthian church as a whole and that the visit from these representatives served to relieve his sadness.

Stephen. stee'vuhn (Gk. *Stephanos G5108*, "crown"). Hellenistic Christian apologist and first Christian MARTYR. Stephen was one of the seven appointed to look after the daily distribution to the poor in the early church (Acts 6:1-6; see DEACON). The need for such men arose out of the complaint of the Hellenists (i.e., Greek-speaking

Jews) that their widows were not receiving a fair share of this relief. Stephen, described as "a man full of faith and of the Holy Spirit" (6:5), and six others were selected by the church and consecrated by the apostles in order to insure an equitable distribution.

Stephen's ministry was not, however, limited to providing for the poor. He did "great wonders and miraculous signs among the people" (Acts 6:8). While this probably brought him into great favor with the people generally, another aspect of his ministry engaged him in bitterest conflict with the adherents of JUDAISM. He taught in the Synagogue of the FREEDMEN and there debated with Jews of the DISPERSION from CYRENE, ALEXANDRIA, CILICIA, and ASIA. When it was evident that they could not refute Stephen's arguments in open debate, these Jews hired informers to misrepresent his arguments. They went around proclaiming, "This fellow never stops speaking against this holy place and against the law. For we have heard him say that this Jesus of Nazareth will destroy this place and change the customs Moses handed down to us" (6:13-14). These accusations were such that the council could be assured of the support of the people of JERUSALEM. Since they were largely dependent on the TEMPLE for their livelihood, any threat to it constituted a threat to them.

Acts 7 records Stephen's remarkable *apologia* before the council, but this speech was not intended to earn him an acquittal; it was rather a vigorous defense of the Christian faith. Stephen's exclamation at the close of his speech is particularly important to a proper understanding of it: "Look ... I see heaven open and the Son of Man standing at the right hand of God" (7:56). This is the only occurrence of the title SON OF MAN in the NT on the lips of anyone other than Jesus himself, and it may reveal that Stephen understood Jesus' significance in a sense greater than a Jewish MESSIAH. Such radical thinking was too much for the listening SANHEDRIN. "They covered their ears and, yelling at the top of their voices, they ... dragged him out of the city and began to stone him." The witnesses, whose responsibility it was to cast the first stones (cf. Deut. 17:7), laid their clothes at Saul's feet (Acts 7:57-58).

steps. See STAIRS.

steward. See OCCUPATIONS AND PROFESSIONS.

stiff-necked. This expression is a literal rendering of the Hebrew phrase *qĕšēh-ʿōrep* (*H7997* + *H6902*), "hard of neck," used especially to describe the intransigence and rebellious spirit of the Israelites in the period of their sojourn in the SINAI desert after the EXODUS from EGYPT (Exod. 32:9 et al.). The SEPTUAGINT rendered the Hebrew literally into Greek with the compound *sklērotrachēlos G5019*, which is used only once in the NT (Acts 7:51, near the conclusion of STEPHEN's speech).

stocks. This English term, referring to an instrument of restraint and punishment, is used primarily to render Hebrew *mahpeket H4551*, which occurs only a few times (Jer. 20:2-3; 29:26; cf. also 2 Chr. 16:10, lit., "house of stocks," that is, "prison"). In Job 13:27 and 33:11 we find the term *sad H6040*, which probably refers to a restraining device like the stock (NIV, "shackles"), but the precise origin and meaning of the term is uncertain. It also occurs in the NT as the translation of Greek *xylon G3833*, which actually means "wood" (thus also the older meaning of English *stock*, cf. KJV at Jer. 2:27 et al.); in the narrative of Acts 16:24, it clearly refers to the posts to which prisoners' limbs were held fast by iron bolts. (The KJV uses the term also in the sense of "family lineage," Lev. 25:47; Acts 13:26; Phil. 3:5.)

Stoic. stoh'ik (Gk. *Stoikos G5121*, from *stoa G5119*, "portico"). In the NT the Stoics are mentioned only once, in Acts 17:18, along with the EPICUREANS. In the same passage (v. 28) PAUL is said to have quoted the words of a Greek poet, "We are his offspring," a line that comes from the Stoic philosopher Aratus. Beyond this quotation and the fact that the Stoics rejected the idea of a bodily RESURRECTION, LUKE gives no information about their views. However, other portions of the NT, especially the epistles of Paul, use language or indirectly allude to concepts associated with Stoicism. (Because one of its tenets was that a person's essential being should not be affected by either pleasure or pain, the English word *stoic* has come

© Dr. James C. Martin. The Eretz Israel Museum. Photographed by permission.

Coin with the image of the Stoic philosopher/emperor, Marcus Aurelius (A.D. 161-180).

to denote someone who is emotionally indifferent to suffering.)

Boasting a galaxy of distinguished exponents, both Greek and Roman—e.g., Zeno, Cleanthes, Seneca, Cicero, Epictetus, and Marcus Aurelius—Stoicism was a system of pantheistic monism. It held that fire is the ultimate substance with God, the active principle of the cosmos, permeating everything as a sort of soul. Nature, it taught, is a hierarchical unity controlled by the universal Logos, an impersonal reason at once immanent and divine. As participants in the Logos, human beings are also participants in deity. Indeed, the true essence of humanity is *nous* or MIND, the capacity to understand the rational order veiled by phenomena. As a logos-being, human beings can perceive and assent to the determinism that makes all events necessary and therefore reduces evil to mere appearance. By assenting to this determinism—indifferently called fate or providence—we are able to live in harmony with nature.

Hence the Stoic ethic often becomes egocentrically negative. Nothing lies within our power except imagination, desire, and emotion; thus by cultivating not only detachment from the world outside but also mastery over our reactions to the world's impingement on us, we achieve freedom, happiness, and self-sufficiency. Impressively noble

and lofty when practiced by, say, a Marcus Aurelius, Stoicism could be aristocratic and austere, rigorously excluding pity, denying pardon, and suppressing genuine feeling. Its view of SIN was hopelessly shallow, since it did not think in terms of obedience to a personal God. Sin was simply an error of judgment, easily rectified by a change of opinion. But among its virtues were cosmopolitanism and egalitarianism. Whatever a person's position or handicap, anyone, Stoicism affirmed, even a slave like Epictetus, can be inwardly free. Moreover, as partakers of a common rational nature, people everywhere are subject to the same law. Implicit in Stoicism, accordingly, was the idea of a universal morality rooted in the universal Logos.

stomach. See BELLY.

stomacher. This English term, referring to the front part of a bodice, is used by the KJV as the rendering of Hebrew *pĕtîgîl H7345*, which occurs only once (Isa. 3:24). The etymology of the Hebrew word is unknown and its meaning is uncertain. Because it stands in contrast to *śaq H8566* (see SACKCLOTH), it is usually rendered "rich robe" (NRSV) or "fine clothing" (NIV).

stone. When entering CANAAN, the Hebrews, who had made bricks in EGYPT (Exod. 5:7), readily turned to the abundant supply of stones, both from quarries and from stream beds. Limestone (Isa. 27:9), gravel (Lam. 3:16), and stones rounded by water in streams (1 Sam. 17:40; Job 14:19) were abundant. Large flat slabs were used as covers for wells (Gen. 29:2-10) and as doors for caves (Josh. 10:18), including for burial caves (Matt. 27:60). Stones were also used as landmarks (2 Sam. 20:8). The stones mentioned in Deut. 19:14; 27:17; and Prov. 22:28 were boundary stones (see Josh. 15:16; 1 Ki. 1:9). Great stones were used in the foundation of the TEMPLE (1 Ki. 6:7). The palace for the PHARAOH's daughter was of high-grade stone (7:8-12). One may today see samples of Israelite stonework in the Wailing Wall of Jerusalem. A stone from the city wall is 14 ft. (over 4 m.) long and 3.75 ft. (over 1 m.) high and wide. Remains of quarries in many places of the land show how widespread the use of stone was in ancient times.

Stones were used in setting up altars and memorials. These objects were of various kinds: monuments, tables, steles or upright slabs, and circular areas enclosed by rocks. After Joshua had led the Hebrews over Jordan, he set up a monument composed of twelve stones taken from the river's bed by representatives of the twelve tribes (Josh. 4:1-9). Jacob set up a monument to commemorate his experience at Bethel (Gen. 28:18). His contract with Laban was sealed by a stele (31:45-46). The miraculous victory over the Philistines called for a memorial (1 Sam. 7:5-12). A heap of stones was placed over one who was executed by stoning, as over the king of Ai (Josh. 8:29) and over Absalom (2 Sam. 18:17-18). Joshua's last official act was to erect a memorial to Israel's covenant with God (Josh. 24:26-28).

Stone weapons were frequently used by the Israelites. The familiar account of David's victory over the giant of Gath reveals the skill of one who had mastered the use of the sling (1 Sam. 17). Among David's warriors were some who could sling stones (1 Chr. 12:2). King Uzziah included in his arsenal stones for slingers and for catapults (2 Chr. 26:14-15). Stones were used in individual conflict (Exod. 21:18; Num. 35:17-23). Certain crimes were punished by stoning (Lev. 20:2, 27; 24:23).

The transition from using an object *in* worship to making it an object *of* worship is never difficult. So Israel was prone to worship stones (see idolatry). Among other pagan evils Isaiah found libations being offered to river stones (Isa. 57:3-7). The law prohibited any such use of stones (Lev. 26:1).

Figurative uses of the word *stone* are frequent in Hebrew writings: Egyptians sank like stones (Exod. 15:5); God's arm could make his enemies still as stones (15:16); Nabal's "heart failed him and he became like a stone" (1 Sam. 25:37); Job spoke of ice as stone (Job 38:30). The hard heart is like stone (Ezek. 11:19), but God has power to change stony hearts into hearts of flesh (Matt. 3:9). Jesus gave a new name to Simon, Peter ("stone"), as an indication of the character that this apostle would have in the days ahead (Jn. 1:42). God is the stone of Israel (Gen. 49:24; Dan. 2:34). The messianic kingdom is a stone that will crush the kingdoms of this world (Dan. 2:34; Matt. 21:44). Jesus Christ is the stone the builders rejected (Ps. 118:22; Matt. 21:42).

Paul presented Jesus as the chief cornerstone of the new dispensation (Eph. 2:20-22). Believers are living stones in God's temple (1 Pet. 2:5-8).

stones, precious. See minerals.

stoning. The act of throwing stones, usually for the purpose of killing a person. The most common form of capital punishment prescribed by biblical law was stoning. It usually took place outside the city (Lev. 24:23; Num. 15:35-36; 1 Ki. 21:13). The prosecution witnesses (the law required two or more, Deut. 17:6) placed their hands on the offender's head (Lev. 24:14) to transfer the guilt of the whole community to the offender. The witnesses then cast the first stones, and the rest of the people followed (Deut. 17:7). All this was done to purge out evil from the community (22:21).

The following ten offenses were punished by stoning: (1) idolatry, that is, the worship of other gods or any heavenly bodies (Deut. 17:2-7); (2) enticement to idolatry (Deut. 13:6-11); (3) blasphemy (Lev. 24:14-23; 1 Ki. 21:10-15); (4) child sacrifice to Molech (Lev. 20:2-5); (5) spirit divination (Lev. 20:27); (6) breaking the Sabbath (Num. 15:32-36); (7) adultery (Deut. 22:21-24); (8) disobedience of a son (Deut. 21:18-21); (9) violation of the ban, or Devoted Thing (Josh. 7:25, burning also occurs here); (10) homicide by an ox (Exod. 21:28-32). The last case is the only one concerning an animal, though Exod. 19:13 threatens both man and beast with stoning if either touches Mount Sinai.

The abundance of stones in Palestine made stoning the most common death penalty. It was also a convenient way to express anger or hatred. It was often threatened (Exod. 17:4; Num. 14:10; 1 Sam. 30:6), especially against Christ and Paul (Jn. 10:31-33; 11:8; Acts 14:5, 19). Actual cases of death by stoning are recorded several times: Adoram (1 Ki. 12:18; see Adoniram), Zechariah (2 Chr. 24:21), and Stephen (Acts 7:58-59).

stool. A three or four-legged seat, used already in ancient times. The Shunammite woman put one in Elisha's room (2 Ki. 4:10 KJV; NIV, "chair"). A stool of peculiar form was used in Egypt for women in childbirth (Exod. 1:16).

storax. See PLANTS (under *poplar*).

store cities. Under the lashes of taskmasters the Israelites built PITHOM and RAMESES as "cities of stores" for PHARAOH (Exod. 1:11). SOLOMON built a number of such supply centers in HAMATH and in other unnamed places throughout his realm (1 Ki. 9:19; 2 Chr. 8:4, 6). During BAASHA's reign, BEN-HADAD concentrated upon and took the store cities of NAPHTALI along with other towns (2 Chr. 16:4). JEHOSHAPHAT, in a program of strengthening JUDAH, built both store-cities and fortresses (17:12). HEZEKIAH too promoted the construction of storage facilities (2 Chr. 32:28). The "store city" apparently had its background in the practice of EGYPT to provide storage for the excessive yield of a "fat" year as a reserve against the poor yield of a "lean" year, as was the case in JOSEPH's time. Beginning with Solomon and throughout the reigns of the later kings, these cities were used for storing grains and oil to be sent later to the palace personnel in JERUSALEM (1 Ki. 4:7, 22-23) or SAMARIA, or to be collected as an important part of government revenue, as is known from the OSTRACA of Samaria and other sources.

storehouse. MALACHI charged that the people of his day had robbed God because they had failed to bring their tithes into the *bēt hāʾôṣār*, literally "house of the treasure," but usually rendered "storehouse" (Mal. 3:10); he evidently had reference to the TEMPLE treasury. The same phrase is used in Neh. 10:38 (Heb. v. 39), which speaks about the

Partial reconstruction of the storehouses at Beersheba.

LEVITES' taking a tenth of the tithes "to the chambers of the storehouse" (NRSV; the NIV here reads, "the storerooms of the treasury").

stork. See BIRDS.

storm. In the Palestinian environment, storms are frequent phenomena. Naturally, they figured prominently in the consciousness of some biblical writers such as the psalmists and the prophet ISAIAH, who saw them variously as a threat to security or a punishment inflicted upon wrongdoers. (Cf. Ps. 55:8; 83:15; Isa. 4:6; 25:4; 28:2.) Three kinds of storm are commonly experienced in PALESTINE. (1) Thunderstorms (see THUNDER) occur mainly at the start of the rainy season, in the autumn when the land is still hot; they are particularly frequent around the Sea of Galilee, where sea air flowing inland passes over the hot basin in which the lake lies. (2) WHIRLWINDS, such as the one by which ELIJAH was caught up (2 Ki. 2), are local vortices with more limited effects. (3) Most important are the desert storms, which occur when the wind blows out from the desert, bringing hot, parching air to the cultivated lands on the desert margins. Often referred to as *sirocco*, these winds blow from the S or E, that is, from the Arabian desert. They are experienced generally at the beginning and at the end of the summer season and frequently are accompanied by choking dust and very high temperatures. Blowing across the land of Palestine, they raise storms as far W as the MEDITERRANEAN (cf. Ps. 48:7). Jesus referred to the characteristics of the desert wind in Lk. 12:55.

storm god. See HADAD #5.

stove. In PALESTINE the stove was usually made of clay. Some were small portable fireplaces, burning charcoal. Others were built outside the house and were heated with dry sticks, grass, and even dung. The hearth or firepot mentioned in Jer. 36:22 was a bronze heater. Only the well-to-do could afford a brazier. For cooking, the stove was molded so as to hold the pot or pan above the fire bowl through which air passed from vents at the bottom. The fire by which PETER warmed himself during the trial of Jesus was probably in a brazier (Mk. 14:67).

© Dr. James C. Martin

Straight Street. This street, the only one identified by name in the NT (Acts 9:11), was located in Damascus, a city within the boundaries of Syria but belonging politically to the Decapolis. The city obtained its freedom from Rome shortly after Christ's death and was under an Arabian ruler during the period covered by Acts 9 (see Aretas). On this street was located the house of a certain Judas, where Saul of Tarsus was a guest (see Paul). It was here that Saul was visited by Ananias, and here that he received his eyesight again, signaling his conversion and call. By current standards, Straight Street (also referred to as *Via Recta*) was probably a lane or alley. A narrow street bearing the same name exists in the modern city of Damascus, and some believe that this is the site of the first-century street.

stranger. The Hebrew term *nokrî H5799* is usually rendered "alien" or "stranger" by the KJV, but "foreigner" in modern translations (Deut. 14:21; Job 19:15; Ps. 69:8; Lam. 5:2). Two other terms, *gēr H1731* and *tôšāb H9369* (KJV, "sojourner"), are sometimes used together in the same passage with no apparent semantic difference (Lev. 25:35; 1 Chr. 29:15; Ps. 39:12), though it has been suggested that in some contexts the latter indicates an individual less assimilated to Israelite society and attached to someone else's household (cf. Exod. 12:445; Lev. 22:10). An additional term, *zār H2424*, has a broad range of meanings, such as "outsider" and "unauthorized," but can also refer to a foreigner (e.g., Isa. 1:7).

Foreigners in Israel enjoyed certain limited religious and civic privileges and were subject to certain laws. They could offer sacrifices (Lev. 17:8; 22:18-19), but were not permitted to enter the sanctuary unless they were circumcised (Ezek. 44:9). They could take part in the three great annual religious festivals attended by all Israelite males (Deut. 16:11, 14). Like the Israelites, they were forbidden to work on the Sabbath and on the Day of Atonement (Exod. 20:10; 23:12; Lev. 16:19; Deut. 5:14; see Atonement, Day of); and like them also they were stoned to death for reviling or blaspheming God's name (Lev. 24:16; Num. 15:30). In general, there was one law for both foreigner and native (Exod. 12:49; Lev. 24:22), and in legal actions aliens were entitled to the same justice as the Israelites (Deut. 1:16) and were liable to the same penalties (Lev. 20:2; 24:16, 22). Israelites were warned not to oppress foreigners, since they themselves had once been strangers in the land of Egypt (Exod. 22:21; 23:9; Lev. 19:33-34). Foreigners were to be loved and treated like native Israelites (Lev. 19:34; Deut. 10:19), for God loves them (Deut. 10:18) and watches over them (Ps. 146:9; Mal. 3:5). Like the Israelites, they were forbidden to eat blood (Lev. 17:10, 12), but, unlike them, they might eat animals that had died a natural death (Deut. 14:21).

In the NT, several Greek words are used with the sense "foreigner" or "stranger," but the most common term is *xenos G3828* (Acts 17:21 et al.). Paul describes Gentiles as "foreigners to the covenants of the promise" (Eph. 2:12); when they come to Christ, however, they are "no longer foreigners and aliens [*paroikos G4230*], but fellow citizens with God's people" (v. 19). On the other hand, Peter refers to his readers as "aliens and strangers [*parepidēmos G4215*] in the world" (1 Pet. 2:11). See also barbarian.

strange woman. This expression is used a number of times by the KJV in the book of Proverbs, usually as the translation of Hebrew *zārâ* (fem. of *zār H2424*, "foreign, unauthorized, illegitimate"), which refers either to a prostitute or to a married Israelite woman involved in an illicit relationship (Prov. 5:3 et al.; NIV, "adulteress"; NRSV, "loose woman"; NJPS, "forbidden woman").

strangle. To deprive of life by choking, and so without bloodshed. Israelites were forbidden to eat flesh from strangled animals because it contained the blood of the animals (Lev. 17:12). At the Jerusalem Council it was decided that even Gentile Christians should not eat such meat (Acts 15:20); some believe that this and the other prohibitions issued at that assembly applied specifically to the churches in Syrian Antioch and surrounding areas (cf. v. 23), but others argue that they are based on the covenant God made with Noah (Gen. 9:3-5) and thus have universal applicability.

straw. The dry residue of stalky plants, such as barley and wheat. It is possible, however, that the straw mentioned in Exod. 5:7-18 was merely the stalks of wild grasses, because the children of Israel were forced to gather what they needed for brick making. In the NT, the term is used only once in a figurative context (1 Cor. 3:12).

stream of Egypt. See EGYPT, WADI OF.

street. In the cities of the ANE the streets were very narrow, often only wide enough to allow for the passage of a CHARIOT. They were also winding and without any plan, although large cities sometimes had one or more avenues. Since refuse was thrown into streets, they were usually very dirty, and scavenger dogs ate a great deal of the garbage. Streets were usually rutted and muddy, since they were not often paved. Herod AGRIPPA I, however, allowed JERUSALEM to be paved with white stones (Jos. *Ant.* 20.9.7 §222). Usually houses abutted directly onto the streets. Each of the houses had a door on the street side, but the windows were on the opposite side, facing courts.

stringed instruments. See MUSIC AND MUSICAL INSTRUMENTS.

stripes. See SCOURGE.

strong drink. See WINE.

stronghold. This English term, referring to a place that has been fortified or that otherwise provides security, is used to render various Hebrew nouns, especially *mĕṣād H5171* (Jdg. 6:2 et al. and see MASADA). It occurs primarily in figurative contexts that speak of God as the protection of his people (Ps. 18:2 et al.). In the NT, Greek *ochyrōma G4065* occurs once with reference to intellectual pretensions that oppose true knowledge and that must be demolished with spiritual weapons (2 Cor. 10:4). See also FORT; ROCK; TOWER.

stubble. The part of the plant stem left standing in the field after the crop has been harvested. The Hebrew term for "stubble" is *qaš H7990*, which in some instances may refer to CHAFF (e.g., Ps. 83:13), that is, the husks or fine particles that are separated from the grain during threshing and win-

nowing. The Israelites were forced to go to the fields to gather stubble because they were not permitted to use STRAW in their brickmaking (Exod. 5:12). God's consuming wrath is depicted in terms of a raging fire sweeping across a field of stubble (15:7). ISAIAH and other later prophets declared that evildoers were the object of God's judgment; they would face a demise like that of fire devouring stubble (Isa. 5:24; 47:14; Joel 2:5; Obad. 18; Nah. 1:10; Mal. 4:1).

stuff. This English term is used a number of times by the KJV, mainly as the rendering of Hebrew *kĕlî H3998* ("vessel, equipment," etc.), which in the plural can mean "goods, possessions" (Gen. 31:37 et al.). The RSV uses the phrase "scarlet stuff" frequently in Exodus to translate a Hebrew phrase that refers to the crimson-colored cloth employed for the curtains of the TABERNACLE (Exod. 26:1 et al.).

stumbling block. This English expression is used a number of times in Bible versions to render Hebrew *mikšōl H4842* ("hindrance") and Greek *skandalon G4998* ("trap"). In the OT the cause of stumbling may be literal, as an obstacle in the path of a blind man (Lev. 19:14), but most often it is used figuratively to picture the judgment of God against the rebellious (Jer. 6:21; Ezek. 3:20). Ethically, the stumbling block is that which causes iniquity, whether gold and silver (Ezek. 7:19) or idols (Ezek. 14:3-4, 7; 44:12). In the NT the idea of "striking against" an object so as to stumble speaks figuratively of a weaker brother who stumbles in his Christian walk (Rom. 14:13; 1 Cor. 8:9). This term is also used in connection with the failure of ISRAEL to recognize her suffering MESSIAH (Rom. 11:9; 1 Cor. 1:23). See OFFENCE.

Suah. soo'uh (Heb. *sûaḥ H6053*, meaning uncertain). Son of Zophah and descendant of ASHER (1 Chr. 7:36).

submission. See OBEDIENCE.

suburbs. This English term—not in its modern meaning of built-up areas surrounding a city center, but in a more general sense—is used frequently by the KJV (esp. in Josh. 21 and 1 Chr. 6) to render

S

Hebrew *migrāš H4494*, which evidently refers to demarcated open lands outside the walls of a CITY. These areas were built over only later as population increased or particular groups were forbidden to settle within the walls. Thus one finds a request for "suburbs … for our cattle" (Josh. 21:2 KJV) and a reference to "the fields of the suburbs" where some priests lived (2 Chr. 31:19 KJV). That such outskirts played an essential part in the life and economy of the urban community in Palestine is shown by their inclusion with each town apportioned to the tribes of Israel. The common rendering "pasturelands" (cf. NIV) seems to fit some contexts, but some believe this meaning arose as a result of a questionable etymology.

Sucathite. soo´kuh-th*i*t (Heb. *śûkātî H8460*, gentilic of the otherwise unattested place name *śûkâ*, meaning unknown). KJV Suchathite. Among the descendants of CALEB (through his son HUR and grandson SALMA) are listed three "clans of scribes who lived at Jabez: the Tirathites, Shimeathites and Sucathites. These are the Kenites who came from Hammath, the father of the house of Recab" (1 Chr. 2:55). Nothing else is known about these clans, and their names cannot be traced to a particular person or place. See KENITE.

Succoth. suhk-uhth´ (Heb. *sukkôt H6111*, "booths"). TNIV Sukkoth. **(1)** A city within the tribal territory of GAD, generally identified with modern Tell Deir ʿAlla, a mound just N of the JABBOK River and about 3 mi. (5 km.) E of the JORDAN. Succoth is first mentioned in connection with JACOB's travels after he wrestled with the angel of the Lord by the Jabbok River and was reconciled to his brother ESAU the next day (Gen. 33:17). The explanation this passage gives for the name Succoth (deriving it from Jacob's cattle booths or stalls) does not necessarily mean that Jacob founded the city. Later, in the days of JOSHUA, Succoth is mentioned along with ZAPHON as part of the inheritance of the tribe of Gad (Josh. 13:27). GIDEON and his army, while pursuing the Midianites to victory, were ill-treated by the elders of Succoth and the neighboring city of Penuel, both of which refused to supply food (Jdg. 8:5-16). See PENUEL (PLACE). SOLOMON found suitable clay ground to

cast the large bronze vessels for the temple near Succoth (1 Ki. 7:46; 2 Chr. 4:17). In the Psalms, Succoth is referred to as the symbol of the victorious occupation of the country of CANAAN E of the Jordan (Ps. 60:6; 108:7).

(2) A city in EGYPT between RAMESES and ETHAM; it was the first stop of the Israelites at the time of the EXODUS (Exod. 12:37; 13:20; Num. 33:5-6). The city is tentatively identified with modern Tell el-Maskhuta, a border fortress in the eastern portion of Wadi Tumilat, W of the bitter lakes. See comments under PITHOM.

Succoth Benoth. suhk´uhth-bee´noth (Heb. *sukkôt bĕnôt H6112*, "booths of daughters," but the form is prob. a corruption of an Akk. name). TNIV Sukkoth Benoth. A Babylonian deity. After defeating the northern kingdom of ISRAEL and carrying away hostages, the Assyrians brought in peoples of various regions of Upper and Lower MESOPOTAMIA and settled them in SAMARIA. There were Babylonians among these peoples who had Succoth Benoth as their god or goddess (2 Ki. 17:30). In extrabiblical sources no such deity is attested, but many scholars have thought that the name may derive from *Ṣarpanitu* ("shining," later *Zēr-bānītu*, "seed-creating"), who was MARDUK's consort; alternatively, the reference could be to ISHTAR, who was sometimes called *Bānītu* ("[female] creator"). Other possibilities have been suggested.

suffering. See PERSECUTION; TRIBULATION.

Suffering Servant. See SERVANT OF THE LORD.

Sukkiim. See SUKKIITES.

Sukkiites. suhk´ee-ites (Heb. *sukkiyyîm H6113*, derivation unknown). Also Sukkiim; KJV Sukkiims (superfluous English pl. form). A people group, evidently from Africa, who along with Libyans and Cushites assisted SHISHAK, king of EGYPT, when he invaded PALESTINE (2 Chr. 12:3). The SEPTUAGINT renders the name as *Trōglodytai* ("cave dwellers"), apparently referring to an Ethiopian tribe mentioned by Herodotus (*Hist.* 4.183; this group is now identified with the Tibboos). The true identity of the Sukkiites is unknown.

S

Sukkoth. suhk-uhth´. (1) TNIV form of SUCCOTH.
(2) The Hebrew name of the Feast of Booths
(Tabernacles). See FEASTS.

sulfur, sulphur. See BRIMSTONE; MINERALS.

Sumer. soo´muhr (from Akk. *šumeru*, although the
Sumerians themselves used the term *kengir* [ki-en-
gi]). The ancient name of the land located in what
is today the southern half of Iraq in the valleys of
the TIGRIS and EUPHRATES Rivers. Other names
used in antiquity to denote this area are Babylonia (see BABYLON) and SHINAR. See also MESO-
POTAMIA. The history of Sumer properly speaking
is the history of her separate cities, such as Kish,
Uruk, Ur, Lagash, Eridu, Nippur, and Sippar. Each
city had its claims to fame: its local god, temples,
monuments, or rulers. The origin of the Sumerians
is unknown, but they evidently reached the Tigris-
Euphrates Valley before the end of the fourth millennium B.C., although the traditional history of
Sumer begins about the year 2800 and ends with
HAMMURABI's conquest of Larsa c. 1720. The
Sumerian language was not Semitic; indeed, it was
apparently unrelated to any other known tongue.
As far as can be determined, they were the inven-
tors of WRITING in the form of the cuneiform
script. They left behind many important literary
works. In language, thought, literary genre, and

© Dr. James C. Martin. The British Museum. Photographed by permission.

This cuneiform tablet, discovered in Nineveh and dating to the
end of the second millennium B.C., contains a list of equivalent
terms in Sumerian and Akkadian.

in other ways the influence of Sumer can be said
to have been immense and lived on through the
Babylonians to the Greeks and the W, not without
leaving an indirect mark on the OT.

summer. The Hebrew word for "summer," *qayiṣ*
H7811, can be used both for the season (Gen. 8:22
et al.) and for its produce (Jer. 40:10 et al.). In PAL-
ESTINE, the months between May and October are
essentially rainless, so that summer is a season of
drought (Ps. 32:4) and often oppressive heat, but
also of field work (Prov. 10:5; Jer. 8:20). The main
business of the season is the HARVEST, first that of
the early crops (cf. Isa. 28:4), then the main crop.
If the harvest is delayed, the produce will become
overripe and spoil, as in the vision of summer fruit
(Amos 8:1-2). In the NT, the Greek word *theros*
G2550 occurs only in Jesus' comment about recognizing the signs of the end times (Matt. 13:28 and
parallels). See also CALENDAR.

sun. Under the titles of various deities, the sun was
worshiped by many peoples of the ancient world
(see RE). In the Bible, the sun (Heb. *šemeš H9087*;
Gk. *hēlios G2463*) is mentioned frequently, especially as part of the imagery of CREATION and in
a number of common Semitic idiomatic expressions. The beneficent nature of the sun was known
among the Hebrews. Sun, moon, and stars determine times and seasons (Gen. 1:14; Jer. 31:35).
Since the location of the sun determined the extent
of heat and light, the day was divided accordingly.
Mid-morning was when the sun grew hot (1 Sam.
11:9); noon was when it was brightest (Gen. 43:16);
beyond noon the heat waned and it was the cool
of the day (3:8). Times and seasons were controlled
by the "laws of the heavens" (Job 38:33; Ps. 119:91).
The sun also determined directions. The direction
of the rising of the sun became EAST (Isa. 45:6); the
direction of its going down (Ps. 50:1) became WEST.
The left hand or darker quarter was NORTH, and the
right hand or brighter quarter SOUTH (Gen. 13:14;
Job 37:17; Ezek. 40:24). The sun also made it possible for humanity to survive, for it produced fruits
(Deut. 33:14). Poetic fancies arose about the sun. It
is like a bridegroom (Ps. 19:4-5), stands in his house
(Hab. 3:11), is ever watchful (Ps. 19:6), dependable
(72:5), and tells of God's continuing care (84:11).

Sun, City of the. See City of Destruction.

Sunday. See Lord's Day.

superscription. This English term is used by the KJV with reference to the legend on a coin (Matt. 22:20; Mk. 12:16; Lk. 20:24; NIV, "inscription"). It is also used of the "written notice" (NIV) attached to the cross (Mk. 15:26; Lk. 23:38). Biblical scholars often use the term *superscription* with reference to the titles of the Psalms.

superstition. Belief in the supernatural that is motivated by fear, proceeds from ignorance, and reflects an irrational view of reality. It may denote also the practices consequent upon such belief. Black magic, witchcraft, spirit-rapping, and the like, may be regarded as manifestations of a superstitious frame of mind. In the OT, the prohibition against divination by consulting a necromancer (one who has a "familiar spirit," Lev. 19:31; Deut. 18:11) and the record of the practice of soothsaying, augury, and the like (2 Ki. 21:6) show that the Israelites were often infected with the superstitious practices of those around them. In NT times the Greek word *deisidaimonia G1272* and the Latin *superstitio* are used in an imprecise way, which makes the exact meaning in a given instance sometimes difficult to determine. For example, Festus reported to Agrippa II that Paul had been involved in disputes with the Jews "about their own superstition" (Acts 25:19 KJV). Considering Agrippa's Jewish connections, it seems unlikely that the newly arrived governor would have paid the king so ill a compliment as to have designated the Jewish faith a superstition in the modern sense of the term (thus the NIV and other versions here translate "religion"). Similarly, when Paul remarked before the Areopagus: "I perceive that in all things you are too superstitious" (Acts 17:22 KJV), he probably meant "most religious." Some believe, however, that in these passages there is the tacit implication of religion to excess, that which is subversive to true religion.

Suph. soof (Heb. *sûp H6069*, "reed[s]"). A place "in the desert east of the Jordan" near which Moses expounded the law to Israel (Deut. 1:1). The Hebrew phrase *môl sûp* ("in front of Suph") is translated by the Septuagint as "near the Red [Sea]," an understanding followed by other ancient translations and the KJV. If this interpretation is correct, the reference would be to the Gulf of Aqabah, and there is indeed some evidence for such a use of the term *yam-sûp* (see Red Sea). Moreover, some argue that the association of Suph in this verse with Paran, Hazeroth, and the Arabah gives support to this identification. Against it is the fact that nowhere else do we find the abbreviation *sûp* for *yam-sûp*; besides, it seems odd that a place in Transjordan should be described as being "in front of" or "near" Aqabah. Others have tried to identify Suph with specific places in Moab (e.g., Suphah).

Suphah. soo'fuh (Heb. *sûpāh H6071*, "reed[s]"). Apparently a place within the territory of Moab, mentioned in parallel with the Arnon River (Num. 21:14). Although some have identified it with modern Khirbet Sufa, a few miles SE of Medeba, its location is unknown. Moreover, the meaning of this verse—a citation from the Book of the Wars of the Lord—is debated. See also Waheb; Wars of the Lord, Book of the.

Supper, Lord's. See Lord's Supper.

supplication. See prayer.

Sur. soor (Heb. *sûr H6075*, possibly from a verb meaning "to depart"). The name of a gate in the city of Jerusalem that probably led from the palace to the environs of the temple (2 Ki. 11:6). See Foundation Gate.

surety. The KJV uses the expression "of a surety" several times as an emphatic expression meaning "surely, for certain" (Gen. 15:13 et al.). Elsewhere it refers to something or someone accepted as security (Gen. 43:9 et al.). See pledge.

surfeiting. This English term, in its archaic sense of "overindulgence," is used once by the KJV to translate Greek *kraipalē G3190*, which refers to uncontrolled drinking (Lk. 21:34). Modern versions usually employ "dissipation" as the rendering of this term. See drunkenness.

S

surname. This English word, as a noun or a verb, is used sixteen times by the KJV (esp. in the book of Acts) to translate various expressions (Acts 1:23 et al.). Modern versions prefer other renderings ("known as," "called," etc.) used in the sense of a name or title applied to someone, thus denoting that person's distinct and individual character.

Susa. soo´suh (Heb. *šûšan H8809*, prob. from Egyp. *sšn*, the name of a plant; Aram. gentilic *šûšankāy H10704* [KJV, "Susanchites"]; in Gk. sources, *Sousa* and *Sousis*). KJV Shushan. One of the oldest cities of the world, Susa became the ancient capital of ELAM and later of PERSIA; known today as Shūsh, it is situated in the plain of Iranian Khuzestan, near the Zagros mountains. The city is mentioned in several postexilic books (Ezra 4:9; Neh. 1:1; Esth. 1:2 [and frequently in this book]). Here Persian kings came to reside for the winter, and here DANIEL had a vision (Dan. 8:1-14; see v. 2). Susa enjoyed a very delightful climate. Many Jews lived here and became prominent in the affairs of the city, as the books of Esther and Nehemiah show. From this city was sent the group who replaced

© Dr. James C. Martin. The British Museum. Photographed by permission.

Calcite jar fragment from Susa, inscribed with the titles of Xerxes king of Persia (5th cent. B.C.).

those removed from SAMARIA (Ezra 4:9). In the last part of the nineteenth century the French carried on extensive excavations at Susa; this archaeological effort uncovered the great palace of King XERXES in which Queen ESTHER lived.

Susanchite. See SUSA.

Susanna. soo-zan´uh (Gk. *Sousanna G5052*, from *šûšan H8808*, "lily"). One of several women who had been healed by Jesus and who helped to support him and his disciples in their travels (Lk. 8:3). Nothing else is known about her, but she was probably among those who witnessed the crucifixion and then returned to the city to prepare spices and ointment for the anointing of the body (23:55-56).

Susanna, History of. See APOCRYPHA.

Susi. soo´si (Heb. *sûsî H6064*, from a word meaning "horse"). Father of Gaddi; the latter, representing the tribe of MANASSEH, was one of the twelve spies sent out to reconnoiter the Promised Land (Num. 13:11).

swaddling band. Strips of cloth (so NIV) in which a newborn baby was wrapped. The child was placed diagonally on a square piece of cloth, which was folded over the infant's feet and sides. Around this bundle bands of cloth were wound. Mary herself wrapped the baby Jesus in swaddling bands (Lk. 2:7, 12 KJV). For a figurative use, see Job 38:9.

swallow. See BIRDS.

swan. See BIRDS.

swearing. See OATH.

sweat. After the FALL, God told ADAM that he would have to work hard enough to cause sweat in order to get his food (Gen. 3:19). Priests in the future temple are not to wear anything that causes them to perspire (Ezek. 44:18).

sweat, bloody. A physical manifestation of the agony of Jesus in GETHSEMANE (Lk. 22:44). Ancient and modern medicine has documented

S

cases of blood extravasated from the capillaries mingling with and coloring the sweat, under severe stress of emotion. See under DISEASES.

swift. See BIRDS.

swine. See ANIMALS (under *pig*).

sword. See ARMS AND ARMOR.

sycamine. See PLANTS.

sycamore, sycomore. See PLANTS.

Sychar. si´kahr (Gk. *Sychar G5373*, either from ʿAskar [a site at the foot of Mt. Ebal] or a corruption of *Sychem G5374* [Shechem]). The one biblical reference to Sychar identifies it as a town in SAMARIA, near the parcel of ground that JACOB gave his son JOSEPH (Jn. 4:5; cf. Gen. 33:19). The precise location of Sychar is open to question. Many modern scholars have identified it with an ancient site named ʿAskar on the eastern slope of Mount EBAL, about half a mile (1 km.) N of JACOB'S WELL and just E of SHECHEM. However, the narrative of Jn. 4:15 suggests the woman of Sychar was in the habit of going to Jacob's well for water, and the village of el-ʿAskar is not sufficiently close to Jacob's well (moreover, at that village there is a copious spring more than adequate to supply the water needs of its inhabitants). Others, following some ancient sources, have argued that Sychar should be identified with Shechem itself. Excavations have revealed that the end of Shechem as a city occurred in 107 B.C., but at the site of the ruins, Tell Balaṭah, there is evidence of occupation from the period of the Samaritans to Roman times. Jacob's well, according to an unbroken tradition, lies about half a mile (1 km.) to the E of the village of Balatah.

Sychem. See SHECHEM.

Syene. si-ee´nee (Heb. *sĕwēnēh H6059*, from Egyp. *swn*). NIV Aswan. An Egyptian city, located on the E bank of the NILE, on the site of modern Aswan, some 550 mi. (885 km.) S of Cairo, at the first cataract of the river an area that and

just opposite the island of Elephantine. This area marked the effective southern boundary of EGYPT during much of the ancient history of that country. As a frontier town, Elephantine was the starting point for expeditions to Nubia, and during the Old Kingdom several of its residents served in official capacities as leaders of caravans or of military missions. The cataract served as a barrier to travel and transport, so the area was strategically and commercially important. Syene itself did not gain prominence until Saite times, but it gradually replaced the island town as the outstanding city of the district. Today its successor, Aswan, is still an important city of S Egypt. Remains of temples can be seen in the city, but excavation has been largely prevented by the presence of modern buildings. Syene appears in the Bible at least twice in prophetic utterances of EZEKIEL against Egypt that allude to the geographic extent of the country (Ezek. 29:10; 30:6). In addition, the city is probably mentioned in Isa. 49:12 (so NIV, following DSS; KJV, "Sinim," following MT).

syllabary. A system of written characters, each of which represents a syllable. See WRITING.

symbol. That which stands for or represents something else; a visible sign or representation of an idea or quality or of another object. Symbolism in its religious application means that an object, action, form, or word has a deeper spiritual meaning than a simple literal interpretation might suggest. A symbol, unlike a type (see TYPOLOGY), is usually not prefigurative but rather represents something that already exists. The Passover, however, was both symbolical and typical, and the symbolic actions of the OT prophets were often predictive in nature.

I. **Interpretation of symbols**. The literature of all the peoples of the world contains symbols. Symbolism was particularly attractive to the oriental mind. Thus the Bible contains many symbols. Some parts of Scripture, of course, contain more (e.g., the prophetic literature and apocalyptic books) than others. Symbols and their meanings arise out of the culture of the peoples that use them. The more remote and obscure the culture, the more difficult the interpretation of the symbols. Bernard Ramm (*Protestant Biblical Interpretation*

S

[1956], 214-15) suggests the following general rules for the interpretation of symbols:

(1) *Those symbols interpreted by the Scriptures are the foundation for all further studies in symbolism.* The book of Revelation interprets many of its symbols; for example, the bowls of incense are the prayers of the saints (Rev. 5:8), the great dragon is SATAN (12:9), the waters are peoples, multitudes, nations, and tongues (17:15). When the Bible interprets its own symbols, we are on sure ground and can often find the same symbols used elsewhere in Scripture in the same or at least similar ways.

(2) *If the symbol is not interpreted:* (a) We should investigate the context thoroughly. (b) By means of a concordance we can check other passages that use the same symbol and see if such cross references will give the clue. (c) Sometimes we may find that the nature of the symbol is a clue to its meaning (although the temptation to read the meanings of our culture into these symbols must be resisted). (d) Sometimes we will find that comparative studies of Semitic culture reveal the meaning of a symbol.

(3) *Beware of double imagery in symbols.* Not all symbols in the Bible have one and only one meaning. The lion is a symbol both for CHRIST ("the Lion of the tribe of Judah") and for the devil (1 Pet. 5:8). Some entities or persons have more than one symbol to represent them; for example, Christ (the lion, the lamb, and the branch) and the Holy Spirit (water, oil, wind, and the dove).

II. Symbolism of numbers. It is evident that certain numbers in the Bible have symbolical significance, some being particularly important. *Seven*, probably the most important number in Scripture (it occurs about six hundred times), has been called the sacred number par excellence. In the literature of ancient Babylonia it is the number of totality or completeness. To speak of the seven gods is to speak of all the gods. This seems to be its primary symbolical meaning in Scripture (cf. the seven creative days in Gen. 1), although other ideas have been proposed.

The book of Revelation makes frequent use of the number seven. There are seven churches (Rev. 1:4), spirits (1:4), lampstands (1:12-13), stars (1:16), lamps (4:5), seals (5:1; 8:1), horns and eyes (5:6), trumpets (8:2), thunders (10:3), heads of the great dragon (12:3), angels with plagues (15:1),

vials (15:7), heads of the beast (13:1), mountains (17:9), and kings (17:10). *Three* appears to be symbolical of "several," "a few," "some," although at times it means "many" or "enough." Some think that it is the number of divine fullness in unity; the three persons of the TRINITY particularly suggest this symbolical meaning. *Four* in the Bible seems to stand for completeness, especially in relation to range or extent. Thus there are four winds (Jer. 49:36; Ezek. 37:9); four directions; four corners of a house (Job 1:19), of the land of Israel (Ezek. 7:2), and of the whole earth (Isa. 11:12). *Ten*, since it is the basis of the decimal system, is also a significant number. In the Bible it is often a round number of indefinite magnitude. *Twelve* seems to be the mystical number of the people of God. The twelve tribes, twelve apostles, and the twelve thousand times twelve thousand sealed in the book of Revelation bear out this symbolical meaning. *Forty* is the round number for a generation and also appears to be symbolical of a period of judgment (cf. the forty days of the flood, the forty years of wilderness wandering, and the forty days and nights of Jesus' temptation). See also NUMBER.

III. Symbolism of colors. Color differentiations were not as exact in the ancient world as they are in modern times. Particularly difficult are the Hebrew words translated blue, purple, and scarlet. No unanimity of opinion exists among biblical scholars with regard to the symbolical meaning of colors. Much care must be taken, therefore, in seeking to assign symbolic meanings to colors. The following are suggestions: *White*, the color of light, is a symbol of purity, holiness, and righteousness (Rev. 7:14). *Blue* is difficult, but perhaps it suggests what is heavenly and divine. *Scarlet*, since it was most often the dress of kings, is regarded as symbolical of royalty. *Black*, the opposite of white, would naturally be associated with evil, such as famine (Rev. 6:5-6) or mourning (Jer. 14:2). *Red* is symbolic of bloodshed and war (Rev. 6:4; 12:3).

IV. Symbolic actions. In addition to objects, names, numbers, and colors, actions may be symbolic. These often are prefigurative and are especially associated with the OT PROPHETS. Behind these actions may lie the conviction that by doing something similar to what is being predicted, the fulfillment is made more certain. Although the prophets themselves did not necessarily believe this, it no doubt made their message more impressive to their audiences. Such symbolical actions by the prophets are found as early as SAMUEL's day. When SAUL took hold of Samuel's robe and tore it, this was understood by Samuel to be symbolic of the tearing away of Saul's kingdom (1 Sam. 15:27-28). By tearing his own garment into twelve pieces, AHIJAH symbolized the breakup of the kingdom of SOLOMON (1 Ki. 11:29-30; cf. also 2 Ki. 13:14-19; 22:11).

Symbolic action is especially frequent in the prophecies of JEREMIAH and EZEKIEL. Jeremiah's smashing of the pot before the elders of the people and the senior priests in the Valley of Ben HINNOM was clearly understood by the people, as their subsequent reaction shows (Jer. 19). Symbolic action was involved in Ezekiel's call to the prophetic office when the Lord commanded him to eat the scroll, inscribed on the front and back with words of lamentation and mourning and woe (Ezek. 2:9-10). Ezekiel was not only thereby informed of the content of his message but also made aware of the importance of assimilating it. Many of Ezekiel's symbolic actions were calculated to gain a hearing for the message God had given him to proclaim. This was particularly true of his drawing on a clay tablet the siege of Jerusalem (Ezek. 4:1-4).

Jesus also used symbolical actions to convey spiritual truth. While all the Gospels attest to our Lord's symbolical actions, the author of the fourth gospel places special stress on them. He calls Jesus' miracles SIGNS. When in the fourth gospel Jesus multiplies the loaves, this is symbolic of the fact that he is himself the Bread of Life (Jn. 6). The blind man healed is symbolic of Christ as the Light of the world (Jn. 9), and LAZARUS's being raised from the dead is symbolic of Jesus as the resurrection and the life (Jn. 11).

Symeon. See SIMEON.

Symmachus. See SEPTUAGINT.

synagogue. A Jewish institution for the reading and exposition of the Holy Scriptures. The Greek noun *synagōgē* G5252 (from the verb *synagō* G5251, "to gather, bring together") can be used generally of any gathering of people for either religious or secular purposes and can also be applied to any gathering place. It is a widely distributed classical term and is used in inscriptions as well as literary texts. In the SEPTUAGINT it is used to render many different Hebrew words and expressions, but in a strong majority of the occurrences it is equivalent to *ʿēdāh H6337*, "assembly, community" (Exod. 12:3 et al.). The next most frequent equivalence is the close synonym *qāhāl H7736*, "company, convocation, assembly" (Gen. 28:3 et al.). The Targums commonly render *ʿēdâ* with ARAMAIC *kĕništāʾ*, which was the standard rabbinic term for "synagogue."

I. History. The synagogue originated perhaps as early as the Babylonian EXILE. It is supposed that the synagogue had its precursor in the spontaneous gatherings of the Jewish people in the lands of their exile on their day of rest and also on special feast days. Since religion stood at the very center of Jewish existence, these gatherings naturally took on a religious significance. The Jews of the exile needed mutual encouragement in the faithful practice of their religion and in the hope of a restoration to the land. These they sought and found in spontaneous assemblies, which proved to be of such religious value that they quickly spread throughout the lands of the DISPERSION.

From about the second century B.C. onward, the sect of the PHARISEES assumed a leading role in the synagogues. It was an institution peculiarly adapted to achieve their ends. By NT times the synagogue was a firmly established institution

Partial reconstruction of the synagogue at Korazin (2nd or 3rd cent. A.D.). (View to the SE.)

© Dr. James C. Martin

among the Jews, who considered it to be an ancient institution, as the words of JAMES in Acts 15:21 show: "For Moses has been preached in every city from the earliest times and is read in the synagogues on every Sabbath." JOSEPHUS, PHILO, and later JUDAISM traced the synagogue back to MOSES. While this tradition has no historical validity, it does reveal that Judaism regarded the synagogue as one of its basic institutions. In the first Christian century synagogues could be found everywhere in the Hellenistic world where there were sufficient Jews to maintain one. In large Jewish centers there would have been many.

II. Purpose. The chief purpose of the synagogue was not primarily public WORSHIP, but instruction in the Holy Scriptures. The very nature of Judaism, a religion of REVELATION, demanded such an institution to survive. All of the rabbis emphasized the importance of knowing the law. Hillel taught, "An ignorant man cannot be truly pious" (*m. ʾAbot* 2:5) and, "The more teaching of the law, the more life; the more school, the more wisdom; the more counsel, the more reasonable action. He who gains a knowledge of the law gains life in the world to come" (2:14). The destiny of both the nation and the individual was dependent on the knowledge of the law. It was the explicit purpose of the synagogue to educate the whole people in the law.

How effectively the synagogue, along with the school, fulfilled this purpose is to be seen (1) from the survival of Judaism, especially in the Dispersion despite the pressures of pagan influences; (2) from the thorough Judaistic nature of GALILEE in the first century, which in the time of Simon MACCABEE was largely pagan; and (3) from the knowledge of the Scriptures, which the apostle PAUL assumes of his hearers in the Hellenistic synagogues.

III. Officials. Although there might be more in some of the larger synagogues, there were always at least two officials. The RULER OF THE SYNAGOGUE (Heb. *rōʾš hakkĕneset*, Gk. *archisynagōgos G801*) was probably elected by the elders of the congregation. He was responsible for (1) the building and property; (2) the general oversight of the public worship, including the maintenance of order (cf. Lk. 13:14); (3) the appointing of persons to read the Scriptures and to pray; and (4) the inviting of strangers to address the congregation. Generally

there was only one ruler for each synagogue, but some synagogues had more (Acts 13:15).

The minister or attendant (Heb. *ḥazzān hakkĕneset*; cf. Lk. 4:20) was a paid officer whose special duty was the care of the synagogue building and its furniture, in particular the rolls of Scripture. During the worship it was the hazan who brought forth the roll from the chest and handed it to the appointed reader. He also returned it to its proper place at the conclusion of the reading (4:20). He had numerous other duties, which included the instruction of children in reading, the administration of scourgings, and the blowing of three blasts on the trumpet from the roof of the synagogue to announce the beginning and end of the SABBATH. Since his work was closely associated with the synagogue building and its equipment, he sometimes lived under its roof.

IV. Building and furniture. Synagogue buildings varied greatly. They were usually built of stone and lay north and south, with the entrance at the south end. Their size and elegance were largely determined by the numerical strength and prosperity of the Jewish communities in which they were built. The principal items of furniture were (1) a chest in which the rolls of Scripture were kept, wrapped in linen cloth; (2) a platform or elevated place on which a reading desk stood; (3) lamps and candelabra, trombones and trumpets; and (4) benches on which the worshipers sat.

V. Worship. The congregation was separated, the men on one side and the women on the other. The more prominent members took the front seats. The service began with the recitation of the Jewish confession of faith, the Shema: "Hear, O Israel: The LORD our God, the LORD is one. Love the LORD your God with all your heart and with all your soul and with all your strength" (Deut. 6:4-5; see SHEMA, THE). This was both preceded and followed by thanksgivings, two before and one after the morning recitation of the confession, and two both before and after the evening recitation. The first of the two that preceded both morning and evening Shema reads: "Blessed art thou, O Lord our God, King of the world, former of light and creator of darkness, author of welfare (peace), and creator of all things."

After the Shema came the prayer (*Tefillah*). The ruler of the synagogue could call on any adult male of the congregation to say this prayer. The person praying usually stood before the chest of the rolls of Scriptures. The oldest form of the Tefillah consisted of a series of ascriptions or petitions, each of which ended in the benedictory response: "Blessed art thou, O Lord." About the close of the first century an arrangement was made in which there were eighteen of these prayers, from which the name "The Eighteen" (*Shemoneh 'Esreh*) was derived, a name that was maintained even when a nineteenth prayer was added. Prayers 1-3 were in praise of God; 4-16 were petitions; and 17-19 were thanksgivings. On Sabbaths and festival days only the first three and last three were recited. A single prayer was substituted for the intervening thirteen petitions, so that the total prayer consisted of seven parts. On New Year's, however, three prayers were substituted for the thirteen.

The Scripture lesson that followed the Tefillah could be read by any member of the congregation, even children. The only exception was that at the Feast of Purim a minor was not allowed to read the book of Esther. If priests or Levites were present in the worship service, they were given precedence. The readers usually stood while reading (cf. Lk. 4:16).

Prescribed lessons out of the PENTATEUCH for special Sabbaths were established early. For other Sabbaths the reader himself chose the passage, but subsequently all the Pentateuchal readings became fixed. Sections, called *sedarim*, were established in order to complete the reading of the Pentateuch within a prescribed time. Babylonian Jews divided the Pentateuch into 154 sections and thus completed reading it in three years, whereas Palestinian Jews read it through once every year.

A lesson from the Prophets immediately followed the reading from the Pentateuch. This custom is mentioned as early as the Mishnah (see TALMUD) and was practiced in NT times. When Jesus came to his hometown of NAZARETH and entered the synagogue, he stood up to read (Lk. 4:16). The book of the prophet Isaiah was given to him, and when he opened the book, he read. It is not clear from this account whether or not Jesus himself chose the portion. He may have, because the readings from the Prophets were not fixed, and either the ruler of the synagogue or the reader could choose them. The prophetical lessons were

usually considerably shorter than those from the Pentateuch. Translations often accompanied both readings. In Palestine the Scriptures were read in Hebrew, accompanied by an extemporaneous and free translation in ARAMAIC, one verse at a time for the Law, three at a time for the Prophets.

The sermon followed the reading from the Prophets (cf. Acts 13:15, where it is called a "message of encouragement"). That this was an important part of the synagogue service is revealed by the many references to teaching in the synagogue in the NT (Matt. 4:23; Mk. 1:21; 6:2; Lk. 4:15; 6:6; 13:10; Jn. 6:59; 18:20). The preacher usually sat (Lk. 4:20), but the Acts account has PAUL standing (Acts 13:16). No single individual was appointed to do the preaching. Any competent worshiper might be invited by the ruler to bring the sermon for the day (Lk. 4:16-17; Acts 13:15). The importance of the "freedom of the synagogue," as this custom was called, to the propagation of the gospel can scarcely be overemphasized. Jesus constantly went into the synagogues to teach, and everywhere Paul went he searched out the synagogue. This was not only that he might preach the Good News to his fellow countrymen but also to reach the God-fearers. These were GENTILES who had become disillusioned with the old pagan religions and were attracted to Judaism because of its high ethical morality and its monotheistic faith. They were not PROSELYTES. Certain requirements in order to attain that status, particularly CIRCUMCISION, kept them out. But they were interested observers. Some even kept the Jewish holy days, observed eating regulations, and were tolerably conversant with the synagogue prayers and Scripture lessons. These God-fearers proved to be ready recipients of the GOSPEL, and it was primarily to reach them that Paul often used the "freedom of the synagogue" to preach Christ.

The worship in the synagogue closed with a blessing that had to be pronounced by a priest and to which the congregation responded with an "Amen." If no priest was present, a prayer was substituted for the blessing. The form of worship of the synagogue was adopted by both the Christian and Muslim religions, and that form in its general outline is to be found today in Jewish places of worship.

S

Synagogue, Great. According to rabbinic tradition, the Great Synagogue or, more accurately, the Great Assembly (*kĕneset haggĕdôlâ, m. ʾAbot* 1:1-2 et al.) was an authoritative body of 120 ELDERS established under EZRA and NEHEMIAH for the purpose of insuring greater obedience to the Mosaic laws. To this institution, which supposedly lasted about two centuries, were attributed various important accomplishments, including the composition of some biblical books, the creation of a liturgy, and the establishment of the canon. Modern scholarship in general regards this tradition as an unhistorical development of Neh. 8-10, which recounts Ezra's reading of the TORAH before a national assembly as well as the positive response of the people. There is no clear reference to such an institution prior to the second century A.D.

Synagogue of the Freedmen. See FREEDMEN, SYNAGOGUE OF THE.

Synoptic Gospels. See GOSPELS.

Syntyche. sin′ti-kee (Gk. *Syntychē G5345,* "fortunate"). A woman in the church at PHILIPPI who, with Euodia, had labored together with PAUL (Phil. 4:2-3). See comments under EUODIA.

Syracuse. sihr′uh-kyooz (Gk. *Syrakousai G5352*). A city on the E coast of SICILY where PAUL spent three days when the ship that carried his party put in en route for PUTEOLI from MALTA (Acts 28:12). Syracuse was the most important Greek city on the island; it boasted two splendid harbors, which contributed substantially to its material prosperity. Corinthian and Dorian Greeks, led by Archias, founded the city in 734 B.C. The Athenians, at the height of their power (413), tried to take the city but were completely routed. In 212 Syracuse came under the control of ROME.

Syria. sihr′ee-uh (Gk. *Syria G5353*). In biblical scholarship, this name is usually applied to the territory N and NE of PALESTINE, covering roughly the area now occupied by the modern state of Syria (and a small part of SE Turkey); some scholars, however, use the term more broadly to include PHOENICIA (modern Lebanon), TRANSJORDAN

(modern Jordan), and even Palestine (modern Israel). In the OT, the KJV and some other modern versions (following the LXX and Vulg.) use the name Syria to translate Hebrew *ʾārām H806,* which most frequently refers to the city-state of DAMASCUS and the neighboring territory (see ARAM).

The territory of Syria/Aram varied considerably, often had vague boundaries, and really never constituted a political unit. Generally speaking, it included the area S of the Taurus Mountains, N of GALILEE and BASHAN, W of the Arabian Desert, and east of the MEDITERRANEAN. This was a territory approximately 300 mi. (500 km.) N to S and 50-150 mi. (80-240 km.) E to W. The chief cities, in addition to Damascus, were ANTIOCH, HAMATH, Biblos (GEBAL), Aleppo, EBLA, Ugarit (RAS SHAMRA), Palmyra (TADMOR), and CARCHEMISH. Two mountain ranges, both running N–S, constitute the most prominent topographical features. The eastern range includes Mount HERMON (over 9,000 ft./2,740 m. high); the western includes Mount Casius and the LEBANON. Between these two ranges is the high plain called Coelesyria, watered by the JORDAN, Leontes, and ORONTES rivers. To the E of Hermon flow the ABANA and the PHARPAR, while in the N of Syria there are tributaries of the EUPHRATES. The many rivers and good soil made Syria generally more prosperous than her neighbor to the south.

In the earliest period of its history Syria was dominated by AMORITES, HITTITES, Mitanni, and especially Egyptians. When, however, the SEA PEOPLES invaded Syria from the N in the twelfth century B.C., an opportunity was afforded the Semitic Aramean tribesmen of the desert to abandon their nomadic way of life and establish themselves in the best areas of Syria.

The Arameans at the time of DAVID and SOLOMON were divided into a number of small kingdoms, the principal ones being Aram of Damascus, Aram of ZOBAH, Aram of MAACAH, Aram of BETH REHOB, and ARAM NAHARAIM. The strongest of these was Zobah, whose king HADADEZER David defeated in battle along with the Syrians of Damascus who came to Hadadezer's aid (2 Sam. 8:3-7). David also subdued Maacah (1 Chr. 19:6-19), Beth Rehob (2 Sam. 10:6), and Aram

Naharaim ("Aram of the two rivers," translated "Mesopotamia" in NRSV, 1 Chr. 19:6). Solomon was unable to hold David's gains in Syria, and the political and military weakness in Israel caused by the disruption afforded the Syrian kingdoms, particularly Damascus, opportunity to further strengthen themselves.

Asa king of JUDAH (911-876 B.C.) appealed to Syria for help against BAASHA king of ISRAEL (909-886); this resulted in an invasion of the northern kingdom by BEN-HADAD I king of Damascus (1 Ki. 15:16-21). OMRI of Israel (885-874), being faced with the growing power of Syria, strategically consummated an alliance with the Phoenicians by the marriage of his son AHAB to JEZEBEL, daughter of ETHBAAL king of the Sidonians (1 Ki. 16:31). Twice during Ahab's reign (874-853) the Syrians under Ben-Hadad I tried to invade Israel but were put to flight, first at SAMARIA (20:1-21) and the following year at APHEK (20:26-34). Three years of peace with Syria followed. Then Ahab, in alliance with JEHOSHAPHAT of Judah, made an attempt to recover RAMOTH GILEAD but was killed on the field of battle.

JEHORAM of Israel (852-841 B.C.) allied himself with AHAZIAH of Judah (852) to war against Ben-Hadad's successor, HAZAEL, and was wounded in battle at Ramoth Gilead (2 Ki. 8:28-29). During Jehu's reign (841-814) Hazael captured the area E of the Jordan (2 Ki. 10:32-33), and during the reign of Jehu's son JEHOAHAZ (814-798) he completely overran Israel and took a number of its cities. These were retaken by Jehoash (798-782) from Hazael's successor, Ben-Hadad II (13:25). The successes of Jehoash were continued by his son JEROBOAM II (782-753), who recovered all of the cities that had been taken by the Syrians from Israel over the years. He even successfully reduced Damascus (2 Ki. 14:25-28).

Nothing is known of Syria from about 773 B.C. until the accession of REZIN in 750. During this time the Assyrian threat, which had been present already for a considerable time, was becoming progressively more real. To meet it, Rezin of Damascus and PEKAH of Israel (740-732) formed a military alliance. In 735 or 736 they attacked JERUSALEM (2 Ki. 16:5; Isa. 7:1), either to eliminate Judah as a possible foe or to force her into

their coalition. Judah's king, AHAZ (735-715), had just come to the throne. He panicked and, despite the prophet ISAIAH's warnings, sent for help from ASSYRIA (Isa. 7:1, 25). This apparently was just the excuse TIGLATH-PILESER III needed to invade Syria-Palestine. He captured the Israelite cities in the tribal territories of DAN and NAPHTALI (2 Ki. 15:29) and took the people captive to Assyria. He then turned his attention to Damascus and in 732 subdued the city and brought an end to the Aramean state, something his predecessors had tried vainly to accomplish for over fifty years.

In subsequent years the Babylonians and Egyptians fought over Syria and with the rise of the Persians it passed into their hands. The Battle of Issus (331 B.C.) brought Syria under the control of ALEXANDER THE GREAT. At his death it became the most important part of the SELEUCID kingdom, which included large areas to the east, including Babylon. By the close of the second century, Syria, with ANTIOCH as its capital, was all that was left of the kingdom of the Seleucids. In 64 the Romans made it a PROVINCE. Its boundaries varied during the following centuries. References to Roman Syria are often paired with its neighboring province to the NW, CILICIA (Acts 15:23, 41; Gal. 1:21). Territories to the S, including ARABIA and JUDEA, were at times regarded to be part of the province of Syria. Under the emperor HADRIAN (ruled A.D. 117-138) it became a consular province named Syria Palaestina.

Syria played a prominent part in the early church. It was at Antioch that the followers of Jesus were first called Christians (Acts 11:26). PAUL was converted in Syria on the road to Damascus (9:1-9) and was commissioned with BARNABAS by the Antioch church to take the gospel to the Gentiles. After the NT period the Syriac-speaking churches, especially the Nestorians, were among the most vibrant and missionary-minded groups of eastern Christianity.

Syriac, Syrian. sihr'ee-ak, -uhn. The KJV uses the form *Syriack* to render *ʾărāmî H811* in Dan. 2:4 ("Then spake the Chaldeans to the king in Syriack"), but *Syrian* in the other occurrences of that Hebrew term (2 Ki. 18:26; Ezra 4:7; Isa. 36:11). In all of these passages the reference is to ARAMAIC,

S

which served as the *lingua franca* of the ANE from about the eighth century B.C. until the Hellenistic period. Modern scholars apply the term *Syriac* to the particular dialect of Aramaic spoken in SYRIA beginning around the NT period. There is a very rich body of Christian literature written in the Syriac language, which is still spoken today (e.g., by a group known as Assyrian Christians).

Syriac versions. See TEXT AND VERSIONS (OT); TEXT AND VERSIONS (NT).

Syrophoenician. si´roh-fi-nish´uhn (Gk. *Syrophoinikissa G5355*, fem. of *Syrophoinix*). This proper adjective describes a woman encountered by CHRIST when he journeyed to the region of TYRE in the territory of PHOENICIA (Mk. 7:24-26 KJV and most versions; NIV, "born in Syrian Phoenicia"). By means of this word her racial extraction is traced to that of the Phoenician stock which resided in the Roman province of SYRIA. Another group of Phoenicians, known as Carthaginians or Libophoenicians, resided in N Africa. The broader category of which she was a part is also given by Mark: she was a Greek or GENTILE, that is, a non-Jew. Matthew refers to her as a Canaanite (Matt. 15:22), an earlier and more general term for residents of CANAAN—and one that would have had negative religious overtones for Jewish readers. Her difficulty in obtaining her request from Christ illustrates quite well the prior claim of the Jews on the ministry of Christ at his first advent.

Syrtis. suhr´tuhs (Gk. *Syrtis G5358*). Name given to the shallow waters of the N coast of Africa between Tunisia and Cyrenaica. Today the Gulf of Sidra forms the SE corner of this bay, which is known as the Greater Syrtis (the Gulf of Gabes, also called the Lesser Syrtis, lies more than 300 mi./480 km. to the W). Always a difficult place for navigation, legend exaggerated the dangers, perhaps to protect Phoenician trade by frightening off other ships. The sailors who were carrying PAUL to ROME, even though they were several hundred miles away from "the Syrtis" (i.e., the Greater Syrtis), did everything to avoid being driven into this dangerous shore (Acts 27:17; KJV, "the quicksands"; NIV, "the sandbars of Syrtis").

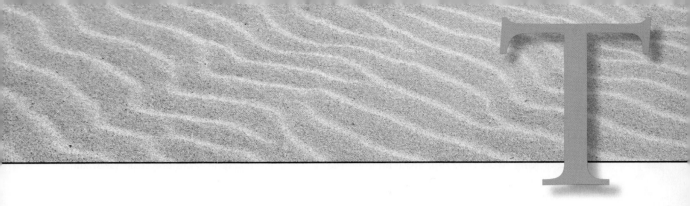

Taanach. tay′uh-nak (Heb. *taʿănak H9505*, derivation uncertain). KJV also Tanach (only Josh. 21:25). One of the royal Canaanite cities defeated by Joshua (Josh. 12:21 et al.). It was situated on the S flank of the Valley of Jezreel (Esdraelon), where the international coastal road or Via Maris struck inland from Sharon. The forested ravines of the northern Ephraim hill country were the most sensitive points of the route for ambush, and Taanach, Megiddo, and Jokneam guarded three important passes. Taanach was assigned to the Levites descended from Kohath (Josh. 21:25), but the Manassites failed to expel the Canaanite inhabitants and instead made them tributary (Jdg. 1:27). There followed a period when the Canaanite cities tried to impose their authority over the Israelite tribes in Galilee, and the Song of Deborah refers to Taanach as the scene of a major battle (5:19). In Solomon's reign the town became an important center (1 Ki. 4:12). Later it was taken by Pharaoh Shishak, who makes allusion to it in his chronicles. Modern Tell Tiʿinnik, the site of the ancient city, is situated on low hills, 5 mi. (8 km.) SE of Megiddo, with which it has been clearly identified in its military history.

Taanath Shiloh. tay′uh-nath-shi′loh (Heb. *taʾănat šilōh H9304*, meaning uncertain). A village that lay between Micmethath and Janoah (Josh. 16:6) on the NE border of the tribal territory of Ephraim. Most scholars identify it with Khirbet Taʿna el-Foqa, some 4.5 (7 km.) SE of Shechem, where there is evidence of an ancient hill fort.

Tabaliah. tab′uh-li′uh (Heb. *ṭĕbalyāhû H3189*, possibly "Yahweh has dipped [*i.e.*, purified]"). Also Tebaliah. Son of Hosah and descendant of Merari; he was a Levite gatekeeper during the time of David (1 Chr. 26:11).

Tabbaoth. tab′ay-oth (Heb. *ṭabbāʿôt H3191*, "signet ring[s]"). Ancestor of a family of temple servants (Nethinim) who returned from the Exile with Zerubbabel (Ezra 2:43; Neh. 7:46; 1 Esd. 5:29).

Tabbath. tab′uhth (Heb. *ṭabbāt H3195*, derivation unknown). A place near Abel Meholah, but probably E of the Jordan, that was the terminal point of Gideon's pursuit of the Midianites (Jdg. 7:22). Some have proposed identifying Tabbath with Ras Abu Ṭabat on the slopes of Jebel ʿAjlun (approximately halfway between Jabesh Gilead and Succoth), but others regard the site as unknown. The Gilead hill country would be the natural rallying point of the defeated host.

Tabeal. See Tabeel.

© Dr. James C. Martin. The Istanbul Archaeological Museum. Photographed by permission.

Pottery from Taanach.

Tabeel. tab´ee-uhl (Heb. *ṭobʾēl H3175*, "God is good"; the form in Isa. 7:6, *ṭobʾal* ["no good"], is thought to be a deliberate disfiguration of the name). **(1)** Father of a man whom REZIN of DAMASCUS and PEKAH of ISRAEL planned to place upon the throne of JUDAH as a puppet king in place of King AHAZ (Isa. 7:6). Some interpret the description "son of Tabel" to mean "native of Tabel" and thus translate "the Tabelite," referring to an area N of GILEAD. Others have thought that the reference is to Tubail king of TYRE, mentioned in a stela of TIGLATH-PILESER III.

(2) One of three Persian officials who wrote a letter of complaint against the Jews to King ARTAXERXES (Ezra 4:7).

taber. An obsolete English verb found only in Nah. 2:7 KJV; it means "to beat (as on a drum)."

Taberah. tab´uh-ruh (Heb. *tabʿērâ H9323*, possibly "burning [place]"). At some unspecified time during the wilderness wanderings, the Israelites "complained about their hardships" and the Lord in anger sent a fire against them. "When the people cried out to Moses, he prayed to the LORD and the fire died down. So that place was called Taberah, because fire from the LORD had burned [Heb. *bāʿărâ*] among them" (Num. 11:1-3; cf. Deut. 9:22). It is not clear whether the burning fire is to be taken literally or as a symbol of some act of judgment. The location of Taberah is unknown.

tabernacle. A transliteration of the Latin word *tabernaculum*, meaning "tent." In the Bible it is used specifically of the sanctuary built under the direction of MOSES in the wilderness. The principal passages dealing with the tabernacle are (1) Exod. 27; (2) Exod. 30-31; (3) Exod. 35-40; and (4) Num. 3:25-38; 4:4-49; 7:1-88. The purpose of the structure is stated in Exod. 25:8, 21-22. The tabernacle was made after the pattern shown to Moses on the mount (25:9; 26:30).

The religious vitality of the Hebrews and the resilience of their social and political organization in the time of JOSHUA would indicate that the period of the wilderness wanderings was the truly creative era from which all that was best in subsequent Israelite history and religion took its rise.

Under the dynamic spiritual leadership of Moses the children of Israel came to worship a cosmic deity whose vitality contrasted sharply with the capricious, decadent gods of ANE religion. The God of SINAI revealed himself as a supremely moral being whose leadership extended over the whole earth. He was the only true God, and he desired to enter into a special spiritual relationship with Israel as a means of his self-expression in the world.

Since this relationship demanded the undivided WORSHIP of the Israelites, it was of supreme importance for a ritual tradition to be established in the wilderness so that Israel could engage in regular spiritual communion with God. The nomadic nature of the sojourn in the Sinai Peninsula precluded the building of a permanent shrine for worship. The only alternative was a portable sanctuary that would embody all that was necessary for the worship of the Lord under nomadic conditions and could also serve as a prototype of a subsequent permanent building.

Such tent-shrines were by no means unknown in the ancient world. For example, in pre-Islamic times the *qubbah* or miniature red leather tent with a dome-shaped top was used for carrying the idols and cultic objects of Arabian tribes. Some *qubbahs* were large enough to erect on the ground, while others were smaller and were mounted on the backs of camels. Such tents were credited with the power of guiding the tribe in its journeys, and in time of war were particularly valuable for the degree of protection they afforded. The *qubbah* possessed an innate sanctity that was only slightly inferior to that of the sacred cultic objects it housed. It was used as a rallying point, a place of worship, and a locale for the giving of oracles. Since the majority of tents in antiquity were dark in color, the fact that the sacred shrine was a conspicuous red (cf. Exod. 25:5) indicates a religious tradition that reaches back to remote antiquity. Other forms of portable tent-shrines have been preserved on bas-reliefs, notably one from the time of RAMSES II (c. 1301-1234 B.C.) that shows the tent of the divine king placed in the center of the Egyptian military camp. Another from the Roman period at Palmyra (TADMOR) in SYRIA depicts a small domed tent erected on the back of a camel.

At Sinai, Moses was given a divine revelation concerning the nature, construction, and furnishings of the tabernacle (Exod. 25:40). The work was carried out by BEZALEEL, OHOLIAB, and their workmen; and when the task was accomplished, the tent was covered by a cloud and was filled with the divine glory (40:34; see SHEKINAH). The descriptions of the tabernacle (chs. 26-27 and 35-38) make it clear that the structure was a portable shrine. Particularly characteristic of its desert origins are the tent curtains, the covering of red leather, and the acacia wood used during the construction. Although there are some problems connected with the terminology used, we can be reasonably certain about the ground plan of the structure.

The tabernacle stood in an outer enclosure or court (Exod. 27:9-18; 38:9-20). Taking the ancient Hebrew cubit to indicate a linear measure of 18 in. (46 cm.), the dimensions of the enclosure were 153 ft. (47 m.) in length and 75 ft. (23 m.) in width. The sides were covered with curtains made from finely woven linen. They were about 7 ft. (2 m.) long and were fastened at the top by hooks and at the bottom by silver clasps to sixty supporting pillars of bronze, placed at intervals of some 7 ft. (2 m.). The enclosure thus formed was uninterrupted apart from an opening in the east wall that was screened by linen curtains embroidered in red, purple, and blue. These hangings were about 30 ft. (9 m.) wide, while those at either side of the entrance were a little over 20 ft. (6 m.) wide. The pillars had capitals (KJV, "chapiters") overlaid with silver and were set in bases (KJV, "sockets") of bronze. They were held in position by bronze pins (27:19; 38:20).

Within this open court the various types of sacrificial offerings were presented and the public acts of worship took place. Near the center was situated the great ALTAR of burnt offering made from acacia wood overlaid with bronze (Exod. 27:1-8). This alter measured nearly 8 ft. (2.5 m.) square and about 5 ft. (1.5 m.) in height. Its corner projections were known as the HORNS OF THE ALTAR. The various sacrificial implements associated with this altar were also made of bronze. A fire that had been miraculously kindled burned continuously on the altar and was tended by the priests (Lev. 6:12; 9:24). Almost in the center of the court was the bronze laver, used by the priests for ritual ablutions (Exod. 30:17-21).

To the W end of the enclosure, parallel to the long walls, stood the tabernacle itself. A rectangular structure about 45 x 15 ft. (14 x 4.5 m.), it was divided into two parts, a Holy Place and a Most Holy Place. The basic constructional material was acacia wood, easily obtainable in the Sinai Peninsula, fashioned into forty-eight "boards" (KJV) some 15 ft. (5 m.) in height and a little over 2 ft. (0.6 m.) in width, overlaid with gold (Exod. 26:15-23). The Hebrew word for "board" is *qereš H7983*, translated "frame" by the NIV; the corresponding Canaanite term is found on a tablet describing the "throne room" (i.e., a trellis pavilion) of the deity EL. When the vertical arms (v. 17; Heb. *yād H3338*, NIV, "projection") were joined to the acacia frames, the same general effect would be produced. The resulting structure would be light in weight yet sufficiently sturdy for ritual purposes. The base of the trellis was set in a silver fixture, and the whole was held together by horizontal bars at the top, middle, and bottom.

The completed tabernacle was divided into two compartments by a CURTAIN on which CHERUBIM were embroidered in red, purple, and blue, and which was suspended on four acacia supports. The outermost of these two areas was known as the Holy Place and was about 30 x 15 ft. (8 x 5 m.) in area. The innermost part of the tabernacle, the Holy of Holies or the Most Holy Place was 15 x 15 ft. (5 x 5 m.). The entrance to the tabernacle was screened by embroidered curtains supported by five acacia pillars overlaid with gold.

The wooden framework of the tabernacle was adorned by ten linen curtains (Exod. 26:1-7) that were embroidered and decorated with figures of cherubim. It measured about 40 ft. (12 m.) in length and 6 ft. (2 m.) in width, being joined in groups of five to make two large curtains. These were then fastened together by means of loops and golden clasps (KJV, "taches") to form one long curtain 60 ft. (18 m.) long and 42 ft. (13 m.) wide. This was draped over the tabernacle proper in such a way that the embroidery was visible from the inside only through the apertures of the trellis work. Three protective coverings were placed over these curtains. The first was made of goat's

T

© Dr. James C. Martin

Modern scholars and artists have attempted various reconstructions of the tabernacle. The one shown here was built at the Timna Nature Reserve, with the front curtain facing due E.

hair and measured 45 ft. (14 m.) long and 6 ft. (2 m.) wide; the second consisted of red-dyed rams' hides, while the third was made of fine leather (v. 14; NIV, "hides of sea cows," but TNIV, "durable leather").

The information furnished in Exodus makes it difficult to decide whether the tabernacle proper had a flat, somewhat sagging drapery roof, or one that was tentlike in shape with a ridgepole and a sloping roof. Present-day models of the tabernacle vary in their interpretation of this question. Historically speaking, if the influence of the desert tent was predominant, there may well have been some peak or apex to the structure. If, however, the tabernacle had anything in common with the design of contemporary Phoenician shrines, it probably had a flat roof.

Exodus 25:10-40 describes the furniture of the sanctuary. The Holy Place, or outer chamber of the tabernacle, contained a table for the bread of the Presence (KJV, "shewbread"), a small acacia-wood structure overlaid with gold. According to Lev. 24:5-9, twelve cakes were placed on this table along with dishes, incense bowls, and pitchers of gold. The bread was renewed each week and was placed in two heaps on the table. Nearby stood the elaborately wrought *menorah* or seven-branched LAMPSTAND of pure gold. A carefully executed floral motif was a feature of its design, and associated with the lampstand were gold wick trimmers and trays (KJV, "snuffers"). The furnishings of the Holy Place were completed by the addition of a small, gold-covered altar of INCENSE. Like the great bronze altar, it had projections on each corner, and like the table of the bread of the Presence, it had golden rings and gold-covered staves to enable it to be moved readily.

The furniture of the innermost shrine, the Most Holy Place, consisted only of the ARK OF THE COVENANT. This was a boxlike structure of acacia wood, whose length was about 4 ft. (120 cm.), while its breadth and height were slightly above 2 ft. (60 cm.). It was covered on the inside and outside with sheet gold and had golden rings and staves like the table of the bread of the Presence and the altar of incense. The lid of the ark, the "mercy seat," was covered with solid gold. On each end was a golden cherub whose wings stretched toward the center of the lid. The precise appearance of the cherubim is a matter of some uncertainty, but in the OT they were generally represented as winged creatures having feet and hands. Some ivory panels unearthed at SAMARIA depict a composite figure having a human face, a four-legged animal body, and two elaborate, conspicuous wings.

The ark was the meeting place of God and his people through Moses, and contained the tablets of the LAW (Exod. 25:16, 22). According to Heb. 9:4, a pot of MANNA and AARON'S STAFF were also placed in the ark. An elaborately worked veil separated the Most Holy Place from the outer compartment of the tabernacle, and when the Israelites journeyed from place to place, the sacred ark was secluded from view by being wrapped in this curtain. Consequently the ark was normally seen only by the high priest, and that on very special ceremonial occasions.

In the tabernacle all the SACRIFICES and acts of public worship commanded by the law took place. A wealth of detail surrounds the legislation for sacrificial offerings in the Mosaic code, but for practical purposes they could be divided into two groups, animal and vegetable. Flour, cakes, parched corn, and libations of wine for the drink offerings constituted the normal vegetable sacrifices and were frequently offered in conjunction with the thanksgivings made by fire (Lev. 4:10-21; Num. 15:11; 28:7-15). Acceptable animals were unblemished oxen, sheep, and goats, not under eight days old and normally not older than three years (cf. Jdg. 6:25). People who were poor were allowed to offer doves as sacrifices (Exod. 12:5; Lev. 5:7; 9:3-4), but fish were not acceptable. Human sacrifice was explicitly prohibited (Lev. 18:21; 20:25). Salt, an emblem of purity, was used in conjunction with both the vegetable and animal offerings. The sacrifices were normally presented to the officiating priests in the outer court of the sanctuary, but on occasion they were offered elsewhere (Jdg. 2:5; 1 Sam. 7:17). In all sacrifices it was necessary for the worshiper to present himself in a condition of ritual purity (Exod. 19:14). In animal sacrifices he then identified himself with his offering by laying his hand on it and dedicating it to the purposes of atonement through vicarious sacrifice. Afterward the blood was sprinkled near the altar and the tabernacle proper. When worshipers ate of a sacrifice in the form of a meal, the idea of communion with God was enhanced. On the Day of Atonement the nation's collective sins of inadvertence were forgiven, and on that occasion only the high priest entered the Most Holy Place (Lev. 16). See ATONEMENT, DAY OF.

According to Exod. 40:2, 17 the tabernacle was set up at Sinai at the beginning of the second year, fourteen days before the Passover celebration of the first anniversary of the EXODUS. When the structure was dismantled during the wanderings, the ark and the the the two altars were carried by the descendants of KOHATH, a LEVITE. The remainder of the tabernacle was transported in six covered wagons, each drawn by two oxen (Num. 7:6-9).

For over thirty-five years during the wilderness period the tabernacle stood at KADESH BARNEA, during which time the ordinary sacrifices were apparently not offered consistently (cf. Amos 5:25). Apart from the comment that the ark preceded the Israelites when they were on the march (Num. 10:33-36), little is said of the tabernacle during the sojourn in the Sinai Peninsula.

Under JOSHUA the first site of the tabernacle in Canaan was probably at GILGAL (Josh. 4:19), though this is not directly mentioned. Probably an early location was at SHECHEM, where the desert covenant was renewed (8:30-35). During Joshua's lifetime, the tabernacle was settled in SHILOH, in Ephraimite territory, to avoid disputes and jealousy on the part of the tribes. Perhaps the degree of permanence associated with this site led to the designation of the structure by the Hebrew term *hêkāl H2121*, "temple" (1 Sam. 1:9; 3:3). This perhaps indicates that the fabric of the original tabernacle had become worn out and that it had been replaced by a more substantial building. In any case, Shiloh was the central sanctuary until the ark was captured by the victorious PHILISTINES after the battle of EBENEZER (c. 1050 B.C.).

The subsequent history of the tabernacle is somewhat obscure. SAUL established it at NOB, close to his home in GIBEAH; but after he massacred the priests there (1 Sam. 22:11-19), the tabernacle was transferred to GIBEON (1 Chr. 16:39; 21:29), perhaps by Saul himself.

When DAVID wished to institute tabernacle religion in his capital city of JERUSALEM, he prepared a place for the ark and pitched a tent in the tradition of the Gibeon tabernacle (2 Sam. 6:17-18). The ark was brought from KIRIATH JEARIM and subsequently lodged in the Davidic tabernacle with due ceremony. This act climaxed David's plan to give the security and legitimacy of religious sanction to his newly established monarchy. The altar of the tabernacle at Gibeon was used for sacrificial worship until the time of SOLOMON, when both it and the Davidic tabernacle were superseded by the building of the TEMPLE. The new edifice incorporated all that remained of earlier tabernacle worship (1 Ki. 8:4), and at that point the history of the tabernacle terminated.

Some of the archaic technical terms associated with the tabernacle call for comment. The designation *'ōhel mô'ēd* (*H185 + H4595*), "tent of meeting," was first applied to a structure that antedated the tabernacle proper (Exod. 33:7). It was pitched outside the camp, and Joshua was its sole attendant (v. 11) in the absence of a formal priesthood. It was a place of REVELATION, where the people met with God. The "tent of meeting" or "tabernacle of

T

the congregation" referred to in Exod. 33 is apparently an interim structure, based on the pattern of a simple desert shrine. It combined political and social functions with the religious revelations given by God to his covenant assembly. However, the expression "the Tent of Meeting" occurs with reference to the tabernacle proper over 140 times.

The word *miškān H5438*, commonly used to designate the tabernacle, is related to the ordinary Canaanite word for "dwelling place" and meant originally a tent, thus reflecting the nomadic background of tabernacle worship. The related verb *šākan H8905* ("to dwell") is used of God's being "tabernacled" with his people (Exod. 25:8; 29:45; et al.). This usage is found in a number of ancient Semitic writings and means "to encamp." The sense is that of God revealing himself on earth in the midst of his chosen people. This concept is reflected by John the apostle when he records that "the Word became flesh and made his dwelling among us" (Jn. 1:14). The Greek verb translated "made his dwelling" is *eskēnōsen*, from *skēnoō G5012*, which means literally "to set up a tent [Gk. *skēnē G5008*], to tabernacle" (though its common meaning is "to live, take up residence"). The doctrine of the Shekinah (from Heb. *šākan*), which developed in the intertestamental period, denotes a local manifestation of the divine glory.

A degree of symbolism was naturally attached by the Hebrews to various aspects of the tabernacle. The structure typified God's living with his people (Exod. 25:8), while the ark of the covenant spoke particularly of his presence and forgiving love. The twelve loaves of the bread of the Presence represented the twelve tribes dedicated to divine service. The *menorah* typified Israel as a people called to be the children of light (cf. Matt. 5:14-16), and the ascending incense symbolized the act of prayer (cf. Rev. 5:8; 8:3). The writer of Hebrews interpreted the tabernacle proper in terms of its twofold division typifying the earthly and heavenly aspects of Christ's ministry. The old tabernacle was but a shadow of the true ideal (Heb. 8:5; 10:1), the latter being pitched by God, not man (8:2). The language of Eph. 5:2 is distinctly reminiscent of Levitical sacrificial terminology, and the Evangelists were sufficiently impressed by the symbolism of the torn veil to

point out that Christ had opened up for all a way into the Most Holy Place (Matt. 27:51; Mk. 15:38; Lk. 23:45). In the early church and in later times, more elaborate, sometimes even fanciful, interpretations were imposed on the structure and ritual of the tabernacle.

Tabernacles, Feast of. See FEASTS.

Tabitha. tab´i-thuh (Gk. *Tabitha G5412*, from Aram. *ṭĕbîtā᾿*). The Jewish name of a Christian woman who was raised from the dead by Peter (Acts 9:36-43). See comments under Dorcas.

table. The common Hebrew term for "table" is *šulḥān H8947* (Exod. 25:23 and frequently), referring originally to a leather mat spread on the ground (Ps. 23:5; 78:19). The table of the bread of the Presence (Exod. 25:23 et al.) was made of acacia wood overlaid with gold (see TABERNACLE). Kings, queens, and governors had dining tables (1 Sam. 20:29; 1 Ki. 18:19; Neh. 5:17); sometimes private persons did as well (1 Ki. 4:10; Job 36:16). Psalm 128:3 provides an attractive picture of a family table. The Greek *trapeza G5544*, a four-legged table, is used of dining furniture (Lk. 22:21; Acts 6:2). To eat under the table was for dogs and the despised (Jdg. 1:7; Matt. 15:27; Lk. 16:21). Moneychangers used tables (Matt. 21:12). Communion is served from the Lord's table (1 Cor. 10:21). See also TABLETS OF THE LAW.

Table of Nations. A term used to designate the genealogical lists in Gen. 10 (cf. also 1 Chr. 1). See JAPHETH; HAM; SHEM.

tablets of the law. KJV, "tables." Stone tablets on which God, with his own finger, engraved the Ten Commandments (Exod. 24:3-4, 12; 31:18; Deut. 4:13; 5:22). When Moses came down from the mountain and saw the worship of the golden calf, he threw down the tablets, breaking them (Exod. 32:15-16, 19; Deut. 9:9-17; 10:1-5). See CALF WORSHIP. At God's command, Moses again went up the mountain with two new tablets and God wrote the law anew (Exod. 34:1-4, 27-29). God gave Moses words in addition to the Ten Commandments and told him to write them down

(34:10-27). Moses put the two tablets in the ARK OF THE COVENANT (Deut. 10:5), where they were in the time of SOLOMON (1 Ki. 8:9; 2 Chr. 5:10). They are referred to in the NT (2 Cor. 3:3; Heb. 9:4). See also COMMANDMENTS, TEN; LAW.

Tabor. tay´buhr (Heb. *tābôr H9314*, possibly "height"). **(1)** Mount Tabor is a hill about 10 mi. (16 km.) SW of the Sea of Galilee in the Valley of JEZREEL (ESDRAELON). The border of the inheritance of ISSACHAR touched Tabor (Josh. 19:22); thus the other tribe to touch it would be ZEBULUN. During the judgeships of DEBORAH and BARAK, Mount Tabor played a principal role (Jdg. 4:6, 12-18; other references include 8:8; Ps. 89:12; Jer. 46:18; Hos. 5:1). It is identified with Jebel et-Tur ("mount of the height"). Although it rises only 1,843 ft. (562 m.) above sea level, it is a prominent feature of the landscape. The mount is rather steep, somewhat symmetrical, and has a rounded top. From the summit one has a lovely view in all directions. The cities of AZNOTH TABOR and KISLOTH TABOR may have derived their name from that of the mountain. Mount Tabor is not mentioned in the NT, yet much of its fame rests in the tradition that the TRANSFIGURATION of our Lord took place on it (most scholars believe the event probably occurred on Mount HERMON).

(2) Tabor is also the name of one of the LEVITICAL CITIES within the tribal territory of ZEBULUN (1 Chr. 6:77; the parallel passage, Josh. 21:34-35, has a different list that omits Tabor). Its identification is uncertain. Some have thought that it was a town associated with Mount Tabor (possibly a settlement on the mountain itself), but if so one would expect the town to have been included within the territory of ISSACHAR, not Zebulun. Others think Tabor is the same as KISLOTH TABOR, which is c. 3 mi. (5 km.) W of the mountain. Another suggestion is DABERATH, on the mountain's NW slope.

(3) Finally, mention is made of a certain "great tree [Heb. *ʾēlôn H471*] of Tabor" that was evidently not far from BETHEL (1 Sam. 10:3; NRSV, "the oak of Tabor"; KJV, wrongly, "the plain of Tabor"). The location is unknown.

tabret. An archaic English term, meaning "timbrel, tambourine," used by the KJV in a number of passages (Gen. 31:27 et al.). See MUSIC AND MUSICAL INSTRUMENTS (sect. I.G).

Tabrimmon. tab-rim´uhn (Heb. *ṭabrimmōn H3193*, an Aram. name meaning "[the god] RIMMON is good"). KJV Tabrimon. Son of HEZION and father of BEN-HADAD I, king of ARAM (1 Ki. 15:18). It is uncertain whether Tabrimmon himself was also a king.

taches. taks. KJV archaism for "clasps" (Exod. 26:2 et al.).

Tachmonite. See TAHKEMONITE.

tackle. This term is used in Acts 27:19 (KJV, "tackling") with reference to a ship's gear or equipment. The KJV has "tacklings" also with reference to the rigging of a ship (Isa. 33:23).

Tadmor. tad´mor (Heb. *tadmōr H9330*, meaning unknown). Also Tadmur. Known in Greek and Latin history as Palmyra, the city of palm trees, Tadmor was an ancient military outpost, trading center, and customs station located in the Syrian desert, half-way between DAMASCUS and the upper EUPHRATES River (see SYRIA). It was a large and pleasant oasis with wonderfully fine mineral springs, fertile soils, and many gardens and palm groves—the only supply station of any consequences on the shorter trade route between Babylonia and Syria. Tadmor's inhabitants are mentioned in extrabiblical inscriptions as early as the nineteenth century B.C. The biblical narratives inform us that when King SOLOMON took N Syria as far N as HAMATH, he not only built "store cities" in the Hamath area, but also "built up Tadmor in the desert" (2 Chr. 8:4; cf. 1 Ki. 9:18, where NRSV and NJPS, following the *Ketib*, read "Tamar") to protect the trade routes and serve the NE boundaries of his extended kingdom. No more is heard of Tadmor until 64 B.C., when Mark Antony raided its merchants who had grown rich through the Babylonian and Indian trade which had passed through there. In early Roman times Tadmor enjoyed considerable commercial prosperity, and splendid buildings were constructed under HADRIAN (A.D. 117-138). Palmyra enjoyed its greatest fame and prosperity in the third century A.D. under its Roman-appointed king Odenathus and his widow Zenobia, who made herself queen and defied the Romans. The ruins include Corinthian columns and a temple to the sun.

Tahan. tay'han (Heb. *taḥan H9380*, derivation uncertain; gentilic *taḥānî H9385*, "Tahanite"). **(1)** Son of EPHRAIM and ancestor of the Tahanite clan (Num. 26:35).

(2) Son of Tela and descendant of Ephraim (1 Chr. 7:25).

Tahapanhes. See TAHPANHES.

Tahash. tay'hash (Heb. *taḥaš H9392*, perhaps "dolphin"). KJV Thahash. Son of NAHOR (brother of ABRAHAM) by his concubine REUMAH (Gen. 22:24). Some have thought that Tahash is a place name, referring to an area near KADESH ON THE ORONTES.

Tahath (person). tay'hath (Heb. *taḥat H9394*, possibly "instead of," i.e., "compensation"). **(1)** Son of Assir, descendant of LEVI through KOHATH, and ancestor of SAMUEL and HEMAN (1 Chr. 6:24, 37).

(2) Son of BERED and great-grandson of EPHRAIM (1 Chr. 7:20a). Some argue that the genealogy is textually corrupt (cf. #3 below).

(3) Son of Eleadah and grandson of #2 above (1 Chr. 7:20b).

Tahath (place). tay'hath (Heb. *taḥat H9395*, possibly "instead of," i.e., "compensation"). A stopping place of the Israelites, between Makheloth and Terah, during their forty years of wilderness wanderings (Num. 33:26-27). The location is unknown.

Tahchemonite. See TAHKEMONITE.

Tahkemonite. tah-kee'muh-nit (Heb. *taḥkĕmōnî H9376*, in form, a gentilic from an unknown name, but widely considered a textual error). Also Tachmonite, Tahchemonite. According to 2 Sam. 23:8, the chief of "the Three" (evidently a special military group within the elite force called "the Thirty") was "Josheb-Basshebeth, a Tahkemonite" (the KJV understands his name as a phrase, "The

Tachmonite that sat in the seat"). The parallel passage, however, reads: "Jashobeam, a Hacmonite [*lit.*, son of Hacmoni], was chief of the officers [*or* of the Thirty]" (1 Chr. 11:11), and many scholars believe that the Samuel passage is textually corrupt. See JASHOBEAM.

Tahpanhes. tah'puhn-heez (Heb. *taḥpanḥēs H9387*, also *taḥpĕnēs* [Jer. 2:16 *Ketib*] and *tĕḥapnĕḥēs* [Ezek. 30:18], possibly from an Egyp. phrase such as *ʾ-ḥt-npʾ-nḥsy*, meaning either "house of the Nubian" or "fortress of Penaḥse"). KJV also Tahapanes (Jer. 2:16), Tehaphnehes (Ezek. 30:18), and Taphnes (Jdt. 1:9). An Egyptian town named with MEMPHIS and MIGDOL as an opponent of ISRAEL (Jer. 2:16; 46:14) and as a place to which Jewish exiles fled after the murder of GEDALIAH following the sack of JUDAH by the Babylonians in 586 B.C., when JEREMIAH was reluctantly compelled to join them (44:1; cf. 43:7-9). Tahpanhes also figures in EZEKIEL's judgment on EGYPT (Ezek. 30:18).

A Phoenician PAPYRUS letter of the sixth century B.C. from EGYPT refers to "Baal Zephon and the gods of Tahpanhes," from which it is thought that the city must have earlier borne the name of BAAL ZEPHON, an Israelite staging post during the EXODUS (Exod. 14:2). The form of the name in extrabiblical Greek literature, *Daphnē*, supports identification with Tell Defneh (Defenneh), 27 mi. (43 km.) SSW of Port Said (9 mi./14 km. W of el-Qanṭara). A recently discovered inscription in NABATEAN, dated to the first century B.C., mentions Tahpahnes (in the form *dpnʾ*) as the site of a shrine devoted to a Nabatean god; evidently the city had broad commercial ties as late as the Roman period.

Tahpenes. tah'puh-neez (Heb. *taḥpĕnēs H9388*, prob. from Egyp. title *ʾ-ḥ(mt)-pʾ-nsw*, "the wife of the king"). An Egyptian queen (1 Ki. 11:19-20). She was the wife of a PHARAOH of the 21st dynasty, perhaps Siamon (c. 979-959 B.C.). The pharaoh gave her sister in marriage to HADAD, the Edomite prince who fled from DAVID to Egypt (1 Ki. 11:17). Tahpenes cared for her sister's son, GENUBATH, in the royal house.

Tahrea. See TAREA.

Tahtim Hodshi. tah´tim-hod´shi (Heb. *taḥtim ḥodšî H9398*, meaning unknown). A district between GILEAD and DAN JAAN, visited by DAVID's commanders in the course of the census (2 Sam. 24:6). Many believe that the text has suffered scribal corruption. Among various proposed emendations, one that has been widely accepted is *ḥaḥittîm qādēšâ*; thus the NRSV rendering, "they came to Gilead, and to Kadesh in the land of the Hittites" (the reference would be either to KEDESH of NAPHTALI or to KADESH ON THE ORONTES).

tale. This noun is used by the KJV a few times in the sense "number, count, total" (Exod. 5:8, 18; 1 Sam. 18:27; 1 Chr. 9:28; cf. the English verb *tell* in the sense "to count," Gen. 15:5; Ps. 22:17 KJV). The English term is sometimes used negatively of a false report, whether slanderous (Ezek. 22:9 KJV) or regarded as incredible (Lk. 24:11 KJV) or simply fictional (1 Tim. 4:7 NIV, NRSV). See FABLE. The KJV also employs "tale" once to translate a Hebrew word that properly means "sigh, moan" (Ps. 90:9).

talebearing. The spreading of gossip or rumors (KJV Lev. 19:16; Prov. 11:13; et al.). See SLANDER.

talent. See MONEY; WEIGHTS AND MEASURES.

talitha cum(i). tal´uh-thuh-koo´mi (Gk. *talitha koum* [or *koumi*] *G5420 + G3182*, from Aram. *ṭĕlîtāʾ*, "girl," and *qûm*, "arise!" [more properly *qûmî*, 2nd person fem. imperative of *qûm*, "to arise"]). Also *talitha k(o)um(i)*. Mark preserves PETER's vivid memory of the exact ARAMAIC words of Jesus when he said to JAIRUS's dead daughter, "Little girl ... get up" (Mk. 5:41). This detail is often used as evidence that Aramaic was the common spoken language of PALESTINE, especially in GALILEE (note other Aram. words of Jesus and of Peter in 7:34; 15:34 Acts 9:40).

Talmai. tal´mi (Heb. *talmay H9440*, prob. from HURRIAN *talm*, "great"). (1) One of three descendants of ANAK who lived in HEBRON when the Israelites spied out the land and who were defeated by the invading Israelites (Num. 13:22; Josh. 15:14; Jdg. 1:10). See AHIMAN.

(2) Son of Ammihud and king of GESHUR, a principality NE of GALILEE; his daughter MAACAH was espoused by DAVID, contrary to the law. The princess became the mother of the passionate ABSALOM (2 Sam. 3:3; 1 Chr. 3:2). It was to Geshur that Absalom fled for refuge after he had murdered his half-brother AMNON (2 Sam. 13:37).

Talmon. tal´muhn (Heb. *ṭalmôn H3236*, possibly "brightness"). A LEVITE listed among the gatekeepers in the postexilic temple; he was evidently the head of a clan of gatekeepers (1 Chr. 9:17; Ezra 2:42; Neh. 7:45; 11:19; 12:25).

Talmud. tal´mood (postbiblical Heb. *talmûd*, "study, teaching," from *lāmad H4340*, "to learn" [in the piel stem, "to teach"]). The authoritative collection of rabbinical legal decisions and Jewish traditions (see JUDAISM). Although not completed until about the sixth century A.D., the Talmud is the culmination of a very long process. The leaders and the generation that returned from BABYLON in 538 B.C. were acutely aware of the necessity of assuring the continuation of Israel's national obedience to the Mosaic LAW. EZRA himself is styled as "a teacher well versed in the Law of Moses" (Ezra 7:6), and there was a popular desire to study and learn the TORAH (Neh. 8:1-18). This historic development brought forth a new social institution among the Jews, the office and service of the "teacher of the law," the rabbinate (see RABBI; SCRIBE). In effect, the local SYNAGOGUE was primarily a setting for

Remains of a synagogue in Tiberias (3rd-4th cent. A.D.), one of the primary centers in the production of the Palestinian Talmud.

© Dr. James C. Martin

T

Torah study. Alongside the written law, however, a great body of TRADITION, the oral law, was in the process of development. According to the Jewish teaching, this oral teaching went back to MOSES himself (*m. ʾAbot* 1:1).

The rise of the sect of the PHARISEES is closely associated with the writing and study of the Jewish traditions that led to the production of the Talmud. JOSEPHUS mentions that "the Pharisees had passed on to the people certain regulations handed down by former generations and not recorded in the Laws of Moses" (*Ant.* 13.10.6 §297). The process involved two distinctive literary forms.

(1) *Mishna.* This Hebrew term (derived from *šānāh H9101*, "to repeat") refers to the oral conversation of the rabbis as they discussed the proper interpretation and course of action requisite upon Jews in regard to the Mosaic law. There is no presentation of evidence but a continual appeal to authority hallowed by age or scriptural foundation. If the discussion produces legal instruction it is known as HALAKAH (in distinction from HAGGADAH, which refers to nonlegal material). The Mishnaic presentation of laws became dominant in Jewish teaching, and its teachers or Tannaim (derived from the corresponding Aram. verb *tēnê* or *tēnāʾ*, "to repeat, hand down") were greatly reverenced. By definition, the oral law was not something to be written down, and it is unclear when the initial attempts at collecting the tradition were made, but undoubtedly some of this work was taking place soon after the destruction of JERUSALEM in A.D. 70. The collections were codified most thoroughly by the famous exponent Rabbi Yehudah ha-Nasi (Judah the Prince), and by about the year 200 it was finally published as an official document. A distinct and parallel collection is known as the *Tosefta*.

(2) *Midrash.* Some use the term *midrashic interpretation* in a derogatory fashion because it is thought to characterize a method filled with folk etymologies, mental gymnastics, and far-fetched connections made on the sheer analogies of the sounds of words. In postbiblical Hebrew, however, the term *midrāš H4535* (from *dāraš H2011*, "to search, inquire") refers simply to the exposition and application of Scripture (see MIDRASH). Often it also refers to a type of literature consisting of such exposition. The Mishnah could be considered a topical method of pronouncement, while the Midrashim were commentaries on continuous texts of Scripture. The midrashic form is traditionally thought to have appeared with Ezra and the "Great Synagogue," passing through two great periods of popularity, the era of the *Sopherim* ("scribes"), which closed about 270 B.C., and the era of the *Zugoth* ("pairs"); it ended with the last pair, Shammai and Hillel, just before the time of Jesus (see HILLEL). The next two centuries, culminating in the publication of the Mishnah, was the period of the *Tannaim* ("repeaters, teachers"). Subsequently, the rabbis who debated or commented on the Mishnah are referred to as the *Amoraim* ("speakers, interpreters"), who were active from the third to sixth centuries.

The work of this latter group issued in the Gemara, and the combination of the Mishnah and the Gemara yielded the Talmud in its entirety. The Mishnah is divided into six major divisions or orders; these in turn are subdivided into tractates, totaling sixty-three in number; each tractate is composed of chapters; and each chapter consists of paragraphs (*mishnayoth*). The Talmud is built on the same organization, citing one paragraph of the Mishna at a time, followed by the Gemara on that paragraph (however, there is no Gemara to many of the tractates). The Talmud was developed in two forms, the Babylonian (Talmud Babli, pronounced Bavli) and the Palestinian (Talmud Yerushalmi). The Babylonian Talmud is fuller and is regarded as the official form.

Tamah. See TEMAH.

Tamar (person). tay´mahr (Heb. *tāmār H9470*, "palm tree"). **(1)** Daughter-in-law of JUDAH (Gen. 38:6-30), included in Matthew's GENEALOGY OF JESUS CHRIST (Matt. 1:3 [KJV, "Thamar"]). Tamar was given in marriage to JUDAH's son, ER, who died because of some unspecified wickedness. Judah then instructed another son, ONAN, to marry Tamar and father children for his brother Er (see LEVIRATE MARRIAGE). Onan married Tamar but avoided having children by her and God took his life as well. Tamar then returned to her Canaanite home after Judah promised that she would marry his third son, SHELAH, when he had grown old enough. Judah, fearing for Shelah's life, did not fulfill his promise. Subsequently, Tamar seduced Judah by hiding her identity and pretending to be a harlot of the heathen worship cult. Twins were born to Tamar by Judah: PEREZ and ZERAH. The former was in the direct line of the ancestry of DAVID, and hence of Christ (Ruth 4:12; Matt. 1:3; Lk. 3:33).

(2) A beautiful daughter of David, sexually assaulted by her infatuated half brother AMNON, who contrived the deed by feigning illness and arranging to have Tamar bring food to him. After this revolting act, Amnon rejected her with loathing. When her brother ABSALOM learned of the deed, he plotted to avenge her and eventually succeeded in having Amnon murdered for his crime (2 Sam. 13).

(3) A beautiful daughter of Absalom, probably named for his beloved sister (2 Sam. 14:27). It is possible that Tamar was Maacah's mother. See discussion under MAACAH #9.

Tamar (place). tay'mahr (Heb. *tāmār H9471*, "palm tree"). A settlement, town, or region mentioned in EZEKIEL's eschatological vision as marking the SE boundary of a future restored Israel (Ezek. 47:19; 48:28; cf. 47:18 NIV, NRSV). "Tamar in the desert" is possibly mentioned also among the towns listed as having been built up by SOLOMON (cf. 1 Ki. 9:18, NRSV and NJPS). If that is the correct reading, it should probably be identified with HAZAZON TAMAR (another name for EN GEDI, 2 Chr. 20:2). Most scholars, however, think Tamar was further S. Some locate it near Qasr el-Juheiniya, where the Romans built a border fort named Tamara (c. 12.5 mi./20 km. WSW of the DEAD SEA). Others think that Tamar is the same as the City of Palms and that the latter name was originally applied to a site now known as Tell ʿAin ʿArus (some 6 mi./10 km. SSE of the Dead Sea); however, there is no compelling reason to deny that the name City of Palms is consistently used with reference to JERICHO. More likely, Tamar should be identified with ʿAin Ḥuṣb (c. 23 mi./37 km. SSW of the Dead Sea in the ARABAH).

tamarisk. See PLANTS.

tambourine. See MUSIC AND MUSICAL INSTRUMENTS (sect. I.G).

Tammuz. tam'uhz (Heb. *tammûz H9452*, from Akk. *Duʾuzu*, which in turn derives from Sumerian *Dumuzi*, "legal [*or* healthy] son"). A Sumerian and Babylonian deity. Tammuz was said to be the husband and brother of Inanna (ISHTAR). He is represented on seals as the protector of flocks against wild beasts. In the Babylonian saga his death and visit to the underworld represents the annual wilting of vegetation in the scorching heat of summer. His return to earth, brought about by the descent of the mourning Ishtar into the nether world, represents the renewal of nature (although some scholars argue that Tammuz is consistently represented as dead, not as having been brought to life). The annual mourning rites for Tammuz took place on the second day of the fourth month (June/July), giving rise to the practice of naming this month Duʾuzu in Babylonia and Tammuz in the postbiblical Jewish CALENDAR. In EZEKIEL's time, a variation of this rite of mourning found women weeping at the N gate of the temple (Ezek. 8:14).

Tanach. See TAANACH.

Tanakh. tah'nahk, tuh-nahch'. Also Tanach, Tanak. A Hebrew name commonly used by Jews as equivalent to "Bible." The word is an acronym based on the first letter of the Hebrew names for the three divisions of the OT: *tôrâ* (Law; see TORAH), *nĕbîʾîm* (Prophets; see NEBIIM), and *kĕtûbîm* (Writings; see KETUBIM).

Tanhumeth. tan-hyoo'mith (Heb. *tanḥumet H9489*, "comfort, consolation"). Father of SERAIAH; the latter was a military officer who remained in JUDAH with GEDALIAH after the destruction of Jerusalem (2 Ki. 25:23; Jer. 40:8). The first passage identifies Tanhumeth as a Netophathite (see NETOPHAH), but the parallel in Jeremiah attaches that description to EPHAI. It seems probable that the words "the sons of Ephai" in Jeremiah are original and that they dropped out in the text of 2 Kings at some point in its transmission.

Tanis. See ZOAR.

tanner, tanning. See OCCUPATIONS AND PROFESSIONS.

Taphath. tay'fath (Heb. *ṭāpat H3264*, possibly from *ṭap H3251*, "little child"). Daughter of SOLOMON and wife of BEN-ABINADAB, who was one of the twelve district governors (1 Ki. 4:11). Another daughter of Solomon is also included in this list (v. 15); see BASEMATH #3.

Tappuah (person). tap'yoo-uh (Heb. *tappûaḥ H9516*, "apple, apple tree"). Son of HEBRON and descendant of JUDAH in the line of CALEB (1 Chr. 2:43). As with a number of other names in the genealogy, Tappuah is no doubt associated with a town, probably BETH TAPPUAH (Josh. 15:52), which was less than 4 mi. (6 km.) from Hebron; another possibility is TAPPUAH (PLACE) #2.

Tappuah (place). tap'yoo-uh (Heb. *tappûaḥ H9517*, "apple, apple tree"). (1) A town on the N boundary of the tribal territory of EPHRAIM (Josh. 16:8). The passage that describes the borders of the tribe of MANASSEH states that its S boundary included the inhabitants of EN TAPPUAH (17:7); then it goes on to say, "Manasseh had the land of Tappuah, but Tappuah itself, on the boundary of Manasseh, belonged to the Ephraimites" (v. 8). This town was apparently the same Tappuah that is described as one of the Canaanite cities whose kings were defeated by JOSHUA (12:17). Its location is not certain, but it is generally identified with modern Sheikh Abu Zarad, about 13 mi. (21 km.) NNW of BETHEL.

(2) A town in the SHEPHELAH within the tribal territory of JUDAH (Josh. 15:34). It was evidently near such towns as ZANOAH and JARMUTH, but the precise location is uncertain.

(3) According to the Lucianic MSS of the SEPTUAGINT, Tappuah (*Taphōe*) was also the name of a city near TIRZAH that was attacked by King MENAHEM (2 Ki. 15:16). Many scholars accept this reading (cf. RSV, NAB, NJB), but others follow the MT, which has the otherwise unknown town of Tiphsah (cf. NIV, NRSV, NJPS). See TIPHSAH #2.

tar. See BITUMEN.

Tarah. See TERAH (PLACE).

Taralah. tair'uh-luh (Heb. *tarʾălâ H9550*, derivation unknown). A town in the tribal territory of BENJAMIN (Josh. 18:27). Since it is associated with such cities as MIZPAH and KEPHIRAH, Taralah must have been located in the W Benjamin plateau, a few miles NW of JERUSALEM, but the precise site is unknown.

Tarea. tair'ee-uh (Heb. *taʾrēaʿ H9308* and *taḥrēaʿ H9390*, meaning unknown). Grandson of MERIBBAAL (i.e., MEPHIBOSHETH) and descendant of King SAUL (1 Chr. 8:35; called "Tahrea" in 9:41).

tares. See PLANTS.

Targum. tahr'guhm (postbiblical Heb. *targûm*, Aram. *targûmāʾ*, "interpretation, translation" [cf. the Aram. verb *tirgēm H9553*, "to proclaim, explain, translate," Ezra 4:7]). Plural *Targums* or *Targumim*. A name applied to translations of the Hebrew Bible into the ARAMAIC language. See TEXT AND VERSIONS (OT).

Tarpelites. tahr'puh-lits (Aram. *ṭarpĕlāyēʾ*, apparently pl. determinative of an otherwise unattested gentilic name, *ṭarpĕlāy H10305*). The KJV transliteration of an ARAMAIC term whose meaning is uncertain (Ezra 4:9). Since the term is gentilic in form, it may indeed mean "people of Tarpel," alluding perhaps to a region in MESOPOTAMIA. The SEPTUAGINT renders it *Tarphallaioi*, referring to an inhabitant of the city of TRIPOLIS, and this interpretation is followed by the NIV. Other modern versions understand the term in the general sense of "officer" (cf. NRSV and NJPS; note that the two preceding terms in the verse, though also gentilic in form, refer to "judges and officials").

Tarshish (person). tahr'shish (Heb. *taršîš H9578*, "topaz" [or some other precious stone]). KJV also Tharshish (1 Chr. 7:10). (1) Son of JAVAN, grandson of JAPHETH, and great-grandson of NOAH (Gen. 10:4; 1 Chr. 1:7). The names of his brothers (ELISHAH, KITTIM, RODANIM) clearly refer to places or people groups, so Tarshish was presumably the progenitor of a Mediterranean people and his name was attached to a geographical area. See TARSHISH (PLACE).

(2) Son of Bilhan and great-grandson of BENJAMIN (1 Chr. 7:10).

(3) One of the seven nobles of PERSIA and MEDIA in the time of XERXES "who had special access to the king and were highest in the kingdom" (Esth. 1:14). Queen VASHTI was banished by Ahasuerus (XERXES) on their advice.

Tarshish (place). tahr′shish (Heb. *taršîš H9576*, "topaz" [or some other precious stone]). KJV also Tharshish (1 Ki. 10:22; 22:48). A region of uncertain location. In some passages the name is associated with ships and ports. Thus HIRAM, king of TYRE, maintained at EZION GEBER, at the head of the Gulf of AQABAH, a refinery and ship-building center from which he and SOLOMON operated "ships of Tarshish" (1 Ki. 10:22; 2 Chr. 9:21; cf. 1 Ki. 9:26-28; 22:48; 2 Chr. 20:36-37). There were perhaps other similar stations maintained by Phoenicians on the Mediterranean coasts and possibly in the E, where cargoes from India could be reshipped. The name Tarshish in such a connection does not seem to indicate destination but rather the nature of the ships, their size and far-voyaging capability; thus in the verses cited above the NIV translates the word as "trading ships" (in 2 Chr. 20:37 [which reads literally, "to go to Tarshish"] the NIV has "to set sail to trade"). A similar idea is shown in other passages (Ps. 48:7; Isa. 2:16 [NIV, "every trading ship"]; 23:1, 6, 10, 14; 60:9; Ezek. 27:25; cf. also Ps. 72:10; Ezek. 38:13).

As a place name, the identification of Tarshish has been debated. The biblical writers clearly viewed it as a very distant place, and it was on a ship headed for Tarshish that JONAH sought to flee from the Lord (Jon. 1:3; 4:2). Suggestions include Carthage and a city on the island of Sardinia, but most scholars see a connection with Tartessus, a city or territory that Herodotus locates in the W Mediterranean region, evidently near Gibraltar (*Hist.* 1.163; 4.152; it seems to have been destroyed in the 6th cent. B.C.). Tartessus, which was possibly founded by Phoenicians, appears to have been located around the lower Guadalquivir River (e.g., Huelva) in Andalucía, SW Spain. Although no specific identification has been confirmed, such a

site is consonant with the data that Tarshish developed trade in minerals (Jer. 10:9; Ezek. 27:12).

Tarsus. tahr′suhs (Gk. *Tarsos G5433*, gentilic *Tarseus G5432*, "of Tarsus"). A city of CILICIA in SE ASIA MINOR; it is modern Tersous, situated in the Cilician plain on the River Cydnus, some 10 mi. (16 km.) inland. This is a common setting for centers of civilization along that coast, once plagued by pirates. A calculation based on the wide extent of its traces suggests that Tarsus once had a population of half a million. The lower reaches of the river were navigable so that Tarsus functioned as a port with a skillfully constructed haven on a lake between the city and the sea. It became the capital of the province of Cilicia in A.D. 72.

Tarsus was the birthplace and early residence of the apostle PAUL, a fact that he himself notes with civic pride in Acts 21:39. During the first century B.C. the city was the home of a philosophical

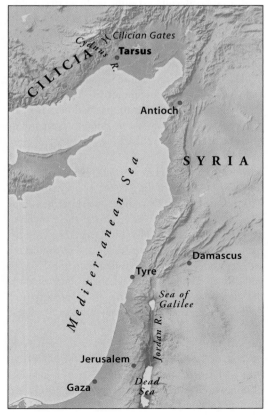

Tarsus.

Excavations at Tarsus.

ian Eponym Texts as the next highest official after the king. See also RABMAG; RABSARIS; RABSHAKEH.

Tartarus. tarh′tuh-ruhs (Gk. *Tartaros*). In Greek mythology, Tartarus was originally the name of a dark abyss where the Titans were confined; later the term became equivalent to HADES. Some Bible versions use this name to translate the verb *tartaroō G5434*, "to cast into Tartarus" (2 Pet. 2:4; NIV, "sent them to hell"). See HELL.

school, a university town, where the intellectual atmosphere was colored by Greek thought. Tarsus stood, like ALEXANDRIA, at the confluence of East and West. The wisdom of the Greeks and the world order of Rome, mingled with the good and ill of oriental mysticism, were deep in its consciousness. A keen-minded Jew, born and bred at Tarsus, would draw the best from more than one world. The Jews had been in Tarsus since ANTIOCHUS Epiphanes' refoundation in 171 B.C., and Paul belonged to a minority that had held Roman CITIZENSHIP probably since POMPEY's organization of the East (66-62 B.C.).

Tartak. tahr′tak (Heb. *tartāq H9581*, meaning unknown). An idol of the Avvites (see IVVAH); along with NIBHAZ, Tartak was introduced by them into SAMARIA when they were relocated there by SARGON II after 722 B.C. (2 Ki. 17:31). A deity with this name is not known in extrabiblical sources, unless Nibhaz and Tartak be identified with the Elamite gods Ibnahaza and Dirtak. Perhaps more likely is the view that the name Tartaq is a corruption of Aramaic ʿtrʿth, that is, the Syrian goddess Atargatis.

Tartan. tahr′tan (Heb. *tartān H9580*, from Akk. *tartānu* or *turtannu*, itself borrowed from HURRIAN). Title of high-ranking Assyrian generals in command of a military force (2 Ki. 19:17; Isa. 20:1 [KJV and other versions]; NIV, "supreme commander"). The Tartan is listed in the Assyr-

taskmasters. See OCCUPATIONS AND PROFESSIONS (under *slave driver*).

tassel. The Israelites were commanded "to make tassels [KJV fringes] on the corners of your garments, with a blue cord on each tassel" (Num. 15:37-39; cf. Deut. 22:12). The purpose of these tassels was to remind the Israelites of the commandments of the Lord, and not to depart from his will. Unfortunately, such injunctions could be misused, and Jesus critiqued the SCRIBES and the PHARISEES: "Everything they do is done for men to see: They make their phylacteries wide and the tassels on their garments long" (Matt. 23:5). See PHYLACTERY.

Tatnai. See TATTENAI.

Tattenai. tat′uh-ni (Aram. *tattĕnay H10779*, meaning unknown). KJV Tatnai. A Persian governor responsible for the province W of the River EUPHRATES during the reign of DARIUS Hystaspes (Ezra 5:3, 6; 6:6, 13). Tattenai, along with SHETHAR-BOZENAI and others, reported to the king on the complaints made regarding the Jewish rebuilding of the temple. His name and title are attested in an extrabiblical document.

tattoo. This term is used by the NIV and some other versions to render the Hebrew *qaʿăqaʿ H7882*, a verb of uncertain meaning; it occurs only once in a passage that prohibits self-mutilation (Lev. 19:28; KJV, "print"; NJPS, "incise"). In the strict sense, a tattoo is an indelible mark, figure, or writing made by pricking and inserting pigment under the skin. Perusal of MOURNING customs in the Bible indicates frequent association of head-shaving with body-cutting and painting (e.g., with clay), but never tattooing. The prohibition in Leviticus likely has to do with some kind of cutting of the skin.

tau. tou (from *tāw* H9338, "mark, sign"). Also *tav*, *taw*. The last (twenty-second) letter of the Hebrew alphabet (ת), with a numerical value of 400. It is named for the shape of the letter, which in its older form looked like an X, that is, a mark. This letter was pronounced *t*, similar to English, although in later times it became spirantized (cf. the *th* sound in English *think*) when it was preceded by a vowel sound.

tavern. See INN.

Taverns, Three. See THREE TAVERNS.

taw. See TAU.

tax booth, tax office. See CUSTOM, RECEIPT OF.

tax collector. See OCCUPATIONS AND PROFESSIONS.

taxes. Charges imposed by governments, either political or ecclesiastical, on the persons or the properties of their members or subjects. In the nomadic period taxes were unknown to the Hebrews. Voluntary presents were given to chieftains in return for protection. The conquered Canaanites were forced to render labor (Josh. 16:10; 17:13; Jdg. 1:28-35). Under the THEOCRACY of ISRAEL every man paid a poll tax of a half-shekel for the support of the TABERNACLE worship (Exod. 30:13; 38:25-26), and this was the only fixed tax. It was equal for rich and poor (30:15). Under the kings, as SAMUEL had warned the people (1 Sam. 8:11-18), heavy taxes were imposed. They amounted to a TITHE of the crops and of the flocks besides the forced military service and other services that were imposed. In the days of SOLOMON, because of his great build-

ing program (the magnificent TEMPLE, the king's palaces, thousands of stables for chariot horses, the navy, etc.), the burden of taxes was made so oppressive that the northern tribes rebelled against his successor, who had threatened even heavier taxation and oppression (1 Ki. 12).

During the days of the divided kingdom, MENAHEM (2 Ki. 15:19-20) bribed the Assyrian king with a thousand talents of silver to support him, raising the amount from the rich men of his kingdom. Similarly HOSHEA (17:3) paid heavy tribute to ASSYRIA, and when he refused to pay further, he lost his kingdom. Later, Pharaoh NECO of EGYPT put JUDAH under heavy tribute, and JEHOIAKIM oppressively taxed Judah (23:33, 35). Under the Persian domination, "taxes, tribute or duty" (Ezra 4:13) were forms of taxation, though ARTAXERXES exempted "priests, Levites," etc. (7:23-24). The Ptolemies, the Seleucids, and later the Romans, all adopted the very cruel but efficient method of "farming out the taxes," each officer extorting more than his share from those under him, and thus adding to the Jewish hatred of the tax collectors (see OCCUPATIONS AND PROFESSIONS), among whom were at one time MATTHEW and ZACCHAEUS, both converts later.

teacher, teaching. See EDUCATION; OCCUPATIONS AND PROFESSIONS; SCHOOL; SYNAGOGUE.

Teacher of Righteousness. See DEAD SEA SCROLLS.

teachers of the law. See SCRIBE.

tears. The secretions of the lacrimal gland. In the Scriptures the emotional aspect of the formation of tears is foremost. Thus DAVID, in referring to his stressful situation before ACHISH (1 Sam. 21:10-15), requests God to put his tears in his bottle (Ps. 56:8), doubtless as a perpetual memorial or reminder of his zeal and suffering for God's righteous cause as he continuously refused to lay his hands on God's anointed. With some hyperbole David says that he waters his couch with his tears, making his bed to swim (Ps. 6:6). JOB also refers to his tears as being poured out unto God (Job 16:20). HEZEKIAH prayed with tears and was

T

rewarded by the addition of fifteen years to his life (Isa. 38:5). JEREMIAH too made frequent reference to his eyes running down with tears (e.g., Jer. 13:17; 14:17). Tears were used by a repentant sinner to wash her Savior's feet (Lk. 7:38). Tears accentuated the earnest plea of the father of the child who had the dumb and deaf spirit (Mk. 9:24). Tears accompanied the prayers of Christ (Heb. 5:7), and tears were associated with PAUL's service for God (Acts 20:19, 31) and TIMOTHY's also (2 Tim. 1:4).

Tebah (person). tee'buh (Heb. ṭebaḥ H3182, "[born at the time of] slaughter"). Son of NAHOR (brother of ABRAHAM) by his concubine REUMAH (Gen. 22:24). See also TEBAH (PLACE).

Tebah (place). tee'buh (Heb. ṭebaḥ H3183 [MT 2 Sam. 8:8, beṭaḥ], variant ṭibḥat H3187 [1 Chr. 18:8], "[place of] slaughter"). A city belonging to the Aramean king HADADEZER and from which DAVID took a great quantity of bronze (2 Sam. 8:8). The KJV and other modern versions have BETAH, following the MT. "Tebah" is the reading of the NIV, which assumes that "Tibhat" in the parallel passage (1 Chr. 18:8) is an alternate form of the name; this reading also has the support of some Greek MSS and of the Syriac version. Many scholars believe that the town received its name from TEBAH (PERSON), who may have been its founder. The town must have been somewhere in the Beqaᶜ Valley in LEBANON, but its precise location is unknown.

Tebaliah. See TABALIAH.

Tebeth. tee'bith (Heb. ṭēbēt H3194, meaning uncertain). The tenth month (December–January) of the Hebrew CALENDAR (Esth. 2:16).

teeth. Isaiah 41:15 tells of "a threshing sledge, new and sharp, with many teeth," literally "possessor of sharp edges," a figure referring to Israel as God's instrument of judgment on the nations. In Ps. 58:6 "teeth," literally "biters," could refer either to teeth or jaws. In Prov. 30:14 "jaws are set with knives" is clearly figurative, referring to the oppressors of the poor, and the same word in Joel 1:6, "the teeth of a lion," is hyperbole, describing the very destruc-

tive habits of the locust. In none of the preceding instances is the ordinary word for tooth used. Some of the more frequent uses of the common words are illustrated in the following passages. In Gen. 49:12 "his teeth whiter than milk" probably refers to the purity and holiness of the MESSIAH; "tooth for tooth" (Exod. 21:24) is of course literal; gnashing with the teeth can be a token of anger (Job 16:9) or of remorse (Matt. 8:12 and several other references to the suffering of the wicked after death) or of contemptuous rage (Lam. 2:16; Acts 7:54). Proverbs 10:26 provides a hint, if one is needed, that the ancients did not have good dental care. Canticles 4:2 speaks of the beauty of teeth.

tefillin. See PHYLACTERY.

Tehillim. See PSALMS, BOOK OF.

Tehinnah. tuh-hin'uh (Heb. tēḥinnāh H9383, "supplication"). Son of Eshton, descendant of JUDAH, and "father" (i.e., founder) of IR NAHASH (1 Chr. 4:12). His place in the Judahite genealogy is not clear.

teil tree. See PLANTS (under *terebinth*).

tekel. See MENE, MENE, TEKEL, PARSIN (UPHARSIN).

Tekoa. tuh-koh'uh (Heb. tĕqôaᶜ H9541, meaning uncertain; gentilic tĕqôᶜi H9542, "from Tekoa, Tekoite"). KJV also Tekoah (2 Sam. 14:2, 4, 9). A town in the hill country within the tribal territory of JUDAH (cf. LXX Josh. 15:59, where many scholars believe that the MT is defective). Tekoa is identified with modern Khirbet Tequᶜ, some 5 mi. (8 km.) S of BETHLEHEM, on a prominent elevation c. 2,700 ft. (820 m.) high, from which the MOUNT OF OLIVES is visible. It looks down on a mass of desert hills. Tekoa was the hometown of the prophet AMOS (Amos 1:1). The scenes that influenced this shepherd of Tekoa are reflected graphically in his book (cf. 4:13; 5:8). The town lies between two valleys cutting deeply down to the DEAD SEA through the wilderness of JUDEA.

Apparently Tekoa was founded at the time of the Hebrew conquest of CANAAN by the Judahite ASHHUR son of HEZRON (1 Chr. 2:24 and 4:5, where "father" undoubtedly means "founder" or "leader"). In 2 Sam. 14:1-22 is the record regarding the wise woman, "the Tekoite," whom Joab, David's general, employed as a ruse to bring back the fugitive Absalom. Tekoa was also the home of Ira son of Ikkesh, one of David's mighty warriors (2 Sam. 23:26). There are several other references to the town (2 Chr. 11:6; 20:20; Neh. 3:5, 27).

Tel, Tell. The Hebrew and Arabic words for "mound." They are frequently found as the first element in the names of archaeological sites, so named because of the accumulated ruins and occupation debris of ancient settlements. See ARCHAEOLOGY.

Tel Abib. tel´uh-beeb´ (Heb. *tēlʾābib H9425*, apparently "mound of ears of grain," but this Heb. form is a modification of Akk. *Til abūbi[m]*, "mound [produced by] the deluge"). Also Tel Aviv. A locality in Babylonia by the great irrigation canal, the Kebar (thus not to be confused with the modern city of Tel Aviv in Israel). It was here that Ezekiel made his first contact with the Jewish exiles in 597 B.C., and he was constrained to share their despair and desolation before being permitted to speak to them (Ezek. 3:15). The Akkadian name *Tel abūbi* suggests that the place was an ancient city reduced to a mound as a result of flooding, followed by decay and long erosion. In exilic times, Tel Abib must have been a Jewish village SE of Babylon and not far from Nippur, but the precise location is unknown.

Telah. tee´luh (Heb. *telaḥ H9436*, perhaps "split"). Son of Resheph and descendant of Ephraim (1 Chr. 7:25). See comments under Resheph (person).

Telaim. tuh-lay´im (Heb. *tĕlāʾim H3230*, possibly "lambs"). A site in S Judah near the ill-defined Amalekite border; it is mentioned only as Saul's concentration point and base for his counterattack on the descendants of Amalek, who had been raiding the area (1 Sam. 15:4; cf. 14:48; 15:2-3). Some modern scholars suggest that "Telaim" may be a variant or corruption of "Telem" (Josh. 15:24), a town in the Negev that, strategically, was a possible assembly point for a desert campaign of this nature. See Telem (place).

Telam. See Telem.

Tel Assar. tel-as´ahr (Heb. *tĕlaʾśśār H9431*, possibly from Akk. *Til-ašuri*, "mound of Asshur"). Also Telassar. A town or region where "the people of Eden" (see Beth Eden) were apparently resettled; it is mentioned by Sennacherib as one of the many places overrun and obliterated by the aggressive hosts of Assyria (2 Ki. 19:12 [KJV, "Thelasar"]; Isa. 37:12). The first element of the name (Akk. *Til*, "mound") suggests a site of ancient habitation (perhaps "ruins of [a town destroyed by the god] Asshur"), but the place is otherwise unknown.

Tel Aviv. See Tel Abib.

Telem (person). tee´luhm (Heb. *ṭelem H3235*, possibly "brightness"). A Levitical gatekeeper who agreed to put away his foreign wife in the time of Ezra (Ezra 10:24).

Telem (place). tee´luhm (Heb. *ṭelem H3234*, possibly "brightness"). A town in the Negev, the extreme S of the tribal territory of Judah, near the border of Edom (Josh. 15:24). It is listed between Ziph and Bealoth and it was possibly some distance SE of Beersheba, but the precise location cannot be determined. By emendation some scholars read "from Telem to Shur" in 1 Sam. 27:8 (NRSV, "Telam"), which would indicate that Telem is the same as Telaim (some read "Telem/Telaim" also in 15:7).

Tel Harsha. tel-hahr´shuh (Heb. *tēl ḥaršāʾ H9426*, possibly "mound of the forest"). One of five Babylonian places from which certain Jewish exiles returned who were unable to prove their Israelite ancestry (Ezra 2:59; Neh. 7:61). The location is unknown.

Tell. See Tel, Tell.

Tell el-Amarna. Tell el-Amarna. See Amarna, Tell el-.

Tel Melah. tel-mee´luh (Heb. *tēl melaḥ H9427*, "mound of salt"). One of five Babylonian places from which certain Jewish exiles returned who

T

were unable to prove their Israelite ancestry (Ezra 2:59; Neh. 7:61). The meaning of the name may suggest that at one time a settlement there had been destroyed and that its ruins had been "sown with salt" (cf. Jdg. 9:45 NRSV), a symbol of permanent infertility (Deut. 29:23). The location is unknown.

Tema. tee´muh (Heb. *têmāʾ H9401*, meaning uncertain; possible gentilic *têmānî H9404*, "Temanite"). Son of ISHMAEL and grandson of ABRAHAM (Gen. 25:15; 1 Chr. 1:31). Tema is also the name of a place that was apparently founded by him or his descendants (Job 6:19; Isa. 21:14; Jer. 25:23), identified with modern Teima (Taymaʾ) in N ARABIA, a large oasis about halfway between DAMASCUS and Mecca. Tema/Teima is on the ancient caravan road connecting the Persian Gulf with the Gulf of AQABAH. It is one of the most attractive oases in Arabia and is still one of the most important trade centers in the land. The biblical references tell of the metropolitan position of Tema in the transdesert trade. In Isa. 21:13-15, its inhabitants are asked to offer refuge and hospitality to Dedanite caravans (see DEDAN) fleeing from a pursuing army. Job 6:19, in a description of the desert, mentions "the caravans of Tema" (some think that Job's friend ELIPHAZ the Temanite [2:11 et al.] was a native of Tema, but see TEMAN). Jeremiah 25:23 prophesied that great trouble would come upon Tema and nearby tribes; this may refer to NEBUCHADNEZZAR's campaign against that region. NABONIDUS, the last king of the Neo-Babylonian, or Chaldean, empire (556-539 B.C.), divided his power with his eldest son BELSHAZZAR and entrusted the kingship to him. He did this that he might proceed with an army against Tema. He conquered the city, slaughtered its inhabitants, rebuilt it so that it recalled the glory of BABYLON, and made it the capital of the western part of his empire.

Temah. tee´muh (Heb. *temaḥ H9457*, meaning unknown). Ancestor of a family of temple servants (NETHINIM) who returned from the captivity with ZERUBBABEL (Ezra 2:53 [KJV, "Thamah"]; Neh. 7:55 [KJV, "Tamah"]).

Teman. tee´muhn (Heb. *têmān H9403*, "south, southern region"; gentilic *têmānî H9404*, "Teman-

ite"). Firstborn son of ELIPHAZ and grandson of ESAU; he was head of an Edomite clan (Gen. 36:11, 15; 42; 1 Chr. 1:36, 53). Teman is also the name of a place in EDOM that was apparently founded by him or his descendants (Jer. 49:7 et al.). According to Gen. 36:34, HUSHAM the Temanite ruled as king in Edom before there were kings in ISRAEL, and one of JOB's comforters, ELIPHAZ, was a Temanite (Job 2:11 et al.); but some scholars argue that either Husham or Job's friend—or both— may have been from a different place, TEMA. The inhabitants of Teman were noted for their WISDOM (Jer. 49:7; Obad. 8-9). Many of the prophets included Teman in their oracles against Edom (Jer. 49:20; Ezek. 25:13; Amos 1:12; Obad. 9), and all declared that Teman would be destroyed. In some of these passages, Teman is virtually a synonym for Edom (this may account for the name, which means something like "southern territory"; Edom was to the S of Israel). However, the association with BOZRAH (Amos 1:12) suggests that Teman designated more specifically the northern parts of Edom. Teman (near the N border) and DEDAN (near the S border) are mentioned together in some of the oracles. One suggestion for the location of Teman is modern Tawilan, about 3 mi. (5 km.) E of PETRA.

Temanite. See TEMA; TEMAN; TEMENI.

Temeni. tem´uh-ni (Heb. *têmĕnî H9405*, gentilic of *yāman H3554*, "right[-hand], south," or *têmān H9403* [see TEMAN], or some otherwise unknown person or place; it is perhaps a variant of *têmānî H9404*, "Temanite"). Son of ASHHUR and descendant of JUDAH (1 Chr. 4:6). Some think that Temeni was an Edomite clan that had been incorporated into the Judahite genealogy.

temperance. The prime meaning is self-control (Acts 24:25; 1 Cor. 9:25; Gal. 5:23; 2 Pet. 1:6). It is not limited to abstinence from liquor. In Acts 24:25 the reference is to chastity. In 1 Tim. 3:2, 11; Tit. 2:2 it is the opposite of "drunken."

temple. The name given to the complex of buildings in JERUSALEM that was the center of the sacrificial cult for the Hebrews. This ritual of sacrifices was the central external service of the ancient people of God and the unifying factor of their religion. Three structures stood successively on Mount MORIAH (2 Chr. 3:1) in Jerusalem. This site is today called the Ḥaram esh-Sharif and is a Muslim holy place. The first temple was built by SOLOMON, the second by ZERUBBABEL and the Jews who returned from the Babylonian EXILE. The third temple, which was in use in the days of Jesus, was begun and largely built by HEROD the Great.

Most ancient religions had temples. Indeed, the Canaanite temples found at MEGIDDO and HAZOR are not unlike that of the Hebrews in ground plan. The Jerusalem temple was distinctive in that it contained no idol in the inner sanctum, but only a box (the ARK OF THE COVENANT) containing the two tablets of the LAW, with the symbolic worshiping CHERUBIM above. The central place of the temple in the religious life of ancient ISRAEL is reflected throughout the Bible. The Psalms abound in references to it (Ps. 42:4; 66:13; 84:1-4; 122:1, 9; 132:5, 7-8, 13-17). The temple was the object of religious aspiration (23:6; 27:4-5). Pilgrimage to the temple brought the people of Israel from the ends of the earth (Ps. 122:1-4; Acts 2:5-11). The visit of Jesus to the temple at the age of twelve is well known (Lk. 2:41-51). Later he exercised some of his ministry there (Matt. 26:55; Lk. 19:45; Jn. 7:28, 37; 10:23). The early Jerusalem Christians also worshiped there until the break between Israel and the CHURCH became final (Acts 3:1; 5:12, 42; 21:26-34).

I. Solomon's temple. The TABERNACLE, the previous sacrificial center (Exod. 35-40), was a simple and impermanent structure brought to PALESTINE by the Hebrews from their desert wanderings. It was natural enough that DAVID should wish God's house to be as grand as his own (2 Sam. 7:2). David, however, was not permitted to undertake the construction of this "house" (2 Sam. 7:5-7; 1 Chr. 22:8). He did prepare for it, however, both in plans and materials (1 Chr. 22:1-19; 28:1-29:9) and more especially by arranging its liturgical service (23:1-26:19).

There are no known remains of Solomon's temple. It clearly was patterned after the tabernacle, but much more complex and ornate. The Phoenicians, who were more advanced culturally than the Hebrews, played a great part in the design and construction of the temple. Recently archaeologists have discovered remains in PHOENICIA and SYRIA that have increased our understanding of the details and motifs of the temple of Jerusalem. Especially useful is the temple found at Tell Tainat in Syria, which was built at about the same time as Solomon's. Its architectural details are believed to be the best guide extant today in reconstructing the details of Solomon's temple, which was noted for lavish beauty of detail rather than for great size. It was accessible only to the priests; the lay Israelites came to it but never entered it. Seven years were required to complete the temple. It was dedicated in Solomon's eleventh year, c. 950 B.C. (1 Ki. 6:38), and was destroyed when the Babylonians burned Jerusalem in 586.

The temple was a prefabricated building. It was made of limestone finished at the quarries (1 Ki. 6:7) in or near Jerusalem. When the stones were brought to the building site, they were built into the wall according to plan. The stone walls were covered with paneling of Lebanese cedar wood, probably finished by skilled Phoenician craftsmen (1 Ki. 5:6; 6:15, 18). The main descriptions of Solomon's temple are found in 1 Ki. 5:1-9:25 and 2 Chr. 2:1-7:22. While many details are uncertain, what can be known of the building with fair certainty is here given.

© Dr. James C. Martin

Aerial view of the remains of an Israelite sanctuary or temple at Arad dating as early as the Solomonic period (10th cent. B.C.). Its building plan bears some striking resemblances to that of Solomon's temple.

T

The temple consisted of three sections: (1) The porch or portico, through which the temple proper was entered (1 Ki. 6:3; Heb. *ʾêlām H395*, also *ʾûlām*). (2) The Holy Place (*haqqōdeš*) or "main hall" (*hêkāl H2121*, although this term is often used of the whole building). Lighted by clerestory windows (vv. 3-4), this hall or nave was 30 ft. wide, 60 long, and 45 high (9 x 18 x 14 m.). It was paneled with cedar, with gold inlay to relieve the wooden monotony and to add grandeur. (3) The Most Holy Place (*bêt-qōdeš haqqōdāšîm*) or "inner sanctuary" (*dĕbîr H1808*), a 30-ft. (9-m.) cube, windowless and overlaid with gold (v. 5; 2 Chr. 3:8-13). It had a raised floor, and the cubicle was reached by steps from the Holy Place. Here God especially manifested his presence by the SHEKINAH glory cloud.

The temple was built on a high platform that was reached by ten steps, a dramatic approach for religious processions. On this platform, before the entrance to the portico, stood two pillars, called JAKIN AND BOAZ (1 Ki. 7:15-22). Possibly these names are the first words of inscriptions carved on the pillars. Just behind them, doors led to the portico, a kind of antechamber to the Holy Place. The cypress doors were carved with cherubim, palm trees, and open flowers inlaid with gold (6:18, 32, 35). These motifs are frequently found in ANE temple structures.

The Holy Place contained ten golden LAMPSTANDS (1 Ki. 7:49; KJV, "candlesticks"). The Arch of Titus in Rome depicts a lampstand from Herod's temple being carried away by the Roman soldiers after the destruction of Jerusalem in A.D. 70. Twelve tables held the twelve loaves of the bread of the Presence (KJV, "shewbread"). The INCENSE altar (7:48), with "horns" (see HORNS OF THE ALTAR), stood near the entrance of the inner sanctuary.

The Most Holy Place contained two guardian cherubim, made of olive wood and adorned with gold. A number of archaeological remains suggest that these were winged sphinxes, with a lion's body, human face, and great wings. They symbolized the majestic presence of God. On the floor beneath them stood the ark of the covenant, the box overlaid with gold, its lid called the mercy seat, on which the atoning blood was sprinkled on the Day of Atonement (Lev. 16:14-15; see ATONEMENT, DAY OF).

At both sides and at the rear of the temple were built three-storied rooms. They were not as high as the central structure and thus the light from the clerestory windows supplied illumination for the Holy Place. This clerestory feature was perhaps an ancestor of the same window arrangement of the medieval cathedrals (recessed window-walls rising above the lower wings or aisle portions). In the chambers around the sanctuary the immense temple treasury was kept (1 Ki. 7:51).

In the courtyard in front of the temple stood two objects intimately connected with the temple worship: the sacrificial altar and the laver, or molten sea. The altar of burnt offering was the central object in the sacrificial service. It was made of brass (2 Chr. 4:1) and probably stood on the great rock that is today covered by the Dome of the Rock on the Ḥaram esh-Sharif.

South of the altar stood the copper alloy laver, or molten sea, or BRONZE SEA (1 Ki. 7:22-26; 2 Ki. 16:17; 2 Chr. 4:2-6). This mammoth cast "sea" was made in the JORDAN Valley, where clay suitable for molding the metal was to be found. It was 3.5 in. (9 cm.) thick, about 15 ft. (4.5 m.) in diameter, and 7.5 ft. (2 m.) high, and stood on the backs of twelve bulls, three facing in each direction. Similar animal supports for thrones are known to have existed among Israel's neighbors. The bull was the Canaanite symbol of fertility and was associated with BAAL (HADAD), the god of rain. The presence of this motif in Solomon's temple suggests that more syncretism may have taken place in the Hebrew religion than is at first evident when one reads the Bible. Some scholars have doubted whether this immense reservoir with a capacity estimated at 10,000 gallons (38,000 liters) could have practically been used for the ceremonial washing, especially since ten small lavers are mentioned (2 Chr. 4:6). They think that its main purpose was to symbolize that WATER or the SEA is the source of life. The Babylonians broke up and carried off this amazing example of ancient metal casting (2 Ki. 25:13).

The temple did not stand alone; it was one of a number of royal buildings constructed by Solomon in the new section of Jerusalem, just N of the old city of David. Solomon's own palace, another for the PHARAOH's daughter, the House of the Forest of Lebanon, the Hall of Pillars, and the Hall of the Throne (1 Ki. 7:1-8) were other buildings in this government quarter. Viewed in this context, the temple appears like a royal chapel. The temple was dedicated by Solomon himself. His prayer on that occasion (8:22-61) shows a great religious spirit reaching out to include even the pagan nations in the WORSHIP of Yahweh.

Certain changes doubtless took place in the temple during the Hebrew kingdom. Pagan IDOL-ATRY was occasionally introduced (2 Ki. 16:10-18; 21:4-9; Ezek. 8:3-18). Pious kings reformed, refurbished, and rededi-cated the temple (2 Chr. 29:3-31:21; 34:8-33). Foreign kings raided it (1 Ki. 14:25-26; 2 Ki. 12:18; 14:14; 18:15-16). When Jerusalem finally fell to the Babylonians in 586 B.C., the temple along with the rest of the city was destroyed and its valuable contents car-ried to BABYLON (2 Ki. 25:8-9, 13-17).

II. Ezekiel's temple. Ezekiel the PROPHET was also a PRIEST. In the early part of his book he predicts that God will judge his idolatrous people by withdrawing his presence from Jerusalem, leaving it to the Gentiles to desolate. But the latter part of the book predicts the reversal of this judg-ment. Judah and Israel reunited will be regathered. The climax of this vision is the proph-et's description of the restored temple of God, with the living waters proceeding from it and the people of God dwelling around it (Ezek. 40-48). *Yahweh Shammah* ("The Lord is there") is the key to this vision; God will yet again live among his people. The temple here described is an ideal construc-tion, both like and unlike Solomon's; none like it ever existed, and it is difficult to see how any such temple could ever be built.

Differing views have been held concerning the meaning of this temple vision. Those interpret-ers who look for a very literal fulfillment of the prophecies believe that this temple will be a part of the millennial kingdom, a great world center of the worship of God, located at Jerusalem. The

sacrifices mentioned (Ezek. 43:18-27) are regarded as commemorative in nature—looking back to Christ's perfect sacrifice rather than forward to it, as did the OT sacrifices.

Other scholars argue that this description can hardly be taken literally. The letter to the Hebrews states that the sacrificial system prefigured Christ, and now that his perfect sacrifice has been made, the imperfect types are done away (Heb. 7:11-10:39). John in the Revelation (Rev. 21:9—22:5) appears to use Ezekiel's temple vision, but he writes, not of a millennial temple, but of the eternal glory of the CHURCH. Thus these interpreters understand

Model of the Jerusalem temple during the NT period. (View to the NW.)

Ezekiel's temple as a highly figurative foreshadow-ing of the new and holy temple of the Lord, which is the BODY OF CHRIST (Eph. 2:11—3:6).

III. The restoration temple of Zerubbabel. The return from Babylonian exile (in 538 B.C.), made possible by the decree of CYRUS, was a small and unpromising one. The returnees were few in number, and their resources were so meager as to need frequent strengthening from the Jews who remained in Babylon. The temple they built is a good example of this. When the foundation was laid, the old men, who had seen the "first house" (Solomon's temple), wept for sorrow (Hag. 2:3), but the young men, who had been born in exile, shouted for joy (Ezra 3:12). Like most of the reconstruction in that first century of the Second

© Dr. James C. Martin. The Holy Land Hotel, Jerusalem. Photographed by permission.

T

© Dr. James C. Martin

The temple mount today. (View to the NW.)

Commonwealth, the temple must have been modest indeed.

Soon after the return, the community began to rebuild the temple. Joshua (JESHUA) the high priest and ZERUBBABEL the governor were the leaders of the movement. Many difficulties kept the builders from completing the temple until 515 B.C. At that time they were urged on in the work by the prophets HAGGAI and ZECHARIAH, and the building was finished. No description of this temple exists. Its dimensions were probably the same as Solomon's, but it was evidently much less ornate and costly.

The Holy Place of the new temple seems to have had a curtain at its front. It had one lampstand, a golden altar of incense, and a table for the bread of the Presence. Another curtain separated the Holy Place from the Most Holy Place. According to JOSEPHUS, the Most Holy Place was empty. Evidently the ark had been destroyed in 586 B.C. and was never replaced. A single slab of stone marked its place. The Babylonian TALMUD asserts that five things were lacking in the new temple: the ark, the sacred fire, the Shekinah, the Holy Spirit, and the URIM AND THUMMIM.

No doubt the temple was repaired and beautified many times in the succeeding centuries, but of this we have no information. Our next knowledge of it comes from the days of ANTIOCHUS Epiphanes. In 168 B.C. this Syrian king sought to

stamp out the Hebrew religion, robbed the temple of its furniture and desecrated it, forcing the high priest to sacrifice a pig on its altar. This action precipitated the Maccabean revolt. In 165 the Jews, led by the MACCABEES, took up arms against the Syrians, eventually recapturing and rededicating the temple. They replaced the stone altar of burnt offering with stones that had not been defiled, meanwhile saving the old stones "until a prophet should come to tell what to do with them" (1 Macc. 4:46) The story of the rededication of the temple and the miraculous supply of oil for the lamps is perpetuated in the Jewish festival of Hanukkah.

Judas Maccabee at this time fortified the temple with walls and towers, making it the citadel of Jerusalem. Sometime during the next century a bridge was built across the Tyropoeon Valley connecting the temple with the Hasmonean palace. The Hasmoneans (Jewish rulers in the line of the Maccabees) were both high priests and kings, and by this bridge they sought to make the temple easier to defend. All of this points up the fact that the Second Commonwealth period was one of uneasy peace at best, and that the temple henceforth was to be both the religious and military center of the Jews. In 63 B.C. the Roman general POMPEY captured Jerusalem and took the temple after a hard struggle, breaking down the Hasmonean bridge. Although Pompey did not harm the temple, the

Roman consul Crassus plundered it of all its gold nine years later.

IV. Herod's temple. Our sources of information concerning Herod's temple are the Jewish historian JOSEPHUS (c. A.D. 38-100) and the tract *Middoth* of the Mishnah written over a century after the final destruction of the temple. Neither can be used uncritically, and many details of the Herodian building and service remain uncertain. HEROD the Great (37-4 B.C.) was an indefatigable builder. Many cities and heathen temples had been rebuilt by him, and it was natural that he should wish to show his own grandeur by replacing the modest restoration temple with a more complex and much more beautiful temple. Other motives probably moved him, especially his desire to ingratiate himself with the more religious Jews, who resented his Idumean origin and his friendliness with the Romans.

Herod began his work in his eighteenth year (20-19 B.C.). The Jews were afraid that the work would interrupt the temple service, but Herod went to great lengths to prevent this, rebuilding the old structure piecemeal, never stopping the ritual observances until an entirely new temple came into being. Since only priests could enter the temple and the inner court, one thousand of them were the masons and the carpenters for that inner area. The "house" itself was finished in a year and a half, but eighty years were spent on the surrounding buildings and court, which were not finally completed until A.D. 64. The Jews said to Jesus that the temple had been under construction forty-six years (Jn. 2:20); more than thirty additional years were to pass before it was really finished, then only to be destroyed. All speak of the grandeur of the building, which was of white marble, its eastern front covered with plates of gold that reflected the rays of the rising sun.

The temple area was probably equivalent to the modern Ḥaram esh-Sharif, except that the N end of the Ḥaram was the location of the fortress ANTONIA. This area, twice as large as that on which Zerubbabel's temple was situated, was artificially built up by underground arches (the present "Solomon's Stables") and fill held in by retaining walls (the Wailing Wall is a part of Herod's western retaining wall). The area, some twenty-six acres in size, was surrounded by a high wall. Gates on each side led into it, but the principal gates were in the S and W walls, leading in from the city. The eastern gate may have been the BEAUTIFUL GATE (Acts 3:2, 10), perhaps located where the Golden Gate stands today. Around the inside of the walls ran porches. The finest one was on the S side—the Royal Porch—having four rows of dazzling white marble columns in the Corinthian style, 162 columns in all. The eastern porch was called SOLOMON'S COLONNADE (Jn. 10:23; Acts 3:11; 5:12). During the FEASTS the Roman guards used to walk on the roofs of the porches to see that order was kept.

Near the NW corner of the temple area was located the fortress Antonia. It dominated the temple and was the headquarters of the guard so often needed to keep the peace. From the stairs that led from the temple precincts to Antonia, PAUL delivered his sermon (Acts 21:31—22:21) after having been rescued by the guard from the mob.

Entering the temple area, one came to four successive walled courts that surrounded the temple, each more exclusive than the one outside it. The first was the Court of the Gentiles. It was not holy ground, and non-Jews were permitted there. Here buying and selling went on; it was here that Jesus cleansed the temple (Jn. 2:14-17). Within the Court of the Gentiles were situated the temple and inner courts, built on a platform 22 ft. (almost 7 m.) above the floor of the outer court. Stairways led up to this platform. Surrounding it was a stone wall on which were placed stones with inscriptions in Greek and Latin forbidding non-Jews from entering on pain of death. Several of these stones have been found (cf. Acts 21:26-28).

On the platform was the inner court. It was the temple precinct and holy ground. Only the covenant people could enter here. It was surrounded by a high wall, and against the inner side of this wall were built storage chambers and colonnades. Ritual paraphernalia was kept in some of the chambers, and the SANHEDRIN is believed to have met in one of them. The inner court was divided into two unequal parts by a cross wall running N–S. The eastern and smaller area was the Women's Court. Here women as well as men were permitted and here were located thirteen chests like inverted trumpets, into which offerings for the expenses of the temple services were placed. In this place the poor widow was commended by Jesus when she gave her two copper coins (Mk. 12:41-44). For reasons of ceremonial purity only men were allowed in the western area, which contained in its center the temple proper. Around the temple was the Court of the Priests, which contained the altar of burnt offering and the laver. Around the Priests' Court was the Court of Israel, accessible to all Jewish males. Here the men gathered when the service was being carried on, to pray and to observe the offering of the sacrifices (Lk. 1:10).

In the center of these many courts within courts stood the temple itself, raised twelve steps above the Court of the Priests. Perhaps the forbidding inaccessibility of the sanctuary was in Paul's mind when he said that Christ "destroyed the barrier, the dividing wall of hostility" to bring the Gentiles into the fellowship of the people of God (Eph. 2:14).

The temple porch—150 ft. (46 m.) in length and breadth and 30 ft. (9 m.) deep—faced east. It projected 22.5 ft. (7 m.) beyond the sides of the temple proper, for the temple was only 105 ft. (32 m.) wide. Above the entrance to the porch (which had no door), Herod had placed a golden eagle, which as a Roman emblem (and an unclean bird) was most distasteful to the Jews. Shortly before his death it was destroyed. In front of the doorway to the Holy Place hung a beautifully colored Babylonian curtain or veil. The inner area of the Holy Place was 60 ft. long, 30 broad, and 90 high (18 x 9 x 27.5 m.), and it contained the altar of incense in the middle, the table of the bread of the Presence on the north, and the lampstand on the south. Only the officiating priests could enter this room, to bring in the incense morning and evening, to trim the lamps daily, and to replace the bread of the Presence every Sabbath.

Between the Holy Place and the Most Holy Place hung two curtains, with 18 in. (46 cm.) space between them. On the Day of Atonement the high priest entered the Most Holy Place with his censer by going to the south side, passing between the curtains to the north side, and thus emerging into the inner sanctuary. The Gospels refer to these as one veil, which was torn in two at the time of Jesus' crucifixion (Matt. 27:51; Mk. 15:38; Lk. 23:45). The Most Holy Place was empty and was entered by the high priest only once a year, on the Day of Atonement.

An upper room, 60 ft. (18 m.) high, covered the two chambers of the temple. From this room workmen were let down in boxes to effect needed repairs. Probably this was to avoid needless walking through the sacred house. As in Solomon's, so in Herod's temple, there were storerooms along the sides, except for the front or east, where the porch stood. These were used for storage and for the residence of officiating priests. No natural light came into this temple from roof or windows. It depended on the lamps for its light.

In front of the temple, in the Courtyard of the Priests, stood the altar of burnt offering. It is believed that this altar stood on the great rock that is covered today by the building called the Dome of the Rock. It was made of unhewn stones. There was always a fire burning on the altar. At the SW corner was located a drainage channel for the blood to the KIDRON Valley. North of the altar were twenty-four rings affixed to the ground. To these were tied the sacrificial victims, and there they were killed by slitting their throats. Still farther to the north were pillars with iron hooks on which the carcasses were hung for dressing. If this reminds us today of a butcher shop rather than a place of worship, we should remember that this antithesis would have been meaningless in the biblical world. Not only did the priests live by eating many of the sacrificial victims, but any killing of an animal for food anywhere was considered a kind of religious act—a sacrifice—and certain rituals were prescribed. South of the sacrificial altar was the bronze laver or wash basin, where the priests washed their hands and feet. The water was supplied by pipes from the temple spring.

The temple was burned when Jerusalem fell to the Roman armies in August A.D. 70. Pictures on the Triumphal Arch of Titus in Rome show the soldiers carrying off the temple furniture as loot. This destruction made complete and final the break between the temple and the church and thus helped to establish for the church a ritual completely separate from Israel. The early Christians saw in this forced cessation of the Jewish ritual a proof of the validity of Christ's claims to be the Redeemer foreshadowed by the OT ceremonial law.

In the NT the term *temple* is used figuratively in a number of ways. Jesus spoke of the temple of his body (Jn. 2:19, 21). The individual believer is a temple (1 Cor. 6:19). So also is the church; but this temple, unlike the earthly one, is equally accessible to all believers (Heb. 6:19; 10:20), now freed by Christ from the ritual limitations of the old covenant (Eph. 2:14). The book of Hebrews (especially Heb. 7-10) in great fullness expounds on Christ as the fulfillment of the typology of the temple and its ritual. The culmination of this idea of the "better covenant" is seen in the new Jerusalem: in his vision John "did not see a temple in the city, because the Lord God Almighty and the Lamb are its temple" (Rev. 21:22).

temptation, testing. The idea of putting to the proof—from either a good or bad intention—is found throughout the Bible. Thus the Lord often tests his people with the purpose of strengthening their faith, while SATAN tempts them because he wishes to undermine their faith. Jesus, true man, faced both testing from God and temptation from Satan.

The reason God tests is provided in Deut. 8:2: "Remember how the LORD your God led you all the way in the desert these forty years, to humble you and to test you in order to know what was in your heart, whether or not you would keep his commandments" (cf. 8:16, "to test you so that in the end it may go well with you"). The Lord tests individuals (e.g., Abraham, Gen. 22:1; Job, Job 23:10; Hezekiah, 2 Chr. 32:31) and nations (Deut. 33:8). Sometimes his testing is severe and painful (1 Cor. 11:32; Heb. 12:4-11; 1 Pet. 1:7; 4:8-13), but it originates in holy love.

Not so with Satan. Until Jesus returns, Satan has freedom to tempt people to sin (2 Sam. 24:11; 1 Chr. 21:1). He is called the tempter (Matt. 4:3; 1 Thess. 3:5) and the adversary of Christians (1 Tim. 5:14; 1 Pet. 5:8). God sometimes uses this tempting as his own testing of believers. Satan afflicted Job within limits imposed by God (Job 1:6-22; 2:1-7). Satan deceived Eve (1 Tim. 2:14); Christians are urged to be constantly alert, watching for his temptation (Mk. 14:38; Lk. 22:40; 2 Cor. 2:11; 1 Pet. 5:8). They can overcome; they need to remember God's promise: "God is faithful; he will not let you be tempted beyond what you can bear. But when you are tempted, he will also provide a way out so that you can stand up under it" (1 Cor. 10:13).

In a different sense, people sometimes test God. When Satan tempted Jesus to jump from the pinnacle of the temple, knowing that angels would come to help (Matt. 4:5-6), he was enticing Jesus to

Traditional site of the Mount of Temptation. (View to the W.)

© Dr. James C. Martin

T

put God to the test. In response Jesus quoted Deut. 6:16 and said, "Do not test the LORD your God." The name of MASSAH ("temptation") constituted a reminder of Israel's testing of God in Sinai (Exod. 17:7; Deut. 6:16). To test God is to assert unbelief and lack of trust in him (see Ps. 95:8-11; Acts 5:9; 15:10; 1 Cor. 10:9).

The words "Lead us not into temptation" (Matt. 6:13) are a part of a prayer to be addressed to the Father by his people. Some translations offer, "Do not bring us to the test/trial." This plea seems to ask that we not be forced into tribulation, extreme testing, or great suffering. The next petition is "but deliver us from the evil one," which recognizes that Satan is active in this world, but that God is greater than Satan. See LORD'S PRAYER.

Ten Commandments. See COMMANDMENTS, TEN.

tenon. This English term is used by the KJV and other versions to render the common Hebrew word *yād H3338* ("hand") in several verses (Exod. 26:17, 19; 36:22, 24). The reference is to some kind of wooden peg or projection on the end of a piece of wood for insertion into a corresponding hole in another piece to form a secure joint. The three sides of the TABERNACLE were made of forty-eight "frames," or boards, each one held in place at the bottom by tenons fitted into sockets of silver to give the boards stability.

tent. A temporary dwelling generally made of strong cloth of goat's hair stretched over poles and held in place by cords reaching out to stakes driven into the ground. It is the typical dwelling of nomadic peoples. Tents are of various shapes—round and tapering, flat and oblong. All of a nomadic family's belongings could normally be carried on one pack animal. A sheik would, of course, have several tents. *Tent* often means any habitation (Gen. 9:27; Job 8:22; Ps. 84:10) and is often used figuratively (Isa. 13:20; 54:2; Jer. 10:20). See also TABERNACLE.

tentmaker. See OCCUPATIONS AND PROFESSIONS.

Tent of Meeting. See TABERNACLE.

Terah (person). ter´uh (Heb. *teraḥ H9561*, perhaps "ibex"; Gk. *Thara G2508*). Son of NAHOR and father of ABRAHAM (Gen. 11:24-32; Josh. 24:2; 1 Chr. 1:26); included in Luke's GENEALOGY OF JESUS CHRIST (Lk. 3:34 [KJV, "Thara"]). STEPHEN made reference to Abraham's father without mentioning his name (Acts 7:2). Terah lived in UR of the Chaldees, identified by most scholars as Tell Muqayyar, on the lower EUPHRATES near the Persian Gulf. From Ur, Terah migrated northward some 500 mi. (800 km.) along the Euphrates to the city of Haran, located about 275 mi. (440 km.) NE of DAMASCUS. See HARAN (PLACE). Terah had two other sons, NAHOR and Haran. See HARAN (PERSON). It was Haran's son LOT who eventually went with Abram to PALESTINE. According to Josh. 24:2 and 15, Terah was an idolater.

Terah (place). ter´uh (Heb. *tāraḥ H9562*). KJV Tarah. A stopping place of the Israelites, between Tahath and Mithcah (Num. 33:25-26). The location is unknown.

teraphim. ter´uh-fim (Heb. *tĕrāpîm H9572*, perhaps "weak [*i.e.*, vile] things" or "demons"). This transliteration is used by the KJV in Jdg. 17:5; 18:14-20; and Hos. 3:4. The NRSV uses it also in 2 Ki. 23:24; Ezek. 21:26; and Zech. 10:2. In addition to these passages, the Hebrew word occurs in Gen. 31:19, 34-35; 1 Sam. 15:23; 19:13, 16. The NIV avoids the transliteration altogether and renders the word as "household gods" (or "idols"). The images referred to by this term ranged from rather small (Gen. 31:34-35), to nearly life-sized (1 Sam. 19:13, 16). Archaeological discoveries at NUZI in Iraq have illuminated the function and significance of these idols. Their possession indicated headship of a household with all of the rights attendant thereto. RACHEL's theft of the teraphim (Gen. 31:19) was an attempt to procure such headship for her husband, although it was rightfully her father LABAN's (whose extreme displeasure is explicable in this light).

It appears that throughout much of their history the Israelites did not find possession of teraphim inconsistent with the worship of Yahweh (cf. Jdg. 17; 18; and esp. 1 Sam. 19:13 and 16, which indicate that they were even found in the household of DAVID). They are spoken of with disapproval from the time of SAMUEL (1 Sam. 15:23) to that of ZECHARIAH (Zech. 10:2). The function of teraphim of which the prophets most disapproved was DIVINATION. As divinatory objects they often are mentioned with EPHODS, which were also used for divination (Jdg. 17:5 and 18:14-20, where they seem to be separate from the idol, and Hos. 3:4). Among the things purged during JOSIAH's reform, teraphim seem to be grouped with mediums and wizards (2 Ki. 23:24).

terebinth. See PLANTS.

Teresh. tihr´esh (Heb. *tereš H9575*, meaning uncertain). One of two EUNUCHS or officers in the court of XERXES (Ahasuerus) who plotted his assassination. MORDECAI found out about it, thus saving the king's life, and the two men were hanged (Esth. 2:21-23; 6:2).

terrace. A term used in the KJV for the "steps" that SOLOMON made of algumwood as an approach to the TEMPLE (2 Chr. 9:11).

terror. In ordinary usage this means extreme fear or dread, or sometimes the one who causes such agitation. The word is a translation of about a dozen Hebrew and Greek words that are rendered also by "dread," "fear," "horror," "terribleness," "ruin." Characteristic are Ps. 55:4, "the terrors of death"; Gen. 35:5, "the terror of God"; and 2 Cor. 5:11 (KJV), "the terror of the Lord."

Terror on Every Side. See MAGOR-MISSABIB.

terrorists. See ZEALOT.

Tertius. tuhr´shee-uhs (Gk. *Tertios G5470*, from Latin *Tertius*, "third"). The SCRIBE or AMANUENSIS to whom PAUL dictated his epistle to the ROMANS. Among Paul's greetings to the Christians in ROME, Tertius inserts his own, "I Tertius, who wrote down this letter, greet you in the Lord" (Rom. 16:22). Some speculate that Tertius was himself a Roman Christian living in CORINTH, from where this letter was written.

Tertullus. tuhr-tuhl´uhs (Gk. *Tertyllos G5472*, from Latin *Tertullus*, diminutive of *tertius*, "third").

The professional orator hired by the Jews to state their case against PAUL before FELIX, Roman governor of JUDEA (Acts 24:1-9). He may have been a Roman, judging from his Latin name. With traditional courtesy Tertullus began his clever rhetoric by flattering the governorship of Felix beyond the facts. He attributed the riot in JERUSALEM to the agitation of Paul, ringleader of an illegal sect who was detained in custody by the Jews for trying to "desecrate the temple" (Acts 24:6). Paul was thus made out to be an enemy of the public peace and of Jewish religion, both of which Felix was charged to uphold. The speech of Tertullus should be compared with the factual account of the incident (21:27-40), with the letter of CLAUDIUS LYSIAS the tribune (23:26-30), and with the reserve of Paul's reply (24:10-21).

test. See TEMPTATION.

testament. This English term (Latin *testamentum*, "last will," from *testari*, "to be a witness") is used by the KJV over a dozen times in the NT as the rendering of Greek *diathēkē G1347* (Matt. 26:28 et al.). In extrabiblical literature this Greek word usually meant "last will," but in the NT (and LXX) it appears to mean COVENANT, and it is so rendered usually in modern versions. In two passages, however, the meaning of the word is disputed. The author of Hebrews links *diathēkē* with the death of the person who has made the disposition (Heb. 9:16-17), and therefore most scholars prefer the translation "will" here. Similarly, it is argued by some that when PAUL uses the illustration of a human *diathēkē* as something that cannot be altered (Gal. 3:15), he has in mind a last will or testament (cf. NRSV).

Testaments of the Twelve Patriarchs. See APOCALYPTIC LITERATURE; PSEUDEPIGRAPHA.

testimonia. This Latin term (sg. *testimonium*) is often used in biblical scholarship to designate collections of OT proof texts, especially those that support Jesus' messiahship (cf. the parallel passages Matt. 21:42; Rom. 9:33; 1 Pet. 2:6-8). Some have even argued that the NT writers had recourse to a "Testimony Book" that brought together such texts.

T

testimony. This English word is used variously in Bible translations to render several terms. The word can bear a number of meanings. (1) It may simply be equivalent to "witness," as in 2 Tim. 1:8 (KJV, NRSV), where PAUL exhorts TIMOTHY not to be ashamed of his testimony to Christ. (2) A second sense is that of "evidence" which witnesses to something, as in Acts 14:3, where the KJV reads, "the Lord … gave testimony to the word of his grace." (3) Frequently in the OT "the Testimony" refers to the Decalogue as a pristine statement of God's will, from which comes the expressions "ark of the Testimony" (Exod. 25:16 et al., or simply "the Testimony," 16:34; see ARK OF THE COVENANT) and "tablets of the Testimony" (31:18; 32:15; 34:29). (4) The expression "testimony" was then extended to cover the whole book of the LAW of God (Ps. 78:5 KJV et al.) or to specific commandments (119:22 KJV et al.). (5) In some instances testimony signifies the word of God given to a prophet (Isa. 8:16, 20). (6) In the book of Revelation, the term refers to the GOSPEL (Rev. 1:2 et al.).

tet. tet (Heb. *têt*, meaning uncertain). Also *teth*. The ninth letter of the Hebrew alphabet (ט), with a numerical value of nine. Its sound in Modern Hebrew corresponds to that of English *t*, but in biblical times it was a so-called "emphatic" consonant, possibly characterized by an additional velar articulation (i.e., with the back of the tongue touching or approaching the soft palate) or by a compression of the pharynx.

Tetragrammaton. tet´ruh-gram´uh-ton. Derived from the Greek words for "four" and "letter," this term refers to the four-consonant name of God, YHWH (prob. pronounced *Yahweh*). See JEHOVAH.

tetrarch. See OCCUPATIONS AND PROFESSIONS.

Tetrateuch. tet´ruh-ty*ook*. This term, derived from the Greek words for "four" and "book," is applied to the first four books of the Bible viewed as a group (cf. PENTATEUCH, "five books"; HEXATEUCH, "six books"). While many scholars use this name as a convenient designation, for others it reflects the view that these books should be distinguished from the book of DEUTERONOMY, the latter being considered part of the so-called "Deuteronomistic History."

text and versions (OT). The OT is a book of sacred literature for Jews and Christians and has no rival in quality or scope of influence among other sacred writings of the world today. It is the focal unit of JUDAISM and the foundation of Christianity's sacred literature. The English OT today is identical with the Hebrew Bible but is arranged differently (see CANONICITY). No autograph (original MS) of any OT writing is known to exist today, but the textual critic tries with all available means to reconstruct documents as nearly like the originals as possible. Until 1947, when the DEAD SEA SCROLLS were discovered, the earliest complete extant MSS of the Hebrew Bible were dated about A.D. 1000. There were, however, fragmentary evidences of considerable value, brought to light from time to time by archaeologists, contributing to the establishment of the biblical text.

The OT was originally written in HEBREW, with the exception of a few passages that were composed in ARAMAIC (Dan. 2:4—7:28; Ezra 4:8—6:18; 7:12-26; Jer. 10:11). The Scriptures were written on animal skins (called vellum or PARCHMENT) or on PAPYRUS (the glutinous pith of a water plant by the same name). The Hebrew Bible is the work of many authors over a period of more than a thousand years, roughly between the fifteenth and fifth centuries B.C. As it grew in size it also grew in sacredness and authority for the Jews.

Several factors have militated against the preservation of the original ancient texts. First, when transcriptions were made onto new scrolls, the old deteriorating ones were sometimes destroyed lest they fall into the hands of profane and unscrupulous people. Second, attempts were made at different times by the enemies of the Jews to destroy their sacred literature. ANTIOCHUS Epiphanes (c. 167 B.C.) burned all the copies he could find, and many rolls were destroyed during the Roman wars (c. A.D. 70). Third, the transmission of the Scriptures was affected by repeated copying. Scribal errors and explanatory marginal notes doubtless resulted in deviations from the original. Fortunately, the Hebrew SCRIBES over time developed

Fragments from a Qumran leather scroll of Exodus written with the older Hebrew script (4QpaleoExod^m or 4Q22).

strict methods for copying the Scriptures, so that from about the second century A.D. through the medieval period the OT text suffered very little change.

I. The Hebrew text. Very little is known about the transmission of the Scriptures prior to the time of the Babylonian EXILE, but presumably copies of the TORAH were available to the PRIESTS and LEVITES who ministered outside JERUSALEM (cf. 2 Chr. 17:7-9). It is generally thought that a more systematic approach arose around the time of EZRA, who is described as "a ready scribe in the law of Moses" (Ezra 7:6 KJV; NIV, "a teacher well versed in the Law of Moses"). In any case, a scribal movement certainly developed during the postexilic period. The scribes (Heb. *sôpĕrîm*) functioned as guardians of the Scriptures. They were professional scholars considered to be experts in the knowledge and interpretation of the LAW, and their functions did include the production and preservation of MSS. (It should be remembered that in the ancient world relatively few people could write well, and

only highly educated men served in a secretarial capacity. See article on SCRIBE.) It is evident that Hebrew scribes, in their endeavor to preserve the text from alteration or addition, counted the number of words in each section of Scripture, and also the number of verses and paragraphs. They sometimes placed marginal notes in their MSS, wrote certain letters in unusual ways, or inserted dots or other marks at various places to provide additional information.

Most of the Hebrew MSS of the OT that have been preserved were produced during the Middle Ages by a class of scholars known as the *Masoretes* (also spelled *Massoretes* and *Masorites*; the name derives from the noun *māsōret H5037*, which in postbiblical Hebrew meant "tradition"). The cognate term *Masorah* refers to a special collection of readings and notes compiled by the Masoretes. For a time there were active groups of Masoretes in both Babylonia and Palestine, but it was the work of those in Tiberias in Palestine that came to be accepted as authoritative throughout the Jewish world. The names of several of the Tiberian Masoretes have been preserved. The most prominent were members of the families of Ben Asher and Ben Naphtali.

The tasks performed by the Masoretes may be arranged under four heads. (1) First and most important was the continuation of the work to which the scribes had already devoted much attention, namely, maintaining the integrity of the text of the Scripture. For this purpose they counted the number of letters, words, verses, and parashahs (paragraphs) in each book and indicated its middle word. They noted all peculiar and unusual forms, indicating how frequently each occurred. (2) A second part of their task was the standardization of the pronunciation of the words in the OT. Prior to their time, Hebrew was written with consonants only (although a few of these could be used occasionally to represent vowels). As time went on, there was a tendency to forget in some instances what vowels should be pronounced with the written consonants, and the grammar tended to become confused as well. The Masoretes set themselves industriously at this highly complicated task and developed a detailed system of vocalization. Performing an immense labor of standardizing

T

the grammar, maintaining the ascertained tradition, and working out a method of indicating precisely how they thought each word would rightly be pronounced, they placed indications of vowel pronunciation on every word of the Hebrew Bible. (3) Another facet of their work involved providing an indication to the reader of the cases in which established tradition favored reading a word in a way that did not seem to fit the accepted consonantal text (see KETIB and QERE). (4) Finally, there was a task that may have been even more time-consuming than the other three: the use of marks to indicate cantillation. For many centuries it had been established practice to chant at least a portion of the synagogue reading of the Scripture. To provide a measure of standardization, the Masoretes invented an extremely complicated system of so-called accents.

With the establishment of their new system of vowels and accents, the Tiberian Masoretes had originated a type of text that soon became standard throughout the Jewish world. This textual form came to be known as the Masoretic Text (MT). Although not completely identical to each other, all Masoretic MSS are remarkably alike. Some of the most important are the following: (1) The Cairo Codex of the Prophets (sometimes designated C); dated in 895, it contains the entire second division of the Hebrew Bible. (2) The Petersburg (or Babylonian) Codex of the Prophets (P, also known as Leningrad B-3); dated to the year 916, this document contains only the Latter Prophets. (3) The Aleppo Codex (sometimes designated A) was also produced in the tenth century; regarded by many as the most important Masoretic MS, it originally contained the entire Bible, but about one fourth of it was destroyed. (4) Leningrad Codex B-19A (designated L), dated to the year 1008, is the MS reproduced in the standard printed edition of the Hebrew Bible, *Biblia Hebraica Stuttgartensia* (a new edition, known as *Biblia Hebraica Quinta*, was introduced in 2004 with the publication of a fascicle that includes the MEGILLOTH).

The study of the Hebrew text, however, was advanced dramatically in 1947, when some Palestinian herdsmen accidentally discovered a cave in the Judean hills that proved to be, among other things, a veritable treasure house of ancient Scriptures. The discovery of these scrolls was acclaimed by biblical scholars as the greatest manuscript discovery in modern times. From this and other caves by the Wadi Qumran, NW of the Dead Sea, came a hoard of OT parchments dated 200 B.C. to the first century A.D. Popularly known as the DEAD SEA SCROLLS, these documents have thus pushed back our knowledge of the Hebrew Bible by over a millennium. Some of the MSS contain a textual form that is different from the MT, that is, they preserve a pattern of readings at variance with that found in Masoretic MSS (e.g., some of the fragments of 1 Samuel found in Qumran show closer alignment to the Hebrew text underlying the Greek SEPTUAGINT). Even these differences, however, do not alter in a substantial way the message of the OT. More important, most of the biblical documents among the DSS present a textual form that is extraordinarily close to the MT, thus confirming in a remarkable way the ancient roots of the standard Hebrew Bible. At the same time, it needs to be appreciated that the DSS often preserve variants that have a greater claim to originality than the corresponding MT readings.

II. Ancient versions. Already in antiquity, the Hebrew Bible was translated into several languages. These ancient translations are of great value for text-critical purposes: occasionally they preserve variant readings that are superior to the MT. In addition, since every translation involves interpretation (an attempt to comprehend the original Hebrew), these versions provide considerable information that helps our understanding of the OT. The most important are the following.

(1) Pride of place belongs to the *Septuagint*, the Greek translation of the Hebrew Bible. Strictly speaking, the name *Septuagint* applies only to a Greek version of the PENTATEUCH that was produced in ALEXANDRIA late in the third century B.C. The rest of the OT was translated during the next century or two by various individuals in different places, and competing Greek translations were carried out from about the first century B.C. to the second century A.D. Because of the importance of the Greek versions, a separate article is devoted to them. See SEPTUAGINT.

(2) Translations of the Hebrew Bible into ARAMAIC are known as *Targums* (alternate pl. form

Targumim). Originally these were oral translations produced in the SYNAGOGUES after Aramaic replaced Hebrew as the spoken language of the Jews. These translations contained religious instructions along with interpretations, which accompanied the reading of Scripture in the synagogues. Compare the procedure followed when Jesus was in the synagogue at NAZARETH (Lk. 4:16-27). Eventually, these oral traditions were put down in writing. The official rabbinic versions in Aramaic were *Targum Onkelos* on the Pentateuch and *Targum of Jonathan* on the Prophets (including the "Former Prophets," i.e., Joshua, Judges, 1-2 Samuel, 1-2 Kings), both of which took final form in Babylonian Judaism. In addition, there are several other Aramaic versions of the Pentateuch, often grouped together under the rubric *Palestinian Targum*. The SAMARITANS had their own Aramaic translation of the Pentateuch, known as the *Samaritan Targum*.

(3) The name *Peshitta* (also *Peshiṭta* and *Peshitto*), meaning "stretched out" or "simple," is applied to the standard translation of the Bible used by Syriac-speaking churches. Syriac is a dialect of Aramaic (usually classed as a form of Eastern Aramaic because it shares features with Jewish Babylonian Aramaic and Mandaic). The designation *Peshitta*, first used c. A.D. 900, perhaps indicates only that it was the "common" or "widely diffused" version (cf. the term *Vulgate*), but possibly it is intended to contrast this translation from others that were accompanied by special textual markings. The origins of the Peshitta of the OT are uncertain. Parts of it, such as the Pentateuch, may have been produced by a Jewish community, and most of it seems to have been completed during the second century A.D.

(4) The Latin translation of the Bible exists in two forms. (a) The *Vetus Latina* or Old Latin (OL) is a translation not of the Hebrew Bible but of the Greek Septuagint; being a "secondary" version, it is thus of lesser value than those based directly on the Hebrew text. The OL was likely produced in N Africa, where Latin was the common and official language. However, the books of both the OT and the NT were translated piecemeal by different people at different times, and by the fourth century the form of the text differed widely from place to place. (b) *Vulgate* is the name applied to the standard Latin translation of the Bible (the Lat. adjective *vulgatus* means "commonly known, in wide circulation"). About the year 382 Pope Damasus commissioned Jerome to revise and standardize the Latin Bible. With regard to the OT, this meant not just a revision of the OL; to a large extent, the work involved a fresh translation directly from the Hebrew. Completed in 405, the Vulgate is a creditable work, and in Western Christianity it was virtually without a rival for a thousand years. Up until the latter part of the twentieth century, modern-language versions of the Bible sponsored by the Roman Catholic Church (e.g., the Rheims-Douay version in English) were based on the Vulgate.

text and versions (NT). The Bible, and especially the NT, occupies a unique place in the literature of ancient times, and part of that uniqueness is the history of its transmission through the centuries: (a) no ancient writing comes close to the Bible in the number of copies made of it from the time it was written until the age of printing; (b) the existing biblical MSS approach the date of its origin far more closely than do the MSS of almost any other piece of ancient literature; and (c) the NT (with the OT) stands virtually alone, among ancient writings, in the extent to which it was translated

Codex Vaticanus, showing Acts 15:25-36.

© Dr. James C. Martin. Sola Scriptura. The Van Kampen Collection on display at the Holy Land Experience in Orlando, Florida. Photographed by permission.

into other languages. In the beginning, of course, there was no "New Testament" as a single volume. The individual books were written over a period of years and afterward were gradually brought together (see CANONICITY).

I. Greek manuscripts. What did a book of the NT look like when it was first written? Its language was GREEK. There doubtless were both written and oral records, probably both in ARAMAIC and in Greek, that lay behind the GOSPELS. Proof is lacking, however, that any of the NT books as such were originally written in Aramaic.

An original copy of a NT book was probably written on PAPYRUS sheets, either folded into a codex, which is the modern book form, or possibly on a papyrus roll (SCROLL). It was long thought that the earliest copies of the NT books were written in roll form, since this was the regular form for both the OT and for other literary writings of the period. However, even the very oldest NT papyrus MSS or fragments that are now known are in the codex form, not the roll. Although the codex form was used for notes, rough drafts of an author's work, etc., the early Christians were evidently pioneers in using the codex form for literary purposes. The codex was far better suited for ready reference to passages and was generally easier to use than the roll. Important papyrus MSS of the NT include several dated to the early third century or even late second century, such as P[46] (Pauline epistles), P[66] (Gospel of John), and P[75] (Luke and John). The earliest known NT papyrus is the Rylands Fragment, P[52], which contains only a few lines from Jn. 18 and is usually dated no later than A.D. 135.

The style of the Greek script in the original of a NT book may have been one of two in common use. Literary works of the period were written in *uncial* or *majuscule* letters: rounded capitals, the letters not connected to each other. A *cursive* or *minuscule* hand, in which the letters were connected, somewhat as in English longhand writing, was used for personal letters, business receipts, and other nonliterary materials. The Greek MSS were written with no separation between words. This was simply an accepted custom (Latin MSS similarly do not separate words, but Hebrew MSS do). The originals of PAUL's epistles were possibly written in the cursive hand if they were regarded as private correspondence; the Gospels would probably have been originally written in uncial letters. Of course, when Paul's letters began to be copied and recopied, they would be thought of as public writings and would doubtless soon be copied in uncial letters. All of the earliest known MSS of the NT are written in uncial letters.

During the first three Christian centuries papyrus was the primary writing material. Sheets were made from thin strips of the papyrus reed, which grew along the NILE and in a very few other places in the MEDITERRANEAN world. The strips were laid side by side, with a second layer placed on top at right angles to the first layer. Pounded together and dried in the sun, these sheets made very serviceable material for writing with a reed pen. In a roll, the side that normally received the writing was the side on which the strips were horizontal. In the codex form, both sides would be used, but the *verso*, where the strips were vertical, would give the writer more difficulty than the *recto*.

At the beginning of the fourth century, a notable change occurred in the production of NT MSS, when vellum or PARCHMENT began to displace papyrus as a writing material. The use of tanned skins for a writing material had long been known and was commonly used for the Hebrew OT. Vellum and parchment, however, are skins that have been treated with lime and made into a thin material having a smooth, firm writing surface. The term *vellum* was applied to the finer skins of calf, kid, or lamb; and *parchment* (from Pergamum, a city prominent in its manufacture) was applied to ordinary skins; but the two terms are now used synonymously. A few papyrus MSS of the NT from the fifth and sixth centuries are known; but apparently papyrus was quickly displaced by the far more durable parchment, and the fourth century may be called the beginning of the parchment period of NT MSS, a period lasting until the introduction of paper as a writing material in the fourteenth century. The earliest NT parchments are often referred to as the "great uncials": Codex Alexandrinus (symbol A) was produced in the fifth century, while Codices Vaticanus (B) and Sinaiticus (‫א‬ or S) are dated to the middle of the fourth century. These three MSS include the books of the SEPTUAGINT.

© Dr. James C. Martin. Sola Scriptura. The Van Kampen Collection on display at the Holy Land Experience in Orlando, Florida. Photographed by permission.

A 9th-cent. Greek MS of the Gospel according to Mark.

In the ninth century another significant change occurred, with the development of the cursive style of handwriting into a literary hand called *minuscule*. By the end of the tenth century the uncial hand had been completely displaced by the minuscule, which remained the regular style of writing until the invention of printing.

We may summarize as follows: from the first to the fourth century, NT MSS were written in uncial letters on papyrus; from the fourth to the tenth, in uncial letters on vellum; from the tenth to the fourteenth, in minuscule letters on vellum; from the fourteenth to the invention of printing in the fifteenth century, in minuscule letters on paper. Over 115 papyrus MSS and fragments are known, about 310 uncials, 2,880 minuscules, and 2,430 lectionaries (MSS that contain NT passages organized for reading on particular days).

II. Variant readings. Since copies were made individually by hand, mistakes and changes inevitably occurred—omissions, additions, changes of words, word order, and spelling—usually unintentionally made, but sometimes intentionally to clarify, explain, or to avoid a doctrinal misunderstanding. In the MSS now known there are thousands of these "variants." The vast majority, however, make no difference in meaning; and the application of accepted principles of textual criticism makes it possible to determine the original form of the text for all practical purposes, though not to verbal perfection. No fundamental Christian doctrine is left in doubt by any textual variant.

These variants, moreover, tended to group themselves into companies. A MS tended to contain the errors of the MS from which it was copied. As MSS were carried to various cities and lands, and as copies were made from accessible documents, the MSS of a given region would tend to contain a similar group of variants, and these would be somewhat different from the variants of MSS in another region. Scholars recognize at least two "text-types" that can be dated as far back as as the third century or even earlier: the Alexandrian (a textual form dominant in EGYPT) and the "Western" (a misleading term that is applied to most Latin witnesses, but also to some evidence from Greek-speaking and Eastern Christianity). Another proposed text-type, the Caesarean, is not accepted by all scholars. After the official recognition of Christianity in the fourth century, with more opportunity to compare MSS, these "local texts" were gradually displaced by a textual form that tended to smooth out rough constructions, harmonize parallel passages, and make for ease of understanding. This text-type, known as "Byzantine" (also "Syrian," "Traditional," "Majority"), became dominant by the eighth century and is found in the majority of surviving MSS. Some time after the invention of printing, it came to be known as the *Textus Receptus* (TR), the "received" or accepted text. The TR was the basis of the KJV and most modern translations until the end of the nineteenth century, at which time the derivative character of the Byzantine text-type was acknowledged by most scholars. (Some, however, argue that this "Majority" text is in fact the earliest form and thus closest to the original.)

III. Patristic quotations. If every MS of the NT itself were destroyed, the NT could virtually be reconstructed from another significant source: the thousands of quotations of NT passages in the writings of the ancient church fathers, principally in Greek, Latin, and Syriac. These quotations must be consulted with care, as they were often given from memory or simply as a scriptural allusion and hence not verbally exact. Yet many are textually reliable; and these are valuable, because readings quoted by a particular church father can usually be assumed to have been current during that person's lifetime and in the region of his activity.

IV. Ancient versions. In the case of most ancient writings, when the MSS in the original language of the work have been consulted, the limits of the field have been reached. The Bible, especially the NT, is therefore virtually unique in ancient literature in this respect, for not only was it translated into other languages in the earliest centuries of its history, but these translations are sufficiently accurate to be of help in textual criticism in determining the original text of the NT. Of course, no original MSS of these ancient translations remain, and the copies that are known must first be examined to determine the original text of the translation. Moreover, certain types of Greek variants would not be reflected in certain versions (e.g., the presence or absence of a definite article in Greek would not normally be reflected in Latin, as Latin has no definite article). Nevertheless, the versions are of great value, not least in helping to show the regions in which certain textual readings were current.

The NT must have been translated into Latin, the official language of the ROMAN EMPIRE, very shortly after the books were written and certainly before the end of the second century. The forty or so extant MSS of this Old Latin (*Vetus Latina*) differ extensively among themselves, and it is not clear whether they represent one or several translations. As a result of these variations, in 382 Pope Damasus commissioned Jerome to undertake a revision of the Latin Bible. In the NT Jerome worked cautiously, making changes only where he felt they were absolutely necessary. This revision, the Latin Vulgate, became the official Bible of the Western church and remains the official Roman Catholic Bible. Probably eight thousand MSS are in existence.

Syriac, a dialect related to ARAMAIC, which was spoken in lands around PALESTINE, likewise received the NT during the second century. The first such translation seems to have been either the original or a translation of a Greek original of a continuous gospel account known as the Diatessaron (meaning "through the four"), constructed by combining elements from all four Gospels. It was composed about 160 by Tatian and seems to have been the Syriac gospel in common use for over a century. There was also made, however, perhaps in the second century, a translation of the four Gospels known as the Old Syriac, which is now known in two MSS, the Sinaitic and the Curetonian.

The Syriac that is still the standard version is the *Peshitta* (meaning "simple"), translated in the fifth century, perhaps by Rabbula, bishop of Edessa. Some 250 MSS are known, none of which contains 2 Peter, 2 and 3 John, Jude, or Revelation. The Peshitta was revised in 508 by authority of Philoxenus, bishop of Mabbog. It is thought by some that this Philoxenian version still exists in or is related to the current Syriac text of the four books named above, which were not in the original Peshitta but are now printed in the Syriac NT. The Philoxenian was in turn revised in 616 by Thomas of Harkel. The Harklean Syriac is such an extremely literal translation from the Greek that it even violates Syriac idiom at times to follow the Greek. It is likewise characterized by numerous marginal alternative readings, often in Greek. About fifty MSS of this version are known. (The Palestinian Syriac version, made about the sixth century, is a distinct work found mainly in lectionaries.)

Likewise significant in textual criticism are the two principal versions of Egypt. The earlier of these is the Sahidic, the dialect of S Egypt, which probably received its NT in the third century; it exists in numerous but fragmentary MSS. The Bohairic, the dialect of Alexandria and the Nile delta, was more literary and later displaced the other dialects to become the current Coptic; about one hundred MSS of the Bohairic NT are known. There are also fragments of versions in three other Egyptian dialects: Fayumic, Middle Egyptian, and Akhmimic.

Although less significant for text-critical purposes, a number of other versions should be noted. The Gothic, translated very accurately from the Greek by the Gothic Bishop Ulfilas, dates from the fourth century and is the earliest version representing the Byzantine text-type. The Armenian originated about A.D. 400, probably made from Syriac;

many MSS of the Armenian version are known, but only one is earlier than the tenth century. The Georgian probably was in existence before the middle of the fifth century, apparently translated from Armenian. The Ethiopic Version originated about the year 600, perhaps translated from Syriac. Versions exist also in Arabic, Persian, Slavonic, and other languages.

Textus Receptus. See TEXT AND VERSIONS (NT).

Thaddaeus. thad'ee-uhs, tha-dee'uhs (Gk. *Thaddaios G2497*, perhaps from Aram. *taddā'*, "breast," but more likely a short form of *Theodosios* or some other name compounded with *Theos G2536*, "God"). One of the twelve apostles (Matt. 10:3; Mk. 3:18). In Matt. 10:3 the KJV follows the Textus Receptus in reading "Lebbaeus, whose surname was Thaddaeus" (both here and in Mk. 3:18 some MSS have LEBBAEUS only instead of Thaddaeus). The parallel lists in Luke-Acts have, instead of Thaddaeus, "Judas son of James" (Lk. 6:16; Acts 1:13; the KJV interprets the text to mean "Judas *the brother* of James"]). See JUDAS #4. Presumably, the names Thaddaeus and Judas refer to the same person. If so, it is uncertain whether Thaddaeus was a secondary name borne by this apostle or whether it (like Lebbaeus?) was a descriptive designation introduced in the Gospels to avoid confusion with JUDAS ISCARIOT.

Thahash. See TAHASH.

Thamah. See TEMAH.

Thamar. See TAMAR.

thankfulness, thanksgiving. See GRATITUDE; PRAYER.

thank offering. See SACRIFICE AND OFFERINGS.

Thara. See TERAH.

Tharshish. See TARSHISH.

theater. In the ancient world, the theater was a structure usually open-air and semicircular, with stone seats. Greek theaters, found as early as the fifth century B.C., were on hillsides to take advantage of natural land formations; these structures were acoustically remarkable. Early Roman theaters were erected as free-standing buildings supported by arch construction. They were used for presentation of dramatic productions, pageants, religious rites, choral singing, games, gladiatorial contests, and public assemblies and forums of citizens. A religious ceremony and drama involving OSIRIS was performed yearly by the Egyptians as early as 2000 B.C., but there is no evidence that ISRAEL ever produced a drama or had theaters. Religious DANCING, however, is found in the OT (Exod. 15:20; 2 Sam. 6:16), and the books of JOB and SONG OF SOLOMON are cast in dramatic dialogue form.

No later civilizations have surpassed the Greek genius for drama. The Greek drama was inextricably bound up with religion, particularly the festival to Dionysus, the wine god, often degenerating into orgies. Menander (342-291 B.C.) was the outstanding figure in the later Greek theater. The Romans introduced the Greek drama as they conquered and assimilated the Hellenistic culture. The growth and proliferation of the Roman theater paralleled the fortunes of the empire. HEROD the Great built theaters in JERUSALEM, CAESAREA, GADARA, and other cities. Theaters were commonly used for public gatherings, since they were likely to provide the largest places of assembly in the city; hence the use of the only theater mentioned in the NT (Acts 19:29), that of EPHESUS.

The theater of ancient Hierapolis in W Asia Minor. (View to the S.)

© Dr. James C. Martin

The ruins of this theater, a most imposing structure seating twenty-five thousand people, have been excavated. Roman theaters tended to be more elaborate than those of the Greeks, contained a more finished stage, and, perhaps in conformity with the needs of a severer climate, were at least in part roofed over.

Thebes. theebz (Gk. *Thēbai*). Greek name given to the ancient capital of Upper EGYPT, corresponding to modern Luxor and Karnak, some 450 mi. (725 km.) S of Cairo. The Egyptians themselves referred to it in several ways, including Weset and City of Amun/Amon (Egyp. *nwt ʾmn*, thus Heb. *nōʾʾāmôn* H5531 [Nah. 3:8; cf. Jer. 46:25] or simply *nōʾ* H5530 [Ezek. 30:14-16]). See AMON #4. It is uncertain why the Greeks gave to it the name Thebes (also the name of several others sites, including an important city in the region of Boeotia, NNW of ATHENS). On the E bank of the NILE, the town focused on the two vast temples of the god Amon at Karnak and Luxor, less than 2 mi. (3 km.) apart. On the W bank, Thebes boasted a row of funerary temples of the kings along the desert edge. Behind these, the tomb chapels of their officials were carved in the rocky hills, whereas the tunnel tombs of the PHARAOHS and their wives were hidden away in the Valleys of the Kings and Queens behind the western cliffs. The temples and tombs on both banks contain a wealth of inscriptions, reliefs, and paintings of the utmost value as background to OT life and times. Unimportant and little known in the third millennium B.C., the city rose into prominence when the Theban 11th and 12th dynasties respectively restored the unity and prosperity of Egypt. The 18th dynasty founded Egypt's empire (18th-20th dynasties, c. 1550-1085 B.C.), to which epoch belong most of the greatest and finest Theban monuments. Amon of Thebes was virtually god of the empire, and in his temples were amassed vast riches. In the time of decline in the first millennium B.C., when royal (and real) power lay in the N, Thebes was still a proud religious center until sacked by the Assyrians in 663 B.C.

Thebez. thee′biz (Heb. *tēbēṣ* H9324, derivation unknown). A fortified town within the tribal territory of MANASSEH, not far from SHECHEM. ABI-MELECH son of GIDEON met his death here when a woman fatally wounded him by throwing an upper millstone from a tower on the wall of the city (Jdg. 9:50). The ignominious death of Abimelech became proverbial in Israel (2 Sam. 11:21). The precise location of Thebez is uncertain, but some scholars identify it with modern Tubas, about 10 mi. (16 km.) NE of Shechem (modern Nablus), on the main highway to BETH SHAN. This geographical area afforded military significance while the fertile valley provided commercial value.

theft. See COMMANDMENTS, TEN; ROBBERY; THIEF.

theism. Belief in the existence of GOD. The terms *atheism*, the dogmatic denial of God, and *agnosticism*, a profession of ignorance, indicate a material distinction from theism. The term *deism* (derived from Latin), though it is the linguistic equivalent of *theism* (derived from Greek), refers to a system of thought based on natural religion and denying that God interferes with the laws of the universe he created.

Thelasar. See TEL ASSAR.

theocracy. Government by divine rule (from Gk. *theos* G2536, "God," and *krateō* G3195, "to control, rule"). The term is distinguished from *democracy*, which places the ultimate power of the government in the hands of all the people; from *hierocracy*, the rule of the priests, which relegates to a religious class unique insight into the will of God; and from *monarchy*, which has a human king or queen to rule over a nation. The word does not appear in the Bible and seems to have been invented by JOSEPHUS, who used *theokratia* to describe the unique character of the Hebrew government (*Against Apion* 2.165). The best and perhaps the only true illustration among nations is ISRAEL from the time that God redeemed them from the power of the PHARAOH and gave them his law at Mount Sinai (Exod. 15:13; 19:5-6), until the time when SAMUEL acceded to their demand, "Now appoint a king to lead us, such as all the other nations have" (1 Sam. 8:5). During this period God ruled through Moses (Exod. 19-Deut. 34), then through JOSHUA (Josh. 1-24), and finally through "judges" whom he raised up from time to time to deliver his people. From the human standpoint, the power was largely in the hands of the priests, who acted on the basis of laws passed by God, in which were united all the powers of the state—legislative, executive, and judicial. Such a government was, of course, possible only because of God's special REVELATION of himself to the nation.

theodicy. This term (from Gk. *theos G2536*, "God," and *dikē G1472*, "judgment") means "the act of justifying God" and refers to defending both his goodness and omnipotence in the face of EVIL. The Bible confronts the problem of evil on nearly all of its pages. While it ultimately gives no rational explanation for the origins of evil, it places it utterly within God's plan and his control. And it presents the most fundamental answer to it—in Jesus Christ.

Theodotion. See SEPTUAGINT.

theophany. This theological term (from Gk. *theos G2536*, "God," and *phainō G5743*, pass. "appear") refers to any temporary, normally visible, manifestation of God. It is to be distinguished from that permanent manifestation of God in Jesus CHRIST called the INCARNATION. Most of its examples must be sought in the OT, though some would include cases mentioned in the NT, such as the heavenly voice and "dove" at Jesus' baptism (Matt. 3:16-17), the voice at the TRANSFIGURATION (17:5) and in the PASSION week (Jn. 12:28), the visible coming of the HOLY SPIRIT (Acts 2:2-3), STEPHEN's vision (7:55-56), and PAUL's Damascus experience (9:3-5). Theophanies are relatively common in GENESIS (e.g., Gen. 3:8; 5:24; 6:9; 18:1-33; 28:10-17). This is easily explicable by the lack of written Scriptures and by the isolated position of the few faithful individuals whose lives are recorded. They are found again in the decisive events of the EXODUS, the conquest of Canaan, and in some of the narratives of the judges. After this they are rare except in the accounts of the PROPHETS, especially in the visions accompanying their call. There is good reason to think that theophanies before the incarnation of Christ were visible manifestations of the preincarnate Son of God. Theophanies of the

Holy Spirit since apostolic times look back to the supreme revelation of Jesus Christ.

Theophilus. thee-of'uh-luhs (Gk. *Theophilos G2541*, "lover [*or* friend] of God"). A man to whom the Gospel of Luke and the Acts of the Apostles were addressed (Lk. 1:3; Acts 1:1). His identity is uncertain and may only be conjectured from the literary conventions of the time and the purposes for which Luke-Acts was written. It has been suggested that LUKE wrote to a Christian audience and that a name with this meaning is a generic term for all of Luke's Christian readers. Appropriately, the book would then be addressed to any "friend of God" who wanted more detailed and accurate information concerning the origin and meaning of his faith. On the other hand, books intended for the general public were sometimes dedicated to a friend and patron who might be able to contribute to the cost of disseminating an otherwise unknown work, or who had suggested its composition. Furthermore, in the gospel Theophilus is described as *kratiste* (vocative of *kratistos G3196*, "most excellent"), a title of conspicuous rank or office (cf. Acts 23:26; 24:3; 26:25). This detail indicates that Luke had a definite person in mind, probably a respected Roman official who had been informed of Christianity and the life of Christ or possibly catechized as a convert. If Theophilus was a questioning catechumen in preparation for Christian baptism, it is understandable why Luke says that he has written his gospel "so that you may have certainty of the things you have been taught" (Lk. 1:4). Others point out that this title can be used in a friendly way as a form of polite or flattering address with no official connotation.

Thessalonians, Letters to the. With the possible exception of GALATIANS, 1 and 2 Thessalonians are the earliest letters surviving from the correspondence of PAUL. They were written to the church in THESSALONICA, which was founded by Paul on his second journey en route from PHILIPPI to ACHAIA. His preaching of Jesus as the MESSIAH aroused such violent controversy in the SYNAGOGUE at Thessalonica that the opposing Jewish faction brought him before the city magistrates, charging him with fomenting insurrection against CAESAR

Overview of 1 THESSALONIANS

Author: The apostle PAUL.

Historical setting: Written from CORINTH during the second missionary journey (c. A.D. 50), in response to a report from TIMOTHY (1 Thess. 3:6).

Purpose: To reassure the recently converted Christians in THESSALONICA of Paul's love for them; to exhort them to holy living; to comfort them by providing instruction concerning Christ's return.

Contents: After an introduction (1 Thess. 1), the apostle explains the nature of his ministry and his concern for the Thessalonians (chs. 2-3), and then proceeds to deal with problems in the church.

(Acts 17:5-9). Paul's friends were placed under bond for his good behavior, and to protect their own security, they sent him away from the city. He proceeded to BEREA, and after a short stay, interrupted by a fanatical group of Jews from Thessalonica, he went on to ATHENS, leaving SILAS and TIMOTHY to continue the preaching (17:10-14). From Athens he sent back instructions that they should join him as quickly as possible (17:15). According to 1 Thessalonians, they did so, and evidently he sent Timothy back again to encourage the Thessalonians while he continued at Athens (1 Thess. 3:2). In the meantime Paul moved on to CORINTH; and there Timothy and Silas found him when they returned with the news of the growth of the Thessalonian church (3:6; Acts 18:5). The first letter was prompted by Timothy's report.

I. 1 Thessalonians. There can be no reasonable doubt concerning the genuineness of this letter. Allusions to it can be found early in the second century, and the earliest direct references attribute it to Paul. As already noted, the information provided by 1 Thessalonians corresponds well with the data on the life of Paul given in Acts. Furthermore, no forger of the second century would have been likely to stress the imminency of the coming of CHRIST as Paul did.

Paul's stay both in Thessalonica and in Athens was brief, and he probably arrived in Corinth about A.D. 50. According to the narrative in Acts,

Paul had begun his ministry there while working at the tentmaker's trade with AQUILA and PRISCILLA (Acts 18:1-3). When Silas and Timothy rejoined him after their stay in MACEDONIA, they brought funds that enabled Paul to stop working and to devote his entire time to evangelism (Acts 18:5; 2 Cor. 11:9). Shortly afterward the Jewish opposition to Paul's preaching became so violent that he was forced out of the synagogue. About a year and a half later he was called before the tribunal of GALLIO, the Roman PROCONSUL (Acts 18:12). Gallio had taken office only a short time previously, in 51 or 52. The first letter, then, must have been written at Corinth about a year prior to that date, in 50 or 51.

Timothy's report included details about problems in the Thessalonian church, and Paul dealt with these in his letter. Some of his Jewish enemies had attacked his character, putting him under obligation to defend himself (1 Thess. 2:1-6, 10, 14-16). A few of the converts were still influenced by the lax morality of the paganism from which they had so recently emerged and in which they had to live (4:3-7). Some of the church members had died, causing the rest to worry whether their departed friends would share in the return of Christ (4:13). Still others, anticipating the second advent, had given up all regular employment and were idly waiting for the Lord to appear (4:9-12). The letter was intended to encourage the Thessalonians' growth as Christians and to settle the

Overview of 2 THESSALONIANS

Author: The apostle PAUL (though some modern scholars dispute this attribution).

Historical setting: Written from CORINTH during the second missionary journey (c. A.D. 51), in response to news of further problems in the church at THESSALONICA.

Purpose: To provide additional instruction regarding the coming of Christ and appropriate Christian living.

Contents: After an introduction (2 Thess. 1), the apostle clarifies that certain events must take place before the coming of the DAY OF THE LORD (ch. 2) and exhorts the Thessalonians to pray, to be industrious, and to exercise church discipline (ch. 3).

questions that were troubling them. The contents may be outlined as follows.

A. The conversion of the Thessalonians (1:1-10)
B. The ministry of Paul (2:1—3:13)
   1. In founding the church (2:1-20)
   2. In concern for the church (3:1-13)
C. The problems of the church (4:1—5:22)
   1. Moral instruction (4:1-12)
   2. The Lord's coming (4:13—5:11)
   3. Ethical duties (5:12-22)
D. Conclusion (5:23-28)

First Thessalonians is a friendly, personal letter. The persecution in Thessalonica and the uncertainty concerning the coming of Christ that Paul had preached had disturbed the believers. Paul devoted the first half of his letter to reviewing his relationship with them in order to counteract the attacks of his enemies. The body of teaching in the second half of the letter dealt with sexual immorality by insisting on standards of holiness. The chief doctrinal topic was the second coming of Christ. Paul assured his readers that those who had died would not perish, but that they would be resurrected at the return of Christ. In company with the living believers, who would be taken up to heaven, all would enter into eternal fellowship with Christ (1 Thess. 4:13-18). Since the exact time of the return was not known, they were urged to be watchful, that they might not be taken unaware.

II. 2 Thessalonians. The genuineness of 2 Thessalonians has been challenged, mainly because of its difference from 1 Thessalonians: the warning of signs preceding the DAY OF THE LORD (2 Thess. 2:1-3) in contrast to a sudden and unannounced appearing (1 Thess. 5:1-3); the teaching on the "man of lawlessness" (2 Thess. 2:3-9; see ANTICHRIST), unique in Paul's letters; and the generally more somber tone of the whole letter have been alleged as reason for rejecting authorship by Paul. None of these is convincing, for the two letters deal with two different aspects of the same general subject, and bear so many resemblances to each other that they are clearly related. Early evidence for the acceptance of 2 Thessalonians is almost as full as for that of 1 Thessalonians. Shadowy references to it appear in the APOSTOLIC FATHERS; later second-century writers mention it definitely as one of the letters of Paul.

The second letter was probably sent from Corinth in A.D. 51, not more than a few months after the first letter. Since Silas and Timothy were still with Paul, it is likely that no great interval elapsed between the writing of the two. Evidently the Thessalonian Christians had been disturbed by the arrival of a letter purporting to come from Paul—a letter he had not authorized (2 Thess. 2:2). Some of them were suffering harsh persecution (1:4-5); others were apprehensive that the last day was about to arrive (2:2); and there were still a few who were idle and disorderly (3:6-12). The second letter serves to clarify further the problems of the first letter and to confirm the confidence of the readers. The contents may be outlined as follows.

A. Salutation (1:1-2)
B. Encouragement in persecution (1:3-12)
C. The signs of the day of Christ (2:1-17)
    1. Warning of false rumors (2:1-2)
    2. The apostasy (2:3)
    3. The revelation of the man of sin (2:4-12)
    4. The preservation of God's people (2:13-17)
D. Spiritual counsel (3:1-15)
E. Conclusion (3:16-18)

Whereas the first letter heralds the RESURRECTION of the righteous dead and the restoration of the living at the return of Christ, the second letter describes the apostasy preceding the coming of Christ to judgment. Paul stated that the "secret power of lawlessness" was already at work and that its climax would be reached with the removal of "the one who now holds it back" (2 Thess. 2:7), who has been variously identified with the HOLY SPIRIT, the power of the ROMAN EMPIRE, and the preaching of Paul himself. With the disappearance of any spiritual restraint, the "man of lawlessness" will be revealed, who will (2:3-10) deceive all people and will be energized by the power of Satan himself.

In view of this prospect, Paul exhorted the Thessalonians to retain their faith and to improve their conduct. He spoke even more vehemently to those who persisted in idleness (2 Thess. 3:6-12), recommending that the Christians withdraw fellowship from them.

Thessalonica. thes'uh-luh-ni'kuh (Gk. *Thessalonikē G2553*; gentilic *Thessalonikeus G2552*, "Thessalonian"). The capital city of the Roman province of MACEDONIA. Thessalonica (modern Thessaloniki, sometimes referred to as Salonica) was founded by Cassander, ALEXANDER THE GREAT's officer who took control of GREECE after Alexander's death in 332 B.C. The city was probably founded toward the end of the century by consolidating small towns at the head of the Thermaic Gulf. It dominated the junction of the northern trade route and the road from the Adriatic to Byzantium, which later became the VIA EGNATIA. Its comparatively sheltered harbor made it the chief port of Macedonia, after Pella yielded to the silting that was the perennial problem of Greek harbors. It was a fortress that withstood a Roman siege, surrendering only after the battle of Pydna sealed Rome's victory in the Macedonian Wars. In 147 B.C. it became the capital of the Roman province and was POMPEY's base a century later in the civil war with Julius CAESAR. Prolific coinage suggests a high level of prosperity. The population included a large Roman element and a Jewish colony. Paul visited Thessalonica after PHILIPPI and appears to have worked among a composite group, comprising the Jews of the synagogue and Greek PROSELYTES, among whom were some women of high social standing (Acts 17:1-9; there was a high degree of emancipation among the women of Macedonia). He then revisited Macedonia during his third journey (19:21). Some years later, while in prison at ROME, Paul entertained a hope of visiting the area again (Phil. 1:25-26; 2:24). After his release, he ministered in the

© Dr. James C. Martin

Excavations of the *cardo* (main street) at Thessalonica.

Thessalonica.

vicinity of Thessalonica and may well have revisited the city (1 Tim. 1:3; 2 Tim. 4:13; Tit. 3:12). A few of the converts of his ministry are mentioned by name: JASON (Acts 17:5-9; cf. Rom. 16:21); possibly DEMAS (2 Tim. 4:10); Gaius (Acts 19:29; cf. 20:4); SECUNDUS and ARISTARCHUS (20:4).

Theudas. thoo´duhs (Gk. *Theudas G2554*, possibly short form of *Theodōros*, "gift of God" or a similar compound). Leader of a rebellion that failed, mentioned by GAMALIEL in a speech before the SANHEDRIN (Acts 5:35-36). Gamaliel cautions the Jewish leadership to be tolerant of the Christian apostles: he reasons that if the apostolic activity were of human origin only, it would fail of itself; but if it were of divine origin, nothing they did could stop it. The death of Theudas and the dispersion of his four hundred followers is cited as a basis for Gamaliel's thesis. JOSEPHUS (*Ant.* 20.5.1) writes of a certain Theudas, a magician who around A.D. 44 led a great band of adherents to the Jordan, promising to divide it for an easy passage of the river, but was caught and beheaded by the soldiers of the procurator Fadus. This cannot have been the same Theudas as the insurgent mentioned in Acts, since Gamaliel's speech would have taken place in the early 30s; moreover, Gamaliel says that Theudas arose before the insurrection led by Judas the Galilean in the days of the taxing under QUIRINIUS about A.D. 6 (see JUDAS #3). It is not necessary to

impugn the historical accuracy of Acts here by assuming that Luke transposed Theudas and Judas, or that he misplaced Gamaliel's speech by moving it from a later section. Nor did Luke misread Josephus (who did not publish his *Antiquities* until A.D. 93). In view of the "ten thousand other disorders" mentioned by Josephus (*Ant.* 17.10.4), there could well have been more than one insurrectionist named Theudas.

thief, thieves. The word is used for anyone who appropriates someone else's property, including petty thieves and highwaymen (Lk. 10:30; Jn. 12:6). Under the law of MOSES, thieves who were caught were expected to restore twice the amount stolen. The thieves crucified with Jesus must have been robbers or brigands, judging by the severity of the punishment and the fact that one of them acknowledged that the death penalty imposed on them was just (Lk. 23:41). See also COMMANDMENTS, TEN; ROBBERY.

thigh. The upper part of a human leg, or the rear leg of a quadruped. To put one's hand under the thigh of another was to enhance the sacredness of an OATH (Gen. 24:2, 9; 47:29). To "smite hip and thigh" (Jdg. 15:8 KJV) implied not only slaughter but slaughter with extreme violence. When the ANGEL of the Lord wrestled with JACOB so that Jacob might know the weakness of his human strength, he touched the hollow (NIV, "socket") of Jacob's thigh and threw it out of joint at the hip, altering Jacob's position from struggling to clinging. When he was thus transformed, God changed his name from Jacob ("supplanter") to ISRAEL ("he struggles with God"); recalling this event, the Israelites "do not eat the tendon attached to the socket of the hip" (Gen. 32:24-32). In oriental feasts the shoulder or the thigh of the meat is often placed before an honored guest (cf. 1 Sam. 9:23-24); he has the privilege of sharing it with those near him. The thigh was the place to strap a sword (Jdg. 3:16; Ps. 45:3; Cant. 3:8). To smite one's thigh (Jer. 31:19; Ezek. 21:12 KJV) was a sign of amazement or of great shame (NIV, "beat your breast").

Thimnathah. See Timnah.

Thirty, the. See champion.

thistle. See plants.

Thomas. tom´uhs (Gk. *Thōmas* G2605, from Aram. *tĕʾômāʾ*, "twin"). One of the twelve apostles (Matt. 10:3; Mk. 3:18; Lk. 6:15; Acts 1:13). In the fourth gospel he is also called Didymus, which is the Greek word for "twin" (Jn. 11:16; 20:24; 21:2). It is possible that Thomas was not a personal name but an epithet (in the later Syriac-speaking churches he was known as Judas Thomas, "Judas the twin"). The Gospel of John gives the most information about him. When the other apostles tried to dissuade Jesus from going to Bethany to heal Lazarus because of the danger involved from hostile Jews, Thomas said to them, "Let us also go, that we may die with him" (11:16). Shortly before the passion, Thomas asked, "Lord, we don't know where you are going, so how can we know the way?" (14:1-6). Thomas was not with the other apostles when Jesus presented himself to them on the evening of the resurrection, and he told them later that he could not believe in Jesus' resurrection (20:24-25). Eight days later he was with the apostles when Jesus appeared to them again, and he exclaimed, "My Lord and my God!" (20:26-29). He was with the six other disciples when Jesus appeared to them at the Sea of Galilee (21:1-8) and was with the rest of the apostles in the upper room at Jerusalem after the ascension (Acts 1:13). According to tradition he afterward labored in Parthia and India; present-day Christians of St. Thomas of India claim spiritual descent from this missionary father, and a place near Madras is called St. Thomas's Mount.

Thomas, Gospel of. This Coptic document, possibly the most important item in the Nag Hammadi Library (NHC II, 2), is probably a translation of a Greek work that was composed in the middle of the second century A.D. It is not a gospel in the ordinary sense of the term, but rather a collection of 114 Logia, that is, sayings and parables attributed to Jesus, usually without a narrative setting. The *Gospel of Thomas* has aroused considerable interest and given rise to an extensive literature. Many of the sayings it preserves have a parallel in the canonical Gospels, but in practically every case there is some modification (e.g., "Whoever is near me is near the fire, and whoever is far from me is far from the kingdom"); frequently, sayings from different Gospels, or different parts of one, are combined. The earliest studies tended to regard *Thomas* as independent of the Synoptics, but many scholars have maintained its dependence on the NT Gospels, the variations being explained as tendentious Gnostic modification or adaptation (see Gnosticism). Not all specialists are convinced of the Gnostic character of the document, and it may be that its history is more complex than has so far been assumed.

thorn. See plants.

thorn in the flesh. The apostle Paul uses this figure with reference to some irritation that troubled him. Described also as "a messenger of Satan," it was apparently a humiliating condition, for the apostle says it "was given" to him so that he might

© Dr. James C. Martin. The Antalya Museum. Photographed by permission.

Byzantine icon of the apostle Thomas. (From Antakya, Turkey.)

not become "conceited because of these surpassingly great revelations" (2 Cor. 12:7). Though the people of CORINTH, no doubt, knew the nature of his problem, that knowledge has been lost. Early conjectures related this passage to some unknown physical ailment that Paul refers to elsewhere (Gal. 4:13). Severe headaches, epilepsy, ophthalmia, and malaria are among the more persistent suggestions. Some ancient writers thought the reference was to times of severe persecution, while the Reformers thought of temptations to spiritual ineffectiveness, and a modern suggestion is that the "thorn" was a person, an enemy. Nearly all modern commentators support the theory of physical malady.

thorns, crown of. See CROWN.

thousand. The Hebrew word for "thousand" (ʾelep H547) developed other meanings, such as "a large military unit" (which originally must have been composed of approximately 1,000 soldiers, e.g., Num. 31:14). But these units were usually tribal subdivisions, and so the word could mean simply "clan" (1 Sam. 10:19 et al.) and possibly even "district" (cf. Mic. 5:2). When the word has these derived meanings, many scholars regard it as a separate term (ʾelep H548). This ambiguity is sometimes used to deal with the extraordinarily large numbers in some OT passages. For example, when we read that the army of the Israelites in the wilderness totaled more than 600,000 (Num. 1:46), it is claimed that the army consisted of 600 troops, with the size of each troop undetermined. Another proposal is that a different Hebrew term with the same consonants is intended (ʾallûp H477, "chieftain"; thus, e.g., Num. 1:39 would read 60 chieftains and 2,700 men from Dan instead of 62,700 men).

thousand years. See ESCHATOLOGY; KINGDOM OF GOD.

Thrace. (Thrakē). Also Thracia. A kingdom and later a Roman PROVINCE in SE Europe, east of MACEDONIA. The name does not appear in the canonical books, but 2 Macc. 12:35 mentions an unnamed Thracian horseman who rescued Gorgias, the governor of Jamnia, from possible Jewish capture.

three. See NUMBER.

Three Hebrew Children, Song of the. See APOCRYPHA.

Three Taverns. (Treis Tabernai G5553, from Latin Tres Tabernae). This name is a misleading rendering of the Latin designation of a staging post on the APPIAN WAY, 33 mi. (53 km.) from ROME (the Latin term taberna means "booth, inn, shop"). It owed its importance to the fact that it was one day's journey from Rome for fast travelers proceeding S from the city to Brundisium, the port for GREECE and intermediate places. Representatives of the Roman Christian community met PAUL's party here (Acts 28:15).

Three Young Men, Song of the. See APOCRYPHA.

threshing. The process of separating seed from the harvested plant. Threshing by treading or trampling is distinguished from beating with a rod as applied to garden plants, such as dill, cummin, and flax (Isa. 28:27-28). For concealment from the Midianites, GIDEON resorted to beating out wheat (Jdg. 6:11) in the winepress rather than on the THRESHING FLOOR. Implements used in threshing were sledges, forks, and shovels. The word also had a figurative use (Isa. 21:10; 41:15; Mic. 4:12-13; 1 Cor. 9:10). See also AGRICULTURE; FARMING.

threshing floor. A level, circular area 25-40 ft. (8-12 m.) in diameter, the threshing floor was constructed in or near the grain field, preferably on an elevated spot exposed to the wind. It was prepared by removing the loose stones (by which a grain-containing border is made), then wetting and tamping the ground, and finally sweeping it. JOSEPH camped at a threshing floor (Gen. 50:10). DAVID built an altar on a former threshing floor, later the site of the TEMPLE (2 Sam. 24:18-25; 2 Chr. 3:1). RUTH visited BOAZ at his threshing floor (Ruth 3:3); and prophets used the term figuratively (Mic. 4:12; cf. Matt. 3:12; Lk. 3:17).

threshold. The stone or wood sill of a doorway, hence the entrance (see DOOR). Foundation

T

sacrifices buried under thresholds confirm that it was often a sacred place. References to thresholds in the OT sometimes related to violent acts (Jdg. 19:27; 1 Sam. 5:4-5; 1 Ki. 14:17). Other passages refer to the thresholds of the TEMPLE, which were lined with gold (2 Chr. 3:7; NIV here and elsewhere, "doorframes"). Priests and Levites served as guardians of the threshold, that is, as doorkeepers (2 Ki. 22:4 et al.). The doorposts and thresholds of the temple "shook" when ISAIAH had his vision (Isa. 6:4). It was a place where God's glory rested (Ezek. 9:3; 10:4) and where the priests worshiped (Ezek. 46:2). In Zeph. 1:9, "I will punish all who avoid stepping on the threshold," the reference is probably to a superstitious cultic practice (cf. 1 Sam. 5:5-6); some think it alludes to those who would mount up a pedestal for idols, or that it has in view rushing through the door for the purposes of plundering the temple.

throne. A chair of state occupied by one in authority or of high position, such as a high priest, judge, governor, or king (Gen. 41:40; 2 Sam. 3:10; Neh. 3:7; Ps. 122:5; Jer. 1:15; Matt. 19:28). SOLOMON's throne was an elaborate one (1 Ki. 10:18-20; 2 Chr. 9:17-19). For ages the throne has been a symbol of authority, exalted position, and majesty (Ps. 9:7; 45:6; 94:20; Prov. 16:12).

thrush. See BIRDS.

thumb. This short, thick digit constitutes the most versatile of the five fingers. Its attachment at the wrist facilitates its rotation into a position in which its tip can directly oppose the tips of any one of the other fingers of the same hand. Experience shows that the loss of the thumb severely cripples the hand (cf. Jdg. 1:6-7; the Heb. word can be applied to the big toe also). It is therefore noteworthy that special prominence is given to the thumbs of AARON's sons in connection with their consecration to the priestly ministry of the tabernacle, since consecration involves the whole being, and especially those parts of the body that are most serviceable (Exod. 29:20; Lev. 8:23-24; cf. also 14:14 et al.).

Thummim. See URIM AND THUMMIM.

thunder. The Hebrew term most often used for "thunder" is *qôl H7754*, a common word that more generally means "sound, voice." It almost always occurs with some other manifestation of storm, such as lightning (Job 28:26), hail (Exod. 9:23), and rain (1 Sam. 12:17). In the narrative of the giving of the law on SINAI it is very clear that the thunder is a demonstration of the divine power (Exod. 19:16; 20:18). In the NT, the common Greek term *brontē G1103* is used throughout exclusively. Like the thunder of the OT, that of the NT is often representative of some divine activity (e.g., Jn. 12:29). The largest number of references by far are in Revelation (Rev. 4:5 et al.). These are in all cases allusions to the scene at Sinai at the giving of the law. In Mk. 3:17, the only other occurrence of the term in the NT, it is used to describe the two disciples, James the son of Zebedee and his brother John. See BOANERGES.

Thunder, Sons of. See BOANERGES.

Thutmose. thy*oot*´mohs, thy*oot*-moh´suh (Egyp. *dḥwty-ms* or Djehutymes, "[the god] Thoth is born" or "born of Thoth"). Variant spellings include Thutmoses (-mosis), Tuthmosis, Thothmes. An Egyptian name popular during the New Kingdom, borne by four kings of the 18th dynasty (see EGYPT). Thutmose I, the third king of the dynasty (c. 1505-1492 B.C.), was the son of Amenhotep I; a vigorous ruler, he engaged in military expeditions in Nubia (see ETHIOPIA) and in Asia, where he crossed the EUPHRATES. His son, Thutmose II, had an unimpressive reign (c. 1492-1479); he married his half-sister, the famous Hatshepsut. The most significant ruler bearing this name was Thutmose III (c. 1479-1425); see below. Thutmose IV, son of Amenhotep II, was the last of the Thutmosids (c. 1400-1390).

Thutmose III was the son of Thutmose II by a concubine. Upon the death of his father c. 1479, the young man was crowned, but Hatshepsut succeeded in becoming regent and "king." Thutmose III remained in a subordinate and obscure position until her death (c. 1457), serving as a priest in the temple of Amon in Karnak (see AMON #4), where an inscription purports to describe how he was divinely chosen for the kingship. His brilliant victory over an Asiatic coalition at MEGIDDO marked the first of seventeen campaigns in Palestine-Syria. Famous as a military strategist and capable as an administrator, Thutmose III created the Egyptian empire. He built extensively at Karnak, at Medinet Habu, and at other sites in Egypt and Nubia. He died c. 1425 and was succeeded by Amenhotep II. The name Thutmose does not appear in the Bible, but Thutmose III has sometimes been regarded as the PHARAOH who was ruling at the time of the Israelite oppression.

Thyatira. thi´uh-ti´ruh (Gk. *Thyateira G2587*). A city some 20 mi. (32 km.) ESE of PERGAMUM and 33 mi. (53 km.) NNW of SARDIS, on a valley road in the alluvial plain between the Hermus and Caicus Rivers. Both in the days of Pergamum's leadership in W ASIA MINOR and later, when international politics drew ROME strongly into the great peninsula, the city derived strength and wealth from the fact that it was a nodal point of communications. The city was founded by SELEUCUS I, the general who, of all four successors of ALEXANDER THE GREAT, inherited the largest area (from far beyond ANTIOCH of Syria to the Hermus Valley). The city was a center of commerce, and the records preserve references to more trade guilds than those listed for any other city in the Roman province of ASIA. Such commercial prosperity attracted a large Jewish minority to Thyatira, for the agricultural Jews began in exile to assume monetary and commercial interests, which were to become their enduring mark (see DIASPORA). LYDIA, whom PAUL met in PHILIPPI, was a Thyatiran seller of PURPLE, a dye from a marine molusk, or "turkey red," the product of the madder root (Acts 16:14).

We do not know when the church of Thyatira was founded, but some decades later the book of Revelation says the Christians there were characterized by "love and faith" as well as "service and perseverance" (Rev. 2:2:18-19). Unfortunately, the church tolerated "that woman Jezebel, who calls herself a prophetess. By her teaching she misleads my servants into sexual immorality and the eating of food sacrificed to idols" (v. 20). The name was deliberately chosen, for the marriage of AHAB with JEZEBEL of TYRE (1 Ki. 16:31 et al.) was a disastrous compromise. John denounced her and pro-

nounced a fierce condemnation: "So I will cast her on a bed of suffering, and I will make those who commit adultery with her suffer intensely, unless they repent of her ways" (v. 22). On the other hand, a great promise of authority is given to those who hold on to the truth (vv. 24-28).

thyine wood. See PLANTS (uncer *citron*).

Tiamat. tee-ah´maht. The name of the goddess of the primordial salt water ocean, the antagonist of the hero-god in the great Babylonian national epic, *Enuma Elish*. Tiamat is a great ugly monster who becomes angry with her own offspring of an innumerable set of lesser gods; these gods select a champion (in the older stories MARDUK, in the later ASSHUR), who then fights a cosmic battle with the chaotic sea. As a result the dead corpse of Tiamat is divided up and separated into the lower and upper cosmos. There are literary allusions to this myth in many ANE traditions. The old proposal that the Hebrew term *tĕhôm H9333* in Gen. 1:2 (see DEEP, THE) derives from the name Tiamat is now generally rejected.

Tiberias. ti-bihr´ee-uhs (Gk. *Tiberias G5500*). A city on the western shore of the Sea of Galilee, halfway down the coast of the lake (see GALILEE, SEA OF). Tiberias itself is mentioned only once in the NT (Jn. 6:23), but the name was extended to the lake, especially in Gentile nomenclature, and John uses it twice in that sense (6:1; 21:1). Modern Tiberias is known in Hebrew as Tebarya (Arab. Ṭabariyeh). Built by HEROD Antipas between the years A.D. 16 and 22, it was named after the reigning emperor, TIBERIUS, reflecting the pro-Roman policy consistently followed by the Herods. The city is said to have occupied the site at RAKKATH, an old town of the tribe of NAPHTALI. Jewish rumor said Tiberias was built over a graveyard, and the place was therefore dubbed unclean (Josephus, *Ant.* 18.2.3). According to some, this information indicates that no earlier city occupied the site, but Herod could easily have included the burial place Rakkath in his larger foundation. Herod built ambitiously. The ruins indicate a wall 3 mi. (5 km.) long. He built a palace, a forum, and a great synagogue, for the foundation illustrates strikingly the

T

© Dr. James C. Martin

A view looking W toward the section of Tiberias that was occupied beginning in NT times.

dual Herodian policy, which sought to combine pro-Roman loyalty with effective patronage of the Jews. Jewish boycott, however, compelled Herod to populate his new town with the lowest elements of the land. Defended by its strong acropolis, Tiberias survived the passing of the other lakeside towns. The hot springs and baths lay S of the city wall, and their healthful nature is mentioned by the Elder Pliny (*Nat. Hist.* 5.15).

Tiberias, Sea of. See GALILEE, SEA OF.

Tiberius. ti-bihr′ee-uhs (Gk. *Tiberios G5501*). Tiberius Claudius Caesar Augustus, second emperor of Rome and ruler at the time of CHRIST's ministry (Lk. 3:1), was born in 42 B.C., the son of Tiberius Claudius Nero and Livia Drusilla. Four years later Livia was divorced in order to marry Octavian, the future emperor AUGUSTUS. Tiberius had a distinguished military career in the East and in Germany, and, in the absence of direct heirs to Augustus, was the logical successor. Augustus, however, did not like Tiberius, whose claims and abilities were bypassed for many years. The experience of disapproval and rejection no doubt contributed to the dourness, secretiveness, ambiguity, and suspicious preoccupations that marred the years of Tiberius's power. A morbid fear of disloyalty led to the heavy incidence of treason trials, which were

a feature of the Roman principate under its worst incumbents. There is no evidence that Tiberius was unduly tyrannous, but aristocrats and writers of their number blamed the prince for features of later tyranny and for precedents of many subsequent incidents of oppression. This, added to the natural unpopularity of a reticent and lonely man, left Tiberius with a reputation that modern scholarship, discounting Tacitus's brilliant and bitter account, has been at some pains to rehabilitate. Tiberius had great ability and some measure of magnanimity; for, in spite of many unhappy memories, he sought loyally to continue Augustus's policies, foreign and domestic. The rumors of senile debauchery on the island of Capri can be listed with the slanders of earlier years, though there is some evidence of mental disturbance in the later period of the principate. The city of TIBERIAS in GALILEE was named after him, and it was his image that would have been imprinted on the coin that Jesus used in his well-known statement about what is due to CAESAR (Matt. 22:19-21 and parallels). Tiberius died on March 16, A.D. 37.

Tibhath. tib′hath. See TEBAH (PLACE).

Tibni. tib′ni (Heb. *tibni H9321*, prob. "strawman"). Son of Ginath and unsuccessful rival for the throne of the kingdom of ISRAEL after the deaths of ELAH and ZIMRI (1 Ki. 16:21-22). Although the struggle with OMRI apparently lasted four years, ending only with Tibni's death, the biblical narrative is largely silent about this period, prompting much speculation among modern scholars.

Tidal. ti′duhl (Heb. *tidʿāl* H9331, prob. from Hittite *Tudḫalia*). King of GOIIM and ally of KEDOR-LAOMER king of ELAM, who with three other rulers led a punitive expedition against SODOM and other cities (Gen. 14:1, 9). Some scholars render the text, "Tidal king of nations," implying either that he ruled a confederacy of city-states or that he bore an honorific title corresponding to the expression common in Akkadian annals, "King of the Four Corners of the Earth." Others identify Goiim with Gutium in MESOPOTAMIA, while still others appeal to the term *gaʾum* (used in MARI texts) and suggest that Tidal ruled a nomadic tribe with no fixed boundaries. It is generally thought that Tidal corresponds to Tudhalia (Tudkhaliyas), the name of several HITTITE rulers, but other proposals have been made. Tidal's identification remains uncertain.

Tiglath-Pileser. tig′lath-pi-lee′zuhr (Heb. *tiglat pilʾeser* H9325 and *tillēgat pilnēʾeser* H9433, from Akk. *Tukulti-apil-ešarra*, "My trust [or help] is in the son of Esharra" [Esharra being the name of the temple of the god ASSHUR]). Also Tilgath-pilneser (KJV and other versions at 1 Chr. 5:6; 2 Chr. 28:20). The name of three kings of ASSYRIA. Tiglath-Pileser I (1115-1077 B.C.) was an important ruler responsible for many military victories and building projects. Tiglath-Pileser II (967-935) receives mention in some documents, but almost nothing is known about him. The rest of this article deals with Tiglath-Pileser III (745-727), the only king of this name that is mentioned in the Bible.

Tiglath-Pileser III injected new vigor into the Assyrian empire, which had suffered another decline after a resurgence of power in the ninth century. He engaged in campaigns to the E and W and was recognized as king even in BABYLON, where he was known as Pulu (thus PUL in 2 Ki. 15:19 and 1 Chr. 5:26). His annals list AZARIAH of JUDAH among the kings from whom he received tribute, but the OT does not relate this account.

He also mentions tribute from MENAHEM of SAMARIA, who bought him off (cf. 2 Ki. 15:19-20). During the reign of the Judean king AHAZ, PEKAH of ISRAEL and REZIN of SYRIA moved against Judah. Ahaz secured the help of Tiglath-Pileser (16:5-8), who captured DAMASCUS, deported its people, and killed Rezin. He took a number of Israelite cities and exiled the inhabitants to Assyria (15:29). He was also responsible for the deportation of Transjordanian Israelites, whom he brought to "Halah, Habor, Hara and the river of Gozan" (1 Chr. 5:6, 26). The transfer of peoples to foreign areas was a practical policy designed to reduce the possibility of revolts in conquered regions. Ahaz also requested military aid from him because of invasions by Edomites and Philistines; he gave gifts from the temple and the palace to Tiglath-Pileser, "but that did not help him" (2 Chr. 28:20-21).

Tigris. ti′gris (Heb. *ḥiddeqel* H2538, from Akk. *Idiqlat*; in Old Pers. the name took the form *Tigrā*, hence Gk. *Tigrēs*). The eastern river of ancient Iraq, which together with the EUPHRATES formed the alluvial plain of MESOPOTAMIA, "[Land] between Rivers." The Tigris is one of the rivers listed to describe the boundaries of EDEN (Gen. 2:14); and it was while "standing on the bank of the great river, the Tigris," that DANIEL received an important vision (Dan. 10:4). The river originates in the Zagros Mountains of W Kurdistan; in its 1,150 mi. (1,850 km.) it receives three principal tributaries from the E: the Great Zab, the Little Zab, and the Diyala. It is difficult for navigation, since for some months it is very shallow, yet it is subject to flooding and during the rainy season ranges outside its banks. In antiquity the Tigris and the Euphrates entered the Persian Gulf by separate mouths, but the shore of the gulf has receded, and today the Tigris joins the Euphrates at Kurna to form the Shatt el-Arab. The rivers of Iran also have been an important factor in the formation of the delta. Through what was ASSYRIA and Babylonia (see BABYLON), the Tigris flows past famous cities, living and dead: Mosul, on the W bank, looks across the river to the mounds of NINEVEH; farther downstream are ASSHUR, Samarra, and Baghdad.

T

Tikvah. tik'vuh (Heb. *tiqwāh H9537*, "hope"; also *toqhat H9534* [2 Chr. 34:22]). **(1)** Son of HARHAS and father of SHALLUM, who was keeper of the royal wardrobe; the latter was married to HULDAH the prophetess (2 Ki. 22:14). In the parallel passage he is called "Tokhath son of Hasrah" (2 Chr. 34:22; KJV, "Tikvath"). The name Tokhath may be a variant form or a copying error, but some believe it was the original (non-Semitic) name of this person, and that it was altered to Tiqvah to make it meaningful in Hebrew.

(2) Father of JAHZEIAH (Ezra 10:15).

Tikvath. See TIKVAH.

tile. Ancient WRITING was done with a stylus on blocks of soft clay, which varied in size according to need. EZEKIEL used such a tile in drawing a prophetic picture of the doom awaiting Jerusalem (Ezek. 4:1-8 KJV; NIV, "tablet"). When a permanent record was desired, the inscribed tile was baked in a furnace. So skilled were scribes of the day that many of their tiles remain in perfect condition after three thousand years. Roofing tiles are mentioned in Lk. 5:19, where the reference is apparently to clay roofing—tiles with which the roof was covered. Clay tiles were not commonly used as roofing material for houses in Palestine, roofs usually being covered with a mixture of clay and straw. It may be that Luke uses the expression "through the tiles" to mean "through the roof," without reference to the material used for the roof.

Tilgath-pilneser. See TIGLATH-PILESER.

tiling. See TILE.

tiller. See OCCUPATIONS AND PROFESSIONS.

Tilon. ti'luhn (Heb. *tîlôn H9400*, meaning unknown). Son of Shimon and descendant of JUDAH (1 Chr. 4:20).

Timaeus. ti-mee'uhs (Gk. *Timaios G5505*). See BARTIMAEUS.

timbrel. See MUSIC AND MUSICAL INSTRUMENTS (sect. I.G).

time. The history of the development of various measurements for time, and the making of instruments for determining them, is an intriguing subject. Before the days of ABRAHAM, the Babylonians had set up a system of days and seasons and had divided the periods of darkness and light into parts. Their seven-day week had been accepted by Egyptians before the time of MOSES. Day and night were determined by the SUN. The week, no doubt, was determined by the phases of the MOON. The month was based on the recurrence of the new moon. In order to provide in the CALENDAR for the extra days of the solar year over the twelve lunar months, the Jews added an intercalary month. They had no way of determining an absolute solar year, so the extra month was added every third year, with adjustments to provide seven extra months each nineteen years. It was added after the spring equinox, hence was called a second ADAR (the preceding month being Adar). This method of keeping the lunar and the solar years synchronized was probably learned by the Israelites during the Babylonian EXILE.

For ages, years were not numbered consecutively as we number them, but were counted for some outstanding event, such as the founding of Rome. The Hebrews had a civil year that began at the vernal equinox, after the custom of BABYLON, and a sacred year that began with the harvest or seventh month (Lev. 25:8-9). They divided the year into two seasons, seedtime or winter, and harvest or summer (Gen. 8:22; 45:6; Exod. 34:21; Prov. 10:5).

The Hebrew word for DAY (*yôm H3427*) may mean a period of daylight or a period of twenty-four hours (in addition to other less definite senses). The Roman day began at midnight and had twelve hours (Jn. 11:9). The Hebrew day was reckoned from sunset. There was the cool of the day (Gen. 3:8) or twilight (Job 24:15). Mid-morning was when the sun had become hot (1 Sam. 11:9). Noon was the heat of the day (Gen. 18:1). Night was divided into WATCHES, so that the length of each varied with changing seasons. The first watch came about 3:30 p.m. Midnight was the middle watch (Jdg. 7:19). The OT also refers to a "morning watch" (Exod. 14:24 KJV; NIV, "last watch of the night"); it was called "cockcrow" in NT times

(Matt. 26:34; Mk. 13:35). The watch was so named because of the changing of watchmen and was not a very definite period (Ps. 90:4; 119:148; Jer. 51:12). Roman influence caused a revision of the watches, so in the days of Christ there were four divisions of the night (Matt. 14:25; Mk. 6:48), these being marked approximately by 7:00 p.m., 9:30 p.m., midnight, 2:30 a.m., and 5:00 a.m.

In the Scriptures the words translated "time" have varied connotations. Temporal existence is "my life" in both Job 7:7 and Ps. 89:47. A period allotted for a special object, task, or cause was its time (Eccl. 3:1; 8:6). A special period of life was "a time," as a period of conception (Gen. 18:10, 14) or the days of pregnancy (1 Sam. 1:20); any special feast or celebration (Ps. 81:3); an occasion for the consummation of divine plans (Job 24:1; Jer. 2:27; Jn. 7:6, 8; Acts 3:21; Rom. 8:22-23; 1 Tim. 6:15). The dispensation of GRACE is the time of SALVATION (Ps. 69:13; Isa. 49:8; 2 Cor. 6:2).

Ancient people had no method of reckoning long periods of time. The Greeks did develop the idea of eras, or connected time elements. The Olympian era dated from 766 B.C.; the SELEUCID era from 312 B.C. Their year began on January 1. In Asia Minor the year began with the autumn equinox. It is, therefore, difficult to determine any precise date for events occurring during NT days. LUKE's dating of events (Lk. 1:5; 2:1-2; 3:1) when JOHN THE BAPTIST began his ministry is the only definite fact on which to determine the times of Jesus with any certainty.

The Hebrews used great and well-known events like the EXODUS, the Babylonian EXILE, the building of the TEMPLE, and an earthquake (Amos 1:1) as fixed points for indicating the time of other events. In the Maccabean age the beginning of the Seleucid era (312 B.C.) became a starting point.

Timna. tim´nuh (Heb. *timnaʿ H9465*, perhaps "protected" or "invincible"). **(1)** Concubine of ELIPHAZ son of ESAU; mother of AMALEK (Gen. 36:12; in 1 Chr. 1:36 MT, Timna appears to be listed as a son of Eliphaz, but the NIV follows LXX [Codex Vaticanus] in rendering "by Timna, Amalek"). She is probably the same person identified as sister of LOTAN, thus a daughter of SEIR the HORITE (Gen. 36:22; 1 Chr. 1:39). Calling attention to Timna's status as a CONCUBINE may have been a way of indicating that the Amalekites were not pure descendants of Esau.

(2) Descendant of Esau, listed among the clan chiefs of EDOM (Gen. 36:40; 1 Chr. 1:51). The KJV spells his name "Timnah" probably to distinguish it from #1 above. Some argue that the names in this list are topographical rather than personal. There is today a region called Timna c. 20 mi. (32 km.) N of the Gulf of AQABAH, but its connection with the biblical name is uncertain.

Timnah. tim´nuh (Heb. *timnâ H9463*, possibly "portion, territory"; gentilic *timnî H9464*, "Timnite"). KJV also Timnath (Gen. 38:12-14; Jdg. 14:1-2, 5) and Thimnathah (Josh. 19:43, misinterpreting the Hebrew locative form). **(1)** A town of uncertain location, noted as the place where JUDAH was headed when he had his encounter with TAMAR (Gen. 38:12-14). It should probably be identified with either #2 or #3 below.

(2) A town located between BETH SHEMESH and EKRON, mentioned in the description of the tribal boundaries of JUDAH (Josh. 15:10), but allotted to the tribe of DAN (19:43, where it is possibly referred to as "Timnah of Ekron"). The Danites were unable to take full possession of Timnah and other towns in this territory (19:47). Timnah was controlled by the PHILISTINES in the time of SAMSON (Jdg. 14:1-2, 5; cf. "Timnite" in 15:6). The region was evidently conquered by Judah at some later point, and during the reign of AHAZ Timnah was one of the towns recaptured and occupied by the Philistines (2 Chr. 28:18). It is generally identified with modern Tell el-Batashi, c. 3 mi. (5 km.) E of Ekron.

(3) A town in the hill country of the tribe of Judah (Josh. 15:57). It was in the same district as MAON and other towns S of HEBRON, but the precise location is unknown.

Timnath. See TIMNAH.

Timnath Heres, Timnath Serah. tim´nath-hee´riz, tim´nath-sihr´uh (Heb. *timnat-ḥeres H9466* [Jdg. 2:9], possibly "portion [*i.e.*, region] of the sun"; *timnat-seraḥ H9467* [Josh. 19:50; 24:30], perhaps "overhanging region" or "leftover

T

portion"). A place in the hill country of Ephraim (see EPHRAIM, HILL COUNTRY OF) given to JOSHUA as his personal inheritance: "he built up the town and settled there" (Josh. 19:50). When he died, he was buried in this city, which is described as being N of GAASH (Josh. 24:30; Jdg. 2:9). Most scholars identify it with modern Khirbet Tibnah, on the W slopes of the hill country, some 18 mi. (29 km.) NW of JERUSALEM and 14 mi. (23 km.) SW of SHECHEM. Many scholars believe that Timnath Heres was the town's original name and that because it alluded (or could be misunderstood to allude) to pagan SUN worship, it was changed to Timnath Serah. The meaning of the latter term is quite uncertain and has given rise to speculation.

Timnath Serah. See TIMNATH HERES.

Timnite. See TIMNAH.

Timon. ti′muhn (Gk. *Timōn G5511*, "precious, valuable"). One of the seven men appointed by the early church to serve tables and thereby relieve the apostles for other duties (Acts 6:5). According to a late tradition, Timon had been among the SEVENTY DISCIPLES (cf. Lk. 10:1 KJV) and subsequently became a bishop in ARABIA. See also DEACON.

Timotheus. See TIMOTHY.

Timothy. tim′oh-thee (Gk. *Timotheos G5510*, prob. "God-honoring" or "God's precious one"). KJV usually Timotheus (but Timothy in the Pastorals and in 2 Cor. 1:1; Phlm. 1; Heb. 13:23; this variation by the KJV has no basis in the Greek text). PAUL's spiritual child (1 Tim. 1:2; 2 Tim. 1:2), later the apostle's travel companion and official representative. His character was apparently a blend of amiability and faithfulness in spite of natural timidity. Paul loved Timothy and admired his outstanding personality traits. One must read Phil. 2:19-22 to know how highly the apostle esteemed this young friend. None of Paul's companions is mentioned as often—or seems to have been with him as constantly—as is Timothy. That this relationship was of an enduring nature is clear from 2 Tim. 4:9, 21. Paul knew that he could count on Timothy. He was the kind of person who, in spite of his youth (1 Tim. 4:12), his natural reserve and timidity (1 Cor. 16:10; 2 Tim. 1:7), and his frequent ailments (1 Tim. 5:23), was willing to leave his home to accompany the apostle on dangerous journeys, to be sent on difficult errands, and to remain to the very end Christ's faithful servant.

Timothy is first mentioned in Acts 16:1, from which passage it may be inferred that he was an inhabitant of LYSTRA (cf. 20:4). He was the offspring of a mixed marriage: he had a GENTILE (presumably pagan) father and a devout Jewish

© Dr. James C. Martin

Theater and forum at Ephesus (looking NE). Timothy shepherded the Christian congregation in this city.

mother (Acts 16:1; 2 Tim. 1:5). From the days of his childhood Timothy had been instructed in the sacred writings of the OT (2 Tim. 3:15). In the manner of devout Israelites his grandmother Lois and mother Eunice had nurtured him (1:5). Then came Paul, who taught this devout family that Jesus Christ is the fulfillment of the OT. First grandmother Lois and mother Eunice became followers of Christ, then, as a result of their cooperation with Paul, Timothy also did so (1:5). These events evidently took place on Paul's first missionary journey. Hence Timothy knew about the persecutions and sufferings that the missionaries (Paul and Barnabas) had experienced on that first journey (3:11), that is, even before Timothy had joined Paul in active missionary labor.

When, on the second journey, Paul and Silas came to Lystra, Timothy became an active member of the group. Paul took Timothy and circumcised him (Acts 16:3). Here it must be remembered that because Timothy's mother was Jewish, he too was legally regarded as a Jew. His case was different, therefore, from that of Titus, whose Gentile identity became a test case in the controversy over circumcision (Gal. 2:3-5). Timothy's situation had nothing to do with determining on what basis Gentiles would be allowed to enter the church. In all probability it was also at this time that Timothy was ordained by the elders of the local church to his new task, Paul himself taking part in this solemn laying on of hands (1 Tim. 4:14; 2 Tim. 1:6).

Timothy then accompanied the missionaries over into Europe—to Philippi and Thessalonica. He also helped the others in the next place to which they went, Berea. Here he and Silas were left behind to give spiritual support to the infant church, while Paul went on to Athens (Acts 17:10-15). At Paul's request Timothy a little later left Berea and met Paul at Athens. Afterward he was sent back to Thessalonica for the purpose of strengthening the brothers there (1 Thess. 3:1-2). After Paul had left Athens and had begun his labors in Corinth, both Silas and Timothy rejoined him (Acts 18:1, 5). At Corinth Timothy worked with Paul. On the third missionary journey Timothy was again with the apostle during the lengthy Ephesus ministry. From there he was sent to Macedonia and to Corinth (Acts 19:21-22; 1 Cor. 4:17;

16:10). When Paul arrived in Macedonia, Timothy rejoined him (2 Cor. 1:1). Afterward he accompanied the apostle to Corinth (Rom. 16:21), was with him on the return to Macedonia (Acts 20:3-4), and was waiting for him at Troas (20:5). He was probably also with Paul in Jerusalem (1 Cor. 16:3). During Paul's first imprisonment at Rome the two were again in close contact (Phil. 1:1; Col. 1:1; Phlm. 1). When Paul expected to be released in a little while, he told the Philippians that he expected to send Timothy to them soon (Phil. 2:19).

Timothy was next found in Ephesus, where the apostle joined him. Paul, on leaving, asked Timothy to remain at this place (1 Tim. 1:3). While there, Timothy one day received a letter from Paul, the letter we now call 1 Timothy. Later, in another letter, Paul, writing from Rome as a prisoner facing death, urged his friend to come to him before winter (2 Tim. 4:9, 21). Whether the two ever actually saw each other again is not recorded. That Timothy tried to see the apostle is certain.

Timothy, Letters to. See Pastoral Letters.

tin. See minerals.

tinkling. This term is used by the KJV in two passages, with reference to (1) the sound of small bells that women wore on a chain fastened to anklets (Isa. 3:16 [NIV, "jingling"]; in v. 18 the Heb. word means "anklet" or "bangle"), and (2) the noise made by a cymbal (1 Cor. 13:1 [NIV, "clanging"]).

Tiphsah. tif′suh (Heb. *tipsaḥ* H9527, perhaps "ford"). (1) A town mentioned as marking the NE boundary of Solomon's kingdom: "he ruled over all the kingdoms west of the River [*i.e.*, the Euphrates], from Tiphsah to Gaza" (1 Ki. 4:24). Tiphsah is generally identified with ancient Thapsacus; called Amphipolis in Seleucid times, it is now known as Dibseh, near the large bend of the Euphrates, 90 mi. (145 km.) NE of Hamath. A great E-W trade route that moved around the Fertile Crescent had a staging post here. There is no means of knowing how strongly the remote frontier was held by Solomon, and some scholars are skeptical that Israel's northern boundaries ever reached that far.

(2) A town of uncertain location that was sacked and brutally treated by MENAHEM (2 Ki. 15:16). Although some scholars think this Tiphsah is the same as #1 above, the text suggests rather a place near TIRZAH and SAMARIA.

Tiras. ti′ruhs (Heb. *tîrās H9410*, meaning unknown, but the name apparently corresponds to Egyptian *tywš*, also spelled *twryš*). Last-named son of JAPHETH and grandson of NOAH (Gen. 10:2; 1 Chr. 1:5). Evidently Tiras was also the name of a people group descended from him, and various identifications have been proposed, including TARSUS and TARSHISH. Many scholars accept a connection with the Tursha, one of the SEA PEOPLES that invaded the Syrian coast and even attacked Egypt in the thirteenth century B.C.; but the identification of the Tursha is also debated. Some think the reference is to THRACIA, others to a place in Italy named Tyrrhenia.

Tirathites. ti′ruh-thits (Heb. *tirʿātîm H9571*, a gentilic form, prob. from an unattested name such as *tirʿâ*). Among the descendants of CALEB (through his son HUR and grandson SALMA) are listed three "clans of scribes who lived at Jabez: the Tirathites, Shimeathites and Sucathites. These are the Kenites who came from Hammath, the father of the house of Recab" (1 Chr. 2:55). Nothing else is known about these clans, and their names cannot be traced to a particular person or place. See KENITE.

tire. An archaic English term used by the KJV both as a verb (meaning "to adorn," 2 Ki. 9:30) and as a noun ("[hair] ornament," Isa. 3:18; Ezek. 24:17, 23).

Tirhakah. tuhr-hay′kuh (Heb. *tirhāqâ H9555*, from Egyp. *tʾhrwq*). Also Taharqa, Tahrqa (and various forms in Greek writers). A PHARAOH of the 25th or Ethiopian dynasty in EGYPT (see ETHIOPIA), identified in the Hebrew Bible as king of CUSH (cf. TNIV, 2 Ki. 19:9; Isa. 37:9; NIV, "the Cushite king of Egypt"). Egypt had been divided into a number of feudal cities and cult centers by the middle of the eighth century B.C. About 730 B.C., however, the Cushite (Nubian) chieftain

Piankhy (Piye) conquered much of Egypt and assumed the unified throne as pharaoh. Tirhakah, who ascended the throne in 690, was the fourth ruler of this dynasty. He carried on campaigns against the pretenders to the throne in the NILE delta region. He was fairly respected by his Egyptian subjects and was able to maintain some degree of order sufficient to build and restore temples and other buildings at Karnak and Medînet Habu.

When the rampaging Assyrian king SENNACHERIB (705-681 B.C.) began his campaigns in SYRIA and threatened HEZEKIAH in JERUSALEM, the Jews evidently appealed to Egypt for aid (cf. 2 Ki. 18:21; Isa. 36:6). The biblical record states that Sennacherib, while besieging Judean cities, heard that Tirhakah was coming against him (2 Ki. 19:9; Isa. 37:9). Sennacherib himself claims to have defeated "the kings of Egypt … and the cavalry of the king of Ethiopia" at ELTEKEH (*ANET*, 287b). Eventually, however, the supernatural loss of his troops forced him back to ASSYRIA (2 Ki. 19:35-36; Isa. 37:36-37). Sennacherib's successor and son, ESARHADDON (680-669), again conquered Syria and "fought daily, without interruption, very bloody battles against Tirhakah (*Tarqû*), king of Egypt and Ethiopia, the one accursed by all the great gods" (from Esarhaddon's stela, *ANET*, 293a). After the death of Esarhaddon, Tirhakah returned to occupy most of his former domain. ASHURBANIPAL, the son and heir of Esarhaddon, had been previously designated the new king. In his first campaign begun in 667 B.C. he again invaded Egypt. After this pursuit Tirhakah does not seem to have recovered his sovereign position and he fled to his native southland, to his city of Napata. There he died in 664, after a long reign of twenty-six years.

Tirhanah. tuhr-hay′nuh (Heb. *tirhānâ H9563*, derivation unknown, possibly a HURRIAN name). Son of CALEB (by his concubine MAACAH), included in the genealogy of JUDAH (1 Chr. 2:48).

Tiria. tihr′ee-uh (Heb. *tîryāʾ H9409*, possibly "might of Yahweh"). Son of JEHALLELEL and descendant of JUDAH (1 Chr. 4:16).

Tirshatha. tuhr-shay′thuh (Heb. *tiršātāʾ H9579*, possibly from a Persian word meaning "respected, excellency"). KJV transliteration of what appears to be a Persian title meaning "governor" or the like. The term is applied to NEHEMIAH (Neh. 8:9; 10:1) and to another unnamed leader, probably SHESH-BAZZAR or ZERUBBABEL (Ezra 2:63; Neh. 7:65, 70). The Persian SATRAP or provincial governor was, in effect, a petty official with no great power whose principal functions included the assessment and collection of taxes.

Tirzah (person). tihr′zuh (Heb. *tirṣāh H9573*, "pleasant" or "obliging"). The youngest of five daughters of ZELOPHEHAD of the tribe of MANASSEH (Num. 26:33). Since Zelophehad had no sons, his daughters requested ELEAZAR the priest that they be allowed to inherit their father's property, and the request was granted on condition that they marry into their father's tribe (27:1-11; 36:11; Josh. 17:3-4). Some think that Tirzah may have settled the town that bears the same name. See TIRZAH (PLACE).

Tirzah (place). tihr′zuh (Heb. *tirṣāh H9574*, "pleasant" or "obliging"). A royal Canaanite city conquered by JOSHUA (Josh. 12:24). It is possible that the town, located within the tribal territory of MANASSEH, was settled by Tirzah, daughter of the Manassite ZELOPHEHAD (cf. 17:1-6, esp. v. 3). See TIRZAH (PERSON). JEROBOAM I maintained a residence at Tirzah (1 Ki. 14:17) and it became the capital of the northern kingdom in the days of BAASHA, ELAH, and ZIMRI (1 Ki. 15:21, 33; 16:6, 8-9, 15). Trapped there by OMRI, Zimri destroyed his residence during a dynastic struggle (16:17-18). Six years later, Omri transferred the capital to SAMARIA (16:23-24), and Tirzah sank into the status of a provincial but still significant town. Toward the end of the northern monarchy of Israel, a citizen of Tirzah, MENAHEM, seized power and usurped the throne from SHALLUM (2 Ki. 15:14, 16). Tirzah is now generally identified with modern Tell el-Farʿah, c. 6 mi. (10 km.) NE of SHECHEM. Noted for the beauty of its environs (Cant. 6:4), the valley where Tirzah was situated is carved out of softer Cenomanian limestones with a good soil cover, in contrast to the rocky Eocene outcrops above the valley. Excavations have revealed a continuous settlement from Chalcolithic times,

before 3000 B.C., to the end of the kingdom of ISRAEL. It flourished as a city in the ninth century B.C., but a burnt level was found terminating the first stratum of the Iron Age occupation that may indicate the civil disorders at the time Omri came to power. There is also evidence of the subsequent reduction of Tirzah from an important fortress to a virtually open town about the time Samaria was created on a new site.

Tishbe. tish′bee (Heb. *tišbê H9586*, conjectured place name; gentilic *tišbî H9585*, "Tishbite"). The hometown of ELIJAH in GILEAD, according to the NIV and some other versions at 1 Ki. 17:1. The KJV, following the Hebrew form found in the MT, has "of the inhabitants of Gilead" (*mittōšābê gilʿād*; cf. NJPS, "an inhabitant of Gilead"). Most scholars, assuming reasonably that the term Tishbite (in the same verse and elsewhere) means "a native of Tishbe," emend the MT vowels to *mittišbê*, "from Tishbe" (other proposals have been made). Some have identified Tishbe with Listib (in Arabic, el-Istib), in E GILEAD, but this town was founded in the Byzantine period, and there is no trace of earlier settlement. Nevertheless, the familiarity of Elijah with this area on the E side of JORDAN is pointed up by the narrative in 1 Ki. 17:2-7 concerning his sojourn at the brook KERITH. The tradition of Elijah's presence in the region about JABESH GILEAD is seen in a place near Listib on the opposite side of the valley called Mar Ilyas (St. Elias). Respect for the spirit of Nebi-Ilyas (the prophet Elias) is given to a grove of oak trees above the ancient ruins. Although "Tishbe in Gilead" cannot be precisely identified, the general location of "Elijah the Tishbite's" homeland seems reasonably secure.

Tishbite. tish′bit. See TISHBE.

Tishri. tish′ree (postbiblical Heb. *tišrî*). The seventh month in the Hebrew sacred CALENDAR (first month in the civil calendar), corresponding to late September and early October. This term is not found in the Bible, which uses instead the Canaanite name ETHANIM (1 Ki. 8:2). According to a rabbinic tradition, Tishri was the month in which the world was created. The Jewish New Year is celebrated on the first and second days of Tishri.

tithe. The tenth part of produce or property for the support of the priesthood or for other religious objectives. References to the tithe are found in both the OT and NT (Heb. *ma'ăśēr H5130*; Gk. *dekatē*, from *dekatos G1281*), but the main teachings are incorporated in three passages in the Mosaic legislation: Lev. 27:30-33; Num. 18:21-32; and Deut. 12:5-18; 14:22-29.

Just when and where the idea arose of making the tenth the rate for paying tribute to rulers and of offering gifts as a religious duty cannot be determined. History reveals that it existed in BABYLON in ancient times, also in PERSIA and EGYPT, even in China. It is quite certain that ABRAHAM knew of it when he migrated from UR (Gen. 14:17-20). Since MELCHIZEDEK was a priest of the Most High, it is certain that by Abraham's day the giving of tithes had been recognized as a holy deed (see Heb. 7:4). Dividing the spoils of war with rulers and religious leaders was widespread (1 Macc. 10:31). SAMUEL warned ISRAEL that the king whom they were demanding would exact tithes of their grain and flocks (1 Sam. 8:10-18). When JACOB made his covenant with God at BETHEL it included payment of tithes (Gen. 28:16-22).

It was a long time before definite legal requirements were set on tithing, hence customs in paying it varied. At first the tither was entitled to share his tithe with the LEVITES (Deut. 14:22-23). After the Levitical code had been completed, tithes belonged exclusively to the Levites (Num. 18:21). If a Hebrew lived too far from the TEMPLE to make taking his tithes practicable, he could sell his animals and use the money gained to buy substitutes at the temple (Deut. 14:24-26). This permit eventually led to gross abuses by priests (Matt. 21:12-13; Mk. 11:15-17). Tithed animals were shared with the Levites (Deut. 15:19-20).

The methods developed for paying the tithes and for their use became somewhat complicated when to the tithes of the FIRSTFRUITS (Prov. 3:9) were added the firstlings of the flocks (Exod. 13:12-13). Then when the Levitical system was established, provision for the upkeep of the sons of Levi was made by tithes (Num. 18:21-24). A penalty of twenty percent of the tithe was exacted from one who sold his tithes and refused to use the money to pay for a substitute (Lev. 27:31).

The Levites in turn gave a tenth to provide for the priests (Num. 18:25-32). The temple was the place to which tithes were taken (Deut. 12:5-12). One could not partake of his tithes at home, but only when delivered at the temple (12:17-18).

To make sure that no deceit would be practiced regarding tithing, each Hebrew was compelled to make a declaration of honesty before the Lord (Deut. 26:13-15). In the tithing of the flocks, every tenth animal that passed under the rod, regardless of its kind, was taken; no substitution was allowed (Lev. 27:32-33). Was there only one tithe each year or was the third-year tithe an extra one? Confusion exists about this, even among Hebrew scholars. As the needs for funds increased with the expansion of the temple service, a third-year tithe (all for the use of the Levites and those in need) was exacted. It seems probable that the increase of temple expenses, due to the number of priests and Levites, made it necessary to impose extra tithes. According to JOSEPHUS, a third tithe was collected (*Ant.* 4.4.3; 8.8.22). MALACHI railed at the Jews for refusing to bring their tithes to the temple storehouse (Mal. 3:8-10). This applied not only to money but also to grains, animals, and fowls, money being deposited in the treasury box (Lk. 21:1-4).

By the time of Christ, Roman rule had greatly affected the economic life of JUDEA, hence it was difficult for people to tithe. But that the laws regarding the tenth were still observed is shown by the fact that the PHARISEES tithed even the herbs that were used in seasoning food (Matt. 23:23; Lk. 11:42).

Titius Justus. tish'ee-uhs-juhs'tuhs'. See JUSTUS #2.

tittle. See DOT.

Titus. ti'tuhs (Gk. *Titos G5519*, from Latin *Titus*). **(1)** A convert, friend, and helper of PAUL (Tit. 1:4), in the NT mentioned only in Paul's letters, especially in 2 Corinthians. He was a Greek, a son of GENTILE parents (Gal. 2:3). After his conversion he accompanied Paul to JERUSALEM, where the apostle rejected the demand of the Judaists that Titus be circumcised. Hence, Titus became a person of significance for the principle of GEN-

© Dr. James C. Martin. On licence Ministero per I Beni e le Attivita Culturali – Soprintendenza Archaeologica di Roma. Rome, Italy.

The Arch of Titus in Rome (W side).

TILE admission to the church solely on the basis of FAITH in Christ. During Paul's third missionary journey Titus was assigned missions to CORINTH to solve its vexing problems (1 Cor. 1-6; 2 Cor. 2:13; 7:5-16) and to encourage material assistance to the needy at Jerusalem (2 Cor. 8). Much later Titus was in CRETE, left behind there by Paul to organize its churches (Tit. 1:4-5). He was requested to meet Paul at NICOPOLIS (3:12). Titus was consecrated, courageous, resourceful. He knew how to handle the quarrelsome Corinthians, the mendacious Cretans, and the pugnacious Dalmatians (2 Tim. 4:10). See also PASTORAL LETTERS.

(2) Titus Flavius Vespasianus was born in A.D. 39 and ruled as emperor of ROME for a short period, 79-81. While still a young man he had served as a tribune of the soldiers in Germany and Britain, and later accompanied his father, VESPASIAN, to Palestine at the time of the Jewish revolt. When the latter was called to ROME and was elevated to the imperial seat, Titus was left in charge of the war and brought it to an end by the capture and destruction of JERUSALEM in the year 70. Upon his return to Rome he celebrated the triumph with his father, and from this time was made a virtual partner in the government, clearly designated for the succession. When Vespasian died in 79 Titus became emperor. In many ways Titus was a contrast to his father. He was the darling of the populace, good looking, affable to everyone. After the parsimonious policy of Vespasian he spent lavishly

and was always remembered with affection in later years. His brief reign was noteworthy mainly for two disasters by which it was visited. In August of 79, Mount Vesuvius erupted and completely destroyed the two towns of Pompeii and Herculaneum, covering the former with a shower of hot ashes and pumice, the latter with a river of lava. In the year 80 there was a plague and disastrous fire at Rome; Titus generously aided the victims of this disaster, and did a great deal to repair the damage to the city. Among other things he finished the Colosseum (begun by Vespasian), and built the baths which bear his name. The reign of Titus was looked upon as a time of ideal happiness, and his untimely death in the year 81 caused universal sorrow.

Titus, Letter to. See PASTORAL LETTERS.

Titus Justus. See JUSTUS #2.

Tizite. ti´zit (Heb. *tiṣî H9407*, apparently the gentilic form of an unattested name such as *tiṣ*). Epithet applied to JOHA son of Shimri, one of DAVID's mighty warriors (1 Chr. 11:45). Presumably this designation identifies him as originating from an otherwise unknown place or tribe named "Tiz" (or the like), but it is unclear why his brother JEDIAEL does not receive the same description.

Toah. toh´uh (Heb. *tôaḥ H9346*, variant *tōḥû H9375*, meaning uncertain). Son of ZUPH, descendant of LEVI through KOHATH, and ancestor of SAMUEL (1 Chr. 6:34; apparently the same as NAHATH in v. 26 and TOHU in 1 Sam. 1:1, but the relationship among these three genealogical lists is debated).

Tob. tob (Heb. *ṭôb H3204*, "good, pleasant"). A town and district of S HAURAN mentioned as the place where JEPHTHAH went when he fled from his brothers (Jdg. 11:3, 5). Later, during the reign of DAVID, the AMMONITES hired twelve thousand mercenaries from Tob to defend themselves from the Israelites (2 Sam. 10:6, 8). Tob is apparently mentioned in Egyptian records, referring to an ARAMEAN state E of the JORDAN River, but NE of the GILEAD hill-country. It is generally identified as eṭ-Ṭayibeh, some 45 mi. (70 km.) NE of modern Amman.

Tob-Adonijah. tob′ad-uh-ni′juh (Heb. *ṭôb ʾădôniyyâ H3207*, "good is the Lord Yahweh"). One of six LEVITES whom King JEHOSHAPHAT sent to teach the LAW in the cities of JUDAH (2 Chr. 17:8). Some Greek MSS and other witnesses omit this name, however, and many scholars believe that it was introduced into the Hebrew text by a scribal mistake (duplicating and conflating the previous two names, Adonijah and Tobijah).

Tobiah. toh-bi′uh (Heb. *ṭôbiyyâ H3209*, short form of TOBIJAH, "Yahweh is good"; see TOBIJAH). **(1)** Ancestor of a family of returned exiles who could not prove their Israelite descent (Ezra 2:60; Neh. 7:62).

(2) An AMMONITE (or less likely a Jew living in AMMON, descendant of #1 above) who served as a Persian official and who joined with SANBAL-LAT and others in persistently opposing the work of NEHEMIAH (Neh. 2:10, 19; 4:3, 7; 6:1, 12-19; 7:62; 13:4, 7). Both he and his son JEHOHANAN bore Jewish names and were married to Jewish women. Tobiah was in high favor with the high priest, ELIASHIB, who gave him a guest room in the TEMPLE compound. He tried to frighten Nehemiah, who regarded him as his chief enemy and cast him and his household goods out of the temple guest chamber (13:4-9). Some scholars think that the family of TOBIAS (#2), which in the 3rd cent. B.C. vied with the family of ONIAS for the high priesthood, was descended from this Tobiah.

Tobias. toh-bi′uhs (Gk. *Tōbias*, from Heb. *ṭôbiyyâ H3209*, "Yahweh is good"; see TOBIAH). **(1)** Son of Tobit (Tob. 1:9 et al.). See APOCRYPHA.

(2) Father or grandfather of a wealthy Jewish man named Hyrcanus (2 Macc. 3:11). This Tobias may have been a descendant of TOBIAH (#2). According to JOSEPHUS (*Ant.* 12.5.1 §§237-

41), the powerful Tobiad family later supported MENELAUS against JASON in the struggle for the high priesthood.

Tobijah. toh-bi′juh (Heb. *ṭôbiyyāhû H3210* and *ṭôbiyyâ H3209*, "Yahweh is good"). **(1)** One of six LEVITES whom King JEHOSHAPHAT sent to teach the LAW in the cities of JUDAH (2 Chr. 17:8). Appointed to the same mission were a number of princes and priests.

(2) One of a group of Jewish exiles who brought gold and silver from BABYLON to help those who had returned under ZERUBBABEL; from these gifts a crown was to be made for Joshua (JESHUA) the high priest (Zech. 6:10, 14). The form of the Hebrew name in this passage is elsewhere rendered TOBIAH in the KJV and other English Bibles (Ezra 2:60 et al.; this inconsistency has no basis in the Hebrew text).

Tobit, Book of. See APOCRYPHA.

Tochen. See TOKEN (PLACE).

Togarmah. toh-gahr′muh (Heb. *tōgarmâ H9328*, meaning unknown). Son of GOMER and grandson of JAPHETH (Gen. 10:3; 1 Chr. 1:6). He was no doubt the eponymous ancestor of a people group that bore his name. In EZEKIEL a nation called BETH TOGARMAH is described as carrying on extensive trade with TYRE in horses and mules (Ezek. 27:14); it is mentioned also as one of the allies of MAGOG in association with Gomer, PERSIA, CUSH, and PUT (38:6). Togarmah is probably to be associated with Til-garimmu, a city located in Urartu (ARMENIA), the eastern part of CAPPADOCIA, SE of the Black Sea.

Tohu. See TOAH.

Toi. See TOU.

Token (place). toh′kuhn (Heb. *tōken H9421*, possibly "measure"). Also Tochen. A town within the tribal territory of SIMEON, listed between RIMMON and ASHAN (1 Chr. 4:32). The parallel list omits Token and has ETHER in its place (Josh. 19:7 MT), but some scholars believe that Token is original and that it dropped out of the Hebrew text (to keep the total number of towns at four, Ain and Rimmon can be read as the name of one town, EN RIMMON). However, this view leaves unexplained the omission of Ether in 1 Chronicles, and so others argue that Token and Ether are alternate names for the same town. If they are different towns, the location of Token is unknown.

token (sign). A word that in the KJV of the OT is used practically synonymously with "sign" (Exod. 13:9, 16). In Num. 17:10 and Josh. 2:12 it means a memorial of something past. In the NT (KJV) "token" is self-explanatory: Mk. 14:44 (NIV, "signal"); Phil. 1:28 (NIV, "sign"); 2 Thess. 1:5; 3:17 (NIV "evidence," "distinguishing mark").

Tokhath. See TIKVAH.

Tola. toh′luh (Heb. *tôlāʿ H9356*, prob. "worm" or "crimson"; gentilic *tôlāʿî H9358*, "Tolaite"). (1) Firstborn son of ISSACHAR, grandson of JACOB, and eponymous ancestor of the Tolaite clan (Gen. 46:13; Num. 26:23). In the time of DAVID, the descendants of Tola who were "fighting men" numbered 22,600 (1 Chr. 7:1-2; some interpret the number to mean 22 muster units totaling 600 soldiers).

(2) Son of Puah, descendant of Issachar, and judge (leader) of Israel for twenty-three years after the time of ABIMELECH (Jdg. 10:1-2). He did not live within the tribal territory of Issachar but rather in the hill country of EPHRAIM in a town called Shamir. See SHAMIR (PLACE). The expression "rose to save Israel" is used only of Tola, but the text does not give additional details about his work.

Tolad. See ELTOLAD.

toll. See TAXES.

tomb. This term may refer to a chamber, vault, or crypt, either underground or above. Sometimes it designates a pretentious burying place on a special site. It may be a beehive structure where many bodies can be placed. In general, any burying place is a tomb. The Hebrews were not impressed by the tombs of EGYPT, hence their burials remained

simple, most burying sites being unmarked. Some kings were interred in a vault in JERUSALEM (1 Ki. 2:10; 11:43); just where this burial place was located has not been determined. Some mention their "father's tomb" (2 Sam. 2:32; Neh. 2:3).

Tombs of NT times were either caves or they were holes dug into stone cliffs. Since only grave clothes are mentioned in connection with tombs, it seems certain that the Jews used neither caskets nor sarcophagi. Tombs carried no inscriptions, no paintings. Embalming, learned in Egypt (Gen. 50:2), was soon a lost art (Jn. 11:39). A general opening gave access to vaults that opened on ledges

Rolling stone at Herod's family tomb.

to provide support for the stone doors. The door to such a grave weighed from one to three tons (.9 to 2.7 metric tons), hence the miracle of the stone being rolled away from Jesus' tomb (Lk. 24:2; Jn. 20:1). See BURIAL.

tongs. This English term is usually the rendering of Hebrew *melqāḥayim H4920* (the dual ending suggests a device consisting of two pieces). Both the NIV and the NRSV use "tongs" in three occurrences of this Hebrew noun (1 Ki. 7:49; 2 Chr. 4:21; Isa. 6:6), but elsewhere the NIV has "wick trimmers" and the NRSV "snuffers" (Exod. 25:38; 37:23; Num. 4:9; the KJV has "tongs" in all but Exod. 37:23, where it uses "snuffers"). In most of the passages, the reference is probably to devices made of gold that were used to dress the wicks of the seven-branched LAMPSTAND in the

TABERNACLE and TEMPLE, the burnt parts of the wicks being placed in snuff trays.

tongue. This term (Heb. *lāšôn H4383*; Gk. *glōssa G1185*) is used in a variety of ways: (1) An organ of the body, used sometimes in drinking (lapping) as GIDEON's men did (Jdg. 7:5; see also Ps. 68:23; Zech. 14:12; Mk. 7:33; Rev. 16:10). (2) An organ of speech (Job 27:4; Ps. 35:28; Prov. 15:2; Mk. 7:35). (3) A language or dialect (Gen. 10:5, 20; Deut. 28:49; Dan. 1:4; Acts 1:19; 2:8; 10:46). (4) A people or race having a common language (Isa. 66:18; Dan. 3:4; Rev. 5:9; 10:11).

The figurative uses, based on (2) above, are interesting. The tongue can be sharpened, that is, made to utter caustic words (Ps. 64:3; 140:3). It is a sharp sword (57:4). It is gentle when it uses quieting language (Prov. 25:15). Ranting is a rage of tongues (Ps. 31:20; Hos. 7:16). The tongue is the pen of an eager writer (Ps. 45:1), a shrewd antagonist (52:2). The tongue of the just is a treasure (Prov. 10:20; 12:18) and a mark of wisdom (Isa. 50:4). It is like a bow (Jer. 9:3), an arrow (9:8), and a lash (18:18). The miracle at PENTECOST included "tongues of fire" (Acts 2:3). The tongue is little but can do great things (Jas. 3:5, 8).

tongues, confusion of. See BABEL.

tongues, gift of. A spiritual gift mentioned in Mk. 16:17; Acts 2:1-13; 10:44-46; 19:6; 1 Cor. 12-14. See GIFTS, SPIRITUAL. The gift appeared on the day of PENTECOST with the outpouring of the HOLY SPIRIT on the assembled believers (Acts 2:1-13). The *external* phenomena heralding the Spirit's coming were followed by the *internal* filling of all those gathered together there. The immediate result was that they "began to speak in other tongues." The context makes clear that "other tongues" means languages different from their own and, by implication, previously unknown to the speakers; for the amazement of the crowd, coming from many lands, was caused by the fact that *Galileans* could speak these varied languages. Under the Spirit's control they spoke "as the Spirit enabled"; the utterances were praise to God (2:11; 10:46). The gift was not designed merely to facilitate the preaching of the GOSPEL; the message in 2:14-36 was not delivered in more than one language. There is no express NT instance of this gift being used to evangelize others. (At LYSTRA, PAUL and BARNABAS preached in Greek, not the native Lycaonian, which they did not understand.) The gift of tongues on Pentecost was a direct witness to God's presence and work in their midst. While the gift came upon all those assembled when the Spirit was poured out (2:4), there is no indication that the three thousand converts at Pentecost received the gift.

It is not explicitly stated that the SAMARITANS received this gift when the Spirit was imparted to them, but the request of SIMON Magus to buy the power to bestow the Spirit indicates that some *external* manifestation did result (Acts 8:14-19). The Pentecostal phenomenon clearly appeared again when the Holy Spirit was poured out on the GENTILES in the house of CORNELIUS (10:44-46). Here again it served as a miraculous token of the divine approval and acceptance of these Gentile believers (11:15-17; 15:7-9). The appearing of the phenomenon in connection with the twelve disciples at EPHESUS (19:6), who dispensationally stood before Pentecost, marked the full incorporation of this group into the church and authenticated Paul's teaching.

The gift of tongues is mentioned by Paul as one of the spiritual gifts so richly bestowed on the Corinthian believers. Their reaction to this gift drew forth Paul's discussion of the varied gifts. They are enumerated, compared, and evaluated by their usefulness to the CHURCH. He lists the gifts twice and places tongues and their interpretation at the end (1 Cor. 12:8-10, 28-30), thus rebuking the Corinthians' improper evaluation of this spectacular gift. He emphasized the comparative value of tongues and prophecy by insisting that "five intelligible words" spoken in the church were of more value than "ten thousand words in a tongue" not understood (14:19). Paul felt it necessary to regulate the use of tongues in their assembly; the ideal place for their exercise was in private (14:28). He insisted that not more than two or three speak in tongues, and that they do so in turn, and one should interpret; no one was to speak in tongues if no interpreter was present (14:27-28). Speaking in tongues was not prohibited (14:39), but intelligent preaching in understandable words was vastly superior.

Two views are held as to the exact nature of the Corinthian "tongues." One view holds that they were foreign languages that the speakers were miraculously enabled to speak without having previously learned them. This view is demanded by Acts 2:1-13, unless it is maintained that the two phenomena are quite distinct. That they were intelligible utterances is urged from the fact that they could be interpreted and were the vehicle of prayer, praise, and thanksgiving (1 Cor. 14:14-17).

Many commentators, however, hold that the Corinthian tongues were not identical with the tongues at Pentecost but were ecstatic outbursts of prayer and praise in which the utterances often became abnormal and incoherent and the connection with the speaker's own conscious intellectual activity was suspended. It is held that the utterances were incomprehensible to the speaker as well as to the audience (1 Cor. 14:14) and that the resultant edification was emotional only (14:4). But 14:4 may only mean that the person's understanding was "unfruitful" to others. Its advocates further hold that this view is indicated in the fact that interpretation was likewise a special gift (12:10).

From 1 Cor. 14:27-28 it is clear that this speaking in tongues was not uncontrollable. It was very different from the religious frenzy that marked some pagan rites in which the worshiper lost control both of reason and the power of will. Any manifestation of tongues that is not under the speaker's control is thereby suspect (14:32).

tongues of fire. One of the phenomena that occurred at the outpouring of the HOLY SPIRIT on the day of PENTECOST. Believers assembled in an upper room saw "what seemed to be tongues of fire that separated and came to rest on each of them" (Acts 2:3) as they were all filled with the Holy Spirit. The tongues of fire were symbolic of the Holy Spirit, who came in power on the church.

tools. The Bible makes reference to tools only incidentally, usually in connection with the arts and crafts (see OCCUPATIONS AND PROFESSIONS). The references to BEZALEL and OHOLIAB, who were especially endowed with skills to build the TABERNACLE (Exod. 31:1-11; 35:30—36:1), and to the importation of Phoenician craftsmen by SOLO-

MON to build the TEMPLE (1 Ki. 7:13), suggest that not many Hebrews were gifted in the use of tools.

Woodworkers made use of metal saws, probably of the Egyptian pull-type, with the teeth pointing toward the handle. They were also used for cutting STONE (cf. 1 Ki. 7:9; Isa. 10:15). Mallets were probably used by the carpenter instead of hammers (Jdg. 4:21; cf. 5:26). At least a half dozen Hebrew words are used with reference to the ax, indicating a variety of these useful tools. The blade might be set parallel, or at right angles to the handle, which itself might be long or short. Stone, bronze, and iron were materials used, and methods of hafting varied considerably (cf. Deut. 20:19 and 19:5 with 2 Ki. 6:5 and Jer. 10:3). Axes also doubled as weapons (Jdg. 9:48; Jer. 46:22). The carpenter used also scrapers, planes, and chisels for cutting (Isa. 44:13), with awls and drills for making holes (Exod. 21:6; Deut. 15:17). The knife was ubiquitous, and used for all types of cutting. For layout and measuring, the line was used, with the plumb-bob, compasses, some kind of square, and rules. Scripture references to these items are numerous.

Agricultural tools included the plowshare, sickle or pruning hook, ox-goad, mattock, forks and shovels, and the ax (1 Sam. 13:21; 1 Ki. 7:40, 45; Joel 3:13). Sharpening was mostly accomplished with stones and files (1 Sam. 13:21). The blacksmith sharpened many tools by heating the metal and hammering out the edges. The potter had his own variety, including the wheel, kiln, tournettes, paddle-and-anvil,

© Dr. James C. Martin. The Eretz Israel Museum. Photographed by permission.

Various tools crafted by carpenters, including plow, threshing sledge, olive press, winnowing fork, and broom.

T

scrapers, and burnishers (see POTTERY). Other crafts, such as weaving, tanning, dyeing, tent-making, painting, jewelry-making, engraving, sculpture, etc., all had their special tools and equipment.

tooth. See TEETH.

topaz. See MINERALS.

Tophel. toh′fuhl (Heb. *tōpel H9523*, meaning uncertain). A town or region "in the desert east of the Jordan," mentioned only in the opening words of Deuteronomy; it is one of several places that help to locate the area where MOSES spoke to Israel (Deut. 1:1). The precise location of Tophel is uncertain. Many scholars tentatively identify it with the modern village of eṭ-Ṭafileh, in a fertile valley some 20 mi. SE (32 km.) of the S tip of the DEAD SEA and 7 mi. (11 km.) NNE of PETRA.

Topheth. toh′fit (Heb. *tōpet H9532* and *topteh H9533* [Isa. 30:33], possibly "hearth, cooking stove"). KJV Tophet. An area in the Valley of HINNOM; the latter was probably part of the Wadi er-Rababi, the deep-sided valley W and S of JERUSALEM that traditionally separated the tribes of BENJAMIN and JUDAH. The Valley of Hinnom served as a sacred grove or garden of the Canaanites, later the center of BAAL worship by apostate Jews (Jer. 32:35). The cultic activity seems to have involved the ritual sacrifice of firstborn infants to the god MOLECH. The name Topheth occurs only in the OT (2 Ki. 23:10; Isa. 30:33; Jer. 7:31-32; 19:6, 11-14). The cult practiced there was most popular in the reigns of AHAZ and MANASSEH, who are said to have sacrificed their own sons in Hinnom, undoubtedly a reference to Tophet (2 Chr. 28:3; 33:6). Under the restoration of JOSIAH, the shrine of Topheth was desecrated and apparently destroyed (2 Ki. 23:10), but the memory of the awesome place lived on and became a symbol of the desolation and judgment of sin. It was filled with refuse from the walled city throughout later antiquity and its precise location is lost.

Torah. toh′ruh (Heb. *tôrâ H9368*, "instruction, rule, law"). The Hebrew name given to the PENTATEUCH, that is, the five books of MOSES. This term, often

rendered "law," must not be interpreted in a solely legal sense—a connotation that was encouraged by the SEPTUAGINT with its rendition of the Hebrew noun with Greek *nomos G3795*. Rather, Torah is primarily a way of life derived from the COVENANT relationship between God and Israel. For example, the word can refer equally well to prophetic utterance (cf. Isa. 1:10; 8:16) and to the counseling of the wise (Prov. 13:4). Even in the Pentateuch, the term sometimes means decisions in respect to equity (Exod. 18:20), instruction in respect to behavior (Gen. 26:5; Exod. 13:9), rules in respect to cult (Lev. 6:9, 14, 25; et al.). It also covers the principle of justice: there shall be one Torah for the native and for the stranger (Exod. 12:49). In rabbinic tradition, Torah connotes the written code plus oral interpretation as codified into the 613 precepts. See TALMUD. Thus Torah is the Jewish way of life, requiring total dedication by reason of the covenant.

torch. See LAMP.

tormentor. This term is used by the KJV as the literal rendering of *basanistēs G991*, which occurs only in Jesus' parable of the two debtors (Matt. 18:34). The Greek term was applied to jailers whose job it was not only to guard prisoners, but also to examine and torture them. Ordinarily, debtors were sold into slavery if they could not pay, but sometimes they were sent to a detention center; here a merciless *basanistēs* would make their lives miserable until restitution was made.

tortoise. See ANIMALS.

Tou. too (Heb. *tōʿû H9495* and *tōʿi H9497*, possibly a HURRIAN name). Also Toi. King of HAMATH on the ORONTES River. All that is known about him is that he sent his son JORAM (Hadoram) to DAVID with gifts, congratulating the Israelite king for his defeat of their common foe HADADEZER of ZOBAH (2 Sam. 8:9-10; 1 Chr. 18:9-10). Some think that Tou's objective was to establish a treaty relationship with David; in any case, a diplomatic relationship would have been beneficial to both parties.

tow. This English term, referring to the short and coarse fibers of flax before spinning, is used by the

KJV in three passages (Jdg. 16:9; Isa. 1:31; 43:17). Modern versions use a variety of equivalents, such as "string, fiber, tinder, wick."

towel. This word is used by English versions only in Jn. 13:4-5, where it renders Greek *lention G3317*, referring to the linen cloth used by Jesus to dry the feet of the apostles in the UPPER ROOM.

tower. A lofty structure used for purposes of protection or attack, such as to defend a city wall, particularly at a gate or a corner in the wall (2 Chr. 14:7; 26:9); to protect flocks and herds and to safeguard roads (2 Ki. 17:9; 2 Chr. 26:10; 27:4); to observe and to attack a city (Isa. 23:13); to protect a vineyard (Matt. 21:33).

town. One normally thinks of the English word *town* as referring to something larger than a VILLAGE but smaller than a CITY, yet in actual usage the distinctions often blur (as when we speak of Chicago as a town). In the Bible it is even more difficult to discriminate clearly between the relevant terms. The primary Hebrew word for "city," *ʿir H6551*, can be applied to a place as large as NINEVEH (Jon. 1:3), but it is also used very frequently of towns whose inhabitants could not have numbered more than a few hundred. The same is true of Greek *polis G4484* (applied, e.g., to JERUSALEM, Matt. 4:5, but also to NAZARETH, 2:23). The Hebrew term for "daughter," *bat H1426*, can refer to the dependent villages of a walled city (e.g., the settlements surrounding HESHBON, Num. 21:25), but it is applied as well to larger cities in figurative language (e.g., "daughter Zion," Isa. 1:8 NRSV). Several other Hebrew terms can be applied to small villages (e.g., Num. 32:41; Neh. 11:25-30; Esth. 9:19). Greek *kōmē G3267* is applied only to small towns (Matt. 9:35 et al.).

According to Lev. 25:31, "villages without walls" come under a different law of redemption: its houses were to be returned to the seller in the JUBILEE Year, whereas city houses could not be redeemed if more than a year passed from the time of sale. In the OT period, the city was distinguished by having a defensive wall as well as being the center of commerce and industry, and in some cases the place where the local governor lived. In

the NT period, the difference between city and town (or village) consisted in the possession of a constitution and law differing from country law, and following the law of the crown. In later times, a city was so designated if it was the bishop's seat. Towns were principally country agricultural centers, dependent on walled cities for protection and for the sale and exchange of farm produce.

town clerk. See OCCUPATIONS AND PROFESSIONS (under *clerk*).

Trachonitis. See TRACONITIS.

Traconitis. trak´uh-ni´tis (Gk. *Trachōnitis G5551*, "rugged region"). Also Trachonitis. A district E of the province of GALILEE and S of the city of DAMASCUS; during the time of Jesus it was part of the tetrarchy of PHILIP (Lk. 3:1). In 23 B.C. HEROD the Great received the task of pacifying Traconitis, Batanea (BASHAN), and Auranitis (HAURAN), unruly tribes to the NE of the JORDAN. After Herod's death in 4 B.C., his domain was divided among his three sons, and Philip was granted this territory, inhabited mainly by non-Jews. Philip died in A.D. 34 and his territory came under the jurisdiction of SYRIA, but in 37 the emperor CALIGULA granted it to AGRIPPA I, grandson of Herod the Great. Traconitis was only a small part of this tetrarchy, located around Tracon in the NE of the territory. It corresponds with the modern el-Lejaᶜ, a plateau of some 350 sq. mi. (900 sq. km.), consisting of volcanic lava beds, intercalated with volcanic necks, ash beds, and sills. The dissected terrain, the thin soils, and its proximity to the desert to the E, all contributed to its poverty, sparsity of population, and the lawless character of the district.

trade and travel.

I. Trade in the OT. ABRAHAM came from a trading port, UR of the Chaldees, which stood in those days at the head of the Persian Gulf, on whose waters humans first learned deep-sea navigation. POTTERY from Ur has been identified in the ruins of Mohenjo-Daro on the Indus, and Ur was no doubt a trading station between the seaborne commerce of the Persian Gulf and the Arabian Sea,

T

T

and the caravan routes of the EUPHRATES Valley. The most negotiable route between E and W ran this way. The fact that Abraham was rich in gold and silver as well as in the nomad assets of flocks and herds (Gen. 13:2; 24:22, 53) is an indication of the wealth of his birthplace and of the commerce that no doubt existed between the desert and the town. The middlemen of this early commerce in the ANE were the people of the desert.

EGYPT, from earliest times, had been a great trading nation. A famous wall painting tells pictorially the story of the exploratory trading expedition sent by Princess Hatshepsut to Punt on the Somali coast fourteen centuries before Christ, and an interesting papyrus speaks of Wen-Amon's quest for fine cedar on the Lebanese shore three centuries later. Hatshepsut's venture had been a quest for myrrh trees, for the embalming practices of the Egyptians needed vast imports of spices and incense. The southern section of the Arabian Peninsula, known as Arabia Felix (Fortunate ARABIA), owed its name to the myrrh and frankincense produced there, and the bulk of this commerce followed the caravan routes NW through the peninsula with Egypt as the chief market. SLAVE trading formed a profitable sideline, and it is significant that JOSEPH was sold to a company of ISHMAELITES carrying myrrh into Egypt (Gen. 37:25). The rich imports of the land were balanced by an export trade in corn, and by tribute money from the neighboring spheres of Egyptian dominance. It is recorded that corn was paid for in weighed silver (41:57; 42:3, 25, 35; 43:11). Egypt was a heavy importer of precious stones and metals, some of which must have been of Indian origin brought up the RED SEA and through the canal, which was periodically open between the head of the waterway and the NILE. Egyptian monuments speak of similar commerce with the N and with the Minoan thalassocracy of CRETE (the Keftiu of early records).

The first organized commerce of the Hebrew people was under SOLOMON, whose farsighted trading ventures were inspired by the Phoenician mercantile cities of TYRE and SIDON. It is possible that the building of the temple first made the Phoenicians aware of the market to be found in their own hinterland, and of the profit to be gained from a partnership with the people who dominated

the land route to the Gulf of AQABAH. Cedar for the architectural projects of David and Solomon was collected at Tyre from the lumbermen in the ranges and rafted down to JOPPA, a distance of 74 mi. (120 km.). It was then hauled 32 mi. (52 km.) up to JERUSALEM (1 Ki. 5:6, 9; 2 Chr. 2:16). The partnership thus begun was extended in a joint venture out of EZION GEBER at the head of the Gulf of Aqabah, down the Red Sea to OPHIR and INDIA. HIRAM king of Tyre supplied the pilots (1 Ki. 9:27-28; 10:11). Ophir was in all probability in S Arabia, but the cargoes mentioned in 1 Ki. 10:22 suggest a trading connection with India.

A larger type of vessel was used in this ocean-going commerce, the "ships of Tarshish" (10:22 KJV; NIV, "trading ships"). TARSHISH was probably Tartessos in Spain, and for such distant and exacting voyaging the Phoenicians had developed a sturdy type of vessel called by this name. An "Indiaman" or a "China clipper" in the days of more recent ocean commerce did not necessarily journey to the lands mentioned in the title. They were types of reliable ocean craft. Similarly the Egyptians called the Phoenician galleys engaged on the Cretan run "Keftiu ships." The text quoted seems to imply that Solomon's traders were speedily throwing off the tutelage of Tyre and venturing forth on their own. Judea supplied Phoenicia with wheat, honey, oil, and balm (1 Ki. 5:11).

Centuries later, Tyrian traders would bring fish into Jerusalem and distress NEHEMIAH by their SABBATH trading (Neh. 13:16). The timber trade too continued into postcaptivity days, and EZRA made arrangements similar to those of Solomon to secure his supplies of Lebanese timber (1 Ki. 5:6, 9; 2 Chr. 2:16; Ezra 3:7). Oil was also exported to Egypt (Hos. 12:1), and a small domestic export trade in woven goods from Judea seems to be implied in Prov. 31:24.

When the Hebrew monarchy fell apart after Solomon's death, it is possible that an interesting commercial situation may have arisen. ISRAEL, the northern kingdom, must have inherited the profitable but seductive alliance with the Phoenician trading towns. JEZEBEL, daughter of the prince of Sidon, married AHAB to seal this partnership. The southern kingdom, however, lay across communication lines to Aqabah and the Red Sea, and there is every evidence that JUDAH had reverted, after Solomon, to an agricultural economy with nothing more than petty trading. Apart from a half-hearted attempt by JEHOSHAPHAT to revive it (1 Ki. 22:48), the eastern trade seems to have vanished with the king who inspired and ordered it. It may have been at this time that Phoenicians, denied the convenient route down the Red Sea, discovered the sea route to India by way of the Cape of Good Hope. A passage in Herodotus (*Hist.* 4.42) seems to imply that the intrepid traders succeeded in this amazing achievement. The prosperity of the Phoenician cities certainly continued, and Ezek. 27 is an eloquent record of the wide and tireless trading activity of Tyre. Ahab's prosperity is also vouched for by archaeological confirmation of the king's "ivory palace" (1 Ki. 22:39).

The commercial consequences of the break with BAAL worship and the death of Jezebel is an interesting speculation. Tyre, without great difficulty, could strangle the economic life of Israel. Tyre's dependence on the hinterland for primary produce would provide a strong deterrent, but there is no doubt that the choice on Mount CARMEL with which ELIJAH confronted the people involved economic as well as theological considerations. The Hebrew kingdoms from this time onward fell into the background as far as commerce was concerned. The EXILE brought vast depopulation, and the restored Israel was a largely agricultural economy. Internal interchange of goods was vigorous enough from earliest times, and provisions in the law lay stress on fairness of dealing, and honesty in WEIGHTS AND MEASURES (Lev. 19:35-36; Deut. 25:13-16). The petty trading in the TEMPLE, castigated by CHRIST, was a sample of the seamier side of this internal commerce; but the foreign trade, which invited investment and brought great wealth, was no more. Palestine at the close of the OT and in the time of Christ was a poor land.

II. Trade in the NT. Trade and commerce have small place in the GOSPELS. The people of Palestine were aware of the activities of merchant and trader, for such parables as those of the talents and the merchant who found a "pearl of great price" were obviously meant to be understood by those to whom they were addressed. Trade, in the wider sense of the word, all through NT times, was

Selling grains and spices is still part of trade and commerce today in Jerusalem's Old City.

supremely in the hands of ROME and of ITALY. There was a growing interference of the state in matters of commerce. The legal machinery by which a "mark on his right hand or on his forehead" could prevent the nonconformist from buying or selling (Rev. 13:16-17) was early apparent.

The foreign trade of the ROMAN EMPIRE was extensive and varied; it was also one-sided, in important cases, for the hoards of Roman coins commonly found in India are an indication of perilously unbalanced trade and great leakage of bullion. Latin and Greek words in early Irish, German, Iranian, and even in Indian and Mongolian tongues, suggest the influence of trade. Archaeology, especially on the S Indian coast, provides similar evidence. Roman merchants were ubiquitous. There was a Roman market at Delphi outside the sacred precincts for the trade in amulets and souvenirs, and this was probably typical of Italian enterprise abroad wherever crowds were gathered for sacred or profane purposes. From the second century B.C. a Roman city stood on Delos, the Aegean center of the slave trade, and when Mithridates in 88 B.C. massacred the Italian residents of ASIA MINOR and the surrounding coasts, twenty-five thousand fell in Delos alone out of a total of one hundred thousand, mostly traders and the agents of commerce.

Rome itself was a vast market, and a grim satiric chapter in the Apocalypse (Rev. 18)—constructed after the fashion of an OT taunt song, partly in imitation of Ezek. 27—speaks of the wealth and volume of the capital's trade and the disruption of the world's economy at the fall and passing of a

T

market so rich. Roman trade extended far beyond the boundaries of the empire. It is certain that merchants from Italy carried their goods into unsubdued Germany, Scandinavia, India, and perhaps China. All this activity sprang from Rome's dominance, the peace that she widely policed, and the absence of political frontiers. There was reason in the merchants' lament predicted in the chapter quoted. Fortunes could be made and lost and made over again. And of AUGUSTUS the merchants said that "through him they sailed the seas in safety, through him they could make their wealth, through him they were happy." The fascinating account of the last journey of PAUL to Rome (Acts 27), first in a ship from ADRAMYTTIUM and then in an Alexandrian freighter, probably under charter to the Roman government for the transport of Egyptian corn to the capital, gives a firsthand picture of the hazards of trade, and of the navigation, the ships, and the management of Mediterranean commerce.

There is not much information about the commodities of export trade. Oysters came to Rome from Britain in barrels of sea water. The tin trade of Cornwall, first exploited by the Phoenicians, doubtless continued under Rome. Northern Gaul seems to have had the rudiments of an exporting textile industry, and Gaul certainly exported Samian pottery. Underwater archaeology on wrecked ships has revealed that large cargoes of wine were carried. A monogram of a double "S" seems to indicate that one such freighter, wrecked near Marseilles, was the property of a shipowner who lived at Delos, one Severus Sestius. On the subject of mass production for such trade there is little information, and none concerning the business organization involved. Certain localities, however, became famous for special commodities, and the commerce implied was no doubt in the hands of specialist traders working a market of their own choice and creation. LYDIA, for example (Acts 16:14), "a dealer in purple cloth from the city of Thyatira" in Asia Minor, was found at PHILIPPI in MACEDONIA in pursuit of her trade. Corinthian bronze and the Cilician cloth that was the raw material of Paul's "tentmaking" were probably distributed, locally or abroad, by similar private enterprise (18:3). The imagery of John's apocalyptic letter to LAODICEA (Rev. 3:14-18) is based partly on trade and industry of the rich Asian town. An important item of trade in EPHESUS, now that the harbor was silting and the port losing its trade and prosperity to SMYRNA, was the manufacture of silver shrines of Artemis to sell to the pilgrims and tourists who visited the famous temple.

Ramsay's illuminating research revealed a Laodicean trade in valuable wool garments of various kinds. Glossy black fleeces were produced in this district and the neighboring COLOSSE by some system of crossbreeding, the genetic effects of which were apparent in the Anatolian flocks of the area until comparatively recent times. There is also evidence of a Laodicean eye salve, based probably on the thermal mud of the nearby HIERAPOLIS. Hence the taunt in the letter about "white garments," and the anointing of the eyes of the spirit with a more effective medicine. Another of the seven churches of the Apocalypse was a center of trade and commerce. More TRADE GUILDS are named in the records of THYATIRA than in those of any other Asian city. Lydia's trade (Acts 16:14) possibly fell under the category of the dyers. They brewed a red dye, perhaps the modern turkey red, from the madder root, which grows abundantly in the district. This PURPLE was nearer in color to scarlet than blue, and Lydia's presence in Macedonia, 500 mi. (800 km.) away, suggests that the commodity was an important export. It is curious to note in this connection that John uses the figure of JEZEBEL, the woman given to AHAB of Israel to seal a commercial and political alliance with PHOENICIA, to describe a "Nicolaitan" of Thyatira, whose fault may have been some spiritually damaging trade association with the surrounding pagan world.

The trade guilds were a major source of difficulty for Christians who sought in their work and in their social activity to emerge from a pagan world with their conscience intact. The guilds or collegia are mentioned in Acts 19 as a source of organized opposition to the preaching of Christianity. The guilds were not trade unions in the modern sense of the word. Their functions were primarily social, and they covered all trades and professions. There are records of guilds of bankers, doctors, architects, producers of linen and woolen goods, workers in metal or stone or clay, builders, carpenters, farmers, fishers, bakers, pastry cooks, embalmers, and transport workers. Like the modern Rotary Club, the guilds satisfied the need for social intercourse, but in the close-knit society of the ancient world they exercised a function and demonstrated an influence unlike that of any comparable organization today.

In Ephesus the guild of silversmiths and allied trades exerted enough pressure on authority and public opinion to check the free activities of Paul in the city. The famous letter of Pliny (*Ep.* 10.96), in which the repression of vigorous Christian activity in BITHYNIA in A.D. 112 is vividly described, is fairly clear indication that the guild of the butchers, alarmed at the falling-off in sales of sacrificial meat, was the ally of the pagan priesthoods in rousing the official persecution of the thriving church. Nor was it easy for Christians to prosper in their trade or business if they attempted to refrain from membership in the appropriate guild or participation in its activities. Since those activities included periodic feasts in the temple of the god or goddess whose patronage was traditionally acknowledged by the trade or calling concerned, what was the faithful Christian to do? Hence the activities of the "Nicolaitans," the "followers of Balaam" and of "Jezebel" of Thyatira, castigated by Jude, Peter, and John. The simple functions and operations of trade and commerce may thus have proved a source of embarrassment, controversy, and division in the early church.

III. Travel. Trade implied travel, and many of the great journeys of the ancient world were made in the pursuit of commerce. Those who pioneered the trade routes from the Euphrates and the Persian Gulf to the Indus civilization and Ceylon must have been intrepid voyagers. The blazing of the "amber route" from Italy to the Baltic coast, the "incense routes" from Arabia Felix through Petra to Palestine, or the Phoenician seaways to Cornwall and the W African coast, not to mention the circumnavigation of the continent, must have been by experienced and determined travelers. All this voyaging was in the interest of ultimate commercial gain. But there were other motives:

A. Colonization. Motivated first by the pressure of increasing population on the limited resources of their homeland, Greek colonies spread around the coasts of the Mediterranean and Black seas, unbroken save for the length of African coastland from the Gulf of Syrtis Major westward. These colonies were places of trade as well as of settlement, and the population often remained distinctive and apart from the natives of the area. Communication was maintained between colony and metropolis, and this was a major occasion of

This aerial view shows a section through which passed the so-called Via Maris, a major trade road of ancient Palestine, connecting Egypt, Europe, and Asia. (View to the W.)

© Dr. James C. Martin

ancient travel. Motives similar to that which sent Abraham's steward to the homeland in search of a bride for Isaac kept people moving over such routes of folk migration.

B. Exploration. Curiosity and a desire for knowledge have always been important objects for human wandering. Curiosity accounted for the journey of the queen of SHEBA to visit Solomon (1 Ki. 10); and if the MAGI, as their gifts imply, also came from Arabia Felix, it was the same SE caravan route that, in a nobler curiosity, brought the Nativity visitors to BETHLEHEM. Curiosity, with historical ends in view, had been the travel motive of the Greek Herodotus in the fifth century B.C. His journeyings covered a wider area even than those of Paul. Exploration was organized by Hatshepsut around the Somali coast, by Alexander around Arabia, and by Nero up the Nile. Trade and conquest were the motives in mind. Less complex were the aims of the daring party from the Bay of Tripoli who, according to Herodotus (*Hist.* 4.174), crossed the Sahara, discovered the Pygmies, and first saw the Niger.

C. Migration. Great folk movements fill all ancient history from neolithic times onward, and the Bible mentions directly and indirectly instances of such mass travel. Abraham left Ur by the NW caravan routes that followed the Fertile Crescent in a great curve up the Euphrates Valley and around into Canaan. The same route continued down the Jordan Valley and by the coast road into Egypt, or by way of the Arabah into the Sinai triangle or Egypt. It was along this southern route that Jacob's family journeyed on their various movements into and out of Egypt. The nomad movements of the Israelites after the Egyptian oppression form a record of mass migration like the "folk-wanderings" of the Indo-European tribes that peopled Europe and determined the character of Iranian and Indian ethnology in the second millennium B.C. Toward the close of the millennium, this movement assumed much more massive shape. A sudden influx of refugees would account for the aggressive imperialism of the Philistines in the time of Saul and David. The movements of conquest and deportation might find a place under this head. It was a policy of Assyria and of Babylon to transfer large masses of subject populations; and such travel,

arduous and enforced though it was, occasioned much movement geographically. There was some freedom of communication between the deportees and those who remained behind, as might be illustrated both from the books of Nehemiah and Ezra and from the apocryphal book of Tobit.

D. Pilgrimage. Religious centers like Jerusalem have always been an occasion of travel. The Gospels mention the annual influx from Galilee into Jerusalem, and the account of the crucifixion speaks of one SIMON from CYRENE in LIBYA who was present in the Holy City as a pilgrim. Paul (Acts 20:16) was anxious to be in Jerusalem in time for Pentecost and was prepared to travel from Greece for the purpose.

E. Preaching. The necessities of preaching and teaching caused widespread travel in both Greek and Roman times; and this, of course, is most strikingly illustrated in the well-defined and admirably recorded journeys of PAUL. The apostle was only one of many people who traveled for that purpose. It is traditionally believed that THOMAS traveled to India, and a large Christian group in that subcontinent is traditionally believed to have descended from his original foundation. APOLLOS (Acts 18:24-28) had moved about, no doubt on teaching missions, between Alexandria, Corinth, and Ephesus. The emperor CLAUDIUS, in a stern communication to the Jews of Alexandria, spoke of troublemakers who had journeyed to the delta town by sea from Syria, and it is likely that this is the first reference in secular literature to the widespread missionary travels of early Christian preachers. Acts 11:19 and 28:15 similarly refer to such unrecorded travelers. It is likely that their journeys were very extensive. The tradition, for example, that JOSEPH of Arimathea traveled to Glastonbury in Britain may not be history, but the story could have arisen only in a world that took for granted the widest and the most distant traveling.

F. Business. Search of a livelihood, as distinct from the pursuit of trade, took thousands on long journeys in the ancient world. Juvenal, at the end of the first century, complains that the ORONTES had long since flowed into the Tiber: Rome had become so cosmopolitan that native merit could find no place, and the needy and the bad from the ends of the earth had sought refuge there. The inhabitants of the Roman ghetto were Jews whose business had brought them from Palestine and the many provincial centers of the DISPERSION, and such uprooted groups were not necessarily static.

G. Service. There were Roman soldiers who had traveled the whole world, and the record of Paul's journey to Rome is an illustration of an official journey of a centurion with an armed escort, engaged on a long and highly responsible courier task. In OT times we find Abraham's steward undertaking a long journey at his master's express command; Tobit acting as agent for the king of Assyria; and Nehemiah adroitly turning a cherished personal project into a royal commission, with all the travel privileges and facilities such a task conferred.

H. Exile. Moses' flight into Midian was an early instance of a journey undertaken to escape from justice, and more formal banishment was an accepted penalty in ancient penology. After the troubles in the ghetto, Claudius banished all the Jews of the capital (Acts 18:2); and Aquila and Priscilla are found in Corinth. It is interesting to note that Aquila had come originally from Pontus in Asia Minor.

Travel was not without its hazards, and Paul in an eloquent passage (2 Cor. 11:25-27), which finds confirmation in more than one ancient writer, speaks of the perils of road and seaway. Luke's superb account of the voyage and wreck of the Alexandrian grain ship is further illustration (Acts 27). In NT times, however, travel was rather safer by land than it has been at most periods in history. Roads were indeed the great contribution of the Romans to Mediterranean civilization, and roads promoted the rapid movement of travelers and contributed substantially to their safety by facilitating the rapid movement of troops. The Persians had invented a swift postal system, but it was used mainly for official communications, and no engineering of any major importance was involved. Persia and Babylon relied on the enforced local labor for the opening of highways, and the imagery of Isa. 40:3-4 is based on the call to such contributions of manpower. The Romans, on the other hand, formed and planned their roads, engineered them boldly, and for the most part paved them. Hence the major contribution to rapid travel. In NT times, in spite of the continuing dangers listed

by Paul from his own experience, the road system was speeding up travel, and the Roman Peace was quelling lawlessness.

Regular passenger services by land or sea were unknown, and there is no evidence that the pattern of procedure changed from OT to Roman times. JONAH, the record runs (Jon. 1:3), "ran away from the LORD and headed for Tarshish. He went down to Joppa, where he found a ship bound for that port. After paying the fare, he went aboard and sailed for Tarshish." Nine centuries after the approximate date of Jonah's flight a similar record reads: "When we had sailed across the open sea off the coast of Cilicia and Pamphylia, we landed at Myra in Lycia. There the centurion found an Alexandrian ship sailing for Italy and put us on board" (Acts 27:5-6). Travelers evidently made their own arrangements, attached themselves to official parties, accompanied caravans, and coordinated their movements with those of trade and commerce.

The relative convenience of travel by land and sea cannot be estimated. In Claudius's communication to the Alexandrians it is expressly stated that the troublesome envoys who came from Syria came by sea. A perfectly good land route S from Palestine existed, for the ETHIOPIAN EUNUCH of Queen CANDACE was using it and riding in a chariot (Acts 8:26-28). On the other hand, the centurion in charge of Paul disembarked his party at PUTEOLI and proceeded to Rome probably via the canal through the Pontine Marshes and certainly by the APPIAN WAY (27:11-15), the route described by the poet Horace who negotiated it a century before. Why Paul decided (20:13) to go afoot across the base of Cape Lectum by the Roman road to Assos in MYSIA is difficult to explain, unless it was because he sought the privacy for meditation impossible aboard a crowded ship. Discomfort must have been the common lot of travelers by sea.

trade guilds. Otherwise known as *collegia*, trade guilds are first mentioned in Acts 19 as a base of organized opposition to the Christian church. These societies were not trade unions in the modern sense. Their functions were primarily social. Records exist of guilds of bakers, bankers, doctors, architects, producers of linen and woolen goods, dyers, workers in metal or stone or clay,

T

builders, carpenters, farmers, pastry cooks, barbers, embalmers, and transport workers. The *collegia* satisfied the need of the humble for the pleasures of social intercourse and the dignity of self-expression. It was the guild of the silversmiths and associated trades that, adroitly led, forced PAUL to withdraw from EPHESUS. It was, it appears, the guild of the butchers that precipitated the persecution of A.D. 112 in BITHYNIA, according to Pliny. The guild banquets, with associated worship of the patron deity and the compromising fellowship involved, were probably the problem of 1 Corinthians. The attempt of certain groups to work out a form of compromise, so essential to the social comfort, and indeed livelihood of many Christians, led to the strong reproaches of 2 Peter, Jude, and Revelation (e.g., Rev. 2:18-29; see THYATIRA).

trades. See OCCUPATIONS AND PROFESSIONS.

tradition. The collective wisdom of any given culture, the notions of its worldview, and the insights of its institutions. The term does not occur in the OT, but the Hebrew Scriptures obviously constitute a rich tradition. In a narrower sense, three types of tradition are mentioned in the NT (Gk. *paradosis G4142*). (1) The most common use refers to the kind of tradition handed down by the Jewish fathers or elders that constituted the oral law, regarded by many of the Jews as of equal authority with the revealed law of MOSES (see TALMUD). Indeed, the PHARISEES tended to make these traditions of even greater authority than the Scriptures (Matt. 15:2-3; Mk. 7:3-4). PAUL refers to his former zeal for the traditions of his fathers (Gal. 1:14), and JOSEPHUS says that "the Pharisees have delivered to the people a great many observances by succession from their fathers which are not written in the law of Moses" (*Ant.* 12.10.6). (2) A second type of tradition is mentioned in Col. 2:8. Some scholars hold that this verse refers to Judaistic heresies, but the emphasis seems to be on the *human*, not necessarily Jewish, origin of these teachings. (3) The third type consists of the GOSPEL truths that the apostles taught. Paul uses *paradosis* in this sense three times (1 Cor. 11:2; 2 Thess. 2:15; 3:6). The meaning of this kind of tradition is "instruction, "teaching." Paul had taught the believers in Corinth and Thes-

salonica the doctrines of the gospel, and he urged them to keep those instructions in mind.

train. As a verb meaning "to instruct, discipline, prepare," this term occurs with some frequency in modern English versions (e.g., 2 Sam. 22:35; 1 Chr. 25:7; Prov. 22:6; Hos. 7:15; 1 Tim. 4:7-8; 2 Tim. 3:16; Heb. 5:14). The word is also used a few times as a noun in the sense of "retinue" (1 Ki. 10:2 KJV [NIV, "caravan"]; Ps. 68:18 = Eph. 4:8), and once with reference to the trailing part of a gown (Isa. 6:1).

Trajan. tray'juhn. Emperor of ROME, A.D. 98-117. Marcus Ulpius Trajanus was born in Spain in the year 53, and after serving in various military and civil capacities was made governor of Germany in 97. While there he learned of his adoption by the then emperor, NERVA, an act which according to the custom of the time assured him of the succession to the throne. Upon Nerva's death in 98, Trajan lingered in Germany on some unfinished business and did not come to Rome until 99. A natural leader, he soon became popular with both army and people. Trajan took upon himself the burden of ruling and manifested an unusual capacity to deal with the complex problems of the huge empire. His policy, however, discouraged initiative on the part of the provinces, which soon learned to look to Rome for the solution of all their problems. He greatly expanded the program of public works, building new baths for the city of Rome, as well as a magnificent forum, and by constructing new roads throughout his domain.

The combined humanity and firmness of Trajan's character is illustrated by his attitude toward the Christians (see Pliny the Younger, *Epistulae* 10.96-97). On the one hand, he ordered that Christians should not be hunted and that those who confessed their faith but then recanted should be let go; on the other hand, he instructed Pliny to execute those who refused to give up their faith. This was in fact the first official policy that Christians should be put to death. His reign was marked by a great military venture against Dacia, the region N of the Danube. His victory is commemorated in the famous Column of Trajan, a 100-ft. (30-m.) marble pillar set on a rectangular base, with a statue of the emperor on top; it includes more than 2,000 finely carved figures.

trance. A state of hypnosis or ecstasy. English versions of the NT use "trance" in three passages in Acts as the rendering of Greek *ekstasis* G1749, which usually means "confusion, astonishment" (Mk. 5:42 et al.). Two of those passages refer to the vision that PETER received in JOPPA (Acts 10:10; 11:5), and the other is an account by PAUL of an experience he had while praying in the TEMPLE (22:17). The English term is rarely used in the OT (though the phrase "into a trance" is supplied by the KJV at Num. 24:4, 16). However, various references to deep sleep in the OT are often interpreted as instances of trance (e.g., Gen. 15:12; 1 Sam. 26:12; Isa. 29:10). In addition, it is often argued that the prophetic experience as well as glossolalia involved some kind of ecstatic trance (cf. 1 Sam. 19:20-24; 1 Cor. 14:14; see TONGUES, GIFT OF).

transfiguration. A change in form or appearance. The term is used specifically with reference to a unique experience of CHRIST recorded in the Synoptic Gospels (Matt. 17:1-8; Mk. 9:2-8; Lk. 9:28-36; alluded to in Jn. 1:14 and 2 Pet. 1:16-18). The use of the noun *transfiguration* in this context derives from the KJV rendering, "he was transfigured before them," which is followed by most versions (Matt. 17:2; Mk. 9:2; the Greek verb here, *metamorphoō* G3565, occurs in two other passages, Rom. 12:2 and 2 Cor. 3:18, where it is rendered by the more common English term "transform"). The accounts portray the transformation as outwardly visible and consisting in an actual physical change in the body of Jesus: "The appearance of his face changed" (Lk. 9:29), "his face shone like the sun" (Matt. 17:2), while "his clothes became dazzling white" (Mk. 9:3). The glory was not caused by the falling of a heavenly light on him from without but by the flashing forth of the radiant splendor within. He had passed into a higher state of existence, his body apparently assuming properties of the RESURRECTION body.

The place where the event occurred is simply described as "a high mountain" (Mk. 9:2). Tradition has identified it with Mount TABOR, but because of its distance from CAESAREA PHILIPPI and the fortification on it at that time, a spur of Mount HERMON seems more probable. Witnessed by PETER, JAMES, and John (see JOHN THE APOS-

Mosaic depicting Jesus' transfiguration (from the Church of Transfiguration on Mt. Tabor).

© Dr. James C. Martin

TLE), the transfiguration occurred while Jesus "was praying" (Lk. 9:29). The natural simplicity of the accounts and their sober insistence on its details powerfully testify to the reality of the event.

While recorded without interpretation, the uniform dating ("after six days" in Matthew and Mark, or inclusively "about eight days after these sayings" in Luke) clearly sets the transfiguration in the context of the crucial events at Caesarea Philippi, Peter's confession, and Christ's announcement of his coming death. The experience gave encouragement to Jesus, who was setting his face to the CROSS. To the shocked disciples it confirmed the necessity of the cross through the conversation of the heavenly visitors about Christ's coming "departure" (Lk. 9:31) as well as the divine endorsement on Christ's teaching. It inseparably linked the suffering with the GLORY. It was the crowning with glory of the perfect human life of Jesus, God's stamp of approval on his sinless humanity. The divine approval established his fitness to be our sinbearer on the cross. It was also an entry for Jesus into the glory in which he would reign, thus constituting a typical manifestation of the king coming into his kingdom (Matt. 16:28; see KINGDOM OF GOD).

transgression. The breaking of the LAW. There is a fine distinction between SIN (Gk. *hamartia* G281) and transgression (*parabasis* G4126), for one who is under no express law may sin (Rom. 5:13), but with the introduction of a law one commits transgression if that law is violated (Rom. 4:15; 5:14; Gal. 3:19). Hence, "sin" causes us to transgress (Rom.

T

7:7, 13). In some cases sin may be implicit disobedience, but transgression indicates explicit disobedience. See also TRESPASS.

Transjordan. trans-jor'duhn. This term, meaning "on the other side of the Jordan" (cf. the common Heb. expression ʿēber hayyardēn, Deut. 1:1 et al.), is used with reference to the territory that lies to the E of the JORDAN River (contrast *Cisjordan*, "on this side of the Jordan," meaning the Land of CANAAN). East PALESTINE as a whole can sometimes be comprehended under the name of the central part of this area, GILEAD (e.g., Josh. 22:9). Generally, Transjordan is reckoned from the region of BASHAN on the N to the RED SEA on the S; the Arabian desert marks an indefinite boundary on the E and SE. Here were the countries of MOAB, EDOM, and AMMON; here too the tribes of REUBEN, GAD, and half of MANASSEH received their inheritance. Cut through by numerous gorges, some with constant water flow, the soil in Transjordan produces abundant crops of grain even without irrigation. It is rugged tableland, 2,000 to 3,000 ft. (600-900 m.) in elevation, with heights of around 5,000 ft. (1,500 m.)

The book of Genesis contains incidental references to this territory (e.g., Gen. 32:10). Later, as the Israelites were approaching Palestine, they sought to use the important KING'S HIGHWAY in Transjordan, but the Edomites would not permit them to do so (Num. 20:17-20). North of Edom lay Moab; there, from Mount Nebo (near the upper end of the Dead Sea), MOSES was granted sight of the land promised to Israel (Deut. 34:1-4; see NEBO, MOUNT). Next, between the rivers ARNON and YARMUK, comes Gilead proper and the AMORITE kingdom of SIHON, who denied Israel passage (Num. 21:21-31; Deut. 12:2). To this district, DAVID a second time fled for sanctuary, escaping his insurrectionist son ABSALOM (2 Sam. 17:21-29). To the E of Gilead and N of the Arnon was the country of Ammon. The northernmost territory was Bashan, of uncertain boundary, remembered for its fat cattle (Amos 4:1) and its King OG of iron bedstead fame (Num. 21:33-35; Deut. 3:1-11; Josh. 12:4-5).

In NT times, PEREA referred to a territory E of JUDEA and SAMARIA across the Jordan, which afforded in part a bypath for strict Jews going from GALILEE in the N to Judea in the S (avoiding contamination by Samaria in between; cf. Jn. 4). To the N lay the Hellenistic DECAPOLIS, a trade federation of ten cities, nine being on the E of Jordan, and one (BETH SHAN) on the W. The grouping secured protection from marauders. Antagonism existed between the Decapolis and both NABATEANS and Jews. Earlier, during the Hasmonean period, the Jews had secured dominance over a large part of Transjordan, from GADARA in the N to MACHAERUS in the S, strongly fortified to resist the Nabateans. ROME, in A.D. 106, made the Nabatean country a part of the province of ARABIA.

translate. This verb, in the sense of "to remove from one place to another," is used by the KJV in three passages (2 Sam. 3:10; Col. 1:13; Heb. 11:5). The last of these refers to ENOCH, who "was translated [NIV, was taken from this life] that he should not see death." Thus it has become common to speak of "Enoch's translation."

translations of the Bible. See BIBLE VERSIONS, ENGLISH; TEXT AND VERSIONS (OT); TEXT AND VERSIONS (NT).

transportation. See TRADE AND TRAVEL.

trap. For the biblical writers the most common form of trap or SNARE was the automatic birdnet, "the snare of the fowler" (Prov. 6:5 et al.). This common form of bird trap or netting device is familiar from Egyptian illustrations. It was a piece of net mounted to spring up and envelop the bird when it alighted on a tripstick or some other form of trigger (Ps. 141:9; Ezek. 12:13; Amos 3:5). Another form of trap was the noose carefully set on the "run" of a bird or an animal and designed to tighten around the neck by the creature's own forward momentum (Job 18:10; 1 Cor. 7:35; this form of trapping device seems to be the metaphor behind Prov. 22:8). Ezekiel 17:20 may refer to a noose falling from above, though it could as likely be a descending net, falling as the victim entangled his feet in some low-lying trigger. Or perhaps the fowler concealed in ambush pulled a releasing string when the birds ventured under the suspended net (Prov. 1:17-18).

A camouflaged pit was an additional form of snare or trap used for the capture of unwary animals (2 Sam. 17:9; Isa. 24:17-18; 42:22; Jer. 18:22; 48:43-44; Lam. 3:47). Psalm 9:15 develops the metaphor; ironically, the hunter fell into the pit designed for his victims. There are numerous other figurative uses (Job 18:8; Ps. 69:22; 91:3; 124:7; 140:5; Prov. 6:5; 7:23; 12:13; Hos. 9:8; Lk. 21:34 [35]; Rom. 11:9; 1 Tim. 3:7; 6:9; 2 Tim. 2:26).

travail. This English term, referring to a woman's labor at birth or more generally to any kind of painful or strenuous work, is used frequently by the KJV to render a variety of words. Most of the uses are figurative. For instance, travail may portray the agonies of divine judgment on the wicked (Babylonians, Isa. 13:8; Zion, Mic. 4:9-10; Israel, Jer. 6:24; Judah, 4:31; Lebanon, 22:23; Damascus, 49:24); the thought of it caused Isaiah anguish like the pains of a woman in labor (Isa. 21:3). Travail may picture the painful exertion necessary to achieve satisfying goals. The Suffering Servant "who makes an offering for sin" shall "see the fruit of the travail of his soul and be satisfied" (Isa. 53:10-11). The apostle PAUL, in the Lord's service, could not forget the "labour and travail" night and day to plant the church at THESSALONICA (1 Thess. 2:9; cf. 2 Thess. 3:8). The Galatians seemed to return to legalistic works, so Paul was "again in travail until Christ be formed" in them (Gal. 4:19). Jesus used the figure of travail to represent the disciples' sorrow (Jn. 16:21-22). Travail also portrays the agony of the world until Christ returns (Rom. 8:22; 1 Thess. 5:3).

travel. See TRADE AND TRAVEL.

Travelers, Valley of the. According to Ezek. 39:11, God "will give to Gog a place for burial in Israel, the Valley of the Travelers east of the sea" (NRSV; similarly NJPS); as a result, the place will be called the Valley of HAMON GOG. The KJV understands the text in a more general sense, "the valley of the passengers on the east of the sea." On the reasonable assumption that "the sea" here is a reference to the DEAD SEA, the NRSV rendering (cf. also TNIV) indicates a place in TRANSJORDAN. It seems strange, however, that a location E of the Dead Sea would be characterized as being "in Israel." The NIV understands the syntax in a slightly different way, "the valley of those who travel east toward the Sea," implying some otherwise unknown place in CANAAN proper. Possibly the passage should be understood symbolically, without reference to a specific geographical location.

treasure. A collection of objects of value, including stores of provisions (e.g., Jer. 41:8; Ezek. 28:4; Dan. 11:43). The "treasure cities" of Exod. 1:11 KJV (NIV, "store cities") were arsenals and depots for provisions (cf. Gen. 41:48, 56). A similar confusion between the precious store and the place of its storing occurs in the NT. For example, Matt. 2:11 and 19:21 refer to the store of precious things, but Matt. 12:35 clearly refers to the storehouses. In Acts 8:27 both notions are incorporated. In Matt. 27:6 the Greek word *korbanas G3168* is derived from Hebrew: the chief priests could not put the polluted silver into the the sacred treasury where the CORBAN gifts were paid. This seems to be distinguished from the *gazophylakion G1126*, the treasury of the temple, simply a collection box into which general offerings were cast (Mk. 12:41; Lk. 21:1). John 8:20 refers to the place where Jesus was teaching in the colonnade, where boxes were placed for the convenient reception of gifts. The metaphorical meaning of treasure is a more common figure of speech in the OT than in the NT (Exod. 19:5; Deut. 28:12; Ps. 17:14; Matt. 13:44; Lk. 12:21; 2 Cor. 4:7). The last reference is to practices such as those illustrated by the DEAD SEA SCROLLS, the preservation of precious possessions in earthenware jars, sealed for safety.

treasurer. See OCCUPATIONS AND PROFESSIONS.

treaty. See COVENANT; DEUTERONOMY.

tree. PALESTINE in ancient times must have been extensively wooded as there are over three hundred references to trees and wood in the Bible. Most of the wooded areas have been cut down, however. Trees were sometimes venerated by pagan people who believed gods inhabited them, and this practice affected the Israelites. SACRIFICES were often offered under trees (Deut. 12:2; 1 Ki. 14:23). Planting a tree near a sacred altar was forbidden (Deut.

16:21). Trees could be used to identify places (Gen. 12:6; Deut. 11:30). Tree limbs were used in celebrating the Feast of Tabernacles (Lev. 23:40). Jesus used fruit-bearing trees as an illustration of believers' bearing fruit (Matt. 7:16-19). See also PLANTS for individual kinds of trees.

tree of knowledge. According to Gen. 2:9, God "made all kinds of trees grow out of the ground" in the Garden of EDEN. The verse continues, "In the middle of the garden were the tree of life and the tree of the knowledge of good and evil." God commanded ADAM not to eat of the tree of knowledge on penalty of death (2:17). The serpent's temptation of EVE (3:1-5) centered on this command, and when he had convinced her that she would not die but become "like God," she ate of it to her sorrow. The precise significance of the tree has been a matter of debate. Elsewhere in the Bible, lack of knowing good and evil is treated as a mark of immaturity (Deut. 1:39; Isa. 7:14-17) and possibly senility (2 Sam. 19:35), but in such passages something different seems to be in mind, namely, moral discernment. In Genesis the phrase "good and evil" possibly indicates the extremes, and thus the totality, of knowledge. If so, the tree may have symbolized God's OMNISCIENCE and the power associated with it. In partaking of its fruit, Adam and Eve reached for divinity but obtained guilt, shame, condemnation, and expulsion instead.

tree of life. Along with "the tree of the knowledge of good and evil" (see TREE OF KNOWLEDGE), the tree of life was originally placed by God in the middle of the Garden of EDEN (Gen. 2:9). At this point in the narrative, nothing is said about the significance of either. There was no command given to ADAM and EVE not to eat of the tree of life. After their sin, when they were expelled from the garden, the reason given was, "The man has now become like one of us, knowing good and evil. He must not be allowed to reach out his hand and take also from the tree of life and eat, and live forever" (Gen. 3:22). Evidently this tree was identified with everlasting LIFE, and as a result of the original SIN, humanity would no longer have access to the tree, but would instead be subject to deterioration and DEATH. In the OT elsewhere, only in Proverbs does the phrase

"tree of life" occur, depicting several virtues (Prov. 3:18; 11:30; 13:12; 15:4; cf. also Ezek. 31:1-12). In the NT, only the book of Revelation has any reference to the tree of life, and in each occurrence it has spiritual, cosmic meaning (Rev. 2:7; 22:1-3).

trench. A long cut in the ground. The term is used by most English versions for the ditch that was dug around the altar in the TEMPLE (1 Ki. 18:32 et al.). The KJV uses it also to render Hebrew terms meaning "encampment" (1 Sam. 17:20 et al.) or "ramp" (2 Sam. 20:15), and a Greek word that the NIV translates "embankment" (Lk. 19:43). In addition, the NIV has "trench" for a Hebrew word that apparently refers to a town moat (Dan. 9:25; KJV, "wall").

trespass. An overstepping of the boundaries, thus an unfaithful or treacherous act that incurs guilt (cf. SIN; TRANSGRESSION). The KJV OT uses this English term frequently, both as a noun and as a verb, to translate several Hebrew words (Lev. 5:15-19 et al.; see SACRIFICE AND OFFERINGS). In the NT, the KJV uses it as a verb a few times to translate Greek *hamartanō G279*, "to sin," when the context has to do with an offense against another person (Matt. 18:15, 35 [following the TR]; Lk. 17:3-4); and it occurs as a noun in five passages to translate Greek *paraptōma G4183*, literally "misstep, fall," but then "offense, wrongdoing, sin" (Matt. 6:14-15; Mk. 11:25-26 [v. 26 missing in important early witnesses]; 2 Cor. 5:19; Eph. 2:1; Col. 2:13). The Greek noun is found in a number of other passages where the KJV has other renderings (Rom. 4:25; 5:15-20; 11:11-12; Gal. 6:1; Eph 1:7; 2:5). The NRSV uses "trespass" consistently (except for Rom. 11:11-12, "stumbling"), whereas the NIV uses it only in Rom. 5. It is difficult to determine whether a sharp distinction is intended between *paraptōma* and *hamartia* (see esp. Rom. 5:20 and Eph. 2:1; and cf. Matt. 6:14-15 [the LORD'S PRAYER] to its parallel, Lk. 11:4).

trespass offering. See SACRIFICE AND OFFERINGS.

trial. See TEMPTATION.

trial of Jesus. The tumultuous proceedings before the Jewish and Roman authorities resulting in the crucifixion of Jesus. All four Gospels record at least part of the twofold trial (Matt. 26:57—27:31; Mk. 14:53—15:20; Lk. 22:54—23:25; Jn. 18:12—19:16), but because of the brief and selective nature of their narratives, the precise chronological order of events is not always certain. It is clear that both parts of the trial were marked by great irregularities, but the writers of the Gospels never assert that this or that in the trial was illegal, for they wrote not as lawyers but as witnesses.

Following his arrest in GETHSEMANE, Jesus was at once taken before the Jewish authorities in JERUSALEM. John alone tells us that he was first brought before the former high priest ANNAS, who conducted a preliminary examination by questioning Jesus about his disciples and teaching. Meanwhile the Sanhedrin members had assembled in the palace of CAIAPHAS, the president of the SANHEDRIN, for an illegal night session, and Annas sent Jesus to them bound (Jn. 18:12-14, 19-24). The attempt to convict Jesus through false witnesses collected and instructed by the Sanhedrin failed because of their contradictory testimony (Matt. 26:59-61; Mk. 14:55-59). Before their charges Jesus maintained a dignified silence, even when blustering Caiaphas demanded an answer (Matt. 26:62), thus denying the validity of the process. Aware that their case had collapsed, Caiaphas brushed aside the witnesses and put Jesus under oath to tell the court if he was "the Christ, the Son of God" (26:63). The answer, in deliberate self-incrimination, was used to condemn Jesus for blasphemy (26:64-66; Mk. 14:61-64). The session broke up in disorder, with indignities being heaped on Jesus (Matt. 26:67-68; Mk. 14:65; Lk. 22:63-65). After dawn the Sanhedrin assembled in its council chamber and reenacted their trial by questioning Jesus on his messianic claims and deity (Lk. 22:66-71). This meeting was held to give a semblance of legality to the condemnation.

Since the Romans had deprived the Sanhedrin of the power of capital punishment, it was necessary to secure a confirmatory death sentence from the Roman governor, who found it expedient to be in Jerusalem during the Passover season. Accordingly, "the whole assembly" (Lk. 23:1) in formal procession brought Jesus, bound, to PILATE. When Pilate asked their charges, they indicated that they wanted him simply to sanction their condemnation of Jesus without a full trial (Jn. 18:29-32). When Pilate's insisted on knowing what the charges were, the people presented three (Lk. 23:2). The charge of treason alone Pilate deemed worthy of investigation. When Jesus explained to him the nature of his kingdom, Pilate concluded that Jesus was harmless and announced a verdict of acquittal (Jn. 18:33-38). This verdict should have ended the trial, but it only evoked a torrent of further charges against Jesus by the Jews, charges that Jesus refused to answer, to Pilate's surprise (Matt. 27:12-14). Having learned that he was a Galilean, Pilate decided to be rid of the unpleasant task by sending Jesus to HEROD Antipas, also present for the Passover, on the plea that Jesus belonged to Herod's jurisdiction. When Jesus refused to amuse Herod with a miracle, maintaining complete silence before him, Herod mocked him and returned him to Pilate uncondemned (Lk. 23:2-12).

With the return of Jesus, Pilate realized that he must handle the trial. Summoning the chief priests "and the people," he reviewed the case to prove the innocence of Jesus, but weakly proposed a compromise by offering to scourge Jesus before releasing him (Lk. 23:13-16). When the multitude requested the customary release of one prisoner (Mk. 15:8), Pilate offered them the choice between the notorious BARABBAS and Jesus (Matt. 27:17). He hoped that the crowd would choose Jesus, thus overruling the chief priests. Before the vote was taken, Pilate received a troublesome warning from his wife (27:19-21). Meanwhile the Jewish leaders persuaded the people to vote for Barabbas. When asked their choice, the people shouted for Barabbas, demanding that Jesus be crucified (Matt. 27:20-21; Lk. 23:18-19). Further remonstrance by Pilate proved useless (Lk. 23:20-22).

According to John's gospel, Pilate, as a last resort to avoid crucifying Jesus, had him scourged, allowed the soldiers to stage a mock coronation, and then brought out the pathetic figure before the people, hoping that the punishment would satisfy them. It only intensified their shouts for his crucifixion (Jn. 19:1-6). A new charge, that Jesus made himself the SON OF GOD, aroused the superstitious fears of Pilate, causing him to make further futile efforts to release him (19:7-11). Using their last weapon, the Jewish leaders threatened to report Pilate to CAESAR if he released Jesus (19:12). This threat, because

T

of Pilate's grievous maladministration, broke all further resistance in the vacillating governor. To his last appeal whether he should crucify their king, the Jews gave the blasphemous answer that they had no king but Caesar (19:15). When Pilate sought to absolve himself of the guilt of Christ's death by publicly washing his hands, the people voluntarily accepted the responsibility (Matt. 27:24-26). Keenly conscious of the gross miscarriage of justice, Pilate yielded by releasing Barabbas and sentencing Jesus to the cross. See also CHRIST, JESUS.

tribe. A large social group composed of families and clans. In the Bible it is applied specifically to the fundamental divisions of the people of ISRAEL. The Hebrew terms for "tribe" are *maṭṭeh H4751* and *šēbeṭ H8657*, both of which mean "staff, rod, scepter," but are applied to people groups under the rule of a chief who holds, literally or figuratively, the scepter of authority. The Greek term *phylē G5876* is used in the NT not only with reference to the Israelite tribes but also more generally to designate GENTILE groups and nations (Matt. 24:30; Rev. 1:7 et al.).

The twelve tribes of Israel (JACOB's new name given in Gen. 32:28) were first mentioned by Jacob in prophecy (49:16, 28). While the Hebrews were in EGYPT they were grouped according to their ancestral houses (Exod. 6:14). After they left Egypt the whole company was conceived of as the twelve tribes of Israel (24:4). The twelve sons of Jacob were REUBEN, SIMEON, LEVI, JUDAH, ISSACHAR, DAN, GAD, ASHER, NAPHTALI, JOSEPH, and BENJAMIN. Although they all had a common father, they had four mothers: LEAH and RACHEL, who were full wives, and BILHAH and ZILPAH, who were CONCUBINES. The tribes were called by these names. On the breastplate of the high priest were twelve precious stones arranged in four rows; each stone had the name of a tribe engraved on it (28:21, 29; 39:14).

When the Israelites were counted to find out the number of men of war in each group, the tribe of Levi was left out of this census because the Lord selected them for the keeping and transporting of the TABERNACLE and its furniture (Num. 1). The whole encampment of the Israelites was organized at SINAI and each tribe assigned its place in which to march and to camp (ch. 2). The withdrawal of the Levites from the group of tribes left only eleven

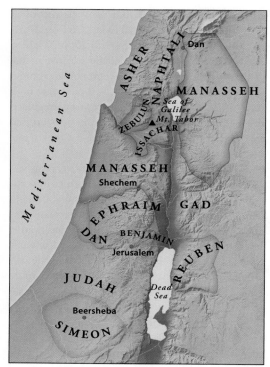

The Tribes of Israel.

tribes. In the list of leaders from each tribe who were to take the census, the children of Joseph are divided between his two sons to make up the tribe of EPHRAIM and the tribe of MANASSEH (Num. 1:10), bringing the total number of tribes back up to twelve. The leadership of Judah among the tribes was prophesied by Jacob (Gen. 49:10), and this tribe was assigned first place in the order of marching (Num. 2:3; 10:14); Judah also was the first tribe to bring an offering after the setting up of the tabernacle (7:12).

Before the Israelites entered the Promised Land, the tribes of Reuben and Gad and half of Manasseh chose to settle on the E side of the Jordan (Num. 32:33). After the land of CANAAN was subdued, the land was divided among the nine and one-half tribes (Josh. 15-19). Judah was given the first lot and received the largest area of land (15:1-62). The tribe of Simeon was assigned territory within Judah (19:1). Judah had all the land W of the DEAD SEA and S of KADESH BARNEA. Just N of Judah were Dan and Benjamin. Ephraim was next to them, Manasseh (half-tribe) was next;

The Hinnom Valley (center of photo) separates the territory of the tribe of Benjamin (N, left) from that of Judah (S, right).

then Issachar, Zebulun, Naphtali, and Asher were situated N of the Valley of JEZREEL, W of the Sea of Galilee, and northward to the LEBANON Mountains. Part of the tribe of Dan went N and seized some territory just S of Mount HERMON, thus settling the farthest N of all the Israelites (Jdg. 18).

During the period of the judges in Israel the tribes were each a law to themselves. The judges' leadership was sectional. When DAVID became king over the whole land, the twelve tribes were again unified. JERUSALEM was conquered and made the capital of the country. There SOLOMON built the TEMPLE. The Lord chose this city as the one place out of all the tribes of Israel where he would put his name (2 Chr. 12:13). David appointed a captain over each tribe (1 Chr. 27:16-22). He also took a census of the tribes (2 Sam. 24:2). Later, when ELIJAH built an altar in the contest with the prophets of BAAL on Mount CARMEL, he used twelve stones to represent the twelve tribes of Israel (1 Ki. 18:31).

The unity of the tribes had a tendency to be disrupted into two factions. After the death of SAUL, David reigned over only Judah at first (2 Sam. 2:4) and did not become king of all the tribes until later (5:3). After the death of Solomon this same division occurred again: Judah and Benjamin became one nation, the kingdom of Judah, and all the area north of them became another nation, the king-

dom of Israel (1 Ki. 12:20). This division continued until both kingdoms went into captivity—Israel in 721 B.C. to ASSYRIA, and Judah in 586 to BABYLON. These catastrophes wiped out tribal distinctions. The tribes are not mentioned by name again except in the devotional literature of the Psalms and in prophecy.

Jesus says that the apostles of Christ will sit on twelve thrones, judging the twelve tribes of Israel (Matt. 19:28; Lk. 22:30). The Holy City, the new Jerusalem, will have twelve gates, each bearing the name of one of the tribes of Israel (Rev. 21:21).

tribulation. This English term, referring to severe distress, usually as the result of oppression, is used by the KJV a few times in the OT (Deut. 4:30 et al.) but more than twenty times in the NT to render the common Greek word *thlipsis* G2568 (Matt. 13:21 et al.). In the many other occurrences of the Greek noun the KJV uses various renderings, especially "affliction" (Mk. 4:17 et al.). The English word *tribulation* is found less frequently in modern versions; the NIV uses it only in the expression "the great tribulation" (Rev. 7:14; the same Gk. phrase, but without the definite article, occurs also in 2:22, as well as in Matt. 24:21 and Acts 7:11).

Clarity requires that a distinction be made regarding the source and the object of tribulation.

For example, God may afflict his people for their unfaithfulness (cf. Deut. 4:30). The unbelieving world, on the other hand, may oppress God's people on account of their faithful testimony. Faced by such oppression, anyone who has no root "quickly falls away" (Matt. 13:21). In the case of true Christians, however, nothing—including "tribulation, or distress, or persecution"—can separate them from the love of God (Rom. 8:35-39 KJV). So believers are "patient in tribulation" (12:12 KJV). After PAUL had been stoned and left for dead at LYSTRA, he returned "exhorting [the disciples] to continue in the faith, and saying that through many tribulations we must enter the kingdom of God" (Acts 14:22 RSV). See PERSECUTION; TRIBULATION, THE GREAT.

tribulation, the great. This phrase, derived from several passages (esp. Dan. 12:1; Matt. 24:21; Rev. 7:14), refers to a definite period of unparalleled suffering sent from God on the earth to accomplish several purposes. It includes intense persecution of God's people by the anti-Christian forces. The period also includes acts of God in pouring out his righteous wrath on the ungodly (Matt. 24:29). Such manifestations of divine WRATH are described in detail by John in Rev. 6-19. On the identity of the people of God in the great tribulation, as well as the time of the rapture, theologians differ. Posttribulationists see the church continuing on earth to the end of the tribulation when the rapture occurs. Midtribulationalists look for the church to survive the first half of the tribulation when the rapture takes place. Pretribulationalists anticipate the rapture prior to the tribulation so that the people of God on earth are members of the restored Jewish nation. See ESCHATOLOGY.

tribune. This term, referring to a Roman military officer in command of a COHORT, is used by the NRSV and other versions in the book of Acts to render Greek *chiliarchos* G5941, which means literally "commander of a thousand" (Acts 21:31-37; 22:24-29; 23:10-22; 24:22; 25:23; NIV, "commander," except for the last reference, "high ranking officers"). The Latin term *tribunus* (lit., "officer of a tribe") was applied primarily to certain officials charged with defending the rights of plebeian citizens, but in the Roman army it referred to the commanders

of *cohortes milliariae*, composed of approximately 1,000 soldiers, thus equivalent to the Greek *chiliarchos*. The latter term, however, occurs also in other passages where the meaning is evidently less precise (Mk. 6:21; Jn. 18:12; Rev. 6:15; 19:18).

tribute. This English term, in the sense of compulsory payment to a superior, occurs frequently in Bible versions, especially in the OT (Jdg. 3:17 et al.). With the establishment of the Hebrew kingdom, the people obligated themselves to the regular exaction of money and services for the support of the court (cf. 1 Sam. 8:10-18). In addition to the payments received from their own people, the kings of ISRAEL and JUDAH received tribute from foreign peoples and rulers (e.g., 2 Sam. 8:2, 6; 1 Ki. 4:21; 2 Ki. 3:4-5; 2 Chr. 17:11; 26:8). More often, particularly after the division of the kingdom, the Israelites found themselves vassals rather than overlords and paid tribute to others. The ARAMEANS collected tribute from Israel, the northern kingdom, as the price for peace (2 Ki. 12:17-18). When later the Assyrians became the dominant power in the E, both Israel and Judah paid tribute to their rulers, including TIGLATH-PILESER III (16:8) and SHALMANESER V (17:3). (The KJV uses "tribute" also as the rendering of a Hebrew word that refers rather to "forced labor," 2 Sam. 20:24 et al.)

When NT history began, ROME was the dominant power. Roman taxation was mainly indirect (see TAXES); but in addition tribute was levied, which was a form of direct tax. Of the three Greek terms translated "tax" or "tribute," the NT usage appears to be as follows: *kēnsos* G3056 refers to the poll tax (the *tributum capitis*), and is mentioned by Jesus when questioned by the PHARISEES (Matt. 22:17, 19; Mk. 12:13-17). Luke in the parallel passage, and again when Jesus is questioned by PILATE, uses the word *phoros* G5843, referring possibly to the *tributum soli* (Lk. 20:22; 23:2), but perhaps the distinction is somewhat blurred here (cf. Rom. 13:6-7). In addition to these exactions, a temple tax was required from all Jewish males above age twenty for support of the TEMPLE (Matt. 17:24-25).

Trinity. According to standard Christian theology, there is one eternal God, the Lord, who is holy love. Through his self-revelation he has disclosed to his people that he is the Father, the Son, and the Holy Spirit. Yet he is not three deities but one Godhead, since all three Persons share the one Deity/Godhead. The biblical teaching of the Trinity is, in a sense, a mystery; and the more we enter into union with God and deepen our understanding of him, the more we recognize how much there is yet to know. The biblical teaching is as follows.

The unity of God. God is one. The OT condemns polytheism and declares that God is one and is to be worshiped and loved as such. "Hear, O Israel: The LORD our God, the LORD is one. Love the LORD your God with all your heart and with all your soul and with all your strength" (Deut. 6:4-5). He said through Isaiah, "There is no God apart from me, a righteous God and a Savior; there is none but me" (Isa. 45:21). And this conviction of the unity of God is continued in the NT (see Mk. 10:18; 12:29; Gal. 3:20; 1 Cor. 8:4; 1 Tim. 2:5).

The Father is God. God is the Father of ISRAEL (Isa. 64:8; Jer. 31:9) and of the anointed king of his people (2 Sam. 7:14; Ps. 2:7; 89:27). Jesus lived in communion with his heavenly Father, always doing his will and recognizing him as truly and eternally God (Matt. 11:25-27; Lk. 10:21-22; Jn. 10:25-28; Rom. 15:6; 2 Cor. 1:3; 11:31). Before his ASCENSION, Jesus said he was going to his Father (with whom he had a unique relation) and to the Father of the disciples (Jn. 20:17). He taught his disciples to pray, "Our Father ..." and to live in communion with him.

Jesus of Nazareth, the Messiah, is the Incarnate Son of God. The disciples came to see that Jesus was the long-expected MESSIAH of Israel (Matt. 16:13-20; Mk. 8:27-30). Later they came to see also that to be the Messiah, Jesus must also be God made man (see Jn. 1:1-2, 18; 20:28; Rom. 9:5; Tit. 2:13; Heb. 1:8; 2 Pet. 1:1). Thus doxologies were offered to him as God (Heb. 13:20-21; 2 Pet. 3:18; Rev. 1:5-6; 5:13; 7:10). See CHRIST, JESUS.

The Spirit is also God. He comes in the name of Jesus Christ, Incarnate Son from the Father in heaven. The way in which the apostles, following Jesus, refer to the HOLY SPIRIT shows that they looked on the Spirit as a Person. In the Acts, the Spirit inspires Scripture, is lied to, is tempted, bears witness, is resisted, directs, carries someone away, informs, commands, calls, sends, thinks a certain

decision is good, forbids, prevents, warns, appoints, and reveals prophetic truth (see Acts 1:16; 5:3, 9, 32; 7:51; 8:29, 39; 10:19; 11:12; 13:2, 4; 15:28; 16:6, 7; 20:23, 28; 28:25). Paul describes the Spirit as bearing witness, speaking, teaching, and acting as guide (Rom. 8:14, 16, 26; Gal. 4:6; Eph. 4:30).

God, the Lord, is Father, Son, and Holy Spirit. This confession and understanding may be said to be basic to the faith of the writers of the NT. There is no systematic explanation of the doctrine of God as Trinity in the NT, but various passages clearly reflect a Trinitarian pattern (Matt. 28:19; Acts 20:28; 1 Cor. 12:4-6; 2 Cor. 13:14; 2 Thess. 2:13-14; Tit. 3:4-6; Heb. 10:29; 1 Pet. 1:2; Rev. 1:4-5). The dogma of the Trinity found in the Nicene Creed may be said to be the systematic presentation of the implications of the Trinitarian suggestions, hints, and patterns of the NT, against the background of the OT. The classic formula is that there is one God and three Persons, and that each Person shares the one Being or Godhead with the two other Persons.

Tripolis. trip′uh-lis (Gk. *Tripolis*, "three-city"). Also Tripoli. This once important seaport in PHOENICIA, some 20 mi. (32 km.) N of Byblos (GEBAL), derived its name from its triple occupancy by citizens of TYRE, SIDON, and ARVAD. Perhaps during the latter Persian period (in the 4th cent. B.C.), it became the center of the conclaves from the neighboring localities. Tripolis was a member of the Phoenician League, and it seems to have been a place of commercial importance, being bounded on three sides by the sea. It is possible that the city is mentioned in the OT (Ezra 4:9 NIV; see TARPELITES).

trireme. See SHIPS.

triumph. This term (as noun or verb) is used variously by English versions to translate several Hebrew words that have different shades of meaning (e.g., Jdg. 8:9 [KJV, "in peace"; NRSV, "victorious"]; Job 17:4 [KJV, "exalt"]; Ps. 9:19 [KJV and NRSV, "prevail"] Prov. 28:12 [KJV, "rejoice"]). See also TRIUMPHAL PROCESSION.

triumphal entry. On the first day of the week in which Jesus was to be rejected and crucified, he entered JERUSALEM like a conqueror and king

T

(Matt. 21:1-11; Mk. 11:1-11; Lk. 19:29-44; Jn. 12:12-19), thus fulfilling, as Matt. 21:4-5 notes, the prophecy of Zech. 9:9. Leaving BETHANY, 2 mi. (3 km.) from Jerusalem, he passed BETHPHAGE where, perhaps by previous arrangement, the donkey with her unbroken colt was obtained. "A great multitude" that had come to the feast were pilgrims, many of them from GALILEE where most of Jesus' ministry had taken place. As they met and then accompanied him with expressions of praise and joy, the natives of Jerusalem, stirred but puzzled, questioned his identity. The impression is gained that Jesus was deliberately presenting himself in such a way that his royal claims would be manifest and Israel brought to a place of decision. Yet for all the acclamation he was not such a MESSIAH as they desired.

triumphal procession. This phrase is used by the NIV and other modern versions in 2 Cor. 2:14: "But thanks be to God, who always leads us in triumphal procession in Christ." The KJV renders, "causeth us to triumph," while the RSV has, "leads us in triumph," which evokes the image of a general *guiding his troops* to victory in combat; there is, however, no clear evidence for such uses of the Greek verb (*thriambeuō G2581*). Many recent interpreters prefer to understand this passage as an allusion to the Roman military *triumphus*, the procession of a victorious general to the Capitoline Hill to offer sacrifice to Jupiter. The honor of a triumph could be granted only by the Roman senate and in accordance with strict rules, among which was one that the victory had to be against foreigners, not in a civil war. Because the captives in such a procession were normally led to their death, PAUL in 2 Cor. 2:14 may be alluding to his sufferings (though the apostle's precise point is debated by scholars). In the other occurrence of this term, Col. 2:15, where the object of the verb certainly refers to Christ's enemies, the meaning may be "triumphing over them" (so most translations).

Troas. troh´az (Gk. *Trōas G5590*). A port on the Aegean coast of W ASIA MINOR, opposite the island of Tenedos, at the mouth of the Dardanelles. It is not to be confused with Homeric Troy, whose fortress ruins stand on an escarpment dominating the coastal plain 10 mi. (16 km.) away. Troas was founded in 300 B.C. in the spate of Greek city building that followed the division of ALEXANDER THE GREAT's short-lived empire. The port was important as the nearest point to Europe, and ROME may have found it sound policy to keep this important haven satisfied and conscious of its importance. Troas figured largely in the story of PAUL (Acts 16:8-11). LUKE recorded in terse narrative how Paul and SILAS had arrived on the Aegean coast under a strange sense of compulsion. Alexan-

Remains of the ancient harbor at Alexandria Troas.

© Dr. James C. Martin

Troas.

in the KJV at Acts 20:15. Almost all early Greek MSS, however, lack the clause "and after remaining in Trogyllium," and thus it is omitted in most modern versions.

Trophimus. trof'uh-muhs (Gk. *Trophimos G5576,* "nourished" [foster child?] or "nourishing"). A Christian from Ephesus who, with other believers, accompanied Paul on his way back to Jerusalem toward the end of the apostle's third missionary journey (Acts 20:4; cf. 21:29). In the light of 2 Cor. 8:18-19 it appears that Trophimus, along with Tychicus, was a delegate from the province of Asia chosen by the churches to bear the collection (see contribution). When they arrived in Jerusalem, Jews from Asia saw Paul and Trophimus together in Jerusalem and hastily supposed that Paul had taken him illegally into the temple proper beyond the outer Court of the Gentiles (21:29). In 2 Tim. 4:20, Paul says that he left Trophimus ill at Miletus. Such a notice does not fit the recorded journeys in Acts since Paul did not leave Trophimus when they were together in Miletus (Acts 20:15), nor did he go to Rome via Miletus. If this is the same man, it shows him traveling again with the apostle, who evidently had been freed from his (first) imprisonment in Rome before 2 Timothy was written.

trumpet. See music and musical instruments (sect. I.H).

Trumpets, Feast of. See feasts.

trustee. This English term, meaning "a person to whom the management of another's property is entrusted," is used once by the NIV and other versions to render the Greek noun *oikonomos G3874:* "as long as the heir is a child," Paul says by way of illustration, that heir "is subject to guardians and trustees until the time set by his father" (Gal. 4:2). The Greek word is more commonly rendered "manager," "steward," and the like (e.g., Lk. 12:42; 16:1 et al.; 1 Cor. 4:1-2 NRSV). See guardian.

dria Troas, to give the port its ancient name, had long since been a Roman colony, but Paul could not accept the city as the goal of his journey. Here he appears to have met Luke, who may indeed have been a certain "man of Macedonia," whom he saw in the dream that compelled him to take the gospel into Europe. The party traveled by sea, from Troas past Imbros and Samothrace, N of Thasos to Neapolis in Thracia, and thence by road to Philippi. Ten years later, after the riot in Ephesus, Paul returned to Troas and established a Christian church (2 Cor. 2:12). After a briefly recorded ministry in Greece (Acts 20:1-3), Paul came again, but Luke confined his narrative to a matter that interested his physician's mind (20:4-12). Perhaps the apostle was in Troas again around the time of his arrest (c. in A.D. 66), for he left essential possessions in that city (2 Tim. 4:13).

Trogyllium. troh-jil'ee-uhm (Gk. *Trōgyllion G5591* [not in NIV]). Some 20 mi. (32 km.) S of Ephesus, a high headland N of the mouth of the Maeander forms a sharply pointed cape called Trogyllium, which protrudes westward and makes a narrow channel between the mainland and the island of Samos. This waterway, barely a mile (0.6 km.) wide, forms a protected roadstead in which a coasting vessel might naturally pass the night before running across the open gulf to Miletus. The pause in the protected anchorage is mentioned

truth. In the OT the word *'ĕmet H622* indicates firmness, stability, fidelity, a reliable basis of support. It is attributed to God as well as creatures, and appears in such expressions as "truly," "of a

T

truth," etc. It is ascribed not only to statements (e.g., Ruth 3:12) but also to behavior (Gen. 24:49) and to promises (2 Sam. 7:28). It is associated with kindness (Gen. 47:29), with justice (Neh. 9:13; Isa. 59:14), with sincerity (Josh. 24:14). The SEPTUAGINT translation, to express the moral aspect, frequently uses Greek *pistis G4411* ("faith, faithfulness, trustworthiness") rather than the usual term for "truth," *alētheia G237* (though this latter word can also indicate "truthfulness, sincerity"). Some have argued that the etymology of *alētheia* is "not concealed," suggesting that something is open, uncovered, revealed for what it indeed is. Although this analysis is uncertain, the word does indicate real and genuine rather than imaginary or spurious, and true rather than false. Hence we read of "the true God" (e.g., Jn. 17:3) and "the true vine" (15:1). NT references to true statements make it evident that the conception of cognitive truth derives from the notions of reliability (e.g., Mk. 5:33; 12:32; Jn. 8:44-46; Rom. 1:25; Eph. 4:25). The cognitive conception, however, is more explicit in the NT than in the OT. Truth is related not only to fidelity and justice but also to KNOWLEDGE and to REVELATION.

The biblical use of the word has rich suggestive meanings. When MOSES refers to "able men, such as fear God, men of truth, hating covetousness" (Exod. 18:21 KJV), there is suggested integrity of character—a kind of reliability that goes beyond the cognitive meaning to include those aspects of personal behavior that seem to be implied by the love of truth. The concept of truth is assumed to be derived from the character of God and is the exact opposite of the concept of lying. "It is impossible for God to lie" (Heb. 6:18; cf. 2 Tim. 2:13; Tit. 1:2). See LIE, LYING.

Jesus prayed, "Sanctify them by the truth; your word is truth" (Jn. 17:17). And he promised, "If you hold to my teaching, you are really my disciples. Then you will know the truth, and the truth will set you free" (Jn. 8:31-32). In such sayings, "*the* truth" means the most important truth, that is, the GOSPEL of the grace of God. One of the saddest scenes in the Bible is the one in which PILATE asks Jesus, "What is truth?" and does not even wait for an answer. Jesus had said, "For this reason I was born, and for this I came into the world, to testify to the truth. Everyone on the side of truth listens to

me" (Jn. 18:37-38). Jesus' words refer not merely to truth, but to *the* truth. Pilate's question omits the definite article and expresses skepticism, not merely as to the gospel but as to the very concept of truth.

The gospel invitation to "believe" is always based on the assumption that the evidence is sufficient, and that it is a moral question whether one will accept the GRACE of God in CHRIST. Those who disbelieve the gospel are morally reprehensible in the sight of God (Jn. 3:18-19, 36; 2 Thess. 2:10-12). Christ is *the truth*, as the sun is *the light*. Those who turn away from Christ, it is assumed, do so willfully and culpably.

Truth, Gospel of. A Gnostic document included in two forms in the NAG HAMMADI LIBRARY (NHC I, 3; XII, 2 [the latter poorly preserved]). In spite of its title, the work contains no narrative, nor does it report the sayings of Jesus, but is rather a kind of homily or meditation on Christ, emphasizing the joy that the GOSPEL gives to "those who have received from the Father of truth the gift of knowing him." Because it uses the NT to give a mild and attractive presentation of Christian GNOSTICISM, many think that it may have been authored by VALENTINUS or more probably by his followers. In any case, the document was likely written in Greek some time before A.D. 200 and subsequently translated into Coptic.

Tryphaena. See TRYPHENA AND TRYPHOSA.

Tryphena and Tryphosa. tri-fee′nuh, tri-foh′suh (Gk. *Tryphaina G5586* and *Tryphōsa G5589*, both from the verb *tryphaō G5587*, "to live delicately *or* luxuriously"). Also Tryphaena. Christian women in ROME to whom PAUL sent greetings (Rom. 16:12). He describes them as "women who work hard in the Lord," possibly a deliberate contrast to their names. Because their names are so similar, it is often thought that they were (twin?) sisters or very close relatives. Both names occur among slaves at the imperial court of CLAUDIUS and have been found in a cemetery used chiefly for the emperor's servants. On that basis, some have thought that Tryphaena and Tryphosa may have been among "the saints … who belong to Caesar's household" (Phil. 4:22).

Tryphosa. See TRYPHENA AND TRYPHOSA.

tsadhe. tsahd´ee (Heb. *ṣādê*, meaning uncertain). Also *ṣade*, *tzaddi*, etc. The eighteenth letter of the Hebrew alphabet (צ), with a numerical value of 90. Its sound in Modern Hebrew corresponds to that of English *ts*, but in biblical times it was a so-called "emphatic" consonant, possibly an *s* accompanied by a compression of the pharynx or by an additional velar articulation (i.e., with the back of the tongue touching or approaching the soft palate).

Tubal. too´buhl (Heb. *tubal* H9317, corresponding to Akk. *Tabāl*). Son of JAPHETH and grandson of NOAH, included in the Table of Nations (Gen. 10:2; 1 Chr. 1:5). Tubal was apparently the eponymous ancestor of a Neo-Hittite confederacy located in the heartland of the Taurus mountains in SE ASIA MINOR. This nation came to prominence during the first millennium B.C. after the decline of the great HITTITE kingdom of Hattusas. EZEKIEL refers to Tubal as the source of slaves and metals (Ezek. 27:13); elsewhere he speaks of GOG as the chief prince of Meshech and Tubal who will fall under God's judgment (38:2-4; 39:1-6). The name Tabal(a) is mentioned in numerous Assyrian records of the punitive campaigns sent into the Taurus. The people of Tabal/Tubal are evidently the ones later referred to as *Tibarēnoi* by Herodotus (*Hist.* 3.94), who states that they supplied troops to the Persian armies of DARIUS and XERXES. Their ferocity was proven by the fact that their defeat and destruction came only after hundreds of years of continual warfare.

Tubal-Cain. too´buhl-kayn´ (Heb. *tûbal qayin* H9340, possibly "Tubal the metal-worker" [cf. CAIN]). Son of LAMECH by his second wife ZILLAH (Gen. 4:22). It is possible that Tubal-Cain was viewed as the ancestor of the KENITES (15:19), often thought to have been metal workers. In any case, he is described as "a sharpener of every artisan of copper and iron" (lit. trans.); this phrase can be understood either in the sense "an instructor of every artificer in brass and iron" (cf. KJV) or, more likely, "a forger of all implements of copper and iron" (cf. NIV and other modern versions).

tumbleweed. See PLANTS.

tumor. See DISEASE (under *plague*).

tunic. See DRESS.

tunnel. See AQUEDUCT; SILOAM.

turban. See DRESS.

turpentine tree. See PLANTS (under *terebinth*).

turquoise. See MINERALS.

turtledove. See BIRDS.

Tuthmosis. See THUTMOSE.

tutor. See GUARDIAN.

Twelve, the. See APOSTLE.

twin. See CASTOR AND POLLUX; DIDYMUS.

Tychicus. tik´uh-kuhs (Gk. *Tychikos* G5608, "fortunate"). A close friend and valued helper of the apostle PAUL. Along with TROPHIMUS, Tychicus was evidently a delegate from the province of ASIA chosen by the churches to accompany the apostle as he took the collection to Jerusalem (cf. Acts 20:4-6 with 2 Cor. 8:18-19; see CONTRIBUTION). Later, Tychicus was with Paul during the latter's first Roman imprisonment and was entrusted with the important mission of delivering the letters to the EPHESIANS and the COLOSSIANS with instructions to inform them of Paul's welfare and to encourage them (Eph. 6:21; Col. 4:7-9). Some time later, Paul purposed to send either ARTEMAS or Tychicus to relieve TITUS in the oversight of the churches on the island of CRETE so that Titus might be free to join the apostle at NICOPOLIS (Tit. 3:12). Loyal and useful to the end, Tychicus was dispatched during Paul's second Roman imprisonment to EPHESUS (2 Tim. 4:12) to care for the churches in and around what was probably his native home (note that Trophimus is identified as an Ephesian in Acts 21:29). This arrangement would free TIMOTHY to rejoin Paul, who desperately wanted to see him before the apostle met his fate as a martyr for the gospel (2 Tim. 4:9, 21).

Tyndale's Version. See BIBLE VERSIONS, ENGLISH.

typology. A form of biblical interpretation which deals with correspondences (e.g., between persons or events) at different periods in the history of salvation. Behind this approach is the belief that God acts in similar ways in both Testaments, and so his action in the NT repeats and thus "fulfills" his action in the OT. The term *typology* stems from Greek *typos G5596*, which means "copy, image, pattern." This Greek word can be used in a general sense of a "pattern" to be copied in a moral or ethical sense (e.g., Phil. 3:17; 1 Thess. 1:7). In certain passages, however, the term is used somewhat technically to depict a salvation-historical correspondence between historical situations like the flood and baptism (1 Pet. 3:21, *antitypos G531*), figures like ADAM and CHRIST (Rom. 5:14), the heavenly pattern and its earthly counterpart (the tent or TABERNACLE, Acts 7:44; Heb. 8:5), Israel's experience in the wilderness (1 Cor. 10:6; in v. 11 the adverb *typikōs G5595* is used), institutions like the Jewish feasts in Jn. 5-10, and priestly imagery like MELCHIZEDEK and Christ in Heb. 7. The "type" is the OT pattern, and the "antitype" (Heb. 9:24; 1 Pet. 3:21) is the NT counterpart or fulfillment. Yet typology is found not just in the NT, for the OT contains examples as well, such as exodus-salvation in Isa. 40:3-5, exodus-exile in Hos. 11:1-2, the rebellion in the wilderness in Ps. 95:7-11, and Melchizedek in Ps. 110:4.

Tyrannus. ti-rah´uhs (Gk. *Tyrannos G5598*, "tyrant" [i.e., a ruler with absolute powers, not necessarily a despot]). An Ephesian in whose hall PAUL lectured (Acts 19:9). When the Jews of EPHESUS opposed Paul's teaching in the synagogue, where he had boldly preached for three months about the KINGDOM OF GOD, he and his followers withdrew to the lecture hall of Tyrannus. Here he reasoned daily for two years. As a result, "all the Jews and Greeks who lived in the province of Asia heard the word of the Lord" (v. 10). It is not certain just who Tyrannus was. Lecture halls could be found in gymnasia in every Greek city (see GYMNASIUM); here a philosopher, orator, or poet could expound his views or give a recitation. Tyrannus may have been a Greek rhetorician living in Ephesus at that time, having his own private lecture hall. It may be that the "hall of Tyrannus" was either a building for hire, named after its owner, or the private residence of a sympathetic donor. Whatever the case, Paul's regular and unmolested use of the room for two years, with such a wide hearing, indicates his exclusive use of a spacious, well-situated room for a period of each day.

Tyre. tir (Heb. ṣôr *H7450*, "rock"; Gk. *Tyros G5602*). A famous port city in PHOENICIA, some 25 mi. (40 km.) S from the sister port of SIDON and 15 mi. (24 km.) N of the modern Lebanese border with Israel. It is a natural geographical frontier. Phoenicia itself is a coastal strip backed by mountains, and Tyre was further defended by rocky promontories (one of them the famous "Ladder of Tyre"), which effectively hampered invasion. Herodotus dates the foundation as early as 2740 B.C., JOSEPHUS as late as 1217. ISAIAH implies that Tyre was a colony of Sidon (Isa. 23:2, 12), and Homer's mention of "Sidonian wares," without reference to Tyre, seems to confirm the greater antiquity of the former city. The AMARNA Letters, apparently refuting Josephus's date, contain an appeal from the ruler of Tyre, dated 1430, imploring help from Amenhotep IV. JOSHUA assigned Tyre to the tribe of ASHER, but in all probability the city was not occupied (Josh. 19:29; 2 Sam. 24:7).

An obscure period of some four centuries follows, and Tyre emerges into history again with the name of HIRAM, friend of DAVID (2 Sam. 5:11). This able monarch seems to have rebuilt and fortified Tyre, taking within its boundaries nearby islands and providing the city with two harbors. The trade of Tyre at this time included the exploitation of the cedar forests of the Lebanon range. Tyrian PURPLE, the product of the murex shellfish, was also a famous export. In addition, the cedar forests provided material for the famous Phoenician galleys (see SHIPS). Accepting the challenge of the sea—the one road to wealth for the narrow little land—the Tyrians, like the rest of their kinfolk, ranged far and wide in the search for the precious shellfish and the metals in which they traded. The copper of CYPRUS, the silver of Spain, and the tin of Cornwall were carried in Tyrian ships. Under SOLOMON, who inherited the partnership with

© Dr. James C. Martin. The British Museum. Photographed by permission.

In this scene of the sack of Tyre by the Assyrians in the 9th cent. B.C., goods from the defeated city are ferried to the mainland, where they are unloaded and then carried as tribute to Shalmaneser III, king of Assyria. (Copy of bronze decoration from the gates of Shalmaneser's palace in Balawat.)

Hiram, the Hebrews participated in Tyrian commerce, provided a southern port at EZION GEBER on the Gulf of AQABAH, and shared the trade with OPHIR and the East. It was probably the loss of this southern outlet to the Red Sea and the East at the division of Israel after Solomon that stimulated the Tyrian exploration of the coast of Africa and led ultimately to the circumnavigation of the continent. Dynastic troubles followed Hiram's death. A certain ETHBAAL emerged victorious after the assassination of his brother. It was Ethbaal's daughter JEZEBEL who became AHAB's notorious queen (1 Ki. 16:31). Renewed troubles after Ethbaal's death led to emigration and to the founding of Carthage.

During the two hundred years of Assyrian aggression, Tyre suffered with the rest of the ANE but, owing to the strength of her position and her sea power, maintained a measure of independence over much of the troubled era. She broke free from NINEVEH a generation before the last stronghold of the Assyrians fell (612 B.C.). These years were the greatest years of Tyrian glory. Ezekiel's account (Ezek. 27-28), set though it is in a context of denunciation and prophecy of ruin, gives a vivid picture of the power and wealth of the great trading port. Ruin eventually came. BABYLON succeeded ASSYRIA, and although Tyre seems successfully to have resisted the long siege of NEBUCHADNEZZAR, the strain of her resistance to Babylon and the damage to her commerce brought the city to poverty. She briefly fell under the power of Egypt and then became a dependency of Babylon, a status she held until Babylon fell to PERSIA.

Persia inherited Babylon's rule. Ezra 3:7 contains an order of Cyrus II to Tyre to supply cedar for the restoration of the TEMPLE in Jerusalem. Cambyses II conscripted a Tyrian fleet against Egypt, and Tyrian ships fought on the Persian side against the Greeks at Salamis. In 332 B.C., in the course of his conquest of the East, ALEXANDER THE GREAT appeared before Tyre. The island stronghold closed her gates, and Alexander was forced to build a causeway. After long months of frustration, he took the city by costly storming. Tyre was broken, and the causeway still remains, now as a place, as Ezekiel foretold, on which fishermen dry their nets (Ezek. 26:5, 14; 47:10). Tyre made a measure of political recovery, and for a period functioned as a republic. She struck an early treaty with ROME, and her independence was respected until 20 B.C., when AUGUSTUS withdrew it. Her remaining history is without significance.

tzaddi. See TSADHE.

U

Ucal. yoo'kuhl (Heb. *ʾukāl H432*, meaning uncertain). TNIV (mg.) Ukal. One of two men—perhaps sons, disciples, or contemporaries—to whom AGUR addressed his oracular sayings; the other was ITHIEL (Prov. 30:1). Many scholars revocalize the Hebrew consonants and, instead of *wĕʾukāl*, read *wāʾēkel* ("and I faint"; cf. NIV mg.) or *wayyûkāl* ("and will I prevail?"; cf. NRSV, TNIV) or the like.

Ukal. yoo'kuhl. TNIV form of UCAL.

Uel. yoo'uhl (Heb. *ʾûʾēl H198*, perhaps "will of God"). One of the descendants of Bani who agreed to put away their foreign wives (Ezra 10:34).

Ugarit. See RAS SHAMRA.

Ulai. yoo'li (Heb. *ʾûlay H217*, from Assyr. *Ulaia*, known to Gk. authors as *Eulaios*, Lat. *Eulaeus*). A stream or artificial irrigation canal near SUSA, capital of ELAM (PLACE) in SW PERSIA, where DANIEL received the vision of a two-horned ram and a goat (Dan. 8:2, 16). Owing to topographical change, which can be swift and confusing in sand and alluvial silt, the identification of Ulai is uncertain. Some think that the reference is to two present-day rivers, the upper Kherkhah and the lower Karun, which in ancient times may have been a single stream debouching into the delta at the head of the Persian Gulf.

Ulam. yoo'luhm (Heb. *ʾûlām H220*, perhaps "first, leader"). **(1)** Son of Peresh (or of Sheresh), grandson of MAKIR, and great-grandson of MANASSEH (1 Chr. 7:16-17).

(2) Firstborn son of ESHEK and descendant of BENJAMIN through SAUL (1 Chr. 8:39). Ulam's sons "were brave warriors who could handle the bow," and his descendants were numerous (v. 40).

ulcer. See DISEASE.

Ulla. uhl'uh (Heb. *ʿullāʾ H6587*, possibly "the small one"). Descendant of ASHER (1 Chr. 7:39). Ulla's place in the genealogy is left unstated, and some scholars believe the name is a textual corruption for some other Asherite mentioned earlier, such as Amal (v. 35).

Ummah. uhm'uh (Heb. *ʿummāh H6646*, possibly "connection" or "near"). A town on the MEDITERRANEAN coast within the tribal territory of ASHER (Josh. 19:30). Ummah was apparently between ACZIB and APHEK on the Plain of ACCO, but its precise location is unknown. Because Acco, an important city allotted to Asher (cf. Jdg. 1:31), is not otherwise included in the list of Asherite towns in Josh. 19:24-31, many scholars believe that Ummah here is a scribal corruption for Acco.

umpire. See DAYSMAN.

uncial. An ancient form of Greek (and Latin) handwriting based on the shapes of capital letters; the term is also applied to MSS written with this type of writing. See TEXT AND VERSIONS (NT).

uncircumcised. In the Bible this word is used both literally and figuratively (in figurative passages, modern versions sometimes use other terms). Uncircumcision represented unbelief and disobedience to the COVENANT of God (Jer. 6:10 KJV; 9:26). Rebellious Israelites have an "uncircumcised heart"; and those whose ears are closed are said to have "uncircumcised ears" (Lev. 26:41; Jer. 6:10). In the NT, unbelieving Jews, though physically circumcised, are said to be spiritually uncircumcised (Rom. 2:28-29); while GENTILES, though physically uncircumcised, are regarded as circumcised if they keep the righteousness of the law (2:25-27). Christ makes no distinction between the circumcised and the uncircumcised (1 Cor. 7:19; Gal. 5:6; 6:15; Col. 3:11); if regenerated, they are united in one body of believers (Eph. 2:11-22). CIRCUMCISION has nothing to do with JUSTIFICATION, for ABRAHAM was justified while still uncircumcised (Rom. 4:9-12).

uncle. This English term renders Hebrew *dôd H1856*, referring specifically to a father's brother (Lev. 20:20 et al.), although in some passages the precise relationship is not made explicit.

unclean, uncleanness. SIN has brought about great changes in both the physical and spiritual realms, making the terms *clean* and *unclean* very common in the thinking of the human race from the earliest times. These words have been factors in determining people's diets, friends, and habits, in fact, their entire deportment. These words took on a new meaning when God began to call the nation of ISRAEL into being. They fall largely into two main divisions: spiritual or moral uncleanness and ceremonial uncleanness.

Some have felt that there is a relation between the forbidden foods of other nations and those that the Lord forbade Israel to eat. This could be true, but it does not take away from the fact that the biblical laws on unclean foods came directly from God. All Israel's restricted foods, unlike those of some other nations, involved the flesh of animals. Leviticus 11 is explicit in differentiating the clean from the unclean mammals (11:1-8, 26-28), sea creatures (11:9-12), birds (11:13-25), and creeping things (11:29-38). Nothing that died of itself was fit for their food, nor were they to eat anything strangled. BLOOD was a forbidden part of their diet. Unclean for Israel were animals that did not chew the cud and part the hoof, fish that did not have both fins and scales, birds that were birds of prey or had unclean habits, and insects that did not have legs above the feet for leaping.

Certain kinds of uncleanness among the Israelites were connected with DEATH. A dead person, regardless of the cause of death, made anyone who touched the body unclean (Num. 19:22). Likewise anything the body touched (19:22) or the enclosure in which the person died was made unclean (19:14). Provisions were made for the cleansing of the unclean in this class by sprinkling his body with the ashes of a red heifer on the third and seventh days (19:17-19). Those who touched the carcass of an animal became unclean and could be cleansed only by washing their clothes in water (Lev. 11:24-28). Certain types of creeping things that died made anything they touched unclean. Some objects thus touched could be cleansed by washing, whereas others had to be destroyed (11:29-37).

Leprosy was looked on as unclean, and God required the person pronounced leprous by the priest to identify himself in a prescribed manner and to separate himself from the rest of the people. Any time anyone drew near, the leper was to cry, "Unclean, unclean." Since this DISEASE was also very contagious, detailed instructions were given for dealing with it (Lev. 13-15).

Anything touched by seminal fluid issuing from the body became unclean. This applied also to certain other kinds of discharges (Lev. 15). Regulations for the cleansing of such persons or things were carefully laid down in the two passages above. According to the law, childbirth made a woman unclean, and this uncleanness lasted for different periods of time, depending on whether the

Burial site on the Mt. of Olives. Human bones were among the items that could make a person ceremonially unclean by contact.

child was male or female. In this case too, special instructions were given for cleansing (ch. 13).

In the PROPHETS there is a deepening of the concept. It is expressed especially in Isaiah's cry, "I am a man of unclean lips" (Isa. 6:5), and in his confession, "All of us have become like one who is unclean, / and all our righteous acts are like filthy rags" (64:6). Similarly, his picture of God's restoration in 35:8, "The unclean will not journey on it [*i.e.*, on the Way of Holiness]," has obviously a moral rather than a ritual implication. Unfortunately, in the postexilic period ever-increasing stress came to be laid on the avoidance of formal uncleanness. It was an obsession both with the Qumran Covenanters (see DEAD SEA SCROLLS) and the PHARISEES. In the later Talmudic developments questions of purity and impurity provide some of the most complex sections of rabbinic legislation.

In the NT the concept of uncleanness is dealt with differently: not that which goes into a person, but what comes out of him, is what defiles him (Mk. 7:18-20); similarly, nothing God has made is essentially unclean (Acts 10:13-15; 1 Tim. 4:4-5). In the CHURCH, CHRIST's teaching was continued. The decisions of the apostolic gathering in Jerusalem were based on regard for those Jews who were law-bound (Acts 15:19-21). Romans 14:14 is PAUL's expression of the fact that uncleanness is something essentially spiritual in its nature (cf. Heb. 12:15). The ritual of washing has become purely pictorial, and WATER becomes a symbol of the word (Eph. 5:26).

unction. This English term, meaning "the act of anointing," is used once by the KJV with reference to the effect of the Spirit's presence upon the believer (1 Jn. 2:20). See ANOINT; HOLY SPIRIT.

undefiled. A person or thing untainted with moral evil (KJV Ps. 119:1; Cant. 5:2; 6:9; Heb. 7:26; 13:4; Jas. 1:27; 1 Pet. 1:4).

undersetter. This archaic English term is used by the KJV in one passage referring to the supports of the laver in Solomon's TEMPLE (1 Ki. 7:30, 34).

underworld. See HADES.

unforgivable sin. See UNPARDONABLE SIN.

unicorn. See ANIMALS (under *cattle*).

union with Christ. While the expression "union with Christ" does not occur in the Bible, it describes the central reality in the salvation revealed there, from its eternal design to its eschatological consummation. This union finds its most prominent NT expression in the phrase "in Christ" or "in the Lord" (with slight variations), occurring frequently and almost exclusively in PAUL's letters (elsewhere, e.g., Jn. 14:20; 15:4-7; 1 Jn. 2:28). Paul's meaning is best gauged by the contrast between ADAM and Christ (the "last Adam" or "second man," Rom. 5:12-19; 1 Cor. 15:20-23; cf. vv. 45, 47). What each does is determinative, respectively, for those "in him." For those "in Christ" this union or solidarity is all-encompassing, extending from eternity to eternity: they are united to Christ not only in their present possession of salvation but also in its past, once-for-all accomplishment (e.g., Rom. 6:3-7; 8:1; Gal. 2:20; Eph. 2:5-6; Col. 3:1-4), in their ELECTION "before the creation of the world" (Eph. 1:4, 9), and in their still future glorification (Rom. 8:17; 1 Cor. 15:22).

Present union (union in the actual appropriation of salvation) is often called "mystical" and "spiritual." But both terms are subject to misunderstanding. Involved is not a mysticism of ecstatic experience at odds with reasoned understanding; rather, it is a mystery in the NT sense of what has been hidden with God in his eternal purposes but now, finally, has been revealed in Christ, particularly through his death and resurrection, and is appropriated by FAITH (Rom. 16:25-26; Col. 1:26-27; 2:2). Certainly, in its full dimensions this mystery is beyond the believer's comprehension. Involved here, as much as in anything pertaining to salvation and the gospel, is that knowledge of Christ's love "that surpasses knowledge" (Eph. 3:18-19; cf. 1 Cor. 2:9). Union with Christ is *spiritual*, not in an immaterial, idealistic sense, but because of the activity and indwelling of the HOLY SPIRIT. In the life of the church and within believers, Christ and the Spirit are inseparable (cf. Jn. 14:18). In Rom. 8:9-10, for example, the phrases "in the Spirit," "the Spirit in you," "belonging to Christ" (equivalent to "in Christ"), and "Christ in you" are all facets of a single union (cf. Eph. 3:16-17: to have "his Spirit in your inner being" is for "Christ … [to] dwell in your hearts"). Union with Christ is reciprocal. Not only are believers "in Christ"—he is "in them" (Jn. 14:20; 17:23, 26; Col. 1:27: "Christ in you, the hope of glory"). Such union, then, is inherently *vital*; Christ indwelling is the very life of the believer (Gal. 2:20; Col. 3:4).

unity. Scripture portrays great richness and variety in its teaching concerning oneness and harmony. There is the unity of the believer with his Lord (see UNION WITH CHRIST), and there is the union manifested in the BODY OF CHRIST, the CHURCH, which rests eventually on a deeper unity of believers in "one Lord, one faith, one baptism." Unity with Christ is illustrated in many ways: that of husband and wife, or the stones and the building. The classic analogy is the vine and the branches (cf. Jn. 15:1-8). Apart from such unity the follower of Christ can "do nothing." The unity is his life and the ground of his action. PAUL took special interest in the unity within the body of believers, and he did not argue for an invisible bond but for a oneness that should characterize the visible body. He recognized unity in diversity and diversity in unity, and he amplified this approach (1 Cor. 12) with the appeal to LOVE as the unifying bond (ch. 13). The apostle looked upon unity as reality already in existence, but also as a reality yet to be attained. As we are "patient, bearing with one another in love," we are then eager "to keep the unity of the Spirit" (Eph. 4:2-3).

unity of the Bible. See BIBLE.

unknown god. When the apostle PAUL addressed the meeting of the AREOPAGUS in ATHENS, he said to his listeners that he had noticed how religious they were, and added: "For as I walked around and looked carefully at your objects of worship, I even found an altar with this inscription: TO AN UNKNOWN GOD. Now what you worship as something unknown I am going to proclaim to you" (Acts 17:23). The existence of such an altar, presumably built in a scrupulous attempt to include every possible deity, was an indication of the Athe-

nians' religious sensitivity. It also betrayed a lack of religious knowledge, which Paul sought to remedy in his address (vv. 24-31).

unknown tongue. See TONGUES, GIFT OF.

unlearned. A word that KJV uses to translate several different Greek terms in the NT (Acts 4:13; 1 Cor. 14:16, 23-24; 2 Tim. 2:23; 2 Pet. 3:16). In the Corinthians passage, the Greek word is *idiōtēs G2626*, which is applied to persons who are not knowledgeable about the distinctive views or customs of a particular group; thus the NRSV translates, "outsider," and the TNIV, "inquirer," both of which are defensible renderings.

unleavened bread. Bread made without yeast. In the preparation of household bread, a piece of fermented dough from a previous baking was placed in the kneading trough along with fresh flour, kneaded into cakes, and then baked. Unleavened bread lacked the fermented dough. See LEAVEN. Unleavened bread or cakes (*maṣṣôt*, pl. of *maṣṣāh H5174*) are associated with the elements eaten at Passover, the feast that commemorates the deliverance of Israel from Egypt. Only unleavened bread was to be eaten for the seven days that followed Passover (Exod. 12:15-20; 13:3-7). By doing so, the Hebrews were reminded of their haste in leaving Egypt during the great EXODUS. They could not wait to bake bread to take with them, but carried dough in their bread troughs in their hurried flight into the desert. They baked their bread as they traveled, as do the desert bedouin today.

Unleavened Bread, Feast of. See FEASTS.

Unni. uhn´i (Heb. *ʿunnî H6716*, possibly "one who has been heard"). **(1)** A LEVITE in the time of DAVID appointed among others to play the lyre (NRSV, harp) as a part of the ministrations before the ARK OF THE COVENANT (1 Chr. 15:18, 20).

(2) A Levite who served after the EXILE; he is described as an associate of MATTANIAH, the director of worship (Neh. 12:9; NRSV, "Unno," following the KETIB).

Unno. uhn´oh. See UNNI #2.

U

U

unpardonable sin. Not a phrase used in the Bible, but the usual way of referring to Jesus' statement that blaspheming or speaking against the HOLY SPIRIT would not be forgiven (Matt. 12:31-32; Mk. 3:29; Lk. 12:10). Other apparent parallels (cf. Heb. 6:4-6; 10:26-27; 1 Jn. 5:16) should be exegeted in the light of that statement. The threat of this sin must be understood against the promise of SALVATION represented always as free and complete. What is the specific sin that is set against this assurance of FORGIVENESS? In the context it must mean that because people, by choice or by habit, confuse the Holy Spirit of God with the unclean spirit of BEELZEBUB, they cannot be reached with the message of salvation and therefore they continue to call his truth a lie. It is not that God *will not forgive* them, but that they, by destroying the very offer of the GOSPEL, place themselves outside the possibility of forgiveness.

untempered morter. This phrase is used by the KJV to render a Hebrew word that refers to plaster or whitewash (Ezek. 13:10-15; 22:28). The prophet uses this word in a metaphorical sense of the false prophets who instead of exposing and denouncing the sinful enterprises of the people weakly acquiesced to them. This is like daubing a stone wall with whitewash to give it the appearance of solidity and strength. A heavy rainstorm will destroy it.

upharsin. See MENE, MENE, TEKEL, PARSIN.

Uphaz. yoo′faz (Heb. ʾûpāz H233, derivation unknown). An unidentified location famous for its GOLD (Jer. 10:9; Dan. 10:5 [KJV, NRSV, TNIV]). In Jer. 10:9, the Aramaic and Syriac versions have OPHIR, a reading accepted by some scholars; others emend "gold from Uphaz" to "fine gold" (cf. 1 Ki. 10:18). In Dan. 10:5, the NIV and NJPS, apparently by emendation, translate "with gold and refined gold" (i.e., very fine gold; cf. Cant. 5:11). It remains uncertain whether a place by the name of Uphaz ever existed.

Upper Gate. KJV, "high gate" and "higher gate." One of the gates of the TEMPLE in JERUSALEM, first mentioned in the time of King Joash (JEHOASH). After the assassination of ATHALIAH, the young monarch was brought "from the temple of the LORD. They went into the palace through the Upper Gate and seated the king on the royal throne" (2 Chr. 23:30; in the parallel it is called "the gate of the runners/guards" [2 Ki. 11:19; cf. v. 6]). This description is interpreted by some to mean that the Upper Gate faced S, but EZEKIEL uses the same name with reference to a gate that "faces north" (Ezek. 9:2, evidently the same as the "north gate" of 8:14). The "Upper Gate" is probably the same as "the Upper Gate of Benjamin at the LORD's temple" (Jer. 20:2), and one of the few things mentioned regarding the reign of JOTHAM is that he "rebuilt the Upper Gate of the temple of the LORD" (2 Ki. 15:35; 2 Chr. 27:3). Some speculate that after this reconstruction it came to be known as the NEW GATE (Jer. 26:10; 36:10). Whether or not these various names refer to the same gate, the precise location is unknown.

upper room. Traditional name given to the room where Jesus celebrated the Last Supper; accordingly, the teaching recorded in Jn. 14-16 is referred to as the Upper Room Discourse. The designation "upper room" derives from the instructions that the Lord gave to the disciples in preparation for the meal (Mk. 14:15; Lk. 22:12). Large upper rooms with outside and inside staircases above the noise and bustle of the city are mentioned in the OT as an architectural feature of Palestinian houses (2 Ki. 1:2 et al.). After the ASCENSION OF CHRIST, the disciples "went up into an upper room" (Acts 1:13 KJV; NIV, "went upstairs to the room"), where the disciples met for prayer (v. 14), MATTHIAS was chosen to replace JUDAS ISCARIOT (vv. 15-26), and the initial events of PENTECOST took place (ch. 2). Many have identified the room where the Last Supper was held with the room mentioned in Acts 1, but there is no evidence that proves (or disproves) this theory.

Ur (place). oor (Heb. ʾûr H243, "light, flame"). Referred to in the Bible as "Ur of the Chaldeans [KJV, Chaldees]," this city in MESOPOTAMIA was the home of ABRAHAM prior to his family's migration to HARAN (Gen. 11:28, 31; 15:7; Neh. 9:7). Until 1850, Ur was considered to be modern

Urfa (Edessa), not far from HARAN, in SE Turkey, which according to a local tradition was the place of Abraham's residence. This view was revived in more recent times by some who suggested that Abraham was a merchant prince who did business in N MESOPOTAMIA. Against this view it must be noted that any tradition of Abraham at Urfa/Edessa goes back only to the eighth century A.D. The OT scarcely implies that Abraham was a merchant or that he moved only a short distance from Ur to Haran. Other pieces of evidence favored a more southerly location, and by 1866 the name *U-ri* was read on several buildings and other inscriptions from the site of Tell el-Muqayyar in S Iraq, 6 mi. (10 km.) SE of Nasiriyah on the EUPHRATES River. This ancient city of Ur certainly lay in territory called Kaldu (Chaldea) from the early first millennium B.C. The southern identification for the biblical Ur is now generally accepted.

The most extensive archaeological work on this site was done by Sir Charles Leonard Woolley between 1922 and 1934. Education was well developed at Ur, for a school was found there with its array of clay tablets. Students learned to read, write, and do varied forms of arithmetic. Further studies have revealed that commerce was well developed and that ships came into Ur from the Persian Gulf, bringing diorite and alabaster used in statue making, copper ore, ivory, gold, and hard woods. Much light has been shed on the worship and religious life of Abraham's day. Nannar was the moon god worshiped there. The temple, ZIGGURAT, and other buildings used in connection with the worship of this pagan deity have been found. Evidences of worship in the homes of the day are revealed by idols found in private niches in the home walls. From this city of idolatry God called Abraham and sent him with a promise to the land of Canaan.

Ur had become a flourishing city in Sumerian times, dominating S Babylonia and sometimes farther afield. See SUMER. The Ur Dynasty founded by Ur-Nammu saw a revival of Sumerian prosperity and the extension of Ur's influence once again to Syria and N Mesopotamia which continued during the reigns of his successors. When the AMORITES overran the S, HAMMURABI (1792-1750 B.C.) controlled Ur for a time, but when it rebelled

This small clay tablet from Ur (3rd dynasty, c. 2046 B.C.) is a commercial text in cuneiform that records the purchase of plough-oxen from various merchants.

© Dr. James C. Martin. The British Museum. Photographed by permission.

against his son it was sacked. Ur's importance as a religious center insured that it was never abandoned for long, and later kings kept it in repair, including NEBUCHADNEZZAR II and NABONIDUS in the sixth cent. The latter rebuilt the ziggurat and other shrines before installing his daughter, Bel-shalti-Nannar, as high priestess in her own new palace.

Ur (person). oor (Heb. *ʾûr H244*, "light, flame"). Father of ELIPHAL; the latter was one of DAVID's mighty warriors (1 Chr. 11:35). The parallel list reads differently (2 Sam. 23:34; see AHASBAI).

Urartu. See ARARAT.

Urbane. uhr´bayn. KJV form of URBANUS.

Urbanus. uhr-bay´nuhs (Gk. *Ourbanos G4042*, from Lat. *Urbanus*, "urbane, refined"). KJV Urbane. A member of the Christian church at Rome to whom PAUL sent greetings (Rom. 16:9). The apostle calls him "our fellow worker in Christ," a description applied also to PRISCILLA and AQUILA in this passage (v. 3), but to no one else. Presumably, Urbanus had assisted Paul in ASIA MINOR or

GREECE and subsequently migrated to the capital of the empire.

Uri. yoor´i (Heb. ʾûrî H247 and ʾurî H788 [1 Ki. 4:19], "light, flame," possibly short form of URIAH or URIEL). **(1)** Son of Hur and father of BEZALEL; the latter was the primary artisan in the building of the TABERNACLE (Exod. 31:2; 35:30; 38:22; 1 Chr. 2:20; 2 Chr. 1:5).

(2) Father of GEBER; the latter was one of SOLOMON's district managers (1 Ki. 4:19).

(3) One of the three Levitical gatekeepers who agreed to put away their foreign wives in the time of EZRA (Ezra 10:24).

Uriah. yoo-ri´uh (Heb. ʾûriyyāhû H250 [only Jer. 26:20-23] and ʾûriyyâ H249, apparently meaning "Yahweh is [my] light" [cf. URIEL]; Gk. Ourias G4043). KJV also Urijah (in 2 Kings, Nehemiah, and Jeremiah) and Urias (NT). **(1)** A HITTITE officer in DAVID's army who was the husband of BATHSHEBA (2 Sam. 11:3-26; 12:9-10, 15; 1 Ki. 15:5); he was included in the elite corps called "the Thirty" (2 Sam. 23:39; 1 Chr. 11:41). Some scholars have suggested that his name is HURRIAN (from *ewir*, "lord," in which case the form reflects the Hittite *-ia* ending rather than the divine name *Yah*), but it seems more likely that he accepted Israelite citizenship and then adopted a Hebrew name to indicate that he was a worshiper of Yahweh. David, in order to cover his adulterous connection with Bathsheba, recalled Uriah from war in order that the latter might visit his wife, but he refused to do so, even though the king tried to make him drunk. When David failed to make this device effective, he gave Uriah a sealed dispatch to JOAB, the commander of the army, requesting that Uriah be placed in a dangerous position and that support be withdrawn. Joab complied and Uriah was killed in battle. Upon his death, David married Bathsheba. The child conceived in adultery was born, but did not survive. Uriah is mentioned in Matthew's GENEALOGY OF JESUS CHRIST (Matt. 1:6).

(2) A priest contemporary with the prophet ISAIAH; Uriah and a certain Zechariah son of Jeberekiah were chosen "as reliable witnesses" of the prophecy concerning MAHER-SHALAL-HASH-BAZ (Isa. 8:2). He is probably the same Uriah who,

at the request of King AHAZ, built a replica of an altar the king had seen in DAMASCUS; this "large new altar" replaced the original bronze altar, and the latter was subsequently used by the king "for seeking guidance" (2 Ki. 16:10-16).

(3) Son of Shemaiah; he was a prophet from KIRJATH JEARIM who protested the policies of King JEHOIAKIM and was sentenced to death. Uriah escaped to Egypt but was captured, brought back to JERUSALEM, and executed (Jer. 26:20-23).

(4) Father of MEREMOTH, who was an important postexilic priest (Ezra 8:33; Neh. 3:4, 21).

(5) One of the prominent men (not identified as priests) who stood near EZRA when the law was read at the great assembly (Neh. 8:4).

Urias. See URIAH.

Uriel. yoor´ee-uhl (Heb. ʾûriʾēl H248, "God is [my] light" [cf. URIAH]). **(1)** Son (or descendant) of Tahath and descendant of LEVI through KOHATH (1 Chr. 6:24; his name is omitted in v. 37). During the reign of DAVID, Uriel was one of the LEVITE leaders who helped to bring the ARK OF THE COVENANT from the house of OBED-EDOM to JERUSALEM (15:5, 11).

(2) A man of GIBEAH whose daughter Micaiah (see MAACAH #9) was the wife of REHOBOAM and the mother of ABIJAH, kings of Judah (2 Chr. 13:2).

Urijah. See URIAH.

Urim and Thummim. yoor´im, thum´im (Heb. ʾûrîm [sg. ûr H242] and tummîm H9460 [sg. uncertain], traditionally understood to mean "lights and perfections," but the derivation of both terms is debated). These words are usually mentioned together as a phrase (Exod. 28:30; Lev. 8:8; Deut. 33:8 [in reverse order]; 1 Sam. 14:41 [NRSV and other versions, following LXX]; Ezra 2:63 = Neh. 7:65), but Urim occurs alone twice (Num. 27:21; 1 Sam. 28:6). Since the definite article is used in the Hebrew text (except for Ezra 2:63 = Neh. 7:65), it is clear they were not strictly proper names (cf. Deut. 33:8, where the words occur with a possessive pronoun). The Urim and Thummim were objects not specifically described, perhaps stones, placed in the BREASTPIECE of the high priest, which he wore when he went into the presence of the Lord and by which he ascertained the will of God in any important matter affecting the nation (Exod. 28:30; Lev. 8:8). It is uncertain what they were and what they looked like and how they were used. One theory is that they were used as the lot and cast like dice, the manner of their fall somehow revealing the Lord's will (1 Sam. 10:19-22; 14:37-42). Another theory is that they served as a symbol of the high priest's authority to seek counsel of the Lord, God's will being revealed to him through inner illumination.

Uruk. See ERECH.

usury. The lending of money at excessive rates of INTEREST. The English term used to mean simply "interest," however, and it is used in that sense by the KJV (Exod. 22:25 et al.).

Uthai. yoo'thi (Heb. *ʿûtay H6433*, perhaps short form of ATHAIAH). **(1)** Son of Ammihud and descendant of JUDAH (1 Chr. 9:4). He was among those who settled in JERUSALEM after the EXILE (v. 3).

(2) A descendant of BIGVAI, part of the company that traveled with EZRA from BABYLON to Jerusalem (Ezra 8:14).

Uz (person). uhz (Heb. *ʿûs H6419*, derivation uncertain). **(1)** Son of ARAM and grandson of SHEM (Gen. 10:23; 1 Chr. 1:17). See also Uz (PLACE).

(2) Son of NAHOR (ABRAHAM's brother) by MILCAH (Gen. 22:21).

(3) Son of Dishan and grandson of SEIR the HORITE (Gen. 36:28; 1 Chr. 1:42).

Uz (place). uhz (Heb. *ʿûs H6420*, derivation unknown). The "land of Uz" was apparently a district or a section of the country E of PALESTINE, on the border of ARABIA. It was the home of JOB (Job 1:1), and the prophet JEREMIAH refers to it twice (Jer. 25:20; Lam. 4:21). The area may have received its name from one of the individuals who bore the same name; see Uz (PERSON). The precise location of the land of Uz is uncertain, and some scholars (associating it with Uz son of ARAM, Gen. 10:23; 1 Chr. 1:17) identify it with HAURAN, an area E of the Sea of Galilee. A region further S is more likely, however, and Wadi Sirhan, SE of Jebel

ed-Druz, seems to fit the biblical description best. This area is a great shallow plain-like depression some 210 mi. (340 km.) long and averaging 20 mi. (32 km.) wide. It begins at the present inland town of Azraq, a typical oasis with many palm groves, some 50 mi. (80 km.) ESE of Amman, and continues in a southeasterly direction to within 10 mi. (16 km.) of Jauf, an important caravan junction of central Arabia. Much of Wadi Sirhan is a vast, flat pasture land, fairly well suited to the raising of camels, donkeys, sheep, and goats. And to this day it sustains wildlife such as gazelle, oryx, ostrich, and the wild ass, though in smaller numbers than in Job's day.

Uzai. yoo'zi (Heb. *ʾûzay H206*, derivation uncertain). Father of PALAL; the latter assisted NEHEMIAH in repairing the JERUSALEM walls (Neh. 3:25).

Uzal. yoo'zuhl (Heb. *ʾûzāl H207*, derivation uncertain). Son of JOKTAN and descendant of SHEM, included in the Table of Nations (Gen. 10:27; 1 Chr. 1:21); he was also the eponymous ancestor of a tribe or country (Ezek. 27:19; however, the text here is uncertain). The two sons of EBER, PELEG and Joktan, represent the two main divisions of the Semitic-speaking people (see SEMITE), and Joktan is considered by some scholars to be the founder of the Arab nation. There is an Arabic tradition that Uzal was the original name of Sanaa (Ṣanʿaʾ), the capital of Yemen in SW ARABIA. Wrought iron is mentioned by Ezekiel as one of the exports of Uzal to TYRE, and Sanaa is still noted for its steel. On the assumption that the SEPTUAGINT of Ezekiel reflects the original reading ("wine" rather than JAVAN), others have suggested Izalla/Aṣalla (cf. TNIV, "Izal"), a city or country known for its wine, located in the hills of NE Syria, between HARAN and the TIGRIS, N of the Khabur River Valley. See also VEDAN.

Uzza. See UZZAH.

Uzzah. uhz'uh (Heb. *ʿuzzāʾ H6438* and *ʿuzzâ H6446*, possibly short form of UZZIAH, "Yahweh is [my] strength"). The KJV has the form Uzzah only in 2 Sam. 6:3, 6-8, and Uzza elsewhere; the NIV and NRSV have Uzzah in this passage as well as in 1 Chr. 6:29; 13:7-11 (Uzza in 2 Ki. 21:18, 26; 1 Chr. 8:7; Ezra 2:49; Neh. 7:51). The spelling in none of the English Bibles corresponds precisely with the Hebrew spellings, mainly because of inconsistency in the latter (note that, according to the Heb., 2 Sam. 6:3 and 6 would require the spelling Uzza, but vv. 7-8 would require Uzzah).

(1) Son of Abinadab (2 Sam. 6:3; see ABINADAB #3). Uzzah was killed while driving the oxcart which carried the ARK OF THE COVENANT to JERUSALEM. The ark had been in the house of Abinadab for some time following the disaster it had occasioned in the PHILISTINE cities and in BETH SHEMESH (1 Sam. 6:19; 7:2). When DAVID decided to bring the ark to JERUSALEM, Uzzah and his brother, AHIO, were assigned to drive the cart. As they reached the threshing floor of NACON, the oxen stumbled and the ark began to slide. Uzzah reached out to steady the ark and was fatally smitten. His death was attributed to the violation of the sacred character of the ark (2 Sam. 6:7; 1 Chr. 13:10). David was greatly distressed at the incident, and immediately canceled his plans to enshrine the ark in Jerusalem. Instead, he deposited it in the home of OBED-EDOM. He named the place PEREZ UZZAH, "the breach of [*or* the breaking out against] Uzzah." The ark remained in the home of Obed-Edom for three months.

(2) Son of Shimei and descendant of LEVI through MERARI (1 Chr. 6:29; Heb. v. 14).

(3) The owner of a garden in which MANASSEH and AMON, kings of JUDAH, were buried (2 Ki. 21:18, 26).

(4) Ancestor of a family of temple servants (NETHINIM) who returned from the EXILE (Ezra 2:49; Neh. 7:51).

Uzzen Sheerah. uhz´uhn-shee´uh-ruh (Heb. *ʾuzzēn šeʾĕrâ H267*, "ear [*or* corner] of Sheerah"). KJV Uzzen-sherah. A village built by SHEERAH, the daughter of EPHRAIM (1 Chr. 7:24). The town must have been near BETH HORON, but its precise location is unknown.

Uzzen-sherah. See UZZEN SHEERAH.

Uzzi. uhz´i (Heb. *ʿuzzî H6454*, prob. short form of UZZIAH or UZZIEL, "Yahweh/God is [my]

strength"). **(1)** Son of Bukki, descendant of LEVI through KOHATH, and ancestor of EZRA (1 Chr. 6:5-6, 51 [Heb. 5:31-32; 6:26]; Ezra 7:4).

(2) Firstborn son of TOLA and grandson of ISSACHAR; he was a family head who had a large progeny, including numerous warriors (1 Chr. 7:2-4).

(3) Son of BELA and grandson of BENJAMIN; a family head (1 Chr. 7:7).

(4) Son of Micri and descendant of Benjamin; his son Elah was among the first to resettle in JERUSALEM (1 Chr. 9:8; cf. v. 3).

(5) Son of Bani, descendant of ASAPH, and "chief officer of the Levites in Jerusalem" at the time of EZRA; he was among "the singers responsible for the service of the house of God" (Neh. 11:22).

(6) Head of the priestly family of JEDAIAH during the days of the high priest JOIAKIM (Neh. 12:19).

(7) A priest or Levite who took part in one of the choirs at the dedication of the wall (Neh. 12:42).

Uzzia. uh-zi´uh (Heb. *ʿuzziyyāʾ H6455*, prob. short form of UZZIAH or UZZIEL, "Yahweh/God is [my] strength"). An "Ashterathite" (i.e., a man from the town of ASHTAROTH in BASHAN) listed among DAVID's mighty warriors (1 Chr. 11:44).

Uzziah. uh-zi´uh (Heb. *ʿuzziyyāhû H6460* and *ʿuzziyyâ H6459*, "Yahweh is [my] strength"; cf. UZZIEL). **(1)** Son of AMAZIAH and his successor as king of JUDAH; also known as AZARIAH (2 Chr. 26 et al.; cf. 2 Ki. 14:21 et al.). At the age of sixteen he became Judah's tenth king (2 Ki. 14:21) and ruled fifty-two years (c. 792-740 B.C.). He came to the throne at a difficult time. His father, because of a military failure, had been killed (14:19). Uzziah was the people's choice as his successor (14:21). He undertook, very early in his career, an expedition against his father's enemies and won battles against the Edomites, Philistines, Arabians, and the Meunites (2 Ki. 14:22; 2 Chr. 26:1-7). He strengthened his kingdom (26:2), and the report of his strength spread as far as Egypt (26:8). He made many improvements on his home front (26:9-10), and he possessed real ability at organization (26:11-15). In spite of these successes, he strayed far from the Lord at the end of his life. Apparently as long as the prophet ZECHARIAH lived, his influence was great on the king and "as long as he sought the

When King Uzziah died, he was buried outside Jerusalem because of his leprosy (2 Chr. 26:23). After the city was expanded under Herod the Great, Uzziah's remains were moved to the Mt. of Olives, and this marble plaque marks the new site. The Aramaic inscription reads: "To this place were brought the bones of Uzziah, the king of Judah. Do not open!"

© Dr. James C. Martin. The Israel Museum, Jerusalem. Photographed by permission.

LORD, God gave him success" (2 Chr. 26:5). However, when he became strong, pride filled his heart, and one day he went into the temple, determined to burn incense to the Lord, a duty to be performed only by the priest. The chief priest AZARIAH with eighty priests went into the temple to reason with him, but he would not listen. Because of his self-will, God struck him with leprosy, which stayed with him until his death (26:16-21).

(2) Son of Uriel and descendant of LEVI through KOHATH (1 Chr. 6:24).

(3) Father of a certain Jonathan who "was in charge of the storehouses" during the reign of DAVID (1 Chr. 27:25).

(4) A postexilic priest; he was one of the descendants of Harim who agreed to put away their foreign wives in the time of EZRA (Ezra 10:21).

(5) Son of Zechariah and descendant of JUDAH; his son Athaiah was a provincial leader who settled in Jerusalem after the EXILE (Neh. 11:4).

Uzziel. uhz'ee-uhl (Heb. *ʿuzzîʾēl* *H6457*, "God is [my] strength"; gentilic *ʿazzîʾēlî* *H6458*, "Uzzielite"). **(1)** Son of KOHATH, grandson of LEVI, and eponymous ancestor of a Kohathite clan (Exod. 6:18, 22; Lev. 10:4; Num. 3:19; 1 Chr. 6:2, 18; 23:12, 20). One of his brothers was AMRAM, the ancestor of MOSES and AARON. One of Uzziel's children, ELZAPHAN (Elizaphan), was the leader of the Kohathite clans "responsible for the care of the ark, the table, the lampstand, the altars, the articles of the sanctuary used in ministering, the curtain, and everything related to their use" (Num. 3:30-31). Members of this family were among the LEVITES who assisted DAVID in bringing the ARK OF THE COVENANT to JERUSALEM (1 Chr. 15:10). They were also given special assignments in David's preparatory arrangements for the temple ritual (1 Chr. 23:12, 20; 24:24).

(2) Son of Ishi and descendant of SIMEON; he was one of the leaders of a band of 500 Simeonites who engaged the AMALEKITES at Mount SEIR in a decisive battle and came out victorious. The Simeonites extended their boundary to include that of the vanquished foe (1 Chr. 4:42-43).

(3) Son of Bela and grandson of BENJAMIN; a family head (1 Chr. 7:7).

(4) Son of HEMAN, the king's seer (1 Chr. 25:4). The fourteen sons of Heman, along with the sons of ASAPH and JEDUTHUN, were set apart "for the ministry of prophesying, accompanied by harps, lyres and cymbals" (v. 1). The assignment of duty was done by lot, and the eleventh lot fell to Uzziel, his sons, and his relatives (25:18, here called AZAREL).

(5) Descendant of JEDUTHUN the musician; he and his brother SHEMAIAH were among the Levites assigned to consecrate the temple in the days of HEZEKIAH (2 Chr. 29:14).

(6) Son of Harhaiah; he was a goldsmith who helped NEHEMIAH in rebuilding the walls of Jerusalem (Neh. 3:8). Some scholars emend the text to read "Uzziel, a son [*i.e.*, member] of the guild of the goldsmiths."

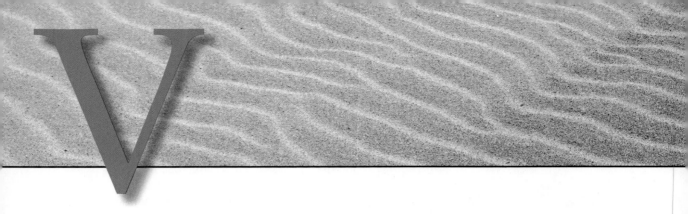

vagabond. This English term is used by the KJV in three passages: with reference to Cain (Gen. 4:12, 14; NIV, "wanderer"); in an imprecatory prayer (Ps. 109:10; NIV, "wandering beggars"); and in a description of itinerant Jewish exorcists (Acts 19:13; NIV, "Jews who went around driving out evil spirits").

Vaheb. See Waheb.

vail. KJV alternate form of "veil"; see Curtain; Dress.

vain. This English term, meaning "worthless" or "futile," is used over a hundred times in the KJV to render a variety of Hebrew and Greek terms; it occurs less frequently in modern versions. For example, God warns the Israelites that if they violate his covenant they will plant seed "in vain" (*lārîq*, "for nothing") because their "enemies will eat it" (Lev. 26:16; the Heb. word *rîq* H8198 means "emptiness"). In the commandment not to take the Lord's name "in vain" (*laššāwʾ*, Exod. 20:7; Deut. 5:11), the word is *šāwʾ* H8736, which also means "emptiness, nothingness," and is often rendered with such adjectives as "worthless" and "false." The NIV renders the Hebrew idiom in the command with the English phrase, "misuses his name" (the NJPS interprets it more specifically, "swears falsely by His name"; see Commandments, Ten). Of several Greek words rendered "vain" in the NT, the most frequent is *kenos* G3031, "empty" (e.g., 1 Cor. 15:58; Gal. 1:2). See also Vanity.

Vaizatha. vi'zuh-thuh (Heb. *wayzātāʾ* H2262, a Persian name of uncertain meaning). KJV Vajezatha. One of the ten sons of Haman who were put to death by the Jews (Esth. 9:9).

Vajezatha. See Vaizatha.

vale. See Valley.

Valentinus. val'uhn-tee'nuhs. An early and influential Christian Gnostic theologian. Probably born early in the second century in Egypt, Valentinus first taught in Alexandria, then moved to Rome c. 135, and eventually became a candidate for the position of bishop. Having been rejected, he seceded from the church, and after some years of living in the eastern parts of the empire he returned to Rome, where he died c. 170. It appears that Valentinus sought to adapt some of the classic myths of non-Christian Gnosticism to the theological framework of Christian orthodoxy, and his popularity gave rise to several Valentinian schools that were severely attacked by the church fathers, especially Irenaeus. In modern times several Valentinian works have been discovered, including the *Gospel of Truth* (see Truth, Gospel of).

valley. The various Hebrew terms that may be translated "vale" or "valley" fall readily into two distinct categories, and in doing so reflect clearly the structure and surface of the Bible lands. (1) The nouns *ʿēmeq* H6677 and *biqʿâ* H1326 indicate a broad vale or lowland, sometimes more than 10 mi. (16 km.) in breadth. In contrast, (2) *naḥal* H5707 ("wadi" or "river valley") and *gayʾ* H1628 indicate a steep-sided valley, that is, a *gorge*. In Palestine the terms in the first category apply primarily to structural features such as the Plain of Esdraelon and the Rift Valley of Jordan (cf. Deut. 34:3). The words in the second category describe valley features that are the result of streams cutting down into the limestones and sandstones of Palestine in

Aerial view from the southern end of the Sea of Galilee looking S along the Jordan Valley.

a dry climate, creating a highly dissected landscape, and in some areas producing a "badland" topography. Such gorges represent serious obstacles to movement and played a prominent part in the military operations of biblical times (cf. Josh. 8:11; 1 Sam. 17:3). See WADI.

Since Israel in OT times was largely a mountain dwelling people, their view of the lowlands which surrounded them (and which were largely occupied by their enemies) was naturally colored by this fact. Consequently, the term SHEPHELAH, often translated "the valley" or "the vale" by the KJV (Deut. 1:7 et al.), was reserved for a specific region, lying between the mountains of JUDEA and the MEDITERRANEAN. It is not a valley at all, but a kind of piedmont zone of low hills lying between the coastal plain proper and the Judean hills, and separated from the latter by a narrow (true) valley. Thus the NIV renders it, "the western foothills." (In the NT, "valley" is the rendering of Gk. *pharanx G5754*, "cleft, ravine" [Lk. 3:5, a citation from the LXX], and *cheimarros G5929*, "[winter] torrent" [Jn. 18:1]).

Valley Gate. A city gate on the SW side of JERUSALEM. The Valley Gate was equipped with towers by UZZIAH, c. 760 B.C. (2 Chr. 26:9). It was the point from which NEHEMIAH began his tour of inspection in 444 B.C. (Neh. 2:13, 15); and it

figured in his work of rebuilding, being located some 500 yards (c. 450 m.) from the DUNG GATE (3:13). If Jerusalem was at this time still confined to the hills E of the central Tyropoeon Valley, the Valley Gate would have been N of the Dung Gate. Otherwise it would have been to the W, opening out from the city onto the slopes of the SW hill. From the Valley Gate the two parties led by EZRA and NEHEMIAH proceeded along the walls for their dedication in 444, in opposite directions, so as to meet at the TEMPLE, on the NE side of the city (Neh. 12:31, 39).

Valley of Ben Hinnom. See HINNOM, VALLEY OF (BEN).

Vaniah. vuh-ni′uh (Heb. *wanyâ H2264*, possibly from Persian *vānya*, "lovable"). One of the descendants of BANI who agreed to put away their foreign wives in the time of EZRA (Ezra 10:36).

vanity. This English term, in the sense of "futility" or "worthlessness" (rather than in its common meaning of "conceit," for which see PRIDE), occurs almost 100 times (13 times pl.) in the KJV, 45 of them in ECCLESIASTES alone. The NRSV preserves the term in this book, but uses it rarely elsewhere (Ps. 89:47 et al.), while in the NIV it does not occur at all. The word is most familiar in the saying, "Vanity of vanities; all is vanity" (Eccl. 1:2 et al. KJV; NIV, "Utterly meaningless! Everything is meaningless!"; NJPS, "Utter futility! All is futile!"). Here and in most other instances, "vanity" translates the Hebrew noun *hebel H2039*, which in some passages is best rendered "breath" (e.g., Isa. 57:13). It is always used with its figurative connotation of that which is weak, ephemeral, transitory. The KJV uses "vanity" also as the rendering of other words (cf. Job 7:3; Prov. 22.8; Rom. 8:20; et al.).

These various terms can refer to that which appears to have meaning, substance, or value, but which turns out to possess none of these elements, and so it is false or deceitful. Those who follow after such things are not only deceived but wicked. Not surprisingly, idols are referred to repeatedly as "vanities" (NIV, "worthless idols," Deut. 32:21; 1 Ki. 16:13; et al.). Other things designated as vanity include: (a) the thoughts and words of the godless (Job 15:35; Ps. 10:7; 144:8); (b) leaving the fruit of one's toil to another (Eccl. 2:19, 21); (c) human fate (2:15; 3:19); life (Eccl. 9:9; 11:10); (d) the message of false prophets (Ezek. 13:6-9 et al.); (e) nations and rulers (Isa. 40:17, 23); (f) pleasure (Eccl. 2:1); (g) wealth (5:10 et al.; cf. Prov. 13:11; 21:6); (h) everyone and everything (Ps. 39:11; 62:9; Eccl. 1:1; 12:8). See IDOLATRY; VAIN.

Vashni. vash′ni (Heb. *wašni H2266* [not in NIV]). Firstborn son of SAMUEL, according to the MT, followed by KJV (1 Chr. 6:28 [Heb., v. 13]). However, since 1 Sam. 8:2 has, "The name of his firstborn son was Joel and the name of his second was Abijah," most scholars believe that the Chronicles passage has suffered textual corruption (due to the same ending of the names "Samuel" and "Joel"). Accordingly, they amend the verse in Chronicles to read, "And the sons of Samuel: Joel the firstborn and the second Abijah" (cf. NIV and NRSV), for which there is support from some ancient versions.

Vashti. vash′ti (Heb. *wašti H2267*, possibly from Persian *vahišta*, "the best"). Queen of PERSIA and wife of Ahasuerus (XERXES I). Vashti refused to exhibit her beauty to his lords on the seventh day of a feast (Esth. 1:9-19; 2:1, 4, 17). The king banished her and made an edict that each man should

be lord over his own house (1:22). Her deposition led to the selection of ESTHER as the new queen. Herodotus (*Hist.* 7.61; 9.108-12) says Xerxes' queen was Amestris and mentions no other wives, leading some scholars to question the reliability of the biblical account. Others believe that Amestris and Vashti are the same woman and that either (1) the names are variant forms or (2) the use of the name Vashti is a literary device calling attention to the woman's beauty. Perhaps more likely is the view that Xerxes had several wives and that Herodotus is interested only in those who bore potential successors to the throne.

vat. See VINE.

Vaticanus, Codex. See SEPTUAGINT; TEXT AND VERSIONS (NT).

vau, vav. See WAW.

Vedan. vee′duhn (Heb. *wĕdān H1968* [not in NIV]). In EZEKIEL's lament over TYRE, the NRSV reads, "Vedan and Javan from Uzal entered into trade for your wares" (Ezek. 27:19; similarly NJPS). If this understanding of the Hebrew text is correct, identification may be made with *Waddan* (also called al-ʾAbwaʾ), a place between Mecca and Medina, involved in Muhammad's first expedition. The name JAVAN normally refers to the Ionians (and thus the NIV has "Greeks"), but because of the context some have thought there was a Javan in ARABIA or that the reference is to a Greek settlement in that area. The phrase "from Uzal" is problematic (see UZAL); if it refers to a place, its location is uncertain, though most scholars look for it somewhere in Arabia. The Hebrew form *wĕdān* has traditionally been understood to mean "and Dan" (thus NIV, "Danites"; cf. KJV), but such a reading is problematic. Many scholars believe that a more accurate text is preserved in the SEPTUAGINT (which instead of "Javan" has *oinon*, "wine," corresponding to Heb. *yayin H3516*), and thus the TNIV translates, "and casks of wine from Izal in exchange for your wares."

vegetables. Modern English versions use this word occasionally in the OT (Deut. 11:10; 1 Ki.

21:2; Prov. 15:17; Dan. 1:12, 16). In addition, the Greek noun *lachanon* G3303, "garden plant, herb," is properly rendered "vegetable" in at least one NT passage (Rom. 14:2). Vegetables are otherwise referred to in various other passages (e.g., Gen. 25:34; Num 11:5). See PLANTS.

veil. See CURTAIN; DRESS.

vein. A word found only in Job 28:1 KJV, "a vein for the silver." The NIV "mine" probably conveys the meaning of the Hebrew more accurately. The Hebrew word, however, is found elsewhere with a much broader meaning ("place of departure, outlet, exit, pronouncement") than is indicated in the passage in Job (e.g., Num. 30:12; Deut. 8:3; Ps. 19:6).

vengeance. Punishment in repayment for injury or offense. In the Bible, different aspects may be discerned through context or parallelism. (1) WRATH as the motivating force in vengeance is prominent in some cases (Prov. 6:34; Isa. 59:17; 63:4; Nah. 1:2; Sir. 5:7; 12:6; Rom. 3:5); human wrath may take the form of malice (Lev. 19:18; 1 Sam. 25:26; Lam. 3:60; Ezek. 25:12, 15). (2) The idea of PUNISHMENT for SIN or injury appears often (Lev. 26:25; Ps. 99:8; Lk. 21:22); this gradually shades over into the concept of recompense or retaliation (Gen. 4:15; Isa. 34:8; Jer. 50:15; Sir. 35:18). (3) The justice of God or the faithfulness of his servants is vindicated by the punishment of enemies (Jdg. 11:36; Ps. 94:1-2 Thess. 1:8); sometimes an individual appeals to God for divine vengeance (Ps. 58:10; Jer. 11:20; 15:15; 20:12). See also AVENGER.

venison. See GAME.

vermilion. A red pigment used for painting walls of palaces (Jer. 22:14 KJV) and for coloring the exotic clothing of the Chaldeans (Ezek. 23:14 KJV). NIV has "red" both times.

versions of the Bible. See BIBLE VERSIONS, ENGLISH; TEXT AND VERSIONS (OT); TEXT AND VERSIONS (NT).

Vespasian. ves-pay´shuhn. Titus Flavius Sabinus Vespasianus was born in A.D. 9 and ruled as emperor of ROME from 69 to 79. Before the age of twenty, Vespasian became military tribune in THRACIA, and he subsequently filled various roles in CRETE. It was not until his forties, however, that he won recognition by his military campaigns in Britain. Little is reported about him during the next two decades, but in the year 67 he was given the responsibility of subduing the Jewish revolt. After the death of NERO in 68, a period of civil war saw the rise and fall of three emperors. In the summer of 69 Vespasian was proclaimed emperor by the eastern legions, and he left his son TITUS in charge of the Jewish war. Before the end of the year, the senate confirmed his emperorship. Vespasian's main task was one of reconstruction after the misrule of Nero and the year of anarchy that had followed it. His blunt, straightforward, and honest character, coupled with simplicity of life and common sense, fitted him perfectly for his task. The successful completion of the war in Palestine by Titus, the suppression of a revolt in Gaul, and the establishment of peace on all frontiers caused a revival of public confidence. In celebration of the new era Vespasian began the rebuilding of the Capitoline temple. He also began construction of the famous Colosseum in the capital city, and throughout the provinces built roads and public buildings where these were needed. Vespasian sponsored the production of works of art, and encouraged educational activity in every way. Although he had a tendency toward autocracy, the general esteem in which he was held is indicated by the fact that upon his death in 79 he was deified by the senate.

vessel. A container for a liquid or some other substance. Vessels were used for storage of food or valuables (e.g., the DEAD SEA SCROLLS). Materials varied from the ubiquitous POTTERY of ancient civilizations to precious metals, glass, and ornamental stone, such as alabaster (Mk. 14:3). BASKETS varied in size from those that could be carried on head or shoulder (Gen. 40:16; Exod. 29:3)—made for holding fruit (Jer. 24:1-2) or for serving as a brickmaker's hod (Ps. 81:6)—to containers large enough to hold a man (Acts 9:25; 2 Cor. 11:33). Baskets are mentioned in connection with the feeding of the 5,000 (Matt. 14:20; Mk. 6:43; Lk. 9:17) and

V

the 4,000 (Matt. 15:37; Mk. 8:8). Other containers included LEATHER bottles, that is, animal skins used for keeping water (Gen. 21:14-15, 19), milk (Jdg. 4:19), and wine (Josh. 9:4, 13; 1 Sam. 1:24; 10:3; 16:20; 2 Sam. 16:1); jars or pitchers used, for example, for drawing water from wells (Gen. 24:14-19; cf. Jn. 4:11); basins or bowls used mainly for libation (e.g., 1 Ki. 7:43, 50), but also in domestic contexts (2 Sam. 17:28; Jn. 13:5); cups of various types (Gen. 44:2 and frequently); and dishes or plates that were often large deep containers commonly of bronze, still used for the common meal of the bedouin (Prov. 19:24 et al.). In Rom. 9:20-24 and 2 Tim. 2:20-21 the term is applied to persons; in 2 Cor. 4:7 it means the person as an instrument of God's will, and in 1 Thess. 4:4 it is used figuratively for a man's own body or for his wife (cf. NIV and mg.; see also 1 Pet. 3:7).

vestibule. See PORCH.

vestment, vesture. See DRESS.

vestry. This English term, in its archaic sense of "wardrobe," is used by the KJV in one passage to render Hebrew *meltāḥâ H4921*, which occurs only once (2 Ki. 10:22).

Via Appia. vee´uh-ah´pee-uh. See APPIAN WAY.

Via Dolorosa. vee´uh-doh-luh-roh´suh. A phrase (Latin for "sorrowful way") used with reference to the traditional route followed by Jesus from the PRAETORIUM or Judgment Hall to GOLGOTHA, the place of his crucifixion. The exact route followed by Jesus after his condemnation to death by PILATE (Matt. 27:26; Mk. 15:15; Lk. 23:25; Jn. 19:16) is debated because of uncertainty regarding those two location. The Praetorium has been placed by some at the Castle of ANTONIA at the NW corner of the TEMPLE area, and by others at the Palace of Herod near the Jaffa Gate. As for Golgotha, it may be located at the site of the present Church of the Holy Sepulchre or at a place known as Gordon's Calvary. The traditional route followed by many pilgrims today begins near the so-called Ecce Homo arch in the vicinity of the Convent of the Sisters of Zion in modern Jerusalem and follows a westerly direc-

tion to the Church of the Holy Sepulchre. On the route there are fourteen stations representing various scenes, some related in the Gospels and others preserved in tradition, which occurred as Jesus made that tragic journey. These fourteen stations are: (1) Jesus is condemned to death; (2) Jesus receives the cross; (3) Jesus falls the first time; (4) Jesus meets his afflicted mother; (5) Simon of Cyrene helps Jesus to carry his cross; (6) Veronica wipes the face of Jesus; (7) Jesus falls the second time; (8) Jesus speaks to the daughters of Jerusalem; (9) Jesus falls the third time; (10) Jesus is stripped of his garments; (11) Jesus is nailed to the cross; (12) Jesus dies on the cross; (13) the body of Jesus is taken down from the cross; (14) Jesus is laid in the sepulchre.

Via Egnatia. vee´uh-eg-nah´teeuh. A major road linking the city of Dyrrhachium, on the W coast of MACEDONIA, to Byzantium, the easternmost city in Europe. Built c. 130 B.C. and named after the Macedonian proconsul Gnaeus Egnatius, the Egnatian Way passed through some of the cities visited by the apostle PAUL, such as THESSALONICA and PHILIPPI.

vial. See BOWL.

Via Maris. vee´uh-mah´ris. This Latin phrase, meaning "the way of the sea" (cf. Isa. 9:1), refers to a major road that ran along the Mediterranean coast in southern Palestine and served as an international route (although some scholars question the appropriateness or historical accuracy of the term). Caravans traveling from EGYPT to either PHOENICIA or SYRIA would often go N through the PHILISTINE coastal towns of GAZA and ASHDOD. At JOPPA the road veered inland to APHEK, then continued N to MEGIDDO. Here one branch took travelers NW to ACCO, TYRE, and SIDON; another branch went NE to HAZOR and thence to DAMASCUS.

vice. See SIN.

victory. The OT associates victory with the God of power and glory and majesty who is in full control of his CREATION (1 Chr. 29:11). That he gives victory in this life to faithful believers is seen throughout Heb. 11. FAITH is the victory that conquers the world (1 Jn. 5:4-5), and through it Christians continually know the victory because of what God has done in Jesus Christ (1 Cor. 15:7). They can look unafraid at the vanquishing of sin and death—and they will not suffer the second death (Rev. 2:11). All the blessings of the new Jerusalem will be inherited by the overcomers (21:1-7).

victual. This English term—especially in the plural, meaning "supplies of food, provisions"—is used more than twenty times by the KJV (e.g., Gen. 14:11; Matt. 14:15). Since the word is uncommon in everyday English, it is seldom found in modern versions. See FOOD.

vigilance. This virtue is most commonly expressed in the Bible in verbal form: Christians are urged to be constantly watchful, on their guard. In GETHSEMANE a particular occasion for watchfulness was stressed by Jesus and was then associated with a rebuke to his sleepy companions (Matt. 26:38-41; Mk. 14:34, 38). More often, however, watchfulness is directed as a general attitude of preparedness in those who await their Lord's return (Matt. 24:42; Mk. 13:33-34, 37; Lk. 21:36; 1 Thess. 5:6; Rev. 3:3).

village. In distinction from a CITY (see also TOWN), the village was unwalled and easy prey for conquest. Villages had no defensive facilities such as moats, towers, or fortified gates (Ezek. 38:11). When threatened, the villagers thronged into the city, increasing the danger of famine (cf. 2 Ki. 6:24-29). Villages increased in number northward from the NEGEV because of greater rainfall. In Chalcolithic times, the Middle Bronze era, and the Iron Age, the Negev was well-occupied, and in the Nabatean-Byzantine era most intensively, when careful conservation of rainfall prevailed. From HEBRON northward a gradual increase of villages occurred toward and beyond JERUSALEM, with the greatest frequency in the territory of ZEBULUN of Lower GALILEE, where rainfall was greatest. Upper Galilee was too broken and too wooded to support the agriculture necessary to village life. TRANSJORDAN was dotted with towns and villages before the nineteenth century B.C., and after the thirteenth century the villages were again mentioned in the record of the conquest. Local village government was administered through the ELDERS who also acted as judges (Ruth 4:2), but the villages were under the larger jurisdiction of the towns (cf. Josh. 15:20-62; 18:24, 28; et al.). The size of villages varied according to whether the country was farmed intensively or not. In the agricultural centers, grain was threshed within the confines of the villages. Activity increased at harvest time, but many of the

Aerial view of the reconstructed Talmudic village of Qatzrin on the Golan Heights.

© Dr. James C. Martin

villagers would be away with the herds at other times.

vine, vineyard. The common grapevine is mentioned throughout Scripture, often in a figurative sense. It was grown in ancient EGYPT and in CANAAN prior to the time of ABRAHAM (Gen. 14:18; Num. 13:20, 24). The mountain regions of JUDEA and SAMARIA, largely unsuited for grain, were well adapted for vine growing. A vineyard was usually surrounded with a protecting wall of stones or thorny hedges to keep out destructive animals (Num. 22:24; Ps. 80:8-13; Prov. 24:30-31; Isa. 5:5). In every vineyard was a tower for the watchman, a winepress hollowed out of a flat rock, and a vat into which the juice flowed from the winepress (Isa. 1:8; 5:1-7; Matt. 21:33-41). The vine branches were usually allowed to lie along the ground or to fall over the terraces, but sometimes they were raised above the ground with sticks or supported on poles to form a bower.

Vines required constant care to keep them productive. They were pruned every spring, and the ground was plowed and kept free of weeds. Pruned branches were gathered and burned (Jn. 15:6). During the harvest season watchmen were stationed in the towers, and sometimes the whole family of the owner took their residence in booths as a protection against thieves. The HARVEST season was always one of special happiness. The treaders of the winepress shouted and sang as they trod the grapes (Jdg. 9:27; Isa. 16:10; Jer. 25:30; 48:33). The gleanings were left to the poor (Lev. 19:10; Deut. 24:21; Jdg. 8:2). The wine was stored in new goatskin bags (Matt. 9:17) or in large pottery containers. Every seventh year the vines were allowed to lie fallow (Exod. 23:11; Lev. 25:3). Grapes were an important part of the diet of the Hebrews. A part of the harvest was preserved in the form of raisin cakes (1 Sam. 25:18). Grapes were also their main source of sugar. The juice of the grapes was drunk fresh and fermented.

Figuratively, the vine symbolized prosperity and peace among the ancient Hebrews (1 Ki. 4:25; Mic. 4:4; Zech. 3:10). The vine also symbolized the chosen people, who instead of producing outstanding fruit yielded only wild grapes (Isa. 5:1-7; cf. Ps. 80:8-16). Some of Jesus' parables relate to vines

and their culture (Matt. 9:17; 20:1-6; 21:28-33; Lk. 13:6-9). Jesus referred to himself as the only true vine with whom his disciples are in organic union (Jn. 15).

vinegar. A sour liquid consisting of acetic acid, produced by the fermentation of WINE or other alcoholic liquors. Faulty methods of manufacture produced in ancient times an inferior wine liable to turn sour rapidly. It was equivalent to the Roman *posca*, a cheap sour wine which, mixed with water, was the common beverage of peasants (cf. Ruth 2:14). The book of Proverbs speaks of its strong acidic taste ("as vinegar to the teeth," Prov. 10:26) and its irritant quality ("like vinegar poured on a wound," 25:20 TNIV). The NAZIRITE's vow of abstinence excluded this form of alcoholic beverage, as well as the intoxicating wine of more common use in higher levels of society, because such a vow could be made in all strata of the community (Num. 6:3). It is uncertain whether the vinegar offered to CHRIST on the CROSS was the soldiers' ration wine, the *posca* brought by the squad on duty, and thus possibly given in kindliness rather than derision (Matt. 27:48; Mk. 15:63; Lk. 23:36; Jn. 19:29).

vineyards, plain of the. See ABEL KERAMIM.

viol. This English term is used by the KJV in four passages (Isa. 5:12; 14:11; Amos 5:23; 6:5) to render a Hebrew term that means "harp" or "lyre." Elsewhere the KJV translates "psaltery" (1 Sam. 10:5 et al.). See MUSIC, MUSICAL INSTRUMENTS (sect. I.C).

viper. See ANIMALS.

virgin. A woman who has not had sexual intercourse. The relevant Hebrew terms are *bĕtûlâ H1435*, which occurs over fifty times (Gen. 24:16; Exod. 22:16-17; et al.), and *ʿalmâ H6625*, which is used only seven times (Gen. 24:43; Exod. 2:8; Ps. 68:25; Prov. 30:19; Cant. 1:3; 6:8; Isa. 7:14). The former term is rendered "virgin" in the standard lexicons, and this translation does seem appropriate in many, or even most, passages. Moreover, the abstract cognate *bĕtûlîm H1436*, a plural form, appears to indicate virginity (Lev. 21:13 [clarified in v. 14]; Jdg. 11:37; in Deut. 22:14-20, it means "evidences of virginity"; but see on Ezek. 23:3 and 8 below).

There are, however, several considerations that should be kept in mind. (a) In a number of passages where *bĕtûlîm* occurs, nothing in the context suggests that virginity is a factor under consideration, and thus the rendering "maiden" or "young woman" is more appropriate (Deut. 32:25 et al.). (b) Sometimes the word *bĕtûlâ* is accompanied by the comment that the woman or women in question had not had sexual relationships (Gen. 24:16; Jdg. 21:12), suggesting that the word by itself did not necessarily indicate virginity. (c) In at least one passage, the word is used of young women who have had sexual intercourse (Esth. 2:19), and Ezekiel uses the term *bĕtûlîm* in his symbolic representation of a woman involved in prostitution (Ezek. 23:3, 8). Thus it is possible that the word had a fairly general meaning, "[marriageable] young woman"; and because in Hebrew society (as in many others) it would be assumed that she was a virgin, the word probably took on the sense of "chaste."

The second Hebrew term, *ʿalmâ*, is clearly the feminine form of *ʿelem H6624*, "young man" (only 1 Sam. 17:56; 20:22), and the abstract plural form *ʿălûmîm H6596* appears to mean "youth" or "youthful vigor" (Job 20:11; 33:25; Ps. 89:45; Isa. 54:4). Thus the lexicons give "young woman" or the like as the meaning of *ʿalmâ*. Similarly, most versions use "maiden" or "young woman" or even "girl" (Exod. 2:8) as the rendering of the word in a majority of its occurrences. The KJV uses "virgin" in four instances (Gen. 24:43; Cant. 1:3; 6:8; Isa. 7:14), the NIV in only two (Cant. 6:8; Isa. 7:14), and the NRSV not at all. The occurrence of *ʿalmâ* in Cant. 6:8 is of lexical significance because in this verse the term is contrasted to "queen" and "concubine"; even here, however, the reference is ambiguous (true virgins? women in the royal harem that have not borne children?). That the term may be applied to virgins is not in doubt (Gen. 24:43 [parallel to *bĕtûlâ*, v. 16]; Exod. 2:8), and no passage requires a reference to someone who is not a virgin (even Prov. 30:19 very likely has in view a woman's initial sexual experience). On the other hand, the evidence does not suggest that the term by itself indicates virginity.

Clearly, the two Hebrew words overlap in meaning, and apart from the fact that the former term is much more frequent, drawing a clear distinction between them is difficult. This factor affects our understanding of *ʿalmâ* in the most controversial passage, Isa. 7:14, which traditionally has been translated, "Behold, a virgin shall conceive, and bear a son" (KJV; similarly NIV); the NRSV and other modern versions, however, use "young woman" in this passage. Some have argued that if Isaiah had intended the meaning "virgin," he would have used *bĕtûlâ* instead, but clearly this argument does not work, for as noted above *bĕtûlâ* too often has a general meaning without reference to sexual experience. On the other hand, it is a fair argument to say that if Isaiah had wanted to stress the woman's virginity, he had other means of doing so (e.g., "a woman who has not known a man," as in Num. 31:35). It may well be that *ʿalmâ*, like *bĕtûlâ*, refers normally to a young woman of sexual maturity who is unmarried and therefore assumed to be a virgin.

In Isa. 7:14, the SEPTUAGINT (followed by Matt. 1:23) translates *ʿalmâ* with Greek *parthenos G4221*, which usually means "virgin." This Greek term too, however, is not free of ambiguity, and in many passages the sense "young [*or* unmarried] woman" is preferable (e.g., . Aristophanes, *Clouds* 530). In later Greek the narrower sense "virgin" is more common, and the LXX normally itself uses *parthenos* to translate *bĕtûlâ*; but occasionally this Greek word is also found as the rendering of *ʿalmâ* and *naʿărāh H5855*, "girl" (cf. Gen. 24:14, 16, 43; Deut. 22:19; et al.). In the NT, *parthenos* is used with reference to MARY, MOTHER OF JESUS (Lk. 1:27), who is explicitly described as not having known a man (v. 34) and as having conceived supernaturally prior to her being joined to Joseph (Matt. 1:18). Thus her virginity does not depend on Matthew's citation from Isaiah, though undoubtedly the evangelist regarded the LXX rendering as singularly appropriate. See VIRGIN BIRTH. Other uses of the word in the NT include the parable of the ten virgins (Matt. 25:1, 7, 11), the reference to PHILIP's "unmarried daughters" (Acts 21:9), PAUL's discussion about whether virgins should marry (1 Cor.

7:25-38), and its occurrence with the masculine definite article referring to chaste men (Rev. 14:4). See also MARRIAGE.

Virgin Birth. The teaching that MARY, MOTHER OF JESUS was a VIRGIN both when she conceived and when she gave birth to Jesus, the child who was IMMANUEL ("God with us"). The source of this doctrine is threefold: (1) The account in Matt. 1:18-25. Here we learn that before Mary and Joseph came together in marriage "she was found to be with child through the Holy Spirit." Further, an angel of the Lord appeared to Joseph to tell him, "Do not be afraid to take Mary home as your wife, because what is conceived in her is from the Holy Spirit." (2) The account in Lk. 1:26-38. Here we learn that the angel told Mary that she had found favor with God and that she would "be with child and give birth to a son." When she asked how this could be since she was a pure virgin, she was told, "The Holy Spirit will come upon you and the power of the Most High will overshadow you. So the holy one to be born will be called the Son of God." (3) The prophecy recorded in Isaiah: "Therefore the Lord himself will give you a sign: The virgin will be with child and will give birth to a son, and will call him Immanuel" (Isa. 7:14; Matt. 1:23).

Although the conception of Jesus was miraculous and unique, his growth within the womb of Mary and his birth were "normal." Matthew and Luke probably got their information from Joseph and Mary, and they recorded it with reverence and reticence. Within their accounts several theological motifs may be recognized. First, they record the facts in such a manner as to convey the idea that conception by a virgin was the appropriate way for the eternal Son to become a man, "bone of our bone, flesh of our flesh." Second, as the HOLY SPIRIT had "hovered" over the old creation (Gen. 1:2), so now the Holy Spirit is present to superintend the origin of a new creation, of which the Incarnate Son will be the center. Third, the virginal conception points to the unique relation of the Incarnate Son to the human race he came to save: There is a basic continuity with us in that he shares our flesh and was born in the "normal" way. There is a basic discontinuity in that he was conceived in regard to his manhood in a unique way—as a new

creation. So he is the same but different, and thus he is one of us, but able to save us, and that is what his name "Jesus" means.

virtue. This English term, meaning "moral excellence," is rarely used in modern Bible versions, but it occurs in the KJV as the rendering of Greek *aretē G746* (Phil. 4:8; 2 Pet. 1:3, 5). Among Greek moralistic writers, especially the STOICS, the term was used very frequently to indicate the highest good, the social uprightness that evokes recognition, merit, and honor. Both PAUL and PETER employ this term in lists of positive moral traits, but they were not merely asking their readers to conduct themselves like well-behaved Greeks. The word rather signifies the moral excellence distinctive of those who have been cleansed from their sins: it builds on faith and generates godliness and love. The KJV uses "virtue" also a few times to translate *dynamis G1539*, "power" (Mk. 5:30; Lk. 6:19; 8:46); and in some OT passages, it uses "virtuous woman" to render a Hebrew phrase that literally means "woman of power" and indicates competence or noble character (Ruth 3:11; Prov. 12:4; 31:10; cf. 31:29, "virtuously").

vision. Although this English word may refer to physical sight, the biblical usage normally focuses on extraphysical dimensions—something seen otherwise than by ordinary sight, something beheld as in a dream or ecstasy, or revealed as to a PROPHET; a visual image without corporeal presence, an object of imaginative contemplation; unusual discernment or foresight. Several Hebrew words can be translated "vision," the most frequent being *ḥāzôn H2606*; the NT writers use *optasia G3965* and other Greek terms. References to visions are especially frequent in the book of Daniel, a factor that, considering the nature of this book, may furnish insight into the peculiar and suggestive connotations of the word. (See DANIEL, BOOK OF.) The references there and elsewhere in the OT seem consistent with the manifest nature of God. Throughout the Scriptures, God is declared as revealing himself and making his ways known through chosen individuals. God commonly communicated his messages to the PATRIARCHS through a vision (e.g., Gen. 15:1). Speaking to AARON and MIRIAM, God said, "When a prophet of the LORD is among you, / I reveal myself to him in visions, / I speak to him in dreams" (Num. 12:6). Although the NT records a few instances of visions during the apostolic period (Acts 9:10, 12; 10:3; et al.), the coming of CHRIST supersedes other means of REVELATION (Heb. 1:1-2a). See also DREAM; TRANCE.

visitation. This English term, in the sense of a special manifestation of divine favor or displeasure, is rarely found in modern versions but is used by the KJV in about a dozen passages (most of them in Jeremiah, e.g., Jer. 8:12; 10:15); in the KJV NT it occurs twice (Lk. 19:44; 1 Pet. 2:12). Similarly, the verbal form is often used of God with reference to his activity, whether gracious or punitive. For example, when recounting that God fulfilled his promise to SARAH that she would bear a child, the biblical text says, "And the LORD visited Sarah as he had said" (Gen. 21:1 KJV; NIV, "was gracious to Sarah"; cf. also 50:24-25; Exod. 3:16; Ruth 1:6; 1 Sam. 2:21; Lk. 1:68 et al.). Conversely, after the Israelites worshiped the golden calf, God said, "in the day when I visit I will visit their sin upon them" (Exod. 32:34 KJV; NIV, "when the time comes for me to punish, I will punish them for their sin"; cf. also Lev. 18:25; Ps. 59:5; Isa. 26:14; et al.).

vocation. See CALL; OCCUPATIONS AND PROFESSIONS.

Vophsi. vof´si (Heb. *wopsî H2265*, derivation uncertain). Father of Nahbi; the latter, representing the tribe of NAPHTALI, was one of the twelve spies sent out to reconnoiter the Promised Land (Num. 13:14).

votive offering. See SACRIFICE AND OFFERINGS.

vow. A voluntary promise to God to perform some service or do something pleasing to him, in return for some hoped-for benefits (Gen. 28:20-22; Lev. 27:2, 8; Num. 30; Jdg. 11:30); or to abstain from certain things (Num. 30:3). In the OT vows were never regarded as a religious duty (Deut. 23:22); but once they were made, they were considered sacred and binding (Deut. 23:21-23; Jdg. 11:35; Ps. 66:13; Eccl. 5:4). Fathers could veto vows made by their daughters, and husbands could veto their wives' vows; but if a husband did not veto a wife's vow and then caused her to break it, the blame was his, not hers (Num. 30). A vow had to be uttered to be binding (Deut. 23:23). Almost anything—people, possessions, oneself—except what was already the Lord's or was an abomination to the Lord (23:18), could be vowed; and all these things could be redeemed with money, their value to be determined by a priest. Houses, lands, and unclean animals that were redeemed had to have a fifth of their value added to make up the redemption money. Jesus referred to vows only once, and that was to condemn the abuse of them (Matt. 15:4-6; Mk. 7:10-13). PAUL's vow in Acts 18:18 was probably a temporary NAZIRITE vow.

Vulgate. vuhl´gayt. Name applied to the standard Latin translation of the Bible (the Lat. adjective *vulgatus* means "commonly known, in wide circulation"). See TEXT AND VERSIONS (OT); TEXT AND VERSIONS (NT).

A page from Nicolas Jenson's edition of the Latin Vulgate (1479).

© Dr. James C. Martin. Sola Scriptura. The Van Kampen Collection on display at the Holy Land Experience in Orlando, Florida. Photographed by permission.

vulture. See BIRDS.

wadi. wah´dee. Sometimes spelled *wady*. The bed of a stream that is usually dry except during the rainy season; the term is also applied to the stream itself. The word is Arabic and is used only of river beds in SW Asia and N Africa; it corresponds to Hebrew *naḥal H5707*, which can be rendered variously ("valley, ravine, brook, river, torrent"). See BROOK; VALLEY.

© Dr. James C. Martin

Wadi Feifa S of the Dead Sea. (View to the NW.)

wafer. This English term is used to render two different Hebrew words. The noun *ṣappîḥit H7613* occurs only once, when the MANNA is said to have "tasted like wafers made with honey" (Exod. 16:31). The second term is *rāqîq H8386*, which refers to a flat cake or thin crisp bread used as part of some offerings (Exod. 29:2 et al.). It usually occurs in combination with *maṣṣāh H5174* (pl. *maṣṣôt*), a flat BREAD made with unleavened dough. See LEAVEN; SACRIFICE AND OFFERINGS.

wages. Compensation to a person hired for performing some work or service. In the nomadic, pastoral society of the patriarchal period there was no wage-earning class. When men worked for others, it was generally for their own maintenance; and often they received some payment in kind for their services. JACOB's service to LABAN was on this basis (Gen. 29:15; 30:32-33; 31:8, 41). With the increasing complexity of a more settled community, once the Israelites were in CANAAN, people were needed to engage in trades and crafts of all kinds. For these services, payment was made, in whole or in part, by weighing out quantities of bronze or silver. Coinage in the standard sense was a later invention, being first used in ASIA MINOR by the Lydians just before 700 B.C. (see MONEY). From here its use spread throughout the Greek world, but it was probably not in common use in the ANE until the Hellenistic period (beginning approx. 300 B.C.).

Bargaining was a common practice. Where there were no set scales for payment, it was usual to negotiate terms in this way in each individual case. The story of Jacob and Laban illustrates such a practice, from the very beginning of the discussion ("Name your wages," Gen. 30:28) down to the last accusation ("you changed my wages ten times," 31:41). The story details the kind of cheating and trickery that both parties practiced. The same tendency to bargain appears in the parable of the vineyard (Matt. 20:1-16), but here the employer was a just and generous man.

The biblical writers make figurative use of the Hebrew and Greek terms with reference to God's dealings with human beings. Thus God's benefits to his people are referred to as recompense (Isa. 40:10; 62:11); and the RETRIBUTION of God is spoken of as REWARD (Ps. 109:20) or gain (2 Pet. 2:15). DEATH is called the wages due for serving sin (Rom. 6:23). In addition, PAUL speaks of his gifts from churches at PHILIPPI as "wages" (2 Cor. 11:8 KJV [NIV, "support"]; cf. Phil. 4:15-18). He earned his living with his hands, and he teaches the right of the laborer to his wages (1 Tim. 5:18).

wagon. See CART.

Waheb. way'heb (Heb. *wāhēb H2259*, possibly "giver"). A place "in Suphah," probably near the ARNON River in MOAB, mentioned in a citation from the Book of the Wars of the Lord (Num. 21:14; TNIV, "Zahab," apparently following the LXX). Some think it refers to the well from which the Arnon flows. The Hebrew text is very difficult, however. See also SUPHAH; WARS OF THE LORD, BOOK OF.

wail. See MOURNING.

walk. The biblical terms for "walk" (mainly Heb. *hālak H2143* and Gk. *peripateō G4344*) are often used in the Bible figuratively to indicate conduct or manner of life (e.g., Gen. 5:22; 1 Ki. 15:3; Ps. 1:1; Eph. 2:2, 10), including the observance of laws or customs (Lev. 26:3; Acts 21:21 [cf. HALAKAH]). Modern versions frequently avoid a literal translation and instead use "live" or other equivalents. See WAY.

wall. The most common Hebrew word for "wall" is *hômâ H2570*, applied mainly to the structures surrounding a CITY (e.g., Josh. 2:15), but sometimes also to those around a building or some other area (e.g., Lam. 2:7). The primary Greek term used in the NT is *teichos G5446*, applied also to city walls (Acts 9:25; 2 Cor. 11:33; Heb. 11:30; Rev. 21:12-19; see also WALL OF PARTITION). House walls were usually made of mud brick set on rubble-stone-base courses, with walls of rubble stone occasionally set

in mud mortar. City walls in early times were built vertically without any outer glacis for protection; down to the beginning of Iron Age II they were casemate type walls and later they were solid and thick to resist the Assyrian battering rams. Thicknesses varied between three and five meters with projecting bastions. The latter were crowned with overhangs to ward off attackers, and crenelations to protect archers.

wall of partition. The KJV uses the phrase "the middle wall of partition" to translate a Greek expression that occurs only once (Eph. 2:14). A literal translation would be, "the partitioning wall, [that is,] the fence," and most modern versions render it simply as "the dividing wall." The following clause has another noun in apposition, "hostility"; thus the NRSV offers the translation, "the dividing wall, that is, the hostility between us," while the NIV has, more simply, "the dividing wall of hostility." In the context, PAUL is addressing Christians of both Jewish and GENTILE backgrounds. Between these Christians there had been a dividing wall, not literally but socially, thus segregating them. The division was seen in the CHURCH in many places (cf. Acts 15; Gal. 2:11-14). In CHRIST, however, this dividing wall was broken down: there was no longer to be any distinction between Jew and Gentile in Christ's kingdom.

wanderings, wilderness. See ISRAEL.

want. See COVETOUSNESS; LUST.

war. Every phase of ISRAEL's life, including their warfare, was bound up with their God. War therefore had religious significance. It was customary for priests to accompany Israel's armies into battle (Deut. 20:1-4). Campaigns were begun and engagements entered into with sacrificial rites (1 Sam. 7:8-10; 13:9) and after consulting the Lord (Jdg. 20:18, 23, 27-28; 1 Sam. 14:37; 23:2; 28:6; 30:8). Prophets were sometimes asked for guidance before a campaign (1 Ki. 22:5; 2 Ki. 3:11).

The blowing of a trumpet throughout the land announced the call to arms (Jdg. 3:27; 1 Sam. 13:3; 2 Sam. 15:10), and priests also used trumpets to sound an alarm (2 Chr. 13:12-16). Weapons

Replica of a catapult used by the Roman army during the siege of Gamla c. A.D. 67.

© Dr. James C. Martin

W

included slings, spears, javelins, bows and arrows, swords, and battering rams. See ARMS AND ARMOR. Strategical movements included the ambush (Josh. 8:3-22), the feint (Jdg. 20:31-34), the flank movement (2 Sam. 5:22-25), the surprise attack (Josh. 11:1-2), the raid (1 Chr. 14:9), the foray (2 Sam. 3:22), and foraging to secure supplies (23:11). Sometimes when opposing armies were drawn up in battle array, champions from each side fought one another (1 Sam. 17). Armies engaged in hand-to-hand combat. Victorious armies pillaged the camp of the enemy, robbed the dead (Jdg. 8:24-26; 1 Sam. 31:9; 2 Chr. 20:25), and often killed or mutilated prisoners (Josh. 8:23, 29; 10:22-27; Jdg. 1:6), though prisoners were usually sold into slavery. Booty was divided equally between those who had taken part in the battle and those who had been left behind in camp (Num. 31:27; Josh. 22:8; 1 Sam. 30:24-25), but some of the spoils were reserved for the LEVITES and for the Lord (Num. 31:28, 30).

When a city was besieged, the besiegers built up huge mounds of earth against the walls, and from these mounds battering rams were used against the walls (2 Sam. 20:15; Ezek. 4:2). The besieged tried to drive off the enemy by throwing darts and stones and shooting arrows at them from the walls. Captured cities were often completely destroyed, and victory was celebrated with song and dance (Exod. 15:1-21; Jdg. 5:1; 1 Sam. 18:6).

Some point out that Jesus accepted war as an inevitable part of the present sinful world order

(Matt. 24:6) but warned that those who take the sword must perish by it (26:52). In the NT Letters the Christian is said to be a soldier (2 Tim. 2:3; 1 Pet. 2:11). The Apocalypse uses the figure of battle and war to describe the final triumph of Christ over SATAN (Rev. 16:14-16; 17:14; 19:14).

wardrobe, keeper of the. See KEEPER.

War of the Sons of Light against the Sons of Darkness. See DEAD SEA SCROLLS.

warrior, divine. The first explicit proclamation of God as a warrior is found in the Song of the Sea, MOSES' hymn celebrating God's victory over the Egyptians at the RED SEA: "The LORD is a warrior; / the LORD is his name. / Pharaoh's chariots and his army / he has hurled into the sea" (Exod. 15:3-4a). This single action of the divine warrior demonstrates the two-sided nature of God's warring activity: SALVATION and JUDGMENT. The theme of the divine warrior is integrally connected to the institution of holy WAR in the Hebrew Scriptures. Indeed, warfare is made holy by the fact that God was with the army in all phases of its activities. In other words, at the heart of holy war is the divine warrior. In early Israelite history, his presence was represented by the ARK OF THE COVENANT, which was a mobile symbol of God's presence.

The appearance of the divine warrior causes convulsions in the creation. Mountains shake; rivers dry up; nature grows impotent (Jdg. 5:4-5; Isa. 24:1-7; Nah. 1:2-6). Furthermore, music ceases from the land (Isa. 24:8-9). When victory comes, however, fertility bursts at the seams and music is jubilant. As a matter of fact, some of the most powerful early songs (Exod. 15; Jdg. 5) and many psalms (e.g., Ps. 24; 98) celebrate God's warring success. Interestingly enough, though God could win any battle on his own, he always insists on Israel's participation—but always as a junior partner. The battle of GIDEON against the Midianites is a prime example (see esp. Jdg. 7); if Israel had gone in with a superior force, then their victory would have led to pride in their own power (cf. also DAVID's words in 1 Sam. 17:45-47).

Finally, the NT picks up the theme of the divine warrior and applies it to CHRIST. However, his warfare has a different object. His battle is against the spiritual powers and principalities, and he wins this battle not with the sword (Matt. 26:47-56), but by his death and resurrection (Col. 2:13-15). PAUL declares that Christ's followers participate in this spiritual warfare (Eph. 6:10-20). The book of Revelation culminates this theme when it pictures Christ's return for the great final battle, when all of God's enemies—physical and spiritual—will be cast into the LAKE OF FIRE (cf. Rev. 19:11-21).

Wars of the Lord, Book of the. One of several books no longer extant which are mentioned in the OT and which played an important, if somewhat obscure, part in Israel's literary history (see also JASHAR, BOOK OF). It is cited by name and quoted in Num. 21:14-15 to substantiate the narrator's statement concerning the boundary cut by the deep ravines of the ARNON River between MOAB and AMMON. The quotation as it stands is obscure (the syntax is apparently incomplete and nothing is known of the names WAHEB and SUPHAH) and sheds little light on the character of the book itself. It is a plausible conjecture, however, that vv. 17-18 and 27-30 are drawn from the same source, not only because of their proximity to the first quotation, but also because of the occurrence (in the case of vv. 27-30) of a number of identical place names as well as the suitability of the taunt itself for the content of the book as suggested by its title. Evidently the book consisted of a number of victory songs written to be sung in celebration of the triumphs of Yahweh in the conquest of CANAAN by Israel. That Yahweh was a "a man of war" (Exod. 15:3 KJV; see WARRIOR, DIVINE) who brought Israel victory in battle was a fact the nation loved to commemorate in song.

Washerman's Field. See FULLER'S FIELD.

washing. Frequent bathing was necessary in the warm climate of the East. In EGYPT, SYRIA, and PALESTINE, people washed the dust from their feet when they entered a house (Gen. 18:4; Jn. 13:10). Ceremonial defilement (see UNCLEAN) was removed by bathing the body and washing the clothing (Lev. 14:8; Num. 19:7-8). The priests washed their hands and feet before entering the sanctuary or offering a sacrifice (Exod. 30:19-21). In the time of Christ the Jews did much ceremonial washing of hands before eating (Mk. 7:3-4) and used public baths as the Greeks and Romans did. Spiritual washing is alluded to in the doctrine of REGENERATION (Jn. 3:5; Tit. 3:5) and the rite of BAPTISM (Acts 22:16).

watch. A man or group of men set to guard a city. NEHEMIAH, when building the walls of Jerusalem, set a watch day and night to warn of enemy approaches (Neh. 4:9), and after the walls were completed, he set watches near the gates (7:3). Even today in the East, when the crops are ripening in the fields and vineyards, one may see watchmen on guard day and night. The temporary shelters set up by the watchmen in the fields are alluded to in Isa. 1:8, for they are deserted as soon as the crops have been gathered. Metaphorically, David prays, "Set a guard over my mouth, O LORD; keep watch [restraint] over the door of my lips" (Ps. 141:3). The Latin word *custodia*, transliterated in Greek, is used three times (Matt. 27:65-66; 28:11) for the Roman watch that was set to guard our Lord's tomb. See also WATCHES OF THE NIGHT.

watches of the night. The divisions into which the hours of the night were divided. The ancient Israelites evidently had a threefold division (cf. "the middle watch" in Jdg. 7:19). The Romans, however, divided the time between sunset and sunrise into four equal watches (Mk. 6:48). When Jesus speaks of "the second or third watch" (Lk. 12.38), it is unclear whether he is referring to the Jewish or Roman system. See also TIME.

watchman. See OCCUPATIONS AND PROFESSIONS.

water. Because of its scarcity in PALESTINE, water is much appreciated there. For its people, absence of water was very serious (Jer. 14:3; Joel 1:20; see FAMINE), and RAIN was a sign of God's favor. The RIVERS of Palestine are mostly small and have little if any water in summer (see WADI). Consequently in Bible times the country depended on rain as its source of water. This supplied springs and fountains. Cisterns were a necessity for the storing of water, but if water was stored too long it became brackish and filthy and a menace to health. In the summer there was no rain, so vegetation was dependent on the heavy dews. Irrigation was carried on where there was sufficient water. When water was scarce, as during a time of siege, it had to be rationed. Drinking water, carried in goatskins, was often sold in the streets. Wells and pools, although comparatively scarce, are often mentioned in the Bible (Gen. 21:19; 24:11; Jn. 4:6; 9:7). Water was used not only for refreshment, but for ceremonial washings before meals and in the Jewish temple ceremony (Lev. 11:32; 16:4; Num. 19:7). The Bible uses it as a symbol of the cleansing of the soul from sin (Ezek. 16:4, 9; 36:25; Jn. 3:5; Eph. 5:26; Heb. 10:22; 1 Jn. 5:6, 8). See also MINERALS (sect. III.G).

watercourse. This English term is used variously in Bible versions to render several Hebrew words or expressions. For example, it occurs a number of times in the NRSV as the translation of a Hebrew word that seems to refer to a stream bed (Ps. 126:4 et al.). The NIV uses it only once to translate a phrase meaning literally, "channels of water" (Prov. 21:1).

Water Gate. A city gate in JERUSALEM, restored by NEHEMIAH, on the E side of Mount ZION. It lay opposite the GIHON spring (Neh. 3:26), or perhaps a little farther N toward the TEMPLE (cf. 12:37). An open square beside the Water Gate furnished a place of assembly for EZRA's reading of the law and for erecting booths for the Feast of Tabernacles in 444 B.C. (8:1, 3, 16).

water hen. See BIRDS.

water for impurity. See WATER OF CLEANSING.

watermelon. See PLANTS (under *melon*).

water of bitterness. See BITTER WATER.

water of cleansing. This phrase is used by the NIV to render Hebrew *mê niddâ* (*H4784 + H5614*), which occurs in only a few contexts (Num. 19:9, 13, 20-21; 31:23). English versions translate this phrase variously: "water of separation" (KJV), "water for impurity" (RSV), "water for cleansing" (NRSV), "water of lustration" (NJPS). Although the precise meaning of the phrase is uncertain, the reference is clearly to a ritually purifying agent for a person or thing that had been defiled, whether by contact with the dead or for other reasons. The ashes of a burned red cow were added to "running water," which was then applied to the defiled person. The burning took place "outside the camp," and the whole animal—even the blood, with the exception of some that was used in sprinkling toward the front of the tent—was reduced to ashes, later to be mixed with the spring water for the specific ceremonies of purification. This "water of impurity" was applied to the defiled person or object by being spilled over it, or sprinkled with branches of hyssop.

waterpot. Term used by the KJV with reference to an earthen jar for carrying or holding water, either for drinking (Jn. 4:28) or for purifying purposes (2:6-7). Modern versions usually have "water jar."

water shaft. This term, referring to an underground conduit for bringing water from a spring into a city, is used by the NIV and other versions to render Hebrew *ṣinnôr H7562* in 2 Sam. 5:8 (this Heb. word occurs in only one other passage with the probable meaning of "waterfall," Ps. 42:7). There is archaeological evidence for water shafts in various cities in PALESTINE from the Canaanite period onward (e.g., JERUSALEM, MEGIDDO, GIBEON, ETHAM). In Jerusalem there is a tunnel to the GIHON spring that brought water to the city, and some scholars have thought that 2 Sam. 5:8

Water shaft connecting to Jerusalem's Gihon Spring.

© Dr. James C. Martin

refers to this tunnel (recent archaeological work has cast doubts on this view).

waterspout. This English term is used by the KJV in one passage (Ps. 42:7), referring to a large rush of water sent by God, perhaps great floods of rain. The NIV renders it "waterfall."

wave offering. See SACRIFICE AND OFFERINGS.

waw. wou (possibly from *wāw H2260*, "hook"). Also *vau, vav*. The sixth letter of the Hebrew alphabet (ו), with a numerical value of six. It represents a bilabial semiconsonant similar to the sound of English *w*, but in later times it acquired a sound more like that of English *v*, which is the current Israeli pronunciation. Before the invention of vowel signs, the *waw* could be used also to represent the sounds *ô* and *û*, and this practice was continued even after the vocalization system was introduced.

wax. This term appears in the Bible only in poetry, where it is used as a simile of melting (Ps. 22:14; 68:2; 97:5; Mic. 1:4). In ancient times wax was used for sealing documents and for making writing tablets, but these uses of wax are not mentioned in the Bible. The English verb *to wax* occurs often in the KJV, but only in the intransitive sense "to grow, increase, become" (e.g., "I am waxed old," Gen. 18:12); the use of this verb is rare in modern versions.

way. This English term is used as the rendering of various biblical words (e.g., Heb. *derek H2006* and Gk. *hodos G3847*). In addition to its use in a literal sense, the word occurs extensively in a figurative sense, denoting behavioral patterns in animal life, movements in nature, varieties of human and divine conduct, action, and intention, as well as attitudes, habits, customs, spirit, and plans in human and divine life. Specific OT examples are the following: (a) of processes in nature (Job 28:26; 38:19, 24; Prov. 6:6; 30:19); (b) of moral conduct, whether good (1 Sam. 12:23; Ps. 119:1) or evil (Jdg. 2:19); (c) of various facets of human experience (Josh. 23:14; Job 3:23; Ps. 142:3; Prov. 3:6); (d) of God's will, command, purposes, providence (Deut. 5:33; Job 36:23; Isa. 2:3; Ezek. 18:25).

In the NT also there are many uses referring to moral conduct (Matt. 21:32; Rom. 3:16-17) and to God's will and purposes (Mk. 12:14; Heb. 3:10). In addition, the book of Acts records that the term "the Way" was used specifically of the Christian faith and manner of life followed by the Lord's disciples and held in contempt by their enemies (Acts 9:2; 19:9, 23; 22:4, 14; 24:22). Most important, the term is used of CHRIST as the final and perfect revealer: in his person and by his sacrificial death, he is the living and personal way to God, his holiness, and salvation. He teaches the way in truth (Matt. 22:16) and is himself the only "way" to God (Jn. 14:4-6) and the one who opens up the way into the holiest by his sacrifice (Heb. 9:8; 10:19-20).

wayfaring man. KJV phrase that translates several Hebrew expressions referring to a traveler (Jdg. 19:17 et al.).

wealth. Abundance of valuable possessions. In the nomadic civilization of the early Hebrews, wealth consisted largely of flocks and herds, silver and gold, brass, iron, and clothing (Josh. 22:8). In the days of JOB, his sons had houses, but their wealth consisted largely of camels, donkeys, flocks, and herds, and "a large number of servants" (Job 1:3). Wealth can come from sinful endeavors (Acts 19:25). From the beginning of ISRAEL, God taught his people that he was the giver of their wealth (Deut. 8:18). He taught them to be liberal: "One man gives freely, yet gains even more; / another withholds unduly, but comes to poverty" (Prov. 11:24). NT teaching goes even further: "Nobody should seek his own good, but the good of others" (1 Cor. 10:24). Some OT passages give the impression that wealth always went with godliness (Ps. 112:3) and that poverty was for the wicked (Prov. 13:18), but other passages prevent such an interpretation (Ps. 73:3-5; Lk. 6:20; 1 Cor. 1:26-28). See also POOR.

wean. To accustom a child to depend on other food than the mother's milk. In ancient times a child was not fully weaned for two or three years, and in some cases probably longer. According to 1 Sam. 1:21-28, HANNAH stopped going up to SHILOH to offer the annual sacrifice until she had

W

weaned SAMUEL, at which time she left the child there in the care of ELI; but it is very unlikely that Samuel would have been left at the sanctuary if he was less than four years old (cf. also 2 Macc. 7:27, which gives the explicit duration of three years). The completion of weaning was sometimes celebrated by a feast (Gen. 21:8). The word is also used in a metaphorical sense (Ps. 131:2; Isa. 28:9).

weapon. See ARMS AND ARMOR.

weasel. See ANIMALS.

weather. See PALESTINE (sect. III).

weaving. The uniting of threads by crossing each other to produce cloth. The art of weaving is well-nigh universal, even among primitive peoples, and its beginnings are lost in the mists of antiquity. JOB complained, "My days are swifter than a weaver's shuttle" (Job 7:6), showing that he not only knew of weaving, but that the art had progressed to the point where the weaver's hands were swift in passing the shuttle back and forth. JABAL, an antediluvian, is called "the father of those who live in tents and raise livestock" (Gen. 4:20), implying that the weaving of tents and the taming of cattle had their beginnings nearly at the same time. Weaving, as a fine art, was in the case of BEZELEL and OHOLIAB a gift from God (Exod. 35:30-35); and their woven work for the TABERNACLE, the curtains and veils, may have surpassed in beauty anything previously known in cloth.

© Dr. James C. Martin

Tent weaving in Turkey.

DAMASCUS, one of the oldest cities of the world, was long known for its woven work; and *damask*, with its beautifully woven figures, takes its name from that city. The lovely acrostic poem on the virtuous woman (Prov. 31:10-31) pictures her as acquainted with the work of spinning and weaving, as well as the work of dressmaking; but the heavier work of weaving tentcloth was often done by men. Acts 18:2-3 mentions PAUL, with AQUILA and his wife PRISCILLA, as tentmakers. The oriental tents were generally woven of goats' hair made so well they were nearly waterproof, and so strong they lasted for a lifetime. In the "doom of Egypt" (Isa. 19) the weavers of both linen and cotton cloth are spoken of as losing hope (19:9), indicating the importance of weaving to the economy of EGYPT in her prosperity. In HEZEKIAH's description of his despair in the days of his sickness (Isa. 38:10-18), he spoke of God as cutting off his life as a weaver cuts the thread when his work is complete (38:12). ISAIAH speaks of the wicked as weaving the spider's web (59:5), thus indicating the futility of their efforts; and 2 Ki. 23:7 speaks with horror of "where women did weaving for Asherah." A giant had a spear like a weaver's rod (1 Chr. 11:23). See also OCCUPATIONS AND PROFESSIONS.

wedding. The ceremony by which a man and a woman are joined together as husband and wife and legally entitled to form a separate family unit. The betrothal was a significant, binding, legal commitment for the forthcoming MARRIAGE (Deut. 20:7), a commitment that could be broken only by death or divorce. At the time of the betrothal, gifts of jewelry (which were often made of gold set with semiprecious stones) would be presented to the girl and sometimes to her mother, and, depending on the society, the bride price, dowry, or contract would also be exchanged. After the invention of coinage it became increasingly common for gold coins to form part of the betrothal gifts. During the period of the betrothal, which normally lasted for one year, the girl was already deemed to belong to her future husband, and the punishment for any man who violated her sexually was death by stoning.

The wedding of patriarchal times was very similar to that found among nomadic bedouin tribes today. Often a separate small tent or hut was erected to be used by the bride and groom for the wedding night (2 Sam. 16:22; Ps. 19:4-5; Cant. 1:16-17). The tent was often round in shape and was pitched in the early evening by the women. To the accompaniment of considerable merriment they also made the bed ready for the bridal pair. For the very poor, who could not afford this privacy, a small section of the groom's parents' tent was partitioned off for the use of the young couple. At sunset, certain female relatives of the groom would go to the tent of the bride's parents and escort the young bride to the nuptial chamber. There the bridegroom would meet her subsequently.

Traditionally, the bride remained veiled and the tent was kept in darkness until after the marriage was consummated. This custom helps to explain the comparative ease with which LABAN was able to substitute LEAH for her younger and more attractive sister RACHEL in the bridal chamber. The public transfer of the bride to the tent of the groom was always a significant part of the wedding ceremony. According to Gen. 24:67, REBEKAH accompanied ISAAC to his tent and she became his wife. This, in its simplest form, was the wedding, without additional ritual.

With the passage of time, changes in lifestyles and habitation, and the increase in wealth and the desire for ostentation, the wedding ceremony became far more elaborate. The entire village or town would participate in this most memorable event. Bride and groom would be dressed in clothing of fine linen, sometimes decorated by means of gold thread that had been woven into the garment. The bride was also prepared for the nuptials by being bathed and groomed with cosmetic preparations and anointed with sweet-smelling perfumes. By tradition she also wore an elaborate headdress heavily encrusted with jewels and often containing gold in the form of small ornaments. After the invention of coinage the headdress was adorned with gold coins, these sometimes forming part of the bride's dowry. In later biblical times there appear to have been separate processions for bride and groom, where each was accompanied by musicians with drums and tambourines, dancers, torchbearers, well-wishers, and friends, all of whom joined with shouts and songs in celebrating the wedding (Jer. 7:34; 16:9; 25:10).

Following the example of King SOLOMON (Cant. 3:11), the bridegroom was crowned king of the festival, and apparently from about the same period (900 B.C.) the bride also submitted to a ceremonial crowning, which in effect made her queen for the period of the celebrations (Ezek. 16:8-13). There seem to have been some occasions when, on arrival at the house of the groom, the men participated in the feast (Gen. 29:22), while the women, including the bride, had a separate feast at the home of the bride's parents. Traditionally, the feasting lasted for seven days (Jdg. 14:12, 17), though this period was sometimes doubled in length and was marked by music and entertainment of all kinds, including special poems and songs proclaiming the praises and extolling the charms of the bride and bridegroom. If some bedouin practices are any guide to the nature of ancient Hebrew marriage proceedings, the songs and poems that were features of the celebrations would be of a decidedly erotic character. The bride would observe all these activities, and might sometimes participate in the dancing with her female attendants. Then, at an approved point in the ceremonies, she was escorted to the specially prepared bridal chamber, to the cheers, laughter, and enthusiasm of the assembled guests.

In the postexilic period, weddings increasingly took place in the middle of the week, so that if, on the wedding night, the bride was found not to be a VIRGIN, her husband could denounce her and bring evidence, or, rather, lack of it, before the magistrates the following day and still have a decision regarding nullity rendered before the Sabbath. The garment stained with hymeneal blood was adopted as the traditional evidence of the bride's virginity and was usually retained as proof by the women of her family.

Although certain aspects of the wedding varied according to the times or local custom, the central theme was the public escorting of the bride to the house of the groom, followed by the celebrating and feasting prior to the wedding night activities in the bridal chamber. As is the practice today in Jewish circles, the wedding ceremony itself was simple and brief, but the accompanying festivities took on an elaborate ritual that varied somewhat according to the social and economic status of the participants.

W

wedge. The phrase "wedge of gold" (lit., "tongue of gold") occurs in connection with the story of ACHAN (Josh. 7:21, 24; TNIV and NRSV, "bar of gold"). In Isa. 13:12, the KJV has "golden wedge" as the rendering of a Hebrew word that means simply "gold."

weeds. See PLANTS.

week. See CALENDAR.

Weeks, Feast of. See FEASTS.

weeks, seventy. See SEVENTY WEEKS.

weights and measures. The modern reader of the Scriptures lives in a world dominated by the scientific method and the reign of "fact"—measurable fact. Meat is weighed in pounds and ounces on scales checked periodically by a bureau of weights and measures. Precise measurements in miles and fractions of miles state the distance between places. Liquids are measured exactly, from the contents of an oil tanker to that of a hypodermic needle. Such precision cannot be expected in the Bible. The ancient Hebrew lived in a different kind of a world. The lack (for most of biblical times) of a strong, paternalistic central government, the simple life of self-sufficient country folk, and the frequent influence of foreign nations whose standards differed from those of the Hebrews help to account for the lack of consistent and specific measurements. One must be content with round numbers in the study of the weights and measures of the Bible.

Our information is gained from two sources—written and archaeological. Written sources include the Bible and other ancient books such as the works of JOSEPHUS, the TALMUD, and references in classical literature. Archaeological information is uncovered by the excavator in the lands of the Bible—labeled weight-stones, jars, and other objects that will be mentioned in this article, which attempts a synthesis of the information from all the sources.

I. Measures of length. Hebrew measures of length arose (as did the English *foot*) from the simple estimating of distance in terms of the body. Farmers today measure the height of horses by *hands*. The ancient Hebrews used the terms *pace* (about a yard), *cubit* (the length of the forearm), *span* (length of a hand; about half a cubit), *palm* (hand-breadth; about one-third of a span), and a *finger* (about one-quarter of a palm). In EGYPT a similar system was used. The *reed*, mainly an instrument for measuring rather than a unit of measurement, was six cubits long (Ezek. 40:5)

The ordinary cubit was equivalent to approximately 18 in. (46 cm.). EZEKIEL mentions a "long cubit," which he equates with a cubit and a hand-breadth (Ezek. 40:5; 43:13), thus roughly equivalent to 21 in. (53 cm.); this longer cubit was used in Ezekiel's measurements and possibly in Solomon's temple (2 Chr. 3:3 may be a reference to it). The length of HEZEKIAH's water tunnel underneath JERUSALEM (see SILOAM) is stated by the inscription in the tunnel to be 1,200 cubits. The tunnel is 1,749 ft. (533 m.) long according to the most reliable measurement, thus the cubit length arrived at is 17.49 in. (45 cm.). This does not mean, however, that the cubit in Hezekiah's time was exactly 17.49 inches long: the figure of 1,200 cubits is a round number, also it is not certain at what point the ancient measuring of the tunnel began. The Siloam inscription, along with other evidence, indicates only that our approximate length for the cubit is not too far off, which is as positive a conclusion as can be hoped for under the circumstances. (The Heb. word *gōmed H1688*, which occurs only once with reference to a sword or dagger [Jdg. 3:16], is translated "cubit" by the KJV and other versions; some scholars consider it to be a "short cubit.")

In OT times distance was usually measured by the length of time necessary to traverse it. Thus we read of the "three-day journey" (Gen. 30:36) and "for seven days" (31:23). About the SABBATH DAY'S WALK there is some uncertainty (see separate article). In addition, the NT mentions two Roman units: the *stadium* ("furlong" KJV, Lk. 24:13; Jn. 6:19), about 606 ft. (185 m.); and the *mile* (Matt. 5:41), about 4,860 ft. (1,480 m.).

II. Measures of area. Land measurements were indicated in terms of the area that a team of oxen could plow in one day (1 Sam. 14:14). This is the meaning of "acre" in Isa. 5:10, where the Hebrew is *ṣemed H7538*, "pair [of oxen]." In MESOPOTAMIA the area a team of oxen could plow in a day was defined as 6,480 sq. cubits or about 4/10 acre. Elsewhere land area was stated as the part of a field that could be seeded with barley in one day (Lev. 27:16).

III. Measures of capacity. Our uncertainty about the units of capacity is understandable when one considers the origin of these terms. They seem to have arisen from common household pots (all handmade locally), or from the farmer's estimate of the carrying ability of a man or beast. The *hin* was a pot and the *ephah* a basket (both words are of Egyptian origin). The *omer* was a sheaf and the *homer* a donkey load.

The *bath* was the standard liquid measure in OT times. Its value is a matter of dispute. At present scholars regard it as equal to 5-6 gallons (19-23 l.), rather than 10 gallons (38 l.) as formerly. The finding of fragments of large jars, inscribed "bath of the king" (perhaps an attempt to standardize the bath for use in tax payments) or simply "bath" have helped to bring about this reduction in size. Unfortunately, these jars cannot be completely restored, hence there is still some uncertainty. Subdivisions of the bath are the hin (1/6 bath) and log (1/12 hin).

The *homer* (donkey load) was the standard dry measure of the OT; it is often thought to equal about 6.25 bushels (208 l.), but some prefer a lower estimate. The homer is to be equated with the *cor*. The *ephah* (about 3/5 bu. or 20 l.) is the dry equivalent of the liquid measure *bath* (Ezek. 45:10). The *lethekh* is mentioned only in Hos. 3:2 and is probably given its correct value in the KJV, which translates it "half homer." Four smaller dry measures are: the *seah*, about 0.2 bu. (7 l.); the *omer*, 4 dry pints (2 l.); the *issaron* (KJV, "tenth deal"; NIV, "a tenth of an ephah"), evidently equivalent to the *omer;* and the *cab*, a little more than 2 dry pints (1 l.). However, modern authorities differ greatly as to the value of the dry measures, some inclining toward a substantially higher value for each.

Of the units used in the OT, the only ones found in the NT are the bath (Lk. 16:6), the seah (Matt. 13:33), and the cor (Lk. 16:7). Other units found in the NT include the *choinix*, a Greek dry measure equal to about two dry pints (Rev. 6:6); the *xestes*, probably equal to just over a pint, but in the NT used in the general sense of "pitcher" (Mk.

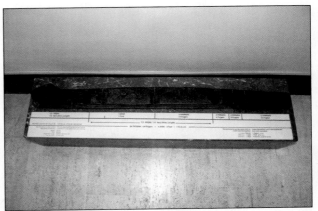

This bronze instrument from Nippur (15th cent. B.C.) was an official linear measure kept in the temple and used as a standard to control other measures in the city.

© Dr. James C. Martin. The Istanbul Archaeological Museum. Photographed by permission.

7:4); the *metretes*, a liquid measure equal to about 39 liters or 9 gallons (Jn. 2:6); the *modius*, a dry measure equal to about 8.49 liters or 7.68 U.S. dry quarts (Matt. 5:15; Mk. 4:21; Lk. 11:33); and the *litra*, the Roman pound of 11.5 oz., used as a measure for both capacity and weight (Jn. 12:3; 19:39).

IV. Measures of weight. Coinage was not used in PALESTINE until after the EXILE (see MONEY). Ezra 2:69 is probably the first mention of coined money in the Bible. During most of OT times, barter (e.g., Gen. 30:27-34; 31:8; 2 Ki. 3:4), value determined by precious metal weighed out, was the means of exchange. The *shekel* is a weight in the OT, not a coin (Ezek. 4:10). Simple balance scales were used, and stones of certain weight (often shekels) were used to determine the weight of the silver or gold involved in the transaction.

In addition to the biblical references to weights, quite a few stone weight-pieces (especially shekels) have been found in the excavations in Palestine, many of them labeled. There is a certain amount of disparity among these. Some have speculated that this is graphic evidence for the necessity of the prophetic indictment of the dishonest merchants who "make the ephah small and the shekel great, and practice deceit with false balances" (Amos 8:5 NRSV). While this explanation is not to be ruled out completely, it must never be forgotten that life in ancient Palestine was simple, rural, and predominantly agricultural. Most of the time there was no strong central government and certainly no bureau

Inscribed Roman bronze weight inlaid with silver (1st cent.). The inscription suggests that it was a standard weight kept at the Temple of Ops (a goddess of plenty and fertility) on the Capitol at Rome.

© Dr. James C. Martin. The British Museum. Photographed by permission.

of weights and measures, although the Israelite monarchy used a "royal standard" (2 Sam. 14:26).

The Hebrews used a modified sexagesimal system of weights modeled on that of the Babylonians. The *shekel* (called by the Babylonians *shiqlu*) was the basic unit: 50 shekels equaled a *maneh* (or *mina;* Babylonian *manû*) and 60 manehs a *talent* (Heb. *kikkār;* Babylonian *biltu*). A *shekel* was made up of twenty *gerahs;* and a *beka* was a half shekel. The Babylonians had 60 shekels in their maneh, but from Exod. 38:25-26 it appears that the Hebrew maneh consisted of only 50. Half a shekel each was paid by 603,550 men, and totaled 100 talents and 1,775 shekels; this means that the talent here equaled 3,000 shekels. Since the talent was almost 60 manehs, the maneh here equals 50 shekels. Ezekiel uses a different system, with 60 shekels to the maneh (45:12).

When one attempts to define the shekel in terms of presently understood weights, the difficulties are formidable. The weight-pieces discovered in Palestine vary greatly. In addition to the double standard mentioned above and the generally unregimented style of ancient Israelite life, the standards themselves may have tended to depreciate, as standards do. The influence of foreign systems may also have been a disturbing factor. The larger weights seem to indicate smaller shekel units than do the smaller weights.

The *beka* or *half shekel* is the only weight named both in the OT and on discovered weights, and of which the relationship to the shekel is given (Exod.

38:26). Several stone weights have been found with Hebrew consonants *BQ* (for *beka*) cut on them, weighing on an average about .21 oz (6 g.), though actual weights vary from .2 to .23 oz. (5.8 to 6.65 g.). One thing these *beka* weights indicated is that the shekel weighed about .4 oz. (12 g.). Therefore the numerous stones bearing a symbol resembling a figure-eight with an open loop, weighing about .4 oz. (12 g.), must be shekel weights. This symbol seems to be a representation of a tied bundle of lump silver. Some conclude that there were three standards for a shekel: the temple shekel of .35 oz. (about 10 g.), the common or commercial shekel of about .4 oz. (11.5 g.), and a "heavy" shekel of about .45 oz. (13 g.). The last of these was probably used in weighing some special commodity.

Certain recent excavations have yielded weights inscribed *pim*, weighing about two-thirds of a shekel. Thus the name of another unit of Hebrew weight is recovered and light is shed on a difficult statement in 1 Sam. 13:21. This verse contains the word *pim*, which was unknown elsewhere and believed to be a textual corruption. Now that *pim* is known to be the name of a weight, the NIV was able to give an improved translation ("two thirds of a shekel"), which indicates that the PHILISTINES, to keep the Hebrews in subjection, made it difficult for the Hebrews to get iron implements and probably overcharged them for repairing them.

Few weights are mentioned in the NT. *Talent* (Matt. 25:15-28) and *pound* (NIV, "mina," Lk. 19:13-25) are sums of money. As mentioned above, the *litra* was used in Jn. 12:3 and 19:39 to indicate an amount of precious oil and may be a weight or a measure of capacity. It was probably the Roman *libra* (pound) of 11.5 oz. (327 g.).

well. Since the RAINS in PALESTINE are concentrated in the winter months, the availability of WATER is a problem through much of the year. Natural sources are springs, streams, rivers, and the Sea of Galilee (see BROOK; FOUNTAIN; RIVER; GALILEE, SEA OF). Artificial sources are wells and CISTERNS. The latter were a problem until after the discovery of waterproof plaster shortly before the EXODUS. The ownership of wells was so important that feuds over them were settled at times only by a unique covenant service, such as the arrangement between ABRAHAM and ABIMELECH (Gen. 21:25-31). This value placed upon wells was in part due to the expense of digging them. Rivals would fight over a well rather than dig a second one. Notice that in Deut. 6:11 wells are listed with other costly items, such as olive groves and vineyards, both of which are very slow growing. The value of wells is seen also in the fact that some bore specific names (Gen. 26:20-22). Cities, in turn, were sometimes known by their wells (e.g., BEERSHEBA).

wen. An abnormal but benign skin growth or cyst. The term is used by the KJV and other versions to render a Hebrew word that occurs only in Lev. 22:22, where the Israelites are instructed not to offer to the LORD any defective sacrifices. The Hebrew term may refer to a wart (cf. NIV).

west. For any nation occupying a Palestinian homeland the W has a threefold significance. (1) It is the direction in which the sun sets, thus "west" is sometimes the translation of a Hebrew word that means literally "the entering of the sun" (Josh. 1:4 et al.). (2) It is the direction in which the MEDITERRANEAN SEA lies; hence Hebrew *yām H3542*, "sea," can mean "west" (Gen. 13:14 et al.) (3) In consequence, it is also the direction from which come the rain-bearing winds (cf. Lk. 12:54). For the Israelites the point of orientation was the EAST (not the N, as it is for us), and therefore the W can sometimes be referred to with the word *ʾaḥărôn H340*, "behind" (esp. in the expression *hayyām hāʾaḥărôn*, "the sea that is behind, the western sea," Deut. 11:24 et al.; see also EASTERN SEA).

western sea. Sea EASTERN SEA; MEDITERRANEAN SEA.

West Gate. According to the NIV, both the West Gate and the (otherwise unknown) SHALLEKETH Gate, on the upper road in the W part of the TEMPLE enclosure, were assigned to SHUPPIM and HOSAH (1 Chr. 26:16). The Hebrew reads literally, "[the lots fell] for the west with the Shalleketh Gate." It is unclear whether in this passage the term for "west" merely indicates direction (cf. NRSV) or whether it designates a gate. If the latter, we have no evidence to determine whether it was an alter-

nate name for the Shalleketh Gate or a different gate altogether (cf. NJPS, "the west [gate], with the Shallecheth gate on the ascending highway").

whale. See ANIMALS.

wheat. See PLANTS.

wheel. Clay models of wheeled vehicles, and some fragments of a potter's wheel (see POTTERY) indicate that both devices were known in ANE countries as early as the fourth millennium B.C. The first wheels, here and elsewhere, were probably suggested to some inventive mind by a rolling log, and were simply slabs cut from a log. The spoked wheel seems to have come with the replacement of the donkey by the horse as a draught animal in the middle of the second millennium B.C. In the description of Solomon's TEMPLE, there is reference to the basins shaped in bronze after the fashion of chariot wheels and are described complete with axles, rims, and spokes (1 Ki. 7:30-33). Probably the model was the heavy Assyrian chariot wheel, rather than the lighter Egyptian model. The northern war chariots were heavily wheeled, and rolled noisily (Jer. 47:3; Nah. 3:2). Both EZEKIEL and DANIEL had APOCALYPTIC visions in which wheels were an image of strength and of rapid movement from place to place (Ezek. 1:15-21; Dan. 7:9).

whelp. The young of various carnivorous mammals; in the Bible it almost always refers to the young of a lion (of a bear in 2 Sam. 17:8). The English term occurs a number of times in the KJV (e.g., Gen. 49:9), but modern versions prefer *cub*. See ANIMALS. Biblical references to whelps or cubs are mainly figurative (Job 4:11; Jer. 51:38; et al.).

whip. See SCOURGE.

whirlwind. A rotating windstorm, usually of limited extent. Although true tornados or severe whirlwinds are rare in PALESTINE, several types of violent storms do occur because of the proximity of mountains and lakes to the hot deserts. Hebrew words translated "whirlwind" include *sĕʿārâ H6194* (used, e.g., of the wind that took ELIJAH up to heaven, 2 Ki. 2:1, 11) and *sûpâh H6070* (Prov. 1:27 et al.).

white. See COLOR.

whole burnt offering. See SACRIFICE AND OFFERINGS.

whore. See PROSTITUTE.

wicked, wickedness. These terms, referring to moral EVIL, are used in the Bible especially of a person that opposes God, his will, his MESSIAH, and his GOSPEL. It can describe a whole people or an individual or the state in which they are (as seen by God). Psalm 37 has many references to wicked or evil people as they are contrasted with the godly or righteous. See RIGHTEOUSNESS. This psalm begins, "Do not fret because of evil men … for like the grass they will soon wither." Wickedness had been in the world since the entrance of SIN, and because of it the Lord sent the great flood (Gen. 6:5), saving only the righteous NOAH and his family.

Only wicked people could have killed Jesus the Messiah (Acts 2:23), but also a generation that did not wholeheartedly accept the gospel must be a wicked generation (Matt. 16:4). In fact, the whole world is constantly in a state of wickedness (Rom. 1:29). The origin and source of wickedness is to be sought in the work and wiles of the devil, who is the "wicked" or "evil" one (Matt. 13:19; Mk. 4:15; Lk. 8:12; Eph. 6:12). See SATAN. Christians are to have nothing to do with the wicked one or wickedness (1 Jn. 2:13; 5:18-19) and are to use the shield of faith (Eph. 6:16). The certainty of punishment for the wicked is often declared (e.g., Matt. 13:49). God permits wickedness in this age but does not condone it, and he will judge those responsible for it. See also MALICE.

widow. In the OT, widows are regarded as being under God's special care (Ps. 68:5; 146:9; Prov. 15:25). From early times they wore a distinctive garb. The Hebrews were commanded to treat them with special consideration and were punished if they did otherwise (Exod. 22:22; Deut. 14:29; Isa. 1:17; Jer. 7:6). The CHURCH looked after poor widows in apostolic times (Acts 6:1; Jas. 1:27). PAUL gives instructions to TIMOTHY about the care of widows by the church (1 Tim. 5:4); but only those were taken care of who were at least sixty years of age, had been married only once, and had a reputation for good works (5:9-10).

wife. See FAMILY; MARRIAGE; WOMAN.

wild ass. See ANIMALS.

wilderness. See DESERT.

wild goat. See ANIMALS (under *ibex*).

Wild Goats, Crags (Rocks) of the. A place in the Judean wilderness at or near EN GEDI, on the W shore of the DEAD SEA, where SAUL went to look for DAVID (1 Sam. 24:2; cf. v. 1).

wild gourd. See PLANTS.

wild grape. See VINE, VINEYARD.

wild ox. See ANIMALS (under *antelope* and *cattle*).

will. See PURPOSE; TESTAMENT.

willow. See PLANTS.

Willows, Brook (Wadi) of the. In his oracle against MOAB, the prophet ISAIAH says that its fugitives carry their wealth "over the Brook of the Willows" (Isa. 5:17 RSV; NRSV, "Wadi of the Willows"; NIV, "Ravine of the Poplars"). Some have identified this brook or ravine with Wadi Abu Gharaba, which flows into the JORDAN just N of the DEAD SEA, but the passage is usually interpreted to indicate that the Moabites are fleeing in a southerly direction. Most recent writers identify it with Wadi el-Ḥesa (see ZERED) because this ravine, located at the SE end of the Dead Sea, served as the boundary between Moab and EDOM. See also ARABAH.

wimple. This English word, referring to a type of hood worn by women in the late Middle Ages, is used by the KJV once (Isa. 3:22; NIV and other versions, "cloak").

wind. The standard word for "wind" in Hebrew is *rûaḥ H8120* (Gen. 8:1 et al.), which can also be rendered "breeze," "breath," "spirit," "courage," and the like. See SPIRIT. The equivalent of *rûaḥ* in Greek is *pneuma G4460*, "breath, spirit" (rendered "wind" in the wordplay at Jn. 3:8, and cf. Heb. 1:7). However, the more common word for "wind" in the NT is *anemos G449*, which occurs about thirty times (Matt. 7:25 et al.).

Winds are important in the Bible, both literally and figuratively. God causes winds, and he created them (Gen. 8:1; Exod. 10:13; Num. 11:31; Ps. 107:25; 135:7; 147:18; Jer. 10:13; Jon. 1:4). The four winds are limits of distance or direction (Jer. 49:36; Ezek. 37:9; Matt. 24:31; et al.). Of the cardinal directions, the E wind is most often mentioned (Gen. 41:6, 23, 27; Exod. 10:13; Ps. 48:7; et al.). Sometimes it is stormy, wrecks ships, withers growing things. The N wind brings rain (Prov. 25:23), is refreshing (Cant. 4:16), or stormy (Ezek. 1:4). The S wind is gentle, helps growth (Job 37:17; Ps. 78:26; Cant. 4:16). The W wind blew away the plague of locusts (Exod. 10:19). Winds brought notable storms (1 Ki. 18:45; 19:11; Job 1:9; Matt. 8:26-27; 14:24, 32; Acts 27:4, 7, 14-15). In Acts there are references to the S wind (Acts 27:13; 28:13), the NW wind (27:12), the SW wind (27:12), and the violent "northeaster" (27:14; see EUROCLYDON). WHIRLWINDS are mentioned several times.

Wind blows chaff (Job 21:18; Ps. 1:4; et al.); fulfills God's commands (Ps. 104:4; 148:8); reveals weakness, transitoriness, worthlessness (Job 15:2; Ps. 18:42; Prov. 11:29; et al.); clears the sky (Job 37:21); drives ships (Jas. 3:4). ELISHA promises water not brought by wind (2 Ki. 3:17). God rides on the wings of the wind (2 Sam. 22:11; Ps. 104:3). The circulation of the wind is recognized (Eccl. 1:6). Wind has a drying effect (Isa. 11:15; Jer. 4:11-12). Princes are to be a hiding place from the wind (Isa. 32:2). Wind has an observable effect on animal life (Jer. 2:24). Ezekiel scattered hair in the wind to symbolize the scattering of the people (Ezek. 5:2, 10, 12; 12:14; 17:21). Winds can be strong and destructive (Jer. 51:16; Ezek. 13:11, 13; Hos. 4:19; 13:15). Wind can represent folly and resulting troubles: "They sow the wind and reap the whirlwind" (Hos. 8:7). God controls the force of the wind (Job 28:25). Believers are warned against evil winds of false doctrine (Eph. 4:4; Jude 12). Stars will fall like figs shaken from the tree by the wind (Rev. 6:13). Wind moved the wings of women carrying a basket (Zech. 5:9). See also PALESTINE (sect. III).

The most controversial passage is in Gen. 1:2, where the phrase *rûaḥ ʾělōhîm*, traditionally understood to mean, "the Spirit of God," is sometimes rendered "a wind from God" (NRSV) or "a mighty wind" (NEB; the use of *ʾělōhîm H466* as a superlative is attested, e.g., in 23:6, "great/mighty prince"). The true meaning is found in the use of the similar phrase *rûaḥ-ʾēl* in parallel with *nišmat šadday* in Job 33:4, "The Spirit of God has made me; / the breath of the Almighty gives me life." Thus the breath or Spirit of God in Gen. 1:2 (not an impersonal natural phenomenon) and God's breathing of the breath of life in 2:7 are properly connected and reflect personal divine activities. See HOLY SPIRIT.

window. See HOUSE.

wine. Several Hebrew words occur, the most frequent of which is *yayin H3516*, mentioned as a common drink (Gen. 14:18); as a drink offering (Lev. 23:13); as intoxicating (Gen. 9:21); and figuratively of wisdom (Prov. 9:2, 5), of wrath (Jer. 25:15), of love (Cant. 1:2; 4:10). Also frequent is *tîrôš H9408*, often translated "new wine" and possibly referring to *must*, that is, grape juice before and during fermentation (Gen. 27:28; Jdg. 9:13; 2 Ki. 18:32; Zech. 9:17), but it too could be intoxicating

A winepress at Masada.

© Dr. James C. Martin

(Hos. 4:11). The Hebrew word translated "strong drink" by the KJV and other versions (NIV, "fermented drink" or "beer") is *šēkār* **H8911** (Lev. 10:9 et al.); it is used to denote any intoxicating drink made from any fruit or grain, and at least in the early period included wine (cf. Num. 28:7 with 28:14; in Isa. 5:11 it occurs in parallel with *yayin* referring to intoxicating beverages in general). Usually, however, the use of the term is restricted to intoxicants other than wine from grapes. It probably refers to beer made from barley. Priests were forbidden to drink wine or strong drink while on duty (Lev. 10:9; Ezek. 44:21). NAZIRITES were not even to touch grapes while under a vow (Num. 6:5, 20; Jdg. 13:4-14; Lk. 1:15). Abuse of wine is condemned in Proverbs (Prov. 4:17; 31:6), also in the Prophets (Isa. 5:11).

In the NT, the primary Greek word is *oinos* **G3885** (Lk. 1:15; Jn. 2:2-11; et al.). The word *gleukos* **G1183** ("new, sweet wine") occurs only once (Act 2:13), where the disciples in their exuberant enthusiasm appeared intoxicated. New wine fermenting would burst old wineskins (Matt. 9:17). Jesus refused the wine offered him on the CROSS because it was drugged (Mk. 15:25). Jesus contrasts himself with JOHN THE BAPTIST (Lk. 7:33-34) as one who ate and drank with others. In OT times wine apparently was not diluted. Before NT times the Hellenistic practice of mixing it with much water was common in Palestine. Wine was a disinfectant (Lk. 10:34) and a medicine (1 Tim. 5:23). It is right for a Christian not to eat meat or drink wine if it causes other believers to stumble (Rom. 14:21). Men (1 Tim. 3:8) and women (Tit. 2:3) church officers were warned against overindulgence. See DRUNKENNESS.

winebibber. This term, referring to someone who drinks wine excessively, is used by the KJV in three passages (Prov. 23:20; Matt. 11:19; Lk. 7:34). See DRUNKENNESS; WINE.

winepress. See VINE, VINEYARD.

wineskin. See BOTTLE; SKIN.

wing. The Bible contains references to literal wings (Gen. 1:21), but most uses are figurative.

The desire of hope is expressed in the psalmist's words, "Oh, that I had the wings of a dove! / I would fly away and be at rest" (Ps. 55:6), and such relief is promised in ISAIAH's statement, "They will soar on wings like eagles" (Isa. 40:31). MOSES assured the Israelites that the Lord cared for them "like an eagle … that spreads out its wings" (Deut. 32:11). RUTH found refuge under the wings of the Lord (Ruth 2:12), and Jesus would have gathered Jerusalem to himself "as a hen gathers her chicks under her wings" (Matt. 23:37). Both the wind and the morning are said to have wings (Ps. 18:10; 139:9), which portray the swift arrival of the Lord's help and accessibility everywhere (cf. also Mal. 4:2). Several symbolic creatures are said to have wings, such as the two women in Zechariah (Zech. 5:9), the lion with eagles' wings in Daniel (Dan. 7:4), and the woman in Revelation (Rev. 12:14). In ancient monuments wings were added to bulls and lions. Isaiah's SERAPHS covered their face with wings in worship, their feet also, but flew with the remaining two (Isa. 6:2). Ezekiel's CHERUBIM, winged living creatures, ascended with glory to God (Ezek. 10:5).

winnowing. See FARMING.

winnowing fork. An implement with two or more prongs used to throw grain into the air after it had been threshed, so that the chaff might be

Winnowing at dusk.

© Garo Nalbandian

blown away (KJV, "fan," Jer. 15:7; Matt. 3:12; Lk. 3:17). The work was done toward evening and at night when a wind came in from the sea and carried away the light chaff. Sometimes a shovel was used for the same purpose.

winter. The Hebrew word translated "winter" is *ḥōrep H3074*, referring to the season for sowing and early growth (Ps. 74:17 et al.), though some think it includes HARVEST time or autumn (another term is *sĕtāw H6255*, only in Cant. 2:11). The NT uses the common Greek word *cheimōn G5930* (Matt. 24:20; Mk. 13:18; Jn. 10:22; 2 Tim. 4:21; cf. the cognate terms in Acts 27:12; 28:11; 1 Cor. 16:6; Tit. 3:12). See also PALESTINE (sect. III).

winter house. Kings and wealthy people had separate residences for hot seasons and residences for cold seasons (Amos 3:15). King JEHOIAKIM had a fire in the brazier in his winter house or apartment (Jer. 36:22).

wisdom. The common Hebrew word for "wisdom" is *ḥokmâ H2683*, which can also be rendered "skill, experience, shrewdness, prudence"; Greek uses *sophia G5053* (also *phronēsis G5860* and cognates). In God wisdom is the infinite, perfect comprehension of all that is or might be (Rom. 11:33-36). God is the source of wisdom as of power, and wisdom is given to people through the fear of the Lord (Job 28:28; Ps. 111:10). In human beings wisdom is an eminently practical attribute, including technical skill (Exod. 28:3), military prowess (Isa. 10:13), and even shrewdness for questionable ends (1 Ki. 2:6). Wisdom is shown in getting desired ends by effective means. People of the world are often wiser in their generation than the children of light (Lk. 16:8). The wisdom of SOLOMON was far ranging in statesmanship (1 Ki. 10:23-24); in understanding of human nature (3:16-25); and in natural history, literature, and popular proverbs (4:29-34). Wisdom is personified in Prov. 8 in a way that provides part of the background for the concept of the Word in Jn. 1:1-18 (see LOGOS).

Wisdom Literature in the OT consists of the books of PROVERBS, ECCLESIASTES, and JOB, but it is also found in shorter passages, such as Ps. 19. In the OT APOCRYPHA, the books of Ecclesiasti-

cus and Wisdom of Solomon belong in the same category. Hebrew wisdom was not all religious; it dealt, as in Proverbs, with everyday conduct in business, family and social relations, and basic morality. Ecclesiastes ranges farther afield to consider the ultimate value of life. Wise men or sages, unlike PROPHETS, claimed no special inspiration. They exercised no priestly functions and were not, like the SCRIBES, devoted exclusively to the study of the sacred writings. Eventually sages and scribes coalesced into one class.

With worsening political conditions and a deepening sense of moral problems in the period of the prophets and later kings, people came to despise worldly wisdom as irreligious and as characteristic of pagans, who might be superior in secular culture, but were inferior from a moral and religious point of view (Isa. 10:12-19). Wisdom is bound up with doing the will of the Lord (Deut. 4:6): to forsake his Word is to forfeit one's wisdom (Jer. 8:8-9). Although Wisdom Literature often seems to equate right with advantage (profit, Eccl. 1:5), there is clear evidence of the controlling hand and moral interest of God in human affairs. The sayings of Jesus, largely proverbial and parabolical, are the crown of biblical wisdom. PAUL calls Jesus "the wisdom of God" (1 Cor. 1:24, 30) and says that in him all the treasures of wisdom are hidden (Col. 2:3). When Paul compares the wisdom of people with the wisdom of God (1 Cor. 2), he is thinking of the former as that of Greek philosophers rather than OT biblical wisdom. The letter of JAMES is Wisdom Literature at its best, a clear mirror of the teaching of Jesus.

Wisdom of Jesus, Son of Sirach. See APOCRYPHA.

Wisdom of Solomon. See APOCRYPHA.

Wise Men. See MAGI.

witch, witchcraft. See DIVINATION; FAMILIAR SPIRIT; MAGIC.

withe (withs). The English term *withe* refers to a flexible twig used as a band. In the plural spelling *withs*, it is used by the KJV in one passage (Jdg.

W

16:7-9), referring to the "seven fresh bowstrings" (NRSV, NIV mg.) with which DELILAH bound SAMSON. Some believe that the objects used by Delilah were animal tendons still wet (cf. NJPS); others suggest that they were simply leather strips (cf. NIV, "thongs").

withered hand. See DISEASES.

witness. One who may be called to testify to an event at which he or she was present. Things may be witnesses: a heap of stones as a sign that God witnessed Jacob and Laban's covenant (Gen. 31:44-52); a song (Deut. 31:19-21); the law (31:26); an altar (Josh. 22:27-34); a stone that has "heard" God speak (24:27); an altar and a pillar on the border of Egypt (Isa. 19:20). Bearing false witness is condemned (Exod. 20:16; 23:2; Deut. 5:20) and punished the same as for the crime of which one accused another (Deut. 19:16-18). True and false witnesses are contrasted (Prov. 14:5). Two or three witnesses were required in legal proceedings (Deut. 19:15; Matt. 18:16; 2 Cor. 13:1; 1 Tim. 5:19; Heb. 10:28). Jeremiah describes the use of witnesses in a transfer of real estate property (Jer. 32:6-25, 44). The tabernacle of witness, or testimony (Num. 17:7-8; 10:2; 2 Chr. 24:6), was so named because the witness of God's presence was in it.

God is called on as a witness (Gen. 31:50; Job 16:19; Jer. 29:23; 42:5; Mic. 1:2; Mal. 3:5; Rom. 1:9; 1 Thess. 2:5, 10). On solemn occasions people acknowledged themselves witnesses (Josh. 24:22; Ruth 4:9-11). God called his people ISRAEL his witnesses (Isa. 43:10, 12; 44:8), and the apostles acknowledged themselves to be such (Lk. 24:48; Acts 1:8; 2:32; 3:15; 5:32; 10:39-41; 1 Thess. 2:10). PETER thought that JUDAS ISCARIOT must be replaced as a witness (Acts 1:22). PAUL had a special appointment as a witness (22:15; 26:16). He reminds TIMOTHY of many witnesses (1 Tim. 6:12; 2 Tim. 2:2). Peter appeals to his readers as a witness of the sufferings of Christ (1 Pet. 5:1). JOHN THE APOSTLE calls Jesus Christ the "faithful witness" (Rev. 1:5; 3:14). The cloud of witnesses of Heb. 12:1 are those who by the lives they lived testify that the life of faith is the only truly worthwhile life. See also MARTYR; TESTIMONY; WITNESS OF THE SPIRIT.

witness, altar of. See ED.

witness of the Spirit. A witness presupposes a person, object, content, or event concerning which TESTIMONY is given. The NT makes it clear that the primary witness of the HOLY SPIRIT is to CHRIST, and not to himself or initially to a body of doctrine (Jn. 14:26; 15:26; 16:7-15; cf. Matt. 16:16-17; 1 Jn. 2:20-22). The Spirit witnesses to the significance of the total redemptive program of God, and believers' eyes are opened to understand (1 Cor. 2:10-16; 2 Cor. 3:12-18). Having inspired selected individuals to write the truth of God (2 Tim. 2:16; 2 Pet. 1:21), the Spirit gives an accompanying inward illumination enabling us to appreciate the objective revelation as God's truth and to apprehend its meaning (1 Cor. 2:10-16; 2 Cor. 3:12-18). The Spirit also convicts people of their sin and of righteousness, warning of coming judgment (Jn. 16:8-11), and ministers to believers, assuring them of their relationship with God (Rom. 8:15-16; Gal. 4:6) and granting them spiritual discernment (1 Cor. 2:15, 16; cf. Rom. 12:2; Phil. 1:10; Col. 1:9).

wizard. See DIVINATION; FAMILIAR SPIRIT; MAGIC.

wolf. See ANIMALS.

woman. The general account of CREATION teaches the full humanity of EVE (Gen. 1:26-27), and this truth is more directly asserted in the special account of her creation (2:18-24), which emphasizes (a) her superiority to all lower animals, (b) ADAM's need of her as helper, (c) her intimate relationship to him as a part of his inmost being, and (d) the nature of MARRIAGE as a "one flesh" relationship. Among OT women that played significant roles are the three patriarchal wives (SARAH, REBEKAH, and RACHEL), MOSES' sister MIRIAM (Exod. 2:1-9; 15:21; Num. 12), the judge DEBORAH (Jdg. 4-5), and the Moabitess RUTH. HANNAH illustrates both the despair of a childless woman and the grace of godly motherhood (1 Sam. 1:1—2:11). The advice of LEMUEL's mother to her son (Prov. 31) pictures an ideal, industrious wife in a prosperous family. Queens, good and bad, and evil women of other classes of society are frankly portrayed in the Bible. The ancient world was a man's world: such promi-

The domestic tasks of women living near ancient Laodicea include processing pomegranates.

nence as women attained was achieved by force of character—sometimes, as in the case of ESTHER, aided by circumstances not of her seeking.

The teaching of Jesus stressed the original monogamous nature of marriage and of a man's obligation of purity in his thoughts and actions toward women (Matt. 5:27-32). Jesus' example in healing (9:18-26) and in social intercourse (Lk. 10:38-42) reinforced his words. The Gospel of Luke is full of evidence of Jesus' understanding and appreciation of women, thus setting a pattern for normal Christian living. Godly women stand out in Jesus' life and ministry: ELIZABETH, mother of his forerunner (Lk. 1); the Virgin Mary (see MARY, MOTHER OF JESUS); ANNA (2:36-38); the sinner of Lk. 7:36-40; MARY Magdalene; MARTHA and Mary of BETHANY; the women who accompanied the disciples on missionary journeys and who provided for them out of their means (8:3). Women remained at the CROSS until the burial and were first at the empty tomb.

Women joined the men in prayer between the ASCENSION and PENTECOST (Acts 1:14). The disciples in JERUSALEM met in the house of Mary, mother of John Mark (12:12). Women were the first converts in Europe, including the prosperous business woman LYDIA at PHILIPPI (16:13-15). PHOEBE, a deaconess, and many other women are greeted in Rom. 16. PAUL (1 Cor. 11:2-16; 14:34-35) urges subordination for Christian women, but he exalts the believing wife as a type of the CHURCH, the bride of Christ (Eph. 5:21-33). He sets high standards for the wives of church officers and for women in official positions (1 Tim. 3:11; Tit. 2:3-5). Likewise, 1 Pet. 3:1-6 urges a subordinate but noble role for married women. To evaluate Bible teaching with regard to women, it is necessary to consider carefully all the pertinent material and to hold firmly to the normative and authoritative character of the words, deeds, and attitude of Jesus Christ.

wood. See FOREST; PLANTS.

wool. The fleece of sheep and some other animals. The wool from the initial shearing was one of the FIRSTFRUITS that the people of ISRAEL were to give to the priests (Deut. 18:4). Israelites were forbidden to wear mixed woolen and linen clothing (22:11). The whiteness of wool as a symbol of purity is contrasted with the crimson of sins (Isa. 1:18) and compared to snow (Ps. 147:16) or the hair of the Ancient of Days (Dan. 7:9) who reappears in John's vision (Rev. 1:14).

word. The Bible contains much that is literally the message of, and from, God—and so it is called "the word of the Lord." That expression occurs hundreds of times in the OT and usually denotes the prophetic word (word from God through the mouth of the PROPHET); however, it also can refer to the LAW of God (Ps. 147:19-20) and to the creative activity of God, who speaks and causes to be (Gen. 1; Ps. 33:6-9). In the case of the prophet, it is never that the prophet chooses to speak a word, but rather that the word from God takes the prophet into its service so that he becomes a mouthpiece for God (Isa. 6; Jer. 1:4-10; Ezek. 1). And, once uttered, God's word does not return to him empty but accomplishes what he purposes (Isa. 55:11).

© Dr. James C. Martin

W

Thus the word of God is the fundamental aspect of God's self-revelation, for by his word he makes known who he is, what he is like, and what his will is for the world. See REVELATION.

In the NT the "word of the Lord" or "word of God" (Acts 4:29; 6:2; 1 Thess. 1:8) is primarily good news from God (Acts 15:7). It is the word concerning Jesus Christ and God's kingdom in and through him (16:31-32; 17:13); and it is also the word of the cross (1 Cor. 1:18), of reconciliation (2 Cor. 5:19), of eternal life (Phil. 2:16), and of salvation (Acts 13:26). Christians are told to abide in this word (Jn. 8:31), to keep it (8:51; 14:23), and serve it (Acts 6:4).

Jesus himself did not speak like an OT prophet. He said, "I say to you," not "The Lord says to you" (see Matt. 5:21-48). The words of Jesus are the words of the heavenly Father, and so to receive and accept them is to receive eternal salvation (Jn. 5:24; 8:51; 12:48; 14:24). But not only is the word spoken by Jesus truly the word from heaven—he himself is the true Word who has come to earth from heaven (1:1-14). As the Word (LOGOS) he is the preexistent Word (SON OF GOD) who exists eternally and so existed before he became the Incarnate Word, when he was rejected by the world he had made. See INCARNATION. But as Incarnate Word, truly sharing our human nature and flesh, he achieved the redemption of the world through his life, death, and resurrection.

work. See LABOR; OCCUPATIONS AND PROFESSIONS.

works. This term is used of deeds done (a) by God out of holy love and (b) by human beings as God's creatures. In the OT the works of God (often in the singular, reflecting that the total activity of the Lord is seen as a unity, one work) refer to his creating and preserving the cosmos (Gen. 2:2; Ps. 8:3), and his deeds of salvation and judgment on behalf of Israel (Ps. 28:5; Isa. 5:12, 19). God's work is "awesome" (Ps. 66:3), is "great" (92:5), is "wonderful" (139:14), and is done in "faithfulness" (33:4). The godly meditate on God's work and works (77:12; 143:5) and praise him for them (72:18; 105:1-2). In the NT God is presented as working in and through the MESSIAH both in CREATION (Jn. 1:1-3) and in REDEMPTION (9:3-4). By his works Jesus reveals his true identity and from whom he comes (Matt. 9:2-5; Jn. 5:36; 10:37-38).

Being made in God's image, human beings perform works as they live in God's world in relationship with other human beings. What deeds they perform cannot be isolated from the state of their hearts and their motivation (Ps. 28:3-4). Works done out of evil motivation are "acts of the sinful nature" (Gal. 5:19). Works done in order to earn the favorable judgment of God at the end of life—seeking JUSTIFICATION by works—are not acceptable for this end (Rom. 3:20; Gal. 2:16; 2 Tim. 1:9). True works, in which God delights, are those that arise from an inward gratitude to God for his goodness and salvation. These spring from FAITH, the faith that holds to Christ as Savior and Lord (Eph. 2:10; Col. 1:10). While PAUL emphasized the need for faith leading to faithfulness to God in good deeds, JAMES (facing a different situation) emphasized that genuine good works are the evidence of true faith (Jas. 2:14-26).

world. This English term can be used not only of the earth in a physical sense, but also of its inhabitants or human existence, of its concerns and

© NASA H0GEv301 in Tarawtula Nebula

"In the beginning God created the heavens and the earth" (Gen. 1:1). Detailed photo of the Tarantula Nebula (NGC 2070) from the Hubble Space Telescope (with star cluster Hodge 301 in lower right). This giant emission nebula, more than 1,000 light-years across, is part of the irregular neighboring galaxy known as the Large Magellanic Cloud.

affairs, of human society, and so forth. The primary Hebrew word for "world" is *'ereṣ H824*, which more frequently is rendered "ground, earth, country." Another term, *tēbēl H9315*, is used as a synonym in some contexts (notice the parallelism in 1 Sam. 2:8; Ps. 24:1; Isa. 24:4; et al.), but it appears to have the distinct sense of "the inhabited and cultivated areas of the mainland" (cf. Job 18:8 et al.). In the NT, the most common term is *kosmos G3180* ("adornment, order, world, universe"), but two other words are relevant. The form *oikoumenē G3876* means literally "inhabited," but because it was often combined with *gē G1178* ("land, earth"), *hē oikoumenē* by itself came to mean "the inhabited world." Finally, the noun *aiōn G172*, which has primarily a temporal reference ("a [long] period of existence, an age"), sometimes by metonymy takes on the spatial meaning "world" (Heb. 1:2; 11:3; cf. also the expressions "the present age" and "this age," where the rendering "world" is just as appropriate).

The term *kosmos* is one of John's favorite words, used of Jesus as Creator (Jn. 1:10; 17:5), Redeemer (1:29; 3:16-17; 4:42; 6:35, 51; 12:47; 1 Jn. 2:2; 4:9, 14), Light of the world (Jn. 1:9, 3:19; 8:12; 9:5; 12:46), Prophet (6:14), he who was to come (11:27), and Judge (9:39; 12:31; 16:11). The contrast between Jesus and his disciples on the one hand, and the world on the other, is drawn in several passages in his gospel (Jn. 8:23; 14:17-22; 15:18-19; 17:9; 18:36) and often in his first epistle. John 17 is rich in references to the relation of believers to the world, considered as a fallen universe hostile to God. In the NT Letters the ethical meaning prevails (e.g., 1 Cor. 1:20-28). Other uses are "since the world began" (Jn. 9:32 KJV); the sun as the light of the world (11:9); the prince of this world, Satan (14:30).

Hebrew cosmology is not tied in with the concept "world" so much as with "heaven and earth" (Gen. 1:1), which embraces the God-oriented universe of sun, moon, planets, stars, and earth, with the abode of God above and SHEOL beneath. The Hebrew words for "world" refer either to the earth itself, or as formed for and inhabited by human beings. In the NT, *kosmos* can include angels, spiritual principalities and powers, human beings, beasts, earth, heavenly bodies, and HADES. It commonly refers to the concerns and affairs of human society, especially in an evil sense, over against the new life in Christ, the KINGDOM OF GOD, the BODY OF CHRIST, the CHURCH. As God is in the world but not of it, so are we: God's mode of being penetrates without mixture the world's mode of being, just as iron is penetrated by magnetism or copper by electricity (cf. Jn. 17:14-18).

worm. See ANIMALS.

wormwood. See PLANTS.

worship. The honor, reverence, and homage paid to superior beings or powers. The English word was originally *weorthscipe* ("worth-ship"), denoting the worthiness of the individual receiving the special honor. While the word is used of human beings, it is especially used of the divine honors paid to a deity, whether of the heathen religions or the true and living God.

When given to God, worship involves an acknowledgment of divine perfections. It may express itself in the form of direct address, as in adoration or thanksgiving, or in service to God; it may be private, or it may be public, involving a cultus. Worship presupposes that God is, that he can be known, and that his perfections set him far above human beings.

The Bible attests to worship from the beginning. In patriarchal times there was both the privacy of prayer (e.g., Gen. 18) and the public act of setting up an altar (e.g., 12:7). From the PATRIARCHS onward, we can divide the Bible into four periods. First, while MOSES established the basis of the public worship of ISRAEL and gave it its focal point in the TABERNACLE, we know little about the actual performance of worship. As 1 Sam. 1:1, for example, shows, the tabernacle remained the center for the pilgrimage festivals with their round of SACRIFICES; at the same time it shows the wealth and depth of private devotion that they represented. In the second period worship became highly organized in the TEMPLE ritual, which had its origin in the tabernacle set up in the wilderness. It was led by PRIESTS assisted by the LEVITES, and included a complex ritual and system of sacrifices. The third stage was that of the SYNAGOGUE, which developed among those who remained in exile.

This greatly differed from worship in the temple. Whereas the latter was centralized in JERUSALEM, the former was found wherever there were Jews. In the synagogues, however, the emphasis was more on instruction than on worship, although the latter was not neglected. The fourth stage was that of the early Christian churches. Jewish Christians continued, as long as they were permitted, to worship in the temple and in the synagogue, though for them the whole ceremonial and sacrificial system ended with the death and resurrection of Jesus. Public Christian worship developed along the lines of the synagogue. It appears that from the first, Christians met in homes for private brotherhood meetings, and the time was the LORD'S DAY (Jn. 20:19, 26; Acts 20:7; 1 Cor. 16:2). Christian public worship consisted of preaching (Acts 20:7; 1 Cor. 14:9), reading of Scripture (Col. 4:16; Jas. 1:22), PRAYER (1 Cor. 14:14-16), singing (Eph. 5:19; Col. 3:16), BAPTISM and the LORD'S SUPPER (Acts 2:41; 1 Cor. 11:18-34), almsgiving (1 Cor. 16:1-2), and sometimes prophesying and tongues.

wrath. The translation of various Hebrew and Greek words, ranging widely in tone, intensity, and effects (Gen. 27:25; 2 Chr. 26:19; Esth. 1:12; Ps. 85:4; Matt. 2:16). The first display of human wrath recorded in the Bible (Gen. 4:5-6) is followed by numerous accounts of disaster wrought by human wrath, which never works the righteousness of God (Jas. 1:20) and is never more than tolerated (Ps. 37:8; Rom. 12:19; Eph. 4:26). The wrath of a just, pure, and holy God is dreadful to evildoers (Num. 11:1-10; Heb. 10:26-31), yet God is slow to anger, eager to forgive (Ps. 103:8-9) and so should we be (Eph. 4:31-32). Less often mentioned in the NT than in the OT, the wrath of God is no less terrible, is revealed most dramatically in the wrath of the Lamb (Jn. 1:29; Rev. 6:16), and abides on "whoever rejects the Son" (Jn. 3:36; cf. Rom. 1:18).

wreath. This English term can refer to an object that is intertwined or that has been arranged in a circular shape. The NIV uses it to render (1) an architectural term that occurs in only one passage (1 Ki. 7:29-30, 36), where it may refer to a spiral design; (2) a Hebrew term usually rendered "crown" (Isa. 28:1, 3, 5), and (3) a Greek term that

the KJV renders "garland" (Acts 14:13). The KJV uses "wreath" also in a number of other passages (Exod. 28:14 et al.). See also CROWN; GARLAND.

wrestling. A contest in which two unarmed individuals seek to subdue each other. Wrestling is a very ancient sport, well illustrated from EGYPT and evidenced from MESOPOTAMIA. In the OT a serious wrestling bout of JACOB is described (Gen. 32:24-25). Wrestling was a popular competition among the Greeks and thus provided NT illustration of spiritual principle. The Greek verb *agōnizomai G76*, "to fight, struggle," is rendered "wrestle" by the NIV and other versions in a passage that speaks about struggling in PRAYER (Col. 4:12). The KJV uses "wrestlings" with reference to RACHEL's emotional contest with LEAH (Gen. 30:8), leading Rachel to name her handmaid's son NAPHTALI ("my struggle"); and it uses "wrestle" to translate Greek *palē G4097*, which occurs only once with reference to the intensity and personal nature of spiritual conflict (Eph. 6:12).

writing. It is generally assumed that the earliest forms of writing were pictographic, not phonetic. That is to say, the ideas were recorded by means of pictures, or sense-symbols, rather than by sound-symbols such as are used in most modern languages. The earliest human beings presumably drew a picture of the idea they wished to represent, rather than using a sign to show how the word in question was to be pronounced. Thus the circle of the sun-disk might indicate either the sun itself (in Egyptian the word *re*, in Sumerian *ud*) or the span of time during which the sun would shine. The concept of "human being" was conveyed in Egyptian by the picture of a person sitting with one leg curled under and the other bent with the knee upright (this figure would be accompanied by a single vertical stroke if only one person was involved or by more strokes according to the number of people referred to). In Sumerian the same concept (*lu*) was conveyed by a triangular head and a turnip-shaped torso; at first it stood up on end, facing right, but later it lay flat on its back facing upward, for all Sumerian signs underwent a ninety-degree shift in direction from vertical to horizontal sometime between 3000 and 2500 B.C.

This earliest stage in writing was marked by the use of the pure *ideogram*. See EGYPT; MESOPOTAMIA; SUMER. (This same principle was operative in primitive Chinese, which developed a system of sign language that has endured to the present day; nearly all of its basic characters, or "radicals," represent pictures of the type of object being referred to. This picture may or may not be accompanied by other strokes that indicate the sound value of the word.)

Evidently the next stage in the history of writing was the introduction of the *phonogram*—the type of sign that indicates a sound. At first this was achieved by the *rebus* principle, that is, by using objects that have a name sounding like the sound of the word that the writer wishes to convey, even though the meaning of the object portrayed is entirely different. Thus in an English *rebus* a person becoming "pale" with fear may be indicated by a picture of a "pail." Similarly in Egyptian the sign for "duck" could also represent "son," because in both cases the word was pronounced *sa*. The Sumerian city of Girsu was spelled by a picture of a dagger (*gir*) followed by a piece of hide or skin (*su*).

Both in Sumerian and in Egyptian there was a very early development of this rebus principle, so that the writing system became equipped with a large number of signs that could convey syllabic sounds, independent of meaning, and thus furnish building blocks for words of two or more syllables. Naturally the number of signs necessary to indicate all possible syllables that could occur in the spoken language was very numerous indeed. Both Egyptian and Sumerian writing retained both ideograms and syllabic phonograms right to the end of their history. Moreover, both languages used signs known as *determinatives*, which had no sound value at all but simply indicated the class of object referred to. In Sumerian the name of a city would often be preceded by the sign for "city" (even though it was not to be pronounced aloud as a separate word); similarly a star (standing for *dingir*, or "god") would precede the name of any deity. On the other hand, these determinatives could follow the rest of the word, rather than precede it; thus the Sumerian name of Babylon was written *ka-dingir-ra KI*. The first element, *ka*, was an ideogram for "gate"; *dingir* was an ideogram for "god"; and *ra*

This terra-cotta foundation peg, mentioning a treaty between the Sumerian king Entemena and the king of Uruk, is a very ancient example of cuneiform writing (c. 2400 B.C.).

© Dr. James C. Martin. The British Museum. Photographed by permission.

was a phonogram indicating that *dingir* ended in an *r* sound and was followed by the genitive particle *-a(k)*; the final *KI* was the sign for "earth" or "land" and served simply as a determinative.

Observe that in this last example the Sumerian name for BABYLON (or Babylonia) means "The Gate of God." When the Semitic-speaking Akkadians and Babylonians conquered the Mesopotamian valley, they took over the writing system of the Sumerians and adapted it to their own language. See ASSYRIA; SEMITE. In some cases they took the Sumerian ideograms and gave them the pronunciation of the appropriate words in their own language. Thus the Babylonian for "gate" was *babum* ("gate of" being pronounced *bab*); the word for "god" was *ilu* (in the genitive *ili*). Hence the very same signs that the Sumerians pronounced as *ka-dingirrak* the Babylonians pronounced as *bab-ili* (which came into Hebrew as *Babel*). Operating on this principle the Babylonians contrived ways of expressing all the necessary sounds in their own language. They would either use the Sumerian phonograms to express the same sound in Akkadian (the language spoken by the Babylonians and Assyrians), or else they would assign new sound values to them. Thus the Sumerian word for "wood" or "tree" was *gish* and was written by four wedges forming a rectangle; the corresponding Akkadian word was *isu*. Hence in Akkadian the sign could furnish the phonetic syllable *gish* (as it did in Sumerian) or else the syllable *is* (derived from the Akkadian word), as for example in the word *is-su-ru* "bird." Thus it was by ingenious adaptation that the Sumerian system of writing was taken over by a nation speaking an entirely different language, and it was used—still in mixed ideographic and phonographic form—to give written expression to their Semitic tongue.

Incidentally, if ABRAHAM's family was residing in UR back in the twentieth century B.C., this would have coincided with the brilliant Sumerian culture that flourished under the 3rd dynasty of Ur. It is quite possible not only that he would have learned both to speak and to read Sumerian but also that this was the only type of writing that he knew about, apart from any writing he encountered during the time he lived in Egypt.

Clay tablet with envelope from S Mesopotamia (late 2nd millennium B.C.). Some differences in cuneiform signs distinguished northern and southern forms of writing in ancient Mesopotamia.

© Dr. James C. Martin

The Egyptian system of writing, at least on its monuments, remained in an artistic pictorial form from its earliest rise about 3000 B.C. until its slow demise in the Roman period, 3,200 years later. Its characters never degenerated into combinations of wedges bearing little resemblance to the original pictographs, as was the case in Sumerian and Akkadian. Of course Egyptian was also (at least as early as the 6th dynasty) written in a cursive, hieratic (abridged) form, especially in business documents, correspondence, and secular literature. But apart from esthetic considerations, Egyptian writing developed peculiarities of its own that were quite different from the Sumerian-Akkadian system. In the first place, it recorded only the consonants of the spoken language, not its vowels. Some of these consonants were like the so-called vowel letters of Hebrew, Aramaic, and Arabic (e.g., ʾaleph or glottal stop, the *y* indicating an *i* sound, and the *w* indicating a *u* sound). On the other hand, the transcriptions of Egyptian names into Akkadian cuneiform and into Greek furnish important evidence as to how Egyptian was vocalized, and these transcriptions do not come out to any consistent pattern of correspondence with these Egyptian "vowel letters." Neither is there any standard relationship between them and their descendants in the Coptic language (which was written in the Greek alphabet and preserved the form of Egyptian as it was spoken in the early Christian centuries). And so it must be recognized that Egyptian hieroglyphic is essentially as consonantal as were the Semitic languages that used the Phoenician alphabet.

A second noteworthy contrast between Egyptian and Sumerian is that it developed genuine alphabetic signs, as well as two-consonant (or three-consonant) syllabic signs. Therefore to the Egyptians goes the credit for being the first to develop an alphabetic system of writing. However, they did not see any need to abandon their ideograms, determinative signs, and syllabic characters just because they had alphabetic letters; and so they simply used all four types of signs in the writing out of their language. Even the more cursive, shorthand type of writing referred to above as *hieratic* introduced virtually no changes in this complicated and cumbersome system; it simply enabled the scribe to write out his four kinds of hieroglyphic signs with a fair degree of rapidity. The same was true of a still more cursive and simplified form of hieratic known as *demotic*, used after 1000 B.C. Not until Egypt was conquered by ALEXANDER THE GREAT (about 332) did the influence of a foreign system of writing make a decisive impact on Egyptian conservatism. By the third century A.D. (the period of the earliest Coptic glosses in the Oxyrhynchus Papyri) the Egyptians were writing out their vernacular, vowels and all, in the letters of the Greek alphabet, to which they soon added seven more alphabetic signs of their own invention, to represent sounds not found in Greek.

The fact that the Egyptians did develop a full set of alphabetic signs had led some scholars to conclude that the most primitive form of the so-called Phoenician alphabet consisted of modifications of various Egyptian consonantal or syllabic signs. See PHOENICIA. This was a reasonable inference, perhaps, but no convincing list of correspondences could be made up by even the most ingenious advocates of this theory. The true origin of the "Phoenician" alphabet is to be sought rather in the alphabetic hieroglyphs of the Sinaitic inscriptions of Serabit el-Khadim (written some time between 1900 and 1500 B.C.). Since they were inscribed by Semitic miners in the employ of Egypt, and since these documents are found side by side with Egyptian hieroglyphic inscriptions (on statues dedicated to the goddess Hathor), it is fair to conclude that these miners got the idea for their alphabet from the Egyptians themselves. But instead of resorting to ideograms and syllabic signs, they contented themselves with alphabetic symbols chosen on the basis of *acrophony*, whereby the first sound of the name of the object represented conveyed the alphabetic unit intended. In Egyptian a sign for "hand" was used as the alphabetic sign for *d*, since the word for "hand" was *dert*. Following this principle, the Semitic miner chose the picture of a hand extended as a sign for *y* (since the word for "hand" was *yadu* in his language). The head of an ox was used for the sound of ʾ*aleph* (the glottal stop) because the word for "ox" was ʾ*alpu* (a name that was preserved in the later Hebrew ʾ*aleph* and in the still later Greek *alpha*). Interestingly enough, this particular letter has been quite well preserved from 1900

B.C. until the present, for if our capital A is turned upside down, it bears a fairly close similarity to that ancient Sinaitic sign for ʾ*aleph*, the ox's head.

During the ensuing centuries this Sinaitic type of script (or modifications of it) was cultivated in CANAAN, for household objects like daggers, rings, ewers, pots, and plaques have been found with short inscriptions, mostly of very uncertain interpretation. But a totally different form of alphabetic writing assumed great importance during this period (1800-1400 B.C.), namely the cuneiform alphabet associated with RAS SHAMRA, ancient Ugarit. Unlike the cuneiform of Babylonia and Assyria, this kind of cuneiform represented an alphabet of about twenty-nine or thirty characters, all of them consonantal (except that three of them indicated the type of vowel occurring after ʾ*aleph*, whether *a*, *i* [or *e*], or *u*). This very early dialect of Canaanite (for Ugaritic seems much closer to biblical Hebrew than to any other known Semitic language) contained several consonants not appearing in any of the NW Semitic scripts; in some cases the sounds are still preserved only in Arabic.

The shapes of characters formed by these wedges bear no consistent similarity to the signs either of Sinaitic letters or the Akkadian syllabary. They are very simple in structure and seem to have no pictographic origin whatever. This type of alphabet flourished not only at Ugarit but also in more southerly localities as well. But after the violent destruction of Ras Shamra in the fifteenth century B.C., the use of the Ugaritic alphabet seems to have declined in favor of the Phoenician.

Several so-called Proto-Phoenician inscriptions have been discovered in Palestinian localities such as GEZER, LACHISH, and SHECHEM, exhibiting forms that could be transitional between the Sinaitic and the authentic Phoenician of the eleventh century B.C. Unfortunately, however, these short lines of writing do not fall into a consistent pattern, and they cannot be deciphered with real certainty. As to the earliest Phoenician inscriptions—those of Shaphatbaal and Ahiram found at GEBAL (Byblos) on the coast N of SIDON—there is still much dispute as to the time when they were written.

The inscription on the sarcophagus (stone coffin) of King Ahiram is dated by various authorities from before 1250 to as late as 1000. This

W

writing has the twenty-two-letter alphabet that was to hold the stage from then on in all the NW Semitic languages (Phoenician, Hebrew, Moabite, and other Canaanite dialects, as well as Aramaic, including its later dialect, Syriac). The earliest Israelite document that has survived in this script is the Gezer Calendar of about 900 B.C. or a few decades earlier. It is a small limestone tablet inscribed with the irregular hand of a schoolboy and containing a list of the successive phases of the agricultural year from season to season. The discovery of this schoolboy's exercise witnesses to the extent of literacy in the reign of SOLOMON. Unfortunately we have no documents from an earlier period to serve as a reliable guide, but it is most likely that MOSES used a Proto-Phoenician type of script rather than any kind of cuneiform (although the use of Akkadian cuneiform for international correspondence is well attested for the time of JOSHUA in PALESTINE). Even in the AMARNA correspondence—which consists of letters in Akkadian addressed by Canaanite princes to the Egyptian court—there were numerous glosses (or explanatory synonyms) in Canaanite or Hebrew, written out in Akkadian cuneiform syllabic signs. Hence this type of writing would also have been known to Moses and available to him. See HEBREW LANGUAGE.

The next important Hebrew inscription after the Gezer Calendar was the SILOAM inscription, incised on the wall of the underground tunnel dug through to the Pool of Siloam in preparation (probably) for the siege of JERUSALEM by SENNACHERIB in 701 B.C. Here we see a trend toward the more freely flowing style of manuscript writing, rather than the stern angularity of monumental style. In particular some of the long-tailed letters (like *mem, nun,* and *kaph*) curve with a bottom swoop to the left. Examples of the rapid brush-stroked type of script are furnished by the Samaritan ostraca of about 770 (containing tax receipts paid to the government of JEROBOAM II; see SAMARIA) and the LACHISH ostraca of 588. These last consist of letters written by the captain of a Jewish outpost to Yaosh, commander of ZEDEKIAH's troops in Lachish. Here the letters are formed in a very compressed or flattened form, but they are still of essentially the same pattern as the old Phoenician.

This Egyptian funerary stela from Thebes (limestone, c. 1800 B.C.) illustrates hieroglyphic writing.

© Dr. James C. Martin. The Cairo Museum. Photographed by permission.

Following the Babylonian exile, this Paleo-Hebrew script (as it is called) was retained for some types of text, such as the books of the PENTATEUCH, for fragments of Leviticus and Exodus have been discovered in the Qumran Caves, dating from the late fourth century B.C. (according to the estimate of some scholars). See DEAD SEA SCHOLARS. The Samaritan sect, which originated from the schism of 535 (when Zerubbabel refused to allow the Samaritan heretics to participate in rebuilding the temple at Jerusalem), for some reason developed a special form of this Paleo-Hebrew script all their own; moreover, they retained it for all their religious literature down through the time of the Muslim conquest and even to this day. Paleo-Hebrew was employed on Jewish coinage of the Maccabean period (second century B.C.; see MACCABEE) and also of the First and Second Revolts (A.D. 67-70 and 132-135). The ARAMAIC-speaking peoples of DAMASCUS, HAMATH, and parts N used pretty much the same style of alphabet, although with minor regional peculiarities.

The so-called Square Hebrew character seems to have developed first on Aramaic soil, possibly during the sixth century B.C. Yet early examples of this script are regrettably sparse, and it remains impossible to trace its rise and development very much prior to the second century B.C. At all events it does not seem to have derived from the epistolary cursive of the Elephantine Papyri (400 B.C.), a set of legal documents and letters written in Aramaic by Jewish mercenaries stationed on an island near the southern border of Egypt. It was an extremely cursive script, but still bore stronger affinity to the Paleo-Hebrew than the Square Hebrew of the Dead Sea Caves.

It is important to observe that the Greeks received their alphabet from the Phoenicians and Arameans, perhaps through contact with their merchants. Through the investigations of Michael Ventris and his colaborers it has now been quite well established that Cretan Linear B, used in Crete during the latter half of the second millennium B.C., consisted of a syllabary somewhat similar to the syllabic writing used in ancient times on the island of CYPRUS. It was an independent invention, so far as we know, and has no relation to any system of writing used in the Semitic lands. The inscriptions themselves were written in a sort of Mycenean dialect of Greek. But these constituted an isolated development without any lasting influence on later times. See GREEK LANGUAGE.

Apart from these special developments in Crete and Cyprus, the Hellenic tribal groups found written expression for their language through the Phoenician alphabet, which supplied the first twenty-two letters of the Greek alphabet (i.e., *alpha* through *tau*). Those Semitic letters that expressed sounds not used by the Greeks were adapted to express vowels. For example, the sign representing a glottal stop, ʾ*aleph*, was used to convey the sound of the vowel *a*; the Semitic *y* of *yod* was simplified to a single vertical stroke as the letter *i* or *iota*; the letter representing the guttural sound Semitic ʿ*ayin* was adapted to express the sound of *o*. The Greeks added new letters, such as the *phi* (at first pronounced liked *ph* in "uphill," but later sounded like *f*) and the *psi* (which rendered the consonant cluster *p-s* as in "capsule").

This, then, was the writing medium that in the providence of God came to be used to convey the message of redemption that is found in the NT Scriptures. From the Western form of the Greek alphabet the Romans derived their Latin alphabet, omitting from it those letters used by the Eastern Greeks that were unnecessary to express the sounds of the Latin tongue. It is this alphabet, therefore, that has descended to us at the present day, ultimately derived from the Semites of the Holy Land.

Wycliffe. See BIBLE VERSIONS, ENGLISH.

Xerxes. zuhrk´seez (Heb. *ʾăḥašwērôš H347*, from Pers. *ḫšayāršā*, possibly "mighty man"; called *Xerxēs* by Gk. writers). KJV and other versions transliterate the Hebrew and read AHASUERUS. (1) Father of DARIUS the Mede (Dan. 9:1).

(2) Son of DARIUS I (Hystaspes) the Great, and ruler of PERSIA (c. 486-465 B.C.; Ezra 4:6; Esth. 1:1 and frequently throughout this book). Xerxes was a man of weak abilities and given to unfortunate reliance upon the advice and opinions of courtiers and harem eunuchs. After suppressing the revolt in EGYPT with great violence and destruction, he levied a navy from EGYPT and his Greek allies, and began to formulate plans to invade Attica. His Phoenician subjects ferried his army across the Hellespont on a double bridge of boats and from there the Persian forces, made up of contingents from nearly fifty nations, marched S and captured ATHENS. However, the tide of war turned swiftly when Xerxes' great fleet was annihilated at the subsequent naval battle of Salamis in 480 B.C., and Xerxes again exhibited his insecurity of character by putting his Phoenician admiral to death and causing the desertion of his naval forces. His commander in Greece, Mardonius, negotiated with Athens to no avail. The war was resumed and Persia was finally defeated at the battle of Plataea in 479/8. The Athenians and many newly won deserters from Persia followed up their success by invading the area of the Eurymedon River, thus ending Persia's hopes for European conquest. The Persian king retired to his palaces at PERSEPOLIS and SUSA, which he expanded and decorated in colossal and ornate style. Of great interest is his religious enthusiasm, for unlike his predecessors he did not accept the validity of the archaic religious cults of Egypt and Babylon but destroyed them both. His inscriptions from Persepolis proclaim his destruction of the temples of the false gods in his dominions and his faithfulness to the deity Ahuram Mazda. The essential personality of Xerxes as presented by Herodotus and his own inscriptions is very similar to that demonstrated in the Bible (see ESTHER, BOOK OF). The career of Xerxes was the preliminary to the collapse of the Achaemenid house under ALEXANDER THE GREAT's conquest.

Yahweh. See JEHOVAH.

Yahweh, day of. See DAY OF THE LORD.

yard. For the sense "courtyard," see TEMPLE. As a unit of measurement, the term is used sometimes in modern versions as the approximate equivalent of two cubits (cf. NIV, Josh. 3:4; Neh. 3:13; Jn. 21:8). See WEIGHTS AND MEASURES (sect. I).

Yarmuk. yahr´muhk. Although not mentioned in the Bible, the Yarmuk has played an important role as the northernmost of the four main rivers in TRANSJORDAN (the others being the JABBOK, the ARNON, and furthest S the ZERED). Sometimes referred to as Canaan's "second river" (after

the JORDAN), the Yarmuk is about 50 mi. (80 km.) long, intermittently draining the BASHAN plateau and cutting a canyon to the Jordan, which it equals at their confluence some 4 mi. (6 km.) S of the Sea of Galilee. Though the scene of a major Muslim triumph against the Byzantine empire in A.D. 636, as well as a current boundary for Israel, Syria, and Jordan, the Yarmuk rarely formed a cultural-historical divide, being renowned rather for therapeutic springs and irrigation.

yarn. A strand of fibers used mainly in weaving and knitting. The term is used by modern English versions (esp. in Exod. 25-28 and 35-39) not as the rendering of a Hebrew word but as an aid in translation. Thus, in the description of the curtains

The Yarmuk River is partly visible in this aerial photograph, just right of center. (View to the S.)

© Dr. James C. Martin

of the TABERNACLE, where the KJV says that they should be made of "fine twined linen, and blue, and purple, and scarlet," the NIV has, "of finely twisted linen and blue, purple and scarlet yarn" (26:1). (The KJV has "linen yarn" in 1 Ki. 10:28 and 2 Chr. 1:16, but the Hebrew form is now understood to mean "from Kue.")

year. See CALENDAR.

yeast. See LEAVEN.

YHWH. See JEHOVAH.

Yiron. See IRON (PLACE).

yod, yodh. yohd (Heb. *yôd*, alternate form of *yād* H3338, "hand"). KJV *jod*. The tenth letter of the Hebrew alphabet (י), with a numerical value of ten. It is named for the shape of the letter, which in its older form resembled the outline of a hand. Its sound corresponds to that of English *y*; in addition, it was used to represent vocalic sounds (*i*, *ê*) prior to the introduction of vowel signs, and this practice was later continued.

yoke. A piece of timber or a heavy wooden pole, shaped to fit over the neck with curved pieces of wood around the neck fastened to the pole, and used to hitch together a team of oxen (or other draft animals) so that they could pull heavy loads evenly. In the Bible, the term is most often used metaphorically to designate a burden, obligation, or SLAVERY (Gen. 27:40; 1 Sam. 11:7; Isa. 58:6, 9; Nah. 1:13; Matt. 11:29; Lk. 14:19; Acts 15:10). When Yahweh delivered Israel from Egyptian slavery, he said, "I broke the bars of your yoke and enabled you to walk with heads held high" (Lev. 26:13; cf. Deut. 28:48). The term is used of affliction and oppression (Lam. 3:27; Isa. 9:4; cf. 10:27), or describe the burden of a person's transgression and its punishment (Lam. 1:14). In the NT the term can also refer to slavery (1 Tim. 6:1), but more significant is the application of the metaphor to the OT LAW, especially CIRCUMCISION (Acts 15:10; . Gal. 5:1). Probably alluding to the use of this figure in JUDAISM with reference to WISDOM (Sir. 51:26), Jesus said: "Take my yoke upon you and learn from me, for I am gentle and humble in heart, and you will find rest for your souls. For my yoke is easy and my burden is light" (Matt. 11:29-30). The Mosaic law forbade the yoking of an ox and a donkey together (Deut. 22:10) because of the inequality of the work, and this rubric no doubt is the source of the familiar mandate of the apostle that Christians should not be "yoked together with unbelievers" (2 Cor. 6:14). See also YOKEFELLOW.

yokefellow. After pleading with EUODIA and SYNTYCHE "to agree with each other in the Lord," PAUL adds, "Yes, and I ask you, loyal yokefellow, help these women …" (Phil. 4:3). The Greek word is *syzygos* G5187, an adjective that literally means "yoked, paired together," but that can also be used, as here, substantively and figuratively, "a person that is joined to another one." In classical literature it is at times equivalent to "wife," and thus some have suggested that the apostle was referring to his own spouse. Others have thought that here the word is a proper name, Syzygus, but evidence is lacking. Most interpreters understand the term in its common figurative sense of "companion" or "comrade," and numerous suggestions have been made in regard to the identity of the person (Luke, Lydia, Epaphroditus, Barnabas, Silas, Timothy). Perhaps it was a way of describing the leader of the church at PHILIPPI.

Yom Kippur. See ATONEMENT, DAY OF.

youth. The ancient concepts of childhood and youth were imprecise. No term exists in Hebrew or Greek for adolescence or puberty as such. Generally a woman is styled a "maiden" (see MAID, MAIDEN) until marriage, regardless of age, and a man is a youth from infancy to manhood (sometime in his twenties). A variety of Hebrew terms are rendered "youth" or the like in the various English versions. See also CHILD.

Zaanaim. See ZAANANNIM.

Zaanan. zay´uh-nan (Heb. *ṣaʾănān H7367*, possibly "place of flocks"). A town against which MICAH prophesied (Mic. 1:11). The imprecation refers to various locations mostly in the SHEPHELAH, and therefore Zaanan is generally considered to be the same as ZENAN (Josh. 15:37).

Zaanannim. zay´uh-na´nim (Heb. *ṣaʿănannîm H7588*, meaning unknown). A place near HELEPH on the S border of the tribe of NAPHTALI known for being the site of a large tree (Josh. 19:33); it was here, not far from KEDESH, that HEBER the Kenite pitched his tent (Jdg. 4:11 [KJV, "Zaanaim"]; his wife, JAEL, killed SISERA in this tent, vv. 17-21). Following the SEPTUAGINT reading in Joshua, some have identified Zaanannim with Khirbet Bessum, 3 mi. (5 km.) NE of TABOR, but several other proposals have been made. The NRSV apparently interprets the two biblical references as indicating different places, for in Joshua it reads, "the oak in Zaanannim," but in Judges, "Elon-bezaanannim" (the latter is the rendering of NJPS in both passages).

Zaavan. zay´uh-vuhn (Heb. *zaʿăwān H2401*, perhaps related to *zaʿăwâ H2400*, "trembling, terror"). Son of EZER and grandson of SEIR the HORITE; he probably became the progenitor of a clan in EDOM (Gen. 36:27; 1 Chr. 1:42 [KJV, "Zavan"]).

Zabad. zay´bad (Heb. *zābād H2274*, "gift" or "[God/Yahweh] has bestowed" [cf. ZABDIEL,

One proposal for the location of Zaanannim is on the plain just SW of the Sea of Galilee. (View to the N.)

© Dr. James C. Martin

ZEBADIAH]). **(1)** Son of Nathan and descendant of JUDAH through JERAHMEEL and ATTAI (1 Chr. 2:36-37); perhaps the same as ZABUD (1 Ki. 4:5).

(2) Son of Tahath and descendant of EPHRAIM (1 Chr. 7:21). Some believe that the genealogy in this passage is textually corrupt. See BERED (PERSON).

(3) Son of AHLAI; he is included among DAVID's mighty warriors (1 Chr. 11:41).

(4) Son of an Ammonite woman named SHIMEATH; he was one of two men who assassinated King Joash/JEHOASH (2 Chr. 24:26). The parallel passage (2 Ki. 12:21) reads differently. See JEHOZABAD.

(5-7) The name of three Israelites—respectively descendants of Zattu, Hashum, and Nebo—who agreed to put away their foreign wives (Ezra 10:27, 33, 43).

Zabbai. zab´i (Heb. *zabbay H2287*, possibly short form of ZEBIDAH, "given, bestowed"). **(1)** One of the descendants of Bebai who agreed to put away their foreign wives (Ezra 10:28).

(2) Father of a certain BARUCH who helped to repair the wall of JERUSALEM (Neh. 3:20; here the *Qere* has ZACCAI).

Zabbud. See ZACCUR.

Zabdi. zab´di (Heb. *zabdi H2275*, "my gift" or short form of a name such as ZABDIEL, "gift of God"). **(1)** Son of Zerah, descendant of JUDAH, and grandfather of ACHAN (Josh. 7:1, 17-18, KJV and other versions). On the basis of the SEPTUAGINT, and of 1 Chr. 2:6-7, some scholars read ZIMRI (cf. NIV).

(2) Son of Shimei and descendant of BENJAMIN (1 Chr. 8:19). He is included among the heads of families who lived in JERUSALEM (v. 28).

(3) A SHIPHMITE who "was in charge of the produce of the vineyards for the wine vats" during the reign of DAVID (1 Chr. 27:27).

(4) Son of ASAPH and ancestor of MATTANIAH; the latter was a postexilic LEVITE who led in worship (Neh. 11:17; apparently called ZACCUR in 1 Chr. 25:2 et al., and ZICRI in 1 Chr. 9:15).

Zabdiel. zab´dee-uhl (Heb. *zabdi'el H2276*, "gift of God" or "my gift is God"). **(1)** Father of JASHO-

BEAM; the latter was a military officer under DAVID in charge of the first division (1 Chr. 27:2).

(2) Son of HAGGEDOLIM; he was chief officer of the priests in the days of NEHEMIAH (Neh. 11:14).

Zabud. zay´buhd (Heb. *zābûd H2280*, "bestowed"). Son of Nathan; he is described as "a priest and personal adviser to the king [SOLOMON]" (1 Ki. 4:5). Some identify Zabud with ZABAD #1; see comments under NATHAN #4.

Zabulon. See ZEBULUN.

Zaccai. zak´i (Heb. *zakkay H2347*, "pure, innocent"; cf. ZACCHAEUS). TNIV Zakkai. **(1)** Ancestor of a family of 760 members who returned from the EXILE (Ezra 2:9; Neh. 7:14).

(2) See ZABBAI #2.

Zacchaeus. za-kee´uhs (Gk. *Zakchaios G2405*, from Heb. *zakkay H2347*, "pure, innocent"; see ZACCAI). Also Zaccheus. A publican or tax collector, referred to only in the Gospel of Luke (Lk. 19:1-10). When Jesus was passing through JERICHO on one occasion, Zacchaeus, a wealthy man who was the chief tax collector in that important city, wished very much to see him. Being short, he climbed a tree by the side of the path. He must have been quite surprised, therefore, when Jesus paused in his journey beneath this very tree and, looking up, urged Zacchaeus to come down. Then he added: "I must stay at your house today" (v. 5). Zacchaeus must have been a district tax commissioner who had purchased the Jericho tax franchise from the Roman or provincial government; he then probably farmed it out to subordinate tax agents who did the actual tax collecting, all of them reaping huge commissions and getting rich off poor and wealthy alike. Jericho was known for its palm groves and balsam and was on the main load of traffic between major commercial centers both W of the Jordan (JOPPA, JERUSALEM) and in TRANSJORDAN. It was easy to amass a fortune there. It is possible he was one of the most hated men in Jericho, and it was natural that the people who witnessed the incident murmured against Jesus: "He has gone to be the guest of a 'sinner'" (v. 7).

Zacchaeus's life was completely transformed through Christ, however. Spontaneously and openly, he confessed the sins of his evil life. His words reveal what his sin was: "Look, Lord! Here and now I give half of my possessions to the poor" (Lk. 19:8). Moreover, because he knew that he had not gotten all his wealth through just means—and how much had not his henchmen stolen from the people through misrepresentation, pressure, and extortion?—he added, "and if I have cheated anybody out of anything, I will pay back four times the amount." According to the law he offered twice the restitution which thieves must make under Jewish law (Exod. 22:1; Num. 5:6). Jesus' pronouncement of remission—"Today salvation has come to this house, because this man, too, is a son of Abraham" (Lk. 19:9)—shows that Zacchaeus should now be regarded as a child of the promise, and that the blessings of ABRAHAM were fulfilled in the forgiving Christ even for those who by their profession were considered heathen (Matt. 18:17).

Zaccheus. See ZACCHAEUS.

Zaccur. zak'uhr (Heb. *zakkûr* H2346, possibly "[God is] mindful"). KJV also Zacchur (1 Chr. 4:26); TNIV Zakkur. (1) Father of SHAMMUA; the latter was one of the spies sent out by MOSES (Num. 13:4).

(2) Son of Hammuel and descendant of SIMEON (1 Chr. 4:26). Some interpret the Hebrew to mean that Zaccur, Hammuel, and Shimei were all sons of MISHMA.

(3) Son of Jaaziah and descendant of LEVI through MERARI (1 Chr. 24:27).

(4) One of the sons of ASAPH who assisted their father in the prophetic ministry of MUSIC; he was the head of the third company of temple musicians appointed by lot under DAVID (1 Chr. 25:2, 10). This Zaccur is apparently the same as ZABDI #4 and ZICRI #5. A descendant of his named Zechariah played the trumpet at the dedication of the wall in postexilic Jerusalem (Neh. 12:35).

(5) A descendant of BIGVAI, part of the company that traveled with EZRA from Babylon to Jerusalem (Ezra 8:14; KJV has ZABBUD following the *Ketib*). See also UTHAI.

(6) Son of Imri; he was one of those who helped NEHEMIAH rebuild the wall of Jerusalem (Neh. 3:2).

(7) A Levite who signed Nehemiah's covenant (Neh. 10:12).

(8) Son of Mattaniah and father of Hanan; the latter was appointed by Nehemiah as assistant to those who were in charge of the temple storerooms (Neh. 13:13).

Zachariah, Zacharias. See ZECHARIAH.

Zacher. See ZEKER.

Zacchur. See ZACCUR.

Zadok. zay'dok (Heb. *ṣādôq* H7401, prob. "righteous"; Gk. *Sadōk* G4882). (1) Son of AHITUB, descendant of LEVI (through KOHATH, AARON, and ELEAZAR), and father of AHIMAAZ (1 Chr. 6:8 [Heb. 5:34]); he was a leading priest during the reigns of DAVID and SOLOMON. He is first mentioned—along with another priest, AHIMELECH son of ABIATHAR—in a list of David's officers (2 Sam. 8:17; cf. 20:25). When David fled from ABSALOM, Zadok started to accompany him, taking along the ARK OF THE COVENANT, but David ordered him to return to JERUSALEM (15:24-29). Zadok always showed unswerving loyalty to David, and his son Ahimaaz served as a courier in the time of conflict (15:36; 17:17-20; 18:19, 22, 27). After the defeat of Absalom, Zadok and Abiathar were bearers of a message encouraging the elders of JUDAH to bring David back to Jerusalem (2 Sam. 19:11-14). These two priests served jointly until the end of David's reign, with Zadok for a time having special responsibility for the worship at the tabernacle in GIBEON (1 Chr. 16:39). When David was close to death, however, Abiathar lent his support to ADONIJAH, whereas Zadok refused to do so (1 Ki. 1:7-8). David then instructed Zadok and other leaders to crown Solomon as king (vv. 32-35), and Zadok himself anointed David's successor (v. 39). As Solomon proceeded to secure his throne, he deposed Abiathar from the priesthood (1 Ki. 2:26-27, 35), thus fulfilling the dire prediction about the house of ELI (1 Sam. 2:27-36). Because of Zadok's prominence during the reign of Solomon, subsequent high priests were chosen only from the Zadokite line. It is significant that in Ezekiel the term "sons of Zadok" is used four times as a designation for the priests (Ezek. 40:46; 43:19; 44:15; 48:11). During the Maccabean and later period, the legitimacy of the Zadokite priesthood played a major role in politics and religion. See further ESSENE; MACCABEE; SADDUCEE.

(2) Son of Ahitub II, descendant of #1 above, and father of SHALLUM (1 Chr. 6:12 [Heb. 5:38]; cf. Ezra 7:2). Because the father and grandfather of this second Zadok bear the same names as those of the first Zadok, some propose that a scribe might at some time have inadvertently copied the same line twice. Elsewhere a Zadok is identified as son of MERAIOTH, grandson of Ahitub, and father of MESHULLAM (1 Chr. 9:11; Neh. 11:11); since Meshullam is likely a variant of Shallum, this lineage probably refers to Zadok II, but some argue that it refers to Zadok I (in which case Ahitub I was his grandfather, not his father).

(3) Father of Jerusha; the latter was the wife of King UZZIAH and mother of King JOTHAM (2 Ki. 15:33; 2 Chr. 27:1).

(4) Son of Baana; he made repairs to a portion of the wall of Jerusalem (Neh. 3:4). He should probably be identified with the Israelite who signed the covenant of NEHEMIAH (10:21; a certain MESHEZABEL is mentioned next to Zadok in both passages).

(5) Son of Immer; he made repairs to the wall of Jerusalem opposite his house (Neh. 3:29).

(6) A scribe whom Nehemiah appointed as one of three men in charge of the storerooms in the temple (Neh. 13:13). Perhaps he should be identified with #4 or #5 above.

(7) Son of Azor, included in Matthew's GENEALOGY OF JESUS CHRIST (Matt. 1:14; KJV, "Sadoc").

Zahab. See WAHEB.

Zaham. zay´ham (Heb. *zaham H2300*, perhaps derived from *zāham H2299*, "to be repulsive"). Son of King REHOBOAM by Mahalath (2 Chr. 11:19).

zain. See ZAYIN.

Zair. zay´uhr (Heb. *ṣāʿir H7583*, possibly "small" or "narrow [path]"). The name of a place where King JEHORAM (Joram) confronted an army from EDOM, which had rebelled against JUDAH (2 Ki. 8:21). The Hebrew text is ambiguous: it can be interpreted to mean that Judah won the battle and that it was the Edomites who fled; on the other hand, we read that the Judean army was surrounded and that subsequently Edom continued in rebellion (v. 22). Modern versions usually understand the text to mean that Jehoram was in straits and attempted an attack, but that his own army fled. Instead of "to Zair," the parallel passage reads, "with his commanders" (2 Chr. 21:9). If the reference to Zair is authentic, the place has never been identified. Proposals include ZIOR (cf. Josh. 15:14), ZOAR (Gen. 13:10 et al.), and SEIR (Gen. 14:6 et al.). It seems likely that the scene of the battle was SE of the DEAD SEA, which makes Zoar the most likely suggestion.

Zakkai. zak´i. TNIV form of ZACCAI.

Zakkur. zak´uhr. TNIV form of ZACCUR.

Zalaph. zay´laf (Heb. *ṣālāp H7523*, "caper" [a prickly shrub]). Father of HANUN; the latter assisted NEHEMIAH in repairing the wall of JERUSALEM (Neh. 3:30).

Zalmon (person). zal´mon (Heb. *ṣalmôn H7514*, possibly "[little] dark one"). An AHOHITE, included among DAVID's mighty warriors (2 Sam. 23:28; called ILAI in 1 Chr. 11:29).

Zalmon (place). zal´mon (Heb. *ṣalmôn H7515*, "black [mountain]"). (1) A mountain near SHECHEM where ABIMELECH and his men cut wood to burn down the stronghold of BAAL-BERITH (Jdg. 9:48). It has not been identified, but many scholars think the name may refer to one of the shoulders of either EBAL or GERIZIM.

(2) A region or mountain mentioned in a poetic passage: "When the Almighty scattered the kings in the land, / it was like snow fallen on Zalmon" (Ps. 68:14; KJV, "it was *white* as snow in Salmon"). The idea seems to be that the enemy and their weapons lay scattered like snowflakes, but the text can be interpreted in other ways. Although this Zalmon may be the same as #1 above, the context (v. 15) suggests that the reference is to a peak in

or near BASHAN, and some commentators identify it with Jebel Druze (c. 60 mi./100 km. SE of DAMASCUS); the mountains in this area are composed of dark volcanic rock and thus may account for the name.

Zalmonah. zal-moh′nuh (Heb. *ṣalmōnâ H7517*, perhaps "dark, gloomy"). The first encampment of the Israelites after leaving Mount HOR (Num. 33:41-42). Its location is unknown, though one possible suggestion is es-Salmaneh, some 22 mi. (35 km.) S of the DEAD SEA.

Zalmunna. See ZEBAH AND ZALMUNNA.

Zamzummim. See ZAMZUMMITES.

Zamzummites. zam-zuh′mits (Heb. *zamzummîm H2368*, possibly from *zāmam H2372*, "to murmur, plan"). Also Zamzummim. The AMMONITE name for the people otherwise called REPHAITES (Deut. 2:20). There is no consensus regarding the meaning or origin of this term, but it may be related to ZUZITES.

Zanoah. zuh-noh′uh (Heb. *zānôḥa H2391*, derivation uncertain). **(1)** A town in the N area of the SHEPHELAH, allotted to the tribe of JUDAH (Josh. 15:34). After the EXILE it was one of the centers where returning exiles settled (Neh. 11:30). When NEHEMIAH rebuilt the walls of JERUSALEM, the men of Zanoah under the leadership of one HANUN were responsible for the VALLEY GATE (3:13). It is generally identified with modern Khirbet Zanuᶜ, 14.5 mi. (23 km.) WSW of JERUSALEM. In the genealogy of Judah, there is mention of "Jekuthiel the father of Zanoah" (1 Chr. 4:18), usually interpreted to be a geographical reference ("father" meaning "founder" or the like). Some scholars believe that this Zanoah is the town in the N Shephelah, but the context (esp. the reference to Soco in the same verse) suggests a different locale; see #2 below.

(2) A town in the hill country of Judah, listed with a group of towns that were S of HEBRON (Josh. 15:56). Some have identified this Zanoah with Khirbet Zanuta (c. 10 mi./16 km. SW of

Hebron, prob. too far W), and others with Khirbet Beit ᶜAmra (just NW of JUTTAH), but neither site can be confirmed. It is likely that 1 Chr. 4:18 refers to this town.

Zaphenath-paaneah. See ZAPHENATH-PANEAH.

Zaphenath-Paneah. zaf′uh-nath-puh-nee′uh (Heb. *ṣopnat paᶜnēaḥ H7624*, meaning disputed). Also Zaphenath-paaneah. The hebraized form of the Egyptian name given to JOSEPH by PHARAOH (Gen. 41:45). Though the Hebrew must represent some transliterated Egyptian name, there is no certainty as to what that name may have been. A widely accepted explanation is that it means, "the god speaks and he lives," but other proposals have been made.

Zaphon. zay′fon (Heb. *ṣāpôn H7601*, "north"). **(1)** A town lying to the E of the JORDAN in the tribal territory of GAD (Josh. 13:27). It was the place where the Ephraimites gathered to meet with JEPHTHAH after he defeated the AMMONITES (Jdg. 12:1; KJV, "northward"). Zaphon is known in Egyptian records, but its location is uncertain. Perhaps the most likely identification is Tell es-Saᶜidiyeh (c. 6 mi./10 km. NW of SUCCOTH).

(2) A mountain near the mouth of the ORONTES River associated with the Canaanite god BAAL and mentioned frequently in Ugaritic literature (see CONGREGATION, MOUNT OF THE). Known to the Romans as Mons Casius, Mount Zaphon is identified with modern Jebel el-ᶜAqra. In several poetic passages in the Bible, it is unclear whether the word should be interpreted as a reference to this mountain or as the noun *ṣāpôn H7600*, "north." For example, the NIV renders Ps. 48:2, "Like the utmost heights of Zaphon is Mount Zion," but the NRSV has, "Mount Zion, in the far north" (cf. also Job 26:7 NRSV and Isa. 14:13 NRSV, TNIV).

Zara, Zarah. See ZERAH.

Zareah, Zareathite. See ZORAH.

Zared. See ZERED.

Z

Zarephath. zair´uh-fath (Heb. *ṣārĕpat H7673*, possibly from *ṣārap H7671*, "to refine"; Gk. *Sarepta G4919*). A Phoenician town to which God instructed ELIJAH to go during a time of drought (1 Ki. 17:9-10). While there, the prophet miraculously provided food for himself and for a widow and her son, and later he raised the son from the dead (vv. 11-24). Jesus referred to that incident as an illustration that "no prophet is accepted in his hometown" (Lk. 4:23-26). The prophet OBADIAH predicted that Israelite exiles would "possess the land as far as Zarephath" (Obad. 20). The city is mentioned in extrabiblical sources; it was a large commercial center, famous for fine glassware, ceramics, textiles, and purple dye. Zarephath is identified with the modern Arab village of Ṣarafand, which lies on a coastal promontory about 8 mi. (13 km.) SSW of Sidon and 13 mi. (21 km.) NNE of Tyre.

Zaretan. See ZARETHAN.

Zarethan. zair´uh-than (Heb. *ṣārētān H7681*, derivation uncertain). A town near Adam; in this vicinity the waters of the JORDAN stopped flowing so that the Israelites could cross the river (Josh. 3:16; KJV, "Zaretan"). See ADAM (PLACE). During the reign of SOLOMON, Zarethan was part of the fourth administrative district (1 Ki. 4:12), and it was in this area that the bronze objects for the TEMPLE were cast (7:46; in the parallel passage, 2 Chr. 4:17, the Hebrew form is *ṣĕrēdātâ* [with locative ending] and thus most English versions read ZEREDAH [KJV, "Zeredathah"], but this is probably a scribal error or an alternate form). The precise location of Zarethan is disputed. Because 1 Ki. 4:12 states that the town was "next to" BETH SHAN, some have looked for a location toward the N, such as Tell es-Saᶜidiyeh, which lies on the E side of the Jordan, some 6 mi. (10 km.) NW of SUCCOTH. Others, pointing out that this site is almost 12 mi. (19 km.) from Adam, prefer to identify Zarethan with Tell Umm Ḥamad, which is only about 3 mi. (5 km.) NE of Adam.

Zareth-shahar. See ZERETH SHAHAR.

Zarhites. See ZERAH.

Zartanah, Zarthan. See ZARETHAN.

Zatthu. See ZATTU.

Zattu. zat´oo (Heb. *zattû᾽ H2456*, derivation unknown). Ancestor of a family that returned to Jerusalem from Babylon with ZERUBBABEL (Ezra 2:8; 8:5; Neh. 7:13). Some members of this family had married foreign women and agreed to put them away (Ezra 10:27). One of the leaders of the people who signed the covenant of NEHEMIAH was named Zattu (Neh. 10:14 [KJV, "Zatthu"]), but it seems probable that here the head of the clan is being referred to by the family name.

Zavan. See ZAAVAN.

zayin. zah´yin (Heb. *zayin*, meaning uncertain; this name is not used in the Bible). The seventh letter of the Hebrew alphabet (ז), with a numerical value of seven. Its sound corresponds to that of English *z*.

Zaza. zay´zuh (Heb. *zāzā᾽ H2321*, derivation uncertain). Son of Jonathan and descendant of JUDAH through JERAHMEEL (1 Chr. 2:33).

zealot. A person characterized by much zeal, enthusiasm, or partisanship. The Greek noun *zēlōtēs G2421* means "enthusiastic adherent," and the NIV usually renders it with "zealous" or "eager" (e.g., Acts 21:20; 22:3; Gal. 1:14; et al.). When capitalized, however, the term Zealot refers to a violent Jewish sect in NT times that opposed Roman domination. The Jewish historian JOSEPHUS lists four sects or parties among the Jews: PHARISEES, SADDUCEES, ESSENES, and a "fourth philosophy" (*Ant.* 18.1.2-6 §§11-25). His description of this "fourth philosophy" is imprecise, but he attributes it to Judas the Galilean, who led a rebellion in A.D. 6 in response to a Roman-ordered census in the land of Israel (cf. Acts 5:37 and see JUDAS #2). It appears that about this time, a biblical interpretation arose that focused upon a new, particularistic emphasis on the KINGDOM OF GOD as concentrated upon Israel and Israel's encounter with the Roman emperor cult. Judas and his followers insisted that no Gentile king could reign over Israel. Violent resistance was the only proper response to foreign overlords. This was at the heart of pure Zealotism.

Often associated with the Zealots were the *Sicarii*. This name comes from Latin *sica*, a curved-shaped dagger (sickle), the weapon favored by these "terrorists" (the NIV rendering of *sikarios G4974* in Acts 21:38). They conducted a campaign of terror—kidnapping, extortion, robbery, and murder, especially against Romans and their sympathizers. The relation between the Sicarii and the Zealots is unclear. Just as there was a connection between the Zealots and Judas's fourth philosophy, the same is true for the Sicarii. With the exception of the battles at MASADA after the fall of JERUSALEM, the Sicarii are never depicted as participating in open conflict. It is possible that as long as this group operated as an undercover force they were designated as Sicarii, but then as Zealots when they joined in pitch battle. If this is true, then we have an aspect of the nature and activity of the Zealots not usually recognized.

In Josephus's writings the Zealots clearly become a discernible group under the leadership of John of Gischala, first in Galilee, and then in Jerusalem. Thus they, along with other groups, were the primary Jewish revolutionary factions in Jerusalem when TITUS began the siege of Jerusalem. These bands or gangs constantly fought each other, even when the Romans were literally at the gates. Although there were many simple folk who were devoted to God with ardent passion and practiced their religion with zeal, those depicted by Josephus as participants in the war of A.D. 66-70 represent zealotism at its worst—fanatical, head-strong, jealous, envious, factional groups, given to party strife. With the temple burned, Jerusalem destroyed, and the entire area in the hands of the Romans, Zealot soldiers were crucified or made to entertain their captors by fighting to the death in games; others were sold as slaves.

In what sense was the apostle Simon called "the Zealot"? He bears this description in Lk. 6:15 and Acts 1:13 (KJV, "Zelotes"), but in Matt. 10:4 and Mk. 6:18 he is designated as the CANANAEAN (NRSV; the NIV translates "Zealot" here as well). This may be an Aramaic word for "zealot" when it was not yet the technical term for the revolutionary party. Matthew and Mark thus avoid the term *zēlōtēs* to avoid confusion with the later revolutionaries. There is no indication that any of the gospel writers imply that Simon was a "Zealot" in the negative sense of the term. He may well have been a "pre-Zealot" who had a strong loyalty to his country. It is more likely, however, that even before his association with Jesus, Simon was simply "zealous" for the law and for God.

Zebadiah. zeb´uh-di´uh (Heb. *zĕbadyāhû H2278* and *zĕbadyâ H2277*, "Yahweh has bestowed"). **(1)** Son of Beriah and descendant of BENJAMIN (1 Chr. 8:15).

(2) Son of Elpaal and descendant of Benjamin (1 Chr. 18:17).

(3) Son of Jehoram from GEDOR; he and his brother Joelah were among the ambidextrous warriors who joined DAVID at ZIKLAG (1 Chr. 12:7).

(4) Son of MESHELEMIAH and descendant of LEVI through KORAH and ASAPH; like his father, he and his brothers were Levitical gatekeepers in the time of DAVID (1 Chr. 26:2).

(5) Son of ASAHEL and nephew of JOAB; he succeeded his father as commander in charge of the division for the fourth month under David (1 Chr. 27:7).

(6) One of six Levites whom King JEHOSHAPHAT sent to teach the law in the cities of Judah (2 Chr. 17:8). Appointed to the same mission were a number of princes and priests.

(7) Son of a certain Ishmael and head of the tribe of Judah during the reign of Jehoshaphat (2 Chr. 19:11).

(8) Son of Michael and descendant of Shephatiah; listed among those who returned from the EXILE in BABYLON to JERUSALEM with EZRA (Ezra 8:8).

(9) One of the two descendants of Immer who agreed to put away their foreign wives (Ezra 10:20).

Zebah and Zalmunna. zee´buh, zal-muhn´uh (Heb. *zebah H2286*, "[born at the time of] sacrifice," and *ṣalmunnāʿ H7518*, derivation uncertain, but perhaps understood to mean, "The Image protects"). Two Midianite kings defeated by GIDEON (Jdg. 8:4-21; Ps. 83:11). The bedouin from MIDIAN, E of the JORDAN, had been plundering the

Israelites and their crops with their camel raids (Jdg. 6:1-6), when the Lord raised up Gideon as a deliverer for Israel. Well known is the military blow which Gideon and his 300 men dealt the Midianite enemy (7:1-22). In the ensuing rout the Midianite princes OREB AND ZEEB were captured and killed by the Ephraimites (7:24-25). Gideon, in his pursuit of the Midianites and their two kings, Zebah and Zalmunna, crossed the Jordan near the JABBOK River, but was refused help by the people of the E MANASSEH areas in SUCCOTH and PENUEL (PLACE) (8.5-9). The two kings were eventually captured (8:10-13). After punishing the people of Succoth and Penuel for failing to help him (8:14-17), Gideon put Zebah and Zalmunna to death on the principle of blood revenge because they had killed his brothers. Psalm 83:11 indicates that both sets of officials, Oreb and Zeeb as well as Zebah and Zalmunna, were important in the conquest of Midian, the former pair possibly being chieftains subordinate to the two kings (cf. Jdg. 7:25 with 8:12).

Zebaim. zuh-bay´im. See POKERETH-HAZZEBAIM.

Zebedee. zeb´uh-dee (Grk. *Zebedaios G2411*, from Heb. *zĕbadyāhû H2278*, "Yahweh has bestowed"; see ZEBADIAH). A Galilean fisherman, father of the apostles James and John (Matt. 4:21; 10:2; Mk. 1:19-20; 3:17; 10:35; Lk. 5:10; Jn. 21:2). See JAMES I; JOHN THE APOSTLE. He was the husband of SALOME and in all probability lived in the vicinity of BETHSAIDA (Matt. 27:56; Mk. 15:40). Because of Mark's reference to his hired servants (Mk. 1:20), one would judge that he had been a man of means and influence. Our only glimpse of him in the Bible is with his sons in their boat mending their nets.

Zebidah. zuh-bi´duh (Heb. *zĕbîdâ H2288*, "bestowed"). Daughter of a certain Pedaiah (from the town of RUMAH), and mother of King JEHOIAKIM (2 Ki. 23:36; KJV and other versions, "Zebudah," following the *Qere*).

Zebina. zuh-bi´nuh (Heb. *zĕbînāʾ H2289*, "bought"). One of the descendants Nebo who agreed to put away their foreign wives (Ezra 10:43).

Zeboiim. zuh-boi´im (Heb. *ṣĕbōʾîm H7375* [with spelling variations], perhaps "[place of] hyenas"; see ZEBOIM]). TNIV Zeboyim. One of the CITIES OF THE PLAIN destroyed by God. It is first mentioned in the OT in reference to the southern border of the Canaanites that ran from the coast inland toward this city as well as SODOM, GOMORRAH, and ADMAH (Gen. 10:19). KEDORLAOMER king of Elam and his three allies attacked these towns during their raid along the ancient KING'S HIGHWAY (14:2). SHEMEBER king of Zeboiim and his allies met the invaders in the Valley of SIDDIM but were defeated (14:8, 10 [KJV, "Zeboim"]). Presumably Zeboiim was destroyed with Sodom and Gomorrah (Gen. 19:24-29; cf. Deut. 29:23; Hos. 11:8). Its exact location is unknown, but presumably it lay at the S end of the DEAD SEA in the area now covered by water.

Zeboim. zuh-boh´im (Heb. *ṣĕbōʿîm H7391*, "[place of] hyenas"). **(1)** A valley within the tribal territory of BENJAMIN, apparently SE of MICMASH (1 Sam. 13:18). PHILISTINE raiders from Micmash traveled the hill road overlooking the Valley of Zeboim with the JORDAN Valley beyond. In that general region there are some wadis that may preserve the meaning of the ancient name (e.g., Abu Ḍabaʿ, Arab. for "father of hyenas"), but the identification of the Valley of Zeboim itself remains uncertain.

(2) A town overlooking the Plain of SHARON; along with HADID, NEBALLAT, LOD, and ONO, Zeboim was settled by Benjamites after the EXILE (Neh. 11:34). The exact site is not known, though some have suggested Khirbet Sabiyeh, N of Lod.

Zeboyim. zuh-boh´yim. TNIV form of ZEBOIIM.

Zebudah. See ZEBIDAH.

Zebul. zee´buhl (Heb. *zĕbul H2291*, "elevation," possibly short form of a theophoric name such as "Baal's lofty dwelling"; some think that Baal-Zebul was the original form of the name BAAL-ZEBUB). Governor of SHECHEM in the days of ABIMELECH son of JERUB-BAAL, that is, GIDEON (Jdg. 9:30). Abimelech had been chosen king by a group of Canaanites in the city (vv. 1-6), and Zebul is referred to as his "deputy" (v. 28). According to the narrative, there was local opposition to Abimelech, and a certain GAAL uttered seditious words during a vintage festival saying that he would get rid of Abimelech (vv. 27-29). Zebul informed Abimelech and advised him to surround Shechem by night (vv. 30-33). In the morning Gaal sallied forth but was quickly routed, and Zebul kept him out of the city (vv. 39-41).

Zebulun. zeb´yuh-luhn (Heb. *zĕbûlûn H2282*, possibly by popular etymology, "honor, exaltation"; gentilic *zĕbûlōnî H2283*, "Zebulunite"; Gk. *Zaboulōn G2404*). KJV NT Zabulon. Tenth son of JACOB and sixth of LEAH (Gen. 30:19; 35:23), and ancestor of the tribe that bears his name. Zebulun was conceived in the context of the rivalry between Leah and RACHEL. When he was born, Leah said, "'This time my husband will treat me with honor [*yizbĕlēnî*; NJPS, will exalt me], because I have borne him six sons.' So she named him Zebulun" (Gen. 30:20; the verb *zābal H2290* occurs only here and its precise meaning is uncertain). Little else is recorded of Zebulun, though we read that his three sons were born before he left CANAAN for EGYPT (Gen. 46:14), where JOSEPH presented his brothers to PHARAOH (47:2). Jacob, in his final blessing, stated that Zebulun (through his descendants) would "live by the seashore / and become a haven for ships," and that the the border of the tribe would "extend toward Sidon" (49:13).

The tribe of Zebulun was subdivided into clans named after his sons, Sered, Elon, and Jahleel (Num. 26:26). GADDIEL son of Sodi was the representative from Zebulun named to help spy out Canaan (13:10), and ELIAB son of Helon was selected to assist MOSES in census-taking (1:9). The two counts, showing that there were 57,400 and 60,500 warriors at the beginning and end of the wanderings (1:31; 26:27), indicate that Zebulun was numerically fourth among the tribes. After Israel conquered Canaan, this tribe received the third allotment (Josh. 19:10-16). The Zebulunites received a northern region that was small, but fruitful and strategically located. The precise territorial boundaries are uncertain, but clear in general. Zebulun's S limit extended from an undetermined stream E of JOKNEAM across the N fringe of ESDRAELON and along the limestone scarp of

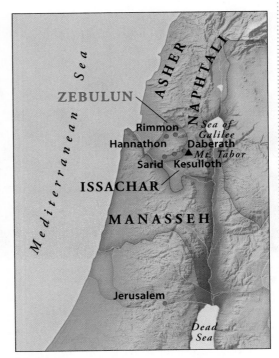

Zebulun.

NAZARETH to the slopes of Tabor. From there it turned irregularly northward, approximately following the Galilean-Mediterranean watershed before bending westward. At least major portions of the basins of Tur'an and Battof (or Asochis) were encompassed before the boundary headed southward across the natural "marchland" of infertile and forested Cenomanian limestone and the margins of the Acco and Esdraelon plains. Thus Zebulun, favored by a generally westward slope toward rain-bearing winds and an E-to-W pattern of fault and fold, presented a varied succession of limestone ridge and rich alluvial valley and yielded olives, grapes, and wheat in particular abundance.

Tribal contributions to DAVID's coronation festivities were generous (1 Chr. 12:40) and characteristically patriotic. Though only ELON among the judges was recorded as a Zebulunite (Jdg. 12:11-12), the tribe played a major role in the defeat of SISERA and MIDIAN (Jdg. 4:6, 10; 5:14, 18; 6:35), and sent 50,000 warriors to David at HEBRON (1 Chr. 12:33). Matthew, recalling Isa. 9:1, saw the MESSIAH from the Zebulunite city of NAZARETH

The prophet Jonah came from Gath Hepher (Khirbet ez-Zurra^c, top of hill) in the tribe of Zebulun.

flooding Zebulun and NAPHTALI with light (Matt. 4:13-16).

Zechariah. zek´uh-ri´uh (Heb. *zĕkaryāhû H2358* and *zĕkaryâ H2357*, "Yahweh has remembered"; Gk. *Zacharias G2408*). KJV also Zachariah (2 Ki. 14:29; 15:8, 11; 18:2) and Zacharias (NT). A very common Hebrew name.

(1) Son of JEROBOAM II and last king of JEHU's dynasty. After ruling in SAMARIA for only six months, Zechariah was murdered at IBLEAM by SHALLUM, who succeeded to the throne (2 Ki. 14:29; 15:8-11). His reign fulfilled the prediction that Jehu's dynasty would rule for four generations (10:30; 15:12).

(2) Father of ABI (ABIJAH), who was the mother of King HEZEKIAH (2 Ki. 18:1-2; 2 Chr. 29:1). Some have thought that this Zechariah may be the same as #29 below.

(3) An important figure from the tribe of REUBEN (1 Chr. 5:7). His genealogical connection as well as the period in which he lived are unclear.

(4) Firstborn son of MESHELEMIAH (= SHELEMIAH) and descendant of LEVI through KORAH and ASAPH; described as "the gatekeeper at the entrance to the Tent of Meeting" (1 Chr. 9:21; 26:2). Elsewhere, in connection with the development of a more permanent organization anticipating the system in the TEMPLE, he is called "a wise

counselor" to whom fell "the lot for the North Gate" (26:14).

(5) Son of JEIEL and descendant of BENJAMIN; his brother NER was the grandfather of SAUL (1 Chr. 9:37 [cf. v. 39]; called ZEKER in 8:31).

(6) A LEVITE and one of the gatekeepers assigned to be a musician when DAVID made preparation to transfer the ARK OF THE COVENANT to JERUSALEM (1 Chr. 15:18, 20; 16:4-5). He is called one of the brothers of the "second order" (NRSV; NIV, "next in rank") who followed HEMAN, ASAPH, and ETHAN.

(7) One of the priests who blew trumpets before the ark (1 Chr. 15:24).

(8) Son of Isshiah and descendant of Levi through KOHATH (1 Chr. 24:25; cf. v. 24 [UZZIEL was son of Kohath]).

(9) Son of Hosah and descendant of Levi through MERARI; he was a gatekeeper in David's reign (1 Chr. 26:11).

(10) Father of Iddo; the latter was an officer appointed by David over the half-tribe of MANASSEH in GILEAD (1 Chr. 27:21).

(11) One of five officials sent by King JEHOSHAPHAT "to teach in the towns of Judah" (2 Chr. 17:7).

(12) Son of Benaiah, descendant of Levi through Asaph, and father of Jahaziel (2 Chr. 20:14); the latter gave King JEHOSHAPHAT a message from the Lord regarding the Moabite and Ammonite invaders (vv. 14-17).

(13) Son of Jehoshaphat (2 Chr. 21:2).

(14) Son of JEHOIADA, who was the high priest during the reign of Joash (JEHOASH) of Judah. A godly man, Zechariah denounced the apostasy of the people from the Lord after his father's death, and Joash ordered him stoned to death in the temple court (2 Chr. 24:20-21). As Zechariah was dying, he uttered a curse on Joash that was soon fulfilled (vv. 22-25). It is often held that this is the Zechariah meant by the Lord's reference in Lk. 11:51, since Scripture mentions no other as slain in this way. Matthew, however, calls the same individual "Zechariah son of Bekariah" (Matt. 23:35), which evidently refers to the writing prophet (#30 below). Various solutions have been proposed, among which is the view that Matthew has deliberately blended the two OT figures for literary and theological reasons. See also #15 below.

(15) A man who instructed King UZZIAH in the ways of God (2 Chr. 26:5). This Zechariah has sometimes been identified with #14 above and with #29 below.

(16) A descendant of Asaph who was among the Levites involved in cleansing the temple during Hezekiah's reign (2 Chr. 29:13).

(17) A descendant of Kohath who oversaw the workmen who repaired the temple in JOSIAH's reign (2 Chr. 34:12).

(18) One of the administrators of the temple in the days of Josiah; he, along with HILKIAH and JEHIEL, contributed "twenty-six hundred Passover offerings and three hundred cattle" (2 Chr. 35:8).

(19) A descendant of Parosh who returned from BABYLON with others under EZRA (Ezra 8:3).

(20) Son of Bebai, also listed among those who returned with Ezra (Ezra 8:11).

(21) One of a group of leaders sent by Ezra to Iddo to get attendants for the house of God (Ezra 8:16).

(22) One of the descendants of Elam who agreed to put away their foreign wives (Ezra 10:26).

(23) One of the prominent men (not identified as priests) who stood near Ezra when the law was read at the great assembly (Neh. 8:4).

(24) Son of Amariah, descendant of PEREZ, and grandfather of Athaiah; the latter was one of the Judahites who after the return from the Babylonian captivity lived in Jerusalem (Neh. 11:4).

(25) Descendant of SHELAH and ancestor of Maaseiah; the latter was another postexilic Judahite who lived in Jerusalem (Neh. 11:5).

(26) Son of Passhur and ancestor of Adaiah; the latter was one of the priests who settled in Jerusalem after the exile (Neh. 11:12).

(27) Son of Jonathan and descendant of Asaph; he led the Levitical musicians at the dedication of the wall of Jerusalem (Neh. 12:35). Probably the same as #28, below.

(28) A priest trumpeter at the dedication of the wall of Jerusalem (Neh. 12:41).

(29) Son of Jeberekiah; he and URIAH the priest were chosen "as reliable witnesses" of the prophecy concerning MAHER-SHALAL-HASH-BAZ (Isa. 8:2). See also #2 above.

(30) Son of Berekiah, grandson of Iddo, descendant of Levi, and one of the writing prophets (Zech. 1:1). His first prophecy was delivered in the second year of DARIUS Hystaspes in 520 B.C. (Ezra 4:24—5:1; Zech. 1:1). He was a contemporary of HAGGAI the prophet, ZERUBBABEL the governor, and Joshua (JESHUA) the high priest (Ezra 5:2; Zech. 3:1; 4:6; 6:11). Born in Babylon, he was a priest as well as a prophet (Neh. 12:16). Ezra calls him the son of Iddo, probably because his father Berekiah died early, and he attained to the position of head of the household and successor to his grandfather. It has been thought by many from Zech. 2:4 that he was a young man at the beginning of his prophetic ministry. See ZECHARIAH, BOOK OF.

(31) Father of JOHN THE BAPTIST (Lk. 3:2) and priest within the division of Abijah during the time of HEROD the Great (Lk. 1:5; cf. 1 Chr. 24:10). Both he and his wife ELIZABETH are described as "upright in the sight of God, observing all the Lord's commandments and regulations blamelessly" (v. 6). They had no children, and when they were aged Zechariah received a vision in the temple at the time of the offering of INCENSE, a ritual that symbolized the prayers of God's people. The angel GABRIEL assured him that Elizabeth would have a child who was to be called John and who would live the separated life of a NAZIRITE, preparing the way of the Lord "in the spirit and power of Elijah" (vv. 7-17). Because Zechariah did not believe the promise, he became mute (vv. 18-22). After the birth of the child, Zechariah confirmed in writing that his name was John, and at that moment "his mouth was opened and his tongue was loosed, and he began to speak, praising God" (vv. 59-64). Filled with the HOLY SPIRIT, Zechariah uttered a prophecy known as the BENEDICTUS (vv. 67-79).

(32) An OT figure who, according to Jesus, was murdered "between the temple and the altar" (Matt. 23:35; similarly Lk. 11:51). See above, #14.

Z

Overview of ZECHARIAH

Author: The prophet Zechariah son of Berekiah (though many scholars think that the last six chapters have a different authorship).

Historical setting: Postexilic JERUSALEM during the reign of the Persian king DARIUS I (c. 520 B.C.), at a time when the Jewish returnees had ceased to rebuild the TEMPLE (cf. HAGGAI, BOOK OF). The second part of the book (Zech. 9-14) may derive from a different, later setting in Zechariah's ministry; those who deny Zechariah's authorship of this section date it as late as the third or even the second century B.C.

Purpose: To rebuke the Israelites for their sins, but also to encourage them in view of the future blessings promised by God.

Contents: Initial call to repentance (Zech. 1:1-6); eight visions and a coronation (1:7-6:15); call to repentance and promise of restoration (chs. 7-8); God's victory over the nations and final deliverance of his people (chs. 9-14).

Zechariah, Book of. The eleventh book in the collection known as the twelve Minor Prophets. The book of Zechariah emerged from the immediate postexilic period and is therefore a valuable source of information about a phase of Jewish history for which extrabiblical documentation is slight.

I. Historical Background. ZECHARIAH was the grandson of Iddo, the head of one of the priestly families that returned from the EXILE (Neh. 12:4, 16). Twenty years after the return, the TEMPLE still lay a blackened ruin, and the discouraged people did not see how it could be restored. At this critical moment God raised up the prophets HAGGAI and Zechariah to encourage the Jews to rebuild the temple. The prophecies of the two men were delivered almost at the same time. Haggai appeared first, in August 520 B.C., and within a month after he made his appeal, the foundation of the temple was laid. Soon after, Zechariah uttered his first prophecy (Zech. 1:1-6). Haggai finished his recorded prophecies the same year. The following year Zechariah gave a message consisting of eight symbolic visions, with an appendix (1:7—6:15). Two years later he gave a third message in answer to an inquiry by the men of BETHEL regarding the

observance of a fast. The two prophecies found in chs. 9-14 are not dated and were probably given at a much later period.

II. Contents

A. Messages delivered on three separate occasions (chs. 1-8).

1. General introduction (1:1-6).

2. Eight symbolic night visions, followed by a coronation scene (1:7—6:15). These visions were intended to encourage the Israelites to complete the temple.

a. The horsemen among the myrtle trees. They patrol the earth for the Lord and bring him reports from all parts of the earth (1:8-17). The purpose of the vision is to assure the Israelites of God's special care for and interest in them.

b. The four horns and the four craftsmen (1:18-21) teach that Israel's enemies are now destroyed and there is no longer any opposition to the building of God's house.

c. The man with a measuring line (ch. 2) teaches that Jerusalem will expand till it outgrows its walls, and God will be its best defense.

d. Joshua (JESHUA), the high priest, clad in filthy garments, which represent the sins of himself and the people, is cleansed and given charge of the temple (ch. 3). He is a type of the future Messiah-Branch who will take away all iniquity.

e. A seven-branched lampstand fed by two olive trees teaches that the people of God will receive God's grace through their spiritual and temporal leaders, through whose efforts the prosperity of the nation will be accomplished (ch. 4).

f. A flying scroll teaches that the land will be purified from wickedness when the temple is built and God's law taught (5:1-4).

g. A woman (typifying the besetting sins of Israel) is carried off in a basket to the land of Babylon, teaching that God not only forgives the sins of his people but carries them away from their land (5:5-11).

h. Four war chariots go forth to protect God's people, teaching God's protective providence (6:1-8).

i. The visions are followed by a scene in which a party of Jews has just come from Babylon with silver and gold for the temple. Zechariah is instructed to take part of it and make a crown for the high priest, a type of the Messiah-Branch who is to be both Priest and King to his people (6:9-15).

3. Two years after the series of visions described above, certain visitors ask whether the fasts observed in memory of the destruction of Jerusalem should still be kept. The reply is no; for God demands not fasts, but observance of moral laws. God has come to dwell with his people; and even the heathen will desire to worship God in Jerusalem (chs. 7-8).

B. Two distinct prophecies, undated (chs. 9-14).

1. God will visit the nations in judgment and his people in mercy. The Prince of Peace will come and confound the evil shepherds, but he will be rejected by the flock, and they will consequently again experience suffering (chs. 9-11).

2. A prophecy describing the victories of the new age and the coming DAY OF THE LORD (chs. 12-14). Three apocalyptic pictures are presented: (a) Jerusalem will be saved from a siege by her enemies by the intervention of the Lord. (b) A REMNANT of Israel will be saved. (c) The nations will come to Jerusalem to share in the joyous Feast of Tabernacles, and all will enjoy the blessings of God's kingdom.

III. Unity of the book. Many scholars hold that chs. 9-14 are not the work of Zechariah and therefore not a part of his prophecy. Some sug-

gest a preexilic date; others, a date after Zechariah, as late as 160 B.C. The main arguments against Zechariah's authorship are the difference in atmosphere between chs. 1-8 and 9-14, the reference to GREECE as an important power in 9:13, and the supposed derogatory reference to the prophecy in ch. 13. The first objection may be answered by pointing to the likelihood that the two sections of the prophecy were given at widely separated times—the second when Zechariah was an old man. The second objection does not take into account that Greece is mentioned long before the time of Zechariah in Isa. 66:19 and Ezek. 27:13, 19; moreover, in Zechariah's time the Greeks were a source of trouble to PERSIA. As for the third objection, one needs to appreciate that it would be impossible for a prophet to belittle prophecy. According to Jewish tradition, these prophecies were written by Zechariah himself, and this is corroborated by internal evidence. It is difficult to see how the makers of the OT canon added these chapters to Zechariah's word if he had nothing to do with them.

Zecher. See ZEKER.

Zedad. zee'dad (Heb. *ṣādād H7398*, meaning uncertain). A town between LEBO HAMATH and ZIPHRON, used to mark the ideal N border of ISRAEL (Num. 34:8; Ezek. 47:15). It is usually identified with modern Ṣadad, some 67 mi. (108 km.) NE of DAMASCUS and 25 mi. (40 km.) SE of RIBLAH.

Zedekiah. zed'uh-ki'uh (Heb. *ṣidqiyyāhû H7409* and *ṣidqiyyâ H7408*, "Yahweh is my justice/righteousness"). **(1)** Son of Kenaanah; he was one of four hundred false prophets who, in opposition to MICAIAH, the true prophet, encouraged AHAB king of JUDAH and JEHOSHAPHAT king of ISRAEL to go to war against the king of ARAM in order to recapture RAMOTH GILEAD (1 Ki. 22:1-38; 2 Chr. 18:1—19:3). The incident is of interest in part for the historical reason that it illuminates group prophecy in ancient Israel. The incident is also of theological interest for several reasons, for it shows that Ahab regarded the prophets as instruments of propaganda to

Z

serve the interests of the state, using their words and actions to influence the deity; Jehoshaphat, on the other hand, regarded the prophet not as an agent of the community to influence the deity by magic, but as the instrument of revelation of the will of God to the community (1 Ki. 22:7-8).

(2) Son of Maaseiah; he was a false prophet whom JEREMIAH predicted would be executed, along with Ahab the son of Kolaiah, by NEBUCHADNEZZAR for immorality and false teaching (Jer. 29:21-23).

(3) Son of Hananiah; he was one of the officials in the court of JEHOIAKIM who heard BARUCH read Jeremiah's scroll (Jer. 36:12).

(4) Third son of JOSIAH (1 Chr. 3:15) and king of Judah from 597 to 586 B.C. His given name was MATTANIAH ("gift of Yahweh"), but it was changed to Zedekiah by Nebuchadnezzar as a mark of vassalage when he made Zedekiah king in place of his eighteen-year-old nephew JEHOIACHIN, who was taken captive to BABYLON along with the cream of the country's leadership. He was twenty-one when he began to reign, and he reigned until the fall of Jerusalem, eleven years of continual agitation and sedition (2 Ki. 24:18). Although the prophet-historian of Kings largely bypasses the events of Zedekiah's reign (cf. 2 Ki. 24:18—25:2), they can be traced through the book of Jeremiah, where he is portrayed as indecisive, torn asunder by conflicting emotions—recognizing Jeremiah as a true prophet, but unable to act in faith on his words. Unable to choose the good by faith he acts perfidiously (cf. Jer. 34; Ezek. 17; 21:25). Because he could not act in faith on the word of God through Jeremiah (cf. Jer. 33:17-23), he brought death upon himself and his people instead of the life offered him.

In the ninth year of his reign (589 B.C.), Zedekiah openly rebelled under the influence of the pro-Egyptian party. Jeremiah predicted death, pestilence, the sword, and the execution of the city's survivors (Jer. 21:1-3). They would be treated like bad figs, unfit to be eaten (Jer. 24:8). Zedekiah himself, however, was not to die by the sword but to die in peace with an honorable burial (34:5). The following summer, July 587, the Babylonians breached the wall and poured in. By this time the food supply was exhausted. Zedekiah with his men of war fled the city by night toward the Jordan. The Babylonians overtook Zedekiah, whose army had become separated from one another. He was brought before Nebuchadnezzar at his headquarters at RIBLAH in central SYRIA. He was shown no mercy. His sons were slain before his eyes; he himself was blinded, bound in fetters, and brought to Babylon (2 Ki. 25:1-7; Jer. 39:1-7; 52:1-11). The prophecies of Jeremiah predicting death if he lacked faith to act resolutely on the word of God's prophet was fulfilled.

(5) Son of Jeconiah/JEHOIACHIN (1 Chr. 3:16). Some have interpreted the text to mean that this Zedekiah is the same as #4, and that he is called "son of Jeconiah" only because he was Jeconiah's successor on the throne.

(6) One of the signatories of the covenant of NEHEMIAH (Neh. 10:1 [Heb. v. 2]; KJV, "Zidkijah"). Although otherwise unknown, he must have been a prominent individual, but probably not a priest (the list of priest signatories appears to begin with Seraiah in v. 2 [Heb. v. 3]).

Zeeb. See OREB AND ZEEB.

Zeker. zee′kuhr (Heb. *zeker* H2353, short form of ZECHARIAH, "Yahweh has remembered"). Also Zecher. Son of JEIEL and descendant of BENJAMIN; his brother NER was the grandfather of SAUL (1 Chr. 8:31 [cf. v. 33]; called "Zechariah" in 9:37).

Zela. zee′luh (Heb. *ṣēlāʿ* H7521, prob. "side"). A city within the tribal territory of BENJAMIN; here, in the tomb of KISH, the bones of SAUL and JONATHAN were buried (2 Sam. 21:14). In Josh. 18:28, Zela (KJV and NIV have the improper transliteration, "Zelah") is mentioned as a part of a group of fourteen Benjamite cities that in general lay a few miles to the NW of JERUSALEM. Zela's exact location is unknown, though some have suggested Khirbet Salah, between Jerusalem and GIBEON, as a possible site. See also ZELZAH.

Zelah. See ZELA.

Zelek. zee′lik (Heb. *ṣeleq* H7530, meaning uncertain). An AMMONITE, included among DAVID's mighty warriors (2 Sam. 23:37; 1 Chr. 11:39).

According to the KETIB in the Samuel passage, both Zelek and Naharai were armor-bearers of JOAB.

Zelophehad. zuh-loh'fuh-had (Heb. *ṣĕlŏpḥād H7524*, possibly "refuge from terror"). Son of Hepher, grandson of GILEAD, and descendant of MANASSEH who died in the wilderness without male descendants (Num. 26:33; 27:1, 7; 36:2, 6, 10-11; Josh. 17:3; 1 Chr. 7:15). His five daughters—Mahlah, Noah, Hoglah, Milcah, and Tirzah—came to MOSES and ELEAZAR to plead for the recognition of women in such cases. As a result it was decided that when a man died without male heirs the inheritance would pass to his daughters.

Zelotes. See ZEALOT.

Zelzah. zel'zuh (Heb. *ṣelṣaḥ H7525*, derivation unknown). A town or landmark on the border (NRSV, "territory") of BENJAMIN near the tomb where RACHEL was buried (1 Sam. 10:2). SAMUEL informed SAUL that two men would providentially meet him here with news about his father's lost donkeys. Aside from this passage, nothing is known of Zelzah (unless it should be equated with ZELA, as some have suggested). It is reasonable to infer that Zelzah was not far from RAMAH, where Samuel lived, but many scholars emend the text in various ways.

Zemaraim. zem'uh-ray'im (Heb. *ṣĕmārayim H7549*, possibly "double peak"). **(1)** A city allotted to the tribe of BENJAMIN (Josh. 18:22). Some identify it with Khirbet es-Samra (c. 4 mi./6 km. NE of JERICHO). Others prefer Ras ez-Zemara (c. 5 mi./8 km. NE of BETHEL) or one of several nearby sites. If Zemaraim was indeed in the vicinity of Bethel, the town should probably be associated with Mount Zemaraim (see #2, below).

(2) A mountain in the hill country of Ephraim (see EPHRAIM, HILL COUNTRY OF) from which ABIJAH of JUDAH addressed JEROBOAM of ISRAEL before a major battle between the two kingdoms (2 Chr. 13:4). Abijah was victorious and captured "the towns of Bethel, Jeshanah and Ephron, with their surrounding villages" (v. 19). It is quite pos-

sible that Mount Zemaraim received its name from the town of Zemaraim or vice versa (see #1, above).

Zemarite. zem'uh-rit (Heb. *ṣĕmārî H7548*, gentilic of the assumed place name *ṣemer*). The Zemarites were a people group descended from CANAAN (Gen. 10:18; 1 Chr. 1:16). They are usually associated with the city of ZEMER.

Zemer. zee'muhr (Heb. *ṣemer*). In Ezek. 27:8, according to some scholars, the words *ḥăkāmayik ṣōr*, "your skilled men, O Tyre," should be emended to *ḥakmê ṣemer*, "skilled men of Zemer" (cf. NRSV). The city of Zemer is mentioned in extrabiblical sources (e.g., Ṣumur in the AMARNA tablets) and is generally identified with modern Ṣumra in Syria (c. 11 mi./18 km. SE of ARVAD, just N of the Syria-Lebanon border). Although the name of this city does not otherwise occur in the Bible, the ZEMARITES included in the Table of Nations (Gen. 10:18; 1 Chr. 1:16) were probably inhabitants of Zemer.

Zemira. See ZEMIRAH.

Zemirah. zuh-mi'ruh (Heb. *zĕmîrâ H2371*, possibly "song"). KJV Zemira. Son of BEKER and grandson of BENJAMIN (1 Chr. 7:8).

Zenan. zee'nuhn (Heb. *ṣĕnān H7569*, meaning uncertain). A town in the SHEPHELAH, within the tribal territory of JUDAH (Josh. 15:37; prob. the same as ZAANAN, Mic. 1:11). It was in the same district as LACHISH and EGLON, but its precise location is unknown.

Zenas. zee'nuhs (Gk. *Zēnas G2424*, prob. short form of *Zēnodōros*, "gift of Zeus"). A lawyer whom PAUL asked TITUS to assist in his journey (Tit. 3:13). He may have been a Christian missionary who worked with Titus on the island of CRETE, or who with APOLLOS was on a mission for Paul that took him to the island. According to some, Titus was being directed to send Zenas and Apollos on to Paul in NICOPOLIS with full provisions, possibly because the apostle had a special need for Zenas's particular expertise as a lawyer (but this view was influenced by the KJV's incorrect rendering,

Z

Overview of ZEPHANIAH

Author: The prophet Zephaniah son of Cushi (though some scholars think that the last two chapters have a different authorship).

Historical setting: The southern kingdom of JUDAH in the days of King JOSIAH (641-609 B.C.), possibly during the early part of his reign, prior to the religious reforms that began in the year 621.

Purpose: To rebuke Judah and warn the nation of future destruction; to announce the coming of the DAY OF THE LORD with both judgment and blessing.

Contents: Divine judgment and call to repentance (Zeph. 1:1—2:3); oracles against various nations (2:4—3:8); promise of purification and restoration (3:9-20).

"Bring"). It is unclear, moreover, whether his legal skills had to do with Roman or with Jewish law. Because the verses just preceding (vv. 9-11) speak of religious legal disputes, it may be that Zenas was an expert in the TORAH.

Zephaniah. zef´uh-ni´uh (Heb. *ṣĕpanyāhû H7623* and *ṣĕpanyâ H7622*, "Yahweh has hidden [*or* treasured]). **(1)** Son of Tahath, descendant of LEVI through KOHATH, and ancestor of SAMUEL and HEMAN (1 Chr. 6:36).

(2) Son of Cushi; a prophet during the early part of the reign of JOSIAH whose prophecy is preserved in the book bearing his name (Zeph. 1:1; see ZEPHANIAH, BOOK OF). He is the only prophet whose ancestry is traced back four generations, and this unique feature may indicate that his great-grandfather HEZEKIAH was the famous king bearing that name. If so he was the only prophet of royal blood, a cousin of Josiah and of the princes to whom he directed much of his prophecy. Apparently he lived in JERUSALEM, for he referred to it as "this place" (1:4) and described its topography with intimate knowledge (1:10-13).

(3) Son of Maaseiah; a priest second in rank during the reign of ZEDEKIAH (Jer. 21:1; 52:24). Some think this Zephaniah may have been JEREMIAH's cousin (cf. 32:7 with 35:4). The false prophet Shemaiah of Nehelam, in a letter from Babylon, appointed Zephaniah priest instead of JEHOIADA

with responsibility to punish pretenders to the gift of prophecy, one of whom, he alleged, was Jeremiah (29:24-28). Zedekiah sent him twice to Jeremiah; once to inquire of Yahweh about the Babylonian siege and once to ask him to pray for the people (21:1-2; 37:3). After the capture of Jerusalem, NEBUZARADAN brought him along with other leaders before the king of BABYLON, who had them killed at RIBLAH (2 Ki. 25:18, 21; Jer. 52:24, 27).

(4) Father of a postexilic Israelite named JOSIAH in whose house the priest Joshua (JESHUA) was crowned (Zech. 6:10). The subsequent reference to HEN son of Zechariah (v. 14) may be an alternate name or title of Josiah.

Zephaniah, Book of. The ninth book in the collection known as the twelve Minor Prophets. Dated in the reign of JOSIAH (Zeph. 1:1), this book was probably written sometime between 640 and 622 B.C., that is, early in that reign, before Josiah's religious reformation began. If ZECHARIAH's ancestor HEZEKIAH (1:1) was the king by that name, the prophet would have been a close relative of Josiah.

The book is concerned throughout with the DAY OF THE LORD. This prophetic concept refers to any intervention of God in history, with its ultimate expression occurring in the end times. See ESCHATOLOGY. In Zeph. 1:2-6 the day of the Lord is seen in its effects on JUDAH and JERUSALEM. It comes as a punishment for the IDOLATRY of the

© Dr. James C. Martin. The British Museum. Photographed by permission.

Philistine pottery (12th cent. B.C.). Zephaniah speaks about God's judgment upon the Philistines.

people (1:4-6). In 1:7-13 the prophet pictures the people as though they were coming to a communal sacrifice, but when they arrive, they are suddenly subject to the devastating punishment of God (1:8-9). The punishment is for social crimes as well as for idolatry.

The eschatological day of the Lord is described in Zeph. 1:14-18. Then in ch. 2 the prophet appeals to the humble to return to God, for that great day will involve universal destruction. The third chapter continues the same message, but there the prophet includes a message of hope that is centered in a REMNANT of God's people, who will be kept secure throughout the turmoil predicted by the prophet (3:12-18).

Zephath. zee´fath (Heb. *ṣĕpat H7634*, prob. "watchtower"). Apparently the earlier, Canaanite name of the city of HORMAH (Jdg. 1:17).

Zephathah. zef´uh-thuh (Heb. *ṣĕpatâ H7635*, prob. "watchtower"). A valley near Mareshah (on the edge of the lowlands NE of LACHISH), where King ASA defeated ZERAH the Cushite (2 Chr. 14:10). See MARESHAH (PLACE). The whole region has such a complex topography of gently sloping

foothills that the exact valley cannot now be identified with certainty.

Zephi. See ZEPHO.

Zepho. zee´foh (Heb. *ṣĕpô H7598* [in 1 Chr. 1:36, *ṣĕpî*], derivation uncertain). Son of ELIPHAZ, grandson of ESAU, and head of an Edomite clan (Gen. 36:11, 15; 1 Chr. 1:36 [KJV and other versions, "Zephi"]).

Zephon. zee´fon (Heb. *ṣĕpôn H7602* [in Gen. 46:16, *ṣipyôn*], derivation uncertain; gentilic *ṣĕpônî H7604*, "Zephonite"). Son of GAD, grandson of JACOB, and eponymous ancestor of the Zephonite clan (Gen. 46:16 [KJV and other versions, "Ziphion"]; Num. 26:15).

Zer. zuhr (Heb. *ṣēr H7643*, perhaps "narrow, restricted"). One of the fortified cities allotted to the tribe of NAPHTALI (Josh. 19:35). Some scholars, however, believe that the first four words of the verse are an erroneous scribal repetition of previous material (in vv. 28-29). Other emendations have been proposed.

Zerah. zihr´uh (Heb. *zerah H2438*, "shining, dawning"; later prob. used as the short form of ZERAHIAH, "Yahweh has shed light"; gentilic *zarḥî H2439*, "Zerahite" [KJV, "Zarhite"]; Gk. *Zara G2406*). KJV also Zarah (Gen. 38:30) and Zara (Matt. 1:3). **(1)** Son of Reuel and grandson of ESAU; a chief in EDOM (Gen. 36:13, 17; 1 Chr. 1:37). Some think this is the same Zerah whose son (or descendant) JOBAB became an Edomite king (Gen. 36:33; 1 Chr. 1:44).

(2) Son of JUDAH by his daughter-in-law TAMAR; his twin brother was PEREZ (Gen. 38:30; 46:12; 1 Chr. 2:4). At birth, his hand came out first and was tied with a scarlet thread to indicate that he was the FIRSTBORN, but through unusual circumstances his brother was born before he was (Gen. 38:28-29). He was called Zerah possibly because he appeared first or as an allusion to the bright (scarlet) thread. His descendants formed the Zerahite clan (Num. 26:20; 1 Chr. 9:6; 27:11, 13; see also IZRAHITE). One of his descendants was ACHAN (Josh. 7:1, 17-18, 24; 22:20); another one was PETHAHIAH, a royal

Z

official after the EXILE (Neh. 11:24). His name is included in Matthew's GENEALOGY OF JESUS CHRIST, which however makes clear that it was his brother Perez who was an ancestor of Jesus (Matt. 1:3).

(3) Son of SIMEON, grandson of JACOB, and eponymous ancestor of the Zerahite clan among the Simeonites (Num. 26:13; 1 Chr. 4:24). In the parallel passages (Gen. 46:10; Exod. 6:15) he is called ZOHAR.

(4) Son of Iddo and descendant of LEVI through GERSHON (1 Chr. 6:21 [Heb. 6:6]).

(5) Son of Adaiah, descendant of Levi through Gershon, and ancestor of the musician ASAPH (1 Chr. 6:41 [MT, 6:26]).

(6) A Cushite (i.e., from ETHIOPIA, but perhaps the leader of a S Arabian tribe) who attacked King ASA of JUDAH with a very large army (2 Chr. 14:9). Zerah was defeated in battle at MARESHAH (PLACE) and pursued to GERAR, where he was completely routed (vv. 10-15). Some have argued that the presence of tents, flocks, and camels among the booty suggests bedouin raiders.

Zerahiah. zer´uh-hi´uh (Heb. *zĕraḥyâ H2440*, "Yahweh has shed light [*or* shone forth]"). **(1)** Son of Uzzi, descendant of LEVI through KOHATH, AARON, and ELEAZAR, and ancestor of ZADOK and EZRA (1 Chr. 6:6, 51 [Heb. 5:32; 6:36]; Ezra 7:4).

(2) Descendant of Pahath-Moab and father of Eliehoenai; the latter was a family head who returned from Babylon with EZRA (Ezra 8:4).

Zerahite. See ZERAH.

Zered. zihr´id (Heb. *zered H2429*, meaning uncertain). KJV also Zared (Num. 21:12). A valley or WADI in TRANSJORDAN where the Israelites, terminating their wanderings and bypassing EDOM, encamped and crossed into MOAB (Num. 21:12; Deut. 2:13). It is often identified with the

The Zered River. (View to the E.)

wadi(s) mentioned in Isa. 15:7 and Amos 6:14; see ARABAH, BROOK (WADI) OF THE, and WILLOWS, BROOK (WADI) OF THE. The Zered may also have been the scene of the flash flood in 2 Ki. 3:16-23. Some identify it with the Wadi Kerak (or some tributary of the Kerak or the ARNON), but most scholars favor Wadi el-Ḥesa. Like other wadis in the area, the Ḥesa flows intermittently in a shallow valley across the plateau; but replenished by rainfall, tributaries, and especially springs, it flows perennially to its terminal oasis through a canyon that cleaves the fault-weakened escarpment. Steep-walled but broad-floored and flanked with cultivable terraces, this wadi formed both the historic divide between Edom and Moab and a difficult but practicable route to the plateau.

Zereda. See ZEREDAH.

Zeredah. zer´uh-duh (Heb. *ṣĕrēdâ H7649*. derivation uncertain). **(1)** A town in the Ephraimite hills (see EPHRAIM, HILL COUNTRY OF) that was the home of JEROBOAM before he rebelled against SOLOMON (1 Ki. 11:26; KJV, "Zereda"). The SEPTUAGINT, in a long addition to 1 Ki. 12:24, has several other references to the town (the name is transcribed as *Sarira*), including the comment that Jeroboam built Zeredah for Solomon. Its location is uncertain, but it is often identified with Deir Ghassaneh, some 15 mi. (24 km.) SW of SHECHEM. See also ZERERAH.

© Dr. James C. Martin

(2) A Transjordanian town near which the bronze objects for the TEMPLE were cast (2 Chr. 4:17 MT, followed by NRSV and other versions; KJV, "Zeredathah"). The name here is a variant for ZARETHAN (1 Ki. 7:46).

Zeredathah. See ZEREDAH #2.

Zererah. zer'uh-rah (Heb. *ṣĕrērâ H7678*, perhaps "narrow, restricted"). KJV Zererath. A town toward which the Midianite army fled after GIDEON and his men blew their trumpets (Jdg. 7:22). The identity and location of Zererah is problematic. The Midianites, who had camped in the Valley of JEZREEL, near the hill of MOREH (6:33; 7:2), must have fled SE, eventually crossing the JORDAN. TABBATH (7:22) almost certainly was in TRANSJORDAN, but it is impossible to determine whether Zererah itself was on the W or E side of the river. Some have thought that Zererah is a mistake for (or a variant of) ZARETHAN, which was probably in Transjordan. Others, following a number of Hebrew MSS, read ZEREDAH, but this town appears to have been SW of SHECHEM and thus not on the path suggested by the text.

Zererath. See ZERERAH.

Zeresh. zihr'ish (Heb. *zereš H2454*, meaning uncertain). Wife of HAMAN, mentioned in two passages in the story of ESTHER. When Haman boasted that Queen Esther had invited him to a banquet with King XERXES, Zeresh and some friends encouraged him to build a gallows so that MORDECAI could be hanged (Esth. 5:10-14). Subsequently, Haman was told by his wife and "advisers" that he would not be able to prevail because Mordecai was a Jew (6:13).

Zereth. zihr'ith (Heb. *ṣeret H7679*, derivation unknown). Son of Asshur (by his wife Helah) and descendant of JUDAH (1 Chr. 4:7; cf. v. 5).

Zereth Shahar. zihr'ith-shay'hahr (Heb. *ṣeret haššaḥar H7680*, meaning uncertain, but see SHAHAR). Also Zereth-shahar. One of the towns in the territory given to the tribe of REUBEN (Josh. 13:19). The town—mentioned in conjunction with

others in MOAB that had formerly belonged to SIHON the Amorite—is described as being "on the hill in the valley," but the precise location is uncertain. Some scholars tentatively identify it with modern ez-Zarat, on the E shore of the DEAD SEA (c. 12 mi./19 km. S of its NE tip; this was the site of Hellenistic Callirrhoe, known for its hot springs, which the ailing HEROD the Great used).

Zeri. zihr'i (Heb. *ṣeri H7662*, "balm"). Son of JEDUTHUN; he and his brothers "prophesied, using the harp in thanking and praising the LORD" (1 Chr. 25:3); the name is probably a variant of IZRI (v. 11).

Zeror. zihr'or (Heb. *ṣerôr H7657*, "stone"). Son of Becorath, descendant of BENJAMIN, and great-grandfather (or more distant ancestor) of King SAUL (1 Sam. 9:1; cf. v. 2). His name is missing from the other genealogies of Saul (1 Chr. 8:33-40; 9:39-44), though some have suggested that Zeror is to be equated with ZUR, who appears there as Saul's uncle (8:30; 9:36).

Zeruah. zuh-roo'uh (Heb. *ṣerûʿâ H7654*, "leprous," perhaps a deliberate scribal distortion of ZERUIAH). The widowed mother of King JEROBOAM (1 Ki. 11:26). It is possible that her Hebrew name was given to her because she had a skin ailment or discoloration, but since the mothers of the kings of Israel (in contrast to those of the kings of Judah) are not otherwise mentioned, some scholars interpret the identification as a way of denigrating Jeroboam. Others suggest that Zeruah is mentioned simply to point out that she was a widow, for some extrabiblical texts use the epithet "a widow's son" with reference to a king who has assumed the throne improperly.

Zerubbabel. zuh-ruhb'uh-buhl (Heb. *zĕrubbābel H2428*, from Akk. *Zēr-Bābili*, "offspring of Babylon"; Gk. *Zorobabel G2431*). KJV NT, Zorobabel. A prominent Israelite who returned to PALESTINE after the EXILE and functioned as the governor of JERUSALEM under the Persian ruler DARIUS Hystaspes I (522-486 B.C.). There are certain difficulties connected with the identification of Zerubbabel, partly because he has sometimes been regarded, without good reason, as identical with

SHESHBAZZAR (Ezra 1:8 et al.), and also because of an apparent discrepancy in the genealogical lists of Ezra and Chronicles. Zerubbabel is usually identified as the son of SHEALTIEL (or Salathiel) and the grandson of King JEHOIACHIN (Ezra 3:2; Hag. 1:1; Matt. 1:12-13; Lk. 3:27), but in one passage the MT describes him as the son of PEDAIAH, who was Shealtiel's brother (1 Chr. 3:19). There are several ways of explaining this discrepancy, the most common of which is the supposition that Shealtiel died without offspring and that his brother Pedaiah married the widow according to ancient Hebrew LEVIRATE law (Deut. 25:5-10). Were Zerubbabel to have been born of such a union he could legally claim to be the son of Shealtiel (alternatively, Shealtiel could well have named his nephew as his heir and thus as his legal son). In any case, Zerubbabel was heir to the throne of JUDAH (1 Chr. 3:17-19) and is listed in the GENEALOGY OF JESUS CHRIST (Matt. 1:13; Lk. 3:27).

When CYRUS allowed the Jews to return to their own land, Joshua (JESHUA) the high priest was the religious leader. When they reached JERUSALEM, they first set up the altar of burnt offering, then they proceeded to lay the foundation of the new TEMPLE. Soon, however, opposition arose. The adversaries of the Jews made an apparently friendly offer of assistance, but Zerubbabel and the other leaders rebuffed them; therefore they wrote to the king and succeeded in stopping the work for a time (Ezra 4). In 520 B.C. the work was resumed and at this point the prophets HAGGAI and ZECHARIAH furnished the necessary moral and spiritual impetus for the rebuilding. Haggai castigated the Jews for their selfishness, indifference, and neglect, spurring Zerubbabel on to give proper oversight to the work in hand (Hag. 2:1-9, 20-23). In the same year Zechariah urged completion of the temple, and promised that earlier opposition would be removed (Zech. 4:6-10). Within four years the new temple was finished, and a great celebration was held at its dedication (Ezra 6:16-22). As far as the record tells, the work of Zerubbabel was complete. It is not known when he died. See RESTORATION.

Zeruiah. zuh-roo´yuh (Heb. *ṣĕrûyâ H7653*, "fragrant" or "balm of Yahweh"). Sister (or step-sister) of DAVID (1 Chr. 2:16); she may have been the daughter of JESSE's wife by a former marriage to NAHASH (2 Sam. 17:25). Zeruiah is known primarily as the mother of ABISHAI, JOAB, and ASAHEL, who were chief officers in David's kingdom (2 Sam. 2:18; 3:39; et al.). Although Zeruiah is mentioned at least twenty-five times in the historical records of Samuel, Kings, and Chronicles, no mention is ever made of her husband.

Zetham. zee´thuhm (Heb. *zētām H2457*, derivation uncertain). Son of LADAN and descendant of LEVI through GERSHON (1 Chr. 23:8; in 26:22 the Heb. can be understood to mean that Zetham was son of Jehieli).

Zethan. zee´thuhn (Heb. *zētān H2340*, possibly "[keeper of] olive trees"). Son of Bilhan and great-grandson of BENJAMIN (1 Chr. 7:10).

Zethar. zee´thahr (Heb. *zētar H2458*, possibly from Pers. *zaitar*, "conqueror"). One of "the seven nobles of Persia and Media who had special access to the king and were highest in the kingdom" (Esth. 1:14). Queen VASHTI was banished by Ahasuerus (XERXES) on their advice.

Zeus. zoos (Gk. *Zeus G2416* [gen. *Dios*, acc. *Dia*]). The chief god of the Greeks. The word comes from an Indo-European root meaning "sky," and its form appears in other Indo-European languages, such as Latin *Jupiter*, the old form of which is *Diespiter* (i.e., *diei pater*, "father of day"), and Teutonic *Ziu* (from which derives *Tuesday*). As the god of the bright sky, Zeus was the lord of thunder and the giver of weather, the "cloud-gatherer" of the Homeric phrase. Since mountain peaks give weather signs, Zeus was enthroned on heights, preeminently on Olympus. Serving the needs of a royal and patriarchal age, he became the protector and ruler of the family. As Zeus Herkeios ("of the household") he ruled the hearth; as Zeus Xenios ("hospitable, defender of strangers") he protected the guest. (According to 2 Macc. 6:2, ANTIOCHUS Epiphanes determined that the temples in Jerusalem and GERIZIM would be called, respectively, the temple of Olympian Zeus and the temple of Zeus Xenios.) Since the state is the larger family and requires a moral framework and foundation similar to that of the smaller unit, Zeus became the protector of law and justice, the supreme god, father of gods and human beings. In the theological dramas of Aeschylus there are concepts of Zeus almost biblical in their loftiness. The name occurs in only one NT passage (Acts 14:12-13; KJV, "Jupiter").

Zia. zi´uh (Heb. *zia͑ H2333*, possibly "one who trembles"). Son of Abihail; he was one of seven relatives from the tribe of GAD who occupied the region E of GILEAD (1 Chr. 5:13; cf. vv. 10, 14).

Ziba. zi´buh (Heb. *ṣibā᾿ H7471*, prob. "twig"). A servant or steward of SAUL whose life and activities are known in the biblical record only during the reign of DAVID. In response to David's request, Ziba introduced to him MEPHIBOSHETH, a crippled son of JONATHAN. By royal provision the land that formerly belonged to King Saul was given to Mephibosheth and placed under the management of Ziba. This may have been an estate of considerable size, since Ziba employed his fifteen sons and twenty servants to cultivate the land (2 Sam. 9:2-12). When David fled during ABSALOM's rebellion, Ziba brought supplies to him and reported that Mephibosheth was disloyal (2 Sam. 16:1-4). The king responded by assigning Mephibosheth's estate to Ziba. Subsequently, Mephibosheth revealed that he had been betrayed by Ziba. By royal decree half of the estate was returned to Mephibosheth while Ziba retained the remainder (19:24-30).

Zibeon. zib´ee-uhn (Heb. *ṣib͑ôn H7390*, "[little] hyena"). (1) A HIVITE whose granddaughter OHOLIBAMAH was married to ESAU (Gen. 36:2, 14). If the gentilic Hivite is equivalent (or should be emended) to HORITE, then this Zibeon is the same as #2 below.

(2) Son of SEIR the Horite; he was a clan chief of EDOM whose son ANAH is credited for discovering certain hot springs in the desert (Gen. 36:20, 24, 29; 1 Chr. 1:38, 40).

Zibia. zib´ee-uh (Heb. *ṣibyā᾿ H7384*, "gazelle"). Son of SHAHARAIM, descendant of BENJAMIN, and family head; he was one of seven children that were born to Shaharaim in MOAB by his wife HODESH

after he had divorced Hushim and Baara (1 Chr. 8:8-10).

Zibiah. zib´ee-uh (Heb. *ṣibyâ H7385*, "[female] gazelle"). A woman of BEERSHEBA who became the wife of King AHAZIAH of JUDAH and mother of King JEHOASH (2 Ki. 12:1; 2 Chr. 24:1).

Zichri. See ZICRI.

Zicri. zik´ri (Heb. *zikrî H2356*, prob. short form of ZECHARIAH, "Yahweh has remembered"). Also Zichri (KJV and other versions); TNIV Zikri. (1) Son of Izhar, grandson of KOHATH, and great-grandson of LEVI (Exod. 6:21); he was MOSES' cousin and the brother of KORAH #3.

(2) Son of Shimei and descendant of BENJAMIN (1 Chr. 8:19). He, as well as #3 and #4 below, is included among the heads of families who lived in JERUSALEM (v. 28).

(3) Son of Shashak and descendant of Benjamin (1 Chr. 8:23).

(4) Son of Jehoram and descendant of Benjamin 1 Chr. (8:27).

(5) Son of ASAPH, descendant of Levi, and ancestor of MATTANIAH; the latter was a prominent LEVITE after the EXILE (1 Chr. 9:15). This Zicri is apparently the same as ZABDI #4 and ZACCUR #4.

(6) Son of Joram and descendant of MOSES through ELIEZER (1 Chr. 26:25).

(7) Father of Eliezer; the latter was an officer over the tribe of REUBEN during the reign of DAVID (27:16).

(8) Descendant of JUDAH and father of Amasiah; the latter was a commander in the days of JEHOSHAPHAT (2 Chr. 17:16).

(9) Father of Elishaphat; the latter was a commander under JEHOIADA the high priest (2 Chr. 23:1).

(10) A warrior from EPHRAIM in the army of King PEKAH of Israel who assassinated Maaseiah son of King AHAZ of Judah and two royal officers (2 Chr. 28:7).

(11) Descendant of Benjamin and father of Joel; the latter was chief officer in the days of NEHEMIAH (Neh. 11:9).

(12) Head of the priestly family of ABIJAH in the days of the high priest JOIAKIM (Neh. 12:17).

Ziddim. zid´im (Heb. *ṣiddîm H7403*, "sides," possibly referring to a location on the slopes of a hill). One of the fortified cities allotted to the tribe of NAPHTALI (Josh. 19:35). The rabbis identified Ziddim with Kephar Ḥittayya, apparently a location just N of the Horns of Hattin, some 6 mi. (10 km.) W of the Sea of Galilee. Few scholars, however, accept this identification, and many believe that the biblical text here has suffered corruption. See ZER.

Zidkijah. See ZEDEKIAH #6.

Zidon, Zidonians. See SIDON.

Zif. See ZIV.

ziggurat. zig´oo-rat (from Akk. *ziqqurratu*, "temple tower"). A staged or stepped temple tower. This architectural form was developed in the third millennium B.C. in Babylonia from a low temenos (a platform supporting a shrine, as at ERECH and ʿUqair) to massive, multiple-story brick towers. The Tower of BABEL (Gen. 11:1-5) might have been a ziggurat, since such buildings are to be found in all principal Mesopotamian cities. The sanctuary of MARDUK at BABYLON was called *Esagil(a)* ("the house whose head is raised up"), and the lofty tower was called *Etemenanki* ("the house of the foundation of heaven and earth"). Of the high tower only the merest fragment, a portion of the lowest story, remains, and it was buried under debris until excavated in modern times. Everything considered, the structure was at least seven stories high, with the dwelling of Marduk erected on the seventh story. The height has been variously estimated up to about 300 ft. (90 m.). The cities of NIPPUR, Larsa, and Sippar each called their ziggurat by the name *Eduranki* ("the house of the bond between heaven and earth"). One of the best preserved of the ziggurats is that in UR of the Chaldees, with a base 200 by 141 ft. (61 x 43 m.) and a bottom terrace 50 ft. (15 m.) high. Jewish and Arab tradition identified the Tower of Babel with the great temple of NEBO in the city of Borsippa, now called Birs-Nimrod. The ruins of this ziggurat, originally seven stories high, still rise over 150 ft. (45 m.) from the plain. The highest preserved ziggurat ruins are those of Dur-kurigalzu (modern ʿAqar Quf, 20 mi./32 km. W of Baghdad), which still towers to a height of 187 ft. (57 m.).

Ziha. zi´huh (Heb. *ṣiḥāʾ H7484*, derivation uncertain). Ancestor of a family of temple servants (NETHINIM) who returned from the Babylonian EXILE (Ezra 2:43; Neh. 7:46). One of two supervisors of the temple servants living on the hill of OPHEL was called Ziha (Neh. 11:21). He was undoubtedly a member of this family, but it is unclear whether Ziha was his own name or whether he is referred to by the clan eponym.

Ziklag. zik´lag (Heb. *ṣiqlag H7637*, derivation unknown). One of the "southernmost towns of the tribe of Judah in the Negev toward the boundary of Edom" (Josh. 15:31; cf. v. 21); it was subsequently allotted to the tribe of SIMEON (Josh. 19:5; 1 Chr. 4:30). In SAUL's time it was under the PHILISTINES (1 Sam. 27:6). King ACHISH of GATH gave Ziklag to DAVID when he was pursued by Saul (1 Sam. 27:6; 1 Chr. 12:1, 20), and David used the town as a base for raids against various groups (1 Sam. 27:8-11). After the last Philistine attack on Saul, David returned to Ziklag and found that it had been raided by the AMALEKITES, on whom he took quick vengeance. The booty was divided with the people in the NEGEV area who had assisted him during his campaigns (1 Sam. 30:1-3; 1 Chr. 12:1-20). The town is mentioned elsewhere (2 Sam. 1:1; 4:10; Neh. 11:28). The location of Ziklag is uncertain. Proposed identifications include modern Tell el-Khuweilifeh (c. 9.5 mi./15 km. NE of BEERSHEBA) and, more likely, Tell esh-Shariʿah (c. 14 mi./23 km. NW of Beersheba).

Zikri. zik´ri. TNIV form of ZICRI.

Zillah. zil´uh (Heb. *ṣillâ H7500*, possibly "shade, protection"). A wife of LAMECH and the mother of TUBAL-CAIN and NAAMAH (Gen. 4:19, 22-23).

Zillethai. zil´uh-thi (Heb. *ṣillĕtay H7531*, possibly "shade [of Yahweh]"). KJV Zilthai. Son of Shimei (see SHEMA [PERSON] #3) and descendant of BENJAMIN (1 Chr. 8:20).

(2) One of several warriors from the tribe of MANASSEH who joined DAVID at ZIKLAG; they are

described as "leaders of units of a thousand" (1 Chr. 12:20).

Zilpah. zil′puh (Heb. *zilpâ H2364*, possibly "small nose"). A maidservant given by LABAN to LEAH on the occasion of her marriage to JACOB. At the request of Leah, Zilpah became Jacob's CONCUBINE, bearing to him GAD and ASHER (Gen. 29:24; 30:9-13; 35:26; 37:2; 46:18). See also BILHAH (PERSON).

Zilthai. See ZILLETHAI.

Zimmah. zim′uh (Heb. *zimmāh H2366*, possibly "plan"). Son or grandson of JAHATH and descendant of LEVI through GERSHON (1 Chr. 6:20, 42; 2 Chr. 29:12).

Zimran. zim′ran (Heb. *zimrān H2383*, derivation uncertain). Son of ABRAHAM and KETURAH (Gen. 25:2; 1 Chr. 1:32). The name Zimran is thought by some to be preserved in modern Zabram, a site W of Mecca.

Zimri (person). zim′ri (Heb. *zimrî H2381*, possibly "[Yahweh is] my protection"). (1) Son of Salu and descendant of SIMEON; he was a tribal leader who was killed by PHINEHAS for his open adultery with a Moabite princess (Num. 25:14).

(2) Son of Zerah, descendant of JUDAH, and grandfather of ACHAN (Josh. 7:1, 17-18 [NIV]; 1 Chr. 2:6). In the Joshua references, most English versions, following the MT, read ZABDI instead of Zimri.

(3) Son of Jehoaddah (Jadah) and descendant of King SAUL through JONATHAN (1 Chr. 8:36; 9:42).

(4) A military official under ELAH of Israel who killed this king and briefly usurped the royal power in 885 B.C. (1 Ki. 16:9-20). Elah had been carousing at TIRZAH while the main army, under OMRI's leadership, was besieging GIBBETHON. When news of the assassination reached the camp, the reaction was so swift that Zimri had only seven days to live. Raising the siege, Omri brought the army to the capital; Zimri, who had perhaps relied on his chariot force, could not hold it. As the troops entered, he retired to the palace and burned it over his own head. The note of his contribution to Israel's apos-

tasy (16:19) may mean that he formally affirmed his adherence to the religious policy of JEROBOAM. His treachery was alluded to by JEZEBEL when she referred to JEHU as "Zimri" (2 Ki. 9:31).

Zimri (place). zim′ri (Heb. *zimri H2382*, derivation uncertain). An unknown country mentioned with ELAM and MEDIA as coming under the judgment of God (Jer. 25:25). Some identify this place with ZIMRAN (also unknown); others believe the text is corrupt (the LXX omits this name).

Zin. zin (Heb. *ṣin H7554*, derivation uncertain). A DESERT that provided the setting for some critical events of biblical history (not to be confused with the Desert of Sin; see SIN, DESERT OF). Possibly named after an unidentified settlement or region (Num. 34:4; Josh. 15:3), the Desert or Wilderness of Zin included KADESH BARNEA, where the Israelites camped (Num. 33:36) and whence they spied out the land (13:21; cf. v. 26). Various incidents are recorded as taking place here (Num. 20:1-13; 27:14; Deut. 32:51). The S border of the Promised Land included a portion of the Desert of Zin (Num. 34:3-4), which was allotted to the tribe of JUDAH (Josh. 15:1-3). It must have extended from somewhere near Kadesh eastward toward the ascent of AKRABBIM and to the border of EDOM. More precise definition is hardly warranted: even in biblical times the Desert of PARAN overlapped (or perchance included) that of Zin (Num. 13:26). However defined, Zin was included in "that vast and dreadful desert" the Israelites experienced (Deut. 1:19; 8:15). With a fickle few inches of rain even in the slightly less arid N, and with its soil bestrewn with rock, flint, and sand, Zin was mostly barren. Yet investigation is disclosing an ancient ebb and flow of settlement based on meticulous utilization of soil and water and the strategy of trade and defense.

Zina. See ZIZA #3.

Zion. zi′uhn (Heb. *ṣiyyôn H7482*, possibly "fortress" or "barren [hill]"; Gk. *Siōn G4994*). KJV also Sion (Ps. 65:1 and NT). The SE hill of JERUSALEM; by extension, the name is applied to the entire city, to its inhabitants, and to the people of God

This elevation in SW Jerusalem is often referred to as Mt. Zion (view to the NE), but the name was originally applied to the City of David, just S of the temple mount.

generally. Zion is first mentioned in the OT as a JEBUSITE fortress (2 Sam. 5:6-9). DAVID captured it and called it the CITY OF DAVID. At this time the citadel probably stood on the long ridge running S of where the TEMPLE would later be located, although not all scholars are agreed on this. This location is near the only known spring; it is suitable for defense; its size is about that of other fortified towns; archaeological remains show that it was inhabited long before David's time; and certain Bible references (1 Ki. 8:1; 2 Chr. 5:2; 32:30; 33:14) indicate that this was the original Zion. (Only in postbiblical times did the name Zion become erroneously transferred to the SW hill of Jerusalem, and this practice prevails today.)

David brought the ARK OF THE COVENANT to Zion, and the hill henceforth became sacred (2 Sam. 6:10-12). When SOLOMON later moved the ark to the temple on nearby Mount MORIAH, the name Zion was evidently extended to take in the temple mount (Isa. 8:18; 18:7; 24:23; Joel 3:17; Mic. 4:7). Zion thus came to stand for the whole of Jerusalem (2 Ki. 19:21; Ps. 48; 69:35; 133:3; Isa. 1:8). The name is frequently used figuratively for the Hebrew nation as God's people. And since Zion is "the joy of all the earth" (Ps. 48:2; cf. Isa. 18:7), the name became synonymous with REDEMPTION

as occurring in any nation; accordingly, to know God and to be written in his book is equated in the Psalms with being "born in Zion" (Ps. 87:4-6). In apostolic usage Mount Zion comes to represent "the heavenly Jerusalem, the city of the living God" (Heb. 12:22). Yet Zion may also refer to the people of Israel (primarily in quotations from the OT, as Rom. 9:33 and 1 Pet. 2:6) and of Jerusalem (Matt. 21:5; Jn. 12:15); or it may identify the mountain on which Christ and his followers will stand in triumph at his second coming (Rev. 14:1; cf. Obad. 21) and from which he will go forth to rule forever (Rom. 11:26; cf. Ps. 132:13-14).

Zion, Daughter of. A figurative expression used in the OT, especially in the Prophets, for JERUSALEM and its inhabitants. The expression "elders of the Daughter of Zion" (Lam. 2:10) clearly shows that the whole population of Jerusalem is thus personified (cf. also "Daughter of Babylon" in Ps. 137:8; "Virgin Daughter of Sidon" in Isa. 23:12; et al.). In several passages (e.g., 2 Ki. 19:21; Isa. 37:22; Lam. 2:13), "Daughter of Zion" is paralleled by "Daughter of Jerusalem," showing their essential equivalence. In the NT "Daughter of Zion" appears only twice in OT quotations (Matt. 21:5 and Jn. 12:15). See also ZION.

© Dr. James C. Martin

Z

Zior. zi′or (Heb. *ṣi‘ōr H7486*, prob. "small"). A town in the hill country within the tribal territory of JUDAH (Josh. 15:54). It was apparently near HEBRON (prob. to its S), but the precise location is unknown. See also ZAIR.

Ziph (person). zif (Heb. *zîp H2334*, derivation unknown). **(1)** Son of Mesha, grandson of CALEB, and descendant of JUDAH (1 Chr. 2:42). The Hebrew text is difficult; see MARESHAH (PERSON) #1. Moreover, Ziph here may be the name of a town whose "father" (i.e., founder) was Mesha; see ZIPH (PLACE) #2.

(2) Son of Jehallelel and descendant of JUDAH (1 Chr. 4:16). Perhaps his name was associated with ZIPH (PLACE) #1.

Ziph (place). zif (Heb. *zîp H2335*, derivation unknown; gentilic *zîpî H2337*, "Ziphite"). **(1)** One of the "southernmost towns of the tribe of Judah in the Negev toward the boundary of Edom" (Josh. 15:24). Possibly this town was named after ZIPH (PERSON) #2 or ZIPHAH (1 Chr. 4:16). Its precise location is uncertain, but some scholars have tentatively identified it with modern Khirbet ez-Zeifeh, some 19 mi. (31 km.) SE of BEERSHEBA.

(2) A town in the hill country within the tribal territory of JUDAH (Josh. 15:55). The open area E of this town was known as the Desert of Ziph, and it was here that DAVID hid from SAUL twice (1 Sam. 23:14-15, 24; 26:2); on both of those occasions the inhabitants of the town, the Ziphites, alerted the king regarding David's whereabouts (2 Sam. 23:19; 26:1; Ps. 54 title [KJV, "Ziphims"]). Ziph was one of the cities fortified by REHOBOAM after the secession of the northern kingdom (2 Chr. 11:8). It is generally identified with modern Tell Zif, 4 mi. (6 km.) SE of HEBRON on a hill some 2,890 ft. (880 m.) above sea level commanding the open country around. Because the Calebites were associated with Hebron, it seems probable that this Ziph was named after ZIPH (PERSON) #1.

Ziph, Desert (Wilderness) of. See ZIPH (PLACE) #2.

Ziphah. zi′fuh (Heb. *zîpâ H2336*, prob. "small"). Son of Jehallelel and descendant of JUDAH (1 Chr.

4:16). Some have thought that Ziphah is an inadvertent scribal repetition of Ziph, which immediately precedes it. Others suggest that Ziphah should be identified with ZIPH (PLACE) #1.

Ziphims. See ZIPH (PLACE) #2.

Ziphion. See ZEPHON.

Ziphite. See ZIPH (PLACE) #2.

Ziphron. zif′ron (Heb. *ziprôn H2412*, derivation unknown). A town between ZEDAD and HAZAR ENAN, used to mark the ideal NE border of ISRAEL (Num. 34:9). Its precise location is uncertain, but some scholars identify it with modern Ḥawwarin, about 75 mi. (120 km.) NE of DAMASCUS.

Zippor. zip′or (Heb. *ṣippôr H7607*, "bird"). Father of King BALAK of MOAB (Num. 22:2, 4, 10, 16; 23:18; Josh. 24:9; Jdg. 11:25).

Zipporah. zi-por′uh (Heb. *ṣippōrâ H7631*, "bird"). Daughter of JETHRO (REUEL), wife of MOSES, and mother of GERSHOM and ELIEZER (Exod. 2:21-22; 18:2-4). After Moses' time in MIDIAN, upon his return to EGYPT, the Lord met "him" (Moses? Moses' son?) and "was about to kill him" (4:24), but Zipporah averted disaster by circumcising the child (vv. 25-26). Apparently Moses sent her back to her father during the unsettled and troublous times connected with the EXODUS.

zither. See MUSIC AND MUSICAL INSTRUMENTS.

Zithri. See SITHRI.

Ziv. ziv (Heb. *ziw H2304*, "blossom"). KJV Zif. The second month in the Jewish religious CALENDAR (corresponding to April-May). The term occurs in only one biblical passage to mark the beginning of SOLOMON's construction of the TEMPLE (1 Ki. 6:1, 37).

Ziz, Pass (Ascent) of. ziz (Heb. *ṣîṣ H7489*, prob. "flowers"). When a vast army from EDOM, MOAB, and AMMON came against JUDAH during the reign of JEHOSHAPHAT, a prophet by the

The Pass of Ziz. (View to the W.)

© Dr. James C. Martin

name of JAHAZIEL revealed that the enemy would be "climbing up by the Pass of Ziz" and that Jehoshaphat's men would "find them at the end of the gorge in the Desert of Jeruel" (2 Chr. 20:16). Evidently the place was near TEKOA, for on the next morning the people of Judah went into the Desert of Tekoa and saw the enemy defeated (vv. 20-23). The exact location of the pass is uncertain, but some identify it with Wadi Ḥaṣaṣa, some 6 mi. (10 km.) N of EN GEDI and 8 mi. (13 km.) SE of Tekoa.

Ziza. zi´zuh (Heb. *zîzāʾ H2330* and *zîzâ H2331* [only 1 Chr. 23:11], meaning uncertain). (**1**) Son of Shiphi and descendant of Shemaiah; he was a clan leader in the tribe of SIMEON (1 Chr. 4:37). Ziza is listed among those whose families increased greatly during the days of King HEZEKIAH and who dispossessed the Hamites and Meunites near GEDOR (vv. 38-41).

(**2**) Son of REHOBOAM (by his favorite wife MAACAH) and descendant of DAVID (2 Chr. 11:20).

(**3**) Son of Shimei and descendant of LEVI through GERSHON (1 Chr. 23:10-11 NIV). The KJV and other versions, following the MT, have "Zina" (v. 10) and "Zizah" (v. 11). The SEPTUAGINT reads *Ziza* in both verses.

Zizah. See ZIZA #3.

Zoan. zoh´uhn (Heb. *ṣōʿan H7586*, from Egyp. *ḏʿnt*, "storm"; LXX, *Tanis*). An ancient Egyptian city, known to classical writers as Tanis, and now represented by the ruins of Ṣan el-Ḥagar el-Qibliya (San al-Hajar) in the NE delta of the NILE, just S of Lake Menzaleh. Before the Ramesside age (c. 1300 B.C.; see RAMSES), the history of Zoan remains obscure, especially as the commonly proposed identification of Zoan-Tanis with the HYKSOS settlement of Avaris and later city of RAMESES is perhaps erroneous. The geographical term "fields of Tanis" (cf. "fields of Zoan" in Ps. 78:12, 43 NRSV) occurs from Ramses II's day onward, while Tanis-Zoan itself is attested from c. 1100 B.C. From the 21st to late 22nd dynasties (c. 1085-715), Tanis-Zoan was the capital of the PHARAOHS, several royal tombs of this period and the ruins of important temples having been discovered there. During the Nubian 25th dynasty (c. 715-664), Tanis was still used as an occasional royal residence and as a northern base, with MEMPHIS as main center. This background lends point to references by ISAIAH to the "officials of Zoan" as "the wise counselors of Pharaoh" (Isa. 19:11, 13; 30:4). In the 26th dynasty (664-525), Zoan was still a major city, and this is reflected in EZEKIEL's denunciation of it with other Egyptian centers (Ezek. 30:14).

Zoar. zoh´ahr (Heb. *ṣō‘ar H7593*, possibly "small"). One of the five CITIES OF THE PLAIN, the others being SODOM, GOMORRAH, ADMAH, and ZEBOIIM. Known biblical facts about Zoar derive from ten references (Gen. 13:10; 14:2, 8; 19:22-23, 30; Deut. 34:3; Isa. 15:5; Jer. 48:34), all quite barren of definite geographical information. Postbiblical historical evidence, indecisive as it is, has strongly influenced most modern scholars, who locate Zoar at the SE corner of the DEAD SEA near the edge of the barren saline plain called the Sebkha, 4-5 mi. (6-8 km.) up the River ZERED from where it empties into the Sea. In particular, it is common to identify ancient Zoar with modern eṣ-Ṣafi, some 5 mi. (8 km.) S of the Dead Sea. The survival of certain place names in the district, such as Jebel Usdum (= Mount Sodom), supports this theory, and the presence of extensive mineral salt deposits is thought to be connected with the story of LOT's wife, who turned to a "pillar of salt" as she walked toward Zoar (Gen. 19:26). Others argue that the Bible seems to locate Zoar specifically at an extremity of the "Plain … the valley of Jericho" in the recital of the dimension of the Promised Land (Deut. 34:3 NRSV); how would Moses have seen the area at the S end of the Dead Sea from Mount Nebo in MOAB opposite JERICHO (34:1)? It is further argued that Gen. 13:10-12 seems to indicate the Valley of Jordan opposite BETHEL and AI. However, a location at the N rather than the S end of the Dead Sea has not won favor.

Zoba. See ZOBAH.

Zobah. zoh´buh (Heb. *ṣōbā’ H7419* [2 Sam. 10:6, 8] and *ṣôbâ H7420*, meaning uncertain). An ARAMEAN kingdom that flourished during the early Hebrew monarchy. Its exact location is not known, but in 2 Sam. 8:8 reference is made to a city in the kingdom of Zobah named BEROTHAI from which DAVID obtained copper. This town may be the same as BEROTHAH and modern Bereitan, about 30 mi. (48 km.) NW of DAMASCUS. SAUL fought against Zobah (1 Sam. 14:47), and subsequently

David, when he sought to establish his northern border, clashed with HADADEZER of Zobah and defeated him (2 Sam. 8:3, 5, 12; 1 Chr. 18:3, 5, 9; Ps. 60 title ["Aram Zobah"]). Later, when AMMON fought David, there were contingents from Zobah and other Aramean towns in the Ammonite forces (2 Sam. 10:6-8; cf. 1 Chr. 19:6). David's general JOAB overwhelmed these allies (2 Sam. 10:9-19; 1 Chr. 19:8-19). In SOLOMON's time, REZON, a fugitive from the king of Zobah, established himself in Damascus and became "Israel's adversary as long as Solomon lived" (1 Ki. 11:23-25).

Zobebah. See HAZZOBEBAH.

Zohar. zoh´hahr (Heb. *ṣōḥar H7468*, possibly "reddish" or "radiant"). **(1)** Father of EPHRON the HITTITE (Gen. 23:8; 25:9).

(2) Son of SIMEON and grandson of JACOB (Gen. 46:10; Exod. 6:15); also called ZERAH (Num. 26:13; 1 Chr. 4:24).

(3) Son of Asshur (by his wife Helah) and descendant of JUDAH (1 Chr. 4:7). See comments under IZHAR #2.

Zoheleth, Stone of. zoh´huh-lith (Heb. *zōḥelet H2325*, "creeping thing"). A stone or boulder near EN ROGEL (a spring just S of JERUSALEM); at this site ADONIJAH offered sacrifices in his abortive attempt to become king (1 Ki. 1:9; RSV, "Serpent's Stone"). The name may indicate either that there was a "crawling" or "sliding" rock (from the overhanging cliffs to the spring) or, more likely, that the stone was associated with the cultic emblem of the serpent. Some have seen a connection between the Zoheleth Stone and the Dragon's Spring (Neh. 2:13; see JACKAL WELL).

Zoheth. zoh´heth (Heb. *zôḥēt H2311*, derivation uncertain). Son of Ishi, included in the genealogy of JUDAH (1 Chr. 4:20).

Zophah. zoh´fuh (Heb. *ṣôpaḥ H7432*, meaning uncertain). Son of Helem; listed among the brave warriors who were heads of families of the tribe of ASHER (1 Chr. 7:35-36; cf. v. 40).

Zophai. See ZUPH (PERSON).

Z

Zophar. zoh′fahr (Heb. *ṣôpar H7436*, meaning uncertain). The third of the three friends of JOB who came to commiserate him (Job 2:11; 11:1; 20:1; 42:9). He came from Naamah, probably a city or region outside PALESTINE (see NAAMATHITE). He was harsh in accusing Job of wickedness and in telling him that he deserved to suffer even more than he had.

Zophim. zoh′fim (Heb. *ṣōpim H7614*, "watchers" or "lookout"). A field on the top of the PISGAH slopes, at the NE end of the DEAD SEA, to which BALAK took BALAAM to see ISRAEL (Num. 23:14). It is uncertain whether the term is a proper name or a common noun (thus possibly "field of watchers" or "lookout field").

Zorah. zor′uh (Heb. *ṣorʿâ H7666*, meaning uncertain; gentilic *ṣorʿātî H7670*, "Zorathite" [1 Chr. 2:53; 4:2], and *ṣorʿî H7668*, "Zorite" [2:54]). KJV also Zoreah (Josh. 15:33), Zareah (Neh. 11:29), Zareathite (1 Chr. 2:53). A city in the SHEPHELAH of the tribe of JUDAH (Josh. 15:33) which formerly belonged to DAN (Josh. 19:41; Jdg. 13:2; 18:2). The town was the home of MANOAH the father of SAMSON (Jdg. 13:2). It was in MAHANEH-DAN, between Zorah and ESHTAOL, that Samson first experienced the constraint of the Spirit of the Lord (13:25); and after his death, he was buried in the same region (16:31). When the Danites decided to

vacate their territory due to PHILISTINE pressure, some of the five men sent out to reconnoiter further N for a new home came from Zorah and Eshtaol (18:2). On their recommendation six hundred warriors from those two towns took LAISH in the N (18:8-11). SOLOMON's son REHOBOAM strengthened the fortifications of Zorah on his southern flank (2 Chr. 11:10). After the EXILE the town was reoccupied by returning exiles (Neh. 11:29). Zorah is confidently identified with modern Ṣarʿah, some 14 mi. (23 km.) W of JERUSALEM (2 mi./3 km. NNE of biblical BETH SHEMESH and about the same distance WSW of Eshtaol); the town sits on a hill overlooking the Wadi eṣ-Ṣarar (SOREK) to its S.

Zorathite. See ZORAH.

Zoreah. See ZORAH.

Zorite. See ZORAH.

Zorobabel. See ZERUBBABEL.

Zuar. zoo′uhr (Heb. *ṣûʿār H7428*, "small"). Father of NETHANEL, who was the leader of the tribe of ISSACHAR during the wilderness wanderings (Num. 1:8; 2:5; 7:18, 23; 10:15).

Zuph. zuhf (Heb. *ṣûp H7431* and *ṣōpay H7433* [1 Chr. 6:26, Heb. v. 11], possibly "flowing honey"). **(1)** Son of ELKANAH, descendant of LEVI through KOHATH, and ancestor of SAMUEL (1 Sam. 1:1; 1 Chr. 6:26 ["Zophai"], 35). See also #2, below.

(2) A region to which SAUL came when he was searching for his father's donkeys (1 Sam. 9:5); the prophet SAMUEL lived in this place (v. 6), so evidently it was near Ramah, though the precise location is unknown. It is very likely that the name of this area was derived from Samuel's ancestor (see #1, above). Samuel's father Elkanah is described as being a native of Ramathaim

This tell or mound is identified as biblical Zorah.

© Dr. James C. Martin

Zuphim (1 Sam. 1:1 NIV mg.), and modern translations usually render the Hebrew phrase "from Ramathaim, a Zuphite" (NJPS, "from Ramathaim of the Zuphites"). See comments under RAMAH #3.

Zuphim, Zuphite. See ZUPH #2.

Zur. zuhr (Heb. *ṣûr H7448*, "rock"). **(1)** A tribal chief from MIDIAN and father of COZBI (Num. 25:15); the latter and her Israelite husband ZIMRI were put to death by PHINEHAS for their part in pagan and immoral behavior (cf. vv. 1-9). In a subsequent battle, the Israelites killed Zur and other Midianite rulers (31:8; Josh. 13:21).

(2) Son of JEIEL and descendant of BENJAMIN; his brother NER was the grandfather of SAUL (1 Chr. 8:30 [cf. v. 33]; 9:36).

Zuriel. zoor'ee-uhl (Heb. *ṣûriʾēl H7452*, "God is my rock"). Son of Abihail and descendant of KEVI through MERARI; he was leader of the Merarites in the wilderness (Num. 3:35).

Zurishaddai. zoor'i-shad'*i* (Heb. *ṣûrîšadday H7453*, "Shaddai is my rock"; see EL SHADDAI). Father of SHELUMIEL; the latter was the leader of the tribe of SIMEON in the wilderness (Num. 1:6; 2:12; 7:36, 41; 10:19).

Zuzim. See ZUZITES.

Zuzites. zoo'zits (Heb. *zûzîm H2309*, derivation uncertain). Also Zuzim (KJV Zuzims, a superfluous English pl. form). A pre-Israelite tribe of Syria-Palestine mentioned in Gen. 14:5 as one of the nations overthrown by the Elamite king KEDORLAOMER. They are said to have lived in Ham, apparently a site located in the N of what is today the country of Jordan. See HAM (PLACE). Most authorities equate the Zuzites with the ZAMZUMMITES of Deut. 2:20, although some object that in the former passage the Zuzites are distinguished from the REPHAITES, while in the latter the Rephaites seem to be identified with the Zamzummites.

Z

Share Your Thoughts

With the Author: Your comments will be forwarded to the author when you send them to *zauthor@zondervan.com*.

With Zondervan: Submit your review of this book by writing to *zreview@zondervan.com*.

Free Online Resources at
www.zondervan.com

Zondervan AuthorTracker: Be notified whenever your favorite authors publish new books, go on tour, or post an update about what's happening in their lives at www.zondervan.com/authortracker.

Daily Bible Verses and Devotions: Enrich your life with daily Bible verses or devotions that help you start every morning focused on God. Visit www.zondervan.com/newsletters.

Free Email Publications: Sign up for newsletters on Christian living, academic resources, church ministry, fiction, children's resources, and more. Visit www.zondervan.com/newsletters.

Zondervan Bible Search: Find and compare Bible passages in a variety of translations at www.zondervanbiblesearch.com.

Other Benefits: Register yourself to receive online benefits like coupons and special offers, or to participate in research.

ZONDERVAN.com/
AUTHORTRACKER
follow your favorite authors